W9-BER-441

Introduction to

HOUGHTON MIFFLIN COMPANY · BOSTON
New York · Atlanta · Geneva, Illinois · Dallas · Palo Alto

American Poetry and Prose

Edited by Norman Foerster

Norman S. Grabo
University of California, Berkeley

Russel B. Nye
Michigan State University

E. Fred Carlisle
Michigan State University

Robert Falk
University of California, Los Angeles

Printed in the U.S.A.

Library of Congress Catalog Card Number: 72-140999
ISBN: 0-395-04457-X

Henry Adams From *The Education of Henry Adams.* Copyright © 1918 by the Massachusetts Historical Society. Reprinted by permission of Houghton Mifflin Company, the authorized publisher.

Sherwood Anderson "Hands," from *Winesburg, Ohio* by Sherwood Anderson; copyright 1919 by B. W. Huebsch, Inc., renewed 1947 by Eleanor Copenhaver Anderson; reprinted by permission of The Viking Press, Inc.

James Baldwin "This Morning, This Evening, So Soon": Copyright © 1960, 1965 by James Baldwin. Reprinted from *Going to Meet the Man* by James Baldwin by permission of the publisher, The Dial Press, Inc.

John Barth "Night-Sea Journey": Copyright © by John Barth from *Lost in the Funhouse* by John Barth. Reprinted by permission of Doubleday & Company, Inc.

Saul Bellow "Leaving the Yellow House," from *Mosby's Memoirs and Other Stories* by Saul Bellow. Copyright © 1958 by Saul Bellow. All rights reserved. Reprinted by permission of The Viking Press, Inc.

William Bradford From *History of Plymouth Plantation 1620–1647*, ed. W. C. Ford, copyright 1912 by the Massachusetts Historical Society; reprinted by permission of the Massachusetts Historical Society.

Cleanth Brooks "The Waste Land: An Analysis," from *Modern Poetry and the Tradition* by Cleanth Brooks; reprinted by permission of The University of North Carolina Press.

William Byrd From *The Secret Diary of William Byrd of Westover, 1709–1712*, ed. Louis B. Wright and Marion Tinling. Copyright 1941 by Louis B. Wright and Marion Tinling.

Hart Crane From *Complete Poems and Selected Letters and Prose of Hart Crane.* Permission of Liveright, Publishers, New York. Copyright 1933, 1958, 1966 by Liveright Publishing Corp.

Stephen Crane Selections from *The Works of Stephen Crane* (1925–1926), ed. Wilson Follett, and from *The Collected Poems of Stephen Crane* (1930), ed. Wilson Follett; reprinted by courtesy of Alfred A. Knopf, Inc.

James Fenimore Cooper From *The American Democrat*, ed. H. L. Mencken; reprinted by courtesy of Alfred A. Knopf, Inc.

E. E. Cummings "in Just-," "Buffalo Bill's," and "The Cambridge ladies": copyright, 1923, 1951, by E. E. Cummings. "Spring is like a perhaps hand": copyright, 1925, by E. E. Cummings. "next to of course god" and "my sweet old etcetera": copyright, 1926, by Horace Liveright; copyright, 1954, by E. E. Cummings. "r-p-o-p-h-e-s-s-a-g-r": copyright, 1935, by E. E. Cummings; renewed, 1963, by Marion Morehouse Cummings. "this little bride and groom": copyright, 1938, by E. E. Cummings; renewed, 1966, by Marion Morehouse Cummings. "plato told" and "pity this busy monster": copyright, 1944, by E. E. Cummings. All reprinted from *Poems 1923–1954* by E. E. Cummings by permission of Harcourt, Brace & World, Inc.

Emily Dickinson Selections reprinted by permission of the publishers and the Trustees of Amherst College from Thomas H. Johnson, Editor, *The Poems of Emily Dickinson*, Cambridge, Mass.: The Belknap Press of Harvard University Press, Copyright, 1951, 1955, by The President and Fellows of Harvard College.

"Papa above": copyright 1914, 1942 by Martha Dickinson Bianchi; "After great pain," "This was a poet," "A Wife—at daybreak," "Within my garden, rides a bird," "Publication is the auction," "My Life had stood—a loaded gun," "Faith—is the pierless bridge": copyright, 1929, © 1957 by Mary L. Hampson; from *The Complete Poems of Emily Dickinson*, edited by Thomas H. Johnson, by permission of Little, Brown and Co.

Jonathan Edwards From *The Philosophy of Jonathan Edwards from His Private Notebooks*, ed. Harvey G. Townsend (University of Oregon Monograph: Studies in Philosophy, no. 2), University of Oregon, 1955; by permission of the University of Oregon.

T. S. Eliot From *Collected Poems 1909–1962* by T. S. Eliot, copyright, 1936, by Harcourt, Brace & World, Inc.; copyright, © 1963, 1964, by T. S. Eliot. Reprinted by permission of the publishers, Harcourt, Brace & World, Inc., and Faber and Faber Ltd.

From *Selected Essays*, New Edition, by T. S. Eliot, copyright, 1932, 1936, 1950, by Harcourt, Brace & World, Inc.; copyright, 1960, 1964, by T. S. Eliot. Reprinted by permission of the publishers, Harcourt, Brace & World, Inc., and Faber and Faber Ltd.

Ralph Ellison "Twentieth-Century Fiction and the Black Mask of Humanity": Copyright 1953 by Ralph Ellison. Reprinted from *Shadow and Act*, by Ralph Ellison, by permission of Random House, Inc.

Ralph Waldo Emerson From *The Journals of Ralph Waldo Emerson*, ed. E. W. Emerson and W. E. Forbes; selections reprinted by permission of the publisher, Houghton Mifflin Company.

William Faulkner "The Bear": copyright 1942 by Curtis Publishing Company; copyright 1942 by William Faulkner. Reprinted from *Go Down, Moses*, by William Faulkner, by permission of Random House, Inc.

F. Scott Fitzgerald "The Rich Boy" (Copyright 1925, 1926 Consolidated Magazines Corporation; renewal copyright 1953, 1954 F. Scott Fitzgerald Lanahan) is reprinted with the permission of Charles Scribner's Sons from *All the Sad Young Men* by F. Scott Fitzgerald.

Robert Frost From *Complete Poems of Robert Frost.* Copyright 1916, 1923, 1928, 1930, 1939, 1947, 1967 by Holt, Rinehart and Winston, Inc. Copyright 1936, 1942, 1944, 1951, © 1956, 1958 by Robert Frost. Copyright © 1964, 1967, 1970 by Lesley Frost Ballantine. Reprinted by permission of Holt, Rinehart and Winston, Inc

Allen Ginsberg From *Howl and Other Poems* by Allen Ginsberg. Copyright © 1956, 1959 by Allen Ginsberg. Reprinted by permission of City Lights Books.

Ernest Hemingway "The Undefeated" is reprinted with the permission of Charles Scribner's Sons from *Men Without Women* by Ernest Hemingway. Copyright 1927 Charles Scribner's Sons; renewal copyright © 1955 Ernest Hemingway.

Langston Hughes "As I Grew Older": copyright 1926 by Alfred A. Knopf, Inc. and renewed 1954 by Langston Hughes. "Song for a Dark Girl": copyright 1927 by Alfred A. Knopf, Inc. and renewed 1955 by Langston Hughes. "American Heartbreak": copyright 1951 by Langston Hughes. All reprinted from

Publisher's Foreword

THIS *Introduction to American Poetry and Prose* presents important and representative works of central figures in our literary tradition and can constitute a full course by itself or can be used with selected separate texts. Like other versions of this distinguished textbook, this one serves both the historical and the critical approaches to our literature. And since the years have narrowed the gap between these two approaches, it has been possible to incorporate elements of a third, which may be called comparative and developmental, focusing attention on certain recurring themes that have grown out of the unique American experience, and on the various ways American writers of different periods have dealt with them. Within the cultural framework provided by this approach, the student is encouraged to look simultaneously in two directions, from the past to the adumbrated future, and from the present to the seminal past, and thereby to gain a deeper insight into the vitality and continuity of American literature. At the same time, the consistent focus on literary concerns, in the structure of the book, the nature of the selections, and the editorial commentary, has made it possible to avoid the pitfall of the purely documentary or sociological; while the ample treatment of major writers within a setting of lesser significant figures averts the temptation to include obscure writers out of the main stream, or to introduce the merely novel or the fashionable and evanescent.

This edition differs from earlier ones in other significant ways. The mere passage of time has shifted the center of gravity toward the contemporary. Relatively less space is devoted to colonial and early federal writing, though the early period now includes Thomas Hooker, exponent of the "plain style" that was to become so important a strain in American writing. The great figures of the nineteenth century receive much the same emphasis as before, but the fifth and contemporary division now begins not at 1900 but at 1914, a genuine break point which gives deeper unity to the sections both before and after, and allows increased space to the ever-growing contemporary.

In subtler ways also this edition has taken the measure of the day and reflects the many and profound changes of the last decade. The editorial materials—the five period introductions, the author introductions, and the selection headnotes—have been revised or rewritten to sharpen the focus on literary trends and developments. This has been done partly by the omission of matter mainly social and historical, and by increased emphasis on interrelations and influences, intellectual and literary. Throughout, every effort has been made to avoid spoonfeeding, on the one hand, and factual cramming on the other, and instead to present background and explanatory material calculated to help the student grasp, interpret, and interrelate for himself the literary works he reads. To this end, also, the texts are footnoted more extensively than before, but not to the point where information assumes a gratuitous and distracting importance for its own sake.

The texts of the selections have been carefully chosen for both their authority and their readability, and are identified throughout. Priority has been given to first editions or first appearance in book form, to standard editions, and to modern critical editions. In the colonial materials, when the verbal sequence of first or early editions is followed, the texts have been generally modernized with respect to italics, abbreviations, capitalization, and spelling. To maintain the rhythms of early American writing, however, the punctuation of the source texts has been generally retained; unusual spellings have been kept when they may be presumed to distinguish colonial pronunciation from modern American English, and special care has been taken not to impair the pronunciation of the poetry. Textual omissions for which the editors of this anthology are responsible are shown by asterisks; titles supplied by the editors are bracketed. The selections from each author are, with few exceptions, in chronological order; dates are given in the headnotes or at the end of a selection (date of publication at the right margin; of composition, if equally or more significant, at the left margin).

Active in the planning and policy-making stages, Professor Foerster was instrumental in soliciting the collaboration of the four distinguished scholars who carried out the actual work of the revision: Norman S. Grabo for the colonial period; Russel B. Nye for the neoclassic and early romantic; E. Fred Carlisle for the romantic; and Robert Falk for the realistic, the recent, and the contemporary. Editors and publisher alike are indebted to the following board of consultants for their advice on the nature of the revision and the editorial materials: Louis J. Budd, Duke University; Hennig Cohen, University of Pennsylvania; Neal F. Doubleday, Millikin University; Richard H. Fogle, University of North Carolina; Ernest E. Sandeen, University of Notre Dame; James Woodress, University of California (Davis); Hyatt H. Waggoner, Brown University. Others whose contributions are gratefully acknowledged are Frank Lentricchia, of the University of California (Irvine), for his work on the contemporary poets; Margaret Linville, of Santa Monica City College, for assistance with the contemporary novelists; and Frank Shuffelton, of the University of Rochester, for assistance with the selection and checking of texts.

Contents

The Colonial Period

The Neoclassic Age

The Romantic Movement

Realism and Naturalism

The Twentieth Century (1914–1970)

INTRODUCTION TO AMERICAN POETRY AND PROSE

The Colonial Period

IN THE BEGINNING was the dream, and the dream was America. Europe was in convulsive transition from the medieval to the modern age: established institutions and patterns of thought were being challenged, and the fabric of society and even of cosmology seemed in danger of dissolution.

> And freely men confess that this world's spent,
> When in the planets and the firmament
> They seek so many new; they see that this
> Is crumbled out again to his atomies.
> 'Tis all in pieces, all coherence gone!

Thus lamented John Donne in 1611. Copernicus and Galileo, Brahe and Kepler had indeed called the Ptolemaic cosmos in doubt. The sixteenth century had done much to throw off the traditions and restraints of medieval learning; in the opening decades of the seventeenth century the growth of a skeptical attitude toward the world, accompanied by new tools for analysis, fractured many traditional concepts and with them much of the era's assurance about the nature of God, man, and the universe. Men were impelled to re-examine and explore their world within and without, to look inside themselves and across immense uncharted seas. The great, hazy, relatively unknown continent of America, already penetrated at its edges by European adventurers, possessed a particular attraction. But the circumstances and motives that thrust Englishmen toward this New World were both varied and confused.

High among these was the assertion of British national pride and honor, especially against the Spanish, Dutch, and French. English sea dogs had plundered galleons returning from South and Central America, where Spaniards and Portuguese had exploited natural riches since the 1490's; and by the end of the sixteenth century, an American base for operations against the Spanish seemed not only a tactical necessity but a patriotic duty.

Economic considerations supplied both a powerful motive and a practical means for colonization. With the substitution of credit for goods and services in the first half of the sixteenth century, financial power tended to concentrate in the hands of the large joint-stock trading companies chartered by the Crown, and the first settlements in the New World were underwritten by London stockholders for whom America represented the hope of a good return on their investment.

Poverty and want in England, especially in the cities, created virtually insoluble social problems. The infant factory system could not hope to accommodate the hosts of unskilled farm workers who streamed cityward, displaced by agricultural reforms. Vagabonds and tramps, thieves and beggars plagued the land; the British government seemed unable to provide for the needy. The colonization of America therefore appeared to furnish an attractive possibility for alleviating England's social problems. As early as 1515, Thomas More's *Utopia* had held out the promise of a New World free of social ills; later writers, both English and American, continued to exploit the Utopian potential as one of the strongest attractions for colonization.

Tying the patriotic, economic, and social motives together was the religious tenor of sixteenth-century England. Henry VIII had made the all-decisive break with the Roman Catholic Church in 1531, but the yeast of Protestantism continued to work within the Church of England, until many who dissented from the established religion came to feel that their only safety and salvation in this world lay across the Atlantic.

Thus out of intellectual, social, economic, and religious unrest and confusion grew seventeenth-century England's dream of a better and more profitable world overseas. Writers like Hakluyt did their best to present America as the cure-all of England's problems and the end-all of her ambitions.

The Virginian Voyage

Shortly after the turn of the century the formation of two new trading companies—the Virginia Company of London and the Virginia Company of Plymouth—fanned fresh interest in establishing plantations across the ocean. Michael Drayton wrote his ode "To the Virginian Voyage"; and in May 1607, Captain Christopher Newport's three ships dropped anchor, supplies, and colonists at the mouth of the James River, where the settlers built a stockade and erected the tents and huts they regally named Jamestown. In spite of their expectations of gold and precious stones, their unwillingness to blister gentlemanly hands with hoe and axe, the squabbles that had erupted among them even before they landed, and the selection of swampy, mosquito-ridden Jamestown "island" as a roosting place, the little band of settlers hung on to become England's first permanent settlement in America. Its success was assured in 1612, when John Rolfe discovered a method of curing Indian tobacco, and the following year, when the home company began making land available to private owners, the settlers cultivated the plant with an energy they had never displayed for company profits alone. But as the colonists dispersed on their newly-gotten farms, rule from the London office became increasingly inadequate and inconvenient. On July 30, 1619, therefore, under Governor George Yeardley's leadership, Virginia's first representative assembly met in Jamestown's Anglican church. From that meeting dates the South's long experience in self-rule that was to prove so valuable in creating an independent America in the following century. Still Virginia's central concern was wealth, which was so anguishingly slow in coming that in 1624 King James annulled the distressed Virginia Company's charter, making the colony a royal dependent, subject to royal governorship.

Though Captain John Smith once wrote in irritation, "I am not so simple to think that ever any other motive than wealth will ever erect there a commonweal," Mammon alone was not capable of sustaining American colonization. Settlers looking for quick riches were discouraged by brutally hard labor, the threat of Indian attacks, quarrels among the colony's leaders, and complaints from England. The John Donne who cried "all coherence gone!" was also a shareholder in the Virginia Company, for whom America was a symptom of unrest and dissolution, rather than a symbol of order. If the coherence Donne sought in politics, religion, and the minds of men was to flower in America, it would have to spring from another quarter and other motives.

The Puritan Migrations

In August 1609 another expedition left England. Unprovided with poets' odes, sent on its way with good riddance, and bound for Holland rather than for America, it nevertheless carried with it the seeds of order, the dedication, and the sense of urgency that would soon characterize America. The men making up this expedition belonged to a group of religious radicals, the extreme left-wing of the Puritan reform movement in England, called Separatists then because they denounced and separated from the established Anglican Church, but now known as Pilgrims.

The origins of Puritanism are quite complex, springing directly from the reform movements on the Continent in the sixteenth century. Martin Luther's dramatic break with the Church of Rome in 1517 marked the beginning, but it was John Calvin who provided a theological and ecclesiastical system to replace the Roman faith. His *Institutes of the Christian Religion* (1536–59), combined with his own extraordinary intellectual and evangelistic talents, gained him a zealous following, not only in his native France, but in Geneva (to which he was banished) and in Holland. Englishmen came to know and respect Calvin's thought, especially when under Mary Tudor (1553–58) England returned to Catholicism and the queen drove hundreds of learned and dedicated English Protestants into exile. Calvin's revival of the relatively uncomplicated theology of St. Augustine, and the practices of the early apostolic church, appealed to them; and when they returned to England after Elizabeth's accession to the throne, they pushed English church reform in the direction of Calvinism.

Almost at once a deep rift developed between those Church of England men to whom the old traditions were valuable and satisfying and those who, while still content to remain within the established church, believed that its reformation had not gone far enough. By 1572 the dissidents were called Puritans, a term applied to any religious group that demonstrated extreme scrupulosity regarding religious behavior. Although there was wide diversity among them, English Puritans generally demanded a literal interpretation of the Bible and its application to the affairs of everyday life. Following Augustine and Calvin, they emphasized God's complete and unquestionable sovereignty, and man's innate weakness, incapacity for good, and perverse habit of dignifying wilfulness by the term "free will." They held that God not only foresaw but predestined all worldly events, controlling even the most minute circumstances by His unceasing providence; that some men were thereby elected to everlasting glory while others were bound for hell. Man's salvation, the Puritans believed, depended not on good works (for how could an innately depraved creature be capable of *any* good?), nor on the externals of elaborate public services and rituals, but solely on full faith in Christ. The high seriousness and missionary zeal with which the English Puritans held and argued their beliefs made them a sober people, and gave them an unshakable reputation (often unwarranted) as enemies of frivolity, humor, and beauty. Although it was possible for Anglo-Catholics to agree with many Puritan principles, they could not accept the Puritan demand that the church give up its episcopal system and adopt Congregational or Presbyterian forms of church government.

One group went too far even for most purists. Robert Browne, an early spokesman, argued in *A Treatise of Reformation* (1582) that since not all who attended and supported the Church of England were godly, the truly pious should meet and worship separately. For their complete repudiation of the Anglican Church, the so-called "Separatists," or "Brownists," were subjected to a great deal of harassment and persecution.

It was one such group of persecuted Separatists in Scrooby, Nottinghamshire, that removed in 1609 from England to Amsterdam and thence to Leyden. They found tolerance in Holland, but not peace. Aliens in a foreign land, their means of livelihood restricted, their young people restive, these English expatriates by 1619 felt it imperative to seek a new land where, under more favorable conditions, they might establish their commonwealth of believers. Accordingly, they negotiated with the Virginia Company of London, secured a leaky ship called the *Speedwell,* abandoned it for the *Mayflower,* and in November 1620 arrived not in Virginia as planned, but at Cape Cod. Knowing they were outside the legal jurisdiction of their patent, and fearing lest the lack of authority completely upset their "plantation," forty-one passengers agreed to create a "civil body politic," just as they had made a covenant to form an independent congregation. This famous Mayflower Compact, or Covenant, has been described as "the fundamental instrument of government for the little democracy which it established without any authority than the wishes of the signers." But it must be remembered that these Pilgrims had not left Europe to found a democracy or to establish a free state. They merely sought a refuge for their own religious society, and they were determined to keep all who differed with them out of their new Jerusalem. In the new continent the Plymouth colony survived the rigors of the wilderness, the ineptitude of its London agents, and the diversions of a few free spirits (such as Thomas Morton of Merrymount) who wandered into it. Under the firm and sagacious leadership of William Bradford and the elders, the Pilgrims sold enough cod, lumber, and furs to find a modest prosperity, maintained their New England foothold, and promised to thrive.

Back in England the non-separatist Puritans found themselves involved in increasingly difficult religious and political conflicts, and they observed the Pilgrim experiment with growing interest. In 1623 the Dorchester Adventurers was formed to maintain fishing and trading operations in New England; in 1628 and 1629, expeditions were sent to what is now Salem to prepare the way for a second colonial venture; and on March 4, 1629, within a week of Charles's dissolution of Parliament, the Dorchester Adventurers, now called the New England Company for a Plantation in Massachusetts Bay, secured a generous charter. The following year, under the leadership of Governor John Winthrop aboard the *Arbella,* the first four ships of what has come to be called the Great Migration arrived and settled at Massachusetts Bay.

As Winthrop told his people, their purpose in the New World was not to amass wealth, but to worship God in their own fashion—to establish a "true" religious society, "to improve our lives to do more service to the Lord, the comfort and increase of the body of Christ whereof we are members, that ourselves and posterity may be the better preserved from the common corruptions of this evil world, to serve the Lord and work out our salvation under the power and purity of His holy ordinances." The Massachusetts Bay Colony had a concept of order and a singleness of purpose that Virginia had lacked. Winthrop was careful to let his company know their holy experiment was being observed by all Christendom: "For we must consider that we shall be as a city upon a hill, the eyes of all people are upon us."

The Puritan-citizen of this city upon a hill found evidences of his progress toward salvation by constant surveillance of the state of his soul. To attain salvation, he believed, a man's soul moved through regular, identifiable stages—an effectual calling, justification (by which a soul knows Christ's sacrifice to be efficacious for itself), sanctification (righteous behavior), and finally, with death, glorification. Self-knowledge, then, was a spiritual necessity; but since God revealed His will through the everyday workings of nature, it became necessary, in order to know one's self, to know the world too. As John Cotton put it, the faithful soul applies its faithfulness to all its worldly activities: "though you may have a godly man busy in his calling from sun rising to sun setting, and may by God's providence fill both his hand and his head with business, yet a living Christian, when he lives a most busy life in this world, yet he lives not a worldly life." Cotton did not mean that the good life was perforce a worldly, materialistic life; yet for many New Englanders, following out Cotton's doctrine often meant substantially that. As a result, New England Puritanism faced two ways. On the one hand, it demanded deep and constant thought about the nature of the universe, about the nature of man and his relation to God, about man's duties to God and his neighbors, and about the high seriousness of life in this world. On the other hand, it hallowed every human activity in the state and in society at large, in government and business, with the sanctity of a religious act. One consequence of the bifurcation was to turn New Englanders into successful businessmen, merchants, and traders, as well as into "saints." And thus it became increasingly difficult to maintain the great dream of a holy commonwealth.

The Colonial Way of Life

Virginia and the New England colonies established the basic patterns of life in seventeenth-century America. New settlements splintered off from Massachusetts to form the colonies of Connecticut, Rhode Island, and New Haven. Expansion was contagious. But the impetus for most new colonization came from abroad. Groups in England and Europe were quick to capitalize on the dreams of land, profit, power, and political and religious refuge that America represented. The newer settlements were made not under the directorship of trade companies but under individual proprietors whose patents gave them virtually royal power in the New World.

Catholic George Calvert, Lord Baltimore, secured a grant north of the Potomac as a refuge for persecuted English Catholics. The colony, tactfully named "Maryland" in honor of King Charles's queen, was settled at St. Mary's City in 1633; careful to offend neither the Massachusetts Puritans nor the Virginia Anglicans, it opened its land to all Christians, excluding only Jews and the forerunners of Unitarianism. Holland, England's most shrewd and powerful economic and colonial rival, moved into the area between Maryland and Connecticut, named it New Netherland, founded the town of New Amsterdam in 1625, and began to penetrate Connecticut territory. Though Swedes settled along the Delaware as early as 1638, neither they nor their Dutch neighbors received substantial support from their homelands. They combined in 1635 to form a population of some ten thousand, but fell easily before English power and were converted into New York in 1664.

By that time, though, the Duke of York was already interested in other holdings. In 1655 he and eight others became Lords Proprietors of land reaching from Virginia to below St. Augustine, Florida. They hoped to oust the Spanish outpost there, develop a tropical economy, and establish a grand aristocracy along lines laid out by the Earl of Shaftesbury, John Locke, and James Harrington's Utopian *Oceana*. But their plan for an American nobility proved desperately impractical for Carolina, and was soon abandoned. While unauthorized settlers congregated at Albemarle Sound, forming the colony to be known after 1719 as North Carolina, the Lords Proprietors sent another expedition to settle the southern part of the colony in 1670. Under Governor William Sayle, they settled along the Ashley River, moving near its mouth a few years later to establish Charleston, which by 1680 became the seat of government and in time the most graceful of southern colonial cities.

To the north another proprietary grant was made in 1665 to Sir George and Philip Carteret and Lord John Berkeley for New Jersey. The venture was not profitable, and in 1679 they sold out to William Penn, who three years later also secured the proprietorship of Pennsylvania from the Lords of Trade. Penn thus controlled the last uncommitted coastal lands, which he opened to religious refugees, especially Quakers, though by this time Swedish Lutherans, Dutch, and Finns were firmly planted along the Delaware, and Penn was obliged by the Lords of Trade to permit Anglican churches to develop as the need arose.

By 1700 the American coast from Florida to Maine was in English hands, either as corporate (trade company), proprietary, or royal colonies. Living under governments much like those in England, and enjoying what Raleigh's charter had called "all the privileges of free denizens, and persons native of England," the colonists were yet not quite Englishmen, nor simply Englishmen living away from home. Nor could they be called Americans, for the alembic of transatlantic life had not yet distilled the type that St. Jean de Crèvecoeur described in 1782. Instead, the colonies were a crazy-quilt of migrants, the rawest of raw materials for the "melting pot." There were even Polish and German laborers and craftsmen as part of the original Jamestown venture, soon joined by Italian glassmakers and French vintners. The Dutch, of course, predominated in early New York, but the area fell increasingly under the influence of French, Germans, Danes, Swedes, Finns, Portuguese, Spanish, Italians, Bohemians, and

Poles. Jews in New York enjoyed surprising freedom, built synagogues, and early in the eighteenth century could amaze young Puritans like Jonathan Edwards, who furtively observed one—"the devoutest person that I ever saw in my life"—from his adjoining window. French Huguenots lived along the coast, concentrated in Pennsylvania, Virginia, and the Carolinas. German Pietists, Mennonites, and Baptists, attracted by the *New-found Eden,* as one propaganda tract described it, made all haste to the New World, especially to Pennsylvania, while Scotsmen joined the oncoming wave early in the eighteenth century, settling largely in the New Jersey area. One class of migrants came involuntarily, without prospects and without hope: in 1619 a Dutch man-of-war brought the first Africans to the colonies, to be sold into servitude ("the great mistake / That Jamestown / Made long ago").

The quarter million Europeans in America by the end of the seventeenth century brought with them their national languages, customs, styles of living, foods, dress, trades and diversions, architecture, and ornamental arts. Even though Anglicanism was the official faith of the royal and proprietary colonies, and Congregationalism deeply ingrained in New England, the religious toleration that accompanied Charles II's return to the throne in 1660 drew Quakers, Baptists, Lutherans, Pietists, and even Roman Catholics and Jews to the colonies. After 1684, when Massachusetts Bay lost its charter, even New England had to suffer the encroachments of other faiths or risk political reprisal from England. Indeed, there was much more variety and contrast in American colonial life in the later seventeenth and early eighteenth centuries than the myths of somber Puritan New England and romantic Cavalier South would indicate.

That there should be very real distinctions between northern and southern life, even in the seventeenth century, was inevitable. The control of immense tobacco lands fell into the hands of the most resourceful and influential settlers quite early, so that Virginia's leading class was largely self-made. Theirs was recently acquired wealth, and though they assumed the *noblesse oblige* of traditional English aristocracy in managing their estates, they resembled English country gentry rather than nobility. The large plantation owner was perforce lawyer, doctor, teacher, farmer, judge, surveyor, and engineer. His immediate concerns were practical and numerous, and though he often yielded to the extravagance of sending his children to England for schooling, he could not on the whole afford a very gay or carefree life. That was usually left to the second or third generation. The diary of William Byrd of Westover provides fascinating glimpses into the life of a Virginia gentleman who had "arrived" as an aristocrat. Carolinians, after surrendering hopes of cultivating tropical fruits, turned to rice, and, using Negro and Indian slaves to work the malarial inland rice fields, escaped whenever they could to the coast. Flocking to Charleston, they soon created a sophisticated miniature of London social life unmatched elsewhere in the colonies.

New England, on the other hand, unsuited for large-scale farming and held tightly together by church as well as social covenants, turned to manufacture and trade in its primarily urban economy. The quick result was a merchant aristocracy that built its own ships, stored them with codfish, wood products, food grains, and salted meats, and sent them to trade along the American coast and to England and Europe. New England grew rich on trade, and as its wealth grew, the bonds of its religious dedication loosened. Whereas the early Puritan assumed that God's favor to a man might be manifested in his life, his grandson, reversing the logic, believed that a man's material success might well be evidence of his saintliness. The homespun-to-riches pattern of a town like Boston had ceased to be a novelty long before Benjamin Franklin grew up there. Increasing prosperity revealed itself in the multiplication of worldly comforts—bigger and fancier houses, imported furniture, expensive books for private libraries, and, by the early eighteenth century, private coaches and footmen.

Economic, religious, and political differences drove Virginia and New England further and further apart in the early eighteenth century. But material prosperity allowed both areas to pursue their happiness with increasing comfort and grace. No sooner were streets laid and houses erected than settlers put aside their drab homespun for colorful and elegant fashions from England and France. By the turn of the century, coffee houses, imitative of those in London, vied with taverns from Charleston to Boston as haunts of idleness. And as leisure increased, so did the variety of diversions—traveling shows and exhibits, clowns, mechanical marvels, cockfights, horse-racing, hunting and fishing, waxworks, and gaming. Those who could afford it, both North and South, fell into the extravagant habit of having their portraits painted by amateur limners. Silversmiths and goldsmiths, furniture-makers and jewelers found their works in constant demand, and by 1716 even Boston had its own bold dancing master. In short, by the second quarter of the eighteenth century, the rude and rugged way of the frontier had practically disappeared from America's major towns. In its place stood a charming, sophisticated life undreamed of in the philosophies of John Smith and William Bradford.

Intellectual and Literary Activity

Largely because of their closer social and economic connections, more highly organized political system, and reasonably good network of roads, the New England colonies developed a distinctive intellectual life much more quickly than the southern colonies. New England's emphasis on learning was closely connected with its religious commitment. The bedrock of the Reformation was its insistence that the faith upon which the salvation of every individual depended was available through the scriptures. Since to "search the scriptures" one had to be able to read, illiteracy was a tool of Satan. Moreover, saving grace came not through miraculous or supernatural means, but through "hearing the word preached." To hear the word intelligently, churchgoers were encouraged to follow the carefully organized delivery of the preacher, to scribble down outlines of his sermons, and to discuss them after meeting with family and neighbors. All this required a high degree of literacy, and much of our knowledge of early American preaching comes from the shorthand notes of avid listeners. Also, New England had from the beginning as great a percentage of university-trained men in proportion to its population as Old England, a fact that encouraged intellectual pursuits. The deep respect in which these Calvinists held learning promoted their desire to maintain a learned ministry and accounts for the promptness with which they established schools and a university, gathered private libraries, and circulated books.

Preaching, of course, forced men to write, but while sermons flowed from their quills, New Englanders turned to other kinds of literary production as well. As early as 1636 plans were under way to turn the Psalms of David into English verse, attending "conscience rather than elegance, fidelity rather than poetry," and early in 1639 Governor John Winthrop noted in his journal that "a printing house was begun at Cambridge by one [Stephen] Day, at the charge of Mr. Glover, who died on sea hitherward. The first thing which was printed was the freeman's oath; the next was an almanac made for New England by Mr. William Pierce, mariner; the next was the Psalms newly turned into meter." This press, even though strictly regulated by the College and by the General Court, immediately groaned under the multitude of informative and edifying works submitted for publication. It was 1681 before a printing press appeared in Virginia, and that was immediately suppressed. In 1683 Virginians were instructed to "allow no person to use a printing press on any occasion whatsoever," and Virginia's lone printing house did not even get started until 1729. There was probably greater need for New Englanders to write: their arguments about theology and church government needed statement and distribution; bothersome differences between the New England Way and English expectations required explanation; and after the revolution of 1642, when victorious English Puritans accused their colonial brethren of deserting the glorious cause by escaping to America, New Englanders wrote to defend their actions. The surprising thing is not that so much was written and printed in the colonies during the seventeenth century, but that out of all the literary activity there grew no great book.

There are probably two reasons for this, neither of which detracts from the intellectual capability or the literary sophistication of colonial writers. In the first place, in keeping with the utilitarian, polemical, and didactic nature of the documents they produced, their style was plain, perspicuous, and (as they liked to say) "spiritual." Its ideals were clarity, logical consistency, general intelligibility, and decorum, and except for the crabbed wit of Nathaniel Ward and the later pomposities of Cotton Mather, early American writing avoided the current fads of Senecan curtness and Ciceronian elaboration. In this the Puritan plain style looked forward to the scientific style idealized by London's Royal Society, described by Bishop Sprat as "a close, naked, natural" style—and admirably adapted to American purposes by Benjamin Franklin. Second, most seventeenth-century colonial writings were occasional, designed to speak to specific problems at particular times. Thus they never display the comprehensive sweep of ideas that marks great books, nor does any single volume synthesize the variety and breadth of colonial thought. Each work stands like a stone in an elaborate building—structurally necessary, sturdy, often interesting in itself, but no real clue to the nature or meaning of the whole structure.

Early New England writing looked two ways simultaneously: outward toward the experience of building a new land, and inward toward the emotional and spiritual life of the individual. Biographies, histories, accounts of exploration, funeral sermons, and elegies expressed the one; autobiographies, diaries, and meditations, the other. William Bradford's consciously constructed *Of Plymouth Plantation* was no simple chronicle of daily events, but a selective and carefully arranged interpretation of the colonial experience coupled with a remarkable awareness of the historical significance of the great new American adventure. To stir emulation and to maintain respect for the worthies of New England, ministers wrote little biographies celebrating the public virtues and private spirituality of eminent divines and magistrates, heedful to point out that godliness often paved the road to public prominence. Sensational accounts of adventures among the Indians, featuring massacres, flights over torturous terrain, horrible torments, and the final joy of returning to civilization, were so popular that they were being issued in anthologies before the end of the seventeenth century. Cotton Mather's ambitious *Magnalia Christi Americana,* so large it had to be sent to London for publication in 1702, incorporated most of the established literary forms, revealing what was implicit in them from the beginning—that this was a literature designed to build saintly heroes and to trace God's support of New England's holy experiment by the favor He showed its individuals. Indeed, from its beginnings, American literature is an individualistic literature, designed to explore the passions and emotions (an aspect of the Puritan character often overlooked) as well as to recount the rigors of life in the wilderness.

When the Puritan turned inward, emphasizing the spiritual, devotional side of his religious experience, his writing tended to become less a part of his distinctly American experience and to partake more fully of the Western, Christian literary tradition. The poetic meditations of Edward Taylor, America's finest seventeenth-century poet, and the prose-poem passages of Jonathan Edwards gain their literary eminence at the same time they cast off their American significance. The amazing thing about colonial literary art as a whole is not, however, that it occasionally achieves real poetic excellence, but that poetry or verse is so dominant.

Theoretically, poetry was to Puritans (as to most contemporary Englishmen and Europeans, no matter how sophisticated) a branch of rhetoric, and a very minor one at that. Like all rhetorical forms, its end was to persuade, and its primary function lay in the decorating or ornamenting of ideas. Similar views of the nature of poetry did not keep English and Continental poets from magnificent literary achievements, and one must not suppose that the Puritans' low view of poetry was peculiar to them or that they held any special animus toward poetry. For poetry—at least verse—is inescapable in colonial writing.

Five main kinds of verse writing predominated. First, writers who took the prevailing poetic theory literally were likely to produce "poems" constructed of rhymed statements whose function was merely to assist the reader's memory. An obvious example would be the *New England Primer*'s alphabet for children, running from "In Adam's Fall/ We sinned all" to "Zaccheus he/ Did climb the Tree/ His Lord to see." Such mnemonic verse was frequently included in histories and treatises to sum up at the ends of chapters. A second kind, closely related to the first, was the long didactic poem, more elaborate in thought and structure, such as Michael Wigglesworth's *The Day of Doom.* A third favorite was historical verse, intended not merely to teach, but to express an action too magnificent for prose (as in Captain Edward Johnson's *Wonder-Working Providence*), or to recount current events (as in Benjamin Tompson's *New England's Crisis*), or to celebrate the greatness of times past (as in Roger Wolcott's outright epic on the founding of Connecticut). A fourth type was the funeral elegy, commemorating the deaths of prominent and obscure persons alike, and reminding readers of the brevity and purposefulness of life. These were printed broadside for distribution at the funeral service, incorporated into formal histories and biographies, as in Cotton Mather's *Magnalia,* or simply recorded in diaries, letter-books, and family papers. By and large, this commemorative verse is without poetic merit, but it provides some useful insights into Puritan emotional values, and occasionally flowers into excellence. Finally, there was the personal, reflective, meditative, and often lyrical poetry best illustrated by Anne Bradstreet and Edward Taylor.

There was, then, no prejudice against literary beauty among early New Englanders. Frivolity, however, was another matter. Ministers were often known for their conversational wit and urbane humor, but a favorable attitude toward such social graces did not extend to the production of literary forms like the novel or drama. French and occasionally English romances made their way to America well before 1700; an edition of John Bunyan's *Pilgrim's Progress* was printed in Boston in 1681, and in that same year *Guy of Warwick,* a pious medieval romance, was sold in Boston's bookstores. But for the most part the New Englander satisfied his natural appetite for fiction through a variety of modes not overtly fictional, each of which, however, contributed to the later development of the American novel. The sermon, for example, frequently offered character sketches, anecdotal exempla, and tales of remarkable providences, all designed to excite interest as well as to edify. The formal character sketches practiced in school also found their way to the pulpit and, in extended form, into biographies and histories. Where fact leaves off and fiction starts cannot be clearly seen. William Bradford and Edward Johnson obviously designed parts of their accounts for literary effect, freely feigning speeches and experimenting with character development. Confessions of faith or personal relations of conversion gave form, conflict, change of fortune, and stupendous consequences to the spiritual life; they could not have been heard without excitement and pleasure. The narrative of captivity, marked by a surprising sentimentality, by psychological probing, and, later, by pure sensationalism, duplicated in frontier reality the great struggles waged in the infinite world of spirit between Satan and the captive soul of man. The romance of a soul's rise from poverty to glorious riches enabled colonial writers to experiment with numerous literary devices, and one can easily see in colonial narratives the seeds of the frontier adventure story, the folk tale, the novel of sensibility, the allegorical romance, and the epistolary and Gothic techniques that came to fruition in the fiction of the late eighteenth and early nineteenth century.

When every natural phenomenon, every qualm of conscience, was assumed to be emblematic of the great dramatic struggle between good and evil, no formal dramatic literature seemed necessary to the early colonist. So, except for dialogues and debates worked into treatises and poems, and sometimes into histories, American literary drama did not develop until after the middle of the eighteenth century. In England, Puritans closed the theaters in 1642, partly because of the licentiousness of the plays, but more because of the social problems endemic to playhouses—the tradition of boys playing the parts of women, the low character of actors (who were lumped with vagabonds and rogues), and the tendency of playgoing to distract men from both business and godliness. This same attitude prevailed in New England. But it is also true, as Louis B. Wright has put it, that "the primary reason that drama did not flourish in seventeenth-century America was the simple fact that no towns were large enough to support theatrical entertainment." Traveling actors occasionally made their ways to the colonies, often to be turned away, and it was approximately 1716 before the first known playhouse was erected in the colonies at Williamsburg, Virginia. Philadelphia, New York, and Charleston all had theaters by the middle of the eighteenth century, though they showed English plays exclusively, and New England college students even presented plays designed to give them practice in Latin and Greek declamation. The first play to be written by a native American was Thomas Godfrey's *The Prince of Parthia*, published in 1765, two years after Godfrey's death; this was a bombastic blank-verse tragedy that strangely and sometimes effectively mingles Elizabethan and Restoration dramatic ideas. But drama did not gain acceptance until after the Revolution, and did not become a distinguished form of American literary art until the twentieth century.

On the whole, while the colonial period provided an excellent apprenticeship for American literature, its products were not of a very high order. The usual explanation—that Puritans were inveterately hostile to beauty and art—is, if not a fiction in itself, at least an oversimplification. The failure of American colonial writing to approach or equal the level of contemporary English or European literature is due rather to other factors. First, the American Puritans represented but one slice of English middle-class society, a class with no very impressive artistic attainments even in England at the time. In the colonies that class was completely removed from contact with the more cultured classes at home. We must remember that the first English settlers in America were born before the golden era of English writing, and that the colonial experience spanned the work of Spenser, Shakespeare, the metaphysical poets, Milton, Dryden, and Pope—a period during which American intellectual life was dominated by one class of people with one overriding concern. Second, the prevailing Calvinism of the American colonists, especially the New England Puritans, contributed to aesthetic barrenness in making art seem impotent if not irrelevant: God's beauty was all-sufficing, and works of nature and of art could be only weak reflections thereof. Moreover, many seventeenth-century Americans believed that the millennium—Christ's second coming—was imminent; with that event all the works of man would pass. This intense conviction of earthly transience further discouraged painstaking artistic creation and concern with form. Emphasis was on ideas and themes rather than on beauty of expression—a fact which may indeed account for the easy acceptance of English literary forms, themselves sometimes inconsistent with American ideas. And finally, Americans of the seventeenth century were simply too busy establishing themselves in the New World to develop and refine a literary culture.

The Decline of Puritanism

At what point the Puritan city upon a hill—and the dominant colonial culture it represented—began to be undermined is not clear. Isolated at first from foreign ideologies, its distinctive theology realized more fully in Massachusetts and Connecticut than anywhere else in the world, Puritanism stiffened into orthodoxy, crystallized, cracked, and began to flake away. The strength derived from adversity in England rigidified in New England to become a fatal defect. More than a religious creed, Puritanism was a way of life that organized all of man's activities, reducing all the arts and sciences to "handmaids" of Theology. As Clarence Faust has pointed out, the Puritan's emphasis on God's sovereignty—with its familiar image of God as a king—hardened into legalism and collapsed in the face of political and social change that everywhere weakened men's trust in monarchical principles. The power of God's providence over man, in the Puritan's view, made him a passive tool in an age when men were—in matters of faith, politics, and ethics—asserting their responsibility and independence; so counter did Calvinism run to eighteenth-century thought and sentiment, that it forced men to look elsewhere for their creeds. The Puritan's concept of an eternal, changeless, static God led him toward an ideal, eternal system of absolutes incapable of adjustment to the new science and the new logic of Descartes, Locke, and Newton. At the same time, the Puritan's emphasis on reason and his respect for human learning opened the door to skepticism, while his glorification of industry slipped almost imperceptibly down the road to materialism. By 1740 the old-fashioned Puritanism was dying, but it went through one last spasm called the Great Awakening.

Religious thought had grown more and more liberal in the last years of the seventeenth century, and many orthodox Calvinists learned to distrust the free-thinking ministers turned out by Harvard. By 1701 they were so dissatisfied that they founded a second college, called Yale, at New Haven, for the express purpose of producing orthodox Calvinist ministers. But "Arminianism," as all liberal thought came to be called, continued to increase. It was not so much that the new breed of ministers spoke against Calvinist doctrines; they simply ignored them, preaching more and more as if man's will were free and his actions had something to do with his salvation. Alarmed by such irresponsible talk, Jonathan Edwards turned aside from intellectual argument to preach a demonstration of the absolutely real and meaningful nature of Calvin's tenets. Preaching to the senses of his congregation, he vivified the consequences of election, damnation, and God's sovereign will, and pictured the depraved condition of their own unconverted souls in such graphic detail that his hearers fell—some literally—before the excitement of his preaching. In 1734 and 1735 his intense sermons brought some to God, many to hysteria, still others to madness and even suicide.

By 1736 Edwards began to moderate his preaching, but religious emotionalism surged up once more when the Reverend George Whitefield, a young English evangelist who had been preaching through the South, arrived in New England in 1740. His intense spirituality and brilliant oratory pierced hardened hearts and melted the religious affections of countless souls as he left a trail of evangelical fire from Georgia to Massachusetts, even joining Edwards for one successful tour. Galleries were packed with hysterical listeners, and a grandstand in Boston collapsed, killing five. Whitefield was succeeded by raving James Davenport, who tore off his clothes as he preached, and by dozens of other itinerant preachers distinguished only by their wild enthusiasm.

By 1745 the Great Awakening was over, but its effects were permanent. Under the lash of its evangelical emotionalism, thirty to forty thousand converts flooded the churches, most of them either distrustful or actively critical of the orthodox clergy whose over-intellectualism and laxity, they believed, had brought religion to its sorry state. Congregations split, church authority and unity almost disappeared, and the range of differences was so great that traditional New England Puritanism was barely recognizable.

The divisions of the Great Awakening drove many people into non-Congregational churches—Anglican, Quaker, Baptist, and Methodist—and also opened the way for the rational religion called "deism," which appeared in America during the latter half of the eighteenth century. Deism served the needs of some of the intellectual, philosophically minded men of the period, but Unitarianism, a somewhat less radical form of religious rationalism, attracted more support. Like the early deists, liberal Congregationalists emphasized the trustworthiness of human reason and moral conscience, but they relied more heavily on the revelations of the Bible, squaring revelation with reason when they could. Because they emphasized the "unity" of God, they were sometimes called "Unitarians," though they did not (until 1826) form a separate church. As the "Unitarian" group developed its theology, it came into greater conflict with traditional Calvinism; it denied Christ's divinity and the whole concept of trinitarianism; it emphasized ethical and humanitarian action as the center of religious worship; and it affirmed man's potential for achieving perfection. Unitarianism, in effect, pointed the way to American Transcendentalism.

When in 1832 Ralph Waldo Emerson surrendered his Unitarian ministry to strike his own original relationship with the universe, he did so from the pulpit of Boston's Second Church, the same pulpit that once held Increase and Cotton Mather. As the impulse that gave seventeenth-century America its most elaborate and distinctive culture, and as a formal movement of serious significance in American life, Puritanism was dead, but its elements were deeply infused into American life and thought.

An Elizabethan Adventurer

JOHN SMITH [1580-1631]

THE SPIRIT OF ADVENTURE and the dreams of wealth, glory, and betterment that characterized the Elizabethan expansion are typified in the life and writings of John Smith. Born in Lincolnshire and raised to trade, young Smith found mercantile life unendurably dull. By his own account, he ran away at fifteen to become a soldier of fortune, spending ten years in Europe and the Near East, years of great trial, marvelous adventure, and high accomplishment—though his veracity is not beyond doubt.

But there is no doubt that he joined the first group of colonists bound for Jamestown in 1607, that he played a major role in holding the colony together by strong leadership and uncompromising discipline, that he went back to England in 1609, returned to America in 1614 on a voyage of exploration to New England, was captured and briefly imprisoned by the French, and thereafter lived out a quiet life in England.

To John Smith, America was an opportunity for England to recapture a golden age of chivalric heroism, to gain great wealth, to frustrate the political ambitions of Catholic Spain, to ease poverty, unemployment, and juvenile delinquency at home, and to bring honor and glory to the English throne. In this heroic context he tirelessly worked and wrote. His various promotional writings, particularly *A True Relation of . . . Virginia* (1608), *A Map of Virginia* (1612), *A Description of New England* (1616), *The General History of Virginia* (1624), and *The True Travels, Adventures, and Observations of Captain John Smith* (1630), form the first substantial body of literature done in and about America.

From a literary point of view, Smith's fabulous and perhaps questionable story of his capture by Powhatan and rescue by Pocahontas may be his most significant contribution. Not only did it supply an enduring and charming legend to American folklore, it marked the beginning of a genre of "captivity" narratives that would have great popularity in the seventeenth and eighteenth centuries as "true adventures," and put its stamp on the historical fiction of the early nineteenth century as well as on the modern Western.

Further reading: *Travels and Works,* ed. E. Arber, 1910. Bradford Smith, *Captain John Smith,* 1953.

FROM *The General History of Virginia*

Smith gave the events he wrote about an egotistic coloring and often a dramatic heightening. In *A True Relation* he had represented Powhatan as uniformly friendly and made no mention of a rescue by an Indian princess. But here, in the *General History,* he puts Powhatan in a very different light, and introduces the Pocahontas episode, of which everyone has heard though few have known it in the original telling. In time it became a favorite bit of American legend adapted by various writers in poetry, fiction, and drama.

Pocahontas married an English gentleman, John Rolfe, went to England with him in the year of Shakespeare's death, and was well received by people and court. Before she reached London, Smith wrote the episode in a petition in her behalf addressed to Queen Anne. Pocahontas died the next year, and later Smith inserted the episode in his *General History.*

Text: Edward Arber, ed., *Travels and Works of Captain John Smith* (2nd edition; Edinburgh, 1910), II, 395-401.

[The Captivity]

But our comedies never endured long without a tragedy; some idle exceptions being muttered against Captain Smith, for not discovering the head of Chickahamania River, and taxed by the Council, to be too slow in so worthy an attempt. The next voyage he proceeded so far, that with much labor by cutting of trees in sunder he made his passage; but when his barge could pass no farther, he left her in a broad bay out of danger of shot, commanding none should go ashore till his return. Himself with two English and two salvages went up higher in a canoe; but he was not long absent, but his men went ashore, whose want of government, gave both occasion and opportunity to the salvages to surprise one George Casson, whom they slew, and much failed not to have cut off the boat and all the rest. Smith, little dreaming of that accident, being got to the marshes at the river's head, twenty miles in the desert, had his two men slain (as is supposed) sleeping by the canoe, whilest himself by fowling sought them victual: who finding he was beset with 200 salvages, two of them he slew, still defending himself with the aid of a salvage his guide, whom he bound to his arm with his garters, and used him as a buckler, yet he was shot in his thigh a little and had many arrows that stuck in his clothes but no great hurt, till at last they took him prisoner. When this news came to Jamestown, much was their sorrow for his loss, few expecting what ensued. Six or seven weeks those barbarians kept him prisoner, many strange triumphs and conjurations they made of him, yet he so demeaned himself amongst them, as he not only diverted them from surprising the fort, but procured his own liberty, and got himself and his company such estimation amongst them, that those salvages admired him more than their own Quiyouckosucks. The manner how they used and delivered him is as follows.

The salvages having drawn from George Casson whither Captain Smith was gone, prosecuting that opportunity they followed him with 300 bowmen, conducted by the King of Pamaunkee, who in divisions searching the turnings of the river, found Robinson and Emry by the fireside: those they shot full of arrows and slew. Then finding the captain as is said, that used the salvage that was his guide as his shield (three of them being slain and divers other so galled) all the rest would not come near him. Thinking thus to have returned to his boat, regarding them, as he marched more then his way, slipped up to the middle in an oozy creek and his salvage with him; yet durst they not come to him, till, being near dead with cold, he threw away his arms. Then according to their composition they drew him forth and led him to the fire, where his men were slain. Diligently they chafed his benumbed limbs.

He demanding for their captain, they shewed him Opechankanough, King of Pamaunkee, to whom he gave a round ivory double compass dial. Much they marveled at the playing of the fly and needle, which they could see so plainly, and yet not touch it, because of the glass that covered them. But when he demonstrated by that globe-like jewel, the roundness of the earth, and skies, the sphere of the sun, moon, and stars, and how the sun did chase the night round about the world continually; the greatness of the land and sea, the diversity of nations, variety of complections, and how we were to them antipodes, and many other such like matters, they all stood as amazed with admiration. Notwithstanding, within an hour after, they tied him to a tree, and as many as could stand about him prepared to shoot him, but the king holding up the compass in his hand, they all laid down their bows and arrows, and in a triumphant manner led him to Orapaks, where he was after their manner kindly feasted, and well used.

Their order in conducting him was thus; drawing themselves all in file, the king in the middest had all their pieces and swords borne before him. Captain Smith was led after him by three great salvages, holding him fast by each arm: and on each side six went in file with their arrows nocked. But arriving at the town (which was but only thirty or forty hunting houses made of mats, which they remove as they please, as we our tents) all the women and children staring to behold him, the soldiers first all in file performed the form of a bissone[1] so well as could be; and on each flank, officers as sergeants to see them keep their orders. A good time they continued this exercise, and then cast themselves in a ring, dancing in such several postures, and singing and yelling out such hellish notes and screeches; being strangely painted, every one his quiver of arrows, and at his back a club; on his arm a fox or an otter's skin, or some such matter for his vambrace;[2] their heads and shoulders painted red, with oil and pocones[3] mingled together, which scarlet-like color made an exceeding handsome shew; his bow in his hand, and the skin of a bird with her wings abroad dried, tied on his head, a piece of copper, a white shell, a long feather, with a small rattle growing at the tails of their snakes tied to it, or some such like toy. All this while Smith and the king stood in the middest guarded, as before is said, and after three

[1] A military formation.

[2] Defensive armor for the forearm.

[3] Bloodroot.

dances they all departed. Smith they conducted to a long house, where thirty or forty tall fellows did guard him; and ere long more bread and venison was brought him then would have served twenty men. I think his stomach at that time was not very good; what he left they put in baskets and tied over his head. About midnight they set the meat again before him, all this time not one of them would eat a bit with him, till the next morning they brought him as much more, and then did they eat all the old, and reserved the new as they had done the other, which made him think they would fat him to eat him. Yet in this desperate estate to defend him from the cold, one Maocassater brought him his gown, in requital of some beads and toys Smith had given him at his first arrival in Virginia.

Two days after, a man would have slain him (but that the guard prevented it) for the death of his son, to whom they conducted him to recover the poor man then breathing his last. Smith told them that at Jamestown he had a water would do it, if they would let him fetch it, but they would not permit that; but made all the preparations they could to assault Jamestown, craving his advice; and for recompense he should have life, liberty, land, and women. In part of a table book he writ his mind to them at the fort, what was intended, how they should follow that direction to affright the messengers, and without fail send him such things as he writ for. And an inventory with them. The difficulty and danger, he told the salvages, of the mines, great guns, and other engines exceedingly affrighted them, yet according to his request they went to Jamestown, in as bitter weather as could be of frost and snow, and within three days returned with an answer.

But when they came to Jamestown, seeing men sally out as he had told them they would, they fled; yet in the night they came again to the same place where he had told them they should receive an answer, and such things as he had promised them, which they found accordingly, and with which they returned with no small expedition, to the wonder of them all that heard it, that he could either divine, or the paper could speak. Then they led him to the Youthtanunds, the Mattapanients, the Payankatanks, the Nantaughtacunds, and Onawmanients upon the rivers of Rapahanock, and Patawomek, over all those rivers, and back again by divers other several nations, to the king's habitation at Pamaunkee, where they entertained him with most strange and fearful conjurations;

As if near led to hell,
Amongst the devils to dwell.

Not long after, early in a morning a great fire was made in a long house, and a mat spread on the one side, as on the other; on the one they caused him to sit, and all the guard went out of the house, and presently came skipping in a great grim fellow, all painted over with coal, mingled with oil; and many snakes and weasels' skins stuffed with moss, and all their tails tied together, so as they met on the crown of his head in a tassel; and round about the tassel was a coronet of feathers, the skins hanging round about his head, back, and shoulders, and in a manner covered his face; with a hellish voice, and a rattle in his hand. With most strange gestures and passions he began his invocation, and environed the fire with a circle of meal; which done, three more such like devils came rushing in with the like antic tricks, painted half black, half red: but all their eyes were painted white, and some red strokes like mutchatos,[4] along their cheeks: round about him those fiends danced a pretty while, and then came in three more as ugly as the rest; with red eyes, and white strokes over their black faces; at last they all sat down right against him; three of them on the one hand of the chief priest, and three on the other. Then all with their rattles began a song, which ended, the chief priest laid down five wheat corns: then straining his arms and hands with such violence that he sweat, and his veins swelled, he began a short oration: at the conclusion they all gave a short groan; and then laid down three grains more. After that, began their song again, and then another oration, ever laying down so many corns as before, till they had twice encircled the fire; that done, they took a bunch of little sticks prepared for that purpose, continuing still their devotion, and at the end of every song and oration, they laid down a stick betwixt the divisions of corn. Till night, neither he nor they did either eat or drink, and then they feasted merrily, with the best provisions they could make. Three days they used this ceremony; the meaning whereof they told him, was to know if he intended them well or no. The circle of meal signified their country, the circles of corn the bounds of the sea, and the sticks his country. They imagined the world to be flat and round, like a trencher, and they in the middest. After this they brought him a bag of gunpowder, which they carefully preserved till the next spring, to plant as they did their corn; because they would be acquainted with the nature of that seed.

Opitchapam the king's brother invited him to his house, where, with as many platters of bread, fowl, and wild beasts, as did environ him, he bid him

[4] Mustachios.

welcome; but not any of them would eat a bit with him, but put up all the remainder in baskets. At his return to Opechankanough's, all the king's women, and their children, flocked about him for their parts, as a due by custom, to be merry with such fragments.

> But his waking mind in hideous dreams did oft see
> wondrous shapes,
> Of bodies strange, and huge in growth, and of
> stupendious makes.

At last they brought him to Meronocomo, where was Powhatan, their emperor. Here more then two hundred of those grim courtiers stood wondering at him, as he had been a monster; till Powhatan and his train had put themselves in their greatest braveries. Before a fire upon a seat like a bedstead, he sat covered with a great robe, made of rarowcun[5] skins, and all the tails hanging by. On either hand did sit a young wench of sixteen or eighteen years, and along on each side the house, two rows of men, and behind them as many women, with all their heads and shoulders painted red; many of their heads bedecked with the white down of birds; but everyone with something: and a great chain of white beads about their necks. At his entrance before the king, all the people gave a great shout. The Queen of Appamatuck was appointed to bring him water to wash his hands, and another brought him a bunch of feathers, instead of a towel, to dry them. Having feasted him after their best barbarous manner they could, a long consultation was held, but the conclusion was, two great stones were brought before Powhatan: then as many as could laid hands on him, dragged him to them, and thereon laid his head, and being ready with their clubs, to beat out his brains, Pocahontas, the king's dearest daughter, when no entreaty could prevail, got his head in her arms, and laid her own upon his to save him from death: whereat the emperor was contented he should live to make him hatchets, and her bells, beads, and copper; for they thought him as well of all occupations as themselves. For the king himself will make his own robes, shoes, bows, arrows, pots; plant, hunt, or do anything so well as the rest.

> They say he bore a pleasant shew,
> But sure his heart was sad.
> For who can pleasant be, and rest,
> That lives in fear and dread:
> And having life suspected, doth
> It still suspected lead.

Two days after, Powhatan, having disguised himself in the most fearful manner he could, caused Captain Smith to be brought forth to a great house in the woods, and there upon a mat by the fire to be left alone. Not long after, from behind a mat that divided the house, was made the most dolefullest noise he ever heard; then Powhatan, more like a devil then a man, with some two hundred more as black as himself, came unto him and told him now they were friends, and presently he should go to Jamestown, to send him two great guns, and a grindstone, for which he would give him the country of Capahowosick, and forever esteem him as his son Nantaquoud. So to Jamestown with twelve guides Powhatan sent him. That night they quartered in the woods, he still expecting (as he had done all this long time of his imprisonment) every hour to be put to one death or other: for all their feasting. But almighty God (by His divine providence) had mollified the hearts of those stern barbarians with compassion. The next morning betimes they came to the fort, where Smith, having used the salvages with what kindness he could, he shewed Rawhunt, Powhatan's trusty servant, two demi-culverings and a millstone to carry Powhatan: they found them somewhat too heavy; but when they did see him discharge them, being loaded with stones, among the boughs of a great tree loaded with icicles, the ice and branches came so tumbling down, that the poor salvages ran away half dead with fear. But at last we regained some conference with them, and gave them such toys; and sent to Powhatan, his women, and children such presents, as gave them in general full content.

1624

[5] Raccoon.

WILLIAM BRADFORD [1590–1657]

"Of Plymouth Plantation, and first of the occasion and inducements thereunto, the which that I may truly unfold, I must begin at the very root and rise of the same. The which I shall endeavor to manifest in a plain style, with singular regard unto the simple truth in all things, at least as near as my slender judgment can attain the same." So in 1630 did William Bradford begin the history he would write until 1650, as he looked back on the events of two decades and more that brought Plymouth colony to a modest prosperity.

No one was in a better position to write that history. Born in Yorkshire, Bradford was raised in the company of Separatists that gathered at the home of William Brewster: religious purists whose consciences would not permit them to participate in the rites and services of the Church of England. He was with the party of Separatists that left England for Holland in 1609, and despite his relative youth, became one of its most respected leaders. Dissatisfied with Dutch surroundings, fearing disintegration as older members of the society died and youths grew into non-English ways, Bradford was one of several who urged emigration to America and helped arrange the voyage of the *Mayflower.* Shortly after the landing in 1620, Governor John Carver died; Bradford was chosen to succeed him, and for the next thirty years, as judge, treasurer, and governor he selflessly directed the colony's fortunes in war, diplomacy, and business.

Bradford's "simple truth" derived from a sense of history embedded in John Foxe's enormously popular *Actes and Monuments.* Seeing the Separatists as the people chosen of God to carry His truth ever westward in what Foxe called an age of "trial and travail," Bradford sought to demonstrate America's manifest destiny by the careful selection of events and the conscious manipulation of a plain, dignified, unpretentious, and often very gripping style. The ruling purpose of illustrating God's providence toward the American venture reveals not only the Puritan's concept of history, but the color of almost day-to-day events: the disturbing presence of wild spirits such as Thomas Morton, the massacre of the Pequot Indians, the negotiations with Dutch and French governors of other settlements, even the scandalous outbreak of sin during the very year in which Nathaniel Hawthorne set Hester Prynne to face her judgment from the scaffold in the Boston marketplace.

Bradford's manuscript was not immediately published, though it was used by such colonial historians as Nathaniel Morton, Cotton Mather, Thomas Prince, and Thomas Hutchinson. During the British occupation of Boston in the Revolutionary War, the manuscript disappeared, and did not come to light again until 1855—in the library of the Bishop of London. The complete work was thereupon printed for the first time, in 1856, and the manuscript was returned to America in 1897.

Further reading: *Of Plymouth Plantation,* ed. S. E. Morison, 1952. Bradford Smith, *Bradford of Plymouth,* 1951. E. F. Bradford, "Conscious Art in Bradford's History of Plymouth Plantation," *New England Quarterly,* April 1928.

FROM *Of Plymouth Plantation*

A long introduction concerns the departure of the Separatists from England, their life for more than a decade in Holland, the decision to remove to America, the voyage in the *Mayflower*, and the landing. The main body of the work is in the form of annals, recording the history of the colony from the settlement of 1620 through the year 1646. By 1692, Plymouth lost its separate identity and was absorbed into Massachusetts; but as early as 1630 Bradford had sensed that his Pilgrims "should be but even as stepping-stones unto others for the performing of so great a work." Text: William Bradford, *History of Plymouth Plantation 1620-1647*, ed. W. C. Ford (Boston, 1912).

[Arrival]

[1620] But to omit other things (that I may be brief), after long beating at sea they fell with that land which is called Cape Cod; the which being made and certainly known to be it, they were not a little joyful. After some deliberation had amongst themselves and with the master of the ship, they tacked about and resolved to stand for the southward (the wind and weather being fair) to find some place about Hudson's River for their habitation. But after they had sailed that course about half the day, they fell amongst dangerous shoals and roaring breakers, and they were so far entangled therewith as they conceived themselves in great danger; and the wind shrinking upon them withal, they resolved to bear up again for the Cape and thought themselves happy to get out of those dangers before night overtook them, as by God's good providence they did. And the next day they got into the cape harbor where they rid in safety. * * *

Being thus arrived in a good harbor, and brought safe to land, they fell upon their knees and blessed the God of heaven who had brought them over the vast and furious ocean, and delivered them from all the perils and miseries thereof, again to set their feet on the firm and stable earth, their proper element. And no marvel if they were thus joyful, seeing wise Seneca was so affected with sailing a few miles on the coast of his own Italy, as he affirmed,[1] that he had rather remain twenty years on his way by land then pass by sea to any place in a short time, so tedious and dreadful was the same unto him.

But here I cannot but stay and make a pause, and stand half amazed at this poor people's present condition; and so I think will the reader, too, when he well considers the same. Being thus passed the vast ocean, and a sea of troubles before in their preparation (as may be remembered by that which went before), they had now no friends to welcome them nor inns to entertain or refresh their weatherbeaten bodies; no houses or much less towns to repair to, to seek for succor. It is recorded in scripture, as a mercy to the Apostle and his shipwrecked company, that the barbarians shewed them no small kindness in refreshing them,[2] but these savage barbarians, when they met with them (as after will appear), were readier to fill their sides full of arrows then otherwise. And for the season it was winter, and they that know the winters of that country know them to be sharp and violent, and subject to cruel and fierce storms, dangerous to travel to known places, much more to search an unknown coast. Besides, what could they see but a hideous and desolate wilderness, full of wild beasts and wild men—and what multitudes there might be of them they knew not. Neither could they, as it were, go up to the top of Pisgah[3] to view from this wilderness a more goodly country to feed their hopes; for which way soever they turned their eyes (save upward to the heavens) they could have little solace or content in respect of any outward objects. For summer being done, all things stand upon them with a weatherbeaten face, and the whole country, full of woods and thickets, represented a wild and savage hue. If they looked behind them, there was the mighty ocean which they had passed and was now as a main bar and gulf to separate them from all the civil parts of the world. If it be said they had a ship to succor them, it is true; but what heard they daily from the master and company? But that with speed they should look out a place (with their shallop) where they would be, at some near distance; for the season was such as he would not stir from thence till a safe harbor was discovered by them, where they would be, and he might go without danger; and that victuals consumed apace but he must and would keep sufficient for themselves and their return. Yea, it was muttered by some that if they got not a place in time, they would turn them and their goods ashore and leave them. Let it also be considered what weak hopes of supply and succor they left behind them, that might bear up their minds in this sad condition and trials they were under; and they could not but be very small. It is true, indeed, the affections and love of their brethren at Leyden was cordial and entire towards them, but they had little power to help them or themselves; and how the case stood between them and the merchants at their coming away hath already been declared. What could now sustain them but the Spirit of God and His grace? May not and ought not the children of these fathers rightly say: "Our fathers were Englishmen which came over this great ocean, and were ready to perish in this wilderness; but they cried

[1] Epistle 53 [*ad Lucilium Epistulae Morales;* Bradford's note].

[2] Acts xxviii.2.

[3] The mountain from which Moses viewed the promised land; Deut. xxxiv.1.

unto the Lord, and He heard their voice and looked on their adversity," etc. "Let them therefore praise the Lord, because He is good: and His mercies endure forever." "Yea, let them which have been redeemed of the Lord, shew how He hath delivered them from the hand of the oppressor. When they wandered in the desert wilderness out of the way, and found no city to dwell in, both hungry and thirsty, their soul was overwhelmed in them. Let them confess before the Lord His loving-kindness and His wonderful works before the sons of men."

[The Mayflower Compact]

[1620] I shall a little return back, and begin with a combination made by them before they came ashore; being the first foundation of their government in this place. Occasioned partly by the discontented and mutinous speeches that some of the strangers[4] amongst them had let fall from them in the ship, that when they came ashore they would use their own liberty, for none had power to command them, the patent they had being for Virginia and not for New England, which belonged to another government, with which the Virginia Company had nothing to do. And partly that such an act by them done, this their condition considered, might be as firm as any patent, and in some respects more sure.

The form was as followeth:

In the name of God, Amen. We whose names are underwritten, the loyal subjects of our dread sovereign lord, King James, by the grace of God of Great Britain, France, and Ireland, king, defender of the faith, etc.

Having undertaken, for the glory of God and advancement of the Christian faith and honor of our king and country, a voyage to plant the first colony in the northern parts of Virginia, do by these presents solemnly and mutually in the presence of God and one of another, covenant and combine ourselves together into a civil body politic, for our better ordering and preservation and furtherance of the ends aforesaid; and by virtue hereof to enact, constitute, and frame such just and equal laws, ordinances, acts, constitutions, and offices, from time to time, as shall be thought most meet and convenient for the general good of the colony, unto which we promise all due submission and obedience. In witness whereof we have hereunder subscribed our names at Cape Cod, the 11th of November, in the year of the reign of our sovereign lord, King James, of England, France and Ireland the eighteenth, and of Scotland the fifty-fourth. *Anno Domini* 1620.

[4] Persons not of the Scrooby-Leyden Separatist group, but "from London and other places," who were added to the *Mayflower* company at the insistence of the financial backers of the enterprise.

After this they chose, or rather confirmed, Mr. John Carver (a man godly and well approved amongst them) their governor for that year. * * *

[Survival]

[1621] They now began to dispatch the ship away which brought them over, which lay till about this time, or the beginning of April. The reason on their part why she stayed so long, was the necessity and danger that lay upon them; for it was well towards the end of December before she could land anything here, or they able to receive anything ashore. Afterwards, the 14th of January, the house which they had made for a general rendezvous by casualty fell afire, and some were fain to retire aboard for shelter; then the sickness began to fall sore amongst them, and the weather so bad as they could not make much sooner any dispatch. Again, the Governor and chief of them, seeing so many die and fall down sick daily, thought it no wisdom to send away the ship, their condition considered and the danger they stood in from the Indians, till they could procure some shelter; and therefore thought it better to draw some more charge upon themselves and friends than hazard all. The master and seamen likewise, though before they hasted the passengers ashore to be gone, now many of their men being dead, and of the ablest of them (as is before noted), and of the rest many lay sick and weak; the master durst not put to sea till he saw his men begin to recover, and the heart of winter over.

Afterwards they (as many as were able) began to plant their corn, in which service Squanto stood them in great stead, showing them both the manner how to set it, and after how to dress and tend it. Also he told them, except they got fish and set with it in these old grounds it would come to nothing. And he showed them that in the middle of April they should have store enough come up the brook by which they began to build, and taught them how to take it, and where to get other provisions necessary for them. All which they found true by trial and experience. Some English seed they sowed, as wheat and pease, but it came not to good, either by the badness of the seed or lateness of the season or both, or some other defect.

In this month of April, whilst they were busy about their seed, their Governor (Mr. John Carver) came out of the field very sick, it being a hot day. He complained greatly of his head and lay down, and within a few hours his senses failed, so as he never spake more till he died, which was within a few days after. Whose death was much lamented and caused great heaviness amongst them, as there was cause. He was buried in the best manner they could, with some volleys of shot by all that bore arms. And his wife, being a weak woman, died within five or six weeks after him.

Shortly after, William Bradford was chosen Governor in his stead, and being not recovered of his illness, in which he had been near the point of death, Isaac Allerton was chosen to be an assistant unto him who, by renewed election every year, continued sundry years together. Which I here note once for all.

May 12 was the first marriage in this place which, according to the laudable custom of the Low Countries, in which they had lived, was thought most requisite to be performed by the magistrate, as being a civil thing, upon which many questions about inheritances do depend, with other things most proper to their cognizance and most consonant to the Scriptures (Ruth iv) and nowhere found in the Gospel to be laid on the ministers as a part of their office.* * *

They began now to gather in the small harvest they had, and to fit up their houses and dwellings against winter, being all well recovered in health and strength and had all things in good plenty. For as some were thus employed in affairs abroad, others were exercised in fishing, about cod and bass and other fish, of which they took good store, of which every family had their portion. All the summer there was no want; and now began to come in store of fowl, as winter approached, of which this place did abound when they came first (but afterward decreased by degrees). And besides waterfowl there was great store of wild turkeys, of which they took many, besides venison, etc. Besides they had about a peck of meal a week to a person, or now since harvest, Indian corn to that proportion. Which made many afterwards write so largely of their plenty here to their friends in England, which were not feigned but true reports. * * *

[1623] All this while no supply was heard of, neither knew they when they might expect any. So they began to think how they might raise as much corn as they could, and obtain a better crop than they had done, that they might not still thus languish in misery. At length, after much debate of things, the Governor (with the advice of the chiefest amongst them) gave way that they should set corn every man for his own particular, and in that regard trust to themselves; in all other things to go on in the general way as before. And so assigned to every family a parcel of land, according to the proportion of their number, for that end, only for present use (but made no division for inheritance) and ranged all boys and youth under some family. This had very good success, for it made all hands very industrious, so as much more corn was planted than otherwise would have been by any means the Governor or any other could use, and saved him a great deal of trouble, and gave far better content. The women now went willingly into the field, and took their little ones with them to set corn; which before would allege weakness and inability; whom to have compelled would have been thought great tyranny and oppression.

The experience that was had in this common course and condition, tried sundry years and that amongst godly and sober men, may well evince the vanity of that conceit of Plato's and other ancients applauded by some of later times; that the taking away of property and bringing in community into a commonwealth would make them happy and flourishing; as if they were wiser than God. For this community (so far as it was) was found to breed much confusion and discontent and retard much employment that would have been to their benefit and comfort. For the young men, that were most able and fit for labour and service, did repine that they should spend their time and strength to work for other men's wives and children without any recompense. The strong, or man of parts, had no more in division of victuals and clothes than he that was weak and not able to do a quarter the other could; this was thought injustice. The aged and graver men to be ranked and equalized in labours and victuals, clothes, etc., with the meaner and younger sort, thought it some indignity and disrespect unto them. And for men's wives to be commanded to do service for other men, as dressing their meat, washing their clothes, etc., they deemed it a kind of slavery, neither could many husbands well brook it. Upon the point all being to have alike, and all to do alike, they thought themselves in the like condition, and one as good as another; and so, if it did not cut off those relations that God hath set amongst men, yet it did at least much diminish and take off the mutual respects that should be preserved amongst them. And would have been worse if they had been men of another condition. Let none object this is men's corruption, and nothing to the course itself. I answer, seeing all men have this corruption in them, God in His wisdom saw another course fitter for them.

[Morton of Merry Mount]

[1628] Hitherto the Indians of these parts had no pieces nor other arms but their bows and arrows, nor of many years after; neither durst they scarce handle a gun, so much were they afraid of them; and the very sight of one (though out of kilter) was a terror unto them. But those Indians to the east parts, which had commerce with the French, got pieces of them, and they in the end made a common trade of it; and in time our English fishermen, led with the like covetousness, followed their example for their own gain; but upon complaint against them, it pleased the King's Majesty to prohibit the same by a strict proclamation, commanding that no sort of arms or munition should by any of his subjects be traded with them.

About some three or four years before this time, there came over one Captain Wollaston (a man of pretty parts), and with him three or four more of some eminency, who brought with them a great many servants with provisions and other implements for to begin a plantation; and pitched themselves in a place within the Massachusetts, which they called, after their captain's name, Mount Wollaston. Amongst whom was one Mr. Morton, who, it should seem, had some small adventure (of his own or other men's) amongst them, but had little respect amongst them, and was slighted by the meanest servants. Having continued there some time, and not finding things to answer their expectations, nor profit to arise as they looked for, Captain Wollaston takes a great part of the servants, and transports them to Virginia, where he puts them off at good rates, selling their time to other men; and writes back to one Mr. Rasdall, one of his chief partners, and accounted their merchant, to bring another part of them to Virginia likewise, intending to put them off there as he had done the rest. And he, with the consent of the said Rasdall, appointed one Fitcher to be his lieutenant and govern the remains of the plantation till he or Rasdall returned to take further order thereabout. But this Morton abovesaid, having more craft then honesty (who had been a kind of pettifogger of Furnival's Inn)[5], in the others' absence watches an opportunity (and commons being but hard amongst them) and got some strong drink and other junkets, and made them a feast; and after they were merry, he began to tell them he would give them good counsel. "You see," saith he, "that many of your fellows are carried to Virginia; and if you stay till this Rasdall return, you will also be carried away and sold for slaves with the rest. Therefore I would advise you to thrust out this Lieutenant Fitcher; and I, having a part in the plantation, will receive you as my partners and consociates; so may you be free from service; and we will converse, trade, plant, and live together as equals, and support and protect one another," or to like effect. This counsel was easily received; so they took opportunity and thrust Lieutenant Fitcher out o' doors and would suffer him to come no more amongst them, but forced him to seek bread to eat and other relief from his neighbors till he could get passages for England.

After this they fell to great licentiousness and led a dissolute life, pouring out themselves into all profaneness. And Morton became lord of misrule and maintained (as it were) a school of atheism. And after they had got some goods into their hands, and got much by trading with the Indians, they spent it as vainly, in quaffing and drinking, both wine and strong waters in great excess and (as some reported) ten pounds' worth in a morning. They also set up a Maypole, drinking and dancing about it many days together, inviting the Indian women for their consorts, dancing and frisking together like so many fairies (or furies rather), and worse practices, as if they had anew revived and celebrated the feasts of the Roman goddess Flora, or the beastly practices of the mad Bacchanalians. Morton likewise (to shew his poetry) composed sundry rhymes and verses, some tending to lasciviousness, and others to the detraction and scandal of some persons, which he affixed to this idle or idol Maypole. They changed also the name of their place; and instead of calling it Mount Wollaston, they call it Merry Mount, as if this jollity would have lasted ever. But this continued not long, for after Morton was sent for England (as follows to be declared), shortly after came over that worthy gentleman, Mr. John Endecott, who brought over a patent under the broad seal for the government of the Massachusetts, who, visiting those parts, caused that Maypole to be cut down and rebuked them for their profaneness and admonished them to look there should be better walking; so they now, or others, changed the name of their place again and called it Mount Dagon.

Now to maintain this riotous prodigality and profuse excess, Morton, thinking himself lawless, and hearing what gain the French and fishermen made by trading of pieces, powder, and shot to the Indians, he, as the head of this consortship, began the practice of the same in these parts. And first he taught them how to use them, to charge and discharge, and what proportion of powder to give the piece, according to the size or bigness of the same; and what shot to use for fowl and what for deer. And having thus instructed them, he employed some of them to hunt and fowl for him, so as they became far more active in that employment then any of the English, by reason of their swiftness of foot and nimbleness of body, being also quick-sighted, and by continual exercise well knowing the haunts of all sorts of game. So as when they saw the execution that a piece would do, and the benefit that might come by the same, they became mad, as it were, after them, and would not stick to give any price

[5] These events came to a head in 1627-28. Thomas Morton may have been a rascally attorney and person, but his association was with Clifford's Inn, and he was instrumental in attempts to revoke the Massachusetts charter. His version of these events was published in Amsterdam in 1637 as *New English Canaan.*

they could attain to for them; accounting their bows and arrows but baubles in comparison of them.

And here I may take occasion to bewail the mischief that this wicked man began in these parts, and which since, base covetousness prevailing in men that should know better, has now at length got the upper hand and made this thing common, notwithstanding any laws to the contrary; so as the Indians are full of pieces all over, both fowling pieces, muskets, pistols, etc. They have also their moulds to make shot of all sorts, as musket bullets, pistol bullets, swan and goose shot, and of smaller sorts. Yes, some have seen them have their screw-plates to make screw-pins themselves, when they want them, with sundry other implements, wherewith they are ordinarily better fitted and furnished then the English themselves. Yea, it is well known that they will have powder and shot when the English want it, nor cannot get it; and that in a time of war or danger, as experience hath manifested, that when lead hath been scarce and men for their own defense would gladly have given a groat a pound, which is dear enough, yet hath it been bought up and sent to other places and sold to such as trade it with the Indians at twelve pence the pound; and it is like they give three or four shillings the pound, for they will have it at any rate. And these things have been done in the same times when some of their neighbors and friends are daily killed by the Indians, or are in danger thereof and live but at the Indians' mercy. Yea, some (as they have acquainted them with all other things) have told them how gunpowder is made, and all the materials in it, and that they are to be had in their own land; and I am confident, could they attain to make saltpeter, they would teach them to make powder. O the horribleness of this villainy! How many both Dutch and English have been lately slain by those Indians, thus furnished, and no remedy provided; nay, the evil more increased, and the blood of their brethren sold for gain, as is to be feared; and in what danger all these colonies are in is too well known. O, that princes and parliaments would take some timely order to prevent this mischief, and at length to suppress it, by some exemplary punishment upon some of these gain-thirsty murderers (for they deserve no better title) before their colonies in these parts be overthrown by these barbarous savages thus armed with their own weapons, by these evil instruments and traitors to their neighbors and country! But I have forgotten myself and have been too long in this digression; but now to return.

This Morton having thus taught them the use of pieces, he sold them all he could spare; and he and his consorts determined to send for many out of England, and had by some of the ships sent for above a score. The which being known, and his neighbors meeting the Indians in the woods armed with guns in this sort, it was a terror unto them who lived stragglingly and were of no strength in any place. And other places (though more remote) saw this mischief would quickly spread over all, if not prevented. Besides, they saw they should keep no servants, for Morton would entertain any, how vile soever, and all the scum of the country or any discontents would flock to him from all places, if this nest was not broken; and they should stand in more fear of their lives and goods in short time from this wicked and debased crew than from the savages themselves.

So sundry of the chief of the straggling plantations, meeting together, agreed by mutual consent to solicit those of Plymouth (who were then of more strength then them all) to join with them to prevent the further growth of this mischief, and suppress Morton and his consorts before they grew to further head and strength. Those that joined in this action (and after contributed to the charge of sending him for England) were from Pascataway, Namkeake, Winisimett, Weesagascusett, Natasco, and other places where any English were seated. Those of Plymouth, being thus sought too by their messengers and letters, and weighing both their reasons and the common danger, were willing to afford them their help, though themselves had least cause of fear or hurt. So, to be short, they first resolved jointly to write to him, and in a friendly and neighborly way to admonish him to forbear those courses, and sent a messenger with their letters to bring his answer. But he was so high as he scorned all advice and asked who had to do with him; he had and would trade pieces with the Indians in despite of all, with many other scurrilous terms full of disdain. They sent to him a second time and bade him be better advised and more temperate in his terms, for the country could not bear the injury he did; it was against their common safety and against the King's proclamation. He answered in high terms as before, and that the King's proclamation was no law, demanding what penalty was upon it. It was answered, more than he could bear, His Majesty's displeasure. But insolently he persisted and said the King was dead and his displeasure with him, and many the like things, and threatened withal that if any came to molest him, let them look to themselves, for he would prepare for them. Upon which they saw there was no way but to take him by force; and having so far proceeded, now to give over would make him far more haughty and insolent. So they mutually resolved to proceed, and obtained of the Governor of Plymouth to send Captain Standish and some other aid with him, to take Morton by force. The which accordingly was done. But they found him to stand stiffly in his defense, having made fast his doors, armed his consorts, set divers dishes of powder and bullets ready on the table; and if they had not been over-armed with drink, more hurt might have been done. They summoned him to yield, but he kept his house, and they could get nothing but scoffs and scorns from him. But at length, fearing they would do some violence to the house, he and some of his crew came out, but not to yield but to shoot; but they were so steeled with drink as their pieces were too heavy for them; himself with a carbine (overcharged and almost half filled with powder and shot, as was after found) had thought to have shot Captain Standish; but he stepped to him and put by his piece and took him. Neither was there any hurt done to any of either side, save that one was so drunk that he ran his own nose upon the point of a sword that one held before him, as he entered the house; but he lost but a little of his hot blood. Morton they brought away to Plymouth, where he was kept till a ship went from the Isle of Shoals for England, with which he was sent to the Council of New England; and letters written to give them information of his course and carriage; and also one was sent at their common charge to inform their Honors more particularly, and to prosecute against him. But he fooled of the messenger, after he was gone from hence, and though he went for England, yet nothing was done to him, not so much as rebuked, for aught was heard; but returned the next year. Some of the worst of the company were dispersed, and some of the more modest kept the house till he should be heard from. But I have been too long about so unworthy a person, and bad a cause.

[War with the Pequots]

[1637] In the fore part of this year, the Pequots fell openly upon the English at Connecticut, in the lower parts of the river, and slew sundry of them as they were at work in the fields, both men and women, to the great terror of the rest, and went away in great pride and triumph, and many high threats. They also assaulted a fort at the river's mouth, though strong and well defended; and though they did not there prevail, yet it struck them with much fear and astonishment to see their bold attempts in the face of danger. Which made them in all places to stand upon their guard and to prepare for resistance, and earnestly to solicit their friends and confederates in the Bay of Massachusetts to send them speedy aid, for they looked for more forcible assaults. Mr. Vane, being then Governor, writ from their General Court to them here to join with them in this war. To which they were cordially willing, but took opportunity to write to them about some former things, as well as present, considerable hereabout. * * *

In the meantime, the Pequots, especially in the winter before, sought to make peace with the Narragansetts, and used very pernicious arguments to move them thereunto: as that the English were strangers and began to overspread their country, and would deprive them thereof in time, if they were suffered to grow and increase. And if the Narragansetts did assist the English to subdue them, they did but make way for their own overthrow, for if they were rooted out, the English would soon take occasion to subjugate them. And if they would hearken to them, they should not need to fear the strength of the English, for they would not come to open battle with them, but fire their houses, kill their cattle, and lie in ambush for them as they went abroad upon their occasions; and all this they might easily do without any or little danger to themselves. The which course being held, they well saw the English could not long subsist, but they would either be starved with hunger or be forced to forsake the country. With many the like things; insomuch that the Narragansetts were once wavering and were half minded to have made peace with them, and joined against the English. But again, when they considered how much wrong they had received from the Pequots, and what an opportunity they now had by the help of the English to right themselves; revenge was so sweet unto them as it prevailed above all the rest, so as they resolved to join with the English against them, and did.

The Court here agreed forthwith to send fifty men at their own charge; and with as much speed as possibly they could, got them armed and had made them ready under sufficient leaders, and provided a bark to carry them provisions and tend upon them for all occasions. But when they were ready to march, with a supply from the Bay, they had word to stay; for the enemy was as good as vanquished and there would be no need.

I shall not take upon me exactly to describe their proceedings in these things, because I expect it will be fully done by themselves who best know the carriage and circumstances of things.[6] I shall therefore but touch them in general. From Connecticut, who were most sensible of the hurt sustained and the present danger, they set out a party of men, and another party met them from the Bay at the Narragansetts', who were to join with them. The Narragansetts were earnest to be gone before the English were well rested and refreshed, especially some of them which came last. It should seem their desire

[6] See John Mason, *A Brief History of the Pequod War*, 1735; John Underhill, *News from America*, 1638; and Philip Vincent, *A True Relation . . .*, 1638.

was to come upon the enemy suddenly and undiscovered. There was a bark of this place, newly put in there, which was come from Connecticut, who did encourage them to lay hold of the Indians' forwardness, and to show as great forwardness as they, for it would encourage them, and expedition might prove to their great advantage. So they went on, and so ordered their march as the Indians brought them to a fort of the enemy's (in which most of their chief men were) before day. They approached the same with great silence and surrounded it both with English and Indians, that they might not break out; and so assaulted them with great courage, shooting amongst them, and entered the fort with all speed. And those that first entered found sharp resistance from the enemy, who both shot at and grappled with them; others ran into their houses and brought out fire and set them on fire, which soon took in their mats; and standing close together, with the wind all was quickly on a flame, and thereby more were burnt to death than was otherwise slain. It burnt their bowstrings and made them unserviceable; those that scaped the fire were slain with the sword, some hewed to pieces, others run through with their rapiers, so as they were quickly dispatched and very few escaped. It was conceived they thus destroyed about 400 at this time. It was a fearful sight to see them thus frying in the fire and the streams of blood quenching the same, and horrible was the stink and scent thereof; but the victory seemed a sweet sacrifice, and they gave the praise thereof to God, who had wrought so wonderfully for them, thus to enclose their enemies in their hands and give them so speedy a victory over so proud and insulting an enemy.

JOHN WINTHROP [1588-1649]

BORN THE SAME YEAR as William Bradford, John Winthrop too was destined to be a major force in the shaping of the colonial experience. He came of a well-to-do Suffolk family, was educated at Cambridge, and after considering the ministry turned instead to law. Intensely Puritan, he was one of the leaders of the group that began the Great Migration to Massachusetts Bay in 1630; in fact, he had been elected governor of the new colony the year before. And from then until his death he served as governor or deputy governor for all but seven years, ever mindful of his admonition to the company aboard the flagship *Arbella:* "to do justly, to love mercy, to walk humbly with our God; . . . for we must consider that we shall be as a city upon a hill, the eyes of all people are upon us. . . ."

Politically astute, and dedicated to fulfilling the dream of a holy commonwealth in the New World, Winthrop dominated the life of Massachusetts Bay as Bradford did that of the less sophisticated and less powerful Plymouth. And like Bradford he kept a journal (from 1630 to 1649) that is a rare and rich account of life during that time. It was published early in the nineteenth century as *The History of New England*, but comparison with *Of Plymouth Plantation* shows the faultiness of that title. For, as much as Winthrop's journal reveals, it lacks the philosophy, the historical perspective, the art, and the conscious dignity of Bradford's work.

Winthrop's course was not always smooth, his politics and diplomacy were often high-handed and arbitrary. But on balance he emerges from the journal a devoted and practical leader who recognized that his infant colony could not survive a gentle leadership. Unauthorized ships entering Boston harbor, heretics and civil dissidents such as Roger Williams and Anne Hutchinson, threatening Indians—all were handled with dispatch, and sometimes with harshness. Once, in a matter involving a deposed militia company commander, Winthrop was actually impeached before the General Court of

Massachusetts on a charge of having exceeded his powers. His position on the rights and liberties of elected authority is summed up in the now famous "little speech" which he made before the Court upon his exoneration.

Further reading: *Journal*, ed. J. K. Hosmer, 1908. A chapter in S. E. Morison, *Builders of the Bay Colony*, 1930, 1964. S. Gray, "The Political Thought of John Winthrop," *New England Quarterly*, 1930. E. Morgan, *The Puritan Dilemma*, 1958.

FROM HIS *Journal*

Winthrop began his journal at Southampton, when the ship *Arbella* was preparing to sail, and continued it till shortly before his death. In both of the following episodes Winthrop raises questions of law, liberty, license, and political dissent and responsibility that still remain vital. Parrington has written of Winthrop's famous "little speech" on liberty, that "No other episode in his varied career reveals so well the admirable poise of the man—the dignity, the self-control, the fair-mindedness, despite an attack that hurt him to the quick." Text: John Winthrop, *The History of New England from 1630 to 1649*, ed. James Savage (2 vols., revised edition; Boston, 1853).

[A Trial for Adultery]

[1644] At this court of assistants, one James Britton, a man ill affected both to our church discipline and civil government, and one Mary Latham, a proper young woman about 18 years of age, whose father was a godly man and had brought her up well, were condemned to die for adultery, upon a law formerly made and published in print. It was thus occasioned and discovered. This woman, being rejected by a young man whom she had an affection unto, vowed she would marry the next that came to her, and accordingly, against her friends' minds, she matched with an ancient man who had neither honesty nor ability, and one whom she had no affection unto. Whereupon, soon after she was married, divers young men solicited her chastity, and drawing her into bad company, and giving her wine and other gifts, easily prevailed with her, and among others this Britton. But God smiting him with a deadly palsy and fearful horror of conscience withal, he could not keep secret, but discovered this, and other the like with other women, and was forced to acknowledge the justice of God in that having often called others fools, &c. for confessing against themselves, he was now forced to do the like. The woman dwelt now in Plymouth patent, and one of the magistrates there, hearing she was detected, &c. sent her to us. Upon her examination, she confessed he did attempt the fact, but did not commit it, and witness was produced that testified (which they both confessed) that in the evening of a day of humiliation through the country for England, &c. a company met at Britton's and there continued drinking sack, &c. till late in the night, and then Britton and the woman were seen upon the ground together, a little from the house. It was reported also that she did frequently abuse her husband, setting a knife to his breast and threatening to kill him, calling him old rogue and cuckold, and said she would make him wear horns as big as a bull. And yet some of the magistrates thought the evidence not sufficient against her, because there were not two direct witnesses; but the jury cast her, and then she confessed the fact, and accused twelve others, whereof two were married men. Five of these were apprehended and committed (the rest were gone), but denying it, and there being no other witness against them than the testimony of a condemned person, there could be no proceeding against them. The woman proved very penitent, and had deep apprehension of the foulness of her sin, and at length attained to hope of pardon by the blood of Christ, and was willing to die in satisfaction to justice. The man also was very much cast down for his sins, but was loth to die, and petitioned the general court for his life, but they would not grant it, though some of the magistrates spake much for it, and questioned the letter, whether adultery was death by God's law now. This Britton had been a professor[1] in England, but coming hither he opposed our church government, &c. and grew dissolute, losing both power and profession of godliness.

They were both executed, they both died very penitently, especially the woman, who had some comfortable hope of pardon of her sin, and gave good exhortation to all young maids to be obedient to their parents, and to take heed of evil company, &c.

[A Little Speech on Liberty]

In 1645 the militia company of Hingham, Massachusetts, dismissed its company commander and elected another in his place. The deposed officer appealed to the colonial government at Boston, which remonstrated with the Hingham citizens to no avail. The case was called to trial, and Deputy Governor Winthrop argued that the citizens of

[1] A religious believer; church member.

Hingham had exceeded their powers; the same accusation was then leveled at Winthrop. After long and bitter debate, the court decided in favor of Winthrop, who concluded with some pertinent remarks on political liberty as the Massachusetts theocracy perceived it.

I suppose something may be expected from me, upon this charge that is befallen me, which moves me to speak now to you; yet I intend not to intermeddle in the proceedings of the court, or with any of the persons concerned therein. Only I bless God, that I see an issue of this troublesome business. I also acknowledge the justice of the court, and, for mine own part, I am well satisfied; I was publicly charged, and I am publicly and legally acquitted, which is all I did expect or desire. And though this be sufficient for my justification before men, yet not so before the God, who hath seen so much amiss in my dispensations (and even in this affair) as calls me to be humble. For to be publicly and criminally charged in this court, is matter of humiliation (and I desire to make a right use of it), notwithstanding I be thus acquitted. If her father had spit in her face (saith the Lord concerning Miriam), should she not have been ashamed seven days?[2] Shame had lien upon her, whatever the occasion had been. I am unwilling to stay you from your urgent affairs, yet give me leave (upon this special occasion) to speak a little more to this assembly. It may be of some good use, to inform and rectify the judgments of some of the people, and may prevent such distempers as have arisen amongst us. The great questions that have troubled the country, are about the authority of the magistrates and the liberty of the people. It is yourselves who have called us to this office, and being called by you, we have our authority from God, in way of an ordinance, such as hath the image of God eminently stamped upon it, the contempt and violation whereof hath been vindicated with examples of divine vengeance. I entreat you to consider, that when you choose magistrates, you take them from among yourselves, men subject to like passions as you are. Therefore when you see infirmities in us, you should reflect upon your own, and that would make you bear the more with us, and not be severe censurers of the failings of your magistrates, when you have continual experience of the like infirmities in yourselves and others. We account him a good servant, who breaks not his covenant. The covenant between you and us is the oath you have taken of us, which is to this purpose, that we shall govern you and judge your causes by the rules of God's laws and our own, according to our best skill. When you agree with a workman to build you a ship or house, etc., he undertakes as well for his skill as for his faithfulness, for it is his profession, and you pay him for both. But when you call one to be a magistrate, he doth not profess nor undertake to have sufficient skill for that office, nor can you furnish him with gifts, etc., therefore you must run the hazard of his skill and ability. But if he fail in faithfulness, which by his oath he is bound unto, that he must answer for. If it fall out that the case be clear to common apprehension, and the rule clear, also, if he transgress here, the error is not in the skill, but in the evil of the will: it must be required of him. But if the cause be doubtful, or the rule doubtful, to men of such understanding and parts as your magistrates are, if your magistrates should err here, yourselves must bear it.

[2] Numbers xii.14.

For the other point concerning liberty, I observe a great mistake in the country about that. There is a twofold liberty, natural (I mean as our nature is now corrupt) and civil or federal. The first is common to man with beasts and other creatures. By this, man, as he stands in relation to man simply, hath liberty to do what he lists; it is a liberty to evil as well as to good. This liberty is incompatible and inconsistent with authority, and cannot endure the least restraint of the most just authority. The exercise and maintaining of this liberty makes men grow more evil, and in time to be worse than brute beasts: *omnes sumus licentia deteriores.*[3] This is that great enemy of truth and peace, that wild beast, which all the ordinances of God are bent against, to restrain and subdue it. The other kind of liberty I call civil or federal; it may also be termed moral, in reference to the covenant between God and man, in the moral law, and the politic covenants and constitutions, amongst men themselves. This liberty is the proper end and object of authority, and cannot subsist without it; and it is a liberty to that only which is good, just, and honest. This liberty you are to stand for, with the hazard (not only of your goods, but) of your lives, if need be. Whatsoever crosseth this, is not authority, but a distemper thereof. This liberty is maintained and exercised in a way of subjection to authority; it is of the same kind of liberty wherewith Christ hath made us free. The woman's own choice makes such a man her husband; yet being so chosen, he is her lord, and she is to be subject to him, yet in a way of liberty, not of bondage; and a true wife accounts her subjection her honor and freedom, and would not think her condition safe and free, but in her subjection to her husband's authority. Such is the liberty of the church under the authority of Christ, her king and husband; His yoke is so easy and sweet to her as a bride's ornaments; and if through frowardness or wantonness, etc., she shake it off, at any

[3] "We are all weakened by liberty."

time, she is at no rest in her spirit, until she take it up again; and whether her lord smiles upon her, and embraceth her in his arms, or whether he frowns, or rebukes, or smites her, she apprehends the sweetness of his love in all, and is refreshed, supported, and instructed by every such dispensation of his authority over her. On the other side, ye know who they are that complain of this yoke and say, let us break their bands, etc., we will not have this man to rule over us. Even so, brethren, it will be between you and your magistrates. If you stand for your natural corrupt liberties, and will do what is good in your own eyes, you will not endure the least weight of authority, but will murmur, and oppose, and be always striving to shake off that yoke; but if you will be satisfied to enjoy such civil and lawful liberties, such as Christ allows you, then will you quietly and cheerfully submit unto that authority which is set over you, in all the administrations of it, for your good. Wherein, if we fail at any time, we hope we shall be willing (by God's assistance) to hearken to good advice from any of you, or in any other way of God; so shall your liberties be preserved, in upholding the honor and power of authority amongst you.

ANNE BRADSTREET [1612–1672]

In a brief autobiography, Anne Bradstreet wrote: "After a short time I changed my condition and was marryed, and came into this country, where I found a new world and new manners, at which my heart rose. But after I was convinced it was the way of God, I submitted to it and joined the church at Boston." Her condition had indeed changed in many ways. Her father was Thomas Dudley, steward to the Earl of Lincoln, in whose elegant and literate estates she was raised; he became one of the leaders of the Great Migration and would alternate with John Winthrop in the governorship of Massachusetts Bay. Her husband, Simon Bradstreet, for a time assisted Dudley in England, and eventually became governor of the Bay himself. Coming to America in 1630 must have been a severe blow to a girl of gentle expectations. Farm life at Ipswich and then Andover gave her time to explore the meaning of her fortunes; she put that time to good use, writing poems of such merit that her brother-in-law took some of them to England for publication, without her knowledge.

In 1650 the poems appeared in London as *The Tenth Muse Lately Sprung Up in America. Or Several Poems, Compiled with Great Variety of Wit and Learning, etc.*, a title she would certainly not have chosen herself. The volume consisted primarily of "quaternions," semi-dramatic pieces dealing with the four elements, the four humours, the four ages of man, and the four seasons of the year. She also versified the history of the four monarchies of the ancient world, most of this work completed before 1643. Well publicized and well received, the poems deserved the efforts at revision that Mistress Bradstreet gave them in time stolen from the raising of eight children and the duties of the wife of a man of public affairs—and against carping tongues that thought a woman's hand more suited to the needle than the pen. Until around 1666 she worked at a second edition, adding yet other poems, but it was not published until after her death as *Several Poems Compiled with Great Variety of Wit and Learning, Full of Delight.* The full range of her writing was not available until the 1867 edition of her *Works* by John Harvard Ellis, from which the texts of the following selections are taken.

Mistress Bradstreet was a studiedly literary poet, rarely original, and never spontaneous. A great admirer of Joshua Sylvester's translation of Guillaume Salluste DuBartas' *Divine Weeks and Works* (an admiration shared by Sidney and Milton), of Francis Quarles, Sir Philip Sidney, and Sir Walter Raleigh, she sought to celebrate and emulate these poets by employing the conventions of the kind of poetry they wrote. Such imitation often led her into dull didacticism and sterile artifice, but it also made possible more ambitious poetic attempts than would otherwise have come about, supporting by tradition what otherwise might have become mere doggerel. And Anne Bradstreet's personal warmth, attention to the homely details of daily life, and sensitivity to the beauties of her frontier surroundings often enough emerge to evince her genuine poetic feeling.

Further reading: *Works*, ed. J. H. Ellis, 1867, 1932. A chapter in S. E. Morison, *Builders of the Bay Colony*, 1930, 1962.

The Author to Her Book

When Chaucer wrote his famous envoy to *Troilus and Criseyde* beginning "Go, litel bok, go, litel myn tragedye"—following Statius and perhaps Boccaccio—he spawned countless similar poems by poets from Lydgate to Skelton and Spenser. Mistress Bradstreet's adaptation, presumably composed after she finally abandoned her attempts to bring her collection of poems into "better dress," masters the convention without sacrificing her own individuality and wry humor.

Thou ill-formed offspring of my feeble brain,
Who after birth did'st by my side remain,
Till snatcht from thence by friends, less wise then true,
Who thee abroad, exposed to public view,
Made thee in rags, halting to th' press to trudge,
Where errors were not lessened (all may judge)
At thy return my blushing was not small,
My rambling brat (in print) should "Mother" call,
I cast thee by as one unfit for light,
Thy visage was so irksome in my sight;
Yet being mine own, at length affection would
Thy blemishes amend, if so I could:
I washed thy face, but more defects I saw,
And rubbing off a spot, still made a flaw.
I stretcht thy joints to make thee even feet,
Yet still thou run'st more hobbling then is meet;
In better dress to trim thee was my mind,
But nought save homespun cloth i' th' house I find.
In this array, 'mongst vulgars mayst thou roam,
In critics' hands, beware thou doth not come;
And take thy way where yet thou art not known,
If for thy father askt, say thou hast none:
And for thy mother, she alas is poor,
Which caused her thus to send thee out of door.

1678

Contemplations

Poetically her most fully realized accomplishment, this poem was written probably between 1660 and 1665. Stimulated by the sublime experience of a brilliant autumnal sunset, the speaker is tempted to imagine the superiority of Nature over Man, until a higher knowledge asserts the supremacy of the human soul whose nature can attain the eternal "security" of everlasting salvation. The first movement of the poem (st. 1-9) presents the effect of natural splendor upon the poet's senses, producing wonder and admiration at God's workmanship and the desire to praise the workman—the natural inclination of a rational creature. The second movement (st. 10-20) leaves sensory responses to ruminate through Fancy and Memory upon the progressive degeneracy of man and the apparent superiority of nature's regenerative powers. The third movement, by a series of emblems (st. 21-28), speculates upon the natural happiness of natural creatures, as the river, fish, and birds all express the joy of existence simply by being what they are. By contrast, the unsatisfied speaker identifies first with one, then another of these natural creatures, clearly changeable and uncertain. And this leads to a view of man as the perplexing middle-term of the universe, existing between the fish and the birds, the lower and upper regions, time and eternity, whose full destiny can only be realized in a supernatural, transcendent realm (st. 29-33).

Despite the praise this poem has received for its sensitivity to natural objects, "Contemplations" is not a nature poem. Its major subject is the mutability of all earthly existence, and it is not therefore surprising that readers will detect echoes of Donne, Herbert, and Spenser. Clearly Mrs. Bradstreet worked at this poem. The rhymes that link stanzas 11-13 show this, as does the interesting stanzaic pattern, which varies the versatile *ababcc* iambic pentameter stanza by adding an extra *c* line in hexameter. It is not accurate to call this, as some have, a modified Spenserian stanza, but the spirit of Spenser, especially of the Mutabilitie Cantos, is obvious.

1

Some time now past in the autumnal tide,
When Phoebus wanted but one hour to bed,
The trees all richly clad, yet void of pride,
Were gilded o'er by his rich golden head.
Their leaves and fruits seemed painted, but was true,
Of green, of red, of yellow, mixed hue;
Rapt were my senses at this delectable view.

2

I wist not what to wish, "Yet sure," thought I,
"If so much excellence abide below,
How excellent is He that dwells on high,
Whose power and beauty by His works we know?
Sure He is goodness, wisdom, glory, light,
That hath this under world so richly dight:
More heaven than earth was here, no winter and no night."

3

Then on a stately oak I cast mine eye,
Whose ruffling top the clouds seemed to aspire;
How long since thou wast in thine infancy?
Thy strength and stature, more thy years admire.
Hath hundred winters passed since thou wast born,
Or thousand since thou brak'st thy shell of horn?
If so, all these as nought eternity doth scorn.

4

Then higher on the glistering sun I gazed,
Whose beams was shaded by the leafy tree;
The more I looked the more I grew amazed,
And softly said, "What glory's like to thee?
Soul of this world, this universe's eye,
No wonder some made thee a deity;
Had I not better known, alas, the same had I.

5

"Thou as a bridegroom from thy chamber rushes
And as a strong man, joys to run a race,[1]
The morn doth usher thee with smiles and blushes,
The earth reflects her glances in thy face.
Birds, insects, animals, with vegetive,
Thy heart from death and dullness doth revive:
And in the darksome womb of fruitful nature dive.

6

"Thy swift annual and diurnal course,
Thy daily straight and yearly oblique path,
Thy pleasing fervor and thy scorching force,
All mortals here the feeling knowledge hath.
Thy presence makes it day, thy absence night,
Quaternal seasons caused by thy might:
Hail, creature full of sweetness, beauty, and delight!

7

"Art thou so full of glory that no eye
Hath strength thy shining rays once to behold?
And is thy splendid throne erect so high
As to approach it can no earthly mould?
How full of glory then must thy Creator be,
Who gave this bright light luster unto thee:
Admired, adored forever, be that majesty!"

Contemplations. [1]Psalms xix.4–6.

8

Silent, alone, where none or saw or heard,
In pathless paths I led my wand'ring feet,
My humble eyes to lofty skies I reared,
To sing some song my mazed Muse thought meet.
My great Creator I would magnify,
That nature had thus decked liberally:
But ah, and ah, again, my imbecility!

9

I heard the merry grasshopper then sing,
The black-clad cricket bear a second part;
They kept one tune and played on the same string,
Seeming to glory in their little art.
Shall creatures abject thus their voices raise,
And in their kind resound their Maker's praise,
Whilst I, as mute, can warble forth no higher lays?

10

When present times look back to ages past,
And men in being fancy those are dead,
It makes things gone perpetually to last
And calls back months and years that long since fled;
It makes a man more aged in conceit
Than was Methuselah or 's grandsire great[2]
While of their persons and their acts his mind doth treat.

11

Sometimes in Eden fair he seems to be,
Sees glorious Adam there made lord of all,
Fancies the apple dangle on the tree
That turned his sovereign to a naked thrall.
Who like a miscreant's driven from that place
To get his bread with pain and sweat of face:
A penalty imposed on his backsliding race.

12

Here sits our grandame in retired place,
And in her lap her bloody Cain new-born;[3]
The weeping imp oft looks her in the face,
Bewails his unknown hap and fate forlorn;
His mother sighs to think of paradise,
And how she lost her bliss to be more wise,
Believing him that was, and is, father of lies.

13

Here Cain and Abel came to sacrifice;
Fruits of the earth and fatlings each do bring;
On Abel's gift the fire descends from skies,

[2]Genesis v.18–27. Adam lived 930 years; Methuselah lived 969 years; his grandfather Jared, 962 years.
[3]Genesis iv.1–16.

But no such sign on false Cain's offering;
With sullen hateful looks he goes his ways,
Hath thousand thoughts to end his brother's days,
Upon whose blood his future good he hopes to raise.

14

There Abel keeps his sheep, no ill he thinks,
His brother comes, then acts his fratricide,
The virgin earth of blood her first draught drinks,
But since that time she often hath been cloyed.
The wretch with ghastly face and dreadful mind
Thinks each he sees will serve him in his kind,
Though none on earth but kindred near then could he find.

15

Who fancies not his looks now at the bar,
His face like death, his heart with horror fraught?
Nor malefactor ever felt like war
When deep despair with wish of life hath fought.
Branded with guilt and crushed with treble woes,
A vagabond to land of Nod he goes;
A city builds, that walls might him secure from foes.

16

Who thinks not oft upon the fathers' ages?
Their long descent, how nephews sons they saw,
The starry observations of those sages,
And how their precepts to their sons were law,
How Adam sighed to see his progeny
Clothed all in his black sinful livery,
Who neither guilt nor yet the punishment could fly.

17

Our life compare we with their length of days;
Who to the tenth of theirs doth now arrive?
And though thus short we shorten many ways,
Living so little while we are alive,
In eating, drinking, sleeping, vain delight.
So unawares comes on perpetual night
And puts all pleasures vain unto eternal flight.

18

When I behold the heavens as in their prime,
And then the earth, though old, still clad in green,
The stones and trees insensible of time,
Nor age nor wrinkle on their front are seen;
If winter come, and greenness then do fade,
A spring returns, and they more youthful made.
But man grows old, lies down, remains where once he's laid.

19

By birth more noble than those creatures all,
Yet seems by nature and by custom cursed;
No sooner born but grief and care makes fall
That state obliterate he had at first:
Nor youth nor strength nor wisdom spring again,
Nor habitations long their names retain,
But in oblivion to the final day remain.

20

Shall I then praise the heavens, the trees, the earth,
Because their beauty and their strength last longer?
Shall I wish there or never to had birth,
Because they're bigger and their bodies stronger?
Nay, they shall darken, perish, fade, and die,
And when unmade so ever shall they lie,
But man was made for endless immortality.

21

Under the cooling shadow of a stately elm
Close sat I by a goodly river's side,
Where gliding streams the rocks did overwhelm;
A lonely place, with pleasures dignified.
I once that loved the shady woods so well,
Now thought the rivers did the trees excel,
And if the sun would ever shine, there would I dwell.

22

While on the stealing stream I fixed mine eye,
Which to the longed-for ocean held its course,
I marked, nor crooks nor rubs that there did lie
Could hinder aught, but still augment its force:
"O happy flood," quoth I, "that holds thy race
Till thou arrive at thy beloved place,
Nor is it rocks or shoals that can obstruct thy pace!

23

"Nor is't enough that thou alone may'st slide,
But hundred brooks in thy clear waves do meet;
So hand in hand along with thee they glide
To Thetis' house,[4] where all embrace and greet:
Thou emblem true of what I count the best,
O could I lead my rivulets to rest,
So may we press to that vast mansion ever blest.

24

"Ye fish which in this liquid region bide,
That for each season have your habitation,
Now salt, now fresh, where you think best to glide,
To unknown coasts to give a visitation,
In lakes and ponds you leave your numerous fry,
So nature taught, and yet you know not why,
You wat'ry folk that know not your felicity.

[4] In Greek mythology, Thetis was the chief of the Nereids and the mother of Achilles. Her house is simply the sea.

25

"Look how the wantons frisk to taste the air,
Then to the colder bottom straight they dive;
Eftsoon to Neptune's glassy hall repair
To see what trade they great ones there do drive,
Who forage o'er the spacious sea-green field,
And take the trembling prey before it yield,
Whose armor is their scales, their spreading fins
their shield."

26

While musing thus with contemplation fed,
And thousand fancies buzzing in my brain,
The sweet-tongued Philomel[5] perched o'er my head,
And chanted forth a most melodious strain,
Which rapt me so with wonder and delight,
I judged my hearing better than my sight,
And wished me wings with her a while to take my
flight.

27

"O merry bird," said I, "that fears no snares,
That neither toils nor hoards up in thy barn,
Feels no sad thoughts, nor cruciating cares
To gain more good or shun what might thee harm;
Thy clothes ne'er wear, thy meat is everywhere,
Thy bed a bough, thy drink the water clear;
Reminds not what is past, nor what's to come doth
fear.

28

"The dawning morn with songs thou dost prevent,[6]
Sets hundred notes unto thy feathered crew,
So each one tunes his pretty instrument
And warbling out the old, begin anew.
And thus they pass their youth in summer season,
Then follow thee into a better region,
Where winter's never felt by that sweet airy legion."

29

Man at the best a creature frail and vain,
In knowledge ignorant, in strength but weak,
Subject to sorrows, losses, sickness, pain,
Each storm his state, his mind, his body break;
From some of these he never finds cessation,
But day or night, within, without, vexation,
Troubles from foes, from friends, from dearest,
near'st relation.

30

And yet this sinful creature, frail and vain,
This lump of wretchedness, of sin and sorrow,
This weather-beaten vessel wracked with pain,
Joys not in hope of an eternal morrow;
Nor all his losses, crosses, and vexation,
In weight, in frequency and long duration,
Can make him deeply groan for that divine
translation.

31

The mariner that on smooth waves doth glide
Sings merrily and steers his bark with ease,
As if he had command of wind and tide,
And now become great master of the seas;
But suddenly a storm spoils all the sport,
And makes him long for a more quiet port,
Which 'gainst all adverse winds may serve for fort.

32

So he that faileth in this world of pleasure,
Feeding on sweets, that never bit of th' sour,
That's full of friends, of honor, and of treasure,
Fond fool, he takes this earth ev'n for heaven's
bower.
But sad affliction comes and makes him see
Here's neither honor, wealth, nor safety;
Only above is found all with security.

33

O Time, the fatal wrack of mortal things,
That draws oblivion's curtains over kings,
Their sumptuous monuments, men know them not,
Their names without a record are forgot,
Their parts, their ports, their pomp's all laid in th'
dust,
Nor wit nor gold nor buildings 'scape time's rust;
But he whose name is graved in the white stone
Shall last and shine when all of these are gone.

1678

[5] The nightingale, which is not native to America, is here strictly a literary convention.

[6] Literally, to come before or anticipate.

To My Dear and Loving Husband

Mrs. Bradstreet's best poems, for many readers, are the short domestic pieces, those concerning her husband, her children, her house. In them, whether she writes directly or figuratively, her thought and feeling strike us as genuine and unforced. In this poem, for instance, the first two couplets give a direct statement on the human level, the next two employ figures (gold mines, riches of the Orient, rivers), the last two give a direct statement culminating on the level of the eternal. Meaning is communicated through the simplest words, generally monosyllabic.

If ever two were one, then surely we.
If ever man were loved by wife, then thee;

If ever wife was happy in a man,
Compare with me, ye women, if you can.
I prize thy love more then whole mines of gold,
Or all the riches that the East doth hold.
My love is such that rivers cannot quench,
Nor ought but love from thee give recompense.
Thy love is such I can no way repay;
The heavens reward thee manifold, I pray.
Then while we live, in love let's so persevere,
That when we live no more, we may live ever.

THOMAS HOOKER [1586-1647]

AMONG PREACHERS of his time, only two rivaled Thomas Hooker in respect and significance—John Cotton, and Hooker's son-in-law Thomas Shepard. Of the three, Shepard has come to represent the spirit of Puritan devotional preaching and writing, while Cotton and Hooker have vied for pre-eminence as architects of New England's social and ecclesiastical thought. Hooker's definitions of the ruling concepts of law, nature, and reason in *A Survey of the Summe of Church Discipline* (1648) have led to a view of Hooker as arch-defender of New England church polity, preacher of the covenant or federal theology, and powerful if inadvertent prophet of democratic principles. But these activities were all part of a later phase of his ministry.

Born in England of middle-class folk, Hooker took his B.A. at Puritan-dominated Emmanuel College, Cambridge, in 1608, his M.A. in 1611. He remained at Cambridge as a tutor until 1618, served as rector of a small community in Surrey until 1620, then became lecturer and assistant minister in Chelmsford, Essex, in 1626. Complaints soon reached his ecclesiastical superiors that he was becoming a dangerously popular preacher, and in 1630 the High Commission arrested him for nonconformity. On the advice of friends who posted bond for him, Hooker escaped to Holland. In 1633 he contrived to sail to New England, where he became pastor of the church of Cambridge. In 1636, with the reluctant approval of Massachusetts Bay officials, he took his congregation to the Connecticut Valley, establishing the new colony of Hartford.

Despite his active involvement in colony affairs, the key to his preaching was not basically political; it was spiritual. Its main endeavor was to spell out and clarify God's plan to redeem fallen and unworthy mankind, and to urge upon men the necessity of coming into an intimate and right relationship with the Lord. God redeemed men by the free distribution of His grace; and while Hooker did not believe that men could earn that grace, he differed from Calvin in arguing that men are obliged to prepare themselves for it. In a series of beautifully written treatises, he taught in practical terms the advantages of self-examination, prayer, and meditation, rigorously intellectual exercises that always involved verbal expression. These spiritual directives began appearing as early as 1632, but Hooker assembled them shortly before his death in the only book he authorized for publication—*The Application of Redemption, By the effectual Work of the Word, and Spirit of Christ, for the bringing home of lost Sinners to God* (London, 1656, 1659).

The scheme of redemption is there stated amply, and in the portion devoted to making ready "a people prepared," Hooker urges the importance of a powerful ministry whose force lies in plain and vigorous preaching. Not only does he teach what was for Puritans an ideal style, he embodies it. Rich in invention of analogies and metaphors, teeming with earthy and commonplace details, terse, pointed, tough-minded, and spiritual—hard talk to crack stubborn spirits—Hooker's style reflects a realistic and practical aesthetic that would mark American writing well beyond his time.

Further reading: Moses C. Tyler, *A History of American Literature*, 1878, 1949. Norman Pettit, *The Heart Prepared*, 1966.

A Plain and Powerful Ministry

Most Puritan preachers believed that the conversion Taylor wrote about came from "hearing the Word preached" and from no other source. Even so, it did not reside in the rhetorical skill of the preacher, but in the mysterious power of grace working through the sermon. For that reason Puritans avoided originality in preaching and subscribed to a set form.

The preacher first read a text (in Hooker's case here, from Luke i.17, "to make ready a people prepared for the Lord"), which he then explicated or "opened" to yield a concise, tersely stated truth called the "doctrine." The doctrine was then proved by a number of reasons, and then the proved doctrine was applied in the "application" or "uses," which normally concluded with an "exhortation" or call to the congregation to accept the truth thus preached.

The advantage of so rigid a form was that the preacher's audience always knew exactly where he was in the sermon; the gain in clarity more than compensated for what was lost of surprise and ingenuity. Hooker's sermon demonstrates that even while his literary judgments are secondary and indirect, they are not insignificant. He is concerned here with the relationships among art (eloquence), language, and truth, as Poe, Emerson, and James will later be. The Bible in this context functions as a *literary* standard as well as a religious authority. In acknowledging the importance of human affections, Hooker counters the popular myth that emotion and beauty had no place in Puritan thought, and his recognition that souls can be deluded by words testifies to a faith in the power of language that was widely shared in the seventeenth century. Even the predominant images of building, carpentry, and houses will emerge in new contexts in the work of Hawthorne, Emerson, and Thoreau. Hooker's is a strong case for the plain businesslike prose that will be fashioned by Franklin and others into a distinctive American language.

Text: The first edition of *The Application of Redemption* (London, 1656).

[Doctrine:] *A plain and powerful ministry, is the only ordinary means to prepare the heart soundly for Christ.*

Hence it is, when our Savior would have this work done, he prepares a workman fit for it, and furnisheth him with abilities, which might enable him to the discharge thereof; the work is great, and the service difficult, and therefore Elias is fitted with a spirit suitable with power answerable unto that purpose for which he was appointed, an instrument as we say for the nonce. John the Baptist he also inherits these abilities, and that minister must be an Elias, i.e., must have his spirit and power in proportion, if ever this great work of preparation followeth his hand with comfort and success. As it was in the material, so also is it in the building of "this spiritual temple, in which the Holy Ghost doth dwell": the Elect of God are like trees of righteousness, the Word is like the axe, that must be lifted by a skillful and strong arm of a cunning minister, who like a spiritual artificer must hew and square, and take off the knotty untowardness in the soul before we can come to couch close and settle upon the Lord Christ as the cornerstone: Paul calls the saints "God's husbandry," I *Cor.* 3.9. A powerful humbling ministry is like the plow, to "plow up the fallow ground, the thorny" sensual hearts of sinful men to receive "the immortal seed of the word of promise" and the spirit of Christ thereby.

For the opening of the point two things are to be attended.

1. What is meant by a plain and powerful ministry, such as that of Elias.

2. How this hath force to effect so great a work.

1. The plainness of the ministry appears, when the language and words are such as those of the meanest capacity have some acquaintance with, and may be able to conceive; when the preacher accommodates his speech to the shallow understanding of the simplest hearer, so far as in him lies, always avoiding the frothy tinkling of quaint and far-fetched phrases, which take off, and blunt as it were the edge of the blessed truth and Word of God. Therefore the Apostle[1] rejects "the wisdom of words" as that which makes the cross of Christ; that is, the doctrine of Christ crucified, revealed in the Gospel, to lose his proper and powerful effect when it is so preached; where let it be observed that it is not only the vanity and emptiness of words which is here condemned, but even that pompous gaudiness, and elegancy of speech, which after an unsuspected manner steals away the mind and affection from the truth, and stays it with itself, when it should be a means both to convey both attention and affection from itself to the truth. He that puts so much sugar into the potion, that he hinders the strength, and the work of it by such a kind of mixture; though he please the palate of the patient, yet thereby he wrongs both the physic, and his health. So here in preaching.

For the excellency of eloquence, and enticing words of human wisdom which in case were com-

[1] St. Paul.

mendable to be used by him who is an orator, or a declaimer in the school,[2] in the pulpit becomes ever fruitless, and many times hurtful and prejudicial to the saving success of the Gospel. Hence the Apostle makes these as opposite, II *Cor.* 2.4: "My speech and my preaching was not with enticing words of man's wisdom, but in the demonstration of the spirit and of power": taking this for granted, as it appears in manner of the speech, the pomp of enticing words must not be discovered if we would have the spirit in the powerful work of it be demonstrated and made to appear; so much sweetness of words as may make way for the efficacy of the Gospel, may be admitted, and no more. And as all kind of curiosity and niceness is to be avoided, so all obscure and unusual phrases, dark sentences and expressions, strange languages are much more to be rejected, as opposite even to the end of speaking, much more to plainness of the preaching of the truth. Words are appointed by God in His providence, to be carriers as it were, by whose help the thoughts of our minds and the savory apprehensions of truth may be communicated, and conveyed over to the understanding of others, whereas by mystical and dark sentences he that comes to hear can by no means profit, because he cannot conceive, and so both hearer and speaker must needs miss their end, and lose their labor, since the one doth no good in his speech, because he so speaks that the other can receive no benefit. He that hath a pastoral heart must be so affected in dispensing the doctrine of grace, as Paul was in writing, *Rom.* 1.7, to all that are, "to all that be at Rome," so should he labor to reach out mercy and comfort to every soul in the congregation, by every sentence he delivers, as much as in him lies, whereas mystical cloudy discourses which exceed the capacity and understanding of most in the assembly, it's not possible they should work powerfully upon their consciences. That which the mind conceives not, the heart affects not: ministers should be, and, if faithful they will be as nurses to the people: they will prepare milk for the meanest and weakest, and meat for all, but never give dry crust or stones instead of bread to any; for that was not to feed, but to starve the child. Hence the Apostle concludes strange languages in the delivery of the truth, to be a curse sent of God upon a people, and therefore the minister that so communicates the Word, he is the messenger that brings a curse to the congregation, I *Cor.* 14.21, 22: "In the Law it is written, with men of other tongues and other lips, will I speak unto this people, wherefore tongues are for a sign not to them that believe, but to them that believe not": whereas prophesying should be in that openness and familiarity of language, that the unbelieving, yea, "unlearned should be convinced, and have the secrets of his heart made manifest to his own conscience," that so he may be truly humbled and acknowledge God's power and presence in the virtue of His own ordinance blessed by Him, I *Cor.* 14.24. It was the complaint of God, *Job* 38.2, "that counsel was darkened by words without knowledge." It was not allowed in Job's conference and debate of questions with his friends, it cannot but be much more condemned in publishing the mysteries of life and salvation to others. It's the scope of the calling and work of the ministry "to give the knowledge of God in the face of Jesus Christ," II *Cor.* 4.8. To darken knowledge therefore, is to cross God's honor, our own callings, the comforts of the people over whom we set, and to be concealers of God's mind, not interpreters and revealers of His will.

Objection: There is only one plea here objected, that carries any appearance of likelihood with it, gathered out of *Eccles.* 12.10, where it is said, "The preacher sought to find out acceptable words, and that that was written, was upright, even words of truth": was it Solomon's care directed by the spirit to study pleasing words to affect his hearers? Should not his practice be a pattern to all to imitate him in like expressions? Dare any affirm but that he did what he ought? And shall any be so careless or presumptuous as not to endeavor to follow that course recorded with so much commendation by the Holy Ghost?

Answer: I yield willingly to all the truths which the text holds out unto us; but it shall appear that nothing from thence by just consequence be collected, that will cross, but rather confirm, and that undoubtedly what hath been affirmed before. That the writings of men should be sound, their speeches acceptable, is granted; but when are they? How shall they be judged to be such? That's the doubt: which once cleared, the objection will be answered fully. Words then must be judged acceptable, not by the foolish fancies, corrupt and carnal humors of men, but from the warrant they have from the scripture, and the work they have in the hearers for their good, as the 11 verse of *Eccles.* 12 discovers; it being added as it were by way of explication, to evidence where that pleasantness of speech lay, "The words of the wise are as goads and nails fastened by the masters of assemblies which are given by one shepherd," as though the preacher should have expressed himself, more freely and fully thus. If any shall ask what these acceptable words formerly mentioned are, and how they may be discerned, it is easy for any thus to know them: by their working upon the heart, as we judge the goodness and virtue of physic by its working upon the

[2] Declamations were customary school and college exercises which all students performed.

body, or in the stomach. Those words which are as goads to awaken and spur on the sluggish and sleepy hearted to the performance of service with greater cheerfulness and speed: those that are as nails to fasten on the precious truths of God, upon the consciences of men, that they are kept within the compass of God's command as sheep within the fold.

Lastly, those words which are indited and taught not by "human wisdom, but by the spirit of Christ," I *Cor.* 2.4, who is the only chief shepherd of his church, and whose voice should only be heard: such words should be sought out by the speaker, such words deserve to be accounted acceptable by those who hear them. Now how far all quaintness and darkness of speech is from this warrant of the Lord, or this powerful work in the hearts of His people, let the sluggish and secure courses, the loose lives and conversations of such persons, parishes, places, and congregations, who have, and love such teachers, and such kind of teaching, proclaim and testify to all the world.

2. Plainness of preaching, appears also in the matter that is spoken: when sin and sinners are set out in their native and natural colors, and carry their proper names, whereby they may be owned suitable to the loathsomeness that is in them, and the danger of those evils which are their undoubted reward: a spade is a spade, and a drunkard is a drunkard, &c, and if he will have his sins, he must and shall have hell with them. It's Satan's policy (who painter or tyre-maker[3] like, cozens all the world with colors) to smut and disfigure the beautiful ways of godliness, and the glorious graces of the spirit, with the soot and dirt of reproaches, and base nick-names: sincerity, he terms singularity; exactness, puritanism and hypocrisy; and so ignorant men (who judge the person by the picture) are brought out of love and liking with those blessed ways of wisdom and holiness. Contrariwise, when he would cast a veil over the ugly and deformed face of Vice, and graceless courses, he is forced to lay some false colors of indifferency, delight, and pleasure: drunkenness is good fellowship, and neighborhood; covetousness comes masked under the vizard of frugality and moderation; cowardliness is trimmed and decked up in the robes of discretion, and wariness. If ministers will not be the devil's brokers, and followers, their manner of proceeding must be expressly contrary. When they come to preach, they must make sin appear truly odious, and fearful to the open view of all, that all may be afraid and endeavor to avoid it. Those secret wipes, and witty jerks, and nips at sin, at which the most profane are pleased, but not reformed, are utterly unsavory and unseeming the place, the person, the office, of the messenger of the Lord of Hosts. What! A minister a jester! O fearful! to make the pulpit a stage, to play with sin, when he should terrify the conscience for it? The Lord abominates the practice; he that knows and fears the Lord should abhor it with detestation. Thus plainly dealt Elias with Ahab, I *Kings* 18.13: "It's thou and thy father's house that have troubled Israel, because ye have forsaken the commandments of the Lord, and followed Baalim." So also with Israel, I *Kings* 18.21: "How long will you halt between two opinions? If the Lord be God, follow Him; but if Baal, then follow him." As if he should have said, away with this patching in profession, either a saint or a devil, make something of it; this is downright dealing. And thus plainly John the Baptist who had the same spirit dealt with Herod. He doth not beat the bush, and go behind the door to tell him his faults, and mince the matter with some intimations, but he speaks out, *Matt.* 14.4: "It is not lawful for thee to have thy brother Philip's wife": either thou must not have that incestuous harlot, or thou must not have grace and glory. Thus again he dealt with the Sadducees and Pharisees when he saw them come to his baptisms. He says to them, *Matt.* 3.7, "Oh ye generation of vipers, who hath forewarned you to flee from the wrath to come?" As if he should have said, eggs and birds, parents and posterity, you are a race of venomous, and poisonful wretches. What? A proud Pharisee to listen to the simplicity of the doctrine of grace, is it possible? If in sincerity and good earnest, you purpose to embrace the doctrine of truth, "bring forth then fruits worthy of amendment of life," verse 8.

We have done with the plainness of the ministry, we are now to inquire wherein the power of a ministry consists: and that appears in two things.

1. There must be soundness of argument, and undeniable evidence of reason out of the Word, which is able to command the conscience; such strength of truth, which like a mighty stream, may carry an understanding hearer. When the Apostle was to come amongst the slanting orators and silken doctors of Corinth, which so excelled in eloquence, he brings the trial of their ministry unto this touch, I *Cor.* 4. 19, 20: "I will know not the speech of them that are puffed up, but the power, for the kingdom of God stands not in word, but in power." It's not the flourishes of words, not the sound and tinkling of a company of fine sentences, like apish toys and rattles, that will commend our ministry in the account of God; there is no kingdom, no power of the work of the spirit; the heavenly majesty of an ordinance is not seen in such empty shells and shadows. A building with painted walls, and no pillars, would be of little use, and less continuance. A body framed

[3]A maker of head-dresses.

out of colors, may be a picture of a bird or beast, but a living creature it cannot be, because it wants the soul and substance which should give life and virtue thereunto. So it is when a multitude of gay sentences are packed together without the sinews and substance of convicting arguments: there may be the picture of a sermon, but the life and power of preaching there will not be in any such expressions.

That a minister may be powerful, an inward heat of heart, and holy affection is required, answerable and suitable to the matter, which is to be communicated; and those add great life and force to the delivery of the truth. "Out of the abundance of the heart the mouth speaks, and a good man out of the good treasure of his heart, brings forth good things," *Matt.* 12.35. Where then there is a heart awanting, the chiefest part of speech, the pith and heart of it is gone; for the several affections out of which the words arise, make an impression, and work a like temper of spirit in him to whom we utter and express ourselves. Thus we speak from heart to heart, and that is the best way to be in the bosom of the hearer, and the only way to make our words take place and prevail. He that mourns in speaking of sin, makes another mourn for sin committed. An exhortation that proceeds from the heart, carries a kind of authority and commission with it, to make way for itself not to return before it confer with the heart of him that will give attendance to it. Brainish discourses talk only with the understanding, they go no further, because they rise no deeper then from the understanding of him that speaks. The doctrine of the Gospel "is like the rain upon the herbs, and the dew upon the grass," *Deut.* 32.2. The strength and stirring of holy affections is like a mighty wind or tempest, makes the truth delivered to press in with more power and speed, and to soak in more deeply, even to the heart root of him that with meekness will receive it. ***

USE 2. The second use discovereth to us the fearful estate and miserable condition of those that lived a long time under a plain and powerful ministry, and yet their hearts have not been fitted and prepared for the Lord Jesus. It is a fearful suspicion that the Lord will never bestow any saving good upon that soul. He that hath lived under a powerful ministry many years, and yet is not wrought upon thereby, it cannot certainly be concluded, but it is greatly to be suspected, that the means of grace will never profit that man. Look as it is with the master carpenter, when he hath turned every piece of timber, and taken what he will for his turn, he tells them that be under him, let this be hewed, and that be framed and made fit for the building. Afterward he finds one piece broken, and another crackt, and another knotty. Why, what says he? There is no squaring of these, they are fit for nothing but for burning; they are not fit for any place in the building. Oh! take heed, when God's ministers have been cutting, and hewing, now exhorting, now persuading, now cutting the heart with reproof, and yet finds here a crackt heart, and there a stubborn soul, that will not be squared by the Word, lest then the Lord should say, these will never be fitted and prepared for me; they are fit for nothing but the fire. Oh! take heed of it, for he that will not be fitted for grace, shall be made a firebrand in Hell forever. Therefore all you that have lived under a powerful ministry, and yet are not prepared, go home and reason with your souls, and plead with your own hearts, and say, Lord, why am not I yet humbled and prepared? Shall I thus be always under the hacking and hewing of the Word, and never be framed? Such a man, and such a man was stubborn, and wicked, and profane, and yet the Lord hath brought him home, and he is become a broken-hearted Christian. What shall I think that am not fitted and prepared for Christ by all the means that I have had? Alas! thou mayest justly suspect God never intends good to thy soul. It is no absolute conclusion, but it is a great suspicion, that those that have lived under a plain and powerful ministry half a dozen years or longer, and have got no good, nor profited under the same, I say, it's a shrewd suspicion, that God will send them down to Hell. Therefore suspect thy own soul and say, Lord, will exhortations never prevail? Will instructions never do me any good? Will terrors, and reproofs never strike my heart? Why, I have heard sermons that would have shaken the very stones I trod on, that would have moved the seat I sat upon; the very fire of Hell hath flashed in my face, I have seen even the very plagues of Hell, I have had many exhortations, instructions, admonitions, and reproofs, and as powerful means as may be, which yet never did me any good. The Lord be merciful to such a poor soul, and turn his heart that he may lay hold of Mercy in due time.

USE 3. Exhortation. Is it so, that a plain and powerful ministry is the means of preparing the soul of a poor sinner for the Lord Jesus? Why then, when you hear the Word plainly and powerfully preached to you, labor that the Word may be so unto you as it is in itself. It is a preparing Word, labor you that it may prepare your hearts to receive Christ. And you that be hearers, everyone labor to save the soul of another; let the father speak concerning his children, and the husband concerning his wife and his family, and the wife concerning her husband. Oh, when will it once be, when will the time come that my child may be fitted for the Lord, when will it be that my poor family, my poor wife, my poor husband shall be prepared for the Lord; the Lord grant, that it may be, if not this sabbath, yet on another; if not this sermon, then at the next. Labor therefore to give way unto the Word of God, and suffer your souls to be wrought upon by it, for the Word is powerful to prepare your hearts, but the minister must hew and square your hearts before they can be prepared for the Lord Jesus, and you must "suffer the words of the exhortation" (as the Apostle says), *Heb.* 13.22. So likewise suffer the words of conviction, of reproof, of admonition, and hold and keep your hearts under the Word, that you may be wrought upon thereby. And as when men have set carpenters awork to build an house, then they come every day, and ask them, how doth the work go on? How doth the building go forward? When you are gone home, do you so reason with yourselves, and ask your own hearts how the work of the Lord goes forward in you? Is my heart yet humbled? Am I yet fitted and prepared for Christ? I thank God I find some work and power of the Word, and therefore I hope the building will go forward.

COTTON MATHER [1663-1728]

His father, Increase Mather, was pastor of the Second Church in Boston, President of Harvard, and perhaps the most powerful intellectual force in New England during his generation. One grandfather was Richard Mather, equally prestigious among first-generation ministers and author of the Cambridge Platform (1649) that established the New England Congregational way; his other grandfather was the famous John Cotton, inventor of the name "Congregational," chief adversary of Roger Williams, and the foremost architect of New England theology. It was a proud lineage, and Cotton Mather was equal to it.

He entered Harvard at twelve, took his B.A. at fifteen and his M.A. at eighteen, was ordained at twenty-two, and quickly emerged as the acknowledged leader of late-seventeenth-century theology, politics, and letters. Tremendously erudite, he wrote nearly five hundred books and pamphlets, mastered a dozen or more languages, dabbled in science, medicine, philanthropy, politics, and literature, was elected to the Royal Society of London, and corresponded with scholars from all over the Western world. He found time for three wives and fifteen children, and he died at the age of sixty-five, only five years after his father.

His writing, as varied as it is abundant, includes devotional tracts, sermons, biographies of New England notables, elegiac poetry, political fables, learned papers on subjects as diverse as hybridization and smallpox inoculation, literary criticism, and most significantly, the history of the culture his family had done so much to create and sustain. Almost all of this variety is contained in his monumental *Magnalia Christi Americana; or, The Ecclesiastical History of New England from Its First Planting,* which he completed in 1697, but had to send to London for publication (1702). In separate parts he therein describes the history of New England's settlement, the lives of governors and magistrates, the lives of sixty eminent divines, the development of Harvard College, the faith and order of the churches, "illustrious providences" affecting the country, and the "Wars of the Lord."

One of these wars, the assaults of Satan through the agency of witches, had long occupied his attention. In 1684 his father had completed a plan formulated some thirty years earlier—to record "such divine judgments, tempests, floods, earthquakes, thunders as are unusual, strange apparitions, or whatever else shall happen that is prodigious, witchcrafts, diabolical possessions, remarkable judgments upon noted sinners, eminent deliverances, and answers of prayer"—in *An Essay for the Recording of Illustrious*

Providences. And young Cotton continued the work in *Memorable Providences Relating to Witchcraft and Possessions* (1689).

In 1691, Satan focused on Salem Village, where the accusations of a few little "bewitched" girls created a panic that did not subside until twenty men and women and two dogs had been executed for witchcraft, fifty-five had confessed, one hundred and fifty were still imprisoned, and some two hundred others stood accused. Although Increase and Cotton Mather urged caution and propriety at the trials that ran from June to September, 1692, their credulity undoubtedly contributed to the catastrophe. Not a participant in the trials, Cotton Mather was commissioned to summarize the events and testimony, which he did under the title *The Wonders of the Invisible World* (London, 1692). The book was answered in 1700 by Robert Calef, a Boston merchant, under the sarcastic title, *More Wonders of the Invisible World*. In terms of the extent of similar events in Europe during the sixteenth and seventeenth centuries, the Salem witchcraft episode was a very minor one. But its impact on provincial New England, and especially on the pre-eminence of the clergy, was enormous; the damage to ministerial prestige contributed to the decline of the orthodoxy that Cotton Mather strove all his life to invigorate.

Further reading: Barrett Wendell, *Cotton Mather: The Puritan Priest*, 1891, 1963. David Levin, *What Happened in Salem?*, 1960. Chadwick Hansen, *Witchcraft at Salem*, 1969.

The Trial of Bridget Bishop

Ichabod Crane's remarkable "appetite for the marvellous" fed on what Washington Irving called Cotton Mather's "History of New England Witchcraft": "No tale was too gross or monstrous for his capacious swallow." And the trial testimony Mather provides here suggests that Crane was not alone among the credulous and superstitious. But the "poppets" found in Bridget Bishop's cellar should also remind us that malefic witchcraft was practiced in seventeenth-century New England as elsewhere. Even concerned ministers knew enough to boil urine with pins in it to drive off a supposed witch—fighting witchcraft with witchcraft; and many persons so profoundly believed in the power of witches to harm them that they succumbed to their own fears, assuming the condition of "bewitched" persons. Text: Cotton Mather, *The Wonders of the Invisible World* (London, 1693 [1692]).

II. The Tryal of Bridget Bishop, alias Oliver, at the Court of Oyer and Terminer, held at Salem, June 2, 1692.

I. She was indicted for bewitching of several persons in the neighborhood, the indictment being drawn up, according to the form in such cases as usual. And pleading, not guilty, there were brought in several persons, who had long undergone many kinds of miseries, which were preternaturally inflicted, and generally ascribed unto an horrible witchcraft. There was little occasion to prove the witchcraft, it being evident and notorious to all beholders. Now to fix the witchcraft on the prisoner of[1] the bar, the first thing used, was the testimony of[1] the bewitched; whereof several testified, that the shape of the prisoner did oftentimes very grievously pinch them, choke them, bite them, and afflict them; urging them to write their names in a book, which the said spectre called, ours. One of them did further testify, that it was the shape of this prisoner, with another, which one day took her from her wheel, and carrying her to the river-side, threatened there to drown her, if she did not sign to the book mentioned: which yet she refused. Others of them did also testify, that the said shape did in her threats brag to them that she had been the death of sundry persons, then by her named; that she had ridden a man then likewise named. Another testified, the apparition of ghosts unto the spectre of Bishop, crying out, you murdered us! About the truth whereof, there was in the matter of fact but too much suspicion.

II. It was testified, that at the examination of the prisoner before the magistrates, the bewitched were extremely tortured. If she did but cast her eyes on them, they were presently struck down; and this in such a manner as there could be no collusion in the business. But upon the touch of her hand upon them, when they lay in their swoons, they would immediately revive; and not upon the touch of any one's else. Moreover, upon some special actions of her body, as the shaking of her head, or the turning of her eyes, they presently and painfully fell into the like postures. And many of the like accidents now fell out, while she was at the bar. One at the same

[1] That is, *about* or *concerning*.

time testifying, that she said, she could not be troubled to see the afflicted thus tormented.

III. There was testimony likewise brought in, that a man striking once at the place, where a bewitched person said, the shape of the Bishop stood, the bewitched cried out, that he had tore her coat, in the place then particularly specified; and the woman's coat was found to be torn in that very place.

IV. One Deliverance Hobbs, who had confessed her being a witch, was now tormented by the spectres, for her confession. And she now testified, that this Bishop tempted her to sign the book again, and to deny what she had confessed. She affirmed, that it was the shape of this prisoner, which whipped her with iron rods, to compel her thereunto. And she affirmed, that this Bishop was at a general meeting of the witches, in a field at Salem-Village, and there partook of a diabolical sacrament in bread and wine then administered.

V. To render it further unquestionable, that the prisoner at the bar, was the person truly charged in this witchcraft, there were produced many evidences of other witchcrafts, by her perpetrated. For instance, John Cook testified, that about five or six years ago, one morning, about sun-rise, he was in his chamber assaulted by the shape of this prisoner: which looked on him, grinned at him, and very much hurt him with a blow on the side of the head: and that on the same day, about noon, the same shape walked in the room where he was, and an apple strangely flew out of his hand, into the lap of his mother, six or eight foot from him.

VI. Samuel Gray testified, that about fourteen years ago, he waked on a night, and saw the room where he lay full of light; and that he then saw plainly a woman between the cradle, and the bed-side, which looked upon him. He rose, and it vanished; tho' he found the doors all fast. Looking out at the entry-door, he saw the same woman, in the same garb again; and said, In God's name, what do you come for? He went to bed, and had the same woman again assaulting him. The child in the cradle gave a great screech, and the woman disappeared. It was long before the child could be quieted; and tho' it were a very likely thriving child, yet from this time it pined away, and after divers months, died in a sad condition. He knew not Bishop, nor her name; but when he saw her after this, he knew by her countenance, and apparel, and all circumstances, that it was the apparition of this Bishop, which had thus troubled him.

VII. John Bly and his wife testified, that he bought a sow of Edward Bishop, the husband of the prisoner; and was to pay the price agreed, unto another person. This prisoner being angry that she was thus hindered from fingering the money, quarrelled with Bly. Soon after which, the sow was taken with strange fits; jumping, leaping, and knocking her head against the fence; she seemed blind and deaf, and would neither eat nor be sucked. Whereupon a neighbor said, she believed the creature was overlooked; and sundry other circumstances concurred, which made the deponents believe that Bishop had bewitched it.

VIII. Richard Coman testified, that eight years ago, as he lay awake in his bed, with a light burning in the room, he was annoyed with the apparition of this Bishop, and of two more that were strangers to him, who came and oppressed him so, that he could neither stir himself, nor wake any one else, and that he was the night after, molested again in the like manner; the said Bishop, taking him by the throat, and pulling him almost out of the bed. His kinsman offered for this cause to lodge with him; and that night, as they were awake, discoursing together, this Coman was once more visited by the guests which had formerly been so troublesome; his kinsman being at the same time strook speechless, and unable to move hand or foot. He had laid his sword by him, which these unhappy spectres did strive much to wrest from him; only he held too fast for them. He then grew able to call the people of his house; but altho' they heard him, yet they had not power to speak or stir; until at last, one of the people crying out, What's the matter? the spectres all vanished.

IX. Samuel Shattock[2] testified, that in the year, 1680, this Bridget Bishop, often came to his house upon such frivolous and foolish errands, that they suspected she came indeed with a purpose of mischief. Presently, whereupon, his eldest child, which was of as promising health and sense, as any child of its age, began to droop exceedingly; and the oftener that Bishop came to the house, the worse grew the child. As the child would be standing at the door, he would be thrown and bruised against the stones, by an invisible hand, and in like sort knock his face against the sides of the house, and bruise it after a miserable manner. After this Bishop would bring him things to dye, and whereof he could not imagine any use; and when she paid him a piece of money, the purse and money were unaccountably conveyed out of a locked box, and never seen more. The child was immediately, hereupon, taken with terrible fits, whereof his friends thought he would have died: indeed he did almost nothing but cry and sleep for several months together; and at length his understanding was utterly taken away. Among other symptoms of an enchantment upon him, one was, that there was a board in the garden, whereon he

[2] Ironically, the same man who in 1661 wrote *The Quaker Petition* seeking legal redress for persecutions then suffered by Quakers in Salem.

would walk; and all the invitations in the world could never fetch him off. About 17 or 18 years after, there came a stranger to Shattock's house, who seeing the child, said, This poor child is bewitched; and you have a neighbor living not far off, who is a witch. He added, your neighbor has had a falling out with your wife; and she said, in her heart, your wife is a proud woman, and she would bring down her pride in this child. He then remembered, that Bishop had parted from his wife in muttering and menacing terms, a little before the child was taken ill. The abovesaid stranger would needs carry the bewitched boy with him, to Bishop's house, on pretence of buying a pot of cider. The woman entertained him in a furious manner; and flew also upon the boy, scratching his face till the blood came; and saying, Thou rogue, what dost thou bring this fellow here to plague me? Now it seems the man had said, before he went, that he would fetch blood of her. Ever after the boy was followed with grievous fits, which the doctors themselves generally ascribed unto witchcraft; and wherein he would be thrown still into the fire or the water, if he were not constantly looked after; and it was verily believed that Bishop was the cause of it.

X. John Louder testified, that upon some little controversy with Bishop about her fowls, going well to bed, he did awake in the night by moonlight, and did see clearly the likeness of this woman grievously oppressing him; in which miserable condition she held him, unable to help himself, till near day. He told Bishop of this; but she denied it, and threatened him very much. Quickly after this, being at home on a Lord's day, with the doors shut about him, he saw a black pig approach him; at which, he going to kick, it vanished away. Immediately after, sitting down, he saw a black thing jump in at the window, and come and stand before him. The body was like that of a monkey, the feet like a cock's, but the face much like a man's. He being so extremely affrighted, that he could not speak; this monster spoke to him, and said, I am a messenger sent unto you, for I understand that you are in some trouble of mind, and if you will be ruled by me, you shall want for nothing in this world. Whereupon he endeavored to clap his hands upon it; but he could feel no substance; and it jumped out of the window again; but immediately came in by the porch, tho' the doors were shut, and said, You had better take my counsel. He then struck at it with a stick, but struck only the ground-sel, and broke the stick: the arm with which he struck was presently disenabled, and it vanished away. He presently went out at the back-door, and spied this Bishop, in her orchard, going toward her house; but he had not power to set one foot forward unto her. Whereupon, returning into the house, he was immediately accosted by the monster he had seen before; which goblin was now going to fly at him; whereat he cry'd out, The whole armor of God be between me and you! So it sprang back, and flew over the apple tree; shaking many apples off the tree, in its flying over. At its leap, it flung dirt with its feet against the stomach of the man; whereon he was then struck dumb, and so continued for three days together. Upon the producing of this testimony, Bishop denied that she knew this deponent: yet their two orchards joined; and they had often had their little quarrels for some years together.

XI. William Stacy testified, that receiving money of this Bishop, for work done by him; he was gone but a matter of three rods from her, and looking for his money, found it unaccountably gone from him. Some time after, Bishop asked him, whether his father would grind her grist for her? He demanded why? She replied, Because folks count me a witch. He answered, No question but he will grind it for you. Being then gone about six rods from her, with a small load in his cart, suddenly the off-wheel slumped; and sunk down into an hole, upon plain ground; so that the deponent was forced to get help for the recovering of the wheel: but stepping back to look for the hole, which might give him this disaster, there was none at all to be found. Some time after, he was waked in the night; but it seemed as light as day; and he perfectly saw the shape of this Bishop in the room, troubling of him; but upon her going out, all was dark again. He charged Bishop afterwards with it, and she denied it not; but was very angry. Quickly after, this deponent having been threatened by Bishop, as he was in a dark night going to the barn, he was very suddenly taken or lifted from the ground, and thrown against a stone wall: after that, he was again hoisted up and thrown down a bank, at the end of his house. After this again, passing by this Bishop, his horse with a small load, striving to draw, all his gears flew to pieces, and the cart fell down; and this deponent going then to lift a bag of corn, of about two bushels, could not budge it with all his might.

Many other pranks of this Bishop's this deponent was ready to testify. He also testified, that he verily believed, the said Bishop was the instrument of his daughter Priscilla's death; of which suspicion, pregnant reasons were assigned.

XII. To crown all, John Bly and William Bly testified, that being employed by Bridget Bishop, to help take down the cellar-wall of the old house wherein she formerly lived, they did in holes of the said old wall, find several poppets, made up of rags and hogs-brussels, with headless pins in them, the points being outward; whereof she could give no account to the court, that was reasonable or tolerable.

XIII. One thing that made against the prisoner was, her being evidently convicted of gross lying in the court, several times, while she was making her plea; but besides this, a jury of women found a preternatural teat upon her body[3]: but upon a second search, within 3 or 4 hours, there was no such thing to be seen. There was also an account of other people whom this woman had afflicted; and there might have been many more, if they had been enquired for; but there was no need of them.

XIV. There was one very strange thing more, with which the court was newly entertained. As this woman was under a guard, passing by the great and spacious meeting-house of Salem, she gave a look towards the house: and immediately a demon invisibly entering the meeting-house, tore down a part of it; so that tho' there was no person to be seen there, yet the people, at the noise, running in, found a board, which was strongly fastened with several nails, transported unto another quarter of the house.
1692

Of Style

Manuductio ad Ministerium: Directions for a Candidate of the Ministry was published in 1726. In the training of a preacher of the Word of God, Mather found a place for poetry, recommending not only Homer and Virgil, despite their pagan idolatries, but even advising scholars to write poetry themselves—"try your young wings now and then." But to the young men of Boston it seemed that Mather's own prose too frequently outdid itself poetically. They found it ornate, overelaborated, pretentiously aureate, while they preferred a direct, economical prose in the service of business, news, and science. Though Mather here defends a richer, more embellished style, he curiously does so in a prose as direct and pointed as Hooker's. Text: T. J. Holmes and K. B. Murdock, eds., *Manuductio ad Ministerium* (New York, 1938; The Facsimile Text Society, no. 42).

There has been a deal of ado about a style; so much, that I must offer you my sentiments upon it. There is a way of writing, wherein the author endeavors, that the reader may have something to the purpose in every paragraph. There is not only a vigor sensible in every sentence, but the paragraph is embellished with profitable references, even to something beyond what is directly spoken. Formal and painful quotations are not studied; yet all that could be learnt from them is insinuated. The writer pretends not unto reading, yet he could not have writ as he does if he had not read very much in his time; and his composures are not only a cloth of gold, but also struck with as many jewels, as the gown of a Russian ambassador. This way of writing has been decried by many, and is at this day more than ever so, for the same reason, that in the old story, the grapes were decried: that they were not ripe. A lazy, ignorant, conceited set of authors, would persuade the whole tribe, to lay aside that way of writing, for the same reason that one would have persuaded his brethren to part with the encumbrance of their bushy tails. But however fashion and humour may prevail, they must not think that the club at their coffee-house is all the world, but there will always be those, who will in this case be governed by indisputable reason: and who will think, that the real excellency of a book will never lie in saying of little; that the less one has for his money in a book, 'tis really the more valuable for it; and that the less one is instructed in a book, and the more of superfluous margin, and superficial harangue, and the less of substantial matter one has in it, the more 'tis to be accounted of? And if a more massy way of writing be never so much disgusted at this day, a better gust will come on, as will some other thing, *quae jam cecidere.* In the meantime, nothing appears to me more impertinent and ridiculous than the modern way (I cannot say rule; for they have none!) of criticizing. The blades that set up for critics, I know not who constituted or commissioned 'em!—they appear to me, for the most part as contemptible, as they are a supercilious generation. For indeed no two of them have the same style; and they are as intolerably cross-grained and severe in their censures one upon another, as they are upon the rest of mankind. But while each of them, conceitedly enough, sets up for the standard of perfection, we are entirely at a loss which fire to follow. Nor can you easily find any one thing wherein they agree for their style, except perhaps a perpetual care to give us jejune and empty pages, without such touches of erudition (so to speak in the style of an ingenious traveler) as may make the discourses less tedious, and more enriching, to the mind of him that peruses them. There is much talk of a florid style, obtaining among the pens, that are most in vogue; but how often would it puzzle one, even with the best glasses to find the flowers! And if they were to be chastised for it, it would be with as much of justice, as Jerome was, for being a Ciceronian. After all, every man will have his own style, which will distinguish him as much as his gait: and if you can attain to that which I have newly described, but always writing so as to give an easy conveyance

[3] Devilish spirits (familiars) appeared to witches to suck on their bodies, leaving behind small marks or teats, which especially in England and New England became primary evidence that persons were indeed leagued with the Devil, and were therefore witches.

unto your ideas, I would not have you by any scourging be driven out of your gait; but if you must confess a fault in it, make a confession like that of the lad unto his father while he was beating him for his versifying.

However, since every man will have his own style, I would pray, that we may learn to treat one another with mutual civilities, and condescensions, and handsomely indulge one another in this, as gentlemen do in other matters.

I wonder what ails people, that they can't let Cicero write in the style of Cicero, and Seneca write in the (much other!) style of Seneca; and own that both may please in their several ways. But I will freely tell you; what has made me consider the humourists that set up for critics upon style, as the most unregardable set of mortals in the world, is this! Far more illustrious critics than any of those to whom I am now bidding defiance, and no less men than your Erasmus's, and your Grotius's, have taxed the Greek style of the New Testament, with I know not what solecisms and barbarisms; and, how many learned folks have obsequiously run away with the notion! Whereas 'tis an ignorant and an insolent whimsy; which they have been guilty of. It may be (and particularly by an ingenious Blackwall, it has been) demonstrated, that the gentlemen are mistaken in every one of their pretended instances; all the unquestionable classics, may be brought in, to convince them of their mistakes. Those glorious oracles are as pure Greek as ever was written in the world; and so correct, so noble, so sublime in their style, that never anything under the cope of heaven, but the Old Testament, has equaled it.

1726

EDWARD TAYLOR [1642?-1729]

The finest poet of the American seventeenth century remained unknown for more than two hundred years. Born and raised in England during the period of Puritan domination, Edward Taylor ventured to New England in 1668, where he immediately entered Harvard College. Three years later he graduated and accepted a call to minister to the frontier town of Westfield, Massachusetts. There he spent the rest of his life, bringing his vigorous intellect to bear on the concerns of that outpost in the wilderness, building its defenses against disease, Indians, civil disorder, heresy, and especially the "apostasy" of such liberal church reformers as Solomon Stoddard of Northampton.

Yet it was not in such worldly activities that Taylor's life found its focus and deepest realization, but rather in the realm of the spirit, which he explored doggedly as he prepared to administer the sacrament of the Lord's Supper (Communion). For a period of over forty years, from 1682 to 1725, he meditated the mysteries of Christ in the sacrament, uttering his pain and delight in 217 "Preparatory Meditations," in a long dramatic narrative poem called "God's Determinations," and in several miscellaneous poems. This solitary singer took great pains with his devotional poetry, seeking homely imagery, intentionally packing his lines and roughing his meters as did the English "metaphysical" poets Donne, Herbert, and Quarles. Except for a few stanzas, his poetry remained unpublished until the late 1930's, when Thomas H. Johnson recognized that the manuscript, in the possession of the Yale University Library, was a literary discovery of the first magnitude.

Taylor's poems prove that a thoroughly orthodox, even conservative, New England Puritan could write real poetry. Of course, to him a poem was less a work of art than an act of religious worship. He never ceased to marvel at the God who took on a human nature and lovingly endured death to save his Elect; the sacrament that symbolized and re-enacted that union of divine and human natures became for Taylor the occasion of both prayer and poetry. "Meditate upon the feast," he urged in his *Treatise Concerning the Lord's Supper* (1694), "its causes, its nature, its guests, its dainties, its reason, and ends: and its benefits, etc. For it carries in its nature and circumstances an umbrage, or epitomized draught of the whole grace of the gospel." The sacrament was central to almost everything he wrote; maintaining and celebrating its purity, against those who valued it less highly than he, became the major effort of his life and art.

Further reading: *Poems,* ed. D. E. Stanford, 1960; abridged edition (paperbound), 1963. Norman S. Grabo, *Edward Taylor,* 1961.

Huswifery

This is Taylor's best-known and most frequently cited poem. In the same form as his *Preparatory Meditations,* "Huswifery" develops its central conceit or brief allegory with unusual consistency. In his *Treatise Concerning the Lord's Supper* (1694), he argued that participating in the sacrament of the Lord's Supper, or Communion, required an appropriate "wedden garment," as in the parable of the wedding feast of the king's son (Matth. xxii.12). "It's such a rich web," he maintained, "that only the gospel markets afford; it's such a web that is only wove in the looms of the gospel, nay, and a richer web and better huswifery it gets not up." Evangelical righteousness is the warp and woof of that garment; with that the poet prays in "Huswifery" to be clothed, so that he may purely and safely partake of the sacrament.

Text: *The Poems of Edward Taylor,* ed. Donald E. Stanford (New Haven, 1960), which for all the poems given below follows the texts established by Thomas H. Johnson in *The Poetical Works of Edward Taylor* (New York, 1939; Princeton, 1943). For this anthology, spelling has been to some extent modernized.

Make me, O Lord, Thy spinning wheel complete.
  Thy holy Word my distaff make for me.
Make mine affections thy swift flyers neat,
  And make my soul Thy holy spool to be.
  My conversation make to be Thy reel,
  And reel the yarn thereon spun of Thy wheel.[1]

Make me Thy loom then, knit therein this twine:
  And make Thy holy Spirit, Lord, wind quills:
Then weave the web Thyself. The yarn is fine.
  Thine ordinances make my fulling mills.[2]
  Then dye the same in heavenly colors choice,
  All pink't with varnish't flowers of paradise.

Then clothe therewith mine understanding, will,
  Affections, judgment, conscience, memory;
My words and actions, that their shine may fill
  My ways with glory and Thee glorify.
  Then mine apparel shall display before Ye
  That I am clothed in holy robes for glory.[3]

1694?

Upon Wedlock and Death of Children

The speaker of most of Taylor's poems is not himself but a representative saint, the personified Church, a collective "I". "Upon Wedlock" is unusual among his poems for its intensely personal subject and emotion. (Twice married, Taylor was father to thirteen children.)

The "knot" of line 1 refers simply to a small plot of flowers, but it quickly expands to include a striking range of meanings. Common to them all is the sense of constriction or tightness residing at the heart of Taylor's sense of loss. When in the fifth stanza Taylor consoles himself for the loss of his second child, the sentiment is touching but acceptable. But when the fourth child also dies (l. 34), amid "torture, vomit, screechings, groans," and again Taylor accepts the loss as God's will, we are made to feel his anguish and resistance as he finds a tense consolation in "I piecemeal pass to glory bright in them." Brave but bitter, the poem shows us a truly human side of seventeenth-century existence.

Taylor had by this time written several verse elegies for prominent New England personages, and showed himself the master of this form of colonial poetry. "Upon Wedlock" belongs among his finest accomplishments.

A curious knot God made in Paradise,
  And drew it out inamled neatly fresh.
It was the true-love knot, more sweet than spice,
  And set with all the flowers of grace's dress.

Huswifery. [1] In spinning, the *distaff* is the forked stick that holds the wool or flax; *flyers* are the revolving arms of the spinning wheel; the *reel* holds the finished thread; *quills* are spindles; *fulling mills* finish or polish the cloth; and *pink't* means decoratively perforated.

[2] Taylor here excludes the ordinance of the Lord's Supper, referring only to those ordained to convert: hearing the Word preached, baptism, and church membership.

[3] "It is the robe of evangelical righteousness constituting the soul complete in the sight of God." See his *Treatise Concerning the Lord's Supper,* 1966.

It's weddens knot, that ne'er can be unti'd:
No Alexander's sword can it divide.[1]

The slips here planted, gay and glorious grow:
Unless an hellish breath do singe their plumes.
Here primrose, cowslips, roses, lillies blow,
With violets and pinks that void perfumes:
Whose beauteous leaves o'erlaid with honey dew,
And chanting birds chirp out sweet music true.

When in this knot I planted was, my stock
Soon knotted, and a manly flower outbrake.[2]
And after it my branch again did knot:
Brought out another flow'r: its sweet-breath'd mate.
One knot gave one tother the tother's place.
Whence checkling smiles fought in each other's face.

But oh! a glorious hand from glory came,
Guarded with angels, soon did crop this flow'r,
Which almost tore the root up of the same,
At that unlookt for, dolesome, darksome hour.
In prayer to Christ perfum'd it did ascend,
And angels bright did it to heaven 'tend.

But pausing on't, this sweet perfum'd my thought,
Christ would in glory have a flow'r, choice, prime,
And having choice, chose this my branch forth brought.
Lord, take't. I thank Thee, Thou tak'st ought of mine;
It is my pledge in glory; part of me
Is now in it, Lord, glorified with Thee.

But praying o'er my branch, my branch did sprout,
And bore another manly flower, and gay,
And after that another sweet brake out,
The which the former hand soon got away.
But oh! the torture, vomit, screechings, groans:
And six weeks' fever would pierce hearts like stones.

Grief o'er doth flow: and nature fault would find
Were not Thy will my spell, charm, joy, and gem:
That as I said, I say, take, Lord, they're Thine:
I piecemeal pass to glory bright in them.
I joy, may I sweet flowers for glory breed,
Whether Thou get'st them green, or lets them seed.

c. 1682

Upon Wedlock. [1]Gordian, King Midas' father, tied a knot so intricate that an oracle declared whoever undid it would rule Asia. Alexander the Great solved the difficulty by cutting the knot with his sword.

[2]Taylor, who first married in 1674, here mentions four children: Samuel, who reached maturity (line 14); Elizabeth, 1676-77 (line 16); James, who also survived childhood (line 32); and Elizabeth, 1681-82 (line 33).

Preparatory Meditations

Taylor described these poems as "Preparatory Meditations before my Approach to the Lord's Supper, Chiefly upon the Doctrine preached upon the Day of Administration." Days of administration came at roughly six-week intervals; for them Taylor prepared a suitable sermon, responding to his own exhortation in poems such as these, a few titled but most of them numbered, both sermons and poems based on the same "doctrine" and both usually drawn from the same scriptural text.

The Reflexion

The soul knows that the Lord is glorious, but by virtue of its "inkfac'd sin" can neither perceive that glory fully nor bring its "sweetness" to itself. At once then a complaint, an act of praise, and a petition for purifying grace, the poem's complexity is accentuated by the surprising, almost surrealistic, changes the central image of the rose undergoes. First a symbol of ultimate beauty, following Solomon, it can stand like a pearl, constitute a bundle of sunbeams, sit most unnaturally carving like the host at a meal, and finally return to its flowery nature. This strange juxtaposition of images makes it impossible to visualize literally what is described in the poem. Taylor, however, wrote in a rich tradition of emblem poems where natural objects in unnatural but symbolically appropriate relationships were usually accompanied by woodcuts or engravings that somewhat clarified the meaning of the poems.

[Canticles ii.1: I am the rose of Sharon]

Lord, art Thou at the table head above
Meat, med'cine, sweetness, sparkling beauties, to
Enamor souls with flaming flakes of love,
And not my trencher, nor my cup o'erflow?
Ben't I a bidden guest? Oh! sweat mine eye:
O'erflow with tears: Oh! draw thy fountains dry.

Shall I not smell thy sweet, oh! Sharon's rose?
Shall not mine eye salute thy beauty? Why?
Shall thy sweet leaves their beauteous sweets upclose?
As half asham'd my sight should on them lie?
Woe's me! For this my sighs shall be in grain
Offer'd on Sorrow's altar for the same.

Had not my soul's, Thy conduit, pipes stopt been
With mud, what ravishment would'st Thou convey?
Let Grace's golden spade dig till the spring
Of tears arise, and clear this filth away.

Lord, let Thy Spirit raise my sighings till
These pipes my soul do with Thy sweetness fill.

Earth once was Paradise of heaven below
Till inkfac'd sin had it with poison stockt;
And chased this Paradise away into
Heav'ns upmost loft, and it in glory lockt.
But Thou, sweet Lord, hast with Thy golden key
Unlockt the door, and made, a golden day.

Once at Thy feast, I saw Thee pearl-like stand
'Tween heaven, and earth, where heaven's bright glory all
In streams fell on Thee, as a floodgate and,
Like sunbeams through Thee on the world to fall.
Oh! Sugar sweet then! My dear sweet Lord, I see
Saints' heaven-lost happiness restor'd by Thee.

Shall heaven and earth's bright glory all up lie,
Like sunbeams bundled in the sun, in Thee?
Dost Thou sit rose at table head, where I
Do sit, and carv'st no morsel sweet for me?
So much before, so little now! Sprindge,[1] Lord,
Thy rosy leaves, and me their glee afford.

Shall not Thy rose my garden fresh perfume?
Shall not Thy beauty my dull heart assail?
Shall not Thy golden gleams run through this gloom?
Shall my black velvet mask Thy fair face veil?
Pass o'er my faults: shine forth, bright sun; arise!
Enthrone Thy rosy-self within mine eyes.
1688

The Experience

When a full sense of real communion with God occurred, "sweet though short," Taylor responded with rapturous confidence. Experiences like this gave him the assurance that he was himself among God's Elect; his delight is appropriate. The claim to be higher than the angels in the order of God's creation borders on heresy, but is carefully kept within the bounds of Puritan orthodoxy, and was asserted also by several of Taylor's contemporaries, including the famous Increase Mather.

Oh! that I always breath'd in such an air,
As I suckt in, feeding on sweet content!
Disht up unto my soul ev'n in that prayer
Pour'd out to God over last sacrament.
What beams of light wrapt up my sight to find
Me nearer God than e'er came in my mind?

Most strange it was! But yet more strange that shine
Which fill'd my soul then to the brim to spy
My nature with Thy nature all divine
Together join'd in Him that's Thou, and I.

The Reflexion. [1] Unfold, spread out.

Flesh of my flesh, bone of my bone. There's run
Thy Godhead, and my manhood in Thy Son.

Oh! that that flame which Thou didst on me cast
Might me enflame, and lighten e'ry where.
Then heaven to me would be less at last,
So much of heaven I should have while here.
Oh! Sweet though short! I'll not forget the same.
My nearness, Lord, to Thee did me enflame.

I'll claim my right: give place, ye angels bright.
Ye further from the Godhead stand than I.
My nature is your lord; and doth unite
Better than yours unto the Deity.
God's throne is first and mine is next: to you
Only the place of waiting-men is due.

Oh! that my heart, thy golden harp might be
Well tun'd by glorious grace, that e'ry string
Screw'd to the highest pitch, might unto Thee
All praises wrapt in sweetest music bring.
I praise Thee, Lord, and better praise Thee would,
If what I had, my heart might ever hold.
1687

I Kenning Through Astronomy

In many ways the most striking of his *Preparatory Meditations,* this poem abounds in emblematic conceptions that, as Austin Warren has observed, simultaneously invite and repel visualization, in shocking imagery as God grinds and kneads Christ into the bread of life, and in packed or strong lines as they had been popularized by the English Metaphysical poets (e.g., "This fill would to the brim/ Heav'n's whelm'd-down crystal meal bowl, yea and higher").

John vi.51: I am the living bread.

I kenning through astronomy divine
The world's bright battlement, wherein I spy
A golden path my pencil cannot line
From that bright throne unto my threshold lie.
And while my puzzled thoughts about it pore,
I find the bread of life in't at my door.

When that this bird of paradise put in
This wicker cage (my corpse) to tweedle praise
Had peckt the fruit forbid: and so did fling
Away its food, and lost its golden days;
It fell into celestial famine sore:
And never could attain a morsel more.

Alas! alas! poor bird, what wilt thou do?
This creatures' field no food for souls e'er gave:
And if thou knock at angels' doors, they show
An empty barrel: they no soul bread have.

Alas! poor bird, the world's white loaf is done,
And cannot yield thee here the smallest crumb.

In this sad state, God's tender bowels[1] run
Out streams of grace: and He to end all strife
The purest wheat in heaven, His dear-dear Son
Grinds, and kneads up into this bread of life:
Which bread of life from heaven down came and stands
Disht on thy table up by angels' hands.

Did God mould up this bread in heaven, and bake,
Which from His table came, and to thine goeth?
Doth He bespeak thee thus: "This soul bread take;
Come, eat thy fill of this, thy God's white loaf!
It's food too fine for angels; yet come, take
And eat thy fill! It's heaven's sugar cake."

What grace is this knead in this loaf? This thing
Souls are but petty things it to admire.
Ye angels, help: this fill would to the brim
Heav'n's whelm'd-down crystal meal bowl, yea and higher.
This bread of life dropt in thy mouth doth cry:
"Eat, eat me, soul, and thou shalt never die."

1688

God's Determinations

Sometime probably between 1685 and 1695, Taylor composed the thirty-five poems that he titled, collectively, *Gods Determinations Touching His Elect: and the Elects Combat in their Conversion, and Coming up to God in Christ together with the Comfortable Effects thereof.* The poem mingles lyric, dramatic, narrative, and meditative modes in tracing man's fall, God's plan to redeem him, man's futile attempts to resist God's grace, and his success, with the help of Christ and the saints, against the accusations of a Satanic conscience, until in the last six lyrics he joyously enters the church and ecstatically rises to partake of the royal feast God has prepared for him.

The Preface

The questions put to Job by the Lord had become a classical *locus* or set-piece for writers in Taylor's time. The freshness of Taylor's treatment lies in his various allusions to human crafts (lathe, bellows, furnace, mould, etc.), which serve to contrast the diminutive capacities of man with the boundless creative power that "spake all things from nothing." Even as he praises God's handiwork, the poet relies upon inadequate, diminishing terms that reduce creation to a pretty trinket or a toy, and so reveals the incapacity of man to appreciate the grandeur of God's accomplishment. Thereby he shows man's weakness and his reliance—unconscious though it may be—upon God, the main theme of the whole of *God's Determinations.* Taylor builds the poem from a series of contrasts between *all* and *nothing,* and indeed it is an all-or-nothing proposition that faces fallen man in the ensuing poems.

Infinity, when all things it beheld
In nothing, and of nothing all did build,
Upon what base was fixt the lathe, wherein
He turn'd this globe, and riggall'd[1] it so trim?
Who blew the bellows of His furnace vast?
Or held the mould wherein the world was cast?
Who laid its corner stone? Or whose command?
Where stand the pillars upon which it stands?
Who lac'd and fillitted the earth so fine,
With rivers like green ribbons smaragdine?[2]
Who made the seas its selvedge, and it locks
Like a quilt ball within a silver box?
Who spread its canopy? Or curtains spun?
Who in this bowling alley bowled the sun?
Who made it always when it rises set
To go at once both down, and up to get?
Who th'curtain rods made for this tapestry?
Who hung the twinkling lanthorns in the sky?[3]
Who? who did this? or who is He? Why, know
It's only Might Almighty this did do.
His hand hath made this noble work which stands
His glorious handiwork not made by hands.
Who spake all things from nothing; and with ease
Can speak all things to nothing, if He please.
Whose little finger at His pleasure can
Outmete ten thousand worlds with half a span;
Whose might almighty can by half a looks
Root up the rocks and rock the hills by th'roots.
Can take this mighty world up in His hand,
And shake it like a squitchen or a wand,
Whose single frown will make the heavens shake
Like as an aspen leaf the wind makes quake.
Oh! what a might is this! Whose single frown
Doth shake the world as it would shake it down?
Which all from nothing fet,[4] from nothing, all:
Hath all on nothing set, lets nothing fall.
Gave all to nothing man indeed, whereby
Through nothing man all might Him glorify.
In nothing then embosst the brightest gem
More precious than all preciousness in them.
But nothing man did throw down all by sin:
And darkened that lightsome gem in him.
That now his brightest diamond is grown
Darker by far than any coalpit stone.

I Kenning. [1] A conventional image for pity or compassion.

The Preface. [1] Grooved.
[2] Emerald.
[3] Lines 1-18 are based upon "The Voice from the Whirlwind," Job xxxviii.1-41.
[4] An old form of "fetched."

The Glory of and Grace in the Church Set Out

In imagery very like that of "Upon Wedlock and Death of Children," Taylor here (near the end of *God's Determinations*) shows the soul who has now accepted her conversion the blessings of being joined to the church. The versatile stanzaic pattern suggests his knowledge of George Herbert, while the refrain inescapably reminds one of John Donne's "A Hymn to God the Father."

Come now behold
Within this knot what flowers do grow:
Spangled like gold:
Whence wreaths of all perfumes do flow.
Most curious colors of all sorts you shall
With all sweet spirits scent. Yet that's not all.

Oh! Look, and find
These choicest flowers most richly sweet
Are disciplin'd
With artificial angels meet.
An heap of pearls is precious: but they shall
When set by art excel. Yet that's not all.

Christ's Spirit showers
Down in His Word, and sacraments
Upon these flowers,
The clouds of grace divine contents.
Such things of wealthy blessings on them fall
As make them sweetly thrive. Yet that's not all.

Yet still behold!
All flourish not at once. We see
While some unfold
Their blushing leaves, some buds there be.
Here's faith, hope, charity in flower, which call
On yonders in the bud. Yet that's not all.

But as they stand
Like beauties reeching in perfume
A divine hand
Doth hand them up to glory's room:
Where each in sweet'ned songs all praises shall
Sing all o're heaven for aye. And that's but all.

The Joy of Church Fellowship Rightly Attended

This is the last poem of *God's Determinations*. The saints, now fully convinced of their salvation and joying in their church membership ("in Christ's coach"), soar heavenward. Some backslide and must be retuned to become "more melodious"; others who were predetermined to be saved, but were kept from church membership, trudge toward glory rather than ride. But all raise their uncontainable joy in song, an apt emblem of Taylor's own sense of poetic motive and purpose.

In heaven soaring up, I dropt an ear
On earth: and oh! sweet melody!
And listening, found it was the saints who were
Encoacht for heaven that sang for joy.
For in Christ's coach they sweetly sing,
As they to glory ride therein.

Oh! joyous hearts! Enfir'd with holy flame!
Is speech thus tasseled with praise?
Will not your inward fire of joy contain,
That it in open flames doth blaze?
For in Christ's coach saints sweetly sing,
As they to glory ride therein.

And if a string do slip, by chance, they soon
Do screw it up again: whereby
They set it in a more melodious tune
And a diviner harmony.
For in Christ's coach they sweetly sing,
As they to glory ride therein.

In all their acts, public, and private, nay
And secret too, they praise impart.
But in their acts divine, and worship, they
With hymns do offer up their heart.
Thus in Christ's coach they sweetly sing,
As they to glory ride therein.

Some few not in; and some whose time and place
Block up this coach's way, do go
As travelers afoot:[1] and so do trace
The road that gives them right thereto;
While in this coach these sweetly sing
As they to glory ride therein.

Joy of Church Fellowship. [1] Those elect souls who through various circumstances did not have access to church membership.

JONATHAN EDWARDS [1703–1758]

No one exemplified the force of the Puritan plain style better than Jonathan Edwards; its proof lay in the startling effects it had upon his hearers. By the time he was eleven or twelve, his precocious essays on natural and supernatural topics clearly revealed his rare ability to observe minutely and reason tightly. As student and instructor at Yale from 1716 to 1722 he formed the basic philosophical positions that underlay his later writings; as his grandfather Solomon Stoddard's assistant at the Northampton church, and later as pastor in his own right, he was able to put those theories into confirming practice.

From Edwards' plain talk, a series of religious revivals radiated from Northampton through the Connecticut Valley in 1734 and 1735. Revitalized by the arrival of the famed English evangelist George Whitefield in 1740, this "Great Awakening" became for five years the most powerful social force of the time. With almost the detachment of Benjamin Franklin, who carefully paced off the distance Whitefield's famous voice would carry, Edwards reported and investigated forces he himself had done much to create in such compelling sermons as *Sinners in the Hands of an Angry God.* His case studies in *A Faithful Narrative of the Surprising Work of God in . . . Conversion* (1736) had been widely published and translated. Further exploring the psychology of religious experience in his brilliant *Treatise Concerning Religious Affections* (1746), he drew a careful distinction between true and false religious emotion and analyzed at length the role of beauty, imagination, and taste.

Convinced by his observations that requirements for church membership had become too lax and that reform was necessary, Edwards attempted to reverse his grandfather's liberal policies and was consequently dismissed from his Northampton pulpit in 1750. He accepted a call to Stockbridge, in the Berkshires, and while ministering to that remote Indian community he returned to the speculations that had occupied him in the "Notes on the Mind" which he had begun as an undergraduate at Yale. Internationally known as a revivalist, he now devoted his energies to the composition of his three greatest intellectual works—*Freedom of the Will* (1754), *The Nature of True Virtue* (1755–58), and *The Great Doctrine of Original Sin Defended* (1757)—in which he asserted more rigorously than ever before the philosophical and psychological bases of fundamental Calvinism. In 1757 he was invited to become president of the College of New Jersey (now Princeton), where he died early the following year from a smallpox inoculation.

Edwards was unremitting in his defense of what are now considered distasteful, anachronistic, and narrow views. He sarcastically and consciously rejected "this age of light and inquiry" because he found it contrary, not only to the Bible, but to logic and experience as well. But he did not retreat into bitter misanthropy; rather, he found mystical rapture and beauty in the stern doctrines of election, predetermination, original sin, and man's absolute dependence on God. Seeking God through experience of and reflections on beauty, he created the first statement of the kind of aesthetic idealism that Emerson, Poe, and Whitman would later urge as the basis for both poetry and morality.

Further reading: *Jonathan Edwards: Representative Selections,* ed. C. H. Faust and T. H. Johnson, 1935, 1962. Ola E. Winslow, *Jonathan Edwards,* 1940. Perry Miller, *Jonathan Edwards,* 1949.

Personal Narrative

During the Great Awakening, Edwards analyzed the religious experiences of many persons, trying to sort out in the frenzy of the period valid signs of saving grace from false signs. His own spiritual autobiography shows him putting his own experience to the test as he traces the four "seasons of awakenings" that brought him to assurance of salvation. The form of the work is therefore not linear but cyclical, each cycle showing an expanding and deepening of his spiritual consciousness, occasionally joined with mystical experiences of complete self-annihilation, of being "swallowed up in Christ." As he tries to communicate the "sweetness" of such experiences, his prose attains a poetic quality that almost matches Edward Taylor's, revealing the lyrical foundation of his tough-minded theology.

For this and the following selections, except as noted, the text is that of the eight-volume edition of *The Works of President Edwards*, ed. Samuel Austin (Worcester, Mass., 1808-9).

I had a variety of concerns and exercises about my soul from my childhood; but had two more remarkable seasons of awakening, before I met with that change, by which I was brought to those new dispositions, and that new sense of things, that I have since had. The first time was when I was a boy, some years before I went to college, at a time of remarkable awakening in my father's congregation. I was then very much affected for many months, and concerned about the things of religion, and my soul's salvation; and was abundant in duties. I used to pray five times a day in secret, and to spend much time in religious talk with other boys; and used to meet with them to pray together. I experienced I know not what kind of delight in religion. My mind was much engaged in it, and had much self-righteous pleasure; and it was my delight to abound in religious duties. I with some of my school-mates joined together, and built a booth in a swamp, in a very retired spot, for a place of prayer. And besides, I had particular secret places of my own in the woods, where I used to retire by myself; and was from time to time much affected. My affections seemed to be lively and easily moved, and I seemed to be in my element when engaged in religious duties. And I am ready to think, many are deceived with such affections, and such a kind of delight as I then had in religion, and mistake it for grace.

But in process of time, my convictions and affections wore off; and I entirely lost all those affections and delights, and left off secret prayer, at least as to any constant performance of it; and returned like a dog to his vomit, and went on in the ways of sin. Indeed I was at times very uneasy, especially towards the latter part of my time at college; when it pleased God, to seize me with a pleurisy; in which he brought me nigh to the grave, and shook me over the pit of hell. And yet, it was not long after my recovery, before I fell again into my old ways of sin. But God would not suffer me to go on with any quietness; I had great and violent inward struggles, till, after many conflicts with wicked inclinations, repeated resolutions, and bonds that I laid myself under by a kind of vows to God, I was brought wholly to break off all former wicked ways and all ways of known outward sin; and to apply myself to seek salvation, and practice many religious duties; but without that kind of affection and delight which I had formerly experienced. My concern now wrought more by inward struggles, and conflicts, and self-reflections. I made seeking my salvation the main business of my life. But yet, it seems to me, I sought after a miserable manner; which has made me sometimes since to question, whether ever it issued in that which was saving; being ready to doubt, whether such miserable seeking ever succeeded. I was indeed brought to seek salvation in a manner that I never was before; I felt a spirit to part with all things in the world, for an interest in Christ. My concern continued and prevailed, with many exercising thoughts and inward struggles; but yet it never seemed to be proper, to express that concern by the name of terror.

From my childhood up, my mind had been full of objections against the doctrine of God's sovereignty, in choosing whom He would to eternal life, and rejecting whom He pleased; leaving them eternally to perish, and be everlastingly tormented in hell. It used to appear like a horrible doctrine to me. But I remember the time very well, when I seemed to be convinced, and fully satisfied, as to this sovereignty of God, and His justice in thus eternally disposing of men, according to His sovereign pleasure. But never could give an account, how, or by what means, I was thus convinced, not in the least imagining at the time, nor a long time after, that there was any extraordinary influence of God's Spirit in it; but only that now I saw further, and my reason apprehended the justice and reasonableness of it. However, my mind rested in it; and it put an end to all those cavils and objections. And there has been a wonderful alteration in my mind, with respect to the doctrine of God's sovereignty, from that day to this; so that I scarce ever have found so much as the rising of an objection against it, in the most absolute sense, in God's shewing mercy to whom He will shew mercy, and hardening whom he will. God's absolute sovereignty and justice, with respect to salvation and damnation, is what my mind seems to rest assured of, as much as of any thing that I see with my eyes; at least it is so at times. But I have often, since that first conviction, had quite another kind of sense of God's sovereignty than I had then. I have often since had not only a conviction, but a delightful conviction. The doctrine has very often appeared exceeding pleasant, bright and sweet. Absolute sovereignty is what I love to ascribe to God. But my first conviction was not so.

The first instance that I remember of that sort of inward, sweet delight in God and divine things that I have lived much in since, was on reading those words, 1 Tim. i:17, *Now unto the King eternal, immortal, invisible, the only wise God, be honor and glory for ever and ever, Amen.* As I read the words, there came into my soul, and was as it were diffused through it, a sense of the glory of the Divine Being; a new sense, quite different from anything I ever experienced before. Never any words of scripture seemed to me as these words did. I thought with myself, how excellent a Being that was, and how happy I should be, if I might enjoy that God, and be rapt up to Him in heaven, and be as it were swallowed up in Him for ever! I kept saying, and as it were singing, over these words of scripture to myself; and went to pray to God that I might enjoy Him, and prayed in a manner quite different from what I used to do; with a new sort of affection. But it never came into my thought, that there was anything spiritual, or of a saving nature in this.

From about that time, I began to have a new kind of apprehensions and ideas of Christ, and the work of redemption and the glorious way of salvation by Him. An inward, sweet sense of these things, at times, came into my heart; and my soul was led away in pleasant views and contemplations of them. And my mind was greatly engaged to spend my time in reading and meditating on Christ, on the beauty and excellency of His person, and the lovely way of salvation by free grace in Him. I found no books so delightful to me, as those that treated of these subjects. Those words Cant. ii:1 used to be abundantly with me, *I am the rose of Sharon, and the lily of the valleys.* The words seemed to me, sweetly to represent the loveliness and beauty of Jesus Christ. The whole book of Canticles used to be pleasant to me, and I used to be much in reading it, about that time; and found, from time to time, an inward sweetness, that would carry me away, in my contemplations. This I know not how to express otherwise, than by a calm, sweet abstraction of soul from all the concerns of this world; and sometimes a kind of vision, or fixed ideas and imaginations, of being alone in the mountains, or some solitary wilderness, far from all mankind, sweetly conversing with Christ, and wrapt and swallowed up in God. The sense I had of divine things, would often of a sudden kindle up, as it were, a sweet burning in my heart; an ardor of soul, that I know not how to express.

Not long after I first began to experience these things, I gave an account to my father of some things that had passed in my mind. I was pretty much affected by the discourse we had together; and when the discourse was ended, I walked abroad alone, in a solitary place in my father's pasture, for contemplation. And as I was walking there, and looking upon the sky and clouds, there came into my mind so sweet a sense of the glorious *majesty* and *grace* of God, as I know not how to express. I seemed to see them both in a sweet conjunction; majesty and meekness joined together; it was a sweet, and gentle, and holy majesty; and also a majestic meekness; an awful sweetness; a high, and great, and holy gentleness.

After this my sense of divine things gradually increased, and became more and more lively, and had more of that inward sweetness. The appearance of everything was altered; there seemed to be, as it were, a calm, sweet cast, or appearance of divine glory, in almost everything. God's excellency, His wisdom, His purity and love, seemed to appear in everything; in the sun, moon, and stars; in the clouds, and blue sky; in the grass, flowers, trees; in the water, and all nature; which used greatly to fix my mind. I often used to sit and view the moon for continuance; and in the day, spent much time in viewing the clouds and sky, to behold the sweet glory of God in these things; in the meantime, singing forth, with a low voice, my contemplations of the Creator and Redeemer. And scarce anything, among all the works of nature, was so sweet to me as thunder and lightning; formerly nothing had been so terrible to me. Before, I used to be uncommonly terrified with thunder, and to be struck with terror when I saw a thunder storm rising; but now, on the contrary, it rejoiced me. I felt God, so to speak, at the first appearance of a thunder storm; and used to take the opportunity, at such times, to fix myself in order to view the clouds, and see the lightnings play, and hear the majestic and awful voice of God's thunder, which oftentimes was exceedingly entertaining, leading me to sweet contemplations of my great and glorious God. While thus engaged, it always seemed natural for me to sing, or chant for my meditations; or, to speak my thoughts in soliloquies with a singing voice.

I felt then great satisfaction, as to my good state, but that did not content me. I had vehement longings of soul after God and Christ, and after more holiness, wherewith my heart seemed to be full, and ready to break; which often brought to my mind the words of the Psalmist, Psal. cxix:28: *My soul breaketh for the longing it hath.* I often felt a mourning and lamenting in my heart, that I had not turned to God sooner, that I might have had more time to grow in grace. My mind was greatly fixed on divine things; almost perpetually in the contemplation of them. I spent most of my time in thinking of divine things, year after year; often walking alone in the woods, and solitary places, for meditation, soliloquy, and prayer, and converse with God; and it was always my manner, at such times, to sing forth my contemplations. I was almost constantly in ejaculatory prayer, wherever I was. Prayer seemed to be natural to me, as the breath by which the inward burnings of my heart had vent. The delights which I now felt in the things of religion, were of an exceeding different kind from those before mentioned, that I had when a boy; and what I then had no more notion of, than one born blind has of pleasant and beautiful colors. They were of a more inward, pure, soul-animating and refreshing nature. Those former delights never reached the heart; and did not arise from any sight of the divine excellency of the things of God; or any taste of the soul-satisfying and life-giving good there is in them.

My sense of divine things seemed gradually to increase, till I went to preach at New York, which was about a year and a half after they began; and while I was there, I felt them, very sensibly, in a much higher degree than I had done before. My longings after God, and holiness, were much increased. Pure and humble, holy and heavenly Christianity appeared exceeding amiable to me. I felt a burning desire to be, in everything, a complete Christian; and conformed to the blessed image of Christ; and that I might live, in all things, according to the pure, sweet, and blessed rules of the gospel. I had an eager thirsting after progress in these things; which put me upon pursuing and pressing after them. It was my continual strife day and night, and constant inquiry, how I should *be* more holy and *live* more holily, and more becoming a child of God, and a disciple of Christ. I now sought an increase of grace and holiness, and a holy life, with much more earnestness, than ever I sought grace before I had it. I used to be continually examining myself, and studying and contriving for likely ways and means, how I should live holily, with far greater diligence and earnestness, than ever I pursued anything in my life; but yet with too great a dependence on my own strength; which afterwards proved a great damage to me. My experience had not then taught me, as it has done since, my extreme feebleness and impotence, every manner of way; and the bottomless depths of secret corruption and deceit there was in my heart. However, I went on with my eager pursuit after more holiness, and conformity to Christ.

The heaven I desired was a heaven of holiness; to be with God, and to spend my eternity in divine love and holy communion with Christ. My mind was very much taken up with contemplations on heaven, and the enjoyments there; and living there in perfect holiness, humility, and love: and it used at that time to appear a great part of the happiness of heaven, that there the saints could express their love to Christ. It appeared to me a great clog and burden, that what I felt within, I could not express as I desired. The inward ardor of my soul, seemed to be hindered and pent up, and could not freely flame out as it would. I used often to think, how in heaven this principle should freely and fully vent and express itself. Heaven appeared exceedingly delightful, as a world of love; and that all happiness consisted in living in pure, humble, heavenly, divine love.

I remember the thoughts I used then to have of holiness; and said sometimes to myself, "I do certainly know that I love holiness, such as the gospel prescribes." It appeared to me, that there was nothing in it but what was ravishingly lovely; the highest beauty and amiableness — a *divine* beauty; far purer than anything here upon earth; and that everything else was like mire and defilement, in comparison of it.

Holiness, as I then wrote down some of my contemplations on it, appeared to me to be of a sweet, pleasant, charming, serene, calm nature; which brought an inexpressible purity, brightness, peacefulness and ravishment to the soul. In other words, that it made the soul like a field or garden of God, with all manner of pleasant flowers; all pleasant, delightful, and undisturbed; enjoying a sweet calm, and the gently vivifying beams of the sun. The soul of a true Christian, as I then wrote my meditations, appeared like such a little white flower as we see in the spring of the year; low and humble on the ground, opening its bosom to receive the pleasant beams of the sun's glory; rejoicing as it were in a calm rapture; diffusing around a sweet fragrancy; standing peacefully and lovingly, in the midst of other flowers round about; all in like manner opening their bosoms, to drink in the light of the sun. There was no part of creature-holiness, that I had so great a sense of its loveliness, as humility, brokenness of heart, and poverty of spirit; and there was nothing that I so earnestly longed for. My heart panted after this—to lie low before God, as in the dust; that I might be nothing, and that God, might be ALL, that I might become as a little child.

While at New York,[1] I was sometimes much af-

[1] From 1722 to 1723 Edwards was minister to a Presbyterian church in New York City.

fected with reflections on my past life, considering how late it was before I began to be truly religious; and how wickedly I had lived till then: and once so as to weep abundantly, and for a considerable time together.

On January 12, 1723, I made a solemn dedication of myself to God, and wrote it down; giving up myself, and all that I had to God; to be for the future in no respect my own; to act as one that had no right to himself, in any respect. And solemnly vowed, to take God for my whole portion and felicity; looking on nothing else as any part of my happiness, nor acting as if it were; and His law for the constant rule of my obedience; engaging to fight with all my might, against the world, the flesh, and the Devil, to the end of my life. But I have reason to be infinitely humbled, when I consider, how much I have failed, of answering my obligation.

I had then abundance of sweet religious conversation in the family where I lived, with Mr. John Smith and his pious mother. My heart was knit in affection to those in whom were appearances of true piety; and I could bear the thoughts of no other companions, but such as were holy, and the disciples of the blessed Jesus. I had great longings for the advancement of Christ's kingdom in the world; and my secret prayer used to be, in great part, taken up in praying for it. If I heard the least hint of any thing that happened, in any part of the world, that appeared, in some respect or other, to have a favorable aspect on the interest of Christ's kingdom, my soul eagerly catched at it; and it would much animate and refresh me. I used to be eager to read public news letters, mainly for that end; to see if I could not find some news favorable to the interest of religion in the world.

I very frequently used to retire into a solitary place, on the banks of Hudson's river, at some distance from the city, for contemplation on divine things, and secret converse with God; and had many sweet hours there. Sometimes Mr. Smith and I walked there together, to converse on the things of God; and our conversation used to turn much on the advancement of Christ's kingdom in the world, and the glorious things that God would accomplish for his church in the latter days. I had then, and at other times, the greatest delight in the holy scriptures, of any book whatsoever. Oftentimes in reading it, every word seemed to touch my heart. I felt a harmony between something in my heart, and those sweet and powerful words. I seemed often to see so much light exhibited by every sentence, and such a refreshing food communicated, that I could not get along in reading; often dwelling long on one sentence, to see the wonders contained in it; and yet almost every sentence seemed to be full of wonders.

I came away from New York in the month of April, 1723, and had a most bitter parting with Madam Smith and her son. My heart seemed to sink within me at leaving the family and city, where I had enjoyed so many sweet and pleasant days. I went from New York to Weathersfield, by water, and as I sailed away, I kept sight of the city as long as I could. However, that night, after this sorrowful parting, I was greatly comforted in God at Westchester, where we went ashore to lodge; and had a pleasant time of it all the voyage to Saybrook. It was sweet to me to think of meeting dear Christians in heaven, where we should never part more. At Saybrook we went ashore to lodge, on Saturday, and there kept the Sabbath; where I had a sweet and refreshing season, walking alone in the fields.

After I came home to Windsor, I remained much in a like frame of mind, as when at New York; only sometimes I felt my heart ready to sink with the thoughts of my friends at New York. My support was in contemplations on the heavenly state; as I find in my Diary of May 1, 1723. It was a comfort to think of that state, where there is fulness of joy; where reigns heavenly, calm, and delightful love, without alloy; where there are continually the dearest expressions of this love; where is the enjoyment of the persons loved, without ever parting; where those persons who appear so lovely in this world, will really be inexpressibly more lovely and full of love to us. And how sweetly will the mutual lovers join together to sing the praises of God and the Lamb! How will it fill us with joy to think, that this enjoyment, these sweet exercises will never cease, but will last to all eternity! I continued much in the same frame, in the general, as when at New York, till I went to New Haven as tutor to the college; particularly once at Bolton, on a journey from Boston, while walking out alone in the fields. After I went to New Haven I sunk in religion; my mind being diverted from my eager pursuits after holiness, by some affairs that greatly perplexed and distracted my thoughts.

In September, 1725, I was taken ill at New Haven, and while endeavoring to go home to Windsor, was so ill at the North Village, that I could go no further; where I lay sick for about a quarter of a year. In this sickness God was pleased to visit me again with the sweet influences of his Spirit. My mind was greatly engaged there in divine, pleasant contemplations, and longings of soul. I observed that those who watched with me, would often be looking out wishfully for the morning; which brought to my mind those words of the Psalmist, and which my soul with delight made its own language, *My soul waiteth for the Lord, more than they that watch for the morning, I say, more than they that watch for the morning;* and when the light of day came in at the windows, it refreshed my soul from one morning to another. It seemed to be some image of the light of God's glory.

I remember, about that time, I used greatly to long for the conversion of some that I was concerned with; I could gladly honor them, and with delight be a servant to them, and lie at their feet, if they were but truly holy. But, some time after this, I was again greatly diverted in my mind with some temporal concerns that exceedingly took up my thoughts, greatly to the wounding of my soul; and went on through various exercises, that it would be tedious to relate, which gave me much more experience of my own heart, than ever I had before.

Since I came to this town,[2] I have often had sweet complacency in God, in views of his glorious perfections and the excellency of Jesus Christ. God has appeared to me a glorious and lovely being, chiefly on the account of his holiness. The holiness of God has always appeared to me the most lovely of all his attributes. The doctrines of God's absolute sovereignty, and free grace, in shewing mercy to whom he would shew mercy; and man's absolute dependence on the operations of God's Holy Spirit, have very often appeared to me as sweet and glorious doctrines. These doctrines have been much my delight. God's sovereignty has ever appeared to me, great part of his glory. It has often been my delight to approach God, and adore him as a sovereign God, and ask sovereign mercy of him.

I have loved the doctrines of the gospel; they have been to my soul like green pastures. The gospel has seemed to me the richest treasure; the treasure that I have most desired, and longed that it might dwell richly in me. The way of salvation by Christ has appeared, in a general way, glorious and excellent, most pleasant and most beautiful. It has often seemed to me, that it would in a great measure spoil heaven, to receive it in any other way. That text has often been affecting and delightful to me, Isa. xxxii:2. *A man shall be an hiding place from the wind, and a covert from the tempest, etc.*

It has often appeared to me delightful, to be united to Christ; to have him for my head, and to be a member of his body; also to have Christ for my teacher and prophet. I very often think with sweetness, and longings, and pantings of soul, of being a little child, taking hold of Christ, to be led by him through the wilderness of this world. That text, Matth. xvii:3, has often been sweet to me, *except ye be converted and become as little children, etc.* I love to think of coming to Christ, to receive salvation of him, poor in spirit, and quite empty of self, humbly exalting him alone; cut off entirely from my own root, in order to grow into, and out of Christ; to have God in Christ to be all in all; and to live by faith on the Son of God, a life of humble unfeigned confidence in him. That scripture has often been sweet to me, Psal. cxv:1. *Not unto us, O Lord, not unto us, but to thy name give glory, for thy mercy and for thy truth's sake.* And those words of Christ, Luke x:21. *In that hour Jesus rejoiced in spirit, and said, I thank thee, O Father, Lord of heaven and earth, that thou hast hid these things from the wise and prudent, and hast revealed them unto babes; even so, Father, for so it seemed good in thy sight.* That sovereignty of God which Christ rejoiced in, seemed to me worthy of such joy; and that rejoicing seemed to show the excellency of Christ, and of what spirit he was.

Sometimes, only mentioning a single word caused my heart to burn within me; or only seeing the name of Christ, or the name of some attribute of God. And God has appeared glorious to me, on account of the Trinity. It has made me have exalting thoughts of God, that he subsists in three persons; Father, Son and Holy Ghost. The sweetest joys and delights I have experienced, have not been those that have arisen from a hope of my own good state; but in a direct view of the glorious things of the gospel. When I enjoy this sweetness, it seems to carry me above the thoughts of my own estate; it seems at such times a loss that I cannot bear, to take off my eye from the glorious pleasant object I behold without me, to turn my eye in upon myself, and my own good estate.

My heart has been much on the advancement of Christ's kingdom in the world. The histories of the past advancement of Christ's kingdom have been sweet to me. When I have read histories of past ages, the pleasantest thing in all my reading has been, to read of the kingdom of Christ being promoted. And when I have expected, in my reading, to come to any such thing, I have rejoiced in the prospect, all the way as I read. And my mind has been much entertained and delighted with the scripture promises and prophecies, which relate to the future glorious advancement of Christ's kingdom upon earth.

I have sometimes had a sense of the excellent fulness of Christ, and his meetness and suitableness as a Saviour; whereby he has appeared to me, far above all, the chief of ten thousands. His blood and atonement have appeared sweet, and his righteousness sweet; which was always accompanied with ardency of spirit; and inward strugglings and breathings, and groanings that cannot be uttered, to be emptied of myself, and swallowed up in Christ.

[2] Edwards returned to Northampton in February 1727.

Once as I rode out into the woods for my health, in 1737, having alighted from my horse in a retired place, as my manner commonly has been, to walk for divine contemplation and prayer, I had a view that for me was extraordinary, of the glory of the Son of God, as Mediator between God and man, and His wonderful, great, full, pure, and sweet grace and love, and meek and gentle condescension. This grace that appeared so calm and sweet, appeared also great above the heavens. The person of Christ appeared ineffably excellent with an excellency great enough to swallow up all thought and conception—which continued, as near as I can judge, about an hour, which kept me the greater part of the time in a flood of tears, and weeping aloud. I felt an ardency of soul to be, what I know not otherwise how to express, emptied and annihilated; to lie in the dust, and to be full of Christ alone; to love Him with a holy and pure love; to trust in Him; to live upon Him; to serve and follow Him; and to be perfectly sanctified and made pure, with a divine and heavenly purity. I have, several other times, had views very much of the same nature, and which have had the same effects.

I have many times had a sense of the glory of the third person in the Trinity, in His office of Sanctifier, in His holy operations, communicating divine light and life to the soul. God, in the communications of His Holy Spirit, has appeared as an infinite fountain of divine glory and sweetness; being full, and sufficient to fill and satisfy the soul; pouring forth itself in sweet communications; like the sun in its glory, sweetly and pleasantly diffusing light and life. And I have sometimes had an affecting sense of the excellency of the Word of God as a Word of life; as the light of life; a sweet, excellent, life-giving Word; accompanied with a thirsting after that Word, that it might dwell richly in my heart.

Often, since I lived in this town, I have had very affecting views of my own sinfulness and vileness; very frequently to such a degree as to hold me in a kind of loud weeping, sometimes for a considerable time together; so that I have often been forced to shut myself up. I have had a vastly greater sense of my own wickedness, and the badness of my own heart, than ever I had before my conversion. It has often appeared to me, that if God should mark iniquity against me, I should appear the very worst of all mankind; of all that have been, since the beginning of the world to this time; and that I should have by far the lowest place in hell. When others, that have come to talk with me about their soul concerns, have expressed the sense they have had of their own wickedness, by saying that it seemed to them, that they were as bad as the Devil himself; I thought their expressions seemed exceeding faint and feeble, to represent my wickedness.

My wickedness, as I am in myself, has long appeared to me perfectly ineffable, and swallowing up all thought and imagination; like an infinite deluge, or mountains over my head. I know not how to express better what my sins appear to me to be, than by heaping infinite upon infinite, and multiplying infinite by infinite. Very often, for these many years, these expressions are in my mind, and in my mouth, "Infinite upon infinite—Infinite upon infinite!" When I look into my heart, and take a view of my wickedness, it looks like an abyss infinitely deeper than hell. And it appears to me, that were it not for free grace, exalted and raised up to the infinite height of all the fulness and glory of the great Jehovah, and the arm of His power and grace stretched forth in all the majesty of His power, and in all the glory of His sovereignty, I should appear sunk down in my sins below hell itself; far beyond the sight of everything but the eye of sovereign grace, that can pierce even down to such a depth. And yet it seems to me, that my conviction of sin is exceeding small, and faint; it is enough to amaze me, that I have no more sense of my sin. I know certainly, that I have very little sense of my sinfulness. When I have had turns of weeping and crying for my sins, I thought I knew at the time, that my repentance was nothing to my sin.

I have greatly longed of late, for a broken heart, and to lie low before God; and, when I ask for humility, I cannot bear the thoughts of being no more humble than other Christians. It seems to me, that though their degrees of humility may be suitable for them, yet it would be a vile self-exaltation in me, not to be the lowest in humility of all mankind. Others speak of their longing to be "humbled to the dust"; that may be a proper expression for them, but I always think of myself, that I ought, and it is an expression that has long been natural for me to use in prayer, "to lie infinitely low before God." And it is affecting to think, how ignorant I was, when a young Christian, of the bottomless, infinite depths of wickedness, pride, hypocrisy, and deceit, left in my heart.

I have a much greater sense of my universal, exceeding dependence on God's grace and strength, and mere good pleasure, of late, than I used formerly to have; and have experienced more of an abhorrence of my own righteousness. The very thought of any joy arising in me, on any consideration of my own amiableness, performances, or experiences, or any goodness of heart or life, is nauseous and detestable to me. And yet I am greatly afflicted with a proud and self-righteous spirit, much more sensibly than I used to be formerly. I see that serpent rising and putting forth its head continually, everywhere, all around me. Though it seems to me, that, in some respects, I was a far better Christian, for two or three years after my first conversion, than I am now; and lived in a more constant delight and pleasure; yet, of late years, I have had a more full and constant sense of the absolute sovereignty of God, and a delight in that sovereignty; and have had more of a sense of the glory of Christ, as a Mediator revealed in the gospel. On one Saturday night, in particular, I had such a discovery of the excellency of the gospel above all other doctrines, that I could not but say to myself, "This is my chosen light, my chosen doctrine"; and of Christ, "This is my chosen prophet." It appeared sweet, beyond all expression, to follow Christ, and to be taught, and enlightened, and instructed by Him; to learn of Him, and live to Him. Another Saturday night (January, 1739), I had such a sense, how sweet and blessed a thing it was to walk in the way of duty; to do that which was right and meet to be done, and agreeable to the holy mind of God; that it caused me to break forth into a kind of loud weeping, which held me some time, so that I was forced to shut myself up, and fasten the doors. I could not but, as it were, cry out, "How happy are they which do that which is right in the sight of God! They are blessed indeed; they are the happy ones!" I had, at the same time, a very affecting sense, how meet and suitable it was that God should govern the world, and order all things according to His own pleasure; and I rejoiced in it, that God reigned and that His will was done.

1742

Notes on the Mind

Emerson's observation that "Beauty is the mark God sets upon virtue" strikes very near the heart of Edwards' philosophy. Edwards, who saw true virtue as indistinguishable from holiness, elaborated the philosophical implications of beauty in *The Nature of True Virtue,* but even as early as his college years he was exploring the aesthetic principles that contribute to that late work. He began his series of seventy-two notes on "The Mind" in his senior year at Yale, intending a treatise on the subject.

His geometrical approach to beauty is akin to Poe's later speculations about poetic unity and also shares the metaphysical implications of Poe's *Eureka.* His emphasis on equality as a principle of beauty bears an interesting relationship to Whitman's principle of Equality in the 1855 preface to *Leaves of Grass.* Never a literary critic, however, even though he did commend both Milton and Richardson, Edwards nonetheless speaks clearly and rigorously about principles relevant to art. And we can see how the terms *excellence* and *excellency,* which occur frequently in his writing, may bear an inconspicuous but significant artistic implication.

Text: From "'The Mind' of Jonathan Edwards: The Reconstructed Manuscript," in Harvey G. Townsend, *The Philosophy of Jonathan Edwards from His Private Notebooks* (University of Oregon Monograph: Studies in Philosophy, no. 2, 1955).

1. EXCELLENCY. There has nothing been more without a definition, than excellency; although it be what we are more concerned with, than any thing else whatsoever: yea, we are concerned with nothing else. But what is this excellency? Wherein is one thing excellent, and another evil; one beautiful, and another deformed? Some have said that all excellency is harmony, symmetry, or proportion; but they have not yet explained it. We would know, why proportion is more excellent than disproportion; that is, why proportion is pleasant to the mind, and disproportion unpleasant? Proportion is a thing that may be explained yet further. It is an equality, or likeness of ratios; so that it is the equality, that makes the proportion. Excellency therefore seems to consist in equality. Thus, if there be two perfect equal circles, or globes, together, there is something more of beauty than if they were of unequal, disproportionate magnitudes. And if two parallel lines be drawn, the beauty is greater, than if they were obliquely inclined without proportion, because there is equality of distance. And if betwixt two parallel lines, two equal circles be placed, each at the same distance from each parallel line, as in Fig. 1, the beauty is greater, than if they stood at irregular distances from the parallel lines. If they stand, each in a perpendicular line, going from the parallel lines, (Fig. 2,) it is requisite that they should each stand at an equal distance from the perpendicular line next to them; otherwise there is no beauty. If there be three of these circles between two parallel lines, and near to a perpendicular line run between them, (Fig. 3,) the most beautiful form perhaps, that they could be placed in, is in an equilateral triangle with the cross line, because there are most equalities. The distance of the two next to the cross line is equal from that, and also equal from the parallel lines. The distance of the third from each parallel is equal, and its distance from each of the other two circles is equal, and is also equal to their distance from one another, and likewise equal to their distance from each end of the cross line. There are two equilateral triangles: one made by the three circles, and the other made by the cross line and two of the sides of the first protracted till they meet that line. And if there be another like it, on the opposite side, to correspond with it and it be taken altogether, the beauty is still greater, where the distances from the lines, in the one, are equal to the distances in the other; also the two next to the cross lines are at equal distances from the other two; or, if you go

crosswise, from corner to corner. The two cross lines are also parallel, so that all parts are at an equal distance, and innumerable other equalities might be found.

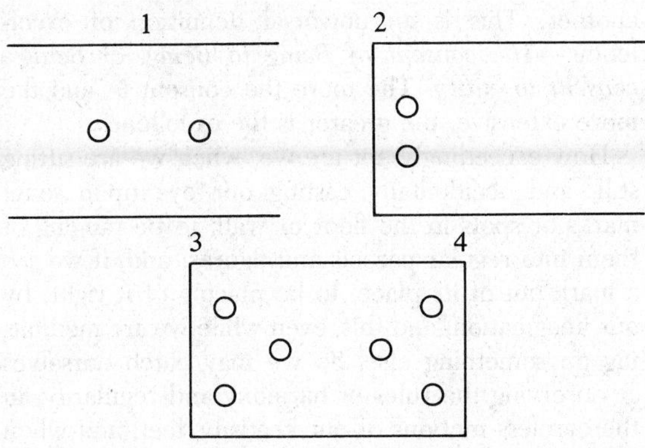

This simple equality, without proportion, is the lowest kind of regularity, and may be called simple beauty. All other beauties and excellencies may be resolved into it. Proportion is complex beauty. Thus, if we suppose that there are two points, A B, placed at two inches distance, and the next, C, one inch farther; (Fig. 1.) it is requisite, in order to regularity and beauty, if there be another, D, that it should be at half an inch distance; otherwise there is no regularity, and the last, D, would stand out of its proper place; because now the relation that the space C D, bears to B C, is equal to the relation that B C, bears to A B; so that B C D, is exactly similar to A B C. It is evident, this is a more complicated excellency than that which consisted in equality, because the terms of the relation are here complex, and before were simple. When there are three points set in a right line, it is requisite, in order to regularity, that they should be set at an equal distance, as A B C, (Fig. 2.) where A B, is similar to B C, or the relation of C to B, is the same as of B to A. But in the other are three terms necessary in each of the parts, between which, is the relation, B C D, is as A B C: so that here more simple beauties are omitted, and yet there is a general complex beauty: that is, B C is not as A B, nor is C D as B C, but yet, B C D is as A B C. It is requisite that the consent or regularity of C D to B C, be omitted, for the sake of the harmony of the whole. For although, if C D was perfectly equal to B C, there would be regularity and beauty with respect to them two; yet, if A B be taken into the idea, there is nothing but confusion. And it might be requisite, if these stood with others, even to omit this proposition,[1] for the sake of one more complex still. Thus, if they stood with other points,

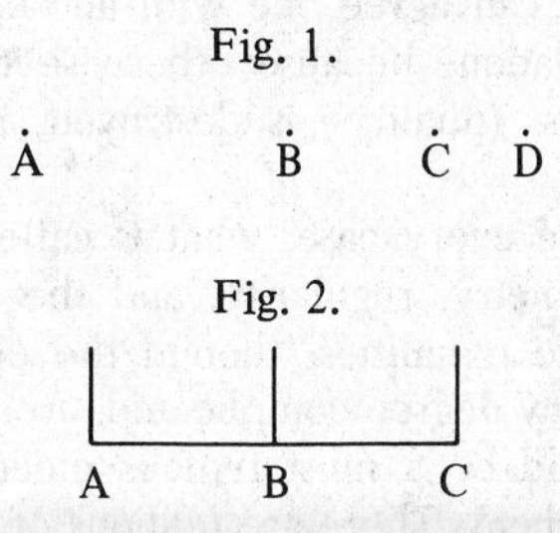

where B stood at four inches distance from A, C at two from B, and D at six from C: the place where D must stand in, if A, B, C, D were alone, viz. one inch from C, must be so as to be made proportionate with the other points beneath;

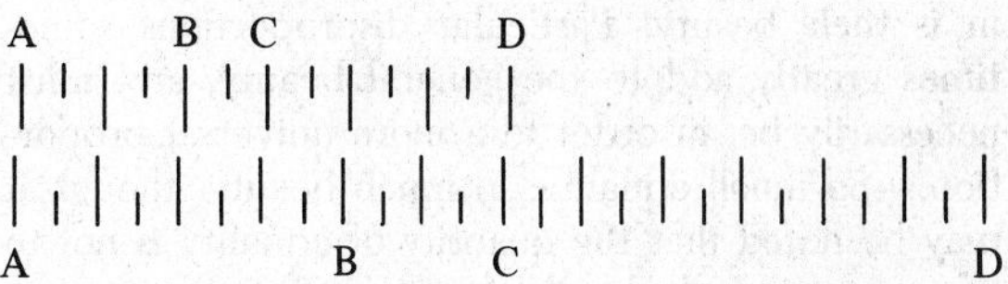

So that although A, B, C, D, are not proportioned, but are confusion among themselves; yet taken with the whole they are proportioned and beautiful.

All beauty consists in similarness or identity of relation. In identity of relation consists all likeness, and all identity between two consists in identity of relation, Thus, when the distance between two is exactly equal, their distance is their relation one to another, the distance is the same, the bodies are two; wherefore this is their correspondency and beauty. So bodies exactly of the same figure, the bodies are two, the relation between the parts of the extremities is the same, and this is their agreement with them. But if there are two bodies of different shapes, having no similarness of relation between the parts of the extremities; this, considered by itself, is a deformity, because being disagrees with being, which must undoubtedly be disagreeable to perceiving being: because what disagrees with Being, must necessarily be disagreeable to Being in general, to every thing that partakes of entity, and of course to perceiving being; and what agrees with Being must be agreeable to Being in general, and therefore to perceiving being. But agreeableness to perceiving being is pleasure, and disagreeableness is pain. Disagreement or contrariety to Being, is evidently an approach to nothing, or a degree of nothing; which is nothing else but disagreement or contrariety of Being, and the greatest and only evil: And entity is the greatest and only good. And by how much more perfect entity is, that is without mixture of nothing, by so much the more excellency.

[1] Proportion?

Two beings can agree one with another in nothing else but relation; because otherwise the notion of their twoness (duality,) is destroyed, and they become one.

And so, in every case, what is called correspondency, symmetry, regularity, and the like, may be resolved into equalities; though the equalities in a beauty, in any degree complicated, are so numerous, that it should be a most tedious piece of work to enumerate them. There are millions of these equalities. Of these consist the beautiful shape of flowers, the beauty of the body of man, and of the bodies of other animals. That sort of beauty which is called natural, as of vines, plants, trees, etc. consists of a very complicated harmony; and all the natural motions, and tendencies, and figures of bodies in the universe are done according to proportion, and therein is their beauty. Particular disproportions sometimes greatly add to the general beauty, and must necessarily be, in order to a more universal proportion:—So much equality, so much beauty; though it may be noted that the quantity of equality is not to be measured only by the number, but the intenseness, according to the quantity of being. As bodies are shadows of being, so their proportions are shadows of proportions.

The pleasures of the senses, where harmony is not the object of judgment, are the result of equality. Thus in music, not only in the proportion which the several notes of a tune bear, one among another, but in merely two notes, there is harmony; whereas it is impossible there should be proportion between only two terms. But the proportion is in the particular vibrations of the air, which strike on the ear. And so, in the pleasantness of light, colours, tastes, smells and touch, all arise from proportion of motion. The organs are so contrived that, upon the touch of such and such particles, there shall be a regular and harmonious motion of the animal spirits.

Spiritual harmonies are of vastly larger extent: i.e. the proportions are vastly oftener redoubled, and respect mere [more?] beings, and require a vastly larger view to comprehend them; as some simple notes do more affect one, who has not a comprehensive understanding of music.

The reason, why equality thus pleases the mind, and inequality is unpleasing, is because disproportion, or inconsistency, is contrary to Being. For Being, if we examine narrowly, is nothing else but proportion. When one being is inconsistent with another being, then Being is contradicted. But contradiction to Being, is intolerable to perceiving being, and the consent to Being, most pleasing.

Excellency consists in the Similarness of one being to another—not merely equality and proportion, but any kind of similarness—thus similarness of direction. Supposing many globes moving in right lines, it is more beautiful, that they should move all the same way, and according to the same direction, than if they moved disorderly; one, one way, and another, another. This is an universal definition of excellency:—*The consent of Being to Being, or Being's consent to entity.* The more the consent is, and the more extensive, the greater is the excellency.

How exceedingly apt are we, when we are sitting still, and accidentally casting our eye upon some marks or spots in the floor or wall, to be ranging of them into regular parcels and figures: and, if we see a mark out of its place, to be placing of it right, by our imagination; and this, even while we are meditating on something else. So we may catch ourselves at observing the rules of harmony and regularity, in the careless motions of our heads or feet, and when playing with our hands, or walking about the room.

Pleasedness, in perceiving being, always rises, either from a perception of consent to Being in general, or of consent to that being that perceives. As we have shown, that agreeableness to entity must be agreeable to perceiving entity; it is as evident that it is necessary that agreeableness to that being must be pleasing to it, if it perceives it. So that pleasedness does not always arise from a perception of excellency; [in general: (Dwight's brackets)] but the greater a Being is, and the more it has of entity, the more will consent to Being in general please it. But God is proper entity itself, and these two therefore, in Him, become the same; for, so far as a thing consents to Being in general, so far it consents to Him; and the more perfect created spirits are, the nearer do they come to their Creator, in this regard.

That, which is often called *self love,* is exceedingly improperly called *love,* for they do not only say that one loves himself, when he sees something amiable in himself, the view of which begets delight. But merely an inclination to pleasure, and averseness to pain, they call self love; so that the devils, and other damned spirits, love themselves, not because they see any thing in themselves, which they imagine to be lovely, but merely, because they do not incline to pain but to pleasure, or merely because they are capable of pain or pleasure; for pain and pleasure include an inclination to agreeableness, and an aversion to disagreeableness. Now how improper is it to say, that one loves himself, because what is agreeable to him is agreeable to him, and what is disagreeable to him is disagreeable to him: which mere entity supposes. So that this, that they call self-love, is no affection, but only the entity of the thing, or his being what he is.

One alone, without any reference to any more, cannot be excellent; for in such case, there can be no manner of relation no way, and therefore no such thing as consent. Indeed what we call *One*, may be excellent because of a consent of parts, or some consent of those in that being, that are distinguished into a plurality some way or other. But in a being that is absolutely without any plurality, there cannot be excellency, for there can be no such thing as consent or agreement.

One of the highest excellencies is love. As nothing else has a proper being but spirits, and as bodies are but the shadow of being, therefore the consent of bodies one to another, and the harmony that is among them, is but the shadow of excellency. The highest excellency therefore must be the consent of spirits one to another. But the consent of spirits consists half in their mutual love one to another. And the sweet harmony between the various parts of the universe, is only an image of mutual love. But yet a lower kind of love may be odious, because it hinders, or is contrary to, a higher and more general. Even a lower proportion is often a deformity, because it is contrary to a more general proportion.

Coroll. 1. If so much of the beauty and excellency of spirits consists in love, then the deformity of evil spirits consists as much in hatred and malice.

Coroll. 2. The more any doctrine, or institution, brings to light of the spiritual world, the more will it urge to love and charity.

Happiness strictly consists in the perception of these three things: of the consent of being to its own being; of its own consent to being; and of being's consent to being.

[14.] EXCELLENCE, to put it in other words, is that which is beautiful and lovely. That which is beautiful, considered by itself separately, and deformed, considered as a part of something else more extended; or beautiful, only with respect to itself and a few other things, and not as a part of that which contains all things—the universe—; is false beauty and a confined beauty. That which is beautiful, with respect to the university of things, has a generally extended excellence and a true beauty; and the more extended, or limited, its system is, the more confined or extended is its beauty.

1719

FROM *Sinners in the Hands of an Angry God*

Thomas Hooker had argued that it was men's hearts that had to be prepared, not their minds, and with this Edwards heartily agreed. But he found—as did Thomas Shepard before him and Edgar Allan Poe a century later—that terror was often a quicker avenue to the heart than pleasure. Intent, as he said, upon "awakening unconverted persons in this congregation" of Enfield, Connecticut, he chose as his grim text Deut. xxxii:35, "Their foot shall slide in due time." He developed his "awful subject" with such inexorable logic and dramatic art—though without flamboyant gestures—that a minister who was present reported, "There was such a breathing of distress, and weeping, that the preacher was obliged to speak to the people and desire silence that he might be heard."

Your wickedness makes you as it were heavy as lead, and to tend downwards with great weight and pressure towards hell; and, if God should let you go, you would immediately sink and swiftly descend and plunge into the bottomless gulf, and your healthy constitution, and your own care and prudence, and best contrivance, and all your righteousness, would have no more influence to uphold you and keep you out of hell, than a spider's web would have to stop a falling rock. Were it not that so is the sovereign pleasure of God, the earth would not bear you one moment; for you are a burden to it; the creation groans with you; the creature is made subject to the bondage of your corruption, not willingly; the sun does not willingly shine upon you to give you light to serve sin and Satan; the earth does not willingly yield her increase to satisfy your lusts; nor is it willingly a stage for your wickedness to be acted upon; the air does not willingly serve you for breath to maintain the flame of life in your vitals, while you spend your life in the service of God's enemies. God's creatures are good, and were made for men to serve God with, and do not willingly subserve to any other purpose, and groan when they are abused to purposes so directly contrary to their nature and end. And the world would spew you out, were it not for the sovereign hand of Him who hath subjected it in hope. There are the black clouds of God's wrath now hanging directly over your heads, full of the dreadful storm, and big with thunder; and were it not for the restraining hand of God, it would immediately burst forth upon you. The sovereign pleasure of God, for the present, stays His rough wind; otherwise it would come with fury, and your destruction would come like a whirlwind, and you would be like the chaff of the summer threshing floor.

The wrath of God is like great waters that are dammed for the present; they increase more and more, and rise higher and higher, till an outlet is given; and, the longer the stream is stopped, the more rapid and mighty is its course, when once it is let loose. It is true, that judgment against your evil work has not been executed hitherto; the floods of God's vengeance have been withheld; but your guilt in the meantime is constantly increasing, and you are every day treasuring up more wrath; the waters are continually rising and waxing more and more mighty; and there is nothing but the mere pleasure of God, that holds the waters back, that are unwilling to be stopped, and press hard to go forward. If God should only withdraw His hand from the floodgate, it would immediately fly open, and the fiery floods of the fierceness and wrath of God, would rush forth with inconceivable fury, and would come upon you with omnipotent power; and if your strength were ten thousand times greater than it is, yea, ten thousand times greater than the strength of the stoutest, sturdiest devil in hell, it would be nothing to withstand or endure it.

The bow of God's wrath is bent, and the arrow made ready on the string, and justice bends the arrow at your heart, and strains the bow, and it is nothing but the mere pleasure of God, and that of an angry God, without any promise or obligation at all, that keeps the arrow one moment from being made drunk with your blood.

Thus are all you that never passed under a great change of heart, by the mighty power of the Spirit of God upon your souls; all that were never born again, and made new creatures, and raised from being dead in sin, to a state of new, and before altogether unexperienced light and life (however you may have reformed your life in many things, and may have had religious affections, and may keep up a form of religion in your families and closets, and in the houses of God, and may be strict in it), you are thus in the hands of an angry God; it is nothing but His mere pleasure that keeps you from being this moment swallowed up in everlasting destruction.

However unconvinced you may now be of the truth of what you hear, by and by you will be fully convinced of it. Those that are gone from being in the like circumstances with you, see that it was so with them; for destruction came suddenly upon most of them; when they expected nothing of it, and while they were saying, Peace and safety: now they see that those things that they depended on for peace and safety were nothing but thin air and empty shadows.

The God that holds you over the pit of hell, much as one holds a spider, or some loathsome insect, over the fire, abhors you, and is dreadfully provoked; His wrath towards you burns like fire; He looks upon you as worthy of nothing else, but to be cast into the fire; He is of purer eyes than to bear to have you in His sight; you are ten thousand times so abominable in His eyes, as the most hateful and venomous serpent is in ours. You have offended him infinitely more than ever a stubborn rebel did his prince. And yet, it is nothing but His hand that holds you from falling into the fire every moment. It is ascribed to nothing else, that you did not go to hell the last night; that you was suffered to awake again in this world, after you closed your eyes to sleep. And there is no other reason to be given why you have not dropped into hell since you arose in the morning, but that God's hand has held you up. There is no other reason to be given why you have not gone to hell, since you have sat here in the house of God, provoking His pure eyes by your sinful wicked manner of attending His solemn worship: yea, there is nothing else that is to be given as a reason why you do not this very moment drop down into hell.

O sinner! consider the fearful danger you are in: it is a great furnace of wrath, a wide and bottomless pit, full of the fire of wrath, that you are held over in the hand of that God, whose wrath is provoked and incensed as much against you, as against many of the damned in hell. You hang by a slender thread, with the flames of divine wrath flashing about it, and ready every moment to singe it, and burn it asunder; and you have no interest in any Mediator, and nothing to lay hold of to save yourself, nothing to keep off the flames of wrath, nothing of your own, nothing that you ever have done, nothing that you can do, to induce God to spare you one moment.

1741

FROM *A Letter to Benjamin Coleman*

The effectiveness of Edwards' "rhetoric of sensation" was evident immediately, as he informed Benjamin Coleman after the first flurry of awakenings in 1734–35. The startling results led Edwards in three significant directions—first toward the series of speculations concerning religious psychology that made him America's foremost religious philosopher of the eighteenth century; second, toward the self-analysis that found a lyric, almost poetic, voice in pieces such as his "Personal Narrative"; and third, toward a series of spiritual biographies, hinted at in this letter, where for the first time an American writer used narrative patterns to test the validity of a character's moral condition by describing his actions. The question raised by these narratives—to what extent can you judge a person's interior moral condition from his observable behavior?—became one of the key concerns of nineteenth-century romancers.

[To the Reverend Benjamin Coleman, May 30, 1735]

* * * A concern about the great things of religion began, about the latter end of December, and the beginning of January, to prevail abundantly in the town, till in a very little time it became universal throughout the town, among old and young, and from the highest to the lowest; all seemed to be

seized with a deep concern about their eternal salvation; all the talk in all companies, and upon all occasions was upon the things of religion, and no other talk was anywhere relished; and scarcely a single person in the whole town was left unconcerned about the great things of the eternal world. Those that were wont to be the vainest, and loosest persons in town seemed in general to be seized with strong convictions. Those that were most disposed to contemn vital and experimental religion, and those that had the greatest conceit of their own reason; the highest families in the town, and the oldest persons in the town, and many little children were affected remarkably; no one family that I know of, and scarcely a person has been exempt and the Spirit of God went on in His saving influences, to the appearance of all human reason and charity, in a truly wonderful and astonishing manner. The news of it filled the neighbouring towns with talk, and there were many in them that scoffed and made a ridicule of the religion that appeared in Northampton. But it was observable that it was very frequent and common that those of other towns that came into this town, and observed how it was here, were greatly affected, and went home with wounded spirits, and were never more able to shake off the impression that it made upon them, till at length there began to appear a general concern in several of the towns in the country. * * *

People are brought off from inordinate engagedness after the world, and have been ready to run into the other extreme of too much neglecting their worldly business and to mind nothing but religion. Those that are under convictions are put upon it earnestly to enquire what they shall do to be saved, and diligently to use appointed means of grace, and apply themselves to all known duty. And those that obtain hope themselves, and the charity of others concerning their good estate, generally seem to be brought to a great sense of their own exceeding misery in a natural condition, and their utter helplessness, and insufficiency for themselves, and their exceeding wickedness and guiltiness in the sight of God; it seldom fails but that each one seems to think himself worse than anybody else, and they are brought to see that they deserve no mercy of God, that all their prayers and pains are exceedingly worthless and polluted, and that God, notwithstanding all that they have done, or can do, may justly execute His eternal wrath upon them, and they seem to be brought to a lively sense of the excellency of Jesus Christ and His sufficiency and willingness to save sinners, and to be much weaned in their affections from the world, and to have their hearts filled with love to God and Christ, and a disposition to lie in the dust before Him. They seem to have given them a lively conviction of the truth of the Gospel, and the divine authority of the holy scriptures; though they can't have the exercise of this at all times alike, nor indeed of any other grace. They seem to be brought to abhor themselves for the sins of their past life, and to long to be holy, and to live holily, and to God's glory; but at the same time complain that they can do nothing, they are poor impotent creatures, utterly insufficient to glorify their Creator and Redeemer. They commonly seem to be much more sensible of their own wickedness after their conversion than before, so that they are often humbled by it; it seems to them that they are really become more wicked, when at the same time they are evidently full of a gracious Spirit. Their remaining sin seems to be their very great burthen, and many of them seem to long after heaven, that there they may be rid of sin. They generally seem to be united in dear love, and affection one to another, and to have a love to all mankind: I never saw the Christian spirit in love to enemies so exemplified, in all my life as I have seen it within this half year. They commonly express a great concern for others' salvation; some say that they think they are far more concerned for others' conversion, after they themselves have been converted, than ever they were for their own; several have thought (though perhaps they might be deceived in it) that they could freely die for the salvation of any soul, of the meanest of mankind, of any Indian in the woods. This town was never so full of love, nor so full of joy, nor so full of distress as it has lately been. Some persons have had those longing desires after Jesus Christ, that have been to that degree as to take away their strength, and very much to weaken them, and make them faint: many have been even overcome with a sense of the dying love of Christ, so that the home of the body has been ready to fail under it; there was once three pious young persons in this town talking together of the dying love of Christ, till they all fainted away; though tis probable the fainting of the two latter was much promoted by the fainting of the first. Many express a sense of the glory of the divine perfections, and of the excellency and fulness of Jesus Christ, and of their own littleness and unworthiness, in a manner truly wonderful, and almost unparalleled; and so likewise of the excellency and wonderfulness of the way of salvation by Jesus Christ. Their esteem of the holy scriptures is exceedingly increased. Many of them say the Bible seems to be a new book to them, as though they never read it before. There have been some instances of persons that by only an accidental sight of the Bible, have been as much moved, it seemed to me, as a lover by the sight of his sweetheart. The preaching of the Word is greatly prized by them; they say they never heard preaching before; and so are God's sabbaths, and ordinances, and opportunities of public worship. The sabbath is longed for before it comes, some by only hearing the bell ring on some occasion in the week time, have been greatly moved, because it has put them in mind of its ringing to call the people together to worship God. But no part of public worship has commonly put an effect on them as singing God's praises. They have a greater respect to ministers than they used to have, there is scarcely a minister preaches here but gets their esteem and affection. The experiences of some persons lately amongst [us] have been beyond almost all that ever I heard or read of. There is a pious woman in this town that is a very modest bashful person, that was moved by what she heard of the experiences of others earnestly to seek to God to give her more clear manifestations of Himself, and evidences of her own good estate, and God answered her request, and gradually gave her more and more of a sense of His glory and love, which she had with intermissions for several days, till one morning the week before last she had it to a more than ordinary degree, and it prevailed more and more till towards the middle of the day, till her nature began to sink under it, as she was alone in the house; but there came somebody into the house, and found her in an unusual, extraordinary frame. She expressed what she saw and felt to him; it came to that at last that they raised the neighbours, they were afraid she would die; I went up to see her and found her perfectly sober and in the exercise of her reason, but having her nature seemingly overborne and sinking, and when she could speak expressing in a manner that can't be described the sense she had of the glory of God, and particularly of such and such perfections, and her own unworthiness, her longing to lie in the dust, sometimes her longing to go to be with Christ, and crying out of the excellency of Christ, and the wonderfulness of His dying love; and so she continued for hours together, though not always in the same degree; at some times she was able to discourse to those about her; but it seemed to me if God had manifested a little more of Himself to her she would immediately have sunk and her frame dissolved under it. She has since been at my house, and continues as full as she can hold, but looks on herself not as an eminent saint, but as the worst of all, and unworthy to go to speak with a minister; but yet now beyond any great doubt of her good estate. There are two persons that belong to other towns that have had such a sense of God's exceeding greatness and majesty, that they were as it were swallowed up; they both of them told me to that purpose that if they in the time of it they had had the least fear that they were not at peace with that great God, they should immediately have died. But there is a very vast variety of degrees of spiritual discoveries, that are made to those that we hope are godly, as there is also in the steps, and method of the Spirit's operation in convincing and converting sinners, and the length of time that persons are under conviction before they have comfort. There is an alteration made in the town in a few months that strangers can scarcely [be] conscious of; our church, I believe, was the largest in New England before, but persons have lately thronged in, so that there are very few adult persons left out. There have been a great multitude hopefully converted, too many, I find, for me to declare abroad with credit to my judgment. The town seems to be full of the presence of God; our young people when they get together instead of frolicking as they used to do are altogether on pious subjects; tis so at weddings and on all occasions. The children in this, and the neighbouring towns have been greatly affected and influenced by the Spirit of God, and many of them hopefully changed; the youngest in this town is between nine and ten years of age; some of them seem to be full of love to Christ and have expressed great longings after Him and willingness to die, and leave father and mother and all things in the world to go to Him, together with a great sense of their unworthiness and admiration of the free grace of God towards them. And there have been many old people, many above fifty and several near seventy, that seem to be wonderfully changed and hopefully new born. The good people that have been formerly converted in the town have many of them been wonderfully enlivened and increased. This work seems to be upon every account an extraordinary dispensation of Providence. Tis extraordinary upon the account of [the] universality of it in affecting all sorts, high and low, rich and poor, wise and unwise, old and young, vicious and moral; tis very extraordinary as to the numbers that are hopefully savingly wrought upon, and particularly the number of aged persons and children and loose livers; and also on the account of the quickness of the work of the Spirit on them, for many seem to have been suddenly taken from a loose way of living, and to be so changed as to become truly holy, spiritual, heavenly persons; tis extraordinary as to the degrees of gracious communications, and the abundant measures in which the Spirit of God has been poured out on many persons; tis extraordinary as to the extent of it, God's Spirit being so remarkably poured out on so many towns at once, and its making such swift progress from place to place. The extraordinariness of the thing has been, I believe, one principal cause that people abroad have suspected it. There have been, as I have heard, many odd and strange stories that have been carried about the country of this affair, which it is a wonder some wise men should be so ready to believe. Some indeed under great terrors of conscience have had impressions on their imaginations; and also under the power of the spiritual discoveries, they have had lively impressed ideas of Christ shedding blood for sinners, His blood running from His veins, and of Christ in His glory in heaven and such like things, but they are always taught, and have been several times taught in public not to lay the weight of their hopes on such things and many have nothing of any such imaginations. There have been several persons that have had their natures overborne under strong convictions, and trembled, and han't been able to stand, they have had such a sense of divine wrath. But there are no new doctrines embraced, but people have been abundantly established in those that we account orthodox; there is no new way of worship affected. There is no oddity of behavior prevails; people are no more superstitious about their clothes, or anything else than they used to be. Indeed there is a great deal of talk when they are together of one another's experiences, and indeed no other is to be expected in a town where the concern of the soul is so universally the concern, and that to so great a degree. And doubtless some persons under the strength of impressions that are made on their minds and under the power of strong affections, are guilty of imprudences, their zeal may need to be regulated by more prudence, and they may need a guide to their assistance; as of old when the church of Corinth had the extraordinary gifts of the Spirit, they needed to be told by the Apostle that the spirit of the prophets were subject to the prophets, and that their gifts were to be exercised with prudence, because God was not the author of confusion but of peace. There is no unlovely oddity in peoples' temper prevailing with this work, but on the contrary the face of things is much changed as to the appearance of a meek, humble, amiable behavior. Indeed the devil has not been idle, but his hand has evidently appeared in several instances endeavoring to mimick the work of the Spirit of God and to cast a slur upon it and no wonder: and there has hereby appeared the need of the watchful eye of skillful guides, and of wisdom from above to direct them. There lately came up hither a couple of ministers from Connecticut, viz., Mr. Lord of Preston, and Mr. Owen of Groton, who had heard of the extraordinary circumstances of this and the neighbouring towns, who had heard the affair well represented by some, and also heard many reports greatly to its disadvantage, who came on purpose to see and satisfy themselves; and that they might thoroughly acquaint themselves, went about, and spent good part of a day, in hearing the accounts of many of our new converts, and examining of them; which was greatly to their satisfaction and they took particular notice, among other things of the modesty with which persons gave account of themselves, and said that the one half was not told them, and could not be told them; and that if they renounced these persons' experiences they must renounce Christianity itself. And Mr. Owens said particularly as to their impressions on their imaginations, they were quite different from what had been represented, and that they were no more than might naturally be expected in such cases.

Thus, Sir, I have given you a particular account of this affair which Satan has so much misrepresented in the country. This is a true account of the matter as far as I have opportunity to know, and I suppose I am under greater advantages to know than any person living. Having been thus long in the account, I forebear to make reflections, or to guess what God is about to do; I leave this to you, and shall only say, as I desire always to say from my heart, "To God be all the glory whose work alone it is"; and let Him have an interest in your prayers, who so much needs divine help at that day, and is your affectionate brother,

& humble servant,

Jth Edwards.

Northampton May 30, 1735

Since I wrote the foregoing letter, there has happened a thing of a very awful nature in the town; my uncle Hawley, the last sabbath morning, laid violent hands on himself, and put an end to his life, by cutting his own throat. He had been for a considerable time greatly concerned about the condition of his soul; till, by the ordering of a sovereign Providence he was suffered to fall into deep melancholy, a distemper that the family are very prone to; he was much overpowered by it; the devil took the advantage and drove him into despairing thoughts: he was kept very much awake a nights, so that he had but very little sleep for two months, till he seemed not to have his faculties in his own power; he was in a great measure past a capacity of receiving advice, or being reasoned with. The coroner's inquest judged him delirious. Satan seems to be in a great rage, at this extraordinary breaking forth of the work of God. I hope it is because he knows that he has but a short time: doubtless he had a great reach, in this violent attack of his against the whole affair. We have appointed a day of fasting in the town this week, by reason of this and other appearances of Satan's rage against poor souls. I yesterday saw a woman that belongs to Durham, who says there is a considerable revival of religion there.

I am yours &c—

J. E.

Northampton, June 3, 1735.

The Quaker Temper

JOHN WOOLMAN [1720–1772]

QUAKERS FIRST ARRIVED in New England in 1656, preaching a personal spiritualism that outspokenly denounced all outward forms of ecclesiastical order and worship, and even, at the beginning, the Bible. Flagrantly eccentric in their behavior, they met with equally extreme repressive measures—fines, warnings, whipping, branding, mutilation, and in some cases death. But with the opening of Pennsylvania and New Jersey to varieties of religious belief in the 1680's, Quakers moderated their behavior, turning more and more to social service, so that established churches and communities found less and less excuse for punitive action against them.

By 1720, when John Woolman was born in New Jersey, the faith of his family was no longer the threat to social order that it once had been. Tailor, shopkeeper, and schoolmaster, Woolman spent most of his life as an itinerant minister for the Society of Friends, preaching the Quaker faith from New England to the Carolinas to all who would hear him. At the same time, in a series of pamphlets, he pleaded for temperance, the abolition of slavery, fairer treatment of the Indians, and relief for the poor. His record of a modest and moving life appeared in his *Journal*, published in Philadelphia two years after his death. John Greenleaf Whittier, who edited it in 1871, called it "a classic of the inner life." In England, Charles Lamb advised readers to get it "by heart"; and Crabb Robinson said of Woolman: "His is a schöne Seele, a beautiful soul. An illiterate tailor, he writes in a style of the most exquisite purity and grace. His moral qualities are transferred to his writings."

Further reading: *The Journal and Essays of John Woolman*, ed. with a biographical introduction by A. M. Gummere, 1922. Janet Whitney, *John Woolman, American Quaker*, 1942. Daniel B. Shea, *Spiritual Autobiography in Early America*, 1968.

FROM HIS *Journal*

Text: *The Journal and Essays of John Woolman*, ed. A. M. Gummere (New York, 1922).

[Youth]

I have often felt a motion of love to leave some hints of my experience of the goodness of God: and pursuant thereto, in the thirty-sixth year of my age, I begin this work.

I was born in Northampton, in Burlington county, in West Jersey, in the year of our Lord 1720; and before I was seven years old I began to be acquainted with the operations of divine love. Through the care of my parents, I was taught to read near as soon as I was capable of it; and as I went from school one seventh-day, I remember, while my companions went to play by the way, I went forward out of sight, and setting down, I read the twenty-second chapter of the Revelations: "He showed me a pure river of water of life, clear as crystal, proceeding out of the throne of God and of the lamb," etc.; and in the reading of it, my mind was drawn to seek after that pure habitation, which I then believed God had prepared for His servants. The place where I sat, and the sweetness that attended my mind, remain fresh in my memory.

This, and the like gracious visitations, had that effect upon me, that when boys used ill language, it troubled me, and through the continued mercies of God, I was preserved from it. The pious instructions of my parents were often fresh in my mind when I happened to be among wicked children, and were of use to me.

My parents, having a large family of children, used frequently, on first days after meeting, to put us to read in the holy scriptures, or some religious books, one after another, the rest sitting by without much conversation; which I have since often thought was a good practice. From what I had read, I believed there had been in past ages, people who walked in uprightness before God in a degree exceeding any that I knew, or heard of, now living; and the apprehension of there being less steadiness and firmness amongst people in this age than in past ages, often troubled me while I was still young.

I had a dream about the ninth year of my age as follows: I saw the moon rise near the West, and run a regular course Eastward, so swift that in about a quarter of an hour, she reached our meridian, when there descended from her a small cloud on a direct line to the earth, which lighted on a pleasant green about twenty yards from the door of my father's house (in which I thought I stood) and was immediately turned into a beautiful green tree. The moon appeared to run on with equal swiftness, and soon set in the East, at which time the sun arose at the place where it commonly doth in the summer, and shining with full radiance in a serene air, it appeared as pleasant a morning as ever I saw.

All this time I stood still in the door, in an awful frame of mind, and I observed that as heat increased by the rising sun, it wrought so powerfully on the little green tree, that the leaves gradually withered, and before noon it appeared dry and dead. There then appeared a being, small of size, moving swift from the North Southward, called a sun worm.

Though I was a child, this dream was instructive to me.

Another thing remarkable in my childhood was, that once, as I went to a neighbor's house, I saw, on the way, a robin sitting on her nest; and as I came near she went off, but having young ones, flew about, and with many cries expressed her concern for them. I stood and threw stones at her, till one striking her, she fell down dead. At first I was pleased with the exploit, but after a few minutes was seized with horror, as having in a sportive way killed an innocent creature while she was careful for her young. I beheld her lying dead, and thought those young ones for which she was so careful must now perish for want of their dam to nourish them; and after some painful considerations on the subject, I climbed up the tree, took all the young birds, and killed them—supposing that better than to leave them to pine away and die miserably: and believed in this case, that scripture proverb was fulfilled, "The tender mercies of the wicked are cruel."[1] I then went on my errand, but, for some hours, could think of little else but the cruelties I had committed, and was much troubled.

Thus He, whose tender mercies are over all His works, hath placed that in the human mind, which incites to exercise goodness towards every living creature, and this being singly attended to, people become tender-hearted and sympathizing; but being frequently and totally rejected, the mind shuts itself up in a contrary disposition.

About the twelfth year of my age, my father being abroad, my mother reproved me for some misconduct, to which I made an undutiful reply; and the next first-day, as I was with my father returning from meeting, he told me he understood I had behaved amiss to my mother, and advised me to be more careful in future. I knew myself blamable, and in shame and confusion remained silent. Being thus awakened to a sense of my wickedness, I felt remorse in my mind, and getting home, I retired and prayed to the Lord to forgive me; and I do not remember that I ever, after that, spoke unhandsomely to either of my parents, however foolish in some other things.

Having attained the age of sixteen, I began to love wanton company: and though I was preserved from profane language or scandalous conduct, still I perceived a plant in me which produced much wild grapes. Yet my merciful Father forsook me not utterly, but at times, through His grace, I was brought seriously to consider my ways; and the sight of my backsliding affected me with sorrow: but for want of rightly attending to the reproofs of instruction, vanity was added to vanity, and repentance. Upon the whole, my mind was more and more alienated from the truth, and I hastened towards destruction. While I meditate on the gulf towards which I traveled, and reflect on my youthful disobedience, my heart is affected with sorrow.

Advancing in age, the number of my acquaintance increased, and thereby my way grew more difficult. Though I had heretofore found comfort in reading the holy scriptures, and thinking on heavenly things, I was now estranged therefrom. I knew I was going from the flock of Christ, and had no resolution to return; hence serious reflections were uneasy to me, and youthful vanities and diversions my greatest pleasure. Running in this road I found many like myself; and we associated in that which is reverse to true friendship. But in this swift race it pleased God to visit me with sickness, so that I doubted of recovering: and then did darkness, horror, and amazement, with full force seize me, even when my pain

[1] Proverbs xii.10.

and distress of body was very great. I thought it would have been better for me never to have had a being, than to see the day which I now saw. I was filled with confusion; and in great affliction both of mind and body, I lay and bewailed myself. I had not confidence to lift up my cries to God, whom I had thus offended; but in a deep sense of my great folly, I was humbled before Him, and at length, that Word which is as a fire and a hammer, broke and dissolved my rebellious heart, and then my cries were put up in contrition, and in the multitude of His mercies I found inward relief, and felt a close engagement, that if He was pleased to restore my health, I might walk humbly before Him.

After my recovery, this exercise remained with me a considerable time, but, by degrees, giving way to youthful vanities, they gained strength, and getting with wanton young people I lost ground. The Lord had been very gracious, and spoke peace to me in the time of my distress, and I now most ungratefully turned again to folly, on which account, at times, I felt sharp reproof, but did not get low enough to cry for help. I was not so hardy as to commit things scandalous, but to exceed in vanity, and promote mirth, was my chief study. Still I retained a love and esteem for pious people, and their company brought an awe upon me. My dear parents several times admonished me in the fear of the Lord, and their admonition entered into my heart, and had a good effect for a season; but not getting deep enough to pray rightly, the tempter, when he came, found entrance. I remember once, having spent a part of a day in wantonness, as I went to bed at night, there lay in a window near my bed a Bible, which I opened, and first cast my eye on the text, "we lie down in our shame, and our confusion covers us."[2] This I knew to be my case, and meeting with so unexpected a reproof, I was somewhat affected with it, and went to bed under remorse of conscience, which I soon cast off again.

Thus time passed on, my heart was replenished with mirth and wantonness, while pleasing scenes of vanity were presented to my imagination, till I attained the age of eighteen years, near which time I felt the judgments of God in my soul like a consuming fire, and looking over my past life, the prospect was moving. I was often sad, and longed to be delivered from those vanities; then again my heart was strongly inclined to them, and there was in me a sore conflict. At times I turned to folly, and then again sorrow and confusion took hold of me. In a while, I resolved totally to leave off some of my vanities, but there was a secret reserve in my heart, of the more refined part of them, and I was not low enough to find true peace. Thus for some months, I had great troubles and disquiet, there remaining in me an unsubjected will, which rendered my labors fruitless, till at length, through the merciful continuance of heavenly visitations, I was made to bow down in spirit before the Most High. I remember one evening I had spent some time in reading a pious author, and walking out alone, I humbly prayed to the Lord for His help, that I might be delivered from those vanities which so ensnared me. . . . Thus, being brought low, He helped me, and as I learned to bear the cross, I felt refreshment to come from His presence: but not keeping in that strength which gave victory, I lost ground again, the sense of which greatly afflicted me; and I sought deserts and lonely places, and there with tears did confess my sins to God, and humbly craved help of Him. And I may say with reverence, He was near to me in my troubles, and in those times of humiliation opened my ear to discipline.

I was now led to look seriously at the means by which I was drawn from the pure truth, and I learned this: that if I would live in the life which the faithful servants of God lived in, I must not go into company as heretofore, in my own will; but all the cravings of sense must be governed by a divine principle. In times of sorrow and abasement, these instructions were sealed upon me, and I felt the power of Christ prevail over all selfish desires, so that I was preserved in a good degree of steadiness; and being young and believing at that time that a single life was best for me, I was strengthened to keep from such company as had often been a snare to me.

I kept steady to meetings; spent first-days in the afternoon chiefly in reading the scriptures and other good books; and was early convinced in my mind that true religion consisted in an inward life, wherein the heart doth love and reverence God the Creator, and learn to exercise true justice and goodness, not only toward all men, but also toward the brute creatures. That as the mind was moved by an inward principle to love God as an invisible, incomprehensible Being, by the same principle it was moved to love Him in all His manifestations in the visible world. That, as by His breath the flame of life was kindled in all animal and sensible creatures, to say we love God as unseen, and at the same time exercise cruelty toward the least creature moving by His life, or by life derived from Him, was a contradiction in itself.

I found no narrowness respecting sects and opinions; but believed that sincere, upright-hearted people, in every society, who truly love God, were accepted of Him.

As I lived under the cross, and simply followed the openings of truth, my mind from day to day was

[2]Jeremiah iii.25.

more enlightened; my former acquaintance were left to judge of me as they would, for I found it safest for me to live in private and keep these things sealed up in my own breast. While I silently ponder on that change which was wrought in me, I find no language equal to it, nor any means to convey to another a clear idea of it. I looked upon the works of God in this visible creation, and an awfulness covered me: my heart was tender and often contrite, and a universal love to my fellow creatures increased in me. This will be understood by such who have trodden in the same path.

Some glances of real beauty is perceivable in their faces, who dwell in true meekness. Some tincture of true harmony in the sound of that voice to which divine love gives utterance, and some appearance of right order in their temper and conduct, whose passions are fully regulated; yet all these do not fully show forth that inward life to such as have not felt it; but this white stone and new name is known rightly to such only who have it.

[Business and Conscience]

Until the year 1756, I continued to retail goods, besides following my trade as a tailor; about which time I grew uneasy on account of my business growing too cumbersome. I began with selling trimmings for garments, and from thence proceeded to sell cloths and linens, and at length having got a considerable shop of goods, my trade increased every year, and the road to large business appeared open: but I felt a stop in my mind.

Through the mercies of the Almighty I had in good degree learned to be content with a plain way of living. I had but a small family, my outward affairs had been prosperous, and, on serious reflection I believed truth did not require me to engage in much cumbering affairs. It had generally been my practice to buy and sell things really useful. Things that served chiefly to please the vain mind in people, I was not easy to trade in; seldom did it, and whenever I did, I found it weaken me as a Christian.

The increase of business became my burthen, for though my natural inclination was towards merchandise, yet I believed truth required me to live more free from outward cumbers. There was now a strife in my mind betwixt the two, and in this exercise my prayers were put up to the Lord, who graciously heard me, and gave me a heart resigned to His holy will; I then lessened my outward business; and as I had opportunity, told my customers of my intention, that they might consider what shop to turn to: and so in a while, wholly laid down merchandise, following my trade as a tailor, myself only, having no prentice. I also had a nursery of apple trees, in which I spent a good deal of time, howing, grafting, trimming, and inoculating.

In merchandise it is the custom, where I lived, to sell chiefly on credit; and poor people often get in debt, and when payment is expected, having not wherewith to pay, and so their creditors often sue for it at law: having often observed occurrences of this kind, I found it good for me to advise poor people to take such as were most useful and not costly.

In the time of trading I had an opportunity of seeing that a too liberal use of spiritous liquors, and the custom of wearing too costly apparel, led some people into great inconveniences: and these two things appear to be often connected one with the other; for by not attending to that use of things which is consistent with universal righteousness, there is a necessary increase of labor which extends beyond what our heavenly Father intends for us: and by great labor, and often by much sweating in the heat, there is, even among such who are not drunkards, a craving of some liquor to revive the spirits: that partly by the wanton, luxurious drinking of some, and partly by the drinking of others, led to it through immoderate labor, very great quantities of rum are annually expended in our colonies, of which we should have no need, did we steadily attend to pure wisdom.

Where men take pleasure in feeling their minds elevated with strong drink, and so indulge this appetite as to disorder their understanding, neglect their duty as members in a family or civil society, and cast off all pretense to religion, their case is much to be pitied. And where such whose lives are for the most part regular, and whose examples have a strong influence on the minds of others, adhere to some customs which powerfully draw toward the use of more strong liquor than pure wisdom directeth the use of, this also, as it hinders the spreading of the spirit of meekness, and strengthens the hands of the more excessive drinkers, is a case to be lamented.

As the least degree of luxury hath some connection with evil, for those who profess to be disciples of Christ, and are looked upon as leaders of the people, to have that mind in them which was also in Him, and so stand separate from every wrong way, is a means of help to the weaker. As I have sometimes been much spent in the heat, and taken spirits to revive me, I have found by experience that the mind is not so calm in such circumstances, nor so fit for divine meditation, as when all such extremes are avoided; and I have felt an increasing care to attend that Holy Spirit which sets right bounds to our desires, and leads those who faithfully follow it to apply all the gifts of divine providence to the purposes for which they were intended. Did such who have the care of great estates attend with singleness of heart to this heavenly instructor, which so opens and enlarges the mind that men love their neighbors as themselves, they would have wisdom given them to manage, without ever finding occasion to employ some people in the luxuries of life, or to make it necessary for others to labor too hard. But for want of regarding steadily this principle of divine love, a selfish spirit takes place in the minds of people, which is attended with darkness and manifold confusions in the world. ***

Though trading in things useful is an honest employ, yet through the great number of superfluities which are commonly bought and sold, and through the corruptions of the times, they who apply to merchandise for a living, have great need to be well experienced in that precept which the prophet Jeremiah laid down for Baruk, his scribe: "Seekest thou great things for thyself? seek them not."

FROM *Considerations on Keeping Negroes*

Negro slavery had been a thorn to Christian consciences for some years before Judge Samuel Sewall of Boston published a broadside entitled *The Selling of Joseph: A Memorial* (1700), which argued that "all men, as they are the sons of Adam, are co-heirs; and have equal right unto liberty, and all other outward comforts of life." Seventy-five years later the first antislavery society was organized in Philadelphia—The Society for the Relief of Free Negroes, Unlawfully Held in Bondage. Quakers had long been outspoken opponents of slavery, Woolman's voice one of the foremost among them following his 1500-mile trip to Virginia and North Carolina in 1746. *Some Considerations* (1754, 1762) is a significant document in the early phase of antislavery agitation. Text: The Gummere edition of *The Journals and Essays.*

[Final Appeal]

If we seriously consider that liberty is the right of innocent men; that the mighty God is a refuge for the oppressed; that in reality we are indebted to them; that they being set free, are still liable to the penalties of our laws, and as likely to have punishment for their crimes as other people: this may answer all our objections. And to retain them in perpetual servitude, without just cause for it, will produce effects, in the event, more grievous than setting them free would do, when a real love to truth and equity was the motive to it.

Our authority over them stands originally in a purchase made from those who, as to the general, obtained theirs by unrighteousness. Whenever we have recourse to such authority, it tends more or less to obstruct the channels through which the perfect plant in us receives nourishment.

There is a principle which is pure, placed in the human mind, which in different places and ages hath had different names; it is, however, pure, and proceeds from God. It is deep, and inward, confined to no forms of religion, nor excluded from any, where the heart stands in perfect sincerity. In whomsoever this takes root and grows, of what nation soever, they become brethren, in the best sense of the expression. Using ourselves to take ways which appear most easy to us, when inconsistent with that purity which is without beginning, we thereby set up a government of our own, and deny obedience to Him whose service is true liberty.

He that hath a servant, made so wrongfully, and knows it to be so, when he treats him otherwise than a free man, when he reaps the benefit of his labor, without paying him such wages as are reasonably due to free men for the like service, clothes excepted; these things, though done in calmness, without any shew of disorder, do yet deprave the mind in like manner, and with as great certainty as prevailing cold congeals water. These steps taken by masters, and their conduct striking the minds of their children, whilst young, leave less room for that which is good to work upon them. The customs of their parents, their neighbors, and the people with whom they converse, working upon their minds; and they, from thence, conceiving ideas of things, and modes of conduct, the entrance into their hearts becomes, in a great measure, shut up against the gentle movings of uncreated purity.

From one age to another, the gloom grows thicker and darker, till error gets established by general opinion: so that whoever attends to perfect goodness, and remains under the melting influence of it, finds a path unknown to many, and sees the necessity to lean upon the arm of divine strength, and dwell alone, or with a few, in the right committing their cause to Him who is a refuge for His people in all their troubles.

Where, through the agreement of a multitude, some channels of justice are stopped, and men may support their characters as just men by being just to a party, there is great danger of contracting an alliance with that spirit which stands in opposition to the God of love, and spreads discord, trouble, and vexation among such who give up to the influence of it.

Negroes are our fellow creatures, and their present condition amongst us requires our serious consideration. We know not the time when those scales in which mountains are weighed may turn. The Parent of mankind is gracious; His care is over His smallest creatures; and a multitude of men escape not His notice. And though many of them are trodden down, and despised, yet He remembers them; He seeth their affliction, and looketh upon the spreading, increasing exaltation of the oppressor. He turns the channels of power, humbles the most haughty people, and gives deliverance to the oppressed, at such periods as are consistent with His infinite justice and goodness. And wherever gain is preferred to equity, and wrong things publicly encouraged, to that degree that wickedness takes root, and spreads wide amongst the inhabitants of a country, there is real cause for sorrow to all such whose love to mankind stands on a true principle, and who wisely consider the end and event of things.

1762

A Virginia Gentleman

WILLIAM BYRD [1674–1744]

Rich in land and equally rich in curiosity and zest for life, Byrd joined a robust temperament to opportunity and means in creating and recording a style of life that has charmed generations of readers. Son of a wealthy and prominent Virginia tobacco planter, he was born near the site of the present city of Richmond, which he himself founded. In 1681 he was sent to England to be educated, and there he spent most of the next twenty years and more. He traveled, read law, dabbled in science, was made a Fellow of the Royal Society, represented Virginia at court, frequented the theater, mingled with literary notables—especially the dramatists William Congreve, Nicholas Rowe, and William Wycherly—and thoroughly absorbed the elegance and sophistication of London.

His father's death in 1704 brought him back to Virginia and to the privileges and responsibilities of a large plantation. At Westover on the James he built one of the finest colonial mansions of the period, filling it with appropriately handsome furniture, glass, and silver from England, as well as with portraits of English noblemen whom he had known and with whom he corresponded. To one of them, the Earl of Orrery, he wrote a description of his life as a rich planter:

> I have a large family of my own, and my doors are open to everybody, yet I have no bills to pay, and half a crown will rest undisturbed in my pocket for many moons together. Like one of the patriarchs, I have my flocks and my herds, my bondmen and bondwomen, and every sort of trade amongst my own servants, so that I live in a kind of independence of everyone but Providence. However, this sort of life is without expense, yet it is attended with a great deal of trouble. I must take care to keep all my people to their duty, to set all the springs in motion, and to make everyone draw his equal share to carry the machine forward. But then'tis an amusement in this silent country.

And even as he increased his estates from the 26,231 acres he inherited to more than 179,000 before his death, he also vigorously pursued the public duties his position entailed. Receiver-general of the King's revenues, he bore a prominent part in the colony's long dispute with Governor Spotswood, and in 1709 he became a member of the Council of State, the aristocratic group that virtually governed Virginia.

Byrd's interests, however, were not exclusively material. His library was distinguished not only by its size (at 3,600 titles it was the largest in Virginia), but by its remarkable balance, ranging from divinity and natural philosophy to history and literature, especially the Elizabethan and Restoration dramatists, and featuring more than five hundred titles in Greek, Latin, and French. In England he tried his hand at verse and polite essay forms, and even published a forty-page *Discourse Concerning the Plague,* but his main literary accomplishment was of another kind.

From 1709 to 1741, Byrd kept a shorthand diary in which he registered with gusto the delights and pangs of the flesh as well as the mind. The brilliance of his observations, the shrewdness of his comments, his ability to vivify characters and places, and the frankness and humor of his approach to everything make the diaries a remarkable portrait of provincial life. The same qualities mark his *History of the Dividing Line Run in the Year 1728,* and another *Secret History,* both of which recount the boundary survey between Virginia and North Carolina (a project which he led), and his account of a visit to Governor Spotswood's iron mines in *A Progress to the Mines in the Year 1732.*

Further reading: *The Writings,* ed. J. S. Bassett, 1901. *William Byrd's Histories of the Dividing Line Betwixt Virginia and North Carolina,* ed. W. K. Boyd, 1929. L. B. Wright, *The First Gentlemen of Virginia,* 1940. R. C. Beatty, *William Byrd of Westover,* 1932.

FROM *Secret Diary*

Undiscovered till well into the twentieth century, a diary for 1709-1712 was published in 1941, one for 1739-1741 in 1942. Our selections are from the former. They provide interesting glimpses of Byrd's life at Westover. Text: *The Secret Diary of William Byrd of Westover, 1709-1712,* ed. Louis B. Wright and Marion Tinling (Richmond, 1941).

[The Life of a Virginia Gentleman]

Dec. 25, 1709. I rose at 7 o'clock and ate milk for breakfast. I neglected to say my prayers because of my company. I ate milk for breakfast. About 11 o'clock the rest of the company ate some broiled turkey for their breakfast. Then we went to church, notwithstanding it rained a little, where Mr. Anderson preached a good sermon for the occasion. I received the sacrament with great devoutness. After church the same company went to dine with me and I ate roast beef for dinner. In the afternoon Dick Randolph and Mr. Jackson went away and Mr. Jackson rode sidelong like a woman. Then we took a walk about the plantation, but a great fog soon drove us into the house again. In the evening we were merry with nonsense and so were my servants. I said my prayers shortly and had good health, good thoughts, and good humor, thanks be to God Almighty.

Dec. 29. I rose at 5 o'clock and read two chapters in Hebrew and some Greek in Cassius.[1] I said my prayers and ate milk for breakfast. I danced my dance.[2] About 9 o'clock I ate again some chocolate with the company. Then we took a walk and I slid on skates, notwithstanding there was a thaw. Then we returned and played at billiards till dinner. I ate boiled beef for dinner. In the afternoon we played at billiards again and in the evening took another walk and gave Mr. Isham Randolph two bits to venture on the ice. He ventured and the ice broke with him and took him up to the mid-leg. Then we came home and played a little at whisk, but I was so sleepy we soon left off.

March 31, 1710. I rose at 7 o'clock and read some Greek in bed. I said my prayers and ate milk for breakfast. Then about 8 o'clock we got a-horseback and rode to Mr. Harrison's and found him very ill but sensible. Here I met Mr. Bland who brought me several letters from England and among the rest two from Colonel Blakiston who had endeavored to procure the Government of Virginia for me at the price of £1000 of my Lady Orkney and that my Lord [agreed], but the Duke of Marlborough declared that no one but soldiers should have the government of a plantation so I was disappointed. God's will be done. From hence I came home where I found all well, thank God. I ate fish for dinner. In the afternoon I went again with my wife to Mr. Harrison's who continued very bad so that I resolved to stay with him all night, which I did with Mr. Anderson and Nat Burwell. He was in the same bad condition till he vomited and then he was more easy. In the morning early I returned home and

[1] Probably the history of Rome by Dion Cassius, a copy of which Byrd owned.

[2] This recurring phrase probably refers to a calisthenic dance, or setting-up exercise, devised by Byrd, who was a bit of a faddist in his lifelong preoccupation with his health.

went to bed. It is remarkable that Mrs. Burwell dreamed this night that she saw a person that with money scales weighed time and declared that there was no more than 18 pennies worth of time to come, which seems to be a dream with some significance either concerning the world or a sick person. In my letters from England I learned that the Bishop of Worcester was of opinion that in the year 1715 the city of Rome would be burnt to the ground, that before the year 1745 the popish religion would be rooted out of the world, that before the year 1790 the Jews and Gentiles would be converted to the Christianity and then would begin the millennium.

April 10. I rose at 6 o'clock and wrote several letters to my overseers. I sent early to inquire after Mr. Harrison and received word that he died about 4 o'clock this morning, which completed the 18th day of his sickness, according to Mrs. Burwell's dream exactly. Just before his death he was sensible and desired Mrs. L— with importunity to open the door because he wanted to go out and could not go till the door was open and as soon as the door was opened he died. The country has lost a very useful man and who was both an advantage and an ornament to it, and I have lost a good neighbor, but God's will be done. I said my prayers and ate caudle[3] for breakfast. I danced my dance. My wife rode to Mrs. Harrison's to comfort her and to assure her that I should be always ready to do her all manner of service. My wife returned before dinner. I ate tripe for dinner. In the afternoon we played at piquet.[4] Then I prepared my matters for the General Court. It rained, with the wind at northeast, and it was very cold, and in the night it snowed.

May 23. I rose at 5 o'clock and read 2 chapters in Hebrew and some Greek in Anacreon. The children were a little better, thank God. I said my prayers and ate milk and strawberries for breakfast. I danced my dance. My daughter was very ill, but the boy had lost his fever, thank God. I settled some accounts and wrote some commonplace. I ate hashed shoat for dinner. In the afternoon Evie had a sweat that worked pretty well, but not long enough, for which I was out of humor with my wife. I read some Italian and some news and then took a walk about the plantation. When I returned I had a great quarrel with my wife, in which she was to blame altogether; however, I made the first step to a reconciliation, to [which] she with much difficulty consented.

June 15. I rose at 5 o'clock and read a chapter in Hebrew and some Greek in Thucydides. I said my prayers and ate milk for breakfast. The weather was very hot. I wrote a letter to England. I ate some broiled pork for dinner. In the afternoon my gripes[5] returned on me and continued till the evening with some violence. Hot things did it no good but in the evening I drank some warm milk from the cow which eased me immediately. It rained this afternoon very hard with a little wind and thunder. This hindered my walking anywhere but in the garden. I foretold by my cellar stinking that it would rain. I impute my gripes to cherry wine, or else pulling my coat off about noon. I said my prayers and had good thoughts, good humor, but indifferent good health, thank God Almighty.

June 16. I rose at 5 o'clock and drank some milk warm from the cow. I read a chapter in Hebrew and some Greek in Thucydides. I said my prayers and danced my dance. About 10 o'clock Captain Drury Stith and his wife came to make us a visit, notwithstanding it was very hot. I was glad to see them because I think them excellent people. We played at billiards till dinner. I ate boiled pork. In the afternoon we passed away the time pleasantly till about 6 o'clock and then they went home. In the evening I took a walk with my wife. We made a little cider of the G-n-t-n apples, which yielded but little juice. I was better of my gripes, thank God. I neglected to say my prayers but had good health, good thoughts, and good humor, thank God Almighty.

June 17. I rose at 5 o'clock and drank some milk hot from the cow. I read a chapter in Hebrew and some Greek in Thucydides. I said my prayers and danced my dance. About 8 o'clock Mr. Anderson came on his way over the river. He told me the quarrel was made up between Parson Slater and his vestry without coming to trial. He stayed about half an hour. Colonel Hill sent his man with a basket of apricots, of which my wife ate twelve immediately and I ate eight which however did not make my gripes return. I set my closet right. I ate tongue and chicken for dinner. In the afternoon I caused L-s-n to be whipped for beating his wife and Jenny was whipped for being his whore. In the evening the sloop came from Appomatox with tobacco. I took a walk about the plantation. I said my prayers and drank some new milk from the cow. I had good health, good thoughts, and good humor, thanks be to God Almighty.

June 18. I rose at 5 o'clock and drank some new milk from the cow. I read a chapter in Hebrew and some Greek in Thucydides. I said my prayers. It was extremely hot. I read a sermon in Dr. Tillotson about angels. I wrote a letter to Williamsburg to

[3]A warm, spiced drink of gruel mixed with wine or ale.

[4]A two-handed card game played with 32 cards.

[5]Intermittent stomach cramps.

send by my sloop which I sent for rum, wine, and sugar from thence and that this might come safely I resolved to send Bannister with the sloop. I ate chicken for dinner but very little because I had no appetite. In the afternoon my wife told me a dream she had two nights. She thought she saw a scroll in the sky in form of a light cloud with writing on it. It ran extremely fast from west to east with great swiftness. The writing she could not read but there was a woman before her that told her there would be a great dearth because of want of rain and after that a pestilence for that the seasons were changed and time inverted. Mr. James Burwell and Charles Doyley came and in the evening I took a walk with them. Our nurse went away in the sloop. I said my prayers and had good health, good thoughts, and good humor, thanks be to God Almighty.

June 19. I rose at 5 o'clock and read a chapter in Hebrew and some Greek in Thucydides. I drank some warm milk from the cow. I said my prayers and danced my dance. About 10 o'clock came Isham Randolph and Mr. Finney to see us. They told me Colonel Randolph was very ill and very melancholy. We played at billiards till dinner. I ate fish for dinner. In the afternoon Mr. Stith came over with my cousin Berkeley, who all stayed here till the evening and then they all went away but Mr. Finney. In the evening we took a walk. Mr. Finney is a sensible man and good natured. He told me that Major Allen died on Thursday last. In our walk we met Mr. C—s who came home with us. I neglected to say my prayers but had good health, good thoughts, and good humor, thank God Almighty.

June 20. I rose at 5 o'clock and drank milk from the cow. I read a chapter in Hebrew and some Greek in Thucydides. I said my prayers and danced my dance. Mr. Finney returned home without any breakfast but I gave him some strong water. Colonel Hill sent us another present of apricots. I wrote a letter to England. I ate five apricots which put my belly out of order. I ate roast mutton for dinner. In the afternoon my belly was griped. I played with my wife at piquet and then I ordered the boat to carry us to my cousin Harrison's where we found my cousin Berkeley and Jimmy Burwell. I was out of order in my belly. About 8 o'clock we returned home where we found all well, thank God. I said my prayers and had good health, good thoughts, and good humor, thanks be to God Almighty.

June 21. I rose at 5 o'clock and drank milk from the cow. I read a chapter in Hebrew and some Greek in Thucydides. I said my prayers and danced my dance. My wife was indisposed. I sent Tom to Appomattox to desire Mr. Mumford to go to the outcry of my uncle's estate. About five nights since I dreamed I saw a flaming star in the air at which I was much frightened and called some others to see it but when they came it disappeared. I fear this portends some judgment to this country or at least to myself. I ate roast mutton for dinner. In the afternoon I settled the closet. About 5 o'clock I received an express from Mr. Clayton that the Governor, Colonel Spotswood, with two men-of-war arrived last night at Kiquotan with several other ships. I sent word of this to Mrs. Harrison and then prepared to go to Williamsburg tomorrow. In the evening I took a walk about the plantation. I said my prayers and had good thoughts, good humor, and good health, thank God Almighty.

July 9. About 11 o'clock we went to church and had a good sermon. After church I invited nobody home because I design to break that custom, that my people may go to church. I ate boiled pork for dinner. In the afternoon my wife and I had a terrible quarrel about the things she had come in [i.e. her goods from England], but at length she submitted because she was in the wrong. For my part I kept my temper very well.

July 15. About 7 o'clock the Negro Betty that ran away was brought home. My wife against my will caused little Jenny to be burned with a hot iron, for which I quarreled with her. It was so hot today that I did not intend to go to the launching of Colonel Hill's ship, but about 9 o'clock the Colonel was so kind as to come and call us. My wife would not go at first but with much entreaty she at last consented. About 12 o'clock we went and found abundance of company at the ship, and about one she was launched and went off very well, notwithstanding several had believed the contrary.

Sept. 20. I rose at 6 o'clock but read nothing because I prepared for the Governor's coming in the evening. I neglected to say my prayers but ate milk for breakfast. I settled several things in my library. All the wood was removed from the place where it used to lay to a better place. I sent John to kill some blue wing[6] and he had good luck. I ate some boiled beef for dinner. In the afternoon all things were put into the best order because Captain Burbydge sent word that the Governor would be here at 4 o'clock but he did not come till 5. Captain Burbydge sent his boat for him and fired as he came up the river. I received at the landing with Mr. C—s and gave him 3 guns. Mr. Clayton and Mr. Robinson came with him. After he had drunk some wine he walked in the garden and into the library till it was dark. Then we went to supper and ate some blue wing. After supper we sat and talked till 9 o'clock,

Sept. 21. I rose at 6 o'clock and read nothing but got ready to receive the company. About 8 o'clock

[6]A North American teal that appeared early every fall.

the Governor came down. I offered him some of my fine water [?]. Then we had milk tea and bread and butter for breakfast. The Governor was pleased with everything and very complaisant. About 10 o'clock Captain Stith came and soon after him Colonel Hill, Mr. Anderson and several others of the militia officers. The Governor was extremely courteous to them. About 12 o'clock Mr. Clayton went to Mrs. Harrison's and then orders were given to bring all the men into the pasture to muster. Just as we got on our horses it began to rain hard; however this did not discourage the Governor but away we rode to the men. It rained half an hour and the Governor mustered them all the while and he presented me to the people to be their Colonel and commander-in-chief. About 3 o'clock we returned to the house and as many of the officers as could sit at the table stayed to dine with the Governor, and the rest went to take part of the hogshead [of punch] in the churchyard. We had a good dinner, well served, with which the Governor seemed to be well pleased. I ate venison for dinner. In the evening all the company went away and we took a walk and found a comic freak of a man that was drunk that hung on the pales. Then we went home and played at piquet and I won the pool. About 9 the Governor went to bed.

Feb. 5, 1711. I rose about eight o'clock and found my cold still worse. I said my prayers and ate milk and potatoes for breakfast. My wife and I quarreled about her pulling her brows. She threatened she would not go to Williamsburg if she might not pull them; I refused, however, and got the better of her, and maintained my authority.

Nov. 23. It was very cold this morning. About 11 o'clock I went to the coffeehouse where the Governor also came and from thence we went to the capitol and read the bill concerning ports the first time. We stayed till 3 o'clock and then went to dinner to Marot's but could get none there and therefore Colonel Lewis and I dined with Colonel Duke and I ate broiled chicken for dinner. After dinner we went to Colonel Carter's room where we had a bowl of punch of French brandy and oranges. We talked very lewdly and were almost drunk and in that condition we went to the coffeehouse and played at dice and I lost £12. We stayed at the coffeehouse till almost 4 o'clock in the morning talking with Major Harrison.

Dec. 29. I rose about 7 o'clock and read two chapters in Hebrew and some Greek in Lucian. I said my prayers and ate boiled milk for breakfast. I had abundance of talk with Mr. G-r-l about the affairs of Falling Creek and he told me some of his wants and so did George Smith, which I endeavored to supply as well as I could. I gave John G-r-l leave to go visit his mother. Poor old Jane died this morning about 9 o'clock and I caused her to be buried as soon as possible because she stank very much. It was not very cold today. I danced my dance. Mr. G-r-l and George Smith went away about 12 o'clock. I ate some broiled goose for dinner. In the afternoon I set my razor, and then went out to shoot with bow and arrow till the evening and then I ran to breathe myself and looked over everything. At night I read some Latin in Terence till about 10 o'clock. I said my prayers and had good health, good thoughts, and good humor, thank God Almighty.

Dec. 30. I rose about 7 o'clock and read a chapter in Hebrew and three chapters in the Greek Testament. I said my prayers very devoutly and ate boiled milk for breakfast. The weather was very clear and warm so that my wife walked out with Mrs. Dunn and forgot dinner, for which I had a little quarrel with her and another afterwards because I was not willing to let her have a book out of the library. About 12 o'clock came Mr. Bland from Williamsburg but brought no news. He stayed to dinner and I ate some roast beef. In the afternoon we sat and talked till about 4 o'clock and then I caused my people to set him over the river and then I walked with the women about the plantation till they were very weary. At night we ate some eggs and drank some Virginia beer and talked very gravely without reading anything. However I said my prayers and spoke with all my people. I had good health, good thoughts, and good humor, thank God Almighty. I danced my dance in the morning.

Dec. 31. I rose about 7 o'clock and read a chapter in Hebrew and six leaves in Lucian. I said my prayers and ate boiled milk for breakfast. The weather continued warm and clear. I settled my accounts and wrote several things till dinner. I danced my dance. I ate some turkey and chine for dinner. In the afternoon I weighed some money and then read some Latin in Terence and then Mr. Mumford came and told me my man Tony had been very sick but he was recovered again, thank God. He told me Robin Bolling had been like to die and that he denied that he was the first to mention the imposition on skins which he certainly did. Then he and I took a walk about the plantation. When I returned I was out of humor to find the Negroes all at work in our chambers. At night I ate some broiled turkey with Mr. Mumford and we talked and were merry all the evening. I said my prayers and had good health, good thoughts, and good humor, thank God Almighty. My wife and I had a terrible quarrel about whipping Eugene while Mr. Mumford was there but she had a mind to show her authority before company but I would not suffer it, which she took very ill; however for peace sake I made the first advance towards a reconciliation which I obtained with some difficulty and after abundance of crying. However it spoiled the mirth of the evening, but I was not conscious that I was to blame in that quarrel.

Jan. 1, 1712. I lay abed till 9 o'clock this morning to bring my wife into temper again and rogered her by way of reconciliation. I read nothing because Mr. Mumford was here, nor did I say my prayers, for the same reason. However I ate boiled milk for breakfast, and after my wife tempted me to eat some pancakes with her. Mr. Mumford and I went to shoot with our bows and arrows but shot nothing, and afterwards we played at billiards till dinner, and when we came we found Ben Harrison there, who dined with us. I ate some partridge for dinner. In the afternoon we played at billiards again and I won two bits. I had a letter from Colonel Duke by H-l the bricklayer who came to offer his services to work for me. Mr. Mumford went away in the evening and John Bannister with him to see his mother. I took a walk about the plantation and at night we drank some mead of my wife's making which was very good. I gave the people some cider and a dram to the Negroes. I read some Latin in Terence and had good health, good thoughts, and good humor, thank God Almighty. I said my prayers.

FROM *History of the Dividing Line*

Surveying the disputed boundary line between Virginia and North Carolina was an arduous undertaking. Byrd's narrative, presumably intended for publication, remained in manuscript form until 1841, nearly a century after his death. In 1929 a rougher version, *A Secret History of the Line,* appeared. The selections below are from the more finished version. Byrd's fresh, lively style, with its flashes of wit, causes us to regard lightly his exaggerations and prejudices. Text: *William Byrd's Histories of the Dividing Line . . .*, ed. William K. Boyd (Raleigh, 1929).

[Life in North Carolina]

March 25 [1728]. The air was chilled this morning with a smart north-west wind, which favored the Dismalites[1] in their dirty march. They returned by the path they had made in coming out, and with great industry arrived in the evening at the spot where the Line had been discontinued.

After so long and laborious a journey, they were glad to repose themselves on their couches of cypress-bark, where their sleep was as sweet as it would have been on a bed of Finland down.

In the mean time, we who stayed behind had nothing to do, but to make the best observations we could upon that part of the country. The soil of our landlord's plantation, though none of the best, seemed more fertile than any thereabouts, where the ground is near as sandy as the deserts of Africa, and consequently barren. The road leading from thence to Edenton, being in distance about 27 miles, lies upon a ridge called Sandy Ridge, which is so wretchedly poor that it will not bring potatoes.

The pines in this part of the country are of a different species from those that grow in Virginia: their bearded leaves are much longer and their cones much larger. Each cell contains a seed of the size and figure of a black-eyed pea, which, shedding in November, is very good mast for hogs, and fattens them in a short time.

The smallest of these pines are full of cones, which are eight or nine inches long, and each affords commonly 60 or 70 seeds. This kind of mast has the advantage of all other by being more constant, and less liable to be nipped by the frost or eaten by the caterpillars. The trees also abound more with turpentine, and consequently yield more tar than either the yellow or the white pine; and for the same reason make more durable timber for building. The inhabitants hereabouts pick up knots of lightwood[2] in abundance, which they burn into tar, and then carry it to Norfolk or Nansimond for a market. The tar made in this method is the less valuable because it is said to burn the cordage, though it is full as good for all other uses as that made in Sweden and Muscovy.

Surely there is no place in the world where the inhabitants live with less labor than in North Carolina. It approaches nearer to the description of Lubberland than any other, by the great felicity of the climate, the easiness of raising provisions, and the slothfulness of the people.

Indian corn is of so great increase that a little pains will subsist a very large family with bread, and then they may have meat without any pains at all, by the help of the low grounds, and the great variety of mast that grows on the high land. The men for their parts, just like the Indians, impose all the work upon the poor women. They make their wives rise out of their beds early in the morning, at the same time that they lie and snore till the sun has run one-third of his course and disperst all the unwholesome damps. Then, after stretching and yawning for half an hour, they light their pipes, and, under the protection of a cloud of smoke, venture out into the open air; though, if it happens to be never so little cold, they quickly return shivering into the chimney corner. When the weather is mild, they stand lean-

[1]A reference to the Dismal Swamp connecting Albemarle Sound with Chesapeake Bay.

[2]A resinous pine-wood.

ing with both their arms upon the cornfield fence, and gravely consider whether they had best go and take a small heat at the hoe: but generally find reasons to put it off till another time.

Thus they loiter away their lives, like Solomon's sluggard,[3] with their arms across, and at the winding up of the year scarcely have bread to eat.

To speak the truth, 'tis a thorough aversion to labor that makes people file off to North Carolina, where plenty and a warm sun confirm them in their disposition to laziness for their whole lives.

March 26. Since we were like to be confined to this place, till the people returned out of the Dismal, 'twas agreed that our chaplain might safely take a turn to Edenton, to preach the Gospel to the infidels there, and christen their children. He was accompanied thither by Mr. Little, one of the Carolina Commissioners, who, to show his regard for the Church, offered to treat him on the road with a fricassee of rum. They fried half a dozen rashers of very fat bacon in a pint of rum, both which being dished up together, served the company at once for meat and drink.

Most of the rum they get in this country comes from New England, and is so bad and unwholesome, that it is not improperly called "kill-devil." It is distilled there from foreign molasses, which, if skilfully managed, yields near gallon for gallon. Their molasses comes from the same country, and has the name of "long sugar" in Carolina, I suppose from the ropiness of it, and serves all the purposes of sugar, both in their eating and drinking.

When they entertain their friends bountifully, they fail not to set before them a capacious bowl of bombo, so called from the Admiral of that name. This is a compound of rum and water in equal parts, made palatable with the said long sugar. As good humor begins to flow, and the bowl to ebb, they take care to replenish it with sheer rum, of which there always is a reserve under the table. But such generous doings happen only when that balsam of life is plenty; for they have often such melancholy times, that neither land-graves nor cassicks[4] can procure one drop for their wives, when they lie in, or are troubled with the colic or vapors. Very few in this country have the industry to plant orchards, which, in a dearth of rum, might supply them with much better liquor.

The truth is, there is one inconvenience that easily discourages lazy people from making this improvement: very often, in autumn, when the apples begin to ripen, they are visited with numerous flights of paraqueets, that bite all the fruit to pieces in a moment, for the sake of the kernels. The havoc they make is sometimes so great, that whole orchards are laid waste in spite of all the noises that can be made, or mawkins that can be dressed up, to fright 'em away. These ravenous birds visit North Carolina only during the warm season, and so soon as the cold begins to come on, retire back towards the sun. They rarely venture so far north as Virginia, except in a very hot summer, when they visit the most southern parts of it. They are very beautiful; but like some other pretty creatures, are apt to be loud and mischievous.

March 27. Betwixt this and Edenton there are many thuckleberry slashes, which afford a convenient harbor for wolves and foxes. The first of these wild beasts is not so large and fierce as they are in other countries more northerly. He will not attack a man in the keenest of his hunger, but run away from him, as from an animal more mischievous than himself.

The foxes are much bolder, and will sometimes not only make a stand, but likewise assault any one that would balk them of their prey. The inhabitants hereabouts take the trouble to dig abundance of wolf-pits, so deep and perpendicular, that when a wolf is once tempted into them, he can no more scramble out again, than a husband who had taken the leap can scramble out of matrimony.

Most of the houses in this part of the country are log-houses, covered with pine or cypress shingles, 3 feet long, and one broad. They are hung upon laths with pegs, and their doors too turn upon wooden hinges, and have wooden locks to secure them, so that the building is finished without nails or other iron-work. They also set up their pales without any nails at all, and indeed more securely than those that are nailed. There are 3 rails mortised into the posts, the lowest of which serves as a sill with a groove in the middle, big enough to receive the end of the pales: the middle part of the pale rests against the inside of the next rail, and the top of it is brought forward to the outside of the uppermost. Such wreathing of the pales in and out makes them stand firm, and much harder to unfix than when nailed in the ordinary way.

Within 3 or 4 miles of Edenton, the soil appears to be a little more fertile, though it is much cut with slashes, which seem all to have a tendency towards the Dismal.

This town is situate on the north side of Albemarle Sound, which is there about 5 miles over. A dirty slash runs all along the back of it, which in the summer is a foul annoyance, and furnishes abundance of that Carolina plague, mosquitoes. They may be 40 or 50 houses, most of them small, and

[3] Proverbs vi.6–11.

[4] Landgraves and Casiques (or Cassocks) were members of the upper house of the Carolina legislature.

built without expense. A citizen here is counted extravagant, if he has ambition enough to aspire to a brick-chimney. Justice herself is but indifferently lodged, the court-house having much the air of a common tobacco-house. I believe this is the only metropolis in the Christian or Mahomedan world, where there is neither church, chapel, mosque, synagogue, or any other place of public worship of any sect or religion whatsoever.

What little devotion there may happen to be is much more private than their vices. The people seem easy without a minister, as long as they are exempted from paying him. Sometimes the Society for Propagating the Gospel has had the charity to send over missionaries to this country; but unfortunately the priest has been too lewd for the people, or, which oftener happens, they too lewd for the priest. For these reasons these reverend gentlemen have always left their flocks as arrant heathen as they found them. Thus much however may be said for the inhabitants of Edenton, that not a soul has the least taint of hypocrisy, or superstition, acting very frankly and aboveboard in all their excesses.

Provisions here are extremely cheap, and extremely good, so that people may live plentifully at trifling expense. Nothing is dear but law, physic, and strong drink, which are all bad in their kind, and the last they get with so much difficulty, that they are never guilty of the sin of suffering it to sour upon their hands. Their vanity generally lies not so much in having a handsome dining-room, as a handsome house of office: in this kind of structure they are really extravagant.

They are rarely guilty of flattering or making any court to their governors, but treat them with all the excesses of freedom and familiarity. They are of opinion their rulers would be apt to grow insolent, if they grew rich, and for that reason take care to keep them poorer, and more dependent, if possible, than the saints in New England used to do their governors. They have very little coin, so they are forced to carry on their home-traffic with paper-money. This is the only cash that will tarry in the country, and for that reason the discount goes on increasing between that and real money, and will do so to the end of the chapter.

[A Visit to the Indians]

April 7. The next day being Sunday, we ordered notice to be sent to all the neighborhood that there would be a sermon at this place, and an opportunity of christening their children. But the likelihood of rain got the better of their devotion, and what perhaps, might still be a stronger motive of their curiosity. In the morning we dispatched a runner to the Nottoway Town, to let the Indians know we intend them a visit that evening, and our honest landlord was so kind as to be our pilot thither, being about 4 miles from his house.

Accordingly in the afternoon we marched in good order to the town, where the female scouts, stationed on an eminence for that purpose, had no sooner spied us, but they gave notice of our approach to their fellow-citizens by continual whoops and cries, which could not possibly have been more dismal at the sight of their most implacable enemies.

This signal assembled all their great men, who received us in a body, and conducted us into the fort. This fort was a square piece of ground, inclosed with substantial puncheons, or strong palisades, about ten feet high, and leaning a little outwards, to make a scalade more difficult.

Each side of the square might be about 100 yards long, with loop-holes at proper distances, through which they may fire upon the enemy.

Within this inclosure we found bark cabins sufficient to lodge all their people, in case they should be obliged to retire thither. These cabins are no other but close arbors made of saplings, arched at the top, and covered so well with bark as to be proof against all weather. The fire is made in the middle, according to the Hibernian fashion, the smoke whereof finds no other vent but at the door, and so keeps the whole family warm, at the expense both of their eyes and complexion.

The Indians have no standing furniture in their cabins but hurdles to repose their persons upon, which they cover with mats or deer-skins. We were conducted to the best apartments in the fort, which just before had been made ready for our reception, and adorned with new mats that were sweet and clean.

The young men had painted themselves in a hideous manner, not so much for ornament as terror. In that frightful equipage they entertained us with sundry war-dances, wherein they endeavored to look as formidable as possible. The instrument they danced to was an Indian-drum, that is, a large gourd with skin braced taut over the mouth of it. The dancers all sang to this music, keeping exact time with their feet, while their heads and arms were screwed into a thousand menacing postures.

Upon this occasion the ladies had arrayed themselves in all their finery. They were wrapt in their red and blue match-coats, thrown so negligently about them that their mahogany skins appeared in several parts, like the Lacedaemonian damsels of old. Their hair was braided with white and blue peak, and hung gracefully in a large roll upon their shoulders.

This peak consists of small cylinders cut out of a conque-shell, drilled through and strung like beads. It serves them both for money and jewels, the blue being of much greater value than the white, for the same reason that Ethiopian mistresses in France are dearer than French, because they are more scarce. The women wear necklaces and bracelets of these precious materials, when they have a mind to appear lovely. Though their complexions be a little sad-colored, yet their shapes are very straight and well proportioned. Their faces are seldom handsome, yet they have an air of innocence and bashfulness, that with a little less dirt would not fail to make them desirable. Such charms might have had their full effect upon men who had been so long deprived of female conversation, but that the whole winter's soil was so crusted on the skins of those dark angels, that it required a very strong appetite to approach them. The bear's oil, with which they anoint their persons all over, makes their skins soft, and at the same time protects them from every species of vermin that use to be troublesome to other uncleanly people.

We were unluckily so many that they could not well make us the complement of bed-fellows, according to the Indian rules of hospitality, though a grave matron whispered one of the Commissioners very civily in the ear, that if her daughter had been but one year older, she should have been at his devotion.

It is by no means a loss of reputation among the Indians, for damsels that are single to have intrigues with the men; on the contrary, they count it an argument of superior merit to be liked by a great number of gallants. However, like the ladies that game they are a little mercenary in their amours, and seldom bestow their favors out of stark love and kindness. But after these women have once appropriated their charms by marriage, they are from thenceforth faithful to their vows, and will hardly ever be tempted by an agreeable gallant, or be provoked by a brutal or even by a fumbling husband to go astray.

The little work that is done among the Indians is done by the poor women, while the men are quite idle, or at most employed only in the gentlemanly diversions of hunting and fishing.

In this, as well as in their wars, they now use nothing but fire-arms, which they purchase of the English for skins. Bows and arrows are grown into disuse, except only amongst their boys. Nor is it ill policy, but on the contrary very prudent, thus to furnish the Indians with fire-arms, because it makes them depend entirely upon the English, not only for their trade, but even for their subsistence. Besides, they were really able to do more mischief while they made use of arrows, of which they would let silently fly several in a minute with wonderful dexterity, whereas now they hardly ever discharge their fire-locks more than once, which they insidiously do from behind a tree, and then retire as nimbly as the Dutch Horse used to do now and then formerly in Flanders.

We put the Indians to no expense, but only of a little corn for our horses, for which in gratitude we cheered their hearts with what rum we had left, which they love better than they do their wives and children.

Though these Indians dwell among the English, and see in what plenty a little industry enables them to live, yet they choose to continue in their stupid idleness, and to suffer all the inconveniences of dirt, cold, and want, rather than to disturb their heads with care, or defile their hands with labor.

The whole number of people belonging to the Nottoway Town, if you include women and children, amount to about 200. These are the only Indians of any consequence now remaining within the limits of Virginia. The rest are either removed, or dwindled to a very inconsiderable number, either by destroying one another, or else by the small-pox and other diseases. Though nothing has been so fatal to them as their ungovernable passion for rum, with which, I am sorry to say it, they have been but too liberally supplied by the English that live near them.

And here I must lament the bad success Mr. Boyle's charity has hitherto had towards converting any of these poor heathens to Christianity.[5] Many children of our neighboring Indians have been brought up in the College of William and Mary. They have been taught to read and write, and have been carefully instructed in the principles of the Christian religion, till they came to be men. Yet after they returned home, instead of civilizing and converting the rest, they have immediately relapsed into infidelity and barbarism themselves.

And some of them too have made the worst use of the knowledge they acquired among the English, by employing it against their benefactors. Besides, as they unhappily forget all the good they learn, and remember the ill, they are apt to be more vicious and disorderly than the rest of their countrymen.

I ought not to quit this subject without doing justice to the great prudence of Col. Spotswood in this affair. That gentleman was lieut. governor of

[5] Robert Boyle, the English physicist, left funds to civilize and Christianize American Indians; the College of William and Mary was the chief beneficiary of his bequest.

Virginia when Carolina was engaged in a bloody war with the Indians. At that critical time it was thought expedient to keep a watchful eye upon our tributary savages, who we knew had nothing to keep them to their duty but their fears.

Then it was that he demanded of each Nation a competent number of their great men's children to be sent to the College, where they served as so many hostages for the good behavior of the rest, and at the same time were themselves principled in the Christian religion. He also placed a school-master among the Saponi Indians, at the salary of fifty pounds per annum, to instruct their children. The person that undertook that charitable work was Mr. Charles Griffin, a man of good family, who by the innocence of his life, and the sweetness of his temper, was perfectly well qualified for that pious undertaking. Besides, he had so much the secret of mixing pleasure with instruction, that he had not a scholar who did not love him affectionately.

Such talents must needs have been blest with a proportionable success, had he not been unluckily removed to the College, by which he left the good work he had begun unfinished. In short, all the pains he had undertaken among the infidels had no other effect but to make them something cleanlier than other Indians are.

The care Col. Spotswood took to tincture the Indian children with Christianity produced the following epigram, which was not published during his administration, for fear it might then have looked like flattery.

Long has the furious priest assay'd in vain,
With sword and faggot, infidels to gain.
But now the milder soldier wisely tries
By gentler methods to unveil their eyes.
Wonders apart, he knew 'twere vain t'engage
The fix'd preventions of misguided age.
With fairer hopes he forms the Indian youth
To early manners, probity and truth.
The lion's whelp thus on the Lybian shore
Is tam'd and gentled by the artful Moor,
Not the grim sire, inured to blood before.

I am sorry I can't give a better account of the state of the poor Indians with respect to Christianity, although a great deal of pains has been and still continues to be taken with them. For my part, I must be of opinion, as I hinted before, that there is but one way of converting these poor infidels, and reclaiming them from barbarity, and that is, charitably to intermarry with them, according to the modern policy of the most Christian King in Canada and Louisiana.

Had the English done this at the first settlement of the Colony, the infidelity of the Indians had been worn out at this day, with their dark complexions, and the country had swarmed with people more than it does with insects.

It was certainly an unreasonable nicety, that prevented their entering into so good-natured an alliance. All nations of men have the same natural dignity, and we all know that very bright talents may be lodged under a very dark skin. The principal difference between one people and another proceeds only from the different opportunities of improvement.

The Indians by no means want understanding, and are in their figure tall and well-proportioned. Even their copper-colored complexion would admit of blanching, if not in the first, at the farthest in the second generation.

I may safely venture to say, the Indian women would have made altogether as honest wives for the first planters, as the damsels they used to purchase from aboard the ships. It is strange, therefore, that any good Christian should have refused a wholesome, straight bed-fellow, when he might have had so fair a portion with her, as the merit of saving her soul.

8. We rested on our clean mats very comfortably, though alone, and the next morning went to the toilet of some of the Indian ladies, where, what with the charms of their persons and the smoke of their apartments, we were almost blinded. They offered to give us silk-grass baskets of their own making, which we modestly refused, knowing that an Indian present, like that of a nun, is a liberality put out to interest, and a bribe placed to the greatest advantage.

Our Chaplain observed with concern that the ruffles of some of our fellow travellers were a little discolored with pochoon,[6] wherewith the good man had been told those Ladies used to improve their invisible charms.

About 10 o'clock we marched out of town in good order, and the war captains saluted us with a volley of small-arms. From thence we proceeded over Black-water Bridge to Col. Henry Harrison's, where we congratulated each other upon our return into Christendom.

[6] Bloodroot, which makes a yellow or deep red stain.

The Neoclassic Age

THE COLONIAL AMERICAN of the early eighteenth century was very much a child of the Age of Reason. John Locke wrote a charter for the Carolinas; Rousseau, Franklin, Montesquieu, Cotton Mather, and Sir Isaac Newton were contemporaries; Voltaire lived to see the signing of the American Declaration of Independence. Puritanism, though still a powerful force, was fast losing its thrust; the new age, in turning away from a God-centered view of life, gave primary allegiance to values it found best exemplified in the classical culture of the ancient Greek world, man-centered and rational, and of the Roman civilization, with its concern for law and form. The Enlightenment, as it arrived in America, was the first nationalized ideological movement in the American experience. Whereas Puritanism was parochial, and largely restricted to New England, the ideas of the Age of Reason permeated the colonies, attracting leaders of thought, from John Adams of Massachusetts, to Benjamin Franklin of Pennsylvania, to Thomas Jefferson of Virginia.

The Intellectual Context

The eighteenth-century philosophical impulse known as the Enlightenment rested on five general beliefs: the inevitability of progress; the perfectibility of man and his institutions; the efficacy of reason; the beneficence of God; and the plenitude and perfection of nature. It stressed the primacy of science over theology, skepticism over authority, reason over faith. The philosophers of the Enlightenment were convinced that it was within man's capacity, by applying reason to his problems, to discover those great laws by which all human and natural activity could be explained. Possessing such knowledge, men could then direct their efforts toward building a society in which progress was certain and continuous. The temper of the Enlightenment was orderly, progressive, hopeful.

American thought, however, much as it drew from Europe, was not simply a transatlantic reflection. The American version of the Enlightenment was late, eclectic, and native. First of all, the natural lag in the transfer of ideas across the ocean meant that patterns of thought conceived in Britain and France were employed to their greatest effect in America a half-century later (or more) under different circumstances, in response to different needs. Americans worked with ideas already old by European standards, in another part of the world, for new purposes, and more often than not with changed meanings attached to them.

Second, the English Enlightenment was a relatively conservative compromise of new and old ideas with current conditions. The British produced a few genuine radicals—William Godwin, Horne Tooke, Thomas Paine, Joseph Priestley (these last two exported to America)—but its Age of Reason was better represented by such reasonable men as Charles James Fox and Edmund Burke. The *philosophes* across the channel—among them Diderot, Holbach, Helvetius, and Voltaire—translated the French version of the Age of Reason into quite un-British extremes. Americans, who needed positive rules to justify a revolution and a new kind of society, found French interpretations of the Enlightenment much more to their satisfaction. American intellectuals read the French and British radicals, praised them, and hoped to turn their thinking to American uses. They took what they needed from British and European thought—using, for example, Locke's explanation of an old English revolution to justify their own against a different England, or adopting French "radicalism," aimed at the long tyranny of royal France, to overthrow a much less tyrannical King and Parliament on another continent. They shaped the Enlightenment to their advantage, and put an American stamp on it.

In literature and art, as in politics, the eighteenth-century American found the temper of the Age of Reason congenial with his own experience and aspirations. Drawing from his education in Enlightened rationalism, he saw a number of analogies between his civilization and that of the classic world; he hoped in his national culture to combine something of the intellectual symmetry and beauty of Greek thought with the Roman sense of law, control, and arrangement. The Newtonian vision of a perfectly machined universe, to his mind, paralleled the classic concept of universal order and beauty. As the classics—and the Puritans—taught him, the eighteenth-century American valued ideas and institutions in terms of their usefulness. Franklin's "Nothing is good or beautiful but in the measure that it is useful" is as much the expression of the American Neoclassic mode as it is of the functional pragmatism of a frontier society. Like their British and French instructors, American writers and artists placed great emphasis on structure, channeling their creative energies within the limits of form established by the masters of the past. And of course, in good Augustan fashion, they believed in the virtues of discipline, reasonableness, clarity, and uniformity, accepting the need for standards of taste, propriety, and decorum.

The rise of Romanticism in England and Europe introduced another factor into later eighteenth-century American thought. The basic concepts of the Romantic movement were not new, but a revival of interest, beginning about 1750, brought about a reexamination and extension of them, which in turn led men on both sides of the Atlantic to question and to alter some of the ideas of the Enlightenment. The Romantics, while never wholly consistent among themselves, tended to agree on three essential principles. First, on the organic nature of life—men, ideas, and institutions were conceived of as wholes or units, each with its own rules of development and governance. Second, on the dynamic quality of life—which was conceived of as fluid, changing, constantly in adaptation and permutation. Third, on the diversity of life—with emphasis on difference in cultures, tastes, societies, principles, and individuals, in contrast to the uniformitarian standards of the Enlightenment. Where the Age of Reason recognized that man was a mixture of passion and reason, and stressed the need for control of the former by the latter power, the Romantics emphasized the validity of human emotions, intuitions, and fancies, or (as they often called it) of the Imagination. Because of this, they believed deeply in the importance of the individual, his private judgment, and his capacity for growth and improvement.

Though the classical tradition remained the cultural anchor of American intellectual life for another generation, American thought after 1780 began to show clear effects of the new Romanticism—its enlargement of man's inward boundaries to include a wider range of imaginative and sensual knowledge; its renewed interest in direct and concrete observation; its awareness of nature and the face of the American land; its emphasis on the validity of ordinary, average, common-held experience; its recognition of nonconformity; its fascination with the exotic, strange, faraway, and "Gothic." Romanticism broadened every man's scope, and opened windows out into the world. Thus Philip Freneau found in the powers of fancy

> Endless images of things,
> Fluttering each on golden wings,
> Ideal objects, such a store,
> The universe could hold no more.

The Revolutionary Experience

The framework of ideas, then, within which the United States achieved its independence was constructed of materials furnished by two great European intellectual movements, Neoclassicism and Romanticism. American thought, as it took shape in the crucial years of its creation between 1765 and 1820, shared in both.

The American people, over these years, confronted three of the most difficult and intricate problems in politics ever faced by any people in the history of the Western world. The first, which occupied their energies to 1776, was how to make and to justify a revolution against the world's greatest military and economic power. The second, paramount during the years 1776 to 1783, was how to execute a revolution and control it. The third, dominating the postwar years, was how to consolidate a revolution—how to bring out of it a just and stable government that would stand in proper relationships to its own citizens and to the rest of a hostile world which (for the most part) did not believe in it. Each phase raised new questions and posed new difficulties on whose solution survival depended; there was little room for error, and everything was being done for the first time. In addition, those involved in this great experiment believed sincerely that everything that was done carried consequences of tremendous importance for the future of the nation, the world, and perhaps for mankind.

At the close of the Seven Years' War in 1763 (known in its American phase as the French and Indian War) Great Britain, having defeated France in India and driven her from North America, was indisputably the master of the Western world. American colonists were proud to have played a crucial role in the victory and equally proud to be British. As Franklin wrote after the victories at Quebec and Montreal, "No one can more sincerely rejoice than I do, on the reduction of Canada, and this is not merely as I am a colonist, but as I am a Briton." Yet in less than twenty years Franklin and thousands of other proud and loyal Britons rejected their King, repudiated their Parliament, and declared war on their fellow Englishmen. Small wonder that John Adams wrote on July 3, 1776, as he paused to reflect on "the whole period from that time to this, and recollect the series of political events, the chain of causes and effect," that "I am surprised at the suddenness as well as the greatness of this revolution." What moved these men from patriotic loyalty to defiance and open rebellion?

There were two complementary sets of reasons, the one political and economic, the other ideological. In the first instance, the argument between Britain and the colonies after 1763 centered on matters of imperial organization and the rights of the colonist within the empire. In the second, the conflict involved different concepts of the rights of man and the contractual nature of governments, both of which were parts of the great intellectual heritage of the Age of Reason.

The period between the French and Indian War and the Declaration of Independence witnessed the shaping of a conflict between a set of colonies that were rapidly beginning to feel like a nation, and a central government that was determined to hold its empire together after the strain of a long, wearisome war. After 1763 the colonies unconsciously began to close ranks against England, as they had against the French danger, and to think of themselves as "Americans." It is impossible to point to a particular year and say, "Here Americanism began," but it is certain that by the middle of the eighteenth century the colonists conceived of themselves as a special kind of Briton, and that they possessed a common outlook and sense of relationship that could only be described as *American.* The term seemed to have, by Franklin's time, a meaning distinct from "British" or "English" that the term "West Indian," for example, clearly did not have. It was quite normal for Franklin's Poor Richard, who was by no means a revolutionary, to refer to his countrymen as "American patriots," or for Dr. William Smith of Philadelphia, long before the Revolution, to speak of the colonies as "our nation," with no sense of disloyalty to England. The growing national spirit provided a wider dimension to the arguments with Britain, and undoubtedly contributed greatly to the colonial will to resist. This is what John Adams meant when he remarked later that "The revolution was effected before the war commenced. The revolution was in the hearts and minds of the people."

The issues at stake, however, were not limited to the rights of Englishmen or colonists. There was also a broader conflict over general political principles, arising from different interpretations of the twin theories of natural rights and government by social contract, both of which stemmed from Enlightenment philosophy. It was assumed that in the beginning man was endowed by his Creator with certain natural rights, which antedated the existence of governments and were superior to them. They were, as Thomas Paine called them, "those rights which always appertain to man in right of his existence." These rights were never exactly enumerated and defined, but they included the protection of life, the acquisition and security of property, freedom of movement, equal justice before law, and the freedom to speak and think within certain limits.

The social contract theory grew from the natural rights concept, for since these rights were not self-enforcing, some form of government seemed necessary to maintain them. To accomplish this, it was also assumed that men consented to a contract with the state for the furtherance and defense of their natural rights. A government was, then, in the definition of the English jurist Blackstone, "a voluntary compact between a ruler and the ruled . . . , liable to such limitations as are necessary for the security of the absolute rights of the latter." The aim of the contract, as James Otis of Pennsylvania explained it, was "above all things to provide for the security, the quiet and happy enjoyment of life, liberty, and property." Implicit in the terms of this contract were three things: that the primary power of government remain with the people; that the authority of government rest on the consent of the governed; and that violations of the contract by the state render that government null and void. The Declaration of Independence defined these theories best, and for all time.

The Revolution forced the colonists to consider much more carefully what "America" and "Americanism" meant, and why they deserved independent existence. They entered the war as a nation, with strong convictions that they knew what they were fighting for; having won, they now had to define that nation. Consistent (and sometimes savage) attacks by British and European critics forced Americans to examine and defend their ideas and ideals, their way of life. Again and again they tried to answer the question of the Frenchman Crèvecoeur, "What is an American?" and in the process they slowly evolved a set of answers to what an American was, and hoped to be.

Americans, at the end of the Revolution, looked ahead with a feeling of fresh beginnings. They held great hope for the future, for they had no record of failure in their past. They were especially conscious of the importance of their actuality as a nation—of existing not simply as England or Europe projected to another continent, but as a different civilization with its own being and futurity. British and European travelers and commentators constantly criticized the United States for being new, different, and un-European (charges which no American could deny)—until Americans gradually began to realize that being so was not necessarily shameful. Indeed, it occurred to them that the United States, because of its very newness, difference, and American-ness, was far superior to Britain or Europe.

Nor was this all. The evidence of history, closely examined, seemed to show that God had willed the United States to be different, so that it might play a special role in the future. It seemed plain to many Americans, as it did to a Connecticut magazine contributor in 1786, that God "had reserved this country to be the last and greatest theater in the improvement of mankind." To fulfill this assignment, it was imperative that America emphasize its nationality, reject the prejudices and patterns of the corrupt Old World, and construct its own civilization to fit the nation's divine purpose. In other words, the United States must be *American,* if it were to succeed in what Jefferson called man's greatest experiment, to determine whether "men may be trusted to govern themselves without a master."

The Acceleration of Social Change

The American colonist in 1760 lived in an environment that was not substantially different from his grandfather's. He owned the same kind of house, traveled in the same fashion, communicated with his fellows in much the same way, drew power for his production from similar sources, and for that matter produced and consumed much the same kinds of goods. The span between the close of the French and Indian War and the Treaty of Ghent measured only fifty-one years—but they were years of incredibly swift change. Between lay two major revolutions, the rise and fall of Napoleon, the attainment of American independence, the ratification of the Constitution, an explosion of scientific knowledge, the culmination of the Industrial Revolution, the formation of modern urban society, and a complete change in methods of transportation and communication. The American of 1820 lived in what was almost literally a new society, so recently built that one man's lifetime might have spanned it all.

At the center of this period of change was the American Revolution, a relatively conservative revolution fought to protect certain rights and practices the colonists believed they already possessed. Its aim was not to destroy an established order, but rather to be allowed to create a new order without interference. American radicals, by European standards, were no more than cautious liberals; yet theirs was a true revolution which wrought irrevocable alterations in American society, in some cases simply by allowing movements already under way to continue without hindrance, in others by initiating wholly new trends.

The Revolution did not create an egalitarian, level, homogeneous American society. The war disturbed but did not substantially rearrange the colonial class structure which, by the mid-eighteenth century, was already different from that of England and Europe. Wealth, talent, education, language, manners, lineage, and such things still counted in the America of 1800 as they had in 1750 (the Jacksonian "common man" had not yet arrived) but never so much as they did abroad, and not quite so much as they had a half-century earlier. Enlightened Americans, like Jefferson, believed in leadership by "a natural aristocracy of worth" and in the social and political guidance of "gentlemen"—which was not the same as the British "gentry." Most would probably have agreed with John Adams, who, though a committed revolutionary, felt that there had to be stability and order in the new society, "decency and respect and veneration introduced for persons in authority, at every rank."

On the other hand, this postwar society was by far the most open and flexible in the world. It included both rich and poor, educated and ignorant, gentleman and boor, but, as Lafayette noted, the gap between them was much narrower than in Europe. In a general way, almost everyone within it had a chance to better himself and his children. There were too many roads to success for any group or class to monopolize them; land, resources, and opportunities were too plentiful to be appropriated for the benefit of a few.

At the time of the Revolution, the American colonies had been settled for more than a century and a half. Since the beginning of the eighteenth century they had shown signs of social and cultural division and a tendency to group themselves along regional lines. Postwar geographers usually identified a central "middle" group of states, a "northern" or "New England" group, a Southern bloc, and occasionally a "coastal" and "back" region. Delegates to the Continental Congress referred to themselves as representing Northern, Middle, or Southern states; likewise, the Continental Army command divided the nation into three military districts, Eastern (New England), Middle, and Southern. After 1800, standard geographies usually identified a fourth or "western" region.

Within these regions there were a number of generally accepted social and cultural divisions—the sweeping into the back counties of the settled states and across the mountains into western Pennsylvania, Kentucky, and Tennessee. Virginia counted 400,000 people in 1775 and 750,000 in 1790, with most of the increase concentrated in its western counties. Kentucky, which had a few hundred people in 1770, listed 73,000 in the 1790 census. This first wave, however, was a mere ripple in comparison with the flood that streamed into the Northwest, the Southwest, and the Mississippi Valley in the years directly ahead. It seemed to the English traveler Morris Birkbeck in 1817 that the entire country was "breaking up and moving westward." By 1821 the nine new Western states contained slightly more than one-quarter of the entire national population. Meanwhile, exploring parties probed beyond the Mississippi into the plains; Lewis and Clark's expedition crossed the continent in 1804-6, and John Jacob Astor set up fur posts on the Pacific coast in 1811 and 1812. For the next century the drive westward and the gradual movement with it of the frontier were facts of primary importance in the development of American society.

"Making Thirteen Clocks Strike Together"

The British governed their colonies under a dual system, that is, by means of a strong central government in London, which made major decisions in colonial affairs, and a subordinate government in the colony itself. The central issue of the Revolution, reduced to its simplest terms, was the degree and quality of subordination that should characterize this relationship. In setting up the government of the newly independent nation, the Founding Fathers retained the dual nature of British policy, replaced the colonial law-making bodies with state legislatures, Parliament with Congress, and wrote new documents spelling out the powers and functions of each.

The Revolutionary leaders agreed that they wanted a government which guaranteed natural rights, states' rights, and all those other individual and political privileges which they believed the British colonial system had denied them. They assumed that, since they had been unable to govern themselves as they wished under a strong centralized British government in London, they could possibly do so under a weaker American government in Philadelphia; furthermore, their whole colonial experience had taught them, long before, to distrust any political authority very far beyond their reach. As inheritors of the Enlightenment, as well as of generations of British political theory, they also believed that government was most effective and trustworthy when kept close to the people, the original source of sovereignty. Thus when the state constitutions were drawn up between 1776 and 1780, they placed the essentials of political control—taxes, currency, militia, voting rights, appointments, guarantees of civil and natural rights—in the state legislatures. These new constitutions translated the principles of the Revolution and the Declaration from general to practical political terms. Not only were these the primary contracts under which the nation governed itself during its first decisive decade; they also established precedents and processes of great usefulness for its later political life. The device of the convention, employed by most of the states in evolving their constitutions, still remains the best political method for the actual making of a social compact. The manner of forming constitutions, as developed in the United States, became the model for establishing or revising constitutional governments all over the Western world. In addition, these documents introduced into politics the American conviction, truly novel to the eighteenth century, that government should be based on a written document, which spelled out the principles on which it was founded, and which must have the approval of those who were to live under it. The careful, specific construction of written instruments of government on such a grand scale was an important contribution to the science of politics.

At the same time that the Continental Congress adopted the Declaration of Independence, it also resolved that "a plan of confederation be prepared and transmitted to the respective colonies for their consideration and approbation." A committee headed by John Dickinson of Pennsylvania prepared a set of Articles of Confederation, which the Congress approved in 1777. After ratification by the necessary number of states, these Articles supplied the machinery by which the United States governed itself as a nation until 1789. With the states exerting control over local matters, and the Congress over national and foreign affairs, the United States, wrote the editor of the *Pennsylvania Packet* in 1781, formed "a well-constructed arch, whose parts, harmonizing and mutually supporting each other, are all the more closely united the greater the pressure is upon them."

The trouble was that the system did not work that way. The Articles of Confederation denied Congress certain indispensable powers over finance, diplomatic affairs, and commerce, distributing them instead among the states. Congress, as a result, became little more than an advisory body, with insufficient authority to act on key national issues or to force cooperation from the reluctant states on domestic ones: in John Adams' pungent phrase, it was the problem of "making thirteen clocks strike together."

Neither Congress, nor the executive, nor the judi-

Boston area as separate from the New England mountain states or the Connecticut Valley; upstate New York as distinct from New York City or the Hudson Valley; the division of Pennsylvania into western (Pittsburgh) and eastern (Philadelphia); the Chesapeake Bay area; the deep South; the Kentucky-Tennessee frontier; and so on. Each of these had its temperamental traits, its personality, its presumably "typical" character such as the canny Yankee, the Dutch New Yorker, the contentious Philadelphian, the cavalier Southerner, the hearty Westerner—who probably did not exist at all except in the popular imagination, but who illustrated the variety of ways by which Americans saw themselves. Even in its youth American society showed great diversity and cultural differentiation. The motto *E Pluribus Unum* had its basis in fact.

One of the most far-reaching consequences of the Revolution was its effect on American economic and industrial life. No longer a colony within an imperial system, the United States at once became an independent unit in the world competition for markets, and rapidly matured, within two generations, into a business civilization. Nowhere was a nation quite so ready as the United States to accept the Industrial Revolution. Lacking any deeply entrenched economic group, it had vast natural resources, a rapidly growing population of producers and consumers, relative political stability and unity, and the protection of a government friendly to business. "All the world," commented Jefferson as he looked about him in 1783, "is becoming commercial." The spread of factories, the introduction of improved machinery and production methods, the establishment of tariffs and other government aids, the growth of banking and credit systems, the opening of the West, and the revolution in transportation combined to make the United States into a burgeoning business society. The conversion from a mercantile to a manufacturing economy was under way, the pattern of nineteenth-century industrial America virtually complete. "We have one material that constitutes aristocracy," John Adams noted in 1808, "and that material is wealth."

The extensive changes wrought in American life during the early decades of independence were accompanied by an astonishing enlargement in the sheer size of the nation. Three states (Vermont, Kentucky, and Tennessee) entered the union between 1789 and 1801; Ohio, Louisiana, Indiana, Illinois, Mississippi, Alabama, Maine, and Missouri joined over the next twenty years. Jefferson's purchase of Louisiana in 1803 more than doubled the size of the country overnight; by a single stroke the United States became proprietor of nearly one-half of North America, master of the continental navigational sys-

tem, and owner of the Western wor
storehouse of untapped natural wealth.
time the population more than doubl
1790 and 1820, rising from 3,900,000 to
thirty years. The West grew even faster
thousand to more than three million ov
period, so that one-third of the people o
States, by 1820, lived beyond the moun

Postwar America was overwhelming
1790 less than five percent of the pop
in towns of more than 8,000, and ev
there were only five cities of more than 1
lation. Philadelphia, the largest (and a
ond largest in the English-speaking
70,000, New York 60,000, Boston 25,000
18,000 and Baltimore 13,000. Within a de
can cities, large and small alike, began
phenomenal expansion. New York pass
phia by adding 36,000 people, and Balti
up to third place, while the western
roomed. It took Boston two hundred ye
30,000; it took Cincinnati only fifty yea
five times that many. Though the Unite
remained a predominantly agrarian nati
and small settlements, the cities pro
points for trade, immigration, and politic
tion that had lasting effects on the conf
American society. It was in the cities t
terns of emergent American culture w
shaped and directed.

The early nineteenth century saw
changes in transportation and communic
tial for the movement of people, goods
mation in a land of immense distances a
population. To unify the country econo
politically, and to join its separate sect
common society under one governmen
United States needed to construct at
east-west lines of travel, each six hundre
sand miles long, across a mountain rang
country inhabited by savages; and a si
south line about a thousand miles long.
rope, where a network of roads and cana
in the making for seven hundred years,
States was expected to accomplish this a
tually, it took less than fifty years. It was
a child who had ridden a packhorse int
to ride within his lifetime from New
Louis on a train.

The effects of this new transportation
American economic life were incalculabl
only goods, but ideas, opinions, and peo
over these roads and waterways. People
the thousands—chiefly westward. Whe
remarked in 1785 on "the rage for emigra
westward country," the first wave w

ciary possessed sufficient jurisdiction where it was needed most, and the worsening situation convinced a number of leaders that a stronger central government was necessary. Some argued that the Articles could be amended into an effective document; others (among them Alexander Hamilton, James Madison, and John Jay) thought that the only solution lay in greater federal control. In 1787 Congress, responding to urgent appeals for action, authorized a convention "for the sole and express purpose of revising the Articles of Confederation and reporting to Congress and the several legislatures therein."

The convention which met in Philadelphia on May 25, 1787, did much more than the charge from Congress suggested. The fifty-five delegates represented a cross-section of the groups that had provided political leadership since the early eighteenth century—landowners, planters, lawyers, businessmen, shippers, bankers. Forty-one of them had served in Congress, seven were former state governors. Washington, who commanded unanimous respect, was chosen presiding officer. In attempting one of the most delicate tasks of political history, the formation of a stable union of independent states under a written body of fundamental law, the delegates had few precedents from which to work; they could draw upon the histories of the Greek confederacies, the colonial charters and state constitutions, the British and classical traditions of law and philosophy, their own colonial past, and little else. The materials which went into the Constitution were not new; the delegates gathered them from the total of Western political experience. But the convention, in an act of creative statesmanship, blended them into new and meaningful combinations, bringing them to bear directly on the specific problems of their place and time.

The delegates did not all agree exactly on what kind of document the convention should produce, but there seemed to be a general consensus on three things. First, the national government would be republican in form and aim, consistent with the substance of the American revolutionary philosophy and the Declaration of Independence. Second, the national government would derive its powers from the consent of the governed and rest on the rights of man. Third, the national authority would be sufficiently increased (and that of the states correspondingly lessened) to meet the requirements of an expanding nation, yet without infringement of the rights of states and individuals. The result was not perfection—the Founding Fathers were, after all, mortal men living in time, subject to circumstance—but it was a very great achievement, and an enduring one. John Adams, assessing what had been done at Philadelphia, found it well done; the American system, he wrote, "will last forever, govern the globe, and introduce the perfection of man."

In one vital respect, however, the Constitution was tragically flawed: its failure to deal forthrightly with the fact of black slavery. Without explicitly recognizing slavery as an institution (the words "slave" and "slavery" were not used, but "person" or "person held to service or labor"), it yet implemented a compromise hammered out between northern and southern delegates whereby five slaves were to be counted as the equivalent of three whites in determining the population count on which a state's Congressional representation was to be based. Without some such compromise, it is true, the Constitution might never have been ratified, nor the Federal Union have come to birth. Moreover, slavery was then on the defensive, even on the decline, and its gradual extinction was rather generally expected. Nevertheless, the great paradox of the American Age of Reason was that the principles of natural rights and equality, so nobly stated in the Declaration of Independence, were not applied to the enslaved Afro-Americans. In the outcome, the additional votes in the House of Representatives that the "three-fifths" provision gave to the slaveholding states weighted the scales toward the perpetuation of slavery, and the invention of the cotton gin in 1793 made the slave system economically viable and ended all prospects of its gradual demise.

When the new Constitution came to the states for ratification, it found strong favor and almost equally strong opposition. Many of its proponents, called "Federalists," were drawn from the same mercantile, financial, and social classes that controlled the convention; a number of the Anti-Federalists, who opposed it, came from the ranks of farmers, laborers, debtors, and small tradesmen, who feared the domination of government by the wealthy groups. One by one, however, the states gave their approval; and when the presidential electors met in 1789 to choose Washington as first President, and John Adams as Vice President, the United States was fully launched as a federal union.

The Frontiers of American Science

The most direct expression of the rationalistic spirit of the Enlightenment came in the advancement of science. The eighteenth-century attitude toward science was founded on four generally accepted principles: the belief that all natural and human problems responded to the application of scientific investigation; a belief in the unity of science, that all knowledge was fundamentally scientific; a belief in a mechanistic universe, governed by consistent natural law which was discoverable by human reason; a belief in the efficacy of the inductive method, and a corresponding distrust of dogmatism and authority. This scientific point of view seemed to provide the best and most understandable pattern by which the affairs of God, man, and nature might be explained; therefore the eighteenth-century philosopher worked outward from this set of beliefs, probing into the social world and the universe in search of laws and principles.

The Neoclassic Age, or Age of Reason, might also be called the Age of Science, for it coincided with the tremendous burst of scientific knowledge that erupted in the late seventeenth century. The American colonies were children of this age, settled in the era of Bacon, Kepler, and Galileo, matured in the era of Newton and Leibnitz. Americans were never far from the stream of scientific knowledge that flowed through the eighteenth century, and men of scientific attainments, such as John Winthrop of Harvard, Cotton Mather, and Benjamin Franklin were representative products of the American Enlightenment. President Thomas Jefferson, for that matter, was a scientist of more than amateur attainments; nor should it be forgotten that the Lewis and Clark expedition, which Jefferson sent westward in 1804, was one of the most significant scientific projects in American history.

Americans believed that science was vitally important to the development of their new continent and new society, for it not only gave man the means to control nature but assisted him in gaining mastery over his own troublesome problems. Thus the poet Joel Barlow hailed the day when

> Science bright
> Through shadowy nature leads with surer light . . . ;
> Gives each effect its own indubious cause,
> Divides her moral from her physic laws,
> Shows where the virtues find their nurturing food,
> And men their motives to be just and good.

It seemed urgent, therefore, that science be encouraged; in fact, there seemed reason to believe that science was peculiarly destined to flourish in America, where, said Samuel Cooper, "liberty unfetters and expands the human mind."

In the process of settling America, there were always new observations to be made, new conditions to be met, new adjustments to the ever-changing frontiers of discovery; hence the American experience proved especially receptive to the implications of scientific method, to the testing and proving of theories by conformity to facts. American conditions, too, favored science that was useful, emphasizing such branches as cartography, surveying, navigational mathematics, astronomy, agriculture, metallurgy, medicine, chemistry, and physics. It was true that American scientists, as they themselves admitted, made fewer theoretical contributions to science than practical ones, and that their main achievements lay in the identification of the flora and fauna of the new continent and the classification of its natural resources. Nevertheless, this was in itself an achievement, for everywhere one looked in the land there were distant horizons of knowledge, so much unknown. In the United States, as in Britain and Europe, these were years of scientific consolidation, rather than discovery. The Reverend Samuel Miller, writing his *Retrospect of the Eighteenth Century* in 1802, concluded that while American science had matured in the half-century just past, it still derived its impetus from abroad, and that it was not yet "properly self-reliant and independent." This would come in time.

The Search for a National Culture

The early years of American independence produced a great deal of writing, of which only a small part could be called artistically distinguished. It was an age of persuasion and argument, rather than of belles-lettres, and much of what was produced seems amateurish and labored. But whatever its literary value, the writing that Americans did in these years is of utmost importance to an understanding of what they thought and felt as their society took shape—as American ideas were germinating, as a national style was forming, as key issues were being hammered out on the anvil of day-to-day experience. The attainments of the age were not small. Within the span of half a century these men knit thirteen disparate colonies into a unit, erected a government, and launched a nation. What they wrote reflects and expresses much of this achievement.

Having won their political independence, Americans searched for ways to create a culture of their own to express the sense and spirit of their new civilization. They were inheritors of the great Western, classical, Christian tradition they shared with Britain and Europe. Yet they were no longer British and European, but American. How, then, might this inheritance be absorbed and used, rather than simply borrowed or imitated? Editors, critics, authors, orators, and politicians alike agreed with those like Nathan Appleton of New England, who after the Revolution reminded his fellow citizens that they must "sing a New song, a Song that neither We nor our Fathers were ever able to sing before," and the historian David Ramsay, who called for "poets, orators, critics and historians equal to the most celebrated of the ancient commonwealths of Greece and Italy."

Exhortations, unfortunately, did not immediately produce great literary accomplishments. Potential

American Homers and Shakespeares faced a number of hurdles and handicaps. A great deal of the creative energy of the times was channeled into political and business life; with a government to construct and a continent to subdue, there was little opportunity to pause for poems. Philip Freneau's advice to young poets to find a job lest they starve had the ring of bitter truth. There were some who felt also that the United States did not have the necessary resources for a distinctive culture and must always lean on Europe. It had no usable past, no tradition of literary patronage, no social diversity; as Washington Irving wrote, it lacked "the charms of storied and poetical associations . . . , the accumulated treasures of age." Neither did the United States have an adequate copyright law. As late as 1830 two of every three books sold came from British or continental presses, and the American market was glutted with cheap, pirated editions of foreign books.

Nevertheless, the outlook for authors was not wholly dark. The American public was literate and well-educated, and, in contrast to Europe, the reading habit was not restricted to the upper classes. Americans, an observer remarked in 1772, had "a taste for books that made almost every man a reader," and foreign travelers rarely failed to note the avidity of newspaper consumption. The cities had numbers of bookstores (Boston alone had fifty in the 1770's) and after 1800 the spread of circulating libraries made books available to almost any American who really wanted to read them. The famous "Coonskin" Library on the Ohio frontier rented books for pelts, and the traveling book-agent poked his way into the remotest log-town hamlet.

To produce its own culture, the United States had first to declare its intellectual independence of Britain. Since no educated American could conceivably wish to reject the great tradition of English letters, his problem became one of what to reject and what to retain that might be made American. As Noah Webster said, no amount of national pride could make him lay aside his beloved Addison. At the outset, the critics decided that Americans should accept Milton, Shakespeare, Addison, Pope, and the rest, but that they must avoid what Webster called "servile imitation" of foreign writing. They must shun anything untrue, immoral, or useless, and things which, in Joel Barlow's phrase, "might prove false and destructive" to American minds.

Simply to avoid European models was not enough. What positive steps might be taken to encourage an *American* artistic tradition? First, though Americans did not have Rob Roy, the Thames, or Cromwell to write about, they decided that they did have a number of things that neither Britain nor Europe could equal. The Indian, the frontier, the Revolution and its heroes, especially the American land itself—these were subjects to challenge and excite the finest artists. The robin, the whippoorwill, and the whispering brook were as inspiring materials for poets, Joseph Dennie thought, "as nightingales, or skylarks, dingles or dells." The Yankee, the Dutchman, the frontiersman, the Southern yeoman, and other national types were as promising literary timber as any of Scott's knights in armor or Germany's young Werthers. The American writer must, then, find the right way to use these unique resources, so that he might create from them a true, correct, and American art. Thus the novelist Charles Brockden Brown advised the American writer to observe his own land directly, to "examine objects with his own eyes, employ European models merely for the improvement of his own taste," and to build his art about "all that is genuine and peculiar in the scene before him." In this way, predicted *The Columbian Orator* (1807), "Columbia's soil" might

> Rear Men as great as Britain's isle;
> Exceed what Greece and Rome have done,
> Or any land beneath the sun.

The post-Revolutionary period was one of intense literary activity, marking the beginnings of a strong (if not always first-rate) belletristic tradition, the emergence of a profession of letters, and the slow recognition by artist and public that literature was art as well as utility. The writing of the period is not easily classifiable. It has been called "late Neoclassic," "pre-Romantic," "transitional," "Federalistic," and other terms, all proper but only partially descriptive. Despite Webster's injunction against imitation, it was heavily derivative, filled with echoes of Addison, Pope, Goldsmith, Richardson, and others, as the writing of a generation later would echo Scott, Wordsworth, Burns, and Byron. It was distinguished by two general trends: first, the dominance of political writing; and second, the decreasing importance of certain older forms and the increased popularity of others.

Politics naturally bulked large, since the overriding issues of the times were centered on political rights, independence, and survival. Government and law (as theology earlier) attracted the best minds of the Revolutionary generation, and the level of their writing was high. Paine's pamphlets and the *Federalist* papers belong in the first rank of political literature in any century. Jefferson's Declaration of Independence, with its adjustment of reason to emotion, its balance of theory with application, and its magnificent rhetoric, cannot be matched.

Among the forms which lost considerable ground after the Revolution were the diary and the journal, both favorite means of self-expression in an earlier, more introspective era. The published sermon rapidly declined in popularity (soon to be replaced by the secular oration), and though travel narratives were still fairly common, they were no longer so widely read as earlier. The promotional tract, its purpose gone, quickly disappeared. The "captivity" tale, favorite American reading since Captain John Smith's adventures, was absorbed into the novel. Such changes were natural reflections of the shifting nature of American society and taste. Those forms of writing of a more direct artistic purpose, in which the ideas of the writer were shaped within the pattern of novel, poem, essay, or play, increased in popularity and their practitioners in skill and sophistication. Also, as one might expect, the postwar drive for nationalism and patriotism caused great activity in both biography and history.

The development of the American essay depended largely on the growth of magazines and newspapers. American writers copied Addison, Steele, Goldsmith, Butler, and the other great English satirists in profusion; few newspapers were without a "Tatler" or a "Scriblerus" imitating their masters. The essay attracted the best authors of the time, as well as the least talented; among those who wrote essays of superior literary quality were Franklin, Freneau, Noah Webster, Joseph Dennie, and James Paulding. The essay was not only an accepted form within which one could imitate or experiment without much risk; it was also a useful vehicle for moral instruction, political comment, satire, burlesque, criticism, or casual pleasure.

Although the novel encountered less public and ecclesiastical opposition after the war than earlier in the century, few men of substance believed it worthy of serious consideration as an art form. Ministers cautioned against fiction that might "inflame the passions and corrupt the heart," and even so sophisticated a poet as John Trumbull expressed distrust of

> . . . books that poison all the mind,
> Novels and plays (where shines display'd
> A world that nature never made.)

For that matter, some believed that there was really very little in America for the novelist to write about. "A novel describing these savage barbarians (*Indians*), their squaws and papooses," wrote one critic (a few years before James Fenimore Cooper), "would not be very interesting." The American who wanted to write a novel also had to compete against the whole established array of British novelists in pirated editions, as well as against the lingering snobbishness and Anglophilia of segments of the reading public. It was easier and safer to imitate Richardson or Scott than to write an American book. Cooper himself found it advisable to foster the rumor that his first novel was by "a prominent Englishman."

Nevertheless, the demand for novels increased so swiftly that bookstores could hardly stock them fast enough, and magazines printed them serially by scores. Following British models, American novels tended to fall into four classes: the novel of morality and sentiment, derived from Richardson and Sterne; the "Gothic" novel of suspense and emotion, modeled on Ann Radcliffe, Walpole, and Godwin; the picaresque-satiric novel, drawn from Smollett, Swift, and Fielding; and the historical romance, inspired by Sir Walter Scott. William Hill Brown's *Power of Sympathy* (1789), the first successful American sentimental novel, was followed by Susannah Rowson's *Charlotte Temple* (1790), which ran subsequently to nearly two hundred editions. After Charlotte opened the floodgates, the magazines were filled with despairing but virtuous heroines, rascally villains, and hapless orphans. Royall Tyler's *Algerine Captive* (1797) and H. H. Brackenridge's *Modern Chivalry* (1792–1815) were satiric novels, but the type never attained popularity. The Gothic tradition attracted Charles Brockden Brown, the most gifted novelist of the pre-Cooper years, whose *Wieland* (1798) and *Ormond* (1799) were excellent if uneven books.

Sir Walter Scott's novels took the United States by storm. Scott's powerful nationalism and his superb use of history represented exactly what Americans hoped to do with their own national experience, and dozens of novelists tried to apply the Scott formula to native materials, with negligible success. James Fenimore Cooper, however, did more than imitate Scott; he naturalized him, so that the historical romance became American. When Leatherstocking walked into fiction with his long rifle, the American novel came of age.

The shift of opinion concerning the theater after 1750 reflected parallel changes in American society. The lessening of religious prejudices against plays, the growth of urban playgoing audiences, the emergence of professional management and the star system, among other things, had much to do with the growing interest in the stage. English companies played fairly regular tours of the colonies, and a few American plays had been produced before the Revolution, notably Thomas Godfrey's pseudo-Jacobean tragedy, *The Prince of Parthia* (1767). However, since the theaters were closed as a wartime measure and the British occupied the major cities, the drama practically vanished until 1783. At the close of the war acting groups quickly reappeared, and within fifteen years several new playhouses were built. Boston's Federal Street Theater and Philadelphia's Chestnut Street Theater opened in 1794, New York's Park Theater in 1798, and both New York and Philadelphia had permanent acting companies by 1800. But the American stage still leaned heavily on imported plays and players, with a few notable exceptions such as Thomas Wignell, who made a career of playing the down-east Yankee, and Lewis Hallam junior, who played everything.

Of the numerous American playwrights who attempted to compete with imported British plays, only Royall Tyler and William Dunlap found much success. Tyler, a Boston lawyer who later sat on the Vermont Supreme Court, wrote a witty comedy of manners, *The Contrast,* first performed in 1787, that merits being called the first American dramatic hit. Dunlap, who wrote at least sixty-five plays, adapted dozens more, and managed two stage companies, wrote and produced *André*, the best tragic play of the period. Despite the popularity of a few dramatists and players, however, the theater found hard going. It had not yet outgrown its dependence on Britain; playgoing audiences, complained the dramatist James Nelson Barker, were still "mental colonists" in the theater. The American stage needed good plays, regular seasons, and solid financing, for all of which it had to wait another generation.

Poets had the most difficult task. "Of all the fools that haunt our coast," wrote Philip Freneau, "the scribbling tribe I pity most." There were no doubt many young men of poetic gifts in the new nation, but the muse attracted few disciples in a climate of revolution and political strife. Some wrote a limited amount of verse, but gave up and turned to law, politics, theology, or education, for, as Freneau commented, "An age employed in edging steel, can no poetic raptures feel." The poetic tradition was trapped in imitation—of Pope, Dryden, Churchill, the "graveyard" school, and later of Scott, Byron, Moore, Leigh Hunt—for it was more convenient and much safer for an American to copy approved models than to strike out for himself, notwithstanding the clamor of critics for "bards of native style."

Since satire was especially suited to the uses of war and politics, lampoons, burlesques, mock epics, hudibrastics, and other combative poetic types flooded out nearly everything else. The contemporary obsession with nationalism led a number of poets, such as Joel Barlow and Timothy Dwight, to expend their limited gifts on awkward patriotic odes and national epics. Yet there were a few authentic American voices. John Trumbull's impish satires showed more than passing talent; Timothy Dwight's inflated pomposities displayed some effective moments of power and dignity; Joel Barlow's "American epic" never came off, but his attempt was not a total failure. Philip Freneau, sea captain, journalist, and poet, produced the best lyric poetry of his generation, combining an unusual freshness and originality with consummate technique. The skill and delicacy of his better verse was unmatched by any American poet of his era and few British, and despite his restlessness and uneven discipline he deserves to be called the first major American poet.

American literature, in the Neoclassic Age, was still only partially American, still to a large extent derivative, imitative, dependent on British models and standards. It was, however, self-consciously searching for a mode and style of its own, testing ways of using its own materials and expressing its own attitudes. The real liberation of American literature was yet to come.

The American in the Age of Reason

BENJAMIN FRANKLIN [1706-1790]

FRANKLIN REPRESENTED perhaps more fully than any other one man the temper and personality of the American eighteenth century: its rationalism and middle-way common sense, its political concerns and its humanitarian activities, its interest in science and the natural world, its belief in individual integrity and its deistic religious tendencies. His life spanned eighty-four years of that century; born and bred in the provincial colonial Boston of Mather and Sewall, he lived on into the new Republic of Washington and Jefferson, alert to and involved in every aspect of its rich, complex, and exciting life.

Son of a tallow chandler and soap boiler, young Franklin was apprenticed in his brother's print shop, but at age seventeen he ran away to New York and Philadelphia to make his fortune, as he recounts in the familiar story told in his *Autobiography.* He soon made it, becoming a wealthy man and Philadelphia's first citizen, and then retired from business in 1748, hoping to spend a quiet, contemplative life in his library and laboratory. However, he was soon appointed deputy postmaster for the colonies, an office he held for nearly twenty years. He also became deeply involved in the argument between the colonies and Britain, and after 1757 served as colonial agent for Pennsylvania in London. From 1770 to 1775 he represented not only Pennsylvania but Georgia, New Jersey, and Massachusetts in their dealings with King and Parliament. In 1775, having given up hope of finding any way to avert the imminent clash between colonies and empire, he returned to America.

At sixty-nine, when he might have retired to his study, Franklin's career in public life was just beginning. He was not a political philosopher like Jefferson; he was rather the practical organizer, the diplomat, the political tactician, but he was no less a believer in liberty, reason, and justice than the Virginian. He served as a member of the Pennsylvania Committee of Correspondence, as a delegate to the Second Continental Congress, as one of the committee appointed to draft the Declaration of Independence, and as the new nation's first representative to France. In 1778 he secured the French alliance, the greatest single factor in the ultimate victory of the American cause, and in 1783 he served with Adams and Jay on the committee that signed the peace treaty at Paris. Franklin then returned to the United States to begin two terms as governor of Pennsylvania, and finally, at eighty-one, he sat in the Philadelphia convention with men half his age to write the American Constitution.

Though science was often crowded out of his life by public service and diplomacy, Franklin was nevertheless one of the dozen or so first-rank scientific scholars of his century, responsible for some of the most notable basic research done in his time. His contributions to the infant science of electricity were especially important: he defined the existence and function of "positive" and "negative" charges (terms which he coined), performed basic research on the battery principle, and proved by his lightning experiment the identity of electricity in natural and manufactured form. He also wrote more than a hundred scientific papers in medicine, botany, hydraulics, physics, engineering, agronomy, chemistry, and ethnology—his first at twenty-three, his last at seventy-nine. A member of the Royal Society of London, Franklin held seven honorary degrees, mastered six languages, and was recognized as one of the world's great scientists by eight foreign governments.

Like Jefferson, Franklin preferred to keep his religious principles to himself, but he held them firmly and practiced them with deep sincerity. He had little interest in theological disputation or speculation, evolved his own set of Christian religious principles, and lived by them. He was, in effect, a deist who found proof of God in His world and works around him. The most acceptable way to worship this deity, he believed, was to serve his fellow men, and to translate the Christian principles he believed in into practical life. He contributed to a Protestant church and a Jewish synagogue, and helped his friend John Carroll to become the first Catholic archbishop in the United States. He attacked no sect, praised or argued with none, and worshipped God in his own way.

Further reading: Carl Van Doren, *Benjamin Franklin,* 1938. A. O. Aldridge, *Benjamin Franklin,* 1965. V. W. Crane, *Benjamin Franklin and a Rising People,* 1954. Bruce Granger, *Benjamin Franklin: American Man of Letters,* 1965. Ralph Ketcham, *The Political Thought of Benjamin Franklin,* 1966.

FROM THE *Autobiography*

Franklin's autobiography brings to the reader some sense of the vitality and energy of Franklin's mind, as well as the variety of his life and the rationality and honesty of his character. He wrote slightly more than half of the manuscript at Twyford, Hampshire, England, in 1771; a small portion at Passy, near Paris, in 1784; and the final portions at Philadelphia in 1788–89. Because it was written at different times over a period of eighteen years, an alert reader may discover over the span certain differences of spirit and attitude. At Twyford Franklin, in his mid-sixties, enjoying good health and obviously pleased at the chance to recall his youth, wrote with quiet satisfaction of his upward climb from runaway apprentice to man of fortune and reputation. When he resumed his task at Passy, however, he was an internationally known celebrity, writing not only the story of his life for his son and family, but a much more formal account for posterity of how he attained eminence, virtue, and wealth. He was much more concerned in this portion with the public record of his career as businessman, civic leader, and scientist, than with his inward life. In 1788, he was eighty-two, ill, and in retirement, and while the writing shows flashes of his old force and spirit, it is for the most part little more than a straightforward account of facts and dates.

The *Autobiography* carries Franklin's life only until 1757, after which came his careers as colonial agent, scientist, Revolutionary leader, diplomat, and statesman. It is therefore an unfortunately incomplete picture of the man, since it omits almost half of his life, and seems to emphasize the "success story" aspects of it. It should be remembered that Franklin retired from business at the age of forty-two, and spent the next forty-two years of his life in the service of his fellowman and his country.

Text: John Bigelow, ed., *The Complete Works of Benjamin Franklin* (New York, 1904; The Federal Edition).

Twyford, at the Bishop of St. Asaph's, 1771

Dear Son: I have ever had pleasure in obtaining any little anecdotes of my ancestors. You may remember the inquiries I made among the remains of my relations when you were with me in England, and the journey I undertook for that purpose. Imagining it may be equally agreeable to you to know the circumstances of my life, many of which you are yet unacquainted with, and expecting the enjoyment of a week's uninterrupted leisure in my present country retirement, I sit down to write them for you. To which I have besides some other inducements. Having emerged from the poverty and obscurity in which I was born and bred, to a state of affluence and some degree of reputation in the world, and having gone so far through life with a considerable share of felicity, the conducing means I made use of, which with the blessing of God so well succeeded, my posterity may like to know, as they may find some of them suitable to their own situations, and therefore fit to be imitated.

That felicity, when I reflected on it, has induced me sometimes to say, that were it offered to my choice, I should have no objection to a repetition of the same life from its beginning, only asking the advantages authors have in a second edition to correct some faults of the first. So I might, besides correcting the faults, change some sinister accidents and events of it for others more favorable. But though this were denied, I should still accept the offer. Since such a repetition is not to be expected, the next thing most like living one's life over again seems to be a recollection of that life, and to make that recollection as durable as possible by putting it down in writing.

Hereby, too, I shall indulge the inclination so natural in old men, to be talking of themselves and their own past actions; and I shall indulge it without being tiresome to others, who, through respect to age, might conceive themselves obliged to give me a hearing, since this may be read or not as any one pleases. And, lastly (I may as well confess it, since my denial of it will be believed by nobody), perhaps I shall a good deal gratify my own *vanity*. Indeed, I scarce ever heard or saw the introductory words, "*Without vanity I may say*," etc., but some vain thing immediately followed. Most people dislike vanity in others, whatever share they have of it themselves; but I give it fair quarter wherever I meet with it, being persuaded that it is often productive of good to the possessor, and to others that are within his sphere of action; and therefore, in many cases, it would not be altogether absurd if a man were to thank God for his vanity among the other comforts of life.

And now I speak of thanking God, I desire with all humility to acknowledge that I owe the mentioned happiness of my past life to His kind providence, which lead me to the means I used and gave them success. My belief of this induces me to *hope*, though I must not *presume*, that the same goodness will still be exercised toward me, in continuing that happiness, or enabling me to bear a fatal reverse, which I may experience as others have done; the complexion of my future fortune being known to Him only in whose power it is to bless to us even our afflictions.

The notes of one of my uncles (who had the same kind of curiosity in collecting family anecdotes) once put into my hands, furnished me with several particulars relating to our ancestors. From these notes I learned that the family had lived in the same village, Ecton, in Northamptonshire, for three hundred years, and how much longer he knew not (perhaps from the time when the name of Franklin, that before was the name of an order of people,[1] was assumed by them as a surname when others took surnames all over the kingdom), on a freehold of about thirty acres, aided by the smith's business, which had continued in the family till his time, the eldest son being always bred to that business, a custom which he and my father followed as to their eldest sons. When I searched the registers at Ecton, I found an account of their births, marriages, and burials, from the year 1555 only, there being no registers kept in that parish at any time preceding. By that register, I perceived that I was the youngest son of the youngest son for five generations back. My grandfather Thomas, who was born in 1598, lived at Ecton till he grew too old to follow business longer, when he went to live with his son John, a dyer at Banbury, in Oxfordshire, with whom my father served an apprenticeship. There my grandfather died and lies buried. We saw his gravestone in 1758. His eldest son Thomas lived in the house at Ecton, and left it with the land to his only child, a daughter, who, with her husband, one Richard Fisher, of Wellingborough, sold it to Mr. Isted, now lord of the manor there. My grandfather had four sons that grew up, viz.: Thomas, John, Benjamin, and Josiah. I will give you what account I can of them at this distance from my papers, and if these are not lost in my absence, you will among them find many more particulars.

Thomas was bred a smith under his father, but being ingenious, and encouraged in learning (as all my brothers were) by an Esquire Palmer, then the principal gentleman in that parish, he qualified himself for the business of scrivener,[2] became a considerable man in the county, was a chief mover of all public-spirited undertakings for the county or town of Northampton, and his own village, of which many instances were related of him, and much taken notice of and patronized by the then Lord Halifax. He died in 1702, January 6, old style, just four years to a day before I was born. The account we received of his life and character from some old people at Ecton, I remember, struck you as something extraordinary, from its similarity to what you knew of mine. "Had he died on the same day," you said, "one might have supposed a transmigration."

John was bred a dyer, I believe, of woollens. Benjamin was bred a silk-dyer, serving an apprenticeship at London. He was an ingenious man. I remember him well, for, when I was a boy, he came over to my father in Boston, and lived in the house with us some years. He lived to a great age. His grandson, Samuel Franklin, now lives in Boston. He left behind him two quarto volumes, MS., of his own poetry, consisting of little occasional pieces addressed to his friends and relations, of which the following, sent to me, is a specimen.[3] He had formed a short-hand of his own, which he taught me, but, never practising it, I have now forgot it. I was named after this uncle, there being a particular affection between him and my father. He was very pious, a great attender of sermons of the best preachers, which he took down in his short-hand, and had with him many volumes of them. He was also much of a politician; too much, perhaps, for his station. There fell lately into my hands in London a collection he had made of all the principal pamphlets relating to public affairs, from 1641 to 1717; many of the volumes are wanting, as appears by the numbering, but there still remain eight volumes in folio, and twenty-four in quarto and in octavo. A dealer in old books met with them, and knowing me by my sometimes buying of him, he brought them to me. It seems my uncle must have left them here when he

[1] That is, those who owned property, or freeholders.

[2] A professional writer, a copyist.

[3] Franklin did not include this poetry in his manuscript.

went to America, which was above fifty years since. There are many of his notes in the margins.

This obscure family of ours was early in the Reformation, and continued Protestants through the reign of Queen Mary, when they were sometimes in danger of trouble on account of their zeal against popery. They had got an English Bible, and to conceal and secure it, it was fastened open with tapes under and within the cover of a joint-stool. When my great-great-grandfather read it to his family, he turned up the joint-stool upon his knees, turning over the leaves then under the tapes. One of the children stood at the door to give notice if he saw the apparitor coming, who was an officer of the spiritual court. In that case the stool was turned down again upon its feet, when the Bible remained concealed under it as before. This anecdote I had from my uncle Benjamin. The family continued all of the Church of England till about the end of Charles the Second's reign, when some of the ministers that had been outed for non-conformity, holding conventicles[4] in Northamptonshire, Benjamin and Josiah adhered to them, and so continued all their lives: the rest of the family remained with the Episcopal Church.

Josiah, my father, married young, and carried his wife with three children into New England, about 1682. The conventicles having been forbidden by law, and frequently disturbed, induced some considerable men of his acquaintance to remove to that country, and he was prevailed with to accompany them thither, where they expected to enjoy their mode of religion with freedom. By the same wife he had four children more; born there, and by a second wife ten more, in all seventeen; of which I remember thirteen sitting at one time at his table, who all grew up to be men and women, and married; I was the youngest son, and the youngest child but two, and was born in Boston, New England. My mother, the second wife, was Abiah Folger, daughter of Peter Folger, one of the first settlers of New England, of whom honorable mention is made by Cotton Mather, in his church history of that country entitled *Magnalia Christi Americana*, as *"a godly, learned Englishman,"* if I remember the words rightly. I have heard that he wrote sundry small occasional pieces, but only one of them was printed, which I saw now many years since. It was written in 1675, in the home-spun verse of that time and people, and addressed to those then concerned in the government there. It was in favor of liberty of conscience, and in behalf of the Baptists, Quakers, and other sectaries that had been under persecution, ascribing the Indian wars, and other distresses that had befallen the country, to that persecution, as so many judgments of God to punish so heinous an offense, and exhorting a repeal of those uncharitable laws. The whole appeared to me as written with a good deal of decent plainness and manly freedom. The six concluding lines I remember, though I have forgotten the two first of the stanza; but the purport of them was, that his censures proceeded from good will, and therefore he would be known to be the author.

"Because to be a libeller (says he)
I hate it with my heart;
From Sherburne town, where now I dwell
My name I do put here;
Without offense your real friend,
It is Peter Folgier."

My elder brothers were all put apprentices to different trades. I was put to the grammar-school at eight years of age, my father intending to devote me, as the tithe[5] of his sons, to the service of the Church. My early readiness in learning to read (which must have been very early, as I do not remember when I could not read), and the opinion of all his friends, that I should certainly make a good scholar, encouraged him in this purpose of his. My uncle Benjamin, too, approved of it, and proposed to give me all his short-hand volumes of sermons, I suppose as a stock to set up with, if I would learn his character. I continued, however, at the grammar-school not quite one year, though in that time I had risen gradually from the middle of the class of that year to be the head of it, and farther was removed into the next class above it, in order to go with that into the third at the end of the year. But my father, in the meantime, from a view of the expense of a college education, which having so large a family he could not well afford, and the mean living many so educated were afterwards able to obtain,—reasons that he gave to his friends in my hearing,—altered his first intention, took me from the grammar-school, and sent me to a school for writing and arithmetic, kept by a then famous man, Mr. George Brownell, very successful in his profession generally, and that by mild, encouraging methods. Under him I acquired fair writing pretty soon, but I failed in the arithmetic, and made no progress in it. At ten years old I was taken home to assist my father in his business, which was that of a tallow-chandler and sope-boiler; a business he was not bred to, but had assumed on his arrival in New England, and on finding his dying trade would not maintain his family, being in little request. Accordingly, I was employed in cutting wick for the candles, filling the dipping mold and the molds for cast candles, attending the shop, going of errands, etc.

I disliked the trade, and had a strong inclination

[4] Meetings of dissenters (here Presbyterians) outlawed by the 1662 Act of Conformity.

[5] The tenth part of income set aside for the church; hence, a gift or contribution.

for the sea, but my father declared against it; however, living near the water, I was much in and about it, learnt early to swim well, and to manage boats; and when in a boat or canoe with other boys, I was commonly allowed to govern, especially in any case of difficulty; and upon other occasions I was generally a leader among the boys, and sometimes led them into scrapes, of which I will mention one instance, as it shows an early projecting public spirit, tho' not then justly conducted.

There was a salt-marsh that bounded part of the mill-pond, on the edge of which, at high water, we used to stand to fish for minnows. By much trampling, we had made it a mere quagmire. My proposal was to build a wharf there fit for us to stand upon, and I showed my comrades a large heap of stones, which were intended for a new house near the marsh, and which would very well suit our purpose. Accordingly, in the evening, when the workmen were gone, I assembled a number of my playfellows, and working with them diligently like so many emmets,[6] sometimes two or three to a stone, we brought them all away and built our little wharf. The next morning the workmen were surprised at missing the stones, which were found in our wharf. Inquiry was made after the removers; we were discovered and complained of; several of us were corrected by our fathers; and, though I pleaded the usefulness of the work, mine convinced me that nothing was useful which was not honest.

I think you may like to know something of his person and character. He had an excellent constitution of body, was of middle stature, but well set, and very strong; he was ingenious, could draw prettily, was skilled a little in music, and had a clear, pleasing voice, so that when he played psalm tunes on his violin and sung withal, as he sometimes did in an evening after the business of the day was over, it was extremely agreeable to hear. He had a mechanical genius too, and, on occasion, was very handy in the use of other tradesmen's tools; but his great excellence lay in a sound understanding and solid judgment in prudential matters, both in private and publick affairs. In the latter, indeed, he was never employed, the numerous family he had to educate and the straitness of his circumstances keeping him close to his trade; but I remember well his being frequently visited by leading people, who consulted him for his opinion in affairs of the town or of the church he belonged to, and showed a good deal of respect for his judgment and advice: he was also much consulted by private persons about their affairs when any difficulty occurred, and frequently chosen an arbitrator between contending parties. At his table he liked to have, as often as he could, some sensible friend or neighbor to converse with, and always took care to start some ingenious or useful topic for discourse, which might tend to improve the minds of his children. By this means he turned our attention to what was good, just, and prudent in the conduct of life; and little or no notice was ever taken of what related to the victuals on the table, whether it was well or ill dressed, in or out of season, of good or bad flavor, preferable or inferior to this or that other thing of the kind, so that I was bro't up in such a perfect inattention to those matters as to be quite indifferent what kind of food was set before me, and so unobservant of it that to this day if I am asked I can scarcely tell a few hours after dinner what I dined upon. This has been a convenience to me in travelling, where my companions have been sometimes very unhappy for want of a suitable gratification of their more delicate, because better instructed, tastes and appetites.

My mother had likewise an excellent constitution: she suckled all her ten children. I never knew either my father or mother to have any sickness but that of which they dy'd, he at eighty-nine, and she at eighty-five years of age. They lie buried together at Boston, where I some years since placed a marble over their grave, with this inscription:

Josiah Franklin,
and
Abiah his wife,
Lie here interred.
They lived lovingly together in wedlock
Fifty-five years.
Without an estate, or any gainful employment,
By constant labor and industry
With God's blessing,
They maintained a large family
Comfortably,
And brought up thirteen children
And seven grandchildren
Reputably.
From this instance, reader,
Be encouraged to diligence in thy calling,
And distrust not Providence.
He was a pious and prudent man;
She, a discreet and virtuous woman.
Their youngest son,
In filial regard to their memory,
Places this stone.
J. F. born 1655, died 1744, Aetat 89.
A. F. born 1667, died 1752,—— 85.

By my rambling digressions I perceive myself to be grown old. I us'd to write more methodically. But one does not dress for private company as for a publick ball. 'T is perhaps only negligence.

To return: I continued thus employed in my father's business for two years, that is, till I was twelve years old; and my brother John, who was bred to

[6]Ants.

that business, having left my father, married, and set up for himself at Rhode Island, there was all appearance that I was destined to supply his place, and become a tallow-chandler. But my dislike to the trade continuing, my father was under apprehensions that if he did not find one for me more agreeable, I should break away and get to sea, as his son Josiah had done, to his great vexation. He therefore sometimes took me to walk with him, and see joiners, bricklayers, turners, braziers, etc., at their work, that he might observe my inclination, and endeavor to fix it on some trade or other on land. It has ever since been a pleasure to me to see good workmen handle their tools; and it has been useful to me, having learnt so much by it as to be able to do little jobs myself in my house when a workman could not readily be got, and to construct little machines for my experiments, while the intention of making the experiment was fresh and warm in my mind. My father at last fixed upon the cutler's trade, and my uncle Benjamin's son Samuel, who was bred to that business in London, being about that time established in Boston, I was sent to be with him some time on liking. But his expectations of a fee with me displeasing my father, I was taken home again.

From a child I was fond of reading, and all the little money that came into my hands was ever laid out in books. Pleased with the *Pilgrim's Progress*, my first collection was of John Bunyan's works in separate little volumes. I afterward sold them to enable me to buy R. Burton's *Historical Collections;* they were small chapmen's books,[7] and cheap, forty or fifty in all. My father's little library consisted chiefly of books in polemic divinity, most of which I read, and have since often regretted that, at a time when I had such a thirst for knowledge, more proper books had not fallen in my way, since it was now resolved I should not be a clergyman. Plutarch's *Lives* there was in which I read abundantly, and I still think that time spent to great advantage. There was also a book of De Foe's, called an *Essay on Projects*, and another of Dr. Mather's, called *Essays to do Good*, which perhaps gave me a turn of thinking that had an influence on some of the principal future events of my life.

This bookish inclination at length determined my father to make me a printer, though he had already one son (James) of that profession. In 1717 my brother James returned from England with a press and letters to set up his business in Boston. I liked it much better than that of my father, but still had a hankering for the sea. To prevent the apprehended effect of such an inclination, my father was impatient to have me bound[8] to my brother. I stood out some time, but at last was persuaded, and signed the indentures when I was yet but twelve years old. I was to serve as an apprentice till I was twenty-one years of age, only I was to be allowed journeyman's wages during the last year. In a little time I made great proficiency in the business, and became a useful hand to my brother. I now had access to better books. An acquaintance with the apprentices of booksellers enabled me sometimes to borrow a small one, which I was careful to return soon and clean. Often I sat up in my room reading the greatest part of the night, when the book was borrowed in the evening and to be returned early in the morning, lest it should be missed or wanted.

And after some time an ingenious tradesman, Mr. Matthew Adams, who had a pretty collection of books, and who frequented our printing-house, took notice of me, invited me to his library, and very kindly lent me such books as I chose to read. I now took a fancy to poetry, and made some little pieces; my brother, thinking it might turn to account, encouraged me, and put me on composing occasional ballads. One was called *The Lighthouse Tragedy*, and contained an account of the drowning of Captain Worthilake, with his two daughters; the other was a sailor's song, on the taking of *Teach* (or Blackbeard) the pirate. They were wretched stuff, in the Grub-street-ballad style; and when they were printed he sent me about the town to sell them. The first sold wonderfully; the event, being recent, having made a great noise. This flattered my vanity; but my father discouraged me by ridiculing my performances, and telling me verse-makers were generally beggars. So I escaped being a poet, most probably a very bad one; but as prose writing has been of great use to me in the course of my life, and was a principal means of my advancement, I shall tell you how, in such a situation, I acquired what little ability I have in that way.

There was another bookish lad in the town, John Collins by name, with whom I was intimately acquainted. We sometimes disputed, and very fond we were of argument, and very desirous of confuting one another, which disputatious turn, by the way, is apt to become a very bad habit, making people often extremely disagreeable in company by the contradiction that is necessary to bring it into practice; and thence, besides souring and spoiling the conversation, is productive of disgusts and, perhaps, enmities where you may have occasion for friendship. I had caught it by reading my father's books of dispute about religion. Persons of good sense, I have since observed, seldom fall into it,

[7] Cheap books sold by street peddlers.

[8] Apprenticed.

except lawyers, university men, and men of all sorts that have been bred at Edinborough.

A question was once, somehow or other, started between Collins and me, of the propriety of educating the female sex in learning, and their abilities for study. He was of opinion that it was improper, and that they were naturally unequal to it. I took the contrary side, perhaps a little for dispute's sake. He was naturally more eloquent, had a ready plenty of words, and sometimes, as I thought, bore me down more by his fluency than by the strength of his reasons. As we parted without settling the point, and were not to see one another again for some time, I sat down to put my arguments in writing, which I copied fair and sent to him. He answered, and I replied. Three or four letters of a side had passed, when my father happened to find my papers and read them. Without entering into the discussion, he took occasion to talk to me about the manner of my writing; observed that, though I had the advantage of my antagonist in correct spelling and pointing[9] (which I ow'd to the printing-house), I fell far short in elegance of expression, in method and in perspicuity, of which he convinced me by several instances. I saw the justice of his remarks, and thence grew more attentive to the manner in writing, and determined to endeavor at improvement.

About this time I met with an odd volume of the *Spectator.* It was the third. I had never before seen any of them. I bought it, read it over and over, and was much delighted with it. I thought the writing excellent, and wished, if possible, to imitate it. With this view I took some of the papers, and, making short hints of the sentiment in each sentence, laid them by a few days, and then, without looking at the book, try'd to compleat the papers again, by expressing each hinted sentiment at length, and as fully as it had been expressed before, in any suitable words that should come to hand. Then I compared my *Spectator* with the original, discovered some of my faults, and corrected them. But I found I wanted a stock of words, or a readiness in recollecting and using them, which I thought I should have acquired before that time if I had gone on making verses; since the continual occasion for words of the same import, but of different length, to suit the measure, or of different sound for the rhyme, would have laid me under a constant necessity of searching for variety, and also have tended to fix that variety in my mind, and make me master of it. Therefore I took some of the tales and turned them into verse; and, after a time, when I had pretty well forgotten the prose, turned them back again. I also sometimes jumbled my collections of hints into confusion, and after some weeks endeavored to reduce them into the best order, before I began to form the full sentences and compleat the paper. This was to teach me method in the arrangement of thoughts. By comparing my work afterwards with the original, I discovered my faults and amended them; but I sometimes had the pleasure of fancying that, in certain particulars of small import, I had been lucky enough to improve the method or the language, and this encouraged me to think I might possibly in time come to be a tolerable English writer, of which I was extremely ambitious. My time for these exercises and for reading was at night, after work or before it began in the morning, or on Sundays, when I contrived to be in the printing-house alone, evading as much as I could the common attendance on public worship which my father used to exact of me when I was under his care, and which indeed I still thought a duty, though I could not, as it seemed to me, afford time to practise it.

When about 16 years of age I happened to meet with a book, written by one Tryon, recommending a vegetable diet. I determined to go into it. My brother, being yet unmarried, did not keep house, but boarded himself and his apprentices in another family. My refusing to eat flesh occasioned an inconveniency, and I was frequently chid for my singularity. I made myself acquainted with Tryon's manner of preparing some of his dishes, such as boiling potatoes or rice, making hasty pudding, and a few others, and then proposed to my brother, that if he would give me, weekly, half the money he paid for my board, I would board myself. He instantly agreed to it, and I presently found that I could save half what he paid me. This was an additional fund for buying books. But I had another advantage in it. My brother and the rest going from the printing-house to their meals, I remained there alone, and, despatching presently my light repast, which often was no more than a bisket or a slice of bread, a handful of raisins, or a tart from the pastry-cook's, and a glass of water, had the rest of the time, till their return, for study, in which I made the greater progress, from that greater clearness of head and quicker apprehension which usually attend temperance in eating and drinking.

And now it was that, being on some occasion made asham'd of my ignorance in figures, which I had twice failed in learning when at school, I took Cocker's book of Arithmetick, and went through the whole by myself with great ease. I also read Seller's and Shermy's books of Navigation, and became acquainted with the little geometry they contain; but never proceeded far in that science. And I read about this time Locke *On Human Understanding,* and the *Art of Thinking,* by Messrs. du Port Royal.

[9] Punctuation.

While I was intent on improving my language, I met with an English grammar (I think it was Greenwood's), at the end of which there were two little sketches of the arts of rhetoric and logic, the latter finishing with a specimen of a dispute in the Socratic method, and soon after I procur'd Xenophon's *Memorable Things of Socrates,* wherein there are many instances of the same method. I was charm'd with it, adopted it, dropt my abrupt contradiction and positive argumentation, and put on the humble inquirer and doubter. And being then, from reading Shaftesbury and Collins,[10] become a real doubter in many points of our religious doctrine, I found this method safest for myself, and very embarrassing to those against whom I used it; therefore I took a delight in it, practis'd it continually, and grew very artful and expert in drawing people, even of superior knowledge, into concessions, the consequences of which they did not foresee, entangling them in difficulties out of which they could not extricate themselves, and so obtaining victories that neither myself nor my cause always deserved. I continu'd this method some few years, but gradually left it, retaining only the habit of expressing myself in terms of modest diffidence, never using, when I advanced any thing that may possibly be disputed, the words *certainly, undoubtedly,* or any others that give the air of positiveness to an opinion, but rather say, I conceive or apprehend a thing to be so and so; it appears to me, or *I should think it so or so;* for such and such reasons; or *I imagine it to be so,* or *it is so, if I am not mistaken.* This habit, I believe, has been of great advantage to me when I have had occasion to inculcate my opinions, and persuade men into measures that I have been from time to time engag'd in promoting; and, as the chief ends of conversation are to *inform* or to be *informed,* to *please* or to *persuade,* I wish well-meaning, sensible men would not lessen their power of doing good by a positive, assuming manner, that seldom fails to disgust, tends to create opposition, and to defeat every one of those purposes for which speech was given to us,—to wit, giving or receiving information or pleasure. For, if you would inform, a positive and dogmatical manner in advancing your sentiments may provoke contradiction and prevent a candid attention. If you wish information and improvement from the knowledge of others, and yet at the same time express yourself as firmly fix'd in your present opinions, modest, sensible men, who do not love disputation, will probably leave you undisturbed in the possession of your error. And by such a manner, you can seldom hope to recommend yourself in *pleasing* your hearers, or to persuade those whose concurrence you desire. Pope says, judiciously:

> *Men should be taught as if you taught them not;*
> *And things unknown propos'd as things forgot;*

farther recommending to us

> To speak, tho' sure, with seeming diffidence.

And he might have coupled with this line that which he has coupled with another, I think, less properly:

> For want of modesty is want of sense.

If you ask, Why less properly? I must repeat the lines:

> Immodest words admit of no defense,
> For want of modesty is want of sense.

Now, is not *want of sense* (where a man is so unfortunate as to want it) some apology for his *want of modesty?* and would not the lines stand more justly thus?

> Immodest words admit *but* this defense,
> That want of modesty is want of sense.

This, however, I should submit to better judgments. * * *

I had been religiously educated as a Presbyterian;[11] and tho' some of the dogmas of that persuasion, such as *the eternal decrees of God, election, reprobation, etc.,* appeared to me unintelligible, others doubtful, and I early absented myself from the public assemblies of the sect, Sunday being my studying day, I never was without some religious principles. I never doubted, for instance, the existence of the Deity; that he made the world, and govern'd it by his Providence; that the most acceptable service of God was the doing good to man; that our souls are immortal; and that all crime will be punished, and virtue rewarded, either here or hereafter. These I esteem'd the essentials of every religion; and, being to be found in all the religions we had in our country, I respected them all, tho' with different degrees of respect, as I found them more or less mix'd with other articles, which, without any tendency to inspire, promote, or confirm morality, serv'd principally to divide us, and make us unfriendly to one another. This respect to all, with an opinion that the worst had some good effects, induc'd me to avoid all discourse that might tend to lessen the good opinion another might have of his own religion; and as our province increas'd in people, and new places of worship were continually

[10] The Earl of Shaftesbury's *Characteristics* (1712, 1714) and Anthony Collins' *Discourse* (1713) were somewhat radical theological treatises.

[11] This portion of the manuscript Franklin wrote in France, after an interval of thirteen years.

wanted, and generally erected by voluntary contribution, my mite for such purpose, whatever might be the sect, was never refused.

Tho' I seldom attended any public worship, I had still an opinion of its propriety, and of its utility when rightly conducted, and I regularly paid my annual subscription for the support of the only Presbyterian minister or meeting we had in Philadelphia. He us'd to visit me sometimes as a friend, and admonish me to attend his administrations, and I was now and then prevail'd on to do so, once for five Sundays successively. Had he been in my opinion a good preacher, perhaps I might have continued, notwithstanding the occasion I had for the Sunday's leisure in my course of study; but his discourses were chiefly either polemic arguments, or explications of the peculiar doctrines of our sect, and were all to me very dry, uninteresting, and unedifying, since not a single moral principle was inculcated or enforc'd, their aim seeming to be rather to make us Presbyterians than good citizens.

At length he took for his text that verse of the fourth chapter of Philippians: *"Finally, brethren, whatsoever things are true, honest, just, pure, lovely, or of good report, if there be any virtue, or any praise, think on these things."* And I imagin'd, in a sermon on such a text, we could not miss of having some morality. But he confin'd himself to five points only, as meant by the apostle, viz.: 1. Keeping holy the Sabbath day. 2. Being diligent in reading the holy Scriptures. 3. Attending duly the publick worship. 4. Partaking of the Sacrament. 5. Paying a due respect to God's ministers. These might be all good things; but, as they were not the kind of good things that I expected from that text, I despaired of ever meeting with them from any other, was disgusted, and attended his preaching no more. I had some years before compos'd a little Liturgy, or form of prayer, for my own private use (viz., in 1728), entitled *Articles of Belief and Acts of Religion.* I return'd to the use of this, and went no more to the public assemblies. My conduct might be blameable, but I leave it, without attempting further to excuse it; my present purpose being to relate facts, and not to make apologies for them.

It was about this time I conceiv'd the bold and arduous project of arriving at moral perfection. I wish'd to live without committing any fault at any time; I would conquer all that either natural inclination, custom, or company might lead me into. As I knew, or thought I knew, what was right and wrong, I did not see why I might not always do the one and avoid the other. But I soon found I had undertaken a task of more difficulty than I had imagined. While my care was employ'd in guarding against one fault, I was often surprised by another; habit took the advantage of inattention; inclination was sometimes too strong for reason. I concluded, at length, that the mere speculative conviction that it was our interest to be completely virtuous, was not sufficient to prevent our slipping; and that the contrary habits must be broken, and good ones acquired and established, before we can have any dependence on a steady, uniform rectitude of conduct. For this purpose I therefore contrived the following method.

In the various enumerations of the moral virtues I had met with in my reading, I found the catalogue more or less numerous, as different writers included more or fewer ideas under the same name. Temperance, for example, was by some confined to eating and drinking, while by others it was extended to mean the moderating every other pleasure, appetite, inclination, or passion, bodily or mental, even to our avarice and ambition. I propos'd to myself, for the sake of clearness, to use rather more names, with fewer ideas annex'd to each, than a few names with more ideas; and I included under thirteen names of virtues all that at that time occurr'd to me as necessary or desirable, and annexed to each a short precept, which fully express'd the extent I gave to its meaning.

These names of virtues, with their precepts, were:

1. Temperance

Eat not to dullness; drink not to elevation.

2. Silence

Speak not but what may benefit others or yourself; avoid trifling conversation.

3. Order

Let all your things have their places; let each part of your business have its time.

4. Resolution

Resolve to perform what you ought; perform without fail what you resolve.

5. Frugality

Make no expense but to do good to others or yourself; *i.e.,* waste nothing.

6. Industry

Lose no time; be always employ'd in something useful; cut off all unnecessary actions.

7. Sincerity

Use no hurtful deceit; think innocently and justly; and, if you speak, speak accordingly.

8. Justice

Wrong none by doing injuries, or omitting the benefits that are your duty.

9. Moderation

Avoid extreams; forbear resenting injuries so much as you think they deserve.

10. Cleanliness

Tolerate no uncleanliness in body, cloaths, or habitation.

11. Tranquillity

Be not disturbed at trifles, or at accidents common or unavoidable.

12. Chastity

Rarely use venery but for health or offspring, never to dulness, weakness, or the injury of your own or another's peace or reputation.

13. Humility

Imitate Jesus and Socrates.

My intention being to acquire the *habitude* of all these virtues, I judg'd it would be well not to distract my attention by attempting the whole at once, but to fix it on one of them at a time; and, when I should be master of that, then proceed to another, and so on till I had gone thro' the thirteen; and, as the previous acquisition of some might facilitate the acquisition of certain others, I arrang'd them with that view, as they stand above. Temperance first, as it tends to procure that coolness and clearness of head, which is so necessary where constant vigilance was to be kept up, and guard maintained against the unremitting attraction of ancient habits, and the force of perpetual temptations. This being acquir'd and establish'd, Silence would be more easy; and my desire being to gain knowledge at the same time that I improv'd in virtue, and considering that in conversation it was obtain'd rather by the use of the ears than of the tongue, and therefore wishing to break a habit I was getting into of prattling, punning, and joking, which only made me acceptable to trifling company, I gave *Silence* the second place. This and the next, *Order*, I expected would allow me more time for attending to my project and my studies. *Resolution*, once become habitual, would keep me firm in my endeavors to obtain all the subsequent virtues; *Frugality* and Industry freeing me from my remaining debt, and producing affluence and independence, would make more easy the practice of Sincerity and Justice, etc., etc. Conceiving, then, that, agreeably to the advice of Pythagoras in his *Golden Verses*, daily examination would be necessary, I contrived the following method for conducting that examination.

I made a little book, in which I allotted a page for each of the virtues. I rul'd each page with red ink, so as to have seven columns, one for each day of the week, marking each column with a letter for the day. I cross'd these columns with thirteen red lines, marking the beginning of each line with the first letter of one of the virtues, on which line, and in its proper column, I might mark, by a little black spot, every fault I found upon examination to have been committed respecting that virtue upon that day.

Form of the Pages

TEMPERANCE.							
EAT NOT TO DULLNESS; DRINK NOT TO ELEVATION.							
	S.	M.	T.	W.	T.	F.	S.
T.							
S.	•	•		•		•	
O.	• •	•	•		•	•	•
R.			•			•	
F.		•			•		
I.			•				
S.							
J.							
M.							
C.							
T.							
C.							
H.							

I determined to give a week's strict attention to each of the virtues successively. Thus, in the first week, my great guard was to avoid every the least offence against *Temperance*, leaving the other virtues to their ordinary chance, only marking every evening the faults of the day. Thus, if in the first week I could keep my first line, marked T, clear of spots, I suppos'd the habit of that virtue so much strengthen'd, and its opposite weaken'd, that I might venture extending my attention to include the next, and for the following week keep both lines clear of spots. Proceeding thus to the last, I could go thro' a course compleat in thirteen weeks, and four courses in a year. And like him who, having a garden to weed, does not attempt to eradicate all the bad herbs at once, which would exceed his reach and his strength, but works on one of the beds at a time, and, having accomplish'd the first, proceeds to a second, so I should have, I hoped, the encouraging pleasure of seeing on my pages the progress I made in virtue, by clearing successively my lines of their spots, till in the end, by a number of courses, I should be happy in viewing a clean book, after a thirteen weeks' daily examination.

This my little book had for its motto these lines from Addison's *Cato:*

> Here will I hold. If there's a power above us
> (And that there is, all nature cries aloud
> Thro' all her works), He must delight in virtue;
> And that which He delights in must be happy.

Another from Cicero,

O vitae Philosophia dux! O virtutum indagatrix expultrixque vitiorum! Unus dies, bene et ex praeceptis tuis actus, peccanti immortalitati est anteponendus.

Another from the Proverbs of Solomon, speaking of wisdom or virtue:

Length of days is in her right hand, and in her left hand riches and honour. Her ways are ways of pleasantness, and all her paths are peace.—iii. 16, 17.

And conceiving God to be the fountain of wisdom, I thought it right and necessary to solicit his assistance for obtaining it; to this end I formed the following little prayer, which was prefix'd to my tables of examination, for daily use.

O powerful Goodness! bountiful Father! merciful Guide! Increase in me that wisdom which discovers my truest interest. Strengthen my resolutions to perform what that wisdom dictates. Accept my kind offices to thy other children as the only return in my power for thy continual favours to me.

I used also sometimes a little prayer which I took from Thomson's *Poems*, viz.:

Father of light and life, thou Good Supreme!
O teach me what is good; teach me Thyself!
Save me from folly, vanity, and vice,
From every low pursuit; and fill my soul
With knowledge, conscious peace, and virtue pure;
Sacred, substantial, never-fading bliss!

The precept of *Order* requiring that *every part of my business should have its allotted time,* one page in my little book contain'd the following scheme of employment for the twenty-four hours of a natural day.

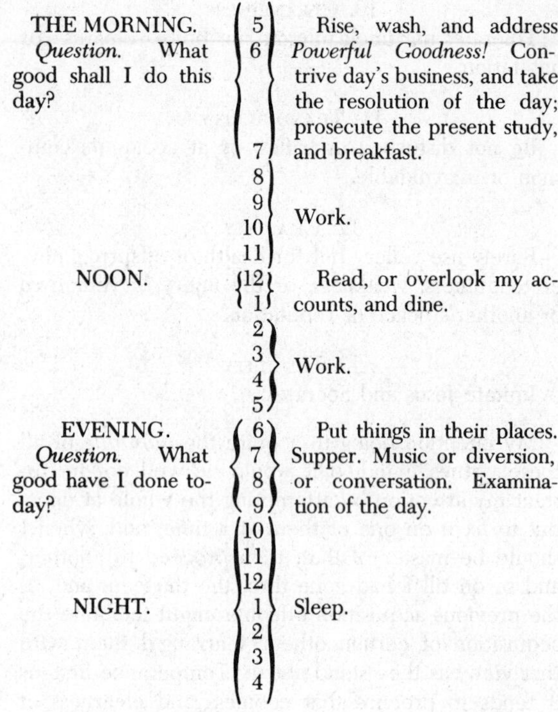

THE MORNING. *Question.* What good shall I do this day?	5 6 7	Rise, wash, and address *Powerful Goodness!* Contrive day's business, and take the resolution of the day; prosecute the present study, and breakfast.
	8 9 10 11	Work.
NOON.	12 1	Read, or overlook my accounts, and dine.
	2 3 4 5	Work.
EVENING. *Question.* What good have I done to-day?	6 7 8 9	Put things in their places. Supper. Music or diversion, or conversation. Examination of the day.
NIGHT.	10 11 12 1 2 3 4	Sleep.

I enter'd upon the execution of this plan for self-examination, and continu'd it with occasional intermissions for some time. I was surpris'd to find myself so much fuller of faults than I had imagined; but I had the satisfaction of seeing them diminish. To avoid the trouble of renewing now and then my little book, which, by scraping out the marks on the paper of old faults to make room for new ones in a new course, became full of holes, I transferr'd my tables and precepts to the ivory leaves of a memorandum book, on which the lines were drawn with red ink, that made a durable stain, and on those lines I mark'd my faults with a black-lead pencil, which marks I could easily wipe out with a wet sponge. After a while I went thro' one course only in a year, and afterward only one in several years, till at length I omitted them entirely, being employ'd in voyages and business abroad, with a multiplicity of affairs that interfered; but I always carried my little book with me.

My scheme of ORDER gave me the most trouble; and I found that, tho' it might be practicable where a man's business was such as to leave him the disposition of his time, that of a journeyman printer, for instance, it was not possible to be exactly observed by a master who must mix with the world and often receive people of business at their own hours. *Order,* too, with regard to places for things, papers, etc., I found extreamly difficult to acquire. I had not been early accustomed to it, and, having an exceeding good memory, I was not so sensible of the inconvenience attending want of method. This article, therefore cost me so much painful attention and my faults in it vexed me so much, and I made so little progress in amendment, and had such frequent relapses that I was almost ready to give up the attempt, and content myself with a faulty character in that respect, like the man who, in buying an ax of a smith, my neighbour, desired to have the whole of its surface as bright as the edge. The smith consented to grind it bright for him if he would turn the wheel; he turn'd while the smith press'd the broad face of the ax hard and heavily on the stone which made the turning of it very fatiguing. The man came every now and then from the wheel to see how the work went on and at length would take his ax as it was, without farther grinding. "No," said the smith, "turn on, turn on; we shall have it bright by and by; as yet, it is only speckled." "Yes," says the man, *"but I think I like a speckled ax best."* And I believe this may have been the case with many who, having, for want of some such means as I employ'd, found the difficulty of obtaining good and breaking bad habits in other points of vice and virtue, have given up the struggle, and concluded that *"a speckled ax was best"*; for something, that pretended to be reason, was every now and then suggesting to me that such extream nicety as I exacted of myself might be a kind of foppery in morals, which, if it were known, would make me ridiculous; that a perfect character might be attended with the inconvenience of being envied and hated; and that a benevolent man should allow a few faults in himself, to keep his friends in countenance.

In truth, I found myself incorrigible with respect to Order; and now I am grown old and my memory bad, I feel very sensibly the want of it. But, on the whole, tho' I never arrived at the perfection I had been so ambitious of obtaining, but fell far short of it, yet I was, by the endeavour, a better and a happier man than I otherwise should have been if I had not attempted it; as those who aim at perfect writing by imitating the engraved copies, tho' they never reach the wish'd-for excellence of those copies, their hand is mended by the endeavour, and is tolerable while it continues fair and legible.

It may be well my posterity should be informed that to this little artifice, with the blessing of God, their ancestor ow'd the constant felicity of his life, down to his 79th year, in which this is written. What reverses may attend the remainder is in the hand of Providence; but, if they arrive, the reflection on past happiness enjoy'd ought to help his bearing them with more resignation. To Temperance he ascribes his long-continued health, and what is still left to him of a good constitution; to Industry and Frugality, the early easiness of his circumstances and acquisition of his fortune, with all that knowledge that enabled him to be a useful citizen, and obtained for him some degree of reputation among the learned; to Sincerity and Justice, the confidence of his country, and the honorable employs it conferred upon him; and to the joint influence of the whole mass of virtues, even in the imperfect state he was able to acquire them, all that evenness of temper, and that cheerfulness in conversation, which makes his company still sought for and agreeable even to his younger acquaintances. I hope, therefore, that some of my descendants may follow the example and reap the benefit.

It will be remark'd that, tho' my scheme was not wholly without religion, there was in it no mark of any of the distinguishing tenets of any particular sect. I had purposely avoided them; for, being fully persuaded of the utility and excellence of my method, and that it might be serviceable to people in all religions, and intending some time or other to publish it, I would not have any thing in it that should prejudice any one, of any sect, against it. I purposed writing a little comment on each virtue, in which I would have shown the advantages of possessing it, and the mischiefs attending its opposite vice; and I should have called my book THE ART OF VIRTUE, because it would have shown the means and manner of obtaining virtue, which would have distinguished it from the mere exhortation to be good, that does not instruct and indicate the means, but is like the apostle's man of verbal charity, who only, without showing to the naked and hungry how or where they might get clothes or victuals, exhorted them to be fed and clothed.—James ii. 15, 16.

But it so happened that my intention of writing and publishing this comment was never fulfilled. I did, indeed, from time to time, put down short hints of the sentiments, reasonings, etc., to be made use of in it, some of which I have still by me; but the necessary close attention to private business in the earlier part of my life, and public business since, have occasioned my postponing it; for, it being connected in my mind with *a great and extensive project* that required the whole man to execute, and which an unforeseen succession of employs prevented my attending to, it has hitherto remain'd unfinish'd.

In this piece it was my design to explain and enforce this doctrine, that vicious actions are not hurtful because they are forbidden, but forbidden because they are hurtful, the nature of man alone considered; that it was, therefore, every one's interest to be virtuous who wish'd to be happy even in this world; and I should, from this circumstance (there being always in the world a number of rich merchants, nobility, states, and princes, who have need of honest instruments for the management of their affairs, and such being rare), have endeavored to convince young persons that no qualities were so likely to make a poor man's fortune as those of probity and integrity.

My list of virtues contain'd at first but twelve; but a Quaker friend having kindly informed me that I was generally thought proud; that my pride show'd itself frequently in conversation; that I was not content with being in the right when discussing any point, but was overbearing, and rather insolent, of which he convinc'd me by mentioning several instances; I determined endeavoring to cure myself, if I could, of this vice or folly among the rest, and I added *Humility* to my list, giving an extensive meaning to the word.

I cannot boast of much success in acquiring the *reality* of this virtue, but I had a good deal with regard to the *appearance* of it. I made it a rule to forbear all direct contradiction to the sentiments of others, and all positive assertion of my own. I even forbid myself, agreeably to the old laws of our Junto, the use of every word or expression in the language that imported[12] a fix'd opinion, such as *certainly, undoubtedly,* etc., and I adopted, instead of them, *I conceive, I apprehend,* or *I imagine* a thing to be so or so; or it *so appears to me at present.* When another asserted something that I thought an error, I deny'd myself the pleasure of contradicting him abruptly, and of showing immediately some absurdity in his proposition; and in answering I began by observing that in certain cases or circumstances his opinion would be right, but in the present case there *appear'd* or *seem'd* to me some difference, etc. I soon found the advantage of this change in my manner; the conversations I engag'd in went on more pleasantly. The modest way in which I propos'd my opinions procur'd them a readier reception and less contradiction; I had less mortification when I was found to be in the wrong, and I more easily prevail'd with others to give up their mistakes and join with me when I happened to be in the right.

And this mode, which I at first put on with some violence to natural inclination, became at length so easy, and so habitual to me, that perhaps for these fifty years past no one has ever heard a dogmatical expression escape me. And to this habit (after my character of integrity) I think it principally owing that I had early so much weight with my fellow-citizens when I proposed new institutions, or alterations in the old, and so much influence in public councils when I became a member; for I was but a bad speaker, never eloquent, subject to much hesitation in my choice of words, hardly correct in language, and yet I generally carried my points.

In reality, there is, perhaps, no one of our natural passions so hard to subdue as *pride.* Disguise it, struggle with it, beat it down, stifle it, mortify it as much as one pleases, it is still alive, and will every now and then peep out and show itself; you will see it, perhaps, often in this history; for, even if I could conceive that I had compleatly overcome it, I should probably be proud of my humility.

[Thus far written at Passy, 1784.][13]

Having mentioned *a great and extensive project* which I had conceiv'd, it seems proper that some account should be here given of that project and its object. Its first rise in my mind appears in the following little paper, accidentally preserv'd, viz.:

Observations on my reading history, in Library, May 19th, 1731.

"That the great affairs of the world, the wars, revolutions, etc., are carried on and effected by parties.

"That the view of these parties is their present general interest, or what they take to be such.

"That the different views of these different parties occasion all confusion.

"That while a party is carrying on a general design, each man has his particular private interest in view.

"That as soon as a party has gain'd its general point, each member becomes intent upon his particular interest; which, thwarting others, breaks that party into divisions, and occasions more confusion.

"That few in public affairs act from a meer view of the good of their country, whatever they may pretend; and, tho' their actings bring real good to their country, yet men primarily considered that their own and their country's interest was united, and did not act from a principle of benevolence.

"That fewer still, in public affairs, act with a view to the good of mankind.

"That seems to me at present to be great occasion for raising a United Party for Virtue, by forming the virtuous and good men of all nations into a regular body, to be govern'd by suitable good and wise rules, which good and wise men may probably be more unanimous in their obedience to, than common people are to common laws.

"I at present think that whoever attempts this aright, and is well qualified, can not fail of pleasing God, and of meeting with success. B. F."

Revolving this project in my mind, as to be undertaken hereafter, when my circumstances should afford me the necessary leisure, I put down from time to time on pieces of paper such thoughts as occurr'd to me respecting it. Most of these are lost; but I find one purporting to be the substance of an intended creed, containing, as I thought, the essentials of every known religion, and being free of every thing that might shock the professors of any religion. It is express'd in these words, viz.:

"That there is one God, who made all things.

"That he governs the world by his providence.

"That he ought to be worshiped by adoration, prayer, and thanksgiving.

"But that the most acceptable service of God is doing good to man.

"That the soul is immortal.

"And that God will certainly reward virtue and punish vice, either here or hereafter."

My ideas at that time were, that the sect should be begun and spread at first among young and single men only; that each person to be initiated should not only declare his assent to such creed, but should

[12] Implied.

[13] Franklin suspended his writing at this point, and resumed it in August 1788 in Philadelphia.

have exercised himself with the thirteen weeks' examination and practice of the virtues, as in the before-mention'd model; that the existence of such a society should be kept a secret till it was become considerable, to prevent solicitations for the admission of improper persons, but that the members should each of them search among his acquaintance for ingenuous, well-disposed youths to whom with prudent caution the scheme should be gradually communicated; that the members should engage to afford their advice, assistance, and support to each other in promoting one another's interests, business, and advancement in life; that, for distinction, we should be call'd *The Society of the Free and Easy:* free, as being, by the general practice and habit of the virtues free from the dominion of vice; and particularly by the practice of industry and frugality, free from debt which exposes a man to confinement and a species of slavery to his creditors.

This is as much as I can now recollect of the project, except that I communicated it in part to two young men, who adopted it with some enthusiasm; but my then narrow circumstances and the necessity I was under of sticking close to my business occasion'd my postponing the further prosecution of it at that time; and my multifarious occupations, public and private, induc'd me to continue postponing, so that it has been omitted till I have no longer strength or activity left sufficient for such an enterprise; tho' I am still of the opinion that it was a practicable scheme, and might have been very useful, by forming a great number of good citizens; and I was not discourag'd by the seeming magnitude of the undertaking, as I have always thought that one man of tolerable abilities may work great changes, and accomplish great affairs among mankind if he first forms a good plan and, cutting off all amusements or other employments that would divert his attention, makes the execution of that same plan his sole study and business.

In 1732 I first publish'd my Almanac, under the name of *Richard Saunders;* it was continu'd by me about twenty-five years, commonly call'd *Poor Richard's Almanac.* I endeavor'd to make it both entertaining and useful, and it accordingly came to be in such demand, that I reap'd considerable profit from it, vending annually near ten thousand. And observing that it was generally read, scarce any neighborhood in the province being without it, I consider'd it as a proper vehicle for conveying instruction among the common people, who bought scarcely any other books; I therefore filled all the little spaces that occurr'd between the remarkable days in the calendar with proverbial sentences, chiefly such as inculcated industry and frugality, as the means of procuring wealth, and thereby securing virtue; it being more difficult for a man in want, to act always honestly, as, to use here one of those proverbs, *it is hard for an empty sack to stand upright.* * * *

I began now to turn my thoughts a little to public affairs, beginning, however, with small matters. The city watch was one of the first things that I conceiv'd to want regulation. It was managed by the constables of the respective wards in turn; the constable warned a number of housekeepers to attend him for the night.[14] Those who chose never to attend, paid him six shillings a year to be excus'd, which was suppos'd to be for hiring substitutes but was, in reality, much more than was necessary for that purpose and made the constableship a place of profit; and the constable, for a little drink, often got such ragamuffins about him as a watch, that respectable housekeepers did not choose to mix with. Walking the rounds, too, was often neglected and most of the nights spent in tippling. I thereupon wrote a paper to be read in Junto, representing these irregularities, but insisting more particularly on the inequality of this six-shilling tax of the constables, respecting the circumstances of those who paid it, since a poor widow housekeeper, all whose property to be guarded by the watch did not perhaps exceed the value of fifty pounds, paid as much as the wealthiest merchant who had thousands of pounds' worth of goods in his stores.

On the whole, I proposed as a more effectual watch, the hiring of proper men to serve constantly in that business; and as a more equitable way of supporting the charge, the levying a tax that should be proportion'd to the property. This idea, being approv'd by the Junto, was communicated to the other clubs, but as arising in each of them; and though the plan was not immediately carried into execution, yet, by preparing the minds of people for the change, it paved the way for the law obtained a few years after when the members of our clubs were grown into more influence.

About this time I wrote a paper (first to be read in Junto but it was afterward publish'd) on the different accidents and carelessnesses by which houses were set on fire, with cautions against them, and means proposed of avoiding them. This was much spoken of as a useful piece and gave rise to a project which soon followed it, of forming a company for the more ready extinguishing of fires and mutual assistance in removing and securing of goods when in danger. Associates in this scheme were presently found, amounting to thirty. Our articles of agreement oblig'd every member to keep always in good order and fit for use, a certain number of leather buckets with strong bags and baskets (for packing and transporting of goods), which were to be

[14] Cities were policed only at night; householders, serving in rotation, assisted the constables and marshals who patrolled the wards.

brought to every fire; and we agreed to meet once a month and spend a social evening together, in discoursing and communicating such ideas as occurred to us upon the subject of fires as might be useful in our conduct on such occasions.

The utility of this institution soon appeared, and many more desiring to be admitted than we thought convenient for one company, they were advised to form another, which was accordingly done; and this went on, one new company being formed after another till they became so numerous as to include most of the inhabitants who were men of property; and now, at the time of my writing this, tho' upward of fifty years since its establishment, that which I first formed, called the Union Fire Company[15] still subsists and flourishes, tho' the first members are all deceas'd but myself and one, who is older by a year than I am. The small fines that have been paid by members for absence at the monthly meetings have been apply'd to the purchase of fire-engines, ladders, fire-hooks, and other useful implements for each company, so that I question whether there is a city in the world better provided with the means of putting a stop to beginning conflagrations; and, in fact, since these institutions, the city has never lost by fire more than one or two houses at a time and the flames have often been extinguished before the house in which they began has been half consumed. * * *

In order of time, I should have mentioned before, that having, in 1742, invented an open stove for the better warming of rooms, and at the same time saving fuel, as the fresh air admitted was warmed in entering, I made a present of the model to Mr. Robert Grace, one of my early friends, who, having an iron-furnace found the casting of the plates for these stoves a profitable thing, as they were growing in demand. To promote that demand, I wrote and published a pamphlet, entitled *An Account of the new-invented Pennsylvania Fireplaces; wherein their Construction and Manner of Operation is particularly explained; their Advantages above every other Method of warming Rooms demonstrated: and all Objections that have been raised against the Use of them answered and obviated,* etc. This pamphlet had a good effect. Gov'r. Thomas was so pleas'd with the construction of this stove, as described in it, that he offered to give me a patent for the sole vending of them for a term of years; but I declin'd it from a principle which has ever weighed with me on such occasions, viz.: *That, as we enjoy great advantages from the inventions of others, we should be glad of an opportunity to serve others by any invention of ours; and this we should do freely and generously.*

[15] Organized December 7, 1736.

An ironmonger in London however, assuming[16] a good deal of my pamphlet, and working it up into his own and making some small changes in the machine, which rather hurt its operation, got a patent for it there and made, as I was told, a little fortune by it. And this is not the only instance of patents taken out for my inventions by others, tho' not always with the same success, which I never contested, as having no desire of profiting by patents myself, and hating disputes. The use of these fireplaces in very many houses, both of this and the neighboring colonies, has been, and is, a great saving of wood to the inhabitants.

Peace being concluded, and the association business therefore at an end, I turn'd my thoughts again to the affair of establishing an academy. The first step I took was to associate in the design a number of active friends, of whom the Junto furnished a good part; the next was to write and publish a pamphlet, entitled *Proposals relating to the Education of Youth in Pennsylvania.* This I distributed among the principal inhabitants gratis; and as soon as I could suppose their minds a little prepared by the perusal of it, I set on foot a subscription for opening and supporting an academy: it was to be paid in quotas yearly for five years; by so dividing it, I judg'd the subscription might be larger and I believe it was so, amounting to no less, if I remember right, than five thousand pounds.

In the introduction to these proposals, I stated their publication, not as an act of mine, but of some *publick-spirited gentlemen,* avoiding as much as I could, according to my usual rule, the presenting myself to the public as the author of any scheme for their benefit.

The subscribers, to carry the project into immediate execution, chose out of their number twenty-four trustees and appointed Mr. Francis, then attorney-general and myself to draw up constitutions for the government of the academy; which being done and signed, a house was hired, masters engag'd, and the schools opened, I think, in the same year, 1749.

The scholars increasing fast, the house was soon found too small and we were looking out for a piece of ground properly situated, with intention to build, when Providence threw into our way a large house ready built which, with a few alterations, might well serve our purpose. This was the building before mentioned, erected by the hearers of Mr. Whitefield,[17] and was obtained for us in the following manner.

It is to be noted that the contributions to this building being made by people of different sects,

[16] Appropriating.

[17] The Rev. George Whitefield, an English Methodist evangelist assisted by Franklin when he earlier visited Pennsylvania.

care was taken in the nomination of trustees, in whom the building and ground were to be vested, that a predominancy should not be given to any sect, lest in time that predominancy might be a means of appropriating the whole to the use of such sect, contrary to the original intention. It was therefore that one of each sect was appointed, viz., one Church-of-England man, one Presbyterian, one Baptist, one Moravian,[18] etc., those, in case of vacancy by death, were to fill it by election from among the contributors. The Moravian happen'd not to please his colleagues and on his death they resolved to have no other of that sect. The difficulty then was, how to avoid having two of some other sect, by means of the new choice.

Several persons were named, and for that reason not agreed to. At length one mention'd me with the observation that I was merely an honest man, and of no sect at all, which prevail'd with them to chuse me. The enthusiasm which existed when the house was built had long since abated, and its trustees had not been able to procure fresh contributions for paying the ground-rent and discharging some other debts the building had occasion'd, which embarrass'd them greatly. Being now a member of both setts of trustees, that for the building and that for the academy, I had a good opportunity of negotiating with both, and brought them finally to an agreement, by which the trustees for the building were to cede it to those of the academy, the latter undertaking to discharge the debt, to keep forever open in the building a large hall for occasional preachers according to the original intention and maintain a free-school for the instruction of poor children. Writings were accordingly drawn and on paying the debts, the trustees of the academy were put into possession of the premises; and by dividing the great and lofty hall into stories, and different rooms above and below for the several schools and purchasing some additional ground the whole was soon made fit for our purpose, and the scholars remov'd into the building. The care and trouble of agreeing with the workmen, purchasing materials and superintending the work, fell upon me; and I went thro' it the more cheerfully, as it did not then interfere with my private business, having the year before taken a very able, industrious, and honest partner, Mr. David Hall with whose character I was well acquainted as he had work'd for me four years. He took off my hands all care of the printing-office, paying me punctually my share of the profits. This partnership continued eighteen years, successfully for us both.

The trustees of the academy, after a while, were incorporated by a charter from the governor; their funds were increas'd by contributions in Britain and grants of land from the proprietaries, to which the Assembly has since made considerable addition; and thus was established the present University of Philadelphia.[19] I have been continued one of its trustees from the beginning, now near forty years, and have had the very great pleasure of seeing a number of the youth who have receiv'd their education in it, distinguished by their improv'd abilities, serviceable in public stations, and ornaments to their country.

When I disengaged myself, as above mentioned, from private business, I flatter'd myself that, by the sufficient tho' moderate fortune I had acquir'd, I had secured leisure during the rest of my life for philosophical studies and amusements. I purchased all Dr. Spence's apparatus, who had come from England to lecture here, and I proceeded in my electrical experiments with great alacrity; but the publick, now considering me as a man of leisure, laid hold of me for their purposes; every part of our civil government, and almost at the same time, imposing some duty upon me. The governor put me into the commission of the peace, the corporation of the city chose me of the common council, and soon after an alderman, and the citizens at large chose me a burgess to represent them in Assembly. This latter station was the more agreeable to me, as I was at length tired with sitting there to hear debates, in which, as clerk, I could take no part, and which were so often unentertaining that I was induc'd to amuse myself with making magic squares or circles, or any thing to avoid weariness; and I conceiv'd my becoming a member would enlarge my power of doing good. I would not, however, insinuate that my ambition was not flatter'd by all these promotions; it certainly was; for, considering my low beginning, they were great things to me and they were still more pleasing as being so many spontaneous testimonies of the public good opinion, and by me entirely unsolicited.

The office of justice of the peace I try'd a little, by attending a few courts, and sitting on the bench to hear causes, but finding that more knowledge of the common law than I possessed was necessary to act in that station with credit, I gradually withdrew from it, excusing myself by my being oblig'd to attend the higher duties of a legislator in the Assembly. My election to this trust was repeated every year for ten years without my ever asking any elector for his vote or signifying, either directly or indirectly, any desire of being chosen. On taking my seat in the House, my son was appointed their clerk.

The year following, a treaty being to be held with the Indians at Carlisle, the governor sent a message to the House, proposing that they should nominate

[18] An evangelical sect which arose in Austria and Germany; large numbers had settled in Pennsylvania.

[19] The present University of Pennsylvania.

some of their members, to be join'd with some members of council, as commissioners for that purpose. The House named the speaker (Mr. Norris) and myself; and, being commission'd, we went to Carlisle, and met the Indians accordingly.

As those people are extreamly apt to get drunk and, when so, are very quarrelsome and disorderly, we strictly forbade the selling any liquor to them; and when they complain'd of this restriction, we told them that if they would continue sober during the treaty we would give them plenty of rum when business was over. They promis'd this and they kept their promise because they could get no liquor, and the treaty was conducted very orderly and concluded to mutual satisfaction. They then claim'd and receiv'd the rum; this was in the afternoon; they were near one hundred men, women, and children, and were lodg'd in temporary cabins built in the form of a square, just without the town. In the evening, hearing a great noise among them, the commissioners walk'd out to see what was the matter. We found they had made a great bonfire in the middle of the square; they were all drunk, men and women, quarreling and fighting. Their dark-colour'd bodies half naked, seen only by the gloomy light of the bonfire, running after and beating one another with firebrands, accompanied by their horrid yellings, form'd a scene the most resembling our ideas of hell that could well be imagin'd; there was no appeasing the tumult, and we retired to our lodging. At midnight a number of them came thundering at our door, demanding more rum, of which we took no notice.

The next day, sensible they had misbehav'd in giving us that disturbance, they sent three of their old counsellors to make their apology. The orator acknowledg'd the fault, but laid it upon the rum; and then endeavored to excuse the rum by saying: *"The Great Spirit, who made all things, made every thing for some use, and whatever use he design'd any thing for, that use it should always be put to. Now, when he made rum, he said, 'Let this be for the Indians to get drunk with,' and it must be so."* And, indeed, if it be the design of Providence to extirpate these savages in order to make room for cultivators of the earth, it seems not improbable that rum may be the appointed means. It has already annihilated all the tribes who formerly inhabited the sea-coast.

In 1751, Dr. Thomas Bond, a particular friend of mine, conceived the idea of establishing a hospital in Philadelphia (a very beneficent design, which has been ascrib'd to me, but was originally his), for the reception and cure of poor sick persons, whether inhabitants of the province or strangers. He was zealous and active in endeavoring to procure subscriptions for it, but the proposal being a novelty in America, and at first not well understood, he met with small success.

At length he came to me with the compliment that he found there was no such thing as carrying a public-spirited project through without my being concern'd in it. "For," says he, "I am often ask'd by those to whom I propose subscribing, Have you consulted Franklin upon this business? And what does he think of it? And when I tell them that I have not (supposing it rather out of your line), they do not subscribe, but say they will consider of it." I enquired into the nature and probable utility of his scheme, and receiving from him a very satisfactory explanation, I not only subscribed to it myself, but engag'd heartily in the design of procuring subscriptions from others. Previously, however, to the solicitation, I endeavoured to prepare the minds of the people by writing on the subject in newspapers, which was my usual custom in such cases but which he had omitted.

The subscriptions afterwards were more free and generous, but beginning to flag, I saw they would be insufficient without some assistance from the Assembly and therefore propos'd to petition for it, which was done. The country members did not at first relish the project; they objected that it could only be serviceable to the city and therefore the citizens alone should be at the expense of it; and they doubted whether the citizens themselves generally approv'd of it. My allegation on the contrary, that it met with such approbation as to leave no doubt of our being able to raise two thousand pounds by voluntary donations, they considered as a most extravagant supposition, and utterly impossible.

On this I form'd my plan and, asking leave to bring in a bill for incorporating the contributors according to the prayer of their petition, and granting them a blank sum of money, which leave was obtained chiefly on the consideration that the House could throw the bill out if they did not like it, I drew it so as to make the important clause a conditional one, viz.: "And be it enacted, by the authority aforesaid, that when the said contributors shall have met and chosen their managers and treasurer, *and shall have raised by their contributions a capital stock of———value* (the yearly interest of which is to be applied to the accommodating of the sick poor in the said hospital, free of charge for diet, attendance, advice, and medicines), *and shall make the same appear to the satisfaction of the speaker of the Assembly for the time being,* that *then* it shall and may be lawful for the said speaker, and he is hereby required, to sign an order on the provincial treasurer for the payment of two thousand pounds, in two yearly payments, to the treasurer of the said hospital, to be applied to the founding, building, and finishing of the same."

This condition carried the bill through; for the members, who had oppos'd the grant and now conceived they might have the credit of being charitable without the expence, agreed to its passage; and then, in soliciting subscriptions among the people, we urg'd the conditional promise of the law as an additional motive to give, since every man's donation would be doubled; thus the clause work'd both ways. The subscriptions accordingly soon exceeded the requisite sum, and we claim'd and receiv'd the public gift, which enabled us to carry the design into execution. A convenient and handsome building was soon erected; the institution has by constant experience been found useful, and flourishes to this day; and I do not remember any of my political manoeuvres, the success of which gave me at the time more pleasure, or wherein, after thinking of it I more easily excus'd myself for having made some use of cunning.

It was about this time that another projector, the Rev. Gilbert Tennent,[20] came to me with a request that I would assist him in procuring a subscription for erecting a new meeting-house. It was to be for the use of a congregation he had gathered among the Presbyterians, who were originally disciples of Mr. Whitefield. Unwilling to make myself disagreeable to my fellow-citizens by too frequently soliciting their contributions, I absolutely refus'd. He then desired I would furnish him with a list of the names of persons I knew by experience to be generous and public-spirited. I thought it would be unbecoming in me, after their kind compliance with my solicitations, to mark them out to be worried by other beggars, and therefore refus'd also to give such a list. He then desir'd I would at least give him my advice. "That I will readily do," said I; "and, in the first place, I advise you to apply to all those whom you know will give something; next to those whom you are uncertain whether they will give any thing or not, and show them the list of those who have given; and, lastly, do not neglect those who you are sure will give nothing, for in some of them you may be mistaken." He laugh'd and thank'd me, and said he would take my advice. He did so, for he ask'd of *everybody*, and he obtain'd a much larger sum than he expected, with which he erected the capacious and very elegant meeting-house that stands in Arch-street.

Our city, tho' laid out with a beautiful regularity, the streets large, straight, and crossing each other at right angles, had the disgrace of suffering those streets to remain long unpav'd, and in wet weather the wheels of heavy carriages plough'd them into a quagmire so that it was difficult to cross them; and in dry weather the dust was offensive. I had liv'd near what was call'd the Jersey Market and saw with pain the inhabitants wading in mud while purchasing their provisions. A strip of ground down the middle of that market was at length pav'd with brick, so that, being once in the market, they had firm footing, but were often over shoes in dirt to get there. By talking and writing on the subject, I was at length instrumental in getting the street pav'd with stone between the market and the brick'd foot-pavement, that was on each side next the houses. This, for some time gave an easy access to the market dry-shod, but, the rest of the street not being pav'd, whenever a carriage came out of the mud upon this pavement it shook off and left its dirt upon it and it was soon cover'd with mire, which was not remov'd, the city as yet having no scavengers.[21]

After some inquiry, I found a poor, industrious man who was willing to undertake keeping the pavement clean by sweeping it twice a week, carrying off the dirt from before all the neighbours' doors, for the sum of sixpence per month to be paid by each house. I then wrote and printed a paper setting forth the advantages to the neighbourhood that might be obtain'd by this small expense; the greater ease in keeping our houses clean, so much dirt not being brought in by people's feet; the benefit to the shops by more custom, etc., etc., as buyers could more easily get at them; and by not having, in windy weather, the dust blown in upon their goods, etc., etc. I sent one of these papers to each house and in a day or two went round to see who would subscribe an agreement to pay these sixpences. It was unanimously sign'd, and for a time well executed. All the inhabitants of the city were delighted with the cleanliness of the pavement that surrounded the market, it being a convenience to all, and this rais'd a general desire to have all the streets paved, and made the people more willing to submit to a tax for that purpose.

After some time I drew a bill for paving the city, and brought it into the Assembly. It was just before I went to England, in 1757, and did not pass till I was gone, and then with an alteration in the mode of assessment, which I thought not for the better, but with an additional provision for lighting as well as paving the streets, which was a great improvement. It was by a private person, the late Mr. John Clifton, his giving a sample of the utility of lamps, by placing one at his door, that the people were first impress'd with the idea of enlighting all the city. The honour of this public benefit has also been

[20] Tennent, a co-worker of Whitefield's, became one of the most influential of American evangelists.

[21] Street cleaners.

ascrib'd to me, but it belongs truly to that gentleman. I did but follow his example, and have only some merit to claim respecting the form of our lamps, as differing from the globe lamps we were at first supply'd with from London. Those we found inconvenient in these respects: they admitted no air below; the smoke, therefore, did not readily go out above, but circulated in the globe, lodg'd on its inside, and soon obstructed the light they were intended to afford; giving, besides, the daily trouble of wiping them clean; and an accidental stroke on one of them would demolish it, and render it totally useless. I therefore suggested the composing them of four flat panes, with a long funnel above to draw up the smoke, and crevices admitting air below, to facilitate the ascent of the smoke; by this means they were kept clean, and did not grow dark in a few hours, as the London lamps do, but continu'd bright till morning, and an accidental stroke would generally break but a single pane, easily repair'd.

I have sometimes wonder'd that the Londoners did not, from the effect holes in the bottom of the globe lamps us'd at Vauxhall[22] have in keeping them clean, learn to have such holes in their street lamps. But, these holes being made for another purpose, viz., to communicate flame more suddenly to the wick by a little flax hanging down thro' them, the other use, of letting in air, seems not to have been thought of; and therefore, after the lamps have been lit a few hours, the streets of London are very poorly illuminated. * * *

1771-1789

The Way to Wealth

These proverbs, which Franklin gathered from many sources, he wrote in his *Autobiography*, "I assembled and formed into a connected discourse prefixed to the Almanac of 175[8], as the harangue of a wise old man to the people attending an auction. The bringing all these scattered counsels thus into a focus enabled them to make greater impression. The piece, being universally approved, was copied in all the newspapers of the [American] Continent; reprinted in Britain on a broadside, to be stuck up in houses; two translations were made of it in French; and great numbers bought by the clergy and gentry, to distribute gratis among their poor parishioners and tenants. In Pennsylvania, . . . some thought it had its share of influence in producing that growing plenty of money which was observable for several years after its publication." The selection was sometimes titled "Father Abraham's Speech." Text: Bigelow edition of *Complete Works* (New York, 1904).

[22] Vauxhall Gardens, a famous London amusement park.

Courteous Reader:

I have heard that nothing gives an author so great pleasure as to find his works respectfully quoted by others. Judge, then, how much I must have been gratified by an incident I am going to relate to you. I stopped my horse lately where a great number of people were collected at an auction of merchants' goods. The hour of the sale not being come, they were conversing on the badness of the times; and one of the company called to a plain, clean, old man, with white locks: "Pray, Father Abraham, what think you of the times? Will not these heavy taxes quite ruin the country? How shall we ever be able to pay them? What would you advise us to do?" Father Abraham stood up and replied: "If you would have my advice, I will give it you in short; for *A word to the wise is enough,* as Poor Richard says." They joined in desiring him to speak his mind, and gathering round him he proceeded as follows:

"Friends," said he, "the taxes are indeed very heavy, and if those laid on by the government were the only ones we had to pay, we might more easily discharge them, but we have many others and much more grievous to some of us. We are taxed twice as much by our idleness, three times as much by our pride, and four times as much by our folly, and from these taxes the commissioners cannot ease or deliver us by allowing an abatement. However, let us hearken to good advice and something may be done for us; *God helps them that help themselves,* as Poor Richard says.

"I. It would be thought a hard government that should tax its people one-tenth part of their time, to be employed in its service, but idleness taxes many of us much more; sloth by bringing on diseases, absolutely shortens life. *Sloth, like rust, consumes faster than labor wears, while the used key is always bright,* as Poor Richard says. *But dost thou love life, then do not squander time, for that is the stuff life is made of,* as Poor Richard says. How much more than is necessary do we spend in sleep, forgetting that *The sleeping fox catches no poultry,* and that *There will be sleeping enough in the grave,* as Poor Richard says.

"*If time be of all things the most precious, wasting time must be,* as Poor Richard says, *the greatest prodigality,* since, as he elsewhere tells us, *Lost time is never found again, and what we call time enough always proves little enough.* Let us then up and be doing, and doing to the purpose; so by diligence shall we do more with less perplexity. *Sloth makes all things difficult, but industry all things easy;* and *He that riseth late must trot all day, and shall scarce overtake his business at night;* while *Laziness travels so slowly that Poverty soon overtakes him. Drive thy business, let not that drive thee;* and *Early to bed and early to rise, makes a man healthy, wealthy, and wise,* as Poor Richard says.

"So what signifies wishing and hoping for better times? We may make these times better if we bestir ourselves. *Industry need not wish, and he that lives upon hopes will die fasting. There are no gains without pains; then help, hands, for I have no lands;* or if I have they are smartly taxed. *He that hath a trade hath an estate, and he that hath a calling hath an office of profit and honor,* as Poor Richard says; but then the trade must be worked at and the calling followed, or neither the estate nor the office will enable us to pay our taxes. If we are industrious we shall never starve, for *At the working man's house hunger looks in but dares not enter.* Nor will the bailiff nor the constable enter, for *Industry pays debts, while despair increaseth them.* What though you have found no treasure, nor has any rich relation left you a legacy, *Diligence is the mother of good luck, and God gives all things to industry. Then plough deep while sluggards sleep, and you shall have corn to sell and to keep.* Work while it is called to-day, for you know not how much you may be hindered to-morrow. *One to-day is worth two to-morrows,* as Poor Richard says; and further, *Never leave that till to-morrow which you can do to-day.* If you were a servant would not you be ashamed that a good master should catch you idle? Are you then your own master? Be ashamed to catch yourself idle when there is so much to be done for yourself, your family, your country, and your king. Handle your tools without mittens; remember that *The cat in gloves catches no mice,* as Poor Richard says. It is true there is much to be done, and perhaps you are weak-handed, but stick to it steadily and you will see great effects; for *Constant dropping wears away stones;* and *By diligence and patience the mouse ate in two the cable;* and *Little strokes fell great oaks.*

"Methinks I hear some of you say, 'Must a man afford himself no leisure?' I will tell thee, my friend, what Poor Richard says: *Employ thy time well, if thou meanest to gain leisure; and, since thou art not sure of a minute, throw not away an hour.* Leisure is time for doing something useful; this leisure the diligent man will obtain, but the lazy man never; for *A life of leisure and a life of laziness are two things. Many, without labor, would live by their wits only, but they break for want of stock;* whereas industry gives comfort and plenty and respect. *Fly pleasures, and they will follow you. The diligent spinner has a large shift; and now I have a sheep and a cow, everybody bids me good morrow.*

"II. But with our industry we must likewise be steady, settled, and careful, and oversee our own affairs with our own eyes, and not trust too much to others; for, as Poor Richard says:

I never saw an oft removed tree,
Nor yet an oft-removed family,
That throve so well as those that settled be.

And again, *Three removes are as bad as a fire;* and again, *Keep thy shop, and thy shop will keep thee;* and again: *If you would have your business done, go; if not, send.* And again:

He that by the plough would thrive,
Himself must either hold or drive.

And again, *The eye of a master will do more work than both his hands;* and again, *Want of care does us more damage than want of knowledge;* and again, *Not to oversee workmen is to leave them your purse open.* Trusting too much to others' care is the ruin of many; for, *In the affairs of this world men are saved, not by faith, but by the want of it;* but a man's own care is profitable; for, *If you would have a faithful servant, and one that you like, serve yourself. A little neglect may breed great mischief; for want of a nail the shoe was lost; for want of a shoe the horse was lost; and for want of a horse the rider was lost, being overtaken and slain by the enemy; all for want of a little care about a horse-shoe nail.*

"III. So much for industry, my friends, and attention to one's own business; but to these we must add frugality, if we would make our industry more certainly successful. A man may, if he knows not how to save as he gets, keep his nose all his life to the grindstone and die not worth a groat at last. *A fat kitchen makes a lean will;* and

Many estates are spent in the getting,
Since women for tea forsook spinning and knitting,
And men for punch forsook hewing and splitting.

If you would be wealthy, think of saving as well as of getting. The Indies have not made Spain rich, because her outgoes are greater than her incomes.

"Away then with your expensive follies, and you will not then have so much cause to complain of hard times, heavy taxes, and chargeable families; for

Women and wine, game and deceit,
Make the wealth small and the want great.

And further, *What maintains one vice would bring up two children.* You may think, perhaps, that a little tea, or a little punch now and then, diet a little more costly, clothes a little finer, and a little entertainment now and then, can be no great matter; but remember, *Many a little makes a mickle.* Beware of little expenses: *A small leak will sink a great ship,* as Poor Richard says; and again, *Who dainties love, shall beggars prove;* and moreover, *Fools make feasts, and wise men eat them.*

"Here you are all got together at this sale of fineries and knick-knacks. You call them *goods;* but if you do not take care they will prove *evils* to some of you. You expect they will be sold cheap, and perhaps they may for less than they cost; but if you have no occasion for them they must be dear to you. Remember what Poor Richard says: *Buy what thou hast no need of, and ere long thou shalt sell thy necessaries.* And again, *At a great pennyworth pause a while.* He means, that perhaps the cheapness is apparent only, and not real; or the bargain, by straitening thee in thy business, may do thee more harm than good. For in another place he says, *Many have been ruined by buying good pennyworths.* Again, *It is foolish to lay out money in a purchase of repentance;* and yet this folly is practised every day at auctions for want of minding the Almanac. Many a one, for the sake of finery on the back, have gone with a hungry belly and half-starved their families. *Silks and satins, scarlet and velvets, put out the kitchen fire,* as Poor Richard says.

"These are not the necessaries of life; they can scarcely be called the conveniences; and yet, only because they look pretty, how many want to have them! By these and other extravagances the genteel are reduced to poverty and forced to borrow of those whom they formerly despised, but who, through industry and frugality, have maintained their standing; in which case it appears plainly that *A ploughman on his legs is higher than a gentleman on his knees,* as Poor Richard says. Perhaps they have had a small estate left them, which they knew not the getting of: they think, *It is day, and will never be night;* that a little to be spent out of so much is not worth minding; but *Always taking out of the meal-tub, and never putting in, soon comes to the bottom,* as Poor Richard says; and then, *When the well is dry, they know the worth of water.* But this they might have known before, if they had taken his advice. *If you would know the value of money, go and try to borrow some; for he that goes a borrowing goes a sorrowing,* as Poor Richard says; and indeed so does he that lends to such people, when he goes to get it again. Poor Dick further advises and says,

Fond pride of dress is sure a very curse;
Ere fancy you consult, consult your purse.

And again, *Pride is as loud a beggar as Want, and a great deal more saucy.* When you have bought one fine thing you must buy ten more, that your appearance may be all of a piece; but Poor Dick says, *It is easier to suppress the first desire than to satisfy all that follow it.* And it is as truly folly for the poor to ape the rich, as for the frog to swell in order to equal the ox.

Vessels large may venture more,
But little boats should keep near shore.

It is, however, a folly soon punished; for, as Poor Richard says, *Pride that dines on vanity sups on contempt. Pride breakfasted with Plenty, dined with Poverty, and supped with Infamy.* And after all, of what use is this pride of appearance, for which so much is risked, so much is suffered? It cannot promote health, nor ease pain; it makes no increase of merit in the person; it creates envy; it hastens misfortune.

"But what madness must it be to *run in debt* for these superfluities! We are offered by the terms of this sale six months' credit; and that, perhaps, has induced some of us to attend it, because we cannot spare the ready money, and hope now to be fine without it. But ah! think what you do when you run in debt; you give to another power over your liberty. If you cannot pay at the time, you will be ashamed to see your creditor; you will be in fear when you speak to him; you will make poor, pitiful, sneaking excuses, and by degrees come to lose your veracity, and sink into base, downright lying; for, *The second vice is lying, the first is running in debt,* as Poor Richard says; and again, to the same purpose, *Lying rides upon Debt's back;* whereas a free-born Englishman ought not to be ashamed nor afraid to see or speak to any man living. But poverty often deprives a man of all spirit and virtue. *It is hard for an empty bag to stand upright.*

"What would you think of that prince or of that government who should issue an edict forbidding you to dress like a gentleman or gentlewoman, on pain of imprisonment or servitude? Would you not say that you were free, have a right to dress as you please, and that such an edict would be a breach of your privileges, and such a government tyrannical? And yet you are about to put yourself under such tyranny when you run in debt for such dress! Your creditor has authority, at his pleasure, to deprive you of your liberty by confining you in gaol till you shall be able to pay him. When you have got your bargain you may perhaps think little of payment, but, as Poor Richard says, *Creditors have better memories than debtors; creditors are a superstitious sect, great observers of set days and times.* The day comes round before you are aware, and the demand is made before you are prepared to satisfy it; or, if you bear your debt in mind, the term, which at first seemed so long, will, as it lessens, appear extremely short. Time will seem to have added wings to his heels as well as his shoulders. *Those have a short Lent who owe money to be paid at Easter.* At present, perhaps, you may think yourselves in thriving circumstances, and that you can bear a little extravagance without injury, but—

For age and want save while you may;
No morning sun lasts a whole day.

Gain may be temporary and uncertain, but ever,

while you live, expense is constant and certain; and *It is easier to build two chimneys than to keep one in fuel*, as Poor Richard says; so, *Rather go to bed supperless than rise in debt.*

Get what you can, and what you get hold;
'T is the stone that will turn all your lead into gold.

And, when you have got the Philosopher's stone, sure you will no longer complain of bad times or the difficulty of paying taxes.

"IV. This doctrine, my friends, is reason and wisdom; but, after all, do not depend too much upon your own industry and frugality and prudence, though excellent things, for they may all be blasted, without the blessing of Heaven; and therefore ask that blessing humbly, and be not uncharitable to those that at present seem to want it, but comfort and help them. Remember Job suffered and was afterwards prosperous.

"And now, to conclude, *Experience keeps a dear school, but fools will learn in no other*, as Poor Richard says, and scarce in that, for it is true *We may give advice, but we cannot give conduct*. However, remember this, *They that will not be counselled cannot be helped;* and further, that *If you will not hear Reason, she will surely rap your knuckles*, as Poor Richard says."

Thus the old gentleman ended his harangue. The people heard it and approved the doctrine, and immediately practised the contrary, just as if it had been a common sermon; for the auction opened, and they began to buy extravagantly. I found the good man had thoroughly studied my Almanacs, and digested all I had dropped on these topics during the course of twenty-five years. The frequent mention he made of me must have tired any one else, but my vanity was wonderfully delighted with it, though I was conscious that not a tenth part of the wisdom was my own which he ascribed to me, but rather the gleanings that I had made of the sense of all ages and nations. However, I resolved to be the better for the echo of it, and though I had at first determined to buy stuff for a new coat, I went away resolved to wear my old one a little longer. Reader, if thou wilt do the same thy profit will be as great as mine. I am, as ever, thine to serve thee,

RICHARD SAUNDERS
1758

Rules for Reducing a Great Empire to a Small One

While serving as agent for several American colonies in London, Franklin wrote this ironic hoax, intended to convince the King and the Ministry of the folly of their attitude toward their American possessions. Its catalogue of grievances, actually a review from the American point of view of British colonial policy from 1768 to 1772, should be compared with that included three years later in the Declaration of Independence. Text: Bigelow edition of *Complete Works* (New York, 1904).

An ancient sage valued himself upon this, that, though he could not fiddle he knew how to make a great city of a little one. The science that I, a modern simpleton, am about to communicate, is the very reverse.

I address myself to all ministers who have the management of extensive dominions, which from their very greatness have become troublesome to govern, because the multiplicity of their affairs leaves no time for fiddling.

1. In the first place, gentlemen, you are to consider that a great empire, like a great cake, is most easily diminished at the edges. Turn your attention, therefore, first to your *remotest* provinces; that, as you get rid of them, the next may follow in order.

2. That the possibility of this separation may always exist, take special care the provinces are *never incorporated with the mother country;* that they do not enjoy the same common rights, the same privileges in commerce; and that they are governed by severer laws, all of your enacting, without allowing them any share in the choice of the legislators. By carefully making and preserving such distinctions, you will (to keep to my simile of the cake) act like a wise gingerbread-baker, who, to facilitate a division, cuts his dough half through in those places where, when baked, he would have it broken to pieces.

3. Those remote provinces have perhaps been acquired, purchased, or conquered, at the sole expense of the settlers, or their ancestors; without the aid of the mother country. If this should happen to increase her strength, by their growing numbers ready to join in her wars; her commerce, by their growing demand for her manufactures; or her naval power, by greater employment for her ships and seamen, they may probably suppose some merit in this, and that it entitles them to some favor; you are therefore to *forget it all, or resent it all*, as if they had done you injury. If they happen to be zealous Whigs, friends of liberty, nurtured in revolution principles, remember all that to their prejudice, and contrive to punish it; for such principles, after a revolution is thoroughly established, are of no more use; they are even odious and abominable.

4. However peaceably your colonies have submitted to your government, shown their affection to your interests, and patiently borne their grievances, you are to suppose them *always inclined to revolt*, and treat them accordingly. Quarter troops among them, who by their insolence may provoke the rising of mobs, and by their bullets and bayonets suppress them. By this means, like the husband who uses his

wife ill from suspicion, you may in time convert your suspicions into realities.

5. Remote provinces must have governors and judges to represent the royal person and execute everywhere the delegated parts of his office and authority. You ministers know that much of the strength of government depends on the opinion of the people, and much of that opinion on the *choice of rulers* placed immediately over them. If you send them wise and good men for governors, who study the interests of the colonists, and advance their prosperity, they will think their king wise and good, and that he wishes the welfare of his subjects. If you send them learned and upright men for judges, they will think him a lover of justice. This may attach your provinces more to his government. You are therefore to be careful whom you recommend to those offices. If you can find prodigals who have ruined their fortunes, broken gamesters or stockjobbers, these may do well as governors; for they will probably be rapacious, and provoke the people by their extortions. Wrangling proctors and pettifogging lawyers, too, are not amiss; for they will be forever disputing and quarrelling with their little Parliaments. If withal they should be ignorant, wrong-headed, and insolent, so much the better. Attorney's clerks and Newgate solicitors[1] will do for chief-justices, especially if they hold their places during your pleasure; and all will contribute to impress those ideas of your government that are proper for a people you would wish to renounce it.

6. To confirm these impressions and strike them deeper, whenever the injured come to the capital with complaints of maladministration, oppression, or injustice, *punish such suitors* with long delay, enormous expense, and a final judgment in favor of the oppressor. This will have an admirable effect every way. The trouble of future complaints will be prevented, and governors and judges will be encouraged to further acts of oppression and injustice; and thence the people may become more disaffected, and at length desperate.

7. When such governors have crammed their coffers and made themselves so odious to the people that they can no longer remain among them with safety to their persons, *recall and reward* them with pensions. You may make them baronets too, if that respectable order should not think fit to resent it. All will contribute to encourage new governors in the same practice, and make the supreme government detestable.

8. If when you are engaged in war, your colonies should vie in liberal aids of men and money against the common enemy, upon your simple requisition, and give far beyond their abilities, reflect that a penny taken from them by your power is more honorable to you than a pound presented by their benevolence; *despise therefore their voluntary grants,* and resolve to harass them with *novel taxes.* They will probably complain to your Parliament, that they are taxed by a body in which they have no representative and that this is contrary to common right. They will petition for redress. Let the Parliament flout their claims, reject their petitions, refuse even to suffer the reading of them, and treat the petitioners with the utmost contempt. Nothing can have a better effect in producing the alienation proposed; for, though many can forgive injuries, none ever forgave contempt.

9. In laying these taxes, *never regard the heavy burdens* those remote people already undergo, in defending their own frontiers, supporting their own provincial government, making new roads, building bridges, churches, and other public edifices; which in old countries have been done to your hands by your ancestors, but which occasion constant calls and demands on the purses of a new people. Forget the restraint you lay on their trade for your own benefit, and the advantage a monoply of this trade gives your exacting merchants. Think nothing of the wealth those merchants and your manufacturers acquire by the colony commerce; their increased ability thereby to pay taxes at home; their accumulating, in the price of their commodities, most of those taxes, and so levying them from their consuming customers; all this, and the employment and support of thousands of your poor by the colonists, you are entirely to forget. But remember to make your arbitrary tax more grievous to your provinces, by public declarations importing that your power of taxing them has *no limits;* so that, when you take from them without their consent a shilling in the pound, you have a clear right to the other nineteen. This will probably weaken every idea of security in their property, and convince them that under such a government they have nothing they can call their own; which can scarce fail of producing the happiest consequences!

10. Possibly, indeed, some of them might still comfort themselves, and say; "Though we have no property, we have yet something left that is valuable; we have constitutional *liberty, both of person and of conscience.* This King, these Lords, and these Commons, who it seems are too remote from us to know us, and feel for us, cannot take from us our Habeas Corpus right, or our right of trial by a jury of our neighbors; they cannot deprive us of the exercise of our religion, alter our ecclesiastical constitution, and compel us to be Papists, if they please, or Mahometans." To annihilate this comfort, begin by laws to perplex their commerce with infinite regulations, impossible to be remembered and ob-

[1] That is, inexpert and scheming lawyers.

served; ordain seizures of their property for every failure; take away the trial of such property by jury, and give it to arbitrary judges of your own appointing, and of the lowest characters in the country, whose salaries and emoluments are to arise out of the duties or condemnations, and whose appointments are during pleasure. Then let there be a formal declaration of both houses, that opposition to your edicts is treason, and that persons suspected of treason in the provinces may, according to some obsolete law, be seized and sent to the metropolis of the empire for trial; and pass an act, that those there charged with certain other offences shall be sent away in chains from their friends and country to be tried in the same manner for felony. Then erect a new court of Inquisition among them, accompanied by an armed force, with instructions to transport all such suspected persons; to be ruined by the expense, if they bring over evidences to prove their innocence, or be found guilty and hanged if they cannot afford it. And, lest the people should think you cannot possibly go any further, pass another solemn declaratory act, "that King, Lords, Commons had, have, and of right ought to have, full power and authority to make statutes of sufficient force and validity to bind the unrepresented provinces *in all cases whatsoever.*"[2] This will include spiritual with temporal, and, taken together, must operate wonderfully to your purpose; by convincing them that they are at present under a power something like that spoken of in the Scriptures, which can not only kill their bodies, but damn their souls to all eternity, by compelling them, if it pleases, to worship the Devil.

11. To make your taxes more odious, and more likely to procure resistance, send from the capital a *board of officers* to superintend the collection, *composed of the most indiscreet,* ill-bred, and insolent you can find. Let these have large salaries out of the extorted revenue, and live in open, grating luxury upon the sweat and blood of the industrious; whom they are to worry continually with groundless and expensive prosecutions before the above-mentioned arbitrary revenue judges; all at the cost of the party prosecuted, though acquitted, because the king is to pay no costs. Let these men, by your order, be exempted from all the common taxes and burdens of the province, though they and their property are protected by its laws. If any revenue officers are suspected of the least tenderness for the people, discard them. If others are justly complained of, protect and reward them. If any of the under officers behave so as to provoke the people to drub them, promote those to better offices; this will encourage others to procure for themselves such profitable drubbings, by multiplying and enlarging such provocations, and all will work towards the end you aim at.

12. Another way to make your tax odious, is to *misapply the produce of it.* If it was originally appropriated for the defence of the provinces, and the better support of government, and the administration of justice, where it may be necessary, then apply none of it to that defence; but bestow it where it is not necessary, in augmenting salaries or pensions to every governor who has distinguished himself by his enmity to the people, and by calumniating them to their sovereign. This will make them pay it more unwillingly, and be more apt to quarrel with those that collect it and those that imposed it; who will quarrel again with them; and all shall contribute to your own purpose, of making them weary of your government.

13. If the people of any province have been accustomed *to support their own governors and judges* to satisfaction, you are to apprehend that such governors and judges may be thereby influenced to treat the people kindly and to do them justice. This is another reason for applying part of that revenue in larger salaries to such governors and judges, given, as their commissions are, during *your* pleasure only; forbidding them to take any salaries from their provinces; that thus the people may no longer hope any kindness from their governors, or (in crown cases)[3] any justice from their judges. And, as the money thus misapplied in one province is extorted from all, probably all will resent the misapplication.

14. If the Parliaments of your provinces should dare to claim rights, or complain of your administration, order them to be harassed with *repeated dissolutions.* If the same men are continually returned by new elections, adjourn their meetings to some country village, where they cannot be accommodated and there keep them during pleasure; for this, you know, is your prerogative; and an excellent one it is, as you may manage it to promote discontents among the people, diminish their respect, and increase their disaffection.

15. Convert the brave, honest officers of your *navy* into pimping tide-waiters and colony officers of the *customs.* Let those who in time of war fought gallantly in defence of the commerce of their countrymen, in peace be taught to prey upon it. Let them learn to be corrupted by great and real smugglers; but (to show their diligence) scour with armed boats every bay, harbor, river, creek, cove, or nook throughout the coast of your colonies; stop and detain every coaster, every wood-boat, every fisherman; tumble their cargoes and even their ballast

[2] The Declaratory Act, passed by Parliament on the same day it repealed the Stamp Act, March 18, 1766, reaffirmed its power over the colonies in no uncertain terms.

[3] Cases in equity, formerly appealed directly to the King.

inside out and upside down; and, if a pennyworth of pins is found unentered, let the whole be seized and confiscated. Thus shall the trade of your colonists suffer more from their friends in time of peace, than it did from their enemies in war. Then let these boats' crews land upon every farm in their way, rob their orchards, steal their pigs and poultry, and insult the inhabitants. If the injured and exasperated farmers, unable to procure other justice, should attack the aggressors, drub them, and burn their boats; you are to call this *high treason and rebellion*, order fleets and armies into their country, and threaten to carry all the offenders three thousand miles to be hanged, drawn and quartered. Oh, this will work admirably!

16. If you are told of *discontents* in your colonies, never believe that they are general, or that you have given occasion for them; therefore do not think of applying any remedy, or of changing any offensive measure. Redress no grievance, lest they should be encouraged to demand the redress of some other grievance. Grant no request that is just and reasonable, lest they should make another that is unreasonable. Take all your informations of the state of the colonies from your governors and officers in enmity with them. Encourage and reward these leasing-makers; secrete their lying accusations, lest they should be confuted; but act upon them as the clearest evidence; and believe nothing you hear from the friends of the people. Suppose all *their* complaints to be invented and promoted by a few factious demagogues, whom if you could catch and hang, all would be quiet. Catch and hang a few of them accordingly; and the blood of the martyrs shall work miracles in favor of your purpose.

17. If you see *rival nations* rejoicing at the prospect of your disunion with your provinces, and endeavoring to promote it; if they translate, publish, and applaud all the complaints of your discontented colonists, at the same time privately stimulating you to severer measures, let not that offend you. Why should it, since you all mean the same thing?

18. If any colony should *at their own charge erect a fortress* to secure their *port* against the fleets of a foreign enemy, get your governor to betray that fortress into your hands.[4] Never think of paying what it costs the country, for that would look at least like some regard for justice; but turn it into a citadel to awe the inhabitants and curb their commerce. If they should have lodged in such fortress the very arms they bought and used to aid you in your conquests, seize them all; it will provoke, like ingratitude added to robbery. One admirable effect of these operations will be to discourage every other colony from erecting such defences, and so their and your enemies may more easily invade them, to the great disgrace of your government, and, of course, the furtherance of your project.

19. Send armies into their country under pretence of protecting the inhabitants; but, instead of garrisoning the forts on their frontiers with those troops to prevent incursions, demolish those forts and order the troops into the heart of the country, that the savages may be encouraged to attack the frontiers, and that the troops may be protected by the inhabitants. This will seem to proceed from your *ill-will or your ignorance*, and contribute further to produce and strengthen an opinion among them that you are no longer fit to govern them.

20. Lastly, invest the *general of your army in the provinces* with great and unconstitutional powers, and free him from the control of even your own civil governors. Let him have troops enough under his command, with all the fortresses in his possession; and who knows but (like some provincial generals in the Roman empire, and encouraged by the universal discontent you have produced) he may take it into his head to set up for himself? If he should, and you have carefully practised the few excellent rules of mine, take my word for it, all the provinces will immediately join him; and you will that day (if you have not done it sooner) get rid of the trouble of governing them, and all the plagues attending their commerce and connection from thenceforth and forever.

Q.E.D.[5]

1773

[4]A reference to Castle William in Boston Harbor, given over to the British forces by Governor Hutchinson in 1770.

[5]"Quod Erat Demonstrandum" ("Which was to be demonstrated"), usually placed at the end of a geometry problem.

The Ephemera

An Emblem of Human Life

During his residence at Passy, near Paris, Franklin amused himself by writing and printing (on his own press) an occasional "bagatelle," a light personal essay, for circulation among his friends. The person addressed is Madame Brillon de Jouy, one of his Passy neighbors and a favorite chess partner. Text: Bigelow edition of *Complete Works* (New York, 1904).

TO MADAME BRILLON, OF PASSY

You may remember, my dear friend, that when we lately spent that happy day in the delightful garden and sweet society of the Moulin Joly,[1] I stopped a little in one of our walks, and stayed some

[1]An island in the Seine, Madame Brillon's home.

time behind the company. We had been shown numberless skeletons of a kind of little fly, called an ephemera, whose successive generations, we were told, were bred and expired within the day. I happened to see a living company of them on a leaf, who appeared to be engaged in conversation. You know I understand all the inferior animal tongues. My too great application to the study of them is the best excuse I can give for the little progress I have made in your charming language. I listened through curiosity to the discourse of these little creatures; but as they, in their national vivacity, spoke three or four together, I could make but little of their conversation. I found, however, by some broken expressions that I heard now and then, they were disputing warmly on the merit of two foreign musicians, one a *cousin*, the other a *moscheto*;[2] in which dispute they spent their time, seemingly as regardless of the shortness of life as if they had been sure of living a month. Happy people! thought I; you are certainly under a wise, just, and mild government, since you have no public grievances to complain of, nor any subject of contention but the perfections and imperfections of foreign music. I turned my head from them to an old gray-headed one, who was single on another leaf, and talking to himself. Being amused with his soliloquy, I put it down in writing, in hopes it will likewise amuse her to whom I am so much indebted for the most pleasing of all amusements, her delicious company and heavenly harmony.

"It was," said he, "the opinion of learned philosophers of our race, who lived and flourished long before my time, that this vast world, the Moulin Joly, could not itself subsist more than eighteen hours; and I think there was some foundation for that opinion, since, by the apparent motion of the great luminary that gives life to all nature, and which in my time has evidently declined considerably towards the ocean at the end of our earth, it must then finish its course, be extinguished in the waters that surround us, and leave the world in cold and darkness, necessarily producing universal death and destruction. I have lived seven of those hours, a great age, being no less than four hundred and twenty minutes of time. How very few of us continue so long! I have seen generations born, flourish, and expire. My present friends are the children and grandchildren of the friends of my youth, who are now, alas, no more! And I must soon follow them; for, by the course of nature, though still in health, I cannot expect to live above seven or eight minutes longer. What now avails all my toil and labor in amassing honey-dew on this leaf, which I cannot live to enjoy! What the political struggles I have been engaged in for the good of my compatriot inhabitants of this bush, or my philosophical studies for the benefit of our race in general! for in politics what can laws do without morals? Our present race of ephemerae will in a course of minutes become corrupt, like those of other and older bushes, and consequently as wretched. And in philosophy how small our progress! Alas! art is long, and life is short! My friends would comfort me with the idea of a name they say I shall leave behind me; and they tell me I have lived long enough to nature and to glory. But what will fame be to an ephemera who no longer exists? And what will become of all history in the eighteenth hour, when the world itself, even the whole Moulin Joly, shall come to its end and be buried in universal ruin?"

To me, after all my eager pursuits, no solid pleasures now remain, but the reflection of a long life spent in meaning well, the sensible conversation of a few good lady ephemerae, and now and then a kind smile and a tune from the ever amiable *Brillante*.[3]

B. Franklin.

1778

[2] One a gnat, the other a mosquito. At the time, Paris was divided over the respective merits of Gluck, a German musician, and Piccini, an Italian.

[3] A pun on "Brillon."

Letters

To Samuel Mather

Samuel Mather, son of Cotton Mather, was himself a noted theologian. Text: Bigelow edition of *Complete Works*.

Passy, 12 May, 1784.

Reverend Sir:—I received your kind letter, with your excellent advice to the people of the United States, which I read with great pleasure, and hope it will be duly regarded. Such writings, though they may be lightly passed over by many readers, yet, if they make a deep impression on one active mind in a hundred, the effects may be considerable. Permit me to mention one little instance, which, though it relates to myself, will not be quite uninteresting to you. When I was a boy, I met with a book entitled *Essays to do Good*, which I think was written by your father. It had been so little regarded by a former possessor, that several leaves of it were torn out; but the remainder gave me such a turn of thinking, as to have an influence on my conduct through life; for I have always set a greater value on the character of a *doer of good*, than on any other kind of reputation; and if I have been, as you seem to think, a useful citizen, the public owes the advantage of it to that book.

You mention your being in your seventy-eighth year; I am in my seventy-ninth; we are grown old together. It is now more than sixty years since I left Boston, but I remember well both your father and grandfather, having heard them both in the pulpit, and seen them in their houses. The last time I saw your father was in the beginning of 1724, when I visited him after my first trip to Pennsylvania. He received me in his library, and on my taking leave showed me a shorter way out of the house, through a narrow passage, which was crossed by a beam overhead. We were all talking as I withdrew, he accompanying me behind, and I turning partly towards him, when he said hastily, *"Stoop, stoop!"* I did not understand him till I felt my head hit against the beam. He was a man that never missed any occasion of giving instruction, and upon this he said to me: *"You are young, and have the world before you;* STOOP *as you go through it, and you will miss many hard thumps."* This advice, thus beat into my head, has frequently been of use to me, and I often think of it when I see pride mortified and misfortunes brought upon people by their carrying their heads too high.

I long much to see my native place, and to lay my bones there. I left it in 1723; I visited it in 1733, 1743, 1753, and 1763. In 1773 I was in England; in 1775 I had a sight of it, but could not enter, it being in possession of the enemy. I did hope to have been there in 1783, but could not obtain my dismission from this employment here, and now I fear I shall never have that happiness. My best wishes, however, attend my dear country. *Esto perpetua.*[1] It is now blest with an excellent constitution; may it last for ever!

This powerful monarchy continues its friendship for the United States. It is a friendship of the utmost importance to our security, and should be carefully cultivated. Britain has not yet well digested the loss of its dominion over us, and has still at times some flattering hopes of recovering it. Accidents may increase those hopes and encourage dangerous attempts. A breach between us and France would infallibly bring the English again upon our backs; and yet we have some wild heads among our countrymen who are endeavoring to weaken that connection! Let us preserve our reputation by performing our engagements, our credit by fulfilling our contracts, and friends by gratitude and kindness; for we know not how soon we may again have occasion for all of them. With great and sincere esteem, I have the honor to be, etc.,

B. FRANKLIN.

To Samuel Mather. [1]"May she endure forever."

To Ezra Stiles

The Rev. Ezra Stiles, President of Yale, wrote Franklin in January 1790, "I wish to know the opinion of my venerable friend concerning Jesus of Nazareth." Text: Albert H. Smyth, ed., *The Works of Benjamin Franklin* (New York, 1905–7).

Philadelphia, March 9, 1790.

REVEREND AND DEAR SIR:—I received your kind Letter of Jan'y 28, and am glad you have at length received the portrait of Gov'r Yale from his Family, and deposited it in the College Library. He was a great and good Man, and had the Merit of doing infinite Service to your Country by his Munificence to that Institution. The Honour you propose doing me by placing mine in the same Room with his, is much too great for my Deserts; but you always had a Partiality for me, and to that it must be ascribed. I am however too much obliged to Yale College, the first learned Society that took Notice of me and adorned me with its Honours,[1] to refuse a Request that comes from it thro' so esteemed a Friend. But I do not think any one of the Portraits you mention, as in my Possession, worthy of the Place and Company you propose to place it in. You have an excellent Artist lately arrived. If he will undertake to make one for you, I shall cheerfully pay the Expence; but he must not delay setting about it, or I may slip thro' his fingers, for I am now in my eighty-fifth year, and very infirm.

I send with this a very learned Work, as it seems to me, on the antient Samaritan Coins, lately printed in Spain, and at least curious for the Beauty of the Impression. Please to accept it for your College Library. I have subscribed for the Encyclopaedia now printing here, with the Intention of presenting it to the College. I shall probably depart before the Work is finished, but shall leave Directions for its Continuance to the End. With this you will receive some of the first numbers.

You desire to know something of my Religion. It is the first time I have been questioned upon it. But I cannot take your Curiosity amiss, and shall endeavour in a few Words to gratify it. Here is my Creed. I believe in one God, Creator of the Universe. That he governs it by his Providence. That he ought to be worshipped. That the most acceptable Service we render to him is doing good to his other Children. That the soul of Man is immortal, and will be treated with Justice in another Life respecting its Conduct in this. These I take to be the fundamental Principles of all sound Religion, and I regard them as you do in whatever Sect I meet with them.

To Stiles. [1]Yale awarded Franklin an honorary Master of Arts degree in 1753.

As to Jesus of Nazareth, my Opinion of whom you particularly desire, I think the System of Morals and his Religion, as he left them to us, the best the World ever saw or is likely to see; but I apprehend it has received various corrupting Changes, and I have, with most of the present Dissenters in England, some Doubts as to his Divinity; tho' it is a question I do not dogmatize upon, having never studied it, and think it needless to busy myself with it now, when I expect soon an Opportunity of knowing the Truth with less Trouble. I see no harm, however, in its being believed, if that Belief has the good Consequence, as probably it has, of making his Doctrines more respected and better observed; especially as I do not perceive, that the Supreme takes it amiss, by distinguishing the Unbelievers in his Government of the World with any peculiar Marks of his Displeasure.

I shall only add, respecting myself, that, having experienced the Goodness of that Being in conducting me prosperously thro' a long life, I have no doubt of its Continuance in the next, though without the smallest Conceit of meriting such Goodness. My Sentiments on this Head you will see in the Copy of an old Letter enclosed, which I wrote in answer to one from a zealous Religionist, whom I had relieved in a paralytic case by electricity, and who, being afraid I should grow proud upon it, sent me his serious though rather impertinent Caution. I send you also the Copy of another Letter, which will shew something of my Disposition relating to Religion. With great and sincere Esteem and Affection, I am, Your obliged old Friend and most obedient humble Servant

B. Franklin.

THOMAS PAINE [1737-1809]

Franklin once said, "Where liberty is, there is my country." Thomas Paine's reply was typical: "Where liberty is not, there is mine." He was born in England, and after failing as a corset-maker, schoolteacher, sailor, and excise officer, he came to America at the age of thirty-seven in 1774 bearing some circumspect letters of recommendation from Franklin. He had already developed a passion for liberty, a clear and forceful pamphlet style, and an excellent command of persuasive techniques. The controversy between colonies and Crown over rights and liberties was exactly fitted to Paine's interests and talents. He plunged into the argument, and in January 1776 published *Common Sense*, which had much to do with crystallizing public support for independence, to Paine "the cause of God and humanity."

Paine served with the Continental Army on General Greene's staff, and at intervals from 1776 to 1783 brought out thirteen pamphlets called "The Crisis," in which he commented on the course of the war and exhorted the populace to greater efforts. After the war, acclaimed by Congress and the people for his services to the nation, he turned his attention to Europe, where other revolutions seemed in the making. He witnessed the early events of the French Revolution, and did his best to assist the beginnings of something similar in England. He was a member of the French Revolutionary Convention, participated in its deliberations, and finally in 1774 he was imprisoned and narrowly escaped the guillotine because he opposed the execution of the king. His American citizenship and the intervention of James Monroe, the American ambassador, saved him, but meanwhile he had published *The Rights of Man* (1791, 1792), had been charged with libel and treason in England, and hanged in effigy by a London mob.

After his release from prison, Paine remained in Paris, in poor health and on the edge of poverty. He continued to write, publishing his strongly deistic *Age of Reason* (1794-96), his political tract *Dissertation on First-Principles of Government* (1795), and his ideas on tax and land reform, *Agrarian Justice* (1797). However, *The Age of Reason* and his bitter attack on the President in his *Letter to Washington* (1796) aroused powerful antagonisms in the United States, and when Paine returned to America in 1802 he found himself discredited and vilified as a drunkard, atheist, and dangerous radical. He lived in obscurity at New Rochelle, New York, stripped of his right to vote and subject to constant abuse and harassment, until he died in 1809. Even in death he remained controversial—the Quakers refused to admit his body to their burial ground, and his bones were finally sent to England, sold at auction as a curiosity, and lost.

Paine, a tactless and often intemperate man of strong feelings, aroused equally strong feelings in others; some of his ideas are still distasteful to large groups of people. He was neither a learned man nor an original thinker, and many of his ideas he borrowed from his contemporaries. But he was one of the most gifted and effective political propagandists who ever lived, and no one did more by his pen for revolutionary America. He was absolutely unafraid, willing to stand up for his principles, and no man fought harder—in three countries—for the freedom he believed in.

Further reading: Moncure D. Conway, *The Life of Thomas Paine*, 2 vols., 1892 (the standard older biography). A. O. Aldridge, *Man of Reason: The Life of Thomas Paine*, 1959. The entry on Paine by Crane Brinton in *The Dictionary of American Biography*.

The American Crisis

(December 19, 1776)

Written in camp (as legend has it, on a drumhead by the light of a campfire) while Washington's army, after a series of defeats, retreated across New Jersey. Washington, who had written his brother, "I think the game is pretty nearly up," ordered the paper read aloud to every regiment of the army, and six days later won a decisive victory at the Battle of Trenton. The famous trumpet call of the opening paragraph is Paine at his brilliant best; seven years later, in the fifteenth issue of the *Crisis* series, he could write exultantly, "The times that tried men's souls are over—and the greatest and completest revolution the world ever knew, gloriously and happily accomplished." The sixteenth and final number of *The Crisis* was published December 9, 1783. Text: Van der Weyde edition of *The Life and Works.*

I

These are the times that try men's souls. The summer soldier and the sunshine patriot will, in this crisis, shrink from the service of their country; but he that stands it *now*, deserves the love and thanks of man and woman. Tyranny, like hell, is not easily conquered; yet we have this consolation with us, that the harder the conflict, the more glorious the triumph. What we obtain too cheap, we esteem too lightly: it is dearness only that gives every thing its value. Heaven knows how to put a proper price upon its goods; and it would be strange indeed if so celestial an article as FREEDOM should not be highly rated. Britain, with an army to enforce her tyranny, has declared that she has a right *(not only to* TAX) but "to BIND *us in* ALL CASES WHATSOEVER," and if being *bound in that manner*, is not slavery, then is there not such a thing as slavery upon earth. Even the expression is impious; for so unlimited a power can belong only to God.

Whether the independence of the continent was declared too soon, or delayed too long, I will not now enter into as an argument; my own simple opinion is, that had it been eight months earlier, it would have been much better. We did not make a proper use of last winter, neither could we, while we were in a dependent state. However, the fault, if it were one, was all our own;[1] we have none to blame but ourselves. But no great deal is lost yet. All that Howe has been doing for this month past, is rather a ravage than a conquest, which the spirit of the Jerseys, a year ago, would have quickly repulsed, and which time and a little resolution will soon recover.

I have as little superstition in me as any man living, but my secret opinion has ever been, and still is, that God Almighty will not give up a people to military destruction, or leave them unsupportedly to perish, who have so earnestly and so repeatedly sought to avoid the calamities of war, by every decent method which wisdom could invent. Neither have I so much of the infidel in me, as to suppose that He has relinquished the government of the world, and given us up to the care of devils; and as I do not, I cannot see on what grounds the king of Britain can look up to heaven for help against us: a

[1] The present winter is worth an age, if rightly employed; but, if lost or neglected, the whole continent will partake of the evil; and there is no punishment that man does not deserve, be he who, or what, or where he will, that may be the means of sacrificing a season so precious and useful. [Paine's note, a citation from his "Common Sense."]

common murderer, a highwayman, or a house-breaker, has as good a pretence as he.

'Tis surprising to see how rapidly a panic will sometimes run through a country. All nations and ages have been subject to them. Britain has trembled like an ague at the report of a French fleet of flat-bottomed boats; and in the fourteenth century the whole English army, after ravaging the kingdom of France, was driven back like men petrified with fear; and this brave exploit was performed by a few broken forces collected and headed by a woman, Joan of Arc. Would that heaven might inspire some Jersey maid to spirit up her countrymen, and save her fair fellow sufferers from ravage and ravishment! Yet panics, in some cases, have their uses; they produce as much good as hurt. Their duration is always short; the mind soon grows through them, and acquires a firmer habit than before. But their peculiar advantage is, that they are the touchstones of sincerity and hypocrisy, and bring things and men to light, which might otherwise have lain forever undiscovered. In fact, they have the same effect on secret traitors, which an imaginary apparition would have upon a private murderer. They sift out the hidden thoughts of man, and hold them up in public to the world. Many a disguised Tory has lately shown his head, that shall penitentially solemnize with curses the day on which Howe arrived upon the Delaware.

As I was with the troops at Fort Lee, and marched with them to the edge of Pennsylvania, I am well acquainted with many circumstances, which those who live at a distance know but little or nothing of.[2] Our situation there was exceedingly cramped, the place being a narrow neck of land between the North River and the Hackensack. Our force was inconsiderable, being not one-fourth so great as Howe could bring against us. We had no army at hand to have relieved the garrison, had we shut ourselves up and stood on our defence. Our ammunition, light artillery, and the best part of our stores, had been removed, on the apprehension that Howe[3] would endeavor to penetrate the Jerseys, in which case Fort Lee could be of no use to us; for it must occur to every thinking man, whether in the army or not, that these kind of field forts are only for temporary purposes, and last in use no longer than the enemy directs his force against the particular object which such forts are raised to defend. Such was our situation and condition at Fort Lee on the morning of the 20th of November, when an officer arrived with information that the enemy with 200 boats had landed about seven miles above; Major General Green, who commanded the garrison, immediately ordered them under arms, and sent express to General Washington at the town of Hackensack, distant by the way of the ferry = six miles. Our first object was to secure the bridge over the Hackensack, which laid up the river between the enemy and us, about six miles from us, and three from them. General Washington arrived in about three-quarters of an hour, and marched at the head of the troops towards the bridge, which place I expected we should have a brush for; however, they did not choose to dispute it with us, and the greatest part of our troops went over the bridge, the rest over the ferry, except some which passed at a mill on a small creek, between the bridge and the ferry, and made their way through some marshy grounds up to the town of Hackensack, and there passed the river. We brought off as much baggage as the wagons could contain, the rest was lost. The simple object was to bring off the garrison, and march them on till they could be strengthened by the Jersey or Pennsylvania militia, so as to be enabled to make a stand. We staid four days at Newark, collected our out-posts with some of the Jersey militia, and marched out twice to meet the enemy, on being informed that they were advancing, though our numbers were greatly inferior to theirs. Howe, in my little opinion, committed a great error in generalship in not throwing a body of forces off from Staten Island through Amboy, by which means he might have seized all our stores at Brunswick, and intercepted our march into Pennsylvania; but if we believe the power of hell to be limited, we must likewise believe that their agents are under some providential control.

I shall not now attempt to give all the particulars of our retreat to the Delaware; suffice it for the present to say, that both officers and men, though greatly harassed and fatigued, frequently without rest, covering, or provision, the inevitable consequences of a long retreat, bore it with a manly and martial spirit. All their wishes centred in one, which was, that the country would turn out and help them to drive the enemy back. Voltaire has remarked that King William never appeared to full advantage but in difficulties and in action; the same remark may be made on General Washington, for the character fits him. There is a natural firmness in some minds which cannot be unlocked by trifles, but which, when unlocked, discovers a cabinet of fortitude; and I reckon it among those kind of public blessings, which we do not immediately see, that God hath

[2] The British General Cornwallis surprised General Nathanael Greene's troops at Fort Lee, New Jersey, on November 20, 1776, and forced the Americans to retreat.

[3] General William Howe, in command of the British forces in the colonies.

blessed him with uninterrupted health, and given him a mind that can even flourish upon care.

I shall conclude this paper with some miscellaneous remarks on the state of our affairs; and shall begin with asking the following question, Why is it that the enemy have left the New England provinces, and made these middle ones the seat of war? The answer is easy: New England is not infested with Tories, and we are. I have been tender in raising the cry against these men, and used numberless arguments to show them their danger, but it will not do to sacrifice a world either to their folly or their baseness. The period is now arrived, in which either they or we must change our sentiments, or one or both must fall. And what is a Tory? Good God! what is he? I should not be afraid to go with a hundred Whigs against a thousand Tories, were they to attempt to get into arms. Every Tory is a coward; for servile, slavish, self-interested fear is the foundation of Toryism; and a man under such influence, though he may be cruel, never can be brave.

But, before the line of irrecoverable separation be drawn between us, let us reason the matter together: Your conduct is an invitation to the enemy, yet not one in a thousand of you has heart enough to join him. Howe is as much deceived by you as the American cause is injured by you. He expects you will all take up arms, and flock to his standard, with muskets on your shoulders. Your opinions are of no use to him, unless you support him personally, for 'tis soldiers, and not Tories, that he wants.

I once felt all that kind of anger, which a man ought to feel, against the mean principles that are held by the Tories: a noted one, who kept a tavern at Amboy,[4] was standing at his door, with as pretty a child in his hand, about eight or nine years old, as I ever saw, and after speaking his mind as freely as he thought was prudent, finished with this unfatherly expression, *"Well! give me peace in my day."* Not a man lives on the continent but fully believes that a separation must some time or other finally take place, and a generous parent should have said, *"If there must be trouble, let it be in my day, that my child may have peace;"* and this single reflection, well applied, is sufficient to awaken every man to duty. Not a place upon earth might be so happy as America. Her situation is remote from all the wrangling world, and she has nothing to do but to trade with them. A man can distinguish himself between temper and principle, and I am as confident, as I am that God governs the world, that America will never be happy till she gets clear of foreign dominion. Wars, without ceasing, will break out till that period arrives, and the continent must in the end be conqueror; for though the flame of liberty may sometimes cease to shine, the coal can never expire.

America did not, nor does not want force; but she wanted a proper application of that force. Wisdom is not the purchase of a day, and it is no wonder that we should err at the first setting off. From an excess of tenderness, we were unwilling to raise an army, and trusted our cause to the temporary defence of a well-meaning militia. A summer's experience has now taught us better; yet with those troops, while they were collected, we were able to set bounds to the progress of the enemy, and, thank God! they are again assembling. I always considered militia as the best troops in the world for a sudden exertion, but they will not do for a long campaign. Howe, it is probable, will make an attempt on this city;[5] should he fail on this side the Delaware, he is ruined. If he succeeds, our cause is not ruined. He stakes all on his side against a part on ours; admitting he succeeds, the consequence will be, that armies from both ends of the continent will march to assist their suffering friends in the middle states; for he cannot go everywhere, it is impossible. I consider Howe as the greatest enemy the Tories have; he is bringing a war into their country, which, had it not been for him and partly for themselves, they had been clear of. Should he now be expelled, I wish with all the devotion of a Christian, that the names of Whig and Tory may never more be mentioned; but should the Tories give him encouragement to come, or assistance if he come, I as sincerely wish that our next year's arms may expel them from the continent, and the Congress appropriate their possessions to the relief of those who have suffered in well-doing. A single successful battle next year will settle the whole. America could carry on a two years' war by the confiscation of the property of disaffected persons, and be made happy by their expulsion. Say not that this is revenge, call it rather the soft resentment of a suffering people, who, having no object in view but the *good* of *all*, have staked their *own all* upon a seemingly doubtful event. Yet it is folly to argue against determined hardness; eloquence may strike the ear, and the language of sorrow draw forth the tear of compassion, but nothing can reach the heart that is steeled with prejudice.

Quitting this class of men, I turn with the warm ardor of a friend to those who have nobly stood, and are yet determined to stand the matter out: I call not upon a few, but upon all: not on *this* state or *that* state, but on *every* state: up and help us; lay your shoulders to the wheel; better have too much force than too little, when so great an object is at

[4] Paine enlisted August 1776 in the Pennsylvania divison of the Flying Camp and was stationed at Amboy, now Perth Amboy, New Jersey.

[5] Philadelphia.

stake. Let it be told to the future world, that in the depth of winter, when nothing but hope and virtue could survive, that the city and the country, alarmed at one common danger, came forth to meet and to repulse it. Say not that thousands are gone, turn out your tens of thousands; throw not the burden of the day upon Providence, but *"show your faith by your works,"* that God may bless you. It matters not where you live, or what rank of life you hold, the evil or the blessing will reach you all. The far and the near, the home counties and the back, the rich and the poor, will suffer or rejoice alike. The heart that feels not now is dead; the blood of his children will curse his cowardice, who shrinks back at a time when a little might have saved the whole, and made *them* happy. I love the man that can smile in trouble, that can gather strength from distress, and grow brave by reflection. 'Tis the business of little minds to shrink; but he whose heart is firm, and whose conscience approves his conduct, will pursue his principles unto death. My own line of reasoning is to myself as straight and clear as a ray of light. Not all the treasures of the world, so far as I believe, could have induced me to support an offensive war, for I think it murder; but if a thief breaks into my house, burns and destroys my property, and kills or threatens to kill me, or those that are in it, and to *"bind me in all cases whatsoever"*[6] to his absolute will, am I to suffer it? What signifies it to me, whether he who does it is a king or a common man; my countryman or not my countryman; whether it be done by an individual villain, or an army of them? If we reason to the root of things we shall find no difference; neither can any just cause be assigned why we should punish in the one case and pardon in the other. Let them call me rebel and welcome, I feel no concern from it; but I should suffer the misery of devils, were I to make a whore of my soul by swearing allegiance to one whose character is that of a sottish, stupid, stubborn, worthless, brutish man. I conceive likewise a horrid idea in receiving mercy from a being, who at the last day shall be shrieking to the rocks and mountains to cover him, and fleeing with terror from the orphan, the widow, and the slain of America.

There are cases which cannot be overdone by language, and this is one. There are persons, too, who see not the full extent of the evil which threatens them; they solace themselves with hopes that the enemy, if he succeed, will be merciful. It is the madness of folly, to expect mercy from those who have refused to do justice; and even mercy, where conquest is the object, is only a trick of war; the cunning of the fox is as murderous as the violence of the wolf, and we ought to guard equally against both. Howe's first object is, partly by threats and partly by promises, to terrify or seduce the people to deliver up their arms and receive mercy. The ministry recommended the same plan to Gage, and this is what the tories call making their peace, *"a peace which passeth all understanding" indeed!* A peace which would be the immediate forerunner of a worse ruin than any we have yet thought of. Ye men of Pennsylvania, do reason upon these things! Were the back counties to give up their arms, they would fall an easy prey to the Indians, who are all armed: this perhaps is what some Tories would not be sorry for. Were the home counties to deliver up their arms, they would be exposed to the resentment of the back counties, who would then have it in their power to chastise their defection at pleasure. And were any one state to give up its arms, *that* state must be garrisoned by all Howe's army of Britons and Hessians to preserve it from the anger of the rest. Mutual fear is the principal link in the chain of mutual love, and woe be to that state that breaks the compact. Howe is mercifully inviting you to barbarous destruction, and men must be either rogues or fools that will not see it. I dwell not upon the vapors of imagination; I bring reason to your ears, and, in language as plain as A, B, C, hold up truth to your eyes.

I thank God, that I fear not. I see no real cause for fear. I know our situation well, and can see the way out of it. While our army was collected, Howe dared not risk a battle; and it is no credit to him that he decamped from the White Plains, and waited a mean opportunity to ravage the defenceless Jerseys; but it is great credit to us, that, with a handful of men, we sustained an orderly retreat for near an hundred miles, brought off our ammunition, all our field pieces, the greatest part of our stores, and had four rivers to pass. None can say that our retreat was precipitate, for we were near three weeks in performing it, that the country might have time to come in. Twice we marched back to meet the enemy, and remained out till dark. The sign of fear was not seen in our camp, and had not some of the cowardly and disaffected inhabitants spread false alarms through the country, the Jerseys had never been ravaged. Once more we are again collected and collecting; our new army at both ends of the continent is recruiting fast, and we shall be able to open the next campaign with sixty thousand men, well armed and clothed. This is our situation, and who will may know it. By perseverance and fortitude we have the prospect of a glorious issue; by cowardice and submission, the sad choice of a variety of evils—a ravaged country—a depopulated city—habitations without safety, and slavery without

[6] Paine is quoting the Declaratory Act of 1766 affirming British authority over the colonies.

hope—our homes turned into barracks and bawdy-houses for Hessians, and a future race to provide for, whose fathers we shall doubt of. Look on this picture and weep over it! and if there yet remains one thoughtless wretch who believes it not, let him suffer it unlamented.

COMMON SENSE.

FROM *The Rights of Man*

Part I

The Rights of Man was Paine's reply to Edmund Burke's *Reflections on the French Revolution* (1790) which cast doubts, Paine believed, on the natural right theory of government, the validity of the right of revolution, and the aspirations of free men everywhere. Part I, published in 1791 in London, where Paine was living, was a direct rebuttal of Burke's interpretation of recent events in France; Part II, which appeared in 1792, was a more general and theoretical exposition of Paine's concept of democratic government. After the appearance of Part II Paine, already under surveillance as a dangerously skilful agitator, was indicted for treason and escaped to France barely an hour ahead of a warrant for his arrest. The book was widely read in the United States, where the struggle between Federalist and Republican was beginning in earnest, and became a kind of handbook for both English and French radicals. The text follows that of the Van der Weyde edition of *The Life and Works.*

[Civil and Natural Rights]

I have now to follow Mr. Burke through a pathless wilderness of rhapsodies, and a sort of descant upon governments, in which he asserts whatever he pleases, on the presumption of its being believed, without offering either evidence or reasons for so doing.

Before anything can be reasoned upon to a conclusion, certain facts, principles, or data, to reason from, must be established, admitted, or denied. Mr. Burke, with his usual outrage, abuses the *Declaration of the Rights of Man*, published by the National Assembly of France,[1] as the basis on which the Constitution of France is built. This he calls "paltry and blurred sheets of paper about the rights of man."

Does Mr. Burke mean to deny that *man* has any rights? If he does, then he must mean that there are no such things as rights any where, and that he has none himself; for who is there in the world but man? But if Mr. Burke means to admit that man has rights, the question then will be, what are those rights, and how came man by them originally?

The error of those who reason by precedents drawn from antiquity, respecting the rights of man, is that they do not go far enough into antiquity. They do not go the whole way. They stop in some of the intermediate stages of an hundred or a thousand years, and produce what was then done as a rule for the present day. This is no authority at all.

If we travel still further into antiquity, we shall find a directly contrary opinion and practise prevailing; and, if antiquity is to be authority, a thousand such authorities may be produced, successively contradicting each other; but if we proceed on, we shall at last come out right; we shall come to the time when man came from the hand of his Maker. What was he then? Man. Man was his high and only title, and a higher cannot be given him. But of titles I shall speak hereafter.

We have now arrived at the origin of man, and at the origin of his rights. As to the manner in which the world has been governed from that day to this, it is no further any concern of ours than to make a proper use of the errors or the improvements which the history of it presents. Those who lived a hundred or a thousand years ago, were then moderns as we are now. They had *their* ancients, and those ancients had others, and we also shall be ancients in our turn.

If the mere name of antiquity is to govern in the affairs of life, the people who are to live an hundred or a thousand years hence, may as well take us for a precedent, as we make a precedent of those who lived an hundred or a thousand years ago.

The fact is, that portions of antiquity, by proving every thing, establish nothing. It is authority against authority all the way, till we come to the divine origin of the rights of man, at the Creation. Here our inquiries find a resting-place, and our reason finds a home.

If a dispute about the rights of man had arisen at a distance of an hundred years from the Creation, it is to this source of authority they must have referred, and it is to the same source of authority that we must now refer.

Though I mean not to touch upon any sectarian principle of religion, yet it may be worth observing, that the genealogy of Christ is traced to Adam. Why then not trace the rights of man to the creation of man? I will answer the question. Because there have been upstart governments, thrusting themselves between, and presumptuously working to *unmake* man.

If any generation of men ever possessed the right of dictating the mode by which the world should be governed for ever, it was the first generation that existed; and if that generation did it not, no succeeding generation can show any authority for doing it, nor can set any up.

The illuminating and divine principle of the equal rights of man (for it has its origin from the Maker of

[1] In August 1789.

man), relates not only to the living individuals, but to generations of men succeeding each other. Every generation is equal in rights to the generations which preceded it, by the same rule that every individual is born equal in rights with his contemporary.

Every history of the Creation, and every traditionary account, whether from the lettered or unlettered world, however they may vary in their opinion or belief of certain particulars, all agree in establishing one point, *the unity of man;* by which I mean that men are all of *one degree,* and consequently that all men are born equal, and with equal natural rights, in the same manner as if posterity had been continued by *creation* instead of *generation,* the latter being only the mode by which the former is carried forward; and consequently, every child born into the world must be considered as deriving its existence from God. The world is as new to him as it was to the first man that existed, and his natural right in it is of the same kind.

The Mosaic account of the Creation, whether taken as divine authority or merely historical, is full to this point, *the unity or equality of man.* The expressions admit of no controversy. "And God said, let us make man in our own image. In the image of God created he him; male and female created he them." The distinction of sexes is pointed out, but no other distinction is even implied. If this be not divine authority, it is at least historical authority, and shows that the equality of man, so far from being a modern doctrine, is the oldest upon record.

It is also to be observed, that all the religions known in the world are founded, so far as they relate to man, on the *unity of man,* as being all of one degree. Whether in heaven or in hell, or in whatever state man may be supposed to exist hereafter, the good and the bad are the only distinctions. Nay, even the laws of governments are obliged to slide into this principle, by making degrees to consist in crimes and not in persons.

It is one of the greatest of all truths, and of the highest advantage to cultivate. By considering man in this light, and by instructing him to consider himself in this light, it places him in a close connection with all his duties, whether to his Creator or to the creation, of which he is a part; and it is only when he forgets his origin, or, to use a more fashionable phrase, his *birth and family,* that he becomes dissolute.

It is not among the least of the evils of the present existing governments in all parts of Europe, that man, considered as man, is thrown back to a vast distance from his Maker, and the artificial chasm filled up by a succession of barriers, or a sort of turnpike gates, through which he has to pass.

I will quote Mr. Burke's catalogue of barriers that he has set up between man and his Maker. Putting himself in the character of a herald, he says—"We fear God—we look with *awe* to kings—with affection to parliaments—with duty to magistrates—with reverence to priests, and with respect to nobility." Mr. Burke has forgotten to put in *"chivalry."* He has also forgotten to put in Peter.

The duty of man is not a wilderness of turnpike gates, through which he is to pass by tickets from one to the other. It is plain and simple, and consists but of two points. His duty to God, which every man must feel; and with respect to his neighbor, to do as he would be done by. If those to whom power is delegated do well, they will be respected; if not, they will be despised; and with regard to those to whom no power is delegated, but who assume it, the rational world can know nothing of them.

Hitherto we have spoken only (and that but in part) of the natural rights of man. We have now to consider the civil rights of man, and to show how the one originates from the other. Man did not enter into society to become *worse* than he was before, nor to have fewer rights than he had before, but to have those rights better secured. His natural rights are the foundation of all his civil rights. But in order to pursue this distinction with more precision, it is necessary to make the different qualities of natural and civil rights.

A few words will explain this. Natural rights are those which appertain to man in right of his existence. Of this kind are all the intellectual rights, or rights of the mind, and also all those rights of acting as an individual for his own comfort and happiness, which are not injurious to the natural rights of others. Civil rights are those which appertain to man in right of his being a member of society.

Every civil right has for its foundation some natural right pre-existing in the individual, but to the enjoyment of which his individual power is not, in all cases, sufficiently competent. Of this kind are all those which relate to security and protection.

From this short review, it will be easy to distinguish between that class of natural rights which man retains after entering into society, and those which he throws into the common stock as a member of society.

The natural rights which he retains, are all those in which the *power* to execute is as perfect in the individual as the right itself. Among this class, as is before mentioned, are all the intellectual rights, or rights of the mind: consequently, religion is one of those rights.

The natural rights which are not retained, are all those in which, though the right is perfect in the individual, the power to execute them is defective. They answer not his purpose. A man, by natural right, has a right to judge in his own cause; and so far as the right of the mind is concerned, he never surrenders it: but what availeth it him to judge, if he has not power to redress? He therefore deposits his right in the common stock of society, and takes the arm of society, of which he is a part, in preference and in addition to his own. Society *grants* him nothing. Every man is proprietor in society, and draws on the capital as a matter of right.

From these premises, two or three certain conclusions will follow.

First, That every civil right grows out of a natural right; or, in other words, is a natural right exchanged.

Secondly, That civil power, properly considered as such, is made up of the aggregate of that class of the natural rights of man, which becomes defective in the individual in point of power, and answers not his purpose, but when collected to a focus, becomes competent to the purpose of every one.

Thirdly, That the power produced from the aggregate of natural rights, imperfect in power in the individual, cannot be applied to invade the natural rights which are retained in the individual, and in which the power to execute is as perfect as the right itself.

We have now, in a few words, traced man from a natural individual to a member of society, and shown, or endeavored to show, the quality of the natural rights retained, and those which are exchanged for civil rights. Let us now apply those principles to governments.

In casting our eyes over the world, it is extremely easy to distinguish the governments which have arisen out of society, or out of the social compact, from those which have not: but to place this in a clearer light than what a single glance may afford, it will be proper to take a review of the several sources from which the governments have arisen, and on which they have been founded.

They may be all comprehended under three heads. First, superstition. Secondly, power. Thirdly, the common interests of society, and the common rights of man.

The first was a government of priestcraft, the second of conquerors, and the third of reason.

When a set of artful men pretended, through the medium of oracles, to hold intercourse with the Deity, as familiarly as they now march up the backstairs in European courts, the world was completely under the government of superstition. The oracles were consulted, and whatever they were made to say, became the law; and this sort of government lasted as long as this sort of superstition lasted.

1791

FROM *The Age of Reason*

In Paris, after his escape from England, Paine wrote *The Age of Reason* (Part I, 1794; Part II, 1796) as an assault on that kind of conservative, organized religion which he believed supported tyranny, superstition, and human misery everywhere. He told Samuel Adams that he hoped by it to stop the people of France, during the violent anticlericalism that characterized the later phases of the French Revolution, from "running into Atheism," and to fix in every man's mind "the first article (as I have said before) of every man's Creed who has any Creed at all, 'I believe in God.'" Unfortunately, his harsh polemics and merciless prose offended the majority of his readers everywhere, who construed the book as an onslaught on Christianity itself and made Paine an object of bitter controversy on both sides of the Atlantic. There were more than thirty-five American replies to *The Age of Reason* within a decade; its author was attacked in press and pulpit as an atheist, Satan's emissary, a drunkard, and a traitor, and he very nearly lost his citizenship. Yet it is clear that in his own fashion Paine considered himself a genuinely religious Christian, and that his book was the most carefully written exposition of deism, or as Paine called it, "the religion of reason," produced during the time. The text follows the Van der Weyde edition of *The Life and Works.*

The Author's Profession of Faith

It has been my intention, for several years past, to publish my thoughts upon religion. I am well aware of the difficulties that attend the subject, and from that consideration, had reserved it to a more advanced period of life. I intended it to be the last offering I should make to my fellow-citizens of all nations, and that at a time when the purity of the motive that induced me to it could not admit of a question, even by those who might disapprove the work. The circumstance that has now taken place in France[1] of the total abolition of the whole national order of priesthood, and of everything appertaining to compulsive systems of religion, and compulsive articles of faith, has not only precipitated my intention, but rendered a work of this kind exceedingly necessary, lest in the general wreck of superstition, of false systems of government and false theology, we lose sight of morality, of humanity and of the theology that is true.

As several of my colleagues, and others of my fellow-citizens of France, have given me the example of making their voluntary and individual profession of faith, I also will make mine; and I do this with all that sincerity and frankness with which the mind of man communicates with itself.

I believe in one God, and no more; and I hope for happiness beyond this life.

I believe in the equality of man; and I believe

[1]Acts of the National Convention since 1792.

that religious duties consist in doing justice, loving mercy, and endeavoring to make our fellow-creatures happy.

But, lest it should be supposed that I believe many other things in addition to these, I shall, in the progress of this work, declare the things I do not believe, and my reasons for not believing them.

I do not believe in the creed professed by the Jewish Church, by the Roman Church, by the Greek Church, by the Turkish Church, by the Protestant Church, nor by any church that I know of. My own mind is my own church.

All national institutions of churches, whether Jewish, Christian or Turkish, appear to me no other than human inventions, set up to terrify and enslave mankind, and monopolize power and profit.

I do not mean by this declaration to condemn those who believe otherwise; they have the same right to their belief as I have to mine. But it is necessary to the happiness of man that he be mentally faithful to himself. Infidelity does not consist in believing, or in disbelieving; it consists in professing to believe what he does not believe.

It is impossible to calculate the moral mischief, if I may so express it, that mental lying has produced in society. When a man has so far corrupted and prostituted the chastity of his mind as to subscribe his professional belief to things he does not believe he has prepared himself for the commission of every other crime.

He takes up the trade of a priest for the sake of gain, and in order to qualify himself for that trade he begins with a perjury. Can we conceive any thing more destructive to morality than this?

Soon after I had published the pamphlet "Common Sense," in America, I saw the exceeding probability that a revolution in the system of government would be followed by a revolution in the system of religion. The adulterous connection of church and state, wherever it has taken place, whether Jewish, Christian or Turkish, has so effectually prohibited by pains and penalties every discussion upon established creeds, and upon first principles of religion, that until the system of government should be changed, those subjects could not be brought fairly and openly before the world; but that whenever this should be done, a revolution in the system of religion would follow. Human inventions and priestcraft would be detected; and man would return to the pure, unmixed and unadulterated belief of one God, and no more.

Building a New Society

MICHEL-GUILLAUME JEAN DE CRÈVECOEUR

[1731–1813]

St. Jean de Crèvecoeur was among the first to perceive the significance of the frontier environment in the development of American society, and the first to observe the "melting pot" at work. He was born into a noble French family in Caen, Normandy, and educated in England. He arrived in Canada in 1754 as a lieutenant with Montcalm's army, specializing in map-making and surveying. About 1759 he came to the American colonies, and in 1765 he took out British citizenship in New York under the name of John Hector St. John. Later he married an American girl, bought a farm in Orange County, sixty miles from New York City, and settled down to an idyllic life as a gentleman farmer.

During the Revolution, however, Crèvecoeur was suspected of Tory sympathies and subjected to such harassment that he returned to France. His *Letters from an American Farmer,* dedicated to the French philosopher Raynal and written in English, was published in London in 1782. In 1783 he returned to New York as French consul to find his wife dead, his house burned, and his three children in a stranger's home. He remained in the United States for nearly ten years, then went back to France where he spent the rest of his life.

Crèvecoeur was an admirer of Rousseau and a child of French romanticism. He found in America exactly what romantic agrarian philosophy prepared him to find—a land of happy husbandmen, living in a free, simple, egalitarian society close to a benevolent nature. "Sentiment and feeling," he once wrote, "are the only guides I know." His portrait of America is both sentimentalized and idealized, but it is nonetheless a perceptive and sympathetic articulation of the feeling that underlay the American dream of the Revolutionary generation.

Further reading: Julia P. Mitchell, *St. Jean de Crèvecoeur,* 1916. S. T. Williams' entry in *The Dictionary of American Biography.* V. L. Parrington, *Main Currents in American Thought,* I (1927), 140–47.

FROM *Letters from an American Farmer*

These "letters," really essays, were written "for the information of a friend in England" and published under the name of "J. Hector St. John, a Farmer in Pennsylvania." Twelve in all, they present a broad and optimistic view of American society, discuss American classes and institutions, and provide information about agriculture, flora, and fauna, under the guise of conversations held with a farmer and his wife. First published in London, the book sold well in both Europe and America; it was reprinted five times in English within ten years, and translated into both French and German. Text: W. B. Trent, ed., *Letters from an American Farmer* (New York, 1904; a reprint of the 1792 edition).

Letter III

What Is an American?

I wish I could be acquainted with the feelings and thoughts which must agitate the heart and present themselves to the mind of an enlightened Englishman, when he first lands on this continent. He must greatly rejoice that he lived at a time to see this fair country discovered and settled; he must necessarily feel a share of national pride, when he views the chain of settlements which embellishes these extended shores. When he says to himself, this is the work of my countrymen, who, when convulsed by factions, afflicted by a variety of miseries and wants, restless and impatient, took refuge here. They brought along with them their national genius, to which they principally owe what liberty they enjoy, and what substance they possess. Here he sees the industry of his native country displayed in a new manner, and traces in their works the embrios of all the arts, sciences, and ingenuity which flourish in Europe. Here he beholds fair cities, substantial villages, extensive fields, an immense country filled with decent houses, good roads, orchards, meadows, and bridges, where an hundred years ago all was wild, woody and uncultivated! What a train of pleasing ideas this fair spectacle must suggest; it is a prospect which must inspire a good citizen with the most heartfelt pleasure. The difficulty consists in the manner of viewing so extensive a scene. He is arrived on a new continent; a modern society offers itself to his contemplation, different from what he had hitherto seen. It is not composed, as in Europe, of great lords who possess every thing, and of a herd of people who have nothing. Here are no aristocratical families, no courts, no kings, no bishops, no ecclesiastical dominion, no invisible power giving to a few a very visible one; no great manufacturers employing thousands, no great refinements of luxury. The rich and the poor are not so far removed from each other as they are in Europe. Some few towns excepted, we are all tillers of the earth, from Nova Scotia to West Florida. We are a people of cultivators, scattered over an immense territory, communicating with each other by means of good roads and navigable rivers, united by the silken bands of mild government, all respecting the laws, without dreading their. power, because they are equitable. We are all animated with the spirit of an industry which is unfettered and unrestrained, because each person works for himself. If he travels through our rural districts he views not the hostile castle, and the haughty mansion, contrasted with the clay-built hut and miserable cabbin, where cattle and men help to keep each other warm, and dwell in meanness, smoke, and indigence. A pleasing uniformity of decent competence appears throughout our habitations. The meanest of our log-houses is a dry and comfortable habitation. Lawyer or merchant are the fairest titles our towns afford; that of a farmer is the only appellation of the rural inhabitants of our country. It must take some time ere he can reconcile himself to our dictionary, which is but short in words of dignity, and names of honour. There, on a Sunday, he sees a congregation of respectable farmers and their wives, all clad in neat homespun, well mounted, or riding in their own humble waggons. There is not among them an esquire, saving the unlettered magistrate. There he sees a parson as simple as his flock, a farmer who does not riot on the labour of others. We have no princes, for whom we toil, starve, and bleed: we are the most perfect society now existing in the world. Here man is free as he ought to be; nor is this pleasing equality so transitory as many others are. Many ages will not see the shores of our great lakes replenished with inland nations, nor the unknown bounds of North America entirely peopled. Who can tell how far it extends? Who can tell the millions of men whom it will feed and contain? for no European foot has as yet travelled half the extent of this mighty continent!

The next wish of this traveller will be to know whence came all these people? they are a mixture of English, Scotch, Irish, French, Dutch, Germans, and Swedes. From this promiscuous breed, that race now called Americans have arisen. The eastern provinces must indeed be excepted, as being the unmixed descendents of Englishmen. I have heard many wish that they had been more intermixed also: for my part, I am no wisher, and think it much better as it has happened. They exhibit a most conspicuous figure in this great and variegated picture; they too enter for a great share in the pleasing perspective displayed in these thirteen provinces. I know it is fashionable to reflect on them, but I respect them for what they have done; for the accuracy and wisdom with which they have settled their territory; for the decency of their manners; for their early love of letters; their ancient college, the first in this hemisphere; for their industry; which to me who am but a farmer, is the criterion of everything. There never was a people, situated as they are, who with so ungrateful a soil have done more in so short a time. Do you think that the monarchical ingredients which are more prevalent in other governments, have purged them from all foul stains? Their histories assert the contrary.

In this great American asylum, the poor of Europe have by some means met together, and in consequence of various causes; to what purpose should they ask one another what countrymen they are? Alas, two thirds of them had no country. Can a wretch who wanders about, who works and starves, whose life is a continual scene of sore affliction or pinching penury; can that man call England or any other kingdom his country? A country that had no bread for him, whose fields procured him no harvest, who met with nothing but the frowns of the rich, the severity of the laws, with jails and punishments; who owned not a single foot of the extensive surface of this planet? No! urged by a variety of motives, here they came. Every thing has tended to regenerate them; new laws, a new mode of living, a new social system; here they are become men: in Europe they were as so many useless plants, wanting vegetative mould, and refreshing showers; they withered, and were mowed down by want, hunger, and war; but now by the power of transplantation, like all other plants they have taken root and flourished! Formerly they were not numbered in any civil lists of their country, except in those of the poor; here they rank as citizens. By what invisible power has this surprising metamorphosis been performed? By that of the laws and that of their industry. The laws, the indulgent laws, protect them as they arrive, stamping on them the symbol of adoption; they receive ample rewards for their labours; these accumulated rewards procure them lands; those lands confer on them the title of freemen, and to that title every benefit is affixed which men can possibly require. This is the great operation daily performed by our laws. From whence proceed these laws? From our government. Whence the government? It is derived from the original genius and strong desire of the people ratified and confirmed by the crown. This is the great chain which links us all, this is the picture which every province exhibits, Nova Scotia excepted. There the crown has done all;[1] either there were no people who had genius, or it was not much attended to: the consequence is, that the province is very thinly inhabited indeed; the power of the crown in conjunction with the musketos has prevented men from settling there. Yet some parts of it flourished once, and it contained a mild harmless set of people. But for the fault of a few leaders, the whole were banished. The greatest political error the crown ever committed in America, was to cut off men from a country which wanted nothing but men!

What attachment can a poor European emigrant have for a country where he had nothing? The knowledge of the language, the love of a few kindred as poor as himself, were the only cords that tied him: his country is now that which gives him land, bread, protection, and consequence: *Ubi panis ibi patria,*[2] is the motto of all emigrants. What then is the American, this new man? He is either an European, or the descendant of an European, hence that strange mixture of blood, which you will find in no other country. I could point out to you a family whose grandfather was an Englishman, whose wife was Dutch, whose son married a French woman, and whose present four sons have now four wives of different nations. *He* is an American, who leaving behind him all his ancient prejudices and manners, receives new ones from the new mode of life he has embraced, the new government he obeys, and the new rank he holds. He becomes an American by being received in the broad lap of our great *Alma Mater.* Here individuals of all nations are melted into a new race of men, whose labours and posterity will one day cause great changes in the world. Americans are the western pilgrims, who are carrying along with them that great mass of arts, sciences, vigour, and industry which began long since in the east; they will finish the great circle. The Americans were once scattered all over Europe; here they are incorporated into one of the finest systems of population which has ever appeared, and which will hereafter become distinct by the power of the different climates they inhabit. The American ought therefore to love this country much better than that wherein either he or his forefathers were born. Here the rewards of his industry follow with equal steps the progress of his labour; his labour is founded on the basis of nature, *self-interest;* can it want a stronger allurement? Wives and children, who before in vain demanded of him a morsel of bread, now, fat and frolicsome, gladly help their father to clear those fields whence exuberant crops are to arise to feed and to clothe them all; without any part being claimed, either by a despotic prince, a rich abbot, or a mighty lord. Here religion demands but little of him; a small voluntary salary to the minister, and gratitude to God; can he refuse these? The American is a new man, who acts upon new principles; he must therefore entertain new ideas, and form new opinions. From involuntary idleness, servile dependence, penury, and useless labour, he has passed to toils of a very different nature, rewarded by ample subsistence.—This is an American.

British America is divided into many provinces, forming a large association, scattered along a coast 1500 miles extent and about 200 wide. This society I would fain examine, at least such as it appears in the middle provinces; if it does not afford that variety of tinges and gradations which may be observed in Europe, we have colours peculiar to ourselves. For instance, it is natural to conceive that those who live near the sea, must be very different from those who live in the woods; the intermediate space will afford a separate and distinct class.

Men are like plants; the goodness and flavour of the fruit proceeds from the peculiar soil and exposition in which they grow. We are nothing but what we derive from the air we breathe, the climate we inhabit, the government we obey, the system of religion we profess, and the nature of our employment. Here you will find but few crimes; these have acquired as yet no root among us. I wish I were able to trace all my ideas; if my ignorance prevents me from describing them properly, I hope I shall be able to delineate a few of the outlines, which are all I propose.

Those who live near the sea, feed more on fish than on flesh, and often encounter that boisterous

[1] The British removed some ten thousand French Acadians from Nova Scotia in 1755 and gave their land to settlers from New England.

[2] "Where the bread is, there is one's country."

element. This renders them more bold and enterprising; this leads them to neglect the confined occupations of the land. They see and converse with a variety of people; their intercourse with mankind becomes extensive. The sea inspires them with a love of traffic, a desire of transporting produce from one place to another; and leads them to a variety of resources which supply the place of labour. Those who inhabit the middle settlements, by far the most numerous, must be very different; the simple cultivation of the earth purifies them, but the indulgences of the government, the soft remonstrances of religion, the rank of independent freeholders, must necessarily inspire them with sentiments, very little known in Europe among people of the same class. What do I say? Europe has no such class of men; the early knowledge they acquire, the early bargains they make, give them a great degree of sagacity. As freemen they will be litigious; pride and obstinacy are often the cause of law suits; the nature of our laws and governments may be another. As citizens it is easy to imagine, that they will carefully read the newspapers, enter into every political disquisition, freely blame or censure governors and others. As farmers they will be careful and anxious to get as much as they can, because what they get is their own. As northern men they will love the chearful cup. As Christians, religion curbs them not in their opinions; the general indulgence leaves every one to think for themselves in spiritual matters; the laws inspect our actions, our thoughts are left to God. Industry, good living, selfishness, litigiousness, country politics, the pride of freemen, religious indifference, are their characteristics. If you recede still farther from the sea, you will come into more modern settlements; they exhibit the same strong lineaments, in a ruder appearance. Religion seems to have still less influence, and their manners are less improved.

Now we arrive near the great woods, near the last inhabited districts; there men seem to be placed still farther beyond the reach of government, which in some measure leaves them to themselves. How can it pervade every corner; as they were driven there by misfortunes, necessity of beginnings, desire of acquiring large tracks of land, idleness, frequent want of oeconomy, ancient debts; the re-union of such people does not afford a very pleasing spectacle. When discord, want of unity and friendship; when either drunkenness or idleness prevail in such remote districts; contention, inactivity, and wretchedness must ensue. There are not the same remedies to these evils as in a long established community. The few magistrates they have, are in general little better than the rest; they are often in a perfect state of war; that of man against man, sometimes decided by blows, sometimes by means of the law; that of man against every wild inhabitant of these venerable woods, of which they are come to dispossess them. There men appear to be no better than carnivorous animals of a superior rank, living on the flesh of wild animals when they can catch them, and when they are not able, they subsist on grain. He who would wish to see America in its proper light, and have a true idea of its feeble beginnings and barbarous rudiments, must visit our extended line of frontiers where the last settlers dwell, and where he may see the first labours of settlement, the mode of clearing the earth, in all their different appearances; where men are wholly left dependent on their native tempers, and on the spur of uncertain industry, which often fails when not sanctified by the efficacy of a few moral rules. There, remote from the power of example, and check of shame, many families exhibit the most hideous parts of our society. They are a kind of forlorn hope, preceding by ten or twelve years the most respectable army of veterans which come after them. In that space, prosperity will polish some, vice and the law will drive off the rest, who uniting again with others like themselves will recede still farther; making room for more industrious people, who will finish their improvements, convert the loghouse into a convenient habitation, and rejoicing that the first heavy labours are finished, will change in a few years that hitherto barbarous country into a fine fertile, well regulated district. Such is our progress, such is the march of the Europeans toward the interior parts of this continent. In all societies there are off-casts; this impure part serves as our precursors or pioneers; my father himself was one of that class, but he came upon honest principles, and was therefore one of the few who held fast; by good conduct and temperance, he transmitted to me his fair inheritance, when not above one in fourteen of his contemporaries had the same good fortune.[3]

Forty years ago this smiling country was thus inhabited; it is now purged, a general decency of manners prevails throughout, and such has been the fate of our best countries.

Exclusive of those general characteristics, each province has its own, founded on the government, climate, mode of husbandry, customs, and peculiarity of circumstances. Europeans submit insensibly to these great powers, and become, in the course of a few generations, not only Americans in general, but either Pennsylvanians, Virginians, or provincials under some other name. Whoever traverses the continent must easily observe those strong differences,

[3] There is some doubt, however, that Crèvecoeur's father was ever in the American colonies.

which will grow more evident in time. The inhabitants of Canada, Massachuset, the middle provinces, the southern ones will be as different as their climates; their only points of unity will be those of religion and language.

As I have endeavoured to shew you how Europeans become Americans; it may not be disagreeable to shew you likewise how the various Christian sects introduced, wear out, and how religious indifference becomes prevalent. When any considerable number of a particular sect happen to dwell contiguous to each other, they immediately erect a temple, and there worship the Divinity agreeably to their own peculiar ideas. Nobody disturbs them. If any new sect springs up in Europe, it may happen that many of its professors will come and settle in America. As they bring their zeal with them, they are at liberty to make proselytes if they can, and to build a meeting and to follow the dictates of their consciences; for neither the government nor any other power interferes. If they are peaceable subjects, and are industrious, what is it to their neighbours how and in what manner they think fit to address their prayers to the Supreme Being? But if the sectaries are not settled close together, if they are mixed with other denominations, their zeal will cool for want of fuel, and will be extinguished in a little time. Then the Americans become as to religion, what they are as to country, allied to all. In them the name of Englishman, Frenchman, and European is lost, and in like manner, the strict modes of Christianity as practised in Europe are lost also. This effect will extend itself still farther hereafter, and though this may appear to you as a strange idea, yet it is a very true one. I shall be able perhaps hereafter to explain myself better, in the meanwhile, let the following example serve as my first justification.

Let us suppose you and I to be travelling; we observe that in this house, to the right, lives a Catholic, who prays to God as he has been taught, and believes in transubstantiation; he works and raises wheat, he has a large family of children, all hale and robust; his belief, his prayers offend nobody. About one mile farther on the same road, his next neighbour may be a good honest plodding German Lutheran, who addresses himself to the same God, the God of all, agreeably to the modes he has been educated in, and believes in consubstantiation; by so doing he scandalizes nobody; he also works in his fields, embellishes the earth, clears swamps, &c. What has the world to do with his Lutheran principles? He persecutes nobody, and nobody persecutes him, he visits his neighbours, and his neighbours visit him. Next to him lives a seceder, the most enthusiastic of all sectaries; his zeal is hot and fiery, but separated as he is from others of the same complexion, he has no congregation of his own to resort to, where he might cabal and mingle religious pride with worldly obstinacy. He likewise raises good crops, his house is handsomely painted, his orchard is one of the fairest in the neighbourhood. How does it concern the welfare of the country, or of the province at large, what this man's religious sentiments are, or really whether he has any at all? He is a good farmer, he is a sober, peaceable, good citizen: William Penn himself would not wish for more. This is the visible character, the invisible one is only guessed at, and is nobody's business. Next again lives a Low Dutchman, who implicitly believes the rules laid down by the synod of Dort. He conceives no other idea of a clergyman than that of an hired man; if he does his work well he will pay him the stipulated sum; if not he will dismiss him, and do without his sermons, and let his church be shut up for years. But notwithstanding this coarse idea, you will find his house and farm to be the neatest in all the country; and you will judge by his waggon and fat horses, that he thinks more of the affairs of this world than of those of the next. He is sober and laborious, therefore he is all he ought to be as to the affairs of this life; as for those of the next, he must trust to the great Creator. Each of these people instruct their children as well as they can, but these instructions are feeble compared to those which are given to the youth of the poorest class in Europe. Their children will therefore grow up less zealous and more indifferent in matters of religion than their parents. The foolish vanity, or rather the fury of making Proselytes, is unknown here; they have no time, the seasons call for all their attention, and thus in a few years, this mixed neighbourhood will exhibit a strange religious medley, that will be neither pure Catholicism nor pure Calvinism. A very perceptible indifference even in the first generation, will become apparent; and it may happen that the daughter of the Catholic will marry the son of the seceder, and settle by themselves at a distance from their parents. What religious education will they give their children? A very imperfect one. If there happens to be in the neighbourhood any place of worship, we will suppose a Quaker's meeting; rather than not shew their fine clothes, they will go to it, and some of them may perhaps attach themselves to that society. Others will remain in a perfect state of indifference; the children of these zealous parents will not be able to tell what their religious principles are, and their grandchildren still less. The neighbourhood of a place of worship generally leads them to it, and the action of going thither, is the strongest evidence they can give of their attachment to any sect. The Quakers are the only people who retain a fondness for their own mode of worship; for be they ever so far separated from each other, they hold a sort of communion with the society, and seldom depart from its rules, at least in this country. Thus all sects are mixed as well as all nations; thus religious indifference is imperceptibly disseminated from one end of the continent to the other; which is at present one of the strongest characteristics of the Americans. Where this will reach no one can tell, perhaps it may leave a vacuum fit to receive other systems. Persecution, religious pride, the love of contradiction, are the food of what the world commonly calls religion. These motives have ceased here: zeal in Europe is confined; here it evaporates in the great distance it has to travel; there it is a grain of powder inclosed, here it burns away in the open air, and consumes without effect.

But to return to our back settlers. I must tell you, that there is something in the proximity of the woods, which is very singular. It is with men as it is with the plants and animals that grow and live in the forests; they are entirely different from those that live in the plains. I will candidly tell you all my thoughts but you are not to expect that I shall advance any reasons. By living in or near the woods, their actions are regulated by the wildness of the neighbourhood. The deer often come to eat their grain, the wolves to destroy their sheep, the bears to kill their hogs, the foxes to catch their poultry. This surrounding hostility, immediately puts the gun into their hands; they watch these animals, they kill some; and thus by defending their property, they soon become professed hunters; this is the progress; once hunters, farewell to the plough. The chase renders them ferocious, gloomy, and unsociable; a hunter wants no neighbour, he rather hates them, because he dreads the competition. In a little time their success in the woods makes them neglect their tillage. They trust to the natural fecundity of the earth, and therefore do little; carelessness in fencing, often exposes what little they sow to destruction; they are not at home to watch; in order therefore to make up the deficiency, they go oftener to the woods. That new mode of life brings along with it a new set of manners, which I cannot easily describe. These new manners being grafted on the old stock, produce a strange sort of lawless profligacy, the impressions of which are indelible. The manners of the Indian natives are respectable, compared with this European medley. Their wives and children live in sloth and inactivity; and having no proper pursuits, you may judge what education the latter receive. Their tender minds have nothing else to contemplate but the example of their parents; like them they grow up a mongrel breed, half civilized, half savage, except nature stamps on them some constitutional propensities. That rich, that voluptuous sentiment is gone that struck them so forcibly; the possession of their freeholds no longer conveys to their minds the same pleasure and pride. To all these reasons you must add, their lonely situation, and you cannot imagine what an effect on manners the great distances they live from each other has! Consider one of the last settlements in it's first view: of what is it composed? Europeans who have not that sufficient share of knowledge they ought to have, in order to prosper; people who have suddenly passed from oppression, dread of government, and fear of laws, into the unlimited freedom of the woods. This sudden change must have a very great effect on most men, and on that class particularly. Eating of wild meat, whatever you may think, tends to alter their temper; though all the proof I can adduce, is, that I have seen it: and having no place of worship to resort to, what little society this might afford, is denied them. The Sunday meetings, exclusive of religious benefits, were the only social bonds that might have inspired them with some degree of emulation in neatness. Is it then surprising to see men thus situated, immersed in great and heavy labours, degenerate a little? It is rather a wonder the effect is not more diffusive. The Moravians and the Quakers are the only instances in exception to what I have advanced. The first never settle singly, it is a colony of the society which emigrates; they carry with them their forms, worship, rules, and decency: the others never begin so hard, they are always able to buy improvements, in which there is a great advantage, for by that time the country is recovered from its first barbarity. Thus our bad people are those who are half cultivators and half hunters; and the worst of them are those who have degenerated altogether into the hunting state. As old ploughmen and new men of the woods, as Europeans and new made Indians, they contract the vices of both; they adopt the moroseness and ferocity of a native, without his mildness, or even his industry at home. If manners are not refined, at least they are rendered simple and inoffensive by tilling the earth; all our wants are supplied by it, our time is divided between labour and rest, and leaves none for the commission of great misdeeds. As hunters it is divided between the toil of the chase, the idleness of repose, or the indulgence of inebriation. Hunting is but a licentious idle life, and if it does not always pervert good dispositions; yet, when it is united with bad luck, it leads to want: want stimulates that propensity to rapacity and injustice, too natural to needy men, which is the fatal gradation. After this explanation of the effects which follow by living in the woods, shall we yet vainly flatter ourselves with the hope of converting the Indians? We should rather begin with converting our back-settlers; and now if I dare mention the name of religion, its sweet accents would be lost in the immensity of these woods. Men thus placed, are not fit either to receive or remember its mild instructions; they want temples and ministers, but as soon as men cease to remain at home, and begin to lead an erratic life, let them be either tawny or white, they cease to be its disciples.

Thus have I faintly and imperfectly endeavoured to trace our society from the sea to our woods! yet you must not imagine that every person who moves back, acts upon the same principles, or falls into the same degeneracy. Many families carry with them all their decency of conduct, purity of morals, and respect of religion; but these are scarce, the power of example is sometimes irresistible. Even among these back-settlers, their depravity is greater or less, according to what nation or province they belong. Were I to adduce proofs of this, I might be accused of partiality. If there happens to be some rich intervals, some fertile bottoms, in those remote districts, the people will there prefer tilling the land to hunting, and will attach themselves to it; but even on these fertile spots you may plainly perceive the inhabitants to acquire a great degree of rusticity and selfishness.

It is in consequence of this straggling situation, and the astonishing power it has on manners, that the back-settlers of both the Carolinas, Virginia, and many other parts, have been long a set of lawless people; it has been even dangerous to travel among them. Government can do nothing in so extensive a country, better it should wink at these irregularities, than that it should use means inconsistent with its usual mildness. Time will efface those stains: in proportion as the great body of population approaches them they will reform, and become polished and subordinate. Whatever has been said of the four New England provinces, no such degeneracy of manners has ever tarnished their annals; their back-settlers have been kept within the bounds of decency, and government, by means of wise laws, and by the influence of religion. What a detestable idea such people must have given to the natives of the Europeans! They trade with them, the worst of people are permitted to do that which none but persons of the best characters should be employed in. They get drunk with them, and often defraud the Indians. Their avarice, removed from the eyes of their superiors, knows no bounds; and aided by a little superiority of knowledge, these traders deceive them, and even sometimes shed blood. Hence those shocking violations, those sudden devastations which have so often stained our frontiers, when hundreds of innocent people have been sacrificed for the crimes of a few. It was in consequence of such behaviour, that the Indians took the hatchet against the Virginians in 1774. Thus are our first steps trod, thus are our first trees felled, in general, by the most vicious of our people; and thus the path is opened for the arrival of a second and better class, the true American freeholders; the most respectable set of people in this part of the world: respectable for their industry, their happy independence, the great share of freedom they possess, the good regulation of their families, and for extending the trade and the dominion of our mother country.

Europe contains hardly any other distinctions but lords and tenants; this fair country alone is settled by freeholders, the possessors of the soil they cultivate, members of the government they obey, and the framers of their own laws, by means of their representatives. This is a thought which you have taught me to cherish; our difference from Europe, far from diminishing, rather adds to our usefulness and consequence as men and subjects. Had our forefathers remained there, they would only have crouded it, and perhaps prolonged those convulsions which had shook it so long. Every industrious European who transports himself here, may be compared to a sprout growing at the foot of a great tree; it enjoys and draws but a little portion of sap; wrench it from the parent roots, transplant it, and it will become a tree bearing fruit also. Colonists are therefore entitled to the consideration due to the most useful subjects; a hundred families barely existing in some parts of Scotland, will here in six years, cause an annual exportation of 10,000 bushels of wheat: 100 bushels being but a common quantity for an industrious family to sell, if they cultivate good land. It is here then that the idle may be employed, the useless become useful, and the poor become rich; but by riches I do not mean gold and silver, we have but little of those metals; I mean a better sort of wealth, cleared lands, cattle, good houses, good cloaths, and an increase of people to enjoy them.

There is no wonder that this country has so many charms, and presents to Europeans so many temptations to remain in it. A traveller in Europe becomes a stranger as soon as he quits his own kingdom; but it is otherwise here. We know, properly speaking, no strangers; this is every person's country; the variety of our soils, situations, climates, governments, and produce, hath something which must please every body. No sooner does an European arrive, no matter of what condition, than his eyes are opened upon the fair prospect; he hears his language spoke, he retraces many of his own country manners, he perpetually hears the names of families and towns with which he is acquainted; he sees happiness and prosperity in all places disseminated; he meets with hospitality, kindness, and plenty every where; he beholds hardly any poor, he seldom hears of punishments and executions; and he wonders at the elegance of our towns, those miracles of industry and freedom. He cannot admire enough our rural districts, our convenient roads, good taverns, and our many accommodations; he involuntarily loves a country where every thing is so lovely. When in England, he was a mere Englishman; here he stands on a larger portion of the globe, not less than its fourth part, and may see the productions of the north, in iron and naval stores; the provisions of Ireland, the grain of Egypt, the indigo, the rice of China. He does not find, as in Europe, a crouded society, where every place is over-stocked; he does not feel that perpetual collision of parties, that difficulty of beginning, that contention which oversets so many. There is room for every body in America; has he any particular talent, or industry? he exerts it in order to procure a livelihood, and it succeeds. Is he a merchant? the avenues of trade are infinite; is he eminent in any respect? he will be employed and respected. Does he love a country life? pleasant farms present themselves; he may purchase what he wants, and thereby become an American farmer. Is he a labourer, sober and industrious? he need not go many miles, nor receive many informations before he will be hired, well fed at the table of his employer, and paid four or five times more than he can get in Europe. Does he want uncultivated lands? thousands of acres present themselves, which he may purchase cheap. Whatever be his talents or inclinations, if they are moderate, he may satisfy them. I do not mean that every one who comes will grow rich in a little time; no, but he may procure an easy, decent maintenance, by his industry. Instead of starving he will be fed, instead of being idle he will have employment; and these are riches enough for such men as come over here. The rich stay in Europe, it is only the middling and the poor that emigrate. Would you wish to travel in independent idleness, from north to south, you will find easy access, and the most chearful reception at every house; society without ostentation, good cheer without pride, and every decent diversion which the country affords, with little expence. It is no wonder that the European who has lived here a few years, is desirous to remain; Europe with all its pomp, is not to be compared to this continent, for men of middle stations, or labourers.

An European, when he first arrives, seems limited in his intentions, as well as in his views; but he very suddenly alters his scale; two hundred miles formerly appeared a very great distance, it is now but a trifle; he no sooner breathes our air than he forms schemes, and embarks in designs he never would have thought of in his own country. There the plenitude of society confines many useful ideas, and often extinguishes the most laudable schemes which here ripen into maturity. Thus Europeans become Americans.

But how is this accomplished in that croud of low, indigent people, who flock here every year from all parts of Europe? I will tell you; they no sooner arrive than they immediately feel the good effects of that plenty of provisions we possess: they fare on our best food, and are kindly entertained; their talents, character, and peculiar industry are immediately inquired into; they find countrymen every where disseminated, let them come from whatever part of Europe. Let me select one as an epitome of the rest; he is hired, he goes to work, and works moderately; instead of being employed by a haughty person, he finds himself with his equal, placed at the substantial table of the farmer, or else at an inferior one as good; his wages are high, his bed is not like that bed of sorrow on which he used to lie: if he behaves with propriety, and is faithful, he is caressed, and becomes as it were a member of the family. He begins to feel the effects of a sort of resurrection; hitherto he had not lived, but simply vegetated; he now feels himself a man, because he is treated as such; the laws of his own country had overlooked him in his insignificancy; the laws of this cover him with their mantle. Judge what an alteration there must arise in the mind and thoughts of this man; he begins to forget his former servitude and dependence, his heart involuntarily swells and glows; this first swell inspires him with those new thoughts which constitute an American. What love can he entertain for a country where his existence was a burthen to him; if he is a generous good man, the love of this new adoptive parent will sink deep into his heart. He looks around, and sees many a prosperous person, who but a few years before was as poor as himself. This encourages him much, he begins to form some little scheme, the first, alas, he ever formed in his life. If he is wise he thus spends two or three years, in which time he acquires knowledge, the use of tools, the modes of working the lands, felling trees, &c. This prepares the foundation of a good name, the most useful acquisition he can make. He is encouraged, he has gained friends; he is advised and directed, he feels bold, he purchases some land; he gives all the money he has brought over, as well as what he has earned, and trusts to the God of harvests for the discharge of the rest. His good name procures him credit. He is now possessed of the deed, conveying to him and his posterity the fee simple and absolute property of two hundred acres of land, situated on such a river. What an epocha in this man's life! He is become a freeholder, from perhaps a German boor—he is now an American, a Pennsylvanian, an English subject. He is naturalized, his name is enrolled with those of the other citizens of the province. Instead of being a vagrant, he has a place of residence; he is called the inhabitant of such a county, or of such a district, and for the first time in his life counts for something; for hitherto he has been a cypher. I only repeat what I have heard many say, and no wonder their hearts should glow, and be agitated with a multitude of feelings, not easy to describe. From nothing to start into being; from a servant to the rank of a master; from being the slave of some despotic prince, to become a free man, invested with lands, to which every municipal blessing is annexed! What a change indeed! It is in consequence of that change that he becomes an American. This great metamorphosis has a double effect, it extinguishes all his European prejudices, he forgets that mechanism of subordination, that servility of disposition which poverty had taught him; and sometimes he is apt to forget too much, often passing from one extreme to the other. If he is a good man, he forms schemes of future prosperity, he proposes to educate his children better than he has been educated himself; he thinks of future modes of conduct, feels an ardor to labour he never felt before. Pride steps in and leads him to every thing that the laws do not forbid: he respects them; with a heart-felt gratitude he looks toward the east, toward that insular government from whose wisdom all his new felicity is derived, and under whose wings and protection he now lives. These reflections constitute him the good man and the good subject. Ye poor Europeans, ye, who sweat, and work for the great—ye, who are obliged to give so many sheaves to the church, so many to your lords, so many to your government, and have hardly any left for yourselves—ye, who are held in less estimation than favourite hunters or useless lap dogs—ye, who only breathe the air of nature, because it cannot be withheld from you; it is here that ye can conceive the possibility of those feelings I have been describing; it is here the laws of naturalization invite every one to partake of our great labours and felicity, to till unrented, untaxed lands! Many, corrupted beyond the power of amendment, have brought with them all their vices, and disregarding the advantages held to them, have gone on in their former career of iniquity, until they have been overtaken and punished by our laws. It is not every emigrant who succeeds; no, it is only the sober, the honest, and industrious: happy those to whom this transition has served as a powerful spur to labour, to prosperity, and to the good establishment of children, born in the days of their poverty; and who had no other portion to expect but the rags of their parents, had it not been for their happy emigration. Others again, have been led astray by this enchanting scene; their new pride, instead of leading them to the fields, has kept them in idleness; the idea of possessing lands is all that satisfies them—though surrounded with fertility, they have mouldered away their time in inactivity, misinformed husbandry, and ineffectual endeavours. How much wiser, in general, the honest Germans than almost all other Europeans; they hire themselves to some of their wealthy landsmen, and in that apprenticeship learn every thing that is necessary. They attentively consider the prosperous industry of others, which imprints in their minds a strong desire of possessing the same advantages. This forcible idea never quits them, they launch forth, and by dint of sobriety, rigid parsimony, and the most persevering industry, they commonly succeed. Their astonishment at their first arrival from Germany is very great—it is to them a dream; the contrast must be powerful indeed; they observe their countrymen flourishing in every place; they travel through whole counties where not a word of English is spoken; and in the names and the language of the people, they retrace Germany. They have been an useful acquisition to this continent, and to Pennsylvania in particular; to them it owes some share of its prosperity: to their mechanical knowledge and patience, it owes the finest mills in all America, the best teams of horses, and many other advantages. The recollection of their former poverty and slavery never quits them as long as they live.

The Scotch and the Irish might have lived in their own country perhaps as poor, but enjoying more civil advantages, the effects of their new situation do not strike them so forcibly, nor has it so lasting an effect. From whence the difference arises I know not, but out of twelve families of emigrants of each country, generally seven Scotch will succeed, nine German, and four Irish. The Scotch are frugal and laborious, but their wives cannot work so hard as German women, who on the contrary vie with their husbands, and often share with them the most severe toils of the field, which they understand better. They have therefore nothing to struggle against, but the common casualties of nature. The Irish do not prosper so well; they love to drink and to quarrel; they are litigious, and soon take to the gun, which is the ruin of every thing; they seem beside to labour under a greater degree of ignorance in husbandry than the others; perhaps it is that their industry had less scope, and was less exercised at home. I have heard many relate, how the land was parcelled out in that kingdom; their ancient conquest has been a great detriment to them, by over-setting their landed property. The lands possessed by a few, are leased down *ad infinitum*, and the occupiers often pay five guineas an acre. The poor are worse lodged there than any where else in Europe; their potatoes, which are easily raised, are perhaps an inducement to laziness: their wages are too low and their whisky too cheap.

There is no tracing observations of this kind, without making at the same time very great allowances, as there are every where to be found, a great many exceptions. The Irish themselves, from different parts of that kingdom, are very different. It is difficult to account for this surprising locality, one would think on so small an island an Irishman must be an Irishman: yet it is not so, they are different in their aptitude to, and in their love of labour.

The Scotch on the contrary are all industrious and saving; they want nothing more than a field to exert themselves in, and they are commonly sure of succeeding. The only difficulty they labour under is, that technical American knowledge which requires some time to obtain; it is not easy for those who seldom saw a tree, to conceive how it is to be felled, cut up, and split into rails and posts.

As I am fond of seeing and talking of prosperous families, I intend to finish this letter by relating to you the history of an honest Scotch Hebridean, who came here in 1774, which will shew you in epitome, what the Scotch can do, wherever they have room for the exertion of their industry. Whenever I hear of any new settlement, I pay it a visit once or twice a year, on purpose to observe the different steps each settler takes, the gradual improvements, the different tempers of each family, on which their prosperity in a great nature depends; their different modifications of industry, their ingenuity, and contrivance; for being all poor, their life requires sagacity and prudence. In an evening I love to hear them tell their stories, they furnish me with new ideas; I sit still and listen to their ancient misfortunes, observing in many of them a strong degree of gratitude to God, and the government. Many a well meant sermon have I preached to some of them. When I found laziness and inattention to prevail, who could refrain from wishing well to these new countrymen; after having undergone so many fatigues. Who could withhold good advice? What a happy change it must be, to descend from the high, sterile, bleak lands of Scotland, where every thing is barren and cold, to rest on some fertile farms in these middle provinces! Such a transition must have afforded the most pleasing satisfaction.

The following dialogue passed at an out-settlement, where I lately paid a visit:

Well, friend, how do you do now; I am come fifty odd miles on purpose to see you; how do you go on with your new cutting and slashing? Very well, good Sir, we learn the use of the axe bravely, we shall make it out; we have a belly full of victuals every day, our cows run about, and come home full of milk, our hogs get fat of themselves in the woods: Oh, this is a good country! God bless the king, and William Penn; we shall do very well by and by, if we keep our healths. Your loghouse looks neat and light, where did you get these shingles? One of our neighbours is a New-England man, and he shewed us how to split them out of chestnut-trees. Now for a barn, but all in good time, here are fine trees to build with. Who is to frame it, sure you don't understand that work yet? A countryman of ours who has been in America these ten years, offers to wait for his money until the second crop is lodged in it. What did you give for your land? Thirty-five shillings per acre, payable in seven years. How many acres have you got? An hundred and fifty. That is enough to begin with; is not your land pretty hard to clear? Yes, Sir, hard enough, but it would be harder still if it was ready cleared, for then we should have no timber, and I love the woods much; the land is nothing without them. Have not you found out any bees yet? No, Sir; and if we had we should not know what to do with them. I will tell you by and by. You are very kind. Farewell, honest man, God prosper you; whenever you travel toward **, enquire for J. S. he will entertain you kindly, provided you bring him good tidings from your family and farm. In this manner I often visit them, and carefully examine their houses, their modes of ingenuity, their different ways; and make them all relate all they know, and describe all they feel. These are scenes which I believe you would willingly share with me. I well remember your philanthropic turn of mind. Is it not better to contemplate under these humble roofs, the rudiments of future wealth and population, than to behold the accumulated bundles of litigious papers in the office of a lawyer? To examine how the world is gradually settled, how the howling swamp is converted into a pleasing meadow, the rough ridge into a fine field; and to hear the chearful whistling, the rural song, where there was no sound heard before, save the yell of the savage, the screech of the owl, or the hissing of the snake? Here an European, fatigued with luxury, riches, and pleasures, may find a sweet relaxation in a series of interesting scenes, as affecting as they are new. England, which now contains so many domes, so many castles, was once like this; a place woody and marshy; its inhabitants, now the favourite nation for arts and commerce, were once painted like our neighbours. The country will flourish in its turn, and the same observations will be made which I have just delineated. Posterity will look back with avidity and pleasure, to trace, if possible, the aera of this or that particular settlement.

Pray, what is the reason that the Scots are in general more religious, more faithful, more honest, and industrious than the Irish? I do not mean to insinuate national reflections, God forbid! It ill becomes any man, and much less an American; but as I know men are nothing of themselves, and that they owe all their different modifications either to government or other local circumstances, there must be some powerful causes which constitute this great national difference.

Agreeable to the account which severale Scotchmen have given me of the north of Britain, of the Orkneys, and the Hebride Islands, they seem, on many accounts, to be unfit for the habitation of men; they appear to be calculated only for great sheep pastures. Who then can blame the inhabitants of these countries for transporting themselves hither? This great continent must in time absorb the poorest part of Europe; and this will happen in proportion as it becomes better known; and as war, taxation, oppression, and misery increase there. The Hebrides appear to be fit only for the residence of malefactors, and it would be much better to send felons there than either to Virginia or Maryland. What a strange compliment has our mother country paid to two of the finest provinces in America! England has entertained in that respect very mistaken ideas; what was intended as a punishment, is become the good fortune of several; many of those who have been transported as felons, are now rich, and strangers to the stings of those wants that urged them to violations of the law: they are become industrious, exemplary, and useful citizens. The English government should purchase the most northern and barren of those islands; it should send over to us the honest, primitive Hebrideans, settle them here on good lands, as a reward for their virtue and ancient poverty; and replace them with a colony of her wicked sons. The severity of the climate, the inclemency of the seasons, the sterility of the soil, the tempestuousness of the sea, would afflict and punish enough. Could there be found a spot better adapted to retaliate the injury it had received by their crimes? Some of those islands might be considered as the hell of Great Britain, where all evil spirits should be sent. Two essential ends would be answered by this simple operation. The good people, by emigration, would be rendered happier; the bad ones would be placed where they ought to be. In a few years the dread of being sent to that wintry region would have a much stronger effect, than that of transportation.—This is no place of punishment; were I a poor hopeless, breadless Englishman, and not restrained by the power of shame, I should be very thankful for the passage. It is of very little importance how, and in what manner an indigent man arrives; for if he is but sober, honest, and industrious, he has nothing more to ask of heaven. Let him go to work, he will have opportunities enough to earn a comfortable support, and even the means of procuring some land; which ought to be the utmost wish of every person who has health and hands to work. I knew a man who came to this country, in the literal sense of the expression, stark naked; I think he was a Frenchman, and a sailor on board an English man of war. Being discontented, he had stripped himself and swam ashore; where finding clothes and friends, he settled afterwards at Maraneck, in the county of Chester, in the province of New-York: he married and left a good farm to each of his sons. I knew another person who was but twelve years old when he was taken on the frontiers of Canada, by the Indians; at his arrival at Albany he was purchased by a gentleman, who generously bound him apprentice to a taylor. He lived to the age of ninety, and left behind him a fine estate and a numerous family, all well settled; many of them I am acquainted with.—Where is then the industrious European who ought to despair?

After a foreigner from any part of Europe is arrived, and become a citizen; let him devoutly listen to the voice of our great parent, which says to him, "Welcome to my shores, distressed European; bless the hour in which thou didst see my verdant fields, my fair navigable rivers, and my green mountains!—If thou wilt work, I have bread for thee; if thou wilt be honest, sober, and industrious, I have greater rewards to confer on thee—ease and independence. I will give thee fields to feed and cloath thee; a comfortable fire-side to sit by, and tell thy children by what means thou hast prospered; and a decent bed to repose on. I shall endow thee beside with the immunities of a freeman. If thou wilt carefully educate thy children, teach them gratitude to God, and reverence to that government, that philanthropic government, which has collected here so many men and made them happy. I will also provide for thy progeny; and to every good man this ought to be the most holy, the most powerful, the most earnest wish he can possibly form, as well as the most consolatory prospect when he dies. Go thou and work and till; thou shalt prosper, provided thou be just, grateful and industrious."

1782

THOMAS JEFFERSON [1743–1826]

Thomas Jefferson was born into one of Virginia's First Families and related by marriage and friendship to most of the others. Educated at William and Mary College, he read law under the great teacher George Wythe and was admitted to the Virginia bar. As a youth he inherited a large family estate and a modest fortune; later, from his wife, he gained forty thousand additional acres and a hundred more slaves. However, he found little to interest him in the life of a wealthy plantation aristocrat or in legal practice, and he soon embarked on the most remarkable public career in American history. He was almost constantly in the service of his colony, state, and nation from 1769, when he entered the Virginia House of Burgesses, until 1809, when he retired from the Presidency after declining a third term. He served as member of the Continental Congress, as governor of Virginia, as Minister to France, as Secretary of State, as Vice President, and as President. After his retirement to his beloved home, Monticello, near Charlottesville, he continued through his correspondence and his circle of friends to serve his nation as adviser, elder statesman, and example. Perhaps no one man, with the possible exception of Washington, had more influence on the early history of the United States.

Jefferson, thirty-seven years younger than Franklin, was like him an excellent representative of the American Enlightenment. He ranged with ease and authority over law, science, history, philosophy, architecture, the classics, art, music, and almost every aspect of the knowledge of his age. He established the design of American public education; he was chiefly responsible for the development of the American two-party system; he bought Louisiana and much of the West from Napoleon and sent Lewis and Clark to open it; he evolved the parliamentary procedures which are still practiced in Congress; his books formed the nucleus of the Library of Congress; and he was most certainly, as his state papers and correspondence show, one of the greatest of American political philosophers.

Jefferson's political creed rested on his ultimate faith that man had "capacity for improvement, for learning and understanding himself and the world." He had too much experience with human nature to trust it completely, but he was confident that under proper conditions, men could be relied upon to think and do the right thing—if they were free, educated, and "habituated to think for themselves and to follow reason as their guides." For this reason he favored a government which diffused political power through an educated, enlightened people, the majority of whom he believed "competent to judge of the facts occurring in ordinary life." His philosophy of government, reduced to a single key idea, was *freedom*, governed by reason and justice. His statement to Benjamin Rush in 1800 expressed it best: "I have sworn," he wrote, "upon the altar of God, eternal hostility against every form of tyranny over the mind of man." Significantly, he chose for his epitaph the three achievements—political, religious, intellectual—for which he wished to be remembered, making no mention of any political office he ever held:

Here was buried Thomas Jefferson
Author of the Declaration of Independence,
of the Statute of Virginia for Religious freedom,
and Father of the University of Virginia.

Jefferson's innate rationalism and his interest in science led him in his religious beliefs toward his own personal variety of deism. Reticent about what he believed, for he thought that religion "is a matter which lies solely between a man and his God," he once remarked that "I am a sect for myself, as far as I know." However, he was an Episcopalian, born, married, and buried under the rites of his church and a lifelong parishioner of it. He believed, as his letters show, in the excellence of New Testament Christianity, feeling that the moral and ethical doctrines of Jesus were "the most pure and perfect" of all teachings and the best possible guides to mankind.

Further reading: Nathan Schachner, *Thomas Jefferson,* 2 vols., 1951. S. G. Brown, *Thomas Jefferson,* 1963. E. T. Martin, *Thomas Jefferson, Scientist,* 1952. Adrienne Koch, *The Philosophy of Thomas Jefferson,* 1943. C. M. Wiltse, *The Jeffersonian Tradition in American Democracy,* 1935. M. D. Peterson, *The Jeffersonian Image in the American Mind,* 1960. Carl Becker, *The Declaration of Independence,* 1922.

The Declaration of Independence

Drafting of the Declaration was initiated by Richard Henry Lee's motion in Continental Congress of June 7, 1776. On June 11 Congress appointed Jefferson, Franklin, Adams, Sherman, and Livingston as a committee to draft the document; Jefferson's copy of the "rough draft" includes changes made by himself, Adams, Franklin, and members of the committee, before its presentation to Congress. It was Jefferson who gave a new direction to the course of American democratic philosophy when in his draft version he altered the customary trio of natural rights, commonly accepted by the English Enlightenment, from "life, liberty, and property," to read "life, liberty, and the pursuit of happiness." Texts: Julian Boyd, editor, *The Papers of Thomas Jefferson* (Princeton, 1950), I, 423-32.

Jefferson's "Original Rough Draught"

A Declaration of the Representatives of the UNITED STATES OF AMERICA, in General Congress assembled.

When in the course of human events it becomes necessary for a people to advance from that subordination in which they have hitherto remained, & to assume among the powers of the earth the equal & independant station to which the laws of nature & of nature's god entitle them, a decent respect to the opinions of mankind requires that they should declare the causes which impel them to the change.

We hold these truths to be sacred & undeniable; that all men are created equal & independant, that from that equal creation they derive rights inherent & inalienable, among which are the preservation of life, & liberty, & the pursuit of happiness; that to secure these ends, governments are instituted among men, deriving their just powers from the consent of the governed; that whenever any form of government shall become destructive of these ends, it is the right of the people to alter or to abolish it, & to institute new government, laying it's foundation on such principles & organising it's powers in such form, as to them shall seem most likely to effect their safety & happiness. prudence indeed will dictate that governments long established should not be changed for light & transient causes: and accordingly all experience hath shewn that mankind are more disposed to suffer while evils are sufferable, than to right themselves by abolishing the forms to which they are accustomed. but when a long train of abuses & usurpations, begun at a distinguished period, & pursuing invariably the same object, evinces a design to subject them to arbitrary power, it is their right, it is their duty, to throw off such government & to provide new guards for their future security. such has been the patient sufferance of these colonies; & such is now the necessity which constrains them to expunge their former systems of government. the history of his present majesty, is a history of unremitting injuries and usurpations, among which no one fact stands single or solitary to contradict the uniform tenor of the rest, all of which have in direct object the establishment of an absolute tyranny over these states. to prove this, let facts be submitted to a candid world, for the truth of which we pledge a faith yet unsullied by falsehood.

he has refused his assent to laws the most wholesome and necessary for the public good:

he has forbidden his governors to pass laws of immediate & pressing importance, unless suspended in their operation till his assent should be obtained; and when so suspended, he has neglected utterly to attend to them.

he has refused to pass other laws for the accomodation of large districts of people unless those people would relinquish the right of representation, a right inestimable to them, & formidable to tyrants alone:

he has dissolved Representative houses repeatedly & continually, for opposing with manly firmness his invasions on the rights of the people:

he has refused for a long space of time to cause others to be elected, whereby the legislative powers, incapable of annihilation, have returned to the people at large for their exercise, the state remaining in the mean time exposed to all the dangers of invasion from without, & convulsions within:

he has endeavored to prevent the population of these states; for that purpose obstructing the laws for naturalization of foreigners; refusing to pass others to encourage their migrations hither; & raising the conditions of new appropriations of lands:

he has suffered the administration of justice totally to cease in some of these colonies, refusing his assent to laws for establishing judiciary powers:

he has made our judges dependant on his will alone, for the tenure of their offices, and amount of their salaries:

he has erected a multitude of new offices by a self-assumed power, & sent hither swarms of officers to harrass our people & eat out their substance:

he has kept among us in times of peace standing armies & ships of war:

he has affected to render the military, independant of & superior to the civil power:

he has combined with others to subject us to a jurisdiction foreign to our constitutions and unacknoleged by our laws; giving his assent to their pretended acts of legislation, for quartering large bodies of armed troops among us;

for protecting them by a mock-trial from punishment for any murders they should commit on the inhabitants of these states;

for cutting off our trade with all parts of the world;

for imposing taxes on us without our consent;

for depriving us of the benefits of trial by jury;

for transporting us beyond seas to be tried for pretended offences:

for taking away our charters, & altering fundamentally the forms of our governments;

for suspending our own legislatures & declaring themselves invested with power to legislate for us in all cases whatsoever:

he has abdicated government here, withdrawing his governors, & declaring us out of his allegiance & protection:

he has plundered our seas, ravaged our coasts, burnt our towns & destroyed the lives of our people:

he is at this time transporting large armies of foreign mercenaries to compleat the works of death, desolation & tyranny, already begun with circumstances of cruelty & perfidy unworthy the head of a civilized nation:

he has endeavored to bring on the inhabitants of our frontiers the merciless Indian savages, whose known rule of warfare is an undistinguished destruction of all ages, sexes, & conditions of existence:

he has incited treasonable insurrections in our fellow-subjects, with the allurements of forfeiture & confiscation of our property:

he has waged cruel war against human nature itself, violating it's most sacred rights of life & liberty in the persons of a distant people who never offended him, captivating & carrying them into slavery in another hemisphere, or to incur miserable death in their transportation thither. this piratical warfare, the opprobrium of *infidel* powers, is the warfare of the CHRISTIAN king of Great Britain, determined to keep open a market where MEN should be bought & sold, he has prostituted his negative for suppressing every legislative attempt to prohibit or to restrain this execrable commerce: and that this assemblage of horrors might want no fact of distinguished die, he is now exciting those very people to rise in arms among us, and to purchase that liberty of which *he* has deprived them, by murdering the people upon whom *he* also obtruded them; thus paying off former crimes committed against the *liberties* of one people, with crimes which he urges them to commit against the *lives* of another.

in every stage of these oppressions we have petitioned for redress in the most humble terms; our repeated petitions have been answered by repeated injury. a prince whose character is thus marked by every act which may define a tyrant, is unfit to be the ruler of a people who mean to be free. future ages will scarce believe that the hardiness of one man, adventured within the short compass of 12 years only, on so many acts of tyranny without a mask, over a people fostered & fixed in principles of liberty.

Nor have we been wanting in attentions to our British brethren. we have warned them from time to time of attempts by their legislature to extend a jurisdiction over these our states. we have reminded them of the circumstances of our emigration & settlement here, no one of which could warrant so strange a pretension: that these were effected at the expence of our own blood & treasure, unassisted by the wealth or the strength of Great Britain: that in constituting indeed our several forms of government, we had adopted one common king, thereby laying a foundation for perpetual league & amity with them: but that submission to their parliament was no part of our constitution, nor ever in idea, if history may be credited: and we appealed to their native justice & magnanimity, as well as to the ties of our common kindred to disavow these usurpations which were likely to interrupt our correspondence & connection. they too have been deaf to the voice of justice & of consanguinity, & when occasions have been given them, by the regular course of their laws, of removing from their councils the disturbers of our harmony, they have by their free election re-established them in power. at this very time too they are permitting their chief magistrate to send over not only soldiers of our common blood, but Scotch & foreign mercenaries to invade & deluge us in blood. these facts have given the last stab to agonizing affection, and manly spirit bids us to renounce for ever these unfeeling brethren. we must endeavor to forget our former love for them, and to hold them as we hold the rest of mankind, enemies in war, in peace friends. we might have been a free & a great people together; but a communication of grandeur & of freedom it seems is below their dignity. be it so, since they will have it: the road to glory & happiness is open to us too; we will climb it in a separate state, and acquiesce in the necessity which pronounces our everlasting Adieu!

We therefore the representatives of the United States of America in General Congress assembled do, in the name & by authority of the good people of these states, reject and renounce all allegiance & subjection to the kings of Great Britain & all others who may hereafter claim by, through, or under them; we utterly dissolve & break off all political connection which may have heretofore subsisted between us & the people or parliament of Great Britain; and finally we do assert and declare these colonies to be free and independant states, and that as free & independant states they shall hereafter have power to levy war, conclude peace, contract alliances, establish commerce, & to do all other acts and things which independant states may of right do. And for the support of this declaration we mutually pledge to each other our lives, our fortunes, & our sacred honour.

As Adopted by Congress

IN CONGRESS, JULY 4, 1776.

THE UNANIMOUS DECLARATION OF THE THIRTEEN UNITED STATES OF AMERICA,

When in the Course of human events, it becomes necessary for one people to dissolve the political bands which have connected them with another, and to assume among the powers of the earth, the separate and equal station to which the Laws of Nature and of Nature's God entitle them, a decent respect to the opinions of mankind requires that they should declare the causes which impel them to the separation. We hold these truths to be self-evident, that all men are created equal, that they are endowed by their Creator with certain unalienable Rights, that among these are Life, Liberty and the pursuit of Happiness. That to secure these rights, Governments are instituted among Men, deriving their just powers from the consent of the governed, That whenever any Form of Government becomes destructive of these ends, it is the Right of the People to alter or to abolish it, and to institute new Government, laying its foundation on such principles and organizing its powers in such form, as to them shall seem most likely to effect their Safety and Happiness. Prudence, indeed, will dictate that Governments long established should not be changed for light and transient causes; and accordingly all experience hath shewn, that mankind are more disposed to suffer, while evils are sufferable, than to right themselves by abolishing the forms to which they are accustomed. But when a long train of abuses and usurpations, pursuing invariably the same Object evinces a design to reduce them under absolute Despotism, it is their right, it is their duty, to throw off such Government, and to provide new Guards for their future security. Such has been the patient sufferance of these Colonies; and such is now the necessity which constrains them to alter their former Systems of Government. The history of the present King of Great Britain is a history of repeated injuries and usurpations, all having in direct object the establishment of an absolute Tyranny over these States. To prove this, let Facts be submitted to a candid world. He has refused his Assent to Laws, the most wholesome and necessary for the public good. He has forbidden his Governors to pass Laws of immediate and pressing importance, unless suspended in their operation till his Assent should be obtained; and when so suspended, he has utterly neglected to attend to them. He has refused to pass other Laws for the accommodation of large districts of people, unless those people would relinquish the right of Representation in the Legislature, a right inestimable to them and formidable to tyrants only. He has called together legislative bodies at places unusual, uncomfortable, and distant from the depository of their public Records, for the sole purpose of fatiguing them into compliance with his measures. He has dissolved Representative Houses repeatedly, for opposing with manly firmness his invasions on the rights of the people. He has refused for a long time, after such dissolutions, to cause others to be elected; whereby the Legislative powers, incapable of Annihilation, have returned to the People at large for their exercise; the State remaining in the mean time exposed to all the dangers of invasion from without, and convulsions within. He has endeavoured to prevent the population of these States; for that purpose obstructing the Laws for Naturalization of Foreigners; refusing to pass others to encourage their migrations hither, and raising the conditions of new Appropriations of Lands. He has obstructed the Administration of Justice, by refusing his Assent to Laws for establishing Judiciary powers. He has made Judges dependent on his Will alone, for the tenure of their offices, and the amount and payment of their salaries. He has erected a multitude of New Offices, and sent hither swarms of Officers to harrass our people, and eat out their substance. He has kept among us, in times of peace, standing Armies without the Consent of our legislatures. He has affected to render the Military independent of and superior to the Civil power. He has combined with others to subject us to a jurisdiction foreign to our constitution, and unacknowledged by our laws; giving his Assent to their Acts of pretended Legislation: For Quartering large bodies of armed troops among us: For protecting them, by a mock Trial, from punishment for any Murders which they should commit on the Inhabitants of these States: For cutting off our Trade with all parts of the world: For imposing Taxes on us without our Consent: For depriving us in many cases of the benefits of Trial by Jury: For transporting us beyond Seas to be tried for pretended offences: For abolishing the free System of English Laws in a neighbouring Province, establishing therein an Arbitrary government, and enlarging its Boundaries so as to render it at once an example and fit instrument for introducing the same absolute rule into these Colonies: For taking away our Charters, abolishing our most valuable Laws, and altering fundamentally the Forms of our Governments: For suspending our own Legislatures, and declaring themselves invested with power to legislate for us in all cases whatsoever. He has abdicated Government here, by declaring us out of his Protection and waging War against us. He has plundered our seas, ravaged our Coasts, burnt our towns, and destroyed the Lives of our people. He is at this time transporting large Armies of foreign Mercenaries to compleat the works of death, desolation and tyranny, already begun with circumstances of Cruelty & perfidy scarcely paralleled in the most barbarous ages, and totally unworthy the Head of a civilized nation. He has constrained our fellow Citizens taken Captive on the high Seas to bear Arms against their Country, to become the executioners of their friends and Brethren, or to fall themselves by their Hands. He has excited domestic insurrections amongst us, and has endeavoured to bring on the inhabitants of our frontiers, the merciless Indian Savages, whose known rule of warfare, is an undistinguished destruction of all ages, sexes and conditions. In every stage of these Oppressions We have Petitioned for Redress in the most humble terms: Our repeated Petitions have been answered only by repeated injury. A Prince, whose character is thus marked by every act which may define a Tyrant, is unfit to be the ruler of a free people. Nor have We been wanting in attentions to our Brittish brethren. We have warned them from time to time of attempts by their legislature to extend an unwarrantable jurisdiction over us. We have reminded them of the circumstances of our emigration and settlement here. We have appealed to their native justice and magnanimity, and we have conjured them by the ties of our common kindred to disavow these usurpations, which would inevitably interrupt our connections and correspondence. They too have been deaf to the voice of justice and of consanguinity. We must, therefore, acquiesce in the necessity, which denounces our Separation, and hold them, as we hold the rest of mankind, Enemies in War, in Peace Friends.

We, therefore, the Representatives of the united States of America, in General Congress, Assembled, appealing to the Supreme Judge of the world for the rectitude of our intentions, do, in the Name, and by Authority of the good People of these Colonies, solemnly publish and declare, That these United Colonies are, and of Right ought to be Free and Independent States; that they are Absolved from all Allegiance to the British Crown, and that all political connection between them and the State of Great Britain, is and ought to be totally dissolved; and that as Free and Independent States, they have full Power to levy War, conclude Peace, contract Alliances, establish Commerce, and to do all other Acts and Things which Independent States may of right do. And for the support of this Declaration, with a firm reliance on the protection of divine Providence, we mutually pledge to each other our Lives, our Fortunes and our sacred Honor.

The Neoclassic Mode in Poetry

JOHN TRUMBULL [1750–1831]

John Trumbull came from a distinguished New England family. Like Jonathan Edwards, who was his mother's cousin, he entered Yale at the age of thirteen (though he had passed his entrance examinations at seven). He took his B.A. in 1767, continued at Yale for three more years and an M.A., then briefly returned as tutor before embarking upon the practice of law. While an undergraduate at Yale he became acquainted with Timothy Dwight and David Humphreys; these three young men formed the nucleus of a group known as "The Connecticut Wits," who specialized in satires of the contemporary scene. Joel Barlow joined the group, as did other "wits," among them Lemuel Hopkins, Richard Alsop, and Theodore Dwight.

Trumbull gained the admiration of his colleagues by his graceful Addisonian essays and his satire on Yale in the Tom Brainless section of *The Progress of Dulness* (1772), written when he was a tutor. To placate the offended college officials, Trumbull added two more sections, which toned down the satire of the first part by generalizing the subjects into the typical eighteenth-century coquette and fop, Harriet Simper and Dick Hairbrain. He also excused himself by pointing out that the ideal end of satire is to "expose vice by general animadversions, and not to brand characters by personal satire."

Trumbull was admitted to the bar in 1773, and entered the Boston law office of John Adams; the following year he moved his practice to New Haven. In 1776 he issued the first two cantos of *M'Fingal*, which quickly became the most popular anti-Tory poem of the Revolution, going through thirty editions in sixty years. A distinguished judge of the Supreme Court of Errors and a state legislator until 1819, Trumbull revised his works in 1820, moved to Detroit five years later, and died there in 1831.

Further reading: Alexander Cowie, *John Trumbull: Connecticut Wit*, 1936. V. L. Parrington, ed., *The Connecticut Wits*, 1926. Leon Howard, *The Connecticut Wits*, 1943.

Prospect of the Future Glory of America

Being the conclusion of an Oration, delivered at the public commencement at Yale-College, September 12, 1770

The rising tide of self-confidence and self-consciousness that swept through the colonies after the French and Indian War elicited numerous demands for and prophecies of a future America that would equal and surpass England and Europe. The term "American," as it was used after 1760 to denote a certain kind of British colonist, began to take on connotations of its own. Although his loyalty to England was not in question, the American colonist became increasingly conscious that he was *American* English, a rather special kind of Englishman with a different future. Thus Franklin could tell Lord Kames in 1767 that the American colonies were destined "to become a great country, populous and mighty," without any thought of separation from the empire. This poem of Trumbull's, prepared for a college commencement and cast in the familiar poetic tradition of the "vision," reflects the nascent nationalism so deeply felt by the young men of his generation who would soon fight a war for independence against England. Text: Arthur H. Nason, ed., *The Writings of John Trumbull*, volume XIV of *The Colonnade*, published by the Andiron Club, New York, 1922; a reprint of the 1820 edition of Trumbull's works.

—And see th' expected hour is on the wing,
With every joy the flight of years can bring;

The splendid scenes the Muse shall dare display,
And unborn ages view the ripen'd day.
 Beneath a sacred grove's inspiring shade,
When Night the world in pleasing glooms array'd,
While the fair moon, that leads the heav'nly train,
With varying brightness dyed the dusky plain,
Entranced I sate; to solemn thought resign'd,
Long visions rising in the raptured mind,
Celestial music charm'd the listening dale,
While these blest sounds my ravish'd ear assail.
 "To views far distant and to scenes more bright,
Along the vale of Time extend thy sight,
Where hours and days and years from yon dim pole,
Wave following wave in long succession roll,
There see, in pomp for ages without end,
The glories of the Western World ascend.
 "See, this blest land in orient morn appears,
Waked from the slumber of six thousand years,
While clouds of darkness veil'd each cheering ray;
To savage beasts and savage men, a prey.
Fair Freedom now her ensigns bright displays,
And peace and plenty bless the golden days.
In radiant state th' imperial realm shall rise,
Her splendor circling to the boundless skies;
Of every Fair she boasts the assembled charms,
The Queen of empires and the nurse of arms.
 "See her bold heroes mark their glorious way,
Arm'd for the fight and blazing on the day!
Blood stains their steps, and o'er th' ensanguined plain,
Mid warring thousands and mid thousands slain,
Their eager swords unsated carnage blend,
And ghastly deaths their raging course attend.
Her dreaded power the subject world shall see,
And laurel'd conquest wait her high decree.
 "And see her navies, rushing to the main,
Catch the swift gales and sweep the wat'ry plain;
Or led by commerce, at the merchant's door
Unlade the treasures of the Asian shore;
Or arm'd with thunder, on the guilty foe
Rush big with death and aim th' unerring blow;
Bid every realm, that hears the trump of fame,
Quake at the distant terror of her name.
 "For pleasing Arts behold her matchless charms,
The first in letters, as the first in arms.
See bolder genius quit the narrow shore,
And realms of science, yet untraced, explore,
Hiding in brightness of superior day,
The fainting gleam of Europe's setting ray.
 "Sublime the Muse shall lift her eagle wing;
Of heavenly themes the sacred bards shall sing,
Tell how the blest Redeemer, man to save,
Thro' the deep mansions of the gloomy grave,
Sought the low shades of night, then rising high
Vanquish'd the powers of hell, and soar'd above the sky;
Or paint the scenes of that funereal day,
When earth's last fires shall mark their dreadful way,
In solemn pomp th' eternal Judge descend,
Doom the wide world and give to nature, end;
Or ope heaven's glories to th' astonish'd eye,
And bid their lays with lofty Milton vie;
Or wake from nature's themes the moral song,
And shine with Pope, with Thompson and with Young.
 "This land her Swift and Addison shall view,
The former honours equall'd by the new;
Here shall some Shakspeare charm the rising age,
And hold in magic chains the listening stage;
A second Watts[1] shall string the heavenly lyre,
And other muses other bards inspire.
 "Her Daughters too the happy land shall grace
With powers of genius, as with charms of face;
Blest with the softness of the female mind,
With fancy blooming and with taste refined,
Some Rowe[2] shall rise, and wrest with daring pen
The pride of science from assuming men;
While each bright line a polish'd beauty wears,
For every muse and every grace are theirs.
 "Nor shall these bounds her rising fame confine,
With equal praise the sister arts shall shine.
 "Behold some new Apelles,[3] skill'd to trace
The varied features of the virgin's face,
Bid the gay landscape rise in rural charms,
Or wake from dust the slumb'ring chief in arms,
Bid art with nature hold a pleasing strife,
And warm the pictured canvas into life.
 "See heaven-born Music strike the trembling string,
Devotion rising on the raptured wing.
 "See the proud dome with lofty walls ascend,
Wide gates unfold, stupendous arches bend,
The spiry turrets, piercing to the skies,
And all the grandeur of the palace rise.
 "The patriot's voice shall Eloquence inspire
With Roman splendor and Athenian fire,
At freedom's call, teach manly breasts to glow,
And prompt the tender tear o'er guiltless woe."
1770

FROM *The Progress of Dulness*

Trumbull chooses the careers of Tom Brainless, a thick-headed parson, Dick Hairbrain, a foppish coxcomb, and Harriet Simper, a silly coquette, as his medium for a satiric

Prospect. [1]Isaac Watts (1674–1748), writer of hymns and popular, heavily moralistic poetry.

[2]Mrs. Elizabeth Rowe (1674–1737), English poetess of eighteenth-century repute.

[3]Greek painter of the fourth century B.C., regarded as the greatest painter of classical antiquity.

commentary on the fashions and foibles of his times, patterned on Samuel Butler's *Hudibras*, which he helped to establish as a popular model for American satiric verse. In the course of the slender plot Harriet, having failed to capture Hairbrain, settles for the stodgy Brainless, a successful small-town minister, thereby bringing poetic justice to all. Text: Arthur H. Nason, ed., *The Writings of John Trumbull.*

Preface

"Pray, what does the author mean?" is the first question most readers will ask, and the last they are able to answer. Therefore in a few words I will explain the subject and design of the following Poem.

The subject is the state of the times in regard to literature and religion. The author was prompted to write, by a hope that it might be of use to point out, in a clear, concise, and striking manner, those general errors, that hinder the advantages of education and the growth of piety. The subject is inexhaustible; nor is my design yet completed. This first part describes the principal mistakes in one course of life, and exemplifies the following well known truths;—that to the frequent scandal, as well of religion, as learning, a fellow, without any share of genius, or application to study, may pass with credit through life, receive the honours of a liberal education, and be admitted to the right hand of fellowship among ministers of the gospel;—that except in one neighboring province, ignorance wanders unmolested at our colleges, examinations are dwindled to mere form and ceremony, and after four years dozing there, no one is ever refused the honors of a degree, on account of dulness and insufficiency;—that the mere knowledge of ancient languages, of the abstruser parts of mathematics, and the dark researches of metaphysics, is of little advantage in any business or profession in life;—that it would be more beneficial, in every place of public education, to take pains in teaching the elements of oratory, the grammar of the English tongue, and the elegancies of style and composition;—that in numberless instances, sufficient care hath not been taken to exclude the ignorant and irreligious from the sacred desk;—that this tenderness to the undeserving tends to debase the dignity of the clergy, and to hinder many worthy men from undertaking the office of the ministry;—and that the virulent controversies of the present day concerning religious, or in many cases, merely speculative opinions, savoring so highly of vanity and ostentation, and breathing a spirit so opposite to christian benevolence, have done more hurt to the cause of religion, than all the malice, the ridicule, and the folly of its enemies.

New-Haven, August 1772.

[Tom Brainless as Student and Preacher]

Two years thus spent in gathering knowledge,
The lad sets forth t' unlade at college,
While down his sire and priest attend him,
To introduce and recommend him;
Or if detain'd, a letter's sent
Of much apocryphal content,
To set him forth, how dull soever,
As very learn'd and very clever;
A genius of the first emission,
With burning love for erudition;
So studious he'll outwatch the moon
And think the planets set too soon.
He had but little time to fit in;
Examination too must frighten.
Depend upon't he must do well,
He knows much more than he can tell;
Admit him, and in little space
He'll beat his rivals in the race;
His father's incomes are but small,
He comes now, if he come at all.
So said, so done, at college now
He enters well, no matter how;
New scenes awhile his fancy please,
But all must yield to love of ease.
In the same round condemn'd each day,
To study, read, recite and pray;
To make his hours of business double—
He can't endure th' increasing trouble;
And finds at length, as times grow pressing,
All plagues are easier than his lesson.
With sleepy eyes and count'nance heavy,
With much excuse of *non paravi*,[1]
Much absence, *tardes* and *egresses*,
The college-evil on him seizes.
Then ev'ry book, which ought to please,
Stirs up the seeds of dire disease;
Greek spoils his eyes, the print's so fine,
Grown dim with study, or with wine;
Of Tully's latin much afraid,
Each page, he calls the doctor's aid;
While geometry, with lines so crooked,
Sprains all his wits to overlook it.
His sickness puts on every name,
Its cause and uses still the same;
'Tis tooth-ache, cholic, gout or stone,

Progress of Dulness. [1] *Non paravi*, I have not prepared for recitation—an excuse commonly given; *tardes* and *egresses*, were terms used at college, for coming in late and going out before the conclusion of service. [Trumbull's note.]

With phases various as the moon;
But though through all the body spread,
Still makes its cap'tal seat, the head.
In all diseases, 'tis expected,
The weakest parts be most infected.

* * * * *

Now in the desk,[2] with solemn air,
Our hero makes his audience stare;
Asserts with all dogmatic boldness,
Where impudence is yoked to dulness;
Reads o'er his notes with halting pace,
Mask'd in the stiffness of his face;
With gestures such as might become
Those statues once that spoke at Rome,
Or Livy's ox, that to the state
Declared the oracles of fate,
In awkward tones, nor said, nor sung,
Slow rumbling o'er the falt'ring tongue,
Two hours his drawling speech holds on,
And names it preaching, when he's done.
With roving tired, he fixes down
For life, in some unsettled town.
People and priest full well agree,
For why—they know no more than he.
Vast tracts of unknown land he gains,
Better than those the moon contains;
There deals in preaching and in prayer,
And starves on sixty pounds a year,
And culls his texts, and tills his farm,
Does little good, and little harm;
On Sunday, in his best array,
Deals forth the dulness of the day,
And while above he spends his breath,
The yawning audience nod beneath.
Thus glib-tongued Merc'ry in his hand
Stretch'd forth the sleep-compelling wand,
Each eye in endless doze to keep—
The God of speaking, and of sleep.

[Dick Hairbrain Learns the Social Graces]

Poor Dick![3] though first thy airs provoke
Th' obstreperous laugh and scornful joke,
Doom'd all the ridicule to stand,
While each gay dunce shall lend a hand;
Yet let not scorn dismay thy hope
To shine a witling and a fop.
Blest impudence the prize shall gain,
And bid thee sigh no more in vain.
Thy varied dress shall quickly show
At once the spendthrift and the beau.
With pert address and noisy tongue,
That scorns the fear of prating wrong,
'Mongst list'ning coxcombs shalt thou shine,
And every voice shall echo thine.
How blest the brainless fop, whose praise
Is doom'd to grace these happy days,
When well-bred vice can genius teach,
And fame is placed in folly's reach,
Impertinence all tastes can hit,
And every rascal is a wit.
The lowest dunce, without despairing,
May learn the true sublime of swearing;
Learn the nice art of jests obscene,
While ladies wonder what they mean;
The heroism of brazen lungs,
The rhetoric of eternal tongues;
While whim usurps the name of spirit,
And impudence takes place of merit,
And every money'd clown and dunce
Commences gentleman at once.
For now, by easy rules of trade,
Mechanic gentlemen are made!
From handicrafts of fashion born;
Those very arts so much their scorn.
To taylors half themselves they owe,
Who make the clothes, that make the beau.
Lo! from the seats, where, fops to bless,
Learn'd artists fix the forms of dress,
And sit in consultation grave,
On folded skirt, or strait'ned sleeve,
The coxcomb trips with sprightly haste,
In all the flush of modern taste;
Oft turning, if the day be fair,
To view his shadow's graceful air;
Well pleased with eager eye runs o'er
The laced suit glitt'ring gay before,[4]
The ruffle, where from open'd vest
The rubied brooch adorns the breast;
The coat with length'ning waist behind,
Whose short skirts dangle in the wind;
The modish hat, whose breadth contains
The measure of its owner's brains;
The stockings gay with various hues;
The little toe-encircling shoes;
The cane, on whose carv'd top is shown
An head, just emblem of his own;
While wrapp'd in self, with lofty stride,
His little heart elate with pride,
He struts in all the joys of show,
That taylors give, or beaux can know.
And who for beauty need repine,
That's sold at every barber's sign;
Nor lies in features or complexion,
But curls disposed in meet direction,

[2] Tom, having graduated, has entered the ministry. The "desk" is a pulpit.

[3] Dick Hairbrain, son of a wealthy farmer, enters college to learn the social graces.

[4] This passage alludes to the modes of dress then in fashion. [Trumbull's note.]

With strong pomatum's grateful odour,
And *quantum sufficit* of powder?
These charms can shed a sprightly grace,
O'er the dull eye and clumsy face;
While the trim dancing-master's art
Shall gestures, trips and bows impart,
Give the gay piece its final touches,
And lend those airs, would lure a dutchess.
Thus shines the form, nor aught behind,
The gifts that deck the coxcomb's mind;
Then hear the daring muse disclose
The sense and piety of beaux.
To grace his speech, let France bestow
A set of compliments for show.
Land of politeness! that affords
The treasure of new-fangled words,
And endless quantities disburses
Of bows and compliments and curses;
The soft address, with airs so sweet,
That cringes at the ladies' feet;
The pert, vivacious, play-house style,
That wakes the gay assembly's smile;
Jests that his brother beaux may hit,
And pass with young coquettes for wit,
And prized by fops of true discerning,
Outface the pedantry of learning.
Yet learning too shall lend its aid,
To fill the coxcomb's spongy head,
And studious oft he shall peruse
The labours of the modern muse.
From endless loads of novels gain
Soft, simp'ring tales of amorous pain,
With double meanings, neat and handy,
From Rochester and Tristram Shandy.[5]
The blund'ring aid of weak reviews,
That forge the fetters of the muse,
Shall give him airs of criticising
On faults of books, he ne'er set eyes on.
The magazines shall teach the fashion,
And common-place of conversation,
And where his knowledge fails, afford
The aid of many a sounding word.
Then least religion he should need,
Of pious Hume he'll learn his creed,
By strongest demonstration shown,
Evince that nothing can be known;
Take arguments, unvex'd by doubt,
On Voltaire's trust, or go without;
'Gainst scripture rail in modern lore,
As thousand fools have rail'd before;
Or pleased a nicer art display
T' expound its doctrines all away,
Suit it to modern tastes and fashions
By various notes and emendations;
The rules the ten commands contain,
With new provisos well explain;
Prove all religion was but fashion,
Beneath the Jewish dispensation.

[5] Sterne's *Tristram Shandy* was then in the highest vogue, and in the zenith of its transitory reputation. [Trumbull's note.]

[Harriet Simper Has Her Day]

Thus HARRIET,[6] rising on the stage,
Learns all the arts, that please the age,
And studies well, as fits her station,
The trade and politics of fashion:
A judge of modes in silks and satins,
From tassels down to clogs and pattens;
A genius, that can calculate
When modes of dress are out of date,
Cast the nativity with ease
Of gowns, and sacks and negligees,
And tell, exact to half a minute,
What's out of fashion and what's in it;
And scanning all with curious eye,
Minutest faults in dresses spy;
(So in nice points of sight, a flea
Sees atoms better far than we;)
A patriot too, she greatly labours,
To spread her arts among her neighbours,
Holds correspondences to learn
What facts the female world concern,
To gain authentic state-reports
Of varied modes in distant courts,
The present state and swift decays
Of tuckers, handkerchiefs and stays,
The colour'd silk that beauty wraps,
And all the rise and fall of caps.
Then shines, a pattern to the fair,
Of mien, address and modish air,
Of every new, affected grace,
That plays the eye, or decks the face,
The artful smile, that beauty warms,
And all th' hypocrisy of charms.
On Sunday, see the haughty maid
In all the glare of dress array'd,
Deck'd in her most fantastic gown,
Because a stranger's come to town.
Heedless at church she spends the day,
For homelier folks may serve to pray,
And for devotion those may go,
Who can have nothing else to do.
Beauties at church must spend their care in
Far other work, than pious hearing;

[6] Harriet Simper, trained in the coquettish arts, pursues Dick, who eludes her.

They've beaux to conquer, bells to rival;
To make them serious were uncivil.
For, like the preacher, they each Sunday
Must do their whole week's work in one day.
  As though they meant to take by blows
Th' opposing galleries of beaux,[7]
To church the female squadron move,
All arm'd with weapons used in love.
Like colour'd ensigns gay and fair,
High caps rise floating in the air;
Bright silk its varied radiance flings,
And streamers wave in kissing-strings;
Each bears th' artill'ry of her charms,
Like training bands at viewing arms.
  So once, in fear of Indian beating,
Our grandsires bore their guns to meeting,
Each man equipp'd on Sunday morn,
With psalm-book, shot and powder-horn;
And look'd in form, as all must grant,
Like th' ancient, true church militant;
Or fierce, like modern deep divines,
Who fight with quills, like porcupines.
  Or let us turn the style and see
Our belles assembled o'er their tea;
Where folly sweetens ev'ry theme,
And scandal serves for sugar'd cream.
  "And did you hear the news? (they cry)
The court wear caps full three feet high,
Built gay with wire, and at the end on't,
Red tassels streaming like a pendant.
Well sure, it must be vastly pretty;
'Tis all the fashion in the city.
And were you at the ball last night?
Well, Chloe look'd like any fright;
Her day is over for a toast;
She'd now do best to act a ghost.
You saw our Fanny; envy must own
She figures, since she came from Boston.
Good company improves one's air—
I think the troops were station'd there.
Poor Coelia ventured to the place;
The small-pox quite has spoil'd her face,
A sad affair, we all confest:
But providence knows what is best.
Poor Dolly, too, that writ the letter
Of love to Dick; but Dick knew better;
A secret that; you'll not disclose it;
There's not a person living knows it.
Sylvia shone out, no peacock finer;
I wonder what the fops see in her.
Perhaps 'tis true what Harry maintains,
She mends on intimate acquaintance."

[7] Young people of different sexes used then to sit in the opposite galleries. [Trumbull's note.]

  Yet that we fairly may proceed,
We own that ladies sometimes read,
And grieve, that reading is confin'd
To books that poison all the mind;
Novels and plays (where shines display'd
A world that nature never made),
Which swell their hopes with airy fancies,
And amorous follies of romances;
Inspire with dreams the witless maiden
On flowery vales and fields Arcadian,
And constant hearts no chance can sever,
And mortal loves, that last for ever.
  For while she reads romance, the fair one
Fails not to think herself the heroine;
For every glance, or smile, or grace,
She finds resemblance in her face,
Expects the world to fall before her,
And every fop she meets adore her.
Thus Harriet reads, and reading really
Believes herself a young Pamela,
The high-wrought whim, the tender strain
Elate her mind and turn her brain:
Before her glass, with smiling grace,
She views the wonders of her face;
There stands in admiration moveless,
And hopes a Grandison, or Lovelace.[8]
  Then shines she forth, and round her hovers,
The powder'd swarm of bowing lovers;
By flames of love attracted thither,
Fops, scholars, dunces, cits, together.
No lamp exposed in nightly skies,
E'er gather'd such a swarm of flies;
Or flame in tube electric draws
Such thronging multitudes of straws.
(For I shall still take similes
From fire electric when I please.)
  With vast confusion swells the sound,
When all the coxcombs flutter round.
What undulation wide of bows!
What gentle oaths and am'rous vows!
What double entendres all so smart!
What sighs hot-piping from the heart!
What jealous leers! what angry brawls
To gain the lady's hand at balls!
What billet-doux, brimful of flame!
Acrostics lined with Harriet's name!
What compliments, o'er-strained with telling
Sad lies of Venus and of Helen!
What wits half-crack'd with commonplaces
On angels, goddesses and graces!
On fires of love what witty puns!

[8] Pamela, Sir Charles Grandison, and Lovelace were all characters in the enormously popular sentimental novels of Samuel Richardson (1689-1761).

What similes of stars and suns!
What cringing, dancing, ogling, sighing,
What languishing for love, and dying!

* * * * *

And here her brightest hopes miscarry;
For Dick was too gallant to marry.
He own'd she'd charms for those who need 'em,
But he, be sure, was all for freedom;
So, left in hopeless flames to burn,
Gay Dick esteem'd her in her turn.
In love, a lady once given over
Is never fated to recover,
Doom'd to indulge her troubled fancies,
And feed her passion by romances;
And always amorous, always changing,
From coxcomb still to coxcomb ranging,
Finds in her heart a void, which still
Succeeding beaux can never fill:
As shadows vary o'er a glass,
Each holds in turn the vacant place;
She doats upon her earliest pain,
And following thousands loves in vain.
Poor HARRIET now hath had her day;
No more the beaux confess her sway;
New beauties push her from the stage;
She trembles at th' approach of age,
And starts to view the alter'd face,
That wrinkles at her in her glass:
So Satan, in the monk's tradition,
Fear'd, when he met his apparition.
At length her name each coxcomb cancels
From standing lists of toasts and angels;
And slighted where she shone before,
A grace and goddess now no more,
Despised by all, and doom'd to meet
Her lovers at her rival's feet,
She flies assemblies, shuns the ball,
And cries out, vanity, on all;
Affects to scorn the tinsel-shows
Of glittering belles and gaudy beaux;
Nor longer hopes to hide by dress
The tracks of age upon her face.
Now careless grown of airs polite,
Her noonday nightcap meets the sight;
Her hair uncomb'd collects together,
With ornaments of many a feather;
Her stays for easiness thrown by,
Her rumpled handkerchief awry,
A careless figure half undress'd,
(The reader's wits may guess the rest;)
All points of dress and neatness carried,
As though she'd been a twelvemonth married;
She spends her breath, as years prevail,
At this sad wicked world to rail,
To slander all her sex *impromptu*,
And wonder what the times will come to.

[An Amorous Temper]

Tom Brainless, at the close of last year,
Had been six years a rev'rend Pastor,
And now resolved, to smooth his life,
To seek the blessing of a wife.
His brethren saw his amorous temper,
And recommended fair Miss Simper,
Who fond, they heard, of sacred truth,
Had left her levities of youth,
Grown fit for ministerial union,
And grave, as Christian's wife in Bunyan.
On this he rigg'd him in his best,
And got his old grey wig new dress'd,
Fix'd on his suit of sable stuffs,
And brush'd the powder from the cuffs,
With black silk stockings, yet in being,
The same he took his first degree in;
Procured a horse of breed from Europe,
And learn'd to mount him by the stirrup,
And set forth fierce to court the maid;
His white-hair'd Deacon went for aid;
And on the right, in solemn mode,
The Reverend Mr. Brainless rode.
Thus grave, the courtly pair advance,
Like knight and squire in famed romance.
The priest then bow'd in sober gesture,
And all in scripture terms address'd her;
He'd found, for reasons amply known,
It was not good to be alone,
And thought his duty led to trying
The great command of multiplying;
So with submission, by her leave,
He'd come to look him out an Eve,
And hoped, in pilgrimage of life,
To find an helpmate in a wife,
A wife discreet and fair withal,
To make amends for Adam's fall.
In short, the bargain finish'd soon,
A reverend Doctor made them one.
And now the joyful people rouze all
To celebrate their priest's espousal;
And first, by kind agreement set,
In case their priest a wife could get,
The parish vote him five pounds clear,
T' increase his salary every year.
Then swift the tag-rag gentry come
To welcome Madam Brainless home;
Wish their good Parson joy; with pride
In order round salute the bride.

1772–73

JOEL BARLOW [1754-1812]

Joel Barlow, born a farmer's son near Redding, Connecticut, in 1754, attended Dartmouth and Yale, graduating from the latter in 1778 as "class poet." Licensed a Congregational minister after a six-week course in theology, he served as chaplain to a Massachusetts line regiment during the war, and afterwards entered law practice in Hartford. During his army years he began work on a long "national" epic, published in 1787 as *The Vision of Columbus,* highly regarded for its patriotism at the time. He was also associated, as one of the conservative group of "Connecticut Wits," with Trumbull, Humphreys, and Hopkins in the series of strongly Federalist satires known as *The Anarchiad* in 1786-87.

Barlow left the law to join the Scioto Company, formed to promote speculative land sales in Ohio, and was sent to England in 1788 as its European agent. When the company was exposed as a swindle, Barlow, who apparently was innocent, immediately resigned. While in London, he met and moved with the political radicals—among them Paine, William Godwin, and Joseph Priestley—and soon he was caught up in the wave of revolutionary excitement sweeping England and Europe. The Connecticut Yankee became a cosmopolite, at home in London and Paris; the Federalist conservative became a Jacobin radical; the New England Congregationalist turned into a deist. His *Advice to the Privileged Orders* (Part I, 1791), an answer to Edmund Burke's criticisms of the French revolutionaries, attacked the church, the monarchy, courts, armies, and all other institutions that subverted justice and oppressed the people:

> The tyrannies of the world, whatever be the appellation of the government under which they are exercised, are all aristocratical tyrannies. An ordinance to plunder and murder, whether it fulminate from the Vatican, or steal silently forth from the Harem; whether it come clothed in the *certain science* of a Bed of Justice, or in the legal solemnities of a bench of lawyers; whether it be purchased by the caresses of a woman, or the treasures of a nation,—never confines its effects to the benefit of a single individual; it goes to enrich the whole combination of conspirators whose business it is to dupe and to govern the nation.

In verse he wrote *The Conspiracy of Kings* (1792), proclaiming that under the leadership of France,

> Freedom at last, with Reason in her train,
> Extends o'er earth her everlasting reign.

For the services of his pen he was made an honorary French citizen and lived through the Reign of Terror in Paris without difficulty. From 1795 to 1797 he was American consul in Algiers, during the naval troubles with the Barbary pirates, with whom he concluded a useful treaty.

Barlow had a talent for money-making and by shrewd speculation built up a comfortable fortune. He returned to the United States in 1805 to purchase a country estate near Washington, where he lived in considerable splendor and maintained a salon for liberal writers and thinkers. He also reworked *The Vision of Columbus* into *The Columbiad,* publishing it in 1807, and planned next to write a history of the United States. In 1811, however, President Madison made him ambassador to France, especially to negotiate favorable trade treaties with Napoleon. The Napoleonic armies were deep in Russia, and Barlow's request for an audience with the Emperor was delayed by the disastrous retreat from Moscow. Finally he received word that Napoleon would see him at Wilna, in

Poland, but Barlow never arrived. He died of pneumonia on December 22, 1812, at a small village near Cracow.

Further reading: James Woodress, *A Yankee's Odyssey*, 1958. Vernon L. Parrington, ed., *The Connecticut Wits*, 1926. Leon Howard, *The Connecticut Wits*, 1943.

The Hasty Pudding

A Poem in Three Cantos

In January 1793 Barlow was in Savoy, near the French Alps, at Chambéry, where unexpectedly (and inexplicably) he was served corn-meal mush, or hasty pudding, at the inn. Suddenly homesick for New England, he wrote this playful dietary epic in memory of the familiar dish of his Yankee boyhood. It was published in the United States three years later, running through five editions in its first year and remaining perennially popular. A mock-heroic pastoral, the poem burlesques the conventions of the epic form, with an invocation to the Muse, learned allusions, rhetorical flights, and inflated diction. Yet it was something more than a humorous burlesque. It not only represents one of the earliest uses of folklore and folk-materials in American poetry, but it is also a sincere affirmation of Jeffersonian agrarian simplicity and a celebration of the honest, homely joys of American country life. Text: The New Haven edition, 1796, with the original preface.

Omne tulit punctum qui miscuit utile dulci,
He makes a good breakfast who mixes pudding with molasses.

To Mrs. Washington

MADAM:—A simplicity in diet, whether it be considered with reference to the happiness of individuals or the prosperity of a nation, is of more consequence than we are apt to imagine. In recommending so great and necessary a virtue to the rational part of mankind, I wish it were in my power to do it in such a manner as would be likely to gain their attention. I am sensible that it is one of those subjects in which example has infinitely more power than the most convincing arguments, or the highest charms of poetry. Goldsmith's *Deserted Village,* though possessing these two advantages in a greater degree than any other work of the kind, has not prevented villages in England from being deserted. The apparent interest of the rich individuals, who form the taste as well as the laws in that country, has been against him; and with that interest it has been vain to contend.

The vicious habits which in this little piece I endeavor to combat, seem to me not so difficult to cure. No class of people has any interest in supporting them, unless it be the interest which certain families may feel in vieing with each other in sumptuous entertainments. There may indeed be some instances of depraved appetites which no arguments will conquer; but these must be rare. There are very few persons but would always prefer a plain dish for themselves, and would prefer it likewise for their guests, if there were no risk of reputation in the case. This difficulty can only be removed by example; and the example should proceed from those whose situation enables them to take the lead in forming the manners of a nation. Persons of this description in America, I should hope, are neither above nor below the influence of truth and reason when conveyed in language suited to the subject.

Whether the manner I have chosen to address my arguments to them be such as to promise any success, is what I cannot decide. But I certainly had hopes of doing some good, or I should not have taken the pains of putting so many rhymes together; and much less should I have ventured to place your name at the head of these observations.

Your situation commands the respect and your character the affections of a numerous people. These circumstances impose a duty upon you, which I believe you discharge to your own satisfaction and that of others. The example of your domestic virtues has doubtless a great effect among your countrywomen. I only wish to rank *simplicity of diet* among the virtues. In that case it will certainly be cherished by you, and I should hope more esteemed by others than it is at present.

THE AUTHOR.

Canto I

Ye Alps audacious, through the heavens that rise,
To cramp the day and hide me from the skies;
Ye Gallic flags, that o'er their heights unfurled,
Bear death to kings, and freedom to the world,
I sing not you. A softer theme I choose,
A virgin theme, unconscious of the Muse,
But fruitful rich, well suited to inspire
The purest frenzy of poetic fire.
  Despise it not, ye bards to terror steel'd,
Who hurl your thunders round the epic field;
Nor ye who strain your midnight throats to sing
Joys that the vineyard and the still-house[1] bring;

The Hasty Pudding. [1] Distillery.

Or on some distant fair your notes employ,
And speak of raptures that you ne'er enjoy.
I sing the sweets I know, the charms I feel,
My morning incense, and my evening meal,
The sweets of Hasty Pudding. Come, dear bowl,
Glide o'er my palate, and inspire my soul.
The milk beside thee, smoking from the kine,
Its substance mingle, married in with thine,
Shall cool and temper thy superior heat,
And save the pains of blowing while I eat.
  Oh! could the smooth, the emblematic song
Flow like thy genial juices o'er my tongue,
Could those mild morsels in my numbers chime,
And, as they roll in substance, roll in rhyme,
No more thy awkward unpoetic name
Should shun the muse, or prejudice thy fame;
But rising grateful to the accustom'd ear,
All bards should catch it, and all realms revere!
  Assist me first with pious toil to trace
Through wrecks of time, thy lineage and thy race;
Declare what lovely squaw, in days of yore,
(Ere great Columbus sought thy native shore)
First gave thee to the world; her works of fame
Have lived indeed, but lived without a name.
Some tawny Ceres,[2] goddess of her days,
First learn'd with stones to crack the well dried maize,
Through the rough sieve to shake the golden shower,
In boiling water stir the yellow flour:
The yellow flour, bestrew'd and stirr'd with haste,
Swells in the flood and thickens to a paste,
Then puffs and wallops, rises to the brim,
Drinks the dry knobs that on the surface swim;
The knobs at last the busy ladle breaks,
And the whole mass its true consistence takes.
  Could but her sacred name, unknown so long,
Rise, like her labors, to the son of song,
To her, to them, I'd consecrate my lays,
And blow her pudding with the breath of praise.
If 'twas Oella[3] whom I sang before
I here ascribe her one great virtue more.
Not through the rich Peruvian realms alone
The fame of Sol's sweet daughter should be known,
But o'er the world's wide clime should live secure,
Far as his rays extend, as long as they endure.
  Dear Hasty Pudding, what unpromised joy
Expands my heart to meet thee in Savoy!
Doom'd o'er the world through devious paths to roam,
Each clime my country, and each house my home,
My soul is soothed, my cares have found an end,
I greet my long lost, unforgotten friend.
  For thee through Paris, that corrupted town,
How long in vain I wandered up and down,
Where shameless Bacchus, with his drenching hoard,
Cold from his cave usurps the morning board.
London is lost in smoke and steep'd in tea;
No Yankee there can lisp the name of thee;
The uncouth word, a libel on the town,
Would call a proclamation from the crown.[4]
From climes oblique, that fear the sun's full rays,
Chill'd in their fogs, exclude the generous maize:
A grain, whose rich, luxuriant growth requires
Short gentle showers, and bright etherial fires.
  But here, though distant from our native shore,
With mutual glee, we meet and laugh once more,
The same! I know thee by that yellow face,
That strong complexion of true Indian race,
Which time can never change, nor soil impair,
Nor Alpine snows, nor Turkey's morbid air;
For endless years, through every mild domain,
Where grows the maize, there thou art sure to reign.
  But man, more fickle, the bold license claims,
In different realms to give thee different names.
Thee the soft nations round the warm Levant
Polenta call, the French of course *Polente*.
E'en in thy native regions, how I blush
To hear the Pennsylvanians call thee *Mush!*
On Hudson's banks, while men of Belgic spawn
Insult and eat thee by the name *Suppawn*.
All spurious appellations, void of truth;
I've better known thee from my earliest youth,
Thy name is *Hasty-Pudding!* thus my sire
Was wont to greet thee fuming from his fire;
And while he argued in thy just defence
With logic clear, he thus explain'd the sense:—
"In *haste* the boiling cauldron, o'er the blaze,
Receives and cooks the ready powder'd maize;
In *haste* 'tis served, and then in equal *haste*,
With cooling milk, we make the sweet repast.
No carving to be done, no knife to grate
The tender ear, and wound the stony plate;
But the smooth spoon, just fitted to the lip,
And taught with art the yielding mass to dip,
By frequent journeys to the bowl well stored,
Performs the *hasty* honors of the board."
Such is thy name, significant and clear,
A name, a sound to every Yankee dear,
But most to me, whose heart and palate chaste
Preserve my pure hereditary taste.

[2] Goddess of grain.

[3] A Peruvian goddess of household arts, to whom Barlow had referred in *The Vision of Columbus*.

[4] A certain king, at the time when this was written, was publishing proclamations to prevent American principles from being propagated in his country. [Barlow's note.]

There are who strive to stamp with disrepute
The luscious food, because it feeds the brute;
In tropes of high-strain'd wit, while gaudy prigs
Compare thy nursling, man, to pamper'd pigs;
With sovereign scorn I treat the vulgar jest,
Nor fear to share thy bounties with the beast.
What though the generous cow gives me to quaff
The milk nutritious: am I then a calf?
Or can the genius of the noisy swine,
Though nursed on pudding, claim a kin to mine?
Sure the sweet song, I fashion to thy praise,
Runs more melodious than the notes they raise.
My song resounding in its grateful glee,
No merit claims: I praise myself in thee.
My father loved thee through his length of days!
For thee his fields were shaded o'er with maize;
From thee what health, what vigor he possess'd,
Ten sturdy freemen from his loins attest;
Thy constellation ruled my natal morn,
And all my bones were made of Indian corn.
Delicious grain! whatever form it take,
To roast or boil, to smother or to bake,
In every dish 'tis welcome still to me,
But most, my *Hasty Pudding*, most in thee.
Let the green succotash with thee contend,
Let beans and corn their sweetest juices blend,
Let butter drench them in its yellow tide,
And a long slice of bacon grace their side;
Not all the plate, how famed soe'er it be,
Can please my palate like a bowl of thee.
Some talk of *Hoe-Cake*, fair Virginia's pride,
Rich *Johnny-Cake*, this mouth has often tried;
Both please me well, their virtues much the same,
Alike their fabric, as allied their fame,
Except in dear New England, where the last
Receives a dash of pumpkin in the paste,
To give it sweetness and improve the taste.
But place them all before me, smoking hot,
The big, round dumpling, rolling from the pot,
The pudding of the bag, whose quivering breast,
With suet lined, leads on the Yankee feast,
The *Charlotte*[5] brown within whose crusty sides
A belly soft the pulpy apple hides;
The yellow bread whose face like amber glows,
And all of Indian that the bake-pan knows,—
You tempt me not—my fav'rite greets my eyes,
To that loved bowl my spoon by instinct flies.

Canto II

To mix the food by vicious rules of art,
To kill the stomach, and to sink the heart
To make mankind to social virtue sour,
Cram o'er each dish, and be what they devour;
For this the kitchen muse first fram'd her book,
Commanding sweats to stream from every cook;
Children no more their antic gambols tried,
And friends to physic wonder'd why they died.
Not so the Yankee—his abundant feast,
With simples furnish'd and with plainness drest,
A numerous offspring gathers round the board,
And cheers alike the servant and the lord;
Whose well-bought hunger prompts the joyous taste,
And health attends them from the short repast.
While the full pail rewards the milk-maid's toil,
The mother sees the morning cauldron boil;
To stir the pudding next demands their care;
To spread the table and the bowls prepare;
To feed the household as their portions cool
And send them all to labor or to school.
Yet may the simplest dish some rules impart,
For nature scorns not all the aids of art.
E'en *Hasty-Pudding*, purest of all food,
May still be bad, indifferent, or good,
As sage experience the short process guides,
Or want of skill, or want of care presides.
Whoe'er would form it on the surest plan,
To rear the child and long sustain the man;
To shield the morals while it mends the size,
And all the powers of every food supplies,
Attend the lesson that the muse shall bring,
Suspend your spoons, and listen while I sing.
But since, O man! thy life and health demand
Not food alone but labor from thy hand,
First in the field, beneath the sun's strong rays,
Ask of thy mother earth the needful maize;
She loves the race that courts her yielding soil,
And gives her bounties to the sons of toil.
When now the ox, obedient to thy call,
Repays the loan that fill'd the winter stall,
Pursue his traces o'er the furrow'd plain,
And plant in measur'd hills the golden grain.
But when the tender germ begins to shoot,
And the green spire declares the sprouting root,
Then guard your nursling from each greedy foe,
The insidious worm, the all-devouring crow.
A little ashes, sprinkled round the spire,
Soon steep'd in rain, will bid the worm retire;
The feather'd robber with his hungry maw
Swift flies the field before your man of straw,
A frightful image, such as schoolboys bring,
When met to burn the pope, or hang the king.[6]
Thrice in the season, through each verdant row
Wield the strong ploughshare and the faithful hoe:
The faithful hoe, a double task that takes,
To till the summer corn, and roast the winter cakes.

[5] A pastry dessert.

[6] A reference perhaps to "Guy Fawkes Day" in England, November 5.

Slow springs the blade, while check'd by chilling rains,
Ere yet the sun the seat of Cancer[7] gains;
But when his fiercest fires emblaze the land,
Then start the juices, then the roots expand;
Then, like a column of Corinthian mould,
The stalk struts upward and the leaves unfold;
The busy branches all the ridges fill,
Entwine their arms, and kiss from hill to hill.
Here cease to vex them, all your cares are done:
Leave the last labors to the parent sun;
Beneath his genial smiles, the well-drest field,
When autumn calls, a plenteous crop shall yield.
Now the strong foliage bears the standards high,
And shoots the tall top-gallants to the sky;
The suckling ears their silky fringes bend,
And pregnant grown, their swelling coats distend;
The loaded stalk, while still the burthen grows,
O'erhangs the space that runs between the rows;
High as a hop-field waves the silent grove,
A safe retreat for little thefts of love,
When the pledged roasting ears invite the maid,
To meet her swain beneath the new-form'd shade;
His generous hand unloads the cumbrous hill,
And the green spoils her ready basket fill;
Small compensation for the two-fold bliss,
The promised wedding, and the present kiss.
Slight depredations these; but now the moon
Calls from his hollow tree the sly raccoon;
And while by night he bears his prize away,
The bolder squirrel labors through the day.
Both thieves alike, but provident of time,
A virtue rare, that almost hides their crime.
Then let them steal the little stores they can,
And fill their gran'ries from the toils of man;
We've one advantage, where they take no part,
With all their wiles they ne'er have found the art
To boil the *Hasty-Pudding;* here we shine
Superior far to tenants of the pine;
This envied boon to man shall still belong,
Unshared by them, in substance or in song.
At last the closing season browns the plain,
And ripe October gathers in the grain;
Deep loaded carts the spacious corn-house fill,
The sack distended marches to the mill;
The lab'ring mill beneath the burthen groans,
And showers the future pudding from the stones;
Till the glad housewife greets the powder'd gold,
And the new crop exterminates the old.
Ah who can sing what every wight must feel,
The joy that enters with the bag of meal,
A general jubilee pervades the house,
Wakes every child and gladdens every mouse.

[7] The sign of the zodiac marking June.

Canto III

The days grow short; but though the falling sun
To the glad swain proclaims his day's work done,
Night's pleasing shades his various tasks prolong,
And yield new subjects to my various song.
For now, the corn-house fill'd, the harvest home,
The invited neighbors to the *husking* come;
A frolic scene, where work, and mirth, and play,
Unite their charms to chase the hours away.
Where the huge heap lies centred in the hall,
The lamp suspended from the cheerful wall,
Brown corn-fed nymphs, and strong hard-handed beaus,
Alternate ranged, extend in circling rows,
Assume their seats, the solid mass attack;
The dry husks rustle, and the corn-cobs crack;
The song, the laugh, alternate notes resound,
And the sweet cider trips in silence round.
The laws of husking every wight can tell;
And sure no laws he ever keeps so well:
For each red ear a general kiss he gains,
With each smut ear he smuts the luckless swains;
But when to some sweet maid a prize is cast,
Red as her lips, and taper as her waist,
She walks the round, and culls one favored beau,
Who leaps, the luscious tribute to bestow.
Various the sport, as are the wits and brains
Of well pleased lasses and contending swains;
Till the vast mound of corn is swept away,
And he that gets the last ear wins the day.
Meanwhile the housewife urges all her care,
The well-earn'd feast to hasten and prepare.
The sifted meal already waits her hand,
The milk is strain'd, the bowls in order stand,
The fire flames high; and, as a pool (that takes
The headlong stream that o'er the mill-dam breaks)
Foams, roars, and rages, with incessant toils,
So the vex'd cauldron rages, roars and boils.
First with clean salt, she seasons well the food,
Then strews the flour, and thickens all the flood.
Long o'er the simmering fire she lets it stand;
To stir it well demands a stronger hand;
The husband takes his turn: and round and round
The ladle flies; at last the toil is crown'd;
When to the board the thronging huskers pour,
And take their seats as at the corn before.
I leave them to their feast. There still belong
More useful matters to my faithful song.
For rules there are, though ne'er unfolded yet,
Nice rules and wise, how pudding should be ate.
Some with molasses grace the luscious treat,
And mix, like bards, the useful and the sweet.
A wholesome dish, and well deserving praise,
A great resource in those bleak wintry days,

When the chill'd earth lies buried deep in snow,
And raging Boreas dries the shivering cow.
 Blest cow! thy praise shall still my notes employ,
Great source of health, the only source of joy;
Mother of Egypt's god,—but sure, for me,
Were I to leave my God, I'd worship thee.
How oft thy teats these pious hands have press'd!
How oft thy bounties prove my only feast!
How oft I've fed thee with my favorite grain!
And roar'd, like thee, to see thy children slain!
 Ye swains who know her various worth to prize,
Ah! house her well from winter's angry skies.
Potatoes, pumpkins, should her sadness cheer,
Corn from your crib, and mashes from your beer;
When spring returns, she'll well acquit the loan,
And nurse at once your infants and her own.
 Milk then with pudding I should always choose;
To this in future I confine my muse,
Till she in haste some further hints unfold,
Good for the young, nor useless to the old.
First in your bowl the milk abundant take,
Then drop with care along the silver lake
Your flakes of pudding; these at first will hide
Their little bulk beneath the swelling tide;
But when their growing mass no more can sink,
When the soft island looms above the brink,
Then check your hand; you've got the portion due,
So taught my sire, and what he taught is true.
 There is a choice in spoons. Though small appear
The nice distinction, yet to me 'tis clear.
The deep bowl'd Gallic spoon, contrived to scoop
In ample draughts the thin diluted soup,
Performs not well in those substantial things,
Whose mass adhesive to the metal clings;
Where the strong labial muscles must embrace,
The gentle curve, and sweep the hollow space.
With ease to enter and discharge the freight,
A bowl less concave, but still more dilate,
Becomes the pudding best. The shape, the size,
A secret rests, unknown to vulgar eyes.
Experienced feeders can alone impart
A rule so much above the lore of art.
These tuneful lips that thousand spoons have tried,
With just precision could the point decide.
Though not in song; the muse but poorly shines
In cones, and cubes, and geometric lines;
Yet the true form, as near as she can tell,
Is that small section of a goose egg shell,
Which in two equal portions shall divide
The distance from the centre to the side.
 Fear not to slaver; 'tis no deadly sin:——
Like the free Frenchman, from your joyous chin
Suspend the ready napkin; or like me,
Poise with one hand your bowl upon your knee;
Just in the zenith your wise head project,
Your full spoon, rising in a line direct,
Bold as a bucket, heed no drops that fall,
The wide mouth'd bowl will surely catch them all![8]

1793 1796

A Song

Why Barlow was regarded as a dangerous revolutionary in England, and by some in the United States, is aptly illustrated by a parody he wrote on England's "God Save the King" for the amusement of his friends, presumably sung at a dinner after the execution of Louis XVI in France in 1793. The text follows the version given in the *Columbian Centinel*, November 16, 1805.

Fame let thy trumpet sound,
Tell all the world around—
 How Capet fell:
And when great George's poll
Shall in the basket roll,
Let mercy then control
 The Guillotine.

When all the sceptered crew
Have paid their homage to
 The Guillotine;
Let Freedom's flag advance,
Till all the world, like France!
O'er tyrants' graves shall dance,
 And peace begin.

1793

On the Discoveries of Captain Lewis

On January 14, 1807, a dinner was given at Washington for Captain Meriwether Lewis, in recognition of his safe return from his journey with William Clark to the Pacific. "At an early period in the entertainment," reported the *National Intelligencer*, "the following elegant and glowing stanzas, from the pen of Mr. Barlow, were recited by Mr.

[8] The following note was added in a later edition: "There are various ways of preparing and eating it; with molasses, butter, sugar, cream, and fried. Why so excellent a thing cannot be eaten alone? Nothing is perfect alone, even man who boasts of so much perfection is nothing without his fellow substance. In eating, beware of the lurking heat that lies deep in the mass; dip your spoon gently, take shallow dips and cool it by degrees. It is sometimes necessary to blow. This is indicated by certain signs which every experienced feeder knows. They should be taught to young beginners. I have known a child's tongue blistered for want of this attention, and then the schooldame would insist that the poor thing had told a lie. A mistake: the falsehood was in the faithless pudding. A prudent mother will cool it for her child with her own sweet breath. The husband, seeing this, pretends his own wants blowing too from the same lips. A sly deceit of love. She knows the cheat, lends her pouting lips, and gives a gentle blast, which warms the husband's heart more than it cools his pudding."

Beckley." Barlow, like others in the Jefferson administration, was fully aware of the implications of the Lewis and Clark expedition for the nation's future, and fascinated by the prospects of westward expansion. Text: *National Intelligencer,* January 16, 1807.

Let the Nile cloak his head in the clouds, and defy
The researches of science and time;
Let the Niger escape the keen traveller's eye,
By plunging or changing his clime.

Columbus! not so shall thy boundless domain
Defraud thy brave sons of their right:
Streams, midlands, and shorelands elude us in vain,
We shall drag their dark regions to light.

Look down, sainted sage, from thy synod of Gods;
See, inspired by thy venturous soul,
Mackenzie roll northward his earth-draining floods,
And surge the broad waves to the pole.

With the same soaring genius thy Lewis ascends,
And seizing the car of the sun,
O'er the sky-propping hills and high waters he bends
And gives the proud earth a new zone.

Potowmak, Ohio, Missouri had felt
Half her globe in their cincture compress;
His long curving course has completed the belt,
And tamed the last tide of the west.

Then hear the loud voice of the nation proclaim,
And all ages resound the decree:
Let our occident stream bear the young hero's name
Who taught him his path to the sea.

These four brother floods, like a garland of flowers,
Shall entwine all our states in a band,
Conform and confederate their wide spreading powers,
And their wealth and their wisdom expand.

From Darien to Davis one garden shall bloom,
Where war's wearied banners are furl'd,
And the far scenting breezes that waft its perfume,
Shall settle the storms of the world.

Then hear the loud voice of the nation proclaim
And all ages resound the decree:
Let our occident stream bear the young hero's name,
Who taught him his path to the sea.

1807

Advice to a Raven in Russia

In early December 1812, at the onset of his fatal illness, Barlow dictated to his secretary a bitterly ironical indictment of the ruin and desolation left by twenty years of war in Europe. Napoleon's army, reeling back from the defeat at Moscow, retreating in the iron cold of Russian winter, was but a day or so away from Barlow's inn near Cracow. To him it seemed that the Emperor had shattered utterly the great eighteenth-century dream of the "everlasting reign" of peace and justice hailed in *The Columbiad,* and that tyranny and oppression once more stalked the world. The poem was copied in diplomatic code and sent to Mrs. Barlow in Paris but never reached her. The manuscript, after Barlow's death, was preserved and published some thirty years later. The text given here is that newly established by Leon Howard from the holograph manuscript and printed in his article "Joel Barlow and Napoleon," *Huntington Library Quarterly,* Vol. II, No. 1 (October 1938).

Black fool, why winter here? These frozen skies,
Worn by your wings and deafen'd by your cries,
Should warn you hence, where milder suns invite,
And day alternates with his mother night.
You fear perhaps your food will fail you there,
Your human carnage, that delicious fare
That lured you hither, following still your friend
The great Napoleon to the world's bleak end.
You fear, because the southern climes pour'd forth
Their clustering nations to infest the north,
Bavarians, Austrians, those who Drink the Po
And those who skirt the Tuscan seas below,
With all Germania, Neustria,[1] Belgia, Gaul,
Doom'd here to wade thro slaughter to their fall,
You fear he left behind no wars, to feed
His feather'd canibals and nurse the breed.
Fear not, my screamer, call your greedy train,
Sweep over Europe, hurry back to Spain,
You'll find his legions there; the valliant crew
Please best their master when they toil for you.
Abundant there they spread the country o'er
And taint the breeze with every nation's gore,
Iberian, Lussian,[2] British widely strown,
But still more wide and copious flows their own.
Go where you will; Calabria, Malta, Greece,
Egypt and Syria still his fame increase,
Domingo's fatten'd isle and India's plains
Glow deep with purple drawn from Gallic veins.
No Raven's wing can stretch the flight so far
As the torn bandrols of Napoleon's war.
Choose then your climate, fix your best abode,
He'll make you deserts and he'll bring you blood.
How could you fear a dearth? have not mankind,
Tho slain by millions, millions left behind?

Advice to a Raven. [1] Part of the Frankish empire of Clovis I, encompassing much of the Seine and Loire valleys.
[2] Lusian; Portuguese.

Has not CONSCRIPTION still the power to weild
Her annual faulchion[3] o'er the human field?
A faithful harvester! or if a man
Escape that gleaner, shall he scape the BAN?
The triple BAN, that like the hound of hell
Gripes with three joles,[4] to hold his victim well.
Fear nothing then, hatch fast your ravenous brood,
Teach them to cry to Bonaparte for food;
They'll be like you, of all his suppliant train,
The only class that never cries in vain.
For see what mutual benefits you lend!
(The surest way to fix the mutual friend)
While on his slaughter'd troops your tribes are fed,
You cleanse his camp and carry off his dead.
Imperial Scavenger! but now you know
Your work is vain amid these hills of snow.
His tentless troops are marbled thro with frost
And change to crystal when the breath is lost.
Mere trunks of ice, tho limb'd like human frames
And lately warm'd with life's endearing flames,
They cannot taint the air, the world impest,
Nor can you tear one fiber from their breast.
No! from their visual sockets, as they lie,

[3] Sword or sickle.
[4] Jowls; that is, jaws.

With beak and claws you cannot pluck an eye.
The frozen orb, preserving still its form,
Defies your talons as it braves the storm,
But stands and stares to God, as if to know
In what curst hands he leaves his world below.
Fly then, or starve; tho all the dreadful road
From Minsk to Moskow with their bodies strow'd
May count some Myriads, yet they can't suffice
To feed you more beneath these dreary skies.
Go back, and winter in the wilds of Spain;
Feast there awhile, and in the next campaign
Rejoin your master; for you'll find him then,
With his new million of the race of men,
Clothed in his thunders, all his flags unfurl'd,
Raging and storming o'er the prostrate world.
War after war his hungry soul requires,
State after State shall sink beneath his fires,
Yet other Spains in victim smoke shall rise
And other Moskows suffocate the skies,
Each land lie reeking with its people's slain
And not a stream run bloodless to the main.
Till men resume their souls, and dare to shed
Earth's total vengeance on the monster's head,
Hurl from his blood-built throne this king of woes,
Dash him to dust, and let the world repose.

1812 1843

PHILLIS WHEATLEY [1754?–1784]

THE LITTLE GIRL who would be Phillis Wheatley was brought from Africa to Boston in 1761 when she was about seven years old (she was then shedding her front teeth) and was purchased at the slave market by John Wheatley, a prosperous tailor, to be trained up as a personal servant for his wife. She apparently retained only one memory of her African life: her mother's custom of pouring a libation of water to the rising sun. Frail, gentle, and affectionate, she immediately won the heart of her mistress; and under the tutelage of the Wheatleys' accomplished daughter Mary, she learned to speak, read, and write English with a quick intelligence that carried teacher and pupil on to a more ambitious program of studies that included astronomy, geography, ancient history, and, more significantly, the Bible, the Latin classical writers (in translation and in the original), and the English poets. Under these literary influences, Phillis was soon writing poetry herself, an endeavor in which she was encouraged by the Wheatleys, who treated her almost as one of the family, assigning her only such light tasks as might be expected of a daughter of the house, and introducing her to their circle of acquaintance. She was sixteen when her first published poem appeared, an elegy on the death of the popular revivalist preacher George Whitefield, issued as a broadside and widely reprinted. As word of her talent spread, she was often asked to compose a memorial poem on some departed worthy, famous or obscure, for the New England tradition of the funeral elegy was still strong in pre-Revolutionary Boston. Several of these were published as broadsides. In 1773 Mr.

Wheatley and others arranged for the publication, in London, of a volume of her poems, which was prefaced by an "attestation" signed by the governor and other dignitaries of Massachusetts. In the same year, as Phillis was in poor health, the Wheatleys sent her on a visit to England, under the escort of their son, Nathaniel, in the hope that the sea voyage would be beneficial. There, through the Countess of Huntington, Whitefield's patroness, to whom Phillis dedicated her book, she met many prominent personages including the Lord Mayor of London, who presented her with a copy of *Paradise Lost.* Plans were under way for her presentation at Court, when word came of the serious illness of Mrs. Wheatley, and Phillis returned home.

Phillis' London triumph marked the high tide of her fortunes. Mrs. Wheatley died in 1774, and Mr. Wheatley four years later. After the break-up of the Wheatley household, Phillis married John Peters, a free Negro of Boston, but the marriage was plagued by poverty and misfortune. The couple lived in the country for a time, and when they returned to Boston, it was to a life radically different from what Phillis had earlier known. Mary Wheatley Lathrop was dead, Nathaniel was living in England, and many family friends had been dispersed by the outbreak of the Revolution and the British occupation of Boston. Perhaps too diffident and too proud to seek out those who had known her in better days, Phillis lapsed into obscurity and died in 1784, survived only a few hours by the last of her three children.

If Phillis Wheatley's work has been both underrated and overpraised, it is perhaps because the story of her life has prejudiced critical evaluations. Like all the American neoclassic poets, she was imitative. Pope's translation of Homer was her favorite work, and the strongest influence on her writing, in combination with the religious piety of her adopted New England culture. Undeniably, much of her poetry is mediocre, but much of it was "occasional" verse written in response to requests which she always obligingly fulfilled. In her better poems she often displays a genuine empathy for the classical mode and a craftsmanship that entitle her to an acknowledged place among the poets of America's Neoclassic Age.

Further reading: *The Poems of Phillis Wheatley,* ed. Julian D. Mason, Jr., 1966. Winthrop D. Jordan, *White Over Black: American Attitudes Toward the Negro, 1550–1812,* 1968.

To the University of Cambridge, in New-England

Exactly what prompted the thirteen-year-old "Ethiop" girl to pen this admonition to the young men of Harvard, it is impossible to say; but the conversation in many a Boston drawing room of the time must often have dealt with the goings-on across the Charles: the escapades of the students, the inroads of liberal theology and deism, and the college's first full-scale rebellion in 1766 (triggered by rancid butter in the commons). This early poem, one of the few she wrote in other than heroic couplets, shows the influence more of Milton than of Pope. Text: The poems reprinted here are from the edition by Julian D. Mason, Jr. (Chapel Hill, 1966).

While an intrinsic ardor prompts to write,
The muses promise to assist my pen;
'Twas not long since I left my native shore
The land of errors, and *Egyptian* gloom:
Father of mercy, 'twas thy gracious hand
Brought me in safety from those dark abodes.[1]
  Students, to you 'tis giv'n to scan the heights
Above, to traverse the ethereal space,
And mark the systems of revolving worlds.
Still more, ye sons of science ye receive
The blissful news by messengers from heav'n,
How *Jesus'* blood for your redemption flows.
See him with hands out-stretcht upon the cross;
Immense compassion in his bosom glows;
He hears revilers, nor resents their scorn:
What matchless mercy in the Son of God!
When the whole human race by sin had fall'n,
He deign'd to die that they might rise again,

To the University. [1] Phillis Wheatley rarely alluded to her condition in her poems. When she does so, here and in lines 24–30 of "To the Earl of Dartmouth" (where she expresses a different view), it is, as Mason has remarked, to strengthen her points.

And share with him in the sublimest skies,
Life without death, and glory without end.

Improve your privileges while they stay,
Ye pupils, and each hour redeem, that bears
Or good or bad report of you to heav'n.
Let sin, that baneful evil to the soul,
By you be shunn'd, nor once remit your guard;
Suppress the deadly serpent in its egg.
Ye blooming plants of human race devine,
An *Ethiop* tells you 'tis your greatest foe;
Its transient sweetness turns to endless pain,
And in immense perdition sinks the soul.

1767 1773

To the Right Honourable William, Earl of Dartmouth

Hail, happy day, when, smiling like the morn,
Fair *Freedom* rose *New-England* to adorn:
The northern clime beneath her genial ray,
Dartmouth,[1] congratulates thy blissful sway:
Elate with hope her race no longer mourns,
Each soul expands, each grateful bosom burns,
While in thine hand with pleasure we behold
The silken reins, and *Freedom's* charms unfold.[2]
Long lost to realms beneath the northern skies
She shines supreme, while hated *faction* dies:
Soon as appear'd the *Goddess* long desir'd,
Sick at the view, she lanquish'd and expir'd;
Thus from the splendors of the morning light
The owl in sadness seeks the caves of night.

No more, *America*, in mournful strain
Of wrongs, and grievance unredress'd complain,
No longer shalt thou dread the iron chain,
Which wanton *Tyranny* with lawless hand
Had made, and with it meant t' enslave the land.

Should you, my lord, while you peruse my song,
Wonder from whence my love of *Freedom* sprung,
Whence flow these wishes for the common good,
By feeling hearts alone best understood,
I, young in life, by seeming cruel fate
Was snatch'd from *Afric's* fancy'd happy seat:
What pangs excruciating must molest,
What sorrows labour in my parent's breast?
Steel'd was that soul and by no misery mov'd
That from a father seiz'd his babe belov'd:
Such, such my case.[3] And can I then but pray
Others may never feel tyrannic sway?

For favours past, great Sir, our thanks are due,
And thee we ask thy favours to renew,
Since in thy pow'r, as in thy will before,
To sooth the griefs, which thou did'st once deplore.
May heav'nly grace the sacred sanction give
To all thy works, and thou for ever live
Not only on the wings of fleeting *Fame*,
Though praise immortal crowns the patriot's name,
But to conduct to heav'ns refulgent fane,
May fiery coursers sweep th' ethereal plain,
And bear thee upwards to that blest abode,
Where, like the prophet, thou shalt find thy God.

1772 1773

To the Earl of Dartmouth. [1] William Legge, Second Earl of Dartmouth (1731-1801), who in August 1772 became Secretary of State for the Colonies and President of the Board of Trade and Foreign Plantations in Lord North's administration. Phillis met him when she was in England in 1773, and he gave her a copy of Smollett's translation of *Don Quixote*. Dartmouth College was named for him.

[2] Phillis' hopes proved to be false ones, as he proved to be a minister not in sympathy with the events which occurred in New England in the following months. (Mason)

[3] Cf. lines 2-6 of "To the University of Cambridge."

PHILIP FRENEAU [1752-1832]

FRENEAU WAS BORN of French Huguenot and Scottish parents in New York State, but the family moved to a large New Jersey estate, within sight of the ocean, when he was ten. He attended Princeton in the same class as James Madison and Hugh Henry Brackenridge, collaborating with the latter on their commencement poem, "The Rising Glory of America." After his graduation Freneau moved restlessly from job to job. He taught school, shipped out as a sailor, visited and dreamed in the West Indies, returned to enlist in the Revolutionary army, was captured and nearly died in a British prison ship, and served as a captain in the coastal trade. After entering politics on the side of the Jeffersonians he was appointed a government clerk of foreign languages, and eked out a precarious living as farmer, sea captain, and journalist. Though he was determined from the first to be a poet ("To write was my sad destiny / The worst of trades, we all agree") circumstances were on the whole against him. Much of his work was elicited by the Revolutionary War or by the political battles of the Federalist period, not the kind of poetry he was naturally drawn to or the kind he wrote best. A large part of his energy was consumed in newspaper work and by some six hundred essays on various topics published in journals. He also suffered from want of an audience to encourage him and to respond to his better verse.

Freneau's poetry, issued in collected editions in 1786, 1788, 1809, and 1815, falls into fairly clear divisions. His wartime verse reflects the heated passions of the times and his hatred of the British, whose treatment on the prison ship he neither forgot nor forgave. His political satires, modeled on the English tradition of Dryden and Churchill, and directed against the Federalists, were expert and effective, so much so that Washington himself called him "that rascal Freneau," and Jefferson affirmed that he "had saved our constitution, which was fast galloping into monarchy." An avowed radical, Freneau threw himself into a number of reform causes and wrote verses about them. His lyric verse, dealing with the themes of nature, transience, the past, and personal experience, shows him to have been a poet of genuine gifts and imagination. Though he echoed Collins, Gray, Akenside, and other English pre-Romantics, there is in his best lyric verse a freshness, originality, and haunting beauty unsurpassed in the poetry of the times. Late in life, Freneau also produced a small body of deist-Unitarian religious verse of excellent quality. Most of all, however, Freneau's importance as a poet lies in the fact that he alone, of his American generation, broke out of the constrictions of neoclassical imitation to look at life around him directly, read it imaginatively, and record it sensitively.

The text of all Freneau poems, unless otherwise noted, is that of Fred L. Pattee, *The Poems of Philip Freneau* (Princeton, 1902-7).

Further reading: *Poems of Freneau*, ed. H. H. Clark, 1929. Lewis Leary, *That Rascal Freneau*, 1941.

The Power of Fancy

Written while he was still a Princeton undergraduate, this poem reflects somewhat self-consciously Freneau's reading of Milton's "Il Penseroso" and of the fashionable English pre-Romantic poets, especially Joseph Warton, whose "Ode to Fancy" (1746) probably served as his model. A number of characteristics of pre-Romantic verse are implicit in the poem—the praise of the "fancy" as a transforming power; the use of the dream device; the interest in the melancholy, the exotic, and the distant; the classical and pastoral reference; and a vaguely deistic concept of the universe. Freneau's rimed tetrameter is a creative departure from the conventional couplet.

Wakeful, vagrant, restless thing,
Ever wandering on the wing,
Who thy wondrous source can find,
Fancy, regent of the mind;
A spark from Jove's resplendent throne,
But thy nature all unknown.
This spark of bright, celestial flame,
From Jove's seraphic altar came,
And hence alone in man we trace,
Resemblance to the immortal race.
Ah! what is all this mighty whole,
These suns and stars that round us roll!
What are they all, where'er they shine,
But Fancies of the Power Divine!
What is this globe, these lands, and seas,
And heat, and cold, and flowers, and trees,
And life, and death, and beast, and man,
And time—that with the sun began—
But thoughts on reason's scale combin'd,
Ideas of the Almighty mind!
On the surface of the brain
Night after night she walks unseen,
Noble fabrics doth she raise
In the woods or on the seas,
On some high, steep, pointed rock,
Where the billows loudly knock
And the dreary tempests sweep
Clouds along the uncivil deep.
Lo! she walks upon the moon,
Listens to the chimy tune
Of the bright, harmonious spheres,
And the song of angels hears;
Sees this earth a distant star,[1]
Pendant, floating in the air;
Leads me to some lonely dome,
Where Religion loves to come,
Where the bride of Jesus dwells,
And the deep ton'd organ swells
In notes with lofty anthems join'd,
Notes that half distract the mind.
Now like lightning she descends
To the prison of the fiends,
Hears the rattling of their chains,
Feels their never ceasing pains—
But, O never may she tell
Half the frightfulness of hell.
Now she views Arcadian rocks,
Where the shepherds guard their flocks,
And, while yet her wings she spreads,
Sees chrystal streams and coral beds,
Wanders to some desert deep,
Or some dark, enchanted steep,
By the full moonlight doth shew
Forests of a dusky blue,
Where, upon some mossy bed,
Innocence reclines her head.
Swift, she stretches o'er the seas
To the far off Hebrides,
Canvas on the lofty mast
Could not travel half so fast—
Swifter than the eagle's flight
Or instantaneous rays of light!
Lo! contemplative she stands
On Norwegia's rocky lands—
Fickle Goddess, set me down
Where the rugged winters frown
Upon Orca's[2] howling steep,
Nodding o'er the northern deep,
Where the winds tumultuous roar,
Vext that Ossian sings no more.
Fancy, to that land repair,
Sweetest Ossian slumbers there;
Waft me far to southern isles
Where the soften'd winter smiles,
To Bermuda's orange shades,
Or Demarara's[3] lovely glades;
Bear me o'er the sounding cape,
Painting death in every shape,
Where daring Anson[4] spread the sail
Shatter'd by the stormy gale—
Lo! she leads me wide and far,
Sense can never follow her—
Shape thy course o'er land and sea,
Help me to keep pace with thee,
Lead me to yon' chalky cliff,
Over rock and over reef,
Into Britain's fertile land,
Stretching far her proud command.
Look back and view, thro' many a year,
Caesar, Julius Caesar, there.
Now to Tempe's verdant wood,
Over the mid-ocean flood

The Power of Fancy. [1]Milton's Paradise Lost, B. ii, v. 1052. [Freneau's note.]

[2]Possibly the Orkney Islands, north of Scotland.

[3]British Guiana.

[4]Commander of a British expedition to the South Pacific, 1740-44.

Lo! the islands of the sea—
Sappho, Lesbos mourns for thee:
Greece, arouse thy humbled head,
Where are all thy mighty dead
Who states to endless ruin hurl'd
And carried vengeance through the world?—
Troy, thy vanish'd pomp resume,
Or, weeping at thy Hector's tomb,
Yet those faded scenes renew,
Whose memory is to Homer due.
Fancy, lead me wandering still
Up to Ida's cloud-topt hill;
Not a laurel there doth grow
But in vision thou shalt show,—
Every sprig on Virgil's tomb
Shall in livelier colours bloom,
And every triumph Rome has seen
Flourish on the years between.
  Now she bears me far away
In the east to meet the day,
Leads me over Ganges' streams,
Mother of the morning beams—
O'er the ocean hath she ran,
Places me on Tinian;[5]
Farther, farther in the east,
Till it almost meets the west,
Let us wandering both be lost
On Taitis sea-beat coast,
Bear me from that distant strand,
Over ocean, over land,
To California's golden shore—
Fancy, stop, and rove no more.
  Now, tho' late, returning home,
Lead me to Belinda's[6] tomb;
Let me glide as well as you
Through the shroud and coffin too,
And behold, a moment, there,
All that once was good and fair—
Who doth here so soundly sleep?
Shall we break this prison deep?—
Thunders cannot wake the maid,
Lightnings cannot pierce the shade,
And tho' wintry tempests roar,
Tempests shall disturb no more.
  Yet must those eyes in darkness stay,
That once were rivals to the day?—
Like heaven's bright lamp beneath the main
They are but set to rise again.
  Fancy, thou the muses' pride,
In thy painted realms reside
Endless images of things,
Fluttering each on golden wings,
Ideal objects, such a store,

[5]Island in the Marianas, in the South Pacific.

[6]A conventional name in 18th-century poetry for a lost sweetheart.

The universe could hold no more:
Fancy, to thy power I owe
Half my happiness below;
By thee Elysian groves were made,
Thine were the notes that Orpheus play'd;
By thee was Pluto charm'd so well
While rapture seiz'd the sons of hell—
Come, O come—perceiv'd by none,
You and I will walk alone.

1770

The Vanity of Existence

To Thyrsis[1]

In youth, gay scenes attract our eyes,
  And not suspecting their decay
Life's flowery fields before us rise,
  Regardless of its winter day.

But vain pursuits and joys as vain,
  Convince us life is but a dream.
Death is to wake, to rise again
  To that true life you best esteem.

So nightly on some shallow tide,
  Oft have I seen a splendid show;
Reflected stars on either side,
  And glittering moons were seen below.

But when the tide had ebbed away,
  The scene fantastic with it fled,
A bank of mud around me lay,
  And sea-weed on the river's bed.

1781

To the Memory of the Brave Americans

Under General Greene, in South Carolina, who fell in the action of September 8, 1781[1]

At Eutaw Springs the valiant died;
  Their limbs with dust are covered o'er—
Weep on, ye springs, your tearful tide;
  How many heroes are no more!

The Vanity of Existence. [1]A conventional dedication adopted from English pastoral poetry; Thyrsis was a shepherd mentioned by Theocritus.

To the Brave Americans. [1]General Nathanael Greene's troops engaged the British under Cornwallis at Eutaw Springs, South Carolina, with a loss of seven hundred men.

If in this wreck of ruin, they
  Can yet be thought to claim a tear,
O smite your gentle breast, and say
  The friends of freedom slumber here!

Thou, who shalt trace this bloody plain,
  If goodness rules thy generous breast,
Sigh for the wasted rural reign;
  Sigh for the shepherds, sunk to rest!

Stranger, their humble graves adorn;
  You too may fall, and ask a tear;
'Tis not the beauty of the morn
  That proves the evening shall be clear.—

They saw their injured country's woe;
  The flaming town, the wasted field;
Then rushed to meet the insulting foe;
  They took the spear—but left the shield.

Led by thy conquering genius, Greene,
  The Britons they compelled to fly;
None distant viewed the fatal plain,
  None grieved, in such a cause to die—

But, like the Parthian, famed of old,
  Who, flying, still their arrows threw,
These routed Britons, full as bold,
  Retreated, and retreating slew.[2]

Now rest in peace, our patriot band;
  Though far from nature's limits thrown,
We trust they find a happier land,
  A brighter sunshine of their own.

1781

The Wild Honey Suckle[1]

Fair flower, that dost so comely grow,
Hid in this silent, dull retreat,
Untouched thy honied blossoms blow,
Unseen thy little branches greet:
    No roving foot shall crush thee here,
    No busy hand provoke a tear.

By Nature's self in white arrayed,
She bade thee shun the vulgar eye,
And planted here the guardian shade,
And sent soft waters murmuring by;
    Thus quietly thy summer goes,
    Thy days declining to repose.

Smit with those charms, that must decay,
I grieve to see your future doom;
They died—nor were those flowers more gay,
The flowers that did in Eden bloom;
    Unpitying frosts, and Autumn's power
    Shall leave no vestige of this flower.

From morning suns and evening dews
At first thy little being came:
If nothing once, you nothing lose,
For when you die you are the same;
    The space between, is but an hour,
    The frail duration of a flower.

1786

To an Author

Your leaves bound up compact and fair,
In neat array at length prepare,
To pass their hour on learning's stage,
To meet the surly critic's rage;
The statesman's slight, the smatterer's sneer—
Were these, indeed, your only fear,
You might be tranquil and resigned:
What most should touch your fluttering mind;
Is that, few critics will be found
To sift your works, and deal the wound.

Thus, when one fleeting year is past
On some bye-shelf your book is cast—
Another comes, with something new,
And drives you fairly out of view:
With some to praise, but more to blame,
The mind returns to—whence it came;
And some alive, who scarce could read
Will publish satires on the dead.

Thrice happy Dryden,[1] who could meet
Some rival bard in every street!
When all were bent on writing well
It was some credit to excel:—

Thrice happy Dryden, who could find
A Milbourne for his sport designed—
And Pope, who saw the harmless rage
Of Dennis bursting o'er his page

[2] After the first engagement the British fled in confusion. Greene, in his eagerness, pursued them too closely, and sheltered by the brick house, they inflicted upon the advancing Americans the greater part of the loss of life incurred during the battle. [Freneau's note.]

The Wild Honey Suckle. [1] The white swamp honeysuckle of the Carolinas.

To an Author. [1] See Johnson's lives of the English Poets. [Freneau's note.]

Might justly spurn the critic's aim,
Who only helped to swell his fame.

On these bleak climes by Fortune thrown,
Where rigid Reason reigns alone,
Where lovely Fancy has no sway,
Nor magic forms about us play—
Nor nature takes her summer hue
Tell me, what has the muse to do?—

An age employed in edging steel
Can no poetic raptures feel;
No solitude's attracting power,
No leisure of the noon day hour,
No shaded stream, no quiet grove
Can this fantastic century move;

The muse of love in no request—
Go—try your fortune with the rest,
One of the nine you should engage,
To meet the follies of the age:—

On one, we fear, your choice must fall—
The least engaging of them all—[2]
Her visage stern—an angry style—
A clouded brow—malicious smile—
A mind on murdered victims placed—
She, only she, can please the taste!

1778

The Indian Burying Ground

Freneau provided a note for this poem: "The North American Indians bury their dead in a sitting posture; decorating the corpse with wampum, the images of birds, quadrupeds, &c. And (if that of a warrior) with bows, arrows, tomahawks, and other military weapons."

In spite of all the learned have said,
  I still my old opinion keep;
The posture, that we give the dead,
  Points out the soul's eternal sleep.

Not so the ancients of these lands—
  The Indian, when from life released,
Again is seated with his friends,
  And shares again the joyous feast.

His imaged birds, and painted bowl,
  And venison, for a journey dressed,
Bespeak the nature of the soul,
  Activity, that knows no rest.

[2] I.e., the muse of satire.

His bow, for action ready bent,
  And arrows, with a head of stone,
Can only mean that life is spent,
  And not the old ideas gone.

Thou, stranger, that shalt come this way,
  No fraud upon the dead commit—
Observe the swelling turf, and say
  They do not lie, but here they sit.

Here still a lofty rock remains,
  On which the curious eye may trace
(Now wasted, half, by wearing rains)
  The fancies of a ruder race.

Here still an aged elm aspires,
  Beneath whose far-projecting shade
(And which the shepherd still admires)
  The children of the forest played!

There oft a restless Indian queen
  (Pale Shebah, with her braided hair)
And many a barbarous form is seen
  To chide the man that lingers there.

By midnight moons, o'er moistening dews;
  In habit for the chase arrayed,
The hunter still the deer pursues,
  The hunter and the deer, a shade!

And long shall timorous fancy see
  The painted chief, and pointed spear,
And Reason's self shall bow the knee
  To shadows and delusions here.

1788

On the Uniformity and Perfection of Nature

This poem and the one that follows are direct statements of Freneau's deism, published after the movement had declined. Freneau presents a familiar set of concepts and attitudes: the First Cause, reason, nature, the Newtonian world machine, law and order, optimism ("all is right," "Heaven below"), a religion of truth and goodness and tolerance. Text: Harry Hayden Clark, *Poems of Freneau* (New York, 1929).

On one fix'd point all nature moves,
Nor deviates from the track she loves;
Her system, drawn from reason's source,
She scorns to change her wonted course.

Could she descend from that great plan
To work unusual things for man,

To suit the insect of an hour—
This would betray a want of power,

Unsettled in its first design
And erring, when it did combine
The parts that form the vast machine,
The figures sketch'd on nature's scene.

Perfections of the great first cause
Submit to no contracted laws,
But all-sufficient, all-supreme,
Include no trivial views in them.

Who looks through nature with an eye
That would the scheme of heaven descry,
Observes her constant, still the same,
In all her laws, through all her frame.

No imperfection can be found
In all that is, above, around,—
All, nature made, in reason's sight
Is order all and all is right.

1815

On the Religion of Nature

Text: H. H. Clark, *Poems of Freneau* (New York, 1929).

The power that gives with liberal hand
  The blessings man enjoys, while here,
And scatters through a smiling land
  The abundant products of the year;
    That power of nature, ever bless'd,
    Bestow'd religion with the rest.

Born with ourselves, her early sway
  Inclines the tender mind to take
The path of right, fair virtue's way
  Its own felicity to make.
    This universally extends
    And leads to no mysterious ends.

Religion, such as nature taught,
  With all divine perfection suits;
Had all mankind this system sought
  Sophists would cease their vain disputes,
    And from this source would nations know
    All that can make their heaven below.

This deals not curses on mankind,
  Or dooms them to perpetual grief,
If from its aid no joys they find,
  It damns them not for unbelief;
    Upon a more exalted plan
    Creatress nature dealt with man—

Joy to the day, when all agree
  On such grand systems to proceed,
From fraud, design, and error free,
  And which to truth and goodness lead:
    Then persecution will retreat
    And man's religion be complete.

1815

WILLIAM ELLERY CHANNING [1780–1842]

THOUGH "infidelity" was fast declining by 1800, the decline did not mean that old-fashioned Calvinist orthodoxy had won the day, for "unitarian" doctrines were already well established in many Congregational and Presbyterian congregations. Kindred movements, both deism and Unitarianism professed to be rational and liberal, and they were at one in opposing Calvinism. Rejecting the doctrine of man's total depravity, they affirmed the exalted nature and unlimited possibilities of man. On the other hand, they differed in that deism was a "natural religion" (a religion based on nature in its scientific aspects) and Unitarianism essentially traditionally Christian in its principles. Numbers of younger ministers, especially in New England, increasingly dissatisfied with the rigors of orthodoxy, turned toward this liberalized theology. They shouted no dissent, but quietly made their churches Unitarian, one after another, without changing pastors or houses of worship, almost without disturbing their parishioners' minds.

The central figure in this development was a Boston minister, William Ellery Channing. Born in Rhode Island, he graduated from Harvard in 1798, tutored in a Virginia family, read the deists and political radicals, studied theology, and in 1803 was installed in Boston's Federal Street Church, where he remained the rest of his life. Though Channing never meant to lead any movement, the Unitarian liberals sought him out. The clarity and conviction of his sermons and essays soon made him a recognized leader of the liberal wing and projected him more and more into the controversy. His sermon on "Unitarian Christianity," preached at the ordination of the Reverend Jared Sparks at Baltimore in 1819, became a rallying point for theological liberals, and his essay-review in *The Christian Examiner* for 1820, "The Moral Argument Against Calvinism," which he characterized as "a false theology," attracted national attention. He opposed the orthodox variety of Calvinism, he once said, "inasmuch as it prostrates the independence of the mind, teaches men that they are naturally incapable of discerning religious truth, generates a timid, superstitious dependence on those who profess to have been brought from darkness into light, and so commonly infuses into its professors a censorious and uncharitable spirit." He later helped to organize a conference of liberal ministers, which in 1825 became the American Unitarian Association. As minister, editor, and lecturer, Channing's influence on his and the next generation was large indeed; his theological, social, and political views filtered through New England's intellectual life. Active in the antislavery, pacifist, and temperance movements, and a friend to reform in all fields, Channing said in the preface to his collected works that there were two master principles which governed him: respect for human nature and reverence for human liberty.

Further reading: Arthur W. Brown, *Always Young for Liberty*, 1956. Madeleine H. Rice, *The Life of W. E. Channing*, 1961. Robert L. Patterson, *The Philosophy of W. E. Channing*, 1952.

FROM *Remarks on National Literature*

Originally written as a review-article for *The Christian Examiner* in 1830; Channing revised and retitled it for inclusion in his collected works in 1841. Despite its title, Channing's use of the term "national" was neither narrow nor chauvinistic. Though he advises American authors to draw inspiration from the American experience and to use American themes, he never conceived of literature as something to be produced in cultural isolation, and was fully aware of the interconnections of all art in all times and places. What he proposes is an American literature that expresses the national character, but since literature reflects the moral qualities of the nation which produces it,

America cannot expect to produce great national literature until the nation itself is great. A call for cultural independence that preceded Emerson's *American Scholar* by seven years, Channing's essay called for national self-cultivation and self-reliance. "A country," he wrote, "like an individual, has dignity and power only in proportion as it is self-founded. There is a great stir to secure to ourselves the manufacturing of our own clothing. We say, let others spin and weave for us, but let them not think for us." Text: *Works,* 1848 edition, Volume I.

* * * Do we possess, indeed, what may be called a national literature? Have we produced eminent writers in the various departments of intellectual effort? Are our chief resources of instruction and literary enjoyment furnished from ourselves? We regret that the reply to these questions is so obvious. The few standard works which we have produced, and which promise to live, can hardly, by any courtesy, be denominated a national literature. On this point, if marks and proofs of our real condition were needed, we should find them in the current apologies for our deficiencies. Our writers are accustomed to plead in our excuse, our youth, the necessities of a newly settled country, and the direction of our best talents to practical life. Be the pleas sufficient or not, one thing they prove, and that is, our consciousness of having failed to make important contributions to the interests of the intellect. We have few names to place by the side of the great names in science and literature on the other side of the ocean. We want those lights which make a country conspicuous at a distance. Let it not be said, that European envy denies our just claims. In an age like this, when the literary world forms a great family, and the products of mind are circulated more rapidly than those of machinery, it is a nation's own fault, if its name be not pronounced with honor beyond itself. We have ourselves heard, and delighted to hear, beyond the Alps, our country designated as the land of Franklin. This name had scaled that mighty barrier, and made us known where our institutions and modes of life were hardly better understood than those of the natives of our forests.

We are accustomed to console ourselves for the absence of a commanding literature, by urging our superiority to other nations in our institutions for the diffusion of elementary knowledge through all classes of the community. We have here just cause for boasting, though perhaps less than we imagine. That there are gross deficiencies in our common schools, and that the amount of knowledge which they communicate, when compared with the time spent in its acquisition, is lamentably small, the community begin to feel. There is a crying need for a higher and more quickening kind of instruction than the laboring part of society have yet received, and we rejoice that the cry begins to be heard. But, allowing our elementary institutions to be ever so perfect, we confess that they do not satisfy us. We want something more. A dead level of intellect, even if it should rise above what is common in other nations, would not answer our wishes and hopes for our country. We want great minds to be formed among us, minds which shall be felt afar, and through which we may act on the world. We want the human intellect to do its utmost here. We want this people to obtain a claim on the gratitude of the human race, by adding strength to the foundation, and fulness and splendor to the developement of moral and religious truth; by originality of thought, by discoveries of science, and by contributions to the refining pleasures of taste and imagination.

With these views we do and must lament, that, however we surpass other nations in providing for, and spreading elementary instruction, we fall behind many in provision for the liberal training of the intellect, for forming great scholars, for communicating that profound knowledge, and that thirst for higher truths, which can alone originate a commanding literature. The truth ought to be known. There is among us much superficial knowledge, but little severe, persevering research; little of that consuming passion for new truth, which makes outward things worthless; little resolute devotion to a high intellectual culture. There is nowhere a literary atmosphere, or such an accumulation of literary influence, as determines the whole strength of the mind to its own enlargement, and to the manifestation of itself in enduring forms. Few among us can be said to have followed out any great subject of thought patiently, laboriously, so as to know thoroughly what others have discovered and taught concerning it, and thus to occupy a ground from which new views may be gained. Of course, exceptions are to be found. This country has produced original and profound thinkers. We have named Franklin, and we may name Edwards, one of the greatest men of his age, though unhappily his mind was lost, in a great degree, to literature, and we fear to religion, by vassalage to a false theology. His work on the Will throws, indeed, no light on human nature, and, notwithstanding the nobleness of the subject, gives no great or elevated thoughts; but, as a specimen of logical acuteness and controversial power, it certainly ranks in the very highest class of metaphysical writings. We might also name living authors who do honor to their country. Still, we may say, we chiefly prize what has been done among us, as a promise of higher and more extensive effort. Patriotism, as well as virtue, forbids us to burn incense to national vanity. The truth should be seen and felt. In an age of great intellectual activity, we rely chiefly for intellectual excitement and enjoyment on foreign minds, nor is our own mind felt abroad. Whilst clamoring against dependence on European manufactures, we contentedly rely on Europe for the nobler and more important fabrics of the intellect. We boast of our political institutions, and receive our chief teachings, books, impressions, from the school of monarchy. True, we labor under disadvantages. But, if our liberty deserves the praise which it receives, it is more than a balance for these. We believe that it is. We believe that it does open to us an indefinite intellectual progress. Did we not so regard it, we should value it little. If hereditary governments minister most to the growth of the mind, it were better to restore them than to cling to a barren freedom. Let us not expose liberty to this reproach. Let us prove, by more generous provisions for the diffusion of elementary knowledge, for the training of great minds, and for the joint culture of the moral and intellectual powers, that we are more and more instructed, by freedom, in the worth and greatness of human nature, and in the obligation of contributing to its strength and glory.

We have spoken of the condition of our literature. We now proceed to the consideration of the causes which obstruct its advancement; and we are immediately struck by one so prevalent, as to deserve distinct notice. We refer to the common doctrine, that we need, in this country, useful knowledge, rather than profound, extensive, and elegant literature, and that this last, if we covet it, may be imported from abroad in such variety and abundance, as to save us the necessity of producing it among ourselves. How far are these opinions just? This question we purpose to answer.

That useful knowledge should receive our first and chief care, we mean not to dispute. * * *

We have said that we prize, as highly as any, useful knowledge. But by this we mean knowledge which answers and ministers to our complex and various nature; we mean that which is useful, not only to the animal man, but to the intellectual, moral, and religious man; useful to a being of spiritual faculties, whose happiness is to be found in their free and harmonious exercise. We grant, that there is primary necessity for that information and skill by which subsistence is earned, and life is preserved; for it is plain that we must live, in order to act and improve. But life is the means; action and improvement the end; and who will deny that the noblest utility belongs to that knowledge, by which the chief purpose of our creation is accomplished? According to these views, a people should honor and cultivate, as unspeakably useful, that literature which corresponds to, and calls forth, the highest faculties; which expresses and communicates energy of thought, fruitfulness of invention, force of moral purpose, a thirst for the true, and a delight in the beautiful. According to these views, we attach special importance to those branches of literature which relate to human nature, and which give it a consciousness of its own powers. History has a noble use, for it shows us human beings in various and opposite conditions, in their strength and weakness, in their progress and relapses, and thus reveals the causes and means by which the happiness and virtue of the race may be enlarged. Poetry is useful, by touching deep springs in the human soul; by giving voice to its more delicate feelings; by breathing out, and making more intelligible, the sympathy which subsists between the mind and the outward universe; by creating beautiful forms of manifestations for great moral truths. Above all, that higher philosophy, which treats of the intellectual and moral constitution of man, of the foundation of knowledge, of duty, of perfection, of our relations to the spiritual world, and especially to God; this has a usefulness so peculiar as to throw other departments of knowledge into obscurity; and a people, among whom this does not find honor, has little ground to boast of its superiority to uncivilized tribes. It will be seen from these remarks, that utility, with us, has a broad meaning. In truth, we are slow to condemn as useless, any researches or discoveries of original and strong minds, even when we discern in them no bearing on any interests of mankind; for all truth is of a prolific nature, and has connexions not immediately perceived; and it may be, that what we call vain speculations, may, at no distant period, link themselves with some new facts or theories, and guide a profound thinker to the most important results. The ancient mathematician, when absorbed in solitary thought, little imagined that his theorems, after the lapse of ages, were to be applied by the mind of Newton to the solution of the mysteries of the universe, and not only to guide the astronomer through the heavens, but the navigator through the pathless ocean. For ourselves, we incline to hope much from truths, which are particularly decried as useless; for the noblest and most useful truth is of an abstract or universal nature; and yet the abstract, though susceptible of infinite application, is generally, as we know, opposed to the practical.

We maintain, that a people, which has any serious purpose of taking a place among improved communities, should studiously promote within itself every variety of intellectual exertion. It should resolve strenuously to be surpassed by none. It should feel that mind is the creative power, through which all the resources of nature are to be turned to account, and by which a people is to spread its influence, and establish the noblest form of empire. It should train within itself men able to understand and to use whatever is thought and discovered over the whole earth. The whole mass of human knowledge should exist among a people, not in neglected libraries, but in its higher minds. Among its most cherished institutions, should be those, which will ensure to it ripe scholars, explorers of ancient learning, profound historians and mathematicians, intellectual laborers devoted to physical and moral science, and to the creation of a refined and beautiful literature.

Let us not be misunderstood. We have no desire to rear in our country a race of pedants, of solemn triflers, of laborious commentators on the mysteries of a Greek accent or a rusty coin. We would have men explore antiquity, not to bury themselves in its dust, but to learn its spirit, and so to commune with its superior minds, as to accumulate on the present age, the influences of whatever was great and wise in former times. What we want is, that those among us, whom God has gifted to comprehend whatever is now known, and to rise to new truths, may find aids and institutions to fit them for their high calling, and may become at once springs of a higher intellectual life to their own country, and joint workers with the great of all nations and times in carrying forward their race.

We know that it will be said, that foreign scholars, bred under institutions which this country cannot support, may do our intellectual work, and send us books and learning to meet our wants. To this we have much to answer. In the first place, we reply, that, to avail ourselves of the higher literature of other nations, we must place ourselves on a level with them. The products of foreign machinery we can use, without any portion of the skill that produced them. But works of taste and genius, and profound investigations of philosophy, can only be estimated and enjoyed through a culture and power corresponding to that from which they sprung.

In the next place, we maintain, that it is an immense gain to a people, to have in its own bosom, among its own sons, men of distinguished intellect. Such men give a spring and life to a community by their presence, their society, their fame; and what deserves remark, such men are nowhere so felt as in a republic like our own; for here the different classes of society flow together and act powerfully on each other, and a free communication, elsewhere unknown, is established between the gifted few and the many. It is one of the many good fruits of liberty, that it increases the diffusiveness of intellect; and accordingly a free country is, above all others, false to itself, in withholding from its superior minds the means of enlargement.

We next observe, and we think the observation important, that the facility with which we receive the literature of foreign countries, instead of being a reason for neglecting our own, is a strong motive for its cultivation. We mean not to be paradoxical, but we believe that it would be better to admit no books from abroad, than to make them substitutes for our own intellectual activity. The more we receive from other countries, the greater the need of an original literature. A people, into whose minds the thoughts of foreigners are poured perpetually, needs an energy within itself to resist, to modify this mighty influence, and, without it, will inevitably sink under the worst bondage, will become intellectually tame and enslaved. We have certainly no desire to complete our restrictive system, by adding to it a literary non-intercourse law. We rejoice in the increasing intellectual connexion between this country and the old world. But sooner would we rupture it, than see our country sitting passively at the feet of foreign teachers. It were better to have no literature, than form ourselves unresistingly on a foreign one. The true sovereigns of a country are those who determine its mind, its modes of thinking, its tastes, its principles; and we cannot consent to lodge this sovereignty in the hands of strangers. A country, like an individual, has dignity and power only in proportion as it is self-formed. There is a great stir to secure to ourselves the manufacturing of our own clothing. We say, let others spin and weave for us, but let them not think for us. A people, whose government and laws are nothing but the embodying of public opinion, should jealously guard this opinion against foreign dictation. We need a literature to counteract, and to use wisely the literature which we import. We need an inward power proportionate to that which is exerted on us, as the means of self-subsistence. It is particularly true of a people, whose institutions demand for their support a free and bold spirit, that they should be able to subject to a manly and independent criticism, whatever comes from abroad. These views seem to us to deserve serious attention. We are more and more a reading people. Books are already among the most powerful influences here. The question is, shall Europe, through these, fashion us after its pleasure? Shall America be only an echo of what is thought and written under the aristocracies beyond the ocean?

Another view of the subject is this. A foreign literature will always, in a measure, be foreign. It has sprung from the soul of another people, which, however like, is still not our own soul. Every people has much in its own character and feelings, which can only be embodied by its own writers, and which, when transfused through literature, makes it touching and true, like the voice of our earliest friend.

We now proceed to an argument in favor of native literature, which, if less obvious, is, we believe, not less sound than those now already adduced. We have hitherto spoken of literature as the expression, the communication, of the higher minds in a community. We now add, that it does much more than is commonly supposed, to *form* such minds, so that, without it, a people wants one of the chief means of educating or perfecting talent and genius. One of the great laws of our nature, and a law singularly important to social beings, is, that the intellect enlarges and strengthens itself by expressing worthily its best views. In this, as in other respects, it is more blessed to give than to receive. Superior minds are formed, not merely by solitary thought, but almost as much by communication. Great thoughts are never fully possessed, till he who has conceived them has given them fit utterance. One of the noblest and most invigorating labors of genius is, to clothe its conceptions in clear and glorious forms, to give them existence in other souls. Thus literature creates, as well as manifests, intellectual power, and, without it, the highest minds will never be summoned to the most invigorating action. * * *

We come now to our last, and what we deem a weighty argument in favor of a native literature. We desire and would cherish it, because we hope from it important aids to the cause of truth and human nature. We believe, that a literature, springing up in this new soil, would bear new fruits, and, in some respects, more precious fruits, than are elsewhere produced. We know that our hopes may be set down to the account of that national vanity, which, with too much reason, is placed by foreigners among our besetting sins. But we speak from calm and deliberate conviction. We are inclined to believe, that, as a people, we occupy a position, from which the great subjects of literature may be viewed more justly than from those which most other nations hold. Undoubtedly we labor under disadvantages. We want the literary apparatus of Europe; her libraries, her universities, her learned institutions, her race of professed scholars, her spots consecrated by the memory of sages, and a thousand stirring associations which hover over ancient nurseries of learning. But the mind is not a local power. Its spring is within itself, and, under the inspiration of liberal and high feeling, it may attain and worthily express nobler truth than outward helps could reveal.

The great distinction of our country is, that we enjoy some peculiar advantages for understanding our own nature. Man is the great subject of literature, and juster and profounder views of man may be expected here, than elsewhere. In Europe, political and artificial distinctions have, more or less, triumphed over and obscured our common nature. In Europe, we meet kings, nobles, priests, peasants. How much rarer is it to meet *men;* by which we mean, human beings conscious of their own nature, and conscious of the utter worthlessness of all outward distinctions, compared with what is treasured up in their own souls. Man does not value himself as man. It is for his blood, his rank, or some artificial distinction, and not for the attributes of humanity, that he holds himself in respect. The institutions of the old world all tend to throw obscurity over what we most need to know, and that is, the worth and claims of a human being. We know that great improvements in this respect are going on abroad. Still the many are too often postponed to the few. The mass of men are regarded as instruments to work with, as materials to be shaped for the use of their superiors. That consciousness of our own nature, which contains, as a germ, all nobler thoughts, which teaches us at once self-respect and respect for others, and which binds us to God by filial sentiment and hope, this has been repressed, kept down by establishments founded in force; and literature, in all its departments, bears, we think, the traces of this inward degradation. We conceive that our position favors a juster and profounder estimate of human nature. We mean not to boast, but there are fewer obstructions to that moral consciousness, that consciousness of humanity, of which we have spoken. Man is not hidden from us by so many disguises as in the old world. The essential equality of all human beings, founded on the possession of a spiritual, progressive, immortal nature, is, we hope, better understood; and nothing more than this single conviction is needed, to work the mightiest changes in every province of human life and of human thought.

We have stated what seems to us our most important distinction. But our position has other advantages. The mere circumstance of its being a new one, gives reason to hope for some new intellectual activity, some fresher views of nature and life. We are not borne down by the weight of antiquated institutions, time-hallowed abuses, and the remnants of feudal barbarism. The absence of a religious establishment is an immense gain, as far as originality of mind is in question; for an establishment, however advantageous in other respects, is, by its nature, hostile to discovery and progress. To keep the mind where it is, to fasten the notions of one age on all future time, is its aim and proper business; and if it happened, as has generally been the case, to grow up in an age of strife and passion, when, as history demonstrates, the church was overrun with error, it cannot but perpetuate darkness and mental bondage. Among us, intellect, though far from being free, has broken some of the chains of other countries, and is more likely, we conceive, to propose to itself its legitimate object, truth,—everlasting and universal truth.

We have no thought of speaking contemptuously of the literature of the old world. It is our daily nutriment. We feel our debt to be immense to the glorious company of pure and wise minds, which in foreign lands have bequeathed us in writing their choicest thoughts and holiest feelings. Still we feel, that all existing literature has been produced under influences, which have necessarily mixed with it much error and corruption; and that the whole of it ought to pass, and must pass, under rigorous review. For example, we think that the history of the human race is to be re-written. Men imbued with the prejudices which thrive under aristocracies and state religions, cannot understand it. Past ages, with their great events, and great men, are to undergo, we think, a new trial, and to yield new results. It is plain, that history is already viewed under new aspects, and we believe, that the true principles for studying and writing it are to be unfolded here, at least as rapidly as in other countries. It seems to us that in literature an immense work is yet to be done. The most interesting questions to mankind are yet in debate. Great principles are yet to be settled in criticism, in morals, in politics; and, above all, the true character of religion is to be rescued from the disguises and corruptions of ages. We want a reformation. We want a literature, in which genius will pay supreme, if not undivided homage, to truth and virtue; in which the childish admiration of what has been called greatness, will give place to a wise moral judgment; which will breathe reverence for the mind, and elevating thoughts of God. The part which this country is to bear in this great intellectual reform, we presume not to predict. We feel, however, that, if true to itself, it will have the glory and happiness of giving new impulses to the human mind. This is our cherished hope. We should have no heart to encourage native literature, did we not hope that it would become instinct with a new spirit. We cannot admit the thought, that this country is to be only a repetition of the old world. We delight to believe that God, in the fulness of time, has brought a new continent to light, in order that the human mind should move here with a new freedom, should frame new social institutions, should explore new paths, and reap new harvests. We are accustomed to estimate nations by their creative energies, and we shall blush for our country, if, in circumstances so peculiar, original, and creative, it shall satisfy itself with a passive reception and mechanical reiteration of the thoughts of strangers.

1830, 1841

FROM *Christianity a Rational Religion*

The development of Channing's theology followed a rather clearly defined course, once he determined its direction. He wanted, he said, to return "spirituality" to religion, and to do so meant that he must re-assess the Calvinism that had driven it out and explain the Unitarianism that would bring it back. His Baltimore sermon of 1819, titled "Unitarian Christianity," set the two opposing systems against each other—new liberalism against old orthodoxy—to assert the superiority of the one over the other. His essay "The Moral Argument Against Calvinism," the following year, showed the basic inconsistencies between the doctrines of Calvinism and the perfections of God; God could not be, Channing argued, what Calvinism had made Him. His sermon of 1826, awkwardly titled "Unitarianism Christianity Most Favorable to Piety," concluded that of the two theologies, Unitarian and orthodox, the former possessed "a superior tendency to form an elevated religious character."

Channing in a sense provided a bridge from the Enlightenment to the Transcendentalists. He believed in the essential goodness and rationality of human nature, the reasonableness of nature and religion, the unity of God, the sufficiency of the individual, the moral emphasis of theology, the need for a social, humanitarian Christianity. The epitaph on his tombstone summarized his faith best—"He breathed into theology a humane spirit." Yet Channing too was a child of romanticism. A friend of Coleridge and an admiring student of *Biographia Literaria* and *The Friend,* he also knew Wordsworth (who read to him from the manuscript of *The Prelude*), Carlyle, Kant, and Cousin, and he moved with the philosophical and psychological currents of the times. He saw religion and poetry as two edges of the same tool, which "pierces beneath the exterior of life to the depths of the soul, and which lays open its mysterious workings, borrowing from the whole outward creation fresh images and correspondences, with which to illuminate the secrets of the world within us." His essay on the uses of reason (in the Romantic sense) in religion provides a preview of a central principle of the Transcendentalist philosophy. Text: *Works,* 1848 edition, Volume IV.

Christianity is a Rational religion. Were it not so, I should be ashamed to profess it. I am aware that it is the fashion with some to decry reason, and to set up revelation as an opposite authority. This error though countenanced by good men, and honestly maintained for the defence of the Christian cause, ought to be earnestly withstood; for it virtually surrenders our religion into the hands of the unbeliever. It saps the foundation to strengthen the building. It places our religion in hostility to human nature, and gives to its adversaries the credit of vindicating the rights and noblest powers of the mind.

We must never forget that our rational nature is the greatest gift of God. For this we owe him our chief gratitude. It is a greater gift than any outward aid or benefaction, and no doctrine which degrades it can come from its Author. The developement of it is the end of our being. Revelation is but a means, and is designed to concur with nature, providence, and God's spirit, in carrying forward reason to its perfection. I glory in Christianity because it enlarges, invigorates, exalts my rational nature. If I could not be a Christian without ceasing to be rational, I should not hesitate as to my choice. I feel myself bound to sacrifice to Christianity property, reputation, life; but I ought not to sacrifice to any religion, that reason which lifts me above the brute and constitutes me a man. I can conceive no sacrilege greater than to prostrate or renounce the highest faculty which we have derived from God. In so doing we should offer violence to the divinity within us. Christianity wages no war with reason, but is one with it, and is given to be its helper and friend.

I wish, in the present discourse, to illustrate and confirm the views now given. My remarks will be arranged under two heads. I propose, first, to show that Christianity is founded on, and supposes, the authority of reason, and cannot therefore oppose it without subverting itself. My object in this part of the discourse will be to expose the error of those who hope to serve revelation by disparaging reason. * * * —Before I begin, let me observe that this discussion, from the nature of the subject, must assume occasionally an abstract form, and will demand serious attention. I am to speak of Reason, the chief faculty of the mind; and no simplicity of language in treating such a topic can exempt the hearer from the necessity of patient effort of thought.

I am to begin with showing that the Christian revelation is founded on the authority of reason, and consequently cannot oppose it; and here it may be proper to settle the meaning of the word Reason. One of the most important steps towards the truth is to determine the import of terms. Very often fierce controversies have sprung from obscurity of language, and the parties, on explaining themselves, have discovered that they have been spending their strength in a war of words. What, then, is reason?

The term Reason is used with so much latitude, that to fix its precise limits is not an easy task. In this respect it agrees with the other words which express the intellectual faculties. One idea, however, is always attached to it. All men understand by reason the highest faculty or energy of the mind. Without laboring for a philosophical definition that will comprehend all its exercises, I shall satisfy myself with pointing out two of its principal characteristics or functions.

First, it belongs to reason to comprehend Universal truths. This is among its most important offices. There are particular and there are universal truths. The last are the noblest, and the capacity of perceiving them is the distinction of intelligent beings; and these belong to reason. Let me give my meaning by some illustrations. I see a stone falling to the ground. This is a particular truth; but I do not stop here. I believe that not only this particular stone falls towards the earth, but that every particle of matter, in whatever world, tends, or, as is sometimes said, is attracted towards all other matter. Here is a universal truth, a principle extending to the whole material creation, and essential to its existence. This truth belongs to reason.—Again, I see a man producing some effect, a manufacture, a house. Here is a particular truth. But I am not only capable of seeing particular causes and effects; I am sure that every thing which begins to exist, no matter when or where, must have a cause, that no change ever has taken place or ever will take place without a cause. Here is a universal truth, something true here and everywhere, true now and through eternity; and this truth belongs to reason.—Again, I see with my eyes, I traverse with my hands, a limited space; but this is not all. I am sure, that, beyond the limits which my limbs or senses reach, there is an unbounded space; that, go where I will, an infinity will spread around me. Here is another universal truth, and this belongs to reason. The idea of Infinity is indeed one of the noblest conceptions of this faculty.—Again, I see a man conferring a good on another. Here is a particular truth or perception. But my mind is not confined to this. I see and feel that it is right for all intelligent beings, exist when or where they may, to do good, and wrong for them to seek the misery of others. Here is a universal truth, a law extending from God to the lowest human being; and this belongs to reason. I trust I have conveyed to you my views in regard to the first characteristic of this highest power of the soul. Its office is to discern universal truths, great and eternal principles. But it does not stop here. Reason is also exercised in applying these universal truths to particular cases, beings, events. For example, reason teaches me, as we have seen, that all changes without exception require a cause; and in conformity to this principle, it prompts me to seek the particular causes of the endless changes and appearances which fall under my observation. Thus reason is perpetually at work on the ideas furnished us by the senses, by consciousness, by memory, associating them with its own great truths, or investing them with its own universality.

I now proceed to the second function of reason, which is indeed akin to the first. Reason is the power which tends, and is perpetually striving, to reduce our various thoughts to Unity or Consistency. Perhaps the most fundamental conviction of reason is, that all truths agree together; that inconsistency is the mark of error. Its intensest, most earnest effort is to bring concord into the intellect, to reconcile what seem to be clashing views. On the observation of a new fact, reason strives to incorporate it with former knowledge. It can allow nothing to stand separate in the mind. It labors to bring together scattered truths, and to give them the strength and beauty of a vital order. Its end and delight is harmony. It is shocked by an inconsistency in belief, just as a fine ear is wounded by a discord. It carries within itself an instinctive consciousness, that all things which exist are intimately bound together; and it cannot rest until it has connected whatever we witness with the infinite whole. Reason, according to this view, is the most glorious form or exercise of the intellectual nature. It corresponds to the unity of God and the universe, and seeks to make the soul the image and mirror of this sublime unity.

I have thus given my views of reason; but, to prevent all perversion, before I proceed to the main discussion, let me offer a word or two more of explanation. In this discourse, when I speak of the accordance of revelation with reason, I suppose this faculty to be used deliberately, conscientiously, and with the love of truth. Men often baptize with the name of reason their prejudices, unexamined notions, or opinions adopted through interest, pride, or other unworthy biasses. It is not uncommon to hear those who sacrifice the plainest dictates of the rational nature to impulse and passion, setting themselves up as oracles of reason. Now when I say revelation must accord with reason, I do not mean by the term the corrupt and superficial opinions of men who have betrayed and debased their rational powers. I mean reason, calmly, honestly exercised for the acquisition of truth and the invigoration of virtue.

After these explanations, I proceed to the discussion of the two leading principles to which this Discourse is devoted.

First, I am to show that revelation is founded on the authority of reason, and cannot therefore oppose or disparage it without subverting itself. Let me state a few of the considerations which convince me of the truth of this position. The first is, that reason alone makes us capable of receiving a revelation. It must previously exist and operate, or we should be wholly unprepared for the communications of Christ. Revelation, then, is built on reason. You will see the truth of these remarks if you will consider to whom revelation is sent. Why is it given to men rather than to brutes? Why have not God's messengers gone to the fields to proclaim his glad tidings to bird and beast? The answer is obvious. These want reason; and, wanting this, they have no capacity or preparation for revealed truth. And not only would revelation be lost on the brute; let it speak to the child, before his rational faculties have been awakened, and before some ideas of duty and his own nature have been developed, and it might as well speak to a stone. Reason is the preparation and ground of revelation.

This truth will be still more obvious, if we consider, not only to whom, but in what way, the Christian revelation is communicated. How is it conveyed? In words. Did it make these words? No. They were in use ages before its birth. Again I ask, Did it make the ideas or thoughts which these words express? No. If the hearers of Jesus had not previously attached ideas to the terms which he employed, they could not have received his meaning. He might as well have spoken to them in a foreign tongue. Thus the ideas which enter into Christianity subsisted before. They were ideas of reason; so that to this faculty revelation owes the materials of which it is composed.

Revelation, we must remember, is not our earliest teacher. Man is not born with the single power of reading God's word, and sent immediately to that guide. His eyes open first on another volume, that of the creation. Long before he can read the Bible, he looks round on the earth and sky. He reads the countenances of his friends, and hears and understands their voices. He looks, too, by degrees within himself, and acquires some ideas of his own soul. Thus his first school is that of nature and reason, and this is necessary to prepare him for a communication from Heaven. Revelation does not find the mind a blank, a void, prepared to receive unresistingly whatever may be offered; but finds it in possession of various knowledge from nature and experience, and, still more, in possession of great principles, fundamental truths, moral ideas, which are derived from itself, and which are the germs of all its future improvement. This last view is peculiarly important. The mind does not receive every thing from abroad. Its great ideas arise from itself, and by those native lights it reads and comprehends the volumes of nature and revelation. We speak, indeed, of nature and revelation as making known to us an intelligent

First Cause; but the ideas of intelligence and causation we derive originally from our own nature. The elements of the idea of God we gather from ourselves. Power, wisdom, love, virtue, beauty, and happiness, words which contain all that is glorious in the universe and interesting in our existence, express attributes of the mind, and are understood by us only through consciousness. It is true, these ideas or principles of reason are often obscured by thick clouds, and mingled with many and deplorable errors. Still they are never lost. Christianity recognises them, is built on them, and needs them as its interpreters. If an illustration of these views be required, I would point you to what may be called the most fundamental idea of religion. I mean the idea of right, of duty. Do we derive this originally and wholly from sacred books? Has not every human being, whether born within or beyond the bounds of revelation, a sense of the distinction between right and wrong? Is there not an earlier voice than revelation, approving or rebuking men according to their deeds? In barbarous ages is not conscience heard? And does it not grow more articulate with the progress of society? Christianity does not create, but presupposes the idea of duty; and the same may be said of other great convictions. Revelation, then, does not stand alone, nor is it addressed to a blank and passive mind. It was meant to be a joint worker with other teachers, with nature, with Providence, with conscience, with our rational powers; and as these all are given us by God, they cannot differ from each other. God must agree with himself. He has but one voice. It is man who speaks with jarring tongues. Nothing but harmony can come from the Creator; and, accordingly, a religion claiming to be from God, can give no surer proof of falsehood than by contradicting those previous truths which God is teaching by our very nature. We have thus seen that reason prepares us for a divine communication, and that it furnishes the ideas or materials of which revelation consists. This is my first consideration.

I proceed to a second. I affirm, then, that revelation rests on the authority of reason, because to this faculty it submits the evidences of its truth, and nothing but the approving sentence of reason binds us to receive and obey it. This is a very weighty consideration. Christianity, in placing itself before the tribunal of reason and in resting its claims on the sanction of this faculty, is one of the chief witnesses to the authority and dignity of our rational nature. That I have ascribed to this faculty its true and proper office, may be easily made to appear. I take the New Testament in hand, and on what ground do I receive its truths as divine? I see nothing on its pages but the same letters in which other books are written. No miraculous voice from Heaven assures me that it is God's word, nor does any mysterious voice within my soul command me to believe the supernatural works of Christ. How, then, shall I settle the question of the origin of this religion? I must examine it by the same rational faculties by which other subjects are tried. I must ask what are its evidences, and I must lay them before reason, the only power by which evidence can be weighed. I have not a distinct faculty given me for judging a revelation. I have not two understandings, one for inquiring into God's word and another into his works. As with the same bodily eye I now look on the earth, now on the heavens, so with the same power of reason I examine now nature, now revelation. Reason must collect and weigh the various proofs of Christianity. It must especially compare this system with those great moral convictions, which are written by the finger of God on the heart, and which make man a law to himself. A religion subverting these, it must not hesitate to reject, be its evidences what they may. A religion, for example, commanding us to hate and injure society, reason must instantly discard, without even waiting to examine its proofs. From these views we learn, not only that it is the province of reason to judge of the truth of Christianity, but, what is still more important, that the rules or tests by which it judges are of its own dictation. The laws which it applies in this case have their origin in itself. No one will pretend, that revelation can prescribe the principles by which the question of its own truth should be settled; for, until proved to be true, it has no authority. Reason must prescribe the tests or standards, to which a professed communication from God should be referred; and among these none are more important than that moral law, which belongs to the very essence, and is the deepest conviction, of the rational nature. Revelation, then, rests on reason, and, in opposing it, would act for its own destruction.

I have given two views. I have shown that revelation draws its ideas or materials from reason, and that it appeals to this power as the judge of its truth. I now assert, thirdly, that it rests on the authority of reason, because it needs and expects this faculty to be its interpreter, and without this aid would be worse than useless. How is the right of interpretation, the real meaning, of Scriptures to be ascertained? I answer, By reason. I know of no process by which the true sense of the New Testament is to pass from the page into my mind without the use of my rational faculties. It will not be pretended that this book is so exceedingly plain, its words so easy, its sentences so short, its meaning so exposed on the surface, that the whole truth may be received in a moment and without any intellectual effort. There is no such miraculous simplicity in the Scriptures. In truth, no book can be written so simply as to need no exercise of reason. Almost every word has more than one meaning, and judgment is required to select the particular sense intended by the writer. Of all books, perhaps the Scriptures need most the use of reason for their just interpretation; and this, not from any imperfection, but from the strength, boldness, and figurative character of their style, and from the distance of the time when they were written. I open the New Testament and my eye lights on this passage; "If thy hand offend thee, cut it off and cast it from thee." Is this language to be interpreted in its plainest and most obvious sense? Then I must mutilate my body, and become a suicide. I look again, and I find Jesus using these words to the Jews; "Fill ye up the measure of your iniquities." Am I to interpret this according to the letter, or the first ideas which it suggests? Then Jesus commanded his hearers to steep themselves in crime, and was himself a minister of sin. It is only by a deliberate use of reason, that we can penetrate beneath the figurative, hyperbolical, and often obscure style of the New Testament, to the real meaning. Let me go to the Bible, dismissing my reason and taking the first impression which the words convey, and there is no absurdity, however gross, into which I shall not fall. I shall ascribe a limited body to God, and unbounded knowledge to man, for I read of God having limbs, and of man knowing all things. Nothing is plainer, than that I must compare passage with passage, and limit one by another, and especially limit all by those plain and universal principles of reason, which are called common sense, or I shall make revelation the patron of every folly and vice. So essential is reason to the interpretation of the Christian records. Revelation rests upon its authority. Can it then oppose it, or teach us to hold it in light esteem?

I have now furnished the proofs of my first position, that revelation is founded on reason; and in discussing this, I have wished not only to support the main doctrine, but to teach you to reverence, more perhaps than you have done, your rational nature. This has been decried by theologians, until men have ceased to feel its sacredness and dignity. It ought to be regarded as God's greatest gift. It is his image within us. To renounce it would be to offer a cruel violence to ourselves, to take our place among the brutes. * * *

The Romantic Movement

Youth, said Emerson, is romantic. It was a circumstance of far-reaching implications for American literature that when our writers were starting to create an independent literary culture, Europe was communicating romantic enthusiasms and America was full of youthful vigor. The first settlers had brought with them from the Old World a mature culture, and later colonials assimilated their American experiences within an intellectual and literary context that was primarily a European import. Now, with political independence won by revolution, and with national confidence and self-consciousness enhanced by the War of 1812, Americans were ready to shape and express a civilization that should be uniquely that of a new people on the face of the earth.

The American Scene

The environment of our writers from Irving to Whitman was a yeasty one. Physical America itself was growing at a spectacular rate. In 1820 the people of the United States numbered 9,638,000; in 1860 they had increased to 31,443,000, owing partly to immigration. Even more amazing was the expansion in territory. By 1821, as many as eleven states had been added to the original thirteen. From New England and the Upper South pioneers moved into the rich valley of the Ohio and Mississippi. Chicago, in 1833, had a population of only 350, but by 1870 about 300,000. When California was annexed from Mexico in 1848, wide open spaces beckoned all the way to the Pacific.

East and Middle West were linked by the Erie Canal, and then came the age of railroads—the Baltimore and Ohio, the Pennsylvania, and others, till by 1860 the iron rails covered 30,000 miles. The general aspect of the country was still agricultural; yet by 1860 the value of its manufactures equaled that of its crops. Sectional differences were so great that, as one historian has said, the civilizations of North and South were as wide apart as those of Canada and Mexico today. The South was now the Cotton Kingdom, with white fields, black slaves, and an attachment to Sir Walter Scott, in whose novels, as S. E. Morison puts it, "the cotton lord and his lady found a romantic mirror of their life and ideals." But it was the democratic West—the land of the advancing frontier—that seemed the America of the future. "Europe," said Emerson, "stretches to the Alleghenies; America lies beyond." The winning of the West was in a sense a romanticism of action, reaching its climax in the discovery of gold in California, from which the fever of sudden riches spread rapidly to the East and even to Europe. The speed with which the West was effectively settled is a main feature of this period. In vain did John Quincy Adams, like Jefferson before him, wish to avoid the evils of a too rapid expansion by preserving the Western lands for a planned development over centuries.

And yet in a very real sense the America of the future was not the agricultural West, but the industrial East. Even before the Civil War, the pattern of a business civilization was well established. The Industrial Revolution arrived in a land as rich in resources as it was vast in extent, a land with a *laissez-faire* economy that made the competition for success and wealth unbridled. A succession of newly invented machines was the means to a tremendous increase in productivity and trade. By 1840 the United States had 1200 cotton textile factories, chiefly in New England, and the pig-iron industry, centered in eastern Pennsylvania, raised its production tenfold in the forty years preceding 1850. The crops of the Middle West were pouring east in ever-growing volume. Assuredly America was the land of opportunity.

Was it also, in Washington Irving's phrase, the "Land of the Almighty Dollar"? If so, it was hardly because Americans were peculiarly sinful in their love of riches, for better examples of unrestrained materialism and its attendant abuses could be found in industrial England. But there is no question that wealth seemed astonishingly easy to attain. "In the seething America of the 1830's and 1840's," says a prominent historian, "both immigrant and old American felt that, with just a little luck, fortune might be waiting for him around the corner. Hadn't Astor made $20,000,000, Girard left $6,000,000, while men in every community were evidently getting rich on a large if less spectacular scale?" There had always, of course, been a materialistic as well as an idealistic aspect to the American dream.

At any rate, Americans pursued business with abandon. A traveler described New York about 1840 as "the busiest community that any man could desire to live in. In the streets all is hurry and bustle; the very carts, instead of being drawn by horses at a walking pace, are often met at a gallop, and always in a brisk trot. The whole of the population seen in the streets seems to enjoy this bustle, and add to it by their own rapid pace." Travelers generally frowned upon this American speed, as in the eighteenth century they had deplored American indolence. Visitors from England, in the East, looked in vain for public parks, games and sports, or walking in the country. As work had been a virtue among the Puritans, so now the making of money was conceived as a patriotic duty, a contribution to the rapid development of the country. A leisure class seemed inappropriate when the man of inherited wealth, as an observer tells us, saw "nobody about him not engaged in business." Cultural activities were commonly disparaged because they reduced the speed of money-making; literature and music were more suitable for women. Everything seemed to conspire to encourage a type of businessman full of drive and zest in his vocation but otherwise empty. A crass plutocracy was taking the place of the old aristocracy.

And the prizes were open to all. The eighteenth century had stressed the "free" in the concept of "free and equal," especially the free, rational mind, and the Revolution brought political freedom. The early national period was zealous not only for the "free" but for the "equal." Equality was dramatized by the Jacksonian upheaval. From this time dates the custom of telling the American boy that someday he may be President of the United States. In many ways the middle-class leadership that took the place of the aristocracy flattered and served the common man, the laborer and farmer. It is significant that the Whig party in 1840 deemed it wise to ignore the patrician origin of William Henry Harrison and to picture him, in the campaign, as seated before a log cabin with a barrel of hard cider. State after state extended the ballot, and an effective public school system was undertaken in earnest. There were many workers for humanitarian reforms: prison reform, temperance, the granting of women's rights, the abolition of slavery, the last of which increasingly cast the others in shadow. To the old conservative families of the East and South, it seemed that they were living out of context in this century of the common man, not to say of commonness. But there were also patricians like Ralph Waldo Emerson who accepted the changing world and welcomed "the near, the low, the common."

While the prosperous were growing in wealth and power and the common man was comfortable and could hope to be prosperous, Americans became brash and boastful. They scorned the Old World monarchies far overseas and feared no nation under the sun. Seeing the rapid progress of the country in material power, in science and technology, apparently in every department of life, they readily transformed the eighteenth-century idea of progress into a religion, and envisaged for their land a resplendent future. The only dark cloud in sight was slavery, but 99 per cent of Northern businessmen, it has been estimated, believed that if the North held its tongue and kept its fingers out, the problem would somehow solve itself without ruining business and breaking up the Union.

The spirit of nationalism throve along with this zest for business expansion and optimism over the future. In America as in Europe, the cosmopolitanism of the eighteenth century was followed by the nationalism of the nineteenth. It emerged symbolically during the War of 1812 in the guise of "Uncle Sam," and was expressed in the patriotic gaiety and bombastic oratory of Fourth of July celebrations. In a mood we would now call isolationist, America turned its back on the Atlantic and in the 1820's announced the Monroe Doctrine that the Americas were for Americans. By the middle of the century the slogan "Manifest Destiny" suggested rather that the Americas were for the Americans of the United States. In their patriotic zeal and their appetite for expansion, many people came to feel that the great American democracy should include territories that nature seemed to have intended for her: Canada, the Caribbean, Mexico, Central America, the islands of the Pacific.

Thus an expansive self-reliance showed itself on the national as on the individual level. It showed itself also, between these two extremes, on the level of the section and the state. A section of the United States, as the historian Turner put it, is a "potential nation," or "the faint image of a European nation." It is a part of our national domain conscious of its own tradition, material interests, social ideals, as different from those of other sections. Before the Civil War the country had four sections: East (the old

North), South, Middle West, and Far West. The secession of the South was a violent assertion of its self-reliance. There was a similar sense of unity and pride within the individual state. It was not so much the South that seceded as one southern state after another. The great war that followed substantially settled the relation of states' rights, sectional interests, and the Union.

Despite young America's growing absorption in business and material progress, an adequate public for the new literary movement was prepared in a number of ways. The romantic impulse from Europe might well have proved fruitless if there had not been strong American roots favoring romanticism. Some of them have already been indicated. One was America's patriotic nationalism, crude but capable of idealistic refinement. Another was its democratic society, with far more liberty, equality, and fraternity than in the aristocratic eighteenth century. Another was the emphasis on the individual man, the self-reliant man, encouraged both by a *laissez-faire* economy and the individualism of the frontier. Another was the mood of optimism natural in a land of opportunity.

But the most vital preparation for such writers as Emerson, Thoreau, Hawthorne, Melville, and Whitman was a religious spirit that goes back to the men and women who settled America. Puritans, Quakers, Anglicans and others had left in the American mind an enduring reverence and a sensitive conscience. The worldliness and rationalism of the age of Franklin could bank the old religious fires, but not quench them. In the early nineteenth century, revivals flamed up afresh; more important perhaps was a piety expressed in day-by-day observances. As we read in an autobiography by S. G. Goodrich, "In most families the first exercise of the morning was reading the Bible, followed by prayer, at which all were assembled, including the servants and helpers of the kitchen and the farm." Calvinists were still far from extinct, especially in the country, while the Unitarians were well established among the upper classes in cities and town. If Unitarianism was related on one side to Locke and eighteenth-century rationalism, it was related on the other to Emerson and the Transcendentalist movement. Already in the words of William Ellery Channing, the great leader of the Unitarians, one can see the thoughts of Emerson and his contemporaries emerging. "We must start in religion," Channing had said, "from our own souls. In these is the fountain of all divine truth. . . . The soul is the spring of our knowledge of God."

Often closely connected with these various types of religious devotion was a hunger of the mind, shown by the Lyceum and other schemes for popular lectures, which spread over the country. In 1834, when this cultural movement was at its height, the local lyceums totaled about 3,000. A favorite speaker was Ralph Waldo Emerson, whose tours took him even beyond the Mississippi in midwinter. Meanwhile, in publications, literary taste had long been nourished, after a fashion, by sentimental and Gothic novels and dramas. Poor though they were in quality, they opened the way for something better by stirring sympathetic feelings and an appetite for the strange and mysterious.

To preserve what was strong in the spiritual and imaginative background, to deepen what was shallow, to refine and diversify what was crude and over-simple, to transform what was faintly felt into a whole new vision of life and art—this was to be the task of the literary artists of the Romantic Movement.

The Romantic Revolt

Since the closing years of the eighteenth century, the more sensitive minds, in America as in Europe, had become increasingly less comfortable in the world of ideas established so long ago by Newton, Locke, and Pope. They were profoundly dissatisfied with a rationalism and neoclassicism daily more remote from their experience. In the political realm there was no real problem, since the democratic ideas of the eighteenth century were still held valid, needing only fuller expression in theory and practice. But in the vast realm of thought and feeling concerning the deity, and nature, and human nature and destiny, and an art suited to a new outlook on life—here a tremendous change seemed called for.

Romanticism provided a new and more relevant set of affirmations, which may be summarized as follows. Man is something more than a thinking machine in a machine universe. We cannot be content with ideas clear and consistent at the expense of truth; something is always left out. Reality is too large and diverse, too vital and fluid, to be compassed by cool reason. Nor is common sense sufficient; it may be the way to wealth and easy living, but not to high thinking or deep feeling. The world we live in is not a dead machine, but rather a living, breathing being. God is not outside the universe, forgetting and forgotten, but in it and in us, an immanent presence. Man does not come into the world as a blank page to be written on, but as a spirit trailing clouds of glory. What then is a poet? Not a polite tailor in words, dressing nature and human nature to advantage, not a wit writing an artificial language for town and court, but a man speaking to all men of our common humanity and the experiences of the heart. He is an inspired bard, a creative, original genius expressing his innermost self, which is always taking new forms, reshaping its world in new visions of truth and beauty. As Josiah Royce was later to sum up the German romantic school, it proclaimed:

> Trust your genius; follow your noble heart; change your doctrine whenever your heart changes, and change your heart often. Such is the practical creed of the romanticists. The world, you see, is after all the world of the inner life. . . . The world is essentially what men of genius make it. Let us be men of genius, and make what we choose.

The secret of life, in the new outlook, lay not in the head but in the heart. Reality was to be sought not through conscious thought but through immediate intuitive perception: the kingdom of God was within. The head brought only doubt and barrenness; man must trust the heart—feeling—desire—the yearning for fulfillment—the Faustian spirit of aspiration. The human spirit had to be emancipated, freed from the tyranny of everything exterior to itself, whether this was a Calvinistic dogma of depravity, or a cramping rationalism, or a commonsense obsession with the pots and pans of practical life. Freed from these it might regain the sense of wonder, the bloom of the world; might dwell upon the strange, the mysterious, the miraculous, might hope for a revelation here and now.

The inner life and its needs, in the romantic view, are not identical in all men. If men are born free and equal in worth as human beings, they are also born different, no two of them alike. Each should therefore be true to himself, express his uniquely valuable self. It is hardly mere accident that the new words compounded with *self* in the nineteenth century were not often like the old *self-conceit, self-esteem, self-denial,* which now seemed unpleasant, but rather *self-expression, self-realization, self-culture, self-help, self-reliance,* which seemed attractive.

The Romantic Movement was strikingly international. In America, as in all the major countries of Europe, it had native roots but was fertilized and brought to fruition by foreign influences. Each country sought a national culture, an organic expression of its special "genius." As a result, differing interests and emphases characterize the romanticisms of England, Germany, France, Spain, Russia, the United States. But the resemblances are at least equally obvious. National self-reliance did not mean isolationism of the mind. The thinkers, artists, and critics who led the way used suggestions wherever they found them, not only in native experience but in any land where a renewal was in progress. In France they looked largely to England, in England to Germany, in Germany to England, for ideas and attitudes, for visions of the good life, for the inspiration of imaginative art. In the United States they looked to many European countries, above all England and Germany, where the movement flourished about two decades earlier than in the New World.

In Germany they saw philosophy given a new start by Immanuel Kant, whose critiques, as they understood, had demolished the Age of Reason at its very foundations and made possible the erection of a new structure in harmony with man's high aspirations. Starting from Kant, Fichte had declared his "world-positing ego"—an inner spiritual activity which enables each individual to build his own world. Then came the poetic philosopher Schelling, with his idea, dear to many romanticists, that spirit within man is the same as spirit within nature. Along with the philosophers were fascinating literary figures: not only the towering Goethe—one of Emerson's "Representative Men"—but a whole Romantic School, bold and brilliant (Tieck, Novalis, the Schlegels, and others). Here, then, was a dazzling array of systematic thinkers and creative writers who had broken with the eighteenth century and at length carried the movement, as Carlyle said, to completion. It is true that Americans often knew them only slightly and understood them ill—much as Marx and Freud fared in the twentieth century. Yet at least they were convinced, by Coleridge and Carlyle, that Germany had led in a direction they wanted to go in their own way.

In England too they saw the old thought and literary art dissolved, the new taking form. If many were convinced that the core of the movement was in Germany, all American writers were naturally drawn to England by habit, sentiment, and language: what they found could be readily assimilated. Wordsworth illustrated for them a poetic sensibility expressed in simple language, profound in feeling and imagination, in contact with the spiritual "Presences" of Nature (instead of the deistic "absentee" Creator) and with the lives of common folk glorified by human dignity. Coleridge, for the Transcendentalists at any rate, made his impression chiefly through his prose writings, in which the new German philosophy and the tradition of Platonism were combined with religious earnestness. He seemed to validate the intuitive and imaginative powers of man that rationalism had so long neglected. And then there was the young romantic Carlyle, escaping from both Scottish Calvinism and the Age of Reason with the aid of his beloved Germans, exemplifying a hatred of artificiality and sham, a love of sincerity and wonder, an awareness of the Infinite, that vast reservoir of power upon which great men draw so much and lesser men too little.

Although Carlyle's *Sartor Resartus* was first published in book form in America, with a preface by his friend Emerson, oddly enough Emerson failed to mention him when, in 1840, he sketched the course of the new movement. "This love of the Infinite," he wrote in *The Dial*, ". . . this new love of the vast, always native in Germany, was imported into France by De Staël, appeared in England in Coleridge, Wordsworth, Byron, Shelley, . . . and finds a most genial climate in the American mind." Many other traits of European romanticism were acclimatized by American writers looking for incitement, doctrine, example. Not content merely to look from afar, many of them made the Atlantic crossing, in days when it was slow and uncomfortable, to see the Old World intimately with their own eyes. Clearly, the War of Independence did not end, among American intellectuals, the sense of an Atlantic community.

Literary Centers of American Romanticism

"Who reads an American book?" Sydney Smith's question in the *Edinburgh Review* of 1820 was painfully galling to Americans. They were, as Irving said, "a young people, necessarily an imitative one," but they were also sensitive and ambitious. They knew only too well how little they had written to merit British approbation in the two hundred years since the Plymouth plantation, or in the thirty-seven years since the recognition of the American Republic. Yet in fact a national literature was beginning in the city of New York at this very time, as witness *The Sketch Book* by Irving in 1819–20 and *The Spy* by Cooper in 1821. Bryant was soon to join them.

These three early romantics, born in the eighteenth century, did most of their best work during the years 1810–35. The genial pen of Irving, schooled in neoclassic prose, made the picturesque past of Europe and America live. Cooper, while no stylist, could tell a story and describe graphically the forest frontier with its rather too noble Indians. Bryant, assimilating the English pre-romantics and Wordsworth, wrote, with poetic dignity and breadth, of nature and death. With these three "Knickerbocker" writers were associated others prominent in their day but now generally forgotten.

Most of the Knickerbocker writers were drawn to New York by advantages it offered the man of letters. Intent though the new metropolis was on commercial enterprise, its wealth made for cultural advance, for publishing houses, magazines, and newspapers (including the *Evening Post* long edited by Bryant). In 1820 the city's population was 123,000; by 1840 it was 312,000. Early in the century it had the air of a country town, with half-built streets—a "hobbledehoy metropolis" Cooper called it. As seen by Charles Dickens in 1842, it was still a straggling city, low and flat, without plumbing, its waterfront bristling with masts, its streets roamed by scavenger hogs; but it also had many stately residences richly furnished and adorned with silverware and oil portraits. Old families, Dutch and English, saw the cherished past fading as the *nouveau riche* took charge. The Hudson Valley market-town was becoming the urban symbol of a fast-moving young America devoted to commerce, industry, and finance.

It is a far cry from the solid materialism of New York to the airy idealism of Concord. The place was only a village, one of thousands in the nation, yet in it was a stir of mind and spirit that affected American life and letters for decades. Less than twenty miles from Boston, Concord was a community of 2,000 when Thoreau was born there—he was the only native in the literary group. The village was on a quietly gliding stream, bordered by dwarf willows and wild grape vines (whence the cultivated Concord grape). Meadows led to uplands and small lakes called ponds. Walden Pond, where Emerson owned woodland, was less than a two-mile walk from his house on the Lexington road at the edge of town. In another part of the rambling white village was the Old Manse, where Emerson and then Hawthorne lived for a time, close to the hallowed spot at the river where

> . . . once the embattled farmers stood
> And fired the shot heard round the world.

In this historic association Concord may symbolize the nationalistic impulse of American romanticism. But its roots go much deeper, to the time when Old Concord was the first inland plantation of the Massachusetts Colony and had as its first minister an ancestor of Emerson. To this pleasant little town, where plain living and high thinking had always seemed natural, Emerson came to reside in 1834, followed after some years by Bronson Alcott, Ellery Channing (poet nephew of the Unitarian leader), and Hawthorne. At times Margaret Fuller lived there, and at all times Concord-born Thoreau.

Before the Concord group began to form, Massachusetts had nothing comparable to the activity of the Connecticut Wits or the New York group of early romantics. In the whole state, Emerson remarked dryly in his journal, "from 1790 to 1820, there was not a book, a speech, a conversation, or a thought," and for the years after 1820 he could name only Channing, Webster, and Edward Everett. But the Transcendental movement, for which Concord was to be famous, was gathering, and by 1836 burst forth with vigor. In September 1836, Emerson, Alcott, George Ripley, F. H. Hedge and two others "chanced to confer together," as Hedge recalled, "on the state of current opinion in theology and philosophy, which we agreed in thinking very unsatisfactory. . . . What we strongly felt was dissatisfaction with the reigning sensuous philosophy, dating from Locke, on which our Unitarian theology was based." Hedge went on to say that, thanks to the writings of Coleridge and Carlyle, "there was a promise in the air of a new era of intellectual life." Later meetings were attended at one time or another by Orestes Brownson, Margaret Fuller, Jones Very, Thoreau, and others of less interest today. These informal gatherings led to a quarterly magazine, *The Dial*, edited by Margaret Fuller and later Emerson, which ran for four years. They also helped to create an atmosphere that produced, in time, such social experiments as the "ideal" communities of Brook Farm and Fruitlands, as well as Thoreau's one-man experiment at Walden Pond.

What was this "Transcendentalism" that everyone was talking about in eastern Massachusetts and few professed to understand? Often described in a single phrase as "Romanticism on Puritan soil," the Transcendental movement was both a spiritual affirmation and an intellectual effort to restore—but in a vastly changed form—the high conception of the human soul and destiny in which Puritan New England had been schooled so long but which a rationalism based on the senses had overlaid with a burden become intolerable. It is a return to something like the flashes of divinity in the poems of Edward Taylor, or Jonathan Edwards' "New Sense," or the Inner Light of the Quakers, or the exalted vision of Being in Plato and the Platonic tradition down to Coleridge. Vague and eclectic, Transcendentalism sought support not only in Kant and other Germans, but in Plato, Plotinus, the Hindu epics, and wherever the sages and the poets seemed to have touched a high reality. It differed from its New England background of Calvinism in celebrating not the omnipotence of God but the limitless possibilities of the self.

Two men of Concord perhaps offer the best way to grasp the significance of Transcendentalism, through their lives and their writings. Emerson was the leader of the movement, yet gathered no disciples. The only way to follow him was, paradoxically, to go one's own way, be wholly one's self and nowise an imitator. Emerson's own way led him to resign his ministry in the Unitarian church and to seek a strictly personal religion, together with a new vocation, that of writing and lecturing to further spiritual ends. In *Nature* he condensed with at least a show of system the doctrine and aspiration of the new movement. His address on the American Scholar was the definitive declaration of cultural independence. In a long stream of lectures and essays on well-nigh every aspect of life, he expressed the optimism, the confident self-reliance of the young Republic, preached the limitless capacities of man, of every man no matter how common. He encouraged the United States of that day to think out the implications of its democratic slogans, and to aim at an achievement in the realm of the spirit equal to its achievement in material prosperity. In his desire to call forth the best that the self might exalt itself to, he magnified the spark of divinity that seems to touch man, till the self appeared to be God. It was only later, in essays not regarded as among the most "Emersonian," that he doubted this bold extension of romantic individualism, and limited it with a respect for actual experience and the concept of a Fate that reminds us that men are but human. On the other hand Emerson came to feel, through faith in progress, a new source of optimism. In general it may fairly be said of him, as James T. Adams has said, that "in no other author can we get so close to the whole of the American spirit."

An even more resolute man of Concord was Emerson's friend Thoreau. Austerely self-sufficient, nonconformist by principle and practice, he led his own life as completely as anyone could without wholly breaking away from society, as he demonstrated by his temporary hermitage at Walden Pond. He followed where the spirit led, had no other vocation, refused to let any deadening routine interfere with his effort to keep himself fresh and alert in his relation with himself and the world. What little he needed to sustain himself, unmarried, he easily earned by doing odd jobs. He loved nature without sentimentalism, sauntered to watch the seasons and entertain thoughts, often alone, often with a companion. In his best writing he described the life of nature sensitively, and examined the values of human existence with honesty and wit. "The transcendental philosophy," he said waggishly, "needs the leaven of humor to render it light and digestible." He inveighed against low aims, stupid conventions, and the meaningless pursuit of material prosperity. The scope of thought in which he lived is indicated well enough by an entry in his journal in 1851: "Perchance this window-seat in which we sit discoursing Transcendentalism, with only Germany and Greece stretching behind our minds, was made so deep because this was a few years ago a garrison-house," i.e., of the Puritans against the Indians. Germany and Greece represent Thoreau's concern with the European tradition, in what he considered its truest moments, from Homer down to his own contemporaries. At the same time he made the Puritan past of New England very real to himself, and persistently studied the Indians, since whatever was wild in nature or man had for him a fundamental value.

Viewed from the abodes of urbanity and scholarship in Boston and Cambridge, the Transcendentalists looked like eccentrics. Lowell pictured Thoreau as mainly an egotist with scant logic and no humor. And he found the group in general, at least its faddist fringe, simply comical:

> Every form of intellectual and physical dyspepsia brought forth its gospel.... No brain but had its private maggot, which must have found pitiably short commons sometimes. Not a few impecunious zealots abjured the use of money (unless earned by other people), professing to live on the internal revenues of the spirit. Some had an assurance of instant millennium so soon as hooks and eyes should be substituted for buttons.... Many foreign revolutionists out of work added to the general misunderstanding their contribution of broken English in every most ingenious form of fracture.

Beside a passage like this we may extract a sentence from the privacy of Emerson's journal, where he speaks of Longfellow in his mansion at Cambridge. "If Socrates were here we could go and talk with him; but Longfellow we cannot go and talk with; there is a palace, and servants, and a row of bottles of different colored wines, and wine glasses, and fine coats." To Concord *that* was oddity; the appropriate thing was plain living. But in truth Longfellow had a gracious, simple nature and was no more spoiled by affluence than the great Virginian who had made this same "palace" his headquarters—George Washington.

Longfellow had probably a wider influence on his own generation than any other American writer save Emerson. He domesticated for the ordinary American the courtly muses of Europe. To a middle-class nation undernourished by Puritan moralism and Neoclassic rationalism, he brought in obvious and familiar rhythms the warmth, the color, the rich variety, the sentiment and magic, of the unfamiliar old cultures abroad, German, Spanish, Portuguese, Italian, Belgian, Scandinavian. He did this, to be sure, romantically, ignoring (as Irving had done) the living present of Europe, slighting the great illuminations of its past, and placing his emphasis rather on the picturesque, the "quaint," a realm of beauty and strangeness, a dream-world offering escape—life being "prosaic in this country to the last degree." From a prosaic present he turned not only to the European but also the American past. As he said, "The dreary old Puritanical times begin to look romantic in the distance." The moralistic twist which he gave his poems made them acceptable to a middle-class nation very definitely on the side of virtue. With that kept in view it was ready, at last, to enter the palace of art.

Longfellow, and Lowell after him, held the professorship of *belles-lettres* at Harvard. Oliver Wendell Holmes was professor of medicine and dean of the medical school. When Lowell entered Harvard as a student in 1834, there were only 220 undergraduates. According to Edward Everett Hale, "The whole drift of fashion, occupation, and habit among the undergraduates ran in lines suggested by literature." The books they bought or took from the library were works of literature—not theology, or politics, or science. "Some Philadelphia publisher had printed in one volume Coleridge's poems, Shelley's, and Keats'... you saw the book pretty much everywhere."

Aside from the three academic writers of Cambridge, Boston had literati of its own. Among them was Thomas W. Parsons, a native of the city, a dentist who wrote accomplished poetry and who loved Dante as Longfellow and Lowell did, translating admirably most of the *Divine Comedy.* There was Orestes Brownson, prominent as editor of the *Democratic Review* and other quarterlies, writer of numerous books including a novel, and successively a Presbyterian, a Universalist, an independent, a Unitarian minister, and finally a Roman Catholic of uncertain orthodoxy. There was Francis Parkman, born in Boston, still regarded today as the greatest of American historians, who applied to the epic struggle of France and England in America a combination of the scientific method of German scholarship and the literary approach of Walter Scott.

The Romantic View of Life

These, then, are the broad facts of American romanticism: its revolt—against the rationalism that dominated the eighteenth century and lingered among the Unitarians; its affirmation—the supremacy of the heart, the inner life of the self; its environment—expansive, optimistic young America from about 1820 to the Civil War; its radial center—Transcendental Concord.

If we have nowhere presented a set definition of romanticism, American or international, this is because its complexities have eluded all scholarly efforts to reduce it to an acceptable formula. The significance of the literature of the period will, however, be clearer if we make some attempt to explore and describe the romantic quest, if not to define it. As a starting point, the phrase "Individualism in feeling and imagination" may serve as a convenient label for the complex elements entering into romantic literature; but only an analysis will make such a label really useful.

The individualism demanded by the romantics was something other than the rational individualism of the age of Franklin and Jefferson. Jefferson had said: "Fix reason firmly in her seat, and call to her tribunal every fact, every opinion. . . . Neither believe nor reject anything because other persons . . . have rejected or believed it. Your own reason is the only oracle given you by heaven." The romantics shared this hostility to authority, but not the deference to reason. They boldly unfixed reason from her seat, and declared that the true oracle is intuition—something they knew without reasoning, something that satisfied the instincts of the heart. The individualism they proclaimed was that of the whole self, in which the affirmation of the feelings and imagination seemed to be central.

"Trust thyself: every heart vibrates to that iron string," said Emerson. He said: "If the single man plant himself indomitably on his instincts, and there abide, the huge world will come round to him." He said: "Whoso would be a man, must be a nonconformist." He said: "The root and seed of democracy is the doctrine, Judge for yourself. Reverence thyself."

Self-reliance has been justified in two opposite ways—because all men are different from each other, and because they are all alike. The view that they are different has been associated with romanticism ever since Rousseau began his *Confessions* by declaring that he was made unlike anybody he had ever seen; different, if not better. All men, it seems, are born free and different, and each should be himself and pursue happiness in his own way. "Is it not the chief disgrace in the world," asked Emerson, "not to yield that peculiar fruit which each man was created to bear?" The dignity of man requires that a man insist on himself and never imitate other men. In the same vein Walt Whitman speaks of the thought that comes to us, a thought calm "like the stars, shining eternal. This is the thought of identity—yours for you, as mine for me." A man, says Whitman, has his "own central idea and purpose," grows from it and to it. While he may gather and absorb influences from outside, he must never imperil "the precious idiocrasy and special nativity and intention that he is, the man's self." This idea of the uniqueness of every man runs, as an assumption if not an assertion, all through the Romantic Movement.

In direct contrast is the idea of the Neoclassic Age that all men are basically the same: not the uniqueness of men but the unity of man, not the particular man but the universal man. The two views do not, of course, exclude each other, but simply emphasize two aspects of humanity. Both views are common in this period, both the romantic sense of difference or novelty and the old classical sense—going back to Socrates and Plato—of sameness or universality. We have quoted Emerson's doctrine of uniqueness, but actually his prevailing emphasis was on unity, though in the end he gave unity itself a romantic twist. In a *Dial* paper he directly contrasted the two views, and left no doubt as to his choice of emphasis. There is, he said, a healthy subjectivism and an unhealthy subjectivism. The danger of subjectivism is shown when it is indulged by the narrow-minded and the selfish, in whom it is a form of personal vanity, or escape from inner sickness. This is the "abominable self." On the other hand, there is an impersonal subjectivism. "A man may say I, and never refer to himself as an individual. . . . The great man, even whilst he relates a private fact personal to him, is really leading us away from him to an universal experience." The reason is, "that there is One Mind, and that all the powers and privileges which lie in any, lie in all." This last quotation, it will be observed, sums up the central drift of essay after essay in Emerson's best-known writings. Thus, in *Essays, First Series*, Emerson prefixed a motto in which he says (as he wants us to say):

> I am owner of the sphere,
> Of the seven stars and the solar year,
> Of Caesar's hand, and Plato's brain,
> Of Lord Christ's heart, and Shakespeare's strain.

Whitman later said much the same thing, beginning his "Song of Myself" with a line that looks purely personal till the second line makes it universal:

> I celebrate myself, and sing myself,
> And what I assume you shall assume.

Harmonious though this kind of thought is with the classical tradition, it takes on, we feel, a romantic cast. Perhaps it is the focus on the ego—the inflated ego—the very notion of a "Song of Myself" in place of, say, Pope's "Essay on Man." Or we may say it is the bold pride of the romantic instead of the ethical moderation inculcated by a classical author like Homer or Sophocles. Or we may say, rather, that a romantic optimism, a too ready slipping into illusion, causes a certain blindness to the facts of life. In sober truth, few individuals who plant themselves indomitably on their instincts will find the huge world coming round to them. Emerson, as usual, suggests his own corrective, remarking upon the "yawning difference" "between men as they ought to be and as they are." His doubts that men have it in their power to bring into being all that is latent but buried in them, begin early in his writings and multiply and deepen as he moves on to scan the meaning of Experience, of Illusions, of Fate. He had called genius "a larger imbibing of the common heart," or "a large infusion of Deity," but his efforts to encourage and confidently call forth in every man the vast riches of humanity—to democratize genius, so to speak—were typical only of Transcendentalism in its heyday.

It was the *feeling* individual, rather, with most romantics. Not developing their outlook, like Emerson, ministerially, they placed at the center of the self feeling and imagination. They sought every kind of experience and responded with sensuous warmth, trusting the heart wherever it led.

Feeling—love—the heart: these were bepraised in the Romantic period as reason had been in the Neoclassic. For a hundred years sentimentalism, reacting against the rule of reason, had proclaimed the goodness of human nature, the virtue of the man of feeling. In the romantic triumph this sentimentalism was changed into something rich and strange. Feeling became far more genuine, complicated, and interesting. It was still at war with the eighteenth-century kind of reason: "that false secondary power," Wordsworth called it, "by which we multiply distinctions," an analytic power by which we divide and divide vital reality till we "break down all grandeur." Feeling, a synthetic power, preserves vital reality, the meaning of things in their wholeness.

Romanticism restored to literature the emotional vitality of the Renaissance, interrupted by the long reign of neo- and pseudo-classicism. But now, in literature as in life, feeling was far more introverted and personal. It was individual joy, rapture, love, longing, regret, fear, hope, faith, enthusiasm, despair, an auto-registration of moods. These feelings were experienced with the keen sensibility and tumult of a youthful spirit—most romantics died early or became less romantic. The feeling perhaps most typical, internationally, was that of longing (in German, *Sehnsucht*), a vague longing for love, beauty, the infinite. The poetry of ancient classicism was the poetry of enjoyment, said A. W. Schlegel, and that of romanticism is the poetry of desire, a desire that can never be satisfied, an indefinite desire that must end in melancholy.

Is the romantic, then, like the sentimentalist, a man of feeling instead of a man of reason or of action? Basically, perhaps; and yet one must recognize a great difference. The feeling of the sentimentalist is weak and shallow; that of the romantic, stronger and deeper. The sentimentalist luxuriates in feeling for its own sake; the romantic, while he may often do this, is engaged in a quest of high truth through imagination. He believes in feeling as a value; he believes also that its value depends on an exertion of imagination. This is one of his key words, an old word which he used in a new way that has been common ever since. Before the romantic period, imagination had been synonymous with memory, a calling up of things past, or, by extension, a creation of something new by a recombination of things remembered. But now it transcended these old uses, came to be thought of as an instrument of insight into a truth above the field of the senses. Truth, it was held, lies in feeling, but it is the imagination that finds it. The really vital meanings of human life cannot be approached by the systematic and external operations of science, but only by an immediate emotional perception, warm flashes of intuition or imagination, a knowledge from within the human spirit.

The concept of imagination is so important that it will be worth while to review a famous statement of it. In his preface to *Lyrical Ballads* Wordsworth announced that the object of this new departure in poetry was to take situations from common life—in which "the essential passions of the heart" are clearest—and "to throw over them a certain coloring of imagination, whereby ordinary things should be presented to the mind in an unusual aspect." That is, the poetic mind does not see nature and life prosaically, as literal fact, but throws over them (as Coleridge put it in one of his poems),

> A light, a glory, a fair luminous cloud
> Enveloping the earth.

How does this happen? First, something that the poet sees or experiences stirs an emotion in him. Secondly, this emotion is recollected in the tranquillity of meditation, till the actual emotion has become a poetic emotion. Thirdly, this poetic emotion, now grown powerful, spontaneously overflows in expression. So far the poet. Other persons, reading the poem, have their feelings strengthened and purified. Most readers, belonging to "the poor loveless ever-anxious crowd," as Coleridge calls them, need to be awakened from "the lethargy of custom" and to see life freshly with eyes of wonder. As moonlight gives an ordinary and familiar scene or experience a new and richer meaning, so the romantic imagination, shedding the light of the human spirit, adds, says Wordsworth,

> the gleam
> The light that never was, on sea or land,
> The consecration and the poet's dream.

The views of the two poets are so close that we may speak of the Wordsworth-Coleridge concept of imagination. Again and again, from Bryant to Whitman, we are reminded of it in American criticism. Poe, for example, maintains that it is not the business of the poet to express passion—what we have called the "actual emotion"—but to "elevate the soul" by an image of Supernal Beauty. In an imaginative poem, he says, at every stroke of the lyre we hear a ghostly echo; in every glimpse of beauty "we catch, through long and wild vistas, dim bewildering visions of a far more ethereal beauty *beyond.*" Poetry should have "the *vagueness* of exaltation," "a certain wild license and *indefiniteness*": "the atmosphere of the mystic," a "breath of faëry." Poe was obviously following, in his own way, the theory as well as the practice of Coleridge and Shelley.

The romantic imagination was not equally satisfactory to all the leaders of the American movement. Lowell, especially, became highly suspicious of "cloud-castles," and called for wisdom, judgment, reason to steady and guide the poet, as in the ethical imagination of the Greeks and Shakespeare and the spiritual imagination of his beloved Dante. While he complained that Wordsworth could not see "beyond the limits of his own consciousness and experience," he held that Dante, though himself the protagonist of the *Divine Comedy*, had for his theme not a man but man, whose highest end was to "climb through every phase of human experience to that transcendental and super-sensual region where the true, the good, and the beautiful blend in the white light of God." Deploring the irresponsibility to which the romantic imagination was inclined, Lowell also condemned its frequent morbidity or "liver-complaint." So did Walt Whitman, and more significantly, because the ground of his criticism was an optimism just as characteristically romantic as the pessimism he brushed aside. Of the modern tendency "to turn everything to pathos, ennui, morbidity, dissatisfaction, death," Whitman remarked abruptly: "I call this thing in our modern literature delirium tremens." Its presence in the wholesome air of the New World he attributed to the influence of the decadent Old World. "Europe, with all its glories," is "a vast abnormal ward or hysterical sick-chamber."

Like the indefinite, the remote and strange attracted the romantic imagination. Perhaps no one has put so neatly as Emerson the contrast between things near seen with realistic eyes and things remote seen by the idealizing imagination: "Every ship is romantic, save that we are sailing in." But it was Poe who most deliberately cultivated the addition of strangeness to beauty, in prose as well as verse. Attracted, as Hawthorne was also, by the horrors and mysteries that the "Gothic" writers had exploited so crudely, he made them shapes of beauty, as in "The Fall of the House of Usher." To the humdrum actual world he opposed visions of Dream-Land, the Valley of Many-Colored Grass, or "ultimate dim Thule." Longfellow was to find inspiration in the Middle Ages; Irving's imagination was similarly captured by early Spain. To some of the Transcendentalists, Asia counted far more than did the European Middle Ages: Emerson found Asia rich in suggestions of a spiritual view of life, and Thoreau immersed himself as in bracing waters in the Bhagavad-Gita, the Vedas, the Vishnu Purana, the Institute of Menu. On one occasion, on meeting Walt Whitman, who struck him as "wonderfully like the Orientals," he asked whether he had read them. "No," replied Whitman, "tell me about them." And for Whitman too the "mystic Orient" became important.

Whatever inspiration American writers found in foreign lands, they derived most of their subject-matter from their native past. A nationalistic, self-reliant America must grow from roots in its own soil, even though that soil was poor when compared (as by Irving) with Europe's "storied and poetical associations." To Emerson at sea, homeward bound from the Old World, "America, my country" was a

> Land without history, . .
> No castles, no cathedrals, and no kings;
> Land of the forest. . . .

Yet it was not therefore to be disowned, but rather prized for whatever it could offer. From Irving to Whitman, American writers explored their domestic heritage.

Irving pictured the Dutch of New Amsterdam in his rollicking *Knickerbocker's History* and the best of his short tales. The Puritan background became foreground in the fine art of Hawthorne's *The Scarlet Letter* and of short pieces like "The Maypole of Merry Mount" and "Young Goodman Brown." The Revolutionary period inspired a life of Washington by Irving and *The Spy* by Cooper. The Indians appear in the novels of Cooper and of William Gilmore Simms, in Longfellow's *Hiawatha,* in the historical writing of Parkman. Whitman gives numerous glimpses of the American past. These are only examples. Through the writers named, and others, one could adumbrate the first two centuries of the American experience.

While re-creating much of the older America, the writers of the romantic period correspondingly slighted contemporary themes, though there were important exceptions such as Lowell's *Biglow Papers* and Melville's *Moby-Dick.* They were even more aloof from the present when dealing with the European scene. Thus, Irving romantically closed his eyes to the England of the Industrial Revolution, with its factories, mines, and social problems, preferring Westminster Abbey, Stratford-on-Avon, and picturesque byways. Even Emerson, shifting his focus from America, found all of his "Representative Men" in the European past.

In one important romantic respect, however, Emerson's "land of the forest" was peerless: the opportunities it afforded for kinship and correspondence with nature. "Never need an American," said Irving, "look beyond his own country for the sublime and beautiful of natural scenery." To Irving nature was just scenery, but to the more typical romantics it was a spiritual resource valid when religion had faded, a living being (not Newton's machine) speaking to the soul in a language that feeling and imagination could understand. Nature, the near thing, was indubitably American, but the new attitude toward it came with the romantic impulse from abroad. Among the early European enthusiasts for wild nature had been Rousseau. To him nature was both a standard of simplicity and virtue and a refuge from harsh actuality. The introspective, complicated Germans went further, and fell into an ambiguity from which romanticism never quite extricated itself. On the one hand, it seemed to them, nature is a personality, a friend—even, perhaps, a divine friend—that sympathizes with man's sorrow, works upon his feelings, speaks to him of beauty, freedom, peace, happiness, touches him with intimations of high truth. On the other hand, when nature comes alive in this manner, it is really man—the poetically endowed man—who gives the life he seems to receive. Does man, as Wordsworth suggests, half create and half perceive?

However this mystery may be resolved, the essential fact, for romanticism, remains the kinship of man and nature. We strike it at once, in the opening lines of the first great poem in the American movement, Bryant's "Thanatopsis":

> To him who in the love of Nature holds
> Communion with her visible forms, she speaks
> A various language.

It was Emerson who formulated most carefully, in his book on *Nature*, the relation of the inner and outer worlds. "The lover of nature," he says, "is he whose inward and outward senses are still truly adjusted to each other." In the fields and woods he finds himself, with delight, "not alone and unacknowledged. They nod to me, and I to them." "It is certain that the power to produce this delight does not reside in nature, but in man, or in a harmony of both," though actually, as Emerson goes on, the human soul seems to be swallowing up nature, assimilating the Not Me to the Me. The harmony of the two, in his theory, depends on the relation of correspondence. "Every appearance in nature corresponds to some state of the mind." He gives familiar examples: an enraged man is a lion, a firm one is a rock, light and darkness are knowledge and ignorance. But "Every natural fact is a symbol of some spiritual fact." In *Nature* Emerson thought of all these symbols as fixed and permanent; later, as changing and transitory—so many brief illuminations. But the important thing is that correspondence meant for him what Providence had meant to his Puritan ancestors; that nature, to the sensitive human spirit, was a revelation taking the place of the Bible. Emerson might have made much of the one Puritan, Jonathan Edwards, who had glimpsed this possibility. Had he had access to Edwards' *Images or Shadows of Divine Things* (unpublished until 1947), he would surely have read with a shock of recognition:

> Why is it not rational to suppose that the corporeal and visible world should be designedly made and constituted in analogy to the more spiritual, noble, and real world? It is certainly agreeable to what is apparently the method of God's working.

To feel kinship with nature in her gentler aspects was not difficult. One could be at home where nature invited the domesticities of hedgerow, orchard, pasture, woodlot—a more or less humanized nature. But what of wild nature? This was America's original distinction. Stretching westward from the ocean, even beyond the Father of Waters, this "land of the forest" powerfully affected the imagination of many romantic writers. Even Irving, with his face toward the Old World, remembers America's "trackless forests, where vegetation puts forth all its magnificence." "The mighty forest" dominates Bryant's "Thanatopsis," "A Forest Hymn," and other poems. Cooper gave a full picture of it: the ancient woods with soaring trees, the black mystery at night, the lakes and mountains, here and there human figures swallowed up in the landscape. Hawthorne restored the old Puritan forest, as in a famous scene of *The Scarlet Letter*, or in the sinister adventures of Young Goodman Brown "in the heart of the dark wilderness." Emerson thought of calling his first collected essays *Forest Essays*, and worshipped the pine gods in "Wood Notes."

But it was Thoreau who best communicated the tonic freedom of the forest, its wildness and beauty in large and small. In *The Maine Woods* he described a nature "savage and awful, though beautiful." *Walden* bore as a subtitle *Life in the Woods;* the life was that of wild creatures and plants as well as his own among them. To get to the heart of reality, it seemed to Thoreau, he must enter deeply into the wild. True, the inner spiritual reality was for him as for Emerson final. Yet, by the doctrine of correspondence, the inner was closely bound up with the outer reality. When the mood of wildness was on, he could "eat the brown earth," or desire to seize and devour a woodchuck raw. He loved rainstorms, and enjoyed wading in cold, bracing swamps—"a sort of baptism." As he might have put it, the Wild made him wild. But such adventures in feeling were matched by an intellectual conviction: that all civilization refers back to primitive nature and from time to time must return to its source of vitality, or decay and die. This was symbolized for him in the old fable of Romulus and Remus. The children of the Roman Empire, not being suckled by wolves, had to yield place to the northern barbarians who were. The continent of America, he goes on to say, is the she-wolf of our time. Here the moribund civilization of Europe can be reinvigorated and found a new Rome. It is not surprising that Thoreau rejoiced when he read Whitman's "very brave and American" *Leaves of Grass:* "Though rude, and sometimes ineffectual, it is a great primitive poem,—an alarum or trumpet-note ringing through the American camp."

With Whitman we come to one more object of romantic enthusiasm: the common man. He is the natural, earthy man. Everything, says Whitman, "comes out of the dirt—everything: everything comes out of the people, the everyday people, the people as you find them and leave them: not university people, not F.F.V. people." The People, yes the People—this has been the cry of the modern world ever since the eighteenth century. Then, as Emerson noted, such poets as Goldsmith *(The Deserted Village),* Burns ("The Cotter's Saturday Night"), and Cowper (*The Task*) had begun to celebrate plain folk and wholesome rustic living. But it was Wordsworth who most memorably celebrated not only the natural world but the common man who lived in it, beginning with the "underprivileged" people of the *Lyrical Ballads* and rising to a climax in the shepherd poem "Michael."

In America, where the equalitarian spirit of the frontier was added to the democratic ideology inherited from the eighteenth century, writers like Bryant, Cooper, and Hawthorne were sympathetic toward the Jacksonian revolution, and Emerson (as Whitman recognized) formed a view of life basically democratic despite his patrician origin and training. No one placed a higher valuation than Emerson on the latent powers of every man: "Each man shall feel the world is his, and man shall treat with man as a sovereign state with a sovereign state." In the main he presented his thought abstractly, as the titles of his essays indicate, leaving to others a more concrete, flesh-and-blood representation. Thus, it was Whittier who gave the dignity of verse to farmers, lumbermen, and shoemakers, and who in *Snow-Bound* dwelt with loving memory upon what Emerson had called "the meaning of household life." It was Whittier also who most passionately espoused the cause of the common man made slave, though Emerson, Thoreau, Longfellow, and Lowell also took part, each in his own way.

But the cause of the common man belonged especially to Whitman. In him the currents of romantic individualism and humanitarian altruism ran strong and ran together, blending self-pride and universal sympathy. Son of a carpenter, brought up in the country and in the "village" of Brooklyn, Whitman lived his life outside the circles of gentility and learning. Common people were, for him, the "divine average," the promise of a future America leading the modern world. United in a "universal democratic comradeship," in "adhesiveness or love, that fuses, ties and aggregates, making the races comrades, and fraternizing all," they must equally possess self-pride, "a rich, luxuriant, varied personalism," "the pride and centripetal isolation of a human being in himself." With Emerson, he conceived that greatness was for each individual, waiting only to be claimed. How far he was inclined to carry romantic egoism is indicated by a notebook entry: "If I walk with Jah in Heaven and he assume to be intrinsically greater than I it offends me, and I shall certainly withdraw from Heaven."

Here was a poet of the people, by the people, and for the people. Ironically, the people themselves preferred Longfellow.

Literary Art

"Trust your genius." The romantics trusted it in art, as in life. For them the essence of literary art, like the essence of living, was self-expression. This meant a pivotal change in the concept of literature. The new concept can be made clearer by glancing back at the old. Through the ages, from Plato and Aristotle down to Dr. Johnson, the classical mind had viewed literature as an imitation of life, a representation of the actions of men.

The romantics rejected this literary theory. The theory, and still more the practice, had been distorted and diminished during the long reign of neo- and pseudo-classicism by the development of conventions and rules. The time seemed ripe for a fresh start. For the old concept of literature as an *imitation* the romantics substituted the concept of literature as an *expression.* It might be the expression of a state of society, or of a national spirit, but characteristically it was assumed to be an expression of self, of the writer's own personality and experience in the world as he knew it or chose to make it. Literature became largely confessional—personal, autobiographic, lyrical. The traditional epic disappeared. The familiar essay became far more personal, as in Lamb. For the first time in the history of literature, the lyric became the typical kind of poetry. The romantic revival was indeed a period of great lyrical poetry, expressing keen and subtle sense impressions and an immense range of emotions—joy, ecstasy, love, yearning, regret—with a spontaneity and intensity reminiscent of the Renaissance. Small wonder that Emerson, while aware of the Puritan in himself, exclaimed approvingly, "This writing is blood-warm." What life might be is shown not by the practical and prudential crowd, whose existence is almost a death-in-life, but by the poet, who lives creatively and freely, building his inner world of beauty and high meaning, and externalizing it in words.

This closeness to personal experience is characteristic of the poetry of Bryant, Poe, Emerson, Longfellow, and many other American writers, but most notably of Walt Whitman. Glancing backward from old age, he himself described *Leaves of Grass* as "an attempt, from first to last, to put a *Person,* a human being (myself, in the latter half of the Nineteenth Century, in America), freely, fully and truly on record." The book was a memorable contribution to that art of the self which is typical of the Romantic Movement. The German romantics were personal on principle: Novalis had declared, "The novel is a life in the form of a book." Whitman went one step further:

> Camerado, this is no book,
> Who touches this touches a man.

The idea that a work of literary art grows out of experience and expresses a life lived brings us to the doctrine of organic form. This favorite romantic doctrine was not new but renovated. It appears in Greek thought as early as Plato, who said that a work of art should be like a living creature. After the middle of the eighteenth century it was affirmed by Edward Young, in whose view a work of original genius "may be said to be of a vegetable nature; it grows, it is not made." Here was an idea highly appropriate to romanticism. As the universe is not a machine but a living entity, so a work of art is not a mechanical construction but an organic structure. Like A. W. Schlegel in Germany, Coleridge wrote: "The organic form is innate; it shapes, as it develops itself from within, and its fullness of development is one and the same with the perfection of its outward form. Such as the life is, such is the form." Mechanical form, on the other hand, is consciously imposed from the outside: "The form is mechanic when on any given material we impress a predetermined form, . . . as when to a mass of wet clay we give whatever shape we wish it to retain when hardened."

Pursuing this biological analogy, romanticism conceives of any excellent work of art as a structure growing in an environment, developing from a living germ. Each part has its proper function, and all the parts work together as a unit. Among the parts that may enter into the complex unity and harmony of a particular work of art are diction, rhythm, image, symbol, ideas, attitude, tone, setting, character, incident, etc. Thus a successful poem, says Coleridge, offers "such delight from the *whole,* as is compatible with a distinct gratification from each component part." The parts "mutually support and explain each other." Successful poetry, in his view, cannot be written by deliberate effort; the organic principle applies to the poet as well as the poem—he is born and not made, though he can cultivate his gift.

Emerson conceives that the eternal power expresses itself in the poet's intuition, and the poet's intuition expresses itself in the words and music of the poem. Spirit gives the divine hint to the poet, and the poet passes it on to all men, in a form that is excellent in proportion as it is determined by the hint itself, not arbitrarily devised by the poet. "For it is not meters, but a meter-making argument that makes a poem—a thought so passionate and alive that like the spirit of a plant or an animal it has an architecture of its own, and adorns nature with a new thing." Like all beauty, it has "fitness," a perfect adaptation of means to end. Form is not "outside embellishment" as the eighteenth century seemed to think, but already dictated by content. "A verse is not a vehicle to carry a sentence as a jewel is carried in a case: the verse must be alive, and inseparable from its contents, as the soul of man inspires and directs the body." The superior poem cannot be analyzed; you cannot separate word and thought. But in the inferior poem they fall apart, and you can distinguish between the vague thought and the awkward or conventional expression. Strictly, in the ideal poem, "There is always a right word, and every other than that is wrong."

Evidently the organic principle could be used to explain any aspect of creation: the man of genius, the intuition that flashed upon his inward eye, the shaping spirit of his imagination, the expression of his vision in an aesthetic order governing even the word. Not only order but disorder, according to A. W. Schlegel. Classical art, he said, reflects "a world submitted to a beautiful order," but romantic art responds to "the secret attraction to a chaos which lies concealed in the very bosom of the ordered universe and is perpetually striving after new and marvellous births."

Yet the wish to escape restraints may explain the presence in romantic art of so much that is experimental, uneven, disproportionate, pretentious, inconsistent, fragmentary, or simply careless. We might attribute romantic disorder to the stress placed upon the values of living rather than the values of art, which made the search for beauty a quest of the poetic life rather than the patient and loving production of works of art. When they did concentrate upon an artifact, the romantics were inclined to value content more than form, despite the theory that the two are inseparable. The wonder is that they nevertheless produced so many shapes of beauty that are contemplated with pleasure today, notably, in our own literature, *Moby-Dick*, which confronts the chaos of life with a powerful aesthetic control, and *The Scarlet Letter*, in which the problem of evil is treated with the tight economy and perfect harmony of mature art.

Tight economy and perfect harmony were deliberately chosen as aesthetic goals in the conscious art of Poe. In this he was closer to the classicists than the romantics. Here was one theorist who, in contrast to Emerson and Whitman, had scant use for the organic view of art, that form grows naturally out of idea. In theory and practice alike, he believed that art should be rational. Yet he was not wholly a classicist. He himself reported, in romantic terms, "My life has been *whim*—impulse—passion—a longing for solitude—a scorn of all things present in an earnest desire for the future." If that was his life, his life and his art were anything but identical. To him the natural man was the rational man: "Man's chief idiosyncracy being reason, it follows that his savage condition—his condition of action *without* reason—is his *un*natural state." Writing a poem or story is a kind of action, requiring in high degree the powers of causality, i.e., a perception of the causes needed to produce a desired effect. Imagination is "never otherwise than analytic." Originality is not "a mere matter of impulse or inspiration" but rather a matter of purposeful construction: "To originate is carefully, patiently, and understandingly to combine." In Poe's view, art is almost a mathematical logic. In many of his tales he used mathematics or discussed its nature, and he was absorbed in problems and puzzles of all sorts, from cryptography to plagiarism, some of which he presented in a new art form, the detective story.

Though Poe was exceptional in displaying his thought concerning external form, we may infer that most romantic writers reflected upon technical problems far more than their published works show. For example, even if some of them had little to say about symbolism, they were generally agreed that it is an invaluable artistic method for expressing a complex and difficult kind of meaning.

Through the symbol, as they conceived, the indefinite could be suggested through a concrete representation, and the abstract thus made tangible. Instead of using familiar symbols such as the crown of monarchy and the cross of Christianity, a writer could devise fresh ones of his own choosing. Some might be made obvious to any reader; others might be left vague, stimulating the imagination to find the most fitting abstract equivalent. Symbolism is not the same as allegory. In an allegory there is a fixed and coherent system of signs, whereas a symbol can stand alone, serve a temporary purpose—a flash of illumination. It may appear once or repeatedly, and the same image may at various times represent quite different things. A good example of a symbol is the ethereal dream-maiden, in Rousseau, Novalis, Shelley, Poe, Melville.

A symbol dominates the masterpiece of Hawthorne, from title—*The Scarlet Letter*—to the very end. And as he showed in one short tale after another, his mind characteristically brooded upon or played with symbols, often with a tantalizing ambiguity. Reality, he felt, was something far too complex and uncertain to be set down in terms of reason and denotative statement. This is why Melville declared that in reading Hawthorne, "It is not the brain that can test such a man; it is only the heart."

Melville himself well exemplified his own belief that "You must have plenty of sea-room to tell the Truth in." There is plenty of sea-room in *Moby-Dick*, a work that owed something to Hawthorne's deep probings, Carlyle's flashes of insight, Shakespeare's grappling with the essence of things, but mainly grew out of his own experience and speculation. Symbols irradiate the whole fable, help to bind it together. Some are used only to enlighten details of the action. The same image may symbolize quite different things in different contexts. The sea can suggest mystery, the source of life, its end, an alien element, or a friendly one. And readers interpreting with both brain and heart are by no means always agreed as to what is symbolized. Like Hawthorne, unlike most romantics, Melville was obsessed with the problem of evil in the universe. To the ship's captain with the Old Testament name of Ahab, the monstrous White Whale symbolizes "that intangible malignity which has been from the beginning; to whose dominion even the modern Christians ascribe one-half of the worlds . . . all the subtle demonisms of life and thought; all evil. . . ." Hating the inscrutable,—"be the white whale agent, or be the white whale principal,"—Ahab defies the universe. "I'd strike the sun if it insulted me. . . . Who's over me?"

Turning now to the question of style, in poetry and prose, we shall find relatively little on the subject in the writings of the two great innovators: Wordsworth in England and Whitman in America. Like romantic writers in general, they were more absorbed in "life values" than in "art values."

In the well-known preface to *Lyrical Ballads* poetic style is treated as mainly a matter of language and diction. As the term *ballad* implies, Wordsworth did not propose to abandon the long-established conventions of meter and rhyme. But he attacked with vigor the neoclassic convention of a "poetic diction" apart from the diction of prose and of actual speech. He pointed out that writers in early times, feeling powerfully, used a daring and figurative language, but that later writers (apparently in the eighteenth century) maintained this language without a correspondence of feeling. They used it mechanically, unconcerned about the contrast between the heightened language and their low-keyed feelings. Wordsworth gives an example from Gray:

> In vain to me the smiling mornings shine,
> And reddening Phoebus lifts his golden fire;
> The birds in vain their amorous descant join
> Or cheerful fields resume their green attire.

Such language he finds artificial and gaudy, without the urgency of genuine feeling. To restore vitality, to bring expression close to real life once more, Wordsworth proposes the experiment of employing "a selection of the real language of men in a state of vivid sensation." It is not to be the language of gentlemen or of the craft of poets, but a "plainer and more emphatic language" suited to "humble and rustic life." Incidentally, he will have scant use for the personifications (Hope, Peace, and the like, with capital letters) by means of which poets had sought an easy elevation. What he wishes to do, in short, is to write like "a man speaking to men."

By the time of Emerson and Longfellow this "blood-warm" manner of writing was common. Poetry was much closer to the currents of real life, its language more concrete, its verse freed from the stylized heroic couplet and diversified to serve many ends. Yet romanticism itself tended to form a poetic diction and style of its own, a vague and too readily flowing eloquence. We can see this style beginning in Wordsworth and Coleridge, established as a pattern by Byron and Shelley, followed in varying degrees by Bryant, Poe, Whittier, Longfellow, and Lowell.

To the bold, independent mind of Walt Whitman, this stylized romantic verse seemed anything but an inevitable expression of modern democratic America. Rhyme, for example—"venerable and heavenly forms of chiming versification"—he regarded as fitting for the feudal order, not for the democratic. Whitman felt, as he declared in his 1855 preface to *Leaves of Grass,* that the genius of the United States lay "most in the common people." The true meaning of simplicity, the "art of art," was perhaps suggested to him by the natural man, the "indescribable freshness and unconsciousness about an illiterate person." But simplicity was suggested even more, in his preface, by lower orders of life: "To speak in literature with the perfect rectitude and insouciance of the movements of animals and the unimpeachableness of the sentiment of trees in the woods and grass by the roadside is the flawless triumph of art." For such simple communication he will need "new free forms" of expression: "The cleanest expression is that which finds no sphere worthy of itself and makes one." In his own poems Whitman proceeded (with hints from various sources including Biblical verse) to create a new form, which came to be called free verse, avowedly if not always actually dispensing with poetic diction, personification, rhyme, stanza, and meter. He retained only the verse line, which, on the organic principle, should tally the substance expressed. The result might be called a free-and-easy, unadorned poetry, fitly illustrated by the daguerreotype used in the first edition—Walt in workingman's clothes, nonchalant and self-sufficient, "me imperturbe." Here was a poetry intended, more truly than in Wordsworth's theory, to be the natural speech of a man speaking to men, an exalted conversational medium. Similar experiments were later to be made by Robert Frost, Carl Sandburg, and T. S. Eliot.

The new view of life also brought a new way of writing prose. The prose desired by the Neoclassic Age had had the formal clarity and order of a Greek temple. Proper words were in proper places, and unity, proportion, and balance produced a design that appealed to the mind. In the Romantic Movement, on the other hand, prose had a more flowing contour, like that of romantic music, appealing to the senses and emotions. There is another significant contrast. Neoclassic prose was thought of as a *human* medium, essentially the same for all who wrote. (In practice, this implied writing with the easy dignity of eighteenth-century gentlemen.) But when emphasis was shifted from the samenesses of men to their differences, it was also shifted from social communication to self-expression. Style became, consciously or unconsciously, a more *personal* medium: the mirror of a man's peculiar individuality, the echo of his uniqueness, the flavor of his special sensibility.

A good American example of what style meant

under romantic auspices is offered by Thoreau. Like Poe and Hawthorne, he wrote a prose blending the old virtues of rational design and the new virtues of emotional imagery and color expressed in terms of a distinct personality. Few writers give us so strong a sense of their own essence. Prominent in the author of *Walden* are his disciplined integrity, his play of mind, his love of beauty, features of his writing that also enter into his conscious reflections on style.

Often he speaks of style in organic terms, as when he says, "It is not in man to determine what his style shall be." But this means no resting on his oars. Only by sustained effort can a man learn to write well, for "Every sentence is the result of a long probation." Mind, body and senses, he says, must work together: "Expression is the act of a whole man." A writer needs intercourse with men and things, and especially labor with his hands, which is "the best method of removing palaver and sentimentality out of one's style." Calluses on the hands will have much to do with the writing of "tougher truth" and the firmness of his sentences. As Thoreau says finely, "A sentence should read as if its author, had he held a plow instead of a pen, could have drawn a furrow deep and straight to the end." He liked to speak with the homely reality of the farmer, being suspicious of genteel literary men and college professors, so often "weak and flimsy." With Puritan integrity and Yankee common sense he proclaims that "the one great rule of composition—and if I were a professor of rhetoric I should insist on this—is to *speak the truth.*"

Nothing is harder than perfect truth, honesty, candor, but if a writer can achieve it, "the rest will follow." Of the rest he says little, but for him, judging from his writing, it included color and warmth, surprise of the mind, a loving precision in shaping the thought, and a "concentrated and nutty" quality—his own was somewhat acrid, like an acorn. Surprise came from the use of paradox, conceits, puns, sundry kinds of wit and humor. Color and warmth came from keen senses and health, faithful observation, sensitive imagery, sympathetic response to the theme. With his reserved temperament, Thoreau generally avoided speaking directly of beauty, but it is prominent in one illuminating passage, which sums up his own notion of prose style:

> In writing, conversation should be folded many times thick. It is the height of art that, on the first perusal, plain common sense should appear; on the second, severe truth; and on a third, beauty; and, having these warrants for its depth and reality, we may then enjoy the beauty for evermore.

Both in life and in art, the extremes of romanticism were avoided in England and the United States. In these countries there was little of the extravagance, the chaos, the license of German romanticism. Though the English had largely started the movement, they were restrained, as in other periods, by their aversion to extremes and their respect for tradition. In America, the strongest restraint came from the old Puritan culture, its discipline still effective even when the sanctioning beliefs had evaporated, as one can readily see in Emerson and Hawthorne. At the same time, common sense—Anglo-Saxon and Yankee—had a sobering effect on men like Emerson, Thoreau, and Lowell. Furthermore, the romantic revolt was moderate because American rationalism and neoclassicism had been moderate, and because the way to a romantic outlook had been gradually prepared by the fluid frontier of a land of opportunity, and by the democratic revolution that preceded the French Revolution by about twenty years. The heady ideas of European romanticism in full tide came to a nation of free men accustomed to belief in human dignity and habituated to self-control no less than to self-assertion.

WASHINGTON IRVING [1783-1859]

WASHINGTON IRVING was born into a wealthy New York City merchant family and educated privately for the law. However, since he preferred to write essays for two newspapers edited by his brother Peter, he soon decided to follow a literary career. In 1802-1803 he wrote a series of delightfully impudent satires on city society for his brother's papers under the pseudonym of "Jonathan Oldstyle, Gent.," and his career was launched. The Irving family sent young Washington to Europe for two years, 1804-1806, and although he was admitted to the bar on his return and taken into the family firm, he showed little interest in either law or business. Instead he joined with his brother William, James Kirke Paulding, and several other young men who called themselves "The Nine Worthies of Cockloft Hall" and lived the pleasant, carefree lives of men-about-town. In 1807 and 1808 they published the series of satiric essays called *Salmagundi*, which enjoyed a good deal of popularity and showed also a great deal of promise. In 1809 Irving's fiancée, Mathilda Hoffman, died, a tragic loss from which he never recovered. He threw himself into the completion of his *History of New York*, published that same year, which gave him an immediate reputation as a burlesque humorist and advanced his career another step.

In 1815, in the prime of life, Irving went to England on business, unaware that he was to make his literary reputation abroad and to remain there for seventeen years. The family firm failed not long after, and Irving for the first time in his life was thrown upon his own resources. His friendship with Sir Walter Scott, publisher John Murray, and the London literati stood him in good stead as he resumed his writing (which he had allowed to lapse for ten years), for it resulted in Murray's publication of *The Sketch Book* (1819-20), which catapulted him into instant fame on both sides of the Atlantic. After *Bracebridge Hall* (1822), a continuation of the *Sketch Book* style, he lived in Germany for a year, published *Tales of a Traveller* (1824), spent some months in London and Paris, and went to Madrid to serve in the American Legation. The appeal of Spain to his imagination produced *The Life of Columbus* (1828) and *The Companions of Columbus* (1831); two historical studies, *The Conquest of Granada* (1829) and *The Conquest of Spain* (1835); and his last volume of tales, *The Alhambra* (1832). After *The Alhambra* Irving turned to history, biography, and travel; his work lost much of the imaginativeness and vitality that marked his Hudson Valley, German, English, and Spanish stories and sketches, though it may have gained in prestige.

Irving returned to the United States in 1832, to find its social, political, and economic complexion drastically changed. This was Jacksonian America, in the full flush of its ebullient and energetic nationalism and there seemed to be little place for an aristocratic Knickerbocker gentleman. However, Irving adjusted to the new society in time; he became interested in the frontier, took an extended tour into the prairies, and wrote three books about the new West—*Astoria* (1834), an account of John Jacob Astor's fur empire; *A Tour on the Prairies* (1835), an expansion of his travel journal; and *The Adventures of Captain Bonneville* (1837), a Rocky Mountain scout and explorer.

Irving's literary fame constantly elicited offers of various political sinecures and finally, in 1842, he accepted the post of Minister to Spain for three years, after which he returned to New York to settle at Sunnyside, his gracious country home at Tarrytown, near "Sleepy Hollow," where he completed his *Life of Mahomet* (1850) and his five-volume *Life of Washington* (1859). Although he wrote no fiction after 1832, Irving's contributions to the development of the American short tale were of great importance; he lent it style, skill, atmosphere, characterization, and respectability, and both Poe and Hawthorne, who perfected the form after him, owed much to Irving's beginnings. Nor should it be forgotten that Irving was America's first internationally-known man of letters, an intermediary between the literary Old and New Worlds who impressed his example on both his own and foreign culture.

Further reading: Edward Wagenknecht, *Washington Irving,* 1962. Van Wyck Brooks, *The World of Washington Irving,* 1934.

FROM *A History of New-York*

Irving in 1808 planned to collaborate with his brother Peter on a parody of a popular guidebook, Dr. Samuel Latham Mitchill's *Picture of New-York* (1807), which would be "written in a serio-comic vein, and treating local errors, follies, and abuses with good-humored satire." Peter, however, left for Europe, and Irving became so fascinated by his study of old Dutch New York that he decided to write a comic history of that period alone. Aside from its burlesque elements, the book contains a good deal of reasonably authentic historical material; it is also tremendously allusive, reflecting on almost every page Irving's readings in Cervantes, Homer, Fielding, Sterne, Swift, Malory, and dozens of other sources. He introduced his book to the public by an intricate literary hoax, first placing advertisements in the papers asking for information concerning "a small, elderly gentleman, dressed in an old black coat and cocked hat," named Diedrich Knickerbocker. Knickerbocker's appearance was reported in several places, until finally his landlord announced that he was selling a manuscript, found in the old man's hotel room, to defray his overdue bills. The *History* appeared shortly afterwards.

Irving's aim, he later wrote, "was to embody the traditions of the city in an amusing form; to illustrate its local humors, customs, and peculiarities; to clothe home scenes and places and familiar names with those imaginative and whimsical associations so seldom met with in our new country, but which live like charms and spells about the cities of the old world, binding the heart of the native inhabitant to his home." He created Diedrich Knickerbocker as a gentle burlesque of the old Dutch New Yorkers and their descendants, but the name was soon adopted by the public at large to designate any New Yorker, and Father Knickerbocker, this "very worthy good sort of old gentleman, though a little queer in his ways," became the city's patron saint. Text: *A History of New-York from the Beginning of the World to the End of the Dutch Dynasty* (New York, 1849). The title page of the original edition in 1809 added: "Containing among many Surprising and Curious Matters, the Unutterable Ponderings of Walter the Doubter, the Disastrous Projects of William the Testy, and the Chivalric Achievements of Peter the Headstrong, the three Dutch Governors of New Amsterdam; being the only Authentic History of the Times that ever hath been, or ever will be Published. By Diedrich Knickerbocker."

The *History* was divided into seven books: Book I treats of the history of the world to the Dutch settlement of New Amsterdam; Book II records the founding of the province; Book III covers the period of Wouter Van Twiller; Book IV records the reign of William the Testy, a rather pointed burlesque of Thomas Jefferson and his administration; Books V, VI, and VII are devoted to the governorship of Peter Stuyvesant.

Book III

In Which Is Recorded the Golden Reign of Wouter Van Twiller

CHAPTER I

OF THE RENOWNED WOUTER VAN TWILLER, HIS UNPARALLELED VIRTUES—AS LIKEWISE HIS UNUTTERABLE WISDOM IN THE LAW CASE OF WANDLE SCOONHOVEN AND BARENT BLEECKER—AND THE GREAT ADMIRATION OF THE PUBLIC THEREAT.

Grievous and very much to be commiserated is the task of the feeling historian, who writes the history of his native land. If it fall to his lot to be the recorder of calamity or crime, the mournful page is watered with his tears—nor can he recall the most prosperous and blissful era, without a melancholy sigh at the reflection, that it has passed away for ever! I know not whether it be owing to an immoderate love for the simplicity of former times, or to that certain tenderness of heart incident to all sentimental historians; but I candidly confess that I cannot look back on the happier days of our city, which I now describe, without great dejection of spirits. With faltering hand do I withdraw the curtain of oblivion, that veils the modest merit of our venerable ancestors, and as their figures rise to my mental vision, humble myself before their mighty shades.

Such are my feelings when I revisit the family mansion of the Knickerbockers, and spend a lonely hour in the chamber where hang the portraits of my forefathers, shrouded in dust, like the forms they represent. With pious reverence do I gaze on the countenances of those renowned burghers, who have preceded me in the steady march of existence—whose sober and temperate blood now meanders through my veins, flowing slower and slower in its feeble conduits, until its current shall soon be stopped for ever!

These, I say to myself, are but frail memorials of the mighty men who flourished in the days of the patriarchs; but who, alas, have long since mouldered in that tomb, towards which my steps are insensibly and irresistibly hastening! As I pace the darkened chamber and lose myself in melancholy musings, the shadowy images around me almost seem to steal once more into existence—their countenances to assume the animation of life—their eyes to pursue me in every movement! Carried away by the delusions of fancy, I almost imagine myself surrounded by the shades of the departed, and holding sweet converse with the worthies of antiquity! Ah, hapless Diedrich! born in a degenerate age, abandoned to the buffetings of fortune—a stranger and a weary pilgrim in thy native land—blest with no weeping wife, nor family of helpless children; but doomed to wander neglected through those crowded streets, and elbowed by foreign upstarts from those fair abodes where once thine ancestors held sovereign empire!

Let me not, however, lose the historian in the man, nor suffer the doting recollections of age to overcome me, while dwelling with fond garrulity on the virtuous days of the patriarchs—on those sweet days of simplicity and ease, which never more will dawn on the lovely island of Manna-hata.

These melancholy reflections have been forced from me by the growing wealth and importance of New-Amsterdam, which, I plainly perceive, are to involve it in all kinds of perils and disasters. Already, as I observed at the close of my last book, they had awakened the attention of the mother country. The usual mark of protection shown by mother countries to wealthy colonies was forthwith manifested; a governor being sent out to rule over the province and squeeze out of it as much revenue as possible. The arrival of a governor of course put an end to the protectorate of Oloffe the Dreamer. He appears, however, to have dreamt to some purpose during his sway, as we find him afterwards living as a patroon on a great landed estate on the banks of the Hudson; having virtually forfeited all right to his ancient appellation of Kortlandt or Lackland.

It was in the year of our Lord 1629 that Mynheer Wouter Van Twiller was appointed governor of the province of Nieuw-Nederlandts, under the commission and control of their High Mightinesses the Lords States General of the United Netherlands, and the privileged West India Company.

This renowned old gentleman arrived at New-Amsterdam in the merry month of June, the sweetest month in all the year; when dan Apollo seems to dance up the transparent firmament—when the robin, the thrush, and a thousand other wanton songsters make the woods to resound with amorous ditties, and the luxurious little boblincon revels among the clover blossoms of the meadows—all which happy coincidence persuaded the old dames of New-Amsterdam, who were skilled in the art of foretelling events, that this was to be a happy and prosperous administration.

The renowned Wouter (or Walter) Van Twiller, was descended from a long line of Dutch burgomasters, who had successively dozed away their lives, and grown fat upon the bench of magistracy in Rotterdam; and who had comported themselves with such singular wisdom and propriety, that they were never either heard or talked of—which, next to being universally applauded, should be the object of ambition of all magistrates and rulers. There are two opposite ways by which some men make a figure in the world; one by talking faster than they think; and the other by holding their tongues and not thinking at all. By the first many a smatterer acquires the reputation of a man of quick parts; by the other many a dunderpate, like the owl, the stupidest of birds, comes to be considered the very type of wisdom. This, by the way, is a casual remark, which I would not for the universe have it thought I apply to Governor Van Twiller. It is true he was a man shut up within himself, like an oyster, and rarely spoke except in monosyllables; but then it was allowed he seldom said a foolish thing. So invincible was his gravity that he was never known to laugh or even to smile through the whole course of a long and prosperous life. Nay if a joke were uttered in his presence, that set light-minded hearers in a roar, it was observed to throw him into a state of perplexity. Sometimes he would deign to inquire into the matter, and when, after much explanation, the joke was made as plain as a pike-staff; he would continue to smoke his pipe in silence, and at length, knocking out the ashes would exclaim, "Well! I see nothing in all that to laugh about."

With all his reflective habits, he never made up his mind on a subject. His adherents accounted for this by the astonishing magnitude of his ideas. He conceived every subject on so grand a scale that he had not room in his head to turn it over and examine both sides of it. Certain it is that if any matter were propounded to him on which ordinary mortals would rashly determine at first glance, he would put on a vague, mysterious look; shake his capacious head; smoke some time in profound silence, and at length observe that "he had his doubts about the matter," which gained him the reputation of a man slow of belief, and not easily imposed upon. What is more, it gained him a lasting name: for to this habit of the mind has been attributed his surname of Twiller; which is said to be a corruption of the original Twijfler, or, in plain English, *Doubter*.

The person of this illustrious old gentleman was formed and proportioned, as though it had been moulded by the hands of some cunning Dutch statuary, as a model of majesty and lordly grandeur. He was exactly five feet six inches in height, and six feet five inches in circumference. His head was a perfect sphere, and of such stupendous dimensions, that dame Nature with all her sex's ingenuity, would have been puzzled to construct a neck capable of supporting it; wherefore she wisely declined the attempt, and settled it firmly on the top of his backbone, just between the shoulders. His body was oblong and particularly capacious at bottom; which was wisely ordered by Providence, seeing that he was a man of sedentary habits, and very averse to the idle labor of walking. His legs were short, but sturdy in proportion to the weight they had to sustain; so that when erect he had not a little the appearance of a beer barrel on skids. His face, that infallible index of the mind, presented a vast expanse, unfurrowed by any of those lines and angles which disfigure the human countenance with what is termed expression. Two small gray eyes twinkled feebly in the midst, like two stars of lesser magnitude in a hazy firmament; and his full-fed cheeks, which seemed to have taken toll of every thing that went into his mouth, were curiously mottled and streaked with dusky red, like a spitzenberg apple.

His habits were as regular as his person. He daily took his four stated meals, appropriating exactly an hour to each; he smoked and doubted eight hours, and he slept the remaining twelve of the four-and-twenty. Such was the renowned Wouter Van Twiller—a true philosopher, for his mind was either elevated above, or tranquilly settled below, the cares and perplexities of this world. He had lived in it for years, without feeling the least curiosity to know whether the sun revolved round it, or it round the sun; and he had watched, for at least half a century, the smoke curling from his pipe to the ceiling, without once troubling his head with any of those numerous theories, by which a philosopher would have perplexed his brain, in accounting for its rising above the surrounding atmosphere.

In his council he presided with great state and solemnity. He sat in a huge chair of solid oak, hewn in the celebrated forest of the Hague, fabricated by an experienced timmerman of Amsterdam, and curiously carved about the arms and feet, into exact imitations of gigantic eagle's claws. Instead of a sceptre he swayed a long Turkish pipe, wrought with jasmin and amber, which had been presented to a stadtholder of Holland, at the conclusion of a treaty with one of the petty Barbary powers. In this stately chair would he sit, and this magnificent pipe would he smoke, shaking his right knee with a constant motion, and fixing his eye for hours together upon a little print of Amsterdam, which hung in a black frame against the opposite wall of the council chamber. Nay, it has even been said, that when any deliberation of extraordinary length and intricacy was on the carpet, the renowned Wouter would shut his eyes for full two hours at a time, that he might not be disturbed by external objects—and at such times the internal commotion of his mind was evinced by certain regular guttural sounds, which his admirers declared were merely the noise of conflict, made by his contending doubts and opinions.

It is with infinite difficulty I have been enabled to collect these biographical anecdotes of the great man under consideration. The facts respecting him were so scattered and vague, and divers of them so questionable in point of authenticity, that I have had to give up the search after many, and decline the admission of still more, which would have tended to heighten the coloring of his portrait.

I have been the more anxious to delineate fully the person and habits of Wouter Van Twiller, from the consideration that he was not only the first, but also the best governor that ever presided over this ancient and respectable province; and so tranquil and benevolent was his reign, that I do not find throughout the whole of it, a single instance of any offender being brought to punishment—a most indubitable sign of a merciful governor, and a case unparalleled, excepting in the reign of the illustrious King Log, from whom, it is hinted, the renowned Van Twiller was a lineal descendant.

The very outset of the career of this excellent magistrate was distinguished by an example of legal acumen, that gave flattering presage of a wise and equitable administration. The morning after he had been installed in office, and at the moment that he was making his breakfast from a prodigious earthen dish, filled with milk and Indian pudding, he was interrupted by the appearance of Wandle Schoonhoven, a very important old burgher of New-Amsterdam, who complained bitterly of one Barent Bleecker, inasmuch as he refused to come to a settlement of accounts, seeing that there was a heavy balance in favor of the said Wandle. Governor Van Twiller, as I have already observed, was a man of few words; he was likewise a mortal enemy to multiplying writings—or being disturbed at his breakfast. Having listened attentively to the statement of Wandle Schoonhoven, giving an occasional grunt, as he shoveled a spoonful of Indian pudding into his mouth—either as a sign that he relished the dish, or comprehended the story—he called unto him his constable, and pulling out of his breeches pocket a huge jack-knife, dispatched it after the defendant as a summons, accompanied by his tobacco-box as a warrant.

This summary process was as effectual in those simple days as was the seal ring of the great Haroun Alraschid among the true believers. The two parties being confronted before him, each produced a book of accounts, written in a language and character that would have puzzled any but a High Dutch commentator, or a learned decipherer of Egyptian obelisks. The sage Wouter took them one after the other, and having poised them in his hands, and attentively counted over the number of leaves, fell straightway into a very great doubt, and smoked for half an hour without saying a word; at length, laying his finger beside his nose, and shutting his eyes for a moment, with the air of a man who has just caught a subtle idea by the tail, he slowly took his pipe from his mouth, puffed forth a column of tobacco smoke, and with marvellous gravity and solemnity pronounced—that having carefully counted over the leaves and weighed the books, it was found, that one was just as thick and as heavy as the other—therefore it was the final opinion of the court that the accounts were equally balanced—therefore Wandle should give Barent a receipt, and Barent should give Wandle a receipt—and the constable should pay the costs.

This decision being straightway made known, diffused general joy throughout New-Amsterdam, for the people immediately perceived, that they had a very wise and equitable magistrate to rule over them. But its happiest effect was, that not another lawsuit took place throughout the whole of his administration—and the office of constable fell into such decay, that there was not one of those losel scouts known in the province for many years. I am the more particular in dwelling on this transaction, not only because I deem it one of the most sage and righteous judgments on record, and well worthy the attention of modern magistrates; but because it was a miraculous event in the history of the renowned Wouter—being the only time he was ever known to come to a decision in the whole course of his life.

1809

FROM *The Sketch Book*

In 1820 the English critic Sydney Smith sneered "And who, the wide world over, reads an American book?" The answer was already forthcoming, for within a few weeks Irving's *Sketch Book*, published by the great London publisher John Murray with Sir Walter Scott's blessing, took the reading public of Great Britain and America by storm. The complete edition contained thirty-two selections, only three—"Rip Van Winkle," "The Spectre Bridegroom," and "The Legend of Sleepy Hollow"—classifiable as tales, all of them reworkings of German legendary stories, provided with American backgrounds. As its name suggested, the book was chiefly composed of sketches of English life ("A Sunday in London"), comments on English customs ("Rural Funerals"), observations on famous places ("Westminster Abbey"), literary musings, anecdotes, and even two essays on the American Indian. The three tales were Irving's first experiments in the literary form soon to become the short story, to whose development he made his own unique and decisive contributions. He wrote later:

"I consider a story merely as a frame on which to stretch my materials. It is the play of thought, and sentiment and language; the weaving in of characters, lightly yet expressively delineated; the familiar and faithful exhibition of scenes in common life; and the half concealed vein of humour that is often playing through the whole—these are among what I aim at, and upon which I felicitate myself in proportion as I think I succeed. . . .

"I have preferred adopting a mode of sketches & short tales rather than long works, because I chose to take a line of writing peculiar to myself; rather than fall into the manner or school of any other writer: and there is a constant activity of thought and nicety of execution required in writings of this kind, more than the world appears to imagine. . . . In these shorter writings every page must have its merit. The author must be continually piquant—woe to him if he makes an awkward sentence or writes a stupid page; the critics are sure to pounce upon it. Yet if he succeed: the very variety and piquancy of his writings; nay their very brevity; makes them frequently recurred to—and when the mere interest of the story is exhausted, he begins to get credit for his touches of pathos or humour; his points of wit or turns of language. . . ."

The text follows that of the Knickerbocker Edition of the *Works*, Philadelphia, 1870-71. The sketches and stories were published originally in seven installments in New York between May 1819 and September 1820, then collected and published in London.

The Author's Account of Himself[1]

"I am of this mind with Homer, that as the snaile that crept out of her shel was turned eftsoons into a toad, and thereby was forced to make a stoole to sit on; so the traveller that straggleth from his owne country is in a short time transformed into so monstrous a shape, that he is faine to alter his mansion with his manners, and to live where he can, not where he would."—Lyly's *Euphues*.

I was always fond of visiting new scenes, and observing strange characters and manners. Even when a mere child I began my travels, and made many tours of discovery into foreign parts and unknown regions of my native city, to the frequent alarm of my parents, and the emolument of the town-crier. As I grew into boyhood, I extended the range of my observations. My holiday afternoons were spent in rambles about the surrounding country. I made myself familiar with all its places famous in history or fable. I knew every spot where a murder or robbery had been committed, or a ghost

[1]Presumably "Geoffrey Crayon, Gent.," the character invented by Irving to serve as author of *The Sketch Book*.

seen. I visited the neighboring villages, and added greatly to my stock of knowledge by noting their habits and customs, and conversing with their sages and great men. I even journeyed one long summer's day to the summit of the most distant hill, whence I stretched my eye over many a mile of *terra incognita,* and was astonished to find how vast a globe I inhabited.

This rambling propensity strengthened with my years. Books of voyages and travels became my passion, and in devouring their contents, I neglected the regular exercises of the school. How wistfully would I wander about the pier-heads in fine weather, and watch the parting ships, bound to distant climes; with what longing eyes would I gaze after their lessening sails, and waft myself in imagination to the ends of the earth!

Further reading and thinking, though they brought this vague inclination into more reasonable bounds, only served to make it more decided. I visited various parts of my own country; and had I been merely a lover of fine scenery, I should have felt little desire to seek elsewhere its gratification, for on no country have the charms of nature been more prodigally lavished. Her mighty lakes, like oceans of liquid silver; her mountains, with their bright aerial tints; her valleys, teeming with wild fertility; her tremendous cataracts, thundering in their solitudes; her boundless plains, waving with spontaneous verdure; her broad deep rivers, rolling in solemn silence to the ocean; her trackless forests, where vegetation puts forth all its magnificence; her skies, kindling with the magic of summer clouds and glorious sunshine;—no, never need an American look beyond his own country for the sublime and beautiful of natural scenery.

But Europe held forth the charms of storied and poetical association. There were to be seen the masterpieces of art, the refinements of highly cultivated society, the quaint peculiarities of ancient and local custom. My native country was full of youthful promise: Europe was rich in the accumulated treasures of age. Her very ruins told the history of times gone by, and every mouldering stone was a chronicle. I longed to wander over the scenes of renowned achievement,—to tread, as it were, in the footsteps of antiquity,—to loiter about the ruined castle,—to meditate on the falling tower,—to escape, in short, from the commonplace realities of the present, and lose myself among the shadowy grandeurs of the past.

I had, beside all this, an earnest desire to see the great men of the earth. We have, it is true, our great men in America: not a city but has an ample share of them. I have mingled among them in my time, and been almost withered by the shade into which they cast me; for there is nothing so baleful to a small man as the shade of a great one, particularly the great man of a city. But I was anxious to see the great men of Europe; for I had read in the works of various philosophers, that all animals degenerated in America, and man among the number.[2] A great man of Europe, thought I, must therefore be as superior to a great man of America, as a peak of the Alps to a highland of the Hudson; and in this idea I was confirmed, by observing the comparative importance and swelling magnitude of many English travellers among us, who, I was assured, were very little people in their own country. I will visit this land of wonders, thought I, and see the gigantic race from which I am degenerated.

It has been either my good or evil lot to have my roving passion gratified. I have wandered through different countries, and witnessed many of the shifting scenes of life. I cannot say that I have studied them with the eye of a philosopher, but rather with the sauntering gaze with which humble lovers of the picturesque stroll from the window of one printshop to another, caught sometimes by the delineations of beauty, sometimes by the distortions of caricature, and sometimes by the loveliness of landscape. As it is the fashion for modern tourists to travel pencil in hand, and bring home their portfolios filled with sketches, I am disposed to get up a few for the entertainment of my friends. When, however, I look over the hints and memorandums I have taken down for the purpose, my heart almost fails me at finding how my idle humor has led me aside from the great objects studied by every regular traveller who would make a book. I fear I shall give equal disappointment with an unlucky landscape-painter, who had travelled on the continent, but, following the bent of his vagrant inclination, had sketched in nooks, and corners, and by-places. His sketchbook was accordingly crowded with cottages, and landscapes, and obscure ruins; but he had neglected to paint St. Peter's, or the Coliseum; the cascade of Terni, or the bay of Naples; and had not a single glacier or volcano in his whole collection.

Rip Van Winkle

A POSTHUMOUS WRITING OF
DIEDRICH KNICKERBOCKER.

By Woden, God of Saxons,
From whence comes Wensday, that is Wodensday,
Truth is a thing that ever I will keep
Unto thylke day in which I creep into
My sepulchre—

—Cartwright.

[The following Tale was found among the papers of the late Diedrich Knickerbocker, an old gentleman of New

[2]A theory expounded especially by the French philosopher the Comte de Buffon.

York, who was very curious in the Dutch history of the province, and the manners of the descendants from its primitive settlers. His historical researches, however, did not lie so much among books as among men; for the former are lamentably scanty on his favorite topics; whereas he found the old burghers, and still more their wives, rich in that legendary lore so invaluable to true history. Whenever, therefore, he happened upon a genuine Dutch family, snugly shut up in its low-roofed farmhouse, under a spreading sycamore, he looked upon it as a little clasped volume of black-letter, and studied it with the zeal of a book-worm.

The result of all these researches was a history of the province during the reign of the Dutch governors, which he published some years since. There have been various opinions as to the literary character of his work, and, to tell the truth, it is not a whit better than it should be. Its chief merit is its scrupulous accuracy, which indeed was a little questioned on its first appearance, but has since been completely established; and it is now admitted into all historical collections as a book of unquestionable authority.

The old gentleman died shortly after the publication of his work; and now that he is dead and gone, it cannot do much harm to his memory to say that his time might have been much better employed in weightier labors. He, however, was apt to ride his hobby his own way; and though it did now and then kick up the dust a little in the eyes of his neighbors, and grieve the spirit of some friends, for whom he felt the truest deference and affection, yet his errors and follies are remembered "more in sorrow than in anger," and it begins to be suspected that he never intended to offend. But however his memory may be appreciated by critics, it is still held dear by many folk whose good opinion is well worth having; particularly by certain biscuit-makers, who have gone so far as to imprint his likeness on their New-Year cakes; and have thus given him a chance for immortality, almost equal to being stamped on a Waterloo Medal, or a Queen Anne's Farthing.[1]]

Whoever has made a voyage up the Hudson must remember the Kaatskill mountains. They are a dismembered branch of the great Appalachian family, and are seen away to the west of the river, swelling up to a noble height, and lording it over the surrounding country. Every change of season, every change of weather, indeed, every hour of the day, produces some change in the magical hues and shapes of these mountains, and they are regarded by all the good wives, far and near, as perfect barometers. When the weather is fair and settled, they are clothed in blue and purple, and print their bold outlines on the clear evening sky; but sometimes, when the rest of the landscape is cloudless, they will gather a hood of gray vapors about their summits, which, in the last rays of the setting sun, will glow and light up like a crown of glory.

[1]All British veterans of the Battle of Waterloo received a medal bearing the likeness of the Prince Regent; the copper farthing bore Queen Anne's.

At the foot of these fairy mountains, the voyager may have descried the light smoke curling up from a village, whose shingle roofs gleam among the trees, just where the blue tints of the upland melt away into the fresh green of the nearer landscape. It is a little village, of great antiquity, having been founded by some of the Dutch colonists in the early times of the province, just about the beginning of the government of the good Peter Stuyvesant (may he rest in peace!), and there were some of the houses of the original settlers standing within a few years, built of small yellow bricks brought from Holland, having latticed windows and gable fronts, surmounted with weathercocks.

In that same village, and in one of these very houses (which, to tell the precise truth, was sadly time-worn and weather-beaten), there lived, many years since, while the country was yet a province of Great Britain, a simple, good-natured fellow, of the name of Rip Van Winkle. He was a descendant of the Van Winkles who figured so gallantly in the chivalrous days of Peter Stuyvesant, and accompanied him to the siege of Fort Christina. He inherited, however, but little of the martial character of his ancestors. I have observed that he was a simple, good-natured man; he was, moreover, a kind neighbor, and an obedient, hen-pecked husband. Indeed, to the latter circumstance might be owing that meekness of spirit which gained him such universal popularity; for those men are most apt to be obsequious and conciliating abroad, who are under the discipline of shrews at home. Their tempers, doubtless, are rendered pliant and malleable in the fiery furnace of domestic tribulation; and a curtain-lecture is worth all the sermons in the world for teaching the virtues of patience and long-suffering. A termagant wife may, therefore, in some respects, be considered a tolerable blessing; and if so, Rip Van Winkle was thrice blessed.

Certain it is, that he was a great favorite among all the good wives of the village, who, as usual with the amiable sex, took his part in all family squabbles; and never failed, whenever they talked those matters over in their evening gossipings, to lay all the blame on Dame Van Winkle. The children of the village, too, would shout with joy whenever he approached. He assisted at their sports, made their playthings, taught them to fly kites and shoot marbles, and told them long stories of ghosts, witches, and Indians. Whenever he went dodging about the village, he was surrounded by a troop of them, hanging on his skirts, clambering on his back, and playing a thousand tricks on him with impunity; and not a dog would bark at him throughout the neighborhood.

The great error in Rip's composition was an insuperable aversion to all kinds of profitable labor. It could not be from the want of assiduity or perseverance; for he would sit on a wet rock, with a rod as long and heavy as a Tartar's lance, and fish all day without a murmur, even though he should not be encouraged by a single nibble. He would carry a fowling-piece on his shoulder for hours together, trudging through woods and swamps, and up hill and down dale, to shoot a few squirrels or wild pigeons. He would never refuse to assist a neighbor even in the roughest toil, and was a foremost man at all country frolics for husking Indian corn, or building stone fences; the women of the village, too, used to employ him to run their errands, and to do such little odd jobs as their less obliging husbands would not do for them. In a word, Rip was ready to attend to anybody's business but his own; but as to doing family duty, and keeping his farm in order, he found it impossible.

In fact, he declared it was of no use to work on his farm; it was the most pestilent little piece of ground in the whole country; everything about it went wrong, and would go wrong, in spite of him. His fences were continually falling to pieces; his cow would either go astray, or get among the cabbages; weeds were sure to grow quicker in his fields than anywhere else; the rain always made a point of setting in just as he had some out-door work to do; so that though his patrimonial estate had dwindled away under his management, acre by acre, until there was little more left than a mere patch of Indian corn and potatoes, yet it was the worst conditioned farm in the neighborhood.

His children, too, were as ragged and wild as if they belonged to nobody. His son Rip, an urchin begotten in his own likeness, promised to inherit the habits, with the old clothes, of his father. He was generally seen trooping like a colt at his mother's heels, equipped in a pair of his father's cast-off galligaskins,[2] which he had much ado to hold up with one hand, as a fine lady does her train in bad weather.

Rip Van Winkle, however, was one of those happy mortals, of foolish, well-oiled dispositions, who take the world easy, eat white bread or brown, whichever can be got with least thought or trouble, and would rather starve on a penny than work for a pound. If left to himself, he would have whistled life away in perfect contentment; but his wife kept continually dinning in his ears about his idleness, his carelessness, and the ruin he was bringing on his family. Morning, noon, and night, her tongue was incessantly going, and everything he said or did was sure to produce a torrent of household eloquence. Rip had but one way of replying to all lectures of the kind, and that, by frequent use, had grown into a habit. He shrugged his shoulders, shook his head, cast up his eyes, but said nothing. This, however, always provoked a fresh volley from his wife; so that he was fain to draw off his forces, and take to the outside of the house—the only side which, in truth, belongs to a hen-pecked husband.

Rip's sole domestic adherent was his dog Wolf, who was as much hen-pecked as his master; for Dame Van Winkle regarded them as companions in idleness, and even looked upon Wolf with an evil eye, as the cause of his master's going so often astray. True it is, in all points of spirit befitting an honorable dog, he was as courageous an animal as ever scoured the woods; but what courage can withstand the ever-enduring and all-besetting terrors of a woman's tongue? The moment Wolf entered the house his crest fell, his tail drooped to the ground, or curled between his legs, he sneaked about with a gallows air, casting many a sidelong glance at Dame Van Winkle, and at the least flourish of a broomstick or ladle he would fly to the door with yelping precipitation.

Times grew worse and worse with Rip Van Winkle as years of matrimony rolled on; a tart temper never mellows with age, and a sharp tongue is the only edged tool that grows keener with constant use. For a long while he used to console himself, when driven from home, by frequenting a kind of perpetual club of the sages, philosophers, and other idle personages of the village, which held its sessions on a bench before a small inn, designated by a rubicund portrait of His Majesty George the Third. Here they used to sit in the shade through a long, lazy summer's day, talking listlessly over village gossip, or telling endless sleepy stories about nothing. But it would have been worth any statesman's money to have heard the profound discussions that sometimes took place, when by chance an old newspaper fell into their hands from some passing traveller. How solemnly they would listen to the contents, as drawled out by Derrick Van Bummel, the schoolmaster, a dapper learned little man, who was not to be daunted by the most gigantic word in the dictionary; and how sagely they would deliberate upon public events some months after they had taken place.

The opinions of this junto were completely controlled by Nicholas Vedder, patriarch of the village, and landlord of the inn, at the door of which he took his seat from morning till night, just moving sufficiently to avoid the sun and keep in the shade of a large tree; so that the neighbors could tell the hour by his movements as accurately as by a sundial. It is true he was rarely heard to speak, but smoked his pipe incessantly. His adherents, however (for every great man has his adherents), perfectly understood him, and knew how to gather his opin-

[2]Trousers.

ions. When anything that was read or related displeased him, he was observed to smoke his pipe vehemently, and to send forth short, frequent, and angry puffs; but when pleased, he would inhale the smoke slowly and tranquilly, and emit it in light and placid clouds; and sometimes, taking the pipe from his mouth, and letting the fragrant vapor curl about his nose, would gravely nod his head in token of perfect approbation.

From even this stronghold the unlucky Rip was at length routed by his termagant wife, who would suddenly break in upon the tranquillity of the assemblage and call the members all to naught; nor was that august personage, Nicholas Vedder himself, sacred from the daring tongue of this terrible virago, who charged him outright with encouraging her husband in habits of idleness.

Poor Rip was at last reduced almost to despair; and his only alternative, to escape from the labor of the farm and clamor of his wife, was to take gun in hand and stroll away into the woods. Here he would sometimes seat himself at the foot of a tree, and share the contents of his wallet with Wolf, with whom he sympathized as a fellow-sufferer in persecution. "Poor Wolf," he would say, "thy mistress leads thee a dog's life of it, but never mind, my lad, whilst I live thou shalt never want a friend to stand by thee!" Wolf would wag his tail, look wistfully in his master's face, and if dogs can feel pity, I verily believe he reciprocated the sentiment with all his heart.

In a long ramble of the kind on a fine autumnal day, Rip had unconsciously scrambled to one of the highest parts of the Kaatskill mountains. He was after his favorite sport of squirrel-shooting, and the still solitudes had echoed and re-echoed with the reports of his gun. Panting and fatigued, he threw himself, late in the afternoon, on a green knoll, covered with mountain herbage, that crowned the brow of a precipice. From an opening between the trees he could overlook all the lower country for many a mile of rich woodland. He saw at a distance the lordly Hudson, far, far below him, moving on its silent but majestic course, with the reflection of a purple cloud, or the sail of a lagging bark, here and there sleeping on its glassy bosom, and at last losing itself in the blue highlands.

On the other side he looked down into a deep mountain glen, wild, lonely, and shagged, the bottom filled with fragments from the impending cliffs, and scarcely lighted by the reflected rays of the setting sun. For some time Rip lay musing on this scene; evening was gradually advancing; the mountains began to throw their long blue shadows over the valleys; he saw that it would be dark long before he could reach the village, and he heaved a heavy sigh when he thought of encountering the terrors of Dame Van Winkle.

As he was about to descend, he heard a voice from a distance, hallooing, "Rip Van Winkle, Rip Van Winkle!" He looked round, but could see nothing but a crow winging its solitary flight across the mountain. He thought his fancy must have deceived him, and turned again to descend, when he heard the same cry ring through the still evening air: "Rip Van Winkle! Rip Van Winkle!"—at the same time Wolf bristled up his back, and giving a low growl, skulked to his master's side, looking fearfully down into the glen. Rip now felt a vague apprehension stealing over him; he looked anxiously in the same direction, and perceived a strange figure slowly toiling up the rocks, and bending under the weight of something he carried on his back. He was surprised to see any human being in this lonely and unfrequented place; but supposing it to be some one of the neighborhood in need of his assistance, he hastened down to yield it.

On nearer approach he was still more surprised at the singularity of the stranger's appearance. He was a short, square-built old fellow, with thick bushy hair, and a grizzled beard. His dress was of the antique Dutch fashion,—a cloth jerkin strapped around the waist—several pair of breeches, the outer one of ample volume, decorated with rows of buttons down the sides, and bunches at the knees. He bore on his shoulders a stout keg, that seemed full of liquor, and made signs for Rip to approach and assist him with the load. Though rather shy and distrustful of this new acquaintance, Rip complied with his usual alacrity; and mutually relieving one another, they clambered up a narrow gully, apparently the dry bed of a mountain torrent. As they ascended, Rip every now and then heard long, rolling peals, like distant thunder, that seemed to issue out of a deep ravine, or rather cleft, between lofty rocks, toward which their rugged path conducted. He paused for an instant, but supposing it to be the muttering of one of those transient thunder-showers which often take place in mountain heights, he proceeded. Passing through the ravine, they came to a hollow, like a small amphitheatre, surrounded by perpendicular precipices, over the brinks of which impending trees shot their branches, so that you only caught glimpses of the azure sky and the bright evening cloud. During the whole time Rip and his companion had labored on in silence; for though the former marvelled greatly what could be the object of carrying a keg of liquor up this wild mountain, yet there was something strange and incomprehensible about the unknown, that inspired awe and checked familiarity.

On entering the amphitheatre, new objects of

wonder presented themselves. On a level spot in the centre was a company of odd-looking personages playing at ninepins. They were dressed in a quaint, outlandish fashion; some wore short doublets, others jerkins, with long knives in their belts, and most of them had enormous breeches, of similar style with that of the guide's. Their visages, too, were peculiar: one had a large beard, broad face, and small piggish eyes; the face of another seemed to consist entirely of nose, and was surmounted by a white sugar-loaf hat, set off with a little red cock's tail. They all had beards, of various shapes and colors. There was one who seemed to be the commander. He was a stout old gentleman, with a weather-beaten countenance; he wore a laced doublet, broad belt and hanger, high crowned hat and feather, red stockings, and high-heeled shoes, with roses[3] in them. The whole group reminded Rip of the figures in an old Flemish painting, in the parlor of Dominie Van Shaick, the village parson, and which had been brought over from Holland at the time of the settlement.

What seemed particularly odd to Rip was, that, though these folks were evidently amusing themselves, yet they maintained the gravest faces, the most mysterious silence, and were, withal, the most melancholy party of pleasure he had ever witnessed. Nothing interrupted the stillness of the scene but the noise of the balls, which, whenever they rolled, echoed along the mountains like rumbling peals of thunder.

As Rip and his companion approached them, they suddenly desisted from their play, and stared at him with such fixed, statue-like gaze, and such strange, uncouth, lack-lustre countenances, that his heart turned within him, and his knees smote together. His companion now emptied the contents of the keg into large flagons, and made signs to him to wait upon the company. He obeyed with fear and trembling; they quaffed the liquor in profound silence, and then returned to their game.

By degrees Rip's awe and apprehension subsided. He even ventured, when no eye was fixed upon him, to taste the beverage, which he found had much of the flavor of excellent Hollands.[4] He was naturally a thirsty soul, and was soon tempted to repeat the draught. One taste provoked another; and he reiterated his visits to the flagon so often that at length his senses were overpowered, his eyes swam in his head, his head gradually declined, and he fell into a deep sleep.

On waking, he found himself on the green knoll whence he had first seen the old man of the glen. He rubbed his eyes—it was a bright sunny morning. The birds were hopping and twittering among the bushes, and the eagle was wheeling aloft, and breasting the pure mountain breeze. "Surely," thought Rip, "I have not slept here all night." He recalled the occurrences before he fell asleep. The strange man with a keg of liquor—the mountain ravine—the wild retreat among the rocks—the woe-begone party at ninepins—the flagon—"Oh! that flagon! that wicked flagon!" thought Rip, "what excuse shall I make to Dame Van Winkle?"

He looked round for his gun, but in place of the clean, well-oiled fowling-piece, he found an old firelock lying by him, the barrel encrusted with rust, the lock falling off, and the stock worm-eaten. He now suspected that the grave roisters of the mountains had put a trick upon him, and, having dosed him with liquor, had robbed him of his gun. Wolf, too, had disappeared, but he might have strayed away after a squirrel or partridge. He whistled after him, and shouted his name, but all in vain; the echoes repeated his whistle and shout, but no dog was to be seen.

He determined to revisit the scene of the last evening's gambol, and if he met with any of the party, to demand his dog and gun. As he rose to walk, he found himself stiff in the joints, and wanting in his usual activity. "These mountain beds do not agree with me," thought Rip, "and if this frolic should lay me up with a fit of the rheumatism, I shall have a blessed time with Dame Van Winkle." With some difficulty he got down into the glen: he found the gully up which he and his companion had ascended the preceding evening; but to his astonishment a mountain stream was now foaming down it, leaping from rock to rock, and filling the glen with babbling murmurs. He, however, made shift to scramble up its sides, working his toilsome way through thickets of birch, sassafras, and witch-hazel, and sometimes tripped up or entangled by the wild grape-vines that twisted their coils or tendrils from tree to tree, and spread a kind of network in his path.

At length he reached to where the ravine had opened through the cliffs to the amphitheatre; but no traces of such opening remained. The rocks presented a high, impenetrable wall, over which the torrent came tumbling in a sheet of feathery foam, and fell into a broad deep basin, black from the shadows of the surrounding forest. Here, then, poor Rip was brought to a stand. He again called and whistled after his dog; he was only answered by the cawing of a flock of idle crows, sporting high in air about a dry tree that overhung a sunny precipice; and who, secure in their elevation, seemed to look down and scoff at the poor man's perplexities. What was to be done? the morning was passing away, and Rip felt famished for want of his breakfast. He

[3]Rosettes.
[4]Gin.

grieved to give up his dog and gun; he dreaded to meet his wife; but it would not do to starve among the mountains. He shook his head, shouldered the rusty firelock, and, with a heart full of trouble and anxiety, turned his footsteps homeward.

As he approached the village he met a number of people, but none whom he knew, which somewhat surprised him, for he had thought himself acquainted with every one in the country round. Their dress, too, was of a different fashion from that to which he was accustomed. They all stared at him with equal marks of surprise, and whenever they cast their eyes upon him, invariably stroked their chins. The constant recurrence of this gesture induced Rip, involuntarily, to do the same, when, to his astonishment, he found his beard had grown a foot long!

He had now entered the skirts of the village. A troop of strange children ran at his heels, hooting after him, and pointing at his gray beard. The dogs, too, not one of which he recognized for an old acquaintance, barked at him as he passed. The very village was altered; it was larger and more populous. There were rows of houses which he had never seen before, and those which had been his familiar haunts had disappeared. Strange names were over the doors—strange faces at the windows—everything was strange. His mind now misgave him; he began to doubt whether both he and the world around him were not bewitched. Surely this was his native village, which he had left but the day before. There stood the Kaatskill mountains—there ran the silver Hudson at a distance—there was every hill and dale precisely as it had always been. Rip was sorely perplexed. "That flagon last night," thought he, "has addled my poor head sadly!"

It was with some difficulty that he found the way to his own house, which he approached with silent awe, expecting every moment to hear the shrill voice of Dame Van Winkle. He found the house gone to decay—the roof fallen in, the windows shattered, and the doors off the hinges. A half-starved dog that looked like Wolf was skulking about it. Rip called him by name, but the cur snarled, showed his teeth, and passed on. This was an unkind cut indeed. "My very dog," sighed poor Rip, "has forgotten me!"

He entered the house, which, to tell the truth, Dame Van Winkle had always kept in neat order. It was empty, forlorn, and apparently abandoned. This desolateness overcame all his connubial fears—he called loudly for his wife and children—the lonely chambers rang for a moment with his voice, and then all again was silence.

He now hurried forth, and hastened to his old resort, the village inn, but it too was gone. A large rickety wooden building stood in its place, with great gaping windows, some of them broken and mended with old hats and petticoats, and over the door was painted, "The Union Hotel, by Jonathan Doolittle." Instead of the great tree that used to shelter the quiet little Dutch inn of yore, there now was reared a tall naked pole, with something on the top that looked like a red night-cap,[5] and from it was fluttering a flag, on which was a singular assemblage of stars and stripes;—all this was strange and incomprehensible. He recognized on the sign, however, the ruby face of King George, under which he had smoked so many a peaceful pipe; but even this was singularly metamorphosed. The red coat was changed for one of blue and buff, a sword was held in the hand instead of a sceptre, the head was decorated with a cocked hat, and underneath was painted in large characters, GENERAL WASHINGTON.

There was, as usual, a crowd of folk about the door, but none that Rip recollected. The very character of the people seemed changed. There was a busy, bustling, disputatious tone about it, instead of the accustomed phlegm and drowsy tranquillity. He looked in vain for the sage Nicholas Vedder, with his broad face, double chin, and fair long pipe, uttering clouds of tobacco-smoke instead of idle speeches; or Van Bummel, the schoolmaster, doling forth the contents of an ancient newspaper. In place of these, a lean, bilious-looking fellow, with his pockets full of handbills, was haranguing vehemently about rights of citizens—elections—members of congress — liberty — Bunker's Hill — heroes of seventy-six—and other words, which were a perfect Babylonish jargon to the bewildered Van Winkle.

The appearance of Rip, with his long, grizzled beard, his rusty fowling-piece, his uncouth dress, and an army of women and children at his heels, soon attracted the attention of the tavern-politicians. They crowded round him, eying him from head to foot with great curiosity. The orator bustled up to him, and, drawing him partly aside, inquired "On which side he voted?" Rip stared in vacant stupidity. Another short but busy little fellow pulled him by the arm, and, rising on tiptoe, inquired in his ear, "Whether he was Federal or Democrat?" Rip was equally at a loss to comprehend the question; when a knowing, self-important old gentleman, in a sharp cocked hat, made his way through the crowd, putting them to the right and left with his elbows as he passed, and planting himself before Van Winkle, with one arm akimbo, the other resting on his cane, his keen eyes and sharp hat penetrating, as it were, into his very soul, demanded in an austere tone, "What brought him to the election with a gun on his

[5]A "liberty cap," symbol of the recent Revolution.

shoulder, and a mob at his heels; and whether he meant to breed a riot in the village?"—"Alas! gentlemen," cried Rip, somewhat dismayed, "I am a poor quiet man, a native of the place, and a loyal subject of the King, God bless him!"

Here a general shout burst from the by-standers—"A tory! a tory! a spy! a refugee! hustle him! away with him!" It was with great difficulty that the self-important man in the cocked hat restored order; and, having assumed a tenfold austerity of brow, demanded again of the unknown culprit, what he came there for, and whom he was seeking? The poor man humbly assured him that he meant no harm, but merely came there in search of some of his neighbors, who used to keep about the tavern.

"Well—who are they?—name them."

Rip bethought himself a moment, and inquired, "Where's Nicholas Vedder?"

There was a silence for a little while, when an old man replied, in a thin piping voice, "Nicholas Vedder! why, he is dead and gone these eighteen years! There was a wooden tombstone in the churchyard that used to tell all about him, but that's rotten and gone too."

"Where's Brom Dutcher?"

"Oh, he went off to the army in the beginning of the war; some say he was killed at the storming of Stony Point—others say he was drowned in a squall at the foot of Antony's Nose.[6] I don't know—he never came back again."

"Where's Van Bummel, the schoolmaster?"

"He went off to the wars too, was a great militia general, and is now in congress."

Rip's heart died away at hearing of these sad changes in his home and friends, and finding himself thus alone in the world. Every answer puzzled him too, by treating of such enormous lapses of time, and of matters which he could not understand: war—congress—Stony Point—he had no courage to ask after any more friends, but cried out in despair, "Does nobody here know Rip Van Winkle?"

"Oh, Rip Van Winkle!" exclaimed two or three, "oh, to be sure! that's Rip Van Winkle yonder, leaning against the tree."

Rip looked, and he beheld a precise counterpart of himself, as he went up the mountain; apparently as lazy, and certainly as ragged. The poor fellow was now completely confounded. He doubted his own identity, and whether he was himself or another man. In the midst of his bewilderment, the man in the cocked hat demanded who he was, and what was his name.

"God knows," exclaimed he, at his wit's end; "I'm not myself—I'm somebody else—that's me yonder—no—that's somebody else got into my shoes—I was myself last night, but I fell asleep on the mountain, and they've changed my gun, and everything's changed, and I'm changed, and I can't tell what's my name, or who I am!"

The by-standers began now to look at each other, nod, wink significantly, and tap their fingers against their foreheads. There was a whisper, also, about securing the gun, and keeping the old fellow from doing mischief, at the very suggestion of which the self-important man in the cocked hat retired with some precipitation. At this critical moment a fresh, comely woman pressed through the throng to get a peep at the gray-bearded man. She had a chubby child in her arms, which, frightened at his looks, began to cry. "Hush, Rip," cried she, "hush, you little fool; the old man won't hurt you." The name of the child, the air of the mother, the tone of her voice, all awakened a train of recollections in his mind. "What is your name, my good woman?" asked he.

"Judith Gardenier."

"And your father's name?"

"Ah, poor man, Rip Van Winkle was his name, but it's twenty years since he went away from home with his gun, and never has been heard of since,—his dog came home without him; but whether he shot himself, or was carried away by the Indians, nobody can tell. I was then but a little girl."

Rip had but one question more to ask; but he put it with a faltering voice:

"Where's your mother?"

"Oh, she too had died but a short time since; she broke a bloodvessel in a fit of passion at a New England pedler."

There was a drop of comfort, at least, in this intelligence. The honest man could contain himself no longer. He caught his daughter and her child in his arms. "I am your father!" cried he—"Young Rip Van Winkle once—old Rip Van Winkle now!—Does nobody know poor Rip Van Winkle?"

All stood amazed, until an old woman, tottering out from among the crowd, put her hand to her brow, and peering under it in his face for a moment, exclaimed, "Sure enough! it is Rip Van Winkle—it is himself! Welcome home again, old neighbor. Why, where have you been these twenty long years?"

Rip's story was soon told, for the whole twenty years had been to him but as one night. The neighbors stared when they heard it; some were seen to wink at each other, and put their tongues in their cheeks: and the self-important man in the cocked hat, who, when the alarm was over, had returned to the field, screwed down the corners of his mouth, and shook his head—upon which there was a general shaking of the head throughout the assemblage.

[6] A headland and mountain near West Point.

It was determined, however, to take the opinion of old Peter Vanderdonk, who was seen slowly advancing up the road. He was a descendant of the historian of that name, who wrote one of the earliest accounts of the province. Peter was the most ancient inhabitant of the village, and well versed in all the wonderful events and traditions of the neighborhood. He recollected Rip at once, and corroborated his story in the most satisfactory manner. He assured the company that it was a fact, handed down from his ancestor the historian, that the Kaatskill mountains had always been haunted by strange beings. That it was affirmed that the great Hendrick Hudson, the first discoverer of the river and country, kept a kind of vigil there every twenty years, with his crew of the *Half-moon;* being permitted in this way to revisit the scenes of his enterprise, and keep a guardian eye upon the river and the great city called by his name.[7] That his father had once seen them in their old Dutch dresses playing at ninepins in a hollow of the mountain; and that he himself had heard, one summer afternoon, the sound of their balls, like distant peals of thunder.

To make a long story short, the company broke up and returned to the more important concerns of the election. Rip's daughter took him home to live with her; she had a snug, well-furnished house, and a stout, cheery farmer for a husband, whom Rip recollected for one of the urchins that used to climb upon his back. As to Rip's son and heir, who was the ditto of himself, seen leaning against the tree, he was employed to work on the farm; but evinced an hereditary disposition to attend to anything else but his business.

Rip now resumed his old walks and habits; he soon found many of his former cronies, though all rather the worse for the wear and tear of time; and preferred making friends among the rising generation, with whom he soon grew into great favor.

Having nothing to do at home, and being arrived at that happy age when a man can be idle with impunity, he took his place once more on the bench at the inn-door, and was reverenced as one of the patriarchs of the village, and a chronicle of the old times "before the war." It was some time before he could get into the regular track of gossip, or could be made to comprehend the strange events that had taken place during his torpor. How that there had been a revolutionary war,—that the country had thrown off the yoke of old England,—and that, instead of being a subject of his Majesty George the Third, he was now a free citizen of the United States. Rip, in fact, was no politician; the changes of states and empires made but little impression on him; but there was one species of despotism under which he had long groaned, and that was—petticoat government. Happily that was at an end; he had got his neck out of the yoke of matrimony, and could go in and out whenever he pleased, without dreading the tyranny of Dame Van Winkle. Whenever her name was mentioned, however, he shook his head, shrugged his shoulders, and cast up his eyes; which might pass either for an expression of resignation to his fate, or joy at his deliverance.

He used to tell his story to every stranger that arrived at Mr. Doolittle's hotel. He was observed, at first, to vary on some points every time he told it, which was, doubtless, owing to his having so recently awaked. It at last settled down precisely to the tale I have related, and not a man, woman, or child in the neighborhood but knew it by heart. Some always pretended to doubt the reality of it, and insisted that Rip had been out of his head, and that this was one point on which he always remained flighty. The old Dutch inhabitants, however, almost universally gave it full credit. Even to this day they never hear a thunderstorm of a summer afternoon about the Kaatskill, but they say Hendrick Hudson and his crew are at their game of ninepins; and it is a common wish of all hen-pecked husbands in the neighborhood, when life hangs heavy on their hands, that they might have a quieting draught out of Rip Van Winkle's flagon.

NOTE.

The foregoing Tale, one would suspect, had been suggested to Mr. Knickerbocker by a little German superstition about the Emperor Frederick *der Rothbart,* and the Kypphäuser mountain: the subjoined note, however, which he had appended to the tale, shows that it is an absolute fact, narrated with his usual fidelity.

"The story of Rip Van Winkle may seem incredible to many, but nevertheless I give it my full belief, for I know the vicinity of our old Dutch settlements to have been very subject to marvellous events and appearances. Indeed, I have heard many stranger stories than this, in the villages along the Hudson; all of which were too well authenticated to admit of a doubt. I have even talked with Rip Van Winkle myself, who, when last I saw him, was a very venerable old man, and so perfectly rational and consistent on every other point, that I think no conscientious person could refuse to take this into the bargain; nay, I have seen a certificate on the subject taken before a country justice and signed with a cross, in the justice's own handwriting. The story, therefore, is beyond the possibility of doubt.

"D. K."

POSTSCRIPT.

The following are travelling notes from a memorandum-book of Mr. Knickerbocker.

The Kaatsberg, or Catskill Mountains, have always been a region full of fable. The Indians considered them the abode of spirits, who influenced the

[7] Hudson, New York, was an important shipping center in Irving's time.

weather, spreading sunshine or clouds over the landscape, and sending good or bad hunting-seasons. They were ruled by an old squaw spirit, said to be their mother. She dwelt on the highest peak of the Catskills, and had charge of the doors of day and night to open and shut them at the proper hour. She hung up the new moons in the skies, and cut up the old ones into stars. In times of drought, if properly propitiated, she would spin light summer clouds out of cobwebs and morning dew, and send them off from the crest of the mountain, flake after flake, like flakes of carded cotton, to float in the air; until, dissolved by the heat of the sun, they would fall in gentle showers, causing the grass to spring, the fruits to ripen, and the corn to grow an inch an hour. If displeased, however, she would brew up clouds black as ink, sitting in the midst of them like a bottle-bellied spider in the midst of its web; and when these clouds broke, woe betide the valleys!

In old times, say the Indian traditions, there was a kind of Manitou or Spirit, who kept about the wildest recesses of the Catskill Mountains, and took a mischievous pleasure in wreaking all kinds of evils and vexations upon the red men. Sometimes he would assume the form of a bear, a panther, or a deer, lead the bewildered hunter a weary chase through tangled forests and among ragged rocks; and then spring off with a loud ho! ho! leaving him aghast on the brink of a beetling precipice or raging torrent.

The favorite abode of this Manitou is still shown. It is a great rock or cliff on the loneliest part of the mountains, and, from the flowering vines which clamber about it, and the wild flowers which abound in its neighborhood, is known by the name of the Garden Rock. Near the foot of it is a small lake, the haunt of the solitary bittern, with water-snakes basking in the sun on the leaves of the pond-lilies which lie on the surface. This place was held in great awe by the Indians, insomuch that the boldest hunter would not pursue his game within its precincts. Once upon a time, however, a hunter who had lost his way, penetrated to the Garden Rock, where he beheld a number of gourds placed in the crotches of trees. One of these he seized and made off with it, but in the hurry of his retreat he let it fall among the rocks, when a great stream gushed forth, which washed him away and swept him down precipices, where he was dashed to pieces, and the stream made its way to the Hudson, and continues to flow to the present day; being the identical stream known by the name of the Kaaterskill.

The Legend of Sleepy Hollow

FOUND AMONG THE PAPERS OF THE LATE DIEDRICH KNICKERBOCKER

A pleasing land of drowsy head it was,
Of dreams that wave before the half-shut eye,
And of gay castles in the clouds that pass,
For ever flushing round a summer sky.

Castle of Indolence.

In the bosom of one of those spacious coves which indent the eastern shore of the Hudson, at that broad expansion of the river denominated by the ancient Dutch navigators the Tappan Zee, and where they always prudently shortened sail, and implored the protection of St. Nicholas when they crossed, there lies a small market-town or rural port, which by some is called Greensburgh, but which is more generally and properly known by the name of Tarry Town. This name was given, we are told, in former days, by the good housewives of the adjacent country, from the inveterate propensity of their husbands to linger about the village tavern on market-days. Be that as it may, I do not vouch for the fact, but merely advert to it for the sake of being precise and authentic. Not far from this village, perhaps about two miles, there is a little valley, or rather lap of land, among high hills, which is one of the quietest places in the whole world. A small brook glides through it, with just murmur enough to lull one to repose; and the occasional whistle of a quail, or tapping of a woodpecker, is almost the only sound that ever breaks in upon the uniform tranquillity.

I recollect that, when a stripling, my first exploit in squirrel-shooting was in a grove of tall walnut-trees that shades one side of the valley. I had wandered into it at noon-time, when all nature is particularly quiet, and was startled by the roar of my own gun, as it broke the Sabbath stillness around, and was prolonged and reverberated by the angry echoes. If ever I should wish for a retreat, whither I might steal from the world and its distractions, and dream quietly away the remnant of a troubled life, I know of none more promising than this little valley.

From the listless repose of the place, and the peculiar character of its inhabitants, who are descendants from the original Dutch settlers, this sequestered glen has long been known by the name of SLEEPY HOLLOW, and its rustic lads are called the Sleepy Hollow Boys throughout all the neighboring country. A drowsy, dreamy influence seems to hang over the land, and to pervade the very atmosphere. Some say that the place was bewitched by a high German doctor,[1] during the early days of the settlement; others, that an old Indian chief, the prophet or wizard of his tribe, held his pow-wows there before the country was discovered by Master Hendrick Hudson. Certain it is, the place still continues under the sway of some bewitching power, that holds a spell over the minds of the good people, causing them to walk in a continual reverie. They are given to all kinds of marvellous beliefs; are subject to trances and visions; and frequently see strange sights, and hear music and voices in the air. The whole neighborhood abounds with local tales,

[1] "High" or southern German.

haunted spots, and twilight superstitions; stars shoot and meteors glare oftener across the valley than in any other part of the country, and the nightmare,[2] with her whole ninefold, seems to make it the favorite scene of her gambols.

The dominant spirit, however, that haunts this enchanted region, and seems to be commander-in-chief of all the powers of the air, is the apparition of a figure on horseback without a head. It is said by some to be the ghost of a Hessian trooper, whose head had been carried away by a cannon-ball, in some nameless battle during the Revolutionary War, and who is ever and anon seen by the country folk, hurrying along in the gloom of night, as if on the wings of the wind. His haunts are not confined to the valley, but extend at times to the adjacent roads, and especially to the vicinity of a church at no great distance. Indeed, certain of the most authentic historians of those parts, who have been careful in collecting and collating the floating facts concerning this spectre, allege that the body of the trooper, having been buried in the churchyard, the ghost rides forth to the scene of battle in nightly quest of his head; and that the rushing speed with which he sometimes passes along the Hollow, like a midnight blast, is owing to his being belated, and in a hurry to get back to the churchyard before daybreak.

Such is the general purport of this legendary superstition, which has furnished materials for many a wild story in that region of shadows; and the spectre is known, at all the country firesides, by the name of the Headless Horseman of Sleepy Hollow.

It is remarkable that the visionary propensity I have mentioned is not confined to the native inhabitants of the valley, but is unconsciously imbibed by every one who resides there for a time. However wide awake they may have been before they entered that sleepy region, they are sure, in a little time, to inhale the witching influence of the air, and begin to grow imaginative, to dream dreams, and see apparitions.

I mention this peaceful spot with all possible laud; for it is in such little retired Dutch valleys, found here and there embosomed in the great State of New York, that population, manners, and customs remain fixed; while the great torrent of migration and improvement, which is making such incessant changes in other parts of this restless country, sweeps by them unobserved. They are like those little nooks of still water which border a rapid stream; where we may see the straw and bubble riding quietly at anchor, or slowly revolving in their mimic harbor, undisturbed by the rush of the passing current. Though many years have elapsed since I trod the drowsy shades of Sleepy Hollow, yet I question whether I should not still find the same trees and the same families vegetating in its sheltered bosom.

In this by-place of nature, there abode, in a remote period of American history, that is to say, some thirty years since, a worthy wight of the name of Ichabod Crane; who sojourned, or, as he expressed it, "tarried," in Sleepy Hollow, for the purpose of instructing the children of the vicinity. He was a native of Connecticut, a State which supplies the Union with pioneers for the mind as well as for the forest, and sends forth yearly its legions of frontier woodsmen and country schoolmasters. The cognomen of Crane was not inapplicable to his person. He was tall, but exceedingly lank, with narrow shoulders, long arms and legs, hands that dangled a mile out of his sleeves, feet that might have served for shovels, and his whole frame most loosely hung together. His head was small, and flat at top, with huge ears, large green glassy eyes, and a long snipe nose, so that it looked like a weathercock perched upon his spindle neck, to tell which way the wind blew. To see him striding along the profile of a hill on a windy day, with his clothes bagging and fluttering about him, one might have mistaken him for the genius of famine descending upon the earth, or some scarecrow eloped from a corn-field.

His school-house was a low building of one large room, rudely constructed of logs; the windows partly glazed, and partly patched with leaves of old copy-books. It was most ingeniously secured at vacant hours by a withe twisted in the handle of the door, and stakes set against the window-shutters; so that, though a thief might get in with perfect ease, he would find some embarrassment in getting out: an idea most probably borrowed by the architect, Yost Van Houten, from the mystery of an eel-pot. The school-house stood in a rather lonely but pleasant situation, just at the foot of a woody hill, with a brook running close by, and a formidable birch-tree growing at one end of it. From hence the low murmur of his pupils' voices, conning over their lessons, might be heard on a drowsy summer's day, like the hum of a bee-hive; interrupted now and then by the authoritative voice of the master, in the tone of menace or command; or, peradventure, by the appalling sound of the birch, as he urged some tardy loiterer along the flowery path of knowledge. Truth to say, he was a conscientious man, and ever bore in mind the golden maxim, "Spare the rod and spoil the child."—Ichabod Crane's scholars certainly were not spoiled.

I would not have it imagined, however, that he was one of those cruel potentates of the school, who joy in the smart of their subjects; on the contrary, he administered justice with discrimination rather than severity, taking the burden off the backs of the

[2]A particular kind of witch, accompanied by nine assistants.

weak, and laying it on those of the strong. Your mere puny stripling, that winced at the least flourish of the rod, was passed by with indulgence; but the claims of justice were satisfied by inflicting a double portion on some little, tough, wrong-headed, broad-skirted Dutch urchin, who sulked and swelled and grew dogged and sullen beneath the birch. All this he called "doing his duty" by their parents; and he never inflicted a chastisement without following it by the assurance, so consolatory to the smarting urchin, that "he would remember it, and thank him for it the longest day he had to live."

When school-hours were over, he was even the companion and playmate of the larger boys; and on holiday afternoons would convoy some of the smaller ones home, who happened to have pretty sisters, or good housewives for mothers, noted for the comforts of the cupboard. Indeed it behooved him to keep on good terms with his pupils. The revenue arising from his school was small, and would have been scarcely sufficient to furnish him with daily bread, for he was a huge feeder, and, though lank, had the dilating powers of an anaconda; but to help out his maintenance, he was, according to country custom in those parts, boarded and lodged at the houses of the farmers, whose children he instructed. With these he lived successively a week at a time; thus going the rounds of the neighborhood, with all his worldly effects tied up in a cotton handkerchief.

That all this might not be too onerous on the purses of his rustic patrons, who are apt to consider the costs of schooling a grievous burden, and schoolmasters as mere drones, he had various ways of rendering himself both useful and agreeable. He assisted the farmers occasionally in the lighter labors of their farms; helped to make hay; mended the fences; took the horses to water; drove the cows from pasture; and cut wood for the winter fire. He laid aside, too, all the dominant dignity and absolute sway with which he lorded it in his little empire, the school, and became wonderfully gentle and ingratiating. He found favor in the eyes of the mothers, by petting the children, particularly the youngest; and like the lion bold, which whilom so magnanimously the lamb did hold, he would sit with a child on one knee, and rock a cradle with his foot for whole hours together.

In addition to his other vocations, he was the singing-master of the neighborhood, and picked up many bright shillings by instructing the young folks in psalmody. It was a matter of no little vanity to him, on Sundays, to take his station in front of the church-gallery, with a band of chosen singers; where, in his own mind, he completely carried away the palm from the parson. Certain it is, his voice resounded far above all the rest of the congregation; and there are peculiar quavers still to be heard in that church, and which may even be heard half a mile off, quite to the opposite side of the mill-pond, on a still Sunday morning, which are said to be legitimately descended from the nose of Ichabod Crane. Thus, by divers little makeshifts in that ingenious way which is commonly denominated "by hook and by crook," the worthy pedagogue got on tolerably enough, and was thought, by all who understood nothing of the labor of headwork, to have a wonderfully easy life of it.

The schoolmaster is generally a man of some importance in the female circle of a rural neighborhood; being considered a kind of idle, gentlemanlike personage, of vastly superior taste and accomplishments to the rough country swains, and, indeed, inferior in learning only to the parson. His appearance, therefore, is apt to occasion some little stir at the tea-table of a farm-house, and the addition of a supernumerary dish of cakes or sweet-meats, or, peradventure, the parade of a silver tea-pot. Our man of letters, therefore, was peculiarly happy in the smiles of all the country damsels. How he would figure among them in the churchyard, between services on Sundays! gathering grapes for them from the wild vines that overrun the surrounding trees; reciting for their amusement all the epitaphs on the tombstones; or sauntering, with a whole bevy of them, along the banks of the adjacent mill-pond; while the more bashful country bumpkins hung sheepishly back, envying his superior elegance and address.

From his half itinerant life, also, he was a kind of travelling gazette, carrying the whole budget of local gossip from house to house: so that his appearance was always greeted with satisfaction. He was, moreover, esteemed by the women as a man of great erudition, for he had read several books quite through, and was a perfect master of Cotton Mather's *History of New England Witchcraft*, in which, by the way, he most firmly and potently believed.

He was, in fact, an odd mixture of small shrewdness and simple credulity. His appetite for the marvellous, and his powers of digesting it, were equally extraordinary; and both had been increased by his residence in this spellbound region. No tale was too gross or monstrous for his capacious swallow. It was often his delight, after his school was dismissed in the afternoon, to stretch himself on the rich bed of clover bordering the little brook that whimpered by his school-house, and there con over old Mather's direful tales, until the gathering dusk of the evening made the printed page a mere mist before his eyes. Then, as he wended his way, by swamp and stream, and awful woodland, to the farm-house where he happened to be quartered, every sound of nature, at that witching hour, fluttered his excited imagination; the moan of the whippoorwill[3] from the hill-side; the boding cry of the treetoad, that harbinger of storm; the dreary hooting of the screech-owl, or the sudden rustling in the thicket of birds frightened from their roost. The fire-flies, too, which sparkled most vividly in the darkest places, now and then startled him, as one of uncommon brightness would stream across his path; and if, by chance, a huge blockhead of a beetle came winging his blundering flight against him, the poor varlet was ready to give up the ghost, with the idea that he was struck with a witch's token. His only resource on such occasions, either to drown thought or drive away evil spirits, was to sing psalm-tunes; and the good people of Sleepy Hollow, as they sat by their doors of an evening, were often filled with awe, at hearing his nasal melody, "in linkèd sweetness long drawn out," floating from the distant hill, or along the dusky road.

Another of his sources of fearful pleasure was, to pass long winter evenings with the old Dutch wives, as they sat spinning by the fire, with a row of apples roasting and spluttering along the hearth, and listen to their marvellous tales of ghosts and goblins, and haunted fields, and haunted brooks, and haunted bridges, and haunted houses, and particularly of the headless horseman, or Galloping Hessian of the Hollow, as they sometimes called him. He would delight them equally by his anecdotes of witchcraft, and of the direful omens and portentous sights and sounds in the air, which prevailed in the earlier times of Connecticut; and would frighten them wofully with speculations upon comets and shooting-stars, and with the alarming fact that the world did absolutely turn round, and that they were half the time topsy-turvy!

But if there was a pleasure in all this, while snugly cuddling in the chimney-corner of a chamber that was all of a ruddy glow from the crackling wood-fire, and where, of course, no spectre dared to show his face, it was dearly purchased by the terrors of his subsequent walk homewards. What fearful shapes and shadows beset his path amidst the dim and ghastly glare of a snowy night!—With what wistful look did he eye every trembling ray of light streaming across the waste fields from some distant window!—How often was he appalled by some shrub covered with snow, which, like a sheeted spectre, beset his very path!—How often did he shrink with curdling awe at the sound of his own steps on a frosty crust beneath his feet; and dread to look over his shoulder, lest he should behold some uncouth being tramping close behind him!—and how often was he thrown into complete dismay by some rushing blast, howling among the trees, in the idea that it was the Galloping Hessian on one of his nightly scourings!

All these, however, were mere terrors of the night, phantoms of the mind that walk in darkness; and though he had seen many spectres in his time, and been more than once beset by Satan in divers shapes, in his lonely perambulations, yet daylight put an end to all these evils; and he would have passed a pleasant life of it, in despite of the devil and all his works, if his path had not been crossed by a being that causes more perplexity to mortal man than ghosts, goblins, and the whole race of witches put together, and that was—a woman.

Among the musical disciples who assembled, one evening in each week, to receive his instructions in psalmody, was Katrina Van Tassel, the daughter and only child of a substantial Dutch farmer. She was a blooming lass of fresh eighteen; plump as a partridge; ripe and melting and rosy-cheeked as one of her father's peaches, and universally famed, not merely for her beauty, but her vast expectations. She was withal a little of a coquette, as might be perceived even in her dress, which was a mixture of ancient and modern fashions, as most suited to set off her charms. She wore the ornaments of pure yellow gold, which her great-great-grandmother had brought over from Saardam; the tempting stomacher of the olden time; and withal a provokingly short petticoat, to display the prettiest foot and ankle in the country round.

Ichabod Crane had a soft and foolish heart towards the sex; and it is not to be wondered at that so tempting a morsel soon found favor in his eyes; more especially after he had visited her in her paternal mansion. Old Baltus Van Tassel was a perfect picture of a thriving, contented, liberal-hearted farmer. He seldom, it is true, sent either his eyes or his thoughts beyond the boundaries of his own farm; but within those everything was snug, happy, and well-conditioned. He was satisfied with his wealth, but not proud of it; and piqued himself upon the hearty abundance rather than the style in which he lived. His stronghold was situated on the banks of the Hudson, in one of those green, sheltered, fertile nooks in which the Dutch farmers are so fond of nestling. A great elm-tree spread its broad branches over it; at the foot of which bubbled up a spring of the softest and sweetest water, in a little well, formed of a barrel; and then stole sparkling away through the grass, to a neighboring brook, that bubbled along among alders and dwarf willows. Hard by the farm-house was a vast barn, that might have served for a church; every window and crevice

[3] The whippoorwill is a bird which is only heard at night. It receives its name from its note, which is thought to resemble those words. [Irving's note.]

of which seemed bursting forth with the treasures of the farm; the flail was busily resounding within it from morning till night; swallows and martins skimmed twittering about the eaves; and rows of pigeons, some with one eye turned up, as if watching the weather, some with their heads under their wings, or buried in their bosoms, and others swelling, and cooing, and bowing about their dames, were enjoying the sunshine on the roof. Sleek unwieldly porkers were grunting in the repose and abundance of their pens; whence sallied forth, now and then, troops of sucking pigs, as if to snuff the air. A stately squadron of snowy geese were riding in an adjoining pond, convoying whole fleets of ducks; regiments of turkeys were gobbling through the farm-yard, and guinea fowls fretting about it, like ill-tempered housewives, with their peevish discontented cry. Before the barn-door strutted the gallant cock, that pattern of a husband, a warrior, and a fine gentleman, clapping his burnished wings, and crowing in the pride and gladness of his heart—sometimes tearing up the earth with his feet, and then generously calling his ever-hungry family of wives and children to enjoy the rich morsel which he had discovered.

The pedagogue's mouth watered, as he looked upon this sumptuous promise of luxurious winter fare. In his devouring mind's eye he pictured to himself every roasting-pig running about with a pudding in his belly, and an apple in his mouth; the pigeons were snugly put to bed in a comfortable pie, and tucked in with a coverlet of crust; the geese were swimming in their own gravy; and the ducks pairing cosily in dishes, like snug married couples, with a decent competency of onion-sauce. In the porkers he saw carved out the future sleek side of bacon, and juicy relishing ham; not a turkey but he beheld daintily trussed up, with its gizzard under its wing, and, peradventure, a necklace of savory sausages; and even bright chanticleer himself lay sprawling on his back, in a side-dish, with uplifted claws, as if craving that quarter which his chivalrous spirit disdained to ask while living.

As the enraptured Ichabod fancied all this, and as he rolled his great green eyes over the fat meadowlands, the rich fields of wheat, of rye, of buckwheat, and Indian corn, and the orchard burdened with ruddy fruit, which surrounded the warm tenement of Van Tassel, his heart yearned after the damsel who was to inherit these domains, and his imagination expanded with the idea how they might be readily turned into cash, and the money invested in immense tracts of wild land, and shingle palaces in the wilderness. Nay, his busy fancy already realized his hopes, and presented to him the blooming Katrina, with a whole family of children, mounted on the top of a wagon loaded with household trumpery, with pots and kettles dangling beneath; and he beheld himself bestriding a pacing mare, with a colt at her heels, setting out for Kentucky, Tennessee, or the Lord knows where.

When he entered the house, the conquest of his heart was complete. It was one of those spacious farm-houses, with high-ridged, but lowly-sloping roofs, built in the style handed down from the first Dutch settlers; the low projecting eaves forming a piazza along the front, capable of being closed up in bad weather. Under this were hung flails, harness, various utensils of husbandry, and nets for fishing in the neighboring river. Benches were built along the sides for summer use; and a great spinning-wheel at one end, and a churn at the other, showed the various uses to which this important porch might be devoted. From this piazza the wandering Ichabod entered the hall, which formed the centre of the mansion and the place of usual residence. Here, rows of resplendent pewter, ranged on a long dresser, dazzled his eyes. In one corner stood a huge bag of wool ready to be spun; in another a quantity of linsey-woolsey just from the loom; ears of Indian corn, and strings of dried apples and peaches, hung in gay festoons along the walls, mingled with the gaud of red peppers; and a door left ajar gave him a peep into the best parlor, where the claw-footed chairs and dark mahogany tables shone like mirrors; and irons,[4] with their accompanying shovel and tongs, glistened from their covert of asparagus tops; mock-oranges and conch-shells decorated the mantel-piece; strings of various colored birds' eggs were suspended above it, a great ostrich egg was hung from the centre of the room, and a corner-cupboard, knowingly left open, displayed immense treasures of old silver and well-mended china.

From the moment Ichabod laid his eyes upon these regions of delight, the peace of his mind was at an end, and his only study was how to gain the affections of the peerless daughter of Van Tassel. In this enterprise, however, he had more real difficulties than generally fell to the lot of a knight-errant of yore, who seldom had anything but giants, enchanters, fiery dragons, and such like easily conquered adversaries, to contend with; and had to make his way merely through gates of iron and brass, and walls of adamant, to the castle-keep, where the lady of his heart was confined; all which he achieved as easily as a man would carve his way to the centre of a Christmas pie; and then the lady gave him her hand as a matter of course. Ichabod, on the contrary, had to win his way to the heart of a country coquette, beset with a labyrinth of whims

[4] Probably a misprint for *andirons*.

and caprices, which were forever presenting new difficulties and impediments; and he had to encounter a host of fearful adversaries of real flesh and blood, the numerous rustic admirers, who beset every portal to her heart; keeping a watchful and angry eye upon each other, but ready to fly out in the common cause against any new competitor.

Among these the most formidable was a burly, roaring, roistering blade, of the name of Abraham, or, according to the Dutch abbreviation, Brom Van Brunt, the hero of the country round, which rang with his feats of strength and hardihood. He was broad-shouldered and double-jointed, with short, curly black hair, and a bluff but not unpleasant countenance, having a mingled air of fun and arrogance. From his Herculean frame and great powers of limb, he had received the nickname of BROM BONES, by which he was universally known. He was famed for great knowledge and skill in horsemanship, being as dexterous on horseback as a Tartar. He was foremost at all races and cockfights; and, with the ascendency which bodily strength acquires in rustic life, was the umpire in all disputes, setting his hat on one side, and giving his decisions with an air and tone admitting of no gainsay or appeal. He was always ready for either a fight or a frolic; but had more mischief than ill-will in his composition; and, with all his overbearing roughness, there was a strong dash of waggish good-humor at the bottom. He had three or four boon companions, who regarded him as their model, and at the head of whom he scoured the country, attending every scene of feud or merriment for miles round. In cold weather he was distinguished by a fur cap, surmounted with a flaunting fox's tail; and when the folks at a country gathering descried this well-known crest at a distance, whisking about among a squad of hard riders, they always stood by for a squall. Sometimes his crew would be heard dashing along past the farmhouses at midnight, with whoop and halloo, like a troop of Don Cossacks; and the old dames, startled out of their sleep, would listen for a moment till the hurry-scurry had clattered by, and then exclaim, "Ay, there goes Brom Bones and his gang!" The neighbors looked upon him with a mixture of awe, admiration and good will; and when any madcap prank, or rustic brawl, occurred in the vicinity, always shook their heads, and warranted Brom Bones was at the bottom of it.

This rantipole[5] hero had for some time singled out the blooming Katrina for the object of his uncouth gallantries; and though his amorous toyings were something like the gentle caresses and endearments of a bear, yet it was whispered that she did not altogether discourage his hopes. Certain it is, his advances were signals for rival candidates to retire, who felt no inclination to cross a line in his amours; insomuch, that, when his horse was seen tied to Van Tassel's paling on a Sunday night, a sure sign that his master was courting, or, as it is termed, "sparking," within, all other suitors passed by in despair, and carried the war into other quarters.

Such was the formidable rival with whom Ichabod Crane had to contend, and, considering all things, a stouter man than he would have shrunk from the competition, and a wiser man would have despaired. He had, however, a happy mixture of pliability and perseverance in his nature; he was in form and spirit like a supple-jack[6]—yielding, but tough; though he bent, he never broke; and though he bowed beneath the slightest pressure yet, the moment it was away—jerk! he was as erect, and carried his head as high as ever.

To have taken the field openly against his rival would have been madness; for he was not a man to be thwarted in his amours, any more than that stormy lover, Achilles. Ichabod, therefore, made his advances in a quiet and gently insinuating manner. Under cover of his character of singing-master, he had made frequent visits at the farm-house; not that he had anything to apprehend from the meddlesome interference of parents, which is so often a stumbling-block in the path of lovers. Balt Van Tassel was an easy, indulgent soul; he loved his daughter better even than his pipe, and, like a reasonable man and an excellent father, let her have her way in everything. His notable little wife, too, had enough to do to attend to her housekeeping and manage her poultry; for, as she sagely observed, ducks and geese are foolish things, and must be looked after, but girls can take care of themselves. Thus while the busy dame bustled about the house, or plied her spinning-wheel at one end of the piazza, honest Balt would sit smoking his evening pipe at the other, watching the achievements of a little wooden warrior, who, armed with a sword in each hand, was most valiantly fighting the wind on the pinnacle of the barn. In the meantime, Ichabod would carry on his suit with the daughter by the side of the spring under the great elm, or sauntering along in the twilight,—that hour so favorable to the lover's eloquence.

I profess not to know how women's hearts are wooed and won. To me they have always been matters of riddle and admiration. Some seem to have but one vulnerable point or door of access, while others have a thousand avenues, and may be captured in a thousand different ways. It is a great triumph of skill to gain the former, but a still greater

[5] Reckless.

[6] A kind of walking stick or cane.

proof of generalship to maintain possession of the latter, for the man must battle for his fortress at every door and window. He who wins a thousand common hearts is therefore entitled to some renown; but he who keeps undisputed sway over the heart of a coquette, is indeed a hero. Certain it is, this was not the case with the redoubtable Brom Bones; and from the moment Ichabod Crane made his advances, the interests of the former evidently declined; his horse was no longer seen tied at the palings on Sunday nights, and a deadly feud gradually arose between him and the preceptor of Sleepy Hollow.

Brom, who had a degree of rough chivalry in his nature, would fain have carried matters to open warfare, and have settled their pretensions to the lady according to the mode of those most concise and simple reasoners, the knights-errant of yore—by single combat; but Ichabod was too conscious of the superior might of his adversary to enter the lists against him: he had overheard a boast of Bones, that he would "double the schoolmaster up, and lay him on a shelf of his own school-house;" and he was too wary to give him an opportunity. There was something extremely provoking in this obstinately pacific system; it left Brom no alternative but to draw upon the funds of rustic waggery in his disposition, and to play off boorish practical jokes upon his rival. Ichabod became the object of whimsical persecution to Bones and his gang of rough riders. They harried his hitherto peaceful domains; smoked out his singing-school, by stopping up the chimney; broke into the school-house at night, in spite of its formidable fastenings of withe and window-stakes, and turned everything topsy-turvy: so that the poor schoolmaster began to think all the witches in the country held their meetings there. But what was still more annoying, Brom took opportunities of turning him into ridicule in presence of his mistress, and had a scoundrel dog whom he taught to whine in the most ludicrous manner, and introduced as a rival of Ichabod's to instruct her in psalmody.

In this way matters went on for some time, without producing any material effect on the relative situation of the contending powers. On a fine autumnal afternoon, Ichabod, in pensive mood, sat enthroned on the lofty stool whence he usually watched all the concerns of his little literary realm. In his hand he swayed a ferule, that sceptre of despotic power; the birch of justice reposed on three nails, behind the throne, a constant terror to evil-doers; while on the desk before him might be seen sundry contraband articles and prohibited weapons, detected upon the persons of idle urchins; such as half-munched apples, popguns, whirligigs, fly-cages, and whole legions of rampant little paper game-cocks. Apparently there had been some appalling act of justice recently inflicted, for his scholars were all busily intent upon their books, or slyly whispering behind them with one eye kept upon the master; and a kind of buzzing stillness reigned throughout the school-room. It was suddenly interrupted by the appearance of a negro, in tow-cloth jacket and trousers, a round-crowned fragment of a hat, like the cap of Mercury, and mounted on the back of a ragged, wild, half-broken colt, which he managed with a rope by way of halter. He came clattering up to the school-door with an invitation to Ichabod to attend a merry-making or "quilting frolic," to be held that evening at Mynheer Van Tassel's; and having delivered his message with that air of importance, and effort at fine language, which a negro is apt to display on petty embassies of the kind, he dashed over the brook, and was seen scampering away up the Hollow, full of the importance and hurry of his mission.

All was now bustle and hubbub in the late quiet school-room. The scholars were hurried through their lessons, without stopping at trifles; those who were nimble skipped over half with impunity, and those who were tardy had a smart application now and then in the rear, to quicken their speed, or help them over a tall word. Books were flung aside without being put away on the shelves, inkstands were overturned, benches thrown down, and the whole school was turned loose an hour before the usual time, bursting forth like a legion of young imps, yelping and racketing about the green, in joy at their early emancipation.

The gallant Ichabod now spent at least an extra half-hour at his toilet, brushing and furbishing up his best and indeed only suit of rusty black, and arranging his locks by a bit of broken looking-glass, that hung up in the school-house. That he might make his appearance before his mistress in the true style of a cavalier, he borrowed a horse from the farmer with whom he was domiciliated, a choleric old Dutchman, of the name of Hans Van Ripper, and, thus gallantly mounted, issued forth, like a knight-errant in quest of adventures. But it is meet I should, in the true spirit of romantic story, give some account of the looks and equipments of my hero and his steed. The animal he bestrode was a broken-down plough-horse, that had outlived almost everything but his viciousness. He was gaunt and shagged, with a ewe neck and a head like a hammer; his rusty mane and tail were tangled and knotted with burrs; one eye had lost its pupil, and was glaring and spectral; but the other had the gleam of a genuine devil in it. Still he must have had fire and mettle in his day, if we may judge from the name he bore of Gunpowder. He had, in fact, been a favorite steed of his master's, the choleric Van Ripper, who was a furious rider, and had infused, very probably, some of his own spirit into the animal; for, old and broken-down as he looked, there was more of the lurking devil in him than in any young filly in the country.

Ichabod was a suitable figure for such a steed. He rode with short stirrups, which brought his knees nearly up to the pommel of the saddle; his sharp elbows stuck out like grasshoppers'; he carried his whip perpendicularly in his hand, like a sceptre, and, as his horse jogged on, the motion of his arms was not unlike the flapping of a pair of wings. A small wool hat rested on the top of his nose, for so his scanty strip of forehead might be called; and the skirts of his black coat fluttered out almost to the horse's tail. Such was the appearance of Ichabod and his steed, as they shambled out of the gate of Hans Van Ripper, and it was altogether such an apparition as is seldom to be met with in broad daylight.

It was, as I have said, a fine autumnal day, the sky was clear and serene, and nature wore that rich and golden livery which we always associate with the idea of abundance. The forests had put on their sober brown and yellow, while some trees of the tenderer kind had been nipped by the frosts into brilliant dyes of orange, purple, and scarlet. Streaming files of wild ducks began to make their appearance high in the air; the bark of the squirrel might be heard from the groves of beech and hickory nuts, and the pensive whistle of the quail at intervals from the neighboring stubble-field.

The small birds were taking their farewell banquets. In the fulness of their revelry, they fluttered, chirping and frolicking, from bush to bush, and tree to tree, capricious from the very profusion and variety around them. There was the honest cockrobin, the favorite game of stripling sportsmen, with its loud querulous notes; and the twittering blackbirds flying in sable clouds; and the golden-winged woodpecker, with his crimson crest, his broad black gorget, and splendid plumage; and the cedarbird, with its red-tipt wings and yellow-tipt tail, and its little monteiro cap[7] of feathers; and the blue jay, that noisy coxcomb, in his gay light-blue coat and white under-clothes, screaming and chattering, nodding and bobbing and bowing, and pretending to be on good terms with every songster of the grove.

As Ichabod jogged slowly on his way, his eye, ever open to every symptom of culinary abundance, ranged with delight over the treasures of jolly autumn. On all sides he beheld vast store of apples; some hanging in oppressive opulence on the trees; some gathered into baskets and barrels for the market; others heaped up in rich piles for the cider-press. Farther on he beheld great fields of Indian corn, with its golden ears peeping from their leafy coverts, and holding out the promise of cakes and hasty-pudding; and the yellow pumpkins lying beneath them, turning up their fair round bellies to the sun, and giving ample prospects of the most luxurious of pies; and anon he passed the fragrant buckwheat fields, breathing the odor of the bee-hive, and as he beheld them, soft anticipations stole over his mind of dainty slapjacks, well buttered, and garnished with honey or treacle, by the delicate little dimpled hand of Katrina Van Tassel.

Thus feeding his mind with many sweet thoughts and "sugared suppositions," he journeyed along the sides of a range of hills which look out upon some of the goodliest scenes of the mighty Hudson. The sun gradually wheeled his broad disk down into the west. The wide bosom of the Tappan Zee lay motionless and glossy, excepting that here and there a gentle undulation waved and prolonged the blue shadow of the distant mountain. A few amber clouds floated in the sky, without a breath of air to move them. The horizon was of a fine golden tint, changing gradually into a pure apple-green, and from that into the deep blue of the mid-heaven. A slanting ray lingered on the woody crests of the precipices that overhung some parts of the river, giving greater depth to the dark-gray and purple of their rocky sides. A sloop was loitering in the distance, dropping slowly down with the tide, her sail hanging uselessly against the mast; and as the reflection of the sky gleamed along the still water, it seemed as if the vessel was suspended in the air.

It was toward evening that Ichabod arrived at the castle of the Heer Van Tassel, which he found thronged with the pride and flower of the adjacent country. Old farmers, a spare leathern-faced race, in homespun coats and breeches, blue stockings, huge shoes, and magnificent pewter buckles. Their brisk withered little dames, in close crimped caps, long-waisted shortgowns, homespun petticoats, with scissors and pincushions, and gay calico pockets hanging on the outside. Buxom lasses, almost as antiquated as their mothers, excepting where a straw hat, a fine ribbon, or perhaps a white frock, gave symptoms of city innovation. The sons, in short square-skirted coats with rows of stupendous brass buttons, and their hair generally queued in the fashion of the times, especially if they could procure an eel-skin for the purpose, it being esteemed, throughout the country, as a potent nourisher and strengthener of the hair.

Brom Bones, however, was the hero of the scene, having come to the gathering on his favorite steed,

[7]A variety of hunting cap.

Daredevil, a creature, like himself, full of mettle and mischief, and which no one but himself could manage. He was, in fact, noted for preferring vicious animals, given to all kinds of tricks, which kept the rider in constant risk of his neck, for he held a tractable well-broken horse as unworthy of a lad of spirit.

Fain would I pause to dwell upon the world of charms that burst upon the enraptured gaze of my hero, as he entered the state parlor of Van Tassel's mansion. Not those of the bevy of buxom lasses, with their luxurious display of red and white; but the ample charms of a genuine Dutch country tea-table, in the sumptuous time of autumn. Such heaped-up platters of cakes of various and almost indescribable kinds, known only to experienced Dutch housewives! There was the doughty doughnut, the tenderer oly koek, and the crisp and crumbling cruller; sweet cakes and short cakes, ginger-cakes and honey-cakes, and the whole family of cakes. And then there were apple-pies and peach-pies and pumpkin-pies; besides slices of ham and smoked beef; and moreover delectable dishes of preserved plums, and peaches, and pears, and quinces; not to mention broiled shad and roasted chickens; together with bowls of milk and cream, all mingled higgledy-piggledy, pretty much as I have enumerated them, with the motherly tea-pot sending up its clouds of vapor from the midst—Heaven bless the mark! I want breath and time to discuss this banquet as it deserves, and am too eager to get on with my story. Happily, Ichabod Crane was not in so great a hurry as his historian, but did ample justice to every dainty.

He was a kind and thankful creature, whose heart dilated in proportion as his skin was filled with good cheer; and whose spirits rose with eating as some men's do with drink. He could not help, too, rolling his large eyes round him as he ate, and chuckling with the possibility that he might one day be lord of all this scene of almost unimaginable luxury and splendor. Then, he thought, how soon he'd turn his back upon the old school-house; snap his fingers in the face of Hans Van Ripper, and every other niggardly patron, and kick any itinerant pedagogue out-of-doors that should dare to call him comrade!

Old Baltus Van Tassel moved about among his guests with a face dilated with content and good-humor, round and jolly as the harvest-moon. His hospitable attentions were brief, but expressive, being confined to a shake of the hand, a slap on the shoulder, a loud laugh, and a pressing invitation to "fall to, and help themselves."

And now the sound of the music from the common room, or hall, summoned to the dance. The musician was an old gray-headed negro, who had been the itinerant orchestra of the neighborhood for more than half a century. His instrument was as old and battered as himself. The greater part of the time he scraped on two or three strings, accompanying every movement of the bow with a motion of the head; bowing almost to the ground, and stamping with his foot whenever a fresh couple were to start.

Ichabod prided himself upon his dancing as much as upon his vocal powers. Not a limb, not a fibre about him was idle; and to have seen his loosely hung frame in full motion, and clattering about the room, you would have thought Saint Vitus himself, that blessed patron of the dance, was figuring before you in person. He was the admiration of all the negroes; who, having gathered, of all ages and sizes, from the farm and the neighborhood, stood forming a pyramid of shining black faces at every door and window, gazing with delight at the scene, rolling their white eyeballs, and showing grinning rows of ivory from ear to ear. How could the flogger of urchins be otherwise than animated and joyous? the lady of his heart was his partner in the dance, and smiling graciously in reply to all his amorous oglings; while Brom Bones, sorely smitten with love and jealousy, sat brooding by himself in one corner.

When the dance was at an end, Ichabod was attracted to a knot of the sager folks, who, with old Van Tassel, sat smoking at one end of the piazza, gossiping over former times, and drawing out long stories about the war.

This neighborhood, at the time of which I am speaking, was one of those highly favored places which abound with chronicle and great men. The British and American line had run near it during the war; it had, therefore, been the scene of marauding, and infested with refugees, cow-boys,[8] and all kinds of border chivalry. Just sufficient time has elapsed to enable each story-teller to dress up his tale with a little becoming fiction, and, in the indistinctness of his recollection, to make himself the hero of every exploit.

There was the story of Doffue Martling, a large blue-bearded Dutchman, who had nearly taken a British frigate with an old iron nine-pounder from a mud breastwork, only that his gun burst at the sixth discharge. And there was an old gentleman who shall be nameless, being too rich a mynheer to be lightly mentioned, who, in the battle of White Plains, being an excellent master of defence, parried a musket-ball with a small sword, insomuch that he absolutely felt it whiz round the blade, and glance off at the hilt; in proof of which he was ready at any time to show the sword, with the hilt a little bent. There were several more that had been equally

[8]Name given to guerrillas during the Revolution.

great in the field, not one of whom but was persuaded that he had a considerable hand in bringing the war to a happy termination.

But all these were nothing to the tales of ghosts and apparitions that succeeded. The neighborhood is rich in legendary treasures of the kind. Local tales and superstitions thrive best in these sheltered long-settled retreats; but are trampled underfoot by the shifting throng that forms the population of most of our country places. Besides, there is no encouragement for ghosts in most of our villages, for they have scarcely had time to finish their first nap, and turn themselves in their graves before their surviving friends have travelled away from the neighborhood; so that when they turn out at night to walk their rounds, they have no acquaintance left to call upon. This is perhaps the reason why we so seldom hear of ghosts, except in our long-established Dutch communities.

The immediate cause, however, of the prevalence of supernatural stories in these parts was doubtless owing to the vicinity of Sleepy Hollow. There was a contagion in the very air that blew from that haunted region; it breathed forth an atmosphere of dreams and fancies infecting all the land. Several of the Sleepy Hollow people were present at Van Tassel's and, as usual, were doling out their wild and wonderful legends. Many dismal tales were told about funeral trains, and mourning cries and wailings heard and seen about the great tree where the unfortunate Major André was taken, and which stood in the neighborhood. Some mention was made also of the woman in white, that haunted the dark glen at Raven Rock, and was often heard to shriek on winter nights before a storm, having perished there in the snow. The chief part of the stories, however, turned upon the favorite spectre of Sleepy Hollow, the headless horseman, who had been heard several times of late, patrolling the country; and, it was said, tethered his horse nightly among the graves in the churchyard.

The sequestered situation of this church seems always to have made it a favorite haunt of troubled spirits. It stands on a knoll, surrounded by locust-trees and lofty elms, from among which its decent whitewashed walls shine modestly forth, like Christian purity beaming through the shades of retirement. A gentle slope descends from it to a silver sheet of water, bordered by high trees, between which, peeps may be caught at the blue hills of the Hudson. To look upon its grass-grown yard, where the sunbeams seem to sleep so quietly, one would think that there at least the dead might rest in peace. On one side of the church extends a wide woody dell, along which raves a large brook among broken rocks and trunks of fallen trees. Over a deep black part of the stream, not far from the church, was formerly thrown a wooden bridge; the road that led to it, and the bridge itself, were thickly shaded by overhanging trees, which cast a gloom about it, even in the daytime, but occasioned a fearful darkness at night. This was one of the favorite haunts of the headless horseman; and the place where he was most frequently encountered. The tale was told of old Brouwer, a most heretical disbeliever in ghosts, how he met the horseman returning from his foray into Sleepy Hollow, and was obliged to get up behind him; how they galloped over bush and brake, over hill and swamp, until they reached the bridge; when the horseman suddenly turned into a skeleton, threw old Brouwer into the brook, and sprang away over the tree-tops with a clap of thunder.

This story was immediately matched by a thrice marvellous adventure of Brom Bones, who made light of the galloping Hessian as an arrant jockey. He affirmed that, on returning one night from the neighboring village of Sing Sing, he had been overtaken by this midnight trooper; that he had offered to race with him for a bowl of punch, and should have won it too, for Daredevil beat the goblin horse all hollow, but, just as they came to the church bridge, the Hessian bolted, and vanished in a flash of fire.

All these tales, told in that drowsy undertone with which men talk in the dark, the countenances of the listeners only now and then receiving a casual gleam from the glare of a pipe, sank deep in the mind of Ichabod. He repaid them in kind with large extracts from his invaluable author, Cotton Mather, and added many marvellous events that had taken place in his native State of Connecticut, and fearful sights which he had seen in his nightly walks about the Sleepy Hollow.

The revel now gradually broke up. The old farmers gathered together their families in their wagons, and were heard for some time rattling along the hollow roads, and over the distant hills. Some of the damsels mounted on pillions behind their favorite swains, and their light-hearted laughter, mingling with the clatter of hoofs, echoed along the silent woodlands, sounding fainter and fainter until they gradually died away—and the late scene of noise and frolic was all silent and deserted. Ichabod only lingered behind, according to the custom of country lovers, to have a *tête-à-tête* with the heiress, fully convinced that he was now on the high road to success. What passed at this interview I will not pretend to say, for in fact I do not know. Something, however, I fear me, must have gone wrong, for he certainly sallied forth, after no very great interval, with an air quite desolate and chop-fallen.—Oh, these women! these women! Could that girl have been playing off any of her coquettish tricks?—Was her encouragement of the poor pedagogue all a mere sham to secure her conquest of his rival?—Heaven only knows, not I!—Let it suffice to say, Ichabod stole forth with the air of one who had been sacking a hen-roost, rather than a fair lady's heart. Without looking to the right or left to notice the scene of rural wealth on which he had so often gloated, he went straight to the stable, and with several hearty cuffs and kicks, roused his steed most uncourteously from the comfortable quarters in which he was soundly sleeping, dreaming of mountains of corn and oats, and whole valleys of timothy and clover.

It was the very witching time of night that Ichabod, heavy-hearted and crestfallen, pursued his travel homewards, along the sides of the lofty hills which rise above Tarry Town, and which he had traversed so cheerily in the afternoon. The hour was as dismal as himself. Far below him, the Tappan Zee spread its dusky and indistinct waste of waters, with here and there the tall mast of a sloop riding quietly at anchor under the land. In the dead hush of midnight he could even hear the barking of the watchdog from the opposite shore of the Hudson; but it was so vague and faint as only to give an idea of his distance from this faithful companion of man. Now and then, too, the long-drawn crowing of a cock, accidentally awakened, would sound far, far off, from some farm-house away among the hills—but it was like a dreaming sound in his ear. No signs of life occurred near him, but occasionally the melancholy chirp of a cricket, or perhaps the gutteral twang of a bull-frog, from a neighboring marsh, as if sleeping uncomfortably, and turning suddenly in his bed.

All the stories of ghosts and goblins that he had heard in the afternoon, now came crowding upon his recollection. The night grew darker and darker; the stars seemed to sink deeper in the sky, and driving clouds occasionally hid them from his sight. He had never felt so lonely and dismal. He was, moreover, approaching the very place where many of the scenes of the ghost-stories had been laid. In the centre of the road stood an enormous tulip-tree, which towered like a giant above all the other trees of the neighborhood, and formed a kind of landmark. Its limbs were gnarled, and fantastic, large enough to form trunks for ordinary trees, twisting down almost to the earth, and rising again into the air. It was connected with the tragical story of the unfortunate Andre, who had been taken prisoner hard by; and was universally known by the name of Major André's tree. The common people regarded it with a mixture of respect and superstition, partly out of sympathy for the fate of its ill-starred namesake, and partly from the tales of strange sights and doleful lamentations told concerning it.

As Ichabod approached this fearful tree, he began to whistle: he thought his whistle was answered,—it was but a blast sweeping sharply through the dry branches. As he approached a little nearer, he thought he saw something white, hanging in the midst of the tree,—he paused and ceased whistling; but on looking more narrowly, perceived that it was a place where the tree had been scathed by lightning, and the white wood laid bare. Suddenly he heard a groan,—his teeth chattered and his knees smote against the saddle: it was but the rubbing of one huge bough upon another, as they were swayed about by the breeze. He passed the tree in safety; but new perils lay before him.

About two hundred yards from the tree a small brook crossed the road, and ran into a marshy and thickly wooded glen, known by the name of Wiley's swamp. A few rough logs, laid side by side, served for a bridge over this stream. On that side of the road where the brook entered the wood, a group of oaks and chestnuts, matted thick with wild grapevines, threw a cavernous gloom over it. To pass this bridge was the severest trial. It was at this identical spot that the unfortunate André was captured, and under the covert of those chestnuts and vines were the sturdy yeomen concealed who surprised him. This has ever since been considered a haunted stream, and fearful are the feelings of the school boy who has to pass it alone after dark.

As he approached the stream, his heart began to thump; he summoned up, however, all his resolution, gave his horse half a score of kicks in the ribs, and attempted to dash briskly across the bridge; but instead of starting forward, the perverse old animal made a lateral movement, and ran broadside against the fence. Ichabod, whose fears increased with the delay, jerked the reins on the other side, and kicked lustily with the contrary foot: it was all in vain; his steed started, it is true, but it was only to plunge to the opposite side of the road into a thicket of brambles and alder bushes. The schoolmaster now bestowed both whip and heel upon the starveling ribs of old Gunpowder, who dashed forward, snuffling and snorting, but came to a stand just by the bridge, with a suddenness that had nearly sent his rider sprawling over his head. Just at this moment a plashy tramp by the side of the bridge caught the sensitive ear of Ichabod. In the dark shadow of the grove, on the margin of the brook, he beheld something huge, misshapen, black and towering. It stirred not, but seemed gathered up in the gloom, like some gigantic monster ready to spring upon the traveller.

The hair of the affrighted pedagogue rose upon his head with terror. What was to be done? To turn and fly was now too late; and besides, what chance was there of escaping ghost or goblin, if such it was, which could ride upon the wings of the wind? Summoning up, therefore, a show of courage, he demanded in stammering accents—"Who are you?" He received no reply. He repeated his demand in a still more agitated voice. Still there was no answer. Once more he cudgelled the sides of the inflexible Gunpowder, and, shutting his eyes, broke forth with involuntary fervor into a psalm-tune. Just then the shadowy object of alarm put itself in motion, and, with a scramble and a bound, stood at once in the middle of the road. Though the night was dark and dismal, yet the form of the unknown might now in some degree be ascertained. He appeared to be a horseman of large dimensions, and mounted on a black horse of powerful frame. He made no offer of molestation or sociability, but kept aloof on one side of the road, jogging along on the blind side of old Gunpowder, who had now got over his fright and waywardness.

Ichabod, who had no relish for this strange midnight companion, and bethought himself of the adventure of Brom Bones with the Galloping Hessian, now quickened his steed, in hopes of leaving him behind. The stranger, however, quickened his horse to an equal pace. Ichabod pulled up, and fell into a walk, thinking to lag behind,—the other did the same. His heart began to sink within him; he endeavored to resume his psalm-tune, but his parched tongue clove to the roof of his mouth, and he could not utter a stave. There was something in the moody and dogged silence of this pertinacious companion, that was mysterious and appalling. It was soon fearfully accounted for. On mounting a rising ground, which brought the figure of his fellow-traveller in relief against the sky, gigantic in height, and muffled in a cloak, Ichabod was horror-struck, on perceiving that he was headless!—but his horror was still more increased, on observing that the head, which should have rested on his shoulders, was carried before him on the pommel of the saddle: his terror rose to desperation; he rained a shower of kicks and blows upon Gunpowder, hoping, by a sudden movement, to give his companion the slip,—but the spectre started full jump with him. Away then they dashed, through thick and thin; stones flying, and sparks flashing at every bound. Ichabod's flimsy garments fluttered in the air, as he stretched his long lank body away over his horse's head, in the eagerness of his flight.

They had now reached the road which turns off to Sleepy Hollow; but Gunpowder, who seemed possessed with a demon, instead of keeping up it, made an opposite turn, and plunged headlong downhill to the left. This road leads through a sandy hollow, shaded by trees for about a quarter of a mile, where it crosses the bridge famous in goblin story, and just beyond swells the green knoll on which stands the whitewashed church.

As yet the panic of the steed had given his unskilful rider an apparent advantage in the chase; but just as he had got half-way through the hollow, the girths of the saddle gave way, and he felt it slipping from under him. He seized it by the pommel, and endeavored to hold it firm, but in vain; and had just time to save himself by clasping old Gunpowder round the neck, when the saddle fell to the earth, and he heard it trampled underfoot by his pursuer. For a moment, the terror of Hans Van Ripper's wrath passed across his mind—for it was his Sunday saddle; but this was no time for petty fears; the goblin was hard on his haunches; and (unskilful rider that he was!) he had much ado to maintain his seat; sometimes slipping on one side, sometimes on another, and sometimes jolted on the high ridge of his horse's backbone, with a violence that he verily feared would cleave him asunder.

An opening in the trees now cheered him with the hopes that the church-bridge was at hand. The wavering reflection of a silver star in the bosom of the brook told him that he was not mistaken. He saw the walls of the church dimly glaring under the trees beyond. He recollected the place where Brom Bones' ghostly competitor had disappeared. "If I can but reach that bridge," thought Ichabod, "I am safe." Just then he heard the black steed panting and blowing close behind him; he even fancied that he felt his hot breath. Another convulsive kick in the ribs, and old Gunpowder sprang upon the bridge; he thundered over the resounding planks; he gained the opposite side; and now Ichabod cast a look behind to see if his pursuer should vanish, according to rule, in a flash of fire and brimstone. Just then he saw the goblin rising in his stirrups, and in the very act of hurling his head at him. Ichabod endeavored to dodge the horrible missile, but too late. It encountered his cranium with a tremendous crash,—he was tumbled headlong into the dust, and Gunpowder, the black steed, and the goblin rider, passed by like a whirlwind.

The next morning the old horse was found without his saddle, and with the bridle under his feet, soberly cropping the grass at his master's gate. Ichabod did not make his appearance at breakfast;—dinner-hour came, but no Ichabod. The boys assembled at the school-house, and strolled idly about the banks of the brook; but no schoolmaster. Hans Van Ripper now began to feel some uneasiness about the fate of poor Ichabod, and his saddle. An inquiry was set on foot, and after diligent investigation they came upon his traces. In one part of the road leading to the church was found the saddle trampled in the dirt; the tracks of horses' hoofs deeply dented in the road, and evidently at furious speed, were traced to the bridge, beyond which, on the bank of a broad part of the brook, where the water ran deep and black, was found the hat of the unfortunate Ichabod, and close beside it a shattered pumpkin.

The brook was searched, but the body of the schoolmaster was not to be discovered. Hans Van Ripper, as executor of his estate, examined the bundle which contained all his worldly effects. They consisted of two shirts and a half; two stocks for the neck; a pair or two of worsted stockings, an old pair of corduroy small-clothes; a rusty razor; a book of psalm-tunes, full of dogs' ears; and a broken pitch-pipe. As to the books and furniture of the school-house, they belonged to the community, excepting Cotton Mather's *History of Witchcraft*, a *New England Almanac,* and a book of dreams and fortune-telling; in which last was a sheet of foolscap much scribbled and blotted in several fruitless attempts to make a copy of verses in honor of the heiress of Van Tassel. These magic books and the poetic scrawl were forthwith consigned to the flames by Hans Van Ripper; who from that time forward determined to send his children no more to school; observing, that he never knew any good come of this same reading and writing. Whatever money the schoolmaster possessed, and he had received his quarter's pay but a day or two before, he must have had about his person at the time of his disappearance.

The mysterious event caused much speculation at the church on the following Sunday. Knots of gazers and gossips were collected in the churchyard, at the bridge, and at the spot where the hat and pumpkin had been found. The stories of Brouwer, of Bones, and a whole budget of others, were called to mind; and when they had diligently considered them all, and compared them with the symptoms of the present case, they shook their heads, and came to the conclusion that Ichabod had been carried off by the Galloping Hessian. As he was a bachelor, and in nobody's debt, nobody troubled his head any more about him. The school was removed to a different quarter of the Hollow, and another pedagogue reigned in his stead.

It is true, an old farmer, who had been down to New York on a visit several years after, and from whom this account of the ghostly adventure was received, brought home the intelligence that Ichabod Crane was still alive; that he had left the neighborhood, partly through fear of the goblin and Hans Van Ripper, and partly in mortification at having been suddenly dismissed by the heiress; that he had changed his quarters to a distant part of the country; had kept school and studied law at the same time, had been admitted to the bar, turned politician, electioneered, written for the newspapers, and finally had been made a justice of the Ten Pound Court.[9] Brom Bones too, who shortly after his rival's disappearance conducted the blooming Katrina in triumph to the altar, was observed to look exceedingly knowing whenever the story of Ichabod was related, and always burst into a hearty laugh at the mention of the pumpkin; which led some to suspect that he knew more about the matter than he chose to tell.

The old country wives, however, who are the best judges of these matters, maintain to this day that Ichabod was spirited away by supernatural means; and it is a favorite story often told about the neighborhood round the winter evening fire. The bridge became more than ever an object of superstitious awe, and that may be the reason why the road has been altered of late years, so as to approach the church by the border of the millpond. The school-house, being deserted, soon fell to decay, and was reported to be haunted by the ghost of the unfortunate pedagogue; and the ploughboy, loitering homeward of a still summer evening, has often fancied his voice at a distance, chanting a melancholy psalm-tune, among the tranquil solitudes of Sleepy Hollow.

POSTSCRIPT, FOUND IN THE HANDWRITING OF MR. KNICKERBOCKER.

The preceding Tale is given, almost in the precise words in which I heard it related at a Corporation meeting of the ancient city of Manhattoes, at which were present many of its sagest and most illustrious burghers. The narrator was a pleasant, shabby, gentlemanly old fellow, in pepper-and-salt clothes, with a sadly humorous face; and one whom I strongly suspected of being poor,—he made such efforts to be entertaining. When his story was concluded, there was much laughter and approbation, particularly from two or three deputy aldermen, who had been asleep the greater part of the time. There was, however, one tall, dry-looking old gentleman, with beetling eyebrows, who maintained a grave and rather severe face throughout; now and then folding his arms, inclining his head, and looking down upon the floor, as if turning a doubt over in his mind. He was one of your wary men, who never laugh, but on good grounds—when they have reason and the law on their side. When the mirth of the rest of the company had subsided and silence was restored, he leaned one arm on the elbow of his chair, and sticking the other akimbo, demanded, with a slight but exceedingly sage motion of the head, and contraction of the brow, what was the moral of the story, and what it went to prove?

The story-teller, who was just putting a glass of wine to his lips, as a refreshment after his toils, paused for a moment, looked at his inquirer with an

[9]Small claims court, restricted to cases involving ten pounds in money value.

air of infinite deference, and, lowering the glass slowly to the table, observed, that the story was intended most logically to prove:

"There is no situation in life but has its advantages and pleasures—provided we will but take a joke as we find it;

"That, therefore, he that runs races with goblin troopers is likely to have rough riding of it.

"*Ergo*, for a country schoolmaster to be refused the hand of a Dutch heiress, is a certain step to high preferment in the state."

The cautious old gentleman knit his brows tenfold closer after this explanation, being sorely puzzled by ratiocination of the syllogism; while, methought, the one in pepper-and-salt eyed him with something of a triumphant leer. At length he observed, that all this was very well, but still he thought the story a little on the extravagant—there were one or two points on which he had his doubts.

"Faith, sir," replied the story-teller, "as to that matter, I don't believe one half of it myself."

D. K.

A Sunday in London

In a preceding paper I have spoken of an English Sunday in the country and its tranquillizing effect upon the landscape; but where is its sacred influence more strikingly apparent than in the very heart of that great Babel, London? On this sacred day the gigantic monster is charmed into repose. The intolerable din and struggle of the week are at an end. The shops are shut. The fires of forges and manufactories are extinguished, and the sun, no longer obscured by murky clouds of smoke, pours down a sober yellow radiance into the quiet streets. The few pedestrians we meet, instead of hurrying forward with anxious countenances, move leisurely along; their brows are smoothed from the wrinkles of business and care; they have put on their Sunday looks and Sunday manners with their Sunday clothes, and are cleansed in mind as well as in person.

And now the melodious clangor of bells from church-towers summons their several flocks to the fold. Forth issues from his mansion the family of the decent tradesman, the small children in the advance; then the citizen and his comely spouse, followed by the grown-up daughters, with small morocco-bound prayer-books laid in the folds of their pocket-handkerchiefs. The house-maid looks after them from the window, admiring the finery of the family, and receiving, perhaps, a nod and smile from her young mistresses, at whose toilet she has assisted.

Now rumbles along the carriage of some magnate of the city, peradventure an alderman or a sheriff, and now the patter of many feet announces a procession of charity scholars in uniforms of antique cut, and each with a prayer-book under his arm.

The ringing of bells is at an end; the rumbling of the carriages has ceased; the pattering of feet is heard no more; the flocks are folded in ancient churches, cramped up in by-lanes and corners of the crowded city, where the vigilant beadle keeps watch, like the shepherd's dog, round the threshold of the sanctuary. For a time everything is hushed, but soon is heard the deep, pervading sound of the organ, rolling and vibrating through the empty lanes and courts, and the sweet chanting of the choir, making them resound with melody and praise. Never have I been more sensible of the sanctifying effect of church music than when I have heard it thus poured forth, like a river of joy, through the inmost recesses of this great metropolis, elevating it, as it were, from all the sordid pollutions of the week, and bearing the poor world-worn soul on a tide of triumphant harmony to heaven.

The morning service is at an end. The streets are again alive with the congregations returning to their homes, but soon again relapse into silence. Now comes on the Sunday dinner, which to the city tradesman is a meal of some importance. There is more leisure for social enjoyment at the board. Members of the family can now gather together who are separated by the laborious occupations of the week. A school-boy may be permitted on that day to come to the paternal home; an old friend of the family takes his accustomed Sunday seat at the board, tells over his well-known stories, and rejoices young and old with his well-known jokes.

On Sunday afternoon the city pours forth its legions to breathe the fresh air and enjoy the sunshine of the parks and rural environs. Satirists may say what they please about the rural enjoyments of a London citizen on Sunday, but to me there is something delightful in beholding the poor prisoner of the crowded and dusty city enabled thus to come forth once a week and throw himself upon the green bosom of Nature. He is like a child restored to the mother's breast, and they who first spread out these noble parks and magnificent pleasure-grounds which surround this huge metropolis have done at least as much for its health and morality as if they had expended the amount of cost in hospitals, prisons, and penitentiaries.

FROM *A Tour on the Prairies*

Irving returned to the United States in 1832 after seventeen years abroad, intending to publish an American book. The accounts of the Western country intrigued him, and that same year he set out with H. L. Ellsworth, commissioner in charge of the removal of the Indians to the southwest, traveling down the Ohio and Mississippi to St. Louis, up the Missouri to Independence, on horseback across Indian country to Fort Gibson, Arkansas, and beyond into Pawnee country. He kept a rather scanty set of notes which he expanded into *A Tour on the Prairies,* published in 1835, his first book written about America since the *Knickerbocker History.* It is clear that Irving simply did not know what to do with such new experiences as buffalo, savages, frontiersmen, and this broad new country. A cultivated, urbanized man, he could not record his observations without romanticizing them so that the picture of the West which emerged was an idealized, Europeanized version of what wild nature should look like. Thus he reacts to what he sees in terms of what he knows—seeing an Indian on horseback as a museum object, a frontier scout and his Indian companion as "preux chevalier" and squire, and Gothic castles in the Arkansas forest. The text follows the London edition of 1835.

Chapter VII

In the morning early, (Oct. 12,) the two Creeks who had been sent express by the commander of Fort Gibson, to stop the company of rangers, arrived at our encampment on their return. They had left the company encamped about fifty miles distant, in a fine place on the Arkansas, abounding in game, where they intended to await our arrival. This news spread animation throughout our party, and we set out on our march, at sunrise, with renewed spirit.

In mounting our steeds, the young Osage attempted to throw a blanket upon his wild horse. The fine, sensitive animal took fright, reared and recoiled. The attitudes of the wild horse and the almost naked savage would have formed studies for a painter or a statuary.

I often pleased myself, in the course of our march, with noticing the appearance of the young Count and his newly enlisted follower, as they rode before me. Never was preux chevalier better suited with an esquire. The Count was well mounted, and, as I have before observed, was a bold and graceful rider. He was fond, too, of caracoling his horse, and dashing about in the buoyancy of youthful spirits. His dress was a gay Indian hunting-frock, of dressed deer-skin, setting well to the shape, dyed of a beautiful purple, and fancifully embroidered with silks of various colors; as if it had been the work of some Indian beauty, to decorate a favorite chief. With this he wore leathern pantaloons and moccasins, a foraging-cap, and a double-barrelled gun slung by a bandoleer athwart his back: so that he was quite a picturesque figure as he managed gracefully his spirited steed.

The young Osage would ride close behind him on his wild and beautifully mottled horse, which was decorated with crimson tufts of hair. He rode, with his finely shaped head and bust naked; his blanket being girt round his waist. He carried his rifle in one hand, and managed his horse with the other, and seemed ready to dash off at a moment's warning, with his youthful leader, on any madcap foray or scamper. The Count, with the sanguine anticipations of youth, promised himself many hardy adventures and exploits in company with his youthful "brave," when we should get among the buffaloes, in the Pawnee hunting-grounds.

After riding some distance, we crossed a narrow, deep stream, upon a solid bridge, the remains of an old beaver dam; the industrious community which had constructed it had all been destroyed. Above us, a streaming flight of wild geese, high in air, and making a vociferous noise, gave note of the waning year.

About half-past ten o'clock we made a halt in a forest, where there was abundance of pea-vine. Here we turned the horses loose to graze. A fire was made, water procured from an adjacent spring, and in a short time our little Frenchman, Tonish, had a pot of coffee prepared for our refreshment. While partaking of it, we were joined by an old Osage, one of a small hunting party who had recently passed this way. He was in search of his horse, which had wandered away, or been stolen. Our half-breed, Beatte, made a wry face on hearing of Osage hunters in this direction. "Until we pass those hunters," said he, "we shall see no buffaloes. They frighten away everything like a prairie on fire."

The morning repast being over, the party amused themselves in various ways. Some shot with their rifles at mark, others lay asleep half buried in the deep bed of foliage, with their heads resting on their saddles; others gossiped round the fire at the foot of a tree, which sent up wreaths of blue smoke among the branches. The horses banqueted luxuriously on the pea-vines, and some lay down and rolled amongst them.

We were overshadowed by lofty trees, with straight, smooth trunks, like stately columns; and as the glancing rays of the sun shone through the transparent leaves, tinted with the many-colored hues of autumn, I was reminded of the effect of sunshine among the stained windows and clustering columns of a Gothic cathedral. Indeed there is a grandeur and solemnity in our spacious forests of the West, that awaken in me the same feeling I have experienced in those vast and venerable piles, and the sound of the wind sweeping through them supplies occasionally the deep breathings of the organ.

About noon the bugle sounded to horse, and we were again on the march, hoping to arrive at the encampment of the rangers before night; as the old Osage had assured us it was not above ten or twelve miles distant. In our course through a forest, we passed by a lonely pool, covered with the most magnificent water-lilies I have ever beheld; among which swam several wood-ducks, one of the most beautiful of water-fowl, remarkable for the gracefulness and brilliancy of its plumage.

After proceeding some distance farther, we came down upon the banks of the Arkansas, at a place where tracks of numerous horses, all entering the water, showed where a party of Osage hunters had recently crossed the river on their way to the buffalo range. After letting our horses drink in the river, we continued along its bank for a space, and then across prairies, where we saw a distant smoke, which we hoped might proceed from the encampment of the rangers. Following what we supposed to be their trail, we came to a meadow in which were a number of horses grazing; they were not, however, the horses of the troop. A little farther on, we reached a straggling Osage village, on the banks of the Arkansas. Our arrival created quite a sensation. A number of old men came forward and shook hands with us all severally; while the women and children huddled together in groups, staring at us wildly, chattering and laughing among themselves. We found that all the young men of the village had departed on a hunting expedition, leaving the women and children and old men behind. Here the Commissioner made a speech from on horseback; informing his hearers of the purport of his mission, to promote a general peace among the tribes of the West, and urging them to lay aside all warlike and bloodthirsty notions, and not to make any wanton attacks upon the Pawnees. This speech being interpreted by Beatte, seemed to have a most pacifying effect upon the multitude, who promised faithfully that, as far as in them lay, the peace should not be disturbed; and indeed their age and sex gave some reason to trust that they would keep their word.

Still hoping to reach the camp of the rangers before nightfall, we pushed on until twilight, when we were obliged to halt on the borders of a ravine. The rangers bivouacked under trees, at the bottom of the dell, while we pitched our tent on a rocky knoll near a running stream. The night came on dark and overcast, with flying clouds, and much appearance of rain. The fires of the rangers burnt brightly in the dell, and threw strong masses of light upon the robber-looking groups that were cooking, eating, and drinking around them. To add to the wildness of the scene, several Osage Indians, visitors from the village we had passed, were mingled among the men. Three of them came and seated themselves by our fire. They watched everything that was going on round them in silence, and looked like figures of monumental bronze. We gave them food, and, what they most relished, coffee; for the Indians partake in the universal fondness for this beverage, which pervades the West. When they had made their supper, they stretched themselves side by side before the fire, and began a low nasal chant, drumming with their hands upon their breasts by way of accompaniment. Their chant seemed to consist of regular staves, every one terminating, not in a melodious cadence, but in the abrupt interjection huh! uttered almost like a hiccup. This chant, we were told by our interpreter, Beatte, related to ourselves, our appearance, our treatment of them, and all that they knew of our plans. In one part they spoke of the young Count, whose animated character and eagerness for Indian enterprise had struck their fancy, and they indulged in some waggery about him and the young Indian beauties, that produced great merriment among our half-breeds.

This mode of improvising is common throughout the savage tribes; and in this way, with a few simple inflections of the voice, they chant all their exploits in war and hunting, and occasionally indulge in a vein of comic humor and dry satire, to which the Indians appear to me much more prone than is generally imagined.

In fact, the Indians that I have had an opportunity of seeing in real life are quite different from those described in poetry. They are by no means the stoics that they are represented: taciturn, unbending, without a tear or a smile. Taciturn they are, it is true, when in company with white men, whose good-will they distrust, and whose language they do not understand; but the white man is equally taciturn under like circumstances. When the Indians are among themselves, however, there cannot be greater gossips. Half their time is taken up in talking over their adventures in war and hunting, and in telling whimsical stories. They are great mimics and buffoons, also, and entertain themselves excessively at the expense of the whites with whom they have associated, and who have supposed them impressed with profound respect for their grandeur and dignity. They are curious observers, noting everything in silence, but with a keen and watchful eye; occasionally exchanging a glance or a grunt with each other, when anything particularly strikes them; but reserving all comments until they are alone. Then it is that they give full scope to criticism, satire, mimicry, and mirth.

In the course of my journey along the frontier I have had repeated opportunities of noticing their excitability and boisterous merriment at their games; and have occasionally noticed a group of Osages sitting round a fire until a late hour at night, engaged in the most animated and lively conversation; and at times making the woods resound with peals of laughter. As to tears, they have them in abundance, both real and affected; at times they make a merit of them. No one weeps more bitterly or profusely at the death of a relative or friend; and they have stated times when they repair to howl and lament at their graves. I have heard doleful wailings at daybreak in the neighboring Indian villages, made by some of the inhabitants, who go out at that hour into the fields to mourn and weep for the dead; at such times, I am told, the tears will stream down their cheeks in torrents.

As far as I can judge, the Indian of poetical fiction is, like the shepherd of pastoral romance, a mere personification of imaginary attributes.

The nasal chant of our Osage guests gradually died away; they covered their heads with their blankets and fell fast asleep, and in a little while all was silent, excepting the pattering of scattered raindrops upon our tent.

In the morning our Indian visitors breakfasted with us, but the young Osage who was to act as esquire to the Count in his knight-errantry on the prairies, was nowhere to be found. His wild horse, too, was missing, and, after many conjectures, we came to the conclusion that he had taken "Indian leave" of us in the night. We afterwards ascertained that he had been persuaded so to do by the Osages we had recently met with; who had represented to him the perils that would attend him in an expedition to the Pawnee hunting-grounds, where he might fall into the hands of the implacable enemies of his tribe; and, what was scarcely less to be apprehended, the annoyances to which he would be subjected from the capricious and overbearing conduct of the white men; who, as I have witnessed in my own short experience, are prone to treat the poor Indians as little better than brute animals. Indeed, he had had a specimen of it himself in the narrow escape he made from the infliction of "Lynch's law," by the hard-winking worthy of the frontier, for the flagitious crime of finding a stray horse.

The disappearance of the youth was generally regretted by our party, for we had all taken a great fancy to him from his handsome, frank, and manly appearance, and the easy grace of his deportment. He was indeed a native-born gentleman. By none, however, was he so much lamented as by the young Count, who thus suddenly found himself deprived of his esquire. I regretted the departure of the Osage for his own sake, for we should have cherished him throughout the expedition, and I am convinced, from the munificent spirit of his patron, he would have returned to his tribe laden with wealth of beads and trinkets and Indian blankets.

1835

JAMES FENIMORE COOPER [1789–1851]

COOPER WAS BORN in New Jersey, but when he was only a little more than a year old he was taken to Cooperstown, New York, in territory only recently claimed from the forest and still surrounded by it. At Cooperstown his father, Judge William Cooper, held almost feudal control over the settlement and huge tracts of wilderness-land; young James (he added Fenimore, his mother's family name, to his own later) grew up as a young baronial aristocrat. He was privately educated by an English tutor at Albany, studied at Yale without much interest or distinction, was dismissed after a student prank, shipped out with the merchant marine, and later entered the United States Navy. After marrying Susan DeLancey, daughter of a wealthy and former Tory family, he resigned his midshipman's commission and assumed his inherited role as cultivated country gentleman on his estate in Westchester County, New York.

Cooper drifted into authorship by accident. To prove to his wife that he could write a better book than the sentimental English society novel she was reading, he wrote one of his own, published as *Precaution* (1820), which was good enough to prove his point, but not to satisfy his taste. Thus he began *The Spy* (1821), an absorbing story of the American Revolution, the best novel yet written in America and a highly popular one. Its chief figure, the shrewd, deceptive, furtive peddler, Harvey Birch, who plays the game of double agent to perfection, is one of the major character creations of early American fiction. Cooper moved his next novel to the life he knew as a boy in Cooperstown, and in 1823 published *The Pioneers,* the first of the famous Leatherstocking Tales, which eventually included *The Last of the Mohicans* (1826), *The Prairie* (1827), *The Pathfinder* (1840), and *The Deerslayer* (1841). *The Pioneers* introduced Cooper's second and greatest character creation, Natty Bumppo the noble frontiersman (whose Indian friends Uncas, Chingachgook, and Hardheart were noble savages too), who in his simplicity and freedom embodied all the virtues of wilderness life. Immediately after *The Pioneers* came *The Pilot* (1824), the first of eleven sea novels and the one which introduced Cooper's third major character creation, Long Tom Coffin, the prototype of the tough, wise, salty Yankee sailor. Within three years, therefore, Cooper opened three great veins of native literary materials—the Revolutionary past, the sea, and the frontier—and American fiction was never the same again.

His literary reputation firmly established, Cooper moved to New York City. During the years 1826–33 he traveled extensively in Europe, and on his return became embroiled in a variety of political and literary controversies and an almost equal number of libel suits, most of which he won. A democrat by conviction and an aristocrat by nature and training, Cooper found much in Jackson's America to criticize. He continued to produce books in a steady stream (thirty-two novels alone during his lifetime) but broadened his range to include social criticism, manners, travel, history, biography, political and social commentaries, and satires and allegories, as well as novels of the sea, the frontier, and the American past. The "Littlepage" series, *Satanstoe* (1845), *The Chainbearer* (1846), and *The Redskins* (1846), for example, dealt with the clash between aristocrat and democrat in upstate New York during the Anti-Rent troubles of the eighteen-forties. *The Monikins* (1835), *The Crater* (1848), *Homeward Bound* and *Home as Found* (both 1848) were satires or allegories. *Notions of the Americans* (1828), *A Letter to his Countrymen* (1834), and *The American Democrat* (1838) were constructive critiques of the American system.

Cooper's fictional techniques, drawn from the historical and sentimental novel traditions of the eighteenth and early nineteenth century, were unfortunately already obsolescent before he finished his work, as compared to those developments in the American novel deriving from more sophisticated and expert practitioners such as Poe, Hawthorne, and Melville. His old-fashioned discursive style and his overly theatrical dramatics no longer attract the modern reader, who is often unwilling to accept the conventions of the older tradition within which Cooper wrote. However, within the limits of his artistic techniques and concepts, Cooper's work can still generate power, and his epic of the wilderness, The Leatherstocking Tales, is so much a part of the mainstream of the American mythos that no student of American literature can afford to lack acquaintance with it.

Further reading: Robert E. Spiller, *Fenimore Cooper: Critic of His Times,* 1931. Donald Ringe, *James Fenimore Cooper,* 1962. Henry Nash Smith, *Virgin Land* (especially chaps. 6 and 21), 1950.

FROM *Notions of the Americans*

Cooper, who resented the condescension and ignorance of many Europeans concerning American life and culture, set himself in this book to the task of informing and correcting them. Built about the device of letters presumably written home by an intelligent English traveler in the United States, it represents the earliest of Cooper's several attempts to explain the United States and to defend its character and institutions against foreign criticism. However, it was not especially well received in England, and detracted from his popularity abroad. Text: From the first edition of 1828, Philadelphia; subtitled "Picked Up by a Travelling Bachelor."

[Problems of a Native Literature]

The literature of the United States has, indeed, two powerful obstacles to conquer before (to use a mercantile expression) it can ever enter the markets of its own country on terms of perfect equality with that of England. Solitary and individual works of genius may, indeed, be occasionally brought to light, under the impulses of the high feeling which has conceived them; but, I fear, a good, wholesome, profitable and continued pecuniary support, is the applause that talent most craves. The fact, that an American publisher can get an English work without money, must, for a few years longer, (unless legislative protection shall be extended to their own authors,) have a tendency to repress a national literature. No man will pay a writer for an epic, a tragedy, a sonnet, a history, or a romance, when he can get a work of equal merit for nothing. I have conversed with those who are conversant on the subject, and, I confess, I have been astonished at the information they imparted.

A capital American publisher has assured me that there are not a dozen writers in this country, whose works he should feel confidence in publishing at all, while he reprints hundreds of English books without the least hesitation. This preference is by no means so much owing to any difference in merit, as to the fact that, when the price of the original author is to be added to the uniform hazard which accompanies all literary speculations, the risk becomes too great. The general taste of the reading world in this country is better than that of England.[1] The fact is both proved and explained by the circumstance that thousands of works that are printed and read in the mother country, are not printed and read here. The publisher on this side of the Atlantic has the advantage of seeing the reviews of every book he wishes to print, and, what is of far more importance, he knows, with the exception of books that he is sure of selling, by means of a name, the decision of the English critics before he makes his choice. Nine times in ten, popularity, which is all he looks for, is a sufficient test of general merit. Thus, while you find every English work of character, or notoriety, on the shelves of an American book-store, you may ask in vain for most of the trash that is so greedily devoured in the circulating libraries of the mother country, and which would be just as eagerly devoured here, had not a better taste been created by a compelled abstinence. That taste must now be overcome before such works could be sold at all.

When I say that books are not rejected here, from any want of talent in the writers, perhaps I ought to explain. I wish to express something a little different. Talent is sure of too many avenues to wealth and honours, in America, to seek, unnecessarily, an unknown and hazardous path. It is better paid in the ordinary pursuits of life, than it would be likely to be paid by an adventure in which an extraordinary and skilful, because practised, foreign competition is certain. Perhaps high talent does not often make the

[1] The writer does not mean that the best taste of America is better than that of England; perhaps it is not quite so good; but, as a whole, the American reading world requires better books than the whole of the English reading world. [Cooper's note.]

trial with the American bookseller; but it is precisely for the reason I have named.

The second obstacle against which American literature has to contend, is in the poverty of materials. There is scarcely an ore which contributes to the wealth of the author, that is found, here, in veins as rich as in Europe. There are no annals for the historian; no follies (beyond the most vulgar and commonplace) for the satirist; no manners for the dramatist; no obscure fictions for the writer of romance; no gross and hardy offences against decorum for the moralist; nor any of the rich artificial auxiliaries of poetry. The weakest hand can extract a spark from the flint, but it would baffle the strength of a giant to attempt kindling a flame with a pudding-stone. I very well know there are theorists who assume that the society and institutions of this country are, or ought to be, particularly favourable to novelties and variety. But the experience of one month, in these States, is sufficient to show any observant man the falsity of their position. The effect of a promiscuous assemblage any where, is to create a standard of deportment; and great liberty permits every one to aim at its attainment. I have never seen a nation so much alike in my life, as the people of the United States, and what is more, they are not only like each other, but they are remarkably like that which common sense tells them they ought to resemble. No doubt, traits of character that are a little peculiar, without, however, being either very poetical, or very rich, are to be found in remote districts; but they are rare, and not always happy exceptions. In short, it is not possible to conceive a state of society in which more of the attributes of plain good sense, or fewer of the artificial absurdities of life, are to be found, than here. There is no costume for the peasant, (there is scarcely a peasant at all,) no wig for the judge, no baton for the general, no diadem for the chief magistrate. The darkest ages of their history are illuminated by the light of truth; the utmost efforts of their chivalry are limited by the laws of God; and even the deeds of their sages and heroes are to be sung in a language that would differ but little from a version of the ten commandments. However useful and respectable all this may be in actual life, it indicates but one direction to the man of genius.

1828

FROM *The American Democrat*

The American Democrat, a careful and incisive analysis of the social and political contexts of contemporary America, remains the clearest statement of Cooper's mature democratic beliefs. In it, he attempted to formulate and to justify his concept of an ideal society in terms of what he considered to be basic American principles. Though nominally a member of Jackson's Democratic party, he was not happy with what he felt were its dangerous "leveling" tendencies, or with the political factionalism and partisanship it seemed to engender. Cooper did not fear democracy, but rather its excesses and abuses, particularly the possibility that the rule of an intelligent majority might degenerate into a tyranny of the masses, and judiciously restrained freedom into unrestrained license. Text: H. L. Mencken, ed., *The American Democrat* (New York, 1931).

[Equality]

Equality, in a social sense, may be divided into that of condition, and that of rights. Equality of condition is incompatible with civilization, and is found only to exist in those communities that are but slightly removed from the savage state. In practice, it can only mean a common misery.

Equality of rights is a peculiar feature of democracies. These rights are properly divided into civil and political, though even these definitions are not to be taken as absolute, or as literally exact.

Under the monarchies of the old world, there exist privileged classes, possessed of exclusive rights. For a long period the nobles were exempted from taxes, and many other charges, advantages that are still enjoyed by them, in certain countries. In England, even, the nobles are entitled to hereditary advantages that are denied to those who are of inferior birth. All these distinctions are done away with in principle, in countries where there exists a professed equality of rights, though there is probably no community that does not make some distinctions between the political privileges of men. If this be true, there is strictly no equality of political rights, any where, although there may be, and is, a nearer approach to an equality of civil rights.

By political rights we understand, the suffrage, eligibility to office, and a condition of things that admits of no distinction between men, unless on principles that are common to all. Thus, though a man is not qualified to vote until he has reached the age of twenty-one, the regulation does not affect political equality, since all are equally subjected to the rule, and all become electors on attaining the same age.

With an equality of civil rights, all men are equal before the law; all classes of the community being liable equally to taxation, military service, jury duties, and to the other impositions attendant on civilization, and no one being exempted from its control, except on general rules, which are dependent on the good of all, instead of the exemption's belonging to the immunities of individuals, estates, or families. An equality of civil rights may be briefly defined to be an absence of privileges.

The distinction between the equality of civil and political rights is material, one implying merely equality before the administration of the law, the other, equality in the power to frame it.

An equality of civil rights is never absolute, but we are to understand by the term, such an equality only, as is compatible with general justice and the relations between the different members of families. Thus, women nowhere possess precisely the same rights as men, or men the same rights as women. The wife, usually, can neither sue nor be sued, while the husband, except in particular cases, is made liable to all legal claims on account of the wife. Minors are deprived of many of their civil rights, or, it would be better to say, do not attain them, until they reach a period of life that has been arbitrarily fixed, and which varies in different countries, according to their several policies.

Neither is equality of political rights ever absolute. In those countries where the suffrage is said to be universal, exceptions exist, that arise from the necessity of things, or from that controlling policy which can never be safely lost sight of in the management of human affairs. The interests of women being thought to be so identified with those of their male relatives as to become, in a great degree, inseparable, females are, almost generally, excluded from the possession of political rights. There can be no doubt that society is greatly the gainer, by thus excluding one half its members, and the half that is best adapted to give a tone to its domestic happiness, from the strife of parties, and the fierce struggles of political controversies. Men are also excluded from political rights previously to having attained the age prescribed by law. Paupers, those who have no fixed abodes, and aliens in law, though their lives may have been principally passed in the country, are also excluded from the enjoyment of political rights, every where. Thus birthright is almost universally made a source of advantage. These exceptions, however, do not very materially affect the principle of political equality, since the rules are general, and have been made solely with a reference to the good of society, or to render the laws less liable to abuses in practice.

It follows, that equality, whether considered in connection with our civil or political rights, must not be taken as a general and absolute condition of society, but as such an equality as depends on principles that are equitable, and which are suited to the actual wants of men.

[Aristocrat and Democrat]

We live in an age when the words aristocrat and democrat are much used, without regard to the real significations. An aristocrat is one of a few who possess the political power of a country; a democrat, one of the many. The words are also properly applied to those who entertain notions favorable to aristocratical or democratical forms of government. Such persons are not necessarily either aristocrats or democrats in fact, but merely so in opinion. Thus a member of a democratical government may have an aristocratical bias, and vice versa.

To call a man who has the habits and opinions of a gentleman, an aristocrat from that fact alone, is an abuse of terms and betrays ignorance of the true principles of government, as well as of the world. It must be an equivocal freedom under which every one is not the master of his own innocent acts and associations; and he is a sneaking democrat indeed who will submit to be dictated to, in those habits over which neither law nor morality assumes a right of control.

Some men fancy that a democrat can only be one who seeks the level, social, mental and moral, of the majority, a rule that would at once exclude all men of refinement, education, and taste from the class. These persons are enemies of democracy, as they at once render it impracticable. They are usually great sticklers for their own associations and habits, too, though unable to comprehend any of a nature that are superior. They are, in truth, aristocrats in principle, though assuming a contrary pretension, the groundwork of all their feelings and arguments being self. Such is not the intention of liberty, whose aim is to leave every man to be the master of his own acts; denying hereditary honors, it is true, as unjust and unnecessary, but not denying the inevitable consequences of civilization.

The law of God is the only rule of conduct in this, as in other matters. Each man should do as he would be done by. Were the question put to the greatest advocate of indiscriminate association, whether he would submit to have his company and habits dictated to him, he would be one of the first to resist the tyranny; for they who are the most rigid in maintaining their own claims in such matters, are usually the loudest in decrying those whom they fancy to be better off than themselves. Indeed, it may be taken as a rule in social intercourse, that he who is the most apt to question the pretensions of others is the most conscious of the doubtful position he himself occupies; thus establishing the very claims he affects to deny, by letting his jealousy of it be seen. Manners, education, and refinement, are positive things, and they bring with them innocent tastes which are productive of high enjoyments; and it is as unjust to deny their possessors their indulgence as it would be to insist on the less fortunate's passing the time they would rather devote to athletic amusements, in listening to operas for which they have no relish, sung in a language they do not understand.

All that democracy means, is as equal a participation in rights as is practicable; and to pretend that social equality is a condition of popular institutions is to assume that the latter are destructive of civilization, for, as nothing is more self-evident than the impossibility of raising all men to the highest standard of tastes and refinement, the alternative would be to reduce the entire community to the lowest. The whole embarrassment on this point exists in the difficulty of making men comprehend qualities they do not themselves possess. We can all perceive the difference between ourselves and our inferiors, but when it comes to a question of the difference between us and our superiors, we fail to appreciate merits of which we have no proper conceptions. In face of this obvious difficulty, there is the safe and just governing rule, already mentioned, or that of permitting every one to be the undisturbed judge of his own habits and associations, so long as they are innocent and do not impair the rights of others to be equally judges for themselves. It follows, that social intercourse must regulate itself, independently of institutions, with the exception that the latter, while they withhold no natural, bestow no factitious advantages beyond those which are inseparable from the rights of property, and general civilization.

In a democracy, men are just as free to aim at the highest attainable places in society, as to attain the largest fortunes; and it would be clearly unworthy of all noble sentiment to say that the grovelling competition for money shall alone be free, while that which enlists all the liberal acquirements and elevated sentiments of the race, is denied the democrat. Such an avowal would be at once a declaration of the inferiority of the system, since nothing but ignorance and vulgarity could be its fruits.

The democratic gentleman must differ in many essential particulars from the aristocratical gentleman, though in their ordinary habits and tastes they are virtually identical. Their principles vary; and, to a slight degree, their deportment accordingly. The democrat, recognizing the right of all to participate in power, will be more liberal in his general sentiments, a quality of superiority in itself; but in conceding this much to his fellow man, he will proudly maintain his own independence of vulgar domination as indispensable to his personal habits. The same principles and manliness that would induce him to depose a royal despot would induce him to resist a vulgar tyrant.

There is no more capital, though more common error, than to suppose him an aristocrat who maintains his independence of habits; for democracy asserts the control of the majority, only, in matters of law, and not in matters of custom. The very object of the institution is the utmost practicable personal liberty, and to affirm the contrary, would be sacrificing the end to the means.

An aristocrat, therefore, is merely one who fortifies his exclusive privileges by positive institutions, and a democrat, one who is willing to admit of a free competition, in all things. To say, however, that the last supposes this competition will lead to nothing, is an assumption that means are employed without any reference to an end. He is the purest democrat who best maintains his rights, and no rights can be dearer to a man of cultivation, than exemptions from unseasonable invasions on his time, by the coarse-minded and ignorant.

PREFACE TO *The Leatherstocking Tales*

Cooper wrote this preface for a new edition of his novels to be published by Putnam's in New York. The novels known as "The Leatherstocking Tales" were not written in order of the development of their chief character, and the series did not begin to display its epic qualities until the third of the five appeared. *The Pioneers* (1823) introduced Leatherstocking, or Natty Bumppo, as an old man living in an upper New York State settlement in 1793, in conflict with the forces of civilization which had already replaced the frontier forest of his youth. In *The Last of the Mohicans* (1826) Cooper returned Natty, now named "Hawkeye," to the French and Indian Wars and Montcalm's siege of Fort Henry in 1757, while in *The Prairie* (1827), laid in the trans-Mississippi West about 1805, he chronicled the aged frontiersman's last days and death. However, in *The Pathfinder* (1840) Cooper returned once more to Natty's youth and the New York State frontier of the 1760's. In *The Deerslayer* (1841), laid there twenty years earlier, he introduced the boy to his first meaningful contact with the Indian and the wilderness, the contact that was to occupy the rest of his life. The text of this and subsequent selections from the novels is that of the Townsend edition of 1859–61, New York, the first definitive edition, also known as the "Darley" edition because of the illustrations by F. O. C. Darley.

This series of Stories, which has obtained the name of "The Leather-Stocking Tales," has been written in a very desultory and inartificial manner. The order in which the several books appeared was essentially different from that in which they would have been presented to the world, had the regular course of their incidents been consulted. In the Pioneers, the first of the series written, the Leather-Stocking is represented as already old, and driven from his early haunts in the forest, by the sound of the axe, and the smoke of the settler. "The Last of the Mohicans," the next book in the order of publication, carried the readers back to a much earlier period in the history of our hero, representing him as middle-aged, and in the fullest vigor of manhood. In the Prairie, his career terminates, and he is laid in his grave. There, it was originally the intention to leave him, in the expectation that, as in the case of the human mass, he would soon be forgotten. But a latent regard for this character induced the author to resuscitate him in "The Pathfinder," a book that was not long after succeeded by "The Deerslayer," thus completing the series as it now exists.

While the five books that have been written were originally published in the order just mentioned, that of the incidents, insomuch as they are connected with the career of their principal character, is, as has been stated, very different. Taking the life of the Leather-Stocking as a guide, "The Deerslayer" should have been the opening book, for in that work he is seen just emerging into manhood; to be succeeded by "The Last of the Mohicans," "The Pathfinder," "The Pioneers," and "The Prairie." This arrangement embraces the order of events, though far from being that in which the books at first appeared. "The Pioneers" was published in 1822; "The Deerslayer" in 1841; making the interval between them nineteen years. Whether these progressive years have had a tendency to lessen the value of the last-named book, by lessening the native fire of its author, or of adding somewhat in the way of improved taste and a more matured judgment, is for others to decide.

If anything from the pen of the writer of these romances is at all to outlive himself, it is, unquestionably, the series of "The Leather-Stocking Tales." To say this, is not to predict a very lasting reputation for the series itself, but simply to express the belief it will outlast any, or all, of the works from the same hand.

It is undeniable that the desultory manner in which "The Leather-Stocking Tales" were written, has, in a measure, impaired their harmony, and otherwise lessened their interest. This is proved by the fate of the two books last published, though probably the two most worthy an enlightened and cultivated reader's notice. If the facts could be ascertained, it is probable the result would show that of all those (in America, in particular) who have read the three first books of the series, not one in ten has a knowledge of the existence even of the two last. Several causes have tended to produce this result. The long interval of time between the appearance of "The Prairie" and that of "The Pathfinder," was itself a reason why the later books of the series should be overlooked. There was no longer novelty to attract attention, and the interest was materially impaired by the manner in which events were necessarily anticipated, in laying the last of the series first before the world. With the generation that is now coming on the stage this fault will be partially removed by the edition contained in the present work, in which the several tales will be arranged solely in reference to their connexion with each other.

The author has often been asked if he had any original in his mind, for the character of Leather-Stocking. In a physical sense, different individuals known to the writer in early life, certainly presented themselves as models, through his recollections; but in a moral sense this man of the forest is purely a creation. The idea of delineating a character that possessed little of civilization but its highest principles as they are exhibited in the uneducated, and all of savage life that is not incompatible with these great rules of conduct, is perhaps natural to the situation in which Natty was placed. He is too proud of his origin to sink into the condition of the wild Indian, and too much a man of the woods not to imbibe as much as was at all desirable, from his friends and companions. In a moral point of view it was the intention to illustrate the effect of seed scattered by the way side. To use his own language, his "gifts" were "white gifts," and he was not disposed to bring on them discredit. On the other hand, removed from nearly all the temptations of civilized life, placed in the best associations of that which is deemed savage, and favorably disposed by nature to improve such advantages, it appeared to the writer that his hero was a fit subject to represent the better qualities of both conditions, without pushing either to extremes.

There was no violent stretch of the imagination, perhaps, in supposing one of civilized associations in childhood, retaining many of his earliest lessons amid the scenes of the forest. Had these early impressions, however, not been sustained by continued, though casual connexion with men of his own color, if not of his own caste, all our information goes to show he would soon have lost every trace of his origin. It is believed that sufficient attention was paid to the particular circumstances in which this individual was placed, to justify the picture of his qualities that has been drawn. The Delawares early attracted the attention of the missionaries, and were a tribe unusually influenced by their precepts and example. In many instances they became Christians, and cases occurred in which their subsequent lives gave proof of the efficacy of the great moral changes that had taken place within them.

A leading character in a work of fiction has a fair right to the aid which can be obtained from a poetical view of the subject. It is in this view, rather than in one more strictly circumstantial, that Leather-Stocking has been drawn. The imagination has no great task in portraying to itself a being removed from the every-day inducements to err, which abound in civilized life, while he retains the best and simplest of his early impressions; who sees God in the forest; hears him in the winds; bows to him in the firmament that o'ercanopies all; submits to his sway in a humble belief of his justice and mercy; in a word, a being who finds the impress of the Deity in all the works of nature, without any of the blots produced by the expedients, and passion, and mistakes of man. This is the most that has been attempted in the character of Leather-Stocking. Had this been done without any of the drawbacks of humanity, the picture would have been, in all probability, more pleasing than just. In order to preserve the *vrai-semblable,* therefore, traits derived from the prejudices, tastes, and even the weaknesses of his youth, have been mixed up with these higher qualities and longings, in a way, it is hoped, to represent a reasonable picture of human nature, without offering to the spectator a "monster of goodness."

It has been objected to these books that they give a more favorable picture of the red man than he deserves. The writer apprehends that much of this objection arises from the habits of those who have made it. One of his critics, on the appearance of the first work in which Indian character was portrayed, objected that its "characters were Indians of the school of Heckewelder, rather than of the school of nature."[1] These words quite probably contain the substance of the true answer to the objection. Heckewelder was an ardent, benevolent missionary, bent on the good of the red man, and seeing in him one who had the soul, reason, and characteristics of a fellow-being. The critic is understood to have been a very distinguished agent of the government, one very familiar with Indians, as they are seen at the councils to treat for the sale of their lands, where little or none of their domestic qualities come in play, and where, indeed, their evil passions are known to have the fullest scope. As just would it be to draw conclusions of the general state of American society from the scenes of the capital, as to suppose that the negotiating of one of these treaties is a fair picture of Indian life.

It is the privilege of all writers of fiction, more particularly when their words aspire to the elevation of romances, to present the *beau-idéal* of their characters to the reader. This it is which constitutes poetry, and to suppose that the red man is to be represented only in the squalid misery or in the degraded moral state that certainly more or less belongs to his condition, is, we apprehend, taking a very narrow view of an author's privileges. Such criticism would have deprived the world of even Homer.

1850

[1] The book by the Moravian missionary, the Reverend John Heckewelder, *Account of the History, Manners, and Customs of the Indian Nations* . . . (1819), was an important source of information for Cooper.

FROM *The Deerslayer*

Deerslayer's killing of his first Indian was a moment of crucial importance in his life, and Cooper prepared for and explored it carefully. There is a ritualistic flavor to the passage, an almost formal treatment of what was, for the boy Natty, his initiation into frontier manhood and the irrevocable loss of his youthful innocence. Each of the antagonists acts out his part in the ceremony according to his nature, with grace, skill, and respect for the other's role. In this passage, as well, Cooper introduces the doctrine of "gifts," the idea that although all men are basically the same in nature, each man has certain "gifts" or propensities, imposed upon him by experience and environment. Thus the white man and the Indian are destined to play out different roles in the wilderness drama, each acting according to his "gifts." (I Corinthians xii.4–13 speaks of the "diversities of gifts . . . , but the same spirit" in all men.)

Chapter VII

"Clear, placid Leman! Thy contrasted lake
With the wild world I dwelt in, is a thing
Which warns me, with its stillness, to forsake
Earth's troubled waters for a purer spring.
This quiet sail is as a noiseless wing
To waft me from distraction: once I loved
Torn ocean's roar, but thy soft murmuring
Sounds sweet as if a sister's voice reproved,
That I with stern delights should e'er have been so moved."
—Byron.

Day had fairly dawned before the young man, whom we have left in the situation described in the last chapter, again opened his eyes. This was no sooner done, than he started up, and looked about him with the eagerness of one who suddenly felt the importance of accurately ascertaining his precise position. His rest had been deep and undisturbed; and when he awoke, it was with a clearness of intellect and a readiness of resources that were much needed at that particular moment. The sun had not risen, it is true, but the vault of heaven was rich with the winning softness that "brings and shuts the day," while the whole air was filled with the carols of birds, the hymns of the feathered tribe. These sounds first told Deerslayer the risks he ran. The air, for wind it could scarce be called, was still light, it is true, but it had increased a little in the course of the night, and as the canoes were mere feathers on the water, they had drifted twice the expected distance; and, what was still more dangerous, had approached so near the base of the mountain that here rose precipitously from the eastern shore, as to render the carols of the birds plainly audible. This was not the worst. The third canoe had taken the same direction, and was slowly drifting towards a point where it must inevitably touch, unless turned aside by a shift of wind, or human hands. In other respects, nothing presented itself to attract attention, or to awaken alarm. The castle stood on its shoal, nearly abreast of the canoes, for the drift had amounted to miles in the course of the night, and the ark lay fastened to its piles, as both had been left so many hours before.

As a matter of course, Deerslayer's attention was first given to the canoe ahead. It was already quite near the point, and a very few strokes of the paddle sufficed to tell him that it must touch before he could possibly overtake it. Just at this moment, too, the wind inopportunely freshened, rendering the drift of the light craft much more rapid and certain. Feeling the impossibility of preventing a contact with the land, the young man wisely determined not to heat himself with unnecessary exertions; but first looking to the priming of his piece, he proceeded slowly and warily towards the point, taking care to make a little circuit, that he might be exposed on only one side, as he approached.

The canoe adrift being directed by no such intelligence, pursued its proper way, and grounded on a small sunken rock, at the distance of three or four yards from the shore. Just at that moment, Deerslayer had got abreast of the point, and turned the bows of his own boat to the land; first casting loose his tow, that his movements might be unencumbered. The canoe hung an instant on the rock; then it rose a hair's-breadth on an almost imperceptible swell of the water, swung round, floated clear, and reached the strand. All this the young man noted, but it neither quickened his pulses nor hastened his hand. If any one had been lying in wait for the arrival of the waif, he must be seen, and the utmost caution in approaching the shore became indispensable; if no one was in ambush, hurry was unnecessary. The point being nearly diagonally opposite to the Indian encampment, he hoped the last, though the former was not only possible, but probable; for the savages were prompt in adopting all the expedients of their particular modes of warfare, and quite likely had many scouts searching the shores for craft to carry them off to the castle. As a glance at the lake from any height or projection would expose the smallest object on its surface, there was little hope that either of the canoes could pass unseen; and Indian sagacity needed no instruction to tell which way a boat or log would drift, when the direction of the wind was known. As Deerslayer drew nearer and nearer to the land, the stroke of his paddle grew slower, his eye became more watchful, and his ears and nostrils almost dilated with the effort to detect any lurking danger. 'Twas a trying moment for a novice, nor was there the encouragement which even the timid sometimes feel, when conscious of being observed and commended. He was entirely alone, thrown on his own resources, and was cheered by no friendly eye, emboldened by no encouraging voice. Notwithstanding all these circumstances, the most experienced veteran in forest warfare could not have behaved better. Equally free from recklessness and hesitation, his advance was marked by a sort of philosophical prudence, that appeared to render him superior to all motives but those which were best calculated to effect his purpose. Such was the commencement of a career in forest exploits, that afterwards rendered this man, in his way, and under the limits of his habits and opportunities, as renowned as many a hero whose name has adorned the pages of works more celebrated than legends simple as ours can ever become.

When about a hundred yards from the shore, Deerslayer rose in the canoe, gave three or four vigorous strokes with the paddle, sufficient of themselves to impel the bark to land, and then quickly laying aside the instrument of labor, he seized that of war. He was in the very act of raising the rifle, when a sharp report was followed by the buzz of a bullet that passed so near his body, as to cause him involuntarily to start. The next instant Deerslayer staggered, and fell his whole length in the bottom of the canoe. A yell—it came from a single voice—followed, and an Indian leaped from the bushes upon the open area of the point, bounding towards the canoe. This was the moment the young man desired. He rose on the instant, and levelled his own rifle at his uncovered foe; but his finger hesitated about pulling the trigger on one whom he held at such a disadvantage. This little delay, probably, saved the life of the Indian, who bounded back into the cover as swiftly as he had broken out of it. In the meantime Deerslayer had been swiftly approaching the land, and his own canoe reached the point just as his enemy disappeared. As its movements had not been directed, it touched the shore a few yards from the other boat; and though the rifle of his foe had to be loaded, there was not time to secure his prize, and to carry it beyond danger, before he would be exposed to another shot. Under the circumstances, therefore, he did not pause an instant, but dashed into the woods and sought a cover.

On the immediate point there was a small open

area, partly in native grass, and partly beach, but a dense fringe of bushes lined its upper side. This narrow belt of dwarf vegetation passed, one issued immediately into the high and gloomy vaults of the forest. The land was tolerably level for a few hundred feet, and then it rose precipitously in a mountain-side. The trees were tall, large, and so free from under-brush, that they resembled vast columns, irregularly scattered, upholding a dome of leaves. Although they stood tolerably close together, for their ages and size, the eye could penetrate to considerable distances; and bodies of men, even, might have engaged beneath their cover, with concert and intelligence.

Deerslayer knew that his adversary must be employed in re-loading, unless he had fled. The former proved to be the case, for the young man had no sooner placed himself behind a tree, than he caught a glimpse of the arm of the Indian, his body being concealed by an oak, in the very act of forcing the leathered bullet home. Nothing would have been easier than to spring forward, and decide the affair by a close assault on his unprepared foe; but every feeling of Deerslayer revolted at such a step, although his own life had just been attempted from a cover. He was yet unpractised in the ruthless expedients of savage warfare, of which he knew nothing except by tradition and theory, and it struck him as an unfair advantage to assail an unarmed foe. His color had heightened, his eye frowned, his lips were compressed, and all his energies were collected and ready; but, instead of advancing to fire, he dropped his rifle to the usual position of a sportsman in readiness to catch his aim, and muttered to himself, unconscious that he was speaking—

"No, no—that may be red-skin warfare, but it's not a Christian's gifts. Let the miscreant charge, and then we'll take it out like men; for the canoe he *must* not, and *shall* not have. No, no; let him have time to load, and God will take care of the right!"

All this time the Indian had been so intent on his own movements, that he was even ignorant that his enemy was in the wood. His only apprehension was, that the canoe would be recovered and carried away before he might be in readiness to prevent it. He had sought the cover from habit, but was within a few feet of the fringe of bushes, and could be at the margin of the forest in readiness to fire in a moment. The distance between him and his enemy was about fifty yards, and the trees were so arranged by nature that the line of sight was not interrupted, except by the particular trees behind which each party stood.

His rifle was no sooner loaded, than the savage glanced around him, and advanced incautiously as regarded the real, but stealthily as respected the fancied position of his enemy, until he was fairly exposed. Then Deerslayer stepped from behind his own cover, and hailed him.

"This-a-way, red-skin; this-a-way, if you're looking for me," he called out. "I'm young in war, but not so young as to stand on an open beach to be shot down like an owl, by daylight. It rests on yourself whether it's peace or war atween us; for my gifts are white gifts, and I'm not one of them that thinks it valiant to slay human mortals, singly, in the woods."

The savage was a good deal startled by this sudden discovery of the danger he ran. He had a little knowledge of English, however, and caught the drift of the other's meaning. He was also too well schooled to betray alarm, but, dropping the butt of his rifle to the earth, with an air of confidence, he made a gesture of lofty courtesy. All this was done with the ease and self-possession of one accustomed to consider no man his superior. In the midst of this consummate acting, however, the volcano that raged within caused his eyes to glare, and his nostrils to dilate, like those of some wild beast that is suddenly prevented from taking the fatal leap.

"Two canoe," he said, in the deep guttural tones of his race, holding up the number of fingers he mentioned, by way of preventing mistakes; "one for you—one for me."

"No, no, Mingo, that will never do. You own neither; and neither shall you have, as long as I can prevent it. I know it's war atween your people and mine, but that's no reason why human mortals should slay each other, like savage creatur's that meet in the woods; go your way, then, and leave me to go mine. The world is large enough for us both; and when we meet fairly in battle, why, the Lord will order the fate of each of us."

"Good!" exclaimed the Indian; "my brother missionary—great talk; all about Manitou."

"Not so—not so, warrior. I'm not good enough for the Moravians, and am too good for most of the other vagabonds that preach about in the woods. No, no, I'm only a hunter, as yet, though afore the peace is made, 'tis like enough there'll be occasion to strike a blow at some of your people. Still, I wish it to be done in fair fight, and not in a quarrel about the ownership of a miserable canoe."

"Good! My brother very young—but he very wise. Little warrior—great talker. Chief, sometimes, in council."

"I don't know this, nor do I say it, Injin," returned Deerslayer, coloring a little at the ill-concealed sarcasm of the other's manner; "I look forward to a life in the woods, and I only hope it may be a peaceable one. All young men must go on the war-path, when there's occasion, but war isn't needfully massacre. I've seen enough of the last, this very night, to know that Providence frowns on it; and I now invite you to go your own way, while I go mine; and hope that we may part fri'nds."

"Good! My brother has two scalp—grey hair under t'other. Old wisdom—young tongue."

Here the savage advanced with confidence, his hand extended, his face smiling, and his whole bearing denoting amity and respect. Deerslayer met his offered friendship in a proper spirit, and they shook hands cordially, each endeavoring to assure the other of his sincerity and desire to be at peace.

"All have his own," said the Indian; "my canoe, mine; your canoe, your'n. Go look; if your'n, you keep; if mine, I keep."

"That's just, red-skin; though you must be wrong in thinking the canoe your property. Howsever, seein' is believin', and we'll go down to the shore, where you may look with your own eyes; for it's likely you'll object to trustin' altogether to mine."

The Indian uttered his favorite exclamation of "good!" and then they walked, side by side, towards the shore. There was no apparent distrust in the manner of either, the Indian moving in advance, as if he wished to show his companion that he did not fear turning his back to him. As they reached the open ground, the former pointed towards Deerslayer's boat, and said emphatically—

"No mine—pale-face canoe. *This* red-man's. No want other man's canoe—want his own."

"You're wrong, red-skin, you're altogether wrong. This canoe was left in old Hutter's keeping, and is his'n according to all law, red or white, till its owner comes to claim it. Here's the seats and the stitching of the bark to speak for themselves. No man ever know'd an Injin to turn off such work."

"Good! My brother little ole—big wisdom. Injin no make him. White man's work."

"I'm glad you think so, for holding out to the contrary might have made ill blood atween us; every one having a right to take possession of his own. I'll just shove the canoe out of reach of dispute at once, as the quickest way of settling difficulties."

While Deerslayer was speaking, he put a foot against the end of the light boat, and giving a vigorous shove, he sent it out into the lake a hundred feet or more, where, taking the true current, it would necessarily float past the point, and be in no further danger of coming ashore. The savage started at this ready and decided expedient, and his companion saw that he cast a hurried and fierce glance at his own canoe, or that which contained the paddles. The change of manner, however, was but momentary, and then the Iroquois resumed his air of friendliness, and a smile of satisfaction.

"Good!" he repeated, with stronger emphasis than ever. "Young head, old mind. Know how to settle quarrel. Farewell, brother. He go to house in water—muskrat house—Injin go to camp; tell chiefs no find canoe."

Deerslayer was not sorry to hear this proposal, for he felt anxious to join the females, and he took the offered hand of the Indian very willingly. The parting words were friendly, and, while the red-man walked calmly towards the wood, with the rifle in the hollow of his arm, without once looking back in uneasiness or distrust, the white man moved towards the remaining canoe, carrying his piece in the same pacific manner, it is true, but keeping his eyes fastened on the movements of the other. This distrust, however, seemed to be altogether uncalled for, and, as if ashamed to have entertained it, the young man averted his look, and stepped carelessly up to his boat. Here he began to push the canoe from the shore, and to make his other preparations for departing. He might have been thus employed a minute, when, happening to turn his face towards the land, his quick and certain eye told him, at a glance, the imminent jeopardy in which his life was placed. The black, ferocious eyes of the savage were glancing on him, like those of the crouching tiger, through a small opening in the bushes, and the muzzle of his rifle seemed already to be opening in a line with his own body.

Then, indeed, the long practice of Deerslayer, as a hunter, did him good service. Accustomed to fire with the deer on the bound, and often when the precise position of the animal's body had in a manner to be guessed at, he used the same expedients here. To cock and poise his rifle were the acts of a single moment and a single motion; then, aiming almost without sighting, he fired into the bushes where he knew a body ought to be, in order to sustain the appalling countenance which alone was visible. There was not time to raise the piece any higher, or to take a more deliberate aim. So rapid were his movements, that both parties discharged their pieces at the same instant, the concussions mingling in one report. The mountains, indeed, gave back but a single echo. Deerslayer dropped his piece, and stood, with head erect, steady as one of the pines in the calm of a June morning, watching the result; while the savage gave the yell that has become historical for its appalling influence, leaped through the bushes and came bounding across the open ground, flourishing a tomahawk. Still Deerslayer moved not, but stood with his unloaded rifle fallen against his shoulders, while, with a hunter's habits, his hands were mechanically feeling for the powder-horn and charger. When about forty feet from his enemy, the savage hurled his keen weapon; but it was with an eye so vacant, and a hand so unsteady and feeble, that the young man caught it by the handle as it was flying past him. At that instant the Indian staggered and fell his whole length on the ground.

"I know'd it—I know'd it!" exclaimed Deerslayer, who was already preparing to force a fresh bullet into his rifle; "I know'd it must come to this, as soon as I had got the range from the creatur's eyes. A man sights suddenly, and fires quick, when his own life's in danger; yes, I know'd it would come to this. I was about the hundredth part of a second too quick for him, or it might have been bad for me! The riptyle's bullet has just grazed my side—but, say what you will for or ag'in 'em, a red-skin is by no means as sartain with powder and ball as a white man. Their gifts don't seem to lie that-a-way. Even Chingachgook, great as he is in other matters, isn't downright deadly with the rifle."

By this time the piece was reloaded, and Deerslayer, after tossing the tomahawk into the canoe, advanced to his victim, and stood over him, leaning on his rifle, in melancholy attention. It was the first instance in which he had seen a man fall in battle—it was the first fellow-creature against whom he had ever seriously raised his own hand. The sensations were novel; and regret, with the freshness of our better feelings, mingled with his triumph. The Indian was not dead, though shot directly through the body. He lay on his back motionless, but his eyes, now full of consciousness, watched each action of his victor—as the fallen bird regards the fowler—jealous of every movement. The man probably expected the fatal blow which was to precede the loss of his scalp; or perhaps he anticipated that this latter act of cruelty would precede his death. Deerslayer read his thoughts; and he found a melancholy satisfaction in relieving the apprehensions of the helpless savage.

"No, no, red-skin," he said; "you've nothing more to fear from me. I am of a Christian stock, and scalping is not of my gifts. I'll just make sartain of your rifle, and then come back and do you what sarvice I can. Though here I can't stay much longer, as the crack of three rifles will be apt to bring some of your devils down upon me."

The close of this was said in a sort of a soliloquy, as the young man went in quest of the fallen rifle. The piece was found where its owner had dropped it, and was immediately put into the canoe. Laying his own rifle at its side, Deerslayer then returned and stood over the Indian again.

"All inmity atween you and me's at an ind, red-skin," he said; "and you may set your heart at rest on the score of the scalp, or any further injury. My gifts are white, as I've told you; and I hope my conduct will be white also!"

Could looks have conveyed all they meant, it is probable Deerslayer's innocent vanity on the subject of color would have been rebuked a little; but he comprehended the gratitude that was expressed in the eyes of the dying savage, without in the least detecting the bitter sarcasm that struggled with the better feeling.

"Water!" ejaculated the thirsty and unfortunate creature; "give poor Injin water."

"Aye, water you shall have, if you drink the lake dry. I'll just carry you down to it, that you may take your fill. This is the way, they tell me, with all wounded people—water is their greatest comfort and delight."

So saying, Deerslayer raised the Indian in his arms, and carried him to the lake. Here he first helped him to take an attitude in which he could appease his burning thirst; after which he seated himself on a stone, and took the head of his wounded adversary in his own lap, and endeavored to soothe his anguish in the best manner he could.

"It would be sinful in me to tell you your time hadn't come, warrior," he commenced, "and therefore I'll not say it. You've passed the middle age already, and, considerin' the sort of lives ye lead, your days have been pretty well filled. The principal thing now, is to look forward to what comes next. Neither red-skin nor pale-face, on the whole, calculates much on sleepin' for ever; but both expect to live in another world. Each has his gifts, and will be judged by 'em, and, I suppose, you've thought these matters over enough, not to stand in need of sarmons when the trial comes. You'll find your happy hunting-grounds, if you've been a just Injin; if an onjust, you'll meet your desarts in another way. I've my own idees about these things; but you're too old and exper'enced to need any explanations from one as young as I."

"Good!" ejaculated the Indian, whose voice retained its depth even as life ebbed away; "young head—ole wisdom!"

"It's sometimes a consolation, when the ind comes, to know that them we've harmed, or *tried* to harm, forgive us. I suppose natur' seeks this relief, by way of getting a pardon on 'arth; as we never can know whether He pardons, who is all in all, till judgment itself comes. It's soothing to know that *any* pardon at such times; and that, I conclude, is the secret. Now, as for myself, I overlook altogether your designs ag'in my life; first, because no harm came of 'em; next, because it's your gifts, and natur', and trainin', and I ought not to have trusted you at all; and, finally and chiefly, because I can bear no ill-will to a dying man, whether heathen or Christian. So put your heart at ease, so far as I'm consarned; you know best what other matters ought to trouble you, or what ought to give you satisfaction in so trying a moment."

It is probable that the Indian had some of the fearful glimpses of the unknown state of being which God in mercy seems at times to afford to all the human race; but they were necessarily in conformity with his habits and prejudices. Like most of his people, and like too many of our own, he thought more of dying in a way to gain applause among those he left than to secure a better state of existence hereafter. While Deerslayer was speaking, his mind was a little bewildered, though he felt that the intention was good; and when he had done, a regret passed over his spirit that none of his own tribe were present to witness his stoicism, under extreme bodily suffering, and the firmness with which he met his end. With the high innate courtesy that so often distinguishes the Indian warrior before he becomes corrupted by too much intercourse with the worst class of the white men, he endeavored to express his thankfulness for the other's good intentions, and to let him understand that they were appreciated.

"Good!" he repeated, for this was an English word much used by the savages—"good—young head; young *heart,* too. *Old* heart tough; no shed tear. Hear Indian when he die, and no want to lie—what he call him?"

"Deerslayer is the name I bear now, though the Delawares have said that when I get back from this war-path, I shall have a more manly title, provided I can 'arn one."

"That good name for boy—poor name for warrior. He get better quick. No fear *there*"—the savage had strength sufficient, under the strong excitement he felt, to raise a hand and tap the young man on his breast—"eye sartain—finger lightning—aim, death—great warrior soon. No Deerslayer—Hawkeye—Hawkeye—Hawkeye. Shake hand."

Deerslayer—or Hawkeye, as the youth was then first named, for in after years he bore the appellation throughout all that region—Deerslayer took the hand of the savage, whose last breath was drawn in that attitude, gazing in admiration at the countenance of a stranger, who had shown so much readiness, skill, and firmness, in a scene that was equally trying and novel. When the reader remembers it is the highest gratification an Indian can receive to see his enemy betray weakness, he will be better able to appreciate the conduct which had extorted so great a concession at such a moment.

"His spirit has fled!" said Deerslayer, in a suppressed, melancholy voice. "Ah's me! Well, to this we must all come, sooner or later; and he is happiest, let his skin be of what color it may, who is best fitted to meet it. Here lies the body of no doubt a brave warrior, and the soul is already flying towards its heaven or hell, whether that be a happy hunting-ground, a place scant of game; regions of glory, according to Moravian doctrine, or flames of fire! So it happens, too, as regards other matters! Here have old Hutter and Hurry Harry got themselves into difficulty, if they hav'n't got themselves into torment and death, and all for a bounty that luck offers to me in what many would think a lawful and suitable manner. But not a farthing of such money shall cross my hand. White I was born, and white will I die; clinging to color to the last, even though the King's Majesty, his governors, and all his councils, both at home and in the Colonies, forget from what they come, and where they hope to go, and all for a little advantage in warfare. No, no—warrior, hand of mine shall never molest your scalp, and so your soul may rest in peace on the p'int of making a decent appearance, when the body comes to join it, in your own land of spirits."

Deerslayer arose as soon as he had spoken. Then he placed the body of the dead man in a sitting posture, with its back against the little rock, taking the necessary care to prevent it from falling or in any way settling into an attitude that might be thought unseemly by the sensitive, though wild notions of a savage. When this duty was performed, the young man stood gazing at the grim countenance of his fallen foe, in a sort of melancholy abstraction. As was his practice, however, a habit gained by living so much alone in the forest, he then began again to give utterance to his thoughts and feelings aloud.

"I didn't wish your life, red-skin," he said, "but you left me no choice atween killing or being killed. Each party acted according to his gifts, I suppose, and blame can light on neither. You were treacherous, according to your natur' in war, and I was a little oversightful, as I'm apt to be in trusting others. Well, this is my first battle with a human mortal, though it's not likely to be the last. I have fou't most of the creatur's of the forest, such as bears, wolves, painters, and catamounts, but this is the beginning with the red-skins. If I was Injin born, now, I might tell of this, or carry in the scalp, and boast of the expl'ite afore the whole tribe; or, if my inimy had only been even a bear, 'twould have been nat'ral and proper to let everybody know what had happened; but I don't well see how I'm to let even Chingachgook into this secret, so long as it can be done only by boasting with a white tongue. And why should I wish to boast of it a'ter all? It's slaying a human, although he was a savage; and how do I know that he was a just Injin; and that he has not been taken away suddenly to anything but happy hunting-grounds. When it's onsartain whether good or evil has been done, the wisest way is not to be boastful—still, I *should* like Chingachgook to know that I haven't discredited the Delawares or my training!"

Part of this was uttered aloud, while part was merely muttered between the speaker's teeth; his more confident opinions enjoying the first advantage, while his doubts were expressed in the latter mode. Soliloquy and reflection received a startling interruption, however, by the sudden appearance of a second Indian on the lake shore, a few hundred yards from the point. This man, evidently another scout, who had probably been drawn to the place by the reports of the rifles, broke out of the forest with so little caution that Deerslayer caught a view of his person before he was himself discovered. When the latter event did occur, as was the case a moment later, the savage gave a loud yell, which was answered by a dozen voices from different parts of the mountain-side. There was no longer any time for delay; in another minute the boat was quitting the shore under long and steady sweeps of the paddle.

As soon as Deerslayer believed himself to be at a safe distance, he ceased his efforts, permitting the little bark to drift, while he leisurely took a survey of the state of things. The canoe first sent adrift was floating before the air, quite a quarter of a mile above him, and a little nearer to the shore than he wished, now that he knew more of the savages were so near at hand. The canoe shoved from the point was within a few yards of him, he having directed his own course towards it on quitting the land. The dead Indian lay in grim quiet where he had left him, the warrior who had shown himself from the forest had already vanished, and the woods themselves were as silent and seemingly deserted as the day they came fresh from the hands of their great Creator. This profound stillness, however, lasted but a moment. When time had been given to the scouts of the enemy to reconnoitre, they burst out of the thicket upon the naked point, filling the air with yells of fury at discovering the death of their companion. These cries were immediately succeeded by shouts of delight when they reached the body and clustered eagerly around it. Deerslayer was a sufficient adept in the usages of the natives to understand the reason of the change. The yell was the customary lamentation at the loss of a warrior, the shout a sign of rejoicing that the conqueror had not been able to secure the scalp; the trophy, without which a victory is never considered complete. The distance at which the canoes lay probably prevented any attempts to injure the conqueror, the American Indian, like the panther of his own woods, seldom making any effort against his foe unless tolerably certain it is under circumstances that may be expected to prove effective.

As the young man had no longer any motive to remain near the point, he prepared to collect his canoes, in order to tow them off to the castle. That nearest was soon in tow, when he proceeded in quest of the other, which was all this time floating up the lake. The eye of Deerslayer was no sooner fastened on this last boat, than it struck him that it was nearer to the shore than it would have been had it merely followed the course of the gentle current of air. He began to suspect the influence of some unseen current in the water, and he quickened his exertions, in order to regain possession of it before it could drift in to a dangerous proximity to the woods. On getting nearer, he thought that the canoe had a perceptible motion through the water, and, as it lay broadside to the air, that this motion was taking it towards the land. A few vigorous strokes of the paddle carried him still nearer, when the mystery was explained. Something was evidently in motion on the off-side of the canoe or that which was furthest from himself, and closer scrutiny showed that it was a naked human arm. An Indian was lying in the bottom of the canoe, and was propelling it slowly, but certainly, to the shore, using his hand as a paddle. Deerslayer understood the whole artifice at a glance. A savage had swum off to the boat while he was occupied with his enemy on the point, got possession, and was using these means to urge it to the shore.

Satisfied that the man in the canoe could have no arms, Deerslayer did not hesitate to dash close alongside of the retiring boat, without deeming it necessary to raise his own rifle. As soon as the wash of the water, which he made in approaching, became audible to the prostrate savage, the latter sprang to his feet, and uttered an exclamation that proved how completely he was taken by surprise.

"If you've enj'yed yourself enough in that canoe, red-skin," Deerslayer coolly observed, stopping his own career in sufficient time to prevent an absolute collision between the two boats—"if you've enj'yed yourself enough in that canoe, you'll do a prudent act by taking to the lake ag'in. I'm reasonable in these matters, and don't crave your blood, though there's them about that would look upon you more as a due-bill for the bounty than a human mortal. Take to the lake this minute, afore we get to hot words."

The savage was one of those who did not understand a word of English, and he was indebted to the gestures of Deerslayer, and to the expression of an eye that did not often deceive, for an imperfect comprehension of his meaning. Perhaps, too, the sight of the rifle that lay so near the hand of the white man quickened his decision. At all events, he crouched like a tiger about to take his leap, uttered a yell, and the next instant his naked body disappeared in the water. When he rose to take breath, it was at the distance of several yards from the canoe, and the hasty glance he threw behind him denoted how much he feared the arrival of a fatal messenger from the rifle of his foe. But the young man made no indication of any hostile intention. Deliberately securing the canoe to the others, he began to paddle from the shore; and by the time the Indian reached the land, and had shaken himself, like a spaniel on quitting the water, his dreaded enemy was already beyond rifle-shot on his way to the castle. As was so much his practice, Deerslayer did not fail to soliloquize on what had just occurred, while steadily pursuing his course towards the point of destination.

"Well, well"—he commenced—" 'twould have been wrong to kill a human mortal without an object. Scalps are of no account with me, and life is sweet, and ought not to be taken marcilessly by them that have white gifts. The savage was a Mingo, it's true; and I make no doubt he is, and will be as long as he lives, a ra'al riptyle and vagabond; but that's no reason I should forget my gifts and color. No, no—let him go; if ever we meet ag'in, rifle in hand, why then 'twill be seen which has the stoutest heart and the quickest eye. Hawkeye! That's not a bad name for a warrior, sounding much more manful and valiant than Deerslayer! 'Twouldn't be a bad title to begin with, and it has been fairly 'arned. If 'twas Chingachgook, now, he might go home and boast of his deeds, and the chiefs would name him Hawkeye in a minute; but it don't become white blood to brag, and 'tisn't easy to see how the matter can be known unless I do. Well, well—everything is in the hands of Providence; this affair as well as another; I'll trust to that for getting my desarts in all things."

Having thus betrayed what might be termed his weak spot, the young man continued to paddle in silence, making his way diligently, and as fast as his tows would allow him, towards the castle. By this time the sun had not only risen, but it had appeared over the eastern mountains, and was shedding a flood of glorious light on this as yet unchristened sheet of water. The whole scene was radiant with beauty; and no one unaccustomed to the ordinary history of the woods would fancy it had so lately witnessed incidents so ruthless and barbarous. As he approached the building of old Hutter, Deerslayer thought, or rather *felt*, that its appearance was in singular harmony with all the rest of the scene. Although nothing had been consulted but strength and security, the rude, massive logs, covered with their rough bark, the projecting roof, and the form, would contribute to render the building picturesque in almost any situation, while its actual position added novelty and piquancy to its other points of interest.

When Deerslayer drew nearer to the castle, however, objects of interest presented themselves that at once eclipsed any beauties that might have distinguished the scenery of the lake, and the site of the singular edifice. Judith and Hetty stood on the platform before the door, Hurry's door-yard, awaiting his approach with manifest anxiety; the former, from time to time, taking a survey of his person and of the canoes through the old ship's spy-glass that has been already mentioned. Never probably did this girl seem more brilliantly beautiful than at that moment; the flush of anxiety and alarm increasing her color to its richest tints, while the softness of her eyes, a charm that even poor Hetty shared with her, was deepened by intense concern. Such, at least, without pausing or pretending to analyse motives, or to draw any other very nice distinctions between cause and effect, were the opinions of the young man, as his canoes reached the side of the ark, where he carefully fastened all three before he put his foot on the platform.

1841

WILLIAM CULLEN BRYANT [1794–1878]

In an autobiographical account of his early years Bryant tells of his birth at Cummington, in the Berkshire hills of Massachusetts; of his father, a poetry-loving physician, and of his mother, descended from John and Priscilla Alden; of his maternal grandfather, a devout Calvinist in whose home he spent much of his childhood; of his enthusiasm over Pope and the great neoclassic writers; and of his early determination to be a poet himself. Born into a conservative Federalist country family, far from Boston and urban sophistication, young Bryant was raised in an atmosphere of old-fashioned New England morality and seriousness. He began writing poems at the age of eight, and at fourteen published his first poem, a neoclassic satire against Jefferson called "The Embargo." After study at Williams College and his admission to the law, his horizons broadened, the range of his poetry widened, his skill at his craft advanced, and his own ideas were modified by his discovery of Wordsworthian romanticism and Jacksonian politics. After the publication of his first volume of *Poems* (1821), young Bryant was regarded, until the rise of Longfellow's popularity, as America's leading poet, and he continued to be second only to Longfellow in public esteem for the next two generations.

In 1825 Bryant moved to New York, entered journalism, and in 1829, after two years as its assistant editor, became editor of the powerful New York *Evening Post,* a position he held for the next forty-nine years. Under his editorship the *Post* became the leading liberal newspaper of the period; in its editorial columns Bryant supported free speech, trade unionism, collective bargaining, legal and penal reform, the abolition of slavery, and Democratic administrations from Jackson to Pierce. He joined the new Republican Party in 1855, supported Lincoln and the Civil War, and after it joined in the reform movements in politics which succeeded the Grant administration.

Bryant's career as a journalist reduced the amount of his poetic output, but never submerged it. He continued to write poetry, to lecture about it, and to edit his own and others' volumes. He also spent years on a translation of the *Iliad* and the *Odyssey,* which appeared in 1870 and 1872, and he never hesitated to lend his support to liberal causes. He died, in fact, after exposing himself to the elements in his eightieth year during an outdoor tribute to the Italian patriot Mazzini in Central Park.

Further reading: *William Cullen Bryant: Representative Selections,* ed. Tremaine McDowell, 1935. Howard H. Peckham, *Gotham Yankee: A Biography of William Cullen Bryant,* 1950.

Thanatopsis

Bryant apparently began this poem, the most famous he ever wrote and one of his most characteristic, when he was sixteen. In its original version it began with "Yet a few days . . ." (line 17) and ended with ". . . and make their bed with thee" (line 66), suggesting that it was a fragment, a fashionable device in contemporary poetry. In 1821 he added the present introduction and conclusion. The text of this and subsequent poems is that of Bryant's own edition of *Poems: Collected and Arranged by the Author* (New York, 1865). The Greek "thanatopsis" means "view of death."

To him who in the love of Nature holds
Communion with her visible forms, she speaks
A various language; for his gayer hours
She has a voice of gladness, and a smile
And eloquence of beauty, and she glides
Into his darker musings, with a mild

And healing sympathy, that steals away
Their sharpness ere he is aware. When thoughts
Of the last bitter hour come like a blight
Over thy spirit, and sad images
Of the stern agony, and shroud, and pall,
And breathless darkness, and the narrow house,
Make thee to shudder, and grow sick at heart;—
Go forth, under the open sky, and list
To Nature's teachings, while from all around—
Earth and her waters, and the depths of air,—
Comes a still voice—Yet a few days, and thee
The all-beholding sun shall see no more
In all his course; nor yet in the cold ground,
Where thy pale form was laid, with many tears,
Nor in the embrace of ocean, shall exist
Thy image. Earth, that nourished thee, shall claim
Thy growth, to be resolved to earth again,
And, lost each human trace, surrendering up
Thine individual being, shalt thou go
To mix for ever with the elements,
To be a brother to the insensible rock
And to the sluggish clod, which the rude swain
Turns with his share, and treads upon. The oak
Shall send his roots abroad, and pierce thy mould.

Yet not to thine eternal resting-place
Shalt thou retire alone,—nor couldst thou wish
Couch more magnificent. Thou shalt lie down
With patriarchs of the infant world—with kings,
The powerful of the earth—the wise, the good,
Fair forms, and hoary seers of ages past,
All in one mighty sepulchre. The hills
Rock-ribbed and ancient as the sun; the vales
Stretching in pensive quietness between;
The venerable woods; rivers that move
In majesty, and the complaining brooks
That make the meadows green; and, poured round all,
Old ocean's gray and melancholy waste,—
Are but the solemn decorations all
Of the great tomb of man. The golden sun,
The planets, all the infinite host of heaven,
Are shining on the sad abodes of death,
Through the still lapse of ages. All that tread
The globe are but a handful to the tribes
That slumber in its bosom.—Take the wings
Of morning, traverse Barca's[1] desert sands,
Or lose thyself in the continuous woods
Where rolls the Oregan,[2] and hears no sound,
Save his own dashings—yet—the dead are there:
And millions in those solitudes, since first
The flight of years began, have laid them down
In their last sleep—the dead reign there alone.
So shalt thou rest, and what if thou withdraw
In silence from the living and no friend
Take note of thy departure? All that breathe
Will share thy destiny. The gay will laugh
When thou art gone, the solemn brood of care
Plod on, and each one as before will chase
His favourite phantom; yet all these shall leave
Their mirth and their employments, and shall come,
And make their bed with thee. As the long train
Of ages glide away, the sons of men,
The youth in life's green spring, and he who goes
In the full strength of years, matron, and maid,
And the sweet babe, and the gray-headed man,—
Shall one by one be gathered to thy side,
By those, who in their turn shall follow them.

So live, that when thy summons comes to join
The innumerable caravan, which moves
To that mysterious realm, where each shall take
His chamber in the silent halls of death,
Thou go not, like the quarry-slave at night,
Scourged to his dungeon, but, sustained and soothed
By an unfaltering trust, approach thy grave
Like one who wraps the drapery of his couch
About him, and lies down to pleasant dreams.

1811 — 1817, 1821

Thanatopsis. [1] Northern Africa.
[2] The Columbia River.

Inscription for the Entrance to a Wood

First published with "Thanatopsis" in the same issue of the *North American Review* in September 1817, under the title "A Fragment." In revising the poem in 1821 Bryant added the closing lines, beginning with "The cool wind . . . ." The actual wood was a grove of trees in front of his boyhood home in Cummington, Massachusetts.

Stranger, if thou hast learned a truth which needs
No school of long experience, that the world
Is full of guilt and misery, and hast seen
Enough of all its sorrows, crimes, and cares,
To tire thee of it, enter this wild wood
And view the haunts of Nature. The calm shade
Shall bring a kindred calm, and the sweet breeze
That makes the green leaves dance, shall waft a balm
To thy sick heart. Thou wilt find nothing here
Of all that pained thee in the haunts of men
And made thee loathe thy life. The primal curse
Fell, it is true, upon the unsinning earth,
But not in vengeance. God hath yoked to guilt
Her pale tormentor, misery. Hence these shades
Are still the abodes of gladness; the thick roof
Of green and stirring branches is alive

And musical with birds, that sing and sport
In wantonness of spirit; while below
The squirrel, with raised paws and form erect,
Chirps merrily. Throngs of insects in the shade
Try their thin wings and dance in the warm beam
That waked them into life. Even the green trees
Partake the deep contentment; as they bend
To the soft winds, the sun from the blue sky
Looks in and sheds a blessing on the scene.
Scarce less the cleft-born wild-flower seems to enjoy
Existence, than the winged plunderer
That sucks its sweets. The mossy rocks themselves,
And the old and ponderous trunks of prostrate trees
That lead from knoll to knoll a causey[1] rude,
Or bridge the sunken brook, and their dark roots,
With all their earth upon them, twisting high,
Breathe fixed tranquillity. The rivulet
Sends forth glad sounds, and tripping o'er its bed
Of pebbly sands, or leaping down the rocks,
Seems, with continuous laughter, to rejoice
In its own being. Softly tread the marge,
Lest from her midway perch thou scare the wren
That dips her bill in water. The cool wind,
That stirs the stream in play, shall come to thee,
Like one that loves thee nor will let thee pass
Ungreeted, and shall give its light embrace.

1815 — 1817, 1821

Inscription. [1] Causeway.

To a Waterfowl

In December 1815, Bryant walked from Cummington to Plainfield, Massachusetts, to inquire into opportunities there for beginning the practice of law. He wrote in a letter "that he felt, as he walked up the hills, very forlorn and desolate indeed, not knowing what was to become of him in the big world. . . . The sun had already set, leaving behind it one of those brilliant seas of chrysolite and opal which often flood the New England skies; and while he was looking upon the rosy splendor with rapt admiration, a solitary bird made wing along the illuminated horizon. He watched the lone wanderer until it was lost in the distance, asking himself whither it had come and to what home it was flying. When he went to the house where he was to stop for the night, his mind was still full of what he had seen and felt, and he wrote these lines." (Parke Godwin, *A Biography of William Cullen Bryant*, 1883)

Whither, midst falling dew,
While glow the heavens with the last steps of day,
Far, through their rosy depths, dost thou pursue
Thy solitary way?

Vainly the fowler's eye
Might mark thy distant flight to do thee wrong,
As, darkly seen against the crimson sky,
Thy figure floats along.

Seek'st thou the plashy brink
Of weedy lake, or marge of river wide,
Or where the rocking billows rise and sink
On the chafed ocean side?

There is a Power whose care
Teaches thy way along that pathless coast,—
The desert and illimitable air,—
Lone wandering, but not lost.

All day thy wings have fanned,
At that far height, the cold thin atmosphere,
Yet stoop not, weary, to the welcome land,
Though the dark night is near.

And soon that toil shall end;
Soon shalt thou find a summer home and rest,
And scream among thy fellows; reeds shall bend,
Soon, o'er thy sheltered nest.

Thou'rt gone, the abyss of heaven
Hath swallowed up thy form; yet, on my heart
Deeply hath sunk the lesson thou hast given,
And shall not soon depart.

He who, from zone to zone,
Guides through the boundless sky thy certain flight,
In the long way that I must tread alone,
Will lead my steps aright.

1815 — 1818

A Winter Piece

The time has been that these wild solitudes,
Yet beautiful as wild, were trod by me
Oftener than now; and when the ills of life
Had chafed my spirit—when the unsteady pulse
Beat with strange flutterings—I would wander forth
And seek the woods. The sunshine on my path
Was to me as a friend. The swelling hills,
The quiet dells retiring far between,
With gentle invitation to explore
Their windings, were a calm society
That talked with me and soothed me. Then the chant
Of birds, and chime of brooks, and soft caress
Of the fresh sylvan air, made me forget
The thoughts that broke my peace, and I began
To gather simples by the fountain's brink,
And lose myself in day-dreams. While I stood
In nature's loneliness, I was with one

With whom I early grew familiar, one
Who never had a frown for me, whose voice
Never rebuked me for the hours I stole
From cares I loved not, but of which the world
Deems highest, to converse with her. When shrieked
The bleak November winds, and smote the woods,
And the brown fields were herbless, and the shades,
That met above the merry rivulet,
Were spoiled, I sought, I loved them still; they seemed
Like old companions in adversity.
Still there was beauty in my walks; the brook,
Bordered with sparkling frost-work, was as gay
As with its fringe of summer flowers. Afar,
The village with its spires, the path of streams,
And dim receding valleys, hid before
By interposing trees, lay visible
Through the bare grove, and my familiar haunts
Seemed new to me. Nor was I slow to come
Among them, when the clouds, from their still skirts,
Had shaken down on earth the feathery snow,
And all was white. The pure keen air abroad,
Albeit it breathed no scent of herb, nor heard
Love-call of bird nor merry hum of bee,
Was not the air of death. Bright mosses crept
Over the spotted trunks, and the close buds,
That lay along the boughs, instinct with life,
Patient, and waiting the soft breath of Spring,
Feared not the piercing spirit of the North.
The snow-bird twittered on the beechen bough,
And 'neath the hemlock, whose thick branches bent
Beneath its bright cold burden, and kept dry
A circle, on the earth, of withered leaves,
The partridge found a shelter. Through the snow
The rabbit sprang away. The lighter track
Of fox, and the racoon's broad path were there,
Crossing each other. From his hollow tree,
The squirrel was abroad, gathering the nuts
Just fallen, that asked the winter cold and sway
Of winter blast, to shake them from their hold.

But winter has yet brighter scenes,—he boasts
Splendors beyond what gorgeous Summer knows;
Or Autumn with his many fruits, and woods
All flushed with many hues. Come when the rains
Have glazed the snow, and clothed the trees with ice;
While the slant sun of February pours
Into the bowers a flood of light. Approach!
The incrusted surface shall upbear thy steps,
And the broad arching portals of the grove
Welcome thy entering. Look! the massy trunks
Are cased in the pure crystal; each light spray,
Nodding and tinkling in the breath of heaven,
Is studded with its trembling water-drops,
That glimmer with an amethystine light.
But round the parent stem the long low boughs
Bend, in a glittering ring, and arbors hide
The glassy floor. Oh! you might deem the spot
The spacious cavern of some virgin mine,
Deep in the womb of earth—where the gems grow,
And diamonds put forth radiant rods and bud
With amethyst and topaz—and the place
Lit up, most royally, with the pure beam
That dwells in them. Or haply the vast hall
Of fairy palace, that outlasts the night,
And fades not in the glory of the sun;—
Where crystal columns send forth slender shafts
And crossing arches; and fantastic aisles
Wind from the sight in brightness, and are lost
Among the crowded pillars. Raise thine eye;
Thou seest no cavern roof, no palace vault;
There the blue sky and the white drifting cloud
Look in. Again the wildered fancy dreams
Of spouting fountains, frozen as they rose,
And fixed, with all their branching jets, in air,
And all their sluices sealed. All, all is light;
Light without shade. But all shall pass away
With the next sun. From numberless vast trunks,
Loosened, the crashing ice shall make a sound
Like the far roar of rivers, and the eve
Shall close o'er the brown woods as it was wont.

And it is pleasant, when the noisy streams
Are just set free, and milder suns melt off
The plashy snow, save only the firm drift
In the deep glen or the close shade of pines,—
'Tis pleasant to behold the wreaths of smoke
Roll up among the maples of the hill,
Where the shrill sound of youthful voices wakes
The shriller echo, as the clear pure lymph,
That from the wounded trees, in twinkling drops,
Falls, mid the golden brightness of the morn,
Is gathered in with brimming pails, and oft,
Wielded by sturdy hands, the stroke of axe
Makes the woods ring. Along the quiet air,
Come and float calmly off the soft light clouds,
Such as you see in summer, and the winds
Scarce stir the branches. Lodged in sunny cleft,
Where the cold breezes come not, blooms alone
The little wind-flower, whose just opened eye
Is blue as the spring heaven it gazes at—
Startling the loiterer in the naked groves
With unexpected beauty, for the time
Of blossoms and green leaves is yet afar.
And ere it comes, the encountering winds shall oft
Muster their wrath again, and rapid clouds
Shade heaven, and bounding on the frozen earth
Shall fall their volleyed stores, rounded like hail

And white like snow, and the loud North again
Shall buffet the vexed forest in his rage.

1820

To Cole, the Painter, Departing for Europe

Thomas Cole (1801–48), born in England, came to the United States in 1819 to become one of the most famous landscape painters of the "Hudson River" school. A close friend of Bryant's, he had similar tastes in art and much in common with his view of American nature.

Thine eyes shall see the light of distant skies:
  Yet, Cole! thy heart shall bear to Europe's strand
  A living image of our own bright land,
Such as upon thy glorious canvas lies;
Lone lakes—savannas where the bison roves—
  Rocks rich with summer garlands—solemn streams—
  Skies, where the desert eagle wheels and screams—
Spring bloom and autumn blaze of boundless groves.
Fair scenes shall greet thee where thou goest—fair,
  But different—every where the trace of men,
  Paths, homes, graves, ruins, from the lowest glen
To where life shrinks from the fierce Alpine air,
  Gaze on them, till the tears shall dim thy sight,
  But keep that earlier, wilder image bright.

1829

The Prairies

Two of Bryant's brothers settled in Illinois, where he visited them in 1832, his first contact with the frontier country. The poem which grew out of his experience combined his consciousness of the great new American West with conventional romantic themes of the transience of life and the ruins of ancient empires.

  These are the gardens of the Desert,[1] these
The unshorn fields, boundless and beautiful,
For which the speech of England has no name—
The Prairies. I behold them for the first,
And my heart swells, while the dilated sight
Takes in the encircling vastness. Lo! they stretch
In airy undulations, far away,
As if the ocean, in his gentlest swell,
Stood still, with all his rounded billows fixed,
And motionless for ever.— Motionless?—
No—they are all unchained again. The clouds
Sweep over with their shadows, and, beneath,
The surface rolls and fluctuates to the eye;
Dark hollows seem to glide along and chase
The sunny ridges. Breezes of the South!
Who toss the golden and the flame-like flowers,
And pass the prairie-hawk that, poised on high,
Flaps his broad wings, yet moves not—ye have played
Among the palms of Mexico and vines
Of Texas, and have crisped the limpid brooks
That from the fountains of Sonora glide
Into the calm Pacific—have ye fanned
A nobler or a lovelier scene than this?
Man hath no part in all this glorious work:
The hand that built the firmament hath heaved
And soothed these verdant swells, and sown their slopes
With herbage, planted them with island groves,
And hedged them round with forests. Fitting floor
For this magnificent temple of the sky—
With flowers whose glory and whose multitude
Rival the constellations! The great heavens
Seem to stoop down upon the scene in love,—
A nearer vault, and of a tenderer blue,
Than that which bends above our eastern hills.

  As o'er the verdant waste I guide my steed,
Among the high rank grass that sweeps his sides,
The hollow beating of his footstep seems
A sacrilegious sound. I think of those
Upon whose rest he tramples. Are they here—
The dead of other days?—and did the dust
Of these fair solitudes once stir with life
And burn with passion? Let the mighty mounds
That overlook the rivers, or that rise
In the dim forest crowded with old oaks,
Answer. A race, that long has passed away,
Built them;—a disciplined and populous race
Heaped, with long toil, the earth, while yet the Greek
Was hewing the Pentelicus[2] to forms
Of symmetry, and rearing on its rock
The glittering Parthenon. These ample fields
Nourished their harvests, here their herds were fed,
When haply by their stalls the bison lowed,
And bowed his maned shoulder to the yoke.
All day this desert murmured with their toils,
Till twilight blushed, and lovers walked, and wooed
In a forgotten language, and old tunes,
From instruments of unremembered form,
Gave the soft winds a voice. The red man came—
The roaming hunter tribes, warlike and fierce,
And the mound-builders vanished from the earth.

The Prairies. [1] Bryant uses the word in its Biblical sense, meaning a vast, uninhabited region.

[2] Mount Pentelicus, in Greece, was noted for its marble quarries.

The solitude of centuries untold
Has settled where they dwelt. The prairie-wolf[3]
Hunts in their meadows, and his fresh-dug den
Yawns by my path. The gopher mines the ground
Where stood their swarming cities. All is gone;
All—save the piles of earth that hold their bones,
The platforms where they worshipped unknown gods,
The barriers which they builded from the soil
To keep the foe at bay—till o'er the walls
The wild beleaguerers broke, and, one by one
The strongholds of the plain were forced, and heaped
With corpses. The brown vultures of the wood
Flocked to those vast uncovered sepulchres,
And sat, unscared and silent, at their feast.
Haply some solitary fugitive,
Lurking in marsh and forest, till the sense
Of desolation and of fear became
Bitterer than death, yielded himself to die.
Man's better nature triumphed then. Kind words
Welcomed and soothed him; the rude conquerors
Seated the captive with their chiefs; he chose
A bride among their maidens, and at length
Seemed to forget—yet ne'er forgot—the wife
Of his first love, and her sweet little ones,
Butchered, amid their shrieks, with all his race.

Thus change the forms of being. Thus arise
Races of living things, glorious in strength,
And perish, as the quickening breath of God
Fills them, or is withdrawn. The red man, too,
Has left the blooming wilds he ranged so long,
And, nearer to the Rocky Mountains, sought
A wider hunting-ground. The beaver builds
No longer by these streams, but far away,
On waters whose blue surface ne'er gave back
The white man's face—among Missouri's springs,
And pools whose issues swell the Oregan,
He rears his little Venice. In these plains
The bison feeds no more. Twice twenty leagues
Beyond remotest smoke of hunter's camp,
Roams the majestic brute, in herds that shake
The earth with thundering steps—yet here I meet
His ancient footprints stamped beside the pool.

Still this great solitude is quick with life.
Myriads of insects, gaudy as the flowers
They flutter over, gentle quadrupeds,
And birds, that scarce have learned the fear of man,
Are here, and sliding reptiles of the ground,
Startlingly beautiful. The graceful deer
Bounds to the wood at my approach. The bee,
A more adventurous colonist than man,
With whom he came across the eastern deep,
Fills the savannas[4] with his murmurings,
And hides his sweets, as in the golden age,
Within the hollow oak. I listen long
To his domestic hum, and think I hear
The sound of that advancing multitude
Which soon shall fill these deserts. From the ground
Comes up the laugh of children, the soft voice
Of maidens, and the sweet and solemn hymn
Of Sabbath worshippers. The low of herds
Blends with the rustling of the heavy grain
Over the dark-brown furrows. All at once
A fresher wind sweeps by, and breaks my dream,
And I am in the wilderness alone.

1832 1833

[3] The coyote.

[4] Treeless, rolling country.

EDGAR ALLAN POE [1809-1849]

"The saddest and the strangest figure in American literary history," Killis Campbell called him. "Few writers have lived a life so full of struggle and disappointment, and none have lived and died more completely out of sympathy with their times." Poe was, nevertheless, deeply indebted to the English romantic writers, and his neurotic personality reminds us of various wayward geniuses in European romanticism.

Edgar Poe was the child of itinerant actors. Within less than three years after his birth in Boston, his father deserted the family and his mother died in poverty at Richmond, Virginia. It may well be that the sight of his mother dying of tuberculosis made an impression that eventually transmuted itself into fictional forms (Berenice, Morella, Eleanora, Ligeia). The child Edgar was taken into the home of a Richmond merchant, Allan, whose name Poe later added to his own. He was never formally adopted, and his relations with his foster-parents were never happy. From 1815 to 1820 he studied at schools in England, and during the next five years in Richmond. In February 1826 he entered the University of Virginia. Apparently in an attempt to supplement an insufficient allowance from his foster-father, Poe resorted to gambling and ran up heavy debts. At this time, too, he acquired a reputation as a hard drinker. Allan refused to pay his debts and took him out of the University in December. They quarreled bitterly and decisively, and in 1827 Poe ran away and enlisted, in Boston, as a private in the U.S. Army under the name of Edgar A. Perry. In Boston, too, he brought out his first book, a thin volume called *Tamerlane and Other Poems. By a Bostonian.*

Within two years the young soldier had found time to produce another book of poems, *Al Aaraaf, Tamerlane, and Minor Poems,* and had risen to the rank of sergeant-major. With Allan's help, virtually the last he was to receive from that source, he secured an appointment to West Point, entering in July 1830. Less than eight months later, he deliberately got himself dismissed for neglect of duty. From this time on, Poe was dependent on his pen for a livelihood.

A volume of poems issued in 1831 showed a new sureness: here were "Israfel," "To Helen," "The City in the Sea." The next four years he spent mostly in Baltimore, boarding there with his aunt, Mrs. Clemm, and writing poems and stories. In 1833 the *Baltimore Saturday Visitor* awarded him a prize of $100 for the best short story submitted in its contest. It was one of his few financial successes. In 1835 he removed to Richmond and became editor of the *Southern Literary Messenger,* an able and successful editor noted for his caustic book reviews in a day when criticism was indulgent.

In 1836 he married his cousin Virginia Clemm, a girl of thirteen, with Mrs. Clemm joining the Poe household to give it some measure of stability throughout its various moves and misfortunes. Poe quit the *Messenger,* partly because he felt that his salary was less than he deserved; spent a year in New York; then settled in Philadelphia, and became editor of *Graham's Magazine.* His *Tales of the Grotesque and Arabesque* were published in 1840, and in 1843 "The Gold Bug" won him another $100 prize. But his wife was ill, he dreaded her death, he drank, he could not make a decent living. In 1844 he returned to New York to seek new opportunities.

The next year "The Raven" brought him fame and ten dollars. He was editor of the *Broadway Journal* for two years, till it failed. In 1847 he was working on his *Eureka: an Essay on the Material and Spiritual Universe,* and his wife was dying. The rest of his story is one of poverty, intoxication, frequent illness, mistaken love affairs, and fine poems. In 1848 he attempted suicide with laudanum. In 1849 he visited Richmond for the last time, and became engaged to a sweetheart of his youth, now a wealthy widow. The remaining events are obscure. In Baltimore he was found unconscious at a ward polling place, and died four days later, at age 40.

Such are the chief external facts of his life. It is still difficult to say what sort of person the man himself was. Unfortunate throughout his life, Poe was also unfortunate in his literary executor, the Reverend Rufus W. Griswold, an editor and compiler who wrote a memoir in which, by a combination of truth, half-truth, and lies, he pictured Poe as an almost diabolic figure. Poe's defenders, in turn, tended to romanticize him as a persecuted genius. The sordid story and the romantic legend were equally unsatisfactory. Partisanship has often dogged even the efforts of careful scholars to give a convincing portrait.

Similarly, critical opinion of Poe's writings has veered between extremes of enthusiasm and distaste. The Irish poet Yeats judged Poe to be "always and for all lands a great lyric poet," and many French authors, such as Maupassant, Baudelaire, and Valéry, extolled him as an original artist of high distinction. In France, indeed, Poe has generally been hailed as the founder of modern poetry, especially Symbolist poetry. In the United States, on the other hand, he has been disparaged by writers in many camps. Emerson once summed him up as "the jingle man," and Henry James pronounced an enthusiasm for Poe's work as "the mark of a decidedly primitive stage of reflection." Still others have dismissed him as vague, disorderly, perverse, or simply monotonous.

Poe's range may be narrow, but within his own dimensions he is a fascinating, important, and at times even a brilliant writer. Edgar Poe was a writer who could not embrace America as Emerson or Whitman could. On the contrary, he rejected a great deal of the contemporary cultural scene: he disliked America's early subservience to British standards, the narrow provincialism that replaced it, and the general anti-poetic quality of American life. Along with the dominant culture, Poe repudiated the scientific spirit and the prevailing commercial values that, according to him, had taken over America. He looked elsewhere for significance and fulfillment. In his writing he explored the possibilities of experience beyond the factual, ordinary world. He sought a transcendent world of inviolate beauty; he explored the chaos and terror of psychological disintegration and madness; and he tried to transform the mundane world with the power of a brilliant critical and analytic mind.

Text: For the poetry reprinted here, the textual source is Floyd Stovall's edition of *The Poems of Edgar Allan Poe* (Charlottesville, 1965); for the criticism, *Selections from the Critical Writings of Edgar Allan Poe,* ed. F. C. Prescott (New York, 1909); for the tales, the Virginia Edition of *The Complete Works of Edgar Allan Poe,* ed. James A. Harrison (New York, 1902).

Further reading: A. H. Quinn, *Edgar Allan Poe: A Critical Biography,* 1941. Edward H. Davidson, *Poe: A Critical Study,* 1959; and *Selected Writings of Edgar Allan Poe,* 1956. Vincent Buranelli, *Edgar Allan Poe,* 1961. Edward Wagenknecht, *Edgar Allan Poe: The Man Behind the Legend,* 1963. *Poe: A Collection of Critical Essays,* ed. Robert Regan, 1967. Richard Wilbur, *Poe: Complete Poems,* 1959.

Dreams

Oh! that my young life were a lasting dream!
My spirit not awak'ning till the beam
Of an Eternity should bring the morrow.
Yes! tho' that long dream were of hopeless sorrow,
'Twere better than the cold reality
Of waking life, to him whose heart must be,
And hath been still, upon the lovely earth,
A chaos of deep passion, from his birth.
But should it be—that dream eternally
Continuing—as dreams have been to me
In my young boyhood—should it thus be giv'n,
'Twere folly still to hope for higher Heav'n.
For I have revell'd when the sun was bright
I' the summer sky, in dreams of living light
And loveliness,—have left my very heart
In climes of mine imagining—apart
From mine own home, with beings that have been
Of mine own thought—what more could I have
 seen?
'Twas once—and only once—and the wild hour
From my remembrance shall not pass—some pow'r
Or spell had bound me—'twas the chilly wind
Came o'er me in the night, and left behind
Its image on my spirit—or the moon
Shone on my slumbers in her lofty noon
Too coldly—or the stars—howe'er it was,
That dream was as that night-wind—let it pass.

I *have been* happy, tho' but in a dream.
I have been happy—and I love the theme:
Dreams! in their vivid colouring of life
As in that fleeting, shadowy, misty strife
Of semblance with reality which brings
To the delirious eye, more lovely things
Of Paradise and Love—and all our own!
Than young Hope in his sunniest hour hath known.

1827

A Dream Within a Dream

Take this kiss upon the brow!
And, in parting from you now,
Thus much let me avow—
You are not wrong, who deem
That my days have been a dream;
Yet if Hope has flown away
In a night, or in a day,
In a vision, or in none,
Is it therefore the less *gone?*
All that we see or seem
Is but a dream within a dream.

I stand amid the roar
Of a surf-tormented shore,
And I hold within my hand
Grains of the golden sand—
How few! yet how they creep
Through my fingers to the deep,
While I weep—while I weep!
O God! can I not grasp
Them with a tighter clasp?
O God! can I not save
One from the pitiless wave?
Is *all* that we see or seem
But a dream within a dream?

1827, 1829, 1849

Romance

Poe chose this poem as the preface to a group of his poems published in 1829, and as the introduction to the entire volume of 1831.

Romance, who loves to nod and sing,
With drowsy head and folded wing,
Among the green leaves as they shake
Far down within some shadowy lake,
To me a painted paroquet
Hath been—a most familiar bird—
Taught me my alphabet to say—
To lisp my very earliest word
While in the wild wood I did lie,
A child—with a most knowing eye.

Of late, eternal Condor years
So shake the very Heaven on high
With tumult as they thunder by,
I have no time for idle cares
Through gazing on the unquiet sky.
And when an hour with calmer wings
Its down upon my spirit flings—
That little time with lyre and rhyme
To while away—forbidden things!
My heart would feel to be a crime
Unless it trembled with the strings.

1829

Sonnet—To Science

The poem served as an introduction to Poe's long poem "Al Aaraaf" (1829, 1845), which is, according to Edward Davidson, "Poe's youthful, inconclusive version of the Fall of Man."

Science! true daughter of Old Time thou art!
Who alterest all things with thy peering eyes.
Why preyest thou thus upon the poet's heart,
Vulture, whose wings are dull realities?
How should he love thee? or how deem thee wise,
Who wouldst not leave him in his wandering
To seek for treasure in the jewelled skies,

Albeit he soared with an undaunted wing?
Hast thou not dragged Diana from her car?
And driven the Hamadryad[1] from the wood
To seek a shelter in some happier star?
Hast thou not torn the Naiad from her flood,
The Elfin from the green grass, and from me
The summer dream beneath the tamarind tree?

1829

To Helen

"To Helen" may have been inspired by Mrs. Jane Stanard, of Richmond, mother of a school friend. She died in 1824, when Poe was fifteen. In letters, he later spoke of her as "the first purely ideal love of my soul," and as "an angel to my forlorn and darkened nature." But more importantly, Helen represents Poe's ideal of beauty. She appears here as an idealized, classical, aesthetic figure (not a human or sexual one at all) who evokes the glory and grandeur of the past.

Helen, thy beauty is to me
  Like those Nicéan[1] barks of yore,
That gently, o'er a perfumed sea,
  The weary, way-worn wanderer bore
  To his own native shore.

On desperate seas long wont to roam,
  Thy hyacinth hair, thy classic face,
Thy Naiad airs have brought me home
  To the glory that was Greece
And the grandeur that was Rome.

Lo! in yon brilliant window-niche
  How statue-like I see thee stand,
  The agate lamp within thy hand!
Ah, Psyche, from the regions which
  Are Holy-Land!

1831, 1845

Israfel

Poe's note: "And the angel Israfel, whose heart-strings are a lute, and who has the sweetest voice of all God's creatures.—KORAN." Apparently Poe quoted not the Koran itself but George Sale's *Discourse* (1734) on the Koran, inserting from Béranger the phrase about the heart-strings.

In Heaven a spirit doth dwell
  "Whose heart-strings are a lute;"
None sing so wildly well
As the angel Israfel,
And the giddy stars (so legends tell)
Ceasing their hymns, attend the spell
  Of his voice, all mute.

Tottering above
  In her highest noon,
  The enamoured moon
Blushes with love,
  While, to listen, the red levin
  (With the rapid Pleiads, even,
  Which were seven,)
  Pauses in Heaven.

And they say (the starry choir
  And the other listening things)
That Israfeli's fire
Is owing to that lyre
  By which he sits and sings—
The trembling living wire
Of those unusual strings.

But the skies that angel trod,
  Where deep thoughts are a duty—
Where Love's a grown-up God—
  Where the Houri glances are
Imbued with all the beauty
  Which we worship in a star.

Therefore, thou art not wrong,
  Israfeli, who despisest
An unimpassioned song;
To thee the laurels belong,
  Best bard, because the wisest!
Merrily live, and long!

The ecstasies above
  With thy burning measures suit—
Thy grief, thy joy, thy hate, thy love,
  With the fervour of thy lute—
  Well may the stars be mute!

Yes, Heaven is thine; but this
  Is a world of sweets and sours;
  Our flowers are merely—flowers,
And the shadow of thy perfect bliss
  Is the sunshine of ours.

If I could dwell
Where Israfel
  Hath dwelt, and he where I,
He might not sing so wildly well
  A mortal melody,
While a bolder note than this might swell
  From my lyre within the sky.

1831

To Science. [1]A figure in "Al Aaraaf."
To Helen. [1]Probably without specific reference—suggestive and evocative, but nothing more.

The Sleeper

At midnight, in the month of June,
I stand beneath the mystic moon.
An opiate vapor, dewy, dim,
Exhales from out her golden rim,
And, softly dripping, drop by drop,
Upon the quiet mountain top,
Steals drowsily and musically
Into the universal valley.
The rosemary nods upon the grave;
The lily lolls upon the wave;
Wrapping the fog about its breast,
The ruin moulders into rest;
Looking like Lethe, see! the lake
A conscious slumber seems to take,
And would not, for the world, awake.
All Beauty sleeps!—and lo! where lies
Irene, with her Destinies!

Oh, lady bright! can it be right—
This window open to the night?
The wanton airs, from the tree-top,
Laughingly through the lattice drop—
The bodiless airs, a wizard rout,
Flit through thy chamber in and out,
And wave the curtain canopy
So fitfully—so fearfully—
Above the closed and fringéd lid
'Neath which thy slumb'ring soul lies hid,
That, o'er the floor and down the wall,
Like ghosts the shadows rise and fall!
Oh, lady dear, hast thou no fear?
Why and what art thou dreaming here?
Sure thou art come o'er far-off seas,
A wonder to these garden trees!
Strange is thy pallor! strange thy dress!
Strange, above all, thy length of tress,
And this all solemn silentness!

The lady sleeps! Oh, may her sleep,
Which is ènduring, so be deep!
Heaven have her in its sacred keep!
This chamber changed for one more holy,
This bed for one more melancholy,
I pray to God that she may lie
Forever with unopened eye,
While the pale sheeted ghosts go by!

My love, she sleeps! Oh, may her sleep,
As it is lasting, so be deep!
Soft may the worms about her creep!
Far in the forest, dim and old,
For her may some tall vault unfold—
Some vault that oft hath flung its black
And wingèd pannels fluttering back,
Triumphant, o'er the crested palls,
Of her grand family funerals—
Some sepulchre, remote, alone,
Against whose portal she hath thrown,
In childhood, many an idle stone—
Some tomb from out whose sounding door
She ne'er shall force an echo more,
Thrilling to think, poor child of sin!
It was the dead who groaned within.

1831, 1845

The City in the Sea

The earlier titles Poe used for this poem suggest its meaning: "The Doomed City," "The City of Sin," "The City in the Sea: a Prophecy." The prototype for the city is obviously Gomorrah. Poe's concern here is not with ideal beauty, but with the creation of a strange, mysterious, unreal world that suggests sin, decay, and death.

Lo! Death has reared himself a throne
In a strange city lying alone
Far down within the dim West,
Where the good and the bad and the worst and the best
Have gone to their eternal rest.
There shrines and palaces and towers
(Time-eaten towers that tremble not!)
Resemble nothing that is ours.
Around, by lifting winds forgot,
Resignedly beneath the sky
The melancholy waters lie.

No rays from the holy heaven come down
On the long night-time of that town;
But light from out the lurid sea
Streams up the turrets silently—
Gleams up the pinnacles far and free—
Up domes—up spires—up kingly halls—
Up fanes—up Babylon-like walls—
Up shadowy long-forgotten bowers
Of sculptured ivy and stone flowers—
Up many and many a marvelous shrine
Whose wreathèd friezes intertwine
The viol, the violet, and the vine.

Resignedly beneath the sky
The melancholy waters lie.
So blend the turrets and shadows there
That all seem pendulous in air,
While from a proud tower in the town
Death looks gigantically down.

There open fanes and gaping graves
Yawn level with the luminous waves;

But not the riches there that lie
In each idol's diamond eye—
Not the gaily-jewelled dead
Tempt the waters from their bed;
For no ripples curl, alas!
Along that wilderness of glass—
No swellings tell that winds may be
Upon some far-off happier sea—
No heavings hint that winds have been
On seas less hideously serene.

But lo, a stir is in the air!
The wave—there is a movement there!
As if the towers had thrust aside,
In slightly sinking, the dull tide—
As if their tops had feebly given
A void within the filmy Heaven.
The waves have now a redder glow—
The hours are breathing faint and low—
And when, amid no earthly moans,
Down, down that town shall settle hence,
Hell, rising from a thousand thrones,
Shall do it reverence.

1831, 1845

Lenore

The poem may refer to the marriage of a woman Poe loved to an older man or to his grief at the death of his foster-mother, but essentially it is a good example of Poe's view that the death of a young and beautiful woman is a peculiarly poetic theme. By combining melancholy with beauty, the theme, supposedly, becomes one of the most effective for realizing ideal beauty.

Ah, broken is the golden bowl![1]—the spirit flown forever!
Let the bell toll!—a saintly soul floats on the Stygian River:—
And, Guy De Vere, hast *thou* no tear?—weep now or never more!
See! on yon drear and rigid bier low lies thy love, Lenore!
Come! let the burial rite be read—the funeral song be sung!—
An anthem for the queenliest dead that ever died so young—
A dirge for her the doubly dead in that she died so young.

"Wretches! ye loved her for her wealth and ye hated her for her pride;
And when she fell in feeble health, ye blessed her—that she died:
How *shall* the ritual, then, be read?—the requiem how be sung
By you—by yours, the evil eye—by yours, the slanderous tongue
That did to death the innocence that died, and died so young?"

Peccavimus:—[2] yet rave not thus! but let a Sabbath song
Go up to God so solemnly the dead may feel no wrong!
The sweet Lenore hath gone before, with Hope that flew beside,
Leaving thee wild for the dear child that should have been thy bride—
For her, the fair and debonair, that now so lowly lies,
The life upon her yellow hair, but not within her eyes—
The life still there upon her hair, the death upon her eyes.

"Avaunt!—avaunt! to friends from fiends the indignant ghost is riven—
From Hell unto a high estate within the utmost Heaven—
From moan and groan to a golden throne beside the King of Heaven:—
Let *no* bell toll, then, lest her soul, amid its hallowed mirth,
Should catch the note as it doth float up from the damned Earth!
And I—to-night my heart is light:—no dirge will I upraise,
But waft the angel on her flight with a Paean of old days!"

1831, 1843, 1845

Lenore. [1] See Ecclesiastes xii.6.

[2] "We have sinned."

The Coliseum

Poe chose the Coliseum as a symbol for the "grandeur, gloom, and glory"—the greatness—of a past civilization which still has a present magical, mysterious meaning.

Type of the antique Rome! Rich reliquary
Of lofty contemplation left to Time
By buried centuries of pomp and power!
At length—at length—after so many days
Of weary pilgrimage and burning thirst,
(Thirst for the springs of lore that in thee lie,)
I kneel, an altered and an humble man,
Amid thy shadows, and so drink within
My very soul thy grandeur, gloom, and glory!

Vastness! and Age! and Memories of Eld!
Silence! and Desolation! and dim Night!
I feel ye now—I feel ye in your strength—
O spells more sure than e'er Judaean king
Taught in the gardens of Gethsemane!
O charms more potent than the rapt Chaldee
Ever drew down from out the quiet stars!

Here, where a hero fell, a column falls!
Here, where the mimic eagle glared in gold,
A midnight vigil holds the swarthy bat!
Here, where the dames of Rome their gilded hair
Waved to the wind, now wave the reed and thistle!
Here, where on golden throne the monarch lolled,
Glides, spectre-like, unto his marble home,
Lit by the wan light of the horned moon,
The swift and silent lizard of the stones!

But stay! these walls—these ivy-clad arcades—
These mouldering plinths—these sad and blackened shafts—
These vague entablatures—this crumbling frieze—
These shattered cornices—this wreck—this ruin—
These stones—alas! these gray stones—are they all—
All of the famed, and the colossal left
By the corrosive Hours to Fate and me?

"Not all"—the Echoes answer me—"not all!
Prophetic sounds and loud, arise forever
From us, and from all Ruin, unto the wise,
As melody from Memnon[1] to the Sun.
We rule the hearts of mightiest men—we rule
With a despotic sway all giant minds.
We are not impotent—we pallid stones.
Not all our power is gone—not all our fame—
Not all the magic of our high renown—
Not all the wonder that encircles us—
Not all the mysteries that in us lie—
Not all the memories that hang upon
And cling around about us as a garment,
Clothing us in a robe of more than glory."

1833, 1845

Dream-Land

Lines 9-20 include particularly effective examples of Poe's imagery that negates or breaks down conventional time and space relationships. Poe approaches the "other world" by negating conventional reality or by placing it in a strange context. "Ultimate" is used in the sense of farthest, as in the Latin *ultima Thule.* Thule was the Greek and Latin name for the northernmost land, but came to be used for any very distant region—even, as here by Poe, a region outside space and time.

By a route obscure and lonely,
Haunted by ill angels only,
Where an Eidolon, named NIGHT,
On a black throne reigns upright,
I have reached these lands but newly
From an ultimate dim Thule—
From a wild weird clime that lieth, sublime,
Out of SPACE—out of TIME.

Bottomless vales and boundless floods,
And chasms, and caves, and Titan woods,
With forms that no man can discover
For the tears that drip all over;
Mountains toppling evermore
Into seas without a shore;
Seas that restlessly aspire,
Surging, unto skies of fire;
Lakes that endlessly outspread
Their lone waters—lone and dead,—
Their still waters—still and chilly
With the snows of the lolling lily.

By the lakes that thus outspread
Their lone waters, lone and dead,—
Their sad waters, sad and chilly
With the snows of the lolling lily,—
By the mountains—near the river
Murmuring lowly, murmuring ever,—
By the grey woods,—by the swamp
Where the toad and the newt encamp,—
By the dismal tarns and pools
Where dwell the Ghouls,—
By each spot the most unholy—
In each nook most melancholy,—
There the traveller meets, aghast,
Sheeted Memories of the Past—
Shrouded forms that start and sigh
As they pass the wanderer by—
White-robed forms of friends long given,
In agony, to the Earth—and Heaven.

For the heart whose woes are legion
'Tis a peaceful, soothing region—
For the spirit that walks in shadow
'Tis—oh 'tis an Eldorado!
But the traveller, travelling through it,
May not—dare not openly view it;
Never its mysteries are exposed
To the weak human eye unclosed;
So wills its King, who hath forbid
The uplifting of the fringéd lid;
And thus the sad Soul that here passes
Beholds it but through darkened glasses.

The Coliseum. [1] A huge statue at Thebes that emitted music when touched by the sun.

By a route obscure and lonely,
Haunted by ill angels only,
Where an Eidolon, named NIGHT,
On a black throne reigns upright,
I have wandered home but newly
From this ultimate dim Thule.

1844

The Raven

"The Raven" provides an obvious transition from the poems to the tales, for its themes are typical of the poems, yet its narrative structure and its narrator are characteristic of the tales. The poem traces the psychological disintegration of a sensitive and initially stable mind.

Poe did not discuss such matters in the essay, "The Philosophy of Composition," in which he presented an analysis of his composition of "The Raven." To what extent one may trust the accuracy of Poe's account of the making of the poem is uncertain. The essay, however, provides useful suggestions about the idea and structure of the poem.

Once upon a midnight dreary, while I pondered, weak and weary,
Over many a quaint and curious volume of forgotten lore—
While I nodded, nearly napping, suddenly there came a tapping,
As of some one gently rapping, rapping at my chamber door.
" 'Tis some visitor," I muttered, "tapping at my chamber door—
Only this and nothing more."

Ah, distinctly I remember it was in the bleak December;
And each separate dying ember wrought its ghost upon the floor.
Eagerly I wished the morrow;—vainly I had sought to borrow
From my books surcease of sorrow—sorrow for the lost Lenore—
For the rare and radiant maiden whom the angels name Lenore—
Nameless *here* for evermore.

And the silken, sad, uncertain rustling of each purple curtain
Thrilled me—filled me with fantastic terrors never felt before;
So that now, to still the beating of my heart, I stood repeating
" 'Tis some visitor entreating entrance at my chamber door—
Some late visitor entreating entrance at my chamber door;—
This it is and nothing more."

Presently my soul grew stronger; hesitating then no longer,
"Sir," said I, "or Madam, truly your forgiveness I implore;
But the fact is I was napping, and so gently you came rapping,
And so faintly you came tapping, tapping at my chamber door,
That I scarce was sure I heard you"—here I opened wide the door;—
Darkness there and nothing more.

Deep into that darkness peering, long I stood there wondering, fearing,
Doubting, dreaming dreams no mortal ever dared to dream before;
But the silence was unbroken, and the stillness gave no token,
And the only word there spoken was the whispered word, "Lenore?"
This I whispered, and an echo murmured back the word, "Lenore!"
Merely this and nothing more.

Back into the chamber turning, all my soul within me burning,
Soon again I heard a tapping somewhat louder than before.
"Surely," said I, "surely that is something at my window lattice;
Let me see, then, what thereat is, and this mystery explore—
Let my heart be still a moment and this mystery explore;—
'Tis the wind and nothing more!"

Open here I flung the shutter, when, with many a flirt and flutter,
In there stepped a stately Raven of the saintly days of yore;
Not the least obeisance made he; not a minute stopped or stayed he;
But, with mien of lord or lady, perched above my chamber door—
Perched upon a bust of Pallas[1] just above my chamber door—
Perched, and sat, and nothing more.

The Raven. [1] Pallas Athene, goddess of wisdom.

Then this ebony bird beguiling my sad fancy into smiling,
By the grave and stern decorum of the countenance it wore,
"Though thy crest be shorn and shaven, thou," I said, "art sure no craven,
Ghastly grim and ancient Raven wandering from the Nightly shore—
Tell me what thy lordly name is on the Night's Plutonian shore!"
Quoth the Raven "Nevermore."

Much I marvelled this ungainly fowl to hear discourse so plainly,
Though its answer little meaning—little relevancy bore;
For we cannot help agreeing that no living human being
Ever yet was blessed with seeing bird above his chamber door—
Bird or beast upon the sculptured bust above his chamber door,
With such name as "Nevermore."

But the Raven, sitting lonely on the placid bust, spoke only
That one word, as if his soul in that one word he did outpour.
Nothing farther then he uttered—not a feather then he fluttered—
Till I scarcely more than muttered "Other friends have flown before—
On the morrow *he* will leave me, as my hopes have flown before."
Then the bird said "Nevermore."

Startled at the stillness broken by reply so aptly spoken,
"Doubtless," said I, "what it utters is its only stock and store
Caught from some unhappy master whom unmerciful Disaster
Followed fast and followed faster till his songs one burden bore—
Till the dirges of his Hope that melancholy burden bore
Of 'Never—nevermore' "

But the Raven still beguiling all my fancy into smiling,
Straight I wheeled a cushioned seat in front of bird, and bust and door;
Then, upon the velvet sinking, I betook myself to linking
Fancy unto fancy, thinking what this ominous bird of yore—
What this grim, ungainly, ghastly, gaunt, and ominous bird of yore
Meant in croaking "Nevermore."

This I sat engaged in guessing, but no syllable expressing
To the fowl whose fiery eyes now burned into my bosom's core;
This and more I sat divining, with my head at ease reclining
On the cushion's velvet lining that the lamp-light gloated o'er,
But whose velvet-violet lining with the lamp-light gloating o'er,
She shall press, ah, nevermore!

Then, methought, the air grew denser, perfumed from an unseen censer
Swung by Seraphim whose foot-falls tinkled on the tufted floor.
"Wretch," I cried, "thy God hath lent thee—by these angels he hath sent thee
Respite—respite and nepenthe from thy memories of Lenore;
Quaff, oh quaff this kind nepenthe and forget this lost Lenore!"
Quoth the Raven "Nevermore."

"Prophet!" said I, "thing of evil!—prophet still, if bird or devil!—
Whether Tempter sent, or whether tempest tossed thee here ashore,
Desolate yet all undaunted, on this desert land enchanted—
On this home by Horror haunted—tell me truly, I implore—
Is there—*is* there balm in Gilead?[2]—tell me—tell me, I implore!"
Quoth the Raven "Nevermore."

"Prophet!" said I, "thing of evil!—prophet still, if bird or devil!
By that Heaven that bends above us—by that God we both adore—
Tell this soul with sorrow laden if, within the distant Aidenn,[3]
It shall clasp a sainted maiden whom the angels name Lenore—

[2]See Jeremiah viii.22; the reference is to a medicinal herb.
[3]The Moslem paradise.

Clasp a rare and radiant maiden whom the angels name Lenore."
  Quoth the Raven "Nevermore."

"Be that word our sign of parting, bird or fiend!" I shrieked, upstarting—
"Get thee back into the tempest and the Night's Plutonian shore!
Leave no black plume as a token of that lie thy soul hath spoken!
Leave my loneliness unbroken!—quit the bust above my door!
Take thy beak from out my heart, and take thy form from off my door!"
  Quoth the Raven "Nevermore."

And the Raven, never flitting, still is sitting, *still* is sitting
On the pallid bust of Pallas just above my chamber door;
And his eyes have all the seeming of a demon's that is dreaming,
And the lamp-light o'er him streaming throws his shadow on the floor;
And my soul from out that shadow that lies floating on the floor
  Shall be lifted—nevermore!

1845

Ulalume

The poem, apparently, describes a region similar to the one through which Poe often walked on his way to his wife's grave in Mamaroneck. Weir refers to Robert Weir, a well-known nineteenth-century "misty" landscape painter. Auber refers to a French composer, Daniel François Auber, who wrote *La Lac des Fées.* Yaanek refers to a then recently discovered volcano in Antarctica, Mt. Erebus. The poem dramatizes the speaker's recognition that he cannot accept human, sexual love and thus reject the ideal love his dead wife represents.

The skies they were ashen and sober;
  The leaves they were crispèd and sere—
  The leaves they were withering and sere;
It was night in the lonesome October
  Of my most immemorial year:
It was hard by the dim lake of Auber,
  In the misty mid region of Weir:—
It was down by the dank tarn of Auber,
  In the ghoul-haunted woodland of Weir.

Here once, through an alley Titanic,
  Of cypress, I roamed with my Soul—
  Of cypress, with Psyche, my Soul.
These were days when my heart was volcanic
  As the scoriac rivers that roll—
  As the lavas that restlessly roll
Their sulphurous currents down Yaanek,
  In the ultimate climes of the pole—
That groan as they roll down Mount Yaanek,
  In the realms of the Boreal Pole.

Our talk had been serious and sober,
  But our thoughts they were palsied and sere—
  Our memories were treacherous and sere;
For we knew not the month was October,
  And we marked not the night of the year—
  (Ah, night of all nights in the year!)
We noted not the dim lake of Auber,
  (Though once we have journeyed down here)
Remembered not the dank tarn of Auber,
  Nor the ghoul-haunted woodland of Weir.

And now, as the night was senescent,
  And star-dials pointed to morn—
  As the star-dials hinted of morn—
At the end of our path a liquescent
  And nebulous lustre was born
Out of which a miraculous crescent
  Arose with a duplicate horn—
Astarte's bediamonded crescent,
  Distinct with its duplicate horn.

And I said—"She is warmer than Dian;
  She rolls through an ether of sighs—
  She revels in a region of sighs.
She has seen that the tears are not dry on
  These cheeks where the worm never dies,
And has come past the stars of the Lion,
  To point us the path to the skies—
  To the Lethean peace of the skies—
Come up, in despite of the Lion,
  To shine on us with her bright eyes—
Come up, through the lair of the Lion,
  With Love in her luminous eyes."

But Psyche, uplifting her finger,
  Said—"Sadly this star I mistrust—
  Her pallor I strangely mistrust—
Ah, hasten!—ah, let us not linger!
  Ah, fly!—let us fly!—for we must."
In terror she spoke; letting sink her
  Wings till they trailed in the dust—
In agony sobbed; letting sink her
  Plumes till they trailed in the dust—
  Till they sorrowfully trailed in the dust.

I replied—"This is nothing but dreaming.
  Let us on, by this tremulous light!
  Let us bathe in this crystalline light!
Its Sibyllic splendor is beaming

With Hope and in Beauty to-night—
See!—it flickers up the sky through the night!
Ah, we safely may trust to its gleaming
And be sure it will lead us aright—
We safely may trust to a gleaming
That cannot but guide us aright
Since it flickers up to Heaven through the night."

Thus I pacified Psyche and kissed her,
And tempted her out of her gloom—
And conquered her scruples and gloom;
And we passed to the end of the vista—
But were stopped by the door of a tomb—
By the door of a legended tomb:—
And I said—"What is written, sweet sister,
On the door of this legended tomb?"
She replied—"Ulalume—Ulalume!—
'Tis the vault of thy lost Ulalume!"

Then my heart it grew ashen and sober
As the leaves that were crispèd and sere—
As the leaves that were withering and sere—
And I cried—"It was surely October,
On *this* very night of last year,
That I journeyed—I journeyed down here!—
That I brought a dread burden down here—
On this night of all nights in the year,
Ah, what demon has tempted me here?
Well I know, now, this dim lake of Auber—
This misty mid region of Weir:—
Well I know, now, this dank tarn of Auber—
This ghoul-haunted woodland of Weir."

Said we, then—the two, then—"Ah, can it
Have been that the woodlandish ghouls—
The pitiful, the merciful ghouls,
To bar up our way and to ban it
From the secret that lies in these wolds—
From the thing that lies hidden in these wolds—
Have drawn up the spectre of a planet
From the limbo of lunary souls—
This sinfully scintillant planet
From the Hell of the planetary souls?"

1847

Annabel Lee

Various suggestions have been made about the "real" woman. Davidson suggests that Mrs. Sarah Royster Shelton (Poe's youthful love) is the intended person. She and Poe were separated for a long time, in part because of interfering relatives. Poe was engaged to her during the last months of his life.

It was many and many a year ago,
In a kingdom by the sea,
That a maiden there lived whom you may know
By the name of Annabel Lee;
And this maiden she lived with no other thought
Than to love and be loved by me.

She was a child and *I* was a child,
In this kingdom by the sea,
But we loved with a love that was more than love—
I and my Annabel Lee—
With a love that the wingèd seraphs of Heaven
Coveted her and me.

And this was the reason that, long ago,
In this kingdom by the sea,
A wind blew out of a cloud by night
Chilling my Annabel Lee;
So that her high-born kinsmen came
And bore her away from me,
To shut her up in a sepulchre
In this kingdom by the sea.

The angels, not half so happy in Heaven,
Went envying her and me:—
Yes! that was the reason (as all men know,
In this kingdom by the sea)
That the wind came out of the cloud chilling
And killing my Annabel Lee.

But our love it was stronger by far than the love
Of those who were older than we—
Of many far wiser than we—
And neither the angels in Heaven above
Nor the demons down under the sea
Can ever dissever my soul from the soul
Of the beautiful Annabel Lee:—

For the moon never beams without bringing me dreams
Of the beautiful Annabel Lee;
And the stars never rise but I feel the bright eyes
Of the beautiful Annabel Lee:
And so all the night-tide, I lie down by the side
Of my darling, my darling, my life and my bride
In her sepulchre there by the sea—
In her tomb by the side of the sea.

1849

Eldorado

The poem doubtless comments on the California gold rush, but its theme is quite typical of Poe's poetry: the contrast between an ideal, unreachable world and the fallen one in which men live.

Gaily bedight,
A gallant knight,

In sunshine and in shadow,
    Had journeyed long,
    Singing a song,
In search of Eldorado.

    But he grew old—
    This knight so bold—
And o'er his heart a shadow
    Fell as he found
    No spot of ground
That looked like Eldorado.

    And, as his strength
    Failed him at length,
He met a pilgrim shadow—
    "Shadow," said he,
    "Where can it be—
This land of Eldorado?"

    "Over the Mountains
    Of the Moon,
Down the Valley of the Shadow,
    Ride, boldly ride,"
    The shade replied,—
"If you seek for Eldorado!"

1849

FROM *The Poetic Principle*

Originally a lecture written in 1848, "The Poetic Principle" was published in 1850, after Poe's death.

To Poe, the end of art is pleasure, not truth. So that pleasure may be intense, the work of art, whether poetry or prose, must have unity and brevity. In poetry, pleasure should be aroused by the creation of beauty—not a mere duplication of the concrete beauties of the world, but a suggestion of a higher order of beauty which may be called supernal. Since music brings us close to the supernal, the musical elements of verse—meter, rhythm, and rhyme—are essential.

In speaking of the Poetic Principle, I have no design to be either thorough or profound. While discussing, very much at random, the essentiality of what we call Poetry, my principal purpose will be to cite for consideration, some few of those minor English or American poems which best suit my own taste, or which, upon my own fancy, have left the most definite impression. By "minor poems" I mean, of course, poems of little length. And here, in the beginning, permit me to say a few words in regard to a somewhat peculiar principle, which, whether rightfully or wrongfully, has always had its influence in my own critical estimate of the poem. I hold that a long poem does not exist. I maintain that the phrase, "a long poem," is simply a flat contradiction in terms.

I need scarcely observe that a poem deserves its title only inasmuch as it excites, by elevating the soul. The value of the poem is in the ratio of this elevating excitement. But all excitements are, through a psychal necessity, transient. That degree of excitement which would entitle a poem to be so called at all, cannot be sustained throughout a composition of any great length. After the lapse of half an hour, at the very utmost, it flags—fails—a revulsion ensues—and then the poem is, in effect, and in fact, no longer such.

There are, no doubt, many who have found difficulty in reconciling the critical dictum that the "Paradise Lost" is to be devoutly admired throughout, with the absolute impossibility of maintaining for it, during perusal, the amount of enthusiasm which that critical dictum would demand. This great work, in fact, is to be regarded as poetical, only when, losing sight of that vital requisite in all works of Art, Unity, we view it merely as a series of minor poems. If, to preserve its Unity—its totality of effect or impression—we read it (as would be necessary) at a single sitting, the result is but a constant alternation of excitement and depression. After a passage of what we feel to be true poetry, there follows, inevitably, a passage of platitude which no critical pre-judgment can force us to admire; but if, upon completing the work, we read it again, omitting the first book—that is to say, commencing with the second—we shall be surprised at now finding that admirable which we before condemned—that damnable which we had previously so much admired. It follows from all this that the ultimate, aggregate, or absolute effect of even the best epic under the sun, is a nullity:—and this is precisely the fact.

In regard to the Iliad, we have, if not positive proof, at least very good reason for believing it intended as a series of lyrics; but, granting the epic intention, I can say only that the work is based in an imperfect sense of art. The modern epic is, of the supposititious ancient model, but an inconsiderate and blindfold imitation. But the day of these artistic anomalies is over. If, at any time, any very long poem *were* popular in reality, which I doubt, it is at least clear that no very long poem will ever be popular again.

That the extent of a poetical work is, *ceteris paribus*,[1] the measure of its merit, seems undoubtedly, when we thus state it, a proposition sufficiently absurd—yet we are indebted for it to the Quarterly Reviews. Surely there can be nothing in mere *size*,

[1] Other things being equal.

abstractly considered—there can be nothing in mere *bulk*, so far as a volume is concerned, which has so continuously elicited admiration from these saturnine pamphlets! A mountain, to be sure, by the mere sentiment of physical magnitude which it conveys, *does* impress us with a sense of the sublime—but no man is impressed after *this* fashion by the material grandeur of even "The Columbiad."[2] Even the Quarterlies have not instructed us to be so impressed by it. *As yet,* they have not *insisted* on our estimating Lamartine[3] by the cubic foot, or Pollok[4] by the pound—but what else are we to *infer* from their continual prating about "sustained effort"? If, by "sustained effort," any little gentleman has accomplished an epic, let us frankly commend him for the effort—if this indeed be a thing commendable—but let us forbear praising the epic on the effort's account. It is to be hoped that common sense, in the time to come, will prefer deciding upon a work of art, rather by the impression it makes, by the effect it produces, than by the time it took to impress the effect, or by the amount of "sustained effort" which has been found necessary in effecting the impression. The fact is, that perseverance is one thing, and genius quite another; nor can all the Quarterlies in Christendom confound them. By and by, this proposition, with many which I have just been urging, will be received as self-evident. In the mean time, by being generally condemned as falsities, they will not be essentially damaged as truths.

On the other hand, it is clear that a poem may be improperly brief. Undue brevity degenerates into mere epigrammatism. A *very* short poem, while now and then producing a brilliant or vivid, never produces a profound or enduring effect. There must be the steady pressing down of the stamp upon the wax. De Béranger[5] has wrought innumerable things, pungent and spirit-stirring; but, in general, they have been too imponderous to stamp themselves deeply into the public attention; and thus, as so many feathers of fancy, have been blown aloft only to be whistled down the wind.

A remarkable instance of the effect of undue brevity in depressing a poem—in keeping it out of the popular view—is afforded by the following exquisite little Serenade:

I arise from dreams of thee
  In the first sweet sleep of night,
When the winds are breathing low,
  And the stars are shining bright;
I arise from dreams of thee,
  And a spirit in my feet
Has led me—who knows how?—
  To thy chamber-window, sweet!

The wandering airs, they faint
  On the dark, the silent stream—
The Champak odors fail
  Like sweet thoughts in a dream;
The nightingale's complaint,
  It dies upon her heart,
As I must die on thine,
  O, beloved as thou art!

O, lift me from the grass!
  I die, I faint, I fail!
Let thy love in kisses rain
  On my lips and eyelids pale.
My cheek is cold and white, alas!
  My heart beats loud and fast:
Oh! press it close to thine again,
  Where it will break at last!

Very few, perhaps, are familiar with these lines—yet no less a poet than Shelley is their author. ° ° °

While the epic mania—while the idea that, to merit in poetry, prolixity is indispensable—has, for some years past, been gradually dying out of the public mind, by mere dint of its own absurdity—we find it succeeded by a heresy too palpably false to be long tolerated, but one which, in the brief period it has already endured, may be said to have accomplished more in the corruption of our Poetical Literature than all its other enemies combined. I allude to the heresy of *The Didactic.* It has been assumed, tacitly and avowedly, directly and indirectly, that the ultimate object of all Poetry is Truth. Every poem, it is said, should inculcate a moral; and by this moral is the poetical merit of the work to be adjudged. We Americans especially have patronized this happy idea; and we Bostonians, very especially, have developed it in full. We have taken it into our heads that to write a poem simply for the poem's sake, and to acknowledge such to have been our design, would be to confess ourselves radically wanting in the true Poetic dignity and force:—but the simple fact is, that, would we but permit ourselves to look into our own souls, we should immediately there discover that under the sun there neither exists nor *can* exist any work more thoroughly dignified—more supremely noble than this very poem—this poem *per se*—this poem which is a poem and nothing more—this poem written solely for the poem's sake.

With as deep a reverence for the True as ever inspired the bosom of man, I would, nevertheless,

[2] Once called America's tin-plated epic; written by Joel Barlow, published in 1807.

[3] Alphonse de Lamartine (1790-1869), French poet.

[4] Robert Pollok (1798-1827), Scottish poet.

[5] Pierre Jean de Béranger (1780-1857), French lyric poet.

limit, in some measure, its modes of inculcation. I would limit to enforce them. I would not enfeeble them by dissipation. The demands of Truth are severe. She has no sympathy with the myrtles. All *that* which is so indispensable in Song is precisely all *that* with which *she* has nothing whatever to do. It is but making her a flaunting paradox, to wreathe her in gems and flowers. In enforcing a truth, we need severity rather than efflorescence of language. We must be simple, precise, terse. We must be cool, calm, unimpassioned. In a word, we must be in that mood which, as nearly as possible, is the exact converse of the poetical. *He* must be blind, indeed, who does not perceive the radical and chasmal differences between the truthful and the poetical modes of inculcation. He must be theory-mad beyond redemption who, in spite of these differences, shall still persist in attempting to reconcile the obstinate oils and waters of Poetry and Truth.

Dividing the world of mind into its three most immediately obvious distinctions, we have the Pure Intellect, Taste, and the Moral Sense. I place Taste in the middle, because it is just this position which, in the mind, it occupies. It holds intimate relations with either extreme; but from the Moral Sense is separated by so faint a difference that Aristotle has not hesitated to place some of its operations among the virtues themselves. Nevertheless, we find the *offices* of the trio marked with a sufficient distinction. Just as the Intellect concerns itself with Truth, so Taste informs us of the Beautiful while the Moral Sense is regardful of Duty. Of this latter, while Conscience teaches the obligation, and Reason the expediency, Taste contents herself with displaying the charms:—waging war upon Vice solely on the ground of her deformity—her disproportion—her animosity to the fitting, to the appropriate, to the harmonious—in a word, to Beauty.

An immortal instinct, deep within the spirit of man, is thus, plainly, a sense of the Beautiful. This it is which administers to his delight in the manifold forms, and sounds, and odors, and sentiments amid which he exists. And just as the lily is repeated in the lake, or the eyes of Amaryllis in the mirror, so is the mere oral or written repetition of these forms, and sounds, and colors, and odors, and sentiments, a duplicate source of delight. But this mere repetition is not poetry. He who shall simply sing, with however glowing enthusiasm, or with however vivid a truth of description, of the sights, and sounds, and odors, and colors, and sentiments, which greet *him* in the common with all mankind—he, I say, has yet failed to prove his divine title. There is still a something in the distance which he has been unable to attain. We have still a thirst unquenchable, to allay which he has not shown us the crystal springs. This thirst belongs to the immortality of Man. It is at once a consequence and an indication of his perennial existence. It is the desire of the moth for the star. It is no mere appreciation of the Beauty before us—but a wild effort to reach the Beauty above. Inspired by an ecstatic prescience of the glories beyond the grave, we struggle, by multiform combinations among the things and thoughts of Time, to attain a portion of that Loveliness whose very elements, perhaps, appertain to eternity alone. And thus when by Poetry—or when by Music, the most entrancing of the Poetic moods—we find ourselves melted into tears—we weep then—not as the Abbaté Gravina[6] supposes—through excess of pleasure, but through a certain, petulant, impatient sorrow at our inability to grasp *now*, wholly, here on earth, at once and forever, those divine and rapturous joys, of which *through* the poem, or *through* the music, we attain to but brief and indeterminate glimpses.

The struggle to apprehend the supernal Loveliness—this struggle, on the part of souls fittingly constituted—has given to the world all *that* which it (the world) has ever been enabled at once to understand and to *feel* as poetic.

The Poetic Sentiment, of course, may develop itself in various modes—in Painting, in Sculpture, in Architecture, in the Dance—very especially in Music—and very peculiarly, and with a wide field, in the composition of the Landscape Garden. Our present theme, however, has regard only to its manifestation in words. And here let me speak briefly on the topic of rhythm. Contenting myself with the certainty that Music, in its various modes of meter, rhythm, and rhyme, is of so vast a moment in Poetry as never to be wisely rejected—is so vitally important an adjunct, that he is simply silly who declines its assistance, I will not now pause to maintain its absolute essentiality. It is in Music, perhaps, that the soul most nearly attains the great end for which, when inspired by the Poetic Sentiment, it struggles—the creation of supernal Beauty. It *may* be, indeed, that here this sublime end is, now and then, attained *in fact*. We are often made to feel, with a shivering delight, that from an earthly harp are stricken notes which *cannot* have been unfamiliar to the angels. And thus there can be little doubt that in the union of Poetry with Music in its popular sense, we shall find the widest field for the Poetic development. The old Bards and Minnesingers had advantages which we do not possess—and Thomas Moore, singing his own songs, was, in the most legitimate manner, perfecting them as poems.

To recapitulate, then:—I would define, in brief, the Poetry of words as *The Rhythmical Creation of*

[6] Giovanni Gravina (1664-1718), Italian critic.

Beauty. Its sole arbiter is Taste. With the Intellect or with the Conscience, it has only collateral relations. Unless incidentally, it has no concern whatever either with Duty or with Truth.

A few words, however, in explanation. *That* pleasure which is at once the most pure, the most elevating, and the most intense, is derived, I maintain, from the contemplation of the Beautiful. In the contemplation of Beauty we alone find it possible to attain that pleasurable elevation, or excitement, *of the soul*, which we recognize as the Poetic Sentiment, and which is so easily distinguished from Truth, which is the satisfaction of the Reason, or from Passion, which is the excitement of the heart. I make Beauty, therefore—using the word as inclusive of the sublime—I make Beauty the province of the poem, simply because it is an obvious rule of Art that effects should be made to spring as directly as possible from their causes:—no one as yet having been weak enough to deny that the peculiar elevation in question is at least *most readily* attainable in the poem. It by no means follows, however, that the incitements of Passion, or the precepts of Duty, or even the lessons of Truth, may not be introduced into a poem, and with advantage; for they may subserve, incidentally, in various ways, the general purposes of the work:—but the true artist will always contrive to tone them down in proper subjection to that *Beauty* which is the atmosphere and the real essence of the poem.[7] * * *

Thus, although in a very cursory and imperfect manner, I have endeavored to convey to you my conception of the Poetic Principle. It has been my purpose to suggest that, while this Principle itself is, strictly and simply, the Human Aspiration for Supernal Beauty, the manifestation of the Principle is always found in *an elevating excitement of the Soul*—quite independent of that passion which is the intoxication of the Heart—or of that Truth which is the satisfaction of the Reason. For in regard to Passion, alas! its tendency is to degrade, rather than to elevate the Soul. Love, on the contrary—Love—the true, the divine Eros—the Uranian, as distinguished from the Dionaean Venus—is unquestionably the purest and truest of all poetical themes. And in regard to Truth—if, to be sure, through the attainment of a truth, we are led to perceive a harmony where none was apparent before, we experience at once the true poetical effect—but this effect is referable to the harmony alone, and not in the least degree to the truth which merely served to render the harmony manifest.

[7] In passages here omitted, Poe presented, and briefly commented on, poems by Longfellow, Bryant, Pinkney, Moore, Hood, Byron, and Tennyson.

We shall reach, however, more immediately a distinct conception of what the true Poetry is, by mere reference to a few of the simple elements which induce in the Poet himself the true poetical effect. He recognizes the ambrosia which nourishes his soul, in the bright orbs that shine in Heaven—in the volutes of the flower—in the clustering of low shrubberies—in the waving of the grain-fields—in the slanting of tall, Eastern trees—in the blue distance of mountains—in the grouping of clouds—in the twinkling of half-hidden brooks—in the gleaming of silver rivers—in the repose of sequestered lakes—in the star-mirroring depths of lonely wells. He perceives it in the songs of birds—in the harp of Aeolus—in the sighing of the night-wind—in the repining voice of the forest—in the surf that complains to the shore—in the fresh breath of the woods—in the scent of the violet—in the voluptuous perfume of the hyacinth—in the suggestive odor that comes to him, at eventide, from far-distant, undiscovered islands, over dim oceans, illimitable and unexplored. He owns it in all noble thoughts—in all unworldly motives—in all holy impulses—in all chivalrous, generous, and self-sacrificing deeds. He feels it in the beauty of woman—in the grace of her step—in the lustre of her eye—in the melody of her voice—in her soft laughter—in her sigh—in the harmony of the rustling of her robes. He deeply feels it in her winning endearments—in her burning enthusiasms—in her gentle charities—in her meek and devotional endurances—but above all—ah, far above all—he kneels to it—he worships it in the faith, in the purity, in the strength, in the altogether divine majesty—of her *love*. * * *

The Philosophy of Composition

First printed in *Graham's Magazine*, April, 1846. Though himself a romantic in the effects produced by his art, Poe rejected the extreme view (common among romantics) that literary works, especially poems, are written unconsciously in a state of inspiration ("ecstatic intuition"). In this essay he embraces the opposite extreme: that they are written with conscious deliberation. Taking "The Raven" as an example, he affirms that he constructed it "with the precision and rigid consequence of a mathematical problem." He presents an analysis of the artistic questions he faced and the arguments he used in answering them. His account of the writing of "The Raven" may exaggerate the calculation and consciousness involved, though he actually worked on the poem for four years. Nevertheless, the essay is valuable because it identifies important elements in the poem and because it develops important aspects of Poe's theory of poetry.

Charles Dickens, in a note now lying before me, alluding to an examination I once made of the mechanism of "Barnaby Rudge," says—"By the way, are you aware that Godwin wrote his "Caleb Williams" backwards? He first involved his hero in a web of difficulties, forming the second volume, and then, for the first, cast about him for some mode of accounting for what had been done."

I cannot think this the *precise* mode of procedure on the part of Godwin—and indeed what he himself acknowledges, is not altogether in accordance with Mr. Dickens' idea—but the author of "Caleb Williams" was too good an artist not to perceive the advantage derivable from at least a somewhat similar process. Nothing is more clear than that every plot, worth the name, must be elaborated to its *dénouement* before anything be attempted with the pen. It is only with the *dénouement* constantly in view that we can give a plot its indispensable air of consequence, or causation, by making the incidents, and especially the tone at all points, tend to the development of the intention.

There is a radical error, I think, in the usual mode of constructing a story. Either history affords a thesis—or one is suggested by an incident of the day—or, at best, the author sets himself to work in the combination of striking events to form merely the basis of his narrative—designing, generally, to fill in with description, dialogue, or autorial comment, whatever crevices of fact, or action, may, from page to page, render themselves apparent.

I prefer commencing with the consideration of an *effect*. Keeping originality *always* in view—for he is false to himself who ventures to dispense with so obvious and so easily attainable a source of interest—I say to myself, in the first place, "Of the innumerable effects, or impressions, of which the heart, the intellect, or (more generally) the soul is susceptible, what one shall I, on the present occasion, select?" Having chosen a novel, first, and secondly a vivid effect, I consider whether it can be best wrought by incident or tone—whether by ordinary incidents and peculiar tone, or the converse, or by peculiarity both of incident and tone—afterward looking about me (or rather within) for such combinations of event, or tone, as shall best aid me in the construction of the effect.

I have often thought how interesting a magazine paper might be written by any author who would—that is to say, who could—detail, step by step, the processes by which any one of his compositions attained its ultimate point of completion. Why such a paper has never been given to the world, I am much at a loss to say—but, perhaps, the autorial vanity has had more to do with the omission than any one other cause. Most writers—poets in especial—prefer having it understood that they compose by a species of fine frenzy—an ecstatic intuition—and would positively shudder at letting the public take a peep behind the scenes, at the elaborate and vacillating crudities of thought—at the true purposes seized only at the last moment—at the innumerable glimpses of idea that arrived not at the maturity of full view—at the fully matured fancies discarded in despair as unmanageable—at the cautious selections and rejections—at the painful erasures and interpolations—in a word, at the wheels and pinions—the tackle for scene-shifting—the step-ladders and demon-traps—the cock's feathers, the red paint and the black patches, which, in ninety-nine cases out of the hundred, constitute the properties of the literary *histrio*.

I am aware, on the other hand, that the case is by no means common, in which an author is at all in condition to retrace the steps by which his conclusions have been attained. In general, suggestions, having arisen pell-mell, are pursued and forgotten in a similar manner.

For my own part, I have neither sympathy with the repugnance alluded to, nor, at any time, the least difficulty in recalling to mind the progressive steps of any of my compositions; and, since the interest of an analysis, or reconstruction, such as I have considered a *desideratum*, is quite independent of any real or fancied interest in the thing analyzed, it will not be regarded as a breach of decorum on my part to show the *modus operandi* by which some one of my own works was put together. I select "The Raven," as the most generally known. It is my design to render it manifest that no one point in its composition is referable either to accident or intuition—that the work proceeded, step by step, to its completion with the precision and rigid consequence of a mathematical problem.

Let us dismiss, as irrelevant to the poem, *per se*, the circumstance—or say the necessity—which, in the first place, gave rise to the intention of composing *a* poem that should suit at once the popular and the critical taste.

We commence, then, with this intention.

The initial consideration was that of extent. If any literary work is too long to be read at one sitting, we must be content to dispense with the immensely important effect derivable from unity of impression—for, if two sittings be required, the affairs of the world interfere, and everything like totality is at once destroyed. But since, *ceteris paribus*, no poet can afford to dispense with *anything* that may advance his design, it but remains to be seen whether there is, in extent, any advantage to counterbalance the loss of unity which attends it. Here I say no, at once. What we term a long poem is, in fact, merely a succession of brief ones—that is to say, of brief poetical effects. It is needless to demonstrate that a poem is such, only inasmuch as it intensely excites, by elevating, the soul; and all intense excitements are, through a psychal necessity, brief. For this reason, at least one half of the "Paradise Lost" is essentially prose—a succession of poetical excitements interspersed, *inevitably*, with corresponding depressions—the whole being deprived, through the extremeness of its length, of the vastly important artistic element, totality, or unity, of effect.

It appears evident, then, that there is a distinct limit, as regards length, to all works of literary art—the limit of a single sitting—and that, although in certain classes of prose composition, such as "Robinson Crusoe" (demanding no unity), this limit may be advantageously overpassed, it can never properly be overpassed in a poem. Within this limit, the extent of a poem may be made to bear mathematical relation to its merit—in other words, to the excitement or elevation—again in other words, to the degree of true poetical effect which it is capable of inducing; for it is clear that the brevity must be in direct ratio of the intensity of the intended effect:—this, with one proviso—that a certain degree of duration is absolutely requisite for the production of any effect at all.

Holding in view these considerations, as well as that degree of excitement which I deemed not above the popular, while not below the critical, taste, I reached at once what I conceived the proper *length* for my intended poem—a length of about one hundred lines. It is, in fact, a hundred and eight.

My next thought concerned the choice of an impression, or effect, to be conveyed: and here I may as well observe that, throughout the construction, I kept steadily in view the design of rendering the work *universally* appreciable. I should be carried too far out of my immediate topic were I to demonstrate a point upon which I have repeatedly insisted, and which, with the poetical, stands not in the slightest need of demonstration—the point, I mean, that Beauty is the sole legitimate province of the poem. A few words, however, in elucidation of my real meaning, which some of my friends have evinced a disposition to misrepresent. That pleasure which is at once the most intense, the most elevating, and the most pure, is, I believe, found in the contemplation of the beautiful. When, indeed, men speak of Beauty, they mean, precisely, not a quality, as is supposed, but an effect—they refer, in short, just to that intense and pure elevation of *soul—not* of intellect, or of heart—upon which I have commented, and which is experienced in consequence of contemplating "the beautiful." Now I designate Beauty as the province of the poem, merely because it is an obvious rule of Art that effects should be made to spring from direct causes—that objects should be attained through means best adapted for their attainment—no one as yet having been weak enough to deny that the peculiar elevation alluded to is *most readily* attained in the poem. Now the object Truth, or the satisfaction of the intellect, and the object Passion, or the excitement of the heart, are, although attainable, to a certain extent, in poetry, far more readily attainable in prose. Truth, in fact, demands a precision, and Passion, a *homeliness* (the truly passionate will comprehend me) which are absolutely antagonistic to that Beauty which, I maintain, is the excitement, or pleasurable elevation, of the soul. It by no means follows from anything here said, that passion, or even truth, may not be introduced, and even profitably introduced, into a poem—for they may serve in elucidation, or aid the general effect, as do discords in music, by contrast—but the true artist will always contrive, first, to tone them into proper subservience to the predominant aim, and, secondly, to enveil them, as far as possible, in that Beauty which is the atmosphere and the essence of the poem.

Regarding, then, Beauty as my province, my next question referred to the *tone* of its highest manifestation—and all experience has shown that this tone is one of *sadness*. Beauty of whatever kind, in its supreme development, invariably excites the sensitive soul to tears. Melancholy is thus the most legitimate of all the poetical tones.

The length, the province, and the tone, being thus determined, I betook myself to ordinary induction, with the view of obtaining some artistic piquancy which might serve me as a key-note in the construction of the poem—some pivot upon which the whole structure might turn. In carefully thinking over all the usual artistic effects—or more properly *points*, in the theatrical sense—I did not fail to perceive immediately that no one had been so universally employed as that of the *refrain*. The universality of its employment sufficed to assure me of its intrinsic value, and spared me the necessity of submitting it to analysis. I considered it, however, with regard to its susceptibility of improvement, and soon saw it to be in a primitive condition. As commonly used, the *refrain*, or burden, not only is limited to lyric verse, but depends for its impression upon the force of monotone—both in sound and thought. The pleasure is deduced solely from the sense of identity—of repetition. I resolved to diversify, and so vastly heighten, the effect, by adhering, in general, to the monotone of sound, while I continually varied that of thought: that is to say, I determined to produce continuously novel effects, by the variation *of the application* of the *refrain*—the *refrain* itself remaining, for the most part, unvaried.

These points being settled, I next bethought me

of the *nature* of my *refrain.* Since its application was to be repeatedly varied, it was clear that the *refrain* itself must be brief, for there would have been an insurmountable difficulty in frequent variations of application in any sentence of length. In proportion to the brevity of the sentence, would, of course, be the facility of the variation. This led me at once to a single word as the best *refrain.*

The question now arose as to the *character* of the word. Having made up my mind to a *refrain,* the division of the poem into stanzas was, of course, a corollary: the *refrain* forming the close to each stanza. That such a close, to have force, must be sonorous and susceptible of protracted emphasis, admitted no doubt: and these considerations inevitably led me to the long *o* as the most sonorous vowel, in connection with *r* as the producible consonant.

The sound of the *refrain* being thus determined, it became necessary to select a word embodying this sound, and at the same time in the fullest possible keeping with that melancholy which I had predetermined as the tone of the poem. In such a search it would have been absolutely impossible to overlook the word "Nevermore." In fact, it was the very first which presented itself.

The next *desideratum* was a pretext for the continuous use of the one word "nevermore." In observing the difficulty which I at once found in inventing a sufficiently plausible reason for its continuous repetition, I did not fail to perceive that this difficulty arose solely from the pre-assumption that the word was to be so continuously or monotonously spoken by a *human* being—I did not fail to perceive, in short, that the difficulty lay in the reconciliation of this monotony with the exercise of reason on the part of the creature repeating the word. Here, then, immediately arose the idea of a *non*-reasoning creature capable of speech; and, very naturally, a parrot, in the first instance, suggested itself, but was superseded forthwith by a Raven, as equally capable of speech, and infinitely more in keeping with the intended *tone.*

I had now gone so far as the conception of a Raven—the bird of ill omen—monotonously repeating the one word, "Nevermore," at the conclusion of each stanza, in a poem of melancholy tone, and in length about one hundred lines. Now, never losing sight of the object *supremeness,* or perfection, at all points, I asked myself—"Of all melancholy topics, what, according to the *universal* understanding of mankind, is the *most* melancholy?" Death—was the obvious reply. "And when," I said, "is this most melancholy of topics most poetical?" From what I have already explained at some length, the answer, here also, is obvious—"When it most closely allies itself to *Beauty:* the death, then, of a beautiful woman is, unquestionably, the most poetical topic in the world—and equally is it beyond doubt that the lips best suited for such topic are those of a bereaved lover."

I had now to combine the two ideas, of a lover lamenting his deceased mistress and a Raven continuously repeating the word "Nevermore"—I had to combine these, bearing in mind my design of varying, at every turn, the *application* of the word repeated; but the only intelligible mode of such combination is that of imagining the Raven employing the word in answer to the queries of the lover. And here it was I saw at once the opportunity afforded for the effect on which I had been depending—that is to say, the effect of the *variation of application.* I saw that I could make the first query propounded by the lover—the first query to which the Raven should reply "Nevermore"—that I could make this first query a commonplace one—the second less so—the third still less, and so on—until at length the lover, startled from his original *nonchalance* by the melancholy character of the word itself—by its frequent repetition—and by a consideration of the ominous reputation of the fowl that uttered it—is at length excited to superstition, and wildly propounds queries of a far different character—queries whose solution he has passionately at heart—propounds them half in superstition and half in that species of despair which delights in self-torture—propounds them not altogether because he believes in the prophetic or demoniac character of the bird (which, reason assures him, is merely repeating a lesson learned by rote) but because he experiences a phrenzied pleasure in so modeling his questions as to receive from the *expected* "Nevermore" the most delicious because the most intolerable of sorrow. Perceiving the opportunity thus afforded me—or, more strictly, thus forced upon me in the progress of the construction—I first established in mind the climax, or concluding query—that query to which "Nevermore" should be in the last place an answer—that in reply to which this word "Nevermore" should involve the utmost conceivable amount of sorrow and despair.

Here then the poem may be said to have its beginning—at the end, where all works of art should begin—for it was here, at this point of my preconsiderations, that I first put pen to paper in the composition of the stanza:

> "Prophet," said I, "thing of evil! prophet still if bird
> or devil!
> By that heaven that bends above us—by that God
> we both adore,

Tell this soul with sorrow laden, if within the
distant Aidenn,
It shall clasp a sainted maiden whom the angels
name Lenore—
Clasp a rare and radiant maiden whom the angels
name Lenore."
Quoth the raven "Nevermore."

I composed this stanza, at this point, first that, by establishing the climax, I might the better vary and graduate, as regards seriousness and importance, the preceding queries of the lover—and, secondly, that I might definitely settle the rhythm, the metre, and the length and general arrangement of the stanza—as well as graduate the stanzas which were to precede, so that none of them might surpass this in rhythmical effect. Had I been able, in the subsequent composition, to construct more vigorous stanzas, I should, without scruple, have purposely enfeebled them, so as not to interfere with the climacteric effect.

And here I may as well say a few words of the versification. My first object (as usual) was originality. The extent to which this has been neglected, in versification, is one of the most unaccountable things in the world. Admitting that there is little possibility of variety in mere *rhythm*, it is still clear that the possible varieties of metre and stanza are absolutely infinite—and yet, *for centuries, no man, in verse, has ever done, or ever seemed to think of doing, an original thing.* The fact is, originality (unless in minds of very unusual force) is by no means a matter, as some suppose, of impulse or intuition. In general, to be found, it must be elaborately sought, and although a positive merit of the highest class, demands in its attainment less of invention than negation.

Of course, I pretend to no originality in either the rhythm or metre of the "Raven." The former is trochaic—the latter is octameter acatalectic, alternating with heptameter catalectic repeated in the *refrain* of the fifth verse, and terminating with tetrameter catalectic. Less pedantically—the feet employed throughout (trochees) consist of a long syllable followed by a short: the first line of the stanza consists of eight of these feet—the second of seven and a half (in effect two-thirds)—the third of eight—the fourth of seven and a half—the fifth the same—the sixth three and a half. Now, each of these lines, taken individually, has been employed before, and what originality the "Raven" has, is in their *combination into stanza;* nothing even remotely approaching this combination has ever been attempted. The effect of this originality of combination is aided by other unusual, and some altogether novel effects, arising from an extension of the application of the principles of rhyme and alliteration.

The next point to be considered was the mode of bringing together the lover and the Raven—and the first branch of this consideration was the *locale.* For this the most natural suggestion might seem to be a forest, or the fields—but it has always appeared to me that a close *circumscription of space* is absolutely necessary to the effect of insulated incident:—it has the force of a frame to a picture. It has an indisputable moral power in keeping concentrated the attention, and, of course, must not be confounded with mere unity of place.

I determined, then, to place the lover in his chamber—in a chamber rendered sacred to him by memories of her who had frequented it. The room is represented as richly furnished—this is mere pursuance of the ideas I have already explained on the subject of Beauty, as the sole true poetical thesis.

The *locale* being thus determined, I had now to introduce the bird—and the thought of introducing him through the window, was inevitable. The idea of making the lover suppose, in the first instance, that the flapping of the wings of the bird against the shutter, is a "tapping" at the door, originated in a wish to increase, by prolonging, the reader's curiosity, and in a desire to admit the incidental effect arising from the lover's throwing open the door, finding all dark, and thence adopting the half-fancy that it was the spirit of his mistress that knocked.

I made the night tempestuous, first, to account for the Raven's seeking admission, and secondly, for the effect of contrast with the (physical) serenity within the chamber.

I made the bird alight on the bust of Pallas, also for the effect of contrast between the marble and the plumage—it being understood that the bust was absolutely *suggested* by the bird—the bust of *Pallas* being chosen, first, as most in keeping with the scholarship of the lover, and, secondly, for the sonorousness of the word, Pallas, itself.

About the middle of the poem, also, I have availed myself of the force of contrast, with a view of deepening the ultimate impression. For example, an air of the fantastic—approaching as nearly to the ludicrous as was admissible—is given to the Raven's entrance. He comes in "with many a flirt and flutter."

Not the *least obeisance made he*—not a moment
stopped or stayed he,
But with mien of lord or lady, perched above my
chamber door.

In the two stanzas which follow, the design is more obviously carried out:—

Then this ebony bird beguiling my sad fancy into
smiling
By the *grave and stern decorum of the countenance
it wore,*
"Though thy *crest be shorn and shaven* thou," I
said, "art sure no craven,
Ghastly grim and ancient Raven wandering from
the nightly shore—
Tell me what thy lordly name is on the Night's
Plutonian shore!"
Quoth the Raven "Nevermore."

Much I marvelled *this ungainly fowl* to hear
discourse so plainly,
Though its answer little meaning—little relevancy
bore;
For we cannot help agreeing that no living human
being
*Ever yet was blessed with seeing bird above his
chamber door—*
*Bird or beast upon the sculptured bust above his
chamber door,*
With such name as "Nevermore."

The effect of the *dénouement* being thus provided for, I immediately drop the fantastic for a tone of the most profound seriousness:—this tone commencing in the stanza directly following the one last quoted, with the line,

But the Raven, sitting lonely on that placid bust,
spoke only, etc.

From this epoch the lover no longer jests—no longer sees anything even of the fantastic in the Raven's demeanor. He speaks of him as a "grim, ungainly, ghastly, gaunt, and ominous bird of yore," and feels the "fiery eyes" burning into his "bosom's core." This revolution of thought, or fancy, on the lover's part, is intended to induce a similar one on the part of the reader—to bring the mind into a proper frame for the *dénouement*—which is now brought about as rapidly and as *directly* as possible.

With the *dénouement* proper—with the Raven's reply, "Nevermore," to the lover's final demand if he shall meet his mistress in another world—the poem, in its obvious phase, that of a simple narrative, may be said to have its completion. So far, everything is within the limits of the accountable—of the real. A raven, having learned by rote the single word "Nevermore," and having escaped from the custody of its owner, is driven at midnight, through the violence of a storm, to seek admission at a window from which a light still gleams—the chamber-window of a student, occupied half in poring over a volume, half in dreaming of a beloved mistress deceased. The casement being thrown open at the fluttering of the bird's wings, the bird itself perches on the most convenient seat out of the immediate reach of the student, who, amused by the incident and the oddity of the visitor's demeanor, demands of it, in jest and without looking for a reply, its name. The raven addressed, answers with its customary word, "Nevermore"—a word which finds immediate echo in the melancholy heart of the student, who, giving utterance aloud to certain thoughts suggested by the occasion, is again startled by the fowl's repetition of "Nevermore." The student now guesses the state of the case, but is impelled, as I have before explained, by the human thirst for self-torture, and in part by superstition, to propound such queries to the bird as will bring him, the lover, the most of the luxury of sorrow, through the anticipated answer "Nevermore." With the indulgence, to the extreme, of this self-torture, the narration, in what I have termed its first or obvious phase, has a natural termination, and so far there has been no overstepping of the limits of the real.

But in subjects so handled, however skilfully, or with however vivid an array of incident, there is always a certain hardness or nakedness, which repels the artistical eye. Two things are invariably required—first, some amount of complexity, or more properly, adaptation; and, secondly, some amount of suggestiveness—some undercurrent, however indefinite, of meaning. It is this latter, in especial, which imparts to a work of art so much of that *richness* (to borrow from colloquy a forcible term) which we are too fond of confounding with *the ideal.* It is the *excess* of the suggested meaning—it is the rendering this the upper instead of the undercurrent of the theme—which turns into prose (and that of the very flattest kind) the so called poetry of the so called transcendentalists.

Holding these opinions, I added the two concluding stanzas of the poem—their suggestiveness being thus made to pervade all the narrative which has preceded them. The undercurrent of meaning is rendered first apparent in the lines—

"Take thy beak from out *my heart,* and take thy
form from off my door!"
Quoth the Raven "Nevermore!"

It will be observed that the words, "from out my heart," involve the first metaphorical expression in the poem. They, with the answer, "Nevermore," dispose the mind to seek a moral in all that has been previously narrated. The reader begins now to regard the Raven as emblematical—but it is not until the very last line of the very last stanza, that the intention of making him emblematical of *Mournful and Never-ending Remembrance* is permitted distinctly to be seen:

And the Raven, never flitting, still is sitting, still is
sitting,
On the pallid bust of Pallas, just above my chamber
door;

And his eyes have all the seeming of a demon's that
is dreaming,
And the lamplight o'er him streaming throws his
shadow on the floor;
And my soul *from out that shadow* that lies floating
on the floor
Shall be lifted—nevermore.

1846

Hawthorne's Twice-Told Tales

The two major Poe essays included here are mainly theoretical. But he also wrote a great bulk of practical criticism, discussing particular authors and books, with a high degree of independence, honesty, and insight. The two kinds often overlap, as in his essay on Hawthorne, where he is reviewing the second edition of *Twice-Told Tales* and at the same time setting forth his theory of the short story. The essay may be read for the light it sheds on his own fiction, examples of which are printed directly after this selection.

We said a few hurried words about Mr. Hawthorne in our last number, with the design of speaking more fully in the present. We are still, however, pressed for room, and must necessarily discuss his volumes more briefly and more at random than their high merits deserve.

The book professes to be a collection of *tales,* yet is, in two respects, misnamed. These pieces are now in their third republication, and, of course, are thrice-told. Moreover, they are by no means *all* tales, either in the ordinary or in the legitimate understanding of the term. Many of them are pure essays; for example, "Sights from a Steeple," "Sunday at Home," "Little Annie's Ramble," "A Rill from the Town Pump," "The Toll-Gatherer's Day," "The Haunted Mind," "The Sister Years," "Snow-Flakes," "Night Sketches," and "Foot-Prints on the Sea-Shore." We mention these matters chiefly on account of their discrepancy with that marked precision and finish by which the body of the work is distinguished.

Of the Essays just named, we must be content to speak in brief. They are each and all beautiful, without being characterized by the polish and adaptation so visible in the tales proper. A painter would at once note their leading or predominant feature, and style it *repose.* There is no attempt at effect. All is quiet, thoughtful, subdued. Yet this repose may exist simultaneously with high originality of thought; and Mr. Hawthorne has demonstrated the fact. At every turn we meet with novel combinations; yet these combinations never surpass the limits of the quiet. We are soothed as we read; and withal is a calm astonishment that ideas so apparently obvious have never occurred or been presented to us before. Herein our author differs materially from Lamb or Hunt or Hazlitt—who, with vivid originality of manner and expression, have less of the true novelty of thought than is generally supposed, and whose originality, at best, has an uneasy and meretricious quaintness, replete with startling effects unfounded in nature, and inducing trains of reflection which lead to no satisfactory result. The Essays of Hawthorne have much of the character of Irving, with more of originality, and less of finish; while, compared with the Spectator, they have a vast superiority at all points. The Spectator, Mr. Irving, and Mr. Hawthorne have in common that tranquil and subdued manner which we have chosen to denominate *repose;* but, in the case of the two former, this repose is attained rather by the absence of novel combination, or of originality, than otherwise, and consists chiefly in the calm, quiet, unostentatious expression of commonplace thoughts, in an unambitious, unadulterated Saxon. In them, by strong effort, we are made to conceive the absence of all. In the essays before us the absence of effort is too obvious to be mistaken, and a strong undercurrent of *suggestion* runs continuously beneath the upper stream of the tranquil thesis. In short, these effusions of Mr. Hawthorne are the product of a truly imaginative intellect, restrained, and in some measure repressed, by fastidiousness of taste, by constitutional melancholy and by indolence.

But it is of his tales that we desire principally to speak. The tale proper, in our opinion, affords unquestionably the fairest field for the exercise of the loftiest talent, which can be afforded by the wide domains of mere prose. Were we bidden to say how the highest genius could be most advantageously employed for the best display of its own powers, we should answer, without hesitation—in the composition of a rhymed poem, not to exceed in length what might be perused in an hour. Within this limit alone can the highest order of true poetry exist. We need only here say, upon this topic, that, in almost all classes of composition, the unity of effect or impression is a point of the greatest importance. It is clear, moreover, that this unity cannot be thoroughly preserved in productions whose perusal cannot be completed at one sitting. We may continue the reading of a prose composition, from the very nature of prose itself, much longer than we can persevere, to any good purpose, in the perusal of a poem. This latter, if truly fulfilling the demands of the poetic sentiment, induces an exaltation of the soul which cannot be long sustained. All high excitements are necessarily transient. Thus a long poem is a paradox. And, without unity of impression, the deepest effects cannot be brought about. Epics were the offspring of an imperfect sense of Art, and their reign is no more. A poem *too* brief may produce a vivid, but never an intense or enduring impression. Without a certain continuity of effort—without a certain duration or repetition of purpose—the soul is never deeply moved. There must be the dropping of the water upon the rock. De Béranger has wrought brilliant things—pungent and spirit-stirring—but, like all immassive bodies, they lack *momentum*, and thus fail to satisfy the Poetic Sentiment. They sparkle and excite, but, from want of continuity, fail deeply to impress. Extreme brevity will degenerate into epigrammatism; but the sin of extreme length is even more unpardonable. *In medio tutissimus ibis.*[1]

Were we called upon, however, to designate that class of composition which, next to such a poem as we have suggested, should best fulfil the demands of high genius—should offer it the most advantageous field of exertion—we should unhesitatingly speak of the prose tale, as Mr. Hawthorne has here exemplified it. We allude to the short prose narrative, requiring from a half-hour to one or two hours in its perusal. The ordinary novel is objectionable, from its length, for reasons already stated in substance. As it cannot be read at one sitting, it deprives itself, of course, of the immense force derivable from *totality*. Worldly interests intervening during the pauses of perusal, modify, annul, or counteract, in a greater or less degree, the impressions of the book. But simple cessation in reading, would, of itself, be sufficient to destroy the true unity. In the brief tale, however, the author is enabled to carry out the fulness of his intention, be it what it may. During the hour of perusal the soul of the reader is at the writer's control. There are no external or extrinsic influences—resulting from weariness or interruption.

A skillful literary artist has constructed a tale. If wise, he has not fashioned his thoughts to accommodate his incidents; but having conceived, with deliberate care, a certain unique or single *effect* to be wrought out, he then invents such incidents—he then combines such events as may best aid him in establishing this preconceived effect. If his very initial sentence tend not to the outbringing of this effect, then he has failed in his first step. In the whole composition there should be no word written, of which the tendency, direct or indirect, is not to the one pre-established design. And by such means, with such care and skill, a picture is at length painted which leaves in the mind of him who contemplates it with a kindred art, a sense of the fullest satisfaction. The idea of the tale has been presented unblemished, because undisturbed; and this is an end unattainable by the novel. Undue brevity is just as exceptionable here as in the poem; but undue length is yet more to be avoided.

We have said that the tale has a point of superiority even over the poem. In fact, while the *rhythm* of this latter is an essential aid in the development of the poem's highest idea—the idea of the Beautiful—the artificialities of this rhythm are an inseparable bar to the development of all points of thought or expression which have their basis in *Truth*. But Truth is often, and in very great degree, the aim of the tale. Some of the finest tales are tales of ratiocination. Thus the field of this species of composition, if not in so elevated a region on the mountain of Mind, is a table-land of far vaster extent than the domain of the mere poem. Its products are never so rich, but infinitely more numerous, and more appreciable by the mass of mankind. The writer of the prose tale, in short, may bring to his theme a vast variety of modes or inflections of thought and expression—(the ratiocinative, for example, the sarcastic, or the humorous) which are not only antagonistical to the nature of the poem, but absolutely forbidden by one of its most peculiar and indispensable adjuncts; we allude, of course, to rhythm. It may be added here, *par parenthèse*, that the author who aims at the purely beautiful in a prose tale is laboring at a great disadvantage. For Beauty can be better treated in the poem. Not so with terror, or passion, or horror, or a multitude of such other points. And here it will be seen how full of prejudice are the usual animadversions against those *tales of effect*, many fine examples of which were found in the earlier numbers of Blackwood.[2] The impressions produced were wrought in a legitimate sphere of action, and constituted a legitimate although sometimes an exaggerated interest. They were relished by every man of genius: although there were found many men of genius who condemned them without just ground. The true critic will but demand that the design intended be accomplished, to the fullest extent, by the means most advantageously applicable.

We have very few American tales of real merit—we may say, indeed, none, with the exception of "The Tales of a Traveller" of Washington Irving, and these "Twice-Told Tales" of Mr. Hawthorne. Some of the pieces of Mr. John Neal[3] abound in vigor and originality; but, in general, his compositions of this class are excessively diffuse, extravagant, and indicative of an imperfect sentiment of Art. Articles at random are, now and then, met with in our periodicals which might be advantageously compared with the best effusions of the British Maga-

[1] "You travel most safely the middle road."

[2] An English periodical started in 1817.

[3] Neal (1793–1876) was an American writer who contributed to *Blackwood's* in the 1820's.

zines; but, upon the whole, we are far behind our progenitors in this department of literature.

Of Mr. Hawthorne's Tales we should say, emphatically, that they belong to the highest region of Art—an Art subservient to genius of a very lofty order. We had supposed, with good reason for so supposing, that he had been thrust into his present position by one of the impudent *cliques* which beset our literature, and whose pretensions it is our full purpose to expose at the earliest opportunity; but we have been most agreeably mistaken. We know of few compositions which the critic can more honestly commend than these "Twice-Told Tales." As Americans, we feel proud of the book.

Mr. Hawthorne's distinctive trait is invention, creation, imagination, originality—a trait which, in the literature of fiction, is positively worth all the rest. But the nature of the originality, so far as regards its manifestation in letters, is but imperfectly understood. The inventive or original mind as frequently displays itself in novelty of *tone* as in novelty of matter. Mr. Hawthorne is original at *all* points.

It would be a matter of some difficulty to designate the best of these tales; we repeat that, without exception, they are beautiful. "Wakefield" is remarkable for the skill with which an old idea—a well-known incident—is worked up or discussed. A man of whims conceives the purpose of quitting his wife and residing *incognito,* for twenty years, in her immediate neighborhood. Something of this kind actually happened in London. The force of Mr. Hawthorne's tale lies in the analysis of the motives which must or might have impelled the husband to such folly, in the first instance, with the possible causes of his perseverance. Upon this thesis a sketch of singular power has been constructed.

"The Wedding Knell" is full of the boldest imagination—an imagination fully controlled by taste. The most captious critic could find no flaw in this production.

"The Minister's Black Veil" is a masterly composition of which the sole defect is that to the rabble its exquisite skill will be *caviare.* The *obvious* meaning of this article will be found to smother its insinuated one. The *moral* put into the mouth of the dying minister will be supposed to convey the *true* import of the narrative; and that a crime of dark dye (having reference to the "young lady") has been committed, is a point which only minds congenial with that of the author will perceive.

"Mr. Higginbotham's Catastrophe" is vividly original and managed most dexterously.

"Dr. Heidegger's Experiment" is exceedingly well imagined, and executed with surpassing ability. The artist breathes in every line of it.

"The White Old Maid" is objectionable, even more than the "Minister's Black Veil," on the score of its mysticism. Even with the thoughtful and analytic, there will be much trouble in penetrating its entire import.

"The Hollow of the Three Hills" we would quote in full had we space;—not as evincing higher talent than any of the other pieces, but as affording an excellent example of the author's peculiar ability. The subject is commonplace. A witch subjects the Distant and the Past to the view of a mourner. It has been the fashion to describe, in such cases, a mirror in which the images of the absent appear; or a cloud of smoke is made to arise, and thence the figures are gradually unfolded. Mr. Hawthorne has wonderfully heightened his effect by making the ear, in place of the eye, the medium by which the fantasy is conveyed. The head of the mourner is enveloped in the cloak of the witch, and within its magic folds there arise sounds which have an all-sufficient intelligence. Throughout this article also, the artist is conspicuous—not more in positive than in negative merits. Not only is all done that should be done, but (what perhaps is an end with more difficulty attained) there is nothing done which should not be. Every word *tells,* and there is not a word which does *not* tell.

In "Howe's Masquerade" we observe something which resembles plagiarism[4]—but which *may be* a very flattering coincidence of thought. We quote the passage in question.

> *With a dark flush of wrath* upon his brow they saw the general *draw his sword* and *advance to meet* the figure *in the cloak* before the latter had stepped one pace upon the floor.
>
> "Villain, *unmuffle yourself,*" cried he, "you pass no farther!"
>
> The figure, without blanching a hair's breadth from the sword which was pointed at his breast, made a solemn pause, and lowered the cape of the cloak from his face, yet not sufficiently for the spectators to catch a glimpse of it. But Sir William Howe had evidently seen enough. The sternness of his countenance gave place to a look of wild amazement, if not horror, while he recoiled several steps from the figure, *and let fall his sword* upon the floor.

The idea here is, that the figure in the cloak is the phantom or reduplication of Sir William Howe; but in an article called "William Wilson," one of the "Tales of the Grotesque and Arabesque," we have not only the same idea, but the same idea similarly presented in several respects. We quote two paragraphs, which our readers may compare with what

[4] Unlikely, since Hawthorne published his tale a year before Poe's.

has been already given. We have italicized, above, the immediate particulars of resemblance.

> The brief moment in which I averted my eyes had been sufficient to produce, apparently, a material change in the arrangement at the upper or farther end of the room. A large mirror, it appeared to me, now stood where none had been perceptible before; and as I stepped up to it in extremity of terror, mine own image, but with features all pale and dabbled in blood, *advanced* with a feeble and tottering gait to meet me.
>
> Thus it appeared I say, but was not. It was Wilson, who then stood before me in the agonies of dissolution. Not a line in all the marked and singular lineaments of that face which was not even identically mine own. *His mask and cloak lay where he had thrown them, upon the floor.*

Here it will be observed that, not only are the two general conceptions identical, but there are various *points* of similarity. In each case the figure seen is the wraith or duplication of the beholder. In each case the scene is a masquerade. In each case the figure is cloaked. In each, there is a quarrel—that is to say, angry words pass between the parties. In each the beholder is enraged. In each the cloak and sword fall upon the floor. The "villain, unmuffle yourself," of Mr. H. is precisely paralleled by a passage at page 56 of "William Wilson."

In the way of objection we have scarcely a word to say of these tales. There is, perhaps, a somewhat too general or prevalent *tone*—a tone of melancholy and mysticism. The subjects are insufficiently varied. There is not so much of *versatility* evinced as we might well be warranted in expecting from the high powers of Mr. Hawthorne. But beyond these trivial exceptions we have really none to make. The style is purity itself. Force abounds. High imagination gleams from every page. Mr. Hawthorne is a man of the truest genius. We only regret that the limits of our Magazine will not permit us to pay him that full tribute of commendation, which, under other circumstances, we should be so eager to pay.

1842

Ligeia

The story contains a number of allusions which Poe hardly expected the reader to recognize. Many of them are little more than decorative and do not clarify or enrich the meaning. It may be worth noting, however, that in the paragraph beginning "For eyes we have no models" is a reference to a proverb that came from the Greek philosopher Democritus: "Truth lies at the bottom of a well." The source of the epigraph has never been identified; Poe may have invented it and attributed it to the English clergyman and philosopher Glanvill (1636–80) who wrote on the occult and supernatural.

> And the will therein lieth, which dieth not. Who knoweth the mysteries of the will, with its vigor? For God is but a great will pervading all things by nature of its intentness. Man doth not yield himself to the angels, nor unto death utterly, save only through the weakness of his feeble will.—*Joseph Glanvill.*

I cannot, for my soul, remember how, when, or even precisely where, I first became acquainted with the lady Ligeia. Long years have since elapsed, and my memory is feeble through much suffering. Or, perhaps, I cannot *now* bring these points to mind, because, in truth, the character of my beloved, her rare learning, her singular yet placid cast of beauty, and the thrilling and enthralling eloquence of her low musical language, made their way into my heart by paces so steadily and stealthily progressive that they have been unnoticed and unknown. Yet I believe that I met her first and most frequently in some large, old, decaying city near the Rhine. Of her family—I have surely heard her speak. That it is of a remotely ancient date cannot be doubted. Ligeia! Ligeia! Buried in studies of a nature more than all else adapted to deaden impressions of the outward world, it is by that sweet word alone—by Ligeia—that I bring before mine eyes in fancy the image of her who is no more. And now, while I write, a recollection flashes upon me that I have *never known* the paternal name of her who was my friend and my betrothed, and who became the partner of my studies, and finally the wife of my bosom. Was it a playful charge on the part of my Ligeia? or was it a test of my strength of affection, that I should institute no inquiries upon this point? or was it rather a caprice of my own—a wildly romantic offering on the shrine of the most passionate devotion? I but indistinctly recall the fact itself—what wonder that I have utterly forgotten the circumstances which originated or attended it? And, indeed, if ever that spirit which is entitled *Romance*—if ever she, the wan and the misty-winged *Ashtophet* of idolatrous Egypt, presided, as they tell, over marriages ill-omened, then most surely she presided over mine.

There is one dear topic, however, on which my memory fails me not. It is the *person* of Ligeia. In stature she was tall, somewhat slender, and, in her latter days, even emaciated. I would in vain attempt to portray the majesty, the quiet ease, of her demeanor, or the incomprehensible lightness and elasticity of her footfall. She came and departed as a shadow. I was never made aware of her entrance into my closed study save by the dear music of her low sweet voice, as she placed her marble hand upon my shoulder. In beauty of face no maiden ever equalled her. It was the radiance of an opium-dream—an airy and spirit-lifting vision more wildly divine than the phantasies which hovered about the slumbering souls of the daughters of Delos. Yet her features were not of that regular mould which we have been falsely taught to worship in the classical labors of the heathen. "There is no exquisite beauty," says Bacon, Lord Verulam, speaking truly of all the forms and *genera* of beauty, "without some *strangeness* in the proportion." Yet, although I saw that the features of Ligeia were not of a classic regularity—although I perceived that her loveliness was indeed "exquisite," and felt that there was much of "strangeness" pervading it, yet I have tried in vain to detect the irregularity and to trace home my own perception of "the strange." I examined the contour of the lofty and pale forehead—it was faultless—how cold indeed that word when applied to a majesty so divine!—the skin rivalling the purest ivory, the commanding extent and repose, the gentle prominence of the regions above the temples; and then the raven-black, the glossy, the luxuriant, and naturally-curling tresses, setting forth the full force of the Homeric epithet, "hyacinthine"! I looked at the delicate outlines of the nose—and nowhere but in the graceful medallions of the Hebrews had I beheld a similar perfection. There were the same luxurious smoothness of surface, the same scarcely perceptible tendency to the aquiline, the same harmoniously curved nostrils speaking the free spirit. I regarded the sweet mouth. Here was indeed the triumph of all things heavenly—the magnificent turn of the short upper lip—the soft, voluptuous slumber of the under—the dimples which sported, and the color which spoke—the teeth glancing back, with a brilliancy almost startling, every ray of the holy light which fell upon them in her serene and placid, yet most exultingly radiant of all smiles. I scrutinized the formation of the chin—and here, too, I found the gentleness of breadth, the softness and the majesty, the fullness and the spirituality, of the Greek—the contour which the god Apollo revealed but in a dream, to Cleomenes, the son of the Athenian. And then I peered into the large eyes of Ligeia.

For eyes we have no models in the remotely antique. It might have been, too, that in these eyes of my beloved lay the secret to which Lord Verulam alludes. They were, I must believe, far larger than the ordinary eyes of our own race. They were even fuller than the fullest of the gazelle eyes of the tribe of the valley of Nourjahad. Yet it was only at intervals—in moments of intense excitement—that this peculiarity became more than slightly noticeable in Ligeia. And at such moments was her beauty—in my heated fancy thus it appeared perhaps—the beauty of beings either above or apart from the earth—the beauty of the fabulous Houri of the Turk. The hue of the orbs was the most brilliant of black, and, far over them, hung jetty lashes of great length. The brows, slightly irregular in outline, had the same tint. The "strangeness," however, which I found in the eyes, was of a nature distinct from the formation, or the color, or the brilliancy of the features, and must, after all, be referred to the *expression.* Ah, word of no meaning! behind whose vast latitude of mere sound we intrench our ignorance of so much of the spiritual. The expression of the eyes of Ligeia! How for long hours have I pondered upon it! How have I, through the whole of a midsummer night, struggled to fathom it! What was it—that something more profound than the well of Democritus—which lay far within the pupils of my beloved? What *was* it? I was possessed with a passion to discover. Those eyes! those large, those shining, those divine orbs! they became to me twin stars of Leda, and I to them devoutest of astrologers.

There is no point, among the many incomprehensible anomalies of the science of mind, more thrillingly exciting than the fact—never, I believe, noticed in the schools—that in our endeavors to recall to memory something long forgotten, we often find ourselves *upon the very verge* of remembrance, without being able, in the end, to remember. And thus how frequently, in my intense scrutiny of Ligeia's eyes, have I felt approaching the full knowledge of their expression—felt it approaching—yet not quite be mine—and so at length entirely depart! And (strange, oh strangest mystery of all!) I found, in the commonest objects of the universe, a circle of analogies to that expression. I mean to say that, subsequently to the period when Ligeia's beauty passed into my spirit, there dwelling as in a shrine, I derived, from many existences in the material world, a sentiment such as I felt always aroused within me by her large and luminous orbs. Yet not the more could I define that sentiment, or analyze, or even steadily view it. I recognized it, let me repeat, sometimes in the survey of a rapidly-growing vine—in the contemplation of a moth, a butterfly, a chrysalis, a stream of running water. I have felt it in the ocean; in the falling of a meteor. I have felt it in the glances of unusually aged people. And there are one or two stars in heaven—(one especially, a star of the sixth magnitude, double and changeable, to be found near the large star in Lyra)—in a telescopic scrutiny of which I have been made aware of the feeling. I have been filled with it by certain sounds from stringed instruments, and not unfrequently by passages from books. Among innumerable other instances, I well remember something in a volume of Joseph Glanvill, which (perhaps merely from its quaintness—who shall say?) never failed to inspire me with the sentiment:—"And the will therein lieth, which dieth not. Who knoweth the mysteries of the will, with its vigor? For God is but a great will pervading all things by nature of its intentness. Man doth not yield him to the angels, nor unto death utterly, save only through the weakness of his feeble will."

Length of years, and subsequent reflection, have enabled me to trace, indeed, some remote connection between this passage in the English moralist and a portion of the character of Ligeia. An *intensity* in thought, action, or speech, was possibly, in her, a result, or at least an index, of that gigantic volition which, during our long intercourse, failed to give other and more immediate evidence of its existence. Of all the women whom I have ever known, she, the outwardly calm, the ever-placid Ligeia, was the most violently a prey to the tumultuous vultures of stern passion. And of such passion I could form no estimate, save by the miraculous expansion of those eyes which at once so delighted and appalled me—by the almost magical melody, modulation, distinctness and placidity of her very low voice—and by the fierce energy (rendered doubly effective by contrast with her manner of utterance) of the wild words which she habitually uttered.

I have spoken of the learning of Ligeia: it was immense—such as I have never known in woman. In the classical tongues was she deeply proficient, and as far as my own acquaintance extended in regard to the modern dialects of Europe, I have never known her at fault. Indeed upon any theme of the most admired, because simply the most abstruse of the boasted erudition of the academy, have I *ever* found Ligeia at fault? How singularly—how thrillingly, this one point in the nature of my wife has forced itself, at this late period only, upon my attention! I said her knowledge was such as I have never known in woman—but where breathes the man who has traversed, and successfully, *all* the wide areas of moral, physical, and mathematical science? I saw not then what I now clearly perceive, that the acquisitions of Ligeia were gigantic, were astounding; yet I was sufficiently aware of her infinite supremacy to resign myself, with a child-like confidence, to her guidance through the chaotic world of metaphysical investigation at which I was most busily occupied during the earlier years of our marriage. With how vast a triumph—with how vivid a delight—with how much of all that is ethereal in hope—did I *feel*, as she bent over me in studies but little sought—but less known—that delicious vista by slow degrees expanding before me, down whose long, gorgeous, and all untrodden path, I might at length pass onward to the goal of a wisdom too divinely precious not to be forbidden!

How poignant, then, must have been the grief with which, after some years, I beheld my well-grounded expectations take wings to themselves and fly away! Without Ligeia I was but as a child groping benighted. Her presence, her readings alone, rendered vividly luminous the many mysteries of the transcendentalism in which we were immersed. Wanting the radiant lustre of her eyes, letters, lambent and golden, grew duller than Saturnian lead. And now those eyes shone less and less frequently upon the pages over which I pored. Ligeia grew ill. The wild eyes blazed with a too—too glorious effulgence; the pale fingers became of the transparent waxen hue of the grave, and the blue veins upon the lofty forehead swelled and sank impetuously with the tides of the most gentle emotion. I saw that she must die—and I struggled desperately in spirit with the grim Azrael. And the struggles of the passionate wife were, to my astonishment, even more energetic than my own. There had been much in her stern nature to impress me with the belief that, to her, death would have come without its terrors;—but not so. Words are impotent to convey any just idea of the fierceness of resistance with which she wrestled with the Shadow. I groaned in anguish at the pitiable spectacle. I would have soothed—I would have reasoned; but, in the intensity of her wild desire for life,—for life—*but* for life—solace and reason were alike the uttermost of folly. Yet not until the last instance, amid the most convulsive writhings of her fierce spirit, was shaken the external placidity of her demeanor. Her voice grew more gentle—grew more low—yet I would not wish to dwell upon the wild meaning of the quietly uttered words. My brain reeled as I hearkened entranced, to a melody more than mortal—to assumptions and aspirations which mortality had never before known.

That she loved me I should not have doubted; and I might have been easily aware that, in a bosom such as hers, love would have reigned no ordinary passion. But in death only, was I fully impressed with the strength of her affection. For long hours, detaining my hand, would she pour out before me the overflowing of a heart whose more than passionate devotion amounted to idolatry. How had I deserved to be so blessed by such confessions?—how had I deserved to be so cursed with the removal of my beloved in the hour of her making them? But upon this subject I cannot bear to dilate. Let me say only, that in Ligeia's more than womanly abandonment to a love, alas! all unmerited, all unworthily bestowed, I at length recognized the principle of her longing with so wildly earnest a desire for the life which was now fleeing so rapidly away. It is this wild longing—it is this eager vehemence of desire for life—*but* for life—that I have no power to portray—no utterance capable of expressing.

At high noon of the night in which she departed,

beckoning me, peremptorily, to her side, she bade me repeat certain verses composed by herself not many days before. I obeyed her. They were these:[1]

Lo! 'tis a gala night
  Within the lonesome latter years!
An angel throng, bewinged, bedight
  In veils, and drowned in tears,
Sit in a theatre, to see
  A play of hopes and fears,
While the orchestra breathes fitfully
  The music of the spheres.

Mimes, in the form of God on high,
  Mutter and mumble low,
And hither and thither fly—
  Mere puppets they, who come and go
At bidding of vast formless things
  That shift the scenery to and fro,
Flapping from out their Condor wings
  Invisible Wo!

That motley drama!—oh, be sure
  It shall not be forgot!
With its Phantom chased forever more,
  By a crowd that seize it not,
Through a circle that ever returneth in
  To the self-same spot,
And much of Madness, and more of Sin,
  And Horror the soul of the plot.

But see, amid the mimic rout
  A crawling shape intrude!
A blood-red thing that writhes from out
  The scenic solitude!
It writhes—it writhes!—with mortal pangs
  The mimes become its food,
And seraphs sob at vermin fangs
  In human gore imbued.

Out—out are the lights—out all!
  And over each quivering form,
The curtain, a funeral pall,
  Comes down with the rush of a storm,
While the angels, all pallid and wan,
  Uprising, unveiling, affirm
That the play is the tragedy, "Man,"
  And its hero the Conqueror Worm.

"O God!" half shrieked Ligeia, leaping to her feet and extending her arms aloft with a spasmodic movement, as I made an end of these lines—"O God! O Divine Father!—shall these things be undeviatingly so?—shall this Conqueror be not once conquered? Are we not part and parcel in Thee? Who—who knoweth the mysteries of the will with its vigor? Man doth not yield him to the angels, *nor unto death utterly*, save only through the weakness of his feeble will."

And now, as if exhausted with emotion, she suffered her white arms to fall, and returned solemnly to her bed of death. And as she breathed her last sighs, there came mingled with them a low murmur from her lips. I bent to them my ear and distinguished, again, the concluding words of the passage in Glanvill—*"Man doth not yield him to the angels, nor unto death utterly, save only through the weakness of his feeble will."*

She died;—and I, crushed into the very dust with sorrow, could no longer endure the lonely desolation of my dwelling in the dim and decaying city by the Rhine. I had no lack of what the world calls wealth. Ligeia had brought me far more, very far more than ordinarily falls to the lot of mortals. After a few months, therefore, of weary and aimless wandering, I purchased, and put in some repair, an abbey, which I shall not name, in one of the wildest and least frequented portions of fair England. The gloomy and dreary grandeur of the building, the almost savage aspect of the domain, the many melancholy and time-honored memories connected with both, had much in unison with the feelings of utter abandonment which had driven me into that remote and unsocial region of the country. Yet although the external abbey, with its verdant decay hanging about it, suffered but little alteration, I gave way, with a child-like perversity, and perchance with a faint hope of alleviating my sorrows, to a display of more than regal magnificence within.—For such follies, even in childhood, I had imbibed a taste and now they came back to me as if in the dotage of grief. Alas, I feel how much even of incipient madness might have been discovered in the gorgeous and fantastic draperies, in the solemn carvings of Egypt, in the wild cornices and furniture, in the Bedlam patterns of the carpets of tufted gold! I had become a bounden slave in the trammels of opium, and my labors and my orders had taken a coloring from my dreams. But these absurdities I must not pause to detail. Let me speak only of that one chamber, ever accursed, whither, in a moment of mental alienation, I led from the altar as my bride—as the successor of the unforgotten Ligeia—the fair-haired and blue-eyed Lady Rowena Trevanion, of Tremaine.

There is no individual portion of the architecture and decoration of that bridal chamber which is not now visibly before me. Where were the souls of the haughty family of the bride, when, through thirst of gold, they permitted to pass the threshold of an apartment *so* bedecked, a maiden and a daughter so beloved? I have said that I minutely remember the details of the chamber—yet I am sadly forgetful on topics of deep moment—and here there was no system, no keeping, in the fantastic display, to take hold upon the memory. The room lay in a high turret of the castellated abbey, was pentagonal in

[1] Poe added the poem to the story in 1845. "Ligeia" appeared originally in 1838, and the poem was published separately in 1843.

shape, and of capacious size. Occupying the whole southern face of the pentagon was the sole window—an immense sheet of unbroken glass from Venice—a single pane, and tinted of a leaden hue, so that the rays of either the sun or moon, passing through it, fell with a ghastly lustre on the objects within. Over the upper portion of this huge window, extended the trellis-work of an aged vine, which clambered up the massy walls of the turret. The ceiling, of gloomy-looking oak, was excessively lofty, vaulted, and elaborately fretted with the wildest and most grotesque specimens of a semi-Gothic, semi-Druidical device. From out the most central recess of this melancholy vaulting, depended, by a single chain of gold with long links, a huge censer of the same metal, Saracenic in pattern, and with many perforations so contrived that there writhed in and out of them, as if endued with a serpent vitality, a continual succession of parti-colored fires.

Some few ottomans and golden candelabra, of Eastern figure, were in various stations about—and there was the couch, too—the bridal couch—of an Indian model, and low, and sculptured of solid ebony, with a pall-like canopy above. In each of the angles of the chamber stood on end a gigantic sarcophagus of black granite, from the tombs of the kings over against Luxor, with their aged lids full of immemorial sculpture. But in the draping of the apartment lay, alas! the chief phantasy of all. The lofty walls, gigantic in height—even unproportionably so—were hung from summit to foot, in vast folds, with a heavy and massive-looking tapestry—tapestry of a material which was found alike as a carpet on the floor, as a covering for the ottomans and the ebony bed, as a canopy for the bed, and as the gorgeous volutes of the curtains which partially shaded the window. The material was the richest cloth of gold. It was spotted all over, at irregular intervals, with arabesque figures, about a foot in diameter, and wrought upon the cloth in patterns of the most jetty black. But these figures partook of the true character of the arabesque only when regarded from a single point of view. By a contrivance now common, and indeed traceable to a very remote period of antiquity, they were made changeable in aspect. To one entering the room, they bore the appearance of simple monstrosities; but upon a farther advance, this appearance gradually departed; and, step by step, as the visitor moved his station in the chamber, he saw himself surrounded by an endless succession of the ghastly forms which belong to the superstition of the Norman, or arise in the guilty slumbers of the monk. The phantasmagoric effect was vastly heightened by the artificial introduction of a strong continual current of wind behind the draperies—giving a hideous and uneasy animation to the whole.

In halls such as these—in a bridal chamber such as this—I passed, with the Lady of Tremaine, the unhallowed hours of the first month of our marriage—passed them with but little disquietude. That my wife dreaded the fierce moodiness of my temper—that she shunned me and loved me but little—I could not help perceiving; but it gave me rather pleasure than otherwise. I loathed her with a hatred belonging more to demon than to man. My memory flew back, (oh, with what intensity of regret!) to Ligeia, the beloved, the august, the beautiful, the entombed. I revelled in recollections of her purity, of her wisdom, of her lofty, her ethereal nature, of her passionate, her idolatrous love. Now, then, did my spirit fully and freely burn with more than all the fires of her own. In the excitement of my opium dreams (for I was habitually fettered in the shackles of the drug), I would call aloud upon her name, during the silence of the night, or among the sheltered recesses of the glens by day, as if, through the wild eagerness, the solemn passion, the consuming ardor of my longing for the departed, I could restore her to the pathway she had abandoned—ah, *could* it be forever?—upon the earth.

About the commencement of the second month of the marriage, the Lady Rowena was attacked with sudden illness, from which her recovery was slow. The fever which consumed her, rendered her nights uneasy; and in her perturbed state of half-slumber, she spoke of sounds, and of motions, in and about the chamber of the turret, which I concluded had no origin save in the distemper of her fancy, or perhaps in the phantasmagoric influences of the chamber itself. She became at length convalescent—finally well. Yet but a brief period elapsed, ere a second more violent disorder again threw her upon a bed of suffering; and from this attack her frame, at all times feeble, never altogether recovered. Her illnesses were, after this epoch, of alarming character, and of more alarming recurrence, defying alike the knowledge and the great exertions of her physicians. With the increase of the chronic disease, which had thus, apparently, taken too sure hold upon her constitution to be eradicated by human means, I could not fail to observe a similar increase in the nervous irritation of her temperament, and in her excitability by trivial causes of fear. She spoke again, and now more frequently and pertinaciously, of the sounds—of the slight sounds—and of the unusual motions among the tapestries, to which she had formerly alluded.

One night, near the closing in of September, she pressed this distressing subject with more than usual emphasis upon my attention. She had just awakened from an unquiet slumber, and I had been watching, with feelings half of anxiety, half of vague terror, the workings of her emaciated countenance. I sat by the side of her ebony bed, upon one of the ottomans of India. She partly arose, and spoke, in an earnest low whisper, of sounds which she *then* heard, but which I could not hear—of motions which she *then* saw, but which I could not perceive. The wind was rushing hurriedly behind the tapestries, and I wished to show her (what, let me confess it, I could not *all* believe) that those almost inarticulate breathings, and those very gentle variations of the figures upon the wall, were but the natural effects of that customary rushing of the wind. But a deadly pallor, overspreading her face, had proved to me that my exertions to reassure her would be fruitless. She appeared to be fainting, and no attendants were within call. I remembered where was deposited a decanter of light wine which had been ordered by her physicians, and hastened across the chamber to procure it. But, as I stepped beneath the light of the censer, two circumstances of a startling nature attracted my attention. I had felt that some palpable although invisible object had passed lightly by my person; and I saw that there lay upon the golden carpet, in the very middle of the rich lustre thrown from the censer, a shadow—a faint, indefinite shadow of angelic aspect—such as might be fancied for the shadow of a shade. But I was wild with the excitement of an immoderate dose of opium, and heeded these things but little, nor spoke of them to Rowena. Having found the wine, I recrossed the chamber, and poured out a gobletful, which I held to the lips of the fainting lady. She had now partially recovered, however, and took the vessel herself, while I sank upon an ottoman near me, with my eyes fastened upon her person. It was then that I became distinctly aware of a gentle foot-fall upon the carpet, and near the couch; and in a second thereafter, as Rowena was in the act of raising the wine to her lips, I saw, or may have dreamed that I saw, fall within the goblet, as if from some invisible spring in the atmosphere of the room, three or four large drops of a brilliant and ruby-colored fluid. If this I saw—not so Rowena. She swallowed the wine unhesitatingly, and I forbore to speak to her of a circumstance which must, after all, I considered, have been but the suggestion of a vivid imagination, rendered morbidly active by the terror of the lady, by the opium, and by the hour.

Yet I cannot conceal it from my own perception that, immediately subsequent to the fall of the ruby-drops, a rapid change for the worse took place in the disorder of my wife; so that, on the third subsequent night, the hands of her menials prepared her for the tomb, and on the fourth, I sat alone, with her shrouded body, in that fantastic chamber which had received her as my bride.—Wild visions, opium-engendered, flitted, shadow-like before me. I gazed with unquiet eye upon the sarcophagi in the angles of the room, upon the varying figures of the drapery, and upon the writhing of the particolored fires in the censer overhead. My eyes then fell, as I called to mind the circumstances of a former night, to the spot beneath the glare of the censer where I had seen the faint traces of the shadow. It was there, however, no longer; and breathing with greater freedom, I turned my glances to the pallid and rigid figure upon the bed. Then rushed upon me a thousand memories of Ligeia—and then came back upon my heart, with the turbulent violence of a flood, the whole of that unutterable wo with which I had regarded *her* thus enshrouded. The night waned; and still, with a bosom full of bitter thoughts of the one only and supremely beloved, I remained gazing upon the body of Rowena.

It might have been midnight, or perhaps earlier, or later, for I had taken no note of time, when a sob, low, gentle, but very distinct, startled me from my revery.—I *felt* that it came from the bed of ebony—the bed of death. I listened in an agony of superstitious terror—but there was no repetition of the sound. I strained my vision to detect any motion in the corpse—but there was not the slightest perceptible. Yet I could not have been deceived. I *had* heard the noise, however faint, and my soul was awakened within me. I resolutely and perseveringly kept my attention riveted upon the body. Many minutes elapsed before any circumstance occurred tending to throw light upon the mystery. At length it became evident that a slight, a very feeble, and barely noticeable tinge of color had flushed up within the cheeks, and along the sunken small veins of the eyelids. Through a species of unutterable horror and awe, for which the language of mortality has no sufficiently energetic expression, I felt my heart cease to beat, my limbs grow rigid where I sat. Yet a sense of duty finally operated to restore my self-possession. I could no longer doubt that we had been precipitate in our preparations—that Rowena still lived. It was necessary that some immediate exertion be made; yet the turret was altogether apart from the portion of the abbey tenanted by the servants—there were none within call—I had no means of summoning them to my aid without leaving the room for many minutes—and this I could not venture to do. I therefore struggled alone in my endeavors to call back the spirit still hovering. In a short period it was certain, however, that a relapse had taken place; the color disappeared from both eyelid and cheek, leaving a wanness even more than that of marble; the lips became doubly shrivelled and pinched up in the ghastly expression of death; a repulsive clamminess and coldness overspread rapidly the surface of the body; and all the usual rigorous stiffness immediately supervened. I fell back with a shudder upon the couch from which I had been so startlingly aroused, and again gave myself up to passionate waking visions of Ligeia.

An hour thus elapsed when (could it be possible?) I was a second time aware of some vague sound issuing from the region of the bed. I listened—in extremity of horror. The sound came again—it was a sigh. Rushing to the corpse, I saw—distinctly saw—a tremor upon the lips. In a minute afterwards they relaxed, disclosing a bright line of the pearly teeth. Amazement now struggled in my bosom with the profound awe which had hitherto reigned there alone. I felt that my vision grew dim, that my reason wandered; and it was only by a violent effort that I at length succeeded in nerving myself to the task which duty thus once more had pointed out. There was now a partial glow upon the forehead and upon the cheek and throat; a perceptible warmth pervaded the whole frame; there was even a slight pulsation at the heart. The lady *lived;* and with redoubled ardor I betook myself to the task of restoration. I chafed and bathed the temples and the hands, and used every exertion which experience, and no little medical reading, could suggest. But in vain. Suddenly, the color fled, the pulsation ceased, the lips resumed the expression of the dead, and, in an instant afterward, the whole body took upon itself the icy chilliness, the livid hue, the intense rigidity, the sunken outline, and all the loathsome peculiarities of that which has been, for many days, a tenant of the tomb.

And again I sunk into visions of Ligeia—and again, (what marvel that I shudder while I write?) *again* there reached my ears a low sob from the region of the ebony bed. But why shall I minutely detail the unspeakable horrors of that night? Why shall I pause to relate how, time after time, until near the period of the gray dawn, this hideous drama of revivification was repeated; how each terrific relapse was only into a sterner and apparently more irredeemable death; how each agony wore the aspect of a struggle with some invisible foe; and how each struggle was succeeded by I know not what of wild change in the personal appearance of the corpse? Let me hurry to a conclusion.

The greater part of the fearful night had worn away, and she who had been dead, once again stirred—and now more vigorously than hitherto, although arousing from a dissolution more appalling in its utter hopelessness than any. I had long ceased to struggle or to move, and remained sitting rigidly upon the ottoman, a helpless prey to a whirl of violent emotions, of which extreme awe was perhaps the least terrible, the least consuming. The corpse, I repeat, stirred, and now more vigorously than before. The hues of life flushed up with unwonted energy into the countenance—the limbs relaxed—and, save that the eyelids were yet pressed heavily together, and that the bandages and draperies of the grave still imparted their charnel character to the figure, I might have dreamed that Rowena had indeed shaken off, utterly, the fetters of Death. But if this idea was not, even then, altogether adopted, I could at least doubt no longer, when, arising from the bed, tottering, with feeble steps, with closed eyes, and with the manner of one bewildered in a dream, the thing that was enshrouded advanced bodily and palpably into the middle of the apartment.

I trembled not—I stirred not—for a crowd of unutterable fancies connected with the air, the stature, the demeanor of the figure, rushing hurriedly through my brain, had paralyzed—had chilled me into stone. I stirred not—but gazed upon the apparition. There was a mad disorder in my thoughts—a tumult unappeasable. Could it, indeed, be the *living* Rowena who confronted me? Could it indeed be Rowena *at all*—the fair-haired, the blue-eyed Lady Rowena Trevanion of Tremaine? Why, *why* should I doubt it? The bandage lay heavily about the mouth—but then might it not be the mouth of the breathing Lady of Tremaine? And the cheeks—there were the roses as in her noon of life—yes, these might indeed be the fair cheeks of the living Lady of Tremaine. And the chin, with its dimples, as in health, might it not be hers? but *had she then grown taller since her malady?* What inexpressible madness seized me with that thought? One bound, and I had reached her feet! Shrinking from my touch, she let fall from her head, unloosened, the ghastly cerements which had confined it, and there streamed forth, into the rushing atmosphere of the chamber, huge masses of long and dishevelled hair; *it was blacker than the raven wings of the midnight!* And now slowly opened *the eyes* of the figure which stood before me. "Here then, at least," I shrieked aloud, "can I never—can I never be mistaken—these are the full, and the black, and the wild eyes—of my lost love—of the lady—of the Lady Ligeia."

1838

The Fall of the House of Usher

The epigraph may be translated: "His heart is a lute held up; as soon as it is touched it resounds." This we may remember when we come to the characterization of Usher, with his "morbid acuteness of the senses" and "excessive nervous agitation." Cf. "Israfel," line 2.

Son coeur est un luth suspendu;
Sitôt qu'on le touche il résonne.

—De Béranger.

During the whole of a dull, dark, and soundless day in the autumn of the year, when the clouds hung oppressively low in the heavens, I had been passing alone, on horseback, through a singularly dreary tract of country; and at length found myself, as the shades of the evening drew on, within view of the melancholy House of Usher. I know not how it was—but, with the first glimpse of the building, a sense of insufferable gloom pervaded my spirit. I say insufferable; for the feeling was unrelieved by any of that half-pleasurable, because poetic, sentiment, with which the mind usually receives even the sternest natural images of the desolate or terrible. I looked upon the scene before me—upon the mere house, and the simple landscape features of the domain—upon the bleak walls—upon the vacant eye-like windows—upon a few rank sedges—and upon a few white trunks of decayed trees—with an utter depression of soul which I can compare to no earthly sensation more properly than to the after-dream of the reveller upon opium—the bitter lapse into everyday life—the hideous dropping off of the veil. There was an iciness, a sinking, a sickening of the heart—an unredeemed dreariness of thought which no goading of the imagination could torture into aught of the sublime. What was it—I paused to think—what was it that so unnerved me in the contemplation of the House of Usher? It was a mystery all insoluble; nor could I grapple with the shadowy fancies that crowded upon me as I pondered. I was forced to fall back upon the unsatisfactory conclusion, that while, beyond doubt, there *are* combinations of very simple natural objects which have the power of thus affecting us, still the analysis of this power lies among considerations beyond our depth. It was possible, I reflected, that a mere different arrangement of the particulars of the scene, of the details of the picture, would be sufficient to modify, or perhaps to annihilate its capacity for sorrowful impression; and acting upon this idea, I reined my horse to the precipitous brink of a black and lurid tarn that lay in unruffled lustre by the dwelling, and gazed down—but with a shudder even more thrilling than before—upon the remodelled and inverted images of the gray sedge, and the ghastly tree-stems, and the vacant and eye-like windows.

Nevertheless, in this mansion of gloom I now proposed to myself a sojourn of some weeks. Its proprietor, Roderick Usher, had been one of my boon companions in boyhood; but many years had elapsed since our last meeting. A letter, however, had lately reached me in a distant part of the country—a letter from him—which in its wildly importunate nature, had admitted of no other than a personal reply. The MS. gave evidence of nervous agitation. The writer spoke of acute bodily illness—of a mental disorder which oppressed him—and of an earnest desire to see me, as his best, and indeed his only personal friend, with a view of attempting, by the cheerfulness of my society, some alleviation of his malady. It was the manner in which all this, and much more, was said—it was the apparent *heart* that went with his request—which allowed me no room for hesitation; and I accordingly obeyed forthwith what I still considered a very singular summons.

Although, as boys, we had been even intimate associates, yet I really knew little of my friend. His reserve had been always excessive and habitual. I was aware, however, that his very ancient family had been noted, time out of mind, for a peculiar sensibility of temperament, displaying itself, through long ages, in many works of exalted art, and manifested, of late, in repeated deeds of munificent yet unobtrusive charity, as well as in a passionate devotion to the intricacies, perhaps even more than to the orthodox and easily recognizable beauties, of musical science. I had learned, too, the very remarkable fact, that the stem of the Usher race, all time-honored as it was, had put forth, at no period, any enduring branch; in other words, that the entire family lay in the direct line of descent, and had always, with very trifling and very temporary variation, so lain. It was this deficiency, I considered, while running over in thought the perfect keeping of the character of the premises with the accredited character of the people, and while speculating upon the possible influence which the one, in the long lapse of centuries, might have exercised upon the other—it was this deficiency, perhaps, of collateral issue, and the consequent undeviating transmission, from sire to son, of the patrimony with the name, which had, at length, so identified the two as to merge the original title of the estate in the quaint and equivocal appellation of the "House of Usher"—an appellation which seemed to include, in the minds of the peasantry who used it, both the family and the family mansion.

I have said that the sole effect of my somewhat childish experiment—that of looking down within the tarn—had been to deepen the first singular impression. There can be no doubt that the consciousness of the rapid increase of my superstition—for why should I not so term it?—served mainly to accelerate the increase itself. Such, I have long known, is the paradoxical law of all sentiments having terror as a basis. And it might have been for this reason only, that, when I again uplifted my eyes to the house itself, from its image in the pool, there grew in my mind a strange fancy—a fancy so ridiculous, indeed, that I but mention it to show the vivid force of the sensations which oppressed me. I had so worked upon my imagination as really to believe that about the whole mansion and domain there hung an atmosphere peculiar to themselves and their immediate vicinity—an atmosphere which had no affinity with the air of heaven, but which had reeked up from the decayed trees, and the gray wall, and the silent tarn—a pestilent and mystic vapour, dull, sluggish, faintly discernible, and leaden-hued.

Shaking off from my spirit what *must* have been a dream, I scanned more narrowly the real aspect of the building. Its principal feature seemed to be that of an excessive antiquity. The discoloration of ages had been great. Minute fungi overspread the whole exterior, hanging in a fine tangled web-work from the eaves. Yet all this was apart from any extraordinary dilapidation. No portion of the masonry had fallen; and there appeared to be a wild inconsistency between its still perfect adaptation of parts, and the crumbling condition of the individual stones. In this there was much that reminded me of the specious totality of old wood-work which has rotted for long years in some neglected vault, with no disturbance from the breath of the external air. Beyond this indication of extensive decay, however, the fabric gave little token of instability. Perhaps the eye of a scrutinising observer might have discovered a barely perceptible fissure, which, extending from the roof of the building in front, made its way down the wall in a zigzag direction, until it became lost in the sullen waters of the tarn.

Noticing these things, I rode over a short causeway to the house. A servant in waiting took my horse, and I entered the Gothic archway of the hall. A valet, of stealthy step, thence conducted me, in silence, through many dark and intricate passages in my progress to the *studio* of his master. Much that I encountered on the way contributed, I know not how, to heighten the vague sentiments of which I have already spoken. While the objects around me—while the carvings of the ceilings, the sombre tapestries of the walls, the ebon blackness of the floors, and the phantasmagoric armorial trophies which rattled as I strode, were but matters to which, or to such as which, I had been accustomed from my infancy—while I hesitated not to acknowledge how familiar was all this—I still wondered to find how unfamiliar were the fancies which ordinary images were stirring up. On one of the staircases, I met the physician of the family. His countenance, I thought, wore a mingled expression of low cunning and perplexity. He accosted me with trepidation and passed on. The valet now threw open a door and ushered me into the presence of his master.

The room in which I found myself was very large and lofty. The windows were long, narrow, and pointed, and at so vast a distance from the black oaken floor as to be altogether inaccessible from within. Feeble gleams of encrimsoned light made their way through the trellised panes, and served to render sufficiently distinct the more prominent objects around; the eye, however, struggled in vain to reach the remoter angles of the chamber, or the recesses of the vaulted and fretted ceiling. Dark draperies hung upon the walls. The general furniture was profuse, comfortless, antique, and tattered. Many books and musical instruments lay scattered about, but failed to give any vitality to the scene. I felt that I breathed an atmosphere of sorrow. An air of stern, deep, and irredeemable gloom hung over and pervaded all.

Upon my entrance, Usher arose from a sofa on which he had been lying at full length, and greeted me with a vivacious warmth which had much in it, I at first thought, of an overdone cordiality—of the constrained effort of the *ennuyé* man of the world. A glance, however, at his countenance convinced me of his perfect sincerity. We sat down; and for some moments, while he spoke not, I gazed upon him with a feeling half of pity, half of awe. Surely, man had never before so terribly altered, in so brief a period, as had Roderick Usher! It was with difficulty that I could bring myself to admit the identity of the wan being before me with the companion of my early boyhood. Yet the character of his face had been at all times remarkable. A cadaverousness of complexion; an eye large, liquid, and luminous beyond comparison; lips somewhat thin and very pallid, but of a surpassingly beautiful curve; a nose of a delicate Hebrew model, but with a breadth of nostril unusual in similar formations; a finely moulded chin, speaking, in its want of prominence, of a want of moral energy; hair of a more than web-like softness and tenuity; these features, with an inordinate expansion above the regions of the temple, made up altogether a countenance not easily to be forgotten. And now in the mere exaggeration of the prevailing character of these features, and of the expression they were wont to convey, lay so much of change that I doubted to whom I spoke. The now ghastly pallor of the skin, and the now miraculous lustre of the eye, above all things startled and even awed me. The silken hair, too, had been suffered to grow all unheeded, and as, in its wild gossamer texture, it floated rather than fell about the face, I could not, even with effort, connect its arabesque expression with any idea of simple humanity.

In the manner of my friend I was at once struck

with an incoherence—an inconsistency; and I soon found this to arise from a series of feeble and futile struggles to overcome an habitual trepidancy—an excessive nervous agitation. For something of this nature I had indeed been prepared, no less by his letter, than by reminiscences of certain boyish traits, and by conclusions deduced from his peculiar physical conformation and temperament. His action was alternately vivacious and sullen. His voice varied rapidly from a tremendous indecision (when the animal spirits seemed utterly in abeyance) to that species of energetic concision—that abrupt, weighty, unhurried, and hollow-sounding enunciation—that leaden, self-balanced and perfectly modulated guttural utterance, which may be observed in the lost drunkard, or the irreclaimable eater of opium, during the periods of his most intense excitement.

It was thus that he spoke of the object of my visit, of his earnest desire to see me, and of the solace he expected me to afford him. He entered, at some length, into what he conceived to be the nature of his malady. It was, he said, a constitutional and a family evil, and one for which he despaired to find a remedy—a mere nervous affection, he immediately added, which would undoubtedly soon pass off. It displayed itself in a host of unnatural sensations. Some of these, as he detailed them, interested and bewildered me; although, perhaps, the terms and the general manner of the narration had their weight. He suffered much from a morbid acuteness of the senses; the most insipid food was alone endurable; he could wear only garments of certain texture; the odours of all flowers were oppressive; his eyes were tortured by even a faint light; and there were but peculiar sounds, and these from stringed instruments, which did not inspire him with horror.

To an anomalous species of terror I found him a bounden slave. "I shall perish," said he, "I *must* perish in this deplorable folly. Thus, thus, and not otherwise, shall I be lost. I dread the events of the future, not in themselves, but in their results. I shudder at the thought of any, even the most trivial, incident, which may operate upon this intolerable agitation of soul. I have, indeed, no abhorrence of danger, except in its absolute effect—in terror. In this unnerved—in this pitiable condition, I feel that the period will sooner or later arrive when I must abandon life and reason together, in some struggle with the grim phantasm, FEAR."

I learned, moreover, at intervals, and through broken and equivocal hints, another singular feature of his mental condition. He was enchained by certain superstitious impressions in regard to the dwelling which he tenanted, and whence, for many years, he had never ventured forth—in regard to an influence whose supposititious force was conveyed in terms too shadowy here to be re-stated—an influence which some peculiarities in the mere form and substance of his family mansion, had, by dint of long sufferance, he said, obtained over his spirit—an effect which the *physique* of the gray walls and turrets, and of the dim tarn into which they all looked down, had, at length, brought about upon the *morale* of his existence.

He admitted, however, although with hesitation, that much of the peculiar gloom which thus afflicted him could be traced to a more natural and far more palpable origin—to the severe and long-continued illness—indeed to the evidently approaching dissolution—of a tenderly beloved sister—his sole companion for long years—his last and only relative on earth. "Her decease," he said, with a bitterness which I can never forget, "would leave him (him the hopeless and the frail) the last of the ancient race of the Ushers." While he spoke, the lady Madeline (for so was she called) passed slowly through a remote portion of the apartment, and, without having noticed my presence, disappeared. I regarded her with an utter astonishment not unmingled with dread—and yet I found it impossible to account for such feelings. A sensation of stupor oppressed me, as my eyes followed her retreating steps. When a door, at length, closed upon her, my glance sought instinctively and eagerly the countenance of the brother—but he had buried his face in his hands, and I could only perceive that a far more than ordinary wanness had overspread the emaciated fingers through which trickled many passionate tears.

The disease of the lady Madeline had long baffled the skill of her physicians. A settled apathy, a gradual wasting away of the person, and frequent although transient affections of a partially cataleptical character, were the unusual diagnosis. Hitherto she had steadily borne up against the pressure of her malady, and had not betaken herself finally to bed; but, on the closing in of the evening of my arrival at the house, she succumbed (as her brother told me at night with inexpressible agitation) to the prostrating power of the destroyer; and I learned that the glimpse I had obtained of her person would thus probably be the last I should obtain—that the lady, at least while living, would be seen by me no more.

For several days ensuing, her name was unmentioned by either Usher or myself: and during this period I was busied in earnest endeavours to alleviate the melancholy of my friend. We painted and read together; or I listened, as if in a dream, to the wild improvisations of his speaking guitar. And thus, as a closer and still closer intimacy admitted me more unreservedly into the recesses of his spirit, the more bitterly did I perceive the futility of all attempt at cheering a mind from which darkness, as if an inherent positive quality, poured forth upon all objects of the moral and physical universe, in one unceasing radiation of gloom.

I shall ever bear about me a memory of the many solemn hours I thus spent alone with the master of the House of Usher. Yet I should fail in any attempt to convey an idea of the exact character of the studies, or of the occupations, in which he involved me, or led me the way. An excited and highly distempered ideality threw a sulphureous lustre over all. His long improvised dirges will ring forever in my ears. Among other things, I hold painfully in mind a certain singular perversion and amplification of the wild air of the last waltz of Von Weber. From the paintings over which his elaborate fancy brooded, and which grew, touch by touch, into vaguenesses at which I shuddered the more thrillingly, because I shuddered knowing not why;—from these paintings (vivid as their images now are before me) I would in vain endeavour to educe more than a small portion which should lie within the compass of merely written words. By the utter simplicity, by the nakedness of his designs, he arrested and overawed attention. If ever mortal painted an idea, that mortal was Roderick Usher. For me at least—in the circumstances then surrounding me—there arose, out of the pure abstractions which the hypochondriac contrived to throw upon his canvas, an intensity of intolerable awe, no shadow of which felt I ever yet in the contemplation of the certainly glowing yet too concrete reveries of Fuseli.

One of the phantasmagoric conceptions of my friend, partaking not so rigidly of the spirit of abstraction, may be shadowed forth, although feebly, in words. A small picture presented the interior of an immensely long and rectangular vault or tunnel, with low walls, smooth, white, and without interruption or device. Certain accessory points of the design served well to convey the idea that this excavation lay at an exceeding depth below the surface of the earth. No outlet was observed in any portion of its vast extent, and no torch, or other artificial source of light was discernible; yet a flood of intense rays rolled throughout, and bathed the whole in a ghastly and inappropriate splendour.

I have just spoken of that morbid condition of the auditory nerve which rendered all music intolerable to the sufferer, with the exception of certain effects of stringed instruments. It was, perhaps, the narrow limits to which he thus confined himself upon the guitar, which gave birth, in great measure, to the fantastic character of his performances. But the fervid *facility* of his *impromptus* could not be so accounted for. They must have been, and were, in the notes, as well as in the words of his wild fantasias (for he not unfrequently accompanied himself with rhymed verbal improvisations), the result of that intense mental collectedness and concentration to which I have previously alluded as observable only in particular moments of the highest artificial excitement. The words of one of these rhapsodies I have easily remembered. I was, perhaps, the more forcibly impressed with it, as he gave it, because, in the under or mystic current of its meaning, I fancied that I perceived, and for the first time, a full consciousness on the part of Usher, of the tottering of his lofty reason upon her throne. The verses, which were entitled "The Haunted Palace,"[1] ran very nearly, if not accurately, thus:

I

In the greenest of our valleys,
  By good angels tenanted,
Once a fair and stately palace—
  Radiant palace—reared its head.
In the monarch Thought's dominion—
  It stood there!
Never seraph spread a pinion
  Over fabric half so fair!

II

Banners yellow, glorious, golden,
  On its roof did float and flow,
(This—all this—was in the olden
  Time long ago)
And every gentle air that dallied,
  In that sweet day,
Along the ramparts plumed and pallid,
  A wingèd odour went away.

III

Wanderers in that happy valley
  Through two luminous windows saw
Spirits moving musically
  To a lute's well-tunèd law,
Round about a throne, where sitting
  (Porphyrogene!)
In state his glory well befitting,
  The ruler of the realm was seen.

IV

And all with pearl and ruby glowing
  Was the fair palace door,
Through which came flowing, flowing, flowing
  And sparkling evermore,
A troop of Echoes, whose sweet duty
  Was but to sing,
In voices of surpassing beauty,
  The wit and wisdom of their king.

V

But evil things, in robes of sorrow,
  Assailed the monarch's high estate;

[1] The poem was first published, separately, in 1839, five months before Poe incorporated it into the story.

(Ah, let us mourn, for never morrow
 Shall dawn upon him, desolate!)
And round about his home, the glory
 That blushed and bloomed
Is but a dim-remembered story
 Of the old time entombed.

VI

And travellers now within that valley,
 Through the red-litten windows, see
Vast forms that move fantastically
 To a discordant melody;
While, like a ghastly rapid river,
 Through the pale door,
A hideous throng rush out forever,
 And laugh—but smile no more.

I well remember that suggestions arising from this ballad, led us into a train of thought, wherein there became manifest an opinion of Usher's which I mention not so much on account of its novelty, (for other men[2] have thought thus,) as on account of the pertinacity with which he maintained it. This opinion, in its general form, was that of the sentience of all vegetable things. But, in his disordered fancy, the idea had assumed a more daring character, and trespassed, under certain conditions, upon the kingdom of inorganization. I lack words to express the full extent, or the earnest *abandon* of his persuasion. The belief, however, was connected (as I have previously hinted) with the gray stones of the home of his forefathers. The conditions of the sentience had been here, he imagined, fulfilled in the method of collocation of these stones—in the order of their arrangement, as well as in that of the many *fungi* which overspread them, and of the decayed trees which stood around—above all, in the long undisturbed endurance of this arrangement, and in its reduplication in the still waters of the tarn. Its evidence—the evidence of the sentience—was to be seen, he said, (and I here started as he spoke,) in the gradual yet certain condensation of an atmosphere of their own about the waters and the walls. The result was discoverable, he added, in that silent, yet importunate and terrible influence which for centuries had moulded the destinies of his family, and which made *him* what I now saw him—what he was. Such opinions need no comment, and I will make none.

Our books[3]—the books which, for years, had formed no small portion of the mental existence of the invalid—were, as might be supposed, in strict keeping with this character of phantasm. We pored together over such works as the *Ververt et Chartreuse* of Gresset; the *Belphegor* of Machiavelli; the *Heaven and Hell* of Swedenborg; the *Subterranean Voyage of Nicholas Klimm* by Holberg; the *Chiromancy* of Robert Flud, of Jean D'Indaginé, and of De la Chambre; the *Journey into the Blue Distance* of Tieck; and the *City of the Sun* of Campanella. One favorite volume was a small octavo edition of the *Directorium Inquisitorum*, by the Dominican Eymeric de Gironne; and there were passages in Pomponius Mela, about the old African Satyrs and Aegipans, over which Usher would sit dreaming for hours. His chief delight, however, was found in the perusal of an exceedingly rare and curious book in quarto Gothic—the manual of a forgotten church—the *Vigiliae Mortuorum secundum Chorum Ecclesiae Maguntinae*.[4]

I could not help thinking of the wild ritual of this work, and of its probable influence upon the hypochondriac, when one evening, having informed me abruptly that the lady Madeline was no more, he stated his intention of preserving her corpse for a fortnight, (previously to its final interment,) in one of the numerous vaults within the main walls of the building. The worldly reason, however, assigned for this singular proceeding, was one which I did not feel at liberty to dispute. The brother had been led to his resolution (so he told me) by consideration of the unusual character of the malady of the deceased, of certain obtrusive and eager inquiries on the part of her medical men, and of the remote and exposed situation of the burial-ground of the family. I will not deny that when I called to mind the sinister countenance of the person whom I met upon the staircase, on the day of my arrival at the house, I had no desire to oppose what I regarded as at best but a harmless, and by no means an unnatural, precaution.

At the request of Usher, I personally aided him in the arrangements for the temporary entombment. The body having been encoffined, we two alone bore it to its rest. The vault in which we placed it (and which had been so long unopened that our torches, half smothered in its oppressive atmosphere, gave us little opportunity for investigation) was small, damp, and entirely without means of admission for light; lying, at great depth, immediately beneath that portion of the building in which was my own sleeping apartment. It had been used, apparently, in remote feudal times, for the worst purposes of a donjon-keep, and in later days as a place of deposit for powder, or some other highly combustible substance, as a portion of its floor, and the whole interior of a long archway through which we

[2] Watson, Dr. Percival, Spallanzani, and especially the Bishop of Llandaff.—See "Chemical Essays," vol. v. [Poe's note.]

[3] Davidson indicates that all the volumes in Usher's library are authentic except for the *Mad Trist*, mentioned later in the story. The works deal mainly with the occult and magical.

[4] Vigils for the Dead according to the Choir of the Church of Mayence.

reached it, were carefully sheathed with copper. The door, of massive iron, had been, also, similarly protected. Its immense weight caused an unusually sharp grating sound, as it moved upon its hinges.

Having deposited our mournful burden upon tressels within this region of horror, we partially turned aside the yet unscrewed lid of the coffin, and looked upon the face of the tenant. A striking similitude between the brother and sister now first arrested my attention; and Usher, divining, perhaps, my thoughts, murmured out some few words from which I learned that the deceased and himself had been twins, and that sympathies of a scarcely intelligible nature had always existed between them. Our glances, however, rested not long upon the dead—for we could not regard her unawed. The disease which had thus entombed the lady in the maturity of youth, had left, as usual in all maladies of a strictly cataleptical character, the mockery of a faint blush upon the bosom and the face, and that suspiciously lingering smile upon the lip which is so terrible in death. We replaced and screwed down the lid, and, having secured the door of iron, made our way, with toil, into the scarcely less gloomy apartments of the upper portion of the house.

And now, some days of bitter grief having elapsed, an observable change came over the features of the mental disorder of my friend. His ordinary manner had vanished. His ordinary occupations were neglected or forgotten. He roamed from chamber to chamber with hurried, unequal, and objectless step. The pallor of his countenance had assumed, if possible, a more ghastly hue—but the luminousness of his eye had utterly gone out. The once occasional huskiness of his tone was heard no more; and a tremulous quaver, as if of extreme terror, habitually characterized his utterance. There were times, indeed, when I thought his unceasingly agitated mind was labouring with some oppressive secret, to divulge which he struggled for the necessary courage. At times, again, I was obliged to resolve all into the mere inexplicable vagaries of madness, for I beheld him gazing upon vacancy for long hours, in an attitude of the profoundest attention, as if listening to some imaginary sound. It was no wonder that his condition terrified—that it infected me. I felt creeping upon me, by slow yet certain degrees, the wild influences of his own fantastic yet impressive superstitions.

It was, especially, upon retiring to bed late in the night of the seventh or eighth day after the placing of the lady Madeline within the donjon, that I experienced the full power of such feelings. Sleep came not near my couch,—while the hours waned and waned away. I struggled to reason off the nervousness which had dominion over me. I endeavoured to believe that much, if not all, of what I felt, was due to the bewildering influence of the gloomy furniture of the room—of the dark and tattered draperies, which, tortured into motion by the breath of a rising tempest, swayed fitfully to and fro upon the walls, and rustled uneasily about the decorations of the bed. But my efforts were fruitless. An irrepressible tremour gradually pervaded my frame; and, at length, there sat upon my very heart an incubus of utterly causeless alarm. Shaking this off with a gasp and a struggle, I uplifted myself upon the pillows, and, peering earnestly within the intense darkness of the chamber, hearkened—I know not why, except that an instinctive spirit prompted me—to certain low and indefinite sounds which came, through the pauses of the storm, at long intervals, I knew not whence. Overpowered by an intense sentiment of horror, unaccountable yet unendurable, I threw on my clothes with haste (for I felt that I should sleep no more during the night), and endeavoured to arouse myself from the pitiable condition into which I had fallen, by pacing rapidly to and fro through the apartment.

I had taken but few turns in this manner, when a light step on an adjoining staircase arrested my attention. I presently recognized it as that of Usher. In an instant afterward he rapped, with a gentle touch, at my door, and entered, bearing a lamp. His countenance was, as usual, cadaverously wan—but, moreover, there was a species of mad hilarity in his eyes—an evidently restrained *hysteria* in his whole demeanour. His air appalled me—but anything was preferable to the solitude which I had so long endured, and I even welcomed his presence as a relief.

"And you have not seen it?" he said abruptly, after having stared about him for some moments in silence—"you have not then seen it?—but, stay! you shall." Thus speaking, and having carefully shaded his lamp, he hurried to one of the casements, and threw it freely open to the storm.

The impetuous fury of the entering gust nearly lifted us from our feet. It was, indeed, a tempestuous yet sternly beautiful night, and one wildly singular in its terror and its beauty. A whirlwind had apparently collected its force in our vicinity; for there were frequent and violent alterations in the direction of the wind; and the exceeding density of the clouds (which hung so low as to press upon the turrets of the house) did not prevent our perceiving the life-like velocity with which they flew careering from all points against each other, without passing away into the distance. I say that even their exceeding density did not prevent our perceiving this—yet we had no glimpse of the moon or stars—nor was there any flashing forth of the lightning. But the under surfaces of the huge masses of agitated vapour, as well as all terrestrial objects immediately around us, were glowing in the unnatural light of a faintly luminous and distinctly visible gaseous exhalation which hung about and enshrouded the mansion.

"You must not—you shall not behold this!" said I, shudderingly, to Usher, as I led him, with a gentle violence, from the window to a seat. "These appearances, which bewilder you, are merely electrical phenomena not uncommon—or it may be that they have their ghastly origin in the rank miasma of the tarn. Let us close this casement;—the air is chilling and dangerous to your frame. Here is one of your favourite romances. I will read, and you shall listen;—and so we will pass away this terrible night together."

The antique volume which I had taken up was the *Mad Trist* of Sir Launcelot Canning; but I had called it a favourite of Usher's more in sad jest than in earnest; for, in truth, there is little in its uncouth and unimaginative prolixity which could have had interest for the lofty and spiritual ideality of my friend. It was, however, the only book immediately at hand; and I indulged a vague hope that the excitement which now agitated the hypochondriac, might find relief (for the history of mental disorder is full of similar anomalies) even in the extremeness of the folly which I should read. Could I have judged, indeed, by the wild overstrained air of vivacity with which he hearkened, or apparently hearkened, to the words of the tale, I might well have congratulated myself upon the success of my design.

I had arrived at that well-known portion of the story where Ethelred, the hero of the *Trist*, having sought in vain for peaceable admission into the dwelling of the hermit, proceeds to make good an entrance by force. Here, it will be remembered, the words of the narrative run thus:

> "And Ethelred, who was by nature of a doughty heart, and who was now mighty withal, on account of the powerfulness of the wine which he had drunken, waited no longer to hold parley with the hermit, who, in sooth, was of an obstinate and maliceful turn, but, feeling the rain upon his shoulders, and fearing the rising of the tempest, uplifted his mace outright, and with blows, made quickly room in the plankings of the door for his gauntleted hand; and now pulling therewith sturdily, he so cracked, and ripped, and tore all asunder, that the noise of the dry and hollow-sounding wood alarumed and reverberated throughout the forest."

At the termination of this sentence I started, and for a moment, paused; for it appeared to me (although I at once concluded that my excited fancy had deceived me)—it appeared to me that, from some very remote portion of the mansion, there came, indistinctly, to my ears, what might have been, in its exact similarity of character, the echo (but a stifled and dull one certainly) of the very cracking and ripping sound which Sir Launcelot had so particularly described. It was, beyond doubt, the coincidence alone which had arrested my attention; for, amid the rattling of the sashes of the casements, and the ordinary commingled noises of the still increasing storm, the sound, in itself, had nothing, surely, which should have interested or disturbed me. I continued the story:

> "But the good champion Ethelred, now entering within the door, was sore enraged and amazed to perceive no signal of the maliceful hermit; but, in the stead thereof, a dragon of a scaly and prodigious demeanour, and of a fiery tongue, which sate in guard before a palace of gold, with a floor of silver; and upon the wall there hung a shield of shining brass with this legend enwritten—
>
> Who entereth herein, a conqueror hath bin;
> Who slayeth the dragon, the shield he shall win.
>
> And Ethelred uplifted his mace, and struck upon the head of the dragon, which fell before him, and gave up his pesty breath, with a shriek so horrid and harsh, and withal so piercing, that Ethelred had fain to close his ears with his hands against the dreadful noise of it, the like whereof was never before heard."

Here again I paused abruptly, and now with a feeling of wild amazement—for there could be no doubt whatever that, in this instance, I did actually hear (although from what direction it proceeded I found it impossible to say) a low and apparently distant, but harsh, protracted, and most unusual screaming or grating sound—the exact counterpart of what my fancy had already conjured up for the dragon's unnatural shriek as described by the romancer.

Oppressed, as I certainly was, upon the occurrence of this second and most extraordinary coincidence, by a thousand conflicting sensations, in which wonder and extreme terror were predominant, I still retained sufficient presence of mind to avoid exciting, by any observation, the sensitive nervousness of my companion. I was by no means certain that he had noticed the sounds in question; although, assuredly, a strange alteration had, during the last few minutes, taken place in his demeanour. From a position fronting my own, he had gradually brought round his chair, so as to sit with his face to the door of the chamber; and thus I could but partially perceive his features, although I saw that his lips trembled as if he were murmuring inaudibly. His head had dropped upon his breast—yet I knew that he was not asleep, from the wide and rigid opening of the eye as I caught a glance of it in profile. The motion of his body, too, was at variance with this idea—for he rocked from side to side with a gentle yet constant and uniform sway. Having rapidly taken notice of all this, I resumed the narrative of Sir Launcelot, which thus proceeded:

> "And now, the champion, having escaped from the terrible fury of the dragon, bethinking himself of the brazen shield, and of the breaking up of the enchantment which was upon it, removed the carcass from out of the way before him, and approached valorously over the silver pavement of the castle to where the shield was upon the wall; which in sooth tarried not for his full coming, but fell down at his feet upon the silver floor, with a mighty great and terrible ringing sound."

No sooner had these syllables passed my lips, than—as if a shield of brass had indeed, at the moment, fallen heavily upon a floor of silver—I became aware of a distinct, hollow, metallic, and clangorous, yet apparently muffled reverberation. Completely unnerved, I leaped to my feet; but the measured rocking movement of Usher was undisturbed. I rushed to the chair in which he sat. His eyes were bent fixedly before him, and throughout his whole countenance there reigned a stony rigidity. But as I placed my hand upon his shoulder, there came a strong shudder over his whole person; a sickly smile quivered about his lips; and I saw that he spoke in a low, hurried, and gibbering murmur, as if unconscious of my presence. Bending closely over him, I at length drank in the hideous import of his words.

"Not hear it?—yes, I hear it, and *have* heard it. Long—long—long—many minutes, many hours, many days, have I heard it—yet I dared not—oh, pity me, miserable wretch that I am!—I dared not—I *dared* not speak! *We have put her living in the tomb!* Said I not that my senses were acute? I *now* tell you that I heard her first feeble movements in the hollow coffin. I heard them—many, many days ago—yet I dared not—*I dared not speak!* And now—to-night—Ethelred—ha! ha!—the breaking of the hermit's door, and the death-cry of the dragon, and the clangour of the shield!—say, rather, the rending of her coffin, and the grating of the iron hinges of her prison, and her struggles within the coppered archway of the vault! Oh whither shall I fly? Will she not be here anon? Is she not hurrying to upbraid me for my haste? Have I not heard her footstep on the stair? Do I not distinguish that heavy and horrible beating of her heart? MADMAN!"—here he sprang furiously to his feet, and shrieked out his syllables, as if in the effort he were giving up his soul—"MADMAN! I TELL YOU THAT SHE NOW STANDS WITHOUT THE DOOR!"

As if in the superhuman energy of his utterance there had been found the potency of a spell—the huge antique panels to which the speaker pointed, threw slowly back, upon the instant, their ponderous and ebony jaws. It was the work of the rushing gust—but then without those doors there DID stand the lofty and enshrouded figure of the lady Madeline of Usher. There was blood upon her white robes, and the evidence of some bitter struggle upon every portion of her emaciated frame. For a moment she remained trembling and reeling to and fro upon the threshold, then, with a low moaning cry, fell heavily inward upon the person of her brother, and, in her violent and now final death-agonies, bore him to the floor a corpse, and a victim to the terrors he had anticipated.

From that chamber, and from that mansion, I fled aghast. The storm was still abroad in all its wrath as I found myself crossing the old causeway. Suddenly there shot along the path a wild light, and I turned to see whence a gleam so unusual could have issued; for the vast house and its shadows were alone behind me. The radiance was that of the full, setting, and blood-red moon, which now shone vividly through that once barely-discernible fissure of which I have before spoken as extending from the roof of the building, in a zigzag direction, to the base. While I gazed, this fissure rapidly widened—there came a fierce breath of the whirlwind—the entire orb of the satellite burst at once upon my sight—my brain reeled as I saw the mighty walls rushing asunder—there was a long tumultuous shouting sound like the voice of a thousand waters—and the deep and dank tarn at my feet closed sullenly and silently over the fragments of the "HOUSE OF USHER."

1839

The Masque of the Red Death

The "Red Death" had long devastated the country. No pestilence had ever been so fatal, or so hideous. Blood was its Avatar and its seal—the redness and the horror of blood. There were sharp pains, and sudden dizziness, and then profuse bleeding at the pores, with dissolution. The scarlet stains upon the body, and especially upon the face of the victim, were the pest ban which shut him out from the aid and from the sympathy of his fellow-men. And the whole seizure, progress and termination of the disease, were the incidents of half an hour.

But the Prince Prospero was happy and dauntless

and sagacious. When his dominions were half depopulated, he summoned to his presence a thousand hale and light-hearted friends from among the knights and dames of his court, and with these retired to the deep seclusion of one of his castellated abbeys. This was an extensive and magnificent structure, the creation of the prince's own eccentric yet august taste. A strong and lofty wall girdled it in. This wall had gates of iron. The courtiers, having entered, brought furnaces and massy hammers and welded the bolts. They resolved to leave means neither of ingress or egress to the sudden impulses of despair or of frenzy from within. The abbey was amply provisioned. With such precautions the courtiers might bid defiance to contagion. The external world could take care of itself. In the meantime it was folly to grieve, or to think. The prince had provided all the appliances of pleasure. There were buffoons, there were improvisatori, there were ballet-dancers, there were musicians, there was Beauty, there was wine. All these and security were within. Without was the "Red Death."

It was toward the close of the fifth or sixth month of his seclusion, and while the pestilence raged most furiously abroad, that the Prince Prospero entertained his thousand friends at a masked ball of the most unusual magnificence.

It was a voluptuous scene, that masquerade. But first let me tell of the rooms in which it was held. There were seven—an imperial suite. In many palaces, however, such suites form a long and straight vista, while the folding-doors slide back nearly to the walls on either hand, so that the view of the whole extent is scarcely impeded. Here the case was very different; as might have been expected from the duke's love of the *bizarre*. The apartments were so irregularly disposed that the vision embraced but little more than one at a time. There was a sharp turn at every twenty or thirty yards, and at each turn a novel effect. To the right and left, in the middle of each wall, a tall and narrow Gothic window looked out upon a closed corridor which pursued the windings of the suite. These windows were of stained glass whose color varied in accordance with the prevailing hue of the decorations of the chamber into which it opened. That at the eastern extremity was hung, for example, in blue—and vividly blue were its windows. The second chamber was purple in its ornaments and tapestries, and here the panes were purple. The third was green throughout, and so were the casements. The fourth was furnished and lighted with orange—the fifth with white—the sixth with violet. The seventh apartment was closely shrouded in black velvet tapestries that hung all over the ceiling and down the walls, falling in heavy folds upon a carpet of the same material and hue. But in this chamber only, the color of the windows failed to correspond with the decorations. The panes here were scarlet—a deep blood color. Now in no one of the seven apartments was there any lamp or candelabrum, amid the profusion of golden ornaments that lay scattered to and fro or depended from the roof. There was no light of any kind emanating from lamp or candle within the suite of chambers. But in the corridors that followed the suite there stood, opposite to each window, a heavy tripod, bearing a brazier of fire that projected its rays through the tinted glass and so glaringly illumined the room. And thus were produced a multitude of gaudy and fantastic appearances. But in the western or black chamber the effect of the fire-light that streamed upon the dark hangings through the blood-tinted panes, was ghastly in the extreme, and produced so wild a look upon the countenances of those who entered, that there were few of the company bold enough to set foot within its precincts at all.

It was in this apartment, also, that there stood against the western wall a gigantic clock of ebony. Its pendulum swung to and fro with a dull, heavy, monotonous clang; and, when the minute-hand made the circuit of the face, and the hour was to be stricken, there came from the brazen lungs of the clock a sound which was clear and loud and deep and exceedingly musical, but of so peculiar a note and emphasis that, at each lapse of an hour, the musicians of the orchestra were constrained to pause, momentarily, in their performance, to hearken to the sound; and thus the waltzers perforce ceased their evolutions; and there was a brief disconcert of the whole gay company; and, while the chimes of the clock yet rang, it was observed that the giddiest grew pale, and the more aged and sedate passed their hands over their brows as if in confused reverie or meditation. But when the echoes had fully ceased, a light laughter at once pervaded the assembly; the musicians looked at each other and smiled as if at their own nervousness and folly, and made whispering vows, each to the other, that the next chiming of the clock should produce in them no similar emotion; and then, after the lapse of sixty minutes, (which embrace three thousand and six hundred seconds of the Time that flies,) there came yet another chiming of the clock, and then were the same disconcert and tremulousness and meditation as before.

But, in spite of these things, it was a gay and magnificent revel. The tastes of the duke were peculiar. He had a fine eye for colors and effects. He disregarded the *decora* of mere fashion. His plans were bold and fiery, and his conceptions glowed with barbaric lustre. There are some who would have thought him mad. His followers felt that he was not. It was necessary to hear and see and touch him to be *sure* that he was not.

He had directed, in great part, the moveable embellishments of the seven chambers, upon occasion of this great *fête;* and it was his own guiding taste which had given character to the masqueraders. Be sure they were grotesque. There were much glare and glitter and piquancy and phantasm—much of what has been since seen in "Hernani."[1] There were arabesque figures with unsuited limbs and appointments. There were delirious fancies such as the madman fashions. There was much of the beautiful, much of the wanton, much of the *bizarre,* something of the terrible, and not a little of that which might have excited disgust. To and fro in the seven chambers there stalked, in fact, a multitude of dreams. And these—the dreams—writhed in and about, taking hue from the rooms, and causing the wild music of the orchestra to seem as the echo of their steps. And, anon, there strikes the ebony clock which stands in the hall of the velvet. And then, for a moment, all is still, and all is silent save the voice of the clock. The dreams are stiff-frozen as they stand. But the echoes of the chime die away—they have endured but an instant—and a light, half-subdued laughter floats after them as they depart. And now again the music swells, and the dreams live, and writhe to and fro more merrily than ever, taking hue from the many tinted windows through which stream the rays from the tripods. But to the chamber which lies most westwardly of the seven, there are now none of the maskers who venture; for the night is waning away; and there flows a ruddier light through the blood-colored panes; and the blackness of the sable drapery appalls; and to him whose foot falls upon the sable carpet, there comes from the near clock of ebony a muffled peal more solemnly emphatic than any which reaches *their* ears who indulge in the more remote gaieties of the other apartments.

But these other apartments were densely crowded, and in them beat feverishly the heart of life. And the revel went whirlingly on, until at length there commenced the sounding of midnight upon the clock. And then the music ceased, as I have told; and the evolutions of the waltzers were quieted; and there was an uneasy cessation of all things as before. But now there were twelve strokes to be sounded by the bell of the clock; and thus it happened, perhaps, that more of thought crept, with more of time, into the meditations of the thoughtful among those who revelled. And thus, too, it happened, perhaps, that before the last echoes of the last chime had utterly sunk into silence, there were many individuals in the crowd who had found leisure to become aware of the presence of a masked figure which had arrested the attention of no single individual before. And the rumor of this new presence having spread itself whisperingly around, there arose at length from the whole company a buzz, or murmur, expressive of disapprobation and surprise—then, finally, of terror, of horror, and of disgust.

In an assembly of phantasms such as I have painted, it may well be supposed that no ordinary appearance could have excited such sensation. In truth the masquerade license of the night was nearly unlimited; but the figure in question had out-Heroded Herod, and gone beyond the bounds of even the prince's indefinite decorum. There are chords in the hearts of the most reckless which cannot be touched without emotion. Even with the utterly lost, to whom life and death are equally jests, there are matters of which no jests can be made. The whole company, indeed, seemed now deeply to feel that in the costume and bearing of the stranger neither wit nor propriety existed. The figure was tall and gaunt, and shrouded from head to foot in the habiliments of the grave. The mask which concealed the visage was made so nearly to resemble the countenance of a stiffened corpse that the closest scrutiny must have had difficulty in detecting the cheat. And yet all this might have been endured, if not approved, by the mad revellers around. But the mummer had gone so far as to assume the type of the Red Death. His vesture was dabbled in *blood*—and his broad brow, with all the features of the face, was besprinkled with the scarlet horror.

When the eyes of Prince Prospero fell upon this spectral image (which with a slow and solemn movement, as if more fully to sustain its *rôle,* stalked to and fro among the waltzers) he was seen to be convulsed, in the first moment, with a strong shudder either of terror or distaste; but, in the next, his brow reddened with rage.

"Who dares?" he demanded hoarsely of the courtiers who stood near him—"who dares insult us with this blasphemous mockery? Seize him and unmask him—that we may know whom we have to hang at sunrise, from the battlements!"

It was in the eastern or blue chamber in which stood the Prince Prospero as he uttered these words. They rang throughout the seven rooms loudly and clearly—for the prince was a bold and robust man, and the music had become hushed at the waving of his hand.

It was in the blue room where stood the prince, with a group of pale courtiers by his side. At first, as he spoke, there was a slight rushing movement of

[1]A play by Victor Hugo, presented in 1830.

this group in the direction of the intruder, who at the moment was also near at hand, and now, with deliberate and stately step, made closer approach to the speaker. But from a certain nameless awe with which the mad assumption of the mummer had inspired the whole party, there were found none who put forth hand to seize him; so that, unimpeded, he passed within a yard of the prince's person; and, while the vast assembly, as if with one impulse, shrank from the centres of the rooms to the walls, he made his way uninterruptedly, but with the same solemn and measured step which had distinguished him from the first, through the blue chamber to the purple—through the purple to the green—through the green to the orange—through this again to the white—and even thence to the violet, ere a decided movement had been made to arrest him. It was then, however, that the Prince Prospero, maddening with rage and the shame of his own momentary cowardice, rushed hurriedly through the six chambers, while none followed him on account of a deadly terror that had seized upon all. He bore aloft a drawn dagger, and had approached, in rapid impetuosity, to within three or four feet of the retreating figure, when the latter, having attained the extremity of the velvet apartment, turned suddenly and confronted his pursuer. There was a sharp cry—and the dagger dropped gleaming upon the sable carpet, upon which, instantly afterwards, fell prostrate in death the Prince Prospero. Then, summoning the wild courage of despair, a throng of the revellers at once threw themselves into the black apartment, and, seizing the mummer, whose tall figure stood erect and motionless within the shadow of the ebony clock, gasped in unutterable horror at finding the grave-cerements and corpse-like mask, which they handled with so violent a rudeness, untenanted by any tangible form.

And now was acknowledged the presence of the Red Death. He had come like a thief in the night. And one by one dropped the revellers in the blood-bedewed halls of their revel, and died each in the despairing posture of his fall. And the life of the ebony clock went out with that of the last of the gay. And the flames of the tripods expired. And Darkness and Decay and the Red Death held illimitable dominion over all.

1842

The Purloined Letter

Very different from the tales of tone or atmosphere are the "tales of ratiocination," or detective stories. "The Purloined Letter" is one of a series concerning M. Dupin, the prototype of Conan Doyle's Sherlock Holmes. The epigraph: "Nothing is more odious to wisdom than too great cleverness." It has not been located in Seneca, however.

Nil sapientiae odiosius acumine nimio.

—Seneca.

At Paris, just after dark one gusty evening in the autumn of 18—, I was enjoying the twofold luxury of meditation and a meerschaum, in company with my friend C. Auguste Dupin, in his little back library, or book-closet, *au troisième, No. 33, Rue Dunôt, Faubourg St. Germain.* For one hour at least we had maintained a profound silence; while each, to any casual observer, might have seemed intently and exclusively occupied with the curling eddies of smoke that oppressed the atmosphere of the chamber. For myself, however, I was mentally discussing certain topics which had formed matter for conversation between us at an earlier period of the evening; I mean the affair of the Rue Morgue, and the mystery attending the murder of Marie Rogêt.[1] I looked upon it, therefore, as something of a coincidence, when the door of our apartment was thrown open and admitted our old acquaintance, Monsieur G—, the Prefect of the Parisian police.

We gave him a hearty welcome; for there was nearly half as much of the entertaining as of the contemptible about the man, and we had not seen him for several years. We had been sitting in the dark, and Dupin now arose for the purpose of lighting a lamp, but sat down again, without doing so, upon G.'s saying that he had called to consult us, or rather to ask the opinion of my friend, about some official business which had occasioned a great deal of trouble.

"If it is any point requiring reflection," observed Dupin, as he forebore to enkindle the wick, "we shall examine it to better purpose in the dark."

"That is another of your odd notions," said the Prefect, who had a fashion of calling every thing "odd" that was beyond his comprehension, and thus lived amid an absolute legion of "oddities."

"Very true," said Dupin, as he supplied his visitor with a pipe, and rolled towards him a comfortable chair.

"And what is the difficulty now?" I asked. "Nothing more in the assassination way, I hope?"

"Oh no; nothing of that nature. The fact is, the business is *very* simple indeed, and I make no doubt that we can manage it sufficiently well ourselves; but then I thought Dupin would like to hear the details of it, because it is so excessively *odd.*"

"Simple and odd," said Dupin.

[1] Cases solved in other Poe stories: "The Murders in the Rue Morgue" and "The Mystery of Marie Roget."

"Why, yes; and not exactly that, either. The fact is, we have all been a good deal puzzled because the affair *is* so simple, and yet baffles us altogether."

"Perhaps it is the very simplicity of the thing which puts you at fault," said my friend.

"What nonsense you *do* talk!" replied the Prefect, laughing heartily.

"Perhaps the mystery is a little *too* plain," said Dupin.

"Oh, good heavens! who ever heard of such an idea?"

"A little *too* self-evident."

"Ha! ha! ha!—ha! ha! ha!—ho! ho! ho!"—roared our visitor, profoundly amused, "oh, Dupin, you will be the death of me yet!"

"And what, after all, *is* the matter on hand?" I asked.

"Why, I will tell you," replied the Prefect, as he gave a long, steady, and contemplative puff, and settled himself in his chair. "I will tell you in a few words; but, before I begin, let me caution you that this is an affair demanding the greatest secrecy, and that I should most probably lose the position I now hold, were it known that I confided it to any one."

"Proceed," said I.

"Or not," said Dupin.

"Well, then; I have received personal information, from a very high quarter, that a certain document of the last importance has been purloined from the royal apartments. The individual who purloined it is known; this beyond a doubt; he was seen to take it. It is known, also, that it still remains in his possession."

"How is this known?" asked Dupin.

"It is clearly inferred," replied the Prefect, "from the nature of the document, and from the non-appearance of certain results which would at once arise from its passing *out* of the robber's possession;—that is to say, from his employing it as he must design in the end to employ it."

"Be a little more explicit," I said.

"Well, I may venture so far as to say that the paper gives its holder a certain power in a certain quarter where such power is immensely valuable." The Prefect was fond of the cant of diplomacy.

"Still I do not quite understand," said Dupin.

"No? Well; the disclosure of the document to a third person, who shall be nameless, would bring in question the honor of a personage of most exalted station; and this fact gives the holder of the document an ascendancy over the illustrious personage whose honor and peace are so jeopardized."

"But this ascendancy," I interposed, "would depend upon the robber's knowledge of the loser's knowledge of the robber. Who would dare—"

"The thief," said G—, "is the Minister D—, who dares all things, those unbecoming as well as those becoming a man. The method of the theft was not less ingenious than bold. The document in question—a letter, to be frank—had been received by the personage robbed while alone in the royal *boudoir.* During its perusal she was suddenly interrupted by the entrance of the other exalted personage from whom especially it was her wish to conceal it. After a hurried and vain endeavor to thrust it in a drawer, she was forced to place it, open as it was, upon a table. The address, however, was uppermost, and, the contents thus unexposed, the letter escaped notice. At this juncture enters the Minister D—. His lynx eye immediately perceives the paper, recognizes the handwriting of the address, observes the confusion of the personage addressed, and fathoms her secret. After some business transactions, hurried through in his ordinary manner, he produces a letter somewhat similar to the one in question, opens it, pretends to read it, and then places it in close juxtaposition to the other. Again he converses, for some fifteen minutes, upon the public affairs. At length, in taking leave, he takes also from the table the letter to which he had no claim. Its rightful owner saw, but, of course, dared not call attention to the act, in the presence of the third personage who stood at her elbow. The minister decamped; leaving his own letter—one of no importance—upon the table."

"Here, then," said Dupin to me, "you have precisely what you demand to make the ascendancy complete—the robber's knowledge of the loser's knowledge of the robber."

"Yes," replied the Prefect; "and the power thus attained has, for some months past, been wielded, for political purposes, to a very dangerous extent. The personage robbed is more thoroughly convinced, every day, of the necessity of reclaiming her letter. But this, of course, cannot be done openly. In fine, driven to despair, she has committed the matter to me."

"Than whom," said Dupin, amid a perfect whirlwind of smoke, "no more sagacious agent could, I suppose, be desired, or even imagined."

"You flatter me," replied the Prefect; "but it is possible that some such opinion may have been entertained."

"It is clear," said I, "as you observe, that the letter is still in possession of the minister; since it is this possession, and not any employment of the letter, which bestows the power. With the employment the power departs."

"True," said G.; "and upon this conviction I proceeded. My first care was to make thorough search of the minister's hotel; and here my chief embarrassment lay in the necessity of searching without his knowledge. Beyond all things, I have been warned of the danger which would result from giving him reason to suspect our design."

"But," said I, "you are quite *au fait* in these investigations. The Parisian police have done this thing often before."

"O yes; and for this reason I did not despair. The habits of the minister gave me, too, a great advantage. He is frequently absent from home all night. His servants are by no means numerous. They sleep at a distance from their master's apartment, and, being chiefly Neapolitans, are readily made drunk. I have keys, as you know, with which I can open any chamber or cabinet in Paris. For three months a night has not passed, during the greater part of which I have not been engaged, personally, in ransacking the D— Hôtel. My honor is interested, and, to mention a great secret, the reward is enormous. So I did not abandon the search until I had become fully satisfied that the thief is a more astute man than myself. I fancy that I have investigated every nook and corner of the premises in which it is possible that the paper can be concealed."

"But is it not possible," I suggested, "that although the letter may be in the possession of the minister, as it unquestionably is, he may have concealed it elsewhere than upon his own premises?"

"This is barely possible," said Dupin. "The present peculiar condition of affairs at court, and especially of those intrigues in which D— is known to be involved, would render the instant availability of the document—its susceptibility of being produced at a moment's notice—a point of nearly equal importance with its possession."

"Its susceptibility of being produced?" said I.

"That is to say, of being *destroyed*," said Dupin.

"True," I observed; "the paper is clearly then upon the premises. As for its being upon the person of the minister, we may consider that as out of the question."

"Entirely," said the Prefect. "He has been twice waylaid, as if by footpads, and his person rigorously searched under my own inspection."

"You might have spared yourself this trouble," said Dupin. "D—, I presume, is not altogether a fool, and, if not, must have anticipated these waylayings, as a matter of course."

"Not *altogether* a fool," said G., "but then he's a poet, which I take to be only one remove from a fool."

"True," said Dupin, after a long and thoughtful whiff from his meerschaum, "although I have been guilty of certain doggerel myself."

"Suppose you detail," said I, "the particulars of your search."

"Why the fact is, we took our time, and we searched *every where*. I have had long experience in these affairs. I took the entire building, room by room; devoting the nights of a whole week to each. We examined, first, the furniture of each apartment. We opened every possible drawer; and I presume you know that, to a properly trained police agent, such a thing as a *secret* drawer is impossible. Any man is a dolt who permits a 'secret' drawer to escape him in a search of this kind. The thing is *so* plain. There is a certain amount of bulk—of space—to be accounted for in every cabinet. Then we have accurate rules. The fiftieth part of a line could not escape us. After the cabinets we took the chairs. The cushions we probed with the fine long needles you have seen me employ. From the tables we removed the tops."

"Why so?"

"Sometimes the top of a table, or other similarly arranged piece of furniture, is removed by the person wishing to conceal an article; then the leg is excavated, the article deposited within the cavity, and the top replaced. The bottoms and tops of bedposts are employed in the same way."

"But could not the cavity be detected by sounding?" I asked.

"By no means, if, when the article is deposited, a sufficient wadding of cotton be placed around it. Besides, in our case, we were obliged to proceed without noise."

"But you could not have removed—you could not have taken to pieces *all* articles of furniture in which it would have been possible to make a deposit in the manner you mention. A letter may be compressed into a thin spiral roll, not differing much in shape or bulk from a large knitting-needle, and in this form it might be inserted into the rung of a chair, for example. You did not take to pieces all the chairs?"

"Certainly not; but we did better—we examined the rungs of every chair in the hotel, and, indeed, the jointings of every description of furniture, by the aid of a most powerful microscope. Had there been any traces of recent disturbance we should not have failed to detect it instantly. A single grain of gimlet-dust, for example, would have been as obvious as an apple. Any disorder in the glueing—any unusual gaping in the joints—would have sufficed to insure detection."

"I presume you looked to the mirrors, between the boards and the plates, and you probed the beds and the bed-clothes, as well as the curtains and carpets."

"That of course; and when we had absolutely completed every particle of the furniture in this way, then we examined the house itself. We divided its entire surface into compartments, which we numbered, so that none might be missed; then we scrutinized each individual square inch throughout the premises, including the two houses immediately adjoining, with the microscope, as before."

"The two houses adjoining!" I exclaimed; "you must have had a great deal of trouble."

"We had; but the reward offered is prodigious."

"You include the *grounds* about the houses?"

"All the grounds are paved with brick. They gave us comparatively little trouble. We examined the moss between the bricks, and found it undisturbed."

"You looked among D—'s papers, of course, and into the books of the library?"

"Certainly; we opened every package and parcel; we not only opened every book, but we turned over every leaf in each volume, not contenting ourselves with a mere shake, according to the fashion of some of our police officers. We also measured the thickness of every book-*cover*, with the most accurate admeasurement, and applied to each the most jealous scrutiny of the microscope. Had any of the bindings been recently meddled with, it would have been utterly impossible that the fact should have escaped observation. Some five or six volumes, just from the hands of the binder, we carefully probed, longitudinally, with the needles."

"You explored the floors beneath the carpets?"

"Beyond doubt. We removed every carpet, and examined the boards with the microscope."

"And the paper on the walls?"

"Yes."

"You looked into the cellars?"

"We did."

"Then," I said, "you have been making a miscalculation, and the letter is *not* upon the premises, as you suppose."

"I fear you are right there," said the Prefect. "And now, Dupin, what would you advise me to do?"

"To make a thorough re-search of the premises."

"That is absolutely needless," replied G—. "I am not more sure that I breathe than I am that the letter is not at the Hôtel."

"I have no better advice to give you," said Dupin. "You have, of course, an accurate description of the letter?"

"Oh yes!"—And here the Prefect, producing a memorandum-book, proceeded to read aloud a minute account of the internal, and especially of the external appearance of the missing document. Soon after finishing the perusal of this description, he took his departure, more entirely depressed in spirits than I had ever known the good gentleman before.

In about a month afterwards he paid us another visit, and found us occupied very nearly as before. He took a pipe and a chair and entered into some ordinary conversation. At length I said,—

"Well, but G—, what of the purloined letter? I presume you have at last made up your mind that there is no such thing as overreaching the Minister?"

"Confound him, say I—yes; I made the re-examination, however, as Dupin suggested—but it was all labor lost, as I knew it would be."

"How much was the reward offered, did you say?" asked Dupin.

"Why, a very great deal—a *very* liberal reward—I don't like to say how much, precisely; but one thing I *will* say, that I wouldn't mind giving my individual check for fifty thousand francs to any one who could obtain me that letter. The fact is, it is becoming of more and more importance every day; and the reward has been lately doubled. If it were trebled, however, I could do no more than I have done."

"Why, yes," said Dupin, drawlingly, between the whiffs of his meerschaum, "I really—think, G—, you have not exerted yourself—to the utmost in this matter. You might—do a little more, I think, eh?"

"How?—in what way?"

"Why—puff, puff—you might—puff, puff—employ counsel in the matter, eh?—puff, puff, puff. Do you remember the story they tell of Abernethy?"

"No; hang Abernethy!"

"To be sure! hang him and welcome. But, once upon a time, a certain rich miser conceived the design of spunging upon this Abernethy for a medical opinion. Getting up, for this purpose, an ordinary conversation in a private company, he insinuated his case to the physician, as that of an imaginary individual.

" 'We will suppose,' said the miser, 'that his symptoms are such and such; now, doctor, what would *you* have directed him to take?' "

" 'Take!' said Abernethy, 'why, take *advice*, to be sure.' "

"But," said the Prefect, a little discomposed, "I am *perfectly* willing to take advice, and to pay for it. I would *really* give fifty thousand francs to any one who would aid me in the matter."

"In that case," replied Dupin, opening a drawer, and producing a check-book, "you may as well fill me up a check for the amount mentioned. When you have signed it, I will hand you the letter."

I was astounded. The Prefect appeared absolutely thunder-stricken. For some minutes he remained speechless and motionless, looking incredulously at my friend with open mouth, and eyes that seemed starting from their sockets; then, apparently recovering himself in some measure, he seized a pen, and after several pauses and vacant stares, finally filled up and signed a check for fifty thousand francs, and handed it across the table to Dupin. The latter examined it carefully and deposited it in his pocket-book; then, unlocking an *escritoire,* took thence a letter and gave it to the Prefect. This functionary grasped it in a perfect agony of joy, opened it with a trembling hand, cast a rapid glance at its contents, and then, scrambling and struggling to the door, rushed at length unceremoniously from the room and from the house, without having uttered a syllable since Dupin had requested him to fill up the check.

When he had gone, my friend entered into some explanations.

"The Parisian police," he said, "are exceedingly able in their way. They are persevering, ingenious, cunning, and thoroughly versed in the knowledge which their duties seem chiefly to demand. Thus, when G— detailed to us his mode of searching the premises at the Hôtel D—, I felt entire confidence in his having made a satisfactory investigation—so far as his labors extended."

"So far as his labors extended?" said I.

"Yes," said Dupin. "The measures adopted were not only the best of their kind, but carried out to absolute perfection. Had the letter been deposited within the range of their search, these fellows would, beyond a question, have found it."

I merely laughed—but he seemed quite serious in all that he said.

"The measures, then," he continued, "were good in their kind, and well executed; their defect lay in their being inapplicable to the case, and to the man. A certain set of highly ingenious resources are, with the Prefect, a sort of Procrustean bed, to which he forcibly adapts his designs. But he perpetually errs by being too deep or too shallow, for the matter in hand; and many a schoolboy is a better reasoner than he. I knew one about eight years of age, whose success at guessing in the game of 'even and odd' attracted universal admiration. This game is simple, and is played with marbles. One player holds in his hand a number of these toys, and demands of another whether that number is even or odd. If the guess is right, the guesser wins one; if wrong, he loses one. The boy to whom I allude won all the marbles of the school. Of course he had some principle of guessing; and this lay in mere observation and admeasurement of the astuteness of his opponents. For example, an arrant simpleton is his opponent, and, holding up his closed hand, asks, 'are they even or odd?' Our schoolboy replies, 'odd,' and loses; but upon the second trial he wins, for he then says to himself, 'the simpleton had them even upon the first trial, and his amount of cunning is just sufficient to make him have them odd upon the second; I will therefore guess odd';—he guesses odd, and wins. Now, with a simpleton a degree above the first, he would have reasoned thus: 'This fellow finds that in the first instance I guessed odd, and, in the second, he will propose to himself upon the first impulse, a simple variation from even to odd, as did the first simpleton; but then a second thought will suggest that this is too simple a variation, and finally he will decide upon putting it even as before. I will therefore guess even';—he guesses even, and wins. Now this mode of reasoning in the schoolboy, whom his fellows termed 'lucky,'—what, in its last analysis, is it?"

"It is merely," I said, "an identification of the reasoner's intellect with that of his opponent."

"It is," said Dupin; "and, upon inquiring of the boy by what means he effected the *thorough* identification in which his success consisted, I received answer as follows: 'When I wish to find out how wise, or how stupid, or how good, or how wicked is any one, or what are his thoughts at the moment, I fashion the expression of my face, as accurately as possible, in accordance with the expression of his, and then wait to see what thoughts or sentiments arise in my mind or heart, as if to match or correspond with the expression.' This response of the schoolboy lies at the bottom of all the spurious profundity which has been attributed to Rochefoucauld, to La Bougive, to Machiavelli, and to Campanella."

"And the identification," I said, "of the reasoner's intellect with that of his opponent, depends, if I understand you aright, upon the accuracy with which the opponent's intellect is admeasured."

"For its practical value it depends upon this," replied Dupin; "and the Prefect and his cohort fail so frequently, first, by default of this identification, and, secondly, by ill-admeasurement, or rather through non-admeasurement of the intellect with which they are engaged. They consider only their *own* ideas of ingenuity; and, in searching for anything hidden, advert only to the modes in which *they* would have hidden it. They are right in this much—that their own ingenuity is a faithful representative of that of *the mass;* but when the cunning of the individual felon is diverse in character from their own, the felon foils them, of course. This always happens when it is above their own, and very usually when it is below. They have no variation of principle in their investigations; at best, when urged by some unusual emergency—by some extraordinary reward—they extend or exaggerate their old modes of *practice,* without touching their principles. What, for example, in this case of D—, has been done to vary the principle of action? What is all this boring, and probing, and sounding, and scrutinizing with the microscope, and dividing the surface of the building into registered square inches—what is it all but an exaggeration *of the application* of the one principle or set of principles of search, which are based upon the one set of notions regarding human ingenuity, to which the Prefect, in the long routine of his duty, has been accustomed? Do you not see he has taken it for granted that *all* men proceed to conceal a letter—not exactly in a gimlet-hole bored in a chair-leg—but, at least, in *some* out-of-the-way hole or corner suggested by the same tenor of thought which would urge a man to secrete a letter in a gimlet-hole bored in a chair-leg? And do you not see also, that such *recherchés* nooks for concealment are adapted only for ordinary occasions, and would be adopted only by ordinary intellects; for, in all cases of concealment, a disposal of the article concealed—a disposal of it in this *recherché* manner,—is, in the very first instance, presumable and presumed; and thus its discovery depends, not at all upon the acumen, but altogether upon the mere care, patience, and determination of the seekers; and where the case is of importance—or, what amounts to the same thing in the policial eyes, when the reward is of magnitude,—the qualities in question have *never* been known to fail. You will now understand what I meant in suggesting that, had the purloined letter been hidden any where within the limits of the Prefect's examination—in other words, had the principle of its concealment been comprehended within the principles of the Prefect—its discovery would have been a matter altogether beyond question. This functionary, however, has been thoroughly mystified; and the remote source of his defeat lies in the supposition that the Minister is a fool, because he has acquired renown as a poet. All fools are poets; this the Prefect *feels;* and he is merely guilty of a *non distributio medii*[2] in thence inferring that all poets are fools."

"But is this really the poet?" I asked. "There are two brothers, I know; and both have attained reputation in letters. The Minister I believe has written learnedly on the Differential Calculus. He is a mathematician, and no poet."

"You are mistaken; I know him well; he is both. As poet *and* mathematician, he would reason well; as mere mathematician, he could not have reasoned at all, and thus would have been at the mercy of the Prefect."

"You surprise me," I said, "by these opinions, which have been contradicted by the voice of the world. You do not mean to set at naught the well-digested idea of centuries. The mathematical reason has long been regarded as *the* reason *par excellence.*"

"'*Il y a à parier,*'" replied Dupin, quoting from Chamfort, "'*que toute idée publique, toute convention reçue, est une sottise, car elle a convenu au plus grand nombre.*'[3] The mathematicians, I grant you, have done their best to promulgate the popular error to which you allude, and which is none the less an error for its promulgation as truth. With an art worthy a better cause, for example, they have insinuated the term 'analysis' into application to algebra. The French are the originators of this particular deception; but if a term is of any importance—if words derive any value from applicability—then 'analysis' conveys 'algebra' about as much as, in Latin, '*ambitus*' implies 'ambition,' '*religio*' 'religion,' or '*homines honesti*' a set of *honorable* men."

"You have a quarrel on hand, I see," said I, "with some of the algebraists of Paris; but proceed."

"I dispute the availability, and thus the value, of that reason which is cultivated in any especial form other than the abstractly logical. I dispute, in particular, the reason educed by mathematical study. The mathematics are the science of form and quantity; mathematical reasoning is merely logic applied to observation upon form and quantity. The great error lies in supposing that even the truths of what is called *pure* algebra, are abstract or general truths. And this error is so egregious that I am confounded at the universality with which it has been received. Mathematical axioms are *not* axioms of general truth. What is true of *relation*—of form and quantity—is often grossly false in regard to morals, for example. In this latter science it is very usually *un*true that the aggregated parts are equal to the whole. In chemistry also the axiom fails. In the consideration of motive it fails; for two motives, each of a given value, have not, necessarily, a value when united, equal to the sum of their values apart. There are numerous other mathematical truths which are only truths within the limits of *relation.* But the mathematician argues, from his *finite truths,* through habit, as if they were of an absolutely general applicability—as the world indeed imagines them to be. Bryant, in his very learned 'Mythology,' mentions an analogous source of error, when he says that 'although the Pagan fables are not believed, yet we forget ourselves continually, and make inferences from them as existing realities.' With the algebraists, however, who are Pagans themselves, the 'Pagan fables' *are* believed, and the inferences are made, not so much through lapse of memory, as through an unaccountable addling of the brains. In short, I nev-

[2] Undistributed middle.

[3] "I'll wager, that every idea which is generally held, every set convention, is a stupidity; for it has suited the majority."

er yet encountered the mere mathematician who could be trusted out of equal roots, or one who did not clandestinely hold it as a point of his faith that $x^2 + px$ was absolutely and unconditionally equal to q. Say to one of these gentlemen, by way of experiment, if you please, that you believe occasions may occur where $x^2 + px$ is *not* altogether equal to q, and, having made him understand what you mean, get out of his reach as speedily as convenient, for, beyond doubt, he will endeavor to knock you down.

"I mean to say," continued Dupin, while I merely laughed at his last observations, "that if the Minister had been no more than a mathematician, the Prefect would have been under no necessity of giving me this check. I knew him, however, as both mathematician and poet, and my measures were adapted to his capacity, with reference to the circumstances by which he was surrounded. I knew him as a courtier, too, and as a bold *intriguant.* Such a man, I considered, could not fail to be aware of the ordinary policial modes of action. He could not have failed to anticipate—and events have proved that he did not fail to anticipate—the waylayings to which he was subjected. He must have foreseen, I reflected, the secret investigations of his premises. His frequent absences from home at night, which were hailed by the Prefect as certain aids to his success, I regarded only as *ruses,* to afford opportunity for thorough search to the police, and thus the sooner to impress them with the conviction to which G—, in fact, did finally arrive—the conviction that the letter was not upon the premises. I felt, also, that the whole train of thought, which I was at some pains in detailing to you just now, concerning the invariable principle of policial action in searches for articles concealed—I felt that this whole train of thought would necessarily pass through the mind of the Minister. It would imperatively lead him to despise all the ordinary *nooks* of concealment. *He* could not, I reflected, be so weak as not to see that the most intricate and remote recess of his hotel would be as open as his commonest closets to the eyes, to the probes, to the gimlets, and to the microscopes of the Prefect. I saw, in fine, that he would be driven, as a matter of course, to *simplicity,* if not deliberately induced to it as a matter of choice. You will remember, perhaps, how desperately the Prefect laughed when I suggested, upon our first interview, that it was just possible this mystery troubled him so much on account of its being *so very* self-evident."

"Yes," said I, "I remember his merriment well. I really thought he would have fallen into convulsions."

"The material world," continued Dupin, "abounds with the very strict analogies to the immaterial; and thus some color of truth has been given to the rhetorical dogma, that metaphor, or simile, may be made to strengthen an argument, as well as to embellish a description. The principle of the *vis inertiae,*[4] for example, seems to be identical in physics and metaphysics. It is not more true in the former, that a large body is with more difficulty set in motion than a smaller one, and that its subsequent *momentum* is commensurate with this difficulty, than it is, in the latter, that intellects of the vaster capacity, while more forcible, more constant, and more eventful in their movements than those of inferior grade, are yet the less readily moved, and more embarrassed and full of hesitation in the first few steps of their progress. Again: have you ever noticed which of the street signs, over the shop doors, are the most attractive of attention?"

"I have never given the matter a thought," I said.

"There is a game of puzzles," he resumed, "which is played upon a map. One party playing requires another to find a given word—the name of town, river, state or empire—any word, in short, upon the motley and perplexed surface of the chart. A novice in the game generally seeks to embarrass his opponents by giving them the most minutely lettered names; but the adept selects such words as stretch, in large characters, from one end of the chart to the other. These, like the over-largely lettered signs and placards of the street, escape observation by dint of being excessively obvious; and here the physical oversight is precisely analogous with the moral inapprehension by which the intellect suffers to pass unnoticed those considerations which are too obtrusively and too palpably self-evident. But this is a point, it appears, somewhat above or beneath the understanding of the Prefect. He never once thought it probable, or possible, that the Minister had deposited the letter immediately beneath the nose of the whole world, by way of best preventing any portion of that world from perceiving it.

"But the more I reflected upon the daring, dashing, and discriminating ingenuity of D—; upon the fact that the document must always have been *at hand,* if he intended to use it to good purpose; and upon the decisive evidence, obtained by the Prefect, that it was not hidden within the limits of that dignitary's ordinary search—the more satisfied I became that, to conceal this letter, the Minister had resorted to the comprehensive and sagacious expedient of not attempting to conceal it at all.

"Full of these ideas, I prepared myself with a pair of green spectacles, and called one fine morning, quite by accident, at the Ministerial hotel. I found D— at home, yawning, lounging, and dawdling, as usual, and pretending to be in the last extremity of

[4] Force of inertia.

ennui. He is, perhaps, the most really energetic human being now alive—but that is only when nobody sees him.

"To be even with him, I complained of my weak eyes, and lamented the necessity of the spectacles, under cover of which I cautiously and thoroughly surveyed the apartment, while seemingly intent only upon the conversation of my host.

"I paid especial attention to a large writing-table near which he sat, and upon which lay confusedly, some miscellaneous letters and other papers, with one or two musical instruments and a few books. Here, however, after a long and very deliberate scrutiny, I saw nothing to excite particular suspicion.

"At length my eyes, in going the circuit of the room, fell upon a trumpery filigree card-rack of pasteboard, that hung dangling by a dirty blue ribbon, from a little brass knob just beneath the middle of the mantel-piece. In this rack, which had three or four compartments, were five or six visiting cards and a solitary letter. This last was much soiled and crumpled. It was torn nearly in two, across the middle—as if a design, in the first instance, to tear it entirely up as worthless, had been altered, or stayed, in the second. It had a large black seal, bearing the D— cipher *very* conspicuously, and was addressed, in a diminutive female hand, to D—, the minister, himself. It was thrust carelessly, and even, as it seemed, contemptuously, into one of the upper divisions of the rack.

"No sooner had I glanced at this letter, than I concluded it to be that of which I was in search. To be sure, it was, to all appearance, radically different from the one of which the Prefect had read us so minute a description. Here the seal was large and black, with the D— cipher; there it was small and red, with the ducal arms of the S— family. Here, the address, to the Minister, was diminutive and feminine; there the superscription, to a certain royal personage, was markedly bold and decided; the size alone formed a point of correspondence. But, then, the *radicalness* of these differences, which was excessive; the dirt; the soiled and torn condition of the paper, so inconsistent with the *true* methodical habits of D—, and so suggestive of a design to delude the beholder into an idea of the worthlessness of the document; these things, together with the hyperobtrusive situation of this document, full in the view of every visitor, and thus exactly in accordance with the conclusions to which I had previously arrived; these things, I say, were strongly corroborative of suspicion, in one who came with the intention to suspect.

"I protracted my visit as long as possible, and, while I maintained a most animated discussion with the Minister, on a topic which I knew well had never failed to interest and excite him, I kept my attention really riveted upon the letter. In this examination, I committed to memory its external appearance and arrangement in the rack; and also fell, at length, upon a discovery which set at rest whatever trivial doubt I might have entertained. In scrutinizing the edges of the paper, I observed them to be more *chafed* than seemed necessary. They presented the *broken* appearance which is manifested when a stiff paper, having been once folded and pressed with a folder, is refolded in a reversed direction, in the same creases or edges which had formed the original fold. This discovery was sufficient. It was clear to me that the letter had been turned, as a glove, inside out, re-directed, and resealed. I bade the Minister good morning, and took my departure at once, leaving a gold snuff-box upon the table.

"The next morning I called for the snuff-box, when we resumed, quite eagerly, the conversation of the preceding day. While thus engaged, however, a loud report, as if of a pistol, was heard immediately beneath the windows of the hotel, and was succeeded by a series of fearful screams, and the shoutings of a mob. D— rushed to a casement, threw it open, and looked out. In the meantime, I stepped to the card-rack, took the letter, put it in my pocket, and replaced it by a *fac-simile* (so far as regards externals,) which I had carefully prepared at my lodgings; imitating the D— cipher, very readily, by means of a seal formed of bread.

"The disturbance in the street had been occasioned by the frantic behavior of a man with a musket. He had fired it among a crowd of women and children. It proved, however, to have been without ball, and the fellow was suffered to go his way as a lunatic or a drunkard. When he had gone, D— came from the window, whither I had followed him immediately upon securing the object in view. Soon afterwards I bade him farewell. The pretended lunatic was a man in my own pay."

"But what purpose had you," I asked, "in replacing the letter by a *fac-simile*? Would it not have been better, at the first visit, to have seized it openly, and departed?"

"D—," replied Dupin, "is a desperate man, and a man of nerve. His hotel, too, is not without attendants devoted to his interests. Had I made the wild attempt you suggest, I might never have left the Ministerial presence alive. The good people of Paris might have heard of me no more. But I had an object apart from these considerations. You know my political prepossessions. In this matter, I act as a partisan of the lady concerned. For eighteen months the Minister has had her in his power. She has now him in hers—since, being unaware that the letter is not in his possession, he will proceed with his exactions as if it was. Thus will he inevitably commit himself, at once, to his political destruction. His downfall, too, will not be more precipitate than awkward. It is all very well to talk about the *facilis descensus Averni;*[5] but in all kinds of climbing, as Catalani said of singing, it is far more easy to get up than to come down. In the present instance I have no sympathy—at least no pity—for him who descends. He is that *monstrum horrendum,*[6] an unprincipled man of genius. I confess, however, that I should like very well to know the precise character of his thoughts, when, being defied by her whom the Prefect terms 'a certain personage,' he is reduced to opening the letter which I left for him in the card-rack."

"How? did you put any thing particular in it?"

[5] Easy descent to Hades.
[6] Horrible monster.

"Why—it did not seem altogether right to leave the interior blank—that would have been insulting. D—, at Vienna once, did me an evil turn, which I told him, quite good-humoredly, that I should remember. So, as I knew he would feel some curiosity in regard to the identity of the person who had outwitted him, I thought it a pity not to give him a clue. He is well acquainted with my MS., and I just copied into the middle of the blank sheet the words—

—Un dessein si funeste,
S'il n'est digne d'Atrée, est digne de Thyeste.[7]

They are to be found in Crébillon's 'Atrée.'"

1845

[7] "So deadly a scheme, if it is not worthy of Atreus, is at least worthy of Thyestes." In Greek legend, Thyestes seduced the wife of his brother Atreus; and Atreus, in revenge, killed Thyestes' sons and served them to their father at a banquet.

Romanticism on Puritan Soil

RALPH WALDO EMERSON [1803-1882]

Like Poe, Emerson was born in Boston. "His soul received its bent," said Charles Eliot Norton, "from the innocent America of before 1830," an America that had a "confident, sweet, morning spirit." (In the opinion of Norton, who was professor of the history of fine art at Harvard in Emerson's later years, the mood of young America limited his mind, encouraged him in an optimism that became a bigotry.)

Along with the buoyant optimism of the new nation, Emerson had the moral enthusiasm of his Puritan heritage. While Poe was the son of wandering actors, grew up in Virginia, and became an advocate of art for art's sake, Emerson was the son of a Unitarian minister, was shaped by his Massachusetts ancestry and environment, and believed in art for life's sake—or morals' sake. Behind him stretched impressively a long line of ministers of the Gospel. His own father, William Emerson, was minister of the First Church, Unitarian, in Boston. He died when the boy was not quite eight years old. Thereafter the widow and her four boys attended the church of William Ellery Channing. Mrs. Emerson was a highly competent mother. His Aunt Mary Moody Emerson was a pious and stimulating woman who held before him, as he put it later, an "immeasurably high standard." He was brought up in poverty; at times he and a brother had to share the use of a winter overcoat. Yet all four managed to go through Harvard. Emerson was messenger for the president, and waited on table; he graduated at the middle of his class. To help his brother William, he spent the next three years in teaching, shyly, in a school for young ladies.

He entered the Harvard divinity school in 1825, his studies handicapped by physical ailments, the care of a brother temporarily insane, and the need of more school teaching. His license to preach, given late in 1826, implied not so much a proof of capacity as a vote of confidence. At this juncture a new ailment, in the lungs, sent him to South Carolina and Florida for a long winter. In 1829 he became pastor of the Second Church, the church of the Mathers, now Unitarian, and in the same year married Ellen Tucker—"17 years old," he reported, "and very beautiful, by universal consent," but of delicate health. Within less than a year and a half her life was taken by tuberculosis. The white plague was almost a family institution: it brought death also to Emerson's two younger brothers, and dogged his own career for about six years, years in what he called the house of Pain.

He was also struggling in the house of doubt. First—as early as 1824—he had questioned whether the ministry, after all, was his true vocation. His love of eloquence boded well for his preaching, but was he not lacking in self-confidence among men, in warmth of heart, in moral worth? As time went on he questioned not so much his own fitness as the Christian ministry itself. Did not even the Unitarian church involve restraints upon the free spiritual life? And was it not a worship of dead forms rather than a vital faith? "The profession," he said, in his journal "is antiquated." In December 1832 he resigned his charge. Disagreement with his congregation over celebration of the Lord's Supper was only the immediate occasion. Bereaved, ill, and adrift in the world, he sailed for Europe on Christmas Day.

When he returned in the following September, he had regained his health and won a new assurance. In the course of his travels, from Italy to Scotland, he had seen his contemporary heroes—Landor, Coleridge, Carlyle, Wordsworth—and found them "all deficient, all these four ... in insight into religious truth. They have no idea of that species of moral truth which I call the first philosophy." He must have meant that he had a better idea of it himself. In November he began giving lectures. In the next year he settled in Concord, thenceforth his home. In 1835 he married Lydia Jackson. In 1836 his son Waldo was born, and his book *Nature* was published.

With this book he launched what turned out to be a series of three great Transcendental challenges. In them we can see the interplay of many forces: the old Puritan spirit, the deistic tendency of Unitarianism, an optimistic nationalism, the doctrines of the Platonic tradition, the impulse of the Romantic Movement. In *Nature* the challenge lay mainly in the field of philosophy. In the address on the American Scholar it was mainly in literature—the fit education of the writer. In his Divinity School address it was in religion. Emerson's years of frustration and groping were at an end. In place of the "antiquated" faith of his fathers, he had achieved a new faith of his own, vital if unorthodox.

He had also achieved a new vocation—that of the lecturer. Two of the three challenges were lectures. His love of eloquence, frustrated when he resigned his pulpit, found expression on the public lecture platform. Why he became one of the most popular lecturers in America is suggested by Lowell's essay "Emerson the Lecturer." In this way he nearly doubled the income he received from the estate of his first wife. He gave hundreds upon hundreds of lectures, ranging repeatedly as far as the West, even beyond the Mississippi. Cheerfully he bore the hardships of travel in those days, and temperatures of 20 below zero. "This climate and people are a new test for the wares of a man of letters."

As a man of letters, he mostly arrived at his published results indirectly, writing in his private journal, writing lectures based largely on his journal, finally writing essays based on both journal and lectures and publishing them as books. His most famous books were the *Essays* of 1841 and a second series in 1844. Most of the essays dealt with abstractions, such as Self-Reliance, Compensation, Love, The Over-Soul, The Poet, Manners, Politics, and were suggestive and inspirational rather than closely reasoned. These two volumes came with the flood-tide of Transcendentalism, far more memorably registered in them than in the four years' run of *The Dial*, the periodical organ of the movement edited by Margaret Fuller and Emerson.

In many of the essays his faith in the religion of the self was at its height, but in a few, such as that on Experience, we begin to see the later Emerson, forced by growing experience to recognize that man is not always a god but a creature limited by heredity, temperament, circumstance, suffering. The later Emerson appears in some of the poems, in *Representative Men* (1850), in *English Traits* (1856), most notably in the essays of *The Conduct of Life* (1860). His old optimism still shone, but the bright light of his faith did not blind him to the dark realities of the human lot.

In his own day and long after, Emerson was regarded as a Yankee Plato, or, in the phrase of Oliver Wendell Holmes, as "a winged Franklin"—"a soaring nature, ballasted with sense." In the cynical period between two world wars, his wings were often clipped by those critics who complained, not without justification, of his bland optimism, or his insistent preaching, or his rhetorical eloquence, or his intangible pantheism and mysticism, or his indifference to reason. In the years that have followed, he has impressed scholars with his important place in the development of American civilization, and interested critics in his qualities of mind and personality, especially in his "psychological ambivalence," i.e. his effort to perceive sharply, and keep himself poised between, the conflicting elements of life, such as free will and fate.

Texts: *The Complete Works of Ralph Waldo Emerson*, Centenary Edition (Boston, 1903–4). *The Journals of Ralph Waldo Emerson*, edited by E. W. Emerson and W. E. Forbes (Boston, 1909–14).

Further reading: R. L. Rusk, *The Life of Ralph Waldo Emerson*, 1949. S. E. Whicher, *Freedom and Fate: an Inner Life of Ralph Waldo Emerson*, 1953. V. C. Hopkins, *Spires of Form: a Study of Emerson's Aesthetic Theory*, 1951. Sherman Paul, *Emerson's Angle of Vision*, 1952. *Emerson: a Collection of Critical Essays*, ed. M. R. Konvitz and S. E. Whicher, 1962. Jonathan Bishop, *Emerson on the Soul*, 1964. Joel Porte, *Emerson and Thoreau: Transcendentalists in Conflict*, 1966.

FROM HIS *Journals*

Emerson began his journals in 1820, when he was a junior in college, and continued them for fifty-five years. When they were published (1909–14; edited by E. W. Emerson and W. E. Forbes) they made a set of ten substantial volumes, from which, in 1926, Bliss Perry extracted *The Heart of Emerson's Journals*. The Journals and Miscellaneous Notebooks are now being brought out in a definitive multi-volume scholarly edition by the Harvard University Press (1960–). The texts of the following selections are from the edition of Emerson and Forbes.

(age 21)

It is my own humor to despise pedigree. I was educated to prize it. The kind Aunt whose cares instructed my youth (and whom may God reward), told me oft the virtues of her and mine ancestors. They have been clergymen for many generations, and the piety of all and the eloquence of many is yet praised in the Churches. But the dead sleep in their moonless night; my business is with the living.

(age 28)

A sect or party is an elegant incognito devised to save a man from the vexation of thinking.

(age 29)

The hour of decision. It seems not worth while for them who charge others with exalting forms above the moon to fear forms themselves with extravagant dislike. * * * I know very well that it is a bad sign in a man to be too conscientious, and stick at gnats. The most desperate scoundrels have been the over-refiners. Without accommodation society is impracticable. But this ordinance [the Lord's Supper] is esteemed the most sacred of religious institutions, and I cannot go habitually to an institution which they esteem holiest with indifference and dislike. [*White Mountains, July 15, 1832*]

Sailed from Boston for Malta, December 25, 1832, in Brig Jasper, Captain Ellis, 236 tons, laden with logwood, mahogany, tobacco, sugar, coffee, beeswax, cheese, etc.

The good Captain rejoices much in my ignorance. He confounded me the other day about the book in the Bible where God was not mentioned, and last night upon St. Paul's shipwreck. Yet I comforted myself at midnight with *Lycidas*. What marble beauty in that classic pastoral.

Perhaps it is a pernicious mistake, yet, rightly seen, I believe it is sound philosophy, that wherever we go, whatever we do, self is the sole subject we study and learn. Montaigne said, himself was all he knew. Myself is much more than I know, and yet I know nothing else. The chemist experiments upon his new salt by trying its affinity to all the various substances he can command, arbitrarily selected, and thereby discloses the most wonderful properties in his subject. And I bring myself to sea, to Malta, to Italy, to find new affinities between me and my fellow men, to observe narrowly the affections, weaknesses, surprises, hopes, doubts, which new sides of the panorama shall call forth in me. Mean, sneakingly mean, would be this philosophy, a reptile unworthy of the name, if *self* be used in the low sense, but as self means Devil, so it means God.

I have been to the Opera, and thought three *taris*, the price of a ticket, rather too much for the whistle. It is doubtless a vice to turn one's eyes inward too much, but I am my own comedy and tragedy. [*Sicily*]

Tonight I heard the *Miserere* sung in St. Peter's and with less effect than yesterday. But what a temple! When night was settling down upon it and a long religious procession moved through a part of the church, I got an idea of its immensity such as I had not before. You walk about on its ample, marble pavement as you would on a common, so free are you of your neighbors; and throngs of people are lost upon it. And what beautiful lights and shades on its mighty gilded arches and vaults and far windows and brave columns, and its rich-clad priests that look as if they were the pictures come down from the walls and walking. [*Rome*]

I ought not to forget the ballet between the acts. Goethe laughs at those who force every work of art into the narrow circle of their own prejudices and cannot admire a picture as a picture, and a tune as a tune. So I was willing to look at this as a ballet, and to see that it was admirable, but I could not help feeling the while that it were better for mankind if there were no such dancers. I have since learned God's decision on the same, in the fact that all the *ballerine* are nearly idiotic.

(age 30)

I collect nothing that can be touched or tasted or smelled, neither cameo, painting, nor medallion; nothing in my trunk but old clothes; but I value much the growing picture which the ages have painted and which I reverently survey.

Pray what brought you here, grave sir? the moving Boulevard seems to say. [*Paris*]

I went this evening into Frascati's, long the most noted of the gambling houses or hells of Paris.

Went into St. Paul's, where service was saying. Poor church. [*London*]

I thank the Great God who has led me through this European scene, this last schoolroom in which he has pleased to instruct me, from Malta's isle, through Sicily, through Italy, through Switzerland, through France, through England, through Scotland, in safety and pleasure, and has now brought me to the shore and the ship that steers westward. He has shown me the men I wished to see,—Landor, Coleridge, Carlyle, Wordsworth; he has thereby comforted and confirmed me in my convictions. Many things I owe to the sight of these men. I shall judge more justly, less timidly, of wise men forevermore. [*Liverpool*]

The men of Europe will say, Expound; let us hear. What is it that is to convince the faithful and at the same time the philosopher? Let us hear this new thing. It is very old. It is the old revelation, that perfect beauty is perfect goodness, it is the development of the wonderful congruities of the moral law of human nature. Let me enumerate a few of the remarkable properties of that nature. A man contains all that is needful to his government within himself. He is made a law unto himself. All real good or evil that can befall him must be from himself. He only can do himself any good or any harm. Nothing can be given to him or taken from him but always there is a compensation. There is a correspondence between the human soul and everything that exists in the world—more properly, everything that is known to man. Instead of studying things without the principles of them, all may be penetrated unto within him. Every act puts the agent in a new condition. The purpose of life seems to be to acquaint a man with himself. He is not to live to the future as described to him, but to live to the real future by living to the real present. The highest revelation is that God is in every man.

(age 31)

Hail to the quiet fields of my fathers! Not wholly unattended by supernatural friendship and favor, let me come hither. Bless my purposes as they are simple and virtuous. Coleridge's fine letter (in London *Literary Gazette,* September 13, 1834) comes in aid of the very thoughts I was revolving. And be it so. Henceforth I design not to utter any speech, poem, or book that is not entirely and peculiarly my work. I will say at public lectures, and the like, those things which I have meditated for their own sake, and not for the first time with a view to that occasion. (*Concord, November 15, 1834.*)

(age 32)

You affirm that the moral development contains all the intellectual, and that Jesus was the perfect man. I bow in reverence unfeigned before that benign man. I know more, hope more, am more, because he has lived. But, if you tell me that in your opinion he has fulfilled all the conditions of man's existence, carried out to the utmost, at least by implication, all man's powers, I suspend my assent. I do not see in him cheerfulness: I do not see in him the love of natural science: I see in him no kindness for art; I see in him nothing of Socrates, of Laplace, of Shakespeare. The perfect man should remind us of all great men. Do you ask me if I would rather resemble Jesus than any other man? If I should say Yes, I should suspect myself of superstition.

I bought my house and two acres six rods of land of John T. Coolidge for 3,500 dollars.

I was married to Lydia Jackson.

(age 33)

Transcendentalism means, says our accomplished Mrs. B.,[1] with a wave of her hand, *a little beyond.*

The grey present, the white future.

Pleasant walk yesterday, the most pleasant of days. At Walden Pond I found a new musical instrument which I call the ice-harp. A thin coat of ice covered a part of the pond, but melted around the edge of the shore. I threw a stone upon the ice which rebounded with a shrill sound, and falling again and again, repeated the note with pleasing modulation. I thought at first it was the "peep, peep" of a bird I had scared. I was so taken with the music that I threw down my stick and spent twenty minutes in throwing stones single or in handfuls on this crystal drum.

Margaret Fuller left us yesterday morning. Among other things that make her visit valuable and memorable, this is not the least, that she gave me five or six lessons in German pronunciation, never by my offer and rather against my will each time, so that now, spite of myself, I shall always have to thank her for a great convenience—which she foresaw.

(age 35)

The unbelief of the age is attested by the loud condemnation of trifles. Look at our silly religious papers. Let a minister wear a cane, or a white hat, go to a theatre, or avoid a Sunday School, let a school-book with a Calvinistic sentence or a Sunday School book without one be heard of, and instantly all the old grannies squeak and gibber and do what they call "sounding an alarm," from Bangor to Mobile. Alike nice and squeamish is its ear. You must on no account say "stink" or "Damn."

"Seek ye first the kingdom of God, and all these things shall be added unto you." What! Art? Hamlets? Ballads?

A *College.*—My College should have Allston, Greenough, Bryant, Irving, Webster, Alcott, summoned for its domestic professors. And if I must send abroad (and, if we send for dancers and singers and actors, why not at the same prices for scholars?), Carlyle, Hallam, Campbell, should come and read lectures on History, Poetry, Letters. I would bid my men come for the love of God and man, promising them an open field and a boundless opportunity, and they should make their own terms. Then I would open my lecture rooms to the wide nation; and they should pay, each man, a fee that should give my professor a remuneration fit and noble. Then I should see the lecture-room, the college, filled with life and hope. Students would come from afar; for who would not ride a hundred miles to hear some one of these men giving his selectest thoughts to those who received them with joy? I should see living learning; the Muse once more in the eye and cheek of the youth.

(age 36)

Nature will not have us fret or fume. When we come out of the Caucus or the Abolition Convention or the Temperance Meeting, she says to us, "So hot,

[1] Probably Almira Penniman Barlow, a family friend (see the Harvard edition of the Journals).

my little Sir!" I fear the criticism of the sun and moon.

I know no means of calming the fret and perturbation into which too much sitting, too much talking, brings me, so perfect as labor. I have no animal spirits; therefore, when surprised by company and kept in a chair for many hours, my heart sinks, my brow is clouded and I think I will run for Acton woods, and live with the squirrels henceforward. But my garden is nearer, and my good hoe, as it bites the ground, revenges my wrongs, and I have less lust to bite my enemies. I confess I work at first with a little venom, lay to a little unnecessary strength. But by smoothing the rough hillocks, I smooth my temper; by extracting the long roots of the piper-grass, I draw out my own splinters; and in a short time I can hear the bobolink's song and see the blessed deluge of light and color that rolls around me.

What Possibilities!—In the country church, I see the cousins of Napoleon, of Wellington, of Wilberforce, of Bentham, of Humboldt. A little air and sunshine, an hour of need, a provoking society, would call out the right fire from these slumbering peasants.

On Sunday we heard sulphurous Calvinism. The preacher railed at Lord Byron. I thought Lord Byron's vice better than Rev. Mr. M.'s virtue.

When I was thirteen years old, my Uncle Samuel Ripley one day asked me, "How is it, Ralph, that all the boys dislike you and quarrel with you, whilst the grown people are fond of you?" Now am I thirty-six and the fact is reversed,—the old people suspect and dislike me, and the young love me.

(age 37)

Yesterday George and Sophia Ripley, Margaret Fuller and Alcott discussed here the Social Plans [Brook Farm]. I wished to be convinced, to be thawed, to be made nobly mad by the kindlings before my eye of a new dawn of human piety. But this scheme was arithmetic and comfort: this was a hint borrowed from the Tremont House and United States Hotel; a rage in our poverty and politics to live rich and gentlemanlike, an anchor to leeward against a change of weather; a prudent forecast on the probable issue of the great questions of Pauperism and Poverty. And not once could I be inflamed, but sat aloof and thoughtless; my voice faltered and fell. It was not the cave of persecution which is the palace of spiritual power, but only a room in the Astor House hired for the Transcendentalists. I do not wish to remove from my present prison to a prison a little larger. I wish to break all prisons. I have not yet conquered my own house. It irks and repents me. Shall I raise the siege of this hencoop, and march baffled away to a pretended siege of Babylon? It seems to me that so to do were to dodge the problem I am set to solve, and to hide my impotency in the thick of a crowd. I can see too, afar,—that I should not find myself more than now,—no, not so much, in that select, but not by me selected, fraternity. Moreover, to join this body would be to traverse all my long trumpeted theory, and the instinct which spoke from it, that one man is a counterpoise to a city,—that a man is stronger than a city, that his solitude is more prevalent and beneficent than the concert of crowds.

(age 38)

I remember, when a child, in the pew on Sundays amusing myself with saying over common words as "black," "white," "board," etc., twenty or thirty times, until the word lost all meaning and fixedness, and I began to doubt which was the right name for the thing, when I saw that neither had any natural relation, but all were arbitrary. It was a child's first lesson in Idealism.

At Cambridge, the last Wednesday, I met twenty members of my college class and spent the day with them. Governor Kent of Maine presided, Upham, Quincy, Lowell, Gardner, Loring, Gorham, Motte, Wood, Blood, Cheney, Withington, Bulfinch, Reed, Burton, Stetson, Lane, Angier, Hilliard, Farnsworth, Dexter, Emerson. It was strange how fast the company returned to their old relation, and the whole mass of college nonsense came back in a flood. They all associated perfectly, were an unit for the day—men who now never meet. Each resumed his old place. The change in them was really very little in twenty years, although every man present was married, and all but one fathers. I too resumed my old place and found myself as of old a spectator rather than a fellow. I drank a great deal of wine (for me) with the wish to raise my spirits to the pitch of good fellowship, but wine produced on me its old effect, and I grew graver with every glass. Indignation and eloquence will excite me, but wine does not.

I saw in Boston Fanny Elssler in the ballet of *Nathalie*. * * * The chief beauty is in the extreme grace of her movement, the variety and nature of her attitude, the winning fun and spirit of all her little coquetries, the beautiful erectness of her body, and the freedom and determination which she can so easily assume, and, what struck me much, the air of perfect sympathy with the house. * * *

I should not think of danger to young women stepping with their father or brother out of happy and guarded parlors into this theatre to return in a few hours to the same; but I can easily suppose that it is not the safest resort for college boys who have left metaphysics, conic sections, or Tacitus to see these tripping satin slippers, and they may not forget this graceful, silvery swimmer when they have retreated again to their baccalaureate cells.

It is a great satisfaction to see the best in each kind, and as a good student of the world, I desire to let pass nothing that is excellent in its own kind unseen, unheard.

The *Dial*[2] is to be sustained or ended, and I must settle the question, it seems, of its life or death. I wish it to live, but do not wish to be its life. Neither do I like to put it in the hands of the Humanity and Reform Men, because they trample on letters and poetry; nor in the hands of the Scholars, for they are dead and dry.

Alcott sees the law of man truer and farther than any one ever did. Unhappily, his conversation never loses sight of his own personality. He never quotes; he never refers; his only illustration is his own biography. His topic yesterday is Alcott on the 17th October; today, Alcott on the 18th October; tomorrow, on the 19th. So will it be always. The poet, rapt into future times or into deeps of nature admired for themselves, lost in their law, cheers us with a lively charm; but this noble genius discredits genius to me. I do not want any more such persons to exist.

If I go into the churches in these days, I usually find the preacher in proportion to his intelligence to be cunning, so that the whole institution sounds hollow. X, the ablest of all the Unitarian clergy, spread popular traps all over the lecture which I heard in the Odeon. But in the days of the Pilgrims and the Puritans, the preachers were the victims of the same faith with which they whipped and persecuted other men, and their sermons are strong, imaginative, fervid, and every word a cube of stone.

(age 39)

I hear with pleasure that a young girl in the midst of rich, decorous Unitarian friends in Boston is well-nigh persuaded to join the Roman Catholic Church. Her friends, who are also my friends, lamented to me the growth of this inclination. But I told them that I think she is to be greatly congratulated on the event. She has lived in great poverty of events. In form and years a woman, she is still a child, having had no experiences, and although of a fine, liberal, susceptible, expanding nature, has never yet found any worthy object of attention; has not been in love, not been called out by any taste, except lately by music, and sadly wants adequate objects. In this church, perhaps, she shall find what she needs, in a power to call out the slumbering religious sentiment. It is unfortunate that the guide who has led her into this path is a young girl of a lively, forcible, but quite external character, who teaches her the historical argument for the Catholic faith. I told A. that I hoped she would not be misled by attaching any importance to that. If the offices of the church attracted her, if its beautiful forms and humane spirit draw her, if St. Augustine and St. Bernard, Jesus and Madonna, cathedral music and masses, then go, for thy dear heart's sake, but do not go out of this icehouse of Unitarianism, all external, into an icehouse again of external. At all events, I charged her to pay no regard to dissenters, but to suck that orange thoroughly.

It is greatest to believe and to hope well of the world, because he who does so, quits the world of experience, and makes the world he lives in.

(age 41)

Be an opener of doors for such as come after thee, and do not try to make the universe a blind alley.

There is not the slightest probability that the college will foster an eminent talent in any youth. If he refuses prayers and recitations, they will torment and traduce and expel him, though he were Newton or Dante.

Even for those whom I really love I have not animal spirits.

I like man, but not men.

(age 44)

Eager, solicitous, hungry, rabid, busy-bodied America attempting many things, vain, ambitious to feel thy own existence, and convince others of thy talent, by attempting and hastily accomplishing much; yes, catch thy breath and correct thyself, and failing here, prosper out there; speed and fever are

[2] Published from July 1840-April 1844; a quarterly magazine of literature, philosophy, and religion; published the work of the Transcendentalists.

never greatness; but reliance and serenity and waiting.

The Superstitions of our Age:
The fear of Catholicism;
The fear of pauperism;
The fear of immigration;
The fear of manufacturing interests;
The fear of radicalism or democracy;
And faith in the steam engine.

(age 46)

Love is temporary and ends with marriage. Marriage is the perfection which love aimed at, ignorant of what it sought. Marriage is a good known only to the parties,—a relation of perfect understanding, aid, contentment, possession of themselves and of the world,—which dwarfs love to green fruit.

(age 48)

This filthy enactment (The Fugitive Slave Law)[3] was made in the nineteenth century, by people who could read and write. I will not obey it, by God.

(age 52)

A *practical man* is the hobby of the age. Well, when I read German philosophy, or wrote verses, I was willing to concede there might be too much of these, and that the Western pioneer with axe on his shoulder, and still moving West as the settlements approached him, had his merits.

Whipple said of the author of "Leaves of Grass" that he had every leaf but the fig leaf.

(age 58)

Why has never the poorest country college offered me a professorship of rhetoric? I think I could have taught an orator, though I am none.

(age 59)

I like people who can do things. When Edward and I struggled in vain to drag our big calf into the barn, the Irish girl put her finger into the calf's mouth, and led her in directly.

[3] The 1850 law providing for the return of escaped Negro slaves to their owners.

(age 60)

I went to Dartmouth College, and found the same old Granny system which I met there twenty-five years ago. The President has an aversion to emulation, as injurious to the character of the pupils. He therefore forbids the election of members into the two literary societies by merit, but arranges that the first scholar alphabetically on the list shall be assigned to the Adelphi, and the second to the Mathesians, and the third to the Adelphi, and the fourth to the Mathesians; and so on. Every student belonging to the one or the other. "Well, but there is a first scholar in the class, is there not, and he has the first oration at Commencement?" "Oh, no, the parts are assigned by lot." The amiable student who explained it added that it tended to remove disagreeable excitement from the societies. I answered, "Certainly, and it would remove more if there were no college at all." I recommended morphine in liberal doses at the College Commons.

(age 65)

A man never gets acquainted with himself, but is always a surprise. We get daily news of the world within, as well as of the world outside, and not less of the central than of the surface facts. A new thought is awaiting him every morning.

(age 66)

Dr. Hedge tells us that the Indian asked John Eliot, "Why God did not kill the Devil?" One would like to know what was Eliot's answer.

(age 67)

In Yosemite, grandeur of these mountains perhaps unmatched in the globe; for here they strip themselves like athletes for exhibition, and stand perpendicular granite walls, showing their entire height, and wearing a liberty cap of snow on their head.

At the request of Galen Clark, our host at Mariposa, and who is, by State appointment, the protector of the trees, and who went with us to the Mammoth Groves, I selected a Sequoia Gigantea, near Galen's Hospice, in the presence of our party, and named it *Samoset,* in memory of the first Indian ally of the Plymouth Colony, and I gave Mr. Clark directions to procure a tin plate, and have the inscription painted thereon in the usual form of the named trees: and paid him its cost.

(age 59–69)

A man's style is his mind's voice. Wooden minds, wooden voices.

Fate.[***] Even the chickens running up and down, and pecking at each white spot and at each other as ridden by chicken nature, seem ever and anon to have a pause of consideration, then hurry on again to be chickens. Men have more pause.

(age 70)

Egypt. Mrs. Helen Bell, it seems, was asked, "What do you think the Sphinx said to Mr. Emerson?" "Why," replied Mrs. Bell, "the Sphinx probably said to him, 'You're another.' "

Thought

I am not poor, but I am proud,
  Of one inalienable right,
Above the envy of the crowd,—
  Thought's holy light.

Better it is than gems or gold,
  And oh! it cannot die,
But thought will glow when the sun grows cold,
  And mix with Deity.

1823

Grace

How much, preventing God, how much I owe
To the defences thou hast round me set;
Example, custom, fear, occasion slow,—
These scorned bondmen were my parapet.
I dare not peep over this parapet
To gauge with glance the roaring gulf below,
The depths of sin to which I had descended,
Had not these me against myself defended.

1833 1842

The Rhodora:

On Being Asked, Whence is the Flower?

Emerson chooses to write about a flower of the American forest rather than the rose or violet of English poetry. Later, in his little book on *Nature*, he formulated in philosophical terms the idea expressed here: that beauty needs no "excuse." When, as in the experience of this poem, he is in the presence of beauty, it seems supreme. But generally he speaks of other ultimate ends; it is equally true for him that goodness needs no excuse, that truth needs no excuse. Unlike Poe, he associates "an interchangeable Truth, Beauty, and Goodness, each wholly interfused in the other," "the eternal trinity of Truth, Goodness, and Beauty, each in its perfection including the three."

In May, when sea-winds pierced our solitudes,
I found the fresh Rhodora in the woods,
Spreading its leafless blooms in a damp nook,
To please the desert and the sluggish brook.
The purple petals, fallen in the pool,
Made the black water with their beauty gay;
Here might the redbird[1] come his plumes to cool,
And court the flower that cheapens his array.
Rhodora! if the sages ask thee why
This charm is wasted on the earth and sky,
Tell them, dear, that if eyes were made for seeing,
Then Beauty is its own excuse for being:[2]
Why thou wert there, O rival of the rose!
I never thought to ask, I never knew:
But, in my simple ignorance, suppose
The self-same Power that brought me there brought
    you.

1834

Each and All

The germ of the poem was probably an 1834 journal entry where Emerson had stated this abstraction in connection with a parable. "I remember when I was a boy going upon the beach and being charmed with the colors and forms of the shells. I picked up many and put them in my pocket. When I got home I could find nothing that I gathered—nothing but some dry, ugly mussel and snail shells. Thence I learned that Composition was more important than the beauty of individual forms to Effect. On the shore they lay wet and social, by the sea and under the sky."

Another journal passage, perhaps a memory of his European trip, gave him the beginning of his poem: "The shepherd or the beggar [the "clown," i.e. rustic, of the poem] in his red cloak little knows what a charm he gives to the wide landscape that charms you on the mountain-top and whereof he makes the most agreeable feature, and I [know] no more the part my individuality plays in the All."

The poem opens with this and three other separate situations, the meaning of which is crystallized in the state-

The Rhodora. [1] Presumably the scarlet tanager.

[2] Cf. *Nature*, the concluding paragraph of Chapter II, "Beauty": "The world thus exists to the soul to satisfy the desire of beauty. This element I call an ultimate end. No reason can be asked or given why the soul seeks beauty. Beauty, in its largest and profoundest sense, is one expression for the universe. God is the all-fair. Truth, and goodness, and beauty, are but different faces of the same All. But beauty in nature is not ultimate. It is the herald of inward and eternal beauty, and is not alone a solid and satisfactory good. It must stand as a part, and not as yet the last or highest expression of the final cause of Nature."

ment of lines 11 and 12. Then come three experiences of enchantment and disillusion—the sparrow, the shells, the maiden. Beauty seems a cheat of the immature; is not truth more to be desired? (Lines 37-39.) The answer, romantically conceived, is given in the rest of the poem. With Emerson, however, the answer represents a poetic mood rather than his prevailing outlook.

There are various awkwardnesses in images, movement of thought and feeling, pattern of meter and rhyme. Yet the lack of conventional design and finish is offset by an intriguing unexpectedness, growing out of free perception. Emerson's "rough" technique will prepare us for Whitman, Emily Dickinson, and many poets of the twentieth century.

Little thinks, in the field, yon red-cloaked clown
Of thee from the hill-top looking down;
The heifer that lows in the upland farm,
Far-heard, lows not thine ear to charm;
The sexton, tolling his bell at noon,
Deems not that great Napoleon
Stops his horse, and lists with delight,
Whilst his files sweep round yon Alpine height;
Nor knowest thou what argument
Thy life to thy neighbor's creed has lent.
All are needed by each one;
Nothing is fair or good alone.
I thought the sparrow's note from heaven,
Singing at dawn on the alder bough;
I brought him home, in his nest, at even;
He sings the song, but it cheers not now,
For I did not bring home the river and sky;—
He sang to my ear,—they sang to my eye.
The delicate shells lay on the shore;
The bubbles of the latest wave
Fresh pearls to their enamel gave,
And the bellowing of the savage sea
Greeted their safe escape to me.
I wiped away the weeds and foam,
I fetched my sea-born treasures home;
But the poor, unsightly, noisome things
Had left their beauty on the shore
With the sun and the sand and the wild uproar.
The lover watched his graceful maid,
As 'mid the virgin train she strayed,
Nor knew her beauty's best attire
Was woven still by the snow-white choir.
At last she came to his hermitage,
Like the bird from the woodlands to the cage;—
The gay enchantment was undone,
A gentle wife, but fairy none.
Then I said, "I covet truth;
Beauty is unripe childhood's cheat;
I leave it behind with the games of youth:"—
As I spoke, beneath my feet
The ground-pine curled its pretty wreath,
Running over the club-moss burrs;
I inhaled the violet's breath;
Around me stood the oaks and firs;
Pine-cones and acorns lay on the ground;
Over me soared the eternal sky,
Full of light and of deity;
Again I saw, again I heard,
The rolling river, the morning bird;—
Beauty through my senses stole;
I yielded myself to the perfect whole.

1834?

Concord Hymn

Sung at the Completion of the Battle Monument, July 4, 1837

By the rude bridge that arched the flood,
  Their flag to April's breeze unfurled,
Here once the embattled farmers stood
  And fired the shot heard round the world.

The foe long since in silence slept;
  Alike the conqueror silent sleeps;
And Time the ruined bridge has swept
  Down the dark stream which seaward creeps.

On this green bank, by this soft stream,
  We set to-day a votive stone;
That memory may their deed redeem,
  When, like our sires, our sons are gone.

Spirit, that made those heroes dare
  To die, and leave their children free,
Bid Time and Nature gently spare
  The shaft we raise to them and thee.

1837

The Problem

Seven years before, Emerson had made his decision to abandon the minister's vocation. But the problem he had faced continued to haunt him. It is stated clearly in the journal: "I dislike to be a clergyman and refuse to be one. Yet how rich a music would be to me a holy clergyman in my town. It seems to me he cannot be a man, quite and whole; yet how plain is the need of one, and how high, yes, highest is the function. Here is division of labor that I like not: a man must sacrifice his manhood for the social good. Something is wrong; I see not what."

I like a church; I like a cowl;
I love a prophet of the soul;
And on my heart monastic aisles
Fall like sweet strains, or pensive smiles;
Yet not for all his faith can see
Would I that cowlèd churchman be.

Why should the vest on him allure,
Which I could not on me endure?

Not from a vain or shallow thought
His awful Jove young Phidias brought;
Never from lips of cunning fell
The thrilling Delphic oracle;
Out from the heart of nature rolled
The burdens of the Bible old;
The litanies of nations came,
Like the volcano's tongue of flame,
Up from the burning core below,—
The canticles of love and woe:
The hand that rounded Peter's dome
And groined the aisles of Christian Rome
Wrought in a sad sincerity:
Himself from God he could not free;
He builded better than he knew;—
The conscious stone to beauty grew.

Know'st thou what wove yon woodbird's nest
Of leaves, and feathers from her breast?
Or how the fish outbuilt her shell,
Painting with morn her annual cell?
Or how the sacred pine-tree adds
To her old leaves new myriads?
Such and so grew these holy piles,
Whilst love and terror laid the tiles.
Earth proudly wears the Parthenon,
As the best gem upon her zone,
And Morning opes with haste her lids
To gaze upon the Pyramids;
O'er England's abbeys bends the sky,
As on its friends, with kindred eye;
For out of Thought's interior sphere
These wonders rose to upper air;
And Nature gladly gave them place,
Adopted them into her race,
And granted them an equal date
With Andes and with Ararat.

These temples grew as grows the grass;
Art might obey, but not surpass.
The passive Master lent his hand
To the vast soul that o'er him planned;
And the same power that reared the shrine
Bestrode the tribes that knelt within.
Ever the fiery Pentecost
Girds with one flame the countless host,
Trances the heart through chanting choirs,
And through the priest the mind inspires.
The word unto the prophet spoken
Was writ on tables yet unbroken;
The word by seers or sibyls told,
In groves of oak, or fanes of gold,
Still floats upon the morning wind,
Still whispers to the willing mind.
One accent of the Holy Ghost
The heedless world hath never lost.
I know what say the fathers wise,—
The Book itself before me lies,
Old *Chrysostom*,[1] best Augustine,
And he who blent both in his line,
The younger *Golden Lips* or mines,
Taylor,[2] the Shakespeare of divines.
His words are music in my ear,
I see this cowlèd portrait dear;
And yet, for all his faith could see,
I would not the good bishop be.

1839

The Sphinx

In 1859 Emerson wrote: "I have often been asked the meaning of "The Sphinx." It is this:—The perception of identity unites all things and explains one by another, and the most rare and strange is equally facile as the most common. But if the mind live only in particulars, and see only differences (wanting the power to see the whole—all in each), then the world addresses to this mind a question it cannot answer, and each new fact tears it to pieces, and it is vanquished by a distracting variety."

The Sphinx is drowsy,
 Her wings are furled:
Her ear is heavy,
 She broods on the world.
"Who'll tell me my secret,
 The ages have kept?—
I awaited the seer
 While they slumbered and slept:—

"The fate of the man-child,
 The meaning of man;
Known fruit of the unknown;
 Daedalian plan;
Out of sleeping a waking,
 Out of waking a sleep;
Life death overtaking;
 Deep underneath deep?

"Erect as a sunbeam,
 Upspringeth the palm;
The elephant browses,
 Undaunted and calm;
In beautiful motion
 The thrush plies his wings;

The Problem. [1] John of Antioch (345?–407), Greek church father, called "Golden Mouth" (Chrysostom) for his *Homilies*.
[2] Jeremy Taylor (1613–67), English theologian and author of *Holy Living* and *Holy Dying*.

Kind leaves of his covert,
Your silence he sings.

"The waves, unashamèd,
In difference sweet,
Play glad with the breezes,
Old playfellows meet;
The journeying atoms,
Primordial wholes,
Firmly draw, firmly drive,
By their animate poles.

"Sea, earth, air, sound, silence,
Plant, quadruped, bird,
By one music enchanted,
One deity stirred,—
Each the other adorning,
Accompany still;
Night veileth the morning,
The vapor the hill.

"The babe by its mother
Lies bathèd in joy;
Glide its hours uncounted,—
The sun is its toy;
Shines the peace of all being,
Without cloud, in its eyes;
And the sum of the world
In soft miniature lies.

"But man crouches and blushes,
Absconds and conceals;
He creepeth and peepeth,
He palters and steals;
Infirm, melancholy,
Jealous glancing around,
An oaf, an accomplice,
He poisons the ground.

"Out spoke the great mother,
Beholding his fear;—
At the sound of her accents
Cold shuddered the sphere:—
'Who has drugged my boy's cup?
Who has mixed my boy's bread?
Who, with sadness and madness,
Has turned my child's head?' "

I heard a poet answer
Aloud and cheerfully,
"Say on, sweet Sphinx! thy dirges
Are pleasant songs to me.
Deep love lieth under
These pictures of time;
They fade in the light of
Their meaning sublime.

"The fiend that man harries
Is love of the Best;
Yawns the pit of the Dragon,[1]
Lit by rays from the Blest.
The Lethe of Nature
Can't trance him again,
Whose soul sees the perfect,
Which his eyes seek in vain.

"To vision profounder,
Man's spirit must dive;
His aye-rolling orb
At no goal will arrive;
The heavens that now draw him
With sweetness untold,
Once found,—for new heavens
He spurneth the old.

"Pride ruined the angels,
Their shame them restores;
Lurks the joy that is sweetest
In stings of remorse.
Have I a lover
Who is noble and free?—
I would he were nobler
Than to love me.

"Eterne alternation
Now follows, now flies;
And under pain, pleasure,—
Under pleasure, pain lies.
Love works at the centre,
Heart-heaving alway;
Forth speed the strong pulses
To the borders of day.

"Dull Sphinx, Jove keep thy five wits;
Thy sight is growing blear;
Rue, myrrh and cummin[2] for the Sphinx,
Her muddy eyes to clear!"
The old Sphinx bit her thick lip,—
Said, "Who taught thee me to name?
I am thy spirit, yoke-fellow;
Of thine eye I am eyebeam.

"Thou art the unanswered question;
Couldst see thy proper eye,
Alway it asketh, asketh;
And each answer is a lie.
So take thy quest through nature,
It through thousand natures ply;
Ask on, thou clothed eternity;
Time is the false reply."

The Sphinx. [1] A reference to Satan.
[2] Presumably healing herbs.

Uprose the merry Sphinx,
And crouched no more in stone;
She melted into purple cloud,
She silvered in the moon;
She spired into a yellow flame;
She flowered in blossoms red;
She flowed into a foaming wave:
She stood Monadnoc's head.

Thorough a thousand voices
Spoke the universal dame;
"Who telleth one of my meanings
Is master of all I am."

1841

The Snow-Storm

Announced by all the trumpets of the sky,
Arrives the snow, and, driving o'er the fields,
Seems nowhere to alight: the whited air
Hides hills and woods, the river, and the heaven,
And veils the farm-house at the garden's end.
The sled and traveller stopped, the courier's feet
Delayed, all friends shut out, the housemates sit
Around the radiant fireplace, enclosed
In a tumultuous privacy of storm.

Come see the north wind's masonry.
Out of an unseen quarry evermore
Furnished with tile, the fierce artificer
Curves his white bastions with projected roof
Round every windward stake, or tree, or door.
Speeding the myriad-handed, his wild work
So fanciful, so savage, nought cares he
For number or proportion. Mockingly,
On coop or kennel he hangs Parian wreaths;
A swan-like form invests the hidden thorn;
Fills up the farmer's lane from wall to wall,
Maugre the farmer's sighs; and at the gate
A tapering turret overtops the work.
And when his hours are numbered, and the world
Is all his own, retiring, as he were not,
Leaves, when the sun appears, astonished Art
To mimic in slow structures, stone by stone,
Built in an age, the mad wind's night-work,
The frolic architecture of the snow.

1841

Ode

Inscribed to W. H. Channing

William Henry Channing, a nephew of the Unitarian leader, William Ellery Channing, was a vigorous political activist, as well as an active Transcendentalist, who had probably urged Emerson to participate in the Abolitionist cause. Emerson's poem not only answers Channing's immediate challenge; it defends, as well, Emerson's whole individualistic position.

Though loath to grieve
The evil time's sole patriot,
I cannot leave
My honeyed thought
For the priest's cant,
Or the statesman's rant.

If I refuse
My study for their politique,
Which at the best is trick,
The angry Muse
Puts confusion in my brain.

But who is he that prates
Of the culture of mankind,
Of better arts and life?
Go, blindworm, go,
Behold the famous States
Harrying Mexico
With rifle and with knife!

Or who, with accent bolder,
Dare praise the freedom-loving mountaineer?
I found by thee, O rushing Contoocook!
And in thy valleys, Agiochook!
The jackals of the negro-holder.

The God who made New Hampshire
Taunted the lofty land
With little men;—
Small bat and wren
House in the oak:—
If earth-fire cleave
The upheaved land, and bury the folk,
The southern crocodile would grieve.
Virtue palters; Right is hence;
Freedom praised, but hid;
Funeral eloquence
Rattles the coffin-lid.

What boots thy zeal,
O glowing friend,
That would indignant rend
The northland from the south?
Wherefore? to what good end?
Boston Bay and Bunker Hill
Would serve things still;—
Things are of the snake.

The horseman serves the horse,
The neatherd serves the neat,
The merchant serves the purse,

The eater serves his meat;
'Tis the day of the chattel,
Web to weave, and corn to grind;
Things are in the saddle,
And ride mankind.

There are two laws discrete,
Not reconciled,—
Law for man, and law for thing;
The last builds town and fleet,
But it runs wild,
And doth the man unking.

'Tis fit the forest fall,
The steep be graded,
The mountain tunnelled,
The sand shaded,
The orchard planted,
The glebe tilled,
The prairie granted,
The steamer built.

Let man serve law for man;
Live for friendship, live for love,
For truth's and harmony's behoof;
The state may follow how it can,
As Olympus follows Jove.

  Yet do not I implore
The wrinkled shopman to my sounding woods,
Nor bid the unwilling senator
Ask votes of thrushes in the solitudes.
Every one to his chosen work;—
Foolish hands may mix and mar;
Wise and sure the issues are.
Round they roll till dark is light,
Sex to sex, and even to odd;—
The over-god
Who marries Right to Might,
Who peoples, unpeoples,—
He who exterminates
Races by stronger races,
Black by white faces,—
Knows to bring honey
Out of the lion;
Grafts gentlest scion
On pirate and Turk.

The Cossack eats Poland,
Like stolen fruit;
Her last noble is ruined,
Her last poet mute:
Straight, into double band
The victors divide;
Half for freedom strike and stand;—
The astonished Muse finds thousands at her side.

1846

Bacchus

In "Bacchus" the "wine which never grew" becomes the symbol for poetic inspiration—for an ideal vision. This poem provides important Emersonian statements about poetry and can be usefully compared to Poe's "Israfel."

Bring me wine, but wine which never grew
In the belly of the grape,
Or grew on vine whose tap-roots, reaching through
Under the Andes to the Cape,
Suffered no savor of the earth to scape.

Let its grapes the morn salute
From a nocturnal root,
Which feels the acrid juice
Of Styx and Erebus;
And turns the woe of Night,
By its own craft, to a more rich delight,

We buy ashes for bread;
We buy diluted wine;
Give me of the true,—
Whose ample leaves and tendrils curled
Among the silver hills of heaven
Draw everlasting dew;
Wine of wine,
Blood of the world,
Form of forms, and mould of statures,
That I intoxicated,
And by the draught assimilated,
May float at pleasure through all natures;
The bird-language rightly spell,
And that which roses say so well.

Wine that is shed
Like the torrents of the sun
Up the horizon walls,
Or like the Atlantic streams, which run
When the South Sea calls.

Water and bread,
Food which needs no transmuting,
Rainbow-flowering, wisdom-fruiting,
Wine which is already man,
Food which teach and reason can.

Wine which Music is,—
Music and wine are one,—
That I, drinking this,
Shall hear far Chaos talk with me;

Kings unborn shall walk with me;
And the poor grass shall plot and plan
What it will do when it is man.
Quickened so, will I unlock
Every crypt of every rock.

I thank the joyful juice
For all I know;—
Winds of remembering
Of the ancient being blow,
And seeming-solid walls of use
Open and flow.

Pour, Bacchus! the remembering wine;
Retrieve the loss of me and mine!
Vine for vine be antidote,
And the grape requite the lote!
Haste to cure the old despair,—
Reason in Nature's lotus drenched,
The memory of ages quenched;
Give them again to shine;
Let wine repair what this undid;
And where the infection slid,
A dazzling memory revive;
Refresh the faded tints,
Recut the aged prints,
And write my old adventures with the pen
Which on the first day drew,
Upon the tablets blue,
The dancing Pleiads and eternal men.

1846

Compensation

The Centenary Edition of the poems prints these lines as a single poem; but the Essays show that each group of lines is a separate motto and separate poem.

The wings of Time are black and white,
Pied with morning and with night,
Mountain tall and ocean deep
Trembling balance duly keep.
In changing moon and tidal wave
Glows the feud of Want and Have.
Gauge of more and less through space,
Electric star or pencil plays,
The lonely Earth amid the balls
That hurry through the eternal halls,
A makeweight flying to the void,
Supplemental asteroid,
Or compensatory spark,
Shoots across the neutral Dark.

Man's the elm, and Wealth the vine;
Stanch and strong the tendrils twine:
Though the frail ringlets thee deceive,
None from its stock that vine can reave.
Fear not, then, thou child infirm,
There's no god dare wrong a worm;
Laurel crowns cleave to deserts,
And power to him who power exerts.
Hast not thy share? On winged feet,
Lo! it rushes thee to meet;
And all that Nature made thy own,
Floating in air or pent in stone,
Will rive the hills and swim the sea,
And, like thy shadow, follow thee.

1847

Give All to Love

Emerson's belief in "compensation" and his belief in a spiritual reality enable him to urge the detachment of the last two stanzas.

Give all to love;
Obey thy heart;
Friends, kindred, days,
Estate, good-fame,
Plans, credit and the Muse,—
Nothing refuse.

'Tis a brave master;
Let it have scope:
Follow it utterly,
Hope beyond hope:
High and more high
It dives into noon,
With wing unspent,
Untold intent;
But it is a god,
Knows its own path
And the outlets of the sky.

It was never for the mean;
It requireth courage stout.
Souls above doubt,
Valor unbending,
It will reward,—
They shall return
More than they were,
And ever ascending.

Leave all for love;
Yet, hear me, yet,
One word more thy heart behoved,
One pulse more of firm endeavor,—
Keep thee to-day,
To-morrow, forever,

Free as an Arab
Of thy beloved.

Cling with life to the maid;
But when the surprise,
First vague shadow of surmise
Flits across her bosom young,
Of a joy apart from thee,
Free be she, fancy-free;
Nor thou detain her vesture's hem,
Nor the palest rose she flung
From her summer diadem.

Though thou loved her as thyself,
As a self of purer clay,
Though her parting dims the day,
Stealing grace from all alive;
Heartily know,
When half-gods go,
The gods arrive.

1847

Ode to Beauty

Who gave thee, O Beauty,
The keys of this breast,—
Too credulous lover
Of blest and unblest?
Say, when in lapsed ages
Thee knew I of old?
Or what was the service
For which I was sold?
When first my eyes saw thee,
I found me thy thrall,
By magical drawings,
Sweet tyrant of all!
I drank at thy fountain
False waters of thirst;
Thou intimate stranger,
Thou latest and first!
Thy dangerous glances
Make women of men;
New-born, we are melting
Into nature again.

Lavish, lavish promiser,
Nigh persuading gods to err!
Guest of million painted forms,
Which in turn thy glory warms!
The frailest leaf, the mossy bark,
The acorn's cup, the raindrop's arc,
The swinging spider's silver line,
The ruby of the drop of wine,
The shining pebble of the pond,
Thou inscribest with a bond,
In thy momentary play,
Would bankrupt nature to repay.

Ah, what avails it
To hide or to shun
Whom the Infinite One
Hath granted his throne?
The heaven high over
Is the deep's lover;
The sun and sea,
Informed by thee,
Before me run
And draw me on,
Yet fly me still,
As Fate refuses
To me the heart Fate for me chooses.
Is it that my opulent soul
Was mingled from the generous whole;
Sea-valleys and the deep of skies
Furnished several supplies;
And the sands whereof I'm made
Draw me to them, self-betrayed?

I turn the proud portfolio
Which holds the grand designs
Of Salvator, of Guercino,
And Piranesi's lines.[1]
I hear the lofty paeans
Of the masters of the shell,[2]
Who heard the starry music
And recount the numbers well;
Olympian bards who sung
Divine Ideas below,
Which always find us young
And always keep us so.[3]
Oft, in streets or humblest places,
I detect far-wandered graces,
Which, from Eden wide astray,
In lowly homes have lost their way.

Thee gliding through the sea of form,
Like the lightning through the storm,
Somewhat not to be possessed,
Somewhat not to be caressed,
No feet so fleet could ever find,
No perfect form could ever bind.
Thou eternal fugitive,
Hovering over all that live,
Quick and skilful to inspire

Ode to Beauty. [1]According to Edward Emerson, Margaret Fuller sent the portfolio. Salvator Rosa, Guercino, and Piranesi were Italian painters of the 17th and 18th centuries.

[2]Apollo formed the lyre, the instrument of music and poetry, from a shell.

[3]These four lines served as the motto for "The Poet."

Sweet, extravagant desire,
Starry space and lily-bell
Filling with thy roseate smell,
Wilt not give the lips to taste
Of the nectar which thou hast.

All that's good and great with thee
Works in close conspiracy;
Thou hast bribed the dark and lonely
To report thy features only,
And the cold and purple morning
Itself with thoughts of thee adorning;
The leafy dell, the city mart,
Equal trophies of thine art;
E'en the flowing azure air
Thou hast touched for my despair;
And, if I languish into dreams,
Again I meet the ardent beams.
Queen of things! I dare not die
In Being's deeps past ear and eye;
Lest there I find the same deceiver
And be the sport of Fate forever.
Dread Power, but dear! if God thou be,
Unmake me quite, or give thyself to me!

1847

Hamatreya

Emerson here adapted to his own poetical use a passage from the Hindu *Vishnu Purana* which he had copied into his journal: "These, and other kings who with perishable frames have possessed this ever-enduring world, and who, blinded with deceptive notions of individual occupation, have indulged the feeling that suggests 'This earth is mine,—it is my son's,—it belongs to my dynasty,'—have all passed away. So, many who reigned before them, many who succeeded them, and many who are yet to come, have ceased or will cease to be. Earth laughs, as if smiling with autumnal flowers to behold her kings unable to effect the subjugation of themselves. I will repeat to you, Maitreya [Emerson's Hamatreya], the stanzas that were chanted by Earth."

The names in the first line of the poem are those of the first settlers of Concord.

Bulkeley, Hunt, Willard, Hosmer, Meriam, Flint,
Possessed the land which rendered to their toil
Hay, corn, roots, hemp, flax, apples, wool and wood.
Each of these landlords walked amidst his farm,
Saying, " 'Tis mine, my children's and my name's.
How sweet the west wind sounds in my own trees!
How graceful climb those shadows on my hill!
I fancy these pure waters and the flags
Know me, as does my dog: we sympathize;
And, I affirm, my actions smack of the soil."
Where are these men? Asleep beneath their
grounds:
And strangers, fond as they, their furrows plough.
Earth laughs in flowers, to see her boastful boys
Earth-proud, proud of the earth which is not theirs;
Who steer the plough, but cannot steer their feet
Clear of the grave.
They added ridge to valley, brook to pond,
And sighed for all that bounded their domain;
"This suits me for a pasture; that's my park;
We must have clay, lime, gravel, granite-ledge,
And misty lowland, where to go for peat.
The land is well,—lies fairly to the south.
'Tis good, when you have crossed the sea and back,
To find the sitfast acres where you left them."
Ah! the hot owner sees not Death, who adds
Him to his land, a lump of mould the more.
Hear what the Earth says:—

EARTH-SONG

"Mine and yours;
Mine, not yours.
Earth endures;
Stars abide—
Shine down in the old sea;
Old are the shores;
But where are old men?
I who have seen much,
Such have I never seen.

"The lawyer's deed
Ran sure,
In tail,
To them, and to their heirs
Who shall succeed,
Without fail,
Forevermore.

"Here is the land,
Shaggy with wood,
With its old valley,
Mound and flood.
But the heritors?—
Fled like the flood's foam.
The lawyer, and the laws,
And the kingdom,
Clean swept herefrom.

"They called me theirs,
Who so controlled me;
Yet every one
Wished to stay, and is gone,
How am I theirs,

If they cannot hold me,
But I hold them?"

When I heard the Earth-song
I was no longer brave;
My avarice cooled
Like lust in the chill of the grave.

1847

The Apology

Think me not unkind and rude
That I walk alone in grove and glen;
I go to the god of the wood
To fetch his word to men.

Tax not my sloth that I
Fold my arms beside the brook;
Each cloud that floated in the sky
Writes a letter in my book.

Chide me not, laborious band,
For the idle flowers I brought;
Every aster in my hand
Goes home loaded with a thought.

There was never mystery
But 'tis figured in the flowers;
Was never secret history
But birds tell it in the bowers.

One harvest from thy field
Homeward brought the oxen strong;
A second crop thine acres yield,
Which I gather in a song.

1846

Fable

The mountain and the squirrel
Had a quarrel,
And the former called the latter "Little Prig;"
Bun replied,
"You are doubtless very big;
But all sorts of things and weather
Must be taken in together,
To make up a year
And a sphere.
And I think it no disgrace
To occupy my place.
If I'm not so large as you,
You are not so small as I,
And not half so spry.
I'll not deny you make
A very pretty squirrel track;
Talents differ; all is well and wisely put;
If I cannot carry forests on my back,
Neither can you crack a nut."

1845

Days

Eleven years earlier, he had written to Margaret Fuller: "Heaven walks among us ordinarily muffled in such triple or tenfold disguises that the wisest are deceived and no one suspects the days to be gods." In 1847, on the eve of his birthday, he wrote in his journal: "The days come and go like muffled and veiled figures sent from a distant friendly party, but they say nothing, and if we do not use the gifts they bring, they carry them as silently away."

Daughters of Time, the hypocritic Days,
Muffled and dumb like barefoot dervishes,
And marching single in an endless file,
Bring diadems and fagots in their hands.
To each they offer gifts after his will,
Bread, kingdoms, stars, and sky that holds them all.
I, in my pleachèd garden, watched the pomp,
Forgot my morning wishes, hastily
Took a few herbs and apples, and the Day
Turned and departed silent. I, too late,
Under her solemn fillet saw the scorn.

1851

Two Rivers

By the doctrine of correspondence, the river flowing through the meadows is a symbol of the unbounded Spirit that flows through all things: through the river itself, all of nature, and man, and time.

Thy summer voice, Musketaquit,[1]
Repeats the music of the rain;
But sweeter rivers pulsing flit
Through thee, as thou through Concord Plain.

Thou in thy narrow banks art pent:
The stream I love unbounded goes
Through flood and sea and firmament;
Through light, through life, it forward flows.

I see the inundation sweet,
I hear the spending of the stream
Through years, through men, through Nature fleet,
Through love and thought, through power and dream.

Musketaquit, a goblin strong,
Of shard and flint makes jewels gay;

Two Rivers. [1] The Concord River.

They lose their grief who hear his song,
And where he winds is the day of day.

So forth and brighter fares my stream,—
Who drink it shall not thirst again;
No darkness stains its equal gleam,
And ages drop in it like rain.

1856

Brahma

Why Emerson was attracted to Oriental thought, as well as to Plato and Neo-Platonism, may be seen in his essay on Plato. "In all nations there are minds which incline to dwell in the conception of the fundamental Unity. . . . This tendency finds its highest expression in the religious writings of the East, and chiefly in the Indian Scriptures."

In its day "Brahma" was ridiculed as incomprehensible. But its difficulties would have vanished, as Emerson remarked, if readers had mentally altered Brahma to Jehovah.

If the red slayer think he slays,
  Or if the slain think he is slain,
They know not well the subtle ways
  I keep, and pass, and turn again.

Far or forgot to me is near;
  Shadow and sunlight are the same;
The vanished gods to me appear;
  And one to me are shame and fame.

They reckon ill who leave me out;
  When me they fly, I am the wings;
I am the doubter and the doubt,
  And I the hymn the Brahmin sings.

The strong gods pine for my abode,
  And pine in vain the sacred Seven;[1]
But thou, meek lover of the good!
  Find me, and turn thy back on heaven.

1856

Water

Unpublished in Emerson's lifetime, these lines and the following quatrain, "Nahant," were first printed in an Appendix to the Riverside Edition of the Poems (1883) in a group of "Fragments on Nature and Life." Hyatt H. Waggoner, in *American Poets from the Puritans to the Present* (1968) treats both fragments as a single poem in two parts, finding the first suggestive of Robert Frost's "Sand Dunes," the second of T. S. Eliot's "The Dry Salvages."

The water understands
Civilization well;
It wets my foot, but prettily,
It chills my life, but wittily,
It is not disconcerted,
It is not broken-hearted:
Well used, it decketh joy,
Adorneth, doubleth joy:
Ill used, it will destroy,
In perfect time and measure
With a face of golden pleasure
Elegantly destroy.

1883

Nahant

A journal entry of 1853 reads: "At Nahant the eternal play of the sea seems the anti-clock, or destroyer of the memory of time." The quatrain is untitled in the Riverside Edition.

All day the waves assailed the rock,
  I heard no church-bell chime,
The sea-beat scorns the minster clock
  And breaks the glass of Time.

1883

Terminus

It is time to be old
To take in sail:—
The god of bounds,
Came to me in his fatal rounds,
And said: "No more!
No farther shoot
Thy broad ambitious branches, and thy root.
Fancy departs: no more invent;
Contract thy firmament
To compass of a tent.
There's not enough for this and that,
Make thy option which of two;
Economize the failing river,
Not the less revere the Giver;
Leave the many and hold the few.
Timely wise, accept the terms,
Soften the fall with wary foot;
A little while
Still plan and smile,
And,—fault of novel germs,—
Mature the unfallen fruit.
Curse, if thou wilt, thy sires,
Bad husbands of their fires,
Who, when they gave thee breath,
Failed to bequeath
The needful sinew stark as once,

Brahma. [1] The highest saints in the Hindu faith.

The Baresark marrow to thy bones,
But left a legacy of ebbing veins,
Inconstant heat and nerveless reins,—
Amid the Muses, left thee deaf and dumb,
Amid the gladiators, halt and numb."

As the bird trims her to the gale,
I trim myself to the storm of time;
I man the rudder, reef the sail,
Obey the voice at eve obeyed at prime:
"Lowly faithful, banish fear,
Right onward drive unharmed;
The port, well worth the cruise, is near,
And every wave is charmed."

1860

Nature

Emerson first published *Nature* in September 1836. It was in effect the manifesto of the Transcendental movement. It was also the summation of Emerson's previous thinking, and a ground-plan for his future work. It stated the case for a philosophy of idealism suggested to Emerson by the romantic Coleridge and, behind him, by the new German philosophers. It was reprinted in 1849.

The book is not easy reading. Despite a show of method, it is the work of a mind impatient of close logical thinking. Emerson does not attempt, in the manner of philosophers, carefully to build a demonstration. He throws out affirmations supported by images rather than arguments, and appeals for an instinctive response rather than rational assent. It is, actually, a meditative prose poem. Only the Introduction and first chapter are included here.

Introduction

Our age is retrospective. It builds the sepulchres of the fathers. It writes biographies, histories, and criticism. The foregoing generations beheld God and nature face to face; we, through their eyes. Why should not we also enjoy an original relation to the universe? Why should not we have a poetry and philosophy of insight and not of tradition, and a religion by revelation to us, and not the history of theirs? Embosomed for a season in nature, whose floods of life stream around and through us, and invite us, by the powers they supply, to action proportioned to nature, why should we grope among the dry bones of the past, or put the living generation into masquerade out of its faded wardrobe? The sun shines to-day also. There is more wool and flax in the fields. There are new lands, new men, new thoughts. Let us demand our own works and laws and worship.

Undoubtedly we have no questions to ask which are unanswerable. We must trust the perfection of the creation so far as to believe that whatever curiosity the order of things has awakened in our minds, the order of things can satisfy. Every man's condition is a solution in hieroglyphic to those inquiries he would put. He acts it as life, before he apprehends it as truth. In like manner, nature is already, in its forms and tendencies, describing its own design. Let us interrogate the great apparition that shines so peacefully around us. Let us inquire, to what end is nature?

All science has one aim, namely, to find a theory of nature. We have theories of races and of functions, but scarcely yet a remote approach to an idea of creation. We are now so far from the road to truth, that religious teachers dispute and hate each other, and speculative men are esteemed unsound and frivolous. But to a sound judgment, the most abstract truth is the most practical. Whenever a true theory appears, it will be its own evidence. Its test is, that it will explain all phenomena. Now many are thought not only unexplained but inexplicable; as language, sleep, madness, dreams, beasts, sex.

Philosophically considered, the universe is composed of Nature and the Soul. Strictly speaking, therefore, all that is separate from us, all which Philosophy distinguishes as the NOT ME, that is, both nature and art, all other men and my own body, must be ranked under this name, NATURE. In enumerating the values of nature and casting up their sum, I shall use the word in both senses;—in its common and in its philosophical import. In inquiries so general as our present one, the inaccuracy is not material; no confusion of thought will occur. *Nature,* in the common sense, refers to essences unchanged by man; space, the air, the river, the leaf. *Art* is applied to the mixture of his will with the same things, as in a house, a canal, a statue, a picture. But his operations taken together are so insignificant, a little chipping, baking, patching, and washing, that in an impression so grand as that of the world on the human mind, they do not vary the result.

I. Nature

To go into solitude, a man needs to retire as much from his chamber as from society. I am not solitary whilst I read and write, though nobody is with me. But if a man would be alone, let him look at the stars. The rays that come from those heavenly worlds will separate between him and what he touches. One might think the atmosphere was made transparent with this design, to give man, in the heavenly bodies, the perpetual presence of the sublime. Seen in the streets of cities, how great they are! If the stars should appear one night in a thousand years, how would men believe and adore; and preserve for many generations the remembrance of the city of God which had been shown! But every night come out these envoys of beauty, and light the universe with their admonishing smile.

The stars awaken a certain reverence, because though always present, they are inaccessible; but all natural objects make a kindred impression, when the mind is open to their influence. Nature never wears a mean appearance. Neither does the wisest man extort her secret, and lose his curiosity by finding out all her perfection. Nature never became a toy to a wise spirit. The flowers, the animals, the mountains, reflected the wisdom of his best hour, as much as they had delighted the simplicity of his childhood.

When we speak of nature in this manner, we have a distinct but most poetical sense in the mind. We mean the integrity of impression made by manifold natural objects. It is this which distinguishes the stick of timber of the wood-cutter from the tree of the poet. The charming landscape which I saw this morning is indubitably made up of some twenty or thirty farms. Miller owns this field, Locke that, and Manning the woodland beyond. But none of them owns the landscape. There is a property in the horizon which no man has but he whose eye can integrate all the parts, that is, the poet. This is the best part of these men's farms, yet to this their warranty-deeds give no title.

To speak truly, few adult persons can see nature. Most persons do not see the sun. At least they have a very superficial seeing. The sun illuminates only the eye of the man, but shines into the eye and heart of the child. The lover of nature is he whose inward and outward senses are still truly adjusted to each other; who has retained the spirit of infancy even into the era of manhood. His intercourse with heaven and earth becomes part of his daily food. In the presence of nature a wild delight runs through the man, in spite of real sorrows. Nature says,—he is my creature, and maugre all his impertinent griefs, he shall be glad with me. Not the sun or the summer alone, but every hour and season yields its tribute of delight; for every hour and change corresponds to and authorizes a different state of the mind, from breathless noon to grimmest midnight. Nature is a setting that fits equally well a comic or a mourning piece. In good health, the air is a cordial of incredible virtue. Crossing a bare common, in snow puddles, at twilight, under a clouded sky, without having in my thoughts any occurrence of special good fortune, I have enjoyed a perfect exhilaration. I am glad to the brink of fear. In the woods, too, a man casts off his years, as the snake his slough, and at what period soever of life is always a child. In the woods is perpetual youth. Within these plantations of God, a decorum and sanctity reign, a perennial festival is dressed, and the guest sees not how he should tire of them in a thousand years. In the woods, we return to reason and faith. There I feel that nothing can befall me in life,—no disgrace, no calamity (leaving me my eyes), which nature cannot repair. Standing on the bare ground,—my head bathed by the blithe air, and uplifted into infinite space,—all mean egotism vanishes. I become a transparent eyeball; I am nothing; I see all; the currents of the Universal Being circulate through me. I am part or parcel of God. The name of the nearest friend sounds then foreign and accidental: to be brothers, to be acquaintances, master or servant, is then a trifle and a disturbance. I am the lover of uncontained and immortal beauty. In the wilderness, I find something more dear and connate than in streets or villages. In the tranquil landscape, and especially in the distant line of the horizon, man beholds somewhat as beautiful as his own nature.

The greatest delight which the fields and woods minister is the suggestion of an occult relation between man and the vegetable. I am not alone and unacknowledged. They nod to me, and I to them. The waving of the boughs in the storm is new to me and old. It takes me by surprise, and yet is not unknown. Its effect is like that of a higher thought or a better emotion coming over me, when I deemed I was thinking justly or doing right.

Yet it is certain that the power to produce this delight does not reside in nature, but in man, or in a harmony of both. It is necessary to use these pleasures with great temperance. For nature is not always tricked in holiday attire, but the same scene which yesterday breathed perfume and glittered as for the frolic of the nymphs is overspread with melancholy to-day. Nature always wears the colors of the spirit. To a man laboring under calamity, the heat of his own fire hath sadness in it. Then there is a kind of contempt of the landscape felt by him who has just lost by death a dear friend. The sky is less grand as it shuts down over less worth in the population.

1836

The American Scholar

(Phi Beta Kappa Address at Harvard, 1837)

Scarcely a year after *Nature* came another challenge, this time concerning "the study of letters." Emerson attacked the conventional scholar-specialist, not "Man Thinking"—the "decent, indolent, complaisant" man, not the "free and brave" one. This was an awkward criticism to present on so decorous an occasion. But Emerson spoke out. He spoke to the hearts of the young, reaching depths they had not been aware of. Oliver Wendell Holmes called the Address "our intellectual Declaration of Independence."

Earlier announcements of American cultural self-reliance had been premature or superficial; Emerson's was timely and profound. It was profound because the independent mind, as he conceived, rested upon principles not simply national but universal, valid for all men. And it was timely because the hope which romanticism had encouraged in the few could be offered to the educated public at a moment when its wise and courageous leadership was badly needed. "The present generation," Emerson had written in his journal, "is bankrupt of principles and hope, as of property." It was the time of the panic of 1837, the most severe business panic the country had yet known. It was a time of economic fear that accented the timidity and conformity in all realms of thought, political, moral, religious, educational. Far from leading the way with courage and wisdom, the scholar class, as Emerson described it, had itself succumbed to timidity and conformity. He felt obliged to state the case for self-reliance strongly, even exaggeratedly, in order to awaken a response.

I greet you on the recommencement of our literary year. Our anniversary is one of hope, and, perhaps, not enough of labor. We do not meet for games of strength or skill, for the recitation of histories, tragedies, and odes, like the ancient Greeks; for parliaments of love and poesy, like the Troubadours; nor for the advancement of science, like our contemporaries in the British and European capitals. Thus far, our holiday has been simply a friendly sign of the survival of the love of letters amongst a people too busy to give to letters any more. As such it is precious as the sign of an indestructible instinct. Perhaps the time is already come when it ought to be, and will be, something else; when the sluggard intellect of this continent will look from under its iron lids and fill the postponed expectation of the world with something better than the exertions of mechanical skill. Our day of dependence, our long apprenticeship to the learning of other lands, draws to a close. The millions that around us are rushing into life, cannot always be fed on the sere remains of foreign harvests. Events, actions arise, that must be sung, that will sing themselves. Who can doubt that poetry will revive and lead in a new age, as the star in the constellation Harp, which now flames in our zenith, astronomers announce, shall one day be the pole-star for a thousand years?

In this hope I accept the topic which not only usage but the nature of our association seem to prescribe to this day,—the American Scholar. Year by year we come up hither to read one more chapter of his biography. Let us inquire what light new days and events have thrown on his character and his hopes.

It is one of those fables which out of an unknown antiquity convey an unlooked-for wisdom, that the gods, in the beginning, divided Man into men, that he might be more helpful to himself; just as the hand was divided into fingers, the better to answer its end.

The old fable[1] covers a doctrine ever new and sublime; that there is One Man,—present to all particular men only partially, or through one faculty; and that you must take the whole society to find the whole man. Man is not a farmer, or a professor, or an engineer, but he is all. Man is priest, and scholar, and statesman, and producer, and soldier. In the *divided* or social state these functions are parcelled out to individuals, each of whom aims to do his stint of the joint work, whilst each other performs his. The fable implies that the individual, to possess himself, must sometimes return from his own labor to embrace all the other laborers. But, unfortunately, this original unit, this fountain of power, has been so distributed to multitudes, has been so minutely subdivided and peddled out, that it is spilled into drops, and cannot be gathered. The state of society is one in which the members have suffered amputation from the trunk, and strut about so many walking monsters,—a good finger, a neck, a stomach, an elbow, but never a man.

Man is thus metamorphosed into a thing, into many things. The planter, who is Man sent out into the field to gather food, is seldom cheered by an idea of the true dignity of his ministry. He sees his bushel and his cart, and nothing beyond, and sinks into the farmer, instead of Man on the farm. The tradesman scarcely ever gives an ideal worth to his work, but is ridden by the routine of his craft, and the soul is subject to dollars. The priest becomes a form; the attorney a statute-book; the mechanic a machine; the sailor a rope of the ship.

In this distribution of functions the scholar is the delegated intellect. In the right state he is *Man Thinking*. In the degenerate state, when the victim of society, he tends to become a mere thinker, or still worse, the parrot of other men's thinking.

In this view of him, as Man Thinking, the theory of his office is contained. Him Nature solicits with all her placid, all her monitory pictures; him the past instructs; him the future invites. Is not indeed every man a student, and do not all things exist for the student's behoof? And, finally is not the true scholar the only true master? But the old oracle said, "All things have two handles: beware of the wrong one." In life, too often, the scholar errs with mankind and forfeits his privilege. Let us see him in his school, and consider him in reference to the main influences he receives.

I. The first in time and the first in importance of the influences upon the mind is that of nature. Every day, the sun; and, after sunset, Night and her

[1] It is told in Plato's *Symposium* and mentioned in "Of Brotherly Love" in Plutarch's *Morals*.

stars. Ever the winds blow; ever the grass grows. Every day, men and women, conversing—beholding and beholden. The scholar is he of all men whom this spectacle most engages. He must settle its value in his mind. What is nature to him? There is never a beginning, there is never an end, to the inexplicable continuity of this web of God, but always circular power returning into itself. Therein it resembles his own spirit, whose beginning, whose ending, he never can find,—so entire, so boundless. Far too as her splendors shine, system on system shooting like rays, upward, downward, without center, without circumference,—in the mass and in the particle, Nature hastens to render account of herself to the mind. Classification begins. To the young mind every thing is individual, stands by itself. By and by, it finds how to join two things and see in them one nature; then three, then three thousand; and so, tyrannized over by its own unifying instinct, it goes on tying things together, diminishing anomalies, discovering roots running under ground whereby contrary and remote things cohere and flower out from one stem. It presently learns that since the dawn of history there has been a constant accumulation and classifying of facts. But what is classification but the perceiving that these objects are not chaotic, and are not foreign, but have a law which is also a law of the human mind? The astronomer discovers that geometry, a pure abstraction of the human mind, is the measure of planetary motion. The chemist finds proportions and intelligible method throughout matter; and science is nothing but the finding of analogy, identity, in the most remote parts. The ambitious soul sits down before each refractory fact; one after another reduces all strange constitutions, all new powers, to their class and their law, and goes on forever to animate the last fibre of organization, the outskirts of nature, by insight.

Thus to him, to this schoolboy under the bending dome of day, is suggested that he and it proceed from one root; one is leaf and one is flower; relation, sympathy, stirring in every vein. And what is that root? Is not that the soul of his soul? A thought too bold; a dream too wild. Yet when this spiritual light shall have revealed the law of more earthly natures,—when he has learned to worship the soul, and to see that the natural philosophy that now is, is only the first gropings of its gigantic hand, he shall look forward to an ever expanding knowledge as to a becoming creator. He shall see that nature is the opposite of the soul, answering to it part for part. One is seal and one is print. Its beauty is the beauty of his own mind. Its laws are the laws of his own mind. Nature then becomes to him the measure of his attainments. So much of nature as he is ignorant of, so much of his own mind does he not yet possess. And, in fine, the ancient precept, "Know thyself," and the modern precept, "Study nature," become at last one maxim.

II. The next great influence into the spirit of the scholar is the mind of the Past,—in whatever form, whether of literature, of art, of institutions, that mind is inscribed. Books are the best type of the influence of the past, and perhaps we shall get at the truth,—learn the amount of this influence more conveniently,—by considering their value alone.

The theory of books is noble. The scholar of the first age received into him the world around; brooded thereon; gave it the new arrangement of his own mind, and uttered it again. It came into him life; it went out from him truth. It came to him short-lived actions; it went out from him immortal thoughts. It came to him business; it went from him poetry. It was a dead fact; now, it is quick thought. It can stand, and it can go. It now endures, it now flies, it now inspires. Precisely in proportion to the depth of mind from which it issued, so high does it soar, so long does it sing.

Or, I might say, it depends on how far the process had gone, of transmuting life into truth. In proportion to the completeness of the distillation, so will the purity and imperishableness of the product be. But none is quite perfect. As no air-pump can by any means make a perfect vacuum, so neither can any artist entirely exclude the conventional, the local, the perishable from his book, or write a book of pure thought, that shall be as efficient, in all respects, to a remote posterity, as to contemporaries, or rather to the second age. Each age, it is found, must write its own books; or rather, each generation for the next succeeding. The books of an older period will not fit this.

Yet hence arises a grave mischief. The sacredness which attaches to the act of creation, the act of thought, is transferred to the record. The poet chanting was felt to be a divine man: henceforth the chant is divine also. The writer was a just and wise spirit: henceforward it is settled the book is perfect; as love of the hero corrupts into worship of his statue. Instantly the book becomes noxious: the guide is a tyrant. The sluggish and perverted mind of the multitude, slow to open to the incursions of Reason, having once so opened, having once received this book, stands upon it, and makes an outcry if it is disparaged. Colleges are built on it. Books are written on it by thinkers, not by Man Thinking; by men of talent, that is, who start wrong, who set out from accepted dogmas, not from their own sight of principles. Meek young men grow up in libraries, believing it their duty to accept the views which Cicero, which Locke, which Bacon, have given; forgetful that Cicero, Locke, and Bacon were only young men in libraries when they wrote these books.

Hence, instead of Man Thinking, we have the bookworm. Hence the book-learned class, who value books, as such; not as related to nature and the human constitution, but as making a sort of Third Estate with the world and the soul. Hence the restorers of readings, the emendators, the bibliomaniacs of all degrees.

Books are the best of things, well used; abused, among the worst. What is the right use? What is the one end which all means go to effect? They are for nothing but to inspire. I had better never see a book than to be warped by its attraction clean out of my own orbit, and made a satellite instead of a system. The one thing in the world, of value, is the active soul. This every man is entitled to; this every man contains within him, although in almost all men obstructed and as yet unborn. The soul active sees absolute truth and utters truth, or creates. In this action it is genius; not the privilege of here and there a favorite, but the sound estate of every man. In its essence it is progressive. The book, the college, the school of art, the institution of any kind, stop with some past utterance of genius. This is good, say they,—let us hold by this. They pin me down. They look backward and not forward. But genius looks foward: the eyes of man are set in his forehead, not in his hindhead: man hopes: genius creates. Whatever talents may be, if the man create not, the pure efflux of the Deity is not his;—cinders and smoke there may be, but not yet flame. There are creative manners, there are creative actions, and creative words; manners, actions, words, that is, indicative of no custom or authority, but springing spontaneous from the mind's own sense of good and fair.

On the other part, instead of being its own seer, let it receive from another mind its truth, though it were in torrents of light, without periods of solitude, inquest, and self-recovery, and a fatal disservice is done. Genius is always sufficiently the enemy of genius by over-influence. The literature of every nation bears me witness. The English dramatic poets have Shakespearized now for two hundred years.

Undoubtedly there is a right way of reading, so it be sternly subordinated. Man Thinking must not be subdued by his instruments. Books are for the scholar's idle times. When he can read God directly, the hour is too precious to be wasted in other men's transcripts of their readings. But when the intervals of darkness come, as come they must,—when the sun is hid and the stars withdraw their shining,—we repair to the lamps which were kindled by their ray, to guide our steps to the East again, where the dawn is. We hear, that we may speak. The Arabian proverb says, "A fig tree, looking on a fig tree, becometh fruitful."

It is remarkable, the character of the pleasure we derive from the best books. They impress us with the conviction that one nature wrote and the same reads. We read the verses of one of the great English poets, of Chaucer, of Marvell, of Dryden, with the most modern joy,—with a pleasure, I mean, which is in great part caused by the abstraction of all *time* from their verses. There is some awe mixed with the joy of our surprise, when this poet, who lived in some past world, two or three hundred years ago, says that which lies close to my own soul, that which I also had well-nigh thought and said. But for the evidence thence afforded to the philosophical doctrine of the identity of all minds, we should suppose some preëstablished harmony, some foresight of souls that were to be, and some preparation of stores for their future wants, like the fact observed in insects, who lay up food before death for the young grub they shall never see.

I would not be hurried by any love of system, by any exaggeration of instincts, to underrate the Book. We all know, that as the human body can be nourished on any food, though it were boiled grass and the broth of shoes, so the human mind can be fed by any knowledge. And great and heroic men have existed who had almost no other information than by the printed page. I only would say that it needs a strong head to bear that diet. One must be an inventor to read well. As the proverb says, "He that would bring home the wealth of the Indies, must carry out the wealth of the Indies." There is then creative reading as well as creative writing. When the mind is braced by labor and invention, the page of whatever book we read becomes luminous with manifold allusion. Every sentence is doubly significant, and the sense of our author is as broad as the world. We then see, what is always true, that as the seer's hour of vision is short and rare among heavy days and months, so is its record, perchance the least part of his volume. The discerning will read, in his Plato or Shakespeare, only that least part,—only the authentic utterances of the oracle;—all the rest he rejects, were it never so many times Plato's and Shakespeare's.

Of course there is a portion of reading quite indispensable to a wise man. History and exact science he must learn by laborious reading. Colleges, in like manner, have their indispensable office,—to teach elements. But they can only highly serve us when they aim not to drill, but to create; when they gather from far every ray of various genius to their hospitable halls, and by the concentrated fires, set the hearts of their youth on flame. Thought and knowledge are natures in which apparatus and pretension avail nothing. Gowns and pecuniary foundations, though of towns of gold, can never countervail the least sentence or syllable of wit.[2] Forget this, and our American colleges will recede in their public importance, whilst they grow richer every year.

III. There goes in the world a notion that the scholar should be a recluse, a valetudinarian,—as unfit for any handiwork or public labor as a penknife for an axe. The so-called "practical men" sneer at speculative men, as if, because they speculate or *see*, they could do nothing. I have heard it said that the clergy,—who are always, more universally than any other class, the scholars of their day,—are addressed as women; that the rough, spontaneous conversation of men they do not hear, but only a mincing and diluted speech. They are often virtually disfranchised; and indeed there are advocates for their celibacy. As far as this is true of the studious classes, it is not just and wise. Action is with the scholar subordinate, but it is essential. Without it he is not yet man. Without it thought can never ripen into truth. Whilst the world hangs before the eye as a cloud of beauty, we cannot even see its beauty. Inaction is cowardice, but there can be no scholar without the heroic mind. The preamble of thought, the transition through which it passes from the unconscious to the conscious, is action. Only so much do I know, as I have lived. Instantly we know whose words are loaded with life, and whose not.

The world,—this shadow of the soul, or *other me*,—lies wide around. Its attractions are the keys which unlock my thoughts and make me acquainted with myself. I run eagerly into this resounding tumult. I grasp the hands of those next to me, and take my place in the ring to suffer and to work, taught by an instinct that so shall the dumb abyss be vocal with speech. I pierce its order; I dissipate its fear; I dispose of it within the circuit of my expanding life. So much only of life as I know by experience, so much of the wilderness have I vanquished and planted, or so far have I extended my being, my dominion. I do not see how any man can afford, for the sake of his nerves and his nap, to spare any action in which he can partake. It is pearls and rubies to his discourse. Drudgery, calamity, exasperation, want, are instructors in eloquence and wisdom. The true scholar grudges every opportunity of action past by, as a loss of power. It is the raw material out of which the intellect moulds her splendid products. A strange process too, this by which experience is converted into thought, as a mulberry leaf is converted into satin. The manufacture goes forward at all hours.

The actions and events of our childhood and youth are now matters of calmest observation. They lie like fair pictures in the air. No so with our recent actions,—with the business which we now have in hand. On this we are quite unable to speculate. Our affections as yet circulate through it. We no more feel or know it than we feel the feet, or the hand, or the brain of our body. The new deed is yet a part of life,—remains for a time immersed in our unconscious life. In some contemplative hour it detaches itself from the life like a ripe fruit, to become a thought of the mind. Instantly it is raised, transfigured; the corruptible has put on incorruption. Henceforth it is an object of beauty, however base its origin and neighborhood. Observe too the impossibility of antedating this act. In its grub state, it cannot fly, it cannot shine, it is a dull grub. But suddenly, without observation, the selfsame thing unfurls beautiful wings, and is an angel of wisdom. So is there no fact, no event, in our private history, which shall not, sooner or later, lose its adhesive, inert form, and astonish us by soaring from our body into the empyrean. Cradle and infancy, school and playground, the fear of boys, and dogs, and ferules, the love of little maids and berries, and many another fact that once filled the whole sky, are gone already; friend and relative, profession and party, town and country, nation and world, must also soar and sing.

Of course, he who has put forth his total strength in fit actions has the richest return of wisdom. I will not shut myself out of this globe of action, and transplant an oak into a flowerpot, there to hunger and pine; nor trust the revenue of some single faculty, and exhaust one vein of thought, much like those Savoyards, who, getting their livelihood by carving shepherds, shepherdesses, and smoking Dutchmen, for all Europe, went out one day to the mountain to find stock, and discovered that they had whittled up the last of their pine trees. Authors we have, in numbers, who have written out their vein, and who, moved by a commendable prudence, sail for Greece or Palestine, follow the trapper into the prairie, or ramble round Algiers, to replenish their merchantable stock.

If it were only for a vocabulary, the scholar would be covetous of action. Life is our dictionary. Years are well spent in country labors; in town; in the insight into trades and manufactures; in frank intercourse with many men and women; in science; in art; to the one end of mastering in all their facts a language by which to illustrate and embody our perceptions. I learn immediately from any speaker how much he has already lived, through the poverty or the splendor of his speech. Life lies behind us as the quarry from whence we get tiles and copestones for the masonry of to-day. This is the way to learn

[2] I.e., intellect or reason.

grammar. Colleges and books only copy the language which the field and the work-yard made.

But the final value of action, like that of books, and better than books, is that it is a resource. The great principle of Undulation in nature, that shows itself in the inspiring and expiring of the breath; in desire and satiety; in the ebb and flow of the sea; in day and night; in heat and cold; and, as yet more deeply ingrained in every atom and every fluid, is known to us under the name of Polarity,—these "fits of easy transmission and reflection," as Newton called them, are the law of nature because they are the law of spirit.

The mind now thinks, now acts, and each fit reproduces the other. When the artist has exhausted his materials, when the fancy no longer paints, when thoughts are no longer apprehended and books are a weariness,—he has always the resource *to live*. Character is higher than intellect. Thinking is the function. Living is the functionary. The stream retreats to its source. A great soul will be strong to live, as well as strong to think. Does he lack organ or medium to impart his truths? He can still fall back on this elemental force of living them. This is a total act. Thinking is a partial act. Let the grandeur of justice shine in his affairs. Let the beauty of affection cheer his lowly roof. Those "far from fame," who dwell and act with him, will feel the force of his constitution in the doings and passages of the day better than it can be measured by any public and designed display. Time shall teach him that the scholar loses no hour which the man lives. Herein he unfolds the sacred germ of his instinct, screened from influence. What is lost in seemliness is gained in strength. Not out of those on whom systems of education have exhausted their culture, comes the helpful giant to destroy the old or to build the new, but out of unhandselled[3] savage nature; out of terrible Druids and Berserkers come at last Alfred and Shakespeare.

I hear therefore with joy whatever is beginning to be said of the dignity and necessity of labor to every citizen. There is virtue yet in the hoe and the spade, for learned as well as for unlearned hands. And labor is everywhere welcome; always we are invited to work; only be this limitation observed, that a man shall not for the sake of wider activity sacrifice any opinion to the popular judgments and modes of action.

I have now spoken of the education of the scholar by nature, by books, and by action. It remains to say somewhat of his duties.

They are such as become Man Thinking. They may all be comprised in self-trust. The office of the scholar is to cheer, to raise, and to guide men by showing them facts amidst appearances. He plies the slow, unhonored, and unpaid task of observation. Flamsteed[4] and Herschel,[5] in their glazed observatories, may catalogue the stars with the praise of all men, and the results being splendid and useful, honor is sure. But he, in his private observatory, cataloguing obscure and nebulous stars of the human mind, which as yet no man has thought of as such,—watching days and months sometimes for a few facts; correcting still his old records;—must relinquish display and immediate fame. In the long period of his preparation he must betray often an ignorance and shiftlessness in popular arts, incurring the disdain of the able who shoulder him aside. Long he must stammer in his speech; often forego the living for the dead. Worse yet, he must accept—how often!—poverty and solitude. For the ease and pleasure of treading the old road, accepting the fashions, the education, the religion of society, he takes the cross of making his own, and, of course, the self-accusation, the faint heart, the frequent uncertainty and loss of time, which are the nettles and tangling vines in the way of the self-relying and self-directed; and the state of virtual hositility in which he seems to stand to society and especially to educated society. For all this loss and scorn, what offset? He is to find consolation in exercising the highest functions of human nature. He is one who raises himself from private considerations and breathes and lives on public and illustrious thoughts. He is the world's eye. He is the world's heart. He is to resist the vulgar prosperity that retrogrades ever to barbarism, by preserving and communicating heroic sentiments, noble biographies, melodious verse, and the conclusions of history. Whatsoever oracles the human heart, in all emergencies, in all solemn hours, has uttered as its commentary on the world of actions,—these he shall receive and impart. And whatsoever new verdict Reason from her inviolable seat pronounces on the passing men and events of to-day,—this he shall hear and promulgate.

These being his functions, it becomes him to feel all confidence in himself, and to defer never to the popular cry. He and he only knows the world. The world of any moment is the merest appearance. Some great decorum, some fetish of a government, some ephemeral trade, or war, or man, is cried up by half mankind and cried down by the other half, as if all depended on this particular up or down. The odds are that the whole question is not worth the poorest thought which the scholar has lost in listening to the controversy. Let him not quit his belief that a popgun is a popgun, though the ancient

[3] Primitive, untouched, unused, or unknown.

[4] John Flamsteed (1646–1718), a British astronomer.

[5] William Herschel (1738–1822), an English astronomer whose son, John Frederick William (1792–1871), was an astronomer and chemist active during Emerson's life.

and honorable of the earth affirm it to be the crack of doom. In silence, in steadiness, in severe abstraction, let him hold by himself; add observation to observation, patient of neglect, patient of reproach, and bide his own time,—happy enough if he can satisfy himself alone that this day he has seen something truly. Success treads on every right step. For the instinct is sure, that prompts him to tell his brother what he thinks. He then learns that in going down into the secrets of his own mind he has descended into the secrets of all minds. He learns that he who has mastered any law in his private thoughts, is master to that extent of all men whose language he speaks, and of all into whose language his own can be translated. The poet, in utter solitude remembering his spontaneous thoughts and recording them, is found to have recorded that which men in crowded cities find true for them also. The orator distrusts at first the fitness of his frank confessions, his want of knowledge of the persons he addresses, until he finds that he is the complement of his hearers;—that they drink his words because he fulfils for them their own nature; the deeper he dives into his privatest, secretest presentiment, to his wonder he finds this is the most acceptable, most public, and universally true. The people delight in it; the better part of every man feels, This is my music; this myself.

In self-trust all the virtues are comprehended. Free should the scholar be,—free and brave. Free even to the definition of freedom, "without any hindrance that does not arise out of his own constitution." Brave; for fear is a thing which a scholar by his very function puts behind him. Fear always springs from ignorance. It is a shame to him if his tranquility, amid dangerous times, arise from the presumption that like children and women his is a protected class; or if he seek a temporary peace by the diversion of his thoughts from politics or vexed questions, hiding his head like an ostrich in the flowering bushes, peeping into microscopes, and turning rhymes, as a boy whistles to keep his courage up. So is the danger a danger still; so is the fear worse. Manlike let him turn and face it. Let him look into its eye and search its nature, inspect its origin,—see the whelping of this lion,—which lies no great way back; he will then find in himself a perfect comprehension of its nature and extent; he will have made his hands meet on the other side, and can henceforth defy it and pass on superior. The world is his who can see through its pretension. What deafness, what stone-blind custom, what overgrown error you behold is there only by sufferance,—by your sufferance. See it to be a lie, and you have already dealt it its mortal blow.

Yes, we are the cowed,—we the trustless. It is a mischievous notion that we are come late into nature; that the world was finished a long time ago. As the world was plastic and fluid in the hands of God, so it is ever to so much of his attributes as we bring to it. To ignorance and sin, it is flint. They adapt themselves to it as they may; but in proportion as a man has any thing in him divine, the firmament flows before him and takes his signet and form. Not he is great who can alter matter, but he who can alter my state of mind. They are the kings of the world who give the color of their present thought to all nature and all art, and persuade men by the cheerful serenity of their carrying the matter, that this thing which they do is the apple which the ages have desired to pluck, now at last ripe, and inviting nations to the harvest. The great man makes the great thing. Wherever Macdonald sits, there is the head of the table.[6] Linnaeus makes botany the most alluring of studies, and wins it from the farmer and the herb-woman; Davy, chemistry; and Cuvier, fossils. The day is always his who works in it with serenity and great aims. The unstable estimates of men crowd to him whose mind is filled with a truth, as the heaped waves of the Atlantic follow the moon.

For this self-trust, the reason is deeper than can be fathomed,—darker than can be enlightened. I might not carry with me the feeling of my audience in stating my own belief. But I have already shown the ground of my hope, in adverting to the doctrine that man is one. I believe man has been wronged; he has wronged himself. He has almost lost the light that can lead him back to his prerogatives. Men are become of no account. Men in history, men in the world of to-day, are bugs, are spawn, and are called "the mass" and "the herd." In a century, in a millennium, one or two men; that is to say, one or two approximations to the right state of every man. All the rest behold in the hero or the poet their own green and crude being,—ripened; yes, and are content to be less, so *that* may attain to its full stature. What a testimony, full of grandeur, full of pity, is borne to the demands of his own nature, by the poor clansman, the poor partisan, who rejoices in the glory of his chief. The poor and the low find some amends to their immense moral capacity, for their acquiescence in a political and social inferiority. They are content to be brushed like flies from the path of a great person, so that justice shall be done by him to that common nature which it is the dearest desire of all to see enlarged and glorified. They sun themselves in the great man's light, and feel it to be their own element. They cast the dignity of man from their downtrod selves upon the shoulders of a hero, and will perish to add one drop of blood to make that great heart beat, those giant

[6] A proverbial saying.

sinews combat and conquer. He lives for us, and we live in him.

Men, such as they are, very naturally seek money or power; and power because it is as good as money,—the "spoils," so called, "of office." And why not? for they aspire to the highest, and this, in their sleep-walking, they dream is highest. Wake them and they shall quit the false good and leap to the true, and leave governments to clerks and desks. This revolution is to be wrought by the gradual domestication of the idea of Culture. The main enterprise of the world for splendor, for extent, is the upbuilding of a man. Here are the materials strewn along the ground. The private life of one man shall be a more illustrious monarchy, more formidable to its enemy, more sweet and serene in its influence to its friend, than any kingdom in history. For a man, rightly viewed, comprehendeth the particular natures of all men. Each philosopher, each bard, each actor has only done for me, as by a delegate, what one day I can do for myself. The books which once we valued more than the apple of the eye, we have quite exhausted. What is that but saying that we have come up with the point of view which the universal mind took through the eyes of one scribe; we have been that man, and have passed on. First, one, then another, we drain all cisterns, and waxing greater by all these supplies, we crave a better and more abundant food. The man has never lived that can feed us ever. The human mind cannot be enshrined in a person who shall set a barrier on any one side to this unbounded, unboundable empire. It is one central fire, which, flaming now out of the lips of Etna, lightens the capes of Sicily, and now out of the throat of Vesuvius, illuminates the towers and vineyards of Naples. It is one light which beams out of a thousand stars. It is one soul which animates all men.

But I have dwelt perhaps tediously upon this abstraction of the Scholar. I ought not to delay longer to add what I have to say of nearer reference to the time and to this country.

Historically, there is thought to be a difference in the ideas which predominate over successive epochs, and there are data for marking the genius of the Classic, of the Romantic, and now of the Reflective or Philosophical age. With the views I have intimated of the oneness or the identity of the mind through all individuals, I do not much dwell on these differences. In fact, I believe each individual passes through all three. The boy is a Greek; the youth, romantic; the adult, reflective. I deny not, however, that a revolution in the leading idea may be distinctly enough traced.

Our age is bewailed as the age of Introversion. Must that needs be evil? We, it seems, are critical; we are embarrassed with second thoughts; we cannot enjoy any thing for hankering to know whereof the pleasure consists; we are lined with eyes; we see with our feet; the time is infected with Hamlet's unhappiness,

> Sicklied o'er with the pale cast of thought.

It is so bad then? Sight is the last thing to be pitied. Would we be blind? Do we fear lest we should outsee nature and God, and drink truth dry? I look upon the discontent of the literary class as a mere announcement of the fact that they find themselves not in the state of mind of their fathers, and regret the coming state as untried; as a boy dreads the water before he has learned that he can swim. If there is any period one would desire to be born in, is it not the age of Revolution; when the old and the new stand side by side and admit of being compared; when the energies of all men are searched by fear and by hope; when the historic glories of the old can be compensated by the rich possibilities of the new era? This time, like all times, is a very good one, if we but know what to do with it.

I read with some joy of the auspicious signs of the coming days, as they glimmer already through poetry and art, through philosophy and science, through church and state.

One of these signs is the fact that the same movement which effected the elevation of what was called the lowest class in the state, assumed in literature a very marked and as benign an aspect. Instead of the sublime and beautiful, the near, the low, the common, was explored and poetized. That which had been negligently trodden under foot by those who were harnessing and provisioning themselves for long journeys into far countries, is suddenly found to be richer than all foreign parts. The literature of the poor, the feelings of the child, the philosophy of the street, the meaning of household life, are the topics of the time. It is a great stride. It is a sign—is it not?—of new vigor when the extremities are made active, when currents of warm life run into the hands and the feet. I ask not for the great, the remote, the romantic; what is doing in Italy or Arabia; what is Greek art, or Provençal minstrelsy; I embrace the common, I explore and sit at the feet of the familiar, the low. Give me insight into to-day, and you may have the antique and future worlds. What would we really know the meaning of? The meal in the firkin; the milk in the pan; the ballad in the street; the news of the boat; the glance of the eye; the form and the gait of the body;—show me the ultimate reason of these matters; show me the sublime presence of the highest spiritual cause lurking, as always it does lurk, in these suburbs and extremities of nature; let me see every trifle bristling with the polarity that ranges it instantly on an eternal law; and the shop, the plough, and the ledger referred to the like cause by which light undulates and poets sing;—and the world lies no longer a dull miscellany and lumber-room, but has form and order; there is no trifle, there is no puzzle, but one design unites and animates the farthest pinnacle and the lowest trench.

This idea has inspired the genius of Goldsmith, Burns, Cowper, and, in a newer time, Goethe, Wordsworth, and Carlyle. This idea they have differently followed and with various success. In contrast with their writing, the style of Pope, of Johnson, of Gibbon, looks cold and pedantic. This writing is blood-warm. Man is surprised to find that things near are not less beautiful and wondrous than things remote. The near explains the far. The drop is a small ocean. A man is related to all nature. This perception of the worth of the vulgar is fruitful in discoveries. Goethe, in this very thing the most modern of the moderns, has shown us as none ever did, the genius of the ancients.

There is one man of genius who has done much for this philosophy of life, whose literary value has never yet been rightly estimated:—I mean Emanuel Swedenborg. The most imaginative of men, yet writing with the precision of a mathematician, he endeavored to engraft a purely philosophical Ethics on the popular Christianity of his time. Such an attempt of course must have difficulty which no genius could surmount. But he saw and showed the connection between nature and the affections of the soul. He pierced the emblematic or spiritual character of the visible, audible, tangible world. Especially did his shade-loving muse hover over and interpret the lower parts of nature; he showed the mysterious bond that allies moral evil to the foul material forms, and has given in epical parables a theory of insanity, of beasts, of unclean and fearful things.

Another sign of our times, also marked by an analogous political movement, is the new importance given to the single person. Every thing that tends to insulate the individual,—to surround him with barriers of natural respect, so that each man shall feel the world is his, and man shall treat with man as a sovereign state with a sovereign state,—tends to true union as well as greatness. "I learned," said the melancholy Pestalozzi, "that no man in God's wide earth is either willing or able to help any other man." Help must come from the bosom alone. The scholar is that man who must take up into himself all the ability of the time, all the contributions of the past, all the hopes of the future. He must be an university of knowledges. If there be one lesson more than another which should pierce his ear, it is, The world is nothing, the man is all; in yourself is the law of all nature, and you know not yet how a globule of sap ascends; in yourself slumbers the whole of Reason; it is for you to know all; it is for you to dare all. Mr. President and Gentlemen, this confidence in the unsearched might of man belongs, by all motives, by all prophecy, by all preparation, to the American Scholar. We have listened too long to the courtly muses of Europe. The spirit of the American freeman is already suspected to be timid, imitative, tame. Public and private avarice make the air we breathe thick and fat. The scholar is decent, indolent, complaisant. See already the tragic consequence. The mind of this country, taught to aim at low objects, eats upon itself. There is no work for any but the decorous and the complaisant. Young men of the fairest promise, who begin life upon our shores, inflated by the mountain winds, shined upon by all the stars of God, find the earth below not in unison with these, but are hindered from action by the disgust which the principles on which business is managed inspire, and turn drudges, or die of disgust, some of them suicides. What is the remedy? They did not yet see, and thousands of young men as hopeful now crowding to the barriers for the career do not yet see, that if the single man plant himself indomitably on his instincts, and there abide, the huge world will come round to him. Patience,—patience; with the shades of all the good and great for company; and for solace the perspective of your own infinite life; and for work the study and the communication of principles, the making those instincts prevalent, the conversion of the world. Is it not the chief disgrace in the world, not to be an unit;—not to be reckoned one character;—not to yield that peculiar fruit which each man was created to bear, but to be reckoned in the gross, in the hundred, or the thousand, of the party, the section, to which we belong; and our opinion predicted geographically, as the north, or the south? Not so, brothers and friends,—please God, ours shall not be so. We will walk on our own feet; we will work with our own hands; we will speak our own minds. The study of letters shall be no longer a name for pity, for doubt, and for sensual indulgence. The dread of man and the love of man shall be a wall of defence and a wreath of joy around all. A nation of men will for the first time exist, because each believes himself inspired by the Divine Soul which also inspires all men.

1837

Self-Reliance

In this essay, Emerson asserts that a good society is a society of good individuals, and the only fundamental reform is the reform of one's self. The aims and effects of those known as reformers and humanitarians are superficial, and social progress is an illusion. Conformity, the virtue most widely valued, is the means by which free men are intimidated into slavery to society.

In affirming self-reliance *vs.* conformity, independence *vs.* subjection, the individual *vs.* society, Emerson had behind him an immense amount of American experience, including the settlement of New England by nonconformists, the stand of Roger Williams in favor of the individual conscience, the Inner Light of the Quakers, the passion of Jefferson for all freedoms, the Jacksonian assertion of the common man. Emerson's was a democratic individualism, but at the same time it was a spiritual individualism deeply related to European traditions reaching far back to early Christianity and the philosophy of Plato.

In "The American Scholar" and the "Divinity School Address" Emerson's art was that of the orator adapting his speech to a dignified occasion. Now he is an informal essayist. He is still, in a sense, addressing an audience ("you"), and he is still in a sense ministerial, seeking to stir unused depths in the listener's experience. Full of his subject and purpose, he sustains them through a lengthy discourse, repeating his main point—"trust thyself"—in many statements and over-statements, testing it by many applications to situations in life, alerting the reader by changes in tone and attitude. The essay is studded with pithy, quotable epigrams and with telling metaphors. And the diction, as Lowell said, is at once rich and homely, "like home-spun cloth-of-gold."

I read the other day some verses written by an eminent painter which were original and not conventional. The soul always hears an admonition in such lines, let the subject be what it may. The sentiment they instil is of more value than any thought they may contain. To believe your own thought, to believe that what is true for you in your private heart is true for all men,—that is genius. Speak your latent conviction, and it shall be the universal sense; for the inmost in due time becomes the outmost, and our first thought is rendered back to us by the trumpets of the Last Judgment. Familiar as the voice of the mind is to each, the highest merit we ascribe to Moses, Plato, and Milton is that they set at naught books and tradition, and spoke not what men, but what *they* thought. A man should learn to detect and watch that gleam of light which flashes across his mind from within, more than the lustre of the firmament of bards and sages. Yet he dismisses without notice his thought, because it is his. In every work of genius we recognize our own rejected thoughts; they come back to us with a certain alienated majesty. Great works of art have no more affecting lesson for us than this. They teach us to abide by our spontaneous impression with good-humored inflexibility then most when the whole cry of voices is on the other side. Else to-morrow a stranger will say with masterly good sense precisely what we have thought and felt all the time, and we shall be forced to take with shame our own opinion from another.

There is a time in every man's education when he arrives at the conviction that envy is ignorance; that imitation is suicide; that he must take himself for better for worse as his portion; that though the wide universe is full of good, no kernel of nourishing corn can come to him but through his toil bestowed on that plot of ground which is given to him to till. The power which resides in him is new in nature, and none but he knows what that is which he can do, nor does he know until he has tried. Not for nothing one face, one character, one fact, makes much impression on him and another none. This sculpture in the memory is not without preëstablished harmony. The eye was placed where one ray should fall, that it might testify of that particular ray. We but half express ourselves, and are ashamed of that divine idea which each of us represents. It may be safely trusted as proportionate and of good issues, so it be faithfully imparted, but God will not have his work made manifest by cowards. A man is relieved and gay when he has put his heart into his work and done his best; but what he has said or done otherwise shall give him no peace. It is a deliverance which does not deliver. In the attempt his genius deserts him; no muse befriends; no invention, no hope.

Trust thyself: every heart vibrates to that iron string. Accept the place the divine providence has found for you, the society of your contemporaries, the connection of events. Great men have always done so, and confided themselves childlike to the genius of their age, betraying their perception that the absolutely trustworthy was seated at their heart, working through their hands, predominating in all their being. And we are now men, and must accept in the highest mind the same transcendent destiny; and not minors and invalids in a protected corner, not cowards fleeing before a revolution, but guides, redeemers, and benefactors, obeying the Almighty effort and advancing on Chaos and the Dark.

What pretty oracles nature yields us on this text in the face and behavior of children, babes, and even brutes! That divided and rebel mind, that distrust of a sentiment because our arithmetic has computed the strength and means opposed to our purpose, these have not. Their mind being whole, their eye is as yet unconquered, and when we look in their faces we are disconcerted. Infancy conforms to nobody; all conform to it; so that one babe commonly makes four or five out of the adults who prattle and play to it. So God has armed youth and puberty and manhood no less with its own piquancy and charm, and made it enviable and gracious and its claims not to be put by, if it will stand by itself. Do not think the youth has no force, because he cannot speak to you and me. Hark! in the next room his voice is sufficiently clear and emphatic. It seems he knows how to speak to his contemporaries. Bashful or bold then, he will know how to make us seniors very unnecessary.

The nonchalance of boys who are sure of a dinner, and would disdain as much as a lord to do or say aught to conciliate one, is the healthy attitude of human nature. A boy is in the parlor what the pit is in the playhouse; independent, irresponsible, looking out from his corner on such people and facts as pass by, he tries and sentences them on their merits, in the swift, summary way of boys, as good, bad, interesting, silly, eloquent, troublesome. He cumbers himself never about consequences, about interests; he gives an independent, genuine verdict. You must court him; he does not court you. But the man is as it were clapped into jail by his consciousness. As soon as he has once acted or spoken with *éclat* he is a committed person, watched by the sympathy or the hatred of hundreds whose affections must now enter into his account. There is no Lethe for this. Ah, that he could pass again into his neutrality! Who can thus avoid all pledges and, having observed, observe again from the same unaffected, unbiased, unbribable, unaffrighted innocence,—must always be formidable. He would utter opinions on all passing affairs, which being seen to be not private but necessary, would sink like darts into the ear of men and put them in fear.

These are the voices which we hear in solitude, but they grow faint and inaudible as we enter into the world. Society everywhere is in conspiracy against the manhood of every one of its members. Society is a joint-stock company, in which the members agree, for the better securing of his bread to each shareholder, to surrender the liberty and culture of the eater. The virtue in most request is conformity. Self-reliance is its aversion. It loves not realities and creators, but names and customs.

Whoso would be a man, must be a noncomformist. He who would gather immortal palms must not be hindered by the name of goodness, but must explore if it be goodness. Nothing is at last sacred but the integrity of your own mind. Absolve you to yourself, and you shall have the suffrage of the world. I remember an answer which when quite young I was prompted to make to a valued adviser who was wont to importune me with the dear old doctrines of the church. On my saying, "What have I to do with the sacredness of traditions, if I live wholly from within?" my friend suggested,—"But these impulses may be from below, not from above." I replied, "They do not seem to me to be such; but if I am the Devil's child, I will live then from the Devil." No law can be sacred to me but that of my nature. Good and bad are but names very readily transferable to that or this; the only right is what is after my constitution; the only wrong what is against it. A man is to carry himself in the presence of all opposition as if everything were titular and ephemeral but he. I am ashamed to think how easily we capitulate to badges and names, to large societies and dead institutions. Every decent and well-spoken individual affects and sways me more than is right. I ought to go upright and vital, and speak the rude truth in all ways. If malice and vanity wear the coat of philanthropy, shall that pass? If an angry bigot assumes this bountiful cause of Abolition, and comes to me with his last news from Barbadoes,[1] why should I not say to him, "Go love thy infant; love thy woodchopper; be good-natured and modest; have that grace; and never varnish your hard, uncharitable ambition with this incredible tenderness for black folk a thousand miles off. Thy love afar is spite at home." Rough and graceless would be such greeting, but truth is handsomer than the affectation of love. Your goodness must have some edge to it,—else it is none. The doctrine of hatred must be preached, as the counteraction of the doctrine of love, when that pules and whines. I shun father and mother and wife and brother when my genius calls me. I would write on the lintels of the door-post, *Whim.* I hope it is somewhat better than whim at last, but we cannot spend the day in explanation. Expect me not to show cause why I seek or why I exclude company. Then again, do not tell me, as a good man did to-day, of my obligation to put all poor men in good situations. Are they *my* poor? I tell thee, thou foolish philanthropist, that I grudge the dollar, the dime, the cent I give to such men as do not belong to me and to whom I do not belong. There is a class of persons to whom by all spiritual affinity I am bought and sold; for them I will go to prison if need be; but your miscellaneous popular charities; the education at college of fools; the building of meeting-houses to the vain end to which many now stand; alms to sots, and the thousand-fold Relief Societies;—though I confess with shame I sometimes succumb and give the dollar, it is a wicked dollar, which by and by I shall have the manhood to withhold.

Virtues are, in the popular estimate, rather the exception than the rule. There is the man *and* his virtues. Men do what is called a good action, as some piece of courage or charity, much as they would pay a fine in expiation of daily non-appearance on parade. Their works are done as an apology or extenuation of their living in the world,—as invalids and the insane pay a high board. Their virtues are penances. I do not wish to expiate, but to live. My life is for itself and not for a spectacle. I much prefer that it should be of a lower strain, so it be genuine and equal, than that it should be glitter-

[1] Probably refers to the abolition of slavery there in 1833.

ing and unsteady. I wish it to be sound and sweet, and not to need diet and bleeding. I ask primary evidence that you are a man and refuse this appeal from the man to his actions. I know that for myself it makes no difference whether I do or forbear those actions which are reckoned excellent. I cannot consent to pay for a privilege where I have intrinsic right. Few and mean as my gifts may be, I actually am, and do not need for my own assurance or the assurance of my fellows any secondary testimony.

What I must do is all that concerns me, not what the people think. This rule, equally arduous in actual and in intellectual life, may serve for the whole distinction between greatness and meanness. It is the harder because you will always find those who think they know what is your duty better than you know it. It is easy in the world to live after the world's opinion; it is easy in solitude to live after our own; but the great man is he who in the midst of the crowd keeps with perfect sweetness the independence of solitude.

The objection to conforming to usages that have become dead to you is that it scatters your force. It loses your time and blurs the impression of your character. If you maintain a dead church, contribute to a dead Bible-society, vote with a great party either for the government or against it, spread your table like base housekeepers,—under all these screens I have difficulty to detect the precise man you are: and of course so much force is withdrawn from all your proper life. But do your work, and I shall know you. Do your work, and you shall reinforce yourself. A man must consider what a blind-man's-buff is this game of conformity. If I know your sect I anticipate your argument. I hear a preacher announce for his text and topic the expediency of one of the institutions of his church. Do I not know beforehand that not possibly can he say a new and spontaneous word? Do I not know that with all this ostentation of examining the grounds of the institution he will do no such thing? Do I not know that he is pledged to himself not to look but at one side, the permitted side, not as a man, but as a parish minister? He is a retained attorney, and these airs of the bench are the emptiest affectation. Well, most men have bound their eyes with one or another handkerchief, and attached themselves to some one of these communities of opinion. This conformity makes them not false in a few particulars, authors of a few lies, but false in all particulars. Their every truth is not quite true. Their two is not the real two, their four not the real four; so that every word they say chagrins us and we know not where to begin to set them right. Meantime nature is not slow to equip us in the prison-uniform of the party to which we adhere. We come to wear one cut of face and figure, and acquire by degrees the gentlest asinine expression. There is a mortifying experience in particular, which does not fail to wreak itself also in the general history; I mean the "foolish face of praise," the forced smile which we put on in company where we do not feel at ease, in answer to conversation which does not interest us. The muscles, not spontaneously moved but moved by a low usurping wilfulness, grow tight about the outline of the face, with the most disagreeable sensation.

For nonconformity the world whips you with its displeasure. And therefore a man must know how to estimate a sour face. The by-standers look askance on him in the public street or in the friend's parlor. If this aversion had its origin in contempt and resistance like his own he might well go home with a sad countenance; but the sour faces of the multitude, like their sweet faces, have no deep cause, but are put on and off as the wind blows and a newspaper directs. Yet is the discontent of the multitude more formidable than that of the senate and the college. It is easy enough for a firm man who knows the world to brook the rage of the cultivated classes. Their rage is decorous and prudent, for they are timid, as being very vulnerable themselves. But when to their feminine rage the indignation of the people is added, when the ignorant and the poor are aroused, when the unintelligent brute force that lies at the bottom of society is made to growl and mow, it needs the habit of magnanimity and religion to treat it godlike as a trifle of no concernment.

The other terror that scares us from self-trust is our consistency; a reverence for our past act or word because the eyes of others have no other data for computing our orbit than our past acts, and we are loth to disappoint them.

But why should you keep your head over your shoulder? Why drag about this corpse of your memory, lest you contradict somewhat you have stated in this or that public place? Suppose you should contradict yourself; what then? It seems to be a rule of wisdom never to rely on your memory alone, scarcely even in acts of pure memory, but to bring the past for judgment into the thousand-eyed present, and live ever in a new day. In your metaphysics you have denied personality to the Deity, yet when the devout motions of the soul come, yield to them heart and life, though they should clothe God with shape and color. Leave your theory, as Joseph his coat in the hand of the harlot, and flee.

A foolish consistency is the hobgoblin of little minds, adored by little statesmen and philosophers and divines. With consistency a great soul has simply nothing to do. He may as well concern himself with his shadow on the wall. Speak what you think now in hard words and to-morrow speak what to-morrow thinks in hard words again, though it contradict everything you said to-day.—"Ah, so you shall be sure to be misunderstood."—Is it so bad then to be misunderstood? Pythagoras was misunderstood, and Socrates, and Jesus, and Luther, and Copernicus, and Galileo, and Newton, and every pure and wise spirit that ever took flesh. To be great is to be misunderstood.

I suppose no man can violate his nature. All the sallies of his will are rounded in by the law of his being, as the inequalities of Andes and Himmaleh are insignificant in the curve of the sphere. Nor does it matter how you gauge and try him. A character is like an acrostic or Alexandrian stanza;—read it forward, backward, or across, it still spells the same thing. In this pleasing contrite woodlife which God allows me, let me record day by day my honest thought without prospect or retrospect, and I cannot doubt, it will be found symmetrical, though I mean it not and see it not. My book should smell of pines and resound with the hum of insects. The swallow over my window should interweave that thread or straw he carries in his bill into my web also. We pass for what we are. Character teaches above our wills. Men imagine that they communicate their virtue or vice only by overt actions, and do not see that virtue or vice emit a breath every moment.

There will be an agreement in whatever variety of actions, so they be each honest and natural in their hour. For of one will, the actions will be harmonious, however unlike they seem. These varieties are lost sight of at a little distance, at a little height of thought. One tendency unites them all. The voyage of the best ship is a zigzag line of a hundred tacks. See the line from a sufficient distance, and it straightens itself to the average tendency. Your genuine action will explain itself and will explain your other genuine actions. Your conformity explains nothing. Act singly, and what you have already done singly will justify you now. Greatness appeals to the future. If I can be firm enough to-day to do right and scorn eyes, I must have done so much right before as to defend me now. Be it how it will, do right now. Always scorn appearances and you always may. The force of character is cumulative. All the foregone days of virtue work their health into this. What makes the majesty of the heroes of the senate and the field, which so fills the imagination? The consciousness of a train of great days and victories behind. They shed a united light on the advancing actor. He is attended as by a visible escort of angels. That is it which throws thunder into Chatham's voice, and dignity into Washington's port, and America into Adams's eye. Honor is venerable to us because it is no ephemera. It is always ancient virtue. We worship it to-day because it is not of to-day. We love it and pay it homage because it is not a trap for our love and homage, but is self-dependent, self-derived, and therefore of an old immaculate pedigree, even if shown in a young person.

I hope in these days we have heard the last of conformity and consistency. Let the words be gazetted and ridiculous henceforward. Instead of the gong for dinner, let us hear a whistle from the Spartan fife. Let us never bow and apologize more. A great man is coming to eat at my house. I do not wish to please him; I wish that he should wish to please me. I will stand here for humanity, and though I would make it kind, I would make it true. Let us affront and reprimand the smooth mediocrity and squalid contentment of the times, and hurl in the face of custom and trade and office, the fact which is the upshot of all history, that there is a great responsible Thinker and Actor working wherever a man works; that a true man belongs to no other time or place, but is the center of things. Where he is there is nature. He measures you and all men and all events. Ordinarily, everybody in society reminds us of somewhat else, or of some other person. Character, reality, reminds you of nothing else; it takes place of the whole creation. The man must be so much that he must make all circumstances indifferent. Every true man is a cause, a country, and an age; requires infinite spaces and numbers and time fully to accomplish his design;—and posterity seem to follow his steps as a train of clients. A man Caesar is born, and for ages after we have a Roman Empire. Christ is born, and millions of minds so grow and cleave to his genius that he is confounded with virtue and the possible of man. An institution is the lengthened shadow of one man; as, Monachism, of the Hermit Antony; the Reformation, of Luther; Quakerism, of Fox; Methodism, of Wesley; Abolition, of Clarkson.[2] Scipio, Milton called "the height of Rome"; and all history resolves itself very easily into the biography of a few stout and earnest persons.

Let a man then know his worth, and keep things under his feet. Let him not peep or steal, or skulk up and down with the air of a charity-boy, a bastard, or an interloper in the world which exists for him. But the man in the street, finding no worth in himself which corresponds to the force which built a tower or sculptured a marble god, feels poor when he looks on these. To him a palace, a statue, or a costly book have an alien and forbidding air, much like a gay equipage, and seem to say like that, "Who are you, Sir?" Yet they are all his, suitors for his notice, petitioners to his faculties that they will

[2] Thomas Clarkson (1760-1846), a British abolitionist.

come out and take possession. The picture waits for my verdict; it is not to command me, but I am to settle its claims to praise. That popular fable of the sot who was picked up dead-drunk in the street, carried to the duke's house, washed and dressed and laid in the duke's bed, and, on his waking, treated with all obsequious ceremony like the duke, and assured that he had been insane, owes its popularity to the fact that it symbolizes so well the state of man, who is in the world a sort of sot, but now and then wakes up, exercises his reason and finds himself a true prince.

Our reading is mendicant and sycophantic. In history our imagination plays us false. Kingdom and lordship, power and estate, are a gaudier vocabulary than private John and Edward in a small house and common day's work; but the things of life are the same to both; the sum total of both is the same. Why all this deference to Alfred and Scanderbeg and Gustavus?[3] Suppose they were virtuous; did they wear out virtue? As great a stake depends on your private act to-day as followed their public and renowned steps. When private men shall act with original views, the lustre will be transferred from the actions of kings to those of gentlemen.

The world has been instructed by its kings, who have so magnetized the eyes of nations. It has been taught by this colossal symbol the mutual reverence that is due from man to man. The joyful loyalty with which men have everywhere suffered the king, the noble, or the great proprietor to walk among them by a law of his own, make his own scale of men and things and reverse theirs, pay for benefits not with money but with honor, and represent the law in his person, was the hieroglyphic by which they obscurely signified their consciousness of their own right and comeliness, the right of every man.

The magnetism which all original action exerts is explained when we inquire the reason of self-trust. Who is the Trustee? What is the aboriginal Self, on which a universal reliance may be grounded? What is the nature and power of that science-baffling star, without parallax, without calculable elements, which shoots a ray of beauty even into trivial and impure actions, if the least mark of independence appear? The inquiry leads us to that source, at once the essence of genius, of virtue, and of life, which we call Spontaneity or Instinct. We denote this primary wisdom as Intuition, whilst all later teachings are tuitions. In that deep force, the last fact behind which analysis cannot go, all things find their common origin. For the sense of being which in calm hours rises, we know not how, in the soul, is not diverse from things, from space, from light, from time, from man, but one with them and proceeds obviously from the same source whence their life and being also proceed. We first share the life by which things exist and afterwards see them as appearances in nature and forget that we have shared their cause. Here is the fountain of action and of thought. Here are the lungs of that inspiration which giveth man wisdom and which cannot be denied without impiety and atheism. We lie in the lap of immense intelligence, which makes us receivers of its truth and organs of its activity. When we discern justice, when we discern truth, we do nothing of ourselves, but allow a passage to its beams. If we ask whence this comes, if we seek to pry into the soul that causes, all philosophy is at fault. Its presence or its absence is all we can affirm. Every man discriminates between the voluntary acts of his mind and his involuntary perceptions, and knows that to his involuntary perceptions a perfect faith is due. He may err in the expression of them, but he knows that these things are so, like day and night, not to be disputed. My wilful actions and acquisitions are but roving;—the idlest reverie, the faintest native emotion, command my curiosity and respect. Thoughtless people contradict as readily the statement of perceptions as of opinions, or rather much more readily; for they do not distinguish between perception and notion. They fancy that I choose to see this or that thing. But perception is not whimsical, but fatal. If I see a trait, my children will see it after me, and in course of time all mankind,—although it may chance that no one has seen it before me. For my perception of it is as much a fact as the sun.

The relations of the soul to the divine spirit are so pure that it is profane to seek to interpose helps. It must be that when God speaketh he should communicate, not one thing, but all things; should fill the world with his voice; should scatter forth light, nature, time, souls, from the center of the present thought; and new date and new create the whole. Whenever a mind is simple and receives a divine wisdom, old things pass away,—means, teachers, texts, temples fall; it lives now, and absorbs past and future into the present hour. All things are made sacred by relation to it,—one as much as another. All things are dissolved to their center by their cause, and in the universal miracle petty and particular miracles disappear. If therefore a man claims to know and speak of God and carries you backward to the phraseology of some old mouldered nation in another country, in another world, believe him not. Is the acorn better than the oak which is its fulness and completion? Is the parent better than the child into whom he has cast his ripened being? Whence then this worship of the past? The centuries

[3]Alfred the Great (849-899), king of England and national hero; Scanderbeg (1403?-1468), Albanian leader and national hero; Gustavus, Swedish king and hero.

are conspirators against the sanity and authority of the soul. Time and space are but physiological colors which the eye makes, but the soul is light: where it is, is day; where it was, is night; and history is an impertinence and an injury if it be anything more than a cheerful apologue or parable of my being and becoming.

Man is timid and apologetic; he is no longer upright; he dares not say "I think," "I am," but quotes some saint or sage. He is ashamed before the blade of grass or the blowing rose. These roses under my window make no reference to former roses or to better ones; they are for what they are; they exist with God to-day. There is no time for them. There is simply the rose; it is perfect in every moment of its existence. Before a leaf-bud has burst, its whole life acts; in the full-blown flower there is no more; in the leafless root there is no less. Its nature is satisfied and it satisfies nature in all moments alike. But man postpones or remembers; he does not live in the present, but with reverted eye laments the past, or, heedless of the riches that surround him, stands on tiptoe to foresee the future. He cannot be happy and strong until he too lives with nature in the present, above time.

This should be plain enough. Yet see what strong intellects dare not yet hear God himself unless he speak the phraseology of I know not what David, or Jeremiah, or Paul. We shall not always set so great a price on a few texts, on a few lives. We are like children who repeat by rote the sentences of grandames and tutors, and, as they grow older, of the men of talents and character they chance to see,—painfully recollecting the exact words they spoke; afterwards, when they come into the point of view which those had who uttered these sayings, they understand them and are willing to let the words go; for at any time they can use words as good when occasion comes. If we live truly, we shall see truly. It is as easy for the strong man to be strong, as it is for the weak to be weak. When we have new perception, we shall gladly disburden the memory of its hoarded treasures as old rubbish. When a man lives with God, his voice shall be as sweet as the murmur of the brook and the rustle of the corn.

And now at last the highest truth on this subject remains unsaid; probably cannot be said: for all that we say is the far-off remembering of the intuition. That thought by what I can now nearest approach to say it, is this. When good is near you, when you have life in yourself, it is not by any known or accustomed way; you shall not discern the footprints of any other; you shall not see face of man; you shall not hear any name;—the way, the thought, the good, shall be wholly strange and new. It shall exclude example and experience. You take the way from man, not to man. All persons that ever existed are its forgotten ministers. Fear and hope are alike beneath it. There is somewhat low even in hope. In the hour of vision there is nothing that can be called gratitude, nor properly joy. The soul raised over passion beholds identity and eternal causation, perceives the self-existence of Truth and Right, and calms itself with knowing that all things go well. Vast spaces of nature, the Atlantic Ocean, the South Sea; long intervals of time, years, centuries, are of no account. This which I think and feel underlay every former state of life and circumstances, as it does underlie my present, and what is called life and what is called death.

Life only avails, not the having lived. Power ceases in the instant of repose; it resides in the moment of transition from a past to a new state, in the shooting of the gulf, in the darting to an aim. This one fact the world hates; that the soul *becomes;* for that forever degrades the past, turns all riches to poverty, all reputation to a shame, confounds the saint with the rogue, shoves Jesus and Judas equally aside. Why then do we prate of self-reliance? Inasmuch as the soul is present there will be power not confident but agent. To talk of reliance is a poor external way of speaking. Speak rather of that which relies because it works and is. Who has more obedience than I masters me, though he should not raise his finger. Round him I must revolve by the gravitation of spirits. We fancy it rhetoric when we speak of eminent virtue. We do not yet see that virtue is Height, and that a man or a company of men, plastic and permeable to principles, by the law of nature must overpower and ride all cities, nations, kings, rich men, poets, who are not.

This is the ultimate fact which we so quickly reach on this, as on every topic, the resolution of all into the ever-blessed One. Self-existence is the attribute of the Supreme Cause, and it constitutes the measure of good by the degree in which it enters into all lower forms. All things real are so by so much virtue as they contain. Commerce, husbandry, hunting, whaling, war, eloquence, personal weight, are somewhat, and engage my respect as examples of its presence and impure action. I see the same law working in nature for conservation and growth. Power is, in nature, the essential measure of right. Nature suffers nothing to remain in her kingdoms which cannot help itself. The genesis and maturation of a planet, its poise and orbit, the bended tree recovering itself from the strong wind, the vital resources of every animal and vegetable, are demonstrations of the self-sufficing and therefore self-relying soul.

Thus all concentrates: let us not rove; let us sit at home with the cause. Let us stun and astonish the intruding rabble of men and books and institutions by a simple declaration of the divine fact. Bid the invaders take the shoes from off their feet, for God is here within. Let our simplicity judge them, and our docility to our own law demonstrate the poverty of nature and fortune beside our native riches.

But now we are a mob. Man does not stand in awe of man, nor is his genius admonished to stay at home, to put itself in communication with the internal ocean, but it goes abroad to beg a cup of water of the urns of other men. We must go alone. I like the silent church before the service begins, better than any preaching. How far off, how cool, how chaste the persons look, begirt each one with a precinct or sanctuary! So let us always sit. Why should we assume the faults of our friend, or wife, or father, or child, because they sit around our hearth, or are said to have the same blood? All men have my blood and I all men's. Not for that will I adopt their petulance or folly, even to the extent of being ashamed of it. But your isolation must not be mechanical, but spiritual, that is, must be elevation. At times the whole world seems to be in conspiracy to importune you with emphatic trifles. Friend, climate, child, sickness, fear, want, charity, all knock at once at thy closet door and say,—"Come out unto us." But keep thy state; come not into their confusion. The power men possess to annoy me I give them by a weak curiosity. No man can come near me but through my act. "What we love that we have, but by desire we bereave ourselves of the love."

If we cannot at once rise to the sanctities of obedience and faith, let us at least resist our temptations; let us enter into the state of war and wake Thor and Woden, courage and constancy, in our Saxon breasts. This is to be done in our smooth times by speaking the truth. Check this lying hospitality and lying affection. Live no longer to the expectation of these deceived and deceiving people with whom we converse. Say to them, "O father, O mother, O wife, O brother, O friend, I have lived with you after appearances hitherto. Henceforward I am the truth's. Be it known unto you that henceforward I obey no law less than the eternal law. I will have no covenants but proximities. I shall endeavor to nourish my parents, to support my family, to be the chaste husband of one wife,—but these relations I must fill after a new and unprecedented way. I appeal from your customs. I must be myself. I cannot break myself any longer for you, or you. If you can love me for what I am, we shall be the happier. If you cannot, I will still seek to deserve that you should. I will not hide my tastes or aversions. I will so trust that what is deep is holy, that I will do strongly before the sun and moon whatever inly rejoices me and the heart appoints. If you are noble, I will love you; if you are not, I will not hurt you and myself by hypocritical attentions. If you are true, but not in the same truth with me, cleave to your companions; I will seek my own. I do this not selfishly but humbly and truly. It is alike your interest, and mine, and all men's, however long we have dwelt in lies, to live in truth. Does this sound harsh to-day? You will soon love what is dictated by your nature as well as mine, and if we follow the truth it will bring us out safe at last."—But so may you give these friends pain. Yes, but I cannot sell my liberty and my power, to save their sensibility. Besides, all persons have their moments of reason, when they look out into the region of absolute truth; then will they justify me and do the same thing.

The populace think that your rejection of popular standards is a rejection of all standard, and mere antinomianism; and the bold sensualist will use the name of philosophy to gild his crimes. But the law of consciousness abides. There are two confessionals, in one or the other of which we must be shriven. You may fulfil your round of duties by clearing yourself in the *direct*, or in the *reflex* way. Consider whether you have satisfied your relations to father, mother, cousin, neighbor, town, cat and dog—whether any of these can upbraid you. But I may also neglect this reflex standard and absolve me to myself. I have my own stern claims and perfect circle. It denies the name of duty to many offices that are called duties. But if I can discharge its debts it enables me to dispense with the popular code. If any one imagines that this law is lax, let him keep its commandment one day.

And truly it demands something godlike in him who has cast off the common motives of humanity and has ventured to trust himself for a taskmaster. High be his heart, faithful his will, clear his sight, that he may in good earnest be doctrine, society, law, to himself, that a simple purpose may be to him as strong as iron necessity is to others!

If any man consider the present aspects of what is called by distinction *society*, he will see the need of these ethics. The sinew and heart of man seem to be drawn out, and we are become timorous, desponding whimperers. We are afraid of truth, afraid of fortune, afraid of death, and afraid of each other. Our age yields no great and perfect persons. We want men and women who shall renovate life and our social state, but we see that most natures are insolvent, cannot satisfy their own wants, have an ambition out of all proportion to their practical force and do lean and beg day and night continually. Our housekeeping is mendicant, our arts, our occupations, our marriages, our religion we have not chosen, but society has chosen for us. We are parlor soldiers. We shun the rugged battle of fate, where strength is born.

If our young men miscarry in their first enterprises they lose all heart. If the young merchant fails, men say he is *ruined.* If the finest genius studies at one of our colleges and is not installed in an office within one year afterwards in the cities or suburbs of Boston or New York, it seems to his friends and to himself that he is right in being disheartened and in complaining the rest of his life. A sturdy lad from New Hampshire or Vermont, who in turn tries all the professions, who *teams it, farms it, peddles,* keeps a school, preaches, edits a newspaper, goes to Congress, buys a township, and so forth, in successive years, and always like a cat falls on his feet, is worth a hundred of these city dolls. He walks abreast with his days and feels no shame in not "studying a profession," for he does not postpone his life, but lives already. He has not one chance, but a hundred chances. Let a Stoic open the resources of man and tell men they are not leaning willows, but can and must detach themselves; that with the exercise of self-trust, new powers shall appear; that a man is the word made flesh, born to shed healing to the nations; that he should be ashamed of our compassion, and that the moment he acts from himself, tossing the laws, the books, idolatries and customs out of the window, we pity him no more but thank and revere him;—and that teacher shall restore the life of man to splendor and make his name dear to all history.

It is easy to see that a greater self-reliance must work a revolution in all the offices and relations of men; in their religion; in their education; in their pursuits; their modes of living; their association; in their property; in their speculative views.

1. In what prayers do men allow themselves! That which they call a holy office is not so much as brave and manly. Prayer looks abroad and asks for some foreign addition to come through some foreign virtue, and loses itself in endless mazes of natural and supernatural, and mediatorial and miraculous. Prayer that craves a particular commodity, anything less than all good, is vicious. Prayer is the contemplation of the facts of life from the highest point of view. It is the soliloquy of a beholding and jubilant soul. It is the spirit of God pronouncing his works good. But prayer as a means to effect a private end is meanness and theft. It supposes dualism and not unity in nature and consciousness. As soon as the man is at one with God, he will not beg. He will then see prayer in all action. The prayer of the farmer kneeling in his field to weed it, the prayer of the rower kneeling with the stroke of his oar, are true prayers heard throughout nature, though for cheap ends. Caratach, in Fletcher's *Bonduca,* when admonished to inquire the mind of the god Audate, replies,—

> His hidden meaning lies in our endeavors;
> Our valors are our best gods.

Another sort of false prayers are our regrets. Discontent is the want of self-reliance: it is infirmity of will. Regret calamities if you can thereby help the sufferer; if not attend your own work and already the evil begins to be repaired. Our sympathy is just as base. We come to them who weep foolishly and sit down and cry for company, instead of imparting to them truth and health in rough electric shocks, putting them once more in communication with their own reason. The secret of fortune is joy in our hands. Welcome evermore to gods and men is the self-helping man. For him all doors are flung wide; him all tongues greet, all honors crown, all eyes follow with desire. Our love goes out to him and embraces him because he did not need it. We solicitously and apologetically caress and celebrate him because he held on his way and scorned our disapprobation. The gods love him because men hated him. "To the persevering mortal," said Zoroaster, "the blessed Immortals are swift."

As men's prayers are a disease of the will, so are their creeds a disease of the intellect. They say with those foolish Israelites, "Let not God speak to us, lest we die. Speak thou, speak any man with us, and we will obey." Everywhere I am hindered of meeting God in my brother, because he has shut his own temple doors and recites fables merely of his brother's, or his brother's brother's God. Every new mind is a new classification. If it prove a mind of uncommon activity and power, a Locke, a Lavoisier, a Hutton,[4] a Bentham, a Fourier, it imposes its classification on other men, and lo! a new system. In proportion to the depth of the thought, and so to the number of the objects it touches and brings within reach of the pupil, is his complacency. But chiefly is this apparent in creeds and churches, which are also classifications of some powerful mind acting on the elemental thought of duty and man's relation to the Highest. Such is Calvinism, Quakerism, Swedenborgism. The pupil takes the same delight in subordinating everything to the new terminology as a girl who has just learned botany in seeing a new earth and new seasons thereby. It will happen for a time that the pupil will find his intellectual power has grown by the study of his master's mind. But in all unbalanced minds the classification

[4] James Hutton (1726-97), a Scottish geologist.

is idolized, passes for the end and not for a speedily exhaustible means, so that the walls of the system blend to their eye in the remote horizon with the walls of the universe; the luminaries of heaven seem to them hung on the arch their master built. They cannot imagine how you aliens have any right to see,—how you can see; "It must be somehow that you stole the light from us." They do not yet perceive that light, unsystematic, indomitable, will break into any cabin, even into theirs. Let them chirp awhile and call it their own. If they are honest and do well, presently their neat new pinfold will be too strait and low, will crack, will lean, will rot and vanish, and the immortal light, all young and joyful, million-orbed, million-colored, will beam over the universe as on the first morning.

2. It is for want of self-culture that the superstition of Travelling, whose idols are Italy, England, Egypt, retains its fascination for all educated Americans. They who made England, Italy, or Greece venerable in the imagination, did so by sticking fast where they were, like an axis of the earth. In manly hours we feel that duty is our place. The soul is no traveller; the wise man stays at home, and when his necessities, his duties, on any occasion call him from his house, or into foreign lands, he is at home still and shall make men sensible by the expression of his countenance that he goes, the missionary of wisdom and virtue, and visits cities and men like a sovereign and not like an interloper or a valet.

I have no churlish objection to the circumnavigation of the globe for the purposes of art, of study, and benevolence, so that the man is first domesticated, or does not go abroad with the hope of finding somewhat greater than he knows. He who travels to be amused, or to get somewhat which he does not carry, travels away from himself, and grows old even in youth among old things. In Thebes, in Palmyra, his will and mind have become old and dilapidated as they. He carries ruins to ruins.

Travelling is a fool's paradise. Our first journeys discover to us the indifference of places. At home I dream that at Naples, at Rome, I can be intoxicated with beauty and lose my sadness. I pack my trunk, embrace my friends, embark on the sea and at last wake up in Naples, and there beside me is the stern fact, the sad self, unrelenting, identical, that I fled from. I seek the Vatican and the palaces. I affect to be intoxicated with sights and suggestions, but I am not intoxicated. My giant goes with me wherever I go.

3. But the rage of travelling is a symptom of a deeper unsoundness affecting the whole intellectual action. The intellect is vagabond, and our system of education fosters restlessness. Our minds travel when our bodies are forced to stay at home. We imitate; and what is imitation but the travelling of the mind? Our houses are built with foreign taste; our shelves are garnished with foreign ornaments; our opinions, our tastes, our faculties, lean, and follow the Past and the Distant. The soul created the arts wherever they have flourished. It was in his own mind that the artist sought his model. It was an application of his own thought to the thing to be done and the conditions to be observed. And why need we copy the Doric or the Gothic model? Beauty, convenience, grandeur of thought and quaint expression are as near to us as to any, and if the American artist will study with hope and love the precise thing to be done by him, considering the climate, the soil, the length of the day, the wants of the people, the habit and form of the government, he will create a house in which all these will find themselves fitted, and taste and sentiment will be satisfied also.

Insist on yourself; never imitate. Your own gift you can present every moment with the cumulative force of a whole life's cultivation; but of the adopted talent of another you have only an extemporaneous half possession. That which each can do best, none but his Maker can teach him. No man yet knows what it is, nor can, till that person has exhibited it. Where is the master who could have taught Shakspeare? Where is the master who could have instructed Franklin, or Washington, or Bacon, or Newton? Every great man is a unique. The Scipionism of Scipio is precisely that part he could not borrow. Shakspeare will never be made by the study of Shakspeare. Do that which is assigned you, and you cannot hope too much or dare too much. There is at this moment for you an utterance brave and grand as that of the colossal chisel of Phidias, or trowel of the Egyptians, or the pen of Moses or Dante, but different from all these. Not possibly will the soul, all rich, all eloquent, with thousand-cloven tongue, deign to repeat itself; but if you can hear what these patriarchs say, surely you can reply to them in the same pitch of voice; for the ear and the tongue are two organs of one nature. Abide in the simple and noble regions of thy life, obey thy heart, and thou shall reproduce the Foreworld again.

4. As our Religion, our Education, our Art look abroad, so does our spirit of society. All men plume themselves on the improvement of society, and no man improves.

Society never advances. It recedes as fast on one side as it gains on the other. It undergoes continual changes; it is barbarous, it is civilized, it is christianized, it is rich, it is scientific; but this change is not amelioration. For everything that is given something is taken. Society acquires new arts and loses old instincts. What a contrast between the well-clad, reading, writing, thinking American, with a watch, a pencil, and a bill of exchange in his pocket, and the naked New Zealander, whose property is a club, a spear, a mat and an undivided twentieth of a shed to sleep under! But compare the health of the two men and you shall see that the white man has lost his aboriginal strength. If the traveller tell us truly, strike the savage with a broad-axe and in a day or two the flesh shall unite and heal as if you struck the blow into soft pitch, and the same blow shall send the white to his grave.

The civilized man has built a coach, but has lost the use of his feet. He is supported on crutches, but lacks so much support of muscle. He has a fine Geneva watch, but he fails of the skill to tell the hour by the sun. A Greenwich nautical almanac he has, and so being sure of the information when he wants it, the man in the street does not know a star in the sky. The solstice he does not observe; the equinox he knows as little; and the whole bright calendar of the year is without a dial in his mind. His notebooks impair his memory; his libraries overload his wit; the insurance-office increases the number of accidents; and it may be a question whether machinery does not encumber; whether we have not lost by refinement some energy, by a Christianity, entrenched in establishments and forms, some vigor of wild virtue. For every Stoic was a Stoic; but in Christendom where is the Christian?

There is no more deviation in the moral standard than in the standard of height or bulk. No greater men are now than ever were. A singular equality may be observed between the great men of the first and of the last ages; nor can all the science, art, religion, and philosophy of the nineteenth century avail to educate greater men than Plutarch's heroes, three or four and twenty centuries ago. Not in time is the race progressive. Phocion, Socrates, Anaxagoras, Diogenes, are great men, but they leave no class. He who is really of their class will not be called by their name, but will be his own man, and in his turn the founder of a sect. The arts and inventions of each period are only its costume and do not invigorate men. The harm of the improved machinery may compensate its good. Hudson and Behring accomplished so much in their fishing-boats as to astonish Parry and Franklin, whose equipment exhausted the resources of science and art. Galileo, with an opera-glass, discovered a more splendid series of celestial phenomena than any one since. Columbus found the New World in an undecked boat. It is curious to see the periodical disuse and perishing of means and machinery which were introduced with loud laudation a few years or centuries before. The great genius returns to essential man. We reckoned the improvements of the art of war among the triumphs of science, and yet Napoleon conquered Europe by the bivouac, which consisted of falling back on naked valor and disencumbering it of all aids. The Emperor held it impossible to make a perfect army, says Las Cases,[5] "without abolishing our arms, magazines, commissaries, and carriages, until, in imitation of the Roman custom, the soldier should receive his supply of corn, grind it in his handmill and bake his bread himself."

Society is a wave. The wave moves onward, but the water of which it is composed does not. The same particle does not rise from the valley to the ridge. Its unity is only phenomenal. The persons who make up a nation to-day, next year die, and their experience dies with them.

And so the reliance on Property, including the reliance on governments which protect it, is the want of self-reliance. Men have looked away from themselves and at things so long that they have come to esteem the religious, learned and civil institutions as guards of property, and they deprecate assaults on these, because they feel them to be assaults on property. They measure their esteem of each other by what each has, and not by what each is. But a cultivated man becomes ashamed of his property, out of new respect for his nature. Especially he hates what he has if he see that it is accidental,—came to him by inheritance, or gift, or crime; then he feels that it is not having; it does not belong to him, has no root in him and merely lies there because no revolution or no robber takes it away. But that which a man is, does always by necessity acquire; and what the man acquires, is living property, which does not wait the beck of rulers, or mobs, or revolutions, or fire, or storm, or bankruptcies, but perpetually renews itself wherever the man breathes. "Thy lot or portion of life," said the Caliph Ali,[6] "is seeking after thee; therefore be at rest from seeking after it." Our dependence on these foreign goods leads us to our slavish respect for numbers. The political parties meet in numerous conventions; the greater the concourse and with each new uproar of announcement, The delegation from Essex! The Democrats from New Hampshire! The Whigs of Maine! the young patriot feels himself stronger than before by a new thousand of eyes and arms. In like manner the reformers summon conventions and vote and resolve in multitude. Not so, O friends! will the God deign to enter and inhabit you, but by a method precisely the reverse. It is only as a man puts off all foreign support and stands alone that I see him to be strong and to prevail. He is

[5] Bartolomé de las Casas (1474-1566), Bishop of Chiapas, Guatemala; known as the "Apostle of the Indies."

[6] Fourth caliph of the Muslim Arab empire, and cousin and son-in-law of Mohammed.

weaker by every recruit to his banner. Is not a man better than a town? Ask nothing of men, and, in the endless mutation, thou only firm column must presently appear the upholder of all that surrounds thee. He who knows that power is inborn, that he is weak because he has looked for good out of him and elsewhere, and, so perceiving, throws himself unhesitatingly on his thought, instantly rights himself, stands in the erect position, commands his limbs, works miracles; just as a man who stands on his feet is stronger than a man who stands on his head.

So use all that is called Fortune. Most men gamble with her, and gain all, and lose all, as her wheel rolls. But do thou leave as unlawful these winnings, and deal with Cause and Effect, the chancellors of God. In the Will work and acquire, and thou hast chained the wheel of Chance, and shall sit hereafter out of fear from her rotations. A political victory, a rise of rents, the recovery of your sick or the return of your absent friend, or some other favorable event raises your spirits, and you think good days are preparing for you. Do not believe it. Nothing can bring you peace but yourself. Nothing can bring you peace but the triumph of principles.

1841

The Poet

Emerson gave a lecture titled "The Poet" in 1841; after that he went on to develop his ideas into this second and almost entirely different statement. This essay, written at the height of Emerson's powers, explains his conception of the new poet who would emerge in America. Although Emerson rejects the conventional poetry based on the past and looks to America for the ideal poet, many of his ideas are consistent with the romantic tradition and, in some respects, with modern poetic theory. Emerson's faith in the poet as seer and sayer, his belief that the poet through language and symbol could bring man and nature together, his concern with organic form, and his certainty that the great poet would liberate men are some of the major convictions that become part of his theory. However, these convictions, and indeed the entire essay, must be understood in the context of Emerson's idealism. "The Poet," Poe's "The Poetic Principle," and Whitman's "1855 Preface" are the most important critical statements about poetry written by American Romantics.

Those who are esteemed umpires of taste are often persons who have acquired some knowledge of admired pictures or sculptures, and have an inclination for whatever is elegant; but if you inquire whether they are beautiful souls, and whether their own acts are like fair pictures, you learn that they are selfish and sensual. Their cultivation is local, as if you should rub a log of dry wood in one spot to produce fire, all the rest remaining cold. Their knowledge of the fine arts is some study of rules and particulars, or some limited judgment of color or form, which is exercised for amusement or for show. It is a proof of the shallowness of the doctrine of beauty as it lies in the minds of our amateurs, that men seem to have lost the perception of the instant dependence of form upon soul. There is no doctrine of forms in our philosophy. We were put into our bodies, as fire is put into a pan to be carried about; but there is no accurate adjustment between the spirit and the organ, much less is the latter the germination of the former. So in regard to other forms, the intellectual men do not believe in any essential dependence of the material world on thought and volition. Theologians think it a pretty air-castle to talk of the spiritual meaning of a ship or a cloud, of a city or a contract, but they prefer to come again to the solid ground of historical evidence; and even the poets are contented with a civil and conformed manner of living, and to write poems from the fancy, at a safe distance from their own experience. But the highest minds of the world have never ceased to explore the double meaning, or shall I say, the quadruple or the centuple or much more manifold meaning, of every sensuous fact; Orpheus, Empedocles, Heraclitus, Plato, Plutarch, Dante, Swedenborg, and the masters of sculpture, picture and poetry. For we are not pans and barrows, nor even porters of the fire and torchbearers, but children of the fire, made of it, and only the same divinity transmuted and at two or three removes, when we know least about it. And this hidden truth, that the fountains whence all this river of Time, and its creatures, floweth are intrinsically ideal and beautiful, draws us to the consideration of the nature and functions of the Poet, or the man of Beauty; to the means and materials he uses, and to the general aspect of the art in the present time.

The breadth of the problem is great, for the poet is representative. He stands among partial men for the complete man, and apprises us not of his wealth, but of the common wealth. The young man reveres men of genius, because, to speak truly, they are more himself than he is. They receive of the soul as he also receives, but they more. Nature enhances her beauty, to the eye of loving men, from their belief that the poet is beholding her shows at the same time. He is isolated among his contemporaries, by truth and by his art, but with this consolation in his pursuits, that they will draw all men sooner or later. For all men live by truth and stand in need of expression. In love, in art, in avarice, in politics, in labor, in games, we study to utter our painful secret.

The man is only half himself, the other half is his expression.

Notwithstanding this necessity to be published, adequate expression is rare. I know not how it is that we need an interpreter, but the great majority of men seem to be minors, who have not yet come into possession of their own, or mutes, who cannot report the conversation they have had with nature. There is no man who does not anticipate a supersensual utility in the sun and stars, earth and water. These stand and wait to render him a peculiar service. But there is some obstruction or some excess of phlegm in our constitution, which does not suffer them to yield the due effect. Too feeble fall the impressions of nature on us to make us artists. Every touch should thrill. Every man should be so much an artist that he could report in conversation what had befallen him. Yet, in our experience, the rays or appulses have sufficient force to arrive at the senses, but not enough to reach the quick and compel the reproduction of themselves in speech. The poet is the person in whom these powers are in balance, the man without impediment, who sees and handles that which others dream of, traverses the whole scale of experience, and is representative of man, in virtue of being the largest power to receive and to impart.

For the Universe has three children, born at one time, which reappear under different names, in every system of thought, whether they be called cause, operation and effect; or, more poetically, Jove, Pluto, Neptune; or, theologically, the Father, the Spirit and the Son; but which we will call here the Knower, the Doer and the Sayer. These stand respectively for the love of truth, for the love of good, and for the love of beauty. These three are equal. Each is that which he is, essentially, so that he cannot be surmounted or analyzed, and each of these three has the power of the others latent in him and his own, patent.

The poet is the sayer, the namer, and represents beauty. He is a sovereign, and stands on the center. For the world is not painted or adorned, but is from the beginning beautiful; and God has not made some beautiful things, but Beauty is the creator of the universe. Therefore the poet is not any permissive potentate, but is emperor in his own right. Criticism is infested with a cant of materialism, which assumes that manual skill and activity is the first merit of all men, and disparages such as say and do not, overlooking the fact, that some men, namely poets, are natural sayers, sent into the world to the end of expression, and confounds them with those whose province is action but who quit it to imitate the sayers. But Homer's words are as costly and admirable to Homer as Agamemnon's victories are to Agamemnon. The poet does not wait for the hero or the sage, but, as they act and think primarily, so he writes primarily what will and must be spoken, reckoning the others, though primaries also, yet, in respect to him, secondaries and servants; as sitters or models in the studio of a painter, or as assistants who bring building-materials to an architect.

For poetry was all written before time was, and whenever we are so finely organized that we can penetrate into that region where the air is music, we hear those primal warblings and attempt to write them down, but we lose ever and anon a word or a verse and substitute something of our own, and thus miswrite the poem. The men of more delicate ear write down these cadences more faithfully, and these transcripts, though imperfect, become the songs of the nations. For nature is as truly beautiful as it is good, or as it is reasonable, and must as much appear as it must be done, or be known. Words and deeds are quite indifferent modes of the divine energy. Words are also actions, and actions are a kind of words.

The sign and credentials of the poet are that he announces that which no man foretold. He is the true and only doctor;[1] he knows and tells; he is the only teller of news, for he was present and privy to the appearance which he describes. He is a beholder of ideas and an utterer of the necessary and causal. For we do not speak now of men of poetical talents, or of industry and skill in metre, but of the true poet. I took part in a conversation the other day concerning a recent writer of lyrics, a man of subtle mind, whose head appeared to be a music-box of delicate tunes and rhythms, and whose skill and command of language we could not sufficiently praise. But when the question arose whether he was not only a lyrist but a poet, we were obliged to confess that he is plainly a contemporary, not an eternal man. He does not stand out of our low limitations, like a Chimborazo under the line, running up from a torrid base through all the climates of the globe, with belts of the herbage of every latitude on its high and mottled sides; but this genius is the landscape-garden of a modern house, adorned with fountains and statues, with well-bred men and women standing and sitting in the walks and terraces. We hear, through all the varied music, the ground-tone of conventional life. Our poets are men of talents who sing, and not the children of music. The argument is secondary, the finish of the verses is primary.

For it is not metres, but a metre-making argument

[1] In the sense of teacher.

that makes a poem,—a thought so passionate and alive that like the spirit of a plant or an animal it has an architecture of its own, and adorns nature with a new thing. The thought and the form are equal in the order of time, but in the order of genesis the thought is prior to the form. The poet has a new thought; he has a whole new experience to unfold; he will tell us how it was with him, and all men will be the richer in his fortune. For the experience of each new age requires a new confession, and the world seems always waiting for its poet. I remember when I was young how much I was moved one morning by tidings that genius had appeared in a youth who sat near me at table. He had left his work and gone rambling none knew whither, and had written hundreds of lines, but could not tell whether that which was in him was therein told; he could tell nothing but that all was changed,—man, beast, heaven, earth and sea. How gladly we listened! how credulous! Society seemed to be compromised. We sat in the aurora of a sunrise which was to put out all the stars. Boston seemed to be at twice the distance it had the night before, or was much farther than that. Rome,—what was Rome? Plutarch and Shakspeare were in the yellow leaf, and Homer no more should be heard of. It is much to know that poetry has been written this very day, under this very roof, by your side. What! that wonderful spirit has not expired! these stony moments are still sparkling and animated! I had fancied that the oracles were all silent, and nature had spent her fires; and behold! all night, from every pore, these fine auroras have been streaming. Every one has some interest in the advent of the poet, and no one knows how much it may concern him. We know that the secret of the world is profound, but who or what shall be our interpreter, we know not. A mountain ramble, a new style of face, a new person, may put the key into our hands. Of course the value of genius to us is in the veracity of its report. Talent may frolic and juggle; genius realizes and adds. Mankind in good earnest have availed so far in understanding themselves and their work, that the foremost watchman on the peak announces his news. It is the truest word ever spoken, and the phrase will be the fittest, most musical, and the unerring voice of the world for that time.

All that we call sacred history attests that the birth of a poet is the principal event in chronology. Man, never so often deceived, still watches for the arrival of a brother who can hold him steady to a truth until he has made it his own. With what joy I begin to read a poem which I confide in as an inspiration! And now my chains are to be broken; I shall mount above these clouds and opaque airs in which I live,—opaque, though they seem transparent,—and from the heaven of truth I shall see and comprehend my relations. That will reconcile me to life and renovate nature, to see trifles animated by a tendency, and to know what I am doing. Life will no more be a noise; now I shall see men and women, and know the signs by which they may be discerned from fools and satans. This day shall be better than my birthday: then I became an animal; now I am invited into the science of the real. Such is the hope, but the fruition is postponed. Oftener it falls that this winged man, who will carry me into the heaven, whirls me into mists, then leaps and frisks about with me as it were from cloud to cloud, still affirming that he is bound heavenward; and I, being myself a novice, am slow in perceiving that he does not know the way into the heavens, and is merely bent that I should admire his skill to rise like a fowl or a flying fish, a little way from the ground or the water; but the all-piercing, all-feeding and ocular air of heaven that man shall never inhabit. I tumble down again soon into my old nooks, and lead the life of exaggerations as before, and have lost my faith in the possibility of any guide who can lead me thither where I would be.

But, leaving these victims of vanity, let us, with new hope, observe how nature, by worthier impulses, has insured the poet's fidelity to his office of announcement and affirming, namely by the beauty of things, which becomes a new and higher beauty when expressed. Nature offers all her creatures to him as a picture-language. Being used as a type, a second wonderful value appears in the object, far better than its old value, as the carpenter's stretched cord, if you hold your ear close enough, is musical in the breeze. "Things more excellent than every image," says Jamblichus, "are expressed through images." Things admit of being used as symbols because nature is a symbol, in the whole, and in every part. Every line we can draw in the sand has expression; and there is no body without its spirit or genius. All form is an effect of character; all condition, of the quality of the life; all harmony, of health; and for this reason a perception of beauty should be sympathetic, or proper only to the good. The beautiful rests on the foundations of the necessary. The soul makes the body, as the wise Spenser teaches:—

> So every spirit, as it is more pure,
> And hath in it the more of heavenly light,
> So it the fairer body doth procure
> To habit in, and it more fairly dight,
> With cheerful grace and amiable sight.
> For, of the soul, the body form doth take,
> For soul is form, and doth the body make.

Here we find ourselves suddenly not in a critical speculation but in a holy place, and should go very warily and reverently. We stand before the secret of the world, there where Being passes into Appearance and Unity into Variety.

The Universe is the externization of the soul. Wherever the life is, that bursts into appearance around it. Our science is sensual,[2] and therefore superficial. The earth and the heavenly bodies, physics and chemistry, we sensually treat, as if they were self-existent; but these are the retinue of that Being we have. "The mighty heaven," said Proclus,[3] "exhibits, in its transfigurations, clear images of the splendor of intellectual perceptions; being moved in conjunction with the unapparent periods of intellectual natures." Therefore science always goes abreast with the just elevation of the man, keeping step with religion and metaphysics; or the state of science is an index of our self-knowledge. Since everything in nature answers to a moral power, if any phenomenon remains brute and dark it is because the corresponding faculty in the observer is not yet active.

No wonder then, if these waters be so deep, that we hover over them with a religious regard. The beauty of the fable proves the importance of the sense; to the poet, and to all others; or, if you please, every man is so far a poet as to be susceptible of these enchantments of nature; for all men have the thoughts whereof the universe is the celebration. I find that the fascination resides in the symbol. Who loves nature? Who does not? Is it poets, and men of leisure and cultivation, who live with her? No; but also hunters, farmers, grooms and butchers, though they express their affection in their choice of life and not in their choice of words. The writer wonders what the coachman or the hunter values in riding, in horses and dogs. It is not superficial qualities. When you talk with him he holds these at as slight a rate as you. His worship is sympathetic; he has no definitions, but he is commanded in nature by the living power which he feels to be there present. No imitation or playing of these things would content him; he loves the earnest of the north wind, of rain, of stone and wood and iron. A beauty not explicable is dearer than a beauty which we can see to the end of. It is nature the symbol, nature certifying the supernatural, body overflowed by life which he worships with coarse, but sincere rites.

The inwardness and mystery of this attachment drives men of every class to the use of emblems. The schools of poets and philosophers are not more intoxicated with their symbols than the populace with theirs. In our political parties, compute the power of badges and emblems. See the great ball which they roll from Baltimore to Bunker Hill![4] In the political processions, Lowell goes in a loom, and Lynn in a shoe, and Salem in a ship. Witness the cider-barrel, the log-cabin, the hickory-stick, the palmetto, and all the cognizances of party. See the power of national emblems. Some stars, lilies, leopards, a crescent, a lion, an eagle, or other figure which came into credit God knows how, on an old rag of bunting, blowing in the wind on a fort at the ends of the earth, shall make the blood tingle under the rudest or the most conventional exterior. The people fancy they hate poetry, and they are all poets and mystics!

Beyond this universality of the symbolic language, we are apprised of the divineness of this superior use of things, whereby the world is a temple whose walls are covered with emblems, pictures and commandments of the Deity,—in this, that there is no fact in nature which does not carry the whole sense of nature; and the distinctions which we make in events and in affairs, of low and high, honest and base, disappear when nature is used as a symbol. Thought makes everything fit for use. The vocabulary of an omniscient man would embrace words and images excluded from polite conversation. What would be base, or even obscene, to the obscene, becomes illustrious, spoken in a new connection of thought. The piety of the Hebrew prophets purges their grossness. The circumcision is an example of the power of poetry to raise the low and offensive. Small and mean things serve as well as great symbols. The meaner the type by which a law is expressed, the more pungent it is, and the more lasting in the memories of men; just as we choose the smallest box or case in which any needful utensil can be carried. Bare lists of words are found suggestive to an imaginative and excited mind; as it is related of Lord Chatham that he was accustomed to read in Bailey's Dictionary when he was preparing to speak in Parliament. The poorest experience is rich enough for all the purposes of expressing thought. Why covet a knowledge of new facts? Day and night, house and garden, a few books, a few actions, serve us as well as would all trades and all spectacles. We are far from having exhausted the significance of the few symbols we use. We can come to use them yet with a terrible simplicity. It does not need that a poem should be long. Every word was once a poem. Every new relation is a new word. Also we use defects and deformities to a sacred purpose, so expressing our sense that the evils of the world are such only to the evil eye. In the old mythology, mythologists observe, defects are ascribed to divine

[2] Having to do with the senses generally; the word does not carry the modern connotation of sexuality.

[3] A Greek philosopher, a Neo-Platonist and follower of Plotinus.

[4] A political publicity stunt performed by the Whigs in 1840 to represent their steadily growing majority.

natures, as lameness to Vulcan, blindness to Cupid, and the like,—to signify exuberances.

For, as it is dislocation and detachment from the life of God that makes things ugly, the poet, who re-attaches things to nature and the Whole,—re-attaching even artificial things and violations of nature, to nature, by a deeper insight,—disposes very easily of the most disagreeable facts. Readers of poetry see the factory-village and the railway, and fancy that the poetry of the landscape is broken up by these; for these works of art are not yet consecrated in their reading; but the poet sees them fall within the great Order not less than the beehive or the spider's geometrical web. Nature adopts them very fast into her vital circles, and the gliding train of cars she loves like her own. Besides, in a centered mind, it signifies nothing how many mechanical inventions you exhibit. Though you add millions, and never so surprising, the fact of mechanics has not gained a grain's weight. The spiritual fact remains unalterable, by many or by few particulars; as no mountain is of any appreciable height to break the curve of the sphere. A shrewd country-boy goes to the city for the first time, and the complacent citizen is not satisfied with his little wonder. It is not that he does not see all the fine houses and know that he never saw such before, but he disposes of them as easily as the poet finds place for the railway. The chief value of the new fact is to enhance the great and constant fact of Life, which can dwarf any and every circumstance, and to which the belt of wampum and the commerce of America, are alike.

The world being thus put under the mind for verb and noun, the poet is he who can articulate it. For though life is great, and fascinates and absorbs; and though all men are intelligent of the symbols through which it is named; yet they cannot originally use them. We are symbols and inhabit symbols; workmen, work, and tools, words and things, birth and death, all are emblems; but we sympathize with the symbols, and, being infatuated with the economical uses of things, we do not know that they are thoughts. The poet, by an ulterior intellectual perception, gives them a power which makes their old use forgotten, and puts eyes, and a tongue, into every dumb and inanimate object. He perceives the independence of the thought on the symbol, the stability of the thought, the accidency and fugacity of the symbol. As the eyes of Lyncaeus were said to see through the earth, so the poet turns the world to glass, and shows us all things in their right series and procession. For through that better perception he stands one step nearer to things, and sees the flowing or metamorphosis; perceives that thought is multiform; that within the form of every creature is a force impelling it to ascend into a higher form; and following with his eyes the life, uses the forms which express that life, and so his speech flows with the flowing of nature. All the facts of the animal economy, sex, nutriment, gestation, birth, growth, are symbols of the passage of the world into the soul of man, to suffer there a change and reappear a new and higher fact. He uses forms according to the life, and not according to the form. This is true science. The poet alone knows astronomy, chemistry, vegetation and animation, for he does not stop at these facts, but employs them as signs. He knows why the plain or meadow of space was strown with these flowers we call suns and moons and stars; why the great deep is adorned with animals, with men, and gods; for, in every word he speaks he rides on them as the horses of thought.

By virtue of this science the poet is the Namer or Language-maker, naming things sometimes after their appearance, sometimes after their essence, and giving to every one its own name and not another's, thereby rejoicing the intellect, which delights in detachment or boundary. The poets made all the words, and therefore language is the archives of history, and, if we must say it, a sort of tomb of the muses. For though the origin of most of our words is forgotten, each word was at first a stroke of genius, and obtained currency because for the moment it symbolized the world to the first speaker and to the hearer. The etymologist finds the deadest word to have been once a brilliant picture. Language is fossil poetry. As the limestone of the continent consists of infinite masses of the shells of animalcules, so language is made up of images or tropes, which now, in their secondary use, have long ceased to remind us of their poetic origin. But the poet names the thing because he sees it, or comes one step nearer to it than any other. This expression or naming is not art, but a second nature, grown out of the first, as a leaf out of a tree. What we call nature is a certain self-regulated motion or change; and nature does all things by her own hands, and does not leave another to baptize her but baptizes herself; and this through the metamorphosis again. I remember that a certain poet[5] described it to me thus:—

Genius is the activity which repairs the decays of things, whether wholly or partly of a material and finite kind. Nature, through all her kingdoms, insures herself. Nobody cares for planting the poor fungus; so she shakes down from the gills of one agaric countless spores, any one of which, being preserved, transmits new billions of spores to-morrow or next day. The new agaric of this hour has a chance which the old one had not. This atom of

[5] Emerson himself is that poet; he is working here with Platonic ideas.

seed is thrown into a new place, not subject to the accidents which destroyed its parent two rods off. She makes a man; and having brought him to ripe age, she will no longer run the risk of losing this wonder at a blow, but she detaches from him a new self, that the kind may be safe from accidents to which the individual is exposed. So when the soul of the poet has come to ripeness of thought, she detaches and sends away from it its poems or songs,—a fearless, sleepless, deathless progeny, which is not exposed to the accidents of the weary kingdom of time; a fearless, vivacious offspring, clad with wings (such was the virtue of the soul out of which they came) which carry them fast and far, and infix them irrecoverably into the hearts of men. These wings are the beauty of the poet's soul. The songs, thus flying immortal from their mortal parent, are pursued by clamorous flights of censures, which swarm in far greater numbers and threaten to devour them; but these last are not winged. At the end of a very short leap they fall plump down and rot, having received from the souls out of which they came no beautiful wings. But the melodies of the poet ascend and leap and pierce into the deeps of infinite time.

So far the bard taught me, using his freer speech. But nature has a higher end, in the production of new individuals, than security, namely *ascension*, or the passage of the soul into higher forms. I knew in my younger days the sculptor who made the statue of the youth which stands in the public garden. He was, as I remember, unable to tell directly what made him happy or unhappy, but by wonderful indirections he could tell. He rose one day, according to his habit, before the dawn, and saw the morning break, grand as the eternity out of which it came, and, for many days after, he strove to express this tranquillity, and lo! his chisel had fashioned out of marble the form of a beautiful youth, Phosphorus, whose aspect is such that it is said all persons who look on it become silent. The poet also resigns himself to his mood, and that thought which agitated him is expressed, but *alter idem*,[6] in a manner totally new. The expression is organic, or the new type which things themselves take when liberated. As, in the sun, objects paint their images on the retina of the eye, so they, sharing the aspiration of the whole universe, tend to paint a far more delicate copy of their essence in his mind. Like the metamorphosis of things into higher organic forms is their change into melodies. Over everything stands its daemon or soul, and, as the form of the thing is reflected by the eye, so the soul of the thing is reflected by a melody. The sea, the mountain-ridge, Niagara, and every flower-bed, pre-exist, or super-exist, in pre-cantations, which sail like odors in the air, and when any man goes by with an ear sufficiently fine, he overhears them and endeavors to write down the notes without diluting or depraving them. And herein is the legitimation of criticism, in the mind's faith that the poems are a corrupt version of some text in nature with which they ought to be made to tally. A rhyme in one of our sonnets should not be less pleasing than the iterated nodes of a seashell, or the resembling difference of a group of flowers. The pairing of the birds is an idyl, not tedious as our idyls are; a tempest is a rough ode, without falsehood or rant; a summer, with its harvest sown, reaped and stored, is an epic song, subordinating how many admirably executed parts. Why should not the symmetry and truth that modulate these, glide into our spirits, and we participate the invention of nature?

This insight, which expresses itself by what is called Imagination, is a very high sort of seeing, which does not come by study, but by the intellect being where and what it sees, by sharing the path or circuit of things through forms, and so making them translucid to others. The path of things is silent. Will they suffer a speaker to go with them? A spy they will not suffer; a lover, a poet, is the transcendency of their own nature,—him they will suffer. The condition of true naming, on the poet's part, is his resigning himself to the divine *aura* which breathes through forms, and accompanying that.

It is a secret which every intellectual man quickly learns, that, beyond the energy of his possessed and conscious intellect he is capable of a new energy (as of an intellect doubled on itself), by abandonment to the nature of things; that beside his privacy of power as an individual man, there is a great public power on which he can draw, by unlocking, at all risks, his human doors, and suffering the ethereal tides to roll and circulate through him: then he is caught up into the life of the Universe, his speech is thunder, his thought is law, and his words are universally intelligible as the plants and animals. The poet knows that he speaks adequately then only when he speaks somewhat wildly, or "with the flower of the mind"; not with the intellect used as an organ, but with the intellect released from all service and suffered to take its direction from its celestial life; or as the ancients were wont to express themselves, not with intellect alone but with the intellect inebriated by nectar. As the traveller who has lost his way throws his reins on his horse's neck and trusts to the instinct of the animal to find his road, so must we do with the divine animal who carries us through this world. For if in any manner we can stimulate this instinct, new passages are opened for us into nature; the mind flows into and

[6] The same, yet different.

through things hardest and highest, and the metamorphosis is possible.

This is the reason why bards love wine, mead, narcotics, coffee, tea, opium, the fumes of sandalwood and tobacco, or whatever other procurers of animal exhilaration. All men avail themselves of such means as they can, to add this extraordinary power to their normal powers; and to this end they prize conversation, music, pictures, sculpture, dancing, theatres, travelling, war, mobs, fires, gaming, politics, or love, or science, or animal intoxication,—which are several coarser or finer *quasi*-mechanical substitutes for the true nectar, which is the ravishment of the intellect by coming nearer to the fact. These are auxiliaries to the centrifugal tendency of a man, to his passage out into free space, and they help him to escape the custody of that body in which he is pent up, and of that jail-yard of individual relations in which he is enclosed. Hence a great number of such as were professionally expressers of Beauty, as painters, poets, musicians and actors, have been more than others wont to lead a life of pleasure and indulgence; all but the few who received the true nectar; and, as it was a spurious mode of attaining freedom, as it was an emancipation not into the heavens but into the freedom of baser places, they were punished for that advantage they won, by a dissipation and deterioration. But never can any advantage be taken of nature by a trick. The spirit of the world, the great calm presence of the Creator, comes not forth to the sorceries of opium or of wine. The sublime vision comes to the pure and simple soul in a clean and chaste body. That is not an inspiration which we owe to narcotics, but some counterfeit excitement and fury. Milton says that the lyric poet may drink wine and live generously, but the epic poet, he who shall sing of the gods and their descent unto men, must drink water out of a wooden bowl. For poetry is not "Devil's wine," but God's wine. It is with this as it is with toys. We fill the hands and nurseries of our children with all manner of dolls, drums and horses; withdrawing their eyes from the plain face and sufficing objects of nature, the sun and the moon, the animals, the water and stones, which should be their toys. So the poet's habit of living should be set on a key so low that the common influences should delight him. His cheerfulness should be the gift of the sunlight; the air should suffice for his inspiration, and he should be tipsy with water. That spirit which suffices quiet hearts, which seems to come forth to such from every dry knoll of sere grass, from every pine-stump and half-imbedded stone on which the dull March sun shines, comes forth to the poor and hungry, and such as are of simple taste. If thou fill thy brain with Boston and New York, with fashion and covetousness, and wilt stimulate thy jaded senses with wine and French coffee, thou shalt find no radiance of wisdom in the lonely waste of the pinewoods.

If the imagination intoxicates the poet, it is not inactive in other men. The metamorphosis excites in the beholder an emotion of joy. The use of symbols has a certain power of emancipation and exhilaration for all men. We seem to be touched by a wand which makes us dance and run about happily, like children. We are like persons who come out of a cave or cellar into the open air. This is the effect on us of tropes, fables, oracles and all poetic forms. Poets are thus liberating gods. Men have really got a new sense, and found within their world another world, or nest of worlds; for, the metamorphosis once seen, we divine that it does not stop. I will not now consider how much this makes the charm of algebra and the mathematics, which also have their tropes, but it is felt in every definition; as, when Aristotle defines *space* to be an immovable vessel in which things are contained;—or when Plato defines a *line* to be a flowing point; or *figure* to be a bound of solid; and many the like. What a joyful sense of freedom we have when Vitruvius announces the old opinion of artists that no architect can build any house well who does not know something of anatomy. When Socrates, in Charmides, tells us that the soul is cured of its maladies by certain incantations, and that these incantations are beautiful reasons, from which temperance is generated in souls; when Plato[7] calls the world an animal, and Timaeus affirms that plants also are animals; or affirms a man to be a heavenly tree, growing with his root, which is his head, upward; and, as George Chapman, following him, writes,—

> So in our tree of man, whose nervie root
> Springs in his top;—

when Orpheus speaks of hoariness as "that white flower which marks extreme old age"; when Proclus calls the universe the statue of the intellect; when Chaucer, in his praise of "Gentilesse," compares good blood in mean condition to fire, which, though carried to the darkest house betwixt this and the mount of Caucasus, will yet hold its natural office and burn as bright as if twenty thousand men did it behold; when John saw, in the Apocalypse, the ruin of the world through evil, and the stars fall from heaven as the fig tree casteth her untimely fruit; when Aesop reports the whole catalogue of common daily relations through the masquerade of birds and beasts;—we take the cheerful hint of the immortality of our essence and its versatile habit and

[7] Both *Charmides* and *Timaeus* were written by Plato.

escapes, as when the gypsies say of themselves, "it is in vain to hang them, they cannot die."

The poets are thus liberating gods. The ancient British bards had for the title of their order, "Those who are free throughout the world." They are free, and they make free. An imaginative book renders us much more service at first, by stimulating us through its tropes, than afterward when we arrive at the precise sense of the author. I think nothing is of any value in books excepting the transcendental and extraordinary. If a man is inflamed and carried away by his thought, to that degree that he forgets the authors and the public and heeds only this one dream which holds him like an insanity, let me read his paper, and you may have all the arguments and histories and criticism. All the value which attaches to Pythagoras, Paracelsus, Cornelius Agrippa,[8] Cardan,[9] Kepler, Swedenborg, Schelling, Oken,[10] or any other who introduces questionable facts into his cosmogony, as angels, devils, magic, astrology, palmistry, mesmerism, and so on, is the certificate we have of departure from routine, and that here is a new witness. That also is the best success in conversation, the magic of liberty, which puts the world like a ball in our hands. How cheap even the liberty then seems; how mean to study, when an emotion communicates to the intellect the power to sap and upheave nature; how great the perspective! nations, times, systems, enter and disappear like threads in tapestry of large figure and many colors; dream delivers us to dream, and while the drunkenness lasts we will sell our bed, our philosophy, our religion, in our opulence.

There is good reason why we should prize this liberation. The fate of the poor shepherd, who, blinded and lost in the snowstorm, perishes in a drift within a few feet of his cottage door, is an emblem of the state of man. On the brink of the waters of life and truth, we are miserably dying. The inaccessibleness of every thought but that we are in, is wonderful. What if you come near to it; you are as remote when you are nearest as when you are farthest. Every thought is also a prison; every heaven is also a prison. Therefore we love the poet, the inventor, who in any form, whether in an ode or in an action or in looks and behavior, has yielded us a new thought. He unlocks our chains and admits us to a new scene.

This emancipation is dear to all men, and the power to impart it, as it must come from greater depth and scope of thought, is a measure of intellect. Therefore all books of the imagination endure, all which ascend to that truth that the writer sees nature beneath him, and uses it as his exponent. Every verse or sentence possessing this virtue will take care of its own immortality. The religions of the world are the ejaculations of a few imaginative men.

But the quality of the imagination is to flow, and not to freeze. The poet did not stop at the color or the form, but read their meaning; neither may he rest in this meaning, but he makes the same objects exponents of his new thought. Here is the difference betwixt the poet and the mystic, that the last nails a symbol to one sense, which was a true sense for a moment, but soon becomes old and false. For all symbols are fluxional; all language is vehicular and transitive, and is good, as ferries and horses are, for conveyance, not as farms and houses are, for homestead. Mysticism consists in the mistake of an accidental and individual symbol for an universal one. The morning-redness happens to be the favorite meteor to the eyes of Jacob Behmen,[11] and comes to stand to him for truth and faith; and, he believes, should stand for the same realities to every reader. But the first reader prefers as naturally the symbol of a mother and child, or a gardener and his bulb, or a jeweller polishing a gem. Either of these, or of a myriad more, are equally good to the person to whom they are significant. Only they must be held lightly, and be very willingly translated into the equivalent terms which others use. And the mystic must be steadily told,—All that you say is just as true without the tedious use of that symbol as with it. Let us have a little algebra, instead of this trite rhetoric,—universal signs, instead of these village symbols,—and we shall both be gainers. The history of hierarchies seems to show that all religious error consisted in making the symbol too stark and solid, and was at last nothing but an excess of the organ of language.

Swedenborg, of all men in the recent ages, stands eminently for the translator of nature into thought. I do not know the man in history to whom things stood so uniformly for words. Before him the metamorphosis continually plays. Every thing on which his eye rests, obeys the impulses of moral nature. The figs become grapes whilst he eats them. When some of his angels affirmed a truth, the laurel twig which they held blossomed in their hands. The noise which at a distance appeared like gnashing and thumping, on coming nearer was found to be the voice of disputants. The men in one of his visions, seen in heavenly light, appeared like dragons, and

[8] Cornelius Agrippa (1486–1535), scholar and writer on occult sciences.

[9] Jerome Cardan (1501–76), Italian mathematician and writer on medicine and occult sciences.

[10] Lorenz Oken (1779–1851), German naturalist and participant in the Naturphilosophie movement.

[11] Jacob Boehme (1575–1624), a German mystic philosopher.

seemed in darkness; but to each other they appeared as men, and when the light from heaven shone into their cabin, they complained of the darkness, and were compelled to shut the window that they might see.

There was this perception in him which makes the poet or seer an object of awe and terror, namely that the same man or society of men may wear one aspect to themselves and their companions, and a different aspect to higher intelligences. Certain priests, whom he describes as conversing very learnedly together, appeared to the children who were at some distance like dead horses; and many the like misappearances. And instantly the mind inquires whether these fishes under the bridge, yonder oxen in the pasture, those dogs in the yard, are immutably fishes, oxen and dogs, or only so appear to me, and perchance to themselves appear upright men; and whether I appear as a man to all eyes. The Brahmins and Pythagoras propounded the same question, and if any poet has witnessed the transformation he doubtless found it in harmony with various experiences. We have all seen changes as considerable in wheat and caterpillars. He is the poet and shall draw us with love and terror, who sees through the flowing vest the firm nature, and can declare it.

I look in vain for the poet whom I describe. We do not with sufficient plainness or sufficient profoundness address ourselves to life, nor dare we chaunt our own times and social circumstance. If we filled the day with bravery, we should not shrink from celebrating it. Time and nature yield us many gifts, but not yet the timely man, the new religion, the reconciler, whom all things await. Dante's praise is that he dared to write his autobiography in colossal cipher, or into universality. We have yet had no genius in America, with tyrannous eye, which knew the value of our incomparable materials, and saw, in the barbarism and materialism of the times, another carnival of the same gods whose picture he so much admires in Homer; then in the Middle Ages; then in Calvinism. Banks and tariffs, the newspaper and caucus, Methodism and Unitarianism, are flat and dull to dull people, but rest on the same foundations of wonder as the town of Troy and the temple of Delphi, and are as swiftly passing away. Our log-rolling, our stumps and their politics, our fisheries, our Negroes and Indians, our boats and our repudiations, the wrath of rogues and the pusillanimity of honest men, the northern trade, the southern planting, the western clearing, Oregon and Texas, are yet unsung. Yet America is a poem in our eyes; its ample geography dazzles the imagination, and it will not wait long for metres. If I have not found that excellent combination of gifts in my countrymen which I seek, neither could I aid myself to fix the idea of the poet by reading now and then in Chalmers's collection of five centuries of English poets. These are wits more than poets, though there have been poets among them. But when we adhere to the ideal of the poet, we have our difficulties even with Milton and Homer. Milton is too literary, and Homer too literal and historical.

But I am not wise enough for a national criticism, and must use the old largeness a little longer, to discharge my errand from the muse to the poet concerning his art.

Art is the path of the creator to his work. The paths or methods are ideal and eternal, though few men ever see them; not the artist himself for years, or for a lifetime, unless he come into the conditions. The painter, the sculptor, the composer, the epic rhapsodist, the orator, all partake one desire, namely to express themselves symmetrically and abundantly, not dwarfishly and fragmentarily. They found or put themselves in certain conditions, as, the painter and sculptor before some impressive human figures; the orator into the assembly of the people; and the others in such scenes as each has found exciting to his intellect; and each presently feels the new desire. He hears a voice, he sees a beckoning. Then he is apprised, with wonder, what herds of daemons hem him in. He can no more rest; he says, with the old painter, "By God it is in me and must go forth of me." He pursues a beauty, half seen, which flies before him. The poet pours out verses in every solitude. Most of the things he says are conventional, no doubt; but by and by he says something which is original and beautiful. That charms him. He would say nothing else but such things. In our way of talking we say, "That is yours, this is mine;" but the poet knows well that it is not his; that it is as strange and beautiful to him as to you; he would fain hear the like eloquence at length. Once having tasted this immortal ichor, he cannot have enough of it, and as an admirable creative power exists in these intellections, it is of the last importance that these things get spoken. What a little of all we know is said! What drops of all the sea of our science are baled up! and by what accident it is that these are exposed, when so many secrets sleep in nature! Hence the necessity of speech and song; hence these throbs and heart-beatings in the orator, at the door of the assembly, to the end namely that thought may be ejaculated as Logos, or Word.

Doubt not, O poet, but persist. Say "It is in me, and shall out." Stand there, balked and dumb, stuttering and stammering, hissed and hooted, stand and strive, until at last rage draw out of thee that *dream*-power which every night shows thee is thine own; a power transcending all limit and privacy, and by virtue of which a man is the conductor of the whole river of electricity. Nothing walks, or creeps, or grows, or exists, which must not in turn arise and walk before him as exponent of his meaning. Comes he to that power, his genius is no longer exhaustible. All the creatures by pairs and by tribes pour into his mind as into a Noah's ark, to come forth again to people a new world. This is like the stock of air for our respiration or for the combustion of our fireplace; not a measure of gallons, but the entire atmosphere if wanted. And therefore the rich poets, as Homer, Chaucer, Shakspeare, and Raphael, have obviously no limits to their works except the limits of their lifetime, and resemble a mirror carried through the street, ready to render an image of every created thing.

O poet! a new nobility is conferred in groves and pastures, and not in castles or by the sword-blade any longer. The conditions are hard, but equal. Thou shalt leave the world, and know the muse only. Thou shalt not know any longer the times, customs, graces, politics, or opinions of men, but shalt take all from the muse. For the time of towns is tolled from the world by funereal chimes, but in nature the universal hours are counted by succeeding tribes of animals and plants, and by growth of joy on joy. God wills also that thou abdicate a manifold and duplex life, and that thou be content that others speak for thee. Others shall be thy gentlemen and shall represent all courtesy and worldly life for thee; others shall do the great and resounding actions also. Thou shalt lie close hid with nature, and canst not be afforded to the Capitol or the Exchange. The world is full of renunciations and apprenticeships, and this is thine; thou must pass for a fool and a churl for a long season. This is the screen and sheath in which Pan has protected his well-beloved flower, and thou shalt be known only to thine own, and they shall console thee with tenderest love. And thou shalt not be able to rehearse the names of thy friends in thy verse, for an old shame before the holy ideal. And this is the reward: that the ideal shall be real to thee, and the impressions of the actual world shall fall like summer rain, copious, but not troublesome to thy invulnerable essence. Thou shalt have the whole land for thy park and manor, the sea for thy bath and navigation, without tax and without envy; the woods and the rivers thou shalt own, and thou shalt possess that wherein others are only tenants and boarders. Thou true land-lord! sea-lord! air-lord! Wherever snow falls or water flows or birds fly, wherever day and night meet in twilight, wherever the blue heaven is hung by clouds or sown with stars, wherever are forms with transparent boundaries, wherever are outlets into celestial space, wherever is danger, and awe, and love,—there is Beauty, plenteous as rain, shed for thee, and though thou shouldst walk the world over, thou shalt not be able to find a condition inopportune or ignoble.

1844

Experience

"Experience" presents a sharp contrast to Emerson's earlier work ("Nature" and "Self-Reliance," e.g.), for he speaks here from the point of view of a skeptic. Emerson is deeply aware of the paradox man lives—he lives in time, yet he conceives of a world beyond—and of the great limiting forces over which man has no control. The essay conveys Emerson's overwhelming sense of being trapped within experience and of being isolated from the ideal or spirit—the thought world, as Emerson refers to it. Nevertheless, Emerson expresses a continued faith in the thought world, even though he knows that it cannot immediately, if ever, be realized. The essay does not express Emerson's final view of experience, but it does show how seriously he grappled with contradiction, limitation, illusion, and change.

Where do we find ourselves? In a series of which we do not know the extremes, and believe that it has none. We wake and find ourselves on a stair; there are stairs below us, which we seem to have ascended; there are stairs above us, many a one, which go upward and out of sight. But the Genius which according to the old belief stands at the door by which we enter, and gives us the lethe to drink, that we may tell no tales, mixed the cup too strongly, and we cannot shake off the lethargy now at noonday. Sleep lingers all our lifetime about our eyes, as night hovers all day in the boughs of the fir-tree. All things swim and glitter. Our life is not so much threatened as our perception. Ghostlike we glide through nature, and should not know our place again. Did our birth fall in some fit of indigence and frugality in nature, that she was so sparing of her fire and so liberal of her earth that it appears to us that we lack the affirmative principle, and though we have health and reason, yet we have no superfluity of spirit for new creation? We have enough to live and bring the year about, but not an ounce to impart or to invest. Ah that our Genius were a little more of a genius! We are like millers on the lower levels of a stream, when the factories above them have exhausted the water. We too fancy that the upper people must have raised their dams.

If any of us knew what we were doing, or where we are going, then when we think we best know! We do not know to-day whether we are busy or idle. In times when we thought ourselves indolent, we have afterwards discovered that much was accomplished and much was begun in us. All our days are so unprofitable while they pass, that 't is wonderful where or when we ever got anything of this which we call wisdom, poetry, virtue. We never got it on any dated calendar day. Some heavenly days must have been intercalated somewhere, like those that Hermes won with dice of the Moon, that Osiris might be born.[1] It is said all martyrdoms looked mean when they were suffered. Every ship is a romantic object, except that we sail in. Embark, and the romance quits our vessel and hangs on every other sail in the horizon. Our life looks trivial, and we shun to record it. Men seem to have learned of the horizon the art of perpetual retreating and reference. "Yonder uplands are rich pasturage, and my neighbor has fertile meadow, but my field," says the querulous farmer, "only holds the world together." I quote another man's saying; unluckily that other withdraws himself in the same way, and quotes me. 'T is the trick of nature thus to degrade to-day; a good deal of buzz, and somewhere a result slipped magically in. Every roof is agreeable to the eye until it is lifted; then we find tragedy and moaning women and hard-eyed husbands and deluges of lethe, and the men ask, "What's the news?" as if the old were so bad. How many individuals can we count in society? how many actions? how many opinions? So much of our time is preparation, so much is routine, and so much retrospect, that the pith of each man's genius contracts itself to a very few hours. The history of literature—take the net result of Tiraboschi, Warton, or Schlegel[2]—is a sum of very few ideas and of very few original tales; all the rest being variation of these. So in this great society wide lying around us, a critical analysis would find very few spontaneous actions. It is almost all custom and gross sense. There are even few opinions, and these seem organic in the speakers, and do not disturb the universal necessity.

What opium is instilled into all disaster! It shows formidable as we approach it, but there is at last no rough rasping friction, but the most slippery sliding surfaces; we fall soft on a thought; *Ate Dea* is gentle,—

"Over men's heads walking aloft,
With tender feet treading so soft."

People grieve and bemoan themselves, but it is not half so bad with them as they say. There are moods in which we court suffering, in the hope that here at least we shall find reality, sharp peaks and edges of truth. But it turns out to be scene-painting and counterfeit. The only thing grief has taught me is to know how shallow it is. That, like all the rest, plays about the surface, and never introduces me into the reality, for contact with which we would even pay the costly price of sons and lovers. Was it Boscovich[3] who found out that bodies never come in contact? Well, souls never touch their objects. An innavigable sea washes with silent waves between us and the things we aim at and converse with. Grief too will make us idealists. In the death of my son, now more than two years ago, I seem to have lost a beautiful estate,—no more.[4] I cannot get it nearer to me. If to-morrow I should be informed of the bankruptcy of my principal debtors, the loss of my property would be a great inconvenience to me, perhaps, for many years; but it would leave me as it found me,—neither better nor worse. So is it with this calamity; it does not touch me; something which I fancied was a part of me, which could not be torn away without tearing me nor enlarged without enriching me, falls off from me and leaves no scar. It was caducous. I grieve that grief can teach me nothing, nor carry me one step into real nature. The Indian[5] who was laid under a curse that the wind should not blow on him, nor water flow to him, nor fire burn him, is a type of us all. The dearest events are summer-rain, and we the Para coats that shed every drop. Nothing is left us now but death. We look to that with a grim satisfaction, saying, There at least is reality that will not dodge us.

I take this evanescence and lubricity of all objects, which lets them slip through our fingers then when we clutch hardest, to be the most unhandsome part of our condition. Nature does not like to be observed, and likes that we should be her fools and playmates. We may have the sphere for our cricket-ball, but not a berry for our philosophy. Direct strokes she never gave us power to make; all our blows glance, all our hits are accidents. Our relations to each other are oblique and casual.

Dream delivers us to dream, and there is no end to illusion. Life is a train of moods like a string of beads, and as we pass through them they prove to be many-colored lenses which paint the world their own hue, and each shows only what lies in its focus.

[1] A legend recounted in Plutarch's *Morals*, "Of Isis and Osiris." Hermes won the extra days so that his child by Rhea could be born. The Sun (Rhea's husband) had forbade the child to be born on any day.

[2] Tiraboschi (1731-94), Italian literary historian. Thomas Warton (1728-90), author of *History of English Poetry*. Schlegel: August (1767-1845), who translated Shakespeare into German, or Friedrich (1772-1829) who wrote on German literature and Hindu poetry.

[3] Guiseppe Boscovich (1711-87), Serbo-Croatian astronomer and mathematician; one of the first to adopt Newton's gravitational theory.

[4] Waldo Emerson, his father's first child, died in 1842 at the age of five.

[5] In Robert Southey's *The Curse of Kehama*.

From the mountain you see the mountain. We animate what we can, and we see only what we animate. Nature and books belong to the eyes that see them. It depends on the mood of the man whether he shall see the sunset or the fine poem. There are always sunsets, and there is always genius; but only a few hours so serene that we can relish nature or criticism. The more or less depends on structure or temperament. Temperament is the iron wire on which the beads are strung. Of what use is fortune or talent to a cold and defective nature? Who cares what sensibility or discrimination a man has at some time shown, if he falls asleep in his chair? or if he laugh and giggle? or if he apologize? or is infected with egotism? or thinks of his dollar? or cannot go by food? or has gotten a child in his boyhood? Of what use is genius, if the organ is too convex or too concave and cannot find a focal distance within the actual horizon of human life? Of what use, if the brain is too cold or too hot, and the man does not care enough for results to stimulate him to experiment, and hold him up in it? or if the web is too finely woven, too irritable by pleasure and pain, so that life stagnates from too much reception without due outlet? Of what use to make heroic vows of amendment, if the same old law-breaker is to keep them? What cheer can the religious sentiment yield, when that is suspected to be secretly dependent on the seasons of the year and the state of the blood? I knew a witty physician who found the creed in the biliary duct, and used to affirm that if there was disease in the liver, the man became a Calvinist, and if that organ was sound, he became a Unitarian. Very mortifying is the reluctant experience that some unfriendly excess or imbecility neutralizes the promise of genius. We see young men who owe us a new world, so readily and lavishly they promise, but they never acquit the debt; they die young and dodge the account; or if they live they lose themselves in the crowd.

Temperament also enters fully into the system of illusions and shuts us in a prison of glass which we cannot see. There is an optical illusion about every person we meet. In truth they are all creatures of given temperament, which will appear in a given character, whose boundaries they will never pass; but we look at them, they seem alive, and we presume there is impulse in them. In the moment it seems impulse; in the year, in the lifetime, it turns out to be a certain uniform tune which the revolving barrel of the music-box must play. Men resist the conclusion in the morning, but adopt it as the evening wears on, that temper prevails over everything of time, place and condition, and is inconsumable in the flames of religion. Some modifications the moral sentiment avails to impose, but the individual texture holds its dominion, if not to bias the moral judgments, yet to fix the measure of activity and of enjoyment.

I thus express the law as it is read from the platform of ordinary life, but must not leave it without noticing the capital exception. For temperament is a power which no man willingly hears any one praise but himself. On the platform of physics we cannot resist the contracting influences of so-called science. Temperament puts all divinity to rout. I know the mental proclivity of physicians. I hear the chuckle of the phrenologists. Theoretic kidnappers and slave-drivers, they esteem each man the victim of another, who winds him round his finger by knowing the law of his being; and, by such cheap signboards as the color of his beard or the slope of his occiput, reads the inventory of his fortunes and character. The grossest ignorance does not disgust like this impudent knowingness. The physicians say they are not materialists; but they are:—Spirit is matter reduced to an extreme thinness: O *so* thin!—But the definition of *spiritual* should be, *that which is its own evidence*. What notions do they attach to love! what to religion! One would not willingly pronounce these words in their hearing, and give them the occasion to profane them. I saw a gracious gentleman who adapts his conversation to the form of the head of the man he talks with! I had fancied that the value of life lay in its inscrutable possibilities; in the fact that I never know, in addressing myself to a new individual, what may befall me. I carry the keys of my castle in my hand, ready to throw them at the feet of my lord, whenever and in what disguise soever he shall appear. I know he is in the neighborhood, hidden among vagabonds. Shall I preclude my future by taking a high seat and kindly adapting my conversation to the shape of heads? When I come to that, the doctors shall buy me for a cent.—"But, sir, medical history; the report to the Institute; the proven facts!"—I distrust the facts and the inferences. Temperament is the veto or limitation-power in the constitution, very justly applied to restrain an opposite excess in the constitution, but absurdly offered as a bar to original equity. When virtue is in presence, all subordinate powers sleep. On its own level, or in view of nature, temperament is final. I see not, if one be once caught in this trap of so-called sciences, any escape for the man from the links of the chain of physical necessity. Given such an embryo, such a history must follow. On this platform one lives in a sty of sensualism, and would soon come to suicide. But it is impossible that the creative power should exclude itself. Into every intelligence there is a door which is never closed, through which the creator passes. The intellect, seeker of absolute truth, or the heart, lover of absolute good, intervenes for our succor, and at one whisper of these high powers we awake from ineffectual struggles with this nightmare. We hurl it into its own hell, and cannot again contract ourselves to so base a state.

The secret of the illusoriness is in the necessity of a succession of moods or objects. Gladly we would anchor, but the anchorage is quicksand. This onward trick of nature is too strong for us: *Pero si muove.*[6] When at night I look at the moon and stars, I seem stationary, and they to hurry. Our love of the real draws us to permanence, but health of body consists in circulation, and sanity of mind in variety or facility of association. We need change of objects. Dedication to one thought is quickly odious. We house with the insane, and must humor them; then conversation dies out. Once I took such delight in Montaigne that I thought I should not need any other book; before that, in Shakspeare; then in Plutarch; then in Plotinus; at one time in Bacon; afterwards in Goethe; even in Bettine; but now I turn the pages of either of them languidly, whilst I still cherish their genius. So with pictures; each will bear an emphasis of attention once, which it cannot retain, though we fain would continue to be pleased in that manner. How strongly I have felt of pictures that when you have seen one well, you must take your leave of it; you shall never see it again. I have had good lessons from pictures which I have since seen without emotion or remark. A deduction must be made from the opinion which even the wise express on a new book or occurrence. Their opinion gives me tidings of their mood, and some vague guess at the new fact, but is nowise to be trusted as the lasting relation between that intellect and that thing. The child asks, "Mamma, why don't I like the story as well as when you told it me yesterday?" Alas! child, it is even so with the oldest cherubim of knowledge. But will it answer thy question to say, Because thou wert born to a whole and this story is a particular? The reason of the pain this discovery causes us (and we make it late in respect to works of art and intellect) is the plaint of tragedy which murmurs from it in regard to persons, to friendship and love.

That immobility and absence of elasticity which we find in the arts, we find with more pain in the artist. There is no power of expansion in men. Our friends early appear to us as representatives of certain ideas which they never pass or exceed. They stand on the brink of the ocean of thought and power, but they never take the single step that would bring them there. A man is like a bit of Labrador spar, which has no lustre as you turn it in your hand until you come to a particular angle; then it shows deep and beautiful colors. There is no adaptation or universal applicability in men, but each has his special talent, and the mastery of successful men consists in adroitly keeping themselves where and when that turn shall be oftenest to be practised. We do what we must, and call it by the best names we can, and would fain have the praise of having intended the result which ensues. I cannot recall any form of man who is not superfluous sometimes. But is not this pitiful? Life is not worth the taking, to do tricks in.

Of course it needs the whole society to give the symmetry we seek. The party-colored wheel must revolve very fast to appear white. Something is earned too by conversing with so much folly and defect. In fine, whoever loses, we are always of the gaining party. Divinity is behind our failures and follies also. The plays of children are nonsense, but very educative nonsense. So it is with the largest and solemnest things, with commerce, government, church, marriage, and so with the history of every man's bread, and the ways by which he is to come by it. Like a bird which alights nowhere, but hops perpetually from bough to bough, is the Power which abides in no man and in no woman, but for a moment speaks from this one, and for another moment from that one.

But what help from these fineries or pedantries? What help from thought? Life is not dialectics. We, I think, in these times, have had lessons enough of the futility of criticism. Our young people have thought and written much on labor and reform, and for all that they have written, neither the world nor themselves have got on a step. Intellectual tasting of life will not supersede muscular activity. If a man should consider the nicety of the passage of a piece of bread down his throat, he would starve. At Education Farm[7] the noblest theory of life sat on the noblest figures of young men and maidens, quite powerless and melancholy. It would not rake or pitch a ton of hay; it would not rub down a horse; and the men and maidens it left pale and hungry. A political orator wittily compared our party promises to western roads, which opened stately enough, with planted trees on either side to tempt the traveller, but soon became narrow and narrower and ended in a squirrel-track and ran up a tree. So does culture with us; it ends in headache. Unspeakably sad and barren does life look to those who a few months ago were dazzled with the splendor of the promise of

[6] "Still, it moves."

[7] Brook Farm (1841–47), a communal-living experiment with which Emerson sympathized during its early years.

the times. "There is now no longer any right course of action nor any self-devotion left among the Iranis."[8] Objections and criticism we have had our fill of. There are objections to every course of life and action, and the practical wisdom infers an indifferency, from the omnipresence of objection. The whole frame of things preaches indifferency. Do not craze yourself with thinking, but go about your business anywhere. Life is not intellectual or critical, but sturdy. Its chief good is for well-mixed people who can enjoy what they find, without question. Nature hates peeping, our mothers speak her very sense when they say, "Children, eat your victuals, and say no more of it." To fill the hour,—that is happiness; to fill the hour and leave no crevice for a repentance or an approval. We live amid surfaces, and the true art of life is to skate well on them. Under the oldest mouldiest conventions a man of native force prospers just as well as in the newest world, and that by skill of handling and treatment. He can take hold anywhere. Life itself is a mixture of power and form, and will not bear the least excess of either. To finish the moment, to find the journey's end in every step of the road, to live the greatest number of good hours, is wisdom. It is not the part of men, but of fanatics, or of mathematicians if you will, to say that, the shortness of life considered, it is not worth caring whether for so short a duration we were sprawling in want or sitting high. Since our office is with moments, let us husband them. Five minutes of to-day are worth as much to me as five minutes in the next millennium. Let us be poised, and wise, and our own, to-day. Let us treat the men and women well; treat them as if they were real; perhaps they are. Men live in their fancy, like drunkards whose hands are too soft and tremulous for successful labor. It is a tempest of fancies, and the only ballast I know is a respect to the present hour. Without any shadow of doubt, amidst this vertigo of shows and politics, I settle myself ever the firmer in the creed that we should not postpone and refer and wish, but do broad justice where we are, by whomsoever we deal with, accepting our actual companions and circumstances, however humble or odious, as the mystic officials to whom the universe has delegated its whole pleasure for us. If these are mean and malignant, their contentment, which is the last victory of justice, is a more satisfying echo to the heart than the voice of poets and the casual sympathy of admirable persons. I think that however a thoughtful man may suffer from the defects and absurdities of his company, he cannot without affectation deny to any set of men and women a sensibility to extraordinary merit. The coarse and frivolous have an instinct of superiority, if they have not a sympathy, and honor it in their blind capricious way with sincere homage.

The fine young people despise life, but in me, and in such as with me are free from dyspepsia, and to whom a day is a sound and solid good, it is a great excess of politeness to look scornful and to cry for company. I am grown by sympathy a little eager and sentimental, but leave me alone and I should relish every hour and what it brought me, the potluck of the day, as heartily as the oldest gossip in the barroom. I am thankful for small mercies. I compared notes with one of my friends who expects everything of the universe and is disappointed when anything is less than the best, and I found that I begin at the other extreme, expecting nothing, and am always full of thanks for moderate goods. I accept the clangor and jangle of contrary tendencies. I find my account in sots and bores also. They give a reality to the circumjacent picture which such a vanishing meteorous appearance can ill spare. In the morning I awake and find the old world, wife, babes and mother, Concord and Boston, the dear old spiritual world and even the dear old devil not far off. If we will take the good we will find, asking no questions, we shall have heaping measures. The great gifts are not got by analysis. Everything good is on the highway. The middle region of our being is the temperate zone. We may climb into the thin and cold realm of pure geometry and lifeless science, or sink into that of sensation. Between these extremes is the equator of life, of thought, of spirit, of poetry,—a narrow belt. Moreover, in popular experience everything good is on the highway. A collector peeps into all the picture-shops of Europe for a landscape of Poussin,[9] a crayon-sketch of Salvator;[10] but the Transfiguration, the Last Judgment, the Communion of Saint Jerome, and what are as transcendent as these, are on the walls of the Vatican, the Uffizi, or the Louvre, where every footman may see them; to say nothing of Nature's pictures in every street, of sunsets and sunrises every day, and the sculpture of the human body never absent. A collector recently bought at public auction, in London, for one hundred and fifty-seven guineas, an autograph of Shakspeare; but for nothing a school-boy can read Hamlet and can detect secrets of highest concernment yet unpublished therein. I think I will never read any but the commonest books,—the Bible, Homer, Dante, Shakspeare and Milton. Then we are impatient of so public a life and planet, and run

[8] Quoted from the *Desatir,* presumably a collection of the writings of ancient Persian prophets, including Zoroaster (Whicher, *Selections,* n. 492).

[9] (1593/94—1665), great French painter of the 17th century; exponent of pictorial classicism.

[10] Salvator Rosa (1615-73), Italian painter known for his wild landscapes and battle scenes.

hither and thither for nooks and secrets. The imagination delights in the woodcraft of Indians, trappers and bee-hunters. We fancy that we are strangers, and not so intimately domesticated in the planet as the wild man and the wild beast and bird. But the exclusion reaches them also; reaches the climbing, flying, gliding, feathered and fourfooted man. Fox and woodchuck, hawk and snipe and bittern, when nearly seen, have no more root in the deep world than man, and are just such superficial tenants of the globe. Then the new molecular philosophy shows astronomical interspaces betwixt atom and atom, shows that the world is all outside; it has no inside.

The mid-world is best. Nature, as we know her, is no saint. The lights of the church, the ascetics, Gentoos and corn-eaters, she does not distinguish by any favor. She comes eating and drinking and sinning. Her darlings, the great, the strong, the beautiful, are not children of our law; do not come out of the Sunday School, nor weigh their food, nor punctually keep the commandments. If we will be strong with her strength we must not harbor such disconsolate consciences, borrowed too from the consciences of other nations. We must set up the strong present tense against all the rumors of wrath, past or to come. So many things are unsettled which it is of the first importance to settle;—and, pending their settlement, we will do as we do. Whilst the debate goes forward on the equity of commerce, and will not be closed for a century or two, New and Old England may keep shop. Law of copyright and international copyright is to be discussed, and in the interim we will sell our books for the most we can. Expediency of literature, reason of literature, lawfulness of writing down a thought, is questioned; much is to say on both sides, and, while the fight waxes hot, thou, dearest scholar, stick to thy foolish task, add a line every hour, and between whiles add a line. Right to hold land, right of property, is disputed, and the conventions convene, and before the vote is taken, dig away in your garden, and spend your earnings as a waif or godsend to all serene and beautiful purposes. Life itself is a bubble and a scepticism, and a sleep within a sleep. Grant it, and as much more as they will,—but thou, God's darling! heed thy private dream; thou wilt not be missed in the scorning and scepticism; there are enough of them; stay there in thy closet and toil until the rest are agreed what to do about it. Thy sickness, they say, and thy puny habit require that thou do this or avoid that, but know that thy life is a flitting state, a tent for a night, and do thou, sick or well, finish that stint. Thou art sick, but shalt not be worse, and the universe, which holds thee dear, shall be the better.

Human life is made up of the two elements, power and form, and the proportion must be invariably kept if we would have it sweet and sound. Each of these elements in excess makes a mischief as hurtful as its defect. Everything runs to excess; every good quality is noxious if unmixed, and, to carry the danger to the edge of ruin, nature causes each man's peculiarity to superabound. Here, among the farms, we adduce the scholars as examples of this treachery. They are nature's victims of expression. You who see the artist, the orator, the poet, too near, and find their life no more excellent than that of mechanics or farmers, and themselves victims of partiality, very hollow and haggard, and pronounce them failures, not heroes, but quacks,—conclude very reasonably that these arts are not for man, but are disease. Yet nature will not bear you out. Irresistible nature made men such, and makes legions more of such, every day. You love the boy reading in a book, gazing at a drawing or a cast; yet what are those millions who read and behold, but incipient writers and sculptors? Add a little more of that quality which now reads and sees, and they will seize the pen and chisel. And if one remembers how innocently he began to be an artist, he perceives that nature joined with his enemy. A man is a golden impossibility. The line he must walk is a hair's breadth. The wise through excess of wisdom is made a fool.

How easily, if fate would suffer it, we might keep forever these beautiful limits, and adjust ourselves, once for all, to the perfect calculation of the kingdom of known cause and effect. In the street and in the newspapers, life appears so plain a business that manly resolution and adherence to the multiplication-table through all weathers will insure success. But ah! presently comes a day, or is it only a half-hour, with its angel-whispering,—which discomfits the conclusions of nations and of years! To-morrow again every thing looks real and angular, the habitual standards are reinstated, common-sense is as rare as genius,—is the basis of genius, and experience is hands and feet to every enterprise;—and yet, he who should do his business on this understanding would be quickly bankrupt. Power keeps quite another road than the turnpikes of choice and will; namely the subterranean and invisible tunnels and channels of life. It is ridiculous that we are diplomatists, and doctors, and considerate people; there are no dupes like these. Life is a series of surprises, and would not be worth taking or keeping if it were not. God delights to isolate us every day, and hide from us the past and the future. We would look about us, but with grand politeness he draws down before us an impenetrable screen of purest sky, and another behind us of purest sky. "You will not remember," he seems to say, "and you will not expect." All good conversation, manners and action come from a spontaneity which forgets usages and makes the moment great. Nature hates calculators; her methods are saltatory and impulsive. Man lives by pulses; our organic movements are such; and the chemical and ethereal agents are undulatory and alternate; and the mind goes antagonizing on, and never prospers but by fits. We thrive by casualties. Our chief experiences have been casual. The most attractive class of people are those who are powerful obliquely and not by the direct stroke; men of genius, but not yet accredited; one gets the cheer of their light without paying too great a tax. Theirs is the beauty of the bird or the morning light, and not of art. In the thought of genius there is always a surprise; and the moral sentiment is well called "the newness," for it is never other; as new to the oldest intelligence as to the young child;—"the kingdom that cometh without observation."[11] In like manner, for practical success, there must not be too much design. A man will not be observed in doing that which he can do best. There is a certain magic about his properest action which stupefies your powers of observation, so that though it is done before you, you wist not of it. The art of life has a pudency, and will not be exposed. Every man is an impossibility until he is born; every thing impossible until we see a success. The ardors of piety agree at last with the coldest scepticism,—that nothing is of us or our works,—that all is of God. Nature will not spare us the smallest leaf of laurel. All writing comes by the grace of God, and all doing and having. I would gladly be moral and keep due metes and bounds, which I dearly love, and allow the most to the will of man; but I have set my heart on honesty in this chapter, and I can see nothing at last, in success or failure, than more or less of vital force supplied from the Eternal. The results of life are uncalculated and uncalculable. The years teach much which the days never know. The persons who compose our company converse, and come and go, and design and execute many things, and somewhat comes of it all, but an unlooked-for result. The individual is always mistaken. He designed many things, and drew in other persons as coadjutors, quarrelled with some or all, blundered much, and something is done; all are a little advanced, but the individual is always mistaken. It turns out somewhat new and very unlike what he promised himself.

The ancients, struck with this irreducibleness of the elements of human life to calculation, exalted Chance into a divinity; but that is to stay too long at the spark, which glitters truly at one point, but the universe is warm with the latency of the same fire. The miracle of life which will not be expounded but will remain a miracle, introduces a new element. In the growth of the embryo, Sir Everard Home[12] I think noticed that the evolution was not from one central point, but coactive from three or more points. Life has no memory. That which proceeds in succession might be remembered, but that which is coexistent, or ejaculated from a deeper cause, as yet far from being conscious, knows not its own tendency. So is it with us, now sceptical or without unity, because immersed in forms and effects all seeming to be of equal yet hostile value, and now religious, whilst in the reception of spiritual law. Bear with these distractions, with this coetaneous growth of the parts; they will one day be *members*, and obey one will. On that one will, on that secret cause, they nail our attention and hope. Life is hereby melted into an expectation or a religion. Underneath the inharmonious and trivial particulars, is a musical perfection; the Ideal journeying always with us, the heaven without rent or seam. Do but observe the mode of our illumination. When I converse with a profound mind, or if at any time being alone I have good thoughts, I do not at once arrive at satisfactions, as when, being thirsty, I drink water; or go to the fire, being cold; no! but I am at first apprised of my vicinity to a new and excellent region of life. By persisting to read or to think, this region gives further sign of itself, as it were in flashes of light, in sudden discoveries of its profound beauty and repose, as if the clouds that covered it parted at intervals and showed the approaching traveller the inland mountains, with the tranquil eternal meadows spread at their base, whereon flocks graze and shepherds pipe and dance. But every insight from this realm of thought is felt as initial, and promises a sequel. I do not make it; I arrive there, and behold what was there already. I make! O no! I clap my hands in infantine joy and amazement before the first opening to me of this august magnificence, old with the love and homage of innumerable ages, young with the life of life, the sunbright Mecca of the desert. And what a future it opens! I feel a new heart beating with the love of the new beauty. I am ready to die out of nature and be born again into this new yet unapproachable America I have found in the West:—

> "Since neither now nor yesterday began
> These thoughts, which have been ever, nor yet can
> A man be found who their first entrance knew."[13]

If I have described life as a flux of moods, I must now add that there is that in us which changes not and which ranks all sensations and states of mind.

[11] See Luke xvii.20.

[12] A Scottish surgeon (1756–1832).

[13] From Sophocles' *Antigone*.

The consciousness in each man is a sliding scale, which identifies him now with the First Cause, and now with the flesh of his body; life above life, in infinite degrees. The sentiment from which it sprung determines the dignity of any deed, and the question ever is, not what you have done or forborne, but at whose command you have done or forborne it.

Fortune, Minerva, Muse, Holy Ghost,—these are quaint names, too narrow to cover this unbounded substance. The baffled intellect must still kneel before this cause, which refuses to be named,—ineffable cause, which every fine genius has essayed to represent by some emphatic symbol, as, Thales by water, Anaximenes by air, Anaxagoras by (Νοῦς) thought, Zoroaster by fire, Jesus and the moderns by love; and the metaphor of each has become a national religion. The Chinese Mencius has not been the least successful in his generalization. "I fully understand language," he said, "and nourish well my vast-flowing vigor."—"I beg to ask what you call vast-flowing vigor?" said his companion. "The explanation," replied Mencius, "is difficult. This vigor is supremely great, and in the highest degree unbending. Nourish it correctly and do it no injury, and it will fill up the vacancy between heaven and earth. This vigor accords with and assists justice and reason, and leaves no hunger."—In our more correct writing we give to this generalization the name of Being, and thereby confess that we have arrived as far as we can go. Suffice it for the joy of the universe that we have not arrived at a wall, but at interminable oceans. Our life seems not present so much as prospective; not for the affairs on which it is wasted, but as a hint of this vast-flowing vigor. Most of life seems to be mere advertisement of faculty; information is given us not to sell ourselves cheap; that we are very great. So, in particulars, our greatness is always in a tendency or direction, not in an action. It is for us to believe in the rule, not in the exception. The noble are thus known from the ignoble. So in accepting the leading of the sentiments, it is not what we believe concerning the immortality of the soul or the like, but *the universal impulse to believe*, that is the material circumstance and is the principal fact in the history of the globe. Shall we describe this cause as that which works directly? The spirit is not helpless or needful of mediate organs. It has plentiful powers and direct effects. I am explained without explaining, I am felt without acting, and where I am not. Therefore all just persons are satisfied with their own praise. They refuse to explain themselves, and are content that new actions should do them that office. They believe that we communicate without speech and above speech, and that no right action of ours is quite unaffecting to our friends, at whatever distance; for the influence of action is not to be measured by miles. Why should I fret myself because a circumstance has occurred which hinders my presence where I was expected? If I am not at the meeting, my presence where I am should be as useful to the commonwealth of friendship and wisdom, as would be my presence in that place. I exert the same quality of power in all places. Thus journeys the mighty Ideal before us; it never was known to fall into the rear. No man ever came to an experience which was satiating, but his good is tidings of a better. Onward and onward! In liberated moments we know that a new picture of life and duty is already possible; the elements already exist in many minds around you of a doctrine of life which shall transcend any written record we have. The new statement will comprise the scepticisms as well as the faiths of society, and out of unbeliefs a creed shall be formed. For scepticisms are not gratuitous or lawless, but are limitations of the affirmative statement, and the new philosophy must take them in and make affirmations outside of them, just as much as it must include the oldest beliefs.

It is very unhappy, but too late to be helped, the discovery we have made that we exist. That discovery is called the Fall of Man. Ever afterwards we suspect our instruments. We have learned that we do not see directly, but mediately, and that we have no means of correcting these colored and distorting lenses which we are, or of computing the amount of their errors. Perhaps these subject-lenses have a creative power; perhaps there are no objects. Once we lived in what we saw; now, the rapaciousness of this new power, which threatens to absorb all things, engages us. Nature, art, persons, letters, religions, objects, successively tumble in, and God is but one of its ideas. Nature and literature are subjective phenomena; every evil and every good thing is a shadow which we cast. The street is full of humiliations to the proud. As the fop contrived to dress his bailiffs in his livery and make them wait on his guests at table, so the chagrins which the bad heart gives off as bubbles, at once take form as ladies and gentlemen in the street, shopmen or barkeepers in hotels, and threaten or insult whatever is threatenable and insultable in us. 'Tis the same with our idolatries. People forget that it is the eye which makes the horizon, and the rounding mind's eye which makes this or that man a type or representative of humanity, with the name of hero or saint. Jesus, the "providential man," is a good man on whom many people are agreed that these optical laws shall take effect. By love on one part and by forbearance to press objection on the other part, it is for a time settled that we will look at him in the centre of the horizon, and ascribe to him the properties that will attach to any man so seen. But the longest love or aversion has a speedy term. The great and crescive self, rooted in absolute nature, supplants all relative existence and ruins the kingdom of mortal friendship and love. Marriage (in what is called the spiritual world) is impossible, because of the inequality between every subject and every object. The subject is the receiver of Godhead, and at every comparison must feel his being enhanced by that cryptic might. Though not in energy, yet by presence, this magazine of substance cannot be otherwise than felt; nor can any force of intellect attribute to the object the proper deity which sleeps or wakes forever in every subject. Never can love make consciousness and ascription equal in force. There will be the same gulf between every me and thee as between the original and the picture. The universe is the bride of the soul. All private sympathy is partial. Two human beings are like globes, which can touch only in a point, and whilst they remain in contact all other points of each of the spheres are inert; their turn must also come, and the longer a particular union lasts the more energy of appetency the parts not in union acquire.

Life will be imaged, but cannot be divided nor doubled. Any invasion of its unity would be chaos. The soul is not twin-born but the only begotten, and though revealing itself as child in time, child in appearance, is of a fatal and universal power, admitting no co-life. Every day, every act betrays the ill-concealed deity. We believe in ourselves as we do not believe in others. We permit all things to ourselves, and that which we call sin in others is experiment for us. It is an instance of our faith in ourselves that men never speak of crime as lightly as they think; or every man thinks a latitude safe for himself which is nowise to be indulged to another. The act looks very differently on the inside and on the outside; in its quality and in its consequences. Murder in the murderer is no such ruinous thought as poets and romancers will have it; it does not unsettle him or fright him from his ordinary notice of trifles; it is an act quite easy to be contemplated; but in its sequel it turns out to be a horrible jangle and confounding of all relations. Especially the crimes that spring from love seem right and fair from the actor's point of view, but when acted are found destructive of society. No man at last believes that he can be lost, or that the crime in him is as black as in the felon. Because the intellect qualifies in our own case the moral judgments. For there is no crime to the intellect. That is antinomian or hypernomian, and judges law as well as fact. "It is worse than a crime, it is a blunder," said Napoleon, speaking the language of the intellect. To it, the world is a problem in mathematics or the science of quantity, and it leaves out praise and blame and all weak emotions. All stealing is comparative. If you come to absolutes, pray who does not steal? Saints are sad, because they behold sin (even when they speculate) from the point of view of the conscience, and not of the intellect; a confusion of thought. Sin, seen from the thought, is a diminution, or *less;* seen from the conscience or will, it is pravity or *bad.* The intellect names it shade, absence of light, and no essence. The conscience must feel it as essence, essential evil. This it is not; it has an objective existence, but no subjective.

Thus inevitably does the universe wear our color, and every object fall successively into the subject itself. The subject exists, the subject enlarges; all things sooner or later fall into place. As I am, so I see; use what language we will, we can never say anything but what we are; Hermes, Cadmus, Columbus, Newton, Bonaparte, are the mind's ministers. Instead of feeling a poverty when we encounter a great man, let us treat the new-comer like a travelling geologist who passes through our estate and shows us good slate, or limestone, or anthracite, in our brush pasture. The partial action of each strong mind in one direction is a telescope for the objects on which it is pointed. But every other part of knowledge is to be pushed to the same extravagance, ere the soul attains her due sphericity. Do you see that kitten chasing so prettily her own tail? If you could look with her eyes you might see her surrounded with hundreds of figures performing complex dramas, with tragic and comic issues, long conversations, many characters, many ups and downs of fate,—and meantime it is only puss and her tail. How long before our masquerade will end its noise of tambourines, laughter and shouting, and we shall find it was a solitary performance? A subject and an object,—it takes so much to make the galvanic circuit complete, but magnitude adds nothing. What imports it whether it is Kepler and the sphere, Columbus and America, a reader and his book, or puss with her tail?

It is true that all the muses and love and religion hate these developments, and will find a way to punish the chemist who publishes in the parlor the secrets of the laboratory. And we cannot say too little of our constitutional necessity of seeing things under private aspects, or saturated with our humors. And yet is the God the native of these bleak rocks. That need makes in morals the capital virtue of self-trust. We must hold hard to this poverty, however scandalous, and by more vigorous self-recoveries, after the sallies of action, possess our axis more firmly. The life of truth is cold and so far mournful; but it is not the slave of tears, contritions and perturbations. It does not attempt another's work, nor adopt another's facts. It is a main lesson of wisdom to know your own from another's. I have learned that I cannot dispose of other people's facts; but I possess such a key to my own as persuades me, against all their denials, that they also have a key to theirs. A sympathetic person is placed in the dilemma of a swimmer among drowning men, who all catch at him, and if he give so much as a leg or finger they will drown him. They wish to be saved from the mischiefs of their vices, but not from their vices. Charity would be wasted on this poor waiting on the symptoms. A wise and hardy physician will say, *Come out of that*, as the first condition of advice.

In this our talking America we are ruined by our good nature and listening on all sides. This compliance takes away the power of being greatly useful. A man should not be able to look other than directly and forthright. A preoccupied attention is the only answer to the importunate frivolity of other people; an attention, and to an aim which makes their wants frivolous. This is a divine answer, and leaves no appeal and no hard thoughts. In Flaxman's[14] drawing of the Eumenides of Aeschylus, Orestes supplicates Apollo, whilst the Furies sleep on the threshold. The face of the god expresses a shade of regret and compassion, but is calm with the conviction of the irreconcilableness of the two spheres. He is born into other politics, into the eternal and beautiful. The man at his feet asks for his interest in turmoils of the earth, into which his nature cannot enter. And the Eumenides there lying express pictorially this disparity. The god is surcharged with his divine destiny.

Illusion, Temperament, Succession, Surface, Surprise, Reality, Subjectiveness—these are threads on the loom of time, these are the lords of life. I dare not assume to give their order, but I name them as I find them in my way. I know better than to claim any completeness for my picture. I am a fragment, and this is a fragment of me. I can very confidently announce one or another law, which throws itself into relief and form, but I am too young yet by some ages to compile a code. I gossip for my hour concerning the eternal politics. I have seen many fair pictures not in vain. A wonderful time I have lived in. I am not the novice I was fourteen, nor yet seven years ago. Let who will ask, Where is the fruit? I find a private fruit sufficient. This is a fruit,—that I should not ask for a rash effect from meditations, counsels and the hiving of truths. I should feel it pitiful to demand a result on this town and county, an overt effect on the instant month and year. The effect is deep and secular as the cause. It works on periods in which mortal lifetime is lost. All I know is reception; I am and I have: but I do not get, and when I have fancied I had gotten anything, I found I did not. I worship with wonder the great Fortune. My reception has been so large, that I am not annoyed by receiving this or that superabundantly. I say to the Genius, if he will pardon the proverb, *In for a mill, in for a million.* When I receive a new gift, I do not macerate my body to make the account square, for if I should die I could not make the account square. The benefit overran the merit the first day, and has overrun the merit ever since. The merit itself, so-called, I reckon part of the receiving.

Also that hankering after an overt or practical effect seems to me an apostasy. In good earnest I am willing to spare this most unnecessary deal of doing. Life wears to me a visionary face. Hardest roughest action is visionary also. It is but a choice between soft and turbulent dreams. People disparage knowing and the intellectual life, and urge doing. I am very content with knowing, if only I could know. That is an august entertainment, and would suffice me a great while. To know a little would be worth the expense of this world. I hear always the law of Adrastia,[15] "that every soul which had acquired any truth, should be safe from harm until another period."

I know that the world I converse with in the city and in the farms, is not the world I *think*. I observe that difference, and shall observe it. One day I shall know the value and law of this discrepance. But I have not found that much was gained by manipular attempts to realize the world of thought. Many eager persons successively make an experiment in this way, and make themselves ridiculous. They acquire democratic manners, they foam at the mouth, they hate and deny. Worse, I observe that in the history of mankind there is never a solitary example of success,—taking their own tests of success. I say this polemically, or in reply to the inquiry, Why not realize your world? But far be from me the despair which prejudges the law by a paltry empiricism;—since there never was a right endeavor but it succeeded. Patience and patience, we shall win at the last. We must be very suspicious of the deceptions of the element of time. It takes a good deal of time to eat or to sleep, or to earn a hundred dollars, and a very little time to entertain a hope and an insight which becomes the light of our life. We dress our garden, eat our dinners, discuss the household with

[14] John Flaxman (1755-1826), English sculptor and draftsman.

[15] Nemesis or Destiny: Greek goddess of retributive justice. The law of Destiny saves only those described in the quote. Emerson paraphrased Plato's *Phaedrus* (Centenary Edition, III, p. 309).

our wives, and these things make no impression, are forgotten next week; but, in the solitude to which every man is always returning, he has a sanity and revelations which in his passage into new worlds he will carry with him. Never mind the ridicule, never mind the defeat; up again, old heart!—it seems to say,—there is victory yet for all justice; and the true romance which the world exists to realize will be the transformation of genius into practical power.

1844

Thoreau

"It was a pleasure and a privilege to walk with him," said Emerson of his Concord friend, fourteen years his junior. The rest of the Emerson family enjoyed him when, at times, he lived in the household, and he enjoyed them. Soon after his death, he was the subject of this engaging prose portrait, one of the best essays ever written on Thoreau.

Henry David Thoreau was the last male descendant of a French ancestor who came to this country from the Isle of Guernsey. His character exhibited occasional traits drawn from this blood, in singular combination with a very strong Saxon genius.

He was born in Concord, Massachusetts, on the 12th of July, 1817. He was graduated at Harvard College in 1837, but without any literary distinction. An iconoclast in literature, he seldom thanked colleges for their service to him, holding them in small esteem, whilst yet his debt to them was important. After leaving the University, he joined his brother in teaching a private school, which he soon renounced. His father was a manufacturer of lead-pencils, and Henry applied himself for a time to this craft, believing he could make a better pencil than was then in use. After completing his experiments, he exhibited his work to chemists and artists in Boston, and having obtained their certificates to its excellence and to its equality with the best London manufacture, he returned home contented. His friends congratulated him that he had now opened his way to fortune. But he replied that he should never make another pencil. "Why should I? I would not do again what I have done once." He resumed his endless walks and miscellaneous studies, making every day some new acquaintance with Nature, though as yet never speaking of zoölogy or botany, since, though very studious of natural facts, he was incurious of technical and textual science.

At this time, a strong, healthy youth, fresh from college, whilst all his companions were choosing their profession, or eager to begin some lucrative employment, it was inevitable that his thoughts should be exercised on the same question, and it required rare decision to refuse all the accustomed paths and keep his solitary freedom at the cost of disappointing the natural expectations of his family and friends: all the more difficult that he had a perfect probity, was exact in securing his own independence, and in holding every man to the like duty. But Thoreau never faltered. He was a born protestant. He declined to give up his large ambition of knowledge and action for any narrow craft or profession, aiming at a much more comprehensive calling, the art of living well. If he slighted and defied the opinions of others, it was only that he was more intent to reconcile his practice with his own belief. Never idle or self-indulgent, he preferred, when he wanted money, earning it by some piece of manual labor agreeable to him, as building a boat or a fence, planting, grafting, surveying, or other short work, to any long engagements. With his hardy habits and few wants, his skill in wood-craft, and his powerful arithmetic, he was very competent to live in any part of the world. It would cost him less time to supply his wants than another. He was therefore secure of his leisure.

A natural skill for mensuration, growing out of his mathematical knowledge and his habit of ascertaining the measures and distances of objects which interested him, the size of trees, the depth and extent of ponds and rivers, the height of mountains, and the air-line distance of his favorite summits,—this, and his intimate knowledge of the territory about Concord, made him drift into the profession of land-surveyor. It had the advantage for him that it led him continually into new and secluded grounds, and helped his studies of Nature. His accuracy and skill in this work were readily appreciated, and he found all the employment he wanted.

He could easily solve the problems of the surveyor, but he was daily beset with graver questions, which he manfully confronted. He interrogated every custom, and wished to settle all his practice on an ideal foundation. He was a protestant *à outrance,*[1] and few lives contain so many renunciations. He was bred to no profession; he never married; he lived alone; he never went to church; he never voted; he refused to pay a tax to the State; he ate no flesh, he drank no wine, he never knew the use of tobacco; and, though a naturalist, he used neither trap nor gun. He chose, wisely no doubt for himself, to be the bachelor of thought and Nature. He had no talent for wealth, and knew how to be poor without the least hint of squalor or inelegance. Perhaps he fell into his way of living without forecasting it much, but approved it with later wisdom. "I am often reminded," he wrote in his journal, "that if I had bestowed on me the wealth of Croe-

[1] To the limit.

sus, my aims must be still the same, and my means essentially the same." He had no temptations to fight against,—no appetites, no passions, no taste for elegant trifles. A fine house, dress, the manners and talk of highly cultivated people, were all thrown away on him. He much preferred a good Indian, and considered these refinements as impediments to conversation, wishing to meet his companion on the simplest terms. He declined invitations to dinner-parties, because there each was in every one's way, and he could not meet the individuals to any purpose. "They make their pride," he said, "in making their dinner cost much; I make my pride in making my dinner cost little." When asked at table what dish he preferred, he answered, "The nearest." He did not like the taste of wine, and never had a vice in his life. He said, "I have a faint recollection of pleasure derived from smoking dried lily-stems, before I was a man. I had commonly a supply of these. I have never smoked anything more noxious."

He chose to be rich by making his wants few, and supplying them himself. In his travels, he used the railroad only to get over so much country as was unimportant to the present purpose, walking hundreds of miles, avoiding taverns, buying a lodging in farmers' and fishermen's houses, as cheaper, and more agreeable to him, and because there he could better find the men and the information he wanted.

There was somewhat military in his nature, not to be subdued, always manly and able, but rarely tender, as if he did not feel himself except in opposition. He wanted a fallacy to oppose, a blunder to pillory, I may say required a little sense of victory, a roll of the drum, to call his powers into full exercise. It cost him nothing to say No; indeed he found it much easier than to say Yes. It seemed as if his first instinct on hearing a proposition was to controvert it, so impatient was he of the limitations of our daily thought. This habit, of course, is a little chilling to the social affections; and though the companion would in the end acquit him of any malice or untruth, yet it mars conversation. Hence, no equal companion stood in affectionate relations with one so pure and guileless. "I love Henry," said one of his friends, "but I cannot like him; and as for taking his arm, I should as soon think of taking the arm of an elm-tree."[2]

Yet, hermit and stoic as he was, he was really fond of sympathy, and threw himself heartily and childlike into the company of young people whom he loved, and whom he delighted to entertain, as he only could, with the varied and endless anecdotes of his experiences by field and river; and he was always ready to lead a huckleberry-party or a search for chestnuts or grapes. Talking, one day, of a public discourse, Henry remarked that whatever succeeded with the audience was bad. I said, "Who would not like to write something which all can read, like *Robinson Crusoe*? and who does not see with regret that his page is not solid with a right materialistic treatment, which delights everybody?" Henry objected, of course, and vaunted the better lectures which reached only a few persons. But, at supper, a young girl, understanding that he was to lecture at the Lyceum, sharply asked him "whether his lecture would be a nice, interesting story, such as she wished to hear, or whether it was one of those old philosophical things that she did not care about." Henry turned to her, and bethought himself, and, I saw, was trying to believe that he had matter that might fit her and her brother, who were to sit up and go to the lecture, if it was a good one for them.

He was a speaker and actor of the truth, born such, and was ever running into dramatic situations from this cause. In any circumstance it interested all bystanders to know what part Henry would take, and what he would say; and he did not disappoint expectation, but used an original judgment on each emergency. In 1845 he built himself a small framed house on the shores of Walden Pond, and lived there two years alone, a life of labor and study. This action was quite native and fit for him. No one who knew him would tax him with affectation. He was more unlike his neighbors in his thought than in his action. As soon as he had exhausted the advantages of that solitude, he abandoned it. In 1847, not approving some uses to which the public expenditure was applied, he refused to pay his town tax, and was put in jail.[3] A friend paid the tax for him, and he was released. The like annoyance was threatened the next year. But as his friends paid the tax, notwithstanding his protest, I believe he ceased to resist. No opposition or ridicule had any weight with him. He coldly and fully stated his opinion without affecting to believe that it was the opinion of the company. It was of no consequence if every one present held the opposite opinion. On one occasion he went to the University Library to procure some books. The librarian refused to lend them. Mr. Thoreau repaired to the President, who stated to him the rules and usages, which permitted the loan of books to resident graduates, to clergymen who were alumni, and to some others resident within a circle of ten miles' radius from the College. Mr. Thoreau explained to the President that the railroad had destroyed the old scale of distance,—that the library was useless, yes, and President and College useless, on the terms of his rules,—that the one benefit he

[2] Emerson's own remark.

[3] Thoreau opposed the Government on the Mexican War issue.

owed to the College was its library,—that, at this moment, not only his want of books was imperative but he wanted a large number of books, and assured him that he, Thoreau, and not the librarian, was the proper custodian of these. In short, the President found the petitioner so formidable, and the rules getting to look so ridiculous, that he ended by giving him a privilege which in his hands proved unlimited thereafter.

No truer American existed than Thoreau. His preference of his country and condition was genuine, and his aversation from English and European manners and tastes almost reached contempt. He listened impatiently to news or *bon-mots* gleaned from London circles; and though he tried to be civil, these anecdotes fatigued him. The men were all imitating each other, and on a small mould. Why can they not live as far apart as possible, and each be a man by himself? What he sought was the most energetic nature; and he wished to go to Oregon, not to London. "In every part of Great Britain," he wrote in his diary, "are discovered traces of the Romans, their funereal urns, their camps, their dwellings. But New England, at least, is not based on any Roman ruins. We have not to lay the foundations of our houses on the ashes of a former civilization."

But idealist as he was, standing for abolition of slavery, abolition of tariffs, almost for abolition of government, it is needless to say he found himself not only unrepresented in actual politics, but almost equally opposed to every class of reformers. Yet he paid the tribute of his uniform respect to the Anti-Slavery party. One man, whose personal acquaintance he had formed, he honored with exceptional regard. Before the first friendly word had been spoken for Captain John Brown, he sent notices to most houses in Concord that he would speak in a public hall on the condition and character of John Brown, on Sunday evening, and invited all people to come. The Republican Committee, the Abolitionist Committee, sent him word that it was premature and not advisable. He replied,—"I did not send to you for advice, but to announce that I am to speak." The hall was filled at an early hour by people of all parties, and his earnest eulogy of the hero was heard by all respectfully, by many with a sympathy that surprised themselves.[4]

It was said of Plotinus that he was ashamed of his body, and 'tis very likely he had good reason for it,—that his body was a bad servant, and he had not skill in dealing with the material world, as happens often to men of abstract intellect. But Mr. Thoreau was equipped with a most adapted and serviceable body. He was of short stature, firmly built, of light complexion, with strong, serious blue eyes, and a grave aspect,—his face covered in the late years with a becoming beard. His senses were acute, his frame well-knit and hardy, his hands strong and skillful in the use of tools. And there was a wonderful fitness of body and mind. He could pace sixteen rods more accurately than another man could measure them with rod and chain. He could find his path in the woods at night, he said, better by his feet than his eyes. He could estimate the measure of a tree very well by his eye; he could estimate the weight of a calf or a pig, like a dealer. From a box containing a bushel or more of loose pencils, he could take up with his hands fast enough just a dozen pencils at every grasp. He was a good swimmer, runner, skater, boatman, and would probably outwalk most countrymen in a day's journey. And the relation of body to mind was still finer than we have indicated. He said he wanted every stride his legs made. The length of his walk uniformly made the length of his writing. If shut up in the house he did not write at all.

He had a strong common sense, like that which Rose Flammock the weaver's daughter in Scott's romance,[5] commends in her father, as resembling a yardstick, which, whilst it measures dowlas and diaper, can equally well measure tapestry and cloth of gold. He had always a new resource. When I was planting forest trees, and had procured half a peck of acorns, he said that only a small portion of them would be sound, and proceeded to examine them and select the sound ones. But finding this took time, he said, "I think if you put them all into water the good ones will sink"; which experiment we tried with success. He could plan a garden or a house or a barn; would have been competent to lead a "Pacific Exploring Expedition"; could give judicious counsel in the gravest private or public affairs.

He lived for the day, not cumbered and mortified by his memory. If he brought you yesterday a new proposition, he would bring you to-day another not less revolutionary. A very industrious man, and setting, like all highly organized men, a high value on his time, he seemed the only man of leisure in town, always ready for any excursion that promised well, or for conversation prolonged into late hours. His trenchant sense was never stopped by his rules of daily prudence, but was always up to the new occasion. He liked and used the simplest food, yet, when some one urged a vegetable diet, Thoreau thought all diets a very small matter, saying that "the man who shoots the buffalo lives better than the man who boards at the Graham House." He said, "You can sleep near the railroad, and never be disturbed: Nature knows very well what sounds are worth at-

[4] Thoreau presented his defense, after the Harpers Ferry raid, on October 30, 1859.

[5] *The Betrothed* (1825).

tending to, and has made up her mind not to hear the railroad-whistle. But things respect the devout mind, and a mental ecstasy was never interrupted." He noted what repeatedly befell him, that, after receiving from a distance a rare plant, he would presently find the same in his own haunts. And those pieces of luck which happen only to good players happened to him. One day, walking with a stranger, who inquired where Indian arrow-heads could be found, he replied, "Everywhere," and, stooping forward, picked one on the instant from the ground. At Mount Washington, in Tuckerman's Ravine, Thoreau had a bad fall, and sprained his foot. As he was in the act of getting up from his fall, he saw for the first time the leaves of the *Arnica mollis*.[6]

His robust common sense, armed with stout hands, keen perceptions, and strong will, cannot yet account for the superiority which shone in his simple and hidden life. I must add the cardinal fact, that there was excellent wisdom in him, proper to a rare class of men, which showed him the material world as a means and symbol. This discovery, which sometimes yields to poets a certain casual and interrupted light, serving for the ornament of their writing, was in him an unsleeping insight; and whatever faults or obstructions of temperament might cloud it, he was not disobedient to the heavenly vision. In his youth, he said, one day, "The other world is all my art; my pencils will draw no other; my jack-knife will cut nothing else; I do not use it as a means." This was the muse and genius that ruled his opinions, conversation, studies, work and course of life. This made him a searching judge of men. At first glance he measured his companion, and, though insensible to some fine traits of culture, could very well report his weight and caliber. And this made the impression of genius which his conversation sometimes gave.

He understood the matter in hand at a glance, and saw the limitations and poverty of those he talked with, so that nothing seemed concealed from such terrible eyes. I have repeatedly known young men of sensibility converted in a moment to the belief that this was the man they were in search of, the man of men, who could tell them all they should do. His own dealing with them was never affectionate, but superior, didactic, scorning their petty ways,—very slowly conceding, or not conceding at all, the promise of his society at their houses, or even at his own. "Would he not walk with them?" "He did not know. There was nothing so important to him as his walk; he had no walks to throw away on company." Visits were offered him from respectful parties, but he declined them. Admiring friends offered to carry him at their own cost to the Yellowstone River,—to the West Indies,—to South America. But though nothing could be more grave or considered than his refusals, they remind one, in quite new relations, of that fop Brummell's reply to the gentleman who offered him his carriage in a shower, "But where will *you* ride, then?"—and what accusing silences, and what searching and irresistible speeches, battering down all defenses, his companions can remember!

Mr. Thoreau dedicated his genius with such entire love to the fields, hills and waters of his native town, that he made them known and interesting to all reading Americans, and to people over the sea. The river[7] on whose banks he was born and died he knew from its springs to its confluence with the Merrimack. He had made summer and winter observations on it for many years, and at every hour of the day and night. The result of the recent survey of the Water Commissioners appointed by the State of Massachusetts he had reached by his private experiments, several years earlier. Every fact which occurs in the bed, on the banks, or in the air over it; the fishes, and their spawning and nests, their manners, their food; the shad-flies which fill the air on a certain evening once a year, and which are snapped at by the fishes so ravenously that many of these die of repletion; the conical heaps of small stones on the river-shallows, the huge nests of small fishes, one of which will sometimes overfill a cart; the birds which frequent the stream, heron, duck, sheldrake, loon, osprey; the snake, muskrat, otter, woodchuck and fox, on the banks; the turtle, frog, hyla and cricket, which made the banks vocal,—were all known to him, and, as it were, townsmen and fellow-creatures; so that he felt an absurdity or violence in any narrative of one of these by itself apart, and still more of its dimensions on an inch-rule, or in the exhibition of its skeleton, or the specimen of a squirrel or a bird in brandy. He liked to speak of the manners of the river, as itself a lawful creature, yet with exactness, and always to an observed fact. As he knew the river, so the ponds in this region.

One of the weapons he used, more important to him than microscope or alcohol-receiver to other investigators, was a whim which grew on him by indulgence, yet appeared in gravest statement, namely, of extolling his own town and neighborhood as the most favored center for natural observation. He remarked that the Flora of Massachusetts embraced almost all the important plants of America,—most of the oaks, most of the willows, the best pines, the ash, the maple, the beech, the nuts. He returned Kane's[8] "Arctic Voyage" to a friend of whom he had

[6] A medicinal plant.

[7] The Concord River.

[8] Elisha Kent Kane, a celebrated Arctic explorer of the time, whose books Thoreau knew.

borrowed it, with the remark, that "Most of the phenomena noted might be observed in Concord." He seemed a little envious of the Pole, for the coincident sunrise and sunset, or five minutes' day after six months: a splendid fact which Annursnuc had never afforded him. He found red snow in one of his walks, and told me that he expected to find yet the *Victoria regia*[9] in Concord. He was the attorney of the indigenous plants, and owned to a preference of the weeds to the imported plants, as of the Indian to the civilized man, and noticed, with pleasure, that the willow bean-poles of his neighbor had grown more than his beans. "See these weeds," he said, "which have been hoed at by a million farmers all spring and summer, and yet have prevailed, and just now come out triumphant over all lanes, pastures, fields and gardens, such is their vigor. We have insulted them with low names, too,—as Pigweed, Wormwood, Chickweed, Shad-blossom." He says, "They have brave names, too,—Ambrosia, Stellaria, Amelanchier, Amaranth, etc."

I think his fancy for referring everything to the meridian of Concord did not grow out of any ignorance or depreciation of other longitudes or latitudes, but was rather a playful expression of his conviction of the indifferency of all places, and that the best place for each is where he stands. He expressed it once in this wise: "I think nothing is to be hoped from you, if this bit of mould under your feet is not sweeter to you to eat than any other in this world, or in any world."

The other weapon with which he conquered all obstacles in science was patience. He knew how to sit immovable, a part of the rock he rested on, until the bird, the reptile, the fish, which had retired from him, should come back and resume its habits, nay, moved by curiosity, should come to him and watch him.

It was a pleasure and a privilege to walk with him. He knew the country like a fox or a bird, and passed through it as freely by paths of his own. He knew every track in the snow or on the ground, and what creature had taken this path before him. One must submit abjectly to such a guide, and the reward was great. Under his arm he carried an old music-book to press plants; in his pocket, his diary and pencil, a spy-glass for birds, microscope, jack-knife, and twine. He wore a straw hat, stout shoes, strong gray trousers, to brave scrub-oaks and smilax, and to climb a tree for a hawk's or a squirrel's nest. He waded into the pool for the water-plants, and his strong legs were no insignificant part of his armor. On the day I speak of he looked for the Menyanthes, detected it across the wide pool, and, on examination of the florets, decided that it had been in flower five days. He drew out of his breast-pocket his diary, and read the names of all the plants that should bloom on this day, whereof he kept account as a banker when his notes fall due. The Cypripedium not due till to-morrow. He thought that, if waked up from a trance, in this swamp, he could tell by the plants what time of the year it was within two days. The redstart was flying about, and presently the fine grosbeaks, whose brilliant scarlet "makes the rash gazer wipe his eye," and whose fine clear note Thoreau compared to that of a tanager which has got rid of its hoarseness. Presently he heard a note which he called that of the night-warbler, a bird he had never identified, had been in search of twelve years, which always, when he saw it, was in the act of diving down into a tree or bush, and which it was in vain to seek; the only bird which sings indifferently by night and by day. I told him he must beware of finding and booking it, lest life should have nothing more to show him. He said, "What you seek in vain for, half your life, one day you come full upon, all the family at dinner. You seek it like a dream, and as soon as you find it you become its prey."

His interest in the flower or the bird lay very deep in his mind, was connected with Nature,—and the meaning of Nature was never attempted to be defined by him. He would not offer a memoir of his observations to the Natural History Society. "Why should I? To detach the description from its connections in my mind would make it no longer true or valuable to me: and they do not wish what belongs to it." His power of observation seemed to indicate additional senses. He saw as with microscope, heard as with ear-trumpet, and his memory was a photographic register of all he saw and heard. And yet none knew better than he that it is not the fact that imports, but the impression or effect of the fact on your mind. Every fact lay in glory in his mind, a type of the order and beauty of the whole.

His determination on Natural History was organic. He confessed that he sometimes felt like a hound or a panther, and, if born among Indians, would have been a fell hunter. But, restrained by his Massachusetts culture, he played out the game in this mild form of botany and ichthyology. His intimacy with animals suggested what Thomas Fuller records of Butler the apiologist, that "either he had told the bees things or the bees had told him." Snakes coiled round his legs; the fishes swam into his hand, and he took them out of the water; he pulled the woodchuck out of its hole by the tail and took the foxes under his protection from the hunters. Our naturalist had perfect magnanimity; he had no secrets; he would carry you to the heron's haunt, or even to his

[9]A South American water lily.

most prized botanical swamp,—possibly knowing that you could never find it again, yet willing to take his risks.

No college ever offered him a diploma, or a professor's chair; no academy made him its corresponding secretary, its discoverer, or even its member. Perhaps these learned bodies feared the satire of his presence. Yet so much knowledge of Nature's secret and genius few others possessed; none in a more large and religious synthesis. For not a particle of respect had he to the opinions of any man or body of men, but homage solely to the truth itself; and as he discovered everywhere among doctors some leaning of courtesy, it discredited them. He grew to be revered and admired by his townsmen, who had at first known him only as an oddity. The farmers who employed him as a surveyor soon discovered his rare accuracy and skill, his knowledge of their lands, of trees, of birds, of Indian remains and the like, which enabled him to tell every farmer more than he knew before of his own farm; so that he began to feel a little as if Mr. Thoreau had better rights in his land than he. They felt, too, the superiority of character which addressed all men with a native authority.

Indian relics abound in Concord,—arrow-heads, stone chisels, pestles, and fragments of pottery; and on the riverbank, large heaps of clam-shells and ashes mark spots which the savages frequented. These, and every circumstance touching the Indian, were important in his eyes. His visits to Maine were chiefly for love of the Indian. He had the satisfaction of seeing the manufacture of the bark-canoe, as well as of trying his hand in its management on the rapids. He was inquisitive about the making of the stone arrow-head, and in his last days charged a youth setting out for the Rocky Mountains to find an Indian who could tell him that: "It was well worth a visit to California to learn it." Occasionally, a small party of Penobscot Indians would visit Concord, and pitch their tents for a few weeks in summer on the river-bank. He failed not to make acquaintance with the best of them; though he well knew that asking questions of Indians is like catechizing beavers and rabbits. In his last visit to Maine he had great satisfaction from Joseph Polis, an intelligent Indian of Oldtown, who was his guide for some weeks.

He was equally interested in every natural fact. The depth of his perception found likeness of law throughout Nature, and I know not any genius who so swiftly inferred universal law from the single fact. He was no pedant of a department. His eye was open to beauty, and his ear to music. He found these, not in rare conditions, but wheresoever he went. He thought the best of music was in single strains; and he found poetic suggestion in the humming of the telegraph-wire.

His poetry might be bad or good; he no doubt wanted a lyric facility and technical skill, but he had the source of poetry in his spiritual perception. He was a good reader and critic, and his judgment on poetry was to the ground of it. He could not be deceived as to the presence or absence of the poetic element in any composition, and his thirst for this made him negligent and perhaps scornful of superficial graces. He would pass by many delicate rhythms, but he would have detected every live stanza or line in a volume, and knew very well where to find an equal poetic charm in prose. He was so enamoured of the spiritual beauty that he held all actual written poems in very light esteem in the comparison. He admired Aeschylus and Pindar; but, when some one was commending them, he said that Aeschylus and the Greeks, in describing Apollo and Orpheus, had given no song, or no good one. "They ought not to have moved trees, but to have chanted to the gods such a hymn as would have sung all their old ideas out of their heads, and new ones in." His own verses are often rude and defective. The gold does not yet run pure, is drossy and crude. The thyme and marjoram are not yet honey. But if he want lyric fineness and technical merits, if he have not the poetic temperament, he never lacks the causal thought, showing that his genius was better than his talent. He knew the worth of the Imagination for the uplifting and consolation of human life, and liked to throw every thought into a symbol. The fact you tell is of no value, but only the impression. For this reason his presence was poetic, always piqued the curiosity to know more deeply the secrets of his mind. He had many reserves, an unwillingness to exhibit to profane eyes what was still sacred in his own, and knew well how to throw a poetic veil over his experience. All readers of Walden will remember his mythical record of his disappointments:—

"I long ago lost a hound, a bay horse and a turtle-dove, and am still on their trail. Many are the travellers I have spoken concerning them, describing their tracks, and what calls they answered to. I have met one or two who have heard the hound, and the tramp of the horse, and even seen the dove disappear behind a cloud; and they seemed as anxious to recover them as if they had lost them themselves."

His riddles were worth the reading, and I confide that if at any time I do not understand the expression, it is yet just. Such was the wealth of his truth that it was not worth his while to use words in vain. His poem entitled "Sympathy" reveals the tenderness under that triple steel of stoicism, and the intellectual subtility it could animate. His classic poem on "Smoke" suggests Simonides, but is better than any poem of Simonides. His biography is in his verses. His habitual thought makes all his poetry a hymn to the Cause of causes, the Spirit which vivifies and controls his own:—

I hearing get, who had but ears,
And sight, who had but eyes before;
I moments live, who lived but years,
And truth discern, who knew but learning's lore.

And still more in these religious lines:

Now chiefly is my natal hour,
And only now my prime of life;
I will not doubt the love untold,
Which not my worth nor want have bought,
Which wooed me young, and wooes me old,
And to this evening hath me brought.[10]

Whilst he used in his writings a certain petulance of remark in reference to churches or churchmen, he was a person of a rare, tender and absolute religion, a person incapable of any profanation, by act or by thought. Of course, the same isolation which belonged to his original thinking and living detached him from the social religious forms. This is neither to be censured nor regretted. Aristotle long ago explained it, when he said, "One who surpasses his fellow-citizens in virtue is no longer a part of the city. Their law is not for him, since he is a law to himself."

Thoreau was sincerity itself, and might fortify the convictions of prophets in the ethical laws by his holy living. It was an affirmative experience which refused to be set aside. A truth-speaker he, capable of the most deep and strict conversation; a physician to the wounds of any soul; a friend, knowing not only the secret of friendship, but almost worshipped by those few persons who resorted to him as their confessor and prophet, and knew the deep value of his mind and great heart. He thought that without religion or devotion of some kind nothing great was ever accomplished: and he thought that the bigoted sectarian had better bear this in mind.

His virtues, of course, sometimes ran into extremes. It was easy to trace to the inexorable demand on all for exact truth that austerity which made this willing hermit more solitary even than he wished. Himself of a perfect probity, he required not less of others. He had a disgust at crime, and no worldly success would cover it. He detected paltering as readily in dignified and prosperous persons as in beggars, and with equal scorn. Such dangerous frankness was in his dealing that his admirers called him "that terrible Thoreau," as if he spoke when silent, and was still present when he had departed. I think the severity of his ideal interfered to deprive him of a healthy sufficiency of human society.

The habit of a realist to find things the reverse of their appearance inclined him to put every statement in a paradox. A certain habit of antagonism defaced his earlier writings,—a trick of rhetoric not quite outgrown in his later, of substituting for the obvious word and thought its diametrical opposite. He praised wild mountains and winter forests for their domestic air, in snow and ice he would find sultriness, and commended the wilderness for resembling Rome and Paris. "It was so dry, that you might call it wet."

The tendency to magnify the moment, to read all the laws of Nature in the one object or one combination under your eye, is of course comic to those who do not share the philosopher's perception of identity. To him there was no such thing as size. The pond was a small ocean; the Atlantic, a large Walden Pond. He referred every minute fact to cosmical laws. Though he meant to be just, he seemed haunted by a certain chronic assumption that the science of the day pretended completeness, and he had just found out that the *savans*[11] had neglected to discriminate a particular botanical variety, had failed to describe the seeds or count the sepals. "That is to say," we replied, "the blockheads were not born in Concord; but who said they were? It was their unspeakable misfortune to be born in London, or Paris, or Rome; but poor fellows, they did what they could, considering that they never saw Bateman's Pond, or Nine-Acre Corner, or Becky Stow's Swamp; besides, what were you sent into the world for, but to add this observation?"

Had his genius been only contemplative, he had been fitted to his life, but with his energy and practical ability he seemed born for great enterprise and for command; and I so much regret the loss of his rare powers of action, that I cannot help counting it a fault in him that he had no ambition. Wanting this, instead of engineering for all America, he was the captain of a huckleberry-party. Pounding beans is good to the end of pounding empires one of these days; but if, at the end of years, it is still only beans!

But these foibles, real or apparent, were fast vanishing in the incessant growth of a spirit so robust and wise, and which effaced its defeats with new triumphs. His study of Nature was a perpetual ornament to him, and inspired his friends with curiosity to see the world through his eyes, and to hear his adventures. They possessed every kind of interest.

He had many elegancies of his own, whilst he scoffed at conventional elegance. Thus, he could not bear to hear the sound of his own steps, the grit of gravel; and therefore never willingly walked in the road, but in the grass, on mountains and in woods. His senses were acute, and he remarked that by

[10] The lines are from Thoreau's "Inspiration."

[11] Savants; men of learning.

night every dwelling-house gives out bad air, like a slaughter-house. He liked the pure fragrance of melilot.[12] He honored certain plants with special regard, and, over all, the pond-lily,—then, the gentian, and the *Mikania scandens,*[13] and "life-everlasting," and a bass-tree which he visited every year when it bloomed, in the middle of July, He thought the scent a more oracular inquisition than the sight,—more oracular and trustworthy. The scent, of course, reveals what is concealed from the other senses. By it he detected earthiness. He delighted in echoes, and said they were almost the only kind of kindred voices that he heard. He loved Nature so well, was so happy in her solitude, that he became very jealous of cities and the sad work which their refinements and artifices made with man and his dwelling. The axe was always destroying his forest. "Thank God," he said, "they cannot cut down the clouds!" "All kinds of figures are drawn on the blue ground with this fibrous white paint."

I subjoin a few sentences taken from his unpublished manuscripts, not only as records of his thought and feeling, but for their power of description and literary excellence:—

"Some circumstantial evidence is very strong, as when you find a trout in the milk."

"The chub is a soft fish, and tastes like boiled brown paper salted."

"The youth gets together his materials to build a bridge to the moon, or, perchance, a palace or temple on the earth, and, at length the middle-aged man concludes to build a woodshed with them."

"The locust z-ing."

"Devil's-needles zigzagging along the Nut-Meadow brook."

"Sugar is not so sweet to the palate as sound to the healthy ear."

"I put on some hemlock-boughs, and the rich salt crackling of their leaves was like mustard to the ear, the crackling of uncountable regiments. Dead trees love the fire."

"The bluebird carries the sky on his back."

"The tanager flies through the green foliage as if it would ignite the leaves."

"If I wish for a horse-hair for my compass-sight I must go to the stable; but the hair-bird, with her sharp eyes, goes to the road."

"Immortal water, alive even to the superficies."

"Fire is the most tolerable third party."

"Nature made ferns for pure leaves, to show what she could do in that line."

"No tree has so fair a bole and so handsome an instep as the beech."

"How did these beautiful rainbow-tints get into the shell of the fresh-water clam, buried in the mud at the bottom of our dark river?"

"Hard are the times when the infant's shoes are second-foot."

"We are strictly confined to our men to whom we give liberty."

"Nothing is so much to be feared as fear. Atheism may comparatively be popular with God himself."

"Of what significance the things you can forget? A little thought is sexton to all the world."

"How can we expect a harvest of thought who have not had a seed-time of character?"

"Only he can be trusted with gifts who can present a face of bronze to expectations."

"I ask to be melted. You can only ask of the metals that they be tender to the fire that melts them. To nought else can they be tender."

There is a flower known to botanists, one of the same genus with our summer plant called "Life-Everlasting," a *Gnaphalium* like that, which grows on the most inaccessible cliffs of the Tyrolese mountains, where the chamois dare hardly venture, and which the hunter, tempted by its beauty, and by his love (for it is immensely valued by the Swiss maidens), climbs the cliffs to gather, and is sometimes found dead at the foot, with the flower in his hand. It is called by botanists the *Gnaphalium leontopodium,* but by the Swiss *Edelweisse,* which signifies *Noble Purity.* Thoreau seemed to me living in the hope to gather this plant, which belonged to him of right. The scale on which his studies proceeded was so large as to require longevity, and we were the less prepared for his sudden disappearance. The country knows not yet, or in the least part, how great a son it has lost. It seems an injury that he should leave in the midst his broken task which none else can finish, a kind of indignity to so noble a soul that he should depart out of Nature before yet he has been really shown to his peers for what he is. But he, at least, is content. His soul was made for the noblest society; he had in a short life exhausted the capabilities of this world; wherever there is knowledge, wherever there is virtue, wherever there is beauty, he will find a home.

1862

[12] Sweet clover.

[13] Climbing hempweed.

HENRY DAVID THOREAU [1817-1862]

To Emerson's account of Thoreau it may be worth while to add this factual summary of his life: Born in Concord, Massachusetts, son of John Thoreau, pencil maker, and Cynthia Dunbar; attended the village academy; at Harvard, mastered Greek and read widely on his own account in English literature; graduated in 1837, the year of "The American Scholar," and thereafter was associated with Emerson; did some teaching, and began giving lectures; contributed to *The Dial,* both verse and prose; tutored William Emerson's children on Staten Island; lived for a time at Walden Pond; published in 1849 the first of his two books, *A Week on the Concord and Merrimack Rivers;* five years later published *Walden;* published essays gathered into books after his death *(The Maine Woods, A Yankee in Canada,* and *Cape Cod);* journeyed to Minnesota in search of health; died of tuberculosis in Concord the next year, age forty-four; between his return from college and his death had been away from Concord less than a year in all.

To outward seeming, it was an uneventful life, disappointing to his family, who had invested in his college education at some sacrifice, and to his friends, who saw it as a negation, a refusal or failure to utilize his talents. And yet, as later generations have more fully recognized, it was a life fraught with inward drama; and if the vocation he pursued was not what society expected of a Harvard graduate, it nevertheless lay at the heart of the Transcendental philosophy: self-realization, through a life lived organically in communion with nature, disciplined by the seasons, by the economy of self-support, and by the tension between the civilized and the primitive. *Walden,* as the distillation of his experience, is Thoreau's great achievement.

Text: *The Writings of Henry David Thoreau,* Walden Edition (Boston, 1906).

Further reading: *The Variorum Walden,* ed. Walter Harding, 1962. *A Week on the Concord and Merrimack Rivers. The Collected Poems of Henry Thoreau,* ed. Carl Bode. Sherman Paul, *The Shores of America: Thoreau's Inward Exploration,* 1958. Walter Harding, *A Thoreau Handbook,* 1959. John H. Hicks, ed., *Thoreau in Our Season,* 1966. Charles R. Anderson, *The Magic Circle of Walden,* 1968.

Sic Vita

I am a parcel of vain strivings tied
By a chance bond together,
Dangling this way and that, their links
Were made so loose and wide,
Methinks,
For milder weather.

A bunch of violets without their roots,
And sorrel intermixed,[1]
Encircled by a wisp of straw
Once coiled about their shoots,
The law
By which I'm fixed.

A nosegay which Time clutched from out
Those fair Elysian fields,
With weeds and broken stems, in haste,
Doth make the rabble rout
That waste
The day he yields.

And here I bloom for a short hour unseen,
Drinking my juices up,
With no root in the land

Sic Vita. [1]At the time Thoreau wrote the poem (1837) flower symbolism was very popular. How much further meaning he intended is unknown, but violets surely stood for modesty, and sorrel for "wit ill-timed." (See Bode, *Collected Poems,* p. 351.)

To keep my branches green,
But stand
In a bare cup.

Some tender buds were left upon my stem
In mimicry of life,
But ah! the children will not know,
Till time has withered them,
The woe
With which they're rife.

But now I see I was not plucked for naught,
And after in life's vase
Of glass set while I might survive,
But by a kind hand brought
Alive
To a strange place.

That stock thus thinned will soon redeem its hours,
And by another year,
Such as God knows, with freer air,
More fruits and fairer flowers
Will bear,
While I droop here.

1841

Winter Memories

Within the circuit of this plodding life
There enter moments of an azure hue,
Untarnished fair as is the violet
Or anemone, when the spring strews them
By some meandering rivulet, which make
The best philosophy untrue that aims
But to console man for his grievances.
I have remembered when the winter came,
High in my chamber in the frosty nights,
When in the still light of the cheerful moon,
On every twig and rail and jutting spout,
The icy spears were adding to their length
Against the arrows of the coming sun,
How in the shimmering noon of summer past
Some unrecorded beam slanted across
The upland pastures where the Johnswort grew;
Or heard, amid the verdure of my mind,
The bee's long smothered hum, on the blue flag
Loitering amidst the mead; or busy rill,
Which now through all its course stands still and dumb
Its own memorial,—purling at its play
Along the slopes, and through the meadows next,
Until its youthful sound was hushed at last
In the staid current of the lowland stream;
Or seen the furrows shine but late upturned,
And where the fieldfare[1] followed in the rear,
When all the fields around lay bound and hoar
Beneath a thick integument of snow.
So by God's cheap economy made rich
To go upon my winter's task again.

1842

The Inward Morning

Packed in my mind lie all the clothes
Which outward nature wears,
And in its fashion's hourly change
It all things else repairs.

In vain I look for change abroad,
And can no difference find,
Till some new ray of peace uncalled
Illumes my inmost mind.

What is it gilds the trees and clouds,
And paints the heavens so gay,
But yonder fast-abiding light
With its unchanging ray?

Lo, when the sun streams through the wood,
Upon a winter's morn,
Where'er his silent beams intrude
The murky night is gone.

How could the patient pine have known
The morning breeze would come,
Or humble flowers anticipate
The insect's noonday hum,—

Till the new light with morning cheer
From far streamed through the aisles,
And nimbly told the forest trees
For many stretching miles?

I've heard within my inmost soul
Such cheerful morning news,
In the horizon of my mind
Have seen such orient hues,

As in the twilight of the dawn,
When the first birds awake,
Are heard within some silent wood,
Where they the small twigs break,

Or in the eastern skies are seen,
Before the sun appears,
The harbingers of summer heats
Which from afar he bears.

1842

Winter Memories. [1]A medium-sized European thrush.

Mist

Low-anchored cloud,
Newfoundland air,
Fountain-head and source of rivers,
Dew-cloth, dream drapery,
And napkin spread by fays;
Drifting meadow of the air,
Where bloom the daisied banks and violets,
And in whose fenny labyrinth
The bittern booms and heron wades;
Spirit of lakes and seas and rivers,
Bear only perfumes and the scent
Of healing herbs to just men's fields!

1842?

Smoke

Published in the *Dial*, April 1843, and republished in *Walden*, in which it is introduced as follows: "When the villagers were lighting their fires beyond the horizon, I too gave notice to the various wild inhabitants of Walden vale, by a smoky streamer from my chimney, that I was awake."

Light-winged smoke, Icarian bird,
Melting thy pinions in thy upward flight,
Lark without song, and messenger of dawn,
Circling above the hamlets as thy nest;
Or else, departing dream, and shadowy form
Of midnight vision, gathering up thy skirts;
By night star-veiling, and by day
Darkening the light and blotting out the sun;
Go thou my incense upward from this hearth,
And ask the Gods to pardon this clear flame.

1843

Inspiration

Whate'er we leave to God, God does,
  And blesses us;
The work we choose should be our own,
  God lets alone.

If with light head erect I sing,
  Though all the muses lend their force,
From my poor love of anything,
  The verse is weak and shallow as its source.

But if with bended neck I grope,
  Listening behind me for my wit,
With faith superior to hope,
  More anxious to keep back than forward it,

Making my soul accomplice there
  Unto the flame my heart hath lit,
Then will the verse forever wear,—
  Time cannot bend the line which God hath writ.

Always the general show of things
  Floats in review before my mind,
And such true love and reverence brings,
  That sometimes I forget that I am blind.

But now there comes unsought, unseen,
  Some clear, divine electuary,
And I who had but sensual been,
  Grow sensible, and as God is, am wary.

I hearing get who had but ears,
  And sight, who had but eyes before,
I moments live who lived but years,
  And truth discern who knew but learning's lore.

I hear beyond the range of sound,
  I see beyond the range of sight,
New earths and skies and seas around,
  And in my day the sun doth pale his light.

A clear and ancient harmony
  Pierces my soul through all its din,
As through its utmost melody,—
  Farther behind than they—farther within.

More swift its bolt than lightning is,
  Its voice than thunder is more loud,
It doth expand my privacies
  To all, and leave me single in the crowd.

It speaks with such authority,
  With so serene and lofty tone,
That idle Time runs gadding by,
  And leaves me with Eternity alone.

Then chiefly is my natal hour,
  And only then my prime of life,
Of manhood's strength it is the flower,
  'Tis peace's end and war's beginning strife.

'T hath come in summer's broadest noon,
  By a grey wall or some chance place,
Unseasoned time, insulted June,
  And vexed the day with its presuming face.

Such fragrance round my couch it makes,
  More rich than are Arabian drugs,

That my soul scents its life and wakes
The body up beneath its perfumed rugs.

Such is the Muse—the heavenly maid,
The star that guides our mortal course,
Which shows where life's true kernel's laid,
Its wheat's fine flower, and its undying force.

She with one breath attunes the spheres,
And also my poor human heart,
With one impulse propels the years
Around, and gives my throbbing pulse its start.

I will not doubt forever more,
Nor falter from a steadfast faith,
For though the system be turned o'er,
God takes not back the word which once he saith.

I will then trust the love untold
Which not my worth nor want has bought,
Which wooed me young and woos me old,
And to this evening hath me brought.

My memory I'll educate
To know the one historic truth,
Remembering to the latest date
The only true and sole immortal youth.

Be but thy inspiration given,
No matter through what danger sought,
I'll fathom hell or climb to heaven,
And yet esteem that cheap which love has bought.

Fame cannot tempt the bard
Who's famous with his God,
Nor laurel him reward
Who hath his Maker's nod.

1848 1863

Civil Disobedience

Thoreau, individualist and lover of beauty, could not ignore the great public problem of slavery. His house in Concord was a station on the underground railroad. He knew and admired Captain John Brown, and spoke for him even though public opinion was virtually solid against Brown. This was in 1859. More than a decade earlier, during the Mexican war, he had written "Resistance to Civil Government," later entitled "Civil Disobedience." It was a protest against slavery: "I cannot for an instant recognize that political organization as *my* government which is the *slave's* government also." At the same time it was a general protest against any form of political injustice and an affirmation of the obligation of passive resistance.

I heartily accept the motto, "That government is best which governs least;"[1] and I should like to see it acted up to more rapidly and systematically. Carried out, it finally amounts to this, which also I believe,—"That government is best which governs not at all;" and when men are prepared for it, that will be the kind of government which they will have. Government is at best but an expedient; but most governments are usually, and all governments are sometimes, inexpedient. The objections which have been brought against a standing army, and they are many and weighty, and deserve to prevail, may also at last be brought against a standing government. The standing army is only an arm of the standing government. The government itself, which is only the mode which the people have chosen to execute their will, is equally liable to be abused and perverted before the people can act through it. Witness the present Mexican war, the work of comparatively a few individuals using the standing government as their tool; for, in the outset, the people would not have consented to this measure.

This American government,—what is it but a tradition, though a recent one, endeavoring to transmit itself unimpaired to posterity, but each instant losing some of its integrity? It has not the vitality and force of a single living man; for a single man can bend it to his will. It is a sort of wooden gun to the people themselves. But it is not the less necessary for this; for the people must have some complicated machinery or other, and hear its din, to satisfy that idea of government which they have. Governments show thus how successfully men can be imposed on, even impose on themselves, for their own advantage. It is excellent, we must all allow. Yet this government never of itself furthered any enterprise, but by the alacrity with which it got out of its way. *It* does not keep the country free. *It* does not settle the West. *It* does not educate. The character inherent in the American people has done all that has been accomplished; and it would have done somewhat more, if the government had not sometimes got in its way. For government is an expedient by which men would fain succeed in letting one another alone; and, as has been said, when it is most expedient, the governed are most let alone by it. Trade and commerce, if they were not made of india-rubber, would never manage to bounce over the obstacles which legislators are continually putting in their way; and, if one were to judge these men wholly by the effects of their actions and not partly by their intentions, they would deserve to be classed and punished with those mischievous persons who put obstructions on the railroads.

Civil Disobedience. [1]Although the motto suggests Jefferson, it actually is from the masthead of the *Democratic Review,* a periodical for which Thoreau occasionally wrote. (Harding)

But, to speak practically and as a citizen, unlike those who call themselves no-government men, I ask for, not at once no government, but *at once* a better government. Let every man make known what kind of government would command his respect, and that will be one step toward obtaining it.

After all, the practical reason why, when the power is once in the hands of the people, a majority are permitted, and for a long period continue, to rule is not because they are most likely to be in the right, nor because this seems fairest to the minority, but because they are physically the strongest. But a government in which the majority rule in all cases cannot be based on justice, even as far as men understand it. Can there not be a government in which majorities do not virtually decide right and wrong, but conscience?—in which majorities decide only those questions to which the rule of expediency is applicable? Must the citizen ever for a moment, or in the least degree, resign his conscience to the legislator? Why has every man a conscience, then? I think that we should be men first, and subjects afterward. It is not desirable to cultivate a respect for the law, so much as for the right. The only obligation which I have a right to assume is to do at any time what I think right. It is truly enough said that a corporation has no conscience; but a corporation of conscientious men is a corporation *with* a conscience. Law never made men a whit more just; and, by means of their respect for it, even the well-disposed are daily made the agents of injustice. A common and natural result of an undue respect for law is, that you may see a file of soldiers, colonel, captain, corporal, privates, powder-monkeys, and all, marching in admirable order over hill and dale to the wars, against their wills, ay, against their common sense and consciences, which makes it very steep marching indeed, and produces a palpitation of the heart. They have no doubt that it is a damnable business in which they are concerned; they are all peaceably inclined. Now, what are they? Men at all? or small movable forts and magazines, at the service of some unscrupulous man in power? Visit the Navy-Yard, and behold a marine, such a man as an American government can make, or such as it can make a man with its black arts,—a mere shadow and reminiscence of humanity, a man laid out alive and standing, and already, as one may say, buried under arms with funeral accompaniments, though it may be,—

> "Not a drum was heard, not a funeral note,
> As his corse to the rampart we hurried;
> Not a soldier discharged his farewell shot
> O'er the grave where our hero we buried." [2]

[2] Charles Wolfe (1791-1823), "Burial of Sir John Moore at Corunna."

The mass of men serve the state thus, not as men mainly, but as machines, with their bodies. They are the standing army, and the militia, jailers, constables, *posse comitatus*, etc. In most cases there is no free exercise whatever of the judgment or of the moral sense; but they put themselves on a level with wood and earth and stones; and wooden men can perhaps be manufactured that will serve the purpose as well. Such command no more respect than men of straw or a lump of dirt. They have the same sort of worth only as horses and dogs. Yet such as these even are commonly esteemed good citizens. Others—as most legislators, politicians, lawyers, ministers, and office-holders—serve the state chiefly with their heads; and, as they rarely make any moral distinctions, they are as likely to serve the devil, without *intending* it, as God. A very few—as heroes, patriots, martyrs, reformers in the great sense, and *men*—serve the state with their consciences also, and so necessarily resist it for the most part; and they are commonly treated as enemies by it. A wise man will only be useful as a man, and will not submit to be "clay," and "stop a hole to keep the wind away," [3] but leave that office to his dust at least:—

> "I am too high-born to be propertied,
> To be a secondary at control,
> Or useful serving-man and instrument
> To any sovereign state throughout the world." [4]

He who gives himself entirely to his fellow-men appears to them useless and selfish; but he who gives himself partially to them is pronounced a benefactor and philanthropist.

How does it become a man to behave toward this American government to-day? I answer, that he cannot without disgrace be associated with it. I cannot for an instant recognize that political organization as *my* government which is the *slave's* government also.

All men recognize the right of revolution; that is, the right to refuse allegiance to, and to resist, the government, when its tyranny or its inefficiency are great and unendurable. But almost all say that such is not the case now. But such was the case, they think, in the Revolution of '75. If one were to tell me that this was a bad government because it taxed certain foreign commodities brought to its ports, it is most probable that I should not make an ado about it, for I can do without them. All machines have their friction; and possibly this does enough good to counterbalance the evil. At any rate, it is a great evil to make a stir about it. But when the friction comes to have its machine, and oppression and robbery are

[3] "Imperious Caesar, dead and turn'd to clay,/Might stop a hole to keep the wind away." Shakespeare, *Hamlet* V.i. 236-37.

[4] Shakespeare, *King John* V.ii. 79-82.

organized, I say, let us not have such a machine any longer. In other words, when a sixth of the population of a nation which has undertaken to be the refuge of liberty are slaves, and a whole country is unjustly overrun and conquered by a foreign army, and subjected to military law, I think that it is not too soon for honest men to rebel and revolutionize. What makes this duty the more urgent is the fact that the country so overrun is not our own, but ours is the invading army.

Paley,[5] a common authority with many on moral questions, in his chapter on the "Duty of Submission to Civil Government," resolves all civil obligation into expediency; and he proceeds to say that "so long as the interest of the whole society requires it, that is, so long as the established government cannot be resisted or changed without public inconveniency, it is the will of God . . . that the established government be obeyed,—and no longer. This principle being admitted, the justice of every particular case of resistance is reduced to a computation of the quantity of the danger and grievance on the one side, and of the probability and expense of redressing it on the other." Of this, he says, every man shall judge for himself. But Paley appears never to have contemplated those cases to which the rule of expediency does not apply, in which a people, as well as an individual, must do justice, cost what it may. If I have unjustly wrested a plank from a drowning man, I must restore it to him though I drown myself. This, according to Paley, would be inconvenient. But he that would save his life, in such a case, shall lose it. This people must cease to hold slaves, and to make war on Mexico, though it cost them their existence as a people.

In their practice, nations agree with Paley; but does any one think that Massachusetts does exactly what is right at the present crisis?

"A drab of state, a cloth-o'-silver slut,
To have her train borne up, and her soul trail in the dirt."[6]

Practically speaking, the opponents to a reform in Massachusetts are not a hundred thousand politicians at the South, but a hundred thousand merchants and farmers here,[7] who are more interested in commerce and agriculture than they are in humanity, and are not prepared to do justice to the slave and to Mexico, *cost what it may*. I quarrel not with far-off foes, but with those who, near at home, coöperate with, and do the bidding of, those far away, and without whom the latter would be harmless. We are accustomed to say, that the mass of men are unprepared; but improvement is slow, because the few are not materially wiser or better than the many. It is not so important that many should be as good as you, as that there be some absolute goodness somewhere; for that will leaven the whole lump. There are thousands who are *in opinion* opposed to slavery and to the war, who yet in effect do nothing to put an end to them; who, esteeming themselves children of Washington and Franklin, sit down with their hands in their pockets, and say that they know not what to do, and do nothing; who even postpone the question of freedom to the question of free trade, and quietly read the prices-current along with the latest advices from Mexico, after dinner, and, it may be, fall asleep over them both. What is the price-current of an honest man and patriot to-day? They hesitate, and they regret, and sometimes they petition; but they do nothing in earnest and with effect. They will wait, well disposed, for others to remedy the evil, that they may no longer have it to regret. At most, they give only a cheap vote, and a feeble countenance and Godspeed, to the right, as it goes by them. There are nine hundred and ninety-nine patrons of virtue to one virtuous man. But it is easier to deal with the real possessor of a thing than with the temporary guardian of it.

All voting is a sort of gaming, like checkers or backgammon, with a slight moral tinge to it, a playing with right and wrong, with moral questions; and betting naturally accompanies it. The character of the voters is not staked. I cast my vote, perchance, as I think right; but I am not vitally concerned that that right should prevail. I am willing to leave it to the majority. Its obligation, therefore, never exceeds that of expediency. Even voting *for the right* is *doing* nothing for it. It is only expressing to men feebly your desire that it should prevail. A wise man will not leave the right to the mercy of chance, nor wish it to prevail through the power of the majority. There is but little virtue in the action of masses of men. When the majority shall at length vote for the abolition of slavery, it will be because they are indifferent to slavery, or because there is but little slavery left to be abolished by their vote. *They* will then be the only slaves. Only *his* vote can hasten the abolition of slavery who asserts his own freedom by his vote.

I hear of a convention to be held at Baltimore,[8] or elsewhere, for the selection of a candidate for the Presidency, made up chiefly of editors, and men who are politicians by profession; but I think, what

[5] William Paley (1743–1805), from *Moral and Political Philosophy*.

[6] Cyril Tourneur, *The Revenger's Tragedy* IV.iv.

[7] Many Northerners resisted abolition because they feared it would damage the economy.

[8] The Democratic Party convention of 1848; it evaded the whole issue of slavery.

is it to any independent, intelligent, and respectable man what decision they may come to? Shall we not have the advantage of his wisdom and honesty, nevertheless? Can we not count upon some independent votes? Are there not many individuals in the country who do not attend conventions? But no: I find that the respectable man, so called, has immediately drifted from his position, and despairs of his country, when his country has more reason to despair of him. He forthwith adopts one of the candidates thus selected as the only *available* one, thus proving that he is himself *available* for any purposes of the demagogue. His vote is of no more worth than that of any unprincipled foreigner or hireling native, who may have been bought. O for a man who is a *man*, and, as my neighbor says, has a bone in his back which you cannot pass your hand through! Our statistics are at fault: the population has been returned too large. How many *men* are there to a square thousand miles in this country? Hardly one. Does not America offer any inducement for men to settle here? The American has dwindled into an Odd Fellow,[9]—one who may be known by the development of his organ of gregariousness, and a manifest lack of intellect and cheerful self-reliance; whose first and chief concern, on coming into the world, is to see that the almshouses are in good repair; and, before yet he has lawfully donned the virile garb, to collect a fund for the support of the widows and orphans that may be; who, in short, ventures to live only by the aid of the Mutual Insurance company, which has promised to bury him decently.

It is not a man's duty, as a matter of course, to devote himself to the eradication of any, even the most enormous, wrong; he may still properly have other concerns to engage him; but it is his duty, at least, to wash his hands of it, and, if he gives it no thought longer, not to give it practically his support. If I devote myself to other pursuits and contemplations, I must first see, at least, that I do not pursue them sitting upon another man's shoulders. I must get off him first, that he may pursue his contemplations too. See what gross inconsistency is tolerated. I have heard some of my townsmen say, "I should like to have them order me out to help put down an insurrection of the slaves, or to march to Mexico;—see if I would go;" and yet these very men have each, directly by their allegiance, and so indirectly, at least, by their money, furnished a substitute. The soldier is applauded who refuses to serve in an unjust war by those who do not refuse to sustain the unjust government which makes the war; is applauded by those whose own act and authority he disregards and sets at naught; as if the state were penitent to that degree that it hired one to scourge it while it sinned, but not to that degree that it left off sinning for a moment. Thus, under the name of Order and Civil Government, we are all made at last to pay homage to and support our own meanness. After the first blush of sin comes its indifference; and from immoral it becomes, as it were, *un*moral, and not quite unnecessary to that life which we have made.

The broadest and most prevalent error requires the most disinterested virtue to sustain it. The slight reproach to which the virtue of patriotism is commonly liable, the noble are most likely to incur. Those who, while they disapprove of the character and measures of a government, yield to it their allegiance and support are undoubtedly its most conscientious supporters, and so frequently the most serious obstacles to reform. Some[10] are petitioning the State to dissolve the Union, to disregard the requisitions of the President. Why do they not dissolve it themselves,—the union between themselves and the State,—and refuse to pay their quota into its treasury? Do not they stand in the same relation to the State that the State does to the Union? And have not the same reasons prevented the State from resisting the Union which have prevented them from resisting the State?

How can a man be satisfied to entertain an opinion merely, and enjoy *it*? Is there any enjoyment in it, if his opinion is that he is aggrieved? If you are cheated out of a single dollar by your neighbor, you do not rest satisfied with knowing that you are cheated, or with saying that you are cheated, or even with petitioning him to pay you your due; but you take effectual steps at once to obtain the full amount, and see that you are never cheated again. Action from principle, the perception and the performance of right, changes things and relations; it is essentially revolutionary, and does not consist wholly with anything which was. It not only divides States and churches, it divides families; ay, it divides the *individual*, separating the diabolical in him from the divine.

Unjust laws exist: shall we be content to obey them, or shall we endeavor to amend them, and obey them until we have succeeded, or shall we transgress them at once? Men generally, under such a government as this, think that they ought to wait until they have persuaded the majority to alter them. They think that, if they should resist, the remedy would be worse than the evil. But it is the fault of the government itself that the remedy *is* worse than the evil. *It* makes it worse. Why is it not

[9] The Independent Order of Odd Fellows, a fraternal society that still exists.

[10] Some radical abolitionists urged the Northern states to withdraw from the Union. (Harding)

more apt to anticipate and provide for reform? Why does it not cherish its wise minority? Why does it cry and resist before it is hurt? Why does it not encourage its citizens to be on the alert to point out its faults, and *do* better than it would have them? Why does it always crucify Christ, and excommunicate Copernicus[11] and Luther,[12] and pronounce Washington and Franklin rebels?

One would think, that a deliberate and practical denial of its authority was the only offence never contemplated by government; else, why has it not assigned its definite, its suitable and proportionate, penalty? If a man who has no property refuses but once to earn nine shillings for the State, he is put in prison for a period unlimited by any law that I know, and determined only by the discretion of those who placed him there; but if he should steal ninety times nine shillings from the State, he is soon permitted to go at large again.

If the injustice is part of the necessary friction of the machine of government, let it go, let it go: perchance it will wear smooth,—certainly the machine will wear out. If the injustice has a spring, or a pulley, or a rope, or a crank, exclusively for itself, then perhaps you may consider whether the remedy will not be worse than the evil; but if it is of such a nature that it requires you to be the agent of injustice to another, then, I say, break the law. Let your life be a counter-friction to stop the machine. What I have to do is see, at any rate, that I do not lend myself to the wrong which I condemn.

As for adopting the ways which the State has provided for remedying the evil, I know not of such ways. They take too much time, and a man's life will be gone. I have other affairs to attend to. I came into this world, not chiefly to make this a good place to live in, but to live in it, be it good or bad. A man has not everything to do, but something; and because he cannot do *everything*, it is not necessary that he should do *something* wrong. It is not my business to be petitioning the Governor or the Legislature any more than it is theirs to petition me; and if they should not hear my petition, what should I do then? But in this case the State has provided no way: its very Constitution is the evil. This may seem to be harsh and stubborn and unconciliatory; but it is to treat with the utmost kindness and consideration the only spirit that can appreciate or deserves it. So is all change for the better, like birth and death, which convulse the body.

I do not hesitate to say, that those who call themselves Abolitionists should at once effectually withdraw their support, both in person and property, from the government of Massachusetts, and not wait till they constitute a majority of one, before they suffer the right to prevail through them. I think that it is enough if they have God on their side, without waiting for that other one. Moreover, any man more right than his neighbors constitutes a majority of one already.

I meet this American government, or its representative, the State government, directly, and face to face, once a year—no more—in the person of its tax-gatherer; this is the only mode in which a man situated as I am necessarily meets it; and it then says distinctly, Recognize me; and the simplest, the most effectual, and, in the present posture of affairs, the indispensablest mode of treating with it on this head, of expressing your little satisfaction with and love for it, is to deny it then. My civil neighbor, the tax-gatherer, is the very man I have to deal with,—for it is, after all, with men and not with parchment that I quarrel,—and he has voluntarily chosen to be an agent of the government. How shall he ever know well what he is and does as an officer of the government, or as a man, until he is obliged to consider whether he shall treat me, his neighbor, for whom he has respect, as a neighbor and well-disposed man, or as a maniac and disturber of the peace, and see if he can get over this obstruction to his neighborliness without a ruder and more impetuous thought or speech corresponding with his action. I know this well, that if one thousand, if one hundred, if ten men whom I could name,—if ten *honest* men only,—ay, if *one* HONEST man, in this State of Massachusetts, *ceasing to hold slaves*, were actually to withdraw from this copartnership, and be locked up in the county jail therefor, it would be the abolition of slavery in America. For it matters not how small the beginning may seem to be: what is once well done is done forever. But we love better to talk about it: that we say is our mission. Reform keeps many scores of newspapers in its service, but not one man. If my esteemed neighbor,[13] the State's ambassador, who will devote his days to the settlement of the question of human rights in the Council Chamber, instead of being threatened with the prisons of Carolina, were to sit down the prisoner of Massachusetts, that State which is so anxious to foist the sin of slavery upon her sister,—though at present she can discover only an act of inhospitality to be the ground of a quarrel with her,—the Legislature would not wholly waive the subject the following winter.

Under a government which imprisons any unjustly, the true place for a just man is also a prison. The proper place to-day, the only place which Massachu-

[11] Copernicus (1473-1543) escaped excommunication because he was dying when his theory was published.

[12] Martin Luther (1483-1546) was excommunicated in 1520.

[13] Samuel Hoar (1778-1856) was sent to South Carolina by Massachusetts in 1844 to protest the arrest of black seamen on Massachusetts ships in South Carolina waters. He was evicted from the state by legislative action. (Harding)

setts has provided for her freer and less desponding spirits, is in her prisons, to be put out and locked out of the State by her own act, as they have already put themselves out by their principles. It is there that the fugitive slave, and the Mexican prisoner on parole, and the Indian come to plead the wrongs of his race should find them; on that separate, but more free and honorable, ground, where the State places those who are not *with* her, but *against* her,—the only house in a slave State in which a free man can abide with honor. If any think that their influence would be lost there, and their voices no longer afflict the ear of the State, that they would not be as an enemy within its walls, they do not know by how much truth is stronger than error, nor how much more eloquently and effectively he can combat injustice who has experienced a little in his own person. Cast your whole vote, not a strip of paper merely, but your whole influence. A minority is powerless while it conforms to the majority; it is not even a minority then; but it is irresistible when it clogs by its whole weight. If the alternative is to keep all just men in prison, or give up war and slavery, the State will not hesitate which to choose. If a thousand men were not to pay their tax-bills this year, that would not be a violent and bloody measure, as it would be to pay them, and enable the State to commit violence and shed innocent blood. This is, in fact, the definition of a peaceable revolution, if any such is possible. If the tax-gatherer, or any other public officer, asks me, as one has done, "But what shall I do?" my answer is, "If you really wish to do anything, resign your office." When the subject has refused allegiance, and the officer has resigned his office, then the revolution is accomplished. But even suppose blood should flow. Is there not a sort of blood shed when the conscience is wounded? Through this wound a man's real manhood and immortality flow out, and he bleeds to an everlasting death. I see this blood flowing now.

I have contemplated the imprisonment of the offender, rather than the seizure of his goods,—though both will serve the same purpose,—because they who assert the purest right, and consequently are most dangerous to a corrupt State, commonly have not spent much time in accumulating property. To such the State renders comparatively small service, and a slight tax is wont to appear exorbitant, particularly if they are obliged to earn it by special labor with their hands. If there were one who lived wholly without the use of money, the State itself would hesitate to demand it of him. But the rich man—not to make any invidious comparison—is always sold to the institution which makes him rich. Absolutely speaking, the more money, the less virtue; for money comes between a man and his objects, and obtains them for him; and it was certainly no great virtue to obtain it. It puts to rest many questions which he would otherwise be taxed to answer; while the only new question which it puts is the hard but superfluous one, how to spend it. Thus his moral ground is taken from under his feet. The opportunities of living are diminished in proportion as what are called the "means" are increased. The best thing a man can do for his culture when he is rich is to endeavor to carry out those schemes which he entertained when he was poor. Christ answered the Herodians according to their condition. "Show me the tribute-money," said he;—and one took a penny out of his pocket;—if you use money which has the image of Caesar on it, and which he has made current and valuable, that is, *if you are men of the State,* and gladly enjoy the advantages of Caesar's government, then pay him back some of his own when he demands it. "Render therefore to Caesar that which is Caesar's, and to God those things which are God's,"[14]—leaving them no wiser than before as to which was which; for they did not wish to know.

When I converse with the freest of my neighbors, I perceive that, whatever they may say about the magnitude and seriousness of the question, and their regard for the public tranquillity, the long and the short of the matter is, that they cannot spare the protection of the existing government, and they dread the consequences to their property and families of disobedience to it. For my own part, I should not like to think that I ever rely on the protection of the State. But, if I deny the authority of the State when it presents its tax-bill, it will soon take and waste all my property, and so harass me and my children without end. This is hard. This makes it impossible for a man to live honestly, and at the same time comfortably, in outward respects. It will not be worth the while to accumulate property; that would be sure to go again. You must hire or squat somewhere, and raise but a small crop, and eat that soon. You must live within yourself, and depend upon yourself always tucked up and ready for a start, and not have many affairs. A man may grow rich in Turkey even, if he will be in all respects a good subject of the Turkish government. Confucius said: "If a state is governed by the principles of reason, poverty and misery are subjects of shame; if a state is not governed by the principles of reason, riches and honors are the subjects of shame."[15] No: until I want the protection of Massachusetts to be extended to me in some distant Southern port, where my liberty is endangered, or until I am bent solely on building up an estate at home by peaceful

[14] Matthew xxii.19-21.

[15] Confucius, *Analects.*

enterprise, I can afford to refuse allegiance to Massachusetts, and her right to my property and life. It costs me less in every sense to incur the penalty of disobedience to the State than it would to obey. I should feel as if I were worth less in that case.

Some years ago, the State met me in behalf of the Church,[16] and commanded me to pay a certain sum toward the support of a clergyman whose preaching my father attended, but never I myself. "Pay," it said, "or be locked up in the jail." I declined to pay. But, unfortunately, another man saw fit to pay it. I did not see why the schoolmaster should be taxed to support the priest, and not the priest the schoolmaster; for I was not the State's schoolmaster, but I supported myself by voluntary subscription. I did not see why the lyceum should not present its tax-bill, and have the State to back its demand, as well as the Church. However, at the request of the selectmen, I condescended to make some such statement as this in writing:—"Know all men by these presents, that I, Henry Thoreau, do not wish to be regarded as a member of any incorporated society which I have not joined." This I gave to the town clerk; and he has it. The State, having thus learned that I did not wish to be regarded as a member of that church, has never made a like demand on me since; though it said that it must adhere to its original presumption that time. If I had known how to name them, I should then have signed off in detail from all the societies which I never signed on to; but I did not know where to find a complete list.

I have paid no poll-tax for six years. I was put into a jail once on this account, for one night;[17] and, as I stood considering the walls of solid stone, two or three feet thick, the door of wood and iron, a foot thick, and the iron grating which strained the light, I could not help being struck with the foolishness of that institution which treated me as if I were mere flesh and blood and bones, to be locked up. I wondered that it should have concluded at length that this was the best use it could put me to, and had never thought to avail itself of my services in some way. I saw that, if there was a wall of stone between me and my townsmen, there was a still more difficult one to climb or break through before they could get to be as free as I was. I did not for a moment feel confined, and the walls seemed a great waste of stone and mortar. I felt as if I alone of all my townsmen had paid my tax. They plainly did not know how to treat me, but behaved like persons who are underbred. In every threat and in every compliment there was a blunder; for they thought that my chief desire was to stand the other side of that stone wall. I could not but smile to see how industriously they locked the door on my meditations, which followed them out again without let or hindrance, and *they* were really all that was dangerous. As they could not reach me, they had resolved to punish my body; just as boys, if they cannot come at some person against whom they have a spite, will abuse his dog. I saw that the State was half-witted, that it was timid as a lone woman with her silver spoons, and that it did not know its friends from its foes, and I lost all my remaining respect for it, and pitied it.

Thus the State never intentionally confronts a man's sense, intellectual or moral, but only his body, his senses. It is not armed with superior wit or honesty, but with superior physical strength. I was not born to be forced. I will breathe after my own fashion. Let us see who is the strongest. What force has a multitude? They only can force me who obey a higher law than I. They force me to become like themselves. I do not hear of *men* being *forced* to live this way or that by masses of men. What sort of life were that to live? When I meet a government which says to me, "Your money or your life," why should I be in haste to give it my money? It may be in a great strait, and not know what to do: I cannot help that. It must help itself; do as I do. It is not worth the while to snivel about it. I am not responsible for the successful working of the machinery of society. I am not the son of the engineer. I perceive that, when an acorn and a chestnut fall side by side, the one does not remain inert to make way for the other, but both obey their own laws, and spring and grow and flourish as best they can, till one, perchance, overshadows and destroys the other. If a plant cannot live according to its nature, it dies; and so a man.

The night in prison was novel and interesting enough. The prisoners in their shirt-sleeves were enjoying a chat and the evening air in the doorway, when I entered. But the jailer[18] said, "Come, boys, it is time to lock up;" and so they dispersed, and I heard the sound of their steps returning into the hollow apartments. My roommate was introduced to me by the jailer as "a first-rate fellow and a clever man." When the door was locked, he showed me where to hang my hat, and how he managed matters there. The rooms were whitewashed once a month; and this one, at least, was the whitest, most simply furnished, and probably the neatest apartment in the town. He naturally wanted to know where I came from, and what brought me there; and, when I had told him, I asked him in my turn how he came

[16] Churches then taxed their congregations. The taxes were billed and collected by town officials. The church (First Parish Church of Concord), which had assumed Thoreau wished to be a member, because his parents were, never billed him again. (Harding)

[17] July 23 or 24, 1846.

[18] Sam Staples—jailer, constable, and tax collector—was a personal friend of Thoreau's.

there, presuming him to be an honest man, of course; and, as the world goes, I believe he was. "Why," said he, "they accuse me of burning a barn; but I never did it." As near as I could discover, he had probably gone to bed in a barn when drunk, and smoked his pipe there; and so a barn was burnt. He had the reputation of being a clever man, had been there some three months waiting for his trial to come on, and would have to wait as much longer; but he was quite domesticated and contented, since he got his board for nothing, and thought that he was well treated.

He occupied one window, and I the other; and I saw that if one stayed there long, his principal business would be to look out the window. I had soon read all the tracts that were left there, and examined where former prisoners had broken out, and where a grate had been sawed off, and heard the history of the various occupants of that room; for I found that even here there was a history and a gossip which never circulated beyond the walls of the jail. Probably this is the only house in the town where verses are composed, which are afterward printed in a circular form, but not published. I was shown quite a long list of verses which were composed by some young men who had been detected in an attempt to escape, who avenged themselves by singing them.

I pumped my fellow-prisoner as dry as I could, for fear I should never see him again; but at length he showed me which was my bed, and left me to blow out the lamp.

It was like traveling into a far country, such as I had never expected to behold, to lie there for one night. It seemed to me that I never had heard the town clock strike before, nor the evening sounds of the village; for we slept with the windows open, which were inside the grating. It was to see my native village in the light of the Middle Ages, and our Concord was turned into a Rhine stream, and visions of knights and castles passed before me. They were the voices of old burghers that I heard in the streets. I was an involuntary spectator and auditor of whatever was done and said in the kitchen of the adjacent village inn,—a wholly new and rare experience to me. It was a closer view of my native town. I was fairly inside of it. I never had seen its institutions before. This is one of its peculiar institutions; for it is a shire town. I began to comprehend what its inhabitants were about.

In the morning, our breakfasts were put through the hole in the door, in small oblong-square tin pans, made to fit, and holding a pint of chocolate, with brown bread, and an iron spoon. When they called for the vessels again, I was green enough to return what bread I had left; but my comrade seized it, and said that I should lay that up for lunch or dinner. Soon after he was let out to work at haying in a neighboring field, whither he went every day, and would not be back till noon; so he bade me good-day, saying that he doubted if he should see me again.

When I came out of prison,—for some one[19] interfered, and paid that tax,—I did not perceive that great changes had taken place on the common, such as he observed who went in a youth and emerged a tottering and gray-headed man; and yet a change had to my eyes come over the scene,—the town, and State, and country,—greater than any that mere time could effect. I saw yet more distinctly the State in which I lived. I saw to what extent the people among whom I lived could be trusted as good neighbors and friends; that their friendship was for summer weather only; that they did not greatly propose to do right; that they were a distinct race from me by their prejudices and superstitions, as the Chinamen and Malays are; that in their sacrifices to humanity they ran no risks, not even to their property; that after all they were not so noble but they treated the thief as he had treated them, and hoped, by a certain outward observance and a few prayers, and by walking in a particular straight though useless path from time to time, to save their souls. This may be to judge my neighbors harshly; for I believe that many of them are not aware that they have such an institution as the jail in their village.

It was formerly the custom in our village, when a poor debtor came out of jail, for his acquaintances to salute him, looking through their fingers, which were crossed to represent the grating of a jail window, "How do ye do?" My neighbors did not thus salute me, but first looked at me, and then at one another, as if I had returned from a long journey. I was put into jail as I was going to the shoemaker's to get a shoe which was mended. When I was let out the next morning, I proceeded to finish my errand, and, having put on my mended shoe, joined a huckleberry party, who were impatient to put themselves under my conduct; and in half an hour,—for the horse was soon tackled,—was in the midst of a huckleberry field, on one of our highest hills, two miles off, and then the State was nowhere to be seen.

This is the whole history of "My Prisons."[20]

I have never declined paying the highway tax, because I am as desirous of being a good neighbor as I am of being a bad subject; and as for supporting schools, I am doing my part to educate my fellow-countrymen now. It is for no particular item in the tax-bill that I refuse to pay it. I simply wish to refuse

[19] Probably his Aunt Maria Thoreau.

[20] Reference to a popular book of that title by Silvio Pellico (1789-1854), an Italian revolutionary.

allegiance to the State, to withdraw and stand aloof from it effectually. I do not care to trace the course of my dollar, if I could, till it buys a man or a musket to shoot one with,—the dollar is innocent,—but I am concerned to trace the effects of my allegiance. In fact, I quietly declare war with the State, after my fashion, though I will still make what use and get what advantage of her I can, as is usual in such cases.

If others pay the tax which is demanded of me, from a sympathy with the State, they do but what they have already done in their own case, or rather they abet injustice to a greater extent than the State requires. If they pay the tax from a mistaken interest in the individual taxed, to save his property, or prevent his going to jail, it is because they have not considered wisely how far they let their private feelings interfere with the public good.

This, then, is my position at present. But one cannot be too much on his guard in such a case, lest his action be biased by obstinacy or an undue regard for the opinions of men. Let him see that he does only what belongs to himself and to the hour.

I think sometimes, Why, this people mean well, they are only ignorant; they would do better if they knew how: why give your neighbors this pain to treat you as they are not inclined to? But I think again, This is no reason why I should do as they do, or permit others to suffer much greater pain of a different kind. Again, I sometimes say to myself, When many millions of men, without heat, without ill will, without personal feeling of any kind, demand of you a few shillings only, without the possibility, such is their constitution, of retracting or altering their present demand, and without the possibility, on your side, of appeal to any other millions, why expose yourself to this overwhelming brute force? You do not resist cold and hunger, the winds and the waves, thus obstinately; you quietly submit to a thousand similar necessities. You do not put your head into the fire. But just in proportion as I regard this as not wholly a brute force, but partly a human force, and consider that I have relations to those millions as to so many millions of men, and not of mere brute or inanimate things, I see that appeal is possible, first and instantaneously, from them to the Maker of them, and, secondly, from them to themselves. But if I put my head deliberately into the fire, there is no appeal to fire or to the Maker of fire, and I have only myself to blame. If I could convince myself that I have any right to be satisfied with men as they are, and to treat them accordingly, and not according, in some respects, to my requisitions and expectations of what they and I ought to be, then, like a good Mussulman and fatalist, I should endeavor to be satisfied with things as they are, and say it is the will of God. And, above all, there is this difference between resisting this and a purely brute or natural force, that I can resist this with some effect; but I cannot expect, like Orpheus,[21] to change the nature of the rocks and trees and beasts.

I do not wish to quarrel with any man or nation. I do not wish to split hairs, to make fine distinctions, or set myself up as better than my neighbors. I seek rather, I may say, even an excuse for conforming to the laws of the land. I am but too ready to conform to them. Indeed, I have reason to suspect myself on this head; and each year, as the tax-gatherer comes round, I find myself disposed to review the acts and position of the general and State governments, and the spirit of the people, to discover a pretext for conformity.

> "We must affect our country as our parents,
> And if at any time we alienate
> Our love or industry from doing it honor,
> We must respect effects and teach the soul
> Matter of conscience and religion,
> And not desire of rule or benefit."[22]

I believe that the State will soon be able to take all my work of this sort out of my hands, and then I shall be no better a patriot than my fellow-countrymen. Seen from a lower point of view, the Constitution, with all its faults, is very good; the law and the courts are very respectable; even this State and this American government are, in many respects, very admirable, and rare things, to be thankful for, such as a great many have described them; but seen from a point of view a little higher, they are what I have described them; seen from a higher still, and the highest, who shall say what they are, or that they are worth looking at or thinking of at all?

However, the government does not concern me much, and I shall bestow the fewest possible thoughts on it. It is not many moments that I live under a government, even in this world. If a man is thought-free, fancy-free, imagination-free, that which *is not* never for a long time appearing *to be* to him, unwise rulers or reformers cannot fatally interrupt him.

I know that most men think differently from myself; but those whose lives are by profession devoted to the study of these or kindred subjects content me as little as any. Statesmen and legislators, standing so completely within the institution, never distinctly and nakedly behold it. They speak of moving society, but have no resting-place without it. They

[21] In Greek mythology, Orpheus played his lyre so well that it affected "rocks and trees and beasts."

[22] From *The Battle of Alcazar* by George Peele (1558?-1597?). Thoreau reworded the passage and changed its meaning by removing it from context.

may be men of a certain experience and discrimination, and have no doubt invented ingenious and even useful systems, for which we sincerely thank them; but all their wit and usefulness lie within certain not very wide limits. They are wont to forget that the world is not governed by policy and expediency. Webster[23] never goes behind government, and so cannot speak with authority about it. His words are wisdom to those legislators who contemplate no essential reform in the existing government; but for thinkers, and those who legislate for all time, he never once glances at the subject. I know of those whose serene and wise speculations on this theme would soon reveal the limits of his mind's range and hospitality. Yet, compared with the cheap professions of most reformers, and the still cheaper wisdom and eloquence of politicians in general, his are almost the only sensible and valuable words, and we thank Heaven for him. Comparatively, he is always strong, original, and, above all, practical. Still, his quality is not wisdom, but prudence. The lawyer's truth is not Truth, but consistency or a consistent expediency. Truth is always in harmony with herself, and is not concerned chiefly to reveal the justice that may consist with wrong-doing. He well deserves to be called, as he has been called, the Defender of the Constitution. There are really no blows to be given by him but defensive ones. He is not a leader, but a follower. His leaders are the men of '87.[24] "I have never made an effort," he says, "and never propose to make an effort; I have never countenanced an effort, and never mean to countenance an effort, to disturb the arrangement as originally made, by which the various States came into the Union."[25] Still thinking of the sanction which the Constitution gives to slavery, he says, "Because it was a part of the original compact,—let it stand." Notwithstanding his special acuteness and ability, he is unable to take a fact out of its merely political relations, and behold it as it lies absolutely to be disposed of by the intellect,—what, for instance, it behooves a man to do here in America to-day with regard to slavery,—but ventures, or is driven, to make some such desperate answer as the following, while professing to speak absolutely, and as a private man,—from which what new and singular code of social duties might be inferred? "The manner," says he, "in which the governments of those States where slavery exists are to regulate it is for their own consideration, under their responsibility to their constituents, to the general laws of propriety, humanity, and justice, and to God. Associations formed elsewhere, springing from a feeling of humanity, or any other cause, have nothing whatever to do with it. They have never received any encouragement from me, and they never will."[26]

They who know of no purer sources of truth, who have traced up its stream no higher, stand, and wisely stand, by the Bible and the Constitution, and drink at it there with reverence and humility; but they who behold where it comes trickling into this lake or that pool, gird up their loins once more, and continue their pilgrimage toward its fountain-head.

No man with a genius for legislation has appeared in America. They are rare in the history of the world. There are orators, politicians, and eloquent men, by the thousand; but the speaker has not yet opened his mouth to speak who is capable of settling the much vexed questions of the day. We love eloquence for its own sake, and not for any truth which it may utter, or any heroism it may inspire. Our legislators have not yet learned the comparative value of free trade and of freedom, of union, and of rectitude, to a nation. They have no genius or talent for comparatively humble questions of taxation and finance, commerce and manufactures and agriculture. If we were left solely to the wordy wit of legislators in Congress for our guidance, uncorrected by the seasonable experience and the effectual complaints of the people, America would not long retain her rank among the nations. For eighteen hundred years, though perchance I have no right to say it, the New Testament has been written; yet where is the legislator who has wisdom and practical talent enough to avail himself of the light which it sheds on the science of legislation?

The authority of government, even such as I am willing to submit to,—for I will cheerfully obey those who know and can do better than I, and in many things even those who neither know nor can do so well,—is still an impure one: to be strictly just, it must have the sanction and consent of the governed. It can have no pure right over my person and property but what I concede to it. The progress from an absolute to a limited monarchy, from a limited monarchy to a democracy, is a progress toward a true respect for the individual. Even the Chinese philosopher was wise enough to regard the individual as the basis of the empire. Is a democracy, such as we know it, the last improvement possible in government? Is it not possible to take a step further towards recognizing and organizing the rights of man? There will never be a really free and enlightened State until the State comes to recognize the individual as a higher and independent power, from which all its own power and authority are derived, and treats him accordingly. I please myself

[23] Daniel Webster (1782–1852).

[24] Those who framed the Constitution.

[25] From an 1845 speech by Webster.

[26] Speech, 1848.

with imagining a State at last which can afford to be just to all men, and to treat the individual with respect as a neighbor; which even would not think it inconsistent with its own repose if a few were to live aloof from it, not meddling with it, nor embraced by it, who fulfilled all the duties of neighbors and fellow-men. A State which bore this kind of fruit, and suffered it to drop off as fast as it ripened, would prepare the way for a still more perfect and glorious State, which also I have imagined, but not yet anywhere seen.

1847

FROM *Walden*

The reputation of Thoreau's masterpiece has grown apace in the twentieth century. The first edition—2,000 copies, published in 1854—probably more than sufficed till the death of Thoreau eight years later. Misrepresentation of his motives and actions by James Russell Lowell and Robert Louis Stevenson, who considered him a morbid solitary, hindered the growth of his fame for decades. But during the literary revival that set in about 1912, he became a major American author, and *Walden* an American classic.

Walden has four main aspects, is almost four simultaneous books. First, it is an account of an actual experience by a remarkable personality. A young man, not yet twenty-eight, undertakes in March 1845 an experiment in living, with a view to discovering what is really important to him and what is not. This aspect is indicated by the subtitle *Life in the Woods.*

The book is also a study of nature: of the lake known as Walden Pond, in summer and in winter; of animals and birds, frogs and turtles, ants and wasps, pickerel and perch; of the ground-nut and the pine tree; of rainstorms and snowstorms and the whole moving picture of the seasons. Close observation in the spirit of science is united with a living literary language.

At the same time, *Walden* is a view of modern society as seen by a critical and radical individualist: men, no longer free and creative, have been enslaved by labor and the division of labor; the Industrial Revolution has tended to produce a mechanized, standardized and conformist society destructive of simplicity, naturalness, integrity, depth, and contentment. Thoreau does not claim universal validity for his way of life, but urges the reader to "find and pursue *his own way,*" not some way derived from ancestors or contemporaries.

Finally, the book is a work of art, a group of substantially unified essays in which the personal experience, the study of nature, and the study of society are closely interrelated. The actual time-span of the Walden experiment was two years, two months, and two days; but, the two years being "similar," they are represented in the book with the unity of a single year, from spring to spring. Yet "Time is but the stream I go a-fishing in. . . . Its thin current slides away, but eternity remains." The tone is set by the sense of eternity, that which does not slide away but remains, that which is timeless, universal, absolute.

Of the eighteen chapters, or essays, five are given here, complete.

II. Where I Lived, and What I Lived For

At a certain season of our life we are accustomed to consider every spot as the possible site of a house. I have thus surveyed the country on every side within a dozen miles of where I live. In imagination I have bought all the farms in succession, for all were to be bought, and I knew their price. I walked over each farmer's premises, tasted his wild apples, discoursed on husbandry with him, took his farm at his price, at any price, mortgaging it to him in my mind; even put a higher price on it,—took everything but a deed of it,—took his word for his deed, for I dearly love to talk,—cultivated it, and him too to some extent, I trust, and withdrew when I had enjoyed it long enough, leaving him to carry it on. This experience entitles me to be regarded as a sort of real-estate broker by my friends. Wherever I sat, there I might live, and the landscape radiated from me accordingly. What is a house but a *sedes,* a seat?—better if a country seat. I discovered many a site for a house not likely to be soon improved, which some might have thought too far from the village, but to my eyes the village was too far from it. Well, there I might live, I said; and there I did live, for an hour, a summer and a winter life; saw how I could let the years run off, buffet the winter through, and see the spring come in. The future inhabitants of this region, wherever they may place their houses, may be sure that they have been anticipated. An afternoon sufficed to lay out the land into orchard, wood-lot, and pasture, and to decide what fine oaks or pines should be left to stand before the door, and whence each blasted tree could be seen to the best advantage; and then I let it lie, fallow perchance, for a man is rich in proportion to the number of things which he can afford to let alone.

My imagination carried me so far that I even had the refusal of several farms,—the refusal was all I wanted,—but I never got my fingers burned by actual possession. The nearest that I came to actual possession was when I bought the Hollowell place,[1] and had begun to sort my seeds, and collected materials with which to make a wheelbarrow to carry it on or off with; but before the owner gave me a deed of it, his wife—every man has such a wife—changed her mind and wished to keep it, and he offered me ten dollars to release him. Now, to speak the truth, I had but ten cents in the world, and it surpassed my arithmetic to tell, if I was that man who had ten cents, or who had a farm, or ten dollars, or all together. However, I let him keep the ten

[1] A farm on the Sudbury River near Concord.

dollars and the farm too, for I had carried it far enough; or rather, to be generous, I sold him the farm for just what I gave for it, and, as he was not a rich man, made him a present of ten dollars, and still had my ten cents, and seeds, and materials for a wheelbarrow left. I found thus that I had been a rich man without any damage to my poverty. But I retained the landscape, and I have since annually carried off what it yielded without a wheelbarrow. With respect to landscapes,—

> "I am monarch of all I *survey*,
> My right there is none to dispute."[2]

I have frequently seen a poet withdraw, having enjoyed the most valuable part of a farm, while the crusty farmer supposed that he had got a few wild apples only. Why, the owner does not know it for many years when a poet has put his farm in rhyme, the most admirable kind of invisible fence, has fairly impounded it, milked it, skimmed it, and got all the cream, and left the farmer only the skimmed milk.

The real attractions of the Hollowell farm, to me, were: its complete retirement, being about two miles from the village, half a mile from the nearest neighbor, and separated from the highway by a broad field; its bounding on the river, which the owner said protected it by its fogs from frosts in the spring, though that was nothing to me; the gray color and ruinous state of the house and barn, and the dilapidated fences, which put such an interval between me and the last occupant; the hollow and lichen-covered apple trees, gnawed by rabbits, showing what kind of neighbors I should have; but above all, the recollection I had of it from my earliest voyages up the river, when the house was concealed behind a dense grove of red maples, through which I heard the house-dog bark. I was in haste to buy it, before the proprietor finished getting out some rocks, cutting down the hollow apple trees, and grubbing up some young birches which had sprung up in the pasture, or, in short, had made any more of his improvements. To enjoy these advantages I was ready to carry it on; like Atlas, to take the world on my shoulders,—I never heard what compensation he received for that,—and do all those things which had no other motive or excuse but that I might pay for it and be unmolested in my possession of it; for I knew all the while that it would yield the most abundant crop of the kind I wanted, if I could only afford to let it alone. But it turned out as I have said.

All that I could say, then, with respect to farming on a large scale—I have always cultivated a garden—was, that I had had my seeds ready. Many think that seeds improve with age. I have no doubt that time discriminates between the good and the bad; and when at last I shall plant, I shall be less likely to be disappointed. But I would say to my fellows, once for all, As long as possible live free and uncommitted. It makes but little difference whether you are committed to a farm or the county jail.

Old Cato, whose "De Re Rusticâ" is my "Cultivator,"[3] says,—and the only translation I have seen makes sheer nonsense of the passage,—"When you think of getting a farm turn it thus in your mind, not to buy greedily; nor spare your pains to look at it, and do not think it enough to go round it once. The oftener you go there the more it will please you, if it is good." I think I shall not buy greedily, but go round and round it as long as I live, and be buried in it first, that it may please me the more at last.

The present was my next experiment of this kind, which I purpose to describe more at length, for convenience putting the experience of two years into one. As I have said, I do not propose to write an ode to dejection,[4] but to brag as lustily as chanticleer in the morning, standing on his roost, if only to wake my neighbors up.

When first I took up my abode in the woods, that is, began to spend my nights as well as days there, which, by accident, was on Independence Day, or the Fourth of July, 1845, my house was not finished for winter, but was merely a defence against the rain, without plastering or chimney, the walls being of rough, weather-stained boards, with wide chinks, which made it cool at night. The upright white hewn studs and freshly planed door and window casings gave it a clean and airy look, especially in the morning, when its timbers were saturated with dew, so that I fancied that by noon some sweet gum would exude from them. To my imagination it retained throughout the day more or less of this auroral character, reminding me of a certain house on a mountain which I had visited a year before. This was an airy and unplastered cabin, fit to entertain a travelling god, and where a goddess might trail her garments. The winds which passed over my dwelling were such as sweep over the ridges of mountains, bearing the broken strains, or celestial parts only, of terrestrial music. The morning wind forever blows, the poem of creation is uninterrupted; but

[2] By William Cowper (1731-1800), from "Verses Supposed to be Written by Alexander Selkirk."

[3] Probably refers to either *The Boston Cultivator* or *The New England Cultivator*, both published in Thoreau's lifetime. (Harding)

[4] The epigraph to *Walden* reads, "I do not propose to write an ode to dejection, but to brag as lustily as Chanticleer in the morning, standing on his roost, if only to wake my neighbors up." "Ode to dejection" refers to a poem of that title by Samuel Taylor Coleridge.

few are the ears that hear it. Olympus is but the outside of the earth everywhere.

The only house I had been the owner of before, if I except a boat, was a tent, which I used occasionally when making excursions in the summer, and this is still rolled up in my garret; but the boat, after passing from hand to hand, has gone down the stream of time. With this more substantial shelter about me, I had made some progress toward settling in the world. This frame, so slightly clad, was a sort of crystallization around me, and reacted on the builder. It was suggestive somewhat as a picture in outlines. I did not need to go outdoors to take the air, for the atmosphere within had lost none of its freshness. It was not so much within-doors as behind a door where I sat, even in the rainiest weather. The Harivansa says, "An abode without birds is like a meat without seasoning." Such was not my abode, for I found myself suddenly neighbor to the birds; not by having imprisoned one, but having caged myself near them. I was not only nearer to some of those which commonly frequent the garden and the orchard, but to those wilder and more thrilling songsters of the forest which never, or rarely, serenade a villager,—the wood thrush, the veery, the scarlet tanager, the field sparrow, the whip-poor-will, and many others.

I was seated by the shore of a small pond, about a mile and a half south of the village of Concord and somewhat higher than it, in the midst of an extensive wood between that town and Lincoln, and about two miles south of that our only field known to fame, Concord Battle Ground;[5] but I was so low in the woods that the opposite shore, half a mile off, like the rest, covered with wood, was my most distant horizon. For the first week, whenever I looked out on the pond it impressed me like a tarn high up on the side of a mountain, its bottom far above the surface of other lakes, and, as the sun arose, I saw it throwing off its nightly clothing of mist, and here and there, by degrees, its soft ripples or its smooth reflecting surface was revealed, while the mists, like ghosts, were stealthily withdrawing in every direction into the woods, as at the breaking up of some nocturnal conventicle. The very dew seemed to hang upon the trees later into the day than usual, as on the sides of mountains.

This small lake was of most value as a neighbor in the intervals of a gentle rain-storm in August, when, both air and water being perfectly still, but the sky overcast, mid-afternoon had all the serenity of evening, and the wood thrush sang around, and was heard from shore to shore. A lake like this is never smoother than at such a time; and the clear portion of the air above it being shallow and darkened by clouds, the water, full of light and reflections, becomes a lower heaven itself so much the more important. From a hill-top near by, where the wood had been recently cut off, there was a pleasing vista southward across the pond, through a wide indentation in the hills which form the shore there, where their opposite sides sloping toward each other suggested a stream flowing out in that direction through a wooded valley, but stream there was none. That way I looked between and over the near green hills to some distant and higher ones in the horizon, tinged with blue. Indeed, by standing on tiptoe I could catch a glimpse of some of the peaks of the still bluer and more distant mountain ranges in the northwest, those true-blue coins from heaven's own mint, and also of some portion of the village. But in other directions, even from this point, I could not see over or beyond the woods which surrounded me. It is well to have some water in your neighborhood, to give buoyancy to and float the earth. One value even of the smallest well is, that when you look into it you see that earth is not continent but insular. This is as important as that it keeps butter cool. When I looked across the pond from this peak toward the Sudbury meadows, which in time of flood I distinguished elevated perhaps by a mirage in their seething valley, like a coin in a basin, all the earth beyond the pond appeared like a thin crust insulated and floated even by this small sheet of intervening water, and I was reminded that this on which I dwelt was but *dry land.*

Though the view from my door was still more contracted, I did not feel crowded or confined in the least. There was pasture enough for my imagination. The low shrub oak plateau to which the opposite shore arose stretched away toward the prairies of the West and the steppes of Tartary, affording ample room for all the roving families of men. "There are none happy in the world but beings who enjoy freely a vast horizon,"—said Damodara,[6] when his herds required new and larger pastures.

Both place and time were changed, and I dwelt nearer to those parts of the universe and to those eras in history which had most attracted me. Where I lived was as far off as many a region viewed nightly by astronomers. We are wont to imagine rare and delectable places in some remote and more celestial corner of the system, behind the constellation of Cassiopeia's Chair, far from noise and disturbance. I discovered that my house actually had its site in such a withdrawn, but forever new and unprofaned, part of the universe. If it were worth the while to settle in those parts near to the Pleiades or

[5] Where the first battle of the American Revolution occurred, April 19, 1775.

[6] Another name for Krishna.

the Hyades, to Aldebaran or Altair,[7] then I was really there, or at an equal remoteness from the life which I had left behind, dwindled and twinkling with as fine a ray to my nearest neighbor, and to be seen only in moonless nights by him. Such was that part of creation where I had squatted;—

> "There was a shepherd that did live,
> And held his thoughts as high
> As were the mounts whereon his flocks
> Did hourly feed him by."[8]

What should we think of the shepherd's life if his flocks always wandered to higher pastures than his thoughts?

Every morning was a cheerful invitation to make my life of equal simplicity, and I may say innocence, with Nature herself. I have been as sincere a worshipper of Aurora as the Greeks. I got up early and bathed in the pond; that was a religious exercise, and one of the best things which I did. They say that characters were engraven on the bathing tub of King Tching-thang to this effect: "Renew thyself completely each day; do it again, and again, and forever again."[9] I can understand that. Morning brings back the heroic ages. I was as much affected by the faint hum of a mosquito making its invisible and unimaginable tour through my apartment at earliest dawn, when I was sitting with door and windows open, as I could be by any trumpet that ever sang of fame. It was Homer's requiem; itself an Iliad and Odyssey in the air, singing its own wrath and wanderings. There was something cosmical about it; a standing advertisement, till forbidden, of the everlasting vigor and fertility of the world. The morning, which is the most memorable season of the day, is the awakening hour. Then there is least somnolence in us; and for an hour, at least, some part of us awakes which slumbers all the rest of the day and night. Little is to be expected of that day, if it can be called a day, to which we are not awakened by our Genius, but by the mechanical nudgings of some servitor, are not awakened by our own newly acquired force and aspirations from within, accompanied by the undulations of celestial music, instead of factory bells, and a fragrance filling the air—to a higher life than we fell asleep from; and thus the darkness bear its fruit, and prove itself to be good, no less than the light. That man who does not believe that each day contains an earlier, more sacred, and auroral hour than he has yet profaned, has despaired of life, and is pursuing a descending and darkening way. After a partial cessation of his sensuous life, the soul of man, or its organs rather, are reinvigorated each day, and his Genius tries again what noble life it can make. All memorable events, I should say, transpire in morning time and in a morning atmosphere. The Vedas say, "All intelligences awake with the morning." Poetry and art, and the fairest and most memorable of the actions of men, date from such an hour. All poets and heroes, like Memnon, are the children of Aurora, and emit their music at sunrise. To him whose elastic and vigorous thought keeps pace with the sun, the day is a perpetual morning. It matters not what the clocks say or the attitudes and labors of men. Morning is when I am awake and there is a dawn in me. Moral reform is the effort to throw off sleep. Why is it that men give so poor an account of their day if they have not been slumbering? They are not such poor calculators. If they had not been overcome with drowsiness, they would have performed something. The millions are awake enough for physical labor; but only one in a million is awake enough for effective intellectual exertion, only one in a hundred millions to a poetic or divine life. To be awake is to be alive. I have never yet met a man who was quite awake. How could I have looked him in the face?

We must learn to reawaken and keep ourselves awake, not by mechanical aids, but by an infinite expectation of the dawn, which does not forsake us in our soundest sleep. I know of no more encouraging fact than the unquestionable ability of man to elevate his life by a conscious endeavor. It is something to be able to paint a particular picture, or to carve a statue, and so to make a few objects beautiful; but it is far more glorious to carve and paint the very atmosphere and medium through which we look, which morally we can do. To affect the quality of the day, that is the highest of arts. Every man is tasked to make his life, even in its details, worthy of the contemplation of his most elevated and critical hour. If we refused, or rather used up, such paltry information as we get, the oracles would distinctly inform us how this might be done.

I went to the woods because I wished to live deliberately, to front only the essential facts of life, and see if I could not learn what it had to teach, and not, when I came to die, discover that I had not lived. I did not wish to live what was not life, living is so dear; nor did I wish to practise resignation, unless it was quite necessary. I wanted to live deep and suck out all the marrow of life, to live so sturdily and Spartan-like as to put to rout all that was not life, to cut a broad swath and shave close, to drive life into a corner, and reduce it to its lowest terms, and, if it proved to be mean, why then to get the whole and genuine meanness of it, and publish its meanness to the world; or if it were sublime, to

[7] Constellations and stars.

[8] Lines from an anonymous poem set to music by Robert Jones in 1611.

[9] Confucius, *The Great Learning.*

know it by experience, and be able to give a true account of it in my next excursion. For most men, it appears to me, are in a strange uncertainty about it, whether it is of the devil or of God, and have *somewhat hastily* concluded that it is the chief end of man here to "glorify God and enjoy him forever."[10]

Still we live meanly, like ants; though the fable[11] tells us that we were long ago changed into men; like pygmies[12] we fight with cranes; it is error upon error, and clout upon clout, and our best virtue has for its occasion a superfluous and evitable wretchedness. Our life is frittered away by detail. An honest man has hardly need to count more than his ten fingers, or in extreme cases he may add his ten toes, and lump the rest. Simplicity, simplicity, simplicity! I say, let your affairs be as two or three, and not a hundred or a thousand; instead of a million count half a dozen, and keep your accounts on your thumb-nail. In the midst of this chopping sea of civilized life, such are the clouds and storms and quicksands and thousand-and-one items to be allowed for, that a man has to live, if he would not founder and go to the bottom and not make his port at all, by dead reckoning, and he must be a great calculator indeed who succeeds. Simplify, simplify. Instead of three meals a day, if it be necessary eat but one; instead of a hundred dishes, five; and reduce other things in proportion. Our life is like a German Confederacy,[13] made up of petty states, with its boundary forever fluctuating, so that even a German cannot tell you how it is bounded at any moment. The nation itself, with all its so-called internal improvements, which, by the way are all external and superficial, is just such an unwieldy and overgrown establishment, cluttered with furniture and tripped up by its own traps, ruined by luxury and heedless expense, by want of calculation and a worthy aim, as the million households in the land; and the only cure for it, as for them, is in a rigid economy, a stern and more than Spartan simplicity of life and elevation of purpose. It lives too fast. Men think that it is essential that the *Nation* have commerce, and export ice, and talk through a telegraph, and ride thirty miles an hour, without a doubt, whether *they* do or not; but whether we should live like baboons or like men, is a little uncertain. If we do not get out sleepers,[14] and forge rails, and devote days and nights to the work, but go to tinkering upon our *lives* to improve *them,* who will build railroads? And if railroads are not built, how shall we get to heaven in season? But if we stay at home and mind our business, who will want railroads? We do not ride on the railroad; it rides upon us. Did you ever think what those sleepers are that underlie the railroad? Each one is a man, an Irishman, or a Yankee man. The rails are laid on them, and they are covered with sand, and the cars run smoothly over them. They are sound sleepers, I assure you. And every few years a new lot is laid down and run over; so that, if some have the pleasure of riding on a rail, others have the misfortune to be ridden upon. And when they run over a man that is walking in his sleep, a supernumerary sleeper in the wrong position, and wake him up, they suddenly stop the cars, and make a hue and cry about it, as if this were an exception. I am glad to know that it takes a gang of men for every five miles to keep the sleepers down and level in their beds as it is, for this is a sign that they may sometime get up again.

Why should we live with such hurry and waste of life? We are determined to be starved before we are hungry. Men say that a stitch in time saves nine, and so they take a thousand stitches to-day to save nine to-morrow. As for *work,* we haven't any of any consequence. We have the Saint Vitus' dance, and cannot possibly keep our heads still. If I should only give a few pulls at the parish bell-rope, as for a fire, that is, without setting the bell, there is hardly a man on his farm in the outskirts of Concord, notwithstanding that press of engagements which was his excuse so many times this morning, nor a boy, nor a woman, I might almost say, but would forsake all and follow that sound, not mainly to save property from the flames, but, if we will confess the truth, much more to see it burn, since burn it must, and we, be it known, did not set it on fire,—or to see it put out, and have a hand in it, if that is done as handsomely; yes, even if it were the parish church itself. Hardly a man takes a half-hour's nap after dinner, but when he wakes he holds up his head and asks, "What's the news?" as if the rest of mankind had stood his sentinels. Some give directions to be waked every half-hour, doubtless for no other purpose; and then, to pay for it, they tell what they have dreamed. After a night's sleep the news is as indispensable as the breakfast. "Pray tell me anything new that has happened to a man anywhere on this globe,"—and he reads it over his coffee and rolls, that a man has had his eyes gouged out this morning on the Wachito River;[15] never dreaming the while that he lives in the dark unfathomed mammoth cave of this world, and has but the rudiment of an eye himself.

For my part, I could easily do without the post-

[10] From the "Shorter Catechism" in *The New England Primer.* Thoreau does not think much of that kind of devotion.

[11] In Greek mythology Aeacus, son of Jupiter and king of Oenopia, asked Jupiter to repeople his kingdom (decimated by pestilence) by changing ants into men. (Harding)

[12] Cf. *Iliad* III, the opening lines.

[13] The separate states were not really unified until 1871.

[14] Railroad ties; a pun, too.

[15] The Washita or Ouachita River flows from Arkansas into Louisiana.

office. I think that there are very few important communications made through it. To speak critically, I never received more than one or two letters in my life—I wrote this some years ago—that were worth the postage. The penny-post is, commonly, an institution through which you seriously offer a man that penny for his thoughts which is so often safely offered in jest. And I am sure that I never read any memorable news in a newspaper. If we read of one man robbed, or murdered, or killed by accident, or one house burned, or one vessel wrecked, or one steamboat blown up, or one cow run over on the Western Railroad,[16] or one mad dog killed, or one lot of grasshoppers in the winter,—we never need read of another. One is enough. If you are acquainted with the principle, what do you care for a myriad instances and applications? To a philosopher all *news*, as it is called, is gossip, and they who edit and read it are old women over their tea. Yet not a few are greedy after this gossip. There was such a rush, as I hear, the other day at one of the offices to learn the foreign news by the last arrival, that several large squares of plate glass belonging to the establishment were broken by the pressure,—news which I seriously think a ready wit might write a twelvemonth, or twelve years, beforehand with sufficient accuracy. As for Spain, for instance, if you know how to throw in Don Carlos and the Infanta, and Don Pedro and Seville and Granada,[17] from time to time in the right proportions,—they may have changed the names a little since I saw the papers,—and serve up a bull-fight when other entertainments fail, it will be true to the letter, and give us as good an idea of the exact state or ruin of things in Spain as the most succinct and lucid reports under this head in the newspapers: and as for England, almost the last significant scrap of news from that quarter was the revolution of 1649;[18] and if you have learned the history of her crops for an average year, you never need attend to that thing again, unless your speculations are of a merely pecuniary character. If one may judge who rarely looks into the newspapers, nothing new does ever happen in foreign parts, a French revolution not excepted.

What news! how much more important to know what that is which was never old! "Kieou-he-yu (great dignitary of the state of Wei) sent a man to Khoung-tseu to know his news. Khoung-tseu caused the messenger to be seated near him, and questioned him in these terms: What is your master doing? The messenger answered with respect: My master desires to diminish the number of his faults, but he cannot come to the end of them. The messenger being gone, the philosopher remarked: What a worthy messenger! What a worthy messenger!"[19] The preacher, instead of vexing the ears of drowsy farmers on their day of rest at the end of the week,—for Sunday is the fit conclusion of an ill-spent week, and not the fresh and brave beginning of a new one,—with this one other draggle-tail of a sermon, should shout with thundering voice, "Pause! Avast! Why so seeming fast, but deadly slow?"

Shams and delusions are esteemed for soundest truths, while reality is fabulous. If men would steadily observe realities only, and not allow themselves to be deluded, life, to compare it with such things as we know, would be like a fairy tale and the Arabian Nights' Entertainments. If we respected only what is inevitable and has a right to be, music and poetry would resound along the streets. When we are unhurried and wise, we perceive that only great and worthy things have any permanent and absolute existence, that petty fears and petty pleasures are but the shadow of the reality. This is always exhilarating and sublime. By closing the eyes and slumbering, and consenting to be deceived by shows, men establish and confirm their daily life of routine and habit everywhere, which still is built on purely illusory foundations. Children, who play life, discern its true law and relations more clearly than men, who fail to live it worthily, but who think that they are wiser by experience, that is, by failure. I have read in a Hindoo book, that "there was a king's son, who, being expelled in infancy from his native city, was brought up by a forester, and, growing up to maturity in that state, imagined himself to belong to the barbarous race with which he lived. One of his father's ministers having discovered him, revealed to him what he was, and the misconception of his character was removed, and he knew himself to be a prince. So soul," continues the Hindoo philosopher, "from the circumstances in which it is placed, mistakes its own character, until the truth is revealed to it by some holy teacher, and then it knows itself to be *Brahme*." I perceive that we inhabitants of New England live this mean life that we do because our vision does not penetrate the surface of things. We think that that *is* which *appears* to be. If a man should walk through this town and see only the reality, where, think you, would the "Mill-dam" go to? If he should give us an account of the realities he beheld there, we should not recognize the place in his description. Look at a meeting-house, or a court-house, or a jail, or a shop, or a dwelling-house, and say what that thing really is before a true gaze, and they would all go to pieces in your account of

[16] Connected Worcester, Massachusetts, and Albany, New York.

[17] Names in the news during the thirties and forties. Pedro and Carlos competed for Ferdinand's crown after he died in 1839. The Infanta became Queen Isabella in 1843.

[18] The year Cromwell abolished the monarchy.

[19] Confucius, *Analects*.

them. Men esteem truth remote, in the outskirts of the system, behind the farthest star, before Adam and after the last man. In eternity there is indeed something true and sublime. But all these times and places and occasions are now and here. God himself culminates in the present moment, and will never be more divine in the lapse of all the ages. And we are enabled to apprehend at all what is sublime and noble only by the perpetual instilling and drenching of the reality that surrounds us. The universe constantly and obediently answers to our conceptions; whether we travel fast or slow, the track is laid for us. Let us spend our lives in conceiving then. The poet or the artist never yet had so fair and noble a design but some of his posterity at least could accomplish it.

Let us spend one day as deliberately as Nature, and not be thrown off the track by every nutshell and mosquito's wing that falls on the rails. Let us rise early and fast, or break fast, gently and without perturbation; let company come and let company go, let the bells ring and the children cry,—determined to make a day of it. Why should we knock under and go with the stream? Let us not be upset and overwhelmed in that terrible rapid and whirlpool called a dinner, situated in the meridian shallows. Weather this danger and you are safe, for the rest of the way is down hill. With unrelaxed nerves, with morning vigor, sail by it, looking another way, tied to the mast like Ulysses.[20] If the engine whistles, let it whistle till it is hoarse for its pains. If the bell rings, why should we run? We will consider what kind of music they are like. Let us settle ourselves, and work and wedge our feet downward through the mud and slush of opinion, and prejudice, and tradition, and delusion, and appearance, that alluvion which covers the globe, through Paris and London, through New York and Boston and Concord, through Church and State, through poetry and philosophy and religion, till we come to a hard bottom and rocks in place, which we can call *reality,* and say, This is, and no mistake; and then begin, having a *point d'appui,* below freshet and frost and fire, a place where you might found a wall or a state, or set a lamp-post safely, or perhaps a gauge, not a Nilometer,[21] but a Realometer, that future ages might know how deep a freshet of shams and appearances had gathered from time to time. If you stand right fronting and face to face to a fact, you will see the sun glimmer on both its surfaces, as if it were a cimeter, and feel its sweet edge dividing you through the heart and marrow, and so you will happily conclude your mortal career. Be it life or death, we crave only reality. If we are really dying, let us hear the rattle in our throats and feel cold in the extremities; if we are alive, let us go about our business.

Time is but the stream I go a-fishing in. I drink at it; but while I drink I see the sandy bottom and detect how shallow it is. Its thin current slides away, but eternity remains. I would drink deeper; fish in the sky, whose bottom is pebbly with stars. I cannot count one. I know not the first letter of the alphabet. I have always been regretting that I was not as wise as the day I was born. The intellect is a cleaver; it discerns and rifts its way into the secret of things. I do not wish to be any more busy with my hands than is necessary. My head is hands and feet. I feel all my best faculties concentrated in it. My instinct tells me that my head is an organ for burrowing, as some creatures use their snout and fore paws, and with it I would mine and burrow my way through these hills. I think that the richest vein is somewhere hereabouts; so by the divining-rod and thin rising vapors I judge; and here I will begin to mine.

IV. Sounds

But while we are confined to books, though the most select and classic, and read only particular written languages, which are themselves but dialects and provincial, we are in danger of forgetting the language which all things and events speak without metaphor, which alone is copious and standard. Much is published, but little printed. The rays which stream through the shutter will be no longer remembered when the shutter is wholly removed. No method nor discipline can supersede the necessity of being forever on the alert. What is a course of history or philosophy, or poetry, no matter how well selected, or the best society, or the most admirable routine of life, compared with the discipline of looking always at what is to be seen? Will you be a reader, a student merely, or a seer? Read your fate, see what is before you, and walk on into futurity.

I did not read books the first summer; I hoed beans. Nay, I often did better than this. There were times when I could not afford to sacrifice the bloom of the present moment to any work, whether of the head or hands. I love a broad margin to my life. Sometimes, in a summer morning, having taken my accustomed bath, I sat in my sunny doorway from sunrise till noon, rapt in a revery, amidst the pines and hickories and sumachs, in undisturbed solitude and stillness, while the birds sang around or flitted noiseless through the house, until by the sun falling in at my west window, or the noise of some travel-

[20] Ulysses had himself tied to his ship's mast so he could hear the Sirens' song but not be tempted to go to them.

[21] An ancient instrument that recorded the rise and fall of the Nile.

ler's wagon on the distant highway, I was reminded of the lapse of time. I grew in those seasons like corn in the night, and they were far better than any work of the hands would have been. They were not time subtracted from my life, but so much over and above my usual allowance. I realized what the Orientals mean by contemplation and the forsaking of works. For the most part, I minded not how the hours went. The day advanced as if to light some work of mine; it was morning, and lo, now it is evening, and nothing memorable is accomplished. Instead of singing like the birds, I silently smiled at my incessant good fortune. As the sparrow had its trill, sitting on the hickory before my door, so had I my chuckle or suppressed warble which he might hear out of my nest. My days were not days of the week, bearing the stamp of any heathen deity, nor were they minced into hours and fretted by the ticking of a clock; for I lived like the Puri Indians, of whom it is said that "for yesterday, to-day, and to-morrow they have only one word, and they express the variety of meaning by pointing backward for yesterday, forward for to-morrow, and overhead for the passing day."[1] This was sheer idleness to my fellow-townsmen, no doubt; but if the birds and flowers had tried me by their standard, I should not have been found wanting. A man must find his occasions in himself, it is true. The natural day is very calm, and will hardly reprove his indolence.

I had this advantage, at least, in my mode of life, over those who were obliged to look abroad for amusement, to society and the theatre, that my life itself was become my amusement and never ceased to be novel. It was a drama of many scenes and without an end. If we were always, indeed, getting our living, and regulating our lives according to the last and best mode we had learned, we should never be troubled with ennui. Follow your genius closely enough, and it will not fail to show you a fresh prospect every hour. Housework was a pleasant pastime. When my floor was dirty I rose early, and, setting all my furniture out of doors on the grass, bed and bedstead making but one budget, dashed water on the floor, and sprinkled white sand from the pond on it, and then with a broom scrubbed it clean and white; and by the time the villagers had broken their fast the morning sun had dried my house sufficiently to allow me to move in again, and my meditations were almost uninterrupted. It was pleasant to see my whole household effects out on the grass, making a little pile like a gypsy's pack, and my three-legged table, from which I did not remove the books and pen and ink, standing amid the pines and hickories. They seemed glad to get out themselves, and as if unwilling to be brought in. I was sometimes tempted to stretch an awning over them and take my seat there. It was worth the while to see the sun shine on these things, and hear the free wind blow on them; so much more interesting most familiar objects look out of doors than in the house. A bird sits on the next bough, life-everlasting grows under the table, and blackberry vines run round its legs; pine cones, chestnut burs, and strawberry leaves are strewn about. It looked as if this was the way these forms came to be transferred to our furniture, to tables, chairs, and bedsteads,—because they once stood in their midst.

My house was on the side of a hill, immediately on the edge of the larger wood, in the midst of a young forest of pitch pines and hickories, and half a dozen rods from the pond, to which a narrow footpath led down the hill. In my front yard grew the strawberry, blackberry, and life-everlasting, johnswort and goldenrod, shrub oaks and sand cherry, blueberry and groundnut. Near the end of May, the sand cherry *(Cerasus pumila)* adorned the sides of the path with its delicate flowers arranged in umbels cylindrically about its short stems, which last, in the fall, weighed down with good-sized and handsome cherries, fell over in wreaths like rays on every side. I tasted them out of compliment to Nature, though they were scarcely palatable. The sumach *(Rhus glabra)* grew luxuriantly about the house, pushing up through the embankment which I had made, and growing five or six feet the first season. Its broad pinnate tropical leaf was pleasant though strange to look on. The large buds, suddenly pushing out late in the spring from dry sticks which had seemed to be dead, developed themselves as by magic into graceful green and tender boughs, an inch in diameter; and sometimes, as I sat at my window, so heedlessly did they grow and tax their weak joints, I heard a fresh and tender bough suddenly fall like a fan to the ground, when there was not a breath of air stirring, broken off by its own weight. In August, the large masses of berries, which, when in flower, had attracted many wild bees, gradually assumed their bright velvety crimson hue, and by their weight again bent down and broke the tender limbs.

As I sit at my window this summer afternoon, hawks are circling about my clearing; the tantivy of wild pigeons, flying by twos and threes athwart my view, or perching restless on the white pine boughs behind my house, gives a voice to the air; a fish hawk dimples the glassy surface of the pond and brings up a fish; a mink steals out of the marsh before my door and seizes a frog by the shore; the sedge is bending under the weight of the reed-birds flitting hither and thither; and for the last half-hour

[1] The Puri Indians are Brazilian. The quotation is from *A Lady's Voyage Round the World* by Ida Pfeiffer. (Harding)

I have heard the rattle of railroad cars, now dying away and then reviving like the beat of a partridge, conveying travellers from Boston to the country. For I did not live so out of the world as that boy who, as I hear, was put out to a farmer in the east part of the town, but ere long ran away and came home again, quite down at the heel and homesick. He had never seen such a dull and out-of-the-way place; the folks were all gone off; why, you couldn't even hear the whistle! I doubt if there is such a place in Massachusetts now:—

> "In truth, our villiage has become a butt
> For one of those fleet railroad shafts, and o'er
> Our peaceful plain its soothing sound is—Concord." [2]

The Fitchburg Railroad[3] touches the pond about a hundred rods south of where I dwell. I usually go to the village along its causeway, and am, as it were, related to society by this link. The men on the freight trains, who go over the whole length of the road, bow to me as to an old acquaintance, they pass me so often, and apparently they take me for an employee; and so I am. I too would fain be a track-repairer somewhere in the orbit of the earth.

The whistle of the locomotive penetrates my woods summer and winter, sounding like the scream of a hawk sailing over some farmer's yard, informing me that many restless city merchants are arriving within the circle of the town, or adventurous country traders from the other side. As they come under one horizon, they shout their warning to get off the track to the other, heard sometimes through the circles of two towns. Here come your groceries, country; your rations, countrymen! Nor is there any man so independent on his farm that he can say them nay. And here's your pay for them! screams the countryman's whistle; timber like long battering-rams going twenty miles an hour against the city's walls, and chairs enough to seat all the weary and heavy-laden that dwell within them. With such huge and lumbering civility the country hands a chair to the city. All the Indian huckleberry hills are stripped, all the cranberry meadows are raked into the city. Up comes the cotton, down goes the woven cloth; up comes the silk, down goes the woollen; up come the books, but down goes the wit that writes them.

When I meet the engine with its train of cars moving off with planetary motion,—or, rather, like a comet, for the beholder knows not if with that velocity and with that direction it will ever revisit this system, since its orbit does not look like a returning curve,—with its steam cloud like a banner streaming behind in golden and silver wreaths, like many a downy cloud which I have seen, high in the heavens, unfolding its masses to the light,—as if this travelling demigod, this cloud-compeller, would ere long take the sunset sky for the livery of his train; when I hear the iron horse make the hills echo with his snort like thunder, shaking the earth with his feet, and breathing fire and smoke from his nostrils (what kind of winged horse or fiery dragon they will put into the new Mythology I don't know), it seems as if the earth had got a race now worthy to inhabit it. If all were as it seems, and men made the elements their servants for noble ends! If the cloud that hangs over the engine were the perspiration of heroic deeds, or as beneficent as that which floats over the farmer's fields, then the elements and Nature herself would cheerfully accompany men on their errands and be their escort.

I watch the passage of the morning cars with the same feeling that I do the rising of the sun, which is hardly more regular. Their train of clouds stretching far behind and rising higher and higher, going to heaven while the cars are going to Boston, conceals the sun for a minute and casts my distant field into the shade, a celestial train[4] beside which the petty train of cars which hugs the earth is but the barb of the spear. The stabler of the iron horse was up early this winter morning by the light of the stars amid the mountains, to fodder and harness his steed. Fire, too, was awakened thus early to put the vital heat in him and get him off. If the enterprise were as innocent as it is early! If the snow lies deep, they strap on his snowshoes, and, with the giant plow, plow a furrow from the mountains to the seaboard, in which the cars, like a following drill-barrow, sprinkle all the restless men and floating merchandise in the country for seed. All day the fire-steed flies over the country, stopping only that his master may rest, and I am awakened by his tramp and defiant snort at midnight, when in some remote glen in the woods he fronts the elements incased in ice and snow; and he will reach his stall only with the morning star, to start once more on his travels without rest or slumber. Or perchance, at evening, I hear him in his stable blowing off the superfluous energy of the day, that he may calm his nerves and cool his liver and brain for a few hours of iron slumber. If the enterprise were as heroic and commanding as it is protracted and unwearied!

Far through unfrequented woods on the confines of towns, where once only the hunter penetrated by day, in the darkest night dart these bright saloons without the knowledge of their inhabitants; this moment stopping at some brilliant station-house in town or city, where a social crowd is gathered, the

[2] From W. E. Channing's "Walden Spring."

[3] Built in the 1840's, it connected Boston and Fitchburg.

[4] Refers to Hawthorne's "The Celestial Railroad."

next in the Dismal Swamp, scaring the owl and fox. The startings and arrivals of the cars are now the epochs in the village day. They go and come with such regularity and precision, and their whistle can be heard so far, that the farmers set their clocks by them, and thus one well-conducted institution regulates a whole country. Have not men improved somewhat in punctuality since the railroad was invented? Do they not talk and think faster in the depot than they did in the stage-office? There is something electrifying in the atmosphere of the former place. I have been astonished at the miracles it has wrought; that some of my neighbors, who, I should have prophesied, once for all, would never get to Boston by so prompt a conveyance, are on hand when the bell rings. To do things "railroad fashion" is now the byword; and it is worth the while to be warned so often and so sincerely by any power to get off its track. There is no stopping to read the riot act, no firing over the heads of the mob, in this case. We have constructed a fate, an *Atropos*, that never turns aside. (Let that be the name of your engine.) Men are advertised that at a certain hour and minute these bolts will be shot toward particular points of the compass; yet it interferes with no man's business, and the children go to school on the other track. We live the steadier for it. We are all educated thus to be sons of Tell. The air is full of invisible bolts. Every path but your own is the path of fate. Keep on your own track, then.

What recommends commerce to me is its enterprise and bravery. It does not clasp its hands and pray to Jupiter. I see these men every day go about their business with more or less courage and content, doing more even than they suspect, and perchance better employed than they could have consciously devised. I am less affected by their heroism who stood up for half an hour in the front line of Buena Vista,[5] than by the steady and cheerful valor of the men who inhabit the snow-plow for their winter quarters; who have not merely the three-o'-clock-in-the-morning courage, which Bonaparte thought was the rarest, but whose courage does not go to rest so early, who go to sleep only when the storm sleeps or the sinews of their iron steed are frozen. On this morning of the Great Snow, perchance, which is still raging and chilling men's blood, I hear the muffled tone of their engine bell from out the fog bank of their chilled breath, which announces that the cars *are coming*, without long delay, notwithstanding the veto of a New England northeast snow-storm, and I behold the plowmen covered with snow and rime, their heads peering above the mould-board which is turning down other than daisies and the nests of field mice, like bowlders of the Sierra Nevada, that occupy an outside place in the universe.

Commerce is unexpectedly confident and serene, alert, adventurous, and unwearied. It is very natural in its methods withal, far more so than many fantastic enterprises and sentimental experiments, and hence its singular success. I am refreshed and expanded when the freight train rattles past me, and I smell the stores which go dispensing their odors all the way from Long Wharf[6] to Lake Champlain, reminding me of foreign parts, of coral reefs, and Indian oceans, and tropical climes, and the extent of the globe. I feel more like a citizen of the world at the sight of the palm-leaf[7] which will cover so many flaxen New England heads the next summer, the Manilla hemp and cocoanut husks, the old junk, gunny bags, scrap iron, and rusty nails. This carload of torn sails is more legible and interesting now than if they should be wrought into paper and printed books. Who can write so graphically the history of the storms they have weathered as these rents have done? They are proof-sheets which need no correction. Here goes lumber from the Maine woods, which did not go out to sea in the last freshet, risen four dollars on the thousand because of what did go out or was split up; pine, spruce, cedar,—first, second, third, and fourth qualities, so lately all of one quality, to wave over the bear, and moose, and caribou. Next rolls Thomaston[8] lime, a prime lot, which will get far among the hills before it gets slacked. These rags in bales, of all hues and qualities, the lowest condition to which cotton and linen descend, the final result of dress,—of patterns which are now no longer cried up, unless it be in Milwaukee, as those splendid articles, English, French, or American prints, ginghams, muslins, etc., gathered from all quarters both of fashion and poverty, going to become paper of one color or a few shades only, on which, forsooth, will be written tales of real life, high and low, and founded on fact! This closed car smells of salt fish, the strong New England and commercial scent, reminding me of the Grand Banks[9] and the fisheries. Who has not seen a salt fish, thoroughly cured for this world, so that nothing can spoil it, and putting the perseverance of the saints to the blush? with which you may sweep or pave the streets, and split your kindlings, and the teamster shelter himself and his lading against sun, wind, and rain behind it,—and the trader, as a Concord trader once did, hang it up by his door for a sign when he commences business, until at last his oldest customer

[5] A battle (1847) in the Mexican War.

[6] A major wharf in Boston harbor; some of the goods received there could have been carried by rail to Lake Champlain.

[7] A summer hat.

[8] In Maine.

[9] A major fishing ground off Newfoundland.

cannot tell surely whether it be animal, vegetable, or mineral, and yet it shall be as pure as a snow-flake, and if it be put into a pot and boiled, will come out an excellent dunfish for a Saturday's dinner. Next Spanish hides, with the tails still preserving their twist and the angle of elevation they had when the oxen that wore them were careering over the pampas of the Spanish Main,—a type of all obstinacy, and evincing how almost hopeless and incurable are all constitutional vices. I confess, that practically speaking, when I have learned a man's real disposition, I have no hopes of changing it for the better or worse in this state of existence. As the Orientals say, "A cur's tail may be warmed, and pressed, and bound round with ligatures, and after a twelve years' labor bestowed upon it, still it will retain its natural form." The only effectual cure for such inveteracies as these tails exhibit is to make glue of them, which I believe is what is usually done with them, and then they will stay put and stick. Here is a hogshead of molasses or of brandy directed to John Smith, Cuttingsville, Vermont, some trader among the Green Mountains, who imports for the farmers near his clearing, and now perchance stands over his bulkhead and thinks of the last arrivals on the coast, how they may affect the price for him, telling his customers this moment, as he has told them twenty times before this morning, that he expects some by the next train of prime quality. It is advertised in the Cuttingsville Times.

While these things go up other things come down. Warned by the whizzing sound, I look up from my book and see some tall pine, hewn on far northern hills, which has winged its way over the Green Mountains and the Connecticut, shot like an arrow through the township within ten minutes, and scarce another eye beholds it; going

> "to be the mast
> Of some great ammiral." [10]

And hark! here comes the cattle-train bearing the cattle of a thousand hills, sheepcots, stables, and cow-yards in the air, drovers with their sticks, and shepherd boys in the midst of their flocks, all but the mountain pastures, whirled along like leaves blown from the mountains by the September gales. The air is filled with the bleating of calves and sheep, and the hustling of oxen, as if a pastoral valley were going by. When the old bell-wether at the head rattles his bell, the mountains do indeed skip like rams and the little hills like lambs. A car-load of drovers, too, in the midst, on a level with their droves now, their vocation gone, but still clinging to their useless sticks as their badge of office. But their dogs, where are they? It is a stampede to them; they are quite thrown out; they have lost the scent. Methinks I hear them barking behind the Peterboro' Hills, or panting up the western slope of the Green Mountains. They will not be in at the death. Their vocation, too, is gone. Their fidelity and sagacity are below par now. They will slink back to their kennels in disgrace, or perchance run wild and strike a league with the wolf and the fox. So is your pastoral life whirled past and away. But the bell rings, and I must get off the track and let the cars go by;—

> What's the railroad to me?
> I never go to see
> Where it ends.
> It fills a few hollows,
> And makes banks for the swallows,
> It sets the sand a-blowing,
> And the blackberries a-growing,[11]

but I cross it like a cart-path in the woods. I will not have my eyes put out and my ears spoiled by its smoke and steam and hissing.

Now that the cars are gone by and all the restless world with them, and the fishes in the pond no longer feel their rumbling. I am more alone than ever. For the rest of the long afternoon, perhaps, my meditations are interrupted only by the faint rattle of a carriage or team along the distant highway.

Sometimes, on Sundays, I heard the bells, the Lincoln, Acton, Bedford,[12] or Concord bell, when the wind was favorable, a faint, sweet, and, as it were, natural melody, worth importing into the wilderness. At a sufficient distance over the woods this sound acquires a certain vibratory hum, as if the pine needles in the horizon were the strings of a harp which it swept. All sound heard at the greatest possible distance produces one and the same effect, a vibration of the universal lyre, just as the intervening atmosphere makes a distant ridge of earth interesting to our eyes by the azure tint it imparts to it. There came to me in this case a melody which the air had strained, and which had conversed with every leaf and needle of the wood, that portion of the sound which the elements had taken up and modulated and echoed from vale to vale. The echo is, to some extent, an original sound, and therein is the magic and charm of it. It is not merely a repetition of what was worth repeating in the bell, but partly the voice of the wood; the same trivial words and notes sung by a wood-nymph.

At evening, the distant lowing of some cow in the horizon beyond the woods sounded sweet and melo-

[10] Milton, *Paradise Lost* I.293-94.

[11] Thoreau.

[12] Towns near Concord.

dious, and at first I would mistake it for the voices of certain minstrels by whom I was sometimes serenaded, who might be straying over hill and dale; but soon I was not unpleasantly disappointed when it was prolonged into the cheap and natural music of the cow. I do not mean to be satirical, but to express my appreciation of those youths' singing, when I state that I perceived clearly that it was akin to the music of the cow, and they were at length one articulation of Nature.

Regularly at half-past seven, in one part of the summer, after the evening train had gone by, the whip-poor-wills chanted their vespers for half an hour, sitting on a stump by my door, or upon the ridge-pole of the house. They would begin to sing almost with as much precision as a clock, within five minutes of a particular time, referred to the setting of the sun, every evening. I had a rare opportunity to become acquainted with their habits. Sometimes I heard four or five at once in different parts of the wood, by accident one a bar behind another, and so near me that I distinguished not only the cluck after each note, but often that singular buzzing sound like a fly in a spider's web, only proportionally louder. Sometimes one would circle round and round me in the woods a few feet distant as if tethered by a string, when probably I was near its eggs. They sang at intervals throughout the night, and were again as musical as ever just before and about dawn.

When other birds are still, the screech owls take up the strain, like mourning women their ancient u-lu-lu. Their dismal scream is truly Ben Jonsonian. Wise midnight hags! It is no honest and blunt tu-whit tu-who of the poets, but, without jesting, a most solemn graveyard ditty, the mutual consolations of suicide lovers remembering the pangs and the delights of supernal love in the infernal groves. Yet I love to hear their wailing, their doleful responses, trilled along the woodside; reminding me sometimes of music and singing birds; as if it were the dark and tearful side of music, the regrets and sighs that would fain be sung. They are the spirits, the low spirits and melancholy forebodings, of fallen souls that once in human shape night-walked the earth and did the deeds of darkness, now expiating their sins with their wailing hymns or threnodies in the scenery of their transgressions. They give me a new sense of the variety and capacity of that nature which is our common dwelling. *Oh-o-o-o-o that I never had been bor-r-r-r-n!* sighs one on this side of the pond, and circles with the restlessness of despair to some new perch on the gray oaks. Then—*that I never had been bor-r-r-r-n!* echoes another on the farther side with tremulous sincerity, and—*bor-r-r-r-n!* comes faintly from far in the Lincoln woods.

I was also serenaded by a hooting owl. Near at hand you could fancy it the most melancholy sound in Nature, as if she meant by this to stereotype and make permanent in her choir the dying moans of a human being,—some poor weak relic of mortality who has left hope behind, and howls like an animal, yet with human sobs, on entering the dark valley, made more awful by a certain gurgling melodiousness,—I find myself beginning with the letters *gl* when I try to imitate it,—expressive of a mind which has reached the gelatinous, mildewy stage in the mortification of all healthy and courageous thought. It reminded me of ghouls and idiots and insane howlings. But now one answers from far woods in a strain made really melodious by distance,—*Hoo hoo hoo, hoorer hoo;* and indeed for the most part it suggested only pleasing associations, whether heard by day or night, summer or winter.

I rejoice that there are owls. Let them do the idiotic and maniacal hooting for men. It is a sound admirably suited to swamps and twilight woods which no day illustrates, suggesting a vast and undeveloped nature which men have not recognized. They represent the stark twilight and unsatisfied thoughts which all have. All day the sun has shone on the surface of some savage swamp, where the single spruce stands hung with usnea lichens, and small hawks circulate above, and the chickadee lisps amid the evergreens, and the partridge and rabbit skulk beneath; but now a more dismal and fitting day dawns, and a different race of creatures awakes to express the meaning of Nature there.

Late in the evening I heard the distant rumbling of wagons over bridges,—a sound heard farther than almost any other at night,—the baying of dogs, and sometimes again the lowing of some disconsolate cow in a distant barn-yard. In the meanwhile all the shore rang with the trump of bullfrogs, the sturdy spirits of ancient wine-bibbers and wassailers, still unrepentant, trying to sing a catch in their Stygian lake,—if the Walden nymphs will pardon the comparison, for though there are almost no weeds, there are frogs there,—who would fain keep up the hilarious rules of their old festal tables, though their voices have waxed hoarse and solemnly grave, mocking at mirth, and the wine has lost its flavor, and become only liquor to distend their paunches, and sweet intoxication never comes to drown the memory of the past, but mere saturation and waterloggedness and distention. The most aldermanic, with his chin upon a heart-leaf, which serves for a napkin to his drooling chaps, under this northern shore quaffs a deep draught of the once scorned water, and passes round the cup with the ejaculation *tr-r-r-oonk, tr-r-r-oonk, tr-r-r-oonk!* and straightway comes over the water from some distant cove the same password repeated, where the next in seniority and girth has gulped down to his mark; and when this observance has made the circuit of the shores, then ejaculates the master of ceremonies, with satisfaction, *tr-r-r-oonk!* and each in his turn repeats the same down to the least distended, leakiest, and flabbiest paunched, that there be no mistake; and then the bowl goes round again and again, until the sun disperses the morning mist, and only the patriarch is not under the pond, but vainly bellowing *troonk* from time to time, and pausing for a reply.

I am not sure that I ever heard the sound of cock-crowing from my clearing, and I thought that it might be worth the while to keep a cockerel for his music merely, as a singing bird. The note of this once wild Indian pheasant is certainly the most remarkable of any bird's, and if they could be naturalized without being domesticated, it would soon become the most famous sound in our woods, surpassing the clangor of the goose and the hooting of the owl; and then imagine the cackling of the hens to fill the pauses when their lords' clarions rested! No wonder that man added this bird to his tame stock,—to say nothing of the eggs and drumsticks. To walk in a winter morning in a wood where these birds abounded, their native woods, and hear the wild cockerels crow on the trees, clear and shrill for miles over the resounding earth, drowning the feebler notes of other birds,—think of it! It would put nations on the alert. Who would not be early to rise, and rise earlier and earlier every successive day of his life, till he became unspeakably healthy, wealthy, and wise? This foreign bird's note is celebrated by the poets of all countries along with the notes of their native songsters. All climates agree with brave Chanticleer. He is more indigenous even than the natives. His health is ever good, his lungs are sound, his spirits never flag. Even the sailor on the Atlantic and Pacific is awakened by his voice; but its shrill sound never roused me from my slumbers. I kept neither dog, cat, cow, pig, nor hens, so that you would have said there was a deficiency of domestic sounds; neither the churn, nor the spinning-wheel, nor even the singing of the kettle, nor the hissing of the urn, nor children crying, to comfort one. An old-fashioned man would have lost his senses or died of ennui before this. Not even rats in the wall, for they were starved out, or rather were never baited in,—only squirrels on the roof and under the floor, a whip-poor-will on the ridge-pole, a blue jay screaming beneath the window, a hare or woodchuck under the house, a screech owl or a cat owl behind it, a flock of wild geese or a laughing loon on the pond, and a fox to bark in the night. Not even a lark or an oriole, those mild plantation birds, ever visited my clearing. No cockerels to crow nor hens to cackle in the yard. No yard! but unfenced nature reaching up to your very sills. A young forest growing up under your windows, and wild sumachs and blackberry vines breaking through into your cellar; sturdy pitch pines rubbing and creaking against the shingles for want of room, their roots reaching quite under the house. Instead of a scuttle or a blind blown off in the gale,—a pine tree snapped off or torn up by the roots behind your house for fuel. Instead of no path to the front-yard gate in the Great Snow,—no gate—no front-yard,—and no path to the civilized world.

XI. Higher Laws

As I came home through the woods with my string of fish, trailing my pole, it being now quite dark, I caught a glimpse of a woodchuck stealing across my path, and felt a strange thrill of savage delight, and was strongly tempted to seize and devour him raw; not that I was hungry then, except for that wildness which he represented. Once or twice, however, while I lived at the pond, I found myself ranging the woods, like a half-starved hound, with a strange abandonment, seeking some kind of venison which I might devour, and no morsel could have been too savage for me. The wildest scenes had become unaccountably familiar. I found in myself, and still find, an instinct toward a higher, or, as it is named, spiritual life, as do most men, and another toward a primitive rank and savage one, and I reverence them both. I love the wild not less than the good. The wildness and adventure that are in fishing still recommended it to me. I like sometimes to take rank hold on life and spend my day more as the animals do. Perhaps I have owed to this employment and to hunting, when quite young, my closest acquaintance with Nature. They early introduce us to and detain us in scenery with which otherwise, at that age, we should have little acquaintance. Fishermen, hunters, woodchoppers, and others, spending their lives in the fields and woods, in a peculiar sense a part of Nature themselves, are often in a more favorable mood for observing her, in the intervals of their pursuits, than philosophers or poets even, who approach her with expectation. She is not afraid to exhibit herself to them. The traveller on the prairie is naturally a hunter, on the head waters of the Missouri and Columbia a trapper, and at the Falls of St. Mary[1] a fisherman. He who is only a traveller learns things at second-hand and by the halves, and is poor authority. We are most interested when science reports what those men already know practically or instinctively, for that alone is a true *humanity*, or account of human experience.

They mistake who assert that the Yankee has few amusements, because he has not so many public

[1] In southeastern British Columbia. (Harding)

holidays, and men and boys do not play so many games as they do in England, for here the most primitive but solitary amusements of hunting, fishing, and the like have not yet given place to the former. Almost every New England boy among my contemporaries shouldered a fowling-piece between the ages of ten and fourteen; and his hunting and fishing grounds were not limited, like the preserves of an English nobleman, but were more boundless even than those of a savage. No wonder, then, that he did not oftener stay to play on the common. But already a change is taking place, owing, not to an increased humanity, but to an increased scarcity of game, for perhaps the hunter is the greatest friend of the animals hunted, not excepting the Humane Society.

Moreover, when at the pond, I wished sometimes to add fish to my fare for variety. I have actually fished from the same kind of necessity that the first fishers did. Whatever humanity I might conjure up against it was all factitious, and concerned my philosophy more than my feelings. I speak of fishing only now, for I had long felt differently about fowling, and sold my gun before I went to the woods. Not that I am less humane than others, but I did not perceive that my feelings were much affected. I did not pity the fishes nor the worms. This was habit. As for fowling, during the last years that I carried a gun my excuse was that I was studying ornithology, and sought only new or rare birds. But I confess that I am now inclined to think that there is a finer way of studying ornithology than this. It requires so much closer attention to the habits of the birds, that, if for that reason only, I have been willing to omit the gun. Yet notwithstanding the objection on the score of humanity, I am compelled to doubt if equally valuable sports are ever substituted for these; and when some of my friends have asked me anxiously about their boys, whether they should let them hunt, I have answered, yes,—remembering that it was one of the best parts of my education,—*make* them hunters, though sportsmen only at first, if possible, mighty hunters at last, so that they shall not find game large enough for them in this or any vegetable wilderness,—hunters as well as fishers of men. Thus far I am of the opinion of Chaucer's nun, who

> "yave not of the text a pulled hen
> That saith that hunters ben not holy men."[2]

There is a period in the history of the individual, as of the race, when the hunters are the "best men," as the Algonquins called them. We cannot but pity the boy who has never fired a gun; he is no more humane, while his education has been sadly neglected. This was my answer with respect to those youths who were bent on this pursuit, trusting that they would soon outgrow it. No humane being, past the thoughtless age of boyhood, will wantonly murder any creature which holds its life by the same tenure that he does. The hare in its extremity cries like a child. I warn you, mothers, that my sympathies do not always make the usual phil-*anthropic* distinctions.

Such is oftenest the young man's introduction to the forest, and the most original part of himself. He goes thither at first as a hunter and fisher, until at last, if he has the seeds of a better life in him, he distinguishes his proper objects, as a poet or naturalist it may be, and leaves the gun and fish-pole behind. The mass of men are still and always young in this respect. In some countries a hunting parson is no uncommon sight. Such a one might make a good shepherd's dog, but is far from being the Good Shepherd. I have been surprised to consider that the only obvious employment, except wood-chopping, ice-cutting, or the like business, which ever to my knowledge detained at Walden Pond for a whole half-day any of my fellow-citizens, whether fathers or children of the town, with just one exception, was fishing. Commonly they did not think that they were lucky, or well paid for their time, unless they got a long string of fish, though they had the opportunity of seeing the pond all the while. They might go there a thousand times before the sediment of fishing would sink to the bottom and leave their purpose pure; but no doubt such a clarifying process would be going on all the while. The Governor and his Council faintly remember the pond, for they went a-fishing there when they were boys; but now they are too old and dignified to go a-fishing, and so they know it no more forever. Yet even they expect to go to heaven at last. If the legislature regards it, it is chiefly to regulate the number of hooks to be used there; but they know nothing about the hook of hooks with which to angle for the pond itself, impaling the legislature for a bait. Thus, even in civilized communities, the embryo man passes through the hunter stage of development.

I have found repeatedly, of late years, that I cannot fish without falling a little in self-respect. I have tried it again and again. I have skill at it, and, like many of my fellows, a certain instinct for it, which revives from time to time, but always when I have done I feel that it would have been better if I had not fished. I think that I do not mistake. It is a faint intimation, yet so are the first streaks of morning. There is unquestionably this instinct in me which belongs to the lower orders of creation; yet with every year I am less a fisherman, though without more humanity or even wisdom; at present I am no fisherman at all. But I see that if I were to live in a wilderness I should again be tempted to become a

[2] Prologue, *Canterbury Tales;* said about the monk, however.

fisher and hunter in earnest. Beside, there is something essentially unclean about this diet and all flesh, and I began to see where housework commences, and whence the endeavor, which costs so much, to wear a tidy and respectable appearance each day, to keep the house sweet and free from all ill odors and sights. Having been my own butcher and scullion and cook, as well as the gentleman for whom the dishes were served up, I can speak from an unusually complete experience. The practical objection to animal food in my case was its uncleanness; and besides, when I had caught and cleaned and cooked and eaten my fish, they seemed not to have fed me essentially. It was insignificant and unnecessary, and cost more than it came to. A little bread or a few potatoes would have done as well, with less trouble and filth. Like many of my contemporaries, I had rarely for many years used animal food, or tea, or coffee, etc.; not so much because of any ill effects which I had traced to them, as because they were not agreeable to my imagination. The repugnance to animal food is not the effect of experience, but is an instinct. It appeared more beautiful to live low and fare hard in many respects; and though I never did so, I went far enough to please my imagination. I believe that every man who has ever been earnest to preserve his higher or poetic faculties in the best condition has been particularly inclined to abstain from animal food, and from much food of any kind. It is a significant fact, stated by entomologists,—I find it in Kirby and Spence,—that "some insects in their perfect state, though furnished with organs of feeding, make no use of them;" and they lay it down as "a general rule, that almost all insects in this state eat much less than in that of larvae. The voracious caterpillar when transformed into a butterfly . . . and the gluttonous maggot when become a fly" content themselves with a drop or two of honey or some other sweet liquid. The abdomen under the wings of the butterfly still represents the larva. This is the tidbit which tempts his insectivorous fate. The gross feeder is a man in the larva state; and there are whole nations in that condition, nations without fancy or imagination, whose vast abdomens betray them.

It is hard to provide and cook so simple and clean a diet as will not offend the imagination; but this, I think, is to be fed when we feed the body; they should both sit down at the same table. Yet perhaps this may be done. The fruits eaten temperately need not make us ashamed of our appetites, nor interrupt the worthiest pursuits. But put an extra condiment into your dish, and it will poison you. It is not worth the while to live by rich cookery. Most men would feel shame if caught preparing with their own hands precisely such a dinner, whether of animal or vegetable food, as is every day prepared for them by others. Yet till this is otherwise we are not civilized, and, if gentlemen and ladies, are not true men and women. This certainly suggests what change is to be made. It may be vain to ask why the imagination will not be reconciled to flesh and fat. I am satisfied that it is not. Is it not a reproach that man is a carnivorous animal? True, he can and does live, in a great measure, by preying on other animals; but this is a miserable way,—as any one who will go to snaring rabbits, or slaughtering lambs, may learn,—and he will be regarded as a benefactor of his race who shall teach man to confine himself to a more innocent and wholesome diet. Whatever my own practice may be, I have no doubt that it is a part of the destiny of the human race, in its gradual improvement, to leave off eating animals, as surely as the savage tribes have left off eating each other when they came in contact with the more civilized.

If one listens to the faintest but constant suggestions of his genius, which are certainly true, he sees not to what extremes, or even insanity, it may lead him; and yet that way, as he grows more resolute and faithful, his road lies. The faintest assured objection which one healthy man feels will at length prevail over the arguments and customs of mankind. No man ever followed his genius till it misled him. Though the result were bodily weakness, yet perhaps no one can say that the consequences were to be regretted, for these were a life in conformity to higher principles. If the day and the night are such that you greet them with joy, and life emits a fragrance like flowers and sweet-scented herbs, is more elastic, more starry, more immortal,—that is your success. All nature is your congratulation, and you have cause momentarily to bless yourself. The greatest gains and values are farthest from being appreciated. We easily come to doubt if they exist. We soon forget them. They are the highest reality. Perhaps the facts most astounding and most real are never communicated by man to man. The true harvest of my daily life is somewhat as intangible and indescribable as the tints of morning or evening. It is a little star-dust caught, a segment of the rainbow which I have clutched.

Yet, for my part, I was never unusually squeamish; I could sometimes eat a fried rat with a good relish, if it were necessary. I am glad to have drunk water so long, for the same reason that I prefer the natural sky to an opium-eater's heaven. I would fain keep sober always; and there are infinite degrees of drunkenness. I believe that water is the only drink for a wise man: wine is not so noble a liquor; and think of dashing the hopes of a morning with a cup of warm coffee, or of an evening with a dish of tea! Ah, how low I fall when I am tempted by them! Even music may be intoxicating. Such apparently slight causes destroyed Greece and Rome, and will destroy England and America. Of all ebriosity, who does not prefer to be intoxicated by the air he breathes? I have found it to be the most serious objection to coarse labors long continued, that they compelled me to eat and drink coarsely also. But to tell the truth, I find myself at present somewhat less particular in these respects. I carry less religion to the table, ask no blessing; not because I am wiser than I was, but, I am obliged to confess, because, however much it is to be regretted, with years I have grown more coarse and indifferent. Perhaps these questions are entertained only in youth, as most believe of poetry. My practice is "nowhere," my opinion is here. Nevertheless I am far from regarding myself as one of those privileged ones to whom the Ved refers when it says, that "he who has true faith in the Omnipresent Supreme Being may eat all that exists," that is, is not bound to inquire what is his food, or who prepares it; and even in their case it is to be observed, as a Hindoo commentator has remarked, that the Vedant limits this privilege to "the time of distress."

Who has not sometimes derived an inexpressible satisfaction from his food in which appetite had no share? I have been thrilled to think that I owed a mental perception to the commonly gross sense of taste, that I have been inspired through the palate, that some berries which I had eaten on a hillside had fed my genius. "The soul not being mistress of herself," says Thseng-tseu, "one looks, and one does not see; one listens, and one does not hear; one eats, and one does not know the savor of food."[3] He who distinguishes the true savor of his food can never be a glutton; he who does not cannot be otherwise. A puritan may go to his brown-bread crust with as gross an appetite as ever an alderman to his turtle. Not that food which entereth into the mouth defileth a man, but the appetite with which it is eaten. It is neither the quality nor the quantity, but the devotion to sensual savors; when that which is eaten is not a viand to sustain our animal, or inspire our spiritual life, but food for the worms that possess us. If the hunter has a taste for mud-turtles, muskrats, and other such savage tidbits, the fine lady indulges a taste for jelly made of a calf's foot, or for sardines from over the sea, and they are even. He goes to the mill-pond, she to her preserve-pot. The wonder is how they, how you and I, can live this slimy, beastly life, eating and drinking.

Our whole life is startlingly moral. There is never an instant's truce between virtue and vice. Goodness is the only investment that never fails. In the music of the harp which trembles round the world it is the insisting on this which thrills us. The harp is the travelling patterer for the Universe's Insurance Company, recommending its laws, and our little goodness is all the assessment that we pay. Though the youth at last grows indifferent, the laws of the universe are not indifferent, but are forever on the side of the most sensitive. Listen to every zephyr for some reproof, for it is surely there, and he is unfortunate who does not hear it. We cannot touch a string or move a stop but the charming moral transfixes us. Many an irksome noise, go a long way off, is heard as music, a proud, sweet satire on the meanness of our lives.

We are conscious of an animal in us, which awakens in proportion as our higher nature slumbers. It is reptile and sensual, and perhaps cannot be wholly expelled; like the worms which, even in life and health, occupy our bodies. Possibly we may withdraw from it, but never change its nature. I fear that it may enjoy a certain health of its own; that we may be well, yet not pure. The other day I picked up the lower jaw of a hog, with white and sound teeth and tusks, which suggested that there was an animal health and vigor distinct from the spiritual. This creature succeeded by other means than temperance and purity. "That in which men differ from brute beasts," says Mencius, "is a thing very inconsiderable; the common herd lose it very soon; superior men preserve it carefully."[4] Who knows what sort of life would result if we had attained to purity? If I knew so wise a man as could teach me purity I would go to seek him forthwith. "A command over our passions, and over the external senses of the body, and good acts, are declared by the Ved to be indispensable in the mind's approximation to God." Yet the spirit can for the time pervade and control every member and function of the body, and transmute what in form is the grossest sensuality into purity and devotion. The generative energy, which, when we are loose, dissipates and makes us unclean, when we are continent invigorates and inspires us. Chastity is the flowering of man; and what are called Genius, Heroism, Holiness, and the like, are but various fruits which succeed it. Man flows at once to God when the channel of purity is open. By turns our purity inspires and our impurity casts us down. He is blessed who is assured that the animal is dying out in him day by day, and the divine being established. Perhaps there is none but has cause for shame on account of the inferior and brutish nature to which he is allied. I fear that we are such gods or demigods only as fauns and satyrs, the divine allied to beasts, the creatures of appetite, and that, to some extent, our very life is our disgrace.—

"How happy's he who hath due place assigned
To his beasts and disafforested his mind!

[3] Confucius, *The Great Learning.*

[4] Meng-tse (372?–289? B.C.), Chinese philosopher and teacher of Confucianism.

. . . .
Can use his horse, goat, wolf, and ev'ry beast,
And is not ass himself to all the rest!
Else man not only is the herd of swine,
But he's those devils too which did incline
Them to a headlong rage, and made them worse."[5]

All sensuality is one, though it takes many forms; all purity is one. It is the same whether a man eat, or drink, or cohabit, or sleep sensually. They are but one appetite, and we only need to see a person do any one of these things to know how great a sensualist he is. The impure can neither stand nor sit with purity. When the reptile is attacked at one mouth of his burrow, he shows himself at another. If you would be chaste, you must be temperate. What is chastity? How shall a man know if he is chaste? He shall not know it. We have heard of this virtue, but we know not what it is. We speak conformably to the rumor which we have heard. From exertion come wisdom and purity; from sloth ignorance and sensuality. In the student sensuality is a sluggish habit of mind. An unclean person is universally a slothful one, one who sits by a stove, whom the sun shines on prostrate, who reposes without being fatigued. If you would avoid uncleanness, and all the sins, work earnestly, though it be at cleaning a stable. Nature is hard to be overcome, but she must be overcome. What avails it that you are Christian, if you are not purer than the heathen, if you deny yourself no more, if you are not more religious? I know of many systems of religion esteemed heathenish whose precepts fill the reader with shame, and provoke him to new endeavors, though it be to the performance of rites merely.

I hesitate to say these things, but it is not because of the subject,—I care not how obscene my *words* are,—but because I cannot speak of them without betraying my impurity. We discourse freely without shame of one form of sensuality, and are silent about another. We are so degraded that we cannot speak simply of the necessary functions of human nature. In earlier ages, in some countries, every function was reverently spoken of and regulated by law. Nothing was too trivial for the Hindoo lawgiver, however offensive it may be to modern taste. He teaches how to eat, drink, cohabit, void excrement and urine, and the like, elevating what is mean, and does not falsely excuse himself by calling these things trifles.

Every man is the builder of a temple, called his body, to the god he worships, after a style purely his own, nor can he get off by hammering marble instead. We are all sculptors and painters, and our material is our own flesh and blood and bones. Any nobleness begins at once to refine a man's features, any meanness or sensuality to imbrute them.

John Farmer sat at his door one September evening, after a hard day's work, his mind still running on his labor more or less. Having bathed, he sat down to re-create his intellectual man. It was a rather cool evening, and some of his neighbors were apprehending a frost. He had not attended to the train of his thoughts long when he heard some one playing on a flute, and that sound harmonized with his mood. Still he thought of his work; but the burden of his thought was, that though this kept running in his head, and he found himself planning and contriving it against his will, yet it concerned him very little. It was no more than the scurf of his skin, which was constantly shuffled off. But the notes of the flute came home to his ears out of a different sphere from that he worked in, and suggested work for certain faculties which slumbered in him. They gently did away with the street, and the village, and the state in which he lived. A voice said to him,—Why do you stay here and live this mean moiling life, when a glorious existence is possible for you? Those same stars twinkle over other fields than these.—But how to come out of this condition and actually migrate thither? All that he could think of was to practise some new austerity, to let his mind descend into his body and redeem it, and treat himself with ever increasing respect.

XII. Brute Neighbors

Sometimes I had a companion[1] in my fishing, who came through the village to my house from the other side of the town, and the catching of the dinner was as much a social exercise as the eating of it.

Hermit. I wonder what the world is doing now. I have not heard so much as a locust over the sweet-fern these three hours. The pigeons are all asleep upon their roosts,—no flutter from them. Was that a farmer's noon horn which sounded from beyond the woods just now? The hands are coming in to boiled salt beef and cider and Indian bread. Why will men worry themselves so? He that does not eat need not work. I wonder how much they have reaped. Who would live there where a body can never think for the barking of Bose?[2] And oh, the housekeeping! to keep bright the devil's door-knobs, and scour his tubs this bright day! Better not keep a house. Say, some hollow tree; and then for morning calls and dinner-parties! Only a woodpecker tapping. Oh, they swarm; the sun is too warm there; they are born too far into life for me. I have water from the

[5] John Donne (1573–1631), "To Sir Edward Herbert at Julyers."

[1] William Ellery Channing the younger. He is the poet in the dialogue.

[2] Dog.

spring, and a loaf of brown bread on the shelf.—Hark! I hear a rustling of the leaves. Is it some ill-fed village hound yielding to the instinct of the chase? or the lost pig which is said to be in these woods, whose tracks I saw after the rain? It comes on apace; my sumachs and sweetbriers tremble.—Eh, Mr. Poet, is it you? How do you like the world to-day?

Poet. See those clouds; how they hang! That's the greatest thing I have seen to-day. There's nothing like it in old paintings, nothing like it in foreign lands,—unless when we were off the coast of Spain. That's a true Mediterranean sky. I thought, as I have my living to get, and have not eaten to-day, that I might go a-fishing. That's the true industry for poets. It is the only trade I have learned. Come, let's along.

Hermit. I cannot resist. My brown bread will soon be gone. I will go with you gladly soon, but I am just concluding a serious meditation. I think that I am near the end of it. Leave me alone, then, for a while. But that we may not be delayed, you shall be digging the bait meanwhile. Angleworms are rarely to be met with in these parts, where the soil was never fattened with manure; the race is nearly extinct. The sport of digging the bait is nearly equal to that of catching the fish, when one's appetite is not too keen; and this you may have all to yourself to-day. I would advise you to set in the spade down yonder among the ground-nuts, where you see the johnswort waving. I think that I may warrant you one worm to every three sods you turn up, if you look well in among the roots of the grass, as if you were weeding. Or, if you choose to go farther, it will not be unwise, for I have found the increase of fair bait to be very nearly as the squares of the distances.

Hermit alone. Let me see; where was I? Methinks I was nearly in this frame of mind; the world lay about at this angle. Shall I go to heaven or a-fishing? If I should soon bring this meditation to an end, would another so sweet occasion be likely to offer? I was as near being resolved into the essence of things as ever I was in my life. I fear my thoughts will not come back to me. If it would do any good, I would whistle for them. When they make us an offer, is it wise to say, We will think of it? My thoughts have left no track, and I cannot find the path again. What was it that I was thinking of? It was a very hazy day. I will just try these three sentences of Confut-see; they may fetch that state about again. I know not whether it was the dumps or a budding ecstasy. Mem. There never is but one opportunity of a kind.

Poet. How now, Hermit, is it too soon? I have got just thirteen whole ones, beside several which are imperfect or undersized; but they will do for the smaller fry; they do not cover up the hook so much. Those village worms are quite too large; a shiner may make a meal off one without finding the skewer.

Hermit. Well, then, let's be off. Shall we to the Concord? There's good sport there if the water be not too high.

Why do precisely these objects which we behold make a world? Why has man just these species of animals for his neighbors; as if nothing but a mouse could have filled this crevice? I suspect that Pilpay & Co.[3] have put animals to their best use, for they are all beasts of burden, in a sense, made to carry some portion of our thoughts.

The mice which haunted my house were not the common ones, which are said to have been introduced into the country, but a wild native kind not found in the village. I sent one to a distinguished naturalist,[4] and it interested him much. When I was building, one of these had its nest underneath the house, and before I had laid the second floor, and swept out the shavings, would come out regularly at lunch time and pick up the crumbs at my feet. It probably had never seen a man before; and it soon became quite familiar, and would run over my shoes and up my clothes. It could readily ascend the sides of the room by short impulses, like a squirrel, which it resembled in its motions. At length, as I leaned with my elbow on the bench one day, it ran up my clothes, and along my sleeve, and round and round the paper which held my dinner, while I kept the latter close, and dodged and played at bopeep with it; and when at last I held still a piece of cheese between my thumb and finger, it came and nibbled it, sitting in my hand, and afterward cleaned its face and paws, like a fly, and walked away.

A phoebe soon built in my shed, and a robin for protection in a pine which grew against the house. In June the partridge *(Tetrao umbellus)*, which is so shy a bird, led her brood past my windows, from the woods in the rear to the front of my house, clucking and calling to them like a hen, and in all her behavior proving herself the hen of the woods. The young suddenly disperse on your approach, at a signal from the mother, as if a whirlwind had swept them away, and they so exactly resemble the dried leaves and twigs that many a traveller has placed his foot in the midst of a brood, and heard the whir of the old bird as she flew off, and her anxious calls and mewing, or seen her trail her wings to attract his attention, without suspecting their neighborhood. The parent will sometimes roll and spin round before you in such a dishabille, that you cannot, for a few moments, detect what kind of creature it is.

[3] Pilpay, or Bidpai, author of a collection of East Indian fables.

[4] Louis Agassiz, at Harvard in the late 1840's.

The young squat still and flat, often running their heads under a leaf, and mind only their mother's directions given from a distance, nor will your approach make them run again and betray themselves. You may even tread on them, or have your eyes on them for a minute without discovering them. I have held them in my open hand at such a time, and still their only care, obedient to their mother and their instinct, was to squat there without fear or trembling. So perfect is this instinct, that once, when I had laid them on the leaves again, and one accidentally fell on its side, it was found with the rest in exactly the same position ten minutes afterward. They are not callow like the young of most birds, but more perfectly developed and precocious even than chickens. The remarkably adult yet innocent expression of their open and serene eyes is very memorable. All intelligence seems reflected in them. They suggest not merely the purity of infancy, but a wisdom clarified by experience. Such an eye was not born when the bird was, but is coeval with the sky it reflects. The woods do not yield another such a gem. The traveller does not often look into such a limpid well. The ignorant or reckless sportsman often shoots the parent at such a time, and leaves these innocents to fall a prey to some prowling beast or bird, or gradually mingle with the decaying leaves which they so much resemble. It is said that when hatched by a hen they will directly disperse on some alarm, and so are lost, for they never hear the mother's call which gathers them again. These were my hens and chickens.

It is remarkable how many creatures live wild and free though secret in the woods, and still sustain themselves in the neighborhood of towns, suspected by hunters only. How retired the otter manages to live here! He grows to be four feet long, as big as a small boy, perhaps without any human being getting a glimpse of him. I formerly saw the raccoon in the woods behind where my house is built, and probably still heard their whinnering at night. Commonly I rested an hour or two in the shade at noon, after planting, and ate my lunch, and read a little by a spring which was the source of a swamp and of a brook, oozing from under Brister's Hill, half a mile from my field. The approach to this was through a succession of descending grassy hollows, full of young pitch pines, into a larger wood about the swamp. There, in a very secluded and shaded spot, under a spreading white pine, there was yet a clean, firm sward to sit on. I had dug out the spring and made a well of clear gray water, where I could dip up a pailful without roiling it, and thither I went for this purpose almost every day in midsummer, when the pond was warmest. Thither, too, the woodcock led her brood, to probe the mud for worms, flying but a foot above them down the bank, while they ran in a troop beneath; but a last, spying me, she would leave her young and circle round and round me, nearer and nearer till within four or five feet, pretending broken wings and legs, to attract my attention, and get off her young, who would already have taken up their march, with faint, wiry peep, single file through the swamp, as she directed. Or I heard the peep of the young when I could not see the parent bird. There too the turtle doves sat over the spring, or fluttered from bough to bough of the soft white pines over my head; or the red squirrel, coursing down the nearest bough, was particularly familiar and inquisitive. You only need sit still long enough in some attractive spot in the woods that all its inhabitants may exhibit themselves to you by turns.

I was witness to events of a less peaceful character. One day when I went out to my wood-pile, or rather my pile of stumps, I observed two large ants, the one red, the other much larger, nearly half an inch long, and black, fiercely contending with one another. Having once got hold they never let go, but struggled and wrestled and rolled on the chips incessantly. Looking farther, I was surprised to find that the chips were covered with such combatants, that it was not a *duellum*, but a *bellum*, a war between two races of ants, the red always pitted against the black, and frequently two red ones to one black. The legions of these Myrmidons[5] covered all the hills and vales in my wood-yard, and the ground was already strewn with the dead and dying, both red and black. It was the only battle which I have ever witnessed, the only battle-field I ever trod while the battle was raging; internecine war; the red republicans on the one hand, and the black imperialists on the other. On every side they were engaged in deadly combat, yet without any noise that I could hear, and human soldiers never fought so resolutely. I watched a couple that were fast locked in each other's embraces, in a little sunny valley amid the chips, now at noonday prepared to fight till the sun went down, or life went out. The smaller red champion had fastened himself like a vice to his adversary's front, and through all the tumblings on that field never for an instant ceased to gnaw at one of his feelers near the root, having already caused the other to go by the board; while the stronger black one dashed him from side to side, and, as I saw on looking nearer, had already divested him of several of his members. They fought with more pertinacity than bulldogs. Neither manifested the least disposition to retreat. It was evident that their battle-cry was "Conquer or die." In the meanwhile there

[5] Soldiers from Thessaly who fought under Achilles in the Trojan War. Myrmes means ant in Greek.

came along a single red ant on the hillside of this valley, evidently full of excitement, who either had despatched his foe, or had not yet taken part in the battle; probably the latter, for he had lost none of his limbs; whose mother had charged him to return with his shield or upon it. Or perchance he was some Achilles,[6] who had nourished his wrath apart, and had now come to avenge or rescue his Patroclus. He saw this unequal combat from afar,—for the blacks were nearly twice the size of the red,—he drew near with rapid pace till he stood on his guard within half an inch of the combatants; then, watching his opportunity, he sprang upon the black warrior, and commenced his operations near the root of his right fore leg, leaving the foe to select among his own members; and so there were three united for life, as if a new kind of attraction had been invented which put all other locks and cements to shame. I should not have wondered by this time to find that they had their respective musical bands stationed on some eminent chip, and playing their national airs the while, to excite the slow and cheer the dying combatants. I was myself excited somewhat even as if they had been men. The more you think of it, the less the difference. And certainly there is not the fight recorded in Concord history, at least, if in the history of America, that will bear a moment's comparison with this, whether for the numbers engaged in it, or for the patriotism and heroism displayed. For numbers and for carnage it was an Austerlitz or Dresden.[7] Concord Fight![8] Two killed on the patriots' side, and Luther Blanchard wounded! Why here every ant was a Buttrick,—"Fire! for God's sake fire!"—and thousands shared the fate of Davis and Hosmer. There was not one hireling there. I have no doubt that it was a principle they fought for, as much as our ancestors, and not to avoid a three-penny tax on their tea; and the results of this battle will be as important and memorable to those whom it concerns as those of the battle of Bunker Hill, at least.

I took up the chip on which the three I have particularly described were struggling, carried it into my house, and placed it under a tumbler on my window-sill, in order to see the issue. Holding a microscope to the first-mentioned red ant, I saw that, though he was assiduously gnawing at the near fore leg of his enemy, having severed his remaining feeler, his own breast was all torn away, exposing what vitals he had there to the jaws of the black warrior, whose breastplate was apparently too thick for him to pierce; and the dark carbuncles of the sufferer's eyes shone with ferocity such as war only could excite. They struggled half an hour longer under the tumbler, and when I looked again the black soldier had severed the heads of his foes from their bodies, and the still living heads were hanging on either side of him like ghastly trophies at his saddle-bow, still apparently as firmly fastened as ever, and he was endeavoring with feeble struggles, being without feelers and with only the remnant of a leg, and I know not how many other wounds, to divest himself of them; which at length, after half an hour more, he accomplished. I raised the glass, and he went off over the window-sill in that crippled state. Whether he finally survived that combat, and spent the remainder of his days in some Hôtel des Invalides,[9] I do not know; but I thought that his industry would not be worth much thereafter. I never learned which party was victorious, nor the cause of the war; but I felt for the rest of that day as if I had had my feelings excited and harrowed by witnessing the struggle, the ferocity and carnage, of a human battle before my door.

Kirby and Spence[10] tell us that the battles of ants have long been celebrated and the date of them recorded, though they say that Huber[11] is the only modern author who appears to have witnessed them. "Aeneas Sylvius," say they, "after giving a very circumstantial account of one contested with great obstinacy by a great and small species on the trunk of a pear tree," adds that " 'this action was fought in the pontificate of Eugenius the Fourth, in the presence of Nicholas Pistoriensis, an eminent lawyer, who related the whole history of the battle with the greatest fidelity.' A similar engagement between great and small ants is recorded by Olaus Magnus, in which the small ones, being victorious, are said to have buried the bodies of their own soldiers, but left those of their giant enemies a prey to the birds. This event happened previous to the expulsion of the tyrant Christiern the Second from Sweden." [12] The battle which I witnessed took place in the Presidency of Polk, five years before the passage of Webster's Fugitive-Slave Bill.

Many a village Bose, fit only to course a mud-turtle in a victualling cellar, sported his heavy quarters in the woods, without the knowledge of his master, and ineffectually smelled at old fox burrows and woodchucks' holes; led perchance by some

[6] Did not participate in the Trojan War until his friend Patroclus was killed.

[7] Sites of Napoleonic battles.

[8] The following names are associated with the battle of Concord.

[9] A hospital in Paris.

[10] William Kirby and William Spence, authors of *An Introduction to Entomology* (1846).

[11] François Huber (1750-1831), a Swiss entomologist.

[12] Aeneas Sylvius (1405-64) was Pope Pius II; Eugenius IV was pope from 1431 to 1447; Magnus (1490-1558) was archbishop of Uppsala; Christiern II was a 16th-century ruler of Denmark and Sweden. (Harding)

slight cur which nimbly threaded the wood, and might still inspire a natural terror in its denizens;—now far behind his guide, barking like a canine bull toward some small squirrel which had treed itself for scrutiny, then, cantering off, bending the bushes with his weight, imagining that he is on the track of some stray member of the jerbilla family. Once I was surprised to see a cat walking along the stony shore of the pond, for they rarely wander so far from home. The surprise was mutual. Nevertheless the most domestic cat, which has lain on a rug all her days, appears quite at home in the woods, and, by her sly and stealthy behavior, proves herself more native there than the regular inhabitants. Once, when berrying, I met with a cat with young kittens in the woods, quite wild, and they all, like their mother, had their backs up and were fiercely spitting at me. A few years before I lived in the woods there was what was called a "winged cat" in one of the farmhouses in Lincoln nearest the pond, Mr. Gilian Baker's. When I called to see her in June, 1842, she was gone a-hunting in the woods, as was her wont (I am not sure whether it was a male or female, and so use the more common pronoun), but her mistress told me that she came into the neighborhood a little more than a year before, in April, and was finally taken into their house; that she was of a dark brownish-gray color, with a white spot on her throat, and white feet, and had a large bushy tail like a fox; that in the winter the fur grew thick and flatted out along her sides, forming strips ten or twelve inches long by two and a half wide, and under her chin like a muff, the upper side loose, the under matted like felt, and in the spring these appendages dropped off. They gave me a pair of her "wings," which I keep still. There is no appearance of a membrane about them. Some thought it was part flying squirrel or some other wild animal, which is not impossible, for, according to naturalists, prolific hybrids have been produced by the union of the marten and domestic cat. This would have been the right kind of cat for me to keep, if I had kept any; for why should not a poet's cat be winged as well as his horse?

In the fall the loon *(Colymbus glacialis)* came, as usual, to moult and bathe in the pond, making the woods ring with his wild laughter before I had risen. At rumor of his arrival all the Mill-dam sportsmen are on the alert, in gigs and on foot, two by two and three by three, with patent rifles and conical balls and spy-glasses. They come rustling through the woods like autumn leaves, at least ten men to one loon. Some station themselves on this side of the pond, some on that, for the poor bird cannot be omnipresent; if he dive here he must come up there. But now the kind October wind rises, rustling the leaves and rippling the surface of the water, so that no loon can be heard or seen, though his foes sweep the pond with spy-glasses, and make the woods resound with their discharges. The waves generously rise and dash angrily, taking sides with all waterfowl, and our sportsmen must beat a retreat to town and shop and unfinished jobs. But they were too often successful. When I went to get a pail of water early in the morning I frequently saw this stately bird sailing out of my cove within a few rods. If I endeavored to overtake him in a boat, in order to see how he would manoeuvre, he would dive and be completely lost, so that I did not discover him again, sometimes, till the latter part of the day. But I was more than a match for him on the surface. He commonly went off in a rain.

As I was paddling along the north shore one very calm October afternoon, for such days especially they settle on to the lakes, like the milkweed down, having looked in vain over the pond for a loon, suddenly one, sailing out from the shore toward the middle a few rods in front of me, set up his wild laugh and betrayed himself. I pursued with a paddle and he dived, but when he came up I was nearer than before. He dived again, but I miscalculated the direction he would take, and we were fifty rods apart when he came to the surface this time, for I had helped to widen the interval; and again he laughed long and loud, and with more reason than before. He manoeuvred so cunningly that I could not get within half a dozen rods of him. Each time, when he came to the surface, turning his head this way and that, he coolly surveyed the water and the land, and apparently chose his course so that he might come up where there was the widest expanse of water and at the greatest distance from the boat. It was surprising how quickly he made up his mind and put his resolve into execution. He led me at once to the widest part of the pond, and could not be driven from it. While he was thinking one thing in his brain, I was endeavoring to divine his thought in mine. It was a pretty game, played on the smooth surface of the pond, a man against a loon. Suddenly your adversary's checker disappears beneath the board, and the problem is to place yours nearest to where his will appear again. Sometimes he would come up unexpectedly on the opposite side of me, having apparently passed directly under the boat. So long-winded was he and so unwearIable, that when he had swum farthest he would immediately plunge again, nevertheless; and then no wit could divine where in the deep pond, beneath the smooth surface, he might be speeding his way like a fish, for he had time and ability to visit the bottom of the pond in its deepest part. It is said that loons have been caught in the New York lakes eighty feet beneath the surface, with hooks set for trout,—though Walden is deeper than that. How surprised must the fishes be to see this ungainly visitor from another sphere speeding his way amid their schools! Yet he appeared to know his course as surely under water as on the surface, and swam much faster there. Once or twice I saw a ripple where he approached the surface, just put his head out to reconnoitre, and instantly dived again. I found that it was as well for me to rest on my oars and wait his reappearing as to endeavor to calculate where he would rise; for again and again, when I was straining my eyes over the surface one way, I would suddenly be startled by his unearthly laugh behind me. But why, after displaying so much cunning, did he invariably betray himself the moment he came up by that loud laugh? Did not his white breast enough betray him? He was indeed a silly loon, I thought. I could commonly hear the plash of the water when he came up, and so also detected him. But after an hour he seemed as fresh as ever, dived as willingly, and swam yet farther than at first. It was surprising to see how serenely he sailed off with unruffled breast when he came to the surface, doing all the work with his webbed feet beneath. His usual note was this demoniac laughter, yet somewhat like that of a waterfowl; but occasionally, when he had balked me most successfully and come up a long way off, he uttered a long-drawn unearthly howl, probably more like that of a wolf than any bird; as when a beast puts his muzzle to the ground and deliberately howls. This was his looning,—perhaps the wildest sound that is ever heard here, making the woods ring far and wide. I concluded that he laughed in derision of my efforts, confident of his own resources. Though the sky was by this time overcast, the pond was so smooth that I could see where he broke the surface when I did not hear him. His white breast, the stillness of the air, and the smoothness of the water were all against him. At length, having come up fifty rods off, he uttered one of those prolonged howls, as if calling on the god of loons to aid him, and immediately there came a wind from the east and rippled the surface, and filled the whole air with misty rain, and I was impressed as if it were the prayer of the loon answered, and his god was angry with me; and so I left him disappearing far away on the tumultuous surface.

For hours, in fall days, I watched the ducks cunningly tack and veer and hold the middle of the pond, far from the sportsman; tricks which they will have less need to practise in Louisiana bayous. When compelled to rise they would sometimes circle round and round and over the pond at a considerable height, from which they could easily see to other ponds and the river, like black motes in the sky; and, when I thought they had gone off thither long since, they would settle down by a slanting flight of a quarter of a mile on to a distant part which was left free; but what beside safety they got by sailing in the middle of Walden I do not know, unless they love its water for the same reason that I do.

XVIII. Conclusion

To the sick the doctors wisely recommend a change of air and scenery. Thank Heaven, here is not all the world. The buckeye does not grow in New England, and the mockingbird is rarely heard here. The wild goose is more of a cosmopolite than we; he breaks his fast in Canada, takes a luncheon in the Ohio, and plumes himself for the night in a southern bayou. Even the bison, to some extent, keeps pace with the seasons, cropping the pastures of the Colorado only till a greener and sweeter grass awaits him by the Yellowstone. Yet we think that if rail fences are pulled down, and stone walls piled up on our farms, bounds are henceforth set to our lives and our fates decided. If you are chosen town clerk, forsooth, you cannot go to Tierra del Fuego this summer: but you may go to the land of infernal fire nevertheless. The universe is wider than our views of it.

Yet we should oftener look over the tafferel of our craft, like curious passengers, and not make the voyage like stupid sailors picking oakum. The other side of the globe is but the home of our correspondent. Our voyaging is only great-circle sailing, and the doctors prescribe for diseases of the skin merely. One hastens to southern Africa to chase the giraffe; but surely that is not the game he would be after. How long, pray, would a man hunt giraffes if he could? Snipes and woodcocks also may afford rare sport; but I trust it would be nobler game to shoot one's self.—

> "Direct your eye right inward, and you'll find
> A thousand regions in your mind
> Yet undiscovered. Travel them, and be
> Expert in home-cosmography."[1]

What does Africa,—what does the West stand for? Is not our own interior white on the chart? black though it may prove, like the coast, when discovered. Is it the source of the Nile, or the Niger, or the Mississippi, or a Northwest Passage around this continent, that we would find? Are these the problems which most concern mankind? Is Franklin[2] the only man who is lost, that his wife should be so earnest to find him? Does Mr. Grinnell[3] know where

[1] William Habington (1605-64), "To My Honoured Friend Sir Ed. P. Knight."

[2] Sir John Franklin (1786-1847), a British explorer who was lost in the Arctic.

[3] Henry Grinnell (1799-1874) of New York organized one of the expeditions that searched for Franklin.

he himself is? Be rather the Mungo Park, the Lewis and Clark and Frobisher,[4] of your own streams and oceans; explore your own higher latitudes,—with shiploads of preserved meats to support you, if they be necessary; and pile the empty cans sky-high for a sign. Were preserved meats invented to preserve meat merely? Nay, be a Columbus to whole new continents and worlds within you, opening new channels, not of trade, but of thought. Every man is the lord of a realm beside which the earthly empire of the Czar is but a petty state, a hummock left by the ice. Yet some can be patriotic who have no *self*-respect, and sacrifice the greater to the less. They love the soil which makes their graves, but have no sympathy with the spirit which may still animate their clay. Patriotism is a maggot in their heads. What was the meaning of that South-Sea Exploring Expedition,[5] with all its parade and expense, but an indirect recognition of the fact that there are continents and seas in the moral world to which every man is an isthmus or an inlet, yet unexplored by him, but that it is easier to sail many thousand miles through cold and storm and cannibals, in a government ship, with five hundred men and boys to assist one, than it is to explore the private sea, the Atlantic and Pacific Ocean of one's being alone.—

> "Erret, et extremos alter scrutetur Iberos.
> Plus habet hic vitae, plus habet ille viae."
>
> Let them wander and scrutinize the outlandish
> Australians.
> I have more of God, they more of the road.[6]

It is not worth the while to go round the world to count the cats in Zanzibar. Yet do this even till you can do better, and you may perhaps find some "Symmes' Hole"[7] by which to get at the inside at last. England and France, Spain and Portugal, Gold Coast and Slave Coast, all front on this private sea; but no bark from them has ventured out of sight of land, though it is without doubt the direct way to India. If you would learn to speak all tongues and conform to the customs of all nations, if you would travel farther than all travellers, be naturalized in all climes, and cause the Sphinx to dash her head against a stone, even obey the precept of the old philosopher, and Explore thyself. Herein are demanded the eye and the nerve. Only the defeated and deserters go to the wars, cowards that run away and enlist. Start now on that farthest western way, which does not pause at the Mississippi or the Pacific, nor conduct toward a worn-out China or Japan, but leads on direct, a tangent to this sphere, summer and winter, day and night, sun down, moon down, and at last earth down too.

It is said that Mirabeau[8] took to highway robbery "to ascertain what degree of resolution was necessary in order to place one's self in formal opposition to the most sacred laws of society." He declared that "a soldier who fights in the ranks does not require half so much courage as a foot-pad,"—"that honor and religion have never stood in the way of a well-considered and a firm resolve." This was manly, as the world goes; and yet it was idle, if not desperate. A saner man would have found himself often enough "in formal opposition" to what are deemed "the most sacred laws of society," through obedience to yet more sacred laws, and so have tested his resolution without going out of his way. It is not for a man to put himself in such an attitude to society, but to maintain himself in whatever attitude he find himself through obedience to the laws of his being, which will never be one of opposition to a just government, if he should chance to meet with such.

I left the woods for as good a reason as I went there. Perhaps it seemed to me that I had several more lives to live, and could not spare any more time for that one. It is remarkable how easily and insensibly we fall into a particular route, and make a beaten track for ourselves. I had not lived there a week before my feet wore a path from my door to the pond-side; and though it is five or six years since I trod it, it is still quite distinct. It is true, I fear, that others may have fallen into it, and so helped to keep it open. The surface of the earth is soft and impressible by the feet of men; and so with the paths which the mind travels. How worn and dusty, then, must be the highways of the world, how deep the ruts of tradition and conformity! I did not wish to take a cabin passage, but rather to go before the mast and on the deck of the world, for there I could best see the moonlight amid the mountains. I do not wish to go below now.

I learned this, at least, by my experiment: that if one advances confidently in the direction of his dreams, and endeavors to live the life which he has imagined, he will meet with a success unexpected in common hours. He will put some things behind, will pass an invisible boundary; new, universal, and more liberal laws will begin to establish themselves around and within him; or the old laws be expanded, and interpreted in his favor in a more liberal sense, and he will live with the license of a higher order of beings. In proportion as he simplifies his life, the laws of the universe will appear less

[4] All famous explorers.

[5] To the antarctic islands of the Pacific, 1838–42.

[6] From Claudian (*fl.* 395–404), "The Old Man of Verona." Note Thoreau's change of "Iberos" to "Australians."

[7] A bizarre theory of Captain John Cleves, advanced in 1818, that the earth was hollow and open at both poles.

[8] Count de Mirabeau (1749–91), statesman of the French Revolution.

complex, and solitude will not be solitude, nor poverty poverty, nor weakness weakness. If you have built castles in the air, your work need not be lost; that is where they should be. Now put the foundations under them.

It is a ridiculous demand which England and America make, that you shall speak so that they can understand you. Neither men nor toadstools grow so. As if that were important, and there were not enough to understand you without them. As if Nature could support but one order of understandings, could not sustain birds as well as quadrupeds, flying as well as creeping things, and *hīsh* and *whoa,* which Bright[9] can understand, were the best English. As if there were safety in stupidity alone. I fear chiefly lest my expression may not be *extravagant* enough, may not wander far enough beyond the narrow limits of my daily experience, so as to be adequate to the truth of which I have been convinced. *Extra vagance!* it depends on how you are yarded. The migrating buffalo, which seeks new pastures in another latitude, is not extravagant like the cow which kicks over the pail, leaps the cowyard fence, and runs after her calf, in milking time. I desire to speak somewhere *without* bounds; like a man in a waking moment, to men in their waking moments; for I am convinced that I cannot exaggerate enough even to lay the foundation of a true expression. Who that has heard a strain of music feared then lest he should speak extravagantly any more forever? In view of the future or possible, we should live quite laxly and undefined in front, our outlines dim and misty on that side; as our shadows reveal an insensible perspiration toward the sun. The volatile truth of our words should continually betray the inadequacy of the residual statement. Their truth is instantly *translated;* its literal monument alone remains. The words which express our faith and piety are not definite; yet they are significant and fragrant like frankincense to superior natures.

Why level downward to our dullest perception always, and praise that as common sense? The commonest sense is the sense of men asleep, which they express by snoring. Sometimes we are inclined to class those who are once-and-a-half-witted with the half-witted, because we appreciate only a third part of their wit. Some would find fault with the morning red, if they ever got up early enough. "They pretend," as I hear, "that the verses of Kabir have four different senses; illusion, spirit, intellect, and the exoteric doctrine of the Vedas;"[10] but in this part of the world it is considered a ground for complaint if a man's writings admit of more than one interpretation. While England endeavors to cure the potato-rot, will not any endeavor to cure the brain-rot, which prevails so much more widely and fatally?

I do not suppose that I have attained to obscurity, but I should be proud if no more fatal fault were found with my pages on this score than was found with the Walden ice. Southern customers objected to its blue color, which is the evidence of its purity, as if it were muddy, and preferred the Cambridge ice, which is white, but tastes of weeds. The purity men love is like the mists which envelop the earth, and not like the azure ether beyond.

Some are dinning in our ears that we Americans, and moderns generally, are intellectual dwarfs compared with the ancients, or even the Elizabethan men. But what is that to the purpose? A living dog is better than a dead lion. Shall a man go and hang himself because he belongs to the race of pygmies, and not be the biggest pygmy that he can? Let every one mind his own business, and endeavor to be what he was made.

Why should we be in such desperate haste to succeed and in such desperate enterprises? If a man does not keep pace with his companions, perhaps it is because he hears a different drummer. Let him step to the music which he hears, however measured or far away. It is not important that he should mature as soon as an apple tree or an oak. Shall he turn his spring into summer? If the condition of things which we were made for is not yet, what were any reality which we can substitute? We will not be shipwrecked on a vain reality. Shall we with pains erect a heaven of blue glass over ourselves, though when it is done we shall be sure to gaze still at the true ethereal heaven far above, as if the former were not?

There was an artist in the city of Kouroo[11] who was disposed to strive after perfection. One day it came into his mind to make a staff. Having considered that in an imperfect work time is an ingredient, but into a perfect work time does not enter, he said to himself, It shall be perfect in all respects, though I should do nothing else in my life. He proceeded instantly to the forest for wood, being resolved that it should not be made of unsuitable material; and as he searched for and rejected stick after stick, his friends gradually deserted him, for they grew old in their works and died, but he grew not older by a moment. His singleness of purpose and resolution, and his elevated piety, endowed him, without his knowledge, with perennial youth. As he made no compromise with Time, Time kept out of his way, and only sighed at a distance because he

[9] Oxen. The terms were used in driving oxen.

[10] From Garcin de Tassy, *Histoire de la Littérature Hindoui* (1839).

[11] A legend probably invented by Thoreau.

could not overcome him. Before he had found a stock in all respects suitable the city of Kouroo was a hoary ruin, and he sat on one of its mounds to peel the stick. Before he had given it the proper shape the dynasty of the Candahars was at an end, and with the point of the stick he wrote the name of the last of that race in the sand, and then resumed his work. By the time he had smoothed and polished the staff Kalpa was no longer the pole-star; and ere he had put on the ferule and the head adorned with precious stones, Brahma had awoke and slumbered many times. But why do I stay to mention these things? When the finishing stroke was put to his work, it suddenly expanded before the eyes of the astonished artist into the fairest of all the creations of Brahma. He had made a new system in making a staff, a world with full and fair proportions; in which, though the old cities and dynasties had passed away, fairer and more glorious ones had taken their places. And now he saw by the heap of shavings still fresh at his feet, that, for him and his work, the former lapse of time had been an illusion, and that no more time had elapsed than is required for a single scintillation from the brain of Brahma to fall on and inflame the tinder of a mortal brain. The material was pure, and his art was pure; how could the result be other than wonderful?

No face which we can give to a matter will stead us so well at last as the truth. This alone wears well. For the most part, we are not where we are, but in a false position. Through an infirmity of our natures, we suppose a case, and put ourselves into it, and hence are in two cases at the same time, and it is doubly difficult to get out. In sane moments we regard only the facts, the case that is. Say what you have to say, not what you ought. Any truth is better than make-believe. Tom Hyde, the tinker, standing on the gallows, was asked if he had anything to say. "Tell the tailors," said he, "to remember to make a knot in their thread before they take the first stitch." His companion's prayer is forgotten.

However mean your life is, meet it and live it; do not shun it and call it hard names. It is not so bad as you are. It looks poorest when you are richest. The faultfinder will find faults even in paradise. Love your life, poor as it is. You may perhaps have some pleasant, thrilling, glorious hours, even in a poorhouse. The setting sun is reflected from the windows of the almshouse as brightly as from the rich man's abode; the snow melts before its door as early in the spring. I do not see but a quiet mind may live as contentedly there, and have as cheering thoughts, as in a palace. The town's poor seem to me often to live the most independent lives of any. Maybe they are simply great enough to receive without misgiving. Most think that they are above being supported by the town; but it oftener happens that they are not above supporting themselves by dishonest means, which should be more disreputable. Cultivate poverty like a garden herb, like sage. Do not trouble yourself much to get new things, whether clothes or friends. Turn the old; return to them. Things do not change; we change. Sell your clothes and keep your thoughts. God will see that you do not want society. If I were confined to a corner of a garret all my days, like a spider, the world would be just as large to me while I had my thoughts about me. The philosopher said: "From an army of three divisions one can take away its general, and put it in disorder; from the man the most abject and vulgar one cannot take away his thought."[12] Do not seek so anxiously to be developed, to subject yourself to many influences to be played on; it is all dissipation. Humility like darkness reveals the heavenly lights. The shadows of poverty and meanness gather around us, "and lo! creation widens to our view."[13] We are often reminded that if there were bestowed on us the wealth of Croesus, our aims must still be the same, and our means essentially the same. Moreover, if you are restricted in your range by poverty, if you cannot buy books and newspapers, for instance, you are but confined to the most significant and vital experiences; you are compelled to deal with the material which yields the most sugar and the most starch. It is life near the bone where it is sweetest. You are defended from being a trifler. No man loses ever on a lower level by magnanimity on a higher. Superfluous wealth can buy superfluities only. Money is not required to buy one necessary of the soul.

I live in the angle of a leaden wall, into whose composition was poured a little alloy of bell-metal. Often, in the repose of my mid-day, there reaches my ears a confused *tintinnabulum* from without. It is the noise of my contemporaries. My neighbors tell me of their adventures with famous gentlemen and ladies, what notabilities they met at the dinner-table; but I am no more interested in such things than in the contents of the Daily Times. The interest and the conversation are about costume and manners chiefly; but a goose is a goose still, dress it as you will. They tell me of California and Texas, of England and the Indies, of the Hon. Mr.—— of Georgia or of Massachusetts, all transient and fleeting phenomena, till I am ready to leap from their court-yard like the Mameluke bey.[14] I delight to come to my bearings,—not walk in procession with

[12] Confucius, *Analects*.

[13] Joseph Blanco White (1775–1841), English Poet, "To Night." "Widened" in the poem.

[14] One man escaped a massacre of the Mamelukes ordered in 1811 by the Pasha of Egypt.

pomp and parade, in a conspicuous place, but to walk even with the Builder of the universe, if I may,—not to live in this restless, nervous, bustling, trivial Nineteenth Century, but stand or sit thoughtfully while it goes by. What are men celebrating? They are all on a committee of arrangements, and hourly expect a speech from somebody. God is only the president of the day, and Webster[15] is his orator. I love to weigh, to settle, to gravitate toward that which most strongly and rightfully attracts me;—not hang by the beam of the scale and try to weigh less,—not suppose a case, but take the case that is; to travel the only path I can, and that on which no power can resist me. It affords me no satisfaction to commence to spring an arch before I have got a solid foundation. Let us not play at kittly-benders.[16] There is a solid bottom everywhere. We read that the traveller asked the boy if the swamp before him had a hard bottom. The boy replied that it had. But presently the traveller's horse sank in up to the girths, and he observed to the boy, "I thought you said that this bog had a hard bottom." "So it has," answered the latter, "but you have not got half way to it yet." So it is with the bogs and quicksands of society; but he is an old boy that knows it. Only what is thought, said, or done at a certain rare coincidence is good. I would not be one of those who will foolishly drive a nail into mere lath and plastering; such a deed would keep me awake nights. Give me a hammer, and let me feel for the furring. Do not depend on the putty. Drive a nail home and clinch it so faithfully that you can wake up in the night and think of your work with satisfaction,—a work at which you would not be ashamed to invoke the Muse. So will help you God, and so only. Every nail driven should be as another rivet in the machine of the universe, you carrying on the work.

Rather than love, than money, than fame, give me truth. I sat at a table where were rich food and wine in abundance, and obsequious attendance, but sincerity and truth were not; and I went away hungry from the inhospitable board. The hospitality was as cold as the ices. I thought that there was no need of ice to freeze them. They talked to me of the age of the wine and the fame of the vintage; but I thought of an older, a newer, and purer wine, of a more glorious vintage, which they had not got, and could not buy. The style, the house and grounds and "entertainment" pass for nothing with me. I called on the king, but he made me wait in his hall, and conducted like a man incapacitated for hospitality. There was a man in my neighborhood who lived in a hollow tree. His manners were truly regal. I should have done better had I called on him.

How long shall we sit in our porticoes practising idle and musty virtues, which any work would make impertinent? As if one were to begin the day with long-suffering, and hire a man to hoe his potatoes; and in the afternoon go forth to practise Christian meekness and charity with goodness aforethought! Consider the China pride and stagnant self-complacency of mankind. This generation inclines a little to congratulate itself on being the last of an illustrious line; and in Boston and London and Paris and Rome, thinking of its long descent, it speaks of its progress in art and science and literature with satisfaction. There are the Records of the Philosophical Societies, and the public Eulogies of *Great Men!* It is the good Adam contemplating his own virtue. "Yes, we have done great deeds, and sung divine songs, which shall never die,"—that is, as long as *we* can remember them. The learned societies and great men of Assyria,—where are they? What youthful philosophers and experimentalists we are! There is not one of my readers who has yet lived a whole human life. These may be but the spring months in the life of the race. If we have had the seven-years' itch, we have not seen the seventeen-year locust yet in Concord. We are acquainted with a mere pellicle of the globe on which we live. Most have not delved six feet beneath the surface, nor leaped as many above it. We know not where we are. Beside, we are sound asleep nearly half our time. Yet we esteem ourselves wise, and have an established order on the surface. Truly, we are deep thinkers, we are ambitious spirits! As I stand over the insect crawling amid the pine needles on the forest floor, and endeavoring to conceal itself from my sight, and ask myself why it will cherish those humble thoughts, and hide its head from me who might, perhaps, be its benefactor, and impart to its race some cheering information, I am reminded of the greater Benefactor and Intelligence that stands over me the human insect.

There is an incessant influx of novelty into the world, and yet we tolerate incredible dulness. I need only suggest what kind of sermons are still listened to in the most enlightened countries. There are such words as joy and sorrow, but they are only the burden of a psalm, sung with a nasal twang, while we believe in the ordinary and mean. We think that we can change our clothes only. It is said that the British Empire is very large and respectable, and that the United States are a first-rate power. We do not believe that a tide rises and falls behind every man which can float the British Empire like a chip, if he should ever harbor it in his mind. Who knows what sort of seventeen-year lo-

[15] Daniel Webster (1782–1852).

[16] A child's game: running out on thin ice and trying to not break through.

cust will next come out of the ground? The government of the world I live in was not framed, like that of Britain, in after-dinner conversations over the wine.

The life in us is like the water in the river. It may rise this year higher than man has ever known it, and flood the parched uplands; even this may be the eventful year, which will drown out all our muskrats. It was not always dry land where we dwell. I see far inland the banks which the stream anciently washed, before science began to record its freshets. Every one has heard the story which has gone the rounds of New England, of a strong and beautiful bug which came out of the dry leaf of an old table of apple-tree wood, which had stood in a farmer's kitchen for sixty years, first in Connecticut, and afterward in Massachusetts,—from an egg deposited in the living tree many years earlier still, as appeared by counting the annual layers beyond it; which was heard gnawing out for several weeks, hatched perchance by the heat of an urn. Who does not feel his faith in a resurrection and immortality strengthened by hearing of this? Who knows what beautiful and winged life, whose egg has been buried for ages under many concentric layers of woodenness in the dead dry life of society, deposited at first in the alburnum of the green and living tree, which has been gradually converted into the semblance of its well-seasoned tomb,—heard perchance gnawing out now for years by the astonished family of man, as they sat round the festive board,—may unexpectedly come forth from amidst society's most trivial and handselled furniture, to enjoy its perfect summer life at last!

I do not say that John or Jonathan[17] will realize all this; but such is the character of that morrow which mere lapse of time can never make to dawn. The light which puts out our eyes is darkness to us. Only that day dawns to which we are awake. There is more day to dawn. The sun is but a morning star.

[17] Slang for an Englishman (John Bull) and an American (Brother Jonathan).

NATHANIEL HAWTHORNE [1804–1864]

Of his Puritan ancestors Hawthorne said, "Strong traits of their nature have intertwined themselves with mine." In the beginning the Hathornes (as they spelled the name) were a prominent family of the seaport town of Salem. The first settler, William Hathorne—"grave, bearded, sable-cloaked and steeple-crowned," as Hawthorne pictured him—was a magistrate who took part in the persecution of the Quakers. His son John was a judge conspicuous in the Salem witch trials. In the eighteenth century the Hathornes were sea-captains—including Nathaniel's father, who died in Dutch Guiana when the boy was four years old.

The widow, at age twenty-eight, shut herself into her own room in a solitude that lasted most of the rest of her life, and the boy, like his two sisters, also fell into solitary ways. When the family went to live for some years at Lake Sebago in Maine, they took their old habits from the city to the wilderness. Nathaniel was normal enough, to be sure, while a student at Bowdoin College, Brunswick, Maine, where he established lifelong friendships with Longfellow, Horatio Bridge, and Franklin Pierce, the future President of the United States. But, returned from college, he drifted into a seclusion that lasted twelve years. Near the end of this period he wrote to Longfellow: "I have secluded myself from society; and yet I never meant any such thing, nor dreamed what sort of life I was going to lead. I have made a captive of myself and put me into a dungeon; and now I cannot find the key to let myself out—and if the door were open, I should be almost afraid to come out." Actually, he did come out, in a raiding sort of fashion: by means of free passes on his uncle's stagecoach line he made a number of summer trips in New

England, experiencing, he said, "as much of life as other people do in the whole year's round." But the bulk of his time he spent in dreaming and reflecting, in reading and writing. Under various assumed names, he published an undistinguished novel (*Fanshawe*) and sketches and stories partially collected, in 1837, in the first group of *Twice-Told Tales*. They did not describe what a later American writer called "the rich thicket of reality." As he said to Longfellow, with some overstatement, "I have seen so little of the world that I have nothing but thin air to concoct my stories of." But that little he commanded with an imaginative insight denied to most writers who have thrown themselves into the tumult of life.

Hawthorne's return to the "living world" (as he had called it in *Fanshawe*) came after he had met and fallen in love with Sophia Peabody. In 1838 he became engaged to her. In 1839–40 he served as weigher and gauger in the Boston Custom House, a position secured for him by his Democratic friends and lost through a change of political parties. Then, oddly enough, he became a member of the Brook Farm community. In 1842 he married and went to Concord, where, in the Old Manse, he spent four happy years. This was the period of the second collection of *Twice-Told Tales* and of *Mosses from an Old Manse*. Again he held a custom house position, this time in Salem, and again lost it through a change in administration. By this time he had the experience of fatherhood—a daughter Una, a son Julian. The family left Salem for good, removed to Lenox, to West Newton, to Concord.

Up to this time he had been a writer of sketches and short tales; now he took up the novel, or "romance": *The Scarlet Letter*, 1850; *The House of the Seven Gables*, 1851; *The Blithedale Romance*, 1853. At this juncture, too late for a full effect, he spent seven years in Europe. His friend Pierce, becoming President, nominated him consul at Liverpool. Resigning after three years, he toured the Continent, wrote *The Marble Faun* while living in Italy and in England, and returned to settle in The Wayside in Concord. Four years later, on a tour with Pierce, he died in New Hampshire.

Hawthorne felt strongly the impulse of the Romantic Movement: he shared its feeling for the strange and mysterious, its symbolical imagination and sportive fancy, and he turned to a regional past for much of his material. Yet he could not accept Transcendental optimism, nor did he celebrate nature, or the natural man, or the supremacy of beauty. Far deeper than his interest in the romanticism of his age was his feeling for the Christianity of New England in an earlier age. While he was skeptical of the Puritan theology and found the old intolerance repugnant, he agreed with his ancestors in focusing attention upon the problem of evil, the nature of sin, the contrast of pride and humility. Perversion, mystery, horror, and the like are never with him, as they were with Poe, merely materials for aesthetic use. On the other hand, he is not the moralist intent upon edification. Rather, he is a psychological type of literary artist, analyzing the inner life, the workings of the human heart and will, in a day when this could still be done as by Dante and Shakespeare (or Spenser and Bunyan, two of his favorites), without the help or the hindrance of the psychological science of the age of Freud. The best example is his own great book, his tragedy in the form of a novel, *The Scarlet Letter*.

Hawthorne's art is above all an art of symbols. Whether his story be a novel or a short tale, he works outward from some inner fact, some truth of the mind or soul, toward the concrete world, using a symbol, oftener a cluster of symbols, to link inner and outer and give body to his spiritual meaning. It may even seem, as W. C. Brownell said, that "everything means something else," or might mean various things. Are we to agree with Brownell and other able critics that this ambiguity is a defect in Hawthorne's art, a sign of weakness and confusion, or with R. H. Fogle and other recent able critics, that it is a source of strength, an enrichment of meaning and effect?

Further reading: *The Scarlet Letter. The House of the Seven Gables.* Randall Stewart, *Nathaniel Hawthorne* (biography), 1948. R. H. Fogle, *Hawthorne's Fiction*, 1952. Roy R. Male, *Hawthorne's Tragic Vision*, 1957. Hubert H. Hoeltje, *Inward Sky: The Mind and*

Heart of Nathaniel Hawthorne, 1962. H. H. Waggoner, *Hawthorne: A Critical Study,* 1963. Roy H. Pearce, ed., *Hawthorne Centenary Essays,* 1964. Frederick C. Crews, *The Sins of the Fathers,* 1966. A. N. Kaul, *Hawthorne: A Collection of Critical Essays,* 1966.

FROM HIS *Notebooks*

Text: *Passages from the American Note-Books,* ed. Sophia Hawthorne (Boston, 1868).

[Hints for Stories]

A change from a gay young girl to an old woman; the melancholy events, the effects of which have clustered around her character, and gradually imbued it with their influence, till she becomes a lover of sick-chambers, taking pleasure in receiving dying breaths and in laying out the dead; also having her mind full of funeral reminiscences, and possessing more acquaintances beneath the burial turf than above it.

The scene of a story or sketch to be laid within the light of a street-lantern; the time, when the lamp is near going out; and the catastrophe to be simultaneous with the last flickering gleam.

In an old house, a mysterious knocking might be heard on the wall, where had formerly been a doorway, now bricked up.

A snake, taken into a man's stomach and nourished there from fifteen years to thirty-five, tormenting him most horribly. A type of envy or some other evil passion.

A Fancy Ball, in which the prominent American writers should appear, dressed in character.

An idle man's pleasures and occupations and thoughts during a day spent by the sea-shore; among them, that of sitting on the top of a cliff, and throwing stones at his own shadow, far below.

Meditations about the main gaspipe of a great city—if the supply were to be stopped, what would happen? How many different scenes it sheds light on? It might be made emblematical of something.

To poison a person or a party of persons with the sacramental wine.

The semblance of a human face to be formed on the side of a mountain, or in the fracture of a small stone, by a *lusus naturae.* The face is an object of curiosity for years or centuries, and by and by a boy is born, whose features gradually assume the aspect of that portrait. At some critical juncture, the resemblance is found to be perfect. A prophecy may be connected.

My Kinsman, Major Molineux

The historical background of the story is important. It enables Hawthorne to write a complex tale that deals with an actual political and social situation (and thus with American history) as well as with a typical introduction of a young man to the city and with a symbolic journey into the underground. Text: From the first American edition of *The Snow-Image and Other Twice-Told Tales* (Boston, 1852).

After the kings of Great Britain had assumed the right of appointing the colonial governors, the measures of the latter seldom met with the ready and general approbation which had been paid to those of their predecessors, under the original charters. The people looked with most jealous scrutiny to the exercise of power which did not emanate from themselves, and they usually rewarded their rulers with slender gratitude for the compliances by which, in softening their instructions from beyond the sea, they had incurred the reprehension of those who gave them. The annals of Massachusetts Bay will inform us, that of six governors in the space of about forty years from the surrender of the old charter, under James II, two were imprisoned by a popular insurrection; a third, as Hutchinson[1] inclines to believe, was driven from the province by the whizzing of a musket-ball; a fourth, in the opinion of the same historian, was hastened to his grave by continual bickerings with the House of Representatives; and the remaining two, as well as their successors, till the Revolution, were favored with few and brief intervals of peaceful sway. The inferior members of the court party, in times of high political excitement, led scarcely a more desirable life. These remarks may serve as a preface to the following adventures, which chanced upon a summer night, not far from a hundred years ago. The reader, in order to avoid a long and dry detail of colonial affairs, is requested to dispense with an account of the train of circumstances that had caused much temporary inflammation of the popular mind.

It was near nine o'clock of a moonlight evening, when a boat crossed the ferry with a single passenger, who had obtained his conveyance at that unusual hour by the promise of an extra fare. While he stood on the landing-place, searching in either pocket for the means of fulfilling his agreement, the ferryman lifted a lantern, by the aid of which, and the newly risen moon, he took a very accurate survey of the stranger's figure. He was a youth of barely eighteen years, evidently country-bred, and now, as it should seem, upon his first visit to town.

[1] Thomas Hutchinson (1711–80), royal governor of Massachusetts, 1769–74, and author of *The History of the Colony of Massachusetts-Bay* (1765).

He was clad in a coarse gray coat, well worn, but in excellent repair; his under garments were durably constructed of leather, and fitted tight to a pair of serviceable and well-shaped limbs; his stockings of blue yarn were the incontrovertible work of a mother or a sister; and on his head was a three-cornered hat, which in its better days had perhaps sheltered the graver brow of the lad's father. Under his left arm was a heavy cudgel, formed of an oak sapling, and retaining a part of the hardened root; and his equipment was completed by a wallet, not so abundantly stocked as to incommode the vigorous shoulders on which it hung. Brown, curly hair, well-shaped features, and bright, cheerful eyes were nature's gifts, and worth all that art could have done for his adornment.

The youth, one of whose names was Robin, finally drew from his pocket the half of a little province bill of five shillings, which, in the depreciation in that sort of currency, did but satisfy the ferryman's demand, with the surplus of a sexangular piece of parchment, valued at three pence. He then walked forward into the town, with as light a step as if his day's journey had not already exceeded thirty miles, and with as eager an eye as if he were entering London city, instead of the little metropolis of a New England colony. Before Robin had proceeded far, however, it occurred to him that he knew not whither to direct his steps; so he paused, and looked up and down the narrow street, scrutinizing the small and mean wooden buildings that were scattered on either side.

"This low hovel cannot be my kinsman's dwelling," thought he, "nor yonder old house, where the moonlight enters at the broken casement; and truly I see none hereabouts that might be worthy of him. It would have been wise to inquire my way of the ferryman, and doubtless he would have gone with me, and earned a shilling from the Major for his pains. But the next man I meet will do as well."

He resumed his walk, and was glad to perceive that the street now became wider, and the houses more respectable in their appearance. He soon discerned a figure moving on moderately in advance, and hastened his steps to overtake it. As Robin drew nigh, he saw that the passenger was a man in years, with a full periwig of gray hair, a wide-skirted coat of dark cloth, and silk stockings rolled above his knees. He carried a long and polished cane, which he struck down perpendicularly before him, at every step; and at regular intervals he uttered two successive hems, of a peculiarly solemn and sepulchral intonation. Having made these observations, Robin laid hold of the skirt of the old man's coat, just when the light from the open door and windows of a barber's shop fell upon both their figures.

"Good evening to you, honored sir," said he, making a low bow, and still retaining his hold of the skirt. "I pray you tell me whereabouts is the dwelling of my kinsman, Major Molineux."

The youth's question was uttered very loudly; and one of the barbers, whose razor was descending on a well-soaped chin, and another who was dressing a Ramillies wig, left their occupations, and came to the door. The citizen, in the mean time, turned a long-favored countenance upon Robin, and answered him in a tone of excessive anger and annoyance. His two sepulchral hems, however, broke into the very center of his rebuke, with most singular effect, like a thought of the cold grave obtruding among wrathful passions.

"Let go my garment, fellow! I tell you, I know not the man you speak of. What! I have authority, I have—hem, hem—authority; and if this be the respect you show for your betters, your feet shall be brought acquainted with the stocks by daylight, tomorrow morning!"

Robin released the old man's skirt, and hastened away, pursued by an ill-mannered roar of laughter from the barber's shop. He was at first considerably surprised by the result of his question, but, being a shrewd youth, soon thought himself able to account for the mystery.

"This is some country representative," was his conclusion, "who has never seen the inside of my kinsman's door, and lacks the breeding to answer a stranger civilly. The man is old, or verily—I might be tempted to turn back and smite him on the nose. Ah, Robin, Robin! even the barber's boys laugh at you for choosing such a guide! You will be wiser in time, friend Robin."

He now became entangled in a succession of crooked and narrow streets, which crossed each other, and meandered at no great distance from the water-side. The smell of tar was obvious to his nostrils, the masts of vessels pierced the moonlight above the tops of the buildings, and the numerous signs, which Robin paused to read, informed him that he was near the center of business. But the streets were empty, the shops were closed, and lights were visible only in the second stories of a few dwelling-houses. At length, on the corner of a narrow lane, through which he was passing, he beheld the broad countenance of a British hero swinging before the door of an inn, whence proceeded the voices of many guests. The casement of one of the lower windows was thrown back, and a very thin curtain permitted Robin to distinguish a party at supper, round a well-furnished table. The fragrance of the good cheer steamed forth into the outer air, and the youth could not fail to recollect that the last remnant of his travelling stock of provision had yielded to his morning appetite, and that noon had found and left him dinnerless.

"O, that a parchment three-penny might give me a right to sit down at yonder table!" said Robin, with a sigh. "But the Major will make me welcome to the best of his victuals; so I will even step boldly in, and inquire my way to his dwelling."

He entered the tavern, and was guided by the murmur of voices and the fumes of tobacco, to the public room. It was a long and low apartment, with oaken walls, grown dark in the continual smoke, and a floor, which was thickly sanded, but of no immaculate purity. A number of persons—the larger part of whom appeared to be mariners, or in some way connected with the sea—occupied the wooden benches, or leather-bottomed chairs, conversing on various matters, and occasionally lending their attention to some topic of general interest. Three or four little groups were draining as many bowls of punch, which the West India trade had long since made a familiar drink in the colony. Others, who had the appearance of men who lived by regular and laborious handicraft, preferred the insulated bliss of an unshared potation, and became more taciturn under its influence. Nearly all, in short, evinced a predilection for the Good Creature in some of its various shapes, for this is a vice to which, as Fast Day sermons of a hundred years ago will testify, we have a long hereditary claim. The only guests to whom Robin's sympathies inclined him were two or three sheepish countrymen, who were using the inn somewhat after the fashion of a Turkish caravansary; they had gotten themselves into the darkest corner of the room, and heedless of the Nicotian[2] atmosphere, were supping on the bread of their own ovens, and the bacon cured in their own chimney-smoke. But though Robin felt a sort of brotherhood with these strangers, his eyes were attracted from them to a person who stood near the door, holding whispered conversation with a group of ill-dressed associates. His features were separately striking almost to grotesqueness, and the whole face left a deep impression on the memory. The forehead bulged out into a double prominence, with a vale between; the nose came boldly forth in an irregular curve, and its bridge was of more than a finger's breadth; the eyebrows were deep and shaggy, and the eyes glowed beneath them like fire in a cave.

While Robin deliberated of whom to inquire respecting his kinsman's dwelling, he was accosted by the innkeeper, a little man in a stained white apron, who had come to pay his professional welcome to the stranger. Being in the second generation from a French Protestant, he seemed to have inherited the courtesy of his parent nation; but no variety of circumstances was ever known to change his voice from the one shrill note in which he now addressed Robin.

"From the country, I presume, sir?" said he, with a profound bow. "Beg leave to congratulate you on your arrival, and trust you intend a long stay with us. Fine town here, sir, beautiful buildings, and much that may interest a stranger. May I hope for the honor of your commands in respect to supper?"

"The man sees a family likeness! the rogue has guessed that I am related to the Major!" thought Robin, who had hitherto experienced little superfluous civility.

All eyes were now turned on the country lad, standing at the door, in his worn three-cornered hat, gray coat, leather breeches, and blue yarn stockings, leaning on an oaken cudgel, and bearing a wallet on his back.

Robin replied to the courteous innkeeper, with such an assumption of confidence as befitted the Major's relative. "My honest friend," he said, "I shall make it a point to patronize your house on some occasion, when"—here he could not help lowering his voice—"when I may have more than a parchment three-pence in my pocket. My present business," continued he, speaking with lofty confidence, "is merely to inquire my way to the dwelling of my kinsman, Major Molineux."

There was a sudden and general movement in the room, which Robin interpreted as expressing the eagerness of each individual to become his guide. But the innkeeper turned his eyes to a written paper on the wall, which he read, or seemed to read, with occasional recurrences to the young man's figure.

"What have we here?" said he, breaking his speech into little dry fragments. " 'Left the house of the subscriber, bounden servant, Hezekiah Mudge,—had on, when he went away, gray coat, leather breeches, master's third-best hat. One pound currency reward to whosoever shall lodge him in any jail of the providence.' Better trudge, boy; better trudge!"

Robin had begun to draw his hand towards the lighter end of the oak cudgel, but a strange hostility in every countenance induced him to relinquish his purpose of breaking the courteous innkeeper's head. As he turned to leave the room, he encountered a sneering glance from the bold-featured personage whom he had before noticed; and no sooner was he beyond the door, than he heard a general laugh, in which the innkeeper's voice might be distinguished, like the dropping of small stones into a kettle.

"Now, is it not strange," thought Robin, with his usual shrewdness, "is it not strange that the confession of an empty pocket should outweigh the name of my kinsman, Major Molineux? O, if I had one of those grinning rascals in the woods, where I and my

[2]The room was smoke-filled: probably a reference to Jacques Nicot, who introduced tobacco into France.

oak sapling grew up together, I would teach him that my arm is heavy, though my purse be light!"

On turning the corner of the narrow lane, Robin found himself in a spacious street, with an unbroken line of lofty houses on each side, and a steepled building at the upper end, whence the ringing of a bell announced the hour of nine. The light of the moon, and the lamps from the numerous shop windows, discovered people promenading on the pavement, and amongst them Robin had hoped to recognize his hitherto inscrutable relative. The result of his former inquiries made him unwilling to hazard another, in a scene of such publicity, and he determined to walk slowly and silently up the street, thrusting his face close to that of every elderly gentleman, in search of the Major's lineaments. In his progress, Robin encountered many gay and gallant figures. Embroidered garments of showy colors, enormous periwigs, gold-laced hats, and silver-hilted swords glided past him, and dazzled his optics. Travelled youths, imitators of the European fine gentlemen of the period, trod jauntily along, half dancing to the fashionable tunes which they hummed, and making poor Robin ashamed of his quiet and natural gait. At length, after many pauses to examine the gorgeous display of goods in the shop-windows, and after suffering some rebukes for the impertinence of his scrutiny into people's faces, the Major's kinsman found himself near the steepled building, still unsuccessful in his search. As yet, however, he had seen only one side of the thronged street; so Robin crossed, and continued the same sort of inquisition down the opposite pavement, with stronger hopes than the philosopher seeking an honest man, but with no better fortune. He had arrived about midway towards the lower end, from which his course began, when he overheard the approach of some one, who struck down a cane on the flag-stones at every step, uttering at regular intervals, two sepulchral hems.

"Mercy on us!" quoth Robin, recognizing the sound.

Turning a corner, which chanced to be close at his right hand, he hastened to pursue his researches in some other part of the town. His patience now was wearing low, and he seemed to feel more fatigue from his rambles since he crossed the ferry, than from his journey of several days on the other side. Hunger also pleaded loudly within him, and Robin began to balance the propriety of demanding, violently, and with lifted cudgel, the necessary guidance from the first solitary passenger whom he should meet. While a resolution to this effect was gaining strength, he entered a street of mean appearance, on either side of which a row of ill-built houses was straggling towards the harbor. The moonlight fell upon no passenger along the whole extent, but in the third domicile which Robin passed there was a half-opened door, and his keen glance detected a woman's garment within.

"My luck may be better here," said he to himself.

Accordingly, he approached the door, and beheld it shut closer as he did so; yet an open space remained, sufficing for the fair occupant to observe the stranger, without a corresponding display on her part. All that Robin could discern was a strip of scarlet petticoat, and the occasional sparkle of an eye, as if the moonbeams were trembling on some bright thing.

"Pretty mistress," for I may call her so with a good conscience, thought the shrewd youth, since I know nothing to the contrary,—"my sweet pretty mistress, will you be kind enough to tell me whereabouts I must seek the dwelling of my kinsman, Major Molineux?"

Robin's voice was plaintive and winning, and the female, seeing nothing to be shunned in the handsome country youth, thrust open the door, and came forth into the moonlight. She was a dainty little figure, with a white neck, round arms, and a slender waist, at the extremity of which her scarlet petticoat jutted out over a hoop, as if she were standing in a balloon. Moreover, her face was oval and pretty, her hair dark beneath the little cap, and her bright eyes possessed a sly freedom, which triumphed over those of Robin.

"Major Molineux dwells here," said this fair woman.

Now, her voice was the sweetest Robin had heard that night, the airy counterpart of a stream of melted silver; yet he could not help doubting whether that sweet voice spoke Gospel truth. He looked up and down the mean street, and then surveyed the house before which they stood. It was a small, dark edifice of two stories, the second of which projected over the lower floor; and the front apartment had the aspect of a shop for petty commodities.

"Now truly I am in luck," replied Robin, cunningly, "and so indeed is my kinsman, the Major, in having so pretty a housekeeper. But I prithee trouble him to step to the door; I will deliver him a message from his friends in the country, and then go back to my lodgings at the inn."

"Nay, the Major has been a-bed this hour or more," said the lady of the scarlet petticoat; "and it would be to little purpose to disturb him to-night, seeing his evening draught was of the strongest. But he is a kind-hearted man, and it would be as much as my life's worth to let a kinsman of his turn away from the door. You are the good old gentleman's very picture, and I could swear that was his rainy-weather hat. Also he has garments very much resembling those leather small-clothes. But come in, I pray, for I bid you hearty welcome in his name."

So saying, the fair and hospitable dame took our hero by the hand; and the touch was light, and the force was gentleness, and though Robin read in her eyes what he did not hear in her words, yet the slender-waisted woman in the scarlet petticoat proved stronger than the athletic country youth. She had drawn his half-willing footsteps nearly to the threshold, when the opening of a door in the neighborhood startled the Major's housekeeper, and, leaving the Major's kinsman, she vanished speedily into her own domicile. A heavy yawn preceded the appearance of a man, who, like the Moonshine of Pyramus and Thisbe,[3] carried a lantern, needlessly aiding his sister luminary in the heavens. As he walked sleepily up the street, he turned his broad, dull face on Robin, and displayed a long staff, spiked at the end.

"Home, vagabond, home!" said the watchman, in accents that seemed to fall asleep as soon as they were uttered. "Home, or we'll set you in the stocks, by peep of day!"

"This is the second hint of the kind," thought Robin. "I wish they would end my difficulties, by setting me there to-night."

Nevertheless, the youth felt an instinctive antipathy towards the guardian of midnight order, which at first prevented him from asking his usual question. But just when the man was about to vanish behind the corner, Robin resolved not to lose the opportunity, and shouted lustily after him,—

"I say, friend! will you guide me to the house of my kinsman, Major Molineux?"

The watchman made no reply, but turned the corner and was gone; yet Robin seemed to hear the sound of drowsy laughter stealing along the solitary street. At that moment, also, a pleasant titter saluted him from the open window above his head; he looked up, and caught the sparkle of a saucy eye; a round arm beckoned to him, and next he heard light footsteps descending the staircase within. But Robin, being of the household of a New England clergyman, was a good youth, as well as a shrewd one; so he resisted temptation, and fled away.

He now roamed desperately, and at random, through the town, almost ready to believe that a spell was on him, like that by which a wizard of his country had once kept three pursuers wandering, a whole winter night, within twenty paces of the cottage which they sought. The streets lay before him, strange and desolate, and the lights were extinguished in almost every house. Twice, however, little parties of men, among whom Robin distinguished individuals in outlandish attire, came hurrying along; but though on both occasions they paused to address him, such intercourse did not at all enlighten his perplexity. They did but utter a few words in some language of which Robin knew nothing, and perceiving his inability to answer, bestowed a curse upon him in plain English, and hastened away. Finally, the lad determined to knock at the door of every mansion that might appear worthy to be occupied by his kinsman, trusting that perseverance would overcome the fatality that had hitherto thwarted him. Firm in this resolve, he was passing beneath the walls of a church, which formed the corner of two streets, when, as he turned into the shade of its steeple, he encountered a bulky stranger, muffled in a cloak. The man was proceeding with the speed of earnest business, but Robin planted himself full before him, holding the oak cudgel with both hands across his body, as a bar to further passage.

"Halt, honest man, and answer me a question," said he, very resolutely. "Tell me, this instant, whereabouts is the dwelling of my kinsman, Major Molineux!"

"Keep your tongue between your teeth, fool, and let me pass!" said a deep, gruff voice, which Robin partly remembered. "Let me pass, I say, or I'll strike you to the earth!"

"No, no, neighbor!" cried Robin, flourishing his cudgel, and then thrusting its larger end close to the man's muffled face. "No, no, I'm not the fool you take me for, nor do you pass till I have an answer to my question. Whereabouts is the dwelling of my kinsman, Major Molineux?"

The stranger, instead of attempting to force his passage, stepped back into the moonlight, unmuffled his face, and stared full into that of Robin.

"Watch here an hour, and Major Molineux will pass by," said he.

Robin gazed with dismay and astonishment on the unprecedented physiognomy of the speaker. The forehead with its double prominence, the broad hooked nose, the shaggy eyebrows, and fiery eyes, were those which he had noticed at the inn, but the man's complexion had undergone a singular, or, more properly, a two-fold change. One side of the face blazed an intense red, while the other was black as midnight, the division line being in the broad bridge of the nose; and a mouth which seemed to extend from ear to ear was black or red, in contrast to the color of the cheek. The effect was as if two individual devils, a fiend of fire and a fiend of darkness, had united themselves to form this in-

[3] Cf. Shakespeare, *A Midsummer Night's Dream* III. i.

fernal visage. The stranger grinned in Robin's face, muffled his parti-colored features, and was out of sight in a moment.

"Strange things we travellers see!" ejaculated Robin.

He seated himself, however, upon the steps of the church-door, resolving to wait the appointed time for his kinsman. A few moments were consumed in philosophical speculations upon the species of man who had just left him; but having settled this point shrewdly, rationally, and satisfactorily, he was compelled to look elsewhere for his amusement. And first he threw his eyes along the street. It was of more respectable appearance than most of those into which he had wandered; and the moon, creating, like the imaginative power, a beautiful strangeness in familiar objects, gave something of romance to a scene that might not have possessed it in the light of day. The irregular and often quaint architecture of the houses, some of whose roofs were broken into numerous little peaks, while others ascended, steep and narrow, into a single point, and others again were square; the pure snow-white of some of their complexions, the aged darkness of others, and the thousand sparklings, reflected from bright substances in the walls of many; these matters engaged Robin's attention for a while, and then began to grow wearisome. Next he endeavored to define the forms of distant objects, starting away, with almost ghostly indistinctness, just as his eye appeared to grasp them; and finally he took a minute survey of an edifice which stood on the opposite side of the street, directly in front of the church-door, where he was stationed. It was a large, square mansion, distinguished from its neighbors by a balcony, which rested on tall pillars, and by an elaborate Gothic window, communicating therewith.

"Perhaps this is the very house I have been seeking," thought Robin.

Then he strove to speed away the time, by listening to a murmur which swept continually along the street, yet was scarcely audible, except to an unaccustomed ear like his; it was a low, dull, dreamy sound, compounded of many noises, each of which was at too great a distance to be separately heard. Robin marvelled at this snore of a sleeping town, and marvelled more whenever its continuity was broken by now and then a distant shout, apparently loud where it originated. But altogether it was a sleep-inspiring sound, and, to shake off its drowsy influence, Robin arose, and climbed a window-frame, that he might view the interior of the church. There the moonbeams came trembling in, and fell down upon the deserted pews, and extended along the quiet aisles. A fainter yet more awful radiance was hovering around the pulpit, and one solitary ray had dared to rest upon the unopened page of the great Bible. Had nature, in that deep hour, become a worshipper in the house which man had builded? Or was that heavenly light the visible sanctity of the place,—visible because no earthly and impure feet were within the walls? The scene made Robin's heart shiver with a sensation of loneliness stronger than he had ever felt in the remotest depths of his native woods; so he turned away, and sat down again before the door. There were graves around the church, and now an uneasy thought obtruded into Robin's breast. What if the object of his search, which had been so often and so strangely thwarted, were all the time mouldering in his shroud? What if his kinsman should glide through yonder gate, and nod and smile to him in dimly passing by?

"O that any breathing thing were here with me!" said Robin.

Recalling his thoughts from this uncomfortable track, he sent them over forest, hill, and stream, and attempted to imagine how that evening of ambiguity and weariness had been spent by his father's household. He pictured them assembled at the door, beneath the tree, the great old tree, which had been spared for its huge twisted trunk, and venerable shade, when a thousand leafy brethren fell. There, at the going down of the summer sun, it was his father's custom to perform domestic worship, that the neighbors might come and join with him like brothers of the family, and that the wayfaring man might pause to drink at that fountain, and keep his heart pure by freshening the memory of home. Robin distinguished the seat of every individual of the little audience; he saw the good man in the midst, holding the Scriptures in the golden light that fell from the western clouds; he beheld him close the book and all rise up to pray. He heard the old thanksgivings for daily mercies, the old supplications for their continuance, to which he had so often listened in weariness, but which were now among his dear remembrances. He perceived the slight inequality of his father's voice when he came to speak of the absent one; he noted how his mother turned her face to the broad and knotted trunk; how his elder brother scorned, because the beard was rough upon his upper lip, to permit his features to be moved; how the younger sister drew down a low hanging branch before her eyes; and how the little one of all, whose sports had hitherto broken the decorum of the scene, understood the prayer for her playmate, and burst into clamorous grief. Then he saw them go in at the door; and when Robin would have entered also, the latch tinkled into its place, and he was excluded from his home.

"Am I here, or there?" cried Robin, starting; for all at once, when his thoughts had become visible and audible in a dream, the long, wide, solitary street shone out before him.

He aroused himself, and endeavored to fix his attention steadily upon the large edifice which he had surveyed before. But still his mind kept vibrating between fancy and reality; by turns, the pillars of the balcony lengthened into the tall, bare stems of pines, dwindled down to human figures, settled again into their true shape and size, and then commenced a new succession of changes. For a single moment, when he deemed himself awake, he could have sworn that a visage—one which he seemed to remember, yet could not absolutely name as his kinsman's—was looking towards him from the Gothic window. A deeper sleep wrestled with and nearly overcame him, but fled at the sound of footsteps along the opposite pavement. Robin rubbed his eyes, discerned a man passing at the foot of the balcony, and addressed him in a loud, peevish, and lamentable cry.

"Hallo, friend! must I wait here all night for my kinsman, Major Molineux?"

The sleeping echoes awoke, and answered the voice; and the passenger, barely able to discern a figure sitting in the oblique shade of the steeple, traversed the street to obtain a nearer view. He was himself a gentleman in his prime, of open, intelligent, cheerful, and altogether prepossessing countenance. Perceiving a country youth, apparently homeless and without friends, he accosted him in a tone of real kindness, which had become strange to Robin's ears.

"Well, my good lad, why are you sitting here?" inquired he. "Can I be of service to you in any way?"

"I am afraid not, sir," replied Robin, despondingly; "yet I shall take it kindly, if you'll answer me a single question. I've been searching, half the night, for one Major Molineux; now, sir, is there really such a person in these parts, or am I dreaming?"

"Major Molineux! The name is not altogether strange to me," said the gentleman, smiling. "Have you any objection to telling me the nature of your business with him?"

Then Robin briefly related that his father was a clergyman, settled on a small salary, at a long distance back in the country, and that he and Major Molineux were brothers' children. The Major, having inherited riches, and acquired civil and military rank, had visited his cousin, in great pomp, a year or two before; had manifested much interest in Robin and an elder brother, and, being childless himself, had thrown out hints respecting the future establishment of one of them in life. The elder brother was destined to succeed to the farm which his father cultivated in the interval of sacred duties; it was therefore determined that Robin should profit by his kinsman's generous intentions, especially as he seemed to be rather the favorite, and was thought to possess other necessary endowments.

"For I have the name of being a shrewd youth," observed Robin, in this part of his story.

"I doubt not you deserve it," replied his new friend, good-naturedly; "but pray proceed."

"Well, sir, being nearly eighteen years old, and well-grown, as you see," continued Robin, drawing himself up to his full height, "I thought it high time to begin in the world. So my mother and sister put me in handsome trim, and my father gave me half the remnant of his last year's salary, and five days ago I started for this place, to pay the Major a visit. But, would you believe it, sir! I crossed the ferry a little after dark, and have yet found nobody that would show me the way to his dwelling;—only, an hour or two since, I was told to wait here, and Major Molineux would pass by."

"Can you describe the man who told you this?" inquired the gentleman.

"O, he was a very ill-favored fellow, sir," replied Robin, "with two great bumps on his forehead, a hook nose, fiery eyes,—and, what struck me as the strangest, his face was of two different colors. Do you happen to know such a man, sir?"

"Not intimately," answered the stranger, "but I chanced to meet him a little time previous to your stopping me. I believe you may trust his word, and that the Major will very shortly pass through this street. In the mean time, as I have a singular curiosity to witness your meeting, I will sit down here upon the steps, and bear you company."

He seated himself accordingly, and soon engaged his companion in animated discourse. It was but of brief continuance, however, for a noise of shouting, which had long been remotely audible, drew so much nearer that Robin inquired its cause.

"What may be the meaning of this uproar?" asked he. "Truly, if your town be always as noisy, I shall find little sleep, while I am an inhabitant."

"Why, indeed, friend Robin, there do appear to be three or four riotous fellows abroad to-night," replied the gentleman. "You must not expect all the stillness of your native woods, here in our streets. But the watch will shortly be at the heels of these lads, and"—

"Ay, and set them in the stocks by peep of day," interrupted Robin, recollecting his own encounter with the drowsy lantern-bearer. "But, dear sir, if I may trust my ears, an army of watchmen would never make head against such a multitude of rioters. There were at least a thousand voices went up to make that one shout."

"May not a man have several voices, Robin, as well as two complexions?" said his friend.

"Perhaps a man may; but Heaven forbid that a woman should!" responded the shrewd youth, thinking of the seductive tones of the Major's housekeeper.

The sounds of a trumpet in some neighboring street now became so evident and continual, that Robin's curiosity was strongly excited. In addition to the shouts, he heard frequent bursts from many instruments of discord, and a wild and confused laughter filled up the intervals. Robin rose from the steps, and looked wistfully towards a point whither people seemed to be hastening.

"Surely some prodigious merry-making is going on," exclaimed he. "I have laughed very little since I left home, sir, and should be sorry to lose an opportunity. Shall we step round the corner by that darkish house, and take our share of the fun?"

"Sit down again, sit down, good Robin," replied the gentleman, laying his hand on the skirt of the gray coat. "You forget that we must wait here for your kinsman; and there is reason to believe that he will pass by, in the course of a very few moments."

The near approach of the uproar had now disturbed the neighborhood; windows flew open on all sides; and many heads, in the attire of the pillow, and confused by sleep suddenly broken, were protruded to the gaze of whoever had leisure to observe them. Eager voices hailed each other from house to house, all demanding the explanation, which not a soul could give. Half-dressed men hurried towards the unknown commotion, stumbling as they went over the stone steps that thrust themselves into the narrow foot-walk. The shouts, the laughter, and the tuneless bray, the antipodes of music, came onwards with increasing din, till scattered individuals, and then denser bodies, began to appear round a corner at the distance of a hundred yards.

"Will you recognize your kinsman, if he passes in this crowd?" inquired the gentleman.

"Indeed, I can't warrant it, sir; but I'll take my stand here, and keep a bright lookout," answered Robin, descending to the outer edge of the pavement.

A mighty stream of people now emptied into the street, and came rolling slowly towards the church. A single horseman wheeled the corner in the midst of them, and close behind him came a band of fearful wind-instruments, sending forth a fresher discord, now that no intervening buildings kept it from the ear. Then a redder light disturbed the moonbeams, and a dense multitude of torches shone along the street, concealing, by their glare, whatever object they illuminated. The single horseman, clad in a military dress, and bearing a drawn sword, rode onward as the leader, and, by his fierce and variegated countenance, appeared like war personified: the red of one cheek was an emblem of fire and sword; the blackness of the other betokened the mourning that attends them. In his train were wild figures in the Indian dress, and many fantastic shapes without a model, giving the whole march a visionary air, as if a dream had broken forth from some feverish brain, and were sweeping visibly through the midnight streets. A mass of people, inactive, except as applauding spectators, hemmed the procession in; and several women ran along the sidewalk, piercing the confusion of heavier sounds with their shrill voices of mirth or terror.

"The double-faced fellow has his eye upon me," muttered Robin, with an indefinite but an uncomfortable idea that he was himself to bear a part in the pageantry.

The leader turned himself in the saddle, and fixed his glance full upon the country youth, as the steed went slowly by. When Robin had freed his eyes from those fiery ones, the musicians were passing before him, and the torches were close at hand; but the unsteady brightness of the latter formed a veil which he could not penetrate. The rattling of wheels over the stones sometimes found its way to his ear, and confused traces of a human form appeared at intervals, and then melted into the vivid light. A moment more, and the leader thundered a command to halt: the trumpets vomited a horrid breath, and then held their peace; the shouts and laughter of the people died away, and there remained only a universal hum, allied to silence. Right before Robin's eyes was an uncovered cart. There the torches blazed the brightest, there the moon shone out like day, and there, in tar-and-feathery dignity, sat his kinsman, Major Molineux!

He was an elderly man, of large and majestic person, and strong, square features, betokening a steady soul; but steady as it was, his enemies had found means to shake it. His face was pale as death, and far more ghastly; the broad forehead was contracted in his agony, so that his eyebrows formed one grizzled line; his eyes were red and wild, and the foam hung white upon his quivering lip. His whole frame was agitated by a quick and continual tremor, which his pride strove to quell, even in those circumstances of overwhelming humiliation. But perhaps the bitterest pang of all was when his eyes met those of Robin; for he evidently knew him on the instant, as the youth stood witnessing the foul disgrace of a head grown gray in honor. They stared at each other in silence, and Robin's knees shook, and his hair bristled, with a mixture of pity and terror. Soon, however, a bewildering excitement began to seize upon his mind; the preceding adventures of the night, the unexpected appearance of the crowd, the torches, the confused din and the hush that followed, the spectre of his kinsman reviled by that great multitude,—all this, and, more than all, a perception of tremendous ridicule in the whole scene, affected him with a sort of mental inebriety. At that moment a voice of sluggish merriment saluted Robin's ears; he turned instinctively, and just behind the corner of the church stood the lantern-bearer, rubbing his eyes, and drowsily enjoying the lad's amazement. Then he heard a peal of laughter like the ringing of silvery bells; a woman twitched his arm, a saucy eye met his, and he saw the lady of the scarlet petticoat. A sharp, dry cachinnation appealed to his memory, and standing on tiptoe in the crowd, with his white apron over his head, he beheld the courteous little innkeeper. And lastly, there sailed over the heads of the multitude a great, broad laugh, broken in the midst by two sepulchral hems; thus, "Haw, haw, haw,—hem, hem,—haw, haw, haw, haw!"

The sound proceeded from the balcony of the opposite edifice, and thither Robin turned his eyes. In front of the Gothic window stood the old citizen, wrapped in a wide gown, his gray periwig exchanged for a night-cap, which was thrust back from his forehead, and his silk stockings hanging about his legs. He supported himself on his polished cane in a fit of convulsive merriment, which manifested itself on his solemn old features like a funny inscription on a tombstone. Then Robin seemed to hear the voices of the barbers, of the guests of the inn, and of all who had made sport of him that night. The contagion was spreading among the multitude, when, all at once, it seized upon Robin, and he sent forth a shout of laughter that echoed through the street,—every man shook his sides, every man emptied his lungs, but Robin's shout was the loudest there. The cloud-spirits peeped from their silvery islands, as the congregated mirth went roaring up the sky! The Man in the Moon heard the far bellow; "Oho," quoth he, "the old earth is frolicsome tonight!"

When there was a momentary calm in that tempestuous sea of sound, the leader gave the sign, the procession resumed its march. On they went, like fiends that throng in mockery around some dead potentate, mighty no more, but majestic still in his agony. On they went, in counterfeited pomp, in senseless uproar, in frenzied merriment, trampling all on an old man's heart. On swept the tumult, and left a silent street behind.

"Well, Robin, are you dreaming?" inquired the gentleman, laying his hand on the youth's shoulder.

Robin started, and withdrew his arm from the stone post to which he had instinctively clung, as the living stream rolled by him. His cheek was somewhat pale, and his eye not quite as lively as in the earlier part of the evening.

"Will you be kind enough to show me the way to the ferry?" said he, after a moment's pause.

"You have, then, adopted a new subject of inquiry?" observed his companion, with a smile.

"Why, yes, sir," replied Robin, rather dryly. "Thanks to you, and to my other friends, I have at last met my kinsman, and he will scarce desire to see my face again. I begin to grow weary of a town life, sir. Will you show me the way to the ferry?"

"No, my good friend Robin,—not to-night, at least," said the gentleman. "Some few days hence, if you wish it, I will speed you on your journey. Or, if you prefer to remain with us, perhaps, as you are a shrewd youth, you may rise in the world without the help of your kinsman, Major Molineux."

1832

Roger Malvin's Burial

Hawthorne makes use of history in this tale to provide a stage whereon the psychological and moral drama of guilt and choice can unfold. The place (the frontier in 1725) and the choice (between the self and an obligation to another) give the story an important political and social meaning; beyond that, Hawthorne is clearly concerned with the psychology of guilt and with a sin-sacrifice-redemption pattern. Text: From the author's revised edition of *Mosses from an Old Manse* (Boston, 1854).

One of the few incidents of Indian warfare naturally susceptible of the moonlight of romance was that expedition undertaken for the defence of the frontiers in the year 1725, which resulted in the well-remembered "Lovell's Fight."[1] Imagination, by casting certain circumstances judicially into the shade, may see much to admire in the heroism of a little band who gave battle to twice their number in the heart of the enemy's country. The open bravery displayed by both parties was in accordance with civilized ideas of valor; and chivalry itself might not blush to record the deeds of one or two individuals. The battle, though so fatal to those who fought, was not unfortunate in its consequences to the country; for it broke the strength of a tribe and conduced to the peace which subsisted during several ensuing years. History and tradition are unusually minute in their memorials of this affair; and the captain of a scouting party of frontier men has acquired as actual

[1] With the Penobscot Indians.

a military renown as many a victorious leader of thousands. Some of the incidents contained in the following pages will be recognized, notwithstanding the substitution of fictitious names, by such as have heard, from old men's lips, the fate of the few combatants who were in a condition to retreat after "Lovell's Fight."

The early sunbeams hovered cheerfully upon the tree-tops, beneath which two weary and wounded men had stretched their limbs the night before. Their bed of withered oak leaves was strewn upon the small level space, at the foot of a rock, situated near the summit of one of the gentle swells by which the face of the country is there diversified. The mass of granite, rearing its smooth, flat surface fifteen or twenty feet above their heads, was not unlike a gigantic gravestone, upon which the veins seemed to form an inscription in forgotten characters. On a tract of several acres around this rock, oaks and other hard-wood trees had supplied the place of the pines, which were the usual growth of the land; and a young and vigorous sapling stood close beside the travellers.

The severe wound of the elder man had probably deprived him of sleep; for, so soon as the first ray of sunshine rested on the top of the highest tree, he reared himself painfully from his recumbent posture and sat erect. The deep lines of his countenance and the scattered gray of his hair marked him as past the middle age; but his muscular frame would, but for the effects of his wound, have been as capable of sustaining fatigue as in the early vigor of life. Languor and exhaustion now sat upon his haggard features; and the despairing glance which he sent forward through the depths of the forest proved his own conviction that his pilgrimage was at an end. He next turned his eyes to the companion who reclined by his side. The youth—for he had scarcely attained the years of manhood—lay, with his head upon his arm, in the embrace of an unquiet sleep, which a thrill of pain from his wounds seemed each moment on the point of breaking. His right hand grasped a musket; and, to judge from the violent action of his features, his slumbers were bringing back a vision of the conflict of which he was one of the few survivors. A shout—deep and loud in his dreaming fancy—found its way in an imperfect murmur to his lips; and, starting even at the slight sound of his own voice, he suddenly awoke. The first act of reviving recollection was to make anxious inquiries respecting the condition of his wounded fellow-traveller. The latter shook his head.

"Reuben, my boy," he said, "this rock beneath which we sit will serve for an old hunter's gravestone. There is many and many a long mile of howling wilderness before us yet; nor would it avail me anything if the smoke of my own chimney were but on the other side of that swell of land. The Indian bullet was deadlier than I thought."

"You are weary with our three days' travel," replied the youth, "and a little longer rest will recruit you. Sit you here while I search the woods for the herbs and roots that must be our sustenance; and, having eaten, you shall lean on me, and we will turn our faces homeward. I doubt not that, with my help, you can attain to some one of the frontier garrisons."

"There is not two days' life in me, Reuben," said the other, calmly, "and I will no longer burden you with my useless body, when you can scarcely support your own. Your wounds are deep and your strength is failing fast; yet, if you hasten onward alone, you may be preserved. For me there is no hope, and I will await death here."

"If it must be so, I will remain and watch by you," said Reuben, resolutely.

"No, my son, no," rejoined his companion. "Let the wish of a dying man have weight with you; give me one grasp of your hand, and get you hence. Think you that my last moments will be eased by the thought that I leave you to die a more lingering death? I have loved you like a father, Reuben; and at a time like this I should have something of a father's authority. I charge you to be gone, that I may die in peace."

"And because you have been a father to me, should I therefore leave you to perish and to lie unburied in the wilderness?" exclaimed the youth. "No; if your end be in truth approaching, I will watch by you and receive your parting words. I will dig a grave here by the rock, in which, if my weakness overcome me, we will rest together; or, if Heaven gives me strength, I will seek my way home."

"In the cities and wherever men dwell," replied the other, "they bury their dead in the earth; they hide them from the sight of the living; but here, where no step may pass perhaps for a hundred years, wherefore should I not rest beneath the open sky, covered only by the oak leaves when the autumn winds shall strew them? And for a monument, here is this gray rock, on which my dying hand shall carve the name of Roger Malvin; and the traveller in days to come will know that here sleeps a hunter and a warrior. Tarry not, then, for a folly like this, but hasten away, if not for your own sake, for hers who will else be desolate."

Malvin spoke the last few words in a faltering voice, and their effect upon his companion was strongly visible. They reminded him that there were other and less questionable duties than that of sharing the fate of a man whom his death could not benefit. Nor can it be affirmed that no selfish feeling strove to enter Reuben's heart, though the consciousness made him more earnestly resist his companion's entreaties.

"How terrible to wait the slow approach of death in this solitude!" exclaimed he. "A brave man does not shrink in the battle; and, when friends stand round the bed, even women may die composedly; but here—"

"I shall not shrink even here, Reuben Bourne," interrupted Malvin. "I am a man of no weak heart; and, if I were, there is a surer support than that of earthly friends. You are young, and life is dear to you. Your last moments will need comfort far more than mine; and when you have laid me in the earth, and are alone, and night is settling on the forest, you will feel all the bitterness of the death that may now be escaped. But I will urge no selfish motive to your generous nature. Leave me for my sake, that, having said a prayer for your safety, I may have space to settle my account undisturbed by worldly sorrows."

"And your daughter,—how shall I dare to meet her eye?" exclaimed Reuben. "She will ask the fate of her father, whose life I vowed to defend with my own. Must I tell her that he travelled three days' march with me from the field of battle, and that then I left him to perish in the wilderness? Were it not better to lie down and die by your side than to return safe and say this to Dorcas?"

"Tell my daughter," said Roger Malvin, "that, though yourself sore wounded, and weak, and weary, you led my tottering footsteps many a mile, and left me only at my earnest entreaty, because I would not have your blood upon my soul. Tell her that through pain and danger you were faithful, and that, if your lifeblood could have saved me, it would have flowed to its last drop; and tell her that you will be something dearer than a father, and that my blessing is with you both, and that my dying eyes can see a long and pleasant path in which you will journey together."

As Malvin spoke he almost raised himself from the ground, and the energy of his concluding words seemed to fill the wild and lonely forest with a vision of happiness; but, when he sank exhausted upon his bed of oak leaves, the light which had kindled in Reuben's eye was quenched. He felt as if it were both sin and folly to think of happiness at such a moment. His companion watched his changing countenance, and sought with generous art to wile him to his own good.

"Perhaps I deceive myself in regard to the time I have to live," he resumed. "It may be that, with speedy assistance, I might recover of my wound. The foremost fugitives must, ere this, have carried tidings of our fatal battle to the frontiers, and parties will be out to succor those in like condition with ourselves. Should you meet one of these and guide them hither, who can tell but that I may sit by my own fireside again?"

A mournful smile strayed across the features of the dying man as he insinuated that unfounded hope; which, however, was not without its effect on Reuben. No merely selfish motive, nor even the desolate condition of Dorcas, could have induced him to desert his companion at such a moment—but his wishes seized on the thought that Malvin's life might be preserved, and his sanguine nature heightened almost to certainty the remote possibility of procuring human aid.

"Surely there is reason, weighty reason, to hope that friends are not far distant," he said, half aloud. "There fled one coward, unwounded, in the beginning of the fight, and most probably he made good speed. Every true man on the frontier would shoulder his musket at the news; and, though no party may range so far into the woods as this, I shall perhaps encounter them in one day's march. Counsel me faithfully," he added, turning to Malvin, in distrust of his own motives. "Were your situation mine, would you desert me while life remained?"

"It is now twenty years," replied Roger Malvin, sighing, however, as he secretly acknowledged the wide dissimilarity between the two cases,—"it is now twenty years since I escaped with one dear friend from Indian captivity near Montreal. We journeyed many days through the woods, till at length, overcome with hunger and weariness, my friend lay down and besought me to leave him; for he knew that, if I remained, we both must perish; and, with but little hope of obtaining succor, I heaped a pillow of dry leaves beneath his head and hastened on."

"And did you return in time to save him?" asked Reuben hanging on Malvin's words as if they were to be prophetic of his own success.

"I did," answered the other. "I came upon the camp of a hunting party before sunset of the same day. I guided them to the spot where my comrade was expecting death; and he is now a hale and hearty man upon his own farm, far within the frontiers, while I lie wounded here in the depths of the wilderness."

This example, powerful in effecting Reuben's decision, was aided, unconsciously to himself, by the hidden strength of many another motive. Roger Malvin perceived that the victory was nearly won.

"Now, go, my son, and Heaven prosper you!" he said. "Turn not back with your friends when you meet them, lest your wounds and weariness overcome you; but send hitherward two or three, that may be spared, to search for me; and believe me,

Reuben, my heart will be lighter with every step you take towards home." Yet there was, perhaps, a change both in his countenance and voice as he spoke thus; for, after all, it was a ghastly fate to be left expiring in the wilderness.

Reuben Bourne, but half convinced that he was acting rightly, at length raised himself from the ground and prepared himself for his departure. And first, though contrary to Malvin's wishes, he collected a stock of roots and herbs, which had been their only food during the last two days. This useless supply he placed within reach of the dying man, for whom, also, he swept together a bed of dry oak leaves. Then climbing to the summit of the rock, which on one side was rough and broken, he bent the oak sapling downward, and bound his handkerchief to the topmost branch. This precaution was not unnecessary to direct any who might come in search of Malvin; for every part of the rock, except its broad, smooth front, was concealed at a little distance by the dense undergrowth of the forest. The handkerchief had been the bandage of a wound upon Reuben's arm; and, as he bound it to the tree, he vowed by the blood that stained it that he would return, either to save his companion's life or to lay his body in the grave. He then descended, and stood, with downcast eyes, to receive Roger Malvin's parting words.

The experience of the latter suggested much and minute advice respecting the youth's journey through the trackless forest. Upon this subject he spoke with calm earnestness, as if he were sending Reuben to the battle or the chase while he himself remained secure at home, and not as if the human countenance that was about to leave him were the last he would ever behold. But his firmness was shaken before he concluded.

"Carry my blessing to Dorcas, and say that my last prayer shall be for her and you. Bid her to have no hard thoughts because you left me here,"—Reuben's heart smote him,—"for that your life would not have weighed with you if its sacrifice could have done me good. She will marry you after she has mourned a little while for her father; and Heaven grant you long and happy days, and may your children's children stand round your death bed! And, Reuben," added he, as the weakness of mortality made its way at last, "return, when your wounds are healed and your weariness refreshed,—return to this wild rock, and lay my bones in the grave, and say a prayer over them."

An almost superstitious regard, arising perhaps from the customs of the Indians, whose war was with the dead as well as the living, was paid by the frontier inhabitants to the rites of sepulture; and there are many instances of the sacrifice of life in the attempt to bury those who had fallen by the "sword of the wilderness." Reuben, therefore, felt the full importance of the promise which he most solemnly made to return and perform Roger Malvin's obsequies. It was remarkable that the latter, speaking his whole heart in his parting words, no longer endeavored to persuade the youth that even the speediest succor might avail to the preservation of his life. Reuben was internally convinced that he should see Malvin's living face no more. His generous nature would fain have delayed him, at whatever risk, till the dying scene were past; but the desire of existence and the hope of happiness had strengthened in his heart, and he was unable to resist them.

"It is enough," said Roger Malvin, having listened to Reuben's promise. "Go, and God speed you!"

The youth pressed his hand in silence, turned and was departing. His slow and faltering steps, however, had borne him but a little way before Malvin's voice recalled him.

"Reuben, Reuben," said he, faintly; and Reuben returned and knelt down by the dying man.

"Raise me, and let me lean against the rock," was his last request. "My face will be turned towards home, and I shall see you a moment longer as you pass among the trees."

Reuben, having made the desired alteration in his companion's posture, again began his solitary pilgrimage. He walked more hastily at first than was consistent with his strength; for a sort of guilty feeling, which sometimes torments men in their most justifiable acts, caused him to seek concealment from Malvin's eyes; but after he had trodden far upon the rustling leaves he crept back, impelled by a wild and painful curiosity, and, sheltered by the earthly roots of an uptorn tree, gazed earnestly at the desolate man. The morning sun was unclouded, and the trees and shrubs imbibed the sweet air of the month of May; yet there seemed a gloom on Nature's face, as if she sympathized with mortal pain and sorrow. Roger Malvin's hands were uplifted in a fervent prayer, some of the words of which stole through the stillness of the woods and entered Reuben's heart, torturing it with an unutterable pang. They were the broken accents of a petition for his own happiness and that of Dorcas; and, as the youth listened, conscience, or something in its similitude, pleaded strongly with him to return and lie down again by the rock. He felt how hard was the doom of the kind and generous being whom he had deserted in his extremity. Death would come like the slow approach of a corpse, stealing gradually towards him through the forest, and showing its ghastly and motionless features from behind a nearer and yet a nearer tree. But such must have been

Reuben's own fate had he tarried another sunset; and who shall impute blame to him if he shrink from so useless a sacrifice? As he gave a parting look, a breeze waved the little banner upon the sapling oak and reminded Reuben of his vow.

Many circumstances combined to retard the wounded traveller in his way to the frontiers. On the second day the clouds, gathering densely over the sky, precluded the possibility of regulating his course by the position of the sun; and he knew not but that every effort of his almost exhausted strength was removing him farther from the home he sought. His scanty sustenance was supplied by the berries and other spontaneous products of the forest. Herds of deer, it is true, sometimes bounded past him, and partridges frequently whirred up before his footsteps; but his ammunition had been expended in the fight, and he had no means of slaying them. His wounds, irritated by the constant exertion in which lay the only hope of life, wore away his strength and at intervals confused his reason. But, even in the wanderings of intellect, Reuben's young heart clung strongly to existence; and it was only through absolute incapacity of motion that he at last sank down beneath a tree, compelled there to await death.

In this situation he was discovered by a party who, upon the first intelligence of the fight, had been despatched to the relief of the survivors. They conveyed him to the nearest settlement, which chanced to be that of his own residence.

Dorcas, in the simplicity of the olden time, watched by the bedside of her wounded lover and administered all those comforts that are in the sole gift of woman's heart and hand. During several days Reuben's recollection strayed drowsily among the perils and hardships through which he had passed, and he was incapable of returning definite answers to the inquiries with which many were eager to harass him. No authentic particulars of the battle had yet been circulated; nor could mothers, wives, and children tell whether their loved ones were detained by captivity or by the stronger chain of death. Dorcas nourished her apprehensions in silence till one afternoon when Reuben awoke from an unquiet sleep, and seemed to recognize her more perfectly than at any previous time. She saw that his intellect had become composed, and she could no longer restrain her filial anxiety.

"My father, Reuben?" she began; but the change in her lover's countenance made her pause.

The youth shrank as if with a bitter pain, and the blood gushed vividly into his wan and hollow cheeks. His first impulse was to cover his face; but, apparently with a desperate effort, he half raised himself and spoke vehemently, defending himself against an imaginary accusation.

"Your father was sore wounded in the battle, Dorcas; and he bade me not burden myself with him, but only to lead him to the lakeside, that he might quench his thirst and die. But I would not desert the old man in his extremity, and, though bleeding myself, I supported him; I gave him half my strength, and led him away with me. For three days we journeyed on together, and your father was sustained beyond my hopes; but, awaking at sunrise on the fourth day, I found him faint and exhausted; he was unable to proceed; his life had ebbed away fast; and—"

"He died!" exclaimed Dorcas, faintly.

Reuben felt it impossible to acknowledge that his selfish love of life had hurried him away before her father's fate was decided. He spoke not; he only bowed his head; and, between shame and exhaustion, sank back and hid his face in the pillow. Dorcas wept when her fears were thus confirmed; but the shock, as it had been long anticipated, was on that account the less violent.

"You dug a grave for my poor father in the wilderness, Reuben?" was the question by which her filial piety manifested itself.

"My hands were weak; but I did what I could," replied the youth in a smothered tone. "There stands a noble tombstone above his head; and I would to Heaven I slept as soundly as he!"

Dorcas, perceiving the wildness of his latter words, inquired no further at the time; but her heart found ease in the thought that Roger Malvin had not lacked such funeral rites as it was possible to bestow. The tale of Reuben's courage and fidelity lost nothing when she communicated it to her friends; and the poor youth, tottering from his sick chamber to breathe the sunny air, experienced from every tongue the miserable and humiliating torture of unmerited praise. All acknowledged that he might worthily demand the hand of the fair maiden to whose father he had been "faithful unto death;" and, as my tale is not of love, it shall suffice to say that in the space of a few months Reuben became the husband of Dorcas Malvin. During the marriage ceremony the bride was covered with blushes; but the bridegroom's face was pale.

There was now in the breast of Reuben Bourne an incommunicable thought—something which he was to conceal most heedfully from her whom he most loved and trusted. He regretted, deeply and bitterly, the moral cowardice that had restrained his words when he was about to disclose the truth to Dorcas; but pride, the fear of losing her affection, the dread of universal scorn forbade him to rectify this falsehood. He felt that for leaving Roger Malvin he deserved no censure. His presence, the gratuitous sacrifice of his own life, would have added only another and a needless agony to the last moments of the dying man; but concealment had imparted to a justifiable act much of the secret effect of guilt; and Reuben, while reason told him that he had done right, experienced in no small degree the mental horrors which punish the perpetrator of undiscovered crime. By a certain association of ideas, he at times almost imagined himself a murderer. For years, also, a thought would occasionally recur, which, though he perceived all its folly and extravagance, he had not power to banish from his mind. It was a haunting and torturing fancy that his father-in-law was yet sitting at the foot of the rock, on the withered forest leaves, alive, and awaiting his pledged assistance. These mental deceptions, however, came and went, nor did he ever mistake them for realities; but in the calmest and clearest moods of his mind he was conscious that he had a deep vow unredeemed, and that an unburied corpse was calling to him out of the wilderness. Yet such was the consequence of his prevarication that he could not obey the call. It was now too late to require the assistance of Roger Malvin's friends in performing his long-deferred sepulture; and superstitious fears, of which none were more susceptible than the people of the outward settlements, forbade Reuben to go alone. Neither did he know where in the pathless and illimitable forest to seek that smooth and lettered rock at the base of which the body lay: his remembrance of every portion of his travel thence was indistinct, and the latter part had left no impression upon his mind. There was, however, a continual impulse, a voice audible only to himself, commanding him to go forth and redeem his vow; and he had a strange impression that, were he to make the trial, he would be led straight to Malvin's bones. But year after year that summons, unheard but felt, was disobeyed. His one secret thought became like a chain binding down his spirit and like a serpent gnawing into his heart; and he was transformed into a sad and downcast yet irritable man.

In the course of a few years after their marriage changes began to be visible in the external prosperity of Reuben and Dorcas. The only riches of the former had been his stout heart and strong arm; but the latter, her father's sole heiress, had made her husband master of a farm, under older cultivation, larger, and better stocked than most of the frontier establishments. Reuben Bourne, however, was a neglectful husbandman; and, while the lands of the other settlers became annually more fruitful, his deteriorated in the same proportion. The discouragements to agriculture were greatly lessened by the cessation of Indian war, during which men held the plough in one hand and the musket in the other, and were fortunate if the products of their dangerous labor were not destroyed, either in the field or in the barn, by the savage enemy. But Reuben did not profit by the altered condition of the country; nor can it be denied that his intervals of industrious attention to his affairs were but scantily rewarded with success. The irritability by which he had recently become distinguished, was another cause of his declining prosperity, as it occasioned frequent quarrels in his unavoidable intercourse with the neighboring settlers. The results of these were innumerable lawsuits; for the people of New England, in the earliest stages and wildest circumstances of the country, adopted, whenever attainable, the legal mode of deciding their differences. To be brief, the world did not go well with Reuben Bourne; and, though not till many years after his marriage, he was finally a ruined man, with but one remaining expedient against the evil fate that had pursued him. He was to throw sunlight into some deep recess of the forest, and seek subsistence from the virgin bosom of the wilderness.

The only child of Reuben and Dorcas was a son, now arrived at the age of fifteen years, beautiful in youth, and giving promise of a glorious manhood. He was peculiarly qualified for, and already began to excel in, the wild accomplishments of frontier life. His foot was fleet, his aim true, his apprehension quick, his heart glad and high; and all who anticipated the return of Indian war spoke of Cyrus Bourne as a future leader in the land. The boy was loved by his father with a deep and silent strength, as if whatever was good and happy in his own nature had been transferred to his child, carrying his affections with it. Even Dorcas, though loving and beloved, was far less dear to him; for Reuben's secret thoughts and insulated emotions had gradually made him a selfish man, and he could no longer love deeply except where he saw or imagined some reflection or likeness of his own mind. In Cyrus he recognized what he had himself been in other days; and at intervals he seemed to partake of the boy's spirit and to be revived with a fresh and happy life. Reuben was accompanied by his son in the expedition, for the purpose of selecting a tract of land and felling and burning the timber, which necessarily preceded the removal of the household gods. Two months of autumn were thus occupied after which Reuben Bourne and his young hunter returned to spend their last winter in the settlements.

It was early in the month of May that the little family snapped asunder whatever tendrils of affections had clung to inanimate objects, and bade farewell to the few who, in the blight of fortune, called themselves their friends. The sadness of the parting moment had, to each of the pilgrims, its peculiar alleviations. Reuben, a moody man, and misanthropic because unhappy, strode onward with his usual stern brow and downcast eye, feeling few regrets and disdaining to acknowledge any. Dorcas, while she wept abundantly over the broken ties by which her simple and affectionate nature had bound itself to every thing, felt that the inhabitants of her inmost heart moved on with her, and that all else would be supplied wherever she might go. And the boy dashed one teardrop from his eye, and thought of the adventurous pleasures of the untrodden forest.

O, who, in the enthusiasm of a daydream, has not wished that he were a wanderer in a world of summer wilderness, with one fair and gentle being hanging lightly on his arm? In youth his free and exulting step would know no barrier but the rolling ocean or the snow-topped mountains; a calmer manhood would choose a home where Nature had strewn a double wealth in the vale of some transparent stream; and when hoary age, after long, long years of that pure life, stole on and found him there, it would find him the father of a race, the patriarch of a people, the founder of a mighty nation yet to be. When death, like the sweet sleep which we welcome after a day of happiness, came over him, his far descendants would mourn over the venerated dust. Enveloped by tradition in mysterious attributes, the men of future generations would call him god-like; and remote posterity would see him standing, dimly glorious, far up the valley of a hundred centuries.

The tangled and gloomy forest through which the personages of my tale were wandering differed widely from the dreamer's land of fantasy; yet there was something in their way of life that Nature asserted as her own, and the gnawing cares which went with them from the world were all that now obstructed their happiness. One stout and shaggy steed, the bearer of all their wealth, did not shrink from the added weight of Dorcas; although her hardy breeding sustained her, during the latter part of each day's journey, by her husband's side. Reuben and his son, their muskets on their shoulders and their axes slung behind them, kept an unwearied pace, each watching with a hunter's eye for the game that supplied their food. When hunger bade, they halted and prepared their meal on the bank of some unpolluted forest brook, which, as they knelt down with thirsty lips to drink, murmured a sweet unwillingness, like a maiden at love's first kiss. They slept beneath a hut of branches, and awoke at peep of light refreshed for the toils of another day. Dorcas and the boy went on joyously, and even Reuben's spirit shone at intervals with an outward gladness; but inwardly there was a cold, cold sorrow, which he compared to the snow-drifts lying deep in the glens and hollows of the rivulets while the leaves were brightly green above.

Cyrus Bourne was sufficiently skilled in the travel of the woods to observe that his father did not adhere to the course they had pursued in their expedition of the preceding autumn. They were now keeping farther to the north, striking out more directly from the settlements, and into a region of which savage beasts and savage men were as yet the sole possessors. The boy sometimes hinted his opinions upon the subject, and Reuben listened attentively, and once or twice altered the direction of their march in accordance with his son's counsel; but, having so done, he seemed ill at ease. His quick and wandering glances were sent forward, apparently in search of enemies lurking behind the tree trunks; and, seeing nothing there, he would cast his eyes backwards as if in fear of some pursuer. Cyrus, perceiving that his father gradually resumed the old direction, forbore to interfere; nor, though something began to weigh upon his heart, did his adventurous nature permit him to regret the increased length and the mystery of their way.

On the afternoon of the fifth day they halted, and made their simple encampment nearly an hour before sunset. The face of the country, for the last few miles, had been diversified by swells of land resembling huge waves of a petrified sea; and in one of the corresponding hollows, a wild and romantic spot, had the family reared their hut and kindled their fire. There is something chilling, and yet heart-warming, in the thought of these three, united by strong bands of love and insulated from all that breathe beside. The dark and gloomy pines looked down upon them, and, as the wind swept through their tops, a pitying sound was heard in the forest; or did those old trees groan in fear that men were come to lay the axe to their roots at last? Reuben and his son, while Dorcas made ready their meal, proposed to wander out in search of game, of which that day's march had afforded no supply. The boy, promising not to quit the vicinity of the encampment, bounded off with a step as light and elastic as that of the deer he hoped to slay; while his father, feeling a transient happiness as he gazed after him, was about to pursue an opposite direction. Dorcas, in the meanwhile, had seated herself near their fire of fallen branches, upon the mossgrown and mouldering trunk of a tree uprooted years before. Her employment, diversified by an occasional glance at the pot, now beginning to simmer over the blaze, was the perusal of the current year's Massachusetts Almanac, which, with the exception of an old black-letter Bible, comprised all the literary wealth of the family. None pay a greater regard to arbitrary divisions of time than those who are excluded from society; and Dorcas mentioned, as if the information were of importance, that it was now the twelfth of May. Her husband started.

"The twelfth of May! I should remember it well," muttered he, while many thoughts occasioned a momentary confusion in his mind. "Where am I? Whither am I wandering? Where did I leave him?"

Dorcas, too well accustomed to her husband's wayward moods to note any peculiarity of demeanor, now laid aside the almanac and addressed him in that mournful tone which the tender hearted appropriate to griefs long cold and dead.

"It was near this time of the month, eighteen years ago, that my poor father left this world for a better. He had a kind arm to hold his head and a kind voice to cheer him, Reuben, in his last moments; and the thought of the faithful care you took of him has comforted me many a time since. O, death would have been awful to a solitary man in a wild place like this!"

"Pray Heaven, Dorcas," said Reuben, in a broken voice,—"pray Heaven that neither of us three dies solitary and lies unburied in this howling wilderness!" And he hastened away, leaving her to watch the fire beneath the gloomy pines.

Reuben Bourne's rapid pace gradually slackened as the pang, unintentionally inflicted by the words of Dorcas, became less acute. Many strange reflections, however, thronged upon him; and, straying onward rather like a sleep walker than a hunter, it was attributable to no care of his own that his devious course kept him in the vicinity of the encampment. His steps were imperceptibly led almost in a circle; nor did he observe that he was on the verge of a tract of land heavily timbered, but not with pine trees. The place of the latter was here supplied by oaks and other of the harder woods; and around their roots clustered a dense and bushy undergrowth, leaving, however, barren spaces between the trees, thick strewn with withered leaves. Whenever the rustling of the branches or the creaking of the trunks made a sound, as if the forest were waking from slumber, Reuben instinctively raised the musket that rested on his arm, and cast a quick, sharp glance on every side; but, convinced by a partial observation that no animal was near, he would again give himself up to his thoughts. He was musing on the strange influence that had led him away from his premeditated course and so far into the depths of the wilderness. Unable to penetrate to the secret place of his soul where his motives lay hidden, he believed that a supernatural voice had called him onward and that a supernatural power had obstructed his retreat. He trusted that it was Heaven's intent to afford him an opportunity of expiating his sin; he hoped that he might find the bones so long unburied; and that, having laid the earth over them, peace would throw its sunlight into the sepulchre of his heart. From these thoughts he was aroused by a rustling in the forest at some distance from the spot to which he had wandered. Perceiving the motion of some object behind a thick veil of undergrowth, he fired, with the instinct of a hunter and the aim of a practiced marksman. A low moan, which told his success, and by which even animals can express their dying agony, was unheeded by Reuben Bourne. What were the recollections now breaking upon him?

The thicket into which Reuben had fired was near the summit of a swell of land, and was clustered around the base of a rock, which, in the shape and smoothness of one of its surfaces, was not unlike a gigantic gravestone. As if reflected in a mirror, its likeness was in Reuben's memory. He even recognized the veins which seemed to form an inscription in forgotten characters; everything remained the same, except that a thick covert of bushes shrouded the lower part of the rock, and would have hidden Roger Malvin had he still been sitting there. Yet in the next moment Reuben's eye was caught by another change that time had effected since he last stood where he was now standing again behind the earthy roots of the uptorn tree. The sapling to which he had bound the blood-stained symbol of his vow had increased and strengthened into an oak, far indeed from its maturity, but with no mean spread of shadowy branches. There was one singularity observable in this tree which made Reuben tremble. The middle and lower branches were in luxuriant life, and an excess of vegetation had fringed the trunk almost to the ground; but a blight had apparently stricken the upper part of the oak, and the very topmost bough was withered, sapless, and utterly dead. Reuben remembered how the little banner had fluttered on that topmost bough, when it was green and lovely, eighteen years before. Whose guilt had blasted it?

Dorcas, after the departure of the two hunters, continued her preparations for their evening repast. Her sylvan table was the moss-covered trunk of a large fallen tree, on the broadest part of which she had spread a snow-white cloth and arranged what were left of the bright pewter vessels that had been her pride in the settlements. It had a strange aspect, that one little spot of homely comfort in the desolate heart of Nature. The sunshine yet lingered upon the higher branches of the trees that grew on rising ground; but the shadows of evening had deepened into the hollow where the encampment was made, and the firelight began to redden as it gleamed up the tall trunks of the pines or hovered on the dense and obscure mass of foliage that circled round the spot. The heart of Dorcas was not sad; for she felt that it was better to journey in the wilderness with two whom she loved than to be a lonely woman in a crowd that cared not for her. As she busied herself in arranging seats of mouldering wood, covered with leaves, for Reuben and her son, her voice danced through the gloomy forest in the measure of a song that she had learned in youth. The rude melody, the production of a bard who won no name, was descriptive of a winter evening in a frontier cottage, when, secured from savage inroad by the high-piled snow-drifts, the family rejoiced by their own fire-side. The whole song possessed the nameless charm peculiar to unborrowed thought; but four continually-recurring lines shone out from the rest like the blaze of the hearth whose joys they celebrated. Into them, working magic with a few simple words, the poet had instilled the very essence of domestic love and household happiness, and they were poetry and picture joined in one. As Dorcas sang, the walls of her forsaken home seemed to encircle her; she no longer saw the gloomy pines, nor heard the wind which still, as she began each verse, sent a heavy breath through the branches, and died away in a hollow moan from the burden of the song. She was aroused by the report of a gun in the vicinity of the encampment; and either the sudden sound or her loneliness by the glowing fire caused her to tremble violently. The next moment she laughed in the pride of a mother's heart.

"My beautiful young hunter! My boy has slain a deer!" she exclaimed, recollecting that in the direction whence the shot proceeded Cyrus had gone to the chase.

She waited a reasonable time to hear her son's light step bounding over the rustling leaves to tell of his success. But he did not immediately appear; and she sent her cheerful voice among the trees in search of him.

"Cyrus! Cyrus!"

His coming was still delayed; and she determined, as the report had apparently been very near, to seek for him in person. Her assistance, also, might be necessary in bringing home the venison which she flattered herself he had obtained. She therefore set forward, directing her steps by the long-past sound, and singing as she went, in order that the boy might be aware of her approach and run to meet her. From behind the trunk of every tree, and from every hiding-place in the thick foliage of the undergrowth she hoped to discover the countenance of her son, laughing with the sportive mischief that is born of affection. The sun was now beneath the horizon, and the light that came down among the leaves was sufficiently dim to create many illusions in her expecting fancy. Several times she seemed indistinctly to see his face gazing out from among the leaves; and once she imagined that he stood beckoning to her at the base of a craggy rock. Keeping her eyes on this object, however, it proved to be no more than the trunk of an oak, fringed to the very ground with little branches, one of which, thrust out farther than the rest, was shaken by the breeze. Making her way round the foot of the rock, she suddenly found herself close to her husband, who had approached in another direction. Leaning upon the butt of his gun, the muzzle of which rested upon the withered leaves, he was apparently absorbed in the contemplation of some object at his feet.

"How is this, Reuben? Have you slain the deer and fallen asleep over him?" exclaimed Dorcas, laughing cheerfully, on her first slight observation of his posture and appearance.

He stirred not, neither did he turn his eyes towards her; and a cold, shuddering fear, indefinite in its source and object, began to creep into her blood. She now perceived that her husband's face was ghastly pale, and his features were rigid, as if incapable of assuming any other expression than the strong despair which had hardened upon them. He gave not the slightest evidence that he was aware of her approach.

"For the love of Heaven, Reuben, speak to me!" cried Dorcas; and the strange sound of her own voice affrighted her even more than the dead silence.

Her husband started, stared into her face, drew her to the front of the rock, and pointed with his finger.

O, there lay the boy, asleep, but dreamless, upon the fallen forest leaves! His cheek rested upon his arm—his curled locks were thrown back from his brow—his limbs were slightly relaxed. Had a sudden weariness overcome the youthful hunter? Would his mother's voice arouse him? She knew that it was death.

"This broad rock is the gravestone of your near kindred, Dorcas," said her husband. "Your tears will fall at once over your father and your son."

She heard him not. With one wild shriek, that seemed to force its way from the sufferer's inmost soul, she sank insensible by the side of her dead boy. At that moment the withered topmost bough of the oak loosened itself in the stilly air, and fell in soft, light fragments upon the leaves, upon Reuben, upon his wife and child, and upon Roger Malvin's bones. Then Reuben's heart was stricken, and the tears gushed out like water from a rock. The vow that the wounded youth had made the blighted man had come to redeem. His sin was expiated—the curse was gone from him; and in the hour when he had shed blood dearer to him than his own, a prayer, the first for years, went up to Heaven from the lips of Reuben Bourne.

1832

The May-pole of Merry Mount

Hawthorne here uses the Puritan past to dramatize and interpret a conflict between "Jollity" and "Gloom." With freedom, saturnalian indulgence, pleasure, growth, and fertility on the one side, and with restraint, order, stability, self-denial, and morality on the other, the conflict may seem simplistic. Hawthorne, however, has written a tale about a complex psychological and moral opposition. As in all his historical tales, his use of the past is essentially an attempt to understand the present through it. His interpretation of Merry Mount should be compared with the account William Bradford gives in his history of Plymouth Plantation. Text: From the author's revised edition of *Twice-Told Tales* (Boston, 1851).

Bright were the days at Merry Mount, when the May-pole was the banner-staff of that gay colony! They who reared it, should their banner be triumphant, were to pour sunshine over New England's rugged hills, and scatter flower-seeds throughout the soil. Jollity and gloom were contending for an empire. Midsummer eve had come, bringing deep verdure to the forest, and roses in her lap, of a more vivid hue than the tender buds of Spring. But May, or her mirthful spirit, dwelt all the year round at Merry Mount, sporting with the Summer months, and revelling with Autumn, and basking in the glow of Winter's fireside. Through a world of toil and care she flitted with a dreamlike smile, and came hither to find a home among the lightsome hearts of Merry Mount.

Never had the May-pole been so gayly decked as at sunset on midsummer eve. This venerated emblem was a pine-tree, which had preserved the slender grace of youth, while it equalled the loftiest height of the old wood monarchs. From its top streamed a silken banner, colored like the rainbow. Down nearly to the ground, the pole was dressed with birchen boughs, and others of the liveliest green, and some with silvery leaves, fastened by ribbons that fluttered in fantastic knots of twenty different colors, but no sad ones. Garden flowers, and blossoms of the wilderness, laughed gladly forth amid the verdure, so fresh and dewy that they must have grown by magic on that happy pine tree. Where this green and flowery splendor terminated, the shaft of the May-pole was stained with the seven brilliant hues of the banner at its top. On the lowest green bough hung an abundant wreath of roses, some that had been gathered in the sunniest spots of the forest, and others, of still richer blush, which the colonists had reared from English seed. O, people of the Golden Age, the chief of your husbandry was to raise flowers!

But what was the wild throng that stood hand in hand about the May-pole? It could not be, that the fauns and nymphs, when driven from their classic groves and homes of ancient fable, had sought refuge, as all the persecuted did, in the fresh woods of the West. These were the Gothic monsters, though perhaps of Grecian ancestry. On the shoulders of a comely youth, uprose the head and branching antlers of a stag; a second, human in all other points, had the grim visage of a wolf; a third, still with the trunk and limbs of a mortal man, showed the beard and horns of a venerable he-goat. There was the likeness of a bear erect, brute in all but his hind legs, which were adorned with pink silk stockings. And here again, almost as wondrous, stood a real bear of the dark forest, lending each of his fore paws to the grasp of a human hand, and as ready for the dance as any in that circle. His inferior nature rose half way, to meet his companions as they stooped. Other faces wore the similitude of man or woman, but distorted or extravagant, with red noses pendulous before their mouths, which seemed of awful depth, and stretched from ear to ear in an eternal fit of laughter. Here might be seen the Salvage Man, well known in heraldry, hairy as a baboon, and girdled with green leaves. By his side, a nobler figure, but still a counterfeit, appeared an Indian hunter, with feathery crest and wampum belt. Many of this strange company wore fools-caps, and had little bells appended to their garments, tinkling with a silvery sound, responsive to the inaudible music of their gleesome spirits. Some youths and maidens were of soberer garb, yet well maintained their places in the irregular throng, by the expression of wild revelry upon their features. Such were the colonists of Merry Mount, as they stood in the broad smile of sunset, round their venerated May-pole.

Had a wanderer, bewildered in the melancholy forest, heard their mirth, and stolen a half-affrighted glance, he might have fancied them the crew of Cómus, some already transformed to brutes, some midway between man and beast, and the others rioting in the flow of tipsy jollity that foreran the change. But a band of Puritans, who watched the scene, invisible themselves, compared the masques to those devils and ruined souls with whom their superstition peopled the black wilderness.

Within the ring of monsters, appeared the two

airiest forms, that had ever trodden on any more solid footing than a purple and golden cloud. One was a youth in glistening apparel, with a scarf of the rainbow pattern crosswise on his breast. His right hand held a gilded staff, the ensign of high dignity among the revellers, and his left grasped the slender fingers of a fair maiden, not less gayly decorated than himself. Bright roses glowed in contrast with the dark and glossy curls of each, and were scattered round their feet, or had sprung up spontaneously there. Behind this lightsome couple, so close to the May-pole that its boughs shaded his jovial face, stood the figure of an English priest, canonically dressed, yet decked with flowers, in heathen fashion, and wearing a chaplet of the native vine leaves. By the riot of his rolling eye, and the pagan decorations of his holy garb, he seemed the wildest monster there, and the very Comus of the crew.

"Votaries of the May-pole," cried the flower-decked priest, "merrily, all day long, have the woods echoed to your mirth. But be this your merriest hour, my hearts! Lo, here stand the Lord and Lady of the May, whom I, a clerk of Oxford, and high priest of Merry Mount, am presently to join in holy matrimony. Up with your nimble spirits, ye morris-dancers, green men, and glee maidens, bears and wolves, and horned gentlemen! Come; a chorus now, rich with the old mirth of Merry England, and the wilder glee of this fresh forest; and then a dance, to show the youthful pair what life is made of, and how airily they should go through it! All ye that love the May-pole, lend your voices to the nuptial song of the Lord and Lady of the May!"

This wedlock was more serious than most affairs of Merry Mount, where jest and delusion, trick and fantasy, kept up a continual carnival. The Lord and Lady of the May, though their titles must be laid down at sunset, were really and truly to be partners for the dance of life, beginning the measure that same bright eve. The wreath of roses, that hung from the lowest green bough of the May-pole, had been twined for them, and would be thrown over both their heads, in symbol of their flowery union. When the priest had spoken, therefore, a riotous uproar burst from the rout of monstrous figures.

"Begin you the stave, reverend Sir," cried they all; "and never did the woods ring to such a merry peal as we of the May-pole shall send up!"

Immediately a prelude of pipe, cithern, and viol, touched with practised minstrelsy, began to play from a neighboring thicket, in such a mirthful cadence, that the boughs of the May-pole quivered to the sound. But the May Lord, he of the gilded staff, chancing to look into his Lady's eyes, was wonderstruck at the almost pensive glance that met his own.

"Edith, sweet Lady of the May," whispered he, reproachfully, "is yon wreath of roses a garland to hang above our graves, that you look so sad? O, Edith, this is our golden time! Tarnish it not by any pensive shadow of the mind; for it may be, that nothing of futurity will be brighter than the mere remembrance of what is now passing."

"That was the very thought that saddened me! How came it in your mind too?" said Edith, in a still lower tone than he; for it was high treason to be sad at Merry Mount. "Therefore do I sigh amid this festive music. And besides, dear Edgar, I struggle as with a dream, and fancy that these shapes of our jovial friends are visionary, and their mirth unreal, and that we are no true Lord and Lady of the May. What is the mystery in my heart?"

Just then, as if a spell had loosened them, down came a little shower of withering rose leaves from the May-pole. Alas, for the young lovers! No sooner had their hearts glowed with real passion than they were sensible of something vague and unsubstantial in their former pleasures, and felt a dreary presentiment of inevitable change. From the moment that they truly loved, they had subjected themselves to earth's doom of care and sorrow, and troubled joy, and had no more a home at Merry Mount. That was Edith's mystery. Now leave we the priest to marry them, and the masquers to sport round the May-pole, till the last sunbeam be withdrawn from its summit, and the shadows of the forest mingle gloomily in the dance. Meanwhile, we may discover who these gay people were.

Two hundred years ago, and more, the old world and its inhabitants became mutually weary of each other. Men voyaged by thousands to the West; some to barter glass beads, and such like jewels, for the furs of the Indian hunter; some to conquer virgin empires; and one stern band to pray. But none of these motives had much weight with the colonists of Merry Mount. Their leaders were men who had sported so long with life, that when Thought and Wisdom came, even these unwelcome guests were led astray by the crowd of vanities which they should have put to flight. Erring Thought and perverted Wisdom were made to put on masques, and play the fool. The men of whom we speak, after losing the heart's fresh gayety, imagined a wild philosophy of pleasure, and came hither to act out their latest day-dream. They gathered followers from all that giddy tribe, whose whole life is like the festal days of soberer men. In their train were minstrels, not unknown in London streets; wandering players, whose theatres had been the halls of noblemen; mummers, rope-dancers, and mountebanks, who would long be missed at wakes, church ales, and fairs; in a word, mirth makers of every sort, such as abounded in that age, but now began to be discountenanced by the rapid growth of Puritanism. Light had their footsteps been on land, and as lightly they came across the sea. Many had been maddened by their previous troubles into a gay despair; others were as madly gay in the flush of youth, like the May Lord and his Lady; but whatever might be the quality of their mirth, old and young were gay at Merry Mount. The young deemed themselves happy. The elder spirits, if they knew that mirth was but the counterfeit of happiness, yet followed the false shadow wilfully, because at least her garments glittered brightest. Sworn triflers of a lifetime, they would not venture among the sober truths of life, not even to be truly blest.

All the hereditary pastimes of Old England were transplanted hither. The King of Christmas was duly crowned, and the Lord of Misrule bore potent sway. On the Eve of St. John, they felled whole acres of the forest to make bonfires, and danced by the blaze all night, crowned with garlands, and throwing flowers into the flame. At harvest time, though their crop was of the smallest, they made an image with the sheaves of Indian corn, and wreathed it with autumnal garlands, and bore it home triumphantly. But what chiefly characterized the colonists of Merry Mount, was their veneration for the May-pole. It has made their true history a poet's tale. Spring decked the hallowed emblem with young blossoms and fresh green boughs; Summer brought roses of the deepest blush, and the perfected foliage of the forest; Autumn enriched it with that red and yellow gorgeousness, which converts each wildwood leaf into a painted flower; and Winter silvered it with sleet, and hung it round with icicles, till it flashed in the cold sunshine, itself a frozen sunbeam. Thus each alternate season did homage to the May-pole, and paid it a tribute of its own richest splendor. Its votaries danced round it, once, at least, in every month; sometimes they called it their religion, or their altar; but always, it was the banner-staff of Merry Mount.

Unfortunately, there were men in the new world, of a sterner faith than these May-pole worshippers. Not far from Merry Mount was a settlement of Puritans, most dismal wretches, who said their prayers before daylight, and then wrought in the forest or the cornfield, till evening made it prayer time again. Their weapons were always at hand, to shoot down the straggling savage. When they met in conclave, it was never to keep up the old English mirth, but to hear sermons three hours long, or to proclaim bounties on the heads of wolves and the scalps of Indians. Their festivals were fast days, and their chief pastime the singing of psalms. Woe to the youth or maiden, who did but dream of a dance! The selectman nodded to the constable; and there sat the light-heeled reprobate in the stocks; or if he danced, it was round the whipping-post, which might be termed the Puritan May-pole.

A party of these grim Puritans, toiling through the difficult woods, each with a horseload of iron armor to burden his footsteps, would sometimes draw near the sunny precincts of Merry Mount. There were the silken colonists, sporting round their May-pole; perhaps teaching a bear to dance, or striving to communicate their mirth to the grave Indian; or masquerading in the skins of deer and wolves, which they had hunted for that especial purpose. Often, the whole colony were playing at blindman's buff, magistrates and all, with their eyes bandaged, except a single scape-goat, whom the blinded sinners pursued by the tinkling of the bells at his garments. Once, it is said, they were seen following a flower-decked corpse, with merriment and festive music, to his grave. But did the dead man laugh? In their quietest times, they sang ballads and told tales, for the edification of their pious visitors; or perplexed them with juggling tricks; or grinned at them through horse-collars; and when sport itself grew wearisome, they made game of their own stupidity, and began a yawning match. At the very least of these enormities, the men of iron shook their heads and frowned so darkly, that the revellers looked up, imagining that a momentary cloud had overcast the sunshine, which was to be perpetual there. On the other hand, the Puritans affirmed, that, when a psalm was pealing from their place of worship, the echo which the forest sent them back, seemed often like the chorus of a jolly catch, closing with a roar of laughter. Who but the fiend, and his bond-slaves, the crew of Merry Mount, had thus disturbed them? In due time, a feud arose, stern and bitter on one side, and as serious on the other as anything could be among such light spirits as had sworn allegiance to the May-pole. The future complexion of New England was involved in this important quarrel. Should the grizzly saints establish their jurisdiction over the gay sinners, then would their spirits darken all the clime, and make it a land of clouded visages, of hard toil, of sermon and psalm forever. But should the banner-staff of Merry Mount be fortunate, sunshine would break upon the hills, and flowers would beautify the forest and late posterity do homage to the May-pole.

After these authentic passages from history, we return to the nuptials of the Lord and Lady of the May. Alas! we have delayed too long, and must darken our tale too suddenly. As we glance again at the May-pole, a solitary sunbeam is fading from the summit, and leaves only a faint, golden tinge, blended with the hues of the rainbow banner. Even that dim light is now withdrawn, relinquishing the whole domain of Merry Mount to the evening gloom, which has rushed so instantaneously from the black surrounding woods. But some of these black shadows have rushed forth in human shape.

Yes, with the setting sun, the last day of mirth had passed from Merry Mount. The ring of gay masquers was disordered and broken; the stag lowered his antlers in dismay; the wolf grew weaker than a lamb; the bells of the morris dancers tinkled with tremulous affright. The Puritans had played a characteristic part in the May-pole mummeries. Their darksome figures were intermixed with the wild shapes of their foes, and made the scene a picture of the moment, when waking thoughts start up amid the scattered fantasies of a dream. The leader of the hostile party stood in the center of the circle, while the route of monsters cowered around him, like evil spirits in the presence of a dread magician. No fantastic foolery could look him in the face. So stern was the energy of his aspect, that the whole man, visage, frame and soul, seemed wrought of iron, gifted with life and thought, yet all of one substance with his headpiece and breastplate. It was the Puritan of Puritans; it was Endicott himself!

"Stand off, priest of Baal!" said he, with a grim frown, and laying no reverent hand upon the surplice. "I know thee, Blackstone![1] Thou art the man, who couldst not abide the rule even of thine own corrupted church, and hast come hither to preach iniquity, and to give example of it in thy life. But now shall it be seen that the Lord hath sanctified this wilderness for his peculiar people. Woe unto them that would defile it! And first, for this flower-decked abomination, the altar of thy worship!"

And with his keen sword, Endicott assaulted the hallowed May-pole. Nor long did it resist his arm. It groaned with a dismal sound; it showered leaves and rosebuds upon the remorseless enthusiast; and finally, with all its green boughs, and ribands, and flowers, symbolic of departed pleasures, down fell the banner-staff of Merry Mount. As it sank, tradition says, the evening sky grew darker, and the woods threw forth a more sombre shadow.

"There," cried Endicott, looking triumphantly on his work, "there lies the only May-pole in New England! The thought is strong within me, that, by its fall, is shadowed forth the fate of light and idle mirth makers, amongst us and our posterity. Amen, saith John Endicott."

"Amen!" echoed his followers

[1]Did Governor Endicott speak less positively, we should suspect a mistake here. The Rev. Mr. Blackstone, though an eccentric, is not known to have been an immoral man. We rather doubt his identity with the priest of Merry Mount. [Hawthorne's note.]

But the votaries of the May-pole gave one groan for their idol. At the sound, the Puritan leader glanced at the crew of Comus, each a figure of broad mirth, yet, at this moment, strangely expressive of sorrow and dismay.

"Valiant captain," quoth Peter Palfrey, the Ancient of the band, "what order shall be taken with the prisoners?"

"I thought not to repent me of cutting down a May-pole," replied Endicott, "yet now I could find in my heart to plant it again, and give each of these bestial pagans one other dance round their idol. It would have served rarely for a whipping-post!"

"But there are pine-trees enow," suggested the lieutenant.

"True, good Ancient," said the leader. "Wherefore, bind the heathen crew, and bestow on them a small matter of stripes apiece, as earnest of our future justice. Set some of the rogues in the stocks to rest themselves, so soon as Providence shall bring us to one of our own well-ordered settlements, where such accommodations may be found. Further penalties, such as branding and cropping of ears, shall be thought of hereafter."

"How many stripes for the priest?" inquired Ancient Palfrey.

"None as yet," answered Endicott, bending his iron frown upon the culprit. "It must be for the Great and General Court to determine, whether stripes and long imprisonment, and other grievous penalty, may atone for his transgressions. Let him look to himself! For such as violate our civil order, it may be permitted us to show mercy. But woe to the wretch that troubleth our religion!"

"And this dancing bear," resumed the officer. "Must he share the stripes of his fellows?"

"Shoot him through the head!" said the energetic Puritan. "I suspect witchcraft in the beast."

"Here be a couple of shining ones," continued Peter Palfrey, pointing his weapon at the Lord and Lady of the May. "They seem to be of high station among these misdoers. Methinks their dignity will not be fitted with less than a double share of stripes."

Endicott rested on his sword, and closely surveyed the dress and aspect of the hapless pair. There they stood, pale, downcast, and apprehensive. Yet there was an air of mutual support, and of pure affection, seeking aid and giving it, that showed them to be man and wife, with the sanction of a priest upon their love. The youth, in the peril of the moment, had dropped his gilded staff, and thrown his arm about the Lady of the May, who leaned against his breast, too lightly to burden him, but with weight enough to express that their destinies were linked together, for good or evil. They looked first at each other, and then into the grim captain's face. There they stood, in the first hour of wedlock, while the idle pleasures of which their companions were the emblems, had given place to the sternest cares of life, personified by the dark Puritans. But never had their youthful beauty seemed so pure and high, as when its glow was chastened by adversity.

"Youth," said Endicott, "ye stand in an evil case, thou and thy maiden wife. Make ready presently; for I am minded that ye shall both have a token to remember your wedding day!"

"Stern man," cried the May Lord, "how can I move thee? Were the means at hand, I would resist to the death. Being powerless, I entreat! Do with me as thou wilt, but let Edith go untouched!"

"Not so," replied the immitigable zealot. "We are not wont to show an idle courtesy to that sex, which requireth the stricter discipline. What sayest thou, maid? Shall thy silken bridegroom suffer thy share of the penalty, besides his own?"

"Be it death," said Edith, "and lay it all on me!"

Truly, as Endicott had said, the poor lovers stood in a woful case. Their foes were triumphant, their friends captive and abased, their home desolate, the benighted wilderness around them, and a rigorous destiny, in the shape of the Puritan leader, their only guide. Yet the deepening twilight could not altogether conceal that the iron man was softened; he smiled at the fair spectacle of early love; he almost sighed for the inevitable blight of early hopes.

"The troubles of life have come hastily on this young couple," observed Endicott, "We will see how they comport themselves under their present trials, ere we burden them with greater. If, among the spoil, there be any garments of a more decent fashion, let them be put upon the May Lord and his Lady, instead of their glistening vanities. Look to it, some of you."

"And shall not the youth's hair be cut?" asked Peter Palfrey, looking with abhorrence at the lovelock and long glossy curls of the young man.

"Crop it forthwith, and that in the true pumpkin shell fashion," answered the captain. "Then bring them along with us, but more gently than their fellows. There be qualities in the youth, which may make him valiant to fight, and sober to toil, and pious to pray; and in the maiden, that may fit her to become a mother in our Israel, bringing up babes in better nurture than her own hath been. Nor think ye, young ones, that they are the happiest, even in our lifetime of a moment, who misspend it in dancing round a May-pole!"

And Endicott, the severest Puritan of all who laid the rock foundation of New England, lifted the wreath of roses from the ruin of the May-pole, and threw it, with his own gauntleted hand, over the heads of the Lord and Lady of the May. It was a deed of prophecy. As the moral gloom of the world overpowers all systematic gayety, even so was their home of wild mirth made desolate amid the sad forest. They returned to it no more. But as their flowery garland was wreathed of the brightest roses that had grown there, so, in the tie that united them, were intertwined all the purest and best of their early joys. They went heavenward, supporting each other along the difficult path which it was their lot to tread, and never wasted one regretful thought on the vanities of Merry Mount.

1835

Young Goodman Brown

Among the persons sentenced to death by Judge Hathorne in the Salem witch trials of 1692 were Goody Cloyse and Goody Cory, who figure in this story. To many contemporaries of Hawthorne's ancestor, witchcraft was a terrible menace. To Hawthorne himself, it was local history and a theme for the art of fiction—an opportunity to image forth the fraternity of Evil.

Like Robin, in "My Kinsman, Major Molineux," Young Goodman Brown makes a night journey; and darkness, for him also, provides "light" or knowledge. He discovers the capacity for evil in all men—"the communion of [his] race." Brown, however, fails to realize that man may "have several voices . . . as well as two complexions." His inability to accept ambiguity and man's complexity separates him from others, and he thereafter leads a life of unforgiving loneliness.

Hawthorne found his material mainly in a work published in the year after the trials, Cotton Mather's *Wonders of the Invisible World: Being an Account of the Trials of Several Witches, Lately Executed in New-England.* He found his technique in the conventions of Gothic romance, which he refined and psychologized, focusing on interior experience.

Text: From the author's revised edition of *Mosses from an Old Manse* (Boston, 1854).

Young Goodman Brown came forth at sunset into the street of Salem village; but put his head back, after crossing the threshold, to exchange a parting kiss with his young wife. And Faith, as the wife was aptly named, thrust her own pretty head into the street, letting the wind play with the pink ribbons of her cap while she called to Goodman Brown.

"Dearest heart," whispered she, softly and rather sadly, when her lips were close to his ear, "prithee put off your journey until sunrise and sleep in your own bed to-night. A lone woman is troubled with such dreams and such thoughts that she's afeard of herself sometimes. Pray tarry with me this night, dear husband, of all nights in the year."

"My love and my Faith," replied young Goodman

Brown, "of all nights in the year, this one night must I tarry away from thee. My journey, as thou callest it, forth and back again, must needs be done 'twixt now and sunrise. What, my sweet, pretty wife, dost thou doubt me already, and we but three months married?"

"Then God bless you!" said Faith, with the pink ribbons; "and may you find all well when you come back."

"Amen!" cried Goodman Brown. "Say thy prayers, dear Faith, and go to bed at dusk, and no harm will come to thee."

So they parted; and the young man pursued his way until, being about to turn the corner by the meeting house, he looked back and saw the head of Faith still peeping after him with a melancholy air, in spite of her pink ribbons.

"Poor little Faith!" thought he, for his heart smote him. "What a wretch am I to leave her on such an errand! She talks of dreams, too. Methought as she spoke there was trouble in her face, as if a dream had warned her what work is to be done to-night. But, no, no; 'twould kill her to think it. Well, she's a blessed angel on earth; and after this one night I'll cling to her skirts and follow her to heaven."

With this excellent resolve for the future, Goodman Brown felt himself justified in making more haste on his present evil purpose. He had taken a dreary road, darkened by all the gloomiest trees of the forest, which barely stood aside to let the narrow path creep through, and closed immediately behind. It was all as lonely as could be; and there is this peculiarity in such a solitude, that the traveller knows not who may be concealed by the innumerable trunks and the thick boughs overhead; so that with lonely footsteps he may yet be passing through an unseen multitude.

"There may be a devilish Indian behind every tree," said Goodman Brown to himself; and he glanced fearfully behind him as he added, "What if the devil himself should be at my very elbow!"

His head being turned back, he passed a crook of the road, and, looking forward again, beheld the figure of a man, in grave and decent attire, seated at the foot of an old tree. He arose at Goodman Brown's approach and walked onward side by side with him.

"You are late, Goodman Brown," said he. "The clock of the Old South was striking as I came through Boston; and that is full fifteen minutes agone."

"Faith kept me back a while," replied the young man, with a tremor in his voice, caused by the sudden appearance of his companion, though not wholly unexpected.

It was now deep dusk in the forest, and deepest in that part of it where these two were journeying. As nearly as could be discerned, the second traveller was about fifty years old, apparently in the same rank of life as Goodman Brown, and bearing a considerable resemblance to him, though perhaps more in expression than features. Still they might have been taken for father and son. And yet, though the elder person was as simply clad as the younger, and as simple in manner too, he had an indescribable air of one who knew the world, and who would not have felt abashed at the governor's dinner table or in King William's court,[1] were it possible that his affairs should call him thither. But the only thing about him that could be fixed upon as remarkable was his staff, which bore the likeness of a great black snake, so curiously wrought that it might almost be seen to twist and wriggle itself like a living serpent. This, of course, must have been an ocular deception, assisted by the uncertain light.

"Come, Goodman Brown," cried his fellow-traveller, "this is a dull pace for the beginning of a journey. Take my staff, if you are so soon weary."

"Friend," said the other, exchanging his slow pace for a full stop, "having kept covenant by meeting thee here, it is my purpose now to return whence I came. I have scruples touching the matter thou wot'st of."

"Sayest thou so?" replied he of the serpent, smiling apart. "Let us walk on, nevertheless, reasoning as we go; and if I convince thee not thou shalt turn back. We are but a little way in the forest yet."

"Too far! too far!" exclaimed the goodman, unconsciously resuming his walk. "My father never went into the woods on such an errand, nor his father before him. We have been a race of honest men and good Christians since the days of the martyrs; and shall I be the first of the name of Brown that ever took this path and kept"—

"Such company, thou wouldst say," observed the elder person, interpreting his pause. "Well said, Goodman Brown! I have been as well acquainted with your family as with ever a one among the Puritans; and that's no trifle to say. I helped your grandfather, the constable, when he lashed the Quaker woman so smartly through the streets of Salem; and it was I that brought your father a pitch-pine knot, kindled at my own hearth, to set fire to an Indian village, in King Philip's war.[2] They were my good friends, both; and many a pleasant walk have we had along this path, and returned merrily after midnight. I would fain be friends with you for their sake."

"If it be as thou sayest," replied Goodman Brown, "I marvel they never spoke of these matters; or, verily, I marvel not, seeing that the least rumor of

[1] William III, king of England, 1689–1702.

[2] A war (1675–76) between New England colonists and a confederation of Indians led by King Philip or Metacomet.

the sort would have driven them from New England. We are a people of prayer, and good works to boot, and abide no such wickedness."

"Wickedness or not," said the traveller with the twisted staff, "I have a very general acquaintance here in New England. The deacons of many a church have drunk the communion wine with me; the selectmen of divers towns make me their chairman; and a majority of the Great and General Court are firm supporters of my interest. The governor and I, too—But these are state secrets."

"Can this be so?" cried Goodman Brown, with a stare of amazement at his undisturbed companion. "Howbeit, I have nothing to do with the governor and council; they have their own ways, and are no rule for a simple husbandman like me. But, were I to go on with thee, how should I meet the eye of that good old man, our minister, at Salem village? O, his voice would make me tremble both Sabbath day and lecture day."

Thus far the elder traveller had listened with due gravity; but now burst into a fit of irrepressible mirth, shaking himself so violently that his snakelike staff actually seemed to wriggle in sympathy.

"Ha! ha! ha!" shouted he again and again; then composing himself. "Well, go on, Goodman Brown, go on; but, prithee, don't kill me with laughing."

"Well, then, to end the matter at once," said Goodman Brown, considerably nettled, "there is my wife, Faith. It would break her dear little heart; and I'd rather break my own."

"Nay, if that be the case," answered the other, "e'en go thy ways, Goodman Brown. I would not for twenty old women like the one hobbling before us that Faith should come to any harm."

As he spoke he pointed his staff at a female figure on the path, in whom Goodman Brown recognized a very pious and exemplary dame, who had taught him his catechism in youth, and was still his moral and spiritual adviser, jointly with the minister and Deacon Gookin.

"A marvel, truly, that Goody Cloyse[3] should be so far in the wilderness at nightfall," said he. "But with your leave, friend, I shall take a cut through the woods until we have left this Christian woman behind. Being a stranger to you, she might ask whom I was consorting with and whither I was going."

"Be it so," said his fellow-traveller. "Betake you to the woods, and let me keep the path."

Accordingly the young man turned aside, but took care to watch his companion, who advanced softly along the road until he had come within a staff's length of the old dame. She, meanwhile, was making the best of her way, with singular speed for so aged a woman, and mumbling some indistinct words—a prayer, doubtless—as she went. The traveller put forth his staff and touched her withered neck with what seemed the serpent's tail.

"The devil!" screamed the pious old lady.

"Then Goody Cloyse knows her old friend?" observed the traveller, confronting her and leaning on his writhing stick.

"Ah, forsooth, and is it your worship indeed?" cried the good dame. "Yea, truly is it, and in the very image of my old gossip, Goodman Brown, the grandfather of the silly fellow that now is. But—would your worship believe it?—my broomstick hath strangely disappeared, stolen, as I suspect, by that unhanged witch, Goody Cory, and that, too, when I was all anointed with the juice of smallage, and cinquefoil, and wolf's bane—"

"Mingled with fine wheat and the fat of a new-born babe," said the shape of old Goodman Brown.

"Ah, your worship knows the recipe," cried the old lady, cackling aloud. "So, as I was saying, being all ready for the meeting, and no horse to ride on, I made up my mind to foot it; for they tell me there is a nice young man to be taken into communion tonight. But now your good worship will lend me your arm, and we shall be there in a twinkling."

"That can hardly be," answered her friend. "I may not spare you my arm, Goody Cloyse; but here is my staff, if you will."

So saying, he threw it down at her feet, where, perhaps, it assumed life, being one of the rods which its owner had formerly lent to the Egyptian magi. Of this fact, however, Goodman Brown could not take cognizance. He had cast up his eyes in astonishment, and, looking down again, beheld neither Goody Cloyse nor the serpentine staff, but his fellow-traveller alone, who waited for him as calmly as if nothing had happened.

"That old woman taught me my catechism," said the young man; and there was a world of meaning in this simple comment.

They continued to walk onward, while the elder traveller exhorted his companion to make good speed and persevere in the path, discoursing so aptly that his arguments seemed rather to spring up in the bosom of his auditor than to be suggested by himself. As they went, he plucked a branch of maple to serve for a walking stick, and began to strip it of the twigs and little boughs, which were wet with evening dew. The moment his fingers touched them they became strangely withered and dried up as with a week's sunshine. Thus the pair proceeded, at a good free pace, until suddenly, in a gloomy hollow of the road, Goodman Brown sat himself down on the stump of a tree and refused to go any farther.

"Friend," said he, stubbornly, "my mind is made up. Not another step will I budge on this errand.

[3] Goody, short for Goodwife, a standard term of address, similar to Goodman. Goody Cloyse, Goody Cory, and Martha Carrier were sentenced as "witches" in Salem in 1692.

What if a wretched old woman do choose to go to the devil when I thought she was going to heaven: is that any reason why I should quit my dear Faith and go after her?"

"You will think better of this by and by," said his acquaintance, composedly. "Sit here and rest yourself a while; and when you feel like moving again, there is my staff to help you along."

Without more words, he threw his companion the maple stick, and was as speedily out of sight as if he had vanished into the deepening gloom. The young man sat a few moments by the roadside, applauding himself greatly, and thinking with how clear a conscience he should meet the minister in his morning walk, nor shrink from the eye of good old Deacon Gookin. And what calm sleep would be his that very night, which was to have been spent so wickedly, but so purely and sweetly now, in the arms of Faith! Amidst these pleasant and praiseworthy meditations, Goodman Brown heard the tramp of horses along the road, and deemed it advisable to conceal himself within the verge of the forest, conscious of the guilty purpose that had brought him thither, though now so happily turned from it.

On came the hoof tramps and the voices of the riders, two grave old voices, conversing soberly as they drew near. These mingled sounds appeared to pass along the road, within a few yards of the young man's hiding-place; but, owing doubtless to the depth of the gloom at that particular spot, neither the travellers nor their steeds were visible. Though their figures brushed the small boughs by the wayside, it could not be seen that they intercepted, even for a moment, the faint gleam from the strip of bright sky athwart which they must have passed. Goodman Brown alternately crouched and stood on tiptoe, pulling aside the branches and thrusting forth his head as far as he durst without discerning so much as a shadow. It vexed him the more, because he could have sworn, were such a thing possible, that he recognized the voices of the minister and Deacon Gookin, jogging along quietly, as they were wont to do, when bound to some ordination or ecclesiastical council. While yet within hearing, one of the riders stopped to pluck a switch.

"Of the two, reverend sir," said the voice like the deacon's, "I had rather miss an ordination dinner than to-night's meeting. They tell me that some of our community are to be here from Falmouth and beyond, and others from Connecticut and Rhode Island, besides several of the Indian powwows, who, after their fashion, know almost as much deviltry as the best of us. Moreover, there is a goodly young woman to be taken into communion."

"Mighty well, Deacon Gookin!" replied the solemn old tones of the minister. "Spur up, or we shall be late. Nothing can be done, you know, until I get on the ground."

The hoofs clattered again; and the voices, talking so strangely in the empty air, passed on through the forest, where no church had ever been gathered or solitary Christian prayed. Whither, then, could these holy men be journeying so deep into the heathen wilderness? Young Goodman Brown caught hold of a tree for support, being ready to sink down on the ground, faint and overburdened with the heavy sickness of his heart. He looked up to the sky, doubting whether there really was a heaven above him. Yet there was the blue arch, and the stars brightening in it.

"With heaven above and Faith below, I will yet stand firm against the devil!" cried Goodman Brown.

While he still gazed upward into the deep arch of the firmament and had lifted his hands to pray, a cloud, though no wind was stirring, hurried across the zenith and hid the brightening stars. The blue sky was still visible, except directly overhead, where this black mass of cloud was sweeping swiftly northward. Aloft in the air, as if from the depths of the cloud, came a confused and doubtful sound of voices. Once the listener fancied that he could distinguish the accents of townspeople of his own, men and women, both pious and ungodly, many of whom he had met at the communion table, and had seen others rioting at the tavern. The next moment, so indistinct were the sounds, he doubted whether he had heard aught but the murmur of the old forest, whispering without a wind. Then came a stronger swell of those familiar tones, heard daily in the sunshine at Salem village, but never until now from a cloud of night. There was one voice, of a young woman, uttering lamentations, yet with an uncertain sorrow, and entreating for some favor, which, perhaps, it would grieve her to obtain; and all the unseen multitude, both saints and sinners, seemed to encourage her onward.

"Faith!" shouted Goodman Brown, in a voice of agony and desperation; and the echoes of the forest mocked him, crying, "Faith! Faith!" as if bewildered wretches were seeking her all through the wilderness.

The cry of grief, rage, and terror, was yet piercing the night, when the unhappy husband held his breath for a response. There was a scream, drowned immediately in a louder murmur of voices, fading into far-off laughter, as the dark cloud swept away, leaving the clear and silent sky above Goodman Brown. But something fluttered lightly down through the air and caught on the branch of a tree. The young man seized it, and beheld a pink ribbon.

"My Faith is gone!" cried he, after one stupefied

moment. "There is no good on earth; and sin is but a name. Come, devil; for to thee is this world given."

And, maddened with despair, so that he laughed loud and long, did Goodman Brown grasp his staff and set forth again, at such a rate that he seemed to fly along the forest path rather than to walk or run. The road grew wilder and drearier and more faintly traced, and vanished at length, leaving him in the heart of the dark wilderness, still rushing onward with the instinct that guides mortal man to evil. The whole forest was peopled with frightful sounds—the creaking of the trees, the howling of wild beasts, and the yell of Indians; while sometimes the wind tolled like a distant church bell, and sometimes gave a broad roar around the traveller, as if all Nature were laughing him to scorn. But he was himself the chief horror of the scene, and shrank not from its other horrors.

"Ha! ha! ha!" roared Goodman Brown when the wind laughed at him. "Let us hear which will laugh loudest. Think not to frighten me with your deviltry. Come witch, come wizard, come Indian powwow, come devil himself, and here comes Goodman Brown. You may as well fear him as he fear you."

In truth, all through the haunted forest there could be nothing more frightful than the figure of Goodman Brown. On he flew among the black pines, brandishing his staff with frenzied gestures, now giving vent to an inspiration of horrid blasphemy, and now shouting forth such laughter as set all the echoes of the forest laughing like demons around him. The fiend in his own shape is less hideous than when he rages in the breast of man. Thus sped the demoniac on his course, until, quivering among the trees, he saw a red light before him, as when the felled trunks and branches of a clearing have been set on fire, and throw up their lurid blaze against the sky, at the hour of midnight. He paused, in a lull of the tempest that had driven him onward, and heard the swell of what seemed a hymn, rolling solemnly from a distance with the weight of many voices. He knew the tune; it was a familiar one in the choir of the village meeting house. The verse died heavily away, and was lengthened by a chorus, not of human voices, but of all the sounds of the benighted wilderness pealing in awful harmony together. Goodman Brown cried out; and his cry was lost to his own ear by its unison with the cry of the desert.

In the interval of silence he stole forward until the light glared full upon his eyes. At one extremity of an open space, hemmed in by the dark wall of the forest, arose a rock, bearing some rude, natural resemblance either to an altar or a pulpit, and surrounded by four blazing pines, their tops aflame, their stems untouched, like candles at an evening meeting. The mass of foliage that had overgrown the summit of the rock was all on fire, blazing high into the night and fitfully illuminating the whole field. Each pendent twig and leafy festoon was in a blaze. As the red light arose and fell, a numerous congregation alternately shone forth, then disappeared in shadow, and again grew, as it were, out of the darkness, peopling the heart of the solitary woods at once.

"A grave and dark-clad company," quoth Goodman Brown.

In truth they were such. Among them, quivering to and fro between gloom and splendor, appeared faces that would be seen next day at the council board of the province, and others which, Sabbath after Sabbath, looked devoutly heavenward, and benignantly over the crowded pews, from the holiest pulpits in the land. Some affirm that the lady of the governor was there. At least there were high dames well known to her, and wives of honored husbands, and widows, a great multitude, and ancient maidens, all of excellent repute, and fair young girls, who trembled lest their mothers should espy them. Either the sudden gleams of light flashing over the obscure field bedazzled Goodman Brown, or he recognized a score of the church members of Salem village famous for their especial sanctity. Good old Deacon Gookin had arrived, and waited at the skirts of that venerable saint, his revered pastor. But, irreverently consorting with these grave, reputable, and pious people, these elders of the church, these chaste dames and dewy virgins, there were men of dissolute lives and women of spotted fame, wretches given over to all mean and filthy vice, and suspected even of horrid crimes. It was strange to see that the good shrank not from the wicked, nor were the sinners abashed by the saints. Scattered also among their palefaced enemies were the Indian priests, or powwows, who had often scared their native forest with more hideous incantations than any known to English witchcraft.

"But where is Faith?" thought Goodman Brown; and, as hope came into his heart, he trembled.

Another verse of the hymn arose, a slow and mournful strain, such as the pious love, but joined to words which expressed all that our nature can conceive of sin, and darkly hinted at far more. Unfathomable to mere mortals is the lore of fiends. Verse after verse was sung; and still the chorus of the desert swelled between like the deepest tone of a mighty organ; and with the final peal of that dreadful anthem there came a sound, as if the roaring wind, the rushing streams, the howling beasts, and every other voice of the unconverted wilderness were mingling and according with the voice of guilty man in homage to the prince of all. The four blazing pines threw up a loftier flame, and obscurely discovered shapes and visages of horror on the smoke wreaths above the impious assembly. At the same moment the fire on the rock shot redly forth and formed a glowing arch above its base, where now appeared a figure. With reverence be it spoken, the figure bore no slight similitude, both in garb and manner, to some grave divine of the New England churches.

"Bring forth the converts!" cried a voice that echoed through the field and rolled into the forest.

At the word, Goodman Brown stepped forth from the shadow of the trees and approached the congregation, with whom he felt a loathful brotherhood by the sympathy of all that was wicked in his heart. He could have well nigh sworn that the shape of his own dead father beckoned him to advance, looking downward from a smoke wreath, while a woman, with dim features of despair, threw out her hand to warn him back. Was it his mother? But he had no power to retreat one step, nor to resist, even in thought, when the minister and good old Deacon Gookin seized his arms and led him to the blazing rock. Thither came also the slender form of a veiled female, led between Goody Cloyse, that pious teacher of the catechism, and Martha Carrier, who had received the devil's promise to be queen of hell. A rampant hag was she. And there stood the proselytes beneath the canopy of fire.

"Welcome, my children," said the dark figure, "to the communion of your race. Ye have found thus young your nature and your destiny. My children, look behind you!"

They turned; and flashing forth, as it were, in a sheet of flame, the fiend worshippers were seen; the smile of welcome gleamed darkly on every visage.

"There," resumed the sable form, "are all whom ye have reverenced from youth. Ye deemed them holier than yourselves, and shrank from your own sin, contrasting it with their lives of righteousness and prayerful aspirations heavenward. Yet here are they all in my worshipping assembly. This night it shall be granted you to know their secret deeds; how hoary-bearded elders of the church have whispered wanton words to the young maids of their households; how many a woman, eager for widow's weeds, has given her husband a drink at bedtime and let him sleep his last sleep in her bosom; how beardless youths have made haste to inherit their father's wealth; and how fair damsels—blush not, sweet ones—have dug little graves in the garden, and bidden me, the sole guest, to an infant's funeral. By the sympathy of your human hearts for sin ye shall scent out all the places—whether in church, bed-chamber, street, field, or forest—where crime has been committed, and shall exult to behold the whole earth one stain of guilt, one mighty blood spot. Far more than this. It shall be yours to penetrate, in every bosom, the deep mystery of sin, the fountain of all wicked arts, and which inexhaustibly supplies more evil impulses than human power—than my power at its utmost—can make manifest in deeds. And now, my children, look upon each other."

They did so; and, by the blaze of the hell-kindled torches, the wretched man beheld his Faith, and the wife her husband, trembling before that unhallowed altar.

"Lo, there ye stand, my children," said the figure, in a deep and solemn tone, almost sad with its despairing awfulness, as if his once angelic nature could yet mourn for our miserable race. "Depending upon one another's hearts, ye had still hoped that virtue were not all a dream. Now are ye undeceived. Evil is the nature of mankind. Evil must be your only happiness. Welcome again, my children, to the communion of your race."

"Welcome," repeated the fiend worshippers, in one cry of despair and triumph.

And there they stood, the only pair, as it seemed, who were yet hesitating on the verge of wickedness in this dark world. A basin was hollowed, naturally, in the rock. Did it contain water, reddened by the lurid light? or was it blood? or, perchance, a liquid flame? Herein did the shape of evil dip his hand and prepare to lay the mark of baptism upon their foreheads, that they might be partakers of the mystery of sin, more conscious of the secret guilt of others, both in deed and thought, than they could now be of their own. The husband cast one look at his pale wife, and Faith at him. What polluted wretches would the next glance show them to each other, shuddering alike at what they disclosed and what they saw!

"Faith! Faith!" cried the husband, "look up to heaven, and resist the wicked one."

Whether Faith obeyed, he knew not. Hardly had he spoken when he found himself amid calm night and solitude, listening to a roar of the wind which died heavily away through the forest. He staggered against the rock, and felt it chill and damp; while a hanging twig, that had been all on fire, besprinkled his cheek with the coldest dew.

The next morning young Goodman Brown came slowly into the street of Salem village, staring around him like a bewildered man. The good old minister was taking a walk along the graveyard to get an appetite for breakfast and meditate his sermon, and bestowed a blessing, as he passed, on Goodman Brown. He shrank from the venerable saint as if to avoid an anathema. Old Deacon Gookin was at domestic worship, and the holy words of his prayer were heard through the open window.

"What God doth the wizard pray to?" quoth Goodman Brown. Goody Cloyse, that excellent old Christian, stood in the early sunshine at her own lattice, catechizing a little girl who had brought her a pint of morning's milk. Goodman Brown snatched away the child as from the grasp of the fiend himself. Turning the corner by the meeting-house, he spied the head of Faith, with the pink ribbons, gazing anxiously forth, and bursting into such joy at the sight of him that she skipped along the street and almost kissed her husband before the whole village. But Goodman Brown looked sternly and sadly into her face, and passed on without a greeting.

Had Goodman Brown fallen asleep in the forest and only dreamed a wild dream of a witch meeting?

Be it so, if you will; but, alas! it was a dream of evil omen for young Goodman Brown. A stern, a sad, a darkly meditative, a distrustful, if not a desperate, man did he become from the night of that fearful dream. On the Sabbath day, when the congregation were singing a holy psalm, he could not listen because an anthem of sin rushed loudly upon his ear and drowned all the blessed strain. When the minister spoke from the pulpit, with power and fervid eloquence and with his hand on the open Bible, of the sacred truths of our religion, and of saintlike lives and triumphant deaths, and of future bliss or misery unutterable, then did Goodman Brown turn pale, dreading lest the roof should thunder down upon the gray blasphemer and his hearers. Often, awaking suddenly at midnight, he shrank from the bosom of Faith; and at morning or eventide, when the family knelt down at prayer, he scowled, and muttered to himself, and gazed sternly at his wife, and turned away. And when he had lived long, and was borne to his grave, a hoary corpse, followed by Faith, an aged woman, and children and grandchildren, a goodly procession, besides neighbors not a few, they carved no hopeful verse upon his tombstone; for his dying hour was gloom.

1835

The Minister's Black Veil

A Parable[1]

Although Hawthorne gives the story a specific setting, he is interested primarily in the symbolic meaning of the Reverend Mr. Hooper's story—a parable, as the subtitle indicates. Mr. Hooper has discovered the inner darkness—the "secret sin"—which every man possesses. For him, however, that reality becomes definitive of life. The resulting loneliness and fear hopelessly separate him from his love and from all others. Like Goodman Brown's fate, Hooper's discovery and his inability to accept it and love, as well, imprison him, as Hawthorne says, "in that saddest of all prisons, his own heart." Text: From the author's revised edition of *Twice-Told Tales* (Boston, 1851).

The sexton stood in the porch of Milford meeting-house, pulling lustily at the bell-rope. The old people of the village came stooping along the street. Children with bright faces, tript merrily beside their parents, or mimicked a graver gait, in the conscious dignity of their Sunday clothes. Spruce bachelors looked sidelong at the pretty maidens, and fancied that the Sabbath sunshine made them prettier than on week-days. When the throng had mostly streamed into the porch, the sexton began to toll the bell, keeping his eye on the Reverend Mr. Hooper's door. The first glimpse of the clergyman's figure, was the signal for the bell to cease its summons.

"But what has good Parson Hooper got upon his face?" cried the sexton in astonishment.

All within hearing immediately turned about, and beheld the semblance of Mr. Hooper, pacing slowly his meditative way towards the meeting-house. With one accord they started, expressing more wonder than if some strange minister were coming to dust the cushions of Mr. Hooper's pulpit.

"Are you sure it is our parson?" inquired Goodman Gray of the sexton.

"Of a certainty it is good Mr. Hooper," replied the sexton. "He was to have exchanged pulpits with Parson Shute, of Westbury; but Parson Shute sent to excuse himself yesterday, being to preach a funeral sermon."

The cause of so much amazement may appear sufficiently slight. Mr. Hooper, a gentlemanly person, of about thirty, though still a bachelor, was dressed with due clerical neatness, as if a careful wife had starched his band, and brushed the weekly dust from his Sunday's garb. There was but one thing remarkable in his appearance. Swathed about his forehead, and hanging down over his face, so low as to be shaken by his breath, Mr. Hooper had on a black veil. On a nearer view, it seemed to consist of two folds of crape, which entirely concealed his features, except the mouth and chin, but probably did not intercept his sight, farther than to give a darkened aspect to all living and inanimate things. With this gloomy shade before him, good Mr. Hooper walked onward, at a slow and quiet pace, stooping somewhat and looking on the ground, as is customary with abstracted men, yet nodding kindly to those of his parishioners who still waited on the meeting-house steps. But so wonder-struck were they, that his greeting hardly met with a return.

[1]Another clergyman in New England, Mr. Joseph Moody, of York, Maine, who died about eighty years since, made himself remarkable by the same eccentricity that is here related of the Reverend Mr. Hooper. In his case, however, the symbol had a different import. In early life he had accidentally killed a beloved friend; and from that day till the hour of his own death, he hid his face from men. [Hawthorne's note.]

"I can't really feel as if good Mr. Hooper's face was behind that piece of crape," said the sexton.

"I don't like it," muttered an old woman, as she hobbled into the meeting-house. "He has changed himself into something awful, only by hiding his face."

"Our parson has gone mad!" cried Goodman Gray, following him across the threshold.

A rumor of some unaccountable phenomenon had preceded Mr. Hooper into the meeting-house, and set all the congregation astir. Few could refrain from twisting their heads towards the door; many stood upright, and turned directly about; while several little boys clambered upon the seats, and came down again with a terrible racket. There was a general bustle, a rustling of the women's gowns and shuffling of the men's feet, greatly at variance with that hushed repose which should attend the entrance of the minister. But Mr. Hooper appeared not to notice the perturbation of his people. He entered with an almost noiseless step, bent his head mildly to the pews on each side, and bowed as he passed his oldest parishioner, a white-haired great-grandsire, who occupied an arm-chair in the centre of the aisle. It was strange to observe, how slowly this venerable man became conscious of something singular in the appearance of his pastor. He seemed not fully to partake of the prevailing wonder, till Mr. Hooper had ascended the stairs, and showed himself in the pulpit, face to face with his congregation, except for the black veil. That mysterious emblem was never once withdrawn. It shook with his measured breath as he gave out the psalm; it threw its obscurity between him and the holy page, as he read the Scriptures; and while he prayed, the veil lay heavily on his uplifted countenance. Did he seek to hide it from the dread Being whom he was addressing?

Such was the effect of this simple piece of crape, that more than one woman of delicate nerves was forced to leave the meeting-house. Yet perhaps the pale-faced congregation was almost as fearful a sight to the minister, as his black veil to them.

Mr. Hooper had the reputation of a good preacher, but not an energetic one: he strove to win his people heavenward, by mild, persuasive influences, rather than to drive them thither by the thunders of the Word. The sermon which he now delivered, was marked by the same characteristics of style and manner, as the general series of his pulpit oratory. But there was something, either in the sentiment of the discourse itself, or in the imagination of the auditors, which made it greatly the most powerful effort that they had ever heard from their pastor's lips. It was tinged, rather more darkly than usual, with the gentle gloom of Mr. Hooper's temperament. The subject had reference to secret sin, and those sad mysteries which we hide from our nearest and dearest, and would fain conceal from our own consciousness, even forgetting that the Omniscient can detect them. A subtle power was breathed into his words. Each member of the congregation, the most innocent girl, and the man of hardened breast, felt as if the preacher had crept upon them, behind his awful veil, and discovered their hoarded iniquity of deed or thought. Many spread their clasped hands on their bosoms. There was nothing terrible in what Mr. Hooper said; at least, no violence; and yet, with every tremor of his melancholy voice, the hearers quaked. An unsought pathos came hand in hand with awe. So sensible were the audience of some unwonted attribute in their minister, that they longed for a breath of wind to blow aside the veil, almost believing that a stranger's visage would be discovered, though the form, gesture, and voice were those of Mr. Hooper.

At the close of the services, the people hurried out with indecorous confusion, eager to communicate their pent-up amazement, and conscious of lighter spirits, the moment they lost sight of the black veil. Some gathered in little circles, huddled closely together, with their mouths all whispering in the centre; some went homeward alone, wrapt in silent meditation; some talked loudly, and profaned the Sabbath-day with ostentatious laughter. A few shook their sagacious heads, intimating that they could penetrate the mystery; while one or two affirmed that there was no mystery at all, but only that Mr. Hooper's eyes were so weakened by the midnight lamp, as to require a shade. After a brief interval, forth came good Mr. Hooper also, in the rear of his flock. Turning his veiled face from one group to another, he paid due reverence to the hoary heads, saluted the middle-aged with kind dignity, as their friend and spiritual guide, greeted the young with mingled authority and love, and laid his hands on the little children's heads to bless them. Such was always his custom on the Sabbath-day. Strange and bewildered looks repaid him for his courtesy. None, as on former occasions, aspired to the honor of walking by their pastor's side. Old Squire Saunders, doubtless by an accidental lapse of memory, neglected to invite Mr. Hooper to his table, where the good clergyman had been wont to bless the food, almost every Sunday since his settlement. He returned, therefore, to the parsonage, and, at the moment of closing the door, was observed to look back upon the people, all of whom had their eyes fixed upon the minister. A sad smile gleamed faintly from beneath the black veil, and flickered about his mouth, glimmering as he disappeared.

"How strange," said a lady, "that a simple black

veil, such as any woman might wear on her bonnet, should become such a terrible thing on Mr. Hooper's face!"

"Something must surely be amiss with Mr. Hooper's intellects," observed her husband, the physician of the village. "But the strangest part of the affair is the effect of this vagary, even on a soberminded man like myself. The black veil, though it covers only our pastor's face, throws its influence over his whole person, and makes him ghostlike from head to foot. Do you not feel it so?"

"Truly do I," replied the lady; "and I would not be alone with him for the world. I wonder he is not afraid to be alone with himself!"

"Men sometimes are so," said her husband.

The afternoon service was attended with similar circumstances. At its conclusion, the bell tolled for the funeral of a young lady. The relatives and friends were assembled in the house, and the more distant acquaintances stood about the door, speaking of the good qualities of the deceased, when their talk was interrupted by the appearance of Mr. Hooper, still covered with his black veil. It was now an appropriate emblem. The clergyman stepped into the room where the corpse was laid, and bent over the coffin, to take a last farewell of his deceased parishioner. As he stooped, the veil hung straight down from his forehead, so that, if her eyelids had not been closed for ever, the dead maiden might have seen his face. Could Mr. Hooper be fearful of her glance, that he so hastily caught back the black veil? A person, who watched the interview between the dead and living, scrupled not to affirm, that, at the instant when the clergyman's features were disclosed, the corpse had slightly shuddered, rustling the shroud and muslin cap, though the countenance retained the composure of death. A superstitious old woman was the only witness of this prodigy. From the coffin, Mr. Hooper passed into the chamber of the mourners, and thence to the head of the staircase, to make the funeral prayer. It was a tender and heart-dissolving prayer, full of sorrow, yet so imbued with celestial hopes, that the music of a heavenly harp, swept by the fingers of the dead, seemed faintly to be heard among the saddest accents of the minister. The people trembled, though they but darkly understood him when he prayed that they, and himself, and all of mortal race, might be ready, as he trusted this young maiden had been, for the dreadful hour that should snatch the veil from their faces. The bearers went heavily forth, and the mourners followed, saddening all the street, with the dead before them, and Mr. Hooper in his black veil behind.

"Why do you look back?" said one in the procession to his partner.

"I had a fancy," replied she, "that the minister and the maiden's spirit were walking hand in hand."

"And so had I, at the same moment," said the other.

That night, the handsomest couple of Milford village were to be joined in wedlock. Though reckoned a melancholy man, Mr. Hooper had a placid cheerfulness for such occasions, which often excited a sympathetic smile, where livelier merriment would have been thrown away. There was no quality of his disposition which made him more beloved than this. The company at the wedding awaited his arrival with impatience, trusting that the strange awe, which had gathered over him throughout the day, would now be dispelled. But such was not the result. When Mr. Hooper came, the first thing that their eyes rested on was the same horrible black veil, which had added deeper gloom to the funeral, and could portend nothing but evil to the wedding. Such was its immediate effect on the guests, that a cloud seemed to have rolled duskily from beneath the black crape, and dimmed the light of the candles. The bridal pair stood up before the minister. But the bride's cold fingers quivered in the tremulous hand of the bridegroom, and her deathlike paleness caused a whisper, that the maiden who had been buried a few hours before, was come from her grave to be married. If ever another wedding were so dismal, it was that famous one, where they tolled the wedding knell. After performing the ceremony, Mr. Hooper raised a glass of wine to his lips, wishing happiness to the new married couple, in a strain of mild pleasantry that ought to have brightened the features of the guests, like a cheerful gleam from the hearth. At that instant, catching a glimpse of his figure in the looking-glass, the black veil involved his own spirit in the horror with which it overwhelmed all others. His frame shuddered—his lips grew white—he spilt the untasted wine upon the carpet—and rushed forth into the darkness. For the Earth, too, had on her Black Veil.

The next day, the whole village of Milford talked of little else than Parson Hooper's black veil. That, and the mystery concealed behind it, supplied a topic for discussion between acquaintances meeting in the street, and good women gossiping at their open windows. It was the first item of news that the tavern-keeper told to his guests. The children babbled of it on their way to school. One imitative little imp covered his face with an old black handkerchief, thereby so affrighting his playmates, that the panic seized himself, and he well nigh lost his wits by his own waggery.

It was remarkable that, of all the busybodies and impertinent people in the parish, not one ventured to put the plain question to Mr. Hooper, wherefore he did this thing. Hitherto, whenever there appeared the slightest call for such interference, he had never lacked advisers, nor shown himself averse to be guided by their judgment. If he erred at all, it was by so painful a degree of self-distrust, that even the mildest censure would lead him to consider an indifferent action as a crime. Yet, though so well acquainted with this amiable weakness, no individual among his parishioners chose to make the black veil a subject of friendly remonstrance. There was a feeling of dread, neither plainly confessed nor carefully concealed, which caused each to shift the responsibility upon another, till at length it was found expedient to send a deputation of the church, in order to deal with Mr. Hooper about the mystery, before it should grow into a scandal. Never did an embassy so ill discharge its duties. The minister received them with friendly courtesy, but became silent, after they were seated, leaving to his visitors the whole burthen of introducing their important business. The topic, it might be supposed, was obvious enough. There was the black veil, swathed round Mr. Hooper's forehead, and concealing every feature above his placid mouth, on which, at times, they could perceive the glimmering of a melancholy smile. But that piece of crape, to their imagination, seemed to hang down before his heart, the symbol of a fearful secret between him and them. Were the veil but cast aside, they might speak freely of it, but not till then. Thus they sat a considerable time, speechless, confused, and shrinking uneasily from Mr. Hooper's eye, which they felt to be fixed upon them with an invisible glance. Finally, the deputies returned abashed to their constituents, pronouncing the matter too weighty to be handled, except by a council of the churches, if, indeed, it might not require a general synod.

But there was one person in the village, unappalled by the awe with which the black veil had impressed all beside herself. When the deputies returned without an explanation, or even venturing to demand one, she, with the calm energy of her character, determined to chase away the strange cloud that appeared to be settling round Mr. Hooper, every moment more darkly than before. As his plighted wife, it should be her privilege to know what the black veil concealed. At the minister's first visit, therefore, she entered upon the subject, with a direct simplicity, which made the task easier both for him and her. After he had seated himself, she fixed her eyes steadfastly upon the veil, but could discern nothing of the dreadful gloom that had so overawed the multitude: it was but a double fold of crape, hanging down from his forehead to his mouth, and slightly stirring with his breath.

"No," said she aloud, and smiling, "there is nothing terrible in this piece of crape, except that it hides a face which I am always glad to look upon. Come, good sir, let the sun shine from behind the cloud. First lay aside your black veil: then tell me why you put it on."

Mr. Hooper's smile glimmered faintly.

"There is an hour to come," said he, "when all of us shall cast aside our veils. Take it not amiss, beloved friend, if I wear this piece of crape till then."

"Your words are a mystery too," returned the young lady. "Take away the veil from them, at least."

"Elizabeth, I will," said he, "so far as my vow may suffer me. Know, then, this veil is a type and a symbol, and I am bound to wear it ever, both in light and darkness, in solitude and before the gaze of multitudes, and as with strangers, so with my familiar friends. No mortal eye will see it withdrawn. This dismal shade must separate me from the world: even you, Elizabeth, can never come behind it!"

"What grievous affliction hath befallen you," she earnestly inquired, "that you should thus darken your eyes for ever?"

"If it be a sign of mourning," replied Mr. Hooper, "I, perhaps, like most other mortals, have sorrows dark enough to be typified by a black veil."

"But what if the world will not believe that it is the type of an innocent sorrow?" urged Elizabeth. "Beloved and respected as you are, there may be whispers, that you hide your face under the consciousness of secret sin. For the sake of your holy office, do away this scandal!"

The color rose into her cheeks, as she intimated the nature of the rumors that were already abroad in the village. But Mr. Hooper's mildness did not forsake him. He even smiled again—that same sad smile, which always appeared like a faint glimmering of light, proceeding from the obscurity beneath the veil.

"If I hide my face for sorrow, there is cause enough," he merely replied; "and if I cover it for secret sin, what mortal might not do the same?"

And with this gentle, but unconquerable obstinacy did he resist all her entreaties. At length Elizabeth sat silent. For a few moments she appeared lost in thought, considering, probably, what new methods might be tried, to withdraw her lover from so dark a fantasy, which, if it had no other meaning, was perhaps a symptom of mental disease. Though of a firmer character than his own, the tears rolled down her cheeks. But, in an instant, as it were, a new feeling took the place of sorrow: her eyes were fixed insensibly on the black veil, when, like a sudden twilight in the air, its terrors fell around her. She arose, and stood trembling before him.

"And do you feel it then at last?" said he mournfully.

She made no reply, but covered her eyes with her hand, and turned to leave the room. He rushed forward and caught her arm.

"Have patience with me, Elizabeth!" cried he passionately. "Do not desert me, though this veil must be between us here on earth. Be mine, and hereafter there shall be no veil over my face, no darkness between our souls! It is but a mortal veil—it is not for eternity! Oh! you know not how lonely I am, and how frightened, to be alone behind my black veil. Do not leave me in this miserable obscurity for ever!"

"Lift the veil but once, and look me in the face," said she.

"Never! It cannot be!" replied Mr. Hooper.

"Then, farewell!" said Elizabeth.

She withdrew her arm from his grasp, and slowly departed, pausing at the door, to give one long, shuddering gaze, that seemed almost to penetrate the mystery of the black veil. But, even amid his grief, Mr. Hooper smiled to think that only a material emblem had separated him from happiness, though the horrors, which it shadowed forth, must be drawn darkly between the fondest of lovers.

From that time no attempts were made to remove Mr. Hooper's black veil, or, by a direct appeal, to discover the secret which it was supposed to hide. By persons who claimed a superiority to popular prejudice, it was reckoned merely an eccentric whim, such as often mingles with the sober actions of men otherwise rational, and tinges them all with its own semblance of insanity. But with the multitude, good Mr. Hooper was irreparably a bugbear. He could not walk the street with any peace of mind, so conscious was he that the gentle and timid would turn aside to avoid him, and that others would make it a point of hardihood to throw themselves in his way. The impertinence of the latter class compelled him to give up his customary walk, at sunset, to the burial-ground; for when he leaned pensively over the gate, there would always be faces behind the grave-stones, peeping at his black veil. A fable went the rounds, that the stare of the dead people drove him thence. It grieved him, to the very depth of his kind heart, to observe how the children fled from his approach, breaking up their merriest sports, while his melancholy figure was yet afar off. Their instinctive dread caused him to feel, more strongly than aught else, that a preternatural horror was interwoven with the threads of the black crape. In truth, his own antipathy to the veil was known to be so great, that he never willingly passed before a mirror, nor stooped to drink at a still fountain, lest, in its peaceful bosom, he should be affrighted by himself. This was what gave plausibility to the whispers, that Mr. Hooper's conscience tortured him for some great crime too horrible to be entirely concealed, or otherwise than so obscurely intimated. Thus, from beneath the black veil, there rolled a cloud into the sunshine, an ambiguity of sin or sorrow, which enveloped the poor minister, so that love or sympathy could never reach him. It was said, that ghost and fiend consorted with him there. With self-shudderings and outward terrors, he walked continually in its shadow, groping darkly within his own soul, or gazing through a medium that saddened the whole world. Even the lawless wind, it was believed, respected his dreadful secret, and never blew aside the veil. But still good Mr. Hooper sadly smiled at the pale visages of the worldly throng as he passed by.

Among all its bad influences, the black veil had the one desirable effect, of making its wearer a very efficient clergyman. By the aid of his mysterious emblem—for there was no other apparent cause—he became a man of awful power, over souls that were in agony for sin. His converts always regarded him with a dread peculiar to themselves, affirming, though but figuratively, that, before he brought them to celestial light, they had been with him behind the black veil. Its gloom, indeed, enabled him to sympathize with all dark affections. Dying sinners cried aloud for Mr. Hooper, and would not yield their breath till he appeared; though ever, as he stooped to whisper consolation, they shuddered at the veiled face so near their own. Such were the terrors of the black veil, even when Death had bared his visage! Strangers came long distances to attend service at his church, with the mere idle purpose of gazing at his figure, because it was forbidden them to behold his face. But many were made to quake ere they departed! Once, during Governor Belcher's administration, Mr. Hooper was appointed to preach the election sermon. Covered with his black veil, he stood before the chief magistrate, the council, and the representatives, and wrought so deep an impression, that the legislative measures of that year were characterized by all the gloom and piety of our earliest ancestral sway.

In this manner Mr. Hooper spent a long life, irreproachable in outward act, yet shrouded in dismal suspicions; kind and loving, though unloved, and dimly feared; a man apart from men, shunned in their health and joy, but ever summoned to their aid in mortal anguish. As years wore on, shedding their snows above his sable veil, he acquired a name throughout the New England churches, and they called him Father Hooper. Nearly all his parishioners, who were of mature age when he was settled, had been borne away by many a funeral: he had one congregation in the church, and a more crowded one in the church-yard; and having wrought so late into the evening, and done his work so well, it was now good Father Hooper's turn to rest.

Several persons were visible by the shaded candle-light, in the death-chamber of the old clergyman. Natural connections he had none. But there was the decorously grave, though unmoved physician, seeking only to mitigate the last pangs of the patient whom he could not save. There were the deacons, and other eminently pious members of his church. There, also, was the Reverend Mr. Clark, of Westbury, a young and zealous divine, who had ridden in haste to pray by the bedside of the expiring minister. There was the nurse, no hired handmaiden of death, but one whose calm affection had endured thus long in secrecy, in solitude, amid the chill of age, and would not perish, even at the dying hour. Who, but Elizabeth! And there lay the hoary head of good Father Hooper upon the death-pillow, with the black veil still swathed about his brow and reaching down over his face, so that each more difficult gasp of his faint breath caused it to stir. All through life that piece of crape had hung between him and the world: it had separated him from cheerful brotherhood and woman's love, and kept him in that saddest of all prisons, his own heart; and still it lay upon his face, as if to deepen the gloom of his darksome chamber, and shade him from the sunshine of eternity.

For some time previous, his mind had been confused, wavering doubtfully between the past and the present, and hovering forward, as it were, at intervals, into the indistinctness of the world to come. There had been feverish turns, which tossed him from side to side, and wore away what little strength he had. But in his most convulsive struggles, and in the wildest vagaries of his intellect, when no other thought retained its sober influence, he still showed an awful solicitude lest the black veil should slip aside. Even if his bewildered soul could have forgotten, there was a faithful woman at his pillow, who, with averted eyes, would have covered that aged face, which she had last beheld in the comeliness of manhood. At length the death-stricken old man lay quietly in the torpor of mental and bodily exhaustion, with an imperceptible pulse, and breath that grew fainter and fainter, except when a long, deep, and irregular inspiration seemed to prelude the flight of his spirit.

The minister of Westbury approached the bedside.

"Venerable Father Hooper," said he, "the moment of your release is at hand. Are you ready for the lifting of the veil, that shuts in time from eternity?"

Father Hooper at first replied merely by a feeble motion of his head; then, apprehensive, perhaps, that his meaning might be doubtful, he exerted himself to speak.

"Yea," said he, in faint accents, "my soul hath a patient weariness until that veil be lifted."

"And is it fitting," resumed the Reverend Mr. Clark, "that a man so given to prayer, of such a blameless example, holy in deed and thought, so far as mortal judgment may pronounce; is it fitting that a father in the church should leave a shadow on his memory, that may seem to blacken a life so pure? I pray you, my venerable brother, let not this thing be! Suffer us to be gladdened by your triumphant aspect, as you go to your reward. Before the veil of eternity be lifted, let me cast aside this black veil from your face!"

And thus speaking, the Reverend Mr. Clark bent forward to reveal the mystery of so many years. But, exerting a sudden energy, that made all the beholders stand aghast, Father Hooper snatched both his hands from beneath the bed-clothes, and pressed them strongly on the black veil, resolute to struggle, if the minister of Westbury would contend with a dying man.

"Never!" cried the veiled clergyman. "On earth, never!"

"Dark old man!" exclaimed the affrighted minister, "with what horrible crime upon your soul are you now passing to the judgment?"

Father Hooper's breath heaved; it rattled in his throat; but, with a mighty effort, grasping forward with his hands, he caught hold of life, and held it back till he should speak. He even raised himself in bed; and there he sat, shivering with the arms of death around him, while the black veil hung down, awful, at that last moment, in the gathered terrors of a lifetime. And yet the faint, sad smile, so often there, now seemed to glimmer from its obscurity, and linger on Father Hooper's lips.

"Why do you tremble at me alone?" cried he, turning his veiled face round the circle of pale spectators. "Tremble also at each other! Have men avoided me, and women shown no pity, and children screamed and fled, only for my black veil? What, but the mystery which it obscurely typifies, has made this piece of crape so awful? When the friend shows his inmost heart to his friend; the lover to his best beloved; when man does not vainly shrink from the eye of his Creator, loathsomely treasuring up the secret of his sin; then deem me a monster, for the symbol beneath which I have lived, and die! I look around me, and, lo! on every visage a Black Veil!"

While his auditors shrank from one another, in mutual affright, Father Hooper fell back upon his pillow, a veiled corpse, with a faint smile lingering on the lips. Still veiled, they laid him in his coffin, and a veiled corpse they bore him to the grave. The grass of many years has sprung up and withered on that grave, the burial-stone is moss-grown, and good Mr. Hooper's face is dust; but awful is still the thought, that it mouldered beneath the Black Veil!

1836

The Artist of the Beautiful

In this story Hawthorne deals with the common romantic theme of the sensitive, idealistic artist in a practical and materialistic society. Note how he works out the contrast through characters that embody it and through incidents that give it dramatic poignancy.

In European life and literature many romantic poets and artists, feeling misunderstood and isolated like Hawthorne's hero, contemplated or committed self-destruction. But Owen Warland, possessing "force of character" along with "delicacy," learns to recognize that "the reward of all high performance must be sought within itself." Self-reliant, "he must stand up against mankind and be his own sole disciple, both as respects his genius and the objects to which it is directed." What is truly valuable to an artist is not a material symbol but his inner vision of beauty.

Text: From the author's revised edition of *Mosses from an Old Manse* (Boston, 1854).

An elderly man, with his pretty daughter on his arm, was passing along the street, and emerged from the gloom of the cloudy evening into the light that fell across the pavement from the window of a small shop. It was a projecting window; and on the inside were suspended a variety of watches, pinchbeck, silver, and one or two of gold, all with their faces turned from the street, as if churlishly disinclined to inform the wayfarers what o'clock it was. Seated within the shop, sidelong to the window, with his pale face bent earnestly over some delicate piece of mechanism on which was thrown the concentrated lustre of a shade lamp, appeared a young man.

"What can Owen Warland be about?" muttered old Peter Hovenden, himself a retired watchmaker and the former master of this same young man whose occupation he was now wondering at. "What can the fellow be about? These six months past I have never come by his shop without seeing him just as steadily at work as now. It would be a flight beyond his usual foolery to seek for the perpetual motion; and yet I know enough of my old business to be certain that what he is now so busy with is no part of the machinery of a watch."

"Perhaps, father," said Annie, without showing much interest in the question, "Owen is inventing a new kind of timekeeper. I am sure he has ingenuity enough."

"Poh, child! He has not the sort of ingenuity to invent anything better than a Dutch toy," answered her father, who had formerly been put to much vexation by Owen Warland's irregular genius. "A plague on such ingenuity! All the effect that ever I knew of it was, to spoil the accuracy of some of the best watches in my shop. He would turn the sun out of its orbit and derange the whole course of time, if, as I said before, his ingenuity could grasp anything bigger than a child's toy!"

"Hush, father! He hears you!" whispered Annie, pressing the old man's arm. "His ears are as delicate as his feelings; and you know how easily disturbed they are. Do let us move on."

So Peter Hovenden and his daughter Annie plodded on without further conversation, until in a by-street of the town they found themselves passing the open door of a blacksmith's shop. Within was seen the forge, now blazing up and illuminating the high and dusky roof, and now confining its lustre to a narrow precinct of the coal-strewn floor, according as the breath of the bellows was puffed forth or again inhaled into its vast leathern lungs. In the intervals of brightness it was easy to distinguish objects in remote corners of the shop and the horseshoes that hung upon the wall; in the momentary gloom the fire seemed to be glimmering amidst the vagueness of unenclosed space. Moving about in this red glare and alternate dusk was the figure of the blacksmith, well worthy to be viewed in so picturesque an aspect of light and shade, where the bright blaze struggled with the black night, as if each would have snatched his comely strength from the other. Anon he drew a whitehot bar of iron from the coals, laid it on the anvil, uplifted his arm of might, and was soon enveloped in the myriads of sparks which the strokes of his hammer scattered into the surrounding gloom.

"Now, that is a pleasant sight," said the old watch-maker. "I know what it is to work in gold; but give me the worker in iron after all is said and done. He spends his labor upon a reality. What say you, daughter Annie?"

"Pray don't speak so loud, father," whispered Annie. "Robert Danforth will hear you."

"And what if he should hear me?" said Peter Hovenden. "I say again, it is a good and a wholesome thing to depend upon main strength and reality, and to earn one's bread with the bare and brawny arm of a blacksmith. A watchmaker gets his brain puzzled by his wheels within a wheel, or loses his health or the nicety of his eyesight, as was my case, and finds himself at middle age, or a little after, past labor at his own trade and fit for nothing else, yet too poor to live at his ease. So I say once again, give me main strength for my money. And then, how it takes the nonsense out of a man! Did you ever hear of a blacksmith being such a fool as Owen Warland yonder?"

"Well said, uncle Hovenden!" shouted Robert Danforth from the forge, in a full, deep, merry voice, that made the roof re-echo. "And what says Miss Annie to that doctrine? She, I suppose, will think it a genteeler business to tinker up a lady's watch than to forge a horseshoe or make a gridiron."

Annie drew her father onward without giving him time for reply.

But we must return to Owen Warland's shop, and spend more meditation upon his history and character than either Peter Hovenden, or probably his daughter Annie, or Owen's old schoolfellow, Robert Danforth, would have thought due to so slight a subject. From the time that his little fingers could grasp a penknife, Owen had been remarkable for a delicate ingenuity, which sometimes produced pretty shapes in wood, principally figures of flowers and birds, and sometimes seemed to aim at the hidden mysteries of mechanism. But it was always for purposes of grace, and never with any mockery of the useful. He did not, like the crowd of schoolboy artisans, construct little windmills on the angle of a barn or watermills across the neighboring brook. Those who discovered such peculiarity in the boy as to think it worth their while to observe him closely, sometimes saw reason to suppose that he was attempting to imitate the beautiful movements of Nature as exemplified in the flight of birds or the activity of little animals. It seemed, in fact, a new development of the love of the beautiful, such as might have made him a poet, a painter, or a sculptor, and which was as completely refined from all utilitarian coarseness as it could have been in either of the fine arts. He looked with singular distaste at the stiff and regular processes of ordinary machinery. Being once carried to see a steam engine, in the expectation that his intuitive comprehension of mechanical principles would be gratified, he turned pale and grew sick, as if something monstrous and unnatural had been presented to him. This horror was partly owing to the size and terrible energy of the iron laborer; for the character of Owen's mind was microscopic, and tended naturally to the minute, in accordance with his diminutive frame and the marvellous smallness and delicate power of his fingers. Not that his sense of beauty was thereby diminished into a sense of prettiness. The beautiful idea has no relation to size, and may be as perfectly developed in a space too minute for any but microscopic investigation as within the ample verge that is measured by the arc of the rainbow. But, at all events, this characteristic minuteness in his objects and accomplishments made the world even more incapable than it might otherwise have been of appreciating Owen Warland's genius. The boy's relatives saw nothing better to be done—as perhaps there was not—than to bind him apprentice to a watchmaker, hoping that his strange ingenuity might thus be regulated and put to utilitarian purposes.

Peter Hovenden's opinion of his apprentice has already been expressed. He could make nothing of the lad. Owen's apprehension of the professional mysteries, it is true, was inconceivably quick; but he altogether forgot or despised the grand object of a watchmaker's business, and cared no more for the measurement of time than if it had been merged into eternity. So long, however, as he remained under his old master's care, Owen's lack of sturdiness made it possible, by strict injunctions and sharp oversight, to restrain his creative eccentricity within bounds; but when his apprenticeship was served out, and he had taken the little shop which Peter Hovenden's failing eyesight compelled him to relinquish, then did people recognize how unfit a person was Owen Warland to lead old blind Father Time along his daily course. One of his most rational projects was to connect a musical operation with the machinery of his watches, so that all the harsh dissonances of life might be rendered tuneful, and each flitting moment fall into the abyss of the past in golden drops of harmony. If a family clock was intrusted to him for repair,—one of those tall, ancient clocks that have grown nearly allied to human nature by measuring out the lifetime of many generations,—he would take upon himself to arrange a dance or funeral procession of figures across its venerable face, representing twelve mirthful or melancholy hours. Several freaks of this kind quite destroyed the young watchmaker's credit with that steady and matter-of-fact class of people who hold the opinion that time is not to be trifled with, whether considered as the medium of advancement and prosperity in this world or preparation for the next. His custom rapidly diminished—a misfortune, however, that was probably reckoned among his better accidents by Owen Warland, who was becoming more and more absorbed in a secret occupation which drew all his science and manual dexterity into itself, and likewise gave full employment to the characteristic tendencies of his genius. This pursuit had already consumed many months.

After the old watchmaker and his pretty daughter had gazed at him out of the obscurity of the street, Owen Warland was seized with a fluttering of the nerves, which made his hand tremble too violently to proceed with such delicate labor as he was now engaged upon.

"It was Annie herself!" murmured he. "I should

have known it, by this throbbing of my heart, before I heard her father's voice. Ah, how it throbs! I shall scarcely be able to work again on this exquisite mechanism to-night. Annie! dearest Annie! thou shouldst give firmness to my heart and hand, and not shake them thus; for, if I strive to put the very spirit of beauty into form and give it motion, it is for thy sake alone. O throbbing heart, be quiet! If my labor be thus thwarted, there will come vague and unsatisfied dreams, which will leave me spiritless to-morrow."

As he was endeavoring to settle himself again to his task, the shop door opened and gave admittance to no other than the stalwart figure which Peter Hovenden had paused to admire, as seen amid the light and shadow of the blacksmith's shop. Robert Danforth had brought a little anvil of his own manufacture, and peculiarly constructed, which the young artist had recently bespoken. Owen examined the article, and pronounced it fashioned according to his wish.

"Why, yes," said Robert Danforth, his strong voice filling the shop as with the sound of a bass viol, "I consider myself equal to anything in the way of my own trade; though I should have made but a poor figure at yours with such a fist as this," added he, laughing, as he laid his vast hand beside the delicate one of Owen. "But what then? I put more main strength into one blow of my sledge hammer than all that you have expended since you were a 'prentice. Is not that the truth?"

"Very probably," answered the low and slender voice of Owen. "Strength is an earthly monster. I make no pretensions to it. My force, whatever there may be of it, is altogether spiritual."

"Well, but, Owen, what are you about?" asked his old school-fellow, still in such a hearty volume of tone that it made the artist shrink, especially as the question related to a subject so sacred as the absorbing dream of his imagination. "Folks do say that you are trying to discover the perpetual motion."

"The perpetual motion? Nonsense!" replied Owen Warland, with a movement of disgust; for he was full of little petulances. "It can never be discovered. It is a dream that may delude men whose brains are mystified with matter, but not me. Besides, if such a discovery were possible, it would not be worth my while to make it only to have the secret turned to such purposes as are now effected by steam and water power. I am not ambitious to be honored with the paternity of a new kind of cotton machine."

"That would be droll enough!" cried the blacksmith, breaking out into such an uproar of laughter that Owen himself and the bell glasses on his workboard quivered in unison. "No, no, Owen! No child of yours will have iron joints and sinews. Well, I won't hinder you any more. Good night, Owen, and success; and if you need any assistance, so far as a downright blow of hammer upon anvil will answer the purpose, I'm your man."

And with another laugh the man of main strength left the shop.

"How strange it is," whispered Owen Warland to himself, leaning his head upon his hand, "that all my musings, my purposes, my passion for the beautiful, my consciousness of power to create it—a finer, more ethereal power, of which this earthly giant can have no conception,—all, all, look so vain and idle whenever my path is crossed by Robert Danforth! He would drive me mad were I to meet him often. His hard, brute force darkens and confuses the spiritual element within me; but I, too, will be strong in my own way. I will not yield to him."

He took from beneath a glass a piece of minute machinery, which he set in the condensed light of his lamp, and, looking intently at it through a magnifying glass, proceeded to operate with a delicate instrument of steel. In an instant, however, he fell back in his chair and clasped his hands, with a look of horror on his face that made its small features as impressive as those of a giant would have been.

"Heaven! What have I done?" exclaimed he. "The vapor, the influence of that brute force,—it has bewildered me and obscured my perception. I have made the very stroke—the fatal stroke—that I have dreaded from the first. It is all over—the toil of months, the object of my life. I am ruined!"

And there he sat, in strange despair, until his lamp flickered in the socket and left the Artist of the Beautiful in darkness.

Thus it is that ideas, which grow up within the imagination and appear so lovely to it and of a value beyond whatever men call valuable, are exposed to be shattered and annihilated by contact with the practical. It is requisite for the ideal artist to possess a force of character that seems hardly compatible with its delicacy; he must keep his faith in himself while the incredulous world assails him with its utter disbelief; he must stand up against mankind and be his own sole disciple, both as respects his genius and the objects to which it is directed.

For a time Owen Warland succumbed to this severe but inevitable test. He spent a few sluggish weeks with his head so continually resting in his hands that the townspeople had scarcely an opportunity to see his countenance. When at last it was again uplifted to the light of day, a cold, dull, nameless change was perceptible upon it. In the opinion of Peter Hovenden, however, and that order of sagacious understandings who think that life should be regulated, like clockwork, with leaden weights, the alteration was entirely for the better. Owen now, indeed, applied himself to business with dogged industry. It was marvellous to witness the obtuse gravity with which he would inspect the wheels of a great, old silver watch; thereby delighting the owner, in whose fob it had been worn till he deemed it a portion of his own life, and was accordingly jealous of its treatment. In consequence of the good report thus acquired, Owen Warland was invited by the proper authorities to regulate the clock in the church steeple. He succeeded so admirably in this matter of public interest that the merchants gruffly acknowledged his merits on 'Change; the nurse whispered his praises as she gave the potion in the sick chamber; the lover blessed him at the hour of appointed interview; and the town in general thanked Owen for the punctuality of dinner time. In a word, the heavy weight upon his spirits kept everything in order, not merely within his own system, but wheresoever the iron accents of the church clock were audible. It was a circumstance, though minute yet characteristic of his present state, that, when employed to engrave names or initials on silver spoons, he now wrote the requisite letters in the plainest possible style, omitting a variety of fanciful flourishes that had heretofore distinguished his work in this kind.

One day, during the era of this happy transformation, old Peter Hovenden came to visit his former apprentice.

"Well, Owen," said he, "I am glad to hear such good accounts of you from all quarters, and especially from the town clock yonder, which speaks in your commendation every hour of the twenty-four. Only get rid altogether of your nonsensical trash about the beautiful, which I nor nobody else, nor yourself to boot, could ever understand,—only free yourself of that, and your success in life is as sure as daylight. Why, if you go on in this way, I should even venture to let you doctor this precious old watch of mine; though, except my daughter Annie, I have nothing else so valuable in the world."

"I should hardly dare touch it, sir," replied Owen, in a depressed tone; for he was weighed down by his old master's presence.

"In time," said the latter,—"in time, you will be capable of it."

The old watchmaker, with the freedom naturally consequent on his former authority, went on inspecting the work which Owen had in hand at the moment, together with other matters that were in progress. The artist, meanwhile, could scarcely lift his head. There was nothing so antipodal to his nature as this man's cold, unimaginative sagacity, by contact with which everything was converted into a dream except the densest matter of the physical world. Owen groaned in spirit and prayed fervently to be delivered from him.

"But what is this?" cried Peter Hovenden abruptly, taking up a dusty bell glass, beneath which appeared a mechanical something, as delicate and minute as the system of a butterfly's anatomy. "What have we here? Owen! Owen! there is witchcraft in these little chains, and wheels, and paddles. See! with one pinch of my finger and thumb I am going to deliver you from all future peril."

"For Heaven's sake," screamed Owen Warland, springing up with wonderful energy, "as you would not drive me mad, do not touch it! The slightest pressure of your finger would ruin me forever."

"Aha, young man! And is it so?" said the old watchmaker, looking at him with just enough of penetration to torture Owen's soul with the bitterness of worldly criticism. "Well, take your own course; but I warn you again that in this small piece of mechanism lives your evil spirit. Shall I exorcise him?"

"You are my evil spirit," answered Owen, much excited,—"you and the hard, coarse world! The leaden thoughts and the despondency that you fling upon me are my clogs, else I should long ago have achieved the task that I was created for."

Peter Hovenden shook his head, with the mixture of contempt and indignation which mankind, of whom he was partly a representative, deem themselves entitled to feel towards all simpletons who seek other prizes than the dusty one along the highway. He then took his leave, with an uplifted finger and a sneer upon his face that haunted the artist's dreams for many a night afterwards. At the time of his old master's visit, Owen was probably on the point of taking up the relinquished task; but, by this sinister event, he was thrown back into the state whence he had been slowly emerging.

But the innate tendency of his soul had only been accumulating fresh vigor during its apparent sluggishness. As the summer advanced he almost totally relinquished his business, and permitted Father Time, so far as the old gentleman was represented by the clocks and watches under his control, to stray at random through human life, making infinite confusion among the train of bewildered hours. He wasted the sunshine, as people said, in wandering through the woods and fields and along the banks of streams. There, like a child, he found amusement in chasing butterflies or watching the motions of water insects. There was something truly mysterious in the intentness with which he contemplated these living playthings as they sported on the breeze or examined the structure of an imperial insect whom he had imprisoned. The chase of butterflies was an apt emblem of the ideal pursuit in which he had spent so many golden hours; but would the beautiful idea ever be yielded to his hand like the butterfly that symbolized it? Sweet, doubtless, were these days, and congenial to the artist's soul. They were full of bright conceptions, which gleamed through his intellectual world as the butterflies gleamed through the outward atmosphere, and were real to him, for the instant, without the toil, and perplexity, and many disappointments of attempting to make them visible to the sensual eye. Alas that the artist, whether in poetry, or whatever other material, may not content himself with the inward enjoyment of the beautiful, but must chase the flitting mystery beyond the verge of his ethereal domain, and crush its frail being in seizing it with a material grasp. Owen Warland felt the impulse to give external reality to his ideas as irresistibly as any of the poets or painters who have arrayed the world in a dimmer and fainter beauty, imperfectly copied from the richness of their visions.

The night was now his time for the slow progress of re-creating the one idea to which all his intellectual activity referred itself. Always at the approach of dusk he stole into the town, locked himself within his shop, and wrought with patient delicacy of touch for many hours. Sometimes he was startled by the rap of the watchman, who, when all the world should be asleep, had caught the gleam of lamplight through the crevices of Owen Warland's shutters. Daylight, to the morbid sensibility of his mind, seemed to have an intrusiveness that interfered with his pursuits. On cloudy and inclement days, therefore, he sat with his head upon his hands, muffling, as it were, his sensitive brain in a mist of indefinite musings; for it was a relief to escape from the sharp distinctness with which he was compelled to shape out his thoughts during his nightly toil.

From one of these fits of torpor he was aroused by the entrance of Annie Hovenden, who came into the shop with the freedom of a customer, and also with something of the familiarity of a childish friend. She had worn a hole through her silver thimble, and wanted Owen to repair it.

"But I don't know whether you will condescend to such a task," said she, laughing, "now that you are so taken up with the notion of putting spirit into machinery."

"Where did you get that idea, Annie?" said Owen, starting in surprise.

"O, out of my own head," answered she, "and from something that I heard you say, long ago, when you were but a boy and I a little child. But come; will you mend this poor thimble of mine?"

"Anything for your sake, Annie," said Owen Warland,—"anything, even were it to work at Robert Danforth's forge."

"And that would be a pretty sight!" retorted Annie, glancing with imperceptible slightness at the artist's small and slender frame. "Well; here is the thimble."

"But that is a strange idea of yours," said Owen, "about the spiritualization of matter."

And then the thought stole into his mind that this young girl possessed the gift to comprehend him better than all the world besides. And what a help and strength would it be to him in his lonely toil if he could gain the sympathy of the only being whom he loved! To persons whose pursuits are insulated from the common business of life—who are either in advance of mankind or apart from it—there often comes a sensation of moral cold that makes the spirit shiver as if it had reached the frozen solitudes around the pole. What the prophet, the poet, the reformer, the criminal, or any other man with human yearnings, but separated from the multitude by a peculiar lot, might feel, poor Owen felt.

"Annie," cried he, growing pale as death at the thought, "how gladly would I tell you the secret of my pursuit! You, methinks, would estimate it rightly. You, I know, would hear it with a reverence that I must not expect from the harsh, material world."

"Would I not? to be sure I would!" replied Annie Hovenden, lightly laughing. "Come; explain to me quickly what is the meaning of this little whirligig, so delicately wrought that it might be a plaything for Queen Mab. See! I will put it in motion."

"Hold!" exclaimed Owen, "hold!"

Annie had but given the slightest possible touch, with the point of a needle, to the same minute portion of complicated machinery which has been more than once mentioned, when the artist seized her by the wrist with a force that made her scream aloud. She was affrighted at the convulsion of intense rage and anguish that writhed across his features. The next instant he let his head sink upon his hands.

"Go, Annie," murmured he; "I have deceived myself, and must suffer for it. I yearned for sympathy and thought, and fancied, and dreamed that you might give it me; but you lack the talisman, Annie, that should admit you into my secrets. That touch has undone the toils of months and the thought of a lifetime! It was not your fault, Annie; but you have ruined me!"

Poor Owen Warland! He had indeed erred, yet pardonably; for if any human spirit could have sufficiently reverenced the process so sacred in his eyes, it must have been a woman's. Even Annie Hovenden, possibly, might not have disappointed him had she been enlightened by the deep intelligence of love.

The artist spent the ensuing winter in a way that

satisfied any persons who had hitherto retained a hopeful opinion of him that he was, in truth, irrevocably doomed to inutility as regarded the world, and to an evil destiny on his own part. The decease of a relative had put him in possession of a small inheritance. Thus freed from the necessity of toil, and having lost the steadfast influence of a great purpose,—great, at least, to him,—he abandoned himself to habits from which it might have been supposed the mere delicacy of his organization would have availed to secure him. But, when the ethereal portion of a man of genius is obscured, the earthly part assumes an influence the more uncontrollable, because the character is now thrown off the balance to which Providence had so nicely adjusted it, and which, in coarser natures, is adjusted by some other method. Owen Warland made proof of whatever show of bliss may be found in riot. He looked at the world through the golden medium of wine, and contemplated the visions that bubble up so gaily around the brim of the glass, and that people the air with shapes of pleasant madness, which so soon grow ghostly and forlorn. Even when this dismal and inevitable change had taken place, the young man might still have continued to quaff the cup of enchantments, though its vapor did but shroud life in gloom and fill the gloom with spectres that mocked at him. There was a certain irksomeness of spirit, which, being real, and the deepest sensation of which the artist was now conscious, was more intolerable than any fantastic miseries and horrors that the abuse of wine could summon up. In the latter case he could remember, even out of the midst of his trouble, that all was but a delusion; in the former, the heavy anguish was his actual life.

From this perilous state he was redeemed by an incident which more than one person witnessed, but of which the shrewdest could not explain or conjecture the operation on Owen Warland's mind. It was very simple. On a warm afternoon of spring, as the artist sat among his riotous companions with a glass of wine before him, a splendid butterfly flew in at the open window and fluttered about his head.

"Ah," exclaimed Owen, who had drank freely, "are you alive again, child of the sun and playmate of the summer breeze, after your dismal winter's nap? Then it is time for me to be at work!"

And, leaving his unemptied glass upon the table, he departed and was never known to sip another drop of wine.

And now, again, he resumed his wanderings in the woods and fields. It might be fancied that the bright butterfly, which had come so spirit-like into the window as Owen sat with the rude revellers, was indeed a spirit commissioned to recall him to the pure, ideal life that had so etherealized him among men. It might be fancied that he went forth to seek this spirit in its sunny haunts; for still, as in the summer time gone by, he was seen to steal gently up wherever a butterfly had alighted, and lose himself in contemplation of it. When it took flight his eyes followed the winged vision, as if its airy track would show the path to heaven. But what could be the purpose of the unseasonable toil, which was again resumed, as the watchman knew by the lines of lamplight through the crevices of Owen Warland's shutters? The townspeople had one comprehensive explanation of all these singularities. Owen Warland had gone mad! How universally efficacious—how satisfactory, too, and soothing to the injured sensibility of narrowness and dulness—is this easy method of accounting for whatever lies beyond the world's most ordinary scope! From St. Paul's days down to our poor little Artist of the Beautiful, the same talisman had been applied to the elucidation of all mysteries in the words or deeds of men who spoke or acted too wisely or too well. In Owen Warland's case the judgment of his townspeople may have been correct. Perhaps he was mad. The lack of sympathy—that contrast between himself and his neighbors which took away the restraint of example—was enough to make him so. Or possibly he had caught just so much of the ethereal radiance as served to bewilder him, in an earthly sense, by its intermixture with the common daylight.

One evening, when the artist had returned from a customary ramble and had just thrown the lustre of his lamp on the delicate piece of work so often interrupted, but still taken up again, as if his fate were embodied in its mechanism, he was surprised by the entrance of old Peter Hovenden. Owen never met this man without a shrinking of the heart. Of all the world he was most terrible, by reason of a keen understanding which saw so distinctly what it did see, and disbelieved so uncompromisingly in what it could not see. On this occasion the old watchmaker had merely a gracious word or two to say.

"Owen, my lad," said he, "we must see you at my house to-morrow night."

The artist began to mutter some excuse.

"O, but it must be so," quoth Peter Hovenden, "for the sake of the days when you were one of the household. What, my boy! don't you know that my daughter Annie is engaged to Robert Danforth? We are making an entertainment, in our humble way, to celebrate the event."

"Ah!" said Owen.

That little monosyllable was all he uttered; its tone seemed cold and unconcerned to an ear like Peter Hovenden's; and yet there was in it the stifled outcry of the poor artist's heart, which he compressed within him like a man holding down an evil spirit. One slight outbreak, however, imperceptible to the old watchmaker, he allowed himself. Raising the instrument with which he was about to begin his work, he let it fall upon the little system of machinery that had, anew, cost him months of thought and toil. It was shattered by the stroke!

Owen Warland's story would have been no tolerable representation of the troubled life of those who strive to create the beautiful, if, amid all other thwarting influences, love had not interposed to steal the cunning from his hand. Outwardly he had been no ardent or enterprising lover; the career of his passion had confined its tumults and vicissitudes so entirely within the artist's imagination that Annie herself had scarcely more than a woman's intuitive perception of it; but, in Owen's view, it covered the whole field of his life. Forgetful of the time when she had shown herself incapable of any deep response, he had persisted in connecting all his dreams of artistical success with Annie's image; she was the visible shape in which the spiritual power that he worshipped, and on whose altar he hoped to lay a not unworthy offering, was made manifest to him. Of course he had deceived himself; there were no such attributes in Annie Hovenden as his imagination had endowed her with. She, in the aspect which she wore to his inward vision, was as much a creature of his own as the mysterious piece of mechanism would be were it ever realized. Had he become convinced of his mistake through the medium of successful love,—had he won Annie to his bosom, and there beheld her fade from angel into ordinary woman,—the disappointment might have driven him back, with concentrated energy, upon his sole remaining object. On the other hand, had he found Annie what he fancied, his lot would have been so rich in beauty that out of its mere redundancy he might have wrought the beautiful into many a worthier type than he had toiled for; but the guise in which his sorrow came to him, the sense that the angel of his life had been snatched away and given to a rude man of earth and iron, who could neither need nor appreciate her ministrations,—this was the very perversity of fate that makes human existence appear too absurd and contradictory to be the scene of one other hope or one other fear. There was nothing left for Owen Warland but to sit down like a man that had been stunned.

He went through a fit of illness. After his recovery his small slender frame assumed an obtuser garniture of flesh than it had ever before worn. His thin cheeks became round; his delicate little hand, so spiritually fashioned to achieve fairy taskwork, grew plumper than the hand of a thriving infant. His aspect had a childishness such as might have induced a stranger to pat him on the head—pausing, however, in the act, to wonder what manner of child was here. It was as if the spirit had gone out of him, leaving the body to flourish in a sort of vegetable existence. Not that Owen Warland was idiotic. He could talk, and not irrationally. Somewhat of a babbler, indeed, did people begin to think him; for he was apt to discourse at wearisome length of marvels of mechanism that he had read about in books, but which he had learned to consider as absolutely fabulous. Among them he enumerated the Man of Brass, constructed by Albertus Magnus, and the Brazen Head of Friar Bacon; and, coming down to later times, the automata of a little coach and horses, which it was pretended had been manufactured for the Dauphin of France; together with an insect that buzzed about the ear like a living fly, and yet was but a contrivance of minute steel springs. There was a story, too, of a duck that waddled, and quacked, and ate; though, had any honest citizen purchased it for dinner, he would have found himself cheated with the mere mechanical apparition of a duck.

"But all these accounts," said Owen Warland, "I am now satisfied are mere impositions."

Then, in a mysterious way, he would confess that he once thought differently. In his idle and dreamy days he had considered it possible, in a certain sense, to spiritualize machinery, and to combine with the new species of life and motion thus produced a beauty that should attain to the ideal which Nature has proposed to herself in all her creatures, but has never taken pains to realize. He seemed, however, to retain no very distinct perception either of the process of achieving this object or of the design itself.

"I have thrown it all aside now," he would say. "It was a dream such as young men are always mystifying themselves with. Now that I have acquired a little common sense, it makes me laugh to think of it."

Poor, poor and fallen Owen Warland! These were the symptoms that he had ceased to be an inhabitant of the better sphere that lies unseen around us. He had lost his faith in the invisible, and now prided himself, as such unfortunates invariably do, in the wisdom which rejected much that even his eye could see, and trusted confidently in nothing but what his hand could touch. This is the calamity of men whose spiritual part dies out of them and leaves the grosser understanding to assimilate them more and more to the things of which alone it can take cognizance; but in Owen Warland the spirit was not dead nor passed away; it only slept.

How it awoke again is not recorded. Perhaps the torpid slumber was broken by a convulsive pain. Perhaps, as in a former instance, the butterfly came and hovered about his head and reinspired him,—as indeed this creature of the sunshine had always a mysterious mission for the artist,—reinspired him with the former purpose of his life. Whether it were pain or happiness that thrilled through his veins, his first impulse was to thank Heaven for rendering him again the being of thought, imagination, and keenest sensibility that he had long ceased to be.

"Now for my task," said he. "Never did I feel such strength for it as now."

Yet, strong as he felt himself, he was incited to toil the more diligently by an anxiety lest death should surprise him in the midst of his labors. This anxiety, perhaps, is common to all men who set their hearts upon anything so high, in their own view of it, that life becomes of importance only as conditional to its accomplishment. So long as we love life for itself, we seldom dread the losing it. When we desire life for the attainment of an object, we recognize the frailty of its texture. But, side by side with this sense of insecurity, there is a vital faith in our invulnerability to the shaft of death while engaged in any task that seems assigned by Providence as our proper thing to do, and which the world would have cause to mourn for should we leave it unaccomplished. Can the philosopher, big with the inspiration of an idea that is to reform mankind, believe that he is to be beckoned from this sensible existence at the very instant when he is mustering his breath to speak the word of light? Should he perish so, the weary ages may pass away—the world's, whose life sand may fall, drop by drop—before another intellect is prepared to develop the truth that might have been uttered then. But history affords many an example where the most precious spirit, at any particular epoch manifested in human shape, has gone hence untimely, without space allowed him, so far as mortal judgment could discern, to perform his mission on the earth. The prophet dies, and the man of torpid heart and sluggish brain lives on. The poet leaves his song half sung, or finishes it, beyond the scope of mortal ears, in a celestial choir. The painter—as Allston[1] did—leaves half his conception on the canvas to sadden us with its imperfect beauty, and goes to picture forth the whole, if it be no irreverence to say so, in the hues of heaven. But rather such incomplete designs of this life will be perfected nowhere. This so frequent abortion of man's dearest projects must be taken as a proof that the deeds of earth, however etherealized by piety or genius, are without value, except as exercises and manifestations of the spirit. In heaven, all ordinary thought is higher and more melodious than Milton's song. Then, would he add another verse to any strain that he had left unfinished here?

But to return to Owen Warland. It was his fortune, good or ill, to achieve the purpose of his life. Pass we over a long space of intense thought, yearning effort, minute toil, and wasting anxiety, succeeded by an instant of solitary triumph: let all this be imagined; and then behold the artist, on a winter evening, seeking admittance to Robert Danforth's fireside circle. There he found the man of iron, with his massive substance thoroughly warmed and attempered by domestic influences. And there was Annie, too, now transformed into a matron, with much of her husband's plain and sturdy nature, but imbued, as Owen Warland still believed, with a finer grace, that might enable her to be the interpreter between strength and beauty. It happened, likewise, that old Peter Hovenden was a guest this evening at his daughter's fireside, and it was his well-remembered expression of keen, cold criticism that first encountered the artist's glance.

"My old friend Owen!" cried Robert Danforth, starting up, and compressing the artist's delicate fingers within a hand that was accustomed to gripe bars of iron. "This is kind and neighborly to come to us at last. I was afraid your perpetual motion had bewitched you out of the remembrance of old times."

"We are glad to see you," said Annie, while a blush reddened her matronly cheek. "It was not like a friend to stay from us so long."

"Well, Owen," inquired the old watchmaker, as his first greeting, "how comes on the beautiful? Have you created it at last?"

The artist did not immediately reply, being startled by the apparition of a young child of strength that was tumbling about on the carpet,—a little personage who had come mysteriously out of the infinite, but with something so sturdy and real in his composition that he seemed moulded out of the densest substance which earth could supply. This hopeful infant crawled towards the newcomer, and setting himself on end, as Robert Danforth expressed the posture, stared at Owen with a look of such sagacious observation that the mother could not help exchanging a proud glance with her husband. But the artist was disturbed by the child's look, as imagining a resemblance between it and Peter Hovenden's habitual expression. He could have fancied that the old watchmaker was compressed into this baby shape, and looking out of those baby eyes, and repeating, as he now did, the malicious question:—

"The beautiful, Owen! How comes on the beautiful? Have you succeeded in creating the beautiful?"

"I have succeeded," replied the artist, with a momentary light of triumph in his eyes and a smile of sunshine, yet steeped in such depth of thought that it was almost sadness. "Yes, my friends, it is the truth. I have succeeded."

"Indeed!" cried Annie, a look of maiden mirthfulness peeping out of her face again. "And is it lawful, now, to inquire what the secret is?"

[1] Washington Allston (1778–1843), an American painter.

"Surely; it is to disclose it that I have come," answered Owen Warland. "You shall know, and see, and touch, and possess the secret! For, Annie,—if by that name I may still address the friend of my boyish years,—Annie, it is for your bridal gift that I have wrought this spiritualized mechanism, this harmony of motion, this mystery of beauty. It comes late indeed; but it is as we go onward in life, when objects begin to lose their freshness of hue and our souls their delicacy of perception, that the spirit of beauty is most needed. If,—forgive me, Annie,—if you know how to value this gift, it can never come too late."

He produced, as he spoke, what seemed a jewel box. It was carved richly out of ebony by his own hand, and inlaid with a fanciful tracery of pearl, representing a boy in pursuit of a butterfly, which, elsewhere, had become a winged spirit, and was flying heavenward; while the boy, or youth, had found such efficacy in his strong desire that he ascended from earth to cloud, and from cloud to celestial atmosphere, to win the beautiful. This case of ebony the artist opened, and bade Annie place her finger on its edge. She did so, but almost screamed as a butterfly fluttered forth, and, alighting on her finger's tip, sat waving the ample magnificence of its purple and gold-speckled wings, as if in prelude to a flight. It is impossible to express by words the glory, the splendor, the delicate gorgeousness which were softened into the beauty of this object. Nature's ideal butterfly was here realized in all its perfection; not in the pattern of such faded insects as flit among earthly flowers, but of those which hover across the meads of paradise for child-angels and the spirits of departed infants to disport themselves with. The rich down was visible upon its wings; the lustre of its eyes seemed instinct with spirit. The firelight glimmered around this wonder—the candles gleamed upon it; but it glistened apparently by its own radiance, and illuminated the finger and outstretched hand on which it rested with a white gleam like that of precious stones. In its perfect beauty, the consideration of size was entirely lost. Had its wings overreached the firmament, the mind could not have been more filled or satisfied.

"Beautiful! beautiful!" exclaimed Annie. "Is it alive? Is it alive?"

"Alive? To be sure it is," answered her husband. "Do you suppose any mortal has skill enough to make a butterfly, or would put himself to the trouble of making one, when any child may catch a score of them in a summer's afternoon? Alive? Certainly! But this pretty box is undoubtedly of our friend Owen's manufacture; and really it does him credit."

At this moment the butterfly waved its wings anew, with a motion so absolutely lifelike that Annie was startled, and even awestricken; for, in spite of her husband's opinion, she could not satisfy herself whether it was indeed a living creature or a piece of wondrous mechanism.

"Is it alive?" she repeated, more earnestly than before.

"Judge for yourself," said Owen Warland, who stood gazing in her face with fixed attention.

The butterfly now flung itself upon the air, fluttered around Annie's head, and soared into a distant region of the parlor, still making itself perceptible to sight by the starry gleam in which the motion of its wings enveloped it. The infant on the floor followed its course with his sagacious little eyes. After flying about the room, it returned in a spiral curve and settled again on Annie's finger.

"But is it alive?" exclaimed she again; and the finger on which the gorgeous mystery had alighted was so tremulous that the butterfly was forced to balance himself with his wings. "Tell me if it be alive, or whether you created it."

"Wherefore ask who created it, so it be beautiful?" replied Owen Warland. "Alive? Yes, Annie; it may well be said to possess life, for it has absorbed my own being into itself; and in the secret of that butterfly, and in its beauty,—which is not merely outward, but deep as its whole system,—is represented the intellect, the imagination, the sensibility, the soul of an Artist of the Beautiful! Yes; I created it. But"—and here his countenance somewhat changed—"this butterfly is not now to me what it was when I beheld it afar off in the daydreams of my youth."

"Be it what it may, it is a pretty plaything," said the blacksmith, grinning with childlike delight. "I wonder whether it would condescend to alight on such a great clumsy finger as mine? Hold it hither, Annie."

By the artist's direction, Annie touched her finger's tip to that of her husband; and, after a momentary delay, the butterfly fluttered from one to the other. It preluded a second flight by a similar, yet not precisely the same, waving of wings as in the first experiment; then, ascending from the blacksmith's stalwart finger, it rose in a gradually enlarging curve to the ceiling, made one wide sweep around the room, and returned with an undulating movement to the point whence it had started.

"Well, that does beat all nature!" cried Robert Danforth, bestowing the heartiest praise that he could find expression for; and, indeed, had he paused there, a man of finer words and nicer perception could not easily have said more. "That goes beyond me, I confess. But what then? There is more real use in one downright blow of my sledge hammer than in the whole five years' labor that our friend Owen has wasted on this butterfly."

Here the child clapped his hands and made a great babble of indistinct utterance, apparently demanding that the butterfly should be given him for a plaything.

Owen Warland, meanwhile, glanced sidelong at Annie, to discover whether she sympathized in her husband's estimate of the comparative value of the beautiful and the practical. There was, amid all her kindness towards himself, amid all the wonder and admiration with which she contemplated the marvelous work of his hands and incarnation of his idea, a secret scorn—too secret, perhaps, for her own consciousness, and perceptible only to such intuitive discernment as that of the artist. But Owen, in the latter stages of his pursuit, had risen out of the region in which such a discovery might have been torture. He knew that the world, and Annie as the representative of the world, whatever praise might be bestowed, could never say the fitting word nor feel the fitting sentiment which should be the perfect recompense of an artist who, symbolizing a lofty moral by a material trifle,—converting what was earthly to spiritual gold,—had won the beautiful into his handiwork. Not at this latest moment was he to learn that the reward of all high performance must be sought within itself, or sought in vain. There was, however, a view of the matter which Annie and her husband, and even Peter Hovenden, might fully have understood, and which would have satisfied them that the toil of years had here been worthily bestowed. Owen Warland might have told them that this butterfly, this plaything, this bridal gift of a poor watchmaker to a blacksmith's wife, was, in truth, a gem of art that a monarch would have purchased with honors and abundant wealth, and have treasured it among the jewels of his kingdom as the most unique and wondrous of them all. But the artist smiled and kept the secret to himself.

"Father," said Annie, thinking that a word of praise from the old watchmaker might gratify his former apprentice, "do come and admire this pretty butterfly."

"Let us see," said Peter Hovenden, rising from his chair, with a sneer upon his face that always made people doubt, as he himself did, in everything but a material existence. "Here is my finger for it to alight upon. I shall understand it better when once I have touched it."

But, to the increased astonishment of Annie, when the tip of her father's finger was pressed against that of her husband, on which the butterfly still rested, the insect drooped its wings and seemed on the point of falling to the floor. Even the bright spots of gold upon its wings and body, unless her eyes deceived her, grew dim, and the glowing purple took a dusky hue, and the starry lustre that gleamed around the blacksmith's hand became faint and vanished.

"It is dying! it is dying!" cried Annie, in alarm.

"It has been delicately wrought," said the artist, calmly. "As I told you, it has imbibed a spiritual essence—call it magnetism, or what you will. In an atmosphere of doubt and mockery its exquisite susceptibility suffers torture, as does the soul of him who instilled his own life into it. It has already lost its beauty; in a few moments more its mechanism would be irreparably injured."

"Take away your hand, father!" entreated Annie, turning pale. "Here is my child; let it rest on his innocent hand. There, perhaps, its life will revive and its colors grow brighter than ever."

Her father, with an acrid smile, withdrew his finger. The butterfly then appeared to recover the power of voluntary motion, while its hues assumed much of their original lustre, and the gleam of starlight, which was its most ethereal attribute, again formed a halo round about it. At first, when transferred from Robert Danforth's hand to the small finger of the child, this radiance grew so powerful that it positively threw the little fellow's shadow back against the wall. He, meanwhile, extended his plump hand as he had seen his father and mother do, and watched the waving of the insect's wings with infantine delight. Nevertheless, there was a certain odd expression of sagacity that made Owen Warland feel as if here were old Peter Hovenden, partially, and but partially, redeemed from his hard scepticism into childish faith.

"How wise the little monkey looks!" whispered Robert Danforth to his wife.

"I never saw such a look on a child's face," answered Annie, admiring her own infant, and with good reason, far more than the artistic butterfly. "The darling knows more of the mystery than we do."

As if the butterfly, like the artist, were conscious of something not entirely congenial in the child's nature, it alternately sparkled and grew dim. At length it arose from the small hand of the infant with an airy motion that seemed to bear it upward without an effort, as if the ethereal instincts with which its master's spirit had endowed it impelled this fair vision involuntarily to a higher sphere. Had there been no obstruction, it might have soared into the sky and grown immortal. But its lustre gleamed upon the ceiling; the exquisite texture of its wings brushed against that earthly medium; and a sparkle or two, as of stardust, floated downward and lay glimmering on the carpet. Then the butterfly came fluttering down, and, instead of returning to the infant, was apparently attracted towards the artist's hand.

"Not so! not so!" murmured Owen Warland, as if his handiwork could have understood him. "Thou hast gone forth out of thy master's heart. There is no return for thee."

With a wavering movement, and emitting a tremulous radiance, the butterfly struggled, as it were, towards the infant, and was about to alight upon his finger; but while it still hovered in the air, the little child of strength, with his grandsire's sharp and shrewd expression in his face, made a snatch at the marvellous insect and compressed it in his hand. Annie screamed. Old Peter Hovenden burst into a cold and scornful laugh. The blacksmith, by main force, unclosed the infant's hand, and found within the palm a small heap of glittering fragments, whence the mystery of beauty had fled forever. And as for Owen Warland, he looked placidly at what seemed the ruin of his life's labor, and which was yet no ruin. He had caught a far other butterfly than this. When the artist rose high enough to achieve the beautiful, the symbol by which he made it perceptible to mortal senses became of little value in his eyes while his spirit possessed itself in the enjoyment of the reality.

1844

Rappaccini's Daughter

Hawthorne's setting for this story is foreign and its source legendary. As his notebooks show, he had been reading in Sir Thomas Browne: "A story there passeth of an Indian king that sent unto Alexander a fair woman fed with aconites and other poisons, with this intent, either by converse or copulation complexionally to destroy him." Nevertheless, like his tales of the American past, "Rappaccini's Daughter" dramatizes the difficulties of perception, the ambiguity of action, and the complexity of character and motive. As the story unfolds, the complex, contradictory nature of each character becomes clearer, and by the end the characters have, in some sense, undergone a reversal of roles. At the beginning, for example, Beatrice seems to be both beautiful and inexpressibly terrible—the evil temptress inviting Giovanni to his doom. But the reader later discovers that Beatrice is the one victimized. Her father manipulates and destroys individuals for knowledge and power; Baglioni, whose antidote is a poison, turns out to be selfish, envious, and vengeful; and Giovanni destroys her love and her desire to live by his selfish, bitter attack. But the situation is not even so simple as that. In this story Hawthorne explores the possibilities of ambiguity, not to confuse, but to dramatize his sense of the tangled, complex web of human experience. Text: From the author's revised edition of *Mosses from an Old Manse* (Boston, 1854).

A young man, named Giovanni Guasconti, came, very long ago, from the more southern region of Italy, to pursue his studies at the University of Padua. Giovanni, who had but a scanty supply of gold ducats in his pocket, took lodgings in a high and gloomy chamber of an old edifice which looked not unworthy to have been the palace of a Paduan noble, and which, in fact, exhibited over its entrance the armorial bearings of a family long since extinct. The young stranger, who was not unstudied in the great poem of his country, recollected that one of the ancestors of this family, and perhaps an occupant of this very mansion, had been pictured by Dante as a partaker of the immortal agonies of his Inferno. These reminiscences and associations, together with the tendency to heartbreak natural to a young man for the first time out of his native sphere, caused Giovanni to sigh heavily as he looked around the desolate and ill-furnished apartment.

"Holy Virgin, signor!" cried old Dame Lisabetta, who, won by the youth's remarkable beauty of person, was kindly endeavoring to give the chamber a habitable air, "what a sigh was that to come out of a young man's heart! Do you find this old mansion gloomy? For the love of Heaven, then, put your head out of the window, and you will see as bright sunshine as you have left in Naples."

Guasconti mechanically did as the old woman advised, but could not quite agree with her that the Paduan sunshine was as cheerful as that of southern Italy. Such as it was, however, it fell upon a garden beneath the window and expended its fostering influences on a variety of plants, which seemed to have been cultivated with exceeding care.

"Does this garden belong to the house?" asked Giovanni.

"Heaven forbid, signor, unless it were fruitful of better pot herbs than any that grow there now," answered old Lisabetta. "No; that garden is cultivated by the own hands of Signor Giacomo Rappaccini, the famous doctor, who, I warrant him, has been heard of as far as Naples. It is said that he distils these plants into medicines that are as potent as a charm. Oftentimes you may see the signor doctor at work, and perchance the signora, his daughter, too, gathering the strange flowers that grow in the garden."

The old woman had now done what she could for the aspect of the chamber; and, commending the young man to the protection of the saints, took her departure.

Giovanni still found no better occupation than to look down into the garden beneath his window. From its appearance, he judged it to be one of those botanic gardens which were of earlier date in Padua than elsewhere in Italy or in the world. Or, not improbably, it might once have been the pleasure-place of an opulent family; for there was the ruin of a marble fountain in the center, sculptured with rare art, but so wofully shattered that it was impossible to trace the original design from the chaos of remaining fragments. The water, however, continued to gush and sparkle into the sunbeams as cheerfully as ever. A little gurgling sound ascended to the young man's window and made him feel as if the fountain were an immortal spirit, that sung its song unceasingly and without heeding the vicissitudes around it, while one century embodied it in marble and another scattered the perishable garniture on the soil. All about the pool into which the water subsided grew various plants, that seemed to require a plentiful supply of moisture for the nourishment of gigantic leaves, and, in some instances, flowers gorgeously magnificent. There was one shrub in particular, set in a marble vase in the midst of the pool, that bore a profusion of purple blossoms, each of which had the lustre and richness of a gem; and the whole together made a show so resplendent that it seemed enough to illuminate the garden, even had there been no sunshine. Every portion of the soil was peopled with plants and herbs, which, if less beautiful, still bore tokens of assiduous care, as if all had their individual virtues, known to the scientific mind that fostered them. Some were placed in urns, rich with old carving, and others in common garden pots; some crept serpent-like along the ground or climbed on high, using whatever means of ascent was offered them. One plant had wreathed itself round a statue of Vertumnus, which was thus quite veiled and shrouded in a drapery of hanging foliage, so happily arranged that it might have served a sculptor for a study.

While Giovanni stood at the window he heard a rustling behind a screen of leaves, and became aware that a person was at work in the garden. His figure soon emerged into view, and showed itself to be that of no common laborer, but a tall, emaciated, sallow, and sickly-looking man, dressed in a scholar's garb of black. He was beyond the middle term of life, with gray hair, a thin, gray beard, and a face singularly marked with intellect and cultivation, but which could never, even in his more youthful days, have expressed much warmth of heart.

Nothing could exceed the intentness with which this scientific gardener examined every shrub which grew in his path: it seemed as if he was looking into their inmost nature, making observations in regard to their creative essence, and discovering why one leaf grew in this shape and another in that, and wherefore such and such flowers differed among themselves in hue and perfume. Nevertheless, in spite of this deep intelligence on his part, there was no approach to intimacy between himself and these vegetable existences. On the contrary, he avoided their actual touch or the direct inhaling of their odors with a caution that impressed Giovanni most disagreeably; for the man's demeanor was that of one walking among malignant influences, such as savage beasts, or deadly snakes, or evil spirits, which, should he allow them one moment of license, would wreak upon him some terrible fatality. It was strangely frightful to the young man's imagination to see this air of insecurity in a person cultivating a garden, that most simple and innocent of human toils, and which had been alike the joy and labor of the unfallen parents of the race. Was this garden, then, the Eden of the present world? And this man, with such perception of harm in what his own hands caused to grow,—was he the Adam?

The distrustful gardener, while plucking away the dead leaves or pruning the too luxuriant growth of the shrubs, defended his hands with a pair of thick gloves. Nor were these his only armor. When, in his walk through the garden, he came to the magnificent plant that hung its purple gems beside the marble fountain, he placed a kind of mask over his mouth and nostrils, as if all this beauty did but conceal a deadlier malice; but, finding his task still too dangerous, he drew back, removed the mask, and called loudly, but in the infirm voice of a person affected with inward disease,—

"Beatrice! Beatrice!"

"Here am I, my father. What would you?" cried a rich and youthful voice from the window of the opposite house—a voice as rich as a tropical sunset, and which made Giovanni, though he knew not why, think of deep hues of purple or crimson and of perfumes heavily delectable, "Are you in the garden?"

"Yes, Beatrice," answered the gardener, "and I need your help."

Soon there emerged from under a sculptured portal the figure of a young girl, arrayed with as much richness of taste as the most splendid of the flowers, beautiful as the day, and with a bloom so deep and vivid that one shade more would have been too much. She looked redundant with life, health, and energy; all of which attributes were bound down and compressed, as it were, and girdled tensely, in their luxuriance, by her virgin zone.[1] Yet Giovanni's fancy must have grown morbid while he looked down into the garden; for the impression which the fair stranger made upon him was as if here were another flower, the human sister of those vegetable ones, as beautiful as they, more beautiful than the richest of them, but still to be touched only with a glove, nor to be approached without a mask. As Beatrice came down the garden path, it was observable that she handled and inhaled the odor of sever-

[1]A belt or girdle worn by unmarried women.

al of the plants which her father had most sedulously avoided.

"Here, Beatrice," said the latter, "see how many needful offices require to be done to our chief treasure. Yet, shattered as I am, my life might pay the penalty of approaching it so closely as circumstances demand. Henceforth, I fear, this plant must be consigned to your sole charge."

"And gladly will I undertake it," cried again the rich tones of the young lady, as she bent towards the magnificent plant and opened her arms as if to embrace it. "Yes, my sister, my splendor, it shall be Beatrice's task to nurse and serve thee; and thou shalt reward her with thy kisses and perfumed breath, which to her is as the breath of life."

Then, with all the tenderness in her manner that was so strikingly expressed in her words, she busied herself with such attentions as the plant seemed to require; and Giovanni, at his lofty window, rubbed his eyes, and almost doubted whether it were a girl tending her favorite flower, or one sister performing the duties of affection to another. The scene soon terminated. Whether Dr. Rappaccini had finished his labors in the garden, or that his watchful eye had caught the stranger's face, he now took his daughter's arm and retired. Night was already closing in; oppressive exhalations seemed to proceed from the plants and steal upward past the open window; and Giovanni, closing the lattice, went to his couch and dreamed of a rich flower and beautiful girl. Flower and maiden were different, and yet the same, and fraught with some strange peril in either shape.

But there is an influence in the light of morning that tends to rectify whatever errors of fancy, or even of judgment, we may have incurred during the sun's decline, or among the shadows of the night, or in the less wholesome glow of moonshine. Giovanni's first movement, on starting from sleep, was to throw open the window and gaze down into the garden which his dreams had made so fertile of mysteries. He was surprised, and a little ashamed, to find how real and matter-of-fact an affair it proved to be, in the first rays of the sun which gilded the dewdrops that hung upon leaf and blossom, and, while giving a brighter beauty to each rare flower, brought everything within the limits of ordinary experience. The young man rejoiced that, in the heart of the barren city, he had the privilege of overlooking this spot of lovely and luxuriant vegetation. It would serve, he said to himself, as a symbolic language to keep him in communion with Nature. Neither the sickly and thoughtworn Dr. Giacomo Rappaccini, it is true, nor his brilliant daughter, were now visible; so that Giovanni could not determine how much of the singularity which he attributed to both was due to their own qualities and how much to his wonder-working fancy; but he was inclined to take a most rational view of the whole matter.

In the course of the day he paid his respects to Signor Pietro Baglioni, professor of medicine in the university, a physician of eminent repute, to whom Giovanni had brought a letter of introduction. The professor was an elderly personage, apparently of genial nature and habits that might almost be called jovial. He kept the young man to dinner, and made himself very agreeable by the freedom and liveliness of his conversation, especially when warmed by a flask or two of Tuscan wine. Giovanni, conceiving that men of science, inhabitants of the same city, must needs be on familiar terms with one another, took an opportunity to mention the name of Dr. Rappaccini. But the professor did not respond with so much cordiality as he had anticipated.

"Ill would it become a teacher of the divine art of medicine," said Professor Pietro Baglioni, in answer to a question of Giovanni, "to withhold due and well-considered praise of a physician so eminently skilled as Rappaccini; but, on the other hand, I should answer it but scantily to my conscience were I to permit a worthy youth like yourself, Signor Giovanni, the son of an ancient friend, to imbibe erroneous ideas respecting a man who might hereafter chance to hold your life and death in his hands. The truth is, our worshipful Dr. Rappaccini has as much science as any member of the faculty—with perhaps one single exception—in Padua, or all Italy; but there are certain grave objections to his professional character."

"And what are they?" asked the young man.

"Has my friend Giovanni any disease of body or heart, that he is so inquisitive about physicians?" said the professor, with a smile. "But as for Rappaccini, it is said of him—and I, who know the man well, can answer for its truth—that he cares infinitely more for science than for mankind. His patients are interesting to him only as subjects for some new experiment. He would sacrifice human life, his own among the rest, or whatever else was dearest to him, for the sake of adding so much as a grain of mustard seed to the great heap of his accumulated knowledge."

"Methinks he is an awful man indeed," remarked Guasconti, mentally recalling the cold and purely intellectual aspect of Rappaccini. "And yet, worshipful professor, is it not a noble spirit? Are there many men capable of so spiritual a love of science?"

"God forbid," answered the professor, somewhat testily; "at least, unless they take sounder views of the healing art than those adopted by Rappaccini. It is his theory that all medicinal virtues are comprised within those substances which we term vegetable poisons. These he cultivates with his own hands, and is said even to have produced new varieties of poison, more horribly deleterious than Nature, without the assistance of this learned person, would ever have plagued the world withal. That the signor doctor does less mischief than might be expected with such dangerous substances is undeniable. Now and then, it must be owned, he has effected, or seemed to effect, a marvellous cure; but, to tell you my private mind, Signor Giovanni, he should receive little credit for such instances of success,—they being probably the work of chance,—but should be held strictly accountable for his failures, which may justly be considered his own work."

The youth might have taken Baglioni's opinions with many grains of allowance had he known that there was a professional warfare of long continuance between him and Dr. Rappaccini, in which the latter was generally thought to have gained the advantage. If the reader be inclined to judge for himself, we refer him to certain black-letter tracts on both sides, preserved in the medical department of the University of Padua.

"I know not, most learned professor," returned Giovanni, after musing on what had been said of Rappaccini's exclusive zeal for science,—"I know not how dearly this physician may love his art; but surely there is one object more dear to him. He has a daughter."

"Aha!" cried the professor, with a laugh. "So now our friend Giovanni's secret is out. You have heard of this daughter, whom all the young men in Padua are wild about, though not half a dozen have ever had the good hap to see her face. I know little of the Signora Beatrice save that Rappaccini is said to have instructed her deeply in his science, and that, young and beautiful as fame reports her, she is already qualified to fill a professor's chair. Perchance her father destines her for mine! Other absurd rumors there be, not worth talking about or listening to. So now, Signor Giovanni, drink off your glass of lachryma."[2]

Guasconti returned to his lodgings somewhat heated with the wine he had quaffed, and which caused his brain to swim with strange fantasies in reference to Dr. Rappaccini and the beautiful Beatrice. On his way, happening to pass by a florist's, he bought a fresh bouquet of flowers.

Ascending to his chamber, he seated himself near the window, but within the shadow thrown by the depth of the wall, so that he could look down into the garden with little risk of being discovered. All beneath his eye was a solitude. The strange plants were basking in the sunshine, and now and then nodding gently to one another, as if in acknowledgment of sympathy and kindred. In the midst, by the shattered fountain, grew the magnificent shrub, with its purple gems clustering all over it; they glowed in the air, and gleamed back again out of the depths of the pool, which thus seemed to overflow with colored radiance from the rich reflection that was steeped in it. At first, as we have said, the garden was a solitude. Soon, however,—as Giovanni had half hoped, half feared, would be the case,—a figure appeared beneath the antique sculptured portal, and came down between the rows of plants, inhaling their various perfumes as if she were one of those beings of old classic fable that lived upon sweet odors. On again beholding Beatrice, the young man was even startled to perceive how much her beauty exceeded his recollection of it; so brilliant, so vivid, was its character, that she glowed amid the sunlight, and, as Giovanni whispered to himself, positively illuminated the more shadowy intervals of the garden path. Her face being now more revealed than on the former occasion, he was struck by its expression of simplicity and sweetness—qualities that had not entered into his idea of her character, and which made him ask anew what manner of mortal she might be. Nor did he fail again to observe, or imagine, an analogy between the beautiful girl and the gorgeous shrub that hung its gemlike flowers over the fountain—a resemblance which Beatrice seemed to have indulged a fantastic humor in heightening, both by the arrangement of her dress and the selection of its hues.

Approaching the shrub, she threw open her arms, as with a passionate ardor, and drew its branches into an intimate embrace—so intimate that her features were hidden in its leafy bosom and her glistening ringlets all intermingled with the flowers.

"Give me thy breath, my sister," exclaimed Beatrice; "for I am faint with common air. And give me this flower of thine, which I separate with gentlest fingers from the stem and place it close beside my heart."

With these words the beautiful daughter of Rappaccini plucked one of the richest blossoms of the shrub, and was about to fasten it in her bosom. But now, unless Giovanni's draughts of wine had bewildered his senses, a singular incident occurred. A small orange-colored reptile, of the lizard or chameleon species, chanced to be creeping along the path, just at the feet of Beatrice. It appeared to Giovanni,—but, at the distance from which he gazed, he could scarcely have seen anything so minute,—it appeared to him, however, that a drop or two of moisture from the broken stem of the flower descended upon the lizard's head. For an instant the reptile contorted itself violently, and then lay motionless in the sunshine. Beatrice observed this remarkable phenomenon, and crossed herself, sadly,

[2] Lachryma Christi, a rich Neapolitan wine.

but without surprise; nor did she therefore hesitate to arrange the fatal flower in her bosom. There it blushed, and almost glimmered with the dazzling effect of a precious stone, adding to her dress and aspect the one appropriate charm which nothing else in the world could have supplied. But Giovanni, out of the shadow of his window, bent forward and shrank back, and murmured and trembled.

"Am I awake? Have I my senses?" said he to himself. "What is this being? Beautiful shall I call her, or inexpressibly terrible?"

Beatrice now strayed carelessly through the garden, approaching closer beneath Giovanni's window, so that he was compelled to thrust his head quite out of its concealment in order to gratify the intense and painful curiosity which she excited. At this moment there came a beautiful insect over the garden wall: it had, perhaps, wandered through the city, and found no flowers or verdure among those antique haunts of men until the heavy perfumes of Dr. Rappaccini's shrubs had lured it from afar. Without alighting on the flowers, this winged brightness seemed to be attracted by Beatrice, and lingered in the air and fluttered about her head. Now, here it could not be but that Giovanni Guasconti's eyes deceived him. Be that as it might, he fancied that, while Beatrice was gazing at the insect with childish delight, it grew faint and fell at her feet; its bright wings shivered; it was dead—from no cause that he could discern, unless it were the atmosphere of her breath. Again Beatrice crossed herself and sighed heavily as she bent over the dead insect.

An impulsive movement of Giovanni drew her eyes to the window. There she beheld the beautiful head of the young man—rather a Grecian than an Italian head, with fair, regular features, and a glistening of gold among his ringlets—gazing down upon her like a being that hovered in mid air. Scarcely knowing what he did, Giovanni threw down the bouquet which he had hitherto held in his hand.

"Signora," said he, "there are pure and healthful flowers. Wear them for the sake of Giovanni Guasconti."

"Thanks, signor," replied Beatrice, with her rich voice, that came forth as it were like a gush of music, and with a mirthful expression half childish and half womanlike. "I accept your gift, and would fain recompense it with this precious purple flower; but, if I toss it into the air, it will not reach you. So Signor Guasconti must even content himself with my thanks."

She lifted the bouquet from the ground, and then, as if inwardly ashamed at having stepped aside from her maidenly reserve to respond to a stranger's greeting, passed swiftly homeward through the garden. But few as the moments were, it seemed to Giovanni, when she was on the point of vanishing beneath the sculptured portal, that his beautiful bouquet was already beginning to wither in her grasp. It was an idle thought; there could be no possibility of distinguishing a faded flower from a fresh one at so great a distance.

For many days after this incident the young man avoided the window that looked into Dr. Rappaccini's garden, as if something ugly and monstrous would have blasted his eyesight had he been betrayed into a glance. He felt conscious of having put himself, to a certain extent, within the influence of an unintelligible power by the communication which he had opened with Beatrice. The wisest course would have been, if his heart were in any real danger, to quit his lodgings and Padua itself at once; the next wiser, to have accustomed himself, as far as possible, to the familiar and daylight view of Beatrice—thus bringing her rigidly and systematically within the limits of ordinary experience. Least of all, while avoiding her sight, ought Giovanni to have remained so near this extraordinary being that the proximity and possibility even of intercourse should give a kind of substance and reality to the wild vagaries which his imagination ran riot continually in producing. Guasconti had not a deep heart—or, at all events, its depths were not sounded now; but he had a quick fancy, and an ardent southern temperament, which rose every instant to a higher fever pitch. Whether or no Beatrice possessed those terrible attributes, that fatal breath, the affinity with those so beautiful and deadly flowers which were indicated by what Giovanni had witnessed, she had at least instilled a fierce and subtle poison into his system. It was not love, although her rich beauty was a madness to him; nor horror, even while he fancied her spirit to be imbued with the same baneful essence that seemed to pervade her physical frame; but a wild offspring of both love and horror that had each parent in it, and burned like one and shivered like the other. Giovanni knew not what to dread; still less did he know what to hope; yet hope and dread kept a continual warfare in his breast, alternately vanquishing one another and starting up afresh to renew the contest. Blessed are all simple emotions, be they dark or bright! It is the lurid intermixture of the two that produces the illuminating blaze of the infernal regions.

Sometimes he endeavored to assuage the fever of his spirit by a rapid walk through the streets of Padua or beyond its gates: his footsteps kept time with the throbbings of his brain, so that the walk was apt to accelerate itself to a race. One day he found himself arrested; his arm was seized by a portly personage, who had turned back on recognizing the young man and expended much breath in overtaking him.

"Signor Giovanni! Stay, my young friend!" cried

he. "Have you forgotten me? That might well be the case if I were as much altered as yourself."

It was Baglioni, whom Giovanni had avoided ever since their first meeting, from a doubt that the professor's sagacity would look too deeply into his secrets. Endeavoring to recover himself, he started forth wildly from his inner world into the outer one and spoke like a man in a dream.

"Yes; I am Giovanni Guasconti. You are Professor Pietro Baglioni. Now let me pass!"

"Not yet, not yet, Signor Giovanni Guasconti," said the professor, smiling, but at the same time scrutinizing the youth with an earnest glance. "What! did I grow up side by side with your father? and shall his son pass me like a stranger in these old streets of Padua? Stand still, Signor Giovanni; for we must have a word or two before we part."

"Speedily, then, most worshipful professor, speedily," said Giovanni, with feverish impatience. "Does not your worship see that I am in haste?"

Now, while he was speaking there came a man in black along the street, stooping and moving feebly like a person in inferior health. His face was all overspread with a most sickly and sallow hue, but yet so pervaded with an expression of piercing and active intellect that an observer might easily have overlooked the merely physical attributes and have seen only this wonderful energy. As he passed, this person exchanged a cold and distant salutation with Baglioni, but fixed his eyes upon Giovanni with an intentness that seemed to bring out whatever was within him worthy of notice. Nevertheless, there was a peculiar quietness in the look, as if taking merely a speculative, not human, interest in the young man.

"It is Dr. Rappaccini!" whispered the professor when the stranger had passed. "Has he ever seen your face before?"

"Not that I know," answered Giovanni starting at the name.

"He *has* seen you! he must have seen you!" said Baglioni, hastily. "For some purpose or other, this man of science is making a study of you. I know that look of his! It is the same that coldly illuminates his face as he bends over a bird, a mouse, or a butterfly, which, in pursuance of some experiment, he has killed by the perfume of a flower; a look as deep as Nature itself, but without Nature's warmth of love. Signor Giovanni, I will stake my life upon it, you are the subject of one of Rappaccini's experiments!"

"Will you make a fool of me?" cried Giovanni, passionately. "*That*, signor professor, were an untoward experiment."

"Patience! patience!" replied the imperturbable professor. "I tell thee, my poor Giovanni, that Rappaccini has a scientific interest in thee. Thou hast fallen into fearful hands! And the Signora Beatrice,—what part does she act in this mystery?"

But Guasconti, finding Baglioni's pertinacity intolerable, here broke away, and was gone before the professor could again seize his arm. He looked after the young man intently and shook his head.

"This must not be," said Baglioni to himself. "The youth is the son of my old friend, and shall not come to any harm from which the arcana of medical science can preserve him. Besides, it is too insufferable an impertinence in Rappaccini thus to snatch the lad out of my own hands, as I may say, and make use of him for his infernal experiments. This daughter of his! It shall be looked to. Perchance, most learned Rappaccini, I may foil you where you little dream of it!"

Meanwhile Giovanni had pursued a circuitous route, and at length found himself at the door of his lodgings. As he crossed the threshold he was met by old Lisabetta, who smirked and smiled, and was evidently desirous to attract his attention; vainly, however, as the ebullition of his feelings had momentarily subsided into a cold and dull vacuity. He turned his eyes full upon the withered face that was puckering itself into a smile, but seemed to behold it not. The old dame, therefore, laid her grasp upon his cloak.

"Signor! signor!" whispered she, still with a smile over the whole breadth of her visage, so that it looked not unlike a grotesque carving in wood, darkened by centuries. "Listen, signor! There is a private entrance into the garden!"

"What do you say?" exclaimed Giovanni, turning quickly about, as if an inanimate thing should start into feverish life. "A private entrance into Dr. Rappaccini's garden?"

"Hush! hush! not so loud!" whispered Lisabetta, putting her hand over his mouth. "Yes, into the worshipful doctor's garden, where you may see all his fine shrubbery. Many a young man in Padua would give gold to be admitted among those flowers."

Giovanni put a piece of gold into her hand.

"Show me the way," said he.

A surmise, probably excited by his conversation with Baglioni, crossed his mind, that this interposition of old Lisabetta might perchance be connected with the intrigue, whatever were its nature, in which the professor seemed to suppose that Dr. Rappaccini was involving him. But such a suspicion, though it disturbed Giovanni, was inadequate to restrain him. The instant that he was aware of the possibility of approaching Beatrice, it seemed an absolute necessity of his existence to do so. It mattered not whether she were angel or demon; he was irrevocably within her sphere, and must obey the law that whirled him onward, in ever-lessening circles, towards a result which he did not attempt to foreshadow; and yet, strange to say, there came across him a sudden doubt whether this intense interest on his part were not delusory; whether it were really of so deep and positive a nature as to justify him in now thrusting himself into an incalculable position; whether it were not merely the fantasy of a young man's brain, only slightly or not at all connected with his heart.

He paused, hesitated, turned half about, but again went on. His withered guide led him along several obscure passages, and finally undid a door, through which, as it was opened, there came the sight and sound of rustling leaves, with the broken sunshine glimmering among them. Giovanni stepped forth, and, forcing himself through the entanglement of a shrub that wreathed its tendrils over the hidden entrance, stood beneath his own window in the open area of Dr. Rappaccini's garden.

How often is it the case that, when impossibilities have come to pass and dreams have condensed their misty substance into tangible realities, we find ourselves calm, and even coldly self-possessed, amid circumstances which it would have been a delirium of joy or agony to anticipate! Fate delights to thwart us thus. Passion will choose his own time to rush upon the scene, and lingers sluggishly behind when an appropriate adjustment of events would seem to summon his appearance. So was it now with Giovanni. Day after day his pulses had throbbed with feverish blood at the improbable idea of an interview with Beatrice, and of standing with her, face to face, in this very garden, basking in the Oriental sunshine of her beauty, and snatching from her full gaze the mystery which he deemed the riddle of his own existence. But now there was a singular and untimely equanimity within his breast. He threw a glance around the garden to discover if Beatrice or her father were present, and, perceiving that he was alone, began a critical observation of the plants.

The aspect of one and all of them dissatisfied him; their gorgeousness seemed fierce, passionate, and even unnatural. There was hardly an individual shrub which a wanderer, straying by himself through a forest, would not have been startled to find growing wild, as if an unearthly face had glared at him out of the thicket. Several also would have shocked a delicate instinct by an appearance of artificialness indicating that there had been such commixture, and, as it were, adultery, of various vegetable species, that the production was no longer of God's making, but the monstrous offspring of man's depraved fancy, glowing with only an evil mockery of beauty. They were probably the result of experiment, which in one or two cases had succeeded in mingling plants individually lovely into a compound possessing the questionable and ominous character that distinguished the whole growth of the garden. In fine, Giovanni recognized but two or three plants in the collection, and those of a kind that he well knew to be poisonous. While busy with these contemplations he heard the rustling of a silken garment, and, turning, beheld Beatrice emerging from beneath the sculptured portal.

Giovanni had not considered with himself what should be his deportment; whether he should apologize for his intrusion into the garden, or assume that he was there with the privity at least, if not by the desire, of Dr. Rappaccini or his daughter; but Beatrice's manner placed him at his ease, though leaving him still in doubt by what agency he had gained admittance. She came lightly along the path and met him near the broken fountain. There was surprise in her face, but brightened by a simple and kind expression of pleasure.

"You are a connoisseur in flowers, signor," said Beatrice, with a smile, alluding to the bouquet which he had flung her from the window "It is no marvel, therefore, if the sight of my father's rare collection has tempted you to take a nearer view. If he were here, he could tell you many strange and interesting facts as to the nature and habits of these shrubs; for he has spent a lifetime in such studies, and this garden is his world."

"And yourself, lady," observed Giovanni, "if fame says true,—you likewise are deeply skilled in the virtues indicated by these rich blossoms and these spicy perfumes. Would you deign to be my instructress, I should prove an apter scholar than if taught by Signor Rappaccini himself."

"Are there such idle rumors?" asked Beatrice, with the music of a pleasant laugh. "Do people say that I am skilled in my father's science of plants? What a jest is there! No; though I have grown up among these flowers, I know no more of them than their hues and perfume; and sometimes methinks I would fain rid myself of even that small knowledge. There are many flowers here, and those not the least brilliant, that shock and offend me when they meet my eye. But pray, signor, do not believe these stories about my science. Believe nothing of me save what you see with your own eyes."

"And must I believe all that I have seen with my own eyes?" asked Giovanni, pointedly, while the recollection of former scenes made him shrink. "No, signora; you demand too little of me. Bid me believe nothing save what comes from your own lips."

It would appear that Beatrice understood him. There came a deep flush to her cheek; but she looked full into Giovanni's eyes, and responded to his gaze of uneasy suspicion with a queenlike haughtiness.

"I do so bid you, signor," she replied. "Forget whatever you may have fancied in regard to me. If true to the outward senses, still it may be false in its essence; but the words of Beatrice Rappaccini's lips are true from the depths of the heart outward. Those you may believe."

A fervor glowed in her whole aspect and beamed upon Giovanni's consciousness like the light of truth itself; but while she spoke there was a fragrance in the atmosphere around her, rich and delightful, though evanescent, yet which the young man, from an indefinable reluctance, scarcely dared to draw into his lungs. It might be the odor of the flowers. Could it be Beatrice's breath which thus embalmed her words with a strange richness, as if by steeping them in her heart? A faintness passed like a shadow over Giovanni and flitted away; he seemed to gaze through the beautiful girl's eyes into her transparent soul, and felt no more doubt or fear.

The tinge of passion that had colored Beatrice's manner vanished; she became gay, and appeared to derive a pure delight from her communion with the youth not unlike what the maiden of a lonely island might have felt conversing with a voyager from the civilized world. Evidently her experience of life had been confined within the limits of that garden. She talked now about matters as simple as the daylight or summer clouds, and now asked questions in reference to the city, or Giovanni's distant home, his friends, his mother, and his sisters—questions indicating such seclusion, and such lack of familiarity with modes and forms, that Giovanni responded as if to an infant. Her spirit gushed out before him like a fresh rill that was just catching its first glimpse of the sunlight and wondering at the reflections of earth and sky which were flung into its bosom. There came thoughts, too, from a deep source, and fantasies of a gemlike brilliancy, as if diamonds and rubies sparkled upward among the bubbles of the fountain. Ever and anon there gleamed across the young man's mind a sense of wonder that he should be walking side by side with the being who had so wrought upon his imagination, whom he had idealized in such hues of terror, in whom he had positively witnessed such manifestations of dreadful attributes—that he should be conversing with Beatrice like a brother, and should find her so human and so maidenlike. But such reflections were only momentary; the effect of her character was too real not to make itself familiar at once.

In this free intercourse they had strayed through the garden, and now, after many turns among its avenues, were come to the shattered fountain, beside which grew the magnificent shrub, with its treasury of glowing blossoms. A fragrance was diffused from it which Giovanni recognized as identical with that which he had attributed to Beatrice's breath, but incomparably more powerful. As her eyes fell upon it, Giovanni beheld her press her hand to her bosom as if her heart were throbbing suddenly and painfully.

"For the first time in my life," murmured she, addressing the shrub, "I had forgotten thee."

"I remember, signora," said Giovanni, "that you once promised to reward me with one of these living gems for the bouquet which I had the happy boldness to fling to your feet. Permit me now to pluck it as a memorial of this interview."

He made a step towards the shrub with extended hand; but Beatrice darted forward, uttering a shriek that went through his heart like a dagger. She caught his hand and drew it back with the whole force of her slender figure. Giovanni felt her touch thrilling through his fibres.

"Touch it not!" exclaimed she, in a voice of agony. "Not for thy life! It is fatal!"

Then, hiding her face, she fled from him and vanished beneath the sculptured portal. As Giovanni followed her with his eyes, he beheld the emaciated figure and pale intelligence of Dr. Rappaccini, who had been watching the scene, he knew not how long, within the shadow of the entrance.

No sooner was Guasconti alone in his chamber than the image of Beatrice came back to his passionate musings, invested with all the witchery that had been gathering around it ever since his first glimpse of her, and now likewise imbued with a tender warmth of girlish womanhood. She was human; her nature was endowed with all gentle and feminine qualities; she was worthiest to be worshipped; she was capable, surely, on her part, of the height and heroism of love. Those tokens which he had hitherto considered as proofs of a frightful peculiarity in her physical and moral system were now either forgotten or by the subtle sophistry of passion transmitted into a golden crown of enchantment, rendering Beatrice the more admirable by so much as she was the more unique. Whatever had looked ugly was now beautiful; or, if incapable of such a change, it stole away and hid itself among those shapeless half ideas which throng the dim region beyond the daylight of our perfect consciousness. Thus did he spend the night, nor fell asleep until the dawn had begun to awake the slumbering flowers in Dr. Rappaccini's garden, whither Giovanni's dreams doubtless led him. Up rose the sun in his due season, and, flinging his beams upon the young man's eyelids, awoke him to a sense of pain. When thoroughly aroused, he became sensible of a burning and tingling agony in his hand—in his right hand—the very hand which Beatrice had grasped in her own when he was on the point of plucking one of the gemlike flowers. On the back of that hand there was now a purple print like that of four small fingers, and the likeness of a slender thumb upon his wrist.

O, how stubbornly does love,—or even that cunning semblance of love which flourishes in the imagination, but strikes no depth of root into the heart,—how stubbornly does it hold its faith until the moment comes when it is doomed to vanish into thin mist! Giovanni wrapped a handkerchief about his hand and wondered what evil thing had stung him, and soon forgot his pain in a reverie of Beatrice.

After the first interview, a second was in the inevitable course of what we call fate. A third; a fourth; and a meeting with Beatrice in the garden was no longer an incident in Giovanni's daily life, but the whole space in which he might be said to live; for the anticipation and memory of that ecstatic hour made up the remainder. Nor was it otherwise with the daughter of Rappaccini. She watched for the youth's appearance and flew to his side with confidence as unreserved as if they had been playmates from early infancy—as if they were such playmates still. If, by any unwonted chance, he failed to come at the appointed moment, she stood beneath the window and sent up the rich sweetness of her tones to float around him in his chamber and echo and reverberate throughout his heart: "Giovanni! Giovanni! Why tarriest thou? Come down!" And down he hastened into that Eden of poisonous flowers.

But, with all this intimate familiarity, there was still a reserve in Beatrice's demeanor, so rigidly and invariably sustained that the idea of infringing it scarcely occurred to his imagination. By all appreciable signs, they loved; they had looked love with eyes that conveyed the holy secret from the depths of one soul into the depths of the other, as if it were too sacred to be whispered by the way; they had even spoken love in those gushes of passion when their spirits darted forth in articulated breath like tongues of long hidden flame; and yet there had been no seal of lips, no clasp of hands, nor any slightest caress such as love claims and hallows. He had never touched one of the gleaming ringlets of her hair; her garment—so marked was the physical barrier between them—had never been waved against him by a breeze. On the few occasions when Giovanni had seemed tempted to overstep the limit, Beatrice grew so sad, so stern, and withal wore such a look of desolate separation, shuddering at itself, that not a spoken word was requisite to repel him. At such times he was startled at the horrible suspicions that rose, monster-like, out of the caverns of his heart and stared him in the face; his love grew thin and faint as the morning mist; his doubts alone had substance. But, when Beatrice's face brightened again after the momentary shadow, she was transformed at once from the mysterious, questionable being whom he had watched with so much awe and horror; she was now the beautiful and unsophisticated girl whom he felt that his spirit knew with a certainty beyond all other knowledge.

A considerable time had now passed since Giovanni's last meeting with Baglioni. One morning, however, he was disagreeably surprised by a visit from the professor, whom he had scarcely thought of for whole weeks, and would willingly have forgotten still longer. Given up, as he had long been to a pervading excitement, he could tolerate no companions except upon condition of their perfect sympathy with his present state of feeling. Such sympathy was not to be expected from Professor Baglioni.

The visitor chatted carelessly for a few moments about the gossip of the city and the university, and then took up another topic.

"I have been reading an old classic author lately," said he, "and met with a story that strangely interested me. Possibly you may remember it. It is of an Indian prince, who sent a beautiful woman as a present to Alexander the Great. She was as lovely as the dawn and gorgeous as the sunset; but what especially distinguished her was a certain rich perfume in her breath—richer than a garden of Persian roses. Alexander, as was natural to a youthful conqueror, fell in love at first sight with this magnificent stranger; but a certain sage physician, happening to be present, discovered a terrible secret in regard to her."

"And what was that?" asked Giovanni, turning his eyes downward to avoid those of the professor.

"That this lovely woman," continued Baglioni, with emphasis, "had been nourished with poisons from her birth upward, until her whole nature was so imbued with them that she herself had become the deadliest poison in existence. Poison was her element of life. With that rich perfume of her breath she blasted the very air. Her love would have been poison—her embrace death. Is not this a marvellous tale?"

"A childish fable," answered Giovanni, nervously starting from his chair. "I marvel how your worship finds time to read such nonsense among your graver studies."

"By the by," said the professor, looking uneasily about him, "what singular fragrance is this in your apartment? Is it the perfume of your gloves? It is faint, but delicious; and yet, after all, by no means agreeable. Were I to breathe it long, methinks it would make me ill. It is like the breath of a flower; but I see no flowers in the chamber."

"Nor are there any," replied Giovanni, who had turned pale as the professor spoke; "nor, I think, is there any fragrance except in your worship's imagination. Odors, being a sort of element combined of the sensual and the spiritual, are apt to deceive us in this manner. The recollection of a perfume, the bare idea of it, may easily be mistaken for a present reality."

"Ay; but my sober imagination does not often play such tricks," said Baglioni; "and, were I to fancy any kind of odor, it would be that of some vile apothecary drug, wherewith my fingers are likely enough to be imbued. Our worshipful friend Rappaccini, as I have heard, tinctures his medicaments with odors richer than those of Araby. Doubtless, likewise, the fair and learned Signora Beatrice would minister to her patients with draughts as sweet as a maiden's breath; but woe to him that sips them!"

Giovanni's face evinced many contending emotions. The tone in which the professor alluded to the pure and lovely daughter of Rappaccini was a torture to his soul; and yet the intimation of a view of her character, opposite to his own, gave instantaneous distinctness to a thousand dim suspicions, which now grinned at him like so many demons. But he strove hard to quell them and to respond to Baglioni with a true lover's perfect faith.

"Signor professor," said he, "you were my father's friend; perchance, too, it is your purpose to act a friendly part towards his son. I would fain feel nothing towards you save respect and deference; but I pray you to observe, signor, that there is one subject on which we must not speak. You know not the Signora Beatrice. You cannot, therefore, estimate the wrong—the blasphemy, I may even say—that is offered to her character by a light or injurious word."

"Giovanni! my poor Giovanni!" answered the professor, with a calm expression of pity, "I know this wretched girl far better than yourself. You shall hear the truth in respect to the poisoner Rappaccini and his poisonous daughter; yes, poisonous as she is beautiful. Listen; for, even should you do violence to my gray hairs, it shall not silence me. That old fable of the Indian woman has become a truth by the deep and deadly science of Rappaccini and in the person of the lovely Beatrice."

Giovanni groaned and hid his face.

"Her father," continued Baglioni, "was not restrained by natural affection from offering up his child in this horrible manner as the victim of his insane zeal for science; for, let us do him justice, he is as true a man of science as ever distilled his own heart in an alembic. What, then, will be your fate? Beyond a doubt you are selected as the material of some new experiment. Perhaps the result is to be death; perhaps a fate more awful still. Rappaccini, with what he calls the interest of science before his eyes, will hesitate at nothing."

"It is a dream," muttered Giovanni to himself; "surely it is a dream."

"But," resumed the professor, "be of good cheer, son of my friend. It is not yet too late for the rescue. Possibly we may even succeed in bringing back this miserable child within the limits of ordinary nature, from which her father's madness has estranged her. Behold this little silver vase! It was wrought by the hands of the renowned Benvenuto Cellini, and is well worthy to be a love gift to the fairest dame in Italy. But its contents are invaluable. One little sip of this antidote would have rendered the most virulent poisons of the Borgias innocuous. Doubt not that it will be as efficacious against those of Rappaccini. Bestow the vase, and the precious liquid within it, on your Beatrice, and hopefully await the result."

Baglioni laid a small, exquisitely wrought silver vial on the table and withdrew, leaving what he had said to produce its effects upon the young man's mind.

"We will thwart Rappaccini yet," thought he, chuckling to himself, as he descended the stairs; "but, let us confess the truth of him, he is a wonderful man—a wonderful man indeed; a vile empiric, however, in his practice, and therefore not to be tolerated by those who respect the good old rules of the medical profession."

Throughout Giovanni's whole acquaintance with Beatrice, he had occasionally, as we have said, been haunted by dark surmises as to her character; yet so thoroughly had she made herself felt by him as a simple, natural, most affectionate, and guileless creature, that the image now held up by Professor Baglioni looked as strange and incredible as if it were not in accordance with his own original conception. True, there were ugly recollections connected with his first glimpses of the beautiful girl; he could not quite forget the bouquet that withered in her grasp, and the insect that perished amid the sunny air, by no ostensible agency save the fragrance of her breath. These incidents, however, dissolving in the pure light of her character, had no longer the efficacy of facts, but were acknowledged as mistaken fantasies, by whatever testimony of the senses they might appear to be substantiated. There is something truer and more real than what we can see with the eyes and touch with the finger. On such better evidence had Giovanni founded his confidence in Beatrice, though rather by the necessary force of her high attributes than by any deep and generous faith on his part. But now his spirit was incapable of sustaining itself at the height to which the early enthusiasm of passion had exalted it; he fell down, grovelling among earthly doubts, and defiled therewith the pure whiteness of Beatrice's image. Not that he gave her up; he did but distrust. He resolved to institute some decisive test that should satisfy him, once for all, whether there were those dreadful peculiarities in her physical nature which could not be supposed to exist without some corresponding monstrosity of soul. His eyes, gazing down afar, might have deceived him as to the lizard, the insect, and the flowers; but if he could witness, at the distance of a few paces, the sudden blight of one fresh and healthful flower in Beatrice's hand, there would be room for no further question. With this idea he hastened to the florist's and purchased a bouquet that was still gemmed with the morning dewdrops.

It was now the customary hour of his daily interview with Beatrice. Before descending into the garden, Giovanni failed not to look at his figure in the mirror—a vanity to be expected in a beautiful young man, yet, as displaying itself at that troubled and feverish moment, the token of a certain shallowness of feeling and insincerity of character. He did gaze, however, and said to himself that his features had never before possessed so rich a grace, nor his eyes such vivacity, nor his cheeks so warm a hue of superabundant life.

"At least," thought he, "her poison has not yet insinuated itself into my system. I am no flower to perish in her grasp."

With that thought he turned his eyes on the bouquet, which he had never once laid aside from his hand. A thrill of indefinable horror shot through his frame on perceiving that those dewy flowers were already beginning to droop; they wore the aspect of things that had been fresh and lovely yesterday. Giovanni grew white as marble, and stood motionless before the mirror, staring at his own reflection there as at the likeness of something frightful. He remembered Baglioni's remark about the fragrance that seemed to pervade the chamber. It must have been the poison in his breath! Then he shuddered—shuddered at himself. Recovering from his stupor, he began to watch with curious eye a spider that was busily at work hanging its web from the antique cornice of the apartment, crossing and recrossing the artful system of interwoven lines—as vigorous and active a spider as ever dangled from an old ceiling. Giovanni bent towards the insect, and emitted a deep, long breath. The spider suddenly ceased its toil; the web vibrated with a tremor originating in the body of the small artisan. Again Giovanni sent forth a breath, deeper, longer, and imbued with a venomous feeling out of his heart: he knew not whether he were wicked, or only desperate. The spider made a convulsive gripe with his limbs and hung dead across the window.

"Accursed! accursed!" muttered Giovanni, addressing himself. "Hast thou grown so poisonous that this deadly insect perishes by thy breath?"

At that moment a rich, sweet voice came floating up from the garden.

"Giovanni! Giovanni! It is past the hour! Why tarriest thou? Come down!"

"Yes," muttered Giovanni again. "She is the only being whom my breath may not slay! Would that it might!"

He rushed down, and in an instant was standing before the bright and loving eyes of Beatrice. A moment ago his wrath and despair had been so fierce that he could have desired nothing so much as to wither her by a glance; but with her actual presence there came influences which had too real an existence to be at once shaken off; recollections of the delicate and benign power of her feminine nature, which had so often enveloped him in a religious calm; recollections of many a holy and passionate outgush of her heart, when the pure fountain had been unsealed from its depths and made visible in its transparency to his mental eye; recollections which, had Giovanni known how to estimate them, would have assured him that all this ugly mystery was but an earthly illusion, and that, whatever mist of evil might seem to have gathered over her, the real Beatrice was a heavenly angel. Incapable as he was of such high faith, still her presence had not utterly lost its magic. Giovanni's rage was quelled into an aspect of sullen insensibility. Beatrice, with a quick spiritual sense, immediately felt that there was a gulf of blackness between them which neither he nor she could pass. They walked on together, sad and silent, and came thus to the marble fountain and to its pool of water on the ground, in the midst of which grew the shrub that bore gemlike blossoms. Giovanni was affrighted at the eager enjoyment—the appetite, as it were—with which he found himself inhaling the fragrance of the flowers.

"Beatrice," asked he, abruptly, "whence came this shrub?"

"My father created it," answered she, with simplicity.

"Created it! created it!" repeated Giovanni. "What mean you, Beatrice?"

"He is a man fearfully acquainted with the secrets of Nature," replied Beatrice; "and at the hour when I first drew breath, this plant sprang from the soil, the offspring of his science, of his intellect, while I was but his earthly child. Approach it not!" continued she, observing with terror that Giovanni was drawing nearer to the shrub. "It has qualities that you little dream of. But I, dearest Giovanni,—I grew up and blossomed with the plant and was nourished with its breath. It was my sister, and I loved it with a human affection; for, alas!—hast thou not suspected it?—there was an awful doom."

Here Giovanni frowned so darkly upon her that Beatrice paused and trembled. But her faith in his tenderness reassured her, and made her blush that she had doubted for an instant.

"There was an awful doom," she continued, "the effect of my father's fatal love of science, which estranged me from all society of my kind. Until Heaven sent thee, dearest Giovanni, O, how lonely was thy poor Beatrice!"

"Was it a hard doom?" asked Giovanni fixing his eyes upon her.

"Only of late have I known how hard it was," answered she, tenderly. "O, yes; but my heart was torpid, and therefore quiet."

Giovanni's rage broke forth from his sullen gloom like a lightning flash out of a dark cloud.

"Accursed one!" cried he, with venomous scorn and anger. "And, finding thy solitude wearisome, thou has severed me likewise from all the warmth of life and enticed me into thy region of unspeakable horror!"

"Giovanni!" exclaimed Beatrice, turning her large bright eyes upon his face. The force of his words had not found its way into her mind; she was merely thunderstruck.

"Yes, poisonous thing!" repeated Giovanni, beside himself with passion. "Thou hast done it! Thou hast blasted me! Thou hast filled my veins with poison! Thou hast made me as hateful, as ugly, as loathsome and deadly a creature as thyself—a world's wonder of hideous monstrosity! Now, if our breath be happily as fatal to ourselves as to all others, let us join our lips in one kiss of unutterable hatred, and so die!"

"What has befallen me?" murmured Beatrice, with a low moan out of her heart. "Holy Virgin, pity me, a poor heart-broken child!"

"Thou,—dost thou pray?" cried Giovanni, still with the same fiendish scorn. "Thy very prayers, as they come from thy lips, taint the atmosphere with death. Yes, yes; let us pray! Let us to church and dip our fingers in the holy water at the portal! They that come after us will perish as by a pestilence! Let us sign crosses in the air! It will be scattering curses abroad in the likeness of holy symbols!"

"Giovanni," said Beatrice, calmly, for her grief was beyond passion, "why dost thou join thyself with me thus in those terrible words? I, it is true, am the horrible thing thou namest me. But thou,—what hast thou to do, save with one other shudder at my hideous misery to go forth out of the garden and mingle with thy race, and forget that there ever crawled on earth such a monster as poor Beatrice?"

"Dost thou pretend ignorance?" asked Giovanni, scowling upon her. "Behold! this power have I gained from the pure daughter of Rappaccini."

There was a swarm of summer insects flitting through the air in search of the food promised by the flower odors of the fatal garden. They circled round Giovanni's head, and were evidently attracted towards him by the same influence which had drawn them for an instant within the sphere of several of the shrubs. He sent forth a breath among them, and smiled bitterly at Beatrice as at least a score of the insects fell dead upon the ground.

"I see it! I see it!" shrieked Beatrice. "It is my father's fatal science! No, no, Giovanni; it was not I! Never! never! I dreamed only to love thee and be with thee a little time, and so to let thee pass away, leaving but thine image in mine heart; for, Giovanni, believe it, though my body be nourished with poison, my spirit is God's creature, and craves love as its daily food. But my father,—he has united us in this fearful sympathy. Yes; spurn me, tread upon me, kill me! O, what is death after such words as thine? But it was not I. Not for a world of bliss would I have done it."

Giovanni's passion had exhausted itself in its outburst from his lips. There now came across him a sense, mournful, and not without tenderness, of the intimate and peculiar relationship between Beatrice and himself. They stood, as it were, in an utter solitude, which would be made none the less solitary by the densest throng of human life. Ought not, then, the desert of humanity around them to press this insulated pair closer together? If they should be cruel to one another, who was there to be kind to them? Besides, thought Giovanni, might there not still be a hope of his returning within the limits of ordinary nature, and leading Beatrice, the redeemed Beatrice, by the hand? O, weak, and selfish, and unworthy spirit, that could dream of an earthly union and earthly happiness as possible, after such deep love had been so bitterly wronged as was Beatrice's love by Giovanni's blighting words! No, no; there could be no such hope. She must pass heavily, with that broken heart, across the borders of Time—she must bathe her hurts in some fount of paradise, and forget her grief in the light of immortality, and *there* be well.

But Giovanni did not know it.

"Dear Beatrice," said he approaching her, while she shrank as always at his approach, but now with a different impulse, "dearest Beatrice, our fate is not yet so desperate. Behold! there is a medicine, potent as a wise physician has assured me, and almost divine in its efficacy. It is composed of ingredients the most opposite to those by which thy awful father has brought this calamity upon thee and me. It is distilled of blessed herbs. Shall we not quaff it together, and thus be purified from evil?"

"Give it me!" said Beatrice, extending her hand to receive the little silver vial which Giovanni took from his bosom. She added, with a peculiar emphasis, "I will drink; but do thou await the result."

She put Baglioni's antidote to her lips; and, at the same moment, the figure of Rappaccini emerged from the portal and came slowly towards the marble fountain. As he drew near, the pale man of science seemed to gaze with a triumphant expression at the beautiful youth and maiden, as might an artist who should spend his life in achieving a picture or a group of statuary and finally be satisfied with his success. He paused; his bent form grew erect with conscious power; he spread out his hands over them in the attitude of a father imploring a blessing upon his children; but those were the same hands that had thrown poison into the stream of their lives. Giovanni trembled. Beatrice shuddered nervously, and pressed her hand upon her heart.

"My daughter," said Rappaccini, "thou art no longer lonely in the world. Pluck one of those precious gems from thy sister shrub and bid thy bridegroom wear it in his bosom. It will not harm him now. My science and the sympathy between thee and him have so wrought within his system that he now stands apart from common men, as thou dost, daughter of my pride and triumph, from ordinary women. Pass on, then, through the world, most dear to one another and dreadful to all besides!"

"My father," said Beatrice, feebly,—and still as she spoke she kept her hand upon her heart,—"wherefore didst thou inflict this miserable doom upon thy child?"

"Miserable!" exclaimed Rappaccini. "What mean you, foolish girl? Dost thou deem it misery to be endowed with marvelous gifts against which no power nor strength could avail an enemy—misery, to be able to quell the mightiest with a breath—misery, to be as terrible as thou art beautiful? Wouldst thou, then, have preferred the condition of a weak woman, exposed to all evil and capable of none?"

"I would fain have been loved, not feared," murmured Beatrice, sinking down upon the ground. "But now it matters not. I am going, father, where the evil which thou hast striven to mingle with my being will pass away like a dream—like the fragrance of these poisonous flowers, which will no longer taint my breath among the flowers of Eden. Farewell, Giovanni! Thy words of hatred are like lead within my heart; but they, too, will fall away as I ascend. O, was there not, from the first, more poison in thy nature than in mine?"

To Beatrice,—so radically had her earthly part been wrought upon by Rappaccini's skill,—as poison had been life, so the powerful antidote was death; and thus the poor victim of man's ingenuity and of thwarted nature, and of the fatality that attends all such efforts of perverted wisdom, perished there, at the feet of her father and Giovanni. Just at that moment Professor Pietro Baglioni looked forth from the window, and called loudly, in a tone of triumph mixed with horror, to the thunderstricken man of science,—

"Rappaccini! Rappaccini! and is *this* the upshot of your experiment!"

1844

Ethan Brand

A Chapter from an Abortive Romance

The idea of an Unpardonable Sin, the theme of this story, goes back to the New Testament: "He that shall blaspheme against the Holy Ghost hath never forgiveness, but is in danger of eternal damnation." (Mark iii. 28-29.)

The immediate germ of Hawthorne's story may be found in his notebooks, 1844: "The Unpardonable Sin might consist in a want of love and reverence for the Human Soul; in consequence of which the investigator pried into its dark depths, not with a hope or purpose of making it better, but from a cold philosophical curiosity—content that it should be wicked in whatever kind or degree, and only desiring to study it out. Would not this, in other words, be a separation of the intellect from the heart?" Another notebook entry reads: "The search of an investigator for the Unpardonable Sin—he at last finds it in his own heart and practice."

As Hawthorne conceives of human nature, a man should, ideally, maintain a balance between intellect and feeling. Ethan Brand (like Dr. Rappaccini) has long since lost this balance. His mind has been developed to the highest point; his heart has contracted, hardened, turned to stone. Intellectual pride and loss of human feeling have brought him to a bleak and terrible solitude, to alienation alike from his fellow human beings, Mother Earth, and God—a solitude signed and sealed in his final dramatic act.

Text: From the first American edition of *The Snow-Image and Other Twice-Told Tales* (Boston, 1852).

Bartram the lime-burner, a rough, heavy-looking man, begrimed with charcoal, sat watching his kiln, at nightfall, while his little son played at building houses with the scattered fragments of marble, when, on the hill-side below them, they heard a roar of laughter, not mirthful, but slow, and even solemn, like a wind shaking the boughs of the forest.

"Father, what is that?" asked the little boy, leaving his play, and pressing betwixt his father's knees.

"O, some drunken man, I suppose," answered the lime-burner; "some merry fellow from the bar-room in the village, who dared not laugh loud enough within doors, lest he should blow the roof of the house off. So here he is, shaking his jolly sides at the foot of Graylock."[1]

"But, father," said the child, more sensitive than the obtuse, middle-aged clown, "he does not laugh like a man that is glad. So the noise frightens me!"

"Don't be a fool, child!" cried his father, gruffly. "You will never make a man, I do believe; there is too much of your mother in you. I have known the rustling of a leaf startle you. Hark! Here comes the merry fellow, now. You shall see that there is no harm in him."

Bartram and his little son, while they were talking thus, sat watching the same lime-kiln that had been the scene of Ethan Brand's solitary and meditative life, before he began his search for the Unpardonable Sin. Many years, as we have seen, had now elapsed, since that portentous night when the IDEA was first developed. The kiln, however, on the mountain-side, stood unimpaired, and was in nothing changed since he had thrown his dark thoughts into the intense glow of its furnace, and melted them, as it were, into the one thought that took possession of his life. It was a rude, round, tower-like structure, about twenty feet high, heavily built of rough stones, and with a hillock of earth heaped about the larger part of its circumference; so that the blocks and fragments of marble might be drawn by cart-loads, and thrown in at the top. There was an opening at the bottom of the tower, like an oven-mouth, but large enough to admit a man in a stooping posture, and provided with a massive iron door. With the smoke and jets of flame issuing from the chinks and crevices of this door, which seemed to give admittance into the hill-side, it resembled nothing so much as the private entrance to the infernal regions, which the shepherds of the Delectable Mountains[2] were accustomed to show to pilgrims.

There are many such lime-kilns in that tract of country, for the purpose of burning the white marble which composes a large part of the substance of the hills. Some of them, built years ago, and long deserted, with weeds growing in the vacant round of the interior, which is open to the sky, and grass and wild-flowers rooting themselves in the chinks of the stones, look already like relics of antiquity, and may yet be overspread with the lichens of centuries to come. Others, where the lime-burner still feeds his daily and night-long fire, afford points of interest to the wanderer among the hills, who seats himself on a log of wood or a fragment of marble, to hold a chat with the solitary man. It is a lonesome, and, when the character is inclined to thought, may be an intensely thoughtful occupation; as it proved in the case of Ethan Brand, who had mused to such strange purpose, in days gone by, while the fire in this very kiln was burning.

The man who now watched the fire was of a different order, and troubled himself with no thoughts save the very few that were requisite to his business. At frequent intervals, he flung back the clashing weight of the iron door, and, turning his face from the insufferable glare, thrust in huge logs of oak, or stirred the immense brands with a long pole. Within the furnace were seen the curling and riotous flames, and the burning marble, almost molten with the intensity of heat; while without, the reflection of the fire quivered on the dark intricacy of the surrounding forest, and showed in the foreground a bright and ruddy little picture of the hut, the spring beside its door, the athletic and coal-begrimed figure of the lime-burner, and the half-frightened child, shrinking into the protection of his father's shadow. And when again the iron door was closed, then reappeared the tender light of the half-full moon, which vainly strove to trace out the indistinct shapes of the neighboring mountains; and, in the upper sky, there was a flitting congregation of clouds, still faintly tinged with the rosy sunset, though thus far down into the valley the sunshine had vanished long and long ago.

The little boy now crept still closer to his father, as footsteps were heard ascending the hill-side, and a human form thrust aside the bushes that clustered beneath the trees.

"Halloo! who is it?" cried the lime-burner, vexed at his son's timidity, yet half infected by it. "Come forward, and show yourself, like a man, or I'll fling this chunk of marble at your head!"

"You offer me a rough welcome," said a gloomy voice, as the unknown man drew nigh. "Yet I neither claim nor desire a kinder one, even at my own fireside."

To obtain a distincter view, Bartram threw open the iron door of the kiln, whence immediately issued a gush of fierce light, that smote full upon the stranger's face and figure. To a careless eye there appeared nothing very remarkable in his aspect, which was that of a man in a coarse, brown, country-made suit of clothes, tall and thin, with the staff and heavy

[1] Mt. Greylock in the Berkshires; the highest point in Massachusetts.

[2] An allusion to the Delectable Mountains of John Bunyan's *The Pilgrim's Progress.*

shoes of a wayfarer. As he advanced, he fixed his eyes—which were very bright—intently upon the brightness of the furnace, as if he beheld, or expected to behold, some object worthy of note within it.

"Good evening, stranger," said the lime-burner; "whence come you, so late in the day?"

"I come from my search," answered the wayfarer; "for, at last, it is finished."

"Drunk!—or crazy!" muttered Bartram to himself. "I shall have trouble with the fellow. The sooner I drive him away, the better."

The little boy, all in a tremble, whispered to his father, and begged him to shut the door of the kiln, so that there might not be so much light; for that there was something in the man's face which he was afraid to look at, yet could not look away from. And, indeed, even the lime-burner's dull and torpid sense began to be impressed by an indescribable something in that thin, rugged, thoughtful visage, with the grizzled hair hanging wildly about it, and those deeply-sunken eyes, which gleamed like fires within the entrance of a mysterious cavern. But, as he closed the door, the stranger turned towards him, and spoke in a quiet, familiar way, that made Bartram feel as if he were a sane and sensible man, after all.

"Your task draws to an end, I see," said he. "This marble has already been burning three days. A few hours more will convert the stone to lime."

"Why, who are you?" exclaimed the lime-burner. "You seem as well acquainted with my business as I am myself."

"And well I may be," said the stranger; "for I followed the same craft many a long year, and here, too, on this very spot. But you are a newcomer in these parts. Did you never hear of Ethan Brand?"

"The man that went in search of the Unpardonable Sin?" asked Bartram, with a laugh.

"The same," answered the stranger. "He has found what he sought, and therefore he comes back again."

"What! then you are Ethan Brand himself?" cried the lime-burner, in amazement. "I am a newcomer here, as you say, and they call it eighteen years since you left the foot of Graylock. But, I can tell you, the good folks still talk about Ethan Brand, in the village yonder, and what a strange errand took him away from his lime-kiln. Well, and so you have found the Unpardonable Sin?"

"Even so!" said the stranger, calmly.

"If the question is a fair one," proceeded Bartram, "where might it be?"

Ethan Brand laid his finger on his own heart.

"Here!" replied he.

And then, without mirth in his countenance, but as if moved by an involuntary recognition of the infinite absurdity of seeking throughout the world for what was the closest of all things to himself, and looking into every heart, save his own, for what was hidden in no other breast, he broke into a laugh of scorn. It was the same slow, heavy laugh, that had almost appalled the lime-burner when it heralded the wayfarer's approach.

The solitary mountain-side was made dismal by it. Laughter, when out of place, mistimed, or bursting forth from a disordered state of feeling, may be the most terrible modulation of the human voice. The laughter of one asleep, even if it be a little child,—the madman's laugh,—the wild, screaming laugh of a born idiot,—are sounds that we sometimes tremble to hear, and would always willingly forget. Poets have imagined no utterance of fiends or hobgoblins so fearfully appropriate as a laugh. And even the obtuse lime-burner felt his nerves shaken, as this strange man looked inward at his own heart, and burst into laughter that rolled away into the night, and was indistinctly reverberated among the hills.

"Joe," said he to his little son, "scamper down to the tavern in the village, and tell the jolly fellows there that Ethan Brand has come back, and that he has found the Unpardonable Sin!"

The boy darted away on his errand, to which Ethan Brand made no objection, nor seemed hardly to notice it. He sat on a log of wood, looking steadfastly at the iron door of the kiln. When the child was out of sight, and his swift and light footsteps ceased to be heard treading first on the fallen leaves and then on the rocky mountain-path, the lime-burner began to regret his departure. He felt that the little fellow's presence had been a barrier between his guest and himself, and that he must now deal, heart to heart, with a man who, on his own confession, had committed the one only crime for which Heaven could afford no mercy. That crime, in its indistinct blackness, seemed to overshadow him. The lime-burner's own sins rose up within him, and made his memory riotous with a throng of evil shapes that asserted their kindred with the Master Sin, whatever it might be, which it was within the scope of man's corrupted nature to conceive and cherish. They were all of one family; they went to and fro between his breast and Ethan Brand's, and carried dark greetings from one to the other.

Then Bartram remembered the stories which had grown traditionary in reference to this strange man, who had come upon him like a shadow of the night, and was making himself at home in his old place, after so long absence that the dead people, dead and buried for years, would have had more right to be at home, in any familiar spot, than he. Ethan Brand, it was said, had conversed with Satan himself in the lurid blaze of this very kiln. The legend had been matter of mirth heretofore, but looked grisly now. According to this tale, before Ethan Brand departed on his search, he had been accustomed to evoke a fiend from the hot furnace of the lime-kiln, night after night, in order to confer with him about the Unpardonable Sin; the man and the fiend each laboring to frame the image of some mode of guilt which could neither be atoned for nor forgiven. And, with the first gleam of light upon the mountain-top, the fiend crept in at the iron door, there to abide the intensest element of fire, until again summoned forth to share in the dreadful task of extending man's possible guilt beyond the scope of Heaven's else infinite mercy.

While the lime-burner was struggling with the horror of these thoughts, Ethan Brand rose from the log, and flung open the door of the kiln. The action was in such accordance with the idea in Bartram's mind, that he almost expected to see the Evil One issue forth, red-hot, from the raging furnace.

"Hold! hold!" cried he, with a tremulous attempt to laugh; for he was ashamed of his fears, although they overmastered him. "Don't, for mercy's sake, bring out your devil now!"

"Man!" sternly replied Ethan Brand, "what need have I of the devil? I have left him behind me, on my track. It is with such half-way sinners as you that he busies himself. Fear not, because I open the door. I do but act by old custom, and am going to trim your fire, like a lime-burner, as I was once."

He stirred the vast coals, thrust in more wood, and bent forward to gaze into the hollow prison-house of the fire, regardless of the fierce glow that reddened upon his face. The lime-burner sat watching him, and half suspected his strange guest of a purpose, if not to evoke a fiend, at least to plunge bodily into the flames, and thus vanish from the sight of man. Ethan Brand, however, drew quietly back, and closed the door of the kiln.

"I have looked," said he, "into many a human heart that was seven times hotter with sinful passions than yonder furnace is with fire. But I found not there what I sought. No, not the Unpardonable Sin!"

"What is the Unpardonable Sin?" asked the lime-burner; and then he shrank farther from his companion, trembling lest his question should be answered.

"It is a sin that grew within my own breast," replied Ethan Brand, standing erect, with a pride that distinguishes all enthusiasts of his stamp. "A sin that grew nowhere else! The sin of an intellect that triumphed over the sense of brotherhood with man and reverence for God, and sacrificed everything to its own mighty claims! The only sin that deserves a recompense of immortal agony! Freely, were it to do again, would I incur the guilt. Unshrinkingly I accept the retribution!"

"The man's head is turned," muttered the lime-burner to himself. "He may be a sinner, like the rest of us,—nothing more likely,—but, I'll be sworn, he is a madman too."

Nevertheless he felt uncomfortable at his situation, alone with Ethan Brand on the wild mountain-side, and was right glad to hear the rough murmur of tongues, and the footsteps of what seemed a pretty numerous party, stumbling over the stones and rustling through the underbrush. Soon appeared the whole lazy regiment that was wont to infest the village tavern, comprehending three or four individuals who had drunk flip beside the bar-room fire through all the winters, and smoked their pipes beneath the stoop through all the summers, since Ethan Brand's departure. Laughing boisterously, and mingling all their voices together in unceremonious talk, they now burst into the moonshine and narrow streaks of fire-light that illuminated the open space before the lime-kiln. Bartram set the door ajar again, flooding the spot with light, that the whole company might get a fair view of Ethan Brand, and he of them.

There, among other old acquaintances, was a once ubiquitous man, now almost extinct, but whom we were formerly sure to encounter at the hotel of every thriving village throughout the country. It was the stage-agent. The present specimen of the genus was a wilted and smoke-dried man, wrinkled and red-nosed, in a smartly-cut, brown, bob-tailed coat, with brass buttons, who, for a length of time unknown, had kept his desk and corner in the bar-room, and was still puffing what seemed to be the same cigar that he had lighted twenty years before. He had great fame as a dry joker, though, perhaps, less on account of any intrinsic humor than from a certain flavor of brandy-toddy and tobacco-smoke, which impregnated all his ideas and expressions, as well as his person. Another well-remembered though strangely-altered face was that of Lawyer Giles, as people still called him in courtesy; an elderly ragamuffin, in his soiled shirt-sleeves and tow-cloth trousers. This poor fellow had been an attorney, in what he called his better days, a sharp practitioner, and in great vogue among the village litigants; but flip, and sling, and toddy, and cocktails, imbibed at all hours, morning, noon, and night, had caused him to slide from intellectual to various kinds and degrees of bodily labor, till at last, to adopt his own phrase, he slid into a soap-vat. In other words, Giles was now a soap-boiler, in a small way. He had come to be but the fragment of a human being, a part of one foot having been chopped off by an axe, and an entire hand torn away by the devilish grip of a steam-engine. Yet, though the corporeal hand was gone, a spiritual member remained; for, stretching forth the stump, Giles steadfastly averred that he felt an invisible thumb and fingers with as vivid a sensation as before the real ones were amputated. A maimed and miserable wretch he was; but one, nevertheless, whom the world could not trample on, and had no right to scorn, either in this or any previous stage of his misfortunes, since he had still kept up the courage and spirit of a man, asked nothing in charity, and with his one hand—and that the left one—fought a stern battle against want and hostile circumstances.

Among the throng, too, came another personage, who, with certain points of similarity to Lawyer Giles, had many more of difference. It was the village doctor; a man of some fifty years, whom, at an earlier period of his life, we introduced as paying a professional visit to Ethan Brand during the latter's supposed insanity. He was now a purple-visaged, rude, and brutal, yet half-gentlemanly figure, with something wild, ruined, and desperate in his talk, and in all the details of his gesture and manners. Brandy possessed this man like an evil spirit, and made him as surly and savage as a wild beast, and as miserable as a lost soul; but there was supposed to be in him such wonderful skill, such native gifts of healing, beyond any which medical science could impart, that society caught hold of him, and would not let him sink out of its reach. So, swaying to and fro upon his horse, and grumbling thick accents at the bedside, he visited all the sick-chambers for miles about among the mountain towns, and sometimes raised a dying man, as it were, by miracle, or quite as often, no doubt, sent his patient to a grave that was dug many a year too soon. The doctor had an everlasting pipe in his mouth, and, as somebody said, in allusion to his habit of swearing, it was always alight with hell-fire.

These three worthies pressed forward, and greeted Ethan Brand each after his own fashion, earnestly inviting him to partake of the contents of a certain black bottle, in which, as they averred, he would find something far better worth seeking for than the Unpardonable Sin. No mind, which has wrought itself by intense and solitary meditation into a high state of enthusiasm, can endure the kind of contact with low and vulgar modes of thought and feeling to which Ethan Brand was now subjected. It made him doubt—and, strange to say, it was a painful doubt—whether he had indeed found the Unpardonable Sin, and found it within himself. The whole question on which he had exhausted life, and more than life, looked like a delusion.

"Leave me," he said bitterly, "ye brute beasts, that have made yourselves so, shrivelling up your souls with fiery liquors! I have done with you. Years and years ago, I groped into your hearts, and found nothing there for my purpose. Get ye gone!"

"Why, you uncivil scoundrel," cried the fierce doctor, "is that the way you respond to the kindness of your best friends? Then let me tell you the truth. You have no more found the Unpardonable Sin than yonder boy Joe has. You are but a crazy fellow,—I told you so twenty years ago,—neither better nor worse than a crazy fellow, and the fit companion of old Humphrey, here!"

He pointed to an old man, shabbily dressed, with long white hair, thin visage, and unsteady eyes. For some years past this aged person had been wandering about among the hills, inquiring of all travelers whom he met for his daughter. The girl, it seemed, had gone off with a company of circus-performers; and occasionally tidings of her came to the village, and fine stories were told of her glittering appearance as she rode on horseback in the ring, or performed marvelous feats on the tight-rope.

The white-haired father now approached Ethan Brand, and gazed unsteadily into his face.

"They tell me you have been all over the earth," said he, wringing his hands with earnestness. "You must have seen my daughter, for she makes a grand figure in the world, and everybody goes to see her. Did she send any word to her old father, or say when she was coming back?"

Ethan Brand's eye quailed beneath the old man's. That daughter, from whom he so earnestly desired a word of greeting, was the Esther of our tale, the very girl whom, with such cold and remorseless purpose, Ethan Brand had made the subject of a psychological experiment, and wasted, absorbed, and perhaps annihilated her soul, in the process.

"Yes," murmured he, turning away from the hoary wanderer; "it is no delusion. There is an Unpardonable Sin!"

While these things were passing, a merry scene was going forward in the area of cheerful light, beside the spring and before the door of the hut. A number of the youth of the village, young men and girls, had hurried up the hill-side, impelled by curiosity to see Ethan Brand, the hero of so many a legend familiar to their childhood. Finding nothing, however, very remarkable in his aspect,—nothing but a sunburnt wayfarer, in plain garb and dusty shoes, who sat looking into the fire, as if he fancied pictures among the coals,—these young people speedily grew tired of observing him. As it happened, there was other amusement at hand. An old German Jew, traveling with a diorama on his back, was passing down the mountain-road towards the village just as the party turned aside from it, and, in hopes of eking out the profits of the day, the showman had kept them company to the lime-kiln.

"Come, old Dutchman," cried one of the young men, "let us see your pictures, if you can swear they are worth looking at!"

"O, yes, Captain," answered the Jew,—whether as a matter of courtesy or craft, he styled everybody Captain,—"I shall show you, indeed, some very superb pictures!"

So, placing his box in a proper position, he invited the young men and girls to look through the glass orifices of the machine, and proceeded to exhibit a series of the most outrageous scratchings and daubings, as specimens of the fine arts, that ever an itinerant showman had the face to impose upon his circle of spectators. The pictures were worn out, moreover, tattered, full of cracks and wrinkles, dingy with tobacco-smoke, and otherwise in a most pitiable condition. Some purported to be cities, public edifices, and ruined castles in Europe; other represented Napoleon's battles and Nelson's sea-fights; and in the midst of these would be seen a gigantic, brown, hairy hand,—which might have been mistaken for the Hand of Destiny, though, in truth, it was only the showman's,—pointing its forefinger to various scenes of the conflict, while its owner gave historical illustrations. When, with much merriment at its abominable deficiency of merit, the exhibition was concluded, the German bade little Joe put his head into the box. Viewed through the magnifying-glasses, the boy's round, rosy visage assumed the strangest imaginable aspect of an immense Titanic child, the mouth grinning broadly, and the eyes and every other feature overflowing with fun at the joke. Suddenly, however, that merry face turned pale, and its expression changed to horror, for this easily impressed and excitable child had become sensible that the eye of Ethan Brand was fixed upon him through the glass.

"You make the little man to be afraid, Captain," said the German Jew, turning up the dark and strong outline of his visage, from his stooping posture. "But look again, and, by chance, I shall cause you to see somewhat that is very fine, upon my word!"

Ethan Brand gazed into the box for an instant, and then starting back, looked fixedly at the German. What had he seen? Nothing, apparently; for a curious youth, who had peeped in almost at the same moment, beheld only a vacant space of canvas.

"I remember you now," muttered Ethan Brand to the showman.

"Ah, Captain," whispered the Jew of Nuremberg, with a dark smile, "I find it to be a heavy matter in my show-box,—this Unpardonable Sin! By my faith, Captain, it has wearied my shoulders, this long day, to carry it over the mountain."

"Peace," answered Ethan Brand, sternly, "or get thee into the furnace yonder!"

The Jew's exhibition had scarcely concluded, when a great, elderly dog—who seemed to be his own master, as no person in the company laid claim to him—saw fit to render himself the object of public notice. Hitherto, he had shown himself a very quiet, well-disposed old dog, going round from one to another, and, by way of being sociable, offering his rough head to be patted by any kindly hand that would take so much trouble. But now, all of a sudden, this grave and venerable quadruped, of his own mere motion, and without the slightest suggestion from anybody else, began to run round after his tail, which, to heighten the absurdity of the proceeding, was a great deal shorter than it should have been. Never was seen such headlong eagerness in pursuit of an object that could not possibly be attained; never was heard such a tremendous outbreak of growling, snarling, barking, and snapping,—as if one end of the ridiculous brute's body were at deadly and most unforgivable enmity with the other. Faster and faster, round about went the cur; and faster and still faster fled the unapproachable brevity of his tail; and louder and fiercer grew his yells of rage and animosity; until, utterly exhausted, and as far from the goal as ever, the foolish old dog ceased his performance as suddenly as he had begun it. The next moment he was as mild, quiet, sensible, and respectable in his deportment, as when he first scraped acquaintance with the company.

As may be supposed, the exhibition was greeted with universal laughter, clapping of hands, and shouts of encore, to which the canine performer responded by wagging all that there was to wag of his tail, but appeared totally unable to repeat his very successful effort to amuse the spectators.

Meanwhile, Ethan Brand had resumed his seat upon the log, and moved, it might be, by a perception of some remote analogy between his own case and that of this self-pursuing cur, he broke into the awful laugh, which, more than any other token, expressed the condition of his inward being. From that moment, the merriment of the party was at an end; they stood aghast, dreading lest the inauspicious sound should be reverberated around the horizon, and that mountain would thunder it to mountain, and so the horror be prolonged upon their ears. Then, whispering one to another that it was late,—that the moon was almost down,—that the August night was growing chill,—they hurried homewards, leaving the lime-burner and little Joe to deal as they might with their unwelcome guest. Save for these three human beings, the open space on the hillside was a solitude, set in a vast gloom of forest. Beyond that darksome verge, the firelight glimmered on the stately trunks and almost black foliage of pines, intermixed with the lighter verdure of sapling oaks, maples, and poplars, while here and there lay the gigantic corpses of dead trees, decaying on the leaf-strewn soil. And it seemed to little Joe—a timorous and imaginative child—that the silent forest was holding its breath, until some fearful thing should happen.

Ethan Brand thrust more wood into the fire, and closed the door of the kiln; then looking over his shoulder at the lime-burner and his son, he bade, rather than advised, them to retire to rest.

"For myself, I cannot sleep," said he. "I have matters that it concerns me to meditate upon. I will watch the fire, as I used to do in the old time."

"And call the devil out of the furnace to keep you company, I suppose," muttered Bartram, who had been making intimate acquaintance with the black bottle above-mentioned. "But watch, if you like, and call as many devils as you like! For my part, I shall be all the better for a snooze. Come, Joe!"

As the boy followed his father into the hut, he looked back at the wayfarer, and the tears came into his eyes, for his tender spirit had an intuition of the bleak and terrible loneliness in which this man had enveloped himself.

When they had gone, Ethan Brand sat listening to the crackling of the kindled wood, and looking at the little spirts of fire that issued through the chinks of the door. These trifles, however, once so familiar, had but the slightest hold of his attention, while deep within his mind he was reviewing the gradual but marvelous change that had been wrought upon him by the search to which he had devoted himself. He remembered how the night dew had fallen upon him,—how the dark forest had whispered to him,—how the stars had gleamed upon him,—a simple and loving man, watching his fire in the years gone by, and ever musing as it burned. He remembered with what tenderness, with what love and sympathy for mankind, and what pity for human guilt and woe, he had first begun to contemplate those ideas which afterwards became the inspiration of his life; with what reverence he had then looked into the heart of man, viewing it as a temple originally divine, and, however desecrated, still to be held sacred by a brother; with what awful fear he had deprecated the success of his pursuit, and prayed that the Unpardonable Sin might never be revealed to him. Then ensued that vast intellectual development, which, in its progress, disturbed the counterpoise between his mind and heart. The Idea that possessed his life had operated as a means of education; it had gone on cultivating his powers to the highest point of which they were susceptible; it had raised him from the level of an unlettered laborer to stand on a star-lit eminence, whither the philosophers of the earth, laden with the lore of universities, might vainly strive to clamber after him. So much for the intellect! But where was the heart? That, indeed, had withered—had contracted—had hardened—had perished! It had ceased to partake of the universal throb. He had lost his hold of the magnetic chain of humanity. He was no longer a brother-man, opening the chambers or the dungeons of our common nature by the key of holy sympathy, which gave him a right to share in all its secrets; he was now a cold observer, looking on mankind as the subject of his experiment, and, at length, converting man and woman to be his puppets, and pulling the wires that moved them to such degrees of crime as were demanded for his study.

Thus Ethan Brand became a fiend. He began to be so from the moment that his moral nature had ceased to keep the pace of improvement with his intellect. And now, as his highest effort and inevitable development,—as the bright and gorgeous flower, and rich, delicious fruit of his life's labor,—he had produced the Unpardonable Sin!

"What more have I to seek? What more to achieve?" said Ethan Brand to himself. "My task is done, and well done!"

Starting from the log with a certain alacrity in his gait, and ascending the hillock of earth that was raised against the stone circumference of the lime-kiln, he thus reached the top of the structure. It was a space of perhaps ten feet across, from edge to edge, presenting a view of the upper surface of the immense mass of broken marble with which the kiln was heaped. All these innumerable blocks and fragments of marble were red-hot and vividly on fire, sending up great spouts of blue flame, which quivered aloft and danced madly, as within a magic circle, and sank and rose again, with continual and multitudinous activity. As the lonely man bent forward over this terrible body of fire, the blasting heat smote up against his person with a breath that, it might be supposed, would have scorched and shrivelled him up in a moment.

Ethan Brand stood erect, and raised his arms on high. The blue flames played upon his face, and imparted the wild and ghastly light which alone could have suited its expression; it was that of a fiend on the verge of plunging into his gulf of intensest torment.

"O Mother Earth," cried he, "who art no more my Mother, and into whose bosom this frame shall never be resolved! O mankind, whose brotherhood I have cast off, and trampled thy great heart beneath my feet! O stars of heaven, that shone on me of old, as if to light me onward and upward!—farewell all, and forever. Come, deadly element of Fire,—henceforth my familiar friend! Embrace me, as I do thee!"

That night the sound of a fearful peal of laughter rolled heavily through the sleep of the lime-burner and his little son; dim shapes of horror and anguish haunted their dreams, and seemed still present in the rude hovel, when they opened their eyes to the daylight.

"Up, boy, up!" cried the lime-burner, staring about him. "Thank Heaven, the night is gone, at last; and rather than pass such another, I would watch my lime-kiln, wide awake, for a twelvemonth. This Ethan Brand, with his humbug of an Unpardonable Sin, has done me no such mighty favor, in taking my place!"

He issued from the hut, followed by little Joe, who kept fast hold of his father's hand. The early sunshine was already pouring its gold upon the mountain-tops; and though the valleys were still in shadow, they smiled cheerfully in the promise of the bright day that was hastening onward. The village, completely shut in by hills, which swelled away gently about it, looked as if it had rested peacefully in the hollow of the great hand of Providence. Every dwelling was distinctly visible; the little spires of the two churches pointed upwards, and caught a foreglimmering of brightness from the sun-gilt skies upon their gilded weather-cocks. The tavern was astir, and the figure of the old, smoke-dried stage-agent, cigar in mouth, was seen beneath the stoop. Old Graylock was glorified with a golden cloud upon his head. Scattered likewise over the breasts of the surrounding mountains, there were heaps of hoary mist, in fantastic shapes, some of them far down into the valley, others high up towards the summits, and still others, of the same family of mist or cloud, hovering in the gold radiance of the upper atmosphere. Stepping from one to another of the clouds that rested on the hills, and thence to the loftier brotherhood that sailed in air, it seemed almost as if a mortal man might thus ascend into the heavenly regions. Earth was so mingled with sky that it was a day-dream to look at it.

To supply that charm of the familiar and homely, which Nature so readily adopts into a scene like this, the stage-coach was rattling down the mountain-road, and the driver sounded his horn, while echo caught up the notes, and intertwined them into a rich and varied and elaborate harmony, of which the original performer could lay claim to little share. The great hills played a concert among themselves, each contributing a strain of airy sweetness.

Little Joe's face brightened at once.

"Dear father," cried he, skipping cheerily to and fro, "that strange man is gone, and the sky and the mountains all seem glad of it!"

"Yes," growled the lime-burner, with an oath, "but he has let the fire go down, and no thanks to him if five hundred bushels of lime are not spoiled. If I catch the fellow hereabouts again, I shall feel like tossing him into the furnace!"

With his long pole in his hand, he ascended to the top of the kiln. After a moment's pause, he called to his son.

"Come up here, Joe!" said he.

So little Joe ran up the hillock, and stood by his father's side. The marble was all burnt into perfect, snow-white lime. But on its surface, in the midst of the circle,—snow-white too, and thoroughly converted into lime,—lay a human skeleton, in the attitude of a person who, after long toil, lies down to long repose. Within the ribs—strange to say—was the shape of a human heart.

"Was the fellow's heart made of marble?" cried Bartram, in some perplexity at this phenomenon. "At any rate, it is burnt into what looks like special good lime; and, taking all the bones together, my kiln is half a bushel the richer for him."

So saying, the rude lime-burner lifted his pole, and, letting it fall upon the skeleton, the relics of Ethan Brand were crumbled into fragments.

1850

HERMAN MELVILLE [1819–1891]

Hawthorne had shown that great fiction could come out of long seclusion; Melville showed that it could come out of intense adventurous experience.

When Melville was born, his father, Allan Melville, of distinguished New England Scottish ancestry, was a cultivated gentleman-merchant in New York, dealing in French fabrics, hose, perfumes, and the like. During a business depression he became bankrupt, and in 1830 tried to rehabilitate himself in Albany. There, two years later, he died, leaving Herman (a boy of thirteen) and seven other children. The widow, who had been Maria Gansevoort, of a notable New Netherland family, managed the domestic economy with skill. From parents in the Dutch Reformed Church she had acquired a piety that she sought to pass on to her children. In later years Melville retained a close knowledge of the Bible and a speculative awareness of the essential problems of religion. His formal schooling ended when he was only fifteen—after that he was educated by varied experience and wide reading.

He worked in a bank, he worked in a store, he worked on a farm, he did some teaching. Then, at age twenty, he had his first taste of sea life, shipping as a cabin-boy on a freighter, and, though he did not know it, beginning to gather the primary subject-matter of his fiction. On this voyage he sampled the hard life of the seaman, and saw, not the famed charms of the Old World, but the waterfront slums of vice-ridden Liverpool. After his return he taught school off and on, then submitted again to what he later called "the everlasting itch for things remote."

After a trip to Illinois in 1840, he shipped, early the next year, on the whaler *Acushnet* ("my Yale College and Harvard") bound for the South Seas, and, as it turned out, was away nearly four years. After eighteen months on the ship, he deserted, and with a companion lived in the society of cannibals, the Typees of the Marquesas Islands. Escaping on an Australian whaler to Tahiti, he shipped on another whaler that sailed in Japanese waters and eventually brought him to Honolulu. He joined the American navy, at length returned home on the frigate *United States,* and was discharged in Boston.

Graduated from the school of the sea, Melville entered the vocation of writing. He turned his wanderings into fiction, drawing into the net what he could find in books (such as Stewart's *A Visit to the South Seas* and Ames's *A Mariner's Sketches*). The result was a series of romances, varying in autobiographic content, all published within five years: *Typee* (1846), his life among the cannibals; *Omoo,* adventures in the South Seas; *Redburn,* the voyage to Liverpool; *Mardi,* the South Seas again, in an allegorical and satirical mode; *White-Jacket,* service in the navy; and *Moby-Dick* (1851), life on a whaling ship.

In 1847, the year of the second of these books, he married Elizabeth Shaw, daughter of the chief justice of Massachusetts. For nearly three years he lived and wrote in New York (visiting London and Paris in winter 1849–50). Then he settled with his wife and first child—he was soon to be father to two sons and two daughters—at Pittsfield, Massachusetts. While Hawthorne, a few miles away at Lenox, was writing *The House of the Seven Gables,* Melville was deep in *Moby-Dick, or The Whale,* a book "broiled," he told Hawthorne, "in hell-fire." In this book Melville did for the South Seas and the whalers what Cooper had done for the frontier and Mark Twain was to do for the great age of the Mississippi steamboats. More important, he created a fine story, an unforgettable character, an impressive wrestling with the problem of evil, and a rich, symphonic style.

Melville had poured his best into *Moby-Dick,* and felt that he had written himself out, though forty years of his life were still before him. For reasons not very clear, his art fell into a long decline. In 1852 he published *Pierre, or The Ambiguities,* a darkly symbolical study of good and evil, and then his last novels, *Israel Potter* and *The Confidence Man.* He tried shorter fiction in *The Piazza Tales,* showing great technical command in "Benito Cereno." He tried poetry: *Battle-Pieces and Aspects of the War* and *Clarel.* Then, surprisingly enough, late in life he achieved one more triumph—*Billy Budd,* a short novel left among his manuscripts and unpublished till 1924. Unlike Ahab and Pierre, his earlier heroes, Billy Budd, in tragic defeat, accepts the inscrutable law of life.

Once his writing career had turned awry, Melville could not expect to support his sizeable family by his pen. He received help from relatives, he tried lecturing, and in 1866 was appointed inspector of customs in New York, a post which he held for nearly twenty years. He died obscure.

Further reading: *Moby-Dick. Selected Poems,* ed. Hennig Cohen, 1964. Leon Howard, *Herman Melville: A Biography,* 1951. F. O. Matthiessen, *American Renaissance* (Book 3), 1941. Newton Arvin, *Herman Melville,* 1950. Edward Rosenberry, *Melville and the Comic Spirit,* 1955. Merlin Bowen, *The Long Encounter,* 1960. Warner Berthoff, *The Example of Melville,* 1963. Richard Chase, ed., *Melville: A Collection of Critical Essays,* 1962.

FROM *Hawthorne and His Mosses*

In July 1850 Melville came upon Hawthorne's *Mosses from an Old Manse.* In excited admiration he wrote a long review-article, concealed his authorship by signing it as "By a Virginian," and had it printed in the *Literary World* in the issues of August 17 and 24. Meanwhile—on August 5—Melville met Hawthorne for the first time, and they soon became friends.

The following paragraphs from the article are interesting not only for what they say about Hawthorne, but also for what they reveal about Melville himself, especially his passionate desire to probe to "the very axis of reality." It happens that at this time he was writing his own great novel, *Moby-Dick,* himself wrestling with "black" Truth. In his enthusiasm over the example of Hawthorne, he declares: "Hawthorne has dropped germinous seeds into my soul. He expands and deepens down, the more I contemplate him; and further and further shoots his strong New England roots in the hot soil of my Southern soul." When *Moby-Dick* was published it was dedicated to Nathaniel Hawthorne.

Text: *The Literary World,* August 17, 1850.

It is the least part of genius that attracts admiration. Where Hawthorne is known, he seems to be deemed a pleasant writer, with a pleasant style,—a sequestered, harmless man, from whom any deep and weighty thing would hardly be anticipated—a man who means no meanings. But there is no man, in whom humor and love, like mountain peaks, soar to such a rapt height as to receive the irradiations of the upper skies;—there is no man in whom humor and love are developed in that high form called genius; no such man can exist without also possessing, as the indispensable complement of these, a great, deep intellect, which drops down into the universe like a plummet. Or, love and humor are only the eyes through which such an intellect views this world. The great beauty in such a mind is but the product of its strength. * * *

Spite of all the Indian-summer sunlight on the hither side of Hawthorne's soul, the other side—like the dark half of the physical sphere—is shrouded in a blackness, ten times black. But this darkness but gives more effect to the ever-moving dawn, that for ever advances through it, and circumnavigates his world. Whether Hawthorne has simply availed himself of this mystical blackness as a means to the wondrous effects he makes it to produce in his lights and shades; or whether there really lurks in him, perhaps unknown to himself, a touch of Puritanic gloom,—this, I cannot altogether tell. Certain it is, however, that this great power of blackness in him derives its force from its appeals to that Calvinistic sense of Innate Depravity and Original Sin, from whose visitations, in some shape or other, no deeply thinking mind is always and wholly free. For, in certain moods, no man can weigh this world without throwing in something, somehow like Original Sin, to strike the uneven balance. At all events, perhaps no writer has ever wielded this terrific thought with greater terror than this same harmless Hawthorne. Still more: this black conceit pervades him through and through. You may be witched by his sunlight,—transported by the bright gildings in the skies he builds over you; but there is the blackness of darkness beyond; and even his bright gildings but fringe and play upon the edges of thunder-clouds. In one word, the world is mistaken in this Nathaniel Hawthorne. He himself must often have smiled at its absurd misconception of him. He is immeasurably deeper than the plummet of the mere critic. For it is not the brain that can test such a man; it is only the heart. You cannot come to know greatness by inspecting it; there is no glimpse to be caught of it, except by intuition; you need not ring it, you but touch it, and you find it is gold.

Now, it is that blackness in Hawthorne, of which I have spoken, that so fixes and fascinates me. It may be, nevertheless, that it is too largely developed in him. Perhaps he does not give us a ray of his light for every shade of his dark. But however this may be, this blackness it is that furnishes the infinite obscure of his back-ground,—that back-ground, against which Shakspeare plays his grandest conceits, the things that have made for Shakspeare his loftiest but most circumscribed renown, as the profoundest of thinkers. For by philosophers Shakspeare is not adored as the great man of tragedy and comedy.—"Off with his head; so much for Buckingham!" This sort of rant, interlined by another hand, brings down the house,—those mistaken souls, who dream of Shakspeare as a mere man of Richard-the-Third humps and Macbeth daggers. But it is those deep far-away things in him; those occasional flashings-forth of the intuitive Truth in him; those short, quick probings at the very axis of reality;—these are the things that make Shakspeare, Shakspeare. Through the mouths of the dark characters of Hamlet, Timon, Lear, and Iago, he craftily says, or sometimes insinuates the things which we feel to be so terrifically true, that it were all but madness for any good man, in his own proper character, to utter, or even hint of them. Tormented into desperation, Lear, the frantic king, tears off the mask, and speaks the same madness of vital truth. But, as I before said, it is the least part of genius that attracts admiration. And so, much of the blind, unbridled admiration that has been heaped upon Shakspeare, has been lavished upon the least part of him. And few of his endless commentators and critics seem to have remembered, or even perceived, that the immediate products of a great mind are not so great as that undeveloped and sometimes undevelopable yet dimly-discernible greatness, to which those immediate products are but the infallible indices. In Shakspeare's tomb lies infinitely more than Shakspeare ever wrote. And if I magnify Shakspeare, it is not so much for what he did do as for what he did not do, or refrained from doing. For in this world of lies, Truth is forced to fly like a scared white doe in the woodlands; and only by cunning glimpses will she reveal herself, as in Shakspeare and other masters of the great Art of Telling the Truth,—even though it be covertly and by snatches.

But if this view of the all-popular Shakspeare be seldom taken by his readers, and if very few who extol him have ever read him deeply, or perhaps, only have seen him on the tricky stage (which alone made, and is still making him his mere mob renown)—if few men have time, or patience, or palate, for the spiritual truth as it is in that great genius;—it is then no matter of surprise, that in a contemporaneous age, Nathaniel Hawthorne is a man as yet almost utterly mistaken among men. Here and there, in some quiet arm-chair in the noisy town, or some deep nook among the noiseless mountains, he may be appreciated for something of what he is. But unlike Shakspeare, who was forced to the contrary course by circumstances, Hawthorne (either from simple disinclination, or else from inaptitude) refrains from all the popularizing noise and show of broad farce and blood-besmeared tragedy; content with the still, rich utterance of a great intellect in repose, and which sends few thoughts into circulation, except they be arterialized at his large warm lungs, and expanded in his honest heart.

1850

Bartleby

The main protagonist of "Bartleby" is not the title character, but the lawyer-narrator. Bartleby's loneliness, despair, and terror disrupt the stable, prudent, affluent world in which the attorney has been so comfortably living and throw him into a state of serious psychological conflict. He is torn between the intolerance and incomprehension manifested by his colleagues and assistants, and his own sympathy for and understanding of the scrivener. The dramatic focus of the story is the manner in which the lawyer handles Bartleby's challenge.

"Bartleby" was Melville's first published short story, appearing anonymously in *Putnam's Monthly Magazine* in 1853. Melville included it in his collection of short pieces, *The Piazza Tales,* 1856. The text reprinted here is from Egbert S. Oliver's edition of *The Piazza Tales* (New York, 1948).

I am a rather elderly man. The nature of my avocations, for the last thirty years, has brought me into more than ordinary contact with what would seem an interesting and somewhat singular set of men, of whom, as yet, nothing, that I know of, has ever been written—I mean, the law-copyists, or scriveners. I have known very many of them, professionally and privately, and, if I pleased, could relate divers histories, at which good-natured gentlemen might smile, and sentimental souls might weep. But I waive the biographies of all other scriveners, for a few passages in the life of Bartleby, who was a scrivener, the strangest I ever saw, or heard of. While, of other law-copyists, I might write the complete life, of Bartleby nothing of that sort can be done. I believe that no materials exist, for a full and satisfactory biography of this man. It is an irreparable loss to literature. Bartleby was one of those beings of whom nothing is ascertainable, except from the original sources, and, in his case, those are very small. What my own astonished eyes saw of Bartleby, *that* is all I know of him, except, indeed, one vague report, which will appear in the sequel.

Ere introducing the scrivener, as he first appeared to me, it is fit I make some mention of myself, my *employés*, my business, my chambers, and general surroundings; because some such description is indispensable to an adequate understanding of the chief character about to be presented. Imprimis: I am a man who, from his youth upwards, has been filled with a profound conviction that the easiest way of life is the best. Hence, though I belong to a profession proverbially energetic and nervous, even to turbulence, at times, yet nothing of that sort have I ever suffered to invade my peace. I am one of those unambitious lawyers who never addresses a jury, or in any way draws down public applause; but, in the cool tranquillity of a snug retreat, do a snug business among rich men's bonds, and mortgages, and title-deeds. All who know me, consider me an eminently *safe* man. The late John Jacob Astor,[1] a personage little given to poetic enthusiasm, had no hesitation in pronouncing my first grand point to be prudence; my next, method. I do not speak it in vanity, but simply record the fact, that I was not unemployed in my profession by the late John Jacob Astor; a name which, I admit, I love to repeat; for it hath a rounded and orbicular sound to it, and rings like unto bullion. I will freely add, that I was not insensible to the late John Jacob Astor's good opinion.

Some time prior to the period at which this little history begins, my avocations had been largely increased. The good old office, now extinct in the State of New York, of a Master in Chancery,[2] had been conferred upon me. It was not a very arduous office, but very pleasantly remunerative. I seldom lose my temper; much more seldom indulge in dangerous indignation at wrongs and outrages; but, I must be permitted to be rash here, and declare, that I consider the sudden and violent abrogation of the office of Master in Chancery, by the new Constitution, as a —— premature act; inasmuch as I had counted upon a life-lease of the profits, whereas I only received those of a few short years. But this is by the way.

My chambers were up stairs, at No. — Wall Street. At one end, they looked upon the white wall of the interior of a spacious sky-light shaft, penetrating the building from top to bottom.

This view might have been considered rather tame than otherwise, deficient in what landscape painters call "life". But, if so, the view from the other end of my chambers offered, at least, a contrast, if nothing more. In that direction, my windows commanded an unobstructed view of a lofty brick wall, black by age and everlasting shade; which wall required no spy-glass to bring out its lurking beauties, but, for the benefit of all near-sighted spectators, was pushed up to within ten feet of my window panes. Owing to the great height of the surrounding buildings, and my chambers being on the second floor, the interval between this wall and mine not a little resembled a huge square cistern.

At the period just preceding the advent of Bartleby, I had two persons as copyists in my employment, and a promising lad as an office-boy. First, Turkey; second, Nippers; third, Ginger Nut. These may seem names, the like of which are not usually found in the Directory. In truth, they were nicknames, mutually conferred upon each other by my three clerks, and were deemed expressive of their respective persons or characters. Turkey was a short, pursy Englishman, of about my own age—that is, somewhere not far from sixty. In the morning, one might say, his face was of a fine florid hue, but after twelve o'clock, meridian—his dinner hour—it blazed like a grate full of Christmas coals; and continued blazing—but, as it were, with a gradual wane—till six o'clock, P.M., or thereabouts; after which, I saw no more of the proprietor of the face, which, gaining its meridian with the sun, seemed to set with it, to rise, culminate, and decline the following day, with the like regularity and undiminished glory. There are many singular coincidences I have known in the course of my life, not the least among which was the fact, that, exactly when Turkey displayed his fullest beams from his red and radiant countenance, just then, too, at that critical moment, began the daily period when I considered his business capacities as seriously disturbed for the remainder of the twenty-four hours. Not that he was absolutely idle, or averse to business, then; far from it. The difficulty was, he was apt to be altogether too energetic. There was a strange, inflamed, flurried, flighty recklessness of activity about him. He would be incautious in dipping his pen into his inkstand. All his blots upon my documents were dropped there after twelve o'clock, meridian. Indeed, not only would he be reckless, and sadly given to making blots in the afternoon, but, some days, he went further, and was rather noisy. At such times, too, his face flamed with augmented blazonry, as if cannel

[1]John Jacob Astor (1763-1848), financier; a symbol of wealth and achievement. The reference helps characterize the narrator's values.

[2]A sinecure that enabled the Master to collect fees regardless of the court decision.

coal had been heaped on anthracite. He made an unpleasant racket with his chair; spilled his sandbox; in mending his pens, impatiently split them all to pieces, and threw them on the floor in a sudden passion; stood up, and leaned over his table, boxing his papers about in a most indecorous manner, very sad to behold in an elderly man like him. Nevertheless, as he was in many ways a most valuable person to me, and all the time before twelve o'clock, meridian, was the quickest, steadiest creature, too, accomplishing a great deal of work in a style not easily to be matched—for these reasons, I was willing to overlook his eccentricities, though, indeed, occasionally, I remonstrated with him. I did this very gently, however, because, though the civilest, nay, the blandest and most reverential of men in the morning, yet, in the afternoon, he was disposed, upon provocation, to be slightly rash with his tongue—in fact, insolent. Now, valuing his morning services as I did, and resolved not to lose them—yet, at the same time, made uncomfortable by his inflamed ways after twelve o'clock—and being a man of peace, unwilling by my admonitions to call forth unseemly retorts from him, I took upon me, one Saturday noon (he was always worse on Saturdays) to hint to him, very kindly, that, perhaps, now that he was growing old, it might be well to abridge his labors; in short, he need not come to my chambers after twelve o'clock, but, dinner over, had best go home to his lodgings, and rest himself till tea-time. But no; he insisted upon his afternoon devotions. His countenance became intolerably fervid, as he oratorically assured me—gesticulating with a long ruler at the other end of the room—that if his services in the morning were useful, how indispensable, then, in the afternoon?

"With submission, sir," said Turkey, on this occasion, "I consider myself your right-hand man. In the morning I but marshal and deploy my columns; but in the afternoon I put myself at their head, and gallantly charge the foe, thus"—and he made a violent thrust with the ruler.

"But the blots, Turkey," intimated I.

"True; but, with submission, sir, behold these hairs! I am getting old. Surely, sir, a blot or two of a warm afternoon is not to be severely urged against gray hairs. Old age—even if it blot the page—is honorable. With submission, sir, we *both* are getting old."

This appeal to my fellow-feeling was hardly to be resisted. At all events, I saw that go he would not. So, I made up my mind to let him stay, resolving, nevertheless, to see to it that, during the afternoon, he had to do with my less important papers.

Nippers, the second on my list, was a whiskered, sallow, and, upon the whole, rather piratical-looking young man, of about five and twenty. I always deemed him the victim of two evil powers—ambition and indigestion. The ambition was evinced by a certain impatience of the duties of a mere copyist, an unwarrantable usurpation of strictly professional affairs, such as the original drawing up of legal documents. The indigestion seemed betokened in an occasional nervous testiness and grinning irritability, causing the teeth to audibly grind together over mistakes committed in copying; unnecessary maledictions, hissed, rather than spoken, in the heat of business; and especially by a continual discontent with the height of the table where he worked. Though of a very ingenious mechanical turn, Nippers could never get this table to suit him. He put chips under it, blocks of various sorts, bits of pasteboard, and at last went so far as to attempt an exquisite adjustment, by final pieces of folded blotting-paper. But no invention would answer. If, for the sake of easing his back, he brought the table lid at a sharp angle well up towards his chin, and wrote there like a man using the steep roof of a Dutch house for his desk, then he declared that it stopped the circulation in his arms. If now he lowered the table to his waistbands, and stooped over it in writing, then there was a sore aching in his back. In short, the truth of the matter was, Nippers knew not what he wanted. Or, if he wanted anything, it was to be rid of a scrivener's table altogether. Among the manifestations of his diseased ambition was a fondness he had for receiving visits from certain ambiguous-looking fellows in seedy coats, whom he called his clients. Indeed, I was aware that not only was he, at times, considerable of a ward-politician, but he occasionally did a little business at the Justices' courts, and was not unknown on the steps of the Tombs.[3] I have good reason to believe, however, that one individual who called upon him at my chambers, and who, with a grand air, he insisted was his client, was no other than a dun, and the alleged title-deed, a bill. But, with all his failings, and the annoyances he caused me, Nippers, like his compatriot Turkey, was a very useful man to me; wrote a neat, swift hand; and, when he chose, was not deficient in a gentlemanly sort of deportment. Added to this, he always dressed in a gentlemanly sort of way; and so, incidentally, reflected credit upon my chambers. Whereas, with respect to Turkey, I had much ado to keep him from being a reproach to me. His clothes were apt to look oily, and smell of eating-houses. He wore his pantaloons very loose and baggy in summer. His coats were execrable; his hat not to be handled. But while the hat was a thing of indifference to me, inasmuch as his natural civility and

[3]A large prison in New York City.

deference, as a dependent Englishman, always led him to doff it the moment he entered the room, yet his coat was another matter. Concerning his coats, I reasoned with him; but with no effect. The truth was, I suppose, that a man with so small an income could not afford to sport such a lustrous face and a lustrous coat at one and the same time. As Nippers once observed, Turkey's money went chiefly for red ink. One winter day, I presented Turkey with a highly respectable-looking coat of my own—a padded gray coat, of a most comfortable warmth, and which buttoned straight up from the knee to the neck. I thought Turkey would appreciate the favor, and abate his rashness and obstreperousness of afternoons. But no; I verily believe that buttoning himself up in so downy and blanket-like a coat had a pernicious effect upon him—upon the same principle that too much oats are bad for horses. In fact, precisely as a rash, restive horse is said to feel his oats, so Turkey felt his coat. It made him insolent. He was a man whom prosperity harmed.

Though, concerning the self-indulgent habits of Turkey, I had my own private surmises, yet, touching Nippers, I was well persuaded that, whatever might be his faults in other respects, he was, at least, a temperate young man. But, indeed, nature herself seemed to have been his vintner, and, at his birth, charged him so thoroughly with an irritable, brandy-like disposition, that all subsequent potations were needless. When I consider how, amid the stillness of my chambers, Nippers would sometimes impatiently rise from his seat, and stooping over his table, spread his arms wide apart, seize the whole desk, and move it, and jerk it, with a grim, grinding motion on the floor, as if the table were a perverse voluntary agent, intent on thwarting and vexing him, I plainly perceive that, for Nippers, brandy-and-water were altogether superfluous.

It was fortunate for me that, owing to its peculiar cause—indigestion—the irritability and consequent nervousness of Nippers were mainly observable in the morning, while in the afternoon he was comparatively mild. So that, Turkey's paroxysms only coming on about twelve o'clock, I never had to do with their eccentricities at one time. Their fits relieved each other, like guards. When Nippers's was on, Turkey's was off; and *vice versa.* This was a good natural arrangement, under the circumstances.

Ginger Nut, the third on my list, was a lad, some twelve years old. His father was a car-man, ambitious of seeing his son on the bench instead of a cart, before he died. So he sent him to my office, as student at law, errand-boy, cleaner and sweeper, at the rate of one dollar a week. He had a little desk to himself, but he did not use it much. Upon inspection, the drawer exhibited a great array of the shells of various sorts of nuts. Indeed, to this quick-witted youth, the whole noble science of the law was contained in a nutshell. Not the least among the employments of Ginger Nut, as well as one which he discharged with the most alacrity, was his duty as cake and apple purveyor for Turkey and Nippers. Copying law-papers being proverbially a dry, husky sort of business, my two scriveners were fain to moisten their mouths very often with Spitzenbergs, to be had at the numerous stalls nigh the Custom House and Post Office. Also, they sent Ginger Nut very frequently for that peculiar cake—small, flat, round, and very spicy—after which he had been named by them. Of a cold morning, when business was but dull, Turkey would gobble up scores of these cakes, as if they were mere wafers—indeed, they sell them at the rate of six or eight for a penny—the scrape of his pen blending with the crunching of the crisp particles in his mouth. Of all the fiery afternoon blunders and flurried rashnesses of Turkey, was his once moistening a ginger-cake between his lips, and clapping it on to a mortgage, for a seal. I came within an ace of dismissing him then. But he mollified me by making an oriental bow, and saying—

"With submission, sir, it was generous of me to find you in stationery on my own account."

Now my original business—that of a conveyancer and title hunter, and drawer-up of recondite documents of all sorts—was considerably increased by receiving the master's office. There was now great work for scriveners. Not only must I push the clerks already with me, but I must have additional help.

In answer to my advertisement, a motionless young man one morning stood upon my office threshold, the door being open, for it was summer. I can see that figure now—pallidly neat, pitiably respectable, incurably forlorn! It was Bartleby.

After a few words touching his qualifications, I engaged him, glad to have among my corps of copyists a man of so singularly sedate an aspect, which I thought might operate beneficially upon the flighty temper of Turkey, and the fiery one of Nippers.

I should have stated before that ground glass folding-doors divided my premises into two parts, one of which was occupied by my scriveners, the other by myself. According to my humor, I threw open these doors, or closed them. I resolved to assign Bartleby a corner by the folding-doors, but on my side of them, so as to have this quiet man within easy call, in case any trifling thing was to be done. I placed his desk close up to a small side-window in that part of the room, a window which originally had afforded a lateral view of certain grimy backyards and bricks, but which, owing to subsequent erections, commanded at present no view at all, though it gave some light. Within three feet of the panes was a wall, and the light came down from far above, between two lofty buildings, as from a very small opening in a dome. Still further to a satisfactory arrangement, I procured a high green folding screen, which might entirely isolate Bartleby from my sight, though not remove him from my voice. And thus, in a manner, privacy and society were conjoined.

At first, Bartleby did an extraordinary quantity of writing. As if long famishing for something to copy, he seemed to gorge himself on my documents. There was no pause for digestion. He ran a day and night line, copying by sun-light and by candle-light. I should have been quite delighted with his application, had he been cheerfully industrious. But he wrote on silently, palely, mechanically.

It is, of course, an indispensable part of a scrivener's business to verify the accuracy of his copy, word by word. Where there are two or more scriveners in an office, they assist each other in this examination, one reading from the copy, the other holding the original. It is a very dull, wearisome, and lethargic affair. I can readily imagine that, to some sanguine temperaments, it would be altogether intolerable. For example, I cannot credit that the mettlesome poet, Byron, would have contentedly sat down with Bartleby to examine a law document of, say five hundred pages, closely written in a crimpy hand.

Now and then, in the haste of business, it had been my habit to assist in comparing some brief document myself, calling Turkey or Nippers for this purpose. One object I had, in placing Bartleby so handy to me behind the screen, was, to avail myself of his services on such trivial occasions. It was on the third day, I think, of his being with me, and before any necessity had arisen for having his own writing examined, that, being much hurried to complete a small affair I had in hand, I abruptly called to Bartleby. In my haste and natural expectancy of instant compliance, I sat with my head bent over the original on my desk, and my right hand sideways, and somewhat nervously extended with the copy, so that, immediately upon emerging from his retreat, Bartleby might snatch it and proceed to business without the least delay.

In this very attitude did I sit when I called him, rapidly stating what it was I wanted him to do—namely, to examine a small paper with me. Imagine my surprise, nay, my consternation, when, without moving from his privacy, Bartleby, in a singularly mild, firm voice, replied, "I would prefer not to."

I sat awhile in perfect silence, rallying my stunned faculties. Immediately it occurred to me that my ears had deceived me, or Bartleby had entirely misunderstood my meaning. I repeated my request in the clearest tone I could assume; but in quite as clear a one came the previous reply, "I would prefer not to."

"Prefer not to," echoed I, rising in high excitement, and crossing the room with a stride. "What do you mean? Are you moon-struck? I want you to help me compare this sheet here—take it," and I thrust it towards him.

"I would prefer not to," said he.

I looked at him steadfastly. His face was leanly composed; his gray eye dimly calm. Not a wrinkle of agitation rippled him. Had there been the least uneasiness, anger, impatience or impertinence in his manner; in other words, had there been any thing ordinarily human about him, doubtless I should have violently dismissed him from the premises. But as it was, I should have as soon thought of turning my pale plaster-of-paris bust of Cicero out of doors. I stood gazing at him awhile, as he went on with his own writing, and then reseated myself at my desk. This is very strange, thought I. What had one best do? But my business hurried me. I concluded to forget the matter for the present, reserving it for my future leisure. So calling Nippers from the other room, the paper was speedily examined.

A few days after this, Bartleby concluded four lengthy documents, being quadruplicates of a week's testimony taken before me in my High Court of Chancery. It became necessary to examine them. It was an important suit, and great accuracy was imperative. Having all things arranged, I called Turkey, Nippers, and Ginger Nut, from the next room, meaning to place the four copies in the hands of my four clerks, while I should read from the original. Accordingly, Turkey, Nippers, and Ginger Nut had taken their seats in a row, each with his document in his hand, when I called to Bartleby to join this interesting group.

"Bartleby! quick, I am waiting."

I heard a slow scrape of his chair legs on the uncarpeted floor, and soon he appeared standing at the entrance of his hermitage.

"What is wanted?" said he, mildly.

"The copies, the copies," said I, hurriedly. "We are going to examine them. There"—and I held towards him the fourth quadruplicate.

"I would prefer not to," he said, and gently disappeared behind the screen.

For a few moments I was turned into a pillar of salt, standing at the head of my seated column of clerks. Recovering myself, I advanced towards the screen, and demanded the reason for such extraordinary conduct.

"*Why* do you refuse?"

"I would prefer not to."

With any other man I should have flown outright into a dreadful passion, scorned all further words, and thrust him ignominiously from my presence. But there was something about Bartleby that not only strangely disarmed me, but, in a wonderful manner, touched and disconcerted me. I began to reason with him.

"These are your own copies we are about to examine. It is labor saving to you, because one examination will answer for your four papers. It is common usage. Every copyist is bound to help examine his copy. Is it not so? Will you not speak? Answer!"

"I prefer not to," he replied in a flutelike tone. It seemed to me that, while I had been addressing him, he carefully revolved every statement that I made; fully comprehended the meaning; could not gainsay the irresistible conclusion; but, at the same time, some paramount consideration prevailed with him to reply as he did.

"You are decided, then, not to comply with my request—a request made according to common usage and common sense?"

He briefly gave me to understand, that on that point my judgment was sound. Yes: his decision was irreversible.

It is not seldom the case that, when a man is browbeaten in some unprecedented and violently unreasonable way, he begins to stagger in his own plainest faith. He begins, as it were, vaguely to surmise that, wonderful as it may be, all the justice and all the reason is on the other side. Accordingly, if any disinterested persons are present, he turns to them for some reinforcement of his own faltering mind.

"Turkey," said I, "what do you think of this? Am I not right?"

"With submission, sir," said Turkey, in his blandest tone, "I think that you are."

"Nippers," said I, "what do *you* think of it?"

"I think I should kick him out of the office."

(The reader, of nice perceptions, will here perceive that, it being morning, Turkey's answer is couched in polite and tranquil terms, but Nippers replies in ill-tempered ones. Or, to repeat a previous sentence, Nippers's ugly mood was on duty, and Turkey's off.)

"Ginger Nut," said I, willing to enlist the smallest suffrage in my behalf, "what do *you* think of it?"

"I think, sir, he's a little *luny*," replied Ginger Nut, with a grin.

"You hear what they say," said I, turning towards the screen, "come forth and do your duty."

But he vouchsafed no reply. I pondered a moment in sore perplexity. But once more business hurried me. I determined again to postpone the consideration of this dilemma to my future leisure. With a little trouble we made out to examine the papers without Bartleby, though at every page or two Turkey deferentially dropped his opinion, that this proceeding was quite out of the common; while Nippers, twitching in his chair with a dyspeptic nervousness, ground out, between his set teeth, occasional hissing maledictions against the stubborn oaf behind the screen. And for his (Nippers's) part, this was the first and the last time he would do another man's business without pay.

Meanwhile Bartleby sat in his hermitage, oblivious to everything but his own peculiar business there.

Some days passed, the scrivener being employed upon another lengthy work. His late remarkable conduct led me to regard his ways narrowly. I observed that he never went to dinner; indeed, that he never went anywhere. As yet I had never, of my personal knowledge, known him to be outside of my office. He was a perpetual sentry in the corner. At about eleven o'clock though, in the morning, I noticed that Ginger Nut would advance toward the opening in Bartleby's screen, as if silently beckoned thither by a gesture invisible to me where I sat. The boy would then leave the office, jingling a few pence, and reappear with a handful of ginger-nuts, which he delivered in the hermitage, receiving two of the cakes for his trouble.

He lives, then, on ginger-nuts, thought I; never eats a dinner, properly speaking; he must be a vegetarian, then; but no; he never eats even vegetables, he eats nothing but ginger-nuts. My mind then ran on in reveries concerning the probable effects upon the human constitution of living entirely on ginger-nuts. Ginger-nuts are so called, because they contain ginger as one of their peculiar constituents, and the final flavoring one. Now, what was ginger? A hot, spicy thing. Was Bartleby hot and spicy? Not at all. Ginger, then, had no effect upon Bartleby. Probably he preferred it should have none.

Nothing so aggravates an earnest person as a passive resistance. If the individual so resisted be of a not inhumane temper, and the resisting one perfectly harmless in his passivity, then, in the better moods of the former, he will endeavor charitably to construe to his imagination what proves impossible to be solved by his judgment. Even so, for the most part, I regarded Bartleby and his ways. Poor fellow! thought I, he means no mischief; it is plain he intends no insolence; his aspect sufficiently evinces that his eccentricities are involuntary. He is useful to me. I can get along with him. If I turn him away, the chances are he will fall in with some less-indulgent employer, and then he will be rudely treated, and perhaps driven forth miserably to starve. Yes. Here I can cheaply purchase a delicious self-approval. To befriend Bartleby; to humor him in his strange willfulness, will cost me little or nothing, while I lay up in my soul what will eventually prove a sweet morsel for my conscience. But this mood was not invariable with me. The passiveness of Bartleby sometimes irritated me. I felt strangely goaded on to encounter him in new opposition—to elicit some angry spark from him answerable to my own. But, indeed, I might as well have essayed to strike fire with my knuckles against a bit of Windsor soap. But one afternoon the evil impulse in me mastered me, and the following little scene ensued:

"Bartleby," said I, "when those papers are all copied, I will compare them with you."

"I would prefer not to."

"How? Surely you do not mean to persist in that mulish vagary?"

No answer.

I threw open the folding-doors near by, and, turning upon Turkey and Nippers, exclaimed:

"Bartleby a second time says, he won't examine his papers. What do you think of it, Turkey?"

It was afternoon, be it remembered. Turkey sat glowing like a brass boiler; his bald head steaming; his hands reeling among his blotted papers.

"Think of it?" roared Turkey; "I think I'll just step behind his screen, and black his eyes for him!"

So saying, Turkey rose to his feet and threw his arms into a pugilistic position. He was hurrying away to make good his promise, when I detained him, alarmed at the effect of incautiously rousing Turkey's combativeness after dinner.

"Sit down, Turkey," said I, "and hear what Nippers has to say. What do you think of it, Nippers? Would I not be justified in immediately dismissing Bartleby?"

"Excuse me, that is for you to decide, sir. I think his conduct quite unusual, and, indeed, unjust, as regards Turkey and myself. But it may only be a passing whim."

"Ah," exclaimed I, "you have strangely changed your mind, then—you speak very gently of him now."

"All beer," cried Turkey; "gentleness is effects of beer—Nippers and I dined together to-day. You see how gentle *I* am, sir. Shall I go and black his eyes?"

"You refer to Bartleby, I suppose. No, not to-day, Turkey," I replied; "pray, put up your fists."

I closed the doors, and again advanced towards Bartleby. I felt additional incentives tempting me to my fate. I burned to be rebelled against again. I remembered that Bartleby never left the office.

"Bartleby," said I, "Ginger Nut is away; just step around to the Post Office, won't you? (it was but a three minutes' walk), and see if there is anything for me."

"I would prefer not to."

"You *will* not?"

"I *prefer* not."

I staggered to my desk, and sat there in a deep study. My blind inveteracy returned. Was there any other thing in which I could procure myself to be ignominiously repulsed by this lean, penniless wight?—my hired clerk? What added thing is there, perfectly reasonable, that he will be sure to refuse to do?

"Bartleby!"

No answer.

"Bartleby," in a louder tone.

No answer.

"Bartleby," I roared.

Like a very ghost, agreeably to the laws of magical invocation, at the third summons, he appeared at the entrance of his hermitage.

"Go to the next room, and tell Nippers to come to me."

"I prefer not to," he respectfully and slowly said, and mildly disappeared.

"Very good, Bartleby," said I, in a quiet sort of serenely-severe self-possessed tone, intimating the unalterable purpose of some terrible retribution very close at hand. At the moment I half intended something of the kind. But upon the whole, as it was drawing towards my dinner-hour, I thought it best to put on my hat and walk home for the day, suffering much from perplexity and distress of mind.

Shall I acknowledge it? The conclusion of this whole business was, that it soon became a fixed fact of my chambers, that a pale young scrivener, by the name of Bartleby, had a desk there; that he copied for me at the usual rate of four cents a folio (one hundred words); but he was permanently exempt from examining the work done by him, that duty being transferred to Turkey and Nippers, out of compliment, doubtless, to their superior acuteness; moreover, said Bartleby was never, on any account, to be dispatched on the most trivial errand of any sort; and that even if entreated to take upon him such a matter, it was generally understood that he would "prefer not to"—in other words, that he would refuse point-blank.

As days passed on, I became considerably reconciled to Bartleby. His steadiness, his freedom from all dissipation, his incessant industry (except when he chose to throw himself into a standing revery behind his screen), his great stillness, his unalterableness of demeanor under all circumstances, made him a valuable acquisition. One prime thing was this—*he was always there*—first in the morning, continually through the day, and the last at night. I had a singular confidence in his honesty. I felt my most precious papers perfectly safe in his hands. Sometimes, to be sure, I could not, for the very soul of me, avoid falling into sudden spasmodic passions with him. For it was exceeding difficult to bear in mind all the time those strange peculiarities, privileges, and unheard of exemptions, forming the tacit stipulations on Bartleby's part under which he remained in my office. Now and then, in the eagerness of dispatching pressing business, I would inadvertently summon Bartleby, in a short, rapid tone, to put his finger, say, on the incipient tie of a bit of red tape with which I was about compressing some papers. Of course, from behind the screen the usual answer, "I prefer not to," was sure to come; and then, how could a human creature, with the common infirmities of our nature, refrain from bitterly exclaiming upon such perverseness—such unreasonableness. However, every added repulse of this sort which I received only tended to lessen the probability of my repeating the inadvertence.

Here it must be said, that according to the custom of most legal gentlemen occupying chambers in densely-populated law buildings, there were several keys to my door. One was kept by a woman residing in the attic, which person weekly scrubbed and daily swept and dusted my apartments. Another was kept by Turkey for convenience sake. The third I sometimes carried in my own pocket. The fourth I knew not who had.

Now, one Sunday morning I happened to go to Trinity Church,[4] to hear a celebrated preacher, and finding myself rather early on the ground I thought I would walk around to my chambers for a while. Luckily I had my key with me; but upon applying it to the lock, I found it resisted by something inserted from the inside. Quite surprised, I called out; when to my consternation a key was turned from within; and thrusting his lean visage at me, and holding the door ajar, the apparition of Bartleby appeared, in his shirt sleeves, and otherwise in a strangely tattered deshabille, saying quietly that he was sorry, but he was deeply engaged just then, and—preferred not admitting me at present. In a brief word or two, he moreover added, that perhaps I had better walk around the block two or three times, and by that time he would probably have concluded his affairs.

Now, the utterly unsurmised appearance of Bartleby, tenanting my law-chambers of a Sunday morning, with his cadaverously gentlemanly *nonchalance*, yet withal firm and self-possessed, had such a strange effect upon me, that incontinently I slunk away from my own door, and did as desired. But not without sundry twinges of impotent rebellion against the mild effrontery of this unaccountable scrivener. Indeed, it was his wonderful mildness chiefly, which not only disarmed me, but unmanned me as it were. For I consider that one, for the time, is a sort of unmanned when he tranquilly permits his hired clerk to dictate to him, and order him away from his own premises. Furthermore, I was full of uneasiness as to what Bartleby could possibly be doing in my office in his shirt sleeves, and in an otherwise dismantled condition of a Sunday morning. Was anything amiss going on? Nay, that was out of the question. It was not to be thought of for a moment that Bartleby was an immoral person. But what could he be doing there?—copying? Nay again, whatever might be his eccentricities, Bartleby was an eminently decorous person. He would be the last man to sit down to his desk in any state approaching to nudity. Besides, it was Sunday; and there was something about Bartleby that forbade the supposition that he would by any secular occupation violate the proprieties of the day.

Nevertheless, my mind was not pacified; and full of a restless curiosity, at last I returned to the door. Without hindrance I inserted my key, opened it, and entered. Bartleby was not to be seen. I looked round anxiously, peeped behind his screen; but it was very plain that he was gone. Upon more closely examining the place, I surmised that for an indefinite period Bartleby must have ate, dressed, and slept in my office, and that, too without plate, mirror, or bed. The cushioned seat of a ricketty old sofa in one corner bore the faint impress of a lean, reclining form. Rolled away under his desk, I found a blanket; under the empty grate, a blacking box and brush; on a chair, a tin basin, with soap and a ragged towel; in a newspaper a few crumbs of ginger-nuts and a morsel of cheese. Yes, thought I, it is evident enough that Bartleby has been making his home here, keeping bachelor's hall all by himself. Immediately then the thought came sweeping across me, what miserable friendlessness and loneliness are here revealed! His poverty is great; but his solitude, how horrible! Think of it. Of a Sunday, Wall Street is deserted as Petra;[5] and every night of every day it is an emptiness. This building, too, which of weekdays hums with industry and life, at nightfall echoes with sheer vacancy, and all through Sunday is forlorn. And here Bartleby makes his home; sole spectator of a solitude which he has seen all populous—a

[4]A fashionable Episcopal Church on Wall Street.

[5]An ancient city in modern Jordan; rediscovered shortly before Melville's lifetime after having been deserted for centuries.

sort of innocent and transformed Marius[6] brooding among the ruins of Carthage!

For the first time in my life a feeling of overpowering stinging melancholy seized me. Before, I had never experienced aught but a not unpleasing sadness. The bond of a common humanity now drew me irresistibly to gloom. A fraternal melancholy! For both I and Bartleby were sons of Adam. I remembered the bright silks and sparkling faces I had seen that day, in gala trim, swan-like sailing down the Mississippi of Broadway; and I contrasted them with the pallid copyist, and thought to myself, Ah, happiness courts the light, so we deem the world is gay; but misery hides aloof, so we deem that misery there is none. These sad fancyings—chimeras, doubtless, of a sick and silly brain—led on to other and more special thoughts, concerning the eccentricities of Bartleby. Presentiments of strange discoveries hovered round me. The scrivener's pale form appeared to me laid out, among uncaring strangers, in its shivering winding sheet.

Suddenly I was attracted by Bartleby's closed desk, the key in open sight left in the lock.

I mean no mischief, seek the gratification of no heartless curiosity, thought I; besides, the desk is mine, and its contents, too, so I will make bold to look within. Everything was methodically arranged, the papers smoothly placed. The pigeon holes were deep, and removing the files of documents, I groped into their recesses. Presently I felt something there, and dragged it out. It was an old bandanna handkerchief, heavy and knotted. I opened it, and saw it was a savings's bank.

I now recalled all the quiet mysteries which I had noted in the man. I remembered that he never spoke but to answer; that, though at intervals he had considerable time to himself, yet I had never seen him reading—no, not even a newspaper; that for long periods he would stand looking out, at his pale window behind the screen, upon the dead brick wall; I was quite sure he never visited any refectory or eating house; while his pale face clearly indicated that he never drank beer like Turkey, or tea and coffee even, like other men; that he never went anywhere in particular that I could learn, never went out for a walk, unless, indeed, that was the case at present; that he had declined telling who he was, or whence he came, or whether he had any relatives in the world; that though so thin and pale, he never complained of ill health. And more than all, I remembered a certain unconscious air of pallid—how shall I call it?—of pallid haughtiness, say, or rather an austere reserve about him, which had positively awed me into my tame compliance with his eccentricities, when I had feared to ask him to do the slightest incidental thing for me, even though I might know, from his long-continued motionlessness, that behind his screen he must be standing in one of those dead-wall reveries of his.

Revolving all these things, and coupling them with the recently discovered fact, that he made my office his constant abiding place and home, and not forgetful of his morbid moodiness; revolving all these things, a prudential feeling began to steal over me. My first emotions had been those of pure melancholy and sincerest pity; but just in proportion as the forlornness of Bartleby grew and grew to my imagination, did that same melancholy merge into fear, that pity into repulsion. So true it is, and so terrible, too, that up to a certain point the thought or sight of misery enlists our best affections; but, in certain special cases, beyond that point it does not. They err who would assert that invariably this is owing to the inherent selfishness of the human heart. It rather proceeds from a certain hopelessness of remedying excessive and organic ill. To a sensitive being, pity is not seldom pain. And when at last it is perceived that such pity cannot lead to effectual succor, common sense bids the soul be rid of it. What I saw that morning persuaded me that the scrivener was the victim of innate and incurable disorder. I might give alms to his body; but his body did not pain him; it was his soul that suffered, and his soul I could not reach.

I did not accomplish the purpose of going to Trinity Church that morning. Somehow, the things I had seen disqualified me for the time from churchgoing. I walked homeward, thinking what I would do with Bartleby. Finally, I resolved upon this—I would put certain calm questions to him the next morning, touching his history, etc., and if he declined to answer them openly and unreservedly (and I supposed he would prefer not), then to give him a twenty dollar bill over and above whatever I might owe him, and tell him his services were no longer required; but that if in any other way I could assist him, I would be happy to do so, especially if he desired to return to his native place, wherever that might be, I would willingly help to defray the expenses. Moreover, if, after reaching home, he found himself at any time in want of aid, a letter from him would be sure of a reply.

The next morning came.

"Bartleby," said I, gently calling to him behind his screen.

No reply.

"Bartleby," said I, in a still gentler tone, "come here; I am not going to ask you to do anything you

[6] Caius Marius (155-86 B.C.), a general and consul of Rome who was exiled after civil war; he fled to Carthage but was forbidden to land. The allusion is to a message Marius sent to the governor of Carthage.

would prefer not to do—I simply wish to speak to you."

Upon this he noiselessly slid into view.

"Will you tell me, Bartleby, where you were born?"

"I would prefer not to."

"Will you tell me *anything* about yourself?"

"I would prefer not to."

"But what reasonable objection can you have to speak to me? I feel friendly towards you."

He did not look at me while I spoke, but kept his glance fixed upon my bust of Cicero, which, as I then sat, was directly behind me, some six inches above my head.

"What is your answer, Bartleby?" said I, after waiting a considerable time for a reply, during which his countenance remained immovable, only there was the faintest conceivable tremor of the white attenuated mouth.

"At present I prefer to give no answer," he said, and retired into his hermitage.

It was rather weak in me I confess, but his manner, on this occasion, nettled me. Not only did there seem to lurk in it a certain calm disdain, but his perverseness seemed ungrateful, considering the undeniable good usage and indulgence he had received from me.

Again I sat ruminating what I should do. Mortified as I was at his behavior, and resolved as I had been to dismiss him when I entered my office, nevertheless I strangely felt something superstitious knocking at my heart, and forbidding me to carry out my purpose, and denouncing me for a villain if I dared to breathe one bitter word against this forlornest of mankind. At last, familiarly drawing my chair behind his screen, I sat down and said: "Bartleby, never mind, then, about revealing your history; but let me entreat you, as a friend, to comply as far as may be with the usages of this office. Say now, you will help to examine papers to-morrow or next day: in short, say now, that in a day or two you will begin to be a little reasonable:—say so, Bartleby."

"At present I would prefer not to be a little reasonable," was his mildly cadaverous reply.

Just then the folding-doors opened, and Nippers approached. He seemed suffering from an unusually bad night's rest, induced by severer indigestion than common. He overheard those final words of Bartleby.

"*Prefer not,* eh?" gritted Nippers—"I'd *prefer* him, if I were you, sir," addressing me—"I'd *prefer* him; I'd give him preferences, the stubborn mule! What is it, sir, pray, that he *prefers* not to do now?"

Bartleby moved not a limb.

"Mr. Nippers," said I, "I'd prefer that you would withdraw for the present."

Somehow, of late, I had got into the way of involuntarily using this word "prefer" upon all sorts of not exactly suitable occasions. And I trembled to think that my contact with the scrivener had already and seriously affected me in a mental way. And what further and deeper aberration might it not yet produce? This apprehension had not been without efficacy in determining me to summary measures.

As Nippers, looking very sour and sulky, was departing, Turkey blandly and deferentially approached.

"With submission, sir," said he, "yesterday I was thinking about Bartleby here, and I think that if he would but prefer to take a quart of good ale every day, it would do much towards mending him, and enabling him to assist in examining his papers."

"So you have got the word, too," said I, slightly excited.

"With submission, what word, sir?" asked Turkey, respectfully crowding himself into the contracted space behind the screen, and by so doing, making me jostle the scrivener. "What word, sir?"

"I would prefer to be left alone here," said Bartleby, as if offended at being mobbed in his privacy.

"*That's* the word, Turkey," said I—"*that's* it."

"Oh, *prefer?* oh yes—queer word. I never use it myself. But sir, as I was saying, if he would but prefer—"

"Turkey," interrupted I, "you will please withdraw."

"Oh, certainly, sir, if you prefer that I should."

As he opened the folding-door to retire, Nippers at his desk caught a glimpse of me, and asked whether I would prefer to have a certain paper copied on blue paper or white. He did not in the least roguishly accent the word prefer. It was plain that it involuntarily rolled from his tongue. I thought to myself, surely I must get rid of a demented man, who already has in some degree turned the tongues, if not the heads of myself and clerks. But I thought it prudent not to break the dismission at once.

The next day I noticed that Bartleby did nothing but stand at his window in his dead-wall revery. Upon asking him why he did not write, he said that he had decided upon doing no more writing.

"Why, how now? what next?" exclaimed I, "do no more writing?"

"No more."

"And what is the reason?"

"Do you not see the reason for yourself," he indifferently replied.

I looked steadfastly at him, and perceived that his eyes looked dull and glazed. Instantly it occurred to me, that his unexampled diligence in copying by his dim window for the first few weeks of his stay with me might have temporarily impaired his vision.

I was touched. I said something in condolence with him. I hinted that of course he did wisely in abstaining from writing for a while; and urged him to embrace that opportunity of taking wholesome exercise in the open air. This, however, he did not do. A few days after this, my other clerks being absent, and being in a great hurry to dispatch certain letters by the mail, I thought that, having nothing else earthly to do, Bartleby would surely be less inflexible than usual, and carry these letters to the post-office. But he blankly declined. So, much to my inconvenience, I went myself.

Still added days went by. Whether Bartleby's eyes improved or not, I could not say. To all appearance, I thought they did. But when I asked him if they did, he vouchsafed no answer. At all events, he would do no copying. At last, in reply to my urgings, he informed me that he had permanently given up copying.

"What!" exclaimed I; "suppose your eyes should get entirely well—better than ever before—would you not copy then?"

"I have given up copying," he answered, and slid aside.

He remained as ever, a fixture in my chamber. Nay—if that were possible—he became still more of a fixture than before. What was to be done? He would do nothing in the office; why should he stay there? In plain fact, he had now become a millstone to me, not only useless as a necklace, but afflictive to bear. Yet I was sorry for him. I speak less than truth when I say that, on his own account, he occasioned me uneasiness. If he would but have named a single relative or friend, I would instantly have written, and urged their taking the poor fellow away to some convenient retreat. But he seemed alone, absolutely alone in the universe. A bit of wreck in the mid Atlantic. At length, necessities connected with my business tyrannized over all other considerations. Decently as I could, I told Bartleby that in six days time he must unconditionally leave the office. I warned him to take measures, in the interval, for procuring some other abode. I offered to assist him in this endeavor, if he himself would but take the first step towards a removal. "And when you finally quit me, Bartleby," added I, "I shall see that you go not away entirely unprovided. Six days from this hour, remember."

At the expiration of that period, I peeped behind the screen, and lo! Bartleby was there.

I buttoned up my coat, balanced myself; advanced slowly towards him, touched his shoulder, and said, "The time has come; you must quit this place; I am sorry for you; here is money; but you must go."

"I would prefer not," he replied, with his back still towards me.

"You *must.*"

He remained silent.

Now I had an unbounded confidence in this man's common honesty. He had frequently restored to me sixpences and shillings carelessly dropped upon the floor, for I am apt to be very reckless in such shirt-button affairs. The proceeding, then, which followed will not be deemed extraordinary.

"Bartleby," said I, "I owe you twelve dollars on account; here are thirty-two; the odd twenty are yours—Will you take it?" and I handed the bills towards him.

But he made no motion.

"I will leave them here, then," putting them under a weight on the table. Then taking my hat and cane and going to the door, I tranquilly turned and added—"After you have removed your things from these offices, Bartleby, you will of course lock the door—since every one is now gone for the day but you—and if you please, slip your key underneath the mat, so that I may have it in the morning. I shall not see you again, so good-by to you. If, hereafter, in your new place of abode, I can be of any service to you, do not fail to advise me by letter. Good-by, Bartleby, and fare you well."

But he answered not a word; like the last column of some ruined temple, he remained standing mute and solitary in the middle of the otherwise deserted room.

As I walked home in a pensive mood, my vanity got the better of my pity. I could not but highly plume myself on my masterly management in getting rid of Bartleby. Masterly I call it, and such it must appear to any dispassionate thinker. The beauty of my procedure seemed to consist in its perfect quietness. There was no vulgar bullying, no bravado of any sort, no choleric hectoring, and striding to and fro across the apartment, jerking out vehement commands for Bartleby to bundle himself off with his beggarly traps. Nothing of the kind. Without loudly bidding Bartleby depart—as an inferior genius might have done—I *assumed* the ground that depart he must; and upon that assumption built all I had to say. The more I thought over my procedure, the more I was charmed with it. Nevertheless, next morning, upon awakening, I had my doubts—I had somehow slept off the fumes of vanity. One of the coolest and wisest hours a man has, is just after he awakes in the morning. My procedure seemed as sagacious as ever—but only in theory. How it would prove in practice—there was the rub. It was truly a beautiful thought to have assumed Bartleby's departure; but, after all, that assumption was simply my own, and none of Bartleby's. The great point was, not whether I had assumed that he would quit me, but whether he would prefer so to do. He was more a man of preferences than assumptions.

After breakfast, I walked down town, arguing the probabilities *pro* and *con.* One moment I thought it would prove a miserable failure, and Bartleby would be found all alive at my office as usual; the next moment it seemed certain that I should find his chair empty. And so I kept veering about. At the corner of Broadway and Canal Street, I saw quite an excited group of people standing in earnest conversation.

"I'll take odds he doesn't," said a voice as I passed.

"Doesn't go?—done!" said I, "put up your money."

I was instinctively putting my hand in my pocket to produce my own, when I remembered that this was an election day. The words I had overheard bore no reference to Bartleby, but to the success or non-success of some candidate for the mayoralty. In my intent frame of mind, I had, as it were, imagined that all Broadway shared in my excitement, and were debating the same question with me. I passed on, very thankful that the uproar of the street screened my momentary absent-mindedness.

As I had intended, I was earlier than usual at my office door. I stood listening for a moment. All was still. He must be gone. I tried the knob. The door was locked. Yes, my procedure had worked to a charm; he indeed must be vanished. Yet a certain melancholy mixed with this: I was almost sorry for my brilliant success. I was fumbling under the door mat for the key, which Bartleby was to have left there for me, when accidentally my knee knocked against a panel, producing a summoning sound, and in response a voice came to me from within—"Not yet; I am occupied."

It was Bartleby.

I was thunderstruck. For an instant I stood like the man who, pipe in mouth, was killed one cloudless afternoon long ago in Virginia, by summer lightning; at his own warm open window he was killed, and remained leaning out there upon the dreamy afternoon, till some one touched him, when he fell.

"Not gone!" I murmured at last. But again obeying that wondrous ascendancy which the inscrutable scrivener had over me, and from which ascendancy, for all my chafing, I could not completely escape, I slowly went down stairs and out into the street, and while walking round the block, considered what I should next do in this unheard-of perplexity. Turn the man out by an actual thrusting I could not; to drive him away by calling him hard names would not do; calling in the police was an unpleasant idea; and yet, permit him to enjoy his cadaverous triumph over me—this, too, I could not think of. What was to be done? or, if nothing could be done, was there anything further that I could *assume* in the matter? Yes, as before I had prospectively assumed that Bartleby would depart, so now I might retrospectively assume that departed he was. In the legitimate carrying out of this assumption, I might enter my office in a great hurry, and pretending not to see Bartleby at all, walk straight against him as if he were air. Such a proceeding would in a singular degree have the appearance of a home-thrust. It was hardly possible that Bartleby could withstand such an application of the doctrine of assumptions. But upon second thoughts the success of the plan seemed rather dubious. I resolved to argue the matter over with him again.

"Bartleby," said I, entering the office, with a quietly severe expression, "I am seriously displeased. I am pained, Bartleby. I had thought better of you. I had imagined you of such a gentlemanly organization, that in any delicate dilemma a slight hint would suffice—in short, an assumption. But it appears I am deceived. Why," I added, unaffectedly starting, "you have not even touched that money yet," pointing to it, just where I had left it the evening previous.

He answered nothing.

"Will you, or will you not, quit me?" I now demanded in a sudden passion, advancing close to him.

"I would prefer *not* to quit you," he replied, gently emphasizing the *not*.

"What earthly right have you to stay here? Do you pay any rent? Do you pay my taxes? Or is this property yours?"

He answered nothing.

"Are you ready to go on and write now? Are your eyes recovered? Could you copy a small paper for me this morning? or help examine a few lines? or step round to the post-office? In a word, will you do anything at all, to give a coloring to your refusal to depart the premises?"

He silently retired into his hermitage.

I was now in such a state of nervous resentment that I thought it but prudent to check myself at present from further demonstrations. Bartleby and I were alone. I remembered the tragedy of the unfortunate Adams and the still more unfortunate Colt in the solitary office of the latter; and how poor Colt, being dreadfully incensed by Adams, and imprudently permitting himself to get wildly excited, was at unawares hurried into his fatal act—an act which certainly no man could possibly deplore more than the actor himself.[7] Often it had occurred to me in my ponderings upon the subject, that had that altercation taken place in the public street, or at a private residence, it would not have terminated as it did. It was the circumstance of being alone in a solitary office, up stairs, of a building entirely unhallowed by humanizing domestic associations—an uncarpeted office, doubtless, of a dusty, haggard sort of appearance—this it must have been, which

[7]An actual murder that occurred in 1842.

greatly helped to enhance the irritable desperation of the hapless Colt.

But when this old Adam of resentment rose in me and tempted me concerning Bartleby, I grappled him and threw him. How? Why, simply by recalling the divine injunction: "A new commandment give I unto you, that ye love one another."[8] Yes, this it was that saved me. Aside from higher considerations, charity often operates as a vastly wise and prudent principle—a great safeguard to its possessor. Men have committed murder for jealousy's sake, and anger's sake, and hatred's sake, and selfishness' sake, and spiritual pride's sake; but no man, that ever I heard of, ever committed a diabolical murder for sweet charity's sake. Mere self-interest, then, if no better motive can be enlisted, should, especially with high-tempered men, prompt all beings to charity and philanthropy. At any rate, upon the occasion in question, I strove to drown my exasperated feelings towards the scrivener by benevolently construing his conduct. Poor fellow, poor fellow! thought I, he don't mean anything; and besides, he has seen hard times, and ought to be indulged.

I endeavored, also, immediately to occupy myself, and at the same time to comfort my despondency. I tried to fancy, that in the course of the morning, at such time as might prove agreeable to him, Bartleby, of his own free accord, would emerge from his hermitage and take up some decided line of march in the direction of the door. But no. Half-past twelve o'clock came; Turkey began to glow in the face, overturn his inkstand, and become generally obstreperous; Nippers abated down into quietude and courtesy; Ginger Nut munched his noon apple; and Bartleby remained standing at his window in one of his profoundest dead-wall reveries. Will it be credited? Ought I to acknowledge it? That afternoon I left the office without saying one further word to him.

Some days now passed, during which, at leisure intervals I looked a little into "Edwards on the Will," and "Priestley on Necessity."[9] Under the circumstances, those books induced a salutary feeling. Gradually I slid into the persuasion that these troubles of mine, touching the scrivener, had been all predestinated from eternity, and Bartleby was billeted upon me for some mysterious purpose of an allwise Providence, which it was not for a mere mortal like me to fathom. Yes, Bartleby, stay there behind your screen, thought I; I shall persecute you no more; you are harmless and noiseless as any of these old chairs; in short, I never feel so private as when I know you are here. At last I see it, I feel it; I penetrate to the predestinated purpose of my life. I am content. Others may have loftier parts to enact; but my mission in this world, Bartleby, is to furnish you with office-room for such period as you may see fit to remain.

I believe that this wise and blessed frame of mind would have continued with me, had it not been for the unsolicited and uncharitable remarks obtruded upon me by my professional friends who visited the rooms. But thus it often is, that the constant friction of illiberal minds wears out at last the best resolves of the more generous. Though to be sure, when I reflected upon it, it was not strange that people entering my office should be struck by the peculiar aspect of the unaccountable Bartleby, and so be tempted to throw out some sinister observations concerning him. Sometimes an attorney, having business with me, and calling at my office, and finding no one but the scrivener there, would undertake to obtain some sort of precise information from him touching my whereabouts; but without heeding his idle talk, Bartleby would remain standing immovable in the middle of the room. So after contemplating him in that position for a time, the attorney would depart, no wiser than he came.

Also, when a reference was going on, and the room full of lawyers and witnesses, and business driving fast, some deeply-occupied legal gentleman present, seeing Bartleby wholly unemployed, would request him to run round to his (the legal gentleman's) office and fetch some papers for him. Thereupon, Bartleby would tranquilly decline, and yet remain idle as before. Then the lawyer would give a great stare, and turn to me. And what could I say? At last I was made aware that all through the circle of my professional acquaintance, a whisper of wonder was running round, having reference to the strange creature I kept at my office. This worried me very much. And as the idea came upon me of his possibly turning out a long-lived man, and keep occupying my chambers, and denying my authority; and perplexing my visitors; and scandalizing my professional reputation; and casting a general gloom over the premises; keeping soul and body together to the last upon his savings (for doubtless he spent but half a dime a day), and in the end perhaps outlive me, and claim possession of my office by right of his perpetual occupancy: as all these dark anticipations crowded upon me more and more, and my friends continually intruded their relentless remarks upon the apparition in my room; a great change was wrought in me. I resolved to gather all my faculties together, and forever rid me of this intolerable incubus.

Ere revolving any complicated project, however,

[8] See John xiii.34.

[9] Jonathan Edwards in *Freedom of the Will* (1754) and Joseph Priestley in *The Doctrine of Philosophic Necessity* (1777) argued for predestination and inevitability but from different perspectives: Edwards supported Calvinism while Priestley rejected it and relied on rationalism.

adapted to this end, I first simply suggested to Bartleby the propriety of his permanent departure. In a calm and serious tone, I commended the idea to his careful and mature consideration. But, having taken three days to meditate upon it, he apprised me, that his original determination remained the same; in short, that he still preferred to abide with me.

What shall I do? I now said to myself, buttoning up my coat to the last button. What shall I do? what ought I to do? what does conscience say I *should* do with this man, or, rather, ghost. Rid myself of him, I must; go, he shall. But how? You will not thrust him, the poor, pale, passive mortal—you will not thrust such a helpless creature out of your door? you will not dishonor yourself by such cruelty? No, I will not, I cannot do that. Rather would I let him live and die here, and then mason up his remains in the wall. What, then, will you do? For all your coaxing, he will not budge. Bribes he leaves under your own paper-weight on your table; in short, it is quite plain that he prefers to cling to you.

Then something severe, something unusual must be done. What! surely you will not have him collared by a constable, and commit his innocent pallor to the common jail? And upon what ground could you procure such a thing to be done?—a vagrant, is he? What! he a vagrant, a wanderer, who refuses to budge? It is because he will *not* be a vagrant, then, that you seek to count him *as* a vagrant. That is too absurd. No visible means of support: there I have him. Wrong again: for indubitably he *does* support himself, and that is the only unanswerable proof that any man can show of his possessing the means so to do. No more, then. Since he will not quit me, I must quit him. I will change my offices; I will move elsewhere, and give him fair notice, that if I find him on my new premises I will then proceed against him as a common trespasser.

Acting accordingly, next day I thus addressed him: "I find these chambers too far from the City Hall; the air is unwholesome. In a word, I propose to remove my offices next week, and shall no longer require your services. I tell you this now, in order that you may seek another place."

He made no reply, and nothing more was said.

On the appointed day I engaged carts and men, proceeded to my chambers, and, having but little furniture, everything was removed in a few hours. Throughout, the scrivener remained standing behind the screen, which I directed to be removed the last thing. It was withdrawn; and, being folded up like a huge folio, left him the motionless occupant of a naked room. I stood in the entry watching him a moment, while something from within me upbraided me.

I re-entered, with my hand in my pocket—and—and my heart in my mouth.

"Good-by, Bartleby; I am going—good-by, and God some way bless you; and take that," slipping something in his hand. But it dropped upon the floor, and then—strange to say—I tore myself from him whom I had so longed to be rid of.

Established in my new quarters, for a day or two I kept the door locked, and started at every footfall in the passages. When I returned to my rooms, after any little absence, I would pause at the threshold for an instant, and attentively listen, ere applying my key. But these fears were needless. Bartleby never came nigh me.

I thought all was going well, when a perturbed-looking stranger visited me, inquiring whether I was the person who had recently occupied rooms at No. — Wall Street.

Full of forebodings, I replied that I was.

"Then, sir," said the stranger, who proved a lawyer, "you are responsible for the man you left there. He refuses to do any copying; he refuses to do anything; he says he prefers not to; and he refuses to quit the premises."

"I am very sorry, sir," said I, with assumed tranquillity, but an inward tremor, "but, really, the man you allude to is nothing to me—he is no relation or apprentice of mine, that you should hold me responsible for him."

"In mercy's name, who is he?"

"I certainly cannot inform you. I know nothing about him. Formerly I employed him as a copyist; but he has done nothing for me now for some time past."

"I shall settle him, then—good morning, sir."

Several days passed, and I heard nothing more; and, though I often felt a charitable prompting to call at the place and see poor Bartleby, yet a certain squeamishness, of I know not what, withheld me.

All is over with him, by this time, thought I, at last, when, through another week, no further intelligence reached me. But, coming to my room the day after, I found several persons waiting at my door in a high state of nervous excitement.

"That's the man—here he comes," cried the foremost one, whom I recognized as the lawyer who had previously called upon me alone.

"You must take him away, sir, at once," cried a portly person among them, advancing upon me, and whom I knew to be the landlord of No. — Wall Street. "These gentlemen, my tenants, cannot stand it any longer; Mr. B——," pointing to the lawyer, "has turned him out of his room, and he now persists in haunting the building generally, sitting upon the banisters of the stairs by day, and sleeping in the entry by night. Everybody is concerned; clients are leaving the offices; some fears are entertained of a mob; something you must do, and that without delay."

Aghast at this torrent, I fell back before it, and would fain have locked myself in my new quarters. In vain I persisted that Bartleby was nothing to me—no more than to any one else. In vain—I was the last person known to have anything to do with him, and they held me to the terrible account. Fearful, then, of being exposed in the papers (as one person present obscurely threatened), I considered the matter, and, at length, said, that if the lawyer would give me a confidential interview with the scrivener, in his (the lawyer's) own room, I would, that afternoon, strive my best to rid them of the nuisance they complained of.

Going up stairs to my old haunt, there was Bartleby silently sitting upon the banister at the landing.

"What are you doing here, Bartleby?" said I.

"Sitting upon the banister," he mildly replied.

I motioned him into the lawyer's room, who then left us.

"Bartleby," said I, "are you aware that you are the cause of great tribulation to me, by persisting in occupying the entry after being dismissed from the office?"

No answer.

"Now one of two things must take place. Either you must do something, or something must be done to you. Now what sort of business would you like to engage in? Would you like to re-engage in copying for some one?"

"No; I would prefer not to make any change."

"Would you like a clerkship in a dry-goods store?"

"There is too much confinement about that. No, I would not like a clerkship; but I am not particular."

"Too much confinement," I cried, "why you keep yourself confined all the time!"

"I would prefer not to take a clerkship," he rejoined, as if to settle that little item at once.

"How would a bar-tender's business suit you? There is no trying of the eye-sight in that."

"I would not like it at all; though, as I said before, I am not particular."

His unwonted wordiness inspirited me. I returned to the charge.

"Well, then, would you like to travel through the country collecting bills for the merchants? That would improve your health."

"No, I would prefer to be doing something else."

"How, then, would going as a companion to Europe, to entertain some young gentleman with your conversation—how would that suit you?"

"Not at all. It does not strike me that there is anything definite about that. I like to be stationary. But I am not particular."

"Stationary you shall be, then," I cried, now losing all patience, and, for the first time in all my exasperating connection with him, fairly flying into a passion. "If you do not go away from these premises before night, I shall feel bound—indeed, I *am* bound—to—to—to quit the premises myself!" I rather absurdly concluded, knowing not with what possible threat to try to frighten his immobility into compliance. Despairing of all further efforts, I was precipitately leaving him, when a final thought occurred to me—one which had not been wholly unindulged before.

"Bartleby," said I, in the kindest tone I could assume under such exciting circumstances, "will you go home with me now—not to my office, but my dwelling—and remain there till we can conclude upon some convenient arrangement for you at our leisure? Come, let us start now, right away."

"No: at present I would prefer not to make any change at all."

I answered nothing; but, effectually dodging every one by the suddenness and rapidity of my flight, rushed from the building, ran up Wall Street towards Broadway, and, jumping into the first omnibus, was soon removed from pursuit. As soon as tranquillity returned, I distinctly perceived that I had now done all that I possibly could, both in respect to the demands of the landlord and his tenants, and with regard to my own desire and sense of duty, to benefit Bartleby, and shield him from rude persecution. I now strove to be entirely carefree and quiescent; and my conscience justified me in the attempt; though, indeed, it was not so successful as I could have wished. So fearful was I of being again hunted out by the incensed landlord and his exasperated tenants, that, surrendering my business to Nippers, for a few days, I drove about the upper part of the town and through the suburbs, in my rockaway; crossed over to Jersey City and Hoboken, and paid fugitive visits to Manhattanville and Astoria. In fact, I almost lived in my rockaway for the time.

When again I entered my office, lo, a note from the landlord lay upon the desk. I opened it with trembling hands. It informed me that the writer had sent to the police, and had Bartleby removed to the Tombs as a vagrant. Moreover, since I knew more about him than any one else, he wished me to appear at that place, and make a suitable statement of the facts. These tidings had a conflicting effect upon me. At first I was indignant; but, at last, almost approved. The landlord's energetic, summary disposition, had led him to adopt a procedure which I do not think I would have decided upon myself; and yet, as a last resort, under such peculiar circumstances, it seemed the only plan.

As I afterwards learned, the poor scrivener, when told that he must be conducted to the Tombs, offered not the slightest obstacle, but, in his pale, unmoving way, silently acquiesced.

Some of the compassionate and curious bystanders joined the party; and headed by one of the constables arm in arm with Bartleby, the silent procession filed its way through all the noise, and heat, and joy of the roaring thoroughfares at noon.

The same day I received the note, I went to the Tombs, or, to speak more properly, the Halls of Justice. Seeking the right officer, I stated the purpose of my call, and was informed that the individual I described was, indeed, within. I then assured the functionary that Bartleby was a perfectly honest man, and greatly to be compassionated, however unaccountably eccentric. I narrated all I knew, and closed by suggesting the idea of letting him remain in as indulgent confinement as possible, till something less harsh might be done—though, indeed, I hardly knew what. At all events, if nothing else could be decided upon, the alms-house must receive him. I then begged to have an interview.

Being under no disgraceful charge, and quite serene and harmless in all his ways, they had permitted him freely to wander about the prison, and, especially, in the inclosed grass-platted yards thereof. And so I found him there, standing all alone in the quietest of the yards, his face towards a high wall, while all around, from the narrow slits of the jail windows, I thought I saw peering out upon him the eyes of murderers and thieves.

"Bartleby!"

"I know you," he said, without looking round—"and I want nothing to say to you."

"It was not I that brought you here, Bartleby," said I, keenly pained at his implied suspicion. "And to you, this should not be so vile a place. Nothing reproachful attaches to you by being here. And see, it is not so sad a place as one might think. Look, there is the sky, and here is the grass."

"I know where I am," he replied, but would say nothing more, and so I left him.

As I entered the corridor again, a broad meat-like man, in an apron accosted me, and jerking his thumb over his shoulder, said—"Is that your friend?"

"Yes."

"Does he want to starve? If he does, let him live on the prison fare, that's all."

"Who are you?" asked I, not knowing what to make of such an unofficially speaking person in such a place.

"I am the grub-man. Such gentlemen as have friends here, hire me to provide them with something good to eat."

"Is this so?" said I, turning to the turnkey.

He said it was.

"Well, then," said I, slipping some silver into the grub-man's hands (for so they called him), "I want you to give particular attention to my friend there; let him have the best dinner you can get. And you must be as polite to him as possible."

"Introduce me, will you?" said the grub-man, looking at me with an expression which seemed to say he was all impatience for an opportunity to give a specimen of his breeding.

Thinking it would prove of benefit to the scrivener, I acquiesced; and, asking the grub-man his name, went up with him to Bartleby.

"Bartleby, this is a friend; you will find him very useful to you."

"Your sarvant, sir, your sarvant," said the grub-man, making a low salutation behind his apron. "Hope you find it pleasant here, sir; nice grounds—cool apartments—hope you'll stay with us some-time—try to make it agreeable. What will you have for dinner to-day?"

"I prefer not to dine to-day," said Bartleby, turning away. "It would disagree with me; I am unused to dinners." So saying, he slowly moved to the other side of the inclosure, and took up a position fronting the dead-wall.

"How's this?" said the grub-man, addressing me with a stare of astonishment. "He's odd, ain't he?"

"I think he is a little deranged," said I, sadly.

"Deranged? deranged is it? Well, now, upon my word, I thought that friend of yourn was a gentleman forger; they are always pale and genteel-like, them forgers. I can't help pity 'em—can't help it, sir. Did you know Monroe Edwards?" he added, touchingly, and paused. Then, laying his hand piteously on my shoulder, sighed, "he died of consumption at Sing-Sing. So you weren't acquainted with Monroe?"

"No, I was never socially acquainted with any forgers. But I cannot stop longer. Look to my friend yonder. You will not lose by it. I will see you again."

Some few days after this, I again obtained admission to the Tombs, and went through the corridors in quest of Bartleby; but without finding him.

"I saw him coming from his cell not long ago," said a turnkey, "may be he's gone to loiter in the yards."

So I went in that direction.

"Are you looking for the silent man?" said another turnkey, passing me. "Yonder he lies—sleeping in the yard there. 'Tis not twenty minutes since I saw him lie down."

The yard was entirely quiet. It was not accessible to the common prisoners. The surrounding walls, of amazing thickness, kept off all sounds behind them. The Egyptian character of the masonry weighed upon me with its gloom. But a soft imprisoned turf grew under foot. The heart of the eternal pyramids, it seemed, wherein, by some strange magic, through the clefts, grass-seed, dropped by birds, had sprung.

Strangely huddled at the base of the wall, his

knees drawn up, and lying on his side, his head touching the cold stones, I saw the wasted Bartleby. But nothing stirred. I paused; then went close up to him; stooped over, and saw that his dim eyes were open; otherwise he seemed profoundly sleeping. Something prompted me to touch him. I felt his hand, when a tingling shiver ran up my arm and down my spine to my feet.

The round face of the grub-man peered upon me now. "His dinner is ready. Won't he dine to-day, either? Or does he live without dining?"

"Lives without dining," said I, and closed the eyes.

"Eh!—He's asleep, ain't he?"

"With kings and counselors,"[10] murmured I.

There would seem little need for proceeding further in this history. Imagination will readily supply the meagre recital of poor Bartleby's interment. But, ere parting with the reader, let me say, that if this little narrative has sufficiently interested him, to awaken curiosity as to who Bartleby was, and what manner of life he led prior to the present narrator's making his acquaintance, I can only reply, that in such curiosity I fully share, but am wholly unable to gratify it. Yet here I hardly know whether I should divulge one little item of rumor, which came to my ear a few months after the scrivener's decease. Upon what basis it rested, I could never ascertain; and hence, how true it is I cannot now tell. But, inasmuch as this vague report has not been without a certain suggestive interest to me, however sad, it may prove the same with some others; and so I will briefly mention it. The report was this: that Bartleby had been a subordinate clerk in the Dead Letter Office at Washington, from which he had been suddenly removed by a change in the administration. When I think over this rumor, hardly can I express the emotions which seize me. Dead letters! does it not sound like dead men? Conceive a man by nature and misfortune prone to a pallid hopelessness, can any business seem more fitted to heighten it than that of continually handling these dead letters, and assorting them for the flames? For by the cart-load they are annually burned. Sometimes from out the folded paper the pale clerk takes a ring—the finger it was meant for, perhaps, moulders in the grave; a bank-note sent in swiftest charity—he whom it would relieve, nor eats nor hungers any more; pardon for those who died despairing; hope for those who died unhoping; good tidings for those who died stifled by unrelieved calamities. On errands of life, these letters speed to death.

Ah, Bartleby! Ah, humanity!

1853

[10]A synonym for death; see Job iii:14. Job wished to be at rest with kings and counselors.

Benito Cereno

Although the story is titled "Benito Cereno," it actually dramatizes the ways in which the three main characters—Cereno, Delano, and Babo—encounter and interpret the human situation. Through his skillful use of irony, ambiguity, and point of view, Melville suggests that each character fails, finally, to comprehend reality. Delano seems to succeed, but in the end he is no more capable of dealing with reality than before: he sails off into a blue sky. Benito Cereno sees only evil and malevolence in the world; he has lost all hope and trust, and thus wastes away physically and psychologically. And although Babo and the slaves have a case for revolt against their white oppressors, their way offers nothing because it leads to violence and death, not to any understanding or solution of a serious social and moral problem. Melville has transformed a bare and matter-of-fact source—Delano's *Narrative of Voyages and Travels in the Northern and Southern Hemispheres* (Boston, 1817)—into a fascinating and complex story. Text: *The Piazza Tales*, ed. Egbert S. Oliver (New York, 1948).

In the year 1799, Captain Amasa Delano, of Duxbury, in Massachusetts, commanding a large sealer and general trader, lay at anchor with a valuable cargo, in the harbor of St. Maria—a small, desert, uninhabited island towards the southern extremity of the long coast of Chili. There he had touched for water.

On the second day, not long after dawn, while lying in his berth, his mate came below, informing him that a strange sail was coming into the bay. Ships were then not so plenty in those waters as now. He rose, dressed, and went on deck.

The morning was one peculiar to that coast. Everything was mute and calm; everything gray. The sea, though undulated into long roods of swells, seemed fixed, and was sleeked at the surface like waved lead that has cooled and set in the smelter's mould. The sky seemed a gray surtout. Flights of troubled gray fowl, kith and kin with flights of troubled gray vapors among which they were mixed, skimmed low and fitfully over the waters, as swallows over meadows before storms. Shadows present, foreshadowing deeper shadows to come.

To Captain Delano's surprise, the stranger, viewed through the glass, showed no colors; though to do so upon entering a haven, however unhabited in its shores, where but a single other ship might be lying, was the custom among peaceful seamen of all nations. Considering the lawlessness and loneliness of the spot, and the sort of stories, at that day, associated with those seas, Captain Delano's surprise might have deepened into some uneasiness had he not been a person of a singularly undistrustful good nature, not liable, except on extraordinary and repeated incentives, and hardly then, to indulge in personal alarms, any way involving the imputation of malign evil in man. Whether, in view of what humanity is capable, such a trait implies, along with a benevolent heart, more than ordinary quickness and accuracy of intellectual perception, may be left to the wise to determine.

But whatever misgivings might have obtruded on first seeing the stranger, would almost, in any seaman's mind, have been dissipated by observing that the ship, in navigating into the harbor, was drawing too near the land; a sunken reef making out off her bow. This seemed to prove her a stranger, indeed, not only to the sealer, but the island; consequently, she could be no wonted freebooter on that ocean. With no small interest, Captain Delano continued to watch her—a proceeding not much facilitated by the vapors partly mantling the hull, through which the far matin light from her cabin streamed equivocally enough; much like the sun—by this time hemisphered on the rim of the horizon, and, apparently, in company with the strange ship entering the harbor—which, wimpled by the same low, creeping clouds, showed not unlike a Lima intriguante's one sinister eye peering across the Plaza from the Indian loop-hole of her rusk *saya-y-manta*.[1]

It might have been but a deception of the vapors, but, the longer the stranger was watched the more singular appeared her manoeuvres. Ere long it seemed hard to decide whether she meant to come in or no—what she wanted, or what she was about. The wind, which had breezed up a little during the night, was now extremely light and baffling, which the more increased the apparent uncertainty of her movements.

Surmising, at last, that it might be a ship in distress, Captain Delano ordered his whale-boat to be dropped, and, much to the wary opposition of his mate, prepared to board her, and, at the least, pilot her in. On the night previous, a fishing-party of the seamen had gone a long distance to some detached rocks out of sight from the sealer, and, an hour or two before daybreak, had returned, having met with no small success. Presuming that the stranger might have been long off soundings, the good captain put several baskets of the fish, for presents, into his boat, and so pulled away. From her continuing too near the sunken reef, deeming her in danger, calling to his men, he made all haste to apprise those on board of their situation. But, some time ere the boat came up, the wind, light though it was, having shifted, had headed the vessel off, as well as partly broken the vapors from about her.

Upon gaining a less remote view, the ship, when made signally visible on the verge of the leaden-hued swells, with the shreds of fog here and there raggedly furring her, appeared like a white-washed monastery after a thunderstorm, seen perched upon some dun cliff among the Pyrenees. But it was no purely fanciful resemblance which now, for a moment, almost led Captain Delano to think that nothing less than a ship-load of monks was before him. Peering over the bulwarks were what really seemed, in the hazy distance, throngs of dark cowls; while, fitfully revealed through the open port-holes, other dark moving figures were grimly described, as of Black Friars[2] pacing the cloisters.

Upon a still nigher approach, this appearance was modified, and the true character of the vessel was plain—a Spanish merchantman of the first class, carrying negro slaves, amongst other valuable freight, from one colonial port to another. A very large, and, in its time, a very fine vessel, such as in those days were at intervals encountered along that main; sometimes superseded Acapulco treasure-ships, or retired frigates of the Spanish king's navy, which, like superannuated Italian palaces, still, under a decline of masters, preserved signs of former state.

As the whale-boat drew more and more nigh, the cause of the peculiar pipe-clayed aspect of the stranger was seen in the slovenly neglect pervading her. The spars, ropes, and great part of the bulwarks, looked woolly, from long unacquaintance with the scraper, tar, and the brush. Her keel seemed laid, her ribs put together, and she launched, from Ezekiel's Valley of Dry Bones.[3]

In the present business in which she was engaged, the ship's general model and rig appeared to have undergone no material change from their original warlike and Froissart[4] pattern. However, no guns were seen.

The tops were large, and were railed about with what had once been octagonal net-work, all now in sad disrepair. These tops hung overhead like three ruinous aviaries, in one of which was seen perched, on a ratlin, a white noddy, a strange fowl, so called from its lethargic, somnambulistic character, being frequently caught by hand at sea. Battered and mouldy, the castellated forecastle seemed some ancient turret, long ago taken by assault, and then left to decay. Toward the stern, two high-raised quarter galleries—the balustrades here and there covered with dry, tindery sea-moss—opening out from the unoccupied state-cabin, whose dead-lights, for all the mild weather, were hermetically closed and calked—these tenantless balconies hung over the sea as if it were the grand Venetian canal. But the prin-

[1] Lima women wore a loose-fitting robe that concealed their figures and heads. They could peer out, undetected, with one eye, and also, undetected, arrange an "intrigue."

[2] Dominican friars.

[3] See Ezekiel xxxvii.1-10.

[4] Jean Froissart (1337-1410), author of the *Chronicles*. Suggests the ship's ancient design.

cipal relic of faded grandeur was the ample oval of the shield-like stern-piece, intricately carved with the arms of Castile and Leon, medallioned about by groups of mythological or symbolical devices; uppermost and central of which was a dark satyr in a mask, holding his foot on the prostrate neck of a writhing figure, likewise masked.

Whether the ship had a figure-head, or only a plain beak, was not quite certain, owing to canvas wrapped about that part, either to protect it while undergoing a re-furbishing, or else decently to hide its decay. Rudely painted or chalked, as in a sailor freak, along the forward side of a sort of pedestal below the canvas, was the sentence, *"Seguid vuestro jefe"* (follow your leader); while upon the tarnished headboards, near by, appeared, in stately capitals, once gilt, the ship's name "SAN DOMINICK," each letter streakingly corroded with tricklings of copper-spike rust; while, like mourning weeds, dark festoons of sea-grass slimily swept to and fro over the name, with every hearse-like roll of the hull.

As, at last, the boat was hooked from the bow along toward the gangway amidship, its keel, while yet some inches separated from the hull, harshly grated as on a sunken coral reef. It proved a huge bunch of conglobated barnacles adhering below the water to the side like a wen—a token of baffling airs and long calms passed somewhere in those seas.

Climbing the side, the visitor was at once surrounded by a clamorous throng of whites and blacks, but the latter outnumbering the former more than could have been expected, negro transportation-ship as the stranger in port was. But, in one language, and as with one voice, all poured out a common tale of suffering; in which the negresses, of whom there were not a few, exceeded the others in their dolorous vehemence. The scurvy, together with the fever, had swept off a great part of their number, more especially the Spaniards. Off Cape Horn they had narrowly escaped shipwreck; then, for days together, they had lain tranced without wind; their provisions were low; their water next to none; their lips that moment were baked.

While Captain Delano was thus made the mark of all eager tongues, his one eager glance took in all the faces, with every other object about him.

Always upon first boarding a large and populous ship at sea, especially a foreign one, with a nondescript crew such as Lascars[5] or Manilla men, the impression varies in a peculiar way from that produced by first entering a strange house with strange inmates in a strange land. Both house and ship—the one by its walls and blinds, the other by its high bulwarks like ramparts—hoard from view their interiors till the last moment; but in the case of the ship there is this addition; that the living spectacle it contains, upon its sudden and complete disclosure, has, in contrast with the blank ocean which zones it, something of the effect of enchantment. The ship seems unreal; these strange costumes, gestures, and faces, but a shadowy tableau just emerged from the deep, which directly must receive back what it gave.

Perhaps it was some such influence, as above is attempted to be described, which, in Captain Delano's mind, heightened whatever, upon a staid scrutiny, might have seemed unusual; especially the conspicuous figures of four elderly grizzled negroes, their heads like black, doddered willow tops, who, in venerable contrast to the tumult below them, were couched sphynx-like, one on the starboard cathead, another on the larboard, and the remaining pair face to face on the opposite bulwarks above the main-chains. They each had bits of unstranded old junk in their hands, and, with a sort of stoical self-content, were picking the junk into oakum, a small heap of which lay by their sides. They accompanied the task with a continuous, low, monotonous chant; droning and druling away like so many gray-headed bag-pipers playing a funeral march.

The quarter-deck rose into an ample elevated poop, upon the forward verge of which, lifted, like the oakum-pickers, some eight feet above the general throng, sat along in a row, separated by regular spaces, the cross-legged figures of six other blacks; each with a rusty hatchet in his hand, which, with a bit of brick and a rag, he was engaged like a scullion in scouring; while between each two was a small stack of hatchets, their rusted edges turned forward awaiting a like operation. Though occasionally the four oakum-pickers would briefly address some person or persons in the crowd below, yet the six hatchet-polishers neither spoke to others, nor breathed a whisper among themselves, but sat intent upon their task, except at intervals, when, with the peculiar love in negroes of uniting industry with pastime, two and two they sideways clashed their hatchets together, like cymbals, with a barbarous din. All six, unlike the generality, had the raw aspect of unsophisticated Africans.

But that first comprehensive glance which took in those ten figures, with scores less conspicuous, rested but an instant upon them, as, impatient of the hubbub of voices, the visitor turned in quest of whomsoever it might be that commanded the ship.

But as if not unwilling to let nature make known her own case among his suffering charge, or else in despair of restraining it for the time, the Spanish captain, a gentlemanly, reserved-looking, and rather young man to a stranger's eye, dressed with singular

[5] East Indian sailors.

richness, but bearing plain traces of recent sleepless cares and disquietudes, stood passively by, leaning against the main-mast, at one moment casting a dreary, spiritless look upon his excited people, at the next an unhappy glance toward his visitor. By his side stood a black of small stature, in whose rude face, as occasionally, like a shepherd's dog, he mutely turned it up into the Spaniard's, sorrow and affection were equally blended.

Struggling through the throng, the American advanced to the Spaniard, assuring him of his sympathies, and offering to render whatever assistance might be in his power. To which the Spaniard returned for the present but grave and ceremonious acknowledgments, his national formality dusked by the saturnine mood of ill-health.

But losing no time in mere compliments, Captain Delano, returning to the gangway, had his basket of fish brought up; and as the wind still continued light, so that some hours at least must elapse ere the ship could be brought to the anchorage, he bade his men return to the sealer, and fetch back as much water as the whale-boat could carry, with whatever soft bread the steward might have, all the remaining pumpkins on board, with a box of sugar, and a dozen of his private bottles of cider.

Not many minutes after the boat's pushing off, to the vexation of all, the wind entirely died away, and the tide turning, began drifting back the ship helplessly seaward. But trusting this would not long last, Captain Delano sought, with good hopes, to cheer up the strangers, feeling no small satisfaction that, with persons in their condition, he could—thanks to his frequent voyages along the Spanish main—converse with some freedom in their native tongue.

While left alone with them, he was not long in observing some things tending to heighten his first impressions; but surprise was lost in pity, both for the Spaniards and blacks, alike evidently reduced from scarcity of water and provisions; while long-continued suffering seemed to have brought out the less good-natured qualities of the negroes, besides, at the same time, impairing the Spaniard's authority over them. But, under the circumstances, precisely this condition of things was to have been anticipated. In armies, navies, cities, or families, in nature herself, nothing more relaxes good order than misery. Still, Captain Delano was not without the idea, that had Benito Cereno been a man of greater energy, misrule would hardly have come to the present pass. But the debility, constitutional or induced by the hardships, bodily and mental, of the Spanish captain, was too obvious to be overlooked. A prey to settled dejection, as if long mocked with hope he would not now indulge it, even when it had ceased to be a mock, the prospect of that day or evening at furthest, lying at anchor, with plenty of water for his people, and a brother captain to counsel and befriend, seemed in no perceptible degree to encourage him. His mind appeared unstrung, if not still more seriously affected. Shut up in these oaken walls, chained to one dull round of command, whose unconditionality cloyed him, like some hypochondriac abbot he moved slowly about, at times suddenly pausing, starting, or staring, biting his lip, biting his finger-nail, flushing, paling, twitching his beard, with other symptoms of an absent or moody mind. This distempered spirit was lodged, as before hinted, in as distempered a frame. He was rather tall, but seemed never to have been robust, and now with nervous suffering was almost worn to a skeleton. A tendency to some pulmonary complaint appeared to have been lately confirmed. His voice was like that of one with lungs half gone—hoarsely suppressed, a husky whisper. No wonder that, as in this state he tottered about, his private servant apprehensively followed him. Sometimes the negro gave his master his arm, or took his handkerchief out of his pocket for him; performing these and similar offices with that affectionate zeal which transmutes into something filial or fraternal acts in themselves but menial; and which has gained for the negro the repute of making the most pleasing body-servant in the world; one, too, whom a master need be on no stiffly superior terms with, but may treat with familiar trust; less a servant than a devoted companion.

Marking the noisy indocility of the blacks in general, as well as what seemed the sullen inefficiency of the whites, it was not without humane satisfaction that Captain Delano witnessed the steady good conduct of Babo.

But the good conduct of Babo, hardly more than the ill-behavior of others, seemed to withdraw the half-lunatic Don Benito from his cloudy languor. Not that such precisely was the impression made by the Spaniard on the mind of his visitor. The Spaniard's individual unrest was, for the present, but noted as a conspicuous feature in the ship's general affliction. Still, Captain Delano was not a little concerned at what he could not help taking for the time to be Don Benito's unfriendly indifference towards himself. The Spaniard's manner, too, conveyed a sort of sour and gloomy disdain, which he seemed at no pains to disguise. But this the American in charity ascribed to the harassing effects of sickness, since, in former instances, he had noted that there are peculiar natures on whom prolonged physical suffering seems to cancel every social instinct of kindness; as if, forced to black bread themselves, they deemed it but equity that each person coming nigh them should, indirectly, by some slight or affront, be made to partake of their fare.

But ere long Captain Delano bethought him that, indulgent as he was at the first, in judging the Spaniard, he might not, after all, have exercised charity enough. At bottom it was Don Benito's reserve which displeased him; but the same reserve was shown towards all but his faithful personal attendant. Even the formal reports which, according to sea-usage, were, at stated times, made to him by some petty underling, either a white, mulatto or black, he hardly had patience enough to listen to, without betraying contemptuous aversion. His manner upon such occasions was, in its degree, not unlike that which might be supposed to have been his imperial countryman's, Charles V,[6] just previous to the anchoritish retirement of that monarch from the throne.

This splenetic disrelish of his place was evinced in almost every function pertaining to it. Proud as he was moody, he condescended to no personal mandate. Whatever special orders were necessary, their delivery was delegated to his body-servant, who in turn transferred them to their ultimate destination, through runners, alert Spanish boys or slave boys, like pages or pilot-fish within easy call continually hovering round Don Benito. So that to have beheld this undemonstrative invalid gliding about, apathetic and mute, no landsman could have dreamed that in him was lodged a dictatorship beyond which, while at sea, there was no earthly appeal.

Thus, the Spaniard, regarded in his reserve, seemed the involuntary victim of mental disorder. But, in fact, his reserve might, in some degree, have proceeded from design. If so, then here was evinced the unhealthy climax of that icy though conscientious policy, more or less adopted by all commanders of large ships, which, except in signal emergencies, obliterates alike the manifestation of sway with every trace of sociality; transforming the man into a block, or rather into a loaded cannon, which, until there is call for thunder, has nothing to say.

Viewing him in this light, it seemed but a natural token of the perverse habit induced by a long course of such hard self-restraint, that, notwithstanding the present condition of his ship, the Spaniard should still persist in a demeanor, which, however harmless, or, it may be, appropriate, in a well-appointed vessel, such as the San Dominick might have been at the outset of the voyage, was anything but judicious now. But the Spaniard, perhaps, thought that it was with captains as with gods: reserve, under all events, must still be their cue. But probably this appearance of slumbering dominion might have been but an attempted disguise to conscious imbecility—not deep policy, but shallow device. But be all this as it might, whether Don Benito's manner was designed or not, the more Captain Delano noted its pervading reserve, the less he felt uneasiness at any particular manifestation of that reserve towards himself.

Neither were his thoughts taken up by the captain alone. Wonted to the quiet orderliness of the sealer's comfortable family of a crew, the noisy confusion of the San Dominick's suffering host repeatedly challenged his eye. Some prominent breaches, not only of discipline but of decency, were observed. These Captain Delano could not but ascribe, in the main, to the absence of those subordinate deck-officers to whom, along with higher duties, is intrusted what may be styled the police department of a populous ship. True, the old oakum-pickers appeared at times to act the part of monitorial constables to their countrymen, the blacks; but though occasionally succeeding in allaying trifling outbreaks now and then between man and man, they could do little or nothing toward establishing general quiet. The San Dominick was in the condition of a transatlantic emigrant ship, among whose multitude of living freight are some individuals, doubtless, as little troublesome as crates and bales; but the friendly remonstrances of such with their ruder companions are of not so much avail as the unfriendly arm of the mate. What the San Dominick wanted was, what the emigrant ship has, stern superior officers. But on these decks not so much as a fourth-mate was to be seen.

The visitor's curiosity was roused to learn the particulars of those mishaps which had brought about such absenteeism, with its consequences; because, though deriving some inkling of the voyage from the wails which at the first moment had greeted him, yet of the details no clear understanding had been had. The best account would, doubtless, be given by the captain. Yet at first the visitor was loth to ask it, unwilling to provoke some distant rebuff. But plucking up courage, he at last accosted Don Benito, renewing the expression of his benevolent interest, adding, that did he (Captain Delano) but know the particulars of the ship's misfortunes, he would, perhaps, be better able in the end to relieve them. Would Don Benito favor him with the whole story.

Don Benito faltered; then, like some somnambulist suddenly interfered with, vacantly stared at his visitor, and ended by looking down on the deck. He maintained this posture so long that Captain Delano, almost equally disconcerted, and involuntarily almost as rude, turned suddenly from him, walking forward to accost one of the Spanish seamen for the

[6] Charles V (1500–1558), Holy Roman Emperor and King of Spain, old and feeble at the time of his retirement.

desired information. But he had hardly gone five paces, when, with a sort of eagerness, Don Benito invited him back, regretting his momentary absence of mind, and professing readiness to gratify him.

While most part of the story was being given, the two captains stood on the after part of the main-deck, a privileged spot, no one being near but the servant.

"It is now a hundred and ninety days," began the Spaniard, in his husky whisper, "that this ship, well officered and well manned, with several cabin passengers—some fifty Spaniards in all—sailed from Buenos Ayres bound to Lima, with a general cargo, Paraguay tea and the like—and," pointing forward, "that parcel of negroes, now not more than a hundred and fifty, as you see, but then numbering over three hundred souls. Off Cape Horn we had heavy gales. In one moment, by night, three of my best officers, with fifteen sailors, were lost, with the main-yard; the spar snapping under them in the slings, as they sought, with heavers, to beat down the icy sail. To lighten the hull, the heavier sacks of mata[7] were thrown into the sea, with most of the water-pipes[8] lashed on deck at the time. And this last necessity it was, combined with the prolonged detentions afterwards experienced, which eventually brought about our chief causes of suffering. When—"

Here there was a sudden fainting attack of his cough, brought on, no doubt, by his mental distress. His servant sustained him, and drawing a cordial from his pocket placed it to his lips. He a little revived. But unwilling to leave him unsupported while yet imperfectly restored, the black with one arm still encircled his master, at the same time keeping his eye fixed on his face, as if to watch for the first sign of complete restoration, or relapse, as the event might prove.

The Spaniard proceeded, but brokenly and obscurely, as one in a dream.

—"Oh, my God! rather than pass through what I have, with joy I would have hailed the most terrible gales; but—"

His cough returned and with increased violence; this subsiding, with reddened lips and closed eyes he fell heavily against his supporter.

"His mind wanders. He was thinking of the plague that followed the gales," plaintively sighed the servant; "my poor, poor master!" wringing one hand, and with the other wiping the mouth. "But be patient, Señor," again turning to Captain Delano, "these fits do not last long; master will soon be himself."

Don Benito reviving, went on; but as this portion of the story was very brokenly delivered, the substance only will here be set down.

It appeared that after the ship had been many days tossed in storms off the Cape, the scurvy broke out, carrying off numbers of the whites and blacks. When at last they had worked round into the Pacific, their spars and sails were so damaged, and so inadequately handled by the surviving mariners, most of whom were become invalids, that, unable to lay her northerly course by the wind, which was powerful, the unmanageable ship, for successive days and nights, was blown northwestward, where the breeze suddenly deserted her, in unknown waters, to sultry calms. The absence of the water-pipes now proved as fatal to life as before their presence had menaced it. Induced, or at least aggravated, by the more than scanty allowance of water, a malignant fever followed the scurvy; with the excessive heat of the lengthened calm, making such short work of it as to sweep away, as by billows, whole families of the Africans, and a yet larger number, proportionably, of the Spaniards, including, by a luckless fatality, every remaining officer on board. Consequently, in the smart west winds eventually following the calm, the already rent sails, having to be simply dropped, not furled, at need, had been gradually reduced to the beggar's rags they were now. To procure substitutes for his lost sailors, as well as supplies of water and sails, the captain, at the earliest opportunity, had made for Baldivia, the southernmost civilized port of Chili and South America; but upon nearing the coast the thick weather had prevented him from so much as sighting that harbor. Since which period, almost without a crew, and almost without canvas and almost without water, and, at intervals, giving its added dead to the sea, the San Dominick had been battle-dored about by contrary winds, inveigled by currents, or grown weedy in calms. Like a man lost in woods, more than once she had doubled upon her own track.

"But throughout these calamities," huskily continued Don Benito, painfully turning in the half embrace of his servant, "I have to thank those negroes you see, who, though to your inexperienced eyes appearing unruly, have, indeed, conducted themselves with less of restlessness than even their owner could have thought possible under such circumstances."

Here he again fell faintly back. Again his mind wandered; but he rallied, and less obscurely proceeded.

"Yes, their owner was quite right in assuring me that no fetters would be needed with his blacks; so that while, as is wont in this transportation, those negroes have always remained upon deck—not

[7] Paraguay tea.
[8] Water casks.

thrust below, as in the Guinea-men[9]—they have, also, from the beginning, been freely permitted to range within given bounds at their pleasure."

Once more the faintness returned—his mind roved—but, recovering, he resumed:

"But it is Babo here to whom, under God, I owe not only my own preservation, but likewise to him, chiefly, the merit is due, of pacifying his more ignorant brethren, when at intervals tempted to murmurings."

"Ah, master," sighed the black, bowing his face, "don't speak of me; Babo is nothing; what Babo has done was but duty."

"Faithful fellow!" cried Captain Delano. "Don Benito, I envy you such a friend; slave I cannot call him."

As master and man stood before him, the black upholding the white, Captain Delano could not but bethink him of the beauty of that relationship which could present such a spectacle of fidelity on the one hand and confidence on the other. The scene was heightened by the contrast in dress, denoting their relative positions. The Spaniard wore a loose Chili jacket of dark velvet; white small-clothes and stockings, with silver buckles at the knee and instep; a high-crowned sombrero, of fine grass; a slender sword, silver mounted, hung from a knot in his sash—the last being an almost invariable adjunct, more for utility than ornament, of a South American gentleman's dress to this hour. Excepting when his occasional nervous contortions brought about disarray, there was a certain precision in his attire curiously at variance with the unsightly disorder around; especially in the belittered Ghetto, forward the main-mast, wholly occupied by the blacks.

The servant wore nothing but wide trowsers, apparently, from their coarseness and patches, made out of some old topsail; they were clean, and confined at the waist by a bit of unstranded rope, which, with his composed, deprecatory air at times, made him look something like a begging friar of St. Francis.

However unsuitable for the time and place, at least in the blunt-thinking American's eyes, and however strangely surviving in the midst of all his afflictions, the toilette of Don Benito might not, in fashion at least, have gone beyond the style of the day among South Americans of his class. Though on the present voyage sailing from Buenos Ayres, he had avowed himself a native and resident of Chili, whose inhabitants had not so generally adopted the plain coat and once plebeian pantaloons; but, with a becoming modification, adhered to their provincial costume, picturesque as any in the world. Still, relatively to the pale history of the voyage, and his own pale face, there seemed something so incongruous in the Spaniard's apparel, as almost to suggest the image of an invalid courtier tottering about London streets in the time of the plague.

The portion of the narrative which, perhaps, most excited interest, as well as some surprise, considering the latitudes in question, was the long calms spoken of, and more particularly the ship's so long drifting about. Without communicating the opinion, of course, the American could not but impute at least part of the detentions both to clumsy seamanship and faulty navigation. Eyeing Don Benito's small, yellow hands, he easily inferred that the young captain had not got into command at the hawse-hole, but the cabin-window; and if so, why wonder at incompetence, in youth, sickness, and gentility united?

But drowning criticism in compassion, after a fresh repetition of his sympathies, Captain Delano, having heard out his story, not only engaged, as in the first place, to see Don Benito and his people supplied in their immediate bodily needs, but, also, now further promised to assist him in procuring a large permanent supply of water, as well as some sails and rigging; and, though it would involve no small embarrassment to himself, yet he would spare three of his best seamen for temporary deck officers; so that without delay the ship might proceed to Conception, there fully to refit for Lima, her destined port.

Such generosity was not without its effect, even upon the invalid. His face lighted up; eager and hectic, he met the honest glance of his visitor. With gratitude he seemed overcome.

"This excitement is bad for master," whispered the servant, taking his arm, and with soothing words gently drawing him aside.

When Don Benito returned, the American was pained to observe that his hopefulness, like the sudden kindling in his cheek, was but febrile and transient.

Ere long, with a joyless mien, looking up towards the poop, the host invited his guest to accompany him there, for the benefit of what little breath of wind might be stirring.

As, during the telling of the story, Captain Delano had once or twice started at the occasional cymballing of the hatchet-polishers, wondering why such an interruption should be allowed, especially in that part of the ship, and in the ears of an invalid; and moreover, as the hatchets had anything but an attractive look, and the handlers of them still less so, it was, therefore, to tell the truth, not without some lurking reluctance, or even shrinking, it may be, that Captain Delano, with apparent complaisance,

[9] Slave ships trading with Guinea.

acquiesced in his host's invitation. The more so, since, with an untimely caprice of punctilio, rendered distressing by his cadaverous aspect, Don Benito, with Castilian bows, solemnly insisted upon his guest's preceding him up the ladder leading to the elevation; where, one on each side of the last step, sat for armorial supporters and sentries two of the ominous file. Gingerly enough stepped good Captain Delano between them, and in the instant of leaving them behind, like one running the gauntlet, he felt an apprehensive twitch in the calves of his legs.

But when, facing about, he saw the whole file, like so many organ-grinders, still stupidly intent on their work, unmindful of everything beside, he could not but smile at his late fidgety panic.

Presently, while standing with his host, looking forward upon the decks below, he was struck by one of those instances of insubordination previously alluded to. Three black boys, with two Spanish boys, were sitting together on the hatches, scraping a rude wooden platter, in which some scanty mess had recently been cooked. Suddenly, one of the black boys, enraged at a word dropped by one of his white companions, seized a knife, and, though called to forbear by one of the oakum-pickers, struck the lad over the head, inflicting a gash from which blood flowed.

In amazement, Captain Delano inquired what this meant. To which the pale Don Benito dully muttered, that it was merely the sport of the lad.

"Pretty serious sport, truly," rejoined Captain Delano. "Had such a thing happened on board the Bachelor's Delight, instant punishment would have followed."

At these words the Spaniard turned upon the American one of his sudden, staring, half-lunatic looks; then, relapsing into his torpor, answered, "Doubtless, doubtless, Señor."

Is it, thought Captain Delano, that this hapless man is one of those paper captains I've known, who by policy wink at what by power they cannot put down? I know no sadder sight than a commander who has little of command but the name.

"I should think, Don Benito," he now said, glancing towards the oakum-picker who had sought to interfere with the boys, "that you would find it advantageous to keep all your blacks employed, especially the younger ones, no matter at what useless task, and no matter what happens to the ship. Why, even with my little band, I find such a course indispensable. I once kept a crew on my quarter-deck thrumming mats for my cabin, when, for three days, I had given up my ship—mats, men, and all—for a speedy loss, owing to the violence of a gale, in which we could do nothing but helplessly drive before it."

"Doubtless, doubtless," muttered Don Benito.

"But," continued Captain Delano, again glancing upon the oakum-pickers and then at the hatchet-polishers, near by, "I see you keep some, at least, of your host employed."

"Yes," was again the vacant response.

"Those old men there, shaking their pows from their pulpits," continued Captain Delano, pointing to the oakum-pickers, "seem to act the part of old dominies to the rest, little heeded as their admonitions are at times. Is this voluntary on their part, Don Benito, or have you appointed them shepherds to your flock of black sheep?"

"What posts they fill, I appointed them," rejoined the Spaniard in an acrid tone, as if resenting some supposed satiric reflection.

"And these others, these Ashantee conjurors here," continued Captain Delano, rather uneasily eying the brandished steel of the hatchet-polishers, where, in spots, it had been brought to a shine, "this seems a curious business they are at, Don Benito?"

"In the gales we met," answered the Spaniard, "what of our general cargo was not thrown overboard was much damaged by the brine. Since coming into calm weather, I have had several cases of knives and hatchets daily brought up for overhauling and cleaning."

"A prudent idea, Don Benito. You are part owner of ship and cargo, I presume; but none of the slaves, perhaps?"

"I am owner of all you see," impatiently returned Don Benito, "except the main company of blacks, who belonged to my late friend Alexandro Aranda."

As he mentioned this name, his air was heartbroken; his knees shook; his servant supported him.

Thinking he divined the cause of such unusual emotion, to confirm his surmise, Captain Delano, after a pause, said: "And may I ask, Don Benito, whether—since awhile ago you spoke of some cabin passengers—the friend, whose loss so afflicts you, at the outset of the voyage accompanied his blacks?"

"Yes."

"But died of the fever?"

"Died of the fever. Oh, could I but—"

Again quivering, the Spaniard paused.

"Pardon me," said Captain Delano, lowly, "but I think that, by a sympathetic experience, I conjecture, Don Benito, what it is that gives the keener edge to your grief. It was once my hard fortune to lose at sea, a dear friend, my own brother, then supercargo. Assured of the welfare of his spirit, its departure I could have borne like a man; but that honest eye, that honest hand—both of which had so often met mine—and that warm heart; all, all—like scraps to the dogs—to throw all to the sharks! It was then I vowed never to have for fellow-voyager a man I loved, unless, unbeknown to him, I had provided every requisite, in case of a fatality, for embalming his mortal part for interment on shore. Were your friend's remains now on board this ship, Don Benito, not thus strangely would the mention of his name affect you."

"On board this ship?" echoed the Spaniard. Then, with horrified gestures, as directed against some spectre, he unconsciously fell into the ready arms of his attendant, who, with a silent appeal toward Captain Delano, seemed beseeching him not again to broach a theme so unspeakably distressing to his master.

This poor fellow now, thought the pained American, is the victim of that sad superstition which associates goblins with the deserted body of man, as ghosts with an abandoned house. How unlike are we made! What to me, in like case, would have been a solemn satisfaction, the bare suggestion, even, terrifies the Spaniard into this trance. Poor Alexandro Aranda! what would you say could you here see your friend—who, on former voyages, when you, for months, were left behind, has, I dare say, often longed, and longed, for one peep at you—now transported with terror at the least thought of having you anyway nigh him.

At this moment, with a dreary grave-yard toll, betokening a flaw, the ship's forecastle bell, smote by one of the grizzled oakum-pickers, proclaimed ten o'clock, through the leaden calm; when Captain Delano's attention was caught by the moving figure of a gigantic black, emerging from the general crowd below, and slowly advancing towards the elevated poop. An iron collar was about his neck, from which depended a chain, thrice wound round his body; the terminating links padlocked together at a broad band of iron, his girdle.

"How like a mute Atufal moves," murmured the servant.

The black mounted the steps of the poop, and, like a brave prisoner, brought up to receive sentence, stood in unquailing muteness before Don Benito, now recovered from his attack.

At the first glimpse of his approach, Don Benito had started, a resentful shadow swept over his face; and, as with the sudden memory of bootless rage, his white lips glued together.

This is some mulish mutineer, thought Captain Delano, surveying, not without a mixture of admiration, the colossal form of the negro.

"See, he waits your question, master," said the servant.

Thus reminded, Don Benito, nervously averting his glance, as if shunning, by anticipation, some rebellious response, in a disconcerted voice, thus spoke:—

"Atufal, will you ask my pardon now?"

The black was silent.

"Again, master," murmured the servant, with bitter upbraiding eyeing his countryman, "again, master; he will bend to master yet."

"Answer," said Don Benito, still averting his glance, "say but the one word, *pardon*, and your chains shall be off."

Upon this, the black, slowly raising both arms, let them lifelessly fall, his links clanking, his head bowed; as much as to say, "No, I am content."

"Go," said Don Benito, with inkept and unknown emotion.

Deliberately as he had come, the black obeyed.

"Excuse me, Don Benito," said Captain Delano, "but this scene surprises me; what means it, pray?"

"It means that that negro alone, of all the band, has given me peculiar cause of offence. I have put him in chains; I—"

Here he paused; his hand to his head, as if there were a swimming there, or a sudden bewilderment of memory had come over him; but meeting his servant's kindly glance seemed reassured, and proceeded:—

"I could not scourge such a form. But I told him he must ask my pardon. As yet he has not. At my command, every two hours he stands before me."

"And how long has this been?"

"Some sixty days."

"And obedient in all else? And respectful?"

"Yes."

"Upon my conscience, then," exclaimed Captain Delano, impulsively, "he has a royal spirit in him, this fellow."

"He may have some right to it," bitterly returned Don Benito, "he says he was king in his own land."

"Yes," said the servant, entering a word, "those slits in Atufal's ears once held wedges of gold; but poor Babo here, in his own land, was only a poor slave; a black man's slave was Babo, who now is the white's."

Somewhat annoyed by these conversational familiarities, Captain Delano turned curiously upon the attendant, then glanced inquiringly at his master; but, as if long wonted to these little informalities, neither master nor man seemed to understand him.

"What, pray, was Atufal's offence, Don Benito?" asked Captain Delano; "if it was not something very serious, take a fool's advice, and, in view of his general docility, as well as in some natural respect for his spirit, remit him his penalty."

"No, no, master never will do that," here murmured the servant to himself, "proud Atufal must first ask master's pardon. The slave there carries the padlock, but master here carries the key."

His attention thus directed, Captain Delano now

noticed for the first time, that, suspended by a slender silken cord, from Don Benito's neck, hung a key. At once, from the servant's muttered syllables, divining the key's purpose, he smiled and said:—"So, Don Benito—padlock and key—significant symbols, truly."

Biting his lip, Don Benito faltered.

Though the remark of Captain Delano, a man of such native simplicity as to be incapable of satire or irony, had been dropped in playful allusion to the Spaniard's singularly evidenced lordship over the black; yet the hypochondriac seemed in some way to have taken it as a malicious reflection upon his confessed inability thus far to break down, at least, on a verbal summons, the entrenched will of the slave. Deploring this supposed misconception, yet despairing of correcting it, Captain Delano shifted the subject; but finding his companion more than ever withdrawn, as if still sourly digesting the lees of the presumed affront above mentioned, by-and-by Captain Delano likewise became less talkative, oppressed, against his own will, by what seemed the secret vindictiveness of the morbidly sensitive Spaniard. But the good sailor, himself of a quite contrary disposition, refrained, on his part, alike from the appearance as from the feeling of resentment, and if silent, was only so from contagion.

Presently the Spaniard, assisted by his servant, somewhat discourteously crossed over from his guest; a procedure which, sensibly enough, might have been allowed to pass for idle caprice of ill-humor, had not master and man, lingering round the corner of the elevated skylight, began whispering together in low voices. This was unpleasing. And more; the moody air of the Spaniard, which at times had not been without a sort of valetudinarian stateliness, now seemed anything but dignified; while the menial familiarity of the servant lost its original charm of simple-hearted attachment.

In his embarrassment, the visitor turned his face to the other side of the ship. By so doing, his glance accidentally fell on a young Spanish sailor, a coil of rope in his hand, just stepped from the deck to the first round of the mizzenrigging. Perhaps the man would not have been particularly noticed, were it not that, during his ascent to one of the yards, he, with a sort of covert intentness, kept his eye fixed on Captain Delano, from whom, presently, it passed, as if by a natural sequence, to the two whisperers.

His own attention thus redirected to that quarter, Captain Delano gave a slight start. From something in Don Benito's manner just then, it seemed as if the visitor had, at least partly, been the subject of the withdrawn consultation going on—a conjecture as little agreeable to the guest as it was little flattering to the host.

The singular alternations of courtesy and ill-breeding in the Spanish captain were unaccountable, except on one of two suppositions—innocent lunacy, or wicked imposture.

But the first idea, though it might naturally have occurred to an indifferent observer, and, in some respects, had not hitherto been wholly a stranger to Captain Delano's mind, yet, now that, in an incipient way, he began to regard the stranger's conduct something in the light of an intentional affront, of course the idea of lunacy was virtually vacated. But if not a lunatic, what then? Under the circumstances, would a gentleman, nay, any honest boor, act the part now acted by his host? The man was an imposter. Some low-born adventurer, masquerading as an oceanic grandee; yet so ignorant of the first requisites of mere gentlemanhood as to be betrayed into the present remarkable indecorum. That strange ceremoniousness, too, at other times evinced, seemed not uncharacteristic of one playing a part above his real level. Benito Cereno—Don Benito Cereno—a sounding name. One, too, at that period, not unknown, in the surname, to supercargoes and sea captains trading along the Spanish Main, as belonging to one of the most enterprising and extensive mercantile families in all those provinces; several members of it having titles; a sort of Castilian Rothschild, with a noble brother, or cousin, in every great trading town of South America. The alleged Don Benito was in early manhood, about twenty-nine or thirty. To assume a sort of roving cadetship in the maritime affairs of such a house, what more likely scheme for a young knave of talent and spirit? But the Spaniard was a pale invalid. Never mind. For even to the degree of simulating mortal disease, the craft of some tricksters had been known to attain. To think that, under the aspect of infantile weakness, the most savage energies might be couched—those velvets of the Spaniard but the velvet paw to his fangs.

From no train of thought did these fancies come; not from within, but from without; suddenly, too, and in one throng, like hoar frost; yet as soon to vanish as the mild sun of Captain Delano's good-nature regained its meridian.

Glancing over once again towards his host—whose side-face, revealed above the skylight, was now turned toward him—he was struck by the profile, whose clearness of cut was refined by the thinness, incident to ill-health, as well as ennobled about the chin by the beard. Away with suspicion. He was a true off-shoot of a true hidalgo Cereno.

Relieved by these and other better thoughts, the visitor, lightly humming a tune, now began indifferently pacing the poop, so as not to betray to Don Benito that he had at all mistrusted incivility, much less duplicity; for such mistrust would yet be proved illusory, and by the event; though, for the present, the circumstance which had provoked that distrust remained unexplained. But when that little mystery should have been cleared up, Captain Delano thought he might extremely regret it, did he allow Don Benito to become aware that he had indulged in ungenerous surmises. In short, to the Spaniard's black-letter text, it was best, for a while, to leave open margin.

Presently, his pale face twitching and overcast, the Spaniard, still supported by his attendant, moved over towards his guest, when, with even more than his usual embarrassment, and a strange sort of intriguing intonation in his husky whisper, the following conversation began:—

"Señor, may I ask how long you have lain at this isle?"

"Oh, but a day or two, Don Benito."

"And from what port are you last?"

"Canton."

"And there, Señor, you exchanged your sealskins for teas and silks, I think you said?"

"Yes. Silks, mostly."

"And the balance you took in specie, perhaps?"

Captain Delano, fidgeting a little, answered—

"Yes; some silver, not a very great deal, though."

"Ah—well. May I ask how many men have you, Señor?"

Captain Delano slightly started, but answered—

"About five-and-twenty, all told."

"And at present, Señor, all on board, I suppose?"

"All on board, Don Benito," replied the Captain, now with satisfaction.

"And will be to-night, Señor?"

At this last question, following so many pertinacious ones, for the soul of him Captain Delano could not but look very earnestly at the questioner, who, instead of meeting the glance, with every token of craven discomposure dropped his eyes to the deck; presenting an unworthy contrast to his servant, who, just then, was kneeling at his feet, adjusting a loose shoe-buckle; his disengaged face meantime, with humble curiosity, turned openly up into his master's downcast one.

The Spaniard, still with a guilty shuffle, repeated his question:

"And—and will be to-night Señor?"

"Yes, for aught I know," returned Captain Delano—"but nay," rallying himself into fearless truth, "some of them talked of going off on another fishing party about midnight."

"Your ships generally go—go more or less armed, I believe, Señor?"

"Oh, a six-pounder or two, in case of emergency," was the intrepidly indifferent reply, "with a small stock of muskets, sealing-spears, and cutlasses, you know."

As he thus responded, Captain Delano again glanced at Don Benito, but the latter's eyes were averted; while abruptly and awkwardly shifting the subject, he made some peevish allusion to the calm, and then, without apology, once more, with his attendant, withdrew to the opposite bulwarks, where the whispering was resumed.

At this moment, and ere Captain Delano could cast a cool thought upon what had just passed, the young Spanish sailor, before mentioned, was seen descending from the rigging. In act of stooping over to spring inboard to the deck, his voluminous, unconfined frock, or shirt, of coarse woolen, much spotted with tar, opened out far down the chest, revealing a soiled under garment of what seemed the finest linen, edged, about the neck, with a narrow blue ribbon, sadly faded and worn. At this moment the young sailor's eye was again fixed on the whisperers, and Captain Delano thought he observed a lurking significance in it, as if silent signs, of some Freemason sort, had that instant been interchanged.

This once more impelled his own glance in the direction of Don Benito, and, as before, he could not but infer that himself formed the subject of the conference. He paused. The sound of the hatchet-polishing fell on his ears. He cast another swift side-look at the two. They had the air of conspirators. In connection with the late questionings, and the incident of the young sailor, these things now begat such return of involuntary suspicion, that the singular guilelessness of the American could not endure it. Plucking up a gay and humorous expression, he crossed over to the two rapidly, saying:—"Ha, Don Benito, your black here seems high in your trust; a sort of privy-counsellor, in fact."

Upon this, the servant looked up with a good-natured grin, but the master started as from a venomous bite. It was a moment or two before the Spaniard sufficiently recovered himself to reply; which he did, at last, with cold constraint:—"Yes, Señor, I have trust in Babo."

Here Babo, changing his previous grin of mere animal humor into an intelligent smile, not ungratefully eyed his master.

Finding that the Spaniard now stood silent and reserved, as if involuntarily, or purposely giving hint that his guest's proximity was inconvenient just then, Captain Delano, unwilling to appear uncivil even to incivility itself, made some trivial remark and moved off; again and again turning over in his mind the mysterious demeanor of Don Benito Cereno.

He had descended from the poop, and, wrapped in thought, was passing near a dark hatchway, leading down into the steerage, when, perceiving motion there, he looked to see what moved. The same instant there was a sparkle in the shadowy hatchway, and he saw one of the Spanish sailors, prowling there, hurriedly placing his hand in the bosom of his frock, as if hiding something. Before the man could have been certain who it was that was passing, he slunk below out of sight. But enough was seen of him to make it sure that he was the same young sailor before noticed in the rigging.

What was that which so sparkled? thought Captain Delano. It was no lamp—no match—no live coal. Could it have been a jewel? But how come sailors with jewels?—or with silk-trimmed undershirts either? Has he been robbing the trunks of the dead cabin-passengers? But if so, he would hardly wear one of the stolen articles on board ship here. Ah, ah—if, now, that was, indeed, a secret sign I saw passing between this suspicious fellow and his captain awhile since; if I could only be certain that, in my uneasiness, my senses did not deceive me, then——

Here, passing from one suspicious thing to another, his mind revolved the strange questions put to him concerning his ship.

By a curious coincidence, as each point was recalled, the black wizards of Ashantee would strike up with their hatchets, as in ominous comment on the white stranger's thoughts. Pressed by such enigmas and portents, it would have been almost against nature, had not, even into the least distrustful heart, some ugly misgivings obtruded.

Observing the ship now helplessly fallen into a current, with enchanted sails, drifting with increased rapidity seaward; and noting that, from a lately intercepted projection of the land, the sealer was hidden, the stout mariner began to quake at thoughts which he barely durst confess to himself. Above all, he began to feel a ghostly dread of Don Benito. And yet, when he roused himself, dilated his chest, felt himself strong on his legs, and coolly considered it—what did all these phantoms amount to?

Had the Spaniard any sinister scheme, it must have reference not so much to him (Captain Delano) as to his ship (the Bachelor's Delight). Hence the present drifting away of the one ship from the other, instead of favoring any such possible scheme, was, for the time at least, opposed to it. Clearly any suspicion, combining such contradictions, must need be delusive. Beside, was it not absurd to think of a vessel in distress—a vessel by sickness almost dismanned of her crew—a vessel whose inmates were parched for water—was it not a thousand times absurd that such a craft should, at present, be of a piratical character; or her commander, either for himself or those under him, cherish any desire but for speedy relief and refreshment? But then, might not general distress, and thirst in particular, be affected? And might not that same undiminished Spanish crew, alleged to have perished off to a remnant, be at that very moment lurking in the hold? On heart-broken pretence of entreating a cup of cold water, fiends in human form had got into lonely dwellings, nor retired until a dark deed had been done. And among the Malay pirates, it was no unusual thing to lure ships after them into their treacherous harbors, or entice boarders from a declared enemy at sea, by the spectacle of thinly manned or vacant decks, beneath which prowled a hundred spears with yellow arms ready to upthrust them through the mats. Not that Captain Delano had entirely credited such things. He had heard of them—and now, as stories, they recurred. The present destination of the ship was the anchorage. There she would be near his own vessel. Upon gaining that vicinity, might not the San Dominick, like a slumbering volcano, suddenly let loose energies now hid?

He recalled the Spaniard's manner while telling his story. There was a gloomy hesitancy and subterfuge about it. It was just the manner of one making up his tale for evil purposes, as he goes. But if that story was not true, what was the truth? That the ship had unlawfully come into the Spaniard's possession? But in many of its details, especially in reference to the more calamitous parts, such as the fatalities among the seamen, the consequent prolonged beating about, the past sufferings from obstinate calms, and still continued suffering from thirst; in all these points, as well as others, Don Benito's story had corroborated not only the wailing ejaculations of the indiscriminate multitude, white and black, but likewise—what seemed impossible to be counterfeit—by the very expression and play of every human feature, which Captain Delano saw. If Don Benito's story was, throughout, an invention, then every soul on board, down to the youngest negress, was his carefully drilled recruit in the plot: an incredible inference. And yet, if there was ground for mistrusting his veracity, that inference was a legitimate one.

But those questions of the Spaniard. There, indeed, one might pause. Did they not seem put with much the same object with which the burglar or assassin, by day-time, reconnoitres the walls of a house? But, with ill purposes, to solicit such information openly of the chief person endangered, and so, in effect, setting him on his guard; how unlikely a procedure was that? Absurd, then, to suppose that those questions had been prompted by evil designs. Thus, the same conduct, which, in this instance, had raised the alarm, served to dispel it. In short, scarce any suspicion or uneasiness, however, apparently reasonable at the time, which was not now, with equal apparent reason, dismissed.

At last he began to laugh at his former forebodings; and laugh at the strange ship for, in its aspect, someway siding with them, as it were; and laugh, too, at the odd-looking blacks, particularly those old scissors-grinders, the Ashantees; and those bed-ridden old knitting women, the oakum-pickers; and almost at the dark Spaniard himself, the central hobgoblin of all.

For the rest, whatever in a serious way seemed enigmatical, was now good-naturedly explained away by the thought that, for the most part, the poor invalid scarcely knew what he was about; either sulking in black vapors, or putting idle questions without sense or object. Evidently, for the present, the man was not fit to be intrusted with the ship. On some benevolent plea withdrawing the command from him, Captain Delano would yet have to send her to Conception, in charge of his second mate, a worthy person and good navigator—a plan not more convenient for the San Dominick than for Don Benito; for, relieved from all anxiety, keeping wholly to his cabin, the sick man, under the good nursing of his servant, would probably, by the end of the passage, be in a measure restored to health, and with that he should also be restored to authority.

Such were the American's thoughts. They were tranquilizing. There was a difference between the idea of Don Benito's darkly pre-ordaining Captain Delano's fate, and Captain Delano's lightly arranging Don Benito's. Nevertheless, it was not without something of relief that the good seaman presently perceived his whale-boat in the distance. Its absence had been prolonged by unexpected detention at the sealer's side, as well as its returning trip lengthened by the continual recession of the goal.

The advancing speck was observed by the blacks. Their shouts attracted the attention of Don Benito, who, with a return of courtesy, approaching Captain Delano, expressed satisfaction at the coming of some supplies, slight and temporary as they must necessarily prove.

Captain Delano responded; but while doing so, his attention was drawn to something passing on the deck below: among the crowd climbing the landward bulwarks, anxiously watching the coming boat, two blacks, to all appearances accidentally incommoded by one of the sailors, violently pushed him aside, which the sailor someway resenting, they dashed him to the deck, despite the earnest cries of the oakum-pickers.

"Don Benito," said Captain Delano quickly, "do you see what is going on there? Look!"

But, seized by his cough, the Spaniard staggered, with both hands to his face, on the point of falling. Captain Delano would have supported him, but the servant was more alert, who, with one hand sustaining his master, with the other applied the cordial. Don Benito restored, the black withdrew his support, slipping aside a little, but dutifully remaining within call of a whisper. Such discretion was here evinced as quite wiped away, in the visitor's eyes, any blemish of impropriety which might have attached to the attendant, from the indecorous conferences before mentioned; showing, too, that if the servant were to blame, it might be more the master's fault than his own, since, when left to himself, he could conduct thus well.

His glance called away from the spectacle of disorder to the more pleasing one before him, Captain Delano could not avoid again congratulating his host upon possessing such a servant, who, though perhaps a little too forward now and then, must upon the whole be invaluable to one in the invalid's situation.

"Tell me, Don Benito," he added, with a smile—"I should like to have your man here, myself—what will you take for him? Would fifty doubloons be any object?"

"Master wouldn't part with Babo for a thousand doubloons," murmured the black, overhearing the offer, and taking it in earnest, and, with the strange vanity of a faithful slave, appreciated by his master, scorning to hear so paltry a valuation put upon him by a stranger. But Don Benito, apparently hardly yet completely restored, and again interrupted by his cough, made but some broken reply.

Soon his physical distress became so great, affecting his mind, too, apparently, that, as if to screen the sad spectacle, the servant gently conducted his master below.

Left to himself, the American, to while away the time till his boat should arrive, would have pleasantly accosted some one of the few Spanish seamen he saw; but recalling something that Don Benito had said touching their ill conduct, he refrained; as a shipmaster indisposed to countenance cowardice or unfaithfulness in seamen.

While, with these thoughts, standing with eye directed forward towards that handful of sailors, suddenly he thought that one or two of them returned the glance and with a sort of meaning. He rubbed his eyes, and looked again; but again seemed to see the same thing. Under a new form, but more obscure than any previous one, the old suspicions recurred, but, in the absence of Don Benito, with less of panic than before. Despite the bad account given of the sailors, Captain Delano resolved forthwith to accost one of them. Descending the poop, he made his way through the blacks, his movement drawing a queer cry from the oakum-pickers, prompted by whom, the negroes, twitching each other aside, divided before him; but, as if curious to see what was the object of this deliberate visit to their Ghetto, closing in behind, in tolerable order, followed the white stranger up. His progress thus proclaimed as by mounted kings-at-arms, and escorted as by a Caffre[10] guard of honor, Captain Delano, assuming a good-humored, off-handed air, continued to advance; now and then saying a blithe word to the negroes, and his eye curiously surveying the white faces, here and there sparsely mixed in with the blacks, like stray white pawns venturously involved in the ranks of the chess-men opposed.

While thinking which of them to select for his purpose, he chanced to observe a sailor seated on the deck engaged in tarring the strap of a large block, a circle of blacks squatted round him inquisitively eying the process.

The mean employment of the man was in contrast with something superior in his figure. His hand, black with continually thrusting it into the tar-pot held for him by a negro, seemed not naturally allied to his face, a face which would have been a very fine one but for its haggardness. Whether this haggardness had aught to do with criminality, could not be determined; since, as intense heat and cold, though unlike, produce like sensations, so innocence and guilt, when, through casual association with mental pain, stamping any visible impress, use one seal—a hacked one.

Not again that this reflection occurred to Captain Delano at the time, charitable man as he was. Rather another idea. Because observing so singular a haggardness combined with a dark eye, averted as in trouble and shame, and then, again recalling Don Benito's confessed ill opinion of his crew, insensibly he was operated upon by certain general notions which, while disconnecting pain and abashment from virtue, invariably link them with vice.

If, indeed, there be any wickedness on board this ship, thought Captain Delano, be sure that man there has fouled his hand in it, even as now he fouls it in the pitch. I don't like to accost him. I will speak to this other, this old Jack here on the windlass.

He advanced to an old Barcelona tar, in ragged red breeches and dirty night-cap, cheeks trenched and bronzed, whiskers dense as thorn hedges. Seated between two sleepy-looking Africans, this mariner, like his younger shipmate, was employed upon some rigging—splicing a cable—the sleepy-looking blacks performing the inferior function of holding the outer parts of the ropes for him.

Upon Captain Delano's approach, the man at once hung his head below its previous level; the one necessary for business. It appeared as if he desired to be thought absorbed, with more than common fidelity, in his task. Being addressed, he glanced up, but with what seemed a furtive, diffident air, which sat strangely enough on his weather-beaten visage, much as if a grizzly bear, instead of growling and biting, should simper and cast sheep's eyes. He was asked several questions concerning the voyage—purposely referring to several particulars in Don Benito's narrative, not previously corroborated by those impulsive cries greeting the visitor on first coming on board. The questions were briefly answered, confirming all that remained to be confirmed of the story. The negroes about the windlass joined in with the old sailor; but, as they became talkative, he by degrees became mute, and at length quite glum, seemed morosely unwilling to answer more questions, and yet, all the while, this ursine air was somehow mixed with his sheepish one.

Despairing of getting into unembarrassed talk with such a centaur, Captain Delano, after glancing round for a more promising countenance, but seeing none, spoke pleasantly to the blacks to make way for him; and so, amid various grins and grimaces, returned to the poop, feeling a little strange at first, he could hardly tell why, but upon the whole with regained confidence in Benito Cereno.

How plainly, thought he, did that old whiskerando yonder betray a consciousness of ill desert. No doubt, when he saw me coming, he dreaded lest I, apprised by his Captain of the crew's general misbehavior, came with sharp words for him, and so down with his head. And yet—and yet, now that I think of it, that very old fellow, if I err not, was one of those who seemed so earnestly eyeing me here awhile since. Ah, these currents spin one's head round almost as much as they do the ship. Ha, there now's a pleasant sort of sunny sight; quite sociable, too.

His attention had been drawn to a slumbering negress, partly disclosed through the lace-work of some rigging, lying, with youthful limbs carelessly disposed, under the lee of the bulwarks, like a doe in the shade of a woodland rock. Sprawling at her lapped breasts, was her wide-awake fawn, stark naked, its black little body half lifted from the deck, crosswise with its dam's; its hands, like two paws, clambering upon her; its mouth and nose ineffectually rooting to get at the mark; and meantime giving a vexatious half-grunt, blending with the composed snore of the negress.

The uncommon vigor of the child at length roused the mother. She started up, at a distance facing Captain Delano. But as if not at all concerned at the attitude in which she had been caught, delightedly she caught the child up, with maternal transports, covering it with kisses.

There's naked nature, now; pure tenderness and love, thought Captain Delano, well pleased.

This incident prompted him to remark the other negresses more particularly than before. He was gratified with their manners: like most uncivilized wom-

[10] Kaffir: South African Bantu.

en, they seemed at once tender of heart and tough of constitution; equally ready to die for their infants or fight for them. Unsophisticated as leopardesses; loving as doves. Ah! thought Captain Delano, there, perhaps, are some of the very women whom Ledyard[11] saw in Africa, and gave such a noble account of.

These natural sights somehow insensibly deepened his confidence and ease. At last he looked to see how his boat was getting on; but it was still pretty remote. He turned to see if Don Benito had returned; but he had not.

To change the scene, as well as to please himself with a leisurely observation of the coming boat, stepping over into the mizzen-chains, he clambered his way into the starboard quarter-gallery—one of those abandoned Venetian-looking water-balconies previously mentioned—retreats cut off from the deck. As his foot pressed the half-damp, half-dry sea-mosses matting the place, and a chance phantom cats-paw—an islet of breeze, unheralded, unfollowed—as this ghostly cats-paw came fanning his cheek; as his glance fell upon the row of small, round dead-lights—all closed like coppered eyes of the coffined—and the state-cabin door, once connecting with the gallery, even as the dead-lights had once looked out upon it, but now calked fast like a sarcophagus lid; and to a purple-black, tarred-over panel, threshold, and post; and he bethought him of the time, when that state-cabin and this state-balcony had heard the voices of the Spanish king's officers, and the forms of the Lima viceroy's daughters had perhaps leaned where he stood—as these and other images flitted through his mind, as the cats-paw through the calm, gradually he felt rising a dreamy inquietude, like that of one who alone on the prairie feels unrest from the repose of the noon.

He leaned against the carved balustrade, again looking off toward his boat; but found his eye falling upon the ribbon grass, trailing along the ship's waterline, straight as a border of green box; and parterres of seaweed, broad ovals and crescents, floating nigh and far, with what seemed long formal alleys between, crossing the terraces of swells, and sweeping round as if leading to the grottoes below. And overhanging all was the balustrade by his arm, which, partly stained with pitch and partly embossed with moss, seemed the charred ruin of some summer-house in a grand garden long running to waste.

Trying to break one charm, he was but becharmed anew. Though upon the wide sea, he seemed in some far inland country; prisoner in some deserted château, left to stare at empty grounds, and peer out at vague roads, where never wagon or wayfarer passed.

But these enchantments were a little disenchanted as his eye fell on the corroded main-chains. Of an ancient style, massy and rusty in link, shackle and bolt, they seemed even more fit for the ship's present business than the one for which she had been built.

Presently he thought something moved nigh the chains. He rubbed his eyes, and looked hard. Groves of rigging were about the chains; and there, peering from behind a great stay, like an Indian from behind a hemlock, a Spanish sailor, a marlingspike in his hand, was seen, who made what seemed an imperfect gesture towards the balcony, but immediately, as if alarmed by some advancing step along the deck within, vanished into the recesses of the hempen forest, like a poacher.

What meant this? Something the man had sought to communicate, unbeknown to any one, even to his captain. Did the secret involve aught unfavorable to his captain? Were those previous misgivings of Captain Delano's about to be verified? Or, in his haunted mood at the moment, had some random, unintentional motion of the man, while busy with the stay, as if repairing it, been mistaken for a significant beckoning?

Not unbewildered, again he gazed off for his boat. But it was temporarily hidden by a rocky spur of the isle. As with some eagerness he bent forward, watching for the first shooting view of its beak, the balustrade gave way before him like charcoal. Had he not clutched an outreaching rope he would have fallen into the sea. The crash, though feeble, and the fall, though hollow, of the rotten fragments, must have been overheard. He glanced up. With sober curiosity peering down upon him was one of the old oakum-pickers, slipped from his perch to an outside boom; while below the old negro, and, invisible to him, reconnoitering from a porthole like a fox from the mouth of its den, crouched the Spanish sailor again. From something suddenly suggested by the man's air, the mad idea now darted into Captain Delano's mind, that Don Benito's plea of indisposition, in withdrawing below, was but a pretense; that he was engaged there maturing his plot, of which the sailor, by some means gaining an inkling, had a mind to warn the stranger against; incited, it may be, by gratitude for a kind word on first boarding the ship. Was it from foreseeing some possible interference like this, that Don Benito had, beforehand, given such a bad character of his sailors, while praising the negroes; though, indeed, the former seemed as docile as the latter the contrary? The whites, too, by nature, were the shrewder race. A man with some evil design, would he not be likely to speak

[11] John Ledyard (1751–89), a famous American traveler.

well of that stupidity which was blind to his depravity, and malign that intelligence from which it might not be hidden? Not unlikely, perhaps. But if the whites had dark secrets concerning Don Benito, could then Don Benito be any way in complicity with the blacks? But they were too stupid. Besides, who ever heard of a white so far a renegade as to apostatize from his very species almost, by leaguing in against it with negroes? These difficulties recalled former ones. Lost in their mazes, Captain Delano, who had now regained the deck, was uneasily advancing along it, when he observed a new face; an aged sailor seated cross-legged near the main hatchway. His skin was shrunk up with wrinkles like a pelican's empty pouch; his hair frosted; his countenance grave and composed. His hands were full of ropes, which he was working into a large knot. Some blacks were about him obligingly dipping the strands for him, here and there, as the exigencies of the operation demanded.

Captain Delano crossed over to him, and stood in silence surveying the knot; his mind, by a not uncongenial transition, passing from its own entanglements to those of the hemp. For intricacy, such a knot he had never seen in an American ship, or indeed any other. The old man looked like an Egyptian priest, making Gordian knots for the temple of Ammon. The knot seemed a combination of double-bowline-knot, treble-crown-knot, back-handed-well-knot, knot-in-and-out-knot, and jamming-knot.

At last, puzzled to comprehend the meaning of such a knot, Captain Delano addressed the knotter:

"What are you knotting there, my man?"

"The knot," was the brief reply, without looking up.

"So it seems; but what is it for?"

"For some one else to undo," muttered back the old man, plying his fingers harder than ever, the knot being now nearly completed.

While Captain Delano stood watching him, suddenly the old man threw the knot towards him, saying in broken English—the first heard in the ship—something to this effect: "Undo it, cut it, quick." It was said lowly, but with such condensation of rapidity, that the long, slow words in Spanish, which had preceded and followed, almost operated as covers to the brief English between.

For a moment, knot in hand, and knot in head, Captain Delano stood mute; while, without further heeding him, the old man was now intent upon other ropes. Presently there was a slight stir behind Captain Delano. Turning, he saw the chained negro, Atufal, standing quietly there. The next moment the old sailor rose, muttering, and, followed by his subordinate negroes, removed to the forward of the ship, where in the crowd he disappeared.

An elderly negro, in a clout like an infant's, and with a pepper and salt head, and a kind of attorney air, now approached Captain Delano. In tolerable Spanish, and with a good-natured, knowing wink, he informed him that the old knotter was simple-witted, but harmless; often playing his old tricks. The negro concluded by begging the knot, for of course the stranger would not care to be troubled with it. Unconsciously, it was handed to him. With a sort of congé, the negro received it, and, turning his back, ferreted into it like a detective custom-house officer after smuggled laces. Soon, with some African word, equivalent to pshaw, he tossed the knot overboard.

All this is very queer now, thought Captain Delano, with a qualmish sort of emotion; but, as one feeling incipient sea-sickness, he strove, by ignoring the symptoms, to get rid of the malady. Once more he looked off for his boat. To his delight, it was now again in view, leaving the rocky spur astern.

The sensation here experienced, after at first relieving his uneasiness, with unforeseen efficacy soon began to remove it. The less distant sight of that well-known boat—showing it, not as before, half blended with the haze, but with outline defined, so that its individuality, like a man's, was manifest; that boat, Rover by name, which, though now in strange seas, had often pressed the beach of Captain Delano's home, and brought to its threshold for repairs, had familiarly lain there, as a Newfoundland dog; the sight of that household boat evoked a thousand trustful associations, which, contrasted with previous suspicions, filled him not only with lightsome confidence, but somehow with half humorous self-reproaches at his former lack of it.

"What, I, Amasa Delano—Jack of the Beach, as they called me when a lad—I, Amasa; the same that, duck-satchel in hand, used to paddle along the waterside to the schoolhouse made from the old hulk—I, little Jack of the Beach, that used to go berrying with cousin Nat and the rest; I to be murdered here at the ends of the earth, on board a haunted pirate-ship by a horrible Spaniard? Too nonsensical to think of! Who would murder Amasa Delano? His conscience is clean. There is some one above. Fie, fie, Jack of the Beach! you are a child indeed; a child of the second childhood, old boy; you are beginning to dote and drule, I'm afraid."

Light of heart and foot, he stepped aft, and there was met by Don Benito's servant, who, with a pleasing expression, responsive to his own present feelings, informed him that his master had recovered from the effects of his coughing fit, and had just ordered him to go present his compliments to his good guest, Don Amasa, and say that he (Don Benito) would soon have the happiness to rejoin him.

There now, do you mark that? again thought Captain Delano, walking the poop. What a donkey I was. This kind gentleman who here sends me his kind compliments, he, but ten minutes ago, dark-lantern in hand, was dodging round some old grindstone in the hold, sharpening a hatchet for me, I thought. Well, well; these long calms have a morbid effect on the mind, I've often heard, though I never believed it before. Ha! glancing towards the boat; there's Rover; good dog; a white bone in her mouth. A pretty big bone though, seems to me.—What? Yes, she has fallen afoul of the bubbling tide-rip there. It sets her the other way, too, for the time. Patience.

It was now about noon, though, from the grayness of everything, it seemed to be getting towards dusk.

The calm was confirmed. In the far distance, away from the influence of land, the leaden ocean seemed laid out and leaded up, its course finished, soul gone, defunct. But the current from landward, where the ship was, increased; silently sweeping her further and further towards the tranced waters beyond.

Still, from his knowledge of those latitudes, cherishing hopes of a breeze, and a fair and fresh one, at any moment, Captain Delano, despite present prospects, buoyantly counted upon bringing the San Dominick safely to anchor ere night. The distance swept over was nothing; since, with a good wind, ten minutes' sailing would retrace more than sixty minutes' drifting. Meantime, one moment turning to mark "Rover" fighting the tide-rip, and the next to see Don Benito approaching, he continued walking the poop.

Gradually he felt a vexation arising from the delay of his boat; this soon merged into uneasiness; and at last—his eye falling continually, as from a stage-box into the pit, upon the strange crowd before and below him, and, by-and-by, recognizing there the face—now composed to indifference—of the Spanish sailor who had seemed to beckon from the main-chains—something of his old trepidations returned.

Ah, thought he—gravely enough—this is like the ague: because it went off, it follows not that it won't come back.

Though ashamed of the relapse, he could not altogether subdue it; and so, exerting his good-nature to the utmost, insensibly he came to a compromise.

Yes, this is a strange craft; a strange history, too, and strange folks on board. But—nothing more.

By way of keeping his mind out of mischief till the boat should arrive, he tried to occupy it with turning over and over, in a purely speculative sort of way, some lesser peculiarities of the captain and crew. Among others, four curious points recurred:

First, the affair of the Spanish lad assailed with a knife by the slave boy; an act winked at by Don Benito. Second, the tyranny in Don Benito's treatment of Atufal, the black; as if a child should lead a bull of the Nile by the ring in his nose. Third, the trampling of the sailor by the two negroes; a piece of insolence passed over without so much as a reprimand. Fourth, the cringing submission to their master of all the ships' underlings, mostly blacks; as if by the least inadvertence they feared to draw down his despotic displeasure.

Coupling these points, they seemed somewhat contradictory. But what then, thought Captain Delano, glancing towards his now nearing boat—what then? Why, Don Benito is a very capricious commander. But he is not the first of the sort I have seen; though it's true he rather exceeds any other. But as a nation—continued he in his reveries—these Spaniards are all an odd set; the very word Spaniard has a curious, conspirator, Guy-Fawkish twang to it. And yet, I dare say, Spaniards in the main are as good folks as any in Duxbury, Massachusetts. Ah good! At last "Rover" has come.

As, with its welcome freight, the boat touched the side, the oakum-pickers, with venerable gestures, sought to restrain the blacks, who, at the sight of three gurried[12] water-casks in its bottom, and a pile of wilted pumpkins in its bow, hung over the bulwarks in disorderly raptures.

Don Benito, with his servant, now appeared; his coming, perhaps, hastened by hearing the noise. Of him Captain Delano sought permission to serve out the water, so that all might share alike, and none injure themselves by unfair excess. But sensible, and, on Don Benito's account, kind as this offer was, it was received with what seemed impatience; as if aware that he lacked energy as a commander, Don Benito, with the true jealousy of weakness, resented as an affront any interference. So, at least, Captain Delano inferred.

In another moment the casks were being hoisted in, when some of the eager negroes accidentally jostled Captain Delano, where he stood by the gangway; so that, unmindful of Don Benito, yielding to the impulse of the moment, with good-natured authority he bade the blacks stand back; to enforce his words making use of a half-mirthful, half-menacing gesture. Instantly the blacks paused, just where they were, each negro and negress suspended in his or her posture, exactly as the word had found them—for a few seconds continuing so—while, as between the responsive posts of a telegraph, an unknown syllable ran from man to man among the perched oakum-pickers. While the visitor's attention was

[12] Dirty.

fixed by this scene, suddenly the hatchet-polishers half rose, and a rapid cry came from Don Benito.

Thinking that at the signal of the Spaniard he was about to be massacred, Captain Delano would have sprung for his boat, but paused, as the oakum-pickers, dropping down into the crowd with earnest exclamations, forced every white and every negro back, at the same moment, with gestures friendly and familiar, almost jocose, bidding him, in substance, not to be a fool. Simultaneously the hatchet-polishers resumed their seats, quietly as so many tailors, and at once, as if nothing had happened, the work of hoisting in the casks was resumed, whites and blacks singing at the tackle.

Captain Delano glanced towards Don Benito. As he saw his meagre form in the act of recovering itself from reclining in the servant's arms, into which the agitated invalid had fallen, he could not but marvel at the panic by which himself had been surprised on the darting supposition that such a commander, who, upon a legitimate occasion, so trivial, too, as it now appeared, could lose all self-command, was, with energetic iniquity, going to bring about his murder.

The casks being on deck, Captain Delano was handed a number of jars and cups by one of the steward's aids, who, in the name of his captain, entreated him to do as he had proposed—dole out the water. He complied, with republican impartiality as to this republican element, which always seeks one level, serving the oldest white no better than the youngest black; excepting, indeed, poor Don Benito, whose condition, if not rank, demanded an extra allowance. To him, in the first place, Captain Delano presented a fair pitcher of the fluid; but, thirsting as he was for it, the Spaniard quaffed not a drop until after several grave bows and salutes. A reciprocation of courtesies which the sight-loving Africans hailed with clapping of hands.

Two of the less wilted pumpkins being reserved for the cabin table, the residue were minced up on the spot for the general regalement. But the soft bread, sugar, and bottled cider, Captain Delano would have given the whites alone, and in chief Don Benito; but the latter objected; which disinterestedness not a little pleased the American; and so mouthfuls all around were given alike to whites and blacks; excepting one bottle of cider, which Babo insisted upon setting aside for his master.

Here it may be observed that as, on the first visit of the boat, the American had not permitted his men to board the ship, neither did he now; being unwilling to add to the confusion of the decks.

Not uninfluenced by the peculiar good-humor at present prevailing, and for the time oblivious of any but benevolent thoughts, Captain Delano, who, from recent indications, counted upon a breeze within an hour or two at furthest, dispatched the boat back to the sealer, with orders for all the hands that could be spared immediately to set about rafting casks to the watering-place and filling them. Likewise he bade word be carried to his chief officer, that if, against present expectation, the ship was not brought to anchor by sunset, he need be under no concern; for as there was to be a full moon that night, he (Captain Delano) would remain on board ready to play the pilot, come the wind soon or late.

As the two Captains stood together, observing the departing boat—the servant, as it happened, having just spied a spot on his master's velvet sleeve, and silently engaged in rubbing it out—the American expressed his regrets that the San Dominick had no boats; none, at least, but the unseaworthy old hulk of the long-boat, which, warped as a camel's skeleton in the desert, and almost as bleached, lay potwise inverted amidships, one side a little tipped, furnishing a subterraneous sort of den for family groups of the blacks, mostly women and small children; who, squatting on old mats below, or perched above in the dark dome, on the elevated seats, were described, some distance within, like a social circle of bats, sheltering in some friendly cave; at intervals, ebon flights of naked boys and girls, three or four years old, darting in and out of the den's mouth.

"Had you three or four boats now, Don Benito," said Captain Delano, "I think that, by tugging at the oars, your negroes here might help along matters some. Did you sail from port without boats, Don Benito?"

"They were stove in the gales, Señor."

"That was bad. Many men, too, you lost then. Boats and men. Those must have been hard gales, Don Benito."

"Past all speech," cringed the Spaniard.

"Tell me, Don Benito," continued his companion with increased interest, "tell me, were these gales immediately off the pitch of Cape Horn?"

"Cape Horn?—who spoke of Cape Horn?"

"Yourself did, when giving me an account of your voyage," answered Captain Delano, with almost equal astonishment at this eating of his own words, even as he ever seemed eating his own heart, on the part of the Spaniard. "You yourself, Don Benito, spoke of Cape Horn," he emphatically repeated.

The Spaniard turned, in a sort of stooping posture, pausing an instant, as one about to make a plunging exchange of elements, as from air to water.

At this moment a messenger-boy, a white, hurried by, in the regular performance of his function carrying the last expired half-hour forward to the forecastle, from the cabin time-piece, to have it struck at the ship's large bell.

"Master," said the servant, discontinuing his work on the coat sleeve, and addressing the rapt Spaniard with a sort of timid apprehensiveness, as one charged with a duty, the discharge of which, it was foreseen, would prove irksome to the very person who had imposed it, and for whose benefit it was intended, "master told me never mind where he was, or how engaged, always to remind him, to a minute, when shaving-time comes. Miguel has gone to strike the half-hour afternoon. It is *now*, master. Will master go into the cuddy?"

"Ah—yes," answered the Spaniard, starting, as from dreams into realities; then turning upon Captain Delano, he said that ere long he would resume the conversation.

"Then if master means to talk more to Don Amasa," said the servant, "why not let Don Amasa sit by master in the cuddy, and master can talk, and Don Amasa can listen, while Babo here lathers and strops."

"Yes," said Captain Delano, not unpleased with this sociable plan, "yes, Don Benito, unless you had rather not, I will go with you."

"Be it so, Señor."

As the three passed aft, the American could not but think it another strange instance of his host's capriciousness, this being shaved with such uncommon punctuality in the middle of the day. But he deemed it more than likely that the servant's anxious fidelity had something to do with the matter; inasmuch as the timely interruption served to rally his master from the mood which had evidently been coming upon him.

The place called the cuddy was a light deck-cabin formed by the poop, a sort of attic to the large cabin below. Part of it had formerly been the quarters of the officers; but since their death all the partitionings had been thrown down, and the whole interior converted into one spacious and airy marine hall; for absence of fine furniture and picturesque disarray of odd appurtenances, somewhat answering to the wide, cluttered hall of some eccentric bachelor-squire in the country, who hangs his shooting-jacket and tobacco-pouch on deer antlers, and keeps his fishing-rod, tongs, and walking-stick in the same corner.

The similitude was heightened, if not originally suggested, by glimpses of the surrounding sea; since, in one aspect, the country and the ocean seem cousins-german.

The floor of the cuddy was matted. Overhead, four or five old muskets were stuck into horizontal holes along the beams. On one side was a claw-footed old table lashed to the deck; a thumbed missal on it, and over it a small, meagre crucifix attached to the bulk-head. Under the table lay a dented cutlass or two, with a hacked harpoon, among some melancholy old rigging, like a heap of poor friars' girdles. There were also two long, sharp-ribbed settees of Malacca cane, black with age, and uncomfortable to look at as inquisitors' racks, with a large, misshapen arm-chair, which, furnished with a rude barber's crotch at the back, working with a screw, seemed some grotesque engine of torment. A flag locker was in one corner, open, exposing various colored bunting, some rolled up, others half unrolled, still others tumbled. Opposite was a cumbrous washstand, of black mahogany, all of one block, with a pedestal, like a font, and over it a railed shelf, containing combs, brushes, and other implements of the toilet. A torn hammock of stained grass swung near; the sheets tossed, and the pillow wrinkled up like a brow, as if whoever slept here slept but illy, with alternate visitations of sad thoughts and bad dreams.

The further extremity of the cuddy, overhanging the ship's stern, was pierced with three openings, windows or port-holes, according as men or cannon might peer, socially and unsocially, out of them. At present neither men nor cannon were seen, though huge ring-bolts and other rusty iron fixtures of the wood-work hinted of twenty-four-pounders.

Glancing towards the hammock as he entered, Captain Delano said, "You sleep here, Don Benito?"

"Yes, Señor, since we got into mild weather."

"This seems a sort of dormitory, sitting-room, sail-loft, chapel, armory, and private closet all together, Don Benito," added Captain Delano, looking round.

"Yes, Señor; events have not been favorable to much order in my arrangements."

Here the servant, napkin on arm, made a motion as if waiting his master's good pleasure. Don Benito signified his readiness, when, seating him in the Malacca arm-chair, and for the guest's convenience drawing opposite one of the settees, the servant commenced operations by throwing back his master's collar and loosening his cravat.

There is something in the negro which, in a peculiar way, fits him for avocations about one's person. Most negroes are natural valets and hair-dressers; taking to the comb and brush congenially as to the castinets, and flourishing them apparently with almost equal satisfaction. There is, too, a smooth tact about them in this employment, with a marvelous, noiseless, gliding briskness, not ungraceful in its way, singularly pleasing to behold, and still more so to be the manipulated subject of. And above all is the great gift of good-humor. Not the mere grin or laugh is here meant. Those were unsuitable. But a certain easy cheerfulness, harmonious in every glance and gesture; as though God had set the whole negro to some pleasant tune.

When to all this is added the docility arising from the unaspiring contentment of a limited mind, and that susceptibility of bland attachment sometimes inhering in indisputable inferiors, one readily perceives why those hypochondriacs, Johnson and Byron—it may be, something like the hypochondriac Benito Cereno—took to their hearts, almost to the exclusion of the entire white race, their serving men, the negroes, Barber and Fletcher. But if there be that in the negro which exempts him from the inflicted sourness of the morbid or cynical mind, how, in his most prepossessing aspects, must he appear to a benevolent one? When at ease with respect to exterior things, Captain Delano's nature was not only benign, but familiarly and humorously so. At home, he had often taken rare satisfaction in sitting in his door, watching some free man of color at his work or play. If on a voyage he chanced to have a black sailor, invariably he was on chatty and half-gamesome terms with him. In fact, like most men of a good, blithe heart, Captain Delano took to negroes, not philanthropically, but genially, just as other men to Newfoundland dogs.

Hitherto, the circumstances in which he found the San Dominick had repressed the tendency. But in the cuddy, relieved from his former uneasiness, and, for various reasons, more sociably inclined than at any previous period of the day, and seeing the colored servant, napkin on arm, so debonair about his master, in a business so familiar as that of shaving, too, all his old weakness for negroes returned.

Among other things, he was amused with an odd instance of the African love of bright colors and fine shows, in the black's informally taking from the flag-locker a great piece of bunting of all hues, and lavishly tucking it under his master's chin for an apron.

The mode of shaving among the Spaniards is a little different from what it is with other nations. They have a basin, specifically called a barber's basin, which on one side is scooped out, so as accurately to receive the chin, against which it is closely held in lathering; which is done, not with a brush, but with soap dipped in the water of the basin and rubbed on the face.

In the present instance salt-water was used for lack of better; and the parts lathered were only the upper lip, and low down under the throat, all the rest being cultivated beard.

These preliminaries being somewhat novel to Captain Delano, he sat curiously eying them, so that no conversation took place, nor, for the present, did Don Benito appear disposed to renew any.

Setting down his basin, the negro searched among the razors, as for the sharpest, and having found it, gave it an additional edge by expertly strapping it on the firm, smooth, oily skin of his open palm; he then made a gesture as if to begin, but midway stood suspended for an instant, one hand elevating the razor, the other professionally dabbling among the bubbling suds on the Spaniard's lank neck. Not unaffected by the close sight of the gleaming steel, Don Benito nervously shuddered; his usual ghastliness was heightened by the lather, which lather, again, was intensified in its hue by the contrasting sootiness of the negro's body. Altogether the scene was somewhat peculiar, at least to Captain Delano, nor, as he saw the two thus postured, could he resist the vagary, that in the black he saw a headsman, and in the white a man at the block. But this was one of those antic conceits, appearing and vanishing in a breath, from which, perhaps, the best regulated mind is not always free.

Meantime the agitation of the Spaniard had a little loosened the bunting from around him, so that one broad fold swept curtain-like over the chair-arm to the floor, revealing, amid a profusion of armorial bars and ground-colors—black, blue, and yellow—a closed castle in a blood-red field diagonal with a lion rampant in a white.

"The castle and the lion," exclaimed Captain Delano—"why, Don Benito, this is the flag of Spain you use here. It's well it's only I, and not the King, that sees this," he added, with a smile, "but"—turning towards the black—"it's all one, I suppose, so the colors be gay;" which playful remark did not fail somewhat to tickle the negro.

"Now, master," he said, readjusting the flag, and pressing the head gently further back into the crotch of the chair; "now, master," and the steel glanced nigh the throat.

Again Don Benito faintly shuddered.

"You must not shake so, master. See, Don Amasa, master always shakes when I shave him. And yet master knows I never yet have drawn blood, though it's true, if master will shake so, I may some of these times. Now, master," he continued. "And now, Don Amasa, please go on with your talk about the gale, and all that; master can hear, and between times, master can answer."

"Ah yes, these gales," said Captain Delano; "but the more I think of your voyage, Don Benito, the more I wonder, not at the gales, terrible as they must have been, but at the disastrous interval following them. For here, by your account, have you been these two months and more getting from Cape Horn to St. Maria, a distance which I myself, with a good wind, have sailed in a few days. True, you had calms, and long ones, but to be becalmed for two months, that is, at least, unusual. Why, Don Benito, had almost any other gentleman told me such a story, I should have been half disposed to a little incredulity."

Here an involuntary expression came over the

Spaniard, similar to that just before on the deck, and whether it was the start he gave, or a sudden gawky roll of the hull in the calm, or a momentary unsteadiness of the servant's hand, however it was, just then the razor drew blood, spots of which stained the creamy lather under the throat; immediately the black barber drew back his steel, and remaining in his professional attitude, back to Captain Delano, and face to Don Benito, held up the trickling razor, saying, with a sort of half humorous sorrow, "See, master—you shook so—here's Babo's first blood."

No sword drawn before James the First of England, no assassination in that timid King's presence, could have produced a more terrified aspect than was now presented by Don Benito.

Poor fellow, thought Captain Delano, so nervous he can't even bear the sight of barber's blood; and this unstrung, sick man, is it credible that I should have imagined he meant to spill all my blood, who can't endure the sight of one little drop of his own? Surely, Amasa Delano, you have been beside yourself this day. Tell it not when you get home, sappy Amasa. Well, well, he looks like a murderer, doesn't he? More like as if himself were to be done for. Well, well, this day's experience shall be a good lesson.

Meantime, while these things were running through the honest seaman's mind, the servant had taken the napkin from his arm, and to Don Benito had said—"But answer Don Amasa, please, master, while I wipe this ugly stuff off the razor, and strop it again."

As he said the words, his face was turned half round, so as to be alike visible to the Spaniard and the American, and seemed, by its expression, to hint, that he was desirous, by getting his master to go on with the conversation, considerately to withdraw his attention from the recent annoying accident. As if glad to snatch the offered relief, Don Benito resumed, rehearsing to Captain Delano, that not only were the calms of unusual duration, but the ship had fallen in with obstinate currents; and other things he added, some of which were but repetitions of former statements, to explain how it came to pass that the passage from Cape Horn to St. Maria had been so exceedingly long; now and then mingling with his words, incidental praises, less qualified than before, to the blacks, for their general good conduct. These particulars were not given consecutively, the servant, at convenient times, using his razor, and so, between the intervals of shaving, the story and panegyric went on with more than usual huskiness.

To Captain Delano's imagination, now again not wholly at rest, there was something so hollow in the Spaniard's manner, with apparently some reciprocal hollowness in the servant's dusky comment of silence, that the idea flashed across him, that possibly master and man, for some unknown purpose, were acting out, both in word and deed, nay, to the very tremor of Don Benito's limbs, some juggling play before him. Neither did the suspicion of collusion lack apparent support, from the fact of those whispered conferences before mentioned. But then, what could be the object of enacting this play of the barber before him? At last, regarding the notion as a whimsy, insensibly suggested, perhaps, by the theatrical aspect of Don Benito in his harlequin ensign, Captain Delano speedily banished it.

The shaving over, the servant bestirred himself with a small bottle of scented waters, pouring a few drops on the head, and then diligently rubbing; the vehemence of the exercise causing the muscles of his face to twitch rather strangely.

His next operation was with comb, scissors, and brush; going round and round, smoothing a curl here, clipping an unruly whisker-hair there, giving a graceful sweep to the temple-lock, with other impromptu touches evincing the hand of a master; while, like any resigned gentleman in barber's hands, Don Benito bore all, much less uneasily, at least, than he had done the razoring; indeed, he sat so pale and rigid now, that the negro seemed a Nubian sculptor finishing off a white statue-head.

All being over at last, the standard of Spain removed, tumbled up, and tossed back into the flag-locker, the negro's warm breath blowing away any stray hair which might have lodged down his master's neck; collar and cravat readjusted; a speck of lint whisked off the velvet lapel; all this being done; backing off a little space, and pausing with an expression of subdued self-complacency, the servant for a moment surveyed his master, as, in toilet at least, the creature of his own tasteful hands.

Captain Delano playfully complimented him upon his achievement; at the same time congratulating Don Benito.

But neither sweet waters, nor shampooing, nor fidelity, nor sociality, delighted the Spaniard. Seeing him relapsing into forbidding gloom, and still remaining seated, Captain Delano, thinking that his presence was undesired just then, withdrew, on pretense of seeing whether, as he had prophesied, any signs of a breeze were visible.

Walking forward to the main-mast, he stood awhile thinking over the scene, and not without some undefined misgivings, when he heard a noise near the cuddy, and turning, saw the negro, his hand to his cheek. Advancing, Captain Delano perceived that the cheek was bleeding. He was about to ask the cause, when the negro's wailing soliloquy enlightened him.

"Ah, when will master get better from his sickness; only the sour heart that sour sickness breeds made him serve Babo so; cutting Babo with the razor, because, only by accident, Babo had given master one little scratch; and for the first time in so many a day, too. Ah, ah, ah," holding his hand to his face.

Is it possible, thought Captain Delano; was it to wreak in private his Spanish spite against this poor friend of his, that Don Benito, by his sullen manner, impelled me to withdraw? Ah, this slavery breeds ugly passions in man.—Poor fellow!

He was about to speak in sympathy to the negro, but with a timid reluctance he now reentered the cuddy.

Presently master and man came forth; Don Benito leaning on his servant as if nothing had happened.

But a sort of love-quarrel, after all, thought Captain Delano.

He accosted Don Benito, and they slowly walked together. They had gone but a few paces, when the steward—a tall, rajah-looking mulatto, orientally set off with a pagoda turban formed by three or four Madras handkerchiefs wound about his head, tier on tier—approaching with a salaam, announced lunch in the cabin.

On their way thither, the two captains were preceded by the mulatto, who, turning round as he advanced, with continual smiles and bows, ushered them on, a display of elegance which quite completed the insignificance of the small bare-headed Babo, who, as if not unconscious of inferiority, eyed askance the graceful steward. But in part, Captain Delano imputed his jealous watchfulness to that peculiar feeling which the full-blooded African entertains for the adulterated one. As for the steward, his manner, if not bespeaking much dignity or self-respect, yet evidenced his extreme desire to please; which is doubly meritorious, as at once Christian and Chesterfieldian.

Captain Delano observed with interest that while the complexion of the mulatto was hybrid, his physiognomy was European—classically so.

"Don Benito," whispered he, "I am glad to see this usher-of-the-golden-rod of yours; the sight refutes an ugly remark once made to me by a Barbados planter; that when a mulatto has a regular European face, look out for him; he is a devil. But see, your steward here has features more regular than King George's of England; and yet there he nods, and bows, and smiles; a king, indeed—the king of kind hearts and polite fellows. What a pleasant voice he has, too?"

"He has, Señor."

"But, tell me, has he not, so far as you have known him, always proved a good, worthy fellow?" said Captain Delano, pausing, while with a final genuflexion the steward disappeared into the cabin; "come, for the reason just mentioned, I am curious to know."

"Francesco is a good man," rather sluggishly responded Don Benito, like a phlegmatic appreciator, who would neither find fault nor flatter.

"Ah, I thought so. For it were strange, indeed, and not very creditable to us white-skins, if a little of our blood mixed with the African's, should, far from improving the latter's quality, have the sad effect of pouring vitriolic acid into black broth; improving the hue, perhaps, but not the wholesomeness."

"Doubtless, doubtless, Señor, but"—glancing at Babo—"not to speak of negroes, your planter's remark I have heard applied to the Spanish and Indian intermixtures in our provinces. But I know nothing about the matter," he listlessly added.

And here they entered the cabin.

The lunch was a frugal one. Some of Captain Delano's fresh fish and pumpkins, biscuit and salt beef, the reserved bottle of cider, and the San Dominick's last bottle of Canary.

As they entered, Francesco, with two or three colored aids, was hovering over the table giving the last adjustments. Upon perceiving their master they withdrew, Francesco making a smiling congé, and the Spaniard, without condescending to notice it, fastidiously remarking to his companion that he relished not superfluous attendance.

Without companions, host and guest sat down, like a childless married couple, at opposite ends of the table, Don Benito waving Captain Delano to his place, and, weak as he was, insisting upon that gentleman being seated before himself.

The negro placed a rug under Don Benito's feet, and a cushion behind his back, and then stood behind, not his master's chair, but Captain Delano's. At first, this a little surprised the latter. But it was soon evident that, in taking his position, the black was still true to his master; since by facing him he could the more readily anticipate his slightest want.

"This is an uncommonly intelligent fellow of yours, Don Benito," whispered Captain Delano across the table.

"You say true, Señor."

During the repast, the guest again reverted to parts of Don Benito's story, begging further particulars here and there. He inquired how it was that the scurvy and fever should have committed such wholesale havoc upon the whites, while destroying less than half of the blacks. As if this question reproduced the whole scene of plague before the Spaniard's eyes, miserably reminding him of his solitude in a cabin where before he had had so many friends and officers round him, his hand shook, his face became hueless, broken words escaped; but directly the sane memory of the past seemed replaced by insane terrors of the present. With starting eyes he stared before him at vacancy. For nothing was to be seen but the hand of his servant pushing the Canary over towards him. At length a few sips served partially to restore him. He made random reference to the different constitution of races, enabling one to offer more resistance to certain maladies than another. The thought was new to his companion.

Presently Captain Delano, intending to say something to his host concerning the pecuniary part of the business he had undertaken for him, especially—since he was strictly accountable to his owners—with reference to the new suit of sails, and other things of that sort; and naturally preferring to conduct such affairs in private, was desirous that the servant should withdraw; imagining that Don Benito for a few minutes could dispense with his attendance. He, however, waited awhile; thinking that, as the conversation proceeded, Don Benito, without being prompted, would perceive the propriety of the step.

But it was otherwise. At last catching his host's eye, Captain Delano, with a slight backward gesture of his thumb, whispered, "Don Benito, pardon me, but there is an interference with the full expression of what I have to say to you."

Upon this the Spaniard changed countenance; which was imputed to his resenting the hint, as in some way a reflection upon his servant. After a moment's pause, he assured his guest that the black's remaining with them could be of no disservice; because since losing his officers he had made Babo (whose original office, it now appeared, had been captain of the slaves) not only his constant attendant and companion, but in all things his confidant.

After this, nothing more could be said; though, indeed, Captain Delano could hardly avoid some little tinge of irritation upon being left ungratified in so inconsiderable a wish, by one, too, for whom he intended such solid services. But it is only his querulousness, thought he; and so filling his glass he proceeded to business.

The price of the sails and other matters was fixed upon. But while this was being done, the American observed that, though his original offer of assistance had been hailed with hectic animation, yet now when it was reduced to a business transaction, indifference and apathy were betrayed. Don Benito, in fact, appeared to submit to hearing the details more out of regard to common propriety, than from any impression that weighty benefit to himself and his voyage was involved.

Soon, his manner became still more reserved. The effort was vain to seek to draw him into social talk. Gnawed by his splenetic mood, he sat twitching his beard, while to little purpose the hand of his servant, mute as that on the wall, slowly pushed over the Canary.

Lunch being over, they sat down on the cushioned transom; the servant placing a pillow behind his master. The long continuance of the calm had now affected the atmosphere. Don Benito sighed heavily, as if for breath.

"Why not adjourn to the cuddy," said Captain Delano; "there is more air there." But the host sat silent and motionless.

Meantime his servant knelt before him, with a large fan of feathers. And Francesco coming in on tiptoes, handed the negro a little cup of aromatic waters, with which at intervals he chafed his master's brow; smoothing the hair along the temples as a nurse does a child's. He spoke no word. He only rested his eye on his master's, as if, amid all Don Benito's distress, a little to refresh his spirit by the silent sight of fidelity.

Presently the ship's bell sounded two o'clock; and through the cabin windows a slight rippling of the sea was discerned; and from the desired direction.

"There," exclaimed Captain Delano, "I told you so, Don Benito, look!"

He had risen to his feet, speaking in a very animated tone, with a view the more to rouse his companion. But though the crimson curtain of the stern-window near him that moment fluttered against his pale cheek, Don Benito seemed to have even less welcome for the breeze than the calm.

Poor fellow, thought Captain Delano, bitter experience has taught him that one ripple does not make a wind, any more than one swallow a summer. But he is mistaken for once. I will get his ship in for him, and prove it.

Briefly alluding to his weak condition, he urged his host to remain quietly where he was, since he (Captain Delano) would with pleasure take upon himself the responsibility of making the best use of the wind.

Upon gaining the deck, Captain Delano started at the unexpected figure of Atufal, monumentally fixed at the threshold, like one of those sculptured porters of black marble guarding the porches of Egyptian tombs.

But this time the start was, perhaps, purely physical. Atufal's presence, singularly attesting docility even in sullenness, was contrasted with that of the hatchet-polishers, who in patience evinced their industry; while both spectacles showed, that lax as Don Benito's general authority might be, still, whenever he chose to exert it, no man so savage or colossal but must, more or less, bow.

Snatching a trumpet which hung from the bulwarks, with a free step Captain Delano advanced to the forward edge of the poop, issuing his orders in his best Spanish. The few sailors and many negroes, all equally pleased, obediently set about heading the ship towards the harbor.

While giving some directions about setting a lower stu'n'-sail, suddenly Captain Delano heard a voice faithfully repeating his orders. Turning, he saw Babo, now for the time acting, under the pilot, his original part of captain of the slaves. This assistance proved valuable. Tattered sails and warped yards were soon brought into some trim. And no brace or halyard was pulled but to the blithe songs of the inspirited negroes.

Good fellows, thought Captain Delano, a little training would make fine sailors of them. Why see, the very women pull and sing too. These must be some of those Ashantee negresses that make such capital soldiers, I've heard. But who's at the helm? I must have a good hand there.

He went to see.

The San Dominick steered with a cumbrous tiller, with large horizontal pullies attached. At each pulley-end stood a subordinate black, and between them, at the tiller-head, the responsible post, a Spanish seaman, whose countenance evinced his due share in the general hopefulness and confidence at the coming of the breeze.

He proved the same man who had behaved with so shame-faced an air on the windlass.

"Ah,—it is you, my man," exclaimed Captain Delano—"well, no more sheep's-eyes now;—look straight forward and keep the ship so. Good hand, I trust? And want to get into the harbor, don't you?"

The man assented with an inward chuckle, grasping the tiller-head firmly. Upon this, unperceived by the American, the two blacks eyed the sailor intently.

Finding all right at the helm, the pilot went forward to the forecastle, to see how matters stood there.

The ship now had way enough to breast the current. With the approach of evening, the breeze would be sure to freshen.

Having done all that was needed for the present, Captain Delano, giving his last orders to the sailors, turned aft to report affairs to Don Benito in the cabin; perhaps additionally incited to rejoin him by the hope of snatching a moment's private chat while the servant was engaged upon deck.

From opposite sides, there were, beneath the poop, two approaches to the cabin; one further forward than the other, and consequently communicating with a longer passage. Marking the servant still above, Captain Delano, taking the nighest entrance—the one last named, and at whose porch Atufal still stood—hurried on his way, till, arrived at the cabin threshold, he paused an instant, a little to recover from his eagerness. Then, with the words of his intended business upon his lips, he entered. As he advanced toward the seated Spaniard, he heard another footstep, keeping time with his. From the opposite door, a salver in hand, the servant was likewise advancing.

"Confound the faithful fellow," thought Captain Delano; "what a vexatious coincidence."

Possibly, the vexation might have been something different, were it not for the brisk confidence inspired by the breeze. But even as it was, he felt a slight twinge, from a sudden indefinite association in his mind of Babo with Atufal.

"Don Benito," said he, "I give you joy; the breeze will hold, and will increase. By the way, your tall man and time-piece, Atufal, stands without. By your order, of course?"

Don Benito recoiled, as if at some bland satirical touch, delivered with such adroit garnish of apparent good breeding as to present no handle for retort.

He is like one flayed alive, thought Captain Delano; where may one touch him without causing a shrink?

The servant moved before his master, adjusting a cushion; recalled to civility, the Spaniard stiffly replied: "you are right. The slave appears where you saw him, according to my command; which is, that if at the given hour I am below, he must take his stand and abide my coming."

"Ah now, pardon me, but that is treating the poor fellow like an ex-king indeed. Ah, Don Benito," smiling, "for all the license you permit in some things, I fear lest, at bottom, you are a bitter hard master."

Again Don Benito shrank; and this time, as the good sailor thought, from a genuine twinge of his conscience.

Again conversation became constrained. In vain Captain Delano called attention to the now perceptible motion of the keel gently cleaving the sea; with lack-lustre eye, Don Benito returned words few and reserved.

By-and-by, the wind having steadily risen, and still blowing right into the harbor, bore the San Dominick swiftly on. Rounding a point of land, the sealer at distance came into open view.

Meantime Captain Delano had again repaired to the deck, remaining there some time. Having at last altered the ship's course, so as to give the reef a wide berth, he returned for a few moments below.

I will cheer up my poor friend, this time, thought he.

"Better and better, Don Benito," he cried as he blithely re-entered: "there will soon be an end to your cares, at least for awhile. For when, after a long, sad voyage, you know, the anchor drops into the haven, all its vast weight seems lifted from the captain's heart. We are getting on famously, Don Benito. My ship is in sight. Look through this side-light here; there she is; all a-taunt-o![13] The Bachelor's Delight, my good friend. Ah, how this wind braces one up. Come, you must take a cup of coffee with me this evening. My old steward will give you as fine a cup as ever any sultan tasted. What say you, Don Benito, will you?"

At first, the Spaniard glanced feverishly up, casting a longing look towards the sealer, while with mute concern his servant gazed into his face. Suddenly the old ague of coldness returned, and dropping back to his cushions he was silent.

"You do not answer. Come, all day you have been my host; would you have hospitality all on one side?"

"I cannot go," was the response.

"What? It will not fatigue you. The ships will lie together as near as they can, without swinging foul. It will be little more than stepping from deck to deck; which is but as from room to room. Come, come, you must not refuse me."

"I cannot go," decisively and repulsively repeated Don Benito.

Renouncing all but the last appearance of courtesy, with a sort of cadaverous sullenness, and biting his thin nails to the quick, he glanced, almost glared, at his guest, as if impatient that a stranger's presence should interfere with the full indulgence of his morbid hour. Meantime the sound of the parted waters came more and more gurglingly and merrily in at the windows; as reproaching him for his dark spleen; as telling him that, sulk as he might, and go mad with it, nature cared not a jot; since, whose fault was it, pray?

But the foul mood was now at its depth, as the fair wind at its height.

There was something in the man so far beyond any mere unsociality or sourness previously evinced, that even the forbearing good-nature of his guest could no longer endure it. Wholly at a loss to account for such demeanor, and deeming sickness with eccentricity, however extreme, no adequate excuse, well satisfied, too, that nothing in his own conduct could justify it, Captain Delano's pride began to be roused. Himself became reserved. But all seemed one to the Spaniard. Quitting him, therefore, Captain Delano once more went to the deck.

The ship was now within less than two miles of the sealer. The whale-boat was seen darting over the interval.

To be brief, the two vessels, thanks to the pilot's skill, ere long in neighborly style lay anchored together.

Before returning to his own vessel, Captain Delano had intended communicating to Don Benito the smaller details of the proposed services to be rendered. But, as it was, unwilling anew to subject himself to rebuffs, he resolved, now that he had seen the San Dominick safely moored, immediately to quit her, without further allusion to hospitality or business. Indefinitely postponing his ulterior plans, he would regulate his future actions according to future circumstances. His boat was ready to receive him; but his host still tarried below. Well, thought Captain Delano, if he has little breeding, the more need to show mine. He descended to the cabin to bid a ceremonious, and, it may be, tacitly rebukeful adieu. But to his great satisfaction, Don Benito, as if he began to feel the weight of that treatment with which his slighted guest had, not indecorously, retaliated upon him, now supported by his servant, rose to his feet, and grasping Captain Delano's hand, stood tremulous; too much agitated to speak. But the good augury hence drawn was suddenly dashed, by his resuming all his previous reserve, with augmented gloom, as, with half-averted eyes, he silently reseated himself on his cushions. With a corresponding return of his own chilled feelings, Captain Delano bowed and withdrew.

He was hardly midway in the narrow corridor, dim as a tunnel, leading from the cabin to the stairs, when a sound, as of the tolling for execution in some jail-yard, fell on his ears. It was the echo of the ship's flawed bell, striking the hour, drearily reverberated in this subterranean vault. Instantly, by a fatality not to be withstood, his mind, responsive to the portent, swarmed with superstitious suspicions. He paused. In images far swifter than these sentences, the minutest details of all his former distrusts swept through him.

Hitherto, credulous good-nature had been too ready to furnish excuses for reasonable fears. Why was the Spaniard, so superfluously punctilious at times, now heedless of common propriety in not accompanying to the side his departing guest? Did indisposition forbid? Indisposition had not forbidden more irksome exertion that day. His last equivocal demeanor recurred. He had risen to his feet, grasped his guest's hand, motioned toward his hat; then, in an instant, all was eclipsed in sinister muteness and gloom. Did this imply one brief, repentant relenting at the final moment, from some iniquitous plot, followed by remorseless return to it? His last glance seemed to express a calamitous, yet acquiescent farewell to Captain Delano forever. Why decline the invitation to visit the sealer that evening? Or was the Spaniard less hardened than the Jew,[14] who refrained not from supping at the board of him whom the same night he meant to betray? What imported all those day-long enigmas and contradictions, except they were intended to mystify, prelimi-

[13] Fully rigged.

[14] Judas Iscariot.

nary to some stealthy blow? Atufal, the pretended rebel, but punctual shadow, that moment lurked by the threshold without. He seemed a sentry, and more. Who, by his own confession, had stationed him there? Was the negro now lying in wait?

The Spaniard behind—his creature before: to rush from darkness to light was the involuntary choice.

The next moment, with clenched jaw and hand, he passed Atufal, and stood unharmed in the light. As he saw his trim ship lying peacefully at anchor, and almost within ordinary call; as he saw his household boat, with familiar faces in it, patiently rising and falling on the short waves by the San Dominick's side; and then, glancing about the decks where he stood, saw the oakum-pickers still gravely plying their fingers; and heard the low, buzzing whistle and industrious hum of the hatchet-polishers, still bestirring themselves over their endless occupation; and more than all, as he saw the benign aspect of nature, taking her innocent repose in the evening; the screened sun in the quiet camp of the west shining out like the mild light from Abraham's tent; as charmed eye and ear took in all these, with the chained figure of the black, clenched jaw and hand relaxed. Once again he smiled at the phantoms which had mocked him, and felt something like a tinge of remorse, that, by indulging them even for a moment, he should, by implication, have betrayed an atheist doubt of the ever-watchful Providence above.

There was a few minutes' delay, while, in obedience to his orders, the boat was being hooked along to the gangway. During this interval, a sort of saddened satisfaction stole over Captain Delano, at thinking of the kindly offices he had that day discharged for a stranger. Ah, thought he, after good actions one's conscience is never ungrateful, however much so the benefited party may be.

Presently, his foot, in the first act of descent into the boat, pressed the first round of the side-ladder, his face presented inward upon the deck. In the same moment, he heard his name courteously sounded; and, to his pleased surprise, saw Don Benito advancing—an unwonted energy in his air, as if, at the last moment, intent upon making amends for his recent discourtesy. With instinctive good feeling, Captain Delano, withdrawing his foot, turned and reciprocally advanced. As he did so, the Spaniard's nervous eagerness increased, but his vital energy failed; so that, the better to support him, the servant, placing his master's hand on his naked shoulder, and gently holding it there, formed himself into a sort of crutch.

When the two captains met, the Spaniard again fervently took the hand of the American, at the same time casting an earnest glance into his eyes, but, as before, too much overcome to speak.

I have done him wrong, self-reproachfully thought Captain Delano; his apparent coldness has deceived me; in no instance has he meant to offend.

Meantime, as if fearful that the continuance of the scene might too much unstring his master, the servant seemed anxious to terminate it. And so, still, presenting himself as a crutch, and walking between the two captains, he advanced with them towards the gangway; while still, as if full of kindly contrition, Don Benito would not let go the hand of Captain Delano, but retained it in his, across the black's body.

Soon they were standing by the side, looking over into the boat, whose crew turned up their curious eyes. Waiting a moment for the Spaniard to relinquish his hold, the now embarrassed Captain Delano lifted his foot, to overstep the threshold of the open gangway; but still Don Benito would not let go his hand. And yet, with an agitated tone, he said, "I can go no further; here I must bid you adieu. Adieu, my dear, dear Don Amasa. Go—go!" suddenly tearing his hand loose, "go, and God guard you better than me, my best friend."

Not unaffected, Captain Delano would now have lingered; but catching the meekly admonitory eye of the servant, with a hasty farewell he descended into his boat, followed by the continual adieus of Don Benito, standing rooted in the gangway.

Seating himself in the stern, Captain Delano, making a last salute, ordered the boat shoved off. The crew had their oars on end. The bowsmen pushed the boat a sufficient distance for the oars to be lengthwise dropped. The instant that was done, Don Benito sprang over the bulwarks, falling at the feet of Captain Delano; at the same time, calling towards his ship, but in tones so frenzied, that none in the boat could understand him. But, as if not equally obtuse, three sailors, from three different and distant parts of the ship, splashed into the sea, swimming after their captain, as if intent upon his rescue.

The dismayed officer of the boat eagerly asked what this meant. To which, Captain Delano, turning a disdainful smile upon the unaccountable Spaniard, answered that, for his part, he neither knew nor cared; but it seemed as if Don Benito had taken it into his head to produce the impression among his people that the boat wanted to kidnap him. "Or else—give way for your lives," he wildly added, starting at a clattering hubbub in the ship, above which rang the tocsin of the hatchet-polishers; and seizing Don Benito by the throat he added, "this plotting pirate means murder!" Here, in apparent verification of the words, the servant, a dagger in his hand, was seen on the rail overhead, poised, in the act of leaping, as if with desperate fidelity to befriend his master to the last; while, seemingly to aid the black, the three white sailors were trying to clamber into the hampered bow. Meantime, the whole host of negroes, as if inflamed at the sight of their jeopardized captain, impended in one sooty avalanche over the bulwarks.

All this, with what preceded, and what followed, occurred with such involutions of rapidity, that past, present, and future seemed one.

Seeing the negro coming, Captain Delano had flung the Spaniard aside, almost in the very act of clutching him, and, by the unconscious recoil, shifting his place, with arms thrown up, so promptly grappled the servant in his descent, that with dagger presented at Captain Delano's heart, the black seemed of purpose to have leaped there as to his mark. But the weapon was wrenched away, and the assailant dashed down into the bottom of the boat, which now, with disentangled oars, began to speed through the sea.

At this juncture, the left hand of Captain Delano, on one side, again clutched the half-reclined Don Benito, heedless that he was in a speechless faint, while his right foot, on the other side, ground the prostrate negro; and his right arm pressed for added speed on the after oar, his eye bent forward, encouraging his men to their utmost.

But here, the officer of the boat, who had at last succeeded in beating off the towing sailors, and was now, with face turned aft, assisting the bowsman at his oar, suddenly called to Captain Delano, to see what the black was about; while a Portuguese oarsman shouted to him to give heed to what the Spaniard was saying.

Glancing down at his feet, Captain Delano saw the freed hand of the servant aiming with a second dagger—a small one, before concealed in his wool—with this he was snakishly writhing up from the boat's bottom, at the heart of his master, his countenance lividly vindictive, expressing the centered purpose of his soul; while the Spaniard, half-choked, was vainly shrinking away, with husky words, incoherent to all but the Portuguese.

That moment, across the long-benighted mind of Captain Delano, a flash of revelation swept, illuminating in unanticipated clearness, his host's whole mysterious demeanor, with every enigmatic event of the day, as well as the entire past voyage of the San Dominick. He smote Babo's hand down, but his own heart smote him harder. With infinite pity he withdrew his hold from Don Benito. Not Captain Delano, but Don Benito, the black, in leaping into the boat, had intended to stab.

Both the black's hands were held, as, glancing up towards the San Dominick, Captain Delano, now with scales dropped from his eyes, saw the negroes, not in misrule, not in tumult, not as if frantically concerned for Don Benito, but with mask torn away, flourishing hatchets and knives, in ferocious piratical revolt. Like delirious black dervishes, the six Ashantees danced on the poop. Prevented by their foes from springing into the water, the Spanish boys were hurrying up to the topmost spars, while such of the few Spanish sailors, not already in the sea, less alert, were described, helplessly mixed in, on deck, with the blacks.

Meantime Captain Delano hailed his own vessel, ordering the ports up, and the guns run out. But by this time the cable of the San Dominick had been cut; and the fag-end, in lashing out, whipped away the canvas shroud about the beak, suddenly revealing, as the bleached hull swung round towards the open ocean, death for the figure-head, in a human skeleton; chalky comment on the chalked words below, *"Follow your leader."*

At the sight, Don Benito, covering his face, wailed out: "'Tis he, Aranda! my murdered, unburied friend!"

Upon reaching the sealer, calling for ropes, Captain Delano bound the negro, who made no resistance, and had him hoisted to the deck. He would then have assisted the now almost helpless Don Benito up the side; but Don Benito, wan as he was, refused to move, or be moved, until the negro should have been first put below out of view. When, presently assured that it was done, he no more shrank from the ascent.

The boat was immediately dispatched back to pick up the three swimming sailors. Meantime, the guns were in readiness, though, owing to the San Dominick having glided somewhat astern of the sealer, only the aftermost one could be brought to bear. With this, they fired six times; thinking to cripple the fugitive ship by bringing down her spars. But only a few inconsiderable ropes were shot away. Soon the ship was beyond the gun's range, steering broad out of the bay; the blacks thickly clustering round the bowsprit, one moment with taunting cries towards the whites, the next with upthrown gestures hailing the now dusky moors of ocean—cawing crows escaped from the hand of the fowler.

The first impulse was to slip the cables and give chase. But, upon second thoughts, to pursue with whale-boat and yawl seemed more promising.

Upon inquiring of Don Benito what fire-arms they had on board the San Dominick, Captain Delano was answered that they had none that could be used; because, in the earlier stages of the mutiny, a cabin-passenger, since dead, had secretly put out of order the locks of what few muskets there were. But with all his remaining strength, Don Benito entreated the American not to give chase, either with ship or boat; for the negroes had already proved themselves such desperadoes, that, in case of a present assault, nothing but a total massacre of the whites could be looked for. But, regarding this warning as coming from one whose spirit had been crushed by misery the American did not give up his design.

The boats were got ready and armed. Captain Delano ordered his men into them. He was going himself when Don Benito grasped his arm.

"What! have you saved my life, Señor, and are you now going to throw away your own?"

The officers also, for reasons connected with their interests and those of the voyage, and a duty owing to the owners, strongly objected against their commander's going. Weighing their remonstrances a moment, Captain Delano felt bound to remain; appointing his chief mate—an athletic and resolute man, who had been a privateer's-man—to head the party. The more to encourage the sailors, they were told, that the Spanish captain considered his ship good as lost; that she and her cargo, including some gold and silver, were worth more than a thousand doubloons. Take her, and no small part should be theirs. The sailors replied with a shout.

The fugitives had now almost gained an offing. It was nearly night; but the moon was rising. After hard, prolonged pulling, the boats came up on the ship's quarters, at a suitable distance laying upon their oars to discharge their muskets. Having no bullets to return, the negroes sent their yells. But, upon the second volley, Indianlike, they hurtled their hatchets. One took off a sailor's fingers. Another struck the whale-boat's bow, cutting off the rope there, and remaining stuck in the gunwale like a woodman's axe. Snatching it, quivering from its lodgment, the mate hurled it back. The returned gauntlet now stuck in the ship's broken quarter-gallery, and so remained.

The negroes giving too hot a reception, the whites kept a more respectful distance. Hovering now just out of reach of the hurtling hatchets, they, with a view to the close encounter which must soon come, sought to decoy the blacks into entirely disarming themselves of their most murderous weapons in a hand-to-hand fight, by foolishly flinging them, as missiles, short of the mark, into the sea. But, ere long, perceiving the stratagem, the negroes desisted, though not before many of them had to replace their lost hatchets with handspikes; an exchange which, as counted upon, proved, in the end, favorable to the assailants.

Meantime, with a strong wind, the ship still clove the water; the boats alternately falling behind, and pulling up, to discharge fresh volleys.

The fire was mostly directed towards the stern, since there, chiefly, the negroes, at present, were clustering. But to kill or maim the negroes was not the object. To take them, with the ship, was the object. To do it, the ship must be boarded; which could not be done by boats while she was sailing so fast.

A thought now struck the mate. Observing the Spanish boys still aloft, high as they could get, he called to them to descend to the yards, and cut adrift the sails. It was done. About this time, owing to causes hereafter to be shown, two Spaniards, in the dress of sailors, and conspicuously showing themselves, were killed; not by volleys, but by deliberate marksman's shots; while, as it afterwards appeared, by one of the general discharges, Atufal, the black, and the Spaniard at the helm likewise were killed. What now, with the loss of the sails, and loss of leaders, the ship became unmanageable to the negroes.

With creaking masts, she came heavily round to the wind; the prow slowly swinging into view of the boats, its skeleton gleaming in the horizontal moonlight, and casting a gigantic ribbed shadow upon the water. One extended arm of the ghost seemed beckoning the whites to avenge it.

"Follow your leader!" cried the mate; and, one on each bow, the boats boarded. Sealing-spears and cutlasses crossed hatchets and hand-spikes. Huddled upon the long-boat amidships, the negresses raised a wailing chant, whose chorus was the clash of the steel.

For a time, the attack wavered; the negroes wedging themselves to beat it back; the half-repelled sailors, as yet unable to gain a footing, fighting as troopers in the saddle, one leg sideways flung over the bulwarks, and one without, plying their cutlasses like carters' whips. But in vain. They were almost overborne, when, rallying themselves into a squad as one man, with a huzza, they sprang inboard, where, entangled, they involuntarily separated again. For a few breaths' space, there was a vague, muffled, inner sound, as of submerged sword-fish rushing hither and thither through shoals of black-fish. Soon, in a reunited band, and joined by the Spanish seamen, the whites came to the surface, irresistibly driving the negroes toward the stern. But a barricade of casks and sacks, from side to side, had been thrown up by the mainmast. Here the negroes faced about, and though scorning peace or truce, yet fain would have had respite. But, without pause, overleaping the barrier, the unflagging sailors again closed. Exhausted, the blacks now fought in despair. Their red tongues lolled, wolf-like, from their black mouths. But the pale sailors' teeth were set; not a word was spoken; and, in five minutes more, the ship was won.

Nearly a score of the negroes were killed. Exclusive of those by the balls, many were mangled; their wounds—mostly inflicted by the long-edged sealing-spears—resembling those shaven ones of the English at Preston Pans,[15] made by the poled scythes of the Highlanders. On the other side, none were killed, though several were wounded; some severely, including the mate. The surviving negroes were temporarily secured, and the ship, towed back into the harbor at midnight, once more lay anchored.

Omitting the incidents and arrangements ensuing, suffice it that, after two days spent in refitting, the two ships sailed in company for Conception, in Chili, and thence for Lima, in Peru; where, before the vice-regal courts, the whole affair, from the beginning, underwent investigation.

Though, midway on the passage, the ill-fated Spaniard, relaxed from constraint, showed some signs of regaining health with free-will; yet, agreeably to his own foreboding, shortly before arriving at Lima, he relapsed, finally becoming so reduced as to be carried ashore in arms. Hearing of his story and plight, one of the many religious institutions of the City of Kings opened an hospitable refuge to him, where both physician and priest were his nurses, and a member of the order volunteered to be his one special guardian and consoler, by night and by day.

The following extracts, translated from one of the official Spanish documents, will, it is hoped, shed light on the preceding narrative, as well as, in the first place, reveal the true port of departure and true history of the San Dominick's voyage, down to the time of her touching at the island of St. Maria.

But, ere the extracts come, it may be well to preface them with a remark.

The document selected, from among many others, for partial translation, contains the deposition of Benito Cereno; the first taken in the case. Some disclosures therein were, at the time, held dubious for both learned and natural reasons. The tribunal inclined to the opinion that the deponent, not undisturbed in his mind by recent events, raved of some things which could never have happened. But subsequent depositions of the surviving sailors, bearing out the revelations of their captain in several of the strangest particulars, gave credence to the rest. So that the tribunal, in its final decision, rested its capital sentences upon statements which, had they lacked confirmation, it would have deemed it but duty to reject.

[15]A battle fought in 1745, where the Scottish Highlanders defeated the English.

I, Don Jose de Abos and Padilla, His Majesty's Notary for the Royal Revenue, and Register of this Province, and Notary Public of the Holy Crusade of this Bishopric, etc.

Do certify and declare, as much as is requisite in law, that, in the criminal cause commenced the twenty-fourth of the month of September, in the year seventeen hundred and ninety-nine, against the negroes of the ship San Dominick, the following declaration before me was made:

Declaration of the first witness, DON BENITO CERENO.

The same day, and month, and year, His Honor, Doctor Juan Martinez de Rozas, Councilor of the Royal Audience of this Kingdom, and learned in the law of this Intendency, ordered the captain of the ship San Dominick, Don Benito Cereno, to appear; which he did in his litter, attended by the monk Infelez; of whom he received the oath, which he took by God, our Lord, and a sign of the Cross; under which he promised to tell the truth of whatever he should know and should be asked;—and being interrogated agreeably to the tenor of the act commencing the process, he said, that on the twentieth of May last, he set sail with his ship from the port of Valparaiso, bound to that of Callao; loaded with the produce of the country beside thirty cases of hardware and one hundred and sixty blacks, of both sexes, mostly belonging to Don Alexandro Aranda, gentleman, of the city of Mendoza; that the crew of the ship consisted of thirty-six men, beside the persons who went as passengers; that the negroes were in part as follows:

Here, in the original, follows a list of some fifty names, descriptions, and ages, compiled from certain recovered documents of Aranda's, and also from recollections of the deponent, from which portions only are extracted.

—One, from about eighteen to nineteen years, named José, and this was the man that waited upon his master, Don Alexandro, and who speaks well the Spanish, having served him four or five years; . . . A mulatto, named Francesco, the cabin steward, of a good person and voice, having sung in the Valparaiso churches, native of the province of Buenos Ayres, aged about thirty-five years. . . . A smart negro, name Dago, who had been for many years a grave-digger among the Spaniards, aged forty-six years. . . . Four old negroes, born in Africa, from sixty to seventy, but sound, calkers by trade, whose names are as follows:—the first was named Muri, and he was killed (as was also his son named Diamelo); the second, Nacta; the third, Yola, likewise killed; the fourth, Ghofan; and six full-grown negroes, aged from thirty to forty-five, all raw, and born among the Ashantees—Matiluqui, Yan, Lecbe, Mapenda, Yambaio, Akim; four of whom were killed; . . . a powerful negro named Atufal, who being supposed to have been a chief in Africa, his owner set great store by him. . . . And a small negro of Senegal, but some years among the Spaniards, aged about thirty, which Negro's name was Babo; . . . that he does not remember the names of the others, but that still expecting the residue of Don Alexandro's papers will be found, will then take due account of them all, and remit to the court; . . . and thirty-nine women and children of all ages.

The catalogue over, the deposition goes on:

. . . That all the negroes slept upon deck, as is customary in this navigation, and none wore fetters, because the owner, his friend Aranda, told him that they were all tractable; . . . that on the seventh day after leaving port, at three o'clock in the morning, all the Spaniards being asleep except the two officers on the watch, who were the boatswain, Juan Robles, and the carpenter, Juan Bautista Gayete, and the helmsman and his boy, the negroes revolted suddenly, wounded dangerously the boatswain and the carpenter, and successively killed eighteen men of those who were sleeping upon deck, some with handspikes and hatchets, and others by throwing them alive overboard, after tying them; that of the Spaniards upon deck, they left about seven, as he thinks, alive and tied, to manoeuvre the ship, and three or four more, who hid themselves, remained also alive. Although in the act of revolt the negroes made themselves masters of the hatchway, six or seven wounded went through it to the cockpit, without any hindrance on their part; that during the act of revolt, the mate and another person, whose name he does not recollect, attempted to come up through the hatchway, but being quickly wounded, were obliged to return to the cabin; that the deponent resolved at break of day to come up the companion-way, where the negro Babo was, being the ringleader, and Atufal, who assisted him, and having spoken to them, exhorted them to cease committing such atrocities, asking them, at the same time, what they wanted and intended to do, offering, himself, to obey their commands; that notwithstanding this, they threw, in his presence, three men, alive and tied, overboard; that they told the deponent to come up, and that they would not kill him; which having done, the negro Babo asked him whether there were in those seas any negro countries where they might be carried, and he answered them, No; that the negro Babo afterwards told him to carry them to Senegal or to the neighbouring islands of St. Nicholas; and he answered, that this was impossible, on account of the great distance, the necessity involved of rounding Cape Horn, the bad condition of the vessel, the want of provisions, sails, and water; but that the negro Babo replied to him he must carry them in any way; that they would do and conform themselves to everything the deponent should require as to eating and drinking; that after a long conference, being absolutely compelled to please them, for they threatened to kill all the whites if they were not, at all events, carried to Senegal, he told them that what was most wanting for the voyage was water; that they would go near the coast to take it, and thence they would proceed on their course; that the negro Babo agreed to it; and the deponent steered towards the intermediate ports, hoping to meet some Spanish or foreign vessel that would save them; that within ten or eleven days they saw the land, and continued by it in the vicinity of Nasca; that the deponent observed that the negroes were now restless and mutinous, because he did not effect the taking in of water, the negro Babo having required, with threats, that it should be done, without fail, the following day; he told him he saw plainly that the coast was steep, and the rivers designated in the maps were not to be found, with other reasons suitable to the circumstances; that the best way would be to go to the island of Santa Maria, where they might water easily, it being a solitary island, as the foreigners did; that the deponent did not go to Pisco, that was near, nor make any other port of the coast, because the negro Babo had intimated to him several times, that he would kill all the whites the very moment he should perceive any city, town, or settlement of any kind on the shores to which they should be carried: that having determined to go to the island of Santa Maria, as the deponent had planned, for the purpose of trying whether, on the passage or near the island itself, they could find any vessel that should favor them, or whether he could escape from it in a boat to the neighboring coast of Arruco, to adopt the necessary means he immediately changed his course, steering for the island; that the negroes Babo and Atufal held daily conferences, in which they discussed what was necessary for their design of returning to Senegal, whether they were to kill all the Spaniards, and particularly the deponent; that eight days after parting from the coast of Nasca, the deponent being on the watch a little after day-break, and soon after the negroes had their meeting, the negro Babo came to the place where the deponent was, and told him that he had determined to kill his master, Don Alexandro Aranda, both because he and his companions could not otherwise be sure of their liberty, and that to keep the seamen in subjection, he wanted to prepare a warning of what road they should be made to take did they or any of them oppose him; and that, by means of the death of Don Alexandro, that warning would best be given; but, that what this last meant, the deponent did not at the time comprehend, nor could not, further than that the death of Don Alexandro was intended; and moreover the negro Babo proposed to the deponent to call the mate Raneds, who was sleeping in the cabin, before the thing was done, for fear, as the deponent understood it, that the mate, who was a good navigator, should be killed with Don Alexandro and the rest; that the deponent, who was the friend, from youth, of Don Alexandro, prayed and conjured, but all was useless; for the negro Babo answered him that the thing could not be prevented, and that all the Spaniards risked their death if they should attempt to frustrate his will in this matter, or any other; that, in this conflict, the deponent called the mate, Raneds, who was forced to go apart, and immediately the negro Babo commanded the Ashantee Martinqui and the Ashantee Lecbe to go and commit the murder; that those two went down with hatchets to the berth of Don Alexandro; that, yet half alive and mangled, they dragged him on deck; that they were going to throw him overboard in that state, but the negro Babo stopped them, bidding the murder be completed on the deck before him, which was done, when, by his orders, the body was carried below, forward; that nothing more was seen of it by the deponent for three days; . . . that Don Alonzo Sidonia, an old man, long resident at Valparaiso, and lately appointed to a civil office in Peru, whither he had taken passage, was at the time sleeping in the berth opposite Don Alexandro's; that awakening at his cries, surprised by them, and at the sight of the negroes with their bloody hatchets in their hands, he threw himself into the sea through a window which was near him, and was drowned, without it being in the power of the deponent to assist or take him up; . . . that a short time after killing Aranda, they brought upon deck his german-cousin, of middle-age, Don Francisco Masa, of Mendoza, and the young Don Joaquin, Marques de Aramboalaza, then lately from Spain, with his Spanish servant Ponce, and the three young clerks of Aranda, José Mozairi, Lorenzo Bargas, and Hermenegildo Gandix, all of Cadiz; that Don Joaquin and Hermenegildo Gandix, the negro Babo, for purposes hereafter to appear, preserved alive; but Don Francisco Masa, José Mozairi, and Lorenzo Bargas, with Ponce the servant, beside the boatswain, Juan Robles, the boatswain's mates, Manuel Viscaya and Roderigo Hurta, and four of the sailors, the negro Babo ordered to be thrown alive into the sea, although they made no resistance, nor begged for anything else but mercy; that the boatswain, Juan Robles, who knew how to swim, kept the longest above water, making acts of contrition, and, in the last words he uttered, charged this deponent to cause mass to be said for his soul to our Lady of Succor: . . . that, during the three days which followed, the deponent, uncertain what fate had befallen the remains of Don Alexandro, frequently asked the negro Babo where they were, and, if still on board, whether they were to be preserved for interment ashore, entreating him so to order it; that the negro Babo answered nothing till the fourth day, when at sunrise, the deponent coming on deck, the negro Babo showed him a skeleton, which had been substituted for the ship's proper figure-head—the image of Christopher Colon, the discoverer of the New World; that the negro Babo asked him whose skeleton that was, and whether, from its whiteness, he should not think it a white's; that, upon discovering his face, the negro Babo, coming close, said words to this effect: "Keep faith with the blacks from here to Senegal, or you shall in spirit, as now in body, follow your leader," pointing to the prow; . . . that the same morning the negro Babo took by succession each Spaniard forward, and asked him whose skeleton that was, and whether, from its whiteness, he should not think it a white's; that each Spaniard covered his face; that then to each the negro Babo repeated the words in the first place said to the deponent; . . . that they (the Spaniards), being then assembled aft, the negro Babo harangued them, saying that he had now done all; that the deponent (as navigator for the negroes) might pursue his course, warning him and all of them that they should, soul and body, go the way of Don Alexandro, if he saw them (the Spaniards) speak or plot anything against them (the negroes)—a threat which was repeated every day; that, before the events last mentioned, they had tied the cook to throw him overboard, for it is not known what thing they heard him speak, but finally the negro Babo spared his life, at the request of the deponent; that a few days after, the deponent, endeavoring not to omit any means to preserve the lives of the remaining whites, spoke to the negroes of peace and tranquillity, and agreed to draw up a paper, signed by the deponent and the sailors who could write, as also by the negro Babo, for himself and all the blacks, in which the deponent obliged himself to carry them to Senegal, and they not to kill any more, and he formally to make over to them the ship, with the cargo, with which they were for that time satisfied and quieted. . . . But the next day, the more surely to guard against the sailors' escape, the negro Babo commanded all the boats to be destroyed but the long-boat, which was unseaworthy, and another, a cutter in good condition, which knowing it would yet be wanted for towing the water casks, he had it lowered down into the hold.

Various particulars of the prolonged and perplexed navigation ensuing here follow, with incidents of a calamitous calm, from which portion one passage is extracted, to wit:

—That on the fifth day of the calm, all on board suffering much from the heat, and want of water, and five having died in fits, and mad, the negroes became irritable, and for a chance gesture, which they deemed suspicious—though it was harmless—made by the mate, Raneds, to the deponent in the act of handing a quadrant, they killed him; but that for this they afterwards were sorry, the mate being the only remaining navigator on board, except the deponent.

. . . .

—That omitting other events, which daily happened, and which can only serve uselessly to recall past misfortunes and conflicts, after seventy-three days' navigation, reckoned from the time they sailed from Nasca, during which they navigated under a scanty allowance of water, and were afflicted with the calms before mentioned, they at last arrived at the island of Santa Maria, on the seventeenth of the month of August, at about six o'clock in the afternoon, at which hour they cast anchor very near the American ship, Bachelor's Delight, which lay in the same bay, commanded by the generous Captain Amasa Delano; but at six o'clock in the morning, they had already described the port, and the negroes became uneasy, as soon as at distance they saw the ship, not having expected to see one there; that the negro Babo pacified them, assuring them that no fear need be had; that straightway he ordered the figure on the bow to be covered with canvas, as for repairs, and had the decks a little set in order; that for a time the negro Babo and the negro Atufal conferred; that the negro Atufal was for sailing away, but the negro Babo would not, and, by himself, cast about what to do; that at last he came to the deponent, proposing to him to say and do all that the deponent declares to have said and done to the American captain;

. . . .

—That the negro Babo warned him that if he varied in the least, or uttered any word, or gave any look that should give the least intimation of the past events or present state, he would instantly kill him, with all his companions, showing a dagger, which he carried hid, saying something which, as he understood it, meant that that dagger would be alert as his eye; that the negro Babo then announced the plan to all his companions, which pleased them; that he then, the better to disguise the truth, devised many expedients, in some of them uniting deceit and defense; that of this sort was the device of the six Ashantees before named, who were his bravoes; that them he stationed on the break of the poop, as if to clean certain hatchets (in cases, which were part of the cargo), but in reality to use them, and distribute them at need, and at a given word he told them; that, among other devices, was the device of presenting Atufal, his right hand man, as chained, though in a moment the chains could be dropped; that in every particular he informed the deponent what part he was expected to enact in every device, and what story he was to tell on every occasion, always threatening him with instant death if he varied in the least: that, conscious that many of the negroes would be turbulent, the negro Babo appointed the four aged negroes, who were calkers, to keep what domestic order they could on the decks; that again and again he harangued the Spaniards and his companions, informing them of his intent, and of his devices, and of the invented story that this deponent was to tell; charging them lest any of them varied from that story; that these arrangements were made and matured during the interval of two or three hours, between their first sighting the ship and the arrival on board of Captain Amasa Delano; that this happened at about half-past seven o'clock in the morning, Captain Amasa Delano coming in his boat, and all gladly receiving him; that the deponent, as well as he could force himself, acting then the part of principal owner, and a free captain of the ship, told Captain Amasa Delano, when called upon, that he came from Buenos Ayres, bound to Lima, with three hundred negroes; that off Cape Horn, and in a subsequent fever, many negroes had died; that also, by similar casualties, all the sea officers and the greatest part of the crew had died.

And so the deposition goes on, circumstantially recounting the fictitious story dictated to the deponent by Babo, and through the deponent imposed upon Captain Delano; and also recounting the friendly offers of Captain Delano, with other things, but all of which is here omitted. After the fictitious story, etc., the deposition proceeds:

—that the generous Captain Amasa Delano remained on board all the day, till he left the ship anchored at six o'clock in the evening, deponent speaking to him always of his pretended misfortunes, under the fore-mentioned principles, without having had it in his power to tell a single word, or give him the least hint, that he might know the truth and state of things; because the negro Babo, performing the office of an officious servant with all the appearance of submission of the humble slave, did not leave the deponent one moment; that this was in order to observe the deponent's actions and words, for the negro Babo understands well the Spanish; and besides, there were thereabout some others who were constantly on the watch, and likewise understood the Spanish; . . . that upon one occasion, while deponent was standing on the deck conversing with Amasa Delano, by a secret sign the negro Babo drew him (the deponent) aside, the act appearing as if originating with the deponent; that then, he being drawn aside, the negro Babo proposed to him to gain from Amasa Delano full particulars about his ship, and crew, and arms; that the deponent asked "For what?" that the negro Babo answered he might conceive; that, grieved at the prospect of what might overtake the generous Captain Amasa Delano, the deponent at first refused to ask the desired questions, and used every argument to induce the negro Babo to give up this new design; that the negro Babo showed the point of his dagger; that, after the information had been obtained the negro Babo again drew him aside, telling him that that very night he (the deponent) would be captain of two ships, instead of one, for that, great part of the American's ship's crew being to be absent fishing, the six Ashantees, without any one else, would easily take it; that at this time he said other things to the same purpose; that no entreaties availed; that, before Amasa Delano's coming on board, no hint had been given touching the capture of the American ship; that to prevent this project the deponent was powerless; . . . —that in some things his memory is confused, he cannot distinctly recall every event; . . . —that as soon as they had cast anchor at six of the clock in the evening, as has before been stated, the American Captain took leave, to return to his vessel; that upon a sudden impulse, which the deponent believes to have come from God and his angels, he, after the farewell had been said, followed the generous Captain Amasa Delano as far as the gunwale, where he stayed, under pretense of taking leave, until Amasa Delano should have been seated in his boat; that on shoving off, the deponent sprang from the gunwale into the boat, and fell into it, he knows not how, God guarding him; that—

Here, in the original, follows the account of what further happened at the escape, and how the San Dominick was retaken, and of the passage to the coast; including in the recital many expressions of "eternal gratitude" to the "generous Captain Amasa Delano." The deposition then proceeds with recapitulatory remarks, and a partial renumeration of the negroes, making record of their individual part in the past events, with a view to furnishing, according to command of the court, the data whereon to found the criminal sentences to be pronounced. From this portion is the following:

—That he believes that all the negroes, though not in the first place knowing to the design of revolt, when it was accomplished, approved it. . . . That the negro, José, eighteen years old, and in the personal service of Don Alexandro, was the one who communicated the information to the negro Babo, about the state of things in the cabin, before the revolt; that this is known, because, in the preceding midnight, he used to come from his berth, which was under his master's, in the cabin, to the deck where the ringleader and his associates were, and had secret conversations with the negro Babo, in which he was several times seen by the mate; that, one night, the mate drove him away twice; . . . that this same negro José was the one who, without being commanded to do so by the negro Babo, as Lecbe and Martinqui were, stabbed his master, Don Alexandro, after he had been dragged half-lifeless to the deck; . . . that the mulatto steward, Francesco, was of the first band of revolters, that he was, in all things, the creature and tool of the negro Babo; that, to make his court, he, just before a repast in the cabin, proposed, to the negro Babo, poisoning a dish for the generous Captain Amasa Delano; this is known and believed, because the negroes have said it; but that the negro Babo, having another design, forbade Francesco; . . . that the Ashantee Lecbe was one of the worst of them; for that, on the day the ship was retaken, he assisted in the defense of her, with a hatchet in each hand, with one of which he wounded, in the breast, the chief mate of Amasa Delano, in the first act of boarding; this all knew; that, in sight of the deponent, Lecbe struck, with a hatchet, Don

Francisco Masa, when, by the negro Babo's orders, he was carrying him to throw him overboard, alive; beside participating in the murder, before mentioned, of Don Alexandro Aranda, and others of the cabin-passengers; that, owing to the fury with which the Ashantees fought in the engagement with the boats, but this Lecbe and Yan survived; that Yan was bad as Lecbe; that Yan was the man who, by Babo's command, willingly prepared the skeleton of Don Alexandro, in a way the negroes afterwards told the deponent, but which he, so long as reason is left him, can never divulge; that Yan and Lecbe were the two who, in a calm by night, riveted the skeleton to the bow; this also the negroes told him; that the negro Babo was he who traced the inscription below it; that the negro Babo was the plotter from first to last; he ordered every murder, and was the helm and keel of the revolt; that Atufal was his lieutenant in all; but Atufal, with his own hand, committed no murder; nor did the negro Babo; . . . that Atufal was shot, being killed in the fight with the boats, ere boarding; . . . that the negresses, of age, were knowing to the revolt, and testified themselves satisfied at the death of their master, Don Alexandro; that, had the negroes not restrained them, they would have tortured to death, instead of simply killing, the Spaniards slain by command of the negro Babo; that the negresses used their utmost influence to have the deponent made away with; that, in the various acts of murder, they sang songs and danced—not gaily, but solemnly; and before the engagement with the boats, as well as during the action, they sang melancholy songs to the negroes, and that this melancholy tone was more inflaming than a different one would have been, and was so intended; that all this is believed because the negroes have said it.

—that of the thirty-six men of the crew, exclusive of the passengers (all of whom are now dead), which the deponent had knowledge of, six only remained alive, with four cabin-boys and ship-boys, not included with the crew; . . . —that the negroes broke an arm of one of the cabin-boys and gave him strokes with hatchets.

Then follow various random disclosures referring to various periods of time. The following are extracted:

—That during the presence of Captain Amasa Delano on board, some attempts were made by the sailors, and one by Hermenegildo Gandix, to convey hints to him of the true state of affairs; but that these attempts were ineffectual, owing to fear of incurring death, and, furthermore, owing to the devices which offered contradictions to the true state of affairs, as well as owing to the generosity and piety of Amasa Delano incapable of sounding such wickedness; . . . that Luys Galgo, a sailor about sixty years of age, and formerly of the king's navy, was one of those who sought to convey tokens to Captain Amasa Delano; but his intent, though undiscovered, being suspected, he was, on a pretense, made to retire out of sight, and at last into the hold, and there was made away with. This the negroes have since said; . . . that one of the ship-boys feeling, from Captain Amasa Delano's presence, some hopes of release, and not having enough prudence, dropped some chance-word respecting his expectations, which being overheard and understood by a slave-boy with whom he was eating at the time, the latter struck him on the head with a knife, inflicting a bad wound, but of which the boy is now healing; that likewise, not long before the ship was brought to anchor, one of the seamen, steering at the time, endangered himself by letting the blacks remark some expression in his countenance, arising from some cause similar to the above; but this sailor, by his heedful after conduct, escaped; . . . that these statements are made to show the court that from the beginning to the end of the revolt, it was impossible for the deponent and his men to act otherwise than they did; . . . —that the third clerk, Hermenegildo Gandix, who before had been forced to live among the seamen, wearing a seaman's habit, and in all respects appearing to be one for the time; he, Gandix, was killed by a musket ball fired through mistake from the boats before boarding; having in his fright run up the mizzenrigging, calling to the boats—"don't board," lest upon their boarding the negroes should kill him; that this inducing the Americans to believe he some way favored the cause of the negroes, they fired two balls at him, so that he fell wounded from the rigging, and was drowned in the sea; . . . —that the young Don Joaquin, Marques de Aramboalaza, like Hermenegildo Gandix, the third clerk, was degraded to the office and appearance of a common seaman; that upon one occasion when Don Joaquin shrank, the negro Babo commanded the Ashantee Lecbe to take tar and heat it, and pour it upon Don Joaquin's hands; . . . —that Don Joaquin was killed owing to another mistake of the Americans, but one impossible to be avoided, as upon the approach of the boats, Don Joaquin, with a hatchet tied edge out and upright to his hand, was made by the negroes to appear on the bulwarks; whereupon, seen with arms in his hands and in a questionable attitude, he was shot for a renegade seaman; . . . —that on the person of Don Joaquin was found secreted a jewel, which, by papers that were discovered, proved to have been meant for the shrine of our Lady of Mercy in Lima; a votive offering, beforehand prepared and guarded, to attest his gratitude, when he should have landed in Peru, his last destination, for the safe conclusion of his entire voyage from Spain; . . . —that the jewel, with the other effects of the late Don Joaquin, is in the custody of the brethren of the Hospital de Sacerdotes, awaiting the disposition of the honorable court; . . . —that, owing to the condition of the deponent, as well as the haste in which the boats departed for the attack, the Americans were not forewarned that there were, among the apparent crew, a passenger and one of the clerks, disguised by the negro Babo; . . . —that, beside the negroes killed in the action, some were killed after the capture and re-anchoring at night, when shackled to the ring-bolts on deck; that these deaths were committed by the sailors, ere they could be prevented. That as soon as informed of it, Captain Amasa Delano used all his authority, and, in particular with his own hand, struck down Martinez Gola, who, having found a razor in the pocket of an old jacket of his, which one of the shackled negroes had on, was aiming it at the negro's throat; that the noble Captain Amasa Delano also wrenched from the hand of Bartholomew Barlo a dagger, secreted at the time of the massacre of the whites, with which he was in the act of stabbing a shackled negro, who, the same day, with another negro, had thrown him down and jumped upon him; . . . —that, for all the events, befalling through so long a time, during which the ship was in the hands of the negro Babo, he cannot here give account; but that, what he has said is the most substantial of what occurs to him at present, and is the truth under the oath which he has taken; which declaration he affirmed and ratified, after hearing it read to him.

He said that he is twenty-nine years of age, and broken in body and mind; that when finally dismissed by the court, he shall not return home to Chili, but betake himself to the monastery on Mount Agonia without; and signed with his honor, and crossed himself, and, for the time, departed as he came, in his litter, with the monk Infelez, to the Hospital de Sacerdotes.

BENITO CERENO

DOCTOR ROZAS.

If the Deposition have served as the key to fit into the lock of the complications which precede it, then, as a vault whose door has been flung back, the San Dominick's hull lies open to-day.

Hitherto the nature of this narrative, besides rendering the intricacies in the beginning unavoidable, has more or less required that many things, instead of being set down in the order of occurrence, should be retrospectively, or irregularly given; this last is the case with the following passages, which will conclude the account:

During the long, mild voyage to Lima, there was, as before hinted, a period during which the sufferer a little recovered his health, or, at least in some degree, his tranquillity. Ere the decided relapse which came, the two captains had many cordial conversations—their fraternal unreserve in singular contrast with former withdrawments.

Again and again it was repeated, how hard it had been to enact the part forced on the Spaniard by Babo.

"Ah, my dear friend," Don Benito once said, "at those very times when you thought me so morose and ungrateful, nay, when, as you now admit, you half thought me plotting your murder, at those very times my heart was frozen; I could not look at you, thinking of what, both on board this ship and your own, hung, from other hands, over my kind benefactor. And as God lives, Don Amasa, I know not whether desire for my own safety alone could have nerved me to that leap into your boat, had it not been for the thought that, did you, unenlightened, return to your ship, you, my best friend, with all who might be with you, stolen upon, that night, in your hammocks, would never in this world have wakened again. Do but think how you walked this deck, how you sat in this cabin, every inch of ground mined into honey-combs under you. Had I dropped the least hint, made the least advance towards an understanding between us, death, explosive death—yours as mine—would have ended the scene."

"True, true," cried Captain Delano, starting, "you have saved my life, Don Benito, more than I yours; saved it, too, against my knowledge and will."

"Nay, my friend," rejoined the Spaniard, courteous even to the point of religion, "God charmed your life, but you saved mine. To think of some things you did—those smilings and chattings, rash pointings and gesturings. For less than these, they slew my mate, Raneds; but you had the Prince of Heaven's safe-conduct through all ambuscades."

"Yes, all is owing to Providence, I know; but the temper of my mind that morning was more than commonly pleasant, while the sight of so much suffering, more apparent than real, added to my good-nature, compassion, and charity, happily interweaving the three. Had it been otherwise, doubtless, as you hint, some of my interferences might have ended unhappily enough. Besides, those feelings I spoke of enabled me to get the better of momentary distrust, at times when acuteness might have cost me my life, without saving another's. Only at the end did my suspicions get the better of me, and you know how wide of the mark they then proved."

"Wide, indeed," said Don Benito, sadly; "you were with me all day; stood with me, sat with me, talked with me, looked at me, ate with me, drank with me; and yet, your last act was to clutch for a monster, not only an innocent man, but the most pitiable of all men. To such degree may malign machinations and deceptions impose. So far may even the best man err, in judging the conduct of one with the recesses of whose condition he is not acquainted. But you were forced to it; and you were in time undeceived. Would that, in both respects, it was so ever, and with all men."

"You generalize, Don Benito; and mournfully enough. But the past is passed; why moralize upon it? Forget it. See, yon bright sun has forgotten it all, and the blue sea, and the blue sky; these have turned over new leaves."

"Because they have no memory," he dejectedly replied; "because they are not human."

"But these mild trades that now fan your cheek, do they not come with a human-like healing to you? Warm friends, steadfast friends are the trades."

"With their steadfastness they but waft me to my tomb, Señor," was the foreboding response.

"You are saved," cried Captain Delano, more and more astonished and pained; "you are saved: what has cast such a shadow upon you?"

"The negro."

There was silence, while the moody man sat, slowly and unconsciously gathering his mantle about him, as if it were a pall.

There was no more conversation that day.

But if the Spaniard's melancholy sometimes ended

in muteness upon topics like the above, there were others upon which he never spoke at all; on which, indeed, all his old reserves were piled. Pass over the worst, and, only to elucidate, let an item or two of these be cited. The dress so precise and costly, worn by him on the day whose events have been narrated, had not willingly been put on. And that silver-mounted sword, apparent symbol of despotic command, was not, indeed, a sword, but the ghost of one. The scabbard, artificially stiffened, was empty.

As for the black—whose brain, not body, had schemed and led the revolt, with the plot—his slight frame, inadequate to that which it held, had at once yielded to the superior muscular strength of his captor, in the boat. Seeing all was over, he uttered no sound, and could not be forced to. His aspect seemed to say, since I cannot do deeds, I will not speak words. Put in irons in the hold, with the rest, he was carried to Lima. During the passage, Don Benito did not visit him. Nor then, nor at any time after, would he look at him. Before the tribunal he refused. When pressed by the judges he fainted. On the testimony of the sailors alone rested the legal identity of Babo.

Some months after, dragged to the gibbet at the tail of a mule, the black met his voiceless end. The body was burned to ashes; but for many days, the head, that hive of subtlety, fixed on a pole in the Plaza, met, unabashed, the gaze of the whites; and across the Plaza looked towards St. Bartholomew's church, in whose vaults slept then, as now, the recovered bones of Aranda: and across the Rimac bridge looked towards the monastery, on Mount Agonia without; where, three months after being dismissed by the court, Benito Cereno, borne on the bier, did, indeed, follow his leader.

1855

JOHN GREENLEAF WHITTIER [1807-1892]

BROUGHT UP ON A FARM tilled by his ancestors as far back as 1647, Whittier lived his span of eighty-five years at Haverhill and Amesbury in northeastern Massachusetts. Life meant to him for many years hard toil and poverty, and always frail health, but also the charms of nature, the happiness of human affection, and the consolation of the Quaker faith of his fathers. It meant, too, dedicated service in the cause of abolition of slavery, and the satisfaction of poetic creation.

At the age of fourteen Whittier read Robert Burns and began to scribble verses. Some of them appeared in *The Free Press*, a weekly edited in Newburyport by William Lloyd Garrison. Garrison became interested in his young contributor and urged the boy's parents to send him to Haverhill Academy. There he studied for only two terms; mainly he was self-educated. By turns he was a shoemaker, a teacher, an editor of journals in Boston and Hartford. In 1831 he published his first book, *Legends of New England*, and two years later entered the lists for abolition with a pamphlet on *Justice and Expediency*.

The next three decades, the most vigorous of his life, Whittier gave to his "opinion mill." He was a delegate to the antislavery convention in 1833 in Philadelphia. He was in the Massachusetts legislature in 1835 and 1836. He argued against slavery in prose, verse, and speech, risked his life before hostile mobs, gave up his political career, edited *The Pennsylvania Freeman*. In 1846 he published *Voices of Freedom*, two years later a collected edition of his *Poems*, and after two more years *Songs of Labor and Other Poems*.

The War of the Secession ended, Whittier settled down to the peaceful years he had earned. *Snow-Bound*, a deservedly popular success, was his first financially rewarding volume. Many other publications followed, including one of his best, *The Pennsylvania Pilgrim*, and at length the Riverside Edition of his verse and prose in seven volumes.

His poetry shows clearly the modern concern with "the near, the low, the common" of which Emerson had spoken. It is largely a poetry of the humble: of the pleasures of labor, of the evil of slavery; a poetry of simple home life on the farm; a poetry of popular, regional legends; a poetry of simple religion, the love of God and of man. The spirit of Whittier was close to that of Burns, Scotland's poet of the people, and to that of John Woolman, the Quaker tailor whose *Journal* he edited. Because his verse was often sentimental and moralistic, as well as facile and diffuse, it now seems to us to have been long overvalued. Yet he rose above his usual mediocrity often enough to achieve a small body of genuine poetry that has latterly been undervalued.

Text: *The Writings of John Greenleaf Whittier,* Riverside Edition, edited by Horace E. Scudder (Boston, 1888–89).

Further reading: Whitman Bennett, *Whittier, Bard of Freedom,* 1941. J. A. Pollard, *Whittier, Friend of Man,* 1949. John B. Pickard, *John Greenleaf Whittier,* 1961. Edward C. Wagenknecht, *John Greenleaf Whittier,* 1967.

First-Day Thoughts

Christian attitudes and allusions enter into many of Whittier's poems, regardless of subject. They also become the subject of a considerable group of poems. In "First-Day Thoughts" we see Whittier take his place in a Quaker meeting. The poem is essentially a prayer.

In calm and cool and silence, once again
I find my old accustomed place among
My brethren, where, perchance, no human tongue
Shall utter words; where never hymn is sung,
Nor deep-toned organ blown, nor censer swung,
Nor dim light falling through the pictured pane!
There, syllabled by silence, let me hear
The still small voice which reached the prophet's ear;
Read in my heart a still diviner law
Than Israel's leader on his tables saw!
There let me strive with each besetting sin,
Recall my wandering fancies, and restrain
The sore disquiet of a restless brain;
And, as the path of duty is made plain,
May grace be given that I may walk therein,
Not like the hireling, for his selfish gain,
With backward glances and reluctant tread,
Making a merit of his coward dread,
But, cheerful, in the light around me thrown,
Walking as one to pleasant service led;
Doing God's will as if it were my own,
Yet trusting not in mine, but in His strength alone!

1852

Laus Deo!

"On hearing the bells ring on the passage of the constitutional amendment abolishing slavery."—Whittier's note.

In *Laus Deo!* (Praise be to God!), Whittier's emotion expressed itself in a strongly marked, trochaic meter and in Old Testament echoes: lines 19–20, Job xxxviii.1; line 24, Psalms cvii.16; lines 27–30, Exodus xv.21; lines 34–36, Isaiah xxiii.11; lines 40–41, Numbers xvii.8.

It is done!
Clang of bell and roar of gun
Send the tidings up and down.
How the belfries rock and reel!
How the great guns, peal on peal,
Fling the joy from town to town!

Ring, O bells!
Every stroke exulting tells
Of the burial hour of crime.
Loud and long, that all may hear,
Ring for every listening ear
Of Eternity and Time!

Let us kneel:
God's own voice is in that peal,
And this spot is holy ground.
Lord, forgive us! What are we,
That our eyes this glory see,
That our ears have heard the sound!

For the Lord
On the whirlwind is abroad;
In the earthquake He has spoken:
He has smitten with His thunder
The iron walls asunder,
And the gates of brass are broken!

Loud and long
Lift the old exulting song;
Sing with Miriam by the sea,
He has cast the mighty down;
Horse and rider sink and drown;
"He hath triumphed gloriously!"

Did we dare,
In our agony of prayer,
Ask for more than He has done?
When was ever His right hand
Over any time or land
Stretched as now beneath the sun?

How they pale,
Ancient myth and song and tale,
In this wonder of our days,
When the cruel rod of war
Blossoms white with righteous law,
And the wrath of man is praise!

Blotted out!
All within and all about
Shall a fresher life begin;
Freer breathe the universe
As it rolls its heavy curse
On the dead and buried sin!

It is done!
In the circuit of the sun
Shall the sound thereof go forth.
It shall bid the sad rejoice,
It shall give the dumb a voice,
It shall belt with joy the earth!

Ring and swing,
Bells of joy! On morning's wing
Send the song of praise abroad!
With a sound of broken chains
Tell the nations that He reigns,
Who alone is Lord and God!

1865

Snow-Bound

A Winter Idyl

This idyl (little picture) of rural New England has the poetic warmth of a long cherished memory. "Out of his loyalty, not alone to vanished faces, but to the fulfillment of personal relationships which his boyhood home symbolized, he wrote *Snow-Bound* (1866), the finest of his Yankee idyls, a faultless integration of precisely remembered detail and tender devotion. In a general way this poem is the New England analogue of Burns' 'The Cotter's Saturday Night,' with which it compares favorably both for its wealth of homely description and for its genuineness of sentiment. But against the background of a nation fast adapting itself to urban ways the poem appears something more than a cold pastoral. It is a quiet tribute to a form of civilized living that was passing. Here embodied in glowing terms was the Jeffersonian dream of the virtuous small landholder, beholden to no one and winning an honest, laborious livelihood from the soil." (G. F. Whicher in *Literary History of the United States)*

As the Spirits of Darkness be stronger in the dark, so Good Spirits, which be Angels of Light, are augmented not only by the Divine light of the Sun, but also by our common VVood Fire: and as the Celestial Fire drives away dark spirits, so also this our Fire of VVood doth the same—COR. AGRIPPA, *Occult Philosophy,* Book I. ch. v.[1]

Announced by all the trumpets of the sky,
Arrives the snow, and, driving o'er the fields,
Seems nowhere to alight: the whited air
Hides hills and woods, the river and the heaven,
And veils the farm-house at the garden's end.
The sled and traveller stopped, the courier's feet
Delayed, all friends shut out, the housemates sit
Around the radiant fireplace, enclosed
In a tumultuous privacy of storm.
—Emerson, *The Snow-Storm*

The sun that brief December day
Rose cheerless over hills of gray,
And, darkly circled, gave at noon
A sadder light than waning moon.
Slow tracing down the thickening sky
Its mute and ominous prophecy,
A portent seeming less than threat,
It sank from sight before it set.
A chill no coat, however stout,
Of homespun stuff could quite shut out,
A hard, dull bitterness of cold,
That checked, mid-vein, the circling race
Of life-blood in the sharpened face,
The coming of the snow-storm told.
The wind blew east; we heard the roar
Of Ocean on his wintry shore,
And felt the strong pulse throbbing there
Beat with low rhythm our inland air.

Meanwhile we did our nightly chores,—
Brought in the wood from out of doors,
Littered the stalls, and from the mows
Raked down the herd's-grass for the cows:
Heard the horse whinnying for his corn;
And, sharply clashing horn on horn,
Impatient down the stanchion rows
The cattle shake their walnut bows;
While, peering from his early perch
Upon the scaffold's pole of birch,
The cock his crested helmet bent
And down his querulous challenge sent.

Snow-Bound. [1] Whittier said in his introduction that he had the book (dated 1651) which a local "sorcerer" used as a "conjuring book." It was apparently the work of Henricus Cornelius Agrippa (1486–1535), a scholar and writer about the occult.

Unwarmed by any sunset light
The gray day darkened into night,
A night made hoary with the swarm
And whirl-dance of the blinding storm,
As zigzag, wavering to and fro,
Crossed and recrossed the wingèd snow:
And ere the early bedtime came
The white drift piled the window-frame,
And through the glass the clothes-line posts
Looked in like tall and sheeted ghosts.

So all night long the storm roared on:
The morning broke without a sun;
In tiny spherule traced with lines
Of Nature's geometric signs,
In starry flake, and pellicle,
All day the hoary meteor fell;
And, when the second morning shone,
We looked upon a world unknown,
On nothing we could call our own.
Around the glistening wonder bent
The blue walls of the firmament,
No cloud above, no earth below,—
A universe of sky and snow!
The old familiar sights of ours
Took marvellous shapes; strange domes and towers
Rose up where sty or corn-crib stood,
Or garden-wall, or belt of wood;
A smooth white mound the brush-pile showed,
A fenceless drift what once was road;
The bridle-post an old man sat
With loose-flung coat and high cocked hat;
The well-curb had a Chinese roof;
And even the long sweep, high aloof,
In its slant splendor, seemed to tell
Of Pisa's leaning miracle.

A prompt, decisive man, no breath
Our father wasted: "Boys, a path!"
Well pleased, (for when did farmer boy
Count such a summons less than joy?)
Our buskins on our feet we drew;
With mittened hands, and caps drawn low,
To guard our necks and ears from snow,
We cut the solid whiteness through.
And, where the drift was deepest, made
A tunnel walled and overlaid
With dazzling crystal: we had read
Of rare Aladdin's wondrous cave,
And to our own his name we gave,
With many a wish the luck were ours
To test his lamp's supernal powers.
We reached the barn with merry din,
And roused the prisoned brutes within.
The old horse thrust his long head out,
And grave with wonder gazed about;
The cock his lusty greeting said,
And forth his speckled harem led;
The oxen lashed their tails, and hooked,
And mild reproach of hunger looked;
The hornèd patriarch of the sheep,
Like Egypt's Amun roused from sleep,
Shook his sage head with gesture mute,
And emphasized with stamp of foot.

All day the gusty north-wind bore
The loosening drift its breath before;
Low circling round its southern zone,
The sun through dazzling snow-mist shone.
No church-bell lent its Christian tone
To the savage air, no social smoke
Curled over woods of snow-hung oak.
A solitude made more intense
By dreary-voicèd elements,
The shrieking of the mindless wind,
The moaning tree-boughs swaying blind,
And on the glass the unmeaning beat
Of ghostly finger-tips of sleet.
Beyond the circle of our hearth
No welcome sound of toil or mirth
Unbound the spell, and testified
Of human life and thought outside.
We minded that the sharpest ear
The buried brooklet could not hear,
The music of whose liquid lip
Had been to us companionship,
And, in our lonely life, had grown
To have an almost human tone.

As night drew on, and, from the crest
Of wooded knolls that ridged the west,
The sun, a snow-blown traveller, sank
From sight beneath the smothering bank,
We piled, with care, our nightly stack
Of wood against the chimney-back,—
The oaken log, green, huge, and thick,
And on its top the stout back-stick;
The knotty forestick laid apart,
And filled between with curious art
The ragged brush; then, hovering near,
We watched the first red blaze appear,
Heard the sharp crackle, caught the gleam
On whitewashed wall and sagging beam,
Until the old, rude-furnished room
Burst, flower-like, into rosy bloom;
While radiant with a mimic flame
Outside the sparkling drift became,
And through the bare-boughed lilac-tree
Our own warm hearth seemed blazing free.
The crane and pendent trammels showed,
The Turks' heads on the andirons glowed:
While childish fancy, prompt to tell

The meaning of the miracle,
Whispered the old rhyme: "*Under the tree,*
When fire outdoors burns merrily,
There the witches are making tea."

The moon above the eastern wood
Shone at its full; the hill-range stood
Transfigured in the silver flood,
Its blown snows flashing cold and keen,
Dead white, save where some sharp ravine
Took shadow, or the sombre green
Of hemlocks turned to pitchy black
Against the whiteness at their back.
For such a world and such a night
Most fitting that unwarming light,
Which only seemed where'er it fell
To make the coldness visible.

Shut in from all the world without,
We sat the clean-winged hearth about,
Content to let the north-wind roar
In baffled rage at pane and door,
While the red logs before us beat
The frost-line back with tropic heat;
And ever, when a louder blast
Shook beam and rafter as it passed,
The merrier up its roaring draught
The great throat of the chimney laughed;
The house-dog on his paws outspread
Laid to the fire his drowsy head,
The cat's dark silhouette on the wall
A couchant tiger's seemed to fall;
And, for the winter fireside meet,
Between the andirons' straddling feet,
The mug of cider simmered slow,
The apples sputtered in a row,
And, close at hand, the basket stood
With nuts from brown October's wood.

What matter how the night behaved?
What matter how the north-wind raved?
Blow high, blow low, not all its snow
Could quench our hearth-fire's ruddy glow.
O Time and Change!—with hair as gray
As was my sire's that winter day,
How strange it seems, with so much gone
Of life and love, to still live on!
Ah, brother![2] only I and thou
Are left of all that circle now,—
The dear home faces whereupon
That fitful firelight paled and shone.
Henceforward, listen as we will,
The voices of that hearth are still;
Look where we may, the wide earth o'er
Those lighted faces smile no more.
We tread the paths their feet have worn,
  We sit beneath their orchard trees,
  We hear, like them, the hum of bees
And rustle of the bladed corn;
We turn the pages that they read,
  Their written words we linger o'er,
But in the sun they cast no shade,
No voice is heard, no sign is made,
  No step is on the conscious floor!
Yet Love will dream, and Faith will trust,
(Since He who knows our need is just,)
That somehow, somewhere, meet we must.
Alas for him who never sees
The stars shine through his cypress-trees!
Who, hopeless, lays his dead away,
Nor looks to see the breaking day
Across the mournful marbles play!
Who hath not learned, in hours of faith,
  The truth to flesh and sense unknown,
That Life is ever lord of Death,
  And Love can never lose its own!

We sped the time with stories old,
Wrought puzzles out, and riddles told,
Or stammered from our school-book lore[3]
"The Chief of Gambia's golden shore."
How often since, when all the land
Was clay in Slavery's shaping hand,
As if a far-blown trumpet stirred
The languorous sin-sick air, I heard:
"*Does not the voice of reason cry,*
  Claim the first right which Nature gave,
From the red scourge of bondage fly,
  Nor deign to live a burdened slave!"[4]
Our father rode again his ride
On Memphremagog's wooded side;
Sat down again to moose and samp
In trapper's hut and Indian camp;
Lived o'er the old idyllic ease
Beneath St. François' hemlock-trees;[5]
Again for him the moonlight shone
On Norman cap and bodiced zone;
Again he heard the violin play
Which led the village dance away,
And mingled in its merry whirl
The grandam and the laughing girl.
Or, nearer home, our steps he led
Where Salisbury's level marshes spread
  Mile-wide as flies the laden bee;

[2] Matthew Franklin Whittier (1812–83), who shared his brother's strong antislavery sentiments.

[3] The book, according to Whittier, was Caleb Bingham's *The American Preceptor.*

[4] The fourth stanza of a poem by Sarah Wentworth Morton called "The African Chief," published in Bingham.

[5] Whittier's father had traveled to Canada as a youth. Memphremagog is a lake between Vermont and Canada. St. Francis is a lake in Quebec.

Where merry mowers, hale and strong,
Swept, scythe on scythe, their swaths along
The low green prairies of the sea.
We shared the fishing off Boar's Head,
And round the rocky Isles of Shoals
The hake-broil on the drift-wood coals;
The chowder on the sand-beach made,
Dipped by the hungry, steaming hot,
With spoons of clam-shell from the pot.
We heard the tales of witchcraft old,
And dream and sign and marvel told
To sleepy listeners as they lay
Stretched idly on the salted hay,
Adrift along the winding shores,
When favoring breezes deigned to blow
The square sail of the gundelow
And idle lay the useless oars.

Our mother, while she turned her wheel
Or run the new-knit stocking-heel,
Told how the Indian hordes came down
At midnight on Cocheco town,
And how her own great-uncle bore
His cruel scalp-mark to fourscore.[6]
Recalling, in her fitting phrase,
So rich and picturesque and free,
(The common unrhymed poetry
Of simple life and country ways,)
The story of her early days,—
She made us welcome to her home;
Old hearths grew wide to give us room;
We stole with her a frightened look
At the gray wizard's conjuring-book,
The fame whereof went far and wide
Through all the simple country side;
We heard the hawks at twilight play,
The boat-horn on Piscataqua,[7]
The loon's weird laughter far away;
We fished her little trout-brook, knew
What flowers in wood and meadow grew,
What sunny hillsides autumn-brown
She climbed to shake the ripe nuts down,
Saw where in sheltered cove and bay
The ducks' black squadron anchored lay,
And heard the wild-geese calling loud
Beneath the gray November cloud.

Then, haply, with a look more grave,
And soberer tone, some tale she gave
From painful Sewel's[8] ancient tome,
Beloved in every Quaker home,
Of faith fire-winged by martyrdom,
Or Chalkley's Journal,[9] old and quaint,—
Gentlest of skippers, rare sea-saint!—
Who, when the dreary calms prevailed,
And water-butt and bread-cask failed,
And cruel, hungry eyes pursued
His portly presence mad for food,
With dark hints muttered under breath
Of casting lots for life or death,
Offered, if Heaven withheld supplies,
To be himself the sacrifice.
Then, suddenly, as if to save
The good man from his living grave,
A ripple on the water grew,
A school of porpoise flashed in view.
"Take, eat," he said, "and be content;
These fishes in my stead are sent
By Him who gave the tangled ram
To spare the child of Abraham."

Our uncle, innocent of books,
Was rich in lore of fields and brooks,
The ancient teachers never dumb
Of Nature's unhoused lyceum.
In moons and tides and weather wise,
He read the clouds as prophecies,
And foul or fair could well divine,
By many an occult hint and sign,
Holding the cunning-warded keys
To all the woodcraft mysteries;
Himself to Nature's heart so near
That all her voices in his ear
Of beast or bird had meanings clear,
Like Apollonius[10] of old,
Who knew the tales the sparrows told,
Or Hermes,[11] who interpreted
What the sage cranes of Nilus said;
A simple, guileless, childlike man,
Content to live where life began;
Strong only on his native grounds,
The little world of sights and sounds
Whose girdle was the parish bounds,
Whereof his fondly partial pride
The common features magnified,
As Surrey hills to mountains grew
In White of Selborne's[12] loving view,—

[6] His mother "was born in the Indian-haunted region of Somerset, New Hampshire." (Whittier)

[7] A river between New Hampshire and Maine.

[8] William Sewel (1653–1720), a Dutch Quaker historian, author of *History of the Rise, Increase, and Progress of the . . . Quakers.*

[9] Thomas Chalkley (1675–1741), a sea captain and Quaker zealot, describes this incident in his *Journal* (1747).

[10] Probably Apollonius of Tyana, a philosopher of the first century A.D., who supposedly had magical and wonder-working powers.

[11] Legendary author of Hermetic Books, supposedly the author of all mystical doctrines.

[12] Gilbert White (1720–93), curate of Selborne, who wrote *The Natural History and Antiquities of Selborne,* published 1789.

He told how teal and loon he shot,
And how the eagle's eggs he got,
The feats on pond and river done,
The prodigies of rod and gun;
Till, warming with the tales he told,
Forgotten was the outside cold,
The bitter wind unheeded blew,
From ripening corn the pigeons flew,
The partridge drummed i' the wood, the mink
Went fishing down the river-brink;
In fields with bean or clover gay,
The woodchuck, like a hermit gray,
  Peered from the doorway of his cell;
The muskrat plied the mason's trade,
And tier by tier his mud-walls laid;
And from the shagbark overhead
  The grizzled squirrel dropped his shell.

Next, the dear aunt, whose smile of cheer
And voice in dreams I see and hear,—
The sweetest woman ever Fate
Perverse denied a household mate,
Who, lonely, homeless, not the less
Found peace in love's unselfishness,
And welcome whereso'er she went,
A calm and gracious element,
Whose presence seemed the sweet income
And womanly atmosphere of home—
Called up her girlhood memories,
The huskings and the apple-bees,
The sleigh-rides and the summer sails,
Weaving through all the poor details
And homespun warp of circumstance
A golden woof-thread of romance.
For well she kept her genial mood
And simple faith of maidenhood;
Before her still a cloud-land lay,
The mirage loomed across her way;
The morning dew, that dries so soon
With others, glistened at her noon;
Through years of toil and soil and care,
From glossy tress to thin gray hair,
All unprofaned she held apart
The virgin fancies of the heart.
Be shame to him of woman born
Who hath for such but thought of scorn.

There, too, our elder sister plied
Her evening task the stand beside;
A full, rich nature, free to trust,
Truthful and almost sternly just,
Impulsive, earnest, prompt to act,
And make her generous thought a fact,
Keeping with many a light disguise
The secret of self-sacrifice.
O heart sore-tried! thou hast the best
That Heaven itself could give thee,—rest,
Rest from all bitter thoughts and things!
  How many a poor one's blessing went
  With thee beneath the low green tent
Whose curtain never outward swings!

As one who held herself a part
Of all she saw, and let her heart
  Against the household bosom lean,
Upon the motley-braided mat
Our youngest and our dearest sat,
Lifting her large, sweet, asking eyes,
  Now bathed in the unfading green
And holy peace of Paradise.[13]
Oh, looking from some heavenly hill,
  Or from the shade of saintly palms,
  Or silver reach of river calms,
Do those large eyes behold me still?
With me one little year ago:—
The chill weight of the winter snow
  For months upon her grave has lain;
And now, when summer south-winds blow
  And brier and harebell bloom again,
I tread the pleasant paths we trod,
I see the violet-sprinkled sod
Whereon she leaned, too frail and weak
The hillside flowers she loved to seek,
Yet following me where'er I went
With dark eyes full of love's content.
The birds are glad; the brier-rose fills
The air with sweetness; all the hills
Stretch green to June's unclouded sky;
But still I wait with ear and eye
For something gone which should be nigh,
A loss in all familiar things,
In flower that blooms, and bird that sings.
And yet, dear heart! remembering thee,
  Am I not richer than of old?
Safe in thy immortality,
  What change can reach the wealth I hold?
  What chance can mar the pearl and gold
Thy love hath left in trust with me?
And while in life's late afternoon,
  Where cool and long the shadows grow,
I walk to meet the night that soon
  Shall shape and shadow overflow,
I cannot feel that thou art far,
Since near at need the angels are;
And when the sunset gates unbar,
  Shall I not see thee waiting stand,
And, white against the evening star,
  The welcome of thy beckoning hand?

Brisk wielder of the birch and rule,

[13] His younger sister, Elizabeth Hussey Whittier, died in 1864.

The master of the district school
Held at the fire his favored place,
Its warm glow lit a laughing face
Fresh-hued and fair, where scarce appeared
The uncertain prophecy of beard.
He teased the mitten-blinded cat,
Played cross-pins on my uncle's hat,
Sang songs, and told us what befalls
In classic Dartmouth's college halls.
Born the wild Northern hills among,
From whence his yeoman father wrung
By patient toil subsistence scant,
Not competence and yet not want,
He early gained the power to pay
His cheerful, self-reliant way;
Could doff at ease his scholar's gown
To peddle wares from town to town;
Or through the long vacation's reach
In lonely lowland districts teach,
Where all the droll experience found
At stranger hearths in boarding round,
The moonlit skater's keen delight,
The sleigh-drive through the frosty night,
The rustic-party, with its rough
Accompaniment of blind-man's-buff,
And whirling-plate, and forfeits paid,
His winter task a pastime made.
Happy the snow-locked homes wherein
He tuned his merry violin,
Or played the athlete in the barn,
Or held the good dame's winding-yarn,
Or mirth-provoking versions told
Of classic legends rare and old,
Wherein the scenes of Greece and Rome
Had all the commonplace of home,
And little seemed at best the odds
'Twixt Yankee pedlers and old gods;
Where Pindus-born Arachthus[14] took
The guise of any grist-mill brook,
And dread Olympus at his will
Became a huckleberry hill.

A careless boy that night he seemed;
  But at his desk he had the look
And air of one who wisely schemed,
  And hostage from the future took
  In trainèd thought and lore of book.
Large-brained, clear-eyed, of such as he
Shall Freedom's young apostles be,
Who, following in War's bloody trail,
Shall every lingering wrong assail;
All chains from limb and spirit strike,
Uplift the black and white alike;
Scatter before their swift advance
The darkness and the ignorance,
The pride, the lust, the squalid sloth,
Which nurtured Treason's monstrous growth,
Made murder pastime, and the hell
Of prison-torture possible;
The cruel lie of caste refute,
Old forms remould, and substitute
For Slavery's lash the freeman's will,
For blind routine, wise-handed skill;
A school-house plant on every hill,
Stretching in radiate nerve-lines thence
The quick wires of intelligence;
Till North and South together brought
Shall own the same electric thought,
In peace a common flag salute,
And, side by side in labor's free
And unresentful rivalry,
Harvest the fields wherein they fought.

[14]A river rising in the Pindus mountains in northern Greece.

Another guest[15] that winter night
Flashed back from lustrous eyes the light.
Unmarked by time, and yet not young,
The honeyed music of her tongue
And words of meekness scarcely told
A nature passionate and bold,
Strong, self-concentred, spurning guide,
Its milder features dwarfed beside
Her unbent will's majestic pride.
She sat among us, at the best,
A not unfeared, half-welcome guest,
Rebuking with her cultured phrase
Our homeliness of words and ways.
A certain pard-like, treacherous grace
Swayed the lithe limbs and drooped the lash,
Lent the white teeth their dazzling flash;
And under low brows, black with night,
Rayed out at times a dangerous light;
The sharp heat-lightnings of her face
Presaging ill to him whom Fate
Condemned to share her love or hate.
A woman tropical, intense
In thought and act, in soul and sense,
She blended in a like degree
The vixen and the devotee,
Revealing with each freak or feint
  The temper of Petruchio's Kate,[16]

[15]Whittier's introduction makes lines 510–589 clear: "Harriet Livermore . . . a young woman of fine natural ability, enthusiastic, eccentric, with slight control over her violent temper. . . . She early embraced the doctrine of the Second Advent, and felt it her duty to proclaim the Lord's speedy coming. With this message she crossed the Atlantic and spent the greater part of a long life in travelling over Europe and Asia. She lived some time with Lady Hester Stanhope, a woman as fantastic and mentally strained as herself, on the slope of Mt. Lebanon. . . ."

[16]In Shakespeare's *The Taming of the Shrew.*

The raptures of Siena's saint.[17]
Her tapering hand and rounded wrist
Had facile power to form a fist;
The warm, dark languish of her eyes
Was never safe from wrath's surprise.
Brows saintly calm and lips devout
Knew every change of scowl and pout;
And the sweet voice had notes more high
And shrill for social battle-cry.

Since then what old cathedral town
Has missed her pilgrim staff and gown,
What convent-gate has held its lock
Against the challenge of her knock!
Through Smyrna's plague-hushed thoroughfares,
Up sea-set Malta's rocky stairs,
Gray olive slopes of hills that hem
  Thy tombs and shrines, Jerusalem,
Or startling on her desert throne
The crazy Queen of Lebanon[18]
With claims fantastic as her own,
Her tireless feet have held their way;
And still, unrestful, bowed, and gray,
She watches under Eastern skies,
  With hope each day renewed and fresh,
  The Lord's quick coming in the flesh,
Whereof she dreams and prophesies!

Where'er her troubled path may be,
  The Lord's sweet pity with her go!
The outward wayward life we see,
  The hidden springs we may not know.
Nor is it given us to discern
  What threads the fatal sisters spun,
  Through what ancestral years has run
The sorrow with the woman born,
What forged her cruel chain of moods,
What set her feet in solitudes,
  And held the love within her mute,
What mingled madness in the blood,
  A life-long discord and annoy,
  Water of tears with oil of joy,
And hid within the folded bud
  Perversities of flower and fruit.
It is not ours to separate
  The tangled skein of will and fate,
To show what metes and bounds should stand
Upon the soul's debatable land,
And between choice and Providence
Divide the circle of events;
But He who knows our frame is just,
Merciful and compassionate,
And full of sweet assurances

[17] St. Catherine of Siena (1347–86), the greatest of 14th-century Italian mystics.

[18] Lady Hester Stanhope.

And hope for all the language is,
That He remembereth we are dust!

At last the great logs, crumbling low,
Sent out a dull and duller glow,
The bull's-eye watch that hung in view,
Ticking its weary circuit through,
Pointed with mutely warning sign
Its black hand to the hour of nine.
That sign the pleasant circle broke:
My uncle ceased his pipe to smoke,
Knocked from its bowl the refuse gray,
And laid it tenderly away;
Then roused himself to safely cover
The dull red brands with ashes over.
And while, with care, our mother laid
The work aside, her steps she stayed
One moment, seeking to express
Her grateful sense of happiness
For food and shelter, warmth and health,
And love's contentment more than wealth,
With simple wishes (not the weak,
Vain prayers which no fulfilment seek,
But such as warm the generous heart,
O'er-prompt to do with Heaven its part)
That none might lack, that bitter night,
For bread and clothing, warmth and light.

Within our beds awhile we heard
The wind that round the gables roared,
With now and then a ruder shock,
Which made our very bedsteads rock.
We heard the loosened clapboards tost,
The board-nails snapping in the frost;
And on us, through the unplastered wall,
Felt the light sifted snow-flakes fall.
But sleep stole on, as sleep will do
When hearts are light and life is new;
Faint and more faint the murmurs grew,
Till in the summer-land of dreams
They softened to the sound of streams,
Low stir of leaves, and dip of oars,
And lapsing waves on quiet shores.

Next morn we wakened with the shout
Of merry voices high and clear;
And saw the teamsters drawing near
To break the drifted highways out.
Down the long hillside treading slow
We saw the half-buried oxen go,
Shaking the snow from heads uptost,
Their straining nostrils white with frost.
Before our door the straggling train
Drew up, an added team to gain.
The elders threshed their hands a-cold,

  Passed, with the cider-mug, their jokes
  From lip to lip; the younger folks
Down the loose snow-banks, wrestling, rolled,
Then toiled again the cavalcade
  O'er windy hill, through clogged ravine,
  And woodland paths that wound between
Low drooping pine-boughs winter-weighed.
From every barn a team afoot,
At every house a new recruit,
Where, drawn by Nature's subtlest law,
Haply the watchful young men saw
Sweet doorway pictures of the curls
And curious eyes of merry girls,
Lifting their hands in mock defence
Against the snow-ball's compliments,
And reading in each missive tost
The charm with Eden never lost.

We heard once more the sleigh-bells' sound;
  And, following where the teamsters led,
The wise old Doctor went his round,
Just pausing at our door to say,
In the brief autocratic way
Of one who, prompt at Duty's call,
Was free to urge her claim on all,
  That some poor neighbor sick abed
At night our mother's aid would need.
For, one in generous thought and deed,
  What mattered in the sufferer's sight
  The Quaker matron's inward light,
The Doctor's mail of Calvin's creed?
All hearts confess the saints elect
  Who, twain in faith, in love agree,
And melt not in an acid sect
  The Christian pearl of charity!

So days went on: a week had passed
Since the great world was heard from last.
The Almanac we studied o'er,
Read and reread our little store
Of books and pamphlets, scarce a score;
One harmless novel, mostly hid
From younger eyes, a book forbid,
And poetry, (or good or bad,
A single book was all we had,)
Where Ellwood's[19] meek, drab-skirted Muse,
  A stranger to the heathen Nine,
  Sang, with a somewhat nasal whine,
The wars of David and the Jews.
At last the floundering carrier bore
The village paper to our door.
Lo! broadening outward as we read,
To warmer zones the horizon spread;
In panoramic length unrolled
We saw the marvels that it told.
Before us passed the painted Creeks,
  And daft McGregor on his raids
  In Costa Rica's everglades.
And up Taygetos winding slow
Rode Ypsilanti's Mainote Greeks,
A Turk's head at each saddle-bow![20]
Welcome to us its week-old news,
Its corner for the rustic Muse,
  Its monthly gauge of snow and rain,
Its record, mingling in a breath
The wedding bell and dirge of death:
Jest, anecdote, and love-lorn tale,
The latest culprit sent to jail;
Its hue and cry of stolen and lost,
Its vendue sales and goods at cost,
  And traffic calling loud for gain.
We felt the stir of hall and street,
The pulse of life that round us beat;
The chill embargo of the snow
Was melted in the genial glow;
Wide swung again our ice-locked door,
And all the world was ours once more!

Clasp, Angel of the backward look
  And folded wings of ashen gray
  And voice of echoes far away,
The brazen covers of thy book;
The weird palimpsest old and vast,
Wherein thou hid'st the spectral past;
Where, closely mingling, pale and glow
The characters of joy and woe;
The monographs of outlived years,
Or smile-illumed or dim with tears,
  Green hills of life that slope to death,
And haunts of home, whose vistaed trees
Shade off to mournful cypresses
  With the white amaranths underneath.
Even while I look, I can but heed
  The restless sands' incessant fall,
Importunate hours that hours succeed,
Each clamorous with its own sharp need,
  And duty keeping pace with all.
Shut down and clasp the heavy lids;
I hear again the voice that bids
The dreamer leave his dream midway
For larger hopes and graver fears;
Life greatens in these later years,
The century's aloe flowers to-day!

[19] Thomas Ellwood (1639–1714), friend of Milton and author of *Davideis* (1712), not to be confused with the better-known *Davideis* (1656) by Abraham Cowley.

[20] Contemporary topical references, no longer very important. Gregor McGregor was an adventurer and pirate; the Ypsilanti were a family of Greeks several of whom were active in movements against Turkish rule and, specifically, in the Greek War of Independence.

Yet, haply, in some lull of life,
Some Truce of God, which breaks its strife,
The worldling's eyes shall gather dew,
 Dreaming in throngful city ways
Of winter joys his boyhood knew;
And dear and early friends—the few
Who yet remain—shall pause to view
 These Flemish[21] pictures of old days;
Sit with me by the homestead hearth,
And stretch the hands of memory forth
 To warm them at the wood-fire's blaze!
And thanks untraced to lips unknown
Shall greet me like the odors blown
From unseen meadows newly mown,
Or lilies floating in some pond,
Wood-fringed, the wayside gaze beyond;
The traveller owns the grateful sense
Of sweetness near, he knows not whence,
And, pausing, takes with forehead bare
The benediction of the air.

1866

Abraham Davenport

In blank verse—a form he rarely used—Whittier here shows a terseness and ironic undertone in keeping with a New England type of character he evidently relished. It is a type that much later found a poetic voice in the "wisdom and grace" and "shrewd dry humor" of Robert Frost.

"The famous Dark Day of New England, May 19, 1780, was a physical puzzle for many years to our ancestors, but its occurrence brought something more than philosophical speculation into the minds of those who passed through it. The incident of Colonel Abraham Davenport's sturdy protest is a matter of history." (Whittier)

In the old days (a custom laid aside
With breeches and cocked hats) the people sent
Their wisest men to make the public laws.
And so, from a brown homestead, where the Sound
Drinks the small tribute of the Mianas,
Waved over by the woods of Rippowams,
And hallowed by pure lives and tranquil deaths,
Stamford sent up to the councils of the State
Wisdom and grace in Abraham Davenport.

'Twas on a May-day of the far old year
Seventeen hundred eighty, that there fell
Over the bloom and sweet life of the Spring,
Over the fresh earth and the heaven of noon,
A horror of great darkness, like the night
In day of which the Norland sagas tell,—
The Twilight of the Gods.[1] The low-hung sky
Was black with ominous clouds, save where its rim
Was fringed with a dull glow, like that which climbs
The crater's sides from the red hell below.
Birds ceased to sing, and all the barn-yard fowls
Roosted; the cattle at the pasture bars
Lowed, and looked homeward; bats on leathern wings
Flitted abroad; the sounds of labor died;
Men prayed, and women wept; all ears grew sharp
To hear the doom-blast of the trumpet[2] shatter
The black sky, that the dreadful face of Christ
Might look from the rent clouds, not as he looked
A loving guest at Bethany, but stern
As Justice and inexorable Law.

Meanwhile in the old State House, dim as ghosts
Sat the lawgivers of Connecticut,
Trembling beneath their legislative robes.
"It is the Lord's Great Day! Let us adjourn,"
Some said; and then, as if with one accord,
All eyes were turned to Abraham Davenport.
He rose, slow cleaving with his steady voice
The intolerable hush. "This well may be
The Day of Judgment which the world awaits;
But be it so or not, I only know
My present duty, and my Lord's command
To occupy till He come. So at the post
Where He hath set me in His providence,
I choose, for one, to meet Him face to face,—
No faithless servant frightened from my task,
But ready when the Lord of the harvest calls;
And therefore, with all reverence, I would say,
Let God do His work, we will see to ours.
Bring in the candles." And they brought them in.

Then by the flaring lights the Speaker read,
Albeit with husky voice and shaking hands,
An act to amend an act to regulate
The shad and alewive fisheries. Whereupon
Wisely and well spake Abraham Davenport,
Straight to the question, with no figures of speech
Save the ten Arab signs,[3] yet not without
The shrewd dry humor natural to the man:
His awe-struck colleagues listening all the while,
Between the pauses of his argument,
To hear the thunder of the wrath of God
Break from the hollow trumpet of the cloud.

And there he stands in memory to this day,
Erect, self-poised, a rugged face, half seen
Against the background of unnatural dark,
A witness to the ages as they pass,
That simple duty hath no place for fear.

1866

[21] Refers to Flemish genre painting of domestic subjects.

Abraham Davenport. [1] Or Götterdämmerung, the end of the world; the time when the gods war with their enemies until all are dead.

[2] The Judgment Day trumpet.

[3] The Arabic numerals.

HENRY WADSWORTH LONGFELLOW

[1807-1882]

LONGFELLOW'S REPUTATION as a poet has been, by turns, inflated and deflated. It was inflated at least until the end of the nineteenth century. He was the most widely read poet in the English language, and the first American poet to be memorialized by a bust in Westminster Abbey. He was translated into a score of foreign tongues, from Russian to Portuguese. In America he brought poetry home to the people as no other poet had done, while at the same time winning the applause of most of the men of letters of his day. Unfortunately Longfellow's renown rested largely on his inferior work. Among critics generally, his fame rapidly subsided after 1900, and in the rebellious 1920's he was mercilessly attacked as Victorian, genteel, preachy, silly, out of touch with the realities of American life. By the early 1930's a critic like Ludwig Lewisohn was saying: "Am I slaying the thrice slain? Who, except wretched schoolchildren, now reads Longfellow? . . . The thing to establish in America is not that Longfellow was a very small poet, but that he did not partake of the poetic character at all."

Now, however, we should be able to read Longfellow justly: to avoid the excesses of both the nineteenth-century inflation and the twentieth-century deflation, and to focus attention upon what seems, in sober afterthought, to be his best achievement.

Longfellow came from Portland, Maine. His mother was a descendant of John Alden, a *Mayflower* Pilgrim, his father a lawyer and trustee of Bowdoin College, where the boy Henry entered as a sophomore. One of his classmates was Hawthorne. When he graduated in 1825 he had already shown enough ability at writing verse to make him desire a literary career, though his father wished him to enter the law. Bowdoin settled the matter by establishing a professorship in modern languages and sending the young man to Europe for three years to prepare himself. He returned with a knowledge of German, French, Italian, and Spanish, and late in 1829 he joined the faculty at his alma mater. He had been teaching at Bowdoin for six years when Harvard offered him the Smith professorship of modern languages, and after another year of further preparation in Europe, he began his long residence at the "Craigie house" in Cambridge.

The professor was soon a successful author. His early Irvingesque prose work, *Outre-Mer: A Pilgrimage Beyond the Sea,* was followed by the Germanic romance *Hyperion.* In the same year (1839) came his first book of poems, *Voices of the Night,* including the vastly popular "Psalm of Life." Other volumes of poems quickly followed, and the first of his long narrative poems, *Evangeline.* By 1854 the poet was chafing at the professor's duties, and he resigned from Harvard after eighteen years of service during which he had introduced thousands of young men to the literatures of Europe. *Hiawatha,* his long Indian poem, appeared in 1855, and three years later *The Courtship of Miles Standish,* in which he used his Puritan background. But the even tenor of his life and writings was tragically broken in 1861 when his wife was burned to death. After bringing out *Tales of a Wayside Inn* (Part I), largely done before his wife's death, he buried himself and his grief in the discipline of translating Dante's *Divina Commedia.* Another trip abroad brought him honorary degrees from Oxford and Cambridge and a private audience with Queen Victoria. The major efforts of his later years went into the second and third parts of the *Tales of a Wayside Inn* and his long-projected trilogy *Christus: A Mystery* (1872), a series of thematically related verse dramas. To Craigie House, as to a shrine, came streams of visitors, notables and schoolchildren alike; and there he died peacefully in his seventy-sixth year.

Text: The Riverside Edition of the *Complete Poetical and Prose Works* (Boston, 1886).

Further reading: Lawrance Thompson, *Young Longfellow,* 1938. H. S. Gorman, *A Victorian American: Henry Wadsworth Longfellow,* 1926. Newton Arvin, *Longfellow: His Life and Work,* 1963. Edward C. Wagenknecht, *Henry Wadsworth Longfellow,* 1966.

Nuremberg

Longfellow visited the old Bavarian city in 1842, and two years later communicated his delight to his readers in the New World.

In the valley of the Pegnitz, where across broad meadow-lands
Rise the blue Franconian mountains, Nuremberg, the ancient, stands.

Quaint old town of toil and traffic, quaint old town of art and song,
Memories haunt thy pointed gables, like the rooks that round them throng:

Memories of the Middle Ages, when the emperors, rough and bold,
Had their dwelling in thy castle, time-defying, centuries old;

And thy brave and thrifty burghers boasted, in their uncouth rhyme,
That their great imperial city stretched its hand through every clime.

In the court-yard of the castle, bound with many an iron band,
Stands the mighty linden planted by Queen Cunigunde's[1] hand;

On the square the oriel window, where in old heroic days
Sat the poet Melchior[2] singing Kaiser Maximilian's praise,

Everywhere I see around me rise the wondrous world of Art:
Fountains wrought with richest sculpture standing in the common mart;

And above cathedral doorways saints and bishops carved in stone,
By a former age commissioned as apostles to our own.

In the church of sainted Sebald[3] sleeps enshrined his holy dust,
And in bronze the Twelve Apostles guard from age to age their trust;

In the church of sainted Lawrence stands a pix of sculpture rare,[4]
Like the foamy sheaf of fountains, rising through the painted air.

Here, when Art was still religion, with a simple, reverent heart,
Lived and labored Albrecht Dürer,[5] the Evangelist of Art;

Hence in silence and in sorrow, toiling still with busy hand,
Like an emigrant he wandered, seeking for the Better Land.

Emigravit[6] is the inscription on the tomb-stone where he lies;
Dead he is not, but departed,—for the artist never dies.

Fairer seems the ancient city, and the sunshine seems more fair,
That he once has trod its pavement, that he once has breathed its air!

Through these streets so broad and stately, these obscure and dismal lanes,
Walked of yore the Mastersingers, chanting rude poetic strains.

Nuremberg. [1] Empress and wife of Henry II, the last Saxon king of Germany (1002-1024).

[2] Melchior Pfinzing was one of the most celebrated poets of the sixteenth century. The hero of his *Teuerdank* was the reigning Emperor, Maximilian. [Longfellow's note.]

[3] The tomb of Saint Sebald, in the church which bears his name, is one of the richest works of art in Nuremberg. [Longfellow's note.]

[4] This pix, or tabernacle for the vessels of the sacrament, is by the hand of Adam Kraft. It is an exquisite piece of sculpture. [Longfellow's note.]

[5] German painter and engraver (1471-1528), noted for his engravings and woodcuts of religious subjects.

[6] He has departed.

From remote and sunless suburbs came they to the friendly guild,
Building nests in Fame's great temple, as in spouts the swallows build.

As the weaver plied the shuttle, wove he too the mystic rhyme,
And the smith his iron measures hammered to the anvil's chime;

Thanking God, whose boundless wisdom makes the flowers of poesy bloom
In the forge's dust and cinders, in the tissues of the loom.

Here Hans Sachs, the cobbler-poet, laureate of the gentle craft,
Wisest of the Twelve Wise Masters, in huge folios sang and laughed.[7]

But his house is now an ale-house, with a nicely sanded floor,
And a garland in the window, and his face above the door;

Painted by some humble artist, as in Adam Puschman's song,[8]
As the old man gray and dove-like, with his great beard white and long.

And at night the swart mechanic comes to drown his cark and care,
Quaffing ale from pewter tankards, in the master's antique chair.

Vanished is the ancient splendor, and before my dreamy eye
Wave these mingled shapes and figures, like a faded tapestry.

Not thy Councils, not thy Kaisers, win for thee the world's regard;
But thy painter, Albrecht Dürer, and Hans Sachs thy cobbler bard.

[7] The Twelve Wise Masters was the title of the original corporation of the Mastersingers. Hans Sachs, the cobbler of Nuremberg, though not one of the original twelve, was the most renowned of the Mastersingers, as well as the most voluminous. [Longfellow's note.]

[8] Adam Puschman, in his poem on the death of Hans Sachs, describes him as he appears in a vision:—

An old man,
Gray and white, and dove-like,
Who had, in sooth, a great beard,
And read in a fair, great book,
Beautiful with golden clasps.

[Longfellow's note.]

Thus, O Nuremberg, a wanderer from a region far away,
As he paced thy streets and court-yards, sang in thought his careless lay:

Gathering from the pavement's crevice, as a floweret of the soil,
The nobility of labor,—the long pedigree of toil.

1844

The Arsenal at Springfield

On his wedding journey Longfellow passed through Springfield, Massachusetts, and visited the United States arsenal in company with Charles Sumner. "While Mr. Sumner was endeavoring," says S. Longfellow, "to impress upon the attendant that the money expended upon these weapons of war would have been much better spent upon a great library, Mrs. Longfellow pleased her husband by remarking how like an organ looked the ranged and shining gun-barrels which covered the walls from floor to ceiling, and suggesting what mournful music Death would bring from them. 'We grew quite warlike against war,' she wrote, 'and I urged H. to write a peace poem.' "

This is the Arsenal. From floor to ceiling,
Like a huge organ, rise the burnished arms;
But from their silent pipes no anthem pealing
Startles the villages with strange alarms.

Ah! what a sound will rise, how wild and dreary,
When the death-angel touches those swift keys!
What loud lament and dismal Miserere[1]
Will mingle with their awful symphonies!

I hear even now the infinite fierce chorus,
The cries of agony, the endless groan,
Which, through the ages that have gone before us,
In long reverberations reach our own.

On helm and harness rings the Saxon hammer,
Through Cimbric forest roars the Norseman's song,
And loud, amid the universal clamor,
O'er distant deserts sounds the Tartar gong.

I hear the Florentine, who from his palace
Wheels out his battle-bell with dreadful din,
And Aztec priests upon their teocallis
Beat the wild war-drums made of serpent's skin;

The tumult of each sacked and burning village;
The shout that every prayer for mercy drowns;
The soldiers' revels in the midst of pillage;
The wail of famine in beleaguered towns;

The Arsenal. [1] "Have mercy": a prayer.

The bursting shell, the gateway wrenched asunder,
  The rattling musketry, the clashing blade;
And ever and anon, in tones of thunder,
  The diapason of the cannonade.

Is it, O man, with such discordant noises,
  With such accursed instruments as these,
Thou drownest Nature's sweet and kindly voices,
  And jarrest the celestial harmonies?

Were half the power, that fills the world with terror,
  Were half the wealth, bestowed on camps and courts,
Given to redeem the human mind from error,
  There were no need of arsenals or forts:

The warrior's name would be a name abhorrèd!
  And every nation, that should lift again
Its hand against a brother, on its forehead
  Would wear forevermore the curse of Cain!

Down the dark future, through long generations,
  The echoing sounds grow fainter and then cease;
And like a bell, with solemn, sweet vibrations,
  I hear once more the voice of Christ say, "Peace!"

Peace! and no longer from its brazen portals
  The blast of War's great organ shakes the skies!
But beautiful as songs of the immortals,
  The holy melodies of love arise.

1844

The Fire of Drift-Wood

Devereux Farm, near Marblehead

Though not widely familiar, this clearly seems to be one of Longfellow's successful poems. It states no obtrusive moral. It manages without the aid of elaborate figures of speech. Within a firmly developed unity, it harmonizes a striking scene, a complex retrospective mood, a sensitively simple diction, and the subdued music of the verse. Less immediately obvious is the use of contrast (the turbulence of sea and wind vs. the quiet talk indoors) and of similarity (the old farmhouse, old wrecks, old times, also the two fires brought together at the end).

We sat within the farm-house old,
  Whose windows, looking o'er the bay,
Gave to the sea-breeze damp and cold,
  An easy entrance, night and day.

Not far away we saw the port,
  The strange, old-fashioned, silent town,
The lighthouse, the dismantled fort,
  The wooden houses, quaint and brown.

We sat and talked until the night,
  Descending, filled the little room;
Our faces faded from the sight,
  Our voices only broke the gloom.

We spake of many a vanished scene,
  Of what we once had thought and said,
Of what had been, and might have been,
  And who was changed, and who was dead;

And all that fills the hearts of friends,
  When first they feel, with secret pain,
Their lives thenceforth have separate ends,
  And never can be one again;

The first slight swerving of the heart,
  That words are powerless to express,
And leave it still unsaid in part,
  Or say it in too great excess.

The very tones in which we spake
  Had something strange, I could but mark;
The leaves of memory seemed to make
  A mournful rustling in the dark.

Oft died the words upon our lips,
  As suddenly, from out the fire
Built of the wreck of stranded ships,
  The flames would leap and then expire.

And, as their splendor flashed and failed,
  We thought of wrecks upon the main,
Of ships dismasted, that were hailed
  And sent no answer back again.

The windows, rattling in their frames,
  The ocean, roaring up the beach,
The gusty blast, the bickering flames,
  All mingled vaguely in our speech;

Until they made themselves a part
  Of fancies floating through the brain,
The long-lost ventures of the heart,
  That send no answers back again.

O flames that glowed! O hearts that yearned!
  They were indeed too much akin,
The drift-wood fire without that burned,
  The thoughts that burned and glowed within.

1848

The Jewish Cemetery at Newport

At Newport, Rhode Island, on July 9, 1852, Longfellow wrote in his diary: "Went this morning into the Jewish burying-ground, with a polite old gentleman who keeps the key. There are few graves; nearly all are low tombstones of marble with Hebrew inscriptions, and a few words added in English or Portuguese."

How strange it seems! These Hebrews in their graves,
Close by the street of this fair seaport town,
Silent beside the never-silent waves,
At rest in all this moving up and down!

The trees are white with dust, that o'er their sleep
Wave their broad curtains in the south-wind's breath,
While underneath these leafy tents they keep
The long, mysterious Exodus of Death.

And these sepulchral stones, so old and brown,
That pave with level flags their burial-place,
Seem like the tablets of the Law, thrown down
And broken by Moses at the mountain's base.

The very names recorded here are strange,
Of foreign accent, and of different climes;
Alvares and Rivera interchange
With Abraham and Jacob of old times.

"Blessed be God! for he created Death!"
The mourners said, "and Death is rest and peace;"
Then added, in the certainty of faith,
"And giveth Life that nevermore shall cease."

Closed are the portals of their Synagogue,
No Psalms of David now the silence break,
No Rabbi reads the ancient Decalogue
In the grand dialect the Prophets spake.

Gone are the living, but the dead remain,
And not neglected; for a hand unseen,
Scattering its bounty, like a summer rain,
Still keeps their graves and their remembrance green.

How came they here? What burst of Christian hate,
What persecution, merciless and blind,
Drove o'er the sea—that desert desolate—
These Ishmaels and Hagars of mankind?[1]

They lived in narrow streets and lanes obscure,
Ghetto and Judenstrass,[2] in mirk and mire;
Taught in the school of patience to endure
The life of anguish and the death of fire.

All their lives long, with the unleavened bread
And bitter herbs of exile and its fears,
The wasting famine of the heart they fed,
And slaked its thirst with marah[3] of their tears.

Anathema maranatha![4] was the cry
That rang from town to town, from street to street;
At every gate the accursed Mordecai[5]
Was mocked and jeered, and spurned by Christian feet.

Pride and humiliation hand in hand
Walked with them through the world where'er they went;
Trampled and beaten were they as the sand,
And yet unshaken as the continent.

For in the background figures vague and vast
Of patriarchs and of prophets rose sublime,
And all the great traditions of the Past
They saw reflected in the coming time.

And thus forever with reverted look
The mystic volume of the world they read,
Spelling it backward, like a Hebrew book,
Till life became a Legend of the Dead.

But ah! what once has been shall be no more!
The groaning earth in travail and in pain
Brings forth its races, but does not restore,
And the dead nations never rise again.

1852

The Jewish Cemetery. [1] Ishmael was the son of Abraham by Hagar; cf. Genesis xvi. Both were exiled and hence the names imply outcast.

[2] Street of Jews: they lived in restricted areas or ghettos.

[3] Bitterness.

[4] Anathema (an accused person or formal curse); Maranatha (O Lord, come). The combination results in an intensified curse, calling on God to destroy the Jews. Cf. I Corinthians xvi.22.

[5] In the book of Esther, Mordecai (Esther's cousin) sat in the king's gate and aroused the anger of the king's chief minister, Haman, by refusing to bow down before him. Haman plotted to kill Mordecai and all the Jews, but Haman instead was executed. Longfellow's allusion to Mordecai is to all the persecutions of the Jews.

In the Churchyard at Cambridge

In the village churchyard she lies,
Dust is in her beautiful eyes,
No more she breathes, nor feels, nor stirs;
At her feet and at her head

Lies a slave to attend the dead,
  But their dust is white as hers.

Was she, a lady of high degree,
So much in love with the vanity
  And foolish pomp of this world of ours?
Or was it Christian charity,
And lowliness and humility,
  The richest and rarest of all dowers?

Who shall tell us? No one speaks;
No color shoots into those cheeks,
  Either of anger or of pride,
At the rude question we have asked;
Nor will the mystery be unmasked
  By those who are sleeping at her side.

Hereafter?—And do you think to look
On the terrible pages of that Book
  To find her failings, faults, and errors?
Ah, you will then have other cares,
In your own shortcomings and despairs,
  In your own secret sins and terrors!

1853

My Lost Youth

Longfellow's *Journal:* "March 29, 1855—A day of pain, cowering over the fire. At night as I lie in bed, a poem comes into my mind,—a memory of Portland,—my native town, the city by the sea. . . ." "March 30—Wrote the poem; and am rather pleased with it, and with the bringing in of the two lines of the old Lapland song:

A boy's will is the wind's will,
And the thoughts of youth are long, long thoughts."

These two lines Longfellow translated literally from the German rendering of the Lapland song by Herder, precursor of the German romantic school.

Often I think of the beautiful town
  That is seated by the sea;
Often in thought go up and down
The pleasant streets of that dear old town,
  And my youth comes back to me.
    And a verse of a Lapland song
    Is haunting my memory still:
    "A boy's will is the wind's will,
And the thoughts of youth are long, long thoughts."

I can see the shadowy lines of its trees,
  And catch, in sudden gleams,
The sheen of the far-surrounding seas,
And islands that were the Hesperides
  Of all my boyish dreams.
    And the burden of that old song,
    It murmurs and whispers still:
    "A boy's will is the wind's will,
And the thoughts of youth are long, long thoughts."

I remember the black wharves and the slips,
  And the sea-tides tossing free;
And Spanish sailors with bearded lips,
And the beauty and mystery of the ships,
  And the magic of the sea.
    And the voice of that wayward song
    Is singing and saying still:
    "A boy's will is the wind's will,
And the thoughts of youth are long, long thoughts."

I remember the bulwarks by the shore,
  And the fort upon the hill;
The sunrise gun, with its hollow roar,
The drum-beat repeated o'er and o'er,
  And the bugle wild and shrill.
    And the music of that old song
    Throbs in my memory still:
    "A boy's will is the wind's will,
And the thoughts of youth are long, long thoughts."

I remember the sea-fight far away,[1]
  How it thundered o'er the tide!
And the dead captains, as they lay
In their graves, o'erlooking the tranquil bay,
  Where they in battle died.
    And the sound of that mournful song
    Goes through me with a thrill:
    "A boy's will is the wind's will,
And the thoughts of youth are long, long thoughts."

I can see the breezy dome of groves,
  The shadows of Deering's Woods;
And the friendships old and the early loves
Come back with a Sabbath sound, as of doves
  In quiet neighborhoods.
    And the verse of that sweet old song,
    It flutters and murmurs still:
    "A boy's will is the wind's will,
And the thoughts of youth are long, long thoughts."

I remember the gleams and glooms that dart
  Across the school-boy's brain;
The song and the silence in the heart,
That in part are prophecies, and in part
  Are longings wild and vain.
    And the voice of that fitful song
    Sings on, and is never still:

My Lost Youth. [1]This refers to a naval engagement of the War of 1812, just outside Portland harbor, in which the *Enterprise* (American) defeated the *Boxer* (British); both captains were killed, and were buried side by side in a hillside cemetery in Portland. Longfellow was six years old at the time.

"A boy's will is the wind's will,
And the thoughts of youth are long, long thoughts."

There are things of which I may not speak;
There are dreams that cannot die;
There are thoughts that make the strong heart weak,
And bring a pallor into the cheek,
And a mist before the eye.
And the words of that fatal song
Come over me like a chill:
"A boy's will is the wind's will,
And the thoughts of youth are long, long thoughts."

Strange to me now are the forms I meet
When I visit the dear old town;
But the native air is pure and sweet,
And the trees that o'ershadow each well-known street,
As they balance up and down,
Are singing the beautiful song,
Are sighing and whispering still:
"A boy's will is the wind's will,
And the thoughts of youth are long, long thoughts."

And Deering's Woods are fresh and fair,
And with joy that is almost pain
My heart goes back to wander there,
And among the dreams of the days that were,
I find my lost youth again.
And the strange and beautiful song,
The groves are repeating it still:
"A boy's will is the wind's will,
And the thoughts of youth are long, long thoughts."

1855

Milton

I pace the sounding sea-beach and behold
How the voluminous billows roll and run,
Upheaving and subsiding, while the sun
Shines through their sheeted emerald far unrolled,
And the ninth wave, slow gathering fold by fold
All its loose-flowing garments into one,
Plunges upon the shore, and floods the dun
Pale reach of sands, and changes them to gold.
So in majestic cadence rise and fall
The mighty undulations of thy song,
O sightless bard, England's Maeonides![1]
And ever and anon, high over all
Uplifted, a ninth wave superb and strong,
Floods all the soul with its melodious seas.

1873

Venice

White swan of cities, slumbering in thy nest
So wonderfully built among the reeds
Of the lagoon, that fences thee and feeds,
As sayeth thy old historian and thy guest!
White water-lily, cradled and caressed
By ocean streams, and from the silt and weeds
Lifting thy golden filaments and seeds,
Thy sun-illumined spires, thy crown and crest!
White phantom city, whose untrodden streets
Are rivers, and whose pavements are the shifting
Shadows of palaces and strips of sky;
I wait to see thee vanish like the fleets
Seen in mirage, or towers of cloud uplifting
In air their unsubstantial masonry.

1875

The Tide Rises, The Tide Falls

The tide rises, the tide falls,
The twilight darkens, the curlew calls;
Along the sea-sands damp and brown
The traveller hastens toward the town,
And the tide rises, the tide falls.

Darkness settles on roofs and walls,
But the sea, the sea in the darkness calls;
The little waves, with their soft, white hands,
Efface the footprints in the sands,
And the tide rises, the tide falls.

The morning breaks; the steeds in their stalls
Stamp and neigh, as the hostler calls;
The day returns, but nevermore
Returns the traveller to the shore,
And the tide rises, the tide falls.

1879

Milton. [1] Homer.

JAMES RUSSELL LOWELL [1819-1891]

LOWELL WAS BORN and bred in Cambridge, and at his pleasant colonial house "Elmwood" spent most of his life. He came of one of the old, distinguished families of New England, and his home was rich in accumulated books. As an undergraduate at Harvard he read, he said, "nearly everything except the books prescribed by the faculty." When a senior he edited the college magazine, *Harvardiana,* and wrote the class poem. After graduation in 1838 he studied law, for no good reason. He was not interested.

Then he engaged to marry Maria White, of Watertown, Mass., who communicated to him her enthusiasms. Miss White wrote good poetry, was an ardent liberal and abolitionist, and inclined to mysticism. "They say," he reported, "that she is 'transcendental.'" Her influence and that of her romantic associates—"the Band"—is clear in two books of verse that Lowell published in the period before their marriage in 1844. Briefly he was an editor of the unsuccessful *Pioneer,* and he did antislavery writing for other periodicals. In 1848 he brought out *Poems* (second series), *The Biglow Papers* (first series), *A Fable for Critics,* and *The Vision of Sir Launfal*—all these in one year. He was now successfully launched as a poet. More than that, he had already written most of his best poetry.

He traveled in Europe, with his wife, two children, a nurse, and a goat, in 1851-52. The next year his wife died. He gave a course of lectures in Boston on the English poets, and this led to his Harvard appointment as Smith professor of French and Spanish and of belles-lettres at age thirty-five. After a second sojourn in Europe, 1855-56, he began the life of a teacher, scholar, critic, and, less frequently, poet. By this time his humanitarian ardors had cooled, and he had moved toward nationalism and a conservative humanism, impressed, as H. H. Clark puts it, with the need of "tradition, permanence, and inner control."

In 1857 he married Frances Dunlap, who had been his daughter's governess, and in the same year was made first editor of the *Atlantic Monthly.* Two years later he shifted to the *North American Review.* During the Civil War he wrote the second series of *The Biglow Papers,* and when the war was over delivered his "Commemoration Ode." Then came his long series of critical essays, beginning with *Among My Books* and *My Study Windows.* Before the middle of the 1870's he had been given honorary degrees by Oxford and Cambridge.

He was appointed Minister to Spain in 1877, as Irving had been thirty-five years before. After three years in Madrid, he was made minister to England, where he served till 1885. "During my reign no ambassador or minister has created so much interest or won so much regard," said Queen Victoria. After 1885 Lowell traveled widely, returned to Elmwood, and died.

It was a good life, and he won fame as poet, critic, essayist, professor, editor, diplomat. But he had never quite integrated his abounding talents.

Like Whittier and Longfellow, Lowell has a diminished reputation. This is partly because he had been overrated, and partly because he does not satisfy twentieth-century attitudes and tastes. Even less than Whittier's and Longfellow's poetry has Lowell's continued to speak across the years. His prose essays on European writers of various periods do impress many readers with his admirable standards and frequent insight. But he is too casual in method greatly to serve the literary intellectuals of today.

Text: *The Writings of James Russell Lowell,* Riverside Edition (Boston, 1890).
Further reading: Leon Howard, *Victorian Knight-Errant,* 1952. Martin Duberman, *James Russell Lowell,* 1966.

FROM *A Fable for Critics*

This piece of high-spirited, often penetrating banter is reminiscent of such earlier satires as Pope's *Dunciad,* Byron's *English Bards and Scotch Reviewers,* and Leigh Hunt's *The Feast of the Poets,* as well as *A Critical Fable* by Amy Lowell in the twentieth century. The "fable" is almost nonexistent. Essentially the poem presents critical sketches of American authors, such as those below.

[Emerson]

"There comes Emerson first, whose rich words, every one,
Are like gold nails in temples to hang trophies on,
Whose prose is grand verse, while his verse, the Lord knows,
Is some of it pr— No, 't is not even prose;
I'm speaking of metres; some poems have welled
From those rare depths of soul that have ne'er been excelled;
They're not epics, but that doesn't matter a pin,
In creating, the only hard thing's to begin;
A grass-blade's no easier to make than an oak;
If you've once found the way, you've achieved the grand stroke;
In the worst of his poems are mines of rich matter.
But thrown in a heap with a crash and a clatter;
Now it is not one thing nor another alone
Makes a poem, but rather the general tone,
The something pervading, uniting the whole,
The before unconceived, unconceivable soul,
So that just in removing this trifle or that, you
Take away, as it were, a chief limb of the statue;
Roots, wood, bark, and leaves singly perfect may be,
But, clapt hodge-podge together, they don't make a tree.

"But, to come back to Emerson (whom, by the way,
I believe we left waiting),—his is, we may say,
A Greek head on right Yankee shoulders, whose range
Has Olympus for one pole, for t' other the Exchange;
He seems, to my thinking (although I'm afraid
The comparison must, long ere this, have been made),
A Plotinus-Montaigne, where the Egyptian's gold mist
And the Gascon's shrewd wit cheek-by-jowl coexist;
All admire, and yet scarcely six converts he's got
To I don't (nor they either) exactly know what;
For though he builds glorious temples, 't is odd
He leaves never a doorway to get in a god.
'T is refreshing to old-fashioned people like me
To meet such a primitive Pagan as he,
In whose mind all creation is duly respected
As parts of himself—just a little projected;
And who's willing to worship the stars and the sun,
A convert to—nothing but Emerson.
So perfect a balance there is in his head,
That he talks of things sometimes as if they were dead;
Life, nature, love, God, and affairs of that sort,
He looks at as merely ideas; in short,
As if they were fossils stuck round in a cabinet,
Of such vast extent that our earth's a mere dab in it;
Composed just as he is inclined to conjecture her,
Namely, one part pure earth, ninety-nine parts pure lecturer;
You are filled with delight at his clear demonstration,
Each figure, word, gesture, just fits the occasion,
With the quiet precision of science he'll sort 'em,
But you can't help suspecting the whole a *post mortem.* * * *

"He has imitators in scores, who omit
No part of the man but his wisdom and wit,—
Who go carefully o'er the sky-blue of his brain,
And when he has skimmed it once, skim it again;
If at all they resemble him, you may be sure it is
Because their shoals mirror his mists and obscurities,
As a mud-puddle seems deep as heaven for a minute,
While a cloud that floats o'er is reflected within it.

[Whittier]

"There is Whittier, whose swelling and vehement heart
Strains the strait-breasted drab of the Quaker apart,
And reveals the live Man, still supreme and erect,
Underneath the bemummying wrappers of sect;
There was ne'er a man born who had more of the swing
Of the true lyric bard and all that kind of thing;
And his failures arise (though he seem not to know it)
From the very same cause that has made him a poet,—

A fervor of mind which knows no separation
'Twixt simple excitement and pure inspiration,
As my Pythoness erst sometimes erred from not knowing
If't were I or mere wind through her tripod was blowing;
Let his mind once get head in its favorite direction
And the torrent of verse bursts the dams of reflection,
While, borne with the rush of the metre along,
The poet may chance to go right or go wrong,
Content with the whirl and delirium of song;
Then his grammar's not always correct, nor his rhymes,
And he's prone to repeat his own lyrics sometimes,
Not his best, though, for those are struck off at white-heats
When the heart in his breast like a trip-hammer beats,
And can ne'er be repeated again any more
Than they could have been carefully plotted before:
Like old what's-his-name[1] there at the battle of Hastings
(Who, however, gave more than mere rhythmical bastings),
Our Quaker leads off metaphorical fights
For reform and whatever they call human rights,
Both singing and striking in front of the war,
And hitting his foes with the mallet of Thor;
Anne haec, one exclaims, on beholding his knocks,
Vestis filii tui,[2] O leather-clad Fox?[3]
Can that be thy son, in the battle's mid din,
Preaching brotherly love and then driving it in
To the brain of the tough old Goliath of sin,
With the smoothest of pebbles from Castaly's[4] spring
Impressed on his hard moral sense with a sling?

"All honor and praise to the right-hearted bard
Who was true to The Voice when such service was hard,
Who himself was so free he dared sing for the slave
When to look but a protest in silence was brave;
All honor and praise to the women and men
Who spoke out for the dumb and the down-trodden then!

Whittier. [1] Taillefer, a minstrel in William the Conqueror's army who supposedly encouraged the Normans at the Battle of Hastings by singing of the deeds of Roland.

[2] Latin version of Genesis xxxvii.32; "Is this thy son's coat?" Asked by Joseph's brothers.

[3] George Fox (1624-91), founder of the Society of Friends, the Quakers. The allusions suggest that Whittier is Fox's spiritual or Quaker "son."

[4] Fountain on Mt. Parnassus, sacred to Apollo; the source of poetic inspiration.

[Hawthorne]

"There is Hawthorne, with genius so shrinking and rare
That you hardly at first see the strength that is there;
A frame so robust, with a nature so sweet,
So earnest, so graceful, so lithe and so fleet,
Is worth a descent from Olympus to meet;
'T is as if a rough oak that for ages had stood,
With his gnarled bony branches like ribs of the wood,
Should bloom, after cycles of struggle and scathe,
With a single anemone trembly and rathe;
His strength is so tender, his wildness so meek,
That a suitable parallel sets one to seek,—
He's a John Bunyan Fouqué, a Puritan Tieck;[1]
When Nature was shaping him, clay was not granted
For making so full-sized a man as she wanted,
So, to fill out her model, a little she spared
From some finer-grained stuff for a woman prepared,
And she could not have hit a more excellent plan
For making him fully and perfectly man.

[Poe and Longfellow]

"There comes Poe, with his raven, like Barnaby Rudge,[1]
Three fifths of him genius and two fifths sheer fudge,
Who talks like a book of iambs and pentameters,
In a way to make people of common sense damn metres,
Who has written some things quite the best of their kind,
But the heart somehow seems all squeezed out by the mind,
Who— But hey-day! What's this? Messieurs Mathews[2] and Poe,
You must n't fling mud-balls at Longfellow so,
Does it make a man worse that his character's such
As to make his friends love him (as you think) too much?
Why, there is not a bard at this moment alive
More willing than he that his fellows should thrive;
While you are abusing him thus, even now

Hawthorne. [1] The allusions suggest a contrast between moral intensity and romantic fantasy: John Bunyan (1628-88), Puritan author of *The Pilgrim's Progress*, 1678; Friedrich, Baron de la Motte Fouqué (1777-1843), who published *Undine*, a fairy romance, in 1811; Ludwig Tieck (1773-1853), a German romantic novelist.

Poe. [1] The title character in the Dickens novel, 1841; Rudge was a murderer, a half-wit, and the owner of a raven.

[2] Cornelius Mathews (1817-89). Both Poe and Mathews criticized Longfellow's poetry.

He would help either one of you out of a slough;
You may say that he's smooth and all that till you're hoarse,
But remember that elegance also is force;
After polishing granite as much as you will,
The heart keeps its tough old persistency still;
Deduct all you can, *that* still keeps you at bay;
Why, he'll live till men weary of Collins and Gray.[3]
I'm not over-fond of Greek metres in English,
To me rhyme's a gain, so it be not too jinglish,
And your modern hexameter verses are no more
Like Greek ones than sleek Mr. Pope[4] is like Homer;
As the roar of the sea to the coo of a pigeon is,
So, compared to your moderns, sounds old Melesigenes;[5]
I may be too partial, the reason, perhaps, o't is
That I've heard the old blind man recite his own rhapsodies,
And my ear with that music impregnate may be,
Like the poor exiled shell with the soul of the sea,
Or as one can't bear Strauss when his nature is cloven
To its deeps within deeps by the stroke of Beethoven;
But, set that aside, and 't is truth that I speak,
Had Theocritus[6] written in English, not Greek,
I believe that his exquisite sense would scarce change a line
In that rare, tender, virgin-like pastoral Evangeline.[7]
That's not ancient nor modern, its place is apart
Where time has no sway, in the realm of pure Art,
'T is a shrine of retreat from Earth's hubbub and strife
As quiet and chaste as the author's own life.

[Lowell]

"There is Lowell, who's striving Parnassus[1] to climb
With a whole bale of *isms* tied together with rhyme,
He might get on alone, spite of brambles and boulders,
But he can't with that bundle he has on his shoulders,
The top of the hill he will ne'er come nigh reaching
Till he learns the distinction 'twixt singing and preaching;

[3] William Collins (1721-59) and Thomas Gray (1716-71), English poets.
[4] Alexander Pope (1688-1744) translated Homer into heroic couplets.
[5] An ancient epithet for Homer.
[6] A Greek pastoral poet of the third century B.C.
[7] A long narrative poem in hexameter by Longfellow.
Lowell. [1] A mountain in Greece sacred to the Muses.

His lyre has some chords that would ring pretty well,
But he'd rather by half make a drum of the shell,
And rattle away till he's old as Methusalem,
At the head of a march to the last new Jerusalem.

1848

FROM *The Biglow Papers*

Lowell published the First Series of *The Biglow Papers* (1848) without his own name, as the verses of a young Yankee farmer, "Hosea Biglow," laboriously edited by "Homer Wilbur, A.M., Pastor of the First Church in Jaalam."

In these poems Lowell used humor and dialect for propagandist ends, with great popular success. He found his verses, he said, "copied everywhere; I saw them pinned up in workshops; I heard them quoted and their authorship debated." Whittier declared that the laugh caused by Hosea Biglow was alone enough to have "shaken half the walls of Slavery down." There had been popular "cracker-box philosophers" before, notably Seba Smith ("Major Downing"), but Lowell showed a grasp of character and a literary skill that gave his work a deeper interest.

The First Series concerned the Mexican War and slavery. Lowell said later: "Thinking the Mexican War, as I think it still, a national crime committed in behoof of slavery, our common sin, and wishing to put the feeling of those who thought as I did in a way that would tell, I imagined to myself such an up-country man as I had often seen at antislavery gatherings, capable of district school English, but always instinctively falling back into the natural stronghold of his homely dialect when heated to the point of self-forgetfulness. . . .

"In choosing the Yankee dialect, I did not act without forethought. It had long seemed to me that the great vice of American writing and speaking was a studied want of simplicity, that we were in danger of coming to look on our mother-tongue as a dead language, to be sought in the grammar and dictionary rather than in the heart, and that our only chance of escape was by seeking it at its living sources among those who were, as Scottowe says of Major-General Gibbons, 'divinely illiterate.' "

A Letter

From Mr. Ezekiel Biglow of Jaalam to the Hon. Joseph T. Buckingham, Editor of the Boston Courier, inclosing a poem of his son, Mr. Hosea Biglow.

Jaylem, june 1846.

Mister Eddyter:—Our Hosea wuz down to Boston last week, and he see a cruetin Sarjunt[1] a struttin round as popler as a hen with 1 chicking, with 2

A Letter. [1] Recruiting sergeant. President Polk had been authorized to employ the militia and call out 50,000 volunteers.

fellers a drummin and fifin arter him like all nater. the sarjunt he thout Hosea hed n't gut his i teeth cut cos he looked a kindo's though he'd jest com down, so he cal'lated to hook him in, but Hosy wood n't take none o' his sarse for all he hed much as 20 Rooster's tales stuck onto his hat and eenamost enuf brass a bobbin up and down on his shoulders and figureed onto his coat and trousis, let alone wut nater hed sot in his featers, to make a 6 pounder out on.

wal, Hosea he com home considerabal riled, and arter I'd gone to bed I heern Him a thrashin round like a short-tailed Bull in fli-time. The old Woman ses she to me ses she, Zekle, ses she, our Hosee's gut the chollery or suthin anuther ses she, don't you Bee skeered, ses I, he 's oney amakin pottery ses i, he's ollers on hand at that ere busynes like Da & martin,[2] and shure enuf, cum mornin, Hosy he cum down stares full chizzle, hare on eend and cote tales flyin, and sot rite of to go reed his varses to Parson Wilbur bein he haint aney grate shows o' book larnin himself, bimeby he cum back and sed the parson wuz dreffle tickled with 'em as i hoop you will Be, and said they wuz True grit.

Hosea ses taint hardly fair to call 'em hisn now, cos the parson kind o' slicked off sum o' the last varses, but he told Hosee he did n't want to put his ore in to tetch to the Rest on 'em, bein they wuz verry well As thay wuz, and then Hosy ses he sed suthin a nuther about Simplex Mundishes[3] or sum sech feller, but I guess Hosea kind o' did n't hear him, for I never hearn o' nobody o' that name in this villadge, and I've lived here man and boy 76 year cum next tater diggin, and thair aint no wheres a kitting spryer 'n I be.

If you print 'em I wish you'd jest let folks know who hosy's father is, cos my ant Keziah used to say it 's nater to be curus ses she, she aint livin though and he's a likely kind o' lad.

EZEKIEL BIGLOW.

Thrash away, you'll *hev* to rattle
  On them kittle-drums o' yourn,—
'Taint a knowin' kind o' cattle
  Thet is ketched with mouldy corn;
Put in stiff, you fifer feller,
  Let folks see how spry you be,—
Guess you 'll toot till you are yeller
  'Fore you git ahold o' me!

Thet air flag's a leetle rotten,
  Hope it aint your Sunday's best;—
Fact! it takes a sight o' cotton
  To stuff out a soger's chest:
Sence we farmers hev to pay fer 't,
  Ef you must wear humps like these,
S'posin' you should try salt hay fer't,
  It would du ez slick ez grease.

'T would n't suit them Southun fellers,
  They're a dreffle graspin' set,
We must ollers blow the bellers
  Wen they want their irons het;
May be it's all right ez preachin',
  But *my* narves it kind o' grates,
Wen I see the overreachin'
  O' them nigger-drivin' States.

Them thet rule us, them slave-traders,
  Haint they cut a thunderin' swarth
(Helped by Yankee renegaders),
  Thru the vartu o' the North!
We begin to think it's nater
  To take sarse an' not be riled;—
Who'd expect to see a tater
  All on eend at bein' biled?

Ez fer war, I call it murder,—
  There you hev it plain an' flat;
I don't want to go no furder
  Than my Testyment fer that;
God hez sed so plump an' fairly,
  It's ez long ez it is broad,
An' you've gut to git up airly
  Ef you want to take in God.

'Taint your eppyletts an' feathers
  Make the thing a grain more right;
'Taint afollerin' your bell-wethers
  Will excuse ye in His sight;
Ef you take a sword an' dror it,
  An' go stick a feller thru,
Guv'ment aint to answer for it,
  God 'll send the bill to you.

Wut's the use o' meetin'-goin'
  Every Sabbath, wet or dry,
Ef it's right to go amowin'
  Feller-men like oats an' rye?
I dunno but wut it's pooty
  Trainin' round in bobtail coats,—
But it's curus Christian dooty
  This 'ere cuttin' folks's throats.

They may talk o' Freedom's airy
  Tell they're pupple in the face,—
It's a grand gret cemetary
  Fer the barthrights of our race;

[2] Day and Martin: makers of shoe polish, who advertised in verse.

[3] The parson was actually calling him a simpleton.

They jest want this Californy[4]
  So's to lug new slave-states in
To abuse ye, an' to scorn ye,
  An' to plunder ye like sin.

Aint it cute to see a Yankee
  Take sech everlastin' pains,
All to git the Devil's thankee
  Helpin' on 'em weld their chains?
Wy, it's jest ez clear ez figgers,
  Clear ez one an' one make two,
Chaps thet make black slaves o' niggers
  Want to make wite slaves o' you.

Tell ye jest the eend I've come to
  Arter cipherin' plaguy smart,
An' it makes a handy sum, tu,
  Any gump[5] could larn by heart;
Laborin' man an' laborin' woman
  Hev one glory an' one shame.
Ev'y thin' thet's done inhuman
  Injers all on 'em the same.

'Taint by turnin' out to hack folks
  You're agoin' to git your right,
Nor by lookin' down on black folks
  Coz you're put upon by wite;
Slavery aint o' nary color,
  'Taint the hide thet makes it wus,
All it keers fer in a feller
  'S jest to make him fill its pus.

Want to tackle *me* in, du ye?
  I expect you'll hev to wait;
Wen cold lead puts daylight thru ye
  You'll begin to kal'late;
S'pose the crows wun't fall to pickin'
  All the carkiss from your bones,
Coz you helped to give a lickin'
  To them poor half-Spanish drones?

Jest go home an' ask our Nancy
  Wether I'd be sech a goose
Ez to jine ye,—guess you'd fancy
  The etarnal bung wuz loose!
She wants me fer home consumption,
  Let alone the hay's to mow,—
Ef you're arter folks o' gumption,
  You've a darned long row to hoe.

Take them editors thet's crowin'
  Like a cockerel three months old,—
Don't ketch any on 'em goin',
  Though they *be* so blasted bold;
Aint they a prime lot o' fellers?
  'Fore they think on 't guess they'll sprout
(Like a peach thet's got the yellers[6]),
  With the meanness bustin' out.

Wal, go 'long to help 'em stealin'
  Bigger pens to cram with slaves,
Help the men thet's ollers dealin'
  Insults on your fathers' graves;
Help the strong to grind the feeble,
  Help the many agin the few,
Help the men thet call your people
  Witewashed slaves an' peddlin' crew!

Massachusetts,[7] God forgive her,
  She's akneelin' with the rest,
She, thet ough' to ha' clung ferever
  In her grand old eagle-nest;
She thet ough' to stand so fearless
  W'ile the wracks are round her hurled,
Holdin' up a beacon peerless
  To the oppressed of all the world!

Ha'n't they sold your colored seamen?[8]
  Ha'n't they made your env'ys w'iz?[9]
Wut'll make ye act like freemen?
  Wut'll git your dander riz?
Come, I'll tell ye wut I'm thinkin'
  Is our dooty in this fix,
They'd ha' done 't ez quick ez winkin'
  In the days o' seventy-six.

Clang the bells in every steeple,
  Call all true men to disown
The tradoocers of our people,
  The enslavers o' their own;
Let our dear old Bay State proudly
  Put the trumpet to her mouth,
Let her ring this messidge loudly
  In the ears of all the South:—

"I'll return ye good fer evil
  Much ez we frail mortils can,
But I wun't go help the Devil
  Makin' man the cus o' man;
Call me coward, call me traiter,
  Jest ez suits your mean idees,—

[4] The Compromise of 1850 admitted California as a free state.

[5] A foolish fellow, a dullard. [Lowell's note.]

[6] A fungus or virus disease.

[7] Two of Massachusetts' representatives supported the bill declaring war.

[8] Several Southern states passed laws preventing free blacks from entering those states. The laws were particularly severe on black seamen.

[9] In 1844 Samuel Hoar and George Hubbard went South to act on behalf of oppressed black citizens of Massachusetts. The two were expelled.

Here I stand a tyrant-hater,
  An' the friend o' God an' Peace!"

Ef I'd *my* way I hed ruther
  We should go to work an' part,
They take one way, we take t' other,
  Guess it wouldn't break my heart;
Man hed ough' to put asunder
  Them thet God has noways jined;
An' I shouldn't gretly wonder
  Ef there's thousands o' my mind.

1848

The Courtin'

"The Courtin'" appeared in a brief form in the First Series. Expanded—as given below—it opened the Second Series, which was launched fourteen years after the First, at the time of the Civil War.

God makes sech nights, all white an' still
  Fur 'z you can look or listen,
Moonshine an' snow on field an' hill,
  All silence an' all glisten.

Zekle crep' up quite unbeknown
  An' peeked in thru' the winder,
An' there sot Huldy all alone,
  'ith no one nigh to hender.

A fireplace filled the room's one side
  With half a cord o' wood in—
There warn't no stoves (tell comfort died)
  To bake ye to a puddin'.

The wa'nut logs shot sparkles out
  Towards the pootiest, bless her,
An' leetle flames danced all about
  The chiny on the dresser.

Agin the chimbley crook-necks hung,
  An' in amongst 'em rusted
The ole queen's-arm[1] thet gran'ther Young
  Fetched back f'om Concord busted.

The very room, coz she was in,
  Seemed warm f'om floor to ceilin',
An' she looked full ez rosy agin
  Ez the apples she was peelin'.

'T was kin' o' kingdom-come to look
  On sech a blessed cretur,
A dogrose blushin' to a brook
  Ain't modester nor sweeter.

The Courtin'. [1]Musket.

He was six foot o' man, A 1,
  Clear grit an' human natur',
None couldn't quicker pitch a ton
  Nor dror a furrer straighter.

He'd sparked it with full twenty gals,
  Hed squired 'em, danced 'em, druv 'em,
Fust this one, an' then thet, by spells—
  All is, he couldn't love 'em.

But long o' her his veins 'ould run
  All crinkly like curled maple,
The side she breshed felt full o' sun
  Ez a south slope in Ap'il.

She thought no v'ice hed sech a swing
  Ez hisn in the choir;
My! when he made Ole Hunderd ring,
  She *knowed* the Lord was nigher.

An' she'd blush scarlit, right in prayer,
  When her new meetin'-bunnet
Felt somehow thru' its crown a pair
  O' blue eyes sot upun it.

Thet night, I tell ye, she looked *some!*
  She seemed to 've gut a new soul,
For she felt sartin-sure he'd come,
  Down to her very shoe-sole.

She heered a foot, an' knowed it tu,
  A-raspin' on the scraper,—
All ways to once her feelins flew
  Like sparks in burnt-up paper.

He kin' o' l'itered on the mat,
  Some doubtfle o' the sekle,
His heart kep' goin' pity-pat,
  But hern went pity Zekle.

An' yit she gin her cheer a jerk
  Ez though she wished him furder,
An' on her apples kep' to work,
  Parin' away like murder.

"You want to see my Pa, I s'pose?"
  "Wal . . . no . . . I come dasignin' "—
"To see my Ma? She's sprinklin' clo'es
  Agin to-morrer's i'nin'."

To say why gals acts so or so,
  Or don't, 'ould be presumin';
Mebby to mean *yes* an' say *no*
  Comes nateral to women.

He stood a spell on one foot fust,
  Then stood a spell on t' other,
An' on which one he felt the wust
  He couldn't ha' told ye nuther.

Says he, "I'd better call agin";
  Says she, "Think likely, Mister":
Thet last word pricked him like a pin,
  An' . . . Wal, he up an' kist her.

When Ma bimeby upon 'em slips,
  Huldy sot pale ez ashes,
All kin' o' smily roun' the lips
  An' teary roun' the lashes.

For she was jes' the quiet kind
  Whose naturs never vary,
Like streams that keep a summer mind
  Snowhid in Jenooary.

The blood clost roun' her heart felt glued
  Too tight for all expressin',
Tell mother see how metters stood,
  An' gin 'em both her blessin'.

Then her red come back like the tide
  Down to the Bay o' Fundy,
An' all I know is they was cried[2]
  In meetin' come nex' Sunday.

1867

[2]Announcement was made of the couple's intention to marry.

Romantic and Realist

WALT WHITMAN [1819-1892]

The pulse of the nation beat strong in New York, a city of over half a million souls in 1855 when Whitman published *Leaves of Grass*. But its literary life could not vie with that of Concord and Cambridge. Whitman was its only great writer, and for many years few recognized his greatness. During the late 1850's and early 1860's he fraternized with the "bohemians" who met at Pfaff's restaurant on—or under—Broadway, among them no writers larger than Fitz James O'Brien and William Winter. They were more congenial to Whitman than another group associated with the city: Taylor, Stedman, Stoddard, Aldrich, poets of romanticism in its decline. But in the decades when the romantic impulse was fading away in a tame conventionality, Whitman gave it a last vigorous expression.

Walter Whitman was born at West Hills, Long Island. His ancestors were English and Dutch, some of them Quakers. The Whitmans moved to Brooklyn when Walt was small, and he felt the dual influence of a large city and a pleasant countryside near enough to be always available. He left school at the age of eleven. Office-boy, type-setter, occasional author, he became an itinerant country school teacher in 1836 and continued in this position until 1841 except for one brief flier in newspaper editing. In his spare time he learned the printing business, and in 1841 he definitely cast his lot with journalism in New York.

In five years he rose to be editor of the *Daily Brooklyn Eagle*, but lost his position in 1848 and was glad to accept another on a paper just starting in New Orleans. Three months in the South and he resigned his position and returned, by way of Chicago, to

Brooklyn. Here he made his headquarters until 1862, as journalist, proprietor of a book store, builder, and poet. In 1855 he collected the verse he had recently been writing and published it in a thin volume.

Whitman himself seems to have expected *Leaves of Grass* to be a bombshell. The book, however, was scarcely noticed. It received one important comment: Emerson wrote, "I greet you at the beginning of a great career." Whitman used this sentence, without permission, to advertise the second edition published the next year. This edition contained thirty-two poems, twenty more than the first edition. All his life Whitman continued to supplement, rewrite, and revise *Leaves of Grass.*

Late in 1862 he went down to Fredericksburg to care for a younger brother who had been slightly wounded. The next three years he gave freely of his health and heart as a nurse among the wounded in hospitals in and near Washington. He still found time to write vivid accounts of what he saw, and occasional poems. He gathered the poems in *Drum Taps* in 1865. The same year he was forced out of a governmental clerkship because a superior thought his poems indecent. His friends came to his aid,—one of them with a pamphlet entitled *The Good Gray Poet,* a name which stuck to Whitman thereafter—and he was established as a clerk in another department.

In 1873, two years after he had issued *Democratic Vistas,* he was stricken with paralysis and settled in Camden, New Jersey, where he lived nearly twenty years until his death. He revised his work, sent out a few articles, received many letters from friends in Europe and America, and made occasional journeys. In 1891-92 he approved the ninth edition of *Leaves of Grass,* the last which he supervised before his death.

Whitman's ideas and attitudes were chiefly those of the Romantic Movement. In his response to nature, his mystical desire for immediacy of experience, his cultivation of the senses, feelings, and imagination, his subjective individualism, his celebration of the common man, he was akin to such predecessors as Rousseau, Wordsworth, Shelley, and Emerson. To Emerson, in fact, he was deeply indebted, saying, "I was simmering, simmering, simmering; Emerson brought me to a boil." Even more than the author of "The American Scholar" he felt the romantic desire for a native experience, a national genius, and he tried to make himself spokesman for all America. With his nationalistic vision he combined a faith in progress, which in his day seemed to be supported by the theory of evolution. Into his romanticism he fused what were later to be traits of the developing realistic movement, such as his quest of a living speech coming out of American life, his generous inclusion of the commonplace and trivial, his incorporation of the ugly, his frank emphasis on sex and on bold sexual terms, and his hearty acceptance of science (though he was not really impregnated with its spirit).

To communicate all this, Whitman felt it necessary to achieve a new poetic form. He rejected the time-hallowed marks of English verse: rhymes, regular meters, stanza patterns, elaborate similes, frequent allusions to the Bible, the classics, the Middle Ages, etc. Instead, he aimed at a freer verse form based on the organic principle, a form not imposed upon but growing out of content. One of his least successful experiments was the cataloguing method, coordinating his materials as if to reflect the equality of all things or the complex miscellaneity of modern life. Most successful are features suggested by the art of music.

The reputation of Whitman grew after his death, till it reached a high point during the lusty literary movement of the 1920's. For example, Lewis Mumford in *The Golden Day* (1926) said that "he is more than a single writer: he is almost a literature," and that his poems "belong to sacred literature." Most critics would be less sweeping in their praise; but however Whitman is rated, there is no question of his profound influence on twentieth-century poets, obviously in the case of Carl Sandburg and Allen Ginsberg, more subtly in the case of many others, European as well as American. As a rule the influence of Whitman has stemmed more from his poetic technique than from his vision of life.

Text: *Leaves of Grass,* "Deathbed Edition" (Philadelphia, 1891-92). *Complete Prose Works* (Philadelphia, 1892).

Further reading: *Leaves of Grass: Comprehensive Reader's Edition,* ed. Harold Blodgett and Sculley Bradley, 1965. G. W. Allen, *The Solitary Singer: A Critical Biography of Walt Whitman,* 1955 (rev. 1968). James E. Miller, Jr., *Critical Guide to Leaves of Grass,* 1957. Howard Waskow, *Walt Whitman: Explorations in Form,* 1966. Edwin H. Miller, *Walt Whitman's Poetry: A Psychological Journey,* 1968.

FROM *Preface to Leaves of Grass* *(1855)*

Leaves of Grass originally contained a dozen untitled poems headed by a long Preface—a ten-page double-column essay. Believing that it was time "to break down the barriers of form between prose and poetry," Whitman wrote poetry with prominent prose qualities, and prose with prominent poetic qualities. Some of the prose of the Preface he actually incorporated later, with slight change, in various poems.

Whether or not the Preface is good prose, it is valuable (like Wordsworth's Preface to *Lyrical Ballads*) as a statement of what the poet was up to: a poetic revolution. The following extracts will prove illuminating, especially if read both before and after the poems. The rows of periods (. . .) are Whitman's, serving a function similar to that of dashes.

The opening paragraphs recall Emerson's desire for a truly American poet and his conception of America as itself a poem (cf. the closing passages of *The Poet*).

America does not repel the past or what it has produced under its forms or amid other politics or the idea of castes or the old religions . . . accepts the lesson with calmness . . . is not so impatient as has been supposed that the slough still sticks to opinions and manners and literature while the life which served its requirements has passed into the new life of the new forms . . . perceives that the corpse is slowly borne from the eating and sleeping rooms of the house . . . perceives that it waits a little while in the door . . . that it was fittest for its days . . . that its action has descended to the stalwart and well-shaped heir who approaches . . . and that he shall be fittest for his days.

The Americans of all nations at any time upon the earth have probably the fullest poetical nature. The United States themselves are essentially the greatest poem. In the history of the earth hitherto the largest and most stirring appear tame and orderly to their ampler largeness and stir. Here at last is something in the doings of man that corresponds with the broadcast doings of the day and night. Here is not merely a nation but a teeming nation of nations. Here is action united from strings necessarily blind to particulars and details magnificently moving in vast masses. Here is the hospitality which forever indicates heroes. . . . Here are the roughs and beards and space and ruggedness and nonchalance that the soul loves. Here the performance disdaining the trivial unapproached in the tremendous audacity of its crowds and groupings and the push of its perspective spreads with crampless and flowing breadth and showers its prolific and splendid extravagance. One sees it must indeed own the riches of the summer and winter, and need never be bankrupt while corn grows from the ground or the orchards drop apples or the bays contain fish or men beget children upon women.

Other states indicate themselves in their deputies . . . but the genius of the United States is not best or most in its executives or legislatures, nor in its ambassadors or authors or colleges or churches or parlors, nor even in its newspapers or inventors . . . but always most in the common people. Their manners speech dress friendships—the freshness and candor of their physiognomy—the picturesque looseness of their carriage . . . their deathless attachment to freedom—their aversion to anything indecorous or soft or mean—the practical acknowledgment of the citizens of one state by the citizens of all other states—the fierceness of their roused resentment—their curiosity and welcome of novelty—their self-esteem and wonderful sympathy—their susceptibility to a slight—the air they have of persons who never knew how it felt to stand in the presence of superiors—the fluency of their speech—their delight in music, the sure symptom of manly tenderness and native elegance of soul . . . their good temper and openhandedness—the terrible significance of their elections—the President's taking off his hat to them not they to him—these too are unrhymed poetry. It awaits the gigantic and generous treatment worthy of it.

The largeness of nature or the nation were monstrous without a corresponding largeness and generosity of the spirit of the citizen. Not nature nor swarming states nor streets and steamships nor prosperous business nor farms nor capital nor learning may suffice for the ideal of man . . . nor suffice the poet.

No reminiscences may suffice either. A live nation can always cut a deep mark and can have the best authority the cheapest . . . namely from its own soul. This is the sum of the profitable uses of individuals or states and of present action and grandeur and of the subjects of poets.—As if it were necessary to trot back generation after generation to the eastern records! As if the beauty and sacredness of the demonstrable must fall behind that of the mythical! As if men do not make their mark out of any times! As if the opening of the western continent by discovery and what has transpired since in North and South America were less than the small theatre of the antique or the aimless sleepwalking of the middle ages! The pride of the United States leaves the wealth and finesse of the cities and all returns of commerce and agriculture and all the magnitude of geography or shows of exterior victory to enjoy the breed of fullsized men or one fullsized man unconquerable and simple.

The American poets are to enclose old and new for America is the race of races. Of them a bard is to be commensurate with a people. To him the other continents arrive as contributions . . . he gives them reception for their sake and his own sake. His spirit responds to his country's spirit . . . he incarnates its geography and natural life and rivers and lakes. Mississippi with annual freshets and changing chutes, Missouri and Columbia and Ohio and Saint Lawrence with the falls and beautiful masculine Hudson, do not embouchure where they spend themselves more than they embouchure into him. The blue breadth over the inland sea of Virginia and Maryland and the sea off Massachusetts and Maine and over Manhattan bay and over Champlain and Erie and over Ontario and Huron and Michigan and Superior, and over the Texan and Mexican and Floridian and Cuban seas and over the seas off California and Oregon, is not tallied by the blue breadth of the waters below more than the breadth of above and below is tallied by him. When the long Atlantic coast stretches longer and the Pacific coast stretches longer he easily stretches with them north or south. He spans between them also from east to west and reflects what is between them. On him rise solid growths that offset the growths of pine and cedar and hemlock and live-oak and locust and chestnut and cypress and hickory and limetree and cottonwood and tuliptree and cactus and wildvine and tamarind and persimmon . . . and tangles as tangled as any canebreak or swamp . . . and forests coated with transparent ice and icicles hanging from the boughs and crackling in the wind . . . and sides and peaks of mountains . . . and pasturage sweet and free as savannah or upland or prairie . . . with flights and songs and screams that answer those of the wildpigeon and highhold and orchard-oriole and coot and surf-duck and redshouldered-hawk and fish-hawk and white-ibis and indian-hen and cat-owl and water-pheasant and qua-bird and pied-sheldrake and blackbird and mockingbird and buzzard and condor and night-heron and eagle. To him the hereditary countenance descends both mother's and father's. To him enter the essences of the real things and past and present events—of the enormous diversity of temperature and agriculture and mines—the tribes of red aborigines—the weather-beaten vessels entering new ports or making landings on rocky coasts—the first settlements north or south—the rapid stature and muscle—the haughty defiance of '76, and the war and peace and formation of the constitution . . . the union always surrounded by blatherers and always calm and impregnable—the perpetual coming of immigrants—the wharfhem'd cities and superior marine—the unsurveyed interior—the loghouses and clearings and wild animals and hunters and trappers . . . the free commerce—the fisheries and whaling and gold-digging—the endless gestation of new states—the convening of Congress every December, the members duly coming up from all climates and the uttermost parts . . . the noble character of the young mechanics and of all free American workmen and workwomen . . . the general ardor and friendliness and enterprise—the perfect equality of the female with the male . . . the large amativeness—the fluid movement of the population—the factories and mercantile life and laborsaving machinery—the Yankee swap—the New-York firemen and the target excursion—the southern plantation life—the character of the northeast and the northwest and southwest—slavery and the tremulous spreading of hands to protect it, and the stern opposition to it which shall never cease till it ceases or the speaking of tongues and the moving of lips cease. For such the expression of the American poet is to be transcendant and new. It is to be indirect and not direct or descriptive or epic. Its quality goes through these to much more. Let the age and wars of other nations be chanted and their eras and characters be illustrated and that finish the verse. Not so the great psalm of the republic. Here the theme is creative and has vista. Here comes one among the wellbeloved stonecutters and plans with decision and science and sees the solid and beautiful forms of the future where there are now no solid forms. * * *

The land and sea, the animals fishes and birds, the sky of heaven and the orbs, the forests mountains and rivers, are not small themes . . . but folks expect of the poet to indicate more than the beauty and dignity which always attach to dumb real objects . . .

they expect him to indicate the path between reality and their souls. Men and women perceive the beauty well enough . . . probably as well as he. The passionate tenacity of hunters, woodmen, early risers, cultivators of gardens and orchards and fields, the love of healthy women for the manly form, seafaring persons, drivers of horses, the passion for light and the open air, all is an old varied sign of the unfailing perception of beauty and of a residence of the poetic in outdoor people. They can never be assisted by poets to perceive . . . some may but they never can. The poetic quality is not marshalled in rhyme or uniformity or abstract addresses to things nor in melancholy complaints or good precepts, but is the life of these and much else and is in the soul. The profit of rhyme is that it drops seeds of a sweeter and more luxuriant rhyme, and of uniformity that it conveys itself into its own roots in the ground out of sight. The rhyme and uniformity of perfect poems show the free growth of metrical laws and bud from them as unerringly and loosely as lilacs or roses on a bush, and take shapes as compact as the shapes of chestnuts and oranges and melons and pears, and shed the perfume impalpable to form. The fluency and ornaments of the finest poems or music or orations or recitations are not independent but dependent. All beauty comes from beautiful blood and a beautiful brain. If the greatnesses are in conjunction in a man or woman it is enough . . . the fact will prevail through the universe . . . but the gaggery and gilt of a million years will not prevail. Who troubles himself about his ornaments or fluency is lost. This is what you shall do: Love the earth and sun and the animals, despise riches, give alms to every one that asks, stand up for the stupid and crazy, devote your income and labor to others, hate tyrants, argue not concerning God, have patience and indulgence toward the people, take off your hat to nothing known or unknown or to any man or number of men, go freely with powerful uneducated persons and with the young and with the mothers of families, read these leaves in the open air every season of every year of your life, reexamine all you have been told at school or church or in any book, dismiss whatever insults your own soul, and your very flesh shall be a great poem and have the richest fluency not only in its words but in the silent lines of its lips and face and between the lashes of your eyes and in every motion and joint of your body. . . . The poet shall not spend his time in unneeded work. He shall know that the ground is always ready plowed and manured . . . others may not know it but he shall. He shall go directly to the creation. His trust shall master the trust of everything he touches . . . and shall master all attachment. * * *

The art of art, the glory of expression and the sunshine of the light of letters is simplicity. Nothing is better than simplicity . . . nothing can make up for excess or for the lack of definiteness. To carry on the heave of impulse and pierce intellectual depths and give all subjects their articulations are powers neither common nor very uncommon. But to speak in literature with the perfect rectitude and insouciance of the movements of animals and the unimpeachableness of the sentiment of trees in the woods and grass by the roadside is the flawless triumph of art. If you have looked on him who has achieved it you have looked on one of the masters of all nations and times. You shall not contemplate the flight of the graygull over the bay or the mettlesome action of the blood horse or the tall leaning of sunflowers on their stalk or the appearance of the sun journeying through heaven or the appearance of the moon afterward with any more satisfaction than you shall contemplate him. The greatest poet has less a marked style and is more the channel of thoughts and things without increase or diminution, and is the free channel of himself. He swears to his art, I will not be meddlesome, I will not have in my writing any elegance or effect or originality to hang in the way between me and the rest like curtains. I will have nothing hang in the way, not the richest curtains. What I tell I tell for precisely what it is. Let who may exalt or startle or fascinate or soothe I will have purposes as health or heat or snow has and be as regardless of observation. What I experience or portray shall go from my composition without a shred of my composition. You shall stand by my side and look in the mirror with me. * * *

The direct trial of him who would be the greatest poet is today. If he does not flood himself with the immediate age as with vast oceanic tides . . . and if he does not attract his own land body and soul to himself and hang on its neck with incomparable love and plunge his semitic muscle into its merits and demerits . . . and if he be not himself the age transfigured . . . and if to him is not opened the eternity which gives similitude to all periods and locations and processes and animate and inanimate forms, and which is the bond of time, and rises up from its inconceivable vagueness and infiniteness in the swimming shape of today, and is held by the ductile anchors of life, and makes the present spot the passage from what was to what shall be, and commits itself to the representation of this wave of an hour and this one of the sixty beautiful children of the wave—let him merge in the general run and wait his development. . . . Still the final test of poems or any character or work remains. The prescient poet projects himself centuries ahead and judges performer or performance after the changes of time. Does it live through them? Does it still hold on untired? Will the same style and the direction of genius to similar points be satisfactory now? Has no new discovery in science or arrival at superior planes of thought and judgment and behaviour fixed him or his so that either can be looked down upon? Have the marches of tens and hundreds and thousands of years made willing detours to the right hand and the left hand for his sake? Is he beloved long and long after he is buried? Does the young man think often of him? and the young woman think often of him? and do the middle-aged and the old think of him?

A great poem is for ages and ages in common and for all degrees and complexions and all departments and sects and for a woman as much as a man and a man as much as a woman. A great poem is no finish to a man or woman but rather a beginning. Has any one fancied he could sit at last under some due authority and rest satisfied with explanations and realize and be content and full? To no such terminus does the greatest poet bring . . he brings neither cessation or sheltered fatness and ease. The touch of him tells in action. Whom he takes he takes with firm sure grasp into live regions previously unattained . . . thenceforward is no rest . . . they see the space and ineffable sheen that turn the old spots and lights into dead vacuums. The companion of him beholds the birth and progress of stars and learns one of the meanings. Now there shall be a man cohered out of tumult and chaos . . . the elder encourages the younger and shows him how . . . they two shall launch off fearlessly together till the new world fits an orbit for itself and looks unabashed on the lesser orbits of the stars and sweeps through the ceaseless rings and shall never be quiet again.

There will soon be no more priests. Their work is done. They may wait awhile . . . perhaps a generation or two . . . dropping off by degrees. A superior breed shall take their place . . . the gangs of kosmos and prophets en masse shall take their place. A new order shall arise and they shall be the priests of man, and every man shall be his own priest. The churches built under their umbrage shall be the churches of men and women. Through the divinity of themselves shall the kosmos and the new breed of poets be interpreters of men and women and of all events and things. They shall find their inspiration in real objects today, symptoms of the past and future . . . They shall not deign to defend immortality or God or the perfection of things or liberty or the exquisite beauty and reality of the soul. They shall arise in America and be responded to from the remainder of the earth.

The English language befriends the grand American expression . . . it is brawny enough and limber and full enough. On the tough stock of a race who through all change of circumstances was never without the idea of political liberty, which is the animus of all liberty, it has attracted the terms of daintier and gayer and subtler and more elegant tongues. It is the powerful language of resistance . . . it is the dialect of common sense. It is the speech of the proud and melancholy races and of all who aspire. It is the chosen tongue to express growth faith self-esteem freedom justice equality friendliness amplitude prudence decision and courage. It is the medium that shall well nigh express the inexpressible.

No great literature nor any like style of behaviour or oratory or social intercourse or household arrangements or public institutions or the treatment by bosses of employed people, nor executive detail or detail of the army or navy, nor spirit of legislation or courts or police or tuition or architecture or songs or amusements of the costumes of young men, can long elude the jealous and passionate instinct of American standards. Whether or no the sign appears from the mouths of the people, it throbs a live interrogation in every freeman's and freewoman's heart after that which passes by or this built to remain. Is it uniform with my country? Are its disposals without ignominious distinctions? Is it for the evergrowing communes of brothers and lovers, large, well-united, proud beyond the old models, generous beyond all models? Is it something grown fresh out of the fields or drawn from the sea for use to me today here? I know that what answers for me an American must answer for any individual or nation that serves for a part of my materials. Does this answer? or is it without reference to universal needs? or sprung of the needs of the less developed society of special ranks? or old needs or pleasure overlaid by modern science and forms? Does this acknowledge liberty with audible and absolute acknowledgement, and set slavery at naught for life and death? Will it help breed one goodshaped and wellhung man, and a woman to be his perfect and independent mate? Does it improve manners? Is it for the nursing of the young of the republic? Does it solve readily with the sweet milk of the nipples of the breasts of the mother of many children? Has it too the old ever-fresh forbearance and impartiality? Does it look with the same love on the last born and on those hardening toward stature, and on the errant, and on those who disdain all strength of assault outside of their own?

The poems distilled from other poems will probably pass away. The coward will surely pass away. The expectation of the vital and great can only be satisfied by the demeanor of the vital and great. The swarms of the polished deprecating and reflectors and the polite float off and leave no remembrance. America prepares with composure and goodwill for the visitors that have sent word. It is not intellect that is to be their warrant and welcome. The talented, the artist, the ingenious, the editor, the statesman, the erudite . . . they are not unappreciated . . . they fall in their place and do their work. The soul of the nation also does its work. No disguise can pass on it . . . . no disguise can conceal from it. It rejects none, it permits all. Only toward as good as itself and toward the like of itself will it advance half-way. An individual is as superb as a nation when he has the qualities which make a superb nation. The soul of the largest and wealthiest and proudest nation may well go half-way to meet that of its poets. The signs are effectual. There is no fear of mistake. If the one is true the other is true. The proof of a poet is that his country absorbs him as affectionately as he has absorbed it.

Song of Myself

The longest of Whitman's poems—here printed unabridged—is a celebration of modern man. For Whitman, modern man is best illustrated by the everyday American, living in democratic comradeship. "Myself" could just as well have been "Yourself." Naturally Whitman often speaks from his own personality and experience, but throughout the poem his object is to picture a typical American, a "divine average" humanity. Why divine? Because the poet has come to see, in the simplest of lives, a limitless grandeur of body and soul. This grandeur was suddenly clear to him in the experience described in section 5, a revelation that transformed the world for him. Now, in his love of all life, he wishes to convert others. Addressing his audience with evangelistic intent, he says:

"Long enough have you dream'd contemptible dreams,
Now I wash the gum from your eyes,
You must habit yourself to the dazzle of the light. . . ."

Whitman was doing in this and other poems what Emerson was doing in his lectures. He himself would have tried the direct method of the lyceum platform if he had been a good speaker. Fascinated by the art of oratory, he adopted a mode of writing closely akin to speaking. He is talking "to you, whoever you are," sometimes as in conversation, more generally as in a public address. It is best to try to *hear* him by reading aloud, not stopping at difficulties but leaving them to be cleared up by what is said later. Until one has grasped his spirit and his drift, it is all but useless to inspect his lines closely. Nor is there much point in looking for the outline the speaker is following, for instead of employing thematic progression, Whitman seems to say, in each of the fifty-two sections, whatever at the moment seems to him to need saying. Aesthetically, the results are not happy: good, bad, and indifferent passages jostle each other, and the bad and indifferent are many. Yet the best passages are superb.

He begins, in the first three lines, by asserting the essential identity of *you* and *me*.

1

I celebrate myself, and sing myself,
And what I assume you shall assume,
For every atom belonging to me as good belongs to you.

I loafe and invite my soul,
I lean and loafe at my ease observing a spear of summer grass.

My tongue, every atom of my blood, form'd from this soil, this air,
Born here of parents born here from parents the same, and their parents the same,
I, now thirty-seven years old in perfect health begin,
Hoping to cease not till death.

Creeds and schools in abeyance,
Retiring back a while sufficed at what they are, but never forgotten,
I harbor for good or bad, I permit to speak at every hazard,
Nature without check with original energy.

2

Houses and rooms are full of perfumes, the shelves are crowded with perfumes,
I breathe the fragrance myself and know it and like it,
The distillation would intoxicate me also, but I shall not let it.

The atmosphere is not a perfume, it has no taste of the distillation, it is odorless,
It is for my mouth forever, I am in love with it,
I will go to the bank by the wood and become undisguised and naked,
I am mad for it to be in contact with me.

The smoke of my own breath,
Echoes, ripples, buzz'd whispers, love-root, silk-thread, crotch and vine,
My respiration and inspiration, the beating of my heart, the passing of blood and air through my lungs,
The sniff of green leaves and dry leaves, and of the shore and dark-color'd sea-rocks, and of hay in the barn,
The sound of the belch'd words of my voice loos'd to the eddies of the wind,
A few light kisses, a few embraces, a reaching around of arms,
The play of shine and shade on the trees as the supple boughs wag,
The delight alone or in the rush of the streets, or along the fields and hill-sides,
The feeling of health, the full-noon trill, the song of me rising from bed and meeting the sun.

Have you reckon'd a thousand acres much? have you reckon'd the earth much?
Have you practis'd so long to learn to read?
Have you felt so proud to get at the meaning of poems?

Stop this day and night with me and you shall possess the origin of all poems,
You shall possess the good of the earth and sun, (there are millions of suns left,)
You shall no longer take things at second or third hand, nor look through the eyes of the dead, nor feed on the spectres in books,
You shall not look through my eyes either, nor take things from me,
You shall listen to all sides and filter them from your self.

3

I have heard what the talkers were talking, the talk of the beginning and the end,
But I do not talk of the beginning or the end.

There was never any more inception than there is now,
Nor any more youth or age than there is now,
And will never be any more perfection than there is now,
Nor any more heaven or hell than there is now.

Urge and urge and urge,
Always the procreant urge of the world.

Out of the dimness opposite equals advance, always substance and increase, always sex,
Always a knit of identity, always distinction, always a breed of life.

To elaborate is no avail, learn'd and unlearn'd feel that it is so.

Sure as the most certain sure, plumb in the uprights, well entretied, braced in the beams,
Stout as a horse, affectionate, haughty, electrical,
I and this mystery here we stand.

Clear and sweet is my soul, and clear and sweet is all that is not my soul.

Lack one lacks both, and the unseen is proved by the seen,
Till that becomes unseen and receives proof in its turn.

Showing the best and dividing it from the worst age vexes age,
Knowing the perfect fitness and equanimity of things, while they discuss I am silent, and go bathe and admire myself.

Welcome is every organ and attribute of me, and of any man hearty and clean,
Not an inch nor a particle of an inch is vile, and none shall be less familiar than the rest.

I am satisfied—I see, dance, laugh, sing;
As the hugging and loving bed-fellow sleeps at my side through the night, and withdraws at the peep of the day with stealthy tread,
Leaving the baskets cover'd with white towels swelling the house with their plenty,
Shall I postpone my acceptation and realization and scream at my eyes,
That they turn from gazing after and down the road,
And forthwith cipher and show me to a cent,
Exactly the value of one and exactly the value of two, and which is ahead?

4

Trippers and askers surround me,
People I meet, the effect upon me of my early life or the ward and city I live in, or the nation,
The latest dates, discoveries, inventions, societies, authors old and new,
My dinner, dress, associates, looks, compliments, dues,
The real or fancied indifference of some man or woman I love,
The sickness of one of my folks or of myself, or ill-doing or loss or lack of money, or depressions or exaltations,
Battles, the horrors of fratricidal war, the fever of doubtful news, the fitful events;
These come to me days and nights and go from me again,
But they are not the Me myself.

Apart from the pulling and hauling stands what I am,
Stands amused, complacent, compassionating, idle, unitary,
Looks down, is erect, or bends an arm on an impalpable certain rest,
Looking with side-curved head curious what will come next,
Both in and out of the game and watching and wondering at it.

Backward I see in my own days where I sweated through fog with linguists and contenders,
I have no mockings or arguments, I witness and wait.

5

I believe in you my soul, the other I am must not abase itself to you,
And you must not be abased to the other.

Loafe with me on the grass, loose the stop from your throat,
Not words, not music or rhyme I want, not custom or lecture, not even the best,
Only the lull I like, the hum of your valvèd voice.

I mind how once we lay such a transparent summer morning,
How you settled your head athwart my hips and gently turn'd over upon me,
And parted the shirt from my bosom-bone, and plunged your tongue to my bare-stript heart,
And reach'd till you felt my beard, and reach'd till you held my feet.

Swiftly arose and spread around me the peace and knowledge that pass all the argument of the earth,
And I know that the hand of God is the promise of my own,
And I know that the spirit of God is the brother of my own,
And that all the men ever born are also my brothers, and the women my sisters and lovers,

And that a kelson of the creation is love,
And limitless are leaves stiff or drooping in the fields,
And brown ants in the little wells beneath them,
And mossy scabs of the worm fence, heap'd stones, elder, mullein and poke-weed.

6

A child said *What is the grass?* fetching it to me with full hands;
How could I answer the child? I do not know what it is any more than he.
I guess it must be the flag of my disposition, out of hopeful green stuff woven.

Or I guess it is the handkerchief of the Lord,
A scented gift and remembrancer designedly dropt,
Bearing the owner's name someway in the corners, that we may see and remark, and say *Whose?*

Or I guess the grass is itself a child, the produced babe of the vegetation.

Or I guess it is a uniform hieroglyphic,
And it means, Sprouting alike in broad zones and narrow zones,
Growing among black folds as among white,
Kanuck,[1] Tuckahoe,[2] Congressman, Cuff,[3] I give them the same, I receive them the same.
And now it seems to me the beautiful uncut hair of graves.

Tenderly will I use you curling grass,
It may be you transpire from the breasts of young men,
It may be if I had known them I would have loved them,
It may be you are from old people, or from offspring taken soon out of their mothers' laps,
And here you are the mothers' laps.

This grass is very dark to be from the white heads of old mothers,
Darker than the colorless beards of old men,
Dark to come from under the faint red roofs of mouths.

O I perceive after all so many uttering tongues,
And I perceive they do not come from the roofs of mouths for nothing.

I wish I could translate the hints about the dead young men and women,
And the hints about old men and mothers, and the offspring taken soon out of their laps.

What do you think has become of the young and old men?
And what do you think has become of the women and children?

They are alive and well somewhere,
The smallest sprout shows there is really no death,
And if ever there was it led forward life, and does not wait at the end to arrest it,
And ceas'd the moment life appear'd.

All goes onward and outward, nothing collapses,
And to die is different from what any one supposed, and luckier.

7

Has any one supposed it lucky to be born?
I hasten to inform him or her it is just as lucky to die, and I know it.

Song of Myself. [1] French Canadian.
[2] Whitman's most recent editors, Blodgett and Bradley, identify Tuckahoe as a "tidewater Virginian who eats tuckahoe."
[3] A Negro.

I pass death with the dying and birth with the new-wash'd babe, and am not contain'd between my hat and boots,
And peruse manifold objects, no two alike and every one good,
The earth good and the stars good, and their adjuncts all good.

I am not an earth nor an adjunct of an earth,
I am the mate and companion of people, all just as immortal and fathomless as myself,
(They do not know how immortal, but I know.)

Every kind for itself and its own, for me mine male and female,
For me those that have been boys and that love women,
For me the man that is proud and feels how it stings to be slighted,
For me the sweet-heart and the old maid, for me mothers and the mothers of mothers,
For me lips that have smiled, eyes that have shed tears,
For me children and the begetters of children.

Undrape! you are not guilty to me, nor stale nor discarded,
I see through the broadcloth and gingham whether or no,
And am around, tenacious, acquisitive, tireless, and cannot be shaken away.

8

The little one sleeps in its cradle,
I lift the gauze and look a long time, and silently brush away flies with my hand.

The youngster and the red-faced girl turn aside up the bushy hill,
I peeringly view them from the top.

The suicide sprawls on the bloody floor of the bedroom,
I witness the corpse with its dabbled hair, I note where the pistol has fallen.

The blab of the pave, tires of carts, sluff of boot-soles, talk of the promenaders,
The heavy omnibus, the driver with his interrogating thumb, the clank of the shod horses on the granite floor,
The snow-sleighs, clinking, shouted jokes, pelts of snow-balls,
The hurrahs for popular favorites, the fury of rous'd mobs,
The flap of the curtain'd litter, a sick man inside borne to the hospital,
The meeting of enemies, the sudden oath, the blows and fall,
The excited crowd, the policeman with his star quickly working his passage to the centre of the crowd,
The impassive stones that receive and return so many echoes,
What groans of over-fed or half-starv'd who fall sunstruck or in fits,
What exclamations of women taken suddenly who hurry home and give birth to babes,
What living and buried speech is always vibrating here, what howls restrain'd by decorum,
Arrests of criminals, slights, adulterous offers made, acceptances, rejections with convex lips,
I mind them or the show or resonance of them—I come and I depart.

9

The big doors of the country barn stand open and ready,
The dried grass of the harvest-time loads the slow-drawn wagon,
The clear light plays on the brown gray and green intertinged,
The armfuls are pack'd to the sagging mow.

I am there, I help, I came stretch'd atop of the load,
I felt its soft jolts, one leg reclined on the other,

I jump from the cross-beams and seize the clover and timothy,
And roll head over heels and tangle my hair full of wisps.

10

Alone far in the wilds and mountains I hunt,
Wandering amazed at my own lightness and glee,
In the late afternoon choosing a safe spot to pass the night,
Kindling a fire and broiling the fresh-kill'd game,
Falling asleep on the gather'd leaves with my dog and gun by my side.

The Yankee clipper is under her sky-sails, she cuts the sparkle and scud,
My eyes settle the land, I bend at her prow or shout joyously from the deck.

The boatmen and clam-diggers arose early and stopt for me,
I tuck'd trowser-ends in my boots and went and had a good time;
You should have been with us that day round the chowder-kettle.

I saw the marriage of the trapper in the open air in the far west, the bride was a red girl,
Her father and his friends sat near cross-legged and dumbly smoking, they had moccasins to their feet and large thick blankets hanging from their shoulders,
On a bank lounged the trapper, he was drest mostly in skins, his luxuriant beard and curls protected his neck, he held his bride by the hand,
She had long eyelashes, her head was bare, her coarse straight locks descended upon her voluptuous limbs and reach'd to her feet.

The runaway slave came to my house and stopt outside,
I heard his motions crackling the twigs of the woodpile,
Through the swung half-door of the kitchen I saw him limpsy and weak,
And went where he sat on a log and led him in and assured him,
And brought water and fill'd a tub for his sweated body and bruis'd feet,
And gave him a room that enter'd from my own, and gave him some coarse clean clothes,
And remember perfectly well his revolving eyes and his awkwardness,
And remember putting plasters on the galls of his neck and ankles;
He staid with me a week before he was recuperated and pass'd north,
I had him sit next me at table, my fire-lock lean'd in the corner.

11

Twenty-eight young men bathe by the shore,
Twenty-eight young men and all so friendly;
Twenty-eight years of womanly life and all so lonesome.

She owns the fine house by the rise of the bank,
She hides handsome and richly drest aft the blinds of the window.

Which of the young men does she like the best?
Ah the homeliest of them is beautiful to her.

Where are you off to, lady? for I see you,
You splash in the water there, yet stay stock still in your room.

Dancing and laughing along the beach came the twenty-ninth bather,
The rest did not see her, but she saw them and loved them.

The beards of the young men glisten'd with wet, it ran from their long hair,
Little streams pass'd all over their bodies.

An unseen hand also pass'd over their bodies,
It descended tremblingly from their temples and ribs.

The young men float on their backs, their white bellies bulge to the sun, they do not ask who seizes fast to them,
They do not know who puffs and declines with pendant and bending arch,
They do not think whom they souse with spray.

12

The butcher-boy puts off his killing-clothes, or sharpens his knife at the stall in the market,
I loiter enjoying his repartee and his shuffle and break-down.

Blacksmiths with grimed and hairy chests environ the anvil,
Each has his main-sledge, they are all out, there is a great heat in the fire.

From the cinder-strew'd threshold I follow their movements,
The lithe sheer of their waists plays even with their massive arms,
Overhand the hammers swing, overhand so slow, overhand so sure,
They do not hasten, each man hits in his place.

13

The Negro holds firmly the reins of his four horses, the block swags underneath on its tied-over chain,
The Negro that drives the long dray of the stone-yard, steady and tall he stands pois'd on one leg on the string-piece,
His blue shirt exposes his ample neck and breast and loosens over his hip-band,
His glance is calm and commanding, he tosses the slouch of his hat away from his forehead,
The sun falls on his crispy hair and mustache, falls on the black of his polish'd and perfect limbs.

I behold the picturesque giant and love him, and I do not stop there,
I go with the team also.

In me the caresser of life wherever moving, backward as well as forward sluing,
To niches aside and junior bending, not a person or object missing,
Absorbing all to myself and for this song.

Oxen that rattle the yoke and chain or halt in the leafy shade, what is that you express in your eyes?
It seems to me more than all the print I have read in my life.

My tread scares the wood-drake and wood-duck on my distant and day-long ramble,
They rise together, they slowly circle around.

I believe in those wing'd purposes,
And acknowledge red, yellow, white, playing within me,
And consider green and violet and the tufted crown intentional,
And do not call the tortoise unworthy because she is not something else,
And the jay in the woods never studied the gamut, yet trills pretty well to me,
And the look of the bay mare shames silliness out of me.

14

The wild gander leads his flock through the cool night,
Ya-honk he says, and sounds it down to me like an invitation,

The pert may suppose it meaningless, but I listening close,
Find its purpose and place up there toward the wintry sky.

The sharp-hoof'd moose of the north, the cat on the house-sill, the chickadee, the prairie-dog,
The litter of the grunting sow as they tug at her teats,
The brood of the turkey-hen and she with her half-spread wings,
I see in them and myself the same old law.

The press of my foot to the earth springs a hundred affections,
They scorn the best I can do to relate them.

I am enamour'd of growing out-doors,
Of men that live among cattle or taste of the ocean or woods,
Of the builders and steerers of ships and the wielders of axes and mauls, and the drivers of horses,
I can eat and sleep with them week in and week out.

What is commonest, cheapest, nearest, easiest, is Me,
Me going in for my chances, spending for vast returns,
Adorning myself to bestow myself on the first that will take me,
Not asking the sky to come down to my good will,
Scattering it freely forever.

15

The pure contralto sings in the organ loft,
The carpenter dresses his plank, the tongue of his foreplane whistles its wild ascending lisp,
The married and unmarried children ride home to their Thanksgiving dinner,
The pilot seizes the king-pin, he heaves down with a strong arm,
The mate stands braced in the whale-boat, lance and harpoon are ready,
The duck-shooter walks by silent and cautious stretches,
The deacons are ordain'd with cross'd hands at the altar,
The spinning-girl retreats and advances to the hum of the big wheel,
The farmer stops by the bars as he walks on a First-day loafe and looks at the oats and rye,
The lunatic is carried at last to the asylum a confirm'd case,
(He will never sleep any more as he did in the cot in his mother's bedroom;)
The jour printer with gray head and gaunt jaws works at his case,
He turns his quid of tobacco while his eyes blurr with the manuscript;
The malform'd limbs are tied to the surgeon's table,
What is removed drops horribly in a pail;
The quadroon girl is sold at the auction-stand, the drunkard nods by the bar-room stove,
The machinists rolls up his sleeves, the policeman travels his beat, the gate-keeper marks who pass,
The young fellow drives the express-wagon, (I love him, though I do not know him;)
The half-breed straps on his light boots to compete in the race,
The western turkey-shooting draws old and young, some lean on their rifles, some sit on logs,
Out from the crowd steps the marksman, takes his position, levels his piece;
The groups of newly-come immigrants cover the wharf or levee,
As the woolly-pates hoe in the sugar-field, the overseer views them from his saddle,
The bugle calls in the ball-room, the gentlemen run for their partners, the dancers bow to each other,
The youth lies awake in the cedar-roof'd garret and harks to the musical rain,
The Wolverine sets traps on the creek that helps fill the Huron,
The squaw wrapt in her yellow-hemm'd cloth is offering moccasins and bead-bags for sale,
The connoisseur peers along the exhibition-gallery with half-shut eyes bent sideways,
As the deck-hands make fast the steamboat the plank is thrown for the shore-going passengers,
The young sister holds out the skein while the elder sister winds it off in a ball, and stops now and then for the knots,

The one-year wife is recovering and happy having a week ago borne her first child,
The clean-hair'd Yankee girl works with her sewing-machine or in the factory or mill,
The paving-man leans on his two-handed rammer, the reporter's lead flies swiftly over the note-book, the sign-painter is lettering with blue and gold,
The canal boy trots on the tow-path, the book-keeper counts at his desk, the shoe-maker waxes his thread,
The conductor beats time for the band and all the performers follow him,
The child is baptized, the convert is making his first professions,
The regatta is spread on the bay, the race is begun, (how the white sails sparkle!)
The drover watching his drove sings out to them that would stray,
The pedler sweats with his pack on his back, (the purchaser higgling about the odd cent;)
The bride unrumples her white dress, the minute-hand of the clock moves slowly,
The opium-eater reclines with rigid head and just-open'd lips,
The prostitute draggles her shawl, her bonnet bobs on her tipsy and pimpled neck,
The crowd laugh at her blackguard oaths, the men jeer and wink to each other,
(Miserable! I do not laugh at your oaths nor jeer you;)
The President holding a cabinet council is surrounded by the great Secretaries,
On the piazza walk three matrons stately and friendly with twined arms,
The crew of the fish-smack pack repeated layers of halibut in the hold,
The Missourian crosses the plains toting his wares and his cattle,
As the fare-collector goes through the train he gives notice by the jingling of loose change,
The floor-men are laying the floor, the tinners are tinning the roof, the masons are calling for mortar,
In single file each shouldering his hod pass onward the laborers;
Seasons pursuing each other the indescribable crowd is gather'd, it is the fourth of Seventh-month, (what salutes of cannon and small arms!)
Seasons pursuing each other the plougher ploughs, the mower mows, and the winter grain falls in the ground;
Off on the lakes the pike-fisher watches and waits by the hole in the frozen surface,
The stumps stand thick round the clearing, the squatter strikes deep with his axe,
Flatboatmen make fast towards dusk near the cotton-wood or pecan-trees,
Coon-seekers go through the regions of the Red river or through those drain'd by the Tennessee, or through those of the Arkansas,
Torches shine in the dark that hangs on the Chattahooche or Altamahaw,[4]
Patriarchs sit at supper with sons and grandsons and great-grandsons around them,
In walls of adobie, in canvas tents, rest hunters and trappers after their day's sport,
The city sleeps and the country sleeps,
The living sleep for their time, the dead sleep for their time,
The old husband sleeps by his wife and the young husband sleeps by his wife;
And these tend inward to me, and I tend outward to them,
And such as it is to be of these more or less I am,
And of these one and all I weave the song of myself.

16

I am of old and young, of the foolish as much as the wise,
Regardless of others, ever regardful of others,
Maternal as well as paternal, a child as well as a man,
Stuff'd with the stuff that is coarse and stuff'd with the stuff that is fine,
One of the Nation of many nations, the smallest the same and the largest the same,
A Southerner soon as a Northerner, a planter nonchalant and hospitable down by the Oconee I live,
A Yankee bound my own way ready for trade, my joints the limberest joints on earth and the sternest joints on earth,
A Kentuckian walking the vale of the Elkhorn in my deer-skin leggings, a Louisianian or Georgian,

[4] Southern rivers.

A boatman over lakes or bays or along coasts, a Hoosier, Badger, Buckeye;
At home on Kanadian snow-shoes or up in the bush, or with fishermen off Newfoundland,
At home in the fleet of ice-boats, sailing with the rest and tacking,
At home on the hills of Vermont or in the woods of Maine, or the Texan ranch,
Comrade of Californians, comrade of free North-Westerners, (loving their big proportions,)
Comrade of raftsmen and coalmen, comrade of all who shake hands and welcome to drink and
meat,
A learner with the simplest, a teacher of the thoughtfullest,
A novice beginning yet experient of myriads of seasons,
Of every hue and caste am I, of every rank and religion,
A farmer, mechanic, artist, gentleman, sailor, quaker,
Prisoner, fancy-man, rowdy, lawyer, physician, priest.

I resist any thing better than my own diversity,
Breathe the air but leave plenty after me,
And am not stuck up, and am in my place.

(The moth and the fish-eggs are in their place,
The bright suns I see and the dark suns I cannot see are in their place,
The palpable is in its place and the impalpable is in its place.)

17

These are really the thoughts of all men in all ages and lands, they are not original with me,
If they are not yours as much as mine they are nothing, or next to nothing,
If they are not the riddle and the untying of the riddle they are nothing,
If they are not just as close as they are distant they are nothing.

This is the grass that grows wherever the land is and the water is,
This is the common air that bathes the globe.

18

With music strong I come, with my cornets and my drums,
I play not marches for accepted victors only, I play marches for conquer'd and slain persons.

Have you heard that it was good to gain the day?
I also say it is good to fall, battles are lost in the same spirit in which they are won.

I beat and pound for the dead,
I blow through my embouchures my loudest and gayest for them.

Vivas to those who have fail'd!
And to those whose war-vessels sank in the sea!
And to those themselves who sank in the sea!
And to all generals that lost engagements, and all overcome heroes!
And the numberless unknown heroes equal to the greatest heroes known!

19

This is the meal equally set, this the meat for natural hunger,
It is for the wicked just the same as the righteous, I make appointments with all,
I will not have a single person slighted or left away,
The kept-woman, sponger, thief, are hereby invited,
The heavy-lipp'd slave is invited, the venerealee is invited;
There shall be no difference between them and the rest.

This is the press of a bashful hand, this the float and odor of hair,
This is the touch of my lips to yours, this the murmur of yearning,
This the far-off depth and height reflecting my own face,
This the thoughtful merge of myself, and the outlet again.

Do you guess I have some intricate purpose?
Well I have, for the Fourth-month showers have, and the mica on the side of a rock has.

Do you take it I would astonish?
Does the daylight astonish? does the early redstart twittering through the woods?
Do I astonish more than they?

This hour I tell things in confidence,
I might not tell everybody, but I will tell you.

20

Who goes there? hankering, gross, mystical, nude;
How is it I extract strength from the beef I eat?

What is a man anyhow? what am I? what are you?

All I mark as my own you shall offset it with your own,
Else it were time lost listening to me.

I do not snivel that snivel the world over,
That months are vacuums and the ground but wallow and filth.

Whimpering and truckling fold with powders for invalids,[5] conformity goes to the fourth-remov'd,
I wear my hat as I please indoors or out.

Why should I pray? why should I venerate and be ceremonious?

Having pried through the strata, analyzed to a hair, counsel'd with doctors and calculated close,
I find no sweeter fat than sticks to my own bones.

In all people I see myself, none more and not one a barley-corn less,
And the good or bad I say of myself I say of them.

I know I am solid and sound,
To me the converging objects of the universe perpetually flow,
All are written to me, and I must get what the writing means.

I know I am deathless,
I know this orbit of mine cannot be swept by a carpenter's compass,
I know I shall not pass like a child's carlacue cut with a burnt stick at night.

I know I am august,
I do not trouble my spirit to vindicate itself or be understood,
I see that the elementary laws never apologize,
(I reckon I behave no prouder than the level I plant my house by, after all.)

I exist as I am, that is enough,
If no other in the world be aware I sit content,
And if each and all be aware I sit content.

[5] Physicians then folded doses of powdered medicine in small papers.

One world is aware and by the far largest to me, and that is myself,
And whether I come to my own to-day or in ten thousand or ten million years,
I can cheerfully take it now, or with equal cheerfulness I can wait.

My foothold is tenon'd and mortis'd in granite,
I laugh at what you call dissolution,
And I know the amplitude of time.

21

I am the poet of the Body and I am the poet of the Soul,
The pleasures of heaven are with me and the pains of hell are with me,
The first I graft and increase upon myself, the latter I translate into a new tongue.

I am the poet of the woman the same as the man,
And I say it is as great to be a woman as to be a man,
And I say there is nothing greater than the mother of men.

I chant the chant of dilation or pride,
We have had ducking and deprecating about enough,
I show that size is only development.

Have you outstript the rest? are you the President?
It is a trifle, they will more than arrive there every one, and still pass on.

I am he that walks with the tender and growing night,
I call to the earth and sea half-held by the night.

Press close bare-bosom'd night—press close magnetic nourishing night!
Night of south winds—night of the large few stars!
Still nodding night—mad naked summer night.

Smile O voluptuous cool-breath'd earth!
Earth of the slumbering and liquid trees!
Earth of departed sunset—earth of the mountains misty-topt!
Earth of the vitreous pour of the full moon just tinged with blue!
Earth of shine and dark mottling the tide of the river!
Earth of the limpid gray of clouds brighter and clearer for my sake!
Far-swooping elbow'd earth—rich apple-blossom'd earth!
Smile, for your lover comes.

Prodigal, you have given me love—therefore I to you give love!
O unspeakable passionate love.

22

You sea! I resign myself to you also—I guess what you mean,
I behold from the beach your crooked inviting fingers,
I believe you refuse to go back without feeling of me,
We must have a turn together, I undress, hurry me out of sight of the land,
Cushion me soft, rock me in billowy drowse,
Dash me with amorous wet, I can repay you.

Sea of stretch'd ground-swells,
Sea breathing broad and convulsive breaths,
Sea of the brine of life and of unshovell'd yet always-ready graves,

Howler and scooper of storms, capricious and dainty sea,
I am integral with you, I too am of one phase and of all phases.

Partaker of influx and efflux, I, extoller of hate and conciliation,
Extoller of armies and those that sleep in each others' arms.

I am he attesting sympathy,
(Shall I make my list of things in the house and skip the house that supports them?)

I am not the poet of goodness only, I do not decline to be the poet of wickedness also.

What blurt is this about virtue and about vice?
Evil propels me and reform of evil propels me, I stand indifferent,
My gait is no fault-finder's or rejecter's gait,
I moisten the roots of all that has grown.

Did you fear some scrofula out of the unflagging pregnancy?
Did you guess the celestial laws are yet to be work'd over and rectified?

I find one side a balance and the antipodal side a balance,
Soft doctrine as steady help as stable doctrine,
Thoughts and deeds of the present our rouse and early start.

This minute that comes to me over the past decillions,
There is no better than it and now.

What behaved well in the past or behaves well to-day is not such a wonder,
The wonder is always and always how there can be a mean man or an infidel.

23

Endless unfolding of words of ages!
And mine a word of the modern, the word En-Masse.

A word of the faith that never balks,
Here or henceforward it is all the same to me, I accept Time absolutely.

It alone is without flaw, it alone rounds and completes all,
That mystic baffling wonder alone completes all.

I accept Reality and dare not question it,
Materialism first and last imbuing.

Hurrah for positive science! long live exact demonstration!
Fetch stonecrop[6] mixt with cedar and branches of lilac,
This is the lexicographer, this the chemist, this made a grammar of the old cartouches,
These mariners put the ship through dangerous unknown seas,
This is the geologist, this works with the scalpel, and this is a mathematician.

Gentlemen, to you the first honors always!
Your facts are useful, and yet they are not my dwelling,
I but enter by them to an area of my dwelling.

Less the reminders of properties told my words,
And more the reminders they of life untold, and of freedom and extrication,

[6]A reference to folk medicine practices.

And make short account of neuters and geldings, and favor men and women fully equipt,
And beat the gong of revolt, and stop with fugitives and them that plot and conspire.

24

Walt Whitman, a kosmos, of Manhattan the son,
Turbulent, fleshy, sensual, eating, drinking and breeding,
No sentimentalist, no stander above men and women or apart from them,
No more modest than immodest.

Unscrew the locks from the doors!
Unscrew the doors themselves from their jambs!

Whoever degrades another degrades me,
And whatever is done or said returns at last to me.

Through me the afflatus surging and surging, through me the current and index.

I speak the pass-word primeval, I give the sign of democracy,
By God! I will accept nothing which all cannot have their counterpart of on the same terms.

Through me many long dumb voices,
Voices of the interminable generations of prisoners and slaves,
Voices of the diseas'd and despairing and of thieves and dwarfs,
Voices of cycles of preparation and accretion,
And of the threads that connect the stars, and of wombs and of the father-stuff,
And of the rights of them the others are down upon,
Of the deform'd, trivial, flat, foolish, despised,
Fog in the air, beetles rolling balls of dung.

Through me forbidden voices,
Voices of sexes and lusts, voices veil'd and I remove the veil,
Voices indecent by me clarified and transfigur'd.

I do not press my fingers across my mouth,
I keep as delicate around the bowels as around the head and heart,
Copulation is no more rank to me than death is.

I believe in the flesh and the appetites,
Seeing, hearing, feeling, are miracles, and each part and tag of me is a miracle.

Divine am I inside and out, and I make holy whatever I touch or am touch'd from,
The scent of these arm-pits aroma finer than prayer,
This head more than churches, bibles, and all the creeds.

If I worship one thing more than another it shall be the spread of my own body, or any part of it,
Translucent mould of me it shall be you!
Shaded ledges and rests it shall be you!
Firm masculine colter it shall be you!
Whatever goes to the tilth of me it shall be you!
You my rich blood! your milky stream pale strippings of my life!
Breast that presses against other breasts it shall be you!
My brain it shall be your occult convolutions!
Root of wash'd sweet-flag! timorous pond-snipe! nest of guarded duplicate eggs! it shall be you!
Mix'd tussled hay of head, beard, brawn, it shall be you!
Trickling sap of maple, fibre of manly wheat, it shall be you!
Sun so generous it shall be you!

Vapors lighting and shading my face it shall be you!
You sweaty brooks and dews it shall be you!
Winds whose soft-tickling genitals rub against me it shall be you!
Broad muscular fields, branches of live oak, loving lounger in my winding paths, it shall be you!
Hands I have taken, face I have kiss'd, mortal I have ever touch'd, it shall be you.

I dote on myself, there is that lot of me and all so luscious,
Each moment and whatever happens thrills me with joy,
I cannot tell how my ankles bend, nor whence the cause of my faintest wish,
Nor the cause of the friendship I emit, nor the cause of the friendship I take again.

That I walk up my stoop, I pause to consider if it really be,
A morning-glory at my window satisfies me more than the metaphysics of books.

To behold the day-break!
The little light fades the immense and diaphanous shadows,
The air tastes good to my palate.

Hefts of the moving world at innocent gambols silently rising, freshly exuding,
Scooting obliquely high and low.

Something I cannot see puts upward libidinous prongs,
Seas of bright juice suffuse heaven.

The earth by the sky staid with, the daily close of their junction,
The heav'd challenge from the east that moment over my head,
The mocking taunt, See then whether you shall be master!

25

Dazzling and tremendous how quick the sun-rise would kill me,
If I could not now and always send sun-rise out of me.

We also ascend dazzling and tremendous as the sun,
We found our own O my soul in the calm and cool of the daybreak.

My voice goes after what my eyes cannot reach,
With the twirl of my tongue I encompass worlds and volumes of worlds.

Speech is the twin of my vision, it is unequal to measure itself,
It provokes me forever, it says sarcastically,
Walt you contain enough, why don't you let it out then?

Come now I will not be tantalized, you conceive too much of articulation,
Do you not know O speech how the buds beneath you are folded?
Waiting in gloom, protected by frost,
The dirt receding before my prophetical screams,
I underlying causes to balance them at last,
My knowledge my live parts, it keeping tally with the meaning of all things,
Happiness, (which whoever hears me let him or her set out in search of this day.)

My final merit I refuse you, I refuse putting from me what I really am,
Encompass worlds, but never try to encompass me,
I crowd your sleekest and best by simply looking toward you.

Writing and talk do not prove me,
I carry the plenum of proof and every thing else in my face,
With the hush of my lips I wholly confound the skeptic.

26

Now I will do nothing but listen,
To accrue what I hear into this song, to let sounds contribute toward it.

I hear bravuras of birds, bustle of growing wheat, gossip of flames, clack of sticks cooking my meals,
I hear the sound I love, the sound of the human voice,
I hear all sounds running together, combined, fused or following,
Sounds of the city and sounds out of the city, sounds of the day and night,
Talkative young ones to those like them, the loud laugh of work-people at their meals,
The angry base of disjointed friendship, the faint tones of the sick,
The judge with hands tight to the desk, his pallid lips pronouncing a death-sentence,
The heave'e'yo of stevedores unlading ships by the wharves, the refrain of the anchor-lifters,
The ring of alarm-bells, the cry of fire, the whirr of swift-streaking engines and hose-carts with premonitory tinkles and color'd lights,
The steam-whistle, the solid roll of the train of approaching cars,
The slow march play'd at the head of the association marching two and two,
(They go to guard some corpse, the flag-tops are draped with black muslin.)

I hear the violoncello, ('tis the young man's heart's complaint,)
I hear the key'd cornet, it glides quickly in through my ears,
It shakes mad-sweet pangs through my belly and breast.

I hear the chorus, it is a grand opera,
Ah this indeed is music—this suits me.

A tenor large and fresh as the creation fills me,
The orbic flex of his mouth is pouring and filling me full.

I hear the train'd soprano (what work with hers is this?)
The orchestra whirls me wider than Uranus flies,
It wrenches such ardors from me I did not know I possess'd them,
It sails me, I dab with bare feet, they are lick'd by the indolent waves,
I am cut by bitter and angry hail, I lose my breath,
Steep'd amid honey'd morphine, my windpipe throttled in fakes of death,
At length let up again to feel the puzzle of puzzles,
And that we call Being.

27

To be in any form, what is that?
(Round and round we go, all of us, and ever come back thither,)
If nothing lay more develop'd the quahaug in its callous shell were enough.

Mine is no callous shell,
I have instant conductors all over me whether I pass or stop,
They seize every object and lead it harmlessly through me.

I merely stir, press, feel with my fingers, and am happy,
To touch my person to some one else's is about as much as I can stand.

28

Is this then a touch? quivering me to a new identity,
Flames and ether making a rush for my veins,
Treacherous tip of me reaching and crowding to help them,
My flesh and blood playing out lightning to strike what is hardly different from myself,
On all sides prurient provokers stiffening my limbs,
Straining the udder of my heart for its withheld drip,
Behaving licentious toward me, taking no denial,
Depriving me of my best as for a purpose,
Unbuttoning my clothes, holding me by the bare waist,
Deluding my confusion with the calm of the sunlight and pasture-fields,
Immodestly sliding the fellow-senses away,
They bribed to swap off with touch and go and graze at the edges of me,
No consideration, no regard for my draining strength or my anger,
Fetching the rest of the herd around to enjoy them a while,
Then all uniting to stand on a headland and worry me.

The sentries desert every other part of me,
They have left me helpless to a red marauder,
They all come to the headland to witness and assist against me.

I am given up by traitors,
I talk wildly, I have lost my wits, I and nobody else am the greatest traitor,
I went myself first to the headland, my own hands carried me there.

You villain touch! what are you doing? my breath is tight in its throat,
Unclench your floodgates, you are too much for me.

29

Blind loving wrestling touch, sheath'd hooded sharp-tooth'd touch!
Did it make you ache so, leaving me?

Parting track'd by arriving, perpetual payment of perpetual loan,
Rich showering rain, and recompense richer afterward.

Sprouts take and accumulate, stand by the curb prolific and vital,
Landscapes projected masculine, full-sized and golden.

30

All truths wait in all things,
They neither hasten their own delivery nor resist it,
They do not need the obstetric forceps of the surgeon,
The insignificant is as big to me as any,
(What is less or more than a touch?)

Logic and sermons never convince,
The damp of the night drives deeper into my soul.

(Only what proves itself to every man and woman is so,
Only what nobody denies it so.)

A minute and a drop of me settle my brain,
I believe the soggy clods shall become lovers and lamps,
And a compend of compends is the meat of a man or woman,
And a summit and flower there is the feeling they have for each other,

And they are to branch boundlessly out of that lesson until it becomes omnific,
And until one and all shall delight us, and we them.

31

I believe a leaf of grass is no less than the journey-work of the stars,
And the pismire is equally perfect, and a grain of sand, and the egg of the wren,
And the tree-toad is a chef-d'oeuvre for the highest,
And the running blackberry would adorn the parlors of heaven,
And the narrowest hinge in my hand puts to scorn all machinery,
And the cow crunching with depress'd head surpasses any statue,
And a mouse is miracle enough to stagger sextillions of infidels.

I find I incorporate gneiss, coal, long-threaded moss, fruits, grains, esculent roots,
And am stucco'd with quadrupeds and birds all over,
And have distanced what is behind me for good reasons,
But call any thing back again when I desire it.

In vain the speeding or shyness,
In vain the plutonic rocks send their old heat against my approach,
In vain the mastodon retreats beneath its own powder'd bones,
In vain objects stand leagues off and assume manifold shapes,
In vain the ocean settling in hollows and the great monsters lying low,
In vain the buzzard houses herself with the sky,
In vain the snake slides through the creepers and logs,
In vain the elk takes to the inner passes of the woods,
In vain the razor-bill'd auk sails far north to Labrador,
I follow quickly, I ascend to the nest in the fissure of the cliff.

32

I think I could turn and live with animals, they are so placid and self-contain'd,
I stand and look at them long and long.

They do not sweat and whine about their condition,
They do not lie awake in the dark and weep for their sins,
They do not make me sick discussing their duty to God,
Not one is dissatisfied, not one is demented with the mania of owning things,
Not one kneels to another, nor to his kind that lived thousands of years ago,
Not one is respectable or unhappy over the whole earth.

So they show their relations to me and I accept them,
They bring me tokens of myself, they evince them plainly in their possession.

I wonder where they get those tokens,
Did I pass that way huge times ago and negligently drop them?

Myself moving forward then and now and forever,
Gathering and showing more always and with velocity,
Infinite and omnigenous, and the like of these among them,
Not too exclusive toward the reachers of my remembrancers,
Picking out here one that I love, and now go with him on brotherly terms.

A gigantic beauty of a stallion, fresh and responsive to my caresses,
Head high in the forehead, wide between the ears,
Limbs glossy and supple, tail dusting the ground,
Eyes full of sparkling wickedness, ears finely cut, flexibly moving.

His nostrils dilate as my heels embrace him,
His well-built limbs tremble with pleasure as we race around and return.

I but use you a minute, then I resign you, stallion,
Why do I need your paces when I myself out-gallop them?
Even as I stand or sit passing faster than you.

33

Space and Time! now I see it is true, what I guess'd at,
What I guess'd when I loaf'd on the grass,
What I guess'd while I lay alone in my bed,
And again as I walk'd the beach under the paling stars of the morning.

My ties and ballasts leave me, my elbows rest in sea-gaps,
I skirt sierras, my palms cover continents,
I am afoot with my vision.

By the city's quadrangular houses—in log huts, camping with lumbermen,
Along the ruts of the turnpike, along the dry gulch and rivulet bed,
Weeding my onion-patch or hoeing rows of carrots and parsnips, crossing savannas, trailing in forests,
Prospecting, gold-digging, girdling the trees of a new purchase,
Scorch'd ankle-deep by the hot sand, hauling my boat down the shallow river,
Where the panther walks to and fro on a limb overhead, where the buck turns furiously at the hunter,
Where the rattlesnake suns his flabby length on a rock, where the otter is feeding on fish,
Where the alligator in his tough pimples sleeps by the bayou,
Where the black bear is searching for roots or honey, where the beaver pats the mud with his paddle-shaped tail;
Over the growing sugar, over the yellow-flower'd cotton plant, over the rice in its low moist field,
Over the sharp-peak'd farm house, with its scallop'd scum and slender shoots[7] from the gutters,
Over the western persimmon, over the long-leav'd corn, over the delicate blue-flower flax,
Over the white and brown buckwheat, a hummer and buzzer there with the rest,
Over the dusky green of the rye as it ripples and shades in the breeze;
Scaling mountains, pulling myself cautiously up, holding on by low scragged limbs,
Walking the path worn in the grass and beat through the leaves of the brush,
Where the quail is whistling betwixt the woods and the wheat-lot,
Where the bat flies in the Seventh-month eve, where the great gold-bug drops through the dark,
Where the brook puts out of the roots of the old tree and flows to the meadow,
Where cattle stand and shake away flies with the tremulous shuddering of their hides,
Where the cheese-cloth hangs in the kitchen, where andirons straddle the hearth-slab, where cobwebs fall in festoons from the rafters;
Where trip-hammers crash, where the press is whirling its cylinders,
Wherever the human heart beats with terrible throes under its ribs,
Where the pear-shaped balloon is floating aloft, (floating in it myself and looking composedly down,)
Where the life-car[8] is drawn on the slip-noose, where the heat hatches pale-green eggs in the dented sand,
Where the she-whale swims with her calf and never forsakes it,
Where the steam-ship trails hind-ways its long pennant of smoke,
Where the fin of the shark cuts like a black chip out of the water,
Where the half-burn'd brig is riding on unknown currents,
Where shells grow to her slimy deck, where the dead are corrupting below;

[7] Sediment washed down the roof by the rain.

[8] A watertight boat or chamber traveling on a rope and usually used to haul persons through surf too heavy for an open boat.

Where the dense-starr'd flag is borne at the head of the regiments,
Approaching Manhattan up by the long-stretching island,
Under Niagara, the cataract falling like a veil over my countenance,
Upon a door-step, upon the horse-block of hard wood outside,
Upon the race-course, or enjoying picnics or jigs or a good game of base-ball,
At he-festivals, with blackguard gibes, ironical license, bull-dances, drinking, laughter,
At the cider-mill tasting the sweets of the brown mash, sucking the juice through a straw,
At apple-peelings wanting kisses for all the red fruit I find,
At musters, beach-parties, friendly bees, huskings, house-raisings;
Where the mocking-bird sounds his delicious gurgles, cackles, screams, weeps,
Where the hay-rick stands in the barn-yard, where the dry-stalks are scatter'd, where the brood-cow waits in the hovel,
Where the bull advances to do his masculine work, where the stud to the mare, where the cock is treading the hen,
Where the heifers browse, where geese nip their food with short jerks,
Where sun-down shadows lengthen over the limitless and lonesome prairie,
Where herds of buffalo make a crawling spread of the square miles far and near,
Where the humming-bird shimmers, where the neck of the long-lived swan is curving and winding,
Where the laughing-gull scoots by the shore, where she laughs her near-human laugh,
Where bee-hives range on a gray bench in the garden half hid by the high weeds,
Where band-neck'd partridges roost in a ring on the ground with their heads out,
Where burial coaches enter the arch'd gates of a cemetery,
Where winter wolves bark amid wastes of snow and icicled trees,
Where the yellow-crown'd heron comes to the edge of the marsh at night and feeds upon small crabs,
Where the splash of swimmers and divers cools the warm noon,
Where the katy-did works her chromatic reed on the walnut-tree over the well,
Through patches of citrons and cucumbers with silver-wired leaves,
Through the salt-lick or orange glade, or under conical firs,
Through the gymnasium, through the curtain'd saloon, through the office or public hall;
Pleas'd with the native and pleas'd with the foreign, pleas'd with the new and old,
Pleas'd with the homely woman as well as the handsome,
Pleas'd with the quakeress as she puts off her bonnet and talks melodiously,
Pleas'd with the tune of the choir of the whitewash'd church,
Pleas'd with the earnest words of the sweating Methodist preacher, impress'd seriously at the camp-meeting;
Looking in at the shop-windows of Broadway the whole forenoon, flatting the flesh of my nose on the thick plate glass,
Wandering the same afternoon with my face turn'd up to the clouds, or down a lane or along the beach,
My right and left arms round the sides of two friends, and I in the middle;
Coming home with the silent and dark-cheek'd bush-boy, (behind me he rides at the drape of the day,)
Far from the settlements studying the print of animals' feet, or the moccasin print,
By the cot in the hospital reaching lemonade to a feverish patient,
Nigh the coffin'd corpse when all is still, examining with a candle;
Voyaging to every port to dicker and adventure,
Hurrying with the modern crowd as eager and fickle as any,
Hot toward one I hate, ready in my madness to knife him,
Solitary at midnight in my back yard, my thoughts gone from me a long while,
Walking the old hills of Judaea with the beautiful gentle God by my side,
Speeding through space, speeding through heaven and the stars,
Speeding amid the seven satellites and the broad ring, and the diameter of eighty thousand miles,
Speeding with tail'd meteors, throwing fire-balls like the rest,
Carrying the crescent child that carries its own full mother in its belly,
Storming, enjoying, planning, loving, cautioning,

Backing and filling, appearing and disappearing,
I tread day and night such roads.

I visit the orchards of spheres and look at the product,
And look at quintillions ripen'd and look at quintillions green.

I fly those flights of a fluid and swallowing soul,
My course runs below the soundings of plummets.

I help myself to material and immaterial,
No guard can shut me off, no law prevent me.

I anchor my ship for a little while only,
My messengers continually cruise away or bring their returns to me.

I go hunting polar furs and the seal, leaping chasms with a pike-pointed staff, clinging to topples of brittle and blue.

I ascend to the foretruck,
I take my place late at night in the crow's nest,
We sail the arctic sea, it is plenty light enough,
Through the clear atmosphere I stretch around on the wonderful beauty,
The enormous masses of ice pass me and I pass them, the scenery is plain in all directions,
The white-topt mountains show in the distance, I fling out my fancies toward them,
We are approaching some great battle-field in which we are soon to be engaged,
We pass the colossal outposts of the encampment, we pass with still feet and caution,
Or we are entering by the suburbs some vast and ruin'd city,
The blocks and fallen architecture more than all the living cities of the globe.

I am a free companion, I bivouac by invading watchfires,
I turn the bridegroom out of bed and stay with the bride myself,
I tighten her all night to my thighs and lips.

My voice is the wife's voice, the screech by the rail of the stairs,
They fetch my man's body up dripping and drown'd.

I understand the large hearts of heroes,
The courage of present times and all times,
How the skipper saw the crowded and rudderless wreck of the steam-ship, and Death chasing it up and down the storm,
How he knuckled tight and gave not back an inch, and was faithful of days and faithful of nights,
And chalk'd in large letters on a board, *Be of good cheer, we will not desert you;*
How he follow'd with them and tack'd with them three days and would not give it up,
How he saved the drifting company at last,
How the lank loose-gown'd women look'd when boated from the side of their prepared graves,
How the silent old-faced infants and the lifted sick, and the sharp-lipp'd unshaven men;
All this I swallow, it tastes good, I like it well, it becomes mine,
I am the man, I suffer'd, I was there.

The disdain and calmness of martyrs,
The mother of old, condemn'd for a witch, burnt with dry wood, her children gazing on,
The hounded slave that flags in the race, leans by the fence, blowing, cover'd with sweat,
The twinges that sting like needles his legs and neck, the murderous buckshot and the bullets,
All these I feel or am.

I am the hounded slave, I wince at the bite of the dogs,
Hell and despair are upon me, crack and again crack the marksmen,
I clutch the rails of the fence, my gore dribs, thinn'd with the ooze of my skin,
I fall on the weeds and stones,
The riders spur their unwilling horses, haul close,
Taunt my dizzy ears and beat me violently over the head with whip-stocks.

Agonies are one of my changes of garments,
I do not ask the wounded person how he feels, I myself become the wounded person,
My hurts turn livid upon me as I lean on a cane and observe.

I am the mash'd fireman with breast-bone broken,
Tumbling walls buried me in their debris,
Heat and smoke I inspired, I heard the yelling shouts of my comrades,
I heard the distant click of their picks and shovels,
They have clear'd the beams away, they tenderly lift me forth.

I lie in the night air in my red shirt, the pervading hush is for my sake,
Painless after all I lie exhausted but not so unhappy,
White and beautiful are the faces around me, the heads are bared of their firecaps,
The kneeling crowd fades with the light of the torches.

Distant and dead resuscitate,
They show as the dial or move as the hands of me, I am the clock myself.

I am an old artillerist, I tell of my fort's bombardment,
I am there again.

Again the long roll of the drummers,
Again the attacking cannon, mortars,
Again to my listening ears the cannon responsive.

I take part, I see and hear the whole,
The cries, curses, roar, the plaudits for well-aim'd shots,
The ambulanza slowly passing trailing its red drip,
Workmen searching after damages, making indispensable repairs,
The fall of grenades through the rent roof, the fan-shaped explosion,
The whizz of limbs, heads, stone, wood, iron, high in the air.

Again gurgles the mouth of my dying general, he furiously waves with his hand,
He gasps through the clot *Mind not me—mind—the entrenchments.*

34

Now I tell what I knew in Texas in my early youth,
(I tell not the fall of Alamo,
Not one escaped to tell the fall of Alamo,
The hundred and fifty are dumb yet at Alamo,)
'Tis the tale of the murder in cold blood of four hundred and twelve young men.

Retreating they had form'd in a hollow square with their baggage for breastworks,
Nine hundred lives out of the surrounding enemy's, nine times their number, was the price they took in advance.
Their colonel was wounded and their ammunition gone,
They treated for an honorable capitulation, receiv'd writing and seal, gave up their arms and march'd back prisoners of war.

They were the glory of the race of rangers,
Matchless with horse, rifle, song, supper, courtship,
Large, turbulent, generous, handsome, proud, and affectionate,
Bearded, sunburnt, drest in the free costume of hunters,
Not a single one over thirty years of age.

The second First-day morning they were brought out in squads and massacred, it was beautiful early summer,
The work commenced about five o'clock and was over by eight.

None obey'd the command to kneel,
Some made a mad helpless rush, some stood stark and straight,
A few fell at once, shot in the temple or heart, the living and dead lay together,
The maim'd and mangled dug in the dirt, the new-comers saw them there,
Some half-kill'd attempted to crawl away,
These were despatch'd with bayonets or batter'd with the blunts of muskets,
A youth not seventeen years old seiz'd his assassin till two more came to release him,
The three were all torn and cover'd with the boy's blood.

At eleven o'clock began the burning of the bodies;
That is the tale of the murder of the four hundred and twelve young men.

35

Would you hear of an old-time sea-fight?
Would you learn who won by the light of the moon and stars?
List to the yarn, as my grandmother's father the sailor told it to me.

Our foe was no skulk in his ship I tell you, (said he,)
His was the surly English pluck, and there is no tougher or truer, and never was, and never will be;
Along the lower'd eve he came horribly raking us.

We closed with him, the yards entangled, the cannon touch'd,
My captain lash'd fast with his own hands.

We had receiv'd some eighteen pound shots under the water,
On our lower-gun-deck two large pieces had burst at the first fire, killing all around and blowing up overhead.

Fighting at sun-down, fighting at dark,
Ten o'clock at night, the full moon well up, our leaks on the gain, and five feet of water reported,
The master-at-arms loosing the prisoners confined in the after-hold to give them a chance for themselves.

The transit to and from the magazine is now stopt by the sentinels,
They see so many strange faces they do not know whom to trust.

Our frigate takes fire,
The other asks if we demand quarter?
If our colors are struck and the fighting done?

Now I laugh content, for I hear the voice of my little captain,
We have not struck, he composedly cries, *we have just begun our part of the fighting.*

Only three guns are in use,
One is directed by the captain himself against the enemy's main-mast,
Two well serv'd with grape and canister silence his musketry and clear his decks.

The tops alone second the fire of this little battery, especially the main-top,
They hold out bravely during the whole of the action.

Not a moment's cease,
The leaks gain fast on the pumps, the fire eats toward the powder-magazine.

One of the pumps has been shot away, it is generally thought we are sinking.

Serene stands the little captain,
He is not hurried, his voice is neither high nor low,
His eyes give more light to us than our battle-lanterns.

Toward twelve there in the beams of the moon they surrender to us.

36

Stretch'd and still lies the midnight,
Two great hulls motionless on the breast of the darkness,
Our vessel riddled and slowly sinking, preparations to pass to the one we have conquer'd,
The captain on the quarter-deck coldly giving his orders through a countenance white as a sheet,
Near by the corpse of the child that serv'd in the cabin,
The dead face of an old salt with long white hair and carefully curl'd whiskers,
The flames spite of all that can be done flickering aloft and below,
The husky voices of the two or three officers yet fit for duty,
Formless stacks of bodies and bodies by themselves, dabs of flesh upon the masts and spars,
Cut of cordage, dangle of rigging, slight shock of the soothe of waves,
Black and impassive guns, litter of powder-parcels, strong scent,
A few large stars overhead, silent and mournful shining,
Delicate sniffs of sea-breeze, smells of sedgy grass and fields by the shore, death-messages given in charge to survivors,
The hiss of the surgeon's knife, the gnawing teeth of his saw,
Wheeze, cluck, swash of falling blood, short wild scream, and long, dull, tapering groan,
These so, these irretrievable.

37

You laggards there on guard! look to your arms!
In at the conquer'd doors they crowd! I am possess'd!
Embody all presences outlaw'd or suffering,
See myself in prison shaped like another man,
And feel the dull unintermitted pain.

For me the keepers of convicts shoulder the carbines and keep watch,
It is I let out in the morning and barr'd at night.

Not a mutineer walks handcuff'd to jail but I am handcuff'd to him and walk by his side,
(I am less the jolly one there, and more the silent one with sweat on my twitching lips.)

Not a youngster is taken for larceny but I go up too, and am tried and sentenced.

Not a cholera patient lies at the last gasp but I also lie at the last gasp,
My face is ash-color'd, my sinews gnarl, away from me people retreat.

Askers embody themselves in me and I am embodied in them,
I project my hat, sit shame-faced, and beg.

38

Enough! enough! enough!
Somehow I have been stunn'd. Stand back!
Give me a little time beyond my cuff'd head, slumbers, dreams, gaping,
I discover myself on the verge of a usual mistake.

That I could forget the mockers and insults!
That I could forget the trickling tears and the blows of the bludgeons and hammers!
That I could look with a separate look on my own crucifixion and bloody crowning.

I remember now,
I resume the overstaid fraction,
The grave of rock multiplies what has been confided to it, or to any graves,
Corpses rise, gashes heal, fastenings roll from me.

I troop forth replenish'd with supreme power, one of an average unending procession,
Inland and sea-coast we go, and pass all boundary lines,
Our swift ordinances on their way over the whole earth,
The blossoms we wear in our hats the growth of thousands of years.

Eleves,[9] I salute you! come forward!
Continue your annotations, continue your questionings.

39

The friendly and flowing savage, who is he?
Is he waiting for civilization, or past it and mastering it?

Is he some Southwesterner rais'd out-doors? is he Kanadian?
Is he from the Mississippi country? Iowa, Oregon, California?
The mountains? prairie-life, bush-life? or sailor from the sea?

Wherever he goes men and women accept and desire him,
They desire he should like them, touch them, speak to them, stay with them.

Behavior lawless as snow-flakes, words simple as grass, uncomb'd head, laughter, and naïveté,
Slow-stepping feet, common features, common modes and emanations,
They descend in new forms from the tips of his fingers,
They are wafted with the odor of his body or breath, they fly out of the glance of his eyes.

40

Flaunt of the sunshine I need not your bask—lie over!
You light surfaces only, I force surfaces and depths also.

Earth! you seem to look for something at my hands,
Say, old top-knot,[10] what do you want?
Man or woman, I might tell how I like you, but cannot,
And might tell what it is in me and what it is in you, but cannot,
And might tell that pining I have, that pulse of my nights and days.

[9] French for pupils or students.
[10] A comic term for an Indian, because of the tuft of hair on top of the head. The address here, of course, is not to an Indian.

Behold, I do not give lectures or a little charity,
When I give I give myself.

You there, impotent, loose in the knees,
Open your scarf'd chops till I blow grit within you,
Spread your palms and lift the flaps of your pockets,
I am not to be denied, I compel, I have stores plenty and to spare,
And any thing I have I bestow.

I do not ask who you are, that is not important to me,
You can do nothing and be nothing but what I will infold you.

To cotton-field drudge or cleaner of privies I lean,
On his right cheek I put the family kiss,
And in my soul I swear I never will deny him.

On women fit for conception I start bigger and nimbler babes,
(This day I am jetting the stuff of far more arrogant republics.)

To any one dying, thither I speed and twist the knob of the door,
Turn the bed-clothes toward the foot of the bed,
Let the physician and the priest go home.

I seize the descending man and raise him with resistless will,
O despairer, here is my neck,
By God, you shall not go down! hang your whole weight upon me.

I dilate you with tremendous breath, I buoy you up,
Every room of the house do I fill with an arm'd force,
Lovers of me, bafflers of graves.

Sleep—I and they keep guard all night,
Not doubt, not decease shall dare to lay finger upon you,
I have embraced you, and henceforth possess you to myself,
And when you rise in the morning you will find what I tell you is so.

41

I am he bringing help for the sick as they pant on their backs,
And for strong upright men I bring yet more needed help.

I heard what was said of the universe,
Heard it and heard it of several thousand years;
It is middling well as far as it goes—but is that all?

Magnifying and applying come I,
Outbidding at the start the old cautious hucksters,
Taking myself the exact dimensions of Jehovah,
Lithographing Kronos,[11] Zeus his son, and Hercules his grandson,
Buying drafts of Osiris, Isis, Belus, Brahma, Buddha,
In my portfolio placing Manito loose, Allah on a leaf, the crucifix engraved,
With Odin and the hideous-faced Mexitli and every idol and image,
Taking them all for what they are worth and not a cent more,
Admitting they were alive and did the work of their days,
(They bore mites as for unfledg'd birds who have now to rise and fly and sing for themselves,)

[11]The list of names suggests gods of all times, places, and religions from the Titan, Kronos, to an Algonquian nature spirit, Manito.

Accepting the rough deific sketches to fill out better in myself, bestowing them freely on each man and woman I see,
Discovering as much or more in a framer framing a house,
Putting higher claims for him there with his roll'd-up sleeves driving the mallet and chisel,
Not objecting to special revelations, considering a curl of smoke or a hair on the back of my hand just as curious as any revelation,
Lads ahold of fire-engines and hook-and-ladder ropes no less to me than the gods of the antique wars,
Minding their voices peal through the crash of destruction,
Their brawny limbs passing safe over charr'd laths, their white foreheads whole and unhurt out of the flames;
By the mechanic's wife with her babe at her nipple interceding for every person born,
Three scythes at harvest whizzing in a row from three lusty angels with shirts bagg'd out at their waists,
The snag-tooth'd hostler with red hair redeeming sins past and to come,
Selling all he possesses, travelling on foot to fee lawyers for his brother and sit by him while he is tried for forgery;
What was strewn in the amplest strewing the square rod about me, and not filling the square rod then,
The bull and the bug never worshipp'd half enough,
Dung and dirt more admirable than was dream'd,
The supernatural of no account, myself waiting my time to be one of the supremes,
The day getting ready for me when I shall do as much good as the best, and be as prodigious;
By my life-lumps! becoming already a creator,
Putting myself here and now to the ambush'd womb of the shadows.

42

A call in the midst of the crowd,
My own voice, orotund sweeping and final.

Come my children,
Come my boys and girls, my women, household and intimates,
Now the performer launches his nerve, he has pass'd his prelude on the reeds within.

Easily written loose-finger'd chords—I feel the thrum of your climax and close.

My head slues round on my neck,
Music rolls, but not from the organ,
Folks are around me, but they are no household of mine.

Ever the hard unsunk ground,
Ever the eaters and drinkers, ever the upward and downward sun, ever the air and the ceaseless tides,
Ever myself and my neighbors, refreshing, wicked, real,
Ever the old inexplicable query, ever that thorn'd thumb, that breath of itches and thirsts,
Ever the vexer's *hoot! hoot!* till we find where the sly one hides and bring him forth,
Ever love, ever the sobbing liquid of life,
Ever the bandage under the chin, ever the trestles of death.

Here and there with dimes on the eyes walking,
To feed the greed of the belly the brains liberally spooning,
Tickets buying, taking, selling, but in to the feast never once going,
Many sweating, ploughing, thrashing, and then the chaff for payment receiving,
A few idly owning, and they the wheat continually claiming.

This is the city and I am one of the citizens,
Whatever interests the rest interests me, politics, wars, markets, newspapers, schools,
The mayor and councils, banks, tariffs, steamships, factories, stocks, stores, real estate and personal estate.

The little plentiful manikins skipping around in collars and tail'd coats,
I am aware who they are, (they are positively not worms or fleas,)
I acknowledge the duplicates of myself, the weakest and shallowest is deathless with me,
What I do and say the same waits for them,
Every thought that flounders in me the same flounders in them.

I know perfectly well my own egotism,
Know my omnivorous lines and must not write any less,
And would fetch you whoever you are flush with myself.

Not words of routine this song of mine,
But abruptly to question, to leap beyond yet nearer bring;
This printed and bound book—but the printer and the printing-office boy?
The well-taken photographs—but your wife or friend close and solid in your arms?
The black ship mail'd with iron, her mighty guns in her turrets—but the pluck of the captain and engineers?
In the houses the dishes and fare and furniture—but the host and hostess, and the look out of their eyes?
The sky up there—yet here or next door, or across the way?
The saints and sages in history—but you yourself?
Sermons, creeds, theology—but the fathomless human brain,
And what is reason? and what is love? and what is life?

43

I do not despise you priests, all time, the world over,
My faith is the greatest of faiths and the least of faiths,
Enclosing worship ancient and modern and all between ancient and modern,
Believing I shall come again upon the earth after five thousand years,
Waiting responses from oracles, honoring the gods, saluting the sun,
Making a fetich of the first rock or stump, powowing with sticks in the circle of obis,[12]
Helping the llama or brahmin as he trims the lamps of the idols,
Dancing yet through the streets in a phallic procession, rapt and austere in the woods a gymnosophist,
Drinking mead from the skull-cup, to Shastas and Vedas admirant, minding the Koran,
Walking the teokallis, spotted with gore from the stone and knife, beating the serpent-skin drum,
Accepting the Gospels, accepting him that was crucified, knowing assuredly that he is divine,
To the mass kneeling or the puritan's prayer rising, or sitting patiently in a pew,
Ranting and frothing in my insane crisis, or waiting dead-like till my spirit arouses me,
Looking forth on pavement and land, or outside of pavement and land,
Belonging to the winders of the circuit of circuits.

One of that centripetal and centrifugal gang I turn and talk like a man leaving charges before a journey.

Down-hearted doubters dull and excluded,
Frivolous, sullen, moping, angry, affected, dishearten'd, atheistical,
I know every one of you, I know the sea of torment, doubt, despair and unbelief.

[12] "obis," "llama," etc.—references to a variety of religious practices.

How the flukes splash!
How they contort rapid as lightning, with spasms and spouts of blood!

Be at peace bloody flukes of doubters and sullen mopers,
I take my place among you as much as among any,
The past is the push of you, me, all, precisely the same,
And what is yet untried and afterward is for you, me, all, precisely the same.

I do not know what is untried and afterward,
But I know it will in its turn prove sufficient, and cannot fail.

Each who passes is consider'd, each who stops is consider'd, not a single one can it fail.

It cannot fail the young man who died and was buried,
Nor the young woman who died and was put by his side,
Nor the little child that peep'd in at the door, and then drew back and was never seen again,
Nor the old man who has lived without purpose, and feels it with bitterness worse than gall,
Nor him in the poor house tubercled by rum and the bad disorder,
Nor the numberless slaughter'd and wreck'd, nor the brutish koboo call'd the ordure of humanity,
Nor the sacs merely floating with open mouths for food to slip in,
Nor any thing in the earth, or down in the oldest graves of the earth,
Nor any thing in the myriads of spheres, nor the myriads of myriads that inhabit them,
Nor the present, nor the least wisp that is known.

44

It is time to explain myself—let us stand up.

What is known I strip away,
I launch all men and women forward with me into the Unknown.

The clock indicates the moment—but what does eternity indicate?

We have thus far exhausted trillions of winters and summers,
There are trillions ahead, and trillions ahead of them.

Births have brought us richness and variety,
And other births will bring us richness and variety.

I do not call one greater and one smaller,
That which fills its period and place is equal to any.

Were mankind murderous or jealous upon you, my brother, my sister?
I am sorry for you, they are not murderous or jealous upon me,
All has been gentle with me, I keep no account with lamentation,
(What have I to do with lamentation?)

I am an acme of things accomplish'd, and I an encloser of things to be.

My feet strike an apex of the apices of the stairs,
On every step bunches of ages, and larger bunches between the steps,
All below duly travel'd, and still I mount and mount.

Rise after rise bow the phantoms behind me,
Afar down I see the huge first Nothing, I know I was even there,
I waited unseen and always, and slept through the lethargic mist,
And took my time, and took no hurt from the fetid carbon.

Long I was hugg'd close—long and long.

Immense have been the preparations for me,
Faithful and friendly the arms that have help'd me.

Cycles ferried my cradle, rowing and rowing like cheerful boatmen,
For room to me stars kept aside in their own rings,
They sent influences to look after what was to hold me.

Before I was born out of my mother generations guided me,
My embryo has never been torpid, nothing could overlay it.

For it the nebula cohered to an orb,
The long slow strata piled to rest it on,
Vast vegetables gave it sustenance,
Monstrous sauroids transported it in their mouths and deposited it with care.

All forces have been steadily employ'd to complete and delight me,
Now on this spot I stand with my robust soul.

45

O span of youth! ever-push'd elasticity.
O manhood, balanced, florid and full.

My lovers suffocate me,
Crowding my lips, thick in the pores of my skin,
Jostling me through streets and public halls, coming naked to me at night,
Crying by day *Ahoy!* from the rocks of the river, swinging and chirping over my head,
Calling my name from flower-beds, vines, tangled underbrush,
Lighting on every moment of my life,
Bussing my body with soft balsamic busses,
Noiselessly passing handfuls out of their hearts and giving them to be mine.

Old age superbly rising! O welcome, ineffable grace of dying days!

Every condition promulges not only itself, it promulges what grows after and out of itself,
And the dark hush promulges as much as any.

I open my scuttle at night and see the far-sprinkled systems,
And all I see multiplied as high as I can cipher edge but the rim of the farther systems.

Wider and wider they spread, expanding, always expanding,
Outward and outward and forever outward.

My sun has his sun and round him obediently wheels,
He joins with his partners a group of superior circuit,
And greater sets follow, making specks of the greatest inside them.

There is no stoppage and never can be stoppage,
If I, you, and the worlds, and all beneath or upon their surfaces, were this moment reduced back
to a pallid float, it would not avail in the long run,
We should surely bring up again where we now stand,
And surely go as much farther, and then farther and farther.

A few quadrillions of eras, a few octillions of cubic leagues, do not hazard the span or make it impatient,
They are but parts, any thing is but a part.

See ever so far, there is limitless space outside of that,
Count ever so much, there is limitless time around that.

My rendezvous is appointed, it is certain,
The Lord will be there and wait till I come on perfect terms,
The great Camerado, the lover true for whom I pine will be there.

46

I know I have the best of time and space, and was never measured and never will be measured.

I tramp a perpetual journey, (come listen all!)
My signs are a rain-proof coat, good shoes, and a staff cut from the woods,
No friend of mine takes his ease in my chair,
I have no chair, no church, no philosophy,
I lead no man to a dinner-table, library, exchange,
But each man and each woman of you I lead upon a knoll,
My left hand hooking you round the waist,
My right hand pointing to landscapes of continents and the public road.

Not I, not any one else can travel that road for you,
You must travel it for yourself.

It is not far, it is within reach,
Perhaps you have been on it since you were born and did not know,
Perhaps it is everywhere on water and on land.

Shoulder your duds dear son, and I will mine, and let us hasten forth,
Wonderful cities and free nations we shall fetch as we go.

If you tire, give me both burdens, and rest the chuff[13] of your hand on my hip,
And in due time you shall repay the same service to me,
For after we start we never lie by again.
This day before dawn I ascended a hill and look'd at the crowded heaven,
And I said to my spirit *When we become the enfolders of those orbs, and the pleasure and knowledge of every thing in them, shall we be fill'd and satisfied then?*
And my spirit said *No, we but level that lift to pass and continue beyond.*

You are also asking me questions and I hear you,
I answer that I cannot answer, you must find out for yourself.

Sit a while dear son,
Here are biscuits to eat and here is milk to drink,
But as soon as you sleep and renew yourself in sweet clothes, I kiss you with a good-by kiss and open the gate for your egress hence.

Long enough have you dream'd contemptible dreams,
Now I wash the gum from your eyes,
You must habit yourself to the dazzle of the light and of every moment of your life.

[13] The fat part, cheek, or heel of the hand.

Long have you timidly waded holding a plank by the shore,
Now I will you to be a bold swimmer,
To jump off in the midst of the sea, rise again, nod to me, shout, and laughingly dash with your hair.

47

I am the teacher of athletes,
He that by me spreads a wider breast than my own proves the width of my own,
He most honors my style who learns under it to destroy the teacher.

The boy I love, the same becomes a man not through derived power, but in his own right,
Wicked rather than virtuous out of conformity or fear,
Fond of his sweetheart, relishing well his steak,
Unrequited love or a slight cutting him worse than sharp steel cuts,
First-rate to ride, to fight, to hit the bull's eye, to sail a skiff, to sing a song or play on the banjo,
Preferring scars and the beard and faces pitted with small-pox over all latherers,
And those well-tann'd to those that keep out of the sun.

I teach straying from me, yet who can stray from me?
I follow you whoever you are from the present hour,
My words itch at your ears till you understand them.

I do not say these things for a dollar or to fill up the time while I wait for a boat,
(It is you talking just as much as myself, I act as the tongue of you,
Tied in your mouth, in mine it begins to be loosen'd.)

I swear I will never again mention love or death inside a house,
And I swear I will never translate myself at all, only to him or her who privately stays with me in the open air.

If you would understand me go to the heights or water-shore,
The nearest gnat is an explanation, and a drop or motion of waves a key,
The maul, the oar, the hand-saw, second my words.

No shutter'd room or school can commune with me,
But roughs and little children better than they.

The young mechanic is closest to me, he knows me well,
The woodman that takes his axe and jug with him shall take me with him all day,
The farm-boy ploughing in the field feels good at the sound of my voice,
In vessels that sail my words sail, I go with fishermen and seamen and love them.

The soldier camp'd or upon the march is mine,
On the night ere the pending battle many seek me, and I do not fail them,
On that solemn night (it may be their last) those that know me seek me.

My face rubs to the hunter's face when he lies down alone in his blanket,
The driver thinking of me does not mind the jolt of his wagon,
The young mother and old mother comprehend me,
The girl and the wife rest the needle a moment and forget where they are,
They and all would resume what I have told them.

48

I have said that the soul is not more than the body,
And I have said that the body is not more than the soul,

And nothing, not God, is greater to one than one's self is,
And whoever walks a furlong without sympathy walks to his own funeral drest in his shroud,
And I or you pocketless of a dime may purchase the pick of the earth,
And to glance with an eye or show a bean in its pod confounds the learning of all times,
And there is no trade or employment but the young man following it may become a hero,
And there is no object so soft but it makes a hub for the wheel'd universe,
And I say to any man or woman, Let your soul stand cool and composed before a million universes.

And I say to mankind, Be not curious about God,
For I who am curious about each am not curious about God,
(No array of terms can say how much I am at peace about God and about death.)

I hear and behold God in every object, yet understand God not in the least,
Nor do I understand who there can be more wonderful than myself.

Why should I wish to see God better than this day?
I see something of God each hour of the twenty-four, and each moment then,
In the faces of men and women I see God, and in my own face in the glass,
I find letters from God dropt in the street, and every one is sign'd by God's name,
And I leave them where they are, for I know that wheresoe'er I go,
Others will punctually come for ever and ever.

49

And as to you Death, and you bitter hug of mortality, it is idle to try to alarm me.

To his work without flinching the accoucheur comes,
I see the elder-hand pressing receiving supporting,
I recline by the sills of the exquisite flexible doors,
And mark the outlet, and mark the relief and escape.

And as to you Corpse I think you are good manure, but that does not offend me,
I smell the white roses sweet-scented and growing,
I reach to the leafy lips, I reach to the polish'd breasts of melons.

And as to you Life I reckon you are the leavings of many deaths,
(No doubt I have died myself ten thousand times before.)

I hear you whispering there O stars of heaven,
O suns—O grass of graves—O perpetual transfers and promotions,
If you do not say any thing how can I say any thing?

Of the turbid pool that lies in the autumn forest,
Of the moon that descends the steeps of the soughing twilight,
Toss, sparkles of day and dusk—toss on the black stems that decay in the muck,
Toss to the moaning gibberish of the dry limbs.

I ascend from the moon, I ascend from the night,
I perceive that the ghastly glimmer is noonday sunbeams reflected,
And debouch to the steady and central from the offspring great or small.

50

There is that in me—I do not know what it is—but I know it is in me.

Wrench'd and sweaty—calm and cool then my body becomes,
I sleep—I sleep long.

I do not know it—it is without name—it is a word unsaid,
It is not in any dictionary, utterance, symbol.

Something it swings on more than the earth I swing on,
To it the creation is the friend whose embracing awakes me.

Perhaps I might tell more. Outlines! I plead for my brothers and sisters.

Do you see O my brothers and sisters?
It is not chaos or death—it is form, union, plan—it is eternal life—it is Happiness.

51

The past and present wilt—I have fill'd them, emptied them,
And proceed to fill my next fold of the future.

Listener up there! what have you to confide to me?
Look in my face while I snuff the sidle[14] of evening,
(Talk honestly, no one else hears you, and I stay only a minute longer.)
Do I contradict myself?
Very well then I contradict myself,
(I am large, I contain multitudes.)

I concentrate toward them that are nigh, I wait on the door-slab.

Who has done his day's work? who will soonest be through with his supper?
Who wishes to walk with me?

Will you speak before I am gone? will you prove already too late?

52

The spotted hawk swoops by and accuses me, he complains of my gab and my loitering.

I too am not a bit tamed, I too am untranslatable,
I sound my barbaric yawp over the roofs of the world.

The last scud of day holds back for me,
It flings my likeness after the rest and true as any on the shadow'd wilds,
It coaxes me to the vapor and the dusk.

I depart as air, I shake my white locks at the runaway sun,
I effuse my flesh in eddies, and drift it in lacy jags.

I bequeath myself to the dirt to grow from the grass I love,
If you want me again look for me under your boot-soles.

You will hardly know who I am or what I mean,
But I shall be good health to you nevertheless,
And filter and fibre your blood.

[14] To snuff out the last light of evening. "Sidle": side-light or sidelong.

Failing to fetch me at first keep encouraged,
Missing me one place search another,
I stop somewhere waiting for you.

1855, 1881

There Was a Child Went Forth

Like "Song of Myself," this poem was among the twelve of the first edition of *Leaves of Grass*. Here, quite evidently, Whitman is speaking of his own experience: his parents, the men and women in the streets, the wonderful life of nature inland and by the sea—the shaping influences on the child that went forth into the world.

There was a child went forth every day,
And the first object he look'd upon, that object he became,
And that object became part of him for the day or a certain part of the day,
Or for many years or stretching cycles of years.

The early lilacs became part of this child,
And grass and white and red morning-glories, and white and red clover, and the song of the phoebe-bird,
And the Third-month lambs and the sow's pink-faint litter, and the mare's foal and the cow's calf,
And the noisy brood of the barnyard or by the mire of the pond-side,
And the fish suspending themselves so curiously below there, and the beautiful curious liquid,
And the water-plants with their graceful flat heads, all became part of him.

The field-sprouts of Fourth-month and Fifth-month became part of him,
Winter-grain sprouts and those of the light-yellow corn, and the esculent roots of the garden,
And the apple-trees cover'd with blossoms and the fruit afterward, and wood-berries, and the commonest weeds by the road,
And the old drunkard staggering home from the outhouse of the tavern whence he had lately risen,
And the schoolmistress that pass'd on her way to the school,
And the friendly boys that pass'd, and the quarrelsome boys,
And the tidy and fresh-cheek'd girls, and the barefoot negro boy and girl,
And all the changes of city and country wherever he went.

His own parents, he that had father'd him and she that had conceiv'd him in her womb and birth'd him,
They gave this child more of themselves than that,
They gave him afterward every day, they became part of him.

The mother at home quietly placing the dishes on the supper-table,
The mother with mild words, clean her cap and gown, a wholesome odor falling off her person and clothes as she walks by,
The father, strong, self-sufficient, manly, mean, anger'd, unjust,
The blow, the quick loud word, the tight bargain, the crafty lure,
The family usages, the language, the company, the furniture, the yearning and swelling heart,
Affection that will not be gainsay'd, the sense of what is real, the thought if after all it should prove unreal,
The doubts of day-time and the doubts of night-time, the curious whether and how,
Whether that which appears so is so, or is it all flashes and specks?
Men and women crowding fast in the streets, if they are not flashes and specks what are they?
The streets themselves and the façades of houses, and goods in the windows,
Vehicles, teams, the heavy-plank'd wharves, the huge crossing at the ferries,
The village on the highland seen from afar at sunset, the river between,

Shadows, aureola and mist, the light falling on roofs and gables of white or brown two miles off,
The schooner near by sleepily dropping down the tide, the little boat slack-tow'd astern,
The hurrying tumbling waves, quick-broken crests, slapping,
The strata of color'd clouds, the long bar of maroon-tint away solitary by itself, the spread of purity it lies motionless in,
The horizon's edge, the flying sea-crow, the fragrance of salt marsh and shore mud,
These became part of that child who went forth every day, and who now goes, and will always go forth every day.

1855, 1871

The Sleepers

"The Sleepers," another of the twelve poems in the first edition of *Leaves of Grass,* is a deeply personal, confessional poem—a night journey in which the confused and "ill-assorted" adolescent self moves through sexual awareness toward wholeness and maturity. "The landscape, in which obscure symbols disguise the latent content and the universal taboos, and in which the protagonist undergoes sudden and seemingly inexplicable personal and sexual transformations, is dreamlike, even surrealistic at times, because it evokes vague memories of almost forgotten rites of cultures which provided meaningful communal ceremonies to celebrate the individual's journey to adulthood, as a modern industrial society does not. Unlike a dream, the poem does not end inconclusively, but as in a rite of adolescence the protagonist experiences the terrors of anticipated initiation, with its physical pain, as well as the attendant joys of entrance into manhood and into society—except that the drama in Whitman's poem, of necessity, is played out in the protagonist's consciousness, and that the conclusion is sublimation." (Edwin H. Miller)

1

I wander all night in my vision,
Stepping with light feet, swiftly and noiselessly stepping and stopping,
Bending with open eyes over the shut eyes of sleepers,
Wandering and confused, lost to myself, ill-assorted, contradictory,
Pausing, gazing, bending, and stopping.

How solemn they look there, stretch'd and still,
How quiet they breathe, the little children in their cradles.

The wretched features of ennuyés, the white features of corpses, the livid faces of drunkards, the sick-gray faces of onanists,
The gash'd bodies on battle-fields, the insane in their strong-door'd rooms, the sacred idiots, the new-born emerging from gates, and the dying emerging from gates,
The night pervades them and infolds them.

The married couple sleep calmly in their bed, he with his palm on the hip of the wife, and she with her palm on the hip of the husband,
The sisters sleep lovingly side by side in their bed,
The men sleep lovingly side by side in theirs,
And the mother sleeps with her little child carefully wrapt.

The blind sleep, and the deaf and dumb sleep,
The prisoner sleeps well in the prison, the runaway son sleeps,
The murderer that is to be hung next day, how does he sleep?
And the murder'd person, how does he sleep?

The female that loves unrequited sleeps,
And the male that loves unrequited sleeps,
The head of the money-maker that plotted all day sleeps,
And the enraged and treacherous dispositions, all, all sleep.

I stand in the dark with drooping eyes by the worst-suffering and the most restless,
I pass my hands soothingly to and fro a few inches from them,
The restless sink in their beds, they fitfully sleep.

Now I pierce the darkness, new beings appear,
The earth recedes from me into the night,
I saw that it was beautiful, and I see that what is not the earth is beautiful.

I go from bedside to bedside, I sleep close with the other sleepers each in turn,
I dream in my dream all the dreams of the other dreamers,
And I become the other dreamers.

I am a dance—play up there! the fit is whirling me fast!

I am the ever-laughing—it is new moon and twilight,
I see the hiding of douceurs,[1] I see nimble ghosts whichever way I look,
Cache and cache again deep in the ground and sea, and where it is neither ground nor sea.

Well do they do their jobs those journeymen divine,
Only from me can they hide nothing, and would not if they could,
I reckon I am their boss and they make me a pet besides,
And surround me and lead me and run ahead when I walk,
To lift their cunning covers to signify me with stretch'd arms, and resume the way;
Onward we move, a gay gang of blackguards! with mirth-shouting music and wild-flapping pennants of joy!

I am the actor, the actress, the voter, the politician,
The emigrant and the exile, the criminal that stood in the box,
He who has been famous and he who shall be famous after to-day,
The stammerer, the well-formed person, the wasted or feeble person.

I am she who adorn'd herself and folded her hair expectantly,
My truant lover has come, and it is dark.

Double yourself and receive me darkness,
Receive me and my lover too, he will not let me go without him.

I roll myself upon you as upon a bed, I resign myself to the dusk.

He whom I call answers me and takes the place of my lover,
He rises with me silently from the bed.

Darkness, you are gentler than my lover, his flesh was sweaty and panting,
I feel the hot moisture yet that he left me.

My hands are spread forth, I pass them in all directions,
I would sound up the shadowy shore to which you are journeying.

Be careful darkness! already what was it touch'd me?
I thought my lover had gone, else darkness and he are one,
I hear the heart-beat, I follow, I fade away.

2

I descend my western course, my sinews are flaccid,
Perfume and youth course through me and I am their wake.

[1] Sweets.

It is my face yellow and wrinkled instead of the old woman's,
I sit low in a straw-bottom chair and carefully darn my grandson's stockings.

It is I too, the sleepless widow looking out on the winter midnight,
I see the sparkles of starshine on the icy and pallid earth.

A shroud I see and I am the shroud, I wrap a body and lie in the coffin,
It is dark here under ground, it is not evil or pain here, it is blank here, for reasons.

(It seems to me that every thing in the light and air ought to be happy,
Whoever is not in his coffin and the dark grave let him know he has enough.)

3

I see a beautiful gigantic swimmer swimming naked through the eddies of the sea,
His brown hair lies close and even to his head, he strikes out with courageous arms, he urges himself with his legs,

I see his white body, I see his undaunted eyes,
I hate the swift-running eddies that would dash him head-foremost on the rocks.

What are you doing you ruffianly red-trickled waves?
Will you kill the courageous giant? will you kill him in the prime of his middle age?

Steady and long he struggles,
He is baffled, bang'd, bruis'd, he holds out while his strength holds out,
The slapping eddies are spotted with his blood, they bear him away, they roll him, swing him, turn him,
His beautiful body is borne in the circling eddies, it is continually bruis'd on rocks,
Swiftly and out of sight is borne the brave corpse.

4

I turn but do not extricate myself,
Confused, a past-reading, another, but with darkness yet.

The beach is cut by the razory ice-wind, the wreck-guns sound.
The tempest lulls, the moon comes floundering through the drifts.

I look where the ship helplessly heads end on, I hear the burst as she strikes, I hear the howls of dismay, they grow fainter and fainter.

I cannot aid with my wringing fingers,
I can but rush to the surf and let it drench me and freeze upon me.

I search with the crowd, not one of the company is wash'd to us alive,
In the morning I help pick up the dead and lay them in rows in a barn.

5

Now of the older war-days, the defeat at Brooklyn,
Washington stands inside the lines, he stands on the intrench'd hills amid a crowd of officers,
His face is cold and damp, he cannot repress the weeping drops,
He lifts the glass perpetually to his eyes, the color is blanch'd from his cheeks,
He sees the slaughter of the southern braves confided to him by their parents.

The same at last and at last when peace is declared,
He stands in the room of the old tavern, the well-belov'd soldiers all pass through,

The officers speechless and slow draw near in their turns,
The chief encircles their necks with his arm and kisses them on the cheek,
He kisses lightly the wet cheeks one after another, he shakes hands and bids good-by to the army.

6

Now what my mother told me one day as we sat at dinner together,
Of when she was a nearly grown girl living home with her parents on the old homestead.

A red squaw came one breakfast-time to the old homestead,
On her back she carried a bundle of rushes for rush-bottoming chairs,
Her hair, straight, shiny, coarse, black, profuse, half-envelop'd her face,
Her step was free and elastic, and her voice sounded exquisitely as she spoke.

My mother look'd in delight and amazement at the stranger,
She look'd at the freshness of her tall-borne face and full and pliant limbs,
The more she look'd upon her she loved her,
Never before had she seen such wonderful beauty and purity,
She made her sit on a bench by the jamb of the fireplace, she cook'd food for her,
She had no work to give her, but she gave her remembrance and fondness.

The red squaw staid all the forenoon, and toward the middle of the afternoon she went away,
O my mother was loth to have her go away,
All the week she thought of her, she watch'd for her many a month,
She remember'd her many a winter and many a summer,
But the red squaw never came nor was heard of there again.

7

A show of the summer softness—a contact of something unseen—an amour of the light and air,
I am jealous and overwhelm'd with friendliness,
And will go gallivant with the light and air myself.

O love and summer, you are in the dreams and in me,
Autumn and winter are in the dreams, the farmer goes with his thrift,
The droves and crops increase, the barns are well-fill'd.

Elements merge in the night, ships make tacks in the dreams,
The sailor sails, the exile returns home,
The fugitive returns unharm'd, the immigrant is back beyond months and years,
The poor Irishman lives in the simple house of his childhood with the well-known neighbors and faces,
They warmly welcome him, he is barefoot again, he forgets he is well off,
The Dutchman voyages home, and the Scotchman and Welshman voyage home, and the native of the Mediterranean voyages home,
To every port of England, France, Spain, enter well-fill'd ships,
The Swiss foots it toward his hills, the Prussian goes his way, the Hungarian his way, and the Pole his way,
The Swede returns, and the Dane and Norwegian return.

The homeward bound and the outward bound,
The beautiful lost swimmer, the ennuyé, the onanist, the female that loves unrequited, the money-maker,
The actor and actress, those through with their parts and those waiting to commence,
The affectionate boy, the husband and wife, the voter, the nominee that is chosen and the nominee that has fail'd,
The great already known and the great any time after to-day,

The stammerer, the sick, the perfect-form'd, the homely,
The criminal that stood in the box, the judge that sat and sentenced him, the fluent lawyers, the jury, the audience,
The laugher and weeper, the dancer, the midnight widow, the red squaw,
The consumptive, the erysipalite, the idiot, he that is wrong'd,
The antipodes, and every one between this and them in the dark,
I swear they are averaged now—one is no better than the other,
The night and sleep have liken'd them and restored them.

I swear they are all beautiful,
Every one that sleeps is beautiful, every thing in the dim light is beautiful,
The wildest and bloodiest is over, and all is peace.

Peace is always beautiful,
The myth of heaven indicates peace and night.

The myth of heaven indicates the soul,
The soul is always beautiful, it appears more or it appears less, it comes or it lags behind,
It comes from its embower'd garden and looks pleasantly on itself and encloses the world,
Perfect and clean the genitals previously jetting, and perfect and clean the womb cohering,
The head well-grown proportion'd and plumb, and the bowels and joints proportion'd and plumb.

The soul is always beautiful,
The universe is duly in order, every thing is in its place,
What has arrived is in its place and what waits shall be in its place,
The twisted skull waits, the watery or rotten blood waits,
The child of the glutton or venerealee waits long, and the child of the drunkard waits long, and the drunkard himself waits long,
The sleepers that lived and died wait, the far advanced are to go on in their turns, and the far behind are to come on in their turns,
The diverse shall be no less diverse, but they shall flow and unite—they unite now.

8

The sleepers are very beautiful as they lie unclothed,
They flow hand in hand over the whole earth from east to west as they lie unclothed,
The Asiatic and African are hand in hand, the European and American are hand in hand,
Learn'd and unlearn'd are hand in hand, and male and female are hand in hand,
The bare arm of the girl crosses the bare breast of her lover, they press close without lust, his lips press her neck,
The father holds his grown or ungrown son in his arms with measureless love, and the son holds the father in his arms with measureless love,
The white hair of the mother shines on the white wrist of the daughter,
The breath of the boy goes with the breath of the man, friend is inarm'd by friend,
The scholar kisses the teacher and the teacher kisses the scholar, the wrong'd is made right,
The call of the slave is one with the master's call, and the master salutes the slave,
The felon steps forth from the prison, the insane becomes sane, the suffering of sick persons is reliev'd,
The sweatings and fevers stop, the throat that was unsound is sound, the lungs of the consumptive are resumed, the poor distress'd head is free,
The joints of the rheumatic move as smoothly as ever, and smoother than ever,
Stiflings and passages open, the paralyzed become supple,
The swell'd and convuls'd and congested awake to themselves in condition,
They pass the invigoration of the night and the chemistry of the night, and awake.

I too pass from the night,
I stay a while away O night, but I return to you again and love you.

Why should I be afraid to trust myself to you?
I am not afraid, I have been well brought forward by you,
I love the rich running day, but I do not desert her in whom I lay so long,
I know not how I came of you and I know not where I go with you, but I know I came well and shall go well.

I will stop only a time with the night, and rise betimes,
I will duly pass the day O my mother, and duly return to you.

1855, 1881

Crossing Brooklyn Ferry

Like "Song of Myself," this poem makes no pretence of developing a logical progress of ideas. But it does have more form. There is a single scene: New York harbor. A single situation: the poet is crossing on the ferry between Manhattan and Brooklyn. And a single dominant idea: the identity of all men—those living in the present and those who will follow in the future. The shared experience of place establishes continuity and the possibility of communication between the poet and others to come after him; their common humanity provides a basic identity; and the inner, spiritual reality Whitman speaks of also joins them.

1

Flood-tide below me! I see you face to face!
Clouds of the west—sun there half an hour high—I see you also face to face.

Crowds of men and women attired in the usual costumes, how curious you are to me!
On the ferry-boats the hundreds and hundreds that cross, returning home, are more curious to me than you suppose,
And you that shall cross from shore to shore years hence are more to me, and more in my meditations, than you might suppose.

2

The impalpable sustenance of me from all things at all hours of the day,
The simple, compact, well-join'd scheme, myself disintegrated, every one disintegrated yet part of the scheme,
The similitudes of the past and those of the future,
The glories strung like beads on my smallest sights and hearings, on the walk in the street and the passage over the river,
The current rushing so swiftly and swimming with me far away,
The others that are to follow me, the ties between me and them,
The certainty of others, the life, love, sight, hearing of others.

Others will enter the gates of the ferry and cross from shore to shore,
Others will watch the run of the flood-tide,
Others will see the shipping of Manhattan north and west, and the heights of Brooklyn to the south and east,
Others will see the islands large and small;
Fifty years hence, others will see them as they cross, the sun half an hour high,
A hundred years hence, or ever so many hundred years hence, others will see them,
Will enjoy the sunset, the pouring-in of the flood-tide, the falling-back to the sea of the ebb-tide.

3

It avails not, time nor place—distance avails not,
I am with you, you men and women of a generation, or ever so many generations hence,

Just as you feel when you look on the river and sky, so I felt,
Just as any of you is one of a living crowd, I was one of a crowd,
Just as you are refresh'd by the gladness of the river and the bright flow, I was refresh'd,
Just as you stand and lean on the rail, yet hurry with the swift current, I stood yet was hurried,
Just as you look on the numberless masts of ships and the thick-stemm'd pipes of steamboats, I look'd.

I too many and many a time cross'd the river of old,
Watched the Twelfth-month sea-gulls, saw them high in the air floating with motionless wings, oscillating their bodies,
Saw how the glistening yellow lit up parts of their bodies and left the rest in strong shadow,
Saw the slow-wheeling circles and the gradual edging toward the south,
Saw the reflection of the summer sky in the water,
Had my eyes dazzled by the shimmering track of beams,
Look'd at the fine centrifugal spokes of light round the shape of my head in the sunlit water,
Look'd on the haze on the hills southward and south-westward,
Look'd on the vapor as it flew in fleeces tinged with violet,
Look'd toward the lower bay to notice the vessels arriving,
Saw their approach, saw aboard those that were near me,
Saw the white sails of schooners and sloops, saw the ships at anchor,
The sailors at work in the rigging or out astride the spars,
The round masts, the swinging motion of the hulls, the slender serpentine pennants,
The large and small steamers in motion, the pilots in their pilot-houses,
The white wake left by the passage, the quick tremulous whirl of the wheels,
The flags of all nations, the falling of them at sunset,
The scallop-edged waves in the twilight, the ladled cups, the frolicsome crests and glistening,
The stretch afar growing dimmer and dimmer, the gray walls of the granite storehouses by the docks,
On the river the shadowy group, the big steam-tug closely flank'd on each side by the barges, the hay-boat, the belated lighter,
On the neighboring shore the fires from the foundry chimneys burning high and glaringly into the night,
Casting their flicker of black contrasted with wild red and yellow light over the tops of houses and down into the clefts of streets.

4

These and all else were to me the same as they are to you,
I loved well those cities, loved well the stately and rapid river,
The men and women I saw were all near to me,
Others the same—others who look back on me because I look'd forward to them,
(The time will come, though I stop here to-day and to-night.)

5

What is it then between us?
What is the count of the scores or hundreds of years between us?

Whatever it is, it avails not—distance avails not, and place avails not,
I too lived, Brooklyn of ample hills was mine,
I too walk'd the streets of Manhattan island, and bathed in the waters around it,
I too felt the curious abrupt questionings stir within me,
In the day among crowds of people sometimes they came upon me,
In my walks home late at night or as I lay in my bed they came upon me,
I too had been struck from the float forever held in solution,
I too had receiv'd identity by my body,
That I was I knew was of my body, and what I should be I knew I should be of my body.

6

It is not upon you alone the dark patches fall,
The dark threw its patches down upon me also,
The best I had done seem'd to me blank and suspicious,
My great thoughts as I supposed them, were they not in reality meagre?
Nor is it you alone who know what it is to be evil,
I am he who knew what it was to be evil,
I too knitted the old knot of contrariety,
Blabb'd, blush'd, resented, lied, stole, grudg'd,
Had guile, anger, lust, hot wishes I dared not speak,
Was wayward, vain, greedy, shallow, sly, cowardly, malignant,
The wolf, the snake, the hog, not wanting in me,
The cheating look, the frivolous word, the adulterous wish, not wanting,
Refusals, hates, postponements, meanness, laziness, none of these wanting,
Was one with the rest, the days and haps of the rest,
Was call'd my nighest name by clear loud voices of young men as they saw me approaching or passing,
Felt their arms on my neck as I stood, or the negligent leaning of their flesh against me as I sat,
Saw many I loved in the street or ferry-boat or public assembly, yet never told them a word,
Lived the same life with the rest, the same old laughing, gnawing, sleeping,
Play'd the part that still looks back on the actor or actress,
The same old role, the role that is what we make it, as great as we like,
Or as small as we like, or both great and small.

7

Closer yet I approach you,
What thought you have of me now, I had as much of you—I laid in my stores in advance,
I consider'd long and seriously of you before you were born.

Who was to know what should come home to me?
Who knows but I am enjoying this?
Who knows, for all the distance, but I am as good as looking at you now, for all you cannot see me?

8

Ah, what can ever be more stately and admirable to me than mast-hemm'd Manhattan?
River and sunset and scallop-edg'd waves of flood-tide?
The sea-gulls oscillating their bodies, the hay-boat in the twilight, and the belated lighter?
What gods can exceed these that clasp me by the hand, and with voices I love call me promptly and loudly by my nighest name as I approach?
What is more subtle than this which ties me to the woman or man that looks in my face?
Which fuses me into you now, and pours my meaning into you?

We understand then do we not?
What I promis'd without mentioning it, have you not accepted?
What the study could not teach—what the preaching could not accomplish is accomplish'd, is it not?

9

Flow on, river! flow with the flood-tide, and ebb with the ebb-tide!
Frolic on, crested and scallop-edg'd waves!
Gorgeous clouds of the sunset! drench with your splendor me, or the men and women generations after me!
Cross from shore to shore, countless crowds of passengers!

Stand up, tall masts of Mannahatta! stand up, beautiful hills of Brooklyn!
Throb, baffled and curious brain! throw out questions and answers!
Suspend here and everywhere, eternal float of solution!
Gaze, loving and thirsting eyes, in the house or street or public assembly!
Sound out, voices of young men! loudly and musically call me by my nighest name!
Live, old life! play the part that looks back on the actor or actress!
Play the old role, the role that is great or small according as one makes it!
Consider, you who peruse me, whether I may not in unknown ways be looking upon you;
Be firm, rail over the river, to support those who lean idly, yet haste with the hasting current;
Fly on, sea-birds! fly sideways, or wheel in large circles high in the air;
Receive the summer sky, you water, and faithfully hold it till all downcast eyes have time to take it
 from you!
Diverge, fine spokes of light, from the shape of my head, or any one's head, in the sunlit water!
Come on, ships from the lower bay! pass up or down, white-sail'd schooners, sloops, lighters!
Flaunt away, flags of all nations! be duly lower'd at sunset!
Burn high your fires, foundry chimneys! cast black shadows at nightfall! cast red and yellow light
 over the tops of the houses!
Appearances, now or henceforth, indicate what you are,
You necessary film, continue to envelop the soul,
About my body for me, and your body for you, be hung our divinest aromas,
Thrive, cities—bring your freight, bring your shows, ample and sufficient rivers,
Expand, being than which none else is perhaps more spiritual,
Keep your places, objects than which none else is more lasting.

You have waited, you always wait, you dumb, beautiful ministers,
We receive you with free sense at last, and are insatiate henceforward,
Not you any more shall be able to foil us, or withhold yourselves from us,
We use you, and do not cast you aside—we plant you permanently within us,
We fathom you not—we love you—there is perfection in you also,
You furnish your parts toward eternity,
Great or small, you furnish your parts toward the soul.

1856, 1881

Out of the Cradle Endlessly Rocking

Here we have Whitman at his best, full of his theme, concentrating on an artistic aim from beginning to end, rich in images, sounds, and symbolic meanings, shaping his verse patterns to fit the sense. Psychologically, the poem relates itself to the group of sex poems, "Children of Adam." It is a reminiscence of a boy's inner turmoil, with meanings infused by maturity.

The scene is the seashore of Long Island (Whitman liked its Indian name Paumanok). The time is May to September (he preferred the Quaker Fifth-Month, Ninth-Month). The "characters" are the boy, a pair of mocking-birds, and the sea ("fierce old Mother"). An introduction, a periodic sentence of 22 lines (with the epic predicate "I . . . sing"), lightly touches upon the happenings and significance we are to find in the poem. The poem proper is in two parts. The first part, extending to line 143, gives the story of the birds. The rest, line 143 to the end, interprets the influence of the male bird's song on the "outsetting bard."

Out of the cradle endlessly rocking,
Out of the mocking-bird's throat, the musical shuttle,
Out of the Ninth-month midnight,
Over the sterile sands and the fields beyond, where the child leaving his bed wander'd alone,
 bareheaded, barefoot,
Down from the shower'd halo,
Up from the mystic play of shadows twining and twisting as if they were alive,
Out from the patches of briers and blackberries,
From the memories of the bird that chanted to me,
From your memories sad brother, from the fitful risings and fallings I heard,
From under that yellow half-moon late-risen and swollen as if with tears,

From those beginning notes of yearning and love there in the mist,
From the thousand responses of my heart never to cease,
From the myriad thence-arous'd words
From the word stronger and more delicious than any,
From such as now they start the scene revisiting,
As a flock, twittering, rising, or overhead passing,
Borne hither, ere all eludes me, hurriedly,
A man, yet by these tears a little boy again,
Throwing myself on the sand, confronting the waves,
I, chanter of pains and joys, uniter of here and hereafter,
Taking all hints to use them, but swiftly leaping beyond them,
A reminiscence sing.

Once Paumanok,
When the lilac-scent was in the air and Fifth-month grass was growing,
Up this seashore in some briers,
Two feather'd guests from Alabama, two together,
And their nest, and four light-green eggs spotted with brown,
And every day the he-bird to and fro near at hand,
And every day the she-bird crouch'd on her nest, silent, with bright eyes,
And every day I, a curious boy, never too close, never disturbing them,
Cautiously peering, absorbing, translating.

Shine! shine! shine!
Pour down your warmth, great sun!
While we bask, we two together.

Two together!
Winds blow south, or winds blow north,
Day come white, or night come black,
Home, or rivers and mountains from home,
Singing all time, minding no time,
While we two keep together.

Till of a sudden.
May-be kill'd, unknown to her mate,
One forenoon that she-bird crouch'd not on the nest,
Nor return'd that afternoon, nor the next,
Nor ever appear'd again.

And thenceforward all summer in the sound of the sea,
And at night under the full of the moon in calmer weather,
Over the hoarse surging of the sea,
Or flitting from brier to brier by day,
I saw, I heard at intervals the remaining one, the he-bird,
The solitary guest from Alabama.

Blow! blow! blow!
Blow up sea-winds along Paumanok's shore;
I wait and I wait till you blow my mate to me.

Yes, when the stars glisten'd,
All night long on the prong of a moss-scallop'd stake,
Down almost amid the slapping waves,
Sat the lone singer wonderful causing tears.

He call'd on his mate,
He pour'd forth the meanings which I of all men know.

Yes my brother I know,
The rest might not, but I have treasur'd every note,
For more than once dimly down to the beach gliding,
Silent, avoiding the moonbeams, blending myself with the shadows,
Recalling now the obscure shapes, the echoes, the sounds and sights after their sorts,
The white arms out in the breakers tirelessly tossing,
I, with bare feet, a child, the wind wafting my hair,
Listen'd long and long.

Listen'd to keep, to sing, now translating the notes,
Following you my brother.

Soothe! soothe! soothe!
Close on its wave soothes the wave behind,
And again another behind embracing and lapping, every one close,
But my love soothes not me, not me.

Low hangs the moon, it rose late,
It is lagging—O I think it is heavy with love, with love.

O madly the sea pushes upon the land,
With love, with love.

O night! do I not see my love fluttering out among the breakers?
What is that little black thing I see there in the white?

Loud! loud! loud!
Loud I call to you, my love!
High and clear I shoot my voice over the waves,
Surely you must know who is here, is here,
You must know who I am, my love.

Low-hanging moon!
What is that dusky spot in your brown yellow?
O it is the shape, the shape of my mate!
O moon do not keep her from me any longer.

Land! land! O land!
Whichever way I turn, O I think you could give me my mate back again if you only would,
For I am almost sure I see her dimly whichever way I look.

O rising stars!
Perhaps the one I want so much will rise, will rise with one of you.

O throat! O trembling throat!
Sound clearer through the atmosphere!
Pierce the woods, the earth,
Somewhere listening to catch you must be the one I want.

Shake out carols!
Solitary here, the night's carols!
Carols of lonesome love! death's carols!
Carols under that lagging, yellow, waning moon!

O under that moon where she droops almost down into the sea!
O reckless despairing carols.

But soft! sink low!
Soft! let me just murmur,
And do you wait a moment you husky-nois'd sea,
For somewhere I believe I heard my mate responding to me,
So faint, I must be still, be still to listen,
But not altogether still, for then she might not come immediately to me.

Hither my love!
Here I am! here!
With this just-sustain'd note I announce myself to you,
This gentle call is for you my love, for you.

Do not be decoy'd elsewhere,
That is the whistle of the wind, it is not my voice,
That is fluttering, the fluttering of the spray,
Those are the shadows of leaves.

O darkness! O in vain!
O I am very sick and sorrowful.

O brown halo in the sky near the moon, drooping upon the sea!
O troubled reflection in the sea!
O throat! O throbbing heart!
And singing uselessly, uselessly all the night.

O past! O happy life! O song of joy!
In the air, in the woods, over fields,
Loved! loved! loved! loved! loved!
But my mate no more, no more with me!
We two together no more.

The aria sinking,
All else continuing, the stars shining,
The winds blowing, the notes of the bird continuous echoing,
With angry moan the fierce old mother incessantly moaning,
On the sands of Paumanok's shore gray and rustling,
The yellow half-moon enlarged, sagging down, drooping, the face of the sea almost touching,
The boy ecstatic, with his bare feet the waves, with his hair the atmosphere dallying,
The love in the heart long pent, now loose, now at last tumultuously bursting,
The aria's meaning, the ears, the soul, swiftly depositing,
The strange tears down the cheeks coursing,
The colloquy there, the trio, each uttering,
The undertone, the savage old mother incessantly crying,
To the boy's soul's questions sullenly timing, some drown'd secret hissing,
To the outsetting bard.

Demon or bird! (said the boy's soul,)
Is it indeed toward your mate you sing? or is it really to me?
For I, that was a child, my tongue's use sleeping, now I have heard you,
Now in a moment I know what I am for, I awake,
And already a thousand singers, a thousand songs, clearer, louder, and more sorrowful than yours,
A thousand warbling echoes have started to life within me, never to die.

O you singer solitary, singing by yourself, projecting me,
O solitary me listening, never more shall I cease perpetuating you,
Never more shall I escape, never more the reverberations,
Never more the cries of unsatisfied love be absent from me,
Never again leave me to be the peaceful child I was before what there in the night,
By the sea under the yellow and sagging moon,
The messenger there arous'd, the fire, the sweet hell within,
The unknown want, the destiny of me.

O give me the clew! (it lurks in the night here somewhere,)
O if I am to have so much, let me have more!

A word then, (for I will conquer it,)
The word final, superior to all,
Subtle, sent up—what is it?—I listen;
Are you whispering it, and have been all the time, you sea-waves?
Is that it from your liquid rims and wet sands?

Whereto answering, the sea,
Delaying not, hurrying not,
Whisper'd me through the night, and very plainly before daybreak,
Lisp'd to me the low and delicious word death,
And again death, death, death, death,
Hissing melodious, neither like the bird nor like my arous'd child's heart,
But edging near as privately for me rustling at my feet,
Creeping thence steadily up to my ears and laving me softly all over,
Death, death, death, death, death.

Which I do not forget,
But fuse the song of my dusky demon and brother,
That he sang to me in the moonlight on Paumanok's gray beach,
With the thousand responsive songs at random,
My own songs awaked from that hour,
And with them the key, the word up from the waves,
The word of the sweetest song and all songs,
That strong and delicious word which, creeping to my feet,
(Or like some old crone rocking the cradle, swathed in sweet garments, bending aside,)
The sea whisper'd me.

1859, 1881

As I Ebb'd with the Ocean of Life

This poem is Whitman's classic expression of alienation and despair. In it the poet speaks of his personal insignificance as a man and as a poet; he identifies himself with the meaningless "little wash'd-up drifts" along the shore; and he ends the poem, as he began it, oppressed by his insignificance and by the mystery of nature and death.

1

As I ebb'd with the ocean of life,
As I wended the shores I know,
As I walk'd where the ripples continually wash you Paumanok,
Where they rustle up hoarse and sibilant,
Where the fierce old mother endlessly cries for her castaways,
I musing late in the autumn day, gazing off southward,

Held by this electric self out of the pride of which I utter poems,
Was seiz'd by the spirit that trails in the lines underfoot,
The rim, the sediment that stands for all the water and all the land of the globe.

Fascinated, my eyes reverting from the south, dropt, to follow those slender windrows,
Chaff, straw, splinters of wood, weeds, and the sea-gluten,
Scum, scales from shining rocks, leaves of salt-lettuce, left by the tide,
Miles walking, the sound of breaking waves the other side of me,
Paumanok there and then as I thought the old thought of likenesses,
These you presented to me you fish-shaped island,
As I wended the shores I know,
As I walk'd with that electric self seeking types.

2

As I wend to the shores I know not,
As I list to the dirge, the voices of men and women wreck'd,
As I inhale the impalpable breezes that set in upon me,
As the ocean so mysterious rolls toward me closer and closer,
I too but signify at the utmost a little wash'd-up drift,
A few sands and dead leaves to gather,
Gather, and merge myself as part of the sands and drift.

O baffled, balk'd, bent to the very earth,
Oppress'd with myself that I have dared to open my mouth,
Aware now that amid all that blab whose echoes recoil upon me I have not once had the least idea who or what I am,
But that before all my arrogant poems the real Me stands yet untouch'd, untold, altogether unreach'd,
Withdrawn far, mocking me with mock-congratulatory signs and bows,
With peals of distant ironical laughter at every word I have written,
Pointing in silence to these songs, and then to the sand beneath.

I perceive I have not really understood any thing, not a single object, and that no man ever can,
Nature here in sight of the sea taking advantage of me to dart upon me and sting me,
Because I have dared to open my mouth to sing at all.

3

You oceans both, I close with you,
We murmur alike reproachfully rolling sands and drift, knowing not why,
These little shreds indeed standing for you and me and all.

You friable shore with trails of debris,
You fish-shaped island, I take what is underfoot,
What is yours is mine my father.

I too Paumanok,
I too have bubbled up, floated the measureless float, and been wash'd on your shores,
I too am but a trail of drift and debris,
I too leave little wrecks upon you, you fish-shaped island.

I throw myself upon your breast my father,
I cling to you so that you cannot unloose me,
I hold you so firm till you answer me something.

Kiss me my father,
Touch me with your lips as I touch those I love,
Breathe to me while I hold you close the secret of the murmuring I envy.

4

Ebb, ocean of life, (the flow will return,)
Cease not your moaning you fierce old mother,
Endlessly cry for your castaways, but fear not, deny not me,
Rustle not up so hoarse and angry against my feet as I touch you or gather from you.

I mean tenderly by you and all,
I gather for myself and for this phantom looking down where we lead, and following me and mine.

Me and mine, loose windrows, little corpses,
Froth, snowy white, and bubbles,
(See, from my dead lips the ooze exuding at last,
See, the prismatic colors glistening and rolling,)
Tufts of straw, sands, fragments,
Buoy'd hither from many moods, one contradicting another,
From the storm, the long calm, the darkness, the swell,
Musing, pondering, a breath, a briny tear, a dab of liquid or soil,
Up just as much out of fathomless workings fermented and thrown,
A limp blossom or two, torn, just as much over waves floating, drifted at random,
Just as much for us that sobbing dirge of Nature,
Just as much whence we come that blare of the cloud-trumpets,
We, capricious, brought hither we know not whence, spread out before you,
You up there walking or sitting,
Whoever you are, we too lie in drifts at your feet.

1860, 1881

Once I Pass'd Through a Populous City

From the group of poems on the body, sex, and love which Whitman collected under the title "Children of Adam," this poem has been of more biographic than poetic interest. In the original unpublished draft, the lover was not a woman but "the man who wandered with me there," "one rude and ignorant man."

Once I pass'd through a populous city imprinting my brain for future use with its shows, architecture, customs, traditions,
Yet now of all that city I remember only a woman I casually met there who detain'd me for love of me,
Day by day and night by night we were together—all else has long been forgotten by me,
I remember I say only that woman who passionately clung to me,
Again we wander, we love, we separate again,
Again she holds me by the hand, I must not go,
I see her close beside me with silent lips sad and tremulous.

1860, 1867

When I Heard at the Close of the Day

When I heard at the close of the day how my name had been receiv'd with plaudits in the capitol, still it was not a happy night for me that follow'd,
And else when I carous'd, or when my plans were accomplish'd, still I was not happy,

But the day when I rose at dawn from the bed of perfect health, refresh'd, singing, inhaling the ripe breath of autumn,
When I saw the full moon in the west grow pale and disappear in the morning light,
When I wander'd alone over the beach, and undressing bathed, laughing with the cool waters, and saw the sun rise,
And when I thought how my dear friend my lover was on his way coming, O then I was happy,
O then each breath tasted sweeter, and all that day my food nourish'd me more, and the beautiful day pass'd well,
And the next came with equal joy, and with the next at evening came my friend,
And that night while all was still I heard the waters roll slowly continually up the shores,
I heard the hissing rustle of the liquid and sands as directed to me whispering to congratulate me,
For the one I love most lay sleeping by me under the same cover in the cool night,
In the stillness in the autumn moonbeams his face was inclined toward me,
And his arm lay lightly around my breast—and that night I was happy.

1860, 1867

A Glimpse

A glimpse through an interstice caught,
Of a crowd of workmen and drivers in a bar-room around the stove late of a winter night, and I unremark'd seated in a corner,
Of a youth who loves me and whom I love, silently approaching and seating himself near, that he may hold me by the hand,
A long while amid the noises of coming and going, of drinking and oath and smutty jest,
There we two, content, happy in being together, speaking little, perhaps not a word.

1860, 1867

A Noiseless Patient Spider

A noiseless patient spider,
I mark'd where on a little promontory it stood isolated,
Mark'd how to explore the vacant vast surrounding,
It lauch'd forth filament, filament, filament, out of itself,
Ever unreeling them, ever tirelessly speeding them.

And you O my soul where you stand,
Surrounded, detached, in measureless oceans of space,
Ceaselessly musing, venturing, throwing, seeking the spheres to connect them,
Till the bridge you will need be form'd, till the ductile anchor hold,
Till the gossamer thread you fling catch somewhere, O my soul.

1862–63, 1881

When I Heard the Learn'd Astronomer

When I heard the learn'd astronomer,
When the proofs, the figures, were ranged in columns before me,
When I was shown the charts and the diagrams, to add, divide, and measure them,
When I sitting heard the astronomer where he lectured with much applause in the lecture-room,
How soon unaccountable I became tired and sick,
Till rising and gliding out I wander'd off by myself,

In the mystical moist night-air, and from time to time,
Look'd up in perfect silence at the stars.

1865, 1867

Cavalry Crossing a Ford

A line in long array where they wind betwixt green islands,
They take a serpentine course, their arms flash in the sun—hark to the musical clank,
Behold the silvery river, in it the splashing horses loitering stop to drink,
Behold the brown-faced men, each group, each person a picture, the negligent rest on the saddles,
Some emerge on the opposite bank, others are just entering the ford—while,
Scarlet and blue and snowy white,
The guidon flags flutter gayly in the wind.

1865, 1871

A March in the Ranks Hard-Prest, and The Road Unknown

A march in the ranks hard prest, and the road unknown,
A route through a heavy wood with muffled steps in the darkness,
Our army foil'd with loss severe, and the sullen remnant retreating,
Till after midnight glimmer upon us the lights of a dim-lighted building,
We come to an open space in the woods, and halt by the dim-lighted building,
'Tis a large old church at the crossing roads, now an impromptu hospital,
Entering but for a minute I see a sight beyond all the pictures and poems ever made,
Shadows of deepest, deepest black, just lit by moving candles and lamps,
And by one great pitchy torch stationary with wild red flame and clouds of smoke,
By these, crowds, groups of forms vaguely I see on the floor, some in the pews laid down,
At my feet more distinctly a soldier, a mere lad, in danger of bleeding to death, (he is shot in the abdomen,)
I stanch the blood temporarily, (the youngster's face is white as a lily,)
Then before I depart I sweep my eyes o'er the scene fain to absorb it all,
Faces, varieties, postures beyond description, most in obscurity, some of them dead,
Surgeons operating, attendants holding lights, the smell of ether, the odor of blood,
The crowd, O the crowd of the bloody forms, the yard outside also fill'd,
Some on the bare ground, some on planks or stretchers, some in the death-spasm sweating,
An occasional scream or cry, the doctor's shouted orders or calls,
The glisten of the little steel instruments catching the glint of the torches,
These I resume as I chant, I see again the forms, I smell the odor,
Then hear outside the orders given, *Fall in, my men, fall in;*
But first I bend to the dying lad, his eyes open, a half-smile gives he me,
Then the eyes close, calmly close, and I speed forth to the darkness,
Resuming, marching, ever in darkness marching, on in the ranks,
The unknown road still marching.

1865

A Sight in Camp in the Daybreak Gray and Dim

A sight in camp in the daybreak gray and dim,
As from my tent I emerge so early sleepless,
As slow I walk in the cool fresh air the path near by the hospital tent,
Three forms I see on stretchers lying, brought out there untended lying,

Over each the blanket spread, ample brownish woolen blanket,
Gray and heavy blanket, folding, covering all.

Curious I halt and silent stand,
Then with light fingers I from the face of the nearest the first just lift the blanket;
Who are you elderly man so gaunt and grim, with well-gray'd hair, and flesh all sunken about the eyes?
Who are you my dear comrade?

Then to the second I step—and who are you my child and darling?
Who are you sweet boy with cheeks yet blooming?

Then to the third—a face nor child nor old, very calm, as of beautiful yellow-white ivory;
Young man I think I know you—I think this face is the face of the Christ himself,
Dead and divine and brother of all, and here again he lies.

1865

The Wound-Dresser

1

An old man bending I come among new faces,
Years looking backward resuming in answer to children,
Come tell us old man, as from young men and maidens that love me,
(Arous'd and angry, I'd thought to beat the alarum, and urge relentless war,
But soon my fingers fail'd me, my face droop'd and I resign'd myself,
To sit by the wounded and soothe them, or silently watch the dead;)
Years hence of these scenes, of these furious passions, these chances,
Of unsurpass'd heroes, (was one side so brave? the other was equally brave;)
Now be witness again, paint the mightiest armies of earth,
Of those armies so rapid so wondrous what saw you to tell us?
What stays with you latest and deepest? of curious panics,
Of hard-fought engagements or sieges tremendous what deepest remains?

2

O maidens and young men I love and that love me,
What you ask of my days those the strangest and sudden your talking recalls,
Soldier alert I arrive after a long march cover'd with sweat and dust,
In the nick of time I come, plunge in the fight, loudly shout in the rush of successful charge,
Enter the captur'd works—yet lo, like a swift-running river they fade,
Pass and are gone they fade—I dwell not on soldiers' perils or soldiers' joys,
(Both I remember well—many of the hardships, few the joys, yet I was content.)

But in silence, in dreams' projections,
While the world of gain and appearance and mirth goes on,
So soon what is over forgotten, and waves wash the imprints off the sand,
With hinged knees returning I enter the doors, (while for you up there,
Whoever you are, follow without noise and be of strong heart.)

Bearing the bandages, water and sponge,
Straight and swift to my wounded I go,
Where they lie on the ground after the battle brought in,
Where their priceless blood reddens the grass the ground,
Or to the rows of the hospital tent, or under the roof'd hospital,

To the long rows of cots up and down each side I return,
To each and all one after another I draw near, not one do I miss,
An attendant follows holding a tray, he carries a refuse pail,
Soon to be fill'd with clotted rags and blood, emptied, and fill'd again.

I onward go, I stop,
With hinged knees and steady hand to dress wounds,
I am firm with each, the pangs are sharp yet unavoidable,
One turns to me his appealing eyes—poor boy! I never knew you,
Yet I think I could not refuse this moment to die for you, if that would save you.

3

On, on I go, (open doors of time! open hospital doors!)
The crush'd head I dress, (poor crazed hand tear not the bandage away,)
The neck of the cavalry-man with the bullet through and through I examine,
Hard the breathing rattles, quite glazed already the eye, yet life struggles hard,
(Come sweet death! be persuaded O beautiful death!
In mercy come quickly.)

From the stump of the arm, the amputated hand,
I undo the clotted lint, remove the slough, wash off the matter and blood,
Back on his pillow the soldier bends with curv'd neck and side-falling head,
His eyes are closed, his face is pale, he dares not look on the bloody stump,
And has not yet look'd on it.

I dress a wound in the side, deep, deep,
But a day or two more, for see the frame all wasted and sinking,
And the yellow-blue countenance see.

I dress the perforated shoulder, the foot with the bullet-wound,
Cleanse the one with a gnawing and putrid gangrene, so sickening, so offensive,
While the attendant stands behind aside me holding the tray and pail.

I am faithful, I do not give out,
The fractur'd thigh, the knee, the wound in the abdomen,
These and more I dress with impassive hand, (yet deep in my breast a fire, a burning flame.)

4

Thus in silence in dreams' projections,
Returning, resuming, I thread my way through the hospitals,
The hurt and wounded I pacify with soothing hand,
I sit by the restless all the dark night, some are so young,
Some suffer so much, I recall the experience sweet and sad,
(Many a soldier's loving arms about this neck have cross'd and rested,
Many a soldier's kiss dwells on these bearded lips.)

1865, 1881

When Lilacs Last in the Dooryard Bloom'd

This is a poem about Lincoln, the best of many in American literature.

In Washington, during the year of Gettysburg, Whitman wrote: "I see the President almost every day, as I happen to live where he passes to or from his lodgings out of town. . . . the deep-cut lines, the eyes, always to me with a deep latent sadness in the expression. We have got so that we exchange bows."

On the second inauguration, March 4, 1865: "I saw him on his return, at three o'clock, after the performance was over. He was in his plain two-horse barouche, and look'd very much worn and tired; . . . yet all the old goodness, tenderness, sadness, and canny shrewdness, underneath the furrows. . . . By his side sat his little boy, of ten years. There were no soldiers."

The next month the President was murdered. It was lilac time in Brooklyn when Whitman heard the news—April 15, early in the morning. "Mother prepared breakfast—and other meals afterward—as usual; but not a mouthful was eaten all day by either of us. We each drank half a cup of coffee; that was all. Little was said. We got every newspaper morning and evening, and the frequent extras of that period, and pass'd them silently to each other." A funeral train left Washington on April 21, carrying Lincoln's body to his home town, Springfield, Illinois, halting on the way at Philadelphia, New York, Chicago, and other cities.

The poem which Whitman was moved to write does not mention Lincoln's name, or dwell upon "the man I love." Instead, it unites two broad themes that absorbed him: America, "my land" (typified by its great President) and death, the "dark mother" of all of us. The solemn sense of bereavement that runs through the poem and the remarkable song to "lovely and soothing death" are not so much personal as national. As the funeral train moves on, and the bells toll in cities draped in black, the poet's emotion is that of a people, his tribute only his "sprig of lilac."

The poem is developed largely through three symbols: the star (Lincoln), the lilac (love), the hermit thrush (the poet singing of death). They keep reappearing, like themes in a musical recitative, and at the end are brought together in one phrase—"Lilac and star and bird."

1

When lilacs last in the dooryard bloom'd
And the great star early droop'd in the western sky in the night,
I mourn'd, and yet shall mourn with ever-returning spring.

Ever-returning spring, trinity sure to me you bring,
Lilac blooming perennial and drooping star in the west,
And thought of him I love.

2

O powerful western fallen star!
O shades of night!—O moody, tearful night!
O great star disappear'd—O the black murk that hides the star!
O cruel hands that hold me powerless—O helpless soul of me!
O harsh surrounding cloud that will not free my soul.

3

In the dooryard fronting an old farm-house near the white-wash'd palings,
Stands the lilac-bush tall-growing with heart-shaped leaves of rich green,
With many a pointed blossom rising delicate, with the perfume strong I love,
With every leaf a miracle—and from this bush in the dooryard,
With delicate-color'd blossoms and heart-shaped leaves of rich green,
A sprig with its flower I break.

4

In the swamp in secluded recesses,
A shy and hidden bird is warbling a song.

Solitary the thrush,
The hermit withdrawn to himself, avoiding the settlements,
Sings by himself a song.

Song of the bleeding throat,
Death's outlet song of life, (for well dear brother I know,
If thou wast not granted to sing thou would'st surely die.)

5

Over the breast of the spring, the land, amid cities,
Amid lanes and through old woods, where lately the violets peep'd from the ground, spotting the gray debris,
Amid the grass in the fields each side of the lanes, passing the endless grass,
Passing the yellow-spear'd wheat, every grain from its shroud in the dark-brown fields uprisen,
Passing the apple-tree blows of white and pink in the orchards,
Carrying a corpse to where it shall rest in the grave,
Night and day journeys a coffin.

6

Coffin that passes through lanes and streets,
Through day and night with the great cloud darkening the land,
With the pomp of the inloop'd flags with the cities draped in black,
With the show of the States themselves as of crape-veil'd women standing,
With processions long and winding and the flambeaus of the night,
With the countless torches lit, with the silent sea of faces and the unbared heads,
With the waiting depot, the arriving coffin, and the sombre faces,
With dirges through the night, with the thousand voices rising strong and solemn,
With all the mournful voices of the dirges pour'd around the coffin,
The dim-lit churches and the shuddering organs—where amid these you journey,
With the tolling tolling bells' perpetual clang,
Here, coffin that slowly passes,
I give you my sprig of lilac.

7

(Nor for you, for one alone,
Blossoms and branches green to coffins all I bring,
For fresh as the morning, thus would I chant a song for you O sane and sacred death.

All over bouquets of roses,
O death, I cover you over with roses and early lilies,
But mostly and now the lilac that blooms the first,
Copious I break, I break the sprigs from the bushes,
With loaded arms I come, pouring for you,
For you and the coffins all of you O death.)

8

O western orb sailing the heaven,
Now I know what you must have meant as a month since I walk'd,
As I walk'd in silence the transparent shadowy night,
As I saw you had something to tell as you bent to me night after night,
As you droop'd from the sky low down as if to my side, (while the other stars all look'd on,)
As we wander'd together the solemn night, (for something I know not what kept me from sleep,)
As the night advanced, and I saw on the rim of the west how full you were of woe,
As I stood on the rising ground in the breeze in the cool transparent night,
As I watch'd where you pass'd and was lost in the netherward black of the night,
As my soul in its trouble dissatisfied sank, as where you sad orb,
Concluded, dropt in the night, and was gone.

9

Sing on there in the swamp,
O singer bashful and tender, I hear your notes, I hear your call,

I hear, I come presently, I understand you,
But a moment I linger, for the lustrous star has detain'd me,
The star my departing comrade holds and detains me.

10

O how shall I warble myself for the dead one there I loved?
And how shall I deck my song for the large sweet soul that has gone?
And what shall my perfume be for the grave of him I love?

Sea-winds blown from east and west,
Blown from the Eastern sea and blown from the Western sea, till there on the prairies meeting,
These and with these and the breath of my chant,
I'll perfume the grave of him I love.

11

O what shall I hang on the chamber walls?
And what shall the pictures be that I hang on the walls,
To adorn the burial-house of him I love?

Pictures of growing spring and farms and homes,
With the Fourth-month eve at sundown, and the gray smoke lucid and bright,
With floods of the yellow gold of the gorgeous indolent, sinking sun, burning, expanding the air,
With the fresh sweet herbage under foot, and the pale green leaves of the trees prolific,
In the distance the flowing glaze, the breast of the river, with a wind-dapple here and there,
With ranging hills on the banks, with many a line against the sky, and shadows,
And the city at hand with dwellings so dense, and stacks of chimneys,
And all the scenes of life and the workshops, and the workmen homeward returning.

12

Lo, body and soul—this land,
My own Manhattan with spires, and the sparkling and hurrying tides, and the ships,
The varied and ample land, the South and the North in the light, Ohio's shores and flashing
Missouri,
And ever the far-spreading prairies cover'd with grass and corn.

Lo, the most excellent sun so calm and haughty,
The violet and purple morn with just-felt breezes,
The gentle soft-brown measureless light,
The miracle spreading bathing all, the fulfill'd noon,
The coming eve delicious, the welcome night and the stars,
Over my cities shining all, enveloping man and land.

13

Sing on, sing on you gray-brown bird,
Sing from the swamps, the recesses, pour your chant from the bushes,
Limitless out of the dusk, out of the cedars and pines.

Sing on dearest brother, warble your reedy song,
Loud human song, with voice of uttermost woe.

O liquid and free and tender!
O wild and loose to my soul—O wondrous singer!
You only I hear—yet the star holds me, (but will soon depart,)
Yet the lilac with mastering odor holds me.

14

Now while I sat in the day and look'd forth,
In the close of the day with its light and the fields of spring, and the farmers preparing their crops,
In the large unconscious scenery of my land with its lakes and forests,
In the heavenly aerial beauty, (after the perturb'd winds and the storms,)
Under the arching heavens of the afternoon swift passing, and the voices of children and women,
The many-moving sea-tides, and I saw the ships how they sail'd,
And the summer approaching with richness, and the fields all busy with labor,
And the infinite separate houses, how they all went on, each with its meals and minutia of daily usages,
And the streets how their throbbings throbb'd, and the cities pent—lo, then and there,
Falling upon them all and among them all, enveloping me with the rest,
Appear'd the cloud, appear'd the long black trail,
And I knew death, its thought, and the sacred knowledge of death.

Then with the knowledge of death as walking one side of me,
And the thought of death close-walking the other side of me,
And I in the middle as with companions, and as holding the hands of companions,
I fled forth to the hiding receiving night that talks not,
Down to the shores of the water, the path by the swamp in the dimness,
To the solemn shadowy cedars and ghostly pines so still.

And the singer so shy to the rest receiv'd me,
The gray-brown bird I know receiv'd us comrades three,
And he sang the carol of death, and a verse for him I love.

From deep secluded recesses,
From the fragrant cedars and the ghostly pines so still,
Came the carol of the bird.

And the charm of the carol rapt me,
As I held as if by their hands my comrades in the night,
And the voice of my spirit tallied the song of the bird.

Come lovely and soothing death,
Undulate round the world, serenely arriving, arriving,
In the day, in the night, to all, to each,
Sooner or later delicate death.

Prais'd be the fathomless universe,
For life and joy, and for objects and knowledge curious,
And for love, sweet love—but praise! praise! praise!
For the sure-enwinding arms of cool-enfolding death.

Dark mother always gliding near with soft feet,
Have none chanted for thee a chant of fullest welcome?
Then I chant it for thee, I glorify thee above all,
I bring thee a song that when thou must indeed come, come unfalteringly.

Approach strong deliveress,
When it is so, when thou hast taken them I joyously sing the dead,
Lost in the loving floating ocean of thee,
Laved in the flood of thy bliss O death.

From me to thee glad serenades,
Dances for thee I propose saluting thee, adornments and feastings for thee,

And the sights of the open landscape and the high-spread sky are fitting,
And life and the fields, and the huge and thoughtful night.

The night in silence under many a star,
The ocean shore and the husky whispering wave whose voice I know,
And the soul turning to thee O vast and well-veil'd death,
And the body gratefully nestling close to thee.

Over the tree-tops I float thee a song,
Over the rising and sinking waves, over the myriad fields and the prairies wide,
Over the dense-pack'd cities all and the teeming wharves and ways,
I float this carol with joy, with joy to thee O death.

15

To the tally of my soul,
Loud and strong kept up the gray-brown bird,
With pure deliberate notes spreading filling the night.

Loud in the pines and cedars dim,
Clear in the freshness moist and swamp-perfume,
And I with my comrades there in the night.

While my sight that was bound in my eyes unclosed,
As to long panoramas of visions.

And I saw askant the armies,
I saw as in noiseless dreams hundreds of battle-flags,
Borne through the smoke of the battles and pierc'd with missiles I saw them,
And carried hither and yon through the smoke, and torn and bloody,
And at last but a few shreds left on the staffs, (and all in silence,)
And the staffs all splinter'd and broken.

I saw battle-corpses, myriads of them,
And the white skeletons of young men, I saw them,
I saw the debris and debris of all the slain soldiers of the war,
But I saw they were not as was thought,
They themselves were fully at rest, they suffer'd not,
The living remain'd and suffer'd, the mother suffer'd,
And the wife and the child and the musing comrade suffer'd,
And the armies that remain'd suffer'd.

16

Passing the visions, passing the night,
Passing, unloosing the hold of my comrades' hands,
Passing the song of the hermit bird and the tallying song of my soul,
Victorious song, death's outlet song, yet varying ever-altering song,
As low and wailing, yet clear the notes, rising and falling, flooding the night,
Sadly sinking and fainting, as warning and warning, and yet again bursting with joy,
Covering the earth and filling the spread of the heaven,
As that powerful psalm in the night I heard from recesses,
Passing, I leave thee lilac with heart-shaped leaves,
I leave thee there in the door-yard, blooming, returning with spring.

I cease from my song for thee,
From my gaze on thee in the west, fronting the west, communing with thee,
O comrade lustrous with silver face in the night.

Yet each to keep and all, retrievements out of the night,
The song, the wondrous chant of the gray-brown bird,
And the tallying chant, the echo arous'd in my soul,
With the lustrous and drooping star with the countenance full of woe,
With the holders holding my hand hearing the call of the bird,
Comrades mine and I in the midst, and their memory ever to keep, for the dead I loved so well,
For the sweetest, wisest soul of all my days and lands—and this for his dear sake,
Lilac and star and bird twined with the chant of my soul,
There in the fragrant pines and the cedars dusk and dim.

1865-66, 1881

On the Beach at Night

On the beach at night,
Stands a child with her father,
Watching the east, the autumn sky.

Up through the darkness,
While ravening clouds, the burial clouds, in black masses spreading,
Lower sullen and fast athwart and down the sky,
Amid a transparent clear belt of ether yet left in the east,
Ascends large and calm the lord-star Jupiter,
And nigh at hand, only a very little above,
Swim the delicate sisters the Pleiades.

From the beach the child holding the hand of her father,
Those burial clouds that lower victorious soon to devour all,
Watching, silently weeps.

Weep not, child,
Weep not, my darling,
With these kisses let me remove your tears,
The ravening clouds shall not long be victorious,
They shall not long possess the sky, they devour the stars only in apparition,
Jupiter shall emerge, be patient, watch again another night, the Pleiades shall emerge,
They are immortal, all those stars both silvery and golden shall shine out again,
The great stars and the little ones shall shine out again, they endure,
The vast immortal suns and the long-enduring pensive moons shall again shine.

Then dearest child mournest thou only for Jupiter?
Considerest thou alone the burial of the stars?

Something there is,
(With my lips soothing thee, adding I whisper,
I give thee the first suggestion, the problem and indirection,)
Something there is more immortal even than the stars,
(Many the burials, many the days and nights, passing away,)
Something that shall endure longer even than lustrous Jupiter,
Longer than sun or any revolving satellite,
Or the radiant sisters the Pleiades.

1871

Passage to India

The main technological achievements Whitman speaks of in this poem are the opening of the Suez Canal, the completion of the transcontinental railroad, and the laying of the transoceanic cable—each an achievement in communications, primarily. Whitman also alludes to many other names, places, and events, both past and present; all develop the main themes of the poem—circumnavigation of the world, journey into the past, journey beyond the past and history.

The burden of the poem, Whitman once remarked, is "evolution—. . . the unfolding of cosmic purposes." For him, evolution meant far more than material development. The world has been welded together

"not for trade or transportation only,
But in God's name, and for thy sake O soul."

Far in the past, India led the way in poetry and religion. This will be the way of the future. The world will be circumnavigated by the soul. "Finally shall come the poet worthy that name." He it is who will show how truly, how deeply, the world is one, that Spirit and Matter, Nature and Men, are one. In section 8 we see Whitman taking ship, launching out on trackless seas in an ecstatic adventure of the soul, a voyage to far more than India, more than stars or suns, a voyage whose destination is God.

1

Singing my days,
Singing the great achievements of the present,
Singing the strong light works of engineers,
Our modern wonders, (the antique ponderous Seven outvied,)
In the Old World the east the Suez canal,
The New by its mighty railroad spann'd,
The seas inlaid with eloquent gentle wires;
Yet first to sound, and ever sound, the cry with thee O soul,
The Past! the Past! the Past!

The Past—the dark unfathom'd retrospect!
The teeming gulf—the sleepers and the shadows!
The past—the infinite greatness of the past!
For what is the present after all but a growth out of the past?
(As a projectile form'd, impell'd, passing a certain line, still keeps on,
So the present, utterly form'd, impell'd by the past,)

2

Passage O soul to India!
Eclaircise the myths Asiatic, the primitive fables.

Not you alone proud truths of the world,
Nor you alone ye facts of modern science,
But myths and fables of eld, Asia's, Africa's fables,
The far-darting beams of the spirit, the unloos'd dreams,
The deep diving bibles and legends,
The daring plots of the poets, the elder religions;
O you temples fairer than lilies pour'd over by the rising sun!
O you fables spurning the known, eluding the hold of the known, mounting to heaven!
You lofty and dazzling towers, pinnacled, red as roses, burnish'd with gold!
Towers of fables immortal fashion'd from mortal dreams!
You too I welcome and fully the same as the rest!
You too with joy I sing.

Passage to India!
Lo, soul, seest thou not God's purpose from the first?
The earth to be spann'd, connected by network,
The races, neighbors, to marry and be given in marriage,

The oceans to be cross'd, the distant brought near,
The lands to be welded together.

A worship new I sing,
You captains, voyagers, explorers, yours,
You engineers, you architects, machinists, yours,
You, not for trade or transportation only,
But in God's name, and for thy sake O soul.

3

Passage to India!
Lo soul for thee of tableaus twain,
I see in one the Suez canal initiated, open'd,
I see the procession of steamships, the Empress Eugenie's leading the van,
I mark from on deck the strange landscape, the pure sky, the level sand in the distance,
I pass swiftly the picturesque groups, the workmen gather'd,
The gigantic dredging machines.

In one again, different, (yet thine, all thine, O soul, the same,)
I see over my own continent the Pacific railroad surmounting every barrier,
I see continual trains of cars winding along the Platte carrying freight and passengers,
I hear the locomotives rushing and roaring, and the shrill steam-whistle,
I hear the echoes reverberate through the grandest scenery in the world,
I cross the Laramie plains, I note the rocks in grotesque shapes, the buttes,
I see the plentiful larkspur and wild onions, the barren, colorless, sage-deserts,
I see in glimpses afar or towering immediately above me the great mountains, I see the Wind river and the Wahsatch mountains,
I see the Monument mountain and the Eagle's Nest, I pass the Promontory, I ascend the Nevadas,
I scan the noble Elk mountain and wind around its base,
I see the Humboldt range, I thread the valley and cross the river,
I see the clear waters of lake Tahoe, I see forests of majestic pines,
Or crossing the great desert, the alkaline plains, I behold enchanting mirages of waters and meadows,
Marking through these and after all, in duplicate slender lines,
Bridging the three or four thousand miles of land travel,
Tying the Eastern to the Western sea,
The road between Europe and Asia.

(Ah Genoese thy dream! thy dream!
Centuries after thou art laid in thy grave,
The shore thou foundest verifies thy dream.)

4

Passage to India!
Struggles of many a captain, tales of many a sailor dead,
Over my mood stealing and spreading they come,
Like clouds and cloudlets in the unreach'd sky.

Along all history, down the slopes,
As a rivulet running, sinking now, and now again to the surface rising,
A ceaseless thought, a varied train—lo, soul, to thee, thy sight, they rise
The plans, the voyages again, the expeditions;
Again Vasco de Gama sails forth,
Again the knowledge gain'd, the mariner's compass,
Lands found and nations born, thou born America,

For purpose vast, man's long probation fill'd,
Thou rondure of the world at last accomplish'd.

5

O vast Rondure, swimming in space,
Cover'd all over with visible power and beauty,
Alternate light and day and the teeming spiritual darkness,
Unspeakable high processions of sun and moon and countless stars above,
Below, the manifold grass and waters, animals, mountains, trees,
With inscrutable purpose, some hidden prophetic intention,
Now first it seems my thought begins to span thee.

Down from the gardens of Asia descending radiating,
Adam and Eve appear, then their myriad progeny after them,
Wandering, yearning, curious, with restless explorations,
With questionings, baffled, formless, feverish, with never-happy hearts.
With that sad incessant refrain, *Wherefore unsatisfied soul?* and *Whither O mocking life?*

Ah who shall soothe these feverish children?
Who justify these restless explorations?
Who speak the secret of impassive earth?
Who bind it to us? what is this separate Nature so unnatural?
What is this earth to our affections? (unloving earth, without a throb to answer ours,
Cold earth, the place of graves.)

Yet soul be sure the first intent remains, and shall be carried out,
Perhaps even now the time has arrived.

After the seas are all cross'd, (as they seem already cross'd,)
After the great captains and engineers have accomplish'd their work,
After the noble inventors, after the scientists, the chemist, the geologist, ethnologist,
Finally shall come the poet worthy that name,
The true son of God shall come singing his songs.

Then not your deeds only O voyagers, O scientists and inventors, shall be justified,
All these hearts as of fretted children shall be sooth'd,
All affection shall be fully responded to, the secret shall be told,
All these separations and gaps shall be taken up and hook'd and link'd together,
The whole earth, this cold, impassive, voiceless earth, shall be completely justified,
Trinitas divine shall be gloriously accomplish'd and compacted by the true son of God, the poet,
(He shall indeed pass the straits and conquer the mountains,
He shall double the cape of Good Hope to some purpose,)
Nature and Man shall be disjoin'd and diffused no more,
The true son of God shall absolutely fuse them.

6

Year at whose wide-flung door I sing!
Year of the purpose accomplish'd!
Year of the marriage of continents, climates and oceans!
(No mere doge of Venice now wedding the Adriatic,)
I see O year in you the vast terraqueous globe given and giving all,
Europe to Asia, Africa join'd, and they to the New World,
The lands, geographies, dancing before you, holding a festival garland,
As brides and bridegrooms hand in hand.

Passage to India!
Cooling airs from Caucasus far, soothing cradle of man,
The river Euphrates flowing, the past lit up again.

Lo soul, the retrospect brought forward,
The old, most populous, wealthiest of earth's lands,
The streams of the Indus and the Ganges and their many affluents,
(I my shores of America walking to-day behold, resuming all,)
The tale of Alexander on his warlike marches suddenly dying,
On one side China and on the other side Persia and Arabia,
To the south the great seas and the bay of Bengal,
The flowing literatures, tremendous epics, religions, castes,
Old occult Brahma interminably far back, the tender and junior Buddha,
Central and southern empires and all their belongings, possessors,
The wars of Tamerlane, the reign of Aurungzebe,
The traders, rulers, explorers, Moslems, Venetians, Byzantium, the Arabs, Portuguese,
The first travelers famous yet, Marco Polo, Batouta the Moor,
Doubts to be solv'd, the map incognita, blanks to be fill'd,
The foot of man unstay'd, the hands never at rest,
Thyself O soul that will not brook a challenge.

The mediaeval navigators rise before me.
The world of 1492, with its awaken'd enterprise,
Something swelling in humanity now like the sap of the earth in spring,
The sunset splendor of chivalry declining.

And who art thou sad shade?
Gigantic, visionary, thyself a visionary,
With majestic limbs and pious beaming eyes,
Spreading around with every look of thine a golden world,
Enhuing it with gorgeous hues.

As the chief histrion,
Down to the footlights walks in some great scena,
Dominating the rest I see the Admiral himself,
(History's type of courage, action, faith,)
Behold him sail from Palos leading his little fleet,
His voyage behold, his return, his great fame,
His misfortunes, calumniators, behold him a prisoner, chain'd,
Behold his dejection, poverty, death.

(Curious in time I stand, noting the efforts of heroes,
Is the deferment long? bitter the slander, poverty, death?
Lies the seed unreck'd for centuries in the ground? lo, to God's due occasion,
Uprising in the night, it sprouts, blooms,
And fills the earth with use and beauty.)

7

Passage indeed O soul to primal thought,
Not lands and seas alone, thy own clear freshness,
The young maturity of brood and bloom,
To realms of budding bibles.

O soul, repressless, I with thee and thou with me,
Thy circumnavigation of the world begin,
Of man, the voyage of his mind's return,
To reason's early paradise,
Back, back to wisdom's birth, to innocent intuitions,
Again with fair creation.

8

O we can wait no longer,
We too take ship O soul,
Joyous we too launch out on trackless seas,
Fearless for unknown shores on waves of ecstasy to sail,
Amid the wafting winds, (thou pressing me to thee, I thee to me, O soul,)
Caroling free, singing our song of God,
Chanting our chant of pleasant exploration.

With laugh and many a kiss,
(Let others deprecate, let others weep for sin, remorse, humiliation,)
O soul thou pleasest me, I thee.

Ah more than any priest O soul we too believe in God,
But with the mystery of God we dare not dally.

O soul thou pleasest me, I thee.
Sailing these seas or on the hills, or waking in the night,
Thoughts, silent thoughts, of Time and Space and Death, like waters flowing,
Bear me indeed as through the regions infinite,
Whose air I breathe, whose ripples hear, lave me all over,
Bathe me O God in thee, mounting to thee,
I and my soul to range in range of thee.

O Thou transcendent,
Nameless, the fibre and the breath,
Light of the light, shedding forth universes, thou centre of them,
Thou mightier centre of the true, the good, the loving,
Thou moral, spiritual fountain—affection's source—thou reservoir,
(O pensive soul of me—O thirst unsatisfied—waitest not there?
Waitest not haply for us somewhere there the Comrade perfect?)
Thou pulse—thou motive of the stars, suns, systems,
That, circling, move in order, safe, harmonious,
Athwart the shapeless vastnesses of space,
How should I think, how breathe a single breath, how speak, if, out of myself,
I could not launch, to those, superior universes?

Swiftly I shrivel at the thought of God,
At Nature and its wonders, Time and Space and Death,
But that I, turning, call to thee O soul, thou actual Me,
And lo, thou gently masterest the orbs,
Thou matest Time, smilest content at Death,
And fillest, swellest full the vastnesses of Space.

Greater than stars or suns,
Bounding O soul thou journeyest forth;
What love than thine and ours could wider amplify?

What aspirations, wishes, outvie thine and ours O soul?
What dreams of the ideal? what plans of purity, perfection, strength?
What cheerful willingness for others' sake to give up all?
For others' sake to suffer all?

Reckoning ahead O soul, when thou, the time achiev'd,
The seas all cross'd, weather'd the capes, the voyage done,
Surrounded, copest, frontest God, yieldest, the aim attain'd,
As fill'd with friendship, love complete, the Elder Brother found,
The Younger melts in fondness in his arms.

9

Passage to more than India!
Are thy wings plumed indeed for such far flights?
O soul, voyagest thou indeed on voyages like those?
Disportest thou on waters such as those?
Soundest below the Sanscrit and the Vedas?
Then have thy bent unleash'd.

Passage to you, your shores, ye aged fierce enigmas!
Passage to you, to mastership of you, ye strangling problems!
You, strew'd with the wrecks of skeletons, that, living, never reach'd you.

Passage to more than India!
O secret of the earth and sky!
Of you O waters of the sea! O winding creeks and rivers!
Of you O woods and fields! of you strong mountains of my land!
Of you O prairies! of you gray rocks!
O morning red! O clouds! O rain and snows!
O day and night, passage to you!

O sun and moon and all you stars! Sirius and Jupiter!
Passage to you!

Passage, immediate passage! the blood burns in my veins!
Away O soul! hoist instantly the anchor!
Cut the hawsers—haul out—shake out every sail!
Have we not stood here like trees in the ground long enough?
Have we not grovel'd here long enough, eating and drinking like mere brutes?
Have we not darken'd and dazed ourselves with books long enough?

Sail forth—steer for the deep waters only,
Reckless O soul, exploring, I with thee, and thou with me,
For we are bound where mariner has not yet dared to go,
And we will risk the ship, ourselves and all.

O my brave soul!
O farther farther sail!
O daring joy, but safe! are they not all the seas of God?
O farther, farther, farther sail!

1871

To a Locomotive in Winter

Thee for my recitative,
Thee in the driving storm even as now, the snow, the winter-day declining,
Thee in thy panoply, thy measur'd dual throbbing and thy beat convulsive,
Thy black cylindric body, golden brass and silvery steel,
Thy ponderous side-bars, parallel and connecting rods, gyrating, shuttling at thy sides,
Thy metrical, now swelling pant and roar, now tapering in the distance,
Thy great protruding head-light fix'd in front,
Thy long, pale, floating vapor-pennants, tinged with delicate purple,
The dense and murky clouds out-belching from thy smoke-stack,
Thy knitted frame, thy springs and valves, the tremulous twinkle of thy wheels,
Thy train of cars behind, obedient, merrily following,
Through gale or calm, now swift, now slack, yet steadily careering;
Type of the modern—emblem of motion and power—pulse of the continent,
For once come serve the Muse and merge in verse, even as here I see thee,
With storm and buffeting gusts of wind and falling snow,
By day thy warning ringing bell to sound its notes,
By night thy silent signal lamps to swing.

Fierce-throated beauty!
Roll through my chant with all thy lawless music, thy swinging lamps at night,
Thy madly-whistled laughter, echoing, rumbling like an earthquake, rousing all,
Law of thyself complete, thine own track firmly holding,
(No sweetness debonair of tearful harp or glib piano thine,)
Thy trills of shrieks by rocks and hills return'd,
Launch'd o'er the prairies wide, across the lakes,
To the free skies unpent and glad and strong.

1876

To the Man-of-War-Bird

At the close Whitman departs, in a striking manner, from the romantic tendency to treat nature as equal or superior to man.

Thou who has slept all night upon the storm,
Waking renew'd on thy prodigious pinions,
(Burst the wild storm? above it thou ascended'st,
And rested on the sky, thy slave that cradled thee,)
Now a blue point, far, far in heaven floating,
As to the light emerging here on deck I watch thee,
(Myself a speck, a point on the world's floating vast.)

Far, far at sea,
After the night's fierce drifts have strewn the shore with wrecks,
With re-appearing day as now so happy and serene,
The rosy and elastic dawn, the flashing sun,
The limpid spread of air cerulean,
Thou also re-appearest.

Thou born to match the gale, (thou art all wings,)
To cope with heaven and earth and sea and hurricane,
Thou ship of air that never furl'st thy sails,
Days, even weeks untired and onward, through spaces, realms gyrating,

At dusk that look'st on Senegal, at morn America,
That sport'st amid the lightning-flash and thunder-cloud,
In them, in thy experiences, had'st thou my soul,
What joys! what joys were thine!

1876, 1881

The Dalliance of the Eagles

Skirting the river road, (my forenoon walk, my rest,)
Skyward in air a sudden muffled sound, the dalliance of the eagles,
The rushing amorous contact high in space together,
The clinching interlocking claws, a living, fierce, gyrating wheel,
Four beating wings, two beaks, a swirling mass tight grappling,
In tumbling turning clustering loops, straight downward falling,
Till o'er the river pois'd, the twain yet one, a moment's lull,
A motionless still balance in the air, then parting, talons loosing,
Upward again on slow-firm pinions slanting, their separate diverse flight,
She hers, he his, pursuing.

1880, 1881

The Dismantled Ship

In some unused lagoon, some nameless bay,
On sluggish, lonesome waters, anchor'd near the shore,
An old, dismasted, gray and batter'd ship, disabled, done,
After free voyages to all the seas of earth, haul'd up at last and hawser'd tight,
Lies rusting, mouldering.

1888

FROM *Democratic Vistas*

After the Civil War, the moral corruption of politics and business, and the low tone of life generally, might well have disillusioned a romantic like Whitman. Instead, he sharply characterized what he saw around him, and bravely offered his specifications for a mature democracy in the future.

[American Democracy, Actual and Ideal]

We had best look our times and lands searchingly in the face, like a physician diagnosing some deep disease. Never was there, perhaps, more hollowness at heart than at present, and here in the United States. Genuine belief seems to have left us. The underlying principles of the States are not honestly believ'd in, (for all this hectic glow, and these melodramatic screamings,) nor is humanity itself believ'd in. What penetrating eye does not everywhere see through the mask? The spectacle is appalling. We live in an atmosphere of hypocrisy throughout. The men believe not in the women, nor the women in the men. A scornful superciliousness rules in literature. The aim of all the *littérateurs* is to find something to make fun of. A lot of churches, sects, etc., the most dismal phantasms I know, usurp the name of religion. Conversation is a mass of badinage. From deceit in the spirit, the mother of all false deeds, the offspring is already incalculable. An acute and candid person, in the revenue department in Washington, who is led by the course of his employment to regularly visit the cities, north, south and west, to investigate frauds, has talk'd much with me about his discoveries. The depravity of the business classes of our country is not less than has been supposed, but infinitely greater. The official services of America, national, state, and municipal, in all their branches and departments, except the judiciary, are saturated in corruption, bribery, falsehood, maladministration; and the judiciary is tainted. The great cities reek with respectable as much as non-respectable robbery and scoundrelism. In fashionable life, flippancy, tepid amours, weak infidelism, small aims, or no aims at all, only to kill time. In business, (this all-devouring modern word, business,) the one sole object is, by any means, pecuniary gain. The magician's serpent in the fable ate up all the other serpents; and money-making is our magician's serpent, remaining to-day sole master of the field. The best class we show, is but a mob of fashionably dress'd speculators and vulgarians. True, indeed, behind this fantastic farce, enacted on the visible stage of society, solid things and stupendous labors are to be discover'd, existing crudely and going on in the background, to advance and tell themselves in time. Yet the truths are none the less terrible. I say that our New World democracy, however great a success in uplifting the masses out of their sloughs, in materialistic development, products, and in certain highly-deceptive superficial popular intellectuality, is, so far, an almost complete failure in its social aspects, and in really grand religious, moral, literary, and esthetic results. In vain do we march with unprecedented strides to empire so colossal, outvying the antique, beyond Alexander's, beyond the proudest sway of Rome. In vain have we annex'd Texas, California, Alaska, and reach north for Canada and south for Cuba. It is as if we were somehow being endow'd with a vast and more and more thoroughly-appointed body, and then left with little or no soul.

Let me illustrate further, as I write, with current observations, localities, etc. The subject is important, and will bear repetition. After an absence, I am now again (September, 1870) in New York city and Brooklyn, on a few weeks' vacation. The splendor, picturesqueness, and oceanic amplitude and rush of these great cities, the unsurpass'd situation, rivers and bay, sparkling sea-tides, costly and lofty new buildings, façades of marble and iron, of original grandeur and elegance of design, with the masses of gay color, the preponderance of white and blue, the flags flying, the endless ships, the tumultuous streets, Broadway, the heavy, low, musical roar, hardly ever intermitted, even at night; the jobbers' houses, the rich shops, the wharves, the great Central Park, and the Brooklyn Park of hills, (as I wander among them this beautiful fall weather, musing, watching, absorbing)—the assemblages of the citizens in their groups, conversations, trades, evening amusements, or along the by-quarters—these, I say, and the like of these, completely satisfy my senses of power, fulness, motion, etc., and give me, through such senses and appetites, and through my esthetic conscience, a continued exaltation and absolute fulfilment. Always and more and more, as I cross the East and North rivers, the ferries, or with the pilots in their pilot-houses, or pass an hour in Wall street, or the gold exchange, I realize, (if we must admit such partialisms,) that not Nature alone is great in her fields of freedom and the open air, in her storms, the shows of night and day, the mountains, forests, seas—but in the artificial, the work of man too is equally great—in this profusion of teeming humanity—in these ingenuities, streets, goods, houses, ships—these hurrying, feverish, electric crowds of men, their complicated business genius, (not least among the geniuses,) and all this mighty, many-threaded wealth and industry concentrated here.

But sternly discarding, shutting our eyes to the glow and grandeur of the general superficial effect, coming down to what is of the only real importance, Personalities, and examining minutely, we question, we ask, Are there, indeed, *men* here worthy the name? Are there athletes? Are there perfect women, to match the generous material luxuriance? Is there a pervading atmosphere of beautiful manners? Are there crops of fine youths, and majestic old persons? Are there arts worthy freedom and a rich people? Is there a great moral and religious civilization—the only justification of a great material one? Confess that to severe eyes, using the moral microscope upon humanity, a sort of dry and flat Sahara appears, these cities, crowded with petty grotesques, malformations, phantoms, playing meaningless antics. Confess that everywhere, in shop, street, church, theatre, barroom, official chair, are pervading flippancy and vulgarity, low cunning, infidelity—everywhere the youth puny, impudent, foppish, prematurely ripe—everywhere an abnormal libidinousness, unhealthy forms, male, female, painted, padded, dyed, chignon'd, muddy complexions, bad blood, the capacity for good motherhood deceasing or deceas'd, shallow notions of beauty, with a range of manners, or rather lack of manners, (considering the advantages enjoy'd,) probably the meanest to be seen in the world.

Of all this, and these lamentable conditions, to breathe into them the breath recuperative of sane and heroic life, I say a new founded literature, not merely to copy and reflect existing surfaces, or pander to what is called taste—not only to amuse, pass away time, celebrate the beautiful, the refined, the past, or exhibit technical, rhythmic, or grammatical dexterity—but a literature underlying life, religious, consistent with science, handling the elements and forces with competent power, teaching and training men—and, as perhaps the most precious of its results, achieving the entire redemption of woman out of these incredible holds and webs of silliness, millinery, and every kind of dyspeptic depletion—and thus insuring to the States a strong and sweet Female Race, a race of perfect Mothers—is what is needed.

And now, in the full conception of these facts and points, and all that they infer, pro and con—with yet unshaken faith in the elements of the American masses, the composites, of both sexes, and even consider'd as individuals—and ever recognizing in them the broadest bases of the best literary and esthetic appreciation—I proceed with my speculations, Vistas.

First, let us see what we can make out of a brief, general, sentimental consideration of political democracy, and whence it has arisen, with regard to some of its current features, as an aggregate, and as the basic structure of our future literature and authorship. We shall, it is true, quickly and continually find the origin-idea of the singleness of man, individualism, asserting itself, and cropping forth, even from the opposite ideas. But the mass, or lump character, for imperative reasons, is to be ever carefully weigh'd, borne in mind, and provided for. Only from it, and from its proper regulation and potency, comes the other, comes the chance of individualism. The two are contradictory, but our task is to reconcile them.

The political history of the past may be summ'd up as having grown out of what underlies the words, order, safety, caste, and especially out of the need of some prompt deciding authority, and of cohesion at all cost. Leaping time, we come to the period within the memory of people now living, when, as from some lair where they had slumber'd long, accumulating wrath, sprang up and are yet active, (1790, and on even to the present, 1870,) those noisy eructations, destructive iconoclasms, a fierce sense of wrongs, amid which moves the form, well known in modern history, in the old world, stain'd with much blood, and mark'd by savage reactionary clamors and demands. These bear, mostly, as on one inclosing point of need.

For after the rest is said—after the many time-honor'd and really true things for subordination, experience, rights of property, etc., have been listen'd to and acquiesced in—after the valuable and well-settled statement of our duties and relations in society is thoroughly conn'd over and exhausted—it remains to bring forward and modify everything else with the idea of that Something a man is, (last precious consolation of the drudging poor,) standing apart from all else, divine in his own right, and a woman in hers, sole and untouchable by any canons of authority, or any rule derived from precedent, state-safety, the acts of legislatures, or even from what is called religion, modesty, or art. The radiation of this truth is the key of the most significant doings of our immediately preceding three centuries, and has been the political genesis and life of America. Advancing visibly, it still more advances invisibly. Underneath the fluctuations of the expressions of society, as well as the movements of the politics of the leading nations of the world, we see steadily pressing ahead and strengthening itself, even in the midst of immense tendencies toward aggregation, this image of completeness in separatism, of individual personal dignity, of a single person, either male or female, characterized in the main, not from extrinsic acquirements or position, but in the pride of himself or herself alone; and, as an eventual conclusion and summing up, (or else the entire scheme of things is aimless, a cheat, a crash,) the simple idea that the last, best dependence is to be upon humanity itself, and its own inherent, normal, full-grown qualities, without any superstitious support whatever.* * *

HENRY TIMROD [1828–1867]

TIMROD WAS a member of the Charleston literary group that flourished in the decade before the war and included the novelist William Gilmore Simms and the poets Paul Hamilton Hayne and J. M. Legaré. In general their views were those common in the Romantic Movement, with a significant exception. Convinced defenders of the slave system and the Southern way of life, they did not share in the aspirations toward the reform or basic renewal of society characteristic of such writers as Wordsworth and Shelley, Emerson and Lowell.

Timrod was a native of Charleston. He studied for a year and a half at the University of Georgia, read enough law to convince him that he was unsuited to the legal profession, then supported himself for several years as a tutor on a Carolina plantation while writing poetry. A book of poems emerged in 1860. He enlisted as a volunteer in the armies of the Confederacy, but his frail constitution soon forced him out of service. He was editing a newspaper in Columbia, S. C., when Sherman's army arrived. His fortunes and his health ruined, he died of tuberculosis two years later.

In the "mood of exalted devotion which characterized the Confederacy at its best" (to use J. B. Hubbell's phrase) Timrod quickly matured as a poet. What he had written by 1860 was thinly romantic; his best poems came in the few years left to him. They showed a fine sensibility, at once passionate and controlled. They endure, as F. O. Matthiessen has said, with a classic hardness.

Further reading: J. B. Hubbell, *The South in American Literature*, 1954, pp. 466–74. Edd Winfield Parks, *Henry Timrod*, 1964.

Ethnogenesis

The Greek title means "The Birth of a Nation." Written in February 1861 while the First Confederate Congress was in session at Montgomery, Alabama, this poem reflects the spirit of the South on the verge of armed conflict. Fort Sumter was bombarded April 12.

This and the following poems are reprinted from the Memorial Edition of *Poems of Henry Timrod* (Richmond, 1901).

I

Hath not the morning dawned with added light?
And shall not evening call another star
Out of the infinite regions of the night,
To mark this day in Heaven? At last, we are
A nation among nations; and the world
Shall soon behold in many a distant port
   Another flag unfurled!
Now, come what may, whose favor need we court?
And, under God, whose thunder need we fear?
   Thank him who placed us here
Beneath so kind a sky—the very sun
Takes part with us; and on our errands run
All breezes of the ocean; dew and rain
Do noiseless battle for us; and the Year,
And all the gentle daughters in her train,
March in our ranks, and in our service wield
   Long spears of golden grain!
A yellow blossom as her fairy shield,
June flings her azure banner to the wind,
   While in the order of their birth
Her sisters pass, and many an ample field
Grows white beneath their steps, till now, behold,
   Its endless sheets unfold

THE SNOW OF SOUTHERN SUMMERS! Let the earth
Rejoice! beneath those fleeces soft and warm
Our happy land shall sleep
In a repose as deep
As if we lay intrenched behind
Whole leagues of Russian ice and Arctic storm!

II

And what if, mad with wrongs themselves have
wrought,
In their own treachery caught,
By their own fears made bold,
And leagued with him of old,
Who long since in the limits of the North
Set up his evil throne, and warred with God—[1]
What if, both mad and blinded in their rage,
Our foes should fling us down their mortal gage,
And with a hostile step profane our sod!
We shall not shrink, my brothers, but go forth
To meet them, marshaled by the Lord of Hosts,
And overshadowed by the mighty ghosts
Of Moultrie and of Eutaw[2]—who shall foil
Auxiliars such as these? Not these alone,
But every stock and stone
Shall help us; but the very soil,
And all the generous wealth it gives to toil,
And all for which we love our noble land,
Shall fight beside, and through us; sea and strand,
The heart of woman, and her hand,
Tree, fruit, and flower, and every influence,
Gentle, or grave, or grand;
The winds in our defence
Shall seem to blow; to us the hills shall lend
Their firmness and their calm;
And in our stiffened sinews we shall blend
The strength of pine and palm!

III

Nor would we shun the battleground,
Though weak as we are strong;
Call up the clashing elements around,
And test the right and wrong!
On one side, creeds that dare to teach
What Christ and Paul refrained to preach;
Codes built upon a broken pledge,
And Charity that whets a poniard's edge;
Fair schemes that leave the neighboring poor
To starve and shiver at the schemer's door,
While in the world's most liberal ranks enrolled,
He turns some vast philanthropy to gold;
Religion, taking every mortal form
But that a pure and Christian faith makes warm,
Where not to vile fanatic passion urged,
Or not in vague philosophies submerged,
Repulsive with all Pharisaic leaven,
And making laws to stay the laws of Heaven!
And on the other, scorn of sordid gain,
Unblemished honor, truth without a stain,
Faith, justice, reverence, charitable wealth,
And, for the poor and humble, laws which give,
Not the mean right to buy the right to live,
But life, and home, and health!
To doubt the end were want of trust in God,
Who, if he has decreed
That we must pass a redder sea[3]
Than that which rang to Miriam's holy glee,
Will surely raise at need
A Moses with his rod!

IV

But let our fears—if fears we have—be still,
And turn us to the future! Could we climb
Some mighty Alp, and view the coming time,
The rapturous sight would fill
Our eyes with happy tears!
Not only for the glories which the years
Shall bring us; not for lands from sea to sea,
And wealth, and power, and peace, though these
shall be;
But for the distant peoples we shall bless,
And the hushed murmurs of a world's distress:
For, to give labor to the poor,
The whole sad planet o'er,
And save from want and crime the humblest door,
Is one among the many ends for which
God makes us great and rich!
The hour perchance is not yet wholly ripe
When all shall own it, but the type
Whereby we shall be known in every land
Is that vast gulf[4] which lips our Southern strand,
And through the cold, untempered ocean pours
Its genial streams, that far off Arctic shores
May sometimes catch upon the softened breeze
Strange tropic warmth and hints of summer seas.

1861, 1862

The Cotton Boll

While I recline
At ease beneath
This immemorial pine,
Small sphere!

Ethnogenesis. [1] Refers to Satan in Milton's *Paradise Lost.*
[2] Revolutionary War conflicts.

[3] Cf. Exodus xiv.15.
[4] Gulf stream.

(By dusky fingers brought this morning here
And shown with boastful smiles),
I turn thy cloven sheath,
Through which the soft white fibres peer,
That, with their gossamer bands,
Unite, like love, the sea-divided lands,
And slowly, thread by thread,
Draw forth the folded strands,
Than which the trembling line,
By whose frail help yon startled spider fled
Down the tall spear-grass from his swinging bed,
Is scarce more fine;
And as the tangled skein
Unravels in my hands,
Betwixt me and the noonday light,
A veil seems lifted, and for miles and miles
The landscape broadens on my sight,
As, in the little boll, there lurked a spell
Like that which, in the ocean shell,
With mystic sound,
Breaks down the narrow walls that hem us round,
And turns some city lane
Into the restless main,
With all his capes and isles!

Yonder bird,
Which floats, as if at rest,
In those blue tracts above the thunder, where
No vapors cloud the stainless air,
And never sound is heard,
Unless at such rare time
When, from the City of the Blest,
Rings down some golden chime,
Sees not from his high place
So vast a cirque of summer space
As widens round me in one mighty field,
Which, rimmed by seas and sands,
Doth hail its earliest daylight in the beams
Of gray Atlantic dawns;
And, broad as realms made up of many lands,
Is lost afar
Behind the crimson hills and purple lawns
Of sunset, among plains which roll their streams
Against the Evening Star!
And lo!
To the remotest point of sight,
Although I gaze upon no waste of snow,
The endless field is white;
And the whole landscape glows,
For many a shining league away,
With such accumulated light
As Polar lands would flash beneath a tropic day!
Nor lack there (for the vision grows,
And the small charm within my hands—
More potent even than the fabled one,
Which oped whatever golden mystery
Lay hid in fairy wood or magic vale,
The curious ointment of the Arabian tale—
Beyond all mortal sense
Doth stretch my sight's horizon, and I see,
Beneath its simple influence,
As if with Uriel's crown,
I stood in some great temple of the Sun,
And looked, as Uriel, down!)
Nor lack there pastures rich and fields all green
With all the common gifts of God,
For temperate airs and torrid sheen
Weave Edens of the sod;
Through lands which look one sea of billowy gold
Broad rivers wind their devious ways;
A hundred isles in their embraces fold
A hundred luminous bays;
And through yon purple haze
Vast mountains lift their plumed peaks cloud-
crowned;
And, save where up their sides the plowman creeps
An unhewn forest girds them grandly round,
In whose dark shades a future navy sleeps!
Ye Stars, which, though unseen, yet with me gaze
Upon this loveliest fragment of the earth!
Thou Sun, that kindlest all thy gentlest rays
Above it, as to light a favorite hearth!
Ye Clouds, that in your temples in the West
See nothing brighter than its humblest flowers!
And you, ye Winds, that on the ocean's breast
Are kissed to coolness ere ye reach its bowers!
Bear witness with me in my song of praise,
And tell the world that, since the world began,
No fairer land hath fired a poet's lays,
Or given a home to man!

But these are charms already widely blown!
His be the meed whose pencil's trace
Hath touched our very swamps with grace,
And round whose tuneful way
All Southern laurels bloom;
The Poet of "The Woodlands,"[1] unto whom
Alike are known
The flute's low breathing and the trumpet's tone,
And the soft west wind's sighs;
But who shall utter all the debt,
O land wherein all powers are met
That bind a people's heart,
The world doth owe thee at this day,
And which it never can repay,
Yet scarcely deigns to own!
Where sleeps the poet who shall fitly sing

The Cotton Boll. [1] The country estate of William Gilmore Simms, novelist and poet.

The source wherefrom doth spring
That mighty commerce which, confined
To the mean channels of no selfish mart,
Goes out to every shore
Of this broad earth, and throngs the sea with ships
That bear no thunders; hushes hungry lips
In alien lands;
Joins with a delicate web remotest strands;
And gladdening rich and poor,
Doth gild Parisian domes,
Or feed the cottage-smoke of English homes,
And only bounds its blessings by mankind!
In offices like these, thy mission lies,
My Country! and it shall not end
As long as rain shall fall and Heaven bend
In blue above thee; though thy foes be hard
And cruel as their weapons, it shall guard
Thy hearth-stones as a bulwark; make thee great
In white and bloodless state;
And haply, as the years increase—
Still working through its humbler reach
With that large wisdom which the ages teach—
Revive the half-dead dream of universal peace!
As men who labor in that mine
Of Cornwall, hollowed out beneath the bed
Of ocean, when a storm rolls overhead,
Hear the dull booming of the world of brine
Above them, and a mighty muffled roar
Of winds and waters, yet toil calmly on,
And split the rock, and pile the massive ore,
Or carve a niche, or shape the archèd roof;
So I, as calmly, weave my woof
Of song, chanting the days to come,
Unsilenced, though the quiet summer air
Stirs with the bruit of battles, and each dawn
Wakes from its starry silence to the hum
Of many gathering armies. Still,
In that we sometimes hear,
Upon the Northern winds, the voice of woe
Not wholly drowned in triumph, though I know
The end must crown us, and a few brief years
Dry all our tears,
I may not sing too gladly. To thy will
Resigned, O Lord! we cannot all forget
That there is much even Victory must regret.
And, therefore, not too long
From the great burthen of our country's wrong
Delay our just release!
And, if it may be, save
These sacred fields of peace
From stain of patriot or of hostile blood!
Oh, help us, Lord! to roll the crimson flood
Back on its course, and while our banners wing
Northward, strike with us! till the Goth shall cling
To his own blasted altar-stones, and crave
Mercy; and we shall grant it, and dictate
The lenient future of his fate
There, where some rotting ships and crumbling quays
Shall one day mark the Port which ruled the Western seas.

1861

Charleston

Calm as that second summer which precedes
The first fall of the snow,
In the broad sunlight of heroic deeds,
The City bides the foe.

As yet, behind their ramparts stern and proud,
Her bolted thunders sleep—
Dark Sumter like a battlemented cloud,
Looms o'er the solemn deep.

No Calpe[1] frowns from lofty cliff or scar
To guard the holy strand;
But Moultrie holds in leash her dogs of war
Above the level sand.

And down the dunes a thousand guns lie couched
Unseen, beside the flood,
Like tigers in some Orient jungle crouched,
That wait and watch for blood.

Meanwhile, through streets still echoing with trade,
Walk grave and thoughtful men,
Whose hands may one day wield the patriot's blade
As lightly as the pen.

And maidens with such eyes as would grow dim
Over a bleeding hound,
Seem each one to have caught the strength of him
Whose sword she sadly bound.

Thus girt without and garrisoned at home,
Day patient following day,
Old Charleston looks from roof, and spire, and dome,
Across her tranquil bay.

Ships, through a hundred foes, from Saxon lands
And spicy Indian ports,
Bring Saxon steel and iron to her hands,
And Summer to her courts.

But still, along yon dim Atlantic line,
The only hostile smoke
Creeps like a harmless mist above the brine,
From some frail, floating oak.

Charleston. [1] Gibraltar.

Shall the Spring dawn, and she still clad in smiles,
  And with an unscathed brow,
Rest in the strong arms of her palm-crowned isles,
  As fair and free as now?

We know not; in the temple of the Fates
  God has inscribed her doom;
And, all untroubled in her faith, she waits
  The triumph or the tomb.

1862

FREDERICK DOUGLASS [1817?–1895]

Son of an unknown white father and a black mother from whom he was separated in infancy, Frederick Augustus Washington Bailey was born into slavery on a plantation at Tuckahoe, Maryland. When he was about eight years old he was sent to Baltimore to be house-boy in the home of relatives of his master. His new mistress kindly yielded to his plea to be taught to read, though it was illegal to instruct slaves and the lessons ended abruptly when the master of the household discovered what was going on. But the seed had been sown: the child now understood what gave the white man his power over the black man, and saw that education was the pathway to freedom. Secretly, painfully, he persevered with his reading and taught himself to write.

Returned to plantation life at fifteen, he showed an independence of spirit that induced his master to turn him over to a "slave-breaker" named Covey, with whom he spent a year that hardened his determination to escape to freedom. After one unsuccessful attempt, he managed in 1838 to reach New York, and then New Bedford, Massachusetts, where he found work as a laborer. To mark his entry on the life of a free man, he now took the name of Douglass, after the fugitive chieftain in Scott's *The Lady of the Lake.*

The public career of Frederick Douglass began in 1841. While attending an antislavery convention at Nantucket, the young ex-slave was unexpectedly called upon to speak, and though trembling with stage-fright before the audience of distinguished New Englanders, he spoke so movingly that the Massachusetts Anti-Slavery Society at once offered him a position as lecturer and agent. From that time on, Douglass committed himself to the antislavery cause, as speaker, writer, and founder and editor of several newspapers and periodicals. He was a naturally endowed orator—six feet tall, broad-shouldered, with fine strong features, a melodious voice, an eloquent command of language, and a sincerity and conviction stemming from twenty-one bitter years of bondage. Because many people found it hard to believe that the literate, polished speaker was actually a fugitive slave, he wrote and published the *Narrative of the Life of Frederick Douglass* in 1845, naming names, dates, and places—and indeed so exposing himself that he found it expedient to spend the next two years in England to avoid possible re-enslavement. Members of the Society of Friends arranged the purchase of his freedom, and in 1847 he returned to America, moving to Rochester, New York. In 1859 he again fled the country to avoid arrest for alleged complicity in John Brown's raid.

Returning to the United States in 1860, he supported Lincoln and was thereafter active in Republican Party counsels and in national affairs. Among other honors and offices, he served as Marshal of the District of Columbia and as Minister to Haiti. No gradualist and no theorist, he fought Jim Crow practices and racism in the same practical, hard-line terms that he had fought slavery. In assessing his career, his most recent biographer, Benjamin Quarles, quotes from a *Memorial* by Albion W. Tourgée, published the year after Douglass's death: "Three classes of the American people are under special obligation to him: the colored bondman whom he helped to free from the chains which he himself had worn; the free persons of color whom he had helped make citizens; the white people of the United States whom he sought to free from the bondage of caste and relieve from the odium of slavery."

Further reading: *Narrative of the Life of Frederick Douglass, an American Slave, written by himself*, ed. Benjamin Quarles (The John Harvard Library), 1960. Benjamin Quarles, *Frederick Douglass,* 1948.

FROM *Narrative of the Life of Frederick Douglass*

Douglass twice rewrote his autobiography, and brought it up to date, in *My Bondage and My Freedom* (1855) and the *Life and Times of Frederick Douglass* (1882). The selection given here is from the first edition (Boston, 1845).

Chapter X

I left Master Thomas's[1] house, and went to live with Mr. Covey, on the 1st of January, 1833. I was now, for the first time in my life, a field hand. In my new employment, I found myself even more awkward than a country boy appeared to be in a large city. I had been at my new home but one week before Mr. Covey gave me a very severe whipping, cutting my back, causing the blood to run, and raising ridges on my flesh as large as my little finger. The details of this affair are as follows: Mr. Covey sent me, very early in the morning of one of our coldest days in the month of January, to the woods, to get a load of wood. He gave me a team of unbroken oxen. He told me which was the in-hand ox, and which the off-hand one. He then tied the end of a large rope around the horns of the in-hand ox, and gave me the other end of it, and told me, if the oxen started to run, that I must hold on upon the rope. I had never driven oxen before, and of course I was very awkward. I, however, succeeded in getting to the edge of the woods with little difficulty; but I had got a very few rods into the woods, when the oxen took fright, and started full tilt, carrying the cart against trees, and over stumps, in the most frightful manner. I expected every moment that my brains would be dashed out against the trees. After running thus for a considerable distance, they finally upset the cart, dashing it with great force against a tree, and threw themselves into a dense thicket. How I escaped death, I do not know. There I was, entirely alone, in a thick wood, in a place new to me. My cart was upset and shattered, my oxen were entangled among the young trees, and there was none to help me. After a long spell of effort, I succeeded in getting my cart righted, my oxen disentangled, and again yoked to the cart. I now proceeded with my team to the place where I had, the day before, been chopping wood, and loaded my cart pretty heavily, thinking in this way to tame my oxen. I then proceeded on my way home. I had now consumed one half of the day. I got out of the woods safely, and now felt out of danger. I stopped my oxen to open the woods gate; and just as I did so, before I could get hold of my ox-rope, the oxen again started, rushed through the gate, catching it between the wheel and the body of the cart, tearing it to pieces, and coming within a few inches of crushing me against the gate-post. Thus twice, in one short day, I escaped death by the merest chance. On my return, I told Mr. Covey what had happened, and how it happened. He ordered me to return to the woods again immediately. I did so, and he followed on after me. Just as I got into the woods, he came up and told me to stop my cart, and that he would teach me how to trifle away my time, and break gates. He then went to a large gum-tree, and with his axe cut three large switches, and, after trimming them up neatly with his pocket-knife, he ordered me to take off my clothes. I made him no answer, but stood with my clothes on. He repeated his order. I still made him no answer, nor did I move to strip myself. Upon this he rushed at me with the fierceness of a tiger, tore off my clothes, and lashed me till he had worn out his switches, cutting me so savagely as to leave the marks visible for a long time after. This whipping was the first of a number just like it, and for similar offences.

I lived with Mr. Covey one year. During the first six months, of that year, scarce a week passed without his whipping me. I was seldom free from a sore back. My awkwardness was almost always his excuse for whipping me. We were worked fully up to the point of endurance. Long before day we were up, our horses fed, and by the first approach of day we were off to the field with our hoes and ploughing teams. Mr. Covey gave us enough to eat, but scarce

[1] Thomas Auld of St. Michael's, Talbot County, Maryland.

time to eat it. We were often less than five minutes taking our meals. We were often in the field from the first approach of day till its last lingering ray had left us; and at saving-fodder time, midnight often caught us in the field binding blades.

Covey would be out with us. The way he used to stand it, was this. He would spend the most of his afternoons in bed. He would then come out fresh in the evening, ready to urge us on with his words, example, and frequently with the whip. Mr. Covey was one of the few slaveholders who could and did work with his hands. He was a hard-working man. He knew by himself just what a man or a boy could do. There was no deceiving him. His work went on in his absence almost as well as in his presence; and he had the faculty of making us feel that he was ever present with us. This he did by surprising us. He seldom approached the spot where we were at work openly, if he could do it secretly. He always aimed at taking us by surprise. Such was his cunning, that we used to call him, among ourselves, "the snake." When we were at work in the cornfield, he would sometimes crawl on his hands and knees to avoid detection, and all at once he would rise nearly in our midst, and scream out, "Ha, ha! Come, come! Dash on, dash on!" This being his mode of attack, it was never safe to stop a single minute. His comings were like a thief in the night. He appeared to us as being ever at hand. He was under every tree, behind every stump, in every bush, and at every window, on the plantation. He would sometimes mount his horse, as if bound to St. Michael's, a distance of seven miles, and in half an hour afterwards you would see him coiled up in the corner of the wood-fence, watching every motion of the slaves. He would, for this purpose, leave his horse tied up in the woods. Again, he would sometimes walk up to us, and give us orders as though he was upon the point of starting on a long journey, turn his back upon us, and make as though he was going to the house to get ready; and, before he would get half way thither, he would turn short and crawl into a fence-corner, or behind some tree, and there watch us till the going down of the sun.

Mr. Covey's *forte* consisted in his power to deceive. His life was devoted to planning and perpetrating the grossest deceptions. Every thing he possessed in the shape of learning or religion, he made conform to his disposition to deceive. He seemed to think himself equal to deceiving the Almighty. He would make a short prayer in the morning, and a long prayer at night; and, strange as it may seem, few men would at times appear more devotional than he. The exercises of his family devotions were always commenced with singing; and, as he was a very poor singer himself, the duty of raising the hymn generally came upon me. He would read his hymn, and nod at me to commence. I would at times do so; at others, I would not. My non-compliance would almost always produce much confusion. To show himself independent of me, he would start and stagger through with his hymn in the most discordant manner. In this state of mind, he prayed with more than ordinary spirit. Poor man! such was his disposition, and success at deceiving, I do verily believe that he sometimes deceived himself into the solemn belief, that he was a sincere worshipper of the most high God; and this, too, at a time when he may be said to have been guilty of compelling his woman slave to commit the sin of adultery. The facts in the case are these: Mr. Covey was a poor man; he was just commencing in life; he was only able to buy one slave; and, shocking as is the fact, he bought her, as he said, for *a breeder.* This woman was named Caroline. Mr. Covey bought her from Mr. Thomas Lowe, about six miles from St. Michael's. She was a large, able-bodied woman, about twenty years old. She had already given birth to one child, which proved her to be just what he wanted. After buying her, he hired a married man of Mr. Samuel Harrison, to live with him one year; and him he used to fasten up with her every night! The result was, that, at the end of the year, the miserable woman gave birth to twins. At this result Mr. Covey seemed to be highly pleased, both with the man and the wretched woman. Such was his joy, and that of his wife, that nothing they could do for Caroline during her confinement was too good, or too hard, to be done. The children were regarded as being quite an addition to his wealth.

If at any one time of my life more than another, I was made to drink the bitterest dregs of slavery, that time was during the first six months of my stay with Mr. Covey. We were worked in all weathers. It was never too hot or too cold; it could never rain, blow, hail, or snow, too hard for us to work in the field. Work, work, work, was scarcely more the order of the day than of the night. The longest days were too short him, and the shortest nights too long for him. I was somewhat unmanageable when I first went there, but a few months of this discipline tamed me. Mr. Covey succeeded in breaking me. I was broken in body, soul, and spirit. My natural elasticity was crushed, my intellect languished, the disposition to read departed, the cheerful spark that lingered about my eye died; the dark night of slavery closed in upon me; and behold a man transformed into a brute!

Sunday was my only leisure time. I spent this in a sort of beast-like stupor, between sleep and wake, under some large tree. At times I would rise up, a flash of energetic freedom would dart through my soul, accompanied with a faint beam of hope that flickered for a moment, and then vanished. I sank down again, mourning over my wretched condition. I was sometimes prompted to take my life, and that of Covey, but was prevented by a combination of hope and fear. My sufferings on this plantation seem now like a dream rather than a stern reality.

Our house stood within a few rods of the Chesapeake Bay, whose broad bosom was ever white with sails from every quarter of the habitable globe. Those beautiful vessels, robed in purest white, so delightful to the eye of freemen, were to me so many shrouded ghosts, to terrify and torment me with thoughts of my wretched condition. I have often, in the deep stillness of a summer's Sabbath, stood all alone upon the lofty banks of that noble bay, and traced, with saddened heart and tearful eye, the countless number of sails moving off to the mighty ocean. The sight of these always affected me powerfully. My thoughts would compel utterance; and there, with no audience but the Almighty, I would pour out my soul's complaint, in my rude way, with an apostrophe to the moving multitude of ships:—

"You are loosed from your moorings, and are free; I am fast in my chains, and am a slave! You move merrily before the gentle gale, and I sadly before the bloody whip! You are freedom's swift-winged angels, that fly round the world; I am confined in bands of iron! O that I were free! O, that I were on one of your gallant decks, and under your protecting wing! Alas! betwixt me and you, the turbid waters roll. Go on, go on. O that I could also go! Could I but swim! If I could fly! O, why was I born a man, of whom to make a brute! The glad ship is gone; she hides in the dim distance. I am left in the hottest hell of unending slavery. O God, save me! God, deliver me! Let me be free! Is there any God? Why am I a slave? I will run away. I will not stand it. Get caught, or get clear, I'll try it. I had as well die with ague as the fever. I have only one life to lose. I had as well be killed running as die standing. Only think of it; one hundred miles straight north, and I am free! Try it? Yes! God helping me, I will. It cannot be that I shall live and die a slave. I will take to the water. This very bay shall yet bear me into freedom. The steamboats steered in a north-east course from North Point. I will do the same; and when I get to the head of the bay, I will turn my canoe adrift, and walk straight through Delaware into Pennsylvania. When I get there, I shall not be required to have a pass; I can travel without being disturbed. Let but the first opportunity offer, and, come what will, I am off. Meanwhile, I will try to bear up under the yoke. I am not the only slave in the world. Why should I fret? I can bear as much as any of them. Besides, I am but a boy, and all boys are bound to some one. It may be that my misery in slavery will only increase my happiness when I get free. There is a better day coming."

Thus I used to think, and thus I used to speak to myself; goaded almost to madness at one moment, and at the next reconciling myself to my wretched lot.

I have already intimated that my condition was much worse, during the first six months of my stay at Mr. Covey's, than in the last six. The circumstances leading to the change in Mr. Covey's course toward me form an epoch in my humble history. You have seen how a man was made a slave; you shall see how a slave was made a man. On one of the hottest days of the month of August, 1833, Bill Smith, William Hughes, a slave named Eli, and myself, were engaged in fanning wheat. Hughes was clearing the fanned wheat from before the fan, Eli was turning, Smith was feeding, and I was carrying wheat to the fan. The work was simple, requiring strength rather than intellect; yet, to one entirely unused to such work, it came very hard. About three o'clock of that day, I broke down; my strength failed me; I was seized with a violent aching of the head, attended with extreme dizziness; I trembled in every limb. Finding what was coming, I nerved myself up, feeling it would never do to stop work. I stood as long as I could stagger to the hopper with grain. When I could stand no longer, I fell, and felt as if held down by an immense weight. The fan of course stopped; every one had his own work to do; and no one could do the work of the other, and have his own go on at the same time.

Mr. Covey was at the house, about one hundred yards from the treading-yard where we were fanning. On hearing the fan stop, he left immediately, and came to the spot where we were. He hastily inquired what the matter was. Bill answered that I was sick, and there was no one to bring wheat to the fan. I had by this time crawled away under the side of the post and rail-fence by which the yard was enclosed, hoping to find relief by getting out of the sun. He then asked where I was. He was told by one of the hands. He came to the spot, and, after looking at me awhile, asked me what was the matter. I told him as well as I could, for I scarce had strength to speak. He then gave me a savage kick in the side, and told me to get up. I tried to do so, but fell back in the attempt. He gave me another kick, and again told me to rise. I again tried, and succeeded in gaining my feet; but, stooping to get the tub with which I was feeding the fan, I again staggered and fell. While down in this situation, Mr. Covey took up the hickory slat with which Hughes had been striking off the half-bushel measure, and with it gave me a heavy blow upon the head, making a large wound, and the blood ran freely; and with this again told me to get up. I made no effort to comply, having now made up my mind to let him do his worst. In a short time after receiving this blow, my head grew better. Mr. Covey had now left me to my fate. At this moment I resolved, for the first time, to go to my master, enter a complaint, and ask his protection. In order to do this, I must that afternoon walk seven miles; and this, under the circumstances, was truly a severe undertaking. I was exceedingly feeble; made so as much by the kicks and blows which I received, as by the severe fit of sickness to which I had been subjected. I, however, watched my chance, while Covey was looking in an opposite direction, and started for St. Michael's. I succeeded in getting a considerable distance on my way to the woods, when Covey discovered me, and called after me to come back, threatening what he would do if I did not come. I disregarded both his calls and his threats, and made my way to the woods as fast as my feeble state would allow; and thinking I might be overhauled by him if I kept the road, I walked through the woods, keeping far enough from the road to avoid detection, and near enough to prevent losing my way. I had not gone far before my little strength again failed me. I could go no farther. I fell down, and lay for a considerable time. The blood was yet oozing from the wound on my head. For a time I thought I should bleed to death; and think now that I should have done so, but that the blood so matted my hair as to stop the wound. After lying there about three quarters of an hour, I nerved myself up again, and started on my way, through bogs and briers, barefooted and bareheaded, tearing my feet sometimes at nearly every step; and after a journey of about seven miles, occupying some five hours to perform it, I arrived at master's store. I then presented an appearance enough to affect any but a heart of iron. From the crown of my head to my feet, I was covered with blood. My hair was all clotted with dust and blood; my shirt was stiff with blood. My legs and feet were torn in sundry places with briers and thorns, and were also covered with blood. I suppose I looked like a man who had escaped a den of wild beasts, and barely escaped them. In this state I appeared before my master, humbly entreating him to interpose his authority for my protection. I told him all the circumstances as well as I could, and it seemed, as I spoke, at times to affect him. He would then walk the floor, and seek to justify Covey by saying he expected I deserved it. He asked me what I wanted. I told him, to let me get a new home; that as sure as I lived with Mr. Covey again, I should live with but to die with him; that Covey would surely kill me; he was in a fair way for it. Master Thomas ridiculed the idea that there was any danger of Mr. Covey's killing me, and said that he knew Mr. Covey; that he was a good man, and that he could not think of taking me from him; that, should he do so, he would lose the whole year's wages; that I belonged to Mr. Covey for one year, and that I must go back to him, come what might; and that I must not trouble him with any more stories, or that he would himself *get hold of me.* After threatening me thus, he gave me a very large dose of salts, telling me that I might remain in St. Michael's that night, (it being quite late,) but that I must be off back to Mr. Covey's early in the morning; and that if I did not, he would *get hold of me,* which meant that he would whip me. I remained all night, and, according to his orders, I started off to Covey's in the morning, (Saturday morning,) wearied in body and broken in spirit. I got no supper that night, or breakfast that morning. I reached Covey's about nine o'clock; and just as I was getting over the fence that divided Mrs. Kemp's fields from ours, out ran Covey with his cowskin, to give me another whipping. Before he could reach me, I succeeded in getting to the cornfield; and as the corn was very high, it afforded me the means of hiding. He seemed very angry, and searched for me a long time. My behavior was altogether unaccountable. He finally gave up the chase, thinking, I suppose, that I must come home for something to eat; he would give himself no further trouble in looking for me. I spent that day mostly in the woods, having the alternative before me,—to go home and be whipped to death, or stay in the woods and be starved to death. That night, I fell in with Sandy Jenkins, a slave with whom I was somewhat acquainted. Sandy had a free wife who lived about four miles from Mr. Covey's; and it being Saturday, he was on his way to see her. I told him my circumstances, and he very kindly invited me to go home with him. I went home with him, and talked this whole matter over, and got his advice as to what course it was best for me to pursue. I found Sandy an old adviser. He told me, with great solemnity, I must go back to Covey; but that before I went, I must go with him into another part of the woods, where there was a certain *root,* which, if I would take some of it with me, carrying it *always on my right side,* would render it impossible for Mr. Covey, or any other white man, to whip me. He said he had carried it for years; and since he had done so, he had never received a blow, and never expected to while he carried it. I at first rejected the idea, that the simple carrying of a root in my pocket would have any such effect as he had said, and was not disposed to take it; but Sandy impressed the necessity with much earnestness, telling me it could do no harm, if it did no good. To please him, I at length took the root, and, according to his direction, carried it upon my right side. This was Sunday morning. I immediately started for home; and upon entering the yard gate, out came Mr. Covey on his way to meeting. He spoke to me very kindly, bade me drive the pigs from a lot near by, and passed on towards the church. Now, this singular conduct of Mr. Covey really made me begin to think that there was something in the *root* which Sandy had given me; and had it been on any other day than Sunday, I could have attributed the conduct to no other cause than the influence of that root; and as it was, I was half inclined to think the *root* to be something more than I at first had taken it to be. All went well till Monday morning. On this morning, the virtue of the *root* was fully tested. Long before daylight, I was called to go and rub, curry, and feed, the horses. I obeyed, and was glad to obey. But whilst thus engaged, whilst in the act of throwing down some blades from the loft, Mr. Covey entered the stable with a long rope; and just as I was half out of the loft, he caught hold of my legs, and was about tying me. As soon as I found what he was up to, I gave a sudden spring, and as I did so, he holding to my legs, I was brought sprawling on the stable floor. Mr. Covey seemed now to think he had me, and could do what he pleased; but at this moment—from whence came the spirit I don't know—I resolved to fight; and, suiting my action to the resolution, I seized Covey hard by the throat; and as I did so, I rose. He held on to me, and I to him. My resistance was so entirely unexpected, that Covey seemed taken all aback. He trembled like a leaf. This gave me assurance, and I held him uneasy, causing the blood to run where I touched him with the ends of my fingers. Mr. Covey soon called out to Hughes for help. Hughes came, and, while Covey held me, attempted to tie my right hand. While he was in the act of doing so, I watched my chance, and gave him a heavy kick close under the ribs. This kick fairly sickened Hughes, so that he left me in the hands of Mr. Covey. This kick had the effect of not only weakening Hughes, but Covey also. When he saw Hughes bending over with pain, his courage quailed. He asked me if I meant to persist in my resistance. I told him I did, come what might; that he had used me like a brute for six months, and that I was determined to be used so no longer. With that, he strove to drag me to a stick that was lying just out of the stable door. He meant to knock me down. But just as he was leaning over to get the stick, I seized him with both hands by his collar, and brought him by a sudden snatch to the ground. By this time, Bill came. Covey called upon him for assistance. Bill wanted to know what he could do. Covey said, "Take hold of him, take hold of him!" Bill said his master hired him out to work, and not to help whip me; so he left Covey and myself to fight our own battle out. We were at it for nearly two hours. Covey at length let me go, puffing and blowing at a great rate, saying that if I had not resisted, he would not have whipped me half so much. The truth was, that he had not whipped me at all. I considered him as getting entirely the worst end of the bargain; for he had drawn no blood from me, but I had from him. The whole six months afterwards, that I spent with Mr. Covey, he never laid the weight of his finger upon me in anger. He would occasionally say, he didn't want to get hold of me again. "No," thought I, "you need not; for you will come off worse than you did before."

This battle with Mr. Covey was the turning-point in my career as a slave. It rekindled the few expiring embers of freedom, and revived within me a sense of my own manhood. It recalled the departed self-confidence, and inspired me again with a determination to be free. The gratification afforded by the triumph was a full compensation for whatever else might follow, even death itself. He only can understand the deep satisfaction which I experienced, who has himself repelled by force the bloody arm of slavery. I felt as I never felt before. It was a glorious resurrection, from the tomb of slavery, to the heaven of freedom. My long-crushed spirit rose, cowardice departed, bold defiance took its place; and I now resolved that, however long I might remain a slave in form, the day had passed forever when I could be a slave in fact. I did not hesitate to let it be known of me, that the white man who expected to succeed in whipping, must also succeed in killing me.

From this time I was never again what might be called fairly whipped, though I remained a slave four years afterwards. I had several fights, but was never whipped.

It was for a long time a matter of surprise to me why Mr. Covey did not immediately have me taken by the constable to the whipping-post, and there regularly whipped for the crime of raising my hand against a white man in defence of myself. And the only explanation I can now think of does not entirely satisfy me; but such as it is, I will give it. Mr. Covey enjoyed the most unbounded reputation for being a first-rate overseer and negro-breaker. It was of considerable importance to him. That reputation was at stake; and had he sent me—a boy about sixteen years old—to the public whipping-post, his reputation would have been lost; so, to save his reputation, he suffered me to go unpunished.***

FROM *Fourth of July Oration, 1852*

Speaking in the sonorous cadences of the nineteenth-century American oratorical tradition, yet varying this at times with an almost conversational tone, Douglass confronted his audience, in Corinthian Hall, Rochester, with the question: What could the Fourth of July mean to the black American, slave or free? The text is from the pamphlet publication of the address, Rochester, N. Y., 1852.

*** My business, if I have any here to-day, is with the present. The accepted time with God and his cause is the ever-living now.

"Trust no future, howe'er pleasant,
Let the dead past bury its dead;
Act, act in the living present,
Heart within, and God o'erhead."[1]

We have to do with the past only as we can make it useful to the present and to the future. To all inspiring motives, to noble deeds which can be gained from the past, we are welcome. But now is the time, the important time. Your fathers have lived, died, and have done their work, and have done much of it well. You live and must die, and you must do your work. You have no right to enjoy a child's share in the labor of your fathers, unless your children are to be blest by your labors. You have no right to wear out and waste the hard-earned fame of your fathers to cover your indolence. Sydney Smith tells us that men seldom eulogize the wisdom and virtues of their fathers, but to excuse some folly or wickedness of their own. This truth is not a doubtful one. There are illustrations of it near and remote, ancient and modern. It was fashionable, hundreds of years ago, for the children of Jacob to boast, we have "Abraham to our father,"[2] when they had long lost Abraham's faith and spirit. That people contented themselves under the shadow of Abraham's great name, while they repudiated the deeds which made his name great. Need I remind you that a similar thing is being done all over this country to-day? Need I tell you that the Jews are not the only people who built the tombs of the prophets, and garnished the sepulchres of the righteous? Washington could not die till he had broken the chains of his slaves. Yet his monument is built up by the price of human blood, and the traders in the bodies and souls of men, shout—"We have Washington to *our father.*"—Alas! that it should be so; yet so it is.

"The evil that men do, lives after them,
The good is oft interred with their bones."[3]

[1] Longfellow, "A Psalm of Life."
[2] Luke iii.8.
[3] Shakespeare, *Julius Caesar* III.ii.80–81.

Fellow-citizens, pardon me, allow me to ask, why am I called upon to speak here to-day? What have I, or those I represent, to do with your national independence? Are the great principles of political freedom and of natural justice, embodied in that Declaration of Independence, extended to us? and am I, therefore, called upon to bring our humble offering to the national altar, and to confess the benefits and express devout gratitude for the blessings resulting from your independence to us?

Would to God, both for your sakes and ours, that an affirmative answer could be truthfully returned to these questions! Then would my task be light, and my burden easy and delightful. For *who* is there so cold, that a nation's sympathy could not warm him? Who so obdurate and dead to the claims of gratitude, that would not thankfully acknowledge such priceless benefits? Who so stolid and selfish, that would not give his voice to swell the hallelujahs of a nation's jubilee, when the chains of servitude had been torn from his limbs? I am not that man. In a case like that, the dumb might eloquently speak, and the "lame man leap as an hart."[4]

But, such is not the state of the case. I say it with a sad sense of the disparity between us. I am not included within the pale of this glorious anniversary! Your high independence only reveals the immeasurable distance between us. The blessings in which you, this day, rejoice, are not enjoyed in common.—The rich inheritance of justice, liberty, prosperity and independence, bequeathed by your fathers, is shared by you, not by me. The sunlight that brought life and healing to you, has brought stripes and death to me. This Fourth July is *yours,* not *mine. You* may rejoice, *I* must mourn. To drag a man in fetters into the grand illuminated temple of liberty, and call upon him to join you in joyous anthems, were inhuman mockery and sacrilegious irony. Do you mean, citizens, to mock me, by asking me to speak to-day? If so, there is a parallel to your conduct. And let me warn you that it is dangerous to copy the example of a nation whose crimes, towering up to heaven, were thrown down by the breath of the Almighty, burying that nation in irrecoverable ruin! I can to-day take up the plaintive lament of a peeled and woe-smitten people!

"By the rivers of Babylon, there we sat down. Yea! we wept when we remembered Zion. We hanged our harps upon the willows in the midst thereof. For there, they that carried us away captive, required of us a song; and they who wasted us required of us mirth, saying, Sing us one of the songs of Zion. How can we sing the Lord's song in a strange land? If I forget thee, O Jerusalem, let my

[4] Isaiah xxxv.6.

right hand forget her cunning. If I do not remember thee, let my tongue cleave to the roof of my mouth."[5]

Fellow citizens; above your national, tumultous joy, I hear the mournful wail of millions! whose chains, heavy and grievous yesterday, are, to-day, rendered more intolerable by the jubilee shouts that reach them. If I do forget, if I do not faithfully remember those bleeding children of sorrow this day, "may my right hand forget her cunning, and may my tongue cleave to the roof of my mouth!" To forget them, to pass lightly over their wrongs, and to chime in with the popular theme, would be treason most scandalous and shocking, and would make me a reproach before God and the world. My subject, then, fellow-citizens, is AMERICAN SLAVERY. I shall see, this day, and its popular characteristics, from the slave's point of view. Standing, there, identified with the American bondman, making his wrongs mine, I do not hesitate to declare, with all my soul, that the character and conduct of this nation never looked blacker to me than on this 4th of July! Whether we turn to the declarations of the past, or to the professions of the present, the conduct of the nation seems equally hideous and revolting. America is false to the past, false to the present, and solemnly binds herself to be false to the future. Standing with God and the crushed and bleeding slave on this occasion, I will, in the name of humanity which is outraged, in the name of liberty which is fettered, in the name of the constitution and the Bible, which are disregarded and trampled upon, dare to call in question and to denounce, with all the emphasis I can command, everything that serves to perpetuate slavery—the great sin and shame of America! "I will not equivocate; I will not excuse;"[6] I will use the severest language I can command; and yet not one word shall escape me that any man, whose judgment is not blinded by prejudice, or who is not at heart a slaveholder, shall not confess to be right and just.

But I fancy I hear some one of my audience say, it is just in this circumstance that you and your brother abolitionists fail to make a favorable impression on the public mind. Would you argue more, and denounce less, would you persuade more, and rebuke less, your cause would be much more likely to succeed. But, I submit, where all is plain there is nothing to be argued. What point in the anti-slavery creed would you have me argue? On what branch of the subject do the people of this country need light? Must I undertake to prove that the slave is a man? That point is conceded already. Nobody doubts it. The slaveholders themselves acknowledge it in the enactment of laws for their government.

[5] Psalms cxxxvii.1-6.

[6] William Lloyd Garrison, in the Salutory of *The Liberator.*

They acknowledge it when they punish disobedience on the part of the slave. There are seventy-two crimes in the State of Virginia, which, if committed by a black man, (no matter how ignorant he be,) subject him to the punishment of death; while only two of the same crimes will subject a white man to the like punishment.—What is this but the acknowledgement that the slave is a moral, intellectual and responsible being. The manhood of the slave is conceded. It is admitted in the fact that Southern statute books are covered with enactments forbidding, under severe fines and penalties, the teaching of the slave to read or to write.—When you can point to any such laws, in reference to the beasts of the field, then I may consent to argue the manhood of the slave. When the dogs in your streets, when the fowls of the air, when the cattle on your hills, when the fish of the sea, and the reptiles that crawl, shall be unable to distinguish the slave from a brute, *then* will I argue with you that the slave is a man!

For the present, it is enough to affirm the equal manhood of the negro race. Is it not astonishing that, while we are ploughing, planting and reaping, using all kinds of mechanical tools, erecting houses, constructing bridges, building ships, working in metals of brass, iron, copper, silver and gold; that, while we are reading, writing and cyphering, acting as clerks, merchants and secretaries, having among us lawyers, doctors, ministers, poets, authors, editors, orators and teachers; that, while we are engaged in all manner of enterprises common to other men, digging gold in California, capturing the whale in the Pacific, feeding sheep and cattle on the hill-side, living, moving, acting, thinking, planning, living in families as husbands, wives and children, and, above all, confessing and worshipping the Christian's God, and looking hopefully for life and immortality beyond the grave, we are called upon to prove that we are men!

Would you have me argue that man is entitled to liberty? that he is the rightful owner of his own body? You have already declared it. Must I argue the wrongfulness of slavery? Is that a question for Republicans? Is it to be settled by the rules of logic and argumentation, as a matter beset with great difficulty, involving a doubtful application of the principle of justice, hard to be understood? How should I look to-day, in the presence of Americans dividing, and subdividing a discourse, to show that men have a natural right to freedom? speaking of it relatively, and positively, negatively, and affirmatively. To do so, would be to make myself ridiculous, and to offer an insult to your understanding.— There is not a man beneath the canopy of heaven, that does not know that slavery is wrong *for him.*

What, am I to argue that it is wrong to make men brutes, to rob them of their liberty, to work them without wages, to keep them ignorant of their relations to their fellow men, to beat them with sticks, to flay their flesh with the lash, to load their limbs with irons, to hunt them with dogs, to sell them at auction, to sunder their families, to knock out their teeth, to burn their flesh, to starve them into obedience and submission to their masters? Must I argue that a system thus marked with blood, and stained with pollution, is *wrong?* No! I will not. I have better employment for my time and strength, than such arguments would imply.

What, then, remains to be argued? Is it that slavery is not divine; that God did not establish it; that our doctors of divinity are mistaken? There is blasphemy in the thought. That which is inhuman, cannot be divine! *Who* can reason on such a proposition? They that can, may; I cannot. The time for such argument is past.

At a time like this, scorching irony, not convincing argument, is needed. O! had I the ability, and could I reach the nation's ear, I would, to day, pour out a fiery stream of biting ridicule, blasting reproach, withering sarcasm, and stern rebuke. For it is not light that is needed, but fire; it is not the gentle shower, but thunder. We need the storm, the whirlwind, and the earthquake. The feeling of the nation must be quickened; the conscience of the nation must be roused; the propriety of the nation must be startled; the hypocrisy of the nation must be exposed; and its crimes against God and man must be proclaimed and denounced.

What, to the American slave, is your 4th of July? I answer; a day that reveals to him, more than all other days in the year, the gross injustice and cruelty to which he is the constant victim. To him, your celebration is a sham; your boasted liberty, an unholy license; your national greatness, swelling vanity; your sounds of rejoicing are empty and heartless; your denunciations of tyrants, brass fronted impudence; your shouts of liberty and equality, hollow mockery; your prayers and hymns, your sermons and thanksgivings, with all your religious parade, and solemnity, are, to him, mere bombast, fraud, deception, impiety, and hypocrisy—a thin veil to cover up crimes which would disgrace a nation of savages. There is not a nation on the earth guilty of practices, more shocking and bloody, than are the people of these United States, at this very hour.

Go where you may, search where you will, roam through all the monarchies and despotisms of the old world, travel through South America, search out every abuse, and when you have found the last, lay your facts by the side of the every day practices of this nation, and you will say with me, that, for revolting barbarity and shameless hypocrisy, America reigns without a rival.***

1852

ABRAHAM LINCOLN [1809-1865]

To THE WELL-KNOWN FACTS of Lincoln's biography—his Kentucky birth, his youth in Indiana, his young manhood in backwoods Illinois, his training in law, his tenure in the state and national legislatures—one might add a few pertinent details. There was the senatorial campaign of 1858, the great debates with Stephen A. Douglas. Lincoln lost the election, but when the Republican national convention met in Chicago two years later he was nominated for the Presidency on the third ballot. With 180 electoral votes to his opponents' 123, he was elected to the office and began four stormy years in the White House.

Lincoln's part in the war need not be discussed here. When the result of the conflict was still in doubt, he was re-elected to the Presidency by an overwhelming majority in the electoral college. Inaugurated March 4, 1865, he had served little more than a month of his second term when an assassin's bullet ended his life.

Lincoln has won a place in American letters by salient ideas expressed in a style free of the bombastic oratory of the frontier, a style that ranged from the simply direct to the quietly firm or the harmoniously elevated.

Text: *The Collected Works of Abraham Lincoln*, Rutgers Edition, (New Brunswick, N. J., 1953).

Further reading: Carl Sandburg, *Abraham Lincoln: The Prairie Years and the War Years* (one-volume abridgement of his six-volume work), 1954. David Donald, *Lincoln Reconsidered*, 1956.

Reply to Horace Greeley

EXECUTIVE MANSION, WASHINGTON,
August 22, 1862

HON. HORACE GREELEY.

Dear Sir: I have just read yours of the 19th addressed to myself through the New-York *Tribune.* If there be in it any statement, or assumptions of fact, which I may know to be erroneous, I do not, now and here, controvert them. If there be in it any inferences which I may believe to be falsely drawn, I do not, now and here, argue against them. If there be perceptible in it an impatient and dictatorial tone, I waive it in deference to an old friend, whose heart I have always supposed to be right.

As to the policy I "seem to be pursuing," as you say, I have not meant to leave any one in doubt.

I would save the Union. I would save it the shortest way under the Constitution. The sooner the national authority can be restored, the nearer the Union will be "the Union as it was." If there be those who would not save the Union, unless they could at the same time *save* slavery, I do not agree with them. If there be those who would not save the Union unless they could at the same time *destroy* slavery, I do not agree with them. My paramount object in this struggle *is* to save the Union, and is *not* either to save or to destroy slavery. If I could save the Union without freeing *any* slave, I would do it; and if I could save it by freeing *all* the slaves, I would do it; and if I could save it by freeing some and leaving others alone, I would also do that. What I do about slavery, and the colored race, I do because I believe it helps to save the Union; and what I forbear, I forbear because I do *not* believe it would help to save the Union. I shall do *less* whenever I shall believe what I am doing hurts the cause, and I shall do *more* whenever I shall believe doing more will help the cause. I shall try to correct errors when shown to be errors, and I shall adopt new views so fast as they shall appear to be the true views.

I have here stated my purpose according to my view of *official* duty; and I intend no modification of my oft-expressed *personal* wish that all men every where could be free.

Yours,
A. LINCOLN

Gettysburg Address

"In a photographer's studio eleven days before delivering the speech at Gettysburg, Lincoln had held in his hands the lengthy address of Edward Everett, the designated orator of the day, the printed two-hour discourse covering nearly two sides of a one-sheet supplement of a Boston newspaper. To a young newspaper correspondent from California he said his own speech at Gettysburg would be 'short, short, short'—as it proved to be, ten sentences spoken in less than five minutes. In its implicative qualities, it stands among the supreme utterances of democratic peoples of the world." (Carl Sandburg, in *Literary History of the United States.)*

Four score and seven years ago our fathers brought forth on this continent, a new nation, conceived in liberty, and dedicated to the proposition that all men are created equal.

Now we are engaged in a great civil war, testing whether that nation, or any nation so conceived and so dedicated, can long endure. We are met on a great battle-field of that war. We have come to dedicate a portion of that field, as a final resting place for those who here gave their lives that that nation might live. It is altogether fitting and proper that we should do this.

But, in a larger sense, we cannot dedicate—we cannot consecrate—we cannot hallow—this ground. The brave men, living and dead, who struggled here, have consecrated it, far above our poor power to add or detract. The world will little note, nor long remember what we say here, but it can never forget what they did here. It is for us the living, rather, to be dedicated here to the unfinished work which they who fought here have thus far so nobly advanced. It is rather for us to be here dedicated to the great task remaining before us—that from these honored dead we take increased devotion to that cause for which they gave the last full measure of devotion—that we here highly resolve that these dead shall not have died in vain—that this nation, under God, shall have a new birth of freedom—and that government of the people, by the people, for the people, shall not perish from the earth.

1863

Letter to Mrs. Bixby

"The War Department records showed a Boston woman to have lost five sons in combat actions. The number was less than five, as later research revealed, but Lincoln spoke through her to all families that had lost a boy or man in the war." (Sandburg)

EXECUTIVE MANSION, WASHINGTON,
November 21, 1864

MRS. BIXBY, Boston, Massachusetts.

Dear Madam,—I have been shown in the files of the War Department a statement of the Adjutant General of Massachusetts that you are the mother of five sons who have died gloriously on the field of battle.

I feel how weak and fruitless must be any words of mine which should attempt to beguile you from the grief of a loss so overwhelming. But I cannot refrain from tendering to you the consolation that may be found in the thanks of the Republic they died to save.

I pray that our Heavenly Father may assuage the anguish of your bereavement, and leave you only the cherished memory of the loved and lost, and the solemn pride that must be yours to have laid so costly a sacrifice upon the altar of Freedom.

Yours, very sincerely and respectfully,
ABRAHAM LINCOLN

Second Inaugural Address

FELLOW-COUNTRYMEN: At this second appearing to take the oath of the presidential office, there is less occasion for an extended address than there was at the first. Then a statement, somewhat in detail, of a course to be pursued, seemed fitting and proper. Now, at the expiration of four years, during which public declarations have been constantly called forth on every point and phase of the great contest which still absorbs the attention and engrosses the energies of the nation, little that is new could be presented. The progress of our arms, upon which all else chiefly depends, is as well known to the public as to myself; and it is, I trust, reasonably satisfactory and encouraging to all. With high hope for the future, no prediction in regard to it is ventured.

On the occasion corresponding to this four years ago, all thoughts were anxiously directed to an impending civil war. All dreaded it—all sought to avert it. While the inaugural address was being delivered from this place, devoted altogether to *saving* the Union without war, insurgent agents were in the city seeking to *destroy* it without war—seeking to dissolve the Union, and divide effects, by negotiation. Both parties deprecated war; but one of them would *make* war rather than let the nation survive; and the other would *accept* war rather than let it perish. And the war came.

One eighth of the whole population were colored slaves, not distributed generally over the Union, but localized in the Southern part of it. These slaves constituted a peculiar and powerful interest. All knew that this interest was, somehow, the cause of the war. To strengthen, perpetuate, and extend this interest was the object for which the insurgents would rend the Union, even by war; while the government claimed no right to do more than to restrict the territorial enlargement of it. Neither party expected for the war, the magnitude, or the duration, which it has already attained. Neither anticipated that the *cause* of the conflict might cease with, or even before, the conflict itself should cease. Each looked for an easier triumph, and a result less fundamental and astounding. Both read the same Bible, and pray to the same God; and each invokes His aid against the other. It may seem strange that any men should dare to ask a just God's assistance in wringing their bread from the sweat of other men's faces; but let us judge not that we be not judged. The prayers of both could not be answered; that of neither has been answered fully. The Almighty has his own purposes. "Woe unto the world because of offences! for it must needs be that offences come; but woe to that man by whom the offence cometh!" If we shall suppose that American Slavery is one of those offences which, in the providence of God, must needs come, but which, having continued through His appointed time, He now wills to remove, and that He gives to both North and South this terrible war, as the woe due to those by whom the offence came, shall we discern therein any departure from those divine attributes which the believers in a Living God always ascribe to him? Fondly do we hope—fervently do we pray—that this mighty scourge of war may speedily pass away. Yet, if God wills that it continue, until all the wealth piled by the bound-man's two hundred and fifty years of unrequited toil shall be sunk, and until every drop of blood drawn with the lash, shall be paid by another drawn with the sword, as was said three thousand years ago, so still it must be said, "the judgments of the Lord are true and righteous altogether."

With malice toward none; with charity for all; with firmness in the right, as God gives us to see the right, let us strive on to finish the work we are in; to bind up the nation's wounds; to care for him who shall have borne the battle, and for his widow, and his orphan—to do all which may achieve and cherish a just, and a lasting peace, among ourselves, and with all nations.

1865

Realism and Naturalism

The Gilded Age and After

THE HALF-CENTURY of American history from the close of the Civil War to the outbreak of World War I was a period in which the industrial revolution, which had made itself felt in England and parts of Europe during the first half of the nineteenth century, began to alter radically the social and economic climate of the United States. To the generation that came of age about 1870, the full implications of the change from an essentially rural, provincial, and agrarian nation to one of growing urban centers, burgeoning factories, and all the attendant adjustments which this change brought with it, were at first only dimly realized. A minority of thoughtful Americans, however, began to speak and write their interpretations of the new dispensation, as did Mark Twain in a novel, *The Gilded Age* (1873), whose title has come to be associated with the period as a whole. "The eight years in America from 1860 to 1868," he said, "uprooted institutions that were centuries old, changed the politics of a people, transformed the social life of half the country, and wrought so profoundly upon the entire national character that the influence cannot be measured." A century later, we can see in clear perspective what Twain's words meant. The surging forces of industrial growth, technological progress, westward expansion, and the aggregation of great fortunes by railroad and oil tycoons presaged a social revolution which was to put the ideals of Jefferson and the framers of the Constitution to tests so severe that the result is still uncertain. What we can say for sure about the social and intellectual character of the decades after 1870 is that there was apparent the beginning of a sharp cleavage between the inherited ideals of the earlier romantic and individualistic period and the hard social facts of the post-Appomattox years.

Inherited political and religious ideals, the principles of equality and freedom, Emersonian self-reliance—the dreams of American romantic idealism—were confronted by a new and disturbing set of conditions. Intellectuals began searching for a new ground from which to comprehend and express these conditions and to explore their implications. It was this effort which established the pattern for the literature and thought behind Realism and Naturalism. Philosophers began to work out pragmatic and relativistic modes of thinking to bridge the widening gulf between traditional religious ideas and the deterministic implications of evolutionary science. Novelists responded to demands for greater psychological realism in the creation of character and greater local and regional authenticity of scene. The fundamental ideological conflict of the period between the Civil War and World War I was a working-out of a middle ground and an effort to harmonize two opposed ways of seeing man and his world. One was the hopeful promise of the eighteenth-century Enlightenment with its faith in a divine destiny for the human race and in the political destiny of the nation. The other was a mechanistic and deterministic outlook based on science and the menacing prospect of a world controlled by powerful natural forces. In official America during the Gilded Age and beyond, rugged individualism, *laissez-faire* economics, and the Gospel of Wealth held sway, despite increasing protests and reform movements directed toward some form of governmental control and responsibility. American thought as a whole moved gradually away from its romantic and idealistic moorings, taking color and shape from the spectacle of Reconstruction politics, the rapid growth of cities, advancing technology, and the concentration of corporate power in the commercial world.

The two administrations of President Grant, 1869–1876, have come to be identified with those tendencies associated with Mark Twain's phrase "The Gilded Age." In politics there were graft, lobbying, and opportunism among legislators who, like the fictional Senator Dilworthy, made a fortune bartering political influence for railroad stock. Leadership seemed suddenly to have shifted away from statesmen like Lincoln to a grasping set of exploiters of the nation's fast-moving economy. The machinations of Tammany Hall under Boss Tweed, for example, managed to bilk the city treasury of New York of millions of dollars. Stock manipulators like Jay Gould and "Jubilee Jim" Fisk attempted to corner the gold market on "Black Friday" in 1869, setting off a panic which brought hardship, suffering, and labor strikes in 1873 and again in 1877. Fisk, who rose from Yankee peddler to millionaire, kept mistresses, and was finally shot by a rival lover, was given a gala funeral on Fifth Avenue with two bands and a police escort, the hearse pulled by six horses as thousands of curious onlookers watched the parade. In 1874 the liberal editor of the *Nation*, E. L. Godkin, summed up the situation in a skillful phrase: "chromo-civilization."

After the disputed Hayes-Tilden election in 1876, a temporary equilibrium was established with the end of "Black Reconstruction" in the South when radical control of the former Confederate states was terminated. Dramatic technological inventions such as the telegraph, the telephone, and the incandescent lamp momentarily concealed the fact that urban progress was bringing with it social and economic dislocations and class conflict. From about 1886, the year of the Haymarket riot in Chicago during which several police were killed by a bomb, a new wave of strikes and violence swept the cities, from the Eastern seaboard to the Middle West. In the nineties, a political coalition of farmers, labor organizations, and Greenback party supporters united behind the leadership of William Jennings Bryan, a liberal and an advocate of free silver. When Bryan was defeated in the election of 1896 by William McKinley, conservatism once more ruled in official Washington.

The closing years of the century and the succeeding decade were marked by an era of relative domestic peace, but the Cuban revolution against Spain touched off a wave of sensational journalism which egged the United States into an imperialistic war with Spain. The war diverted the nation from class struggles and established a climate of rugged individualism and the "muscular" philosophy of Teddy Roosevelt, whose dynamic personality and progressive policies provided strong leadership. Roosevelt glorified the strenuous life, carried a "big stick," and despised the weak and ineffective, lending the energy of his zesty philosophy to an era of big business, but at the same time tempering the excesses of expansionism by his policy of trust-busting. During the first decade of the new century, "muckrakers" like Lincoln Steffens were exposing the corruption of municipal governments, and labor was becoming more firmly organized under Samuel Gompers, Eugene Debs, and other leaders. Political liberals like Robert M. La Follette and William Jennings Bryan continued to agitate against the alliance of big business and machine politics. The opposed forces were gathering for future political and economic struggles; but until the outbreak of war in Europe in 1914, the developing industries in the East and the rapid settlement of frontier communities went on apace in an era of progress and expansion.

Science and Evolution

Gilded Age politics and economic conflicts provided the background and affected the cultural tone of the period, but literature was more immediately responsive to the intellectual currents of the age, and especially to the new science and the evolutionary philosophy of Herbert Spencer, Charles Darwin, and their American followers and popularizers. Darwin's *Origin of Species* (1859) was one of the books that changed a world, summing up for the nineteenth century, as did Newton's physics for the eighteenth and Freud's psychology for the twentieth, a new way of thinking about man and his universe. His name has become synonymous with the doctrine of biological evolution and natural selection, but it was the English philosopher Spencer who coined the phrase "survival of the fittest" and who applied the principles of evolution to a wide range of social and philosophical considerations. Spencer's sociology seemed to provide the perfect rationale for the burgeoning, inchoate society of America in the 1870's and 1880's. He proposed that civilizations were subject to an inevitable law of progress and development from simplicity to complexity and that, like a given species, a society would evolve out of struggle and competition toward the preservation of the fittest and best. The American lecturer and historian John Fiske eagerly devoured Spencer's ideas as stated in *First Principles* (1862), *The Study of Sociology* (1873), and other books, and dedicated himself to the task of translating them into a theistic form of cosmic evolution and positivism. His *Outlines of Cosmic Philosophy* (1874) sought to heal the breach between religious orthodoxy and evolutionary thought, suggesting a divine purpose in the process of natural selection. Some went further in the attempt to explain the phenomenon of rugged individualism and big business, defending capitalism on the grounds of the survival of the strong. William Graham Sumner, professor of social science at Yale, proposed that the principle of competition in the natural world showed that social classes did not necessarily owe each other anything, and Andrew Carnegie, the steel magnate, wrote such books as *Triumphant Democracy* (1886) and *The Gospel of Wealth* (1889) glorifying the achievements of capitalistic enterprise.

But these roseate optimisms and apologias for the way things were going somehow failed to account for the disadvantaged classes of society burdened by poverty, low incomes, and slum living in the cities. If biological evolution accounted for the large sweep of progress and for the favored few who emerged at the top of the heap, what about those who, determined by unfavorable environmental conditions, inevitably slipped backward on the scale of evolution toward their ape-like forefathers? If a single individual could become brutalized by the wrong set of circumstances, whole civilizations might likewise retrogress if circumstances so directed. After 1890, less sanguine observers began to see the possibilities for catastrophe if one looked back down the evolutionary scale instead of upward toward some millennial perfection. Henry Adams and his brother Brooks prophesied the "degradation" of democratic ideals and, interpreting Spencerian principles in a gloomy light, saw energy dissipated by the material forces of society symbolized by the dynamo, according to the second law of thermodynamics. Literary magazines in the nineties reverberated with articles about the decline of Western civilization, many of them stemming from a work by a Hungarian writer, *Degeneration* (translated in 1895), whose author, Max Nordau, predicted a general decay of society on evidence of a lowered ethical tone and such debilitating tendencies as bohemianism, *fin-de-siècle* aestheticism, and pre-Raphaelitism. Thorstein Veblen's *The Theory of the Leisure Class* (1899), an attack on the moneyed classes for their idleness and "conspicuous waste," and Lincoln Steffens' *The Shame of the Cities* (1904), which mercilessly exposed corruption in city governments, were American books likewise symptomatic of the time, revealing some of the hollowness of a sanguine belief in an upward law of progress through competition and conflict.

A few distinguished voices took a mediating stand in the question of freedom of will versus a deterministic reading of man's moral and ethical life. William James in *The Will to Believe* (1897) and *Pragmatism* (1907) held that religious faith was a relative matter dependent upon the will of the individual. Arguing from the principle of the biological variation of species, he defended the values of the individual against a mechanistic interpretation of behavior. Man may be conditioned, but he is not wholly shaped by his natural origins if such semi-conscious states as love, feeling, desire, aspiration, and habit are properly directed to serve his best interests. John Dewey, a disciple of James, shifted the emphasis from the individual to the group, conceiving of ideas as "instruments" for shaping conduct and suggesting that social problems could be solved by directing the experience and the education of people into channels useful and desirable to the nation. Still others, like the Harvard philosopher Josiah Royce, sought to reaffirm the idealistic basis of belief, but the two main streams of evolutionary thought which gradually emerged from the many and varied discussions were the new sociology and the new psychology. Novelists of the period were influenced by both these tendencies. The earlier realists became more concerned with the psychology of character and with human relationships, while the naturalists more often either placed man at the mercy of large impersonal forces of the universe or made him the victim of socio-economic pressures.

Writers like James and Howells began to explore character-change under environmental conditions and to discover and analyze the "complex" character and especially that of the young American woman as a product of peculiarly American social conditions. Scientific methods thus undermined the pre-Darwinian stereotypes of romance in which the origins of character were supernatural and the hero of a novel was always brave and the heroine virtuous. In the novels of De Forest, James, Howells, Henry Adams, and others the young American woman was portrayed in a variety of unconventional roles: nervous invalid, jealous lover, scheming adventuress, beautiful cynic, and innocent flirt. Most of all, of course, she was shown as morally "innocent," but subjected to a sophisticated situation in which her innocence was severely tested. The novelists, too, were scientists, testing in the laboratories of their fiction the moral potential of their characters to see what a hundred years of democratic idealism had brought about in the formation of an American type.

Morals, Manners, and Literature

In morals, manners, taste in architecture and interior decoration, as well as in dress and social habits, the large urban middle class and aspiring plutocracy of the Gilded Age has come to be called "genteel," "innocent," and, for want of a more precise term, "Victorian." The American Victorians were heirs of the Puritans. They were respectable (at least outwardly), sober, and morally proper to the point of prudishness; they were afraid of sex and suspicious of all forms of license and all evidences of devious conduct. The widely circulated periodicals like *Harper's*, the *Century*, and *Scribner's* systematically censored materials which were regarded as extreme or "improper," and most readers were shocked at literary expressions of violence, brutality, drunkenness, illegitimacy, and the like. Howells, as editor of the *Atlantic Monthly,* felt it necessary to protect the delicate sensibilities of the young ladies who perused that magazine, and he frequently cautioned Mark Twain to soften his bursts of profanity or vulgarity. The reading audience in this "Age of Innocence" wanted an underlying romance or idealism in their fictional portraits of contemporary life. Like May Welland in Edith Wharton's novel of that title, they preferred to see no evil, hear no evil, speak no evil.

George Santayana saw behind this social phenomenon a fundamental philosophical conflict which he called "The Genteel Tradition." He sensed a schizophrenia in the American mind of the period, divided against itself as between the cruder facts of life in the Gilded Age and the ideals and high-mindedness inherited from Calvinism and Protestant evangelicism, later refined still further by Emersonian transcendentalism. In its worst social manifestations this disparity of things produced some of the awkwardness, the provincialism, and the mingling of genteel manners and bad taste which typified the society of the barons of business and the social elite. The wealthy were unabashedly imitative of the structured arrangements of English or Continental upper classes. And they were given to vulgar displays of money and position. Boston had its Beacon Street aristocracy, New York its Four Hundred of the social register, Chicago its Gold Coast where the kings of dry goods and real estate lived in Gothic splendor, and San Francisco its Nob Hill. So eager were the newly rich "swells" to demonstrate their right to membership in the best circles of society that they built English castles, French chateaux, and Italian palazzos for their dwellings at endless cost and without any functional plan except that of display. These they stuffed with imported Mediterranean and Renaissance treasures—ivory statuettes, marble mantels, stained-glass windows and such—and, to wait upon the captains of industry and their wives who presided over this Napoleonic magnificence, they provided staffs of liveried servants in pumps and silk stockings and powdered hair. Where a million dollars was a fortune in the 1870's, ten, fifty, or a hundred million was considered necessary by the eighties or nineties in this new thrusting aristocracy of wealth.

The degree to which literature responded to these evidences of awkwardness and provincial displays of dubious taste and manners is difficult to assess exactly. Serious novelists like Howells, James, and Edith Wharton reflected the domestic mores of the age in varying shades of realism and satire producing an American version of the English or French "novel of manners." James in *The Europeans* (1878) and Mrs. Wharton in *The House of Mirth* (1905) and the still later *The Age of Innocence* (1920) are among the most skillful practitioners of this fictional genre. In popular fiction gentility and "innocence" took the form of sentimentalism or romance, melodramatic themes and situations, and books written for or about the young. What Mark Twain handled with humor and realism in *Tom Sawyer,* others treated with sentiment and prettiness or an indulgence in nostalgia. Frances Hodgson Burnett's *Little Lord Fauntleroy* (1886) romanticized childhood and bordered on snob-appeal. Thomas Bailey Aldrich's *The Story of a Bad Boy* (1870) was a lesser *Tom Sawyer.* Dime-novel romances poured from the presses of Beadle and Adams, Street and Smith, and other cheap-book publishers. The best-selling stories of Horatio Alger, called "juveniles," had a vast circulation with their dreams of success and rising in society through hard work and sound morals, usually accompanied by luck, pluck, and hairbreadth escapes.

Poetry after the Civil War was for the most part derivative, echoing the sentiments and attitudes of Poe or Longfellow or Tennyson. Whitman's best work had been written by 1870, but *Leaves of Grass* was considered scandalous and his influence remained dormant until much later. Emily Dickinson and Stephen Crane wrote original and experimental poetry expressive of some of the attitudes of realism and naturalism, but their work was not published until the nineties and made little impact upon the generally traditional verse forms of the poets of the Gilded Age. Today, Dickinson's poetry has been recognized as that of a major figure. Her many metaphorical flights of fancy, couched in hymnlike rhythms and elliptical syntax, explored such universal themes as love and death and the sources of poetic inspiration. Almost the complete antithesis of her contemporary, Walt Whitman, she was as important a poet. Withdrawn into her own private world, she became a New England nun, but the range of her imagination and the variety of imagery she used was great. In the history of American poetry, she is nearly unclassifiable. She reminds one of Emerson in ideas and her cryptic form, but she could be compared as well to Edward Taylor or John Donne. Commonplace household chores, a walk in the garden, a bee, a robin, a hummingbird were for her emblems of eternity, of life, of death, of truth, and of God.

Among the precursors of serious realistic fiction the name of John William De Forest must be mentioned. His romantically entitled *Miss Ravenel's Conversion from Secession to Loyalty* (1867) was actually the only novel of the postwar period to describe battle conditions of the Civil War, and the chaotic situation in the South following it, with the vigor and realism of one who had experienced them at first hand. De Forest was the first important novelist to appear after 1865. He was traveled and informed, knew the European writers of his time, and he came near to writing in *Kate Beaumont* (1872) the kind of epic narrative of the struggle over slavery that Stendhal had written about the Napoleonic wars in *The Red and the Black.* Furthermore, he was an outspoken social critic of political corruption during the Gilded Age, satirizing in fiction the collusion between senators and big business in his *Honest John Vane* (1875) and other novels. In general the age produced relatively few reformist novels of high quality. Edward Bellamy's *Looking Backward: 2000-1887* (1888) and Howells' *A Traveler from Altruria* (1894) were successful and popular Utopian novels, and after 1900 the books of Upton Sinclair and Jack London dealt trenchantly with factory conditions and class warfare and propagandized for socialist reforms.

With the increasing consciousness of new regions rapidly opening up in the Middle and Far West after the war, writers began to exploit the differences of setting, dialect, and manners which the new conditions created. New England, the South, California, and other sections began to become aware of themselves in the school of writers, mostly in the short story, which has been called the "local color movement." From the mining country around San Francisco came the clever stories of Bret Harte, *The Luck of Roaring Camp and Other Sketches* (1870), in which frontier scamps and idealistic vagabonds, card sharks with the manners of gentlemen, and prostitutes with hearts of gold struck the fancy of a reading public that did not differentiate between the real and the meretricious. Harte managed to combine Dickensian sentiment with barroom realism and thus mirror in an accurate way the mixture of gentility and awkwardness that marked the period as a whole. Less sensational and more genuinely "local" in feeling and character were Sarah Orne Jewett and Mary Wilkins Freeman in their stories of New England life, George Washington Cable and Joel Chandler Harris writing about the South, and Edward Eggleston whose *The Hoosier Schoolmaster* (1871) realistically depicted backwoods life in Indiana.

If we set aside the major novelists of realism and naturalism, literature during this fifty-year span of American history revealed flashes of talent and occasional undoubted successes. Yet the accomplishment on the whole was modest. There was lacking, for one thing, a serious current of criticism and discussion of principles by which the novel, as a form, could develop and become more conscious of itself. Too few writers were aware of the experimental techniques and new attitudes in evidence in the French and Continental novels of Balzac, Zola, Flaubert, Turgenev, and others. A prevailing provincialism and the lack of an international copyright law compelled American writers to draw their inspiration from a few American and English models such as Hawthorne, Dickens, and George Eliot. Furthermore, the influence of the greater names of the romantic age—Holmes, Whittier, Longfellow, Lowell, and Emerson—was still strong, and the younger writers were impelled to adapt the methods of realism to the idealism of the earlier period. From this cultural lag came a kind of Victorian compromise of morals, tastes, and literary methods.

Realism and Fiction

In the prose fiction of the three most important American novelists of the period—Mark Twain, William Dean Howells, and Henry James—many of the points of view, literary techniques, and attitudes of realism found their finest expression. Of the three, Howells is most easily understood in terms of an aesthetic of realism, difficult as that word is to define. In the literary history of his age, he takes his place somewhere between his two major contemporaries. Like Mark Twain, he was staunchly "American" in his western origin and in the themes and characters of his fiction. He was concerned with the social and psychological problems of the Gilded Age—love, divorce, business, labor, social injustice—and as a prominent editor and critic he took seriously his role as Victorian arbiter of taste to a generation of readers. A close personal friend of his two fellow writers, Howells recognized the rare qualities in their work, encouraged and published their books, and supported them with endless generosity and enthusiasm. Like James he was a conscious craftsman seeking to formulate a philosophy of realism, and also like James he was interested in the psychological springs of conduct in the American character as viewed from a cosmopolitan standpoint. Like Mark Twain he was an acute observer of local manners and colloquial speech tones. To give a capsule comparison of these three masters of fiction: Howells' fiction closely mirrored the age and shared some of its weaknesses; Mark Twain embodied many of the paradoxes of the period in himself and raised the methods of western humor to the level of enduring literature; Henry James, drawing his inspiration from Europe and the Continental novel, made so distinguished and original a contribution to the art of fiction that its influence is yet to be fully measured.

Mark Twain's relation to realism is best understood as part of a reaction against the outworn aspects of a declining romantic tradition and against the effete conventions and "polite" language of gentility. He used the methods of the tall tale, western dialect, parody and burlesque, to produce a broadside against pretension, prudishness, and all kinds of pomp and circumstance. His earliest successes, *The Innocents Abroad* (1869) and *Roughing It* (1872), debunked the glories of the European past and the culture-seekers, and effectively juxtaposed a rough "western" character as vernacular spokesman of the author against a smooth-talking "dude" of the polite East. Mark Twain's famous humor of exaggeration, understatement, and deflation had in it an element of brashness and a "show me" skepticism toward most forms of high seriousness. But if this form of realism was negative, it was all the more effective, phrased as it was in the accents of common American speech and enjoyed by the average middlebrow reader. Mark Twain was much more than a funny man, however. He was a gifted artist in his own special way. *Adventures of Huckleberry Finn* is a masterpiece in adapting the vernacular style to a work of fiction with a serious social theme and in holding consistently to the narrating viewpoint of its shrewd but morally "innocent" young hero who is at odds with the corrupt, pious, slaveholding society of the mid-South. The river itself signifies freedom, independence, honesty—many things Twain felt were ebbing away from the American scene. It is a romantic symbol, almost a god of primitive life on the frontier in contrast to the actuality of life in the shore towns where hypocritical piety and acquisitiveness rule. In the contrast between the romantic Tom and the realistic Huck, Mark Twain expressed the two sides of his own personality, suggesting that reality for him, as in varying ways for other realists, was a matter of balancing off idealistic and pragmatic modes of thought.

His early iconoclastic gaiety turned more serious in the mid-eighties, when his creative powers were at their peak. The youthful exuberance was tempered and mellowed, without the bitterness of his later years. Mark Twain never recaptured the harmony of realism and romance achieved in *Life on the Mississippi* (1883) and *Huckleberry Finn* (1885), though *Pudd'nhead Wilson* (1894) was a remarkable case of transforming a travesty into a problem novel of slavery and racial injustice. He did essay a final powerful work of fiction (never completed by Mark Twain, though posthumously published as *The Mysterious Stranger):* a bitter and misanthropic yet strangely beautiful narrative of man's inhumanity and perversity, deterministic in philosophy, Swiftian in the intensity of its rage, yet shaped and controlled by the method of fable and fantasy and by the medieval setting. The dream motif ("Life itself is only a vision, a dream") carried Mark Twain beyond realism and romance into a Goya-like world of strange forms and distorted shapes in which reality remains only as a vagrant thought and man is reduced to a mere speck in a vast and incomprehensible universe.

For William Dean Howells, realism belonged more nearly to the average experience of middle-class America and to the external world of the Gilded Age. His measure of truth and reality was a due respect for the received decencies and the normal round of life, "fidelity to experience and probability of motive," not violence or extreme passion, murder, hate, or sexual excess. Howells' models were the writers of moderation like Jane Austen or Anthony Trollope or George Eliot. He distrusted the naturalists, Zola and Flaubert, and the harsh realities of *Crime and Punishment;* and though he admired and emulated Hawthorne, he could never have written a novel of the order of *The Scarlet Letter.* His Swedenborgian training and abiding faith in the tradition of democratic idealism kept him, even in his most despairing moods, from abandoning hope for the ultimate realization of the older American dream. His early books showed his belief in the innate moral health of his heroines, who triumphed over perversity and settled everything by their native judgment. His mature works of the 1880's, however, began to reveal penetrating insights into the psychological conflicts of his characters and an increasingly anti-romantic handling of love and marriage. *A Modern Instance* (1882), conceived as a story of sexual jealousy and revenge, became a narrative of the ways in which ordinary misunderstandings and commonplace human foibles could result in a divorce of two weak but otherwise well-meaning young people.

Howells' themes were often of greater significance than his capacity to bring them off. His best balanced novel, *The Rise of Silas Lapham* (1885), was a sympathetic portrait, edged with satire, of a newly rich business tycoon and a sharp examination of the delusions of the romantic love convention. Neither a Jay Gould nor a George Babbitt, Silas Lapham is a successful, boorish entrepreneur with a conscience. Some of Howells' most distinctive fiction was in the realm of social criticism. *A Traveler from Altruria* (1894) shows him as a Christian Socialist, a keen observer of the disparities and injustices of American society whereby the professions of democratic equality from the mouths of complacent professional and business men sound hollow and hypocritical when tested by the existing facts of exploited workers and class-conscious attitudes. The narrative device of a visitor from a remote land,

Altruria, judging America on Christian and moral grounds alone, provides satiric point to a novel which convinces by virtue of its author's absolute honesty. The theme verged on those of the naturalists, whose work Howells disliked, but the method and tone were within the moderate range of Howellsian realism.

Like all writers of major stature, Henry James is not easily classified under any label, such as realism, especially since so much of his life was Europe-oriented and since he was only indirectly affected by American currents of thought. He was, nonetheless, both a realistic novelist and a Victorian of sorts. His aesthetic theories were aimed at resolving some of the critical antitheses of the age, moving toward a synthesis of such opposed ideas as realism *vs.* idealism, truth and actuality *vs.* moral purpose in fiction, art for art's sake *vs.* art with a social purpose, realism *vs.* romance in the novel. Out of such oppositions James the critic sought a mediating position which he described in a later story, looking back to the 1870's with its climate of intellectual hesitation: "It's all tears and laughter as I look back upon that admirable time in which nothing was so romantic as our intense vision of the real." As James grew away from doctrinaire approaches to a literary creed of realism, he began to apply a method of impressionism and literary portraiture influenced by Sainte-Beuve and by his lifelong interest in portrait painting. The art of criticism, he believed, like that of the novel, could be enriched by the use of the typifying and generalizing techniques of the portrait painter.

Europe and the transatlantic contrast provided the theme of many of James's best novels and short stories. He placed his young American heroines in European situations, and by closely observing their moral assumptions and psychological reactions, he illuminated certain deep cross-currents of two continents. The early books like *Daisy Miller* (1878) handled this contrast largely in terms of manners and taste, but on the large canvas of his finest early novel, *The Portrait of a Lady* (1881), James probed deeply into the sources of American innocence and European experience. The surface plot of this story, like many of James's, contains elements of melodrama and international intrigue, but the handling of character is profound and true. He distinguished his characters as "free spirits" and "fixed constituents" or fools, the former open to the chances and often the tragedies of life (his heroes and heroines), the latter closed to the larger possibilities and either dangerous or merely comic in their fixity. His most important contribution to the craft of fiction was his complex use of point of view, what he called the "center of consciousness." Combining this device with new techniques of dramatic action derived from his experience with the stage, he revived his international theme in three remarkable novels written at the turn of the century. In these novels, often called his "major" works, his method became more and more symbolic and indirect. The reader discovers the story through the mind of the central observer who is at the same time the main character. The narrative proceeds by "scenic" episodes, frequently in conversations such as in a play, and the action is conveyed dramatically to the reader through "ficelles" or reflectors. The central plot is paralleled by "the story of the story," as the hero slowly gropes his way through a tangle of deceptions and delusions toward some final illumination and a deeper awareness of himself.

Such complexities at the heart of James's fiction were realistic, indeed, but not "realism" in any simple definition. In his late years he attempted to formulate his method in Prefaces written for the collected edition of his works. These Prefaces, when read along with the novels they discuss, have provided for readers and critics a guidebook of the psychological techniques and dramatic methods which James used and which greatly widened the bounds of fictional art. The novel of realism, as James practiced it, became a new and subtle instrument for the revelation of character.

Literary Naturalism

Literary naturalism in America had its origins in European theory, in scientific thought, and in the movement of social protest at home. Social Darwinism was its matrix, but French fictional methods helped provide it with a literary rationale and a technique. Balzac's *Human Comedy* had first practiced a kind of fiction in which man was merged in his social milieu and treated as a passive product of his environment. It was Emile Zola, however, who first outlined the principles of a full-blown form of scientific naturalism in *The Experimental Novel* (1881). Following Darwin and the French physiologist Claude Bernard, he saw man as the product of a social condition, a mechanism that responded to behavioristic stimuli in the circumstances around him. The function of the novelist for Zola was like that of the scientist, to study the phenomena of man's social life and to observe and report impartially on his findings. Heredity and environment were the key determining factors in his Rougon-Macquart series of novels about the class struggle in which the declining bourgeoisie was giving place to an emerging proletariat. Much influenced by the historians Comte and Marx, Zola maintained the pose of the detached recorder and, like his fellow naturalist Flaubert, believed that the author should entirely efface himself from his material and simply report without sentiment or moralizing. Zola and Flaubert became the advance guard of Continental naturalism. They were pessimistic and deterministic, and they chose materials from the sordid, ugly side of life: sex, hunger, poverty, disease. In *Madame Bovary,* for example, the instinct of sex was the determining force in the degeneration and death of a weak young woman compulsively seeking escape from the monotonous round of everyday life in the French provinces.

The American naturalists of the 1890's absorbed these assumptions and adapted them to the conditions of social unrest and the special variety of social Darwinism identified with the cultural climate of that decade. Stephen Crane, Frank Norris, and Theodore Dreiser became the leading spokesmen of the fiction of naturalism, each with a style distinctly his own, but all three sharing the fundamental premises of a literary creed which included (1) a biological determinism in which man was conceived of as controlled by his primitive, animal instincts; (2) a sociological determinism whereby the weak were destroyed and the strong survived in a world of struggle and chance; (3) a scientific detachment and the impartial role of the newspaperman toward the author's material; and (4) the search for reality, not in the average, but in the violent and the sensational, in war, murder, disaster, poverty and strife, and among the lower orders of mankind. The literary tastes of the period, the Mauve Decade or the Yellow Nineties, fluctuated uncertainly between the extremes of a romantic idealism and a hard-boiled facing-up to the facts of natural selection and jungle ethics. The naturalists found it difficult to espouse a wholly consistent philosophy of materialistic determinism in their novels, nor did they win a popular following until the next century. But there existed in their work as a whole a cohesive body of theory and a serious search for a technique which characterized the novel of naturalism and established the pattern of American fiction for a generation of their successors.

In the work of Stephen Crane, American naturalism received its most artistic expression. His early stories, *Maggie, a Girl of the Streets, The Men in the Storm,* and *An Experiment in Misery,* shocked genteel readers with their candid exposure of slum and tenement life in the Bowery. Crane did not moralize the story of Maggie Johnson, a young girl of drunken and brutal parents, a weak flower that "blossomed in a mud puddle" and then withered under the blows of poverty. She is seduced by a bartender, abandoned by him, and finally drowns herself. No lines could better indicate Crane's point of view than these from the closing section:

> In a room a woman sat at a table eating like a fat monk in a picture.
>
> A soiled, unshaven man pushed open the door and entered.
>
> "Well," said he, "Mag's dead."

In *The Red Badge of Courage* Crane achieved his greatest success, bringing to his behavioristic interpretation of man's helplessness under conditions of battle the brilliant impressionism of his technique. Henry Fleming is the victim of external forces and inward fears too strong for him as he runs wildly from combat, then returns to vindicate himself in an act of heroism equally instinctive. The structural device of a wave-like rhythm alternating between the hope and the despair of the men in battle, the symbolic use of color and religious allusions, the animal imagery to point up primitive instincts and reactions, the short, staccato sentences with the impact of regimental rifle fire—all contribute to a narrative method which became the perfect instrument for a work of naturalistic fiction. In *The Open Boat,* another account of men at the mercy of powerful natural forces, Crane again used the interplay of hopes and fears of the men in the boat as a structural pattern and underlined the indifference of nature to the fate of man by the use of memorable poetic passages and a symbolic suggestiveness. Crane's people are often seen as generic figures of fear, hope, courage, in a bleak world of hostile intent or vast indifference.

Frank Norris brought to American naturalistic fiction the painstaking documentation and the "scientism" of Zola and Flaubert and their fascination for the bizarre and the sensational. Unlike Crane, he preserved the outlines of the conventional novel form, even a traditional treatment of love and marriage, though much transformed from its romantic and sentimental attachments. The structure of his plots was conditioned by the downward movement of the evolutionary cycle in which, under pressures of inherited weaknesses and environmental strains, man reels backward into the beast. In *The Responsibilities of the Novelist* and other essays he described the literary creed from which his novels had been written as a combination of romance and realism, but he rejected the colorless realism and "teacup tragedies" of Howells and his followers for the stronger medicine of violence and melodramatic action. The characters in a naturalistic novel, he said, must be "flung into the throes of a vast and terrible drama of unleashed passions, in blood and sudden death."

In his best novels, *McTeague* and *The Octopus,* Norris anticipated Dreiser by his careful and effective use of realistic details to establish the milieu for his characters, but he differed from Dreiser in the choice of materials and the grandiose sweep of his imagination. He was drawn to vast panoramic and scenic effects, theatrical episodes, fights, murders, and bloody battles. In *The Octopus* he employed all the instruments of the orchestra in a style full of superlatives, mounting periods, capital letters, exclamation points, and such rhetorical devices. Where Crane and Dreiser were content with revealing sexual motivations mainly in the social and moral prejudices of a prudish generation, Norris treated sex as a powerful, biological stirring in the blood of the male animal and the responsive submission of the female. McTeague is shown bending with desire over the prostrate figure of Trina in his dentist's chair and crushing her in his huge arms in a display of sudden bestial urgings. Money, too, is a powerful incentive. The gold tooth on a sign hanging outside his dental parlor, the gold canary in its cage, Trina's hoard of dollars won in a raffle, Maria's imaginary gold plates—these recur in *McTeague* with the insistence of a theme in a musical composition. Norris only rarely reflected in his novels the theme of social protest, though *The Octopus* shows his sympathy with some of the doctrines of Populism. He was primarily fascinated by the cult of muscular Darwinism and the role of man in the scale of evolution. His writing is powerful, rhetorical, sensational, sometimes too doctrinal in its expression of naturalistic methods, but at its best an authentic and impressive body of naturalism, of the Zola variety, adapted to American conditions.

Other less distinctive expressions of the naturalistic mode were the novels and stories of Hamlin Garland, Upton Sinclair, Robert Herrick, and Jack London. Garland's *Main-Travelled Roads* (1891) was naturalistic in the mood of despair and frustration he evoked in the drab lives of midwestern farmers and small-townspeople, but he was more typically realistic in his manner and method. London and Sinclair were both concerned with the class struggle and the panacea of a socialist form of society, and London in *The Call of the Wild* (1903) and *The Sea-Wolf* (1904) explored in a fresh way the Darwinian concept of the brute nature of man and the thin line of demarcation between humanity and the animal world.

Compared with the work of Crane and Norris, the naturalistic novels of Theodore Dreiser seem almost devoid of either style or form. They read like a straightforward diary of day-to-day events which fascinates by its candid realism and nearly embarrasses by its intimacy. Authenticity is achieved by the powerfully cumulative array of circumstances woven into the destinies of the characters. It is this quality of lifelike conviction, together with a compassion for the human predicament and a great sympathy for the victims of industrial and urban society, which has come to be associated with Dreiser's naturalism and which so profoundly influenced the twentieth-century novel. He was not "literary." His stories were case histories drawn from the struggle for survival in his own poverty-ridden family, or from newspaper accounts of such orphans of society as Clyde Griffiths in *The American Tragedy:* creatures of chance driven by the hope of pleasure and the fear of pain, and defeated by inward "chemic compulsions" and by the closed doors of the affluent classes for whom the social structure seemed especially designed. From his reading of Tyndall, Huxley, and Herbert Spencer, Dreiser evolved a "philosophy" in which man was a helpless product of natural forces that crushed the weak and selected the strong to be tossed upward where they became Nietzschean symbols of power and success—like Frank Cowperwood in the trilogy of novels about a robber baron of the business world.

Dreiser's "success novels" employed the same massive circumstantiality as did his stories of immigrant families and young seekers like Carrie Meeber, Jennie Gerhardt, or Clyde Griffiths, but it was these latter characters who moved him more deeply. A strain of romanticism and sentiment in his temperament underlay the more doctrinaire theories of naturalism which he had learned from books and prompted him to touch a deeper note in his tracing out of their destinies. Of Jennie Gerhardt he wrote in an epilogue, later removed from the book:

> But this daughter of the poor felt something—the beauty of trees, the wonder of the rains, the color of existence. . . . Jennie loved and loving, gave. Is there a superior wisdom?

He came to deny any meaning in the mystery and chaos of a purposeless universe, though in many of his essays and autobiographical books he became a moralist, attacking social conventions such as marriage and religious prejudice as interfering with the free expression of sexual instincts and primitive emotions. He was never able to achieve the impassive amoralism of Crane or the disinterest of the French naturalists. Often he stepped out of his narratives to comment and philosophize in the manner of the evolutionary scientist on the fate and hardships of his heroes and heroines. Dreiser's style has been called flat and platitudinous and his novels "inartistic," yet they retain a power and conviction which even his two contemporary naturalists, Crane and Norris, never quite achieved.

Masters of Fiction

SAMUEL L. CLEMENS (MARK TWAIN)

[1835–1910]

THERE WERE many sides to the complex literary personality we know as Mark Twain. Young Sam Clemens, reared in Missouri in a small Mississippi River community in the slaveholding time, had little schooling before he went to work at twelve as a printer's apprentice. He lived through the ebullient, adolescent years of the Republic in its plunge westward, absorbing the rhythms and discords of the nation into his very language and style. A newspaper printer and traveler at the age of eighteen, he worked at his trade in cities from St. Louis to New York. Then longing to get beyond this horizon, he shipped to New Orleans en route to South America, but was diverted by the offer of the pilot Horace Bixby to teach him the art of piloting a steamboat on the Mississippi. For Sam Clemens this was the dream of his youth come true. For eighteen months, perhaps the most impressionable period of his life, he "learned the river," an experience brilliantly recalled years later in his *Atlantic Monthly* series "Old Times on the Mississippi." He called it his "brief, sharp schooling."

The Civil War interrupted these halcyon years and opened a new phase of his life, in the Far West. Journeying by stagecoach to the Nevada Territory, he tried silver and gold mining without success and took up his pen to record the rough, exciting life of Virginia City for the *Enterprise*. Meanwhile he met Artemus Ward and Bret Harte in San Francisco and learned some of their literary methods. One of his stories brought national acclaim: his "Jumping Frog" tale, written under his newly acquired pseudonym "Mark Twain" (which derived from the leadsman's call for safe water) and published in the New York *Saturday Press* in 1865. The tall tale of native folklore provided the inspiration for this style of humorous writing, but Twain added to it the device of the unconsciously funny narrator who is more amusing than the tale he tells. Two journeys out of the country, one to Hawaii and another to the Near East and the Holy Land, gave him material for still another literary genre, the travel letter, which he made over into his own by the admixture of guidebook information with the skeptical, deflationary, frontier bumptiousness of his manner. *The Innocents Abroad* (1869) was his first important success in this field. *Roughing It* (1872), at first named "Innocents at Home," recalled in half-journalese, half-history his trip out West and further demonstrated the humorous mingling of tall stories, exaggeration, understatement, and a rich use of Western dialect. The device of the earthy, vernacular character juxtaposed against the effete, polite Easterner or "dude" was his most effective technique in these early works.

The decade of the seventies was a testing ground for the methods and materials that were to produce his greatest books. After "Old Times on the Mississippi" (1875), which revived his steamboating days, he wrote *The Adventures of Tom Sawyer* (1876), going back still further into his boyhood in a mood of romantic nostalgia saved from sentiment by looking at boy-life through adult eyes. It is a kind of *Treasure Island* of mid-century America. In the eighties he refined upon the techniques used in these works in *Life on the Mississippi* (1883) and *Adventures of Huckleberry Finn* (1885), striking in the latter masterpiece his most profound note of poetry and symbolism, realism and romance, humor and reminiscence. Almost unconsciously he adopted the device of telling the story wholly from a single point of view, gaining dramatic irony and suspense and anticipating the later novelistic methods of Henry James.

This was the peak of Mark Twain's career as a writer, though he was to write other distinguished books, such as *A Connecticut Yankee in King Arthur's Court* (1889) and *Pudd'nhead Wilson* (1894), which with the "Mysterious Stranger" manuscripts show different facets of his mind: the fantasist, the social reformer and believer in the rights of men, the social critic, and finally the misanthropist and the lay philosopher in search of the source of evil in the world. For in his later years misfortune struck Mark Twain and his family. His daughter Susy died, his wife was invalided, his own health began to fail, and he lost a fortune in a typesetting-machine venture. The gay humor and iconoclasm of his youth turned to bitterness and despair while he strove to find a literary form by which to control and somehow come to terms with the growing disillusionment of his life. *Pudd'nhead Wilson* evolved from a grotesque farce about a pair of attached twins into a serious novel with a racial theme and a comment on the corruptive force of slaveholding. But it was in the haunting, unfinished "Chronicle of Young Satan" *(The Mysterious Stranger)* that he came the nearest to recapturing his best manner, discovering in the fairy tale a technique to embody personal tragedies in a lasting literary form.

By the turn of the century Mark Twain's best writing was completed. The two volumes, *What Is Man?* and *The Man That Corrupted Hadleyburg* registered once more his misanthropy and his rage at "the damned human race." He spent his remaining years dictating his autobiography and lecturing—in a white panama suit, a cigar in his mouth, and with the impressive shock of hair, turned white, which marked his appearance at seventy. He could still amuse audiences with his skillful timing and his barbed, iconoclastic remarks, yet the eternal youth in him was slowly drained as the country he represented with such authenticity lost its own youth and innocence and moved toward the industrialized, urban complexities of the twentieth century. He died at Redding, Connecticut, in 1910.

Only the most discerning of his contemporaries, such as William Dean Howells, were able to recognize in Mark Twain, beyond the façade of wild humorist and platform entertainer, the literary mastery which was ultimately to place him among the great practitioners of American literature. His genius was a natural gift, but he added to it the trained methods of a writer who knew his audience and knew how to capture it. Recent criticism has shown him to be a much more conscious craftsman than casual readers might suspect. To mention only one of his original contributions to fictional prose, he took the native tradition of dialect humor from his predecessor-journalists and merged the vernacular spokesman of his earlier books ("Mr. Brown," for example, of *The Innocents Abroad*) with the sympathetic young hero-narrator in *Huckleberry Finn,* to create a truly American voice speaking out against prejudice and bigotry.

Further reading: *The Portable Mark Twain,* ed. Bernard DeVoto, 1946. *Adventures of Huckleberry Finn,* ed. H. N. Smith, 1959. Kenneth Lynn, *Mark Twain and Southwestern Humor,* 1959. H. N. Smith, *Mark Twain: The Development of a Writer,* 1962.

FROM *A Tramp Abroad*

[Baker's Blue-jay Yarn]

The framed story, the tall tale, and the device of the animal to satirize man are all combined here: "Yes, sir, a jay is everything that a man is." The text is that of the first edition (Hartford, 1880).

One never tires of poking about in the dense woods that clothe all these lofty Neckar hills to their tops. The great deeps of a boundless forest have a beguiling and impressive charm in any country; but German legends and fairy tales have given these an added charm. They have peopled all that region with gnomes, and dwarfs, and all sorts of mysterious and uncanny creatures. At the time I am writing of, I had been reading so much of this literature that sometimes I was not sure but I was beginning to believe in the gnomes and fairies as realities.

One afternoon I got lost in the woods about a mile from the hotel, and presently fell into a train of dreamy thought about animals which talk, and kobolds, and enchanted folk, and the rest of the pleasant legendary stuff; and so, by stimulating my fancy, I finally got to imagining I glimpsed small flitting shapes here and there down the columned aisles of the forest. It was a place which was peculiarly meet for the occasion. It was a pine wood, with so thick and soft a carpet of brown needles that one's footfall made no more sound than if he was treading on wool; the tree-trunks were as round and straight and smooth as pillars, and stood close together; they were bare of branches to a point about twenty-five feet above ground, and from there upward so thick with boughs that not a ray of sunlight could pierce through. The world was bright with sunshine outside, but a deep and mellow twilight reigned in there, and also a silence so profound that I seemed to hear my own breathings.

When I had stood ten minutes, thinking and imagining, and getting my spirit in tune with the place, and in the right mood to enjoy the supernatural, a raven suddenly uttered a hoarse croak over my head. It made me start; and then I was angry because I started. I looked up, and the creature was sitting on a limb right over me, looking down at me. I felt something of the same sense of humiliation and injury which one feels when he finds that a human stranger has been clandestinely inspecting him in his privacy and mentally commenting upon him. I eyed the raven, and the raven eyed me. Nothing was said during some seconds. Then the bird stepped a little way along his limb to get a better point of observation, lifted his wings, stuck his head far down below his shoulders toward me, and croaked again—a croak with a distinctly insulting expression about it. If he had spoken in English he could not have said any more plainly than he did say in raven, "Well, what do *you* want here?" I felt as foolish as if I had been caught in some mean act by a responsible being, and reproved for it. However, I made no reply; I would not bandy words with a raven. The adversary waited a while, with his shoulders still lifted, his head thrust down between them, and his keen bright eye fixed on me; then he threw out two or three more insults, which I could not understand, further than that I knew a portion of them consisted of language not used in church.

I still made no reply. Now the adversary raised his head and called. There was an answering croak from a little distance in the wood,—evidently a croak of inquiry. The adversary explained with enthusiasm, and the other raven dropped everything and came. The two sat side by side on the limb and discussed me as freely and offensively as two great naturalists might discuss a new kind of bug. The thing became more and more embarrassing. They called in another friend. This was too much. I saw that they had the advantage of me, and so I concluded to get out of the scrape by walking out of it. They enjoyed my defeat as much as any low white people could have done. They craned their necks and laughed at me, (for a raven *can* laugh, just like a man,) they squalled insulting remarks after me as long as they could see me. They were nothing but ravens—I knew that,—what they thought about me could be a matter of no consequence,—and yet when even a raven shouts after you, "What a hat!" "O, pull down your vest!" and that sort of thing, it hurts you and humiliates you, and there is no getting around it with fine reasoning and pretty arguments.

Animals talk to each other, of course. There can be no question about that; but I suppose there are very few people who can understand them. I never knew but one man who could. I knew he could, however, because he told me so himself. He was a middle-aged, simple-hearted miner, who had lived in a lonely corner of California, among the woods and mountains, a good many years, and had studied the ways of his only neighbors, the beasts and the birds, until he believed he could accurately translate any remark which they made. This was Jim Baker. According to Jim Baker, some animals have only a limited education, and use only very simple words, and scarcely ever a comparison or a flowery figure; whereas, certain other animals have a large vocabulary, a fine command of language and a ready and fluent delivery; consequently these latter talk a great deal; they like it; they are conscious of their talent, and they enjoy "showing off." Baker said, that after long and careful observation, he had come to the conclusion that the blue-jays were the best talkers he had found among birds and beasts. Said he:—

"There's more *to* a blue-jay than any other creature. He has got more moods, and more different kinds of feelings than other creatures; and mind you, whatever a blue-jay feels, he can put into language. And no mere commonplace language, either, but rattling, out-and-out book-talk—and bristling with metaphor, too—just bristling! And as for command of language—why *you* never see a blue-jay get stuck for a word. No man ever did. They just boil out of him! And another thing: I've noticed a good deal, and there's no bird, or cow, or anything that uses as good grammar as a blue-jay. You may say a cat uses good grammar. Well, a cat does—but you let a cat get excited, once; you let a cat get to pulling fur with another cat on a shed, nights, and you'll hear grammar that will give you the lockjaw. Ignorant people think it's the *noise* which fighting cats make that is so aggravating, but it ain't so; it's the sickening grammar they use. Now I've never heard a jay use bad grammar but very seldom; and when they do, they are as ashamed as a human; they shut right down and leave.

"You may call a jay a bird. Well, so he is, in a measure—because he's got feathers on him, and don't belong to no church, perhaps; but otherwise he is just as much a human as you be. And I'll tell you for why. A jay's gifts, and instincts, and feelings, and interests, cover the whole ground. A jay hasn't got any more principle than a Congressman. A jay will lie, a jay will steal, a jay will deceive, a jay will betray; and four times out of five, a jay will go back on his solemnest promise. The sacredness of an obligation is a thing which you can't cram into no blue-jay's head. Now, on top of all this, there's another thing: a jay can out-swear any gentleman in the mines. You think a cat can swear. Well, a cat can; but you give a blue-jay a subject that calls for his reserve-powers, and where is your cat? Don't talk to *me*—I know too much about this thing. And there's yet another thing: in the one little particular of scolding—just good, clean, out-and-out scolding—a blue-jay can lay over anything, human or divine. Yes, sir, a jay is everything that a man is. A jay can cry, a jay can laugh, a jay can feel shame, a jay can reason and plan and discuss, a jay likes gossip and scandal, a jay has got a sense of humor, a jay knows when he is an ass just as well as you do—maybe better. If a jay ain't human, he better take in his sign, that's all. Now I'm going to tell you a perfectly true fact about some blue-jays.

"When I first begun to understand jay language correctly, there was a little incident that happened here. Seven years ago, the last man in this region but me, moved away. There stands his house,—been empty ever since; a log house, with a plank roof—just one big room, and no more; no ceiling—nothing between the rafters and the floor. Well, one Sunday morning I was sitting out here in front of my cabin, with my cat, taking the sun, and looking at the blue hills, and listening to the leaves rustling so lonely in the trees, and thinking of the home away yonder in the States, that I hadn't heard from in thirteen years, when a blue-jay lit on that house, with an acorn in his mouth, and says, 'Hello, I reckon I've struck something!' When he spoke, the acorn dropped out of his mouth and rolled down the roof, of course, but he didn't care; his mind was all on the thing he had struck. It was a knot-hole in the roof. He cocked his head to one side, shut one eye and put the other one to the hole, like a 'possum looking down a jug; then he glanced up with his bright eyes, gave a wink or two with his wings—which signifies gratification, you understand,—and says, 'It looks like a hole, it's located like a hole,—blamed if I don't believe it *is* a hole!'

"Then he cocked his head down and took another look; he glances up perfectly joyful, this time; winks his wings and his tail both, and says, 'O, no, this ain't no fat thing, I reckon! If I ain't in luck!—why it's a perfectly elegant hole!' So he flew down and got that acorn, and fetched it up and dropped it in, and was just tilting his head back, with the heavenliest smile on his face, when all of a sudden he was paralyzed into a listening attitude and that smile faded gradually out of his countenance like breath off'n a razor, and the queerest look of surprise took its place. Then he says, 'Why I didn't hear it fall!' He cocked his eye at the hole again, and took a long look; raised up and shook his head; stepped around to the other side of the hole and took another look from that side; shook his head again. He studied a while, then he just went into the *de*tails—walked round and round the hole and spied into it from every point of the compass. No use. Now he took a thinking attitude on the comb of the roof and scratched the back of his head with his right foot for a minute, and finally says, 'Well, it's too many for *me*, that's certain; must be a mighty long hole; however, I ain't got no time to fool around here, I got to 'tend to business; I reckon it's all right—chance it, anyway.'

"So he flew off and fetched another acorn and dropped it in, and tried to flirt his eye to the hole quick enough to see what become of it, but he was too late. He held his eye there as much as a minute; then he raised up and sighed, and says, 'Consound it, I don't seem to understand this thing, no way; however, I'll tackle her again.' He fetched another acorn, and done his level best to see what become of it, but he couldn't. He says, 'Well, *I* never struck no such a hole as this, before; I'm of the opinion it's a totally new kind of a hole.' Then he begun to get mad. He held in for a spell, walking up and down the comb of the roof and shaking his head and muttering to himself; but his feelings got the upper hand of him, presently, and he broke loose and cussed himself black in the face. I never see a bird take on so about a little thing. When he got through he walks to the hole and looks in again for half a minute; then he says, 'Well, you're a long hole, and a deep hole, and a mighty singular hole altogether—but I've started in to fill you, and I'm d—d if I *don't* fill you, if it takes a hundred years!'

"And with that, away he went. You never see a bird work so since you was born. He laid into his work like a nigger, and the way he hove acorns into that hole for about two hours and a half was one of the most exciting and astonishing spectacles I ever struck. He never stopped to take a look any more—he just hove 'em in and went for more. Well, at last he could hardly flop his wings, he was so tuckered out. He comes a-drooping down, once more, sweating like an ice-pitcher, drops his acorn in and says, '*Now* I guess I've got the bulge on you by this time!' So he bent down for a look. If you'll believe me, when his head come up again he was just pale with rage. He says, 'I've shoveled acorns enough in there to keep the family thirty years, and if I can see a sign of one of 'em I wish I may land in a museum with a belly full of sawdust in two minutes!'

"He just had strength enough to crawl up on to the comb and lean his back agin the chimbly, and then he collected his impressions and begun to free his mind. I see in a second that what I had mistook for profanity in the mines was only just the rudiments, as you may say.

"Another jay was going by, and heard him doing his devotions, and stops to inquire what was up. The sufferer told him the whole circumstance, and says, 'Now yonder's the hole, and if you don't believe me, go and look for yourself.' So this fellow went and looked, and comes back and says, 'How many did you say you put in there?' 'Not any less than two tons,' says the sufferer. The other jay went and looked again. He couldn't seem to make it out, so he raised a yell, and three more jays come. They all examined the hole, they all made the sufferer tell it over again, then they all discussed it, and got off as many leather-headed opinions about it as an average crowd of humans could have done.

"They called in more jays; then more and more, till pretty soon this whole region 'peared to have a blue flush about it. There must have been five thousand of them; and such another jawing and disputing and ripping and cussing, you never heard. Every jay in the whole lot put his eye to the hole and delivered a more chuckle-headed opinion about the mystery than the jay that went there before him. They examined the house all over, too. The door was standing half open, and at last one old jay happened to go and light on it and look in. Of course that knocked the mystery galley-west in a second. There lay the acorns, scattered all over the floor. He flopped his wings and raised a whoop. 'Come here!' he says, 'Come here, everybody; hang'd if this fool hasn't been trying to fill up a house with acorns!' They all came a-swooping down like a blue cloud, and as each fellow lit on the door and took a glance, the whole absurdity of the contract that that first jay had tackled hit him home and he fell over backwards suffocating with laughter, and the next jay took his place and done the same.

"Well, sir, they roosted around here on the housetop and the trees for an hour, and guffawed over that thing like human beings. It ain't any use to tell me a blue-jay hasn't got a sense of humor, because I know better. And memory, too. They brought jays here from all over the United States to look down that hole, every summer for three years. Other birds too. And they could all see the point, except an owl that come from Nova Scotia to visit the Yo Semite, and he took this thing in on his way back. He said he couldn't see anything funny in it. But then he was a good deal disappointed about Yo Semite, too."

1880

FROM *Life on the Mississippi*

Chapters 4–9

In these chapters on learning the river, Mark Twain achieved the peak of his literary style: vigorous and effortless with the flash and sparkle of actual life. They are part of a sequence published in the *Atlantic Monthly* (January–June, 1875) under the title "Old Times on the Mississippi," and later incorporated, essentially unchanged, in *Life on the Mississippi* (1883). In preparing for the later book, Mark Twain visited his home town and other places along the river, reviving his memories of the past. He then combined his *Atlantic* series on piloting with historical and legendary material about the Mississippi to form, as his biographer said, "a memorial seemingly as enduring as the river itself," brilliantly recapturing the humor and the danger of steamboating at the period when the river was alive with commerce and activity and was a symbol to all young boys of the excitements of venturing upon life.

Text: From *Selected Shorter Writings of Mark Twain* (Riverside Editions; Boston, 1962), for which Walter Blair collated the *Atlantic* series with the corresponding chapters from the first edition of *Life on the Mississippi*.

The Boys' Ambition

When I was a boy, there was but one permanent ambition among my comrades in our village[1] on the west bank of the Mississippi River. That was, to be a steamboatman. We had transient ambitions of other sorts, but they were only transient. When a circus came and went, it left us all burning to become clowns; the first negro minstrel show that ever came to our section left us all suffering to try that kind of life; now and then we had a hope that, if we lived and were good, God would permit us to be pirates. These ambitions faded out, each in its turn; but the ambition to be a steamboatman always remained.

Once a day a cheap, gaudy packet arrived upward from St. Louis, and another downward from Keokuk. Before these events, the day was glorious with expectancy; after them, the day was a dead and empty thing. Not only the boys, but the whole village, felt this. After all these years I can picture that old time to myself now, just as it was then: the white town drowsing in the sunshine of a summer's

[1] Hannibal, Missouri. [Twain's note.]

morning; the streets empty, or pretty nearly so; one or two clerks sitting in front of the Water Street stores, with their splint-bottomed chairs tilted back against the wall, chins on breasts, hats slouched over their faces, asleep—with shingle-shavings enough around to show what broke them down; a sow and a litter of pigs loafing along the sidewalk, doing a good business in watermelon rinds and seeds; two or three lonely little freight piles scattered about the "levee;" a pile of "skids" on the slope of the stone-paved wharf, and the fragrant town drunkard asleep in the shadow of them; two or three wood flats at the head of the wharf, but nobody to listen to the peaceful lapping of the wavelets against them; the great Mississippi, the majestic, the magnificent Mississippi, rolling its mile-wide tide along, shining in the sun; the dense forest away on the other side; the "point" above the town, and the "point" below, bounding the river-glimpse and turning it into a sort of sea, and withal a very still and brilliant and lonely one. Presently a film of dark smoke appears above one of those remote "points;" instantly a negro drayman, famous for his quick eye and prodigious voice, lifts up the cry, "S-t-e-a-m-boat a-comin'!" and the scene changes! The town drunkard stirs, the clerks wake up, a furious clatter of drays follows, every house and store pours out a human contribution, and all in a twinkling the dead town is alive and moving. Drays, carts, men, boys, all go hurrying from many quarters to a common centre, the wharf. Assembled there, the people fasten their eyes upon the coming boat as upon a wonder they are seeing for the first time. And the boat *is* rather a handsome sight, too. She is long and sharp and trim and pretty; she has two tall, fancy-topped chimneys, with a gilded device of some kind swung between them; a fanciful pilot-house, all glass and "gingerbread," perched on top of the "texas" deck behind them; the paddle-boxes are gorgeous with a picture or with gilded rays above the boat's name; the boiler deck, the hurricane deck, and the texas deck are fenced and ornamented with clean white railings; there is a flag gallantly flying from the jack-staff; the furnace doors are open and the fires glaring bravely; the upper decks are black with passengers; the captain stands by the big bell, calm, imposing, the envy of all; great volumes of the blackest smoke are rolling and tumbling out of the chimneys—a husbanded grandeur created with a bit of pitch pine just before arriving at a town; the crew are grouped on the forecastle; the broad stage is run far out over the port bow, and an envied deck-hand stands picturesquely on the end of it with a coil of rope in his hand; the pent steam is screaming through the gauge-cocks; the captain lifts his hand, a bell rings, the wheels stop; then they turn back, churning the water to foam, and the steamer is at rest. Then such a scramble as there is to get aboard, and to get ashore, and to take in freight and to discharge freight, all at one and the same time; and such a yelling and cursing as the mates facilitate it all with! Ten minutes later the steamer is under way again, with no flag on the jack-staff and no black smoke issuing from the chimneys. After ten more minutes the town is dead again, and the town drunkard asleep by the skids once more.

My father was a justice of the peace, and I supposed he possessed the power of life and death over all men and could hang anybody that offended him. This was distinction enough for me as a general thing; but the desire to be a steamboatman kept intruding, nevertheless. I first wanted to be a cabin-boy, so that I could come out with a white apron on and shake a table-cloth over the side, where all my old comrades could see me; later I thought I would rather be the deck-hand who stood on the end of the stage-plank with the coil of rope in his hand, because he was particularly conspicuous. But these were only day-dreams,—they were too heavenly to be contemplated as real possibilities. By and by one of our boys went away. He was not heard of for a long time. At last he turned up as apprentice engineer or "striker" on a steamboat. This thing shook the bottom out of all my Sunday-school teachings. That boy had been notoriously worldly, and I just the reverse; yet he was exalted to this eminence, and I left in obscurity and misery. There was nothing generous about this fellow in his greatness. He would always manage to have a rusty bolt to scrub while his boat tarried at our town, and he would sit on the inside guard and scrub it, where we all could see him and envy him and loathe him. And whenever his boat was laid up he would come home and swell around the town in his blackest and greasiest clothes, so that nobody could help remembering that he was a steamboatman; and he used all sorts of steamboat technicalities in his talk, as if he were so used to them that he forgot common people could not understand them. He would speak of the "labboard" side of a horse in an easy, natural way that would make one wish he was dead. And he was always talking about "St. Looey" like an old citizen; he would refer casually to occasions when he was "coming down Fourth Street," or when he was "passing by the Planter's House," or when there was a fire and he took a turn on the brakes of "the old Big Missouri;" and then he would go on and lie about how many towns the size of ours were burned down there that day. Two or three of the boys had long been persons of consideration among us because they had been to St. Louis once and had a vague general knowledge of its wonders, but the day of their glory was over now. They lapsed into a humble silence, and learned to disappear when the ruthless "cub"-engineer approached. This fellow had money, too, and hair oil. Also an ignorant silver watch and a showy brass watch-chain. He wore a leather belt and used no suspenders. If ever a youth was cordially admired and hated by his comrades, this one was. No girl could withstand his charms. He "cut out" every boy in the village. When his boat blew up at last, it diffused a tranquil contentment among us such as we had not known for months. But when he came home the next week, alive, renowned, and appeared in church all battered up and bandaged, a shining hero, stared at and wondered over by everybody, it seemed to us that the partiality of Providence for an undeserving reptile had reached a point where it was open to criticism.

This creature's career could produce but one result, and it speedily followed. Boy after boy managed to get on the river. The minister's son became an engineer. The doctor's and the postmaster's sons became "mud clerks;" the wholesale liquor dealer's son became a barkeeper on a boat; four sons of the chief merchant, and two sons of the county judge, became pilots. Pilot was the grandest position of all. The pilot, even in those days of trivial wages, had a princely salary—from a hundred and fifty to two hundred and fifty dollars a month, and no board to pay. Two months of his wages would pay a preacher's salary for a year. Now some of us were left disconsolate. We could not get on the river—at least our parents would not let us.

So by and by I ran away. I said I would never come home again till I was a pilot and could come in glory. But somehow I could not manage it. I went meekly aboard a few of the boats that lay packed together like sardines at the long St. Louis wharf, and very humbly inquired for the pilots, but got only a cold shoulder and short words from mates and clerks. I had to make the best of this sort of treatment for the time being, but I had comforting day-dreams of a future when I should be a great and honored pilot, with plenty of money, and could kill some of these mates and clerks and pay for them.

I Want to Be a Cub-Pilot

Months afterward the hope within me struggled to a reluctant death, and I found myself without an ambition. But I was ashamed to go home. I was in Cincinnati, and I set to work to map out a new career. I had been reading about the recent exploration of the river Amazon by an expedition sent out by our government. It was said that the expedition, owing to difficulties, had not thoroughly explored a part of the country lying about the head-waters, some four thousand miles from the mouth of the river. It was only about fifteen hundred miles from Cincinnati to New Orleans, where I could doubtless get a ship. I had thirty dollars left; I would go and complete the exploration of the Amazon. This was all the thought I gave to the subject. I never was great in matters of detail. I packed my valise, and took passage on an ancient tub called the "Paul Jones," for New Orleans. For the sum of sixteen dollars I had the scarred and tarnished splendor of "her" main saloon principally to myself, for she was not a creature to attract the eye of wiser travelers.

When we presently got under way and went poking down the broad Ohio, I became a new being, and the subject of my own admiration. I was a traveller! A word never had tasted so good in my mouth before. I had an exultant sense of being bound for mysterious lands and distant climes which I never have felt in so uplifting a degree since. I was in such a glorified condition that all ignoble feelings departed out of me, and I was able to look down and pity the untravelled with a compassion that had hardly a trace of contempt in it. Still, when we stopped at villages and wood-yards, I could not help lolling carelessly upon the railings of the boiler deck to enjoy the envy of the country boys on the bank. If they did not seem to discover me, I presently sneezed to attract their attention, or moved to a position where they could not help seeing me. And as soon as I knew they saw me I gaped and stretched, and gave other signs of being mightily bored with travelling.

I kept my hat off all the time, and stayed where the wind and the sun could strike me, because I wanted to get the bronzed and weather-beaten look of an old traveller. Before the second day was half gone, I experienced a joy which filled me with the purest gratitude; for I saw that the skin had begun to blister and peel off my face and neck. I wished that the boys and girls at home could see me now.

We reached Louisville in time—at least the neighborhood of it. We stuck hard and fast on the rocks in the middle of the river, and lay there four days. I was now beginning to feel a strong sense of being a part of the boat's family, a sort of infant son to the captain and younger brother to the officers. There is no estimating the pride I took in this grandeur, or the affection that began to swell and grow in me for those people. I could not know how the lordly steamboatman scorns that sort of presumption in a mere landsman. I particularly longed to acquire the least trifle of notice from the big stormy mate, and I was on the alert for an opportunity to do him a service to that end. It came at last. The riotous powwow of setting a spar was going on down on the forecastle, and I went down there and stood around in the way—or mostly skipping out of it—till the mate suddenly roared a general order for somebody to bring him a capstan bar. I sprang to his side and said: "Tell me where it is—I'll fetch it!"

If a rag-picker had offered to do a diplomatic service for the Emperor of Russia, the monarch could not have been more astounded than the mate was. He even stopped swearing. He stood and stared down at me. It took him ten seconds to scrape his disjointed remains together again. Then he said impressively: "Well, if this don't beat hell!" and turned to his work with the air of a man who had been confronted with a problem too abstruse for solution.

I crept away, and courted solitude for the rest of the day. I did not go to dinner; I stayed away from supper until everybody else had finished. I did not feel so much like a member of the boat's family now as before. However, my spirits returned, in instalments, as we pursued our way down the river. I was sorry I hated the mate so, because it was not in (young) human nature not to admire him. He was huge and muscular, his face was bearded and whiskered all over; he had a red woman and a blue woman tattooed on his right arm,—one on each side of a blue anchor with a red rope to it; and in the matter of profanity he was sublime. When he was getting out cargo at a landing, I was always where I could see and hear. He felt all the majesty of his great position, and made the world feel it, too. When he gave even the simplest order, he discharged it like a blast of lightning, and sent a long, reverberating peal of profanity thundering after it. I could not help contrasting the way in which the average landsman would give an order, with the mate's way of doing it. If the landsman should wish the gang-plank moved a foot farther forward, he would probably say: "James, or William, one of you push the plank forward, please;" but put the mate in his place, and he would roar out: "Here, now, start that gang-plank for'ard! Lively, now! *What* 're you about! Snatch it! *snatch* it! There! there! Aft again! aft again! Don't you hear me? Dash it to dash! are you going to *sleep* over it! *'Vast* heaving. 'Vast heaving, I tell you! Going to heave it clear astern? WHERE 're you going with that barrel! *for'ard* with it 'fore I make you swallow it, you dash-dash-dash-*dashed* split between a tired mud-turtle and a crippled hearse-horse!"

I wished I could talk like that.

When the soreness of my adventure with the mate had somewhat worn off, I began timidly to make up to the humblest official connected with the boat—the night watchman. He snubbed my advances at first, but I presently ventured to offer him a new chalk pipe, and that softened him. So he allowed me to sit with him by the big bell on the hurricane deck, and in time he melted into conversation. He could not well have helped it, I hung with such homage on his words and so plainly showed that I felt honored by his notice. He told me the names of dim capes and shadowy islands as we glided by them in the solemnity of the night, under the winking stars, and by and by got to talking about himself. He seemed over-sentimental for a man whose salary was six dollars a week—or rather he might have seemed so to an older person than I. But I drank in his words hungrily, and with a faith that might have moved mountains if it had been applied judiciously. What was it to me that he was soiled and seedy and fragrant with gin? What was it to me that his grammar was bad, his construction worse, and his profanity so void of art that it was an element of weakness rather than strength in his conversation? He was a wronged man, a man who had seen trouble, and that was enough for me. As he mellowed into his plaintive history his tears dripped upon the lantern in his lap, and I cried, too, from sympathy. He said he was the son of an English nobleman—either an earl or an alderman, he could not remember which, but believed he was both; his father, the nobleman, loved him, but his mother hated him from the cradle; and so while he was still a little boy he was sent to "one of them old, ancient colleges"—he couldn't remember which; and by and by his father died and his mother seized the property and "shook" him, as he phrased it. After his mother shook him, members of the nobility with whom he was acquainted used their influence to get him the position of "loblolly-boy in a ship;" and from that point my watchman threw off all trammels of date and locality and branched out into a narrative that bristled all along with incredible adventures; a narrative that was so reeking with bloodshed, and so crammed with hair-breadth escapes and the most engaging and unconscious personal villanies, that I sat speechless, enjoying, shuddering, wondering, worshipping.

It was a sore blight to find out afterwards that he was a low, vulgar, ignorant, sentimental, half-witted humbug, an untravelled native of the wilds of Illinois, who had absorbed wildcat literature and appropriated its marvels, until in time he had woven odds and ends of the mess into this yarn, and then gone on telling it to fledglings like me, until he had come to believe it himself.

A Cub-Pilot's Experience

What with lying on the rocks four days at Louisville, and some other delays, the poor old "Paul Jones" fooled away about two weeks in making the voyage from Cincinnati to New Orleans. This gave me a chance to get acquainted with one of the pilots, and he taught me how to steer the boat, and thus made the fascination of river life more potent than ever for me.

It also gave me a chance to get acquainted with a youth who had taken deck passage—more's the pity; for he easily borrowed six dollars of me on a promise to return to the boat and pay it back to me the day after we should arrive. But he probably died or forgot, for he never came. It was doubtless the former, since he had said his parents were wealthy, and he only travelled deck passage because it was cooler.[2]

I soon discovered two things. One was that a vessel would not be likely to sail for the mouth of the Amazon under ten or twelve years; and the other was that the nine or ten dollars still left in my pocket would not suffice for so impossible an exploration as I had planned, even if I could afford to wait for a ship. Therefore it followed that I must contrive a new career. The "Paul Jones" was now bound for St. Louis. I planned a siege against my pilot, and at the end of three hard days he surrendered. He agreed to teach me the Mississippi River from New Orleans to St. Louis for five hundred dollars, payable out of the first wages I should receive after graduation. I entered upon the small enterprise of "learning" twelve or thirteen hundred miles of the great Mississippi River with the easy confidence of my time of life. If I had really known what I was about to require of my faculties, I should not have had the courage to begin. I supposed that all a pilot had to do was to keep his boat in the river, and I did not consider that that could be much of a trick, since it was so wide.

The boat backed out from New Orleans at four in the afternoon, and it was "our watch" until eight. Mr. Bixby, my chief, "straightened her up," plowed her along past the sterns of the other boats that lay at the Levee, and then said, "Here, take her; shave those steamships as close as you'd peel an apple." I took the wheel, and my heart-beat fluttered up into the hundreds; for it seemed to me that we were about to scrape the side off every ship in the line, we were so close. I held my breath and began to claw the boat away from the danger; and I had my own opinion of the pilot who had known no better than to get us into such peril, but I was too wise to express it. In half a minute I had a wide margin of safety intervening between the "Paul Jones" and the ships; and within ten seconds more I was set aside in disgrace, and Mr. Bixby was going into danger again and flaying me alive with abuse of my cowardice. I was stung, but I was obliged to admire the easy confidence with which my chief loafed from side to side of his wheel, and trimmed the ships so closely that disaster seemed ceaselessly imminent. When he had cooled a little he told me that the easy water was close ashore and the current outside, and therefore we must hug the bank, up-stream, to get the benefit of the former, and stay well out, down-stream, to take advantage of the latter. In my own mind I resolved to be a down-stream pilot and leave the up-streaming to people dead to prudence.

Now and then Mr. Bixby called my attention to certain things. Said he, "This is Six-Mile Point." I assented. It was pleasant enough information, but I could not see the bearing of it. I was not conscious that it was a matter of any interest to me. Another time he said, "This is Nine-Mile Point." Later he said, "This is Twelve-Mile Point." They were all about level with the water's edge; they all looked about alike to me; they were monotonously unpicturesque. I hoped Mr. Bixby would change the subject. But no; he would crowd up around a point, hugging the shore with affection, and then say: "The slack water ends here, abreast this bunch of China trees; now we cross over." So he crossed over. He gave me the wheel once or twice, but I had no luck. I either came near chipping off the edge of a sugar-plantation, or I yawed too far from shore, and so dropped back into disgrace again and got abused.

The watch was ended at last, and we took supper and went to bed. At midnight the glare of a lantern shone in my eyes, and the night watchman said:—

"Come! turn out!"

And then he left. I could not understand this extraordinary procedure; so I presently gave up trying to, and dozed off to sleep. Pretty soon the watchman was back again, and this time he was gruff. I was annoyed. I said:—

"What do you want to come bothering around here in the middle of the night for? Now, as like as not, I'll not get to sleep again to-night."

The watchman said:—

"Well, if this an't good, I'm blest."

The "off-watch" was just turning in, and I heard some brutal laughter from them and such remarks as "Hello, watchman! an't the new cub turned out yet? He's delicate, likely. Give him some sugar in a rag, and send for the chambermaid to sing rock-a-by-baby to him."

About this time Mr. Bixby appeared on the scene. Something like a minute later I was climbing the pilot-house steps with some of my clothes on and the rest in my arms. Mr. Bixby was close behind, commenting. Here was something fresh—this thing of getting up in the middle of the night to go to work. It was a detail in piloting that had never occurred to me at all. I knew that boats ran all night, but somehow I had never happened to reflect that somebody had to get up out of a warm bed to run them. I began to fear that piloting was not quite

[2] "Deck" passage—*i.e.*, steerage passage. [Twain's note.]

so romantic as I had imagined it was; there was something very real and worklike about this new phase of it.

It was a rather dingy night, although a fair number of stars were out. The big mate was at the wheel, and he had the old tub pointed at a star and was holding her straight up the middle of the river. The shores on either hand were not much more than half a mile apart, but they seemed wonderfully far away and ever so vague and indistinct. The mate said:—

"We've got to land at Jones's plantation, sir."

The vengeful spirit in me exulted. I said to myself, I wish you joy of your job, Mr. Bixby; you'll have a good time finding Mr. Jones's plantation such a night as this; and I hope you never *will* find it as long as you live.

Mr. Bixby said to the mate:—

"Upper end of the plantation, or the lower?"

"Upper."

"I can't do it. The stumps there are out of water at this stage. It's no great distance to the lower, and you'll have to get along with that."

"All right, sir. If Jones don't like it, he'll have to lump it, I reckon."

And then the mate left. My exultation began to cool and my wonder to come up. Here was a man who not only proposed to find this plantation on such a night, but to find either end of it you preferred. I dreadfully wanted to ask a question, but I was carrying about as many short answers as my cargo-room would admit of, so I held my peace. All I desired to ask Mr. Bixby was the simple question whether he was ass enough to really imagine he was going to find that plantation on a night when all plantations were exactly alike and all of the same color. But I held in. I used to have fine inspirations of prudence in those days.

Mr. Bixby made for the shore and soon was scraping it, just the same as if it had been daylight. And not only that, but singing—

"Father in heaven, the day is declining," etc.

It seemed to me that I had put my life in the keeping of a peculiarly reckless outcast. Presently he turned on me and said:—

"What's the name of the first point above New Orleans?"

I was gratified to be able to answer promptly, and I did. I said I didn't know.

"Don't *know*?"

This manner jolted me. I was down at the foot again, in a moment. But I had to say just what I had said before.

"Well, you're a smart one," said Mr. Bixby. "What's the name of the *next* point?"

Once more I didn't know.

"Well, this beats anything. Tell me the name of *any* point or place I told you."

I studied a while and decided that I couldn't.

"Look here! What do you start out from, above Twelve-Mile Point, to cross over?"

"I—I—don't know."

"You—you—don't know?" mimicking my drawling manner of speech. "What *do* you know?"

"I—I—nothing, for certain."

"By the great Caesar's ghost, I believe you! You're the stupidest dunderhead I ever saw or heard of, so help me Moses! The idea of *you* being a pilot—*you!* Why, you don't know enough to pilot a cow down a lane."

Oh, but his wrath was up! He was a nervous man, and he shuffled from one side of his wheel to the other as if the floor was hot. He would boil awhile to himself, and then overflow and scald me again.

"Look here! What do you suppose I told you the names of those points for?"

I tremblingly considered a moment, and then the devil of temptation provoked me to say:—

"Well to—to—be entertaining, I thought."

This was a red rag to the bull. He raged and stormed so (he was crossing the river at the time) that I judged it made him blind, because he ran over the steering-oar of a trading-scow. Of course the traders sent up a volley of red-hot profanity. Never was a man so grateful as Mr. Bixby was: because he was brim full, and here were subjects who would *talk back*. He threw open a window, thrust his head out, and such an irruption followed as I never had heard before. The fainter and farther away the scowmen's curses drifted, the higher Mr. Bixby lifted his voice and the weightier his adjectives grew. When he closed the window he was empty. You could have drawn a seine through his system and not caught curses enough to disturb your mother with. Presently he said to me in the gentlest way:—

"My boy, you must get a little memorandum-book; and every time I tell you a thing, put it down right away. There's only one way to be a pilot, and that is to get this entire river by heart. You have to know it just like A B C."

That was a dismal revelation to me; for my memory was never loaded with anything but blank cartridges. However, I did not feel discouraged long. I judged that it was best to make some allowances, for doubtless Mr. Bixby was "stretching." Presently he pulled a rope and struck a few strokes on the big bell. The stars were all gone now, and the night was as black as ink. I could hear the wheels churn along the bank, but I was not entirely certain that I could see the shore. The voice of the invisible watchman called up from the hurricane deck:—

"What's this, sir?"

"Jones's plantation."

I said to myself, I wish I might venture to offer a small bet that it isn't. But I did not chirp. I only waited to see. Mr. Bixby handled the engine bells, and in due time the boat's nose came to the land, a torch glowed from the forecastle, a man skipped ashore, a darky's voice on the bank said, "Gimme de k'yarpet-bag, Mars' Jones," and the next moment we were standing up the river again, all serene. I reflected deeply a while, and then said,—but not aloud,—Well, the finding of that plantation was the luckiest accident that ever happened; but it couldn't happen again in a hundred years. And I fully believed it *was* an accident, too.

By the time we had gone seven or eight hundred miles up the river, I had learned to be a tolerably plucky upstream steersman, in daylight, and before we reached St. Louis I had made a trifle of progress in night-work, but only a trifle. I had a note-book that fairly bristled with the names of towns, "points," bars, islands, bends, reaches, etc.; but the information was to be found only in the note-book—none of it was in my head. It made my heart ache to think I had only got half of the river set down; for as our watch was four hours off and four hours on, day and night, there was a long four-hour gap in my book for every time I had slept since the voyage began.

My chief was presently hired to go on a big New Orleans boat, and I packed my satchel and went with him. She was a grand affair. When I stood in her pilot-house I was so far above the water that I seemed perched on a mountain; and her decks stretched so far away, fore and aft, below me, that I wondered how I could ever have considered the little "Paul Jones" a large craft. There were other differences, too. The "Paul Jones's" pilot-house was a cheap, dingy, battered rattle-trap, cramped for room: but here was a sumptuous glass temple; room enough to have a dance in; showy red and gold window-curtains; an imposing sofa; leather cushions and a back to the high bench where visiting pilots sit, to spin yarns and "look at the river;" bright, fanciful "cuspadores," instead of a broad wooden box filled with sawdust; nice new oilcloth on the floor; a hospitable big stove for winter; a wheel as high as my head, costly with inlaid work; a wire tiller-rope; bright brass knobs for the bells; and a tidy, white-aproned, black "texas-tender," to bring up tarts and ices and coffee during mid-watch, day and night. Now this was "something like;" and so I began to take heart once more to believe that piloting was a romantic sort of occupation after all. The moment we were under way I began to prowl about the great steamer and fill myself with joy. She was as clean and as dainty as a drawing-room; when I looked down her long, gilded saloon, it was like gazing through a splendid tunnel; she had an oil-picture, by some gifted sign-painter, on every stateroom door; she glittered with no end of prism-fringed chandeliers; the clerk's office was elegant, the bar was marvellous, and the bar-keeper had been barbered and upholstered at incredible cost. The boiler deck (*i.e.*, the second story of the boat, so to speak), was as spacious as a church, it seemed to me; so with the forecastle; and there was no pitiful handful of deck-hands, firemen, and roustabouts down there, but a whole battalion of men. The fires were fiercely glaring from a long row of furnaces, and over them were eight huge boilers! This was unutterable pomp. The mighty engines—but enough of this. I had never felt so fine before. And when I found that the regiment of natty servants respectfully "sir'd" me, my satisfaction was complete.

A Daring Deed

When I returned to the pilot-house St. Louis was gone, and I was lost. Here was a piece of river which was all down in my book, but I could make neither head nor tail of it: you understand, it was turned around. I had seen it when coming upstream, but I had never faced about to see how it looked when it was behind me. My heart broke again, for it was plain that I had got to learn this troublesome river *both ways*.

The pilot-house was full of pilots, going down to "look at the river." What is called the "upper river" (the two hundred miles between St. Louis and Cairo, where the Ohio comes in) was low; and the Mississippi changes its channel so constantly that the pilots used to always find it necessary to run down to Cairo to take a fresh look, when their boats were to lie in port a week; that is, when the water was at a low stage. A deal of this "looking at the river" was done by poor fellows who seldom had a berth, and whose only hope of getting one lay in their being always freshly posted and therefore ready to drop into the shoes of some reputable pilot, for a single trip, on account of such pilot's sudden illness, or some other necessity. And a good many of them constantly ran up and down inspecting the river, not because they ever really hoped to get a berth, but because (they being guests of the boat) it was cheaper to "look at the river" than stay ashore and pay board. In time these fellows grew dainty in their tastes, and only infested boats that had an established reputation for setting good tables. All visiting pilots were useful, for they were always ready and willing, winter or summer, night or day, to go out in the yawl and help buoy the channel or assist the boat's pilot in any way they could. They were likewise welcome because all pilots are tireless talkers, when gathered together, and as they talk only about the river they are always understood and are always interesting. Your true pilot cares nothing about anything on earth but the river, and his pride in his occupation surpasses the pride of kings.

We had a fine company of these river inspectors along this trip. There were eight or ten; and there was abundance of room for them in our great pilot-house. Two or three of them wore polished silk hats, elaborate shirt-fronts, diamond breastpins, kid gloves, and patent-leather boots. They were choice in their English, and bore themselves with a dignity proper to men of solid means and prodigious reputation as pilots. The others were more or less loosely clad, and wore upon their heads tall felt cones that were suggestive of the days of the Commonwealth.

I was a cipher in this august company, and felt subdued, not to say torpid. I was not even of sufficient consequence to assist at the wheel when it was necessary to put the tiller hard down in a hurry; the guest that stood nearest did that when occasion required—and this was pretty much all the time, because of the crookedness of the channel and the scant water. I stood in a corner; and the talk I listened to took the hope all out of me. One visitor said to another:—

"Jim, how did you run Plum Point, coming up?"

"It was in the night, there, and I ran it the way one of the boys on the 'Diana' told me; started out about fifty yards above the wood pile on the false point, and held on the cabin under Plum Point till I raised the reef—quarter less twain—then straightened up for the middle bar till I got well abreast the old one-limbed cotton-wood in the mend, then got my stern on the cotton-wood and head on the low place above the point, and came through a-booming—nine and a half."

"Pretty square crossing, an't it?"

"Yes, but the upper bar's working down fast."

Another pilot spoke up and said:—

"I had better water than that, and ran it lower down; started out from the false point—mark twain—raised the second reef abreast the big snag in the bend, and had quarter less twain."

One of the gorgeous ones remarked:—

"I don't want to find fault with your leadsmen, but that's a good deal of water for Plum Point, it seems to me."

There was an approving nod all around as this quiet snub dropped on the boaster and "settled" him. And so they went on talk-talk-talking. Meantime, the thing that was running in my mind was, "Now, if my ears hear aright, I have not only to get the names of all the towns and islands and bends, and so on, by heart, but I must even get up a warm personal acquaintanceship with every old snag and one-limbed cotton-wood and obscure wood pile that ornaments the banks of this river for twelve hundred miles; and more than that, I must actually know where these things are in the dark, unless these guests are gifted with eyes that can pierce through two miles of solid blackness. I wish the piloting business was in Jericho and I had never thought of it."

At dusk Mr. Bixby tapped the big bell three times (the signal to land), and the captain emerged from his drawing-room in the forward end of the texas, and looked up inquiringly. Mr. Bixby said:—

"We will lay up here all night, captain."

"Very well, sir."

That was all. The boat came to shore and was tied up for the night. It seemed to me a fine thing that the pilot could do as he pleased, without asking so grand a captain's permission. I took my supper and went immediately to bed, discouraged by my day's observations and experiences. My late voyage's note-booking was but a confusion of meaningless names. It had tangled me all up in a knot every time I had looked at it in the daytime. I now hoped for respite in sleep; but no, it revelled all through my head till sunrise again, a frantic and tireless nightmare.

Next morning I felt pretty rusty and low-spirited. We went booming along, taking a good many chances, for we were anxious to "get out of the river" (as getting out to Cairo was called) before night should overtake us. But Mr. Bixby's partner, the other pilot, presently grounded the boat, and we lost so much time getting her off that it was plain the darkness would overtake us a good long way above the mouth. This was a great misfortune, especially to certain of our visiting pilots, whose boats would have to wait for their return, no matter how long that might be. It sobered the pilot-house talk a good deal. Coming up-stream, pilots did not mind low water or any kind of darkness; nothing stopped them but fog. But down-stream work was different; a boat was too nearly helpless, with a stiff current pushing behind her; so it was not customary to run down-stream at night in low water.

There seemed to be one small hope, however: if we could get through the intricate and dangerous Hat Island crossing before night, we could venture the rest, for we would have plainer sailing and better water. But it would be insanity to attempt Hat Island at night. So there was a deal of looking at watches all the rest of the day, and a constant ciphering upon the speed we were making; Hat Island was the eternal subject; sometimes hope was high and sometimes we were delayed in a bad crossing, and down it went again. For hours all hands lay under the burden of this suppressed excitement; it was even communicated to me, and I got to feeling so solicitous about Hat Island, and under such an awful pressure of responsibility, that I wished I might have five minutes on shore to draw a good, full, relieving breath, and start over again. We were standing no regular watches. Each of our pilots ran such portions of the river as he had run when coming up-stream, because of his greater familiarity with it; but both remained in the pilot-house constantly.

An hour before sunset Mr. Bixby took the wheel, and Mr. W—— stepped aside. For the next thirty minutes every man held his watch in his hand and was restless, silent, and uneasy. At last somebody said, with a doomful sigh,—

"Well yonder's Hat Island—and we can't make it."

All the watches closed with a snap, everybody sighed and muttered something about its being "too bad, too bad—ah, if we could *only* have got here half an hour sooner!" and the place was thick with the atmosphere of disappointment. Some started to go out, but loitered, hearing no bell-tap to land. The sun dipped behind the horizon, the boat went on. Inquiring looks passed from one guest to another; and one who had his hand on the door-knob and had turned it, waited, then presently took away his hand and let the knob turn back again. We bore steadily down the bend. More looks were exchanged, and nods of surprised admiration—but no words. Insensibly the men drew together behind Mr. Bixby, as the sky darkened and one or two dim stars came out. The dead silence and sense of waiting became oppressive. Mr. Bixby pulled the cord, and two deep, mellow notes from the big bell floated off on the night. Then a pause, and one more note was struck. The watchman's voice followed, from the hurricane-deck:—

"Labboard lead, there! Stabboard lead!"

The cries of the leadsmen began to rise out of the distance, and were gruffly repeated by the word-passers on the hurricane deck.

"M-a-r-k three! . . . . M-a-r-k three! . . . . Quarter-less-three! . . . . Half twain! . . . . Quarter twain! . . . . M-a-r-k twain! . . . . Quarter-less"—

Mr. Bixby pulled two bell-ropes, and was answered by faint jinglings far below in the engine room, and our speed slackened. The steam began to whistle through the gauge-cocks. The cries of the leadsmen went on—and it is a weird sound, always, in the night. Every pilot in the lot was watching now, with fixed eyes, and talking under his breath. Nobody was calm and easy but Mr. Bixby. He would put his wheel down and stand on a spoke, and as the steamer swung into her (to me) utterly invisible marks—for we seemed to be in the midst of a wide and gloomy sea—he would meet and fasten her there. Out of the murmur of half-audible talk, one caught a coherent sentence now and then—such as:

"There; she's over the first reef all right!"

After a pause, another subdued voice:—

"Her stern's coming down just *exactly* right, by *George!*"

"Now she's in the marks; over she goes!"

Somebody else muttered:—

"Oh, it was done beautiful—*beautiful!*"

Now the engines were stopped altogether, and we drifted with the current. Not that I could see the boat drift, for I could not, the stars being all gone by this time. This drifting was the dismalest work; it held one's heart still. Presently I discovered a blacker gloom than that which surrounded us. It was the head of the island. We were closing right down upon it. We entered its deeper shadow, and so imminent seemed the peril that I was likely to suffocate; and I had the strongest impulse to do *something*, anything, to save the vessel. But still Mr. Bixby stood by his wheel, silent, intent as a cat, and all the pilots stood shoulder to shoulder at his back.

"She'll not make it!" somebody whispered.

The water grew shoaler and shoaler, by the leadsman's cries, till it was down to:—

"Eight-and-a-half! . . . . E-i-g-h-t feet! . . . . E-i-g-h-t feet! . . . . Seven-and"—

Mr. Bixby said warningly through his speaking-tube to the engineer:—

"Stand by, now!"

"Aye-aye, sir!"

"Seven-and-a-half! Seven feet! *Six* and"—

We touched bottom! Instantly Mr. Bixby set a lot of bells ringing, shouted through the tube, "*Now*, let her have it—every ounce you've got!" then to his partner, "Put her hard down! snatch her! snatch her!" The boat rasped and ground her way through the sand, hung upon the apex of disaster a single tremendous instant, and then over she went! And such a shout as went up at Mr. Bixby's back never loosened the roof of a pilot-house before!

There was no more trouble after that. Mr. Bixby was a hero that night; and it was some little time, too, before his exploit ceased to be talked about by river men.

Fully to realize the marvellous precision required in laying the great steamer in her marks in that murky waste of water, one should know that not only must she pick her intricate way through snags and blind reefs, and then shave the head of the island so closely as to brush the overhanging foliage with her stern, but at one place she must pass almost within arm's reach of a sunken and invisible wreck that would snatch the hull timbers from under her if she should strike it, and destroy a quarter of a million dollars' worth of steamboat and cargo in five minutes, and maybe a hundred and fifty human lives into the bargain.

The last remark I heard that night was a compliment to Mr. Bixby, uttered in soliloquy and with unction by one of our guests. He said:—

"By the Shadow of Death, but he's a lightning pilot!"

Perplexing Lessons

At the end of what seemed a tedious while, I had managed to pack my head full of islands, towns, bars, "points," and bends; and a curiously inanimate mass of lumber it was, too. However, inasmuch as I could shut my eyes and reel off a good long string of these names without leaving out more than ten miles of river in every fifty, I began to feel that I could take a boat down to New Orleans if I could make her skip those little gaps. But of course my complacency could hardly get start enough to lift my nose a trifle into the air, before Mr. Bixby would think of something to fetch it down again. One day he turned on me suddenly with this settler:—

"What is the shape of Walnut Bend?"

He might as well have asked me my grandmother's opinion of protoplasm. I reflected respectfully, and then said I didn't know it had any particular shape. My gunpowdery chief went off with a bang, of course, and then went on loading and firing until he was out of adjectives.

I had learned long ago that he only carried just so many rounds of ammunition, and was sure to subside into a very placable and even remorseful old smooth-bore as soon as they were all gone. That word "old" is merely affectionate; he was not more than thirty-four. I waited. By and by he said:—

"My boy, you've got to know the *shape* of the river perfectly. It is all there is left to steer by on a very dark night. Everything else is blotted out and gone. But mind you, it hasn't the same shape in the night that it has in the day-time."

"How on earth am I ever going to learn it, then?"

"How do you follow a hall at home in the dark? Because you know the shape of it. You can't see it."

"Do you mean to say that I've got to know all the million trifling variations of shape in the banks of this interminable river as well as I know the shape of the front hall at home?"

"On my honor, you've got to know them *better* than any man ever did know the shapes of the halls in his own house."

"I wish I was dead!"

"Now I don't want to discourage you, but"—

"Well, pile it on me; I might as well have it now as another time."

"You see, this has got to be learned; there isn't any getting around it. A clear starlight night throws such heavy shadows that, if you didn't know the shape of a shore perfectly, you would claw away from every bunch of timber, because you would take the black shadow of it for a solid cape; and you see you would be getting scared to death every fifteen minutes by the watch. You would be fifty yards from shore all the time when you ought to be within fifty feet of it. You can't see a snag in one of those shadows, but you know exactly where it is, and the shape of the river tells you when you are coming to it. Then there's your pitch-dark night; the river is a very different shape on a pitch-dark night from what it is on a starlight night. All shores seem to be straight lines, then, and mighty dim ones, too; and you'd *run* them for straight lines, only you know better. You boldly drive your boat right into what seems to be a solid, straight wall (you knowing very well that in reality there is a curve there), and that wall falls back and makes way for you. Then there's your gray mist. You take a night when there's one of these grisly, drizzly, gray mists, and then there isn't *any* particular shape to a shore. A gray mist would tangle the head of the oldest man that ever lived. Well, then, different kinds of *moonlight* change the shape of the river in different ways. You see"—

"Oh, don't say any more, please! Have I got to learn the shape of the river according to all these five hundred thousand different ways? If I tried to carry all that cargo in my head it would make me stoop-shouldered."

"*No!* you only learn *the* shape of the river; and you learn it with such absolute certainty that you can always steer by the shape that's *in your head,* and never mind the one that's before your eyes."

"Very well, I'll try it; but, after I have learned it, can I depend on it? Will it keep the same form and not go fooling around?"

Before Mr. Bixby could answer, Mr. W—— came in to take the watch, and he said,—

"Bixby, you'll have to look out for President's Island, and all that country clear away up above the Old Hen and Chickens. The banks are caving and the shape of the shores changing like everything. Why, you wouldn't know the point above 40. You can go up inside the old sycamore snag, now."[3]

So that question was answered. Here were leagues of shore changing shape. My spirits were down in the mud again. Two things seemed pretty apparent to me. One was, that in order to be a pilot a man had got to learn more than any one man

[3] It may not be necessary, but still it can do no harm to explain that "inside" means between the snag and the shore. [Twain's note.]

ought to be allowed to know; and the other was, that he must learn it all over again in a different way every twenty-four hours.

That night we had the watch until twelve. Now it was an ancient river custom for the two pilots to chat a bit when the watch changed. While the relieving pilot put on his gloves and lit his cigar, his partner, the retiring pilot, would say something like this:—

"I judge the upper bar is making down a little at Hale's Point; had quarter twain with the lower lead and mark twain[4] with the other."

"Yes, I thought it was making down a little, last trip. Meet any boats?"

"Met one abreast the head of 21, but she was away over hugging the bar, and I couldn't make her out entirely. I took her for the 'Sunny South'—hadn't any skylight forward of the chimneys."

And so on. And as the relieving pilot took the wheel his partner[5] would mention that we were in such-and-such a bend, and say we were abreast of such-and-such a man's wood-yard or plantation. This was courtesy; I supposed it was *necessity*. But Mr. W—— came on watch full twelve minutes late on this particular night,—a tremendous breach of etiquette; in fact, it is the unpardonable sin among pilots. So Mr. Bixby gave him no greeting whatever, but simply surrendered the wheel and marched out of the pilot-house without a word. I was appalled; it was a villanous night for blackness, we were in a particularly wide and blind part of the river, where there was no shape or substance to anything, and it seemed incredible that Mr. Bixby should have left that poor fellow to kill the boat trying to find out where he was. But I resolved that I would stand by him any way. He should find that he was not wholly friendless. So I stood around, and waited to be asked where we were. But Mr. W—— plunged on serenely through the solid firmament of black cats that stood for an atmosphere, and never opened his mouth. Here is a proud devil, thought I; here is a limb of Satan that would rather send us all to destruction than put himself under obligations to me, because I am not yet one of the salt of the earth and privileged to snub captains and lord it over everything dead and alive in a steamboat. I presently climbed up on the bench; I did not think it was safe to go to sleep while this lunatic was on watch.

However, I must have gone to sleep in the course of time, because the next thing I was aware of was the fact that day was breaking, Mr. W—— gone, and Mr. Bixby at the wheel again. So it was four o'clock and all well—but me; I felt like a skinful of dry bones and all of them trying to ache at once.

Mr. Bixby asked me what I had stayed up there for. I confessed that it was to do Mr. W—— a benevolence,—tell him where he was. It took five minutes for the entire preposterousness of the thing to filter into Mr. Bixby's system, and then I judge it filled him nearly up to the chin; because he paid me a compliment—and not much of a one either. He said,—

"Well, taking you by-and-large, you do seem to be more different kinds of an ass than any creature I ever saw before. What did you suppose he wanted to know for?"

I said I thought it might be a convenience to him.

"Convenience! D—nation! Didn't I tell you that a man's got to know the river in the night the same as he'd know his own front hall?"

"Well, I can follow the front hall in the dark if I know it *is* the front hall; but suppose you set me down in the middle of it in the dark and not tell me which hall it is; how am *I* to know?"

"Well, you've *got* to, on the river!"

"All right. Then I'm glad I never said anything to Mr. W——"

"I should say so! Why, he'd have slammed you through the window and utterly ruined a hundred dollars' worth of window-sash and stuff."

I was glad this damage had been saved, for it would have made me unpopular with the owners. They always hated anybody who had the name of being careless, and injuring things.

I went to work now to learn the shape of the river; and of all the eluding and ungraspable objects that ever I tried to get mind or hands on, that was the chief. I would fasten my eyes upon a sharp, wooden point that projected far into the river some miles ahead of me, and go to laboriously photographing its shape upon my brain; and just as I was beginning to succeed to my satisfaction, we would draw up toward it and the exasperating thing would begin to melt away and fold back into the bank! If there had been a conspicuous dead tree standing upon the very point of the cape, I would find that tree inconspicuously merged into the general forest, and occupying the middle of a straight shore, when I got abreast of it! No prominent hill would stick to its shape long enough for me to make up my mind what its form really was, but it was as dissolving and changeful as if it had been a mountain of butter in the hottest corner of the tropics. Nothing ever had the same shape when I was coming down-stream that it had borne when I went up. I mentioned these little difficulties to Mr. Bixby. He said,—

"That's the very main virtue of the thing. If the shapes didn't change every three seconds they wouldn't be of any use. Take this place where we are now, for instance. As long as that hill over yonder is only one hill, I can boom right along the way

[4] Two fathoms. Quarter twain is 2-1/4 fathoms, 13-1/2 feet. Mark three is three fathoms. [Twain's note.]

[5] "Partner" is technical for "the other pilot." [Twain's note.]

I'm going; but the moment it splits at the top and forms a V, I know I've got to scratch to starboard in a hurry, or I'll bang this boat's brains out against a rock; and then the moment one of the prongs of the V swings behind the other, I've got to waltz to larboard again, or I'll have a misunderstanding with a snag that would snatch the keelson out of this steamboat as neatly as if it were a sliver in your hand. If that hill didn't change its shape on bad nights there would be an awful steamboat grave-yard around here inside of a year."

It was plain that I had got to learn the shape of the river in all the different ways that could be thought of,—upside down, wrong end first, inside out, fore-and-aft, and "thort-ships,"—and then know what to do on gray nights when it hadn't any shape at all. So I set about it. In the course of time I began to get the best of this knotty lesson, and my self-complacency moved to the front once more. Mr. Bixby was all fixed, and ready to start it to the rear again. He opened on me after this fashion:—

"How much water did we have in the middle crossing at Hole-in-the-Wall, trip before last?"

I considered this an outrage. I said:—

"Every trip, down and up, the leadsmen are singing through that tangled place for three quarters of an hour on a stretch. How do you reckon I can remember such a mess as that?"

"My boy, you've got to remember it. You've got to remember the exact spot and the exact marks the boat lay in when we had the shoalest water, in every one of the five hundred shoal places between St. Louis and New Orleans; and you mustn't get the shoal soundings and marks of one trip mixed up with the shoal soundings and marks of another, either, for they're not often twice alike. You must keep them separate."

When I came to myself again, I said,—

"When I get so that I can do that, I'll be able to raise the dead, and then I won't have to pilot a steamboat to make a living. I want to retire from this business. I want a slush-bucket and a brush; I'm only fit for a roustabout. I haven't got brains enough to be a pilot; and if I had I wouldn't have strength enough to carry them around, unless I went on crutches."

"Now drop that! When I say I'll learn[6] a man the river, I mean it. And you can depend on it, I'll learn him or kill him."

Continued Perplexities

There was no use in arguing with a person like this. I promptly put such a strain on my memory that by and by even the shoal water and the countless crossing-marks began to stay with me. But the result was just the same. I never could more than get one knotty thing learned before another presented itself. Now I had often seen pilots gazing at the water and pretending to read it as if it were a book; but it was a book that told me nothing. A time came at last, however, when Mr. Bixby seemed to think me far enough advanced to bear a lesson on water-reading. So he began:—

"Do you see that long, slanting line on the face of the water? Now, that's a reef. Moreover, it's a bluff reef. There is a solid sandbar under it that is nearly as straight up and down as the side of a house. There is plenty of water close up to it, but mighty little on top of it. If you were to hit it you would knock the boat's brains out. Do you see where the line fringes out at the upper end and begins to fade away?"

"Yes, sir."

"Well, that is a low place; that is the head of the reef. You can climb over there, and not hurt anything. Cross over, now, and follow along close under the reef—easy water there—not much current."

I followed the reef along till I approached the fringed end. Then Mr. Bixby said,—

"Now get ready. Wait till I give the word. She won't want to mount the reef; a boat hates shoal water. Stand by—wait—*wait*—keep her well in hand. *Now* cramp her down! Snatch her! snatch her!"

He seized the other side of the wheel and helped to spin it around until it was hard down, and then we held it so. The boat resisted, and refused to answer for a while, and next she came surging to starboard, mounted the reef, and sent a long, angry ridge of water foaming away from her bows.

"Now watch her; watch her like a cat, or she'll get away from you. When she fights strong and the tiller slips a little, in a jerky, greasy sort of way, let up on her a trifle; it is the way she tells you at night that the water is too shoal; but keep edging her up, little by little, toward the point. You are well up on the bar, now; there is a bar under every point, because the water that comes down around it forms an eddy and allows the sediment to sink. Do you see those fine lines on the face of the water that branch out like the ribs of a fan? Well, those are little reefs; you want to just miss the ends of them, but run them pretty close. Now look out—look out! Don't you crowd that slick, greasy-looking place; there ain't nine feet there; she won't stand it. She begins to smell it; look sharp, I tell you! Oh, blazes, there you go! Stop the starboard wheel! Quick! Ship up to back! Set her back!"

The engine bells jingled and the engines answered promptly, shooting white columns of steam far aloft out of the 'scape pipes, but it was too late. The boat

[6] "Teach" is not in the river vocabulary. [Twain's note.]

had "smelt" the bar in good earnest; the foamy ridges that radiated from her bows suddenly disappeared, a great dead swell came rolling forward, and swept ahead of her, she careened far over to larboard, and went tearing away toward the other shore as if she were about scared to death. We were a good mile from where we ought to have been, when we finally got the upper hand of her again.

During the afternoon watch the next day, Mr. Bixby asked me if I knew how to run the next few miles. I said:—

"Go inside the first snag above the point, outside the next one, start out from the lower end of Higgins's wood-yard, make a square crossing, and"—

"That's all right. I'll be back before you close up on the next point."

But he wasn't. He was still below when I rounded it and entered upon a piece of the river which I had some misgivings about. I did not know that he was hiding behind a chimney to see how I would perform. I went gayly along, getting prouder and prouder, for he had never left the boat in my sole charge such a length of time before. I even got to "setting" her and letting the wheel go, entirely, while I vaingloriously turned my back and inspected the stern marks and hummed a tune, a sort of easy indifference which I had prodigiously admired in Bixby and other great pilots. Once I inspected rather long, and when I faced to the front again my heart flew into my mouth so suddenly that if I hadn't clapped my teeth together I should have lost it. One of those frightful bluff reefs was stretching its deadly length right across our bows! My head was gone in a moment; I did not know which end I stood on; I gasped and could not get my breath; I spun the wheel down with such rapidity that it wove itself together like a spider's web; the boat answered and turned square away from the reef, but the reef followed her! I fled, but still it followed still it kept—right across my bows! I never looked to see where I was going, I only fled. The awful crash was imminent. Why didn't that villain come? If I committed the crime of ringing a bell, I might get thrown overboard. But better that than kill the boat. So in blind desperation I started such a rattling "shivaree" down below as never had astounded an engineer in this world before, I fancy. Amidst the frenzy of the bells the engines began to back and fill in a furious way, and my reason forsook its throne—we were about to crash into the woods on the other side of the river. Just then Mr. Bixby stepped calmly into view on the hurricane deck. My soul went out to him in gratitude. My distress vanished; I would have felt safe on the brink of Niagara, with Mr. Bixby on the hurricane deck. He blandly and sweetly took his tooth-pick out of his mouth between his fingers, as if it were a cigar,—we were just in the act of climbing an overhanging big tree, and the passengers were scudding astern like rats,—and lifted up these commands to me ever so gently:—

"Stop the starboard. Stop the larboard. Set her back on both."

The boat hesitated, halted, pressed her nose among the boughs a critical instant, then reluctantly began to back away.

"Stop the larboard. Come ahead on it. Stop the starboard. Come ahead on it. Point her for the bar."

I sailed away as serenely as a summer's morning. Mr. Bixby came in and said, with mock simplicity,—

"When you have a hail, my boy, you ought to tap the big bell three times before you land, so that the engineers can get ready."

I blushed under the sarcasm, and said I hadn't had any hail.

"Ah! Then it was for wood, I suppose. The officer of the watch will tell you when he wants to wood up."

I went on consuming, and said I wasn't after wood.

"Indeed? Why, what could you want over here in the bend, then? Did you ever know of a boat following a bend up-stream at this stage of the river?"

"No, sir,—and *I* wasn't trying to follow it. I was getting away from a bluff reef."

"No, it wasn't a bluff reef; there isn't one within three miles of where you were."

"But I saw it. It was as bluff as that one yonder."

"Just about. Run over it!"

"Do you give it as an order?"

"Yes. Run over it!"

"If I don't, I wish I may die."

"All right; I am taking the responsibility."

I was just as anxious to kill the boat, now, as I had been to save it before. I impressed my orders upon my memory, to be used at the inquest, and made a straight break for the reef. As it disappeared under our bows I held my breath; but we slid over it like oil.

"Now, don't you see the difference? It wasn't anything but a *wind* reef. The wind does that."

"So I see. But it is exactly like a bluff reef. How am I ever going to tell them apart?"

"I can't tell you. It is an instinct. By and by you will just naturally *know* one from the other, but you never will be able to explain why or how you know them apart."

It turned out to be true. The face of the water, in time, became a wonderful book—a book that was a dead language to the uneducated passenger, but which told its mind to me without reserve, delivering its most cherished secrets as clearly as if it uttered them with a voice. And it was not a book to be read once and thrown aside, for it had a new story to tell every day. Throughout the long twelve hundred miles there was never a page that was void of interest, never one that you could leave unread without loss, never one that you would want to skip, thinking you could find higher enjoyment in some other thing. There never was so wonderful a book written by man; never one whose interest was so absorbing, so unflagging, so sparklingly renewed with every re-perusal. The passenger who could not read it was charmed with a peculiar sort of faint dimple on its surface (on the rare occasions when he did not overlook it altogether); but to the pilot that was an *italicized* passage; indeed, it was more than that, it was a legend of the largest capitals, with a string of shouting exclamation points at the end of it; for it meant that a wreck or a rock was buried there that could tear the life out of the strongest vessel that ever floated. It is the faintest and simplest expression the water ever makes, and the most hideous to a pilot's eye. In truth, the passenger who could not read this book saw nothing but all manner of pretty pictures in it, painted by the sun and shaded by the clouds, whereas to the trained eye these were not pictures at all, but the grimmest and most dead-earnest of reading-matter.

Now when I had mastered the language of this water and had come to know every trifling feature that bordered the great river as familiarly as I knew the letters of the alphabet, I had made a valuable acquisition. But I had lost something, too. I had lost something which could never be restored to me while I lived. All the grace, the beauty, the poetry, had gone out of the majestic river! I still keep in mind a certain wonderful sunset which I witnessed when steamboating was new to me. A broad expanse of the river was turned to blood; in the middle distance the red hue brightened into gold, through which a solitary log came floating, black and conspicuous; in one place a long, slanting mark lay sparkling upon the water; in another the surface was broken by boiling, tumbling rings, that were as many-tinted as an opal; where the ruddy flush was faintest, was a smooth spot that was covered with graceful circles and radiating lines, ever so delicately traced; the shore on our left was densely wooded, and the sombre shadow that fell from this forest was broken in one place by a long ruffled trail that shone like silver; and high above the forest wall a clean-stemmed dead tree waved a single leafy bough that glowed like a flame in the unobstructed splendor that was flowing from the sun. There were graceful curves, reflected images, woody heights, soft distances; and over the whole scene, far and near, the dissolving lights drifted steadily, enriching it, every passing moment, with new marvels of coloring.

I stood like one bewitched. I drank it in, in a speechless rapture. The world was new to me, and I had never seen anything like this at home. But as I have said, a day came when I began to cease from noting the glories and the charms which the moon and the sun and the twilight wrought upon the river's face; another day came when I ceased altogether to note them. Then, if that sunset scene had been repeated, I should have looked upon it without rapture, and should have commented upon it, inwardly, after this fashion: This sun means that we are going to have wind to-morrow; that floating log means that the river is rising, small thanks to it; that slanting mark on the water refers to a bluff reef which is going to kill somebody's steamboat one of these nights, if it keeps on stretching out like that; those tumbling "boils" show a dissolving bar and a changing channel there; the lines and circles in the slick water over yonder are a warning that that troublesome place is shoaling up dangerously; that silver streak in the shadow of the forest is the "break" from a new snag, and he has located himself in the very best place he could have found to fish for steamboats; that tall dead tree, with a single living branch, is not going to last long, and then how is a body ever going to get through this blind place at night without the friendly old landmark?

No, the romance and beauty were all gone from the river. All the value any feature of it had for me now was the amount of usefulness it could furnish toward compassing the safe piloting of a steamboat. Since those days, I have pitied doctors from my heart. What does the lovely flush in a beauty's cheek mean to a doctor but a "break" that ripples above some deadly disease? Are not all her visible charms sown thick with what are to him the signs and symbols of hidden decay? Does he ever see her beauty at all, or doesn't he simply view her professionally, and comment upon her unwholesome condition all to himself? And doesn't he sometimes wonder whether he has gained most or lost most by learning his trade?

1875, 1883

Frescoes from the Past

As the text itself explains, Mark Twain intended this "raft-passage" for use in *Huckleberry Finn,* which he had begun in 1876 but did not finish until 1885. It was included instead in *Life on the Mississippi,* as Chapter 3, even though Huck and Jim are the main characters involved. The episode illustrates the tradition of the Old Southwest when the keelboatmen plied their flat-bottomed scows along the Ohio and Mississippi rivers in the 1830's and 1840's. The humor of boasting and chest-thumping heroics was typical of the stories told about Davy Crockett and Mike Fink, who was called king of the keelboatmen. Text: *Life on the Mississippi* (Boston, 1883).

By way of illustrating keelboat talk and manners, and that now-departed and hardly-remembered raft-life, I will throw in, in this place, a chapter from a book which I have been working at, by fits and starts, during the past five or six years, and may possibly finish in the course of five or six more. The book is a story which details some passages in the life of an ignorant village boy, Huck Finn, son of the town drunkard of my time out west, there. He has run away from his persecuting father, and from a persecuting good widow who wishes to make a nice, truth-telling, respectable boy of him; and with him a slave of the widow's has also escaped. They have found a fragment of a lumber-raft (it is high water and dead summer time), and are floating down the river by night, and hiding in the willows by day,—bound for Cairo whence the negro will seek freedom in the heart of the free States. But in a fog, they pass Cairo without knowing it. By and by they begin to suspect the truth, and Huck Finn is persuaded to end the dismal suspense by swimming down to a huge raft which they have seen in the distance ahead of them, creeping aboard under cover of the darkness, and gathering the needed information by eavesdropping:—

But you know a young person can't wait very well when he is impatient to find a thing out. We talked it over, and by and by Jim said it was such a black night, now, that it wouldn't be no risk to swim down to the big raft and crawl aboard and listen,—they would talk about Cairo, because they would be calculating to go ashore there for a spree, maybe; or anyway they would send boats ashore to buy whiskey or fresh meat or something. Jim had a wonderful level head, for a nigger: he could most always start a good plan when you wanted one.

I stood up and shook my rags off and jumped into the river, and struck out for the raft's light. By and by, when I got down nearly to her, I eased up and went slow and cautious. But everything was all right—nobody at the sweeps. So I swum down along the raft till I was most abreast the camp fire in the middle, then I crawled aboard and inched along and got in among some bundles of shingles on the weather side of the fire. There was thirteen men there—they was the watch on deck of course. And a mighty rough-looking lot, too. They had a jug, and tin cups, and they kept the jug moving. One man was singing—roaring, you may say; and it wasn't a nice song—for a parlor anyway. He roared through his nose, and strung out the last word of every line very long. When he was done they all fetched a kind of Injun war-whoop, and then another was sung. It begun:—

"There was a woman in our towdn,
In our towdn did dwed'l (dwell,)
She loved her husband dear-i-lee,
But another man twyste as wed'l.

Singing too, riloo, riloo, riloo,
Ri-too, riloo, rilay - - - e,
She loved her husband dear-i-lee,
But another man twyste as wed'l."

And so on—fourteen verses. It was kind of poor, and when he was going to start on the next verse one of them said it was the tune the old cow died on; and another one said: "Oh, give us a rest." And another one told him to take a walk. They made fun of him till he got mad and jumped up and begun to cuss the crowd, and said he could lam any thief in the lot..

They was all about to make a break for him, but the biggest man there jumped up and says:—

"Set whar you are, gentlemen. Leave him to me; he's my meat."

Then he jumped up in the air three times, and cracked his heels together every time. He flung off a buckskin coat that was all hung with fringes, and says, "You lay thar tell the chawin-up's done;" and flung his hat down, which was all over ribbons, and says, "You lay thar tell his sufferin's is over."

Then he jumped up in the air and cracked his heels together again, and shouted out:—

"Whoo-oop! I'm the old original iron-jawed, brass-mounted, copper-bellied corpse-maker from the wilds of Arkansaw!—Look at me! I'm the man they call Sudden Death and General Desolation! Sired by a hurricane, dam'd by an earthquake, half-brother to the cholera, nearly related to the small-pox on the mother's side! Look at me! I take nineteen alligators and a bar'l of whiskey for breakfast when I'm in robust health, and a bushel of rattlesnakes and a dead body when I'm ailing! I split the everlasting rocks with my glance, and I squench the thunder when I speak! Whoo-oop! Stand back and give me room according to my strength! Blood's my natural drink, and the wails of the dying is music to my ear! Cast your eye on me, gentlemen!—and lay low and hold your breath, for I'm bout to turn myself loose!"

All the time he was getting this off, he was shaking his head and looking fierce, and kind of swelling around in a little circle, tucking up his wrist-bands, and now and then straightening up and beating his breast with his fist, saying, "Look at me, gentlemen!" When he got through, he jumped up and cracked his heels together three times, and let off a roaring "whoo-oop! I'm the bloodiest son of a wildcat that lives!"

Then the man that had started the row tilted his old slouch hat down over his right eye; then he bent stooping forward, with his back sagged and his south end sticking out far, and his fists a-shoving out and drawing in in front of him, and so went around in a little circle about three times, swelling himself up and breathing hard. Then he straightened, and jumped up and cracked his heels together three times before he lit again (that made them cheer), and he began to shout like this:

"Whoo-oop! bow your neck and spread, for the kingdom of sorrow's a-coming! Hold me down to the earth, for I feel my powers a-working! whoo-oop! I'm a child of sin, *don't* let me get a start! Smoked glass, here, for all! Don't attempt to look at me with the naked eye, gentlemen! When I'm playful I use the meridians of longitude and parallels of latitude for a seine, and drag the Atlantic Ocean for whales! I scratch my head with the lightning and purr myself to sleep with the thunder! When I'm cold, I bile the Gulf of Mexico and bathe in it; when I'm hot I fan myself with an equinoctial storm; when I'm thirsty I reach up and suck a cloud dry like a sponge; when I range the earth hungry, famine follows in my tracks! Whoo-oop! Bow your neck and spread! I put my hand on the sun's face and make it night in the earth; I bite a piece out of the moon and hurry the seasons; I shake myself and crumble the mountains! Contemplate me through leather—*don't* use the naked eye! I'm the man with a petrified heart and biler-iron bowels! The massacre of isolated communities is the pastime of my idle moments, the destruction of nationalities the serious business of my life! The boundless vastness of the great American desert is my enclosed property, and I bury my dead on my own premises!" He jumped up and cracked his heels together three times before he lit (they cheered him again), and as he come down he shouted out: "Whoo-oop! bow your neck and spread, for the pet child of calamity's a-coming!"

Then the other one went to swelling around and blowing again—the first one—the one they called Bob; next, the Child of Calamity chipped in again, bigger than ever; then they both got at it at the same time, swelling round and round each other and punching their fists most into each other's faces, and whooping and jawing like Injuns; then Bob called the Child names, and the Child called him names back again; next, Bob called him a heap rougher names, and the Child come back at him with the very worst kind of language; next, Bob knocked the Child's hat off, and the Child picked it up and kicked Bob's ribbony hat about six foot; Bob went and got it and said never mind, this warn't going to be the last of this thing, because he was a man that never forgot and never forgive, and so the Child better look out, for there was a time a-coming, just as sure as he was a living man, that he would have to answer to him with the best blood in his body. The Child said no man was willinger than he for that time to come, and he would give Bob fair warning, *now*, never to cross his path again, for he could never rest till he had waded in his blood, for such was his nature, though he was sparing him now on account of his family, if he had one.

Both of them was edging away in different directions, growling and shaking their heads and going on about what they was going to do; but a little black-whiskered chap skipped up and says:—

"Come back here, you couple of chicken-livered cowards, and I'll thrash the two of ye!"

And he done it, too. He snatched them, he jerked them this way and that, he booted them around, he knocked them sprawling faster than they could get up. Why, it warn't two minutes till they begged like dogs—and how the other lot did yell and laugh and clap their hands all the way through, and shout "Sail in, Corpse-Maker!" "Hi! at him again, Child of Calamity!" "Bully for you, little Davy!" Well, it was a perfect pow-wow for a while. Bob and the Child had red noses and black eyes when they got through. Little Davy made them own up that they was sneaks and cowards and not fit to eat with a dog or drink with a nigger; then Bob and the Child shook hands with each other, very solemn, and said they had always respected each other and was willing to let bygones be bygones. So then they washed their faces in the river; and just then there was a loud order to stand by for a crossing, and some of them went forward to man the sweeps there, and the rest went aft to handle the after-sweeps.

I laid still and waited for fifteen minutes, and had a smoke out of a pipe that one of them left in reach; then the crossing was finished, and they stumped back and had a drink around and went to talking and singing again. Next they got out an old fiddle, and one played, and another patted juba, and the rest turned themselves loose on a regular old-fashioned keel-boat breakdown. They couldn't keep that up very long without getting winded, so by and by they settled around the jug again.

They sung "jolly, jolly raftsman's the life for me," with a rousing chorus, and then they got to talking about differences betwixt hogs, and their different kind of habits; and next about women and their different ways; and next about the best ways to put out houses that was afire; and next about what ought to be done with the Injuns; and next about what a king had to do, and how much he got; and next about how to make cats fight; and next about what to do when a man has fits; and next about differences betwixt clear-water rivers and muddy-water ones. The man they called Ed said the muddy Mississippi water was wholesomer to drink than the clear water of the Ohio; he said if you let a pint of this yaller Mississippi water settle, you would have about a half to three-quarters of an inch of mud in the bottom, according to the stage of the river, and then it warn't no better than Ohio water—what you wanted to do was to keep it stirred up—and when the river was low, keep mud on hand to put in and thicken the water up the way it ought to be.

The Child of Calamity said that was so; he said there was nutritiousness in the mud, and a man that drunk Mississippi water could grow corn in his stomach if he wanted to. He says:—

"You look at the graveyards; that tells the tale. Trees won't grow worth shucks in a Cincinnati graveyard, but in a Sent Louis graveyard they grow upwards of eight hundred foot high. It's all on account of the water the people drunk before they laid up. A Cincinnati corpse don't richen a soil any."

And they talked about how Ohio water didn't like to mix with Mississippi water. Ed said if you take the Mississippi on a rise when the Ohio is low, you'll find a wide band of clear water all the way down the east side of the Mississippi for a hundred mile or more, and the minute you get out a quarter of a mile from shore and pass the line, it is all thick and yaller the rest of the way across. Then they talked about how to keep tobacco from getting mouldy, and from that they went into ghosts and told about a lot that other folks had seen; but Ed says:—

"Why don't you tell something that you've seen yourselves? Now let me have a say. Five years ago I was on a raft as big as this, and right along here it was a bright moonshiny night, and I was on watch and boss of the stabboard oar forrard, and one of my pards was a man named Dick Allbright, and he come along to where I was sitting, forrard—gaping and stretching, he was—and stooped down on the edge of the raft and washed his face in the river, and come and set down by me and got out his pipe, and had just got it filled, when he looks up and says,—

" 'Why looky-here,' he says, 'ain't that Buck Miller's place, over yander in the bend?'

" 'Yes,' says I, 'it is—why?' He laid his pipe down and leaned his head on his hand, and says,—

" 'I thought we'd be furder down.' I says,—

" 'I thought it too, when I went off watch'—we was standing six hours on and six off—'but the boys told me,' I says, 'that the raft didn't seem to hardly move, for the last hour,'—says I, 'though she's a slipping along all right, now,' says I. He give a kind of groan, and says,—

" 'I've seed a raft act so before, along here,' he says, ' 'pears to me the current has most quit above the head of this bend durin' the last two years,' he says.

"Well, he raised up two or three times, and looked away off and around on the water. That started me at it, too. A body is always doing what he sees somebody else doing, though there mayn't be no sense in it. Pretty soon I see a black something floating on the water away off to stabboard and quartering behind us. I see he was looking at it, too. I says,—

" 'What's that?' He says, sort of pettish,—

" ' 'Tain't nothing but an old empty bar'l.'

" 'An empty bar'l!' says I, 'why,' says I, 'a spy-glass is a fool to *your* eyes. How can you tell it's an empty bar'l?' He says,—

" 'I don't know; I reckon it ain't a bar'l, but I thought it might be,' says he.

" 'Yes,' I says, 'so it might be, and it might be anything else, too; a body can't tell nothing about it, such a distance as that,' I says.

"We hadn't nothing else to do, so we kept on watching it. By and by I says,—

" 'Why, looky-here, Dick Allbright, that thing's a-gaining on us, I believe.'

"He never said nothing. The thing gained and gained, and I judged it must be a dog that was about tired out. Well, we swung down into the crossing, and the thing floated across the bright streak of the moonshine, and, by George, it *was* a bar'l. Says I,—

" 'Dick Allbright, what made you think that thing was a bar'l, when it was half a mile off,' says I. Says he,—

" 'I don't know.' Says I,—

" 'You tell me, Dick Allbright.' Says he,—

" 'Well, I knowed it was a bar'l; I've seen it before; lots has seen it; they says it's a hanted bar'l.'

"I called the rest of the watch, and they come and stood there, and I told them what Dick said. It floated right along abreast, now, and didn't gain any more. It was about twenty foot off. Some was for having it aboard, but the rest didn't want to. Dick Allbright said rafts that had fooled with it had got bad luck by it. The captain of the watch said he didn't believe in it. He said he reckoned the bar'l gained on us because it was in a little better current than what we was. He said it would leave by and by.

"So then we went to talking about other things, and we had a song, and then a breakdown; and after that the captain of the watch called for another song; but it was clouding up, now, and the bar'l stuck right thar in the same place, and the song didn't seem to have much warm-up to it, somehow, and so they didn't finish it, and there warn't any cheers, but it sort of dropped flat, and nobody said anything for a minute. Then everybody tried to talk at once, and one chap got off a joke, but it warn't no use, they didn't laugh, and even the chap that made the joke didn't laugh at it, which ain't usual. We all just settled down glum, and watched the bar'l, and was oneasy and oncomfortable. Well, sir, it shut down black and still, and then the wind begin to moan around, and next the lightning begin to play and the thunder to grumble. And pretty soon there was a regular storm, and in the middle of it a man that was running aft stumbled and fell and sprained his ankle so that he had to lay up. This made the boys shake their heads. And every time the lightning come, there was that bar'l with the blue lights winking around it. We was always on the look-out for it. But by and by, towards dawn, she was gone. When the day come we couldn't see her anywhere, and we warn't sorry, neither.

"But next night about half-past nine, when there was songs and high jinks goin on, here she comes again, and took her old roost on the stabboard side. There warn't no more high jinks. Everybody got solemn; nobody talked; you couldn't get anybody to do anything but set around moody and look at the bar'l. It begun to cloud up again. When the watch changed, the off watch stayed up, 'stead of turning in. The storm ripped and roared around all night, and in the middle of it another man tripped and sprained his ankle, and had to knock off. The bar'l left towards day, and nobody see it go.

"Everybody was sober and down in the mouth all day. I don't mean the kind of sober that comes of leaving liquor alone,—not that. They was quiet, but they all drunk more than usual,—not together, but each man sidled off and took it private, by himself.

"After dark the off watch didn't turn in; nobody sung, nobody talked; the boys didn't scatter around, neither; they sort of huddled together, forrard; and for two hours they set there, perfectly still, looking steady in the one direction, and heaving a sigh once in a while. And then, here comes the bar'l again. She took up her old place. She staid there all night; nobody turned in. The storm come on again, after midnight. It got awful dark; the rain poured down; hail, too; the thunder boomed and roared and bellowed; the wind blowed a hurricane; and the lightning spread over everything in big sheets of glare, and showed the whole raft as plain as day; and the river lashed up white as milk as far as you could see for miles, and there was that bar'l jiggering along, same as ever. The captain ordered the watch to man the after sweeps for a crossing, and nobody would go,—no more sprained ankles for them, they said. They wouldn't even *walk* aft. Well then, just then the sky split wide open, with a crash, and the lightning killed two men of the after watch, and crippled two more. Crippled them how, say you? Why, *sprained their ankles!*

"The bar'l left in the dark betwixt lightnings, toward dawn. Well, not a body eat a bite at breakfast that morning. After that the men loafed around, in twos and threes, and talked low together. But none of them herded with Dick Allbright. They all give him the cold shake. If he come around where any of the men was, they split up and sidled away. They wouldn't man the sweeps with him. The captain had all the skiffs hauled up on the raft, alongside of his wigwam, and wouldn't let the dead men be took ashore to be planted; he didn't believe a man that got ashore would come back; and he was right.

"After night come, you could see pretty plain that there was going to be trouble if that bar'l come again; there was such a muttering going on. A good many wanted to kill Dick Allbright, because he'd seen the bar'l on other trips, and that had an ugly look. Some wanted to put him ashore. Some said, let's all go ashore in a pile, if the bar'l comes again.

"This kind of whispers was still going on, the men being bunched together forrard watching for the bar'l, when, lo and behold you! here she comes again. Down she comes, slow and steady, and settles into her old tracks. You could a heard a pin drop. Then up comes the captain, and says:—

"Boys, don't be a pack of children and fools; I don't want this bar'l to be dogging us all the way to Orleans, and *you* don't; well, then, how's the best way to stop it? Burn it up,—that's the way. I'm going to fetch it aboard,' he says. And before anybody could say a word, in he went.

"He swum to it, and as he come pushing it to the raft, the men spread to one side. But the old man got it aboard and busted in the head, and there was a baby in it! Yes sir; a stark-naked baby. It was Dick Allbright's baby; he owned up and said so.

" 'Yes,' he says, a-leaning over, 'yes, it is my own lamented darling, my poor lost Charles William Allbright deceased,' says he,—for he could curl his tongue around the bulliest words in the language when he was a mind to, and lay them before you without a jint started, anywheres. Yes, he said he used to live up at the head of this bend, and one night he choked his child, which was crying, not intending to kill it,—which was prob'ly a lie,—and then he was scared, and buried it in a bar'l, before his wife got home, and off he went, and struck the northern trail and went to rafting; and this was the third year that the bar'l had chased him. He said the bad luck always begun light, and lasted till four men was killed, and then the bar'l didn't come any more after that. He said if the men would stand it one more night,—and was a-going on like that,—but the men had got enough. They started to get out a boat to take him ashore and lynch him, but he grabbed the little child all of a sudden and jumped overboard with it hugged up to his breast and shedding tears, and we never see him again in this life, poor old suffering soul, nor Charles William neither."

"*Who* was shedding tears?" says Bob; "was it Allbright or the baby?"

"Why, Allbright, of course; didn't I tell you the baby was dead? Been dead three years—how could it cry?"

"Well, never mind how it could cry—how could

it *keep* all that time?" says Davy. "You answer me that."

"I don't know how it done it," says Ed. "It done it, though—that's all I know about it."

"Say—what did they do with the bar'l?" says the Child of Calamity.

"Why, they hove it overboard, and it sunk like a chunk of lead."

"Edward, did the child look like it was choked?" says one.

"Did it have its hair parted?" says another.

"What was the brand on that bar'l, Eddy?" says a fellow they called Bill.

"Have you got the papers for them statistics, Edmund?" says Jimmy.

"Say, Edwin, was you one of the men that was killed by the lightning?" says Davy.

"Him? O, no, he was both of 'em," says Bob. Then they all haw-hawed.

"Say, Edward, don't you reckon you'd better take a pill? You look bad—don't you feel pale?" says the Child of Calamity.

"O, come, now, Eddy," says Jimmy, "show up; you must a kept part of that bar'l to prove the thing by. Show us the bunghole—*do*—and we'll all believe you."

"Say, boys," says Bill, "less divide it up. Thar's thirteen of us. I can swaller a thirteenth of the yarn, if you can worry down the rest."

Ed got up mad and said they could all go to some place which he ripped out pretty savage, and then walked off aft cussing to himself, and they yelling and jeering at him, and roaring and laughing so you could hear them a mile.

"Boys, we'll split a watermelon on that," says the Child of Calamity; and he came rummaging around in the dark amongst the shingle bundles where I was, and put his hand on me. I was warm and soft and naked; so he says "Ouch!" and jumped back.

"Fetch a lantern or a chunk of fire here, boys—there's a snake here as big as a cow!"

So they run there with a lantern, and crowded up and looked in on me.

"Come out of that, you beggar!" says one.

"Who are you?" says another.

"What are you after here? Speak up prompt, or overboard you go."

"Snake him out, boys. Snatch him out by the heels."

I began to beg, and crept out amongst them trembling. They looked me over, wondering, and the Child of Calamity says:—

"A cussed thief! Lend a hand and less heave overboard!"

"No," says Big Bob, "less get out the paint-pot and paint him a sky-blue all over from head to heel, and *then* heave him over."

"Good! that's it. Go for the paint, Jimmy."

When the paint come, and Bob took the brush and was just going to begin, the others laughing and rubbing their hands, I begun to cry, and that sort of worked on Davy, and he says:—

"'Vast there! He's nothing but a cub. I'll paint the man that teches him!"

So I looked around on them, and some of them grumbled and growled, and Bob put down the paint, and the others didn't take it up.

"Come here to the fire, and less see what you're up to here," says Davy. "Now set down there and give an account of yourself. How long have you been aboard here?"

"Not over a quarter of a minute, sir," says I.

"How did you get dry so quick?"

"I don't know, sir. I'm always that way, mostly."

"Oh, you are, are you? What's your name?"

I warn't going to tell my name. I didn't know what to say, so I just says:

"Charles William Allbright, sir."

Then they roared—the whole crowd; and I was mighty glad I said that, because maybe laughing would get them in a better humor.

When they got done laughing, Davy says:—

"It won't hardly do, Charles William. You couldn't have growed this much in five year, and you was a baby when you come out of the bar'l, you know, and dead at that. Come, now, tell a straight story, and nobody'll hurt you, if you ain't up to anything wrong. What *is* your name?"

"Aleck Hopkins, sir. Aleck James Hopkins."

"Well, Aleck, where did you come from, here?"

"From a trading-scow. She lays up the bend yonder. I was born on her. Pap has traded up and down here all his life; and he told me to swim off here, because when you went by he said he would like to get some of you to speak to a Mr. Jonas Turner, in Cairo, and tell him—"

"Oh, come!"

"Yes, sir, it's as true as the world; Pap he says—"

"Oh, your grandmother!"

They all laughed, and I tried again to talk, but they broke in on me and stopped me.

"Now, looky-here," says Davy; "you're scared, and so you talk wild. Honest, now, do you live in a scow, or is it a lie?"

"Yes, sir, in a trading scow. She lays up at the head of the bend. But I warn't born in her. It's our first trip."

"Now you're talking! What did you come aboard here, for? To steal?"

"No, sir, I didn't.—It was only to get a ride on the raft. All boys does that."

"Well, I know that. But what did you hide for?"

"Sometimes they drive the boys off."

"So they do. They might steal. Looky-here; if we

let you off this time, will you keep out of these kind of scrapes hereafter?"

" 'Deed I will, boss. You try me."

"All right, then. You ain't but little ways from shore. Overboard with you, and don't you make a fool of yourself another time this way.—Blast it, boy, some raftsmen would rawhide you till you were black and blue!"

I didn't wait to kiss good-bye, but went overboard and broke for shore. When Jim come along by and by, the big raft was away out of sight around the point. I swum out and got aboard, and was mighty glad to see home again.

The boy did not get the information he was after, but his adventure has furnished the glimpse of the departed raftsman and keelboatman which I desire to offer in this place.

1883

FROM *The Chronicle of Young Satan*

The selection contains most of Chapter 2 of "The Chronicle of Young Satan," an incompleted story which provided the basis for the text of the posthumously published *The Mysterious Stranger* (1916). It was written in 1897–98 during a period of bitterness and discouragement for Mark Twain and contained some of his strongest indictments of "the damned human race." Six years after his death his literary executor, A. B. Paine, together with F. A. Duneka of Harper and Brothers, edited the unpublished manuscript, making many changes and deletions in Mark Twain's text, particularly in the iconoclastic passages aimed at orthodox Christianity and organized religion. The result was *The Mysterious Stranger,* which has been read ever since as the authentic Mark Twain text. Recent scholarship has shown that fully 25 per cent of Mark Twain's wordage was altered, that one entirely new character was invented (the astrologer), and that the conclusion of a different manuscript version of the story was joined to "The Chronicle of Young Satan" to give the tale a completed form never achieved by Twain himself in his various manuscript states. (See J. S. Tuckey, *Mark Twain and Little Satan, The Writing of The Mysterious Stranger,* 1963.) In 1969 W. M. Gibson edited all the existing states of the story under the title *Mark Twain's Mysterious Stranger Manuscripts,* further demonstrating the spurious nature of the Paine-Duneka version. The present text is from this volume.

"The Chronicle of Young Satan" was at first planned as a story with a Hannibal, Missouri, setting in which the boys were to be slightly altered portraits of Tom Sawyer and his friends. The change to a medieval Austrian scene provided the remoteness necessary for the theme of magic and supernatural powers. The character of the mysterious stranger derived from Mark Twain's interest in apparitional phenomena and dream experience reflected in his reading during the 1890's. Some of the language describing the degraded nature of man parallels Mark Twain's essay "The Lowest Animal," written about 1897 and published in 1962 in *Mark Twain, Letters from the Earth,* edited by Bernard DeVoto.

Three of us boys were always together, and had been so from the cradle, being fond of each other from the beginning, and this affection deepening as the years went on—Nikolaus Baumann, son of the principal judge of the local court; Seppi Wohlmeyer, son of the keeper of the principal inn, the "Golden Stag," which had a nice garden, with shade trees, reaching down to the river-side, and pleasure-boats for hire; and I was the third—Theodor Fischer, son of the church organist, who was also leader of the village band, teacher of the violin, composer, tax collector of the commune, sexton, and in other ways a useful citizen and respected by all. We knew the hills and the woods as well as the birds knew them; for we were always roaming them when we had leisure—at least when we were not swimming or boating or fishing, or playing on the ice or sliding down hill.

And we had the run of the castle park, and very few had that. It was because we were pets of the oldest serving-man in the castle—Felix Brandt; and often we went there, nights, to hear him talk about old times and strange things, and smoke with him (he taught us that), and drink coffee; for he had served in the wars, and was at the siege of Vienna; and there, when the Turks were defeated and driven away, among the captured things were bags of coffee, and the Turkish prisoners explained the character of it and how to make a pleasant drink out of it, and now he always kept coffee by him, to drink himself, and also to astonish the ignorant with. When it stormed he kept us all night; and while it thundered and lightened outside he told about ghosts and horrors of every kind, and of battles and murders and mutilations, and such things, and made it pleasant and cosy inside; and he told these things from his own experience largely. He had seen many ghosts in his time, and witches and enchanters, and once he was lost in a fierce storm at midnight in the mountains, and by the glare of the lightning had seen the Wild Huntsman rage by on the blast with his spectre dogs chasing after him through the driving cloud-rack. Also he had seen an incubus once, and several times he had seen the great bat that sucks the blood from the necks of people while they are asleep, fanning them softly with its wings and so keeping them drowsy till they die. He encouraged us not to fear supernatural things, such as ghosts, and said they did no harm, but only wandered about because they were lonely and distressed and wanted kindly notice and compassion; and in time we learned to not be afraid, and even went down with him in the night to the haunted chamber in the dungeons of the castle. The ghost appeared only once, and it went by very dim to the sight and floating noiseless through the air, and then disappeared; and we scarcely trembled, he had taught us so well. He said it came up sometimes in the night and woke him up by passing its clammy hand over his face, but it did him no hurt, it only wanted sympathy and notice. But the strangest thing was, that he had seen angels; actual angels out of heaven, and had talked with them. They had no wings, and wore clothes, and talked and looked and acted just like any natural person, and you would never know them for angels, except for the wonderful things they did which a mortal could not do, and the way they suddenly disappeared while you were talking with them, which was also a thing which no mortal could do. And he said they were pleasant and cheerful, not gloomy and melancholy, like ghosts.

It was after that kind of a talk, one May night, that we got up next morning and had a good breakfast with him and then went down and crossed the bridge and went away up into the hills on the left to a woody hill-top which was a favorite place of ours, and there we stretched out on the grass in the shade to rest and smoke and talk over those strange things, for they were in our minds yet, and impressing us. But we couldn't smoke, because we had been heedless and left our flint and steel behind.

Soon there came a youth strolling towards us through the trees, and he sat down and began to talk in a friendly way, just as if he knew us. But we did not answer him, for he was a stranger and we were not used to strangers and were shy of them. He had new and good clothes on, and was handsome and had a winning face and a pleasant voice, and was easy and graceful and unembarrassed, not slouchy and awkward and diffident like other boys. We wanted to be friendly with him, but didn't know how to begin. Then I thought of the pipe, and wondered if it would be taken as kindly meant if I offered it to him. But I remembered that we had no fire; so I was sorry and disappointed. But he looked up bright and pleased, and said—

"Fire? Oh, that is easy—I will furnish it."

I was so astonished I couldn't speak; for I had not said anything. He took the pipe and blew his breath on it, and the tobacco glowed red and spirals of blue smoke rose up. We jumped up and were going to run, for that was natural; and we did run a few steps, although he was yearningly pleading for us to stay, and giving us his word that he would not do us any harm, but only wanted to be friends with us and have company. So we stopped and stood, and wanted to go back, being full of curiosity and wonder, but afraid to venture. He went on coaxing, in his soft persuasive way; and when we saw that the pipe did not blow up and nothing happened, our confidence returned by little and little, and presently our curiosity got to be stronger than our fear, and we ventured back—but slowly, and ready to fly, at any alarm.

He was bent on putting us at ease, and he had the right art; one could not remain timorous and doubtful where a person was so earnest and simple and gentle and talked so alluringly as he did; no, he won us over, and it was not long before we were content and comfortable and chatty, and glad we had found this new friend. When the feeling of constraint was all gone, we asked him how he had learned to do that strange thing, and he said he hadn't learned it at all, it came natural to him—like other things—other curious things.

"What ones?"

"Oh, a number; I don't know how many."

"Will you let us see you do them?"

"Do—please!" the others said.

"You won't run away again?"

"No—indeed we won't. Please do, won't you?"

"Yes, with pleasure; but you mustn't forget your promise, you know."

We said we wouldn't, and he went to a puddle and came back with water in a cup which he had made out of a leaf, and blew upon it and threw it out; and it was a lump of ice, the shape of the cup. We were astonished and charmed, but not afraid any more; we were very glad to be there, and asked him to go on and do some more things. And he did. He said he would give us any kind of fruit we liked, whether it was in season or not. We all spoke at once—

"Orange!"

"Apple!"

"Grapes!"

"They are in your pockets," he said, and it was true. And they were of the best, too, and we ate them and wished we had more, though none of us said so.

"You will find them where those came from," he said, "and everything else your appetites call for; and you need not name the thing you wish; as long as I am with you, you have only to wish and find."

And he said true. There was never anything so wonderful and so interesting. Bread, cakes, sweets, nuts—whatever one wanted, it was there. He ate nothing himself, but sat and chatted, and did one curious thing after another to amuse us. He made a toy squirrel out of clay, and it ran up a tree and sat on a limb overhead and barked down at us. Then he made a dog that was not much larger than a mouse, and it treed the squirrel and danced about the tree, excited and barking, and was as alive as any dog could be. It frightened the squirrel from tree to tree and followed it up until both were out of sight in the forest. He made birds out of clay and set them free and they flew away singing.

At last I made bold to ask him to tell us who he was.

"An angel," he said, quite simply, and set another clay bird free and clapped his hands and made it fly away.

A kind of awe fell upon us when we heard him say that, and we were afraid again; but he said we need not be troubled, there was no occasion for us to be afraid of an angel, and he liked us anyway. He went on chatting as simply and unaffectedly as ever; and while he talked he made a crowd of little men and women the size of your finger, and they went diligently to work and cleared and leveled off a space a couple of yards square in the grass and began to build a cunning little castle in it, the women mixing the mortar and carrying it up the scaffoldings in pails on their heads, just as our workwomen have always done, and the men laying the courses of masonry—five hundred of those toy people swarming briskly about and working diligently and wiping the sweat off their faces as natural as life. In the absorbing interest of watching those five hundred little people make the castle grow step by step and course by course and take shape and symmetry, that feeling of awe soon passed away, and we were quite comfortable and at home again. We asked if we might make some people, and he said yes, and told Seppi to make some cannon for the walls, and told Nikolaus to make some halberdiers with breastplates and greaves and helmets, and I was to make some cavalry, with horses; and in allotting these tasks he called us by our names, but did not say how he knew them. Then Seppi asked him what his own name was, and he said tranquilly—

"*Satan*," and held out a chip and caught a little woman on it who was falling from the scaffolding and put her back where she belonged, and said "she is an idiot to step backward like that and not notice what she is about."

It caught us suddenly, that name did, and our work dropped out of our hands and broke to pieces—a cannon, a halberdier and a horse. Satan laughed, and asked what was the matter. It was a natural laugh, and pleasant and sociable, not boisterous, and had a reassuring influence upon us; so I said there was nothing much the matter, only it seemed a strange name for an angel. He asked why.

"Because it's—it's—well, it's *his* name, you know."

"Yes—he is my uncle."

He said it placidly, but it took our breath, for a moment, and made our hearts beat hard. He did not seem to notice that, but partly mended our halberdiers and things with a touch, handed them to us to finish, and said—

"Don't you remember?—he was an angel himself once."

"Yes—it's true," said Seppi, "I didn't think of that."

"Before the Fall he was blameless."

"Yes," said Nikolaus, "he was without sin."

"It is a good family—ours," said Satan; "there is not a better. He is the only member of it that has ever sinned."

I should not be able to make any one understand how exciting it all was. You know that kind of quiver that trembles around through you when you are seeing something that is so strange and enchanting and wonderful that it is just a fearful joy to be alive and look at it; and you know how you gaze, and your lips turn dry and your breath comes short, but you wouldn't be anywhere but there, not for the world. I was bursting to ask one question—I had it on my tongue's end and could hardly hold it back—but I was ashamed to ask it, it might be a rudeness. Satan set an ox down that he had been making, and smiled up at me and said—

"It wouldn't be a rudeness; and I should forgive it if it was. Have I *seen* him? Millions of times. From the time that I was a little child a thousand years old I was his second-best favorite among the nursery-angels of our blood and lineage—to use a human phrase—yes, from that time till the Fall; eight thousand years, measured as you count time."

"Eight—*thousand?*"

"Yes." He turned to Seppi, and went on as if answering something that was in Seppi's mind, "Why, naturally I look like a boy, for that is what I am. With us, what you call time is a spacious thing; it takes a long stretch of it to grow an angel to full age." There was a question in my mind, and he turned to me and answered it: "I am sixteen thousand years old—counting as you count." Then he turned to Nikolaus and said, "No, the Fall did not affect me nor the rest of the relationship. It was only he that I was named for who ate of the fruit of the tree and then beguiled the man and the woman with it. We others are still ignorant of sin; we are not able to commit it; we are without blemish, and shall abide in that estate always. We—" Two of the little workmen were quarreling, and in buzzing little bumble-bee voices they were cursing and swearing at each other; now came blows and blood, then they locked themselves together in a life-and-death struggle. Satan reached out his hand and crushed the life out of them with his fingers, threw them away, wiped the red from his fingers on his handkerchief and went on talking where he had left off: "We cannot do wrong; neither have we any disposition to do it, for we do not know what it is."

It seemed a strange speech, in the circumstances, but we barely noticed that, we were so shocked and grieved at the wanton murder he had committed—for murder it was, it was its true name, and it was without palliation or excuse, for the men had not wronged him in any way. It made us miserable; for we loved him, and had thought him so noble and beautiful and gracious, and had honestly *believed* he was an angel; and to have him do this cruel thing—ah, it lowered him so, and we had had such pride in him. He went right on talking, just as if nothing had happened: telling about his travels, and the interesting things he had seen in the big worlds of our solar system and of other solar systems far away in the remotenesses of space, and about the customs of the immortals that inhabit them, somehow fascinating us, enchanting us, charming us in spite of the pitiful scene that was now under our eyes: for the wives of the little dead men had found the crushed and shapeless bodies and were crying over them and sobbing and lamenting, and a priest was kneeling there with his hands crossed upon his breast praying, and crowds and crowds of pitying friends were massed about them, reverently uncovered, with their bare heads bowed, and many with the tears running down—a scene which Satan paid no attention to until the small noise of the weeping and praying began to annoy him, then he reached out and took the heavy board seat out of our swing and brought it down and mashed all those people into the earth just as if they had been flies, and went on talking just the same.

An angel, and kill a priest! an angel who did not know how to do wrong, and yet destroys in cold blood a hundred helpless poor men and women who had never done him any harm! It made us sick to see that awful deed, and to think that none of those poor creatures was prepared except the priest, for none of them had ever heard a mass or seen a church. And we were witnesses; we could not get away from that thought; we had seen these murders done and it was our duty to tell, and let the law take its course.

But he went talking right along, and worked his enchantments upon us again with that fatal music of his voice. He *made* us forget everything; we could only listen to him, and love him and be his slaves, to do with as he would. He made us drunk with the joy of being with him, and of looking into the heaven of his eyes, and of feeling the ecstasy that thrilled along our veins from the touch of his hand.

He had seen everything, he had been everywhere, he knew everything, and he forgot nothing. What another must study, he learned at a glance; there were no difficulties for him. And he made things live before you when he told about them. He saw the world made; he saw Adam created; he saw Samson surge against the pillars and bring the temple down in ruins about him; he saw Caesar's death; he told of the daily life in heaven, he had seen the damned writhing in the red waves of hell; and he made us see all these things, and it was as if we were on the spot and looking at them with our own eyes. And we *felt* them, too, but there was no sign that they were anything to him, beyond being mere entertainments. Those visions of hell, those poor babes and women and girls and lads and men shrieking and supplicating in anguish—why, we could hardly bear it, but he was as bland about it as if it had been so many imitation rats in an artificial fire.

And always when he was talking about men and women here in the earth and their doings—even their grandest and sublimest—we were secretly ashamed, for his manner showed that to him they and their doings were of paltry poor consequence; often you would think he was talking about flies, if you didn't know. Once he even said, in so many words, that our people down here were quite interesting to him, notwithstanding they were so dull and ignorant and trivial and conceited, and so diseased and rickety, and such a shabby poor worthless lot all around. He said it in a quite matter-of-course way and without any bitterness, just as a person might talk about bricks or manure or any other thing that was of no consequence and hadn't feelings. I could see he meant no offence, but in my thoughts I set it down as not very good manners.

"Manners!" he said, "why it is merely the truth, and truth is good manners; manners are a fiction. The castle is done! Do you like it?"

Any one would have been obliged to like it. It was lovely to look at, it was so shapely and fine, and so cunningly perfect in all its particulars, even to the little flags waving from the turrets. Satan said we must put the artillery in place, now, and station the halberdiers and deploy the cavalry. Our men and horses were a spectacle to see, they were so little like what they were intended for; for of course we had no art in making such things. Satan said they were the worst he had seen; and when he touched them and made them alive, it was just ridiculous the way they acted, on account of their legs not being of uniform lengths. They reeled and sprawled around as if they were drunk, and endangered everybody's lives around them, and finally fell over and lay helpless and kicking. It made us all laugh, though it was a shameful thing to see. The guns were charged with dirt, to fire a salute; but they were so crooked and so badly made that they all burst when they went off, and killed some of the gunners and crippled the others. Satan said we would have a storm, now, and an earthquake, if we liked, but we must stand off a piece, out of danger. We wanted to call the people away, too, but he said never mind them, they were of no consequence and we could make more, some time or other if we needed them.

A small storm-cloud began to settle down black

over the castle, and the miniature lightning and thunder began to play and the ground to quiver and the wind to pipe and wheeze and the rain to fall, and all the people flocked into the castle for shelter. The cloud settled down blacker and blacker and one could see the castle only dimly through it; the lightnings blazed out flash upon flash and they pierced the castle and set it on fire and the flames shone out red and fierce through the cloud, and the people came flying out, shrieking, but Satan brushed them back, paying no attention to our begging and crying and imploring; and in the midst of the howling of the wind and volleying of the thunder the magazine blew up, the earthquake rent the ground wide and the castle's wreck and ruin tumbled into the chasm, which swallowed it from sight and closed upon it, with all that innocent life, not one of the five hundred poor creatures escaping.

Our hearts were broken, we could not keep from crying.

"Don't cry," Satan said, "they were of no value."

"But they are gone to hell!"

"Oh, it is no matter, we can make more."

It was of no use to try to move him; evidently he was wholly without feeling, and could not understand. He was full of bubbling spirits, and as gay as if this were a wedding instead of a fiendish massacre. And he was bent on making us feel as he did, and of course his magic accomplished his desire. It was no trouble to him, he did whatever he pleased with us. In a little while we were dancing on that grave, and he was playing to us on a strange sweet instrument which he took out of his pocket; and the music—there is no music like that, unless perhaps in heaven, and that was where he brought it from, he said. It made one mad, for pleasure; and we could not take our eyes from him, and the looks that went out of our eyes came from our hearts, and their dumb speech was worship. He brought the dance from heaven, too, and the bliss of paradise was in it.

Presently he said he must go away on an errand. But we could not bear the thought of it, and clung to him, and pleaded with him to stay; and that pleased him, and he said so; and said he would not go yet, but would wait a little while and we would sit down and talk a few minutes longer; and he told us Satan was only his *real* name and he was to be known by it to us alone, but he had chosen another one to be called by in presence of others; just a common one, such as people have—Philip Traum.

It sounded so odd and mean for such a being! But it was his decision, and we said nothing; his decision was sufficient.

We had seen wonders this day; and my thoughts began to run on the pleasure it would be to tell of them when I got home; but he noticed those thoughts, and said—

"No, all these matters are a secret between us four. I do not mind your *trying* to tell them, if you like, but I will protect your tongues, and nothing of the secret will escape from them."

It was a disappointment, but it couldn't be helped, and it cost us a sigh or two. We talked pleasantly along, and he was always reading our thoughts and responding to them, and it seemed to me that this was the most wonderful of all the things he did; but he interrupted my musings, and said—

"No, it would be wonderful for you, but it is not wonderful for me. I am not limited, like you. I am not subject to human conditions; I can measure and understand your human weaknesses, for I have studied them; but I have none of them. My flesh is not real, although it is firm to the touch, my clothes are not real, I am a spirit. Father Peter is coming." We looked around, but did not see any one. "He is not in sight yet, but you will see him presently."

"Do you know him, Satan?"

"No."

"Won't you talk with him when he comes? He is not ignorant and dull, like us, and he would so like to talk with you. Will you?"

"Another time, yes, but not now. I must go on my errand after a little. There he is; now you can see him. Sit still, and don't say anything."

We looked up and saw Father Peter approaching through the chestnuts. We three were sitting together in the grass, and Satan sat in front of us in the path. Father Peter came slowly along with his head down, thinking, and stopped within a couple of yards of us and took off his hat and got out his silk handkerchief and stood there mopping his face and looking as if he was going to speak to us, but he didn't. Presently he muttered, "I can't think what brought me here; it seems as if I was in my study a minute ago—but I suppose I have been dreaming along for an hour and have come all this stretch without noticing; for I am not myself in these troubled days." Then he went mumbling along to himself and walked *straight through* Satan, just as if nothing was there. It made us catch our breath to see it. We had the impulse to cry out, the way you nearly always do when a startling thing happens, but something mysteriously restrained us and we remained quiet, only breathing fast. Then the trees hid Father Peter after a little, and Satan said—

"It is as I told you—I am only a spirit."

"Yes, one perceives it now," said Nikolaus, "but *we* are not spirits. It is plain he did not see you, but were we invisible too? He looked at us, but he didn't seem to see us."

"No, none of us was visible to him, for I wished it so."

It seemed almost too good to be true, that we were actually seeing these romantic and wonderful things, and that it was not a dream. And there he sat, looking just like anybody—so natural, and simple, and charming, and chatting along again the same as ever, and—well, words cannot make you understand what we felt. It was an ecstasy; and an ecstasy is a thing that will not go into words; it feels like music, and one cannot tell about music so that another person can get the feeling of it. He was back in the old ages once more, now, and making them live before us. He had seen so much, so much! It was just a wonder to look at him and try to think how it must seem to have such experiences behind one.

But it made you seem sorrowfully trivial, and the creature of a day, and such a short and paltry day, too. And he didn't say anything to raise up your drooping pride any—no, not a word. He always spoke of men in the same old indifferent way—just as one speaks of bricks and manure-piles and such things; you could see that they were of no consequence to him, one way or the other. He didn't mean to hurt us, you could see that; just as we don't mean to insult a brick when we disparage it; a brick's emotions are nothing to us; it never occurs to us to think whether it has any or not.

Once when he was bunching the most illustrious kings and conquerors and poets and prophets and pirates and beggars together—just a brick-pile—I was shamed into putting in a word for man, and asked him why he made so much difference between men and himself. He had to struggle with that a moment; he didn't seem to understand how I could ask such a strange question. Then he said—

"The *difference* between man and *me?* The *difference* between a mortal and an immortal? between a clod and a spirit?" He picked up a wood-louse that was creeping along a piece of bark: "What is the difference between Homer and this? between Caesar and this?"

I said—

"One cannot compare things which by their nature and by the interval between them are not comparable."

"You have answered your own question," he said. "I will expand it. Man is made of dirt—I *saw* him made. I am not made of dirt. Man is a museum of disgusting diseases, a home of impurities; he comes to-day and is gone to-morrow, he begins as dirt and departs as a stench; I am of the aristocracy of the Imperishables. And man has the *Moral Sense.* You understand? he has the *Moral Sense.* That would seem to be difference enough between us, all by itself."

He stopped there, as if that settled the matter. I was sorry, for at that time I had but a dim idea of what the moral sense was. I merely knew that we were proud of having it, and when he talked like that about it it wounded me and I felt as a girl feels who thinks her dearest finery is being admired, and then overhears strangers making fun of it. For a while we were all silent, and I, for one, was depressed. Then Satan began to chat again, and soon he was sparkling along in such a cheerful and vivacious vein that my spirits rose once more. He told some very cunning things that put us in a gale of laughter; and when he was telling about the time that Samson tied the torches to the foxes' tails and set them loose in the Philistines' corn and was sitting on the fence slapping his thighs and laughing, with the tears running down his cheeks, and lost his balance and fell off the fence, the memory of that picture got *him* to laughing, too, and we did have a most lovely and jolly time. By and by he said—

"I am going on my errand, now."

"Don't!" we all said, "don't go; stay with us. You won't come back."

"Yes, I will, I give you my word."

"When? To-night? To-morrow? Say when?"

"It won't be long. You will see."

"We like you."

"And I you. And as a proof of it I will show you something fine to see. Usually when I go, I merely vanish; but now I will dissolve myself and let you see me do it."

He stood up, and it was quickly finished. He thinned away and thinned away until he was a soap-bubble, except that he kept his shape. You could see the bushes through him as clearly as you see things through a soap-bubble, and all over him played and flashed the delicate iridescent colors of the bubble, and along with them was that thing shaped like a window-sash which you always see on the globe of the bubble. You have seen a bubble strike the carpet and lightly bound along two or three times before it bursts. He did that. He sprang—touched the grass—bounded—floated along—touched again—and so on, and presently exploded,—*puff!* and in his place was vacancy.

It was a strange and beautiful thing to see. We did not say anything, but sat wondering, and dreaming, and blinking; and finally Seppi roused up and said, mournfully and sighing—

"I reckon none of it has happened." * * *

c. 1897–98

WILLIAM DEAN HOWELLS [1837–1920]

"Between 1860, the date of his first published book, and 1921, over a hundred volumes of poems, plays, short stories, essays, novels, travel sketches, biographies, and autobiographies had accumulated on the Howells shelf," writes one of his biographers. In his own time, however, Howells was known primarily as a novelist of realism whose books were avidly read by the same lady-intellectuals who perused the *Atlantic Monthly* when he was its editor. He was regarded in publishing circles as a critic, reviewer, and champion of a fiction which turned away from conventional romancing and love-making toward psychological analysis of character-motives. Today, his forward-looking ideas seem somewhat "Victorian" and moderate, but a knowledge of his career and his most important work is equivalent to a knowledge of his time, the last half of the nineteenth century. He was its most accurate fictional recorder, almost a literary movement in himself, and his influence was enormous. The "Dean" of American letters, he was guide, philosopher, and friend to many of the best writers of the period. A man of wide sympathies, a Swedenborgian mystic by inheritance, a romantic in temper, and a gifted stylist, Howells was in fact "the reporter of his age."

Like both Lincoln and Mark Twain, Howells was born and brought up in the log-cabin West. His Ohio boyhood offered little chance for formal schooling. Like Mark Twain, he learned the art of writing as a printer's apprentice, setting type for his father's newspaper in small towns near Cincinnati and Columbus. Later he became a newspaperman and editor of the *Ohio State Journal* in Columbus. Early in life he steeped himself in the English poets and novelists. *My Literary Passions* (1895) gave testimony to his love and knowledge of the world's greatest literature from Dante and Cervantes down to his own time. In *Literary Friends and Acquaintance* (1900) he described his first trip to the literary shrines of New England where he met his American peers, such men as Lowell, Holmes, Emerson, Hawthorne, and Whitman. In 1861 he was appointed vice-consul to Venice (a political reward for his campaign biography of Lincoln); here he lived for four years, observing Italian life and reading Dante and Goldoni, the latter an important influence on his later realism. He published two travel books, *Venetian Life* (1866) and *Italian Journeys* (1867).

Back in America in 1865, he became assistant editor of the *Atlantic Monthly*, succeeding to the editorship in 1871. While championing realistic methods in his editorial policy, he was writing sharply observant sketches of American manners, scenes, dress, and accents, which verged on fiction: he called them romances. He noted the differences between regional types as he saw them on railroad trains between western and eastern towns; and finding the contrast a good source of fictional material, he wrote *Their Wedding Journey* (1871) and *A Chance Acquaintance* (1873). These novels brought him to his "discovery" of the American girl for fiction: he was the first to place her innocence in more sophisticated situations, thereby opening the way for the novel of international contrast which Henry James was to explore even more fully. Howells' *A Foregone Conclusion* (1875) and *The Lady of the Aroostook* (1879) were his best efforts in this genre. During this period he met Henry James and Mark Twain, admired them both and encouraged their writing, even when he was a bit shocked at Clemens' flamboyant personality.

The 1880's were years of great success for Howells as a novelist, and of sharp change and challenge in his social and intellectual life. Resigning his editorship, he devoted himself to European travel and to broadening the themes of his fiction to include divorce (*A Modern Instance*, 1882), the ethics of business (*The Rise of Silas Lapham*, 1885), and social strife and inequality (*Annie Kilburn*, 1887, and *A Hazard of New Fortunes*, 1890). In 1886 he became a columnist for *Harper's Magazine* ("The Editor's Study"), and in that role he battled for realism in fiction and attacked romantic sentimentalism. He likewise spoke out for the "Chicago anarchists" of the Haymarket affair and championed the cause of labor and the underprivileged, finding support in the doctrines of Tolstoy and in the Christian Socialist philosophy. His new sensitiveness to economic ills forced him to revise his former belief that America was a place mainly of "the smiling aspects of life," and led him to write his most trenchant criticism of American society in the Utopian novel *A Traveler from Altruria* (1894). In his later years Howells wrote other successful novels, criticism, and books of reminiscence of his boyhood in Ohio. Outliving his two great contemporaries, Mark Twain and Henry James, he died in New York City in 1920.

During the 1930's it was Howells' social criticism that revived interest in his work. Today he is read for his psychological studies of character, his acute notations of manners, and his unerring ear for speech tones. If his realism now seems dated, and if he was too anxious to defer to the reticences and tastes of his lady readers, he can be re-studied for his exposures of certain underlying social tensions and conflicts of personality in fiction. His deft penetration into the feminine psyche approached that of James, and he surpassed James in his closer knowledge and deeper feeling for American scenes and people. Less original than James and less gifted than Twain at his best, Howells shared something of the talents of both. James once said that Howells was a "great American naturalist," but that he did not "go far enough." Yet today Howellsians are discovering new sources of interest in his pre-Freudian delineations of passion and frustration, and in his recognition of the latent strains of Puritanism in the American life of his time.

Further reading: *A Modern Instance*, ed. W. M. Gibson, 1957. *The Rise of Silas Lapham*, ed. E. H. Cady, 1957. E. H. Cady, *The Road to Realism: The Early Years, 1837–1885, of William Dean Howells*, 1956, and *The Realist at War*, 1958.

FROM *Criticism and Fiction*

The essays comprising *Criticism and Fiction* were written when Howells was conducting "The Editor's Study" column of *Harper's Magazine* in the years 1886–92. They were gathered together in 1891 and rearranged to make a coherent volume, the central theme of which was a defense of Howells' concept of realism in fiction and an attack on romantic conventions in the novel. During those years Howells was undergoing a crucial change in his thinking about social problems, reading Tolstoy and becoming associated with the Christian Socialists. Thus his theory of literary realism was closely connected with his humanitarian ideas. At the same time, he was reviewing the European naturalists like Dostoevsky, Zola, and Flaubert and seeking to formulate a "realism" which was less extreme than theirs and more suited to American conditions. But his new radicalism brought down upon him much abuse from conservatives and attacks from abroad, especially England. The significance of the book, however, was in its prophetic quality. It was a manifesto of the need for fiction to seek the truth in the light of science and democratic ideas of social equality. The volume contained twenty-eight chapters, or sections, three of which are reprinted here. The text is that of the 1891 edition.

II

*** "As for those called critics," the author [Burke] says, "they have generally sought the rule of the arts in the wrong place; they have sought among poems, pictures, engravings, statues, and buildings; but art can never give the rules that make an art. This is, I believe, the reason why artists in general, and poets principally, have been confined in so narrow a circle; they have been rather imitators of one another than of nature. Critics follow them, and therefore can do little as guides. I can judge but poorly of anything while I measure it by no other standard than itself. The true standard of the arts is in every man's power; and an easy observation of the most common, sometimes of the meanest things, in nature will give the truest lights, where the greatest sagacity and industry that slights such observation must leave us in the dark, or, what is worse, amuse and mislead us by false lights."[1]

[1] The quotation is from Edmund Burke's *Philosophical Inquiry into the Origin of our Ideas on the Sublime and the Beautiful* (1756).

If this should happen to be true—and it certainly commends itself to acceptance—it might portend an immediate danger to the vested interests of criticism, only that it was written a hundred years ago; and we shall probably have the "sagacity and industry that slights the observation" of nature long enough yet to allow most critics the time to learn some more useful trade than criticism as they pursue it. Nevertheless, I am in hopes that the communistic era in taste foreshadowed by Burke is approaching, and that it will occur within the lives of men now overawed by the foolish old superstition that literature and art are anything but the expression of life, and are to be judged by any other test than that of their fidelity to it. The time is coming, I hope, when each new author, each new artist, will be considered, not in his proportion to any other author or artist, but in his relation to the human nature, known to us all, which it is his privilege, his high duty, to interpret. "The true standard of the artist is in every man's power" already, as Burke says; Michelangelo's "light of the piazza," the glance of the common eye, is and always was the best light on a statue; Goethe's "boys and blackbirds" have in all ages been the real connoisseurs of berries; but hitherto the mass of common men have been afraid to apply their own simplicity, naturalness, and honesty to the appreciation of the beautiful. They have always cast about for the instruction of some one who professed to know better, and who browbeat wholesome common-sense into the self-distrust that ends in sophistication. They have fallen generally to the worst of this bad species, and have been "amused and misled" (how pretty that quaint old use of amuse is!) "by the false lights" of critical vanity and self-righteousness. They have been taught to compare what they see and what they read, not with the things that they have observed and known, but with the things that some other artist or writer has done. Especially if they have themselves the artistic impulse in any direction they are taught to form themselves, not upon life, but upon the masters who became masters only by forming themselves upon life. The seeds of death are planted in them, and they can produce only the still-born, the academic. They are not told to take their work into the public square and see if it seems true to the chance passer, but to test it by the work of the very men who refused and decried any other test of their own work. The young writer who attempts to report the phrase and carriage of every-day life, who tries to tell just how he has heard men talk and seen them look, is made to feel guilty of something low and unworthy by the stupid people who would like to have him show how Shakespeare's men talked and looked, or Scott's, or Thackeray's, or Balzac's, or Hawthorne's, or Dickens's; he is instructed to idealize his personages, that is, to take the life-likeness out of them, and put the book-likeness into them. He is approached in the spirit of wretched pedantry into which learning, much or little, always decays when it withdraws itself and stands apart from experience in an attitude of imagined superiority, and which would say with the same confidence to the scientist: "I see that you are looking at a grasshopper there which you have found in the grass, and I suppose you intend to describe it. Now don't waste your time and sin against culture in that way. I've got a grasshopper here, which has been evolved at considerable pains and expense out of the grasshopper in general; in fact, it's a type. It's made up of wire and card-board, very prettily painted in a conventional tint, and it's perfectly indestructible. It isn't very much like a real grasshopper, but it's a great deal nicer, and it's served to represent the notion of a grasshopper ever since man emerged from barbarism. You may say that it's artificial. Well, it is artificial; but then it's ideal too; and what you want to do is to cultivate the ideal. You'll find the books full of my kind of grasshopper, and scarcely a trace of yours in any of them. The thing that you are proposing to do is commonplace; but if you say that it isn't commonplace, for the very reason that it hasn't been done before, you'll have to admit that it's photographic."[2]

As I said, I hope the time is coming when not only the artist, but the common, average man, who always "has the standard of the arts in his power," will have also the courage to apply it, and will reject the ideal grasshopper wherever he finds it, in science, in literature, in art, because it is not "simple, natural, and honest," because it is not like a real grasshopper. But I will own that I think the time is yet far off, and that the people who have been brought up on the ideal grasshopper, the heroic grasshopper, the impassioned grasshopper, the self-devoted, adventureful, good old romantic card-board grasshopper, must die out before the simple, honest, and natural grasshopper can have a fair field. I am in no haste to compass the end of these good people, whom I find in the mean time very amusing. It is delightful to meet one of them, either in print or out of it—some sweet elderly lady or excellent gentleman whose youth was pastured on the literature of thirty or forty years ago—and to witness the confidence with which they preach their favorite authors as all the law and the prophets. They have commonly read little or nothing since, or,

[2] Louis Agassiz, Professor of Natural History at Harvard, an anti-Darwinist, once lectured on grasshoppers in refutation of certain ideas about the origin of species. Howells knew Agassiz' work.

if they have, they have judged it by a standard taken from these authors, and never dreamed of judging it by nature; they are destitute of the documents in the case of the later writers; they suppose that Balzac was the beginning of realism, and that Zola is its wicked end; they are quite ignorant, but they are ready to talk you down, if you differ from them, with an assumption of knowledge sufficient for any occasion. The horror, the resentment, with which they receive any question of their literary saints is genuine; you descend at once very far in the moral and social scale, and anything short of offensive personality is too good for you; it is expressed to you that you are one to be avoided, and put down even a little lower than you have naturally fallen.

These worthy persons are not to blame; it is part of their intellectual mission to represent the petrifaction of taste, and to preserve an image of a smaller and cruder and emptier world than we now live in, a world which was feeling its way towards the simple, the natural, the honest, but was a good deal "amused and misled" by lights now no longer mistakable for heavenly luminaries. They belong to a time, just passing away, when certain authors were considered authorities in certain kinds, when they must be accepted entire and not questioned in any particular. Now we are beginning to see and to say that no author is an authority except in those moments when he held his ear close to Nature's lips and caught her very accent. These moments are not continuous with any authors in the past, and they are rare with all. Therefore I am not afraid to say now that the greatest classics are sometimes not at all great, and that we can profit by them only when we hold them, like our meanest contemporaries, to a strict accounting, and verify their work by the standard of the arts which we all have in our power, the simple, the natural, and the honest.

Those good people, those curious and interesting if somewhat musty back-numbers, must always have a hero, an idol of some sort, and it is droll to find Balzac, who suffered from their sort such bitter scorn and hate for his realism while he was alive, now become a fetich in his turn, to be shaken in the faces of those who will not blindly worship him. But it is no new thing in the history of literature: whatever is established is sacred with those who do not think. At the beginning of the century, when romance was making the same fight against effete classicism which realism is making to-day against effete romanticism, the Italian poet Monti[3] declared that "the romantic was the cold grave of the Beautiful," just as the realistic is now supposed to be. The romantic of that day and the real of this are in certain degree the same. Romanticism then sought, as realism seeks now, to widen the bounds of sympathy, to level every barrier against aesthetic freedom, to escape from the paralysis of tradition. It exhausted itself in this impulse; and it remained for realism to assert that fidelity to experience and probability of motive are essential conditions of a great imaginative literature. It is not a new theory, but it has never before universally characterized literary endeavor. When realism becomes false to itself, when it heaps up facts merely, and maps life instead of picturing it, realism will perish too. Every true realist instinctively knows this, and it is perhaps the reason why he is careful of every fact, and feels himself bound to express or to indicate its meaning at the risk of over-moralizing. In life he finds nothing insignificant; all tells for destiny and character; nothing that God has made is contemptible. He cannot look upon human life and declare this thing or that thing unworthy of notice, any more than the scientist can declare a fact of the material world beneath the dignity of his inquiry. He feels in every nerve the equality of things and the unity of men; his soul is exalted, not by vain shows and shadows and ideals, but by realities, in which alone the truth lives. In criticism it is his business to break the images of false gods and misshapen heroes, to take away the poor silly toys that many grown people would still like to play with. He cannot keep terms with Jack the Giant-killer or Puss in Boots, under any name or in any place, even when they reappear as the convict Vautrec, or the Marquis de Montrivaut, or the Sworn Thirteen Noblemen. He must say to himself that Balzac, when he imagined these monsters, was not Balzac, he was Dumas; he was not realistic, he was romantic.

XVIII

In General Grant's confession of novel-reading there is a sort of inference that he had wasted his time, or else the guilty conscience of the novelist in me imagines such an inference. But however this may be, there is certainly no question concerning the intention of a correspondent who once wrote to me after reading some rather bragging claims I had made for fiction as a mental and moral means. "I have very grave doubts," he said, "as to the whole list of magnificent things that you seem to think novels have done for the race, and can witness in myself many evil things which they have done for me. Whatever in my mental make-up is wild and visionary, whatever is untrue, whatever is injurious, I can trace to the perusal of some work of fiction. Worse than that, they beget such high-strung and

[3] Vicenzo Monti (1754-1828). Howells translated the phrase which follows from Monti's *Sulla Mitologia. Sermone* (1825).

supersensitive ideas of life that plain industry and plodding perseverance are despised, and matter-of-fact poverty, or every-day, commonplace distress, meets with no sympathy, if indeed noticed at all, by one who has wept over the impossibly accumulated sufferings of some gaudy hero or heroine."

I am not sure that I had the controversy with this correspondent that he seemed to suppose; but novels are now so fully accepted by every one pretending to cultivated taste—and they really form the whole intellectual life of such immense numbers of people, without question of their influence, good or bad, upon the mind—that it is refreshing to have them frankly denounced, and to be invited to revise one's ideas and feelings in regard to them. A little honesty, or a great deal of honesty, in this quest will do the novel, as we hope yet to have it, and as we have already begun to have it, no harm; and for my own part I will confess that I believe fiction in the past to have been largely injurious, as I believe the stage play to be still almost wholly injurious, through its falsehood, its folly, its wantonness, and its aimlessness. It may be safely assumed that most of the novel-reading which people fancy an intellectual pastime is the emptiest dissipation, hardly more related to thought or the wholesome exercise of the mental faculties than opium-eating; in either case the brain is drugged, and left weaker and crazier for the debauch. If this may be called the negative result of the fiction habit, the positive injury that most novels work is by no means so easily to be measured in the case of young men whose character they help so much to form or deform, and the women of all ages whom they keep so much in ignorance of the world they misrepresent. Grown men have little harm from them, but in the other cases, which are the vast majority, they hurt because they are not true—not because they are malevolent, but because they are idle lies about human nature and the social fabric, which it behooves us to know and to understand, that we may deal justly with ourselves and with one another. One need not go so far as our correspondent, and trace in the fiction habit "whatever is wild and visionary, whatever is untrue, whatever is injurious," in one's life; bad as the fiction habit is it is probably not responsible for the whole sum of evil in its victims, and I believe that if the reader will use care in choosing from this fungus-growth with which the fields of literature teem every day, he may nourish himself as with the true mushroom, at no risk from the poisonous species.

The tests are very plain and simple, and they are perfectly infallible. If a novel flatters the passions, and exalts them above the principles, it is poisonous; it may not kill, but it will certainly injure; and this test will alone exclude an entire class of fiction, of which eminent examples will occur to all. Then the whole spawn of so-called unmoral romances, which imagine a world where the sins of sense are unvisited by the penalties following, swift or slow, but inexorably sure, in the real world, are deadly poison: these do kill. The novels that merely tickle our prejudices and lull our judgment, or that coddle our sensibilities or pamper our gross appetite for the marvelous are not so fatal, but they are innutritious, and clog the soul with unwholesome vapors of all kinds. No doubt they too help to weaken the moral fibre, and make their readers indifferent to "plodding perseverance and plain industry," and to "matter-of-fact poverty and commonplace distress."

Without taking them too seriously, it still must be owned that the "gaudy hero and heroine" are to blame for a great deal of harm in the world. That heroine long taught by example, if not precept, that Love, or the passion or fancy she mistook for it, was the chief interest of a life, which is really concerned with a great many other things; that it was lasting in the way she knew it; that it was worthy of every sacrifice, and was altogether a finer thing than prudence, obedience, reason; that love alone was glorious and beautiful, and these were mean and ugly in comparison with it. More lately she has begun to idolize and illustrate Duty, and she is hardly less mischievous in this new role, opposing duty, as she did love, to prudence, obedience, and reason. The stock hero, whom, if we met him, we could not fail to see was a most deplorable person, has undoubtedly imposed himself upon the victims of the fiction habit as admirable. With him, too, love was and is the great affair, whether in its old romantic phase of chivalrous achievement or manifold suffering for love's sake, or its more recent development of the "virile," the bullying, and the brutal, or its still more recent agonies of self-sacrifice, as idle and useless as the moral experiences of the insane asylums. With his vain posturings and his ridiculous splendor he is really a painted barbarian, the prey of his passions and his delusions, full of obsolete ideals, and the motives and ethics of a savage, which the guilty author of his being does his best—or his worst—in spite of his own light and knowledge, to foist upon the reader as something generous and noble. I am not merely bringing this charge against that sort of fiction which is beneath literature and outside of it, "the shoreless lakes of ditch-water," whose miasmas fill the air below the empyrean where the great ones sit; but I am accusing the work of some of the most famous, who have, in this instance or in that, sinned against the truth, which can alone exalt and purify men. I do not say that they have constantly done so, or even commonly done so; but that they have done so at all marks them as of the past, to be read with the due historical allowance for their epoch and their conditions. For I believe that, while inferior writers will and must continue to imitate them in their foibles and their errors, no one hereafter will be able to achieve greatness who is false to humanity, either in its facts or its duties. The light of civilization has already broken even upon the novel, and no conscientious man can now set about painting an image of life without perpetual question of the verity of his work, and without feeling bound to distinguish so clearly that no reader of his may be misled, between what is right and what is wrong, what is noble and what is base, what is health and what is perdition, in the actions and the characters he portrays.

The fiction that aims merely to entertain—the fiction that is to serious fiction as the opera-bouffe, the ballet, and the pantomime are to the true drama—need not feel the burden of this obligation so deeply; but even such fiction will not be gay or trivial to any reader's hurt, and criticism will hold it to account if it passes from painting to teaching folly.

More and more not only the criticism which prints its opinions, but the infinitely vaster and powerfuler criticism which thinks and feels them merely, will make this demand. I confess that I do not care to judge any work of the imagination without first of all applying this test to it. We must ask ourselves before we ask anything else, Is it true?—true to the motives, the impulses, the principles that shape the life of actual men and women? This truth, which necessarily includes the highest morality and the highest artistry—this truth given, the book cannot be wicked and cannot be weak; and without it all graces of style and feats of invention and cunning of construction are so many superfluities of naughtiness. It is well for the truth to have all these, and shine in them, but for falsehood they are merely meretricious, the bedizenment of the wanton; they atone for nothing, they count for nothing. But in fact they come naturally of truth, and grace it without solicitation; they are added unto it. In the whole range of fiction we know of no true picture of life—that is, of human nature—which is not also a masterpiece of literature, full of divine and natural beauty. It may have no touch or tint of this special civilization or of that; it had better have this local color well ascertained; but the truth is deeper and finer than aspects, and if the book is true to what men and women know of one another's souls it will be true enough, and it will be great and beautiful. It is the conception of literature as something apart from life, superfinely aloof, which makes it really unimportant to the great mass of mankind, without a message or a meaning for them; and it is the notion that a novel may be false in its portrayal of causes and effects that makes literary art contemptible even to those whom it amuses, that forbids them to regard the novelist as a serious or right-minded person. If they do not in some moment of indignation cry out against all novels, as my correspondent does, they remain besotted in the fume of the delusions purveyed to them, with no higher feeling for the author than such maudlin affection as the habitué of an opium-joint perhaps knows for the attendant who fills his pipe with the drug.

Or, as in the case of another correspondent who writes that in his youth he "read a great many novels, but always regarded it as an amusement, like horse-racing and card-playing," for which he had no time when he entered upon the serious business of life, it renders them merely contemptuous. His view of the matter may be commended to the brotherhood and sisterhood of novelists as full of wholesome if bitter suggestion; and we urge them not to dismiss it with high literary scorn as that of some Boeotian dull to the beauty of art. Refuse it as we may, it is still the feeling of the vast majority of people for whom life is earnest, and who find only a distorted and misleading likeness of it in our books. We may fold ourselves in our scholars' gowns, and close the doors of our studies, and affect to despise this rude voice; but we cannot shut it out. It comes to us from wherever men are at work, from wherever they are truly living, and accuses us of unfaithfulness, of triviality, of mere stage-play; and none of us can escape conviction except he prove himself worthy of his time—a time in which the great masters have brought literature back to life, and filled its ebbing veins with the red tides of reality. We cannot all equal them; we need not copy them; but we can all go to the sources of their inspiration and their power; and to draw from these no one need go far—no one need really go out of himself.

Fifty years ago, Carlyle, in whom the truth was always alive, but in whom it was then unperverted by suffering, by celebrity, and by despair, wrote in his study of Diderot: "Were it not reasonable to prophesy that this exceeding great multitude of novel-writers and such like must, in a new generation, gradually do one of two things: either retire into the nurseries, and work for children, minors, and semi-fatuous persons of both sexes, or else, what were far better, sweep their novel-fabric into the dust-cart, and betake themselves with such faculty as they have to understand and record what is true, of which surely there is, and will forever be, a whole infinitude unknown to us of infinite importance to us? Poetry, it will more and more come to be understood, is nothing but higher knowledge; and the only genuine Romance (for grown persons), Reality."

If, after half a century, fiction still mainly works for "children, minors, and semi-fatuous persons of both sexes," it is nevertheless one of the hopefulest signs of the world's progress that it has begun to work for "grown persons," and if not exactly in the way that Carlyle might have solely intended in urging its writers to compile memoirs instead of building the "novel-fabric," still it has, in the highest and widest sense, already made Reality its Romance. I cannot judge it, I do not even care for it, except as it has done this; and I can hardly conceive of a literary self-respect in these days compatible with the old trade of make-believe, with the production of the kind of fiction which is too much honored by classification with card-playing and horse-racing. But let fiction cease to lie about life; let it portray men and women as they are, actuated by the motives and the passions in the measure we all know; let it leave off painting dolls and working them by springs and wires; let it show the different interests in their true proportions; let it forbear to preach pride and revenge, folly and insanity, egotism and prejudice, but frankly own these for what they are, in whatever figures and occasions they appear; let it not put on fine literary airs; let it speak the dialect, the language, that most Americans know—the language of unaffected people everywhere—and there can be no doubt of an unlimited future, not only of delightfulness but of usefulness, for it.

XXIV

One of the great newspapers[1] the other day invited the prominent American authors to speak their minds upon a point in the theory and practice of fiction which had already vexed some of them. It was the question of how much or how little the American novel ought to deal with certain facts of life which are not usually talked of before young people, and especially young ladies. Of course the question was not decided, and I forget just how far the balance inclined in favor of a larger freedom in the matter. But it certainly inclined that way; one or two writers of the sex which is somehow supposed to have purity in its keeping (as if purity were a thing that did not practically concern the other sex, preoccupied with serious affairs) gave it a rather vigorous tilt to that side. In view of this fact it would not be the part of prudence to make an effort to dress the balance; and indeed I do not know that I was going to make any such effort. But there are some things to say, around and about the subject, which I should like to have some one else say, and which I may myself possibly be safe in suggesting.

One of the first of these is the fact, generally lost sight of by those who censure the Anglo-Saxon novel for its prudishness, that it is really not such a prude after all; and that if it is sometimes apparently anxious to avoid those experiences of life not spoken of before young people, this may be an appearance only. Sometimes a novel which has this shuffling air, this effect of truckling to propriety, might defend itself, if it could speak for itself, by saying that such experiences happened not to come within its scheme, and that, so far from maiming or mutilating itself in ignoring them, it was all the more faithfully representative of the tone of modern life in dealing with love that was chaste, and with passion so honest that it could be openly spoken of before the tenderest society bud at dinner. It might say that the guilty intrigue, the betrayal, the extreme flirtation even, was the exceptional thing in life, and unless the scheme of the story necessarily involved it, that it would be bad art to lug it in, and as bad taste as to introduce such topics in a mixed company. It could say very justly that the novel in our civilization now always addresses a mixed company, and that the vast majority of the company are ladies, and that very many, if not most, of these ladies are young girls. If the novel were written for men and for married women alone, as in continental Europe, it might be altogether different. But the simple fact is that it is not written for them alone among us, and it is a question of writing, under cover of our universal acceptance, things for young girls to read which you would be put out-of-doors for saying to them, or frankly giving notice of your intention, and so cutting yourself off from the pleasure—and it is a very high and sweet one—of appealing to these vivid, responsive intelligences, which are none the less brilliant and admirable because they are innocent.

One day a novelist who liked, after the manner of other men, to repine at his hard fate, complained to his friend, a critic, that he was tired of the restriction he had put upon himself in this regard; for it is a mistake, as can be readily shown, to suppose that others impose it. "See how free those French fellows are!" he rebelled. "Shall we always be shut up to our tradition of decency?"

"Do you think it's much worse than being shut up to their tradition of indecency?" said his friend.

Then that novelist began to reflect, and he remembered how sick the invariable motive of the French novel made him. He perceived finally that, convention for convention, ours was not only more tolerable, but on the whole was truer to life, not only to its complexion, but also to its texture. No

[1] The *New York Herald*, March 24, 1889, had questioned some American authors on the subject of the effects of the Young Girl reader inhibiting writers from dealing frankly with the passions in novels. Howells' reply was the basis of this passage.

one will pretend that there is not vicious love beneath the surface of our society; if he did, the fetid explosions of the divorce trials would refute him; but if he pretended that it was in any just sense characteristic of our society, he could be still more easily refuted. Yet it exists, and it is unquestionably the material of tragedy, the stuff from which intense effects are wrought. The question, after owning this fact, is whether these intense effects are not rather cheap effects. I incline to think they are, and I will try to say why I think so, if I may do so without offence. The material itself, the mere mention of it, has an instant fascination; it arrests, it detains, till the last word is said, and while there is anything to be hinted. This is what makes a love intrigue of some sort all but essential to the popularity of any fiction. Without such an intrigue the intellectual equipment of the author must be of the highest, and then he will succeed only with the highest class of readers. But any author who will deal with a guilty love intrigue holds all readers in his hand, the highest with the lowest, as long as he hints the slightest hope of the smallest potential naughtiness. He need not at all be a great author; he may be a very shabby wretch, if he has but the courage or the trick of that sort of thing. The critics will call him "virile" and "passionate"; decent people will be ashamed to have been limed by him; but the low average will only ask another chance of flocking into his net. If he happens to be an able writer, his really fine and costly work will be unheeded, and the lure to the appetite will be chiefly remembered. There may be other qualities which make reputations for other men, but in his case they will count for nothing. He pays this penalty for his success in that kind; and every one pays some such penalty who deals with some such material. It attaches in like manner to the triumphs of the writers who now almost form a school among us, and who may be said to have established themselves in an easy popularity simply by the study of erotic shivers and fervors. They may find their account in the popularity, or they may not; there is no question of the popularity.

But I do not mean to imply that their case covers the whole ground. So far as it goes, though, it ought to stop the mouths of those who complain that fiction is enslaved to propriety among us. It appears that of a certain kind of impropriety it is free to give us all it will, and more. But this is not what serious men and women writing fiction mean when they rebel against the limitations of their art in our civilization. They have no desire to deal with nakedness, as painters and sculptors freely do in the worship of beauty; or with certain facts of life, as the stage does, in the service of sensation. But they ask why, when the conventions of the plastic and histrionic arts liberate their followers to the portrayal of almost any phase of the physical or of the emotional nature, an American novelist may not write a story on the lines of Anna Karenina or Madame Bovary. Sappho they put aside,[2] and from Zola's work they avert their eyes. They do not condemn him or Daudet, necessarily, or accuse their motives; they leave them out of the question; they do not want to do that kind of thing. But they do sometimes wish to do another kind, to touch one of the most serious and sorrowful problems of life in the spirit of Tolstoi and Flaubert, and they ask why they may not. At one time, they remind us, the Anglo-Saxon novelist did deal with such problems—De Foe in his spirit, Richardson in his, Goldsmith in his. At what moment did our fiction lose the privilege? In what fatal hour did the Young Girl arise and seal the lips of Fiction, with a touch of her finger, to some of the most vital interests of life?

Whether I wished to oppose them in their aspiration for greater freedom, or whether I wished to encourage them, I should begin to answer them by saying that the Young Girl had never done anything of the kind. The manners of the novel have been improving with those of its readers; that is all. Gentlemen no longer swear or fall drunk under the table, or abduct young ladies and shut them up in lonely country-houses, or so habitually set about the ruin of their neighbors' wives, as they once did. Generally, people now call a spade an agricultural implement; they have not grown decent without having also grown a little squeamish, but they have grown comparatively decent; there is no doubt about that. They require of a novelist whom they respect unquestionable proof of his seriousness, if he proposes to deal with certain phases of life; they require a sort of scientific decorum. He can no longer expect to be received on the ground of entertainment only; he assumes a higher function, something like that of a physician or a priest, and they expect him to be bound by laws as sacred as those of such professions; they hold him solemnly pledged not to betray them or abuse their confidence. If he will accept the conditions, they give him their confidence, and he may then treat to his greater honor, and not at all to his disadvantage, of such experiences, such relations of men and women as George Eliot treats in Adam Bede, in Daniel Deronda, in Romola, in almost all her books; such as Hawthorne treats in the Scarlet Letter; such as Dickens treats in David Copperfield; such as Thackeray treats in Pendennis, and glances at in every one of his fictions; such as most of the masters of English fiction have at some time treated more or less openly. It is quite

[2] Daudet's novel *Sappho* was dedicated: "To my sons when they shall have arrived at the age of twenty-one."

false or quite mistaken to suppose that our novels have left untouched these most important realities of life. They have only not made them their stock in trade; they have kept a true perspective in regard to them; they have relegated them in their pictures of life to the space and place they occupy in life itself, as we know it in England and America. They have kept a correct proportion, knowing perfectly well that unless the novel is to be a map, with everything scrupulously laid down in it, a faithful record of life in far the greater extent could be made to the exclusion of guilty love and all its circumstances and consequences.

I justify them in this view not only because I hate what is cheap and meretricious, and hold in peculiar loathing the cant of the critics who require "passion" as something in itself admirable and desirable in a novel, but because I prize fidelity in the historian of feeling and character. Most of these critics who demand "passion" would seem to have no conception of any passion but one. Yet there are several other passions: the passion of grief, the passion of avarice, the passion of pity, the passion of ambition, the passion of hate, the passion of envy, the passion of devotion, the passion of friendship; and all these have a greater part in the drama of life than the passion of love, and infinitely greater than the passion of guilty love. Wittingly or unwittingly, English fiction and American fiction have recognized this truth, not fully, not in the measure it merits, but in greater degree than most other fiction.

1891

Mark Twain: An Inquiry

Appearing in the *North American Review*, February 1901, this essay was occasioned by the publication of a uniform edition of Mark Twain's writings. It was later incorporated into *My Mark Twain* (1910), a warm and human portrait of Howells' lifelong friend. This essay was Howells' mature estimate of Twain's literary stature, interesting for its prediction of his future reputation. The text is that of the *North American Review*.

Two recent events have concurred to offer criticism a fresh excuse, if not a fresh occasion, for examining the literary work of Mr. Samuel L. Clemens, better known to the human family by his pseudonym of Mark Twain. One of these events is the publication of his writings in a uniform edition, which it is to be hoped will remain indefinitely incomplete; the other is his return to his own country after an absence so long as to form a psychological perspective in which his characteristics make a new appeal.

I

The uniform edition of Mr. Clemens's writings is of that dignified presence which most of us have thought their due in moments of high pleasure with their quality, and high dudgeon with their keeping in the matchlessly ugly subscription volumes of the earlier issues. Yet now that we have them in this fine shape, fit every one, in its elect binding, paper and print, to be set on the shelf of a gentleman's library, and not taken from it without some fear of personal demerit, I will own a furtive regret for the hideous blocks and bricks of which the visible temple of the humorist's fame was first builded. It was an advantage to meet the author in a guise reflecting the accidental and provisional moods of a unique talent finding itself out; and the pictures which originally illustrated the process were helps to the imagination such as the new uniform edition does not afford. In great part it could not retain them, for reasons which the recollection of their uncouth vigor will suggest, but these reasons do not hold in all cases, and especially in the case of Mr. Dan Beard's extraordinarily sympathetic and interpretative pictures for "The Connecticut Yankee at King Arthur's Court." The illustrations of the uniform edition, in fact, are its weak side, but it can be said that they do not detract from one's delight in the literature; no illustrations could do that; and, in compensation for their defect, the reader has the singularly intelligent and agreeable essay of Mr. Brander Matthews on Mr. Clemens's work, by way of introduction to the collection. For the rest one may acquit one's self of one's whole duty to the uniform edition by reminding the reader that in the rich variety of its inclusion are those renowning books, "The Innocents Abroad" and "Roughing It;" the first constructive fiction on the larger scale, "Tom Sawyer" and "Huckleberry Finn;" the later books of travel, "A Tramp Abroad" and "Following the Equator," the multiplicity of tales, sketches, burlesques, satires and speeches, together with the spoil of Mr. Clemens's courageous forays in the region of literary criticism, and his later romances, "The Connecticut Yankee," "The American Claimant," and the "Joan of Arc." These complete an array of volumes which the most unconventional reviewer can hardly keep from calling goodly, and which is responsive to the spirit of the literature in a certain desultory and insuccessive arrangement.

II

So far as I know Mr. Clemens is the first writer to use in extended writing the fashion we all use in thinking, and to set down the thing that comes into his mind without fear or favor of the thing that went before, or the thing that may be about to follow. I, for instance, in putting this paper together, am anxious to observe some sort of logical order, to discipline such impressions and notions as I have of the subject into a coherent body which shall march column-wise to a conclusion obvious if not inevitable from the start. But Mr. Clemens, if he were writing it, would not be anxious to do any such thing. He would take whatever offered itself to his hand out of that mystical chaos, that divine ragbag, which we call the mind, and leave the reader to look after relevancies and sequences for himself. These there might be, but not of that hard and fast sort which I am eager to lay hold of, and the result would at least be satisfactory to the author, who would have shifted the whole responsibility to the reader, with whom it belongs, at least as much as with the author. In other words, Mr. Clemens uses in work on the larger scale the method of the elder essayists, and you know no more where you are going to bring up in "The Innocents Abroad" or "Following the Equator" than in an essay of Montaigne. The end you arrive at is the end of the book, and you reach it amused but edified, and sorry for nothing but to be there. You have noted the author's thoughts, but not his order of thinking; he has not attempted to trace the threads of association between the things that have followed one another; his reason, not his logic, has convinced you, or rather it has persuaded you, for you have not been brought under conviction. It is not certain that this method is of design with Mr. Clemens; that might spoil it; and possibly he will be as much surprised as any one to know that it is his method. It is imaginable that he pursues it from no wish but to have pleasure of his work, and not to fatigue either himself or his reader; and his method may be the secret of his vast popularity, but it cannot be the whole secret of it. Any one may compose a scrap-book, and offer it to the public with nothing of Mark Twain's good fortune. Everything seems to depend upon the nature of the scraps, after all; his scraps might have been consecutively arranged, in a studied order, and still have immensely pleased; but there is no doubt that people like things that have at least the appearance of not having been drilled into line. Life itself has that sort of appearance as it goes on; it is an essay with moments of drama in it, rather than a drama; it is a lesson, with the precepts appearing haphazard, and not precept upon precept; it is a school, but not always a school-room; it is a temple, but the priests are not always in their sacerdotal robes; sometimes they are eating the sacrifice behind the altar and pouring the libations for the god through the channels of their dusty old throats. An instinct of something chaotic, ironic, empiric in the order of experience seems to have been the inspiration of our humorist's art, and what finally remains with the reader, after all the joking and laughing, is not merely the feeling of having had a mighty good time, but the conviction that he has got the worth of his money. He has not gone through the six hundred pages of "The Innocents Abroad," or "Following the Equator," without having learned more of the world as the writer saw it than any but the rarest traveller is able to show for his travel; and possibly with his average, practical American public, which was his first tribunal, and must always be his court of final appeal, Mark Twain justified himself for being so delightful by being so instructive. If this bold notion is admissible it seems the moment to say that no writer ever imparted information more inoffensively.

But his great charm is his absolute freedom in a region where most of us are fettered and shackled by immemorial convention. He saunters out into the trim world of letters, and lounges across its neatly kept paths, and walks about on the grass at will, in spite of all the signs that have been put up from the beginning of literature, warning people of dangers and penalties for the slightest trespass.

One of the characteristics I observe in him is his single-minded use of words, which he employs as Grant did to express the plain, straight meaning their common acceptance has given them with no regard to their structural significance or their philological implications. He writes English as if it were a primitive and not a derivative language, without Gothic or Latin or Greek behind it, or German and French beside it. The result is the English in which the most vital works of English literature are cast, rather than the English of Milton, and Thackeray, and Mr. Henry James. I do not say that the English of the authors last named is less than vital, but only that it is not the most vital. It is scholarly and conscious; it knows who its grandfather was; it has the refinement and subtlety of an old patriciate. You will not have with it the widest suggestion, the largest human feeling, or perhaps the loftiest reach of imagination, but you will have the keen joy that exquisite artistry in words can alone impart, and that you will not have in Mark Twain. What you will have in him is a style which is as personal, as biographical as the style of any one who has written, and expresses a civilization whose courage of the chances, the preferences, the duties, is not the measure of its essential modesty. It has a thing to say, and it says it in the word that may be the first, or second, or third choice, but will not be the instrument of the most fastidious ear, the most delicate and exacting sense, though it will be the word that surely and strongly conveys intention from the author's mind to the reader's. It is the Abraham Lincolnian word, not the Charles Sumnerian; it is American, Western.

III

Now that Mark Twain has become a fame so world-wide, we should be in some danger of forgetting, but for his help, how entirely American he is, and we have already forgotten, perhaps, how truly Western he is, though his work, from first to last, is always reminding us of the fact. But here I should like to distinguish. It is not alone in its generous humor, with more honest laughter in it than humor ever had in the world till now, that his work is so Western. Any one who has really known the West (and really to know it one must have lived it), is aware of the profoundly serious, the almost tragical strain which is the fundamental tone in the movement of such music as it has. Up to a certain point, in the presence of the mystery which we call life, it trusts and hopes and laughs; beyond that it doubts and fears, but it does not cry. It is more likely to laugh again, and in the work of Mark Twain there is little of the pathos which is supposed to be the ally of humor, little suffusion of apt tears from the smiling eyes. It is too sincere for that sort of play; and if after the doubting and the fearing it laughs again, it is with a suggestion of that resentment which youth feels when the disillusion from its trust and hope comes, and which is the grim second-mind of the West in the presence of the mystery. It is not so much the race-effect as the region-effect; it is not the Anglo-American finding expression, it is the Westerner, who is not more thoroughly the creature of circumstances, of conditions, but far more dramatically their creature, than any prior man. He found himself placed in them and under them, so near to a world in which the natural and primitive was obsolete, that while he could not escape them, neither could he help challenging them. The inventions, the appliances, the improvements of the modern world invaded the hoary eld of his rivers and forests and prairies, and while he was still a pioneer, a hunter, a trapper, he found himself confronted with the financier, the scholar, the gentleman. They seemed to him, with the world they represented, at first very droll, and he laughed. Then they set him thinking, and as he never was afraid of anything, he thought over the whole field, and demanded explanations of all his prepossessions, of equality, of humanity, of representative government and revealed religion. When they had not their answers ready, without accepting the conventions of the modern world as solutions or in any manner final, he laughed again, not mockingly, but patiently, compassionately. Such, or somewhat like this, was the genesis and evolution of Mark Twain.

Missouri was Western, but it was also Southern, not only in the institution of slavery, to the custom and acceptance of which Mark Twain was born and bred without any applied doubt of its divinity, but in the peculiar social civilization of the older South from which his native State was settled. It would be reaching too far out to claim that American humor, of the now prevailing Western type, is of Southern origin, but without staying to attempt it I will say that I think the fact could be established; and I think one of the most notably Southern traits of Mark Twain's humor is its power of seeing the fun of Southern seriousness, but this vision did not come to him till after his liberation from neighborhood in the vaster far West. He was the first, if not the only man of his section, to betray a consciousness of the grotesque absurdities in the Southern inversion of the civilized ideals in behalf of slavery, which must have them upside down in order to walk over them safely. No American of Northern birth or breeding could have imagined the spiritual struggle of Huck Finn in deciding to help the negro Jim to his freedom, even though he should be forever despised as a negro thief in his native town, and perhaps eternally lost through the blackness of his sin. No Northerner could have come so close to the heart of a Kentucky feud, and revealed it so perfectly, with the whimsicality playing through its carnage, or could have so brought us into the presence of the sardonic comi-tragedy of the squalid little river town where the store-keeping magnate shoots down his drunken tormentor in the arms of the drunkard's daughter, and then cows with bitter mockery the mob that comes to lynch him. The strict religiosity compatible in the Southwest with savage precepts of conduct is something that could make itself known in its amusing contrast only to the native Southwesterner, and the revolt against it is as constant in Mark Twain as the enmity to New England orthodoxy is in Dr. Holmes. But he does not take it with such serious resentment as Dr. Holmes is apt to take his inherited Puritanism, and it may be therefore that he is able to do it more perfect justice, and impart it more absolutely. At any rate there are no more vital passages in his fiction than those which embody character as it is affected for good as well as evil by the severity of the local Sunday-schooling and church-going.

IV

I find myself, in spite of the discipline I intend for this paper, speaking first of the fiction, which by no means came first in Mark Twain's literary development. It is true that his beginnings were in short sketches, more or less inventive, and studies of life in which he let his imagination play freely; but it was not till he had written "Tom Sawyer" that he could be called a novelist. Even now I think he should rather be called a romancer, though such a book as "Huckleberry Finn" takes itself out of the order of romance and places itself with the great things in picaresque fiction. Still it is more poetic than picaresque, and of a deeper psychology. The probable and credible soul that the author divines in the son of the town drunkard is one which we might each own brother, and the art which portrays this nature at first hand in the person and language of the hero, without pose or affectation, is fine art. In the boy's history the author's fancy works realistically to an end as high as it has reached elsewhere, if not higher; and I who like "The Connecticut Yankee at King Arthur's Court" so much, have half a mind to give my whole heart to "Huckleberry Finn."

Both "Huckleberry Finn" and "Tom Sawyer" wander in episodes loosely related to the main story, but they are of a closer and more logical advance from the beginning to the end than the fiction which preceded them, and which I had almost forgotten to name before them. We owe to "The Gilded Age" a type in Colonel Mulberry Sellers which is as likely to endure as any fictitious character of our time. It embodies the sort of Americanism which survived through the civil war, and characterized in its boundlessly credulous, fearlessly adventurous, unconsciously burlesque excess the period of political and economic expansion which followed the war. Colonel Sellers was, in some rough sort, the America of that day, which already seems so remote, and is best imaginable through him. Yet the story itself was of the fortuitous structure of what may be called the autobiographical books, such as "The Innocents Abroad" and "Roughing It." Its desultory and accidental character was heightened by the cooperation of Mr. Clemens's fellow humorist, Charles Dudley Warner, and such coherence as it had was weakened by the diverse qualities of their minds and their irreconcilable ideals in literature. These never combined to a sole effect or to any variety of effects that left the reader very clear what the story was all about; and yet from the cloudy solution was precipitated at least one character which, as I have said, seems of as lasting substance and lasting significance as any which the American imagination has evolved from the American environment.

If Colonel Sellers is Mr. Clemens's supreme invention, as it seems to me, I think that his "The Connecticut Yankee" is his greatest achievement in the way of a greatly imagined and symmetrically developed romance. Of all the fanciful schemes in fiction it pleases me most, and I give myself with absolute delight to its notion of a keen East Hartford Yankee finding himself, by a retroactionary spell, at the court of King Arthur of Britain, and becoming part of the sixth century with all the customs and ideas of the nineteenth in him and about him. The field for humanizing satire which this scheme opens is illimitable; but the ultimate achievement, the last poignant touch, the most exquisite triumph of the book, is the return of the Yankee to his own century, with his look across the gulf of the ages at the period of which he had been a part and his vision of the sixth century woman he had loved holding their child in her arms.

It is a great fancy, transcending in aesthetic beauty the invention in "The Prince and Pauper," with all the delightful and affecting implications of that charming fable, and excelling the heartrending story in which Joan of Arc lives and prophesies and triumphs and suffers. She is indeed realized to the modern sense as few figures of the past have been realized in fiction; and is none the less of her time and of all time because her supposititious historian is so recurrently of ours. After Sellers, and Huck Finn, and Tom Sawyer, and the Connecticut Yankee she is the author's finest creation; and if he had succeeded in portraying no other woman nature, he would have approved himself its fit interpreter in her. I do not think he succeeds so often with that nature as with the boy nature or the man nature, apparently because it does not interest him so much. He will not trouble himself to make women talk like women at all times; oftentimes they talk too much like him, though the simple, homely sort express themselves after their kind; and Mark Twain does not always write men's dialogue so well as he might. He is apt to burlesque the lighter colloquiality, and it is only in the more serious and most tragical junctures that his people utter themselves with veracious simplicity and dignity. That great, burly fancy of his is always tempting him to the exaggeration which is the condition of so much of his personal humor, but which when it invades the drama spoils the illusion. The illusion renews itself in the great moments, but I wish it could be kept infract in the small, and I blame him that he does not rule his fancy better. His imagination is always dramatic in its conceptions, but not always in its expressions; the talk of his people is often inadequate caricature in the ordinary exigencies, and his art contents itself with makeshift in the minor action. Even in "Huck Finn," so admirably proportioned and honestly studied, you find a piece of lawless extravagance hurled in, like the episode of the two strolling actors in the flatboat; their broad burlesque is redeemed by their final tragedy—a prodigiously real and moving passage—but the friend of the book cannot help wishing the burlesque was not there. One laughs, and then despises oneself for laughing, and this is not what Mark Twain often makes you do. There are things in him that shock, and more things that we think shocking, but this may not be so much because of their nature, as because of our want of naturalness; they wound our conventions rather than our convictions. As most women are more the subjects of convention than men, his humor is not for most women; but I have a theory that when women like it they like it far beyond men. Its very excess must satisfy that demand of their insatiate nerves for something that there is enough of; but I offer this conjecture with instant readiness to withdraw it under correction. What I feel rather surer of is that there is something finally feminine in the inconsequence of his ratiocination, and his beautiful confidence that we shall be able to follow him to his conclusion in all those turnings and twistings and leaps and bounds, by which his mind carries itself to any point but that he seems aiming at. Men, in fact, are born of women, and possibly Mark Twain owes his literary method to the colloquial style of some far ancestress who was more concerned in getting there, and amusing herself on the way, than in ordering her steps.

Possibly also it is to this ancestress that he owes the instinct of right and wrong which keeps him clear as to the conditions that formed him, and their injustice. Slavery in a small Missouri river town could not have been the dignified and patriarchal institution which Southerners of the older South are fond of remembering or imagining. In the second generation from Virginia ancestry of this sort, Mark Twain was born to the common necessity of looking out for himself, and while making himself practically of another order of things he felt whatever was fine in the old and could regard whatever was ugly and absurd more tolerantly, more humorously than those who bequeathed him their enmity to it. Fortunately for him, and for us who were to enjoy his humor, he came to his intellectual consciousness in a world so large and free and safe that he could be fair to any wrong while seeing the right so unfailingly; and nothing is finer in him than his gentleness with the error which is simply passive and negative. He gets fun out of it, of course, but he deals almost tenderly with it, and hoards his violence for the superstitions and traditions which are arrogant and active. His pictures of that old river-town, Southwestern life, with its faded and tattered aristocratic ideals and its squalid democratic realities, are pathetic, while they are so unsparingly true and so inapologetically and unaffectedly faithful.

The West, when it began to put itself into literature, could do so without the sense, or the apparent sense, of any older or politer world outside of it; whereas the East was always looking fearfully over its shoulder at Europe, and anxious to account for itself as well as represent itself. No such anxiety as this entered Mark Twain's mind, and it is not claiming too much for the Western influence upon American literature to say that the final liberation of the East from this anxiety is due to the West, and to its ignorant courage or its indifference to its difference from the rest of the world. It would not claim to be superior, as the South did, but it could claim to be humanly equal, or rather it would make no claim at all, but would simply be, and what it was, show itself without holding itself responsible for not being something else.

The Western boy of forty or fifty years ago grew up so close to the primeval woods or fields that their inarticulate poetry became part of his being, and he was apt to deal simply and uncritically with literature when he turned to it, as he dealt with nature. He took what he wanted, and left what he did not like; he used it for the playground, not the workshop of his spirit. Something like this I find true of Mark Twain in peculiar and uncommon measure. I do not see any proof in his books that he wished at any time to produce literature, or that he wished to reproduce life. When filled up with an experience that deeply interested him, or when provoked by some injustice or absurdity that intensely moved him, he burst forth, and the outbreak might be altogether humorous, but it was more likely to be humorous with a groundswell of seriousness carrying it profoundly forward. In all there is something curiously, not very definably, elemental, which again seems to me Western. He behaves himself as if he were the first man who was ever up against the proposition in hand. He deals as newly, for instance, with the relations of Shelley to his wife, and with as personal and direct an indignation as if they had never attracted critical attention before; and this is the mind or the mood which he brings to all literature. Life is another affair with him; it is not a discovery, not a surprise; every one else knows how it is; but here is a new world, and he explores it with a ramping joy, and shouts for the reader to come on and see how, in spite of all the lies about it, it is the same old world of men and women, with really nothing in it but their passions and prejudices and hypocrisies. At heart he was always deeply and essentially romantic, and once must have expected life itself to be a fairy dream. When it did not turn out so he found it tremendously amusing still, and his expectation not the least amusing thing in it, but without rancour, without grudge or bitterness in his disillusion, so that his latest word is as sweet as his first. He is deeply and essentially romantic in his literary conceptions, but when it comes to working them out he is helplessly literal and real; he is the impassioned lover, the helpless slave of the concrete. For this reason, for his wish, his necessity, first to ascertain his facts, his logic is as irresistible as his laugh.

V

All life seems, when he began to find it out, to have the look of a vast joke, whether the joke was on him or on his fellow beings, or if it may be expressed without any irreverence, on their common creator. But it was never wholly a joke, and it was not long before his literature began to own its pathos. The sense of this is not very apparent in "Innocents Abroad," but in "Roughing It" we began to be distinctly aware of it, and in the successive books it is constantly imminent, not as a clutch at the heart-strings, but as a demand of common justice, common sense, the feeling of proportion. It is not sympathy with the under dog merely as under dog that moves Mark Twain; for the under dog is sometimes rightfully under. But the probability is that it is wrongfully under, and has a claim to your inquiry into the case which you cannot ignore without atrocity. Mark Twain never ignores it; I know nothing finer in him than his perception that in this curiously contrived mechanism men suffer for their sorrows rather oftener than they suffer for their sins; and when they suffer for their sorrows they have a right not only to our pity but to our help. He always gives his help, even when he seems to leave the pity to others, and it may be safely said that no writer has dealt with so many phases of life with more unfailing justice. There is no real telling how any one comes to be what he is; all speculation concerning the fact is more or less impudent or futile conjecture; but it is conceivable that Mark Twain took from his early environment the custom of clairvoyance in things in which most humorists are purblind, and that being always in the presence of the under dog, he came to feel for him as under with him. If the knowledge and vision of slavery did not tinge all life with potential tragedy, perhaps it was this which lighted in the future humorist the indignation at injustice which glows in his page. His indignation relieves itself as often as not in a laugh; injustice is the most ridiculous thing in the world, after all, and indignation with it feels its own absurdity.

It is supposable, if not more than supposable, that the ludicrous incongruity of a slaveholding democracy nurtured upon the Declaration of Independence, and the comical spectacle of white labor owning black labor, had something to do in quickening the sense of contrast which is the mountain of humor, or is said to be so. But not to drive too hard a conjecture which must remain conjecture, we may reasonably hope to find in the untrammelled, the almost unconditional life of the later and farther West, with its individualism limited by nothing but individualism, the outside causes of the first overflow of the spring. We are so fond of classification, which we think is somehow interpretation, that one cannot resist the temptation it holds out in the case of the most unclassifiable things; and I must yield so far as to note that the earliest form of Mark Twain's work is characteristic of the greater part of it. The method used in "Innocents Abroad" and in "Roughing It" is the method used in "Life on the Mississippi," in "A Tramp Abroad" and in "Following the Equator," which constitute in bulk a good half of all his writings, as they express his dominant aesthetics. If he had written the fictions alone, we should have had to recognize a rare inventive talent, a great imagination and dramatic force; but I think it must be allowed that the personal books named overshadow the fictions. They have the qualities that give character to the fictions, and they have advantages that the fictions have not and that no fiction can have. In them, under cover of his pseudonym, we come directly into the presence of the author, which is what the reader is always longing and seeking to do; but unless the novelist is a conscienceless and tasteless recreant to the terms of his art, he cannot admit the reader to his intimacy. The personal books of Mark Twain have not only the charm of the essay's inconsequent and desultory method, in which invention, fact, reflection and philosophy wander in after one another in any following that happens, but they are of an immediate and most informal hospitality which admits you at once to the author's confidence, and makes you frankly welcome not only to his thought but to his way of thinking. He takes no trouble in the matter, and he asks you to take none. All that he requires is that you will have common sense, and be able to tell a joke when you see it. Otherwise the whole furnishing of his mental mansion is at your service, to make such use as you can of it, but he will not be always directing your course, or requiring you to enjoy yourself in this or that order.

In the case of the fictions, he conceives that his first affair is to tell a story, and a story when you are once launched upon it does not admit of deviation without some hurt to itself. In Mark Twain's novels, whether they are for boys or for men, the episodes are only those that illustrate the main narrative or relate to it, though he might have allowed himself somewhat larger latitude in the old-fashioned tradition which he has oftenest observed in them. When it comes to the critical writings, which again are personal, and which, whether they are criticisms of literature or of life, are always so striking, he is quite relentlessly logical and coherent. Here there is no lounging or sauntering, with entertaining or edifying digressions. The object is in view from the first, and the reasoning is straightforwardly to it throughout. This is as notable in the admirable paper on the Jews, or on the Austrian situation, as in that on Harriet Shelley, or that on Cooper's novels. The facts are first ascertained with a conscience uncommon in critical writing of any kind, and then they are handled with vigor and precision till the polemic is over. It does not so much matter whether you agree with the critic or not; what you have to own is that here is a man of strong convictions, clear ideas and ardent sentiments, based mainly upon common sense of extraordinary depth and breadth.

VI

In fact, what finally appeals to you in Mark Twain, and what may hereafter be his peril with his readers, is his common sense. It is well to eat humble pie when one comes to it at the *table d'hôte* of life, and I wish here to offer my brother literary men a piece of it that I never refuse myself. It is true that other men do not really expect much common sense of us, whether we are poets or novelists or humorists. They may enjoy our company, and they may like us or pity us, but they do not take us very seriously, and they would as soon we were fools as not if we will only divert or comfort or inspire them. Especially if we are humorists do they doubt our practical wisdom; they are apt at first sight to take our sense for a part of the joke, and the humorist who convinces them that he is a man of as much sense as any of them, and possibly more, is in the parlous case of having given them hostages for seriousness which he may not finally be able to redeem.

I should say in the haste to which every inquiry of this sort seems subject, that this was precisely the case with Mark Twain. The exceptional observer must have known from the beginning that he was a thinker of courageous originality and penetrating sagacity, even when he seemed to be joking; but in the process of time it has come to such a pass with him that the wayfaring man can hardly shirk knowledge of the fact. The fact is thrown into sudden and picturesque relief by his return to his country after the lapse of time long enough to have let a new generation grow up in knowledge of him. The projection of his reputation against a background of foreign appreciation, more or less luminous, such as no other American author has enjoyed, has little or nothing to do with his acceptance on the new terms. Those poor Germans, Austrians, Englishmen and Frenchmen who have been, from time to time in the last ten years, trying to show their esteem for his peculiar gifts could never come as close to the heart of his humor as we could; we might well doubt if they could fathom all his wisdom, which begins and ends in his humor; and if ever they seemed to chance upon his full significance, we naturally felt a kind of grudge, when we could not call it their luck, and suspected him of being less significant in the given instances than they supposed. The danger which he now runs with us is neither heightened nor lessened by the spread of his fame, but is an effect from intrinsic causes. Possibly it might not have been so great if he had come back comparatively forgotten; it is certain only that in coming back more remembered than ever, he confronts a generation which began to know him not merely by his personal books and his fiction, but by those criticisms of life and literature which have more recently attested his interest in the graver and weightier things.

Graver and weightier, people call them, but whether they are really more important than the lighter things, I am by no means sure. What I am amused with, independently of the final truth, is the possibility that his newer audience will exact this serious mood of Mr. Clemens, whereas we of his older world only suffered it, and were of a high conceit with our liberality in allowing a humorist sometimes to be a philosopher. Some of us indeed, not to be invidiously specific as to whom, were always aware of potentialities in him, which he seemed to hold in check, or to trust doubtfully to his reader as if he thought they might be thought part of the joke. Looking back over his work now, the later reader would probably be able to point out to earlier readers the evidence of a constant growth in the direction of something like recognized authority in matters of public import, especially those that were subject to the action of the public conscience as well as the public interest, until now hardly any man writing upon such matters is heard so willingly by all sorts of men. All of us, for instance, have read somewhat of the conditions in South Africa which have eventuated in the present effort of certain British politicians to destroy two free Republics in the interest of certain British speculators; but I doubt if we have found the case anywhere so well stated as in the closing chapters of Mark Twain's "Following the Equator." His estimate of the military character of the belligerents on either side is of the prophetic cast which can come only from the thorough assimilation of accomplished facts; and in those passages the student of the actual war can spell its anticipative history. It is by such handling of such questions, unpremeditated and almost casual as it seems, that Mark Twain has won his claim to be heard on any public matter, and achieved the odd sort of primacy which he now enjoys.

But it would be rather awful if the general recognition of his prophetic function should implicate the renunciation of the humor that has endeared him to mankind. It would be well for his younger following to beware of reversing the error of the elder, and taking everything in earnest, as these once took nothing in earnest from him. To reverse that error would not be always to find his true meaning, and perhaps we shall best arrive at this by shunning each other's mistakes. In the light of the more modern appreciation, we elders may be able to see some things seriously that we once thought pure drolling, and from our experience his younger admirers may learn to receive as drolling some things that they might otherwise accept as preaching. What we all should wish to do is to keep Mark Twain what he has always been: a comic force unique in the power of charming us out of our cares and troubles, united with as potent an ethic sense of the duties, public and private, which no man denies in himself without being false to other men. I think we may hope for the best he can do to help us deserve our self-respect, without forming Mark Twain societies to read philanthropic meanings into his jokes, or studying the Jumping Frog as the allegory of an imperializing Republic. I trust the time may be far distant when the Meditation at the Tomb of Adam shall be memorized and declaimed by ingenuous youth as a mystical appeal for human solidarity.

1901

HENRY JAMES [1843–1916]

Henry James was born in New York City near Washington Square, the second son of a well-to-do, liberal-minded father who was a writer of philosophical treatises, a friend of Emerson and Carlyle, and a follower of Swedenborgian beliefs. Henry and his older brother, William, later to become a famous philosopher and pragmatist, were educated in the Continental manner, exposed to enlightening influences and to European travel. From an early age they were taken to England, France, Germany, and Switzerland, where they studied French and absorbed the artistic atmosphere of the Old World. In Henry's case this background engendered a lifelong interest in art and prepared him for his career as an international novelist. In an early story, "A Passionate Pilgrim" (1871), he described some of his experiences in the character of Clement Searle, a young American who discovered the delights and also the disappointments of an older culture when he visited England to claim an inheritance. In 1875 James declared his "irresistible longing" to live and to write in Europe. The remainder of his life was dedicated to this end. He wrote more than sixty-five volumes—novels, plays, travel books, *nouvelles,* books of art and literary criticism, biography and personal reminiscence. His was a quiet existence of observation, traveling on the Continent, living in England, and writing constantly. He did not marry. He once called himself "that queer monster, the artist" with an "inexhaustible sensibility."

James is one of the few American writers whose career shows steady growth in the depth of his concerns and the enlargement of his themes. Three main periods are recognizable: (1) the apprentice years, from 1870 to 1882, when he explored the possibilities of the transatlantic contrast of manners in terms of American "innocence" and European "experience"; (2) the middle years, extending to about 1895, when he wrote three long social novels, a sequence of tales of artists and stories on the theme of "missed experience," travel books, literary criticism and portraiture; and (3) his final, "complex" phase, when he returned to the international theme with a deeper penetration into its moral and psychological implications and when he wrote tales of the supernatural like

"The Turn of the Screw" or psychological ghost stories like "The Jolly Corner." In this third period, also, his novels explored the baneful influence of evilly disposed minds over young and adolescent ones. His last years saw the publication of his collected works, for which he wrote the now-famous Prefaces discussing the techniques and theories of fiction that have influenced a generation of writers including Joseph Conrad, Edith Wharton, Virginia Woolf, Willa Cather, and D. H. Lawrence.

His first long novel, *Roderick Hudson* (1875), narrated the career of a talented young sculptor who becomes corrupted by the influence of an exotic woman and loses his artistic gift. It is a vividly authentic account of expatriate artists in the Italian atmosphere of beauty and moral decay. It recalls Hawthorne's *The Marble Faun* and shows a breadth of canvas worthy of Balzac. James's literary models in these years were George Eliot, Balzac, Turgenev, and Flaubert. *The American* (1877) was another international novel of manners in which a rich but "innocent" American businessman is subjected to intrigue and moral deviation at the hands of a French family of aristocratic pretensions. *Daisy Miller* (1878), James's "poetic" study of a young girl who violates the social codes of the Old World, achieved a success of scandal when outraged nativist readers interpreted it as an insult to American womanhood. Though not one of his best novels, it brought him his one moment of popularity. It was followed by *The Europeans* (1879), a social comedy which reversed the international contrast by bringing some Europeans to Boston, where the two different cultures are cleverly dramatized. But it was in the long novel, *The Portrait of a Lady* (1881) that the theme of the two cultures was pushed to the limits of tragedy: Isabel Archer, one of James's romantically idealistic and naive heroines, is betrayed into an international marriage that proves to be a tragic mistake. Here James extended the basically melodramatic plot of international marriage into a profound study of American innocence vis-à-vis European intrigue and made of it an exemplum of freedom and fate. George Eliot and Turgenev were again his literary models, but at the heart of the novel were James's anguished memories of his cousin Minny Temple, whose early death haunted his imagination and marked, as he said, the death of his own youth.

His three "big" novels of the middle period were *The Bostonians* (1886), *The Princess Casamassima* (1886), and *The Tragic Muse* (1890), each exploring different social phenomena, and all rich with a variety of scenes and people. The first was a satire on the woman's suffrage movement in Boston; the second, a handling of the underground world of the anarchists in London; and the third, a portrait of an actress who achieves fame on the stage but whose private inclinations are frustrated by the Philistine upper-class society in which she is thrown. During the eighties James lived in London. He had lost favor with the reading public in both America and England, and had to confess that the demand for his books had fallen to a low state. In "The Art of Fiction," an essay on his craft, he had discussed the analogy of fiction with portrait painting. Now he looked to the art of the stage for further ways to extend the bounds of the novel. His strong sense of form ("I delight in a deep-breathing economy and organic form") brought him into conflict with the loosely contrived narratives of Victorian fiction. He began to think of his novels as composed of "picture" and "scene." More and more he cultivated the dramatic methods of objectivity and dialogue, and depended increasingly upon a "central consciousness," or observer, through whose vision the story is unfolded. He later employed poetic symbols, extended metaphors, and key scenes of betrayal and revelation—an unguarded moment, a half-spoken word, or a retreating figure on a dark street marked climactic points in these novels.

The 1890's were the dramatic years. James's plays were not successful, partly because he tried to apply the neat structures of the French classical drama and the "well-made" play to his own subjective themes and psychological interests. He failed to please thrill-hungry audiences. After 1895 he returned to his old form, the novel, but with many new dramatic techniques to experiment with. *What Maisie Knew* (1897) was one of these staged-novels employing the ironic center of a young girl's consciousness as the narrative device, exposing the adult world around her. *The Awkward Age* (1899) was even more experimental. Entirely objective, it attempted with considerable success to deal with a problem of manners and marriage almost wholly in dialogue and in a symmetrical form that suggests a geometrical problem.

At the turn of the century James wrote three long novels in which he returned to the international theme. These represent his most "complex" style. *The Wings of the Dove* (1902), *The Ambassadors* (1903), and *The Golden Bowl* (1904), each one a separate technical feat, form a trio in which the contrast of manners is handled respectively in terms of tragedy, realism and comedy, and philosophical resolution. In the first, Milly Theale, dying of an illness, is victimized by an English couple scheming to deceive her and inherit her wealth. In the second, Lambert Strether is sent to Paris to save a young man from what his family at home regard as an immoral liaison with a Frenchwoman. He finds the situation not what he had expected, fails as an ambassador, but learns so much about the rich, complex, aesthetic world of Paris that the defeat becomes for him almost an education. Finally, in *The Golden Bowl*, Maggie Verver transforms her inheritance of vast wealth and moral innocence into an instrument of forgiveness and maturity when, in recovering her errant Italian nobleman-husband from an affair with her best friend, she succeeds in reconciling the New World to the Old.

"It is a complex fate to be an American," James once wrote, "and one of the responsibilities it entails is fighting against a superstitious valuation of Europe." This paradox lay at the heart of James's life and career, and his remarkable achievement in fiction is largely a commentary on it.

Further reading: *The Ambassadors*, ed. Leon Edel, 1960. *The Portrait of a Lady*, ed. Leon Edel, 1963. R. P. Blackmur, *The Art of the Novel: Critical Prefaces*, 1934. *The Notebooks of Henry James*, ed. F. O. Matthiessen and K. B. Murdock, 1947.

The Real Thing

First published in *Black and White* (April 16, 1892), this clever parable on the artist's craft was included by James in Vol. XVIII of his New York Edition. The text used here is that of its first book publication, *The Real Thing and Other Tales* (1893). For the source and early plans for this story, see the *Notebook* entry below. In addition to the pathos of the English couple who were "utterly unable to *do* anything" except "*show* themselves," James makes a subtle point about the artist's choice of materials. In creating an illusion of reality, should he depend upon such models as the Monarchs, who represent the real thing, or should he adapt to his own shaping imagination less rigid examples like the professional models, Oronte and Miss Churm, who "had had, for dear life, to *know how* to do something"?

I

When the porter's wife (she used to answer the house-bell), announced "A gentleman—with a lady, sir," I had, as I often had in those days, for the wish was father to the thought, an immediate vision of sitters. Sitters my visitors in this case proved to be; but not in the sense I should have preferred. However, there was nothing at first to indicate that they might not have come for a portrait. The gentleman, a man of fifty, very high and very straight, with a moustache slightly grizzled and a dark grey walking-coat admirably fitted, both of which I noted professionally—I don't mean as a barber or yet as a tailor—would have struck me as a celebrity if celebrities often were striking. It was a truth of which I had for some time been conscious that a figure with a good deal of frontage was, as one might say, almost never a public institution. A glance at the lady helped to remind me of this paradoxical law: she also looked too distinguished to be a "personality." Moreover one would scarcely come across two variations together.

Neither of the pair spoke immediately—they only prolonged the preliminary gaze which suggested that each wished to give the other a chance. They were visibly shy; they stood there letting me take them in—which, as I afterwards perceived, was the most practical thing they could have done. In this way their embarrassment served their cause. I had seen people painfully reluctant to mention that they desired anything so gross as to be represented on canvas; but the scruples of my new friends appeared almost insurmountable. Yet the gentleman might have said "I should like a portrait of my wife," and the lady might have said "I should like a portrait of my husband." Perhaps they were not husband and wife—this naturally would make the matter more delicate. Perhaps they wished to be done together—

in which case they ought to have brought a third person to break the news.

"We come from Mr. Rivet," the lady said at last, with a dim smile which had the effect of a moist sponge passed over a "sunk" piece of painting, as well as of a vague allusion to vanished beauty. She was as tall and straight, in her degree, as her companion, and with ten years less to carry. She looked as sad as a woman could look whose face was not charged with expression; that is, her tinted oval mask showed friction as an exposed surface shows it. The hand of time had played over her freely, but only to simplify. She was slim and stiff, and so well-dressed, in dark blue cloth, with lappets and pockets and buttons, that it was clear she employed the same tailor as her husband. The couple had an indefinable air of prosperous thrift—they evidently got a good deal of luxury for their money. If I was to be one of their luxuries it would behove me to consider my terms.

"Ah, Claude Rivet recommended me?" I inquired; and I added that it was very kind of him, though I could reflect that, as he only painted landscape, this was not a sacrifice.

The lady looked very hard at the gentleman, and the gentleman looked round the room. Then staring at the floor a moment and stroking his moustache, he rested his pleasant eyes on me with the remark: "He said you were the right one."

"I try to be, when people want to sit."

"Yes, we should like to," said the lady anxiously.

"Do you mean together?"

My visitors exchanged a glance. "If you could do anything with *me*, I suppose it would be double," the gentleman stammered.

"Oh, yes, there's naturally a higher charge for two figures than for one."

"We should like to make it pay," the husband confessed.

"That's very good of you," I returned, appreciating so unwonted a sympathy—for I supposed he meant pay the artist.

A sense of strangeness seemed to dawn on the lady. "We mean for the illustrations—Mr. Rivet said you might put one in."

"Put one in—an illustration?" I was equally confused.

"Sketch her off, you know," said the gentleman, colouring.

It was only then that I understood the service Claude Rivet had rendered me; he had told them that I worked in black and white, for magazines, for story-books, for sketches of contemporary life, and consequently had frequent employment for models. These things were true, but it was not less true (I may confess it now—whether because the aspiration was to lead to everything or to nothing I leave the reader to guess), that I couldn't get the honours, to say nothing of the emoluments, of a great painter of portraits out of my head. My "illustrations" were my pot-boilers; I looked to a different branch of art (far and away the most interesting it had always seemed to me), to perpetuate my fame. There was no shame in looking to it also to make my fortune; but that fortune was by so much further from being made from the moment my visitors wished to be "done" for nothing. I was disappointed; for in the pictorial sense I had immediately *seen* them. I had seized their type—I had already settled what I would do with it. Something that wouldn't absolutely have pleased them, I afterwards reflected.

"Ah, you're—you're—a—?" I began, as soon as I had mastered my surprise. I couldn't bring out the dingy word "models"; it seemed to fit the case so little.

"We haven't had much practice," said the lady.

"We've got to *do* something, and we've thought than an artist in your line might perhaps make something of us," her husband threw off. He further mentioned that they didn't know many artists and that they had gone first, on the off-chance (he painted views of course, but sometimes put in figures—perhaps I remembered), to Mr. Rivet, whom they had met a few years before at a place in Norfolk where he was sketching.

"We used to sketch a little ourselves," the lady hinted.

"It's very awkward, but we absolutely *must* do something," her husband went on.

"Of course, we're not so *very* young," she admitted, with a wan smile.

With the remark that I might as well know something more about them, the husband had handed me a card extracted from a neat new pocket-book (their appurtenances were all of the freshest) and inscribed with the words "Major Monarch." Impressive as these words were they didn't carry my knowledge much further; but my visitor presently added: "I've left the army, and we've had the misfortune to lose our money. In fact our means are dreadfully small."

"It's an awful bore," said Mrs. Monarch.

They evidently wished to be discreet—to take care not to swagger because they were gentlefolks. I perceived they would have been willing to recognise this as something of a drawback, at the same time that I guessed at an underlying sense—their consolation in adversity—that they *had* their points. They certainly had; but these advantages struck me as preponderantly social; such for instance as would help to make a drawing-room look well. However, a drawing-room was always, or ought to be, a picture.

In consequence of his wife's allusion to their age Major Monarch observed: "Naturally, it's more for the figure that we thought of going in. We can still hold ourselves up." On the instant I saw that the figure was indeed their strong point. His "naturally" didn't sound vain, but it lighted up the question. "*She* has got the best," he continued, nodding at his wife, with a pleasant after-dinner absence of circumlocution. I could only reply, as if we were in fact sitting over our wine, that this didn't prevent his own from being very good; which led him in turn to rejoin: "We thought that if you ever have to do people like us, we might be something like it. *She*, particularly—for a lady in a book, you know."

I was so amused by them that, to get more of it, I did my best to take their point of view; and though it was an embarrassment to find myself appraising physically, as if they were animals on hire or useful blacks, a pair whom I should have expected to meet only in one of the relations in which criticism is tacit, I looked at Mrs. Monarch judicially enough to be able to exclaim, after a moment, with conviction: "Oh yes, a lady in a book!" She was singularly like a bad illustration.

"We'll stand up, if you like," said the Major; and he raised himself before me with a really grand air.

I could take his measure at a glance—he was six feet two and a perfect gentleman. It would have paid any club in process of formation and in want of a stamp to engage him at a salary to stand in the principal window. What struck me immediately was that in coming to me they had rather missed their vocation; they could surely have been turned to better account for advertising purposes. I couldn't of course see the thing in detail, but I could see them make someone's fortune—I don't mean their own. There was something in them for a waistcoat-maker, an hotel-keeper or a soap-vendor. I could imagine "We always use it" pinned on their bosoms with the greatest effect; I had a vision of the promptitude with which they would launch a table d'hôte.

Mrs. Monarch sat still, not from pride but from shyness, and presently her husband said to her: "Get up my dear and show how smart you are." She obeyed, but she had no need to get up to show it. She walked to the end of the studio, and then she came back blushing, with her fluttered eyes on her husband. I was reminded of an incident I had accidentally had a glimpse of in Paris—being with a friend there, a dramatist about to produce a play—when an actress came to him to ask to be intrusted with a part. She went through her paces before him, walked up and down as Mrs. Monarch was doing. Mrs. Monarch did it quite as well, but I abstained from applauding. It was very odd to see such people apply for such poor pay. She looked as if she had ten thousand a year. Her husband had used the word that described her: she was, in the London current jargon, essentially and typically "smart." Her figure was, in the same order of ideas, conspicuously and irreproachably "good." For a woman of her age her waist was surprisingly small; her elbow moreover had the orthodox crook. She held her head at the conventional angle; but why did she come to *me?* She ought to have tried on jackets at a big shop. I feared my visitors were not only destitute, but "artistic"—which would be a great complication. When she sat down again I thanked her, observing that what a draughtsman most valued in his model was the faculty of keeping quiet.

"Oh, *she* can keep quiet," said Major Monarch. Then he added, jocosely: "I've always kept her quiet."

"I'm not a nasty fidget, am I?" Mrs. Monarch appealed to her husband.

He addressed his answers to me. "Perhaps it isn't out of place to mention—because we ought to be quite business-like, oughtn't we?—that when I married her she was known as the Beautiful Statue."

"Oh dear!" said Mrs. Monarch, ruefully.

"Of course I should want a certain amount of expression," I rejoined.

"Of *course!*" they both exclaimed.

"And then I suppose you know that you'll get awfully tired."

"Oh, we *never* get tired!" they eagerly cried.

"Have you had any kind of practice?"

They hesitated—they looked at each other. "We've been photographed, *immensely*," said Mrs. Monarch.

"She means the fellows have asked us," added the Major.

"I see—because you're so good-looking."

"I don't know what they thought, but they were always after us."

"We always got our photographs for nothing," smiled Mrs. Monarch.

"We might have brought some, my dear," her husband remarked.

"I'm not sure we have any left. We've given quantities away," she explained to me.

"With our autographs and that sort of thing," said the Major.

"Are they to be got in the shops?" I inquired, as a harmless pleasantry.

"Oh, yes; *hers*—they used to be."

"Not now," said Mrs. Monarch, with her eyes on the floor.

II

I could fancy the "sort of thing" they put on the presentation-copies of their photographs, and I was sure they wrote a beautiful hand. It was odd how quickly I was sure of everything that concerned them. If they were now so poor as to have to earn shillings and pence, they never had had much of a margin. Their good looks had been their capital, and they had good-humouredly made the most of the career that this resource marked out for them. It was in their faces, the blankness, the deep intellectual repose of the twenty years of country-house visiting which had given them pleasant intonations. I could see the sunny drawing-rooms, sprinkled with periodicals she didn't read, in which Mrs. Monarch had continuously sat; I could see the wet shrubberies in which she had walked, equipped to admiration for either exercise. I could see the rich covers the Major had helped to shoot and the wonderful garments in which, late at night, he repaired to the smoking-room to talk about them. I could imagine their leggings and waterproofs, their knowing tweeds and rugs, their rolls of sticks and cases of tackle and neat umbrellas; and I could evoke the exact appearance of their servants and the compact variety of their luggage on the platforms of country stations.

They gave small tips, but they were liked; they didn't do anything themselves, but they were welcome. They looked so well everywhere; they gratified the general relish for stature, complexion and "form." They knew it without fatuity or vulgarity, and they respected themselves in consequence. They were not superficial; they were thorough and kept themselves up—it had been their line. People with such a taste for activity had to have some line. I could feel how, even in a dull house, they could have been counted upon for cheerfulness. At present something had happened—it didn't matter what, their little income had grown less, it had grown least—and they had to do something for pocket-money. Their friends liked them, but didn't like to support them. There was something about them that represented credit—their clothes, their manners, their type; but if credit is a large empty pocket in which an occasional chink reverberates, the chink at least must be audible. What they wanted of me was to help to make it so. Fortunately they had no children—I soon divined that. They would also perhaps wish our relations to be kept secret: this was why it was "for the figure"—the reproduction of the face would betray them.

I liked them—they were so simple; and I had no objection to them if they would suit. But, somehow, with all their perfections I didn't easily believe in them. After all they were amateurs, and the ruling passion of my life was the detestation of the amateur. Combined with this was another perversity—an innate preference for the represented subject over the real one: the defect of the real one was so apt to be a lack of representation. I liked things that appeared; then one was sure. Whether they *were* or not was a subordinate and almost a profitless question. There were other considerations, the first of which was that I already had two or three people in use, notably a young person with big feet, in alpaca, from Kilburn, who for a couple of years had come to me regularly for my illustrations and with whom I was still—perhaps ignobly—satisfied. I frankly explained to my visitors how the case stood; but they had taken more precautions than I supposed. They had reasoned out their opportunity, for Claude Rivet had told them of the projected *édition de luxe* of one of the writers of our day—the rarest of the novelists—who, long neglected by the multitudinous vulgar and dearly prized by the attentive (need I mention Philip Vincent?) had had the happy fortune of seeing, late in life, the dawn and then the full light of a higher criticism—an estimate in which, on the part of the public, there was something really of expiation. The edition in question, planned by a publisher of taste, was practically an act of high reparation; the wood-cuts with which it was to be enriched were the homage of English art to one of the most independent representatives of English letters. Major and Mrs. Monarch confessed to me that they had hoped I might be able to work *them* into my share of the enterprise. They knew I was to do the first of the books, "Rutland Ramsay," but I had to make clear to them that my participation in the rest of the affair—this first book was to be a test—was to depend on the satisfaction I should give. If this should be limited my employers would drop me without a scruple. It was therefore a crisis for me, and naturally I was making special preparations, looking about for new people, if they should be necessary, and securing the best types. I admitted however that I should like to settle down to two or three good models who would do for everything.

"Should we have often to—a—put on special clothes?" Mrs. Monarch timidly demanded.

"Dear, yes—that's half the business."

"And should we be expected to supply our own costumes?"

"Oh, no; I've got a lot of things. A painter's models put on—or put off—anything he likes."

"And do you mean—a—the same?"

"The same?"

Mrs. Monarch looked at her husband again.

"Oh, she was just wondering," he explained, "if the costumes are in *general* use." I had to confess that they were, and I mentioned further that some of them (I had a lot of genuine, greasy last-century things), had served their time, a hundred years ago, on living, world-stained men and women. "We'll put on anything that *fits*," said the Major.

"Oh, I arrange that—they fit in the pictures."

"I'm afraid I should do better for the modern books. I would come as you like," said Mrs. Monarch.

"She has got a lot of clothes at home: they might do for contemporary life," her husband continued.

"Oh, I can fancy scenes in which you'd be quite natural." And indeed I could see the slipshod rearrangements of stale properties—the stories I tried to produce pictures for without the exasperation of reading them—whose sandy tracts the good lady might help to people. But I had to return to the fact that for this sort of work—the daily mechanical grind—I was already equipped; the people I was working with were fully adequate.

"We only thought we might be more like *some* characters," said Mrs. Monarch mildly, getting up.

Her husband also rose; he stood looking at me with a dim wistfulness that was touching in so fine a man. "Wouldn't it be rather a pull sometimes to have—a—to have—?" He hung fire; he wanted me to help him by phrasing what he meant. But I couldn't—I didn't know. So he brought it out, awkwardly: "The *real* thing; a gentleman, you know, or a lady." I was quite ready to give a general assent—I admitted that there was a great deal in that. This encouraged Major Monarch to say, following up his appeal with an unacted gulp: "It's awfully hard—we've tried everything." The gulp was communicative; it proved too much for his wife. Before I knew it Mrs. Monarch had dropped again upon a divan and burst into tears. Her husband sat down beside her, holding one of her hands; whereupon she quickly dried her eyes with the other, while I felt embarrassed as she looked up at me. "There isn't a confounded job I haven't applied for—waited for—prayed for. You can fancy we'd be pretty bad first. Secretaryships and that sort of thing? You might as well ask for a peerage. I'd be *anything*—I'm strong; a messenger or a coalheaver. I'd put on a gold-laced cap and open carriage-doors in front of the haberdasher's; I'd hang about a station, to carry portmanteaus; I'd be a postman. But they won't *look* at you; there are thousands, as good as yourself, already on the ground. *Gentlemen*, poor beggars, who have drunk their wine, who have kept their hunters!"

I was as reassuring as I knew how to be, and my visitors were presently on their feet again while, for the experiment, we agreed on an hour. We were discussing it when the door opened and Miss Churm came in with a wet umbrella. Miss Churm had to take the omnibus to Maida Vale and then walk half-a-mile. She looked a trifle blowsy and slightly splashed. I scarcely ever saw her come in without thinking afresh how odd it was that, being so little in herself, she should yet be so much in others. She was a meagre little Miss Churm, but she was an ample heroine of romance. She was only a freckled cockney, but she could represent everything, from a fine lady to a shepherdess; she had the faculty, as she might have had a fine voice or long hair. She couldn't spell, and she loved beer, but she had two or three "points," and practice, and a knack, and mother-wit, and a kind of whimsical sensibility, and a love of the theatre, and seven sisters, and not an ounce of respect, especially for the *h*. The first thing my visitors saw was that her umbrella was wet, and in their spotless perfection they visibly winced at it. The rain had come on since their arrival.

"I'm all in a soak; there *was* a mess of people in the 'bus. I wish you lived near a stytion," said Miss Churm. I requested her to get ready as quickly as possible, and she passed into the room in which she always changed her dress. But before going out she asked me what she was to get into this time.

"It's the Russian princess, don't you know?" I answered; "the one with the 'golden eyes,' in black velvet, for the long thing in the *Cheapside*."

"Golden eyes? I *say!*" cried Miss Churm, while my companions watched her with intensity as she withdrew. She always arranged herself, when she was late, before I could turn round; and I kept my visitors a little, on purpose, so that they might get an idea, from seeing her, what would be expected of themselves. I mentioned that she was quite my notion of an excellent model—she was really very clever.

"Do you think she looks like a Russian princess?" Major Monarch asked, with lurking alarm.

"When I make her, yes."

"Oh, if you have to *make* her—!" he reasoned, acutely.

"That's the most you can ask. There are so many that are not makeable."

"Well now, *here's* a lady"—and with a persuasive smile he passed his arm into his wife's—"who's already made!"

"Oh, I'm not a Russian princess," Mrs. Monarch protested, a little coldly. I could see that she had known some and didn't like them. There, immediately, was a complication of a kind that I never had to fear with Miss Churm.

This young lady came back in black velvet—the gown was rather rusty and very low on her lean shoulders—and with a Japanese fan in her red hands. I reminded her that in the scene I was doing she had to look over someone's head. "I forget whose it is; but it doesn't matter. Just look over a head."

"I'd rather look over a stove," said Miss Churm; and she took her station near the fire. She fell into position, settled herself into a tall attitude, gave a certain backward inclination to her head and a certain forward droop to her fan, and looked, at least to my prejudiced sense, distinguished and charming, foreign and dangerous. We left her looking so, while I went downstairs with Major and Mrs. Monarch.

"I think I could come about as near it as that," said Mrs. Monarch.

"Oh, you think she's shabby, but you must allow for the alchemy of art."

However, they went off with an evident increase of comfort, founded on their demonstrable advantage in being the real thing. I could fancy them shuddering over Miss Churm. She was very droll about them when I went back, for I told her what they wanted.

"Well, if *she* can sit I'll tyke to bookkeeping," said my model.

"She's very lady-like," I replied, as an innocent form of aggravation.

"So much the worse for *you*. That means she can't turn round."

"She'll do for the fashionable novels."

"Oh yes, she'll *do* for them!" my model humorously declared. "Ain't they bad enough without her?" I had often sociably denounced them to Miss Churm.

III

It was for the elucidation of a mystery in one of these works that I first tried Mrs. Monarch. Her husband came with her, to be useful if necessary—it was sufficiently clear that as a general thing he would prefer to come with her. At first I wondered if this were for "propriety's" sake—if he were going to be jealous and meddling. The idea was too tiresome, and if it had been confirmed it would speedily have brought our acquaintance to a close. But I soon saw there was nothing in it and that if he accompanied Mrs. Monarch it was (in addition to the chance of being wanted), simply because he had nothing else to do. When she was away from him his occupation was gone—she never *had* been away from him. I judged, rightly, that in their awkward situation their close union was their main comfort and that this union had no weak spot. It was a real marriage, an encouragement to the hesitating, a nut for pessimists to crack. Their address was humble (I remember afterwards thinking it had been the only thing about them that was really professional), and I could fancy the lamentable lodgings in which the Major would have been left alone. He could bear them with his wife—he couldn't bear them without her.

He had too much tact to try and make himself agreeable when he couldn't be useful; so he simply sat and waited, when I was too absorbed in my work to talk. But I liked to make him talk—it made my work, when it didn't interrupt it, less sordid, less special. To listen to him was to combine the excitement of going out with the economy of staying at home. There was only one hindrance: that I seemed not to know any of the people he and his wife had known. I think he wondered extremely, during the term of our intercourse, whom the deuce I *did* know. He hadn't a stray sixpence of an idea to fumble for; so we didn't spin it very fine—we confined ourselves to questions of leather and even of liquor (saddlers and breeches-makers and how to get good claret cheap), and matters like "good trains" and the habits of small game. His lore on these last subjects was astonishing, he managed to interweave the station-master with the ornithologist. When he couldn't talk about greater things he could talk cheerfully about smaller, and since I couldn't accompany him into reminiscences of the fashionable world he could lower the conversation without a visible effort to my level.

So earnest a desire to please was touching in a man who could so easily have knocked one down. He looked after the fire and had an opinion on the draught of the stove, without my asking him, and I could see that he thought many of my arrangements not half clever enough. I remember telling him that if I were only rich I would offer him a salary to come and teach me how to live. Sometimes he gave a random sigh, of which the essence was: "Give me even such a bare old barrack as *this*, and I'd do something with it!" When I wanted to use him he came alone; which was an illustration of the superior courage of women. His wife could bear her solitary second floor, and she was in general more discreet; showing by various small reserves that she was alive to the propriety of keeping our relations markedly professional—not letting them slide into sociability. She wished it to remain clear that she and the Major were employed, not cultivated, and if she approved of me as a superior, who could be kept in his place, she never thought me quite good enough for an equal.

She sat with great intensity, giving the whole of her mind to it, and was capable of remaining for an hour almost as motionless as if she were before a photographer's lens. I could see she had been photographed often, but somehow the very habit that made her good for that purpose unfitted her for mine. At first I was extremely pleased with her lady-like air, and it was a satisfaction, on coming to follow her lines, to see how good they were and how far they could lead the pencil. But after a few times I began to find her too insurmountably stiff; do what I would with it my drawing looked like a photograph or a copy of a photograph. Her figure had no variety of expression—she herself had no sense of variety. You may say that this was my business, was only a question of placing her. I placed her in every conceivable position, but she managed to obliterate their differences. She was always a lady certainly, and into the bargain was always the same lady. She was the real thing, but always the same thing. There were moments when I was oppressed by the serenity of her confidence that she *was* the real thing. All her dealings with me and all her husband's were an implication that this was lucky for *me*. Meanwhile I found myself trying to invent types that approached her own, instead of making her own transform itself—in the clever way that was not impossible, for instance, to poor Miss Churm. Arrange as I would and take the precautions I would, she always, in my pictures, came out too tall—landing me in the dilemma of having represented a fascinating woman as seven feet high, which, out of respect perhaps to my own very much scantier inches, was far from my idea of such a personage.

The case was worse with the Major—nothing I could do would keep *him* down, so that he became useful only for the representation of brawny giants. I adored variety and range, I cherished human accidents, the illustrative note; I wanted to characterise closely, and the thing in the world I most hated was the danger of being ridden by a type. I had quarrelled with some of my friends about it—I had parted company with them for maintaining that one *had* to be, and that if the type was beautiful (witness Raphael and Leonardo), the servitude was only a gain. I was neither Leonardo nor Raphael; I might only be a presumptuous young modern searcher, but I held that everything was to be sacrificed sooner than character. When they averred that the haunting type in question could easily *be* character, I retorted, perhaps superficially: "Whose?" It couldn't be everybody's—it might end in being nobody's.

After I had drawn Mrs. Monarch a dozen times I perceived more clearly than before that the value of such a model as Miss Churm resided precisely in the fact that she had no positive stamp, combined of course with the other fact that what she did have was a curious and inexplicable talent for imitation. Her usual appearance was like a curtain which she could draw up at request for a capital performance. This performance was simply suggestive; but it was a word to the wise—it was vivid and pretty. Sometimes, even, I thought it, though she was plain herself, too insipidly pretty; I made it a reproach to her that the figures drawn from her were monotonously (*bêtement,* as we used to say) graceful. Nothing made her more angry: it was so much her pride to feel that she could sit for characters that had nothing in common with each other. She would accuse me at such moments of taking away her "reputytion."

It suffered a certain shrinkage, this queer quantity, from the repeated visits of my new friends. Miss Churm was greatly in demand, never in want of employment, so I had no scruple in putting her off occasionally, to try them more at my ease. It was certainly amusing at first to do the real thing—it was amusing to do Major Monarch's trousers. They *were* the real thing, even if he did come out colossal. It was amusing to do his wife's back hair (it was so mathematically neat,) and the particular "smart" tension of her tight stays. She lent herself especially to positions in which the face was somewhat averted or blurred; she abounded in ladylike back views and *profils perdus.* When she stood erect she took naturally one of the attitudes in which court-painters represent queens and princesses; so that I found myself wondering whether, to draw out this accomplishment, I couldn't get the editor of the *Cheapside* to publish a really royal romance, "A Tale of Buckingham Palace." Sometimes, however, the real thing and the make-believe came into contact; by which I mean that Miss Churm, keeping an appointment or coming to make one on days when I had much work in hand, encountered her invidious rivals. The encounter was not on their part, for they noticed her no more than if she had been the housemaid; not from intentional loftiness, but simply because, as yet, professionally, they didn't know how to fraternise, as I could guess that they would have liked—or at least that the Major would. They couldn't talk about the omnibus—they always walked; and they didn't know what else to try—she wasn't interested in good trains or cheap claret. Besides, they must have felt—in the air—that she was amused at them, secretly derisive of their ever knowing how. She was not a person to conceal her scepticism if she had had a chance to show it. On the other hand Mrs. Monarch didn't think her tidy; for why else did she take pains to say to me (it was going out of the way, for Mrs. Monarch), that she didn't like dirty women?

One day when my young lady happened to be present with my other sitters (she even dropped in, when it was convenient, for a chat), I asked her to be so good as to lend a hand in getting tea—a service with which she was familiar and which was one of a class that, living as I did in a small way, with slender domestic resources, I often appealed to my models to render. They liked to lay hands on my property, to break the sitting, and sometimes the china—I made them feel Bohemian. The next time I saw Miss Churm after this incident she surprised me greatly by making a scene about it—she accused me of having wished to humiliate her. She had not resented the outrage at the time, but had seemed obliging and amused, enjoying the comedy of asking Mrs. Monarch, who sat vague and silent, whether she would have cream and sugar, and putting an exaggerated simper into the question. She had tried intonations—as if she too wished to pass for the real thing; till I was afraid my other visitors would take offence.

Oh, *they* were determined not to do this; and their touching patience was the measure of their great need. They would sit by the hour, uncomplaining, till I was ready to use them; they would come back on the chance of being wanted and would walk away cheerfully if they were not. I used to go to the door with them to see in what magnificent order they retreated. I tried to find other employment for them—I introduced them to several artists. But they didn't "take," for reasons I could appreciate, and I became conscious, rather anxiously, that after such disappointments they fell back upon me with a heavier weight. They did me the honour to think that it was I who was most *their* form. They were not picturesque enough for the painters, and in those days there were not so many serious workers in black and white. Besides, they had an eye to the great job I had mentioned to them—they had secretly set their hearts on supplying the right essence for my pictorial vindication of our fine novelist. They knew that for this undertaking I should want no costume-effects, none of the frippery of past ages—that it was a case in which everything would be contemporary and satirical and, presumably, genteel. If I could work them into it their future would be assured, for the labour would of course be long and the occupation steady.

One day Mrs. Monarch came without her husband—she explained his absence by his having had to go to the City. While she sat there in her usual anxious stiffness there came, at the door, a knock which I immediately recognised as the subdued appeal of a model out of work. It was followed by the entrance of a young man whom I easily perceived to be a foreigner and who proved in fact an Italian acquainted with no English word but my name, which he uttered in a way that made it seem to include all others. I had not then visited his country, nor was I proficient in his tongue; but as he was not so meanly constituted—what Italian is?—as to depend only on that member for expression he conveyed to me, in familiar but graceful mimicry, that he was in search of exactly the employment in which the lady before me was engaged. I was not struck with him at first, and while I continued to draw I emitted rough sounds of discouragement and dismissal. He stood his ground, however, not importunately, but with a dumb, dog-like fidelity in his eyes which amounted to innocent impudence—the manner of a devoted servant (he might have been in the house for years), unjustly suspected. Suddenly I saw that this very attitude and expression made a picture, whereupon I told him to sit down and wait till I should be free. There was another picture in the way he obeyed me, and I observed as I worked that there were others still in the way he looked wonderingly, with his head thrown back, about the high studio. He might have been crossing himself in St. Peter's. Before I finished I said to myself: "The fellow's a bankrupt orange-monger, but he's a treasure."

When Mrs. Monarch withdrew he passed across the room like a flash to open the door for her, standing there with the rapt, pure gaze of the young Dante spellbound by the young Beatrice. As I never insisted, in such situations, on the blankness of the British domestic, I reflected that he had the making of a servant (and I needed one, but couldn't pay him to be only that), as well as of a model; in short I made up my mind to adopt my bright adventurer if he would agree to officiate in the double capacity. He jumped at my offer, and in the event my rashness (for I had known nothing about him) was not brought home to me. He proved a sympathetic though a desultory ministrant, and had in a wonderful degree the *sentiment de la pose*. It was uncultivated, instinctive; a part of the happy instinct which had guided him to my door and helped him to spell out my name on the card nailed to it. He had had no other introduction to me than a guess, from the shape of my high north window, seen outside, that my place was a studio and that as a studio it would contain an artist. He had wandered to England in search of fortune, like other itinerants, and had embarked, with a partner and a small green handcart, on the sale of penny ices. The ices had melted away and the partner had dissolved in their train. My young man wore tight yellow trousers with reddish stripes and his name was Oronte. He was sallow but fair, and when I put him into some old clothes of my own he looked like an Englishman. He was as good as Miss Churm, who could look, when required, like an Italian.

IV

I thought Mrs. Monarch's face slightly convulsed when, on her coming back with her husband, she found Oronte installed. It was strange to have to recognise in a scrap of a lazzarone a competitor to her magnificent Major. It was she who scented danger first, for the Major was anecdotically unconscious. But Oronte gave us tea, with a hundred eager confusions (he had never seen such a queer process), and I think she thought better of me for having at last an "establishment." They saw a couple of drawings that I had made of the establishment, and Mrs. Monarch hinted that it never would have struck her that he had sat for them. "Now the drawings you make from *us*, they look exactly like us," she reminded me, smiling in triumph; and I recognised that this was indeed just their defect. When I drew the Monarchs I couldn't, somehow, get away from them—get into the character I wanted to represent; and I had not the least desire my model should be discoverable in my picture. Miss Churm never was, and Mrs. Monarch thought I hid her, very properly, because she was vulgar; whereas if she was lost it was only as the dead who go to heaven are lost—in the gain of an angel the more.

By this time I had got a certain start with "Rutland Ramsay," the first novel in the great projected series; that is I had produced a dozen drawings, several with the help of the Major and his wife, and I had sent them in for approval. My understanding with the publishers, as I have already hinted, had been that I was to be left to do my work, in this particular case, as I liked, with the whole book committed to me; but my connection with the rest of the series was only contingent. There were moments when, frankly, it *was* a comfort to have the real thing under one's hand; for there were characters in "Rutland Ramsay" that were very much like it. There were people presumably as straight as the Major and women of as good a fashion as Mrs. Monarch. There was a great deal of country-house life—treated, it is true, in a fine, fanciful, ironical, generalised way—and there was a considerable implication of knickerbockers and kilts. There were certain things I had to settle at the outset; such things for instance as the exact appearance of the hero, the particular bloom of the heroine. The author of course gave me a lead, but there was a margin for interpretation. I took the Monarchs into my confidence, I told them frankly what I was about, I mentioned my embarrassments and alternatives. "Oh, take *him!*" Mrs. Monarch murmured sweetly, looking at her husband; and "What could you want better than my wife?" the Major inquired, with the comfortable candour that now prevailed between us.

I was not obliged to answer these remarks—I was only obliged to place my sitters. I was not easy in mind, and I postponed, a little timidly perhaps, the solution of the question. The book was a large canvas, the other figures were numerous, and I worked off at first some of the episodes in which the hero and the heroine were not concerned. When once I had set *them* up I should have to stick to them—I couldn't make my young man seven feet high in one place and five feet nine in another. I inclined on the whole to the latter measurement, though the Major more than once reminded me that *he* looked about as young as anyone. It was indeed quite possible to arrange him, for the figure, so that it would have been difficult to detect his age. After the spontaneous Oronte had been with me a month, and after I had given him to understand several different times that his native exuberance would presently constitute an insurmountable barrier to our further intercourse, I waked to a sense of his heroic capacity. He was only five feet seven, but the remaining inches were latent. I tried him almost secretly at first, for I was really rather afraid of the judgment my other models would pass on such a choice. If they regarded Miss Churm as little better than a snare, what would they think of the representation by a person so little the real thing as an Italian street-vendor of a protagonist formed by a public school?

If I went a little in fear of them it was not because they bullied me, because they had got an oppressive foothold, but because in their really pathetic decorum and mysteriously permanent newness they counted on me so intensely. I was therefore very glad when Jack Hawley came home: he was always of such good counsel. He painted badly himself, but there was no one like him for putting his finger on the place. He had been absent from England for a year; he had been somewhere—I don't remember where—to get a fresh eye. I was in a good deal of dread of any such organ, but we were old friends; he had been away for months and a sense of emptiness was creeping into my life. I hadn't dodged a missile for a year.

He came back with a fresh eye, but with the same old black velvet blouse, and the first evening he spent in my studio we smoked cigarettes till the small hours. He had done no work himself, he had only got the eye; so the field was clear for the production of my little things. He wanted to see what I had done for the *Cheapside,* but he was disappointed in the exhibition. That at least seemed the meaning of two or three comprehensive groans which, as he lounged on my big divan, on a folded leg, looking at my latest drawings, issued from his lips with the smoke of the cigarette.

"What's the matter with you?" I asked.

"What's the matter with *you!*"

"Nothing save that I'm mystified."

"You are indeed. You're quite off the hinge. What's the meaning of this new fad?" And he tossed me, with visible irreverence, a drawing in which I happened to have depicted both my majestic models. I asked if he didn't think it good, and he replied that it struck him as execrable, given the sort of thing I had always represented myself to him as wishing to arrive at; but I let that pass, I was so anxious to see exactly what he meant. The two figures in the picture looked colossal, but I supposed this was *not* what he meant, inasmuch as, for aught he knew to the contrary, I might have been trying for that. I maintained that I was working exactly in the same way as when he last had done me the honour to commend me. "Well, there's a big hole somewhere," he answered; "wait a bit and I'll discover it." I depended upon him to do so: where else was the fresh eye? But he produced at last nothing more luminous than "I don't know—I don't like your types." This was lame, for a critic who had never consented to discuss with me anything but the question of execution, the direction of strokes and the mystery of values.

"In the drawings you've been looking at I think my types are very handsome."

"Oh, they won't do!"

"I've had a couple of new models."

"I see you have. *They* won't do."

"Are you very sure of that?"

"Absolutely—they're stupid."

"You mean *I* am—for I ought to get round that."

"You *can't*—with such people. Who are they?"

I told him, as far as was necessary, and he declared, heartlessly: *"Ce sont des gens qu'il faut mettre à la porte."*

"You've never seen them; they're awfully good," I compassionately objected.

"Not seen them? Why, all this recent work of yours drops to pieces with them. It's all I want to see of them."

"No one else has said anything against it—the *Cheapside* people are pleased."

"Everyone else is an ass, and the *Cheapside* people the biggest asses of all. Come, don't pretend, at this time of day, to have pretty illusions about the public, especially about publishers and editors. It's not for *such* animals you work—it's for those who know, *coloro chè sanno;* so keep straight for *me* if you can't keep straight for yourself. There's a certain sort of thing you tried for from the first—and a very good thing it is. But this twaddle isn't *in* it." When I talked with Hawley later about "Rutland Ramsay" and its possible successors he declared that I must get back into my boat again or I would go to the bottom. His voice in short was the voice of warning.

I noted the warning, but I didn't turn my friends out of doors. They bored me a good deal; but the very fact that they bored me admonished me not to sacrifice them—if there was anything to be done with them—simply to irritation. As I look back at this phase they seem to me to have pervaded my life not a little. I have a vision of them as most of the time in my studio, seated, against the wall, on an old velvet bench to be out of the way, and looking like a pair of patient courtiers in a royal ante-chamber. I am convinced that during the coldest weeks of the winter they held their ground because it saved them fire. Their newness was losing its gloss, and it was impossible not to feel that they were objects of charity. Whenever Miss Churm arrived they went away, and after I was fairly launched in "Rutland Ramsay" Miss Churm arrived pretty often. They managed to express to me tacitly that they supposed I wanted her for the low life of the book, and I let them suppose it, since they had attempted to study the work—it was lying about the studio—without discovering that it dealt only with the highest circles. They had dipped into the most brilliant of our novelists without deciphering many passages. I still took an hour from them, now and again, in spite of Jack Hawley's warning: it would be time enough to dismiss them, if dismissal should be necessary, when the rigour of the season was over. Hawley had made their acquaintance—he had met them at my fireside—and thought them a ridiculous pair. Learning that he was a painter they tried to approach him, to show him too that they were the real thing; but he looked at them, across the big room, as if they were miles away: they were a compendium of everything that he most objected to in the social system of his country. Such people as that, all convention and patent-leather, with ejaculations that stopped conversation, had no business in a studio. A studio was a place to learn to see, and how could you see through a pair of feather beds?

The main inconvenience I suffered at their hands was that, at first, I was shy of letting them discover how my artful little servant had begun to sit to me for "Rutland Ramsay." They knew that I had been odd enough (they were prepared by this time to allow oddity to artists,) to pick a foreign vagabond out of the streets, when I might have had a person with whiskers and credentials; but it was some time before they learned how high I rated his accomplishments. They found him in an attitude more than once, but they never doubted I was doing him as an organ-grinder. There were several things they never guessed, and one of them was that for a striking scene in the novel, in which a footman briefly figured, it occurred to me to make use of Major Monarch as the menial. I kept putting this off, I didn't like to ask him to don the livery—besides the difficulty of finding a livery to fit him. At last, one day late in the winter, when I was at work on the despised Oronte (he caught one's idea in an instant), and was in the glow of feeling that I was going very straight, they came in, the Major and his wife, with their society laugh about nothing (there was less and less to laugh at), like country-callers—they always reminded me of that—who have walked across the park after church and are presently persuaded to stay to luncheon. Luncheon was over, but they could stay to tea—I knew they wanted it. The fit was on me, however, and I couldn't let my ardour cool and my work wait, with the fading daylight, while my model prepared it. So I asked Mrs. Monarch if she would mind laying it out—a request which, for an instant, brought all the blood to her face. Her eyes were on her husband's for a second, and some mute telegraphy passed between them. Their folly was over the next instant; his cheerful shrewdness put an end to it. So far from pitying their wounded pride, I must add, I was moved to give it as complete a lesson as I could. They bustled about together and got out the cups and saucers and made the kettle boil. I know they felt as if they were waiting on my servant, and when the tea was prepared I said: "He'll have a cup, please—he's tired." Mrs. Monarch brought him one where he stood, and he took it from her as if he had been a gentleman at a party, squeezing a crush-hat with an elbow.

Then it came over me that she had made a great effort for me—made it with a kind of nobleness—and that I owed her a compensation. Each time I saw her after this I wondered what the compensation could be. I couldn't go on doing the wrong thing to oblige them. Oh, it *was* the wrong thing, the stamp of the work for which they sat—Hawley was not the only person to say it now. I sent in a large number of the drawings I had made for "Rutland Ramsay," and I received a warning that was more to the point than Hawley's. The artistic adviser of the house for which I was working was of opinion that many of my illustrations were not what had been looked for. Most of these illustrations were the subjects in which the Monarchs had figured. Without going into the question of what *had* been looked for, I saw at this rate I shouldn't get the other books to do. I hurled myself in despair upon Miss Churm, I put her through all her paces. I not only adopted Oronte publicly as my hero, but one morning when the Major looked in to see if I didn't require him to finish a figure for the *Cheapside*, for which he had begun to sit the week before, I told him that I had changed my mind—I would do the drawing from my man. At this my visitor turned pale and stood looking at me. "Is *he* your idea of an English gentleman?" he asked.

I was disappointed, I was nervous, I wanted to get on with my work; so I replied with irritation: "Oh, my dear Major—I can't be ruined for *you!*"

He stood another moment; then, without a word, he quitted the studio. I drew a long breath when he was gone, for I said to myself that I shouldn't see him again. I had not told him definitely that I was in danger of having my work rejected, but I was vexed at his not having felt the catastrophe in the air, read with me the moral of our fruitless collaboration, the lesson that, in the deceptive atmosphere of art, even the highest respectability may fail of being plastic.

I didn't owe my friends money, but I did see them again. They re-appeared together, three days later, and under the circumstances there was something tragic in the fact. It was a proof to me that they could find nothing else in life to do. They had threshed the matter out in a dismal conference—they had digested the bad news that they were not in for the series. If they were not useful to me even for the *Cheapside* their function seemed difficult to determine, and I could only judge at first that they had come, forgivingly, decorously, to take a last leave. This made me rejoice in secret that I had little leisure for a scene; for I had placed both my other models in position together and I was pegging away at a drawing from which I hoped to derive glory. It had been suggested by the passage in which Rutland Ramsay, drawing up a chair to Artemisia's piano-stool, says extraordinary things to her while she ostensibly fingers out a difficult piece of music. I had done Miss Churm at the piano before—it was an attitude in which she knew how to take on an absolutely poetic grace. I wished the two figures to "compose" together, intensely, and my little Italian had entered perfectly into my conception. The pair were vividly before me, the piano had been pulled out; it was a charming picture of blended youth and murmured love, which I had only to catch and keep. My visitors stood and looked at it, and I was friendly to them over my shoulder.

They made no response, but I was used to silent company and went on with my work, only a little disconcerted (even though exhilarated by the sense that *this* was at least the ideal thing), at not having got rid of them after all. Presently I heard Mrs.

Monarch's sweet voice beside, or rather above me: "I wish her hair was a little better done." I looked up and she was staring with a strange fixedness at Miss Churm whose back was turned to her. "Do you mind my just touching it?" she went on—a question which made me spring up for an instant, as with the instinctive fear that she might do the young lady a harm. But she quieted me with a glance I shall never forget—I confess I should like to have been able to paint *that*—and went for a moment to my model. She spoke to her softly, laying a hand upon her shoulder and bending over her; and as the girl, understandingly, gratefully assented, she disposed her rough curls, with a few quick passes, in such a way as to make Miss Churm's head twice as charming. It was one of the most heroic personal services I have ever seen rendered. Then Mrs. Monarch turned away with a low sigh and, looking about her as if for something to do, stooped to the floor with a noble humility and picked up a dirty rag that had dropped out of my paint-box.

The Major meanwhile had also been looking for something to do and, wandering to the other end of the studio, saw before him my breakfast things, neglected, unremoved. "I say, can't I be useful *here?*" he called out to me with an irrepressible quaver. I assented with a laugh that I fear was awkward and for the next ten minutes, while I worked, I heard the light clatter of china and the tinkle of spoons and glass. Mrs. Monarch assisted her husband—they washed up my crockery, they put it away. They wandered off into my little scullery, and I afterwards found that they had cleaned my knives and that my slender stock of plate had an unprecedented surface. When it came over me, the latent eloquence of what they were doing, I confess that my drawing was blurred for a moment—the picture swam. They had accepted their failure, but they couldn't accept their fate. They had bowed their heads in bewilderment to the perverse and cruel law in virtue of which the real thing could be so much less precious than the unreal; but they didn't want to starve. If my servants were my models, my models might be my servants. They would reverse the parts—the others would sit for the ladies and gentlemen, and *they* would do the work. They would still be in the studio—it was an intense dumb appeal to me not to turn them out. "Take us on," they wanted to say—"we'll do *anything.*"

When all this hung before me the *afflatus* vanished—my pencil dropped from my hand. My sitting was spoiled and I got rid of my sitters, who were also evidently rather mystified and awestruck. Then, alone with the Major and his wife, I had a most uncomfortable moment. He put their prayer into a single sentence: "I say, you know—just let *us* do for you, can't you?" I couldn't—it was dreadful to see them emptying my slops; but I pretended I could, to oblige them, for about a week. Then I gave them a sum of money to go away; and I never saw them again. I obtained the remaining books, but my friend Hawley repeats that Major and Mrs. Monarch did me a permanent harm, got me into a second-rate trick. If it be true I am content to have paid the price—for the memory.

1892, 1893

Greville Fane

For an account of the origin of this story, see the selection from James's *Notebooks,* below. It belongs to a group of tales of writers and artists, most of them written in the key of satire. This one reflects James's disappointment at the poor reception of some of his own novels and his attitude toward readers who prefer the kind of popular trash which Greville Fane wrote. The story first appeared in the *Illustrated London News* (September 1892) and was reprinted in *The Real Thing and Other Tales* (1893). James revised it slightly for the New York Edition, Vol. XVI, the text followed here.

Coming in to dress for dinner I found a telegram: "Mrs. Stormer dying; can you give us half a column for to-morrow evening? Let her down easily, but not too easily." I was late; I was in a hurry; I had very little time to think; but at a venture I dispatched a reply: "Will do what I can." It was not till I had dressed and was rolling away to dinner that, in the hansom, I bethought myself of the difficulty of the condition attached. The difficulty was not of course in letting her down easily but in qualifying that indulgence. "So I simply won't qualify it," I said. I didn't admire but liked her, and had known her so long that I almost felt heartless in sitting down at such an hour to a feast of indifference. I must have seemed abstracted, for the early years of my acquaintance with her came back to me. I spoke of her to the lady I had taken down, but the lady I had taken down had never heard of Greville Fane. I tried my other neighbour, who pronounced her books "too vile." I had never thought them very good, but I should let her down more easily than that.

I came away early, for the express purpose of driving to ask about her. The journey took time, for she lived in the northwest district, in the neighbourhood of Primrose Hill. My apprehension that I should be too late was justified in a fuller sense than I had attached to it—I had only feared that the house would be shut up. There were lights in the windows, and the temperate tinkle of my bell brought a servant immediately to the door; but poor

Mrs. Stormer had passed into a state in which the resonance of no earthly knocker was to be feared. A lady hovering behind the servant came forward into the hall when she heard my voice. I recognised Lady Luard, but she had mistaken me for the doctor.

"Pardon my appearing at such an hour," I said; "it was the first possible moment after I heard."

"It's all over," Lady Luard replied. "Dearest mamma!"

She stood there under the lamp with her eyes on me; she was very tall, very stiff, very cold, and always looked as if these things, and some others beside, in her dress, in her manner and even in her name, were an implication that she was very admirable. I had never been able to follow the argument, but that's a detail. I expressed briefly and frankly what I felt, while the little mottled maidservant flattened herself against the wall of the narrow passage and tried to look detached without looking indifferent. It was not a moment to make a visit, and I was on the point of retreating when Lady Luard arrested me with a queer casual drawling "Would you—a—would you perhaps be *writing* something?" I felt for the instant like an infamous interviewer, which I wasn't. But I pleaded guilty to this intention, on which she returned: "I'm so very glad—but I think my brother would like to see you." I detested her brother, but it wasn't an occasion to act this out; so I suffered myself to be inducted, to my surprise, into a small back room which I immediately recognised as the scene, during the later years, of Mrs. Stormer's imperturbable industry. Her table was there, the battered and blotted accessory to innumerable literary lapses, with its contracted space for the arms (she wrote only from the elbow down) and the confusion of scrappy scribbled sheets which had already become literary remains. Leolin was also there, smoking a cigarette before the fire and looking impudent even in his grief, sincere as it well might have been.

To meet him, to greet him, I had to make a sharp effort; for the air he wore to me as he stood before me was quite that of his mother's murderer. She lay silent for ever upstairs—as dead as an unsuccessful book, and his swaggering erectness was a kind of symbol of his having killed her. I wondered if he had already, with his sister, been calculating what they could get for the poor papers on the table; but I hadn't long to wait to learn, since in reply to the few words of sympathy I addressed him he puffed out: "It's miserable, miserable, yes; but she has left three books complete." His words had the oddest effect; they converted the cramped little room into a seat of trade and made the "book" wonderfully feasible. He would certainly get all that could be got for the three. Lady Luard explained to me that her husband had been with them, but had had to go down to the House. To her brother she mentioned that I was going to write something, and to me again made it clear that she hoped I would "do mamma justice." She added that she didn't think this had ever been done. She said to her brother: "Don't you think there are some things he ought thoroughly to understand?" and on his instantly exclaiming "Oh thoroughly, thoroughly!" went on rather austerely: "I mean about mamma's birth."

"Yes and her connexions," Leolin added.

I professed every willingness, and for five minutes I listened; but it would be too much to say I clearly understood. I don't even now, but it's not important. My vision was of other matters than those they put before me, and while they desired there should be no mistake about their ancestors I became keener and keener about themselves. I got away as soon as possible and walked home through the great dusky empty London—the best of all conditions for thought. By the time I reached my door my little article was practically composed—ready to be transferred on the morrow from the polished plate of fancy. I believe it attracted some notice, was thought "graceful" and was said to be by some one else. I had to be pointed without being lively, and it took some doing. But what I said was much less interesting than what I thought—especially during the half-hour I spent in my armchair by the fire, smoking the cigar I always light before going to bed. I went to sleep there, I believe; but I continued to moralise about Greville Fane. I'm reluctant to lose that retrospect altogether, and this is a dim little memory of it, a document not to "serve." The dear woman had written a hundred stories, but none so curious as her own.

When first I knew her she had published half a dozen fictions, and I believe I had also perpetrated a novel. She was more than a dozen years my elder, but a person who always acknowledged her comparative state. It wasn't so very long ago, but in London, amid the big waves of the present, even a near horizon gets hidden. I met her at some dinner and took her down, rather flattered at offering my arm to a celebrity. She didn't look like one, with her matronly mild inanimate face, but I supposed her greatness would come out in her conversation. I gave it all the opportunities I could, but was nevertheless not disappointed when I found her only a dull kind woman. This was why I liked her—she rested me so from literature. To myself literature was an irritation, a torment; but Greville Fane slumbered in the intellectual part of it even as a cat on a hearthrug or a Creole in a hammock. She wasn't a woman of genius, but her faculty was so special, so much a gift out of hand, that I've often wondered why she fell below that distinction. This was doubtless because the transaction, in her case, had remained incomplete; genius always pays for the gift, feels the debt, and she was placidly unconscious of a call. She could invent stories by the yard, but couldn't write a page of English. She went down to her grave without suspecting that though she had contributed volumes to the diversion of her contemporaries she hadn't contributed a sentence to the language. This hadn't prevented bushels of criticism from being heaped on her head; she was worth a couple of columns any day to the weekly papers, in which it was shown that her pictures of life were dreadful but her style superior. She asked me to come and see her and I complied. She lived then in Montpellier Square; which helped me to see how dissociated her imagination was from her character.

An industrious widow, devoted to her daily stint, to meeting the butcher and baker and making a home for her son and daughter, from the moment she took her pen in her hand she became a creature of passion. She thought the English novel deplorably wanting in that element, and the task she had cut out for herself was to supply the deficiency. Passion in high life was the general formula of this work, for her imagination was at home only in the most exalted circles. She adored in truth the aristocracy, and they constituted for her the romance of the world or, what is more to the point, the prime material of fiction. Their beauty and luxury, their loves and revenges, their temptations and surrenders, their immoralities and diamonds were as familiar to her as the blots on her writing-table. She was not a belated producer of the old fashionable novel, but, with a cleverness and a modernness of her own, had freshened up the fly-blown tinsel. She turned off plots by the hundred and—so far as her flying quill could convey her—was perpetually going abroad. Her types, her illustrations, her tone were nothing if not cosmopolitan. She recognised nothing less provincial than European society, and her fine folk knew each other and made love to each other from Doncaster to Bucharest. She had an idea that she resembled Balzac, and her favourite historical characters were Lucien de Rubempré and the Vidame de Pamiers. I must add that when I once asked her who the latter personage was she was unable to tell me. She was very brave and healthy and cheerful, very abundant and innocent and wicked. She was expert and vulgar and snobbish, and never so intensely British as when she was particularly foreign.

This combination of qualities had brought her early success, and I remember having heard with wonder and envy of what she "got," in those days, for a novel. The revelation gave me a pang: it was such a proof that, practising a totally different style, I should never make my fortune. And yet when, as I knew her better she told me her real tariff and I saw how rumour had quadrupled it, I liked her enough to be sorry. After a while I discovered too that if she got less it was not that *I* was to get any more. My failure never had what Mrs. Stormer would have called the banality of being relative—it was always admirably absolute. She lived at ease however in those days—ease is exactly the word, though she produced three novels a year. She scorned me when I spoke of difficulty—it was the only thing that made her angry. If I hinted at the grand licking into shape that a work of art required she thought it a pretension and a *pose.* She never recognised the "torment of form"; the furthest she went was to introduce into one of her books (in satire her hand was heavy) a young poet who was always talking about it. I couldn't quite understand her irritation on this score, for she had nothing at stake in the matter. She had a shrewd perception that form, in prose at least, never recommended any one to the public we were condemned to address; according to which she lost nothing (her private humiliation not counted) by having none to show. She made no pretence of producing works of art, but had comfortable tea-drinking hours in which she freely confessed herself a common pastrycook, dealing in such tarts and puddings as would bring customers to the shop. She put in plenty of sugar and of cochineal, or whatever it is that gives these articles a rich and attractive colour. She had a calm independence of observation and opportunity which constituted an inexpugnable strength and would enable her to go on indefinitely. It's only real success that wanes, it's only solid things that melt. Greville Fane's ignorance of life was a resource still more unfailing than the most approved receipt. On her saying once that the day would come when she should have written herself out I answered: "Ah you open straight into fairyland, and the fairies love you and *they* never change. Fairyland's always there; it always was from the beginning of time and always will be to the end. They've given you the key and you can always open the door. With me it's different; I try, in my clumsy way, to be in some direct relation to life." "Oh bother your direct relation to life!" she used to reply, for she was always annoyed by the phrase—which wouldn't in the least prevent her using it as a note of elegance. With no more prejudices than an old sausage-mill, she would give forth again with patient punctuality any poor verbal scrap that had been dropped into her. I cheered her with saying that the dark day, at the end, would be for the 'likes' of *me;* since, proceeding in our small way by experience and study—priggish we!—we depended not on a revelation but on a little tiresome process. Attention depended on occasion, and where should we be when occasion failed?

One day she told me that as the novelist's life was so delightful and, during the good years at least, such a comfortable support—she had these staggering optimisms—she meant to train up her boy to follow it. She took the ingenious view that it was a profession like another and that therefore everything was to be gained by beginning young and serving an apprenticeship. Moreover the education would be less expensive than any other special course, inasmuch as she could herself administer it. She didn't profess to keep a school, but she could at least teach her own child. It wasn't that she had such a gift, but—she confessed to me as if she were afraid I should laugh at her—that *he* had. I didn't laugh at her for that, because I thought the boy sharp—I had seen him sundry times. He was well-grown and good-looking and unabashed, and both he and his sister made me wonder about their defunct papa, concerning whom the little I knew was that he had been a country vicar and brother to a small squire. I explained them to myself by suppositions and imputations possibly unjust to the departed; so little were they—superficially at least—the children of their mother. There used to be on an easel in her drawing-room an enlarged photograph of her husband, done by some horrible posthumous "process" and draped, as to its florid frame, with a silken scarf which testified to the candour of Greville Fane's bad taste. It made him look like an unsuccessful tragedian, but it wasn't a thing to trust. He may have been a successful comedian. Of the two children the girl was the elder, and struck me in all her younger years as singularly colourless. She was only long, very long, like an undecipherable letter. It wasn't till Mrs. Stormer came back from a protracted residence abroad that Ethel (which was this young lady's name) began to produce the effect, large and stiff and afterwards eminent in her, of a certain kind of resolution, something as public and important as if a meeting and a chairman had passed it. She gave one to understand she meant to do all she could for herself. She was long-necked and near-sighted and striking, and I thought I had never seen sweet seventeen in a form so hard and high and dry. She was cold and affected and ambitious, and she carried an eyeglass with a long handle, which she put up whenever she wanted not to see. She had come out, as the phrase is, immensely; and yet I felt as if she were surrounded with a spiked iron railing. What she meant to do for herself was to marry, and it was the only thing, I think, that she meant to do for any one else; yet who would be inspired to clamber over that bristling barrier? What flower of tenderness or of intimacy would such an adventurer conceive as his reward?

This was for Sir Baldwin Luard to say; but he naturally never confided me the secret. He was a joyless jokeless young man, with the air of having other secrets as well, and a determination to get on politically that was indicated by his never having been known to commit himself—as regards any proposition whatever—beyond an unchallengeable "Oh!" His wife and he must have conversed mainly in prim ejaculations, but they understood sufficiently that they were kindred spirits. I remember being angry with Greville Fane when she announced these nuptials to me as magnificent; I remember asking her what splendour there was in the union of the daughter of a woman of genius with an irredeemable mediocrity. "Oh he has immense ability," she said; but she blushed for the maternal fib. What she meant was that though Sir Baldwin's estates were not vast—he had a dreary house in South Kensington and a still drearier "Hall" somewhere in Essex, which was let—the connexion was a "smarter" one than a child of hers could have aspired to form. In spite of the social bravery of her novels she took a very humble and dingy view of herself, so that of all her productions "my daughter Lady Luard" was quite the one she was proudest of. That personage thought our authoress vulgar and was distressed and perplexed by the frequent freedoms of her pen, but had a complicated attitude for this indirect connexion with literature. So far as it was lucrative her ladyship approved of it and could compound with the inferiority of the pursuit by practical justice to some of its advantages. I had reason to know—my reason was simply that poor Mrs. Stormer told me—how she suffered the inky fingers to press an occasional bank-note into her palm. On the other hand she deplored the "peculiar style" to which Greville Fane had devoted herself, and wondered where a spectator with the advantage of so ladylike a daughter could have picked up such views about the best society. "She might know better, with Leolin and me," Lady Luard had been heard to remark; but it appeared that some of Greville Fane's superstitions were incurable. She didn't live in Lady Luard's society, and the best wasn't good enough for her—she must improve on it so prodigiously.

I could see this necessity increase in her during the years she spent abroad, when I had glimpses of her in the shifting sojourns that lay in the path of my annual ramble. She betook herself from Germany to Switzerland and from Switzerland to Italy; she favoured cheap places and set up her desk in the smaller capitals. I took a look at her whenever I could, and I always asked how Leolin was getting on. She gave me beautiful accounts of him, and, occasion favouring, the boy was produced for my advantage. I had entered from the first into the joke of his career—I pretended to regard him as a consecrated child. It had been a joke for Mrs. Stormer at first, but the youth himself had been shrewd enough to make the matter serious. If his parent accepted the principle that the intending novelist can't begin too early to see life, Leolin wasn't interested in hanging back from the application of it. He was eager to qualify himself and took to cigarettes at ten on the highest literary grounds. His fond mother gazed at him with extravagant envy and, like Desdemona, wished heaven had made *her* such a man. She explained to me more than once that in her profession she had found her sex a dreadful drawback. She loved the story of Madame George Sand's early rebellion against this hindrance, and believed that if she had worn trousers she could have written as well as that lady. Leolin had for the career at least the qualification of trousers, and as he grew older he recognised its importance by laying in ever so many pair. He grew up thus in gorgeous apparel, which was his way of interpreting his mother's system. Whenever I met her, accordingly, I found her still under the impression that she was carrying this system out and that the sacrifices made him were bearing heavy fruit. She was giving him experience, she was giving him impressions, she was putting a *gagne-pain* into his hand. It was another name for spoiling him with the best conscience in the world. The queerest pictures come back to me of this period of the good lady's life and of the extraordinarily virtuous muddled bewildering tenor of it. She had an idea she was seeing foreign manners as well as her petticoats would allow; but in reality she wasn't seeing anything, least of all, fortunately, how much she was laughed at. She drove her whimsical pen at Dresden and at Florence—she produced in all places and at all times the same romantic and ridiculous fictions. She carried about her box of properties, tumbling out promptly the familiar tarnished old puppets. She believed in them when others couldn't, and as they were like nothing that was to be seen under the sun it was impossible to prove by comparison that they were wrong. You can't compare birds and fishes; you could only feel that, as Greville Fane's characters had the fine plumage of the former species, human beings must be of the latter.

It would have been droll if it hadn't been so exemplary to see her tracing the loves of the duchesses beside the innocent cribs of her children. The immoral and the maternal lived together, in her diligent days, on the most comfortable terms, and she stopped curling the moustaches of her Guardsmen to pat the heads of her babes. She was haunted by solemn spinsters who came to tea from Continental pensions, and by unsophisticated Americans who told her she was just loved in *their* country. "I had rather be just paid there," she usually replied; for this tribute of transatlantic opinion was the only thing that galled her. The Americans went away thinking her coarse; though as the author of so many beautiful love-stories she was disappointing to most of these pilgrims, who hadn't expected to find a shy stout ruddy lady in a cap like a crumbled pyramid. She wrote about the affections and the impossibility of controlling them, but she talked of the price of pension and the convenience of an English chemist. She devoted much thought and many thousands of francs to the education of her daughter, who spent three years at a very superior school at Dresden, receiving wonderful instruction in sciences, arts and tongues, and who, taking a different line from Leolin, was to be brought up wholly as a *femme du monde.* The girl was musical and philological; she went in for several languages and learned enough about them to be inspired with a great contempt for her mother's artless accents. Greville Fane's French and Italian were droll; the imitative faculty had been denied her, and she had an unequalled gift, especially pen in hand, of squeezing big mistakes into small opportunities. She knew it but didn't care; correctness was the virtue in the world that, like her heroes and heroines, she valued least. Ethel, who had noted in her pages some remarkable lapses, undertook at one time to revise her proofs; but I remember her telling me a year after the girl had left school that this function had been very briefly exercised. "She can't read me," said Mrs. Stormer; "I offend her taste. She tells me that at Dresden—at school—I was never allowed." The good lady seemed surprised at this, having the best conscience in the world about her lucubrations. She had never meant to fly in the face of anything, and considered that she grovelled before the Rhadamanthus of the English literary tribunal, the celebrated and awful Young Person. I assured her, as a joke, that she was frightfully indecent—she had in fact that element of truth as little as any other—my purpose being solely to prevent her guessing that her daughter had dropped her not because she was immoral but because she was vulgar. I used to figure her children closeted together and putting it to each other with a gaze of dismay: "Why should she *be* so—and so *fearfully* so—when she has the advantage of our society? Shouldn't *we* have taught her better?" Then I imagined their recognising with a blush and a shrug that she was unteachable, irreformable. Indeed she was, poor lady, but it's never fair to read by the light of taste things essentially not written in it. Greville Fane kept through all her riot of absurdity a witless confidence that should have been as safe from criticism as a stutter or a squint.

She didn't make her son ashamed of the profession to which he was destined, however; she only made him ashamed of the way she herself exercised it. But he bore his humiliation much better than his sister, being ready to assume he should one day restore the balance. A canny and far-seeing youth, with appetites and aspirations, he hadn't a scruple in his composition. His mother's theory of the happy knack he could pick up deprived him of the wholesome discipline required to prevent young idlers from becoming cads. He enjoyed on foreign soil a casual tutor and the common snatch or two of a Swiss school, but addressed himself to no consecutive study nor to any prospect of a university or a degree. It may be imagined with what zeal, as the years went on, he entered into the pleasantry of there being no manual so important to him as the massive book of life. It was an expensive volume to peruse, but Mrs. Stormer was willing to lay out a sum in what she would have called her *premiers frais*. Ethel disapproved—she found this education irregular for an English gentleman. Her voice was for Eton and Oxford or for any public school—she would have resigned herself to one of the scrubbier—with the army to follow. But Leolin never was afraid of his sister, and they visibly disliked, though they sometimes agreed to assist, each other. They could combine to work the oracle—to keep their mother at her desk.

When she reappeared in England, telling me she had "secured" all the Continent could give her, Leolin was a broad-shouldered red-faced young man with an immense wardrobe and an extraordinary assurance of manner. She was fondly, quite aggressively certain she had taken the right course with him, and addicted to boasting of all he knew and had seen. He was now quite ready to embark on the family profession, to commence author, as they used to say, and a little while later she told me he had started. He had written something tremendously clever which was coming out in the *Cheapside*. I believe it came out; I had no time to look for it; I never heard anything about it. I took for granted that if this contribution had passed through his mother's hands it would virtually rather illustrate *her* fine facility, and it was interesting to consider the poor lady's future in the light of her having to write her son's novels as well as her own. This wasn't the way she looked at it herself—she took the charming ground that he'd help her to write hers. She used to assure me he supplied passages of the greatest value to these last—all sorts of telling technical things, happy touches about hunting and yachting and cigars and wine, about City slang and the way men talk at clubs—that she couldn't be expected to get very straight. It was all so much practice for him and so much alleviation for herself. I was unable to identify such pages, for I had long since ceased to "keep up" with Greville Fane; but I could quite believe at least that the wine-question had been put by Leolin's good offices on a better footing, for the dear woman used to mix her drinks—she was perpetually serving the most splendid suppers—in the queerest fashion. I could see him quite ripe to embrace regularly that care. It occurred to me indeed, when she settled in England again, that she might by a shrewd use of both her children be able to rejuvenate her style. Ethel had come back to wreak her native, her social yearning, and if she couldn't take her mother into company would at least go into it herself. Silently, stiffly, almost grimly, this young lady reared her head, clenched her long teeth, squared her lean elbows and found her way up the staircases she had marked. The only communication she ever made, the only effusion of confidence with which she ever honoured me, was when she said "I don't want to know the people mamma knows, I mean to know others." I took due note of the remark, for I wasn't one of the "others." I couldn't trace therefore the steps and stages of her climb; I could only admire it at a distance and congratulate her mother in due course on the results. The results, the gradual, the final, the wonderful, were that Ethel went to "big" parties and got people to take her. Some of them were people she had met abroad, and others people the people she had met abroad had met. They ministered alike to Miss Ethel's convenience, and I wondered how she extracted so many favours without the expenditure of a smile. Her smile was the dimmest thing in nature, diluted, unsweetened, inexpensive lemonade, and she had arrived precociously at social wisdom, recognising that if she was neither pretty enough nor rich enough nor clever enough, she could at least, in her muscular youth, be rude enough. Therefore, so placed to give her parent tips, to let her know what really occurred in the mansions of the great, to supply her with local colour, with *data* to work from, she promoted the driving of the well-worn quill, over the brave old battered blotting book, to a still lustier measure and precisely at the moment when most was to depend on this labour. But if she became a great critic it appeared that the labourer herself was constitutionally inapt for the lesson. It was late in the day for Greville Fane to learn, and I heard nothing of her having developed a new manner. She was to have had only one manner, as Leolin would have said, from start to finish.

She was weary and spent at last, but confided to me that she couldn't afford to pause. She continued to speak of her son's work as the great hope of their future—she had saved no money—though the young man wore to my sense an air more and more professional if you like, but less and less literary. There was at the end of a couple of years something rare in the impudence of his playing of his part in the comedy. When I wondered how she could play hers it was to feel afresh the fatuity of her fondness, which was proof, I believed—I indeed saw to the end—against any interference of reason. She loved the young impostor with a simple blind benighted love, and of all the heroes of romance who had passed before her eyes he was by far the brightest. He was at any rate the most real—she could touch him, pay for him, suffer for him, worship him. He made her think of her princes and dukes, and when she wished to fix these figures in her mind's eye she thought of her boy. She had often told me she was herself carried away by her creations, and she was certainly carried away by Leolin. He vivified—by what romantically might have been at least—the whole question of youth and passion. She held, not unjustly, that the sincere novelist should feel the whole flood of life; she acknowledged with regret that she hadn't had time to feel it herself, and the lapse in her history was in a manner made up by the sight of its rush through this magnificent young man. She exhorted him, I suppose, to encourage the rush; she wrung her own flaccid little sponge into the torrent. What passed between them in her pedagogic hours was naturally a blank to me, but I gathered that she mainly impressed on him that the great thing was to live, because that gave you material. He asked nothing better; he collected material, and the recipe served as a universal pretext. You had only to look at him to see that, with his rings and breastpins, his cross-barred jackets, his early *embonpoint,* his eyes that looked like imitation jewels, his various indications of a dense full-blown temperament, his idea of life was singularly vulgar; but he was so far auspicious as that his response to his mother's expectations was in a high degree practical. If she had imposed a profession on him from his tenderest years it was exactly a profession that he followed. The two were not quite the same, inasmuch as the one he had adopted was simply to live at her expense; but at least she couldn't say he hadn't taken a line. If she insisted on believing in him he offered himself to the sacrifice. My impression is that her secret dream was that he should have a *liaison* with a countess, and he persuaded her without difficulty that he had one. I don't know what countesses are capable of, but I've a clear notion of what Leolin was.

He didn't persuade his sister, who despised him—she wished to work her mother in her own way; so that I asked myself why the girl's judgement of him didn't make me like her better. It was because it didn't save her after all from the mute agreement with him to go halves. There were moments when I couldn't help looking hard into his atrocious young eyes, challenging him to confess his fantastic fraud and give it up. Not a little tacit conversation passed between us in this way, but he had always the best of the business. If I said: "Oh come now, with *me* you needn't keep it up; plead guilty and I'll let you off," he wore the most ingenuous, the most candid expression, in the depths of which I could read: "Ah yes, I know it exasperates you—that's just why I do it." He took the line of earnest enquiry, talked about Balzac and Flaubert, asked me if I thought Dickens *did* exaggerate and Thackeray *ought* to be called a pessimist. Once he came to see me, at his mother's suggestion he declared, on purpose to ask me how far, in my opinion, in the English novel, one really might venture to "go." He wasn't resigned to the usual pruderies, the worship of childish twaddle; he suffered already from too much bread and butter. He struck out the brilliant idea that nobody knew how far we might go, since nobody had ever tried. Did I think *he* might safely try—would it injure his mother if he did? He would rather disgrace himself by his timidities than injure his mother, but certainly some one ought to try. Wouldn't *I* try—couldn't I be prevailed upon to look at it as a duty? Surely the ultimate point ought to be fixed—he was worried, haunted by the question. He patronised me unblushingly, made me feel a foolish amateur, a helpless novice, enquired into my habits of work and conveyed to me that I was utterly *vieux jeu* and hadn't had the advantage of an early training. I hadn't been brought up from the egg, I knew nothing of life— didn't go at it on *his* system. He had dipped into French feuilletons and picked up plenty of phrases, and he made a much better show in talk than his poor mother, who never had time to read anything and could only be showy with her pen. If I didn't kick him downstairs it was because he would have landed on her at the bottom.

When she went to live at Primrose Hill I called there and found her wasted and wan. It had visibly dropped, the elation caused the year before by Ethel's marriage; the foam on the cup had subsided and there was bitterness in the draught. She had had to take a cheaper house—and now had to work still harder to pay even for that. Sir Baldwin was obliged to be close; his charges were fearful, and the dream of her living with her daughter—a vision she had never mentioned to me—must be renounced. "I'd have helped them with things, and could have lived perfectly in one room," she said; "I'd have paid for everything, and—after all—I'm some one, ain't I? But I don't fit in, and Ethel tells me there are tiresome people she *must* receive. I can help them from here, no doubt, better than from there. She told me once, you know, what she thinks of my picture of life. 'Mamma, your picture of life's preposterous!' No doubt it is, but she's vexed with me for letting my prices go down; and I had to write three novels to pay for all her marriage cost me. I did it very well—I mean the outfit and the wedding; but that's why I'm here. At any rate she doesn't want a dingy old woman at Blicket. I should give the place an atmosphere of literary prestige, but literary prestige is only the eminence of nobodies. Besides, she knows what to think of my glory—she knows I'm glorious only at Peckham and Hackney. She doesn't want her friends to ask if I've never known nice people. She can't tell them I've never been in society. She tried to teach me better once, but I couldn't catch on. It would seem too as if Peckham and Hackney had had enough of me; for (don't tell any one!) I've had to take less for my last than I ever took for anything." I asked her how little this had been, not from curiosity, but in order to upbraid her, more disinterestedly than Lady Luard had done, for such concessions. She answered "I'm ashamed to tell you" and then began to cry.

I had never seen her break down and I was proportionately moved; she sobbed like a frightened child over the extinction of her vogue and the exhaustion of her vein. Her little workroom seemed indeed a barren place to grow flowers for the market, and I wondered in the after years (for she continued to produce and publish) by what desperate and heroic process she dragged them out of the soil. I remember asking her on that occasion what had become of Leolin and how much longer she intended to allow him to amuse himself at her cost. She retorted with spirit, wiping her eyes, that he was down at Brighton hard at work—he was in the midst of a novel—and that he *felt* life so, in all its misery and mystery, that it was cruel to speak of such experiences as a pleasure. "He goes beneath the surface," she said, "and he *forces* himself to look at things from which he'd rather turn away. Do you call that amusing yourself? You should see his face sometimes! And he does it for me as much as for himself. He tells me everything—he comes home to me with his *trouvailles*. We're artists together, and to the artist all things are pure. I've often heard you say so yourself." The novel Leolin was engaged in at Brighton never saw the light, but a friend of mine and of Mrs. Stormer's who was staying there happened to mention to me later that he had seen the young apprentice to fiction driving, in a dog-cart, a young lady with a very pink face. When I suggested that she was perhaps a woman of title with whom he was conscientiously flirting my informant replied: "She is indeed, but do you know what her title is?" He pronounced it—it was familiar and descriptive—but I won't reproduce it here. I don't know whether Leolin mentioned it to his mother: she would have needed all the purity of the artist to forgive him. I hated so to come across him that in the very last years I went rarely to see her, though I knew she had come pretty well to the end of her rope. I didn't want her to tell me she had fairly to give her books away; I didn't want to see her old and abandoned and derided; I didn't want, in a word, to see her terribly cry. She still, however, kept it up amazingly, and every few months, at my club, I saw three new volumes, in green, in crimson, in blue, on the book-table that groaned with light literature. Once I met her at the Academy soirée, where you meet people you thought were dead, and she vouchsafed the information, as if she owed it to me in candour, that Leolin had been obliged to recognise the insuperable difficulties of the question of *form*—he was so fastidious; but that she had now arrived at a definite understanding with him (it was such a comfort!) that *she* would do the form if he would bring home the substance. That was now his employ—he foraged for her in the great world at a salary. "He's my 'devil,' don't you see? as if I were a great lawyer: he gets up the case and I argue it." She mentioned further that in addition to his salary he was paid by the piece: he got so much for a striking character, so much for a pretty name, so much for a plot, so much for an incident, and had so much promised him if he would invent a new crime.

"He *has* invented one," I said, "and he's paid every day of his life."

"What is it?" she asked, looking hard at the picture of the year, "Baby's Tub," near which we happened to be standing.

I hesitated a moment. "I myself will write a little story about it, and then you'll see."

But she never saw; she had never seen anything, and she passed away with her fine blindness unimpaired. Her son published every scrap of scribbled paper that could be extracted from her table-drawers, and his sister quarrelled with him mortally about the proceeds, which showed her only to have wanted a pretext, for they can't have been great. I don't know what Leolin lives on unless on a queer lady many years older than himself, whom he lately married. The last time I met him he said to me with his infuriating smile: "Don't you think we can go a little further still—just a little?" *He* really—with me at least—goes too far.

1892, 1893, 1909

Maud-Evelyn

One wonders why James omitted this bizarre and skillfully-narrated tale from his collected edition. It first appeared in the *Atlantic Monthly* in April 1900; was reprinted the same year in the volume called *The Soft Side;*

and was included by Percy Lubbock in the 35-volume edition of James's works published in London, 1921-23, from which the present text is taken. In his *Notebooks*, James indicated the source-idea for the story as that of a childless couple, or one which had lost a daughter, meeting a young man they like and gradually accepting the illusion that he *might* have married their daughter. He succumbs to the suggestion and ends by believing it. James writes: "He lives with the parents. They leave him their money. I see him later. *He is a widower.* He dies to rejoin his wife. He leaves their fortune to the girl he doesn't marry." In writing the story, James added the narrator, Lady Emma, and complicated his *donnée* still further by her relationship with Lavinia and her attitude toward Marmaduke.

On some allusion to a lady who, though unknown to myself, was known to two or three of the company, it was asked by one of these if we had heard the odd circumstance of what she had just "come in for"—the piece of luck suddenly overtaking, in the grey afternoon of her career, so obscure and lonely a personage. We were at first, in our ignorance, mainly reduced to crude envy; but old Lady Emma, who for a while had said nothing, scarcely even appearing to listen and letting the chatter, which was indeed plainly beside the mark, subside of itself, came back from a mental absence to observe that if what had happened to Lavinia was wonderful, certainly, what had for years gone before it, led up to it, had likewise not been without some singular features. From this we perceived that Lady Emma had a story—a story moreover out of the ken even of those of her listeners acquainted with the quiet person who was the subject of it. Almost the oddest thing—as came out afterwards—was that such a situation should, for the world, have remained so in the background of this person's life. By "afterwards" I mean simply before we separated; for what came out came on the spot, under encouragement and pressure, our common, eager solicitation. Lady Emma, who always reminded me of a fine old instrument that has first to be tuned, agreed, after a few of our scrapings and fingerings, that, having said so much, she couldn't, without wantonly tormenting us, forbear to say all. She had known Lavinia, whom she mentioned throughout only by that name, from far away, and she had also known—— But what she had known I must give as nearly as possible as she herself gave it. She talked to us from her corner of the sofa, and the flicker of the firelight in her face was like the glow of memory, the play of fancy, from within.

I

"Then why on earth don't you take him?" I asked. I think that was the way that, one day when she was about twenty—before some of you perhaps were born—the affair, for me, must have begun. I put the question because I knew she had had a chance, though I didn't know how great a mistake her failure to embrace it was to prove. I took an interest because I liked them both—you see how I like young people still—and because, as they had originally met at my house, I had in a manner to answer to each for the other. I'm afraid I'm thrown baldly back on the fact that if the girl was the daughter of my earliest, almost my only governess, to whom I had remained much attached and who, after leaving me, had married—for a governess—"well," Marmaduke (it isn't *his* real name!) was the son of one of the clever men who had—I was charming then, I assure you I was—wanted, years before, and this one as a widower, to marry me. I hadn't cared, somehow, for widowers, but even after I had taken somebody else I was conscious of a pleasant link with the boy whose stepmother it had been open to me to become and to whom it was perhaps a little a matter of vanity with me to show that I should have been for him one of the kindest. This was what the woman his father eventually did marry was not, and that threw him upon me the more.

Lavinia was one of nine, and her brothers and sisters, who have never done anything for her, help, actually, in different countries and on something, I believe, of that same scale, to people the globe. There were mixed in her then, in a puzzling way, two qualities that mostly exclude each other—an extreme timidity and, as the smallest fault that could qualify a harmless creature for a world of wickedness, a self-complacency hard in tiny, unexpected spots, for which I used sometimes to take her up, but which, I subsequently saw, would have done something for the flatness of her life had they not evaporated with everything else. She was at any rate one of those persons as to whom you don't know whether they might have been attractive if they had been happy, or might have been happy if they had been attractive. If I was a trifle vexed at her not jumping at Marmaduke, it was probably rather less because I expected wonders of him than because I thought she took her own prospect too much for granted. She had made a mistake and, before long, admitted it; yet I remember that when she expressed to me a conviction that he would ask her again, I also thought this highly probable, for in the meantime I had spoken to him. "She does care for you," I declared; and I can see at this moment, long ago though it be, his handsome empty young face look, on the words, as if, in spite of itself for a little, it really thought. I didn't press the matter, for he had, after all, no great things to offer; yet my conscience was easier, later on, for having not said less. He had three hundred and fifty a year from his mother, and one of his uncles had promised him something—I don't mean an allowance, but a place, if I recollect, in a business. He assured me that he loved as a man loves—a man of twenty-two!—but once. He said it, at all events, as a man says it but once.

"Well, then," I replied, "your course is clear."

"To speak to her again, you mean?"

"Yes—try it."

He seemed to try it a moment in imagination; after which, a little to my surprise, he asked: "Would it be very awful if she should speak to *me*?"

I stared. "Do you mean pursue you—overtake you? Ah, if you're running away——"

"I'm not running away!"—he was positive as to that. "But when a fellow has gone so far——"

"He can't go any further? Perhaps," I replied dryly. "But in that case he shouldn't talk of 'caring.'"

"Oh, but I do, I do."

I shook my head. "Not if you're too proud!" On which I turned away, looking round at him again, however, after he had surprised me by a silence that seemed to accept my judgement. Then I saw he had not accepted it; I perceived it indeed to be essentially absurd. He expressed more, on this, than I had yet seen him do—had the queerest, frankest, and, for a young man of his conditions, saddest smile.

"I'm *not* proud. It isn't *in* me. If you're not, you're not, you know. I don't think I'm proud enough."

It came over me that this was, after all, probable; yet somehow I didn't at the moment like him the less for it, though I spoke with some sharpness. "Then what's the matter with you?"

He took a turn or two about the room, as if what he had just said had made him a little happier. "Well, how can a man say more?" Then, just as I was on the point of assuring him that I didn't know what he had said, he went on: "I swore to her that I would never marry. Oughtn't that to be enough?"

"To make her come after you?"

"No—I suppose scarcely that; but to make her feel sure of me—to make her wait."

"Wait for what?"

"Well, till I come back."

"Back from where?"

"From Switzerland—haven't I told you? I go there next month with my aunt and my cousin."

He was quite right about not being proud—this was an alternative distinctly humble.

II

And yet see what it brought forth—the beginning of which was something that, early in the autumn, I learned from poor Lavinia. He had written to her, they were still such friends; and thus it was that she knew his aunt and his cousin to have come back without him. He had stayed on—stayed much longer and travelled much further: he had been to the Italian lakes and to Venice; he was now in Paris. At this I vaguely wondered, knowing that he was always short of funds and that he must, by his uncle's beneficence, have started on the journey on a basis of expenses paid. "Then whom has he picked up?" I asked; but feeling sorry, as soon as I had spoken, to have made Lavinia blush. It was almost as if he had picked up some improper lady, though in this case he wouldn't have told her, and it wouldn't have saved him money.

"Oh, he makes acquaintance so quickly, knows people in two minutes," the girl said. "And every one always wants to be nice to him."

This was perfectly true, and I saw what she saw in it. "Ah, my dear, he will have an immense circle ready for you!"

"Well," she replied, "if they do run after us I'm not likely to suppose it will ever be for me. It will be for *him*, and they may do to me what they like. My pleasure will be—but you'll see." I already saw—saw at least what she supposed she herself saw: her drawing-room crowded with female fashion and her attitude angelic. "Do you know what he said to me again before he went?" she continued.

I wondered; he *had* then spoken to her. "That he will never, never marry——"

"Any one but *me*!" She ingenuously took me up. "Then you knew?"

It might be. "I guessed."

"And don't you believe it?"

Again I hesitated. "Yes." Yet all this didn't tell me why she had changed colour. "Is it a secret—whom he's with?"

"Oh no, they seem so nice. I was only struck with the way you know him—your seeing immediately that it must be a new friendship that has kept him over. It's the devotion of the Dedricks," Lavinia said. "He's travelling with them."

Once more I wondered. "Do you mean they're taking him about?"

"Yes—they've invited him."

No, indeed, I reflected—he wasn't proud. But what I said was: "Who in the world are the Dedricks?"

"Kind, good people whom, last month, he accidentally met. He was walking some Swiss pass—a long, rather stupid one, I believe, without his aunt and his cousin, who had gone round some other way and were to meet him somewhere. It came on to rain in torrents, and while he was huddling under a shelter he was overtaken by some people in a carriage, who kindly made him get in. They drove him,

I gather, for several hours; it began an intimacy, and they've continued to be charming to him."

I thought a moment. "Are they ladies?"

Her own imagination meanwhile had also strayed a little. "I think about forty."

"Forty ladies?"

She quickly came back. "Oh no; I mean Mrs. Dedrick is."

"About forty? Then Miss Dedrick——"

"There isn't any Miss Dedrick."

"No daughter?"

"Not with them, at any rate. No one but the husband."

I thought again. "And how old is *he?*"

Lavinia followed my example. "Well, about forty, too."

"About forty-two?" We laughed, but "That's all right!" I said; and so, for the time, it seemed.

He continued absent, none the less, and I saw Lavinia repeatedly, and we always talked of him, though this represented a greater concern with his affairs than I had really supposed myself committed to. I had never sought the acquaintance of his father's people, nor seen either his aunt or his cousin, so that the account given by these relatives of the circumstances of their separation reached me at last only through the girl, to whom, also—for she knew them as little—it had circuitously come. They considered, it appeared, the poor ladies he had started with, that he had treated them ill and thrown them over, sacrificing them selfishly to company picked up on the road—a reproach deeply resented by Lavinia, though about the company too I could see she was not much more at her ease. "How can he help it if he's so taking?" she asked; and to be properly indignant in one quarter she had to pretend to be delighted in the other. Marmaduke *was* "taking"; yet it also came out between us at last that the Dedricks must certainly be extraordinary. We had scant added evidence, for his letters stopped, and that naturally was one of our signs. I had meanwhile leisure to reflect—it was a sort of study of the human scene I always liked—on what to be taking consisted of. The upshot of my meditations, which experience has only confirmed, was that it consisted simply of itself. It was a quality implying no others. Marmaduke *had* no others. What indeed was his need of any?

III

He at last, however, turned up; but then it happened that if, on his coming to see me, his immediate picture of his charming new friends quickened even more than I had expected my sense of the variety of the human species, my curiosity about them failed to make me respond when he suggested I should go to see them. It's a difficult thing to explain, and I don't pretend to put it successfully, but doesn't it often happen that one may think well enough of a person without being inflamed with the desire to meet—on the ground of any such sentiment—other persons who think still better? Somehow—little harm as there was in Marmaduke—it was but half a recommendation of the Dedricks that they were crazy about him. I didn't say this—I was careful to say little; which didn't prevent his presently asking if he mightn't then bring them to *me*. "If not, why not?" he laughed. He laughed about everything.

"Why not? Because it strikes me that your surrender doesn't require any backing. Since you've done it you must take care of yourself."

"Oh, but they're as safe," he returned, "as the Bank of England. They're wonderful—for respectability and goodness."

"Those are precisely qualities to which my poor intercourse can contribute nothing." He hadn't, I observed, gone so far as to tell me they would be "fun," and he *had*, on the other hand, promptly mentioned that they lived in Westbourne Terrace. They were not forty—they were forty-five; but Mr. Dedrick had already, on considerable gains, retired from some primitive profession. They were the simplest, kindest, yet most original and unusual people, and nothing could exceed, frankly, the fancy they had taken to him. Marmaduke spoke of it with a placidity of resignation that was almost irritating. I suppose I should have despised him if, after benefits accepted, he had said they bored him; yet their not boring him vexed me even more than it puzzled. "Whom do they know?"

"No one but me. There are people in London like that."

"Who know no one but you?"

"No—I mean no one at all. There are extraordinary people in London, and awfully nice. You haven't an idea. You people don't know every one. They lead their lives—they go their way. One finds—what do you call it?—refinement, books, cleverness, don't you know, and music, and pictures, and religion, and an excellent table—all sorts of pleasant things. You only come across them by chance; but it's all perpetually going on."

I assented to this: the world was very wonderful, and one must certainly see what one could. In my own quarter too I found wonders enough. "But are you," I asked, "as fond of them——"

"As they are of *me?*" He took me up promptly, and his eyes were quite unclouded. "I'm quite sure I shall become so."

"Then are you taking Lavinia——?"

"Not to see them—no." I saw, myself, the next minute, of course, that I had made a mistake. "On what footing *can* I?"

I bethought myself. "I keep forgetting you're not engaged."

"Well," he said after a moment, "I shall never marry another."

It somehow, repeated again, gave on my nerves. "Ah, but what good will that do her, or me either, if you don't marry *her?*"

He made no answer to this—only turned away to look at something in the room; after which, when he next faced me, he had a heightened colour. "She ought to have taken me that day," he said gravely and gently; fixing me also as if he wished to say more.

I remember that his very mildness irritated me; some show of resentment would have been a promise that the case might still be righted. But I dropped it, the silly case, without letting him say more, and, coming back to Mr. and Mrs. Dedrick, asked him how in the world, without either occupation or society, they passed so much of their time. My question appeared for a moment to leave him at a loss, but he presently found light; which, at the same time, I saw on my side, really suited him better than further talk about Lavinia. "Oh, they live for Maud-Evelyn."

"And who's Maud-Evelyn?"

"Why, their daughter."

"Their daughter?" I had supposed them childless.

He partly explained. "Unfortunately they've lost her."

"Lost her?" I required more.

He hesitated again. "I mean that a great many people would take it that way. But *they* don't—they won't."

I speculated. "Do you mean other people would have given her up?"

"Yes—perhaps even tried to forget her. But the Dedricks can't."

I wondered what she had done: had it been anything very bad? However, it was none of my business, and I only said: "They communicate with her?"

"Oh, all the while."

"Then why isn't she with them?"

Marmaduke thought. "She *is*—now."

" 'Now?' Since when?"

"Well, this last year."

"Then why do you say they've lost her?"

"Ah," he said, smiling sadly, "I should call it that. I, at any rate," he went on, "don't see her."

Still more I wondered. "They keep her apart?"

He thought again. "No, it's not that. As I say, they live for her."

"But they don't want *you* to—is that it?"

At this he looked at me for the first time, as I thought, a little strangely. "How *can* I?"

He put it to me as if it were bad of him, somehow, that he shouldn't; but I made, to the best of my ability, a quick end of that. "You can't. Why in the world *should* you? Live for *my* girl. Live for Lavinia."

IV

I had unfortunately run the risk of boring him again with that idea, and, though he had not repudiated it at the time, I felt in my having returned to it the reason why he never reappeared for weeks. I saw "my girl," as I had called her, in the interval, but we avoided with much intensity the subject of Marmaduke. It was just this that gave me my perspective for finding her constantly full of him. It determined me, in all the circumstances, not to rectify her mistake about the childlessness of the Dedricks. But whatever I left unsaid, her naming the young man was only a question of time, for at the end of a month she told me he had been twice to her mother's and that she had seen him on each of these occasions.

"Well then?"

"Well then, he's very happy."

"And still taken up——"

"As much as ever, yes, with those people. He didn't tell me so, but I could see it."

I could too, and her own view of it. "What, in that case, did he tell you?"

"Nothing—but I think there's something he wants to. Only not what *you* think," she added.

I wondered then if it were what I had had from him the last time. "Well, what prevents him?" I asked.

"From bringing it out? I don't know."

It was in the tone of this that she struck, to my ear, the first note of an acceptance so deep and a patience so strange that they gave me, at the end, even more food for wonderment than the rest of the business. "If he can't speak, why does he come?"

She almost smiled. "Well, I think I *shall* know."

I looked at her; I remember that I kissed her. "You're admirable; but it's very ugly."

"Ah," she replied, "he only wants to be kind!"

"To *them?* Then he should let others alone. But what I call ugly is his being content to be so 'beholden'——"

"To Mr. and Mrs. Dedrick?" She considered as if

there might be many sides to it. "But mayn't he do them some good?"

The idea failed to appeal to me. "What good can Marmaduke do? There's one thing," I went on, "in case he should want you to know them. Will you promise me to refuse?"

She only looked helpless and blank. "Making their acquaintance?"

"Seeing them, going near them—ever, ever."

Again she brooded. "Do you mean *you* won't?"

"Never, never."

"Well, then, I don't think I want to."

"Ah, but that's not a promise." I kept her up to it. "I want your word."

She demurred a little. "But why?"

"So that at least he shan't make use of you," I said with energy.

My energy overbore her, though I saw how she would really have given herself. "I promise, but it's only because it's something I know he will never ask."

I differed from her at the time, believing the proposal in question to have been exactly the subject she had supposed him to be wishing to broach; but on our very next meeting I heard from her of quite another matter, upon which, as soon as she came in, I saw her to be much excited.

"You know then about the daughter without having told me? He called again yesterday," she explained as she met my stare at her unconnected plunge, "and now I know that he *has* wanted to speak to me. He at last brought it out."

I continued to stare. "Brought what?"

"Why, everything." She looked surprised at my face. "Didn't he tell you about Maud-Evelyn?"

I perfectly recollected, but I momentarily wondered. "He spoke of there being a daughter, but only to say that there's something the matter with her. What is it?"

The girl echoed my words. "What 'is' it?—you dear, strange thing! The matter with her is simply that she's dead."

"Dead?" I was naturally mystified. "When, then, did she die?"

"Why, years and years ago—fifteen, I believe. As a little girl. Didn't you understand it so?"

"How *should* I?—when he spoke of her as 'with' them and said that they lived for her!"

"Well," my young friend explained, "that's just what he meant—they live for her memory. She *is* with them in the sense that they think of nothing else."

I found matter for surprise in this correction, but also, at first, matter for relief. At the same time it left, as I turned it over, a fresh ambiguity. "If they think of nothing else, how can they think so much of Marmaduke?"

The difficulty struck her, though she gave me even then a dim impression of being already, as it were, rather on Marmaduke's side, or, at any rate—almost as against herself—in sympathy with the Dedricks. But her answer was prompt: "Why, that's just their reason—that they can talk to him so much about her."

"I see." Yet still I wondered. "But what's *his* interest——?"

"In being drawn into it?" Again Lavinia met her difficulty. "Well, that she was so interesting! It appears she was lovely."

I doubtless fairly gaped. "A little girl in a pinafore?"

"She was out of pinafores; she was, I believe, when she died, about fourteen. Unless it was sixteen! She was at all events wonderful for beauty."

"That's the rule. But what good does it do him if he has never seen her?"

She thought a moment, but this time she had no answer. "Well, you must ask him!"

I determined without delay to do so; but I had before me meanwhile other contradictions. "Hadn't I better ask him on the same occasion what he means by their 'communicating'?"

Oh, this was simple. "They go in for 'mediums,' don't you know, and raps, and sittings. They began a year or two ago."

"Ah, the idiots!" I remember, at this, narrow-mindedly exclaiming. "Do they want to drag *him* in——?"

"Not in the least; they don't desire it, and he has nothing to do with it."

"Then where does his fun come in?"

Lavinia turned away; again she seemed at a loss. At last she brought out: "Make him show you her little photograph."

But I remained unenlightened. "Is her little photograph his fun?"

Once more she coloured for him. "Well, it represents a young loveliness!"

"That he goes about showing?"

She hesitated. "I think he has only shown it to *me*."

"Ah, you're just the last one!" I permitted myself to observe.

"Why so, if I'm also struck?"

There was something about her that began to escape me, and I must have looked at her hard. "It's very good of you to be struck!"

"I don't only mean by the beauty of the face," she went on; "I mean by the whole thing—by that also of the attitude of the parents, their extraordinary fidelity and the way that, as he says, they have made of her memory a real religion. That was what, above all, he came to tell me about."

I turned away from her now, and she soon afterwards left me; but I couldn't help its dropping from me before we parted that I had never supposed him to be *that* sort of fool.

V

If I were really the perfect cynic you probably think me I should frankly say that the main interest of the rest of this matter lay for me in fixing the sort of fool I *did* suppose him. But I'm afraid, after all, that my anecdote amounts mainly to a presentation of my own folly. I shouldn't be so in possession of the whole spectacle had I not ended by accepting it, and I shouldn't have accepted it had it not, for my imagination, been saved somehow from grotesqueness. Let me say at once, however, that grotesqueness, and even indeed something worse, did at first appear to me strongly to season it. After that talk with Lavinia I immediately addressed to our friend a request that he would come to see me; when I took the liberty of challenging him outright on everything she had told me. There was one point in particular that I desired to clear up and that seemed to me much more important even than the colour of Maud-Evelyn's hair or the length of her pinafores: the question, I of course mean, of my young man's good faith. Was he altogether silly or was he only altogether mercenary? I felt my choice restricted for the moment to these alternatives.

After he had said to me "It's as ridiculous as you please, but they've simply adopted me," I had it out with him, on the spot, on the issue of common honesty, the question of what he was conscious, so that his self-respect should be saved, of being able to give such benefactors in return for such bounty. I'm obliged to say that to a person so inclined at the start to quarrel with him his amiability could yet prove persuasive. His contention was that the equivalent he represented was something for his friends alone to measure. He didn't for a moment pretend to sound deeper than the fancy they had taken to him. He had not, from the first, made up to them in any way: it was all their own doing, their own insistence, their own eccentricity, no doubt, and even, if I liked, their own insanity. Wasn't it enough that he was ready to declare to me, looking me straight in the eye, that he was "really and truly" fond of them and that they didn't bore him a mite? I had evidently—didn't I see?—an ideal for him that he wasn't at all, if I didn't mind, the fellow to live up to. It was he himself who put it so, and it drew from me the pronouncement that there *was* something irresistible in the refinement of his impudence. "I don't go near Mrs. Jex," he said—Mrs. Jex was their favourite medium: "I do find *her* ugly and vulgar and tiresome, and I hate that part of the business. Besides," he added in words that I afterwards remembered, "I don't require it: I do beautifully without it. But my friends themselves," he pursued, "though they're of a type you've never come within miles of, are not ugly, are not vulgar, are not in any degree whatever any sort of a 'dose.' They're, on the contrary, in their own unconventional way, the very best company. They're endlessly amusing. They're delightfully queer and quaint and kind—they're like people in some old story or of some old time. It's at any rate our own affair—mine and theirs—and I beg you to believe that I should make short work of a remonstrance on the subject from any one but you."

I remember saying to him three months later: "You've never yet told me what they really want of you"; but I'm afraid this was a form of criticism that occurred to me precisely because I had already begun to guess. By that time indeed I had had great initiations, and poor Lavinia had had them as well—hers in fact throughout went further than mine—and we shared them together, and I had settled down to a tolerably exact sense of what I was to see. It was what Lavinia added to it that really made the picture. The portrait of the little dead girl had evoked something attractive, though one had not lived so long in the world without hearing of plenty of little dead girls; and the day came when I felt as if I had actually sat with Marmaduke in each of the rooms converted by her parents—with the aid not only of the few small, cherished relics, but that of the fondest figments and fictions, ingenious imaginary mementoes and tokens, the unexposed make-believes of the sorrow that broods and the passion that clings—into a temple of grief and worship. The child, incontestably beautiful, had evidently been passionately loved, and in the absence from their lives—I suppose originally a mere accident—of such other elements, either new pleasures or new pains, as abound for most people, their feeling had drawn to itself their whole consciousness: it had become mildly maniacal. The idea was fixed, and it kept others out. The world, for the most part, allows no leisure for such a ritual, but the world had consistently neglected this plain, shy couple, who were sensitive to the wrong things and whose sincerity and fidelity, as well as their tameness and twaddle, were of a rigid, antique pattern.

I must not represent that either of these objects of interest, or my care for their concerns, took up all my leisure; for I had many claims to meet and many complications to handle, a hundred preoccupations and much deeper anxieties. My young woman, on her side, had other contacts and contingencies—other troubles too, poor girl; and there were stretches of time in which I neither saw Marmaduke nor heard a word of the Dedricks. Once, only once, abroad, in Germany at a railway-station, I met him in their company. They were colourless, commonplace, elderly Britons, of the kind you identify by the livery of their footman or the labels of their luggage, and the mere sight of them justified me to my conscience in having avoided, from the first, the stiff problem of conversation with them. Marmaduke saw me on the spot and came over to me. There was no doubt whatever of *his* vivid bloom. He had grown fat—or almost, but not with grossness—and might perfectly have passed for the handsome, happy, full-blown son of doting parents who couldn't let him out of view and to whom he was a model of respect and solicitude. They followed him with placid, pleased eyes when he joined me, but asking nothing at all for themselves and quite fitting into his own manner of saying nothing about them. It had its charm, I confess, the way he could be natural and easy, and yet intensely conscious too, on such a basis. What he was conscious of was that there were things I by this time knew; just as, while we stood there and good-humouredly sounded each other's faces—for, having accepted everything at last, I was only a little curious—I knew that he measured my insight. When he returned again to his doting parents I had to admit that, doting as they were, I felt him not to have been spoiled. It was incongruous in such a career, but he was rather more of a man. There came back to me with a shade of regret after I had got on this occasion into my train, which was not theirs, a memory of some words that, a couple of years before, I had uttered to poor Lavinia. She had said to me, speaking in reference to what was then our frequent topic and on some fresh evidence that I have forgotten: "He feels now, you know, about Maud-Evelyn quite as the old people themselves do."

"Well," I had replied, "it's only a pity he's paid for it!"

"Paid?" She had looked very blank.

"By all the luxuries and conveniences," I had explained, "that he comes in for through living with them. For that's what he practically does."

At present I saw how wrong I had been. He was paid, but paid differently, and the mastered wonder of that was really what had been between us in the waiting-room of the station. Step by step, after this, I followed.

VI

I can see Lavinia, for instance, in her ugly new mourning immediately after her mother's death. There had been long anxieties connected with this event, and she was already faded, already almost old. But Marmaduke, on her bereavement, had been to her, and she came straightway to me.

"Do you know what he thinks now?" she soon began. "He thinks he knew her."

"Knew the child?" It came to me as if I had half expected it.

"He speaks of her now as if she hadn't been a child." My visitor gave me the strangest fixed smile. "It appears that she wasn't so young—it appears she had grown up."

I stared. "How can it 'appear'? They *know* at least! There were the facts."

"Yes," said Lavinia, "but they seem to have come to take a different view of them. He talked to me a long time, and all about *her*. He told me things."

"What kind of things? Not trumpery stuff, I hope, about 'communicating'—about his seeing or hearing her?"

"Oh no, he doesn't go in for that; he leaves it to the old couple, who, I believe, cling to their mediums, keep up their sittings and their rappings and find in it all a comfort, an amusement, that he doesn't grudge them and that he regards as harmless. I mean anecdotes—memories of his own. I mean things she said to him and that they did together—places they went to. His mind is full of them."

I turned it over. "Do you think he's decidedly mad?"

She shook her head with her bleached patience. "Oh no, it's too beautiful!"

"Then are *you* taking it up? I mean the preposterous theory——"

"It *is* a theory," she broke in, "but it isn't necessarily preposterous. Any theory has to suppose something," she sagely pursued, "and it depends at any rate on what it's a theory *of*. It's wonderful to see this one work."

"Wonderful always to see the growth of a legend!" I laughed. "This is a rare chance to watch one in formation. They're all three in good faith building it up. Isn't that what you made out from him?"

Her tired face fairly lighted. "Yes—you understand it; and you put it better than I. It's the gradual effect of brooding over the past; the past, that way, grows and grows. They make it and make it. They've persuaded each other—the parents—of so many things that they've at last also persuaded *him*. It has been contagious."

"It's you who put it well," I returned. "It's the oddest thing I ever heard of, but it is, in its way, a reality. Only we mustn't speak of it to others."

She quite accepted that precaution. "No—to nobody. *He* doesn't. He keeps it only for me."

"Conferring on you thus," I again laughed, "such a precious privilege!"

She was silent a moment, looking away from me. "Well, he has kept his vow."

"You mean of not marrying? Are you very sure?" I asked. "Didn't he perhaps——?" But I faltered at the boldness of my joke.

The next moment I saw I needn't. "He *was* in love with her," Lavinia brought out.

I broke now into a peal which, however provoked, struck even my own ear at the moment as rude almost to profanity. "He literally tells you outright that he's making believe?"

She met me effectively enough. "I don't think he *knows* he is. He's just completely in the current."

"The current of the old people's twaddle?"

Again my companion hesitated; but she knew what she thought. "Well, whatever we call it, I like it. It isn't so common, as the world goes, for any one—let alone for two or three—to feel and to care for the dead as much as that. It's self-deception, no doubt, but it comes from something that—well," she faltered again, "is beautiful when one does hear of it. They make her out older, so as to imagine they had her longer; and they make out that certain things really happened to her, so that she shall have had more life. They've invented a whole experience for her, and Marmaduke has become a part of it. There's one thing, above all, they want her to have had." My young friend's face, as she analysed the mystery, fairly grew bright with her vision. It came to me with a faint dawn of awe that the attitude of the Dedricks *was* contagious. "And she did have it!" Lavinia declared.

I positively admired her, and if I could yet perfectly be rational without being ridiculous, it was really, more than anything else, to draw from her the whole image. "She had the bliss of knowing Marmaduke? Let us agree to it, then, since she's not here to contradict us. But what I don't get over is the scant material for *him!*" It may easily be conceived how little, for the moment, I could get over it. It was the last time my impatience was to be too much for me, but I remember how it broke out. "A man who might have had *you!*"

For an instant I feared I had upset her—thought I saw in her face the tremor of a wild wail. But poor Lavinia was magnificent. "It wasn't that he might have had 'me'—that's nothing: it was, at the most, that I might have had *him*. Well, isn't that just what has happened? He's mine from the moment no one else has him. I give up the past, but don't you see what it does for the rest of life? I'm surer than ever that he won't marry."

"Of course, he won't—to quarrel, with those people!"

For a minute she answered nothing; then, "Well, for whatever reason!" she simply said. Now, however, I had gouged out of her a couple of still tears, and I pushed away the whole obscure comedy.

VII

I might push it away, but I couldn't really get rid of it; nor, on the whole, doubtless, did I want to, for to have in one's life, year after year, a particular question or two that one couldn't comfortably and imposingly make up one's mind about was just the sort of thing to keep one from turning stupid. There had been little need of my enjoining reserve upon Lavinia: she obeyed, in respect to impenetrable silence save with myself, an instinct, an interest of her own. We never therefore gave poor Marmaduke, as you call it, "away"; we were much too tender, let alone that she was also too proud; and, for himself, evidently, there was not, to the end, in London, another person in his confidence. No echo of the queer part he played ever came back to us; and I can't tell you how this fact, just by itself, brought home to me little by little a sense of the charm he was under. I met him "out" at long intervals—met him usually at dinner. He had grown like a person with a position and a history. Rosy and rich-looking, fat, moreover, distinctly fat at last, there was almost in him something of the bland—yet not too bland—young head of an hereditary business. If the Dedricks had been bankers he might have constituted the future of the house. There was none the less a long middle stretch during which, though we were all so much in London, he dropped out of my talks with Lavinia. We were conscious, she and I, of his absence from them; but we clearly felt in each quarter that there are things after all unspeakable, and the fact, in any case, had nothing to do with her seeing or not seeing our friend. I was sure, as it happened, that she did see him. But there were moments that for myself still stand out.

One of these was a certain Sunday afternoon when it was so dismally wet that, taking for granted I should have no visitors, I had drawn up to the fire with a book—a successful novel of the day—that I promised myself comfortably to finish. Suddenly, in my absorption, I heard a firm rat-tat-tat; on which I remember giving a groan of inhospitality. But my visitor proved in due course Marmaduke, and Marmaduke proved—in a manner even less, at the point we had reached, to have been counted on—still more attaching than my novel. I think it was only an accident that he became so; it would have been the turn of a hair either way. He hadn't come to speak—he had only come to talk, to show once more that we could continue good old friends without his speaking. But somehow there were the circumstances: the insidious fireside, the things in the room, with their reminders of his younger time; perhaps even too the open face of my book, looking at him from where I had laid it down for him and giving him a chance to feel that he could supersede Wilkie Collins. There was at all events a promise of intimacy, of opportunity for him in the cold lash of the windows by the storm. We should be alone; it was cosy; it was safe.

The action of these impressions was the more marked that what was touched by them, I afterwards saw, was not at all a desire for an effect—was just simply a spirit of happiness that needed to overflow. It had finally become too much for him. His past, rolling up year after year, had grown too interesting. But he was, all the same, directly stupefying. I forget what turn of our preliminary gossip brought it out, but it came, in explanation of something or other, as it had not yet come: "When a man has had for a few months what *I* had, you know!" The moral appeared to be that nothing in the way of human experience of the exquisite could again particularly matter. He saw, however, that I failed immediately to fit his reflexion to a definite case, and he went on with the frankest smile: "You look as bewildered as if you suspected me of alluding to some sort of thing that isn't usually spoken of; but I assure you I mean nothing more reprehensible than our blessed engagement itself."

"Your blessed engagement?" I couldn't help the tone in which I took him up; but the way he disposed of that was something of which I feel to this hour the influence. It was only a look, but it put an end to my tone for ever. It made me, on my side, after an instant, look at the fire—look hard and even turn a little red. During this moment I saw my alternatives and I chose; so that when I met his eyes again I was fairly ready. "You still feel," I asked with sympathy, "how much it did for you?"

I had no sooner spoken than I saw that that would be from that moment the right way. It instantly made all the difference. The main question would be whether I could keep it up. I remember that only a few minutes later, for instance, this question gave a flare. His reply had been abundant and imperturbable—had included some glance at the way death brings into relief even the faintest things that have preceded it; on which I felt myself suddenly as restless as if I had grown afraid of him. I got up to ring for tea; he went on talking—talking about Maud-Evelyn and what she had been for him; and when the servant had come up I prolonged, nervously, on purpose, the order I had wished to give. It made time, and I could speak to the footman sufficiently without thinking: what I thought of really was the risk of turning right round with a little outbreak. The temptation was strong; the same influences that had worked for my companion just worked, in their way, during that minute or two, for me. *Should* I, taking him unaware, flash at him a plain "I say, just settle it for me once for all. *Are* you the boldest and basest of fortune-hunters, or have you only, more innocently and perhaps more pleasantly, suffered your brain slightly to soften?" But I missed the chance—which I didn't in fact afterwards regret. My servant went out, and I faced again to my visitor, who continued to converse. I met his eyes once more, and their effect was repeated. If anything had happened to his brain this effect was perhaps the domination of the madman's stare. Well, he was the easiest and gentlest of madmen. By the time the footman came back with tea I was in for it; I was in for everything. By "everything" I mean my whole subsequent treatment of the case. It *was*—the case was—really beautiful. So, like all the rest, the hour comes back to me: the sound of the wind and the rain; the look of the empty, ugly, cabless square and of the stormy spring light; the way that, uninterrupted and absorbed, we had tea together by my fire. So it was that he found me receptive and that I found myself able to look merely grave and kind when he said, for example: "Her father and mother, you know, really, that first day—the day they picked me up on the Splügen—recognised me as the proper one."

"The proper one?"

"To make their son-in-law. They wanted her so," he went on, "to have had, don't you know, just everything."

"Well, if she did have it"—I tried to be cheerful—"isn't the whole thing then all right?"

"Oh, it's all right *now*," he replied—"now that we've got it all there before us. You see, they couldn't like me so much"—he wished me thoroughly to understand—"without wanting me to have been the man."

"I see—that was natural."

"Well," said Marmaduke, "it prevented the possibility of any one else."

"Ah, that would never have done!" I laughed.

His own pleasure at it was impenetrable, splendid. "You see, they couldn't do much, the old people—and they can do still less now—with the future; so they had to do what they could with the past."

"And they seem to have done," I concurred, "remarkably much."

"Everything, simply. Everything," he repeated. Then he had an idea, though without insistence or importunity—I noticed it just flicker in his face. "If you *were* to come to Westbourne Terrace——."

"Oh, don't speak of that!" I broke in. "It wouldn't be decent now. I should have come, if at all, ten years ago."

But he saw, with his good humour, further than this. "I see what you mean. But there's much more in the place now than then."

"I daresay. People get new things. All the same——!" I was at bottom but resisting my curiosity.

Marmaduke didn't press me, but he wanted me to know. "There are our rooms—the whole set; and I don't believe you ever saw anything more charming, for *her* taste was extraordinary. I'm afraid too that I myself have had much to say to them." Then as he made out that I was again a little at sea, "I'm talking," he went on, "of the suite prepared for her marriage." He "talked" like a crown prince. "They were ready, to the last touch—there was nothing more to be done. And they're just as they were—not an object moved, not an arrangement altered, not a person but ourselves coming in: they're only exquisitely kept. All our presents are there—I should have liked you to see them."

It had become a torment by this time—I saw that I had made a mistake. But I carried it off. "Oh, I couldn't have borne it!"

"They're not sad," he smiled—"they're too lovely to be sad. They're happy. And the things——!" He seemed, in the excitement of our talk, to have them before him.

"They're so very wonderful?"

"Oh, selected with a patience that makes them almost priceless. It's really a museum. There was nothing they thought too good for her."

I had lost the museum, but I reflected that it could contain no object so rare as my visitor. "Well, you've helped them—you could do *that*."

He quite eagerly assented. "I could do that, thank God—I could do that! I felt it from the first, and it's what I *have* done." Then as if the connexion were direct: "All *my* things are there."

I thought a moment. "Your presents?"

"Those I made her. She loved each one, and I remember about each the particular thing she said. Though I do say it," he continued, "none of the others, as a matter of fact, come near mine. I look at them every day, and I assure you I'm not ashamed." Evidently, in short, he had spared nothing, and he talked on and on. He really quite swaggered.

VIII

In relation to times and intervals I can only recall that if this visit of his to me had been in the early spring it was one day in the late autumn—a day, which couldn't have been in the same year, with the difference of hazy, drowsy sunshine and brown and yellow leaves—that, taking a short-cut across Kensington Gardens, I came, among the untrodden ways, upon a couple occupying chairs under a tree, who immediately rose at the sight of me. I had been behind them at recognition, the fact that Marmaduke was in deep mourning having perhaps, so far as I had observed it, misled me. In my desire both not to look flustered at meeting them and to spare their own confusion I bade them again be seated and asked leave, as a third chair was at hand, to share a little their rest. Thus it befell that after a minute Lavinia and I had sat down, while our friend, who had looked at his watch, stood before us among the fallen foliage and remarked that he was sorry to have to leave us. Lavinia said nothing, but I expressed regret; I couldn't, however, as it struck me, without a false or a vulgar note speak as if I had interrupted a tender passage or separated a pair of lovers. But I could look him up and down, take in his deep mourning. He had not made, for going off, any other pretext than that his time was up and that he was due at home. "Home," with him now, had but one meaning: I knew him to be completely quartered in Westbourne Terrace. "I hope nothing has happened," I said—"that you've lost no one whom *I* know."

Marmaduke looked at my companion, and she looked at Marmaduke. "He has lost his wife," she then observed.

Oh, this time, I fear, I had a small quaver of brutality; but it was at him I directed it. "Your wife? I didn't know you had *had* a wife!"

"Well," he replied, positively gay in his black suit, his black gloves, his high hatband, "the more we live in the past, the more things we find in it. That's a literal fact. You would see the truth of it if your life had taken such a turn."

"*I* live in the past," Lavinia put in gently and as if to help us both.

"But with the result, my dear," I returned, "of not making, I hope, such extraordinary discoveries!" It seemed absurd to be afraid to be light.

"May none of her discoveries be more fatal than mine!" Marmaduke wasn't uproarious, but his treatment of the matter had the good taste of simplicity. "They've wanted it so for her," he continued to me wonderfully, "that we've at last seen our way to it—I mean to what Lavinia has mentioned." He hesitated but three seconds—he brought it brightly out. "Maud-Evelyn had *all* her young happiness."

I stared, but Lavinia was, in her peculiar manner, as brilliant. "The marriage *did* take place," she quietly, stupendously explained to me.

Well, I was determined not to be left. "So you're a widower," I gravely asked, "and these are the signs?"

"Yes; I shall wear them always now."

"But isn't it late to have begun?"

My question had been stupid, I felt the next instant; but it didn't matter—he was quite equal to the occasion. "Oh, I had to wait, you know, till all the facts about my marriage had given me the right." And he looked at his watch again. "Excuse me—I *am* due. Good-bye, good-bye." He shook hands with each of us, and as we sat there together watching him walk away I was struck with his admirable manner of looking the character. I felt indeed as our eyes followed him that we were at one on this, and I said nothing till he was out of sight. Then by the same impulse we turned to each other.

"I thought he was never to marry!" I exclaimed to my friend.

Her fine wasted face met me gravely. "He isn't—ever. He'll be still more faithful."

"Faithful this time to whom?"

"Why, to Maud-Evelyn." I said nothing—I only checked an ejaculation; but I put out a hand and took one of hers, and for a minute we kept silence. "Of course it's only an idea," she began again at last, "but it seems to me a beautiful one." Then she continued resignedly and remarkably: "And now *they* can die."

"Mr. and Mrs. Dedrick?" I pricked up my ears. "Are they dying?"

"Not quite, but the old lady, it appears, is failing, steadily weakening; less, as I understand it, from any definite ailment than because she just feels her work done and her little sum of passion, as Marmaduke calls it, spent. Fancy, with her convictions, all her reasons for wanting to die! And if she goes, he says, Mr. Dedrick won't long linger. It will be quite 'John Anderson my jo.' "

"Keeping her company down the hill, to lie beside her at the foot?"

"Yes, having settled all things."

I turned these things over as we walked away, and how they had settled them—for Maud-Evelyn's dignity and Marmaduke's high advantage; and before we parted that afternoon—we had taken a cab in the Bayswater Road and she had come home with me—I remember saying to her: "Well then, when they die won't he be free?"

She seemed scarce to understand. "Free?"

"To do what he likes."

She wondered. "But he does what he likes now."

"Well then, what *you* like!"

"Oh, you know what *I* like——!"

Ah, I closed her mouth! "You like to tell horrid fibs—yes, I know it!"

What she had then put before me, however, came in time to pass: I heard in the course of the next year of Mrs. Dedrick's extinction, and some months later, without, during the interval, having seen a sign of Marmaduke, wholly taken up with his bereaved patron, learned that her husband had touchingly followed her. I was out of England at the time; we had had to put into practice great economies and let our little place; so that, spending three winters successively in Italy, I devoted the periods between, at home, altogether to visits among people, mainly relatives, to whom these friends of mine were not known. Lavinia of course wrote to me—wrote, among many things, that Marmaduke was ill and had not seemed at all himself since the loss of his "family," and this in spite of the circumstance, which she had already promptly communicated, that they had left him, by will, "almost everything." I knew before I came back to remain that she now saw him often and, to the extent of the change that had overtaken his strength and his spirits, greatly ministered to him. As soon as we at last met I asked for news of him; to which she replied: "He's gradually going." Then on my surprise: "He has had his life."

"You mean that, as he said of Mrs. Dedrick, his sum of passion is spent?"

At this she turned away. "You've never understood."

I *had*, I conceived; and when I went subsequently to see him I was moreover sure. But I only said to Lavinia on this first occasion that I would immediately go; which was precisely what brought out the climax, as I feel it to be, of my story. "He's not now, you know," she turned round to admonish me, "in Westbourne Terrace. He has taken a little old house in Kensington."

"Then he hasn't kept the things?"

"He has kept everything." She looked at me still more as if I had never understood.

"You mean he has moved them?"

She was patient with me. "He has moved nothing. Everything is as it was, and kept with the same perfection."

I wondered. "But if he doesn't live there?"

"It's just what he does."

"Then how can he be in Kensington?"

She hesitated, but she had still more than her old grasp of it. "He's in Kensington—without living."

"You mean that at the other place——?"

"Yes, he spends most of his time. He's driven over there every day—he remains there for hours. He keeps it for that."

"I see—it's still the museum."

"It's still the temple!" Lavinia replied with positive austerity.

"Then why did he move?"

"Because, you see, there"—she faltered again—"I could come to him. And he wants me," she said with admirable simplicity.

Little by little I took it in. "After the death of the parents, even, you never went?"

"Never."

"So you haven't seen anything?"

"Anything of hers? Nothing."

I understood, oh perfectly; but I won't deny that I was disappointed: I had hoped for an account of his wonders and I immediately felt that it wouldn't be for me to take a step that she had declined. When, a short time later, I saw them together in Kensington Square—there were certain hours of the day that she regularly spent with him—I observed that everything about him was new, handsome and simple. They were, in their strange, final union—if union it could be called—very natural and very touching; but he was visibly stricken—he had his ailment in his eyes. She moved about him like a sister of charity—at all events like a sister. He was neither robust nor rosy now, nor was his attention visibly very present, and I privately and fancifully asked myself where it wandered and waited. But poor Marmaduke was a gentleman to the end—he wasted away with an excellent manner. He died twelve days ago; the will was opened; and last week, having meanwhile heard from her of its contents, I saw Lavinia. He leaves her everything that he himself had inherited. But she spoke of it all in a way that caused me to say in surprise: "You haven't yet been to the house?"

"Not yet. I've only seen the solicitors, who tell me there will be no complications."

There was something in her tone that made me ask more. "Then you're not curious to see what's there?"

She looked at me with a troubled—almost a pleading—sense, which I understood; and presently she said: "Will you go with me?"

"Some day, with pleasure—but not the first time. You must go alone then. The 'relics' that you'll find there," I added—for I had read her look—"you must think of now not as hers——"

"But as his?"

"Isn't that what his death—with his so close relation to them—has made them for you?"

Her face lighted—I saw it was a view she could thank me for putting into words. "I see—I see. They *are* his. I'll go."

She went, and three days ago she came to me. They're really marvels, it appears, treasures extraordinary, and she has them all. Next week I go with her—I shall see them at last. Tell *you* about them, you say? My dear man, everything.

1900

The Jolly Corner

This story grew from a suggestion to James that he follow up his tale "The Turn of the Screw" by writing an international ghost story. It was first published in *The English Review* for December 1908, then included in the New York Edition, Vol. XVII, with a group of stories dealing with apparitional experiences and psychic states. James had returned to America in 1904 after twenty years in Europe. In his effort to re-orient himself to his home country, he wrote *The American Scene*, traveling and lecturing to gather material for it. He wandered through Washington Square, his old neighborhood, and his thoughts suggested a story which would reverse the "international theme" of his earlier fiction, but with a psychological treatment. Some critics see in the story a reflection of buried elements in James's own psychic life. In theme, it is related to James's novel *The Sense of the Past*, in which a young American finds himself at night in his ancestral home in England, his identity exchanged for that of a forebear whose portrait he had admired. The text used here is that of the New York Edition.

I

"Every one asks me what I 'think' of everything," said Spencer Brydon; "and I make answer as I can—begging or dodging the question, putting them off with any nonsense. It wouldn't matter to any of them really," he went on, "for, even were it possible to meet in that stand-and-deliver way so silly a demand on so big a subject, my 'thoughts' would still be almost altogether about something that concerns only myself." He was talking to Miss Staverton, with whom for a couple of months now he had availed himself of every possible occasion to talk; this disposition and this resource, this comfort and support, as the situation in fact presented itself, having promptly enough taken the first place in the considerable array of rather unattenuated surprises attending his so strangely belated return to America. Everything was somehow a surprise; and that might be natural when one had so long and so consistently neglected everything, taken pains to give surprises so much margin for play. He had given them more than thirty years—thirty-three, to be exact; and they now seemed to him to have organised their performance quite on the scale of that licence. He had been twenty-three on leaving New York—he was fifty-six to-day: unless indeed he were to reckon as he had sometimes, since his repatriation, found himself feeling; in which case he would have lived longer than is often allotted to man. It would have taken a century, he repeatedly said to himself, and said also to Alice Staverton, it would have taken a longer absence and a more averted mind than those even of which he had been guilty, to pile up the differences, the newnesses, the queernesses, above all the bignesses, for the better or the worse, that at present assaulted his vision wherever he looked.

The great fact all the while however had been the incalculability; since he *had* supposed himself, from decade to decade, to be allowing, and in the most liberal and intelligent manner, for brilliancy of change. He actually saw that he had allowed for nothing; he missed what he would have been sure of finding, he found what he would never have imagined. Proportions and values were upside-down; the ugly things he had expected, the ugly things of his far-away youth, when he had too promptly waked up to a sense of the ugly—these uncanny phenomena placed him rather, as it happened, under the charm; whereas the "swagger" things, the modern, the monstrous, the famous things, those he had more particularly, like thousands of ingenuous enquirers every year, come over to see, were exactly his sources of dismay. They were as so many set traps for displeasure, above all for reaction, of which his restless tread was constantly pressing the spring. It was interesting, doubtless, the whole show, but it would have been too disconcerting hadn't a certain finer truth saved the situation. He had distinctly not, in this steadier light, come over *all* for the monstrosities; he had come, not only in the last analysis but quite on the face of the act, under an impulse with which they had nothing to do. He had come—putting the thing pompously—to look at his "property," which he had thus for a third of a century not been within four thousand miles of; or, expressing it less sordidly, he had yielded to the humour of seeing again his house on the jolly corner, as he usually, and quite fondly, described it—the one in which he had first seen the light, in which various members of his family had lived and had died, in which the holidays of his overschooled boyhood had been passed and the few social flowers of his chilled adolescence gathered, and which, alienated then for so long a period, had, through the successive deaths of his two brothers and the termination of old arrangements, come wholly into his hands. He was the owner of another, not quite so "good"—the jolly corner having been, from far back, superlatively extended and consecrated; and the value of the pair represented his main capital, with an income consisting, in these later years, of their respective rents which (thanks precisely to their original excellent type) had never been depressingly low. He could live in "Europe," as he had been in the habit of living, on the product of these flourishing New York leases, and all the better since, that of the second structure, the mere number in its long row, having within a twelvemonth fallen in, renovation at a high advance had proved beautifully possible.

These were items of property indeed, but he had found himself since his arrival distinguishing more than ever between them. The house within the street, two bristling blocks westward, was already in course of reconstruction as a tall mass of flats; he had acceded, some time before, to overtures for this conversion—in which, now that it was going forward, it had been not the least of his astonishments to find himself able, on the spot, and though without a previous ounce of such experience, to participate with a certain intelligence, almost with a certain authority. He had lived his life with his back so turned to such concerns and his face addressed to those of so different an order that he scarce knew what to make of this lively stir, in a compartment of his mind never yet penetrated, of a capacity for business and a sense for construction. These virtues, so common all round him now, had been dormant in his own organism—where it might be said of them perhaps that they had slept the sleep of the just. At present, in the splendid autumn weather—the autumn at least was a pure boon in the terrible place—he loafed about his "work" undeterred, secretly agitated; not in the least "minding" that the whole proposition, as they said, was vulgar and sordid, and ready to climb ladders, to walk the plank, to handle materials and look wise about them, to ask questions, in fine, and challenge explanations and really "go into" figures.

It amused, it verily quite charmed him; and, by the same stroke, it amused, and even more, Alice Staverton, though perhaps charming her perceptibly less. She wasn't however going to be better-off for it, as *he* was—and so astonishingly much: nothing was now likely, he knew, ever to make her better-off than she found herself, in the afternoon of life, as the delicately frugal possessor and tenant of the small house in Irving Place to which she had subtly managed to cling through her almost unbroken New York career. If he knew the way to it now better than to any other address among the dreadful multiplied numberings which seemed to him to reduce the whole place to some vast ledger-page, overgrown, fantastic, of ruled and criss-crossed lines and figures—if he had formed, for his consolation, that habit, it was really not a little because of the charm of his having encountered and recognised, in the vast wilderness of the wholesale, breaking through the mere gross generalisation of wealth and force and success, a small still scene where items and shades, all delicate things, kept the sharpness of the notes of a high voice perfectly trained, and where economy hung about like the scent of a garden. His old friend lived with one maid and herself dusted her relics and trimmed her lamps and polished her silver; she stood off, in the awful modern crush, when she could, but she sallied forth and did battle when the challenge was really to "spirit," the spirit she after all confessed to, proudly and a little shyly, as to that of the better time, that of *their* common, their quite far-away and antediluvian social period and order. She made use of the street-cars when need be, the terrible things that people scrambled for as the panic-stricken at sea scramble for the boats; she affronted, inscrutably, under stress, all the public concussions and ordeals; and yet, with that slim mystifying grace of her appearance, which defied you to say if she were a fair young woman who looked older through trouble, or a fine smooth older one who looked young through successful indifference; with her precious reference, above all, to memories and histories into which he could enter, she was as exquisite for him as some pale pressed flower (a rarity to begin with), and, failing other sweetnesses, she was a sufficient reward of his effort. They had communities of knowledge, "their" knowledge (this discriminating possessive was always on her lips) of presences of the other age, presences all overlaid, in his case, by the experience of a man and the freedom of a wanderer, overlaid by pleasure, by infidelity, by passages of life that were strange and dim to her, just by "Europe" in short, but still unobscured, still exposed and cherished, under that pious visitation of the spirit from which she had never been diverted.

She had come with him one day to see how his "apartment-house" was rising; he had helped her over gaps and explained to her plans, and while they were there had happened to have, before her, a brief but lively discussion with the man in charge, the representative of the building-firm that had undertaken his work. He had found himself quite "standing-up" to this personage over a failure on the latter's part to observe some detail of one of their noted conditions, and had so lucidly argued his case that, besides ever so prettily flushing, at the time, for sympathy in his triumph, she had afterwards said to him (though to a slightly greater effect of irony) that he had clearly for too many years neglected a real gift. If he had but stayed at home he would have anticipated the inventor of the sky-scraper. If he had but stayed at home he would have discovered his genius in time really to start some new variety of awful architectural hare and run it till it burrowed in a gold-mine. He was to remember these words, while the weeks elapsed, for the small silver ring they had sounded over the queerest and deepest of his own lately most disguised and most muffled vibrations.

It had begun to be present to him after the first fortnight, it had broken out with the oddest abruptness, this particular wanton wonderment: it met him there—and this was the image under which he himself judged the matter, or at least, not a little, thrilled and flushed with it—very much as he might have been met by some strange figure, some unexpected occupant, at a turn of one of the dim passages of an empty house. The quaint analogy quite hauntingly remained with him, when he didn't indeed rather improve it by a still intenser form: that of his opening a door behind which he would have made sure of finding nothing, a door into a room shuttered and void, and yet so coming, with a great suppressed start, on some quite erect confronting presence, something planted in the middle of the place and facing him through the dusk. After that visit to the house in construction he walked with his companion to see the other and always so much the better one, which in the eastward direction formed one of the corners, the "jolly" one precisely, of the street now so generally dishonoured and disfigured in its westward reaches, and of the comparatively conservative Avenue. The Avenue still had pretensions, as Miss Staverton said, to decency; the old people had mostly gone, the old names were unknown, and here and there an old association seemed to stray, all vaguely, like some very aged person, out too late, whom you might meet and feel the impulse to watch or follow, in kindness, for safe restoration to shelter.

They went in together, our friends; he admitted himself with his key, as he kept no one there, he explained, preferring, for his reasons, to leave the place empty, under a simple arrangement with a good woman living in the neighbourhood and who came for a daily hour to open windows and dust and sweep. Spencer Brydon had his reasons and was growingly aware of them; they seemed to him better each time he was there, though he didn't name them all to his companion, any more than he told her as yet how often, how quite absurdly often, he himself came. He only let her see for the present, while they walked through the great blank rooms, that absolute vacancy reigned and that, from top to bottom, there was nothing but Mrs. Muldoon's broomstick, in a corner, to tempt the burglar. Mrs. Muldoon was then on the premises, and she loquaciously attended the visitors, preceding them from room to room and pushing back shutters and throwing up sashes—all to show them, as she remarked, how little there was to see. There was little indeed to see in the great gaunt shell where the main dispositions and the general apportionment of space, the style of an age of ampler allowances, had nevertheless for its master their honest pleading message, affecting him as some good old servant's, some lifelong retainer's appeal for a character, or even for a retiring-pension; yet it was also a remark of Mrs. Muldoon's that, glad as she was to oblige him by her noonday round, there was a request she greatly hoped he would never make of her. If he should wish her for any reason to come in after dark she would just tell him, if he "plased," that he must ask it of somebody else.

The fact that there was nothing to see didn't militate for the worthy woman against what one *might* see, and she put it frankly to Miss Staverton that no lady could be expected to like, could she? "craping up to thim top storeys in the ayvil hours." The gas and the electric light were off the house, and she fairly evoked a gruesome vision of her march through the great grey rooms—so many of them as there were too!—with her glimmering taper. Miss Staverton met her honest glare with a smile and the profession that she herself certainly would recoil from such an adventure. Spencer Brydon meanwhile held his peace—for the moment; the question of the "evil" hours in his old home had already become too grave for him. He had begun some time since to "crape," and he knew just why a packet of candles addressed to that pursuit had been stowed by his own hand, three weeks before, at the back of a drawer of the fine old sideboard that occupied, as a "fixture," the deep recess in the dining-room. Just now he laughed at his companions—quickly however changing the subject; for the reason that, in the first place, his laugh struck him even at that moment as starting the odd echo, the conscious human resonance (he scarce knew how to qualify it) that sounds made while he was there alone sent back to his ear or his fancy; and that, in the second, he imagined Alice Staverton for the instant on the point of asking him, with a divination, if he ever so prowled. There were divinations he was unprepared for, and he had at all events averted enquiry by the time Mrs. Muldoon had left them, passing on to other parts.

There was happily enough to say, on so consecrated a spot, that could be said freely and fairly; so that a whole train of declarations was precipitated by his friend's having herself broken out, after a yearning look round: "But I hope you don't mean they want you to pull *this* to pieces!" His answer came, promptly, with his re-awakened wrath: it was of course exactly what they wanted, and what they were "at" him for, daily, with the iteration of people who couldn't for their life understand a man's liability to decent feelings. He had found the place, just as it stood and beyond what he could express, an interest and a joy. There were values other than the beastly rent-values, and in short, in short—! But it was thus Miss Staverton took him up. "In short you're to make so good a thing of your sky-scraper that, living in luxury on *those* ill-gotten gains, you can afford for a while to be sentimental here!" Her smile had for him, with the words, the particular mild irony with which he found half her talk suffused; an irony without bitterness and that came, exactly, from her having so much imagination—not, like the cheap sarcasms with which one heard most people, about the world of "society," bid for the reputation of cleverness, from nobody's really having any. It was agreeable to him at this very moment to be sure that when he had answered, after a brief demur, "Well yes: so, precisely, you may put it!" her imagination would still do him justice. He explained that even if never a dollar were to come to him from the other house he would nevertheless cherish this one; and he dwelt, further, while they lingered and wandered, on the fact of the stupefaction he was already exciting, the positive mystification he felt himself create.

He spoke of the value of all he read into it, into the mere sight of the walls, mere shapes of the rooms, mere sound of the floors, mere feel, in his hand, of the old silver-plated knobs of the several mahogany doors, which suggested the pressure of the palms of the dead; the seventy years of the past in fine that these things represented, the annals of nearly three generations, counting his grandfather's, the one that had ended there, and the impalpable ashes of his long-extinct youth, afloat in the very air like microscopic motes. She listened to everything; she was a woman who answered intimately but who utterly didn't chatter. She scattered abroad therefore no cloud of words; she could assent, she could agree, above all she could encourage, without doing that. Only at the last she went a little further than he had done himself. "And then how do you know? You may still, after all, want to live here." It rather indeed pulled him up, for it wasn't what he had been thinking, at least in her sense of the words. "You mean I may decide to stay on for the sake of it?"

"Well, *with* such a home—!" But, quite beautifully, she had too much tact to dot so monstrous an *i*, and it was precisely an illustration of the way she didn't rattle. How could any one—of any wit—insist on any one else's "wanting" to live in New York?

"Oh," he said, "I *might* have lived here (since I had my opportunity early in life); I might have put in here all these years. Then everything would have been different enough—and, I dare say, 'funny' enough. But that's another matter. And then the beauty of it—I mean of my perversity, of my refusal to agree to a 'deal'—is just in the total absence of a reason. Don't you see that if I had a reason about the matter at all it would *have* to be the other way, and would then be inevitably a reason of dollars? There are no reasons here *but* of dollars. Let us therefore have none whatever—not the ghost of one."

They were back in the hall then for departure, but from where they stood the vista was large, through an open door, into the great square main saloon, with its almost antique felicity of brave spaces between windows. Her eyes came back from that reach and met his own a moment. "Are you very sure the 'ghost' of one doesn't, much rather, serve—?"

He had a positive sense of turning pale. But it was as near as they were then to come. For he made answer, he believed, between a glare and a grin: "Oh ghosts—of course the place must swarm with them! I should be ashamed of it if it didn't. Poor Mrs. Muldoon's right, and it's why I haven't asked her to do more than look in."

Miss Staverton's gaze again lost itself, and things she didn't utter, it was clear, came and went in her mind. She might even for the minute, off there in the fine room, have imagined some element dimly gathering. Simplified like the death-mask of a handsome face, it perhaps produced for her just then an effect akin to the stir of an expression in the "set" commemorative plaster. Yet whatever her impression may have been she produced instead a vague platitude. "Well, if it were only furnished and lived in—!"

She appeared to imply that in case of its being still furnished he might have been a little less opposed to the idea of a return. But she passed straight into the vestibule, as if to leave her words behind her, and the next moment he had opened the house-door and was standing with her on the steps. He closed the door and, while he re-pocketed his key, looking up and down, they took in the comparatively harsh actuality of the Avenue, which reminded him of the assault of the outer light of the Desert on the traveller emerging from an Egyptian tomb. But he risked before they stepped into the street his gathered answer to her speech. "For me it *is* lived in. For me it *is* furnished." At which it was easy for her to sigh "Ah yes—!" all vaguely and discreetly; since his parents and his favourite sister, to say nothing of other kin, in numbers, had run their course and met their end there. That represented, within the walls, ineffaceable life.

It was a few days after this that, during an hour passed with her again, he had expressed his impatience of the too flattering curiosity—among the people he met—about his appreciation of New York. He had arrived at none at all that was socially producible, and as for that matter of his "thinking" (thinking the better or the worse of anything there) he was wholly taken up with one subject of thought. It was mere vain egoism, and it was moreover, if she liked, a morbid obsession. He found all things come back to the question of what he personally might have been, how he might have led his life and "turned out," if he had not so, at the outset, given it up. And confessing for the first time to the intensity within him of this absurd speculation—which but proved also, no doubt, the habit of too selfishly thinking—he affirmed the impotence there of any other source of interest, any other native appeal. "What would it have made of me, what would it have made of me? I keep for ever wondering, all idiotically; as if I could possibly know! I see what it has made of dozens of others, those I meet, and it positively aches within me, to the point of exasperation, that it would have made something of me as well. Only I can't make out *what*, and the worry of it, the small rage of curiosity never to be satisfied, brings back what I remember to have felt, once or twice, after judging best, for reasons, to burn some important letter unopened. I've been sorry, I've hated it—I've never known what was in the letter. You may of course say it's a trifle—!"

"I don't say it's a trifle," Miss Staverton gravely interrupted.

She was seated by her fire, and before her, on his feet and restless, he turned to and fro between this intensity of his idea and a fitful and unseeing inspection, through his single eye-glass, of the dear little old objects on her chimney-piece. Her interruption made him for an instant look at her harder. "I shouldn't care if you did!" he laughed, however; "and it's only a figure, at any rate, for the way I now feel. *Not* to have followed my perverse young course—and almost in the teeth of my father's curse, as I may say; not to have kept it up, so, 'over there,' from that day to this, without a doubt or a pang; not, above all, to have liked it, to have loved it, so much, loved it, no doubt, with such an abysmal conceit of my own preference: some variation from *that*, I say, must have produced some different effect for my life and for my 'form.' I should have stuck here—if it had been possible; and I was too young, at twenty-three, to judge, *pour deux sous*, whether it *were* possible. If I had waited I might have seen it was, and then I might have been, by staying here, something nearer to one of these types who have been hammered so hard and made so keen by their conditions. It isn't that I admire them so much—the question of any charm in them, or of any charm, beyond that of the rank money-passion, exerted by their conditions *for* them, has nothing to do with the matter: it's only a question of what fantastic, yet perfectly possible, development of my own nature I mayn't have missed. It comes over me that I had then a strange *alter ego* deep down somewhere within me, as the full-blown flower is in the small tight bud, and that I just took the course, I just transferred him to the climate, that blighted him for once and for ever."

"And you wonder about the flower," Miss Staverton said. "So do I, if you want to know; and so I've been wondering these several weeks. I believe in the flower," she continued, "I feel it would have been quite splendid, quite huge and monstrous."

"Monstrous above all!" her visitor echoed; "and I imagine, by the same stroke, quite hideous and offensive."

"You don't believe that," she returned; "if you did you wouldn't wonder. You'd know, and that would be enough for you. What you feel—and what I feel *for* you—is that you'd have had power."

"You'd have liked me that way?" he asked.

She barely hung fire. "How should I not have liked you?"

"I see. You'd have liked me, have preferred me, a billionaire!"

"How should I not have liked you?" she simply again asked.

He stood before her still—her question kept him motionless. He took it in, so much there was of it; and indeed his not otherwise meeting it testified to that. "I know at least what I am," he simply went on; "the other side of the medal's clear enough. I've not been edifying—I believe I'm thought in a hundred quarters to have been barely decent. I've followed strange paths and worshipped strange gods; it must have come to you again and again—in fact you've admitted to me as much—that I was leading, at any time these thirty years, a selfish frivolous scandalous life. And you see what it has made of me."

She just waited, smiling at him. "You see what it has made of *me*."

"Oh, you're a person whom nothing can have altered. You were born to be what you are, anywhere, anyway; you've the perfection nothing else could have blighted. And don't you see how, without my exile, I shouldn't have been waiting till now—?" But he pulled up for the strange pang.

"The great thing to see," she presently said, "seems to me to be that it has spoiled nothing. It hasn't spoiled your being here at last. It hasn't spoiled this. It hasn't spoiled your speaking—" She also however faltered.

He wondered at everything her controlled emotion might mean. "Do you believe then—too dreadfully!—that I *am* as good as I might ever have been?"

"Oh no! Far from it!" With which she got up from her chair and was nearer to him. "But I don't care," she smiled.

"You mean I'm good enough?"

She considered a little. "Will you believe it if I say so? I mean will you let that settle your question for you?" And then as if making out in his face that he drew back from this, that he had some idea which, however absurd, he couldn't yet bargain away: "Oh you don't care either—but very differently: you don't care for anything but yourself."

Spencer Brydon recognised it—it was in fact what he had absolutely professed. Yet he importantly qualified. "*He* isn't myself. He's the just so totally other person. But I do want to see him," he added. "And I can. And I shall."

Their eyes met for a minute while he guessed from something in hers that she divined his strange sense. But neither of them otherwise expressed it, and her apparent understanding, with no protesting shock, no easy derision, touched him more deeply than anything yet, constituting for his stifled perversity, on the spot, an element that was like breatheable air. What she said however was unexpected. "Well, *I've* seen him."

"You—?"

"I've seen him in a dream."

"Oh a 'dream'—!" It let him down.

"But twice over," she continued. "I saw him as I see you now."

"You've dreamed the same dream—?"

"Twice over," she repeated. "The very same."

This did somehow a little speak to him, as it also gratified him. "You dream about me at that rate?"

"Ah about *him!*" she smiled.

His eyes again sounded her. "Then you know all about him." And as she said nothing more: "What's the wretch like?"

She hesitated, and it was as if he were pressing her so hard that, resisting for reasons of her own, she had to turn away. "I'll tell you some other time!"

II

It was after this that there was most of a virtue for him, most of a cultivated charm, most of a preposterous secret thrill, in the particular form of surrender to his obsession and of address to what he more and more believed to be his privilege. It was what in these weeks he was living for—since he really felt life to begin but after Mrs. Muldoon had retired from the scene and, visiting the ample house from attic to cellar, making sure he was alone, he knew himself in safe possession and, as he tacitly expressed it, let himself go. He sometimes came twice in the twenty-four hours; the moments he liked best were those of gathering dusk, of the short autumn twilight; this was the time of which, again and again, he found himself hoping most. Then he could, as seemed to him, most intimately wander and wait, linger and listen, feel his fine attention, never in his life before so fine, on the pulse of the great vague place: he preferred the lampless hour and only wished he might have prolonged each day the deep crepuscular spell. Later—rarely much before midnight, but then for a considerable vigil—he watched with his glimmering light; moving slowly, holding it high, playing it far, rejoicing above all, as much as he might, in open vistas, reaches of communication between rooms and by passages; the long straight chance or show, as he would have called it, for the revelation he pretended to invite. It was a practice he found he could perfectly "work" without exciting remark; no one was in the least the wiser for it; even Alice Staverton, who was moreover a well of discretion, didn't quite fully imagine.

He let himself in and let himself out with the assurance of calm proprietorship; and accident so far favoured him that, if a fat Avenue "officer" had happened on occasion to see him entering at eleven-thirty, he had never yet, to the best of his belief, been noticed as emerging at two. He walked there on the crisp November nights, arrived regularly at the evening's end; it was as easy to do this after dining out as to take his way to a club or to his hotel. When he left his club, if he hadn't been dining out, it was ostensibly to go to his hotel; and when he left his hotel, if he had spent a part of the evening there, it was ostensibly to go to his club. Everything was easy in fine; everything conspired and promoted: there was truly even in the strain of his experience something that glossed over, something that salved and simplified, all the rest of consciousness. He circulated, talked, renewed, loosely and pleasantly, old relations—met indeed, so far as he could, new expectations and seemed to make out on the whole that in spite of the career, of such different contacts, which he had spoken of to Miss Staverton as ministering so little, for those who might have watched it, to edification, he was positively rather liked than not. He was a dim secondary social success—and all with people who had truly not an idea of him. It was all mere surface sound, this murmur of their welcome, this popping of their corks—just as his gestures of response were the extravagant shadows, emphatic in proportion as they meant little, of some game of *ombres chinoises.* He projected himself all day, in thought, straight over the bristling line of hard unconscious heads and into the other, the real, the waiting life; the life that, as soon as he had heard behind him the click of his great house-door, began for him, on the jolly corner, as beguilingly as the slow opening bars of some rich music follows the tap of the conductor's wand.

He always caught the first effect of the steel point of his stick on the old marble of the hall pavement, large black-and-white squares that he remembered as the admiration of his childhood and that had then made in him, as he now saw, for the growth of an early conception of style. This effect was the dim reverberating tinkle as of some far-off bell hung who should say where?—in the depths of the house, of the past, of that mystical other world that might have flourished for him had he not, for weal or woe, abandoned it. On this impression he did ever the same thing; he put his stick noiselessly away in a corner—feeling the place once more in the likeness of some great glass bowl, all precious concave crystal, set delicately humming by the play of a moist finger round its edge. The concave crystal held, as it were, this mystical other world, and the indescribably fine murmur of its rim was the sigh there, the scarce audible pathetic wail to his strained ear, of all the old baffled forsworn possibilities. What he did therefore by this appeal of his hushed presence was to wake them into such measure of ghostly life as they might still enjoy. They were shy, all but unappeasably shy, but they weren't really sinister; at least they weren't as he had hitherto felt them—before they had taken the Form he so yearned to make them take, the Form he at moments saw himself in the light of fairly hunting on tiptoe, the points of his evening-shoes, from room to room and from storey to storey.

That was the essence of his vision—which was all rank folly, if one would, while he was out of the house and otherwise occupied, but which took on the last verisimilitude as soon as he was placed and posted. He knew what he meant and what he wanted; it was as clear as the figure on a cheque presented in demand for cash. His *alter ego* "walked"—that was the note of his image of him, while his image of his motive for his own odd pastime was the desire to waylay him and meet him. He roamed, slowly, warily, but all restlessly, he himself did—Mrs. Muldoon had been right, absolutely, with her figure of their "craping"; and the presence he watched for would roam restlessly too. But it would be as cautious and as shifty; the conviction of its probable, in fact its already quite sensible, quite audible evasion of pursuit grew for him from night to night, laying on him finally a rigour to which nothing in his life had been comparable. It had been the theory of many superficially-judging persons, he knew, that he was wasting that life in a surrender to sensations, but he had tasted of no pleasure so fine as his actual tension, had been introduced to no sport that demanded at once the patience and the nerve of this stalking of a creature more subtle, yet at bay perhaps more formidable, than any beast of the forest. The terms, the comparisons, the very practices of the chase positively came again into play; there were even moments when passages of his occasional experience as a sportsman, stirred memories, from his younger time, of moor and mountain and desert, revived for him—and to the increase of his keenness—by the tremendous force of analogy. He found himself at moments—once he had placed his single light on some mantel-shelf or in some recess—stepping back into shelter or shade, effacing himself behind a door or in an embrasure, as he had sought of old the vantage of rock and tree; he found himself holding his breath and living in the joy of the instant, the supreme suspense created by big game alone.

He wasn't afraid (though putting himself the question as he believed gentlemen on Bengal tiger-shoots or in close quarters with the great bear of the Rockies had been known to confess to having put it); and this indeed—since here at least he might be frank!—because of the impression, so intimate and so strange, that he himself produced as yet a dread, produced certainly a strain, beyond the liveliest he was likely to feel. They fell for him into categories, they fairly became familiar, the signs, for his own perception, of the alarm his presence and his vigilance created; though leaving him always to remark, portentously, on his probably having formed a relation, his probably enjoying a consciousness, unique in the experience of man. People enough, first and last, had been in terror of apparitions, but who had ever before so turned the tables and become himself, in the apparitional world, an incalculable terror? He might have found this sublime had he quite dared to think of it; but he didn't too much insist, truly, on that side of his privilege. With habit and repetition he gained to an extraordinary degree the power to penetrate the dusk of distances and the darkness of corners, to resolve back into their innocence the treacheries of uncertain light, the evil-looking forms taken in the gloom by mere shadows, by accidents of the air, by shifting effects of perspective; putting down his dim luminary he could still wander on without it, pass into other rooms and, only knowing it was there behind him in case of need, see his way about, visually project for his purpose a comparative clearness. It made him feel, this acquired faculty, like some monstrous stealthy cat; he wondered if he would have glared at these moments with large shining yellow eyes, and what it mightn't verily be, for the poor hard-pressed *alter ego*, to be confronted with such a type.

He liked however the open shutters; he opened everywhere those Mrs. Muldoon had closed, closing them as carefully afterwards, so that she shouldn't notice: he liked—oh this he did like, and above all in the upper rooms!—the sense of the hard silver of the autumn stars through the window-panes, and scarcely less the flare of the street-lamps below, the white electric lustre which it would have taken curtains to keep out. This was human actual social; this was of the world he had lived in, and he was more at his ease certainly for the countenance, coldly general and impersonal, that all the while and in spite of his detachment it seemed to give him. He had support of course mostly in the rooms at the wide front and the prolonged side; it failed him considerably in the central shades and the parts at the back. But if he sometimes, on his rounds, was glad of his optical reach, so none the less often the rear of the house affected him as the very jungle of his prey. The place was there more subdivided; a large "extension" in particular, where small rooms for servants had been multiplied, abounded in nooks and corners, in closets and passages, in the ramifications especially of an ample back staircase over which he leaned, many a time, to look far down—not deterred from his gravity even while aware that he might, for a spectator, have figured some solemn simpleton playing at hide-and-seek. Outside in fact he might himself make that ironic *rapprochement;* but within the walls, and in spite of the clear windows, his consistency was proof against the cynical light of New York.

It had belonged to that idea of the exasperated consciousness of his victim to become a real test for him; since he had quite put it to himself from the first that, oh distinctly! he could "cultivate" his whole perception. He had felt it as above all open to cultivation—which indeed was but another name for his manner of spending his time. He was bringing it on, bringing it to perfection, by practice; in consequence of which it had grown so fine that he was now aware of impressions, attestations of his general postulate, that couldn't have broken upon him at once. This was the case more specifically with a phenomenon at last quite frequent for him in the upper rooms, the recognition—absolutely unmistakeable, and by a turn dating from a particular hour, his resumption of his campaign after a diplomatic drop, a calculated absence of three nights—of his being definitely followed, tracked at a distance carefully taken and to the express end that he should the less confidently, less arrogantly, appear to himself merely to pursue. It worried, it finally quite broke him up, for it proved, of all the conceivable impressions, the one least suited to his book. He was kept in sight while remaining himself—as regards the essence of his position—sightless, and his only recourse then was in abrupt turns, rapid recoveries of ground. He wheeled about, retracing his steps, as if he might so catch in his face at least the stirred air of some other quick revolution. It was indeed true that his fully dislocalised thought of these manoeuvres recalled to him Pantaloon, at the Christmas farce, buffeted and tricked from behind by ubiquitous Harlequin; but it left intact the influence of the conditions themselves each time he was re-exposed to them, so that in fact this association, had he suffered it to become constant, would on a certain side have but ministered to his intenser gravity. He had made, as I have said, to create on the premises the baseless sense of a reprieve, his three absences; and the result of the third was to confirm the after-effect of the second.

On his return, that night—the night succeeding his last intermission—he stood in the hall and looked up the staircase with a certainty more intimate than any he had yet known. "He's *there,* at the top, and waiting—not, as in general, falling back for disappearance. He's holding his ground, and it's the first time—which is a proof, isn't it? that something has happened for him." So Brydon argued with his hand on the banister and his foot on the lowest stair; in which position he felt as never before the air chilled by his logic. He himself turned cold in it, for he seemed of a sudden to know what now was involved. "Harder pressed?—yes, he takes it in, with its thus making clear to him that I've come, as they say, 'to stay.' He finally doesn't like and can't bear it, in the sense, I mean, that his wrath, his menaced interest, now balances with his dread. I've hunted him till he has 'turned': that, up there, is what has happened—he's the fanged or the antlered animal brought at last to bay." There came to him, as I say—but determined by an influence beyond my notation!—the acuteness of this certainty; under which however the next moment he had broken into a sweat that he would as little have consented to attribute to fear as he would have dared immediately to act upon it for enterprise. It marked none the less a prodigious thrill, a thrill that represented sudden dismay, no doubt, but also represented, and with the selfsame throb, the strangest, the most joyous, possibly the next minute almost the proudest, duplication of consciousness.

"He has been dodging, retreating, hiding, but now, worked up to anger, he'll fight!"—this intense impression made a single mouthful, as it were, of terror and applause. But what was wondrous was that the applause, for the felt fact, was so eager, since, if it was his other self he was running to earth, this ineffable identity was thus in the last resort not unworthy of him. It bristled there—somewhere near at hand, however unseen still—as the hunted thing, even as the trodden worm of the adage *must* at last bristle; and Brydon at this instant tasted probably of a sensation more complex than had ever before found itself consistent with sanity. It was as if it would have shamed him that a character so associated with his own should triumphantly succeed in just skulking, should to the end not risk the open; so that the drop of this danger was, on the spot, a great lift of the whole situation. Yet with another rare shift of the same subtlety he was already trying to measure by how much more he himself might now be in peril of fear; so rejoicing that he could, in another form, actively inspire that fear, and simultaneously quaking for the form in which he might passively know it.

The apprehension of knowing it must after a little have grown in him, and the strangest moment of his adventure perhaps, the most memorable or really most interesting, afterwards, of his crisis, was the lapse of certain instants of concentrated conscious *combat,* the sense of a need to hold on to something, even after the manner of a man slipping and slipping on some awful incline; the vivid impulse, above all, to move, to act, to charge, somehow and upon something—to show himself, in a word, that he wasn't afraid. The state of "holding-on" was thus the state to which he was momentarily reduced; if there had been anything, in the great vacancy, to seize, he would presently have been aware of having clutched it as he might under a shock at home have clutched the nearest chair-back. He had been surprised at any rate—of this he *was* aware—into something unprecedented since his original appropriation of the place; he had closed his eyes, held them tight, for a long minute, as with that instinct of dismay and that terror of vision. When he opened them the room, the other contiguous rooms, extraordinarily, seemed lighter—so light, almost, that at first he took the change for day. He stood firm, however that might be, just where he had paused; his resistance had helped him—it was as if there were something he had tided over. He knew after a little what this was—it had been in the imminent danger of flight. He had stiffened his will against going; without this he would have made for the stairs, and it seemed to him that, still with his eyes closed, he would have descended them, would have known how, straight and swiftly, to the bottom.

Well, as he had held out, here he was—still at the top, among the more intricate upper rooms and with the gauntlet of the others, of all the rest of the house, still to run when it should be his time to go. He would go at his time—only at his time: didn't he go every night very much at the same hour? He took out his watch—there was light for that: it was scarcely a quarter past one, and he had never withdrawn so soon. He reached his lodgings for the most part at two—with his walk of a quarter of an hour.

He would wait for the last quarter—he wouldn't stir till then; and he kept his watch there with his eyes on it, reflecting while he held it that this deliberate wait, a wait with an effort, which he recognised, would serve perfectly for the attestation he desired to make. It would prove his courage—unless indeed the latter might most be proved by his budging at last from his place. What he mainly felt now was that, since he hadn't originally scuttled, he had his dignities—which had never in his life seemed so many—all to preserve and to carry aloft. This was before him in truth as a physical image, an image almost worthy of an age of greater romance. That remark indeed glimmered for him only to glow the next instant with a finer light; since what age of romance, after all, could have matched either the state of his mind or, "objectively," as they said, the wonder of his situation? The only difference would have been that, brandishing his dignities over his head as in a parchment scroll, he might then—that is in the heroic time—have proceeded downstairs with a drawn sword in his other grasp.

At present, really, the light he had set down on the mantel of the next room would have to figure his sword; which utensil, in the course of a minute, he had taken the requisite number of steps to possess himself of. The door between the rooms was open, and from the second another door opened to a third. These rooms, as he remembered, gave all three upon a common corridor as well, but there was a fourth, beyond them, without issue save through the preceding. To have moved, to have heard his step again, was appreciably a help; though even in recognising this he lingered once more a little by the chimney-piece on which his light had rested. When he next moved, just hesitating where to turn, he found himself considering a circumstance that, after his first and comparatively vague apprehension of it, produced in him the start that often attends some pang of recollection, the violent shock of having ceased happily to forget. He had come into sight of the door in which the brief chain of communication ended and which he now surveyed from the nearer threshold, the one not directly facing it. Placed at some distance to the left of this point, it would have admitted him to the last room of the four, the room without other approach or egress, had it not, to his intimate conviction, been closed *since* his former visitation, the matter probably of a quarter of an hour before. He stared with all his eyes at the wonder of the fact, arrested again where he stood and again holding his breath while he sounded its sense. Surely it had been *subsequently* closed—that is it had been on his previous passage indubitably open!

He took it full in the face that something had happened between—that he couldn't not have noticed before (by which he meant on his original tour of all the rooms that evening) that such a barrier had exceptionally presented itself. He had indeed since that moment undergone an agitation so extraordinary that it might have muddled for him any earlier view; and he tried to convince himself that he might perhaps then have gone into the room and, inadvertently, automatically, on coming out, have drawn the door after him. The difficulty was that this exactly was what he never did; it was against his whole policy, as he might have said, the essence of which was to keep vistas clear. He had them from the first, as he was well aware, quite on the brain: the strange apparition, at the far end of one of them, of his baffled "prey" (which had become by so sharp an irony so little the term now to apply!) was the form of success his imagination had most cherished, projecting into it always a refinement of beauty. He had known fifty times the start of perception that had afterwards dropped; had fifty times gasped to himself "There!" under some fond brief hallucination. The house, as the case stood, admirably lent itself; he might wonder at the taste, the native architecture of the particular time, which could rejoice so in the multiplication of doors—the opposite extreme to the modern, the actual almost complete proscription of them; but it had fairly contributed to provoke this obsession of the presence encountered telescopically, as he might say, focussed and studied in diminishing perspective and as by a rest for the elbow.

It was with these considerations that his present attention was charged—they perfectly availed to make what he saw portentous. He *couldn't*, by any lapse, have blocked that aperture; and if he hadn't, if it was unthinkable, why what else was clear but that there had been another agent? Another agent?—he had been catching, as he felt, a moment back, the very breath of him; but when had he been so close as in this simple, this logical, this completely personal act? It was so logical, that is, that one might have *taken* it for personal; yet for what did Brydon take it, he asked himself, while, softly panting, he felt his eyes almost leave their sockets. Ah this time at last they *were*, the two, the opposed projections of him, in presence; and this time, as much as one would, the question of danger loomed. With it rose, as not before, the question of courage—for what he knew the blank face of the door to say to him was "Show us how much you have!" It stared, it glared back at him with that challenge; it put to him the two alternatives: should he just push it open or not? Oh to have this consciousness was to *think*—and to think, Brydon knew, as he stood there, was, with the lapsing moments, not to have acted! Not to have acted—that was the misery and the pang—was even still not to act; was in fact *all* to feel the thing in another, in a new and terrible way. How long did he pause and how long did he debate? There was presently nothing to measure it; for his vibration had already changed—as just by the effect of its intensity. Shut up there, at bay, defiant, and with the prodigy of the thing palpably proveably *done*, thus giving notice like some stark signboard—under that accession of accent the situation itself had turned; and Brydon at last remarkably made up his mind on what it had turned to.

It had turned altogether to a different admonition; to a supreme hint, for him, of the value of Discretion! This slowly dawned, no doubt—for it could take its time; so perfectly, on his threshold, had he been stayed, so little as yet had he either advanced or retreated. It was the strangest of all things that now when, by his taking ten steps and applying his hand to a latch, or even his shoulder and his knee, if necessary, to a panel, all the hunger of his prime need might have been met, his high curiosity crowned, his unrest assuaged—it was amazing, but it was also exquisite and rare, that insistence should have, at a touch, quite dropped from him. Discretion—he jumped at that; and yet not, verily, at such a pitch, because it saved his nerves or his skin, but because, much more valuably, it saved the situation. When I say he "jumped" at it I feel the consonance of this term with the fact that—at the end indeed of I know not how long—he did move again, he crossed straight to the door. He wouldn't touch it—it seemed now that he might *if* he would: he would only just wait there a little, to show, to prove, that he wouldn't. He had thus another station, close to the thin partition by which revelation was denied him; but with his eyes bent and his hands held off in a mere intensity of stillness. He listened as if there had been something to hear, but this attitude, while it lasted, was his own communication. "If you won't then—good: I spare you and I give up. You affect me as by the appeal positively for pity: you convince me that for reasons rigid and sublime—what do I know?—we both of us should have suffered. I respect them then, and, though moved and privileged as, I believe, it has never been given to man, I retire, I renounce—never, on my honour, to try again. So rest forever—and let *me!*"

That, for Brydon was the deep sense of this last demonstration—solemn, measured, directed, as he felt it to be. He brought it to a close, he turned away; and now verily he knew how deeply he had been stirred. He retraced his steps, taking up his candle, burnt, he observed, well-nigh to the socket, and marking again, lighten it as he would, the distinctness of his footfall; after which, in a moment, he knew himself at the other side of the house. He did here what he had not yet done at these hours—he opened half a casement, one of those in the front, and let in the air of the night; a thing he would have taken at any time previous for a sharp rupture of his spell. His spell was broken now, and it didn't matter—broken by his concession and his surrender, which made it idle henceforth that he should ever come back. The empty street—its other life so marked even by the great lamplit vacancy—was within call, within touch; he stayed there as to be in it again, high above it though he was still perched; he watched as for some comforting common fact, some vulgar human note, the passage of a scavenger or a thief, some night-bird however base. He would have blessed that sign of life; he would have welcomed positively the slow approach of his friend the policeman, whom he had hitherto only sought to avoid, and was not sure that if the patrol had come into sight he mightn't have felt the impulse to get into relation with it, to hail it, on some pretext, from his fourth floor.

The pretext that wouldn't have been too silly or too compromising, the explanation that would have saved his dignity and kept his name, in such a case, out of the papers, was not definite to him: he was so occupied with the thought of recording his Discretion—as an effect of the vow he had just uttered to his intimate adversary—that the importance of this loomed large and something had overtaken all ironically his sense of proportion. If there had been a ladder applied to the front of the house, even one of the vertiginous perpendiculars employed by painters and roofers and sometimes left standing overnight, he would have managed somehow, astride of the window-sill, to compass by outstretched leg and arm that mode of descent. If there had been some such uncanny thing as he had found in his room at hotels, a workable fire-escape in the form of notched cable or a canvas shoot, he would have availed himself of it as a proof—well, of his present delicacy. He nursed that sentiment, as the question stood, a little in vain, and even—at the end of he scarce knew, once more, how long—found it, as by the action on his mind of the failure of response of the outer world, sinking back to vague anguish. It seemed to him he had waited an age for some stir of the great grim hush; the life of the town was itself under a spell—so unnaturally, up and down the whole prospect of known and rather ugly objects, the blankness and the silence lasted. Had they ever, he asked himself, the hard-faced houses, which had begun to look livid in the dim dawn, had they ever spoken so little to any need of his spirit? Great builded voids, great crowded stillnesses put on, often, in the heart of cities, for the small hours, a sort of sinister mask, and it was of this large collective negation that Brydon presently became conscious—all the more that the break of day was, almost incredibly, now at hand, proving to him what a night he had made of it.

He looked again at his watch, saw what had become of his time-values (he had taken hours for minutes—not, as in other tense situations, minutes for hours) and the strange air of the streets was but the weak, the sullen flush of a dawn in which everything was still locked up. His choked appeal from his own open window had been the sole note of life, and he could but break off at last as for a worse despair. Yet while so deeply demoralised he was capable again of an impulse denoting—at least by his present measure—extraordinary resolution; of retracing his steps to the spot where he had turned cold with the extinction of his last pulse of doubt as to there being in the place another presence than his own. This required an effort strong enough to sicken him; but he had his reason, which overmastered for the moment everything else. There was the whole of the rest of the house to traverse, and how should he screw himself to that if the door he had seen closed were at present open? He could hold to the idea that the closing had practically been for him an act of mercy, a chance offered him to descend, depart, get off the ground and never again profane it. This conception held together, it worked; but what it meant for him depended now clearly on the amount of forbearance his recent action, or rather his recent inaction, had engendered. The image of the "presence," whatever it was, waiting there for him to go—this image had not yet been so concrete for his nerves as when he stopped short of the point at which certainty would have come to him. For, with all his resolution, or more exactly with all his dread, he did stop short—he hung back from really seeing. The risk was too great and his fear too definite: it took at this moment an awful specific form.

He knew—yes, as he had never known anything—that, *should* he see the door open, it would all too abjectly be the end of him. It would mean that the agent of his shame—for his shame was the deep abjection—was once more at large and in general possession; and what glared him thus in the face was the act that this would determine for him. It would send him straight about to the window he had left open, and by that window, be long ladder and dangling rope as absent as they would, he saw himself uncontrollably insanely fatally take his way to the street. The hideous chance of this he at least could avert; but he could only avert it by recoiling in time from assurance. He had the whole house to deal with, this fact was still there; only he now knew that uncertainty alone could start him. He stole back from where he had checked himself—merely to do so was suddenly like safety—and, making blindly for the greater staircase, left gaping rooms and sounding passages behind. Here was the top of the stairs, with a fine large dim descent and three spacious landings to mark off. His instinct was all for mildness, but his feet were harsh on the floors, and, strangely, when he had in a couple of minutes become aware of this, it counted somehow for help. He couldn't have spoken, the tone of his voice would have scared him, and the common conceit or resource of "whistling in the dark" (whether literally or figuratively) have appeared basely vulgar; yet he liked none the less to hear himself go, and when he had reached his first landing—taking it all with no rush, but quite steadily—that stage of success drew from him a gasp of relief.

The house, withal, seemed immense, the scale of space again inordinate; the open rooms, to no one of which his eyes deflected, gloomed in their shuttered state like mouths of caverns; only the high skylight that formed the crown of the deep well created for him a medium in which he could advance, but which might have been, for queerness of colour, some watery under-world. He tried to think of something noble, as that his property was really grand, a splendid possession; but this nobleness took the form too of the clear delight with which he was finally to sacrifice it. They might come in now, the builders, the destroyers—they might come as soon as they would. At the end of two flights he had dropped to another zone, and from the middle of the third, with only one more left, he recognised the influence of the lower windows, of half-drawn blinds, of the occasional gleam of street-lamps, of the glazed spaces of the vestibule. This was the bottom of the sea, which showed an illumination of its own and which he even saw paved—when at a given moment he drew up to sink a long look over the banisters—with the marble squares of his childhood. By that time indubitably he felt, as he might have said in a commoner cause, better; it had allowed him to stop and draw breath, and the ease increased with the sight of the old black-and-white slabs. But what he most felt was that now surely, with the element of impunity pulling him as by hard firm hands, the case was settled for what he might have seen above had he dared that last look. The closed door, blessedly remote now, was still closed—and he had only in short to reach that of the house.

He came down further, he crossed the passage forming the access to the last flight; and if here again he stopped an instant it was almost for the sharpness of the thrill of assured escape. It made him shut his eyes—which opened again to the straight slope of the remainder of the stairs. Here was impunity still, but impunity almost excessive; inasmuch as the side-lights and the high fan-tracery of the entrance were glimmering straight into the hall; an appearance produced, he the next instant saw, by the fact that the vestibule gaped wide, that the hinged halves of the inner door had been thrown far back. Out of that again the *question* sprang at him, making his eyes, as he felt, half-start from his head, as they had done, at the top of the house, before the sign of the other door. If he had left that one open, hadn't he left this one closed, and wasn't he now in *most* immediate presence of some inconceivable occult activity? It was as sharp, the question, as a knife in his side, but the answer hung fire still and seemed to lose itself in the vague darkness to which the thin admitted dawn, glimmering archwise over the whole outer door, made a semicircular margin, a cold silvery nimbus that seemed to play a little as he looked—to shift and expand and contract.

It was as if there had been something within it, protected by indistinctness and corresponding in extent with the opaque surface behind, the painted panels of the last barrier to his escape, of which the key was in his pocket. The indistinctness mocked him even while he stared, affected him as somehow shrouding or challenging certitude, so that after faltering an instant on his step he let himself go with the sense that here *was* at last something to meet, to touch, to take, to know—something all unnatural and dreadful, but to advance upon which was the condition for him either of liberation or of supreme defeat. The penumbra, dense and dark, was the virtual screen of a figure which stood in it as still as some image erect in a niche or as some black-vizored sentinel guarding a treasure. Brydon was to know afterwards, was to recall and make out, the particular thing he had believed during the rest of his descent. He saw, in its great grey glimmering margin, the central vagueness diminish, and he felt it to be taking the very form toward which, for so many days, the passion of his curiosity had yearned. It gloomed, it loomed, it was something, it was somebody, the prodigy of a personal presence.

Rigid and conscious, spectral yet human, a man of his own substance and stature waited there to measure himself with his power to dismay. This only could it be—this only till he recognised, with his advance, that what made the face dim was the pair of raised hands that covered it and in which, so far from being offered in defiance, it was buried as for dark deprecation. So Brydon, before him, took him in; with every fact of him now, in the higher light, hard and acute—his planted stillness, his vivid truth, his grizzled bent head and white masking hands, his queer actuality of evening-dress, of dangling double eye-glass, of gleaming silk lappet and white linen, of pearl button and gold watch-guard and polished shoe. No portrait by a great modern master could have presented him with more intensity, thrust him out of his frame with more art, as if there had been "treatment," of the consummate sort, in his every shade and salience. The revulsion, for our friend, had become, before he knew it, immense—this drop, in the act of apprehension, to the sense of his adversary's inscrutable manoeuvre. That meaning at least, while he gaped, it offered him; for he could but gape at his other self in this other anguish, gape as a proof that *he*, standing there for the achieved, the enjoyed, the triumphant life, couldn't be faced in his triumph. Wasn't the proof in the splendid covering hands, strong and completely spread?—so spread and so intentional that, in spite of a special verity that surpassed every other, the fact that one of these hands had lost two fingers, which were reduced to stumps, as if accidentally shot away, the face was effectually guarded and saved.

"Saved," though, *would* it be?—Brydon breathed his wonder till the very impunity of his attitude and the very insistence of his eyes produced, as he felt, a sudden stir which showed the next instant as a deeper portent, while the head raised itself, the betrayal of a braver purpose. The hands, as he looked, began to move, to open; then, as if deciding in a flash, dropped from the face and left it uncovered and presented. Horror, with the sight, had leaped into Brydon's throat, gasping there in a sound he couldn't utter; for the bared identity was too hideous as *his*, and this glare was the passion of his protest. The face, *that* face, Spencer Brydon's?—he searched it still, but looking away from it in dismay and denial, falling straight from his height of sublimity. It was unknown, inconceivable, awful, disconnected from any possibility—! He had been "sold," he inwardly moaned, stalking such game as this: the presence before him was a presence, the horror within him a horror, but the waste of his nights had been only grotesque and the success of his adventure an irony. Such an identity fitted his at *no* point, made its alternative monstrous. A thousand times yes, as it came upon him nearer now—the face was the face of a stranger. It came upon him nearer now, quite as one of those expanding fantastic images projected by the magic lantern of childhood; for the stranger, whoever he might be, evil, odious, blatant, vulgar, had advanced as for aggression, and he knew himself give ground. Then harder pressed still, sick with the force of his shock, and falling back as under the hot breath and the roused passion of a life larger than his own, a rage of personality before which his own collapsed, he felt the whole vision turn to darkness and his very feet give way. His head went round; he was going; he had gone.

III

What had next brought him back, clearly—though after how long?—was Mrs. Muldoon's voice, coming to him from quite near, from so near that he seemed presently to see her as kneeling on the ground before him while he lay looking up at her; himself not wholly on the ground, but half-raised and upheld—conscious, yes, of tenderness of support and, more particularly, of a head pillowed in extraordinary softness and faintly refreshing fragrance. He considered, he wondered, his wit but half at his service; then another face intervened, bending more directly over him, and he finally knew that Alice Staverton had made her lap an ample and perfect cushion to him, and that she had to this end seated herself on the lowest degree of the staircase, the rest of his long person remaining stretched on his old black-and-white slabs. They were cold, these marble squares of his youth; but *he* somehow was not, in this rich return of consciousness—the most wonderful hour, little by little, that he had ever known, leaving him, as it did, so gratefully, so abysmally passive, and yet as with a treasure of intelligence waiting all round him for quiet appropriation; dissolved, he might call it, in the air of the place and producing the golden glow of a late autumn afternoon. He had come back, yes—come back from further away than any man but himself had ever travelled; but it was strange how with this sense what he had come back *to* seemed really the great thing, and as if his prodigious journey had been all for the sake of it. Slowly but surely his consciousness grew, his vision of his state thus completing itself: he had been miraculously *carried* back—lifted and carefully borne as from where he had been picked up, the uttermost end of an interminable grey passage. Even with this he was suffered to rest, and what had now brought him to knowledge was the break in the long mild motion.

It had brought him to knowledge, to knowledge—yes, this was the beauty of his state; which came to resemble more and more that of a man who has gone to sleep on some news of a great inheritance, and then, after dreaming it away, after profaning it with matters strange to it, has waked up again to serenity of certitude and has only to lie and watch it grow. This was the drift of his patience—that he had only to let it shine on him. He must moreover, with intermissions, still have been lifted and borne; since why and how else should he have known himself, later on, with the afternoon glow intenser, no longer at the foot of his stairs—situated as these now seemed at that dark other end of his tunnel—but on a deep window-bench of his high saloon, over which had been spread, couch-fashion, a mantle of soft stuff lined with grey fur that was familiar to his eyes and that one of his hands kept fondly feeling as for its pledge of truth. Mrs. Muldoon's face had gone, but the other, the second he had recognised, hung over him in a way that showed how he was still propped and pillowed. He took it all in, and the more he took it the more it seemed to suffice: he was as much at peace as if he had had food and drink. It was the two women who had found him, on Mrs. Muldoon's having plied, at her usual hour, her latch-key—and on her having above all arrived while Miss Staverton still lingered near the house. She had been turning away, all anxiety, from worrying the vain bell-handle—her calculation having been of the hour of the good woman's visit; but the latter, blessedly, had come up while she was still there, and they had entered together. He had then lain, beyond the vestibule, very much as he was lying now—quite, that is, as he appeared to have fallen, but all so wondrously without bruise or gash; only in a depth of stupor. What he most took in, however, at present, with the steadier clearance, was that Alice Staverton had for a long unspeakable moment not doubted he was dead.

"It must have been that I *was.*" He made it out as she held him. "Yes—I can only have died. You brought me literally to life. Only," he wondered, his eyes rising to her, "only, in the name of all the benedictions, how?"

It took her but an instant to bend her face and kiss him, and something in the manner of it, and in the way her hands clasped and locked his head while he felt the cool charity and virtue of her lips, something in all this beatitude somehow answered everything. "And now I keep you," she said.

"Oh keep me, keep me!" he pleaded while her face still hung over him: in response to which it dropped again and stayed close, clingingly close. It was the seal of their situation—of which he tasted the impress for a long blissful moment in silence. But he came back. "Yet how did you know—?"

"I was uneasy. You were to have come, you remember—and you had sent no word."

"Yes, I remember—I was to have gone to you at one to-day." It caught on to their "old" life and relation—which were so near and so far. "I was still out there in my strange darkness—where was it, what was it? I must have stayed there so long." He could but wonder at the depth and the duration of his swoon.

"Since last night?" she asked with a shade of fear for her possible indiscretion.

"Since this morning—it must have been: the cold dim dawn of to-day. Where have I been," he vaguely wailed, "where have I been?" He felt her hold him close, and it was as if this helped him now to make in all security his mild moan. "What a long dark day!"

All in her tenderness she had waited a moment. "In the cold dim dawn?" she quavered.

But he had already gone on piecing together the parts of the whole prodigy. "As I didn't turn up you came straight—?"

She barely cast about. "I went first to your hotel—where they told me of your absence. You had dined out last evening and hadn't been back since. But they appeared to know you had been at your club."

"So you had the idea of *this*—?"

"Of what?" she asked in a moment.

"Well—of what has happened."

"I believed at least you'd have been here. I've known, all along," she said, "that you've been coming."

" 'Known' it—?"

"Well, I've believed it. I said nothing to you after that talk we had a month ago—but I felt sure. I knew you *would*," she declared.

"That I'd persist, you mean?"

"That you'd see him."

"Ah but I didn't!" cried Brydon with his long wail. "There's somebody—an awful beast; whom I brought, too horribly, to bay. But it's not me."

At this she bent over him again, and her eyes were in his eyes. "No—it's not you." And it was as if, while her face hovered, he might have made out in it, hadn't it been so near, some particular meaning blurred by a smile. "No, thank heaven," she repeated—"it's not you! Of course it wasn't to have been."

"Ah but it *was*," he gently insisted. And he stared before him now as he had been staring for so many weeks. "I was to have known myself."

"You couldn't!" she returned consolingly. And then reverting, and as if to account further for what she had herself done, "But it wasn't only *that*, that you hadn't been at home," she went on. "I waited till the hour at which we had found Mrs. Muldoon that day of my going with you; and she arrived, as I've told you, while, failing to bring any one to the door, I lingered in my despair on the steps. After a little, if she hadn't come, by such a mercy, I should have found means to hunt her up. But it wasn't," said Alice Staverton, as if once more with her fine intention—"it wasn't only that."

His eyes, as he lay, turned back to her. "What more then?"

She met it, the wonder she had stirred. "In the cold dim dawn, you say? Well, in the cold dim dawn of this morning I too saw you."

"Saw *me*—?"

"Saw *him*," said Alice Staverton. "It must have been at the same moment."

He lay an instant taking it in—as if he wished to be quite reasonable. "At the same moment?"

"Yes—in my dream again, the same one I've named to you. He came back to me. Then I knew it for a sign. He had come to you."

At this Brydon raised himself; he had to see her better. She helped him when she understood his movement, and he sat up, steadying himself beside her there on the window-bench and with his right hand grasping her left. "*He* didn't come to me."

"You came to yourself," she beautifully smiled.

"Ah I've come to myself now—thanks to you, dearest. But this brute, with his awful face—this brute's a black stranger. He's none of *me*, even as I *might* have been," Brydon sturdily declared.

But she kept the clearness that was like the breath of infallibility. "Isn't the whole point that you'd have been different?"

He almost scowled for it. "As different as *that*—?"

Her look again was more beautiful to him than the things of this world. "Haven't you exactly wanted to know *how* different? So this morning," she said, "you appeared to me."

"Like *him*?"

"A black stranger!"

"Then how did you know it was I?"

"Because, as I told you weeks ago, my mind, my imagination, had worked so over what you might, what you mightn't have been—to show you, you see, how I've thought of you. In the midst of that you came to me—that my wonder might be answered. So I knew," she went on; "and believed that, since the question held you too so fast, as you told me that day, you too would see for yourself. And when this morning I again saw I knew it would be because you had—and also then, from the first moment, because you somehow wanted me. *He* seemed to tell me of that. So why," she strangely smiled, "shouldn't I like him?"

It brought Spencer Brydon to his feet. "You 'like' that horror—?"

"I *could* have liked him. And to me," she said, "he was no horror. I had accepted him."

" 'Accepted'—?" Brydon oddly sounded.

"Before, for the interest of his difference—yes.

And as *I* didn't disown him, as *I* knew him—which you at last, confronted with him in his difference, so cruelly didn't, my dear—well, he must have been, you see, less dreadful to me. And it may have pleased him that I pitied him."

She was beside him on her feet, but still holding his hand—still with her arm supporting him. But though it all brought for him thus a dim light, "You 'pitied' him?" he grudgingly, resentfully asked.

"He has been unhappy, he has been ravaged," she said.

"And haven't I been unhappy? Am not I—you've only to look at me!—ravaged?"

"Ah I don't say I like him *better*," she granted after a thought. "But he's grim, he's worn—and things have happened to him. He doesn't make shift, for sight, with your charming monocle."

"No"—it struck Brydon: "I couldn't have sported mine 'downtown.' They'd have guyed me there."

"His great convex pince-nez—I saw it, I recognised the kind—is for his poor ruined sight. And his poor right hand—!"

"Ah!" Brydon winced—whether for his proved identity or for his lost fingers. Then, "He has a million a year," he lucidly added. "But he hasn't you."

"And he isn't—no, he isn't—*you!*" she murmured as he drew her to his breast.

1908, 1909

FROM HIS *Notebooks*

Beginning in 1878, James kept an account of the first hints of plots for his stories and the early plans for developing them. The following excerpts are from *The Notebooks of Henry James,* edited by F. O. Matthiessen and K. B. Murdock (1947).

[Greville Fane]

February 27th, 1889. * * *

There comes back to me with a certain vividness of solicitation, an idea that I noted a long time ago, suggested by something that Jennie Thackeray once said or repeated to me. That is, her story of Trollope's having had the plan of bringing up his son to write novels, as a lucrative trade. She added (as Mrs. R. Ritchie) that she and her husband had the same idea with regard to her little girl. They would train her up to it as to a regular profession. This suggested to me the figure of a weary battered labourer in the field of fiction attempting to carry out this project with a child and meeting, by the irony of fate, the strangest discomfiture. All sorts of possibilities vaguely occur to one as latent in it. The child is given a chance to 'see life,' etc., that it may have material, and sees life to such a tune that he (or she) is swamped and destroyed. That is one element. Then the mother (this especially if it be a 'lady-novelist') tries to enable the son to go out into the world for *her own* purposes—to see society, hear things, etc. The poor mother describes fashionable life and the upper classes—and wants data and material. She is frowsy and dingy herself—she can't go—and she is too busy. The stupidity of the children, who bring home nothing—have no observation, etc. But there must be an *action,* of some little sort—and this occurs to me. There is a daughter and she has appeared pretty and clever—she is the one (there is a son beside), whom there has been this attempt to *form,* to train. In the early years there must be the dim vision of a handsome, idle father, living upon his wife. The expense of the girl's education, etc.—and also the boy's, who is good-looking and unaddicted to any literary pursuit. The particular drama to be that the girl proves quite useless as a novelist, but grows up, marries a snob on the edge of good society, is worldly and hard and would be smart, and is ashamed of her mother. Thinks her novels are vulgar rubbish—keeps her at a distance—almost ignores her—makes her very unhappy. The poor lady is obliged to go on writing, meanwhile, to meet the demands of her son—whom she has thrown into the world to pick up information for her, and who has simply become idle, selfish, extravagant and vicious. She has all sorts of <lurking?> romanticisms and *naïvetés*—make a very vivid amusing pathetic picture of her mixture of queer qualities, etc.—her immorality, her natural penchant to license *à la Ouida,* of which her priggish daughter is ashamed. Her love of splendour, of the aristocracy, of high society—the wealth and beauty which she attributes to her people, etc.—contrasted with the small shabby facts of her own life. She dies at the end, worn out, disappointed, poor. The thing had much best be told by a witness of her life—a friend—a critic, a journalist, etc.: in the 1st person: rapid notes. I speak of the telegram from the editor of one of the big papers when she dies, asking for 1/2 a column about her. I saw and wrote the 1/2 column and made it kinder. Then for myself I wrote these other notes—kinder still.—The thing to be called by the *nom de plume* of the poor lady—some rather smart *man's* name.

This little sketch of which I think very well on the whole (Feb. 28th) would gain in effect by the supposititious narrator being himself a novelist but of the younger generation and of the modern psychological type. There would be touches there which might throw the poor woman's funny old art into contrast with his point of view—touches of bewilderment at his work on *her* side and of indulgence and humour on his.

[The Real Thing]

Paris, Hotel Westminster, February 22d, 1891.

In pursuance of my plan of writing some very short tales—things of from 7000 to 10,000 words, the easiest length to 'place,' I began yesterday the little story that was suggested to me some time ago by an incident related to me by George du Maurier—the lady and gentleman who called upon him with a word from Frith, an oldish, faded, ruined pair—he an officer in the army—who unable to turn a penny in any other way, were trying to find employment as models. I was struck with the pathos, the oddity and typicalness of the situation—the little tragedy of good-looking gentlefolk, who had been all their life stupid and well-dressed, living, on a fixed income, at country-houses, watering places and clubs, like so many others of their class in England, and were now utterly unable to do anything, had no cleverness, no art nor craft to make use of as a *gagne-pain*—could only *show* themselves, clumsily, for the fine, clean, well-groomed animals that they were, only hope to make a little money by—in this manner—just simply *being*. I thought I saw a subject for very brief treatment in the *donnée*—and I think I do still; but to do anything worth while with it I must (as always, great Heavens!) be very clear as to what is in it and what I wish to get out of it. I tried a beginning yesterday, but I instantly became conscious that I must straighten out the little idea. It must be an idea—it can't be a 'story' in the vulgar sense of the word. It must be a picture; it must illustrate something. God knows that's enough—if the thing *does* illustrate. To make little anecdotes of this kind real *morceaux de vie* is a plan quite inspiring enough. *Voyons un peu,* therefore, what one can put into this one—I mean how much of life. One must put a little action—not a stupid, mechanical, arbitrary action, but something that is of the real essence of the subject. I thought of representing the husband as jealous of the wife—that is, jealous of the artist employing her, from the moment that, in point of fact, she begins to sit. But this is vulgar and obvious—worth nothing. What I wish to represent is the baffled, ineffectual, incompetent character of their attempt, and how it illustrates once again the everlasting English amateurishness—the way superficial, untrained, unprofessional effort goes to the wall when confronted with trained, competitive, intelligent, *qualified* art—in whatever line it may be a question of. It is out of *that* element that my little action and movement must come; and now I begin to see just how—as one always *does*—Glory be to the Highest—when one begins to look at a thing hard and straight and seriously—to fix it—as I am so sadly lax and desultory about doing. What subjects I should find—for *everything*—if I could only achieve this more as a habit! Let my contrast and complication here come from the opposition—to my melancholy Major and his wife—of a couple of little vulgar professional people *who know*, with the consequent bewilderment, vagueness, depression of the former—their failure to understand how such people can be better than *they*—their failure, disappointment, disappearance—going forth into the vague again. *Il y a bien quelque chose à tirer de ça.* They have no pictorial sense. They are only clean and stiff and stupid. The others are dirty, even—the melancholy Major and his wife remark on it, wondering. The artist is beginning a big illustrated book, a new edition of a famous novel—say *Tom Jones:* and he is willing to try to work them in—for he takes an interest in their predicament, and feels—sceptically, but, with his flexible artistic sympathy—the appeal of their type. He is willing to give them a trial. Make it out that *he* himself is on trial—he is young and 'rising,' but he has still his golden spurs to win. He can't afford, *en somme,* to make many mistakes. He has regular work in drawing every week for a serial novel in an illustrated paper; but the great project—that of a big house—of issuing an illustrated Fielding promises him a big lift. He has been intrusted with (say) *Joseph Andrews,* experimentally; he will have to do this brilliantly in order to have the engagement for the rest confirmed. He has already 2 models in his service—the 'complication' must come from *them.* One is a common, clever, London girl, of the smallest origin and without conventional beauty, but of aptitude, of perceptions—knowing thoroughly *how.* She says 'lydy' and 'plice,' but she has the pictorial sense; and can look like anything he wants her to look like. She poses, in short, in perfection. So does her colleague, a professional Italian, a little fellow—ill dressed, smelling of garlic, but admirably serviceable, quite universal. They must be contrasted, confronted, *juxtaposed* with the others; whom they take for people who *pay,* themselves, till they learn the truth when they are overwhelmed with derisive amazement. The denouement simply that the melancholy Major and his wife won't do—they're not 'in it.' Their surprise—their helpless, proud assent—without other prospects: yet at the same time *their* degree of more silent amazement at the success of the two inferior people—who are so much less nice-looking than themselves. Frankly, however, is this contrast enough of a *story,* by itself? It seems to me Yes—for it's an IDEA—and how the deuce should I get *more* into 7000 words? It must be simply 50 pp. of my manuscript. The little tale of *The Servant (Brooksmith)* which I did the other day for *Black and White* and which I thought of at the same time as this, proved a very tight squeeze into the same tiny number of words, and I probably shall find that there is much more to be done with this than the compass will admit of. Make it tremendously succinct—with a very short pulse or rhythm—and the closest selection of detail—in other words *summarize* intensely and keep down the lateral development. It *should* be a little gem of bright, quick, vivid form. I shall get every grain of 'action' that the space admits of if I make something, for the artist, hang in the balance—depend on the way he does this particular work. It's when he finds that he shall lose his great opportunity if he keeps on with them, that he has to tell the gentlemanly couple, that, frankly, they won't serve his turn—and make them wander forth into the cold world again. I must keep them the age I've made them—50 and 40—because it's more touching; but I must bring up the age of the 2 real models to almost the same thing. That increases the incomprehensibility (to the amateurs) of their usefulness. Picture the immanence, in the latter, of the idle, provided-for, country-house habit—the blankness of the *manière d'être.* But in how tremendously few words I must do it. This is a lesson—a *magnificent* lesson—if I'm to do a good many. Something as admirably compact and *selected* as Maupassant.

Regional Writing

BRET HARTE [1836–1902]

BRET HARTE was an Easterner who struck literary pay dirt in the mining camps of the Sierras during the exciting years of the Gold Rush. He was born in Albany and lived in the East until he was nineteen, when he went to California where his widowed mother had settled and remarried. He remained a dude in the frontier settlement, a small, neat, fashionably dressed man described by a contemporary as a "dandy" and "a dainty man: too much like a woman to rough it in the mines." At first he made a meager living in Humboldt County, teaching, working as a printer's devil and as a messenger for the Wells Fargo express. His literary gift began to show itself in contributions to San Francisco magazines, *The Golden Era* and the *Californian.* As editor of the latter he wrote clever parodies and imitations of Dickens, Cooper, Poe, Whittier, and others (later collected in *Condensed Novels and Other Papers,* 1867), skillfully deflating sentiment and pretentious writing and thus contributing to the techniques of American humor and realism. He encouraged contributions from Mark Twain, who later acknowledged his indebtedness to Harte for having polished and improved his apprentice writing.

It was while he was editor of the *Overland Monthly* that Harte wrote the stories and poems which made his reputation. In August 1868 "The Luck of Roaring Camp" appeared, perhaps his best-known story; in 1869, "The Outcasts of Poker Flat"; and in 1870, his dialect poem of the inscrutable Chinese card shark, "Plain Language from Truthful James" (often titled "The Heathen Chinee"). These three works were perfectly timed for a popular response. The California "legend" had drifted back East. The Argonauts of the Gold Rush were invested with an aura of romance, combined with earthy humor, which hinted at the emergence of a new American hero. Harte was the first to depict them in literature: outlaws, gamblers, miners, stagecoach drivers, prostitutes and pretty schoolmarms. His uninhibited yet delicately phrased portrayals of ungenteel frontier types satisfied the public craving for something fresh and Western.

The Luck of Roaring Camp and Other Sketches (1870) spread Bret Harte's name across the continent. Returning East, he capitalized on his popularity by signing an unprecedented $10,000 contract to contribute twelve stories to the *Atlantic Monthly* in the course of a year. Though he continued to write steadily and well for the rest of his life, he mainly imitated his own formula of the Western dialect story as he had perfected it in the late 1860's and early 1870's. Somehow he was unable to develop any new strain after he had left the scenes of Roaring Camp and Simpson's Bar. In 1878 he sailed for Europe, without his family, and never returned to America, continuing to produce fiction and serving in diplomatic posts in Germany and Scotland. His later years were lived in London, where he died in 1902.

Harte's literary success was due to both talent and timing. Yet, for all his stylistic flair, we cannot say that his writing has much depth or originality. His frontier people are a mixture of the real thing and the literary type: his gamblers have hearts of gold, and his degenerate characters show the unmistakable manners of ladies and gentlemen. His best work, however, continues to be read here and abroad for its brilliant evocation of an epoch in American history and its mingling of local authenticity with a Dickensian eye for picturesque character types. He was the first and one of the best of the local colorists; but more than that, he was largely responsible for the creation of the Western "legend." A hundred years of popular fictions, films, and television have now familiarized and stereotyped this legend; Bret Harte almost single-handedly invented it.

Further reading: Joseph B. Harrison, ed., *Bret Harte: Representative Selections,* 1941. G. R. Stewart, Jr., *Bret Harte: Argonaut and Exile,* 1931.

The Luck of Roaring Camp

In an essay, "The Rise of the American Short Story" (1899), Bret Harte maintained that humor was the basis of the local color story. The humor was at first orally transmitted and then polished in the press. It consisted, among other things, of understatement, extravagance, slang, and paradox, and derived its special quality from "a peculiar atmosphere of locality"—in this case, the western mining camp. He also called the short story "irreverent," "devoid of all moral responsibility," and voicing "not only the dialect but the habits of a people or locality." Text: From *The Luck of Roaring Camp and Other Sketches* (1870).

There was commotion in Roaring Camp. It could not have been a fight, for in 1850 that was not novel enough to have called together the entire settlement. The ditches and claims were not only deserted, but "Tuttle's grocery" had contributed its gamblers, who, it will be remembered, calmly continued their game the day that French Pete and Kanaka Joe shot each other to death over the bar in the front room. The whole camp was collected before a rude cabin on the outer edge of the clearing. Conversation was carried on in a low tone, but the name of a woman was frequently repeated. It was a name familiar enough in the camp,—"Cherokee Sal."

Perhaps the less said of her the better. She was a coarse, and, it is to be feared, a very sinful woman. But at that time she was the only woman in Roaring Camp, and was just then lying in sore extremity, when she most needed the ministration of her own sex. Dissolute, abandoned, and irreclaimable, she was yet suffering a martyrdom hard enough to bear even when veiled by sympathizing womanhood, but now terrible in her loneliness. The primal curse had come to her in that original isolation which must have made the punishment of the first transgression so dreadful. It was, perhaps, part of the expiation of her sin, that, at a moment when she most lacked her sex's intuitive tenderness and care, she met only the half-contemptuous faces of her masculine associates. Yet a few of the spectators were, I think, touched by her sufferings. Sandy Tipton thought it was "rough on Sal," and, in the contemplation of her condition, for a moment rose superior to the fact that he had an ace and two bowers in his sleeve.

It will be seen, also, that the situation was novel. Deaths were by no means uncommon in Roaring Camp, but a birth was a new thing. People had been dismissed the camp effectively, finally, and with no possibility of return; but this was the first time that anybody had been introduced *ab initio.* Hence the excitement.

"You go in there, Stumpy," said a prominent citizen known as "Kentuck," addressing one of the loungers. "Go in there, and see what you kin do. You've had experience in them things."

Perhaps there was a fitness in the selection. Stumpy, in other climes, had been the putative head of two families; in fact, it was owing to some legal informality in these proceedings that Roaring Camp—a city of refuge—was indebted to his company. The crowd approved the choice, and Stumpy was wise enough to bow to the majority. The door closed on the extempore surgeon and midwife, and Roaring Camp sat down outside, smoked its pipe, and awaited the issue.

The assemblage numbered about a hundred men. One or two of these were actual fugitives from justice, some were criminal, and all were reckless. Physically, they exhibited no indication of their past lives and character. The greatest scamp had a Raphael face, with a profusion of blond hair; Oakhurst, a gambler, had the melancholy air and intellectual abstraction of a Hamlet; the coolest and most courageous man was scarcely over five feet in height, with a soft voice and an embarrassed, timid manner. The term "roughs" applied to them was a distinction rather than a definition. Perhaps in the minor details of fingers, toes, ears, etc., the camp may have been deficient, but these slight omissions did not detract from their aggregate force. The strongest man had but three fingers on his right hand; the best shot had but one eye.

Such was the physical aspect of the men that were dispersed around the cabin. The camp lay in a triangular valley, between two hills and a river. The only outlet was a steep trail over the summit of a hill that faced the cabin, now illuminated by the rising moon. The suffering woman might have seen it from the rude bunk whereon she lay,—seen it winding like a silver thread until it was lost in the stars above.

A fire of withered pine-boughs added sociability to the gathering. By degrees the natural levity of Roaring Camp returned. Bets were freely offered and taken regarding the result. Three to five that "Sal would get through with it"; even, that the child would survive; side bets as to the sex and complexion of the coming stranger. In the midst of an excited discussion an exclamation came from those nearest the door, and the camp stopped to listen. Above the swaying and moaning of the pines, the swift rush of the river, and the crackling of the fire, rose a sharp, querulous cry,—a cry unlike anything heard before in the camp. The pines stopped moaning, the river ceased to rush, and the fire to crackle. It seemed as if Nature had stopped to listen too.

The camp rose to its feet as one man! It was proposed to explode a barrel of gunpowder, but, in consideration of the situation of the mother, better counsels prevailed, and only a few revolvers were discharged; for, whether owing to the rude surgery of the camp, or some other reason, Cherokee Sal was sinking fast. Within an hour she had climbed, as it were, that rugged road that led to the stars, and so passed out of Roaring Camp, its sin and shame forever. I do not think that the announcement disturbed them much, except in speculation as to the fate of the child. "Can he live now?" was asked of Stumpy. The answer was doubtful. The only other being of Cherokee Sal's sex and maternal condition in the settlement was an ass. There was some conjecture as to fitness, but the experiment was tried. It was less problematical than the ancient treatment of Romulus and Remus, and apparently as successful.

When these details were completed, which exhausted another hour, the door was opened, and the anxious crowd of men who had already formed themselves into a queue, entered in single file. Beside the low bunk or shelf, on which the figure of the mother was starkly outlined below the blankets stood a pine table. On this a candle-box was placed, and within it, swathed in staring red flannel, lay the last arrival at Roaring Camp. Beside the candle-box was placed a hat. Its use was soon indicated. "Gentlemen," said Stumpy, with a singular mixture of authority and *ex officio* complacency,—"Gentlemen will please pass in at the front door, round the table, and out at the back door. Them as wishes to contribute anything toward the orphan will find a hat handy." The first man entered with his hat on; he uncovered, however, as he looked about him, and so, unconsciously, set an example to the next. In such communities good and bad actions are catching. As the procession filed in, comments were audible,—criticisms addressed, perhaps, rather to Stumpy, in the character of showman,—"Is that him?" "mighty small specimen"; "hasn't mor'n got the color"; "ain't bigger nor a derringer." The contributions were as characteristic: A silver tobacco-box; a doubloon; a navy revolver, silver mounted; a gold specimen; a very beautifully embroidered lady's handkerchief (from Oakhurst the gambler); a diamond breastpin; a diamond ring (suggested by the pin, with the remark from the giver that he "saw that pin and went two diamonds better"); a slung shot; a Bible (contributor not detected); a golden spur; a silver teaspoon (the initials, I regret to say, were not the giver's); a pair of surgeon's shears; a lancet; a Bank of England note for £5; and about $200 in loose gold and silver coin. During these proceedings Stumpy maintained a silence as impassive as the dead on his left, a gravity as inscrutable as that of the newly born on his right. Only one incident occurred to break the monotony of the curious procession. As Kentuck bent over the candle-box half curiously, the child turned, and, in a spasm of pain, caught at his groping finger, and held it fast for a moment. Kentuck looked foolish and embarrassed. Something like a blush tried to assert itself in his weather-beaten cheek. "The d—d little cuss!" he said, as he extricated his finger, with, perhaps, more tenderness and care than he might have been deemed capable of showing. He held that finger a little apart from its fellows as he went out, and examined it curiously. The examination provoked the same original remark in regard to the child. In fact, he seemed to enjoy repeating it. "He rastled with my finger," he remarked to Tipton, holding up the member, "the d—d little cuss!"

It was four o'clock before the camp sought repose. A light burnt in the cabin where the watchers sat, for Stumpy did not go to bed that night. Nor did Kentuck. He drank quite freely, and related with great gusto his experience, invariably ending with his characteristic condemnation of the new-comer. It seemed to relieve him of any unjust implication of sentiment, and Kentuck had the weaknesses of the nobler sex. When everybody else had gone to bed, he walked down to the river, and whistled reflectingly. Then he walked up the gulch, past the cabin, still whistling with demonstrative unconcern. At a large redwood tree he paused and retraced his steps, and again passed the cabin. Half-way down to the river's bank he again paused, and then returned and knocked at the door. It was opened by Stumpy. "How goes it?" said Kentuck, looking past Stumpy toward the candle-box. "All serene," replied Stumpy. "Anything up?" "Nothing." There was a pause—an embarrassing one—Stumpy still holding the door. Then Kentuck had recourse to his finger, which he held up to Stumpy. "Rastled with it,—the d—d little cuss," he said, and retired.

The next day Cherokee Sal had such rude sepulture as Roaring Camp afforded. After her body had been committed to the hillside, there was a formal meeting of the camp to discuss what should be done with her infant. A resolution to adopt it was unanimous and enthusiastic. But an animated discussion in regard to the manner and feasibility of providing for its wants at once sprung up. It was remarkable that the argument partook of none of those fierce personalities with which discussions were usually conducted at Roaring Camp. Tipton proposed that they should send the child to Red Dog,—a distance of forty miles,—where female attention could be procured. But the unlucky suggestion met with fierce and unanimous opposition. It was evident that no plan which entailed parting from their new acquisition would for a moment be entertained. "Besides," said Tom Ryder, "them fellows at Red Dog would swap it, and ring in somebody else on us." A disbelief in the honesty of other camps prevailed at Roaring Camp as in other places.

The introduction of a female nurse in the camp also met with objection. It was argued that no decent woman could be prevailed to accept Roaring Camp as her home; and the speaker urged that "they didn't want any more of the other kind." This unkind allusion to the defunct mother, harsh as it may seem, was the first spasm of propriety,—the first symptom of the camp's regeneration. Stumpy advanced nothing. Perhaps he felt a certain delicacy in interfering with the selection of a possible successor in office. But when questioned, he averred stoutly that he and "Jinny"—the mammal before alluded to—could manage to rear the child. There was something original, independent, and heroic about the plan that pleased the camp. Stumpy was retained. Certain articles were sent for to Sacramento. "Mind," said the treasurer, as he pressed a bag of gold-dust into the expressman's hand, "the best that can be got,—lace, you know, and filigree-work and frills,—d—m the cost!"

Strange to say, the child thrived. Perhaps the invigorating climate of the mountain camp was compensation for material deficiencies. Nature took the foundling to her broader breast. In that rare atmosphere of the Sierra foot-hills,—that air pungent with balsamic odor, that ethereal cordial at once bracing and exhilarating,—he may have found food and nourishment, or a subtle chemistry that transmuted asses' milk to lime and phosphorus. Stumpy inclined to the belief that it was the latter and good nursing. "Me and that ass," he would say, "has been father and mother to him! Don't you," he would add, apostrophizing the helpless bundle before him, "never go back on us."

By the time he was a month old, the necessity of giving him a name became apparent. He had generally been known as "the kid," "Stumpy's boy," "the Cayote" (an allusion to his vocal powers), and even by Kentuck's endearing diminutive of "the d—d little cuss." But these were felt to be vague and unsatisfactory, and were at last dismissed under another influence. Gamblers and adventurers are generally superstitious, and Oakhurst one day declared that the baby had brought "the luck" to Roaring Camp. It was certain that of late they had been successful. "Luck" was the name agreed upon, with the prefix of Tommy for greater convenience. No allusion was made to the mother, and the father was unknown. "It's better," said the philosophical Oakhurst, "to take a fresh deal all round. Call him Luck, and start him fair." A day was accordingly set apart for the christening. What was meant by this ceremony the reader may imagine, who has already gathered some idea of the reckless irreverence of Roaring Camp. The master of ceremonies was one "Boston," a noted wag, and the occasion seemed to promise the greatest facetiousness. This ingenious satirist had spent two days in preparing a burlesque of the church service, with pointed local allusions. The choir was properly trained, and Sandy Tipton was to stand godfather. But after the procession had marched to the grove with music and banners, and the child had been deposited before a mock altar, Stumpy stepped before the expectant crowd. "It ain't my style to spoil fun, boys," said the little man, stoutly, eying the faces around him, "but it strikes me that this thing ain't exactly on the squar. It's playing it pretty low down on this yer baby to ring in fun on him that he ain't going to understand. And ef there's going to be any godfathers round, I'd like to see who's got any better rights than me." A silence followed Stumpy's speech. To the credit of all humorists be it said, that the first man to acknowledge its justice was the satirist, thus stopped of his fun. "But," said Stumpy, quickly, following up his advantage, "we're here for a christening, and we'll have it. I proclaim you Thomas Luck, according to the laws of the United States and the State of California, so help me God." It was the first time that the name of the Deity had been uttered otherwise than profanely in the camp. The form of christening was perhaps even more ludicrous than the satirist had conceived; but, strangely enough, nobody saw it and nobody laughed. "Tommy" was christened as seriously as he would have been under a Christian roof, and cried and was comforted in as orthodox fashion.

And so the work of regeneration began in Roaring Camp. Almost imperceptibly a change came over the settlement. The cabin assigned to "Tommy Luck"—or "The Luck," as he was more frequently called—first showed signs of improvement. It was kept scrupulously clean and white-washed. Then it was boarded, clothed, and papered. The rosewood cradle—packed eighty miles by mule—had, in Stumpy's way of putting it, "sorter killed the rest of the furniture." So the rehabilitation of the cabin became a necessity. The men who were in the habit of lounging in at Stumpy's to see "how The Luck got on" seemed to appreciate the change, and, in self-defence, the rival establishment of "Tuttle's grocery" bestirred itself, and imported a carpet and mirrors. The reflections of the latter on the appearance of Roaring Camp tended to produce stricter habits of personal cleanliness. Again, Stumpy imposed a kind of quarantine upon those who aspired to the honor and privilege of holding "The Luck." It was a cruel mortification to Kentuck—who, in the carelessness of a large nature and the habits of frontier life, had begun to regard all garments as a second cuticle, which, like a snake's, only sloughed off through decay—to be debarred this privilege from certain prudential reasons. Yet such was the subtle influence of innovation that he thereafter appeared regularly every afternoon in a clean shirt, and face still shining from his ablutions. Nor were moral and social sanitary laws neglected. "Tommy," who was supposed to spend his whole existence in a persistent attempt to repose, must not be disturbed by noise. The shouting and yelling which had gained the camp its infelicitous title were not permitted within hearing distance of Stumpy's. The men conversed in whispers, or smoked with Indian gravity. Profanity was tacitly given up in these sacred precincts, and throughout the camp a popular form of expletive, known as "D—n the luck!" and "Curse the luck!" was abandoned, as having a new personal bearing. Vocal music was not interdicted, being supposed to have a soothing, tranquillizing quality, and one song, sung by "Man-o'-War Jack," an English sailor, from her Majesty's Australian colonies, was quite popular as a lullaby. It was a lugubrious recital of the exploits of "the Arethusa, Seventy-four," in a muffled minor, ending with a prolonged dying fall at the burden of each verse, "On b-o-o-o-ard of the Arethusa." It was a fine sight to see Jack holding The Luck, rocking from side to side as if with the motion of a ship, and crooning forth this naval ditty. Either through the peculiar rocking of Jack or the length of his song,—it contained ninety stanzas, and was continued with conscientious deliberation to the bitter end,—the lullaby generally had the desired effect. At such times the men would lie at full length under the trees, in the soft summer twilight, smoking their pipes and drinking in the melodious utterances. An indistinct idea that this was pastoral happiness pervaded the camp. "This 'ere kind o' think," said the Cockney Simmons, meditatively reclining on his elbow, "is 'evingly." It reminded him of Greenwich.

On the long summer days The Luck was usually carried to the gulch, from whence the golden store of Roaring Camp was taken. There, on a blanket spread over pine-boughs, he would lie while the men were working in the ditches below. Latterly, there was a rude attempt to decorate this bower with flowers and sweet-smelling shrubs, and generally some one would bring him a cluster of wild honeysuckles, azaleas, or the painted blossoms of Las Mariposas. The men had suddenly awakened to the fact that there were beauty and significance in these trifles, which they had so long trodden carelessly beneath their feet. A flake of glittering mica, a fragment of variegated quartz, a bright pebble from the bed of the creek, became beautiful to eyes thus cleared and strengthened and were invariably put aside for "The Luck." It was wonderful how many treasures the woods and hillsides yielded that "would do for Tommy." Surrounded by playthings such as never child out of fairy-land had before, it is to be hoped that Tommy was content. He appeared to be securely happy, albeit there was an infantine gravity about him, a contemplative light in his round gray eyes that sometimes worried Stumpy. He was always tractable and quiet, and it is recorded that once having crept beyond his "corral,"—a hedge of tessellated pine-boughs, which surrounded his bed,—he dropped over the bank on his head in the soft earth, and remained with his mottled legs in the air in that position for at least five minutes with unflinching gravity. He was extricated without a murmur. I hesitate to record the many other instances of his sagacity, which rest, unfortunately, upon the statements of prejudiced friends. Some of them were not without a tinge of superstition. "I crep' up the bank just now," said Kentuck one day, in a breathless state of excitement, "and dern my skin if he wasn't a talking to a jaybird as was a sittin' on his lap. There they was, just as free and sociable as anything you please, a jawin' at each other just like two cherry-bums." Howbeit, whether creeping over the pine-boughs or lying lazily on his back blinking at the leaves above him, to him the birds sang, the squirrels chattered, and the flowers bloomed. Nature was his nurse and playfellow. For him she would let slip between the leaves golden shafts of sunlight that fell just within his grasp; she would send wandering breezes to visit him with the balm of bay and resinous gums; to him the tall redwoods nodded familiarly and sleepily, the bumblebees buzzed, and the rooks cawed a slumbrous accompaniment.

Such was the golden summer of Roaring Camp. They were "flush times,"—and the Luck was with them. The claims had yielded enormously. The camp was jealous of its privileges and looked suspiciously on strangers. No encouragement was given to immigration, and, to make their seclusion more perfect, the land on either side of the mountain wall that surrounded the camp they duly preempted. This, and a reputation for singular proficiency with the revolver, kept the reserve of Roaring Camp inviolate. The expressman—their only connecting link with the surrounding world—sometimes told wonderful stories of the camp. He would say, "They've a street up there in 'Roaring,' that would lay over any street in Red Dog. They've got vines and flowers round their houses, and they wash themselves twice a day. But they're mighty rough on strangers, and they worship an Ingin baby."

With the prosperity of the camp came a desire for further improvement. It was proposed to build a hotel in the following spring, and to invite one or two decent families to reside there for the sake of "The Luck,"—who might perhaps profit by female companionship. The sacrifice that this concession to the sex cost these men, who were fiercely sceptical in regard to its general virtue and usefulness, can only be accounted for by their affection for Tommy. A few still held out. But the resolve could not be carried into effect for three months, and the minority meekly yielded in the hope that something might turn up to prevent it. And it did.

The winter of 1851 will long be remembered in the foot-hills. The snow lay deep on the Sierras, and every mountain creek became a river, and every river a lake. Each gorge and gulch was transformed into a tumultuous watercourse that descended the hillsides, tearing down giant trees and scattering its drift and debris along the plain. Red Dog had been twice under water, and Roaring Camp had been forewarned. "Water put the gold into them gulches," said Stumpy. "It's been here once and will be here again!" And that night the North Fork suddenly leaped over its banks, and swept up the triangular valley of Roaring Camp.

In the confusion of rushing water, crushing trees, and crackling timber, and the darkness which seemed to flow with the water and blot out the fair valley, but little could be done to collect the scattered camp. When the morning broke, the cabin of Stumpy nearest the river-bank was gone. Higher up the gulch they found the body of its unlucky owner; but the pride, the hope, the joy, the Luck, of Roaring Camp had disappeared. They were returning with sad hearts, when a shout from the bank recalled them.

It was a relief-boat from down the river. They had picked up, they said, a man and an infant, nearly exhausted, about two miles below. Did anybody know them, and did they belong here?

It needed but a glance to show them Kentuck lying there, cruelly crushed and bruised, but still holding the Luck of Roaring Camp in his arms. As they bent over the strangely assorted pair, they saw that the child was cold and pulseless. "He is dead," said one. Kentuck opened his eyes. "Dead?" he repeated feebly. "Yes, my man, and you are dying too." A smile lit the eyes of the expiring Kentuck. "Dying," he repeated, "he's a taking me with him,—tell the boys I've got the Luck with me now"; and the strong man, clinging to the frail babe as a drowning man is said to cling to a straw, drifted away into the shadowy river that flows forever to the unknown sea.

1868

HAMLIN GARLAND [1860-1940]

GARLAND WAS one of the literary regionalists of the Middle West, a spokesman for the silent, struggling pioneer farmers of Wisconsin, South Dakota, and Iowa where he spent his boyhood. In 1884, he escaped a lifetime of such toil by "back-trailing" to Boston, where he lived for several years at near-starvation level, educating himself by hard study and teaching in the Boston School of Oratory. In 1887 and again in 1889 he returned to his father's farm on the middle border, where he became deeply impressed by the conditions of poverty, unremitting labor, and cultural starvation on such farms, and he determined to write stories expressing both the bitterness and the heroism of the people who worked them. In the best of his early volumes, *Main-Travelled Roads* (1891) and *Prairie Folks* (1893), he wrote a series of brief, poignant studies of the harsh and narrow lives of men and women like his own parents. A persistent strain of indignation and evangelical wrath marked much of Garland's work, having its source partly in his personal feelings and partly in the political atmosphere of the 1890's, when the Farmer's Alliance and the Granger Movement had organized to express their resentment against the industrial East.

While in Boston, Garland eagerly read the poetry of Walt Whitman, absorbing the poet's sense of a spiritual brotherhood of workers and much of his nationalistic feeling. He also studied Darwin and Herbert Spencer in an effort to understand the evolutionary and biological processes in nature leading from simple to complex forms and thus perhaps to rationalize his own intellectual ambitions to rise above his parents' destiny. Garland learned from Taine the all-importance of environment as a determining agent in the fate of man, and he absorbed his ideas of economics from Henry George's theory of the "single tax" to correct the injustice of the "unearned increment" that favored property owners at the expense of the laboring farmer. His novels *Jason Edwards* (1892) and *A Spoil of Office* (1892) dealt with political corruption and land speculation.

In 1891 Garland published a volume of literary theory called *Crumbling Idols*, an argument for what he termed "Veritism," calling for a forward-looking literature which would be true to contemporary America. Like Emerson and Whitman, he prophesied a revival of the nationalistic spirit in letters. He also defined the significance of "localism" in the novel. But as a statement of an aesthetics of realism, the book was not original, nor was Garland ever to embody his own material in a genuinely deterministic framework, as did Dreiser, or in a meaningful form, as did James. He remained the practitioner of Howellsian realism, faithful to detail and documentation and the effects of environment, but without Howells's psychological insight, and with a tendency to veer off into romantic conventions. As he became known and in demand by the popular magazines, he lost much of his earlier radicalism and fervor. When he returned later to the subject of the middle border in his autobiographical works, *A Son of the Middle Border* (1917) and *A Daughter of the Middle Border* (1921), it was with a more mature perspective and a mellower mood. In these summings-up of his younger years he wrote more naturally and easily, not restrained by the formal demands of the long novel. These two books, together with his later literary reminiscences (from his championship of Stephen Crane to his efforts to advance the "Chicago Renaissance"), have become valuable sources of memorabilia for the literary historian.

Further reading: *A Son of the Middle Border. Main-Travelled Roads,* ed. B. R. McElderry, Jr., 1956. Jean Holloway, *Hamlin Garland,* 1960. D. Pizer, *Hamlin Garland's Early Work and Career,* 1960.

Under the Lion's Paw

Written in 1889 and included in *Main-Travelled Roads* (1891), this story expressed the revolt of farmers in the Middle West against land speculators and absentee owners who profited from the labor of tenants. Populist political philosophy and Henry George's single-tax theory are both motivating influences on Garland here. How successfully does he combine the two elements of art and propaganda?

"Along this main-travelled road trailed an endless line of prairie-schooners, coming into sight at the east, and passing out of sight over the swell to the west. We children used to wonder where they were going and why they went."

It was the last of autumn and first day of winter coming together. All day long the ploughmen on their prairie farms had moved to and fro on their wide level field through the falling snow, which melted as it fell, wetting them to the skin—all day, notwithstanding the frequent squalls of snow, the dripping, desolate clouds, and the muck of the furrows, black and tenacious as tar.

Under their dripping harness the horses swung to and fro silently, with that marvellous uncomplaining patience which marks the horse. All day the wild geese, honking wildly, as they sprawled sidewise down the wind, seemed to be fleeing from an enemy behind, and with neck outthrust and wings extended, sailed down the wind, soon lost to sight.

Yet the ploughman behind his plough, though the snow lay on his ragged great-coat, and the cold clinging mud rose on his heavy boots, fettering him like gyves, whistled in the very beard of the gale. As day passed, the snow, ceasing to melt, lay along the ploughed land, and lodged in the depth of the stubble, till on each slow round the last furrow stood out black and shining as jet between the ploughed land and the gray stubble.

When night began to fall, and the geese, flying low, began to alight invisibly in the near cornfield, Stephen Council was still at work "finishing a land." He rode on his sulky-plough when going with the wind, but walked when facing it. Sitting bent and cold but cheery under his slouch hat, he talked encouragingly to his four-in-hand.

"Come round there, boys!—round agin! We got t' finish this land. Come in there, Dan! *Stiddy,* Kate!—stiddy! None o' y'r tantrums, Kittie. It's purty tuff, but got a be did. *Tchk! tchk!* Step along, Pete! Don't let Kate git y'r single-tree on the wheel. *Once* more!"

They seemed to know what he meant, and that this was the last round, for they worked with greater vigor than before.

"Once more, boys, an' sez I oats an' a nice warm stall, an' sleep f'r all."

By the time the last furrow was turned on the land it was too dark to see the house, and the snow changing to rain again. The tired and hungry man could see the light from the kitchen shining through the leafless hedge, and lifting a great shout, he yelled, "Supp*er* f'r a half a dozen!"

It was nearly eight o'clock by the time he had finished his chores and started for supper. He was picking his way carefully through the mud, when the tall form of a man loomed up before him with a premonitory cough.

"Waddy ye want?" was the rather startled question of the farmer.

"Well, ye see," began the stranger in a deprecating tone, "we'd like t' git in f'r the night. We've tried every house f'r the last two miles, but they hadn't any room f'r us. My wife's jest about sick, 'n' the children are cold and hungry—"

"Oh, y' want a stay all night, eh?"

"Yes, sir; it 'ud be a great accom—"

"Waal, I don't make it a practice t' turn anybuddy away hungry, not on sech nights as this. Drive right in. We ain't got much, but sech as it is—"

But the stranger had disappeared. And soon his steaming, weary team, with drooping heads and swinging single-trees, moved past the well to the block beside the path. Council stood at the side of the "schooner" and helped the children out—two little half-sleeping children—and then a small woman with a babe in her arms.

"There ye go!" he shouted, jovially, to the children. "*Now* we're all right. Run right along to the house there, an' tell Mam' Council you wants sumpthin' t' eat. Right this way, Mis'—keep right off t' the right there. I'll go an' git a lantern. Come," he said to the dazed and silent group at his side.

"Mother," he shouted, as he neared the fragrant

and warmly-lighted kitchen, "here are some wayfarers an' folks who need sumpthin t' eat an' a place t' snooze." He ended by pushing them all in.

Mrs. Council, a large, jolly, rather coarse-looking woman, took the children in her arms. "Come right in, you little rabbits. 'Most asleep, hay? Now here's a drink o' milk f'r each o' ye. I'll have s'm tea in a minute. Take off y'r things and set up t' the fire."

While she set the children to drinking milk, Council got out his lantern and went out to the barn to help the stranger about his team, where his loud, hearty voice could be heard as it came and went between the hay-mow and the stalls.

The woman came to light as a small, timid, and discouraged-looking woman, but still pretty, in a thin and sorrowful way.

"Land sakes! An' you've travelled all the way from Clear Lake t'-day in this mud! Waal! waal! No wonder you're all tired out. Don't wait f'r the men, Mis'—" She hesitated, waiting for the name.

"Haskins."

"Mis' Haskins, set right up to the table an' take a good swig o' tea, whilst I make y' s'm toast. It's green tea, an' it's good. I tell Council as I git older I don't seem t' enjoy Young Hyson n'r Gunpowder. I want the reel green tea, jest as it comes off'n the vines. Seems t' have more heart in it some way. Don't s'pose it has. Council says it's all in m' eye."

Going on in this easy way, she soon had the children filled with bread and milk and the woman thoroughly at home, eating some toast and sweet-melon pickles, and sipping the tea.

"See the little rats!" she laughed at the children. "They're full as they can stick now, and they want to go to bed. Now don't git up, Mis' Haskins; set right where you are an' let me look after 'em. I know all about young ones, though I am all alone now. Jane went an' married last fall. But, as I tell Council, it's lucky we keep our health. Set right there, Mis' Haskins; I won't have you stir a finger."

It was an unmeasured pleasure to sit there in the warm, homely kitchen, the jovial chatter of the housewife driving out and holding at bay the growl of the impotent, cheated wind.

The little woman's eyes filled with tears which fell down upon the sleeping baby in her arms. The world was not so desolate and cold and hopeless, after all.

"Now I hope Council won't stop out there and talk politics all night. He's the greatest man to talk politics an, read the *Tribune*. How old is it?"

She broke off and peered down at the face of the babe.

"Two months 'n' five days," said the mother, with a mother's exactness.

"Ye don't say! I want t' know! The dear little pudzy-wudzy!" she went on, stirring it up in the neighborhood of the ribs with her fat forefinger.

"Pooty tough on 'oo to go gallivant'n' 'cross lots this way."

"Yes, that's so; a man can't lift a mountain," said Council, entering the door. "Sarah, this is Mr. Haskins from Kansas. He's been eat up 'n' drove out by grasshoppers."

"Glad t' see yeh! Pa, empty that wash-basin 'n' give him a chance t' wash."

Haskins was a tall man, with a thin, gloomy face. His hair was a reddish brown, like his coat, and seemed equally faded by the wind and sun. And his sallow face, though hard and set, was pathetic somehow. You would have felt that he had suffered much by the line of his mouth showing under his thin, yellow mustache.

"Hain't Ike got home yet, Sairy?"

"Hain't seen 'im."

"W-a-a-l, set right up, Mr. Haskins; wade right into what we've got; 'tain't much, but we manage to live on it—she gits fat on it," laughed Council, pointing his thumb at his wife.

After supper, while the women put the children to bed, Haskins and Council talked on, seated near the huge cooking-stove, the steam rising from their wet clothing. In the Western fashion, Council told as much of his own life as he drew from his guest. He asked but few questions; but by and by the story of Haskins's struggles and defeat came out. The story was a terrible one, but he told it quietly, seated with his elbows on his knees, gazing most of the time at the hearth.

"I didn't like the looks of the country, anyhow," Haskins said, partly rising and glancing at his wife. "I was ust t' northern Ingyannie, where we have lots a timber 'n' lots o' rain, 'n' I didn't like the looks o' that dry prairie. What galled me the worst was goin' s' far away acrosst so much fine land layin' all through here vacant."

"And the 'hoppers eat ye four years hand running, did they?"

"Eat! They wiped us out. They chawed everything that was green. They jest set around waitin' f'r us to die t' eat us too. My God! I ust t' dream of 'em sitt'n' 'round on the bedpost, six feet long, workin' their jaws. They eet the fork-handles. They got worse 'n' worse till they jest rolled on one another, piled up like snow in winter. Well, it ain't no use; if I was t' talk all winter I couldn't tell nawthin'. But all the while I couldn't help thinkin' of all that land back here that nobuddy was usin', that I ought a had 'stead o' bein' out there in that cussed country."

"Waal, why didn't ye stop an' settle here?" asked Ike, who had come in and was eating his supper.

"Fer the simple reason that you fellers wantid ten

'r fifteen dollars an acre fer the bare land, and I hadn't no money fer that kind o' thing."

"Yes, I do my own work," Mrs. Council was heard to say in the pause which followed. "I'm a-gettin' purty heavy t' be on m' laigs all day, but we can't afford t' hire, so I keep rackin' around somehow, like a foundered horse. S' lame—I tell Council he can't tell how lame I am f'r I'm jest as lame in one laig as t'other." And the good soul laughed at the joke on herself as she took a handful of flour and dusted the biscuit-board to keep the dough from sticking.

"Well, I hain't *never* been very strong," said Mrs. Haskins. "Our folks was Canadians an' small-boned, and then since my last child I hain't got up again fairly. I don't like t' complain—Tim has about all he can bear now—but they was days this week when I jest wanted to lay right down an' die."

"Waal, now, I'll tell ye," said Council from his side of the stove, silencing everybody with his good-natured roar, "I'd go down and *see* Butler, *anyway*, if I was you. I guess he'd let you have his place purty cheap; the farm's all run down. He's ben anxious t' let t' somebuddy next year. It 'ud be a good chance fer you. Anyhow, you go to bed, and sleep like a babe. I've got some ploughin' t' do anyhow, an' we'll see if somethin' can't be done about your case. Ike, you go out an' see if the horses is all right, an' I'll show the folks t' bed."

When the tired husband and wife were lying under the generous quilts of the spare bed, Haskins listened a moment to the wind in the eaves, and then said, with a slow and solemn tone:

"There are people in this world who are good enough t' be angels, an' only haff t' die to *be* angels."

II

Jim Butler was one of those men called in the west "land poor." Early in the history of Rock River he had come into the town and started in the grocery business in a small way, occupying a small building in a mean part of the town. At this period of his life he earned all he got, and was up early and late, sorting beans, working over butter, and carting his goods to and from the station. But a change came over him at the end of the second year, when he sold a lot of land for four times what he paid for it. From that time forward he believed in land speculation as the surest way of getting rich. Every cent he could save or spare from his trade he put into land at forced sale, or mortgages on land, which were "just as good as the wheat," he was accustomed to say.

Farm after farm fell into his hands, until he was recognized as one of the leading land-owners of the county. His mortgages were scattered all over Cedar County, and as they slowly but surely fell in he sought usually to retain the former owner as tenant.

He was not ready to foreclose; indeed, he had the name of being one of the "easiest" men in the town. He let the debtor off again and again, extending the time whenever possible.

"I don't want y'r land," he said. "All I'm after is the int'rest on my money—that's all. Now if y' want 'o stay on the farm, why, I'll give y' a good chance. I can't have the land layin' vacant." And in many cases the owner remained as tenant.

In the mean time he had sold his store; he couldn't spend time in it; he was mainly occupied now with sitting around town on rainy days, smoking and "gassin' with the boys," or in riding to and from his farms. In fishing time he fished a good deal. Doc Grimes, Ben Ashley, and Cal Cheatham were his cronies on these fishing excursions or hunting trips in the time of chickens or partridges. In winter they went to northern Wisconsin to shoot deer.

In spite of all these signs of easy life, Butler persisted in saying he "hadn't money enough to pay taxes on his land," and was careful to convey the impression that he was poor in spite of his twenty farms. At one time he was said to be worth fifty thousand dollars, but land had been a little slow of sale of late, so that he was not worth so much. A fine farm, known as the Higley place, had fallen into his hands in the usual way the previous year, and he had not been able to find a tenant for it. Poor Higley, after working himself nearly to death on it, in the attempt to lift the mortgage, had gone off to Dakota, leaving the farm and his curse to Butler.

This was the farm which Council advised Haskins to apply for; and the next day Council hitched up his team and drove down town to see Butler.

"You jest lem *me* do all the talkin'," he said. "We'll find him wearin' out his pants on some salt-barrel somewe'rs; and if he thought you *wanted* a place, he'd sock it to you hot and heavy. You jest keep quiet; I'll fix 'im."

Butler was seated in Ben Ashley's store, telling "fish yarns," when Council sauntered in casually.

"Hello, But; lyin' agin, hay?"

"Hello, Steve! how goes it?"

"Oh, so-so. Too dang much rain these days. I thought it was goin' t' freeze f'r good last night. Tight squeak if I git m' ploughin' done. How's farmin' with *you* these days?"

"Bad. Ploughin' ain't half done."

"It 'ud be a religious idee f'r you t' go out an' take a hand y'rself."

"I don't haff to," said Butler, with a wink.

"Got anybody on the Higley place?"

"No. Know of anybody?"

"Waal, no; not eggsackly. I've got a relation back t' Michigan who's ben hot an' cold on the idee o' comin' West f'r some time. *Might* come if he could get a good lay-out. What do you talk on the farm?"

"Well, I d' know. I'll rent it on shares or I'll rent it money rent."

"Waal, how much money, say?"

"Well, say ten per cent on the price—two-fifty."

"Waal, that ain't bad. Wait on 'im till 'e thrashes?"

Haskins listened eagerly to his important question, but Council was coolly eating a dried apple which he had speared out of a barrel with his knife. Butler studied him carefully.

"Well, knocks me out of twenty-five dollars interest."

"My relation 'll need all he's got t' git his crops in," said Council, in the same indifferent way.

"Well, all right; *say* wait," concluded Butler.

"All right; this is the man. Haskins, this is Mr. Butler—no relation to Ben—the hardest working man in Cedar county."

On the way home Haskins said: "I ain't much better off. I'd like that farm; it's a good farm, but it's all run down, an' so 'm I. I could make a good farm of it if I had half a show. But I can't stock it n'r seed it."

"Waal, now, don't you worry," roared Council in his ear. "We'll pull y' through somehow till next harvest. He's agreed t' hire it ploughed, an' you can earn a hundred dollars ploughin' an' y' c'n git the seed o' me, an' pay me back when y' can."

Haskins was silent with emotion, but at last he said, "I ain't got nothin' t' live on."

"Now don't you worry 'bout that. You jest make your headquarters at ol' Steve Council's. Mother'll take a pile o' comfort in havin' y'r wife an' children 'round. Y' see Jane's married off lately, an' Ike's away a good 'eal, so we'll be darn glad t' have ye stop with us this winter. Nex' spring we'll see if y' can't git a start agin;" and he chirruped to the team, which sprang forward with the rumbling, clattering wagon.

"Say, looky here, Council, you can't do this. I never saw—" shouted Haskins in his neighbor's ear.

Council moved about uneasily in his seat, and stopped his stammering gratitude by saying: "Hold on, now; don't make such a fuss over a little thing. When I see a man down, an' things all on top of 'm, I jest like t' kick em off an' help 'm up. That's the kind of religion I got, an' it's about the *only* kind."

They rode the rest of the way home in silence. And when the red light of the lamp shone out into the darkness of the cold and windy night, and he thought of this refuge for his children and wife, Haskins could have put his arm around the neck of his burly companion and squeezed him like a lover; but he contented himself with saying: "Steve Council, you'll git y'r pay f'r this some day."

"Don't want any pay. My religion ain't run on such business principles."

The wind was growing colder, and the ground was covered with a white frost, as they turned into the gate of the Council farm, and the children came rushing out, shouting "Papa's come!" They hardly looked like the same children who had sat at the table the night before. Their torpidity under the influence of sunshine and Mother Council had given way to a sort of spasmodic cheerfulness, as insects in winter revive when laid on the earth.

III

Haskins worked like a fiend, and his wife, like the heroic woman that she was, bore also uncomplainingly the most terrible burdens. They rose early and toiled without intermission till the darkness fell on the plain, then tumbled into bed, every bone and muscle aching with fatigue, to rise with the sun next morning to the same round of the same ferocity of labor.

The eldest boy, now nine years old, drove a team all through the spring, ploughing and seeding, milked the cows, and did chores innumerable, in most ways taking the place of a man; an infinitely pathetic but common figure—this boy—on the American farm, where there is no law against child labor. To see him in his coarse clothing, his huge boots, and his ragged cap, as he staggered with a pail of water from the well, or trudged in the cold and cheerless dawn out into the frosty field behind his team, gave the city-bred visitor a sharp pang of sympathetic pain. Yet Haskins loved his boy, and would have saved him from this if he could, but he could not.

By June the first year the result of such Herculean toil began to show on the farm. The yard was cleaned up and sown to grass, the garden ploughed and planted, and the house mended. Council had given them four of his cows.

"Take 'em an' run 'em on shares. I don't want a milk s' many. Ike's away s' much now, Sat'd'ys an' Sund'ys, I can't stand the bother anyhow."

Other men, seeing the confidence of Council in the new-comer, had sold him tools on time; and as he was really an able farmer, he soon had round him many evidences of his care and thrift. At the advice of Council he had taken the farm for three years, with the privilege of re-renting or buying at the end of the term.

"It's a good bargain, an' y' want 'o nail it," said

Council. "If you have any kind ov a crop, you can pay y'r debts, an' keep seed an' bread."

The new hope which now sprang up in the heart of Haskins and his wife grew great almost as a pain by the time the wide field of wheat began to wave and rustle and swirl in the winds of July. Day after day he would snatch a few moments after supper to go and look at it.

"Have ye seen the wheat t'-day, Nettie?" he asked one night as he rose from supper.

"No, Tim, I ain't had time."

"Well, take time now. Le's go look at it."

She threw an old hat on her head—Tommy's hat—and looking almost pretty in her thin sad way, went out with her husband to the hedge.

"Ain't it grand, Nettie? Just look at it."

It was grand. Level, russet here and there, heavy-headed, wide as a lake, and full of multitudinous whispers and gleams of wealth, it stretched away before the gazers like the fabled field of the cloth of gold.

"Oh, I think—I *hope* we'll have a good crop, Tim; and oh, how good the people have been to us!"

"Yes; I don't know where we'd be t'-day if it hadn't ben f'r Council and his wife."

"They're the best people in the world," said the little woman, with a great sob of gratitude.

"We'll be in the field on Monday, sure," said Haskins, griping the rail on the fence as if already at the work of the harvest.

The harvest came, bounteous, glorious, but the winds came and blew it into tangles, and the rain matted it here and there close to the ground, increasing the work of gathering it threefold.

Oh, how they toiled in those glorious days! Clothing dripping with sweat, arms aching, filled with briers, fingers raw and bleeding, backs broken with the weight of heavy bundles, Haskins and his man toiled on. Tommy drove the harvester while his father and a hired man bound on the machine. In this way they cut ten acres every day, and almost every night after supper, when the hand went to bed, Haskins returned to the field, shocking the bound grain in the light of the moon. Many a night he worked till his anxious wife came out to call him in to rest and lunch.

At the same time she cooked for the men, took care of the children, washed and ironed, milked the cows at night, made the butter, and sometimes fed the horses and watered them while her husband kept at the shocking. No slave in the Roman galleys could have toiled so frightfully and lived, for this man thought himself a free man, and that he was working for his wife and babes.

When he sank into his bed with a deep groan of relief, too tired to change his grimy, dripping clothing, he felt that he was getting nearer and nearer to a home of his own, and pushing the wolf of want a little farther from his door.

There is no despair so deep as the despair of a homeless man or woman. To roam the roads of the country or the streets of the city, to feel there is no rood of ground on which the feet can rest, to halt weary and hungry outside lighted windows and hear laughter and song within—these are the hungers and rebellions that drive men to crime and women to shame.

It was the memory of this homelessness, and the fear of its coming again, that spurred Timothy Haskins and Nettie, his wife, to such ferocious labor during that first year.

IV

"'M, yes; 'm, yes; first-rate," said Butler, as his eye took in the neat garden, the pigpen, and the well-filled barn-yard. "You're git'n' quite a stock around yer. Done well, eh?"

Haskins was showing Butler around the place. He had not seen it for a year, having spent the year in Washington and Boston with Ashley, his brother-in-law, who had been elected to Congress.

"Yes, I've laid out a good deal of money during the last three years. I've paid out three hundred dollars f'r fencin'."

"Um—h'm! I see, I see," said Butler, while Haskins went on.

"The kitchen there cost two hundred; the barn ain't cost much in money, but I've put a lot o' time on it. I've dug a new well, and I—"

"Yes, yes. I see! You've done well. Stalk worth a thousand dollars," said Butler, picking his teeth with a straw.

"About that," said Haskins, modestly. "We begin to feel's if we wuz git'n' a home f'r ourselves; but we've worked hard. I tell ye we begin to feel it, Mr. Butler, and we're goin' t' begin t' ease up purty soon. We've been kind o' plannin' a trip back t' *her* folks after the fall ploughin's done."

"*Eggs*-actly!" said Butler, who was evidently thinking of something else. "I suppose you've kine o' kalklated on stayin' here three years more?"

"Well, yes. Fact is, I think I c'n buy the farm this fall, if you'll give me a reasonable show."

"Um—m! What do you call a reasonable show?"

"Waal; say a quarter down and three years' time."

Butler looked at the huge stacks of wheat which filled the yard, over which the chickens were fluttering and crawling, catching grasshoppers, and out of which the crickets were singing innumerably. He smiled in a peculiar way as he said, "Oh, I won't be hard on yer. But what did you expect to pay f'r the place?"

"Why, about what you offered it for before, two thousand five hundred, or *possibly* the three thousand dollars," he added quickly, as he saw the owner shake his head.

"This farm is worth five thousand and five hundred dollars," said Butler, in a careless but decided voice.

"*What!*" almost shrieked the astounded Haskins. "What's that? Five thousand? Why, that's double what you offered it for three years ago."

"Of course; and it's worth it. It was all run down then; now it's in good shape. You've laid out fifteen hundred dollars in improvements, according to your own story."

"But *you* had nothin' t' do about that. It's my work an' my money."

"You bet it was; but it's my land."

"But what's to pay me for all my—?"

"Ain't you had the use of 'em?" replied Butler, smiling calmly into his face.

Haskins was like a man struck on the head with a sand-bag; he couldn't think; he stammered as he tried to say: "But—I never 'd git the use—You'd rob me. More'n that: you agreed—you promised that I could buy or rent at the end of three years at—"

"That's all right. But I didn't say I'd let you carry off the improvements, nor that I'd go on renting the farm at two-fifty. The land is doubled in value, it don't matter how; it don't enter into the question; an' now you can pay me five hundred dollars a year rent, or take it on your own terms at fifty-five hundred, or—git out."

He was turning away when Haskins, the sweat pouring from his face, fronted him, saying again:

"But *you've* done nothing to make it so. You hain't added a cent. I put it all there myself, expectin' to buy. I worked an' sweat to improve it. I was workin' f'r myself an' babes—"

"Well, why didn't you buy when I offered to sell? What y' kickin' about?"

"I'm kickin' about payin' you twice f'r my own things—my own fences, my own kitchen, my own garden."

Butler laughed. "You're too green t' eat, young feller. *Your* improvements! The law will sing another tune."

"But I trusted your word."

"Never trust anybody, my friend. Besides, I didn't promise not to do this thing. Why, man, don't look at me like that. Don't take me for a thief. It's the law. The reg'lar thing. Everybody does it."

"I don't care if they do. It's stealin' jest the same. You take three thousand dollars of my money. The work o' my hands and my wife's." He broke down at this point. He was not a strong man mentally. He could face hardship, ceaseless toil, but he could not face the cold and sneering face of Butler.

"But I don't take it," said Butler, coolly. "All you've got to do is to go on jest as you've been a-doin', or give me a thousand dollars down, and a mortgage at ten per cent on the rest."

Haskins sat down blindly on a bundle of oats near by, and with staring eyes and drooping head went over the situation. He was under the lion's paw. He felt a horrible numbness in his heart and limbs. He was hid in a mist, and there was no path out.

Butler walked about, looking at the huge stacks of grain, and pulling now and again a few handfuls out, shelling the heads in his hands and blowing the chaff away. He hummed a little tune as he did so. He had an accommodating air of waiting.

Haskins was in the midst of the terrible toil of the last year. He was walking again in the rain and the mud behind his plough, he felt the dust and dirt of the threshing. The ferocious husking time, with its cutting wind and biting, clinging snows, lay hard upon him. Then he thought of his wife, how she had cheerfully cooked and baked, without holiday and without rest.

"Well, what do you think of it?" inquired the cool, mocking, insinuating voice of Butler.

"I think you're a thief and a liar!" shouted Haskins, leaping up. "A black-hearted houn'!" Butler's smile maddened him; with a sudden leap he caught a fork in his hands, and whirled it in the air. "You'll never rob another man, damn ye!" he grated through his teeth, a look of pitiless ferocity in his accusing eyes.

Butler shrank and quivered, expecting the blow; stood, held hypnotized by the eyes of the man he had a moment before despised—a man transformed into an avenging demon. But in the deadly hush between the lift of the weapon and its fall there came a gush of faint, childish laughter, and then across the range of his vision, far away and dim, he saw the sun-bright head of his baby girl, as, with the pretty tottering run of a two-year-old, she moved across the grass of the door-yard. His hands relaxed; the fork fell to the ground; his head lowered.

"Make out y'r deed an' morgige, an' git off'n my land, an' don't ye never cross my line agin; if y' do, I'll kill ye."

Butler backed away from the man in wild haste, and climbing into his buggy with trembling limbs, drove off down the road, leaving Haskins seated dumbly on the sunny pile of sheaves, his head sunk into his hands.

1889

CHARLES WADDELL CHESNUTT [1858–1932]

IT HAS BEEN SAID that the appearance of "The Goophered Grapevine," by Charles W. Chesnutt, in the August 1887 issue of the *Atlantic Monthly* "broke the color line" in American fiction. For the first time, and in one of the most prestigious literary vehicles of the day, the work of a Negro writer was presented without reference to his race, to be judged solely on its merits by the prevailing standards of criticism.

Charles Waddell Chesnutt was born in Cleveland, Ohio, of free Negro parents who had moved North from Fayetteville, North Carolina. After the war, when he was eight years old, the family returned to Fayetteville, and there he grew up. He produced his first short story when he was fourteen years old, and saw it published in a local newspaper. At fourteen, too, he became a pupil-teacher, then went on to teach at various country schools, and in 1880 became principal of the State Normal School at Fayetteville. But what he most wanted to do was to write—"not so much," he said, "for the elevation of the colored people as the elevation of the whites; for I consider the unjust spirit of caste . . . a barrier to the moral progress of the American people." Chafing under the limited opportunities open to him in the South, he learned shorthand in order to have a marketable skill and went back to Cleveland, where he found employment as a stenographer in the accounting and legal departments of the Nickel Plate Railroad Company. He later became a court reporter and established his own bureau of legal stenography. In his free time he studied law and wrote stories, some of which he sold to the McClure syndicate. The year 1887 was a significant one for him: he was admitted to the bar, and "The Goophered Grapevine" was published in the *Atlantic*. At about this time he considered going to live in Europe, perhaps London, to escape the race prejudice of his native land, and to make a new life for himself and his family through his law and his writing. He decided, however, that success in his own country against heavy odds would have more meaning for him than success in a foreign country.

Encouraged by Howells, Cable, Walter Hines Page, and other literary men, Chesnutt gathered a selection of his dialect stories into a volume entitled *The Conjure Woman* (1899). These southern regional tales, drawing on folkways and folk lore, had an authenticity and an absence of sentimentality that distinguished them from the work of Joel Chandler Harris, Thomas Nelson Page, and others who were writing in a similar vein. But Chesnutt was not exclusively a regional writer. He was more interested in exploring through fiction the problems—both interracial and intraracial—of Afro-Americans of mixed blood, especially those who were, as he described himself, without "visible admixture." *The Wife of His Youth and Other Stories* (1899) brought together his best short stories on this theme, and he further addressed himself to it in two novels, *The House Behind the Cedars* (1900) and *The Marrow of Tradition* (1901). These, together with his third and last novel, *The Colonel's Dream* (1905), on the plight of the black laboring man in the South, were less well received than his short stories, partly because American readers were not responsive to his material and treatment, but also because Chesnutt's thematic and technical control was less firm in his novels than in his shorter fiction.

Disappointed at the reception of his novels, Chesnutt thereafter wrote little and published less, turning his attention to his court reporting business, which yielded him a comfortable living. His reputation as a literary spokesman for his race was overtaken by the Harlem Renaissance of the 1920's; but his achievement in American letters was recognized in 1928, four years before his death, by the Spingarn gold medal and citation for his "pioneer work as a literary artist depicting the life and struggle of Americans of African descent."

Further reading: H. M. Chesnutt, *Charles Waddell Chesnutt: Pioneer of the Color Line*, 1952. H. M. Gloster, *Negro Voices in American Fiction*, 1948, 1965.

The Goophered Grapevine

First published in the *Atlantic Monthly* (August 1887), this story was included in *The Conjure Woman* (1899). The text followed here is that of the *Atlantic*.

About ten years ago my wife was in poor health, and our family doctor, in whose skill and honesty I had implicit confidence, advised a change of climate. I was engaged in grape-culture in northern Ohio, and decided to look for a locality suitable for carrying on the same business in some Southern State. I wrote to a cousin who had gone into the turpentine business in central North Carolina, and he assured me that no better place could be found in the South than the State and neighborhood in which he lived: climate and soil were all that could be asked for, and land could be bought for a mere song. A cordial invitation to visit him while I looked into the matter was accepted. We found the weather delightful at that season, the end of the summer, and were most hospitably entertained. Our host placed a horse and buggy at our disposal, and himself acted as guide until I got somewhat familiar with the country.

I went several times to look at a place which I thought might suit me. It had been at one time a thriving plantation, but shiftless cultivation had well-nigh exhausted the soil. There had been a vineyard of some extent on the place, but it had not been attended to since the war, and had fallen into utter neglect. The vines—here partly supported by decayed and broken-down arbors, there twining themselves among the branches of the slender saplings which had sprung up among them—grew in wild and unpruned luxuriance, and the few scanty grapes which they bore were the undisputed prey of the first comer. The site was admirably adapted to grape-raising; the soil, with a little attention, could not have been better; and with the native grape, the luscious scuppernong, mainly to reply upon, I felt sure that I could introduce and cultivate successfully a number of other varieties.

One day I went over with my wife, to show her the place. We drove between the decayed gate-posts—the gate itself had long since disappeared—and up the straight, sandy lane to the open space where a dwelling-house had once stood. But the house had fallen a victim to the fortunes of war, and nothing remained of it except the brick pillars upon which the sills had rested. We alighted, and walked about the place for a while; but on Annie's complaining of weariness I led the way back to the yard, where a pine log, lying under a spreading elm, formed a shady though somewhat hard seat. One end of the log was already occupied by a venerable-looking colored man. He held on his knees a hat full of grapes, over which he was smacking his lips with great gusto, and a pile of grape-skins near him indicated that the performance was no new thing. He respectfully rose as we approached, and was moving away, when I begged him to keep his seat.

"Don't let us disturb you," I said. "There's plenty of room for us all."

He resumed his seat with somewhat of embarrassment.

"Do you live around here?" I asked, anxious to put him at his ease.

"Yas, suh. I lives des ober yander, behine de nex' san'-hill, on de Lumberton plank-road."

"Do you know anything about the time when this vineyard was cultivated?"

"Lawd bless yer, suh, I knows all about it. Dey ain' na'er a man in dis settlement w'at won' tell yer ole Julius McAdoo 'uz bawn an' raise' on dis yer same plantation. Is you de Norv'n gemman w'at's gwine ter buy de ole vimya'd?"

"I am looking at it," I replied; "but I don't know that I shall care to buy unless I can be reasonably sure of making something out of it."

"Well, suh, you is a stranger ter me, en I is a stranger ter you, en we is bofe strangers ter one anudder, but 'f I 'uz in yo' place, I wouldn' buy dis vimya'd."

"Why not?" I asked.

"Well, I dunner whe'r you b'lieves in cunj'in er not,—some er de w'ite folks don't, er says dey don't,—but de truf er de matter is dat dis yer ole vimya'd is goophered."

"Is what?" I asked, not grasping the meaning of this unfamiliar word.

"Is goophered, cunju'd, bewitch'."

He imparted this information with such solemn earnestness, and with such an air of confidential mystery, that I felt somewhat interested, while Annie was evidently much impressed, and drew closer to me.

"How do you know it is bewitched?" I asked.

"I wouldn' spec' fer you ter b'lieve me 'less you know all 'bout de fac's. But ef you en young miss dere doan' min' lis'n'in' ter a ole nigger run on a minute er two w'ile you er restin', I kin 'splain to yer how it all happen'."

We assured him that we would be glad to hear how it all happened, and he began to tell us. At first the current of his memory—or imagination—seemed somewhat sluggish; but as his embarrassment wore off, his language flowed more freely, and the story acquired perspective and coherence. As he became more and more absorbed in the narrative, his eyes assumed a dreamy expression, and he seemed to lose sight of his auditors, and to be living over again in monologue his life on the old plantation.

"Ole Mars Dugal' McAdoo bought dis place long many years befo' de wah, en I 'member well w'en he sot out all dis yer part er de plantation in scuppernon's. De vimes growed monst'us fas', en Mars Dugal' made a thousan' gallon er scuppernon' wine eve'y year.

"Now, ef dey's an'thing a nigger lub, nex' ter 'possum, en chick'n, en watermillyums, it's scuppernon's. Dey ain' nuffin dat kin stan' up side'n de scuppernon' fer sweetness; sugar ain't a suckumstance ter scuppernon'. W'en de season is nigh 'bout ober, en de grapes begin ter swivel up des a little wid de wrinkles er ole age,—w'en de skin git sof' en brown,—den de scuppernon' make you smack yo' lip en roll yo' eye en wush fer mo'; so I reckon it ain' very 'stonishin' dat niggers lub scuppernon'.

"Dey wuz a sight er niggers in de naberhood er de vimya'd. Dere wuz ole Mars Henry Brayboy's niggers, en ole Mars Dunkin McLean's niggers, en Mars Dugal's own niggers; den dey wuz a settlement er free niggers en po' buckrahs down by de Wim'l'ton Road, en Mars Dugal' had de only vimya'd in de naberhood. I reckon it ain' so much so nowadays, but befo' de wah, in slab'ry times, er nigger didn' mine goin' fi' er ten mile in a night, w'en dey wuz sump'n good ter eat at de yuther een.

"So atter a w'ile Mars Dugal' begin ter miss his scuppernon's. Co'se he 'cuse' de niggers er it, but dey all 'nied it ter de las'. Mars Dugal' sot spring guns en steel traps, en he en de oberseah sot up nights once't er twice't, tel one night Mars Dugal'—he 'uz a monst'us keerless man—got his leg shot full er cow-peas. But somehow er nudder dey couldn' nebber ketch none er de niggers. I dunner how it happen, but it happen des like I tell yer, en de grapes kep' on a-goin des de same.

"But bimeby ole Mars Dugal' fix' up a plan ter stop it. Dey 'uz a cunjuh 'ooman livin' down mongs' de free niggers on de Wim'l'ton Road, en all de darkies fum Rockfish ter Beaver Crick wuz feared uv her. She could wuk de mos' powerfulles' kind er goopher,—could make people hab fits er rheumatiz, er make 'em des dwinel away en die; en dey say she went out ridin' de niggers at night, for she wuz a witch 'sides bein' a cunjuh 'ooman. Mars Dugal' hearn 'bout Aun' Peggy's doin's, en begun ter 'flect whe'r er no he couldn' git her ter he'p him keep de niggers off'n de grapevimes. One day in de spring er de year, ole miss pack' up a basket er chick'n en poun'-cake, en a bottle er scuppernon' wine, en Mars Dugal' tuk it in his buggy en driv ober ter Aun' Peggy's cabin. He tuk de basket in, en had a long talk wid Aun' Peggy. De nex' day Aun' Peggy come up ter de vimya'd. De niggers seed her slippin' 'roun', en dey soon foun' out what she 'uz doin' dere. Mars Dugal' had hi'ed her ter goopher de grapevimes. She sa'ntered 'roun' mongs' de vimes, en tuk a leaf fum dis one, en a grape-hull fum dat one, en a grape-seed fum anudder one; en den a little twig fum here, en a little pinch er dirt fum dere,—en put it all in a big black bottle, wid a snake's toof en a speckle' hen's gall en some ha'rs fum a black cat's tail, en den fill' de bottle wid scuppernon' wine. W'en she got de goopher all ready en fix', she tuk 'n went out in de woods en buried it under de root uv a red oak tree, en den come back en tole one er de niggers she done goopher de grapevimes, en a'er a nigger w'at eat dem grapes 'ud be sho ter die inside'n twel' mont's.

"Atter dat de niggers let de scuppernon's 'lone, en Mars Dugal' didn' hab no 'casion ter fine no mo' fault; en de season wuz mos' gone, w'en a strange gemman stop at de plantation one night ter see Mars Dugal' on some business; en his coachman, seein' de scuppernon's growin' so nice en sweet, slip 'roun' behine de smoke-house, en et all de scuppernon's he could hole. Nobody didn' notice it at de time, but dat night, on de way home, de gemman's hoss runned away en kill' de coachman. W'en we hearn de noos, Aun' Lucy, de cook, she up 'n say she seed de strange nigger eat'n' er de scuppernon's behine de smoke-house; en den we knowed de goopher had b'en er wukkin. Den one er de nigger chilluns runned away fum de quarters one day, en got in de scuppernon's, en died de nex' week. W'ite folks say he die' er de fevuh, but de niggers knowed it wuz de goopher. So you k'n be sho de darkies didn' hab much ter do wid dem scuppernon' vimes.

"W'en de scuppernon' season 'uz ober fer dat year, Mars Dugal' foun' he had made fifteen hund'ed gallon er wine; en one er de niggers hearn him laffin' wid de oberseah fit ter kill, en sayin' dem fifteen hund'ed gallon er wine wuz monst'us good intrus' on de ten dollars he laid out on de vimya'd. So I 'low ez he paid Aun' Peggy ten dollars fer to goopher de grapevimes.

"De goopher didn' wuk no mo' tel de nex' summer, w'en 'long to'ds de middle er de season one er de fiel' han's died; en ez dat lef' Mars Dugal' sho't er han's, he went off ter town fer ter buy anudder. He fotch de noo nigger home wid 'im. He wuz er ole nigger, er de color er a gingy-cake, en ball ez a hossapple on de top er his head. He wuz a peart ole nigger, do', en could do a big day's wuk.

"Now it happen dat one er de niggers on de nex' plantation, one er ole Mars Henry Brayboy's niggers, had runned away de day befo', en tuk ter de swamp, en old Mars Dugal' en some er de yuther nabor w'ite folks had gone out wid dere guns en dere dogs fer ter he'p 'em hunt fer de nigger; en de han's on our own plantation wuz all so flusterated dat we fuhgot ter tell de noo han' 'bout de goopher on de scuppernon' vimes. Co'se he smell de grapes en see de vimes, an atter dahk de fus' thing he done wuz ter slip off ter de grapevimes 'dout sayin' nuffin ter nobody. Nex' mawnin' he tole some er de niggers 'bout de fine bait er scuppernon' he et de night befo'.

"W'en dey tole 'im 'bout de goopher on de grapevimes, he 'uz dat tarrified dat he turn pale, en look des like he gwine ter die right in his tracks. De oberseah come up an axed w'at 'uz de matter; en w'en dey tole 'im Henry be'n eatin' er de scuppernon's, en got de goopher on 'im, he gin Henry a big drink er w'iskey, en 'low dat de nex' rainy day he take 'im ober ter Aun' Peggy's, en see ef she wouldn' take de goopher off'n him, seein' ez he didn' know nuffin erbout it tel he done et de grapes.

"Sho nuff, it rain de nex' day, en de oberseah went ober ter Aun' Peggy's wid Henry. En Aun' Peggy say dat bein' ez Henry didn' know 'bout de goopher, en et de grapes in ign'ance er de quinseconces, she reckon she mought be able fer ter take de goopher off'n him. So she fotch out er bottle wid some cunjuh medicine in it, en po'd some out in a go'd fer Henry ter drink. He manage ter git it down; he say it tas'e like whiskey wid sump'n bitter in it. She 'lowed dat 'ud keep de goopher off'n him tel de spring; but w'en de sap begin ter rise in de grapevimes he ha' ter come en see her agin, en she tell him w'at e's ter do.

"Nex' spring, w'en de sap commence' ter rise in de scuppernon' vime, Henry tuk a ham one night. Whar'd he git de ham? *I* doan know; dey wa'nt no hams on de plantation 'cep'n' w'at 'uz in de smoke-house, but *I* never see Henry 'bout de smoke-house. But ez I wuz a-sayin', he tuk de ham ober ter Aun' Peggy's; en Aun' Peggy tole 'im dat w'en Mars Dugal' begin ter prume de grapevimes, he mus' go en take 'n scrape off de sap whar it ooze out'n de cut een's er de vimes, en 'n'int his ball head wid it; en ef he do dat once't a year de goopher wouldn' wuk agin 'im long ez he done it. En bein' ez he fotch her de ham, she fix' it so he kin eat all de scuppernon' he want.

"So Henry 'n'int his head wid de sap out'n de big grapevime des ha'f way 'twix' de quarters en de big house, en de goopher nebber wuk agin him dat summer. But de beatenes' thing you eber see happen ter Henry. Up ter dat time he wuz ez ball ez a sweeten' 'tater, but des ez soon ez de young leaves begun ter come out on de grapevimes de ha'r begun ter grow out on Henry's head, en by de middle er de summer he had de bigges' head er ha'r on de plantation. Befo' dat, Henry had tol'able good ha'r 'roun' de aidges, but soon ez de young grapes begun ter come Henry's ha'r begun ter quirl all up in little balls, des like dis yer reg'lar grapy ha'r, en by de time de grapes got ripe his head look des like a bunch er grapes. Combin' it didn' do no good; he wuk at it ha'f de night wid er Jim Crow,[1] en think he git it straighten' out, but in de mawnin' de grapes 'ud be dere des de same. So he gin it up, en tried ter keep de grapes down by havin' his ha'r cut sho't.

"But dat wa'nt de quares' thing 'bout de goopher. When Henry come ter de plantation, he wuz gittin' a little ole an stiff in de j'ints. But dat summer he got des ez spry en libely ez any young nigger on de plantation; fac' he got so biggity dat Mars Jackson, de oberseah, ha' ter th'eaten ter whip 'im, ef he didn' stop cuttin' up his didos en behave hisse'f. But de mos' cur'ouses' thing happen' in de fall, when de sap begin ter go down in de grapevimes. Fus', when de grapes 'uz gethered, de knots begun ter straighten out'n Henry's h'ar; en w'en de leaves begin ter fall, Henry's ha'r begin ter drap out; en w'en de vimes 'uz b'ar, Henry's head wuz baller 'n it wuz in de spring, en he begin ter git ole en stiff in de j'ints ag'in, en paid no mo' tention ter de gals dyoin' er de whole winter. En nex' spring, w'en he rub de sap on ag'in, he got young ag'in, en so soopl en libely dat none er de young niggers on de plantation couldn' jump, ner dance, ner hoe ez much cotton ez Henry. But in de fall er de year his grapes begun ter straighten out, en his j'ints ter git stiff, en his ha'r drap off, en de rheumatiz begin ter wrastle wid 'im.

"Now, ef you'd a knowed old Mars Dugal' McAdoo, you'd a knowed dat it ha' ter be a mighty rainy day when he couldn' fine sump'n fer his niggers ter do, en it ha' ter be a mighty little hole he couldn' crawl thoo, en ha' ter be a monst'us cloudy night w'en a dollar git by him in de dahkness; en w'en he see how Henry git young in de spring en ole in de fall, he 'lowed ter hisse'f ez how he could make mo' money outen Henry dan by wukkin' him in de cotton fiel'. 'Long de nex' spring, atter de sap com-

[1] A small card, resembling a curry-comb in construction, and used by negroes in the rural districts instead of a comb. [Chesnutt's note.]

mence' ter rise, en Henry 'n'int 'is head en commence fer ter git young en soopl, Mars Dugal' up'n tuk Henry ter town, en sole 'im fer fifteen hunder' dollars. Co'se de man w'at bought Henry didn' know nuffin 'bout de goopher, en Mars Dugal' didn' see no 'casion fer ter tell 'im. Long to'ds de fall, w'en de sap went down, Henry begin ter git ole again same ez yuzhal, en his noo marster begin ter git skeered les'n he gwine ter lose his fifteen-hunder'-dollar nigger. He sent fer a mighty fine doctor, but de med'cine didn' 'pear ter do no good; de goopher had a good holt. Henry tole de doctor 'bout de goopher, but de doctor des laff at 'im.

"One day in de winter Mars Dugal' went ter town, en wuz santerin' long de Main Street, when who should he meet but Henry's noo marster. Dey said 'Hoddy,' en Mars Dugal' ax 'im ter hab a seegyar; en atter dey run on awhile 'bout de craps en de weather, Mars Dugal' ax 'im, sorter keerless, like ez ef he des thought of it,—

" 'How you like de nigger I sole you las' spring?'

"Henry's marster shuck his head en knock de ashes off'n his seegyar.

" 'Spec' I made a bad bahgin when I bought dat nigger. Henry done good wuk all de summer, but sence de fall set in he 'pears ter be sorter pinin' away. Dey ain' nuffin pertickler de matter wid 'im—leastways de doctor say so—'cept'n' a tech er de rheumatiz; but his ha'r is all fell out, en ef he don't pick up his strenk mighty soon, I spec' I'm gwine ter lose 'im.'

"Dey smoked on awhile, en bimeby ole mars say, 'Well, a bahgin's a bahgin, but you en me is good fren's, en I doan wan' ter see you lose all de money you paid fer dat nigger; en ef w'at you say is so, en I ain't 'sputin' it, he ain't wuf much now. I spec's you wukked him too ha'd dis summer, er e'se de swamps down here don't agree wid de san'-hill nigger. So you des lemme know, en ef he gits any wusser I'll be willin' ter gib yer five hund'ed dollars fer 'im, en take my chances on his livin'.'

"Sho nuff, when Henry begun ter draw up wid de rheumatiz en it look like he gwine ter die fer sho, his noo marster sen' fer Mars Dugal', en Mars Dugal' gin him what he promus, en brung Henry home ag'in. He tuk good keer uv 'im dyoin' er de winter,—give 'im w'iskey ter rub his rheumatiz, en terbacker ter smoke, en all he want ter eat,—'caze a nigger w'at he could make a thousan' dollars a year off'n didn' grow on eve'y huckleberry bush.

"Nex' spring, w'en de sap ris en Henry's ha'r commence' ter sprout, Mars Dugal' sole 'im ag'in, down in Robeson County dis time; en he kep' dat sellin' business up fer five year er mo'. Henry nebber say nuffin 'bout de goopher ter his noo marsters, 'caze he know he gwine ter be tuk good keer uv de nex' winter, w'en Mars Dugal' buy him back. En Mars Dugal' made 'nuff money off'n Henry ter buy anudder plantation ober on Beaver Crick.

"But long 'bout de een' er dat five year dey come a stranger ter stop at de plantation. De fus' day he 'uz dere he went out wid Mars Dugal' en spent all de mawnin' lookin' ober de vimya'd, en atter dinner dey spent all de evenin' playin' kya'ds. De niggers soon 'skiver' dat he wuz a Yankee, en dat he come down ter Norf C'lina fer ter learn de w'ite folks how to raise grapes en make wine. He promus Mars Dugal' he cud make de grapevimes ba'r twice't ez many grapes, en dat de noo wine-press he wuz a-sellin' would make mo' d'n twice't ez many gallons er wine. En ole Mars Dugal' des drunk it all in, des 'peared ter be bewitched wid dat Yankee. W'en de darkies see dat Yankee runnin' 'roun de vimya'd en diggin' under de grapevimes, dey shuk dere heads, en 'lowed dat dey feared Mars Dugal' losin' his min'. Mars Dugal' had all de dirt dug away fum under de roots er all de scuppernon' vimes, an' let 'em stan' dat away fer a week er mo'. Den dat Yankee made de niggers fix up a mixtry er lime en ashes en manyo, en po' it roun' de roots er de grapevimes. Den he 'vise' Mars Dugal' fer ter trim de vimes close't, en Mars Dugal' tuck 'n done eve'ything de Yankee tole him ter do. Dyoin' all er dis time, mind yer, 'e wuz libbin' off'n de fat er de lan', at de big house, en playin' kyards wid Mars Dugal' eve'y night; en dey say Mars Dugal' los' mo'n a thousan' dollars dyoin' er de week dat Yankee wuz a runnin' de grapevimes.

"W'en de sap ris nex' spring, ole Henry 'n'inted his head ez yuzhal, en his ha'r commence' ter grow des de same ez it done eve'y year. De scuppernon' vimes growed monst's fas', en de leaves wuz greener en thicker dan dey eber be'n dyowin my rememb'ance; en Henry's ha'r growed out thicker dan eber, en he 'peared ter git younger 'n younger, en soopler 'n soopler; en seein' ez he wuz sho't er han's dat spring, havin' tuk in consid'able noo groun', Mars Dugal' 'cluded he wouldn' sell Henry 'tel he git de crap in en de cotton chop'. So he kep' Henry on de plantation.

"But 'long 'bout time fer de grapes ter come on de scuppernon' vimes, dey 'peared ter come a change ober dem; de leaves wivered en swivel' up, en de young grapes turn' yaller, en bimeby eve'y-body on de plantation could see dat de whole vimya'd wuz dyin'. Mars Dugal' tuck 'n water de vimes en done all he could, but 't wan' no use: dat Yankee done bus' de watermillyum. One time de vimes picked up a bit, en Mars Dugal' thought dey wuz gwine ter come out ag'in; but dat Yankee done dug too close unde' de roots, en prune de branches too close ter de vime, en all dat lime en ashes done burn' de life outen de vimes, en dey des kep' a with'in' en a swivelin'.

"All dis time de goopher wuz a-wukkin'. W'en de vimes commence' ter wither, Henry commence' ter complain er his rheumatiz, en when de leaves begin ter dry up his ha'r commence' ter drap out. When de vimes fresh up a bit Henry 'ud git peart agin, en when de vimes wither agin Henry 'ud git ole agin, en des kep' gittin' mo' en mo' fitten fer nuffin; he des pined away, en fine'ly tuk ter his cabin; en when de big vime whar he got de sap ter 'n'int his head withered en turned yaller en died, Henry died too,—des went out sorter like a cannel. Dey didn't 'pear ter be nuffin de matter wid 'im, 'cep'n' de rheumatiz, but his strenk des dwinel' away 'tel he didn' hab ernuff lef' ter draw his bref. De goopher had got de under holt, en th'owed Henry fer good en all dat time.

"Mars Dugal' tuk on might'ly 'bout losin' his vimes en his nigger in de same year; en he swo' dat ef he could git holt er dat Yankee he'd wear 'im ter a frazzle, en den chaw up de frazzle; en he'd done it, too, for Mars Dugal' 'uz a monst'us brash man w'en he once git started. He sot de vimya'd out ober agin, but it wuz th'ee er fo' year befo' de vimes got ter b'arin' any scuppernon's.

"W'en de wah broke out, Mars Dugal' raise' a comp'ny, en went off ter fight de Yankees. He say he wuz mighty glad dat wah come, en he des want ter kill a Yankee fer eve'y dollar he los' 'long er dat grape-raisin' Yankee. En I 'spec' he would a done it, too, ef de Yankees hadn' s'picioned sump'n, en killed him fus'. Atter de s'render ole miss move' ter town, de niggers all scattered 'way fum de plantation, en de vimya'd ain' be'n cultervated sence."

"Is that story true?" asked Annie, doubtfully, but seriously, as the old man concluded his narrative.

"It's des ez true ez I'm a-settin' here, miss. Dey's a easy way ter prove it: I kin lead de way right ter Henry's grave ober yander in de plantation buryin'-groun'. En I tell yer w'at, marster, I wouldn' 'vise yer to buy dis yer ole vimya'd 'caze de goopher 's on it yit, en dey ain' no tellin' w'en it's a gwine ter crap out."

"But I thought you said all the old vines died."

"Dey did 'pear ter die, but a few ov 'em come out ag'in, en is mixed in mongs' de yuthers. I ain' skeered ter eat de grapes 'caze I knows de old vimes fum de noo ones; but wid strangers dey ain' no tellin' w'at might happen. I wouldn' 'vise yer ter buy dis vimya'd."

I bought the vineyard, nevertheless, and it has been for a long time in a thriving condition, and is referred to by the local press as a striking illustration of the opportunities open to Northern capital in the development of Southern industries. The luscious scuppernong holds first rank among our grapes, though we cultivate a great many other varieties, and our income from grapes packed and shipped to the Northern markets is quite considerable. I have not noticed any developments of the goopher in the vineyard, although I have a mild suspicion that our colored assistants do not suffer from want of grapes during the season.

I found, when I bought the vineyard, that Uncle Julius had occupied a cabin on the place for many years, and derived a respectable revenue from the neglected grapevines. This, doubtless, accounted for his advice to me not to buy the vineyard, though whether it inspired the goopher story I am unable to state. I believe, however, that the wages I pay him for his services are more than an equivalent for anything he lost by the sale of the vineyard.

1887

New Voices in Poetry

SIDNEY LANIER [1842–1881]

Lanier's was the first poetic work of high promise to emerge from the desolate South of the Reconstruction days. Henry Timrod was dead, Paul Hamilton Hayne's powers were frustrate through disease, and Lanier, a dozen years younger than they, found himself at the close of the war with impaired health and without a career. Born in Macon, Georgia, graduated from Oglethorpe College, Georgia, in 1860, he had served four years in the Confederate army, had been captured running a blockade, and emerged from a Federal prison at the end of the war with tuberculosis. He tried schoolteaching, he tried the law, he wrote a novel (*Tiger Lilies,* 1867), he wrote and printed poems. An excellent musician, he was appointed first flutist of the Peabody Symphony Orchestra of Baltimore in 1873, and two years later he drew considerable attention to his writing with the poem "Corn," which he published in *Lippincott's Magazine.*

He published a volume of *Poems* in 1877, and was made lecturer on English Literature in Johns Hopkins University in 1879. The next year appeared *The Science of English Verse.* But tuberculosis was upon him. He fled to the Carolina mountains, and died there at the age of thirty-nine.

Like Poe and Whitman and many other moderns, Lanier held music to be the supreme art. His flute-playing vied with his writing as a medium of expression; the relation of music to verse was the theme of *The Science of English Verse;* and his own experiments in the writing of musical poetry are noteworthy.

Further reading: A. H. Starke, *Sidney Lanier,* 1933. J. B. Hubbell, *The South in American Literature,* 1954, pp. 758–77.

The Symphony

In letters written before the poem Lanier had said: "I have so many fair dreams and hopes about music in these days. It is a gospel whereof the people are in great need. As Christ gathered up the ten commandments and re-distilled them into the clear liquid of that wondrous eleventh—Love God utterly, and thy neighbor as thyself—so I think the time will come when music, rightly developed to its now-little-foreseen grandeur, will be found to be a later revelation of all gospels in one."

"Trade, Trade, Trade: pah, are we not all sick? A man cannot walk down a green alley of woods, in these days, without unawares getting his mouth and nose and eyes covered with some web or other that Trade has stretched across, to catch some gain or other. 'Tis an old spider that has crawled all over our modern life, and covered it with a flimsy web that conceals the Realities."

The text followed, for these poems, is that of the Centennial Edition of Lanier's works (Baltimore, 1945).

"O Trade! O Trade! would thou wert dead!
The Time needs heart—'tis tired of head:
We're all for love," the violins said.
"Of what avail the rigorous tale
Of bill for coin and box for bale?
Grant thee, O Trade! thine uttermost hope:
Level red gold with blue sky-slope,
And base it deep as devils grope:
When all's done, what hast thou won

Of the only sweet that's under the sun?
Ay, canst thou buy a single sigh
Of true love's least, least ecstasy?"
Then, with a bridegroom's heart-beats trembling,
All the mightier strings assembling
Ranged them on the violins' side
As when the bridegroom leads the bride,
And, heart in voice, together cried:
"Yea, what avail the endless tale
Of gain by cunning and plus by sale?
Look up the land, look down the land—
The poor, the poor, the poor, they stand
Wedged by the pressing of Trade's hand
Against an inward-opening door
That pressure tightens evermore:
They sigh a monstrous foul-air sigh
For the outside leagues of liberty,
Where Art, sweet lark, translates the sky
Into a heavenly melody.
'Each day, all day' (these poor folks say),
'In the same old year-long, drear-long way,
We weave in the mills and heave in the kilns,
We sieve mine-meshes under the hills,
And thieve much gold from the Devil's bank tills,
To relieve, O God, what manner of ills?—
The beasts, they hunger, and eat, and die;
And so do we, and the world's a sty;
Hush, fellow-swine: why nuzzle and cry?
Swinehood hath no remedy
Say many men, and hasten by,
Clamping the nose and blinking the eye.
But who said once, in the lordly tone,
Man shall not live by bread alone
But all that cometh from the Throne?
    Hath God said so?
    But Trade saith *No:*
And the kilns and the curt-tongued mills say *Go!*
There's plenty that can, if you can't: we know.
Move out, if you think you're underpaid.
The poor are prolific; we're not afraid;
    Trade is trade.'"
Thereat this passionate protesting
    Meekly changed, and softened till
It sank to sad requesting
    And suggesting sadder still:
"And oh, if men might some time see
How piteous-false the poor decree
That trade no more than trade must be!
Does business mean, *Die, you—live, I?*
Then 'Trade is trade' but sings a lie:
'Tis only war grown miserly.
If business is battle, name it so:
War-crimes less will shame it so,
And widows less will blame it so.
Alas: for the poor to have some part
In yon sweet living lands of Art,
Makes problem not for head, but heart.
Vainly might Plato's brain revolve it:
Plainly the heart of a child could solve it."

And then, as when from words that seem but rude
We pass to silent pain that sits abrood
Back in our heart's great dark and solitude,
So sank the strings to gentle throbbing
Of long chords change-marked with sobbing—
Motherly sobbing, not distinctlier heard
Than half wing-openings of the sleeping bird,
Some dream of danger to her young hath stirred.

Then stirring and demurring ceased, and lo!
Every least ripple of the strings' song-flow
Died to a level with each level bow
And made a great chord tranquil-surfaced so,
As a brook beneath his curving bank doth go
To linger in the sacred dark and green
Where many boughs the still pool overlean
And many leaves make shadow with their sheen.
    But presently
A velvet flute-note fell down pleasantly
Upon the bosom of that harmony,
And sailed and sailed incessantly,
As if a petal from a wild-rose blown
Had fluttered down upon that pool of tone
And boatwise dropped o' the convex side
And floated down the glassy tide
And clarified and glorified
The solemn spaces where the shadows bide.
From the warm concave of that fluted note
Somewhat, half song, half odor, forth did float,
As if a rose might somehow be a throat:
"When Nature from her far-off glen
Flutes her soft messages to men,
The flute can say them o'er again;
Yea, Nature, singing sweet and lone,
Breathes through life's strident polyphone
The flute-voice in the world of tone.
    Sweet friends,
    Man's love ascends
To finer and diviner ends
Than man's mere thought e'er comprehends.
    For I, e'en I,
    As here I lie,
A petal on a harmony,
Demand of Science whence and why
Man's tender pain, man's inward cry,
When he doth gaze on earth and sky?
I am not overbold:
    I hold
Full powers from Nature manifold.
I speak for each no-tonguèd tree

That, spring by spring, doth nobler be,
And dumbly and most wistfully
His mighty prayerful arms outspreads
Above men's oft-unheeding heads,
And his big blessing downward sheds.
I speak for all-shaped blooms and leaves,
Lichens on stones and moss on eaves,
Grasses and grains in ranks and sheaves;
Broad-fronded ferns and keen-leaved canes,
And briery mazes bounding lanes,
And marsh-plants, thirsty-cupped for rains,
And milky stems and sugary veins;
For every long-armed woman-vine
That round a piteous tree doth twine;
For passionate odors, and divine
Pistils, and petals crystalline;
All purities of shady springs,
All shynesses of film-winged things
That fly from tree-trunks and bark-rings;
All modesties of mountain-fawns
That leap to covert from wild lawns,
And tremble if the day but dawns;
All sparklings of small beady eyes
Of birds, and sidelong glances wise
Wherewith the jay hints tragedies;
All piquancies of prickly burs,
And smoothnesses of downs and furs,
Of eiders and of minevers;
All limpid honeys that do lie
At stamen-bases, nor deny
The humming-birds' fine roguery,
Bee-thighs, nor any butterfly;
All gracious curves of slender wings,
Bark-mottlings, fibre-spiralings,
Fern-wavings and leaf-flickerings;
Each dial-marked leaf and flower-bell
Wherewith in every lonesome dell
Time to himself his hours doth tell;
All tree-sounds, rustlings of pine-cones,
Wind-sighings, doves' melodious moans,
And night's unearthly under-tones;
All placid lakes and waveless deeps,
All cool reposing mountain-steeps,
Vale-calms and tranquil lotos-sleeps;—
Yea, all fair forms, and sounds, and lights,
And warmths, and mysteries, and nights,
Of Nature's utmost depths and heights.
—These doth my timid tongue present,
Their mouthpiece and leal instrument
And servant, all love-eloquent.
I heard, when *'All for love'* the violins cried:
So, Nature calls through all her system wide,
Give me thy love, O man, so long denied.
Much time is run, and man hath changed his ways,
Since Nature, in the antique fable-days,
Was hid from man's true love by proxy fays,
False fauns and rascal gods that stole her praise.
The nymphs, cold creatures of man's colder brain,
Chilled Nature's streams till man's warm heart was fain
Never to lave its love in them again.
Later, a sweet Voice *Love thy neighbor* said;
Then first the bounds of neighborhood outspread
Beyond all confines of old ethnic dread.
Vainly the Jew might wag his covenant head:
'All men are neighbors,' so the sweet Voice said.
So, when man's arms had circled all man's race,
The liberal compass of his warm embrace
Stretched bigger yet in the dark bounds of space;
With hands a-grope he felt smooth Nature's grace,
Drew her to breast and kissed her sweetheart face:
Yea, man found neighbors in great hills and trees
And streams and clouds and suns and birds and bees,
And throbbed with neighbor-loves in loving these.
But oh, the poor! the poor! the poor!
That stand by the inward-opening door
Trade's hand doth tighten ever more,
And sigh their monstrous foul-air sigh
For the outside hills of liberty,
Where Nature spreads her wild blue sky
For Art to make into melody!
Thou Trade! thou king of the modern days!
Change thy ways,
Change thy ways;
Let the sweaty laborers file
A little while,
A little while,
Where Art and Nature sing and smile.
Trade! is thy heart all dead, all dead?
And hast thou nothing but a head?
I'm all for heart," the flute-voice said,
And into sudden silence fled,
Like as a blush that while 'tis red
Dies to a still, still white instead.

Thereto a thrilling calm succeeds,
Till presently the silence breeds
A little breeze among the reeds
That seems to blow by sea-marsh weeds:
Then from the gentle stir and fret
Sings out the melting clarionet,
Like as a lady sings while yet
Her eyes with salty tears are wet.
"O Trade! O Trade!" the Lady said,
"I too will wish thee utterly dead
If all thy heart is in thy head.
For O my God! and O my God!
What shameful ways have women trod
At beckoning of Trade's golden rod!
Alas when sighs are traders' lies,
And heart's-ease eyes and violet eyes

Are merchandise!
O purchased lips that kiss with pain!
O cheeks coin-spotted with smirch and stain!
O trafficked hearts that break in twain!
—And yet what wonder at my sisters' crime?
So hath Trade withered up Love's sinewy prime,
Men love not women as in olden time.
Ah, not in these cold merchantable days
Deem men their life an opal gray, where plays
The one red Sweet of gracious ladies'-praise.
Now, comes a suitor with sharp prying eye—
Says, *Here, you Lady, if you'll sell, I'll buy:*
Come, heart for heart—a trade? What! weeping?
why?
Shame on such wooers' dapper mercery!
I would my lover kneeling at my feet
In humble manliness should cry, *O sweet!*
I know not if thy heart my heart will greet;
I ask not if thy love my love can meet:
Whate'er thy worshipful soft tongue shall say,
I'll kiss thine answer, be it yea or nay:
I do but know I love thee, and I pray
To be thy knight until my dying day.
Woe him that cunning trades in hearts contrives!
Base love good women to base loving drives.
If men loved larger, larger were our lives;
And wooed they nobler, won they nobler wives."

There thrust the bold straightforward horn
To battle for that lady lorn,
With heartsome voice of mellow scorn,
Like any knight in knighthood's morn.
"Now comfort thee," said he,
"Fair Lady.
For God shall right thy grievous wrong,
And man shall sing thee a true-love song,
Voiced in act his whole life long,
Yea, all thy sweet life long,
Fair Lady.
Where's he that craftily hath said,
The day of chivalry is dead?
I'll prove that lie upon his head,
Or I will die instead,
Fair Lady.
Is Honor gone into his grave?
Hath Faith become a caitiff knave,
And Selfhood turned into a slave
To work in Mammon's cave,
Fair Lady?
Will Truth's long blade ne'er gleam again?
Hath Giant Trade in dungeons slain
All great contempts of mean-got gain
And hates of inward stain,
Fair Lady?
For aye shall name and fame be sold,
And place be hugged for the sake of gold,
And smirch-robed Justice feebly scold
At Crime all money-bold,
Fair Lady?
Shall self-wrapt husbands aye forget
Kiss-pardons for the daily fret
Wherewith sweet wifely eyes are wet—
Blind to lips kiss-wise set—
Fair Lady?
Shall lovers higgle, heart for heart,
Till wooing grows a trading mart
Where much for little, and all for part,
Make love a cheapening art,
Fair Lady?
Shall woman scorch for a single sin
That her betrayer can revel in,
And she be burnt, and he but grin
When that the flames begin,
Fair Lady?
Shall ne'er prevail the woman's plea,
We maids would far, far whiter be
If that our eyes might sometimes see
Men maids in purity,
Fair Lady?
Shall Trade aye salve his conscience-aches
With jibes at Chivalry's old mistakes—
The wars that o'erhot knighthood makes
For Christ's and ladies' sakes,
Fair Lady?
Now by each knight that e'er hath prayed
To fight like a man and love like a maid,
Since Pembroke's life, as Pembroke's blade,
I' the scabbard, death, was laid,
Fair Lady,
I dare avouch my faith is bright
That God doth right and God hath might.
Nor time hath changed His hair to white,
Nor His dear love to spite,
Fair Lady.
I doubt no doubts: I strive, and shrive my clay,
And fight my fight in the patient modern way
For true love and for thee—ah me! and pray
To be thy knight until my dying day,
Fair Lady."
Made end that knightly horn, and spurred away
Into the thick of the melodious fray.

And then the hautboy played and smiled,
And sang like any large-eyed child,
Cool-hearted and all undefiled.
"Huge Trade!" he said,
"Would thou wouldst lift me on thy head,
And run where'er my finger led!
Once said a Man—and wise was He—
Never shalt thou the heavens see,

Save as a little child thou be."
Then o'er sea-lashings of commingling tunes
The ancient wise bassoons,
    Like weird,
    Gray-beard
Old harpers sitting on the high sea-dunes,
    Chanted runes:
"Bright-waved gain, gray-waved loss,
The sea of all doth lash and toss,
One wave forward and one across:
But now 'twas trough, now 'tis crest,
And worst doth foam and flash to best,
    And curst to blest.

"Life! Life! thou sea-fugue, writ from east to west,
    Love, Love alone can pore
    On thy dissolving score
    Of harsh half-phrasings,
        Blotted ere writ,
    And double erasings
        Of chords most fit.
Yea, Love, sole music-master blest,
May read thy weltering palimpsest.
To follow Time's dying melodies through,
And never to lose the old in the new,
And ever to solve the discords true—
    Love alone can do.
And ever Love hears the poor-folks' crying,
And ever Love hears the women's sighing,
And ever sweet knighthood's death-defying,
And ever wise childhood's deep implying,
But never a trader's glozing and lying.

"And yet shall Love himself be heard,
Though long deferred, though long deferred:
O'er the modern waste a dove hath whirred:
Music is Love in search of a word."
1875

The Stirrup-Cup

Death, thou'rt a cordial old and rare:
Look how compounded, with what care!
Time got his wrinkles reaping thee
Sweet herbs from all antiquity.

David to thy distillage went,
Keats, and Gotama excellent,
Omar Khayyám, and Chaucer bright,
And Shakspere for a king-delight.

Then, Time, let not a drop be spilt:
Hand me the cup whene'er thou wilt;
'Tis thy rich stirrup-cup to me;
I'll drink it down right smilingly.
1877

The Marshes of Glynn

Glooms of the live-oaks, beautiful-braided and woven
With intricate shades of the vines that myriad-cloven
  Clamber the forks of the multiform boughs,—
      Emerald twilights,—
      Virginal shy lights,
Wrought of the leaves to allure to the whisper of vows,
When lovers pace timidly down through the green colonnades
Of the dim sweet woods, of the dear dark woods,
  Of the heavenly woods and glades,
That run to the radiant marginal sand-beach within
    The wide sea-marshes of Glynn;—

Beautiful glooms, soft dusks in the noonday fire,—
Wildwood privacies, closets of lone desire,
Chamber from chamber parted with wavering arras of leaves,—
Cells for the passionate pleasure of prayer to the soul that grieves,
Pure with a sense of the passing of saints through the wood,
Cool for the dutiful weighing of ill with good;—

O braided dusks of the oak and woven shades of the vine,
While the riotous noon-day sun of the June-day long did shine,
Ye held me fast in your heart and I held you fast in mine;
But now when the noon is no more, and riot is rest,
And the sun is a-wait at the ponderous gate of the West,
And the slant yellow beam down the wood-aisle doth seem
Like a lane into heaven that leads from a dream,—
Ay, now, when my soul all day hath drunken the soul of the oak,
And my heart is at ease from men, and the wearisome sound of the stroke
  Of the scythe of time and the trowel of trade is low,
  And belief overmasters doubt, and I know that I know,
  And my spirit is grown to a lordly great compass within,

That the length and the breadth and the sweep of the Marshes of Glynn
Will work me no fear like the fear they have wrought me of yore
When length was fatigue, and when breadth was but bitterness sore,
And when terror and shrinking and dreary unnamable pain
Drew over me out of the merciless miles of the plain,—
Oh, now, unafraid, I am fain to face
The vast sweet visage of space.
To the edge of the wood I am drawn, I am drawn,
Where the gray beach glimmering runs, as a belt of the dawn,
For a mete and a mark
To the forest-dark:—
So:
Affable live-oak, leaning low,—
Thus—with your favor—soft, with a reverent hand
(Not lightly touching your person, Lord of the land!),
Bending your beauty aside, with a step I stand
On the firm-packed sand,
Free
By a world of marsh that borders a world of sea.
Sinuous southward and sinuous northward the shimmering band
Of the sand-beach fastens the fringe of the marsh to the folds of the land.
Inward and outward to northward and southward the beach-lines linger and curl
As a silver-wrought garment that clings to and follows the firm sweet limbs of a girl.
Vanishing, swerving, evermore curving again into sight,
Softly the sand-beach wavers away to a dim gray looping of light.
And what if behind me to westward the wall of the woods stands high?
The world lies east: how ample, the marsh and the sea and the sky!
A league and a league of marsh-grass, waist-high, broad in the blade,
Green, and all of a height, and unflecked with a light or a shade,
Stretch leisurely off, in a pleasant plain,
To the terminal blue of the main.

Oh, what is abroad in the marsh and the terminal sea?
Somehow my soul seems suddenly free
From the weighing of fate and the sad discussion of sin,
By the length and the breadth and the sweep of the marshes of Glynn.

Ye marshes, how candid and simple and nothing-withholding and free
Ye publish yourselves to the sky and offer yourselves to the sea!
Tolerant plains, that suffer the sea and the rains and the sun,
Ye spread and span like the catholic man who hath mightily won
God out of knowledge and good out of infinite pain
And sight out of blindness and purity out of a stain.

As the marsh-hen secretly builds on the watery sod,
Behold I will build me a nest on the greatness of God:
I will fly in the greatness of God as the marsh-hen flies
In the freedom that fills all the space 'twixt the marsh and the skies:
By so many roots as the marsh-grass sends in the sod
I will heartily lay me a-hold on the greatness of God:
Oh, like to the greatness of God is the greatness within
The range of the marshes, the liberal marshes of Glynn.

And the sea lends large, as the marsh: lo, out of his plenty the sea
Pours fast: full soon the time of the flood-tide must be:
Look how the grace of the sea doth go
About and about through the intricate channels that flow
Here and there,
Everywhere,
Till his waters have flooded the uttermost creeks and the low-lying lanes,
And the marsh is meshed with a million veins,
That like as with rosy and silvery essences flow
In the rose-and-silver evening glow.
Farewell, my lord Sun!
The creeks overflow: a thousand rivulets run
'Twixt the roots of the sod; the blades of the marsh-grass stir;
Passeth a hurrying sound of wings that westward whirr;
Passeth, and all is still; and the currents cease to run;
And the sea and the marsh are one.

How still the plains of the waters be!
The tide is in his ecstasy.
The tide is at his highest height:
And it is night.

And now from the Vast of the Lord will the waters of sleep
Roll in on the souls of men,
But who will reveal to our waking ken
The forms that swim and the shapes that creep
Under the waters of sleep?
And I would I could know what swimmeth below when the tide comes in
On the length and the breadth of the marvellous marshes of Glynn.

1878

EMILY DICKINSON [1830–1886]

The emergence of Emily Dickinson from a provincial New England spinsterhood in Amherst, Massachusetts, to the stature of "one of the great poets of all time" is one of the most dramatic stories of our literary history. The discovery of her unpublished poems, written on the backs of envelopes and on brown paper bags, neatly wrapped in bunches, tied with thread, and stowed away in dresser drawers, came only after her death—though it had always been well-known in the family that she wrote. Most of them were enclosed with letters to family and friends, expressing her joy in the changing seasons and her consolations over the death of friends. Her sister Lavinia found many of them in a locked box and sought the help of Mabel Loomis Todd, wife of a professor at Amherst College, to bring them to light. They were first published in 1890.

Emily Dickinson's mind was shaped by the romantic and Transcendental "liberation" of the first half of the nineteenth century, the same forces that had kindled the intellectual life of Emerson and so many others. The difference in Emily's case was the strong pull of Puritan theology, enforced by the limitations of her personal life and restricted education. She had little formal schooling. When she was twenty a friend gave her a copy of Emerson's *Poems*. Her reading included the Bible, Shakespeare, Sir Thomas Browne, George Eliot, Keats, Carlyle, and the Brownings, and, as she said, her lexicon was her constant companion. When the severe post-Calvinist theology to which she was subjected proved too dogmatic, she turned to the life of the imagination and the discipline of lyric poetry. At the same time she consciously renounced the world, becoming a kind of village eccentric, living within the narrow confines of her father's house and grounds.

With seven generations of solid New Englanders behind her, Emily was born in Amherst, Massachusetts, in the Connecticut Valley, where the shadow of Jonathan Edwards was still firm. Her lawyer father, treasurer of Amherst College, was a pillar of the First Church, with a heart, said Emily, "pure and terrible." Describing the family, her sister Lavinia said that Emily "had to think—she was the only one of us that had that to do. Father believed; and mother loved; and Austin had Amherst; and I had the family to keep track of." The family observed morning devotions, and on Sundays attended church twice. After schooling at Amherst Academy, Emily went for a year to Mount Holyoke Female Seminary, where young ladies were divided into three groups: those who were professed Christians, those who "had hope," and those "without hope." Emily belonged, uncomfortably, in the third group; nor in later years did her preoccupation with the soul bring her into the fold. Yet she remained immersed, like her forebears, in the Word of God. As Thomas H. Johnson ventures to say, "in almost every poem she wrote, there are echoes of her sensitivity to the idiom of the Bible, and of her dependence upon its imagery for her own striking figures of speech." And her verse meters were based on the old English hymns of Isaac Watts, familiar to her as a child.

After her return from Mount Holyoke, she lived all her days in Amherst, except for some rare visits to Washington, Philadelphia, and Boston. Like her sister, she never married. In Ben Newton, a student in her father's law office, she found "a friend, who taught me Immortality," and who, till his early death, encouraged her ambition to write poetry. A few years later came an experience of love that, says her biographer, "may well have been the single most important event in her life"—her love of Charles Wadsworth, of Philadelphia, a married minister with a family. There seems to have been correspondence, and in 1860 he called on her in Amherst. The next year, when he accepted a pastorate in San Francisco, she was in a tumult of misery. It was at this time that she began to dress exclusively in immaculate white. The Queen Recluse (as her friend Bowles called her) was writing "bridal" poems, and many others: two-thirds of all her poems seem to have been composed within eight years.

By 1870 Miss Dickinson, isolated in her "dear home," saw only family and friends. "I do not cross my father's ground to any house or town." If not wide, her experience was deep and intense. "I find ecstasy in living," she said, and she found it also in writing about living, about the great themes: nature, love, death, immortality. As early as 1862 she had understood that, instead of seeking publication, she must confine herself to an audience of a few correspondents, among whom only one, Helen Hunt Jackson, poet and novelist, recognized her stature—"You are a great poet." In her lifetime only seven poems appeared in print, anonymously, but the total number eventually gathered into an authoritative edition amounted to 1775 poems.

Like the seventeenth-century metaphysical poets to whom she has been compared, Emily Dickinson's technique was witty, epigrammatic, elliptical, and rich in the devices of paradox, irony, and ambiguity. She sought to express the life of the spirit through commonplace things: bees, spiders, moths, the sunrise and the sunset. She flouted conventional meters and regular rimes, cultivating off-rimes, dissonance, and unorthodox syntax and punctuation. She had an elfish humor about serious matters, calling God "a noted clergyman" or "Papa above." She played a poetic role of childlike simplicity and dependence, seeming to need a father-figure like Wadsworth or her lifelong correspondent Thomas Wentworth Higginson to steady her volatile flights of fancy.

Further reading: *Emily Dickinson: Selected Poems,* ed. John Brinnin, 1960. *Selected Poems and Letters of Emily Dickinson,* ed. Robert Linscott, 1959. George Whicher, *This Was a Poet,* 1938 (reissued 1952). Thomas H. Johnson, *Emily Dickinson, An Interpretative Biography,* 1955, 1967. Charles Anderson, *Emily Dickinson's Poetry: Stairway of Surprise,* 1960.

Poems

The text given here for the poems is that established by Thomas H. Johnson in *The Poems of Emily Dickinson* (3 vols.; Cambridge, Mass., 1955). The order (chronological) and numbering are Johnson's.

61

Papa above!
Regard a Mouse
O'erpowered by the Cat!
Reserve within thy kingdom
A "Mansion" for the Rat!

Snug in seraphic Cupboards
To nibble all the day,
While unsuspecting Cycles
Wheel solemnly away!

160

Emily Dickinson seldom referred to her poems with titles. A few, like this one, were given titles when published after her death. This was named "Called Back." Lines 13-14 echo I Corinthians ii.9. The day before her death she wrote a letter: "Little cousins,—Called Back. Emily."

Just lost, when I was saved!
Just felt the world go by!
Just girt me for the onset with Eternity,
When breath blew back,
And on the other side
I heard recede the disappointed tide!

Therefore, as One returned, I feel,
Odd secrets of the line to tell!
Some Sailor, skirting foreign shores—
Some pale Reporter, from the awful doors
Before the Seal!

Next time, to stay!
Next time, the things to see
By Ear unheard,
Unscrutinized by Eye—

Next time, to tarry,
While the Ages steal—
Slow tramp the Centuries,
And the Cycles wheel!

185

"Faith" is a fine invention
When Gentlemen can *see*—
But *Microscopes* are prudent
In an Emergency.

187

"Requiescat" and "Troubled About Many Things" were two titles for this poem given by later editors.

How many times these low feet staggered—
Only the soldered mouth can tell—
Try—can you stir the awful rivet—
Try—can you lift the hasps of steel!

Stroke the cool forehead—hot so often—
Lift—if you care—the listless hair—
Handle the adamantine fingers
Never a thimble—more—shall wear—

Buzz the dull flies—on the chamber window—
Brave—shines the sun through the freckled pane—
Fearless—the cobweb swings from the ceiling—
Indolent Housewife—in Daisies—lain!

210

The thought beneath so slight a film—
Is more distinctly seen—
As laces just reveal the surge—
Or Mists—the Appenine—

214

The final line has two variants, both probably by editors and not Emily's own. In 1861 the poem was printed in the *Springfield Daily Republican*, the line reading: "Come staggering toward the sun." In the first edition of the poems, edited by T. W. Higginson and Mabel Todd, the line read: "Leaning against the sun."

I taste a liquor never brewed—
From Tankards scooped in Pearl—
Not all the Frankfort Berries
Yield such an Alcohol!

Inebriate of Air—am I—
And Debauchee of Dew—
Reeling—thro endless summer days—
From inns of Molten Blue—

When "Landlords" turn the drunken Bee
Out of the Foxglove's door—
When Butterflies—renounce their "drams"—
I shall but drink the more!

Till Seraphs swing their snowy Hats—
And Saints—to windows run—
To see the little Tippler
From Manzanilla come!

216

Emily wrote several different forms of this poem. In editing it for publication, Higginson liked the final stanza of the 1861 version so well that he printed it together with the two original stanzas. Emily apparently meant it as a variant reading of the second stanza and not as an additional one.

Safe in their Alabaster Chambers—
Untouched by Morning
And untouched by Noon—
Sleep the meek members of the Resurrection—
Rafter of satin,
And Roof of stone.

Light laughs the breeze
In her Castle above them—
Babbles the Bee in a stolid Ear,
Pipe the Sweet Birds in ignorant cadence—
Ah, what sagacity perished here!

1859 version

Safe in their Alabaster Chambers—
Untouched by Morning—
And untouched by Noon—

Lie the meek members of the Resurrection—
Rafter of Satin—and Roof of Stone!

Grand go the Years—in the Crescent—above them—
Worlds scoop their Arcs—
And Firmaments—row—
Diadems—drop—and Doges—surrender—
Soundless as dots—on a Disc of Snow—

1861 version

249

Higginson said of this poem: "One poem only I dread a little to print—that wonderful 'Wild Nights,'—lest the malignant read into it more than that virgin recluse ever dreamed of putting there. . . . Yet what a loss to omit it!"

Wild Nights—Wild Nights!
Were I with thee
Wild Nights should be
Our luxury!

Futile—the Winds—
To a Heart in port—
Done with the Compass—
Done with the Chart!

Rowing in Eden—
Ah, the Sea!
Might I but moor—Tonight—
In Thee!

254

"Hope" is the thing with feathers—
That perches in the soul—
And sings the tune without the words—
And never stops—at all—

And sweetest—in the Gale—is heard—
And sore must be the storm—
That could abash the little Bird
That kept so many warm—

I've heard it in the chillest land—
And on the strangest Sea—
Yet, never, in Extremity,
It asked a crumb—of Me.

258

There's a certain Slant of light,
Winter Afternoons—
That oppresses, like the Heft
Of Cathedral Tunes—

Heavenly Hurt, it gives us—
We can find no scar,
But internal difference,
Where the Meanings, are—

None may teach it—Any—
'Tis the Seal Despair—
An imperial affliction
Sent us of the Air—

When it comes, the Landscape listens—
Shadows—hold their breath—
When it goes, 'tis like the Distance
On the look of Death—

280

The metaphor of the funeral here is intended to express the theme of spiritual death. The burial details are vividly realistic.

I felt a Funeral, in my Brain,
And Mourners to and fro
Kept treading—treading—till it seemed
That Sense was breaking through—

And when they all were seated,
A Service, like a Drum—
Kept beating—beating—till I thought
My Mind was going numb—

And then I heard them lift a Box
And creak across my Soul
With those same Boots of Lead, again,
Then Space—began to toll,

As all the Heavens were a Bell,
And Being, but an Ear,
And I, and Silence, some strange Race
Wrecked, solitary, here—

And then a Plank in Reason, broke,
And I dropped down, and down—
And hit a World, at every plunge,
And Finished knowing—then—

287

In *Emily Dickinson's Poetry: Stairway of Surprise* (1960) Charles Anderson writes: "The soul of the clock passes out of the decimals of human time into 'Degreeless Noon' of eternity. . . ." He identifies "Him" in the last line as God or the soul of the trinket, Man.

A Clock stopped—
Not the Mantel's—
Geneva's farthest skill
Cant put the puppet bowing—
That just now dangled still—

An awe came on the Trinket!
The Figures hunched, with pain—
Then quivered out of Decimals—
Into Degreeless Noon—

It will not stir for Doctor's—
This Pendulum of snow—
The Shopman importunes it—
While cool—concernless No—

Nods from the Gilded pointers—
Nods from the Seconds slim
Decades of Arrogance between
The Dial life—
And Him—

288

I'm Nobody! Who are you?
Are you—Nobody—too?
Then there's a pair of us!
Dont tell! they'd banish us—you know!

How dreary—to be—Somebody!
How public—like a Frog—
To tell your name—the livelong June—
To an admiring Bog!

303

In *Poems* (1890) this was titled "Exclusion." Written in 1862 when Emily apparently made a decision to withdraw into her private world, the poem states the theme of living by her own choice.

The Soul selects her own Society—
Then—shuts the Door—
To her divine Majority—
Present no more—

Unmoved—she notes the Chariots—pausing—
At her low Gate—
Unmoved—an Emperor be kneeling
Upon her Mat—

I've known her—from an ample nation—
Choose One—
Then—close the Valves of her attention—
Like Stone—

318

I'll tell you how the Sun rose—
A Ribbon at a time—
The Steeples swam in Amethyst—
The news, like Squirrels, ran—
The Hills untied their Bonnets—
The Bobolinks—begun—
Then I said softly to myself—
"That must have been the Sun"!
But how he set—I know not—
There seemed a purple stile
That little Yellow boys and girls
Were climbing all the while—
Till when they reached the other side,
A Dominie in Gray—
Put gently up the evening Bars—
And led the flock away—

328

A Bird came down the Walk—
He did not know I saw—
He bit an Angleworm in halves
And ate the fellow, raw,

And then he drank a Dew
From a convenient Grass—
And then hopped sidewise to the Wall
To let a Beetle pass—

He glanced with rapid eyes
That hurried all around—
They looked like frightened Beads, I thought—
He stirred his Velvet Head

Like one in danger, Cautious,
I offered him a Crumb,
And he unrolled his feathers
And rowed him softer home—

Than Oars divide the Ocean,
Too silver for a seam—

Or Butterflies, off Banks of Noon
Leap, plashless as they swim.

341

After great pain, a formal feeling comes—
The Nerves sit ceremonious, like Tombs—
The stiff Heart questions was it He, that bore,
And Yesterday, or Centuries before?

The Feet, mechanical, go round—
Of Ground, or Air, or Ought—
A Wooden way
Regardless grown,
A Quartz contentment, like a stone—

This is the Hour of Lead—
Remembered, if outlived,
As Freezing persons, recollect the Snow—
First—Chill—then Stupor—then the letting go—

401

What Soft—Cherubic Creatures—
These Gentlewomen are—
One would as soon assault a Plush—
Or violate a Star—

Such Dimity Convictions—
A Horror so refined
Of freckled Human Nature—
Of Deity—ashamed—

It's such a common—Glory—
A Fisherman's—Degree—
Redemption—Brittle Lady—
Be so—ashamed of Thee—

435

Much Madness is divinest Sense—
To a discerning Eye—
Much Sense—the starkest Madness—
'Tis the Majority
In this, as All, prevail—
Assent—and you are sane—
Demur—you're straightway dangerous—
And handled with a Chain—

441

This is my letter to the World
That never wrote to Me—
The simple News that Nature told—
With tender Majesty

Her Message is committed
To Hands I cannot see—
For love of Her—Sweet—countrymen—
Judge tenderly—of Me

448

This was a Poet—It is That
Distills amazing sense
From ordinary Meanings—
And Attar so immense

From the familiar species
That perished by the Door—
We wonder it was not Ourselves
Arrested it—before—

Of Pictures, the Discloser—
The Poet—it is He—
Entitles Us—by Contrast—
To ceaseless Poverty—

Of Portion—so unconscious—
The Robbing—could not harm—
Himself—to Him—a Fortune—
Exterior—to Time—

461

A Wife—at Daybreak I shall be—
Sunrise—Hast thou a Flag for me?
At Midnight, I am but a Maid,
How short it takes to make it Bride—
Then—Midnight, I have passed from thee
Unto the East, and Victory—

Midnight—Good Night! I hear them call,
The Angels bustle in the Hall—
Softly my Future climbs the Stair,
I fumble at my Childhood's prayer
So soon to be a Child no more—
Eternity, I'm coming—Sir,
Savior—I've seen the face—before!

465

I heard a Fly buzz—when I died—
The Stillness in the Room
Was like the Stillness in the Air—
Between the Heaves of Storm—

The Eyes around—had wrung them dry—
And Breaths were gathering firm
For that last Onset—when the King
Be witnessed—in the Room—

I willed my Keepsakes—Signed away
What portion of me be
Assignable—and then it was
There interposed a Fly—

With Blue—uncertain stumbling Buzz—
Between the light—and me—
And then the Windows failed—and then
I could not see to see—

500

Within my Garden, rides a Bird
Upon a single Wheel—
Whose spokes a dizzy Music make
As 'twere a travelling Mill—

He never stops, but slackens
Above the Ripest Rose—
Partakes without alighting
And praises as he goes,

Till every spice is tasted—
And then his Fairy Gig
Reels in remoter atmospheres—
And I rejoin my Dog,

And He and I, perplex us
If positive, 'twere we—
Or bore the Garden in the Brain
This Curiosity—

But He, the best Logician,
Refers my clumsy eye—
To just vibrating Blossoms!
An Exquisite Reply!

511

Grouped with the "Love" poems in the 1890 edition, this one has been connected with the departure of the Rev. Charles Wadsworth for California in 1861.

If you were coming in the Fall,
I'd brush the Summer by
With half a smile, and half a spurn,
As Housewives do, a Fly.

If I could see you in a year,
I'd wind the months in balls—
And put them each in separate Drawers,
For fear the numbers fuse—

If only Centuries, delayed,
I'd count them on my Hand,
Subtracting, till my fingers dropped
Into Van Dieman's Land.

If certain, when this life was out—
That your's and mine, should be—
I'd toss it yonder, like a Rind,
And take Eternity—

But, now, uncertain of the length
Of this, that is between,
It goads me, like the Goblin Bee—
That will not state—it's sting.

520

I started Early—Took my Dog—
And visited the Sea—
The Mermaids in the Basement
Came out to look at me—

And Frigates—in the Upper Floor
Extended Hempen Hands—
Presuming Me to be a Mouse—
Aground—upon the Sands—

But no Man moved Me—till the Tide
Went past my simple Shoe—
And past my Apron—and my Belt
And past my Boddice—too—

And made as He would eat me up—
As wholly as a Dew
Upon a Dandelion's Sleeve—
And then—I started—too—

And He—He followed—close behind—
I felt His Silver Heel
Upon my Ancle—Then my Shoes
Would overflow with Pearl—

Until We met the Solid Town—
No One He seemed to know—

And bowing—with a Mighty look—
At me—The Sea withdrew—

536

The Heart asks Pleasure—first—
And then—Excuse from Pain—
And then—those little Anodynes
That deaden suffering—

And then—to go to sleep—
And then—if it should be
The will of it's Inquisitor
The privilege to die—

547

I've seen a Dying Eye
Run round and round a Room—
In search of Something—as it seemed—
Then Cloudier become—
And then—obscure with Fog—
And then—be soldered down
Without disclosing what it be
'Twere blessed to have seen—

664

Of all the Souls that stand create—
I have elected—One—
When Sense from Spirit—files away—
And Subterfuge—is done—
When that which is—and that which was—
Apart—intrinsic—stand—
And this brief Tragedy of Flesh—
Is shifted—like a Sand—
When Figures show their royal Front—
And Mists—are carved away,
Behold the Atom—I preferred—
To all the lists of Clay!

675

The distilling of perfume as a metaphor for poetry was similarly used in No. 448.

Essential Oils—are wrung—
The Attar from the Rose
Be not expressed by Suns—alone—
It is the gift of Screws—
The General Rose—decay—
But this—in Lady's Drawer
Make Summer—When the Lady lie
In Ceaseless Rosemary—

709

Publication—is the Auction
Of the Mind of Man—
Poverty—be justifying
For so foul a thing

Possibly—but We—would rather
From Our Garret go
White—Unto the White Creator—
Than invest—Our Snow—

Thought belong to Him who gave it—
Then—to Him Who bear
It's Corporeal illustration—Sell
The Royal Air—

In the Parcel—Be the Merchant
Of the Heavenly Grace—
But reduce no Human Spirit
To Disgrace of Price—

712

The gown in the fourth stanza seems to be a bridal gown. "Tippet" is a scarf or stole worn by those in holy orders. The concept of celestial marriage is likely, since Emily used the metaphor in other poems of death; see No. 461.

Because I could not stop for Death—
He kindly stopped for me—
The Carriage held but just Ourselves—
And Immortality.

We slowly drove—He knew no haste
And I had put away
My labor and my leisure too,
For His Civility—

We passed the School, where Children strove
At Recess—in the Ring—
We passed the Fields of Gazing Grain—
We passed the Setting Sun—

Or rather—He passed Us—
The Dews drew quivering and chill—
For only Gossamer, my Gown—
My Tippet—only Tulle—

We paused before a House that seemed
A Swelling of the Ground—
The Roof was scarcely visible—
The Cornice—in the Ground—

Since then—'tis Centuries—and yet
Feels shorter than the Day
I first surmised the Horses Heads
Were toward Eternity—

729

Alter! When the Hills do—
Falter! When the Sun
Question if His Glory
Be the Perfect One—

Surfeit! When the Daffodil
Doth of the Dew—
Even as Herself—Sir—
I will—of You—

754

My Life had stood—a Loaded Gun—
In Corners—till a Day
The Owner passed—identified—
And carried Me away—

And now We roam in Sovreign Woods—
And now We hunt the Doe—
And every time I speak for Him—
The Mountains straight reply—

And do I smile, such cordial light
Upon the Valley glow—
It is as a Vesuvian face
Had let it's pleasure through—

And when at Night—Our good Day done—
I guard My Master's Head—
'Tis better than the Eider-Duck's
Deep Pillow—to have shared—

To foe of His—I'm deadly foe—
None stir the second time—
On whom I lay a Yellow Eye—
Or an emphatic Thumb—

Though I than He—may longer live
He longer must—than I—
For I have but the power to kill,
Without—the power to die—

915

Faith—is the Pierless Bridge
Supporting what We see
Unto the Scene that We do not—
Too slender for the eye

It bears the Soul as bold
As it were rocked in Steel
With Arms of Steel at either side—
It joins—behind the Vail

To what, could We presume
The Bridge would cease to be
To Our far, vascillating Feet
A first Necessity.

986

A narrow Fellow in the Grass
Occasionally rides—
You may have met Him—did you not
His notice sudden is—

The Grass divides as with a Comb—
A spotted shaft is seen—
And then it closes at your feet
And opens further on—

He likes a Boggy Acre
A Floor too cool for Corn—
Yet when a Boy, and Barefoot—
I more than once at Noon
Have passed, I thought, a Whip lash
Unbraiding in the Sun
When stooping to secure it
It wrinkled, and was gone—

Several of Nature's People
I know, and they know me—
I feel for them a transport
Of cordiality—

But never met this Fellow
Attended, or alone
Without a tighter breathing
And Zero at the Bone—

1068

Further in Summer than the Birds
Pathetic from the Grass
A minor Nation celebrates
It's unobtrusive Mass.

No Ordinance be seen
So gradual the Grace
A pensive Custom it becomes
Enlarging Loneliness.

Antiquest felt at Noon
When August burning low
Arise this spectral Canticle
Repose to typify

Remit as yet no Grace
No Furrow on the Glow
Yet a Druidic Difference
Enhances Nature now

1129

Tell all the Truth but tell it slant—
Success in Circuit lies
Too bright for our infirm Delight
The Truth's superb surprise
As Lightning to the Children eased—
With explanation kind
The Truth must dazzle gradually
Or every man be blind—

1207

He preached upon "Breadth" till it argued him
narrow—
The Broad are too broad to define
And of "Truth" until it proclaimed him a Liar—
The Truth never flaunted a Sign—

Simplicity fled from his counterfeit presence
As Gold the Pyrites would shun—
What confusion would cover the innocent Jesus
To meet so enabled a Man!

1732

My life closed twice before its close;
It yet remains to see
If Immortality unveil
A third event to me,

So huge, so hopeless to conceive
As these that twice befel.
Parting is all we know of heaven,
And all we need of hell.

The Fiction of Naturalism

STEPHEN CRANE [1871-1900]

Stephen Crane's life, like much of his writing, was brief and intense, full of excitement, danger, and publicity, like a continuous headline in one of the newspapers for which he reported. His literary output of more than twelve volumes was crowded into less than a single decade, the Nineties, but during that period he experienced and wrote about virtually the whole spectrum of life: poverty and the slums, fear, cowardice and the mystery of heroism in war, love, God, shipwreck, foreign travel, small-town prejudice, the West. His themes were universalized into the basic emotions surrounding violent action. Yet Crane was less concerned with such actions as he portrayed in *Maggie* or *The Red Badge of Courage* than with the psychological states of the actors, observed under stress, and with the artistic ways to render them convincing. He was one of the first to use impressionist techniques of painting in prose, combining a hard-boiled realism of subject and a keen ear for colloquial speech with a haziness of outline and a suggestive symbolism. The love of color which marks his writing has also sometimes been referred to his interest in neo-impressionist effects. His unusual literary style, at its best, adapted such methods to the subject matter of realism and naturalism.

Crane's early life and education scarcely seem to account for the *avant garde* nature of his art. Born the fourteenth child of a Methodist minister and schoolmaster in Newark, New Jersey, in 1871, he had a typical American boyhood and school life, though in hard-pressed economic circumstances. The family lived in small New Jersey towns like the Whilomville of his later fiction, settling in 1882 in Asbury Park. Crane was sent to school nearby and later attended the Hudson River military academy at Claverock, New York. His brother Townley ran a news agency in Asbury Park where Crane gained his first apprentice experience as a cub reporter. In school and later during his two terms at Lafayette College and Syracuse University, he was more interested in playing baseball and watching college football than in his studies, and he later said that his knowledge of battle came from such gridiron struggles. He left college for lack of money and became a full-time reporter for the New York *Tribune* until his strongly worded account of a labor demonstration in Asbury Park proved too loaded with implied criticism of middle-class complacency toward working classes, and he lost his job. He spent the next year, 1891-92, free-lancing and living in poverty-areas of New York City, acquainting himself with Bowery flophouses, saloons, and police stations, learning at first hand how the other half lived.

Maggie: A Girl of the Streets, written first about 1890 and published in pamphlet form under the pseudonym "Johnston Smith," with money borrowed from his brother, described slum life and prostitution in the Bowery and revealed the powerful irony of Crane's pen. The established publishers would not touch it, but it brought him recognition and encouragement from Hamlin Garland and Howells, and Crane's literary career was thus launched. In 1895 *The Red Badge of Courage* brought Crane immediate success and proved a best-seller. Though he was too young to have known of battle-scenes in the Civil War at first hand, his convincing account of the emotions of a raw recruit under fire had the scientific authenticity of the French naturalists and reflected Crane's reading of Tolstoy. Just as *Maggie* anticipated Norris, Dreiser, and later naturalists and determinists, and even surpassed them in its factual honesty, *The Red Badge* was a full generation in advance of Dos Passos, Hemingway, and others in its depiction of the realities of modern war. Crane was immediately hailed as a young genius whose literary models and precursors were unaccountable. Actually his sources consisted of Mathew Brady's photographs of Chancellorsville, magazine accounts of the war, and the reminiscences of a teacher who had served in combat.

While *The Red Badge* demonstrated Crane's ability to write powerfully without direct exposure to the event, he seems to have adopted a contrary theory that immersion in experience and on-the-spot reporting was the soundest basis for achieving the authenticity he desired. His newly won fame brought him an assignment to travel in the West and in Mexico in search of material for a newspaper syndicate. Making of his life a tale of heroism and adventure in a period of fervid journalism, the Spanish-American War, and the Teddy Roosevelt cult of athleticism, he joined a risky filibustering expedition carrying arms to the Cuban revolutionaries. The ship foundered off the Florida coast, but Crane managed to escape in a dinghy with three crewmen and was dragged from the surf, half-dead from exhaustion. He then transformed the experience into a story, "The Open Boat," in which his use of a carefully controlled point of view, together with a bleak sense of the futility of man's plight amid natural forces and with suggestively symbolic coloring, raised the piece from its journalistic setting to the level of enduring art. It is worthy to be compared to the work of Melville and Conrad. After this, Crane again set out, despite failing health, to report the Greek-Turkish War. When the war ended, he went to England for the few remaining years of his life, a respected figure now, with a circle of literary friends such as Henry James, Conrad, and H. G. Wells. When his lung-disease weakened him further, he left for a sanitarium in Germany with his common-law wife, Cora Crane, but died within a week at Badenweiler, on June 5, 1900.

Crane's productions included more than just the urban naturalism and the war tales for which he is best known. He wrote effective western stories such as "The Bride Comes to Yellow Sky" and "The Blue Hotel"; two volumes of verse, *The Black Riders and Other Lines* (1895) and *War Is Kind* (1899); several collections of short stories with small-town settings not unlike those of Sherwood Anderson—notably, *The Monster and Other Stories* (1899) and *Whilomville Stories* (1900). He wrote one unsuccessful novel and much else that was second-rate. One critic says: "He produced too much, he kept repeating himself, and he never developed." But his half-dozen best things are enough to rank him high in American literature. Like Poe, he was most effective in the short tale or story. His people tended to type—the young soldier, the correspondent, a girl of the streets, a wounded man, etc.—often referred to without names because they were representative of certain primitive emotions or states of mind. Complexity of characterization was not Crane's forte. Yet within his limitations he possessed great stylistic gifts. He shared, for instance, Henry James's sense of dramatic form and his method of telling the story both from inside and outside of the observing narrator. Crane's war reporting and war fiction has been compared to that of Kipling, though it revealed more conscious craftsmanship, and in his tight-lipped understatement and irony he bears comparison with Ambrose Bierce. In poetic technique Crane's verse has some of the curt rhythms of Emily Dickinson, but it has more in common with the later work of T. S. Eliot, Ezra Pound, and the Imagists. His most famous prose sentence, "The red sun was pasted in the sky like a wafer," is close in feeling to Eliot's image of evening "spread out against the sky like a patient etherized upon a table." Crane was a master of language and striking effects, but perhaps most of all his work is marked by a creed of honest reporting: "I understand," he said, "that a man is born into the world with his own pair of eyes, and he is not at all responsible for his vision—he is merely responsible for his personal honesty. To keep close to this personal honesty is my supreme ambition."

Further reading: *Stephen Crane: An Omnibus,* ed. R. W. Stallman, 1952. *Stephen Crane: Stories and Tales,* ed. R. W. Stallman, 1955. *The Poems of Stephen Crane,* ed. Joseph Katz, 1966. John Berryman, *Stephen Crane,* 1950.

The Upturned Face

This brief but powerful example of Crane's war stories was first published in *Ainslee's Magazine*, March 1900, and posthumously in *Last Words* (1902). The terse military conversation and the uncertainty of the two officers over the burial procedure indicate Crane's effort to get at the soldiers' state of mind. The story is similar to certain scenes in *The Red Badge of Courage*, as well as to Ambrose Bierce's "Occurrence at Owl Creek Bridge." Crane said he was "wonderfully keen" on this small tale and wanted to see it produced on the stage so as "to curdle the blood of the British public" and "be the sensation of the year." But it was never staged.

"What will we do now?" said the adjutant, troubled and excited.

"Bury him," said Timothy Lean.

The two officers looked down close to their toes where lay the body of their comrade. The face was chalk-blue; gleaming eyes stared at the sky. Over the two upright figures was a windy sound of bullets, and on the top of the hill Lean's prostrate company of Spitzbergen infantry was firing measured volleys.

"Don't you think it would be better—" began the adjutant. "We might leave him until to-morrow."

"No," said Lean. "I can't hold that post an hour longer. I've got to fall back, and we've got to bury old Bill."

"Of course," said the adjutant, at once. "Your men got entrenching tools?"

Lean shouted back to his little line, and two men came slowly, one with a pick, one with a shovel. They started in the direction of the Rostina sharpshooters. Bullets cracked near their ears. "Dig here," said Lean gruffly. The men, thus caused to lower their glances to the turf, became hurried and frightened, merely because they could not look to see whence the bullets came. The dull beat of the pick striking the earth sounded amid the swift snap of close bullets. Presently the other private began to shovel.

"I suppose," said the adjutant, slowly, "we'd better search his clothes for—things."

Lean nodded. Together in curious abstraction they looked at the body. Then Lean stirred his shoulders suddenly, arousing himself.

"Yes," he said, "we'd better see what he's got." He dropped to his knees, and his hands approached the body of the dead officer. But his hands wavered over the buttons of the tunic. The first button was brick-red with drying blood, and he did not seem to dare touch it.

"Go on," said the adjutant, hoarsely.

Lean stretched his wooden hand, and his fingers fumbled the bloodstained buttons. At last he rose with ghastly face. He had gathered a watch, a whistle, a pipe, a tobacco-pouch, a handkerchief, a little case of cards and papers. He looked at the adjutant. There was a silence. The adjutant was feeling that he had been a coward to make Lean do all the grisly business.

"Well," said Lean, "that's all, I think. You have his sword and revolver?"

"Yes," said the adjutant, his face working, and then he burst out in a sudden strange fury at the two privates. "Why don't you hurry up with that grave? What are you doing, anyhow? Hurry, do you hear? I never saw such stupid—"

Even as he cried out in his passion the two men were labouring for their lives. Ever overhead the bullets were spitting.

The grave was finished. It was not a masterpiece—a poor little shallow thing. Lean and the adjutant again looked at each other in a curious silent communication.

Suddenly the adjutant croaked out a weird laugh. It was a terrible laugh, which had its origin in that part of the mind which is first moved by the singing of the nerves. "Well," he said humorously to Lean, "I suppose we had best tumble him in."

"Yes," said Lean. The two privates stood waiting, bent over their implements. "I suppose," said Lean, "it would be better if we laid him in ourselves."

"Yes," said the adjutant. Then, apparently remembering that he had made Lean search the body, he stooped with great fortitude and took hold of the dead officer's clothing. Lean joined him. Both were particular that their fingers should not feel the corpse. They tugged away; the corpse lifted, heaved, toppled, flopped into the grave, and the two officers, straightening, looked again at each other—they were always looking at each other. They sighed with relief.

The adjutant said, "I suppose we should—we should say something. Do you know the service, Tim?"

"They don't read the service until the grave is filled in," said Lean, pressing his lips to an academic expression.

"Don't they?" said the adjutant, shocked that he had made the mistake. "Oh, well," he cried, suddenly, "let us—let us say something—while he can hear us."

"All right," said Lean. "Do you know the service?"

"I can't remember a line of it," said the adjutant.

Lean was extremely dubious. "I can repeat two lines, but—"

"Well, do it," said the adjutant. "Go as far as you can. That's better than nothing. And the beasts have got our range exactly."

Lean looked at his two men. "Attention," he barked. The privates came to attention with a click, looking much aggrieved. The adjutant lowered his helmet to his knee. Lean, bareheaded, stood over the grave. The Rostina sharpshooters fired briskly.

"O Father, our friend has sunk in the deep waters of death, but his spirit has leaped toward Thee as the bubble arises from the lips of the drowning. Perceive, we beseech, O Father, the little flying bubble, and—"

Lean, although husky and ashamed, had suffered no hesitation up to this point, but he stopped with a hopeless feeling and looked at the corpse.

The adjutant moved uneasily. "And from Thy superb heights—" he began, and then he too came to an end.

"And from Thy superb heights," said Lean.

The adjutant suddenly remembered a phrase in the back of the Spitzbergen burial service, and he exploited it with the triumphant manner of a man who has recalled everything, and can go on.

"O God, have mercy—"

"O God, have mercy—" said Lean.

"Mercy," repeated the adjutant, in quick failure.

"Mercy," said Lean. And then he was moved by some violence of feeling, for he turned upon his two men and tigerishly said, "Throw the dirt in."

The fire of the Rostina sharpshooters was accurate and continuous.

One of the aggrieved privates came forward with his shovel. He lifted his first shovel-load of earth, and for a moment of inexplicable hesitation it was held poised above this corpse, which from its chalk-blue face looked keenly out from the grave. Then the soldier emptied his shovel on—on the feet.

Timothy Lean felt as if tons had been swiftly lifted from off his forehead. He had felt that perhaps the private might empty the shovel on—on the face. It had been emptied on the feet. There was a great point gained there—ha, ha!—the first shovelful had been emptied on the feet. How satisfactory!

The adjutant began to babble. "Well, of course—a man we've messed with all these years—impossible—you can't, you know, leave your intimate friends rotting on the field. Go on, for God's sake, and shovel, you."

The man with the shovel suddenly ducked, grapped his left arm with his right hand, and looked at his officer for orders. Lean picked the shovel from the ground. "Go to the rear," he said to the wounded man. He also addressed the other private. "You get under cover, too; I'll finish this business."

The wounded man scrambled hard still for the top of the ridge without devoting any glances to the direction from whence the bullets came, and the other man followed at an equal pace; but he was different, in that he looked back anxiously three times.

This is merely the way—often—of the hit and unhit.

Timothy Lean filled the shovel, hesitated, and then, in a movement which was like a gesture of abhorrence, he flung the dirt into the grave, and as it landed it made a sound—plop. Lean suddenly stopped and mopped his brow—a tired labourer.

"Perhaps we have been wrong," said the adjutant. His glance wavered stupidly. "It might have been better if we hadn't buried him just at this time. Of course, if we advance to-morrow the body would have been—"

"Damn you," said Lean, "shut your mouth." He was not the senior officer.

He again filled the shovel and flung the earth. Always the earth made that sound—plop. For a space Lean worked frantically, like a man digging himself out of danger.

Soon there was nothing to be seen but the chalk-blue face. Lean filled the shovel. "Good God," he cried to the adjutant. "Why didn't you turn him somehow when you put him in? This—" Then Lean began to stutter.

The adjutant understood. He was pale to the lips. "Go on, man," he cried, beseechingly, almost in a shout.

Lean swung back the shovel. It went forward in a pendulum curve. When the earth landed it made a sound—plop.

1900

The Open Boat

A Tale Intended to be after the Fact: Being the Experience of Four Men From the Sunk Steamer "Commodore"

First published in *Scribner's Magazine,* June 1897, the story appeared the next year in *The Open Boat and Other Tales of Adventure,* the text reprinted here. Crane had gone aboard the *Commodore,* January 1, 1897, to report the Cuban rebellion. Loaded with munitions for the rebels and carrying a crew of about twenty-eight men, the ship sprang a leak and the pumps failed. Crane and three of the crew managed to get ashore in a dinghy, but William Higgins, a sailor, was killed in the surf, as in the story. The New York *Press* and the Florida *Times-Union* headlined the story of the wreck, and Crane's courage was featured in the reports. He was interviewed: "Brilliant Author Not of the Sort to Give Up His Cuban Letters Because of Shipwreck," one liner said. The captain testified to Crane's bravery; and "That newspaper feller was a nervy man," said the cook. The dinghy was at sea for twenty-seven hours. For complete newspaper accounts of the shipwreck see R. W. Stallman, *Stephen Crane: An Omnibus* (1952). In creating a work of art from his experience, Crane employed the structural device of alternating moods, hope and despair, and he stressed the theme of brotherhood. Details of the sea—the gulls, the waves, the shore—are transposed into symbols of life, death, and survival.

I

None of them knew the color of the sky. Their eyes glanced level, and were fastened upon the waves that swept toward them. These waves were of the hue of slate, save for the tops, which were of foaming white, and all of the men knew the colors of the sea. The horizon narrowed and widened, and dipped and rose, and at all times its edge was jagged with waves that seemed thrust up in points like rocks.

Many a man ought to have a bath-tub larger than the boat which here rode upon the sea. These waves were most wrongfully and barbarously abrupt and tall, and each froth-top was a problem in small-boat navigation.

The cook squatted in the bottom, and looked with both eyes at the six inches of gunwale which separated him from the ocean. His sleeves were rolled over his fat forearms, and the two flaps of his unbuttoned vest dangled as he bent to bail out the boat. Often he said, "Gawd! that was a narrow clip." As he remarked it he invariably gazed eastward over the broken sea.

The oiler, steering with one of the two oars in the boat, sometimes raised himself suddenly to keep clear of water that swirled in over the stern. It was a thin little oar, and it seemed often ready to snap.

The correspondent, pulling at the other oar, watched the waves and wondered why he was there.

The injured captain, lying in the bow, was at this time buried in that profound dejection and indifference which comes, temporarily at least, to even the bravest and most enduring when, willy-nilly, the firm fails, the army loses, the ship goes down. The mind of the master of a vessel is rooted deep in the timbers of her, though he command for a day or a decade; and this captain had on him the stern impression of a scene in the grays of dawn of seven turned faces, and later a stump of a topmast with a white ball on it, that slashed to and fro at the waves, went low and lower, and down. Thereafter there was something strange in his voice. Although steady, it was deep with mourning, and of a quality beyond oration or tears.

"Keep 'er a little more south, Billie," said he.

"A little more south, sir," said the oiler in the stern.

A seat in this boat was not unlike a seat upon a bucking broncho, and, by the same token, a broncho is not much smaller. The craft pranced and reared and plunged like an animal. As each wave came, and she rose for it, she seemed like a horse making at a fence outrageously high. The manner of her scramble over these walls of water is a mystic thing, and, moreover, at the top of them were ordinarily these problems in white water, the foam racing down from the summit of each wave, requiring a new leap, and a leap from the air. Then, after scornfully bumping a crest, she would slide and race and splash down a long incline, and arrive bobbing and nodding in front of the next menace.

A singular disadvantage of the sea lies in the fact that, after successfully surmounting one wave, you discover that there is another behind it, just as important and just as nervously anxious to do something effective in the way of swamping boats. In a ten-foot dinghy one can get an idea of the resources of the sea in the line of waves that is not probable to the average experience, which is never at sea in a dinghy. As each slaty wall of water approached, it shut all else from the view of the men in the boat, and it was not difficult to imagine that this particular wave was the final outburst of the ocean, the last effort of the grim water. There was a terrible grace in the move of the waves, and they came in silence, save for the snarling of the crests.

In the wan light the faces of the men must have been gray. Their eyes must have glinted in strange ways as they gazed steadily astern. Viewed from a balcony, the whole thing would, doubtless, have been weirdly picturesque. But the men in the boat had no time to see it, and if they had had leisure, there were other things to occupy their minds. The sun swung steadily up the sky, and they knew it was broad day because the color of the sea changed from slate to emerald-green streaked with amber lights, and the foam was like tumbling snow. The process of the breaking day was unknown to them. They were aware only of this effect upon the color of the waves that rolled toward them.

In disjointed sentences the cook and the correspondent argued as to the difference between a life-saving station and a house of refuge. The cook had said: "There's a house of refuge just north of the Mosquito Inlet Light, and as soon as they see us they'll come off in their boat and pick us up."

"As soon as who see us?" said the correspondent.

"The crew," said the cook.

"Houses of refuge don't have crews," said the correspondent. "As I understand them, they are only places where clothes and grub are stored for the benefit of shipwrecked people. They don't carry crews."

"Oh, yes, they do," said the cook.

"No, they don't," said the correspondent.

"Well, we're not there yet, anyhow," said the oiler in the stern.

"Well," said the cook, "perhaps it's not a house of

refuge that I'm thinking of as being near Mosquito Inlet Light; perhaps it's a life-saving station."

"We're not there yet," said the oiler in the stern.

II

As the boat bounced from the top of each wave the wind tore through the hair of the hatless men, and as the craft plopped her stern down again the spray slashed past them. The crest of each of these waves was a hill, from the top of which the men surveyed for a moment a broad, tumultuous expanse, shining and wind-riven. It was probably splendid, it was probably glorious, this play of the free sea, wild with lights of emerald and white and amber.

"Bully good thing it's an on-shore wind," said the cook. "If not, where would we be? Wouldn't have a show."

"That's right," said the correspondent.

The busy oiler nodded his assent.

Then the captain, in the bow, chuckled in a way that expressed humor, contempt, tragedy, all in one. "Do you think we've got much of a show now, boys?" said he.

Whereupon the three were silent, save for a trifle of hemming and hawing. To express any particular optimism at this time they felt to be childish and stupid, but they all doubtless possessed this sense of the situation in their minds. A young man thinks doggedly at such times. On the other hand, the ethics of their condition was decidedly against any open suggestion of hopelessness. So they were silent.

"Oh, well," said the captain, soothing his children, "we'll get ashore all right."

But there was that in his tone which made them think; so the oiler quoth, "Yes! if this wind holds."

The cook was bailing. "Yes! if we don't catch hell in the surf."

Canton-flannel gulls flew near and far. Sometimes they sat down on the sea, near patches of brown seaweed that rolled over the waves with a movement like carpets on a line in a gale. The birds sat comfortably in groups, and they were envied by some in the dinghy, for the wrath of the sea was no more to them than it was to a covey of prairie-chickens a thousand miles inland. Often they came very close and stared at the men with black, bead-like eyes. At these times they were uncanny and sinister in their unblinking scrutiny, and the men hooted angrily at them, telling them to be gone. One came, and evidently decided to alight on the top of the captain's head. The bird flew parallel to the boat, and did not circle, but made short sidelong jumps in the air in chicken fashion. His black eyes were wistfully fixed upon the captain's head. "Ugly brute," said the oiler to the bird. "You look as if you were made with a jack-knife." The cook and the correspondent swore darkly at the creature. The captain naturally wished to knock it away with the end of the heavy painter, but he did not dare do it, because anything resembling an emphatic gesture would have capsized this freighted boat; and so, with his open hand, the captain gently and carefully waved the gull away. After it had been discouraged from the pursuit the captain breathed easier on account of his hair, and others breathed easier because the bird struck their minds at this time as being somehow gruesome and ominous.

In the meantime the oiler and the correspondent rowed; and also they rowed. They sat together in the same seat, and each rowed an oar. Then the oiler took both oars; then the correspondent took both oars; then the oiler; then the correspondent. They rowed and they rowed. The very ticklish part of the business was when the time came for the reclining one in the stern to take his turn at the oars. By the very last star of truth, it is easier to steal eggs from under a hen than it was to change seats in the dinghy. First the man in the stern slid his hand along the thwart and moved with care, as if he were of Sèvres. Then the man in the rowing-seat slid his hand along the other thwart. It was all done with the most extraordinary care. As the two sidled past each other, the whole party kept watchful eyes on the coming wave, and the captain cried: "Look out, now! Steady, there!"

The brown mats of seaweed that appeared from time to time were like islands, bits of earth. They were traveling, apparently, neither one way nor the other. They were, to all intents, stationary. They informed the men in the boat that it was making progress slowly toward the land.

The captain, rearing cautiously in the bow after the dinghy soared on a great swell, said that he had seen the lighthouse at Mosquito Inlet. Presently the cook remarked that he had seen it. The correspondent was at the oars then, and for some reason he too wished to look at the lighthouse; but his back was toward the far shore, and the waves were important, and for some time he could not seize an opportunity to turn his head. But at last there came a wave more gentle than the others, and when at the crest of it he swiftly scoured the western horizon.

"See it?" said the captain.

"No," said the correspondent, slowly; "I didn't see anything."

"Look again," said the captain. He pointed. "It's exactly in that direction."

At the top of another wave the correspondent did as he was bid, and this time his eyes chanced on a small, still thing on the edge of the swaying horizon.

It was precisely like the point of a pin. It took an anxious eye to find a lighthouse so tiny.

"Think we'll make it, Captain?"

"If this wind holds and the boat don't swamp, we can't do much else," said the captain.

The little boat, lifted by each towering sea and splashed viciously by the crests, made progress that in the absence of seaweed was not apparent to those in her. She seemed just a wee thing wallowing miraculously, top up, at the mercy of five oceans. Occasionally a great spread of water, like white flames, swarmed into her.

"Bail her, cook," said the captain, serenely.

"All right, Captain," said the cheerful cook.

III

It would be difficult to describe the subtle brotherhood of men that was here established on the seas. No one said that it was so. No one mentioned it. But it dwelt in the boat, and each man felt it warm him. They were a captain, an oiler, a cook, and a correspondent, and they were friends—friends in a more curiously iron-bound degree than may be common. The hurt captain, lying against the water-jar in the bow, spoke always in a low voice and calmly; but he could never command a more ready and swiftly obedient crew than the motley three of the dinghy. It was more than a mere recognition of what was best for the common safety. There was surely in it a quality that was personal and heartfelt. And after this devotion to the commander of the boat, there was this comradeship, that the correspondent, for instance, who had been taught to be cynical of men, knew even at the time was the best experience of his life. But no one said that it was so. No one mentioned it.

"I wish we had a sail," remarked the captain. "We might try my overcoat on the end of an oar, and give you two boys a chance to rest." So the cook and the correspondent held the mast and spread wide the overcoat; the oiler steered; and the little boat made good way with her new rig. Sometimes the oiler had to scull sharply to keep a sea from breaking into the boat, but otherwise sailing was a success.

Meanwhile the lighthouse had been growing slowly larger. It had now almost assumed color, and appeared like a little gray shadow on the sky. The man at the oars could not be prevented from turning his head rather often to try for a glimpse of this little gray shadow.

At last, from the top of each wave, the men in the tossing boat could see land. Even as the lighthouse was an upright shadow on the sky, this land seemed but a long black shadow on the sea. It certainly was thinner than paper. "We must be about opposite New Smyrna," said the cook, who had coasted this shore often in schooners. "Captain, by the way, I believe they abandoned that life-saving station there about a year ago."

"Did they?" said the captain.

The wind slowly died away. The cook and the correspondent were not now obliged to slave in order to hold high the oar; but the waves continued their old impetuous swooping at the dinghy, and the little craft, no longer under way, struggled woundily over them. The oiler or the correspondent took the oars again.

Shipwrecks are *apropos* of nothing. If men could only train for them and have them occur when the men had reached pink condition, there would be less drowning at sea. Of the four in the dinghy none had slept any time worth mentioning for two days and two nights previous to embarking in the dinghy, and in the excitement of clambering about the deck of a foundering ship they had also forgotten to eat heartily.

For these reasons, and for others, neither the oiler nor the correspondent was fond of rowing at this time. The correspondent wondered ingenuously how in the name of all that was sane could there be people who thought it amusing to row a boat. It was not an amusement; it was a diabolical punishment, and even a genius of mental aberrations could never conclude that it was anything but a horror to the muscles and a crime against the back. He mentioned to the boat in general how the amusement of rowing struck him, and the weary-faced oiler smiled in full sympathy. Previously to the foundering, by the way, the oiler had worked double watch in the engine-room of the ship.

"Take her easy now, boys," said the captain. "Don't spend yourselves. If we have to run a surf you'll need all your strength, because we'll sure have to swim for it. Take your time."

Slowly the land arose from the sea. From a black line it became a line of black and a line of white—trees and sand. Finally the captain said that he could make out a house on the shore. "That's the house of refuge, sure," said the cook. "They'll see us before long, and come out after us."

The distant lighthouse reared high. "The keeper ought to be able to make us out now, if he's looking through a glass," said the captain. "He'll notify the life-saving people."

"None of those other boats could have got ashore to give word of the wreck," said the oiler, in a low voice, "else the life-boat would be out hunting us."

Slowly and beautifully the land loomed out of the sea. The wind came again. It had veered from the northeast to the southeast. Finally a new sound struck the ears of the men in the boat. It was the low thunder of the surf on the shore. "We'll never be able to make the lighthouse now," said the captain. "Swing her head a little more north, Billie."

"A little more north, sir," said the oiler.

Whereupon the little boat turned her nose once more down the wind, and all but the oarsman watched the shore grow. Under the influence of this expansion doubt and direful apprehension were leaving the minds of the men. The management of the boat was still most absorbing, but it could not prevent a quiet cheerfulness. In an hour, perhaps, they would be ashore.

Their backbones had become thoroughly used to balancing in the boat, and they now rode this wild colt of a dinghy like circus men. The correspondent thought that he had been drenched to the skin, but happening to feel in the top pocket of his coat, he found therein eight cigars. Four of them were soaked with sea-water; four were perfectly scatheless. After a search, somebody produced three dry matches; and thereupon the four waifs rode in their little boat and, with an assurance of an impending rescue shining in their eyes, puffed at the big cigars, and judged well and ill of all men. Everybody took a drink of water.

IV

"Cook," remarked the captain, "there don't seem to be any signs of life about your house of refuge."

"No," replied the cook. "Funny they don't see us!"

A broad stretch of lowly coast lay before the eyes of the men. It was of low dunes topped with dark vegetation. The roar of the surf was plain, and sometimes they could see the white lip of a wave as it spun up the beach. A tiny house was blocked out black upon the sky. Southward, the slim lighthouse lifted its little gray length.

Tide, wind, and waves were swinging the dinghy northward. "Funny they don't see us," said the men.

The surf's roar was here dulled, but its tone was nevertheless thunderous and mighty. As the boat swam over the great rollers the men sat listening to this roar. "We'll swamp sure," said everybody.

It is fair to say here that there was not a life-saving station within twenty miles in either direction; but the men did not know this fact, and in consequence they made dark and opprobrious remarks concerning the eyesight of the nation's life-savers. Four scowling men sat in the dinghy, and surpassed records in the invention of epithets.

"Funny they don't see us."

The light-heartedness of a former time had completely faded. To their sharpened minds it was easy to conjure pictures of all kinds of incompetency and blindness and, indeed, cowardice. There was the shore of the populous land, and it was bitter and bitter to them that from it came no sign.

"Well," said the captain, ultimately, "I suppose we'll have to make a try for ourselves. If we stay out here too long, we'll none of us have strength left to swim after the boat swamps."

And so the oiler, who was at the oars, turned the boat straight for the shore. There was a sudden tightening of muscles. There was some thinking.

"If we don't all get ashore," said the captain,—"if we don't all get ashore, I suppose you fellows know where to send news of my finish?"

They then briefly exchanged some addresses and admonitions. As for the reflections of the men, there was a great deal of rage in them. Perchance they might be formulated thus: "If I am going to be drowned—if I am going to be drowned—if I am going to be drowned, why, in the name of the seven mad gods who rule the sea, was I allowed to come thus far and contemplate sand and trees? Was I brought here merely to have my nose dragged away as I was about to nibble the sacred cheese of life? It is preposterous! If this old ninnywoman, Fate, cannot do better than this, she should be deprived of the management of men's fortunes. She is an old hen who knows not her intention. If she has decided to drown me, why did she not do it in the beginning, and save me all this trouble? The whole affair is absurd. . . . But no; she cannot mean to drown me. She dare not drown me. She cannot drown me. Not after all this work!" Afterward the man might have had an impulse to shake his fist at the clouds. "Just you drown me, now, and then hear what I call you!"

The billows that came at this time were more formidable. They seemed always just about to break and roll over the little boat in a turmoil of foam. There was a preparatory and long growl in the speech of them. No mind unused to the sea would have concluded that the dinghy could ascend these sheer heights in time. The shore was still afar. The oiler was a wily surfman. "Boys," he said swiftly, "she won't live three minutes more, and we're too far out to swim. Shall I take her to sea again, Captain?"

"Yes; go ahead!" said the captain.

This oiler, by a series of quick miracles and fast and steady oarsmanship, turned the boat in the middle of the surf and took her safely to sea again.

There was a considerable silence as the boat bumped over the furrowed sea to deeper water. Then somebody in gloom spoke: "Well, anyhow, they must have seen us from the shore by now."

The gulls went in slanting flight up the wind toward the gray, desolate east. A squall, marked by dingy clouds, and clouds brick-red, like smoke from a burning building, appeared from the southeast.

"What do you think of those life-saving people? Ain't they peaches?"

"Funny they haven't seen us."

"Maybe they think we're out here for sport! Maybe they think we're fishin'. Maybe they think we're damned fools."

It was a long afternoon. A changed tide tried to force them southward, but wind and wave said northward. Far ahead, where coast-line, sea, and sky formed their mighty angle, there were little dots which seemed to indicate a city on the shore.

"St. Augustine?"

The captain shook his head. "Too near Mosquito Inlet."

And the oiler rowed, and then the correspondent rowed; then the oiler rowed. It was a weary business. The human back can become the seat of more aches and pains than are registered in books for the composite anatomy of a regiment. It is a limited area, but it can become the theater of innumerable muscular conflicts, tangles, wrenches, knots, and other comforts.

"Did you ever like to row, Billie?" asked the correspondent.

"No," said the oiler; "hang it!"

When one exchanged the rowing-seat for a place in the bottom of the boat, he suffered a bodily depression that caused him to be careless of everything save an obligation to wiggle one finger. There was cold sea-water swashing to and fro in the boat, and he lay in it. His head, pillowed on a thwart, was within an inch of the swirl of a wave-crest, and sometimes a particularly obstreperous sea came inboard and drenched him once more. But these matters did not annoy him. It is almost certain that if the boat had capsized he would have tumbled comfortably out upon the ocean as if he felt sure that it was a great, soft mattress.

"Look! There's a man on the shore!"

"Where?"

"There! See 'im? See 'im?"

"Yes, sure! He's walking along."

"Now he's stopped. Look! He's facing us!"

"He's waving at us!"

"So he is! By thunder!"

"Ah, now we're all right! Now we're all right! There'll be a boat out here for us in half an hour."

"He's going on. He's running. He's going up to that house there."

The remote beach seemed lower than the sea, and it required a searching glance to discern the little black figure. The captain saw a floating stick, and they rowed to it. A bath towel was by some weird chance in the boat, and tying this on the stick, the captain waved it. The oarsman did not dare turn his head, so he was obliged to ask questions.

"What's he doing now?"

"He's standing still again. He's looking, I think. . . . There he goes again—toward the house. . . . Now he's stopped again."

"Is he waving at us?"

"No, not now; he was, though."

"Look! There comes another man!"

"He's running."

"Look at him go, would you!"

"Why, he's on a bicycle. Now he's met the other man. They're both waving at us. Look!"

"There comes something up the beach."

"What the devil is that thing?"

"Why, it looks like a boat."

"Why, certainly, it's a boat."

"No; it's on wheels."

"Yes, so it is. Well, that must be the life-boat. They drag them along shore on a wagon."

"That's the life-boat, sure."

"No, by——, it's—it's an omnibus."

"I tell you it's a life-boat."

"It is not! It's an omnibus. I can see it plain. See? One of these big hotel omnibuses."

"By thunder, you're right. It's an omnibus, sure as fate. What do you suppose they are doing with an omnibus? Maybe they are going around collecting the life-crew, hey?"

"That's it, likely. Look! There's a fellow waving a little black flag. He's standing on the steps of the omnibus. There come those other two fellows. Now they're all talking together. Look at the fellow with the flag. Maybe he ain't waving it!"

"That ain't a flag, is it? That's his coat. Why, certainly, that's his coat."

"So it is; it's his coat. He's taken it off and is waving it around his head. But would you look at him swing it!"

"Oh, say, there isn't any life-saving station there. That's just a winter-resort hotel omnibus that has brought over some of the boarders to see us drown."

"What's that idiot with the coat mean? What's he signaling, anyhow?"

"It looks as if he were trying to tell us to go north. There must be a life-saving station up there."

"No; he thinks we're fishing. Just giving us a merry hand. See? Ah, there, Willie!"

"Well, I wish I could make something out of those signals. What do you suppose he means?"

"He don't mean anything; he's just playing."

"Well, if he'd just signal us to try the surf again, or to go to sea and wait, or go north, or go south, or go to hell, there would be some reason in it. But look at him! He just stands there and keeps his coat revolving like a wheel. The ass!"

"There come more people."

"Now there's quite a mob. Look! Isn't that a boat?"

"Where? Oh, I see where you mean. No, that's no boat."

"That fellow is still waving his coat."

"He must think we like to see him do that. Why don't he quit it? It don't mean anything."

"I don't know. I think he is trying to make us go north. It must be that there's a life-saving station there somewhere."

"Say, he ain't tired yet. Look at 'im wave!"

"Wonder how long he can keep that up. He's been revolving his coat ever since he caught sight of us. He's an idiot. Why aren't they getting men to bring a boat out? A fishing-boat—one of those big yawls—could come out here all right. Why don't he do something?"

"Oh, it's all right now."

"They'll have a boat out here for us in less than no time, now that they've seen us."

A faint yellow tone came into the sky over the low land. The shadows on the sea slowly deepened. The wind bore coldness with it, and the men began to shiver.

"Holy smoke!" said one, allowing his voice to express his impious mood, "if we keep on monkeying out here! If we've got to flounder out here all night!"

"Oh, we'll never have to stay here all night! Don't you worry. They've seen us now, and it won't be long before they'll come chasing out after us."

The shore grew dusky. The man waving a coat blended gradually into this gloom, and it swallowed in the same manner the omnibus and the group of people. The spray, when it dashed uproariously over the side, made the voyagers shrink and swear like men who were being branded.

"I'd like to catch the chump who waved the coat. I feel like soaking him one, just for luck."

"Why? What did he do?"

"Oh, nothing, but then he seemed so damned cheerful."

In the meantime the oiler rowed, and then the correspondent rowed, and then the oiler rowed. Gray-faced and bowed forward, they mechanically, turn by turn, plied the leaden oars. The form of the lighthouse had vanished from the southern horizon, but finally a pale star appeared, just lifting from the sea. The streaked saffron in the west passed before the all-merging darkness, and the sea to the east was black. The land had vanished, and was expressed only by the low and drear thunder of the surf.

"If I am going to be drowned—if I am going to be drowned—if I am going to be drowned, why, in the name of the seven mad gods who rule the sea, was I allowed to come thus far and contemplate sand and trees? Was I brought here merely to have my nose dragged away as I was about to nibble the sacred cheese of life?"

The patient captain, drooped over the water-jar, was sometimes obliged to speak to the oarsman.

"Keep her head up! Keep her head up!"

"Keep her head up, sir." The voices were weary and low.

This was surely a quiet evening. All save the oarsman lay heavily and listlessly in the boat's bottom. As for him, his eyes were just capable of noting the tall black waves that swept forward in a most sinister silence, save for an occasional subdued growl of a crest.

The cook's head was on a thwart, and he looked without interest at the water under his nose. He was deep in other scenes. Finally he spoke. "Billie," he murmured dreamfully, "what kind of pie do you like best?"

V

"Pie!" said the oiler and the correspondent, agitatedly. "Don't talk about those things, blast you!"

"Well," said the cook, "I was just thinking about ham sandwiches, and—"

A night on the sea in an open boat is a long night. As darkness settled finally, the shine of the light, lifting from the sea in the south, changed to full gold. On the northern horizon a new light appeared, a small bluish gleam on the edge of the waters. These two lights were the furniture of the world. Otherwise there was nothing but waves.

Two men huddled in the stern, and distances were so magnificent in the dinghy that the rower was enabled to keep his feet partly warm by thrusting them under his companions. Their legs indeed extended far under the rowing-seat until they touched the feet of the captain forward. Sometimes, despite the efforts of the tired oarsman, a wave came piling into the boat, an icy wave of the night, and the chilling water soaked them anew. They would twist their bodies for a moment and groan, and sleep the dead sleep once more, while the water in the boat gurgled about them as the craft rocked.

The plan of the oiler and the correspondent was for one to row until he lost the ability, and then arouse the other from his sea-water couch in the bottom of the boat.

The oiler plied the oars until his head drooped

forward and the overpowering sleep blinded him; and he rowed yet afterward. Then he touched a man in the bottom of the boat, and called his name. "Will you spell me for a little while?" he said meekly.

"Sure, Billie," said the correspondent, awaking and dragging himself to a sitting position. They exchanged places, carefully, and the oiler, cuddling down in the sea-water at the cook's side, seemed to go to sleep instantly.

The particular violence of the sea had ceased. The waves came without snarling. The obligation of the man at the oars was to keep the boat headed so that the tilt of the rollers would not capsize her, and to preserve her from filling when the crests rushed past. The black waves were silent and hard to be seen in the darkness. Often one was almost upon the boat before the oarsman was aware.

In a low voice the correspondent addressed the captain. He was not sure that the captain was awake, although this iron man seemed to be always awake. "Captain, shall I keep her making for that light north, sir?"

The same steady voice answered him. "Yes. Keep it about two points off the port bow."

The cook had tied a life-belt around himself in order to get even the warmth which this clumsy cork contrivance could donate, and he seemed almost stove-like when a rower, whose teeth invariably chattered wildly as soon as he ceased his labor, dropped down to sleep.

The correspondent, as he rowed, looked down at the two men sleeping under foot. The cook's arm was around the oiler's shoulders, and, with their fragmentary clothing and haggard faces, they were the babes of the sea—a grotesque rendering of the old babes in the wood.

Later he must have grown stupid at his work, for suddenly there was a growling of water, and a crest came with a roar and a swash into the boat, and it was a wonder that it did not set the cook afloat in his life-belt. The cook continued to sleep, but the oiler sat up, blinking his eyes and shaking with the new cold.

"Oh, I'm awful sorry, Billie," said the correspondent, contritely.

"That's all right, old boy," said the oiler, and lay down again and was asleep.

Presently it seemed that even the captain dozed, and the correspondent thought that he was the one man afloat on all the oceans. The wind had a voice as it came over the waves, and it was sadder than the end.

There was a long, loud swishing astern of the boat, and a gleaming trail of phosphorescence, like blue flame, was furrowed on the black waters. It might have been made by a monstrous knife.

Then there came a stillness, while the correspondent breathed with the open mouth and looked at the sea.

Suddenly there was another swish and another long flash of bluish light, and this time it was alongside the boat, and might almost have been reached with an oar. The correspondent saw an enormous fin speed like a shadow through the water, hurling the crystalline spray and leaving the long glowing trail.

The correspondent looked over his shoulder at the captain. His face was hidden, and he seemed to be asleep. He looked at the babes of the sea. They certainly were asleep. So, being bereft of sympathy, he leaned a little way to one side and swore softly into the sea.

But the thing did not then leave the vicinity of the boat. Ahead or astern, on one side or the other, at intervals long or short, fled the long sparkling streak, and there was to be heard the whiroo of the dark fin. The speed and power of the thing was greatly to be admired. It cut the water like a gigantic and keen projectile.

The presence of this biding thing did not affect the man with the same horror that it would if he had been a picnicker. He simply looked at the sea dully and swore in an undertone.

Nevertheless, it is true that he did not wish to be alone with the thing. He wished one of his companions to awake by chance and keep him company with it. But the captain hung motionless over the water-jar, and the oiler and the cook in the bottom of the boat were plunged in slumber.

VI

"If I am going to be drowned—if I am going to be drowned—if I am going to be drowned, why, in the name of the seven mad gods who rule the sea, was I allowed to come thus far and contemplate sand and trees?"

During this dismal night, it may be remarked that a man would conclude that it was really the intention of the seven mad gods to drown him, despite the abominable injustice of it. For it was certainly an abominable injustice to drown a man who had worked so hard, so hard. The man felt it would be a crime most unnatural. Other people had drowned at sea since galleys swarmed with painted sails, but still—

When it occurs to a man that nature does not regard him as important, and that she feels she would not maim the universe by disposing of him, he at first wishes to throw bricks at the temple, and he hates deeply the fact that there are no bricks and no temples. Any visible expression of nature would surely be pelleted with his jeers.

Then, if there be no tangible thing to hoot, he feels, perhaps, the desire to confront a personification and indulge in pleas, bowed to one knee, and with hands supplicant, saying, "Yes, but I love myself."

A high cold star on a winter's night is the word he feels that she says to him. Thereafter he knows the pathos of his situation.

The men in the dinghy had not discussed these matters, but each had, no doubt, reflected upon them in silence and according to his mind. There was seldom any expression upon their faces save the general one of complete weariness. Speech was devoted to the business of the boat.

To chime the notes of his emotion, a verse mysteriously entered the correspondent's head. He had even forgotten that he had forgotten this verse, but it suddenly was in his mind.

A soldier of the Legion lay dying in Algiers;
There was lack of woman's nursing, there was dearth of woman's tears;
But a comrade stood beside him, and he took that comrade's hand,
And he said, "I never more shall see my own, my native land."

In his childhood the correspondent had been made acquainted with the fact that a soldier of the Legion lay dying in Algiers, but he had never regarded it as important. Myriads of his school-fellows had informed him of the soldier's plight, but the dinning had naturally ended by making him perfectly indifferent. He had never considered it his affair that a soldier of the Legion lay dying in Algiers, nor had it appeared to him as a matter for sorrow. It was less to him than breaking of a pencil's point.

Now, however, it quaintly came to him as a human, living thing. It was no longer merely a picture of a few throes in the breast of a poet, meanwhile drinking tea and warming his feet at the grate; it was an actuality—stern, mournful, and fine.

The correspondent plainly saw the soldier. He lay on the sand with his feet out straight and still. While his pale left hand was upon his chest in an attempt to thwart the going of his life, the blood came between his fingers. In the far Algerian distance, a city of low square forms was set against a sky that was faint with the last sunset hues. The correspondent, plying the oars and dreaming of the slow and slower movements of the lips of the soldier, was moved by a profound and perfectly impersonal comprehension. He was sorry for the soldier of the Legion who lay dying in Algiers.

The thing which had followed the boat and waited had evidently grown bored at the delay. There was no longer to be heard the slash of the cutwater, and there was no longer the flame of the long trail. The light in the north still glimmered, but it was apparently no nearer to the boat. Sometimes the boom of the surf rang in the correspondent's ears, and he turned the craft seaward then and rowed harder. Southward, some one had evidently built a watch-fire on the beach. It was too low and too far to be seen, but it made a shimmering, roseate reflection upon the bluff back of it, and this could be discerned from the boat. The wind came stronger, and sometimes a wave suddenly raged out like a mountain-cat, and there was to be seen the sheen and sparkle of a broken crest.

The captain, in the bow, moved on his water-jar and sat erect. "Pretty long night," he observed to the correspondent. He looked at the shore. "Those life-saving people take their time."

"Did you see that shark playing around?"

"Yes, I saw him. He was a big fellow, all right."

"Wish I had known you were awake."

Later the correspondent spoke into the bottom of the boat.

"Billie!" There was a slow and gradual disentanglement. "Billie, will you spell me?"

"Sure," said the oiler.

As soon as the correspondent touched the cold, comfortable sea-water in the bottom of the boat and had huddled close to the cook's life-belt he was deep in sleep, despite the fact that his teeth played all the popular airs. This sleep was so good to him that it was but a moment before he heard a voice call his name in a tone that demonstrated the last stages of exhaustion. "Will you spell me?"

"Sure, Billie."

The light in the north had mysteriously vanished, but the correspondent took his course from the wide-awake captain.

Later in the night they took the boat farther out to sea, and the captain directed the cook to take one oar at the stern and keep the boat facing the seas. He was to call out if he should hear the thunder of the surf. This plan enabled the oiler and the correspondent to get respite together. "We'll give those boys a chance to get into shape again," said the captain. They curled down and, after a few preliminary chatterings and trembles, slept once more the dead sleep. Neither knew they had bequeathed to the cook the company of another shark, or perhaps the same shark.

As the boat caroused on the waves, spray occasionally bumped over the side and gave them a fresh soaking, but this had no power to break their repose. The ominous slash of the wind and the water affected them as it would have affected mummies.

"Boys," said the cook, with the notes of every reluctance in his voice, "she's drifted in pretty close. I guess one of you had better take her to sea again." The correspondent, aroused, heard the crash of the toppled crests.

As he was rowing, the captain gave him some whisky and water, and this steadied the chills out of him. "If I ever get ashore and anybody shows me even a photograph of an oar—"

At last there was a short conversation.

"Billie! . . . Billie, will you spell me?"

"Sure," said the oiler.

VII

When the correspondent again opened his eyes, the sea and the sky were each of the gray hue of the dawning. Later, carmine and gold was painted upon the waters. The morning appeared finally, in its splendor, with a sky of pure blue, and the sunlight flamed on the tips of the waves.

On the distant dunes were set many little black cottages, and a tall white windmill reared above them. No man, nor dog, nor bicycle appeared on the beach. The cottages might have formed a deserted village.

The voyagers scanned the shore. A conference was held in the boat. "Well," said the captain, "if no help is coming, we might better try a run through the surf right away. If we stay out here much longer we will be too weak to do anything for ourselves at all." The others silently acquiesced in this reasoning. The boat was headed for the beach. The correspondent wondered if none ever ascended the tall wind-tower, and if then they never looked seaward. This tower was a giant, standing with its back to the plight of the ants. It represented in a degree, to the correspondent, the serenity of nature amid the struggles of the individual—nature in the wind, and nature in the vision of men. She did not seem cruel to him then, nor beneficent, nor treacherous, nor wise. But she was indifferent, flatly indifferent. It is, perhaps, plausible that a man in this situation, impressed with the unconcern of the universe, should see the innumerable flaws of his life and have them taste wickedly in his mind and wish for another chance. A distinction between right and wrong seems absurdly clear to him, then, in this new ignorance of the grave-edge, and he understands that if he were given another opportunity he would mend his conduct and his words, and be better and brighter during an introduction or at a tea.

"Now, boys," said the captain, "she is going to swamp sure. All we can do is to work her in as far as possible, and then when she swamps, pile out and scramble for the beach. Keep cool now, and don't jump until she swamps sure."

The oiler took the oars. Over his shoulders he scanned the surf. "Captain," he said, "I think I'd better bring her about, and keep her head-on to the seas, and back her in."

"All right, Billie," said the captain. "Back her in." The oiler swung the boat then, and, seated in the stern, the cook and the correspondent were obliged to look over their shoulders to contemplate the lonely and indifferent shore.

The monstrous inshore rollers heaved the boat high until the men were again enabled to see the white sheets of water scudding up the slanted beach. "We won't get in very close," said the captain. Each time a man could wrest his attention from the rollers, he turned his glance toward the shore, and in the expression of the eyes during this contemplation there was a singular quality. The correspondent, observing the others, knew that they were not afraid, but the full meaning of their glances was shrouded.

As for himself, he was too tired to grapple fundamentally with the fact. He tried to coerce his mind into thinking of it, but the mind was dominated at this time by the muscles, and the muscles said they did not care. It merely occurred to him that if he should drown it would be a shame.

There were no hurried words, no pallor, no plain agitation. The men simply looked at the shore. "Now, remember to get well clear of the boat when you jump," said the captain.

Seaward the crest of a roller suddenly fell with a thunderous crash, and the long white comber came roaring down upon the boat.

"Steady now," said the captain. The men were silent. They turned their eyes from the shore to the comber and waited. The boat slid up the incline, leaped at the furious top, bounced over it, and swung down the long back of the wave. Some water had been shipped, and the cook bailed it out.

But the next crest crashed also. The tumbling, boiling flood of white water caught the boat and whirled it almost perpendicular. Water swarmed in from all sides. The correspondent had his hands on the gunwale at this time, and when the water entered at that place he swiftly withdrew his fingers, as if he objected to wetting them.

The little boat, drunken with this weight of water, reeled and snuggled deeper into the sea.

"Bail her out, cook! Bail her out!" said the captain.

"All right, Captain," said the cook.

"Now, boys, the next one will do for us sure," said the oiler. "Mind to jump clear of the boat."

The third wave moved forward, huge, furious, implacable. It fairly swallowed the dinghy, and almost simultaneously the men tumbled into the sea. A piece of life-belt had lain in the bottom of the boat, and as the correspondent went overboard he held this to his chest with his left hand.

The January water was icy, and he reflected immediately that it was colder than he had expected to find it off the coast of Florida. This appeared to his dazed mind as a fact important enough to be noted at the time. The coldness of the water was sad; it was tragic. This fact was somehow mixed and confused with his opinion of his own situation so that it seemed almost a proper reason for tears. The water was cold.

When he came to the surface he was conscious of little but the noisy water. Afterward he saw his companions in the sea. The oiler was ahead in the race. He was swimming strongly and rapidly. Off to the correspondent's left, the cook's great white and corked back bulged out of the water; and in the rear the captain was hanging with his one good hand to the keel of the overturned dinghy.

There is a certain immovable quality to a shore, and the correspondent wondered at it amid the confusion of the sea.

It seemed also very attractive; but the correspondent knew that it was a long journey, and he paddled leisurely. The piece of life-preserver lay under him, and sometimes he whirled down the incline of a wave as if he were on a hand-sled.

But finally he arrived at a place in the sea where travel was beset with difficulty. He did not pause swimming to inquire what manner of current had caught him, but there his progress ceased. The shore was set before him like a bit of scenery on a stage, and he looked at it, and understood with his eyes each detail of it.

As the cook passed, much farther to the left, the captain was calling to him, "Turn over on your back, cook! Turn over on your back and use the oar."

"All right, sir." The cook turned on his back, and, paddling with an oar, went ahead as if he were a canoe.

Presently the boat also passed to the left of the correspondent, with the captain clinging with one hand to the keel. He would have appeared like a man raising himself to look over a board fence if it were not for the extraordinary gymnastics of the boat. The correspondent marveled that the captain could still hold to it.

They passed on nearer to shore,—the oiler, the cook, the captain,—and following them went the water-jar, bouncing gaily over the seas.

The correspondent remained in the grip of this strange new enemy, a current. The shore, with its white slope of sand and its green bluff, topped with little silent cottages, was spread like a picture before him. It was very near to him then, but he was impressed as one who, in a gallery, looks at a scene from Brittany or Algiers.

He thought: "I am going to drown? Can it be possible? Can it be possible? Can it be possible?" Perhaps an individual must consider his own death to be the final phenomenon of nature.

But later a wave perhaps whirled him out of this small deadly current, for he found suddenly that he could again make progress toward the shore. Later still he was aware that the captain, clinging with one hand to the keel of the dinghy, had his face turned away from the shore and toward him, and was calling his name. "Come to the boat! Come to the boat!"

In his struggle to reach the captain and the boat, he reflected that when one gets properly wearied drowning must really be a comfortable arrangement—a cessation of hostilities accompanied by a large degree of relief; and he was glad of it, for the main thing in his mind for some moments had been horror of the temporary agony; he did not wish to be hurt.

Presently he saw a man running along the shore. He was undressing with most remarkable speed. Coat, trousers, shirt, everything flew magically off him.

"Come to the boat!" called the captain.

"All right, Captain." As the correspondent paddled, he saw the captain let himself down to bottom and leave the boat. Then the correspondent performed his one little marvel of the voyage. A large wave caught him and flung him with ease and supreme speed completely over the boat and far beyond it. It struck him even then as an event in gymnastics and a true miracle of the sea. An overturned boat in the surf is not a plaything to a swimming man.

The correspondent arrived in water that reached only to his waist, but his condition did not enable him to stand for more than a moment. Each wave knocked him into a heap, and the undertow pulled at him.

Then he saw the man who had been running and undressing, and undressing and running, come bounding into the water. He dragged ashore the cook, and then waded toward the captain; but the captain waved him away and sent him to the correspondent. He was naked—naked as a tree in winter; but a halo was about his head, and he shone like a saint. He gave a strong pull, and a long drag, and a bully heave at the correspondent's hand. The correspondent, schooled in the minor formulae, said, "Thanks, old man." But suddenly the man cried, "What's that?" He pointed a swift finger. The correspondent said, "Go."

In the shallows, face downward, lay the oiler. His forehead touched sand that was periodically, between each wave, clear of the sea.

The correspondent did not know all that transpired afterward. When he achieved safe ground he fell, striking the sand with each particular part of his body. It was as if he had dropped from a roof, but the thud was grateful to him.

It seems that instantly the beach was populated with men with blankets, clothes, and flasks, and women with coffee-pots and all the remedies sacred to their minds. The welcome of the land to the men from the sea was warm and generous; but a still and dripping shape was carried slowly up the beach, and the land's welcome for it could only be the different and sinister hospitality of the grave.

When it came night, the white waves paced to and fro in the moonlight, and the wind brought the sound of the great sea's voice to the men on shore, and they felt that they could then be interpreters.

1897

Poems

FROM *The Black Riders*

These three poems are from *The Black Riders and Other Lines* (1895); text taken from *The Collected Poems of Stephen Crane* (1930). The first poem derives from a love letter Crane wrote Helen Trent, September 20, 1891: "You have the most beautiful arms I ever saw. . . . It would not matter if there was nothing else to hope for in the world or if there was no more world." Of the third poem Thomas Beer, Crane's biographer, wrote: "In the Bowery he had seen a young streetwalker cover the head of a drunken procurer with her body while the fellow's assailants were trying to stamp his face to pieces. Crane ran to bring help and the police arrested the girl for cursing."

Should the wide world roll away,
Leaving black terror,
Limitless night,
Nor God, nor man, nor place to stand
Would be to me essential,
If thou and thy white arms were there,
And the fall to doom a long way.

I saw a man pursuing the horizon;
Round and round they sped.
I was disturbed at this;
I accosted the man.
"It is futile," I said,
"You can never —"

"You lie," he cried,
And ran on.

God lay dead in heaven;
Angels sang the hymn of the end;
Purple winds went moaning,
Their wings drip-dripping
With blood
That fell upon the earth.
It, groaning thing,
Turned black and sank.
Then from the far caverns
Of dead sins
Came monsters, livid with desire.
They fought,
Wrangled over the world,
A morsel.
But of all sadness this was sad,—
A woman's arms tried to shield
The head of a sleeping man
From the jaws of the final beast.

FROM *War Is Kind*

This and the following poems are from *War Is Kind* (1899); text from *The Collected Poems of Stephen Crane* (1930). Since Crane did not give titles to his poems, the editors have thought best not to add them.

Do not weep, maiden, for war is kind.
Because your lover threw wild hands toward the sky
And the affrighted steed ran on alone,
Do not weep.
War is kind.

Hoarse, booming drums of the regiment,
Little souls who thirst for fight,
These men were born to drill and die.
The unexplained glory flies above them,
Great is the battle-god, great, and his
kingdom—
A field where a thousand corpses lie.

Do not weep, babe, for war is kind.
Because your father tumbled in the yellow trenches,
Raged at his breast, gulped and died,
Do not weep.
War is kind.

Swift blazing flag of the regiment,
Eagle with crest of red and gold,
These men were born to drill and die.
Point for them the virtue of slaughter,
Make plain to them the excellence of killing
And a field where a thousand corpses lie.

Mother whose heart hung humble as a button
On the bright splendid shroud of your son,

Do not weep.
War is kind.

The wayfarer,
Perceiving the pathway to truth,
Was struck with astonishment.
It was thickly grown with weeds.
"Ha," he said,
"I see that none has passed here
In a long time."
Later he saw that each weed
Was a singular knife.
"Well," he mumbled at last,
"Doubtless there are other roads."

A man said to the universe:
"Sir, I exist!"
"However," replied the universe,
"The fact has not created in me
A sense of obligation."

A newspaper is a collection of half-injustices
Which, bawled by boys from mile to mile,
Spreads its curious opinion
To a million merciful and sneering men,
While families cuddle the joys of the fireside
When spurred by tale of dire lone agony.
A newspaper is a court
Where everyone is kindly and unfairly tried
By a squalor of honest men.
A newspaper is a market
Where wisdom sells its freedom
And melons are crowned by the crowd.
A newspaper is a game
Where his error scores the player victory
While another's skill wins death.
A newspaper is a symbol;
It is feckless life's chronicle,
A collection of loud tales
Concentrating eternal stupidities,
That in remote ages lived unhaltered,
Roaming through a fenceless world.

THEODORE DREISER [1871–1945]

THEODORE DREISER is identified with literary naturalism more totally than either Crane or Norris, who preceded him, because the entire social and intellectual milieu of the late nineteenth and early twentieth centuries, when naturalism became a way of life, was embodied in his personal history. When he wrote of the biological "chemisms" which controlled his characters and described the struggle for existence in Darwinian terms, he was writing of himself and his family's struggle against poverty and want. Clyde Griffiths in *An American Tragedy* was, like Dreiser himself, a young man in the big city going from job to job, observing the extremes of rich and poor, dreaming of wealth and success in a world of chance. Although he later read Tyndall and Spencer, where he found scientific explanations for the mysteries of life, Dreiser was never quite convincing in his novels when he became doctrinaire or philosophic. But he was wholly convincing in his portrayals of working girls adrift in Chicago or New York at the mercy of callous employers and men ready to exploit their susceptibility. If Dreiser became the Balzac or Zola of American fiction, it was not so much because he followed a conscious creed of art or economic determinism as because he was himself a helpless instrument, as H. L. Mencken said, "of that inchoate flow of forces which he himself is so fond of depicting."

Dreiser was born in Terre Haute, Indiana, in 1871, one of thirteen children of honest, hard-working, but uneducated and underprivileged German-immigrant parents. His father was a religious fanatic, a rigid Catholic believing literally in hell-fire punishment for sins in this world. The family moved from town to town seeking work to escape from miserable poverty, but it was the big city, Chicago, that lured the children as they grew up. Dreiser's sisters both experienced the things he described in *Sister Carrie* (1901) and *Jennie Gerhardt* (1911), and Dreiser himself finally began to "rise" in the field of newspaper reporting. Pounding the pavements in Chicago, St. Louis, and Pittsburgh looking for feature stories for the supplements was the training ground for his city-novels. Later as chief-editor of a chain of popular women's magazines he achieved financial success and security, but he never lost the quality that distinguished him from other writers of his time: his vast sympathy for and understanding of the plight of the social outcast.

Sister Carrie was withdrawn from publication because genteel-minded readers could not accept the fact that a woman who had transgressed the moral code should go unpunished. It was later reissued. Now, along with *Jennie Gerhardt,* another novel of a young girl who becomes the mistress of a wealthy man under pressures of poverty, it is regarded as Dreiser's best work. Fascinated by the business-ethics and the power-psychology of the financial magnate Charles T. Yerkes, Dreiser next wrote two novels, *The Financier* (1912) and *The Titan* (1914), exploring the great financial empire-building of America of the Gilded Age. These novels lacked something of the authenticity of the earlier books, but they were effective in their accumulation of documentary facts and in Dreiser's refusal to sentimentalize the career of Frank Cowperwood into a symbol of evil. He simply reported the facts with the detachment of a case-historian. Another novel with autobiographical overtones, *The Genius* (1915), about a rising young artist, was attacked as scandalous. Mingling erotic episodes with accounts of the commercial and publishing world in New York, it was Dreiser's least satisfying application of the superman theme. In *An American Tragedy* (1925), his greatest success, Dreiser returned to his earlier theme to describe the fall of a young man lacking religious or ethical sanctions and unable to withstand the combined assaults of his own biological drives and the economic pressures of the business world.

Besides novels, Dreiser wrote books of autobiographical reminiscence, social tracts, plays, a volume of poetry, and several collections of short stories. In such books as *A Traveller at Forty* (1913) and *A Hoosier Holiday* (1916) he reported his travels at home and abroad, and in *Hey Rub-a-dub-dub* (1920) he speculated on the world which seemed to him too strange and puzzling to submit to easy economic or scientific theories. "As yet," he wrote in 1916, "we do not understand life, we do not know what it is, what the laws are that govern it." During the 1930's he traveled in Russia, and wrote *Tragic America* (1931) in which he pronounced capitalism a failure and adopted a Marxist philosophy of collectivism. Yet this was not a final solution for him. More and more he was impressed by life's mystery and complexity. He read Thoreau, whose living thoughts he collected for a book in 1939. His last novel, *The Bulwark* (1946), shows him returning to religion and a mystical faith in divinity. Solon Barnes, a prosperous Quaker holding to his inherited principles, watches his family gradually succumb to moral decay and worldly influences, yet despite personal sorrows he reaffirms his faith and expresses a Thoreau-like love for all creatures and a belief in personal revelation.

Thus, by the end of his life Dreiser had returned to the compassion and humanitarianism of his early novels when he recorded the lives of the poor and friendless, like his own family. From this theme he had turned to the other side of social Darwinism, the amoral struggle for power in the business world; but this and his later communist phase were parts of a larger quest for meaning in the "supersensual chaos" of life. The web of forces that entangled man seemed to him planless, changeful, ugly and beautiful, brutal and tender, but essentially inscrutable and more appropriate for the novelist's pen than the philosopher's diagnosis.

Dreiser's style has been termed dull and prosaic, full of clichés, lacking in grace, polish, or form. Admittedly his prose is flat, often platitudinous, when subjected to analysis or compared with that of writers like Henry James or Stephen Crane. Yet to *read* Dreiser is to forget about style and technique. One is swept along in his impressive tide of everyday details which shape the lives of his characters and place them in their surroundings so convincingly that they become almost more real and memorable than the people we encounter in our own daily living.

Further reading: Among the novels: *Sister Carrie, Jennie Gerhardt, The Financier, An American Tragedy.* F. O. Matthiessen, *Theodore Dreiser,* 1951. W. A. Swanberg, *Dreiser,* 1965.

FROM *Sister Carrie*

The publishing history of *Sister Carrie* is itself a capsule history of the revolution in taste of the American reading public between 1900 and 1917. When Frank Norris was a manuscript reader for Doubleday, Page and Company, he enthusiastically recommended Dreiser's novel for publication. *Sister Carrie* appeared in 1901; but when Mrs. Doubleday strongly objected to the frank treatment of sex, the book was withdrawn. Meanwhile it had been published in London and had gained considerable publicity. Not until 1907 could Dreiser find another publisher, but even then the book drew protests from genteel circles. Later, in 1911, Harper and Brothers issued *Sister Carrie* along with Dreiser's second novel, *Jennie Gerhardt.* The present text is from the Riverside Edition edited by Claude Simpson (Boston, 1959), which reprints the first edition but corrects some misprints.

Carrie herself further offended early readers by rising in the world despite her transgression of the moral code. She emerges as a stronger character than either of her lovers, first Drouet and later Hurstwood, and achieves some success as an actress in New York. She is finally shown to be a lover of life and a dreamer of better things who pursues "beauty" by taking a short cut and violating established conventions.

I. The Magnet Attracting: A Waif Amid Forces

When Caroline Meeber boarded the afternoon train for Chicago, her total outfit consisted of a small trunk, a cheap imitation alligator-skin satchel, a small lunch in a paper box, and a yellow leather snap purse, containing her ticket, a scrap of paper with her sister's address in Van Buren Street, and four dollars in money. It was in August, 1889. She was eighteen years of age, bright, timid, and full of the illusions of ignorance and youth. Whatever touch of regret at parting characterised her thoughts, it was certainly not for advantages now being given up. A gush of tears at her mother's farewell kiss, a touch in her throat when the cars clacked by the flour mill where her father worked by the day, a pathetic sigh as the familiar green environs of the village passed in review, and the threads which bound her so lightly to girlhood and home were irretrievably broken.

To be sure there was always the next station, where one might descend and return. There was the great city, bound more closely by these very trains which came up daily. Columbia City was not so very far away, even once she was in Chicago. What, pray, is a few hours—a few hundred miles? She looked at the little slip bearing her sister's address and wondered. She gazed at the green landscape, now passing in swift review, until her swifter thoughts replaced its impression with vague conjectures of what Chicago might be.

When a girl leaves her home at eighteen, she does one of two things. Either she falls into saving hands and becomes better, or she rapidly assumes the cosmopolitan standard of virtue and becomes worse. Of an intermediate balance, under the circumstances, there is no possibility. The city has its cunning wiles, no less than the infinitely smaller and more human tempter. There are large forces which allure with all the soulfulness of expression possible in the most cultured human. The gleam of a thousand lights is often as effective as the persuasive light in a wooing and fascinating eye. Half the undoing of the unsophisticated and natural mind is accomplished by forces wholly superhuman. A blare of sound, a roar of life, a vast array of human hives, appeal to the astonished senses in equivocal terms. Without a counsellor at hand to whisper cautious interpretations, what falsehoods may not these things breathe into the unguarded ear! Unrecognised for what they are, their beauty, like music, too often relaxes, then weakens, then perverts the simpler human perceptions.

Caroline, or Sister Carrie, as she had been half affectionately termed by the family, was possessed of a mind rudimentary in its power of observation and analysis. Self-interest with her was high, but not strong. It was, nevertheless, her guiding characteristic. Warm with the fancies of youth, pretty with the insipid prettiness of the formative period, possessed of a figure promising eventual shapeliness and an eye alight with certain native intelligence, she was a fair example of the middle American class—two generations removed from the emigrant. Books were beyond her interest—knowledge a sealed book. In the intuitive graces she was still crude. She could scarcely toss her head gracefully. Her hands were almost ineffectual. The feet, though small, were set flatly. And yet she was interested in her charms, quick to understand the keener pleasures of life, ambitious to gain in material things. A half-equipped little knight she was, venturing to reconnoitre the mysterious city and dreaming wild dreams of some vague, far-off supremacy, which should make it prey and subject—the proper penitent, grovelling at a woman's slipper.

"That," said a voice in her ear, "is one of the prettiest little resorts in Wisconsin."

"Is it?" she answered nervously.

The train was just pulling out of Waukesha. For some time she had been conscious of a man behind. She felt him observing her mass of hair. He had been fidgeting, and with natural intuition she felt a certain interest growing in that quarter. Her maidenly reserve, and a certain sense of what was conventional under the circumstances, called her to forestall and deny this familiarity, but the daring and magnetism of the individual, born of past experiences and triumphs, prevailed. She answered.

He leaned forward to put his elbows upon the back of her seat and proceeded to make himself volubly agreeable.

"Yes, that is a great resort for Chicago people. The hotels are swell. You are not familiar with this part of the country, are you?"

"Oh, yes, I am," answered Carrie. "That is, I live at Columbia City. I have never been through here, though."

"And so this is your first visit to Chicago," he observed.

All the time she was conscious of certain features out of the side of her eye. Flush, colourful cheeks, a light moustache, a grey fedora hat. She now turned and looked upon him in full, the instincts of self-protection and coquetry mingling confusedly in her brain.

"I didn't say that," she said.

"Oh," he answered, in a very pleasing way and with an assumed air of mistake, "I thought you did."

Here was a type of the travelling canvasser for a manufacturing house—a class which at that time was first being dubbed by the slang of the day "drummers." He came within the meaning of a still newer term, which had sprung into general use among Americans in 1880, and which concisely expressed the thought of one whose dress or manners are calculated to elicit the admiration of susceptible young women—a "masher." His suit was of a striped and crossed pattern of brown wool, new at that time, but since become familiar as a business suit. The low crotch of the vest revealed a stiff shirt bosom of white and pink stripes. From his coat sleeves protruded a pair of linen cuffs of the same pattern, fastened with large, gold plate buttons, set with the common yellow agates known as "cat's-eyes." His fingers bore several rings—one, the ever-enduring heavy seal—and from his vest dangled a neat gold watch chain, from which was suspended the secret insignia of the Order of Elks. The whole suit was rather tight-fitting, and was finished off with heavy-soled tan shoes, highly polished, and the grey fedora hat. He was, for the order of intellect represented, attractive, and whatever he had to recommend him, you may be sure was not lost upon Carrie, in this, her first glance.

Lest this order of individual should permanently pass, let me put down some of the most striking characteristics of his most successful manner and method. Good clothes, of course, were the first essential, the things without which he was nothing. A strong physical nature, actuated by a keen desire for the feminine, was the next. A mind free of any consideration of the problems or forces of the world and actuated not by greed, but an insatiable love of variable pleasure. His method was always simple. Its principal element was daring, backed, of course, by an intense desire and admiration for the sex. Let him meet with a young woman once and he would approach her with an air of kindly familiarity, not unmixed with pleading, which would result in most cases in a tolerant acceptance. If she showed any tendency to coquetry he would be apt to straighten her tie, or if she "took up" with him at all, to call her by her first name. If he visited a department store it was to lounge familiarly over the counter and ask some leading questions. In more exclusive circles, on the train or in waiting stations, he went slower. If some seemingly vulnerable object appeared he was all attention—to pass the compliments of the day, to lead the way to the parlor car, carrying her grip, or, failing that, to take a seat next her with the hope of being able to court her to her destination. Pillows, books, a footstool, the shade lowered; all these figured in the things which he could do. If, when she reached her destination he did not alight and attend her baggage for her, it was because, in his own estimation, he had signally failed.

A woman should some day write the complete philosophy of clothes. No matter how young, it is one of the things she wholly comprehends. There is an indescribably faint line in the matter of man's apparel which somehow divides for her those who are worth glancing at and those who are not. Once an individual has passed this faint line on the way downward he will get no glance from her. There is another line at which the dress of a man will cause her to study her own. This line the individual at her elbow now marked for Carrie. She became conscious of an inequality. Her own plain blue dress, with its black cotton tape trimmings, now seemed to her shabby. She felt the worn state of her shoes.

"Let's see," he went on, "I know quite a number of people in your town. Morgenroth the clothier and Gibson the dry goods man."

"Oh, do you?" she interrupted, aroused by memories of longings their show windows had cost her.

At last he had a clew to her interest, and followed it deftly. In a few minutes he had come about into her seat. He talked of sales of clothing, his travels, Chicago, and the amusements of that city.

"If you are going there, you will enjoy it immensely. Have you relatives?"

"I am going to visit my sister," she explained.

"You want to see Lincoln Park," he said, "and Michigan Boulevard. They are putting up great buildings there. It's a second New York—great. So much to see—theatres, crowds, fine houses—oh, you'll like that."

There was a little ache in her fancy of all he described. Her insignificance in the presence of so much magnificence faintly affected her. She realised that hers was not to be a round of pleasure, and yet there was something promising in all the material prospect he set forth. There was something satisfactory in the attention of this individual with his good clothes. She could not help smiling as he told her of some popular actress of whom she reminded him. She was not silly, and yet attention of this sort had its weight.

"You will be in Chicago some little time, won't you?" he observed at one turn of the now easy conversation.

"I don't know," said Carrie vaguely—a flash vision of the possibility of her not securing employment rising in her mind.

"Several weeks, anyhow," he said, looking steadily into her eyes.

There was much more passing now than the mere words indicated. He recognised the indescribable thing that made up for fascination and beauty in her. She realised that she was of interest to him from the one standpoint which a woman both delights in and fears. Her manner was simple, though for the very reason that she had not yet learned the many little affectations with which women conceal their true feelings. Some things she did appeared bold. A clever companion—had she ever had one—would have warned her never to look a man in the eyes so steadily.

"Why do you ask?" she said.

"Well, I'm going to be there several weeks. I'm going to study stock at our place and get new samples. I might show you 'round."

"I don't know whether you can or not. I mean I don't know whether I can. I shall be living with my sister, and——"

"Well, if she minds, we'll fix that." He took out his pencil and a little pocket note-book as if it were all settled. "What is your address there?"

She fumbled her purse which contained the address slip.

He reached down in his hip pocket and took out a fat purse. It was filled with slips of paper, some mileage books, a roll of greenbacks. It impressed her deeply. Such a purse had never been carried by any one attentive to her. Indeed, an experienced traveller, a brisk man of the world, had never come within such close range before. The purse, the shiny tan shoes, the smart new suit, and the *air* with which he did things, built up for her a dim world of fortune, of which he was the centre. It disposed her pleasantly toward all he might do.

He took out a neat business card, on which was engraved Bartlett, Caryoe & Company, and down in the left-hand corner, Chas. H. Drouet.

"That's me," he said, putting the card in her hand and touching his name. "It's pronounced Drew-eh. Our family was French, on my father's side."

She looked at it while he put up his purse. Then he got out a letter from a bunch in his coat pocket. "This is the house I travel for," he went on, pointing to a picture on it, "corner of State and Lake." There was pride in his voice. He felt that it was something to be connected with such a place, and he made her feel that way.

"What is your address?" he began again, fixing his pencil to write.

She looked at his hand.

"Carrie Meeber," she said slowly. "Three hundred and fifty-four West Van Buren Street, care S. C. Hanson."

He wrote it carefully down and got out the purse again. "You'll be at home if I come around Monday night?" he said.

"I think so," she answered.

How true it is that words are but the vague shadows of the volumes we mean. Little audible links, they are, chaining together great inaudible feelings and purposes. Here were these two, bandying little phrases, drawing purses, looking at cards, and both unconscious of how inarticulate all their real feelings were. Neither was wise enough to be sure of the working of the mind of the other. He could not tell how his luring succeeded. She could not realise that she was drifting, until he secured her address. Now she felt that she had yielded something—he, that he had gained a victory. Already they felt that they were somehow associated. Already he took control in directing the conversation. His words were easy. Her manner was relaxed.

They were nearing Chicago. Signs were everywhere numerous. Trains flashed by them. Across wide stretches of flat, open prairie they could see lines of telegraph poles stalking across the fields toward the great city. Far away were indications of suburban towns, some big smoke-stacks towering high in the air.

Frequently there were two-story frame houses standing out in the open fields, without fence or trees, lone outposts of the approaching army of homes.

To the child, the genius with imagination, or the wholly untravelled, the approach to a great city for the first time is a wonderful thing. Particularly if it be evening—that mystic period between the glare and gloom of the world when life is changing from one sphere or condition to another. Ah, the promise of the night. What does it not hold for the weary! What old illusion of hope is not here forever repeated! Says the soul of the toiler to itself, "I shall soon be free. I shall be in the ways and the hosts of the merry. The streets, the lamps, the lighted chamber set for dining, are for me. The theatre, the halls, the parties, the ways of rest and the paths of song—these are mine in the night." Though all humanity be still enclosed in the shops, the thrill runs abroad. It is in the air. The dullest feel something which they may not always express or describe. It is the lifting of the burden of toil.

Sister Carrie gazed out of the window. Her companion, affected by her wonder, so contagious are all things, felt anew some interest in the city and pointed out its marvels.

"This is Northwest Chicago," said Drouet. "This is the Chicago River," and he pointed to a little muddy creek, crowded with the huge masted wanderers from far-off waters nosing the black-posted banks. With a puff, a clang, and a clatter of rails it was gone. "Chicago is getting to be a great town," he went on. "It's a wonder. You'll find lots to see here."

She did not hear this very well. Her heart was troubled by a kind of terror. The fact that she was alone, away from home, rushing into a great sea of life and endeavour, began to tell. She could not help but feel a little choked for breath—a little sick as her heart beat so fast. She half closed her eyes and tried to think it was nothing, that Columbia City was only a little way off.

"Chicago! Chicago!" called the brakeman, slamming open the door. They were rushing into a more crowded yard, alive with the clatter and clang of life. She began to gather up her poor little grip and closed her hand firmly upon her purse. Drouet arose, kicked his legs to straighten his trousers, and seized his clean yellow grip.

"I suppose your people will be here to meet you?" he said. "Let me carry your grip."

"Oh, no," she said. "I'd rather you wouldn't. I'd rather you wouldn't be with me when I meet my sister."

"All right," he said in all kindness. "I'll be near, though, in case she isn't here, and take you out there safely."

"You're so kind," said Carrie, feeling the goodness of such attention in her strange situation.

"Chicago!" called the brakeman, drawing the word out long. They were under a great shadowy train shed, where the lamps were already beginning to shine out, with passenger cars all about and the train moving at a snail's pace. The people in the car were all up and crowding about the door.

"Well, here we are," said Drouet, leading the way to the door. "Good-bye, till I see you Monday."

"Good-bye," she answered, taking his proffered hand.

"Remember, I'll be looking till you find your sister."

She smiled into his eyes.

They filed out, and he affected to take no notice of her. A lean-faced, rather commonplace woman recognised Carrie on the platform and hurried forward.

"Why, Sister Carrie!" she began, and there was a perfunctory embrace of welcome.

Carrie realised the change of affectional atmosphere at once. Amid all the maze, uproar, and novelty she felt cold reality taking her by the hand. No world of light and merriment. No round of amusement. Her sister carried with her most of the grimness of shift and toil.

"Why, how are all the folks at home?" she began; "how is father, and mother?"

Carrie answered, but was looking away. Down the aisle, toward the gate leading into the waiting-room and the street, stood Drouet. He was looking back. When he saw that she saw him and was safe with her sister he turned to go, sending back the shadow of a smile. Only Carrie saw it. She felt something lost to her when he moved away. When he disappeared she felt his absence thoroughly. With her sister she was much alone, a lone figure in a tossing, thoughtless sea.

II. What Poverty Threatened:

Of Granite and Brass

Minnie's flat, as the one-floor resident apartments were then being called, was in a part of West Van Buren Street inhabited by families of labourers and clerks, men who had come, and were still coming, with the rush of population pouring in at the rate of

50,000 a year. It was on the third floor, the front windows looking down into the street, where, at night, the lights of grocery stores were shining and children were playing. To Carrie, the sound of the little bells upon the horse-cars, as they tinkled in and out of hearing, was as pleasing as it was novel. She gazed into the lighted street when Minnie brought her into the front room, and wondered at the sounds, the movement, the murmur of the vast city which stretched for miles and miles in every direction.

Mrs. Hanson, after the first greetings were over, gave Carrie the baby and proceeded to get supper. Her husband asked a few questions and sat down to read the evening paper. He was a silent man, American born, of a Swede father, and now employed as a cleaner of refrigerator cars at the stock-yards. To him the presence or absence of his wife's sister was a matter of indifference. Her personal appearance did not affect him one way or the other. His one observation to the point was concerning the chances of work in Chicago.

"It's a big place," he said. "You can get in somewhere in a few days. Everybody does."

It had been tacitly understood beforehand that she was to get work and pay her board. He was of a clean, saving disposition, and had already paid a number of monthly instalments on two lots far out on the West Side. His ambition was some day to build a house on them.

In the interval which marked the preparation of the meal Carrie found time to study the flat. She had some slight gift of observation and that sense, so rich in every woman—intuition.

She felt the drag of a lean and narrow life. The walls of the rooms were discordantly papered. The floors were covered with matting and the hall laid with a thin rag carpet. One could see that the furniture was of that poor, hurriedly patched together quality sold by the instalment houses.

She sat with Minnie, in the kitchen, holding the baby until it began to cry. Then she walked and sang to it, until Hanson, disturbed in his reading, came and took it. A pleasant side to his nature came out here. He was patient. One could see that he was very much wrapped up in his offspring.

"Now, now," he said, walking. "There, there," and there was a certain Swedish accent noticeable in his voice.

"You'll want to see the city first, won't you?" said Minnie, when they were eating. "Well, we'll go out Sunday and see Lincoln Park."

Carrie noticed that Hanson had said nothing to this. He seemed to be thinking of something else.

"Well," she said, "I think I'll look around to-morrow. I've got Friday and Saturday, and it won't be any trouble. Which way is the business part?"

Minnie began to explain, but her husband took this part of the conversation to himself.

"It's that way," he said, pointing east. "That's east." Then he went off into the longest speech he had yet indulged in, concerning the lay of Chicago. "You'd better look in those big manufacturing houses along Franklin Street and just the other side of the river," he concluded. "Lots of girls work there. You could get home easy, too. It isn't very far."

Carrie nodded and asked her sister about the neighbourhood. The latter talked in a subdued tone, telling the little she knew about it, while Hanson concerned himself with the baby. Finally he jumped up and handed the child to his wife.

"I've got to get up early in the morning, so I'll go to bed," and off he went, disappearing into the dark little bedroom off the hall, for the night.

"He works way down at the stock-yards," explained Minnie, "so he's got to get up at half-past five."

"What time do you get up to get breakfast?" asked Carrie.

"At about twenty minutes of five."

Together they finished the labour of the day, Carrie washing the dishes while Minnie undressed the baby and put it to bed. Minnie's manner was one of trained industry, and Carrie could see that it was a steady round of toil with her.

She began to see that her relations with Drouet would have to be abandoned. He could not come here. She read from the manner of Hanson, in the subdued air of Minnie, and, indeed, the whole atmosphere of the flat, a settled opposition to anything save a conservative round of toil. If Hanson sat every evening in the front room and read his paper, if he went to bed at nine, and Minnie a little later, what would they expect of her? She saw that she would first need to get work and establish herself on a paying basis before she could think of having company of any sort. Her little flirtation with Drouet seemed now an extraordinary thing.

"No," she said to herself, "he can't come here."

She asked Minnie for ink and paper, which were upon the mantel in the dining-room, and when the latter had gone to bed at ten, got out Drouet's card and wrote him.

"I cannot have you call on me here. You will have to wait until you hear from me again. My sister's place is so small."

She troubled herself over what else to put in the letter. She wanted to make some reference to their relations upon the train, but was too timid. She concluded by thanking him for his kindness in a crude way, then puzzled over the formality of signing her name, and finally decided upon the severe, winding up with a "Very truly," which she subsequently changed to "Sincerely." She sealed and addressed the letter, and going in the front room, the alcove of which contained her bed, drew the one small rocking-chair up to the open window, and sat looking out upon the night and streets in silent wonder. Finally, wearied by her own reflections, she began to grow dull in her chair, and feeling the need of sleep, arranged her clothing for the night and went to bed.

When she awoke at eight the next morning, Hanson had gone. Her sister was busy in the dining-room, which was also the sitting-room, sewing. She worked, after dressing, to arrange a little breakfast for herself, and then advised with Minnie as to which way to look. The latter had changed considerably since Carrie had seen her. She was now a thin, though rugged, woman of twenty-seven, with ideas of life coloured by her husband's, and fast hardening into narrower conceptions of pleasure and duty than had ever been hers in a thoroughly circumscribed youth. She had invited Carrie, not because she longed for her presence, but because the latter was dissatisfied at home, and could probably get work and pay her board here. She was pleased to see her in a way but reflected her husband's point of view in the matter of work. Anything was good enough so long as it paid—say, five dollars a week to begin with. A shop girl was the destiny prefigured for the newcomer. She would get in one of the great shops and do well enough until—well, until something happened. Neither of them knew exactly what. They did not figure on promotion. They did not exactly count on marriage. Things would go on, though, in a dim kind of way until the better thing would eventuate, and Carrie would be rewarded for coming and toiling in the city. It was under such auspicious circumstances that she started out this morning to look for work.

Before following her in her round of seeking, let us look at the sphere in which her future was to lie. In 1889 Chicago had the peculiar qualifications of growth which made such adventuresome pilgrimages even on the part of young girls plausible. Its many and growing commercial opportunities gave it widespread fame, which made of it a giant magnet, drawing to itself, from all quarters, the hopeful and the hopeless—those who had their fortune yet to make and those whose fortunes and affairs had reached a disastrous climax elsewhere. It was a city of over 500,000, with the ambition, the daring, the activity of a metropolis of a million. Its streets and houses were already scattered over an area of seventy-five square miles. Its population was not so much thriving upon established commerce as upon the industries which prepared for the arrival of others. The sound of hammer engaged upon the erection of new structures was everywhere heard. Great industries were moving in. The huge railroad corporations which had long before recognised the prospects of the place had seized upon vast tracts of land for transfer and shipping purposes. Street-car lines had been extended far out into the open country in anticipation of rapid growth. The city had laid miles and miles of streets and sewers through regions where, perhaps, one solitary house stood out alone—a pioneer of the populous ways to be. There were regions open to the sweeping winds and rain, which were yet lighted throughout the night with long, blinking lines of gas-lamps, fluttering in the wind. Narrow board walks extended out, passing here a house, and there a store, at far intervals, eventually ending on the open prairie.

In the central portion was the vast wholesale and shopping district, to which the uninformed seeker for work usually drifted. It was a characteristic of Chicago then, and one not generally shared by other cities, that individual firms of any pretension occupied individual buildings. The presence of ample ground made this possible. It gave an imposing appearance to most of the wholesale houses, whose offices were upon the ground floor and in plain view of the street. The large plates of window glass, now so common, were then rapidly coming into use, and gave to the ground floor offices a distinguished and prosperous look. The casual wanderer could see as he passed a polished array of office fixtures, much frosted glass, clerks hard at work, and genteel business men in "nobby" suits and clean linen lounging about or sitting in groups. Polished brass or nickel signs at the square stone entrances announced the firm and the nature of the business in rather neat and reserved terms. The entire metropolitan centre possessed a high and mighty air calculated to overawe and abash the common applicant, and to make the gulf between poverty and success seem both wide and deep.

Into this important commercial region the timid Carrie went. She walked east along Van Buren Street through a region of lessening importance, until it deteriorated into a mass of shanties and coal-yards, and finally verged upon the river. She walked bravely forward, led by an honest desire to find employment and delayed at every step by the interest of the unfolding scene, and a sense of helplessness amid so much evidence of power and force which she did not understand. These vast buildings, what were they? These strange energies and huge interests, for what purposes were they there? She could have understood the meaning of a little stone-cutter's yard at Columbia City, carving little pieces of marble for individual use, but when the yards of some huge stone corporation came into view, filled with spur tracks and flat cars, transpierced by docks from the river and traversed overhead by immense trundling cranes of wood and steel, it lost all significance in her little world.

It was so with the vast railroad yards, with the crowded array of vessels she saw at the river, and the huge factories over the way, lining the water's edge. Through the open windows she could see the figures of men and women in working aprons, moving busily about. The great streets were wall-lined mysteries to her; the vast offices, strange mazes which concerned far-off individuals of importance. She could only think of people connected with them as counting money, dressing magnificently, and riding in carriages. What they dealt in, how they laboured, to what end it all came, she had only the vaguest conception. It was all wonderful, all vast, all far removed, and she sank in spirit inwardly and fluttered feebly at the heart as she thought of entering any one of these mighty concerns and asking for something to do—something that she could do—anything.

1901

A Literary Spokesman of Ideas

HENRY ADAMS [1838-1918]

Henry Adams was born in Boston in 1838, heir to a family of wealth and great distinction in American history. His great-grandfather was John Adams, who helped draft the Declaration of Independence and became second President of the United States. When he was a boy, Henry Adams spent his summers at Quincy, the home of his grandfather, John Quincy Adams, sixth President of the nation. His father, Charles Francis Adams, distinguished himself as minister to England during the Civil War where he was influential in representing the Northern cause. All were Harvard graduates, gifted men, patriots—but none was more naturally endowed for the life of the mind than Henry Adams, who was diverted from politics to become a historian, writer, and philosopher, and the author of one of the most remarkable books of the present century, *The Education of Henry Adams*. Written in the third person with both a scientific and an ironic detachment, this autobiography is a masterpiece. It portrays "Adams" as an intellectual alien in the progressive, optimistic, evolutionary period of the late nineteenth century. It describes his "education" as a failure, and it calls the age an age of "chaos" doomed to decline as surely as the second law of thermodynamics proved the gradual dissipation of the rays of energy from the sun.

Conservative by temperament, yet far too intelligent to share the complacent views of Spencerian evolution then current, Adams possessed a strong sense of the past. He could see nothing but ultimate catastrophe for a civilization fast enslaving itself by its own scientific discoveries. He predicted the power struggles of the twentieth century with uncanny accuracy. The final contest for world power would culminate in China, he said in 1903, and the world would divide between two poles, Russia and the United States.

Science would control man, and the human race would "commit suicide by blowing up the world."

Adams' actual education was far from the failure he termed it. He studied law at Harvard, then traveled in Europe in the leisurely fashion of an older time, finishing his studies at the University of Berlin in preparation for a career in statesmanship which he never had. Instead, he became an observer and commentator. In 1862 he accompanied his father to London as a secretary to the American legation there. His first literary efforts were exposés of political corruption in the age of the railroad barons, published in *Chapters of Erie, and Other Essays* (1871). When he returned to America after the war, Adams was discouraged at the course of Washington politics under Grant. Ignored by politicians, he accepted a professorship at Harvard where he taught medieval history and devoted himself to searching for a theory to explain human history, reading Turgot, Comte, Lyell, and other evolutionary thinkers of that time.

In 1872 Adams married Marian Hooper, an accomplished woman, the daughter of a distinguished Boston physician. During the seventies he edited the *North American Review,* lectured on the rights of women, and wrote biographies of Albert Gallatin and John Randolph, in addition to his teaching duties. But in 1877 he moved to Washington to observe the political scene. His spacious home on H Street (now the site of the Hay-Adams Hotel) became a salon for such choice friends as Clarence King, John Hay, William H. Evarts, a circle called "The Five of Hearts"; all were talented men. In 1880 Adams wrote his first novel, *Democracy,* published anonymously, its authorship kept secret even from his closest associates because of its sharp satire on certain political figures like Senator Blaine. This was followed by a second novel, *Esther* (1884), whose heroine, perhaps modeled on Mrs. Adams, experienced a conflict between her love for a religious man and her own skepticism and independence of thought. Marian Adams suffered a nervous breakdown in 1885 and committed suicide, a tragedy from which Adams never fully recovered. He immersed himself in his monumental, nine volume *History of the United States During the Administrations of Jefferson and Madison* (1889–1891), traveled to Japan with his painter friend John La Farge, and tried to imbibe something of the quietism of Oriental religion. A trip to Tahiti resulted in his study of the royal family, *Memoirs of Marau Taaroa, Last Queen of Tahiti* (1893, 1901).

In the nineties Adams' interests shifted away from reason and American political history to more subjective and artistic concerns. In Japan he had studied water coloring and the Buddhist religion. In Europe he speculated on the power of Christianity behind the building of the great French medieval cathedrals. This led to one of Adams' most original works, *Mont-Saint-Michel and Chartres* (1904), subtitled "A Study of Thirteenth-Century Unity." His lifelong interest in the role of women in history combined in this book with his study of the mystical aspect of Virgin adoration to explain the architectural miracle of Chartres. In 1907 Adams privately printed *The Education of Henry Adams* (published later, 1918) which pursued further his theory of "force" in history as symbolized by the dynamo he had watched at the Paris Exposition in 1900. He called this book "A Study of Twentieth-Century Multiplicity"—a materialistic and negative force as compared to the unifying influence of the Virgin of Chartres.

His final statements on the direction of world history were gloomy prognostications of despair. In "The Rule of Phase Applied to History" (1909) he again explored the parallel between science and history and prophesied the collapse of the world by precisely 1921. And in *A Letter to American Teachers of History* (1910) he again predicted the end of civilization on the basis of the dissipation of energy and the physical laws of decay and degeneration. As a literary artist Adams was eagerly read by such poetic prophets of pessimism as the early T. S. Eliot and others of the 1920's, but it must be said that he never quite found his proper form. Always the inspired amateur, he was a sometime historian, biographer, scholar, and letter-writer *par excellence.* His greatest forte lay in his ability to see himself objectively and to examine his own complex mind. He outlived his closest friends and relatives, living on until 1918 with increasing agnosticism and despair. But beneath it all there was a glimmer of hope in a mysticism which was religious, if not religion. Found in his wallet after his death was a poem called "Prayer to the Virgin of Chartres" which voiced his faith "not in the future science, but in you!"

Further reading: *The Education of Henry Adams*. Elizabeth Stevenson, ed., *A Henry Adams Reader*, 1959. Elizabeth Stevenson, *Henry Adams: A Biography*, 1955.

FROM *The Education of Henry Adams*

The Editor's Preface, signed by Henry Cabot Lodge, was written by Adams himself, before his death, and given to Lodge to print as his own. Adams died in March 1918. *The Education* was published in September of that year, though it had been privately printed and circulated to friends in 1907. In the original preface Adams cited Jean Jacques Rousseau's *Confessions* and Franklin's *Autobiography* as modern examples of autobiographies, but mostly he wanted to emulate St. Augustine's *Confessions* as a model of a man's account of his education and the role it played in his later experience of life. The book opened as a conventional autobiography, but as Adams says it became "unmanageable" and ended with the famous chapters outlining his dynamic theory of history, complementing his earlier study of *Mont-Saint-Michel and Chartres* (1904). The concept of "force" as determining both thirteenth-century unity and twentieth-century multiplicity was Adams' pose of being a totally disinterested scientist. "History is not obliged to decide," he wrote, "whether the Ultimate tends to a purpose or not." Yet basically the two books expressed his conviction of medieval harmony and modern disaster.

Editor's Preface

This volume, written in 1905 as a sequel to the same author's "Mont-Saint-Michel and Chartres," was privately printed, to the number of one hundred copies, in 1906, and sent to the persons interested, for their assent, correction, or suggestion. The idea of the two books was thus explained at the end of Chapter XXIX:—

"Any schoolboy could see that man as a force must be measured by motion from a fixed point. Psychology helped here by suggesting a unit—the point of history when man held the highest idea of himself as a unit in a unified universe. Eight or ten years of study had led Adams to think he might use the century 1150–1250, expressed in Amiens Cathedral and the Works of Thomas Aquinas, as the unit from which he might measure motion down to his own time, without assuming anything as true or untrue, except relation. The movement might be studied at once in philosophy and mechanics. Setting himself to the task, he began a volume which he mentally knew as 'Mont-Saint-Michel and Chartres: a Study of Thirteenth-Century Unity.' From that point he proposed to fix a position for himself, which he could label: 'The Education of Henry Adams: a Study of Twentieth-Century Multiplicity.' With the help of these two points of relation, he hoped to project his lines forward and backward indefinitely, subject to correction from any one who should know better."

The "Chartres" was finished and privately printed in 1904. The "Education" proved to be more difficult. The point on which the author failed to please himself, and could get no light from readers or friends, was the usual one of literary form. Probably he saw it in advance, for he used to say, half in jest, that his great ambition was to complete St. Augustine's "Confessions," but that St. Augustine, like a great artist, had worked from multiplicity to unity, while he, like a small one, had to reverse the method and work back from unity to multiplicity. The scheme became unmanageable as he approached his end.

Probably he was, in fact, trying only to work into it his favorite theory of history, which now fills the last three or four chapters of the "Education," and he could not satisfy himself with his workmanship. At all events, he was still pondering over the problem in 1910, when he tried to deal with it in another way which might be more intelligible to students. He printed a small volume called "A Letter to American Teachers," which he sent to his associates in the American Historical Association, hoping to provoke some response. Before he could satisfy himself even on this minor point, a severe illness in the spring of 1912 put an end to his literary activity forever.

The matter soon passed beyond his control. In 1913 the Institute of Architects published the "Mont-Saint-Michel and Chartres." Already the "Education" had become almost as well known as the "Chartres," and was freely quoted by every book whose author requested it. The author could no longer withdraw either volume; he could no longer rewrite either, and he could not publish that which he thought unprepared and unfinished, although in his opinion the other was historically purposeless without its sequel. In the end, he preferred to leave the "Education" unpublished, avowedly incomplete, trusting that it might quietly fade from memory. According to his theory of history as explained in Chapters XXXIII and XXXIV, the teacher was at best helpless, and, in the immediate future, silence next to good-temper was the mark of sense. After midsummer, 1914, the rule was made absolute.

The Massachusetts Historical Society now publishes the "Education" as it was printed in 1907, with only such marginal corrections as the author made, and it does this, not in opposition to the author's judgment, but only to put both volumes equally within reach of students who have occasion to consult them.

HENRY CABOT LODGE

September, 1918

I. Quincy (1838–1848)

Under the shadow of Boston State House, turning its back on the house of John Hancock, the little passage called Hancock Avenue runs, or ran, from Beacon Street, skirting the State House grounds, to Mount Vernon Street, on the summit of Beacon Hill; and there, in the third house below Mount Vernon Place, February 16, 1838, a child was born, and christened later by his uncle, the minister of the First Church after the tenets of Boston Unitarianism, as Henry Brooks Adams.[1]

Had he been born in Jerusalem under the shadow of the Temple and circumcised in the Synagogue by his uncle the high priest, under the name of Israel Cohen, he would scarcely have been more distinctly branded, and not much more heavily handicapped in the races of the coming century, in running for such stakes as the century was to offer; but, on the other hand, the ordinary traveller, who does not enter the field of racing, finds advantage in being, so to speak, ticketed through life, with the safeguards of an old, established traffic. Safeguards are often irksome, but sometimes convenient, and if one needs them at all, one is apt to need them badly. A hundred years earlier, such safeguards as his would have secured any young man's success; and although in 1838 their value was not very great compared with what they would have had in 1738, yet the mere accident of starting a twentieth-century career from a nest of associations so colonial—so troglodytic[2]—as the First Church, the Boston State House, Beacon Hill, John Hancock and John Adams, Mount Vernon Street and Quincy, all crowding on ten pounds of unconscious babyhood, was so queer as to offer a subject of curious speculation to the baby long after he had witnessed the solution. What could become of such a child of the seventeenth and eighteenth centuries, when he should wake up to find himself required to play the game of the twentieth? Had he been consulted, would he have cared to play the game at all, holding such cards as he held, and suspecting that the game was to be one of which neither he nor any one else back to the beginning of time knew the rules or the risks or the stakes? He was not consulted and was not responsible, but had he been taken into the confidence of his parents, he would certainly have told them to change nothing as far as concerned him. He would have been astounded by his own luck. Probably no child, born in the year, held better cards than he. Whether life was an honest game of chance, or whether the cards were marked and forced, he could not refuse to play his excellent hand. He could never make the usual plea of irresponsibility. He accepted the situation as though he had been a party to it, and under the same circumstances would do it again, the more readily for knowing the exact values. To his life as a whole he was a consenting, contracting party and partner from the moment he was born to the moment he died. Only with that understanding—as a consciously assenting member in full partnership with the society of his age—had his education an interest to himself or to others.

As it happened, he never got to the point of playing the game at all; he lost himself in the study of it, watching the errors of the players; but this is the only interest in the story, which otherwise has no moral and little incident. A story of education—seventy years of it—the practical value remains to the end in doubt, like other values about which men have disputed since the birth of Cain and Abel; but the practical value of the universe has never been stated in dollars. Although every one cannot be a Gargantua-Napoleon-Bismarck[3] and walk off with the great bells of Notre Dame, every one must bear his own universe, and most persons are moderately interested in learning how their neighbors have managed to carry theirs.

This problem of education, started in 1838, went on for three years, while the baby grew, like other babies, unconsciously, as a vegetable, the outside world working as it never had worked before, to get his new universe ready for him. Often in old age he puzzled over the question whether, on the doctrine of chances, he was at liberty to accept himself or his world as an accident. No such accident had ever happened before in human experience. For him, alone, the old universe was thrown into the ash-heap

[1] Adams ceased using his middle name after 1870.

[2] Primitive, prehistoric. Adams writes ironically.

[3] The reference is to Gargantua's stealing the bells of Notre Dame and tying them to his horse in Rabelais' *Gargantua and Pantagruel.*

and a new one created. He and his eighteenth-century, troglodytic Boston were suddenly cut apart—separated forever—in act if not in sentiment, by the opening of the Boston and Albany Railroad; the appearance of the first Cunard steamers in the bay; and the telegraphic messages which carried from Baltimore to Washington the news that Henry Clay and James K. Polk were nominated for the Presidency. This was in May, 1844; he was six years old; his new world was ready for use, and only fragments of the old met his eyes.

Of all this that was being done to complicate his education, he knew only the color of yellow. He first found himself sitting on a yellow kitchen floor in strong sunlight. He was three years old when he took this earliest step in education; a lesson of color. The second followed soon; a lesson of taste. On December 3, 1841, he developed scarlet fever. For several days he was as good as dead, reviving only under the careful nursing of his family. When he began to recover strength, about January 1, 1842, his hunger must have been stronger than any other pleasure or pain, for while in after life he retained not the faintest recollection of his illness, he remembered quite clearly his aunt entering the sick-room bearing in her hand a saucer with a baked apple.

The order of impressions retained by memory might naturally be that of color or taste, although one would rather suppose that the sense of pain would be first to educate. In fact, the third recollection of the child was that of discomfort. The moment he could be removed, he was bundled up in blankets and carried from the little house in Hancock Avenue to a larger one which his parents were to occupy for the rest of their lives in the neighboring Mount Vernon Street. The season was midwinter, January 10, 1842, and he never forgot his acute distress for want of air under his blankets, or the noises of moving furniture.

As a means of variation from a normal type, sickness in childhood ought to have a certain value not to be classed under any fitness or unfitness of natural selection; and especially scarlet fever affected boys seriously, both physically and in character, though they might through life puzzle themselves to decide whether it had fitted or unfitted them for success; but this fever of Henry Adams took greater and greater importance in his eyes, from the point of view of education, the longer he lived. At first, the effect was physical. He fell behind his brothers two or three inches in height, and proportionally in bone and weight. His character and processes of mind seemed to share in this fining-down process of scale. He was not good in a fight, and his nerves were more delicate than boys' nerves ought to be. He exaggerated these weaknesses as he grew older. The habit of doubt; of distrusting his own judgment and of totally rejecting the judgment of the world; the tendency to regard every question as open; the hesitation to act except as a choice of evils; the shirking of responsibility; the love of line, form, quality; the horror of ennui; the passion for companionship and the antipathy to society—all these are well known qualities of New England character in no way peculiar to individuals but in this instance they seemed to be stimulated by the fever, and Henry Adams could never make up his mind whether, on the whole, the change of character was morbid or healthy, good or bad for his purpose. His brothers were the type; he was the variation.

As far as the boy knew, the sickness did not affect him at all, and he grew up in excellent health, bodily and mental, taking life as it was given; accepting its local standards without a difficulty, and enjoying much of it as keenly as any other boy of his age. He seemed to himself quite normal, and his companions seemed always to think him so. Whatever was peculiar about him was education, not character, and came to him, directly and indirectly, as the result of that eighteenth-century inheritance which he took with his name.

The atmosphere of education in which he lived was colonial, revolutionary, almost Cromwellian,[4] as though he were steeped, from his greatest grandmother's birth, in the odor of political crime. Resistance to something was the law of New England nature; the boy looked out on the world with the instinct of resistance; for numberless generations his predecessors had viewed the world chiefly as a thing to be reformed, filled with evil forces to be abolished, and they saw no reason to suppose that they had wholly succeeded in the abolition; the duty was unchanged. That duty implied not only resistance to evil, but hatred of it. Boys naturally look on all force as an enemy, and generally find it so, but the New Englander, whether boy or man, in his long struggle with a stingy or hostile universe, had learned also to love the pleasure of hating; his joys were few.

Politics, as a practice, whatever its professions, had always been the systematic organization of hatreds, and Massachusetts politics had been as harsh as the climate. The chief charm of New England was harshness of contrasts and extremes of sensibility—a cold that froze the blood, and a heat that boiled it—so that the pleasure of hating—one's self if no better victim offered—was not its rarest amusement; but the charm was a true and natural child of the soil, not a cultivated weed of the ancients. The violence

[4] Oliver Cromwell (1599-1658), leader of the Puritan revolution which resulted in the execution of Charles I in 1649. He ruled England until his death.

of the contrast was real and made the strongest motive of education. The double exterior nature gave life its relative values. Winter and summer, cold and heat, town and country, force and freedom, marked two modes of life and thought, balanced like lobes of the brain. Town was winter confinement, school, rule, discipline; straight, gloomy streets, piled with six feet of snow in the middle; frosts that made the snow sing under wheels or runners; thaws when the streets became dangerous to cross; society of uncles, aunts, and cousins who expected children to behave themselves, and who were not always gratified; above all else, winter represented the desire to escape and go free. Town was restraint, law, unity. Country, only seven miles away, was liberty, diversity, outlawry, the endless delight of mere sense impressions given by nature for nothing, and breathed by boys without knowing it.

Boys are wild animals, rich in the treasures of sense, but the New England boy had a wider range of emotions than boys of more equable climates. He felt his nature crudely, as it was meant. To the boy Henry Adams, summer was drunken. Among senses, smell was the strongest—smell of hot pine-woods and sweet-fern in the scorching summer noon; of new-mown hay; of ploughed earth; of box hedges; of peaches, lilacs, syringas; of stables, barns, cow-yards; of salt water and low tide on the marshes; nothing came amiss. Next to smell came taste, and the children knew the taste of everything they saw or touched, from pennyroyal and flagroot to the shell of a pignut and the letters of a spelling-book—the taste of A-B, AB, suddenly revived on the boy's tongue sixty years afterwards. Light, line, and color as sensual pleasures, came later and were as crude as the rest. The New England light is glare, and the atmosphere harshens color. The boy was a full man before he ever knew what was meant by atmosphere; his idea of pleasure in light was the blaze of a New England sun. His idea of color was a peony, with the dew of early morning on its petals. The intense blue of the sea, as he saw it a mile or two away, from the Quincy hills; the cumuli in a June afternoon sky; the strong reds and greens and purples of colored prints and children's picture-books, as the American colors then ran; these were ideals. The opposites or antipathies, were the cold grays of November evenings, and the thick, muddy thaws of Boston winter. With such standards, the Bostonian could not but develop a double nature. Life was a double thing. After a January blizzard, the boy who could look with pleasure into the violent snow-glare of the cold white sunshine, with its intense light and shade, scarcely knew what was meant by tone. He could reach it only by education.

Winter and summer, then, were two hostile lives, and bred two separate natures. Winter was always the effort to live; summer was tropical license. Whether the children rolled in the grass, or waded in the brook, or swam in the salt ocean, or sailed in the bay, or fished for smelts in the creeks, or netted minnows in the salt-marshes, or took to the pine-woods and the granite quarries, or chased muskrats and hunted snapping-turtles in the swamps, or mushrooms or nuts on the autumn hills, summer and country were always sensual living, while winter was always compulsory learning. Summer was the multiplicity of nature; winter was school.

The bearing of the two seasons on the education of Henry Adams was no fancy; it was the most decisive force he ever knew; it ran though life, and made the division between its perplexing, warring, irreconcilable problems, irreducible opposites, with growing emphasis to the last year of study. From earliest childhood the boy was accustomed to feel that, for him, life was double. Winter and summer, town and country, law and liberty, were hostile, and the man who pretended they were not, was in his eyes a schoolmaster—that is, a man employed to tell lies to little boys. Though Quincy was but two hours' walk from Beacon Hill, it belonged in a different world. For two hundred years, every Adams, from father to son, had lived within sight of State Street, and sometimes had lived in it, yet none had ever taken kindly to the town, or been taken kindly by it. The boy inherited his double nature. He knew as yet nothing about his great-grandfather, who had died a dozen years before his own birth: he took for granted that any great-grandfather of his must have always been good, and his enemies wicked; but he divined his great-grandfather's character from his own. Never for a moment did he connect the two ideas of Boston and John Adams; they were separate and antagonistic; the idea of John Adams went with Quincy. He knew his grandfather John Quincy Adams only as an old man of seventy-five or eighty who was friendly and gentle with him, but except that he heard his grandfather always called "the President," and his grandmother "the Madam," he had no reason to suppose that his Adams grandfather differed in character from his Brooks grandfather who was equally kind and benevolent. He liked the Adams side best, but for no other reason than that it reminded him of the country, the summer, and the absence of restraint. Yet he felt also that Quincy was in a way inferior to Boston, and that socially Boston looked down on Quincy. The reason was clear enough even to a five-year old child. Quincy had no Boston style. Little enough style had either; a simpler manner of life and thought could hardly exist, short of cave-dwelling. The flint-and-steel with which his grandfather Adams used to light his own fires in the early morning was still on the mantelpiece of his study. The idea of a livery or even a dress for servants, or of an evening toilette, was next to blasphemy. Bathrooms, water-supplies, lighting, heating, and the whole array of domestic comforts, were unknown at Quincy. Boston had already a bathroom, a water-supply, a furnace, and gas. The superiority of Boston was evident, but a child liked it no better for that.

The magnificence of his grandfather Brooks's house in Pearl Street or South Street has long ago disappeared, but perhaps his country house at Medford may still remain to show what impressed the mind of a boy in 1845 with the idea of city splendor. The President's place at Quincy was the larger and older and far the more interesting of the two; but a boy felt at once its inferiority in fashion. It showed plainly enough its want of wealth. It smacked of colonial age, but not of Boston style or plush curtains. To the end of his life he never quite overcame the prejudice thus drawn in with his childish breath. He never could compel himself to care for nineteenth-century style. He was never able to adopt it, any more than his father or grandfather or great-grandfather had done. Not that he felt it as particularly hostile, for he reconciled himself to much that was worse; but because, for some remote reason, he was born an eighteenth-century child. The old house at Quincy was eighteenth century. What style it had was in its Queen Anne mahogany panels and its Louis Seize chairs and sofas. The panels belonged to an old colonial Vassall who built the house; the furniture had been brought back from Paris in 1789 or 1801 or 1817, along with porcelain and books and much else of old diplomatic remnants; and neither of the two eighteenth-century styles—neither English Queen Anne nor French Louis Seize—was comfortable for a boy, or for any one else. The dark mahogany had been painted white to suit daily life in winter gloom. Nothing seemed to favor, for a child's objects, the older forms. On the contrary, most boys, as well as grown-up people, preferred the new, with good reason, and the child felt himself distinctly at a disadvantage for the taste.

Nor had personal preference any share in his bias. The Brooks grandfather was as amiable and as sympathetic as the Adams grandfather. Both were born in 1767, and both died in 1848. Both were kind to children, and both belonged rather to the eighteenth than to the nineteenth centuries. The child knew no difference between them except that one was associated with winter and the other with summer; one with Boston, the other with Quincy. Even with Medford, the association was hardly easier. Once as a very young boy he was taken to pass a few days with his grandfather Brooks under charge of his aunt, but became so violently homesick that within twenty-four hours he was brought back in disgrace. Yet he could not remember ever being seriously homesick again.

The attachment to Quincy was not altogether sentimental or wholly sympathetic. Quincy was not a bed of thornless roses. Even there the curse of Cain set its mark. There as elsewhere a cruel universe combined to crush a child. As though three or four vigorous brothers and sisters, with the best will, were not enough to crush any child, every one else conspired towards an education which he hated. From cradle to grave this problem of running order through chaos, direction through space, discipline through freedom, unity through multiplicity, has always been, and must always be, the task of education, as it is the moral of religion, philosophy, science, art, politics, and economy; but a boy's will is his life, and he dies when it is broken, as the colt dies in harness, taking a new nature in becoming tame. Rarely has the boy felt kindly towards his tamers. Between him and his master has always been war. Henry Adams never knew a boy of his generation to like a master, and the task of remaining on friendly terms with one's own family, in such a relation, was never easy.

All the more singular it seemed afterwards to him that his first serious contact with the President should have been a struggle of will, in which the old man almost necessarily defeated the boy, but instead of leaving, as usual in such defeats, a lifelong sting, left rather an impression of as fair treatment as could be expected from a natural enemy. The boy met seldom with such restraint. He could not have been much more than six years old at the time—seven at the utmost—and his mother had taken him to Quincy for a long stay with the President during the summer. What became of the rest of the family he quite forgot; but he distinctly remembered standing at the house door one summer morning in a passionate outburst of rebellion against going to school. Naturally his mother was the immediate victim of his rage; that is what mothers are for, and boys also; but in this case the boy had his mother at unfair disadvantage, for she was a guest, and had no means of enforcing obedience. Henry showed a certain tactical ability by refusing to start, and he met all efforts at compulsion by successful, though too vehement protest. He was in fair way to win, and was holding his own, with sufficient energy, at the bottom of the long staircase which led up to the door of the President's library, when the door opened, and the old man slowly came down. Putting on his hat, he took the boy's hand without a word, and walked with him, paralyzed by awe, up the road to the town. After the first moments of consternation at this interference in a domestic dispute, the boy reflected that an old gentleman close on eighty would never trouble himself to walk near a mile on a hot summer morning over a shadeless road to take a boy to school, and that it would be strange if a lad imbued with the passion of freedom could not find a corner to dodge around, somewhere before reaching the school door. Then and always, the boy insisted that this reasoning justified his apparent submission; but the old man did not stop, and the boy saw all his strategical points turned, one after another, until he found himself seated inside the school, and obviously the centre of curious if not malevolent criticism. Not till then did the President release his hand and depart.

The point was that this act, contrary to the inalienable rights of boys, and nullifying the social compact, ought to have made him dislike his grandfather for life. He could not recall that it had this effect even for a moment. With a certain maturity of mind, the child must have recognized that the President, though a tool of tyranny, had done his disreputable work with a certain intelligence. He had shown no temper, no irritation, no personal feeling, and had made no display of force. Above all, he had held his tongue. During their long walk he had said nothing; he had uttered no syllable of revolting cant about the duty of obedience and the wickedness of resistance to law; he had shown no concern in the matter; hardly even a consciousness of the boy's existence. Probably his mind at that moment was actually troubling itself little about his grandson's iniquities, and much about the iniquities of President Polk, but the boy could scarcely at that age feel the whole satisfaction of thinking that President Polk was to be the vicarious victim of his own sins, and he gave his grandfather credit for intelligent silence. For this forbearance he felt instinctive respect. He admitted force as a form of right; he admitted even temper, under protest; but the seeds of a moral education would at that moment have fallen on the stoniest soil in Quincy, which is, as every one knows, the stoniest glacial and tidal drift known in any Puritan land.

Neither party to this momentary disagreement can have felt rancor, for during these three or four summers the old President's relations with the boy were friendly and almost intimate. Whether his older brothers and sisters were still more favored he failed to remember, but he was himself admitted to a sort of familiarity which, when in his turn he had reached old age, rather shocked him, for it must have sometimes tried the President's patience. He hung about the library; handled the books; deranged the papers; ransacked the drawers; searched the old purses and pocket-books for foreign coins; drew the sword-cane; snapped the travelling-pistols; upset everything in the corners, and penetrated the President's dressing-closet where a row of tumblers, inverted on the shelf, covered caterpillars which were supposed to become moths or butterflies, but never did. The Madam bore with fortitude the loss of the tumblers which her husband purloined for these hatcheries; but she made protest when he carried off her best cut-glass bowls to plant with acorns or peachstones that he might see the roots grow, but which, she said, he commonly forgot like the caterpillars.

At that time the President rode the hobby of tree-culture, and some fine old trees should still remain to witness it, unless they have been improved off the ground; but his was a restless mind, and although he took his hobbies seriously and would have been annoyed had his grandchild asked whether he was bored like an English duke, he probably cared more for the processes than for the results, so that his grandson was saddened by the sight and smell of peaches and pears, the best of their kind, which he brought up from the garden to rot on his shelves for seed. With the inherited virtues of his Puritan ancestors, the little boy Henry conscientiously brought up to him in his study the finest peaches he found in the garden, and ate only the less perfect. Naturally he ate more by way of compensation, but the act showed that he bore no grudge. As for his grandfather, it is even possible that he may have felt a certain self-reproach for his temporary rôle of schoolmaster—seeing that his own career did not offer proof of the worldly advantages of docile obedience—for there still exists somewhere a little volume of critically edited Nursery Rhymes with the boy's name in full written in the President's trembling hand on the fly-leaf. Of course there was also the Bible, given to each child at birth, with the proper inscription in the President's hand on the fly-leaf; while their grandfather Brooks supplied the silver mugs.

So many Bibles and silver mugs had to be supplied, that a new house, or cottage, was built to hold them. It was "on the hill," five minutes' walk above "the old house," with a far view eastward over Quincy Bay, and northward over Boston. Till his twelfth year, the child passed his summers there, and his pleasures of childhood mostly centred in it. Of education he had as yet little to complain. Country schools were not very serious. Nothing stuck to the mind except home impressions, and the sharpest were those of kindred children; but as influences that warped a mind, none compared with the mere effect of the back of the President's bald head, and he sat in his pew on Sundays, in line with that of

President Quincy, who, though some ten years younger, seemed to children about the same age. Before railways entered the New England town, every parish church showed half-a-dozen of these leading citizens, with gray hair, who sat on the main aisle in the best pews, and had sat there, or in some equivalent dignity, since the time of St. Augustine, if not since the glacial epoch. It was unusual for boys to sit behind a President grandfather, and to read over his head the tablet in memory of a President great-grandfather, who had "pledged his life, his fortune, and his sacred honor" to secure the independence of his country and so forth; but boys naturally supposed, without much reasoning, that other boys had the equivalent of President grandfathers, and that churches would always go on, with the bald-headed leading citizens on the main aisle, and Presidents or their equivalents on the walls. The Irish gardener once said to the child: "You'll be thinkin' you'll be President too!" The casuality of the remark made so strong an impression on his mind that he never forgot it. He could not remember ever to have thought on the subject; to him, that there should be a doubt of his being President was a new idea. What had been would continue to be. He doubted neither about Presidents nor about Churches, and no one suggested at that time a doubt whether a system of society which had lasted since Adam would outlast one Adams more.

The Madam was a little more remote than the President, but more decorative. She stayed much in her own room with the Dutch tiles, looking out on her garden with the box walks, and seemed a fragile creature to a boy who sometimes brought her a note or a message, and took distinct pleasure in looking at her delicate face under what seemed to him very becoming caps. He liked her refined figure; her gentle voice and manner; her vague effect of not belonging there, but to Washington or to Europe, like her furniture, and writing-desk with little glass doors above and little eighteenth-century volumes in old binding, labelled "Peregrine Pickle" or "Tom Jones" or "Hannah More."[5] Try as she might, the Madam could never be Bostonian, and it was her cross in life, but to the boy it was her charm. Even at that age, he felt drawn to it. The Madam's life had been in truth far from Boston. She was born in London in 1775, daughter of Joshua Johnson, an American merchant, brother of Governor Thomas Johnson of Maryland; and Catherine Nuth, of an English family in London. Driven from England by the Revolutionary War, Joshua Johnson took his family to Nantes, where they remained till the peace. The girl Louisa Catherine was nearly ten years old when brought back to London, and her sense of nationality must have been confused; but the influence of the Johnsons and the services of Joshua obtained for him from President Washington the appointment of Consul in London on the organization of the Government in 1790. In 1794 President Washington appointed John Quincy Adams Minister to The Hague. He was twenty-seven years old when he returned to London, and found the Consul's house a very agreeable haunt. Louisa was then twenty.

At that time, and long afterwards, the Consul's house, far more than the Minister's, was the centre of contact for travelling Americans, either official or other. The Legation was a shifting point, between 1785 and 1815; but the Consulate, far down in the City, near the Tower, was convenient and inviting; so inviting that it proved fatal to young Adams. Louisa was charming, like a Romney portrait,[6] but among her many charms that of being a New England woman was not one. The defect was serious. Her future mother-in-law, Abigail, a famous New England woman whose authority over her turbulent husband, the second President, was hardly so great as that which she exercised over her son, the sixth to be, was troubled by the fear that Louisa might not be made of stuff stern enough, or brought up in conditions severe enough, to suit a New England climate, or to make an efficient wife for her paragon son, and Abigail was right on that point, as on most others where sound judgment was involved; but sound judgment is sometimes a source of weakness rather than of force, and John Quincy already had reason to think that his mother held sound judgments on the subject of daughters-in law which human nature, since the fall of Eve, made Adams helpless to realize. Being three thousand miles away from his mother, and equally far in love, he married Louisa in London, July 26, 1797, and took her to Berlin to be the head of the United States Legation. During three or four exciting years, the young bride lived in Berlin; whether she was happy or not, whether she was content or not, whether she was socially successful or not, her descendants did not surely know; but in any case she could by no chance have become educated there for a life in Quincy or Boston. In 1801 the overthrow of the Federalist[7] Party drove her and her husband to America, and she became at last a member of the Quincy household, but by that time her children needed all her attention, and she remained there with occasional winters

[5] The first two are titles of well-known eighteenth-century novels by Smollett and Fielding. Adams mistakenly recalled "Hannah More" as a novel. She was a writer on subjects of practical piety and an English bluestocking (1745-1833).

[6] George Romney (1734-1802), British portrait painter of the school of Reynolds and Gainsborough.

[7] The election of Jefferson to the presidency.

in Boston and Washington, till 1809. Her husband was made Senator in 1803, and in 1809 was appointed Minister to Russia. She went with him to St. Petersburg, taking her baby, Charles Francis, born in 1807; but broken-hearted at having to leave her two older boys behind. The life at St. Petersburg was hardly gay for her; they were far too poor to shine in that extravagant society; but she survived it, though her little girl baby did not, and in the winter of 1814-15, alone with the boy of seven years old, crossed Europe from St. Petersburg to Paris, in her travelling-carriage, passing through the armies, and reaching Paris in the *Cent Jours*[8] after Napoleon's return from Elba. Her husband next went to England as Minister, and she was for two years at the Court of the Regent. In 1817 her husband came home to be Secretary of State, and she lived for eight years in F Street, doing her work of entertainer for President Monroe's administration. Next she lived four miserable years in the White House. When that chapter was closed in 1829, she had earned the right to be tired and delicate, but she still had fifteen years to serve as wife of a Member of the House, after her husband went back to Congress in 1833. Then it was that the little Henry, her grandson, first remembered her, from 1843 to 1848, sitting in her panelled room, at breakfast, with her heavy silver teapot and sugar-bowl and cream-jug, which still exist somewhere as an heirloom of the modern safety-vault. By that time she was seventy years old or more, and thoroughly weary of being beaten about a stormy world. To the boy she seemed singularly peaceful, a vision of silver gray, presiding over her old President and her Queen Anne mahogany; an exotic, like her Sèvres china; an object of deference to every one, and of great affection to her son Charles; but hardly more Bostonian than she had been fifty years before, on her wedding-day, in the shadow of the Tower of London.

Such a figure was even less fitted than that of her old husband, the President, to impress on a boy's mind, the standards of the coming century. She was Louis Seize, like the furniture. The boy knew nothing of her interior life, which had been, as the venerable Abigail, long since at peace, foresaw, one of severe stress and little pure satisfaction. He never dreamed that from her might come some of those doubts and self-questionings, those hesitations, those rebellions against law and discipline, which marked more than one of her descendants; but he might even then have felt some vague instinctive suspicion that he was to inherit from her the seeds of the primal sin, the fall from grace, the curse of Abel, that he was not of pure New England stock, but half exotic. As a child of Quincy he was not a true Bostonian, but even as a child of Quincy he inherited a quarter taint of Maryland blood. Charles Francis, half Marylander by birth, had hardly seen Boston till he was ten years old, when his parents left him there at school in 1817, and he never forgot the experience. He was to be nearly as old as his mother had been in 1845, before he quite accepted Boston, or Boston quite accepted him.

A boy who began his education in these surroundings, with physical strength inferior to that of his brothers, and with a certain delicacy of mind and bone, ought rightly to have felt at home in the eighteenth century and should, in proper self-respect, have rebelled against the standards of the nineteenth. The atmosphere of his first ten years must have been very like that of his grandfather at the same age, from 1767 till 1776, barring the battle of Bunker Hill, and even as late as 1846, the battle of Bunker Hill remained actual. The tone of Boston society was colonial. The true Bostonian always knelt in self-abasement before the majesty of English standards; far from concealing it as a weakness, he was proud of it as his strength. The eighteenth century ruled society long after 1850. Perhaps the boy began to shake it off rather earlier than most of his mates.

Indeed this prehistoric stage of education ended rather abruptly with his tenth year. One winter morning he was conscious of a certain confusion in the house in Mount Vernon Street, and gathered, from such words as he could catch, that the President, who happened to be then staying there, on his way to Washington, had fallen and hurt himself. Then he heard the word paralysis. After that day he came to associate the word with the figure of his grandfather, in a tall-backed, invalid armchair, on one side of the spare bedroom fireplace, and one of his old friends, Dr. Parkman or P. P. F. Degrand, on the other side, both dozing.

The end of this first, or ancestral and Revolutionary, chapter came on February 21, 1848—and the month of February brought life and death as a family habit—when the eighteenth century, as an actual and living companion, vanished. If the scene on the floor of the House, when the old President fell, struck the still simple-minded American public with a sensation unusually dramatic, its effect on a ten-year-old boy, whose boy-life was fading away with the life of his grandfather, could not be slight. One had to pay for Revolutionary patriots; grandfathers and grandmothers; Presidents; diplomats; Queen Anne mahogany and Louis Seize chairs, as well as for Stuart portraits. Such things warp young life. Americans commonly believed that they ruined it, and perhaps the practical common-sense of the American mind judged right. Many a boy might be ruined by much less than the emotions of the funer-

[8] The hundred days following Napoleon's return from exile on Elba until his defeat at Waterloo, July 14, 1815.

al service in the Quincy church, with its surroundings of national respect and family pride. By another dramatic chance it happened that the clergyman of the parish, Dr. Lunt, was an unusual pulpit orator, the ideal of a somewhat austere intellectual type, such as the school of Buckminster and Channing[9] inherited from the old Congregational clergy. His extraordinarily refined appearance, his dignity of manner, his deeply cadenced voice, his remarkable English and his fine appreciation, gave to the funeral service a character that left an overwhelming impression on the boy's mind. He was to see many great functions—funerals and festivals—in after-life, till his only thought was to see no more, but he never again witnessed anything nearly so impressive to him as the last services at Quincy over the body of one President and the ashes of another.

The effect of the Quincy service was deepened by the official ceremony which afterwards took place in Faneuil Hall[10] when the boy was taken to hear his uncle, Edward Everett,[11] deliver a Eulogy. Like all Mr. Everett's orations, it was an admirable piece of oratory, such as only an admirable orator and scholar could create; too good for a ten-year-old boy to appreciate at its value; but already the boy knew that the dead President could not be in it, and had even learned why he would have been out of place there; for knowledge was beginning to come fast. The shadow of the War of 1812 still hung over State Street; the shadow of the Civil War to come had already begun to darken Faneuil Hall. No rhetoric could have reconciled Mr. Everett's audience to his subject. How could he say there, to an assemblage of Bostonians in the heart of mercantile Boston, that the only distinctive mark of all the Adamses,[12] since old Sam Adams's father a hundred and fifty years before, had been their inherited quarrel with State Street, which had again and again broken out into riot, bloodshed, personal feuds, foreign and civil war, wholesale banishments and confiscations, until the history of Florence was hardly more turbulent than that of Boston? How could he whisper the word Hartford Convention before the men who had made it? What would have been said had he suggested the chance of Secession and Civil War?

Thus already, at ten years old, the boy found himself standing face to face with a dilemma that might have puzzled an early Christian. What was he?—where was he going? Even then he felt that something was wrong, but he concluded that it must be Boston. Quincy had always been right, for Quincy represented a moral principle—the principle of resistance to Boston. His Adams ancestors must have been right, since they were always hostile to State Street. If State Street was wrong, Quincy must be right! Turn the dilemma as he pleased, he still came back on the eighteenth century and the law of Resistance; of Truth; of Duty, and of Freedom. He was a ten-year-old priest and politician. He could under no circumstances have guessed what the next fifty years had in store, and no one could teach him; but sometimes, in his old age, he wondered—and could never decide—whether the most clear and certain knowledge would have helped him. Supposing he had seen a New York stock-list of 1900, and had studied the statistics of railways, telegraphs, coal, and steel—would he have quitted his eighteenth-century, his ancestral prejudices, his abstract ideals, his semi-clerical training, and the rest, in order to perform an expiatory pilgrimage to State Street, and ask for the fatted calf of his grandfather Brooks and a clerkship in the Suffolk Bank?

Sixty years afterwards he was still unable to make up his mind. Each course had its advantages, but the material advantages, looking back, seemed to lie wholly in State Street.

[9] Joseph Buckminster (1784-1812) and William Ellery Channing (1780-1842), Boston Unitarian ministers.

[10] Town hall of Boston, famous as the place of many patriotic meetings during and after the War of Independence.

[11] Edward Everett (1794-1865), an American statesman, president of Harvard, and a noted orator of the florid school.

[12] The tradition of liberal thought in the Adams family went back to Samuel Adams (1722-1803), an agitator against all forms of authority and an active revolutionist. State Street was the symbol of financial and religious conservatism in Boston.

XXV. The Dynamo and the Virgin (1900)

Until the Great Exposition of 1900[1] closed its doors in November, Adams haunted it, aching to absorb knowledge, and helpless to find it. He would have liked to know how much of it could have been grasped by the best-informed man in the world. While he was thus meditating chaos, Langley came by, and showed it to him.[2] At Langley's behest, the Exhibition dropped its superfluous rags and stripped itself to the skin, for Langley knew what to study, and why, and how; while Adams might as well have stood outside in the night, staring at the Milky Way. Yet Langley said nothing new, and taught nothing that one might not have learned from Lord Bacon, three hundred years before; but though one should have known the "Advancement of Science"[3] as well as one knew the "Comedy of Errors," the literary

[1] The Paris Exposition in 1900 held at the Trocadero exhibition palace.

[2] Samuel Pierpont Langley (1834-1906), American physicist and astronomer who pioneered the science of aerodynamics and solar energy.

[3] Francis Bacon (1561-1626), author of *The Advancement of Learning* (1605), often called the father of inductive reasoning from known facts to general truths; 1620 was the date of his *Novum Organum*.

knowledge counted for nothing until some teacher should show how to apply it. Bacon took a vast deal of trouble in teaching King James I and his subjects, American or other, towards the year 1620, that true science was the development or economy of forces; yet an elderly American in 1900 knew neither the formula nor the forces; or even so much as to say to himself that his historical business in the Exposition concerned only the economies or developments of force since 1893, when he began the study at Chicago.[4]

Nothing in education is so astonishing as the amount of ignorance it accumulates in the form of inert facts. Adams had looked at most of the accumulations of art in the storehouses called Art Museums; yet he did not know how to look at the art exhibits of 1900. He had studied Karl Marx and his doctrines of history with profound attention, yet he could not apply them at Paris. Langley, with the ease of a great master of experiment, threw out of the field every exhibit that did not reveal a new application of force, and naturally threw out, to begin with, almost the whole art exhibit. Equally, he ignored almost the whole industrial exhibit. He led his pupil directly to the forces. His chief interest was in new motors to make his airship feasible, and he taught Adams the astonishing complexities of the new Daimler[5] motor, and of the automobile, which, since 1893, had become a nightmare at a hundred kilometres an hour, almost as destructive as the electric tram which was only ten years older; and threatening to become as terrible as the locomotive steam-engine itself, which was almost exactly Adams's own age.

Then he showed his scholar the great hall of dynamos, and explained how little he knew about electricity or force of any kind, even of his own special sun, which spouted heat in inconceivable volume, but which, as far as he knew, might spout less or more, at any time, for all the certainty he felt in it. To him, the dynamo itself was but an ingenious channel for conveying somewhere the heat latent in a few tons of poor coal hidden in a dirty engine-house carefully kept out of sight; but to Adams the dynamo became a symbol of infinity. As he grew accustomed to the great gallery of machines, he began to feel the forty-foot dynamos as a moral force, much as the early Christians felt the Cross. The planet itself seemed less impressive, in its old-fashioned, deliberate, annual or daily revolution, than this huge wheel, revolving within arm's-length at some vertiginous speed, and barely murmuring—scarcely humming an audible warning to stand a hair's-breadth further for respect of power—while it would not wake the baby lying close against its frame. Before the end, one began to pray to it; inherited instinct taught the natural expression of man before silent and infinite force. Among the thousand symbols of ultimate energy, the dynamo was not so human as some, but it was the most expressive.

Yet the dynamo, next to the steam-engine, was the most familiar of exhibits. For Adams's objects its value lay chiefly in its occult mechanism. Between the dynamo in the gallery of machines and the engine-house outside, the break of continuity amounted to abysmal fracture for a historian's objects. No more relation could he discover between the steam and the electric current than between the Cross and the cathedral. The forces were interchangeable if not reversible, but he could see only an absolute *fiat* in electricity as in faith. Langley could not help him. Indeed, Langley seemed to be worried by the same trouble, for he constantly repeated that the new forces were anarchical, and especially that he was not responsible for the new rays, that were little short of parricidal in their wicked spirit towards science. His own rays, with which he had doubled the solar spectrum, were altogether harmless and beneficent; but Radium denied its God—or, what was to Langley the same thing, denied the truths of his Science. The force was wholly new.

A historian who asked only to learn enough to be as futile as Langley or Kelvin,[6] made rapid progress under this teaching, and mixed himself up in the tangle of ideas until he achieved a sort of Paradise of ignorance vastly consoling to his fatigued senses. He wrapped himself in vibrations and rays which were new, and he would have hugged Marconi and Branly had he met them, as he hugged the dynamo; while he lost his arithmetic in trying to figure out the equation between the discoveries and the economies of force. The economies, like the discoveries, were absolute, supersensual, occult; incapable of expression in horse-power. What mathematical equivalent could he suggest as the value of a Branly coherer?[7] Frozen air, or the electric furnace, had some scale of measurement, no doubt, if somebody could invent a thermometer adequate to the purpose; but X-rays had played no part whatever in man's con-

[4] Adams had attended the Columbian Exposition at Chicago in 1893 where he first became interested in the dynamo and other scientific exhibits.

[5] Gottlieb Daimler (1834–1900), German inventor who produced the first gas-combustion engine in 1884.

[6] William Thompson, Lord Kelvin (1824–1907), English physicist who interested Adams because of his formulations of the principle of the dissipation of energy and the second law of thermodynamics.

[7] Edouard Branly (1846–1940) invented the Branly coherer for detecting radio waves, providing the basis for wireless telegraphy. Marconi (1874–1937), Italian inventor of the wireless telegraph.

sciousness, and the atom itself had figured only as a fiction of thought. In these seven years man had translated himself into a new universe which had no common scale of measurement with the old. He had entered a supersensual world, in which he could measure nothing except by chance collisions of movements imperceptible to his senses, perhaps even imperceptible to his instruments, but perceptible to each other, and so to some known ray at the end of the scale. Langley seemed prepared for anything, even for an indeterminable number of universes interfused—physics stark mad in metaphysics.

Historians undertake to arrange sequences,—called stories, or histories—assuming in silence a relation of cause and effect. These assumptions, hidden in the depths of dusty libraries, have been astounding, but commonly unconscious and childlike; so much so, that if any captious critic were to drag them to light, historians would probably reply, with one voice, that they had never supposed themselves required to know what they were talking about. Adams, for one, had toiled in vain to find out what he meant. He had even published a dozen volumes of American history for no other purpose than to satisfy himself whether, by the severest process of stating, with the least possible comment, such facts as seemed sure, in such order as seemed rigorously consequent, he could fix for a familiar moment a necessary sequence of human movement. The result had satisfied him as little as at Harvard College. Where he saw sequence, other men saw something quite different, and no one saw the same unit of measure. He cared little about his experiments and less about his statesmen, who seemed to him quite as ignorant as himself and, as a rule, no more honest; but he insisted on a relation of sequence, and if he could not reach it by one method, he would try as many methods as science knew. Satisfied that the sequence of men led to nothing and that the sequence of their society could lead no further, while the mere sequence of time was artificial, and the sequence of thought was chaos, he turned at last to the sequence of force; and thus it happened that, after ten years' pursuit, he found himself lying in the Gallery of Machines at the Great Exposition of 1900, his historical neck broken by the sudden irruption of forces totally new.

Since no one else showed much concern, an elderly person without other cares had no need to betray alarm. The year 1900 was not the first to upset schoolmasters. Copernicus and Galileo[8] had broken many professorial necks about 1600; Columbus had stood the world on its head towards 1500; but the nearest approach to the revolution of 1900 was that of 310, when Constantine set up the Cross.[9] The rays that Langley disowned, as well as those which he fathered, were occult, supersensual, irrational; they were a revelation of mysterious energy like that of the Cross; they were what, in terms of mediaeval science, were called immediate modes of the divine substance.

The historian was thus reduced to his last resources. Clearly if he was bound to reduce all these forces to a common value, this common value could have no measure but that of their attraction on his own mind. He must treat them as they had been felt; as convertible, reversible, interchangeable attractions on thought. He made up his mind to venture it; he would risk translating rays into faith. Such a reversible process would vastly amuse a chemist, but the chemist could not deny that he, or some of his fellow physicists, could feel the force of both. When Adams was a boy in Boston, the best chemist in the place had probably never heard of Venus except by way of scandal, or of the Virgin except as idolatry; neither had he heard of dynamos or automobiles or radium; yet his mind was ready to feel the force of all, though the rays were unborn and the women were dead.

Here opened another totally new education, which promised to be by far the most hazardous of all. The knife-edge along which he must crawl, like Sir Lancelot[10] in the twelfth century, divided two kingdoms of force which had nothing in common but attraction. They were as different as a magnet is from gravitation, supposing one knew what a magnet was, or gravitation, or love. The force of the Virgin was still felt at Lourdes,[11] and seemed to be as potent as X-rays; but in America neither Venus nor Virgin ever had value as force—at most as sentiment. No American had ever been truly afraid of either.

This problem in dynamics gravely perplexed an American historian. The Woman had once been supreme; in France she still seemed potent, not merely as a sentiment, but as a force. Why was she unknown in America? For evidently America was ashamed of her, and she was ashamed of herself, otherwise they would not have strewn fig-leaves so profusely all over her. When she was a true force, she was ignorant of fig-leaves, but the monthly-magazine-made American female had not a feature that

[8] Copernicus (1473-1543), Polish scientist whose theory that the earth revolved about the sun shook the religious world. Galileo (1564-1642), Italian astronomer, was also convinced of the Copernican theory, but was deterred from expressing his beliefs by ecclesiastical censure.

[9] Adams refers to the miracle by which Constantine I (288?-337) saw a vision of the flaming cross which led to his conversion to Christianity.

[10] In Chrétien de Troyes' *Chevalier de la Charrette* Lancelot rescued Guinevere in this fashion.

[11] City in southern France, the site of a miracle in which a peasant girl, Bernadette, had a vision of the Virgin Mary.

would have been recognized by Adam. The trait was notorious and often humorous, but any one brought up among Puritans knew that sex was sin. In any previous age, sex was strength. Neither art nor beauty was needed. Every one, even among Puritans, knew that neither Diana of the Ephesians[12] nor any of the Oriental goddesses was worshipped for her beauty. She was goddess because of her force; she was the animated dynamo; she was reproduction—the greatest and most mysterious of all energies; all she needed was to be fecund. Singularly enough, not one of Adams's many schools of education had ever drawn his attention to the opening lines of Lucretius, though they were perhaps the finest in all Latin literature, where the poet invoked Venus exactly as Dante invoked the Virgin:—

"Quae quoniam rerum naturam *sola* gubernas." [13]

The Venus of Epicurean philosophy survived in the Virgin of the Schools:—

"Donna, sei tanto grande, e tanto vali,
Che qual vuol grazia, e a te non ricorre,
Sua disianza vuol volar senz' ali." [14]

All this was to American thought as though it had never existed. The true American knew something of the facts, but nothing of the feelings; he read the letter, but he never felt the law. Before this historical chasm, a mind like that of Adams felt itself helpless; he turned from the Virgin to the Dynamo as though he were a Branly coherer. On one side, at the Louvre and at Chartres, as he knew by the record of work actually done and still before his eyes, was the highest energy ever known to man, the creator of four-fifths of his noblest art, exercising vastly more attraction over the human mind than all the steam-engines and dynamos ever dreamed of; and yet this energy was unknown to the American mind. An American Virgin would never dare command; an American Venus would never dare exist.

The question, which to any plain American of the nineteenth century seemed as remote as it did to Adams, drew him almost violently to study, once it was posed; and on this point Langleys were as useless as though they were Herbert Spencers[15] or dynamos. The idea survived only as art. There one turned as naturally as though the artist were himself a woman. Adams began to ponder, asking himself whether he knew of any American artist who had ever insisted on the power of sex, as every classic had always done; but he could think only of Walt Whitman; Bret Harte, as far as the magazines would let him venture; and one or two painters, for the flesh-tones. All the rest had used sex for sentiment, never for force; to them, Eve was a tender flower, and Herodias[16] an unfeminine horror. American art, like the American language and American education, was as far as possible sexless. Society regarded this victory over sex as its greatest triumph, and the historian readily admitted it, since the moral issue, for the moment, did not concern one who was studying the relations of unmoral force. He cared nothing for the sex of the dynamo until he could measure its energy.

Vaguely seeking a clue, he wandered through the art exhibit, and, in his stroll, stopped almost every day before St. Gaudens's General Sherman,[17] which had been given the central post of honor. St. Gaudens himself was in Paris, putting on the work his usual interminable last touches, and listening to the usual contradictory suggestions of brother sculptors. Of all the American artists who gave to American art whatever life it breathed in the seventies, St. Gaudens was perhaps the most sympathetic, but certainly the most inarticulate. General Grant or Don Cameron had scarcely less instinct of rhetoric than he. All the others—the Hunts, Richardson, John La Farge, Stanford White[18]—were exuberant; only St. Gaudens could never discuss or dilate on an emotion, or suggest artistic arguments for giving to his work the forms that he felt. He never laid down the law, or affected the despot, or became brutalized like Whistler[19] by the brutalities of his world. He required no incense; he was no egoist; his simplicity of thought was excessive; he could not imitate, or give any form but his own to the creations of his hand. No one felt more strongly than he the strength of other men, but the idea that they could affect him never stirred an image in his mind.

[12] Ephesus was the place of the sacred temple of Artemis (Diana): Acts xix.24-41.

[13] "Since thou alone governs the nature of things." Lucretius' *De Rerum Natura,* from the invocation. Lucretius was a Roman poet and philosopher.

[14] "Lady, thou art so great and hast such worth, that if there be who would have grace yet betaketh not himself to thee, his longing seeketh to fly without wings." *Paradiso* xxxiii (Carlyle-Wicksteed transl.).

[15] Herbert Spencer (1820-1903), English evolutionary philosopher and positivist. Adams turned away from the progessivist element of his philosophy in his later years.

[16] Mother of Salome and envious wife of Herod. She disliked John the Baptist for his opposition to her marriage and wanted his head cut off and brought in on a platter. Mark vi. 17-28.

[17] Augustus Saint-Gaudens (1848-1907), American sculptor who did the statue of General Sherman, now in Central Park, New York. He created for Henry Adams a mystic, hooded figure in the Rock Creek Cemetery, Washington, D.C., where Mrs. Adams was buried.

[18] William Morris Hunt (1824-79), painter, and his brother Richard Morris Hunt (1828-95), an architect; H. H. Richardson (1838-1886), architect who built Adams' home in Washington; John La Farge (1835-1910), artist who accompanied Adams to Japan and the Far East; Stanford White (1853-1906), architect.

[19] James Abbott McNeill Whistler (1834-1903), American expatriate portrait-painter and impressionist.

This summer his health was poor and his spirits were low. For such a temper, Adams was not the best companion, since his own gaiety was not *folle;* but he risked going now and then to the studio on Mont Parnasse to draw him out for a stroll in the Bois de Boulogne, or dinner as pleased his moods, and in return St. Gaudens sometimes let Adams go about in his company.

Once St. Gaudens took him down to Amiens, with a party of Frenchmen, to see the cathedral. Not until they found themselves actually studying the sculpture of the western portal, did it dawn on Adams's mind that, for his purposes, St. Gaudens on that spot had more interest to him than the cathedral itself. Great men before great monuments express great truths, provided they are not taken too solemnly. Adams never tired of quoting the supreme phrase of his idol Gibbon,[20] before the Gothic cathedrals: "I darted a contemptuous look on the stately monuments of superstition." Even in the footnotes of his history, Gibbon had never inserted a bit of humor more human than this, and one would have paid largely for a photograph of the fat little historian, on the background of Notre Dame of Amiens, trying to persuade his readers—perhaps himself—that he was darting a contemptuous look on the stately monument, for which he felt in fact the respect which every man of his vast study and active mind always feels before objects worthy of it; but besides the humor, one felt also the relation. Gibbon ignored the Virgin, because in 1789 religious monuments were out of fashion. In 1900 his remark sounded fresh and simple as the green fields to ears that had heard a hundred years of other remarks, mostly no more fresh and certainly less simple. Without malice, one might find it more instructive than a whole lecture of Ruskin. One sees what one brings, and at that moment Gibbon brought the French Revolution. Ruskin brought reaction against the Revolution. St. Gaudens had passed beyond all. He liked the stately monuments much more than he liked Gibbon or Ruskin;[21] he loved their dignity; their unity; their scale; their lines; their lights and shadows; their decorative sculpture; but he was even less conscious than they of the force that created it all—the Virgin, the Woman—by whose genius "the stately monuments of superstition" were built, through which she was expressed. He would have seen more meaning in Isis[22] with the cow's horns, at Edfoo, who expressed the same thought. The art remained, but the energy was lost even upon the artist.

Yet in mind and person St. Gaudens was a survival of the 1500; he bore the stamp of the Renaissance, and should have carried an image of the Virgin round his neck, or stuck in his hat, like Louis XI. In mere time he was a lost soul that had strayed by chance into the twentieth century, and forgotten where it came from. He writhed and cursed at his ignorance, much as Adams did at his own, but in the opposite sense. St. Gaudens was a child of Benvenuto Cellini,[23] smothered in an American cradle. Adams was a quintessence of Boston, devoured by curiosity to think like Benvenuto. St. Gaudens's art was starved from birth, and Adams's instinct was blighted from babyhood. Each had but half of a nature, and when they came together before the Virgin of Amiens they ought both to have felt in her the force that made them one; but it was not so. To Adams she became more than ever a channel of force; to St. Gaudens she remained as before a channel of taste.

For a symbol of power, St. Gaudens instinctively preferred the horse, as was plain in his horse and Victory of the Sherman monument. Doubtless Sherman also felt it so. The attitude was so American that, for at least forty years, Adams had never realized that any other could be in sound taste. How many years had he taken to admit a notion of what Michael Angelo and Rubens[24] were driving at? He could not say; but he knew that only since 1895 had he begun to feel the Virgin or Venus as force, and not everywhere even so. At Chartres—perhaps at Lourdes—possibly at Cnidos[25] if one could still find there the divinely naked Aphrodite of Praxiteles—but otherwise one must look for force to the goddesses of Indian mythology. The idea died out long ago in the German and English stock. St. Gaudens at Amiens was hardly less sensitive to the force of the female energy than Matthew Arnold at the Grande Chartreuse.[26] Neither of them felt goddesses as power—only as reflected emotion, human expression, beauty, purity, taste, scarcely even as sympathy. They felt a railway train as power; yet they, and all other artists, constantly complained that the power embodied in a railway train could never be embodied in art. All the steam in the world could not, like the Virgin, build Chartres.

Yet in mechanics, whatever the mechanicians might think, both energies acted as interchangeable

[20] Edward Gibbon (1737-94), author of *The Decline and Fall of the Roman Empire.*

[21] John Ruskin (1819-1900), English writer and art critic.

[22] Pagan goddess of fertility. Edfu, a city on the Nile River.

[23] Italian sculptor of gold and bronze works and author of *The Memoirs of Benvenuto Cellini* about his amours and lusty adventures (1500-1571).

[24] Peter Paul Rubens (1577-1640), Flemish painter of rich flesh tones.

[25] Praxiteles, a fourth-century Greek sculptor, whose statue of Aphrodite was in the Temple of Cnidos in Asia Minor.

[26] The reference is to Arnold's poem "Stanzas from the Grande Chartreuse," a Carthusian monastery in France. The poem expressed Adams's sense of the waning of religious values.

forces on man, and by action on man all known force may be measured. Indeed, few men of science measured force in any other way. After once admitting that a straight line was the shortest distance between two points, no serious mathematician cared to deny anything that suited his convenience, and rejected no symbol, unproved or unproveable, that helped him to accomplish work. The symbol was force, as a compass-needle or a triangle was force, as the mechanist might prove by losing it, and nothing could be gained by ignoring their value. Symbol or energy, the Virgin had acted as the greatest force the Western world ever felt, and had drawn man's activities to herself more strongly than any other power, natural or supernatural, had ever done; the historian's business was to follow the track of the energy; to find where it came from and where it went to; its complex source and shifting channels; its values, equivalents, conversions. It could scarcely be more complex than radium; it could hardly be deflected, diverted, polarized, absorbed more perplexingly than other radiant matter. Adams knew nothing about any of them, but as a mathematical problem of influence on human progress, though all were occult, all reacted on his mind, and he rather inclined to think the Virgin easiest to handle.

The pursuit turned out to be long and tortuous, leading at last into the vast forests of scholastic science. From Zeno to Descartes, hand in hand with Thomas Aquinas, Montaigne, and Pascal,[27] one stumbled as stupidly as though one were still a German student of 1860. Only with the instinct of despair could one force one's self into this old thicket of ignorance after having been repulsed at a score of entrances more promising and more popular. Thus far, no path had led anywhere, unless perhaps to an exceedingly modest living. Forty-five years of study had proved to be quite futile for the pursuit of power; one controlled no more force in 1900 than in 1850, although the amount of force controlled by society had enormously increased. The secret of education still hid itself somewhere behind ignorance, and one fumbled over it as feebly as ever. In such labyrinths, the staff is a force almost more necessary than the legs; the pen becomes a sort of blind-man's dog, to keep him from falling into the gutters. The pen works for itself, and acts like a hand, modelling the plastic material over and over again to the form that suits it best. The form is never arbitrary, but is a sort of growth like crystallization, as any artist knows too well; for often the pencil or pen runs into side-paths and shapelessness, loses its relations, stops or is bogged. Then it has to return on its trail, and recover, if it can, its line of force. The result of a year's work depends more on what is struck out than on what is left in; on the sequence of the main lines of thought, than on their play or variety. Compelled once more to lean heavily on this support, Adams covered more thousands of pages with figures as formal as though they were algebra, laboriously striking out, altering, burning, experimenting, until the year had expired, the Exposition had long been closed, and winter drawing to its end, before he sailed from Cherbourg, on January 19, 1901, for home.

[27]Zeno, Greek philosopher of the fourth century, founder of the Stoic school; Thomas Aquinas (1225?-1274), Italian theologian and philosopher; Michel de Montaigne (1533-92), French essayist and skeptic; Blaise Pascal (1623-62), French philosopher and mathematician.

XXXIII. A Dynamic Theory of History (1904)

A dynamic theory, like most theories, begins by begging the question: it defines Progress as the development and economy of Forces. Further, it defines force as anything that does, or helps to do work. Man is a force; so is the sun; so is a mathematical point, though without dimensions or known existence.

Man commonly begs the question again by taking for granted that he captures the forces. A dynamic theory, assigning attractive force to opposing bodies in proportion to the law of mass, takes for granted that the forces of nature capture man. The sum of force attracts; the feeble atom or molecule called man is attracted; he suffers education or growth; he is the sum of the forces that attract him; his body and his thought are alike their product; the movement of the forces controls the progress of his mind, since he can know nothing but the motions which impinge on his senses, whose sum makes education.

For convenience as an image, the theory may liken man to a spider in its web, watching for chance prey. Forces of nature dance like flies before the net, and the spider pounces on them when it can; but it makes many fatal mistakes, though its theory of force is sound. The spider-mind acquires a faculty of memory, and, with it, a singular skill of analysis and synthesis, taking apart and putting together in different relations the meshes of its trap. Man had in the beginning no power of analysis or synthesis approaching that of the spider, or even of the honey-bee; but he had acute sensibility to the higher forces. Fire taught him secrets that no other animal could learn; running water probably taught him even more, especially in his first lessons of mechanics; the animals helped to educate him, trusting themselves into his hands merely for the sake of their food, and carrying his burdens or supplying his clothing; the grasses and grains were academies of study. With little or no effort on his part, all these forces formed his thought, induced his action, and even shaped his figure.

Long before history began, his education was complete, for the record could not have been started until he had been taught to record. The universe that had formed him took shape in his mind as a reflection of his own unity, containing all forces except himself. Either separately, or in groups, or as a whole, these forces never ceased to act on him, enlarging his mind as they enlarged the surface foliage of a vegetable, and the mind needed only to respond, as the forests did, to these attractions. Susceptibility to the highest forces is the highest genius; selection between them is the highest science; their mass is the highest educator. Man always made, and still makes, grotesque blunders in selecting and measuring forces, taken at random from the heap, but he never made a mistake in the value he set on the whole, which he symbolized as unity and worshipped as God. To this day, his attitude towards it has never changed, though science can no longer give to force a name.

Man's function as a force of nature was to assimilate other forces as he assimilated food. He called it the love of power. He felt his own feebleness, and he sought for an ass or a camel, a bow or a sling, to widen his range of power, as he sought a fetish or a planet in the world beyond. He cared little to know its immediate use, but he could afford to throw nothing away which he could conceive to have possible value in this or any other existence. He waited for the object to teach him its use, or want of use, and the process was slow. He may have gone on for hundreds of thousands of years, waiting for Nature to tell him her secrets; and, to his rivals among the monkeys, Nature has taught no more than at their start; but certain lines of force were capable of acting on individual apes, and mechanically selecting types of race or sources of variation. The individual that responded or reacted to lines of new force then was possibly the same individual that reacts on it now, and his conception of the unity seems never to have changed in spite of the increasing diversity of forces; but the theory of variation is an affair of other science than history, and matters nothing to dynamics. The individual or the race would be educated on the same lines of illusion, which, according to Arthur Balfour,[1] had not essentially varied down to the year 1900.

To the highest attractive energy, man gave the name of divine, and for its control he invented the science called Religion, a word which meant, and still means, cultivation of occult force whether in detail or mass. Unable to define Force as a unity, man symbolized it and pursued it, both in himself, and in the infinite, as philosophy and theology; the mind is itself the subtlest of all known forces, and its self-introspection necessarily created a science which had the singular value of lifting his education, at the start, to the finest, subtlest, and broadest training both in analysis and synthesis, so that, if language is a test, he must have reached his highest powers early in his history; while the mere motive remained as simple an appetite for power as the tribal greed which led him to trap an elephant. Hunger, whether for food or for the infinite, sets in motion multiplicity and infinity of thought, and the sure hope of gaining a share of infinite power in eternal life would lift most minds to effort.

He had reached this completeness five thousand years ago, and added nothing to his stock of known forces for a very long time. The mass of nature exercised on him so feeble an attraction that one can scarcely account for his apparent motion. Only a historian of very exceptional knowledge would venture to say at what date between 3000 B.C. and 1000 A.D., the momentum of Europe was greatest; but such progress as the world made consisted in economies of energy rather than in its development; it was proved in mathematics, measured by names like Archimedes, Aristarchus, Ptolemy, and Euclid;[2] or in Civil Law, measured by a number of names which Adams had begun life by failing to learn; or in coinage, which was most beautiful near its beginning, and most barbarous at its close; or it was shown in roads, or the size of ships, or harbors; or by the use of metals, instruments, and writing; all of them economies of force, sometimes more forceful than the forces they helped; but the roads were still travelled by the horse, the ass, the camel, or the slave; the ships were still propelled by sails or oars; the lever, the spring, and the screw bounded the region of applied mechanics. Even the metals were old.

Much the same thing could be said of religious or supernatural forces. Down to the year 300 of the Christian era they were little changed, and in spite of Plato and the sceptics were more apparently chaotic than ever. The experience of three thousand years had educated society to feel the vastness of Nature, and the infinity of her resources of power, but even this increase of attraction had not yet caused economies in its methods of pursuit.

There the Western world stood till the year A.D. 305, when the Emperor Diocletian abdicated; and there it was that Adams broke down on the steps of

[1]Arthur Balfour (1848–1930), British statesman and Conservative party leader. He wrote on *The Foundations of Belief* (1895) and scientific subjects which interested Adams.

[2]Archimedes (2nd century B.C.), Greek mathematician and inventor of mechanical devices, such as the lever for lifting weights; Aristarchus of Samos (2nd century B.C.) Greek astronomer who anticipated Copernicus in the theory that the earth revolves about the sun; Ptolemy (2nd century B.C.) Greek astronomer and mathematician; Euclid (3rd century B.C.), Greek mathematician, founder of modern geometry.

Ara Coeli, his path blocked by the scandalous failure of civilization at the moment it had achieved complete success. In the year 305 the empire had solved the problems of Europe more completely than they have ever been solved since. The Pax Romana,[3] the Civil Law, and Free Trade should, in four hundred years, have put Europe far in advance of the point reached by modern society in the four hundred years since 1500, when conditions were less simple.

The efforts to explain, or explain away, this scandal had been incessant, but none suited Adams unless it were the economic theory of adverse exchanges and exhaustion of minerals; but nations are not ruined beyond a certain point by adverse exchanges, and Rome had by no means exhausted her resources. On the contrary, the empire developed resources and energies quite astounding. No other four hundred years of history before A.D. 1800 knew anything like it; and although some of these developments, like the Civil Law, the roads, aqueducts, and harbors, were rather economies than force, yet in northwestern Europe alone the empire had developed three energies—France, England, and Germany—competent to master the world. The trouble seemed rather to be that the empire developed too much energy, and too fast.

A dynamic law requires that two masses—nature and man—must go on, reacting upon each other, without stop, as the sun and a comet react on each other, and that any appearance of stoppage is illusive. The theory seems to exact excess, rather than deficiency, of action and reaction to account for the dissolution of the Roman Empire, which should, as a problem of mechanics, have been torn to pieces by acceleration. If the student means to try the experiment of framing a dynamic law, he must assign values to the forces of attraction that caused the trouble; and in this case he has them in plain evidence. With the relentless logic that stamped Roman thought, the empire, which had established unity on earth, could not help establishing unity in heaven. It was induced by its dynamic necessities to economize the gods.

The Church has never ceased to protest against the charge that Christianity ruined the empire, and, with its usual force, has pointed out that its reforms alone saved the State. Any dynamic theory gladly admits it. All it asks is to find and follow the force that attracts. The Church points out this force in the Cross, and history needs only to follow it. The empire loudly asserted its motive. Good taste forbids saying that Constantine the Great speculated as audaciously as a modern stock-broker on values of which he knew at the utmost only the volume; or that he merged all uncertain forces into a single trust, which he enormously over-capitalized, and forced on the market; but this is the substance of what Constantine himself said in his Edict of Milan in the year 313, which admitted Christianity into the Trust of State Religions. Regarded as an Act of Congress, it runs: "We have resolved to grant to Christians as well as all others the liberty to practise the religion they prefer, in order that whatever exists of divinity or celestial power may help and favor us and all who are under our government." The empire pursued power—not merely spiritual but physical—in the sense in which Constantine issued his army order the year before, at the battle of the Milvian Bridge: *In hoc signo vinces!*[4] using the Cross as a train of artillery, which, to his mind, it was. Society accepted it in the same character. Eighty years afterwards, Theodosius marched against his rival Eugene with the Cross for physical champion; and Eugene raised the image of Hercules to fight for the pagans;[5] while society on both sides looked on, as though it were a boxing-match, to decide a final test of force between the divine powers. The Church was powerless to raise the ideal. What is now known as religion affected the mind of old society but little. The laity, the people, the million, almost to a man, bet on the gods as they bet on a horse.

No doubt the Church did all it could to purify the process, but society was almost wholly pagan in its point of view, and was drawn to the Cross because, in its system of physics, the Cross had absorbed all the old occult or fetish-power. The symbol represented the sum of nature—the Energy of modern science—and society believed it to be as real as X-rays; perhaps it was! The emperors used it like gunpowder in politics; the physicians used it like rays in medicine; the dying clung to it as the quintessence of force, to protect them from the forces of evil on their road to the next life.

Throughout these four centuries the empire knew that religion disturbed economy, for even the cost of heathen incense affected the exchanges; but no one could afford to buy or construct a costly and complicated machine when he could hire an occult force at trifling expense. Fetish-power was cheap and satisfactory, down to a certain point. Turgot and Auguste Comte long ago fixed this stage of economy as a necessary phase of social education, and historians seem now to accept it as the only gain yet

[3] The peace imposed on the Roman Empire during the peak of its power.

[4] "In this sign we conquer."

[5] Theodosius, one of the Roman emperors of the East who fought and conquered Eugenius of the West in 394, becoming sole emperor.

made towards scientific history. Great numbers of educated people—perhaps a majority—cling to the method still, and practise it more or less strictly; but, until quite recently, no other was known. The only occult power at man's disposal was fetish. Against it, no mechanical force could compete except within narrow limits.

Outside of occult or fetish-power, the Roman world was incredibly poor. It knew but one productive energy resembling a modern machine—the slave. No artificial force of serious value was applied to production or transportation, and when society developed itself so rapidly in political and social lines, it had no other means of keeping its economy on the same level than to extend its slave-system and its fetish-system to the utmost.

The result might have been stated in a mathematical formula as early as the time of Archimedes, six hundred years before Rome fell. The economic needs of a violently centralizing society forced the empire to enlarge its slave-system until the slave-system consumed itself and the empire too, leaving society no resource but further enlargement of its religious system in order to compensate for the losses and horrors of the failure. For a vicious circle, its mathematical completeness approached perfection. The dynamic law of attraction and reaction needed only a Newton to fix it in algebraic form.

At last, in 410, Alaric sacked Rome, and the slave-ridden, agricultural, uncommercial Western Empire—the poorer and less Christianized half—went to pieces. Society, though terribly shocked by the horrors of Alaric's storm, felt still more deeply the disappointment in its new power, the Cross, which had failed to protect its Church.[6] The outcry against the Cross became so loud among Christians that its literary champion, Bishop Augustine of Hippo[7]—a town between Algiers and Tunis—was led to write a famous treatise in defence of the Cross, familiar still to every scholar, in which he defended feebly the mechanical value of the symbol—arguing only that pagan symbols equally failed—but insisted on its spiritual value in the *Civitas Dei* which had taken the place of the *Civitas Romae* in human interest. "Granted that we have lost all we had! Have we lost faith? Have we lost piety? Have we lost the wealth of the inner man who is rich before God? These are the wealth of Christians!" The *Civitas Dei*, in its turn, became the sum of attraction for the Western world, though it also showed the same weakness in mechanics that had wrecked the *Civitas Romae*. St. Augustine and his people perished at Hippo towards 430, leaving society in appearance dull to new attraction.

Yet the attraction remained constant. The delight of experimenting on occult force of every kind is such as to absorb all the free thought of the human race. The gods did their work; history has no quarrel with them; they led, educated, enlarged the mind; taught knowledge; betrayed ignorance; stimulated effort. So little is known about the mind—whether social, racial, sexual or heritable; whether material or spiritual; whether animal, vegetable or mineral—that history is inclined to avoid it altogether; but nothing forbids one to admit, for convenience, that it may assimilate food like the body, storing new force and growing, like a forest, with the storage. The brain has not yet revealed its mysterious mechanism of gray matter. Never has Nature offered it so violent a stimulant as when she opened to it the possibility of sharing infinite power in eternal life, and it might well need a thousand years of prolonged and intense experiment to prove the value of the motive. During these so-called Middle Ages, the Western mind reacted in many forms, on many sides, expressing its motives in modes, such as Romanesque and Gothic architecture, glass windows and mosaic walls, sculpture and poetry, war and love, which still affect some people as the noblest work of man, so that, even to-day, great masses of idle and ignorant tourists travel from far countries to look at Ravenna and San Marco, Palermo and Pisa, Assisi, Cordova, Chartres, with vague notions about the force that created them, but with a certain surprise that a social mind of such singular energy and unity should still lurk in their shadows.

The tourist more rarely visits Constantinople or studies the architecture of Sancta Sofia,[8] but when he does, he is distinctly conscious of forces not quite the same. Justinian has not the simplicity of Charlemagne. The Eastern Empire showed an activity and variety of forces that classical Europe had never possessed. The navy of Nicephoras Phocas[9] in the tenth century would have annihilated in half an hour any navy that Carthage or Athens or Rome ever set afloat. The dynamic scheme began by asserting rather recklessly that between the Pyramids (B.C. 3000), and the Cross (A.D. 300), no new force affected Western progress, and antiquarians may easily dispute the fact; but in any case the motive influence, old or new, which raised both Pyramids and Cross was the same attraction of power in a future life that raised the dome of Sancta Sofia and the Cathedral at Amiens, however much it was

[6]Alaric (370-410), a Gothic conqueror of Rome in 410 after a long siege.

[7]St. Augustine (354-430), author of the *Confessions* which influenced Adams in his *Education*.

[8]Historic Christian church in Constantinople, built under Justinian about 558-563. It became a mosque, then was changed back to a Christian church. It has a vast dome.

[9]An emperor of the Eastern Roman Empire, about 900-969.

altered, enlarged, or removed to distance in space. Therefore, no single event has more puzzled historians than the sudden, unexplained appearance of at least two new natural forces of the highest educational value in mechanics, for the first time within record of history. Literally, these two forces seemed to drop from the sky at the precise moment when the Cross on one side and the Crescent[10] on the other, proclaimed the complete triumph of the *Civitas Dei.* Had the Manichean doctrine of Good and Evil as rival deities been orthodox, it would alone have accounted for this simultaneous victory of hostile powers.

Of the compass, as a step towards demonstration of the dynamic law, one may confidently say that it proved, better than any other force, the widening scope of the mind, since it widened immensely the range of contact between nature and thought. The compass educated. This must prove itself as needing no proof.

Of Greek fire and gunpowder, the same thing cannot certainly be said, for they have the air of accidents due to the attraction of religious motives. They belong to the spiritual world; or to the doubtful ground of Magic which lay between Good and Evil. They were chemical forces, mostly explosives, which acted and still act as the most violent educators ever known to man, but they were justly feared as diabolic, and whatever insolence man may have risked towards the milder teachers of his infancy, he was an abject pupil towards explosives. The Sieur de Joinville left a record of the energy with which the relatively harmless Greek fire educated and enlarged the French mind in a single night in the year 1249, when the crusaders were trying to advance on Cairo. The good king St. Louis and all his staff dropped on their knees at every fiery flame that flew by, praying—"God have pity on us!" and never had man more reason to call on his gods than they, for the battle of religion between Christian and Saracen was trifling compared with that of education between gunpowder and the Cross.

The fiction that society educated itself, or aimed at a conscious purpose, was upset by the compass and gunpowder which dragged and drove Europe at will through frightful bogs of learning. At first, the apparent lag for want of volume in the new energies lasted one or two centuries, which closed the great epochs of emotion by the Gothic cathedrals and scholastic theology. The moment had Greek beauty and more than Greek unity, but it was brief; and for another century or two, Western society seemed to float in space without apparent motion. Yet the attractive mass of nature's energy continued to attract, and education became more rapid than ever before. Society began to resist, but the individual showed greater and greater insistence, without realizing what he was doing. When the Crescent drove the Cross in ignominy from Constantinople in 1453, Gutenberg and Fust[11] were printing their first Bible at Mainz under the impression that they were helping the Cross. When Columbus discovered the West Indies in 1492, the Church looked on it as a victory of the Cross. When Luther and Calvin upset Europe half a century later, they were trying, like St. Augustine, to substitute the *Civitas Dei* for the *Civitas Romae.* When the Puritans set out for New England in 1620, they too were looking to found a *Civitas Dei* in State Street; and when Bunyan made his Pilgrimage in 1678, he repeated St. Jerome.[12] Even when, after centuries of license, the Church reformed its discipline, and, to prove it, burned Giordano Bruno in 1600,[13] besides condemning Galileo in 1630—as science goes on repeating to us every day—it condemned anarchists, not atheists. None of the astronomers were irreligious men; all of them made a point of magnifying God through his works; a form of science which did their religion no credit. Neither Galileo nor Kepler, neither Spinoza[14] nor Descartes, neither Leibnitz[15] nor Newton, any more than Constantine the Great—if so much—doubted Unity. The utmost range of their heresies reached only its personality.

This persistence of thought-inertia is the leading idea of modern history. Except as reflected in himself, man has no reason for assuming unity in the universe, or an ultimate substance, or a prime-motor. The *a priori* insistence on this unity ended by fatiguing the more active—or reactive—minds; and Lord Bacon tried to stop it. He urged society to lay aside the idea of evolving the universe from a thought, and to try evolving thought from the universe. The mind should observe and register forces—take them apart and put them together—without assuming unity at all. "Nature, to be commanded, must be obeyed." "The imagination must be given not wings but weights." As Galileo re-

[10] Symbol of the Mohammedan religion.

[11] Johann Gutenberg (1400-1468) and his partner Johann Fust (1400-1466) were German inventors of printing by movable type.

[12] St. Jerome (340-420), great Biblical scholar and translator of the Scriptures into Latin. Called the Vulgate, this version was a vital step in making the Scriptures available to Western thought.

[13] Italian philosopher burned at the stake for heresy by the Inquisition.

[14] Johannes Kepler (1571-1630), founder of a school of astronomy based on the celestial harmony of the solar system; Benedictus Spinoza (1632-77), Dutch metaphysician and rationalist, regarded as atheistical by the orthodox thinkers of his time.

[15] Gottfried Wilhelm Leibnitz (1646-1716), German systematic philosopher and mathematician, inventor of differential calculus.

versed the action of earth and sun, Bacon reversed the relation of thought to force. The mind was thenceforth to follow the movement of matter, and unity must be left to shift for itself.

The revolution in attitude seemed voluntary, but in fact was as mechanical as the fall of a feather. Man created nothing. After 1500, the speed of progress so rapidly surpassed man's gait as to alarm every one, as though it were the acceleration of a falling body which the dynamic theory takes it to be. Lord Bacon was as much astonished by it as the Church was, and with reason. Suddenly society felt itself dragged into situations altogether new and anarchic—situations which it could not affect, but which painfully affected it. Instinct taught it that the universe in its thought must be in danger when its reflection lost itself in space. The danger was all the greater because men of science covered it with "larger synthesis," and poets called the undevout astronomer mad. Society knew better. Yet the telescope held it rigidly standing on its head; the microscope revealed a universe that defied the senses; gunpowder killed whole races that lagged behind; the compass coerced the most imbruted mariner to act on the impossible idea that the earth was round; the press drenched Europe with anarchism. Europe saw itself, violently resisting, wrenched into false positions, drawn along new lines as a fish that it caught on a hook; but unable to understand by what force it was controlled. The resistance was often bloody, sometimes humorous, always constant. Its contortions in the eighteenth century are best studied in the wit of Voltaire, but all history and all philosophy from Montaigne and Pascal to Schopenhauer and Nietzsche[16] deal with nothing else; and still, throughout it all, the Baconian law held good; thought did not evolve nature, but nature evolved thought. Not one considerable man of science dared face the stream of thought; and the whole number of those who acted, like Franklin, as electric conductors of the new forces from nature to man, down to the year 1800, did not exceed a few score, confined to a few towns in western Europe. Asia refused to be touched by the stream, and America, except for Franklin, stood outside.

Very slowly the accretion of these new forces, chemical and mechanical, grew in volume until they acquired sufficient mass to take the place of the old religious science, substituting their attraction for the attractions of the *Civitas Dei,* but the process remained the same. Nature, not mind, did the work that the sun does on the planets. Man depended more and more absolutely on forces other than his own, and on instruments which superseded his senses. Bacon foretold it: "Neither the naked hand nor the understanding, left to itself, can effect much. It is by instruments and helps that the work is done." Once done, the mind resumed its illusion, and society forgot its impotence; but no one better than Bacon knew its tricks, and for his true followers science always meant self-restraint, obedience, sensitiveness to impulse from without. "Non fingendum aut excogitandum sed inveniendum quid Natura faciat aut ferat."[17]

The success of this method staggers belief, and even to-day can be treated by history only as a miracle of growth, like the sports of nature. Evidently a new variety of mind had appeared. Certain men merely held out their hands—like Newton, watched an apple; like Franklin, flew a kite; like Watt, played with a tea-kettle—and great forces of nature stuck to them as though she were playing ball. Governments did almost nothing but resist. Even gunpowder and ordnance, the great weapon of government, showed little development between 1400 and 1800. Society was hostile or indifferent, as Priestley and Jenner,[18] and even Fulton, with reason complained in the most advanced societies in the world, while its resistance became acute wherever the Church held control; until all mankind seemed to draw itself out in a long series of groups, dragged on by an attractive power in advance, which even the leaders obeyed without understanding, as the planets obeyed gravity, or the trees obeyed heat and light.

The influx of new force was nearly spontaneous. The reaction of mind on the mass of nature seemed not greater than that of a comet on the sun; and had the spontaneous influx of force stopped in Europe, society must have stood still, or gone backward, as in Asia or Africa. Then only economies of process would have counted as new force, and society would have been better pleased; for the idea that new force must be in itself a good is only an animal or vegetable instinct. As Nature developed her hidden energies, they tended to become destructive. Thought itself became tortured, suffering reluctantly, impatiently, painfully, the coercion of new method. Easy thought had always been movement of inertia, and mostly mere sentiment; but even the processes of mathematics measured feebly the needs of force.

The stupendous acceleration after 1800 ended in 1900 with the appearance of the new class of supersensual forces, before which the man of science

[16] Arthur Schopenhauer (1788-1860), German philosopher and exponent of anti-rational, deterministic ideas; Friedrich Nietzsche (1844-1900), German writer who influenced modern materialistic thought with a philosophy of the "Overman" and doctrine of power.

[17] "One should not invent or assume what Nature produces or brings us, but investigate it."

[18] Edward Jenner (1749-1823), inventor of a vaccine for smallpox, giving rise to much religious and popular opposition.

stood at first as bewildered and helpless as, in the fourth century, a priest of Isis before the Cross of Christ.

This, then, or something like this, would be a dynamic formula of history. Any schoolboy knows enough to object at once that it is the oldest and most universal of all theories. Church and State, theology and philosophy, have always preached it, differing only in the allotment of energy between nature and man. Whether the attractive energy has been called God or Nature, the mechanism has been always the same, and history is not obliged to decide whether the Ultimate tends to a purpose or not, or whether ultimate energy is one or many. Every one admits that the will is a free force, habitually decided by motives. No one denies that motives exist adequate to decide the will; even though it may not always be conscious of them. Science has proved that forces, sensible and occult, physical and metaphysical, simple and complex, surround, traverse, vibrate, rotate, repel, attract, without stop; that man's senses are conscious of few, and only in a partial degree; but that, from the beginning of organic existence, his consciousness has been induced, expanded, trained in the lines of his sensitiveness; and that the rise of his faculties from a lower power to a higher, or from a narrower to a wider field, may be due to the function of assimilating and storing outside force or forces. There is nothing unscientific in the idea that, beyond the lines of force felt by the senses, the universe may be—as it has always been—either a supersensuous chaos or a divine unity, which irresistibly attracts, and is either life or death to penetrate. Thus far, religion, philosophy, and science seem to go hand in hand. The schools begin their vital battle only there. In the earlier stages of progress, the forces to be assimilated were simple and easy to absorb, but, as the mind of man enlarged its range, it enlarged the field of complexity, and must continue to do so, even into chaos, until the reservoirs of sensuous or supersensuous energies are exhausted, or cease to affect him, or until he succumbs to their excess.

For past history, this way of grouping its sequences may answer for a chart of relations, although any serious student would need to invent another, to compare or correct its errors; but past history is only a value of relation to the future, and this value is wholly one of convenience, which can be tested only by experiment. Any law of movement must include, to make it a convenience, some mechanical formula of acceleration.

1907, 1918

The Twentieth Century: 1914–1970

Marx, Freud, and the Twentieth Century

THE LITERATURE of the late nineteenth century cannot be read intelligently without reference to Social Darwinism and the principles of sociological and biological evolution of Herbert Spencer and his American followers. Similarly, American writing in the twentieth century cannot be understood without some knowledge of the body of doctrine derived from two towering figures of European origin, Karl Marx and Sigmund Freud. Marx's theories of economic determinism, the class struggle, and the ultimate proletarian revolution were slow to take hold in individualistic and capitalistic America, yet they became increasingly influential, especially in theoretical criticism and in the work of such novelists as Upton Sinclair, Jack London, John Dos Passos, James Farrell, Erskine Caldwell, John Steinbeck, and Richard Wright. Literary Marxism in the United States was more often than not motivated by humanitarian, reformist, or utopian ideals, and with few exceptions stopped well short of dialectical materialism or the rule of the working class. Even at the worst phase of the depression decade of the 1930's, "Reds" were distrusted by the average American as products of an alien culture. Authors and intellectuals of a pinkish hue were given a cold or hostile reception in the press, while Franklin D. Roosevelt's "brain trust" of advisers from the academic world were criticized for bringing socialist ideas into Washington politics. "Freudianism," on the other hand, pervaded almost every level of the American mind after about 1920, from the flappers of the Jazz Age to serious literary figures such as Sherwood Anderson, Eugene O'Neill, William Faulkner, Edmund Wilson, and many other poets, critics, and writers of fiction.

The great popularity of the ideas associated with the name of Freud was in part the result of the promise of new freedoms of behavior, uninhibited pleasure, and sexual hedonism, the intellectual roots of which were only dimly understood, if at all, by the general mind. Freud's system of psychoanalysis, with its corollary theories of repression and sublimation, the sexual motivation of conduct, and the supremacy of the unconscious, was introduced to America through a series of lectures at Clark University in 1909, published as *Five Lectures on Psychoanalysis* the following year. But the scientific significance of these ideas and their antecedents in earlier psychology was largely lost in the popular furor of the 1920's when everything from lipstick, bobbed hair, and short skirts to syncopated music and the petting party was given a pseudo-Freudian implication. To the younger generation, as social historians have described it, all restraints whether of religion, morality, or social manners were repressive, and the answer to all such "puritan" controls was simply to give free rein to the libido. "I'm hipped on Freud and all that," says one of Fitzgerald's flaming youths in *This Side of Paradise.* Such terms as "neurosis," "sublimation," "inhibition," and "Oedipus complex" were glibly used in journalistic writing and cocktail-party conversation mainly as a means to discredit the sexual mores of Victorian America and to justify the moral letdown of the postwar decade.

Serious-minded intellectuals gathered in Greenwich Village apartments and exchanged ideas about dream analysis, dream symbolism, and the psychological origins of art forms. A Freudian-oriented approach to literary criticism emerged to place the emphasis on neurotic antecedents in the author's life or circumstances to explain the mystery of creative art and literary motivation. In the free-wheeling, flamboyant criticism of H. L. Mencken, editor of the *Smart Set* and the *American Mercury,* Freudian ideas were blended with an iconoclastic attack on the literary past, on Puritanism, and on the genteel tradition. A champion of Dreiser and the new realism in which sex and money dominated human motives, Mencken pronounced the creative impulse a mere egocentric and cathartic action not unlike that of a hen laying an egg. George Santayana in *The Genteel Tradition in American Philosophy* (1910) and Van Wyck Brooks in *America's Coming of Age* (1915) applied psychological methods to literary history, both seeing a schizophrenic division in the American mind in the conflict, for example, between the idealism of Emerson (weakened by the genteel tradition) and the pragmatic, workaday world of the average American conditioned by frontier ethics. Brooks also interpreted the work of Mark Twain and Henry James in neo-Freudian terms as having been determined by childhood experiences.

After 1920 a battle of the bookmen took place in which the professors, speaking for conservatism and Academia, were ranged against the journalists, the literary radicals, and the ideals of Bohemia. Irving Babbitt and Paul Elmer More as spokesmen for the New Humanism called for a repudiation of "the cold and clammy facts" of realism and science and a return to the literature of the past and the ethical values of the classics. Babbitt instructed his students at Harvard in the evils of "Menckenism" and pointed to the need for inner checks and controls on the waywardness of the instincts and passions of men. The radicals, on the other hand, including Randolph Bourne, Brooks, Mencken, and the Marxist critics, retaliated with the charge that Humanism was reactionary and academic, looking backward to the Puritans or to the genteel tradition for its models. They took advantage of the appeal to modernism and the examples of the new realists to enforce the principle of vitality and contemporary relevance as essential to good literature. Both schools suffered somewhat from generalization. They were literary theorists, not critics, and both indulged in dogmatism and rhetorical assertion. Neither looked closely at a given work of poetry or prose to assess its literary strategies, its form, or its symbolic or metaphorical significance. This remained for the school of analytical criticism whose founder was J. E. Spingarn, a follower of the Italian critic Benedetto Croce. Spingarn's "expressionism" emphasized the author's intentions, the creative act, and the work of art itself. This tendency, merging with the textual analysis which had its start in the essays of T. S. Eliot, later came to be called the "New Criticism," and in the thirties and forties it emerged as the most influential critical method, partly because of its great effect on the teaching of literature in the classroom.

Marxist criticism began slowly in the late twenties with the founding of periodicals of the left such as the *New Masses* in 1926. V. L. Parrington's influential intellectual history, *Main Currents in American Thought* (1927), a brilliant though one-sided account of the economic determinist position, displayed the inherent weakness of proletarian criticism—the tendency to allow ideological opinions to override aesthetic judgments. After the financial panic of 1929, pro-Marxist criticism spread more rapidly. V. F. Calverton (*The Liberation of American Literature,* 1933) and Granville Hicks (*The Great Tradition,* 1933) both sought to explain literature in terms of social forces and the class struggle. But the increasingly doctrinaire aspect of Marxist ideology led critics like Edmund Wilson to react against the excesses of the method. "The Leftist critic with no literary competence is always trying to measure works of literature by tests which have no validity in that field," he wrote in his essay "Marxism and Literature." And James T. Farrell, in *A Note on Literary Criticism* (1936), warned against the simplistic application of economic or political measures to art and literature. By 1940 the movement had passed its peak; in the new moderation that replaced it Marxist ideas receded in importance, to be balanced by aesthetic considerations, textual and analytical criticism, and standards of taste. This balance was best represented by the work of Edmund Wilson, in whose *Axel's Castle* and *The Triple Thinkers* both Marxist and Freudian principles were subordinated to a broader form of historical interpretation.

The attraction, as well as the weakness, of Marxist criticism was its over-explicit formulation of a ready-made doctrine of social evolution. This was not the case with the criticism deriving from Freud and Carl Jung, in which multiple approaches were somewhat confusingly mingled. Should the critic direct his attention to the mystery of the creative process itself, or should he apply his premises to an analysis of the psychic motivations of the individual author? What relative importance should he ascribe to literary biography? to the "collective unconscious" of the group or race? to intrinsic matters of form, structure, or symbolism within the given novel or poem? Such questions remained largely unresolved while at the same time the new psychology became an increasingly powerful force in both criticism and literature. The elusive meaning and the literary relevance of such concepts as psychoanalysis, the unconscious, myth, Gestalt psychology, psychoanalytic criticism, the neurotic origin of art, and archetypes were slow to be understood and even slower to be formulated into a comprehensible body of critical theory and method. Before World War II one finds only hints and indirections, such as Edmund Wilson's Freudian analysis of the governess in James's *The Turn of the Screw* as a case of neurotic sex-frustration, first published in 1934 and later partially repudiated. Wilson's essays in *The Wound and the Bow* (1941) provided a more complete theoretical discussion of the concept of the neurotic artist, and the method was further extended during the fifties and sixties when the works of earlier American writers like Melville and Hawthorne became the subjects for psychological interpretation.

Much earlier in the century, before 1910, Gertrude Stein was engaged in an intellectual experiment with the nature of experience and the psychological uses of language which had implications for both criticism and fiction. Her studies, starting from William James's discovery of the "flow" or "stream" of consciousness, led her to investigate the possibilities of simplified syntax and "automatic writing" as a means of portraying instinctive or primitive motions of the mind. Combining these ideas with impressionistic and abstract art (Cézanne and Picasso were among her favorites) she evolved a new style of nonrepresentational fiction which depended on repetition and what she called a "continuous present." Gertrude Stein's reputation today rests chiefly on her ability to germinate ideas which influenced writers more successful than herself. In her *Three Lives,* however, especially the story "Melanctha," about a Negro girl's inner life and progress toward self-knowledge, she managed to bring her theories of language and her primitivistic sentence structure to the service of a successful work of fiction. She herself called *Three Lives* the earliest example of the change from nineteenth to twentieth-century writing.

Both Ernest Hemingway and Sherwood Anderson were influenced by Gertrude Stein's blend of primitivism and Freudian motifs in fiction. In Hemingway simple language and repetition were used for behavioristic effects, while in Anderson the same tendency resulted in a style so primitive and mystical as to border on folklore. In *Winesburg, Ohio,* he became the first American to make conscious use of psychoanalysis in fiction. The book was a study of repressions in a group of villagers (he called them "grotesques") living in a small midwestern town. They all suffer from some inner torment brought on by a need for passion and an incapacity to communicate it. Each experiences a "catharsis" which brings the source of his trouble to the surface by means of a spiritual crisis, but which somehow fails to resolve it. Homosexuality, incest, sex symbolism, abnormal and subnormal characters and states of mind, repressive instincts, and the search for a father were pervasive themes in the writing of the twenties and thirties as attested by the fiction of Scott Fitzgerald, Thomas Wolfe, and William Faulkner, and the poetry of Robinson Jeffers. Fitzgerald made the leading character of *Tender Is the Night* a psychoanalyst attempting to cure his wife's neurotic symptoms. The Compson family in Faulkner's *The Sound and the Fury* was interpreted by some critics as flesh-and-blood equivalents of the id, the ego, and the superego.

In the drama of Eugene O'Neill, Freudian themes combined with the influence of Strindberg and ideas stemming from the psychology of Jung to produce a new kind of literary theater called "expressionism." O'Neill's early experimental plays such as *The Emperor Jones* and *The Hairy Ape* owed much to the Jungian concept of the racial unconscious, in which man, stripped of the superficial layers of civilization under extreme experience, is slowly reduced to a primitive state of savagery or animalism. *Strange Interlude,* with its use of asides to differentiate the private and public roles of the characters, reflected Jung's theory of the dialectical interplay of the *persona* and the *anima* (the outward and inward personalities), and in its dominating heroine, Nina Leeds, the play recalled the powerful female-vampires of Strindberg. *Mourning Becomes Electra* dramatized in the Mannon family a case history of a series of oedipal relationships as a means of substituting a modern motivation for the Greek sense of tragedy in the original Agamemnon story as written by Sophocles. O'Neill's great contribution to American drama was his use of new techniques, such as expressionism and symbolism, and his adaptation of tragic themes to the new psychology. His successors, Arthur Miller, Tennessee Williams, and Edward Albee, relied on Freudian psychology and sexual perversion not so much for sensationalism as for symbolic dimension. The rape of Blanche in *A Streetcar Named Desire* and the glass unicorn in *The Glass Menagerie* illustrate Williams' use of sex elements for symbolic purposes. And in *Who's Afraid of Virginia Woolf?* Albee made ambiguous connections between his characters' sexual lives and his exposé of patriotic myths and shibboleths in the American past. In *Death of a Salesman* Arthur Miller combined Marxist criticism of the business ethic with symbolic stage settings, Freudian dream sequences, interior monologues, unusual stage-lighting, and music to reveal the subconscious mind of his tragic hero, Willy Loman, the salesman.

After World War II, American literature as a whole was diverted to still further experimentation with the techniques of expression, and it continued to exploit Freudian motivations and to extend the boundaries of freedom in the use of sex scenes in homosexual as well as heterosexual relationships. The Marxist novel declined as the "cold war" with Russia diminished the idealism that had earlier infused it. The business novel, too, receded in importance. Race relations, the boredom of suburban life, the alienated hero and his relation to established society, and the continued erosion of the

American middle-class success-dream—these were the themes that pervaded fiction after 1945.

The Revival of Poetry, 1920-1945

The "new poetry" movement can be dated, for convenience, with the appearance in Chicago in 1912 of *Poetry: A Magazine of Verse*, edited by Harriet Monroe. In its first years of publication *Poetry* printed Carl Sandburg's "Chicago," T. S. Eliot's "The Love Song of J. Alfred Prufrock," and poems of Ezra Pound, Robert Frost, Hart Crane, and William Carlos Williams. But the immediacy, realism, vigor, and concentration of language that characterized this modern verse were not confined to a single periodical or publishing event. Robinson and Frost, both traditional in their use of rhyme and meter, had previously broken new ground by the introduction of a language adapted from their native New England, at once colloquial, concrete, direct, and free from the conventional prettiness of the Romantic poets and the lyric sweetness of Tennyson. Both found poetry in the rhythms of common Yankee speech. Similarly, but with a harsher midwestern accent and more flamboyant style, Sandburg and Lindsay introduced the sounds and motions of city and prairie. Chicago, "Hog Butcher for the World" and a symbol of the raw industrialism of the nation, somehow became a suitable subject for poetry. At almost the same time, Ezra Pound, who had abandoned his midwestern background and moved to London, was enunciating the principles of "Imagism." Around 1912, he and Richard Aldington, Hilda Doolittle ("H.D."), and the English don T. E. Hulme formed a school in which precise statement, exact meaning, concentration, and the "image" became the basis of a poetics which aimed to discredit conventional abstract diction and unnecessary decoration. Thus, New England, Chicago, and London together participated in a general revitalization of American poetry in the early years of the century.

During his London years, from 1908 to 1919, Pound directed the new movement with the energy of a tyro. He edited *Des Imagistes*, advised Harriet Monroe to publish the work of Frost, Eliot, Crane, H.D., and Williams; translated Provençal poetry and Japanese drama; and produced essays and manifestoes in behalf of *vers libre.* Both Pound and Eliot combined the roles of poet and critic, and both insisted on literary standards drawn from the tradition of classical poetry, the troubadours of medieval times, Renaissance drama, seventeenth-century metaphysical verse, and nineteenth-century symbolism, especially French. To these Pound added Japanese *haiku*, which he saw as a form of imagism. Where Robinson, Frost, Lindsay, and Sandburg emphasized landscape, character, and ethical or social concerns, Eliot and Pound loaded their long poems like *The Waste Land* and the *Cantos* with allusions to many foreign tongues and blended historical or mythological themes in a complex pattern to illustrate contemporary attitudes. A new international poetry thus emerged in the second decade of the century alongside the more "American." Also, taking hints from the dramatic analogy which Henry James had applied to fiction, they both created "personae," or imagined sensibilities, as angles of vision by which the experience of the poem was communicated. Eliot's Prufrock and Pound's Mauberley were such spokesmen. They were twentieth-century antiheroes, modern counterparts of Homer's Ulysses or the Faustian hero of the Renaissance. Their doubts and self-questionings were suggestive of the increasingly self-effacing, oblique stance which the artist was forced to adopt in a world dominated by powerful forces of materialism, where science was ascendant and religious values were disappearing.

The poetry of Pound and Eliot was not without significant social and intellectual content, but the values expressed were indirectly revealed. Both poets were in revolt against the liberal, progressive, humanitarian thought that had been carried over from the nineteenth century. During the 1920's Eliot especially was searching for new values either in the rituals of the established church or in Greek mythology, Buddhism, pagan cults of worship, and fertility rites. In their expatriate situation, both poets seemed to prophesy the doom of Western civilization to follow upon the catastrophe of World War I. Eliot echoed Oswald Spengler's gloomy predictions of the decline of the West: "Falling towers/ Jerusalem Athens Alexandria/ Vienna London. . . ." The mood was not unlike that in E. A. Robinson's poem, "The Man Against the Sky," where humanity is portrayed as dwarfed by a hostile naturalistic cosmos. Comparable, too, was Robinson Jeffers' persistent pessimism for the fate of mankind in its pitiful, self-destructive struggles to assert itself in a universe of vast materialistic forces.

But it was not such expressions of mood or feeling that were to be the hallmark of the new poetry, however naturalistic or "modern" they may have sounded in 1920. Eliot, in his influential essay "The Metaphysical Poets," distinguished between the *intellectual* poetry of Donne and the *reflective* poetry of Tennyson in defining the essence of the new and "difficult" manner. In a now-famous phrase, "dissociation of sensibility," he suggested that English poetry since the seventeenth century had suffered from a failure to fuse thought and feeling, idea and sensation, into a unified expression of "disparate experience." In the metaphysical poets Donne and Marvell and in the French symbolists Baudelaire, Verlaine, Laforgue, and Corbière, he saw methods and techniques peculiarly relevant to the expression of twentieth-century experience in all its variety and complexity. The established language of poetry, moreover, would no longer serve; it had failed to keep pace with changing ideas and ways of thinking. One could not write about the postwar generation in America or Europe in the accents of Tennyson or Swinburne, or even Whitman. New accents were needed, and these in turn led to new attitudes, rhythms, syntax, symbols, and, indeed, a new poetics. Thus the major effort of Pound, Eliot, and others during the twenties and thirties—whether we call it Imagism or Symbolism or Surrealism—was to purify the language of poetry and make it express the realities of the age. What the age demanded, Pound said, was "an image of its accelerated grimace."

In the work of E. E. Cummings, Wallace Stevens, William Carlos Williams, and Marianne Moore the results of this effort may be studied. The poetry between World Wars was a sophisticated poetry, in which a cardinal principle was, in the words of George Whicher, "its insistence on freeing the poem from dependence on anything outside itself. A poem in essence is not a report of an action, emotion, or thought which has previously taken place; it is itself a taking place, a unique experience, a construction with an entity all its own." Readers were not to read poetry as a footnote to history, or as a substitute sermon, or as verbal music. They were asked to adopt the viewpoint of the speaker, often one of irony or detachment, and frequently shifting during the course of the poem. Poetry does not "explain" anything or depend on anything. Thus Williams can describe a red wheelbarrow in a sixteen-word eight-line poem that is a water-color painting, imagistic, having the severe economy of a few strokes, complete in itself. In Wallace Stevens' "Domination of Black" we are not told why the color of the hemlock trees at night recalls to the poet "the cry of peacocks," nor why he is afraid. It is a tone-poem of sound and light which eludes rational meaning.

In the work of these poets, poetry itself frequently became the subject of a poem. MacLeish, for instance, defined the nature of poetry in "Ars Poetica," concluding with the summary lines: "A poem should not mean/ But be." Stevens examined the function of imagination in "The Man with the Blue Guitar" and other poems, and experimented with angles of seeing in "Thirteen Ways of Looking at a Blackbird." In "Of Modern Poetry" he discussed the problem facing the modern poet, who must "construct a new stage" and develop an acute, self-conscious sensitivity to his audience in searching for new ways of statement—a search in which Stevens and others drew on the methods of modern painting, abstract and post-impressionist. The "barbaric yawp" of Whitman was not to be the characteristic accent of this new poetry. The voice of the frontier, of the city or small town, was being replaced by a new sophistication. Irony, wit, paradox, ambiguity, sudden juxtapositions of imagery and restructurings of memory and time, broken syntax, and exotic allusions are some of the devices which the modern poet employs and the modern critic discusses. Metaphor, once used as a source of romantic or Platonic association, becomes the instrument of deflationary or bathetic effect. Eliot, for example, deliberately mocks romantic imagery in the lines: "The evening is spread out against the sky/ Like a patient etherized upon a table." Or Stevens: "The only emperor is the emperor of ice-cream."

If abstract painting and surrealism were sources of inspiration for Williams' "The Yachts," Stevens' "Anecdote of the Jar," and other poems, Cummings introduced typography, acrostics, and other verbal acrobatics in the general attack on conventional modes of expression. Behind this façade of tricks and mannerisms in Cummings' verse was a lyric mood that he might have been chagrined to hear called romantic. His little boys and girls, his joy in the changes of seasons, his love of flowers, trees, and country sounds, and his primitive rhythms give him away as a latter-day Wordsworth. What makes him modern is his prevailing humor and cynicism, a steady erotic strain, and the fresh "look" of his poetry on the page. The lyrical impulse was strong, even when he was resisting the traditional lyricism of the nineteenth century. Like Stevens, who returned to Coleridge's post-Kantian aesthetics as the precedent for his own belief that the poet must make over reality by the creative and ordering power of imagination, Cummings was both an innovator and an artist whose lineage can be traced back to the mainstream of English and American romantic thought.

One should be careful of such terms as "romantic" in speaking of poetry. While much of the new poetry of the twentieth century can be viewed in terms of its reaction to the conventions of the Fireside Poets of New England—Lowell, Longfellow, and Whittier—and likewise to the intellectual milieu that produced Whitman, it is also true that a romantic mood (if we define it as enthusiastic, affirmative, having joy of life, and love of natural things) is a part of the poetry of any period. Where the new poetry diverged from its antecedents was in language and craftsmanship, in the changed temper of its audience, and in the subjective, "private" world in which artists sought refuge from the overpowering incursions of science and scientism. Where Whitman was oratorical, these poets were conversational. Where he was expansive, they were introverted, drawing on the motions of the unconscious mind or dream-images.

As mass-circulation media, television, and other forms of communication gradually usurped the functions of information and entertainment for the larger public, the modern poet was forced to invent the conditions and the poetic theories by which his work could be read. Great public events no longer stimulated his muse. It is a strange fact that little significant poetry was produced as a reaction to World War I, the economic crash, the depression, or the rise of Nazism in Germany. Hart Crane's attempt to synthesize the American experience in an epic poem, *The Bridge,* resulted instead in a kind of mysticism and obscurantism at odds with the poet's grandiose plan for a poem on "The Myth of America." The structural defects of Crane's most ambitious work or of William Carlos Williams' *Paterson* are symptomatic of the dilemma of the American poet bent on carrying on the vision of Whitman in the manner of Eliot or Pound. Eliot himself only partially succeeded in encompassing large world issues with imagistic and symbolistic methods in *The Waste Land,* and Pound was even less successful in the *Cantos* insofar as they were intended as commentaries on contemporary social problems. For despite their alienation from America, both these poets were unable to escape completely from the "American" cast of mind. Eliot's later poetry, especially the *Four Quartets,* if more obscure than his early work, was more successful in blending the techniques of symbolism with a philosophy that was private, leaving "loopholes of retreat" from the broader world outside his own mind. A musical notation provided the formal ordering of these complex, highly subjective poems on such abstract themes as past, present, time, timelessness, and the mysteries of Christian theological doctrines.

The poetic revival covering two or three decades of the twentieth century was a blend of experiment and tradition and of new poetic modes brought to bear on the American scene. Like the criticism and fiction of the same period, poetry was in revolt against both the objects and the means of expression inherited from the nineteenth century. The powerful example of Walt Whitman remained to leave its mark on those poets who accepted, in part at least, the continuing significance of democratic hopes and national ideals. But more and more, poetry withdrew into a private world of its own making.

Fiction Between World Wars

The interest and excitement that greeted the fiction of Howells and James, and the critical controversies about romance and realism during the 1880's and 1890's, made the novel of realism by far the leading literary type of the post-Civil War years. This interest continued into the twentieth century, in which two main streams deriving from the earlier period can be recognized. The tradition of James was carried on by Edith Wharton, Willa Cather, Sinclair Lewis, and F. Scott Fitzgerald, all of whom wrote short stories and novels in which the morals and manners of the middle-class provided the central interest. The naturalist school of Crane, Norris, and Dreiser developed into the proletarian fiction of the new century concerned with political and social problems, the underprivileged, Marxist ideas, and class conflicts. Such writers-on-the-left as Dos Passos, Steinbeck, and Nathanael West were the major exponents of this tradition with its critique of the system of capitalistic finance and its sympathy for the common man. After 1900, Dreiser became the leading practitioner of the long novel of social significance in the naturalistic mode. *Jennie Gerhardt* (1911) was a successor to *Sister Carrie.* Dreiser then published *The Financier* and *The Titan,* two studies of the Darwinian superman and business tycoon, and followed these in 1925 with the monumental *An American Tragedy,* perhaps his most complete realization of the documentary novel combined with a philosophy of materialistic determination. Though naturalism continued to be the prevailing method of fiction, after 1920 there were clear indications that new techniques derived from such European sources as James Joyce, Conrad, Proust, and Dostoevsky were transforming the novel as a form. The influence of Freud was a powerful factor, and the introduction of nonrealistic devices, symbolism, stream-of-consciousness narration, mythic elements, and the like, gave the novel as written by Hemingway, Wolfe, Faulkner, and Sherwood Anderson an entirely new dimension.

By 1945, the end of World War II, it was apparent that the period since about 1920 had witnessed a literary florescence of fiction, poetry, and drama of such variety and originality that historians were beginning to describe it as the "second renaissance" of American letters. The first renaissance—brought to flower by Emerson, Thoreau, Melville, Hawthorne, and their contemporaries—had resulted from the spirit of cultural nationalism and the ferment of romantic thought. Anti-authoritarian in spirit, its major spokesmen (Whitman excepted) still expressed themselves in the voice and accents of British literature. On the other hand, American writers of the 1920's, with the example of Whitman and Mark Twain behind them, evolved an entirely new style by which to express the disillusioning facts of life after World War I. Blending this native realism with the new psychology, the revolutionary technique of Joyce's *Ulysses* (1922), and the quickening tempo of existence in the Jazz Age, they greatly widened the bounds of fiction and literary form. When Woodrow Wilson's dreams for a League of Nations and world peace had begun to fade into the "normalcy" of Warren Harding, artists and intellectuals found themselves in a world they had never made. A sense of alienation from the past and disaffection from the present prevailed, and they could find nothing in the tradition they had inherited from the Victorian age or in the moral assumptions of their own time on which they could build.

But this feeling of "lostness" and disinheritance does not explain the creative vigor and energy, the eager experimentation with new literary methods, or the skill and talent of the generation that produced so much original poetry, drama, and fiction. Artists and writers who flocked to Paris and the Left Bank to escape, or indulge in self-pity, or nurse the wounds of war, found fresh sources of nourishment and literary sustenance. The atmosphere crackled with talk of writing and publishing—poems, novels, stories, little magazines of criticism and commentary. Among the expatriates everyone carried a manuscript which was to be "a novel" and which he was eager to have read or to discuss with fellow writers. Literary salons like that of Gertrude Stein became the meeting ground for artistic innovators like Matisse and Picasso and for American writers like Hemingway, Fitzgerald, and Sherwood Anderson. Sylvia Beach, the publisher of *Ulysses*, kept her famous Shakespeare and Co. bookshop on the Rue de l'Odéon where writers and artists of different nations congregated and exchanged ideas. Surrealism, expressionism, Dadaism, new ways of manipulating and re-ordering language, became the subjects of excited interchange. Paris, for the time, was the literary capital of the world. The fortunate Americans who shared this exiled circle found a new international point of view from which to revalue outworn or provincial ideas.

For one thing, Hemingway, Fitzgerald, Eliot, Pound, and others derived a certain grim satisfaction from the general wreck of traditional landmarks and beliefs. *The Waste Land* was, of course, the classic poetic statement of this tone of decline and defeat, but the novel of the 1920's likewise gained an undercurrent of seriousness and a dimension of tragedy from the mood of the period. This feeling motivated Hemingway, for example, to evolve his characteristic stoicism, the need to "face facts" and learn to live under the new rules of the game in an altered world. "You did not know what it was all about. You never had time to learn. They threw you in and told you the rules and the first time they caught you off base they killed you."

A spirit of bravado, mingled with a romantic preoccupation with the self, was characteristic of the 1920's, and it was so brilliantly embodied in the earlier fiction of Hemingway as to seem almost his special trademark. By the magic of style, derived from Mark Twain and refined by Gertrude Stein and Sherwood Anderson, he made himself the mouthpiece of the generation that matured after the war. Hemingway's forte was both an attitude of mind and a way of putting it. Nick Adams, Jake Barnes, Frederic Henry, all innocents of a prewar America, thrust into a world of violence and exposed to the shock of evil and war, were forced to evolve their own private codes of behavior. It was a philosophy for their time, without benefit of the comforts of religion or the wisdom of the past, a philosophy in which one lived for the moment and developed one's own inner defenses. Personal honor was a cardinal principle of the code, learning to live with "grace under pressure." As Brett Ashley put it, morality is "what we feel good after"; it is what we have "instead of God." Enemies and friends are determined according to this code: those who "belong" and those outside the circle. Hemingway's colloquialisms, his reportorial style, tricks of repetition, understatement, and laconic language expressed the mood of a still-provincial nation suddenly asked to assume the world's burden of evil, and not really prepared to come of age. The Hemingway hero spends much time talking to himself, disciplining himself. The novels were private novels, yet deeply in the currents of the time.

More directly in contact with the American scene and such particular expressions of it as the small-town mentality, the "Rotarianism" of the businessman in a midwestern city, the narrow horizons of what Mencken called "the booboisie" of the Harding-Coolidge era, Sinclair Lewis won a tremendous following both in Europe and in America. Lewis did not contribute notably to the novel as a form, but his iconoclasm in exposing the shallow conventions and provincialisms of his compatriots, together with his assault on such citadels of respectability as the medical profession *(Arrowsmith)* and the Protestant clergy *(Elmer Gantry)*, brought to fiction something of the satiric power it badly needed. During the thirties, Lewis turned to social prophecy and timely themes—the race question *(Kingsblood Royal)* and the fear of totalitarianism which Hitler's rise had spread through the world *(It Can't Happen Here)*, but his gifts of mimicry and his ability to mirror contemporary history constituted his special form of genius, and these did not change appreciably in his later work.

John Dos Passos and John Steinbeck, in quite different ways, carried on the proletarian novel begun by Crane and Dreiser. Dos Passos transformed the documented method of the naturalists by introducing new narrative techniques derived from Joyce's use of stream-of-consciousness and from Sergei Eisenstein's experiments with "montage" in film-making. In *Manhattan Transfer* (1925) and the trilogy called *U.S.A.* (1937) Dos Passos evolved a kind of epic portrayal of American life in the period between wars. Such devices as "the camera eye," the impressionistic use of newspaper headlines, and interspersed biographical sketches of entrepreneurs, labor leaders, and intellectual figures of the time provided a running commentary on contemporary events, always with a Marxian coloration. Steinbeck, on the other hand, idealized the common man (the Mexican-Americans of the Salinas Valley in California or the Okies and migrant workers of the Middle West) from the viewpoint of a mystic and latter-day romantic. His anti-capitalism and his distrust of industrialized society took the form of a primitivistic glorification of the naive and the unspoiled. He was less innovative in method than Dos Passos; his originality lay in the untouched California area and people he portrayed. His most ambitious work, *The Grapes of Wrath* (1939), became one of the most powerful and characteristic novels of the depression decade and stands with *U.S.A.* as an epic of American fiction. If we add Nathanael West's *A Cool Million* and *The Day of the Locust* to a consideration of the social fiction of the 1930's, we can find in the work of these three novelists the best of the proletarian novel of naturalism of that decade. In *The Day of the Locust*, a serio-comic picture of the artificial world of Hollywood, West indeed went beyond realism to bring some of the methods of surrealism and abstract painting to the novel of social prophecy.

Thomas Wolfe and William Faulkner carried on and greatly transformed the tradition of Southern fiction begun early in the century by James Branch Cabell and Ellen Glasgow, who had themselves moved sharply away from the sentimentalized myth of the South in popular novels. Wolfe and Faulkner wrote some of their most characteristic fiction around 1930, late enough for them to have absorbed the influence of Joyce and Proust, as well as Freudian ideas. Wolfe's "torrent of recollection" revealed largely the Faustian appetites and disenchantments of his own experience, coming to focus on the theme of "lostness" and the search of modern man, the young American, for a father-image in the confusion and complexity of the postwar scene. Later criticism called his novels formless and excessively rhetorical, yet his powerful evocations and vast, romantic outpourings, his rhapsodic prose, and his sense of the flowing of time were used to make his central figure (Eugene Gant-George Webber-Thomas Wolfe) somehow symbolic of modern man's loneliness and potential for tragedy. Faulkner, on the other hand, directed his stylistic fury and narrative power toward the creation of a myth of Southern history, tragic in import, fascinating in its psychological depths, its violence, its complexity of Negro-Indian-White relationships, and its elusive Christian symbolism. Perhaps more than any other novelist between the wars, Faulkner experimented with narrative methods: stylistic and thematic symbols, montage, dreams, fragments of memories, interior monologue, blocks of narrative, the psychologic manipulation of past-present-future time, and point of view. More than that, he was unique among American writers of fiction in his creation of a saga or legend out of the materials of Southern history, a myth stretching from book to book, including generations of families, white and black, and involving the guilt and suffering brought upon the entire South by the original sin of slavery. Like Balzac's *Comédie Humaine*, Faulkner's separate novels are really a single "Book," as he himself came to refer to his work.

In 1923 T. S. Eliot, in one of his many prophetic statements, pointed out that the publication of James Joyce's *Ulysses* marked the death of the novel in the form in which it had been received from the nineteenth century. Joyce had demonstrated something new which Eliot called "myth."

> In using myth, [Eliot wrote], in manipulating a continuous parallel between contemporaneity and antiquity, Mr. Joyce is pursuing a method which others must pursue after him. The novel is a form which will no longer serve; it is because the novel, instead of being a form, was simply the expression of an age which had not sufficiently lost all form to feel the need of something stricter.

This prediction anticipated by several decades the criticism of the novel in which, since about 1950, such matters as form and technique have been increasingly emphasized, with such terms as "poetry," "romance," "symbol," and "myth" replacing the earlier and less technical designations of realism, naturalism, or representational fiction. The earlier slice-of-life method in which journalistic truth-telling and straight narration were brought to bear on a central character or group of characters involved in a large social problem—poverty, slums, class struggle, big business, and such—gradually became fused with the newer narrative techniques which Eliot's words suggested. The twentieth-century novelist was impelled to invent new ways of confronting the complexity of his material or to create new systems of value and meaning from the fragments of the past in order to shape and control the chaos of modern civilization. Dreiser's novels, for all their massive accumulation of facts and their convincing representation of social history and fate, failed to explain the irrational modes of experience and the individual "inwardness" that fascinated the younger generation of novelists.

In *My Ántonia* (1918) Willa Cather used some of the newer techniques of poetry and symbolism in her portrait of an immigrant Nebraska girl framed by an observer-narrator in the manner of Henry James. In her later comments on writing fiction, she described her method in that and other books as the antithesis of the social novel in that it would discard all the paraphernalia of naturalistic documentation, throw the "furniture" out the window, and strive for purity and simplicity on a stage as bare as the stage of a Greek theater. She relied on pictorial qualities, symbolic landscapes, inserted narratives, and the sense of the past, repudiating the tradition handed down from Balzac and Zola.

Another writer who followed in the wake of Henry James and Edith Wharton was F. Scott Fitzgerald, whose *This Side of Paradise* (1920) and *The Great Gatsby* (1925) were novels of manners as much as they were pictures of conditions. When he chose to tell the half-tragic story of Jay Gatsby through the eyes of an only partially reliable narrator, Fitzgerald gained a dimension of irony and ambiguity akin to that of Conrad. Thus well before Faulkner's experimentation with the uses of myth, legend, symbolic prose, and psychological time, there were evidences of a trend away from the representational methods of naturalism. In his delineation of flappers, rich boys, and the sad young men of the Jazz Age, Fitzgerald was both social historian and novelist of manners; but he penetrated the darker currents of his time when, in the mistaken dreams of Jay Gatsby for youth and beauty and success, he revealed the hollowness of an American myth which time had rendered a mockery and a pretense.

By 1950 most critics could agree with Eliot that the naturalistic novel had had its day and performed its function of purging fiction of "the beautiful lie" of romanticism. Its older concern with subjects of social significance had yielded well before World War II to a different orientation, a revived interest in the "inwardness" of the individual, his mental processes and sub-rational levels of experience. During the period between wars, the conflict between the naturalistic and the psychological novel was being fought out, and many writers showed the influence of both schools. But it was the element of style and language, form and structure—technique as discovery, to apply Mark Schorer's phrase—that would primarily engage later critics and readers of these novels. One cannot dismiss the contention of Richard Chase, in *The American Novel and Its Tradition*, that the main difference between the novel and other literary types is its effort to achieve a sense of reality in a contemporary setting. Nonetheless, this substratum of reality is now seen as most interestingly communicated through nonrealistic techniques such as romance, symbolism, mythic forces, and the blending of past and present by the means of stream-of-consciousness and the experimental handling of time. The writers of fiction in the twenties and thirties accurately and realistically reflected their milieu, but they were also sensitive to the new developments in narrative method. And their successors after 1945 moved even further away from the naturalistic and the representational in order to experiment more fully with nonrealistic techniques and with existential ideas as these applied to the novel as an art form.

The New Criticism

It has become a truism to describe the twentieth century as an age of criticism. The recovery of "the usable past," the revaluation of older literary reputations, and the discovery of new ones have been distinguishing features of the literary revival that began about 1912. Like poetry, fiction, and the drama, criticism shared the revolt and the excitement of the 1920's, took Marx and Freud to its bosom, and adapted to its own uses the scientific insights of psychology, anthropology, and sociology. In a deeper sense than in any previous period, criticism became a shaping force in the contemporary literary scene. In their effort to restore some of the authority and centrality that literature had enjoyed in the past, critics attempted to define and distinguish the special character of literary expression, poetry and prose, from other kinds of communication. Gradually, in the twenties and thirties, a loosely related body of doctrine, derived from various sources and influences, coalesced into something which was less than a "school" and more than a movement, and which came to be called "The New Criticism." The basis of this criticism, which attracted talents as different as Allen Tate, Yvor Winters, Lionel Trilling,

R. P. Blackmur, and Cleanth Brooks, among others, was its concentration on the nature and function of the separate literary work of art. The new critics differed from one another in training, and even in purpose, yet they had in common a neoclassic interest in literary forms and "kinds," a distrust of impressionistic criticism, and a contempt for the social and moral anarchy of twentieth-century civilization. Ultimately, they were seeking not only a new methodology for criticism but at the same time a new conservatism and orthodoxy of thought and belief.

The name "The New Criticism," used by John Crowe Ransom for a volume he published in 1941, seems to go back to a lecture of that title given by Joel E. Spingarn in 1910 at Columbia University. Foreshadowing the later criticism, Spingarn discarded extrinsic standards for judging literature, and substituted instead a relativism which asked only two questions: "What has the poet tried to do, and how has he fulfilled his intention?" Spingarn left it for others to demonstrate how this principle worked in practice, but the English psychologist and semanticist I. A. Richards began to investigate the scientific basis of literary communication in *The Principles of Literary Criticism* (1924) by examining the language of poetry and "the meaning of meaning." In this and other studies Richards became the first to study objectively the process of reading itself as a preliminary to literary interpretation and judgment. Even earlier, T. E. Hulme, Eliot, and Ezra Pound had been publishing essays in which poetry was described as a classical discipline, an intellectual exercise in technique and form. In his influential "Tradition and the Individual Talent" Eliot rejected Wordsworth's concept of the spontaneous overflow of powerful feelings and his preoccupation with the self, and defined poetry as the participation in a timeless tradition, made up of the sum of all great literary art, in which the personality of the individual poet was submerged, not displayed.

Meanwhile, a group of Southern writers and critics seeking to restore to the modern scene a sense of order, harmony, and tradition which they felt existed in the agrarian life of the prewar South, published jointly a volume entitled *I'll Take My Stand* (1930). Protesting against the mechanistic, culturally chaotic, and anarchic tendencies of Northern industrialism, these Nashville Agrarians outlined a conservative social position and spoke for a return to the leadership of the intellect. The Nashville group, which included some of the influential "Fugitive" poets, also invented a body of formalist principles for analyzing poetry, promulgated their system, and practiced its ideas in their own verse. John Crowe Ransom, a founder and philosopher of the Agrarian movement, defined the nature of the new criticism and illustrated its methods in *The World's Body* (1939) and *The New Criticism* (1941), as well as in the critical quarterly, *The Kenyon Review*, of which he was editor. Ransom, like Eliot, rejected "Platonic" poetry as no longer suitable for modern subtlety and complexity and preferred the metaphysical school in which metaphor, figurative language, and "texture" were the true elements of the poem. Allen Tate's criticism appeared in several volumes, of which *Reactionary Essays* (1936) and *On the Limits of Poetry* (1948) were representative. In an essay called "Tension in Poetry" he discarded the rhetoric of mass communication as a vehicle for the poet and emphasized the "private" nature of poetic language. Poetry, he said, is not simply paraphrasable prose but a complex structure of meaning deriving from a "tension" between external form and internal emotion. Robert Penn Warren and Cleanth Brooks collaborated in disseminating the methods of this school through their influential texts, *Understanding Poetry* and *Understanding Fiction*, which made comprehensible to students such concepts as paradox, irony, intellectuality, and wit as major components of poetic expression. As this new aestheticism gathered force, critics such as Yvor Winters, R. P. Blackmur, and Kenneth Burke demonstrated in a variety of analytical books and essays the special qualities of literary work which differentiated it from other kinds of communication. Winters attacked romantic obscurantism in nineteenth-century American writing and espoused a rationalistic-moralistic approach. Blackmur carried analysis of poetry and prose farther in the direction of a highly intricate discipline, and Burke explored language as "symbolic action" and in *The Philosophy of Literary Form* (1941) developed a new epistemology for criticism.

The rigor with which these critics pursued their goal of providing literature with its own special qualities resulted in a kind of academic scholasticism almost as difficult to comprehend as the "scientism" against which they set themselves. But in the process they accomplished something that American criticism had never achieved—an awareness of the need to study literature as a craft with disciplines of its own as exacting as those of the psychological or social sciences. If they went far toward preciosity and cultism, they pointed to the undoubted values of a close reading of the work and examination of the text. Criticism was recovered as a legitimate part of the university curriculum and a serious art in itself. No longer could either teacher or student be content with having "felt" the beauty of a poem without first having intellectually and imaginatively shared the experience of the artist in writing it. No longer was it enough to pigeon-hole a poem or a novel with broad labels such as "romantic," "realistic," or "naturalistic"—designations which had often been used as course descriptions and only vaguely understood as applied to a specific work of art. In the hands of a younger generation of critics, including F. O. Matthiessen, Lionel Trilling, Richard Chase, and Philip Rahv, the new methods produced skillful and balanced works revaluating the significance of such classic American writers as Thoreau, Whitman, Melville, Hawthorne, Emily Dickinson, Mark Twain, and Henry James. Matthiessen's *American Renaissance,* for example, combined the methods of textual analysis with literary and intellectual history in one of the most balanced studies of a period of American literature to be written by an academic critic.

As David Daiches has put it: "The new criticism has taught a whole generation to read. If it sometimes taught it to read out of the human context which alone gave meaning to what was written, the fault was perhaps inevitable in a movement which sprang in large measure in reaction against romantic gush." In the new dispensation every student became a potential critic. Publishers, alert to the commercial aspects of the situation, began to issue new editions of separate works with critical introductions. This development spread so rapidly as to amount to a "paperback revolution," almost an embarrassment of riches for the reader and student confronted by the multiplication of critical points of view. Books about books, collections of criticism, and bibliographies swelled publishers' lists. The application to literature of close, analytical methods had the effect of focusing attention on the short poem and short story as more manageable units for the exercise of new-critical techniques. The lyric, the sonnet with modern variations, the dramatic poem, and short fiction were types most often anthologized and edited in the many critical textbooks inspired by the success of Brooks and Warren. Intellectual poetry placed the largest demands upon editor and student, especially the poetry of the metaphysical school of seventeenth-century English literature and the symbolist tradition of the nineteenth—Rimbaud, Verlaine, Valéry, Rilke. Modern "difficult" poets such as Hopkins and Yeats became the models for younger practitioners. Editor-critics and teachers of literature began to explicate this poetry, illustrating the complexities of imagery, syntax, figurative language, symbol, metaphor, paradox, and ambiguities of style.

Meanwhile, the literary form which was most difficult to approach by the methods of the formalist critic—the novel—slowly developed a body of theoretical criticism of its own. In *The Craft of Fiction* (1921) Percy Lubbock, a "Jamesian" critic, made the first attempt to apply the principles of James's Prefaces to the modern novel. This work, together with Blackmur's edition of James's Prefaces, *The Art of the Novel* (1934), centered on the study of "point of view" in the novel, and its relation to form and meaning. English critics, especially F. R. Leavis in *The Great Tradition* (1954), were influential exponents of the new criticism of fiction, and in America both independent and academic critics contributed to the growing preoccupation with the novel as form and to the steady reassessment of American novels and novelists. Among these, one can mention a few: Malcolm Cowley (on Faulkner); Robert Penn Warren (on Hemingway and Faulkner); Lionel Trilling, Edmund Wilson, and R. P. Blackmur (all on James and others); Kenneth Burke (on form); Leon Edel (on the psychological novel and on Henry James); Richard Chase (on Melville and on the American novel); Mark Schorer (on technique as discovery); and Wayne Booth (on the rhetoric of fiction and the use of point of view). The term "psychological novel" was at first applied to European novelists like Joyce, Conrad, and Proust whose work was complex, poetic, and experimental. Later the new methods were directed toward a general revaluation of American fiction from Hawthorne to Faulkner and beyond. The investigation of point of view became the single most important discovery of twentieth-century criticism of fiction. Critics revealed the variety of ways in which authors manipulated the dramatic narrator both as a "reliable" and an "unreliable" spokesman. Huck Finn was seen as a vernacular hero and also as the narrative *persona* for the interpretation of Mark Twain's attitude toward the events of that novel. Stephen Crane's use of the technique opened up fresh ways of reading *The Red Badge of Courage, The Open Boat,* and other stories. Henry James's Prefaces had suggested how far a self-conscious novelist could exploit point of view to extend the range of meaning of long novels like *The Wings of the Dove, The Ambassadors,* and *The Golden Bowl,* and Faulkner no less deliberately experimented with multiple points of view in *The Sound and the Fury.*

Parallel with the formal and structural criticism of the novel, yet quite different in orientation, was the school of myth-criticism whose methods derived from modern studies in anthropology. Myth and symbol were the instruments by which the novel was viewed as an evolution from ancient folk epics, fairy tales, and medieval romances. A pioneer book in this field was Constance Rourke's *American Humor* (1931), in which folk heroes like Davy Crockett and Mike Fink were regarded as minor culture-deities created by the need for myth and magic in an otherwise prosaic and pragmatic society. Miss Rourke likewise saw a substratum of folk humor and mythic significance in more formal literature, in the novels of Hawthorne, Melville, and James. Critics began to discover primitive and fabulous elements such as dream-analogies, ritual sacrifice, and fertility rites as shaping-qualities in modern literature, particularly in the novel. T. S. Eliot had been greatly influenced by Sir James Frazer's study of mythology and nature-worship in *The Golden Bough.* Further studies by Malinowski and others led critics to investigate the impact on the novel of "archetypes," the mysterious forces which Jung called "the collective unconscious" of the race. Richard Chase's *Quest for Myth* (1949) attempted to comprehend the significance of the work of Ernst Cassirer, Suzanne K. Langer, and Maud Bodkin for the interpretation of fiction. In another essay Chase distinguished between "nature myths," which had their origin in antiquity—seasonal cycles, harvest rituals, and like phenomena—and "culture myths" of more modern origin. Thus, the symbolism of Melville's white whale, the motif of death and rebirth in *Moby-Dick* and *Billy Budd,* and the initiation ritual and the killing of the bear in Faulkner's famous story seemed to go back to nature myths. On the other hand, the saga of Leatherstocking, the Horatio Alger dream of success, and the Faulkner legend of the South were considered culture myths. In stressing sociological elements and the elusive forces of the racial past of mankind as motivations for literature, the myth critics moved in a direction quite different from that of the critics of structure and point of view. Myth and symbol were difficult to define and to demonstrate, and the reliance of such criticism on the specialized knowledge of anthropological science placed it beyond the reach of most readers. Nonetheless, it has had a profound effect as an approach to serious fiction and to literature in general.

Thus, the new criticism which began slowly and hesitatingly in the early 1900's developed into a highly specialized technique for analyzing and elucidating literature. The influences that went into its making were many and diverse, ranging from the new sciences of psychology, semantics, and sociology to the new literary techniques arising from experimental poetry and prose. French, English, and Oriental theories of art and aesthetics contributed to the movement. To trace all the intellectual sources of the new criticism is a task for professional scholars; but to read intelligently the poetry and prose of the present century (and of the previous century, as well) the student needs some conception of this critical movement and its relation to the modern temper.

Fiction of the Fifties and Sixties: Existentialism

After the holocaust of World War II, ending with atom bombs over Hiroshima and Nagasaki, the world divided into two nuclear-armed camps in a prolonged "cold war" of ideologies, with the Soviet Union at one pole and the United States at the other. The bewildering maze of bureaucratic machinery in business and politics and the new automated society ruled by computers and red tape left the "simple separate person" (as Whitman called him) hopelessly removed from the centers of power and from the possibility of influencing his own threatened fate. Writers viewed the new dispensation with jaundiced eye, some reacting with bitterness and gloom, others with a sense of the futility and absurdity of man's dilemma. Older ways of fictional expression were found inadequate to cope with the new conditions. Fresh techniques of anti-naturalism, fantasy, oblique narrative, and discontinuous or fragmented forms of telling continued to preoccupy the experimental novelist. It seemed no longer possible to handle themes of national or social significance. Writers of fiction, taking their cue from European innovators such as Joyce, Kafka, Beckett, and Genêt, turned to the central problem of man's very existence and the inadequacy of accepted moral codes to cope with reality.

Themes which have prevailed in recent fiction and drama include the following: (1) war and military life as a microcosm of bureaucratic impersonality and the indifference of authority toward the individual; (2) the search for racial identity and the relation of minorities, especially Negro and Jewish, to the white, Protestant establishment; (3) the victimized hero at odds with his environment and helpless to alter it; (4) the role of chance and absurdity in human actions; (5) the continued exposé of the success-dream of the middle-class business ethic, and the emptiness of the suburban "Utopia" of material comfort; (6) psychological maladjustments in the affluent society; (7) the delineation of sexual indulgence and sexual deviation, partly in pursuit of what was felt to be one of the few remaining freedoms left to the private individual in a faceless, dehumanized environment.

The decline of straight, naturalistic narration can be charted in the war fiction after 1945. Norman Mailer's *The Naked and the Dead* (1948) was a first novel by a young writer who was influenced by Dos Passos and Hemingway, but whose own work had more shock-content and a greater feeling for the injustices and antagonisms between ranking officers and common soldiers. Both Mailer and James Jones, whose *From Here to Eternity* was published in 1951, were concerned with the bureaucratic blundering of military decisions, the meaningless violence of war, and the dehumanizing effects of extended army service on the serviceman. Both these writers relied in the main on straightforward narrative; but a later war novelist, Joseph Heller, diverged from this tradition to write his *Catch-22* (1961) in the new vogue of "the absurd," following the lead of Kafka and others, in which bureaucratic officialdom is a vast power-structure with effects both serious and comic. Heller's grotesque and incongruous world of the army is exaggerated beyond reality, yet contains enough fact to keep the reader amused and horrified by turns: "I wanted people to laugh and then look back in horror at what they were laughing at." Mailer, in *The American Dream* (1965), employed the theme of the returning war hero to mock once more the much-frayed dream of success and honor in one's own country. Mailer's anti-hero follows a reverse pattern from ticker-tape and medals of honor to crooked politics, violence, surrealist sexual encounters, and even murder. Like Heller, Mailer here adopted some of the methods of distortion and absurdity to make his ironic point. With the intensification of the Vietnam War in 1966, writers such as Mary McCarthy and Gore Vidal attacked the political powers and impugned American motives, but to do so they abandoned fiction for journalism and polemical diatribes.

During the fifties the "Beat" generation gained notoriety and headlines, bringing a number of novelists to public attention, notably Jack Kerouac, Henry Miller, and William Burroughs, along with the Beat poets. Kerouac's *On the Road* (1957) is the classic novel of the beatnik-bohemian. It is a picaresque account of light-hearted vagabondage in which the main character hitchhikes and drives back and forth across the country, bumming, thieving, having sexual encounters, taking "pot," and relating to other Beats. Kerouac's *The Subterraneans* (1958) and *The Dharma Bums* (1960) reflected the current vogue of Zen Buddhism in the characters' incessant talk of their need for spiritual truth, or "dharma." William Burroughs' *The Naked Lunch* (Paris, 1959) went beyond mere Beat writing in its callous and uninhibited revelation of a sick imagination and in the depraved mentality which wallowed in scatology for its own sake; and the novels of Henry Miller went to such extremes of exhibitionism as to become almost a parody of the Beat style.

Ralph Ellison's *Invisible Man* (1952) marked a new beginning for the black novelist in quest of "visibility" in a white-dominated society, but the novel was more notable for the use of certain comic and surrealist effects than it was as a continuance of the repressed-black theme which it carried forward from earlier writers, notably Richard Wright, whose *Native Son* (1940) had been a landmark. Ellison, like James Baldwin, was an essayist, a novelist, and a short-story writer. In the work of both, one finds autobiography thinly disguised as fiction, Baldwin especially employing a confessional style in his handling of the themes of the alienated black intellectual, the expatriate, and the admitted homosexual. *Another Country* (1962), his most important novel, uses a fairly straightforward narrative method to record the experience of a Negro musician who encounters the inevitable prejudices against his race and whose sexual life and expatriation in Paris result in his eventual suicide (Baldwin's projection of his own case). Baldwin is not concerned with new techniques of narration, but he has a compelling style and exerts an almost hypnotic effect on his readers, so powerfully authentic and convincing is his fictional recounting of his own experiences.

Since about 1950 at least five Jewish novelists have won recognition for their original contributions to American fiction: Norman Mailer, Bernard Malamud, Saul Bellow, Joseph Heller, and Philip Roth. All have excelled both in the long novel and in shorter forms of fiction. Malamud's brilliantly evocative mingling of realism and fantasy centers mainly on his native locale of Lower-East-Side New York, Brooklyn, and the Bronx. Saul Bellow, born in Canada of Russian immigrant parents, has gained a wide audience with his several novels depicting the comic and pathetic adventures of an anti-hero who survives the bewildering and conflicting pressures of modern existence. Bellow's work reflects something of the existential style in his sense of the absurdity of existence and in the loose, episodic form of his writing, yet he is quoted as saying that the writer begins with disharmony and works toward order by a process of the imagination. *Henderson the Rain King* (1959) and *Herzog* (1964) are two of his most successful books. The Jewish novelist is largely preoccupied by the dilemma of the younger generation in conflict with the orthodoxies of its parents and with the inhibiting disciplines of its inherited religious and moral standards. Often the theme is handled with satire or comedy, as in the writing of Philip Roth, whose *Goodbye, Columbus* (1959), a short novel and five stories, contains some felicitous satire on the newly-rich, country-club set in New Jersey. The title story, a portrayal of a love affair between two college-age people of contrasting backgrounds, ends unhappily with the question: "What was it inside me that had turned pursuit and clutching into love, and then turned it inside out again?"

The term "existential" is hard to define precisely in its literary context. Yet in many of the recent writers of fiction there is an increasing use of offbeat, indirect, unreal or surreal effects, and a calculated disorder of form for which either "absurd" or "existential" or both are appropriate designations. A dictionary definition of "existential" is: "the doctrine that man forms his essence in the course of the life he chooses to lead." In popular parlance the word has come to mean little more than "not knowing what will happen next." *Existenzphilosophie* is the German term for a philosophical attitude which developed after World War I and was derived primarily from the writings of the nineteenth-century Danish thinker, Sören Kierkegaard (1813–55). Kierkegaard and his followers rejected the whole idea that a rational or predictable solution to the meaning of reality was possible, and they regarded as absurd the pretension that man's existence was either moving by itself or could be directed toward desirable or ascertainable goals. The only certain reality was the immediate and obvious fact of existence itself, and even that was small cause for comfort since the purpose and direction of life was unknowable. In France, Jean-Paul Sartre was practicing a literary form of existentialism in which uncertainty as to one's future course was inevitable. Sartre's work seemed to lead to a complete nihilism and negation of belief, yet he did retain the sole affirmation that existence itself was real and that a man does have freedom of choice among alternatives, though he chooses in the dark. Existentialism was opposed to such deterministic ideologies as Marxism, which proposed identifiable goals for the human condition. It also stood for a delimited form of individualism as against collectivist ideas, but denied that freedom of choice could result in anything other than loneliness, despair, or a blind groping toward partial self-realization or at least self-expression.

The "absurd drama" of Samuel Beckett, Jean Genêt, Eugene Ionesco, and other European writers influenced American fiction and drama in the 1950's and 1960's. In various ways the work of Ralph Ellison, Flannery O'Connor, Donald Barthelme, John Hawkes, Paul Bowles, Joseph Heller, James Purdy, John Barth, Thomas Pynchon, Edward Albee, and others can be characterized as either "absurd" or "existential" or both. A general feeling of alienation and disillusion pervades much of their writing. The characters exist in a self-enclosed state of isolation from their surroundings, often scarcely able to communicate the most banal things to their fellow human beings. Violent or comic effects result from this state of affairs. In a given novel or short story, the form is fragmented and seemingly incoherent, consisting of a succession of surprises or minor epiphanies in place of the older device of a single climactic event placed near the end. The events of the story usually lead nowhere except to an intensification of the absurdity of the original situation. The direction the story follows is not known even to the author, much less to the main character or characters. The narrative voice of the existential story is rarely "reliable." Emphasis is on symbolic rather than naturalistic effects. The protagonist (more anti-hero than hero) is often depicted in revolt against his circumstances, but there is a strong feeling of hopelessness and uncertainty concerning the object or purpose of the revolt. Among the recognizable traits of existential writing are violence, morbidity, "black" humor, and comedy derived from the extreme and irrelevant situations in which the characters find themselves.

American Poetry Since 1945

When the literary history of twentieth-century America gets written, the first fifty years or so might be seen by the historian as embracing two deeply opposed traditions, inaugurated by literary revolutions espousing apparently antithetical aesthetic and philosophical values. Very simply stated: What we used to call the "new" modernist poetry and criticism of Hulme and the Imagists, Pound and Eliot, Richards and Ransom, Brooks and Warren, was an attack on nineteenth-century Romanticism proper, and on the diluted romanticism of the Victorians. To what extent the critical ideas of the "Symbolist" or "Modernist" group were in fact anti-romantic is problematic, particularly since critics like Richards, Brooks, and Warren, for example, often quoted—and with great enthusiasm—Coleridge's definition of imaginative power as that which reconciles or balances opposite and discordant elements. The romantic metaphor of the poem as organism was also seized upon by the Modernists as essentially and profoundly a definition of the nature of poetic structure.

But Coleridge is complex, and the problem of his influence on modern critical thought is a difficult and technical one. What can be said without reservation, however, is that the moderns were rejecting the idea, commonly held by the Romantics (including Coleridge) that art ought to be subordinated to nature, linguistic architectonics to unfettered expression. The real focal point for Wordsworth was his own personality, the development of *his* mind, the projection of *his* emotions. The poetry of romanticism was a poetry of self: "I celebrate myself, and sing myself," wrote Whitman, who in many ways was the ultimate Romantic, manifesting in his poems the best and the worst qualities generated by the romantic idea of poetry. A rereading of Whitman's Preface to *Leaves of Grass* would be a good way of introducing oneself to the poetry of Robert Lowell, Roethke, Wilbur, Levertov, and Ginsberg.

With the rise of science and scientism (the substituting of scientific values for religious ones) in the last decades of the nineteenth century, the poetry of self underwent a tremendous devaluation. Buttressed by a militant naturalistic philosophy, and an evolutionary view of biology, and a concomitant demoting of the German idealistic philosophy which had fed Emerson's thought, the scientistic enthusiasts made total, dogmatic, and unyielding claims for an objective grasp of truth. Poetry, since it was an admittedly subjective affair dealing with the emotions, was quickly relegated to whatever was the nineteenth-century equivalent of a recreation room: O.K. if you have time for it, but essentially dispensable for mature human beings. The frequent complaint against the encroachments of science, the expressed fear that their occupation was gone—these were familiar themes of later-nineteenth-century poets. The New Poets and the New Critics rejected romanticism, did mighty battle against the scientific enemy, and ended, finally, by positing a whole new set of aesthetic values, the primary one being the notion that poems, because they have their own special way of being and meaning, present us with special ways of knowing the world. Poetry attempted to get on an equal footing with science by claiming for itself a realm of knowledge.

In very large measure, the poetry and the criticism published since 1945 in this country represent a movement that returns (often in a guarded way) to the romantic values that our earlier generation of Modernists rejected. Poetry and criticism since 1945, then, is a reaction against Modernism itself, a new revolution spawning its own manifestoes, its own excesses. T. S. Eliot has become the favorite whipping boy of the neo-romantics; Blake and Whitman, the new gods. If it is true that the first generation of Modernists were creating straw men, in effect, by reacting against the debased forms of romanticism, then it is also true that the younger generation are creating their own straw man in Eliot. There is, now, a new prizing of personality, of lyric straightforwardness and confessional modes of utterance; and in some, there is a seeking of transcendental visions. And with it all, there is a pleasing absence of what might be called "occupational defensiveness," a diminishing of obsessive theoretical self-awareness, a devil-may-care attitude toward the once extravagant claims of science.

In the 1950's it used to be said that American poets could be divided into two groups: pale-faced, academic, formalistic traditionalists; and red-skinned, beat-bohemian, anti-establishment experimenters with the poetry of spontaneity. The dynamic flux of personality, the trauma-ridden psyche, the things of this world, temporality, visionary intuition—these are, variously, the concerns of the neo-romantics who would seem to be carrying the day: poets like Robert Lowell and Richard Wilbur, who in their earlier work seemed to represent a second wave of the earlier Modernism, have turned in their later poems toward a neo-romantic mode. In Lowell, particularly, the student might trace this development through the arc of his career as it moves from a symbolist posture in *Lord Weary's Castle* to the neo-romantic voice of *Life Studies.*

The poet W. D. Snodgrass has made a very useful summary of the new attitude:

> We seek becoming, and find it in all ranges of experience. The Symbolist poem, in its decline, became a terrible temptation to conspicuous admirability. Now, I want my poems to have more and more of my own absurdity, pomposity, monstrousness, silliness. This need considerably lengthens my poems (if you only write your brilliant or moral thoughts, you will write short poems, indeed)—and it leads to something much more dramatic. Instead of having its attitudes always balanced, each part of the poem may now have its own opinions, and you can get from part to part only by changing your mind. Or your heart.

In a word, the chief criterion of the new poetry is sincerity. There is here, in theory at any rate, a subordination of the manner to the matter, of art to nature, to echo Coleridge again. The focal point becomes the flux of existence itself, human subjectivity in its ever-changing forms. The need of the neo-romantic is to break through the artfulness of art—the poem as linguistic object—into that which gave life to the poem. The neo-romantic thus raises all over again the problem of a form-and-content split. The tonal quality of such poems is of a man speaking to men. They have an openness, an immediacy, and a vitalism that suggests we are confronting experience in its purity. At their worst, these poems tend to degenerate into flat, formless banalities, or into chunks of the interior life made external, but so private and so rawly delivered as to be meaningless. The *effect* of these poems at their best is that the poet has somehow got behind language to pulsing actualities. Our postwar trauma-obsessed poets are deceptively simple when they are at their highest creative pitch. But their poems repay careful analysis, especially the good ones, because these reveal the technical strategies of poets who are often contemptuous of technique.

The Revival of Poetry

EDWIN ARLINGTON ROBINSON

[1869–1935]

Gardiner, Maine, the home of the poet and the "Tilbury Town" of Robinson's poetic portraits of broken lives and sensitive, suffering souls, was a New England village in the tradition of Old England, dominated by a manor house that overlooked the town from a hill. In Robinson's youth the house was in disrepair, seldom lived in by the Gardiner family, a monument to the past glory of a once-thriving town of the China trade. The poet's father, a prosperous merchant, had allowed his fortune to wither away by the time his youngest son became of age, so that the solitary, bookish young man, already determined to write poetry, was faced with the threat of poverty. His father's death in 1893 came in a year of economic depression. His mother died shortly after of "black diphtheria," and the grim circumstances of her final illness and burial left a permanent scar on his memory. An ear infection afflicted Robinson during this period, while he was attempting to write and attend college, and he felt at times as if he would lose his sanity. His poems were steadily returned by publishers, but in 1896 he decided to collect and publish them with borrowed funds in a volume entitled *The Torrent and the Night Before.* Some of the best of these early poems were incorporated into a second volume, also privately printed, *The Children of the Night* (1897). Reviewers considered these verses too grim and pessimistic, though a few critics recognized in the reticence of style and astringent irony of the portraits the mark of a genuine poetic voice.

After two years at Harvard—all the higher education he could afford—he moved to Greenwich Village in New York City, where he lived a celibate existence, though not without the friendship and encouragement of other artists and poets such as his former classmate William Vaughn Moody, E. C. Stedman, Hermann Hagedorn, and Percy Mackaye. His reading tended toward the severe school of naturalists—Thomas Hardy, Zola, and the English poet George Crabbe—but temperamentally he had inherited a Puritan strain of self-discipline and idealism going back to his New England ancestress, Anne Bradstreet. He also greatly admired the individualism, ethicism, and mystical transcendentalism of Emerson. From the beginning Robinson displayed a surprising command of his techniques: skillfully rhymed quatrains, a studied avoidance of "poetic" language, and a reliance on the rhythms of colloquial speech heightened by the discipline of form. Later, in his long narrative poems he developed a highly flexible blank verse, but in the earlier poems he relied on established forms like the sonnet and the ballad, putting them to such new uses as psychological realism and the ironic portrait. In his laconic, understated sketches, laced with irony, of such Tilbury Town inhabitants as Richard Cory, Luke Havergal, and Miniver Cheevy, Robinson depicted the disillusionment, frustration, or despair of alienated New Englanders. In this genre he anticipated the Freudian portraits of the small towns of Edgar Lee Masters and Sherwood Anderson.

On the appearance of Robinson's next volume, *Captain Craig* (1902), his work caught the attention of Theodore Roosevelt, who offered the poet a salaried position in the New York Custom House, an act of patronage intended to free him from his drudging job as a subway inspector and permit him to devote his full time to poetry. *Captain Craig* had been subsidized by some of Robinson's friends, at first without his knowledge, and while the volume contained several fine pieces, it failed to bring in any money and received little critical attention. It was followed by *The Town Down the River* (1910), but not until some years later, after he had experimented unsuccessfully with the drama *(Van Zorn* and *The Porcupine),* did Robinson reach the high-water mark of his accomplishment. In *The Man Against the Sky* (1916) the title poem was a meditation on the destiny of man, written in somber tones and a style of high seriousness equal to some of the best of the English Victorians, Arnold or Browning. In "Ben Jonson Entertains a Man from Stratford," one of the most convincingly human portraits of Shakespeare ever written, Robinson brought together all the resources of his art: the dramatic monologue, a conversational blank verse, a wealth of humor and humanity, and a prevailing mood of cynicism and disillusion. Here he succeeded in suppressing his characteristic poetic voice and mannerism, heretofore strongly present even in the dramatic poems, and allowed the characters to speak for themselves. A new note of affirmation is sounded in these poems, a faint but hopeful sign of a permanence behind the flux of life, a "light" dimly seen in the darkened landscape of his imagination.

From this point on, Robinson began to win a recognition long denied him. He wrote steadily and produced long psychological narratives that brought him both fame and security. He spent his summers at the MacDowell artist-colony in Peterborough, New Hampshire, where he turned out his series of poems on the Arthurian story, beginning with *Merlin* (1917). In 1921 his collected poems won the Pulitzer award. *Lancelot* (1920) and *Tristram* (1927), another prize poem, completed the series on the familiar legend of the Round Table in which Robinson cut away the supernatural elements of Malory and the allegorizing of Tennyson to concentrate on the inner conflicts of the characters, thus revealing their sufferings as extensions of their own natures and of the prevailing tragedy of mankind. A tendency, however, to garrulous monologue deprived these blank-verse narratives of the force and impact of his shorter poems. One feels, even in the best of them, that the material is better suited to the psychological novel than to the somewhat monotonous, if brilliant, cadences of Robinson's verse-talk. This criticism applies also to much of his later work, such long narratives as *Roman Bartholow* (1923), *Cavender's House* (1929), *Matthias at the Door* (1931), or *Talifer* (1933).

As Robert Frost put it: "Robinson stayed content with the old way to be new." Like Frost in his use of traditional verse patterns, his latter-day Puritanism, his individualism and his concern with ethical conflicts, he was both conservative and experimental. Both poets handled universal themes with a teasing symbolism and in clipped Yankee speech-idioms. In a different way Robinson might be compared, in certain of his attitudes and themes, to Henry James. Like James he was a literary portraitist and psychologist, and both were concerned with the role of the artist in contemporary American society. "Flammonde," *The Man Who Died Twice,* and other poems deal with the artist in a materialistic and indifferent world. Many of Robinson's heroes are frustrated artists, outcasts from society, egocentric individuals like Robinson himself, enduring a sickness of soul in a godless world, yet restraining themselves from indulgence in self-pity or fashionable cynicism.

Further reading: *Collected Poems of Edwin Arlington Robinson,* 1937. *Selected Poems,* ed. M. D. Zabel, 1965. E. S. Fussell, *Edwin Arlington Robinson: The Literary Background of a Traditional Poet,* 1954. W. L. Anderson, *Edwin Arlington Robinson: A Critical Introduction,* 1967.

Luke Havergal

This and the following two poems were published in *The Children of the Night* (1897). The text of all poems reprinted here is that of the *Collected Poems* (1937), the most complete collection of Robinson's poetry and the last of a series of collections that began in 1921.

Go to the western gate, Luke Havergal,
There where the vines cling crimson on the wall,
And in the twilight wait for what will come.

The leaves will whisper there of her, and some,
Like flying words, will strike you as they fall;
But go, and if you listen she will call.
Go to the western gate, Luke Havergal—
Luke Havergal.

No, there is not a dawn in eastern skies
To rift the fiery night that's in your eyes;
But there, where western glooms are gathering,
The dark will end the dark, if anything:
God slays Himself with every leaf that flies,
And hell is more than half of paradise.
No, there is not a dawn in eastern skies—
In eastern skies.

Out of a grave I come to tell you this,
Out of a grave I come to quench the kiss
That flames upon your forehead with a glow
That blinds you to the way that you must go.
Yes, there is yet one way to where she is,
Bitter, but one that faith may never miss.
Out of a grave I come to tell you this—
To tell you this.

There is the western gate, Luke Havergal,
There are the crimson leaves upon the wall.
Go, for the winds are tearing them away,—
Nor think to riddle the dead words they say,
Nor any more to feel them as they fall;
But go, and if you trust her she will call.
There is the western gate, Luke Havergal—
Luke Havergal.

Richard Cory

Whenever Richard Cory went down town,
We people on the pavement looked at him:
He was a gentleman from sole to crown,
Clean favored, and imperially slim.

And he was always quietly arrayed,
And he was always human when he talked;
But still he fluttered pulses when he said,
"Good-morning," and he glittered when he walked.

And he was rich—yes, richer than a king—
And admirably schooled in every grace:
In fine, we thought that he was every thing
To make us wish that we were in his place.

So on we worked, and waited for the light,
And went without the meat, and cursed the bread;
And Richard Cory, one calm summer night,
Went home and put a bullet through his head.

Credo

I cannot find my way: there is no star
In all the shrouded heavens anywhere;
And there is not a whisper in the air
Of any living voice but one so far
That I can hear it only as a bar
Of lost, imperial music, played when fair
And angel fingers wove, and unaware,
Dead leaves to garlands where no roses are.

No, there is not a glimmer, nor a call,
For one that welcomes, welcomes when he fears,
The black and awful chaos of the night;
For through it all—above, beyond it all—
I know the far-sent message of the years,
I feel the coming glory of the Light.

Miniver Cheevy

First published in *Scribner's Magazine*, March 1907. Later reprinted in *The Town Down the River* (1910).

Miniver Cheevy, child of scorn,
  Grew lean while he assailed the seasons;
He wept that he was ever born,
  And he had reasons.

Miniver loved the days of old
  When swords were bright and steeds were
    prancing;
The vision of a warrior bold
  Would set him dancing.

Miniver sighed for what was not,
  And dreamed, and rested from his labors;
He dreamed of Thebes and Camelot,
  And Priam's neighbors.[1]

Miniver mourned the ripe renown
  That made so many a name so fragrant;
He mourned Romance, now on the town,
  And Art, a vagrant.

Miniver loved the Medici,[2]
  Albeit he had never seen one;
He would have sinned incessantly
  Could he have been one.

Miniver Cheevy. [1] In linking the ancient Greek fortress-city of Thebes with the legendary Camelot of King Arthur's Round Table, and with Priam, King of Troy during the siege of Troy, Robinson is evoking literary echoes suggestive of war and military heroism.

[2] Powerful rulers of Florence during the Renaissance, noted for their wealth, cruelty, and licentiousness.

Miniver cursed the commonplace
And eyed a khaki suit with loathing:
He missed the mediaeval grace
Of iron clothing.

Miniver scorned the gold he sought,
But sore annoyed was he without it;
Miniver thought, and thought, and thought,
And thought about it.

Miniver Cheevy, born too late,
Scratched his head and kept on thinking;
Miniver coughed, and called it fate,
And kept on drinking.

Ben Jonson Entertains a Man from Stratford

First published in *The Drama,* V. Reprinted in *The Man Against the Sky* (1916).

You are a friend then, as I make it out,
Of our man Shakespeare, who alone of us
Will put an ass's head in Fairyland[1]
As he would add a shilling to more shillings,
All most harmonious,—and out of his
Miraculous inviolable increase
Fills Ilion,[2] Rome, or any town you like
Of olden time with timeless Englishmen;
And I must wonder what you think of him—
All you down there where your small Avon flows
By Stratford, and where you're an Alderman.
Some, for a guess, would have him riding back
To be a farrier there, or say a dyer;
Or maybe one of your adept surveyors;
Or like enough the wizard of all tanners.
Not you—no fear of that; for I discern
In you a kindling of the flame that saves—
The nimble element, the true caloric;
I see it, and was told of it, moreover,
By our discriminate friend himself, no other.
Had you been one of the sad average,
As he would have it,—meaning, as I take it,
The sinew and the solvent of our Island,
You'd not be buying beer for this Terpander's[3]
Approved and estimated friend Ben Jonson;
He'd never foist it as a part of his
Contingent entertainment of a townsman
While he goes off rehearsing, as he must,
If he shall ever be the Duke of Stratford.
And my words are no shadow on your town—
Far from it; for one town's as like another
As all are unlike London. Oh, he knows it,—
And there's the Stratford in him; he denies it,
And there's the Shakespeare in him. So, God help him!
I tell him he needs Greek; but neither God
Nor Greek will help him. Nothing will help that man.
You see the fates have given him so much,
He must have all or perish,—or look out
Of London, where he sees too many lords.
They're part of half what ails him: I suppose
There's nothing fouler down among the demons
Than what it is he feels when he remembers
The dust and sweat and ointment of his calling
With his lords looking on and laughing at him.
King as he is, he can't be king *de facto,*
And that's as well, because he wouldn't like it;
He'd frame a lower rating of men then
Than he has now; and after that would come
An abdication or an apoplexy.
He can't be king, not even king of Stratford,—
Though half the world, if not the whole of it,
May crown him with a crown that fits no king
Save Lord Apollo's homesick emissary:[4]
Not there on Avon, or on any stream
Where Naiads[5] and their white arms are no more,
Shall he find home again. It's all too bad.
But there's a comfort, for he'll have that House—
The best you ever saw; and he'll be there
Anon, as you're an Alderman. Good God!
He makes me lie awake o'nights and laugh.

And you have known him from his origin,
You tell me; and a most uncommon urchin
He must have been to the few seeing ones—
A trifle terrifying, I dare say,
Discovering a world with his man's eyes,
Quite as another lad might see some finches,
If he looked hard and had an eye for nature.
But this one had his eyes and their foretelling,
And he had you to fare with, and what else?
He must have had a father and a mother—
In fact I've heard him say so—and a dog,
As a boy should, I venture; and the dog,
Most likely, was the only man who knew him.
A dog, for all I know, is what he needs
As much as anything right here to-day,
To counsel him about his disillusions,
Old aches, and parturitions of what's coming,—
A dog of orders, an emeritus,
To wag his tail at him when he comes home,
And then to put his paws up on his knees
And say, "For God's sake, what's it all about?"

Ben Jonson Entertains. [1] Bottom, the weaver, wears an ass's head in a masque in *A Midsummer Night's Dream.*
[2] Troy. The reference may be to *Troilus and Cressida.*
[3] Greek musician and poet. The allusion is to Shakespeare.
[4] Apollo was the god of song and prophecy, often a symbol of poetic creativity.
[5] Nymphs of rivers and water, said to signify life-giving powers.

I don't know whether he needs a dog or not—
Or what he needs. I tell him he needs Greek;
I'll talk of rules and Aristotle with him,
And if his tongue's at home he'll say to that,
"I have your word that Aristotle knows,
And you mine that I don't know Aristotle."
He's all at odds with all the unities,
And what's yet worse, it doesn't seem to matter;
He treads along through Time's old wilderness
As if the tramp of all the centuries
Had left no roads—and there are none, for him;
He doesn't see them, even with those eyes,—
And that's a pity, or I say it is.
Accordingly we have him as we have him—
Going his way, the way that he goes best,
A pleasant animal with no great noise
Or nonsense anywhere to set him off—
Save only divers and inclement devils
Have made of late his heart their dwelling place.
A flame half ready to fly out sometimes
At some annoyance may be fanned up in him,
But soon it falls, and when it falls goes out;
He knows how little room there is in there
For crude and futile animosities,
And how much for the joy of being whole,
And how much for long sorrow and old pain.
On our side there are some who may be given
To grow old wondering what he thinks of us
And some above us, who are, in his eyes,
Above himself,—and that's quite right and English.
Yet here we smile, or disappoint the gods
Who made it so: the gods have always eyes
To see men scratch; and they see one down here
Who itches, manor-bitten to the bone,
Albeit he knows himself—yes, yes, he knows—
The lord of more than England and of more
Than all the seas of England in all time
Shall ever wash. D'ye wonder that I laugh?
He sees me, and he doesn't seem to care;
And why the devil should he? I can't tell you.

I'll meet him out alone of a bright Sunday,
Trim, rather spruce, and quite the gentleman.
"What ho, my lord!" say I. He doesn't hear me;
Wherefore I have to pause and look at him.
He's not enormous, but one looks at him.
A little on the round if you insist,
For now, God save the mark, he's growing old;
He's five and forty, and to hear him talk
These days you'd call him eighty; then you'd add
More years to that. He's old enough to be
The father of a world, and so he is.
"Ben, you're a scholar, what's the time of day?"
Says he; and there shines out of him again
An aged light that has no age or station—
The mystery that's his—a mischievous
Half-mad serenity that laughs at fame
For being won so easy, and at friends
Who laugh at him for what he wants the most,
And for his dukedom down in Warwickshire;—
By which you see we're all a little jealous. . . .
Poor Greene! I fear the color of his name
Was even as that of his ascending soul;[6]
And he was one where there are many others,—
Some scrivening to the end against their fate,
Their puppets all in ink and all to die there;
And some with hands that once would shade an eye
That scanned Euripides and Aeschylus
Will reach by this time for a pot-house mop
To slush their first and last of royalties.
Poor devils! and they all play to his hand;
For so it was in Athens and old Rome.
But that's not here or there; I've wandered off.
Greene does it, or I'm careful. Where's that boy?

Yes, he'll go back to Stratford. And we'll miss
him?
Dear sir, there'll be no London here without him.
We'll all be riding, one of these fine days,
Down there to see him—and his wife won't like us;
And then we'll think of what he never said
Of women—which, if taken all in all
With what he did say, would buy many horses.
Though nowadays he's not so much for women:
"So few of them," he says, "are worth the guessing."
But there's a worm at work when he says that,
And while he says it one feels in the air
A deal of circumambient hocus-pocus.
They've had him dancing till his toes were tender,
And he can feel 'em now, come chilly rains.
There's no long cry for going into it,
However, and we don't know much about it.
But you in Stratford, like most here in London,
Have more now in the *Sonnets* than you paid for;
He's put one there with all her poison on,
To make a singing fiction of a shadow
That's in his life a fact, and always will be.
But she's no care of ours, though Time, I fear,
Will have a more reverberant ado
About her than about another one
Who seems to have decoyed him, married him,
And sent him scuttling on his way to London,—
With much already learned, and more to learn,
And more to follow. Lord! how I see him now,
Pretending, maybe trying, to be like us.
Whatever he may have meant, we never had him;
He failed us, or escaped, or what you will,—
And there was that about him (God knows what,—

[6] Robert Greene (1560-92), contemporary of Shakespeare and playwright whose jealousy of Shakespeare's success prompted him to call him an "upstart crowe" who decked himself out in borrowed feathers.

We'd flayed another had he tried it on us)
That made as many of us as had wits
More fond of all his easy distances
Than one another's noise and clap-your-shoulder.
But think you not, my friend, he'd never talk!
Talk? He was eldritch[7] at it; and we listened—
Thereby acquiring much we knew before
About ourselves, and hitherto had held
Irrelevant, or not prime to the purpose.
And there were some, of course, and there be now,
Disordered and reduced amazedly
To resignation by the mystic seal
Of young finality the gods had laid
On everything that made him a young demon;
And one or two shot looks at him already
As he had been their executioner;
And once or twice he was, not knowing it,—
Or knowing, being sorry for poor clay
And saying nothing. . . . Yet, for all his engines,
You'll meet a thousand of an afternoon
Who strut and sun themselves and see around 'em
A world made out of more that has a reason
Than his, I swear, that he sees here to-day;
Though he may scarcely give a Fool an exit
But we mark how he sees in everything
A law that, given we flout it once too often,
Brings fire and iron down on our naked heads.
To me it looks as if the power that made him,
For fear of giving all things to one creature,
Left out the first,—faith, innocence, illusion,
Whatever 'tis that keeps us out o' Bedlam,—
And thereby, for his too consuming vision,
Empowered him out of nature; though to see him,
You'd never guess what's going on inside him.
He'll break out some day like a keg of ale
With too much independent frenzy in it;
And all for cellaring what he knows won't keep,
And what he'd best forget—but that he can't.
You'll have it, and have more than I'm foretelling;
And there'll be such a roaring at the Globe
As never stunned the bleeding gladiators.
He'll have to change the color of its hair
A bit, for now he calls it Cleopatra.
Black hair would never do for Cleopatra.

But you and I are not yet two old women,
And you're a man of office. What he does
Is more to you than how it is he does it,—
And that's what the Lord God has never told him.
They work together, and the Devil helps 'em;
They do it of a morning, or if not,
They do it of a night; in which event
He's peevish of a morning. He seems old;
He's not the proper stomach or the sleep—
And they're two sovran agents to conserve him
Against the fiery art that has no mercy
But what's in that prodigious grand new House.
I gather something happening in his boyhood
Fulfilled him with a boy's determination
To make all Stratford 'ware of him. Well, well,
I hope at last he'll have his joy of it,
And all his pigs and sheep and bellowing beeves,
And frogs and owls and unicorns, moreover,
Be less than hell to his attendant ears.
Oh, past a doubt we'll all go down to see him.

He may be wise. With London two days off,
Down there some wind of heaven may yet revive him;
But there's no quickening breath from anywhere
Shall make of him again the poised young faun
From Warwickshire, who'd made, it seems, already
A legend of himself before I came
To blink before the last of his first lightning.
Whatever there be, there'll be no more of that;
The coming on of his old monster Time
Has made him a still man; and he has dreams
Were fair to think on once, and all found hollow.
He knows how much of what men paint themselves
Would blister in the light of what they are;
He sees how much of what was great now shares
An eminence transformed and ordinary;
He knows too much of what the world has hushed
In others, to be loud now for himself;
He knows now at what height low enemies
May reach his heart, and high friends let him fall;
But what not even such as he may know
Bedevils him the worst: his lark may sing
At heaven's gate how he will, and for as long
As joy may listen, but *he* sees no gate,
Save one whereat the spent clay waits a little
Before the churchyard has it, and the worm.
Not long ago, late in an afternoon,
I came on him unseen down Lambeth way,
And on my life I was afear'd of him:
He gloomed and mumbled like a soul from Tophet,
His hands behind him and his head bent solemn.
"What is it now," said I,—"another woman?"
That made him sorry for me, and he smiled.
"No, Ben," he mused; "it's Nothing. It's all Nothing.
We come, we go; and when we're done, we're done.
Spiders and flies—we're mostly one or t'other—
We come, we go; and when we're done, we're done."
"By God, you sing that song as if you knew it!"
Said I, by way of cheering him; "what ails ye?"
"I think I must have come down here to think,"
Says he to that, and pulls his little beard;
"Your fly will serve as well as anybody,

[7] Uncanny.

And what's his hour? He flies, and flies, and flies,
And in his fly's mind has a brave appearance;
And then your spider gets him in her net,
And eats him out, and hangs him up to dry.
That's Nature, the kind mother of us all.
And then your slattern housemaid swings her broom,
And where's your spider? And that's Nature, also.
It's Nature, and it's Nothing. It's all Nothing.
It's all a world where bugs and emperors
Go singularly back to the same dust,
Each in his time; and the old, ordered stars
That sang together, Ben, will sing the same
Old stave to-morrow."

When he talks like that,
There's nothing for a human man to do
But lead him to some grateful nook like this
Where we be now, and there to make him drink.
He'll drink, for love of me, and then be sick;
A sad sign always in a man of parts,
And always very ominous. The great
Should be as large in liquor as in love,—
And our great friend is not so large in either:
One disaffects him, and the other fails him;
Whatso he drinks that has an antic in it,
He's wondering what's to pay in his insides;
And while his eyes are on the Cyprian
He's fribbling all the time with that damned House.
We laugh here at his thrift, but after all
It may be thrift that saves him from the devil;
God gave it, anyhow,—and we'll suppose
He knew the compound of his handiwork.
To-day the clouds are with him, but anon
He'll out of 'em enough to shake the tree
Of life itself and bring down fruit unheard-of,—
And, throwing in the bruised and whole together,
Prepare a wine to make us drunk with wonder;
And if he live, there'll be a sunset spell
Thrown over him as over a glassed lake
That yesterday was all a black wild water.

God send he live to give us, if no more,
What now's a-rampage in him, and exhibit,
With a decent half-allegiance to the ages
An earnest of at least a casual eye
Turned once on what he owes to Gutenberg,[8]
And to the fealty of more centuries
Than are as yet a picture in our vision.
"There's time enough,—I'll do it when I'm old,
And we're immortal men," he says to that;
And then he says to me, "Ben, what's 'immortal'?
Think you by any force of ordination
It may be nothing of a sort more noisy
Than a small oblivion of component ashes
That of a dream-addicted world was once
A moving atomy much like your friend here?"
Nothing will help that man. To make him laugh,
I said then he was a mad mountebank,—
And by the Lord I nearer made him cry.
I could have eat an eft then, on my knees,
Tail, claws, and all of him; for I had stung
The king of men, who had no sting for me,
And I had hurt him in his memories;
And I say now, as I shall say again,
I love the man this side idolatry.

He'll do it when he's old, he says. I wonder.
He may not be so ancient as all that.
For such as he, the thing that is to do
Will do itself,—but there's a reckoning;
The sessions that are now too much his own,
The roiling inward of a stilled outside,
The churning out of all those blood-fed lines,
The nights of many schemes and little sleep,
The full brain hammered hot with too much thinking,
The vexed heart over-worn with too much aching,—
This weary jangling of conjoined affairs
Made out of elements that have no end,
And all confused at once, I understand,
Is not what makes a man to live forever.
O no, not now! He'll not be going now:
There'll be time yet for God knows what explosions
Before he goes. He'll stay awhile. Just wait:
Just wait a year or two for Cleopatra,
For she's to be a balsam and a comfort;
And that's not all a jape of mine now, either.
For granted once the old way of Apollo
Sings in a man, he may then, if he's able,
Strike unafraid whatever strings he will
Upon the last and wildest of new lyres;
Nor out of his new magic, though it hymn
The shrieks of dungeoned hell, shall he create
A madness or a gloom to shut quite out
A cleaving daylight, and a last great calm
Triumphant over shipwreck and all storms.
He might have given Aristotle creeps,
But surely would have given him his *katharsis.*

He'll not be going yet. There's too much yet
Unsung within the man. But when he goes,
I'd stake ye coin o' the realm his only care
For a phantom world he sounded and found wanting
Will be a portion here, a portion there,
Of this or that thing or some other thing
That has a patent and intrinsical
Equivalence in those egregious shillings.

[8] Johann Gutenberg (c.1400-1468), German inventor of printing from movable type.

And yet he knows, God help him! Tell me, now,
If ever there was anything let loose
On earth by gods or devils heretofore
Like this mad, careful, proud, indifferent Shakespeare!
Where was it, if it ever was? By heaven,
'Twas never yet in Rhodes or Pergamon—
In Thebes or Nineveh, a thing like this![9]
No thing like this was ever out of England;
And that he knows. I wonder if he cares.
Perhaps he does. . . . O Lord, that House in Stratford!

Flammonde

First published in the *Outlook*, CIX (1915). Reprinted in *Anthology of Magazine Verse* for 1915, and again in *The Man Against the Sky* (1916).

The man Flammonde, from God knows where,
With firm address and foreign air,
With news of nations in his talk
And something royal in his walk,
With glint of iron in his eyes,
But never doubt, nor yet surprise,
Appeared, and stayed, and held his head
As one by kings accredited.

Erect, with his alert repose
About him, and about his clothes,
He pictured all tradition hears
Of what we owe to fifty years.
His cleansing heritage of taste
Paraded neither want nor waste;
And what he needed for his fee
To live, he borrowed graciously.

He never told us what he was,
Or what mischance, or other cause,
Had banished him from better days
To play the Prince of Castaways.
Meanwhile he played surpassing well
A part, for most, unplayable;
In fine, one pauses, half afraid
To say for certain that he played.

For that, one may as well forego
Conviction as to yes or no;
Nor can I say just how intense
Would then have been the difference
To several, who, having striven
In vain to get what he was given,
Would see the stranger taken on
By friends not easy to be won.

Moreover, many a malcontent
He soothed and found munificent;
His courtesy beguiled and foiled
Suspicion that his years were soiled;
His mien distinguished any crowd,
His credit strengthened when he bowed;
And women, young and old, were fond
Of looking at the man Flammonde.

There was a woman in our town
On whom the fashion was to frown;
But while our talk renewed the tinge
Of a long-faded scarlet fringe,
The man Flammonde saw none of that,
And what he saw we wondered at—
That none of us, in her distress,
Could hide or find our littleness.

There was a boy that all agreed
Had shut within him the rare seed
Of learning. We could understand,
But none of us could lift a hand.
The man Flammonde appraised the youth,
And told a few of us the truth;
And thereby, for a little gold,
A flowered future was unrolled.

There were two citizens who fought
For years and years, and over nought;
They made life awkward for their friends,
And shortened their own dividends.
The man Flammonde said what was wrong
Should be made right; nor was it long
Before they were again in line,
And had each other in to dine.

And these I mention are but four
Of many out of many more.
So much for them. But what of him—
So firm in every look and limb?
What small satanic sort of kink
Was in his brain? What broken link
Withheld him from the destinies
That came so near to being his?

What was he, when we came to sift
His meaning, and to note the drift
Of incommunicable ways
That make us ponder while we praise?
Why was it that his charm revealed
Somehow the surface of a shield?

[9] Rhodes, Aegean island once a center of culture and trade between East and West; Pergamon, ancient capital of the Byzantine Empire; Thebes, capital of ancient Egypt; Nineveh, capital of the Assyrian Empire.

What was it that we never caught?
What was he, and what was he not?

How much it was of him we met
We cannot ever know; nor yet
Shall all he gave us quite atone
For what was his, and his alone;
Nor need we now, since he knew best,
Nourish an ethical unrest:
Rarely at once will nature give
The power to be Flammonde and live.

We cannot know how much we learn
From those who never will return,
Until a flash of unforeseen
Remembrance falls on what has been.
We've each a darkening hill to climb;
And this is why, from time to time
In Tilbury Town, we look beyond
Horizons for the man Flammonde.

Mr. Flood's Party

First published in the *Nation,* CXI (1920). Reprinted in *Avon's Harvest* (1921).

Old Eben Flood, climbing alone one night
Over the hill between the town below
And the forsaken upland hermitage
That held as much as he should ever know
On earth again of home, paused warily.
The road was his with not a native near;
And Eben, having leisure, said aloud,
For no man else in Tilbury Town to hear:

"Well, Mr. Flood, we have the harvest moon
Again, and we may not have many more;
The bird is on the wing, the poet says,[1]
And you and I have said it here before.
Drink to the bird." He raised up to the light
The jug that he had gone so far to fill,
And answered huskily: "Well, Mr. Flood,
Since you propose it, I believe I will."

Alone, as if enduring to the end
A valiant armor of scarred hopes outworn,
He stood there in the middle of the road
Like Roland's ghost winding a silent horn.[2]

Below him, in the town among the trees,
Where friends of other days had honored him,
A phantom salutation of the dead
Rang thinly till old Eben's eyes were dim.

Then, as a mother lays her sleeping child
Down tenderly, fearing it may awake,
He set the jug down slowly at his feet
With trembling care, knowing that most things break.
And only when assured that on firm earth
It stood, as the uncertain lives of men
Assuredly did not, he paced away,
And with his hand extended paused again:

"Well, Mr. Flood, we have not met like this
In a long time; and many a change has come
To both of us, I fear, since last it was
We had a drop together. Welcome home!"
Convivially returning with himself,
Again he raised the jug up to the light;
And with an acquiescent quaver said:
"Well, Mr. Flood, if you insist, I might.

"Only a very little, Mr. Flood—
For auld lang syne. No more, sir; that will do."
So, for the time, apparently it did,
And Eben evidently thought so too;
For soon amid the silver loneliness
Of night he lifted up his voice and sang,
Secure, with only two moons listening,
Until the whole harmonious landscape rang—

"For auld lang syne." The weary throat gave out,
The last word wavered; and the song being done,
He raised again the jug regretfully
And shook his head, and was again alone.
There was not much that was ahead of him,
And there was nothing in the town below—
Where strangers would have shut the many doors
That many friends had opened long ago.

Mr. Flood's Party. [1]The theme of life's brevity and the wording here echo Edward FitzGerald's *The Rubáiyát of Omar Khayyám* (1859): "The Bird of Time has but a little way / To flutter and the Bird is on the Wing."

[2]At Roncevaux in the Pyrenees when part of Charlemagne's army was cut off during the retreat from Spain (A.D. 778), Roland blew his horn for help, but he died. His story became legend in the songs of the troubadours.

Karma

First published in *Dionysius in Doubt* (1925).

Christmas was in the air and all was well
With him, but for a few confusing flaws
In divers of God's images. Because
A friend of his would neither buy nor sell,
Was he to answer for the axe that fell?
He pondered; and the reason for it was,

Partly, a slowly freezing Santa Claus
Upon the corner, with his beard and bell.

Acknowledging an improvident surprise,
He magnified a fancy that he wished
The friend whom he had wrecked were here again.
Not sure of that, he found a compromise;
And from the fulness of his heart he fished
A dime for Jesus who had died for men.

ROBERT FROST [1874-1963]

THE POETRY of Robert Frost is both personal and universal. Rooted in New England, it comes to flower in an art which is at once modern and traditional—modern in its ambivalent formulations of the truth, traditional in its use of established metrical conventions such as the couplet, the sonnet, the rhymed quatrain, the ballad, and blank verse. Romantic in his symbolic expression of local speech, plain people, and the New England regional scene, Frost voiced the twentieth-century conflict between reason and unreason, doubt and faith. He was too honest and too stubborn to take sides. He could doubt without denying; believe without affirming; see the bad without wanting to make it worse; and see the good without wishing, sentimentally, to make it better. Conservative in temper, experimental in mind, always prepared to test life by trial and discovery rather than by tradition alone, he sustained his art by a kindliness of spirit, a shrewd common sense, and a pervading and self-effacing humor. Frost was not afraid to be didactic; but he was never dogmatic. He was a philosophical poet who was suspicious of intellectuality, and a part-time professor always a little defensive about the ways of academic learning. If he seems to some a bit old-fashioned or puritanical in his ethicism and Emersonian individualism, he was also a psychologist, a naturalist, and an early existential-humanist. He was, he said, neither a "prude" nor a "puke," but if he must choose he would rather be "a plain New Hampshire farmer/ With an income in cash of say a thousand/ (From say a publisher in New York City)."

The first of many anomalies in the career of this indigenous New Englander was the fact of his birth and early life in the raw, frontier community of San Francisco during the 1870's, where his adventurous and unconventional father, having abandoned his native Massachusetts in a flurry of sympathy for the postwar South, went to take up newspaper work. When Frost was ten years old his father died. His mother, a schoolteacher with literary talents, returned to New England (Lawrence, Massachusetts) where, with some help from Frost's grandfather, she supported her two children and gave them an education. In 1892 Frost graduated from Lawrence High School, valedictorian of his class, and entered Dartmouth, but shortly withdrew. With something of his father's restless spirit, he tried various odd jobs, shoemaking, journalism, farming, even schoolteaching. Perversely, the one occupation he steadily pursued was writing poetry, which did not pay and which gained him a harvest of rejection slips. In 1895 he married his high-school classmate and co-valedictorian, Elinor White. With a growing family, Frost taught in a private school and in 1897 made another attempt at college as a special student at Harvard. This time he stayed two years, but decided once again that an academic career was not for him. Later, however, when his reputation as a poet was established, he was to spend much of his life as a poet-in-residence and teacher of literature and philosophy, prodding and stimulating students with wisdom, wit, and understanding. He taught at Amherst, Michigan, and Dartmouth in various intervals between 1917 and 1938, always returning to his farms in

New Hampshire and Vermont to write. In 1920 he helped found the Bread Loaf School of English at Middlebury, Vermont, and became an annual lecturer there.

The year 1912 became a turning point of his life when Frost and his wife decided to gamble and make a new start. They sold their farm at Derry, New Hampshire, and moved the family of four children to England, renting a house in Beaconsfield, Buckinghamshire, where Frost felt he could share in the atmosphere of the new poetry movement and "write and be poor without further scandal in the family." The gamble was a success. *A Boy's Will* (1913), his first volume of verse, was immediately accepted. It was followed in 1914 by *North of Boston,* now a landmark in the history of American poetry. Frost won the respect of his fellow Georgian poets, Wilfred Gibson, Lascelles Abercrombie, Edward Thomas, and Rupert Brooke. He met the ubiquitous Ezra Pound, who promptly wrote a review of his poems for Harriet Monroe's *Poetry* magazine, making Frost known in his native country. Thus, like so many American writers, Frost made his reputation in England, and when both of his books were published in the United States in 1915, he told his wife: "My book has gone home. We must go too."

The Frost family, now numbering five children, settled in Franconia, New Hampshire, the farm which gave title to his next volume, *Mountain Interval* (1916). He began public readings of his poetry, giving "unpoetic" renderings of the now familiar lines from "Mending Wall," "Birches," and other poems with the laconic New England idioms and understated rhythms so essential to his meaning. In 1923 *New Hampshire: A Poem with Notes and Grace Notes* won him the first of his four Pulitzer Prizes. Invitations for lectureships, fellowships, readings, and writers' conferences now came rapidly. He received honorary degrees from more than forty colleges and universities, including Oxford and Cambridge in 1957. Gradually Frost came to be acknowledged as a kind of unofficial American poet laureate. He was twice honored on his birthday by resolutions of the United States Senate. He was invited to read "The Gift Outright" at the inauguration of President John F. Kennedy in 1961. In 1949 *The Complete Poems of Robert Frost* gathered all of his work to date in one volume, including such volumes as *West-Running Brook* (1928), *A Further Range* (1936), *A Witness Tree* (1942), *Steeple Bush* (1947), and his two verse-dramas, *A Masque of Reason* (1945) and *A Masque of Mercy* (1947). One later volume, *A Clearing Range* (1962), appeared before his death in Boston in 1963.

Frost's poetry is modern in its complexity of thought and in its awareness of the confusion of belief and the fragmentization of earlier human values. His style is deceptively simple, drawing on images of nature and regional materials. But Frost was no retrospective romantic poet. Social and economic problems, industrial and urban dislocations, are not his surface subjects, but the twentieth-century mind is nonetheless fully exposed in his poetry, as effectively as in the work of such symbolistic poets as Yeats and Eliot, if in quite different terms.

Further reading: *Complete Poems,* 1949. *Selected Poems,* ed. Robert Graves, 1963. Elizabeth Sargeant, *Robert Frost: The Trial by Existence,* 1960.

The Death of the Hired Man

The prevailing poetic method of *North of Boston* (1914), in which this poem (written a decade earlier) appeared, is that of narrative and dramatic dialogue. The form is blank verse, the setting rural New England, and interest focuses on psychological characterization of local, Yankee types. In the conversation between Mary and Warren, Frost portrays the hired man as a mixture of pride, ignorance, self-respect, and servility. Sentiment is avoided because of this human factor, as by the laconic speech of the farmer and his wife. Silas is both pathetic and a little ludicrous, while retaining the sympathy of the poet. He is a type of the New England hired hand of that time, and also, in his blend of pride and dependency, an analogue of workingmen generally.

Mary sat musing on the lamp-flame at the table
Waiting for Warren. When she heard his step,
She ran on tip-toe down the darkened passage
To meet him in the doorway with the news
And put him on his guard. "Silas is back."
She pushed him outward with her through the door

And shut it after her. "Be kind," she said.
She took the market things from Warren's arms
And set them on the porch, then drew him down
To sit beside her on the wooden steps.

"When was I ever anything but kind to him?
But I'll not have the fellow back," he said.
"I told him so last haying, didn't I?
'If he left then,' I said, 'that ended it.'
What good is he? Who else will harbour him
At his age for the little he can do?
What help he is there's no depending on.
Off he goes always when I need him most.
'He thinks he ought to earn a little pay,
Enough at least to buy tobacco with,
So he won't have to beg and be beholden.'
'All right,' I say, 'I can't afford to pay
Any fixed wages, though I wish I could.'
'Someone else can.' 'Then someone else will have to.'
I shouldn't mind his bettering himself
If that was what it was. You can be certain,
When he begins like that, there's someone at him
Trying to coax him off with pocket-money,—
In haying time, when any help is scarce.
In winter he comes back to us. I'm done."
"Sh! not so loud: he'll hear you," Mary said.

"I want him to: he'll have to soon or late."

"He's worn out. He's asleep beside the stove.
When I came up from Rowe's I found him here,
Huddled against the barn-door fast asleep,
A miserable sight, and frightening, too—
You needn't smile—I didn't recognise him—
I wasn't looking for him—and he's changed.
Wait till you see."

"Where did you say he'd been?"

"He didn't say. I dragged him to the house,
And gave him tea and tried to make him smoke.
I tried to make him talk about his travels.
Nothing would do: he just kept nodding off."

"What did he say? Did he say anything?"

"But little."

"Anything? Mary, confess
He said he'd come to ditch the meadow for me."

"Warren!"

"But did he? I just want to know."

"Of course he did. What would you have him say?
Surely you wouldn't grudge the poor old man
Some humble way to save his self-respect.
He added, if you really care to know,
He meant to clear the upper pasture, too.
That sounds like something you have heard before?
Warren, I wish you could have heard the way
He jumbled everything. I stopped to look
Two or three times—he made me feel so queer—
To see if he was talking in his sleep.
He ran on Harold Wilson—you remember—
The boy you had in haying four years since.
He's finished school, and teaching in his college.

"Silas declares you'll have to get him back.
He says they two will make a team for work:
Between them they will lay this farm as smooth!
The way he mixed that in with other things.
He thinks young Wilson a likely lad, though daft
On education—you know how they fought
All through July under the blazing sun,
Silas up on the cart to build the load,
Harold along beside to pitch it on."

"Yes, I took care to keep well out of earshot."

"Well, those days trouble Silas like a dream.
You wouldn't think they would. How some things linger!
Harold's young college boy's assurance piqued him.
After so many years he still keeps finding
Good arguments he sees he might have used.
I sympathise. I know just how it feels
To think of the right thing to say too late.
Harold's associated in his mind with Latin.
He asked me what I thought of Harold's saying
He studied Latin like the violin
Because he liked it—that an argument!
He said he couldn't make the boy believe
He could find water with a hazel prong—
Which showed how much good school had ever done him.
He wanted to go over that. But most of all
He thinks if he could have another chance
To teach him how to build a load of hay—"

"I know, that's Silas' one accomplishment.
He bundles every forkful in its place,
And tags and numbers it for future reference,
So he can find and easily dislodge it
In the unloading. Silas does that well.
He takes it out in bunches like birds' nests.
You never see him standing on the hay
He's trying to lift, straining to lift himself."

"He thinks if he could teach him that, he'd be
Some good perhaps to someone in the world.
He hates to see a boy the fool of books.
Poor Silas, so concerned for other folks,
And nothing to look backward to with pride,
And nothing to look forward to with hope,
So now and never any different."

Part of a moon was falling down the west,
Dragging the whole sky with it to the hills.
Its light poured softly in her lap. She saw
And spread her apron to it. She put out her hand
Among the harp-like morning-glory strings,
Taut with the dew from garden bed to eaves,
As if she played unheard the tenderness
That wrought on him beside her in the night.
"Warren," she said, "he has come home to die:
You needn't be afraid he'll leave you this time."

"Home," he mocked gently.

"Yes, what else but home?
It all depends on what you mean by home.
Of course he's nothing to us, any more
Than was the hound that came a stranger to us
Out of the woods, worn out upon the trail."

"Home is the place where, when you have to go there,
They have to take you in."

"I should have called it
Something you somehow haven't to deserve."

Warren leaned out and took a step or two,
Picked up a little stick, and brought it back
And broke it in his hand and tossed it by.
"Silas has better claim on us you think
Than on his brother? Thirteen little miles
As the road winds would bring him to his door.
Silas has walked that far no doubt to-day.
Why didn't he go there? His brother's rich,
A somebody—director in the bank."

"He never told us that."

"We know it though."

"I think his brother ought to help, of course.
I'll see to that if there is need. He ought of right
To take him in, and might be willing to—
He may be better than appearances.
But have some pity on Silas. Do you think
If he'd had any pride in claiming kin
Or anything he looked for from his brother,
He'd keep so still about him all this time?"

"I wonder what's between them."

"I can tell you.
Silas is what he is—we wouldn't mind him—
But just the kind that kinsfolk can't abide.
He never did a thing so very bad.
He don't know why he isn't quite as good
As anyone. He won't be made ashamed
To please his brother, worthless though he is."

"*I* can't think Si ever hurt anyone."

"No, but he hurt my heart the way he lay
And rolled his old head on that sharp-edged chair-back.
He wouldn't let me put him on the lounge.
You must go in and see what you can do.
I made the bed up for him there to-night.
You'll be surprised at him—how much he's broken.
His working days are done; I'm sure of it."

"I'd not be in a hurry to say that."

"I haven't been. Go, look, see for yourself.
But, Warren, please remember how it is:
He's come to help you ditch the meadow.
He has a plan. You mustn't laugh at him.
He may not speak of it, and then he may.
I'll sit and see if that small sailing cloud
Will hit or miss the moon."

It hit the moon.
Then there were three there, making a dim row,
The moon, the little silver cloud, and she.

Warren returned—too soon, it seemed to her, 169
Slipped to her side, caught up her hand and waited.

"Warren?" she questioned.

"Dead," was all he answered.

The Road Not Taken

This and the following poem are from *Mountain Interval* (1916).

Two roads diverged in a yellow wood,
And sorry I could not travel both
And be one traveler, long I stood
And looked down one as far as I could
To where it bent in the undergrowth;

Then took the other, as just as fair,
And having perhaps the better claim,
Because it was grassy and wanted wear;

Though as for that the passing there
Had worn them really about the same,

And both that morning equally lay
In leaves no step had trodden black.
Oh, I kept the first for another day!
Yet knowing how way leads on to way,
I doubted if I should ever come back.

I shall be telling this with a sigh
Somewhere ages and ages hence:
Two roads diverged in a wood, and I—
I took the one less traveled by,
And that has made all the difference.

The Oven Bird

There is a singer everyone has heard,
Loud, a mid-summer and a mid-wood bird,
Who makes the solid tree trunks sound again.
He says that leaves are old and that for flowers
Mid-summer is to spring as one to ten.
He says the early petal-fall is past
When pear and cherry bloom went down in showers
On sunny days a moment overcast;
And comes that other fall we name the fall.
He says the highway dust is over all.
The bird would cease and be as other birds
But that he knows in singing not to sing.
The question that he frames in all but words
Is what to make of a diminished thing.

Fire and Ice

This and the following two poems were published in *New Hampshire* (1923).

Some say the world will end in fire,
Some say in ice.
From what I've tasted of desire
I hold with those who favor fire.
But if it had to perish twice,
I think I know enough of hate
To say that for destruction ice
Is also great
And would suffice.

Stopping by Woods on a Snowy Evening

Whose woods these are I think I know.
His house is in the village though;
He will not see me stopping here
To watch his woods fill up with snow.

My little horse must think it queer
To stop without a farmhouse near
Between the woods and frozen lake
The darkest evening of the year.

He gives his harness bells a shake
To ask if there is some mistake.
The only other sound's the sweep
Of easy wind and downy flake.

The woods are lovely, dark and deep.
But I have promises to keep,
And miles to go before I sleep,
And miles to go before I sleep.

Nothing Gold Can Stay

Nature's first green is gold,
Her hardest hue to hold.
Her early leaf's a flower;
But only so an hour.
Then leaf subsides to leaf.
So Eden sank to grief,
So dawn goes down to day.
Nothing gold can stay.

Spring Pools

From the volume *West-Running Brook* (1928).

These pools that, though in forests, still reflect
The total sky almost without defect,
And like the flowers beside them, chill and shiver,
Will like the flowers beside them soon be gone,
And yet not out by any brook or river,
But up by roots to bring dark foliage on.

The trees that have it in their pent-up buds
To darken nature and be summer woods—
Let them think twice before they use their powers
To blot out and drink up and sweep away
These flowery waters and these watery flowers
From snow that melted only yesterday.

Neither Out Far Nor In Deep

This poem and the two following ones appeared in *A Further Range* (1936).

The people along the sand
All turn and look one way.
They turn their back on the land.
They look at the sea all day.

As long as it takes to pass
A ship keeps raising its hull;
The wetter ground like glass
Reflects a standing gull.

The land may vary more;
But wherever the truth may be—
The water comes ashore,
And the people look at the sea.

They cannot look out far.
They cannot look in deep.
But when was that ever a bar
To any watch they keep?

Desert Places

Snow falling and night falling fast, oh, fast
In a field I looked into going past,
And the ground almost covered smooth in snow,
But a few weeds and stubble showing last.

The woods around it have it—it is theirs.
All animals are smothered in their lairs.
I am too absent-spirited to count;
The loneliness includes me unawares.

And lonely as it is that loneliness
Will be more lonely ere it will be less—
A blanker whiteness of benighted snow
With no expression, nothing to express.

They cannot scare me with their empty spaces
Between stars—on stars where no human race is.
I have it in me so much nearer home
To scare myself with my own desert places.

Provide, Provide

The witch that came (the withered hag)
To wash the steps with pail and rag,
Was once the beauty Abishag,

The picture pride of Hollywood.
Too many fall from great and good
For you to doubt the likelihood.

Die early and avoid the fate.
Or if predestined to die late,
Make up your mind to die in state.

Make the whole stock exchange your own!
If need be occupy a throne,
Where nobody can call *you* crone.

Some have relied on what they knew;
Others on being simply true.
What worked for them might work for you.

No memory of having starred
Atones for later disregard,
Or keeps the end from being hard.

Better to go down dignified
With boughten friendship at your side
Than none at all. Provide, provide!

The Silken Tent

This and the following two poems are from *A Witness Tree* (1942).

She is as in a field a silken tent
At midday when a sunny summer breeze
Has dried the dew and all its ropes relent,
So that in guys it gently sways at ease,
And its supporting central cedar pole,
That is its pinnacle to heavenward
And signifies the sureness of the soul,
Seems to owe naught to any single cord,
But strictly held by none, is loosely bound
By countless silken ties of love and thought
To everything on earth the compass round,
And only by one's going slightly taut
In the capriciousness of summer air
Is of the slightest bondage made aware.

Come In

As I came to the edge of the woods,
Thrush music—hark!
Now if it was dusk outside,
Inside it was dark.

Too dark in the woods for a bird
By sleight of wing
To better its perch for the night,
Though it still could sing.

The last of the light of the sun
That had died in the west
Still lived for one song more
In a thrush's breast.

Far in the pillared dark
Thrush music went—
Almost like a call to come in
To the dark and lament.

But no, I was out for stars:
I would not come in.
I meant not even if asked;
And I hadn't been.

The Gift Outright

The land was ours before we were the land's.
She was our land more than a hundred years
Before we were her people. She was ours
In Massachusetts, in Virginia,
But we were England's, still colonials,
Possessing what we still were unpossessed by,
Possessed by what we now no more possessed.
Something we were withholding made us weak
Until we found out that it was ourselves
We were withholding from our land of living,
And forthwith found salvation in surrender.
Such as we were we gave ourselves outright
(The deed of gift was many deeds of war)
To the land vaguely realizing westward,
But still unstoried, artless, unenhanced,
Such as she was, such as she would become.

Directive

From *Steeple Bush* (1947).

Back out of all this now too much for us,
Back in a time made simple by the loss
Of detail, burned, dissolved, and broken off
Like graveyard marble sculpture in the weather,
There is a house that is no more a house
Upon a farm that is no more a farm
And in a town that is no more a town.
The road there, if you'll let a guide direct you
Who only has at heart your getting lost,
May seem as if it should have been a quarry—
Great monolithic knees the former town
Long since gave up pretense of keeping covered.
And there's a story in a book about it:
Besides the wear of iron wagon wheels
The ledges show lines ruled southeast northwest,
The chisel work of an enormous Glacier
That braced his feet against the Arctic Pole.
You must not mind a certain coolness from him
Still said to haunt this side of Panther Mountain.
Nor need you mind the serial ordeal
Of being watched from forty cellar holes
As if by eye pairs out of forty firkins.
As for the woods' excitement over you
That sends light rustle rushes to their leaves,
Charge that to upstart inexperience.
Where were they all not twenty years ago?
They think too much of having shaded out
A few old pecker-fretted apple trees.
Make yourself up a cheering song of how
Someone's road home from work this once was,
Who may be just ahead of you on foot
Or creaking with a buggy load of grain.
The height of the adventure is the height
Of country where two village cultures faded
Into each other. Both of them are lost.
And if you're lost enough to find yourself
By now, pull in your ladder road behind you
And put a sign up CLOSED to all but me.
Then make yourself at home. The only field
Now left's no bigger than a harness gall.
First there's the children's house of make believe,
Some shattered dishes underneath a pine,
The playthings in the playhouse of the children.
Weep for what little things could make them glad.
Then for the house that is no more a house,
But only a belilaced cellar hole,
Now slowly closing like a dent in dough.
This was no playhouse but a house in earnest.
Your destination and your destiny's
A brook that was the water of the house,
Cold as a spring as yet so near its source,
Too lofty and original to rage.
(We know the valley streams that when aroused
Will leave their tatters hung on barb and thorn.)
I have kept hidden in the instep arch
Of an old cedar at the waterside
A broken drinking goblet like the Grail
Under a spell so the wrong ones can't find it,
So can't get saved, as Saint Mark says they mustn't.
(I stole the goblet from the children's playhouse.)
Here are your waters and your watering place.
Drink and be whole again beyond confusion.

CARL SANDBURG [1878–1967]

By the time of his death at eighty-nine, Sandburg had won so many literary honors and had become such a fixture in the American pantheon as to seem almost beyond criticism. He was a twentieth-century reincarnation of the American dream, an admirer of Lincoln and Walt Whitman, and a spokesman of the workingman as the symbol of American democratic idealism. Back in 1914, however, before he had become known and when Harriet Monroe published "Chicago" and eight other brief, imagist poems in *Poetry: A Magazine of Verse,* his work was greeted with disdain as crude and impudent. At first, he was identified with the "Chicago Renaissance" of poetry and grouped with Vachel Lindsay and Edgar Lee Masters as one of the prairie poets, a new voice from the Midwest. Even more than Lindsay, Sandburg emulated Whitman's barbaric yawp and shared his sense of democratic brotherhood and his mystical vision of America as the nation of the common man, and he joined to this a proletarian feeling for the industrial worker and the field hand. Thus his poetry built a bridge over the widening gulf in twentieth-century America between rural and urban civilization. His verse is rich in the idiom of ordinary folk. Slang, folk songs, tall tales, and proverbial wisdom were converted into the stuff of his writing.

Born in Galesburg, Illinois, of hard-working, uneducated Swedish-immigrant parents, Sandburg was over thirty years old before he established himself as a poet. In *Always the Young Strangers* (1953), he described the first twenty years of his vagrant life. Leaving school after the eighth grade, he worked at an astonishing variety of odd jobs—milkman, porter in a barber shop, brickmaker, dishwasher, sign painter, stage hand, migrant field worker, salesman of stereoscopic views—as well as just plain hobo-riding the rails. In 1898 he served six months as a soldier in Puerto Rico, then failed to pass the examinations for West Point. Returning to Galesburg, he enrolled at Lombard College. He studied there for four years and was active in college journalism, but withdrew within months of getting his diploma and took to wandering once more, this time doing work as a police reporter in New York and elsewhere in the East. Writing poetry had been an ambition from his earliest years. In 1904 his first pamphlet saw the light when it was printed on a hand press by Sandburg's professor and admirer, Philip Wright of Lombard College.

Backtrailing to the Middle West, Sandburg became an organizer for the Social-Democratic party in Wisconsin and later private secretary to the socialist mayor of Milwaukee. There he met Lillian Steichen whom he married in 1908, and the couple were active in socialist politics and reformist activities. Still a drifter, Sandburg moved to Chicago and worked as a reporter for several liberal newspapers, but his poetry now began to appear in the magazines. Ezra Pound acknowledged him, and Ben Hecht noted his resemblance to Whitman's humanity and *vers libre. Chicago Poems,* his first important volume, appeared in 1916, followed in succeeding years by *Cornhuskers* (1918), *Smoke and Steel* (1920), *Slabs of the Sunburnt West* (1922), *Good Morning America* (1926), and his tribute to the common man *The People, Yes* (1936), a poetic grab-bag of folk wisdom written in the native humor tradition. He had long since begun collecting folk songs. Now to his poetry-readings he added music, accompanying his renditions on the guitar. In 1927 he published his collection as *The American Songbag.* Sandburg's prose works were largely journalistic, but his one masterwork was his life of Lincoln, a monumental study in six volumes divided into *The Prairie Years* (1926) and *The War Years* (1939). Other publications were several biographies, a number of children's books, and a long historical novel, *Remembrance Rock* (1948).

The newer criticism has not been easy with Sandburg. His weaknesses as a poet were a lack of serious craftsmanship, no recognizable intellectual growth from his earliest work, and a poetry based on feeling, with a somewhat limited range of sympathies from the political left. His best poetry came from his humanitarian and patriotic instincts, with little sense of form. He once said that people were uncertain "whether I was a poet, a biographer, a wandering troubadour with a guitar, a mid-west Hans Christian Andersen, or a historian of current events." But his place in American poetry will probably rest on a few poems written, as Louis Untermeyer pointed out, in two quite different moods—"the muscular, hard-hitting son of the streets, and his almost unrecognizable twin, the shadow painter, the haunter of mists, the lover of implications and overtones."

Further reading: *Complete Poems*, 1950. *Harvest Poems, 1910-1960*, 1960. Richard Crowder, *Carl Sandburg*, 1964.

Chicago

From *Chicago Poems* (1916), this poem appeared two years earlier in *Poetry* magazine. In its use of long free-verse lines with initial repetitions, it recalls Whitman's "Song of Myself." At first considered by conventional critics as crude and formless, it is now seen as having careful design in its closing restatement of the opening apostrophe to the city, but with the significant shift of attitude in the words "proud to be." The text for all the poems reprinted here is that of the *Complete Poems* (1950).

Hog Butcher for the World,
Tool Maker, Stacker of Wheat,
Player with Railroads and the Nations' Freight Handler;
Stormy, husky, brawling,
City of the Big Shoulders:

They tell me you are wicked and I believe them, for I have seen your painted women under the gas lamps luring the farm boys.
And they tell me you are crooked and I answer: Yes, it is true I have seen the gunman kill and go free to kill again.
And they tell me you are brutal and my reply is: On the faces of women and children I have seen the marks of wanton hunger.
And having answered so I turn once more to those who sneer at this my city, and I give them back the sneer and say to them:
Come and show me another city with lifted head singing so proud to be alive and coarse and strong and cunning.
Flinging magnetic curses amid the toil of piling job on job, here is a tall bold slugger set vivid against the little soft cities;
Fierce as a dog with tongue lapping for action, cunning as a savage pitted against the wilderness,
Bareheaded,
Shoveling,
Wrecking,
Planning,
Building, breaking, rebuilding,
Under the smoke, dust all over his mouth, laughing with white teeth,
Under the terrible burden of destiny laughing as a young man laughs,
Laughing even as an ignorant fighter laughs who has never lost a battle,
Bragging and laughing that under his wrist is the pulse, and under his ribs the heart of the people,
Laughing!

Laughing the stormy, husky, brawling laughter of Youth, half-naked, sweating, proud to be Hog Butcher, Tool Maker, Stacker of Wheat, Player with Railroads and Freight Handler to the Nation.

Fog

This famous imagist poem is an almost perfect example of the Japanese *haiku* in mood and in its approximation of the traditional seventeen-syllable form. It conforms also to the rules for imagist poetry laid down by T. E. Hulme and Ezra Pound in its use of common speech and in the single impression and fresh metaphor. From *Chicago Poems* (1916).

The fog comes
on little cat feet.
It sits looking
over harbor and city
on silent haunches
and then moves on.

Lost

This and the following poem are from *Chicago Poems* (1916).

Desolate and lone
All night long on the lake
Where fog trails and mist creeps,
The whistle of a boat
Calls and cries unendingly,
Like some lost child
In tears and trouble
Hunting the harbor's breast
And the harbor's eyes.

I Am the People, the Mob

I am the people—the mob—the crowd—the mass.
Do you know that all the great work of the world is done through me?
I am the workingman, the inventor, the maker of the world's food and clothes.
I am the audience that witnesses history. The Napoleons come from me and the Lincolns. They die. And then I send forth more Napoleons and Lincolns.
I am the seed ground. I am a prairie that will stand for much plowing. Terrible storms pass over me. I forget. The best of me is sucked out and wasted. I forget. Everything but Death comes to me and makes me work and give up what I have. And I forget.
Sometimes I growl, shake myself and spatter a few red drops for history to remember. Then—I forget.
When I, the People, learn to remember, when I, the People, use the lessons of yesterday and no longer forget who robbed me last year, who played me for a fool,—then there will be no speaker in all the world say the name: "The People," with any fleck of a sneer in his voice or any far-off smile of derision.
The mob—the crowd—the mass—will arrive then.

Cool Tombs

From *Cornhuskers* (1918).

When Abraham Lincoln was shoveled into the tombs, he forgot the copperheads and the assassin
. . . in the dust, in the cool tombs.

And Ulysses Grant lost all thought of con men and Wall Street, cash and collateral turned ashes
. . . in the dust, in the cool tombs.

Pocahontas' body, lovely as a poplar, sweet as a red haw in November or a pawpaw in May, did
she wonder? does she remember? . . . in the dust, in the cool tombs?

Take any streetful of people buying clothes and groceries, cheering a hero or throwing confetti and
blowing tin horns . . . tell me if the lovers are losers . . . tell me if any get more than the
lovers . . . in the dust . . . in the cool tombs.

Broken-face Gargoyles

From *Smoke and Steel* (1920).

All I can give you is broken-face gargoyles.
It is too early to sing and dance at funerals,
Though I can whisper to you I am looking for an undertaker humming a lullaby and throwing his
feet in a swift and mystic buck-and-wing, now you see it and now you don't.

Fish to swim a pool in your garden flashing a speckled silver,
A basket of wine-saps filling your room with flame-dark for your eyes and the tang of valley
orchards for your nose,
Such a beautiful pail of fish, such a beautiful peck of apples, I cannot bring you now.
It is too early and I am not footloose yet.

I shall come in the night when I come with a hammer and saw.
I shall come near your window, where you look out when your eyes open in the morning,
And there I shall slam together bird-houses and bird-baths for wingloose wrens and hummers to
live in, birds with yellow wing tips to blur and buzz soft all summer,
So I shall make little fool homes with doors, always open doors for all and each to run away when
they want to.
I shall come just like that even though now it is early and I am not yet footloose,
Even though I am still looking for an undertaker with a raw, windbitten face and a dance in his
feet.
I make a date with you (put it down) for six o'clock in the evening a thousand years from now.

All I can give you now is broken-face gargoyles.
All I can give you now is a double gorilla head with two fish mouths and four eagle eyes hooked on
a street wall, spouting water and looking two ways to the ends of the street for the new
people, the young strangers, coming, coming, always coming.

It is early.
I shall yet be footloose.

LANGSTON HUGHES [1902–1967]

"WHEN I WAS in the second grade," Langston Hughes wrote in *The Big Sea* (1940), "my grandmother took me to Lawrence to raise me. And I was unhappy for a long time, and very lonesome, living with my grandmother. Then it was that books began to happen to me, and I began to believe in nothing but books and the wonderful world in books—where if people suffered, they suffered in beautiful language, not in monosyllables, as we did in Kansas." The boy who began seeing life in that way was born in Joplin, Missouri. His parents separated when he was a small child, and in consequence he was shuttled from place to place, living for a time with his grandmother in Kansas and later with his mother in Illinois and Ohio. He went to high school in Cleveland, and began writing poems and short stories. After graduation, he spent a year in Mexico, where his father had settled and prospered. The father-son relationship was antagonistic, but the visit had at least one good result: the older man agreed to finance his son's education at Columbia.

Though Hughes left Columbia after a year, a new period of his life had begun. He worked at a number of odd jobs and then sailed for Africa as a seaman on a merchant ship. It was not only college he wanted to leave behind, he later explained, "but everything unpleasant and miserable out of my past: the memory of my father, the poverty and uncertainties of my mother's life, the stupidities of color-prejudice, black in a white world, the fear of not finding a job, the bewilderment of no one to talk to about things that trouble you, the feeling of always being controlled by others—by parents, by employers, by some outer necessity not your own. All those things I wanted to throw away. To be free of. To escape from. I wanted to be a man on my own, control my own life, and go my own way." Hughes of course never wholly escaped these things, but he did escape for a time the necessity of dealing with them. When he returned to the United States he continued at menial jobs, but he also continued doing what satisfied him most: writing. His poems began to attract notice, and he received help and encouragement from men like Vachel Lindsay, whom he met while working as a busboy. He returned to college (Lincoln University in Pennsylvania) on a scholarship, published a novel, and then began in earnest the writing career that continued for nearly forty years.

Hughes was more prolific than any other black American author has yet been. He produced a stream of writing that included ten volumes of poetry, sixty-six published short stories, four volumes of the "Simple" tales, two volumes of autobiography, and over twenty dramas, operas, musicals, and gospel song-plays. He was also responsible for numerous essays, songs, translations, and miscellaneous works of nonfiction; he edited several collections of the writings of other black authors; and at the time of his death he was planning still another volume of autobiography.

Hughes's poems will probably continue to be his most appealing work. Along with the short stories and the tales of Jesse Semple, known as "Simple," they form a nearly complete record of his insights into his world and personality. He wrote mainly of scenes familiar to all American blacks, of every background, but as an artist and a man Hughes returned most often to the world of Harlem. The poems reflect his changing views of a changing Harlem from the time he first went there in the early twenties. For Hughes, as for many others, the Harlem of the Negro Renaissance was for a while bright with a kind of success, and much of his early poetry reflects its sound and glitter. Later, the economic depression of the thirties exerted its influence on his work, as did the new militancy of the late fifties and sixties. Hughes knew as well as anyone the realities of a world where "it's easier to get dope / than to get a job," where a man "strikes up a tune all gay and bright and glad / To keep the gall from biting in his mouth."

In the "Simple" tales, the author creates a fully developed personality, one that appears closely to resemble his own. Hughes called him "my ace-boy," and said that "Simple might be laughing to keep from crying." Simple is one of those whose "incongruous humor," as Hughes put it, "becomes ironic laughter," and his irony in turn betrays a certain wisdom. People never see "beyond the *surface* of Negro color," Hughes once complained, and beneath Simple's wisdom may be sensed a deeper level of meaning. But as in Hughes himself, it remains only half-revealed.

Further reading: *Selected Poems,* 1959. *The Best of Simple,* 1957. James A. Emanuel, *Langston Hughes,* 1967.

American Heartbreak

This and the following poems are reprinted from *Selected Poems of Langston Hughes* (1959).

I am the American heartbreak—
Rock on which Freedom
Stumps its toe—
The great mistake
That Jamestown
Made long ago.

1926

As I Grew Older

It was a long time ago.
I have almost forgotten my dream.
But it was there then,
In front of me,
Bright like a sun—
My dream.

And then the wall rose,
Rose slowly,
Slowly,
Between me and my dream.
Rose slowly, slowly,
Dimming,
Hiding,
The light of my dream.
Rose until it touched the sky—
The wall.

Shadow.
I am black.

I lie down in the shadow.
No longer the light of my dream before me,
Above me.
Only the thick wall.
Only the shadow.

My hands!
My dark hands!
Break through the wall!
Find my dream!
Help me to shatter this darkness,
To smash this night,
To break this shadow
Into a thousand lights of sun,
Into a thousand whirling dreams
Of sun!

1926

Song for a Dark Girl

Way Down South in Dixie
  (Break the heart of me)
They hung my black young lover
  To a cross roads tree.

Way Down South in Dixie
  (Bruised body high in air)
I asked the white Lord Jesus
  What was the use of prayer.

Way Down South in Dixie
  (Break the heart of me)
Love is a naked shadow
  On a gnarled and naked tree.

1927

Dream Boogie

Good morning, daddy!
Ain't you heard
The boogie-woogie rumble
Of a dream deferred?

Listen closely:
You'll hear their feet
Beating out and beating out a—

  You think
  It's a happy beat?

Listen to it closely:
Ain't you heard
something underneath
like a—

What did I say?

Sure,
I'm happy!
Take it away!

Hey, pop!
Re-bop!
Mop!

Y-e-a-h!

1951

Harlem

What happens to a dream deferred?

Does it dry up
like a raisin in the sun?
Or fester like a sore—
And then run?
Does it stink like rotten meat?
Or crust and sugar over—
like a syrupy sweet?

Maybe it just sags
like a heavy load.

Or does it explode?

1951

EZRA POUND [1885-]

In 1949 Ezra Pound was awarded the Bollingen Foundation prize for the best book of poetry written in the preceding year. The choice was made by a committee of poets and scholars who were also Fellows of the Library of Congress, and the quasi-official nature of the award set off a controversy which tested some of the fundamental faiths of a democratic government as well as those of the world of art and letters. The prize committee found itself in the position of offering one of the nation's highest awards for artistic achievement to a man who had been indicted for treason, adjudged of unsound mind and unfit for trial, and committed to a federal hospital for the insane. Various imponderable issues were at stake: the relation of the state to a leading poet who had transgressed the bounds of loyalty; the relation between genius and sanity, between the artist and the established morality; and, equally perplexing, the value of the poetry itself *(The Pisan Cantos)* which combines technical brilliance and learning with bad public manners and dubious taste.

Pound's achievement as a poet, critic, friend of genius, tireless espouser of literary causes and nagging persuader of publishers and editors to recognize fresh talent is now almost unquestioned. From 1914 on, he gave advice to and gained hearings for writers and artists whose later reputations fully vindicated his judgment, among them Yeats, T. S. Eliot, James Joyce, D. H. Lawrence, Robert Frost, and Hart Crane. Pound's own poetry, though it lacked thematic control and firm direction, revealed remarkable skill in versification and in the transposition into English of an astonishing variety of tongues and rhythmic patterns, including Greek, Latin, Anglo-Saxon, Provençal, Chinese, Japanese, and French poetry. His literary stance was anti-romantic and anti-Victorian. At various times he was an exponent for Imagism, Vorticism, abstract art, the Japanese *haiku* and *tanka,* the Confucian ode, *vers libre,* the Italian *sestina,* and the French *ballade.* Like

T. S. Eliot, he created out of a prodigious memory for classical, medieval, and modern literature a new poetry and a live tradition. "There are few living poets," wrote W. H. Auden, "even if they are not conscious of having been influenced by Pound, who could say, 'My work would be exactly the same if Mr. Pound had never lived.' "

Born in Idaho and educated at Hamilton College and the University of Pennsylvania, where he took an M.A. in Romance Languages in 1906, Pound traveled and studied in London, Paris, and Italy before taking up a teaching position at Wabash College in Crawfordsville, Indiana. Four months later he was dismissed on a charge of immoral behavior, and his future career as an irreconcilable expatriate was begun. He went to London and established himself as the crusty monarch of other alienated writers. Between 1908 and 1920 he produced seven volumes of poetry, a number of books of essays, and a biography of the unknown abstractionist sculptor, Gaudier-Brzeska, who was one of his finds. He became the literary executor of the Fenollosa manuscripts of Oriental poetry, and from this important collection he issued translations of Nō-plays and other classical Japanese drama. He offered himself as foreign correspondent to Harriet Monroe's *Poetry* magazine, a role in which he made significant discoveries of unrecognized poetic talents: for example, he saw the originality of Eliot's "Prufrock" and had it published in *Poetry* and reviewed. From 1914 to 1920 Pound edited *Des Imagistes,* calling for a poetry without sentiment, cliché, or "emotional slither." He helped found *Blast,* a Vorticist periodical. His own work showed the influences of Yeats, Browning, and the Pre-Raphaelites, but he always disavowed literary labels for himself.

By 1920 Pound was announcing his final self-exile from English-speaking countries with a farewell to the "obstinate isle" (England) of his autobiographical poem, *Hugh Selwyn Mauberley.* Now in Paris, he continued his activities as impresario. In 1921 he "midwived" Eliot's *The Waste Land,* reducing the long manuscript by almost half and earning Eliot's gratitude in the dedication. The Paris period ended in 1924, and Pound lived thereafter in Italy, though he did not abandon his United States citizenship. In the seaside village of Rapallo, he pursued his lifetime project, *The Cantos,* the Joycean, free-associating, personalized epic into which he poured his store of literary references, his ironic humor, his prejudices, and his extreme economic and political doctrines. Usury and high interest rates became his *idée fixe.* He assumed a martyr's complex toward America and sought to save his native country from its errors by lecturing it on Marxist economic theories derived from the work of Sylvio Gesell and by rewriting history so as to place Mussolini side by side with Thomas Jefferson as a politicial leader. He even visited America in 1939 to press his views of "social credit," but he got such a poor reception that he shortly returned to Italy. In 1941, under the aegis of the Mussolini regime, he began the wartime series of anti-American broadcasts from Rome that led to his arrest on the charge of treason in 1945. Instead of being brought to trial, however, he was found legally insane by court psychiatrists, and placed in St. Elizabeth's Hospital, Washington, D.C., where he remained for twelve years. When in 1958 Pound was finally released through the efforts of Robert Frost, Eliot, and other fellow-poets and friends (some of whom had served on the Bollingen Prize committee), he again took up his life in Italy. Unbroken by his experience and still cocky, he lives at Merano, in the Italian Alps, with his wife, Dorothy Shakespear, whom he married in 1915.

Always a poseur, Pound in his palmier days affected flagrant costumery. In London he wore a monocle, a Byronic cape, and a Renaissance mustache and beard to set off flowing red hair. He possessed a pungent and acid humor directed against the establishment and wittily phrased in a kind of shorthand invective; he was a master of the devastating *bon mot.* But considered as poet and critic, he was the single most influential figure of the new poetry beginning about 1914. Along with Eliot, he effected a revolution in poetic standards and taste in the English-speaking world.

Further reading: *Personae: The Collected Poems of Ezra Pound,* 1926, reissued 1950. *Ezra Pound: Selected Poems,* ed. T. S. Eliot, 1928 and 1959. Hugh Kenner, *The Poetry of Ezra Pound,* 1951. John Espy, *Ezra Pound's Mauberley: A Study in Composition,* 1955.

The Return

From *Ripostes* (1912). Inspired by a French poem, *"J'ai feint que des dieux m'aient parlé,"* from Henri de Régnier's *Médailles d'Argile,* it indicates the influence of French symbolism upon Pound. He has compressed 51 lines into a brief poem, using only hints from the original, and has caught the classical tone and strophe form to perfection. A moment of weary exhaustion, following the excitements of the hunt, or a vision of rare beauty, is captured on canvas in these few lines.

See, they return; ah, see the tentative
Movements, and the slow feet,
The trouble in the pace and the uncertain
Wavering!

See, they return, one, and by one,
With fear, as half-awakened;
As if the snow should hesitate
And murmur in the wind,
        and half turn back;
These were the "Wing'd-with-Awe,"
        Inviolable.

Gods of the wingèd shoe!
With them the silver hounds,
        sniffing the trace of air!

Haie! Haie!
    These were the swift to harry;
These the keen-scented;
These were the souls of blood.

Slow on the leash,
        pallid the leash-men!

The River Merchant's Wife

A Letter

From *Cathay: Translations by Ezra Pound* (1915). When Pound received the manuscripts of Ernest Fenollosa containing many literal translations from the Chinese, he reworked them to catch both the visual and rhythmical qualities of the Chinese poems. This was from Li Po, a Chinese poet of the T'ang dynasty (*Rihaku* is the Japanese form of the name), and it illustrates Pound's theory of "the exact word" to render a visual image.

While my hair was still cut straight across my
        forehead
I played about the front gate, pulling flowers.
You came by on bamboo stilts, playing horse,
You walked about my seat, playing with blue plums.
And we went on living in the village of Chokan:
Two small people, without dislike or suspicion.

At fourteen I married My Lord you.
I never laughed, being bashful.
Lowering my head, I looked at the wall.
Called to, a thousand times, I never looked back.[1]

At fifteen I stopped scowling,
I desired my dust to be mingled with yours
For ever and for ever and for ever.
Why should I climb the lookout?

At sixteen you departed,
You went into far Ku-to-yen, by the river of swirling
        eddies,
And you have been gone five months.
The monkeys make sorrowful noise overhead.
You dragged your feet when you went out.
By the gate now, the moss is grown, the different
        mosses,
Too deep to clear them away!

The leaves fall early this autumn, in wind.
The paired butterflies are already yellow with
        August
Over the grass in the West garden;
They hurt me. I grow older.
If you are coming down through the narrows of the
        river Kiang,
Please let me know beforehand,
And I will come out to meet you
        As far as Cho-fu-sa.

By Rihaku.

In a Station at the Metro

From *Lustra* (1916). This brief imagistic poem was first written in 36 lines, then reduced to 18, then to just two. Pound's account of its inception and composition reveals much about his dislike for verbal excess, as well as his

The River Merchant's Wife. [1]A reference to the teasing of the bride in a Chinese wedding ceremony. Her eyes lowered, she makes no reply to bawdy remarks made to her.

interest in Japanese poetry and the association in his mind between poetry and painting.

Once on getting out of a "metro" train in Paris, Pound says, he saw a beautiful face, then others, a woman's and a child's, and he sought all that day for words to express his sudden and lovely emotion. None offered until at length there came to him an "equation"—not in speech, but in "little splotches of color." This he called an "image," or "vortex." An image he defined as "that which presents an intellectual and emotional complex in an instant of time." A vortex, similarly, comes to the consciousness in some "primary form." In this case it was felt in color as a single image, like the Japanese *hokku,* which Pound described as "one idea set on top of another." Like Japanese verse, vorticism is art before it has spread itself into flaccidity:

"The fallen blossom flies
back to its branch:
A butterfly."

That, Pound says, is the substance of a well-known *hokku.* His experience in Paris belonged to that kind of inspiration and should have gone into paint. "In a poem of this sort," he wrote, "one is trying to record the precise instant when a thing outward and objective transforms itself into a thing inward and subjective."

The apparition of these faces in the crowd;
Petals on a wet, black bough.

The Rest

This and the following poem, both from *Lustra* (1916), illustrate different viewpoints on the expatriate theme. The first reflects Pound's revolt against the materialism of America—the exiled artist. The second finds him in a more conciliatory mood toward his fellow American poet.

O helpless few in my country,
O remnant enslaved!

Artists broken against her,
Astray, lost in the villages,
Mistrusted, spoken against,

Lovers of beauty, starved,
Thwarted with systems,
Helpless against the control;

You who cannot wear yourselves out
By persisting to successes,
You who can only speak,
Who cannot steel yourselves into reiteration;

You of the finer sense,
Broken against false knowledge,
You who can know at first hand,
Hated, shut in, mistrusted:

Take thought:
I have weathered the storm,
I have beaten out my exile.

A Pact

I make a pact with you, Walt Whitman—
I have detested you long enough.
I come to you as a grown child
Who has had a pig-headed father;
I am old enough now to make friends.
It was you that broke the new wood,
Now is a time for carving.
We have one sap and one root—
Let there be commerce between us.

FROM *Hugh Selwyn Mauberley*

(Life and Contacts)

In this poem Pound again, in a far more complex way, deals with the theme of the exiled artist out of tune with the times. E.P. is Pound himself; Mauberley, a sort of alter ego of Pound and a minor artist, reflecting the failure of genuine devotion to art in a diseased age. The full poem contains eighteen separate sections, of which the first twelve and "Envoi" are reprinted here. The poem marks the final expatriation of Pound from America and England and the beginning of his life in Rapallo, Italy, where he was to spend many years of alienation. *Mauberley* depicts various phases of the poet's "life" and his literary "contacts"—both living and dead. The subject of the poet, ignored by his age and rebellious against it, is held together by a parallel with the journey of Odysseus through temptations and dangers toward his ultimate goal, "Penelope." It is a kind of summing up, midway in his career, of his relation to the aestheticism of the 1890's and the cultural sterility of the era of World War I. A further aim of Pound, here and elsewhere, was to purge poetry of excessively romantic diction and rhetoric and to restore the exact word—an aim of the Imagists and new poets of the 1912 movement—"to purify the dialect of the tribe." The epitaph to himself, quoted from a Carthaginian poet, suggest Pound's and Mauberley's withdrawal from the world and may be translated: "The heat calls us into the shade."

Vocat Aestus in Umbram

Nemesianus Ec. IV.

I
E. P. Ode Pour L'Election De Son Sepulchre[1]

For three years, out of key with his time,
He strove to resuscitate the dead art
Of poetry; to maintain "the sublime"
In the old sense. Wrong from the start—

Hugh Selwyn Mauberley. [1]"Ode on the Choice of his Tomb"—from an ode by Ronsard, French poet (1534-85).

No, hardly, but seeing he had been born
In a half-savage country, out of date;
Bent resolutely on wringing lilies from the acorn;
Capaneus; trout for factitious bait;[2]

Ἴδμεν γάρ τοι πάνθ', ὅσ' ἐνὶ Τροίῃ
Caught in the unstopped ear;
Giving the rocks small lee-way
The chopped seas held him, therefore, that year.

His true Penelope was Flaubert,
He fished by obstinate isles;
Observed the elegance of Circe's hair
Rather than the mottoes on sun-dials.[3]

Unaffected by "the march of events,"
He passed from men's memory in *l'an trentiesme*
De son eage; the case presents
No adjunct to the Muses' diadem.[4]

II

The age demanded an image
Of its accelerated grimace,
Something for the modern stage,
Not, at any rate, an Attic grace;

Not, not certainly, the obscure reveries
Of the inward gaze;
Better mendacities
Than the classics in paraphrase!

The "age demanded" chiefly a mould in plaster,
Made with no loss of time,
A prose kinema, not, not assuredly, alabaster
Or the "sculpture" of rhyme.

III

The tea-rose tea-gown, etc.
Supplants the mousseline of Cos,
The pianola "replaces"
Sappho's barbitos.

Christ follows Dionysus,
Phallic and ambrosial
Made way for macerations;
Caliban casts out Ariel.[5]

All things are a flowing,
Sage Heracleitus says;[6]
But a tawdry cheapness
Shall outlast our days.

Even the Christian beauty
Defects—after Samothrace;[7]
We see *τὸ καλὸν*[8]
Decreed in the market-place.

Faun's flesh is not to us,
Nor the saint's vision.
We have the Press for wafer;
Franchise for circumcision.

All men, in law are equals.
Free of Pisistratus,[9]
We choose a knave or an eunuch
To rule over us.

O bright Apollo,
τίν' ἄνδρα, τίν' ἥρωα, τίνα θεὸν[1]
What god, man, or hero
Shall I place a tin wreath upon!

IV

These fought in any case,
and some believing,
pro domo, in any case . . .

Some quick to arm,
some for adventure,
some from fear of weakness,
some from fear of censure,
some for love of slaughter, in imagination,

[2] Pound says that two opposing views of his career may be the heroic one (like Capaneus, one of the Seven Against Thebes, who was struck down by Zeus for his rebellion) or the ridiculous view (like that of a fish taking an artificial bait).

[3] The above two stanzas portray the poet as Odysseus who heard the Siren's song ("For we know all the things that are in Troy") and who has fished in "obstinate isles"—the many languages of Pound's study (and possibly a satiric reference to the British Isles)—and who admired the beauty of Circe's hair, despite its danger, instead of reading the clichés found on sundials. Penelope was Odysseus' wife who remained faithful to him for many years of his absence. Flaubert, French novelist and author of *Madame Bovary,* whom Pound admired for the purity of his diction—*le mot juste.*

[4] Pound points up the irony of contrast between his wasted life and that of François Villon whose *Grand Testament* began with the line "In the thirtieth year of my age."

[5] In above two stanzas "mousseline" is a costly silk from the Greek island of Cos, used in the tunic; "barbitos"—lyre; Dionysus—Greek god worshipped in phallic rites; Ariel and Caliban—ethereal beauty and bestial ignorance (see Shakespeare's *The Tempest*).

[6] Greek philosopher whose work emphasized the concept of an eternally changing universe.

[7] The Nike of Samothrace, a statue which Pound uses as the essence of classic beauty, as opposed to Christian beauty (or beauties?).

[8] "The Beautiful."

[9] Athenian dictator who enforced rigid conformity to the law.

[1] From Pindar's *Second Olympian Ode,* meaning: "What man, what hero, what god . . ." Pound disliked Pindar as the "prize windbag of all ages," and the lines which follow are contemptuous: i.e., a "tin" god.

learning later . . .
some in fear, learning love of slaughter;
Died some, pro patria,
non "dulce" non "et decor"[2] . . .
walked eye-deep in hell
believing in old men's lies, then unbelieving
came home, home to a lie,
home to many deceits,
home to old lies and new infamy;
usury age-old and age-thick
and liars in public places.
Daring as never before, wastage as never before.
Young blood and high blood,
fair cheeks, and fine bodies;

fortitude as never before,

frankness as never before,
disillusions as never told in the old days,
hysterias, trench confessions,
laughter out of dead bellies.

V

There died a myriad,
And of the best, among them,
For an old bitch gone in the teeth,
For a botched civilization,

Charm, smiling at the good mouth,
Quick eyes gone under earth's lid,

For two gross of broken statues,
For a few thousand battered books.

Yeux Glauques[3]

Gladstone was still respected,
When John Ruskin produced
"King's Treasuries"; Swinburne
And Rossetti still abused.

Foetid Buchanan lifted up his voice
When that faun's head of hers
Became a pastime for
Painters and adulterers.

The Burne-Jones cartons
Have preserved her eyes;
Still, at the Tate, they teach
Cophetua to rhapsodize;

Thin like brook-water,
With a vacant gaze.
The English Rubaiyat was still-born
In those days.

The thin, clear gaze, the same
Still darts out faun-like from the half-ruin'd face,
Questing and passive. . . .
"Ah, poor Jenny's case" . . .

Bewildered that a world
Shows no surprise
At her last maquero's
Adulteries.

"Siena Mi Fe; Disfecemi Maremma"[4]

Among the pickled foetuses and bottled bones,
Engaged in perfecting the catalogue,
I found the last scion of the
Senatorial families of Strasbourg, Monsieur Verog.[5]

For two hours he talked of Gallifet;[6]
Of Dowson; of the Rhymers' Club;
Told me how Johnson (Lionel) died
By falling from a high stool in a pub . . .[7]

But showed no trace of alcohol
At the autopsy, privately performed—
Tissue preserved—the pure mind
Arose toward Newman as the whisky warmed.

[2] That is, they died, but not as Horace wrote: *"Dulce et decorum est pro patria mori"* ("It is sweet and appropriate to die for one's country").

[3] This section returns to the 19th century suggesting that the beginning of the present "botched civilization" lay in the period of Gladstone and Ruskin. In the '90's pre-Raphaelite poets like Swinburne and Rossetti were indifferently received and harshly treated by critics like Buchanan who especially singled out "Jenny," a London harlot and the subject of a Rossetti poem. The girl with the *yeux glauques* ("glaucous eyes") was Elizabeth Siddal, an English model and later Rossetti's wife. Pound says she was painted by Burne-Jones in his "Cophetua and the Beggar Maid" (1884). FitzGerald translated the *Rubáiyát of Omar Khayyám* (1859).

[4] Dante's *Purgatorio.* Among those violently slain who repented before death was Pia de Tolomei whose husband, in love with another woman, had her murdered in his castle at Maremma. "Siena made me; Maremma unmade me."

[5] Identified as Victor Plarr, biographer of Dowson and author of a book of poems, *In the Dorian Mood* (1896).

[6] French general of the Franco-Prussian War at the battle of Sedan.

[7] Ernest Dowson and Lionel Johnson were poets of the '90's and members of the Rhymers' Club whom Pound admired. Strongly addicted to drugs and alcohol, both died young.

Dowson found harlots cheaper than hotels;
Headlam[8] for uplift; Image[9] impartially imbued
With raptures for Bacchus, Terpsichore and the Church.
So spoke the author of "The Dorian Mood,"
M. Verog, out of step with the decade,
Detached from his contemporaries,
Neglected by the young,
Because of these reveries.

Brennbaum[1]

The sky-like limpid eyes,
The circular infant's face,
The stiffness from spats to collar
Never relaxing into grace;

The heavy memories of Horeb, Sinai and the forty years,
Showed only when the daylight fell
Level across the face
Of Brennbaum "The Impeccable."

Mr. Nixon[2]

In the cream gilded cabin of his steam yacht
Mr. Nixon advised me kindly, to advance with fewer
Dangers of delay. "Consider
Carefully the reviewer.

"I was as poor as you are;
When I began I got, of course,
Advance on royalties, fifty at first," said Mr. Nixon,
"Follow me and take a column,
Even if you have to work free.

"Butter reviewers. From fifty to three hundred
I rose in eighteen months;
The hardest nut I had to crack
Was Dr. Dundas.[3]

"I never mentioned a man but with the view
Of selling my own works.
The tip's a good one, as for literature
It gives no man a sinecure.

[8] Rev. Stewart Headlam of Gloucester, who held festive parties with dancers and revelry for church and literary people.

[9] Professor Selwyn Image co-edited *The Hobby Horse*, literary periodical of the '90's.

[1] Literary portrait of a Jewish intellectual of the '90's. J. J. Espey suggests he was modeled after Max Beerbohm, though the Beerbohm family is not Jewish.

[2] Portrait of a literary man who publicly stated that his real interest in letters was to make money. A fictitious name, he was probably, in real life, the novelist, Arnold Bennett (see Studies by H. Kenner and J. J. Espey).

[3] A literary editor—a type name.

"And no one knows, at sight, a masterpiece.
And give up verse, my boy,
There's nothing in it."

* * * *

Likewise a friend of Bloughram's[4] once advised me:
Don't kick against the pricks,
Accept opinion. The "Nineties" tried your game
And died, there's nothing in it.

X

Beneath the sagging roof
The stylist has taken shelter,
Unpaid, uncelebrated,
At last from the world's welter

Nature receives him;
With a placid and uneducated mistress
He exercises his talents
And the soil meets his distress.

The haven from sophistications and contentions
Leaks through its thatch;
He offers succulent cooking;
The door has a creaking latch.[5]

XI

"Conservatrix of Milésien"
Habits of mind and feeling,
Possibly. But in Ealing
With the most bank-clerkly of Englishmen?

No, "Milesian" is an exaggeration.
No instinct has survived in her
Older than those her grandmother
Told her would fit her station.[6]

XII

"Daphne with her thighs in bark
Stretches toward me her leafy hands,"—
Subjectively. In the stuffed-satin drawing room
I await The Lady Valentine's[7] commands,

[4] See Browning's "Bishop Blougram's Apology" for Pound's original. He misspells "Blougram."

[5] The true artist is forced to retire from a commercial world and live in a Bohemian way in the country.

[6] These two stanzas are an ironic statement of the tame love-making of the modern woman, "conservatrix Milésien." The *Milésien Tales* were highly erotic stories by Aristides of Milesia, an ancient city of Asia Minor. The stories are mostly lost, as is their tradition of eroticism, in such "proper" surroundings as Ealing (or any other small town) near the city of London. Pound takes the quotation from Rémy de Gourmont's *Histoires Magiques* (1894) where, as J. J. Espey has shown, the meaning is frankly sexual.

[7] Pound compares the legend of Daphne, a nymph changed into a laurel tree while pursued by Apollo, to the modern society patroness of the artist—Lady Valentine. The quotation is from Gautier's "Le Château de Souvenir."

Knowing that my coat has never been
Of precisely the fashion
To stimulate, in her,
A durable passion;

Doubtful, somewhat, of the value
Of well-gowned approbation
Of literary effort,
But never of The Lady Valentine's vocation:

Poetry, her border of ideas,
The edge, uncertain, but a means of blending
With other strata
Where the lower and higher have ending:

A hook to catch the Lady Jane's attention,
A modulation toward the theatre,
Also, in case of revolution,
A possible friend and comforter.

* * * *

Conduct, on the other hand, the soul
"Which the highest cultures have nourished"
To Fleet St. where
Dr. Johnson flourished;

Beside this thoroughfare
The sale of half-hose has
Long since superseded the cultivation
Of Pierian roses.[8]

[8] The theme of patronage is carried further by the reference to Dr. Johnson, whose famous letter to Chesterfield marked the end of the earlier tradition of support for the artist by the wealthy. Johnson retired to Fleet Street, now a purely business section unconcerned with art. Haberdashery shops have taken the place of the worship of Muses, as once in Pieria, Greece, where art was celebrated. The quotation is a translation by Pound of a line from a poem by Laforgue, "*Complainte des Pianos qu'on Entend dans les Quartiers Aisés.*"

Envoi (1919)[9]

Go, dumb-born book,
Tell her that sang me once that song of Lawes:
Hadst thou but song
As thou hast subjects known,
Then were there cause in thee that should condone
Even my faults that heavy upon me lie,
And build her glories their longevity.

Tell her that sheds
Such treasure in the air,
Recking naught else but that her graces give
Life to the moment,
I would bid them live
As roses might, in magic amber laid,
Red overwrought with orange and all made
One substance and one colour
Braving time.

Tell her that goes
With song upon her lips
But sings not out the song, nor knows
The maker of it, some other mouth,
May be as fair as hers,
Might, in new ages, gain her worshippers,
When our two dusts with Waller's shall be laid,
Siftings on siftings in oblivion,
Till change hath broken down
All things save Beauty alone.

1920

[9] The "Farewell" sings the triumph of beauty and love over all material things in the accents of Edmund Waller's "Go, Lovely Rose!", set to music by the English composer Henry Lawes.

THOMAS STEARNS ELIOT [1888–1965]

THE POEMS OF T. S. Eliot, together with his critical essays written mainly in the 1920's, are now regarded as among the most influential literary documents of the twentieth century. An American by birth and early training, Eliot settled in England in 1914, became a British citizen in 1927, and declared himself a "royalist in politics, a classicist in literature, and an Anglo-Catholic in religion." His voice had a strongly British intonation, and in manner and dress he was the image of an upper-class English gentleman with a black bowler hat and an umbrella. Yet he always affirmed the fundamental American quality of his mind. His poetry and criticism adhered to cosmopolitan-international standards of thought, embracing a tradition from Homer to Dante and Shakespeare and including a special preference for the seventeenth-century English metaphysical poets and the French symbolists. Almost single-handedly Eliot was responsible for a revolutionary shift in the direction of critical taste. He substituted new literary gods for old and led an abrupt departure from the liberal-democratic conventions of the nineteenth century. From the first, his poetry pointed toward a new kind of authoritarianism. His technique was formed out of learned references and echoes from Ecclesiastes, Shakespeare, Dante, Homer, and classical myths mingling strangely with slang, scraps of popular music, parody, and scenes from high and low life in contemporary London. *The Waste Land,* "Gerontion," "Ash Wednesday," the *Four Quartets,* and other poems were baffling in their cultural and stylistic complexity, yet they somehow blended theme and meaning to produce a profound critique of the modern world.

Eliot's roots were thoroughly American. He was born in St. Louis of a family of New England ancestry going back to Massachusetts Puritans of the seventeenth century. His grandfather had moved to St. Louis to become a founder of the first Unitarian Church there and also of Washington University. Eliot attended preparatory school in New England and went on to Harvard, where he took his baccalaureate degree in 1910. His studies were in philosophy and literature, and he was an editor of the *Harvard Advocate* and class poet. Two further years at Harvard under the tutelage of Irving Babbitt, who taught him the New Humanist's distrust of romanticism, and under Josiah Royce and Santayana, gave Eliot further philosophical training both as a student and as a teaching assistant. After a year in Paris at the Sorbonne (he was much impressed by the lectures of Henri Bergson) he went to Germany on a fellowship. His travels were interrupted by the outbreak of war in Europe, and he moved to Merton College, Oxford. In 1915 he married Vivienne Haigh-Wood, a ballet dancer, from whom he was later separated. He tried private-school teaching, disliked it, and became a clerk in Lloyd's Bank, a position he kept from 1918 to 1925 while writing much of the poetry and criticism that made him famous.

Eliot was an editor of the *Egoist* from 1917 to 1920, then chief editor of the *Criterion,* in which *The Waste Land* appeared in 1922 after considerable blue-penciling by his friend and admirer, Ezra Pound, to whom the poem was dedicated. He became a member of the publishing firm of Faber and Faber, with which he was associated most of his life. His first critical volume, *The Sacred Wood* (1920), formulated the aesthetic philosophy underlying his poetry and established guidelines for the "new criticism" which emphasized analysis of the text of a poet's work rather than biography or antecedent literary influences. In this volume, too, he stated his belief that poetry was "not a turning loose of emotion, but an escape from emotion," and he defined his term "objective correlative" as "a set of objects, a situation, a chain of events which shall be the formula for that emotion." The direction of Eliot's thought was steadily toward the authority of the early Church and a mystical Christianity. He became increasingly ascetic and contemplative, searching for meaning and belief in Oriental religion, in the history of Christian martyrdom, and in the metaphysics of Christian doctrine.

In 1932 Eliot returned for the first time to America. His earlier associations now began to blend with his deracinated method in a series of poems on New England "places." These prefigured the volume often considered his mature masterpiece, *Four Quartets* (1943), based on the poet's memories of certain locales in America and England which became the starting points for his probings into the mysteries of time, history, eternity, and the meaning of life. Another development of this period was Eliot's turn from lyric poetry to the drama. From 1935 *(Murder in the Cathedral)* until about 1958 *(The Elder Statesman)* he experimented with a verse-drama which was concerned with psychological themes of modern relevance while still preserving something of the symbolic quality of older poetic plays. *Murder in the Cathedral* was the most powerfully conceived of these plays, based on the martyrdom of Thomas à Becket and containing a Greek-like chorus of commentary on the theme of guilt and temptation.

Eliot received the Nobel Prize for literature in 1948, with a citation recognizing his innovations in modern poetry. In 1957 he married his secretary, Valerie Fletcher. He lived his last years in relative seclusion, the elder statesman of a cult which was no longer a cult, and which continues to produce aftershocks in the literary world. Always interested in philosophy, he wrote many books of speculation on the meaning of such abstractions as culture, politics, and religion, but his greatest genius will probably continue to be manifest in his highly original poetic technique, his prophetic quality, and the germinal nature of his criticism. Eliot died in London in 1965.

Further reading: *The Complete Poems and Plays of T. S. Eliot,* 1952. *Collected Poems of T. S. Eliot, 1909-1962,* 1963. F. O. Matthiessen, *The Achievement of T. S. Eliot,* 3rd ed., 1958. Grover Smith, *T. S. Eliot's Poetry and Plays,* 1956.

The Love Song of J. Alfred Prufrock

First published in *Poetry* magazine in 1915, this poem was included in *Prufrock and Other Observations* (1917). The text used here, and for all the Eliot selections, is *T. S. Eliot: Collected Poems, 1909-1962* (1963).

S'io credesse che mia risposta fosse
A persona che mai tornasse al mondo,
Questa fiamma staria senza piu scosse.
Ma perciocche giammai di questo fondo
Non torno vivo alcun, s'i'odo il vero,
Senza tema d'infamia ti rispondo.[1]

Let us go then, you and I,[2]
When the evening is spread out against the sky
Like a patient etherised upon a table;
Let us go, through certain half-deserted streets,
The muttering retreats
Of restless nights in one-night cheap hotels
And sawdust restaurants with oyster-shells:
Streets that follow like a tedious argument
Of insidious intent
To lead you to an overwhelming question . . .

Prufrock. [1] Dante, *Inferno,* xxvii: "If I thought my answer were to one who ever could return to the world, this flame should shake no more [that is, my spirit would speak no more]; but since if what I hear be true, none ever did return alive from this depth, without fear of infamy I answer thee." Spoken by the shade of Guido de Montefeltro who, although he had become a monk regretting his warlike life, still betrayed the Colonna family to their enemy Pope Boniface VIII. Punished in Hades for his sins, he confesses his errors to Dante in this passage. How does the epigraph relate to Eliot's poem?

[2] Much of the meaning in this difficult, widely-reprinted poem depends upon the interpretation given the "you" and "I". They have been identified with Prufrock's outer and his inner selves, perhaps in Freudian language his ego (I) and id (you). The "I" or speaker is a timid, hypersensitive, self-scrutinizing anti-hero afraid to risk a decision (the "overwhelming question") or a proposal (to the woman in the poem called "one"). The "you" is his subconscious self, his buried emotional life, and his wishful existence. Note the prevalence of imagery denoting the twilight world: sleep, fog, cats, the sea—a world of instinct and passion. On the other hand, there are the details of his petty, dull, and insipid outward life, the "human voices" which destroy him just as surely as his submerged emotions. The use of sudden contrasts, ironic self-mockings, and reversals of mood mark the poem as written under the influence of the French symbolist poet, Jules Laforgue. Query: Why is the poem called a "love song"?

Oh, do not ask, "What is it?"
Let us go and make our visit.

In the room the women come and go
Talking of Michelangelo.

The yellow fog that rubs its back upon the window-panes,
The yellow smoke that rubs its muzzle on the window-panes
Licked its tongue into the corners of the evening,
Lingered upon the pools that stand in drains,
Let fall upon its back the soot that falls from chimneys,
Slipped by the terrace, made a sudden leap,
And seeing that it was a soft October night,
Curled once about the house, and fell asleep.

And indeed there will be time
For the yellow smoke that slides along the street,
Rubbing its back upon the window-panes;
There will be time, there will be time
To prepare a face to meet the faces that you meet;
There will be time to murder and create,
And time for all the works and days of hands
That lift and drop a question on your plate;
Time for you and time for me,
And time yet for a hundred indecisions,
And for a hundred visions and revisions,
Before the taking of a toast and tea.

In the room the women come and go
Talking of Michelangelo.

And indeed there will be time
To wonder, "Do I dare?" and, "Do I dare?"
Time to turn back and descend the stair,[3]
With a bald spot in the middle of my hair—
(They will say: "How his hair is growing thin!")
My morning coat, my collar mounting firmly to the chin,
My necktie rich and modest, but asserted by a simple pin—
(They will say: "But how his arms and legs are thin!")
Do I dare
Disturb the universe?

[3]The figure of the ascending stairway, frequently used by Eliot (cf. "Ash Wednesday," section 3, originally published under the title "The Summit of the Stairway") is drawn from Dante. In *Purgatorio*, xxvi, the Provençal poet Arnaut Daniel, who has sinned in lust, speaks to Dante: "Now I pray you, by that Goodness which guideth you to the summit of the stairway, be mindful in due time of my pain." In Dante, climbing the stairs marks various stages of purification of the soul in its ascent to Paradise. Here the emphasis is placed on *descending* the stair, perhaps indicative of Prufrock's lapse toward spiritual sterility and of the emptiness of modern society generally.

In a minute there is time
For decisions and revisions which a minute will reverse.

For I have known them all already, known them all:
Have known the evenings, mornings, afternoons,
I have measured out my life with coffee spoons;
I know the voices dying with a dying fall
Beneath the music from a farther room.
So how should I presume?

And I have known the eyes already, known them all—
The eyes that fix you in a formulated phrase,
And when I am formulated, sprawling on a pin,
When I am pinned and wriggling on the wall,
Then how should I begin
To spit out all the butt-ends of my days and ways?
And how should I presume?

And I have known the arms already, known them all—
Arms that are braceleted and white and bare
(But in the lamplight, downed with light brown hair!)
Is it perfume from a dress
That makes me so digress?
Arms that lie along a table, or wrap about a shawl.
And should I then presume?
And how should I begin?

. . . .

Shall I say, I have gone at dusk through narrow streets
And watched the smoke that rises from the pipes
Of lonely men in shirt-sleeves, leaning out of windows? . . .

I should have been a pair of ragged claws
Scuttling across the floors of silent seas.

. . . .

And the afternoon, the evening, sleeps so peacefully!
Smoothed by long fingers,
Asleep . . . tired . . . or it malingers,
Stretched on the floor, here beside you and me.
Should I, after tea and cakes and ices,
Have the strength to force the moment to its crisis?
But though I have wept and fasted, wept and prayed,
Though I have seen my head (grown slightly bald) brought in upon a platter,[4]
I am no prophet—and here's no great matter;
I have seen the moment of my greatness flicker,

[4]In Matthew xiv.3-11, King Herod orders John the Baptist to be beheaded and his head presented to the Queen's daughter, Salome, upon a platter. Note the various allusions to the dead returning to the world throughout the poem.

And I have seen the eternal Footman hold my coat, and snicker,
And in short, I was afraid.

And would it have been worth it, after all,
After the cups, the marmalade, the tea,
Among the porcelain, among some talk of you and me,
Would it have been worth while,
To have bitten off the matter with a smile,
To have squeezed the universe into a ball,
To roll it toward some overwhelming question,
To say: "I am Lazarus, come from the dead,[5]
Come back to tell you all, I shall tell you all"—
If one, settling a pillow by her head,
  Should say: "That is not what I meant at all.
  That is not it, at all."

And would it have been worth it, after all,
Would it have been worth while,
After the sunsets and the dooryards and the sprinkled streets,
After the novels, after the teacups, after the skirts that trail along the floor—
And this, and so much more?—
It is impossible to say just what I mean!
But as if a magic lantern threw the nerves in patterns on a screen:
Would it have been worth while
If one, settling a pillow or throwing off a shawl,
And turning toward the window, should say:
  "That is not it at all,
  That is not what I meant, at all."

. . . .

No! I am not Prince Hamlet, nor was meant to be;
Am an attendant lord, one that will do
To swell a progress, start a scene or two,
Advise the prince; no doubt, an easy tool,
Deferential, glad to be of use,
Politic, cautious, and meticulous;
Full of high sentence, but a bit obtuse;
At times, indeed, almost ridiculous—
Almost, at times, the Fool.[6]

I grow old . . . I grow old . . .
I shall wear the bottoms of my trousers rolled.

Shall I part my hair behind? Do I dare to eat a peach?
I shall wear white flannel trousers, and walk upon the beach.
I have heard the mermaids singing, each to each.

I do not think that they will sing to me.

I have seen them riding seaward on the waves
Combing the white hair of the waves blown back
When the wind blows the water white and black.

We have lingered in the chambers of the sea
By sea-girls wreathed with seaweed red and brown
Till human voices wake us, and we drown.

[5] Lazarus was restored to life from the tomb by a miracle of Christ (John x.1-44).

[6] The reference is to one of the minor characters in *Hamlet*, Rosencrantz or Guildenstern, or possibly Polonius who is full of windy and "obtuse" advice often spoken in "high sentence" or pompous language.

The Waste Land

First published in the *Criterion* in 1922 and shortly thereafter in book form as *The Waste Land* (1922), this has been one of the most discussed and most influential poems of our time. In it Eliot makes his most complex use of allusions, fitting together quotations from many sources in order to bring to bear upon his present statements numerous literary associations in a medley of parallels and ironic contrasts. Many of these references are explained in Eliot's own "Notes on 'The Waste Land,'" in his *Collected Poems.* Eliot stated: "Not only the title, but the plan and a good deal of the incidental symbolism of the poem were suggested by Miss Jessie L. Weston's book on the Grail legend: *From Ritual to Romance.*" He also used parts of Frazer's *The Golden Bough* for certain references to vegetation ceremonies. Miss Weston had connected the Fisher King of the fertility cults with the Grail legend in which the Lance and the Grail, the sacred vessel of the Last Supper, were sex symbols similar to those found in the Tarot pack. The interweaving of these symbols constitutes the central meaning of the poem, as they are applied to the modern waste land.

The poet is concerned with the problem of spiritual barrenness, or dryness—the loss of religion—but also with the remedies to this condition, represented variously as death and liberation, and as suffering followed by liberation and transformation. The inhabitants of the Waste Land, which is the present-day world, are at present incapable of these experiences. By mingling references to the Christian rites, to the legend of the Fisher King (a king who was sexually maimed and whose land was put under a curse and made a Waste Land), and to other fertility myths, the death act of liberation is further associated with the liberating of life-giving forces of water, which would relieve the drought of the Waste Land, while spiritual sterility is associated with sexual sterility. In the act of drowning—death by water—two of these symbols are fused into a major symbol. Other frequent symbols are roots, rocks, winter, spring, rubbish, rats, broken images, blindness, burial, bones, thunder. In addition, Eliot half-quotes or echoes many literary sources, especially Dante, Shakespeare, and the Bible.

"NAM Sibyllam quidem Cumis ego ipse oculis meis vidi in ampulla pendere, et cum illi pueri dicerent: Σίβυλλα τί θέλεις; respondebat illa: ἀποθανεῖν θέλω." [1]

For Ezra Pound
il miglior fabbro[2]

I. The Burial of the Dead

Here we see present day society, deprived of God's grace, sterile, torpid, reluctant to awaken from its torpidity (lines 1-7), and afraid of death. A series of literary, Biblical, and historical allusions add parallels to this spiritual situation, and develop the symbols outlined above. The spurious Madame Sosostris, like Madame de Tornquist, appears to be a fraudulent substitute for true spiritual vision. The last lines (60-70) suggest parallels between the Waste Land and London, Baudelaire's Paris, and Dante's Limbo, and sound the theme of the fertility myths.

April is the cruelest month, breeding
Lilacs out of the dead land,[3] mixing
Memory and desire, stirring
Dull roots with spring rain.
Winter kept us warm, covering
Earth in forgetful snow, feeding
A little life with dried tubers.
Summer surprised us, coming over the
    Starnbergersee
With a shower of rain; we stopped in the colonnade,
And went on in sunlight, into the Hofgarten,
And drank coffee, and talked for an hour.
Bin gar keine Russin, stamm' aus Litauen, echt
    deutsch.[4]
And when we were children, staying at the
    archduke's,
My cousin's, he took me out on a sled,
And I was frightened. He said, Marie,
Marie, hold on tight. And down we went.
In the mountains, there you feel free.
I read, much of the night, and go south in the
    winter.

What are the roots that clutch, what branches grow
Out of this stony rubbish? Son of man,
You cannot say, or guess, for you know only
A heap of broken images, where the sun beats,
And the dead tree gives no shelter, the cricket no
    relief,
And the dry stone no sound of water.[5] Only
There is shadow under this red rock,
(Come in under the shadow of this red rock),
And I will show you something different from either
Your shadow at morning striding behind you
Or your shadow at evening rising to meet you;
I will show you fear in a handful of dust.
    Frisch weht der Wind
    Der Heimat zu
    Mein Irisch Kind,
    Wo weilest du?[6]
"You gave me hyacinths first a year ago;
"They called me the hyacinth girl."
—Yet when we came back, late, from the Hyacinth
    garden,
Your arms full, and your face wet, I could not
Speak, and my eyes failed, I was neither
Living nor dead, and I knew nothing,
Looking into the heart of light, the silence.[7]
Oed' und leer das Meer.

Madame Sosostris,[8] famous clairvoyante,
Had a bad cold, nevertheless

The Waste Land. [1] The epigraph, from Petronius' *Satyricon,* tells of a dinner party presided over by the drunken Trimalchio in which he tells the guests he has seen the Cumaean Sybil (a prophetess) hanging in a cage with boys taunting her. When the boys cried: "Sybil, what do you want?" she replied: "I long to die." The Sybil had been granted eternal life, but had forgotten to ask for eternal youth. In Eliot's poem she is associated with Madame Sosostris, another false prophetess of the Waste Land, and Tiresias, the blind prophet, who has experienced love of both sexes. G. Williamson says: "Reduced to its simplest terms, *The Waste Land* is a statement of the experience that drives a character to the fortune-teller, the fortune that is told, and the unfolding of that fortune."

[2] The Italian dedication (taken from Dante's description of Arnaut Daniel) to Ezra Pound may be rendered: "the better craftsman." Eliot indicated his debt to Pound who helped him revise the poem.

[3] An ironic reversal of the Vegetation rites where spring restored the Fisher King to potency. Lilacs symbolized fertility in the primitive legends.

[4] Chance talk overheard in a café in Munich, reflecting post-World War I conditions in Germany: "I am not a Russian, but pure German from Lithuania."

[5] Cf. Ecclesiastes xii.5. The Preacher warns of the days to come when "the almond tree shall flourish, and the grasshopper shall be a burden, and the desire shall fail. . . . Then shall the dust return to the earth as it was."

[6] From Wagner's *Tristan und Isolde,* Act I: "Fresh blows the wind / To home, and now / My Irish maid / Where waitest thou?" The song is a light-hearted love song. But the passage about the hyacinth girl is an unhappy recollection of love, and the following quotation, "Oed' und leer das Meer" (Wide and empty the sea), is again from Wagner's opera, Act III, when Tristan is desolately watching for Isolde's return.

[7] Describes the effect of the vision of the Holy Grail (a symbol of purity and holiness) upon the impure.—G. Williamson.

[8] Madame Sosostris is an example of the way true prophecy has been perverted in the Waste Land to mere fortune-telling. The Tarot cards, once used for purposes of divining the coming of the waters, have now fallen into disuse, their significance forgotten. "The Hanged Man, a member of the traditional pack, fits my purpose in two ways: because he is associated in my mind with the Hanged God of Frazer, and because I associate him with the hooded figure in the passage of the disciples to Emmaus in Part V. The Phoenician Sailor and the Merchant appear later. . . . The Man with Three Staves (an authentic member of the Tarot pack) I associate, quite arbitrarily, with the Fisher King himself" (Eliot's note). He has also noted that "all the women are one woman," suggesting the connection between Marie (l. 15), Belladonna (l. 49), and the various ladies of "situations" in Part II.

Is known to be the wisest woman in Europe,
With a wicked pack of cards. Here, said she,
Is your card, the drowned Phoenician Sailor,
(Those are pearls that were his eyes.[9] Look!)
Here is Belladonna, the Lady of the Rocks,
The lady of situations.
Here is the man with three staves, and here the
 Wheel,
And here is the one-eyed merchant, and this card,
Which is blank, is something he carries on his back,
Which I am forbidden to see. I do not find
The Hanged Man. Fear death by water.
I see crowds of people, walking round in a ring.
Thank you. If you see dear Mrs. Equitone,
Tell her I bring the horoscope myself:
One must be so careful these days.

Unreal City,[10]
Under the brown fog of a winter dawn,
A crowd flowed over London Bridge, so many,
I had not thought death had undone so many.[11]
Sighs, short and infrequent, were exhaled,
And each man fixed his eyes before his feet.
Flowed up the hill and down King William Street
To where Saint Mary Woolnoth kept the hours
With a dead sound on the final stroke of nine.
There I saw one I knew, and stopped him crying:
 "Stetson![12]
"You who were with me in the ships at Mylae![13]
"That corpse you planted last year in your garden,
"Has it begun to sprout? Will it bloom this year?
"Or has the sudden frost disturbed its bed?
"Oh keep the Dog far hence, that's friend to men,
"Or with his nails he'll dig it up again![14]
"You! hypocrite lecteur!—mon semblable,—mon
 frère!"[15]

II. A Game of Chess[1]

The opening description of material ("synthetic") splendor and the references to the Philomela legend, which presents one aspect of the theme of suffering and transformation—of beauty out of violence, suffering, or death—lead to the two concluding scenes, in which modern sexual and intellectual sterility image the spiritual sterility of the modern world.

The Chair she sat in, like a burnished throne,[2]
Glowed on the marble, where the glass
Held up by standards wrought with fruited vines
From which a golden Cupidon peeped out
(Another hid his eyes behind his wing)
Doubled the flames of sevenbranched candelabra
Reflecting light upon the table as
The glitter of her jewels rose to meet it,
From satin cases poured in rich profusion;
In vials of ivory and colored glass
Unstoppered, lurked her strange synthetic perfumes,
Unguent, powdered, or liquid—troubled, confused
And drowned the sense in odors; stirred by the air
That freshened from the window, these ascended
In fattening the prolonged candle-flames,
Flung their smoke into the laquearia,
Stirring the pattern on the coffered ceiling.
Huge sea-wood fed with copper
Burned green and orange, framed by the colored
 stone,
In which sad light a carvèd dolphin swam.
Above the antique mantel was displayed
As though a window gave upon the sylvan scene
The change of Philomel, by the barbarous king
So rudely forced; yet there the nightingale
Filled all the desert with inviolable voice

[9] Shakespeare's *The Tempest*, I, ii, 398, in which there is also a death and transformation by drowning.

[10] Cleanth Brooks has shown that the "Unreal City" has become identified in the passage which follows with modern London, the waste land of medieval legends, Dante's Purgatory, and Baudelaire's Paris.

[11] Dante, *Inferno*, iii, 55-57. Watching a crowd of people crossing London Bridge, the poet is reminded of Dante, seeing a crowd in hell and saying: "So great a crowd of people. I had not believed Death had undone so many."

[12] Stetson is any man in the Waste Land, a friend of the protagonist, or one of the crowd of damned whom Dante recognizes in purgatory.

[13] At the battle of Mylae (260 B.C.) the Romans defeated the Carthaginians on the sea. By linking Stetson with the ancient battle, Eliot associates modern wars with all wars, equally destructive.

[14] In Webster's *The White Devil*, a play of murder, passion, fratricide, and betrayal, a mad woman, Cornelia, sings a dirge while burying her son who has been murdered by his brother: "But keep the wolf far thence that's foe to men/Or with his nails he'll dig them [i.e. the friendless bodies of unburied men] up again." Eliot alters "wolf" to "Dog," capitalizing the word to refer to Sirius, the Dogstar which, according to Frazer's *The Golden Bough*, appeared at its brightest at the rising of the waters of the Nile—hence a *friend* to man.

[15] In Baudelaire's *Les Fleurs du Mal*, the poet describes himself as sunk in suffering and boredom and addresses the reader as like himself: "You, hypocrite reader, my likeness, my brother!"

II. [1] The title and later references in this section to a chess-game draw on the play of Middleton, *Women Beware Women*, Act II, in which a mother is kept playing chess in one room while her daughter is being seduced in another. Middleton has both scenes take place at once on the stage and arranges for the mother to be checkmated at the same moment the daughter, Bianca, is seduced by the Duke. See ll. 137-8 below.

[2] Cf. Shakespeare's *Antony and Cleopatra*, II, ii, 199 ff., where Cleopatra is described lying in splendor on a barge "like a burnished throne" going to meet Antony. The lady is Belladonna, "lady of situations," a woman of the Waste Land. Eliot alters "barge" to "Chair," suggesting the constellation Cassiopeia, shaped like a chair, and named for a mythical queen whose vanity brought destruction to her country.

And still she cried, and still the world pursues,
"Jug Jug" to dirty ears.[3]
And other withered stumps of time
Were told upon the walls; staring forms
Leaned out, leaning, hushing the room enclosed.
Footsteps shuffled on the stair.
Under the firelight, under the brush, her hair
Spread out in fiery points
Glowed into words, then would be savagely still.

"My nerves are bad tonight. Yes, bad. Stay with me.
"Speak to me. Why do you never speak. Speak.
"What are you thinking of? What thinking? What?
"I never know what you are thinking. Think."

I think we are in rats' alley[4]
Where the dead men lost their bones.

"What is that noise?"
The wind under the door.
"What is that noise now? What is the wind doing?"
Nothing again nothing.[5]
"Do
"You know nothing? Do you see nothing? Do you remember
"Nothing?"

I remember
Those are pearls that were his eyes.[6]
"Are you alive or not? Is there nothing in your head?"

But
O O O O that Shakespeherian Rag—[7]
It's so elegant
So intelligent
"What shall I do now? What shall I do?"
"I shall rush out as I am, and walk the street
"With my hair down, so. What shall we do tomorrow?
"What shall we ever do?"
The hot water at ten.
And if it rains, a closed car at four.
And we shall play a game of chess,
Pressing lidless eyes and waiting for a knock upon the door.[8]

When Lil's husband got demobbed, I said—
I didn't mince my words, I said to her myself,
HURRY UP PLEASE ITS TIME[9]
Now Albert's coming back, make yourself a bit smart.
He'll want to know what you done with that money he gave you
To get yourself some teeth. He did, I was there.
You have them all out, Lil, and get a nice set,
He said, I swear, I can't bear to look at you.
And no more can't I, I said, and think of poor Albert,
He's been in the army four years, he wants a good time,
And if you don't give it him, there's others will, I said.
Oh is there, she said. Something o'that, I said.
Then I'll know who to thank, she said, and give me a striaght look.
HURRY UP PLEASE ITS TIME
If you don't like it you can get on with it, I said.
Others can pick and choose if you can't.
But if Albert makes off, it won't be for lack of telling.
You ought to be ashamed, I said, to look so antique
(And her only thirty-one.)
I can't help it, she said, pulling a long face,
It's them pills I took, to bring it off, she said.
(She's had five already, and nearly died of young George.)
The chemist said it would be all right, but I've never been the same.
You *are* a proper fool, I said.
Well, if Albert won't leave you alone, there it is, I said,
What you get married for if you don't want children?
HURRY UP PLEASE ITS TIME

[3] Ovid, *Metamorphoses*, VI, 412 ff., describes the rape of Philomela by King Tereus of Thrace who then cut out her tongue to silence her. The gods, in pity, changed her into a nightingale. The "jug-jug" was common in Elizabethan songs comparing a ravished woman to Philomela. "Tereu" is Tereus. See Part III, ll. 203-206.

[4] Another image of the sterility and spiritual death of the Waste Land.

[5] Echoes of lines in two of Webster's plays. In *The Devil's Law Case,* the dying Duke is saved when his enemy stabs him a second time, opening the wound to allow it to drain. The surgeon, hearing him breathe, says: "Is the wind in that doore still?"—i.e. is he still living? In *The White Devil*, when Flamineo is about to be killed, his murderer asks: "What dost think on?" and he replies: "Nothing; of nothing."

[6] Shakespeare's *The Tempest*. Cf. note to l. 48.

[7] Eliot parodies a popular song of 1912, "The Shakespearian Rag," by way of comment on the modern distortion of the classics.

[8] The lady, neurotic and bored, like the woman in Webster's play, waits for some similar experience or sign. Cf. note to "A Game of Chess" (Part II).

[9] The customary call of the bartender in a London pub telling the customers that it is closing time.

Well, that Sunday Albert was home, they had a hot gammon,[10]
And they asked me in to dinner, to get the beauty of it hot—
HURRY UP PLEASE ITS TIME
HURRY UP PLEASE ITS TIME
Goonight Bill. Goonight Lou. Goonight May. Goonight.
Ta ta. Goonight. Goonight.
Good night, ladies, good night, sweet ladies, good night, good night.[11]

III. The Fire Sermon[1]

Here references to Spenser's *Prothalamion* appear among scenes in the Waste Land and scenes along the twentieth-century river bank, and among references to *The Tempest,* to the nightingale, and to the Grail rituals and their vulgar parallel in the Mrs. Porter song. Then present-day society is adumbrated again in the dubious proposition of Mr. Eugenides and the scenes of sterile, casual, joyless lust, with interjections of the themes of spiritual regeneration (lines 257-65) and the songs of the Rhine Daughters. The conclusion cites the writings of Buddha and Augustine on lust.

The river's tent is broken: the last fingers of leaf
Clutch and sink into the wet bank. The wind
Crosses the brown land, unheard. The nymphs are departed.
Sweet Thames, run softly, till I end my song.[2]
The river bears no empty bottles, sandwich papers,
Silk handkerchiefs, cardboard boxes, cigarette ends
Or other testimony of summer nights. The nymphs are departed.
And their friends, the loitering heirs of city directors;
Departed, have left no addresses.
By the waters of Leman I sat down and wept[3] . . .
Sweet Thames, run softly till I end my song,
Sweet Thames, run softly, for I speak not loud or long.
But at my back in a cold blast I hear
The rattle of the bones, and chuckle spread from ear to ear.

A rat crept softly through the vegetation
Dragging its slimy belly on the bank
While I was fishing in the dull canal
On a winter evening round behind the gashouse
Musing upon the king my brother's wreck
And on the king my father's death before him.
White bodies naked on the low damp ground
And bones cast in a little low dry garret,
Rattled by the rat's foot only, year to year.
But at my back from time to time I hear[4]
The sound of horns and motors, which shall bring
Sweeney to Mrs. Porter in the spring.
O the moon shone bright on Mrs. Porter
And on her daughter
They wash their feet in soda water[5]
Et O ces voix d'enfants, chantant dans la coupole![6]

Twit twit twit
Jug jug jug jug jug jug
So rudely forc'd
Tereu

Unreal City
Under the brown fog of a winter noon
Mr. Eugenides, the Smyrna merchant
Unshaven, with a pocket full of currants
C.i.f. London:[7] documents at sight,
Asked me in demotic French
To luncheon at the Cannon Street Hotel
Followed by a weekend at the Metropole.

[10] A side of ham.

[11] In *Hamlet,* IV, v, 67 ff., Ophelia, out of her mind, sings songs and ends her wild talk with: "Good-night, ladies; good-night, sweet ladies; good-night, good-night."

III. [1] Cf. note to l. 308.

[2] Eliot compares the tawdry scene along the Thames river at present (c. 1920) with the beautiful wedding hymn of Edmund Spenser's "Prothalamion" (1596) describing a procession of nymphs on the same river. This is one line from the poem.

[3] In Psalm 137, the Jews weep over their exile from Palestine: "By the rivers of Babylon, there we sat down, yea, we wept, when we remembered Zion." Lac Leman is the French name for Lake Geneva in Switzerland.

[4] This and the following lines contain a medley of quotations and echoes. In Marvell's "To His Coy Mistress" are the lines: "But at my back I always hear/Time's winged chariot hurrying near." The poet urges his mistress not to be coy, as time is passing and beauty fades.

[5] Sweeney appears in a number of Eliot's poems, always as a type of the debased human animal, living on the lowest plane of sex and appetite. Mrs. Porter and her daughter were part of a vulgar ballad sung by soldiers in World War I. They kept a bawdy house in Cairo and practiced precautionary ablutions.

[6] From Paul Verlaine's sonnet, "Parsifal," which translated reads: "And, O those children's voices chanting in the dome!" In the story of the Grail, Parsifal, having resisted the seductions of the temptress, Kundry, is granted power to enter the castle and to heal the wounds of the king with his lance. First, however, his feet are washed by Kundry, whose taint is thus cleansed. Parsifal becomes king and receives the Holy Grail. In celebration, the children sing from the choir loft, as in the lines from Verlaine's poem. Eliot ironically places this line alongside the vulgar foot-washing of Mrs. Porter.

[7] "Carriage and insurance free to London"—a banking phrase. Mr. Eugenides, Eliot says in a note, "melts into the Phoenician sailor, and the latter is not wholly distinct from Ferdinand Prince of Naples." He is a "one-eyed businessman, making the protagonist an indecent proposal—thus bringing the ideas of lust, perversion, and profit into a single character.

At the violet hour, when the eyes and back
Turn upward from the desk, when the human engine waits
Like a taxi throbbing waiting,
I Tiresias,[8] though blind, throbbing between two lives,
Old man with wrinkled female breasts, can see
At the violet hour, the evening hour that strives
Homeward, and brings the sailor home from the sea,
The typist home at teatime, clears her breakfast, lights
Her stove, and lays out food in tins.
Out of the window perilously spread
Her drying combinations touched by the sun's last rays,
On the divan are piled (at night her bed)
Stockings, slippers, camisoles, and stays.
I Tiresias, old man with wrinkled dugs
Perceived the scene, and foretold the rest—
I too awaited the expected guest.
He, the young man carbuncular, arrives,
A small house agent's clerk, with one bold stare,
One of the low on whom assurance sits
As a silk hat on a Bradford millionaire.
The time is now propitious, as he guesses,
The meal is ended, she is bored and tired,
Endeavors to engage her in caresses
Which still are unreproved, if undesired.
Flushed and decided, he assaults at once;
Exploring hands encounter no defense;
His vanity requires no response,
And makes a welcome of indifference.
(And I Tiresias have foresuffered all
Enacted on this same divan or bed;
I who have sat by Thebes below the wall
And walked among the lowest of the dead.)
Bestows one final patronizing kiss,
And gropes his way, finding the stairs unlit . . .

She turns and looks a moment in the glass,
Hardly aware of her departed lover;
Her brain allows one half-formed thought to pass:
"Well now that's done: and I'm glad it's over."
When lovely woman stoops to folly[9] and
Paces about her room again, alone,
She smooths her hair with automatic hand,
And puts a record on the gramophone.

"This music crept by me upon the waters"[10]
And along the Strand, up Queen Victoria Street.
O City city, I can sometimes hear
Beside a public bar in Lower Thames Street,
The pleasant whining of a mandolin
And a clatter and a chatter from within
Where fishermen lounge at noon: where the walls
Of Magnus Martyr[11] hold
Inexplicable splendor of Ionian white and gold.

The river sweats[12]
Oil and tar
The barges drift
With the turning tide
Red sails
Wide
To leeward, swing on the heavy spar.
The barges wash
Drifting logs
Down Greenwich reach
Past the Isle of Dogs.
Weialala leia
Wallala leialala

Elizabeth and Leicester[13]
Beating oars

[8] Eliot explains that the two sexes meet in Tiresias, the blind prophet, and "what Tiresias *sees*, in fact, is the substance of the poem." He cites the passage from Ovid's *Metamorphoses*, III, 316 ff., describing how Tiresias was turned into a woman when he struck two serpents coupling in the forest. Seven years later, seeing the same serpents, he struck them again and was restored to manhood. Having experienced both sexes, he was asked to judge an argument between Jove and Juno as to which sex experienced most pleasure in love. When he supported Jove, Juno punished him by blinding him. Jove, in compensation, gave him the gift of prophecy. Thus Eliot places Tiresias in a central position in the poem, as one who sees the lust and boredom of such scenes as the following between the typist and the young man carbuncular. Tiresias lived at Thebes and was consulted where he sat near the wall. After his death he went to Hades, still retaining his powers, and was visited by Ulysses. Cf. ll. 245–46.

[9] The phrase comes from Goldsmith's *The Vicar of Wakefield* where Olivia, who has been seduced, sings a song which says that "when lovely woman stoops to folly" her only course is to die. Eliot makes the contrast between her thought and the resigned acceptance of the typist.

[10] This line, like ll. 48, 191–92, is from Shakespeare's *The Tempest:* "Sitting on a bank/ Weeping again the king my father's wrack/ This music crept by me upon the waters."

[11] Church built by Christopher Wren which was regarded by Eliot as having a particularly fine interior. It is located near London Bridge among bars where fishermen congregate.

[12] "The Song of the (three) Thames-daughters begins here. From line 292 to 306 inclusive they speak in turn. V. *Götterdämmerung,* III, i: the Rhine-daughters" (Eliot's note). In the Wagner opera the three Rhine-daughters lament the theft of their gold and the loss of the beauty of the river. The two introductory stanzas describe the Thames in the present time and at the time of Elizabeth.

[13] The scene depicted here is taken by Eliot from Froude's life of *Elizabeth,* Vol. I, Ch. iv, in which the Bishop De Quadra, ambassador of Spain to England, writes a letter recounting Elizabeth's love for Lord Robert Leicester. Eliot, in a note, quotes the De Quadra letter: "In the afternoon we were in a barge, watching the games on the river. (The queen) was alone with Lord Robert and myself on the poop, when they began to talk nonsense, and went so far that Lord Robert at last said, as I was on the spot there was no reason why they should not be married if the queen pleased." Eliot places this courtly flirtation alongside the three episodes of seduction which follow.

The stern was formed
A gilded shell
Red and gold
The brisk swell
Rippled both shores
Southwest wind
Carried down stream
The peal of bells
White towers
        Weialala leia
        Wallala leialala

"Trams and dusty trees.
Highbury bore me. Richmond and Kew
Undid me.[14] By Richmond I raised my knees
Supine on the floor of a narrow canoe."

"My feet are at Moorgate, and my heart
Under my feet. After the event
He wept. He promised 'a new start.'
I made no comment. What should I resent?"

"On Margate Sands.
I can connect
Nothing with nothing
The broken fingernails of dirty hands.
My people humble people who expect
Nothing."
        la la

To Carthage then I came[15]

Burning burning burning burning[16]
O Lord Thou pluckest me out
O Lord Thou pluckest

burning

[14] The three stanzas which follow are the laments of three daughters of the Thames, Waste Land counterparts of the Rhine maidens, recounting their love-experiences in the park and resort areas near London such as Richmond and Kew. Highbury is a working-class neighborhood; Moorgate, a warehouse district near London Bridge. Margate Sands is a popular resort on the Thames estuary.

[15] From St. Augustine's *Confessions,* III, i. Carthage, notorious as a place of lust and unholy love, was the scene of Augustine's confession of his own impure desires. He called on God's help to pluck him out of the cauldron of passions of his youth; cf. ll. 309–310.

[16] Eliot refers the reader to the complete text of Buddha's Fire Sermon from which this line is taken. The passage (which Eliot says "corresponds in importance to the Sermon on the Mount") calls for a life free from burning passions and all depravity and a dedication to the pure and holy way. Eliot adds: "The collocation of these two representatives of eastern and western asceticism, as the culmination of this part of the poem, is not an accident."

IV. Death by Water[1]

Death by water brings a kind of peace, brings an end to the lust, fear, and pettiness of the first three parts.

Phlebas the Phoenician, a fortnight dead,
Forgot the cry of gulls, and the deep sea swell
And the profit and loss.
                    A current under sea
Picked his bones in whispers. As he rose and fell
He passed the stages of his age and youth
Entering the whirlpool.
                    Gentile or Jew
O you who turn the wheel[2] and look to
        windward,
Consider Phlebas, who was once handsome and tall
        as you.

V. What the Thunder Said

We return here to the Christ theme. Christ is not yet risen, but there is thunder over distant mountains. Then the arid Waste Land is again described. Abruptly we are on the journey to Emmaus, with Christ risen but not yet seen or recognized. Nightmare visions of the decay of eastern Europe and of death and destruction and aridity lead to a vision of the long awaited rain. The thunder speaks the formula for the removal of the curse—give, sympathise, control. But this formula has not yet been satisfied by the society. The protagonist sits by his still arid plain, considering the task of setting at least his own affairs in order. He sees the problem clearly enough now, but the great task, the great ordeal lies before him. The last line signifies the peace to be achieved through the formula.

After the torchlight red on sweaty faces
After the frosty silence in the gardens[1]
After the agony in stony places
The shouting and the crying
Prison and palace and reverberation
Of thunder of spring over distant mountains
He who was living is now dead

IV. [1] Part IV is an adaptation of part of an earlier poem by Eliot in French called *Dans le Restaurant* in which an old waiter describes to a patron his earliest sex experience at the age of seven. The lecherous waiter is identified with Phlebas the Phoenician, the drowned sailor of Madame Sosostris' Tarot cards. Both are purified by death in water, as was the fertility god of the pagan rituals whose image was thrown into the water as a symbol of fertility and resurrected again in the spring. Here the waiter, Phlebas, and Ferdinand of *The Tempest* seem to represent the purification of the lust depicted in Part III.

[2] The wheel: one of the Tarot cards allegorizing the wheel of fortune. The god, Anubis, in the figure of a jackal, is represented on one side and Typhon, as a serpent, on the other. The wheel itself is turned by a figure holding a sword and a crown. The "whirlpool" is the mystery of man's fate, his death and cleansing in the water.

V. [1] The Garden of Gethsemane and that of Golgotha, scenes of Christ's betrayal, crucifixion, and burial.

We who were living are now dying
With a little patience

Here is no water but only rock[2]
Rock and no water and the sandy road
The road winding above among the mountains
Which are mountains of rock without water
If there were water we should stop and drink
Amongst the rock one cannot stop or think
Sweat is dry and feet are in the sand
If there were only water amongst the rock
Dead mountain mouth of carious teeth that cannot spit
Here one can neither stand nor lie nor sit
There is not even silence in the mountains
But dry sterile thunder without rain
There is not even solitude in the mountains
But red sullen faces sneer and snarl
From doors of mudcracked houses
If there were water
And no rock
If there were rock
And also water
And water
A spring
A pool among the rock
If there were the sound of water only
Not the cicada
And the dry grass singing
But sound of water over a rock
Where the hermit-thrush sings in the pine trees
Drip drop drip drop drop drop drop
But there is no water

Who is the third who walks always beside you?[3]
When I count, there are only you and I together
But when I look ahead up the white road
There is always another one walking beside you
Gliding wrapped in a brown mantle, hooded
I do not know whether a man or woman
—But who is that on the other side of you?

What is that sound high in the air[4]
Murmur of maternal lamentation

[2] The Journey to Emmaus begins here and proceeds through a bleak and sterile country in which images of the Waste Land and echoes of Ecclesiastes prevail, relieved only by the song of the thrush (l. 357) and the illusion of dripping water to relieve the drought.

[3] Christ, risen from the dead, accompanies the disciples to Emmaus, but (cf. Luke) "their eyes were holden that they should not know him." Eliot's note cites one of the Antarctic expeditions of the time in which the explorers, nearly exhausted, had a delusion that there was one more member with them than could actually be counted.

[4] This passage depicts a nightmare vision of the decay of eastern Europe, stimulated by Eliot's reading of Hermann Hesse's German book, *A Glimpse into Chaos.* The passage records the fear of Europe over the turbulence of the Russian revolution, presaging a general cracking up of western civilization.

Who are those hooded hordes swarming
Over endless plains, stumbling in cracked earth
Ringed by the flat horizon only
What is the city over the mountains
Cracks and reforms and bursts in the violet air
Falling towers
Jerusalem Athens Alexandria
Vienna London
Unreal

A woman drew her long black hair out tight[5]
And fiddled whisper music on those strings
And bats with baby faces in the violet light
Whistled, and beat their wings
And crawled head downward down a blackened wall
And upside down in air were towers
Tolling reminiscent bells, that kept the hours
And voices singing out of empty cisterns and exhausted wells.

In this decayed hole among the mountains
In the faint moonlight, the grass is singing
Over the tumbled graves, about the chapel[6]
There is the empty chapel, only the wind's home.
It has no windows, and the door swings,
Dry bones can harm no one.
Only a cock stood on the rooftree
Co co rico co co rico
In a flash of lightning. Then a damp gust
Bringing rain

Ganga was sunken,[7] and the limp leaves
Waited for rain, while the black clouds
Gathered far distant, over Himavant
The jungle crouched, humped in silence.

[5] This and the following lines contain a series of macabre images perhaps prophetic of the Day of Judgment, recalling Renaissance paintings of doomsday by various artists and also echoing lines from the twelfth chapter of Ecclesiastes. Cleanth Brooks identified the woman who plays music on her long hair with the earlier lady of "A Game of Chess" (ll. 132–33).

[6] To the theme of Christ's trial and agony is now added the strange initiation of the knight of the Grail legends approaching the Chapel Perilous and the Perilous Cemetery, prior to his vision of the Grail. In the legends recounted in *From Ritual to Romance* there is a storm and great wind, an altar in the chapel, a dead body upon it, sometimes candles and a Black Hand which extinguishes them. The significance of the knight's ordeal seems lost in the Waste Land where only an empty chapel is seen with a weathercock in place of the prophetic crowing of the cock in Luke xxii, which announces Peter's denial of Christ.

[7] The Ganges River, scene of the early vegetation myths, had its source in the Himalaya mountains ("Himavant"). The thunder and rain were the promise of spring and fertility over the land.

Then spoke the thunder
DA
Datta:[8] what have we given?
My friend, blood shaking my heart
The awful daring of a moment's surrender
Which an age of prudence can never retract
By this, and this only, we have existed[9]
Which is not to be found in our obituaries
Or in memories draped by the beneficent spider
Or under seals broken by the lean solicitor
In our empty rooms
DA
Dayadhvam: I have heard the key
Turn in the door once and turn once only[10]
We think of the key, each in his prison
Thinking of the key, each confirms a prison
Only at nightfall, ethereal rumors
Revive for a moment a broken Coriolanus[11]
DA
Damyata: The boat responded
Gaily, to the hand expert with sail and oar
The sea was calm, your heart would have responded
Gaily, when invited, beating obedient
To controlling hands

I sat upon the shore
Fishing,[12] with the arid plain behind me
Shall I at least set my lands in order?[13]
London Bridge is falling down falling down falling
down
Poi s'ascose nel foco che gli affina[14]
Quando fiam uti chelidon—O swallow swallow[15]
Le Prince d' Aquitaine à la tour abolie[16]
These fragments I have shored against my ruins
Why then Ile fit you. Hieronymo's mad againe.[17]
Datta. Dayadhvam. Damyata.
Shantih shantih shantih[18]

[8] "'Datta, dayadhvam, damyata' (Give, sympathise, control). The fable of the meaning of the Thunder is found in the *Brihadaranyaka—Upanishad,* 5, 1" (Eliot's note). Here the thunder speaks the words of the wise man to the protagonist of the poem: self-giving, self-control, and compassion.

[9] Giving in the Waste Land has been only a momentary surrender, that of sex, but even that is some evidence of existence and a sign of forgiveness.

[10] Eliot cites Dante, *Inferno,* xxxiii, 46: "And below I heard the door of the horrible tower being locked." Count Ugolino had been imprisoned by Archbishop Ruggieri along with his sons and grandsons. The door was locked and the keys of the prison thrown away. In the ninth circle of hell, he is found gnawing upon the head of the archbishop. The incident is a type of all self-imprisonment.

[11] Coriolanus of Shakespeare's play is another type of self-pride and self-interest told under the admonishment of "sympathise."

[12] Eliot's note here refers the reader to Miss Weston's chapter "The Fisher King" in which Christian symbolism of "fish," as applied to Christ and the Apostles, is likewise derived from pagan symbols in which the fish is a life-force and indicates fertility and birth.

[13] Cf. Isaiah xxxviii.1: "Set thine house in order: for thou shalt die, not live."

[14] The quotation is from Dante, *Purgatorio,* xxvi, 148. Arnaut Daniel, a Provençal poet who has sinned in lust, asks Dante to remember his pain when he ascends the stairway leading to Paradise. Then, says Dante, "he disappeared into the purifying flame."

[15] Eliot's note on the swallow refers to a medieval poem called "Pervigilium Veneris" ("Nights of Venus") in which all nature celebrates the time of love. The nightingale (symbol of betrayed beauty, and likewise the voiceless artist) cries: "When shall I be as the swallow and cease to be voiceless?"

[16] Eliot's note refers to a sonnet by Gerard de Nerval, entitled *El Desdichado,* in which the poet, bereaved and inconsolable, bewails his fate in melancholy strain and compares himself to "the Prince of Aquitaine in the ruined tower."

[17] From Thomas Kyd's *Spanish Tragedy,* an Elizabethan play of murder, madness, and violence, subtitled "Hieronymo Is Mad Again." Hieronymo is asked by the king to perform a play. Seeking revenge for the murder of his son, he says to the king: "Why, then, I'll fit you!"—i.e. he will do the play and revenge himself at the same time, which he does, but is killed himself during the performance. Earlier, he has bitten off his tongue to avoid confessing, an incident which recalls the theme of the nightingale, Philomela, referred to in the lines about the swallow, above.

[18] "Shantih. Repeated as here, a formal ending to an Upanishad. 'The Peace which passeth understanding' is our equivalent to this word" (Eliot's note).

The Metaphysical Poets

At the time this essay was written, the metaphysical poets were doubtless "more often named than read," and, when read, were likely to be abused with prejudice, or relished merely with "antiquarian affection." But for Eliot they counted importantly. If he could make them count importantly for others, he would be doing much toward justifying the difficult and complex poets of his own time.

Eliot rests his case for the seventeenth-century poets on their technique. He does not concern himself with their philosophical truth or ethical values. He concerns himself with the processes of historical change, only to argue that what happened should not have happened—that the virtue of these poets "ought not to have disappeared."

The essay first appeared in 1921. The text is from the volume *Homage to John Dryden* (1924).

By collecting these poems[1] from the work of a generation more often named than read, and more often read than profitably studied, Professor Grierson has rendered a service of some importance. Certainly the reader will meet with many poems already preserved in other anthologies, at the same time that he discovers poems such as those of Aurelian Townshend or Lord Herbert of Cherbury here included. But the function of such an anthology as this is neither that of Professor Saintsbury's admi-

The Metaphysical Poets. [1] *Metaphysical Lyrics and Poems of the Seventeenth Century:* Donne to Butler. Selected and edited, with an Essay, by Herbert J. C. Grierson (Oxford: Clarendon Press. London: Milford). [Eliot's note.]

rable edition of Caroline poets nor that of the *Oxford Book of English Verse.* Mr. Grierson's book is in itself a piece of criticism and a provocation of criticism; and we think that he was right in including so many poems of Donne, elsewhere (though not in many editions) accessible, as documents in the case of "metaphysical poetry." The phrase has long done duty as a term of abuse or as the label of a quaint and pleasant taste. The question is to what extent the so-called metaphysicals formed a school (in our own time we should say a "movement"), and how far this so-called school or movement is a digression from the main current.

Not only is it extremely difficult to define metaphysical poetry, but difficult to decide what poets practice it and in which of their verses. The poetry of Donne (to whom Marvell and Bishop King are sometimes nearer than any of the other authors) is late Elizabethan, its feeling often very close to that of Chapman. The "courtly" poetry is derivative from Jonson, who borrowed liberally from the Latin; it expires in the next century with the sentiment and witticism of Prior. There is finally the devotional verse of Herbert, Vaughan, and Crashaw (echoed long after by Christina Rossetti and Francis Thompson); Crashaw, sometimes more profound and less sectarian than the others, has a quality which returns through the Elizabethan period to the early Italians. It is difficult to find any precise use of metaphor, simile, or other conceit, which is common to all the poets and at the same time important enough as an element of style to isolate these poets as a group. Donne, and often Cowley, employ a device which is sometimes considered characteristically "metaphysical"; the elaboration (contrasted with the condensation) of a figure of speech to the farthest stage to which ingenuity can carry it. Thus Cowley develops the commonplace comparison of the world to a chess-board through long stanzas ("To Destiny"), and Donne, with more grace, in "A Valediction," the comparison of two lovers to a pair of compasses. But elsewhere we find, instead of the mere explication of the content of a comparison, a development by rapid association of thought which requires considerable agility on the part of the reader.

> On a round ball
> A workman that hath copies by, can lay
> An Europe, Afrique, and an Asia,
> And quickly make that, which was nothing, All,
> So doth each teare,
> Which thee doth weare,
> A globe, yea, world by that impression grow,
> Till thy tears mixt with mine doe overflow
> This world, by waters sent from thee, my heaven
> dissolved so.

Here we find at least two connections which are not implicit in the first figure, but are forced upon it by the poet: from the geographer's globe to the tear, and the tear to the deluge. On the other hand, some of Donne's most successful and characteristic effects are secured by brief words and sudden contrasts:

> A bracelet of bright hair about the bone,

where the most powerful effect is produced by the sudden contrast of associations of "bright hair" and of "bone." This telescoping of images and multiplied associations is characteristic of the phrase of some of the dramatists of the period which Donne knew: not to mention Shakespeare, it is frequent in Middleton, Webster, and Tourneur, and is one of the sources of the vitality of their language.

Johnson, who employed the term "metaphysical poets," apparently having Donne, Cleveland, and Cowley chiefly in mind, remarks of them that "the most heterogeneous ideas are yoked by violence together." The force of this impeachment lies in the failure of the conjunction, the fact that often the ideas are yoked but not united; and if we are to judge of styles of poetry by their abuse, enough examples may be found in Cleveland to justify Johnson's condemnation. But a degree of heterogeneity of material compelled into unity by the operation of the poet's mind is omnipresent in poetry. We need not select for illustration such a line as:

> Notre âme est un trois-mâts cherchant son Icarie;

we may find it in some of the best lines of Johnson himself ("The Vanity of Human Wishes"):

> His fate was destined to a barren strand,
> A petty fortress, and a dubious hand;
> He left a name at which the world grew pale,
> To point a moral, or adorn a tale—

where the effect is due to a contrast of ideas, different in degree but the same in principle, as that which Johnson mildly reprehended. And in one of the finest poems of the age (a poem which could not have been written in any other age), the "Exequy" of Bishop King, the extended comparison is used with perfect success: the idea and the simile become one in the passage in which the Bishop illustrates his impatience to see his dead wife, under the figure of a journey:

> Stay for me there; I will not faile
> To meet thee in that hollow Vale.
> And think not much of my delay;
> I am already on the way,
> And follow thee with all the speed
> Desire can make, or sorrows breed.
> Each minute is a short degree,
> And ev'ry houre a step towards thee.
> At night when I betake to rest,
> Next morn I rise nearer my West
> Of life, almost by eight houres sail,

Than when sleep breath'd his drowsy gale . . .
But heark! My Pulse, like a soft Drum
Beats my approach, tells Thee I come;
And slow howere my marches be,
I shall at last sit down by Thee.

(In the last few lines there is that effect of terror which is several times attained by one of Bishop King's admirers, Edgar Poe.) Again, we may justly take these quatrains from Lord Herbert's "Ode," stanzas which would, we think, be immediately pronounced to be of the metaphysical school:

So when from hence we shall be gone,
And be no more, nor you, nor I,
As one another's mystery,
Each shall be both, yet both but one.

This said, in her up-lifted face,
Her eyes, which did that beauty crown,
Were like two stars, that having faln down,
Look up again to find their place:

While such a moveless silent peace
Did seize on their becalmed sense,
One would have thought some influence
Their ravished spirits did possess.

There is nothing in these lines (with the possible exception of the stars, a simile not at once grasped, but lovely and justified) which fits Johnson's general observations on the metaphysical poets in his essay on Cowley. A good deal resides in the richness of association which is at the same time borrowed from and given to the word "becalmed"; but the meaning is clear, the language simple and elegant. It is to be observed that the language of these poets is as a rule simple and pure; in the verse of George Herbert this simplicity is carried as far as it can go—a simplicity emulated without success by numerous modern poets. The *structure* of the sentences, on the other hand, is sometimes far from simple, but this is not a vice; it is a fidelity to thought and feeling. The effect, at its best, is far less artificial than that of an ode by Gray. And as this fidelity induces variety of thought and feeling, so it induces variety of music. We doubt whether, in the eighteenth century, could be found two poems in nominally the same metre, so dissimilar as Marvell's "Coy Mistress" and Crashaw's "Saint Teresa"; the one producing an effect of great speed by the use of short syllables, and the other an ecclesiastical solemnity by the use of long ones:

Love, thou art absolute sole lord
Of life and death.

If so shrewd and sensitive (though so limited) a critic as Johnson failed to define metaphysical poetry by its faults, it is worth while to inquire whether we may not have more success by adopting the opposite method: by assuming that the poets of the seventeenth century (up to the Revolution) were the direct and normal development of the precedent age; and, without prejudicing their case by the adjective "metaphysical," consider whether their virtue was not something permanently valuable, which subsequently disappeared, but ought not to have disappeared. Johnson has hit, perhaps by accident, on one of their peculiarities, when he observes that "their attempts were always analytic"; he would not agree that, after the dissociation, they put the material together again in a new unity.

It is certain that the dramatic verse of the later Elizabethan and early Jacobean poets expresses a degree of development of sensibility which is not found in any of the prose, good as it often is. If we except Marlowe, a man of prodigious intelligence, these dramatists were directly or indirectly (it is at least a tenable theory) affected by Montaigne. Even if we except also Jonson and Chapman, these two were notably erudite, and were notably men who incorporated their erudition into their sensibility: their mode of feeling was directly and freshly altered by their reading and thought. In Chapman especially there is a direct sensuous apprehension of thought, or a re-creation of thought into feeling, which is exactly what we find in Donne:

in this one thing, all the discipline
Of manners and of manhood is contained;
A man to join himself with th' Universe
In his main sway, and make in all things fit
One with that All, and go on, round as it;
Not plucking from the whole his wretched part,
And into straits, or into nought revert,
Wishing the complete Universe might be
Subject to such a rag of it as he;
But to consider great Necessity.

We compare this with some modern passage:

No, when the fight begins within himself,
A man's worth something. God stoops o'er his head.
Satan looks up between his feet—both tug—
He's left, himself, i' the middle; the soul wakes
And grows. Prolong that battle through his life!

It is perhaps somewhat less fair, though very tempting (as both poets are concerned with the perpetuation of love by offspring), to compare with the stanzas already quoted from Lord Herbert's "Ode" the following from Tennyson:

One walked between his wife and child,
With measured footfall firm and mild,
And now and then he gravely smiled.
The prudent partner of his blood
Leaned on him, faithful, gentle, good,
Wearing the rose of womanhood.
And in their double love secure,
The little maiden walked demure,
Pacing with downward eyelids pure.
These three made unity so sweet,

My frozen heart began to beat,
Remembering its ancient heat.

The difference is not a simple difference of degree between poets. It is something which had happened to the mind of England between the time of Donne or Lord Herbert of Cherbury and the time of Tennyson and Browning; it is the difference between the intellectual poet and the reflective poet. Tennyson and Browning are poets, and they think; but they do not feel their thought as immediately as the odour of a rose. A thought to Donne was an experience; it modified his sensibility. When a poet's mind is perfectly equipped for its work, it is constantly amalgamating disparate experience; the ordinary man's experience is chaotic, irregular, fragmentary. The latter falls in love, or reads Spinoza, and these two experiences have nothing to do with each other, or with the noise of the typewriter or the smell of cooking; in the mind of the poet these experiences are always forming new wholes.

We may express the difference by the following theory: The poets of the seventeenth century, the successors of the dramatists of the sixteenth, possessed a mechanism of sensibility which could devour any kind of experience. They are simple, artificial, difficult, or fantastic, as their predecessors were; no less nor more than Dante, Guido Cavalcanti, Guinizelli, or Cino. In the seventeenth century a dissociation of sensibility set in, from which we have never recovered; and this dissociation, as is natural, was aggravated by the influence of the two most powerful poets of the century, Milton and Dryden. Each of these men performed certain poetic functions so magnificently well that the magnitude of the effect concealed the absence of others. The language went on and in some respects improved; the best verse of Collins, Gray, Johnson, and even Goldsmith satisfies some of our fastidious demands better than that of Donne or Marvell or King. But while the language became more refined, the feeling became more crude. The feeling, the sensibility, expressed in the "Country Churchyard" (to say nothing of Tennyson and Browning) is cruder than that in the "Coy Mistress."

The second effect of the influence of Milton and Dryden followed from the first, and was therefore slow in manifestation. The sentimental age began early in the eighteenth century, and continued. The poets revolted against the ratiocinative, the descriptive; they thought and felt by fits, unbalanced; they reflected. In one or two passages of Shelley's "Triumph of Life," in the second "Hyperion," there are traces of a struggle toward unification of sensibility. But Keats and Shelley died, and Tennyson and Browning ruminated.

After this brief exposition of a theory—too brief, perhaps, to carry conviction—we may ask, what would have been the fate of the "metaphysical" had the current of poetry descended in a direct line from them, as it descended in a direct line to them? They would not, certainly, be classified as metaphysical. The possible interests of a poet are unlimited; the more intelligent he is the better; the more intelligent he is the more likely that he will have interests: our only condition is that he turn them into poetry, and not merely meditate on them poetically. A philosophical theory which has entered into poetry is established, for its truth or falsity in one sense ceases to matter, and its truth in another sense is proved. The poets in question have, like other poets, various faults. But they were, at best, engaged in the task of trying to find the verbal equivalent for states of mind and feeling. And this means both that they are more mature, and that they wear better, than later poets of certainly not less literary ability.

It is not a permanent necessity that poets should be interested in philosophy, or in any other subject. We can only say that it appears likely that poets in our civilization, as it exists at present, must be *difficult*. Our civilization comprehends great variety and complexity, and this variety and complexity, playing upon a refined sensibility, must produce various and complex results. The poet must become more and more comprehensive, more allusive, more indirect, in order to force, to dislocate if necessary, language into his meaning. (A brilliant and extreme statement of this view, with which it is not requisite to associate oneself, is that of M. Jean Epstein, "La Poésie d'aujourd'hui.") Hence we get something which looks very much like the conceit—we get, in fact, a method curiously similar to that of the "metaphysical poets," similar also in its use of obscure words of simple phrasing.

O géraniums diaphanes, guerroyeurs sortilèges,
Sacrilèges monomanes!
Emballages, dévergondages, douches! O pressoirs
Des vendanges des grands soirs!
Layettes aux abois,
Thyrses au fond des bois!
Transfusions, représailles,
Relevailles, compresses et l'éternal potion,
Angélus! n'en pouvoir plus
De débâcles nuptiales! de débâcles nuptiales!

The same poet could write also simply:

Elle est bien loin, elle pleure,
Le grand vent se lamente aussi . . .

Jules Laforgue, and Tristan Corbière in many of his poems, are nearer to the "school of Donne" than any modern English poet. But poets more classical than they have the same essential quality of transmuting ideas into sensations, of transforming an observation into a state of mind.

Pour l'enfant, amoureux de cartes et d'estampes,
L'univers est égal à son vaste appétit.
Ah, que le monde est grand à la clarté des lampes!
Aux yeux du souvenir que le monde est petit!

In French literature the great master of the seventeenth century—Racine—and the great master of the nineteenth—Baudelaire—are in some ways more like each other than they are like any one else. The greatest two masters of diction are also the greatest two psychologists, the most curious explorers of the soul. It is interesting to speculate whether it is not a misfortune that two of the greatest masters of diction in our language, Milton and Dryden, triumph with a dazzling disregard of the soul. If we continued to produce Miltons and Drydens it might not so much matter, but as things are it is a pity that English poetry has remained so incomplete. Those who object to the "artificiality" of Milton or Dryden sometimes tell us to "look into our hearts and write." But that is not looking deep enough; Racine or Donne looked into a good deal more than the heart. One must look into the cerebral cortex, the nervous system, and the digestive tracts.

May we not conclude, then, that Donne, Crashaw, Vaughan, Herbert and Lord Herbert, Marvell, King, Cowley at his best, are in the direct current of English poetry, and that their faults should be reprimanded by this standard rather than coddled by antiquarian affection? They have been enough praised in terms which are implicit limitations because they are "metaphysical" or "witty," "quaint" or "obscure," though at their best they have not these attributes more than other serious poets. On the other hand, we must not reject the criticism of Johnson (a dangerous person to disagree with) without having mastered it, without having assimilated the Johnsonian canons of taste. In reading the celebrated passage in his essay on Cowley we must remember that by wit he clearly means something more serious than we usually mean today; in his criticism of their versification we must remember in what a narrow discipline he was trained, but also how well trained; we must remember that Johnson tortures chiefly the chief offenders, Cowley and Cleveland. It would be a fruitful work, and one requiring a substantial book, to break up the classification of Johnson (for there has been none since) and exhibit these poets in all their difference of kind and of degree, from the massive music of Donne to the faint, pleasing tinkle of Aurelian Townshend—whose "Dialogue Between a Pilgrim and Time" is one of the few regrettable omissions from the excellent anthology of Professor Grierson.

ROBINSON JEFFERS [1887-1962]

THE TYPICAL SITUATION in one of Jeffers' poetic narratives is somewhat as follows: A ranch isolated among the rocks and redwoods along the rugged coast of northern California is the scene of a human melodrama involving macabre and violent incidents—madness, idiocy, incest, murder, racial degeneracy. The story frequently follows the grim plot of a Greek tragedy or a Biblical tale and is played against a background of vast, silent boulders and remote stars. Jeffers' poetry is almost uniquely imbued with his chosen region of Carmel, where immemorial granite cliffs overlook the surf-beaten shore and circling hawks symbolize the wild, destructive nature of man. This non-human universe shaped Jeffers' bleakly nihilistic view of man as a fleeting excrescence on the boundless and inanimate indifference of stone and sea and stars. Incest, a prevailing theme in his poetry, is exploited both for its shock-effect and, more significantly, as a symbol of modern life turned inward, feeding upon itself, perverted and self-destructive. Civilization was for him a sickness, and he looked forward to a time when man, the animal "Christ was rumored to have died for," would be erased altogether from the earth.

Jeffers' intellectual roots lay in the scientific pessimism of the 1890's, with its view of the vastness of the solar system and the littleness of mankind, and in the social Freudianism of the 1920's, which saw only cause, not cure, in the depths of man's inner world.

His own life offers little explanation for the violence of his poetry or the disillusion of his thought. He was the son of a professor of Biblical language and literature in a theological seminary in Pittsburgh. His education included boarding schools in Germany and Switzerland, a term at the University of Pittsburgh, and a B.A. degree from Occidental College in Los Angeles where his family had moved. Another year abroad, at Zurich University, was followed by an M.A. in literature at the University of Southern California, then three years of medicine at the same institution and a year studying forestry at the University of Washington. Trained in modern languages and the classics, he decided to write poetry when, about 1914, he inherited a sufficient income to permit him to withdraw with his wife to Carmel, where he built with his own hands a tower of rocks, called "Tor House." Here he lived most of his life writing his poems in "Hawk Tower," now a literary landmark. He printed his first poems privately. His work shows little of the technical preoccupation or social concern of the expatriate poets of his generation. There is not much change or development in his themes or methods from decade to decade. Jeffers reiterated in succeeding volumes the same tragic episodes and the same dark reading of human destiny that marked his work from almost the beginning.

To understand and appreciate Jeffers one should read one or two of his long narrative poems such as *Roan Stallion, Tamar,* or *The Tower Beyond Tragedy,* all written about 1925. The first of these, based on a Monterey County incident of a man killed by his own horse, is a powerful story of lust and sexuality in which the primitive strength and beauty of a stallion are pitted against the pathological cruelty and viciousness of man. In *The Tower Beyond Tragedy* Jeffers reworked the Aeschylean drama of the revenge-murder of their mother by Orestes and Electra. Orestes, refusing the crown of his father, Agamemnon, and rejecting the love offered him by his sister, vows to cut humanity ("the wound which festers") out of his being and seek in the inanimate world a forgetfulness of the curse of humanity.

Jeffers' poetic style is one of great power and rhythmic beauty, the long blank-verse and free-verse lines embodying the natural speech tones of his characters, yet having a quality of tragic elevation and high seriousness. Among his important volumes are *Thurso's Landing* (1932), *Give Your Heart to the Hawks* (1933), and *Be Angry at the Sun* (1941). The dramatic aspect of his narratives was demonstrated when *The Tower Beyond Tragedy* and *Medea* (1946), the latter based on Euripides' play, were performed on the stage with Judith Anderson in the leading roles. A late poem, *The Cretan Woman* (1954), was similarly played on the stage. His shorter lyrics gave skillful expression to his misanthropy and his need to create poetry from gloom and defeat ("I can tell lies in prose"). On these and his longer narratives of classical and Biblical origins his reputation will continue to rest.

Further reading: *The Selected Poetry of Robinson Jeffers,* 1938. *Roan Stallion, Tamar, and Other Poems,* 1925. F. I. Carpenter, *Robinson Jeffers,* 1962.

To the Stone-Cutters

From *Tamar and Other Poems* (1924). To what extent do the closing lines qualify the earlier statement of man's "foredefeated" struggle against time? The text for this and the following poems is *The Selected Poetry of Robinson Jeffers* (1938).

Stone-cutters fighting time with marble, you foredefeated
Challengers of oblivion
Eat cynical earnings, knowing rock splits, records fall down,
The square-limbed Roman letters
Scale in the thaws, wear in the rain. The poet as well
Builds his monument mockingly;

For man will be blotted out, the blithe earth die, the brave sun
Die blind, his heart blackening:
Yet stones have stood for a thousand years, and pained thoughts found
The honey peace in old poems.

Hurt Hawks

From *Cawdor and Other Poems* (1928).

I

The broken pillar of the wing jags from the clotted shoulder,
The wing trails like a banner in defeat,
No more to use the sky forever but live with famine
And pain a few days: cat nor coyote
Will shorten the week of waiting for death, there is game without talons.
He stands under the oak-bush and waits
The lame feet of salvation; at night he remembers freedom
And flies in a dream, the dawns ruin it.
He is strong and pain is worse to the strong, incapacity is worse.
The curs of the day come and torment him
At distance, no one but death the redeemer will humble that head,
The intrepid readiness, the terrible eyes.
The wild God of the world is sometimes merciful to those
That ask mercy, not often to the arrogant.
You do not know him, you communal people, or you have forgotten him;
Intemperate and savage, the hawk remembers him;
Beautiful and wild, the hawks, and men that are dying, remember him.

II

I'd sooner, except the penalties, kill a man than a hawk; but the great redtail
Had nothing left but unable misery
From the bone too shattered for mending, the wing that trailed under his talons when he moved.
We had fed him six weeks, I gave him freedom,
He wandered over the foreland hill and returned in the evening, asking for death,
Not like a beggar, still eyed with the old
Implacable arrogance. I gave him the lead gift in the twilight.
What fell was relaxed,
Owl-downy, soft feminine feathers; but what
Soared: the fierce rush: the night-herons by the flooded river cried fear at its rising
Before it was quite unsheathed from reality.

Self-Criticism in February

From *Such Counsels You Gave to Me* (1937).

The bay is not blue but somber yellow
With wrack from the battered valley, it is speckled with violent foam-heads
And tiger-striped with long lovely storm-shadows.
You love this better than the other mask; better eyes than yours
Would feel the equal beauty in the blue.
It is certain you have loved the beauty of storm disproportionately.
But the present time is not pastoral, but founded

On violence, pointed for more massive violence: perhaps it is not
Perversity but need that perceives the storm-beauty.
Well, bite on this: your poems are too full of ghosts and demons,
And people like phantoms—how often life's are—
And passion so strained that the clay mouths go praying for destruction—
Alas, it is not unusual in life;
To every soul at some time. *But why insist on it? And now*
For the worst fault: you have never mistaken
Demon nor passion nor idealism for the real God.
Then what is most disliked in those verses
Remains most true. *Unfortunately. If only you could sing*
That God is love, or perhaps that social
Justice will soon prevail. I can tell lies in prose.

EDWARD ESTLIN CUMMINGS [1894-1962]

"e. e. cummings' " distrust of the capital letter, his tricks with ordinary syntax, his outrageous punctuation, verbal surgery, and typographical acrostics can be explained as sheer literary exhibitionism. But they were also a warning to the reader not to expect conformity to the established world of the Protestant ethic and Warren Harding's America. One of the disillusioned generation of World War I, Cummings shocked conservative critics and readers with his eccentric verses, richly spiced with eroticism and lightly veiled affronts to the conventional morality and Rotarian materialism of the time. As a literary expatriate in Paris, he painted, wrote poetry and plays, and moved in *avant garde* circles. Among his literary generation were Malcolm Cowley, William Carlos Williams, Ernest Hemingway, Gertrude Stein, and Marianne Moore. After the Paris years he lived for several decades in a studio in Patchin Place, Greenwich Village, writing for the *Dial* and enjoying the spectacle of life, the foreign people and restaurants, the colorful sights and sounds of New York City.

Edward Estlin Cummings was born in Cambridge, Massachusetts. His father taught English and the social sciences at Harvard, and later became minister of the Congregational Old South Church of Boston. The future poet graduated from Harvard in 1915, and in 1917 he went with the Norton Harjes Ambulance Corps to France, where he endured one of the memorable experiences of his life—three months in a grim hospital-prison, through the blundering of the French military intelligence. He was mistakenly suspected of pro-German sentiments, partly because of his friendship with William S. Brown, (another young American ambulance driver, who had run afoul of the French censors), and partly because of the defiantly ambiguous answers he gave to the questions put to him. Released through the efforts of his father and the U.S. Department of State, he wrote of the ordeal in *The Enormous Room* (1922), likening himself to John Bunyan, who came forth from prison to glimpse the Delectable Mountains. For Cummings the Delectable Mountains represented the freedom of the human spirit from coercion and misused authority of all kinds. Some years later, in 1930, he made a month's visit to Russia to see for himself the results of the Soviet experiment and came away disillusioned with Marxist totalitarianism, as described in his narrative-diary EIMI (pronounced "ay-mee" and meaning "Am").

Cummings' poetry ranged from clever experiments in word-play to exquisite love poems, and from razor-sharp thrusts at Philistinism to expressions of the joy of living and the pleasures of children, love, flowers, spring, and natural things. His poems competed, he said, "with roses and locomotives (not to mention acrobats Spring electricity Coney Island the fourth of July the eyes of mice and Niagara Falls)." Also "with elephants and El Greco." For him there were mainly two conflicting sets of values: "Is" and "Un." "Is-people" were kind, sensitive, innocent, accepting life and loving the natural, elemental gifts of life. On the other hand stood the world of "un" (or "non") which included all the social taboos and prohibitions, governmental restrictions, money, science, wars, and other authoritarian forces that stifle the individual human spirit. Cummings' shorthand titles suggest the originality and freshness of his outlook: *Tulips and Chimneys* (1923); *&* [And] (1925); *is 5* (1926); *VV* [ViVa] (1931); *no thanks* (1935); *1 x 1* [One Times One] (1944); and XAIPE [Hail!] (1950). Besides poetry he wrote *Him*, a play (1927), *Tom: A Ballet* (1935), and prose works on poetry and art. His taste in painting ran to surrealism and Picasso; his own drawings, oils, and sketches were impressionistic in style.

In 1952-53 Cummings was appointed Norton Professor at Harvard, where he delivered lectures to enthusiastic audiences. Later published as *i: six nonlectures* (1953), these described his own life and literary enthusiasms. He was a skillful and dramatic reader, and large crowds always gathered to hear the handsome, expressive poet, with his Harvard accent and face "like a sensitive truck driver," give the oral equivalent of his strangely printed, lower-case poems. He was awarded the Bollingen Prize in 1957 for his collected verse.

Further reading: *e. e. cummings: Poems, 1923-1954* (the most complete collection), 1954. *100 Selected Poems*, 1959. Charles Norman, *The Magic-Maker: E. E. Cummings*, 1958, rev. 1965.

in Just-

This and the two following poems are from Cummings' first volume, *Tulips and Chimneys* (1923). The text followed for all the Cummings selections is *Poems 1923-1954;* titles are supplied here from the table of contents in that edition.

in Just-
spring   when the world is mud-
luscious the little
lame balloonman

whistles   far   and wee

and eddieandbill come
running from marbles and
piracies and it's
spring

when the world is puddle-wonderful

the queer
old balloonman whistles
far   and   wee
and bettyandisbel come dancing

from hop-scotch and jump-rope and

it's
spring
and
the
goat-footed

balloonMan whistles
far
and
wee

Buffalo Bill's

Buffalo Bill's
defunct
who used to
ride a watersmooth-silver
stallion
and break onetwothreefourfive pigeonsjustlikethat
Jesus
he was a handsome man
and what i want to know is
how do you like your blueeyed boy
Mister Death

the Cambridge ladies

the Cambridge ladies who live in furnished souls
are unbeautiful and have comfortable minds
(also, with the church's protestant blessings
daughters, unscented shapeless spirited)
they believe in Christ and Longfellow, both dead,
are invariably interested in so many things—
at the present writing one still finds
delighted fingers knitting for the is it Poles?
perhaps. While permanent faces coyly bandy
scandal of Mrs. N and Professor D
. . . . the Cambridge ladies do not care, above
Cambridge if sometimes in its box of
sky lavender and cornerless, the
moon rattles like a fragment of angry candy

Spring is like a perhaps hand

From *&* [And] (1925).

Spring is like a perhaps hand
(which comes carefully
out of Nowhere)arranging
a window,into which people look(while
people stare
arranging and changing placing

carefully there a strange
thing and a known thing here)and

changing everything carefully

spring is like a perhaps
Hand in a window
(carefully to
and fro moving New and
Old things,while
people stare carefully
moving a perhaps
fraction of flower here placing
an inch of air there)and

without breaking anything.

"next to of course god america i

This and the following poem appeared in *is 5* (1926).

"next to of course god america i
love you land of the pilgrims' and so forth oh
say can you see by the dawn's early my
country 'tis of centuries come and go
and are no more what of it we should worry
in every language even deafanddumb
thy sons acclaim your glorious name by gorry
by jingo by gee by gosh by gum
why talk of beauty what could be more beautiful than these heroic happy dead
who rushed like lions to the roaring slaughter
they did not stop to think they died instead
then shall the voice of liberty be mute?"

He spoke. And drank rapidly a glass of water

my sweet old etcetera

my sweet old etcetera
aunt lucy during the recent

war could and what
is more did tell you just
what everybody was fighting

for,
my sister
isabel created hundreds
(and
hundreds)of socks not to
mention shirts fleaproof earwarmers

etcetera wristers etcetera, my
mother hoped that

i would die etcetera
bravely of course my father used
to become hoarse talking about how it was
a privilege and if only he
could meanwhile my

self etcetera lay quietly
in the deep mud et

cetera
(dreaming,
et
    cetera, of
Your smile
eyes knees and of your Etcetera)

r-p-o-p-h-e-s-s-a-g-r

From *no thanks* (1935).

                        r-p-o-p-h-e-s-s-a-g-r
            who
a)s w(e loo)k
upnowgath
            PPEGORHRASS
                                eringint(o-
aThe):l
        eA
            !p:
S   a
                        (r
rIvInG   .gRrEaPsPhOs)
                                        to
rea(be)rran(com)gi(e)ngly
,grasshopper;

this little bride & groom are

From *Collected Poems* (1938).

this little bride & groom are
standing)in a kind
of crown he dressed
in black candy she

veiled with candy white
carrying a bouquet of
pretend flowers this
candy crown with this candy

little bride & little
groom in it kind of stands on
a thin ring which stands on a much
less thin very much more

big & kinder of ring & which
kinder of stands on a
much more than very much
biggest & thickest & kindest

of ring & all one two three rings
are cake & everything is protected by
cellophane against anything(because
nothing really exists

plato told

This and the following poem were published in *1 x 1* [One Times One] (1944).

plato told

him:he couldn't
believe it(jesus

told him;he
wouldn't believe
it)lao

tsze
certainly told
him,and general
(yes

mam)
sherman;
and even
(believe it
or

not)you
told him:i told
him;we told him
(he didn't believe it,no

sir)it took
a nipponized bit of
the old sixth

avenue
el;in the top of his head:to tell

him

pity this busy monster,manunkind

pity this busy monster,manunkind,

not. Progress is a comfortable disease:
your victim(death and life safely beyond)

plays with the bigness of his littleness
—electrons deify one razorblade
into a mountainrange;lenses extend

unwish through curving wherewhen till unwish
returns on its unself.
A world of made
is not a world of born—pity poor flesh

and trees,poor stars and stones,but never this
fine specimen of hypermagical

ultraomnipotence. We doctors know

a hopeless case if—listen:there's a hell
of a good universe next door;let's go

WALLACE STEVENS [1879–1955]

A SUCCESSFUL LAWYER and corporation executive, a conservative Republican in politics, a quiet, dignified, middle-class citizen who became vice-president of the Hartford (Connecticut) Accident and Insurance Company—Wallace Stevens was a living, breathing contradiction of the stereotype of the aesthetic sensibility alienated from the commercial society of America. He came from a Pennsylvania Dutch family, his father a lawyer and a Presbyterian. The son was duly educated at Harvard and New York University law school, was admitted to the bar in 1904, and practiced law in New York until 1916, when he joined the legal department of the insurance company with which he remained throughout his life. Poetry, art, and philosophy came to dominate his interests, but he always kept his business and intellectual lives in separate, sealed compartments and was not at all disturbed over their possible contradiction. "It gives a man character as a poet to have daily contact with a job," he said. "I doubt whether I've lost a thing by leading an exceedingly regular and well-disciplined life." A collector of post-impressionist and abstract paintings, he read modern French poetry and criticism and the philosophy of Plato, Aristotle, Coleridge, and Henri Bergson. He was much influenced by the French philosopher Henri Focillon and the doctrine of ideas as form.

Reading Stevens' poetry, one is suddenly immersed in a world of aesthetics. The Jazz Age, the depression decade, World War II, social and economic problems are nowhere touched. No expatriate or patriot, he did not join the caravan of intellectuals leading to Paris or Rome. In 1923, at the age of forty-four, Stevens quietly produced his first volume of poetry, *Harmonium,* "new poetry" of the advanced order, complex, syntactically radical, symbolic, and richly dressed in sensuous coloration and gaudy rhetoric. The poems had ironic and clever titles frequently suggestive of the surrealist or impressionist paintings in his collection: "Anecdote of the Jar," "Study of Two Pears," "Two Figures in Dense Violet Night," "Lions in Sweden."

Stevens' first poems appeared in 1914 in *Poetry* magazine, where they won a prize. He won another award for his experimental, symbolic play, *Three Travellers at Sunrise,* written in the vein of the classical Japanese drama which had interested Yeats and Pound. With the publication of *Harmonium* Stevens was at once recognized as a serious artist, a poet's poet for whom art and aesthetics substituted for religious faith in a world without belief. In an age of disbelief, he said, "it is for the poet to supply the satisfactions of belief, in his measure and style." The prevailing theme of Stevens' poetry is poetry itself: its nature and function, the role of the poet, the creative mind, and the power of the imagination to define reality. His literary models were Laforgue, Mallarmé, Verlaine, and the symbolists in general, as well as Yeats, Pound, and Eliot. In art he admired Cézanne, Matisse, Manet, and, beyond them, Picasso.

The poetry defies rational explication. When Stevens speaks of reality, he means reality that has been made over by the imagination of the poet. His work as a whole is suggested by the title of his second volume, *Ideas of Order* (1935), where one immediately senses affinities with a version of the Coleridgean concept of the transcending imagination, but with a difference. Stevens discarded metaphysical teleology for a kind of existential view of the world of things. "It is Not Ideas About the Thing, But the Thing Itself," as one of his titles has it. The artist's imagination is the center of meaning. It is "the necessary angel" which can evolve beauty out of chaos and death. Poetry is "the supreme fiction." The poet is a Noble Rider or a Virile Youth because he "gives to life the supreme fictions without which we are unable to conceive of it." In his *The Necessary Angel,* a collection of prose essays given as lectures to academic audiences at Harvard, Yale, Princeton, and Columbia (and delivered in a dry, uninflected manner), Stevens offered an aesthetic rationale for his highly subjective view of the poet's function. Though provocative and learned, the volume is unsystematic, sending the reader once more back to the poetry itself with its vivid colors and its metaphoric parrots, peacocks, firecats, lions in Sweden, pears, and pineapples. There we find that the poet is both a philosopher and a clown, a "Comedian as the Letter C," a man with a blue guitar, or a connoisseur of chaos. He is a well-dressed gentleman with a monocle or a beard, or he is an artist placing gay colors on canvas in carefully arranged sequences. To understand Stevens is to suspend one's rational faculties and to read him as "pure poetry."

His work was officially acknowledged by the National Institute of Arts and Letters in 1946. He was awarded the Bollingen Prize in Poetry in 1950 and his *Collected Poems* (1954) received the Pulitzer Prize. Stevens died at Hartford, Connecticut, in 1955.

Further reading: *The Collected Poems of Wallace Stevens,* 1954. *Poems by Wallace Stevens,* ed. S. F. Morse, 1959. Robert Pack, *Wallace Stevens,* 1958. Frank Kermode, *Wallace Stevens,* 1960.

Domination of Black

This poem should be read as an impressionist painting in words. There is only meaning enough to be faintly suggestive of the idea of fear or impending disaster ("night," "I felt afraid"). The poet seems to be exploring the symbolic content of color and sound. It has been interpreted by Frank Doggett as a poetic expression of Stevens' theory that resemblances of things are a part of the structure of reality. Each color and figuration in the poem is repeated in another: colors and shadows, leaves and peacocks' tails, leaves and planets, etc. Stevens wrote: "Perhaps the whole field of connotation is based on resemblance." Thus reality is composed of a continuity based on the resemblances of dissimilar things.

This and the five following poems appeared in Stevens' first volume, *Harmonium* (1923). The text for all poems reprinted here is that of *The Collected Poems of Wallace Stevens* (1954).

At night, by the fire,
The colors of the bushes
And of the fallen leaves,
Repeating themselves,
Turned in the room,
Like the leaves themselves
Turning in the wind.
Yes: but the color of the heavy hemlocks
Came striding.
And I remembered the cry of the peacocks.

The colors of their tails
Were like the leaves themselves
Turning in the wind,
In the twilight wind.
They swept over the room,
Just as they flew from the boughs of the hemlocks
Down to the ground.
I heard them cry—the peacocks.
Was it a cry against the twilight
Or against the leaves themselves
Turning in the wind,
Turning as the flames
Turned in the fire,
Turning as the tails of the peacocks
Turned in the loud fire,
Loud as the hemlocks
Full of the cry of the peacocks?
Or was it a cry against the hemlocks?

Out of the window,
I saw how the planets gathered
Like the leaves themselves
Turning in the wind.
I saw how the night came,
Came striding like the color of the heavy hemlocks.
I felt afraid.
And I remembered the cry of the peacocks.

The Emperor of Ice-Cream

Stevens called this poem his favorite because it "wears a deliberately commonplace costume, and yet seems to me to contain something of the essential gaudiness of poetry." There have been many attempts to reduce it to rational meaning, though Stevens himself commented that it was not possible to attach a single, rational meaning to a thing (poem) which has its origin in the imagination. One may guess that ice-cream is a kind of universally accepted fact of life to which even death must yield its sway. It may represent the "be" while the funeral or wake taking place may only "seem." But details such as the roller of cigars, the wenches, and the boys cannot all be separately explained. It might be noted that the artistic arrangement of the body, with boys offering flowers wrapped in newspapers, closely parallels that of Manet's impressionist painting of a nude, "Olympia," which Stevens must have known.

Call the roller of big cigars,
The muscular one, and bid him whip
In kitchen cups concupiscent curds.
Let the wenches dawdle in such dress
As they are used to wear, and let the boys
Bring flowers in last month's newspapers.
Let be be finale of seem.
The only emperor is the emperor of ice-cream.

Take from the dresser of deal,
Lacking the three glass knobs, that sheet
On which she embroidered fantails once
And spread it so as to cover her face.
If her horny feet protrude, they come
To show how cold she is, and dumb.
Let the lamp affix its beam.
The only emperor is the emperor of ice-cream.

Sunday Morning

The religious-philosophical meditation in verse has been a tradition in English poetry from Milton and Donne through Wordsworth, Tennyson, Arnold, and others. "Sunday Morning" belongs in this tradition of high-serious reflections on ultimate questions of the meaning of existence. Robinson and Eliot are other exponents of the genre in the twentieth century. The reader should search the poem, therefore, for the basis of Stevens' philosophical ideas concerning man, nature, God, and the origins of belief.

In the course of the dialogue between the woman and the poet, there takes place a gradual and beautifully expressed triumph of a form of pantheistic naturalism over traditional Christian doctrine. Supernatural faith in a life beyond this life is rejected. Thus poetry, not God, is the supreme fiction and the ultimate reality. The poem is a working-out of Stevens' belief, stated in *The Necessary Angel* (1951), that the poet's function is "to make his imagination become the light in the minds of others." The "ring of men" worshipping the sun in a savage ritual (section VII) affirms Stevens' abandonment of formal religion for a primitive faith in nature as shaped and guided by the imagination of the poet.

I

Complacencies of the peignoir, and late
Coffee and oranges in a sunny chair,
And the green freedom of a cockatoo
Upon a rug mingle to dissipate
The holy hush of ancient sacrifice.
She dreams a little, and she feels the dark
Encroachment of that old catastrophe,
As a calm darkens among water-lights.
The pungent oranges and bright, green wings
Seem things in some procession of the dead,

Winding across wide water, without sound.
The day is like wide water, without sound,
Stilled for the passing of her dreaming feet
Over the seas, to silent Palestine,
Dominion of the blood and sepulchre.

II

Why should she give her bounty to the dead?
What is divinity if it can come
Only in silent shadows and in dreams?
Shall she not find in comforts of the sun,
In pungent fruit and bright, green wings, or else
In any balm or beauty of the earth,
Things to be cherished like the thought of heaven?
Divinity must live within herself:
Passions of rain, or moods in falling snow;
Grievings in loneliness, or unsubdued
Elations when the forest blooms; gusty
Emotions on wet roads on autumn nights;
All pleasures and all pains, remembering
The bough of summer and the winter branch.
These are the measures destined for her soul.

III

Jove in the clouds had his inhuman birth.
No mother suckled him, no sweet land gave
Large-mannered motions to his mythy mind.
He moved among us, as a muttering king,
Magnificent, would move among his hinds,
Until our blood, commingling, virginal,
With heaven, brought such requital to desire
The very hinds discerned it, in a star.
Shall our blood fail? Or shall it come to be
The blood of paradise? And shall the earth
Seem all of paradise that we shall know?
The sky will be much friendlier then than now,
A part of labor and a part of pain,
And next in glory to enduring love,
Not this dividing and indifferent blue.

IV

She says, "I am content when wakened birds,
Before they fly, test the reality
Of misty fields, by their sweet questionings;
But when the birds are gone, and their warm fields
Return no more, where, then, is paradise?"
There is not any haunt of prophecy,
Nor any old chimera of the grave,
Neither the golden underground, nor isle
Melodious, where spirits gat them home,
Nor visionary south, nor cloudy palm
Remote on heaven's hill, that has endured
As April's green endures; or will endure
Like her remembrance of awakened birds,
Or her desire for June and evening, tipped
By the consummation of the swallow's wings.

V

She says, "But in contentment I still feel
The need of some imperishable bliss."
Death is the mother of beauty; hence from her,
Alone, shall come fulfilment to our dreams
And our desires. Although she strews the leaves
Of sure obliteration on our paths,
The path sick sorrow took, the many paths
Where triumph rang its brassy phrase, or love
Whispered a little out of tenderness,
She makes the willow shiver in the sun
For maidens who were wont to sit and gaze
Upon the grass, relinquished to their feet.
She causes boys to pile new plums and pears
On disregarded plate. The maidens taste
And stray impassioned in the littering leaves.

VI

Is there no change of death in paradise?
Does ripe fruit never fall? Or do the boughs
Hang always heavy in that perfect sky,
Unchanging, yet so like our perishing earth,
With rivers like our own that seek for seas
They never find, the same receding shores
That never touch with inarticulate pang?
Why set the pear upon those river-banks
Or spice the shores with odors of the plum?
Alas, that they should wear our colors there,
The silken weavings of our afternoons,
And pick the strings of our insipid lutes!
Death is the mother of beauty, mystical,
Within whose burning bosom we devise
Our earthly mothers waiting, sleeplessly.

VII

Supple and turbulent, a ring of men
Shall chant in orgy on a summer morn
Their boisterous devotion to the sun,
Not as a god, but as a god might be,
Naked among them, like a savage source.
Their chant shall be a chant of paradise,
Out of their blood, returning to the sky;
And in their chant shall enter, voice by voice,
The windy lake wherein their lord delights,
The trees, like serafin, and echoing hills,
That choir among themselves long afterward.
They shall know well the heavenly fellowship

Of men that perish and of summer morn.
And whence they came and whither they shall go
The dew upon their feet shall manifest.

VIII

She hears, upon that water without sound,
A voice that cries, "The tomb in Palestine
Is not the porch of spirits lingering.
It is the grave of Jesus, where he lay."
We live in an old chaos of the sun,
Or old dependency of day and night,
Or island solitude, unsponsored, free,
Of that wide water, inescapable.
Deer walk upon our mountains, and the quail
Whistle about us their spontaneous cries;
Sweet berries ripen in the wilderness;
And, in the isolation of the sky,
At evening, casual flocks of pigeons make
Ambiguous undulations as they sink,
Downward to darkness, on extended wings.

Anecdote of the Jar

Not literally paraphrasable, this anecdote hints at the idea that the artist re-shapes nature and actually creates it. The jar, a still-life painting, placed in a "slovenly wilderness," dominates the landscape and alters its character.

I placed a jar in Tennessee,
And round it was, upon a hill.
It made the slovenly wilderness
Surround that hill.

The wilderness rose up to it,
And sprawled around, no longer wild.
The jar was round upon the ground
And tall and of a port in air.

It took dominion everywhere.
The jar was gray and bare.
It did not give of bird or bush,
Like nothing else in Tennessee.

Peter Quince at the Clavier

The story of Susanna and the Elders in the Old Testament Apocrypha tells of the judgment of Daniel against two lusting elders who spied on the beautiful and virtuous Susanna, wife of Joachim, while she was bathing. When she refused their advances, they were angry and told a lie that she had committed adultery with a young man. About to be executed, Susanna was saved by Daniel's proof of the perjury of the elders, who were then put to death. Stevens transforms this tale into a lyric praise of beauty—not Platonic beauty, but the immortality of "flesh." Here poetry is music, whereas it is more often allied with art in Stevens' aesthetic. Peter Quince, who plays music for Bottom's farce of Pyramus and Thisbe in *A Midsummer Night's Dream,* here adapts the keyboard of the clavier to the four parts of a sonata: exposition, development of the theme, recapitulation, and final coda. Note the shifts from rapid rhythms to slow ones, expressing different phases of the story.

I

Just as my fingers on these keys
Make music, so the selfsame sounds
On my spirit make a music, too.

Music is feeling, then, not sound;
And thus it is that what I feel,
Here in this room, desiring you,

Thinking of your blue-shadowed silk,
Is music. It is like the strain
Waked in the elders by Susanna.

Of a green evening, clear and warm,
She bathed in her still garden, while
The red-eyed elders, watching, felt

The basses of their beings throb
In witching chords, and their thin blood
Pulse pizzicati of Hosanna.

II

In the green water, clear and warm,
Susanna lay.
She searched
The touch of springs,
And found
Concealed imaginings.
She sighed,
For so much melody.

Upon the bank, she stood
In the cool
Of spent emotions.
She felt, among the leaves,
The dew
Of old devotions.

She walked upon the grass,
Still quavering.
The winds were like her maids,
On timid feet,
Fetching her woven scarves,
Yet wavering.

A breath upon her hand
Muted the night.
She turned—
A cymbal crashed,
And roaring horns.

III

Soon, with a noise like tambourines,
Came her attendant Byzantines.

They wondered why Susanna cried
Against the elders by her side;

And as they whispered, the refrain
Was like a willow swept by rain.

Anon, their lamps' uplifted flame
Revealed Susanna and her shame.

And then, the simpering Byzantines
Fled, with a noise like tambourines.

IV

Beauty is momentary in the mind—
The fitful tracing of a portal;
But in the flesh it is immortal.

The body dies; the body's beauty lives.
So evenings die, in their green going,
A wave, interminably flowing.
So gardens die, their meek breath scenting
The cowl of winter, done repenting.
So maidens die, to the auroral
Celebration of a maiden's choral.

Susanna's music touched the bawdy strings
Of those white elders; but, escaping,
Left only Death's ironic scraping.
Now, in its immortality, it plays
On the clear viol of her memory,
And makes a constant sacrament of praise.

Sea Surface Full of Clouds

I

In that November off Tehuantepec,
The slopping of the sea grew still one night
And in the morning summer hued the deck

And made one think of rosy chocolate
And gilt umbrellas. Paradisal green
Gave suavity to the perplexed machine

Of ocean, which like limpid water lay.
Who, then, in that ambrosial latitude
Out of the light evolved the moving blooms,

Who, then, evolved the sea-blooms from the clouds
Diffusing balm in that Pacific calm?
C'était mon enfant, mon bijou, mon âme.

The sea-clouds whitened far below the calm
And moved, as blooms move, in the swimming green
And in its watery radiance, while the hue

Of heaven in an antique reflection rolled
Round those flotillas. And sometimes the sea
Poured brilliant iris on the glistening blue.

II

In that November off Tehuantepec
The slopping of the sea grew still one night.
At breakfast jelly yellow streaked the deck

And made one think of chop-house chocolate
And sham umbrellas. And a sham-like green
Capped summer-seeming on the tense machine

Of ocean, which in sinister flatness lay.
Who, then, beheld the rising of the clouds
That strode submerged in that malevolent sheen,

Who saw the mortal massives of the blooms
Of water moving on the water-floor?
C'était mon frère du ciel, ma vie, mon or.

The gongs rang loudly as the windy booms
Hoo-hooed it in the darkened ocean-blooms.
The gongs grew still. And then blue heaven spread

Its crystalline pendentives on the sea
And the macabre of the water-glooms
In an enormous undulation fled.

III

In that November off Tehuantepec,
The slopping of the sea grew still one night
And a pale silver patterned on the deck

And made one think of porcelain chocolate
And pied umbrellas. An uncertain green,
Piano-polished, held the tranced machine

Of ocean, as a prelude holds and holds.
Who, seeing silver petals of white blooms
Unfolding in the water, feeling sure

Of the milk within the saltiest spurge, heard, then,
The sea unfolding in the sunken clouds?
Oh! C'était mon extase et mon amour.

So deeply sunken were they that the shrouds,
The shrouding shadows, made the petals black
Until the rolling heaven made them blue,

A blue beyond the rainy hyacinth,
And smiting the crevasses of the leaves
Deluged the ocean with a sapphire blue.

IV

In that November off Tehuantepec
The night-long slopping of the sea grew still.
A mallow morning dozed upon the deck

And made one think of musky chocolate
And frail umbrellas. A too-fluent green
Suggested malice in the dry machine

Of ocean, pondering dank stratagem.
Who then beheld the figures of the clouds
Like blooms secluded in the thick marine?

Like blooms? Like damasks that were shaken off
From the loosed girdles in the spangling must.
C'était ma foi, la nonchalance divine.

The nakedness would rise and suddenly turn
Salt masks of beard and mouths of bellowing,
Would—But more suddenly the heaven rolled

Its bluest sea-clouds in the thinking green,
And the nakedness became the broadest blooms,
Mile-mallows that a mallow sun cajoled.

V

In that November off Tehuantepec
Night stilled the slopping of the sea. The day
Came, bowing and voluble, upon the deck,

Good clown. . . . One thought of Chinese chocolate
And large umbrellas. And a motley green
Followed the drift of the obese machine

Of ocean, perfected in indolence.
What pistache one, ingenious and droll,
Beheld the sovereign clouds as jugglery

And the sea as turquoise-turbaned Sambo, neat
At tossing saucers—cloudy-conjuring sea?
C'était mon esprit bâtard, l'ignominie.

The sovereign clouds came clustering. The conch
Of loyal conjuration trumped. The wind
Of green blooms turning crisped the motley hue

To clearing opalescence. Then the sea
And heaven rolled as one and from the two
Came fresh transfigurings of freshest blue.

So-and-So Reclining on Her Couch

From *Transport to Summer* (1947). The light, satiric tone embodies a serious theme of the relation of the artist to his subject. The model is "half who made her," but she is likewise real—young, innocent, desirable—and even, as the mischievous last line hints, more to the sculptor than a geometric projection.

On her side, reclining on her elbow.
This mechanism, this apparition,
Suppose we call it Projection A.

She floats in air at the level of
The eye, completely anonymous,
Born, as she was, at twenty-one,

Without lineage or language, only
The curving of her hip, as motionless gesture,
Eyes dripping blue, so much to learn.

If just above her head there hung,
Suspended in air, the slightest crown
Of Gothic prong and practick bright,

The suspension, as in solid space,
The suspending hand withdrawn, would be
An invisible gesture. Let this be called

Projection B. To get at the thing
Without gestures is to get at it as
Idea. She floats in the contention, the flux

Between the thing as idea and
The idea as thing. She is half who made her.
This is the final Projection, C.

The arrangement contains the desire of
The artist. But one confides in what has no
Concealed creator. One walks easily

The unpainted shore, accepts the world
As anything but sculpture. Good-bye,
Mrs. Pappadopoulos, and thanks.

WILLIAM CARLOS WILLIAMS [1883-1963]

AN EARLY "modern" in American poetry whose work mingles influences from Whitman to James Joyce, Pound, and Stevens, William Carlos Williams evolved a method distinctively his own. He was by profession a physician, a pediatrician in a small New Jersey town. At the same time he was a dedicated and serious poet, a writer of fiction, prose essays, and criticism, who published nearly forty volumes during his busy lifetime.

Such an unusual combination of talent and energy could only be the product of an unusual background. Williams' father was English-born. He married a Puerto Rican woman of Dutch-Spanish-Jewish origins. Both parents had literary and artistic tastes. Williams grew up in Rutherford, New Jersey, and was educated at private schools in New York, Paris, and Geneva. He spoke fluent French and some Spanish, studied medicine at the University of Pennsylvania, interned in New York, and spent a year at Leipzig specializing in pediatrics before settling in Rutherford, where he married and brought up a family. There he remained, practicing his two professions of medicine and literature. While at Pennsylvania he had met Ezra Pound and Hilda Doolittle, both of whom were to influence Williams in the direction of Imagist verse. His first commercially published book, *The Tempers* (1913), with a favorable introductory note by Pound, showed him moving away from traditional rhyme and diction toward free verse and a subjective view of experience beyond realism.

Williams admired the symbolism of Pound and Stevens, yet he could not accept their separation of poetry from the lives of ordinary American people, especially the poor and disadvantaged whom he knew from his medical practice. Metaphysics did not interest him, but the drab and often ugly lives of his sick and suffering patients appealed to his sense of humanity and reality. He wanted to deal with local themes and native experience, as Whitman had, and at the same time he saw the value of re-ordering and arranging his material in new ways to provide freshness and immediacy. In this he was influenced by two artist-friends, Charles Sheeler and Charles Demuth, both of whom had absorbed into their still-life paintings and water colors the methods of cubism from the work of Marcel Duchamp. Color, texture, and light-and-shadow became Williams' ways of poetic expression. He admired Wallace Stevens for bringing a new artistic order out of the chaos of reality. His credo, "No ideas but in things," voiced the spirit of Imagism with its surface simplicity and attention to exactness of language.

Williams felt two needs, somewhat opposed: the need for a tight and controlled form, and the need to express the life around him accurately in the essential American speech-idiom. The poems in *Al Que Quiere!* (1917) and *Sour Grapes* (1921) showed several of his special preoccupations: experimentation with techniques of painting, a feeling for the beauty of harsh and shocking material, a neo-romanticism toward women and sexuality, and free verse. His natural lust for life often remained somewhat out of focus with his search for a poetry of order and symbol. In his long epic poem *Paterson*, written in five parts between 1946 and 1958, he made a valiant attempt to synthesize the disparate elements of his poetic creed. Williams invented the term "variable foot" to explain the rhythmic unit of this work, used to catch the feel of American speech and to break away from the syllable-counting of older English verse. *Paterson* is a poem about an industrial city fused with the entire life of a man—Williams himself, alias "Paterson." Something of Joyce's use of Dublin in *Ulysses* went into it, together with a whole congeries of material: the early origins and colonial history of Paterson, snatches of memories, letters, impressions of scenes and people, scandal, sex, and the symbolic use of the Passaic River running its course to the sea. It is an American epic for the twentieth century, as was *Leaves of Grass* for the nineteenth. Williams' conception is both grandiose and confusing.

Besides poetry, Williams produced novels and short fiction, a verse-play, translations from the Spanish, a volume of "improvisations" called *Kora in Hell* (1920), and a long *Autobiography,* rich in memorabilia of his literary friends and associations. His numerous awards included the Bollingen Poetry Award in 1953 and the National Book Prize for *Paterson, Book Two.* He also received several honorary degrees. His place in modern poetry lies somewhere between the symbolism of Pound or Stevens and the "American grain" of Whitman or Sandburg.

Further reading: *The Collected Earlier Poems of William Carlos Williams,* 1951. *Paterson,* 1963. Vivienne Koch, *William Carlos Williams,* 1950.

Portrait of a Lady

From *The Tempers* (1913). Williams refers to two French painters, Jean Antoine Watteau (1684-1721) and Jean Honoré Fragonard (1732-1806), both of whom did highly romantic, idealized scenes of courtly love in outdoor settings of lush beauty. Fragonard actually painted "The Swing" showing a lady in flowing dress kicking off her slipper while being swung high in the trees (appletrees?) and revealing her "thighs" in risqué fashion, for the period. In Watteau's famous "Embarkation for Cythera," showing couples setting out in a gilded boat for the island of love, there is a Venus-like figure standing amid the trees, her limbs enveloped in rose petals. The woman-tree image was also a pre-Raphaelite motif, perhaps recalling Provençal poetry. See Ezra Pound's "A Virginal."

The text used here is that of *The Collected Earlier Poems of William Carlos Williams* (1951).

Your thighs are appletrees
whose blossoms touch the sky.
Which sky? The sky
where Watteau hung a lady's
slipper. Your knees
are a southern breeze—or
a gust of snow. Agh! what
sort of man was Fragonard?
—as if that answered
anything. Ah, yes—below
the knees, since the tune
drops that way, it is
one of those white summer days,
the tall grass of your ankles
flickers upon the shore—
Which shore?—
the sand clings to my lips—
Which shore?
Agh, petals maybe. How
should I know?
Which shore? Which shore?
I said petals from an appletree.

Pastoral

From *Al Que Quiere!* [To Him Who Wants It] (1917).

When I was younger
it was plain to me
I must make something of myself.
Older now
I walk back streets
admiring the houses
of the very poor:
roof out of line with sides
the yards cluttered
with old chicken wire, ashes,
furniture gone wrong;
the fences and outhouses
built of barrel-staves
and parts of boxes, all,
if I am fortunate,
smeared a bluish green
that properly weathered
pleases me best
of all colors.

No one
will believe this
of vast import to the nation.

Queen-Ann's-Lace

From *Sour Grapes* (1921). The flower, wild carrot, to which the poet likens the woman, is called "Queen Anne's Lace" because of the delicate white clusters, umbrella-shaped, that rise from a single stem. A purple floret at the center often occurs, as Williams describes.

Her body is not so white as
anemone petals nor so smooth—nor
so remote a thing. It is a field
of the wild carrot taking

the field by force; the grass
does not raise above it.
Here is no question of whiteness,
white as can be, with a purple mole
at the center of each flower.
Each flower is a hand's span
of her whiteness. Wherever
his hand has lain there is
a tiny purple blemish. Each part
is a blossom under his touch
to which the fibers of her being
stem one by one, each to its end,
until the whole field is a
white desire, empty, a single stem,
a cluster, flower by flower,
a pious wish to whiteness gone over
or nothing.

The Botticellian Trees

From *Collected Poems, 1921-1931* (1934).

The alphabet of
the trees

is fading in the
song of the leaves

the crossing
bars of the thin

letters that spelled
winter

and the cold
have been illumined

with
pointed green

by the rain and sun—
The strict simple

principles of
straight branches

are being modified
by pinched out

ifs of color, devout
conditions

the smiles of love—
. . . .

until the stript
sentences

move as a woman's
limbs under cloth

and praise from secrecy
with hot ardor

love's ascendancy
in summer—

In summer the song
sings itself

above the muffled words—

The Yachts

From *An Early Martyr and Other Poems* (1935). The reader would profit from a comparison of this poem with the water-color painting by Williams' friend, Charles Sheeler, called "Pertaining to Yachts and Yachting," which may well have inspired it. Sheeler's style was abstract, delineating the sharp outlines of the sails, emphasized by gradations of light, having the effect of camera angles in modern photography. Note the shift in the poem from objective description in the beginning to a subjective interpretation of the scene in the closing lines.

contend in a sea which the land partly encloses
shielding them from the too heavy blows
of an ungoverned ocean which when it chooses

tortures the biggest hulls, the best man knows
to pit against its beating, and sinks them pitilessly.
Mothlike in mists, scintillant in the minute

brilliance of cloudless days, with broad bellying sails
they glide to the wind tossing green water
from their sharp prows while over them the crew
crawls

ant-like, solicitously grooming them, releasing,
making fast as they turn, lean far over and having
caught the wind again, side by side, head for the
mark.

In a well guarded arena of open water surrounded
by
lesser and greater craft which, sycophant, lumbering
and flittering follow them, they appear youthful,
rare

as the light of a happy eye, live with the grace
of all that in the mind is fleckless, free and
naturally to be desired. Now the sea which holds
them

is moody, lapping their glossy sides, as if feeling
for some slightest flaw but fails completely.
Today no race. Then the wind comes again. The
yachts

move, jockeying for a start, the signal is set and they
are off. Now the waves strike at them but they are
too
well made, they slip through, though they take in
canvas.

Arms with hands grasping seek to clutch at the
prows.
Bodies thrown recklessly in the way are cut aside.
It is a sea of faces about them in agony, in despair

until the horror of the race dawns staggering the
mind,
the whole sea become an entanglement of watery
bodies
lost to the world bearing what they cannot hold.
Broken,
beaten, desolate, reaching from the dead to be taken
up
they cry out, failing, failing! their cries rising
in waves still as the skillful yachts pass over.

The Dance

Pieter Breughel (c. 1525–1569) was a Flemish painter famous for his great canvases depicting peasant life—harvesting, hunting, eating, drinking, and dancing. The "kermess" or "kermis" was a church fair, or dance. Here Williams catches the gusto and earthiness of the scene in one of Breughel's best and most colorful paintings. From *The Collected Later Poems* (1950).

In Breughel's great picture, The Kermess,
the dancers go round, they go round and
around, the squeal and the blare and the
tweedle of bagpipes, a bugle and fiddles
tipping their bellies (round as the thick-
sided glasses whose wash they impound)
their hips and their bellies off balance
to turn them. Kicking and rolling about
the Fair Grounds, swinging their butts, those
shanks must be sound to bear up under such
rollicking measures, prance as they dance
in Breughel's great picture, The Kermess.

HART CRANE [1899–1932]

In "Voyages: I" Hart Crane wrote: "The bottom of the sea is cruel." Six years later his suicidal plunge from a ship into the Gulf of Mexico ended his brief, turbulent life—a life dedicated to poetry and marked by family disturbances, homosexual love affairs, and alcoholic excesses. Crane's undoubted talents never quite equaled his overriding artistic visions. As in one of his literary models, Poe, a pattern of instability underlay his natural gifts and hindered their full realization.

Crane was born in Garrettsville, Ohio. He was the only son of a successful candy manufacturer who was impatient with "poetry nonsense" and urged him to follow a business career. He dropped out of school at thirteen, but the lack of formal education did not prevent him from embarking on a course of wide if unsystematic reading in earlier American literature, especially Melville and Whitman. He was impressed by the new poetic techniques of Eliot, Pound, and Stevens, and he eagerly read the French symbolists—Rimbaud in particular—and also the Elizabethan dramatists.

In 1916 Crane lived for a year on a fruit ranch owned by his mother's family at the Isle of Pines in Cuba, where he discovered the sea and the exotic beauty of the tropics. When his parents were divorced, Crane sided with his mother and struck out on his own, working in New York, Cleveland, and Akron as a mechanic, a soda-jerk, and a writer of advertising copy. In New York he began to publish his poems and found a literary circle among poets and writers who published in the *Dial*, the *Little Review*, the *Seven Arts*, and other of the little magazines. Allen Tate, Gorham Munson, and Waldo Frank were his closest friends and admirers. Crane's first volume of verse, *White Buildings* (1926), showed his creative talent, but lacked a unifying theme. It was a series of imagistic lyrics, closing with six love poems ("Voyages") in which, as Waldo Frank noted, Crane began to explore one of his dominating symbols, the sea, as a mystic and sexual force, somewhat in the manner of Whitman. Crane's restless life carried him from New York to California, then to England, to France, and back to Cuba—finally to Mexico, where he had gone on a Guggenheim fellowship to write an epic poem on Montezuma. There he lived his last year, hoping to regain his psychic balance, but unable to write the poem.

Crane had already achieved a measure of fame when he took his own life. In 1930 he had won the *Poetry* prize for his symbolic epic of America, *The Bridge*. This, his masterwork, had its inception when he was living in a small room in Brooklyn Heights within view of the inspiring span of Brooklyn Bridge. Gradually there formed in his mind an epic poem, with the Bridge as the central symbol, encompassing the history of the American continent from the vision of Columbus to the machine age. It was to be a twentieth-century "Passage to India." Crane was convinced of the value of a mythic technique, based on cultural memory, such as that in *The Waste Land*, but he also considered Eliot's poem "spiritually dead." Turning away from the pessimism of Eliot, he visualized a poem embodying the earlier, idealistic dream of Whitman and fusing past, present, and future into a mystic whole. Among the many strands of influence in *The Bridge* were the allusive symbolism of Rimbaud, the mysticism of P. D. Ouspensky, and the spiritual pioneering of the novelist Waldo Frank.

Aided by a grant from the philanthropist Otto H. Kahn, Crane began to write his new-world epic on "The Myth of America." It was designed to trace the westward movement across the continent, from Brooklyn Bridge, in a layered symbolic method, telescoping time and history, panoramic in extent. River, city, and sea were inanimate symbols;

Pocahontas, the Indian princess, was a pervasive figure as fertility-goddess of the land; and Rip Van Winkle and Walt Whitman became symbolic personages. The poem divides into eight sections, roughly parallel to a musical score, and loosely held together by the figure of the poet walking the streets and riding the subways of Manhattan. The obscurity of the poem, and of Crane in general, derives partly from his eclecticism and partly from his metaphorical leaps beyond conventional syntax—what Crane called "the logic of metaphor" originating in subconscious thought.

The Bridge is neither fully realized nor structurally resolved, but it bears the mark of genius in individual lines and extended metaphors, and its overall conception is in the grand manner. Some readers find Crane's shorter, personally motivated poems more genuine in feeling and more satisfying in structure. "Voyages," "Royal Palm," "The Broken Tower," and a few others represent his lyric technique at its best.

Further reading: *The Collected Poems of Hart Crane,* ed. Waldo Frank, 1933, 1946. Brom Weber, *Hart Crane: A Biographical and Critical Study,* 1948. R. W. B. Lewis, *The Poetry of Hart Crane: A Critical Study,* 1967.

FROM *The Bridge*

Sections of the poem appeared in magazines between 1927 and 1930. The "Proem" and eight numbered sections make up the whole, which appeared in 1930. The present text is taken from the *Collected Poems,* edited by Waldo Frank (1946). The eight sections are as follows: I, Ave Maria; II, Powhatan's Daughter; III, Cutty Sark; IV, Cape Hatteras; V, Three Songs; VI, Quaker Hill; VII, The Tunnel; VIII, Atlantis. Crane meant *The Bridge* to be a "mystical synthesis of America." He intended not a chronological account of American history, which could be found in any history book, but "a more organic panorama, showing the continuous and living evidence of the past in . . . the present." The "Proem" invokes the Bridge as a mythic force and contrasts its freedom with counter-images of the commercialized (Wall Street) and mechanized life of modern America.

Proem: To Brooklyn Bridge

How many dawns, chill from his rippling rest
The seagull's wings shall dip and pivot him,
Shedding white rings of tumult, building high
Over the chained bay waters Liberty—

Then, with inviolate curve, forsake our eyes
As apparitional as sails that cross
Some page of figures to be filed away;
—Till elevators drop us from our day . . .

I think of cinemas, panoramic sleights
With multitudes bent toward some flashing scene
Never disclosed, but hastened to again,
Foretold to other eyes on the same screen;

And Thee, across the harbor, silver-paced
As though the sun took step of thee, yet left
Some motion ever unspent in thy stride,—
Implicitly thy freedom staying thee!

Out of some subway scuttle, cell or loft
A bedlamite speeds to thy parapets,
Tilting there momently, shrill shirt ballooning,
A jest falls from the speechless caravan.

Down Wall, from girder into street noon leaks,
A rip-tooth of the sky's acetylene;
All afternoon the cloud-flown derricks turn . . .
Thy cables breathe the North Atlantic still.

And obscure as that heaven of the Jews,
Thy guerdon . . . Accolade thou dost bestow
Of anonymity time cannot raise:
Vibrant reprieve and pardon thou dost show.

O harp and altar, of the fury fused,
(How could mere toil align thy choiring strings!)
Terrific threshold of the prophet's pledge,
Prayer of pariah, and the lover's cry,—

Again the traffic lights that skim thy swift
Unfractioned idiom, immaculate sigh of stars,
Beading thy path—condense eternity:
And we have seen night lifted in thine arms.

Under thy shadow by the piers I waited;
Only in darkness is thy shadow clear.
The City's fiery parcels all undone,
Already snow submerges an iron year . . .

O Sleepless as the river under thee,
Vaulting the sea, the prairies' dreaming sod,
Unto us lowliest sometime sweep, descend
And of the curveship lend a myth to God.

II. Powhatan's Daughter

This section is in five parts, of which "Van Winkle" is the second and "The River" the third. The parts omitted here are concerned with Powhatan's daughter, Pocahontas, who Crane said was "the mythological nature-symbol chosen to represent the physical body of the continent, or the soil." Throughout the section the original text has marginal notes apostrophizing Pocahontas and recalling her memory as an earth-goddess of the past; these notes are omitted here.

Van Winkle

Crane said that in this part the protagonist is walking to the subway, reminiscing of his childhood. Rip Van Winkle becomes identified with the protagonist as a symbol of the youth of America and "guardian angel" of the journey into the past.

Macadam, gun-gray as the tunny's belt,
Leaps from Far Rockaway to Golden Gate:
Listen! the miles a hurdy-gurdy grinds—
Down gold arpeggios mile on mile unwinds.

Times earlier, when you hurried off to school,
—It is the same hour though a later day—
You walked with Pizarro in a copybook,
And Cortes rode up, reining tautly in—
Firmly as coffee grips the taste,—and away!

There was Priscilla's cheek close in the wind,
And Captain Smith, all beard and certainty,
And Rip Van Winkle, bowing by the way,—
"Is this Sleepy Hollow, friend—?" And he—

And Rip forgot the office hours,
and he forgot the pay;
Van Winkle sweeps a tenement
down town on Avenue A,—

The grind-organ says . . . Remember, remember
The cinder pile at the end of the backyard
Where we stoned the family of young
Garter snakes under . . . And the monoplanes
We launched—with paper wings and twisted
Rubber bands. . . . Recall—
the rapid tongues
That flittered from under the ash heap day
After day whenever your stick discovered
Some sunning inch of unsuspecting fiber—
It flashed back at your thrust, as clean as fire.

And Rip was slowly made aware
that he, Van Winkle, was not here
Nor there. He woke and swore he'd seen Broadway a
Catskill daisy chain in May—

So memory, that strikes a rhyme out of a box,
Or splits a random smell of flowers through glass—
Is it the whip stripped from the lilac tree
One day in spring my father took to me,
Or is it the Sabbatical, unconscious smile
My mother almost brought me once from church
And once only, as I recall—?

It flickered through the snow screen, blindly
It forsook her at the doorway; it was gone
Before I had left the window. It
Did not return with the kiss in the hall.

Macadam, gun-gray as the tunny's belt,
Leaps from Far Rockaway to Golden Gate . . .
Keep hold of that nickel for car-change, Rip,—
Have you got your paper—?
And hurry along, Van Winkle—it's getting late!

The River

The opening lines express "the cultural confusion of the present," from modern science and business to race-memories of the Virgin Birth of Christ. The subway merges into a railroad going west toward the Mississippi River, and alongside the tracks are the hoboes who are the inheritors of the pioneer spirit at least in their closeness to the land beneath which sleeps Pocahontas. The endless flow of time moves westward to the great River, which, in turn, "tortured with history," flows into the sea.

Stick your patent name on a signboard
brother—all over—going west—young man
Tintex—Japalac—Certain-teed Overalls ads
and lands sakes! under the new playbill ripped
in the guaranteed corner—see Bert Williams what?
Minstrels when you steal a chicken just
save me the wing, for if it isn't
Erie it ain't for miles around a
Mazda—and the telegraphic night coming on
Thomas
a Ediford—and whistling down the tracks
a headlight rushing with the sound—can you
imagine—while an EXPRESS makes time like
SCIENCE—COMMERCE and the HOLYGHOST
RADIO ROARS IN EVERY HOME WE HAVE THE
NORTHPOLE
WALLSTREET AND VIRGINBIRTH WITHOUT STONES OR
WIRES OR EVEN RUNning brooks connecting ears
and no more sermons windows flashing roar
Breathtaking—as you like it . . . eh?

So the 20th Century—so
whizzed the Limited—roared by and left
three men, still hungry on the tracks, ploddingly
watching the tail lights wizen and converge,

slipping gimleted and neatly out of sight.
The last bear, shot drinking in the Dakotas,
Loped under wires that span the mountain stream.
Keen instruments, strung to a vast precision
Bind town to town and dream to ticking dream.
But some men take their liquor slow—and count—
Though they'll confess no rosary nor clue—
The river's minute by the far brook's year.
Under a world of whistles, wires and steam
Caboose-like they go ruminating through
Ohio, Indiana—blind baggage—
To Cheyenne tagging . . . Maybe Kalamazoo.

Time's renderings, time's blendings they construe
As final reckonings of fire and snow;
Strange bird-wit, like the elemental gist
Of unwalled winds they offer, singing low
My Old Kentucky Home and Casey Jones,
Some Sunny Day. I heard a road-gang chanting
so.
And afterwards, who had a colt's eyes—one said,
"Jesus! Oh I remember watermelon days!" And
sped
High in a cloud of merriment, recalled
"—And when my Aunt Sally Simpson smiled," he
drawled—
"It was almost Louisiana, long ago."

"There's no place like Booneville though, Buddy,"
One said, excising a last burr from his vest,
"—For early trouting." Then peering in the can,
"—But I kept on the tracks." Possessed, resigned,
He trod the fire down pensively and grinned,
Spreading dry shingles of a beard. . . .

Behind
My father's cannery works I used to see
Rail-squatters ranged in nomad raillery,
The ancient men—wifeless or runaway
Hobo-trekkers that forever search
An empire wilderness of freight and rails.
Each seemed a child, like me, on a loose perch.
Holding to childhood like some termless play.
John, Jake, or Charley, hopping the slow freight
—Memphis to Tallahassee—riding the rods,
Blind fists of nothing, humpty-dumpty clods.

Yet they touch something like a key perhaps.
From pole to pole across the hills, the states
—They know a body under the wide rain;
Youngsters with eyes like fjords, old reprobates
With racetrack jargon,—dotting immensity
They lurk across her, knowing her yonder breast
Snow-silvered, sumac-stained or smoky blue,
Is past the valley-sleepers, south or west.
—As I have trod the rumorous midnights, too.

And past the circuit of the lamp's thin flame
(O Nights that brought me to her body bare!)
Have dreamed beyond the print that bound her
name.
Trains sounding the long blizzards out—I heard
Wail into distances I knew were hers.
Papooses crying on the wind's long mane
Screamed redskin dynasties that fled the brain,
—Dead echoes! But I knew her body there,
Time like a serpent down her shoulder, dark,
And space, an eaglet's wing, laid on her hair.
Under the Ozarks, domed by Iron Mountain,
The old gods of the rain lie wrapped in pools
Where eyeless fish curvet a sunken fountain
And re-descend with corn from querulous crows.
Such pilferings make up their timeless eatage,
Propitiate them for their timber torn
By iron, iron—always the iron dealt cleavage!
They doze now, below axe and powder horn.

And Pullman breakfasters glide glistening steel
From tunnel into field—iron strides the dew—
Straddles the hill, a dance of wheel on wheel.
You have a half-hour's wait at Siskiyou,
Or stay the night and take the next train through.
Southward, near Cairo passing, you can see
The Ohio merging,—borne down Tennessee;
And if it's summer and the sun's in dusk
Maybe the breeze will lift the River's musk
—As though the waters breathed that you might
know
Memphis Johnny, Steamboat Bill, Missouri Joe.
Oh, lean from the window, if the train slows down,
As though you touched hands with some ancient
clown,
—A little while gaze absently below
And hum *Deep River* with them while they go.

Yes, turn again and sniff once more—look see,
O Sheriff, Brakeman and Authority—
Hitch up your pants and crunch another quid,
For you, too, feed the River timelessly.
And few evade full measure of their fate;
Always they smile out eerily what they seem.
I could believe he joked at heaven's gate—
Dan Midland—jolted from the cold brake-beam.

Down, down—born pioneers in time's despite,
Grimed tributaries to an ancient flow—
They win no frontier by their wayward plight,
But drift in stillness, as from Jordan's brow.

You will not hear it as the sea; even stone
Is not more hushed by gravity . . . But slow,
As loth to take more tribute—sliding prone
Like one whose eyes were buried long ago

The River, spreading, flows—and spends your
dream.
What are you, lost within this tideless spell?
You are your father's father, and the stream—
A liquid theme that floating niggers swell.

Damp tonnage and alluvial march of days—
Nights turbid, vascular with silted shale
And roots surrendered down of moraine clays:
The Mississippi drinks the farthest dale.

O quarrying passion, undertowed sunlight!
The basalt surface drags a jungle grace
Ochreous and lynx-barred in lengthening might;
Patience! and you shall reach the biding place!

Over DeSoto's bones the freighted floors
Throb past the City storied of three thrones.
Down two more turns the Mississippi pours
(Anon tall ironsides up from salt lagoons)

And flows within itself, heaps itself free.
All fades but one thin skyline 'round . . . Ahead
No embrace opens but the stinging sea;
The River lifts itself from its long bed,

Poised wholly on its dream, a mustard glow,
Tortured with history, its one will—flow!
—The Passion spreads in wide tongues, chocked and
slow,
Meeting the Gulf, hosannas silently below.

Voyages: I

Crane called the series of six sea "Voyages" which were published in *White Buildings* (1926) "love poems." In the first, the menace of the sea is stressed; in the second, the danger gives way to love—"sleep, death, desire"—and love and death are joined.

Above the fresh ruffles of the surf
Bright striped urchins flay each other with sand.
They have contrived a conquest for shell shucks,
And their fingers crumble fragments of baked weed
Gaily digging and scattering.

And in answer to their treble interjections
The sun beats lightning on the waves,
The waves fold thunder on the sand;
And could they hear me I would tell them:

O brilliant kids, frisk with your dog,
Fondle your shells and sticks, bleached
By time and the elements; but there is a line
You must not cross nor ever trust beyond it
Spry cordage of your bodies to caresses
Too lichen-faithful from too wide a breast.
The bottom of the sea is cruel.

Voyages: II

—And yet this great wink of eternity,
Of rimless floods, unfettered leewardings,
Samite sheeted and processioned where
Her undinal[1] vast belly moonward bends,
Laughing the wrapt inflections of our love;

Take this Sea, whose diapason knells
On scrolls of silver snowy sentences,
The sceptered terror of whose sessions rends
As her demeanors motion well or ill,
All but the pieties of lovers' hands.

And onward, as bells off San Salvador
Salute the crocus lusters of the stars,
In these poinsettia meadows of her tides,—
Adagios[2] of islands, O my Prodigal,
Complete the dark confessions her veins spell.

Mark how her turning shoulders wind the hours,
And hasten while her penniless rich palms
Pass superscription of bent foam and wave,—
Hasten, while they are true,—sleep, death, desire,
Close round one instant in one floating flower.

Bind us in time, O seasons clear, and awe.
O minstrel galleons of Carib fire,
Bequeath us to no earthly shore until
Is answered in the vortex of our grave
The seal's wide spindrift gaze toward paradise.

The Broken Tower

Crane's last poem was completed less than a year before his death in 1933. The poet is bidding farewell to the "lofty tower" of song (perhaps his life's greatest work, *The Bridge)* and expressing a need to return to more personal themes—love and "sweet mortality." The cathedral tower is contrasted with "the quiet lake" as the poem concludes on a note of resignation and hope for another and lesser tower of song "within."

Voyages II. [1] Undine was a goddess of the moon who yearned for a mortal lover.

[2] Crane explained this word as a metaphorical way of depicting "the motion of a boat through islands clustered thickly, the rhythm of the motion, etc." He felt it was both a more "direct" and a more "creative" way of describing a complex of feelings than the more logical and grammatical "coasting slowly through the islands" would have been.

The bell-rope that gathers God at dawn
Dispatches me as though I dropped down the knell
Of a spent day—to wander the cathedral lawn
From pit to crucifix, feet chill on steps from hell.

Have you not heard, have you not seen that corps
Of shadows in the tower, whose shoulders sway
Antiphonal carillons launched before
The stars are caught and hived in the sun's ray?

The bells, I say, the bells break down their tower;
And swing I know not where. Their tongues
    engrave
Membrane through marrow, my long-scattered score
Of broken intervals. . . . And I, their sexton slave!

Oval encyclicals in canyons heaping
The impasse high with choir. Banked voices slain!
Pagodas, campaniles with reveilles outleaping—
O terraced echoes prostrate on the plain! . . .

And so it was I entered the broken world
To trace the visionary company of love, its voice
An instant in the wind (I know not whither hurled)
But not for long to hold each desperate choice.

My word I poured. But was it cognate, scored
Of that tribunal monarch of the air
Whose thigh embronzes earth, strikes crystal Word
In wounds pledged once to hope—cleft to despair?

The steep encroachments of my blood left me
No answer (could blood hold such a lofty tower
As flings the question true?)—or is it she
Whose sweet mortality stirs latent power?—

And through whose pulse I hear, counting the
    strokes
My veins recall and add, revived and sure
The angelus of wars my chest evokes:
What I hold healed, original now, and pure . . .

And builds, within, a tower that is not stone
(Not stone can jacket heaven)—but slip
Of pebbles—visible wings of silence sown
In azure circles, widening as they dip

The matrix of the heart, lift down the eye
That shrines the quiet lake and swells a tower . . .
The commodious, tall decorum of that sky
Unseals her earth, and lifts love in its shower.

ARCHIBALD MacLEISH [1892-]

In 1926 MacLeish, then living in Paris and reading the French symbolists, Eliot, and Pound, defined poetry as "motionless in time," not having *meaning*, but simply *being*. In 1958, he wrote: "The nature of art is action, and there is no part of human experience, public or private, on which it cannot act, or should not." The shift indicated between these two statements of his poetic creed, from aesthetics to social action, is suggested by the outward events of his career as soldier, lawyer, editor, historian, and civil servant. Abandoning the legal profession in 1923, MacLeish went to France, where he read and wrote poetry under the influence of the "lost generation" of expatriate artists. Returning to America in 1929, he rediscovered his native land and centered his interests on social and political problems: the historical origins of poverty, the threat of Fascism, the perils of war. His poetry reflected his increasing commitment to public life, as he sought the reasons for the decline of a pristine democracy of the past and the loss of certainty in the face of the trials besetting the nation in the twentieth century. Though he had learned and applied many of the techniques of the new poetry, he turned from private poetry to address the public at large in the semi-official voice of the poet-turned-statesman, and much of his later work is polemic in purpose and nostalgic in manner.

Born in Glencoe, Illinois, MacLeish graduated from Yale University and Harvard Law School (1917). He was captain of an artillery battalion in World War I, then returned to

Boston to practice law. Giving up a career in law for literature, he lived in France from 1923 to 1928. During these years he published several volumes of poetry, including *Streets of the Moon* (1926), a verse-play entitled *Nobodaddy* (1926), and a long, self-questioning poem, *The Hamlet of A. MacLeish,* which signaled his break from the mood of disillusion of the expatriate writers. His volume *New Found Land* (1930) marked his return to America and his awakened patriotism. He traveled to Mexico where, to prepare himself to write *Conquistador* (1932), he followed the route of Cortez. This long epic poem of the Spanish conqueror who was defeated in the end by the tenacious Aztec civilization, with its implied parallel to the problem of twentieth-century dictators, won him a Pulitzer Prize. During the 1930's as a staff writer for *Fortune* magazine he addressed himself to such topical issues as public housing, minorities, and the rising spectre of war in Europe. In 1939 MacLeish was appointed Librarian of Congress by President Roosevelt. He then served for several years under the Roosevelt administration as Director of War Information and as Assistant Secretary of State. After the war he became one of the founders of UNESCO.

Besides poetry, MacLeish wrote a series of verse-plays adapted for radio broadcast. *Panic* (1935), *The Fall of the City* (1937), and *Air Raid* (1938) were successfully dramatized warnings of the need for Americans to face up to such threats to freedom as social and financial irresponsibility, mob hysteria, dictators, and the prospect of destruction from enemy air attacks. He followed these works with *The Irresponsibles: A Declaration* (1940), a warning addressed to fellow poets and intellectuals, whom he charged with detachment and indifference on national issues. In 1948, in *Actfive,* MacLeish returned once more to the manner of his earlier, subjective poetry, asking in an Eliot-like vein: "Who will give meaning to these broken stones these/Broken bodies violated brains/Corrupted spirits shriveled hearts?"

MacLeish became a professor of writing at Harvard in 1949. His *Collected Poems, 1917-1952* won him his second Pulitzer Prize, and in 1958 he again achieved this distinction with his philosophical verse-play, *J.B.* Based on the trials of Job, the play posed the question whether man in the twentieth century could summon the patience and the forgiveness to rise above the God-created suffering and injustice of the universe. The play succeeded on Broadway and in theaters across the country.

MacLeish has won a permanent place in the poetry of our time. Evaluating his work from the point of view of the new criticism, Cleanth Brooks wrote that his poetry "is essentially a poetry of the noun, not of the verb. His images . . . do tend to become symbols; but the symbols are relatively static, lack dynamic quality." Especially in his poetry of declamation and exhortation, it is true that one feels a want of the irony, complexity, and indirectness of poets like Yeats and Eliot. Yet MacLeish adapted those models to his own kind of verse. He modified their techniques to suit his poetry of public stance and prophecy.

Further reading: *Collected Poems, 1917-1952,* 1952. Cleanth Brooks, *Modern Poetry and the Tradition,* 1939.

Ars Poetica

The title comes from Horace's *De Arte Poetica* in which he defines poetry as a difficult, exacting art like painting. MacLeish was at this time studying the work of the French symbolist school in which technique and aesthetics were valued more highly than didacticism.

From *Streets of the Moon* (1926). The text followed for all selections from MacLeish is the *Collected Poems* (1952).

A poem should be palpable and mute
As a globed fruit,

Dumb
As old medallions to the thumb,

Silent as the sleeve-worn stone
Of casement ledges where the moss has grown—

A poem should be wordless
As the flight of birds.

A poem should be motionless in time
As the moon climbs,

Leaving, as the moon releases
Twig by twig the night-entangled trees,

Leaving, as the moon behind the winter leaves,
Memory by memory the mind—

A poem should be motionless in time
As the moon climbs.

A poem should be equal to:
Not true.

For all the history of grief
An empty doorway and a maple leaf.

For love
The leaning grasses and two lights above the sea—

A poem should not mean
But be.

American Letter

For Gerald Murphy

From *New Found Land* (1930), this poem marks MacLeish's return to America from five years of living in Europe and his weighing in the balance the values of his native country with those of an older civilization.

The wind is east but the hot weather continues,
Blue and no clouds, the sound of the leaves thin,
Dry like the rustling of paper, scored across
With the slate-shrill screech of the locusts.
The tossing of
Pines is the low sound. In the wind's running
The wild carrots smell of the burning sun.
Why should I think of the dolphins at Capo di Mele?[1]
Why should I see in my mind the taut sail
And the hill over St.-Tropez and your hand on the tiller?
Why should my heart be troubled with palms still?
I am neither a sold boy nor a Chinese official
Sent to sicken in Pa for some Lo-Yang dish.
This is my own land, my sky, my mountain:
This—not the humming pines and the surf and the sound
At the Ferme Blanche, nor Port Cros in the dusk and the harbor
Floating the motionless ship and the sea-drowned star.
I am neither Po Chü-i[2] nor another after
Far from home, in a strange land, daft
For the talk of his own sort and the taste of his lettuces.
This land is my native land. And yet
I am sick for home for the red roofs and the olives,
And the foreign words and the smell of the sea fall.
How can a wise man have two countries?
How can a man have the earth and the wind and want
A land far off, alien, smelling of palm-trees
And the yellow gorse at noon in the long calms?

It is a strange thing—to be an American.
Neither an old house it is with the air
Tasting of hung herbs and the sun returning
Year after year to the same door and the churn
Making the same sound in the cool of the kitchen
Mother to son's wife, and the place to sit
Marked in the dusk by the worn stone at the well-head—
That—nor the eyes like each other's eyes and the skull
Shaped to the same fault and the hands' sameness.
Neither a place it is nor a blood name.
America is West and the wind blowing.
America is a great word and the snow,
A way, a white bird, the rain falling,
A shining thing in the mind and the gulls' call.
America is neither a land nor a people,
A word's shape it is, a wind's sweep—
America is alone: many together,
Many of one mouth, of one breath,
Dressed as one—and none brothers among them:
Only the taught speech and the aped tongue.
America is alone and the gulls calling.

It is a strange thing to be an American.
It is strange to live on the high world in the stare
Of the naked sun and the stars as our bones live.
Men in the old lands housed by their rivers.
They built their towns in the vales in the earth's shelter.
We first inhabit the world. We dwell
On the half earth, on the open curve of a continent.
Sea is divided from sea by the day-fall. The dawn
Rides the low east with us many hours;
First are the capes, then are the shorelands, now
The blue Appalachians faint at the day rise;

American Letter. [1]An Italian spa on the Mediterranean coast. St.-Tropez, Ferme Blanche, Port Cros, and Cette (below) are French towns.

[2]A Chinese poet, exiled from his homeland, who wrote lyrics full of nostalgic memories of his native place.

The willows shudder with light on the long Ohio:
The Lakes scatter the low sun: the prairies
Slide out of the dark: in the eddy of clean air
The smoke goes up from the high plains of Wyoming:
The steep Sierras rise: the struck foam
Flames at the wind's heel on the far Pacific:
Already the noon leans to the eastern cliff:
The elms darken the door and the dust-heavy lilacs.

It is strange to sleep in the bare stars and to die
On an open land where few bury before us:
(From the new earth the dead return no more.)
It is strange to be born of no race and no people.
In the old lands they are many together. They keep
The wise past and the words spoken in common.
They remember the dead with their hands, their mouths dumb.
They answer each other with two words in their meeting.
They live together in small things. They eat
The same dish, their drink is the same and their proverbs.
Their youth is like. They are like in their ways of love.
They are many men. There are always others beside them.
Here it is one man and another and wide
On the darkening hills the faint smoke of the houses.
Here it is one man and the wind in the boughs.

Therefore our hearts are sick for the south water.
The smell of the gorse comes back to our night thought.
We are sick at heart for the red roofs and the olives;
We are sick at heart for the voice and the foot-fall...

Therefore we will not go though the sea call us.

This, this is our land, this is our people,
This that is neither a land nor a race. We must reap
The wind here in the grass for our soul's harvest:
Here we must eat our salt or our bones starve.
Here we must live or live only as shadows.
This is our race, we that have none, that have had
Neither the old walls nor the voices around us,
This is our land, this is our ancient ground—
The raw earth, the mixed bloods and the strangers,
The different eyes, the wind, and the heart's change.
These we will not leave though the old call us.
This is our country-earth, our blood, our kind.
Here we will live our years till the earth blind us—
The wind blows from the east. The leaves fall.
Far off in the pines a jay rises.
The wind smells of haze and the wild ripe apples.
I think of the masts at Cette and the sweet rain.

FROM *Frescoes for Mr. Rockefeller's City*

Frescoes for Mr. Rockefeller's City (1933) consists of six poems conceived as mural paintings for Rockefeller Center, a cluster of buildings begun in 1931 and completed in 1947, now comprising a "city" of skyscrapers in itself. The poem given here shows MacLeish having surmounted the hesitation of "American Letter" and now prepared to rediscover with new eyes the symbols and values of his native land.

Landscape as a Nude

She lies on her left side her flank golden:
Her hair is burned black with the strong sun.
The scent of her hair is of rain in the dust on her shoulders:
She has brown breasts and the mouth of no other country.

Ah she is beautiful here in the sun where she lies:
She is not like the soft girls naked in vineyards
Nor the soft naked girls of the English islands
Where the rain comes in with the surf on an east wind:

Hers is the west wind and the sunlight: the west
Wind is the long clean wind of the continents—
The wind turning with earth, the wind descending
Steadily out of the evening and following on:

The wind here where she lies is west: the trees
Oak ironwood cottonwood hickory: standing in
Great groves they roll on the wind as the sea would:
The grasses of Iowa Illinois Indiana

Run with the plunge of the wind as a wave tumbling.

Under her knees there is no green lawn of the Florentines:
Under her dusty knees is the corn stubble:
Her belly is flecked with the flickering light of the corn.

She lies on her left side her flank golden:
Her hair is burned black with the strong sun.
The scent of her hair is of dust and of smoke on her shoulders:
She has brown breasts and the mouth of no other country.

MARIANNE MOORE [1887-]

For several years a librarian in a branch of the New York Public Library, Miss Moore cultivated an antiquarian curiosity for recondite facts gleaned from encyclopedias, old newspapers, government leaflets, advertising brochures, scholarly books and magazines, and other forms of reference material. Her range of interests includes Oriental art, plant and sea life, major league baseball, antique clocks, and esoteric birds and animals, often more read about than actually observed. As Morton D. Zabel said of her: "She mixes the statistics of newspapers with the casual hints and cross references of a mind constructed like a card catalogue." She herself said, "My writing is, if not like a cabinet of fossils, a kind of collection of flies in amber." Like the sub-sub-librarian of Melville's *Moby-Dick*, or like T. S. Eliot (who admired Miss Moore's poetry), she annotates her poems both seriously and with a sly wink at academic scholarship. Her quotations, however, are scrupulously enclosed in quotation marks. The strange and seemingly irrelevant bits of scientific and technical lore she collects are then woven into the fabric of intricately patterned poems which, as Eliot remarked, "move with the elegance of a minuet." There are no overriding ideas or preoccupations in her work. She is not concerned with large serious themes, or with reforming the race. A lover of words, especially rare and Latinized scientific names, she develops her poems in a cool, detached, unemotional style, extending her subjects into a series of conceits somewhat after the fashion of John Donne and the metaphysicals. Always one finds "wit" and serious humor.

The essential rhythmic unit in a typical Moore poem is the stanza, which is shaped by typography and by light, though persistent, rhyme. The stanzas are parallel in form, containing a like number of syllables and line-lengths. She uses lower-case letters and oddly-separated words, giving an effect of spontaneity. Despite her dry manner there is a fluidity of style which results from her conviction that poetry has much in common with instrumental music. The slight, factual materials from which she fashions her verses are thus set off as if within a richly embossed frame, a device which intensifies the impression of a fresh approach to reality without actually distorting or rearranging it. She aimed, as she put it, at "imaginary gardens with real toads in them."

Marianne Moore's now fully acknowledged reputation was slow in arriving. Her emergence as a poet was almost accidental. She was born near St. Louis, attended Bryn Mawr College, prepared herself for a business career at a commercial college in Carlisle, Pennsylvania, and taught in the Indian school in Carlisle from 1911 to 1915. Moving to New Jersey, and then to New York, where she was a librarian for four years, she took up writing seriously after her first poems appeared in 1915 in *Poetry: A Magazine of Verse* and in the London *Egoist*. Her poetry attracted the attention of Hilda Doolittle, Robert McAlmon, and others of the Imagist group, and her first volume, *Poems* (1921), was published in England by these admirers and without her knowledge. In 1924 a reprint of this book, with additional poems, was published in America as *Observations*, winning for her a poetry award from the *Dial* magazine. This led to her appointment as an editor of the *Dial*, a position which brought her in close touch with many of the poets and writers of that important publication, among them Pound, Eliot, Stevens, Williams, Yeats, and Auden. Her *Selected Poems* (1935), with an introduction by Eliot, signaled her arrival as one of the significant poets of her generation. *The Pangolin and Other Verse* (1936), *Nevertheless* (1946), and *Collected Poems* (1951) are some of her important volumes, the latter bringing her a Pulitzer Prize. She has translated *The Fables of La Fontaine* (1954) and has written a book of critical essays, *Predilections* (1955). She has lived quietly in Brooklyn for many years, enjoying the limited but durable reputation of an original talent whose work is admired by connoisseurs, and practicing her art of "pure" poetry without the need for didactics, polemics, or controversy.

Further reading: *Collected Poems,* 1951. T. S. Eliot's Introduction to the *Selected Poems,* 1935. R. P. Blackmur, *The Double Agent,* 1935. B. F. Engle, *Marianne Moore,* 1964.

The Fish

This and the two following poems are from *Selected Poems* (1935). For all poems given here the text is that of *Collected Poems* (1951).

wade
through black jade.
   Of the crow-blue mussel-shells, one keeps
   adjusting the ash-heaps;
      opening and shutting itself like

an
injured fan.
   The barnacles which encrust the side
   of the wave, cannot hide
      there for the submerged shafts of the

sun,
split like spun
   glass, move themselves with spotlight swiftness
   into the crevices—
      in and out, illuminating

the
turquoise sea
   of bodies. The water drives a wedge
   of iron through the iron edge
      of the cliff; whereupon the stars,

pink
rice-grains, ink-
   bespattered jelly-fish, crabs like green
   lilies, and submarine
      toadstools, slide each on the other.

All
external
   marks of abuse are present on this
   defiant edifice—
      all the physical features of

ac-
cident—lack
of cornice, dynamite grooves, burns, and
hatchet strokes, these things stand
out on it; the chasm-side is

dead.
Repeated
evidence has proved that it can live
on what can not revive
its youth. The sea grows old in it.

Poetry

Author's note: "*Diary of Tolstoy* (Dutton), p. 84. 'Where the boundary between prose and poetry lies, I shall never be able to understand. The question is raised in manuals of style, yet the answer to it lies beyond me. Poetry is verse: prose is not verse. Or else poetry is everything with the exception of business documents and school books.'

" 'Literalists of the imagination.' Yeats: *Ideas of Good and Evil* (A. H. Bullen), p. 182. 'The limitation of his view was from the very intensity of his vision; he was a too literal realist of imagination, as others are of nature; and because he believed that the figures seen by the mind's eye, when exalted by inspiration, were "eternal existences," symbols of divine essences, he hated every grace of style that might obscure their lineaments.' "

I, too, dislike it: there are things that are important beyond
all this fiddle.
Reading it, however, with a perfect contempt for it, one
discovers in
it after all, a place for the genuine.
Hands that can grasp, eyes
that can dilate, hair that can rise
if it must, these things are important not because a

high-sounding interpretation can be put upon them but because they are
useful. When they become so derivative as to become
unintelligible,
the same thing may be said for all of us, that we
do not admire what
we cannot understand: the bat
holding on upside down or in quest of something to

eat, elephants pushing, a wild horse taking a roll, a tireless
wolf under
a tree, the immovable critic twitching his skin like a horse
that feels a flea, the base-
ball fan, the statistician—
nor is it valid
to discriminate against "business documents and

school-books"; all these phenomena are important. One
must make a distinction
however: when dragged into prominence by half poets,
the result is not poetry,

nor till the poets among us can be
"literalists of
the imagination"—above
insolence and triviality and can present

for inspection, "imaginary gardens with real toads in them,"
shall we have
it. In the meantime, if you demand on the one hand,
the raw material of poetry in
all its rawness and
that which is on the other hand
genuine, you are interested in poetry.

Critics and Connoisseurs

There is a great amount of poetry in unconscious
fastidiousness. Certain Ming
products, imperial floor-coverings of coach-
wheel yellow, are well enough in their way but I have
seen something
that I like better—a
mere childish attempt to make an imperfectly ballasted animal stand up,
similar determination to make a pup
eat his meat from the plate.

I remember a swan under the willows in Oxford,
with flamingo-coloured, maple-
leaflike feet. It reconnoitred like a battle-
ship. Disbelief and conscious fastidiousness were the
staple
ingredients in its
disinclination to move. Finally its hardihood was
not proof against its
proclivity to more fully appraise such bits
of food as the stream

bore counter to it; it made away with what I gave it
to eat. I have seen this swan and
I have seen you; I have seen ambition without
understanding in a variety of forms. Happening to stand
by an ant-hill, I have
seen a fastidious ant carrying a stick north, south,
east, west, till it turned on
itself, struck out from the flower-bed into the
lawn,
and returned to the point

from which it had started. Then abandoning the stick as
useless and overtaxing its
jaws with a particle of whitewash—pill-like but
heavy, it again went through the same course of procedure.
What is
there in being able

to say that one has dominated the stream in an
attitude of self-defence;
in proving that one has had the experience
of carrying a stick?

Four Quartz Crystal Clocks

From *What Are Years?* (1941). Author's note: "Bell T. Leaflet, 1939, *'The World's Most Accurate Clocks:* In the Bell Telephone Laboratories in New York, in a "time vault" whose temperature is maintained within 1/100 of a degree at 41° centigrade, are the most accurate clocks in the world—the four quartz crystal clocks. . . . When properly cut and inserted in a suitable circuit, they will control the rate of electric vibration to an accuracy of one part in a million. . . . When you call MEridian 7-1212 for correct time you get it every 15 seconds.'

"Jean Giraudoux: 'Appeler à l'aide d'un camouflage ces instruments faits pour la vérité qui sont la radio, le cinéma, la presse?' 'J'ai traversé voilà un an des pays arabes où l'on ignorait encore que Napoléon était mort.' *Une allocation radiodiffusée de M. Giraudoux aux Françaises à propos de Sainte Catherine;* the *Figaro*, November 1939.

"The cannibal Chronos. Rhea, mother of Zeus, hid him from Chronos who 'devoured all his children except Jupiter (air), Neptune (water), and Pluto (the grave). These, Time cannot consume.' Brewer's *Dictionary of Phrase and Fable.*"

There are four vibrators, the world's exactest clocks;
and these quartz time-pieces that tell
time intervals to other clocks,
these worksless clocks work well;
independently the same, kept in
the 41° Bell
Laboratory time

vault. Checked by a comparator with Arlington,
they punctualize the "radio,
cinema," and "presse,"—a group the
Giraudoux truth-bureau
of hoped-for accuracy has termed
"instruments of truth". We know—
as Jean Giraudoux says

certain Arabs have not heard—that Napoleon
is dead; that a quartz prism when
the temperature changes, feels
the change and that the then
electrified alternate edges
oppositely charged, threaten
careful timing; so that

this water-clear crystal as the Greeks used to say,
this "clear ice" must be kept at the
same coolness. Repetition, with
the scientist, should be
synonymous with accuracy.
The lemur-student can see
that an aye-aye is not

an angwan-tibo, potto, or loris. The seaside burden should not embarrass
the bell-boy with the buoy-ball
endeavouring to pass
hotel patronesses; nor could a
practised ear confuse the glass
eyes for taxidermists

with eye-glasses from the optometrist. And as
MEridian-7 one-two
one-two gives, each fifteenth second
in the same voice, the new
data—"The time will be" so and so—
you realize that "when you
hear the signal", you'll be

hearing Jupiter or jour pater, the day god—
the salvaged son of Father Time—
telling the cannibal Chronos
(eater of his proxime
newborn progeny) that punctuality
is not a crime.

Fiction of the Twenties and Thirties

EDITH WHARTON [1862–1937]

THE SMALL, select social world of "old New York," a society rigidly controlled by a combination of money and matriarchal grandmothers, was the scene of Edith Wharton's childhood and youth. When she came to write about it in her fiction, she approached it, as one critic has said, "half in the cool spirit of the anthropologist studying the death of a tribe and half with the nostalgia of a survivor mourning the loss of vanished graces." This kind of ambivalence caused her to write from inner tensions and helped make of her a psychological novelist. Further contributing to her high reputation as an artist in fiction were her knowledge of social manners, her sense of social history, her keen satirical thrust, and her innate good taste. She has been compared, not unfavorably, with Jane Austen and George Eliot. Her long and close friendship with Henry James and her many years' residence in France strengthened her handling of the American character as viewed from a European perspective. Like James, she used a dramatic method, seeing her material through the eyes of a sensitive observer who is both judge and victim of the society around him. Marriage, divorce, the socially acceptable and the ostracized, the insider and the stranger, inherited wealth versus the rising plutocracy—such were her major themes. If she lacked James's subtlety and his rage for technique, she was better informed than he about the special society she chose to depict: the narrow world of the leading families in New York during the seventies and eighties, the Joneses, the Schermerhorns, and the Rhinelanders, who owned great houses and entertained lavishly, but in good taste.

Edith Newbold Jones was brought up with the standards of lawyers and bankers of inherited wealth and much leisure. In her circle, "foreign" influences were viewed with distrust, divorce was scandalous, and money was valued only when it had been kept for at least two generations. Religion was reduced to a form. The proper role of a woman was to marry well and to become a charming hostess at parties for the "right" people. Edith Jones was surrounded by servants, trained by tutors and by European travel. In the summers the family went to Newport with the other best people. After "coming out" at the age of seventeen, she was married in 1885 to Edward Wharton, a Boston banker thirteen years older than she. Edith Wharton now duly settled into the routine of social life—with one great exception: she began to write. Her first volume of fiction, *The Greater Inclination*, appeared in 1899. *The House of Mirth* (1905), one of her finest novels, portrayed the life of Lily Bart, an American Emma Bovary who is slowly strangled by her lack of money and her unwillingness to conform to the rigid social code of the circle to which she belonged.

In 1907 the Whartons went to France, where Edward Wharton's health broke and a mental collapse followed. After some years, Edith Wharton obtained a divorce (1913), and with the outbreak of war in Europe she devoted herself to her writing and to charitable work with refugees and children, for which she was decorated by the French government. She now chose to remain in France, separating herself from her former life; she divided her time between a home near Paris and a villa on the French Riviera. She was seen by her friends as a woman of charm, elegant in dress and manners, formal in mien, inwardly shy, but a *grande dame* of the world of letters and a formidable personality.

Her best work in the Jamesian manner included the novelette, *Madame de Treymes* (1907), based on a contrast of French and American codes of conduct. *The Custom of the Country* (1913) concerned the career of a social-climbing, ambitious girl, Undine Spragg, who sacrifices husbands and lovers on both sides of the Atlantic in her drive for success. Her prize-winning novel, *The Age of Innocence* (1920), handles the international theme in terms of a Europeanized woman, about whom there is a faint aroma of scandal, who is sacrificed to the god of propriety by the tribal laws of the old New York social establishment. These novels, together with *The Reef* (1912), show Edith Wharton's use of the transatlantic theme. On the other hand are her books with purely American settings and characters, *Ethan Frome* (1911) and *Summer* (1917), both among her best work, though more in the naturalistic vein of American fiction, in which the narrowness and poverty of small-town life are the determining forces.

Mrs. Wharton's other writing, though prolific, fails to equal the power of these books. Her short stories, however, are uniformly good, and a few of them are brilliantly done. In such tales as "Autres Temps," "Roman Fever," and "After Holbein," she displayed a master's touch in selecting "crucial instances" in which subconscious impulses are let loose and entire lives exposed. She also wrote—again like James—ghost stories of psychological interest, *Tales of Men and Ghosts* (1910). Though she too wrote on the art of the novel (*The Writing of Fiction*, 1925), she somehow fails to take the reader into her workshop, as James generally succeeds in doing in his discussions of technique. In 1934 she published a charming and nostalgic memoir of her earlier years, *A Backward Glance*, but her reserved temper prevented her from intimate self-revelation. She preferred to adumbrate her own inner conflicts in the lives of her fictional characters.

Further reading: A. H. Quinn, ed., *An Edith Wharton Treasury*, 1950 (includes *The Age of Innocence*). *The House of Mirth*, ed. R. W. B. Lewis (Riverside Editions), 1963. Percy Lubbock, *Portrait of Edith Wharton*, 1947. Blake Nevius, *Edith Wharton: A Study of Her Fiction*, 1953.

Autres Temps . . .

From *Xingu and Other Stories* (1916), this story was written around 1913, the year of Mrs. Wharton's own divorce. She may have been contemplating her own possible return to America and the reception she could expect from her family and friends. It has been called one of her best two or three short stories.

I

Mrs. Lidcote, as the huge menacing mass of New York defined itself far off across the waters, shrank back into her corner of the deck and sat listening with a kind of unreasoning terror to the steady onward drive of the screws.

She had set out on the voyage quietly enough,—in what she called her "reasonable" mood,—but the week at sea had given her too much time to think of things and had left her too long alone with the past.

When she was alone, it was always the past that occupied her. She couldn't get away from it, and she didn't any longer care to. During her long years of exile she had made her terms with it, had learned to accept the fact that it would always be there, huge, obstructing, encumbering, bigger and more dominant than anything the future could ever conjure up. And, at any rate, she was sure of it, she understood it, knew how to reckon with it; she had learned to screen and manage and protect it as one does an afflicted member of one's family.

There had never been any danger of her being allowed to forget the past. It looked out at her from the face of every acquaintance, it appeared suddenly in the eyes of strangers when a word enlightened them: "Yes, *the* Mrs. Lidcote, don't you know?" It had sprung at her the first day out, when, across the dining-room, from the captain's table, she had seen Mrs. Lorin Boulger's revolving eye-glass pause and the eye behind it grow as blank as a dropped blind. The next day, of course, the captain had asked: "You know your ambassadress, Mrs. Boulger?" and she had replied that, No, she seldom left Florence, and hadn't been to Rome for more than a day since the Boulgers had been sent to Italy. She was so used to these phrases that it cost her no effort to repeat them. And the captain had promptly changed the subject.

No, she didn't, as a rule, mind the past, because she was used to it and understood it. It was a great concrete fact in her path that she had to walk around every time she moved in any direction. But now, in the light of the unhappy event that had summoned her from Italy,—the sudden unanticipated news of her daughter's divorce from Horace Pursh and remarriage with Wilbour Barkley—the past, her own poor miserable past, started up at her with eyes of accusation, became, to her disordered fancy, like the afflicted relative suddenly breaking away from nurses and keepers and publicly parading the horror and misery she had, all the long years, so patiently screened and secluded.

Yes, there it had stood before her through the agitated weeks since the news had come—during her interminable journey from India, where Leila's letter had overtaken her, and the feverish halt in her apartment in Florence, where she had had to stop and gather up her possessions for a fresh start—there it had stood grinning at her with a new balefulness which seemed to say: "Oh, but you've got to look at me *now*, because I'm not only your own past but Leila's present."

Certainly it was a master-stroke of those arch-ironists of the shears and spindle to duplicate her own story in her daughter's. Mrs. Lidcote had always somewhat grimly fancied that, having so signally failed to be of use to Leila in other ways, she would at least serve her as a warning. She had even abstained from defending herself, from making the best of her case, had stoically refused to plead extenuating circumstances, lest Leila's impulsive sympathy should lead to deductions that might react disastrously on her own life. And now that very thing had happened, and Mrs. Lidcote could hear the whole of New York saying with one voice: "Yes, Leila's done just what her mother did. With such an example what could you expect?"

Yet if she had been an example, poor woman, she had been an awful one; she had been, she would have supposed, of more use as a deterrent than a hundred blameless mothers as incentives. For how could any one who had seen anything of her life in the last eighteen years have had the courage to repeat so disastrous an experiment?

Well, logic in such cases didn't count, example didn't count, nothing probably counted but having the same impulses in the blood; and that was the dark inheritance she had bestowed upon her daughter. Leila hadn't consciously copied her; she had simply "taken after" her, had been a projection of her own long-past rebellion.

Mrs. Lidcote had deplored, when she started, that the *Utopia* was a slow steamer, and would take eight full days to bring her to her unhappy daughter; but now, as the moment of reunion approached, she would willingly have turned the boat about and fled back to the high seas. It was not only because she felt still so unprepared to face what New York had in store for her, but because she needed more time to dispose of what the *Utopia* had already given her. The past was bad enough, but the present and future were worse, because they were less comprehensible, and because, as she grew older, surprises and inconsequences troubled her more than the worst certainties.

There was Mrs. Boulger, for instance. In the light, or rather the darkness, of new developments, it might really be that Mrs. Boulger had not meant to cut her, but had simply failed to recognize her. Mrs. Lidcote had arrived at this hypothesis simply by listening to the conversation of the persons sitting next to her on deck—two lively young women with the latest Paris hats on their heads and the latest New York ideas in them. These ladies, as to whom it would have been impossible for a person with Mrs. Lidcote's old-fashioned categories to determine whether they were married or unmarried, "nice" or "horrid," or any one or other of the definite things which young women, in her youth and her society, were conveniently assumed to be, had revealed a familiarity with the world of New York that, again according to Mrs. Lidcote's traditions, should have implied a recognized place in it. But in the present fluid state of manners what did anything imply except what their hats implied—that no one could tell what was coming next?

They seemed, at any rate, to frequent a group of idle and opulent people who executed the same gestures and revolved on the same pivots as Mrs. Lidcote's daughter and her friends: their Coras, Matties and Mabels seemed at any moment likely to reveal familiar patronymics, and once one of the speakers, summing up a discussion of which Mrs. Lidcote had missed the beginning, had affirmed with headlong confidence: "Leila? Oh, *Leila's* all right."

Could it be *her* Leila, the mother had wondered, with a sharp thrill of apprehension? If only they would mention surnames! But their talk leaped elliptically from allusion to allusion, their unfinished sentences dangled over bottomless pits of conjecture, and they gave their bewildered hearer the impression not so much of talking only of their intimates, as of being intimate with every one alive.

Her old friend Franklin Ide could have told her, perhaps; but here was the last day of the voyage, and she hadn't yet found courage to ask him. Great as had been the joy of discovering his name on the passenger-list and seeing his friendly bearded face in the throng against the taffrail at Cherbourg, she had as yet said nothing to him except, when they had met: "Of course I'm going out to Leila."

She had said nothing to Franklin Ide because she had always instinctively shrunk from taking him into her confidence. She was sure he felt sorry for her, sorrier perhaps than any one had ever felt; but he had always paid her the supreme tribute of not showing it. His attitude allowed her to imagine that compassion was not the basis of his feeling for her, and it was part of her joy in his friendship that it was the one relation seemingly unconditioned by her state, the only one in which she could think and feel and behave like any other woman.

Now, however, as the problem of New York loomed nearer, she began to regret that she had not spoken, had not at least questioned him about the hints she had gathered on the way. He did not know the two ladies next to her, he did not even, as it chanced, know Mrs. Lorin Boulger; but he knew New York, and New York was the sphinx whose riddle she must read or perish.

Almost as the thought passed through her mind his stooping shoulders and grizzled head detached themselves against the blaze of light in the west, and he sauntered down the empty deck and dropped into the chair at her side.

"You're expecting the Barkleys to meet you, I suppose?" he asked.

It was the first time she had heard any one pronounce her daughter's new name, and it occurred to her that her friend, who was shy and inarticulate, had been trying to say it all the way over and had at last shot it out at her only because he felt it must be now or never.

"I don't know. I cabled, of course. But I believe she's at—they're at—*his* place somewhere."

"Oh, Barkley's; yes, near Lenox, isn't it? But she's sure to come to town to meet you."

He said it so easily and naturally that her own constraint was relieved, and suddenly, before she knew what she meant to do, she had burst out: "She may dislike the idea of seeing people."

Ide, whose absent short-sighted gaze had been fixed on the slowly gliding water, turned in his seat to stare at his companion.

"Who? Leila?" he said with an incredulous laugh.

Mrs. Lidcote flushed to her faded hair and grew pale again. "It took *me* a long time—to get used to it," she said.

His look grew gently commiserating. "I think you'll find—" he paused for a word—"that things are different now—altogether easier."

"That's what I've been wondering—ever since we started." She was determined now to speak. She moved nearer, so that their arms touched, and she could drop her voice to a murmur. "You see, it all came on me in a flash. My going off to India and Siam on that long trip kept me away from letters for weeks at a time; and she didn't want to tell me beforehand—oh, I understand *that,* poor child! You know how good she's always been to me; how she's tried to spare me. And she knew, of course, what a state of horror I'd be in. She knew I'd rush off to her at once and try to stop it. So she never gave me a hint of anything, and she even managed to muzzle

Susy Suffern—you know Susy is the one of the family who keeps me informed about things at home. I don't yet see how she prevented Susy's telling me; but she did. And her first letter, the one I got up at Bangkok, simply said the thing was over—the divorce, I mean—and that the very next day she'd—well, I suppose there was no use waiting; and *he* seems to have behaved as well as possible, to have wanted to marry her as much as—"

"Who? Barkley?" he helped her out. "I should say so! Why what do you suppose—" He interrupted himself. "He'll be devoted to her, I assure you."

"Oh, of course; I'm sure he will. He's written me—really beautifully. But it's a terrible strain on a man's devotion. I'm not sure that Leila realizes—"

Ide sounded again his little reassuring laugh. "I'm not sure that you realize. *They're* all right."

It was the very phrase that the young lady in the next seat had applied to the unknown "Leila," and its recurrence on Ide's lips flushed Mrs. Lidcote with fresh courage.

"I wish I knew just what you mean. The two young women next to me—the ones with the wonderful hats—have been talking in the same way."

"What? About Leila?"

"About *a* Leila; I fancied it might be mine. And about society in general. All their friends seem to be divorced; some of them seem to announce their engagements before they get their decree. One of them—*her* name was Mabel—as far as I could make out, her husband found out that she meant to divorce him by noticing that she wore a new engagement-ring."

"Well, you see Leila did everything 'regularly,' as the French say," Ide rejoined.

"Yes; but are these people in society? The people my neighbours talk about?"

He shrugged his shoulders. "It would take an arbitration commission a good many sittings to define the boundaries of society nowadays. But at any rate they're in New York; and I assure you you're *not;* you're farther and farther from it."

"But I've been back there several times to see Leila." She hesitated and looked away from him. Then she brought out slowly: "And I've never noticed—the least change—in—in my own case—"

"Oh," he sounded deprecatingly, and she trembled with the fear of having gone too far. But the hour was past when such scruples could restrain her. She must know where she was and where Leila was. "Mrs. Boulger still cuts me," she brought out with an embarrassed laugh.

"Are you sure? You've probably cut *her;* if not now, at least in the past. And in a cut if you're not first you're nowhere. That's what keeps up so many quarrels."

The word roused Mrs. Lidcote to a renewed sense of realities. "But the Purshes," she said—"the Purshes are so strong! There are so many of them, and they all back each other up, just as my husband's family did. I know what it means to have a clan against one. They're stronger than any number of separate friends. The Purshes will *never* forgive Leila for leaving Horace. Why, his mother opposed his marrying her because of—of me. She tried to get Leila to promise that she wouldn't see me when they went to Europe on their honeymoon. And now she'll say it was my example."

Her companion, vaguely stroking his beard, mused a moment upon this; then he asked, with seeming irrelevance, "What did Leila say when you wrote that you were coming?"

"She said it wasn't the least necessary, but that I'd better come, because it was the only way to convince me that it wasn't."

"Well, then, that proves she's not afraid of the Purshes."

She breathed a long sigh of remembrance. "Oh, just at first, you know—one never is."

He laid his hand on hers with a gesture of intelligence and pity. "You'll see, you'll see," he said.

A shadow lengthened down the deck before them, and a steward stood there, proffering a Marconigram.

"Oh, now I shall know!" she exclaimed.

She tore the message open, and then let it fall on her knees, dropping her hands on it in silence.

Ide's enquiry roused her: "It's all right?"

"Oh, quite right. Perfectly. She can't come; but she's sending Susy Suffern. She says Susy will explain." After another silence she added, with a sudden gush of bitterness: "As if I needed any explanation!"

She felt Ide's hesitating glance upon her. "She's in the country?"

"Yes. 'Prevented last moment. Longing for you, expecting you. Love from both.' Don't you *see,* the poor darling, that she couldn't face it?"

"No, I don't." He waited. "Do you mean to go to her immediately?"

"It will be too late to catch a train this evening; but I shall take the first to-morrow morning." She considered a moment. "Perhaps it's better. I need a talk with Susy first. She's to meet me at the dock, and I'll take her straight back to the hotel with me."

As she developed this plan, she had the sense that Ide was still thoughtfully, even gravely, considering her. When she ceased, he remained silent a moment; then he said almost ceremoniously: "If your talk with Miss Suffern doesn't last too late, may I come and see you when it's over? I shall be dining at my club, and I'll call you up at about ten, if I may. I'm off to Chicago on business to-morrow morning, and it would be a satisfaction to know, before I start, that your cousin's been able to reassure you, as I know she will."

He spoke with a shy deliberateness that, even to Mrs. Lidcote's troubled perceptions, sounded a long-silenced note of feeling. Perhaps the breaking down of the barrier of reticence between them had released unsuspected emotions in both. The tone of his appeal moved her curiously and loosened the tight strain of her fears.

"Oh, yes, come—do come," she said, rising. The huge threat of New York was imminent now, dwarfing, under long reaches of embattled masonry, the great deck she stood on and all the little specks of life it carried. One of them, drifting nearer, took the shape of her maid, followed by luggage-laden stewards, and signing to her that it was time to go below. As they descended to the main deck, the throng swept her against Mrs. Lorin Boulger's shoulder, and she heard the ambassadress call out to some one, over the vexed sea of hats: "So sorry! I should have been delighted, but I've promised to spend Sunday with some friends at Lenox."

II

Susy Suffern's explanation did not end till after ten o'clock, and she had just gone when Franklin Ide, who, complying with an old New York tradition, had caused himself to be preceded by a long white box of roses, was shown into Mrs. Lidcote's sitting-room.

He came forward with his shy half-humorous smile and, taking her hand, looked at her for a moment without speaking.

"It's all right," he then pronounced.

Mrs. Lidcote returned his smile. "It's extraordinary. Everything's changed. Even Susy has changed; and you know the extent to which Susy used to represent the old New York. There's no old New York left, it seems. She talked in the most amazing way. She snaps her fingers at the Purshes. She told me—*me*, that every woman had a right to happiness and that self-expression was the highest duty. She accused me of misunderstanding Leila; she said my point of view was conventional! She was bursting with pride at having been in the secret, and wearing a brooch that Wilbour Barkley'd given her!"

Franklin Ide had seated himself in the arm-chair she had pushed forward for him under the electric chandelier. He threw back his head and laughed. "What did I tell you?"

"Yes; but I can't believe that Susy's not mistaken. Poor dear, she has the habit of lost causes; and she may feel that, having stuck to me, she can do no less than stick to Leila."

"But she didn't—did she?—openly defy the world for you? She didn't snap her fingers at the Lidcotes?"

Mrs. Lidcote shook her head, still smiling. "No. It was enough to defy *my* family. It was doubtful at one time if they would tolerate her seeing me, and she almost had to disinfect herself after each visit. I believe that at first my sister-in-law wouldn't let the girls come down when Susy dined with her."

"Well, isn't your cousin's present attitude the best possible proof that times have changed?"

"Yes, yes; I know." She leaned forward from her sofa-corner, fixing her eyes on his thin kindly face, which gleamed on her indistinctly through her tears. "If it's true, it's—it's dazzling. She says Leila's perfectly happy. It's as if an angel had gone about lifting gravestones, and the buried people walked again, and the living didn't shrink from them."

"That's about it," he assented.

She drew a deep breath, and sat looking away from him down the long perspective of lamp-fringed streets over which her windows hung.

"I can understand how happy you must be," he began at length.

She turned to him impetuously. "Yes, yes; I'm happy. But I'm lonely, too—lonelier than ever. I didn't take up much room in the world before; but now—where is there a corner for me? Oh, since I've begun to confess myself, why shouldn't I go on? Telling you this lifts a gravestone from *me!* You see, before this, Leila needed me. She was unhappy, and I knew it, and though we hardly ever talked of it I felt that, in a way, the thought that I'd been through the same thing, and down to the dregs of it, helped her. And her needing me helped *me*. And when the news of her marriage came my first thought was that now she'd need me more than ever, that she'd have no one but me to turn to. Yes, under all my distress there was a fierce joy in that. It was so new and wonderful to feel again that there was one person who wouldn't be able to get on without me! And now what you and Susy tell me seems to have taken my child from me; and just at first that's all I can feel."

"Of course it's all you feel." He looked at her musingly. "Why didn't Leila come to meet you?"

"That was really my fault. You see, I'd cabled that I was not sure of being able to get off on the *Utopia*, and apparently my second cable was delayed, and when she received it she'd already asked some people over Sunday—one or two of her old friends, Susy says. I'm so glad they should have wanted to go to her at once; but naturally I'd rather have been alone with her."

"You still mean to go, then?"

"Oh, I must. Susy wanted to drag me off to Ridgefield with her over Sunday, and Leila sent me word that of course I might go if I wanted to, and that I was not to think of her; but I know how disappointed she would be. Susy said she was afraid I might be upset at her having people to stay, and that, if I minded, she wouldn't urge me to come. But if *they* don't mind, why should I? And of course, if they're willing to go to Leila it must mean—"

"Of course. I'm glad you recognize that," Franklin Ide exclaimed abruptly. He stood up and went over to her, taking her hand with one of his quick gestures. "There's something I want to say to you," he began—

The next morning, in the train, through all the other contending thoughts in Mrs. Lidcote's mind there ran the warm undercurrent of what Franklin Ide had wanted to say to her.

He had wanted, she knew, to say it once before, when, nearly eight years earlier, the hazard of meeting at the end of a rainy autumn in a deserted Swiss hotel had thrown them for a fortnight into unwonted propinquity. They had walked and talked together, borrowed each other's books and newspapers, spent the long chill evenings over the fire in the dim lamplight of her little pitch-pine sitting-room; and she had been wonderfully comforted by his presence, and hard frozen places in her had melted, and she had known that she would be desperately sorry when he went. And then, just at the end, in his odd indirect way, he had let her see that it rested with her to have him stay. She could still relive the sleepless night she had given to that discovery. It was preposterous, of course, to think of repaying his devotion by accepting such a sacrifice; but how find reasons to convince him? She could not bear to let him think her less touched, less inclined to him than she was: the generosity of his love deserved that she should repay it with the truth. Yet how let him see what she felt, and yet refuse what he offered? How confess to him what had been on her lips when he made the offer: "I've seen what it did to one man; and there must never, never be another"? The tacit ignoring of her past had been the element in which their friendship lived, and she could not suddenly, to him of all men, begin to talk of herself like a guilty woman in a play. Somehow, in the end, she had managed it, had averted a direct explanation, had made him understand that her life was over, that she existed only for her daughter, and that a more definite word from him would have been almost a breach of delicacy. She was so used to behaving as if her life were over! And, at any rate, he had taken her hint, and she had been able to spare her sensitiveness and his. The next year, when he came to Florence to see her, they met again in the old friendly way; and that till now had continued to be the tenor of their intimacy.

And now, suddenly and unexpectedly, he had brought up the question again, directly this time, and in such a form that she could not evade it: putting the renewal of his plea, after so long an interval, on the ground that, on her own showing, her chief argument against it no longer existed.

"You tell me Leila's happy. If she's happy, she doesn't need you—need you, that is, in the same way as before. You wanted, I know, to be always in reach, always free and available if she should suddenly call you to her or take refuge with you. I understood that—I respected it. I didn't urge my case because I saw it was useless. You couldn't, I understood well enough, have felt free to take such happiness as life with me might give you while she was unhappy, and, as you imagined, with no hope of release. Even then I didn't feel as you did about it; I understood better the trend of things here. But ten years ago the change hadn't really come; and I had no way of convincing you that it was coming. Still, I always fancied that Leila might not think her case was closed, and so I chose to think that ours wasn't either. Let me go on thinking so, at any rate, till you've seen her, and confirmed with your own eyes what Susy Suffern tells you."

III

All through what Susy Suffern told and retold her during their four-hours' flight to the hills this plea of Ide's kept coming back to Mrs. Lidcote. She did not yet know what she felt as to its bearing on her own fate, but it was something on which her confused thoughts could stay themselves amid the welter of new impressions, and she was inexpressibly glad that he had said what he had, and said it at that particular moment. It helped her to hold fast to her identity in the rush of strange names and new categories that her cousin's talk poured out on her.

With the progress of the journey Miss Suffern's communications grew more and more amazing. She was like a cicerone preparing the mind of an inexperienced traveller for the marvels about to burst on it.

"You won't know Leila. She's had her pearls re-set. Sargent's to paint her. Oh, and I was to tell you that she hopes you won't mind being the least bit squeezed over Sunday. The house was built by Wilbour's father, you know, and it's rather old-fashioned—only ten spare bedrooms. Of course that's small for what they mean to do, and she'll show you the new plans they've had made. Their idea is to keep the present house as a wing. She told me to explain—she's so dreadfully sorry not to be able to give you a sitting-room just at first. They're thinking of Egypt for next winter, unless, of course, Wilbour gets his appointment. Oh, didn't she write you about that? Why, he wants Rome, you know—the second secretaryship. Or, rather, he wanted England; but Leila insisted that if they went abroad she must be near you. And of course what she says is law. Oh, they quite hope they'll get it. You see Horace's uncle is in the Cabinet,—one of the assistant secretaries,—and I believe he has a good deal of pull—"

"Horace's uncle? You mean Wilbour's, I suppose," Mrs. Lidcote interjected, with a gasp of which a fraction was given to Miss Suffern's flippant use of the language.

"Wilbour's? No, I don't. I mean Horace's. There's no bad feeling between them, I assure you. Since Horace's engagement was announced—you didn't know Horace was engaged? Why, he's marrying one of Bishop Thorbury's girls: the red-haired one who wrote the novel that every one's talking about, 'This Flesh of Mine.' They're to be married in the cathedral. Of course Horace *can*, because it was Leila who—but, as I say, there's not the *least* feeling, and Horace wrote himself to his uncle about Wilbour."

Mrs. Lidcote's thoughts fled back to what she had said to Ide the day before on the deck of the *Utopia*. "I didn't take up much room before, but now where is there a corner for me?" Where indeed in this crowded, topsy-turvey world, with its headlong changes and helter-skelter readjustments, its new tolerances and indifferences and accommodations, was there room for a character fashioned by slower sterner processes and a life broken under their inexorable pressure? And then, in a flash, she viewed the chaos from a new angle, and order seemed to move upon the void. If the old processes were changed, her case was changed with them; she, too, was a part of the general readjustment, a tiny fragment of the new pattern worked out in bolder freer harmonies. Since her daughter had no penalty to pay, was not she herself released by the same stroke? The rich arrears of youth and joy were gone; but was there not time enough left to accumulate new stores of happiness? That, of course, was what Franklin Ide had felt and had meant her to feel. He had seen at once what the change in her daughter's situation would make in her view of her own. It was almost—wondrously enough!—as if Leila's folly had been the means of vindicating hers.

Everything else for the moment faded for Mrs. Lidcote in the glow of her daughter's embrace. It was unnatural, it was almost terrifying, to find herself standing on a strange threshold, under an unknown roof, in a big hall full of pictures, flowers, firelight, and hurrying servants, and in this spacious unfamiliar confusion to discover Leila, bareheaded, laughing, authoritative, with a strange young man jovially echoing her welcome and transmitting her orders; but once Mrs. Lidcote had her child on her breast, and her child's "It's all right, you old darling!" in her ears, every other feeling was lost in the deep sense of well-being that only Leila's hug could give.

The sense was still with her, warming her veins and pleasantly fluttering her heart, as she went up to her room after luncheon. A little constrained by the presence of visitors, and not altogether sorry to defer for a few hours the "long talk" with her daughter for which she somehow felt herself tremulously unready, she had withdrawn, on the plea of fatigue, to the bright luxurious bedroom into which Leila had again and again apologized for having been obliged to squeeze her. The room was bigger and finer than any in her small apartment in Florence; but it was not the standard of affluence implied in her daughter's tone about it that chiefly struck her, nor yet the finish and complexity of its appointments. It was the look it shared with the rest of the house, and with the perspective of the gardens beneath its windows, of being part of an "establishment"—of something solid, avowed, founded on sacraments and precedents and principles. There was nothing about the place, or about Leila and Wilbour, that suggested either passion or peril: their relation seemed as comfortable as their furniture and as respectable as their balance at the bank.

This was, in the whole confusing experience, the thing that confused Mrs. Lidcote most, that gave her at once the deepest feeling of security for Leila and the strongest sense of apprehension for herself. Yes, there was something oppressive in the completeness and compactness of Leila's well-being. Ide had been right: her daughter did not need her. Leila, with her first embrace, had unconsciously attested the fact in the same phrase as Ide himself and as the two young women with the hats. "It's all right, you old darling!" she had said: and her mother sat alone, trying to fit herself into the new scheme of things which such a certainty betokened.

Her first distinct feeling was one of irrational resentment. If such a change was to come, why had it not come sooner? Here was she, a woman not yet old, who had paid with the best years of her life for the theft of the happiness that her daughter's contemporaries were taking as their due. There was no sense, no sequence, in it. She had had what she wanted, but she had had to pay too much for it. She had had to pay the last bitterest price of learning that love has a price: that it is worth so much and no more. She had known the anguish of watching the man she loved discover this first, and of reading the discovery in his eyes. It was a part of her history that she had not trusted herself to think of for a long time past: she always took a big turn about that haunted corner. But now, at the sight of the young man downstairs, so openly and jovially Leila's, she was overwhelmed at the senseless waste of her own adventure, and wrung with the irony of perceiving that the success or failure of the deepest human experiences may hang on a matter of chronology.

Then gradually the thought of Ide returned to her. "I chose to think that our case wasn't closed," he had said. She had been deeply touched by that. To every one else her case had been closed so long! *Finis* was scrawled all over her. But here was one man who had believed and waited, and what if what he believed in and waited for were coming true? If Leila's "all right" should really foreshadow hers?

As yet, of course, it was impossible to tell. She had fancied, indeed, when she entered the drawing-room before luncheon, that a too-sudden hush had fallen on the assembled group of Leila's friends, on the slender vociferous young women and the lounging golf-stockinged young men. They had all received her politely, with the kind of petrified politeness that may be either a tribute to age or a protest at laxity; but to them, of course, she must be an old woman because she was Leila's mother, and in a society so dominated by youth the mere presence of maturity was a constraint.

One of the young girls, however, had presently emerged from the group, and, attaching herself to Mrs. Lidcote, had listened to her with a blue gaze of admiration which gave the older woman a sudden happy consciousness of her long-forgotten social graces. It was agreeable to find herself attracting this young Charlotte Wynn, whose mother had been among her closest friends, and in whom something of the soberness and softness of the earlier manners had survived. But the little colloquy, broken up by the announcement of luncheon, could of course result in nothing more definite than this reminiscent emotion.

No, she could not yet tell how her own case was to be fitted into the new order of things; but there were more people—"older people" Leila had put it—arriving by the afternoon train, and that evening at dinner she would doubtless be able to judge. She began to wonder nervously who the new-comers might be. Probably she would be spared the embarrassment of finding old acquaintances among them; but it was odd that her daughter had mentioned no names.

Leila had proposed that, later in the afternoon, Wilbour should take her mother for a drive: she said she wanted them to have a "nice, quiet talk." But Mrs. Lidcote wished her talk with Leila to come first, and had, moreover, at luncheon, caught stray allusions to an impending tennis-match in which her son-in-law was engaged. Her fatigue had been a sufficient pretext for declining the drive, and she had begged Leila to think of her as peacefully resting in her room till such time as they could snatch their quiet moment.

"Before tea, then, you duck!" Leila with a last kiss had decided; and presently Mrs. Lidcote, through her open window, had heard the fresh loud voices of her daughter's visitors chiming across the gardens from the tennis-court.

IV

Leila had come and gone, and they had had their talk. It had not lasted as long as Mrs. Lidcote wished, for in the middle of it Leila had been summoned to the telephone to receive an important message from town, and had sent word to her mother that she couldn't come back just then, as one of the young ladies had been called away unexpectedly and arrangements had to be made for her departure. But the mother and daughter had had almost an hour together, and Mrs. Lidcote was happy. She had never seen Leila so tender, so solicitous. The only thing that troubled her was the very excess of this solicitude, the exaggerated expression of her daughter's annoyance that their first moments together should have been marred by the presence of strangers.

"Not strangers to me, darling, since they're friends of yours," her mother had assured her.

"Yes; but I know your feeling, you queer wild mother. I know how you've always hated people." (*Hated people!* Had Leila forgotten why?) "And that's why I told Susy that if you preferred to go with her to Ridgefield on Sunday I should perfectly understand, and patiently wait for our good hug. But you didn't really mind them at luncheon, did you, dearest?"

Mrs. Lidcote, at that, had suddenly thrown a startled look at her daughter. "I don't mind things of that kind any longer," she had simply answered.

"But that doesn't console me for having exposed

you to the bother of it, for having let you come here when I ought to have *ordered* you off to Ridgefield with Susy. If Susy hadn't been stupid she'd have made you go there with her. I hate to think of you up here all alone."

Again Mrs. Lidcote tried to read something more than a rather obtuse devotion in her daughter's radiant gaze. "I'm glad to have had a rest this afternoon, dear; and later—"

"Oh, yes, later, when all this fuss is over, we'll more than make up for it, sha'n't we, you precious darling?" And at this point Leila had been summoned to the telephone, leaving Mrs. Lidcote to her conjectures.

These were still floating before her in cloudy uncertainty when Miss Suffern tapped at the door.

"You've come to take me down to tea? I'd forgotten how late it was," Mrs. Lidcote exclaimed.

Miss Suffern, a plump peering little woman, with prim hair and a conciliatory smile, nervously adjusted the pendent bugles of her elaborate black dress. Miss Suffern was always in mourning, and always commemorating the demise of distant relatives by wearing the discarded wardrobe of their next of kin. "It isn't *exactly* mourning," she would say; "but it's the only stitch of black poor Julia had—and of course George was only my mother's step-cousin."

As she came forward Mrs. Lidcote found herself humorously wondering whether she were mourning Horace Pursh's divorce in one of his mother's old black satins.

"Oh, *did* you mean to go down for tea?" Susy Suffern peered at her, a little fluttered. "Leila sent me up to keep you company. She thought it would be cozier for you to stay here. She was afraid you were feeling rather tired."

"I was; but I've had the whole afternoon to rest in. And this wonderful sofa to help me."

"Leila told me to tell you that she'd rush up for a minute before dinner, after everybody had arrived; but the train is always dreadfully late. She's in despair at not giving you a sitting-room; she wanted to know if I thought you really minded."

"Of course I don't mind. It's not like Leila to think I should." Mrs. Lidcote drew aside to make way for the housemaid, who appeared in the doorway bearing a table spread with a bewildering variety of tea-cakes.

"Leila saw to it herself," Miss Suffern murmured as the door closed. "Her one idea is that you should feel happy here."

It struck Mrs. Lidcote as one more mark of the subverted state of things that her daughter's solicitude should find expression in the multiplicity of sandwiches and the piping-hotness of muffins; but then everything that had happened since her arrival seemed to increase her confusion.

The note of a motor-horn down the drive gave another turn to her thoughts. "Are those the new arrivals already?" she asked.

"Oh, dear, no; they won't be here till after seven." Miss Suffern craned her head from the window to catch a glimpse of the motor. "It must be Charlotte leaving."

"Was it the little Wynn girl who was called away in a hurry? I hope it's not on account of illness."

"Oh, no; I believe there was some mistake about dates. Her mother telephoned her that she was expected at the Stepleys, at Fishkill, and she had to be rushed over to Albany to catch a train."

Mrs. Lidcote meditated. "I'm sorry. She's a charming young thing. I hoped I should have another talk with her this evening after dinner."

"Yes; it's too bad." Miss Suffern's gaze grew vague. "You *do* look tired, you know," she continued, seating herself at the tea-table and preparing to dispense its delicacies. "You must go straight back to your sofa and let me wait on you. The excitement has told on you more than you think, and you mustn't fight against it any longer. Just stay quietly up here and let yourself go. You'll have Leila to yourself on Monday."

Mrs. Lidcote received the tea-cup which her cousin proffered, but showed no other disposition to obey her injunctions. For a moment she stirred her tea in silence; then she asked: "Is it your idea that I should stay quietly up here till Monday?"

Miss Suffern set down her cup with a gesture so sudden that it endangered an adjacent plate of scones. When she had assured herself of the safety of the scones she looked up with a fluttered laugh. "Perhaps, dear, by to-morrow you'll be feeling differently. The air here, you know—"

"Yes, I know." Mrs. Lidcote bent forward to help herself to a scone. "Who's arriving this evening?" she asked.

Miss Suffern frowned and peered. "You know my wretched head for names. Leila told me—but there are so many—"

"So many? She didn't tell me she expected a big party."

"Oh, not big: but rather outside of her little group. And of course, as it's the first time, she's a little excited at having the older set."

"The older set? Our contemporaries, you mean?"

"Why—yes." Miss Suffern paused as if to gather herself up for a leap. "The Ashton Gileses," she brought out.

"The Ashton Gileses? Really? I shall be glad to see

Mary Giles again. It must be eighteen years," said Mrs. Lidcote steadily.

"Yes," Miss Suffern gasped, precipitately refilling her cup.

"The Ashton Gileses; and who else?"

"Well, the Sam Fresbies. But the most important person, of course, is Mrs. Lorin Boulger."

"Mrs. Boulger? Leila didn't tell me she was coming."

"Didn't she? I suppose she forgot everything when she saw you. But the party was got up for Mrs. Boulger. You see, it's very important that she should—well, take a fancy to Leila and Wilbour; his being appointed to Rome virtually depends on it. And you know Leila insists on Rome in order to be near you. So she asked Mary Giles, who's intimate with the Boulgers, if the visit couldn't possibly be arranged; and Mary's cable caught Mrs. Boulger at Cherbourg. She's to be only a fortnight in America; and getting her to come directly here was rather a triumph."

"Yes; I see it was," said Mrs. Lidcote.

"You know, she's rather—rather fussy; and Mary was a little doubtful if—"

"If she would, on account of Leila?" Mrs. Lidcote murmured.

"Well, yes. In her official position. But luckily she's a friend of the Barkleys. And finding the Gileses and Fresbies here will make it all right. The times have changed!" Susy Suffern indulgently summed up.

Mrs. Lidcote smiled. "Yes; a few years ago it would have seemed improbable that I should ever again be dining with Mary Giles and Harriet Fresbie and Mrs. Lorin Boulger."

Miss Suffern did not at the moment seem disposed to enlarge upon this theme; and after an interval of silence Mrs. Lidcote suddenly resumed: "Do they know I'm here, by the way?"

The effect of her question was to produce in Miss Suffern an exaggerated access of peering and frowning. She twitched the tea-things about, fingered her bugles, and, looking at the clock, exclaimed amazedly: "Mercy! Is it seven already?"

"Not that it can make any difference, I suppose," Mrs. Lidcote continued. "But did Leila tell them I was coming?"

Miss Suffern looked at her with pain. "Why, you don't suppose, dearest, that Leila would do anything—"

Mrs. Lidcote went on: "For, of course, it's of the first importance, as you say, that Mrs. Lorin Boulger should be favorably impressed, in order that Wilbour may have the best possible chance of getting Rome."

"I *told* Leila you'd feel that, dear. You see, it's actually on *your* account—so that they may get a post near you—that Leila invited Mrs. Boulger."

"Yes, I see that." Mrs. Lidcote, abruptly rising from her seat, turned her eyes to the clock. "But, as you say, it's getting late. Oughtn't we to dress for dinner?"

Miss Suffern, at the suggestion, stood up also, an agitated hand among her bugles. "I do wish I could persuade you to stay up here this evening. I'm sure Leila'd be happier if you would. Really, you're much too tired to come down."

"What nonsense, Susy!" Mrs. Lidcote spoke with sudden sharpness, her hand stretched to the bell. "When do we dine? At half-past eight? Then I must really send you packing. At my age it takes time to dress."

Miss Suffern, thus projected toward the threshold, lingered there to repeat: "Leila'll never forgive herself if you make an effort you're not up to." But Mrs. Lidcote smiled on her without answering, and the icy light-wave propelled her through the door.

V

Mrs. Lidcote, though she had made the gesture of ringing for her maid, had not done so.

When the door closed, she continued to stand motionless in the middle of her soft spacious room. The fire which had been kindled at twilight danced on the brightness of silver and mirrors and sober gilding; and the sofa toward which she had been urged by Miss Suffern heaped up its cushions in inviting proximity to a table laden with new books and papers. She could not recall having ever been more luxuriously housed, or having ever had so strange a sense of being out alone, under the night, in a wind-beaten plain. She sat down by the fire and thought.

A knock on the door made her lift her head, and she saw her daughter on the threshold. The intricate ordering of Leila's fair hair and the flying folds of her dressing-gown showed that she had interrupted her dressing to hasten to her mother; but once in the room she paused a moment, smiling uncertainly, as though she had forgotten the object of her haste.

Mrs. Lidcote rose to her feet. "Time to dress, dearest? Don't scold! I sha'n't be late."

"To dress?" Leila stood before her with a puzzled look. "Why, I thought, dear—I mean, I hoped you'd decided just to stay here quietly and rest."

Her mother smiled. "But I've been resting all the afternoon!"

"Yes, but—you know you *do* look tired. And

when Susy told me just now that you meant to make the effort—"

"You came to stop me?"

"I came to tell you that you needn't feel in the least obliged—"

"Of course. I understand that."

There was a pause during which Leila, vaguely averting herself from her mother's scrutiny, drifted toward the dressing-table and began to disturb the symmetry of the brushes and bottles laid out on it.

"Do your visitors know that I'm here?" Mrs. Lidcote suddenly went on.

"Do they— Of course—why, naturally," Leila rejoined, absorbed in trying to turn the stopper of a salts-bottle.

"Then won't they think it odd if I don't appear?"

"Oh, not in the least, dearest. I assure you they'll *all* understand." Leila laid down the bottle and turned back to her mother, her face alight with reassurance.

Mrs. Lidcote stood motionless, her head erect, her smiling eyes on her daughter's. "Will they think it odd if I *do*?"

Leila stopped short, her lips half parted to reply. As she paused, the colour stole over her bare neck, swept up to her throat, and burst into flame in her cheeks. Thence it sent its devastating crimson up to her very temples, to the lobes of her ears, to the edges of her eye-lids, beating all over her in fiery waves, as if fanned by some imperceptible wind.

Mrs. Lidcote silently watched the conflagration; then she turned away her eyes with a slight laugh. "I only meant that I was afraid it might upset the arrangement of your dinner-table if I didn't come down. If you can assure me that it won't, I believe I'll take you at your word and go back to this irresistible sofa." She paused, as if waiting for her daughter to speak; then she held out her arms. "Run off and dress, dearest; and don't have me on your mind." She clasped Leila close, pressing a long kiss on the last afterglow of her subsiding blush. "I do feel the least bit overdone, and if it won't inconvenience you to have me drop out of things, I believe I'll basely take to my bed and stay there till your party scatters. And now run off, or you'll be late; and make my excuses to them all."

VI

The Barkleys' visitors had dispersed, and Mrs. Lidcote, completely restored by her two days' rest, found herself, on the following Monday alone with her children and Miss Suffern.

There was a note of jubilation in the air, for the party had "gone off" so extraordinarily well, and so completely, as it appeared, to the satisfaction of Mrs. Lorin Boulger, that Wilbour's early appointment to Rome was almost to be counted on. So certain did this seem that the prospect of a prompt reunion mitigated the distress with which Leila learned of her mother's decision to return almost immediately to Italy. No one understood this decision; it seemed to Leila absolutely unintelligible that Mrs. Lidcote should not stay on with them till their own fate was fixed, and Wilbour echoed her astonishment.

"Why shouldn't you, as Leila says, wait here till we can all pack up and go together?"

Mrs. Lidcote smiled her gratitude with her refusal. "After all, it's not yet sure that you'll be packing up."

"Oh, you ought to have seen Wilbour with Mrs. Boulger," Leila triumphed.

"No, you ought to have seen Leila with her," Leila's husband exulted.

Miss Suffern enthusiastically appended: "I *do* think inviting Harriet Fresbie was a stroke of genius!"

"Oh, we'll be with you soon," Leila laughed. "So soon that it's really foolish to separate."

But Mrs. Lidcote held out with the quiet firmness which her daughter knew it was useless to oppose. After her long months in India, it was really imperative, she declared, that she should get back to Florence and see what was happening to her little place there; and she had been so comfortable on the *Utopia* that she had a fancy to return by the same ship. There was nothing for it, therefore, but to acquiesce in her decision and keep her with them till the afternoon before the day of the *Utopia's* sailing. This arrangement fitted in with certain projects which, during her two days' seclusion, Mrs. Lidcote had silently matured. It had become to her of the first importance to get away as soon as she could, and the little place in Florence, which held her past in every fold of its curtains and between every page of its books, seemed now to her the one spot where that past would be endurable to look upon.

She was not unhappy during the intervening days. The sight of Leila's well-being, the sense of Leila's tenderness, were, after all, what she had come for; and of these she had had full measure. Leila had never been happier or more tender; and the contemplation of her bliss, and the enjoyment of her affection, were an absorbing occupation for her mother. But they were also a sharp strain on certain overtightened chords, and Mrs. Lidcote, when at last she found herself alone in the New York hotel to which she had returned the night before embarking, had the feeling that she had just escaped with her life from the clutch of a giant hand.

She had refused to let her daughter come to town with her; she had even rejected Susy Suffern's company. She wanted no viaticum but that of her own thoughts; and she let these come to her without shrinking from them as she sat in the same high-hung sitting-room in which, just a week before, she and Franklin Ide had had their memorable talk.

She had promised her friend to let him hear from her, but she had not kept her promise. She knew that he had probably come back from Chicago, and that if he learned of her sudden decision to return to Italy it would be impossible for her not to see him before sailing; and as she wished above all things not to see him she had kept silent, intending to send him a letter from the steamer.

There was no reason why she should wait till then to write it. The actual moment was more favorable, and the task, though not agreeable, would at least bridge over an hour of her lonely evening. She went up to the writing-table, drew out a sheet of paper and began to write his name. And as she did so, the door opened and he came in.

The words she met him with were the last she could have imagined herself saying when they had parted. "How in the world did you know that I was here?"

He caught her meaning in a flash. "You didn't want me to, then?" He stood looking at her. "Suppose I ought to have taken your silence as meaning that. But I happened to meet Mrs. Wynn, who is stopping here, and she asked me to dine with her and Charlotte, and Charlotte's young man. They told me they'd seen you arriving this afternoon, and I couldn't help coming up."

There was a pause between them, which Mrs. Lidcote at last surprisingly broke with the exclamation: "Ah, she *did* recognize me, then!"

"Recognize you?" He stared. "Why—"

"Oh, I saw she did, though she never moved an eyelid. I saw it by Charlotte's blush. The child has the prettiest blush. I saw that her mother wouldn't let her speak to me."

Ide put down his hat with an impatient laugh. "Hasn't Leila cured you of your delusions?"

She looked at him intently. "Then you don't think Margaret Wynn meant to cut me?"

"I think your ideas are absurd."

She paused for a perceptible moment without taking this up; then she said, at a tangent: "I'm sailing tomorrow early. I meant to write to you—there's the letter I'd begun."

Ide followed her gesture, and then turned his eyes back to her face. "You didn't mean to see me, then, or even to let me know that you were going till you'd left?"

"I felt it would be easier to explain to you in a letter—"

"What in God's name is there to explain?" She made no reply, and he pressed on: "It can't be that you're worried about Leila, for Charlotte Wynn told me she'd been there last week, and there was a big party arriving when she left: Fresbies and Gileses, and Mrs. Lorin Boulger—all the board of examiners! If Leila has passed *that*, she's got her degree."

Mrs. Lidcote had dropped down into a corner of the sofa where she had sat during their talk of the week before. "I was stupid," she began abruptly. "I ought to have gone to Ridgefield with Susy. I didn't see till afterward that I was expected to."

"You were expected to?"

"Yes. Oh, it wasn't Leila's fault. She suffered—poor darling; she was distracted. But she'd asked her party before she knew I was arriving."

"Oh, as to that—" Ide drew a deep breath of relief. "I can understand that it must have been a disappointment not to have you to herself just at first. But, after all, you were among old friends or their children: the Gileses and Fresbies—and little Charlotte Wynn." He paused a moment before the last name, and scrutinized her hesitatingly. "Even if they came at the wrong time, you must have been glad to see them all at Leila's."

She gave him back his look with a faint smile. "I didn't see them."

"You didn't see them?"

"No. That is, excepting little Charlotte Wynn. That child is exquisite. We had a talk before luncheon the day I arrived. But when her mother found out that I was staying in the house she telephoned her to leave immediately, and so I didn't see her again."

The colour rushed to Ide's sallow face. "I don't know where you get such ideas!"

She pursued, as if she had not heard him: "Oh, and I saw Mary Giles for a minute too. Susy Suffern brought her up to my room the last evening, after dinner, when all the others were at bridge. She meant it kindly—but it wasn't much use."

"But what were you doing in your room in the evening after dinner?"

"Why, you see, when I found out my mistake in coming,—how embarrassing it was for Leila, I mean—I simply told her I was very tired, and preferred to stay upstairs till the party was over."

Ide, with a groan, struck his hand against the arm of his chair. "I wonder how much of all this you simply imagined!"

"I didn't imagine the fact of Harriet Fresbie's not

even asking if she might see me when she knew I was in the house. Nor of Mary Giles's getting Susy, at the eleventh hour, to smuggle her up to my room when the others wouldn't know where she'd gone; nor poor Leila's ghastly fear lest Mrs. Lorin Boulger, for whom the party was given, should guess I was in the house, and prevent her husband's giving Wilbour the second secretaryship because she'd been obliged to spend a night under the same roof with his mother-in-law!"

Ide continued to drum on his chair-arm with exasperated fingers. "You don't *know* that any of the acts you describe are due to the causes you suppose."

Mrs. Lidcote paused before replying, as if honestly trying to measure the weight of this argument. Then she said in a low tone: "I know that Leila was in an agony lest I should come down to dinner the first night. And it was for me she was afraid, not for herself. Leila is never afraid for herself."

"But the conclusions you draw are simply preposterous. There are narrow-minded women everywhere, but the women who were at Leila's knew perfectly well that their going there would give her a sort of social sanction, and if they were willing that she should have it, why on earth should they want to withhold it from you?"

"That's what I told myself a week ago, in this very room, after my first talk with Susy Suffern." She lifted a misty smile to his anxious eyes. "That's why I listened to what you said to me the same evening, and why your arguments half convinced me, and made me think that what had been possible for Leila might not be impossible for me. If the new dispensation had come, why not for me as well as for the others? I can't tell you the flight my imagination took!"

Franklin Ide rose from his seat and crossed the room to a chair near her sofa-corner. "All I cared about was that it seemed—for the moment—to be carrying you toward me," he said.

"I cared about that, too. That's why I meant to go away without seeing you." They gave each other grave look for look. "Because, you see, I was mistaken," she went on. "We were both mistaken. You say it's preposterous that the women who didn't object to accepting Leila's hospitality should have objected to meeting me under her roof. And so it is; but I begin to understand why. It's simply that society is much too busy to revise its own judgments. Probably no one in the house with me stopped to consider that my case and Leila's were identical. They only remembered that I'd done something which, at the time I did it, was condemned by society. My case has been passed on and classified: I'm the woman who has been cut for nearly twenty years. The older people have half forgotten why, and the younger ones have never really known: it's simply become a tradition to cut me. And traditions that have lost their meaning are the hardest of all to destroy."

Ide sat motionless while she spoke. As she ended, he stood up with a short laugh and walked across the room to the window. Outside, the immense black prospect of New York, strung with its myriad lines of light, stretched away into the smoky edges of the night. He showed it to her with a gesture.

"What do you suppose such words as you've been using—'society,' 'tradition,' and the rest—mean to all the life out there?"

She came and stood by him in the window. "Less than nothing, of course. But you and I are not out there. We're shut up in a little tight round of habit and association, just as we're shut up in this room. Remember, I thought I'd got out of it once; but what really happened was that the other people went out, and left me in the same little room. The only difference was that I was there alone. Oh, I've made it habitable now, I'm used to it; but I've lost any illusions I may have had as to an angel's opening the door."

Ide again laughed impatiently. "Well, if the door won't open, why not let another prisoner in? At least it would be less of a solitude—"

She turned from the dark window back into the vividly lighted room.

"It would be more of a prison. You forget that I know all about that. We're all imprisoned, of course—all of us middling people, who don't carry our freedom in our brains. But we've accommodated ourselves to our different cells, and if we're moved suddenly into new ones we're likely to find a stone wall where we thought there was thin air, and to knock ourselves senseless against it. I saw a man do that once."

Ide, leaning with folded arms against the window-frame, watched her in silence as she moved restlessly about the room, gathering together some scattered books and tossing a handful of torn letters into the paper-basket. When she ceased, he rejoined: "All you say is based on preconceived theories. Why didn't you put them to the test by coming down to meet your old friends? Don't you see the inference they would naturally draw from your hiding yourself when they arrived? It looked as though you were afraid of them—or as though you hadn't forgiven them. Either way, you put them in the wrong instead of waiting to let them put you in the right. If Leila had buried herself in a desert do you suppose society would have gone to fetch her out? You say you were afraid for Leila and that she was afraid for you. Don't you see what all these complications of feeling mean? Simply that you were too nervous at the moment to let things happen naturally, just as you're too nervous now to judge them rationally." He paused and turned his eyes to her face. "Don't try to just yet. Give yourself a little more time. Give *me* a little more time. I've always known it would take time."

He moved nearer, and she let him have her hand. With the grave kindness of his face so close above her she felt like a child roused out of frightened dreams and finding a light in the room.

"Perhaps you're right—" she heard herself begin; then something within her clutched her back, and her hand fell away from him.

"I know I'm right: trust me," he urged. "We'll talk of this in Florence soon."

She stood before him, feeling with despair his kindness, his patience and his unreality. Everything he said seemed like a painted gauze let down between herself and the real facts of life; and a sudden desire seized her to tear the gauze into shreds.

She drew back and looked at him with a smile of superficial reassurance. "You *are* right—about not talking any longer now. I'm nervous and tired, and it would do no good. I brood over things too much. As you say, I must try not to shrink from people." She turned away and glanced at the clock. "Why, it's only ten! If I send you off I shall begin to brood again; and if you stay we shall go on talking about the same thing. Why shouldn't we go down and see Margaret Wynn for half an hour?"

She spoke lightly and rapidly, her brilliant eyes on his face. As she watched him, she saw it change, as if her smile had thrown a too vivid light upon it.

"Oh, no—not to-night!" he exclaimed.

"Not to-night? Why, what other night have I, when I'm off at dawn? Besides, I want to show you at once that I mean to be more sensible—that I'm not going to be afraid of people any more. And I should really like another glimpse of little Charlotte." He stood before her, his hand in his beard, with the gesture he had in moments of perplexity. "Come!" she ordered him gaily, turning to the door.

He followed her and laid his hand on her arm. "Don't you think—hadn't you better let me go first and see? They told me they'd had a tiring day at the dressmaker's. I daresay they have gone to bed."

"But you said they'd a young man of Charlotte's dining with them. Surely he wouldn't have left by ten? At any rate, I'll go down with you and see. It takes so long if one sends a servant first." She put him gently aside, and then paused as a new thought struck her. "Or wait; my maid's in the next room. I'll tell her to go and ask if Margaret will receive me. Yes, that's much the best way."

She turned back and went toward the door that led to her bedroom; but before she could open it she felt Ide's quick touch again.

"I believe—I remember now—Charlotte's young man was suggesting that they should all go out—to a music-hall or something of the sort. I'm sure—I'm positively sure that you won't find them."

Her hand dropped from the door, his dropped from her arm, and as they drew back and faced each other she saw the blood rise slowly through his sallow skin, redden his neck and ears, encroach upon the edges of his beard, and settle in dull patches under his kind troubled eyes. She had seen the same blush on another face, and the same impulse of compassion she had then felt made her turn her gaze away again.

A knock on the door broke the silence, and a porter put his head into the room.

"It's only just to know how many pieces there'll be to go down to the steamer in the morning."

With the words she felt that the veil of painted gauze was torn in tatters, and that she was moving again among the grim edges of reality.

"Oh, dear," she exclaimed, "I never *can* remember! Wait a minute; I shall have to ask my maid."

She opened her bedroom door and called out: "Annette!"

GERTRUDE STEIN [1874–1946]

GERTRUDE STEIN became a celebrity in her own time. In her Paris apartment she was hostess to two generations of American writers, artists, soldiers, and tourists. She was a literary expatriate who admired her native America, but chose to live in France. In her own writing she was a radical innovator in her theories of language and in new and "difficult" ways of expression. In 1903 she moved into rooms at 27 rue de Fleurus, Paris, and began collecting the paintings of Picasso, Braque, Cézanne, and Matisse. These artists profoundly influenced her theories of art and literature. Some of her portraits have been called "verbal still-lifes," and like Picasso she learned the values of reducing reality to primary forms. Her experimental narratives, word-ballets, depictions of people, places, and events became increasingly non-representational. The primitive and gnomic-reiterative aspect of her prose won her the title of "the Mother Goose of Montparnasse"; but as one critic put it, she was a Mother Goose with a mind. "When I said, A rose is a rose is a rose, and then later made that into a ring, I made poetry and what did I do I caressed completely caressed and addressed a noun."

Miss Stein was born in Allegheny, Pennsylvania, of German-Jewish stock. Her family had prospered in America, and like Henry James, whose work she admired, she was educated both in America and in Europe. Also like James, she turned away from the literature of naturalism and social protest. Comparing herself with him, she claimed they together had initiated the modern tendency in literature. As an undergraduate at Radcliffe studying under William James, she became interested in the motions of the mind and what James had termed the "stream" of consciousness. From Harvard she entered the Johns Hopkins Medical School, but after four years became bored with academic routine, refused to take examinations, and left for Europe to join her brother Leo. Together they spent a year in London, then moved to Paris where she began her long career as a collector and patron of the Spanish cubist painters and as guide, philosopher, and friend of artists and writers. Here she was joined by Alice B. Toklas, who became her lifelong companion, chef, secretary, and alter ego. In her most famous and most readable book, *The Autobiography of Alice B. Toklas* (1933), Gertrude Stein wrote her own diary of the Paris years during the 1920's, a kind of Jamesian indirect narration through the voice of Miss Toklas that allowed her to comment more freely on the many contemporaries who visited her salon, as well as to assess without modesty her own undoubted literary talents. The book is rich in literary gossip and anecdote. Eliot, Pound, Fitzgerald, and Hemingway were among the Americans who came to exchange ideas with the author of *Three Lives* (1909), *Tender Buttons* (1914), and *The Making of Americans* (1924), while she sat under her own portrait painted by Picasso and talked about art and literature.

Her technique was evident from the first. In an early story, "Melanctha," analyzing the mental and psychological behavior of a young Negro girl and her lover, she employed simple language and verbal repetition (she called it "insistence") to maintain "a continuous present." By eliminating past time and most of the aids of the traditional novelist, concentrating on words alone as if they contained the same spatial and plastic qualities as pigment in a painting, she accomplished a fresh, if puzzling, result. Her later writing went even further in rejecting conventional syntax and punctuation. One critic described the style as "art by subtraction." Another described *Tender Buttons* as "thought-in-the-process-of-being-recorded." In her plays, such as *Four Saints in Three Acts* (1929), she relied on words arranged in patterns and rhythmic groupings, recurring structures of sounds and words producing the effect of a musical ballet rather than a dramatic performance.

To explain and illustrate her literary experiments, Miss Stein wrote a number of volumes of aesthetic and compositional theory. Perhaps in the long run she will be valued more for her definitions of art and language than for her creative work. In both, however, there is the same cryptic, repetitive style. In *Composition as Explanation* (1926), first delivered as a lecture at Oxford and Cambridge, she discusses her ideas of time, composition, history, and the "continuous present." *How to Write* (1931), *Lectures in America* (1935), *The Geographical History of America* (1936), *Picasso* (1939), and *What Are Masterpieces* (1940) are among her theoretical books with oblique comments on her own writing. Some of her creative work cannot be considered entirely apart from the theories it was written to illustrate; it may be that interest in her most difficult writing will be limited to those who subscribe to the Stein cult. For others, Gertrude Stein may be one of those fascinating figures of literature whom it is more interesting to read about than to read.

During World War II she and Miss Toklas lived in the south of France. Two books of this period were *Wars I Have Seen* (1944) and *Brewsie and Willie* (1946). After her return to Paris she was visited by many American soldiers who regarded her as a generous hostess and a tourist attraction. She died in Paris in 1946. Her last words were two questions: "What is the answer?" and failing to hear a reply, "In that case, what is the question?" The precise nature of her reputation is still a question, but with the modern emphasis on the anti-naturalistic in literature, her innovations seem to have gained contemporary relevance and significance.

Further reading: *Selected Writings of Gertrude Stein* (Modern Library). J. M. Brinnin, *The Third Rose: Gertrude Stein and Her World*, 1959. Elizabeth Sprigge, *Gertrude Stein: Her Life and Her Work*, 1957.

The Life and Death of Juan Gris

Juan Gris, the Spanish cubist painter who died in 1927, was greatly admired by Gertrude Stein. Speaking as if by Miss Toklas, she wrote in *The Autobiography:* "The most moving thing Gertrude Stein has ever written is The Life and Death of Juan Gris." The piece was first printed in *transition.* The present text is from *Portraits and Prayers* (1934).

Juan Gris was one of the younger children of a well-to-do merchant of Madrid. The earliest picture he has of himself is at about five years of age dressed in a little lace dress standing beside his mother who was very sweet and pleasantly maternal-looking. When he was about seven years old his father failed in business honorably and the family fell upon very hard times but in one way and another two sons and a daughter lived to grow up well educated and on the whole prosperous. Juan went to the school of engineering at Madrid and when about seventeen came to Paris to study. He tells delightful stories of his father and Spanish ways which strangely enough he never liked. He had very early a very great attraction and love for French culture. French culture has always seduced me he was fond of saying. It seduces me and then I am seduced over again. He used to tell how Spaniards love not to resist temptation. In order to please them the better class merchants such as his father would always have to leave many little things about everything else being packages carefully tied up and in the back on shelves. He used to dwell upon the lack of trust and comradeship in Spanish life. Each one is a general or does not fight and if he does not fight each one is a general. No one that is no Spaniard can help any one because no one no Spaniard can help any one. And this being so and it is so Juan Gris was a brother and comrade to every one being one as no one ever had been one. That is the proportion. One to any one number of millions. That is any proportion. Juan Gris was that one. French culture was always a seduction. Bracque who was such a one was always a seduction seducing French culture seducing again and again. Josette equable intelligent faithful spontaneous delicate courageous delightful forethoughtful the school of Fontainebleau delicate deliberate measured and free all these things seduced. I am seduced and then I am seduced over again he was fond of saying. He had his own Spanish gift of intimacy. We were intimate. Juan knew what he did. In the beginning he did all sorts of things he used to draw for humorous illustrated papers he had a child a boy named George he lived about he was not young and enthusiastic. The first serious exhibition of his pictures was at the Galerie Kahnweiler rue Vignon in 1914. As a Spaniard he knew cubism and had stepped through into it. He had stepped through it. There was beside this perfection. To have it shown you. Then came the war and desertion. There was little aid. Four years partly illness much perfection and rejoining beauty and perfection and then at the end there came a definite creation of something. This is what is to be measured. He made something that is to be measured. And that is that something.

Therein Juan Gris is not everything but more than anything. He made that thing. He made the thing. He made a thing to be measured. Later having done it he could be sorry it was not why they like it. And so he made it very well loving and he made it with plainly playing. And he liked a knife and all but reasonably. This is what is made to be and he then did some stage setting. We liked it but nobody else could see that something is everything. It is everything if it is what is it. Nobody can ask about measuring. Unfortunately. Juan could go on living. No one can say that Henry Kahnweiler can be left out of him. I remember he said Kahnweiler goes on but no one buys anything and I said it to him and he smiled so gently and said I was everything. This is the history of Juan Gris.

FROM *The Autobiography of Alice B. Toklas*

Miss Stein said that she wrote the book in six weeks while staying at Bilginin in southern France in 1932. Published the following year, it became a best-seller, the first time her writing had brought her an income. The present text is that of the Random House edition (1960).

[Ernest Hemingway]

The first thing that happened when we were back in Paris was Hemingway with a letter of introduction from Sherwood Anderson.

I remember very well the impression I had of Hemingway that first afternoon. He was an extraordinarily good-looking young man, twenty-three years old. It was not long after that that everybody was twenty-six. It became the period of being twenty-six. During the next two or three years all the young men were twenty-six years old. It was the right age apparently for that time and place. There were one or two under twenty, for example George Lynes but they did not count as Gertrude Stein carefully explained to them. If they were young men they were twenty-six. Later on, much later on they were twenty-one and twenty-two.

So Hemingway was twenty-three, rather foreign looking, with passionately interested, rather than interesting eyes. He sat in front of Gertrude Stein and listened and looked.

They talked then, and more and more, a great deal together. He asked her to come and spend an evening in their apartment and look at his work. Hemingway had then and has always a very good instinct for finding apartments in strange but pleasing localities and good femmes de ménage and good food. This his first apartment was just off the place du Tertre. We spent the evening there and he and Gertrude Stein went over all the writing he had done up to that time. He had begun the novel that it was inevitable he would begin and there were the little poems afterwards printed by McAlmon in the Contract Edition. Gertrude Stein rather liked the poems, they were direct, Kiplingesque, but the novel she found wanting. There is a great deal of description in this, she said, and not particularly good description. Begin over again and concentrate, she said.

Hemingway was at this time Paris correspondent for a canadian newspaper. He was obliged there to express what he called the canadian viewpoint.

He and Gertrude Stein used to walk together and talk together a great deal. One day she said to him, look here, you say you and your wife have a little money between you. Is it enough to live on if you live quietly. Yes, he said. Well, she said, then do it. If you keep on doing newspaper work you will never see things, you will only see words and that will not do, that is of course if you intend to be a writer. Hemingway said he undoubtedly intended to be a writer. He and his wife went away on a trip and shortly after Hemingway turned up alone. He came to the house about ten o'clock in the morning and he stayed, he stayed for lunch, he stayed all afternoon, he stayed for dinner and he stayed until about ten o'clock at night and then all of a sudden he announced that his wife was enceinte and then with great bitterness, and I, I am too young to be a father. We consoled him as best we could and sent him on his way.

When they came back Hemingway said that he had made up his mind. They would go back to America and he would work hard for a year and with what he would earn and what they had they would settle down and he would give up newspaper work and make himself a writer. They went away and well within the prescribed year they came back with a new born baby. Newspaper work was over.

The first thing to do when they came back was as they thought to get the baby baptised. They wanted

Gertrude Stein and myself to be god-mothers and an english war comrade of Hemingway was to be god-father. We were all born of different religions and most of us were not practising any, so it was rather difficult to know in what church the baby could be baptised. We spent a great deal of time that winter, all of us, discussing the matter. Finally it was decided that it should be baptised episcopalian and episcopalian it was. Just how it was managed with the assortment of god-parents I am sure I do not know, but it was baptised in the episcopalian chapel.

Writer or painter god-parents are notoriously unreliable. That is, there is certain before long to be a cooling of friendship. I know several cases of this, poor Paulot Picasso's god-parents have wandered out of sight and just as naturally it is a long time since any of us have seen or heard of our Hemingway god-child.

However in the beginning we were active god-parents, I particularly. I embroidered a little chair and I knitted a gay coloured garment for the god-child. In the meantime the god-child's father was very earnestly at work making himself a writer.

Gertrude Stein never corrects any detail of anybody's writing, she sticks strictly to general principles, the way of seeing what the writer chooses to see, and the relation between that vision and the way it gets down. When the vision is not complete the words are flat, it is very simple, there can be no mistake about it, so she insists. It was at this time that Hemingway began the short things that afterwards were printed in a volume called In Our Time.

One day Hemingway came in very excited about Ford Madox Ford and the Transatlantic. Ford Madox Ford had started the Transatlantic some months before. A good many years before, indeed before the war, we had met Ford Madox Ford who was at that time Ford Madox Hueffer. He was married to Violet Hunt and Violet Hunt and Gertrude Stein were next to each other at the tea table and talked a great deal together. I was next to Ford Madox Hueffer and I liked him very much and I liked his stories of Mistral and Tarascon and I liked his having been followed about in that land of the french royalist, on account of his resemblance to the Bourbon claimant. I had never seen the Bourbon claimant but Ford at that time undoubtedly might have been a Bourbon.

We had heard that Ford was in Paris, but we had not happened to meet. Gertrude Stein had however seen copies of the Transatlantic and found it interesting but had thought nothing further about it.

Hemingway came in then very excited and said that Ford wanted something of Gertrude Stein's for the next number and he, Hemingway, wanted The Making of Americans to be run in it as a serial and he had to have the first fifty pages at once. Gertrude Stein was of course quite overcome with her excitement at this idea, but there was no copy of the manuscript except the one that we had had bound. That makes no difference, said Hemingway, I will copy it. And he and I between us did copy it and it was printed in the next number of the Transatlantic. So for the first time a piece of the monumental work which was the beginning, really the beginning of modern writing, was printed, and we were very happy. Later on when things were difficult between Gertrude Stein and Hemingway, she always remembered with gratitude that after all it was Hemingway who first caused to be printed a piece of The Making of Americans. She always says, yes sure I have a weakness for Hemingway. After all he was the first of the young men to knock at my door and he did make Ford print the first piece of The Making of Americans.

I myself have not so much confidence that Hemingway did do this. I have never known what the story is but I have always been certain that there was some other story behind it all. That is the way I feel about it.

Gertrude Stein and Sherwood Anderson are very funny on the subject of Hemingway. The last time that Sherwood was in Paris they often talked about him. Hemingway had been formed by the two of them and they were both a little proud and a little ashamed of the work of their minds. Hemingway had at one moment, when he had repudiated Sherwood Anderson and all his works, written him a letter in the name of american literature which he, Hemingway, in company with his contemporaries was about to save, telling Sherwood just what he, Hemingway thought about Sherwood's work, and, that thinking, was in no sense complimentary. When Sherwood came to Paris Hemingway naturally was afraid. Sherwood as naturally was not.

As I say he and Gertrude Stein were endlessly amusing on the subject. They admitted that Hemingway was yellow, he is, Gertrude Stein insisted, just like the flat-boat men on the Mississippi river as described by Mark Twain. But what a book, they both agreed, would be the real story of Hemingway, not those he writes but the confessions of the real Ernest Hemingway. It would be for another audience than the audience Hemingway now has but it would be very wonderful. And then they both agreed that they have a weakness for Hemingway because he is such a good pupil. He is a rotten pupil, I protested. You don't understand, they both said, it is so flattering to have a pupil who does it without understanding it, in other words he takes training and anybody who takes training is a favourite pupil. They both admit it to be a weakness.

Gertrude Stein added further, you see he is like Derain. You remember Monsieur de Tuille said, when I did not understand why Derain was having the success he was having that it was because he looks like a modern and he smells of the museums. And that is Hemingway, he looks like a modern and he smells of the museums. But what a story that of the real Hem, and one he should tell himself but alas he never will. After all, as he himself once murmured, there is the career, the career.

But to come back to the events that were happening.

Hemingway did it all. He copied the manuscript and corrected the proof. Correcting proofs is, as I said before, like dusting, you learn the values of the thing as no reading suffices to teach it to you. In correcting these proofs Hemingway learned a great deal and he admired all that he learned. It was at this time that he wrote to Gertrude Stein saying that it was she who had done the work in writing The Making of Americans and he and all his had but to devote their lives to seeing that it was published.

He had hopes of being able to accomplish this. Some one, I think by the name of Sterne, said that he could place it with a publisher. Gertrude Stein and Hemingway believed that he could, but soon Hemingway reported that Sterne had entered into his period of unreliability. That was the end of that.

In the meantime and sometime before this Mina Loy had brought McAlmon to the house and he came from time to time and be brought his wife and brought William Carlos Williams. And finally he wanted to print The Making of Americans in the Contact Edition and finally he did. I will come to that.

In the meantime McAlmon had printed the three poems and ten stories of Hemingway and William Bird had printed In Our Time and Hemingway was getting to be known. He was coming to know Dos Passos and Fitzgerald and Bromfield and George Antheil and everybody else and Harold Loeb was once more in Paris. Hemingway had become a writer. He was also a shadow-boxer, thanks to Sherwood, and he heard about bull-fighting from me. I have always loved spanish dancing and spanish bull-fighting and I loved to show the photographs of bull-fighters and bull-fighting. I also loved to show the photograph where Gertrude Stein and I were in the front row and had our picture taken there accidentally. In these days Hemingway was teaching some young chap how to box. The boy did not know how, but by accident he knocked Hemingway out. I believe this sometimes happens. At any rate in these days Hemingway although a sportsman was easily tired. He used to get quite worn out walking from his house to ours. But then he had been worn by the war. Even now he is, as Hélène says all men are, fragile. Recently a robust friend of his said to Gertrude Stein, Ernest is very fragile, whenever he does anything sporting something breaks, his arm, his leg, or his head.

In those early days Hemingway liked all his contemporaries except Cummings. He accused Cummings of having copied everything, not from anybody but from somebody. Gertrude Stein who had been much impressed by The Enormous Room said that Cummings did not copy, he was the natural heir of the New England tradition with its aridity and its sterility, but also with its individuality. They disagreed about this. They also disagreed about Sherwood Anderson. Gertrude Stein contended that Sherwood Anderson had a genius for using a sentence to convey a direct emotion, this was in the great american tradition, and that really except Sherwood there was no one in America who could write a clear and passionate sentence. Hemingway did not believe this, he did not like Sherwood's taste. Taste has nothing to do with sentences, contended Gertrude Stein. She also added that Fitzgerald was the only one of the younger writers who wrote naturally in sentences.

Gertrude Stein and Fitzgerald are very peculiar in their relation to each other. Gertrude Stein had been very much impressed by This Side of Paradise. She read it when it came out and before she knew any of the young american writers. She said of it that it was this book that really created for the public the new generation. She has never changed her opinion about this. She thinks this equally true of *The Great Gatsby*. She thinks Fitzgerald will be read when many of his well known contemporaries are forgotten. Fitzgerald always says that he thinks Gertrude Stein says these things just to annoy him by making him think that she means them, and he adds in his favourite way, and her doing it is the cruellest thing I ever heard. They always however have a very good time when they meet. And the last time they met they had a good time with themselves and Hemingway.

Then there was McAlmon. McAlmon had one quality that appealed to Gertrude Stein, abundance, he could go on writing, but she complained that it was dull.

There was also Glenway Wescott but Glenway Wescott at no time interested Gertrude Stein. He has a certain syrup but it does not pour.

So then Hemingway's career was begun. For a little while we saw less of him and then he began to come again. He used to recount to Gertrude Stein the conversations that he afterwards used in The Sun Also Rises and they talked endlessly about the character of Harold Loeb. At this time Hemingway was preparing his volume of short stories to submit to publishers in America. One evening after we had not seen him for a while he turned up with Shipman. Shipman was an amusing boy who was to inherit a few thousand dollars when he came of age. He was not of age. He was to buy the Transatlantic Review when he came of age, so Hemingway said. He was to support a surrealist review when he came of age, André Masson said. He was to buy a house in the country when he came of age, Josette Gris said. As a matter of fact when he came of age nobody who had known him then seemed to know what he did do with his inheritance. Hemingway brought him with him to the house to talk about buying the Transatlantic and incidentally he brought the manuscript he intended sending to America. He handed it to Gertrude Stein. He had added to his stories a little story of meditations and in these he said that The Enormous Room was the greatest book he had ever read. It was then that Gertrude Stein said, Hemingway, remarks are not literature.

After this we did not see Hemingway for quite a while and then we went to see some one, just after The Making of Americans was printed, and Hemingway who was there came up to Gertrude Stein and began to explain why he would not be able to write a review of the book. Just then a heavy hand fell on his shoulder and Ford Madox Ford said, young man it is I who wish to speak to Gertrude Stein. Ford then said to her, I wish to ask your permission to dedicate my new book to you. May I. Gertrude Stein and I were both awfully pleased and touched.

For some years after this Gertrude Stein and Hemingway did not meet. And then we heard that he was back in Paris and telling a number of people how much he wanted to see her. Don't you come home with Hemingway on your arm, I used to say when she went out for a walk. Sure enough one day she did come back bringing him with her.

They sat and talked a long time. Finally I heard her say, Hemingway, after all you are ninety percent Rotarian. Can't you, he said, make it eighty percent. No, said she regretfully, I can't. After all, as she always says, he did, and I may say, he does have moments of disinterestedness.

After that they met quite often. Gertrude Stein always says she likes to see him, he is so wonderful. And if he could only tell his own story. In their last conversation she accused him of having killed a great many of his rivals and put them under the sod. I never, said Hemingway, seriously killed anybody but one man and he was a bad man and, he deserved it, but if I killed anybody else I did it unknowingly, and so I am not responsible.

It was Ford who once said of Hemingway, he comes and sits at my feet and praises me. It makes me nervous. Hemingway also said once, I turn my flame which is a small one down and down and then suddenly there is a big explosion. If there were nothing but explosions my work would be so exciting nobody could bear it.

However, whatever I say, Gertrude Stein always says, yes I know but I have a weakness for Hemingway. ° ° °

SHERWOOD ANDERSON [1876-1941]

SHERWOOD ANDERSON was a born poet and story-teller whose natural genius was frustrated and delayed in its development by the industrial and business-minded society around him. It was not only the midwestern small-town environment of his boyhood with its narrow horizons, or even his lack of schooling, which sent him in his early life into the world of business to make money, but also the overpowering dream of success in the Horatio Alger tradition which seemed the only incentive for a young idealist. In 1912, when he was nearing forty, living a middle-class life in Elyria, Ohio, married and prospering in his own business, Anderson finally rebelled against the life he was leading. From his own account of this epiphany or spiritual illumination, he was "called" to leave his family and business to enter the world of art and writing. It was a Gauguin-like apotheosis. Later biographers relating the facts of this experience have described it more accurately as a mental collapse in which Anderson left his office and was found dazed and ill in the streets of Cleveland some days later. He had written both poetry and fiction before that episode, but thenceforth he decided to devote his life to literature. He separated from the first of his wives (he was married four times) and moved to Chicago.

Anderson quickly found a circle of writers and critics who formed the "Chicago Renaissance" and who gave him both counsel and encouragement. Among them were Waldo Frank, Floyd Dell, Ben Hecht, and Van Wyck Brooks. He began to publish in avant-garde magazines such as the *Little Review*, the *New Republic*, and the *Seven Arts*. His first novel, *Windy McPherson's Son* (1916) was a book about himself. Sam McPherson receives a "call" to escape from his job and family and follow his star toward the "truth" by living a vagabond life as a carpenter and socialist. Anderson's own gradual acceptance of his new life and conversion is suggested in the fact that Sam is in the end convinced he cannot run away from life. Anderson's next book, *Winesburg, Ohio* (1919), was his most successful work of fiction, brilliantly original, and now a literary landmark. He had found his special form in the short portrait of small-town people whose lives are blunted by both their environment and their own inability to express the tortured thoughts and emotions within them.

Anderson's early life was spent in Clyde, Ohio, and other small towns where his wandering family lived just ahead of the bill collector. His father, a ne'er-do-well harness-maker and village "character" with a gift for story-telling, was unable to provide a living for the family, and Anderson went to work at fourteen, taking various jobs as delivery boy, newsboy, stable-hand, and warehouse worker. In 1898 he served some months as a soldier in the Spanish-American War. He went into advertising in order to be able to write and make a living at the same time, but found himself unable to continue this divided life. After his first literary success he traveled to Europe, where he met Gertrude Stein. Her influence and that of D. H. Lawrence, Turgenev, and Walt Whitman helped form the style of simplicity, clarity, and mystical poetic-prose for which he is famous. Biblical rhythms are likewise apparent in his work, and the influence of Freud underlay almost all his writing. "If there is anything you do not understand in human life," he said, "consult the works of Dr. Freud."

Anderson wrote novels, plays, poetry, impressionistic and journalistic vignettes of American life, and short stories. As a novelist he was inclined to transpose his own problems into fictional form. *Poor White* (1920), *Many Marriages* (1923), *Dark Laughter* (1925), and *Kit Brandon* (1936) were all concerned with the central experience of his own life, the search for aesthetic fulfillment and sexual freedom in a society dominated by the myth of business success. He was at his best in the short sketch or portrait, as in *Winesburg, Ohio*, with its Freudian concern for the "well" of the subconscious in confused and groping people, and its special tenderness for adolescents and the sensitive but frustrated inhabitants of small midwestern towns. His autobiographical books such as *A Story Teller's Story* (1924) and *Tar: A Midwest Childhood* (1926) subtly evoked the inner consciousness and uncertainties of a young boy trying to understand the adult world and the mysteries of sex. A mood of wonder, strangeness, and awe pervades his finest characterizations, whether of himself or his fictional people, and it is this element that sets Anderson apart from the naturalists and realists of his day. "Realism," he said, "in so far as it means reality to life, is always bad art."

All his life a wanderer, impatient with regular life, he lived his late years on a farm, tried to settle down, and published two newspapers in the town of Marion in southwestern Virginia. He died in Panama in 1941 while at the start of a tour of South America. His literary reputation has grown since his death with the recognition of his originality and his gift for a prose style that verged upon poetry and for a realism that went beyond the representational.

Further reading: *The (Viking) Portable Sherwood Anderson*, ed. Horace Gregory, 1949. Cleveland Chase, *Sherwood Anderson*, 1927. Waldo Frank's essay on *Winesburg, Ohio* in *Story* magazine, September-October, 1941. Brom Weber, *Sherwood Anderson*, 1964.

Hands

First published in the *Masses* (March 1916), this story became the opening chapter of *Winesburg, Ohio* (1919), from which the present text is taken. It is one of Anderson's most skillful delineations of loneliness, isolation, and defeat, yet it should be noted that any overt statement of the "theme" of the story is qualified by the subtle, elusive nature of the style and organization. Why does Anderson avoid a straightforward chronological, cause-and-effect development? What is the artistic purpose of the final scene? Note Anderson's use of contradictory effects in his depiction of Wing Biddlebaum's hands. His use of the hands as a central image transcends realism and approaches a surrealistic method. In his introduction to *Winesburg, Ohio*, Anderson explained that people become "grotesques" when they withdraw into themselves through fear, shame, or social pressures, or when, attempting to grasp one of the many "truths" which the world offers, they become false to themselves.

(CONCERNING WING BIDDLEBAUM)

Upon the half-decayed veranda of a small frame house that stood near the edge of a ravine near the town of Winesburg, Ohio, a fat little old man walked nervously up and down. Across a long field that had been seeded for clover but that had produced only a dense crop of yellow mustard weeds, he could see the public highway along which went a wagon filled with berry pickers returning from the fields. The berry pickers, youths and maidens, laughed and shouted boisterously. A boy clad in a blue shirt leaped from the wagon and attempted to drag after him one of the maidens who screamed and protested shrilly. The feet of the boy in the road kicked up a cloud of dust that floated across the face of the departing sun. Over the long field came a thin girlish voice. "Oh, you Wing Biddlebaum, comb your hair, it's falling into your eyes," commanded the voice to the man, who was bald and whose nervous little hands fiddled about the bare white forehead as though arranging a mass of tangled locks.

Wing Biddlebaum, forever frightened and beset by a ghostly band of doubts, did not think of himself as in any way a part of the life of the town where he had lived for twenty years. Among all the people of Winesburg but one had come close to him. With George Willard, son of Tom Willard, the proprietor of the new Willard House, he had formed something like a friendship. George Willard was the reporter on the *Winesburg Eagle* and sometimes in the evenings he walked out along the highway to Wing Biddlebaum's house. Now as the old man walked up and down on the veranda, his hands moving nervously about, he was hoping that George Willard would come and spend the evening with him. After the wagon containing the berry pickers had passed, he went across the field through the tall mustard weeds and climbing a rail fence peered anxiously along the road to the town. For a moment he stood thus, rubbing his hands together and looking up and down the road, and then, fear overcoming him, ran back to walk again upon the porch on his own house.

In the presence of George Willard, Wing Biddlebaum, who for twenty years had been the town mystery, lost something of his timidity, and his shadowy personality, submerged in a sea of doubts, came forth to look at the world. With the young reporter at his side, he ventured in the light of day into Main Street or strode up and down on the rickety front porch of his own house, talking excitedly. The voice that had been low and trembling became shrill and loud. The bent figure straightened. With a kind of wriggle, like a fish returned to the brook by the fisherman, Biddlebaum the silent began to talk, striving to put into words the ideas that had been accumulated by his mind during long years of silence.

Wing Biddlebaum talked much with his hands. The slender expressive fingers, forever active, forever striving to conceal themselves in his pockets or behind his back, came forth and became the piston rods of his machinery of expression.

The story of Wing Biddlebaum is a story of hands. Their restless activity, like unto the beating of the wings of an imprisoned bird, had given him his name. Some obscure poet of the town had thought of it. The hands alarmed their owner. He wanted to keep them hidden away and looked with amazement at the quiet inexpressive hands of other men who worked beside him in the fields, or passed, driving sleepy teams on country roads.

When he talked to George Willard, Wing Biddlebaum closed his fists and beat with them upon a table or on the walls of his house. The action made him more comfortable. If the desire to talk came to him when the two were walking in the fields, he sought out a stump or the top board of a fence and with his hands pounding busily talked with renewed ease.

The story of Wing Biddlebaum's hands is worth a book in itself. Sympathetically set forth it would tap many strange, beautiful qualities in obscure men. It is a job for a poet. In Winesburg the hands had attracted attention merely because of their activity. With them Wing Biddlebaum had picked as high as a hundred and forty quarts of strawberries in a day. They became his distinguishing feature, the source of his fame. Also they made more grotesque an already grotesque and elusive individuality. Winesburg was proud of the hands of Wing Biddlebaum in the same spirit in which it was proud of Banker White's new stone house and Wesley Moyer's bay stallion, Tony Tip, that had won the two-fifteen trot at the fall races in Cleveland.

As for George Willard, he had many times wanted to ask about the hands. At times an almost overwhelming curiosity had taken hold of him. He felt that there must be a reason for their strange activity and their inclination to keep hidden away and only a growing respect for Wing Biddlebaum kept him from blurting out the questions that were often in his mind.

Once he had been on the point of asking. The two were walking in the fields on a summer afternoon and had stopped to sit upon a grassy bank. All afternoon Wing Biddlebaum had talked as one inspired. By a fence he had stopped and beating like a giant woodpecker upon the top board had shouted at George Willard, condemning his tendency to be too much influenced by the people about him. "You are destroying yourself," he cried. "You have the inclination to be alone and to dream and you are afraid of dreams. You want to be like others in town here. You hear them talk and you try to imitate them."

On the grassy bank Wing Biddlebaum had tried again to drive his point home. His voice became soft and reminiscent, and with a sigh of contentment he launched into a long rambling talk, speaking as one lost in a dream.

Out of the dream Wing Biddlebaum made a picture for George Willard. In the picture men lived again in a kind of pastoral golden age. Across a green open country came clean-limbed young men, some afoot, some mounted upon horses. In crowds the young men came to gather about the feet of an old man who sat beneath a tree in a tiny garden and who talked to them.

Wing Biddlebaum became wholly inspired. For once he forgot the hands. Slowly they stole forth and lay upon George Willard's shoulders. Something new and bold came into the voice that talked. "You must try to forget all you have learned," said the old man. "You must begin to dream. From this time on you must shut your ears to the roaring of the voices."

Pausing in his speech, Wing Biddlebaum looked long and earnestly at George Willard. His eyes glowed. Again he raised the hands to caress the boy and then a look of horror swept over his face.

With a convulsive movement of his body, Wing Biddlebaum sprang to his feet and thrust his hands deep into his trousers pockets. Tears came to his eyes. "I must be getting along home. I can talk no more with you," he said nervously.

Without looking back, the old man had hurried down the hillside and across a meadow, leaving George Willard perplexed and frightened upon the grassy slope. With a shiver of dread the boy arose and went along the road toward town. "I'll not ask him about his hands," he thought, touched by the memory of the terror he had seen in the man's eyes. "There's something wrong, but I don't want to know what it is. His hands have something to do with his fear of me and of everyone."

And George Willard was right. Let us look briefly

into the story of the hands. Perhaps our talking of them will arouse the poet who will tell the hidden wonder story of the influence for which the hands were but fluttering pennants of promise.

In his youth Wing Biddlebaum had been a school teacher in a town in Pennsylvania. He was not then known as Wing Biddlebaum, but went by the less euphonic name of Adolph Myers. As Adolph Myers he was much loved by the boys of his school.

Adolph Myers was meant by nature to be a teacher of youth. He was one of those rare, little-understood men who rule by a power so gentle that it passes as a lovable weakness. In their feeling for the boys under their charge such men are not unlike the finer sort of women in their love of men.

And yet that is but crudely stated. It needs the poet there. With the boys of his school, Adolph Myers had walked in the evening or had sat talking until dusk upon the schoolhouse steps lost in a kind of dream. Here and there went his hands, caressing the shoulders of the boys, playing about the tousled heads. As he talked his voice became soft and musical. There was a caress in that also. In a way the voice and the hands, the stroking of the shoulders and the touching of the hair was a part of the schoolmaster's effort to carry a dream into the young minds. By the caress that was in his fingers he expressed himself. He was one of those men in whom the force that creates life is diffused, not centralized. Under the caress of his hands doubt and disbelief went out of the minds of the boys and they began also to dream.

And then the tragedy. A half-witted boy of the school became enamored of the young master. In his bed at night he imagined unspeakable things and in the morning went forth to tell his dreams as facts. Strange hideous accusations fell from his loose-hung lips. Through the Pennsylvania town went a shiver. Hidden, shadowy doubts that had been in men's minds concerning Adolph Myers were galvanized into beliefs.

The tragedy did not linger. Trembling lads were jerked out of bed and questioned. "He put his arms about me," said one. "His fingers were always playing in my hair,' said another.

One afternoon a man of the town, Henry Bradford, who kept a saloon, came to the schoolhouse door. Calling Adolph Myers into the school yard he began to beat him with his fists. As his hard knuckles beat down into the frightened face of the schoolmaster, his wrath became more and more terrible. Screaming with dismay, the children ran here and there like disturbed insects. "I'll teach you to put your hands on my boy, you beast," roared the saloon keeper, who, tired of beating the master, had begun to kick him about the yard.

Adolph Myers was driven from the Pennsylvania town in the night. With lanterns in their hands a dozen men came to the door of the house where he lived alone and commanded that he dress and come forth. It was raining and one of the men had a rope in his hands. They had intended to hang the schoolmaster, but something in his figure, so small, white, and pitiful, touched their hearts and they let him escape. As he raw away into the darkness they repented of their weakness and ran after him, swearing and throwing sticks and great balls of soft mud at the figure that screamed and ran faster and faster into the darkness.

For twenty years Adolph Myers had lived alone in Winesburg. He was but forty but looked sixty-five. The name of Biddlebaum he got from a box of goods seen at a freight station as he hurried through an eastern Ohio town. He had an aunt in Winesburg, a black-toothed old woman who raised chickens, and with her he lived until she died. He had been ill for a year after the experience in Pennsylvania, and after his recovery worked as a day laborer in the fields, going timidly about and striving to conceal his hands. Although he did not understand what had happened he felt that the hands must be to blame. Again and again the fathers of the boys had talked of the hands. "Keep your hands to yourself," the saloon keeper had roared, dancing with fury in the schoolhouse yard.

Upon the veranda of his house by the ravine, Wing Biddlebaum continued to walk up and down until the sun had disappeared and the road beyond the field was lost in the gray shadows. Going into his house he cut slices of bread and spread honey upon them. When the rumble of the evening train that took away the express cars loaded with the day's harvest of berries had passed and restored the silence of the summer night, he went again to walk upon the veranda. In the darkness he could not see the hands and they became quiet. Although he still hungered for the presence of the boy, who was the medium through which he expressed his love of man, the hunger became again a part of his loneliness and his waiting. Lighting a lamp, Wing Biddlebaum washed the few dishes soiled by his simple meal and, setting up a folding cot by the screen door that led to the porch, prepared to undress for the night. A few stray white bread crumbs lay on the cleanly washed floor by the table; putting the lamp on a low stool he began to pick up the crumbs, carrying them to his mouth one by one with unbelievable rapidity. In the dense blotch of light beneath the table, the kneeling figure looked like a priest engaged in some service of his church. The nervous expressive fingers, flashing in and out of the light, might well have been mistaken for the fingers of the devotee going swiftly through decade after decade of his rosary.

JEAN TOOMER [1894–1967]

JEAN TOOMER's reputation as a writer and his place in modern American literature rest on a single book, *Cane,* published in 1923. Though this strange, scintillating work failed to achieve a popular success in its day, it was acclaimed by a perceptive few, including Sherwood Anderson and Hart Crane, for its bold experimentation with an idiom beyond realism, as well as for its intensity of racial expression; and it was "rediscovered" in the 1960's for the same qualities. In its impact on the emerging black writers of the twenties, *Cane* may have been the most significant book of the Harlem Renaissance.

Toomer's ancestry was as mixed as that of many of his countrymen. He himself identified seven strains: French, Dutch, Welsh, Negro, German, Jewish, and Indian. He was born in Washington, D. C., of a family whose fortunes had dwindled since the Reconstruction years when his maternal grandfather was lieutenant-governor of Louisiana. He was educated in the Washington public schools, then briefly attended the University of Wisconsin and the City College of New York, but found what he wanted at neither. He taught in rural Georgia for a time, and there his contact with the black community sparked his talent.

Cane, a collection of stories, poems, and sketches, eludes formal classification. Prose merges into poetry, novella into play, meaning into sound, realism into impressionism and other nonrepresentational modes. It is not without design, as Arna Bontemps has pointed out, but the pattern is adumbrated by scene and mood: through the movement of the three parts from rural Georgia to the black ghetto of Washington, D. C., and finally back to Georgia; through the consciousness of the poet-observer; and through the pride of race that informs the whole.

After *Cane* came a series of discouragements, including an unsuccessful attempt at playwriting, and thereafter Toomer's rage for experiment seemed to turn from literary expression to a search for a philosophy and a life-style. He moved restlessly about the country, studied in France for a time under the Russian mystic Gurdjieff, and in 1931 joined an experiment in communal living in Wisconsin. There he met and married the young novelist Marjorie Latimer, a descendant of John Cotton and Anne Bradstreet, who died in childbirth the following year. After another period of wandering, in the Southwest, Toomer married the daughter of a member of the New York Stock Exchange and settled into a tranquil life in Bucks County, Pennsylvania, allying himself with the Society of Friends, writing for the *Friends' Intelligencer,* and giving lectures. He never had another book accepted for commercial publication, and what writing he did was almost wholly devoted to the philosophical questions that increasingly preoccupied him.

Perhaps Toomer himself best summed up both the tensions and the wellsprings of his creativity in an autobiographical note written in 1922: "My position in America has been a curious one. I have lived equally amid the two race groups. Now white, now colored. From my own point of view I am naturally and inevitably an American. I have strived for a spiritual fusion analogous to the fact of racial intermingling. Without denying a single element in me, with no desire to subdue one to the other, I have sought to let them function as complements. I have tried to let them live in harmony. Within the last two or three years, however, my growing need for artistic expression has pulled me deeper and deeper into the Negro group. And as my powers of receptivity increased, I found myself loving it in a way that I could never love the other. It has stimulated and fertilized whatever creative talent I may contain within me."

Further reading: *Cane*, 1923; reissued with an introduction by Arna Bontemps, 1969.

Esther

From *Cane* (1923), this is one of the Georgia cycle of pieces that make up the first third of the book.

1

Nine.

Esther's hair falls in soft curls about her high-cheek-boned chalk-white face. Esther's hair would be beautiful if there were more gloss to it. And if her face were not prematurely serious, one would call it pretty. Her cheeks are too flat and dead for a girl of nine. Esther looks like a little white child, starched, frilled, as she walks slowly from her home towards her father's grocery store. She is about to turn in Broad from Maple Street. White and black men loafing on the corner hold no interest for her. Then a strange thing happens. A clean-muscled, magnificent, black-skinned Negro, whom she had heard her father mention as King Barlo, suddenly drops to his knees on a spot called the Spittoon. White men, unaware of him, continue squirting tobacco juice in his direction. The saffron fluid splashes on his face. His smooth black face begins to glisten and to shine. Soon, people notice him, and gather round. His eyes are rapturous upon the heavens. Lips and nostrils quiver. Barlo is in a religious trance. Town folks know it. They are not startled. They are not afraid. They gather round. Some beg boxes from the grocery stores. From old McGregor's notion shop. A coffin-case is pressed into use. Folks line the curb-stones. Business men close shop. And Banker Warply parks his car close by. Silently, all await the prophet's voice. The sheriff, a great florid fellow whose leggings never meet around his bulging calves, swears in three deputies. "Wall, y cant never tell what a nigger like King Barlo might be up t." Soda bottles, five fingers full of shine, are passed to those who want them. A couple of stray dogs start a fight. Old Goodlow's cow comes flopping up the street. Barlo, still as an Indian fakir, has not moved. The town bell strikes six. The sun slips in behind a heavy mass of horizon cloud. The crowd is hushed and expectant. Barlo's under jaw relaxes, and his lips begin to move.

"Jesus has been awhisperin strange words deep down, O way down deep, deep in my ears."

Hums of awe and of excitement.

"He called me to His side an said, 'Git down on your knees beside me, son, Ise gwine t whisper in your ears.' "

An old sister cries, "Ah, Lord."

" 'Ise agwine t whisper in your ears,' he said, an I replied, 'Thy will be done on earth as it is in heaven.' "

"Ah, Lord. Amen. Amen."

"An Lord Jesus whispered strange good words deep down, O way down deep, deep in my ears. An He said, 'Tell em till you feel your throat on fire.' I saw a vision. I saw a man arise, an he was big an black an powerful—"

Some one yells, "Preach it, preacher, preach it!"

"—but his head was caught up in th clouds. An while he was agazin at th heavens, heart filled up with th Lord, some little white-ant biddies came an tied his feet to chains. They led him t th coast, they led him t th sea, they led him across th ocean an they didnt set him free. The old coast didnt miss him, an th new coast wasnt free, he left the old-coast brothers, t give birth t you an me. O Lord, great God Almighty, t give birth t you an me."

Barlo pauses. Old gray mothers are in tears. Fragments of melodies are being hummed. White folks are touched and curiously awed. Off to themselves, white and black preachers confer as to how best to rid themselves of the vagrant, usurping fellow. Barlo looks as though he is struggling to continue. People are hushed. One can hear weevils work. Dusk is falling rapidly, and the customary store lights fail to throw their feeble glow across the gray dust and flagging of the Georgia town. Barlo rises to his full height. He is immense. To the people he assumes the outlines of his visioned African. In a mighty voice he bellows:

"Brothers an sisters, turn your faces t th sweet face of the Lord, an fill your hearts with glory. Open your eyes an see th dawnin of th mornin light. Open your ears—"

Years afterwards Esther was told that at that very moment a great, heavy, rumbling voice actually was heard. That hosts of angels and of demons paraded up and down the streets all night. That King Barlo rode out of town astride a pitch-black bull that had a glowing gold ring in its nose. And that old Limp Underwood, who hated niggers, woke up next morning to find that he held a black man in his arms.

This much is certain: an inspired Negress, of wide reputation for being sanctified, drew a portrait of a black madonna on the court-house wall. And King Barlo left town. He left his image indelibly upon the mind of Esther. He became the starting point of the only living patterns that her mind was to know.

2

Sixteen.

Esther begins to dream. The low evening sun sets the windows of McGregor's notion shop aflame. Esther makes believe that they really are aflame. The town fire department rushes madly down the road. It ruthlessly shoves black and white idlers to one side. It whoops. It clangs. It rescues from the second-story window a dimpled infant which she claims for her own. How had she come by it? She thinks of it immaculately. It is a sin to think of it immaculately. She must dream no more. She must repent her sin. Another dream comes. There is no fire department. There are no heroic men. The fire starts. The loafers on the corner form a circle, chew their tobacco faster, and squirt juice just as fast as they can chew. Gallons on top of gallons they squirt upon the flames. The air reeks with the stench of scorched tobacco juice. Women, fat chunky Negro women, lean scrawny white women, pull their skirts up above their heads and display the most ludicrous underclothes. The women scoot in all directions from the danger zone. She alone is left to take the baby in her arms. But what a baby! Black, singed, woolly, tobacco-juice baby—ugly as sin. Once held to her breast, miraculous thing: its breath is sweet and its lips can nibble. She loves it frantically. Her joy in it changes the town folks' jeers to harmless jealousy, and she is left alone.

Twenty-two.

Esther's schooling is over. She works behind the counter of her father's grocery store. "To keep the money in the family," so he said. She is learning to make distinctions between the business and the social worlds. "Good business comes from remembering that the white folks dont divide the niggers, Esther. Be just as black as any man who has a silver dollar." Esther listlessly forgets that she is near white, and that her father is the richest colored man in town. Black folk who drift in to buy lard and snuff and flour of her, call her a sweet-natured, accommodating girl. She learns their names. She forgets them. She thinks about men. "I dont appeal to them. I wonder why." She recalls an affair she had with a little fair boy while still in school. It had ended in her shame when he as much as told her that for sweetness he preferred a lollipop. She remembers the salesman from the North who wanted to take her to the movies that first night he was in town. She refused, of course. And he never came back, having found out who she was. She thinks of Barlo. Barlo's image gives her a slightly stale thrill. She spices it by telling herself his glories. Black. Magnetically so. Best cotton picker in the county, in the state, in the whole world for that matter. Best man with his fists, best man with dice, with a razor. Promoter of church benefits. Of colored fairs. Vagrant preacher. Lover of all the women for miles and miles around. Esther decides that she loves him. And with a vague sense of life slipping by, she resolves that she will tell him so, whatever people say, the next time he comes to town. After the making of this resolution which becomes a sort of wedding cake for her to tuck beneath her pillow and go to sleep upon, she sees nothing of Barlo for five years. Her hair thins. It looks like the dull silk on puny corn ears. Her face pales until it is the color of the gray dust that dances with dead cotton leaves.

3

Esther is twenty-seven.

Esther sells lard and snuff and flour to vague black faces that drift in her store to ask for them. Her eyes hardly see the people to whom she gives change. Her body is lean and beaten. She rests listlessly against the counter, too weary to sit down. From the street some one shouts, "King Barlo has come back to town." He passes her window, driving a large new car. Cut-out open. He veers to the curb, and steps out. Barlo has made money on cotton during the war. He is as rich as anyone. Esther suddenly is animate. She goes to her door. She sees him at a distance, the center of a group of credulous men. She hears the deep-bass rumble of his talk. The sun swings low. McGregor's windows are aflame again. Pale flame. A sharply dressed white girl passes by. For a moment Esther wishes that she might be like her. Not white; she has no need for being that. But sharp, sporty, with get-up about her. Barlo is connected with that wish. She mustnt wish. Wishes only make you restless. Emptiness is a thing that grows by being moved. "I'll not think. Not wish. Just set my mind against it." Then the thought comes to her that those purposeless, easy-going men will possess him, if she doesnt. Purpose is not dead in her, now that she comes to think of it. That loose women will have their arms around him at Nat

Bowle's place to-night. As if her veins are full of fired sun-bleached southern shanties, a swift heat sweeps them. Dead dreams, and a forgotten resolution are carried upward by the flames. Pale flames. "They shant have him. Oh, they shall not. Not if it kills me they shant have him." Jerky, aflutter, she closes the store and starts home. Folks lazing on store window-sills wonder what on earth can be the matter with Jim Crane's gal, as she passes them. "Come to remember, she always was a little off, a little crazy, I reckon." Esther seeks her own room, and locks the door. Her mind is a pink mesh-bag filled with baby toes.

Using the noise of the town clock striking twelve to cover the creaks of her departure, Esther slips into the quiet road. The town, her parents, most everyone is sound asleep. This fact is a stable thing that comforts her. After sundown a chill wind came up from the west. It is still blowing, but to her it is a steady, settled thing like the cold. She wants her mind to be like that. Solid, contained, and blank as a sheet of darkened ice. She will not permit herself to notice the peculiar phosphorescent glitter of the sweet-gum leaves. Their movement would excite her. Exciting too, the recession of the dull familiar homes she knows so well. She doesnt know them at all. She closes her eyes, and holds them tightly. Wont do. Her being aware that they are closed recalls her purpose. She does not want to think of it. She opens them. She turns now into the deserted business street. The corrugated iron canopies and mule- and horse-gnawed hitching posts bring her a strange composure. Ghosts of the commonplaces of her daily life take stride with her and become her companions. And the echoes of her heels upon the flagging are rhythmically monotonous and soothing. Crossing the street at the corner of McGregor's notion shop, she thinks that the windows are a dull flame. Only a fancy. She walks faster. Then runs. A turn into a side street brings her abruptly to Nat Bowle's place. The house is squat and dark. It is always dark. Barlo is within. Quietly she opens the outside door and steps in. She passes through a small room. Pauses before a flight of stairs down which people's voices, muffled, come. The air is heavy with fresh tobacco smoke. It makes her sick. She wants to turn back. She goes up the steps. As if she were mounting to some great height, her head spins. She is violently dizzy. Blackness rushes to her eyes. And then she finds that she is in a large room. Barlo is before her.

"Well, I'm sholy damned—skuse me, but what, what brought you here, lil milk-white gal?"

"You." Her voice sounds like a frightened child's that calls homeward from some point miles away.

"Me?"

"Yes, you Barlo."

"This aint th place fer y. This aint th place fer y."

"I know. I know. But I've come for you."

"For me for what?"

She manages to look deep and straight into his eyes. He is slow at understanding. Guffaws and giggles break out from all around the room. A coarse woman's voice remarks, "So thats how th dictie niggers does it." Laughs. "Mus give em credit fo their gall."

Esther doesnt hear. Barlo does. His faculties are jogged. She sees a smile, ugly and repulsive to her, working upward through thick licker fumes. Barlo seems hideous. The thought comes suddenly, that conception with a drunken man must be a mighty sin. She draws away, frozen. Like a somnambulist she wheels around and walks stiffly to the stairs. Down them. Jeers and hoots pelter bluntly upon her back. She steps out. There is no air, no street, and the town has completely disappeared.

ERNEST HEMINGWAY [1899–1961]

VIOLENT ACTION and constant exposure to danger and death became Hemingway's way of life. In his fiction, a code of sportsmanship and war was a thematic center and a powerful symbol. His incredible career, and the legend which developed around his impressive figure and personality, was that of a man of action, a devil-may-care adventurer and expatriate news correspondent, an amateur boxer, lusty brawler and drinker, *aficionado* of the bullfights, big-game hunter and deep-sea fisherman, front-line correspondent in two wars (in one of which he was severely wounded), the victim of three automobile accidents and two plane crashes (from which he miraculously recovered), a man of four wives and many loves, but above all a writer of stories and novels of so new and fresh an order as to make him the leading spokesman of the mood of America between World Wars. The Hemingway legend and the Hemingway life have been so intertwined as to make it difficult to separate fact from fiction. His writing was a fictional commentary on this remarkable biography. Yet he did not portray violence for its sensational effects; he wanted to record exactly, without false rhetoric or sentiment, "what you really felt, not what you were supposed to feel." He was concerned with the way a man lives in a world of violence and destruction, with man's inward defenses against fate, his cultivation of a code of honor, courage and endurance. It is not surprising, therefore, that he died, as he lived, by violence and by a code: he took his own life with a shotgun blast in his home in Idaho at the age of sixty-one.

Hemingway was born in Oak Park, Illinois, a middle-class suburb of Chicago, the son of a doctor who initiated the boy into the outdoor life of hunting, camping, and fishing. In high school Hemingway played football and wrote for the school paper. In 1917 he left home and schooling to become a young reporter for the Kansas City *Star.* Restless to enlist for the war, he was rejected because of an eye injury from football, but finally managed to go overseas as an ambulance driver for the Red Cross. Attached to the Italian army on the Austrian front, he was hit in the leg and chest by mortar fire, requiring many operations and months of recovery before returning to the front to serve out the war with an Italian regiment. Back in America, he joined the news staff of the Toronto *Star,* married, and soon took off once more for Europe and Paris as a correspondent. There Hemingway joined the circle of expatriate intellectuals, named "the lost generation" by Gertrude Stein and including such notables as Pound, Eliot, James Joyce, and Scott Fitzgerald. In a posthumous book, *A Moveable Feast* (1964), Hemingway described these Paris years.

He began his literary career with the volume of stories called *In Our Time* (1924) centering on the experiences of young Nick Adams (Hemingway's youthful alter ego) who learns about life in raw and brutal circumstances from his travels with his physician father. Nick goes to war and is severely wounded and shell-shocked, but recovers to vow for himself a "separate peace" and life apart from the established order of society. This book and his first novel, *The Sun Also Rises* (1926), are Hemingway at his best. Jake Barnes, the hero of the novel, has been wounded in the war and is incapacitated for physical love. He is living in Paris in a circle of artists and writers whose lives are lived for drink and promiscuous sex. In love with Brett Ashley, he can only suffer while she has affairs with his friends and runs off during the Pamplona fiesta with a Spanish bullfighter. Jake learns to live by the "code," to endure and to avoid making a "show." He drowns his pain in drink. "I did not care what it was all about. All I wanted to know was how to live in it."

Hemingway's short stories are among the best written in this century. *Men Without Women* (1927) and *Winner Take Nothing* (1933) were collections of his short fiction. His second novel, *A Farewell to Arms* (1929), which he developed from two early sketches about Nick Adams, became a best-seller and a successful film. Frederic Henry, wounded in the war, has an ill-fated love affair with Catherine Barkley, an English nurse. After the defeat at Caparetto, the couple escape to Switzerland where she dies in childbirth. He is left to brood over the indifference of fate and the senselessness of life which is like a war-game played for keeps.

In 1929 Hemingway settled in Key West, Florida, devoting himself to sea fishing and writing. He traveled to Spain and discovered in the bullfights another symbol for his credo of risking one's life in a destructive element. *Death in the Afternoon* (1932) was the record of this experience. His love of Spain made Hemingway a strong partisan of the Loyalist cause during the Civil War. He covered this war, and in *For Whom the Bell Tolls* (1940) recounted in fiction his part in an incident of blowing up a bridge, writing once again an immensely successful novel of war, love, and death. It marked what one critic called Hemingway's "reconversion to the world." He turned away from the individualistic code of his earlier career to one of devotion to a cause, citing John Donne's words that no man can exist as an "island."

During World War II Hemingway continued to live the dangerous life. He flew missions over France with the R.A.F., fought in Normandy and France, and helped liberate Paris with a one-man "army." After the war he was partially paralyzed in a plane accident in Africa while on a hunting safari. He recovered to read obituaries already prepared by the newspapers. In the 1950's Hemingway lived on a farm near Havana, Cuba, until Castro's regime forced him to leave. He was awarded the Nobel Prize for literature in 1954 with a citation for his "powerful style-performing mastery of the art of narration." In 1960 and 1961 he spent months of hospitalization at the Mayo Clinic for hypertension and complications. Returning with his wife, Mary Welsh, to their Idaho home, he took his own life, repeating the act of his father who had killed himself with his Civil War revolver in 1929.

The magic of Hemingway's style is difficult to analyze. Like Mark Twain and Stephen Crane (Hemingway rated them high in American literature), he transformed the language of reporting into a fictional art. His style was formed from them and from the primitive rhythms of Gertrude Stein and Sherwood Anderson. It was a prose stripped clean of artificial rhetoric—spare, simple, terse, laconic. Americanisms like "nice," "funny," and "fine" provided an almost choric effect disguising strong feelings and the stresses of life. Tension vibrates underneath his staccato dialogues, and the characters appear to be speaking a code-language designed to preserve their sanity in the face of certain catastrophe. Hemingway's last distinguished work was a short novel, *The Old Man and the Sea* (1952), another testament to courage in the face of great odds, this time about an old fisherman who hooks a giant marlin and seeks to protect his catch against the sea and the sharks. Hemingway said: "I tried to make a real old man, a real boy, a real sea and a real fish and real sharks. But if I made them good and true enough they would mean many things." He was not a novelist of ideas or an experimenter in new techniques of fiction, but in his special forte of revealing men and women struggling to retain "grace under pressure" he was a master. Hemingway's sensitivity to the spirit of his age made him for many years its most admired spokesman in fiction. His best novels and short stories will remain a permanent heritage of American letters.

Further reading: *The Sun Also Rises. The (Viking) Portable Hemingway,* ed. Malcolm Cowley. Philip Young, *Ernest Hemingway,* 1952, rev. 1967. Carlos Baker, *Ernest Hemingway: A Life Story,* 1969.

The Undefeated

First published in *This Quarter* (Milan) in 1925, this story was included in *Men Without Women* (1927) from which the present text is taken.

Manuel Garcia climbed the stairs to Don Miguel Retana's office. He set down his suitcase and knocked on the door. There was no answer. Manuel, standing in the hallway, felt there was some one in the room. He felt it through the door.

"Retana," he said, listening.

There was no answer.

He's there, all right, Manuel thought.

"Retana," he said and banged the door.

"Who's there?" said some one in the office.

"Me, Manolo," Manuel said.

"What do you want?" asked the voice.

"I want to work," Manuel said.

Something in the door clicked several times and it swung open. Manuel went in, carrying his suitcase.

A little man sat behind a desk at the far side of the room. Over his head was a bull's head, stuffed by a Madrid taxidermist; on the walls were framed photographs and bull-fight posters.

The little man sat looking at Manuel.

"I thought they'd killed you," he said.

Manuel knocked with his knuckles on the desk. The little man sat looking at him across the desk.

"How many corridas[1] you had this year?" Retana asked.

"One," he answered.

"Just that one?" the little man asked.

"That's all."

"I read about it in the papers," Retana said. He leaned back in the chair and looked at Manuel.

Manuel looked up at the stuffed bull. He had seen it often before. He felt a certain family interest in it. It had killed his brother, the promising one, about nine years ago. Manuel remembered the day. There was a brass plate on the oak shield the bull's head was mounted on. Manuel could not read it, but he imagined it was in memory of his brother. Well, he had been a good kid.

The plate said: "The Bull 'Mariposa' of the Duke of Veragua, which accepted 9 varas for 7 caballos, and caused the death of Antonio Garcia, Novillero, April 27, 1909."[2]

Retana saw him looking at the stuffed bull's head. "The lot the Duke sent me for Sunday will make a scandal," he said. "They're all bad in the legs. What do they say about them at the Café?"

"I don't know," Manuel said. "I just got in."

"Yes," Retana said. "You still have your bag."

He looked at Manuel, leaning back behind the big desk.

"Sit down," he said. "Take off your cap."

Manuel sat down; his cap off, his face was changed. He looked pale, and his coleta pinned forward on his head, so that it would not show under the cap, gave him a strange look.

"You don't look well," Retana said.

"I just got out of the hospital," Manuel said.

"I heard they'd cut your leg off," Retana said.

"No," said Manuel. "It got all right."

Retana leaned forward across the desk and pushed a wooden box of cigarettes toward Manuel.

"Have a cigarette," he said.

"Thanks."

Manuel lit it.

"Smoke?" he said, offering the match to Retana.

"No," Retana waved his hand, "I never smoke."

Retana watched him smoking.

"Why don't you get a job and go to work?" he said.

"I don't want to work," Manuel said. "I am a bull-fighter."

"There aren't any bull-fighters any more," Retana said.

"I'm a bull-fighter," Manuel said.

"Yes, while you're in there," Retana said.

Manuel laughed.

Retana sat, saying nothing and looking at Manuel.

"I'll put you in a nocturnal[3] if you want," Retana offered.

"When?" Manuel asked.

"To-morrow night."

"I don't like to substitute for anybody," Manuel said. That was the way they all got killed. That was the way Salvador got killed. He tapped with his knuckles on the table.

"It's all I've got," Retana said.

"Why don't you put me on next week?" Manuel suggested.

"You wouldn't draw," Retana said. "All they want is Litri and Rubito and La Torre. Those kids are good."

"They'd come to see me get it," Manuel said, hopefully.

"No, they wouldn't. They don't know who you are any more."

"I've got a lot of stuff," Manuel said.

"I'm offering to put you on to-morrow night,"

[1] From *corridas de toros*, bullfights.

[2] *Varas*, lances used by the picadors. *Caballos*, horses ridden by picadors, frequently gored by bulls during the fight. *Novillero*, apprentice or semi-professional matador.

[3] A night bullfight.

Retana said. "You can work with young Hernandez and kill two novillos after the Charlots."[4]

"Whose novillos?" Manuel asked.

"I don't know. Whatever stuff they've got in the corrals. What the veterinaries won't pass in the daytime."

"I don't like to substitute," Manuel said.

"You can take it or leave it," Retana said. He leaned forward over the papers. He was no longer interested. The appeal that Manuel had made to him for a moment when he thought of the old days was gone. He would like to get him to substitute for Larita because he could get him cheaply. He could get others cheaply too. He would like to help him though. Still he had given him the chance. It was up to him.

"How much do I get?" Manuel asked. He was still playing with the idea of refusing. But he knew he could not refuse.

"Two hundred and fifty pesetas," Retana said. He had thought of five hundred, but when he opened his mouth it said two hundred and fifty.

"You pay Villalta seven thousand," Manuel said.

"You're not Villalta," Retana said.

"I know it," Manuel said.

"He draws it, Manolo," Retana said in explanation.

"Sure," said Manuel. He stood up. "Give me three hundred, Retana."

"All right," Retana agreed. He reached in the drawer for a paper.

"Can I have fifty now?" Manuel asked.

"Sure," said Retana. He took a fifty peseta note out of his pocket-book and laid it, spread out flat, on the table.

Manuel picked it up and put it in his pocket.

"What about a cuadrilla?"[5] he asked.

"There's the boys that always work for me nights," Retana said. "They're all right."

"How about picadors?"[6] Manuel asked.

"They're not much," Retana admitted.

"I've got to have one good pic," Manuel said.

"Get him then," Retana said. "Go and get him."

"Not out of this," Manuel said. "I'm not paying for any cuadrilla out of sixty duros."

Retana said nothing but looked at Manuel across the big desk.

"You know I've got to have one good pic," Manuel said.

Retana said nothing but looked at Manuel from a long way off.

"It isn't right," Manuel said.

Retana was still considering him, leaning back in his chair, considering him from a long way away.

"There're the regular pics," he offered.

"I know," Manuel said. "I know your regular pics."

Retana did not smile. Manuel knew it was over.

"All I want is an even break," Manuel said reasoningly. "When I go out there I want to be able to call my shots on the bull. It only takes one good picador."

He was talking to a man who was no longer listening.

"If you want something extra," Retana said, "go and get it. There will be a regular cuadrilla out there. Bring as many of your own pics as you want. The charlotada[7] is over by 10.30."

"All right," Manuel said. "If that's the way you feel about it."

"That's the way," Retana said.

"I'll see you to-morrow night," Manuel said.

"I'll be out there," Retana said.

Manuel picked up his suitcase and went out.

"Shut the door," Retana called.

Manuel looked back. Retana was sitting forward looking at some papers. Manuel pulled the door tight until it clicked.

He went down the stairs and out of the door into the hot brightness of the street. It was very hot in the street and the light on the white buildings was sudden and hard on his eyes. He walked down the shady side of the steep street toward the Puerta del Sol.[8] The shade felt solid and cool as running water. The heat came suddenly as he crossed the intersecting streets. Manuel saw no one he knew in all the people he passed.

Just before the Puerta del Sol he turned into a café.

It was quiet in the café. There were a few men sitting at tables against the wall. At one table four men played cards. Most of the men sat against the wall smoking, empty coffee-cups and liqueur-glasses before them on the tables. Manuel went through the long room to a small room in back. A man sat at a table in the corner asleep. Manuel sat down at one of the tables.

A waiter came in and stood beside Manuel's table.

"Have you seen Zurito?" Manuel asked him.

[4] *Novillos*, bulls. The "Charlots" were clowns who performed comic acts before the bullfight; named after Charlie Chaplin.

[5] *Cuadrilla*, troupe consisting of two or three bandilleros (fighters who help draw the bull with the cape and who place the barbs in the bull) and two or three picadors. Each matador has his own *cuadrilla*.

[6] *Picadors*, men on horseback who "pic" the bull with shafts or lances.

[7] The burlesque or "Charlie Chaplin."

[8] Gate of the Sun, a monument in Madrid.

"He was in before lunch," the waiter answered. "He won't be back before five o'clock."

"Bring me some coffee and milk and a shot of the ordinary," Manuel said.

The waiter came back into the room carrying a tray with a big coffee-glass and a liqueur-glass on it. In his left hand he held a bottle of brandy. He swung these down to the table and a boy who had followed him poured coffee and milk into the glass from two shiny, spouted pots with long handles.

Manuel took off his cap and the waiter noticed his pigtail pinned forward on his head. He winked at the coffee-boy as he poured out the brandy into the little glass beside Manuel's coffee. The coffee-boy looked at Manuel's pale face curiously.

"You fighting here?" asked the waiter, corking up the bottle.

"Yes," Manuel said. "To-morrow."

The waiter stood there, holding the bottle on one hip.

"You in the Charlie Chaplins?" he asked.

The coffee-boy looked away, embarrassed.

"No. In the ordinary."

"I thought they were going to have Chaves and Hernandez," the waiter said.

"No. Me and another."

"Who? Chaves or Hernandez?"

"Hernandez, I think."

"What's the matter with Chaves?"

"He got hurt."

"Where did you hear that?"

"Retana."

"Hey, Looie," the waiter called to the next room, "Chaves got cogida."[9]

Manuel had taken the wrapper off the lumps of sugar and dropped them into his coffee. He stirred it and drank it down, sweet, hot, and warming in his empty stomach. He drank off the brandy.

"Give me another shot of that," he said to the waiter.

The waiter uncorked the bottle and poured the glass full, slopping another drink into the saucer. Another waiter had come up in front of the table. The coffee-boy was gone.

"Is Chaves hurt bad?" the second waiter asked Manuel.

"I don't know," Manuel said, "Retana didn't say."

"A hell of a lot he cares," the tall waiter said. Manuel had not seen him before. He must have just come up.

"If you stand in with Retana in this town, you're a made man," the tall waiter said. "If you aren't in with him, you might just as well go out and shoot yourself."

"You said it," the other waiter who had come in said. "You said it then."

"You're right I said it," said the tall waiter. "I know what I'm talking about when I talk about that bird."

"Look what he's done for Villalta," the first waiter said.

"And that ain't all," the tall waiter said. "Look what he's done for Marcial Lalanda. Look what he's done for Nacional."

"You said it, kid," agreed the short waiter.

Manuel looked at them, standing talking in front of his table. He had drunk his second brandy. They had forgotten about him. They were not interested in him.

"Look at that bunch of camels," the tall waiter went on. "Did you ever see this Nacional II?"

"I seen him last Sunday didn't I?" the original waiter said.

"He's a giraffe," the short waiter said.

"What did I tell you?" the tall waiter said. "Those are Retana's boys."

"Say, give me another shot of that," Manuel said. He had poured the brandy the waiter had slopped over in the saucer into his glass and drank it while they were talking.

The original waiter poured his glass full mechanically, and the three of them went out of the room talking.

In the far corner the man was still asleep, snoring slightly on the intaking breath, his head back against the wall.

Manuel drank his brandy. He felt sleepy himself. It was too hot to go out into the town. Besides there was nothing to do. He wanted to see Zurito. He would go to sleep while he waited. He kicked his suitcase under the table to be sure it was there. Perhaps it would be better to put it back under the seat, against the wall. He leaned down and shoved it under. Then he leaned forward on the table and went to sleep.

When he woke there was some one sitting across the table from him. It was a big man with a heavy brown face like an Indian. He had been sitting there some time. He had waved the waiter away and sat reading the paper and occasionally looking down at Manuel, asleep, his head on the table. He read the paper laboriously, forming the words with his lips as he read. When it tired him he looked at Manuel. He sat heavily in the chair, his black Cordoba hat tipped forward.

Manuel sat up and looked at him.

"Hello, Zurito," he said.

"Hello, kid," the big man said.

"I've been asleep." Manuel rubbed his forehead with the back of his fist.

[9] *Cogida,* tossing or goring by the bull.

"I thought maybe you were."

"How's everything?"

"Good. How is everything with you?"

"Not so good."

They were both silent. Zurito, the picador, looked at Manuel's white face. Manuel looked down at the picador's enormous hands folding the paper to put away in his pocket.

"I got a favor to ask you, Manos," Manuel said.

Manosduros was Zurito's nickname. He never heard it without thinking of his huge hands. He put them forward on the table self-consciously.

"Let's have a drink," he said.

"Sure," said Manuel.

The waiter came and went and came again. He went out of the room looking back at the two men at the table.

"What's the matter, Manolo?" Zurito set down his glass.

"Would you pic two bulls for me to-morrow night?" Manuel asked, looking up at Zurito across the table.

"No," said Zurito. "I'm not pic-ing."

Manuel looked down at his glass. He had expected that answer; now he had it. Well, he had it.

"I'm sorry, Manolo, but I'm not pic-ing." Zurito looked at his hands.

"That's all right," Manuel said.

"I'm too old," Zurito said.

"I just asked you," Manuel said.

"Is it the nocturnal to-morrow?"

"That's it. I figured if I had just one good pic, I could get away with it."

"How much are you getting?"

"Three hundred pesetas."

"I get more than that for pic-ing."

"I know," said Manuel. "I didn't have any right to ask you."

"What do you keep on doing it for?" Zurito asked. "Why don't you cut off your coleta, Manolo?"[10]

"I don't know," Manuel said.

"You're pretty near as old as I am," Zurito said.

"I don't know," Manuel said. "I got to do it. If I can fix it so that I get an even break, that's all I want. I got to stick with it, Manos."

"No, you don't."

"Yes, I do. I've tried keeping away from it."

"I know how you feel. But it isn't right. You ought to get out and stay out."

"I can't do it. Besides, I've been going good lately."

Zurito looked at his face.

"You've been in the hospital."

[10] Cutting the *coleta*, or pigtail, of the fighter signified his retirement.

"But I was going great when I got hurt."

Zurito said nothing. He tipped the cognac out of his saucer into his glass.

"The papers said they never saw a better faena,"[11] Manuel said.

Zurito looked at him.

"You know when I get going I'm good," Manuel said.

"You're too old," the picador said.

"No," said Manuel. "You're ten years older than I am."

"With me it's different."

"I'm not too old," Manuel said.

They sat silent, Manuel watching the picador's face.

"I was going great till I got hurt," Manuel offered.

"You ought to have seen me, Manos," Manuel said, reproachfully.

"I don't want to see you," Zurito said. "It makes me nervous."

"You haven't seen me lately."

"I've seen you plenty."

Zurito looked at Manuel, avoiding his eyes.

"You ought to quit it, Manolo."

"I can't," Manuel said. "I'm going good now, I tell you."

Zurito leaned forward, his hands on the table.

"Listen. I'll pic for you and if you don't go big to-morrow night, you'll quit. See? Will you do that?"

"Sure."

Zurito leaned back, relieved.

"You got to quit," he said. "No monkey business. You got to cut the coleta."

"I won't have to quit," Manuel said. "You watch me. I've got the stuff."

Zurito stood up. He felt tired from arguing.

"You got to quit," he said. "I'll cut your coleta myself."

"No, you won't," Manuel said. "You won't have a chance."

Zurito called the waiter.

"Come on," said Zurito. "Come on up to the house."

Manuel reached under the seat for his suitcase. He was happy. He knew Zurito would pic for him. He was the best picador living. It was all simple now.

"Come on up to the house and we'll eat," Zurito said.

Manuel stood in the patio de caballos[12] waiting for

[11] *Faena*, a complete cycle of a bullfight, which consists of three parts, called *tercios*. The final third is called The Hour of Truth.

[12] *Patio de caballos*, stableyard where the horses are kept.

the Charlie Chaplins to be over. Zurito stood beside him. Where they stood it was dark. The high door that led into the bull-ring was shut. Above them they heard a shout, then another shout of laughter. Then there was silence. Manuel liked the smell of the stables about the patio de caballos. It smelt good in the dark. There was another roar from the arena and then applause, prolonged applause, going on and on.

"You ever seen these fellows?" Zurito asked, big and looming beside Manuel in the dark.

"No," Manuel said.

"They're pretty funny," Zurito said. He smiled to himself in the dark.

The high, double, tight-fitting door into the bull-ring swung open and Manuel saw the ring in the hard light of the arc-lights, the plaza, dark all the way around, rising high; around the edge of the ring were running and bowing two men dressed like tramps, followed by a third in the uniform of a hotel bell-boy who stooped and picked up the hats and canes thrown down onto the sand and tossed them back up into the darkness.

The electric light went on in the patio.

"I'll climb onto one of those ponies while you collect the kids," Zurito said.

Behind them came the jingle of the mules, coming out to go into the arena and be hitched onto the dead bull.

The members of the cuadrilla, who had been watching the burlesque from the runway between the barrera[13] and the seats, came walking back and stood in a group talking, under the electric light in the patio. A good-looking lad in a silver-and-orange suit came up to Manuel and smiled.

"I'm Hernandez," he said and put out his hand.

Manuel shook it.

"They're regular elephants we've got tonight," the boy said cheerfully.

"They're big ones with horns," Manuel agreed.

"You drew the worst lot," the boy said.

"That's all right," Manuel said. "The bigger they are, the more meat for the poor."

"Where did you get that one?" Hernandez grinned.

"That's an old one," Manuel said. "You line up your cuadrilla, so I can see what I've got."

"You've got some good kids," Hernandez said. He was very cheerful. He had been on twice before in nocturnals and was beginning to get a following in Madrid. He was happy the fight would start in a few minutes.

"Where are the pics?" Manuel asked.

"They're back in the corrals fighting about who gets the beautiful horses," Hernandez grinned.

[13] Wooden fence around the bullring.

The mules came through the gate in a rush, the whips snapping, bells jangling and the young bull ploughing a furrow of sand.

They formed up for the paseo[14] as soon as the bull had gone through.

Manuel and Hernandez stood in front. The youths of the cuadrillas were behind, their heavy capes furled over their arms. In back, the four picadors, mounted, holding their steel-tipped push-poles erect in the half-dark of the corral.

"It's a wonder Retana wouldn't give us enough light to see the horses by," one picador said.

"He knows we'll be happier if we don't get too good a look at these skins," another pic answered.

"This thing I'm on barely keeps me off the ground," the first picador said.

"Well, they're horses."

"Sure, they're horses."

They talked, sitting their gaunt horses in the dark.

Zurito said nothing. He had the only steady horse of the lot. He had tried him, wheeling him in the corrals and he responded to the bit and the spurs. He had taken the bandage off his right eye and cut the strings where they had tied his ears tight shut at the base. He was a good, solid horse, solid on his legs. That was all he needed. He intended to ride him all through the corrida. He had already, since he had mounted, sitting in the half-dark in the big, quilted saddle, waiting for the paseo, pic-ed through the whole corrida in his mind. The other picadors went on talking on both sides of him. He did not hear them.

The two matadors stood together in front of their three peones,[15] their capes furled over their left arms in the same fashion. Manuel was thinking about the three lads in back of him. They were all three Madrilenos,[16] like Hernandez, boys about nineteen. One of them, a gypsy, serious, aloof, and dark-faced, he liked the look of. He turned.

"What's your name, kid?" he asked the gypsy.

"Fuentes," the gypsy said.

"That's a good name," Manuel said.

The gypsy smiled, showing his teeth.

"You take the bull and give him a little run when he comes out," Manuel said.

"All right," the gypsy said. His face was serious. He began to think about just what he would do.

"Here she goes," Manuel said to Hernandez.

"All right. We'll go."

Heads up, swinging with the music, their right arms swinging free, they stepped out, crossing the sanded arena under the arc-lights, the cuadrillas

[14] Ceremonial parade of bullfighters preceding the bullfight.

[15] The star performers were *matadors,* the men who kill the bull. Two matadors took part, assisted by *peones,* who work under them.

[16] Natives of Madrid.

opening out behind, the picadors riding after, behind came the bull-ring servants and the jingling mules. The crowd applauded Hernandez as they marched across the arena. Arrogant, swinging, they looked straight ahead as they marched.

They bowed before the president, and the procession broke up into its component parts. The bull-fighters went over to the barrera and changed their heavy mantles for the light fighting capes. The mules went out. The picadors galloped jerkily around the ring, and two rode out the gate they had come in by. The servants swept the sand smooth.

Manuel drank a glass of water poured for him by one of Retana's deputies, who was acting as his manager and sword-handler. Hernandez came over from speaking with his own manager.

"You got a good hand, kid," Manuel complimented him.

"They like me," Hernandez said happily.

"How did the paseo go?" Manuel asked Retana's man.

"Like a wedding," said the handler. "Fine. You came out like Joselito and Belmonte."

Zurito rode by, a bulky equestrian statue. He wheeled his horse and faced him toward the toril[17] on the far side of the ring where the bull would come out. It was strange under the arc-light. He pic-ed in the hot afternoon sun for big money. He didn't like this arc-light business. He wished they would get started.

Manuel went up to him.

"Pic him, Manos," he said. "Cut him down to size for me."

"I'll pic him, kid," Zurito spat on the sand. "I'll make him jump out of the ring."

"Lean on him, Manos," Manuel said.

"I'll lean on him," Zurito said. "What's holding it up?"

"He's coming now," Manuel said.

Zurito sat there, his feet in the box-stirrups, his great legs in the buckskin-covered armor gripping the horse, the reins in his left hand, the long pic held in his right hand, his broad hat well down over his eyes to shade them from the lights, watching the distant door of the toril. His horse's ears quivered. Zurito patted him with his left hand.

The red door of the toril swung back and for a moment Zurito looked into the empty passageway far across the arena. Then the bull came out in a rush, skidding on his four legs as he came out under the lights, then charging in a gallop, moving softly in a fast gallop, silent except as he woofed through wide nostrils as he charged, glad to be free after the dark pen.

In the first row of seats, slightly bored, leaning forward to write on the cement wall in front of his knees, the substitute bull-fight critic of *El Heraldo* scribbled: "Campagnero, Negro, 42, came out at 90 miles an hour with plenty of gas——"

Manuel, leaning against the barrera, watching the bull, waved his hand and the gypsy ran out, trailing his cape. The bull, in full gallop, pivoted and charged the cape, his head down, his tail rising. The gypsy moved in a zigzag, and as he passed, the bull caught sight of him and abandoned the cape to charge the man. The gyp sprinted and vaulted the red fence of the barrera as the bull struck it with his horns. He tossed into it twice with his horns, banging into the wood blindly.

The critic of *El Heraldo* lit a cigarette and tossed the match at the bull, then wrote in his note-book, "large and with enough horns to satisfy the cash customers, Campagnero showed a tendency to cut into the terrane of the bull-fighters."

Manuel stepped out on the hard sand as the bull banged into the fence. Out of the corner of his eye he saw Zurito sitting the white horse close to the barrera, about a quarter of the way around the ring to the left. Manuel held the cape close in front of him, a fold in each hand, and shouted at the bull. "Huh! Huh!" The bull turned, seemed to brace against the fence as he charged in a scramble, driving into the cape as Manuel side-stepped, pivoted on his heels with the charge of the bull, and swung the cape just ahead of the horns. At the end of the swing he was facing the bull again and held the cape in the same position close in front of his body, and pivoted again as the bull recharged. Each time, as he swung, the crowd shouted.

Four times he swung with the bull, lifting the cape so it billowed full, and each time bringing the bull around to charge again. Then, at the end of the fifth swing, he held the cape against his hip and pivoted, so the cape swung out like a ballet dancer's skirt and wound the bull around himself like a belt, to step clear, leaving the bull facing Zurito on the white horse, come up and planted firm, the horse facing the bull, its ears forward, its lips nervous, Zurito, his hat over his eyes, leaning forward, the long pole sticking out before and behind in a sharp angle under his right arm, held halfway down, the triangular iron point facing the bull.

El Heraldo's second-string critic, drawing on his cigarette, his eyes on the bull, wrote: "the veteran Manolo designed a series of acceptable veronicas, ending in a very Belmontistic recorte that earned applause from the regulars, and we entered the tercio of the cavalry."[18]

Zurito sat his horse, measuring the distance between the bull and the end of the pic. As he looked,

[17] Place where the bull is enclosed.

[18] *Veronicas*, passes with the cape. A *recorte* is a special move in which the matador flicks the cape in rapid motions.

the bull gathered himself together and charged, his eyes on the horse's chest. As he lowered his head to hook, Zurito sunk the point of the pic in the swelling hump of muscle above the bull's shoulder, leaned all his weight on the shaft, and with his left hand pulled the white horse into the air, front hoofs pawing, and swung him to the right as he pushed the bull under and through so the horns passed safely under the horse's belly and the horse came down, quivering, the bull's tail brushing his chest as he charged the cape Hernandez offered him.

Hernandez ran sideways, taking the bull out and away with the cape, toward the other picador. He fixed him with a swing of the cape, squarely facing the horse and rider, and stepped back. As the bull saw the horse he charged. The picador's lance slid along his back, and as the shock of the charge lifted the horse, the picador was already half-way out of the saddle, lifting his right leg clear as he missed with the lance and falling to the left side to keep the horse between him and the bull. The horse, lifted and gored, crashed over with the bull driving into him, the picador gave a shove with his boots against the horse and lay clear, waiting to be lifted and hauled away and put on his feet.

Manuel let the bull drive into the fallen horse; he was in no hurry, the picador was safe; besides, it did a picador like that good to worry. He'd stay on longer next time. Lousy pics! He looked across the sand at Zurito a little way out from the barrera, his horse rigid, waiting.

"Huh!" he called to the bull, "Tomar!" holding the cape in both hands so it would catch his eye. The bull detached himself from the horse and charged the cape, and Manuel, running sideways and holding the cape spread wide, stopped, swung on his heels, and brought the bull sharply around facing Zurito.

"Campagnero accepted a pair of varas for the death of one rosinante,[19] with Hernandez and Manolo at the quites,"[20] *El Heraldo's* critic wrote. "He pressed on the iron and clearly showed he was no horse-lover. The veteran Zurito resurrected some of his old stuff with the pike-pole, notably the suerte——"[21]

"Olé! Olé!" the man sitting beside him shouted. The shout was lost in the roar of the crowd, and he slapped the critic on the back. The critic looked up to see Zurito, directly below him, leaning far out over his horse, the length of the pic rising in a sharp angle under his armpit, holding the pic almost by the point, bearing down with all his weight, holding the bull off, the bull pushing and driving to get at the horse, and Zurito, far out, on top of him, holding him, holding him, and slowly pivoting the horse against the pressure, so that at last he was clear. Zurito felt the moment when the horse was clear and the bull could come past, and relaxed the absolute steel lock of his resistance, and the triangular steel point of the pic ripped in the bull's hump of shoulder muscle as he tore loose to find Hernandez's cape before his muzzle. He charged blindly into the cape and the boy took him out into the open arena.

Zurito sat patting his horse and looking at the bull charging the cape that Hernandez swung for him out under the bright light while the crowd shouted.

"You see that one?" he said to Manuel.

"It was a wonder," Manuel said.

"I got him that time," Zurito said. "Look at him now."

At the conclusion of a closely turned pass of the cape the bull slid to his knees. He was up at once, but far out across the sand Manuel and Zurito saw the shine of the pumping flow of blood, smooth against the black of the bull's shoulder.

"I got him that time," Zurito said.

"He's a good bull," Manuel said.

"If they gave me another shot at him, I'd kill him," Zurito said.

"They'll change the thirds on us," Manuel said.

"Look at him now," Zurito said.

"I got to go over there," Manuel said, and started on a run for the other side of the ring, where the monos were leading a horse out by the bridle toward the bull, whacking him on the legs with rods and all, in a procession, trying to get him toward the bull, who stood, dropping his head, pawing, unable to make up his mind to charge.

Zurito, sitting his horse, walking him toward the scene, not missing any detail, scowled.

Finally the bull charged, the horse leaders ran for the barrera, the picador hit too far back, and the bull got under the horse, lifted him, threw him onto his back.

Zurito watched. The monos, in their red shirts, running out to drag the picador clear. The picador, now on his feet, swearing and flopping his arms. Manuel and Hernandez standing ready with their capes. And the bull, the great, black bull, with a horse on his back, hooves dangling, the bridle caught in the horns. Black bull with a horse on his back, staggering short-legged, then arching his neck and lifting, thrusting, charging to slide the horse off, horse sliding down. Then the bull into a lunging charge at the cape Manuel spread for him.

The bull was slower now, Manuel felt. He was bleeding badly. There was a sheen of blood all down his flank.

[19]An old horse, so named from Don Quixote's nag, Rosinante.

[20]*Quites,* the technique of diverting the bull, turning him away from any of the fighters endangered.

[21]*Suerte,* one of the formal maneuvers performed by the matador.

Manuel offered him the cape again. There he came, eyes open, ugly, watching the cape. Manuel stepped to the side and raised his arms, tightening the cape ahead of the bull for the veronica.

Now he was facing the bull. Yes, his head was going down a little. He was carrying it lower. That was Zurito.

Manuel flopped the cape; there he comes; he side-stepped and swung in another veronica. He's shooting awfully accurately, he thought. He's had enough fight, so he's watching now. He's hunting now. Got his eye on me. But I always give him the cape.

He shook the cape at the bull; there he comes; he side-stepped. Awful close that time. I don't want to work that close to him.

The edge of the cape was wet with blood where it had swept along the bull's back as he went by.

All right, here's the last one.

Manuel, facing the bull, having turned with him each charge, offered the cape with his two hands. The bull looked at him. Eyes watching, horns straight forward, the bull looked at him, watching.

"Huh!" Manuel said, "Toro!" and leaning back, swung the cape forward. Here he comes. He side-stepped, swung the cape in back of him, and pivoted, so the bull followed a swirl of cape and then was left with nothing, fixed by the pass, dominated by the cape. Manuel swung the cape under his muzzle with one hand, to show the bull was fixed, and walked away.

There was no applause.

Manuel walked across the sand toward the barrera, while Zurito rode out of the ring. The trumpet had blown to change the act to the planting of the banderillos while Manuel had been working with the bull. He had not consciously noticed it. The monos were spreading canvas over the two dead horses and sprinkling sawdust around them.

Manuel came up to the barrera for a drink of water. Retana's man handed him the heavy porous jug.

Fuentes, the tall gypsy, was standing holding a pair of banderillos, holding them together, slim, red sticks, fish-hook points out. He looked at Manuel.

"Go on out there," Manuel said.

The gypsy trotted out. Manuel set down the jug and watched. He wiped his face with his handkerchief.

The critic of *El Heraldo* reached for the bottle of warm champagne that stood between his feet, took a drink, and finished his paragraph.

"—the aged Manolo rated no applause for a vulgar series of lances with the cape and we entered the third of the palings."

Alone in the centre of the ring the bull stood, still fixed. Fuentes, tall, flat-backed, walking toward him arrogantly, his arms spread out, the two slim, red sticks, one in each hand, held by the fingers, points straight forward. Fuentes walked forward. Back of him and to one side was a peon with a cape. The bull looked at him and was no longer fixed.

His eyes watched Fuentes, now standing still. Now he leaned back, calling to him. Fuentes twitched the two banderillos and the light on the steel points caught the bull's eye.

His tail went up and he charged.

He came straight, his eyes on the man. Fuentes stood still, leaning back, the banderillos pointing forward. As the bull lowered his head to hook, Fuentes leaned backward, his arms came together and rose, his two hands touching, the banderillos two descending red lines, and leaning forward drove the points into the bull's shoulder, leaning far in over the bull's horns and pivoting on the two upright sticks, his legs tight together, his body curving to one side to let the bull pass.

"Olé!" from the crowd.

The bull was hooking wildly, jumping like a trout, all four feet off the ground. The red shaft of the banderillos tossed as he jumped.

Manuel standing at the barrera, noticed that he hooked always to the right.

"Tell him to drop the next pair on the right," he said to the kid who started to run out to Fuentes with the new banderillos.

A heavy hand fell on his shoulder. It was Zurito.

"How do you feel, kid?" he asked.

Manuel was watching the bull.

Zurito leaned forward on the barrera, leaning the weight of his body on his arms. Manuel turned to him.

"You're going good," Zurito said.

Manuel shook his head. He had nothing to do now until the next third. The gypsy was very good with the banderillos. The bull would come to him in the next third in good shape. He was a good bull. It had all been easy up to now. The final stuff with the sword was all he worried over. He did not really worry. He did not even think about it. But standing there he had a heavy sense of apprehension. He looked out at the bull, planning his faena, his work with the red cloth that was to reduce the bull, to make him manageable.

The gypsy was walking out toward the bull again, walking heel-and-toe, insultingly, like a ball-room dancer, the red shafts of the banderillos twitching with his walk. The bull watched him, not fixed now, hunting him, but waiting to get close enough so he could be sure of getting him, getting the horns into him.

As Fuentes walked forward the bull charged. Fuentes ran across the quarter of a circle as the bull charged and, as he passed running backward, stopped, swung forward, rose on his toes, arms straight out, and sunk the banderillos straight down into the tight of the big shoulder muscles as the bull missed him.

The crowd were wild about it.

"That kid won't stay in this night stuff long," Retana's man said to Zurito.

"He's good," Zurito said.

"Watch him now."

They watched.

Fuentes was standing with his back against the barrera. Two of the cuadrilla were back of him, with their capes ready to flop over the fence to distract the bull.

The bull, with his tongue out, his barrel heaving, was watching the gypsy. He thought he had him now. Back against the red planks. Only a short charge away. The bull watched him.

The gypsy bent back, drew back his arms, the banderillos pointing at the bull. He called to the bull, stamped one foot. The bull was suspicious. He wanted the man. No more barbs in the shoulder.

Fuentes walked a little closer to the bull. Bent back. Called again. Somebody in the crowd shouted a warning.

"He's too damn close," Zurito said.

"Watch him," Retana's man said.

Leaning back, inciting the bull with the banderillos, Fuentes jumped, both feet off the ground. As he jumped the bull's tail rose and he charged. Fuentes came down on his toes, arms straight out, whole body arching forward, and drove the shafts straight down as he swung his body clear of the right horn.

The bull crashed into the barrera where the flopping capes had attracted his eye as he lost the man.

The gypsy came running along the barrera toward Manuel, taking the applause of the crowd. His vest was ripped where he had not quite cleared the point of the horn. He was happy about it, showing it to the spectators. He made the tour of the ring. Zurito saw him go by, smiling, pointing at his vest. He smiled.

Somebody else was planting the last pair of banderillos. Nobody was paying any attention.

Retana's man tucked a baton inside the red cloth of a muleta,[22] folded the cloth over it, and handed it over the barrera to Manuel. He reached in the leather sword-case, took out a sword, and holding it by its leather scabbard, reached it over the fence to Manuel. Manuel pulled the blade out by the red hilt and the scabbard fell limp.

He looked at Zurito. The big man saw he was sweating.

"Now you get him, kid," Zurito said.

Manuel nodded.

"He's in good shape," Zurito said.

"Just like you want him," Retana's man assured him.

Manuel nodded.

The trumpeter, up under the roof, blew for the final act, and Manuel walked across the arena toward where, up in the dark boxes, the president must be.

In the front row of seats the substitute bull-fight critic of *El Heraldo* took a long drink of the warm champagne. He had decided it was not worth while to write a running story and would write up the corrida back in the office. What the hell was it anyway? Only a nocturnal. If he missed anything he would get it out of the morning papers. He took another drink of the champagne. He had a date at Maxim's at twelve. Who were these bull-fighters anyway? Kids and bums. A bunch of bums. He put his pad of paper in his pocket and looked over toward Manuel, standing very much alone in the ring, gesturing with his hat in a salute toward a box he could not see high up in the dark plaza. Out in the ring the bull stood quiet, looking at nothing.

"I dedicate this bull to you, Mr. President, and to the public of Madrid, the most intelligent and generous of the world," was what Manuel was saying. It was a formula. He said it all. It was a little long for nocturnal use.

He bowed at the dark, straightened, tossed his hat over his shoulder, and, carrying the muleta in his left hand and the sword in his right, walked out toward the bull.

Manuel walked toward the bull. The bull looked at him; his eyes were quick. Manuel noticed the way the banderillos hung down on his left shoulder and the steady sheen of blood from Zurito's pic-ing. He noticed the way the bull's feet were. As he walked forward, holding the muleta in his left hand and the sword in his right, he watched the bull's feet. The bull could not charge without gathering his feet together. Now he stood square on them, dully.

Manuel walked toward him, watching his feet. This was all right. He could do this. He must work to get the bull's head down, so he could go in past the horns and kill him. He did not think about the sword, not about killing the bull. He thought about one thing at a time. The coming things oppressed him, though. Walking forward, watching the bull's feet, he saw successively his eyes, his wet muzzle, and the wide, forward-pointing spread of his horns. The bull had light circles about his eyes. His eyes watched Manuel. He felt he was going to get this little one with the white face.

Standing still now and spreading the red cloth of

[22] The red flag used by the bullfighters. Contrary to popular belief, it is not used to enrage the bull, because all cattle are color-blind. It functions to minimize the sight of blood.

the muleta with the sword, pricking the point into the cloth so that the sword, now held in his left hand, spread the red flannel like the jib of a boat, Manuel noticed the points of the bull's horns. One of them was splintered from banging against the barrera. The other was sharp as a porcupine quill. Manuel noticed while spreading the muleta that the white base of the horn was stained red. While he noticed these things he did not lose sight of the bull's feet. The bull watched Manuel steadily.

He's on the defensive now, Manuel thought. He's reserving himself. I've got to bring him out of that and get his head down. Always get his head down. Zurito had his head down once, but he's come back. He'll bleed when I start him going and that will bring it down.

Holding the muleta, with the sword in his left hand widening it in front of him, he called to the bull.

The bull looked at him.

He leaned back insultingly and shook the wide-spread flannel.

The bull saw the muleta. It was a bright scarlet under the arc-light. The bull's legs tightened.

Here he comes. Whoosh! Manuel turned as the bull came and raised the muleta so that it passed over the bull's horns and swept down his broad back from head to tail. The bull had gone clean up in the air with the charge. Manuel had not moved.

At the end of the pass the bull turned like a cat coming around a corner and faced Manuel.

He was on the offensive again. His heaviness was gone. Manuel noted the fresh blood shining down the black shoulder and dripping down the bull's leg. He drew the sword out of the muleta and held it in his right hand. The muleta held low down in his left hand, leaning toward the left, he called to the bull. The bull's legs tightened, his eyes on the muleta. Here he comes, Manuel thought. Yuh!

He swung with the charge, sweeping the muleta ahead of the bull, his feet firm, the sword following the curve, a point of light under the arcs.

The bull recharged as the pase natural finished and Manuel raised the muleta for a pase de pecho.[23] Firmly planted, the bull came by his chest under the raised muleta. Manuel leaned his head back to avoid the clattering banderillo shafts. The hot, black bull body touched his chest as it passed.

Too damn close, Manuel thought. Zurito, leaning on the barrera, spoke rapidly to the gypsy, who trotted out toward Manuel with a cape. Zurito pulled his hat down low and looked out across the arena at Manuel.

Manuel was facing the bull again, the muleta held low and to the left. The bull's head was down as he watched the muleta.

"If it was Belmonte doing that stuff, they'd go crazy," Retana's man said.

Zurito said nothing. He was watching Manuel out in the centre of the arena.

"Where did the boss dig this fellow up?" Retana's man asked.

"Out of the hospital," Zurito said.

"That's where he's going damn quick," Retana's man said.

Zurito turned on him.

"Knock on that," he said, pointing to the barrera.

"I was just kidding, man," Retana's man said.

"Knock on the wood."

Retana's man leaned forward and knocked three times on the barrera.

"Watch the faena," Zurito said.

Out in the centre of the ring, under the lights, Manuel was kneeling, facing the bull, and as he raised the muleta in both hands the bull charged, tail up.

Manuel swung his body clear and, as the bull recharged, brought around the muleta in a half-circle that pulled the bull to his knees.

"Why, that one's a great bull-fighter," Retana's man said.

"No, he's not," said Zurito.

Manuel stood up and, the muleta in his left hand, the sword in his right, acknowledged the applause from the dark plaza.

The bull had humped himself up from his knees and stood waiting, his head hung low.

Zurito spoke to two of the other lads of the cuadrilla and they ran out to stand back of Manuel with their capes. There were four men back of him now. Hernandez had followed him since he first came out with the muleta. Fuentes stood watching, his cape held against his body, tall, in repose, watching lazy-eyed. Now the two came up. Hernandez motioned them to stand one at each side. Manuel stood alone, facing the bull.

Manuel waved back the men with the capes. Stepping back cautiously, they saw his face was white and sweating.

Didn't they know enough to keep back? Did they want to catch the bull's eye with the capes after he was fixed and ready? He had enough to worry about without that kind of thing.

The bull was standing, his four feet square, looking at the muleta. Manuel furled the muleta in his left hand. The bull's eyes watched it. His body was heavy on his feet. He carried his head low, but not too low.

[23] *Pase natural* is performed with the cape in the left hand. *Pase de pecho* is a maneuver to make the bull pass before the matador's chest.

Manuel lifted the muleta at him. The bull did not move. Only his eyes watched.

He's all lead, Manuel thought. He's all square. He's framed right. He'll take it.

He thought in bull-fight terms. Sometimes he had a thought and the particular piece of slang would not come into his mind and he could not realize the thought. His instincts and his knowledge worked automatically, and his brain worked slowly and in words. He knew all about bulls. He did not have to think about them. He just did the right thing. His eyes noted things and his body performed the necessary measures without thought. If he thought about it, he would be gone.

Now, facing the bull, he was conscious of many things at the same time. There were the horns, the one splintered, the other smoothly sharp, the need to profile himself toward the left horn, lance himself short and straight, lower the muleta so the bull would follow it, and, going in over the horns, put the sword all the way into a little spot about as big as a five-peseta piece straight in back of the neck, between the sharp pitch of the bull's shoulders. He must do all this and must then come out from between the horns. He was conscious he must do all this, but his only thought was in words: "Corto y derecho."[24]

"Corto y derecho," he thought, furling the muleta. Short and straight. Corto y derecho, he drew the sword out of the muleta, profiled on the splintered left horn, dropped the muleta across his body, so his right hand with the sword on the level with his eye made the sign of the cross, and, rising on his toes, sighted along the dipping blade of the sword at the spot high up between the bull's shoulders.

Corto y derecho he lanced himself on the bull.

There was a shock, and he felt himself go up in the air. He pushed on the sword as he went up and over, and it flew out of his hand. He hit the ground and the bull was on him. Manuel, lying on the ground, kicked at the bull's muzzle with his slippered feet. Kicking, kicking, the bull after him, missing him in his excitement, bumping him with his head, driving the horns into the sand. Kicking like a man keeping a ball in the air, Manuel kept the bull from getting a clean thrust at him.

Manuel felt the wind on his back from the capes flopping at the bull, and then the bull was gone, gone over him in a rush. Dark, as his belly went over. Not even stepped on.

Manuel stood up and picked up the muleta. Fuentes handed him the sword. It was bent where it had struck the shoulder-blade. Manuel straightened it on his knee and ran toward the bull, standing now beside one of the dead horses. As he ran, his jacket flopped where it had been ripped under his armpit.

"Get him out of there," Manuel shouted to the gypsy. The bull had smelled the blood of the dead horse and ripped into the canvas-cover with his horns. He charged Fuentes's cape, with the canvas hanging from his splintered horn, and the crowd laughed. Out in the ring, he tossed his head to rid himself of the canvas. Hernandez, running up from behind him, grabbed the end of the canvas and neatly lifted it off the horn.

The bull followed it in a half-charge and stopped still. He was on the defensive again. Manuel was walking toward him with the sword and muleta. Manuel swung the muleta before him. The bull would not charge.

Manuel profiled toward the bull, sighting along the dipping blade of the sword. The bull was motionless, seemingly dead on his feet, incapable of another charge.

Manuel rose to his toes, sighting along the steel, and charged.

Again there was the shock and he felt himself being borne back in a rush, to strike hard on the sand. There was no chance of kicking this time. The bull was on top of him. Manuel lay as though dead, his head on his arms, and the bull bumped him. Bumped his back, bumped his face in the sand. He felt the horn go into the sand between his folded arms. The bull hit him in the small of the back. His face drove into the sand. The horn drove through one of his sleeves and the bull ripped it off. Manuel was tossed clear and the bull followed the capes.

Manuel got up, found the sword and muleta, tried the point of the sword with his thumb, and then ran toward the barrera for a new sword.

Retana's man handed him the sword over the edge of the barrera.

"Wipe off your face," he said.

Manuel, running again toward the bull, wiped his bloody face with his handkerchief. He had not seen Zurito. Where was Zurito?

The cuadrilla had stepped away from the bull and waited with their capes. The bull stood, heavy and dull again after the action.

Manuel walked toward him with the muleta. He stopped and shook it. The bull did not respond. He passed it right and left, left and right before the bull's muzzle. The bull's eyes watched it and turned with the swing, but he would not charge. He was waiting for Manuel.

Manuel was worried. There was nothing to do but go in. Corto y derecho. He profiled close to the bull, crossed the muleta in front of his body and charged. As he pushed in the sword, he jerked his body to the left to clear the horn. The bull passed

[24] *Corto y derecho,* short and straight.

him and the sword shot up in the air, twinkling under the arc-lights, to fall red-hilted on the sand.

Manuel ran over and picked it up. It was bent and he straightened it over his knee.

As he came running toward the bull, fixed again now, he passed Hernandez standing with his cape.

"He's all bone," the boy said encouragingly.

Manuel nodded, wiping his face. He put the bloody handkerchief in his pocket.

There was the bull. He was close to the barrera now. Damn him. Maybe he was all bone. Maybe there was not any place for the sword to go in. The hell there wasn't! He'd show them.

He tried a pass with the muleta and the bull did not move. Manuel chopped the muleta back and forth in front of the bull. Nothing doing.

He furled the muleta, drew the sword out, profiled and drove in on the bull. He felt the sword buckle as he shoved it in, leaning his weight on it, and then it shot high in the air, end-over-ending into the crowd. Manuel had jerked clear as the sword jumped.

The first cushions thrown down out of the dark missed him. Then one hit him in the face, his bloody face looking toward the crowd. They were coming down fast. Spotting the sand. Somebody threw an empty champagne-bottle from close range. It hit Manuel on the foot. He stood there watching the dark, where the things were coming from. Then something whished through the air and struck by him. Manuel leaned over and picked it up. It was his sword. He straightened it over his knee and gestured with it to the crowd.

"Thank you," he said. "Thank you."

Oh, the dirty bastards! Dirty bastards! Oh, the lousy, dirty bastards! He kicked into a cushion as he ran.

There was the bull. The same as ever. All right, you dirty, lousy bastard!

Manuel passed the muleta in front of the bull's black muzzle.

Nothing doing.

You won't! All right. He stepped close and jammed the sharp peak of the muleta into the bull's damp muzzle.

The bull was on him as he jumped back and as he tripped on a cushion he felt the horn go into him, into his side. He grabbed the horn with his two hands and rode backward, holding tight onto the place. The bull tossed him and he was clear. He lay still. It was all right. The bull was gone.

He got up coughing and feeling broken and gone. The dirty bastards!

"Give me the sword," he shouted. "Give me the stuff."

Fuentes came up with the muleta and the sword.

Hernandez put his arm around him.

"Go on to the infirmary, man," he said. "Don't be a damn fool."

"Get away from me," Manuel said. "Get to hell away from me."

He twisted free. Hernandez shrugged his shoulders. Manuel ran toward the bull.

There was the bull standing, heavy, firmly planted.

All right, you bastard! Manuel drew the sword out of the muleta, sighted with the same movement, and flung himself onto the bull. He felt the sword go in all the way. Right up to the guard. Four fingers and his thumb into the bull. The blood was hot on his knuckles, and he was on top of the bull.

The bull lurched with him as he lay on, and seemed to sink; then he was standing clear. He looked at the bull going down slowly over on his side, then suddenly four feet in the air.

Then he gestured at the crowd, his hand warm from the bull blood.

All right, you bastards! He wanted to say something, but he started to cough. It was hot and choking. He looked down for the muleta. He must go over and salute the president. President hell! He was sitting down looking at something. It was the bull. His four feet up. Thick tongue out. Things crawling around on his belly and under his legs. Crawling where the hair was thin. Dead bull. To hell with the bull! To hell with them all! He started to get to his feet and commenced to cough. He sat down again, coughing. Somebody came and pushed him up.

They carried him across the ring to the infirmary, running with him across the sand, standing blocked at the gate as the mules came in, then around under the dark passageway, men grunting as they took him up the stairway, and then laid him down.

The doctor and two men in white were waiting for him. They laid him out on the table. They were cutting away his shirt. Manuel felt tired. His whole chest felt scalding inside. He started to cough and they held something to his mouth. Everybody was very busy.

There was an electric light in his eyes. He shut his eyes.

He heard some one coming very heavily up the stairs. Then he did not hear it. Then he heard a noise far off. That was the crowd. Well, somebody would have to kill his other bull. They had cut away all his shirt. The doctor smiled at him. There was Retana.

"Hello, Retana!" Manuel said. He could not hear his voice.

Retana smiled at him and said something. Manuel could not hear it.

Zurito stood beside the table, bending over where the doctor was working. He was in his picador clothes, without his hat.

Zurito said something to him. Manuel could not hear it.

Zurito was speaking to Retana. One of the men in white smiled and handed Retana a pair of scissors. Retana gave them to Zurito. Zurito said something to Manuel. He could not hear it.

To hell with this operating-table! He'd been on plenty of operating-tables before. He was not going to die. There would be a priest if he was going to die.

Zurito was saying something to him. Holding up the scissors.

That was it. They were going to cut off his coleta. They were going to cut off his pigtail.

Manuel sat up on the operating-table. The doctor stepped back, angry. Some one grabbed him and held him.

"You couldn't do a thing like that, Manos," he said.

He heard suddenly, clearly, Zurito's voice.

"That's all right," Zurito said. "I won't do it. I was joking."

"I was going good," Manuel said. "I didn't have any luck. That was all."

Manuel lay back. They had put something over his face. It was all familiar. He inhaled deeply. He felt very tired. He was very, very tired. They took the thing away from his face.

"I was going good," Manuel said weakly. "I was going great."

Retana looked at Zurito and started for the door.

"I'll stay here with him," Zurito said.

Retana shrugged his shoulders.

Manuel opened his eyes and looked at Zurito.

"Wasn't I going good, Manos?" he asked, for confirmation.

"Sure," said Zurito. "You were going great."

The doctor's assistant put the cone over Manuel's face and he inhaled deeply. Zurito stood awkwardly, watching.

F. SCOTT FITZGERALD [1896-1940]

THE HIGH-PITCHED, pleasure-seeking era of the 1920's with its jazz rhythms, its flappers and rich boys, bootleggers and speakeasies—a Trimalchio's feast of irresponsible social behavior and moral letdown—was born in 1919 in the early stories of F. Scott Fitzgerald even more vividly than it was recognizable in fact. When, after 1929, the bubble burst with the collapse of the stock market, he knew that he had lived through its worst excesses and suffered its moral bankruptcy. He had also given it a name—The Jazz Age. As a writer, Fitzgerald belongs in the tradition of Henry James, Edith Wharton, and Conrad as a novelist of manners and morals. He was also a social historian of prophetic instincts who, even at the height of his own youthful gaiety and success, was able to see that "the greatest, gaudiest spree in history" could not last. In the mid-thirties when he came to analyze his own emotional crack-up in a series of confessional articles for *Esquire* magazine, he described the Jazz Age as a nightmare and a delusion both for himself and for the nation. His own happiness, he realized, had been as unnatural as the Boom, and his personal tragedy a counterpart of "the wave of despair that swept the nation when the Boom was over." The strain of his double life, living hedonistically and at the same time measuring with the objective eye of a serious artist the inevitable cost of such living, was too great. Fitzgerald died at 44, but not before he had written the novel (*The Great Gatsby*, 1925) and the succession of short stories which captured brilliantly and authentically the overwrought temper of that decade of American life.

Fitzgerald was born in the Middle West, in St. Paul, Minnesota, of a family conscious of declining fortunes, but not without social status and a moderate income. He went to private schools and then to Princeton, where he wrote librettos for the Triangle Club and mingled with the undergraduate intelligentsia. Leaving Princeton in 1917, he enlisted in the army and was sent to training camps, but never got overseas. In Georgia he met his future wife, Zelda Sayre, a party-loving debutante, dancer, and *belle dame sans merci* who was to become the prototype for the siren-heroines of Fitzgerald's novels and stories. Later she became a permanent invalid in a sanitarium for the insane. While Fitzgerald was in the army, he wrote his first novel, *This Side of Paradise* (1920), the book that ushered in the Jazz Age and became a success of scandal by reporting from inside the excitements of petting parties, flirts, and baby vamps who shocked their Victorian parents. It earned Fitzgerald $18,000 in one year and enabled him to marry Zelda and embark on a spree of spending and riotous living. In New York, in Paris, on the French Riviera, the Fitzgeralds recklessly expended themselves while he wrote for the popular magazines to pay the bills. *The Beautiful and Damned* (1922) was a novelized record of the dissipated life Scott and Zelda had been leading, and of his sense of the disaster toward which they and their generation were moving. Money as the road to pleasure and the high-life preoccupied him. He both admired and resented his Princeton classmates who possessed inherited wealth. They seemed to him to have the power to win "the top girl" and the means to prolong the dream of beauty and youth.

But with the darker side of his mind Fitzgerald sensed an impending tragedy which exposed to his artistic imagination the falseness of the illusion of perpetual youth. In his best novel, *The Great Gatsby,* one of the enduring books of this century, he succeeded in embodying the essential tragedy of a generation in a controlled, artistic work. Using a Conradian narrator who is both an objective observer and a participant in the events of the story, Fitzgerald allowed the theme—a critique of the American dream of success—to emerge gradually and dramatically from a sequence of violent and bizarre actions. A young man, unable to grasp the enormity of his delusion, allows his dream of love and beauty to destroy his life. His fate brilliantly exposed the anachronism of the nineteenth-century myth of innocence when transposed into the wasteland of twentieth-century America.

Fitzgerald's great urge for popularity led him to write stories for the wide-circulation periodicals like the *Saturday Evening Post.* He collected this body of fiction in several volumes, including *Flappers and Philosophers* (1920), *Tales of the Jazz Age* (1922), and *All the Sad Young Men* (1926). Taken together they constitute one of the best pictures we have of the high spirits and the darker currents of that time. It was the latter mood which gradually prevailed in his own life. Zelda's illness became increasingly serious. While she was in a hospital in Baltimore, Fitzgerald wrote his most ambitious novel, *Tender is the Night* (1934), a story of a young psychiatrist who marries a wealthy heiress and cures her of mental illness, but in doing so exhausts his own emotional resources and becomes a broken man trying to recover his balance. Fitzgerald himself had reached this point. His books went unsold, he drank heavily, he tried desperately to write another serious novel. In Hollywood, where he went to restore his income and his career, he met Sheilah Graham, a society columnist, whose devotion helped him, but his death from a heart attack ended the promising start he had made in an unfinished novel, *The Last Tycoon,* a novel of a movie producer whose struggle against the deteriorating influences of Hollywood is portrayed in heroic and martyred terms. In style and execution this work showed flashes of Fitzgerald's best writing.

Scott Fitzgerald almost literally and cruelly wrote his own death-warrant in his stories and novels of that schizophrenic age. As playboy and serious artist he deliberately exploited his own life and recorded his own emotional bankruptcy and despair. He was—like his characters Jay Gatsby, Dick Diver, Anson Hunter, and the others—a young man beckoned by the green light of youth and beauty and fame, yet conscious all along of the dark current which carried both himself and his generation toward disillusion and defeat.

Further reading: *The (Viking) Portable F. Scott Fitzgerald,* ed. Dorothy Parker and John O'Hara, 1945. *The Crack-up: F. Scott Fitzgerald,* ed. Edmund Wilson, 1945. Arthur Mizener, *The Far Side of Paradise,* 1951. Andrew Turnbull, *Scott Fitzgerald,* 1962.

The Rich Boy

Originally published in the *Red Book* (January and February 1926), this story was included in the collection *All the Sad Young Men* (1926), from which the present text is taken.

Begin with an individual, and before you know it you find that you have created a type; begin with a type, and you find that you have created—nothing. That is because we are all queer fish, queerer behind our faces and voices than we want any one to know or than we know ourselves. When I hear a man proclaiming himself an "average, honest, open fellow," I feel pretty sure that he has some definite and perhaps terrible abnormality which he has agreed to conceal—and his protestation of being average and honest and open is his way of reminding himself of his misprision.

There are no types, no plurals. There is a rich boy, and this is his and not his brothers' story. All my life I have lived among his brothers but this one has been my friend. Besides, if I wrote about his brothers I should have to begin by attacking all the lies that the poor have told about the rich and the rich have told about themselves—such a wild structure they have erected that when we pick up a book about the rich, some instinct prepares us for unreality. Even the intelligent and impassioned reporters of life have made the country of the rich as unreal as fairy-land.

Let me tell you about the very rich. They are different from you and me. They possess and enjoy early, and it does something to them, makes them soft where we are hard, and cynical where we are trustful, in a way that, unless you were born rich, it is very difficult to understand. They think, deep in their hearts, that they are better than we are because we had to discover the compensations and refuges of life for ourselves. Even when they enter deep into our world or sink below us, they still think that they are better than we are. They are different. The only way I can describe young Anson Hunter is to approach him as if he were a foreigner and cling stubbornly to my point of view. If I accept his for a moment I am lost—I have nothing to show but a preposterous movie.

II

Anson was the eldest of six children who would some day divide a fortune of fifteen million dollars, and he reached the age of reason—is it seven?—at the beginning of the century when daring young women were already gliding along Fifth Avenue in electric "mobiles." In those days he and his brother had an English governess who spoke the language very clearly and crisply and well, so that the two boys grew to speak as she did—their words and sentences were all crisp and clear and not run together as ours are. They didn't talk exactly like English children but acquired an accent that is peculiar to fashionable people in the city of New York.

In the summer the six children were moved from the house on Seventy-first Street to a big estate in northern Connecticut. It was not a fashionable locality—Anson's father wanted to delay as long as possible his children's knowledge of that side of life. He was a man somewhat superior to his class, which composed New York society, and to his period, which was the snobbish and formalized vulgarity of the Gilded Age, and he wanted his sons to learn habits of concentration and have sound constitutions and grow up into right-living and successful men. He and his wife kept an eye on them as well as they were able until the two older boys went away to school, but in huge establishments this is difficult—it was much simpler in the series of small and medium-sized houses in which my own youth was spent—I was never far out of the reach of my mother's voice, of the sense of her presence, her approval or disapproval.

Anson's first sense of his superiority came to him when he realized the half-grudging American deference that was paid to him in the Connecticut village. The parents of the boys he played with always inquired after his father and mother, and were vaguely excited when their own children were asked to the Hunters' house. He accepted this as the natural state of things, and a sort of impatience with all groups of which he was not the center—in money, in position, in authority—remained with him for the rest of his life. He disdained to struggle with other boys for precedence—he expected it to be given him freely, and when it wasn't he withdrew into his family. His family was sufficient, for in the East money is still a somewhat feudal thing, a clan-forming thing. In the snobbish West, money separates families to form "sets."

At eighteen, when he went to New Haven, Anson was tall and thick-set, with a clear complexion and a healthy color from the ordered life he had led in school. His hair was yellow and grew in a funny way on his head, his nose was beaked—these two things kept him from being handsome—but he had a confident charm and a certain brusque style, and the upper-class men who passed him on the street knew without being told that he was a rich boy and had gone to one of the best schools. Nevertheless, his very superiority kept him from being a success in college—the independence was mistaken for egotism, and the refusal to accept Yale standards with the proper awe seemed to belittle all those who had. So, long before he graduated, he began to shift the center of his life to New York.

He was at home in New York—there was his own house with "the kind of servants you can't get any more"—and his own family, of which, because of his good humor and a certain ability to make things go, he was rapidly becoming the centre, and the débutante parties, and the correct manly world of the men's clubs, and the occasional wild spree with the gallant girls whom New Haven only knew from the fifth row. His aspirations were conventional enough—they included even the irreproachable shadow he would some day marry, but they differed from the aspirations of the majority of young men in that there was no mist over them, none of that quality which is variously known as "idealism" or "illusion." Anson accepted without reservation the world of high finance and high extravagance, of divorce and dissipation, of snobbery and of privilege. Most of our lives end as a compromise—it was as a compromise that his life began.

He and I first met in the late summer of 1917 when he was just out of Yale, and, like the rest of us, was swept up into the systematized hysteria of the war. In the blue-green uniform of the naval aviation he came down to Pensacola, where the hotel orchestras played "I'm sorry, dear," and we young officers danced with the girls. Every one liked him, and though he ran with the drinkers and wasn't an especially good pilot, even the instructors treated him with a certain respect. He was always having long talks with them in his confident, logical voice—talks which ended by his getting himself, or more frequently, another officer, out of some impending trouble. He was convivial, bawdy, robustly avid for pleasure, and we were all surprised when he fell in love with a conservative and rather proper girl.

Her name was Paula Legendre, a dark, serious beauty from somewhere in California. Her family kept a winter residence just outside of town, and in spite of her primness she was enormously popular; there is a large class of men whose egotism can't endure humor in a woman. But Anson wasn't that sort, and I couldn't understand the attraction of her "sincerity"—that was the thing to say about her—for his keen and somewhat sardonic mind.

Nevertheless, they fell in love—and on her terms. He no longer joined the twilight gathering at the De Sota bar, and whenever they were seen together they were engaged in a long, serious dialogue, which must have gone on several weeks. Long afterward he told me that it was not about anything in particular but was composed on both sides of immature and even meaningless statements—the emotional content that gradually came to fill it grew up not out of the words but out of its enormous seriousness. It was a sort of hypnosis. Often it was interrupted, giving way to that emasculated humor we call fun; when they were alone it was resumed again, solemn, low-keyed, and pitched so as to give each other a sense of unity in feeling and thought. They came to resent any interruptions of it, to be unresponsive to facetiousness about life, even to the mild cynicism of their contemporaries. They were only happy when the dialogue was going on, and its seriousness bathed them like the amber glow of an open fire. Toward the end there came an interruption they did not resent—it began to be interrupted by passion.

Oddly enough, Anson was as engrossed in the dialogue as she was and as profoundly affected by it, yet at the same time aware that on his side much was insincere, and on hers much was merely simple. At first, too, he despised her emotional simplicity as well, but with his love her nature deepened and blossomed, and he could despise it no longer. He felt that if he could enter into Paula's warm safe life he would be happy. The long preparation of the dialogue removed any constraint—he taught her some of what he had learned from more adventurous women, and she responded with a rapt holy intensity. One evening after a dance they agreed to marry, and he wrote a long letter about her to his mother. The next day Paula told him that she was rich, that she had a personal fortune of nearly a million dollars.

III

It was exactly as if they could say "Neither of us has anything: we shall be poor together"—just as delightful that they should be rich instead. It gave them the same communion of adventure. Yet when Anson got leave in April, and Paula and her mother accompanied him North, she was impressed with the standing of his family in New York and with the scale on which they lived. Alone with Anson for the first time in the rooms where he had played as a boy, she was filled with a comfortable emotion, as though she were preeminently safe and taken care of. The pictures of Anson in a skull cap at his first school, of Anson on horseback with the sweetheart of a mysterious forgotten summer, of Anson in a gay group of ushers and bridesmaids at a wedding, made her jealous of his life apart from her in the past, and so completely did his authoritative person seem to sum up and typify these possessions of his that she was inspired with the idea of being married immediately and returning to Pensacola as his wife.

But an immediate marriage wasn't discussed—even the engagement was to be secret until after the war. When she realized that only two days of his leave remained, her dissatisfaction crystallized in the intention of making him as unwilling to wait as she was. They were driving to the country for dinner, and she determined to force the issue that night.

Now a cousin of Paula's was staying with them at the Ritz, a severe, bitter girl who loved Paula but was somewhat jealous of her impressive engagement, and as Paula was late in dressing, the cousin, who wasn't going to the party, received Anson in the parlor of the suite.

Anson had met friends at five o'clock and drunk freely and indiscreetly with them for an hour. He left the Yale Club at a proper time, and his mother's chauffeur drove him to the Ritz, but his usual capacity was not in evidence, and the impact of the steam-heated sitting-room made him suddenly dizzy. He knew it, and he was both amused and sorry.

Paula's cousin was twenty-five, but she was exceptionally naïve, and at first failed to realize what was up. She had never met Anson before, and she was surprised when he mumbled strange information and nearly fell off his chair, but until Paula appeared it didn't occur to her that what she had taken for the odor of a dry-cleaned uniform was really whisky. But Paula understood as soon as she appeared; her only thought was to get Anson away before her mother saw him, and at the look in her eyes the cousin understood too.

When Paula and Anson descended to the limousine they found two men inside, both asleep; they were the men with whom he had been drinking at the Yale Club, and they were also going to the party. He had entirely forgotten their presence in the car. On the way to Hempstead they awoke and sang. Some of the songs were rough, and though Paula tried to reconcile herself to the fact that Anson had few verbal inhibitions, her lips tightened with shame and distaste.

Back at the hotel the cousin, confused and agitated, considered the incident, and then walked into Mrs. Legendre's bedroom, saying: "Isn't he funny?"

"Who is funny?"

"Why—Mr. Hunter. He seemed so funny."

Mrs. Legendre looked at her sharply.

"How is he funny?"

"Why, he said he was French. I didn't know he was French."

"That's absurd. You must have misunderstood." She smiled: "It was a joke."

The cousin shook her head stubbornly.

"No. He said he was brought up in France. He said he couldn't speak any English, and that's why he couldn't talk to me. And he couldn't!"

Mrs. Legendre looked away with impatience just as the cousin added thoughtfully, "Perhaps it was because he was so drunk," and walked out of the room.

This curious report was true. Anson, finding his voice thick and uncontrollable, had taken the unusual refuge of announcing that he spoke no English. Years afterward he used to tell that part of the story, and he invariably communicated the uproarious laughter which the memory aroused in him.

Five times in the next hour Mrs. Legendre tried to get Hempstead on the phone. When she succeeded there was a ten-minute delay before she heard Paula's voice on the wire.

"Cousin Jo told me Anson was intoxicated."

"Oh, no. . . ."

"Oh, yes. Cousin Jo says he was intoxicated. He told her he was French, and fell off his chair and behaved as if he was very intoxicated. I don't want you to come home with him."

"Mother, he's all right! Please don't worry about——"

"But I do worry. I think it's dreadful. I want you to promise me not to come home with him."

"I'll take care of it, mother. . . ."

"I don't want you to come home with him."

"All right, mother. Good-by."

"Be sure now, Paula. Ask some one to bring you."

Deliberately Paula took the receiver from her ear and hung it up. Her face was flushed with helpless annoyance. Anson was stretched asleep out in a bedroom upstairs, while the dinner-party below was proceeding lamely toward conclusion.

The hour's drive had sobered him somewhat—his arrival was merely hilarious—and Paula hoped that the evening was not spoiled, after all, but two imprudent cocktails before dinner completed the disaster. He talked boisterously and somewhat offensively to the party at large for fifteen minutes, and then slid silently under the table; like a man in an old print—but, unlike an old print, it was rather horrible without being at all quaint. None of the young girls present remarked upon the incident—it seemed to merit only silence. His uncle and two other men carried him upstairs, and it was just after this that Paula was called to the phone.

An hour later Anson awoke in a fog of nervous agony, through which he perceived after a moment the figure of his uncle Robert standing by the door.

". . . I said are you better?"

"What?"

"Do you feel better, old man?"

"Terrible," said Anson.

"I'm going to try you on another Bromo-seltzer. If you can hold it down, it'll do you good to sleep."

With an effort Anson slid his legs from the bed and stood up.

"I'm all right," he said dully.

"Take it easy."

"I thin' if you gave me a glassbrandy I could go downstairs."

"Oh, no——"

"Yes, that's the only thin'. I'm all right now. . . . I suppose I'm in dutch dow' there."

"They know you're a little under the weather," said his uncle deprecatingly. "But don't worry about it. Schuyler didn't even get here. He passed away in the locker-room over at the Links."

Indifferent to any opinion, except Paula's, Anson was nevertheless determined to save the débris of the evening, but when after a cold bath he made his appearance most of the party had already left. Paula got up immediately to go home.

In the limousine the old serious dialogue began. She had known that he drank, she admitted, but she had never expected anything like this—it seemed to her that perhaps they were not suited to each other, after all. Their ideas about life were too different, and so forth. When she finished speaking, Anson spoke in turn, very soberly. Then Paula said she'd have to think it over; she wouldn't decide tonight; she was not angry but she was terribly sorry. Nor would she let him come into the hotel with her, but just before she got out of the car she leaned and kissed him unhappily on the cheek.

The next afternoon Anson had a long talk with Mrs. Legendre while Paula sat listening in silence. It was agreed that Paula was to brood over the incident for a proper period and then, if mother and daughter thought it best, they would follow Anson to Pensacola. On his part he apologized with sincerity and dignity—that was all; with every card in her hand Mrs. Legendre was unable to establish any advantage over him. He made no promises, showed no humility, only delivered a few serious comments on life which brought him off with rather a moral superiority at the end. When they came South three weeks later, neither Anson in his satisfaction nor Paula in her relief at the reunion realized that the psychological moment had passed forever.

IV

He dominated and attracted her, and at the same time filled her with anxiety. Confused by his mixture of solidity and self-indulgence, of sentiment and cynicism—incongruities which her gentle mind was unable to resolve—Paula grew to think of him as two alternating personalities. When she saw him alone, or at a formal party, or with his casual inferiors, she felt a tremendous pride in his strong, attractive presence, the paternal, understanding stature of his mind. In other company she became uneasy when what had been a fine imperviousness to mere gentility showed its other face. The other face was gross, humorous, reckless of everything but pleasure. It startled her mind temporarily away from him, even led her into a short covert experiment with an old beau, but it was no use—after four months of Anson's enveloping vitality there was an anaemic pallor in all other men.

In July he was ordered abroad, and their tenderness and desire reached a crescendo. Paula considered a last-minute marriage—decided against it only because there were always cocktails on his breath now, but the parting itself made her physically ill with grief. After his departure she wrote him long letters of regret for the days of love they had missed by waiting. In August Anson's plane slipped down into the North Sea. He was pulled onto a destroyer after a night in the water and sent to hospital with pneumonia; the armistice was signed before he was finally sent home.

Then, with every opportunity given back to them, with no material obstacle to overcome, the secret weavings of their temperaments came between them, drying up their kisses and their tears, making their voices less loud to one another, muffling the intimate chatter of their hearts until the old communication was only possible by letters, from far away. One afternoon a society reporter waited for two hours in the Hunters' house for a confirmation of their engagement. Anson denied it; nevertheless an early issue carried the report as a leading paragraph—they were "constantly seen together at Southampton, Hot Springs, and Tuxedo Park." But the serious dialogue had turned a corner into a long-sustained quarrel, and the affair was almost played out. Anson got drunk flagrantly and missed an engagement with her, whereupon Paula made certain behavioristic demands. His despair was helpless before his pride and his knowledge of himself: the engagement was definitely broken.

"Dearest," said their letters now, "Dearest, Dearest, when I wake up in the middle of the night and realize that after all it was not to be, I feel that I want to die. I can't go on living any more. Perhaps when we meet this summer we may talk things over and decide differently—we were so excited and sad that day, and I don't feel that I can live all my life without you. You speak of other people. Don't you know there are no other people for me, but only you. . . ."

But as Paula drifted here and there around the East she would sometimes mention her gaieties to make him wonder. Anson was too acute to wonder. When he saw a man's name in her letters he felt more sure of her and a little disdainful—he was always superior to such things. But he still hoped that they would some day marry.

Meanwhile he plunged vigorously into all the movement and glitter of post-bellum New York, entering a brokerage house, joining half a dozen clubs, dancing late, and moving in three worlds—his own world, the world of young Yale graduates, and that section of the half-world which rests one end on Broadway. But there was always a thorough and infractible eight hours devoted to his work in Wall Street, where the combination of his influential family connection, his sharp intelligence, and his abundance of sheer physical energy brought him almost immediately forward. He had one of those invaluable minds with partitions in it; sometimes he appeared at his office refreshed by less than an hour's sleep, but such occurrences were rare. So early as 1920 his income in salary and commissions exceeded twelve thousand dollars.

As the Yale tradition slipped into the past he became more and more of a popular figure among his classmates in New York, more popular than he had ever been in college. He lived in a great house, and had the means of introducing young men into other great houses. Moreover, his life already seemed secure, while theirs, for the most part, had arrived again at precarious beginnings. They commenced to turn to him for amusement and escape, and Anson responded readily, taking pleasure in helping people and arranging their affairs.

There were no men in Paula's letters now, but a note of tenderness ran through them that had not been there before. From several sources he heard that she had "a heavy beau," Lowell Thayer, a Bostonian of wealth and position, and though he was sure she still loved him, it made him uneasy to think that he might lose her, after all. Save for one unsatisfactory day she had not been in New York for almost five months, and as the rumors multiplied he became increasingly anxious to see her. In February he took his vacation and went down to Florida.

Palm Beach sprawled plump and opulent between the sparkling sapphire of Lake Worth, flawed here and there by houseboats at anchor, and the great turquoise bar of the Atlantic Ocean. The huge bulks of the Breakers and the Royal Poinciana rose as twin paunches from the bright level of the sand, and around them clustered the Dancing Glade, Bradley's House of Chance, and a dozen modistes and milliners with goods at triple prices from New York. Upon the trellissed veranda of the Breakers two hundred women stepped right, stepped left, wheeled, and slid in that then celebrated calisthenic known as the double-shuffle, while in half-time to the music two thousand bracelets clicked up and down on two hundred arms.

At the Everglades Club after dark Paula and Lowell Thayer and Anson and a casual fourth played bridge with hot cards. It seemed to Anson that her kind, serious face was wan and tired—she had been around now for four, five, years. He had known her for three.

"Two spades."

"Cigarette? . . . Oh, I beg your pardon. By me."

"By."

"I'll double three spades."

There were a dozen tables of bridge in the room, which was filling up with smoke. Anson's eyes met Paula's, held them persistently even when Thayer's glance fell between them. . . .

"What was bid?" he asked abstractedly.

"Rose of Washington Square"

sang the young people in the corners:

"I'm withering there
In basement air——"

The smoke banked like fog, and the opening of a door filled the room with blown swirls of ectoplasm. Little Bright Eyes streaked past the tables seeking Mr. Conan Doyle among the Englishmen who were posing as Englishmen about the lobby.

"You could cut it with a knife."

". . . cut it with a knife."

". . . a knife."

At the end of the rubber Paula suddenly got up and spoke to Anson in a tense, low voice. With scarcely a glance at Lowell Thayer, they walked out the door and descended a long flight of stone steps—in a moment they were walking hand in hand along the moonlit beach.

"Darling, darling. . . ." They embraced recklessly, passionately, in a shadow. . . . Then Paula drew back her face to let his lips say what she wanted to hear—she could feel the words forming as they kissed again. . . . Again she broke away, listening, but as he pulled her close once more she realized that he had said nothing—only "*Darling! Darling!*" in that deep, sad whisper that always made her cry. Humbly, obediently, her emotions yielded to him and the tears streamed down her face, but her heart kept on crying: "Ask me—oh, Anson, dearest, ask me!"

"Paula. . . . *Paula!*"

The words wrung her heart like hands, and Anson, feeling her tremble, knew that emotion was enough. He need say no more, commit their destinies to no practical enigma. Why should he, when he might hold her so, biding his own time, for another year—forever? He was considering them both, her more than himself. For a moment, when she said suddenly that she must go back to her hotel, he hesitated, thinking, first, "This is the moment, after all," and then: "No, let it wait—she is mine. . . ."

He had forgotten that Paula too was worn away inside with the strain of three years. Her mood passed forever in the night.

He went back to New York next morning filled with a certain restless dissatisfaction. Late in April, without warning, he received a telegram from Bar Harbor in which Paula told him that she was engaged to Lowell Thayer, and that they would be married immediately in Boston. What he never really believed could happen had happened at last.

Anson filled himself with whisky that morning, and going to the office, carried on his work without a break—rather with a fear of what would happen if he stopped. In the evening he went out as usual, saying nothing of what had occurred; he was cordial, humorous, unabstracted. But one thing he could not help—for three days, in any place, in any company, he would suddenly bend his head into his hands and cry like a child.

V

In 1922 when Anson went abroad with the junior partner to investigate some London loans, the journey intimated that he was to be taken into the firm. He was twenty-seven now, a little heavy without being definitely stout, and with a manner older than his years. Old people and young people liked him and trusted him, and mothers felt safe when their daughters were in his charge, for he had a way, when he came into a room, of putting himself on a footing with the oldest and most conservative people there. "You and I," he seemed to say, "we're solid. We understand."

He had an instinctive and rather charitable knowledge of the weaknesses of men and women, and, like a priest, it made him the more concerned for the maintenance of outward forms. It was typical of him that every Sunday morning he taught in a fashionable Episcopal Sunday school—even though a cold shower and a quick change into a cutaway coat were all that separated him from the wild night before.

After his father's death he was the practical head of his family, and, in effect, guided the destinies of the younger children. Through a complication his authority did not extend to his father's estate, which was administrated by his Uncle Robert, who was the horsy member of the family, a good-natured, hard-drinking member of that set which centers about Wheatley Hills.

Uncle Robert and his wife, Edna, had been great friends of Anson's youth, and the former was disappointed when his nephew's superiority failed to take a horsey form. He backed him for a city club which was the most difficult in America to enter—one could only join if one's family had "helped to build up New York" (or, in other words, were rich before 1880)—and when Anson, after his election, neglected it for the Yale Club, Uncle Robert gave him a little talk on the subject. But when on top of that Anson declined to enter Robert Hunter's own conservative and somewhat neglected brokerage house, his manner grew cooler. Like a primary teacher who has taught all he knew, he slipped out of Anson's life.

There were so many friends in Anson's life—scarcely one for whom he had not done some unusual kindness and scarcely one whom he did not occasionally embarrass by his bursts of rough conversation or his habit of getting drunk whenever and however he liked. It annoyed him when any one else blundered in that regard—about his own lapses he was always humorous. Odd things happened to him and he told them with infectious laughter.

I was working in New York that spring, and I used to lunch with him at the Yale Club, which my university was sharing until the completion of our own. I had read of Paula's marriage, and one afternoon, when I asked him about her, something moved him to tell me the story. After that he frequently invited me to family dinners at his house and behaved as though there was a special relation between us, as though with his confidence a little of that consuming memory had passed into me.

I found that despite the trusting mothers, his attitude toward girls was not indiscriminately protective. It was up to the girl—if she showed an inclination toward looseness, she must take care of herself, even with him.

"Life," he would explain sometimes, "has made a cynic of me."

By life he meant Paula. Sometimes, especially when he was drinking, it became a little twisted in his mind, and he thought that she had callously thrown him over.

This "cynicism," or rather his realization that naturally fast girls were not worth sparing, led to his affair with Dolly Karger. It wasn't his only affair in those years, but it came nearest to touching him deeply, and it had a profound effect upon his attitude toward life.

Dolly was the daughter of a notorious "publicist" who had married into society. She herself grew up into the Junior League, came out at the Plaza, and went to the Assembly; and only a few old families like the Hunters could question whether or not she "belonged," for her picture was often in the papers, and she had more enviable attention than many girls who undoubtedly did. She was dark-haired, with carmine lips and a high, lovely color, which she concealed under pinkish-gray powder all through the first year out, because high color was unfashionable—Victorian-pale was the thing to be. She wore black, severe suits and stood with her hands in her pockets leaning a little forward, with a humorous restraint on her face. She danced exquisitely—better than anything she liked to dance—better than anything except making love. Since she was ten she had always been in love, and, usually, with some boy who didn't respond to her. Those who did—and there were many—bored her after a brief encounter, but for her failures she reserved the warmest spot in her heart. When she met them she would always try once more—sometimes she succeeded, more often she failed.

It never occurred to this gypsy of the unattainable that there was a certain resemblance in those who refused to love her—they shared a hard intuition that saw through to her weakness, not a weakness of emotion but a weakness of rudder. Anson perceived this when he first met her, less than a month after Paula's marriage. He was drinking rather heavily, and he pretended for a week that he was falling in love with her. Then he dropped her abruptly and forgot—immediately he took up the commanding position in her heart.

Like so many girls of that day Dolly was slackly and indiscreetly wild. The unconventionality of a slightly older generation had been simply one facet of a post-war movement to discredit obsolete manners—Dolly's was both older and shabbier, and she saw in Anson the two extremes which the emotionally shiftless woman seeks, an abandon to indulgence alternating with a protective strength. In his character she felt both the sybarite and the solid rock, and these two satisfied every need of her nature.

She felt that it was going to be difficult, but she mistook the reason—she thought that Anson and his family expected a more spectacular marriage, but she guessed immediately that her advantage lay in his tendency to drink.

They met at the large débutante dances, but as her infatuation increased they managed to be more and more together. Like most mothers, Mrs. Karger believed that Anson was exceptionally reliable, so she allowed Dolly to go with him to distant country clubs and suburban houses without inquiring closely into their activities or questioning her explanations when they came in late. At first these explanations might have been accurate, but Dolly's worldly ideas of capturing Anson were soon engulfed in the rising sweep of her emotion. Kisses in the back of taxis and motor-cars were no longer enough; they did a curious thing:

They dropped out of their world for a while and made another world just beneath it where Anson's tippling and Dolly's irregular hours would be less noticed and commented on. It was composed, this world, of varying elements—several of Anson's Yale friends and their wives, two or three young brokers and bond salesmen and a handful of unattached men, fresh from college, with money and a propensity to dissipation. What this world lacked in spaciousness and scale it made up for by allowing them a liberty that it scarcely permitted itself. Moreover, it centered around them and permitted Dolly the pleasure of a faint condescension—a pleasure which Anson, whose whole life was a condescension from the certitudes of his childhood, was unable to share.

He was not in love with her, and in the long feverish winter of their affair he frequently told her so. In the spring he was weary—he wanted to renew his life at some other source—moreover, he saw that either he must break with her now or accept the responsibility of a definite seduction. Her family's encouraging attitude precipitated his decision—one evening when Mr. Karger knocked discreetly at the library door to announce that he had left a bottle of old brandy in the dining-room, Anson felt that life was hemming him in. That night he wrote her a short letter in which he told her that he was going on his vacation, and that in view of all the circumstances they had better meet no more.

It was June. His family had closed up the house and gone to the country, so he was living temporarily at the Yale Club. I had heard about his affair with Dolly as it developed—accounts salted with humor, for he despised unstable women, and granted them no place in the social edifice in which he believed—and when he told me that night that he was definitely breaking with her I was glad. I had seen Dolly here and there, and each time with a feeling of pity at the hopelessness of her struggle, and of shame at knowing so much about her that I had no right to know. She was what is known as "a pretty little thing," but there was a certain recklessness which rather fascinated me. Her dedication to the goddess of waste would have been less obvious had she been less spirited—she would most certainly throw herself away, but I was glad when I heard that the sacrifice would not be consummated in my sight.

Anson was going to leave the letter of farewell at her house next morning. It was one of the few houses left open in the Fifth Avenue district, and he knew that the Kargers, acting upon erroneous information from Dolly, had foregone a trip abroad to give their daughter her chance. As he stepped out the door of the Yale Club into Madison Avenue the postman passed him, and he followed back inside. The first letter that caught his eye was in Dolly's hand.

He knew what it would be—a lonely and tragic monologue, full of the reproaches he knew, the invoked memories, the "I wonder if's"—all the immemorial intimacies that he had communicated to Paula Legendre in what seemed another age. Thumbing over some bills, he brought it on top again and opened it. To his surprise it was a short, somewhat formal note, which said that Dolly would be unable to go to the country with him for the week-end, because Perry Hull from Chicago had unexpectedly come to town. It added that Anson had brought this on himself: "—if I felt that you loved me as I love you I would go with you at any time, any place, but Perry is *so* nice, and he so much wants me to marry him——"

Anson smiled contemptuously—he had had experience with such decoy epistles. Moreover, he knew how Dolly had labored over this plan, probably sent for the faithful Perry and calculated the time of his arrival—even labored over the note so that it would make him jealous without driving him away. Like most compromises, it had neither force nor vitality but only a timorous despair.

Suddenly he was angry. He sat down in the lobby and read it again. Then he went to the phone, called Dolly and told her in his clear, compelling voice that he had received her note and would call for her at five o'clock as they had previously planned. Scarcely waiting for the pretended uncertainty of her "Perhaps I can see you for an hour," he hung up the receiver and went down to his office. On the way he tore his own letter into bits and dropped it in the street.

He was not jealous—she meant nothing to him—but at her pathetic ruse everything stubborn and self-indulgent in him came to the surface. It was a presumption from a mental inferior and it could not be overlooked. If she wanted to know to whom she belonged she would see.

He was on the door-step at quarter past five. Dolly was dressed for the street, and he listened in silence to the paragraph of "I can only see you for an hour," which she had begun on the phone.

"Put on your hat, Dolly," he said, "we'll take a walk."

They strolled up Madison Avenue and over to Fifth while Anson's shirt dampened upon his portly body in the deep heat. He talked little, scolding her, making no love to her, but before they had walked six blocks she was his again, apologizing for the note, offering not to see Perry at all as an atonement, offering anything. She thought that he had come because he was beginning to love her.

"I'm hot," he said when they reached 71st Street. "This is a winter suit. If I stop by the house and change, would you mind waiting for me downstairs? I'll only be a minute."

She was happy; the intimacy of his being hot, of any physical fact about him, thrilled her. When they came to the iron-grated door and Anson took out his key she experienced a sort of delight.

Downstairs it was dark, and after he ascended in the lift Dolly raised a curtain and looked out through opaque lace at the houses over the way. She heard the lift machinery stop, and with the notion of teasing him pressed the button that brought it down. Then on what was more than an impulse she got into it and sent it up to what she guessed was his floor.

"Anson," she called, laughing a little.

"Just a minute," he answered from his bedroom . . . then after a brief delay: "Now you can come in."

He had changed and was buttoning his vest. "This is my room," he said lightly. "How do you like it?"

She caught sight of Paula's picture on the wall and stared at it in fascination, just as Paula had stared at the pictures of Anson's childish sweethearts five years before. She knew something about Paula—sometimes she tortured herself with fragments of the story.

Suddenly she came close to Anson, raising her arms. They embraced. Outside the area window a soft artificial twilight already hovered, though the sun was still bright on a back roof across the way. In half an hour the room would be quite dark. The uncalculated opportunity overwhelmed them, made them both breathless, and they clung more closely. It was eminent, inevitable. Still holding one another, they raised their heads—their eyes fell together upon Paula's picture, staring down at them from the wall.

Suddenly Anson dropped his arms, and sitting down at his desk tried the drawer with a bunch of keys.

"Like a drink?" he asked in a gruff voice.

"No, Anson."

He poured himself half a tumbler of whisky, swallowed it, and then opened the door into the hall.

"Come on," he said.

Dolly hesitated.

"Anson—I'm going to the country with you tonight, after all. You understand that, don't you?"

"Of course," he answered brusquely.

In Dolly's car they rode on to Long Island, closer in their emotions than they had ever been before. They knew what would happen—not with Paula's face to remind them that something was lacking, but when they were alone in the still, hot Long Island night they did not care.

The estate in Port Washington where they were to spend the week-end belonged to a cousin of Anson's who had married a Montana copper operator. An interminable drive began at the lodge and twisted under imported poplar saplings toward a huge, pink, Spanish house. Anson had often visited there before.

After dinner they danced at the Linx Club. About midnight Anson assured himself that his cousins would not leave before two—then he explained that

Dolly was tired; he would take her home and return to the dance later. Trembling a little with excitement, they got into a borrowed car together and drove to Port Washington. As they reached the lodge he stopped and spoke to the night-watchman.

"When are you making a round, Carl?"

"Right away."

"Then you'll be here till everybody's in?"

"Yes, sir."

"All right. Listen: if any automobile, no matter whose it is, turns in at this gate, I want you to phone the house immediately." He put a five-dollar bill into Carl's hand. "Is that clear?"

"Yes, Mr. Anson." Being of the Old World, he neither winked nor smiled. Yet Dolly sat with her face turned slightly away.

Anson had a key. Once inside he poured a drink for both of them—Dolly left hers untouched—then he ascertained definitely the location of the phone, and found that it was within easy hearing distance of their rooms, both of which were on the first floor.

Five minutes later he knocked at the door of Dolly's room.

"Anson?" He went in, closing the door behind him. She was in bed, leaning up anxiously with elbows on the pillow; sitting beside her he took her in his arms.

"Anson, darling."

He didn't answer.

"Anson. . . . Anson! I love you. . . . Say you love me. Say it now—can't you say it now? Even if you don't mean it?"

He did not listen. Over her head he perceived that the picture of Paula was hanging here upon this wall.

He got up and went close to it. The frame gleamed faintly with thrice-reflected moonlight—within was a blurred shadow of a face that he saw he did not know. Almost sobbing, he turned around and stared with abomination at the little figure on the bed.

"This is all foolishness," he said thickly. "I don't know what I was thinking about. I don't love you and you'd better wait for somebody that loves you. I don't love you a bit, can't you understand?"

His voice broke, and he went hurriedly out. Back in the salon he was pouring himself a drink with uneasy fingers, when the front door opened suddenly, and his cousin came in.

"Why, Anson, I hear Dolly's sick," she began solicitously. "I hear she's sick. . . ."

"It was nothing," he interrupted, raising his voice so that it would carry into Dolly's room. "She was a little tired. She went to bed."

For a long time afterward Anson believed that a protective God sometimes interfered in human affairs. But Dolly Karger, lying awake and staring at the ceiling, never again believed in anything at all.

VI

When Dolly married during the following autumn, Anson was in London on business. Like Paula's marriage, it was sudden, but it affected him in a different way. At first he felt that it was funny, and had an inclination to laugh when he thought of it. Later it depressed him—it made him feel old.

There was something repetitive about it—why, Paula and Dolly had belonged to different generations. He had a foretaste of the sensation of a man of forty who hears that the daughter of an old flame has married. He wired congratulations and, as was not the case with Paula, they were sincere—he had never really hoped that Paula would be happy.

When he returned to New York, he was made a partner in the firm, and, as his responsibilities increased, he had less time on his hands. The refusal of a life-insurance company to issue him a policy made such an impression on him that he stopped drinking for a year, and claimed that he felt better physically, though I think he missed the convivial recounting of those Celliniesque adventures which, in his early twenties, had played such a part of his life. But he never abandoned the Yale Club. He was a figure there, a personality, and the tendency of his class, who were now seven years out of college, to drift away to more sober haunts was checked by his presence.

His day was never too full nor his mind too weary to give any sort of aid to any one who asked it. What had been done at first through pride and superiority had become a habit and a passion. And there was always something—a younger brother in trouble at New Haven, a quarrel to be patched up between a friend and his wife, a position to be found for this man, an investment for that. But his specialty was the solving of problems for young married people. Young married people fascinated him and their apartments were almost sacred to him—he knew the story of their love-affair, advised them where to live and how, and remembered their babies' names. Toward young wives his attitude was circumspect: he never abused the trust which their husbands—strangely enough in view of his unconcealed irregularities—invariably reposed in him.

He came to take a vicarious pleasure in happy marriages, and to be inspired to an almost equally pleasant melancholy by those that went astray. Not a season passed that he did not witness the collapse of an affair that perhaps he himself had fathered. When Paula was divorced and almost immediately remarried to another Bostonian, he talked about her to me all one afternoon. He would never love any one as he had loved Paula, but he insisted that he no longer cared.

"I'll never marry," he came to say; "I've seen too much of it, and I know a happy marriage is a very rare thing. Besides, I'm too old."

But he did believe in marriage. Like all men who spring from a happy and successful marriage, he believed in it passionately—nothing he had seen would change his belief, his cynicism dissolved upon it like air. But he did really believe he was too old. At twenty-eight he began to accept with equanimity the prospect of marrying without romantic love; he resolutely chose a New York girl of his own class, pretty, intelligent, congenial, above reproach—and set about falling in love with her. The things he had said to Paula with sincerity, to other girls with grace, he could no longer say at all without smiling, or with the force necessary to convince.

"When I'm forty," he told his friends, "I'll be ripe. I'll fall for some chorus girl like the rest."

Nevertheless, he persisted in his attempt. His mother wanted to see him married, and he could now well afford it—he had a seat on the Stock Exchange, and his earned income came to twenty-five thousand a year. The idea was agreeable: when his friends—he spent most of his time with the set he and Dolly had evolved—closed themselves in behind domestic doors at night, he no longer rejoiced in his freedom. He even wondered if he should have married Dolly. Not even Paula had loved him more, and he was learning the rarity, in a single life, of encountering true emotion.

Just as this mood began to creep over him a disquieting story reached his ear. His aunt Edna, a woman just this side of forty, was carrying on an open intrigue with a dissolute, hard-drinking young man named Cary Sloane. Every one knew of it except Anson's Uncle Robert, who for fifteen years had talked long in clubs and taken his wife for granted.

Anson heard the story again and again with increasing annoyance. Something of his old feeling for his uncle came back to him, a feeling that was more than personal, a reversion toward that family solidarity on which he had based his pride. His intuition singled out the essential point of the affair, which was that his uncle shouldn't be hurt. It was his first experiment in unsolicited meddling, but with his knowledge of Edna's character he felt that he could handle the matter better than a district judge or his uncle.

His uncle was in Hot Springs. Anson traced down the sources of the scandal so that there should be no possibility of mistake and then he called Edna and asked her to lunch with him at the Plaza next day. Something in his tone must have frightened her, for she was reluctant, but he insisted, putting off the date until she had no excuse for refusing.

She met him at the appointed time in the Plaza lobby, a lovely, faded, gray-eyed blonde in a coat of Russian sable. Five great rings, cold with diamonds and emeralds, sparkled on her slender hands. It occurred to Anson that it was his father's intelligence and not his uncle's that had earned the fur and the stones, the rich brilliance that buoyed up her passing beauty.

Though Edna scented his hostility, she was unprepared for the directness of his approach.

"Edna, I'm astonished at the way you've been acting," he said in a strong, frank voice. "At first I couldn't believe it."

"Believe what?" she demanded sharply.

"You needn't pretend with me, Edna. I'm talking about Cary Sloane. Aside from any other consideration, I didn't think you could treat Uncle Robert———"

"Now look here, Anson—" she began angrily, but his peremptory voice broke through hers:

"—and your children in such a way. You've been married eighteen years, and you're old enough to know better."

"You can't talk to me like that! You———"

"Yes, I can. Uncle Robert has always been my best friend." He was tremendously moved. He felt a real distress about his uncle, about his three young cousins.

Edna stood up, leaving her crab-flake cocktail untasted.

"This is the silliest thing———"

"Very well, if you won't listen to me I'll go to Uncle Robert and tell him the whole story—he's bound to hear it sooner or later. And afterward I'll go to old Moses Sloane."

Edna faltered back into her chair.

"Don't talk so loud," she begged him. Her eyes blurred with tears. "You have no idea how your voice carries. You might have chosen a less public place to make all these crazy accusations."

He didn't answer.

"Oh, you never liked me, I know," she went on. "You're just taking advantage of some silly gossip to try and break up the only interesting friendship I've ever had. What did I ever do to make you hate me so?"

Still Anson waited. There would be the appeal to his chivalry, then to his pity, finally to his superior sophistication—when he had shouldered his way through all these there would be admissions, and he could come to grips with her. By being silent, by being impervious, by returning constantly to his main weapon, which was his own true emotion, he bullied her into frantic despair as the luncheon hour slipped away. At two o'clock she took out a mirror and a handkerchief, shined away the marks of her tears and powdered the slight hollows where they had lain. She had agreed to meet him at her own house at five.

When he arrived she was stretched on a chaise longue which was covered with cretonne for the summer, and the tears he had called up at luncheon seemed still to be standing in her eyes. Then he was aware of Cary Sloane's dark anxious presence upon the cold hearth.

"What's this idea of yours?" broke out Sloane immediately. "I understand you invited Edna to lunch and then threatened her on the basis of some cheap scandal."

Anson sat down.

"I have no reason to think it's only scandal."

"I hear you're going to take it to Robert Hunter, and to my father."

Anson nodded.

"Either you break it off—or I will," he said.

"What God damned business is it of yours, Hunter?"

"Don't lose your temper, Cary," said Edna nervously. "It's only a question of showing him how absurd——"

"For one thing, it's my name that's being handed around," interrupted Anson. "That's all that concerns you, Cary."

"Edna isn't a member of your family."

"She most certainly is!" His anger mounted. "Why—she owes this house and the rings on her fingers to my father's brains. When Uncle Robert married her she didn't have a penny."

They all looked at the rings as if they had a significant bearing on the situation. Edna made a gesture to take them from her hand.

"I guess they're not the only rings in the world," said Sloane.

"Oh, this is absurd," cried Edna. "Anson, will you listen to me? I've found out how the silly story started. It was a maid I discharged who went right to the Chilicheffs—all these Russians pump things out of their servants and then put a false meaning on them." She brought down her fist angrily on the table: "And after Tom lent them the limousine for a whole month when we were South last winter——"

"Do you see?" demanded Sloane eagerly. "This maid got hold of the wrong end of the thing. She knew that Edna and I were friends, and she carried it to the Chilicheffs. In Russia they assume that if a man and a woman——"

He enlarged the theme to a disquisition upon social relations in the Caucasus.

"If that's the case it better be explained to Uncle Robert," said Anson dryly, "so that when the rumors do reach him he'll know they're not true."

Adopting the method he had followed with Edna at luncheon he let them explain it all away. He knew that they were guilty and that presently they would cross the line from explanation into justification and convict themselves more definitely than he could ever do. By seven they had taken the desperate step of telling him the truth—Robert Hunter's neglect, Edna's empty life, the casual dalliance that had flamed up into passion—but like so many true stories it had the misfortune of being old, and its enfeebled body beat helplessly against the armor of Anson's will. The threat to go to Sloane's father sealed their helplessness, for the latter, a retired cotton broker out of Alabama, was a notorious fundamentalist who controlled his son by a rigid allowance and the promise that at his next vagary the allowance would stop forever.

They dined at a small French restaurant, and the discussion continued—at one time Sloane resorted to physical threats, a little later they were both imploring him to give them time. But Anson was obdurate. He saw that Edna was breaking up, and that her spirit must not be refreshed by any renewal of their passion.

At two o'clock in a small night-club on 53d Street, Edna's nerves suddenly collapsed, and she cried to go home. Sloane had been drinking heavily all evening, and he was faintly maudlin, leaning on the table and weeping a little with his face in his hands. Quickly Anson gave them his terms. Sloane was to leave town for six months, and he must be gone within forty-eight hours. When he returned there was to be no resumption of the affair, but at the end of a year Edna might, if she wished, tell Robert Hunter that she wanted a divorce and go about it in the usual way.

He paused, gaining confidence from their faces for his final word.

"Or there's another thing you can do," he said slowly, "if Edna wants to leave her children, there's nothing I can do to prevent your running off together."

"I want to go home!" cried Edna again. "Oh, haven't you done enough to us for one day?"

Outside it was dark, save for a blurred glow from Sixth Avenue down the street. In that light those two who had been lovers looked for the last time into each other's tragic faces, realizing that between them there was not enough youth and strength to avert their eternal parting. Sloane walked suddenly off down the street and Anson tapped a dozing taxi-driver on the arm.

It was almost four; there was a patient flow of cleaning water along the ghostly pavement of Fifth Avenue, and the shadows of two night women flitted over the dark façade of St. Thomas's church. Then the desolate shrubbery of Central Park where Anson had often played as a child, and the mounting numbers, significant as names, of the marching streets. This was his city, he thought, where his name had flourished through five generations. No change could alter the permanence of its place here, for change itself was the essential substratum by which he and those of his name identified themselves with the spirit of New York. Resourcefulness and a powerful will—for his threats in weaker hands would have been less than nothing—had beaten the gathering dust from his uncle's name, from the name of his family, from even this shivering figure that sat beside him in the car.

Cary Sloane's body was found next morning on the lower shelf of a pillar of Queensboro Bridge. In the darkness and in his excitement he had thought that it was the water flowing black beneath him, but in less than a second it made no possible difference—unless he had planned to think one last thought of Edna, and call out her name as he struggled feebly in the water.

VII

Anson never blamed himself for his part in this affair—the situation which brought it about had not been of his making. But the just suffer with the unjust, and he found that his oldest and somehow his most precious friendship was over. He never knew what distorted story Edna told, but he was welcome in his uncle's house no longer.

Just before Christmas Mrs. Hunter retired to a select Episcopal heaven, and Anson became the responsible head of his family. An unmarried aunt who had lived with them for years ran the house, and attempted with helpless inefficiency to chaperone the younger girls. All the children were less self-reliant than Anson, more conventional both in their virtues and in their shortcomings. Mrs. Hunter's death had postponed the début of one daughter and the wedding of another. Also it had taken something deeply material from all of them, for with her passing the quiet, expensive superiority of the Hunters came to an end.

For one thing, the estate, considerably diminished by two inheritance taxes and soon to be divided among six children, was not a notable fortune any more. Anson saw a tendency in his youngest sisters to speak rather respectfully of families that hadn't "existed" twenty years ago. His own feeling of precedence was not echoed in them—sometimes they were conventionally snobbish, that was all. For another thing, this was the last summer they would spend on the Connecticut estate; the clamor against it was too loud: "Who wants to waste the best months of the year shut up in that dead old town?" Reluctantly he yielded—the house would go into the market in the fall, and next summer they would rent a smaller place in Westchester County. It was a step down from the expensive simplicity of his father's idea, and, while he sympathized with the revolt, it also annoyed him; during his mother's lifetime he had gone up there at least every other week-end—even in the gayest summers.

Yet he himself was part of this change, and his strong instinct for life had turned him in his twenties from the hollow obsequies of that abortive leisure class. He did not see this clearly—he still felt that there was a norm, a standard of society. But there was no norm, it was doubtful if there had ever been a true norm in New York. The few who still paid and fought to enter a particular set succeeded only to find that as a society it scarcely functioned—or, what was more alarming, that the Bohemia from which they fled sat above them at table.

At twenty-nine Anson's chief concern was his own growing loneliness. He was sure now that he would never marry. The number of weddings at which he had officiated as best man or usher was past all counting—there was a drawer at home that bulged with the official neckties of this or that wedding-party, neckties standing for romances that had not endured a year, for couples who had passed completely from his life. Scarf-pins, gold pencils, cuff-buttons, presents from a generation of grooms had passed through his jewel-box and been lost—and with every ceremony he was less and less able to imagine himself in the groom's place. Under his hearty good-will toward all those marriages there was despair about his own.

And as he neared thirty he became not a little depressed at the inroads that marriage, especially lately, had made upon his friendships. Groups of people had a disconcerting tendency to dissolve and disappear. The men from his own college—and it was upon them he had expended the most time and affection—were the most elusive of all. Most of them were drawn deep into domesticity, two were dead, one lived abroad, one was in Hollywood writing continuities for pictures that Anson went faithfully to see.

Most of them, however, were permanent commuters with an intricate family life centering around some suburban country club, and it was from these that he felt his estrangement most keenly.

In the early days of their married life they had all needed him; he gave them advice about their slim finances, he exorcised their doubts about the advisability of bringing a baby into two rooms and a bath, especially he stood for the great world outside. But now their financial troubles were in the past and the fearfully expected child had evolved into an absorbing family. They were always glad to see old Anson, but they dressed up for him and tried to impress him with their present importance, and kept their troubles to themselves. They needed him no longer.

A few weeks before his thirtieth birthday the last of his early and intimate friends was married. Anson acted in his usual rôle of best man, gave his usual silver tea-service, and went down to the usual *Homeric* to say good-by. It was a hot Friday afternoon in May, and as he walked from the pier he realized that Saturday closing had begun and he was free until Monday morning.

"Go where?" he asked himself.

The Yale Club, of course; bridge until dinner, then four or five raw cocktails in somebody's room and a pleasant confused evening. He regretted that this afternoon's groom wouldn't be along—they had always been able to cram so much into such nights: they knew how to attach women and how to get rid of them, how much consideration any girl deserved from their intelligent hedonism. A party was an adjusted thing—you took certain girls to certain places and spent just so much on their amusement; you drank a little, not much, more than you ought to drink, and at a certain time in the morning you stood up and said you were going home. You avoided college boys, sponges, future engagements, fights, sentiment, and indiscretions. That was the way it was done. All the rest was dissipation.

In the morning you were never violently sorry—you made no resolutions, but if you had overdone it and your heart was slightly out of order, you went on the wagon for a few days without saying anything about it, and waited until an accumulation of nervous boredom projected you into another party.

The lobby of the Yale Club was unpopulated. In the bar three very young alumni looked up at him, momentarily and without curiosity.

"Hello there, Oscar," he said to the bartender. "Mr. Cahill been around this afternoon?"

"Mr. Cahill's gone to New Haven."

"Oh . . . that so?"

"Gone to the ball game. Lot of men gone up."

Anson looked once again into the lobby, considered for a moment, and then walked out and over to Fifth Avenue. From the broad window of one of his clubs—one that he had scarcely visited in five years—a gray man with watery eyes stared down at him. Anson looked quickly away—that figure sitting in vacant resignation, in supercilious solitude, depressed him. He stopped and, retracing his steps, started over 47th Street toward Teak Warden's apartment. Teak and his wife had once been his most familiar friends—it was a household where he and Dolly Karger had been used to go in the days of their affair. But Teak had taken to drink, and his wife had remarked publicly that Anson was a bad influence on him. The remark reached Anson in an exaggerated form—when it was finally cleared up, the delicate spell of intimacy was broken, never to be renewed.

"Is Mr. Warden at home?" he inquired.

"They've gone to the country."

The fact unexpectedly cut at him. They were gone to the country and he hadn't known. Two years before he would have known the date, the hour, come up at the last moment for a final drink, and planned his first visit to them. Now they had gone without a word.

Anson looked at his watch and considered a week-end with his family, but the only train was a local that would jolt through the aggressive heat for three hours. And tomorrow in the country, and Sunday—he was in no mood for porch-bridge with polite undergraduates, and dancing after dinner at a rural road-house, a diminutive of gaiety which his father had estimated too well.

"Oh, no," he said to himself. . . . "No."

He was a dignified, impressive young man, rather stout now, but otherwise unmarked by dissipation. He could have been cast for a pillar of something—at times you were sure it was not society, at others nothing else—for the law, for the church. He stood for a few minutes motionless on the sidewalk in front of a 47th Street apartment-house; for almost the first time in his life he had nothing whatever to do.

Then he began to walk briskly up Fifth Avenue, as if he had just been reminded of an important engagement there. The necessity of dissimulation is one of the few characteristics that we share with dogs, and I think of Anson on that day as some well-bred specimen who had been disappointed at a familiar back door. He was going to see Nick, once a fashionable bartender in demand at all private dances, and now employed in cooling non-alcoholic champagne among the labyrinthine cellars of the Plaza Hotel.

"Nick," he said, "what's happened to everything?"

"Dead," Nick said.

"Make me a whisky sour." Anson handed a pint bottle over the counter. "Nick, the girls are different; I had a little girl in Brooklyn and she got married last week without letting me know."

"That a fact? Ha-ha-ha," responded Nick diplomatically. "Slipped it over on you."

"Absolutely," said Anson. "And I was out with her the night before."

"Ha-ha-ha," said Nick, "ha-ha-ha!"

"Do you remember the wedding, Nick, in Hot Springs where I had the waiters and the musicians singing 'God save the King'?"

"Now where was that, Mr. Hunter?" Nick concentrated doubtfully. "Seems to me that was——"

"Next time they were back for more, and I began to wonder how much I'd paid them," continued Anson.

"—seems to me that was at Mr. Trenholm's wedding."

"Don't know him," said Anson decisively. He was offended that a strange name should intrude upon his reminiscences; Nick perceived this.

"Naw—aw—" he admitted, "I ought to know that. It was one of *your* crowd—Brakins. . . . Baker——"

"Bicker Baker," said Anson responsively. "They put me in a hearse after it was over and covered me up with flowers and drove me away."

"Ha-ha-ha," said Nick. "Ha-ha-ha."

Nick's simulation of the old family servant paled presently and Anson went upstairs to the lobby. He looked around—his eyes met the glance of an unfamiliar clerk at the desk, then fell upon a flower from the morning's marriage hesitating in the mouth of a brass cuspidor. He went out and walked slowly toward the blood-red sun over Columbus Circle. Suddenly he turned around and, retracing his steps to the Plaza, immured himself in a telephone-booth.

Later he said that he tried to get me three times that afternoon, that he tried every one who might be in New York—men and girls he had not seen for years, an artist's model of his college days whose faded number was still in his address book—Central told him that even the exchange existed no longer. At length his quest roved into the country, and he held brief disappointing conversations with emphatic butlers and maids. So-and-so was out, riding, swimming, playing golf, sailed to Europe last week. Who shall I say phoned?

It was intolerable that he should pass the evening alone—the private reckonings which one plans for a moment of leisure lose every charm when the solitude is enforced. There were always women of a sort, but the ones he knew had temporarily vanished, and to pass a New York evening in the hired company of a stranger never occurred to him—he would have considered that that was something shameful and secret, the diversion of a traveling salesman in a strange town.

Anson paid the telephone bill—the girl tried unsuccessfully to joke with him about its size—and for the second time that afternoon started to leave the Plaza and go he knew not where. Near the revolving door the figure of a woman, obviously with child, stood sideways to the light—a sheer beige cape fluttered at her shoulders when the door turned and, each time, she looked impatiently toward it as if she were weary of waiting. At the first sight of her a strong nervous thrill of familiarity went over him, but not until he was within five feet of her did he realize that it was Paula.

"Why, Anson Hunter!"

His heart turned over.

"Why, Paula——"

"Why, this is wonderful. I can't believe it, *Anson!*"

She took both his hands, and he saw in the freedom of the gesture that the memory of him had lost poignancy to her. But not to him—he felt that old mood that she evoked in him stealing over his brain, that gentleness with which he had always met her optimism as if afraid to mar its surface.

"We're at Rye for the summer. Pete had to come East on business—you know of course I'm Mrs. Peter Hagerty now—so we brought the children and took a house. You've got to come out and see us."

"Can I?" he asked directly. "When?"

"When you like. Here's Pete." The revolving door functioned, giving up a fine tall man of thirty with a tanned face and a trim mustache. His immaculate fitness made a sharp contrast with Anson's increasing bulk, which was obvious under the faintly tight cutaway coat.

"You oughtn't to be standing," said Hagerty to his wife. "Let's sit down here." He indicated lobby chairs, but Paula hesitated.

"I've got to go right home," she said. "Anson, why don't you—why don't you come out and have dinner with us tonight? We're just getting settled, but if you can stand that——"

Hagerty confirmed the invitation cordially.

"Come out for the night."

Their car waited in front of the hotel, and Paula with a tired gesture sank back against silk cushions in the corner.

"There's so much I want to talk to you about," she said, "it seems hopeless."

"I want to hear about you."

"Well"—she smiled at Hagerty—"that would take a long time too. I have three children—by my first marriage. The oldest is five, then four, then three." She smiled again. "I didn't waste much time having them, did I?"

"Boys?"

"A boy and two girls. Then—oh, a lot of things happened, and I got a divorce in Paris a year ago and married Pete. That's all—except that I'm awfully happy."

In Rye they drove up to a large house near the Beach Club, from which there issued presently three dark, slim children who broke from an English governess and approached them with an esoteric cry. Abstractedly and with difficulty Paula took each one into her arms, a caress which they accepted stiffly, as they had evidently been told not to bump into Mummy. Even against their fresh faces Paula's skin showed scarcely any weariness—for all her physical languor she seemed younger than when he had last seen her at Palm Beach seven years ago.

At dinner she was preoccupied, and afterward, during the homage to the radio, she lay with closed eyes on the sofa, until Anson wondered if his presence at this time were not an intrusion. But at nine o'clock, when Hagerty rose and said pleasantly that he was going to leave them by themselves for a while, she began to talk slowly about herself and the past.

"My first baby," she said—"the one we call Darling, the biggest little girl—I wanted to die when I knew I was going to have her, because Lowell was like a stranger to me. It didn't seem as though she could be my own. I wrote you a letter and tore it up. Oh, you were *so* bad to me, Anson."

It was the dialogue again, rising and falling. Anson felt a sudden quickening of memory.

"Weren't you engaged once?" she asked—"a girl named Dolly something?"

"I wasn't ever engaged. I tried to be engaged, but I never loved anybody but you, Paula."

"Oh," she said. Then after a moment: "This baby is the first one I ever really wanted. You see, I'm in love now—at last."

He didn't answer, shocked at the treachery of her remembrance. She must have seen that the "at last" bruised him, for she continued:

"I was infatuated with you, Anson—you could make me do anything you liked. But we wouldn't have been happy. I'm not smart enough for you. I don't like things to be complicated like you do." She paused. "You'll never settle down," she said.

The phrase struck at him from behind—it was an accusation that of all accusations he had never merited.

"I could settle down if women were different," he said. "If I didn't understand so much about them, if women didn't spoil you for other women, if they had only a little pride. If I could go to sleep for a while and wake up into a home that was really mine—why, that's what I'm made for, Paula, that's what women have seen in me and liked in me. It's only that I can't get through the preliminaries any more."

Hagerty came in a little before eleven; after a whisky Paula stood up and announced that she was going to bed. She went over and stood by her husband.

"Where did you go, dearest?" she demanded.

"I had a drink with Ed Saunders."

"I was worried. I thought maybe you'd run away."

She rested her head against his coat.

"He's sweet, isn't he, Anson?" she demanded.

"Absolutely," said Anson, laughing.

She raised her face to her husband.

"Well, I'm ready," she said. She turned to Anson: "Do you want to see our family gymnastic stunt?"

"Yes," he said in an interested voice.

"All right. Here we go!"

Hagerty picked her up easily in his arms.

"This is called the family acrobatic stunt," said Paula. "He carries me upstairs. Isn't it sweet of him?"

"Yes," said Anson.

Hagerty bent his head slightly until his face touched Paula's.

"And I love him," she said. "I've just been telling you, haven't I, Anson?"

"Yes," he said.

"He's the dearest thing that ever lived in this world; aren't you, darling? . . . Well, good night. Here we go. Isn't he strong?"

"Yes," Anson said.

"You'll find a pair of Pete's pajamas laid out for you. Sweet dreams—see you at breakfast."

"Yes," Anson said.

VIII

The older members of the firm insisted that Anson should go abroad for the summer. He had scarcely had a vacation in seven years, they said. He was stale and needed a change. Anson resisted.

"If I go," he declared, "I won't come back any more."

"That's absurd, old man. You'll be back in three months with all this depression gone. Fit as ever."

"No." He shook his head stubbornly. "If I stop, I won't go back to work. If I stop, that means I've given up—I'm through."

"We'll take a chance on that. Stay six months if you like—we're not afraid you'll leave us. Why, you'd be miserable if you didn't work."

They arranged his passage for him. They liked Anson—every one liked Anson—and the change that had been coming over him cast a sort of pall over the office. The enthusiasm that had invariably signaled up business, the consideration toward his equals and his inferiors, the lift of his vital presence—within the past four months his intense nervousness had melted down these qualities into the fussy pessimism of a man of forty. On every transaction in which he was involved he acted as a drag and a strain.

"If I go I'll never come back," he said.

Three days before he sailed Paula Legendre Hagerty died in childbirth. I was with him a great deal then, for we were crossing together, but for the first time in our friendship he told me not a word of how he felt, nor did I see the slightest sign of emotion. His chief preoccupation was with the fact that he was thirty years old—he would turn the conversation to the point where he could remind you of it and then fall silent, as if he assumed that the statement would start a chain of thought sufficient to itself. Like his partners, I was amazed at the change in him, and I was glad when the *Paris* moved off into the wet space between the worlds, leaving his principality behind.

"How about a drink?" he suggested.

We walked into the bar with that defiant feeling that characterizes the day of departure and ordered four Martinis. After one cocktail a change came over him—he suddenly reached across and slapped my knee with the first joviality I had seen him exhibit for months.

"Did you see that girl in the red tam?" he demanded, "the one with the high color who had the two police dogs down to bid her good-by."

"She's pretty," I agreed.

"I looked her up in the purser's office and found out that she's alone. I'm going down to see the steward in a few minutes. We'll have dinner with her tonight."

After a while he left me, and within an hour he was walking up and down the deck with her, talking to her in his strong, clear voice. Her red tam was a bright spot of color against the steel-green sea, and from time to time she looked up with a flashing bob of her head, and smiled with amusement and interest, and anticipation. At dinner we had champagne, and were very joyous—afterward Anson ran the pool with infectious gusto, and several people who had seen me with him asked me his name. He and the girl were talking and laughing together on a lounge in the bar when I went to bed.

I saw less of him on the trip than I had hoped. He wanted to arrange a foursome, but there was no one available, so I saw him only at meals. Sometimes, though, he would have a cocktail in the bar, and he told me about the girl in the red tam, and his adventures with her, making them all bizarre and amusing, as he had a way of doing, and I was glad that he was himself again, or at least the self that I knew, and with which I felt at home. I don't think he was ever happy unless some one was in love with him, responding to him like filings to a magnet, helping him to explain himself, promising him something. What it was I do not know. Perhaps they promised that there would always be women in the world who would spend their brightest, freshest, rarest hours to nurse and protect that superiority he cherished in his heart.

WILLIAM FAULKNER [1897–1962]

In 1950, when he accepted the Nobel Prize for literature in Stockholm and spoke of the duties of the writer in serious terms, Faulkner placed "Yoknapatawpha County" (the fictional name for his home territory of northern Mississippi) authoritatively on the world literary map and at the same time succeeded, in his own laconic phrase, in making a small "scratch on the face of anonymity." Behind his modest words lies a brilliant, if uneven, record of some sixteen novels and enough short fiction to fill seven volumes.

Faulkner came of an old and proud Mississippi family which included a governor, a colonel in the Confederate army, bankers, and railroad builders, all of whom helped build Lafayette County and the town of Oxford. He portrays them and the other "old families" with mingled pride and scorn in his books—the Sartorises, the Compsons, the Sutpens, the De Spains, the Benbows—once-aristocratic planters whose present descendants are reduced to a genteel poverty and worse, alcoholism, insanity, despair. Although cultivated and well-born, these families are weak and have suffered deeply from the sin of slavery on their land. They expiate this sin by watching the country being invaded by the pushing and lower-class Snopeses who have appropriated to themselves and their children the rivers, forests, and farms, wasting and abusing their newly-won title. Faulkner's Negro and Indian characters are mostly treated with sympathy and respect and a feeling that both, having been deprived of their birthright by the whites, have won from suffering a measure of dignity and peace.

Most of Faulkner's life was lived in Oxford, where he went to school through the fifth grade, and spasmodically attended high school and later, 1919–21, the University of Mississippi. His education, like his personality, was private and independent. His early reading was in romantic poetry of the Swinburne kind; later came the modern Imagists and the standard classics, such as Shakespeare, Keats, Dickens, Thackeray, and Balzac. He also read Joyce, whose work has left a mark upon his own. During the First World War he joined the Canadian Air Force but was not sent to France. He returned to Oxford, working at odd jobs in desultory fashion, painting university buildings, and acting as postmaster at the university. He preferred to regard himself as a poet turning out quantities of verse in the Imagist manner; some of it was later published. In 1925 en route to Europe, he went to New Orleans, where he met Sherwood Anderson and decided to stay and write novels. His first novel, *Soldiers' Pay,* was written there and published through Anderson's help. Now embarked on a writing career he produced sketches, poetry, and criticism in the *Times-Picayune* and the *Double Dealer,* an experimental magazine of writers and artists in the bohemian group of the French Quarter.

After a short trip to Europe, Faulkner settled again to writing. He finished *Sartoris* and *The Sound and the Fury* (1921), the latter a critical success, but neither book brought any financial return. In need of money to finance his marriage, he deliberately undertook to produce a pot-boiling "shocker," *Sanctuary,* which brought him instant popularity, huge sales, a Hollywood contract, and notoriety.

Sartoris had introduced the pattern of his later work, the "Yoknapatawpha Saga," a kind of microcosm of the South in which the pattern of the old and new people, the town of "Jefferson," and the geographical details form a mythical domain and family tree. His succeeding work filled in, incompletely but with the fascination of a puzzle, further episodes and periods in this legend extending from before the Civil War down to the 1930's. This tapestry seems to have been woven without a deliberate plan, but Faulkner gradually came to regard all his work as a single "book." With one or two exceptions his novels contributed to the story—notably *Light in August* (1932), *Absalom, Absalom!* (1936), *The Unvanquished* (1938), *Intruder in the Dust* (1959). Outside the saga was *The Fable* (1954), a story of the First World War in France and an allegory of the crucifixion. In 1957 he returned to the Snopes-story with *The Town*, part of a trilogy with *The Hamlet* (1940). His last book, *The Reivers* (1962) was a humorous reminiscence of boyhood adventure, showing a kinship with Mark Twain.

Faulkner's fiction is "as Southern as Bourbon whiskey," yet in its mythic and symbolic qualities it goes far beyond localism. It is concerned with the destinies of a race and a civilization. A born story-teller, Faulkner transformed family gossip and old wives' tales (a woman murders her lover and sleeps with his corpse, a spinster accuses a Negro of rape, a local druggist is suspected of being a dope addict, etc.) into the permanence of literary art. He likewise employed experimental devices of style and form. *The Sound and the Fury* began as a short story and developed into a complex narrative using interior monologues to reveal different angles of vision toward the same set of events in the history of the Compson family. Violence, perversion, sex, murder, racial hatred are his themes. The sins of the past and the guilt of the present are steadily in the foreground of his works, revealed through dream, revery, stream-of-consciousness, and montage. Normal time-sequences give way to flashbacks and "psychological time." Thematic symbols suggest Biblical parallels and analogues to contemporary characters and scenes. Faulkner's prose is in two contrasting modes: one is racy, realistic, richly humorous, employing dialect and speech tones; the other is poetic, rhetorical, using complex syntax and sentences running to several pages in length. Despite his tendency to over-write and a certain obscurity deriving from symbolic effects, his work struck a chord in the modern mind and has found readers in many languages besides English.

In his last years Faulkner traveled to Europe and Japan on cultural missions for the United States. He was also writer-in-residence at the University of Virginia. His talks to students and foreign audiences have been published in *Faulkner at Nagano* (1956) and *Faulkner in the University* (1959). He died in Oxford, Mississippi, at the age of sixty-five.

Further reading: *Light in August. The (Viking) Portable Faulkner*, ed. Malcolm Cowley, 1946. *Collected Short Stories of William Faulkner*, 1961. F. J. Hoffman and O. W. Vickery, eds., *William Faulkner: Three Decades of Criticism*, 1960.

The Bear

Like *Moby-Dick*, "The Bear" is an epic story of a hunt for a legendary beast. It is also a symbolic tale of man's relation to the land which has been cursed by the traffic in slaves and the fierce economic strife among men. Published in its final form in *Go Down, Moses*, 1942 (the text reprinted here), it had appeared in two earlier versions: in *Harper's* (1935) as "Lion," and in the *Saturday Evening Post* (1942) as "The Bear." The central theme of the young Ike McCaslin learning to be faithful to the wilderness and finding his heritage of manhood in a "pageant-rite" of the hunt has its beginnings in the earlier stories, but its full development in the final version involves the secondary theme of white injustice to the Negro and a Faulknerian interpretation of the entire tragic history of the South. The first three sections and the fifth are concerned primarily with the hunt for Old Ben and the wisdom to be learned from the wilderness under the tutelage of Sam Fathers. The long fourth section moves ahead in time to Ike McCaslin's twenty-first year when he refuses to inherit the property bequeathed to him by his grandfather, Carothers McCaslin, because it is stained by the guilt of slavery and mixed blood.

The "wilderness theme" contains two contrasting strands. It is the source of moral and spiritual knowledge, Ike's "college," where he learns courage, humility, pity, and pride—in short, his heritage of responsible manhood. The wilderness is likewise the victim of man's greed and the encroachment of a corrupt civilization. Old Ben's death signalizes the end of an era, corresponding in time to the defeat of the South and the beginning of its decline. Thus Ike fatalistically takes part in God's predestined plan when he abandons his watch, gun, and compass and submits himself, almost sacrificially, to the forces which will teach him humanity through suffering.

It is a mistake to search too pointedly for a symbolic reading of the story. As in all profound literature, the meanings are suggested, not stated. Sam Fathers, by his name, his part-Negro, part-Indian blood, bears several relationships to the story and to his young "novitiate," Ike. Boon Hogganbeck, the half-savage hunter; Lion, the dog whom Ike "should have hated and feared"; the one-eyed mule "which would not spook at the smell of blood"; and the taste of brass in Ike's mouth at the sight of Old Ben—

all these have overtones of meaning to the reader. In the end when Ike finds Boon frenziedly hammering at the parts of his gun beneath the Gum Tree full of squirrels and shouting, "Don't touch a one of them! They're mine!" the reader senses that Boon, as a blind and ignorant part of humanity, has helped to destroy the spirit of the wilderness and hastened the coming of the new age, fiercely competitive and devoted to trivial and possessive ends.

1

There was a man and a dog too this time. Two beasts, counting Old Ben, the bear, and two men, counting Boon Hogganbeck, in whom some of the same blood ran which ran in Sam Fathers, even though Boon's was a plebeian strain of it and only Sam and Old Ben and the mongrel Lion were taintless and incorruptible.

He was sixteen. For six years now he had been a man's hunter. For six years now he had heard the best of all talking. It was of the wilderness, the big woods, bigger and older than any recorded document; of white man fatuous enough to believe he had bought any fragment of it, of Indian ruthless enough to pretend that any fragment of it had been his to convey; bigger than Major de Spain and the scrap he pretended to, knowing better; older than old Thomas Sutpen of whom Major de Spain had had it and who knew better; older even than old Ikkemotubbe, the Chickasaw chief, of whom old Sutpen had had it and who knew better in his turn. It was of the men, not white nor black nor red but men, hunters, with the will and hardihood to endure and the humility and skill to survive, and the dogs and the bear and deer juxtaposed and reliefed against it, ordered and compelled by and within the wilderness in the ancient and unremitting contest according to the ancient and immitigable rules which voided all regrets and brooked no quarter;—the best game of all, the best of all breathing and forever the best of all listening, the voices quiet and weighty and deliberate for retrospection and recollection and exactitude among the concrete trophies—the racked guns and the heads and skins—in libraries of town houses or the offices of plantation houses or (and best of all) in the camps themselves where the intact and still-warm meat yet hung, the men who had slain it sitting before the burning logs on hearths when there were houses and hearths or about the smoky blazing of piled wood in front of stretched tarpaulins when there were not. There was always a bottle present, so that it would seem to him that those fine fierce instants of heart and brain and courage and wiliness and speed were concentrated and distilled into that brown liquor which not women, not boys and children, but only hunters drank, drinking not of the blood they spilled but some condensation of the wild immortal spirit, drinking it moderately, humbly even, not with the pagan's base and baseless hope of acquiring thereby the virtues of cunning and strength and speed but in salute to them. Thus it seemed to him on this December morning not only natural but actually fitting that this should have begun with whisky.

He realized later that it had begun long before that. It had already begun on that day when he first wrote his age in two ciphers and his cousin McCaslin brought him for the first time to the camp, the big woods, to earn for himself from the wilderness the name and state of hunter provided he in his turn were humble and enduring enough. He had already inherited then, without ever having seen it, the big old bear with one trap-ruined foot that in an area almost a hundred miles square had earned for himself a name, a definite designation like a living man:—the long legend of corn-cribs broken down and rifled, of shoats and grown pigs and even calves carried bodily into the woods and devoured and traps and deadfalls overthrown and dogs mangled and slain and shotgun and even rifle shots delivered at point-blank range yet with no more effect than so many peas blown through a tube by a child—a corridor of wreckage and destruction beginning back before the boy was born, through which sped, not fast but rather with the ruthless and irresistible deliberation of a locomotive, the shaggy tremendous shape. It ran in his knowledge before he ever saw it. It loomed and towered in his dreams before he even saw the unaxed woods where it left its crooked print, shaggy, tremendous, red-eyed, not malevolent but just big, too big for the dogs which tried to bay it, for the horses which tried to ride it down, for the men and the bullets they fired into it; too big for the very country which was its constricting scope. It was as if the boy had already divined what his senses and intellect had not encompassed yet: that doomed wilderness whose edges were being constantly and punily gnawed at by men with plows and axes who feared it because it was wilderness, men myriad and nameless even to one another in the land where the old bear had earned a name, and through which ran not even a mortal beast but an anachronism indomitable and invincible out of an old dead time, a phantom, epitome and apotheosis of the old wild life which the little puny humans swarmed and hacked at in a fury of abhorrence and fear like pygmies about the ankles of a drowsing elephant;—the old bear, solitary, indomitable, and alone; widowered childless and absolved of mortality—old Priam reft of his old wife and outlived all his sons.

Still a child, with three years then two years then one year yet before he too could make one of them, each November he would watch the wagon containing the dogs and the bedding and food and guns and his cousin McCaslin and Tennie's Jim and Sam Fathers too until Sam moved to the camp to live, depart for the Big Bottom, the big woods. To him, they were going not to hunt bear and deer but to keep yearly rendezvous with the bear which they did not even intend to kill. Two weeks later they would return, with no trophy, no skin. He had not expected it. He had not even feared that it might be in the wagon this time with the other skins and heads. He did not even tell himself that in three years or two years or one year more he would be present and that it might even be his gun. He believed that only after he had served his apprenticeship in the woods which would prove him worthy to be a hunter, would he even be permitted to distinguish the crooked print, and that even then for two November weeks he would merely make another minor one, along with his cousin and Major de Spain and General Compson and Walter Ewell and Boon and the dogs which feared to bay it and the shotguns and rifles which failed even to bleed it, in the yearly pageant-rite of the old bear's furious immortality.

His day came at last. In the surrey with his cousin and Major de Spain and General Compson he saw the wilderness through a slow drizzle of November rain just above the ice point as it seemed to him later he always saw it or at least always remembered it—the tall and endless wall of dense November woods under the dissolving afternoon and the year's death, sombre, impenetrable (he could not even discern yet how, at what point they could possibly hope to enter it even though he knew that Sam Fathers was waiting there with the wagon), the surrey moving through the skeleton stalks of cotton and corn in the last of open country, the last trace of man's puny gnawing at the immemorial flank, until, dwarfed by that perspective into an almost ridiculous diminishment, the surrey itself seemed to have ceased to move (this too to be completed later, years later, after he had grown to a man and had seen the sea) as a solitary small boat hangs in a lonely immobility, merely tossing up and down, in the infinite waste of the ocean while the water and then the apparently impenetrable land which it nears without appreciable progress, swings slowly and opens the widening inlet which is the anchorage. He entered it. Sam was waiting, wrapped in a quilt on the wagon seat behind the patient and steaming mules. He entered his novitiate to the true wilderness with Sam beside him as he had begun his apprenticeship in miniature to manhood after the rabbits and such with Sam beside him, the two of them wrapped in the damp, warm, Negro-rank quilt, while the wilderness closed behind his entrance as it had opened momentarily to accept him, opening before his advancement as it closed behind his progress, no fixed path the wagon followed but a channel non-existent ten yards ahead of it and ceasing to exist ten yards after it had passed, the wagon progressing not by its own volition but by attrition of their intact yet fluid circumambiance, drowsing, earless, almost lightless.

It seemed to him that at the age of ten he was witnessing his own birth. It was not even strange to him. He had experienced it all before, and not merely in dreams. He saw the camp—a paintless six-room bungalow set on piles above the spring high-water—and he knew already how it was going to look. He helped in the rapid orderly disorder of their establishment in it and even his motions were familiar to him, foreknown. Then for two weeks he ate the coarse, rapid food—the shapeless sour bread, the wild strange meat, vension and bear and turkey and coon which he had never tasted before—which men ate, cooked by men who were hunters first and cooks afterward; he slept in harsh sheetless blankets as hunters slept. Each morning the gray of dawn found him and Sam Fathers on the stand, the crossing, which had been allotted him. It was the poorest one, the most barren. He had expected that; he had not dared yet to hope even to himself that he would even hear the running dogs this first time. But he did hear them. It was on the third morning—a murmur, sourceless, almost indistinguishable, yet he knew what it was although he had never before heard that many dogs running at once, the murmur swelling into separate and distinct voices until he could call on the five dogs which his cousin owned from among the others. "Now," Sam said, "slant your gun up a little and draw back the hammers and then stand still."

But it was not for him, not yet. The humility was there; he had learned that. And he could learn the patience. He was only ten, only one week. The instant had passed. It seemed to him that he could actually see the deer, the buck, smoke-colored, elongated with speed, vanished, the woods, the gray solitude still ringing even when the voices of the dogs had died away; from far away across the sombre woods and the gray half-liquid morning there came two shots. "Now let your hammers down," Sam said.

He did so. "You knew it too," he said.

"Yes," Sam said. "I want you to learn how to do when you didn't shoot. It's after the chance for the bear or the deer has done already come and gone that men and dogs gets killed."

"Anyway, it wasn't him," the boy said. "It wasn't even a bear. It was just a deer."

"Yes," Sam said, "it was just a deer."

Then one morning, it was in the second week, he heard the dogs again. This time before Sam even spoke he readied the too-long, too-heavy, man-size gun as Sam had taught him, even though this time he knew the dogs and the deer were coming less close than ever, hardly within hearing even. They didn't sound like any running dogs he had ever heard before even. Then he found that Sam, who had taught him first of all to cock the gun and take position where he could see best in all directions and then never to move again, had himself moved up beside him. "There," he said. "Listen." The boy listened, to no ringing chorus strong and fast on a free scent but, a moiling yapping an octave too high and with something more than indecision and even abjectness in it which he could not yet recognize, reluctant, not even moving very fast, taking a long time to pass out of hearing, leaving even then in the air that echo of thin and almost human hysteria, abject, almost humanly grieving, with this time nothing ahead of it, no sense of a fleeing unseen smoke-colored shape. He could hear Sam breathing at his shoulder. He saw the arched curve of the old man's inhaling nostrils.

"It's Old Ben!" he cried, whispering.

Sam didn't move save for the slow gradual turning of his head as the voices faded on and the faint steady rapid arch and collapse of his nostrils. "Hah," he said. "Not even running. Walking."

"But up here!" the boy cried. "Way up here!"

"He do it every year," Sam said. "Once. Ash and Boon say he comes up here to run the other little bears away. Tell them to get to hell out of here and stay out until the hunters are gone. Maybe." The boy no longer heard anything at all, yet still Sam's head continued to turn gradually and steadily until the back of it was toward him. Then it turned back and looked down at him—the same face, grave, familiar, expressionless until it smiled, the same old man's eyes from which as he watched there faded slowly a quality darkly and fiercely lambent, passionate and proud. "He don't care no more for bears than he does for dogs or men neither. He come to see who's here, who's new in camp this year, whether he can shoot or not, can stay or not. Whether we got the dog yet that can bay and hold him until a man gets there with a gun. Because he's the head bear. He's the man." It faded, was gone; again they were the eyes as he had known them all his life. "He'll let them follow him to the river. Then he'll send them home. We might as well go too; see how they look when they get back to camp."

The dogs were there first, ten of them huddled back under the kitchen, himself and Sam squatting to peer back into the obscurity where they crouched, quiet, the eyes rolling and luminous, vanishing, and no sound, only that effluvium which the boy could not quite place yet, of something more than dog, stronger than dog and not just animal, just beast even. Because there had been nothing in front of the abject and painful yapping except the solitude, the wilderness, so that when the eleventh hound got back about mid-afternoon and he and Tennie's Jim held the passive and still trembling bitch while Sam daubed her tattered ear and raked shoulder with turpentine and axle-grease, it was still no living creature but only the wilderness which, leaning for a moment, had patted lightly once her temerity. "Just like a man," Sam said. "Just like folks. Put off as long as she could having to be brave, knowing all the time that sooner or later she would have to be brave once so she could keep on calling herself a dog, and knowing beforehand what was going to happen when she done it."

He did not know just when Sam left. He only knew that he was gone. For the next three mornings he rose and ate breakfast and Sam was not waiting for him. He went to his stand alone; he found it without help now and stood on it as Sam had taught him. On the third morning he heard the dogs again, running strong and free on a true scent again, and he readied the gun as he had learned to do and heard the hunt sweep past on since he was not ready yet, had not deserved other yet in just one short period of two weeks as compared to all the long life which he had already dedicated to the wilderness with patience and humility; he heard the shot again, one shot, the single clapping report of Walter Ewell's rifle. By now he could not only find his stand and then return to camp without guidance, by using the compass his cousin had given him he reached Walter, waiting beside the buck and the moiling of dogs over the cast entrails before any of the others except Major de Spain and Tennie's Jim on the horses, even before Uncle Ash arrived with the one-eyed wagon-mule which did not mind the smell of blood or even, so they said, of bear.

It was not Uncle Ash on the mule. It was Sam, returned. And Sam was waiting when he finished his dinner and, himself on the one-eyed mule and Sam on the other one of the wagon team, they rode for more than three hours through the rapid shortening sunless afternoon, following no path, no trail even that he could discern, into a section of country he had never seen before. Then he understood why Sam had made him ride the one-eyed mule which would not spook at the smell of blood, of wild animals. The other one, the sound one, stopped short and tried to whirl and bolt even as Sam got down, jerking and wrenching at the rein while Sam held it, coaxing it forward with his voice since he did not dare risk hitching it, drawing it forward while the boy dismounted from the marred one which would stand. Then, standing beside Sam in the thick great gloom of ancient woods and the winter's dying afternoon, he looked quietly down at the rotted log scored and gutted with claw-marks and, in the wet earth beside it, the print of the enormous warped two-toed foot. Now he knew what he had heard in the hounds' voices in the woods that morning and what he had smelled when he peered under the kitchen where they huddled. It was in him too, a little different because they were brute beasts and he was not, but only a little different—an eagerness, passive; an abjectness, a sense of his own fragility and impotence against the timeless woods, yet without doubt or dread; a flavor like brass in the sudden run of saliva in his mouth, a hard sharp constriction either in his brain or his stomach, he could not tell which and it did not matter; he knew only that for the first time he realized that the bear which had run in his listening and loomed in his dreams since before he could remember and which therefore must have existed in the listening and the dreams of his cousin and Major de Spain and even old General Compson before they began to remember in their turn, was a mortal animal and that they had departed for the camp each November with no actual intention of slaying it, not because it could not be slain but because so far they had no actual hope of being able to. "It will be tomorrow," he said.

"You mean we will try tomorrow," Sam said. "We aint got the dog yet."

"We've got eleven," he said. "They ran him Monday."

"And you heard them," Sam said. "Saw them too. We aint got the dog yet. It won't take but one. But he aint there. Maybe he aint nowhere. The only other way will be for him to run by accident over somebody that had a gun and knowed how to shoot it."

"That wouldn't be me," the boy said. "It would be Walter or Major or—"

"It might," Sam said. "You watch close tomorrow. Because he's smart. That's how come he has lived this long. If he gets hemmed up and has got to pick out somebody to run over, he will pick out you."

"How?" he said. "How will he know . . ." He ceased. "You mean he already knows me, that I aint never been to the big bottom before, aint had time to find out yet whether I . . ." He ceased again, staring at Sam; he said humbly, not even amazed: "It was me he was watching. I dont reckon he did need to come but once."

"You watch tomorrow," Sam said. "I reckon we better start back. It'll be long after dark now before we get to camp."

The next morning they started three hours earlier than they had ever done. Even Uncle Ash went, the cook, who called himself by profession a camp cook and who did little else save cook for Major de Spain's hunting and camping parties, yet who had been marked by the wilderness from simple juxtaposition to it until he responded as they all did, even the boy who until two weeks ago had never even seen the wilderness, to a hound's ripped ear and shoulder and the print of a crooked foot in a patch of wet earth. They rode. It was too far to walk: the boy and Sam and Uncle Ash in the wagon with the dogs, his cousin and Major de Spain and General Compson and Boon and Walter and Tennie's Jim riding double on the horses; again the first gray light found him, as on that first morning two weeks ago, on the stand where Sam had placed and left him. With the gun which was too big for him, the breech-loader which did not even belong to him but to Major de Spain and which he had fired only once, at a stump on the first day to learn the recoil and how to reload it with the paper shells, he stood against a big gum tree beside a little bayou whose black still water crept without motion out of a canebrake, across a small clearing and into the cane again, where, invisible, a bird, the big woodpecker called Lord-to-God by Negroes, clattered at a dead trunk. It was a stand like any other stand, dissimilar only in incidentals to the one where he had stood each morning for two weeks; a territory new to him yet no less familiar than that other one which after two weeks he had come to believe he knew a little—the same solitude, the same loneliness through which frail and timorous man had merely passed without altering it, leaving no mark or scar, which looked exactly as it must have looked when the first ancestor of Sam Fathers' Chickasaw predecessors crept into it and looked about him, club or stone axe or bone arrow drawn and ready, different only because, squatting at the edge of the kitchen, he had smelled the dogs huddled and cringing beneath it and saw the raked ear and side of the bitch that, as Sam had said, had to be brave once in order to keep on calling herself a dog, and saw yesterday in the earth beside the gutted log, the print of the living foot. He heard no dogs at all. He never did certainly hear them. He only heard the drumming of the woodpecker stop short off, and knew that the bear was looking at him. He never saw it. He did not know whether it was facing him from the cane or behind him. He did not move, holding the useless gun which he knew now he would never fire at it, now or ever, tasting in his saliva that taint of brass which he had smelled in the huddled dogs when he peered under the kitchen.

Then it was gone. As abruptly as it had stopped, the woodpecker's dry hammering set up again, and after a while he believed he even heard the dogs—a murmur, scarce a sound even, which he had probably been hearing for a time, perhaps a minute or two, before he remarked it, drifting into hearing and then out again, dying away. They came nowhere near him. If it was dogs he heard, he could not have sworn to it; if it was a bear they ran, it was another bear. It was Sam himself who emerged from the cane and crossed the bayou, the injured bitch following at heel as a bird dog is taught to walk. She came and crouched against his leg, trembling. "I didn't see him," he said. "I didn't, Sam."

"I know it," Sam said. "He done the looking. You didn't hear him neither, did you?"

"No," the boy said. "I—"

"He's smart," Sam said. "Too smart." Again the boy saw in his eyes that quality of dark and brooding lambence as Sam looked down at the bitch trembling faintly and steadily against the boy's leg. From her raked shoulder a few drops of fresh blood clung like bright berries. "Too big. We aint got the dog yet. But maybe some day."

Because there would be a next time, after and after. He was only ten. It seemed to him that he could see them, the two of them, shadowy in the limbo from which time emerged and became time: the old bear absolved of mortality and himself who shared a little of it. Because he recognised now what he had smelled in the huddled dogs and tasted in his own saliva, recognised fear as a boy, a youth, recognises the existence of love and passion and experience which is his heritage but not yet his patrimony, from entering by chance the presence or perhaps even merely the bedroom of a woman who has loved and been loved by many men. *So I will have to see him,* he thought, without dread or even hope. *I will have to look at him.* So it was in June of the next summer. They were at the camp again, celebrating Major de Spain's and General Compson's birthdays. Although the one had been born in September and the other in the depth of winter and almost thirty years earlier, each June the two of them and McCaslin and Boon and Walter Ewell (and the boy too from now on) spent two weeks at the camp, fishing and shooting squirrels and turkey and running coons and wildcats with the dogs at night. That is, Boon and the Negroes (and the boy too now) fished and shot squirrels and ran the coons and cats, because the proven hunters, not only Major de Spain and old General Compson (who spent those two weeks sitting in a rocking chair before a tremendous iron pot of Brunswick stew, stirring and tasting, with Uncle Ash to quarrel with about how he was making it and Tennie's Jim to pour whisky into the tin dipper from which he drank it), but even McCaslin and Walter Ewell who were still young enough, scorned such other shooting the wild gobblers with pistols for wagers or to test their marksmanship.

That is, his cousin McCaslin and the others thought he was hunting squirrels. Until the third evening he believed that Sam Fathers thought so too. Each morning he would leave the camp right after breakfast. He had his own gun now, a new breech-loader, a Christmas gift; he would own and shoot it for almost seventy years, through two new pairs of barrels and locks and one new stock, until all that remained of the original gun was the silver-inlaid trigger-guard with his and McCaslin's engraved names and the date in 1878. He found the tree beside the little bayou where he had stood that morning. Using the compass he ranged from that point; he was teaching himself to be better than a fair woodsman without even knowing he was doing it. On the third day he even found the gutted log where he had first seen the print. It was almost completely crumbled now, healing with unbelievable speed, a passionate and almost visible relinquishment, back into the earth from which the tree had grown. He ranged the summer woods now, green with gloom, if anything actually dimmer than they had been in November's gray dissolution, where even at noon the sun fell only in windless dappling upon the earth which never completely dried and which crawled with snakes—moccasins and watersnakes and rattlers, themselves the color of the dappled gloom so that he would not always see them until they moved; returning to camp later and later and later, first day, second day, passing in the twilight of the third evening the little log pen enclosing the log barn where Sam was putting up the stock for the night. "You aint looked right yet," Sam said.

He stopped. For a moment he didn't answer. Then he said peacefully, in a peaceful rushing burst, as when a boy's miniature dam in a little brook gives way: "All right. Yes. But how? I went to the bayou. I even found that log again. I—"

"I reckon that was all right. Likely he's been watching you. You never saw his foot?"

"I . . ." the boy said. "I didn't . . . I never thought . . ."

"It's the gun," Sam said. He stood beside the fence, motionless, the old man, son of a Negro slave and a Chickasaw chief, in the battered and faded overalls and the frayed five-cent straw hat which had been the badge of the Negro's slavery and was now the regalia of his freedom. The camp—the clearing, the house, the barn and its tiny lot with which Major de Spain in his turn had scratched punily and evanescently at the wilderness—faded in the dusk, back into the immemorial darkness of the woods. *The gun,* the boy thought. *The gun.* "You will have to choose," Sam said.

He left the next morning before light, without breakfast, long before Uncle Ash would wake in his quilts on the kitchen floor and start the fire. He had only the compass and a stick for the snakes. He could go almost a mile before he would need to see the compass. He sat on a log, the invisible compass in his hand, while the secret night-sounds which had ceased at his movements, scurried again and then fell still for good and the owls ceased and gave over to the waking day birds and there was light in the gray wet woods and he could see the compass. He went fast yet still quietly, becoming steadily better and better as a woodsman without yet having time to realise it; he jumped a doe and a fawn, walked them out of the bed, close enough to see them—the crash of undergrowth, the white scut, the fawn scudding along behind her, faster than he had known it could have run. He was hunting right, upwind, as Sam had taught him, but that didn't matter now. He had left the gun; by his own will and relinquishment he had accepted not a gambit, not a choice, but a condition in which not only the bear's heretofore inviolable anonymity but all the ancient rules and balances of hunter and hunted had been abrogated. He would not even be afraid, not even in the moment when the fear would take him completely: blood, skin, bowels, bones, memory from the long time before it even became his memory—all save that thin clear quenchless lucidity which alone differed him from this bear and from all the other bears and bucks he would follow during almost seventy years, to which Sam had said: "Be scared. You cant help that. But dont be afraid. Aint nothing in the woods going to hurt you if you dont corner it or it dont smell that you are afraid. A bear or a deer has got to be scared of a coward the same as a brave man has got to be."

By noon he was far beyond the crossing on the little bayou, farther into the new and alien country than he had ever been, travelling now not only by the compass but by the old, heavy, biscuit-thick silver watch which had been his father's. He had left the camp nine hours ago; nine hours from now, dark would already have been an hour old. He stopped, for the first time since he had risen from the log when he could see the compass face at last, and looked about, mopping his sweating face on his sleeve. He had already relinquished, of his will, because of his need, in humility and peace and without regret, yet apparently that had not been enough, the leaving of the gun was not enough. He stood for a moment—a child, alien and lost in the green and soaring gloom of the markless wilderness. Then he relinquished completely to it. It was the watch and the compass. He was still tainted. He removed the linked chain of the one and the looped thong of the other from his overalls and hung them on a bush and leaned the stick beside them and entered it.

When he realised he was lost, he did as Sam had coached and drilled him: made a cast to cross his back-track. He had not been going very fast for the last two or three hours, and he had gone even less fast since he left the compass and watch on the bush. So he went slower till now, since the tree could not be very far; in fact, he found it before he really expected to and turned and went to it. But there was no bush beneath it, no compass nor watch, so he did next as Sam had coached and drilled him: made this next circle in the opposite direction and much larger, so that the pattern of the two of them would bisect his track somewhere, but crossing no trace nor mark anywhere of his feet or any feet, and now he was going faster though still not panicked, his heart beating a little more rapidly but strong and steady enough, and this time it was not even the tree because there was a down log beside it which he had never seen before and beyond the log a little swamp, a seepage of moisture somewhere between earth and water, and he did what Sam had coached and drilled him as the next and the last, seeing as he sat down on the log the crooked print, the warped indentation in the wet ground which while he looked at it continued to fill with water until it was level full and the water began to overflow and the sides of the print began to dissolve away. Even as he looked up he saw the next one, and, moving, the one beyond it; moving, not hurrying, running, but merely keeping pace with them as they appeared before him as though they were being shaped out of thin air just one constant pace short of where he would lose them forever and be lost forever himself, tireless, eager, without doubt or dread, panting a little above the strong rapid little hammer of his heart, emerging suddenly into a little glade, and the wilderness coalesced. It rushed, soundless, and solidified—the tree, the bush, the compass and the watch glinting where a ray of sunlight touched them. Then he saw the bear. It did not emerge, appear: it was just there, immobile, fixed in the green and windless noon's hot dappling, not as big as he had dreamed it but as big as he had expected, bigger, dimensionless against the dappled obscurity, looking at him. Then it moved. It crossed the glade without haste, walking for an instant into the sun's full glare and out of it, and stopped again and looked back at him across one shoulder. Then it was gone. It didn't walk into the woods. It faded, sank back into the wilderness without motion as he had watched a fish, a huge old bass, sink back into the dark depths of its pool and vanish without even any movement of its fins.

2

So he should have hated and feared Lion. He was thirteen then. He had killed his buck and Sam Fathers had marked his face with the hot blood, and in the next November he killed a bear. But before that accolade he had become as competent in the woods as many grown men with the same experience. By now he was a better woodsman than most grown men with more. There was no territory within twenty-five miles of the camp that he did not know—bayou, ridge, landmark trees and path; he could have led anyone direct to any spot in it and brought him back. He knew game trails that even Sam Fathers had never seen; in the third fall he found a buck's bedding-place by himself and unbeknown to his cousin he borrowed Walter Ewell's rifle and lay in wait for the buck at dawn and killed it when it walked back to the bed as Sam had told him how the old Chickasaw fathers did.

By now he knew the old bear's footprint better than he did his own, and not only the crooked one. He could see any one of the three sound prints and distinguish it at once from any other, and not only because of its size. There were other bears within that fifty miles which left tracks almost as large, or at least so near that the one would have appeared larger only by juxtaposition. It was more than that. If Sam Fathers had been his mentor and the backyard rabbits and squirrels his kindergarten, then the wilderness the old bear ran was his college and the old male bear itself, so long unwifed and childless as to have become its own ungendered progenitor, was his alma mater.

He could find the crooked print now whenever he wished, ten miles or five miles or sometimes closer than that, to the camp. Twice while on stand during the next three years he heard the dogs strike its trail and once even jump it by chance, the voices high, abject, almost human in their hysteria. Once, still-hunting with Walter Ewell's rifle, he saw it cross a long corridor of down timber where a tornado had passed. It rushed through rather than across the tangle of trunks and branches as a locomotive would, faster than he had ever believed it could have moved, almost as fast as a deer even because the deer would have spent most of that distance in the air; he realised then why it would take a dog not only of abnormal courage but size and speed too ever to bring it to bay. He had a little dog at home, a mongrel, of the sort called fyce by Negroes, a ratter, itself not much bigger than a rat and possessing that sort of courage which had long since stopped being bravery and had become foolhardiness. He brought it with him one June and, timing them as if they were meeting an appointment with another human being, himself carrying the fyce with a sack over its head and Sam Fathers with a brace of the hounds on a rope leash, they lay downwind of the trail and actually ambushed the bear. They were so close that it turned at bay although he realised later this might have been from surprise and amazement at the shrill and frantic uproar of the fyce. It turned at bay against the trunk of a big cypress, on its hind feet; it seemed to the boy that it would never stop rising, taller and taller, and even the two hounds seemed to have taken a kind of desperate and despairing courage from the fyce. Then he realised that the fyce was actually not going to stop. He flung the gun down and ran. When he overtook and grasped the shrill, frantically pinwheeling little dog, it seemed to him that he was directly under the bear. He could smell it, strong and hot and rank. Sprawling, he looked up where it loomed and towered over him like a thunderclap. It was quite familiar, until he remembered: this was the way he had used to dream about it.

Then it was gone. He didn't see it go. He knelt, holding the frantic fyce with both hands, hearing the abased wailing of the two hounds drawing further and further away, until Sam came up, carrying the gun. He laid it quietly down beside the boy and stood looking down at him. "You've done seed him twice now, with a gun in your hands," he said. "This time you couldn't have missed him."

The boy rose. He still held the fyce. Even in his arms it continued to yap frantically, surging and straining toward the fading sound of the hounds like a collection of live-wire springs. The boy was panting a little. "Neither could you," he said. "You had the gun. Why didn't you shoot him?"

Sam didn't seem to have heard. He put out his hand and touched the little dog in the boy's arms which still yapped and strained even though the two hounds were out of hearing now. "He's done gone," Sam said. "You can slack off and rest now, until next time." He stroked the little dog until it began to grow quiet under his hand. "You's almost the one we wants," he said. "You just aint big enough. We aint got that one yet. He will need to be just a little bigger than smart, and a little braver than either." He withdrew his hand from the fyce's head and stood looking into the woods where the bear and the hounds had vanished. "Somebody is going to, some day."

"I know it," the boy said. "That's why it must be one of us. So it wont be until the last day. When even he dont want it to last any longer."

So he should have hated and feared Lion. It was in the fourth summer, the fourth time he had made one in the celebration of Major de Spain's and General Compson's birthday. In the early spring Major de Spain's mare had foaled a horse colt. One evening when Sam brought the horses and mules up to stable them for the night, the colt was missing and it was all he could do to get the frantic mare into the lot. He had thought at first to let the mare lead him back to where she had become separated from the foal. But she would not do it. She would not even feint toward any particular part of the woods or even in any particular direction. She merely ran, as if she couldn't see, still frantic with terror. She whirled and ran at Sam once, as if to attack him in some ultimate desperation, as if she could not for the moment realise that he was a man and a long-familiar one. He got her into the lot at last. It was too dark by that time to back-track her, to unravel the erratic course she had doubtless pursued.

He came to the house and told Major de Spain. It was an animal, of course, a big one, and the colt was dead now, wherever it was. They all knew that. "It's a panther," General Compson said at once. "The same one. That doe and fawn last March." Sam had sent Major de Spain word of it when Boon Hogganbeck came to the camp on a routine visit to see how the stock had wintered—the doe's throat torn out, and the beast had run down the helpless fawn and killed it too.

"Sam never did say that was a panther," Major de Spain said. Sam said nothing now, standing behind Major de Spain where they sat at supper, inscrutable, as if he were just waiting for them to stop talking so he could go home. He didn't even seem to be looking at anything. "A panther might jump a doe, and he wouldn't have much trouble catching the fawn afterward. But no panther would have jumped that colt with the dam right there with it. It was Old Ben," Major de Spain said. "I'm disappointed in him. He has broken the rules. I didn't think he would have done that. He has killed mine and McCaslin's dogs, but that was all right. We gambled the dogs against him; we gave each other warning. But now he has come into my house and destroyed my property, out of season too. He broke the rules. It was Old Ben, Sam." Still Sam said nothing, standing there until Major de Spain should stop talking. "We'll back-track her tomorrow and see," Major de Spain said.

Sam departed. He would not live in the camp; he had built himself a little hut something like Joe Baker's, only stouter, tighter, on the bayou a quarter-mile away, and a stout log crib where he stored a little corn for the shoat he raised each year. The next morning he was waiting when they waked. He had already found the colt. They did not even wait for breakfast. It was not far, not five hundred yards from the stable—the three-months' colt lying on its side, its throat torn out and the entrails and one ham partly eaten. It lay not as if it had been dropped but as if it had been struck and hurled, and no cat-mark, no claw-mark where a panther would have gripped it while finding its throat. They read the tracks where the frantic mare had circled and at last rushed in with that same ultimate desperation with which she had whirled on Sam Fathers yesterday evening, and the long tracks of dead and terrified running and those of the beast which had not even rushed at her when she advanced but had merely walked three or four paces toward her until she broke, and General Compson said, "Good God, what a wolf!"

Still Sam said nothing. The boy watched him while the men knelt, measuring the tracks. There was something in Sam's face now. It was neither exultation nor joy nor hope. Later, a man, the boy realised what it had been, and that Sam had known all the time what had made the tracks and what had torn the throat out of the doe in the spring and killed the fawn. It had been foreknowledge in Sam's face that morning. *And he was glad,* he told himself. *He was old. He had no children, no people, none of his blood anywhere above earth that he would ever meet again. And even if he were to, he could not have touched it, spoken to it, because for seventy years now he had had to be a Negro. It was almost over now and he was glad.*

They returned to camp and had breakfast and came back with guns and the hounds. Afterward the boy realised that they also should have known then who killed the colt as well as Sam Fathers did. But that was neither the first nor the last time he had seen men rationalise from and even act upon their misconceptions. After Boon, standing astride the colt, had whipped the dogs away from it with his belt, they snuffed at the tracks. One of them, a young dog hound without judgment yet, bayed once, and they ran for a few feet on what seemed to be a trail. Then they stopped, looking back at the men, eager enough, not baffled, merely questioning, as if they were asking, "Now what?" Then they rushed back to the colt, where Boon, still astride it, slashed at them with the belt.

"I never knew a trail to get cold that quick," General Compson said.

"Maybe a single wolf big enough to kill a colt with the dam right there beside it dont leave scent," Major de Spain said.

"Maybe it was a hant," Walter Ewell said. He looked at Tennie's Jim. "Hah, Jim?"

Because the hounds would not run it, Major de Spain had Sam hunt out and find the tracks a hundred yards further on and they put the dogs on it again and again the young one bayed and not one of them realised then that the hound was not baying like a dog striking game but was merely bellowing like a country dog whose yard has been invaded. General Compson spoke to the boy and Boon and Tennie's Jim: to the squirrel hunters. "You boys keep the dogs with you this morning. He's probably hanging around somewhere, waiting to get his breakfast off the colt. You might strike him."

But they did not. The boy remembered how Sam stood watching them as they went into the woods with the leashed hounds—the Indian face in which he had never seen anything until it smiled except that faint arching of the nostrils on that first morning when the hounds had found Old Ben. They took the hounds with them on the next day, though when they reached the place where they hoped to strike a fresh trail, the carcass of the colt was gone. Then on the third morning Sam was waiting again, this time until they had finished breakfast. He said, "Come." He led them to his house, his little hut, to the corn-crib beyond it. He had removed the corn and had made a dead-fall of the door, baiting it with the colt's carcass; peering between the logs, they saw an animal almost the color of a gun or pistol barrel, what little time they had to examine its color or shape. It was not crouched nor even standing. It was in motion, in the air, coming toward them—a heavy body crashing with tremendous force against the door so that the thick door jumped and clattered in its frame, the animal, whatever it was, hurling itself against the door again seemingly before it could have touched the floor and got a new purchase to spring from. "Come away," Sam said, "fore he break his neck." Even when they retreated the heavy and measured crashes continued, the stout door jumping and clattering each time, and still no sound from the beast itself—no snarl, no cry.

"What in hell's name is it?" Major de Spain said.

"It's a dog," Sam said, his nostrils arching and collapsing faintly and steadily and that faint, fierce milkiness in his eyes again as on that first morning when the hounds had struck the old bear. "It's the dog."

"*The* dog?" Major de Spain said.

"That's gonter hold Old Ben."

"Dog the devil," Major de Spain said. "I'd rather have Old Ben himself in my pack than that brute. Shoot him."

"No," Sam said.

"You'll never tame him. How do you ever expect to make an animal like that afraid of you?"

"I don't want him tame," Sam said; again the boy watched his nostrils and the fierce milky light in his eyes. "But I almost rather he be tame than scared, of me or any man or any thing. But he won't be neither, of nothing."

"Then what are you going to do with it?"

"You can watch," said Sam.

Each morning through the second week they would go to Sam's crib. He had removed a few shingles from the roof and had put a rope on the colt's carcass and had drawn it out when the trap fell. Each morning they would watch him lower a pail of water into the crib while the dog hurled itself tirelessly against the door and dropped back and leaped again. It never made any sound and there was nothing frenzied in the act but only a cold and grim indomitable determination. Toward the end of the week it stopped jumping at the door. Yet it had not weakened appreciably and it was not as if it had rationalised the fact that the door was not going to give. It was as if for that time it simply disdained to jump no longer. It was not down. None of them had ever seen it down. It stood, and they could see it now—part mastiff, something of Airedale and something of a dozen other strains probably, better than thirty inches at the shoulders and weighing as they guessed almost ninety pounds, with cold yellow eyes and a tremendous chest and over all that strange color like a blued gun-barrel.

Then the two weeks were up. They prepared to break camp. The boy begged to remain and his cousin let him. He moved into the little hut with Sam Fathers. Each morning he watched Sam lower the pail of water into the crib. By the end of that week the dog was down. It would rise and half stagger, half crawl to the water and drink and collapse again. One morning, it could not even reach the water, could not raise its forequarters even from the floor. Sam took a short stick and prepared to enter the crib. "Wait," the boy said. "Let me get the gun—"

"No," Sam said. "He cant move now." Nor could it. It lay on its side while Sam touched it, its head and the gaunted body, the dog lying motionless, the yellow eyes open. They were not fierce and there was nothing of petty malevolence in them, but a cold and almost impersonal malignance like some natural force. It was not even looking at Sam nor at the boy peering at it between the logs.

Sam began to feed it again. The first time he had to raise its head so it could lap the broth. That night he left a bowl of broth containing lumps of meat where the dog could reach it. The next morning the bowl was empty and the dog was lying on its belly, its head up, the cold yellow eyes watching the door as Sam entered, no change whatever in the cold yellow eyes and still no sound from it even when it sprang, its aim and co-ordination still bad from weakness so that Sam had time to strike it down with the stick and leap from the crib and slam the door as the dog, still without having had time to get its feet under it to jump again seemingly, hurled itself against the door as if the two weeks of starving had never been.

At noon that day someone came whooping through the woods from the direction of the camp. It was Boon. He came and looked for a while between the logs, at the tremendous dog lying again on its belly, its head up, the yellow eyes blinking sleepily at nothing: the indomitable and unbroken spirit. "What we better do," Boon said, "is to let that son of a bitch go and catch Old Ben and run him on the dog." He turned to the boy his weather-reddened and beetling face. "Get your traps together. Cass says for you to come on home. You been in here fooling with that horse-eating varmint long enough."

Boon had a borrowed mule at the camp; the buggy was waiting at the edge of the bottom. He was at home that night. He told McCaslin about it. "Sam's going to starve him again until he can go in and touch him. Then he will feed him again. Then he will starve him again, if he has to."

"But why?" McCaslin said. "What for? Even Sam will never tame that brute."

"We dont want him tame. We want him like he is. We just want him to find out at last that the only way he can get out of that crib and stay out of it is to do what Sam or somebody tells him to do. He's the dog that's going to stop Old Ben and hold him. We've already named him. His name is Lion."

Then November came at last. They returned to the camp. With General Compson and Major de Spain and his cousin and Walter and Boon he stood in the yard among the guns and bedding and boxes of food and watched Sam Fathers and Lion come up the lane from the lot—the Indian, the old man in battered overalls and rubber boots and a worn sheepskin coat and a hat which had belonged to the boy's father; the tremendous dog pacing gravely beside him. The hounds rushed out to meet them and stopped, except the young one which still had but little of judgment. It ran up to Lion, fawning. Lion didn't snap at it. He didn't even pause. He struck it rolling and yelping for five or six feet with a blow of one paw as a bear would have done and came on into the yard and stood, blinking sleepily at nothing, looking at no one, while Boon said, "Jesus. Jesus.—Will he let me touch him?"

"You can touch him," Sam said. "He dont care. He dont care about nothing or nobody."

The boy watched that too. He watched it for the next two years from that moment when Boon touched Lion's head and then knelt beside him, feeling the bones and muscles, the power. It was as if Lion were a woman—or perhaps Boon was the woman. That was more like it—the big, grave, sleepy-seeming dog which, as Sam Fathers said, cared about no man and no thing; and the violent, insensitive, hard-faced man with his touch of remote Indian blood and the mind almost of a child. He watched Boon take over Lion's feeding from Sam and Uncle Ash both. He would see Boon squatting in the cold rain beside the kitchen while Lion ate. Because Lion neither slept nor ate with the other dogs though none of them knew where he did sleep until in the second November, thinking until then that Lion slept in his kennel beside Sam Fathers' hut, when the boy's cousin McCaslin said something about it to Sam by sheer chance and Sam told him. And that night the boy and Major de Spain and McCaslin with a lamp entered the back room where Boon slept—the little, tight, airless room rank with the smell of Boon's unwashed body and his wet hunting-clothes—where Boon, snoring on his back, choked and waked and Lion raised his head beside him and looked back at them from his cold, slumbrous yellow eyes.

"Damn it, Boon," McCaslin said. "Get that dog out of here. He's got to run Old Ben tomorrow morning. How in hell do you expect him to smell anything fancier than a skunk after breathing you all night?"

"The way I smell aint hurt my nose none that I ever noticed," Boon said.

"It wouldn't matter if it had," Major de Spain said. "We're not depending on you to trail a bear. Put him outside. Put him under the house with the other dogs."

Boon began to get up. "He'll kill the first one that happens to yawn or sneeze in his face or touches him."

"I reckon not," Major de Spain said. "None of them are going to risk yawning in his face or touching him either, even asleep. Put him outside. I want his nose right tomorrow. Old Ben fooled him last year. I dont think he will do it again."

Boon put on his shoes without lacing them; in his long soiled underwear, his hair still tousled from sleep, he and Lion went out. The others returned to the front room and the poker game where McCaslin's and Major de Spain's hands waited for them on the table. After a while McCaslin said, "Do you want me to go back and look again?"

"No," Major de Spain said. "I call," he said to Walter Ewell. He spoke to McCaslin again. "If you do, dont tell me. I am beginning to see the first sign of my increasing age: I dont like to know that my orders have been disobeyed, even when I knew when I gave them that they would be.—A small pair," he said to Walter Ewell.

"How small?" Walter said.

"Very small," Major de Spain said.

And the boy, lying beneath his piled quilts and blankets waiting for sleep, knew likewise that Lion was already back in Boon's bed, for the rest of that night and the next one and during all the nights of the next November and the next one. He thought then: *I wonder what Sam thinks. He could have Lion with him, even if Boon is a white man. He could ask Major or McCaslin either. And more than that. It was Sam's hand that touched Lion first and*

Lion knows it. Then he became a man and he knew that too. It had been all right. That was the way it should have been. Sam was the chief, the prince; Boon, the plebeian, was his huntsman. Boon should have nursed the dogs.

On the first morning that Lion led the pack after Old Ben, seven strangers appeared in the camp. They were swampers: gaunt, malaria-ridden men appearing from nowhere, who ran trap-lines for coons or perhaps farmed little patches of cotton and corn along the edge of the bottom, in clothes but little better than Sam Fathers' and nowhere near as good as Tennie's Jim's, with worn shotguns and rifles, already squatting patiently in the cold drizzle in the side yard when day broke. They had a spokesman; afterward Sam Fathers told Major de Spain how all during the past summer and fall they had drifted into the camp singly or in pairs and threes, to look quietly at Lion for a while and then go away: "Mawnin, Major. We heerd you was aimin to put that ere blue dawg on that old two-toed bear this mawnin. We figgered we'd come up and watch, if you dont mind. We wont do no shooting, lessen he runs over us."

"You are welcome," Major de Spain said. "You are welcome to shoot. He's more your bear than ours."

"I reckon that aint no lie. I done fed him enough cawn to have a sheer in him. Not to mention a shoat three years ago."

"I reckon I got a sheer too," another said. "Only it aint in the bear." Major de Spain looked at him. He was chewing tobacco. He spat. "Hit was a heifer calf. Nice un too. Last year. When I finally found her, I reckon she looked about like that colt of yourn looked last June."

"Oh," Major de Spain said. "Be welcome. If you see game in front of my dogs, shoot it."

Nobody shot Old Ben that day. No man saw him. The dogs jumped him within a hundred yards of the glade where the boy had seen him that day in the summer of his eleventh year. The boy was less than a quarter-mile away. He heard the jump but he could distinguish no voice among the dogs that he did not know and therefore would be Lion's, and he thought, believed, that Lion was not among them. Even the fact that they were going much faster than he had ever heard them run behind Old Ben before and that the high thin note of hysteria was missing now from their voices was not enough to disabuse him. He didn't comprehend until that night, when Sam told him that Lion would never cry on a trail. "He gonter growl when he catches Old Ben's throat," Sam said. "But he aint gonter never holler, no more than he ever done when he was jumping at that two-inch door. It's that blue dog in him. What you call it?"

"Airedale," the boy said.

Lion was there; the jump was just too close to the river. When Boon returned with Lion about eleven that night, he swore that Lion had stopped Old Ben once but that the hounds would not go in and Old Ben broke away and took to the river and swam for miles down it and he and Lion went down one bank for about ten miles and crossed and came up the other but it had begun to get dark before they struck any trail where Old Ben had come up out of the water, unless he was still in the water when he passed the ford where they crossed. Then he fell to cursing the hounds and ate the supper Uncle Ash had saved for him and went off to bed and after a while the boy opened the door of the little stale room thunderous with snoring and the great grave dog raised its head from Boon's pillow and blinked at him for a moment and lowered its head again.

When the next November came and the last day, the day which it was now becoming traditional to save for Old Ben, there were more than a dozen strangers waiting. They were not all swampers this time. Some of them were townsmen, from other county seats like Jefferson, who had heard about Lion and Old Ben and had come to watch the great blue dog keep his yearly rendezvous with the old two-toed bear. Some of them didn't even have guns and the hunting-clothes and boots they wore had been on a store shelf yesterday.

This time Lion jumped Old Ben more than five miles from the river and bayed and held him and this time the hounds went in, in a sort of desperate emulation. The boy heard them; he was that near. He heard Boon whooping; he heard the two shots when General Compson delivered both barrels, one containing five buckshot, the other a single ball, into the bear from as close as he could force his almost unmanageable horse. He heard the dogs when the bear broke free again. He was running now; panting, stumbling, his lungs bursting, he reached the place where General Compson had fired and where Old Ben had killed two of the hounds. He saw the blood from General Compson's shots, but he could go no further. He stopped, leaning against a tree for his breathing to ease and his heart to slow, hearing the sound of the dogs as it faded on and died away.

In camp that night—they had as guests five of the still terrified strangers in new hunting coats and boots who had been lost all day until Sam Fathers went out and got them—he heard the rest of it: how Lion had stopped and held the bear again but only the one-eyed mule which did not mind the smell of wild blood would approach and Boon was riding the mule and Boon had never been known to hit anything. He shot at the bear five times with his pump gun, touching nothing, and Old Ben killed another hound and broke free once more and reached the river and was gone. Again Boon and Lion hunted as far down one bank as they dared. Too far; they crossed in the first of dusk and dark overtook them within a mile. And this time Lion found the broken trail, the blood perhaps in the darkness where Old Ben had come up out of the water, but Boon had him on a rope, luckily, and he got down from the mule and fought Lion hand-to-hand until he got him back to camp. This time Boon didn't even curse. He stood in the door, muddy, spent, his huge gargoyle's face tragic and still amazed. "I missed him," he said. "I was in twenty-five feet of him and I missed him five times."

"But we have drawn blood," Major de Spain said. "General Compson drew blood. We have never done that before."

"But I missed him," Boon said. "I missed him five times. With Lion looking right at me."

"Never mind," Major de Spain said. "It was a damned fine race. And we drew blood. Next year we'll let General Compson or Walter ride Katie, and we'll get him."

Then McCaslin said, "Where is Lion, Boon?"

"I left him at Sam's," Boon said. He was already turning away. "I aint fit to sleep with him."

So he should have hated and feared Lion. Yet he did not. It seemed to him that there was a fatality in it. It seemed to him that something, he didn't know what, was beginning; had already begun. It was like the last act on a set stage. It was the beginning of the end of something, he didn't know what except that he would not grieve. He would be humble and proud that he had been found worthy to be a part of it too or even just to see it too.

3

It was December. It was the coldest December he had ever remembered. They had been in camp four days over two weeks, waiting for the weather to soften so that Lion and Old Ben could run their yearly race. Then they would break camp and go home. Because of these unforeseen additional days which they had had to pass waiting on the weather, with nothing to do but play poker, the whisky had given out and he and Boon were being sent to Memphis with a suitcase and a note from Major de Spain to Mr Semmes, the distiller, to get more. That is, Major de Spain and McCaslin were sending Boon to get the whisky and sending him to see that Boon got back with it or most of it or at least some of it.

Tennie's Jim waked him at three. He dressed rapidly, shivering, not so much from the cold because a fresh fire already boomed and roared on the hearth, but in that dead winter hour when the blood and the heart are slow and sleep is incomplete. He crossed the gap between house and kitchen, the gap of iron earth beneath the brilliant and rigid night where dawn would not begin for three hours yet, tasting, tongue, palate, and to the very bottom of his lungs, the searing dark, and entered the kitchen, the lamp-lit warmth where the stove glowed, fogging the windows, and where Boon already sat at the table at breakfast, hunched over his plate, almost in his plate, his working jaws blue with stubble and his face innocent of water and his coarse, horse-mane hair innocent of comb—the quarter Indian, grandson of a Chickasaw squaw, who on occasion resented with his hard and furious fists the intimation of one single drop of alien blood and on others, usually after whisky, affirmed with the same fists and the same fury that his father had been the full-blood Chickasaw and even a chief and that even his mother had been only half white. He was four inches over six feet; he had the mind of a child, the heart of a horse, and little hard shoe-button eyes without depth or meanness or generosity or viciousness or gentleness or anything else, in the ugliest face the boy had ever seen. It looked like somebody had found a walnut a little larger than a football and with a machinist's hammer had shaped features into it and then painted it, mostly red; not Indian red but a fine bright ruddy color which whisky might have had something to do with but which was mostly just happy and violent out-of-doors, the wrinkles in it not the residue of the forty years it had survived but from squinting into the sun or into the gloom of cane-brakes where game had run, baked into it by the camp fires before which he had lain trying to sleep on the cold November or December ground while waiting for daylight so he could rise and hunt again, as though time were merely something he walked through as he did through air, aging him no more than air did. He was brave, faithful, improvident and unreliable; he had neither profession job nor trade and owned one vice and one virtue: whisky, and that absolute and unquestioning fidelity to Major de Spain and the boy's cousin McCaslin. "Sometimes I'd call them both virtues," Major de Spain said once. "Or both vices," McCaslin said.

He ate his breakfast, hearing the dogs under the kitchen, wakened by the smell of frying meat or perhaps by the feet overhead. He heard Lion once, short and peremptory, as the best hunter in any camp has only to speak once to all save the fools, and none other of Major de Spain's and McCaslin's dogs were Lion's equal in size and strength and perhaps even in courage, but they were not fools; Old Ben had killed the last fool among them last year.

Tennie's Jim came in as they finished. The wagon was outside. Ash decided he would drive them over to the log-line where they would flag the outbound log-train and let Tennie's Jim wash the dishes. The boy knew why. It would not be the first time he had listened to old Ash badgering Boon.

It was cold. The wagon wheels banged and clattered on the frozen ground; the sky was fixed and brilliant. He was not shivering, he was shaking, slow and steady and hard, the food he had just eaten still warm and solid inside him while his outside shook slow and steady around it as though his stomach floated loose. "They wont run this morning," he said. "No dog will have any nose today."

"Cep Lion," Ash said. "Lion dont need no nose. All he need is a bear." He had wrapped his feet in towsacks and he had a quilt from his pallet bed on the kitchen floor drawn over his head and wrapped around him until in the thin brilliant starlight he looked like nothing at all that the boy had ever seen before. "He run a bear through a thousand-acre icehouse. Catch him too. Them other dogs dont matter because they aint going to keep up with Lion nohow, long as he got a bear in front of him."

"What's wrong with the other dogs?" Boon said. "What the hell do you know about it anyway? This is the first time you've had your tail out of that kitchen since we got here except to chop a little wood."

"Aint nothing wrong with them," Ash said. "And long as it's left up to them, aint nothing going to be. I just wish I had knowed all my life how to take care of my health good as them hounds knows."

"Well, they aint going to run this morning," Boon said. His voice was harsh and positive. "Major promised they wouldn't until me and Ike get back."

"Weather gonter break today. Gonter soft up. Rain by night." Then Ash laughed, chuckled, somewhere inside the quilt which concealed even his face. "Hum up here, mules!" he said, jerking the reins so that the mules leaped forward and snatched the lurching and banging wagon for several feet before they slowed again into their quick, short-paced, rapid plodding. "Sides, I like to know why Major need to wait on you. It's Lion he aiming to use. I aint never heard tell of you bringing no bear nor no other kind of meat into this camp."

Now Boon's going to curse Ash or maybe even hit him, the boy thought. But Boon never did, never had; the boy knew he never would even though four years ago Boon had shot five times with a borrowed pistol at a Negro on the street in Jefferson, with the same result as when he had shot five times at Old Ben last fall. "By God," Boon said, "he aint going to put Lion or no other dog on nothing until I get back tonight. Because he promised me. Whip up them mules and keep them whipped up. Do you want me to freeze to death?"

They reached the log-line and built a fire. After a while the log-train came up out of the woods under the paling east and Boon flagged it. Then in the warm caboose the boy slept again while Boon and the conductor and brakeman talked about Lion and Old Ben as people later would talk about Sullivan and Kilrain and, later still, about Dempsey and Tunney. Dozing, swaying as the springless caboose lurched and clattered, he would hear them still talking, about the shoats and calves Old Ben had killed and the cribs he had rifled and the traps and deadfalls he had wrecked and the lead he probably carried under his hide—Old Ben, the two-toed bear in a land where bears with trap-ruined feet had been called Two-Toe or Three-Toe or Cripple-Foot for fifty years, only Old Ben was an extra bear (the head bear, General Compson called him) and so had earned a name such as a human man could have worn and not been sorry.

They reached Hoke's at sunup. They emerged from the warm caboose in their hunting clothes, the muddy boots and stained khaki and Boon's blue unshaven jowls. But that was all right. Hoke's was a sawmill and commissary and two stores and a loading-chute on a sidetrack from the main line, and all the men in it wore boots and khaki too. Presently the Memphis train came. Boon bought three packages of popcorn-and-molasses and a bottle of beer from the news butch and the boy went to sleep again to the sound of his chewing.

But in Memphis it was not all right. It was as if the high buildings and the hard pavements, the fine carriages and the horse cars and the men in starched collars and neckties made their boots and khaki look a little rougher and a little muddier and made Boon's beard look worse and more unshaven and his face look more and more like he should never have brought it out of the woods at all or at least out of reach of Major de Spain or McCaslin or someone who knew it and could have said, "Dont be afraid. He wont hurt you." He walked through the station, on the slick floor, his face moving as he worked the popcorn out of his teeth with his tongue, his legs spraddled and stiff in the hips as if he were walking on buttered glass, and that blue stubble on his face like the filings from a new gun-barrel. They passed the first saloon. Even through the closed doors the boy could seem to smell the sawdust and the reek of old drink. Boon began to cough. He coughed for something less than a minute. "Damn this cold," he said. "I'd sure like to know where I got it."

"Back there in the station," the boy said.

Boon had started to cough again. He stopped. He looked at the boy. "What?" he said.

"You never had it when we left camp nor on the train either." Boon looked at him, blinking. Then he stopped blinking. He didn't cough again. He said quietly:

"Lend me a dollar. Come on. You've got it. If you ever had one, you've still got it. I dont mean you are tight with your money because you aint. You just dont never seem to ever think of nothing you want. When I was sixteen a dollar bill melted off of me before I even had time to read the name of the bank that issued it." He said quietly: "Let me have a dollar, Ike."

"You promised Major. You promised McCaslin. Not till we get back to camp."

"All right," Boon said in that quiet and patient voice. "What can I do on just one dollar? You aint going to lend me another."

"You're damn right I aint," the boy said, his voice quiet too, cold with rage which was not at Boon, remembering: Boon snoring in a hard chair in the kitchen so he could watch the clock and wake him and McCaslin and drive them the seventeen miles in to Jefferson to catch the train to Memphis; the wild, never-bridled Texas paint pony which he had persuaded McCaslin to let him buy and which he and Boon had bought at auction for four dollars and seventy-five cents and fetched home wired between two gentle old mares with pieces of barbed wire and which had never even seen shelled corn before and didn't even know what it was unless the grains were bugs maybe and at last (he was ten and Boon had been ten all his life) Boon said the pony was gentled and with a towsack over its head and four Negroes to hold it they backed it into an old two-wheeled cart and hooked up the gear and he and Boon got up and Boon said, "All right, boys. Let him go" and one of the Negroes—it was Tennie's Jim—snatched the towsack off and leaped for his life and they lost the first wheel against a post of the open gate only at that moment Boon caught him by the scruff of the neck and flung him into the roadside ditch so he only saw the rest of it in fragments: the other wheel as it slammed through the side gate and crossed the back yard and leaped up onto the gallery and scraps of the cart here and there along the road and Boon vanishing rapidly on his stomach in the leaping and spurting dust and still holding the reins until they broke too and two days later they finally caught the pony seven miles away still wearing the hames and the headstall of the bridle around its neck like a duchess with two necklaces at one time. He gave Boon the dollar.

"All right," Boon said. "Come on in out of the cold."

"I aint cold," he said.

"You can have some lemonade."

"I dont want any lemonade."

The door closed behind him. The sun was well up now. It was a brilliant day, though Ash had said it would rain before night. Already it was warmer; they could run tomorrow. He felt the old lift of heart, as pristine as ever, as on the first day; he would never lose it, no matter how old in hunting and pursuit: the best, the best of all breathing, the humility and the pride. He must stop thinking about it. Already it seemed to him that he was running, back to the station, to the tracks themselves: the first train going south, he must stop thinking about it. The street was busy. He watched the big Norman draft horses, the Percherons; the trim carriages from which the men in the fine overcoats and the ladies rosy in furs descended and entered the station. (They were still next door to it but one.) Twenty years ago his father had ridden into Memphis as a member of Colonel Sartoris' horse in Forrest's command, up Main street and (the tale told) into the lobby of the Gayoso Hotel where the Yankee officers sat in the leather chairs spitting into the tall bright cuspidors and then out again, scot-free—

The door opened behind him. Boon was wiping his mouth on the back of his hand. "All right," he said. "Let's go tend to it and get the hell out of here."

They went and had the suitcase packed. He never knew where or when Boon got the other bottle. Doubtless Mr Semmes gave it to him. When they reached Hoke's again at sundown, it was empty. They could get a return train to Hoke's in two hours; they went straight back to the station as Major de Spain and then McCaslin had told Boon to do and then ordered him to do and had sent the boy along to see that he did. Boon took the first drink from his bottle in the wash room. A man in a uniform cap came to tell him he couldn't drink there and looked at Boon's face once and said nothing. The next time he was pouring into his water glass beneath the edge of a table in the restaurant when the manager (she was a woman) did tell him he couldn't drink there and he went back to the washroom. He had been telling the Negro waiter and all the other people in the restaurant who couldn't help but hear him and who had never heard of Lion and didn't want to, about Lion and Old Ben. Then he happened to think of the zoo. He had found out that there was another train to Hoke's at three oclock and so they would spend the time at the zoo and take the three oclock train until he came back from the washroom for the third time. Then they would take the first train back to camp, get Lion and come back to the zoo where, he said, the bears were fed on ice cream and lady fingers and he would match Lion against them all.

So they missed the first train, the one they were supposed to take, but he got Boon onto the three oclock train and they were all right again, with Boon not even going to the washroom now but drinking in the aisle and talking about Lion and the men he buttonholed no more daring to tell Boon he couldn't drink there than the man in the station had dared.

When they reached Hoke's at sundown, Boon was asleep. The boy waked him at last and got him and the suitcase off the train and he even persuaded him to eat some supper at the sawmill commissary. So he was all right when they got in the caboose of the log-train to go back into the woods, with the sun going down red and the sky already overcast and the ground would not freeze tonight. It was the boy who slept now, sitting behind the ruby stove while the springless caboose jumped and clattered and Boon and the brakeman and the conductor talked about Lion and Old Ben because they knew what Boon was talking about because this was home. "Overcast and already thawing," Boon said. "Lion will get him tomorrow."

It would have to be Lion, or somebody. It would not be Boon. He had never hit anything bigger than a squirrel that anybody ever knew, except the Negro woman that day when he was shooting at the Negro man. He was a big Negro and not ten feet away but Boon shot five times with the pistol he had borrowed from Major de Spain's Negro coachman and the Negro he was shooting at outed with a dollar-and-a-half mail-order pistol and would have burned Boon down with it only it never went off, it just went snicksnicksnicksnicksnick five times and Boon still blasting away and he broke a plate-glass window that cost McCaslin forty-five dollars and hit a Negro woman who happened to be passing in the leg only Major de Spain paid for that; he and McCaslin cut cards, the plate-glass window against the Negro woman's leg. And the first day on stand this year, the first morning in camp, the buck ran right over Boon; he heard Boon's old pump gun go whow. whow. whow. whow. whow. and then his voice: "God damn, here he comes! Head him! Head him!" and when he got there the buck's tracks and the five exploded shells were not twenty paces apart.

There were five guests in camp that night from Jefferson: Mr. Bayard Sartoris and his son and General Compson's son and two others. And the next morning he looked out the window, into the gray thin drizzle of daybreak which Ash had predicted, and there they were, standing and squatting beneath the thin rain, almost two dozen of them who had fed Old Ben corn and shoats and even calves for ten years, in their worn hats and hunting coats and overalls which any town Negro would have thrown away or burned and only the rubber boots strong and sound, and the worn and blueless guns, and some even without guns. While they ate breakfast a dozen more arrived, mounted and on foot: loggers from the camp thirteen miles below and sawmill men from Hoke's and the only gun among them that one which the log-train conductor carried: so that when they went into the woods this morning Major de Spain led a party almost as strong, excepting that some of them were not armed, as some he had led in the last darkening days of '64 and '65. The little yard would not hold them. They overflowed it, into the lane where Major de Spain sat his mare while Ash in his dirty apron thrust the greasy cartridges into his carbine and passed it up to him and the great grave blue dog stood at his stirrup not as a dog stands but as a horse stands, blinking his sleepy topaz eyes at nothing, deaf even to the yelling of the hounds which Boon and Tennie's Jim held on leash.

"We'll put General Compson on Katie this morning," Major de Spain said. "He drew blood last year; if he'd had a mule then that would have stood, he would have—"

"No," General Compson said. "I'm too old to go helling through the woods on a mule or a horse or anything else any more. Besides, I had my chance last year and missed it. I'm going on a stand this morning. I'm going to let that boy ride Katie."

"No, wait," McCaslin said. "Ike's got the rest of his life to hunt bears in. Let somebody else—"

"No," General Compson said. "I want Ike to ride Katie. He's already a better woodsman than you or me either and in another ten years he'll be as good as Walter."

At first he couldn't believe it, not until Major de Spain spoke to him. Then he was up, on the one-eyed mule which would not spook at wild blood, looking down at the dog motionless at Major de Spain's stirrup, looking in the gray streaming light bigger than a calf, bigger than he knew it actually was—the big head, the chest almost as big as his own, the blue hide beneath which the muscles flinched or quivered to no touch since the heart which drove blood to them loved no man and no thing, standing as a horse stands yet different from a horse which infers only weight and speed while Lion inferred not only courage and all else that went to make up the will and desire to pursue and kill, but endurance, the will and desire to endure beyond all imaginable limits of flesh in order to overtake and slay. Then the dog looked at him. It moved its head and looked at him across the trivial uproar of the hounds, out of the yellow eyes as depthless as Boon's, as free as Boon's of meanness or generosity or gentleness or viciousness. They were just cold and sleepy. Then it blinked, and he knew it was not looking at him and never had been, without even bothering to turn its head away.

That morning he heard the first cry. Lion had already vanished while Sam and Tennie's Jim were putting saddles on the mule and horse which had drawn the wagon and he watched the hounds as they crossed and cast, snuffing and whimpering, until they too disappeared. Then he and Major de Spain and Sam and Tennie's Jim rode after them and heard the first cry out of the wet and thawing woods not two hundred yards ahead, high, with that abject, almost human quality he had come to know, and the other hounds joining in until the gloomed woods rang and clamored. They rode then. It seemed to him that he could actually see the big blue dog boring on, silent, and the bear too: the thick, locomotive-like shape which he had seen that day four years ago crossing the blow-down, crashing on ahead of the dogs faster than he had believed it could have moved, drawing away even from the running mules. He heard a shotgun, once. The woods had opened, they were going fast, the clamor faint and fading on ahead; they passed the man who had fired—a swamper, a pointing arm, a gaunt face, the small black orifice of his yelling studded with rotten teeth.

He heard the changed note in the hounds' uproar and two hundred yards ahead he saw them. The bear had turned. He saw Lion drive in without pausing and saw the bear strike him aside and lunge into the yelling hounds and kill one of them almost in its tracks and whirl and run again. Then they were in a streaming tide of dogs. He heard Major de Spain and Tennie's Jim shouting and the pistol sound of Tennie's Jim's leather thong as he tried to turn them. Then he and Sam Fathers were riding alone. One of the hounds had kept on with Lion though. He recognised its voice. It was the young hound which even a year ago had had no judgment and which, by the lights of the other hounds anyway, still had none. *Maybe that's what courage is,* he thought. "Right," Sam said behind him. "Right. We got to turn him from the river if we can."

Now they were in cane: a brake. He knew the path through it as well as Sam did. They came out of the undergrowth and struck the entrance almost exactly. It would traverse the brake and come out onto a high open ridge above the river. He heard the flat clap of Walter Ewell's rifle, then two more. "No," Sam said. "I can hear the hound. Go on."

They emerged from the narrow roofless tunnel of snapping and hissing cane, still galloping, onto the open ridge below which the thick yellow, river reflectionless in the gray and streaming light, seemed not to move. Now he could hear the hound too. It was not running. The cry was a high frantic yapping and Boon was running along the edge of the bluff, his old gun leaping and jouncing against his back on its sling made of a piece of cotton plow-line. He whirled and ran up to them, wild-faced, and flung himself onto the mule behind the boy. "That damn boat!" he cried. "It's on the other side! He went straight across! Lion was too close to him! That little hound too! Lion was so close I couldn't shoot! Go on!" he cried, beating his heels into the mule's flanks. "Go on!"

They plunged down the bank, slipping and sliding in the thawed earth, crashing through the willows and into the water. He felt no shock, no cold, he on one side of the swimming mule, grasping the pommel with one hand and holding his gun above the water with the other, Boon opposite him. Sam was behind them somewhere, and then the river, the water about them, was full of dogs. They swam faster than the mules; they were scrabbling up the bank before the mules touched bottom. Major de Spain was whooping from the bank they had just left and, looking back, he saw Tennie's Jim and the horse as they went into the water.

Now the woods ahead of them and the rain-heavy air were one uproar. It rang and clamored; it echoed and broke against the bank behind them and reformed and clamored and rang until it seemed to the boy that all the hounds which had ever bayed game in this land were yelling down at him. He got his leg over the mule as it came up out of the water. Boon didn't try to mount again. He grasped one stirrup as they went up the bank and crashed through the undergrowth which fringed the bluff and saw the bear, on its hind feet, its back against a tree while the bellowing hounds swirled around it and once more Lion drove in, leaping clear of the ground.

This time the bear didn't strike him down. It caught the dog in both arms, almost lover-like, and they both went down. He was off the mule now. He drew back both hammers of the gun but he could see nothing but moiling spotted houndbodies until the bear surged up again. Boon was yelling something, he could not tell what; he could see Lion still clinging to the bear's throat and he saw the bear, half erect, strike one of the hounds with one paw and hurl it five or six feet and then, rising and rising as though it would never stop, stand erect again and begin to rake at Lion's belly with its forepaws. Then Boon was running. The boy saw the gleam of the blade in his hand and watched him leap among the hounds, hurdling them, kicking them aside as he ran, and fling himself astride the bear as he had hurled himself onto the mule, his legs locked around the bear's belly, his left arm under the bear's throat where Lion clung, and the glint of the knife as it rose and fell.

It fell just once. For an instant they almost resembled a piece of statuary: the clinging dog, the bear, the man astride its back, working and probing the buried blade. Then they went down, pulled over backward by Boon's weight, Boon underneath. It was the bear's back which reappeared first but at once Boon was astride it again. He had never released the knife and again the boy saw the almost infinitesimal movement of his arm and shoulder as he probed and sought; then the bear surged erect, raising with it the man and the dog too, and turned and still carrying the man and the dog it took two or three steps toward the woods on its hind feet as a man would have walked and crashed down. It didn't collapse, crumple. It fell all of a piece, as a tree falls, so that all three of them, man, dog, and bear, seemed to bounce once.

He and Tennie's Jim ran forward. Boon was kneeling at the bear's head. His left ear was shredded, his left coat sleeve was completely gone, his right boot had been ripped from knee to instep; the bright blood thinned in the thin rain down his leg and hand and arm and down the side of his face which was no longer wild but was quite calm. Together they prized Lion's jaws from the bear's throat. "Easy, goddamn it," Boon said. "Can't you see his guts are all out of him?" He began to remove his coat. He spoke to Tennie's Jim in that calm voice: "Bring the boat up. It's about a hundred yards down the bank there. I saw it." Tennie's Jim rose and went away. Then, and he could not remember if it had been a call or an exclamation from Tennie's Jim or if he had glanced up by chance, he saw Tennie's Jim stooping and saw Sam Fathers lying motionless on his face in the trampled mud.

The mule had not thrown him. He remembered that Sam was down too even before Boon began to run. There was no mark on him whatever and when he and Boon turned him over, his eyes were open and he said something in that tongue which he and Joe Baker had used to speak together. But he couldn't move. Tennie's Jim brought the skiff up; they could hear him shouting to Major de Spain across the river. Boon wrapped Lion in his hunting coat and carried him down to the skiff and they carried Sam down and returned and hitched the bear to the one-eyed mule's saddle-bow with Tennie's Jim's leash-thong and dragged him down to the skiff and got him into it and left Tennie's Jim to swim the horse and the two mules back across. Major de Spain caught the bow of the skiff as Boon jumped out and past him before it touched the bank. He looked at Old Ben and said quietly: "Well." Then he walked into the water and leaned down and touched Sam and Sam looked up at him and said something in that old tongue he and Joe Baker spoke. "You dont know what happened?" Major de Spain said.

"No, sir," the boy said. "It wasn't the mule. It wasn't anything. He was off the mule when Boon ran in on the bear. Then we looked up and he was lying on the ground." Boon was shouting at Tennie's Jim, still in the middle of the river.

"Come on, goddam it!" he said. "Bring me that mule!"

"What do you want with a mule?" Major de Spain said.

Boon didn't even look at him. "I'm going to Hoke's to get the doctor," he said in that calm voice, his face quite calm beneath the steady thinning of the bright blood.

"You need a doctor yourself," Major de Spain said. "Tennie's Jim—"

"Damn that," Boon said. He turned on Major de Spain. His face was still calm, only his voice was a pitch higher. "Can't you see his goddamn guts are all out of him?"

"Boon!" Major de Spain said. They looked at one another. Boon was a good head taller than Major de Spain; even the boy was taller now than Major de Spain.

"I've got to get the doctor," Boon said. "His goddamn guts—"

"All right," Major de Spain said. Tennie's Jim came up out of the water. The horse and the sound mule had already scented Old Ben; they surged and plunged all the way up to the top of the bluff, dragging Tennie's Jim with them, before he could stop them and tie them and come back. Major de Spain unlooped the leather thong of his compass from his button-hole and gave it to Tennie's Jim. "Go straight to Hoke's," he said. "Bring Doctor Crawford back with you. Tell him there are two men to be looked at. Take my mare. Can you find the road from here?"

"Yes, sir," Tennie's Jim said.

"All right," Major de Spain said. "Go on." He turned to the boy. "Take the mules and the horse and go back and get the wagon. We'll go on down the river in the boat to Coon bridge. Meet us there. Can you find it again?"

"Yes, sir," the boy said.

"All right. Get started."

He went back to the wagon. He realised then how far they had run. It was already afternoon when he put the mules into the traces and tied the horse's lead-rope to the tail-gate. He reached Coon bridge at dusk. The skiff was already there. Before he could see it and almost before he could see the water he had to leap from the tilting wagon, still holding the reins, and work around to where he could grasp the bit and then the ear of the plunging sound mule and dig his heels and hold it until Boon came up the bank. The rope of the led horse had already snapped and it had already disappeared up the road toward camp. They turned the wagon around and took the mules out and he led the sound mule a hundred yards up the road and tied it. Boon had already brought Lion up to the wagon and Sam was sitting up in the skiff now and when they raised him he tried to walk, up the bank and to the wagon and he tried to climb into the wagon but Boon did not wait; he picked Sam up bodily and set him on the seat. Then they hitched Old Ben to the one-eyed mule's saddle again and dragged him up the bank and set two skid-poles into the open tail-gate and got him into the wagon and he went and got the sound mule and Boon fought it into the traces, striking it across its hard hollow-sounding face until it came into position and stood trembling. Then the rain came down, as though it had held off all day waiting on them.

They returned to camp through it, through the streaming and sightless dark, hearing long before they saw any light the horn and the spaced shots to guide them. When they came to Sam's dark little hut he tried to stand up. He spoke again in the tongue of the old fathers; then he said clearly: "Let me out. Let me out."

"He hasn't got any fire," Major said. "Go on!" he said sharply.

But Sam was struggling now, trying to stand up. "Let me out, master," he said. "Let me go home."

So he stopped the wagon and Boon got down and lifted Sam out. He did not wait to let Sam try to walk this time. He carried him into the hut and Major de Spain got light on a paper spill from the buried embers on the hearth and lit the lamp and Boon put Sam on his bunk and drew off his boots and Major de Spain covered him and the boy was not there, he was holding the mules, the sound one which was trying again to bolt since when the wagon stopped Old Ben's scent drifted forward again along the streaming blackness of air, but Sam's eyes were probably open again on that profound look which saw further than them or the hut, further than the death of a bear and the dying of a dog. Then they went on, toward the long wailing of the horn and the shots which seemed each to linger intact somewhere in the thick streaming air until the next spaced report joined and blended with it, to the lighted house, the bright streaming windows, the quiet faces as Boon entered, bloody and quite calm, carrying the bundled coat. He laid Lion, blood coat and all, on his stale sheetless pallet bed which not even Ash, as deft in the house as a woman, could ever make smooth.

The sawmill doctor from Hoke's was already there. Boon would not let the doctor touch him until he had seen to Lion. He wouldn't risk giving Lion chloroform. He put the entrails back and sewed him up without it while Major de Spain held his head and Boon his feet. But he never tried to move. He lay there, the yellow eyes open upon nothing while the quiet men in the new hunting clothes and in the old ones crowded into the little airless room rank with the smell of Boon's body and garments, and watched. Then the doctor cleaned and disinfected Boon's face and arm and leg and bandaged them and, the boy in front with a lantern and the doctor and McCaslin and Major de Spain and General Compson following, they went to Sam Fathers' hut. Tennie's Jim had built up the fire; he squatted before it, dozing. Sam had not moved since Boon had put him in the bunk and Major de Spain had covered him with the blankets, yet he opened his eyes and looked from one to another of the faces and when McCaslin touched his shoulder and said, "Sam. The doctor wants to look at you," he even drew his hands out of the blanket and began to fumble at his shirt buttons until McCaslin said, "Wait. We'll do it." They undressed him. He lay there—the copper-brown, almost hairless body, the old man's body, the old man, the wild man not even one generation from the woods, childless, kinless, peopleless—motionless, his eyes open but no longer looking at any of them, while the doctor examined him and drew the blankets up and put the stethoscope back into his bag and snapped the bag and only the boy knew that Sam too was going to die.

"Exhaustion," the doctor said. "Shock maybe. A man his age swimming rivers in December. He'll be all right. Just make him stay in bed for a day or two. Will there be somebody here with him?"

"There will be somebody here," Major de Spain said.

They went back to the house, to the rank little room where Boon still sat on the pallet bed with Lion's head under his hand while the men, the ones who had hunted behind Lion and the ones who had never seen him before today, came quietly in to look at him and went away. Then it was dawn and they all went out into the yard to look at Old Ben, with his eyes open too and his lips snarled back from his worn teeth and his mutilated foot and the little hard lumps under his skin which were the old bullets (there were fifty-two of them, buckshot rifle and ball) and the single almost invisible slit under his left shoulder where Boon's blade had finally found his life. Then Ash began to beat on the bottom of the dishpan with a heavy spoon to call them to breakfast and it was the first time he could remember hearing no sound from the dogs under the kitchen while they were eating. It was as if the old bear, even dead there in the yard, was a more potent terror still than they could face without Lion between them.

The rain had stopped during the night. By midmorning the thin sun appeared, rapidly burning away mist and cloud, warming the air and the earth; it would be one of those windless Mississippi December days which are a sort of Indian summer's Indian summer. They moved Lion out to the front gallery, into the sun. It was Boon's idea. "Goddamn it," he said, "he never did want to stay in the house until I made him. You know that." He took a crowbar and loosened the floor boards under his pallet bed so it could be raised, mattress and all, without disturbing Lion's position, and they carried him out to the gallery and put him down facing the woods.

Then he and the doctor and McCaslin and Major de Spain went to Sam's hut. This time Sam didn't open his eyes and his breathing was so quiet, so peaceful that they could hardly see that he breathed. The doctor didn't even take out his stethoscope nor even touch him. "He's all right," the doctor said. "He didn't even catch cold. He just quit."

"Quit?" McCaslin said.

"Yes. Old people do that sometimes. Then they get a good night's sleep or maybe it's just a drink of whisky, and they change their minds."

They returned to the house. And then they began to arrive—the swamp-dwellers, the gaunt men who ran trap-lines and lived on quinine and coons and river water, the farmers of little corn- and cotton-patches along the bottom's edge whose fields and cribs and pig-pens the old bear had rifled, the loggers from the camp and the sawmill men from Hoke's and the town men from further away than that, whose hounds the old bear had slain and whose traps and deadfalls he had wrecked and whose lead he carried. They came up mounted and on foot and in wagons, to enter the yard and look at him and then go on to the front where Lion lay, filling the little yard and overflowing it until there were almost a hundred of them squatting and standing in the warm and drowsing sunlight, talking quietly of hunting, of the game and the dogs which ran it, of hounds and bear and deer and men of yesterday vanished from the earth, while from time to time the great blue dog would open his eyes, not as if he were listening to them but as though to look at the woods for a moment before closing his eyes again, to remember the woods or to see that they were still there. He died at sundown.

Major de Spain broke camp that night. They carried Lion into the woods, or Boon carried him that is, wrapped in a quilt from his bed, just as he had refused to let anyone else touch Lion yesterday until the doctor got there; Boon carrying Lion, and the boy and General Compson and Walter and still almost fifty of them following with lanterns and lighted pine-knots—men from Hoke's and even further, who would have to ride out of the bottom in the dark, and swampers and trappers who would have to walk even, scattering toward the little hidden huts where they lived. And Boon would let nobody else dig the grave either and lay Lion in it and cover him and then General Compson stood at the head of it while the blaze and smoke of the pine-knots streamed away among the winter branches and spoke as he would have spoken over a man. Then they returned to camp. Major de Spain and McCaslin and Ash had rolled and tied all the bedding. The mules were hitched to the wagon and pointed out of the bottom and the wagon was already loaded and the stove in the kitchen was cold and the table was set with scraps of cold food and bread and only the coffee was hot when the boy ran into the kitchen where Major de Spain and McCaslin had already eaten. "What?" he cried. "What? I'm not going."

"Yes," McCaslin said, "we're going out tonight. Major wants to get on back home."

"No!" he said. "I'm going to stay."

"You've got to be back in school Monday. You've already missed a week more than I intended. It will take you from now until Monday to catch up. Sam's all right. You heard Doctor Crawford. I'm going to leave Boon and Tennie's Jim both to stay with him until he feels like getting up."

He was panting. The others had come in. He looked rapidly and almost frantically around at the other faces. Boon had a fresh bottle. He upended it and started the cork by striking the bottom of the bottle with the heel of his hand and drew the cork with his teeth and spat it out and drank. "You're damn right you're going back to school," Boon said. "Or I'll burn the tail off of you myself if Cass dont, whether you are sixteen or sixty. Where in hell do you expect to get without education? Where would Cass be? Where in hell would I be if I hadn't never went to school?"

He looked at McCaslin again. He could feel his breath coming shorter and shorter and shallower and shallower, as if there were not enough air in the kitchen for that many to breathe. "This is just Thursday. I'll come home Sunday night on one of the horses. I'll come home Sunday, then. I'll make up the time I lost studying Sunday night, McCaslin," he said, without even despair.

"No, I tell you," McCaslin said. "Sit down here and eat your supper. We're going out to—"

"Hold up, Cass," General Compson said. The boy did not know General Compson had moved until he put his hand on his shoulder. "What is it, bud?" he said.

"I've got to stay," he said. "I've got to."

"All right," General Compson said. "You can stay. If missing an extra week of school is going to throw you so far behind you'll have to sweat to find out what some hired pedagogue put between the covers of a book, you better quit altogether.—And you shut up, Cass," he said, though McCaslin had not spoken. "You've got one foot straddled into a farm and the other foot straddled into a bank; you aint even got a good hand-hold where this boy was already an old man long before you damned Sartorises and Edmondses invented farms and banks to keep yourselves from having to find out this boy was born knowing and fearing too maybe but without being afraid, that could go ten miles on a compass because he wanted to look at a bear none of us had ever got near enough to put a bullet in and looked at the bear and came the ten miles back on the compass in the dark; maybe by God that's the why and the wherefore of farms and banks.—I reckon you still aint going to tell what it is?"

But still he could not. "I've got to stay," he said.

"All right," General Compson said. "There's plenty of grub left. And you'll come home Sunday, like you promised McCaslin? Not Sunday night: Sunday."

"Yes, sir," he said.

"All right," General Compson said. "Sit down and eat, boys," he said. "Let's get started. It's going to be cold before we get home."

They ate. The wagon was already loaded and ready to depart; all they had to do was to get into it. Boon would drive them out to the road, to the farmer's stable where the surrey had been left. He stood beside the wagon, in silhouette on the sky, turbaned like a Paythan and taller than any there, the bottle tilted. Then he flung it, spinning and glinting in the faint starlight, empty. "Them that's going," he said, "get in the goddamn wagon. Them that aint, get out of the goddamn way." The others got in. Boon mounted to the seat beside General Compson and the wagon moved, on into the obscurity until the boy could no longer see it, even the moving density of it amid the greater night. But he could still hear it, for a long while: the slow deliberate banging of the wooden frame as it lurched from rut to rut. And he could hear Boon even when he could no longer hear the wagon. He was singing, harsh, tuneless, loud.

That was Thursday. On Saturday morning Tennie's Jim left on McCaslin's woods-horse which had not been out of the bottom one time now in six years, and late that afternoon rode through the gate on the spent horse and on to the commissary where McCaslin was rationing the tenants and the wage-hands for the coming week, and this time McCaslin forestalled any necessity or risk of having to wait while Major de Spain's surrey was being horsed and harnessed. He took their own, and with Tennie's Jim already asleep in the back seat he drove in to Jefferson and waited while Major de Spain changed to boots and put on his overcoat, and they drove the thirty miles in the dark of that night and at daybreak on Sunday morning they swapped to the waiting mare and mule and as the sun rose they rode out of the jungle and onto the low ridge where they had buried Lion: the low mound of unannealed earth where Boon's spade-marks still showed, and beyond the grave the platform of freshly cut saplings bound between four posts and the blanket-wrapped bundle upon the platform and Boon and the boy squatting between the platform and the grave until Boon, the bandage removed, ripped from his head so that the long scoriations of Old Ben's claws resembled crusted tar in the sunlight, sprang up and threw down upon them with the old gun with which he had never been known to hit anything although McCaslin was already off the mule, kicked both feet free of the irons and vaulted down before the mule had stopped, walking toward Boon.

"Stand back," Boon said. "By God, you wont touch him. Stand back, McCaslin." Still McCaslin came on, fast yet without haste.

"Cass!" Major de Spain said. Then he said, "Boon! You, Boon!" and he was down too and the boy rose too, quickly, and still McCaslin came on not fast but steady and walked up to the grave and reached his hand steadily out, quickly yet still not fast, and took hold the gun by the middle so that he and Boon faced one another across Lion's grave, both holding the gun, Boon's spent indomitable amazed and frantic face almost a head higher than McCaslin's beneath the black scoriations of beast's claws and then Boon's chest began to heave as though there were not enough air in all the woods, in all the wilderness, for all of them, for him and anyone else, even for him alone.

"Turn it loose, Boon," McCaslin said.

"You damn little spindling—" Boon said. "Dont you know I can take it away from you? Dont you know I can tie it around your neck like a damn cravat?"

"Yes," McCaslin said. "Turn it loose, Boon."

"This is the way he wanted it. He told us. He told

us exactly how to do it. And by God you aint going to move him. So we did it like he said, and I been sitting here ever since to keep the damn wildcats and varmints away from him and by God—" Then McCaslin had the gun, downslanted while he pumped the slide, the five shells snicking out of it so fast that the last one was almost out before the first one touched the ground and McCaslin dropped the gun behind him without once having taken his eyes from Boon's.

"Did you kill him, Boon?" he said. Then Boon moved. He turned, he moved like he was still drunk and then for a moment blind too, one hand out as he blundered toward the big tree and seemed to stop walking before he reached the tree so that he plunged, fell toward it, flinging up both hands and catching himself against the tree and turning until his back was against it, backing with the tree's trunk his wild spent scoriated face and the tremendous heave and collapse of his chest, McCaslin following, facing him again, never once having moved his eyes from Boon's eyes. "Did you kill him, Boon?"

"No!" Boon said. "No!"

"Tell the truth," McCaslin said. "I would have done it if he had asked me to." Then the boy moved. He was between them, facing McCaslin; the water felt as if it had burst and sprung not from his eyes alone but from his whole face, like sweat.

"Leave him alone!" he cried. "Goddamn it! Leave him alone!"

4

[The long Part 4, omitted here, moves ahead in time to Ike McCaslin's twenty-first year when he refuses to inherit the property bequeathed to him by his grandfather, Carothers McCaslin, because it is stained by the guilt of slavery and mixed blood. Ike broods over his family history, the sufferings of mulatto kindred and descendants of Carothers McCaslin who were bought and sold and freed and who suffered with their freedom, his father and uncle who likewise refused to live in the family mansion. He recalls his marriage which was tainted by his wife's desire for the property he has disclaimed. In this section Faulkner appears to draw a parallel between the fall of man, his loss of Eden, and the sin of the McCaslin family and indeed of the South as a whole. "Don't you see? This whole land, the whole South, is cursed, and all of us who derive from it, whom it ever suckled, white and black both, lie under the curse?" Ike's relinquishment of his lands, the wisdom learned from the wilderness, may be a beginning of a slow regeneration.]

5

He went back to the camp one more time before the lumber company moved in and began to cut the timber. Major de Spain himself never saw it again. But he made them welcome to use the house and hunt the land whenever they liked, and in the winter following the last hunt when Sam Fathers and Lion died, General Compson and Walter Ewell invented a plan to corporate themselves, the old group, into a club and lease the camp and the hunting privileges of the woods—an invention doubtless of the somewhat childish old General but actually worthy of Boon Hogganbeck himself. Even the boy, listening, recognised it for the subterfuge it was: to change the leopard's spots when they could not alter the leopard, a baseless and illusory hope to which even McCaslin seemed to subscribe for a while, that once they had persuaded Major de Spain to return to the camp he might revoke himself, which even the boy knew he would not do. And he did not. The boy never knew what occurred when Major de Spain declined. He was not present when the subject was broached and McCaslin never told him. But when June came and the time for the double birthday celebration there was no mention of it and when November came no one spoke of using Major de Spain's house and he never knew whether or not Major de Spain knew they were going on the hunt though without doubt old Ash probably told him: he and McCaslin and General Compson (and that one was the General's last hunt too) and Walter and Boon and Tennie's Jim and old Ash loaded two wagons and drove two days and almost forty miles beyond any country the boy had ever seen before and lived in tents for the two weeks. And the next spring they heard (not from Major de Spain) that he had sold the timber-rights to a Memphis lumber company and in June the boy came to town with McCaslin one Saturday and went to Major de Spain's office—the big, airy, book-lined, second-storey room with windows at one end opening upon the shabby hinder purlieus of stores and at the other a door giving onto the railed balcony above the Square, with its curtained alcove where sat a cedar water-bucket and a sugar-bowl and spoon and tumbler and a wicker-covered demijohm of whisky, and the bamboo-and-paper punkah swinging back and forth above the desk while old Ash in a tilted chair beside the entrance pulled the cord.

"Of course," Major de Spain said. "Ash will probably like to get off in the woods himself for a while, where he wont have to eat Daisy's cooking. Complain about it, anyway. Are you going to take anybody with you?"

"No sir," he said. "I thought that maybe Boon—" For six months now Boon had been town-marshal at Hoke's; Major de Spain had compounded with the lumber company—or perhaps compromised was closer, since it was the lumber company who had decided that Boon might be better as a town-marshal than head of a logging gang.

"Yes," Major de Spain said. "I'll wire him today. He can meet you at Hoke's. I'll send Ash on by the train and they can take some food in and all you will have to do will be to mount your horse and ride over."

"Yes sir," he said. "Thank you." And he heard his voice again. He didn't know he was going to say it yet he did know, he had known it all the time: "Maybe if you . . ." His voice died. It was stopped, he never knew how because Major de Spain did not speak and it was not until his voice ceased that Major de Spain moved, turned back to the desk and the papers spread on it and even that without moving because he was sitting at the desk with a paper in his hand when the boy entered, the boy standing there looking down at the short plumpish gray-haired man in sober fine broadcloth and an immaculate glazed shirt whom he was used to seeing in boots and muddy corduroy, unshaven, sitting the shaggy powerful long-hocked mare with the worn Winchester carbine across the saddlebow and the great blue dog standing motionless as bronze at the stirrup, the two of them in that last year and to the boy anyway coming to resemble one another somehow as two people competent for love or for business who have been in love or in business together for a long time sometimes do. Major de Spain did not look up again.

"No. I will be too busy. But good luck to you. If you have it, you might bring me a young squirrel."

"Yes sir," he said. "I will."

He rode his mare, the three-year-old filly he had bred and raised and broken himself. He left home a little after midnight and six hours later, without even having sweated her, he rode into Hoke's, the tiny log-line junction which he had always thought of as Major de Spain's property too although Major de Spain had merely sold the company (and that many years ago) the land on which the sidetracks and loading-platforms and the commissary store stood, and looked about in shocked and grieved amazement even though he had had forewarning and had believed himself prepared: a new planing-mill already half completed which would cover two or three acres and what looked like miles and miles of stacked steel rails red with the light bright rust of newness and of piled crossties sharp with creosote, and wire corrals and feeding-troughs for two hundred mules at least and the tents for the men who drove them; so that he arranged for the care and stabling of his mare as rapidly as he could and did not look any more, mounted into the log-train caboose with his gun and climbed into the cupola and looked no more save toward the wall of wilderness ahead within which he would be able to hide himself from it once more anyway.

Then the little locomotive shrieked and began to move: a rapid churning of exhaust, a lethargic deliberate clashing of slack couplings traveling backward along the train, the exhaust changing to the deep slow clapping bites of power as the caboose too began to move and from the cupola he watched the train's head complete the first and only curve in the entire line's length and vanish into the wilderness, dragging its length of train behind it so that it resembled a small dingy harmless snake vanishing into weeds, drawing him with it too until soon it ran once more at its maximum clattering speed between the twin walls of unaxed wilderness as of old. It had been harmless once. Not five years ago Walter Ewell had shot a six-point buck from this same moving caboose, and there was the story of the half-grown bear: the train's first trip in to the cutting thirty miles away, the bear between the rails, its rear end elevated like that of a playing puppy while it dug to see what sort of ants or bugs they might contain or perhaps just to examine the curious symmetrical squared barkless logs which had appeared apparently from nowhere in one endless mathematical line overnight, still digging until the driver on the braked engine not fifty feet away blew the whistle at it, whereupon it broke frantically and took the first tree it came to: an ash sapling not much bigger than a man's thigh and climbed as high as it could and clung there, its head ducked between its arms as a man (a woman perhaps) might have done while the brakeman threw chunks of ballast at it, and when the engine returned three hours later with the first load of outbound logs the bear was halfway down the tree and once more scrambled back up as high as it could and clung again while the train passed and was still there when the engine went in again in the afternoon and still there when it came back out at dusk; and Boon had been in Hoke's with the wagon after a barrel of flour that noon when the train-crew told about it and Boon and Ash, both twenty years younger then, sat under the tree all that night to keep anybody from shooting it and the next morning Major de Spain had the log-train held at Hoke's and just before sundown on the second day, with not only Boon and Ash but Major de Spain and General Compson and Walter and McCaslin, twelve then, watching, it came down the tree after almost thirty-six hours without even water and McCaslin told him how for a minute they thought it was going to stop right there at the barrow-pit where they were standing and drink, how it looked at the water and paused and looked at them and at the water again, but did not, gone, running, as bears run, the two sets of feet, front and back, tracking two separate though parallel courses.

It had been harmless then. They would hear the passing log-train sometimes from the camp; sometimes, because nobody bothered to listen for it or not. They would hear it going in, running light and fast, the light clatter of the trucks, the exhaust of the diminutive locomotive and its shrill peanut-parcher whistle flung for one petty moment and absorbed by the brooding and inattentive wilderness without even an echo. They would hear it going out, loaded, not quite so fast now yet giving its frantic and toylike illusion of crawling speed, not whistling now to conserve steam, flinging its bitten laboring miniature puffing into the immemorial woodsface with frantic and bootless vainglory, empty and noisy and puerile, carrying to no destination or purpose sticks which left nowhere any scar or stump as the child's toy loads and transports and unloads its dead sand and rushes back for more, tireless and unceasing and rapid yet never quite so fast as the Hand which plays with it moves the toy burden back to load the toy again. But it was different now. It was the same train, engine cars and caboose, even the same enginemen brakeman and conductor to whom Boon, drunk then sober then drunk again then fairly sober once more all in the space of fourteen hours, had bragged that day two years ago about what they were going to do to Old Ben tomorrow, running with its same illusion of frantic rapidity between the same twin walls of impenetrable and impervious woods, passing the old landmarks, the old game crossings over which he had trailed bucks wounded and not wounded and more than once seen them, anything but wounded, bolt out of the woods and up and across the embankment which bore the rails and ties then down and into the woods again as the earth-bound supposedly move but crossing as arrows travel, groundless, elongated, three times its actual length and even paler, different in color, as if there were a point between immobility and absolute motion where even mass chemically altered, changing without pain or agony not only in bulk and shape but in color too, approaching the color of wind, yet this time it was as though the train (and not only the train but himself, not only his vision which had seen it and his memory which remembered it but his clothes too, as garments carry back into the clean edgeless blowing of air the lingering effluvium of a sick-room or of death) had brought with it into the doomed wilderness even before the actual axe the shadow and portent of the new mill not even finished yet and the rails and ties which were not even laid; and he knew now what he had known as soon as he saw Hoke's this morning but had not yet thought into words: why Major de Spain had not come back, and that after this time he himself, who had had to see it one time other, would return no more.

Now they were near. He knew it before the engine-driver whistled to warn him. Then he saw Ash and the wagon, the reins without doubt wrapped once more about the brake-lever as within the boy's own memory Major de Spain had been forbidding him for eight years to do, the train slowing, the slackened couplings jolting and clashing again from car to car, the caboose slowing past the wagon as he swung down with his gun, the conductor leaning out above him to signal the engine, the caboose still slowing, creeping, although the engine's exhaust was already slatting in mounting tempo against the unechoing wilderness, the crashing of drawbars once more traveling backward along the train, the caboose picking up speed at last. Then it was gone. It had not been. He could no longer hear it. The wilderness soared, musing, inattentive, myriad, eternal, green; older than any mill-shed, longer than any spurline. "Mr. Boon here yet?" he said.

"He beat me in," Ash said. "Had the wagon loaded and ready for me at Hoke's yistiddy when I got there and setting on the front steps at camp last night when I got in. He already been in the woods since fo daylight this morning. Said he gwine up to the Gum Tree and for you to hunt up that way and meet him." He knew where that was: a single big sweet-gum just outside the woods, in an old clearing; if you crept up to it very quietly this time of year and then ran suddenly into the clearing, sometimes you caught as many as a dozen squirrels in it, trapped, since there was no other tree near they could jump to. So he didn't get into the wagon at all.

"I will," he said.

"I figured you would," Ash said, "I fotch you a box of shells." He passed the shells down and began to unwrap the lines from the brake-pole.

"How many times up to now do you reckon Major has told you not to do that?" the boy said.

"Do which?" Ash said. Then he said: "And tell Boon Hogganbeck dinner gonter be on the table in a hour and if yawl want any to come on and eat it."

"In an hour?" he said. "It aint nine oclock yet." He drew out his watch and extended it face-toward Ash. "Look." Ash didn't even look at the watch.

"That's town time. You aint in town now. You in the woods."

"Look at the sun then."

"Nemmine the sun too," Ash said. "If you and Boon Hogganbeck want any dinner, you better come on in and get it when I tole you. I aim to get done in that kitchen because I got my wood to chop. And watch your feet. They're crawling."

"I will," he said.

Then he was in the woods, not alone but solitary; the solitude closed about him, green with summer. They did not change, and, timeless, would not, any more than would the green of summer and the fire and rain of fall and the iron cold and sometimes even snow

The day, the morning when he killed the buck and Sam marked his face with its hot blood, they returned to camp and he remembered old Ash's blinking and disgruntled and even outraged disbelief until at last McCaslin had had to affirm the fact that he had really killed it: and that night Ash sat snarling and unapproachable behind the stove so that Tennie's Jim had to serve the supper and waked them with breakfast already on the table the next morning and it was only half-past one oclock and at last out of Major de Spain's angry cursing and Ash's snarling and sullen rejoinders the fact emerged that Ash not only wanted to go into the woods and shoot a deer also but be intended to and Major de Spain said, "By God, if we dont let him we will probably have to do the cooking from now on:" and Walter Ewell said, "Or get up at midnight to eat what Ash cooks:" and since he had already killed his buck for this hunt and was not to shoot again unless they needed meat, he offered his gun to Ash until Major de Spain took command and allotted that gun to Boon for the day and gave Boon's unpredictable pump gun to Ash, with two buckshot shells but Ash said, "I got shells:" and showed them, four: one buck, one of number three shot for rabbits, two of bird-shot and told one by one their history and their origin and he remembered not Ash's face alone but Major de Spain's and Walter's and General Compson's too, and Ash's voice: "Shoot? In course they'll shoot! Genl Cawmpson guv me this un"—the buckshot—"right outen the same gun he kilt that big buck with eight years ago. And this un"—it was rabbit shell: triumphantly——"is oldern thisyer boy!" And that morning he loaded the gun himself, reversing the order: the bird-shot, the rabbit, then the buck so that the buckshot would feed first into the chamber, and himself without a gun, he and Ash walked beside Major de Spain's and Tennie's Jim's horses and the dogs (that was the snow) until they cast and struck, the sweet strong cries ringing away into the muffled falling air and gone almost immediately, as if the constant and unmurmuring flakes had already buried even the unformed echoes beneath their myriad and weightless falling, Major de Spain and Tennie's Jim gone too, whooping on into the woods; and then it was all right, he knew as plainly as if Ash had told him that Ash had now hunted his deer and that even his tender years had been forgiven for having killed one, and they turned back toward home through the falling snow—that is, Ash said, "Now whut?" and he said, "This way"—himself in front because, although they were less than a mile from camp, he knew that Ash, who had spent two weeks of his life in the camp each year for the last twenty, had no idea whatever where they were, until quite soon the manner in which Ash carried Boon's gun was making him a good deal more than just nervous and he made Ash walk in front, striding on, talking now, an old man's garrulous monologue beginning with where he was at the moment then of the woods and of camping in the woods and of eating in camps then of eating then of cooking it and of his wife's cooking then briefly of his old wife and almost at once and at length of a new light-colored woman who nursed next door to Major de Spain's and if she didn't watch out who she was switching her tail at he would show her how old was an old man or not if his wife just didn't watch him all the time, the two of them in a game trail through a dense brake of cane and brier which would bring them out within a quarter-mile of camp, approaching a big fallen tree-trunk lying athwart the path and just as Ash, still talking, was about to step over it the bear, the yearling, rose suddenly beyond the log, sitting up, its forearms against its chest and its wrists limply arrested as if it had been surprised in the act of covering its face to pray: and after a certain time Ash's gun yawed jerkily up and he said, "You haven't got a shell in the barrel yet. Pump it:" but the gun already snicked and he said, "Pump it. You haven't got a shell in the barrel yet:" and Ash pumped the action and in a certain time the gun steadied again and snicked and he said, "Pump it:" and watched the buckshot shell jerk, spinning heavily, into the cane. This is the rabbit shot: he thought and the gun snicked and he thought: The next is bird-shot: and he didn't have to say Pump it; he cried, "Dont shoot! Dont shoot!" but that was already too late too, the light dry vicious snick! before he could speak and the bear turned and dropped to all-fours and then was gone and there was only the log, the cane, the velvet and constant snow and Ash said, "Now whut?" and he said, "This way. Come on:" and began to back away down the path and Ash said, "I got to find my shells:" and he said, "Goddamn it, goddamn it, come on:" but Ash leaned the gun against the log and returned and stooped and fumbled among the cane roots until he came back and stooped and found the shells and they rose and at that moment the gun, untouched, leaning against the log six feet away and for that while even forgotten by both of them, roared, bellowed and flamed, and ceased: and he carried it now, pumped out the last mummified shell and gave that one also to Ash and, the action still open, himself carried the gun until he stood it in the corner behind Boon's bed at the camp

—; summer, and fall, and snow, and wet and saprife spring in their ordered immortal sequence, the deathless and immemorial phases of the mother who had shaped him if any had toward the man he almost was, mother and father both to the old man born of a Negro slave and a Chickasaw chief who had been his spirit's father if any had, whom he had revered and harkened to and loved and lost and grieved: and he would marry someday and they too would own for their brief while that brief unsubstanced glory which inherently of itself cannot last and hence why glory: and they would, might, carry even the remembrance of it into the time when flesh no longer talks to flesh because memory at least does last: but still the woods would be his mistress and his wife.

He was not going toward the Gum Tree. Actually he was getting farther from it. Time was and not so long ago either when he would not have been allowed here without someone with him, and a little later, when he had begun to learn how much he did not know, he would not have dared be here without someone with him, and later still, beginning to ascertain, even if only dimly, the limits of what he did not know, he could have attempted and carried it through with a compass, not because of any increased belief in himself but because McCaslin and Major de Spain and Walter and General Compson too had taught him at last to believe the compass regardless of what it seemed to state. Now he did not even use the compass but merely the sun and that only subconsciously, yet he could have taken a scaled map and plotted at any time to within a hundred feet of where he actually was; and sure enough, at almost the exact moment when he expected it, the earth began to rise faintly, he passed one of the four concrete markers set down by the lumber company's surveyor to establish the four corners of the plot which Major de Spain had reserved out of the sale, then he stood on the crest of the knoll itself, the four corner-markers all visible now, blanched still even beneath the winter's weathering, lifeless and shockingly alien in that place where dissolution itself was a seething turmoil of ejaculation tumescence conception and birth, and death did not even exist. After two winters' blanketings of leaves and the flood-waters of two springs, there was no trace of the two graves any more at all. But those who would have come this far to find them would not need headstones but would have found them as Sam Fathers himself had taught him to find such: by bearings on trees: and did, almost the first thrust of the hunting knife finding (but only to see if it was still there) the round tin box manufactured for axle-grease and containing now Old Ben's dried mutilated paw, resting above Lion's bones.

He didn't disturb it. He didn't even look for the other grave where he and McCaslin and Major de Spain and Boon had laid Sam's body, along with his hunting horn and his knife and his tobacco-pipe, that Sunday morning two years ago; he didn't have to. He had stepped over it, perhaps on it. But that was all right. *He probably knew I was in the woods this morning long before I got here,* he thought, going on to the tree which had supported one end of the platform where Sam lay when McCaslin and Major de Spain found them—the tree, the other axle-grease tin nailed to the trunk, but weathered, rusted, alien too yet healed already into the wilderness' concordant generality, raising no tuneless note, and empty, long since empty of the food and tobacco he had put into it that day, as empty of that as it would presently be of this which he drew from his pocket—the twist of tobacco, the new bandanna handkerchief, the small paper sack of the peppermint candy which Sam had used to love; that gone too, almost before he had turned his back, not vanished but merely translated into the myriad life which printed the dark mold of these secret and sunless places with delicate fairy tracks, which, breathing and biding and immobile, watched him from beyond every twig and leaf until he moved, moving again, walking on; he had not stopped, he had only paused, quitting the knoll which was no abode of the dead because there was no death, not Lion and not Sam: not held fast in earth but free in earth and not in earth but of earth, myriad yet undiffused of every myriad part, leaf and twig and particle, air and sun and rain and dew and night, acorn oak and leaf and acorn again, dark and dawn and dark and dawn again in their immutable progression and, being myriad, one: and Old Ben too, Old Ben too; they would give him his paw back even, certainly they would give him his paw back: then the long challenge and the long chase, no heart to be driven and outraged, no flesh to be mauled and bled—Even as he froze himself, he seemed to hear Ash's parting admonition. He could even hear the voice as he froze, immobile, one foot just taking his weight, the toe of the other just lifted behind him, not breathing, feeling again and as always the sharp shocking inrush from when Isaac McCaslin long yet was not, and so it was fear all right but not fright as he looked down at it. It had not coiled yet and the buzzer had not sounded either, only one thick rapid contraction, one loop cast sideways as though merely for purchase from which the raised head might start slightly backward, not in fright either, not in threat quite yet, more than six feet of it, the head raised higher than his knee and less than his knee's length away, and old, the once-bright markings of its youth dulled now to a monotone concordant too with the wilderness it crawled and lurked: the old one, the ancient and accursed about the earth, fatal and solitary and he could smell it now: the thin sick smell of rotting cucumbers and something else which had no name, evocative of all knowledge and an old weariness and of pariah-hood and of death. At last it moved. Not the head. The elevation of the head did not change as it began to glide away from him, moving erect yet off the perpendicular as if the head and that elevated third were complete and all: an entity walking on two feet and free of all laws of mass and balance and should have been because even now he could not quite believe that all that shift and flow of shadow behind that walking head could have been one snake: going and then gone; he put the other foot down at last and didn't know it, standing with one hand raised as Sam had stood that afternoon six years ago when Sam led him into the wilderness and showed him and he ceased to be a child, speaking the old tongue which Sam had spoken that day without premeditation either: "Chief," he said: "Grandfather."

He couldn't tell when he first began to hear the sound, because when he became aware of it, it seemed to him that he had been already hearing it for several seconds—a sound as though someone were hammering a gun-barrel against a piece of railroad iron, a sound loud and heavy and not rapid yet with something frenzied about it, as the hammerer were not only a strong man and an earnest one but a little hysterical too. Yet it couldn't be on the log-line because, although the track lay in that direction, it was at least two miles from him and this sound was not three hundred yards away. But even as he thought that, he realised where the sound must be coming from: whoever the man was and whatever he was doing, he was somewhere near the edge of the clearing where the Gum Tree was and where he was to meet Boon. So far, he had been hunting as he advanced, moving slowly and quietly and watching the ground and the trees both. Now he went on, his gun unloaded and the barrel slanted up and back to facilitate its passage through brier and undergrowth, approaching as it grew louder and louder that steady savage somehow queerly hysterical beating of metal on metal, emerging from the woods, into the old clearing, with the solitary gum tree directly before him. At first glance the tree seemed to be alive with frantic squirrels. There appeared to be forty or fifty of them leaping and darting from branch to branch until the whole tree had become one green maelstrom of mad leaves, while from time to time, singly or in twos and threes, squirrels would dart down the trunk then whirl without stopping and rush back up again as though sucked violently back by the vacuum of their fellows' frenzied vortex. Then he saw Boon, sitting, his back against the trunk, his head bent, hammering furiously at something on his lap. What he hammered with was the barrel of his dismembered gun, what he hammered at was the breech of it. The rest of the gun lay scattered about him in a half-dozen pieces while he bent over the piece on his lap his scarlet and streaming walnut face, hammering the disjointed barrel against the gun-breech with the frantic abandon of a madman. He didn't even look up to see who it was. Still hammering, he merely shouted back at the boy in a hoarse strangled voice:

"Get out of here! Dont touch them! Dont touch a one of them! They're mine!"

JOHN STEINBECK [1902–1968]

THE SELECTION of Steinbeck in 1962 by the Nobel Prize Committee for Literature in Stockholm came as a surprise to some people who felt that his reputation had reached its peak twenty years earlier and had been in virtual eclipse since the acclaim which followed the appearance in 1939 of *The Grapes of Wrath*. Steinbeck has been labeled a naturalist, a mystic, and a primitive—and he was all three. The Nobel committee noted his total achievement (more than twelve novels, collections of short stories, plays, nonfiction, scientific lore), his sense of joy in life, his vast sympathetic humanity, social perception, and feeling for outcasts and working people.

Steinbeck's artistic goals were always high. Once he withdrew a completed book before publication, knowing it would sell on his name alone, because he sensed it had been a popular "cheat," not written from the heart but "smart and cagy." His best work belongs to the depression decade. It was his special gift to portray the forgotten man who, despite the pressures of industrial civilization, retains the charm of an unspoiled naturalness. In the early thirties he found his special theme and locale—the Mexican-Americans of the Salinas Valley and the little seaport town of Monterey nearby. The "long valley" called by the picturesque Spanish name *Las Pasturas del Cielo* (the pastures of heaven) yielded him the literary material he wanted in the simple, kindly, ill-educated and morally eccentric farmers and fishermen of that community.

Steinbeck was born in Salinas, California. His favorite youthful reading included Malory's *Le Morte d'Arthur*, Dostoevsky's *Crime and Punishment*, and the King James Version of the Bible. He spent four years at Stanford, taking random courses, especially marine biology and Old English, the latter influencing his primitivistic style. In 1925 he took a freighter to New York, worked as a reporter and a bricklayer, then returned to California to write and earn a living at odd jobs: chemist, migratory fruit-picker, caretaker of an estate in the High Sierras—all lonely jobs. For a time he lived on his own small boat, fishing for his food. His first three books attracted little attention, though *The Pastures of Heaven* (1932) first revealed his interest in "simple" uncorrupted children of nature living in a world apart from the established society. This theme carried over to his first successful work, *Tortilla Flat* (1935), a book of sketches of the *paisanos* of the Monterey country whose naive ways, Robin Hood morality, and cheerfulness appealed to his sense of the romantic and the real. Few readers or critics saw that it was a comic burlesque of the Arthurian romances complete with latter-day knights, a battered round-table, and a search for the holy grail. *In Dubious Battle* (1936) was a dramatic account of a strike among California fruit-pickers and a significant proletarian novel of the 1930's. Next came *Of Mice and Men* (1937), successful both as a novel and a play. It won the Drama Critics Award for its season on Broadway and was notable for its portrayal of a huge, half-witted character, Lennie, who recalled Norris's McTeague in his strength and his frustration, a symbol of the "powerful yearning of all men." *The Long Valley* (1938), a group of Steinbeck's finest short fiction, concerned the theme of a young boy growing up into the world of social responsibility and human suffering, a volume comparable to Hemingway's *In Our Time*.

Steinbeck's first phase ended climactically with the monumental and controversial *The Grapes of Wrath* (1939), a kind of *Uncle Tom's Cabin* of the migrant worker. It was a powerful, documented novel of "Okies" traveling westward from the drouth-destroyed farms in Oklahoma to find relief from starvation by picking California fruit. The book caused a national furor, so compelling was its authenticity and its mingling of the harsh and the gentle: readers were shocked and could hardly believe such things existed. This novel, Steinbeck's masterpiece, won a Pulitzer Prize and became a highly successful film.

He continued to write film scripts. During World War II he was a war correspondent in Africa and Italy, and out of this experience he wrote several volumes of nonfiction as well as the strong drama-novel, *The Moon Is Down* (1942), about the Nazi occupation of a Scandinavian country. After 1945 Steinbeck returned to his California setting in *Cannery Row* (1945) and *The Pearl* (1947). These books and *Sweet Thursday* (1954) harked back to his earlier fiction about the unsophisticated people of the long valley whose happy indigence was an effective commentary on the acquisitive world of business and money-making. In his later novels Steinbeck sought to move in a new direction and treat the normal adult world of American society, but both *East of Eden* (1952) and *The Winter of Our Discontent* (1961) had mixed receptions. The former began as a family chronicle and became a too-elaborate allegory of the Cain-Abel theme. The latter adopted a New England setting to make a comment on manners and morals in modern society. More to the popular taste was *Travels with Charley* (1962), a light and amusing documentary based on a cross-country trip in a truck camper with his French poodle, Charley, in search of the essential American character and image.

Always one recognizes Steinbeck's serious purpose, his unflagging productivity, his love of experience, and his epic sense of the American character and the common people during a period of wars and turbulent change. His originality and literary skill are most evident in his discovery of the Salinas Valley as literary material and in the charming *paisanos* of his early and middle periods.

Further reading: *The (Viking) Portable Steinbeck*, ed. Pascal Covici, 1946. *The Short Novels of John Steinbeck*, 1953, new ed. 1963. Warren French, *John Steinbeck*, 1961.

Flight

First printed in *The Long Valley* (1938), from which the text used here is taken.

About fifteen miles below Monterey, on the wild coast, the Torres family had their farm, a few sloping acres above a cliff that dropped to the brown reefs and to the hissing white waters of the ocean. Behind the farm the stone mountains stood up against the sky. The farm buildings huddled like little clinging aphids on the mountain skirts, crouched low to the ground as though the wind might blow them into the sea. The little shack, the rattling, rotting barn were gray-bitten with sea salt, beaten by the damp wind until they had taken on the color of the granite hills. Two horses, a red cow and a red calf, half a dozen pigs and a flock of lean, multicolored chickens stocked the place. A little corn was raised on the sterile slope, and it grew short and thick under the wind, and all the cobs formed on the landward sides of the stalks.

Mama Torres, a lean, dry woman with ancient eyes, had ruled the farm for ten years, ever since her husband tripped over a stone in the field one day and fell full length on a rattlesnake. When one is bitten on the chest there is not much that can be done.

Mama Torres had three children, two undersized black ones of twelve and fourteen, Emilio and Rosy, whom Mama kept fishing on the rocks below the farm when the sea was kind and when the truant officer was in some distant part of Monterey County. And there was Pepé, the tall smiling son of nineteen, a gentle, affectionate boy, but very lazy. Pepé had a tall head, pointed at the top, and from its peak, coarse black hair grew down like a thatch all around. Over his smiling little eyes Mama cut a straight bang so he could see. Pepé had sharp Indian cheek bones and an eagle nose, but his mouth was as sweet and shapely as a girl's mouth, and his chin was fragile and chiseled. He was loose and gangling, all legs and feet and wrists, and he was very lazy. Mama thought him fine and brave, but she never told him so. She said, "Some lazy cow must have got into thy father's family, else how could I have a son like thee." And she said, "When I carried thee, a sneaking lazy coyote came out of the brush and looked at me one day. That must have made thee so."

Pepé smiled sheepishly and stabbed at the ground with his knife to keep the blade sharp and free from rust. It was his inheritance, that knife, his father's knife. The long heavy blade folded back into the black handle. There was a button on the handle. When Pepé pressed the button, the blade leaped out ready for use. The knife was with Pepé always, for it had been his father's knife.

One sunny morning when the sea below the cliff was glinting and blue and the white surf creamed on the reef, when even the stone mountains looked kindly, Mama Torres called out the door of the shack, "Pepé, I have a labor for thee."

There was no answer. Mama listened. From behind the barn she heard a burst of laughter. She lifted her full long skirt and walked in the direction of the noise.

Pepé was sitting on the ground with his back against a box. His white teeth glistened. On either side of him stood the two black ones, tense and expectant. Fifteen feet away a redwood post was set in the ground. Pepé's right hand lay limply in his lap, and in the palm the big black knife rested. The blade was closed back into the handle. Pepé looked smiling at the sky.

Suddenly Emilio cried, "Ya!"

Pepé's wrist flicked like the head of a snake. The blade seemed to fly open in mid-air, and with a thump the point dug into the redwood post, and the black handle quivered. The three burst into excited laughter. Rosy ran to the post and pulled out the knife and brought it back to Pepé. He closed the blade and settled the knife carefully in his listless palm again. He grinned self-consciously at the sky.

"Ya!"

The heavy knife lanced out and sunk into the post again. Mama moved forward like a ship and scattered the play.

"All day you do foolish things with the knife, like a toy-baby," she stormed. "Get up on thy huge feet that eat up shoes. Get up!" She took him by one loose shoulder and hoisted at him. Pepé grinned sheepishly and came half-heartedly to his feet. "Look!" Mama cried. "Big lazy, you must catch the horse and put on him thy father's saddle. You must ride to Monterey. The medicine bottle is empty. There is no salt. Go thou now, Peanut! Catch the horse."

A revolution took place in the relaxed figure of Pepé. "To Monterey, me? Alone? *Sí*, Mama."

She scowled at him. "Do not think, big sheep, that you will buy candy. No, I will give you only enough for the medicine and the salt."

Pepé smiled. "Mama, you will put the hatband on the hat?"

She relented then. "Yes, Pepé. You may wear the hatband."

His voice grew insinuating, "And the green handkerchief, Mama?"

"Yes, if you go quickly and return with no trouble, the silk green handkerchief will go. If you make sure to take off the handkerchief when you eat so no spot may fall on it. . . ."

"*Sí*, Mama. I will be careful. I am a man."

"Thou? A man? Thou art a peanut."

He went into the rickety barn and brought out a rope, and he walked agilely enough up the hill to catch the horse.

When he was ready and mounted before the door, mounted on his father's saddle that was so old that the oaken frame showed through torn leather in many places, then Mama brought out the round black hat with the tooled leather band, and she reached up and knotted the green silk handkerchief about his neck. Pepé's blue denim coat was much darker than his jeans, for it had been washed much less often.

Mama handed up the big medicine bottle and the silver coins. "That for the medicine," she said, "and that for the salt. That for a candle to burn for the papa. That for *dulces* for the little ones. Our friend Mrs. Rodriguez will give you dinner and maybe a bed for the night. When you go to the church say only ten Paternosters and only twenty-five Ave Marias. Oh! I know, big coyote. You would sit there flapping your mouth over Aves all day while you looked at the candles and the holy pictures. That is not good devotion to stare at the pretty things."

The black hat, covering the high pointed head and black thatched hair of Pepé, gave him dignity and age. He sat the rangy horse well. Mama thought how handsome he was, dark and lean and tall. "I would not send thee now alone, thou little one, except for the medicine," she said softly. "It is not good to have no medicine, for who knows when the toothache will come, or the sadness of the stomach. These things are."

"Adios, Mama," Pepé cried. "I will come back soon. You may send me often alone. I am a man."

"Thou art a foolish chicken."

He straightened his shoulders, flipped the reins against the horse's shoulder and rode away. He turned once and saw that they still watched him, Emilio and Rosy and Mama. Pepé grinned with pride and gladness and lifted the tough buckskin horse to a trot.

When he had dropped out of sight over a little dip in the road, Mama turned to the black ones, but she spoke to herself. "He is nearly a man now," she said. "It will be a nice thing to have a man in the house again." Her eyes sharpened on the children. "Go to the rocks now. The tide is going out. There will be abalones to be found." She put the iron hooks into their hands and saw them down the steep trail to the reefs. She brought the smooth stone *metate* to the doorway and sat grinding her corn to flour and looking occasionally at the road over which Pepé had gone. The noonday came and then the afternoon, when the little ones beat the abalones on a rock to make them tender and Mama patted the tortillas to make them thin. They ate their dinner as the red sun was plunging down toward the ocean. They sat on the doorsteps and watched the big white moon come over the mountain tops.

Mama said, "He is now at the house of our friend Mrs. Rodriguez. She will give him nice things to eat and maybe a present."

Emilio said, "Some day I too will ride to Monterey for medicine. Did Pepé come to be a man today?"

Mama said wisely, "A boy gets to be a man when a man is needed. Remember this thing. I have known boys forty years old because there was no need for a man."

Soon afterwards they retired, Mama in her big oak bed on one side of the room, Emilio and Rosy in their boxes full of straw and sheepskins on the other side of the room.

The moon went over the sky and the surf roared on the rocks. The roosters crowed the first call. The surf subsided to a whispering surge against the reef. The moon dropped toward the sea. The roosters crowed again.

The moon was near down to the water when Pepé rode on a winded horse to his home flat. His dog bounced out and circled the horse yelping with pleasure. Pepé slid off the saddle to the ground. The weathered little shack was silver in the moonlight and the square shadow of it was black to the north and east. Against the east the piling mountains were misty with light; their tops melted into the sky.

Pepé walked wearily up the three steps and into the house. It was dark inside. There was a rustle in the corner.

Mama cried out from her bed. "Who comes? Pepé, is it thou?"

"*Sí*, Mama."

"Did you get the medicine?"

"*Sí*, Mama."

"Well, go to sleep, then. I thought you would be sleeping at the house of Mrs. Rodriguez." Pepé stood silently in the dark room. "Why do you stand there, Pepé? Did you drink wine?"

"*Sí*, Mama."

"Well, go to bed then and sleep out the wine."

His voice was tired and patient, but very firm. "Light the candle, Mama. I must go away into the mountains."

"What is this, Pepé? You are crazy." Mama struck a sulphur match and held the little blue burr until the flame spread up the stick. She set light to the candle on the floor beside her bed. "Now, Pepé, what is this you say?" She looked anxiously into his face.

He was changed. The fragile quality seemed to have gone from his chin. His mouth was less full than it had been, the lines of the lips were straighter, but in his eyes the greatest change had taken place. There was no laughter in them any more, nor any bashfulness. They were sharp and bright and purposeful.

He told her in a tired monotone, told her everything just as it had happened. A few people came into the kitchen of Mrs. Rodriguez. There was wine to drink. Pepé drank wine. The little quarrel—the man started toward Pepé and then the knife—it went almost by itself. It flew, it darted before Pepé knew it. As he talked, Mama's face grew stern, and it seemed to grow more lean. Pepé finished. "I am a man now, Mama. The man said names to me I could not allow."

Mama nodded. "Yes, thou art a man, my poor little Pepé. Thou art a man. I have seen it coming on thee. I have watched you throwing the knife into the post, and I have been afraid." For a moment her face had softened, but now it grew stern again. "Come! We must get you ready. Go. Awaken Emilio and Rosy. Go quickly."

Pepé stepped over to the corner where his brother and sister slept among the sheepskins. He leaned down and shook them gently. "Come, Rosy! Come, Emilio! The mama says you must arise."

The little black ones sat up and rubbed their eyes in the candlelight. Mama was out of bed now, her long black skirt over her nightgown. "Emilio," she cried. "Go up and catch the other horse for Pepé. Quickly, now! Quickly." Emilio put his legs in his overalls and stumbled sleepily out the door.

"You heard no one behind you on the road?" Mama demanded.

"No, Mama. I listened carefully. No one was on the road."

Mama darted like a bird about the room. From a nail on the wall she took a canvas water bag and threw it on the floor. She stripped a blanket from her bed and rolled it into a tight tube and tied the ends with string. From a box beside the stove she lifted a flour sack half full of black stringy jerky. "Your father's black coat, Pepé. Here, put it on."

Pepé stood in the middle of the floor watching her activity. She reached behind the door and brought out the rifle, a long 38-56, worn shiny the whole length of the barrel. Pepé took it from her and held it in the crook of his elbow. Mama brought a little leather bag and counted the cartridges into his hand. "Only ten left," she warned. "You must not waste them."

Emilio put his head in the door. "*'Qui 'st 'l caballo*, Mama."

"Put on the saddle from the other horse. Tie on the blanket. Here, tie the jerky to the saddle horn."

Still Pepé stood silently watching his mother's frantic activity. His chin looked hard, and his sweet mouth was drawn and thin. His little eyes followed Mama about the room almost suspiciously.

Rosy asked softly, "Where goes Pepé?"

Mama's eyes were fierce. "Pepé goes on a journey. Pepé is a man now. He has a man's thing to do."

Pepé straightened his shoulders. His mouth changed until he looked very much like Mama.

At last the preparation was finished. The loaded horse stood outside the door. The water bag dripped a line of moisture down the bay shoulder.

The moonlight was being thinned by the dawn and the big white moon was near down to the sea. The family stood by the shack. Mama confronted Pepé. "Look, my son! Do not stop until it is dark again. Do not sleep even though you are tired. Take care of the horse in order that he may not stop of weariness. Remember to be careful with the bullets—there are only ten. Do not fill thy stomach with jerky or it will make thee sick. Eat a little jerky and fill thy stomach with grass. When thou comest to the high mountains, if thou seest any of the dark watching men, go not near to them nor try to speak to them. And forget not thy prayers." She put her lean hands on Pepé's shoulders, stood on her toes and kissed him formally on both cheeks, and Pepé kissed her on both cheeks. Then he went to Emilio and Rosy and kissed both of their cheeks.

Pepé turned back to Mama. He seemed to look for a little softness, a little weakness in her. His eyes were searching, but Mama's face remained fierce. "Go now," she said. "Do not wait to be caught like a chicken."

Pepé pulled himself into the saddle. "I am a man," he said.

It was the first dawn when he rode up the hill toward the little canyon which let a trail into the mountains. Moonlight and daylight fought with each other, and the two warring qualities made it difficult to see. Before Pepé had gone a hundred yards, the outlines of his figure were misty; and long before he entered the canyon, he had become a gray, indefinite shadow.

Mama stood stiffly in front of her doorstep, and on either side of her stood Emilio and Rosy. They cast furtive glances at Mama now and then.

When the gray shape of Pepé melted into the hillside and disappeared, Mama relaxed. She began the high, whining keen of the death wail. "Our beautiful—our brave," she cried. "Our protector, our son is gone." Emilio and Rosy moaned beside her. "Our beautiful—our brave, he is gone." It was the formal wail. It rose to a high piercing whine and subsided to a moan. Mama raised it three times and then she turned and went into the house and shut the door.

Emilio and Rosy stood wondering in the dawn. They heard Mama whimpering in the house. They went out to sit on the cliff above the ocean. They touched shoulders. "When did Pepé come to be a man?" Emilio asked.

"Last night," said Rosy. "Last night in Monterey." The ocean clouds turned red with the sun that was behind the mountains.

"We will have no breakfast," said Emilio. "Mama will not want to cook." Rosy did not answer him. "Where is Pepé gone?" he asked.

Rosy looked around at him. She drew her knowledge from the quiet air. "He has gone on a journey. He will never come back."

"Is he dead? Do you think he is dead?"

Rosy looked back at the ocean again. A little steamer, drawing a line of smoke sat on the edge of the horizon. "He is not dead," Rosy explained. "Not yet."

Pepé rested the big rifle across the saddle in front of him. He let the horse walk up the hill and he didn't look back. The stony slope took on a coat of short brush so that Pepé found the entrance to a trail and entered it.

When he came to the canyon opening, he swung once in his saddle and looked back, but the houses were swallowed in the misty light. Pepé jerked forward again. The high shoulder of the canyon closed in on him. His horse stretched out its neck and sighed and settled to the trail.

It was a well-worn path, dark soft leaf-mould earth strewn with broken pieces of sandstone. The trail rounded the shoulder of the canyon and dropped steeply into the bed of the stream. In the shallows the water ran smoothly, glinting in the first morning sun. Small round stones on the bottom were as brown as rust with sun moss. In the sand along the edges of the stream the tall, rich wild mint grew, while in the water itself the cress, old and tough, had gone to heavy seed.

The path went into the stream and emerged on the other side. The horse sloshed into the water and stopped. Pepé dropped his bridle and let the beast drink of the running water.

Soon the canyon sides became steep and the first giant sentinel redwoods guarded the trail, great round red trunks bearing foliage as green and lacy as ferns. Once Pepé was among the trees, the sun was lost. A perfumed and purple light lay in the pale green of the underbrush. Gooseberry bushes and blackberries and tall ferns lined the stream, and overhead the branches of the redwoods met and cut off the sky.

Pepé drank from the water bag, and he reached into the flour sack and brought out a black string of jerky. His white teeth gnawed at the string until the tough meat parted. He chewed slowly and drank occasionally from the water bag. His little eyes were slumberous and tired, but the muscles of his face were hard set. The earth of the trail was black now. It gave up a hollow sound under the walking hoofbeats.

The stream fell more sharply. Little waterfalls splashed on the stones. Five-fingered ferns hung over the water and dripped spray from their finger-tips. Pepé rode half over in his saddle, dangling one leg loosely. He picked a bay leaf from a tree beside the way and put it into his mouth for a moment to flavor the dry jerky. He held the gun loosely across the pommel.

Suddenly he squared in his saddle, swung the horse from the trail and kicked it hurriedly up behind a big redwood tree. He pulled up the reins tight against the bit to keep the horse from whinnying. His face was intent and his nostrils quivered a little.

A hollow pounding came down the trail, and a horseman rode by, a fat man with red cheeks and a white stubble beard. His horse put down its head and blubbered at the trail when it came to the place where Pepé had turned off. "Hold up!" said the man and he pulled up his horse's head.

When the last sound of the hoofs died away, Pepé came back into the trail again. He did not relax in the saddle any more. He lifted the big rifle and swung the lever to throw a shell into the chamber, and then he let down the hammer to half cock.

The trail grew very steep. Now the redwood trees were smaller and their tops were dead, bitten dead where the wind reached them. The horse plodded on; the sun went slowly overhead and started down toward the afternoon.

Where the stream came out of a side canyon, the trail left it. Pepé dismounted and watered his horse and filled up his water bag. As soon as the trail had parted from the stream, the trees were gone and only the thick brittle sage and manzanita and chaparral edged the trail. And the soft black earth was gone, too, leaving only the light tan broken rock for the trail bed. Lizards scampered away into the brush as the horse rattled over the little stones.

Pepé turned in his saddle and looked back. He was in the open now: he could be seen from a distance. As he ascended the trail the country grew more rough and terrible and dry. The way wound about the bases of great square rocks. Little gray rabbits skittered in the brush. A bird made a monotonous high creaking. Eastward the bare rock mountaintops were pale and powder-dry under the dropping sun. The horse plodded up and up the trail toward a little V in the ridge which was the pass.

Pepé looked suspiciously back every minute or so, and his eyes sought the tops of the ridges ahead. Once, on a white barren spur, he saw a black figure for a moment, but he looked quickly away, for it was one of the dark watchers. No one knew who the watchers were, nor where they lived, but it was better to ignore them and never to show interest in them. They did not bother one who stayed on the trail and minded his own business.

The air was parched and full of light dust blown by the breeze from the eroding mountains. Pepé drank sparingly from his bag and corked it tightly and hung it on the horn again. The trail moved up the dry shale hillside, avoiding rocks, dropping under clefts, climbing in and out of old water scars. When he arrived at the little pass he stopped and looked back for a long time. No dark watchers were to be seen now. The trail behind was empty. Only the high tops of the redwoods indicated where the stream flowed.

Pepé rode on through the pass. His little eyes were nearly closed with weariness, but his face was stern, relentless and manly. The high mountain wind coasted sighing through the pass and whistled on the edges of the big blocks of broken granite. In the air, a red-tailed hawk sailed over close to the ridge and screamed angrily. Pepé went slowly through the broken jagged pass and looked down on the other side.

The trail dropped quickly, staggering among broken rock. At the bottom of the slope there was a dark crease, thick with brush, and on the other side of the crease a little flat, in which a grove of oak trees grew. A scar of green grass cut across the flat. And behind the flat another mountain rose, desolate with dead rocks and starving little black bushes. Pepé drank from the bag again for the air was so dry that it encrusted his nostrils and burned his lips. He put the horse down the trail. The hooves slipped and struggled on the steep way, starting little stones that rolled off into the brush. The sun was gone behind the westward mountain now, but still it glowed brilliantly on the oaks and on the grassy flat. The rocks and the hillsides still sent up waves of the heat they had gathered from the day's sun.

Pepé looked up to the top of the next dry withered ridge. He saw a dark form against the sky, a man's figure standing on top of a rock, and he glanced away quickly not to appear curious. When a moment later he looked up again, the figure was gone.

Downward the trail was quickly covered. Sometimes the horse floundered for footing, sometimes set his feet and slid a little way. They came at last to the bottom where the dark chaparral was higher than Pepé's head. He held up his rifle on one side and his arm on the other to shield his face from the sharp brittle fingers of the brush.

Up and out of the crease he rode, and up a little cliff. The grassy flat was before him, and the round comfortable oaks. For a moment he studied the trail down which he had come, but there was no movement and no sound from it. Finally he rode out over the flat, to the green streak, and at the upper end of the damp he found a little spring welling out of the earth and dropping into a dug basin before it seeped out over the flat.

Pepé filled his bag first, and then he let the thirsty horse drink out of the pool. He led the horse to the clump of oaks, and in the middle of the grove, fairly protected from sight on all sides, he took off the saddle and the bridle and laid them on the ground. The horse stretched his jaws sideways and yawned. Pepé knotted the lead rope about the horse's neck and tied him to a sapling among the oaks, where he could graze in a fairly large circle.

When the horse was gnawing hungrily at the dry grass, Pepé went to the saddle and took a black string of jerky from the sack and strolled to an oak tree on the edge of the grove, from under which he could watch the trail. He sat down in the crisp dry oak leaves and automatically felt for his big black knife to cut the jerky, but he had no knife. He leaned back on his elbow and gnawed at the tough strong meat. His face was blank, but it was a man's face.

The bright evening light washed the eastern ridge, but the valley was darkening. Doves flew down from the hills to the spring, and the quail came running out of the brush and joined them, calling clearly to one another.

Out of the corner of his eye Pepé saw a shadow grow out of the bushy crease. He turned his head slowly. A big spotted wildcat was creeping toward the spring, belly to the ground, moving like thought.

Pepé cocked his rifle and edged the muzzle slowly around. Then he looked apprehensively up the trail and dropped the hammer again. From the ground beside him he picked an oak twig and threw it toward the spring. The quail flew up with a roar and the doves whistled away. The big cat stood up: for a long moment he looked at Pepé with cold yellow eyes, and then fearlessly walked back into the gulch.

The dusk gathered quickly in the deep valley. Pepé muttered his prayers, put his head down on his arm and went instantly to sleep.

The moon came up and filled the valley with cold blue light, and the wind swept rustling down from the peaks. The owls worked up and down the slopes looking for rabbits. Down in the brush of the gulch a coyote gabbled. The oak trees whispered softly in the night breeze.

Pepé started up, listening. His horse had whinnied. The moon was just slipping behind the western ridge, leaving the valley in darkness behind it. Pepé sat tensely gripping his rifle. From far up the trail he heard an answering whinny and the crash of shod hooves on the broken rock. He jumped to his feet, ran to his horse and led it under the trees. He threw on the saddle and cinched it tight for the steep trail, caught the unwilling head and forced the bit into the mouth. He felt the saddle to make sure the water bag and the sack of jerky were there. Then he mounted and turned up the hill.

It was velvet dark. The horse found the entrance to the trail where it left the flat, and started up, stumbling and slipping on the rocks. Pepé's hand rose up to his head. His hat was gone. He had left it under the oak tree.

The horse had struggled far up the trail when the first change of dawn came into the air, a steel grayness as light mixed thoroughly with dark. Gradually the sharp snaggled edge of the ridge stood out above them, rotten granite tortured and eaten by the winds of time. Pepé had dropped his reins on the horn, leaving direction to the horse. The brush grabbed at his legs in the dark until one knee of his jeans was ripped.

Gradually the light flowed down over the ridge. The starved brush and rocks stood out in the half light, strange and lonely in high perspective. Then there came warmth into the light. Pepé drew up and looked back, but he could see nothing in the darker valley below. The sky turned blue over the coming sun. In the waste of the mountainside, the poor dry brush grew only three feet high. Here and there, big outcroppings of unrotted granite stood up like mouldering houses. Pepé relaxed a little. He drank from his water bag and bit off a piece of jerky. A single eagle flew over, high in the light.

Without warning Pepé's horse screamed and fell on its side. He was almost down before the rifle crash echoed up from the valley. From a hole behind the struggling shoulder, a stream of bright crimson blood pumped and stopped and pumped and stopped. The hooves threshed on the ground. Pepé lay half stunned beside the horse. He looked slowly down the hill. A piece of sage clipped off beside his head and another crash echoed up from side to side of the canyon. Pepé flung himself frantically behind a bush.

He crawled up the hill on his knees and one hand. His right hand held the rifle up off the ground and pushed it ahead of him. He moved with the instinctive care of an animal. Rapidly he wormed his way toward one of the big outcroppings of granite on the hill above him. Where the brush was high he doubled up and ran, but where the cover was slight he wriggled forward on his stomach, pushing the rifle ahead of him. In the last little distance there was no cover at all. Pepé poised and then he darted across the space and flashed around the corner of the rock.

He leaned panting against the stone. When his breath came easier he moved along behind the big rock until he came to a narrow split that offered a thin section of vision down the hill. Pepé lay on his stomach and pushed the rifle barrel through the slit and waited.

The sun reddened the western ridges now. Already the buzzards were settling down toward the place where the horse lay. A small brown bird scratched in the dead sage leaves directly in front of the rifle muzzle. The coasting eagle flew back toward the rising sun.

Pepé saw a little movement in the brush far below. His grip tightened on the gun. A little brown doe stepped daintily out on the trail and crossed it and disappeared into the brush again. For a long time Pepé waited. Far below he could see the little flat and the oak trees and the slash of green. Suddenly his eyes flashed back at the trail again. A quarter of a mile down there had been a quick movement in the chaparral. The rifle swung over. The front sight nestled in the v of the rear sight. Pepé studied for a moment and then raised the rear sight a notch. The little movement in the brush came again. The sight settled on it. Pepé squeezed the trigger. The explosion crashed down the mountain and up the other side, and came rattling back. The whole side of the slope grew still. No more movement. And then a white streak cut into the granite of the slit and a bullet whined away and a crash sounded up from below. Pepé felt a sharp pain in his right hand. A sliver of granite was sticking out from between his first and second knuckles and the point protruded from his palm. Carefully he pulled out the sliver of stone. The wound bled evenly and gently. No vein nor artery was cut.

Pepé looked into a little dusty cave in the rock and gathered a handful of spider web, and he pressed the mass into the cut, plastering the soft web into the blood. The flow stopped almost at once.

The rifle was on the ground. Pepé picked it up, levered a new shell into the chamber. And then he slid into the brush on his stomach. Far to the right he crawled, and then up the hill, moving slowly and carefully, crawling to cover and resting and then crawling again.

In the mountains the sun is high in its arc before it penetrates the gorges. The hot face looked over the hill and brought instant heat with it. The white light beat on the rocks and reflected from them and rose up quivering from the earth again, and the rocks and bushes seemed to quiver behind the air.

Pepé crawled in the general direction of the ridge peak, zig-zagging for cover. The deep cut between his knuckles began to throb. He crawled close to a rattlesnake before he saw it, and when it raised its dry head and made a soft beginning whirr, he backed up and took another way. The quick gray lizards flashed in front of him, raising a tiny line of dust. He found another mass of spider web and pressed it against his throbbing hand.

Pepé was pushing the rifle with his left hand now. Little drops of sweat ran to the ends of his coarse black hair and rolled down his cheeks. His lips and tongue were growing thick and heavy. His lips writhed to draw saliva into his mouth. His little dark eyes were uneasy and suspicious. Once when a gray lizard paused in front of him on the parched ground and turned its head sideways he crushed it flat with a stone.

When the sun slid past noon he had not gone a mile. He crawled exhaustedly a last hundred yards to a patch of high sharp manzanita, crawled desperately, and when the patch was reached he wriggled in among the tough gnarly trunks and dropped his head on his left arm. There was little shade in the meager brush, but there was cover and safety. Pepé went to sleep as he lay and the sun beat on his back. A few little birds hopped close to him and peered and hopped away. Pepé squirmed in his sleep and he raised and dropped his wounded hand again and again.

The sun went down behind the peaks and the cool evening came, and then the dark. A coyote yelled from the hillside, Pepé started awake and looked about with misty eyes. His hand was swollen and heavy; a little thread of pain ran up the inside of his arm and settled in a pocket in his armpit. He peered about and then stood up, for the mountains were black and the moon had not yet risen. Pepé stood up in the dark. The coat of his father pressed on his arm. His tongue was swollen until it nearly filled his mouth. He wriggled out of the coat and dropped it in the brush, and then he struggled up the hill, falling over rocks and tearing his way through the brush. The rifle knocked against stones as he went. Little dry avalanches of gravel and shattered stone went whispering down the hill behind him.

After a while the old moon came up and showed the jagged ridge top ahead of him. By moonlight Pepé traveled more easily. He bent forward so that his throbbing arm hung away from his body. The journey uphill was made in dashes and rests, a frantic rush up a few yards and then a rest. The wind coasted down the slope rattling the dry stems of the bushes.

The moon was at meridian when Pepé came at last to the sharp backbone of the ridge top. On the last hundred yards of the rise no soil had clung under the wearing winds. The way was on solid rock. He clambered to the top and looked down on the other side. There was a draw like the last below him, misty with moonlight, brushed with dry struggling sage and chaparral. On the other side the hill rose up sharply and at the top the jagged rotten teeth of the mountain showed against the sky. At the bottom of the cut the brush was thick and dark.

Pepé stumbled down the hill. His throat was almost closed with thirst. At first he tried to run, but immediately he fell and rolled. After that he went more carefully. The moon was just disappearing behind the mountains when he came to the bottom. He crawled into the heavy brush feeling with his fingers for water. There was no water in the bed of the stream, only damp earth. Pepé laid his gun down and scooped up a handful of mud and put it in his mouth, and then he spluttered and scraped the earth from his tongue with his finger, for the mud drew at his mouth like a poultice. He dug a hole in the stream bed with his fingers, dug a little basin to catch water; but before it was very deep his head fell forward on the damp ground and he slept.

The dawn came and the heat of the day fell on the earth, and still Pepé slept. Late in the afternoon his head jerked up. He looked slowly around. His eyes were slits of wariness. Twenty feet away in the heavy brush a big tawny mountain lion stood looking at him. Its long thick tail waved gracefully, its ears were erect with interest, not laid back dangerously. The lion squatted down on its stomach and watched him.

Pepé looked at the hole he had dug in the earth. A half inch of muddy water had collected in the bottom. He tore the sleeve from his hurt arm, with his teeth ripped out a little square, soaked it in the water and put it in his mouth. Over and over he filled the cloth and sucked it.

Still the lion sat and watched him. The evening came down but there was no movement on the hills. No birds visited the dry bottom of the cut. Pepé looked occasionally at the lion. The eyes of the yellow beast drooped as though he were about to sleep. He yawned and his long thin red tongue curled out. Suddenly his head jerked around and his nostrils quivered. His big tail lashed. He stood up and slunk like a tawny shadow into the thick brush.

A moment later Pepé heard the sound, the faint far crash of horses' hooves on gravel. And he heard something else, a high whining yelp of a dog.

Pepé took his rifle in his left hand and he glided into the brush almost as quietly as the lion had. In the darkening evening he crouched up the hill toward the next ridge. Only when the dark came did he stand up. His energy was short. Once it was dark he fell over the rocks and slipped to his knees on the steep slope, but he moved on and on up the hill, climbing and scrabbling over the broken hillside.

When he was far up toward the top, he lay down and slept for a little while. The withered moon, shining on his face, awakened him. He stood up and moved up the hill. Fifty yards away he stopped and turned back, for he had forgotten his rifle. He walked heavily down and poked about in the brush, but he could not find his gun. At last he lay down to rest. The pocket of pain in his armpit had grown more sharp. His arm seemed to swell out and fall with every heartbeat. There was no position lying down where the heavy arm did not press against his armpit.

With the effort of a hurt beast, Pepé got up and moved again toward the top of the ridge. He held his swollen arm away from his body with his left hand. Up the steep hill he dragged himself, a few steps and a rest, and a few more steps. At last he was nearing the top. The moon showed the uneven sharp back of it against the sky.

Pepé's brain spun in a big spiral up and away from him. He slumped to the ground and lay still. The rock ridge top was only a hundred feet above him.

The moon moved over the sky. Pepé half turned on his back. His tongue tried to make words, but only a thick hissing came from between his lips.

When the dawn came, Pepé pulled himself up. His eyes were sane again. He drew his great puffed arm in front of him and looked at the angry wound. The black line ran up from his wrist to his armpit. Automatically he reached in his pocket for the big black knife, but it was not there. His eyes searched the ground. He picked up a sharp blade of stone and scraped at the wound, sawed at the proud flesh and then squeezed the green juice out in big drops.

Instantly he threw back his head and whined like a dog. His whole right side shuddered at the pain, but the pain cleared his head.

In the gray light he struggled up the last slope to the ridge and crawled over and lay down behind a line of rocks. Below him lay a deep canyon exactly like the last, waterless and desolate. There was no flat, no oak trees, not even heavy brush in the bottom of it. And on the other side a sharp ridge stood up, thinly brushed with starving sage, littered with broken granite. Strewn over the hill there were giant outcroppings, and on the top the granite teeth stood out against the sky.

The new day was light now. The flame of the sun came over the ridge and fell on Pepé where he lay on the ground. His coarse black hair was littered with twigs and bits of spider web. His eyes had retreated back into his head. Between his lips the tip of his black tongue showed.

He sat up and dragged his great arm into his lap and nursed it, rocking his body and moaning in his throat. He threw back his head and looked up into the pale sky. A big black bird circled nearly out of sight, and far to the left another was sailing near.

He lifted his head to listen, for a familiar sound had come to him from the valley he had climbed out of; it was the crying yelp of hounds, excited and feverish, on a trail.

Pepé bowed his head quickly. He tried to speak rapid words but only a thick hiss came from his lips. He drew a shaky cross on his breast with his left hand. It was a long struggle to get to his feet. He crawled slowly and mechanically to the top of a big rock on the ridge peak. Once there, he arose slowly, swaying to his feet, and stood erect. Far below he could see the dark brush where he had slept. He braced his feet and stood there, black against the morning sky.

There came a ripping sound at his feet. A piece of stone flew up and a bullet droned off into the next gorge. The hollow crash echoed up from below. Pepé looked down for a moment and then pulled himself straight again.

His body jarred back. His left hand fluttered helplessly toward his breast. The second crash sounded from below. Pepé swung forward and toppled from the rock. His body struck and rolled over and over, starting a little avalanche. And when at last he stopped against a bush, the avalanche slid slowly down and covered up his head.

NATHANAEL WEST [1903-1940]

Nathanael West was born in New York City as Nathan Weinstein, the son of Jewish immigrants from Russia. Later he changed his name to "West" in a gesture of assimilation suggested by Horace Greeley's injunction to "Go West, young man." Ultimately, having a contract to write movie scripts in Hollywood, he literally went West where he lived and died, at the age of 37 in an automobile accident near Los Angeles. West wrote four novels, two plays, and some short stories, all published during the 1930's. At his death he was known only to a few fellow-writers and a very limited reading audience, but since about 1950 he has been "discovered" and much admired by *avant-garde* critics who see him as an original in fiction, well ahead of his time in his use of poetic and surrealist techniques and in his mingling of comedy with serious social commentary in the novel. His preoccupation with violence as a part of modern society and his use of sexual perversion both for its shocking effect and as a metaphor for the distortion of values in modern life remind one of Faulkner, Eliot, and Joyce. Though he wrote in the heyday of the naturalistic novel of social criticism, he disliked the realists of the Dreiser school and turned away from documentary fiction. He read Dostoevsky, Henry James, and Joyce, liked the French symbolists Rimbaud and Verlaine, and such exotics as Huysmans, James Branch Cabell, and Arthur Machen. During a year in Paris (1925-26) he was attracted to Dadaism and Surrealism in art and to the fictional methods of André Breton. By background and disposition West was a loner; by natural gift he tended to see life in caricature and parody; and by conviction he was a rebel against middle-class conformity and the religious and economic establishment.

A complex writer, with his Russian-Jewish background, his satirical bent, and his compulsion to write about America, West wrote his first novel, he said, "as a protest against writing books." He was both attracted and repelled by Catholic mysticism and Judaic mythology, and some of his most powerful scenes satirize the Eucharist, the Incarnation, the Immaculate Conception, and religious martyrdom and sacrifice. In *The Dream of Balso Snell* (1931) he mocked Christianity by inventing a saint, Saint Puce, a flea who was fertilized, lived, and died in the armpit of Jesus. One critic described this fantastic book as follows: "A poet named Balso Snell finds a wooden Trojan horse and has a picaresque journey up its alimentary canal." *Miss Lonelyhearts* (1933) contains a bizarre scene in which some boys attempt to sacrifice a lamb, but the knife breaks when they try to cut its throat. It runs away, then one of the boys crushes its head with a rock.

West went to school in New York City, but was indifferent to study and never graduated from high school. Later, on a forged transcript, he managed to enter college, posing as another "Nathan Weinstein" whose credits in science courses enabled West to devote himself to his own reading interests and to graduate in two years. He liked aesthetic subjects and dabbled in mysticism and medieval Catholicism. He read Joyce and admired Nietzsche and was talented in art. During his year in Paris he hobnobbed with artists on the Left Bank, grew a beard, and affected the costume and cane of a boulevardier. Forced to return to New York when his father, a contractor, lost his money in the crash, West managed a hotel, spending his time reading and giving free rooms to indigent writers. In 1931, determined to write, he rented a shack in the Adirondacks where he worked slowly and painstakingly on the manuscript that was to become *Miss Lonelyhearts,* parts of which appeared in *Contact.* He earned only a meager income until he sold the novel to a movie studio and secured a contract to write scripts at $350 a week. Meanwhile he had begun a third novel, *A Cool Million* (1934), a grimly serio-comic narrative about the vulnerability of the innocent, middle-class American type to the violent pressures of Communism, Fascism, and Wall Street as West saw them during the decade of the depression and the rise of Hitler.

In Hollywood, West joined the Screen Writers Guild and associated himself with leftist groups and fellow travelers, picketed some stores, and was jailed for a time. In 1937 *The Day of the Locust* was published, West's most finished novel. Ostensibly a satire on the flimsy pretensions of Hollywood hangers-on, freaks, and movie extras, it revealed his ability to expose the potential dangers of modern society generally in the metaphor of the film city. Surrealist techniques, parody, caricature, and skillful satire were joined in this novel.

The world of West's novels is a wasteland in which older values have become half-comic, half-tragic distortions of their original meanings. Love becomes lust and sex, compassion turns to cynicism, democracy to totalitarianism. Latent homosexuality and outright pornography pervade his books. The lonely crowd stands on the brink of some catastrophic and nightmarish apocalypse. West excelled in the portrayal of grotesque people and shockingly repulsive episodes: ill-tempered dwarfs, cripples, sex perverts, drugstore cowboys, a starlet turned call girl, a hateful child actor, a riot in Hollywood, a weird painting of the Burning of Los Angeles. Such people are West's mechanical monsters, created from the chaos of the twentieth-century megalopolis, hollow men and women who act their parts in a monstrous mockery of sanity and common humanity.

Further reading: *The Complete Works of Nathanael West,* 1957. James F. Light, *Nathanael West, An Interpretive Study,* 1961.

A Cool Million

First published in 1934. The present text is taken from *The Complete Works of Nathanael West* (1957).

A Cool Million, or the Dismantling of Lemuel Pitkin is mock-melodrama, parodying the classic Horatio Alger style and the rags-to-riches success story of such boy-novels as *Ragged Dick, Onward and Upward,* and others. West narrates the adventures of Lem Pitkin and his girl counterpart, Betty Prail, in a series of violent and shocking episodes each contributing to the downfall of the hero and heroine. The novel opens with the conventional scene of the hero and his widowed mother being evicted from their home by a grasping landlord. Lem meets Shagpoke Whipple, an ex-president of the United States, a flag-waving, America-first caricature of the patriotic American. In the course of the novel, Lem joins Whipple's National Revolutionary Party, a neo-Fascist organization which seeks to defeat Wall Street and the Communists. Almost every American shibboleth is satirized. Lem loses his teeth, an eye, a leg, and his scalp; Betty is forced into prostitution; yet neither loses faith in the clichés preached by Shagpoke. The style ranges from slapstick and bathroom humor to genuine mock-heroic. The epilogue (Chapter 31) describes a future national holiday dedicated to the memory of Lemuel Pitkin, the All-American Boy.

Chapter 13

One wintry morning, several weeks after the incident in the park, Lem was dismissed from the hospital minus his right eye. It had been so severely damaged that the physicians had thought best to remove it.

He had no money, for, as we have recounted, Snodgrasse's henchmen had robbed him. Even the teeth that Warden Purdy had given him were gone. They had been taken from him by the hospital authorities, who claimed that they did not fit properly and were therefore a menace to his health.

The poor lad was standing on a windy corner, not knowing which way to turn, when he saw a man in a coonskin hat. This remarkable headgear made Lem stare, and the more he looked the more the man seemed to resemble Shagpoke Whipple.

It was Mr. Whipple. Lem hastened to call out to him, and the ex-President stopped to shake hands with his young friend.

"About those inventions," Shagpoke said immediately after they had finished greeting each other. "It was too bad that you left the penitentiary before I could hand them over to you. Not knowing your whereabouts, I perfected them myself.

"But let us repair to a coffee place," he added, changing the subject, "where we can talk over your prospects together. I am still very much interested in your career. In fact, my young friend, America has never had a greater need for her youth than in these parlous times."

After our hero had thanked him for his interest and good wishes, Mr. Whipple continued to talk. "Speaking of coffee," he said, "did you know that the fate of our country was decided in the coffee shops of Boston during the hectic days preceding the late rebellion?"

As they paused at the door of a restaurant, Mr. Whipple asked Lem still another question. "By the way," he said "I am temporarily without funds. Are you able to meet the obligation we will incur in this place?"

"No," replied Lem, sadly, "I am penniless."

"That's different," said Mr. Whipple with a profound sigh. "In that case we will go where I have credit."

Lem was conducted by his fellow townsman to an extremely poor section of the city. After standing on line for several hours, they each received a doughnut and a cup of coffee from the Salvation Army lassie in charge. They then sat down on the curb to eat their little snack.

"You are perhaps wondering," Shagpoke began, "how it is that I stand on line with these homeless vagrants to obtain bad coffee and soggy doughnuts. Be assured that I do it of my own free will and for the good of the state."

Here he paused long enough to skillfully "shoot a snipe" that was still burning. He puffed contentedly on his catch.

"When I left jail, it was my intention to run for office again. But I discovered to my great amazement and utter horror that my party, the Democratic Party, carried not a single plank in its platform that I could honestly endorse. Rank socialism was and is rampant. How could I, Shagpoke Whipple, ever bring myself to accept a program which promised to take from American citizens their inalienable birthright; the right to sell their labor and their children's labor without restrictions as to either price or hours?

"The time for a new party with the old American principles was, I realized, overripe. I decided to form it; and so the National Revolutionary Party, popularly known as the 'Leather Shirts,' was born. The uniform of our 'Storm Troops' is a coonskin cap like the one I am wearing, a deerskin shirt and a pair of moccasins. Our weapon is the squirrel rifle."

He pointed to the long queue of unemployed who stood waiting before the Salvation Army canteen. "These men," he said, "are the material from which I must fill the ranks of my party."

With all the formality of a priest, Shagpoke turned to our hero and laid his hand on his shoulder.

"My boy," he said, and his voice broke under the load of emotion it was forced to bear, "my boy, will you join me?"

"Certainly, sir," said Lem, a little unsurely.

"Excellent!" exclaimed Mr. Whipple. "Excellent! I herewith appoint you a commander attached to my general staff."

He drew himself up and saluted Lem, who was startled by the gesture.

"Commander Pitkin," he ordered briskly, "I desire to address these people. Please obtain a soapbox."

Our hero went on the errand required of him, and soon returned with a large box, which Mr. Whipple immediately mounted. He then set about attracting the attention of the vagrants collected about the Salvation Army canteen by shouting:

"Remember the River Raisin!

"Remember the Alamo!

"Remember the Maine!"

and many other famous slogans.

When a large group had gathered, Shagpoke began his harangue.

"I'm a simple man," he said with great simplicity, "and I want to talk to you about simple things. You'll get no high-falutin talk from me.

"First of all, you people want jobs. Isn't that so?"

An ominous rumble of assent came from the throats of the poorly dressed gathering.

"Well, that's the only and prime purpose of the National Revolutionary Party—to get jobs for everyone. There was enough work to go around in 1927, why isn't there enough now? I'll tell you; because of the Jewish international bankers and the Bolshevik labor unions, that's why. It was those two agents that did the most to hinder American business and to destroy its glorious expansion. The former because of their hatred of America and love for Europe and the latter because of their greed for higher and still higher wages.

"What is the role of the labor union today? It is a privileged club which controls all the best jobs for its members. When one of you applies for a job, even if the man who owns the plant wants to hire you, do you get it? Not if you haven't got a union card. Can any tyranny be greater? Has Liberty ever been more brazenly despised?"

These statements were received with cheers by his audience.

"Citizens, Americans," Mr. Whipple continued, when the noise had subsided, "we of the middle class are being crushed between two gigantic millstones. Capital is the upper stone and Labor the lower, and between them we suffer and die, ground out of existence.

"Capital is international; its home is in London and in Amsterdam. Labor is international; its home is in Moscow. We alone are American; and when we die, America dies.

"When I say that, I make no idle boast, for history bears me out. Who but the middle class left aristocratic Europe to settle on these shores? Who but the middle class, the small farmers and storekeepers, the clerks and petty officials, fought for freedom and died that America might escape from British tyranny?

"This is our country and we must fight to keep it so. If America is ever again to be great, it can only be through the triumph of the revolutionary middle class.

"We must drive the Jewish international bankers out of Wall Street! We must destroy the Bolshevik labor unions! We must purge our country of all the alien elements and ideas that now infest her!

"America for Americans! Back to the principles of Andy Jackson and Abe Lincoln!"

Here Shagpoke paused to let the cheers die down, then called for volunteers to join his "Storm Battalions."

A number of men came forward. In their lead was a very dark individual, who had extra-long black hair of an extremely coarse quality, and on whose head was a derby hat many sizes too small for him.

"Me American mans," he announced proudly. "Me got heap coon hat, two maybe six. By, by catchum plenty more coon maybe." With this he grinned from ear to ear.

But Shagpoke was a little suspicious of his complexion, and looked at him with disfavor. In the South, where he expected to get considerable support for his movement, they would not stand for Negroes.

The good-natured stranger seemed to sense what was wrong, for he said, "Me Injun, mister, me chief along my people. Gotum gold mine, oil well. Name of Jake Raven. Ugh!"

Shagpoke grew cordial at once. "Chief Jake Raven," he said, holding out his hand, "I am happy to welcome you into our organization. We 'Leather Shirts' can learn much from your people, fortitude, courage and relentless purpose among other things."

After taking down his name, Shagpoke gave the Indian a card which read as follows:

EZRA SILVERBLATT
Official Tailor
to the
NATIONAL REVOLUTIONARY PARTY

Coonskin hats with extra long tails, deerskin shirts with or without fringes, blue jeans, moccasins, squirrel rifles, everything for the American Fascist at rock bottom prices. 30% off for Cash.

But let us leave Mr. Whipple and Lem busy with their recruiting to observe the actions of a certain member of the crowd.

The individual in question would have been remarkable in any gathering, and among the starved, ragged men that surrounded Shagpoke, he stuck out like the proverbial sore thumb. For one thing he was fat, enormously fat. There were other fat men present to be sure, but they were yellow, unhealthy, while this man's fat was pink and shone with health.

On his head was a magnificent bowler hat. It was a beautiful jet in color, and must have cost more than twelve dollars. He was snugly encased in a tight-fitting Chesterfield overcoat with a black velvet collar. His stiff-bosomed shirt had light gray bars, and his tie was of some rich but sober material in black and white pin-checks. Spats, rattan stick and yellow gloves completed his outfit.

This elaborate fat man tiptoed out of the crowd and made his way to a telephone booth in a nearby drug store, where he called two numbers.

His conversation with the person answering his first call, a Wall Street exchange, went something like this:

"Operative 6384XM, working out of the Bourse, Paris, France. Middle-class organizers functioning on unemployed front, corner of Houston and Bleecker Streets."

"Thank you, 6384XM, what is your estimate?"

"Twenty men and a fire hose."

"At once, 6384XM, at once."

His second call was to an office near Union Square.

"Comrade R, please. . . . Comrade R?"

"Yes."

"Comrade R, this is Comrade Z speaking. Gay Pay Oo, Moscow, Russia. Middle-class organizers recruiting on the corner of Houston and Bleecker Streets."

"Your estimate, comrade, for liquidation of said activities?"

"Ten men with lead pipes and brass knuckles to cooperate with Wall Street office of the I.J.B."

"No bombs required?"

"No, comrade."

"Der Tag!"

"Der Tag!"

Mr. Whipple had just enrolled his twenty-seventh recruit, when the forces of both the international Jewish bankers and the Communists converged on his meeting. They arrived in high-powered black limousines and deployed through the streets with a skill which showed long and careful training in that type of work. In fact their officers were all West Point graduates.

Mr. Whipple saw them coming, but like a good general his first thoughts were for his men.

"The National Revolutionary Party will now go underground!" he shouted.

Lem, made wary by his past experiences with the police, immediately took to his heels, followed by Chief Raven. Shagpoke, however, was late in getting started. He still had one foot on the soapbox when he was hit a terrific blow on the head with a piece of lead pipe.

Chapter 31

One day a stranger came to the theater to see Lem. He addressed our hero as Commander Pitkin and said that he was Storm Trooper Zachary Coates.

Lem made him welcome and asked eagerly for news of Mr. Whipple. He was told that that very night Shagpoke would be in the city. Mr. Coates then went on to explain that because of its large foreign population New York was still holding out against the National Revolutionary Party.

"But tonight," he said, "this city will be filled with thousands of 'Leather Shirts' from upstate and an attempt will be made to take it over."

While talking he stared hard at our hero. Apparently satisfied with what he saw, he saluted briskly and said, "As one of the original members of the party, you are being asked to cooperate."

"I'll be glad to do anything I can to help," Lem replied.

"Good! Mr. Whipple will be happy to hear that, for he counted on you."

"I am something of a cripple," Lem added with a brave smile. "I may not be able to do much."

"We of the party know how your wounds were acquired. In fact one of our prime purposes is to prevent the youth of this country from being tortured as you were tortured. Let me add, Commander Pitkin, that in my humble opinion you are well on your way to being recognized as one of the martyrs of our cause." Here he saluted Lem once more.

Lem was embarrassed by the man's praise and hurriedly changed the subject. "What are Mr. Whipple's orders?" he asked.

"Tonight, wherever large crowds gather, in the parks, theaters, subways, a member of our party will make a speech. Scattered among his listeners will be numerous 'Leather Shirts' in plain clothes, who will aid the speaker stir up the patriotic fury of the crowd. When this fury reaches its proper height, a march on the City Hall will be ordered. There a monster mass meeting will be held which Mr. Whipple will address. He will demand and get control of the city."

"It sounds splendid," said Lem. "I suppose you want me to make a speech in this theater?"

"Yes, exactly."

"I would if I could," replied Lem, "but I'm afraid

I can't. I have never made a speech in my life. You see, I'm not a real actor but only a 'stooge.' And besides, Riley and Robbins wouldn't like it if I tried to interrupt their act."

"Don't worry about those gentlemen," Mr. Coates said with a smile. "They will be taken care of. As for your other reason, I have a speech in my pocket that was written expressly for you by Mr. Whipple. I have come here to rehearse you in it."

Zachary Coates reached into his pocket and brought out a sheaf of papers. "Read this through first," he said firmly, "then we will begin to study it."

That night Lem walked out on the stage alone. Although he was not wearing his stage costume, but the dress uniform of the "Leather Shirts," the audience knew from the program that he was a comedian and roared with laughter.

This unexpected reception destroyed what little self-assurance the poor lad had and for a minute it looked as though he were going to run. Fortunately, however, the orchestra leader, who was a member of Mr. Whipple's organization, had his wits about him and made his men play the national anthem. The audience stopped laughing and rose soberly to its feet.

In all that multitude one man alone failed to stand up. He was our old friend, the fat fellow in the Chesterfield overcoat. Secreted behind the curtains of a box, he crouched low in his chair and fondled an automatic pistol. He was again wearing a false beard.

When the orchestra had finished playing, the audience reseated itself and Lem prepared to make his speech.

"I am a clown," he began, "but there are times when even clowns must grow serious. This is such a time. I . . ."

Lem got no further. A shot rang out and he fell dead, drilled through the heart by an assassin's bullet.

Little else remains to be told, but before closing this book there is one last scene which I must describe.

It is Pitkin's Birthday, a national holiday, and the youth of America is parading down Fifth Avenue in his honor. They are a hundred thousand strong. On every boy's head is a coonskin hat complete with jaunty tail, and on every shoulder rests a squirrel rifle.

Hear what they are singing. It is *The Lemuel Pitkin Song.*

"Who dares?"—this was L. Pitkin's cry,
As striding on the Bijou stage he came—
"Surge out with me in Shagpoke's name,
For him to live, for him to die!"
A million hands flung up reply,
A million voices answered, "I!"

Chorus

A million hearts for Pitkin, oh!
To do and die with Pitkin, oh!
To live and fight with Pitkin, oh!
Marching for Pitkin.

The youths pass the reviewing stand and from it Mr. Whipple proudly returns their salute. The years have dealt but lightly with him. His back is still as straight as ever and his gray eyes have not lost their keenness.

But who is the little lady in black next to the dictator? Can it be the Widow Pitkin? Yes, it is she. She is crying, for with a mother glory can never take the place of a beloved child. To her it seems like only yesterday that Lawyer Slemp threw Lem into the open cellar.

And next to the Widow Pitkin stands still another woman. This one is young and beautiful, yet her eyes too are full of tears. Let us look closer, for there is something vaguely familiar about her. It is Betty Prail. She seems to have some official position, and when we ask, a bystander tells us that she is Mr. Whipple's secretary.

The marchers have massed themselves in front of the reviewing stand and Mr. Whipple is going to address them.

"Why are we celebrating this day above other days?" he asked his hearers in a voice of thunder. "What made Lemuel Pitkin great? Let us examine his life.

"First we see him as a small boy, light of foot, fishing for bullheads in the Rat River of Vermont. Later, he attends the Ottsville High School, where he is captain of the nine and an excellent outfielder. Then, he leaves for the big city to make his fortune. All this is in the honorable tradition of his country and its people, and he has the right to expect certain rewards.

"Jail is his first reward. Poverty his second. Violence is his third. Death is his last.

"Simple was his pilgrimage and brief, yet a thousand years hence, no story, no tragedy, no epic poem will be filled with greater wonder, or be followed by mankind with deeper feeling, than that which tells of the life and death of Lemuel Pitkin.

"But I have not answered the question. Why is Lemuel Pitkin great? Why does the martyr move in triumph and the nation rise up at every stage of his coming? Why are cities and states his pallbearers?

"Because, although dead, yet he speaks.

"Of what is it that he speaks? Of the right of every American boy to go into the world and there receive fair play and a chance to make his fortune by industry and probity without being laughed at or conspired against by sophisticated aliens.

"Alas, Lemuel Pitkin himself did not have this chance, but instead was dismantled by the enemy. His teeth were pulled out. His eye was gouged from his head. His thumb was removed. His scalp was torn away. His leg was cut off. And, finally, he was shot through the heart.

"But he did not live or die in vain. Through his martyrdom the National Revolutionary Party triumphed, and by that triumph this country was delivered from sophistication, Marxism and International Capitalism. Through the National Revolution its people were purged of alien diseases and America became again American."

"Hail the Martyrdom in the Bijou Theater!" roar Shagpoke's youthful hearers when he is finished.

"Hail, Lemuel Pitkin!"

"All hail, the American boy!"

RICHARD WRIGHT [1908-1960]

When Richard Wright died an expatriate in Paris, an obituary in *Le Monde* recalled the admiration and applause France had given him. But it was the American South that held him, the newspaper observed, "and the South will never let him go." To the extent that any writer is the creation of his past, the South never did let Wright go. His early experience seems to have formed and implanted in his writings the core of violence and bitterness that was both a shock and a revelation to his readers. "I had slowly learned," he explained in *Black Boy*, "that the South could recognize but a part of a man, could accept but a fragment of his personality, and all the rest—the best and deepest things of heart and mind—were tossed away in blind ignorance and hate." This indictment he would later extend to American society as a whole.

He was born near Natchez, Mississippi; his father was a sharecropper. His boyhood was shadowed by a broken home, poverty, and the rootlessness of moving from place to place as his mother struggled to support her two sons. His schooling was irregular and ended with the ninth grade; he was almost wholly self-educated. He struck out on his own in his teens and slowly made his way North, arriving in Chicago in 1927, only to find that he had exchanged the repression of the South for the frustration of the urban ghetto. By this time he was determined to be a writer, and in the writings of H. L. Mencken, Theodore Dreiser, Sinclair Lewis, and other social critics he found voices that spoke to his own experience. Like many of the intellectuals and the dispossessed of the early 1930's, Wright was attracted to the radical left. He began writing for left-wing periodicals and joined the John Reed Club, but later withdrew in disenchantment with political Communism, though he retained Marxist sympathies. During the depression he worked on the Federal Writers' Project in Chicago.

Wright's career was fully launched with the winning of *Story* magazine's prize for the best book-length manuscript submitted by anyone connected with the Federal Writers' Project. This was *Uncle Tom's Children*, published in 1938, a collection of four novellas about the black sharecroppers of the South in their desperate relationship to the white power structure. This work brought him critical recognition and a Guggenheim Fellowship. It was followed in 1940 by *Native Son*, a harsh naturalistic novel in which Wright re-created a powerful sense of the victimization of the black in American society. He explored this same theme in movingly personal terms in *Black Boy* (1945), an autobiography that ended at his seventeenth year with his decision to leave the South forever and seek in the North a life that "could be lived with dignity." By this time, however, Wright had reached the bitter conclusion that he could never realize his dream in his own country, and in 1946 he accepted the invitation of the French Government to live and work in France. There he lived for the rest of his life. In his books of this later period—and especially in his "existential" novel *The Outsider* (1953)—he moved toward a fundamental criticism of the values of American society, whereas his earlier and more characteristic stance was an indictment of that society for denying the Negro full participation in its value system.

In combining the elements of the social-protest novel with the theme of racial injustice, Wright virtually created a new genre, or at least gave new direction and force to the fiction of naturalism. *Native Son,* his masterwork, violent and brutal beyond anything American fiction had yet produced, reached a wide reading audience as a best-seller and brought Negro writing fully into the mainstream of American literature. Wright's influence on his younger contemporaries was enormous, as Ralph Ellison, James Baldwin, and Le Roi Jones, among others, have attested. For good or ill, he has been the measure by which a whole generation of black writers have been judged.

Further reading: *Native Son.* Constance Webb, *Richard Wright: A Biography,* 1968. Edward Margolies, *The Art of Richard Wright,* 1969.

Fire and Cloud

From *Uncle Tom's Children* (1938; new and enlarged edition, 1940). The text reprinted here is from the edition of 1940.

I

"A naughts a naught..."

As he walked his eyes looked vacantly on the dusty road, and the words rolled without movement from his lips, each syllable floating softly up out of the depths of his body.

"N five a figger..."

He pulled out his pocket handkerchief and mopped his brow without lessening his pace.

"All fer the white man..."

He reached the top of the slope and paused, head down.

"N none fer the nigger...."

His shoulders shook in half-laugh and half-shudder. He finished mopping his brow and spat, as though to rid himself of some bitter thing. He thought. Thas the way its awways been! Wistfully he turned and looked back at the dim buildings of the town lying sprawled mistily on the crest of a far hill. Seems like the white folks jus erbout owns this whole worl! Looks like they done conquered *everything.* We black folks is jus los in one big white fog. ... With his eyes still on the hazy buildings, he flexed his lips slowly and spoke under his breath:

"They could do something! They could do *something,* awright! Mabbe ef fiv er six thousan of us marched downtown we could *scare* em inter doin something! Lawd, mabbe them Reds *is* right!"

He walked again and tucked his handkerchief back into his pocket. He could feel the heat of the evening over all his body, not strongly, but closely and persistently, as though he were holding his face over a tub of steaming suds. Far below him at the bottom of the valley lay a cluster of bleak huts with window panes red-lit from dying sunlight. Those huts were as familiar to his eyes as a nest is to the eyes of a bird, for he had lived among them all his life. He knew by sight or sound every black man, woman and child living within those huddled walls. For a moment an array of soft black faces hovered before his eyes. N whut kin Ah tell em? Whut kin Ah say t em? He stopped, looked at the ground and sighed. And then he saw himself as he had stood but a few moments ago, facing the white woman who sat behind the brown, gleaming desk: her arms had been round, slender, snow-white, like cold marble; her hair had been the color of flowing gold and had glinted in the sunlight; her eyes had been wide and grey behind icily white spectacles. It seemed he could hear her saying in her dry, metallic voice: I'm sorry, Taylor. You'll just have to do the best you can. Explain it to them, make them understand that we cant do anything. Everybodys hongry, and after all, it's no harder on your people than it is on ours. Tell them they'll just have to wait....

He wagged his head and his lips broke in a slow, sick smile. Whut she know erbout being hongry? Whut she know erbout it? He walked again, thinking, Here Ah is a man called by Gawd t preach n whut kin Ah do? Hongry folks looking t me fer hep n whut kin Ah do? Ah done tried everything n cant do *nuthin!* Shucks, mabbe Hadley n Greens right? They *might* be right. Gawd knows, they *might* be right.

He lifted his head and saw the wide fields plunging before him, down the hillside. The grass was dark and green. All this! he thought. All *this* n folks hongry! Good Gawd, whuts *wrong!* He saw the road running before him, winding, vanishing, the soft yellow dust filled with the ruts of wagon wheels and tiny threads of auto tires. He threw back his head and spoke out loud:

"The good Lawds gonna clean up this ol worl some day! Hes gonna make a new Heaven n a new Earth! N Hes gonna do it in a eye-twinkle change; Hes gotta do it! Things cant go on like this ferever! Gawd knows they cant!" He pulled off his coat and slung it under his left arm. "Waal, there ain nothing t do but go back n tell em. . . . Tell em the white folks wont let em eat. . . ."

The road curved, descending among the green fields that tumbled to a red sky. This was the land on which the Gread God Almighty had first let him see the light of His blessed day. This was the land on which he had first taken unto himself a wife, leaving his mother and father to cleave to her. And it was on the green slopes of these struggling hills that his first-born son, Jimmy, had romped and played, growing to a strong, upright manhood. He wagged his head, musing: Lawd, them wuz the good ol days. . . . There had been plenty to eat; the blessings of God had been overflowing. He had toiled from sunup to sundown, and in the cool of the evenings his wife, May, had taught him to read and write. Then God had spoken to him, a quiet, deep voice coming out of the black night; God had called him to preach His word, to spread it to the four corners of the earth, to save His black people. And he had obeyed God and had built a church on a rock which the very gates of Hell could not prevail against. Yes, he had been like Moses, leading his people out of the wilderness into the Promised Land. He sighed, walking and taking his coat from his left arm and tucking it under his right. Yes, things had been clear-cut then. In those days there had stretched before his eyes a straight and narrow path and he had walked in it, with the help of a Gracious God. On Sundays he had preached God's Word, and on Mondays and Tuesdays and Wednesdays and Thursdays and Fridays and Saturdays he had taken old Bess, his mule, and his plow and had broke God's ground. For a moment while walking through the dust and remembering his hopes of those early years he seemed to feel again the plow handles trembling in his calloused hands and hear the earth cracking and breaking open, black, rich and damp; it seemed he could see old Bess straining forward with the plow, swishing her tail and tossing her head and snorting now and then. Yes, there had been something in those good old days when he had walked behind his plow, between the broad green earth and a blue sweep of sunlit sky; there had been in it all a surge of will, clean, full, joyful; the earth was his and he was the earth's; they were one; and it was that joy and will and oneness in him that God had spoken to when He had called him to preach His word, to save His black people, to lead them, to guide them, to be a shepherd to His flock. But now the whole thing was giving way, crumbling in his hands, right before his eyes. And every time he tried to think of some way out, of some way to stop it, he saw wide grey eyes behind icily white spectacles. He mopped his brow again. Mabbe Hadley n Greens right. . . . Lawd, Ah don know whut t do! Ef Ah fight fer things the white folk say Ahma bad nigger stirrin up trouble. N ef Ah don do nothin, we starve. . . . But somethings *gotta* be done! Mabbe ef we hada demonstration like Hadley n Green said, we could *scare* them white folks inter doin something. . . .

He looked at the fields again, half wistfully, half curiously. Lawd, we could make them ol fields bloom ergin. We could make em feed us. Thas whut Gawd put em there fer. Plows could break and hoes could chop and hands could pick and arms could carry. . . . On and on that could happen and people could eat and feel as he had felt with the plow handles trembling in his hands, following old Bess, hearing the earth cracking and breaking because he wanted it to crack and break; because he willed it, because the earth was his. And they could sing as he had sung when he and May were first married; sing about picking cotton, fishing, hunting, about sun and rain. They could. . . . But whuts the usa thinkin erbout stuff like this? Its all gone now. . . . And he had to go and tell his congregation, the folks the Great God Almighty had called him to lead to the Promised Land—he had to tell them that the relief would give them no food.

That morning he had sent a committee of ten men and women from his congregation to see the mayor. Wondah how they come out? The mayor tol em something, sho! So fer hes been pretty wid me even if he is a white man. As his feet sank softly into the dust he saw Mayor Bolton; he saw the red chin that always had a short, black stubble of beard; he saw the cigar glowing red in front of a pink, fat face. But he needs something t scare im now, he thought. Hes been running over us too long. . . .

He reached the bottom of the slope, turned into a cinder path, and approached the huts. N Lawd, when Ah do try t do somethin mah own folks wont stan by me, wont stick wid me. Theres old Deacon Smith a-schemin n a-plottin, just a-watchin me lika hawk, just a-waitin fer me t tak mah eyes off the groun sos he kin trip me up, sos he kin run t the white folks n tell em Ahm doin something wrong! A black snake in the grass! A black Judas! Thas all he is! Lawd, the Devils sho busy in this world. . . .

He was walking among the crowded huts now.

hello reveren

"How yuh tonight, sonny!" Let ol Deacon Smith tell it, no matter whut Ah *do*, Ahm wrong. . . .

good evenin reveren

"Good evenin, Sistah!" Hes been a-tryin t cheat me outta mah church ever since hes been erroun here. . . .

how yuh tonight reveren Taylor

"Jus fine. N how yuh tonight, Brother?" Hes aw-ways a-whisperin berhin mah back, a-tryin t take mah congregation erway from me. . . . N when he ain doin that hes a-tryin his best t give me wrong advice, jus like the Devil a-tryin t tempt Jesus. But Ahm gonna march on wida hepa Gawd. . . . Yeah, Ah might preach a sermon erbout tha nex Sunday.

As he turned into the street leading to his home and church he saw a tall brown-skinned boy hurrying towards him. Here comes Jimmy! Ah bet hes lookin fer me. . . . Lawd, Ah hope ain nothin wrong. . . .

II

"Pa!" said Jimmy breathlessly when he was some twenty feet away.

Taylor stopped.

"Whuts the mattah, son?"

Jimmy came close.

"The mayors at home, waitin t see yuh," he whispered.

"The *mayor?*"

"Yeah, n two mo white men. One of em is the Chiefa Police."

"They there *now?*"

"Yeah; in the parlor."

"How long they been there?"

"Bout two-three minutes, Ah reckon. N lissen, Pa . . . Sam wuz by jus now. He say the white folks is ridin up n down the streets in their cars warning all the black folks t stay off the streets cause theres gonna be trouble. . . ."

"Sam say tha?"

"Thas whut he tol me. N lissen, Pa . . . Ahma git Sam n Pete n Bob n Jack n some mo boys together sos ef anything happens. . . ."

Taylor gripped Jimmy's shoulders.

"Naw, son! Yuh fixin t git us *all* inter trouble now! Yuh cant do nothing like tha! Yuh gotta be careful! If them white folks just *thought* we wuz doin somethin like that theyd crack down on us! Wed hava riot!"

"But we cant let em ride erroun n talk big n we do nothin!"

"Lissen here, son! Yuh do whut Ah tell yuh t do!" He shook Jimmy's shoulders and his voice was husky. "Yuh go tell them boys t do *nothin* till Ah see em, yuh hear me? Yuh young fools fixin t git us *all* murdered!"

"We jus as waal git killed fightin as t git killed doing nothin," said Jimmy sullenly.

"Yuh go n do whut Ah tol yuh, *hear* me? Ah gotta go n see tha mayor. . . ."

"Hes here t see yuh erbout tha demonstration," said Jimmy.

"How yuh know?"

"Cause thas whut everybodys sayin."

"Who yuh hear say tha?"

"Deacon Smiths spreadin the word."

Taylor winced as though struck by a blow and looked at the dust.

"Hes tellin alla deacons n the church membahs tha the mayors here t stop yuh," said Jimmy. "Hes tellin em yuhs mixed up wid the Reds."

"Deacon Smith there now, *too?*"

"Yeah; hes in the basement wida other deacons. Theys waitin t see yuh."

"How long they been there?"

"Bout hafa hour. N Hadley n Greens in the Bible Room, waitin t talk wid yuh, too. . . ."

Fear gripped Taylor and he stammered:

"Dddid the mmmmayor ssssee em?"

"Naw, ain nobody seen em yit. Ah brought em in thu the back do and tol em t wait fer yuh. Ahm mighty scared wid them Reds waitin fer yuh in the Bible Room and that Chiefa Police waitin fer yuh in the parlor. Ef ol Deacon Smith knowed tha he sho would make a lotta trouble. . . ."

"Where you ma?"

"She upstairs, sewin."

"She know whuts happenin?"

"Naw, Pa."

Taylor stood still, barely breathing.

"Whut yuh gonna do, Pa?" asked Jimmy.

"Yuh go n tell them boys not t do nothin wrong, son. Go on n tell em now! Ah got too much on mah hands now widout yuh boys stirrin up mo trouble!"

"Yessuh."

"Yuh bettah go n do it *now!*"

"Yessuh."

He watched Jimmy hurry down the street. Lawd, Ah hope tha boy don go n git inter trouble. . . .

"Yuh do whut Ah tol yuh, Jimmy!" he yelled.

"Yessuh!" Jimmy hollered back.

He saw Jimmy turn a dusty corner, and go out of sight. Hadley n Greens there in the Bible Room n the Chiefa Police is waitin in the parlor! Ah cant let them white folks see them Reds! N ef Deacon Smith tells on me they'll lynch me. . . . Ah gotta git em out of tha church widout em seein each other. . . . Good Gawd, whut a mess!

III

No sooner had he opened the door of his church than he heard a crescendo of voices. They back awready! Tha committees back! Aw, Ah bet the mayor followed em here. . . . He walked down the hall, turned into the church's waiting room, and saw a roomful of black faces.

"Reveren Taylor! The mayor run us out!"

"He put the police on us!"

The black brothers and sisters ran to Taylor and surrounded him.

"The mayor tol us t git out n don come back no mo!"

A thin black woman swung onto Taylor's arm, crying:

"Whut Ahm gonna do? Ah ain gotta mouthful of bread at home!"

"Sistahs n Brothers, jusa minute," said Taylor. "Firs, tell me whut the mayor said. . . ."

"He say he cant do *nuthin!* N say fer us not t come back t his office no *mo!* N say ef we do hes gonna put us in jail!"

"In *jail?*" asked Taylor.

"Thas whut he said."

"N he tol us not t march, Reveren. He said ef we demonstrated hed put us *all* in jail."

"Who tol em yuh wuz gonna march?" asked Taylor.

"Ah bet it wuz tha ol Deacon Smith," said Sister Harris.

"The Bible says testify whut yuh see n speak whut yuh know," said Sister Davis to Sister Harris.

"Ah knows whut Ahm talkin erbout!" blazed Sister Harris.

"Sistahs n Brothers, les don start no fuss," said Taylor, sighing and dropping his shoulders.

"Whut they tell yuh at the relief station, Reveren Taylor?" asked Sister James.

"They say they cant do nothin," said Taylor.

The thin black woman came and knelt at Taylor's feet, her face in her hands.

"Reveren Taylor, it ain fer me Ahm astin! Its fer mah chillun! Theys hongry! It ain fer me, its fer them! Gawd, have mercy, theys hongry. . . ."

Taylor stepped back, ran his hand into his pocket and pulled out a palmful of loose coins.

"Here, Sistahs n Brothers, split this up between yuh all. Its ever cent Ah got in this worl, so hep me Gawd!"

He laid the coins on a small table. Brother Booker divided them as far as they would go. Then they swarmed around him again.

"Reveren, whut we gonna do?"

"Cant we make the white folks do something fer us?"

"Ahm tireda bein hongry!"

"Reveren, mah babys sick n Ah cant git her no milk!"

"Reveren, whut kin Ah tell mah wife?"

"Lawd knows, Ahm jus erbout sick of this!"

"Whut kin we do, Reveren?"

Taylor looked at them and was ashamed of his own helplessness and theirs.

"Sistahs n Brothers, les call on the great Gawd who made us n put us in this world. . . ."

He clasped his hands in front of him, closed his eyes, and bowed his head. The room grew still and silent.

"Lawd Gawd Awmighty, Yuh made the sun n the moon n the stars n the earth n the seas n mankind n the beasts of the fields!"

yes jesus

"Yuh made em all, Lawd, n Yuh tol em whut t do!"

yuh made em lawd

"Yuhs strong n powerful n Yo will rules this worl!"

yuh rules it lawd

"Yuh brought the chillun of Israel outta the lan of Egypt!"

yuh sho did

"Yuh made the dry bones rise up outta the valley of death n live!"

yuh made em live lawd

"Yuh saved the Hebrew chillun in the fiery furnace!"

yes jesus

"Yuh stopped the storm n Yuh made the sun stan still!"

yuh stopped it lawd

"Yuh knocked down the walls of Jericho n Yuh kept Jona in the belly of the whale!"

yuh kept im lawd

"Yuh let Yo son Jesus walk on watah n Yuh brought Im back from the dead!"

have mercy jesus

"Yuh made the lame walk!"

yuh did it lawd

"Yuh made the blin see!"

help us now lawd

"Yuh made the deaf hear!"

glory t the mos high

"Lawd, Yuhs a rock in the tima trouble n Yuhs a shelter in the tima storm!"

he is he is

"Lawd, Yuh said Yuhd strike down the wicked men who plagued Yo chillun!"

glory t gawd

"Yuh said Yuhd destroy this ol worl n create a new Heaven n a new Earth!"

wes waitin on yuh jesus

"Lawd, Yuh said call on Yo name n Yuhd answer!"

yuh said it lawd n now wes callin

"Yuh made us n put the breatha life in us!"

yuh did lawd

"Now look down on us, Lawd! Speak t our hearts n let us know what Yo will is! Speak t us like Yuh spoke t Jacob!"

speak lawd n our souls will be clay in yo hans

"Lawd, ack in us n well obey! Try us, Lawd, try us n watch us move t Yo will! Wes helpless at Yo feet, a-waitin fer Yo sign!"

send it lawd

"The white folks say we cant raise nothin on Yo earth! They done put the lans of the worl in their pockets! They done fenced em off n nailed em down! Theys a-trying t take Yo place, Lawd!"

speak t em lawd

"Yuh put us in this worl n said we could live in it! Yuh said this worl wuz Yo own! Now show us the sign like Yuh showed Saul! Show us the sign n well ack! We ast this in the name of Yo son Jesus who died tha we might live! Amen!"

amen amen

Taylor stopped and opened his eyes. The room was quiet; he could hear the clock ticking softly above his head, and from the rear came the sound of children playing back of the church. The sisters and brothers rose from their knees and began talking in subdued tones.

"But, Reveren, whut kin we *do?*"

"The issues wid Gawd now, Sistahs n Brothers."

"Is we gonna march?"

"Is yuh goin wid us t the mayor?"

"Have faith, Sistahs n Brothers. Gawd takes care of His own."

"But Ahm hongry, Reveren. . . ."

"Now, Sistahs n Brothers, Ah got t go. Ah got business t tend t. . . ."

He pushed ahead of the black hands that clung to his sleeve.

"Reveren Taylor. . . ."

The thin black woman wailed, kneeling:

"Please, Reveren, cant yuh do *somethin. . . .*"

He pushed through the door, closed it, and stood for a moment with his eyes shut and his fingers slowly loosening on the knob, his ears filled with the sound of wailing voices.

IV

How come all this gotta happen at *once?* Folks a-beggin fer bread n the mayor here t see me n them Reds a-waitin in the Bible Room. . . . Ef Deacon Smith knowed that hed ruin me sho! Ah cant let the mayor see them Reds. . . . Now, Gawd! He looked at a door at the far end of the room, then hurried to it and opened it softly.

"May!" he called in a hoarse whisper.

"Hunh?"

"C mere, quick!"

"Whutcha wan, Dan?"

"C mon in the *room,* May!"

She edged through the half-opened door and stood in front of him, wide-eyed.

"Whutcha wan, Dan?"

"Now, lissen. . . ."

"Ain nothin wrong, is it, Dan? Ain nothin happened, is it?"

He grabbed her arm.

"Naw, n don git scared!"

"Ah ain scared!"

"Yuh cant do whut Ah wan yuh t do ef yuhs scared!"

"Ah *ain* scared, Dan!"

"Lissen. . . ."

"Yeah?"

"The mayors here, in the parlor. N the Chiefa Police. . . ."

She stood stock still and seemed not to breathe.

"The *mayor?*"

"Yeah. . . ."

"*Ain* nothing wrong, is it, Dan?"

"There wont be ef yuh lissen n try to do right."

"Be careful, Dan!"

"Yeah," he said, his voice low and husky. "Go in and tell them white folks Ahm sick, hear?"

She stepped back from him and shook her head.

"Gawd *ain* wid yuh when yuh lie, Dan!"

"We *gotta* lie t white folks! Theys on our necks! They *make* us lie t them! Whut kin we do but lie!"

"*Dan!*"

"Lissen t whut Ahm telling yuh, May! Tell the mayor Ahm gittin outta bed t see him. Tell im Ahm dressin, see? Tell im t wait a few minutes."

"Yeah?"

"Then go t the basement n tell Deacon Smith Ahm wid the mayor. Tell im n the other deacons t wait."

"Now?"

"Yeah; but Ah ain thru yit. Yuh know Hadley n Green?"

"Them *Reds?*"

"Yeah. . . ."

"Dan!" said May, her lungs suspiring in one gasp of amazed helplessness.

"May, fer Chrissakes!"

She began to cry.

"Don do nothin wrong, Dan, please! Don't fergit Jimmy! Hes jus a young boy n hes gotta grow up in this town wid these white folks. Don go n do nothin n fix it so he wont have a chance. . . . Me n yuh don mattah, but thinka him."

Taylor swallowed and looked hard at her.

"Dan, please. . . ."

"May, yuh do whut Ah tell yuh t do! Ah know whut Ahm doin. Hadley n Green downstairs, in the Bible Room. Tell em so nobody kin hear yuh, hear?—tell em aftah yuh done tol the others—tell em t come in here. Let em in thru yo room. . . ."

"Naw!"

She tried to get through the door. He ran to her and caught her hand again.

"Yuh do whut Ah tell yuh, May!"

"Ah ain gonna have them Reds in *here* wid tha mayor n Chiefa Police out *there!* Ah *ain!*"

"Go on do whut Ah tell yuh, May!"

"Dan!"

"Go *ahead,* May!"

He pushed her. She went through the door, slowly, looking back at him. When the door was closed he rammed his hands deep into his pants' pockets, turned to the open window, and looked out into the street. It was profoundly quiet, save for the silvery sound of children's voices back of the church. The air was soft, warm, and full of the scent of magnolias and violets. Window panes across the street were blood-red from dying sunlight. A car sped past, lifting a great cloud of yellow-brown dust. He went to the center of the room and stood over a table littered with papers. He cocked his head, listening. He heard a door slam; footsteps echoed and ceased. A big eight-day clock above his head boomed six times; he looked and his eyes strayed up and rested on a gleaming, brass cross. Gawd, hep me now! Jus hep me t go thru wid this! Again he heard a door slam. Lawd, Ah hope May do right now. . . . N Ah hope Jimmy don go n ack a fool. . . . He crossed the floor on tiptoe, opened the door, and peeped into May's room. It was empty. A slender prism of dust-filled sunlight cut across the air. He closed the door, turned, pulled off his coat and threw it across the table. Then he loosened his collar and tie. He went to the window again and leaned with his back against the ledge, watching the door of May's room. He heard a hoarse voice rise and die. Footsteps again sounded and ceased. He frowned, listening. How come its takin May so long? He started when a timid knock came. He hurried to the door and cracked it.

V

"Hello, Reverend Taylor!" said Hadley, a white man.

"How yuh, Brother Hadley?"

"N how yuh, Reveren?" asked Green, a black man.

"Ahm fine, Brother Green. C mon in, yuh all."

Hadley and Green edged through the door.

"Say, whuts alla mystery?" asked Green.

"Ssssh! Don't talk so loud," cautioned Taylor. "The mayor n the Chiefa Police is out there."

The Negro and the white man stood stone still.

"Do they know wes here?" asked Green.

"Naw, n don git scared. They done come t see me erbout tha demonstration. . . ."

Hadley and Green looked at each other.

"Pull down tha shade," whispered Green, pointing a shaking, black finger.

Quickly, Hadley moved to one side, out of range of the window. His cheeks flushed pink. Taylor lowered the shade and faced them in the semi-darkness. The eyes of the white man and the black man were upon him steadily.

"Waal?" said Green.

"Ah spose yuh know whuts up," said Taylor.

"Theyre here to scare you," said Hadley.

"Ahm trustin Gawd," sighed Taylor.

"Whut yuh gonna tell em?" asked Green.

"Thas whut Ah wanna see yuh all erbout," said Taylor.

"O.K. Whut kin we do?" asked Green.

Taylor looked around and motioned toward two chairs.

"Set down, Brothers."

"Naw, this is awright," said Green, still standing.

"Come on," said Hadley. "What's on your mind?"

Taylor folded his arms and half sat and half leaned on the edge of the table.

"Yuh all think wes gonna have many folks out in the mawnin fer the demonstration?"

"Whut yuh mean?" asked Green.

"When Ahm talkin wid the mayor and Chiefa Police Ah wanna know how many folks Ahm talkin fer. There ain no use in us havin a demonstration ef ain but a few of us is gonna be out there. The police will try t kill us then. . . ."

"How many folks we can get out tomorrow depends a great deal on you, Reverend," said Hadley.

"Hows that?" asked Taylor.

"If you had let us use your name on those handbills, we could say five thousand easily. . . ."

Taylor turned sharply to Hadley.

"Lissen, Brother, Ah done tol yuh Ah cant do tha! N there ain no use in us talkin erbout it no mo! Ah done told yuh Ah cant let them white folks know Ahm callin folks t demonstrate. Aftah all, Ahma preacher. . . ."

"Its yo duty, Reveren," said Green. "We owes it our black folks."

"Ahm doin mah duty as Gawd lets me see it," said Taylor.

"All right, Reverend," said Hadley. "Heres what happened: Weve covered the city with fifteen thousand leaflets. Weve contacted every organization we could think of, black and white. In other words, weve done all *we* could. The rest depends on the leaders of each group. If we had their active endorsement, none of us would have to worry about a crowd tomorrow. And if we had a crowd we would not have to worry about the police. If they see the whole town turning out, they'll not start any trouble. Now, youre known. White and black in this town respect you. If you let us send out another leaflet with your name on it calling for. . . ."

Taylor turned from them and drew his hand nervously across his face. Hadley and Green were silent, watching him. Taylor went to the window and pulled back the curtain slightly and peeped out. Without turning he said softly:

"Ah done tol yuh all Ah ain scareda lettin yuh use mah name."

"We don mean *that,*" said Green hastily.

"Ef it wuz jus me who wuz takin the chance," said Taylor, "Ah wouldn't care none. But Gawd knows it ain right fer me to send them po folks out inter the streets in fronta police. Gawd knows, Ah cant do tha!"

"Honest, Reveren," said Green, touching Taylor's arm. "Ah don understan. Yuh done been thu harder things than this befo."

"N Ahll go thu wid em ergin," said Taylor proudly.

"All right!" said Hadley. "You can say the word that can make this thing a success. If you don't and we have no crowd, then youre to blame. . . ."

Taylor's eyes narrowed and when he spoke there was a note of anger in his voice.

"Gawd hep yuh ef yuhs a-tryin t say yuh gonna blame me ef things don go right!"

"Naw, Reveren!" said Green, coming hurriedly forward and spreading his black hands softly upon the air. "Don feel that way! Wes all jus in a jam. We got t do either two things: Call off this demonstration and let the folks stay hongry, er git as many as we kin together n go downtown in the mawnin. Ef we git five thousan down there the police wont bother us. Ef yuh let us send out yo name tellin the black folks. . . ."

"Naw, Brother!" said Taylor emphatically.

"Then the demonstrations going to be smashed," said Hadley. "*You* can stop it! You have the responsibility and the blame!"

Taylor sighed.

"Gawd knows Ah ain t blame. Ahm doin what mah heart tells me t do. . . ."

"Then whats keeping you from working with us?" asked Hadley. "Im a white man and Im here willing to fight for your peoples rights!"

"Ahm wid yuh, Brother!" said Taylor in a voice which carried a deep note of pleading. "Ahm wid yuh no mattah whut yuh *think!* But yuh *cant* use mah name! Ef them white folks knowed Ah wuz callin mah folks in the streets to demonstrate, they wouldn't never gimme a chance t git something fer mah folks ergin. . . ."

"Thats just it, Reverend," said Hadley. "Don't be afraid of their turning you down because youre fighting for your people. If they knew youd really fight, theyd dislike you; yes? But you can *make* them give something to *all* of your people, not just to *you.* Dont you see, Taylor, youre standing *between* your people and the white folks. You can make them give something to *all* of them. And the poor, hungry white folks will be with you."

"Ah cant lead mah folks t go ergin them white folks like tha," said Taylor. "Thas *war!*"

Hadley came close to Taylor.

"Reverend, cant you see thats just the way the white folks *want* you to feel? Are you leading your folks just because the white folks *say* you should, or are you leading them because you *want* to? Dont you believe in what youre doing? What kind of leaders are black people to have if the white folks pick them and tell them what to do?"

"Brothers, Ahma Christian, n whut yuhs asting fer is something tha makes blood!" thundered Taylor.

Hadley and Green looked at each other.

"Waal, whut yuh gonna tell the mayor?" asked Green.

Taylor stood in the center of the room with his hands in his pockets, looking down at his feet. His voice came low, as though he were talking to himself, trying to convince himself.

"Ahma tell em mah folks is hongry. Ahma tell em they wanna march. Ahma tell em if they march Ahma march wid em. Ahma tell em they wan bread. . . ."

"Reverend," asked Hadley, "why do you feel that

this is so different from all the other times you've gone straight to the white folks and *demanded* things for your people?"

"It is different!" said Taylor.

"You didn't say that when you saved Scott from that *mob!*"

"Tha wuz different, Brother Hadley."

"I dont see it."

Taylor's voice came low.

"Ah feels differently erbout it, Brothers."

"You saved Scotts life. All right, youre saving the lives of your congregation now. Scott was one man, but there are five hundred starving people in your church."

"We ain facin no mob now, Brother Hadley."

"Then what in Gods name are we facin, Reverend? If those police wholl be out there in the morning with their guns and clubs arent a *legal* mob, then what. . . ."

"Its more than a mob, Brother Hadley."

Hadley and Green shook their heads.

"Ah don understand yuh, Reveren," said Green.

"When Ah saved Scott from tha mob, Ah wuz goin ergin *some* of the white folks. But this thing is going ergin em *all!* This is too much like war!"

"You mean youre going against the ones with *money* now!" said Hadley. "Over three thousand of the poor white folks will be with *us*. . . ."

"But, Brother Hadley, the white folks whos got moneys got *everything!* This is jus like civil war!"

"Reverend," said Hadley, "cant you see that if they were not afraid they wouldn't be here asking to *talk* with you? Go in and talk with them, speak to them in the name of five thousand hungry people. Tell the mayor and the Chief of Police that if they dont give the relief back we will demonstrate."

"Ah cant do tha, Brothers. Ah cant let these white folks think Ahm leadin mah folks tha way. Ah tol yuh Brothers when Ah ergreed t work wid yuh Ahd go as fer as Ah could. Waal, Ah done tha. Now, yuh here astin me t threaten this whole town n Ah ain gonna do tha!" said Taylor.

"Yuh astin fer bread, Reveren," said Green.

"Its threatenin, Brothers," said Taylor. "N tha ain Gawds way!"

"So youll let your folks starve before youll stand up and talk to those white folks?" asked Hadley.

"Ahm ackin as Gawd gives me the light to see," said Taylor.

There was silence. Then Hadley laughed, noiselessly.

"Well," he said. "I didn't know you felt this way, Reverend. I thought we could count on you. You know the Party will stand behind you no matter what happens."

"Ahm sorry, Brother Hadley," said Taylor.

"When kin we see yuh t fin out whut the mayor n Chiefa Police say?" asked Green.

Taylor looked at his watch.

"Its a little aftah six now. Make it half-pas six. Thall gimme time t see the Deacon Board."

Green sighed.

"O.K."

"O.K."

Taylor held the door for them. Then he stood in the center of the room and looked miles through the floor. Lawd, Ah hope Ahm doin right. N they think Ahm scared. . . . He flushed hot with shame and anger. He sat in a chair for a moment, then got right up. He drummed his fingers on the corner of the table. Shucks, Ah jus as waal see them white folks now n git it over wid. Ah knowed this wuz comin up! Ah knowed it! He went through May's room, walking slowly, softly, seeing in his mind the picture of the fat, pink face of Mayor Bolton and the lean, red face of Chief of Police Bruden. As he turned into the narrow hall that led to the parlor he heard children yelling in the playground. He went down a stairway, opened a door, and walked through his hushed, dim-lit church. Pale rose light fell slantwise through stained windows and glinted on mahogany pews. He lifted his eyes and saw the figure of Christ on a huge snow-white cross. Gawd, hep me now! Lemme do the right thing! He followed a red carpet to a door that opened into the parlor. He paused and passed his tongue over his dry lips. He could feel his heart beating. Ahll let them do all the talkin. Ahll just tell em mah folks is hongry. Thas all Ah kin do. Slowly, he turned the knob, his lips half parted in dread.

VI

"Why, hello, Dan!"

"Good evenin, Mistah Mayor."

"Howve you been, Dan?"

"Fairly well, wid de hepa Gawd, suh."

Taylor shook hands with a tall, fat white man in a blue serge suit.

"Its been a long time since Ive seen you, Dan."

"Yessuh. It sho has, yo Honah."

"Hows Jimmy?"

"Jus fine, suh."

"Thats a fine boy youve got, Dan."

"Ahm sho glad yuh think so, suh."

"If you raise that boy right he will be a leader of his people some day, Dan."

"Thas the one hope of mah life, suh," said Taylor with deep emotion.

"May was tellin me youre sick," said the mayor.

"Aw, it ain nothin, suh. Jusa summer col, suh."

"I didn't mean to bother you if youre sick, Dan."

"Thas awright, suh. Ahm feelin much bettah now, suh."

"Oh, youll pull through all right; itll take a lot more than a summer cold to kill old war-horses like you and me, eh, Dan?"

The mayor laughed and winked.

"Ahm hopin Gawd spares me a few mo years, suh," said Taylor.

"But at least you look all right now," said the mayor. "Say, Dan, I want you to meet Chief Bruden. This is Dan, Chief, the boy I was telling you about."

"How yuh, Mistah Chief?" asked Taylor.

A black cigar burned red in Bruden's mouth. He shifted his thin body and growled:

"Hello, boy."

"And, Dan, this is Mr. Lowe, head of our fine Industrial Squad."

"How yuh, suh?" asked Taylor.

Lowe nodded with half-closed eyes.

"Sit down, Dan," said the mayor.

"Yessuh."

Taylor sat on the edge of a chair and rested his palms lightly on his knees.

"Maybe our little visit is a surprise, hunh?" asked the mayor.

"Yessuh. It is. But Ahm glad to be of any hep Ah kin, suh."

"Good; I knew youd talk that way. Now, Dan, we want you to help us. Youre a responsible man in this community; that's why we are here."

"Ah tries t do mah duty as Gawd shows it t me, suh."

"That's the spirit, Dan!" The mayor patted Taylor's knee. "Now, Im going to be perfectly frank with you, Dan." The mayor peeled a wrapper from a black cigar. "Here, have one."

"Thank yuh, suh." Taylor put the cigar into his vest pocket. "Ahll smoke it aftah dinner, suh."

There was a silence during which the three white men looked at Taylor.

"Dan," began the mayor, "its not every nigger Id come to and talk this way. Its not every nigger Id trust as Im about to trust you." The mayor looked straight at Taylor. "Im doing this because Ive faith in you. Ive known you for twenty-five years, Dan. During that time I think Ive played pretty fair with you, havent I?"

Taylor swallowed.

"Ahll have t say yuh have, yo Honah."

"Mister Lowe and the Chief here had another plan," said the mayor. "But I wouldn't hear of it. I told them Id work this thing *my* way. I thought *my* way would be much better. After all, Dan, you and I have worked together in the past and I dont see why we cant work together now. Ive backed you up in a lot of things, Dan. Ive backed you even when other white folks said you were wrong. But I believe in doing the right thing. After all, we are human beings, arent we?"

"Yessuh."

"What Ive done for you in the past Im willing to do again. You remember Scott, dont you?"

"Yessuh. Yuhs been a big hep t me n mah folks, suh."

"Well, Dan, my office is always open to you when you want to see me about any of your problems or the problems of your people," said the mayor.

"N Gawd knows Ah sho thanks yuh, suh."

The mayor bit off the tip of his cigar and spat it into a brass spittoon.

"I'm not going to beat about the bush, Dan."

The mayor paused again. There was silence. Taylor felt called upon to say something.

"Yessuh. Ah sho preciates tha, suh."

"You know these Goddam Reds are organizing a demonstration for tomorrow, dont you?" asked the mayor.

Taylor licked his lips before he answered.

"Yessuh. Ah done heard a lotta folks talkin erbout it, suh."

"That's too bad, Dan," said the mayor.

"Folks is talking erbout it everywhere. . . ." began Taylor.

"What *folks?*" interjected Bruden.

"Waal, mos everbody, suh."

Bruden leaned forward and shook his finger in Taylor's face.

"Listen, boy! I want you to get this straight! Reds aint *folks!* Theyre Goddam sonofabitching lousy bastard rats trying to wreck our country, see? Theyre stirring up race hate! Youre old enough to understand that!"

"Hes telling you straight, boy," said Lowe. "And furthermore. . . ."

"Say, whats all this?" demanded the mayor, turning to Lowe and Bruden. "Wait a minute! Whats the big idea of talking to Dan like that? Hes not mixed up in anything like that. Save that kind of talk for bad niggers. . . ."

"The quicker all you niggers get sense enough in your Goddam thick skulls to keep away from them Reds the better off you'll be!" said Bruden, ignoring the mayor.

"Aw, c mon," said the mayor. "Dans all right. Aint that right, Dan?"

Taylor looked down and saw at his feet a sharp

jutting angle of sunshine falling obliquely through a window. His neck felt hot. This is the show-down, he thought. Theys tryin t trap me. . . . He cleared his throat and looked up slowly and saw the mayor gazing at him with cold grey eyes. He shifted his body slightly and saw the glint of Chief Bruden's police star; he saw Lowe's red lips twisted in half-smile and half-leer.

"Isnt that right, Dan?" the mayor asked again.

"Yessuh. Whut yuh white folks say is right. N Ah ergrees wid yuh. But Ah ain foolin wid nobody thas tryin t stir up race hate; naw, *suh!* Ah ain never done nothin like that n Ah never will, so hep me Gawd! Now, erbout this demonstration: Yessuh, Ah heard erbout it. Thas all everbodys been talking erbout erroun here fer a week, yo Honah. Waal, suh, Ahll tell yuh. Theys jus hongry. Theys marchin cause they don know whut else t do, n thas the truth from here t Heaven! Mistah Mayor, theys hongry! Jus plain *hongry!* Ah give mah las dime today t a woman wid eight chillun. . . ."

"We know all about that, Dan," said the mayor.

"Everybodys hungry," said Bruden.

"Boy, cant you see we are all in the *same* boat?" asked Lowe.

"Waal. . . ." drawled Taylor.

"Thingsll be straightened out soon, Dan," interjected the mayor soothingly. "We will see that nobody starves."

"Ah beg yo pardon, suh. A man died jus the other day from starvation. . . ."

Taylor's voice died in his throat and he looked at the floor. He knew that he had said too much.

"I reckon that makes you out a liar, don't it?" Bruden asked the mayor.

"Aw, naw, suh" said Taylor eagerly. "Ah ain disputin nobodys word, suh. Ah jus thought yuh hadnt heard erbout it. . . ."

"We know all about it," said Bruden, turning his head away and looking out of the window, as though he was through with the conversation, as though his mind was made up.

"What do they think theyre going to get by marching?" asked Lowe.

"They think they kin git some bread," said Taylor.

"It wont get em a Goddam crumb!" said Lowe.

There was silence. Taylor looked again at the jutting angle of sunshine and heard the mayor's shoes shifting uneasily on the brown carpet. A match struck; he heard it drop with an angry hiss into the spittoon.

"I dont see why we cant get along, Dan," drawled the mayor.

"Ahm willin t git erlong, Mistah Mayor!" protested Taylor.

"Dan, here we all are, living in good old Dixie. There are twenty-five thousand people in this town. Ten thousand of those people are black, Dan. Theyre your people. Now, its our job to keep order among the whites, and we would like to think of you as being a responsible man to keep order among the blacks. Lets get together, Dan. You know these black people better than we do. We want to feel we can depend on you. Why dont you look at this thing the right way? You know Ill never turn you down if you do the right thing. . . ."

"Mistah Mayor, as Gawds mah judge, Ahm doin right when Ah tell yuh mah folks is hongry. . . ."

"Youre not doing right when you act like a God-dam Red!" said Lowe.

"These niggers around here trust you, Dan," said the mayor. "They'll do what you tell them to do."

"Speak to them," urged Lowe. "Tell them whats right."

"Mistah Mayor, Gawd in Heaven knows mah people is hongry," said Taylor humbly.

The mayor threw his body forward in the chair and rested his hands on his knees.

"Listen, Dan. I know just how you feel. We *all* feel that way. White people are hungry, too. But weve got to be prudent and do this thing right. Dan, youre a leader and youve got great influence over your congregation here." The mayor paused to let the weight of his words sink in. "Dan, I helped you to get that influence by doing your people a lot of favors through *you* when you came into my office a number of times." The mayor looked at Taylor solemnly. "I'm asking you now to use that influence and tell your people to stay *off* the streets tomorrow!"

When Taylor spoke he seemed to be outside of himself, listening to his own words, aghast and fearful.

"Ahm sho thankful as Gawd knows fer all yuh done done fer me n mah people, suh. But mah word don go so fer in times likes these, yo Honah. These folks is lookin t me fer bread n Ah cant give it t em. They hongry n Ah cant tell em where t eat. Theys gonna march no mattah whut Ah say. . . ."

"Youve got influence here, Dan, and you can use it!"

"They wouldnt be marchin ef they wuznt hongry, yo Honah!"

"Thats Red talk, nigger!" said Lowe, standing.

"Aw, thats all right, Lowe," said the mayor, placatingly.

"Im not going to sit here and let this Goddam nigger insult me to my face!" said Lowe.

Taylor stood up.

"Ahm sorry, suh!"

"You *will* be sorry when you find a Goddam rope around your neck!" said Lowe.

"Now, now," said the mayor, laying his hand on Lowe's arm. He turned to Taylor. "You dont mean you wont speak to em, do you, Dan?"

"There ain nothin Ah kin say t em, Mistah Mayor. . . ."

"Youre doing the wrong thing, Dan!"

"Ahm lettin Gawd be mah judge, suh!"

"If you dont do the right thing *we* will be your judges!" said Lowe.

"Ahm trustin Gawd, suh."

"Well, Goddammit, you better let Him guide you right!" said Bruden, jumping to his feet.

"But white folks!" pleaded Taylor. "Mah folks cant plant nothin! Its ergin the law! They cant git no work! Whut they gonna do? They don wan no trouble. . . ."

"Youre heading for a plenty right now!" said Bruden.

The mayor spoke and his voice was low and resigned.

"Ive done all I could, Dan. You wouldn't follow my advice, now the rest is up to Mister Lowe and Chief Bruden here."

Bruden's voice came with a shout:

"A niggers a nigger! I was against coming here talking to this nigger like he was a white man in the first place. He needs his teeth kicked down his throat!" Bruden poked the red tip of his cigar at Taylor's face. "Im the Chief of Police of this town, and Im here to see that orders kept! The Chamber of Commerce says therell be no demonstration tomorrow. Therell be three hundred police downtown in the morning to see that thats done. If you send them niggers down there, or if you let these Goddam Reds fool you into it, Ill not be responsible for whatll happen! Weve never had a riot in this town, but youre plotting one right now when you act like this! And you know wholl get the worst of it!"

"Cant yuh do something, Mistah Mayor? Cant yuh fix it sos we kin git some relief?"

The mayor did not answer; Lowe came close to him.

"We know youve been seeing Hadley and Green! We know whats going on! So watch yourself, nigger!"

"Suh?"

They went out. Taylor stood at the window and saw them get into their car and disappear in a cloud of dust around a corner. He sat down, feeling sweat over all his body. Gawd knows what t do. . . . He brought Lowe n Bruden here t threaten me. . . N they know erbout Hadley and Green. . . . Somebody tol. . . . He looked up, hearing the soft boom of a clock. Hadley n Greens comin back here at six-thirty. . . . He went down the hall thinking, Lawd, ef Ah only knowed whut t do. . . .

VII

May met him in the hall.

"Whut they say, Dan?" she asked with suppressed hysteria.

"Don bother me now, May!"

"There wont be no trouble, will it, Dan?"

"Naw, May! Now, please! Yuh worrin me!"

"Yuhll spoil things fer Jimmy, Dan! Don do nothin wrong! Its fer Jimmy Ahm astin!"

"Itll be awright! Now, lemme go!"

He hurried down the hallway, leaving her crying. Good Gawd! How come she wont leave me erlone. Firs, its Jimmy; then its her. . . . Ef it ain one its the other. . . . He went to the end of the hall, down the steps, turned, and came to the door of the Deacon Room. He heard subdued voices. He knew that the deacons were waiting for him, waiting for some definite word. Shucks, Ahm willin t go thu wid tha march ef they is. Them white folks cant kill us *all*. . . . He pushed the door in. The voices ceased. He saw a dense cloud of tobacco smoke and a circle of black faces. He forced a wan smile.

"Good evenin, Brothers!" he said.

"How yuh, Reveren?" asked Deacon Bonds.

"Ahm sorry Ahm late," said Taylor.

"Wuz tha the mayor out there?" asked Deacon Williams.

Taylor paused and pulled out his handkerchief.

"Yeah, Brothers, it wuz the mayor. N the Chiefa Police n tha man Lowe from the Red Squad. . . ."

"RED SQUAD!" shouted Deacon Smith, jumping to his feet with an outraged look.

"Whut they say, Reveren?" asked Deacon Williams quietly, ignoring Deacon Smith.

Taylor sighed and looked at the floor. For a moment he loathed them because he knew they were expecting an answer to their questions. They were expecting him to speak now as he had always spoken, to the point, confidently, and finally. He had wanted them to do the talking, and now they were silent, waiting for him to speak. Lawd, Ah hope Ahm doin right. Ah don wanna lead these folks wrong. . . .

"They know all erbout tha demonstration," he said.

"But whut they *say?*" asked Deacon Bonds.

"Shucks, man! Yuh *know* whut they said!" said Deacon Smith. "Yuh *know* how them white folks feel erbout this thing!"

"They don wan us t march," said Taylor. "They said ef we march theyll put the police on us. . . ."

Deacon Smith leveled his forefinger at Taylor and intoned:

"AH TOL YUH SO!"

"They said therell be a riot," Taylor went on stubbornly.

"Yessuh! Brothers, wes gotta do *right!*" said Deacon Smith, banging his open palm down on the table. "Ah awways said wes gotta do *right,* Reveren!"

"Ahm prayin t Gawd t guide us right," said Taylor.

"Yuh sho don ack like it!" said Deacon Smith.

"Let the Reveren finish, will yuh?" asked Deacon Bonds.

"Wes gotta do right!" said Deacon Smith again, sitting down, folding his arms, crossing his legs and turning his face sternly away.

"Whut else they say, Reveren?" asked Deacon Bonds.

Taylor sighed.

"They say wes mixed up with the Reds. . . ."

"N by Gawd we *is!*" bawled Deacon Smith. "At least *yuh* is! Ah tol yuh t leave them Reds erlone! They don mean *no*body *no* good! When men starts t deny Gawd, nothin good kin come from em!"

"Brother Smith, let the Reveren talk, will yuh?" asked Deacon Williams.

"He ain talkin *sense!*" said Deacon Smith.

"They say therell be three hundred police downtown in the mawnin," said Taylor, ignoring Smith. "They say only Washington kin do something erbout relief, n tha we must wait. . . ."

"N Gawd Awmighty knows thas all we kin do: wait!" said Deacon Smith.

"Fer Chrissakes, Brother Smith, let im talk!" said Deacon Williams. "We all know *yuhs* scared!"

"Ah ain scared! Ah got *sense!* Ah. . . ."

"Yuh sho don ack like it, the way yuh shoot off yo mouth!" said Deacon Williams.

Deacon Smith stood up.

"Yuh cant talk tha way t me!"

"Then keep yo big mouth shut!" said Deacon Williams.

"Whos gonna make me?"

"Brothers, please!" begged Taylor.

"A fool kin see tha the white folks is scared!" said Deacon Williams.

"N jus cause theys *scared,* theyll kill *anybody* whuts fool ernuff t go downtown in the mawnin," said Deacon Smith.

"Shucks, Ahm willin t taka chance," said Deacon Hilton.

"Me too!"

"We ain got nothin to lose!"

"Any *fool* kin git his head busted!" said Deacon Smith.

"Brothers, fer the lova Gawd, quit fussin!" said Taylor.

They were silent. Taylor looked at them, letting his eyes rove from face to face.

"Brothers, this is the case," he said finally. "They threatenin us not t march, but they ain saying our folks kin git no relief. Now, Ah figgers ef we hada big crowd downtown in the mawnin they wont bother us . . ."

"Thas whut *yuh* think," sneered Deacon Smith.

"N ef we don hava big crowd, theyll smash us. Now, its up t us. . . ."

"Reveren, do the *po* white folks say they gonna be *wid* us?" asked Deacon Jones.

"Brother Hadley tol me theys gonna be wid us," said Taylor.

"Tha Hadley is a lie n the trutha Gawd ain in im!" shouted Deacon Smith. "Tha white man is jus tryin t trick yuh, Ahm telling yuh!"

"Waal, we kin never know less we try n see," said Deacon Bonds.

"Yeah, but they ain gonna let yuh try but *once,*" said Deacon Smith.

"Waal, Ah ain got but *one* time t die!" said Deacon Bonds.

"Ah think the white folksll be there," said Taylor. "Theys hongry, too. . . ."

"Yuhll wake up *some* day!" said Deacon Smith.

"Whut yuh gonna do, Reveren?" asked Deacon Williams.

"Do the congregation wanna march?" asked Taylor.

"They say theys *gonna* march!"

"Waal, Ahll march wid em," said Taylor quietly. "They wont march erlone. . . ."

Deacon Smith waved his arms and screamed.

"Yeah, yuhll march! But yuhs scared t let em use yo name! Whut kinda leader *is* yuh? Ef yuhs gonna ack a fool n be a Red, then how come yuh wont come on out n say so sos we kin all hear it? Naw, you ain man ernuff t say whut yuh is! Yuh wanna stan in wid the white folks! Yuh wanna stan in wid the Reds! Yuh wanna stan in wid the congregation! Yuh wanna stan in wid the Deacon Board! Yuh wanna stan in wid *ever*body n yuh stan in wid *no*body!"

"Ahm ackin accordin t mah lights!" said Taylor.

"Waal, they ain lettin yuh see fer!" said Deacon Smith.

"Ef yuh gotta plan bettah than mine, Brother Smith, tell us erbout it!"

"AH SAY WE OUGHTNT MARCH!"

"Then, whut we gonna do?"

"Wait n see how things come out!"

"Ahm tireda waitin," said Taylor.

"How come yuh didnt send yo name out on them

leaflets?" demanded Deacon Smith. Without waiting for Taylor to answer, he flared: "Ahll tell yuh why yuh didn't! Yuh *scared!* Yuh didnt wan them white folks t know yuhs mixed up in this demonstration. Yuh wanted em t think yuh wuz being pushed erlong by other folks n yuh couldn't help whut wuz happenin! But, Reveren, as sho as theres a Gawd in Heaven yuh ain foolin nobody!"

Taylor stood up.

"Brother Smith, Ah knows whut yuhs up t! Yuh tryin t run me outta mah church, but yuh cant! Gawd Awmighty Himself put me here n Ahm stayin till He says fer me t go! Yuh been schemin t git me out, but yuh cant do it this way! It ain right n Gawd knows it ain! Yeah; ef mah folks marches in the mawnin Ahm marchin wid em!"

"Thas the time, Reveren!"

"We kin show tha ol mayor something!"

"N therell be white folks wid us, too!"

"Ahll go wid the Reveren n the congregation!"

"Ahll go!"

"N me too!"

"Gawd ain wid yuh when yuh ain in the right!" said Deacon Smith.

"Gawd didnt mean fer folks t be hongry!" said Deacon Bonds.

"But He ain wid yuh when yuh stirrin up trouble, makin blood n riots!" said Deacon Smith. "N any man whut sets here n calls himself a leader called by Gawd t preach n leads his folks the wrong way is a fool n the spirita Gawd ain in him!"

"Now, wait a minute there, Brother Smith!" said Taylor. "Yuhs talkin *dangerous!*"

"Ah say any man whut leads his folks inter guns n police. . . ."

"Ain nobody leading us *nowhere!*" said Deacon Bonds.

"We gwine *ourselves!*" said Deacon Williams.

"Ah ain in this!" said Deacon Smith, jumping again to his feet. "Ah ain in this n Ahm gonna do whut Ah kin t hep mah people!"

The room grew quiet.

"Whut yuh mean, Brother Smith?" asked Taylor.

"Ah say Ahm gonna hep mah people!" said Deacon Smith again.

Taylor walked over to him.

"Is yuh gonna tell the white folks on us?"

Deacon Smith did not answer.

"Talk, Brother Smith!" said Taylor. "Tell us whut yuh mean!"

"Ah means whut Ah means!" said Deacon Smith; and he clamped his teeth tight, sat again, crossed his legs, folded his arms and stared at the blank wall.

Taylor swallowed and looked at the floor. Lawd, Ah don know whut to do! Ah wish this wuz over. . . . This niggers gonna tell on us! Hes gonna tell the white folks sos he kin stan in wid em. . . .

"Brother Smith. . . ." began Taylor.

The door opened and Jimmy stepped into the room.

"Say, Pa!"

"Whut yuh wan, son?"

"Somebodys out front t see yuh. Theys in a car. Theys white folks."

"Scuse me, Brothers," said Taylor. "Ahll be right back."

"Wes gonna set right here till yuh git back," said Deacon Smith.

When outside the door, Taylor turned to Jimmy.

"Who is they, Jimmy? How come they wouldnt come in?"

"Ah dunno, Pa. The car drove up just as Ah wuz comin thu the gate. They white men. They said fer yuh t come right out."

"Awright. N, son, yuh betta go see about yo ma."

"Whuts the mattah?"

"Shes jus upset erbout the demonstration."

"Is they gonna march, Pa?"

"Ah reckon so."

"Is many gonna be out?"

"Ah dunno, son. Ah hope so. Yuh bettah go see erbout yo ma now."

"Yessuh."

"Yuh tell them boys whut Ah tol yuh?"

"Yessuh."

Taylor paused at the front door and peeped out from behind a curtain. In front of his gate was a long black car. Who kin tha be? For a moment he thought the mayor had come back. But his cars grey. . . . He opened the door and walked slowly down the steps. Lawd, mabbe we oughtnt go thu wid this demonstration aftah all? We might all be sorry ef somebodys killed in the mawnin. . . . He walked along a flower-bordered path that smelt of violets and magnolias. Dust rested filmily on tree leaves. The sun was almost gone. As he came to the car a white face looked out.

"Yuh Taylor?"

"Yessuh," answered Taylor, smiling.

The rear door of the car opened and the white man stepped to the ground.

"So youre Taylor, hunh?"

"Yessuh," said Taylor again, still smiling, but puzzled. "Kin Ah be of service t yuh, suh?"

Taylor saw it coming, but could do nothing. He remembered afterward that he had wanted to ask, What yuh doin? The blow caught him flush on the point of the jaw, sending him flying backward. His head struck the edge of the runningboard; a flash of red shot before his eyes. He rolled, face downward, into a bed of thick violets. Dazed, he turned his head, trying to speak. He felt a hand grab the back of his collar and jerk him up.

"Get in the car, nigger!"

"Say, whut yuh. . . ."

"Shut up and get in the car, Goddam you!"

A blow came to his right eye. There were three white men now. They lifted him and rammed him down on the floor in the back of the car.

"Say, yuh cant do this!"

"Get your Goddam mouth shut, you bastard!"

A hard palm slapped him straight across his face. He struggled up, protesting.

"You. . . ."

The heel of a shoe came hard into his solar plexus. He doubled up, like a jackknife. His breath left, and he was rigid, half-paralyzed.

"You think you can run this whole Goddam town, don't you? You think a nigger can run over white folks and get away with it?"

He lay still, barely breathing, looking at blurred white faces in the semi-darkness of the roaring car.

VIII

The moment he tried to tell the direction in which the car was moving, he knew he had waited too long. He remembered dimly that they had turned corners at least three times. He lay with closed eyes and wondered what they were going to do with him. She gonna be worried t death, he thought, thinking of May. And then he thought of Jimmy and said to himself, Ah hope he don go n ack a fool now. . . . The numbness which had deadened most of his stomach and chest was leaving. He felt sweat on his back and forehead. The car slowed, turned; then it ran fast again. He knew by the way the rocks crunched beneath the humming rubber tires that they were speeding over gravel. Whut roads this? He could not tell. There were so many gravel roads leading out of town. He tried to recall how long he had lain there half-paralyzed from that kick in the solar plexus. He was confused; it might have been five minutes or it might have been an hour. The car slowed again, turning. He smelt the strong scent of a burning cigarette and heard the toll of a far off church bell. The car stopped; he heard the sound of other cars, gears shifting and motors throbbing. We mus be at some crossroads. But he could not guess which one. He had an impulse to call for help. But there would not be any use in his doing that now. Mabbe they white folks anyhow. He would be better off as he was; even six white men were better than a mob of white men. The car was speeding again, lurching. He smelt dust, clay dust. Then he heard a hard, rasping voice:

"How is he?"

"O.K."

"Keep im quiet!"

"O.K."

He said nothing. He began to wonder how many of them were in the car. Yes, he should have been watching for something like this. They been threatening me fer a long time. Now this is it. The car was gradually slowing with that long slow slowing preceding a final stop. He felt the rubber tires turning over rough ground; his head rocked from side to side, hitting against the lower back of the front seat. Then the car stopped; the motor stopped; for a moment there was complete silence. Then he heard wind sighing in trees. Wes out in the country somewhere. In the woods, he thought.

"O.K.?"

"O.K.!"

He heard a door open.

"C mon, nigger! Get up and watch yourself!"

He pulled up and caught a glimpse of starry sky. As his feet hit the ground his head began to ache. He had lain cramped so long the blood had left his limbs; he took a step, kicking out his legs to restore circulation. His arms were grabbed from behind and he felt the pressure of a kneecap in the center of his spine. He gasped and reeled backward.

"Where you think youre going?"

He rested on his knees, his body full of pain. He heard a car door slam.

"Awright, nigger! Lets go! Straight ahead!"

He got up and twisted his head about to see who had spoken. He saw four blurred white faces and then they were blotted out. He reeled backward again, his head striking the ground. A pain knotted in his temple.

"Get up, nigger! Keep your eyes in front, and walk, Goddammit!"

He pulled up and limped off, his head down. Mabbe they gonna shoot me? His feet and the feet behind him made a soft *cush-cush* in the dew-wet grass and leaves.

"Aw right, nigger!"

He stopped. Slowly he raised his eyes; he saw a tall white man holding a plaited leather whip in his hand, hitting it gently against his trousers' leg.

"You know what this is, nigger?"

He said nothing.

"Wont talk, hunh? Well, this is a nigger-lesson!"

The whip flashed in faint starlight. The blow numbed his lips. He tasted blood.

"You know what this is? Im asking you again, nigger!"

"Nawsuh," he whispered.

"This is a nigger-whip!"

The leather whacked across his shoulders.

"Mistah, Ah ain done nothin!"

"Aw, naw! You aint done nothin! You aint never done a Goddam thing, have you?" White men were standing close around him now. "All you ever do is play around with Reds, dont you? All you ever do is get crowds of niggers together to threaten white folks, dont you? When we get through with you tonight youll know how to stay in a niggers place! C mon! Get that Goddam vest off!"

He did not move. The whip wrapped itself around his neck, leaving a ring of fire.

"You want me to *beat* it off you?"

He pulled off the vest and held it in his hands.

"C mon! Get that shirt and undershirt off!"

He stripped to his waist and stood trembling. A night wind cooled his sweaty body; he was conscious of his back as he had never been before, conscious of every square inch of black skin there. One of the white men walked off a few paces and stopped.

"Bring im over here!"

"O.K.!"

They guided him with prods and kicks.

"On your knees, nigger!"

He did not move. Again his arms were caught from behind and a kneecap came into the center of his back. Breathless, he dropped, his hands and knees cooling in the wet grass. He lifted his fingers to feel his swelling lips; he felt his wrists being grabbed and carried around the trunk of a tree. He held stiffly and struggled against a rope.

"Let go!"

His arms went limp. He rested his face against a cold tree-trunk. A rope cut into his wrists. They tied his feet together, drawing the rope tight about his ankles. He looked around; they stood watching.

"Well, nigger, what do you know?"

"Nothin, suh."

"Youre a preacher, aint you?"

"Yessuh."

"Well, lets hear you pray some!"

He said nothing. The whip lashed across his bare back, *whick!* He flinched and struggled against the rope that cut his wrists to the bone. The leather thong hummed again, *whick!* and his spine arched inward, like a taut bow.

"Goddam your black soul, pray!"

He twisted his face around, pleading:

"Please, Mistah! Don whip me! Ah ain done nothin. . . ."

Another lash came across his half-turned cheek, *whick!* He jerked around and sheltered his face against the tree-trunk. The lash hit his back, *whick!*

"*Hit* that black bastard, Bob!"

"Let me have that whip!"

"Naw, wait a minute!"

He said nothing. He clenched his teeth, his whole body quivering and waiting. A split second after each blow his body would lurch, as though absorbing the shock.

"You going to pray? You want me to beat you till you *cant* pray?"

He said nothing. He was expecting each blow now; he could almost feel them before they came, stinging, burning. Each flick came straight on his back and left a streak of fire, a streak that merged with the last streak, making his whole back a sheet of living flame. He felt his strength ebbing; he could not clench his teeth any more. His mouth hung open.

"Let me have it, Bob?"

"Naw, its my turn!"

There was a pause. Then the blows came again; the pain burned its way into his body, wave upon wave. It seemed that when he held his muscles taut the blows hurt less; but he could not hold taut long. Each blow weakened him; each blow told him that soon he would give out. Warm blood seeped into his trousers, ran down his thighs. He felt he could not stand it any longer; he held his breath, his lungs swelling. Then he sagged, his back a leaping agony of fire; leaping as of itself, as though it were his but he could not control it any longer. The weight of his body rested on his arms; his head dropped to one side.

"Ahhlll ppppray," he sobbed.

"Pray, then! Goddam you, pray!"

He tried to get his breath, tried to form words, hearing trees sighing somewhere. The thong flicked again, *whick!*

"Ain't you going to pray!"

"Yyyyyessuh. . . ."

He struggled to draw enough air into his lungs to make his words sound.

"Ooour Ffather. . . ."

The whip cut hard, *whick!* pouring fire and fire again.

"Have mercy, Lawd!" he screamed.

"Pray, nigger! Pray like you *mean* it!"

". . wwwhich aaaaart in hheaven . . . hhhallowed bbe Ttthy nname. . . ." The whip struck, *whick!* "Ahm prayin, Mmmmistah!"

"Goddam your black heart, *pray!*"

". . . Tttthine kkkindom ccome . . . Tthy wwill bbe ddddone. . . ."

He sobbed, his breath leaving his lungs, going out from him, not wanting to stay to give sound to his words. The whip brought more fire and he could not stand it any longer; his heart seemed about to burst. He screamed, stretched his knees out and twisted his arms till he lay sideways, half on his stomach. The whip came into his stomach, *whick!* He turned over; it came on his back again, *whick!* He stopped struggling and hung limply, his weight suspended on arms he could not feel. Then fire flamed over all his body; he stiffened, glaring upward, wild-eyed.

"Whats the matter, nigger? You hurt?"

"Awright, kill me! Tie me n kill me! Yuh white trash cowards, kill me!"

"Youre tough, aint you? Just wait! Well kill you, you black sonofabitch!"

"Lemme have that whip!"

"C mon, now! Its my turn"

"Give me that whip, Ellis!"

He was taut, but not feeling the effort to be taut.

"Well git yuh white trash some day! So hep me Gawd, well git yuh!"

The whip stopped.

"Say that again, Goddam you!"

The whip lashed, *whick!* but there was no streak of fire now; there was only one sheet of pain stretching all over his body, leaping, jumping, blazing in his flesh.

"Say it!"

He relaxed and closed his eyes. He stretched his legs out, slowly, not listening, not waiting for the whip to fall, *say it whick! say it whick! say it whick!* He groaned. Then he dropped his head and could not feel any more.

IX

Moonlight pained his eyeballs and the rustle of tree leaves thundered in his ears. He seemed to have only a head that hurt, a back that blazed, and eyes that ached. In him was a feeling that some power had sucked him deep down into the black earth, had drained all strength from him. He was waiting for that power to go away so he could come back to life, to light. His eyes were half-open, but his lids did not move. He was thirsty; he licked his lips, wanting water. Then the thunder in his ears died, rolling away. He moved his hand and touched his forehead; his arm fell limply in the wet grass and he lay waiting to feel that he wanted to move. As his blood began to flow swiftly again he felt sweat breaking out over his body. It seemed he could hear a tiny, faraway sound whispering over and over like a voice in an empty room: Ah got fever. . . . His back rested on a bed of fire, the imprint of leaves and grass searing him with a scalding persistence. He turned over on his stomach and groaned. Then he jerked up, half-sitting. He was fully conscious now, fighting for his strength, remembering the curses, the prayer and the whip. The voice whispered again, this time louder: Ah gotta git home. . . . With fumbling fingers he untied the rope from his ankles and wrists. They didnt kill me, he thought. He stood up and the dark earth swayed and the stars blurred. Lawd, have mercy! He found himself on his knees; he had not known when he had started falling; he just found himself on his knees. Lawd, Ahm weak! He stood up again, more slowly this time, holding onto a tree. He would have to get his shirt; he could not go through the streets with a naked and bleeding back. He put one foot in front of the other with conscious effort, holding his body stiffly. Each slight twist of his shoulders sent a wave of liquid metal over him. In the grass at his feet his shirt was smeared like a white blur. He touched it; it was wet. He held it, instinctively fearing to put it on. When it did touch, his whole back blazed with a pain so intense that it seemed to glow white hot. No, he could not put it on now. Stiffly, he went among the trees, holding the shirt in his hands, looking at the ground.

He stopped at the edge of a dirt road, conscious of the cool steady stars and the fire that smoldered in his back. What roads this? He could not tell. Then he heard a clock striking so faintly that it seemed to be tolling in his own mind. He counted, Wun, Tuh. . . . Its tuh erclock, he thought. He could not stay here all night; he had to go in one direction or another. He watched the brown dusty road winding away in the darkness, like a twisting ribbon. Then he ducked his head, being seared again with fire and feeling a slight rush of air brush across his face. A small bird wheeled past his eyes and fluttered dizzily in the starlight. He watched it veer and dip, then crash softly into a tree limb. It fell to the ground, flapping tiny wings blindly. Then the bird twittered in fright and sailed straight upward into the starlight, vanishing. He walked northward, not going anywhere in particular, but walked northward because the bird had darted in that direction.

The road curved, turned to gravel, crunching under his shoes. This mus be the way, he thought. There were fences along the sides of the road now. He went faster, holding his legs stiffly to avoid pulling the muscles in his back. A church steeple loomed in the starlight, slender and faint. Yeah, thas Houstons church. N Ah gotta go thu a white neighborhood, he thought with despair. He saw houses, white, serene and cool in the night. Spose Ah go to Houston? Naw, hes white. *White.* . . . Even tho he preaches the gospel Ah preaches, he might not take me in. . . . He passed a small graveyard surrounded by a high iron picket fence. A *white* graveyard, he thought and snickered bitterly. Lawd God in Heaven, even the dead cant be together! He stopped and held his shirt in his hands. He dreaded trying to put it on, but he had to. Ah cant go thu the streets like this. Gingerly, he draped the shirt over his shoulders; the whole mass of bruised and mangled flesh flamed, glowed white. With a convulsive movement he rammed his arms into the sleeves, thinking that the faster he did it the less pain there would be. The fire raged so he had a wild impulse to run, feeling that he would have no time to suffer. But he could not run in a white neighborhood. To run would mean to be shot, for a burglar, or anything. Stiff-legged, he went down a road that turned from brown dust to black asphalt. Ahead street lamps glowed in round, rosy hazes.

Far down the shadow-dappled pavement he heard the sound of feet. He walked past a white man, then he listened to the white man's footsteps dying away behind him. He stopped at a corner and held onto a telephone pole. It would be better to keep in the residential district than to go through town. He would be stopped and questioned in town surely. And jailed maybe. Three blocks later on a white boy came up on him so softly and suddenly that he started in panic. After the boy had gone he turned to look; he saw the boy turning, looking at him. He walked on hurriedly. A block later a white woman appeared. When she was some fifty feet away she crossed to the other side of the street. Hate tightened his throat, then he emptied his lungs in a short, silent, bitter laugh. Ah ain gonna bother yuh, white lady. Ah only wan t git home. . . .

Like a pillar of fire he went through the white neighborhood. Some days theys gonna burn! Some days theys gonna burn in Gawd Awmightys fire! How come they make us suffer so? The worls got too mucha everything! Yit they bleed us! They fatten on us like leeches! There ain no groun yuh kin walk on that they don own! N Gawd knows tha ain right! He made the earth fer us all! He ain tol no lie when He put us in this worl n said be fruitful n multiply. . . . Fire fanned his hate; he stopped and looked at the burning stars. "Gawd, ef yuh gimme the strength Ahll tear this ol buildin down! Tear it down, Lawd! Tear it down like ol Samson tore the temple down!" He walked again, mumbling. "Lawd, tell me whut t do! Speak t me, Lawd!" He caught his breath; a dark figure came out of the shadows in front of him. He saw a glint of metal; it was a policeman. He held erect and walked rapidly. Ahll stop, he thought. He wont have t ast me t stop. . . . He saw the white face drawing closer. He stopped and waited.

"Put your hands up, nigger!"

"Yessuh."

He lifted his arms. The policeman patted his hips, his sides. His back blazed, but he bit his lips and held still.

"Who you work for?"

"Ahma preacher, suh."

"A *preacher?*"

"Yessuh."

"What you doing out here this time of night?"

"Ah wuz visitin a sick man, a janitah, suh, whut comes t mah church. He works fer Miz Harvey. . . ."

"Who?"

"Miz Harvey, suh."

"Never heard of her, and I've been on this beat for ten years."

"She lives right back there, suh," he said, half turning and pointing.

"Well, you look all right. You can go on. But keep out of here at night."

"Yessuh."

He was near his own people now. Across a grassy square he could see the top of the round-house glinting dully in the moonlight. The black asphalt turned to cinders and the houses were low, close together, squatting on the ground as though hiding in fear. He saw his church and relaxed. He came to the steps. Caught hold of a banister and rested a moment.

When inside he went quietly down a hall, mounted the stairs, and came to the door of his room. He groped in the dark and felt the bed. He tried to pull off the shirt. It had stuck. He peeled it. Then he eased onto the bed and lay on his stomach. In the darkness his back seemed to take new fire. He went to the kitchen and wet a cloth with cold water. He lay down again with the cloth spread over him. That helped some. Then he began to shake. He was crying.

X

The door creaked.

"Tha yuh, Pa?"

"Son?"

"Good Gawd, wes been lookin all over fer yuh! Where yuh been? Mas worried t death!"

"C mon in, son, n close the do."

"Don yuh wanna light?"

"Naw; close the do."

There was a short silence.

"Whuts the mattah, Pa? Yuh sick?"

"Close the do n sit down, son!"

Taylor could hear Jimmy's breathing, then a chair scraping over the floor and the soft rustle of Jimmy's clothes as he sat.

"Whuts the mattah, Pa? Whut happened?"

Taylor stared in the darkness and slowly licked his

swollen lips. He wanted to speak, but somehow could not. Then he stiffened, hearing Jimmy rise.

"Set *down*, son!"

"But, Pa. . . ."

Fire seethed not only in Taylor's back, but all over, inside and out. It was the fire of shame. The questions that fell from Jimmy's lips burned as much as the whip had. There rose in him a memory of all the times he had given advice, counsel, and guidance to Jimmy. And he wanted to talk to him now as he had in the past. But his impulses were deadlocked. Then suddenly he heard himself speaking, hoarsely, faintly. His voice was like a whisper rising from his whole body.

"They whipped me, son. . . ."

"Whipped yuh? Who?"

Jimmy ran to the bed and touched him.

"Son, set *down!*"

Taylor's voice was filled with a sort of tense despair. He felt Jimmy's fingers leaving him slowly. There was a silence in which he could hear only his own breath struggling in his throat.

"Yuh mean the *white folks?*"

Taylor buried his face in his pillow and tried to still the heaving in his chest.

"They beat me, son. . . ."

"Ahll git a doctah!"

"Naw!"

"But yuhs hurt!"

"Naw; lock the do! Don let May in here. . . ."

"Goddam them white bastards!"

"Set down, son!"

"Who wuz they, Pa?"

"Yuh cant do nothin, son. Yuhll have t wait. . . ."

"Wes been waitin too long! All we do is wait, *wait!*"

Jimmy's footsteps scuffed across the floor. Taylor sat up.

"Son?"

"Ahma git mah gun n git Pete n Bob n Joe n Sam! Theyll see they cant do this t us!"

Taylor groped in the darkness; he found Jimmy's shoulders.

"C mon son! Ahm awright. . . ."

"Thas the reason why they kill us! We take everthing they put on us! We take everthing! *Everthing!*"

"Yuh cant do nothing *erlone*, Jimmy!"

Jimmy's voice was tense, almost hysterical.

"But we kin *make* em know they cant do this t us widout us doin *something!* Aw, hell, Pa! Is we gonna be dogs *all* the time?"

"But theyll kill yuh, son!"

"Somebody *has* t die!"

Taylor wanted to tell Jimmy something, but he could not find the words. What he wanted to say boiled in him, but it seemed too big to come out. He flinched from pain, pressing his fingers to his mouth, holding his breath.

"Pa?"

"Yeah, son?"

"Hadley n Green wuz here t see yuh three-fo times."

"Yeah?"

Jimmy said nothing. Taylor twisted around, trying to see his son's face in the darkness.

"Whut they say, son?"

"Aw, hell! It don mattah. . . ."

"Tell me whut they *said!*"

"Ttthey ssaid. . . . Aw, Paw, they didnt know!"

"Whut they *say?*"

"They said yuh had done run out on em. . . ."

"Run *out?*"

"Everbody wuz astin where yuh wuz," said Jimmy. "Nobody knowed. So they tol em yuh run out. N Brother Smith had the Deacon Board t vote yuh outta the church. . . ."

"Vote me *out?*"

"They said they didnt wan yuh fer pastah no mo. It was Smith who made em do it. He tol em yuh had planned a demonstration n lef em holdin the bag. He fussed n stormed at em. They thought they wuz doin right. . . ."

Taylor lay on his bed of fire in the darkness and cried. He felt Jimmy's fingers again on his face.

"Its awright, Pa. Well git erlong somehow. . . ."

"Seems like Gawds don lef me! Ahd die fer mah people ef Ah only knowed how. . . ."

"Pa. . . ."

"How come Ah cant never do nothin? All mah life Ah done tried n cant do nothin! *Nothin!*"

"Its awright, Pa!"

"Ah done lived all mah life on mah knees, a-beggin n a-pleadin wid the white folks. N all they gimme wuz crumbs! All they did wuz kick me! N then they come wida gun n ast me t give mah own soul! N ef Ah so much as talk lika man they try t kill me. . . ."

He buried his face in the pillow, trying to sink himself into something so deeply that he could never feel again. He heard Jimmy turning the key in the lock.

"Son!"

Again he ran to Jimmy and held him.

"*Don* do tha, son!"

"Thingsll awways be like this less we *fight!*"

"Set down, son! Yo po ol pas a-*beggin* yuh t set down!"

He pulled Jimmy back to the bed. But even then it did not seem he could speak as he wanted to. He felt what he wanted to say, but it was elusive and hard to formulate.

"Son. . . ."

"Ah ain gonna live this way, Pa!"

He groped for Jimmy's shoulders in the darkness and squeezed them till the joints of his fingers cracked. And when words came they seemed to be tearing themselves from him, as though they were being pushed upward like hot lava out of a mountain from deep down.

"Don be a fool, son! Don thow yo life erway! We cant do nothin erlone."

"But theys gonna treat us this way as long as we *let* em!"

He had to make Jimmy understand; for it seemed that in making him understand, in telling him, he, too, would understand.

"We gotta git wid the *people*, son. Too long we done tried t do this thing our way n when we failed we wanted t turn out n pay-off the white folks. Then they kill us up like flies. Its the *people*, son! Wes too much erlone this way! Wes los when wes erlone! Wes gonna be wid our folks. . . ."

"But theys killin us!"

"N theyll keep on killin us less we learn how t fight! Son, its the people we mus gid wid us! Wes empty n weak this way! The reason we cant do nothin is cause wes so much erlone. . . ."

"Them Reds wuz right," said Jimmy.

"Ah dunno," said Taylor, "But let nothin come tween yuh n yo people. Even the Reds cant do nothin ef yuh lose yo people. . . ." Fire burned him as he talked, and he talked as though trying to escape it. "Membah whut Ah tol yuh prayer wuz, son?"

There was silence, then Jimmy answered slowly:

"Yuh mean lettin Gawd be so real in yo life tha everthing yuh do is cause of Im?"

"Yeah, but its different now, son. Its the *people!* Theys the ones whut mus be real t us! Gawds wid the people! N the peoples gotta be real as Gawd t us! We cant hep ourselves er the people when wes erlone. Ah been wrong erbout a lotta things Ah tol yuh, son. Ah tol yuh them things cause Ah thought they wuz right. Ah told yuh t work hard n climb t the top. Ah told yuh folks would lissen t yuh then. But they wont, son! All the will, all the strength, all the power, all the numbahs is in the people! Yuh cant live by yoself! When they beat me tonight, they beat *me*. . . . There wuznt nothin Ah could do but lay there n hate n pray n cry. . . . Ah couldnt *feel* mah people, Ah couldnt *see* mah people, Ah couldnt *hear* mah people. . . . All Ah could feel wuz tha whip cuttin mah blood out. . . ."

In the darkness he imagined he could see Jimmy's face as he had seen it a thousand times, looking eagerly, his eyes staring before him, fashioning his words into images, into life. He hoped Jimmy was doing that now.

"Ahll awways hate them bastards! Ahll *aw*ways hate em!"

"Theres other ways, son."

"Yuhs sick, Pa. . . ."

"Wes all sick, son. Wes gotta think erbout the people, night n day, think erbout em so hard tha our po selves is fergotten. . . . Whut they suffer is whut Ah suffered las night when they whipped me. Wes gotta keep the people wid us."

Jimmy was silent. A soft knock came at the door.

XI

"Dan!"

"Thas Ma," said Jimmy.

Taylor heard Jimmy rise to his feet; he gripped Jimmy's hands.

"Please, Pa! Let her come in n hep yuh!"

"Naw."

"Dan!"

Jimmy broke from him; he heard the key turn in the lock. The door opened.

"Dan! Fer Gawds sake, whuts the mattah?"

Jimmy switched on the light. Taylor lay blinking at May's anxious face. He felt shame again, knowing that he should not feel it, but feeling it anyway. He turned over and buried his face in his hands.

"Dan!"

She ran and knelt at the side of the bed.

"They tried t kill im, Ma! They beat im!" said Jimmy.

"Ah knowed them white folks wuz gonna do something like this! Ah knowed it," sobbed May.

Taylor sat up.

"Yuh be still! Lay down!" said May.

She pushed him back onto the bed.

"Cant yuh do something fer im, Ma? Hes sufferin tha way."

Taylor heard May leave the room and come back.

"Hol still, Dan. This ain gonna hurt yuh. . . ."

He felt warm water laving him, then something cool that smelled of oil. He heard Jimmy moving to and fro, getting things for May. When his back was dressed he felt the bed had somehow changed. He wondered at the strange peace that seeped into his mind and body there in the room with May and Jimmy, with the white folks far off in the darkness.

"Feel bettah, Dan?"

"Ahm awright."

"Yuh hongry?"

"Naw."

He wanted to talk to Jimmy again, to tell him

about the black people. But he could not think of words that would say what the wanted to say. He would tell it somehow later on. He began to toss, moving jerkily, more now from restlessness of mind than from the dying fire still lingering in his body.

XII

Suddenly the doorbell pealed. Taylor turned and saw May and Jimmy looking at each other.

"Somebody at the do," said Jimmy in a tense voice.

"Yuh reckon they white folks?" asked May.

"Yuh bettah go down, Jimmy," said Taylor.

"Ef its any white folks tell em Dans out," said May.

Jimmy's footsteps died away on the stairs. A door slammed. There were faint sounds of voices. Footsteps echoed, came on the stairs, grew loud. Taylor knew that more than one person was coming up. He lifted himself and sat on the edge of the bed.

"Dan, yuh cant git up! Yuhll make yoself sick!"

He ignored her. The door opened and Jimmy ran in.

"Its Brother Bonds, Pa!"

Bonds stood in the doorway with his head wrapped in blood-stained bandages. His face twitched and eyes stared at something beyond the walls of the room, as though his attention had been riveted once and for always upon one fixed spot.

"Whut happened, Brother?" asked Taylor.

Bonds stared, dazed, with hunched and beaten shoulders. Then he sank to the floor, sobbing softly: "They beat me! They beat mah chillun! They beat mah wife! They beat us all cause Ah tol em t git outta mah house! Lawd, how long Yuh gonna let em treat us this way? How long Yuh gonna let em make us suffer?"

May sobbed. Jimmy ran out of the room. Taylor caught him on the stairs.

"Don be a fool, boy! Yuh c mon back here, *now!*"

Jimmy flopped on the edge of a chair and mumbled to himself. The room was quiet save for the rustle of tree leaves that drifted in from the outside and the sound of Bonds sobbing on the floor. As Taylor stood his own suffering was drowned in a sense of widening horror. There was in his mind a vivid picture of all the little dingy huts where black men and women were crouched, afraid to stir out of doors. Bonds stopped crying and looked at Taylor; again that sense of shame spread over Taylor, inside and out. It stirred him to speech.

"Who else they beat, Brother?"

"Seem like everbody, Reveren! Them two Communists got beat something terrible n they put em in jail. N Ah heard they kilt one black man whut tried t fight back. They ketched everbody they kin on the streets n lettin em have it. They ridin up n down in cars. . . ."

Jimmy cursed. The doorbell pealed again.

"Git me a shirt, May!"

"Dan, yuh ain able t do nothin!"

The doorbell pealed again, then again. Taylor started toward the dresser; but May got there before he did and gave him a shirt.

"Dan, be careful!"

"C mon downstairs, Brother Bonds. N yuh, too, Jimmy," said Taylor.

XIII

The church's waiting room was full. Black men and women sat and stood, saying nothing, waiting. Arms were in slings; necks were wrapped in white cloth; legs were bound in bloodstained rags.

"LOOK AT WHUT YUH DONE DONE!" a voice bawled.

It was Deacon Smith. Taylor's eyes went from face to face; he knew them all. Every Sunday they sat in the pews of his church, praying, singing, and trusting the God he gave them. The mute eyes and silent lips pinned him to a fiery spot of loneliness. He wanted to protest that loneliness, wanted to break it down; but he did not know how. No parables sprang to his lips now to give form and meaning to his words; alone and naked, he stood ashamed. Jimmy came through the door and placed his hand on his shoulder.

"Its daylight, Pa. The folks is gatherin in the playground! Theys waiten fer yuh. . . ."

Taylor went into the yard with the crowd at his heels. It was broad daylight and the sun shone. The men in their overalls and the women with children stood about him on all sides, silent. A fat black woman elbowed her way in and faced him.

"Waal, Reveren, we done got beat up. Now, is we gonna march?"

"Yuh wanna march?" asked Taylor.

"It don make no difference wid me," she said. "Them white folks cant do no mo than theys already done."

The crowd chimed in.

"N Gawd knows they cant!"

"Ahll go ef the nex one goes!"

"Ah gotta die sometime, so Ah just as waal die now!"

"They cant kill us but once!"

"Ahm tired anyhow! Ah don care!"

"The white folks says theys gonna meet us at the park!"

Taylor turned to Jimmy.

"Son, git yo boys together n tell em t roun up everbody!"

"Yessuh!"

May was pulling at his sleeve.

"Dan, yuh *cant* do this. . . ."

Deacon Smith pushed his way in and faced him.

"Yuhll never set foot in a church ergin ef yuh lead them po black folks downtown t be killed!"

The crowd surged.

"Ain nobody leadin us nowhere!"

"We goin ourselves!"

"Is we gonna march, Reveren?"

"Yeah; soon as the crowd gits together," said Taylor.

"Ain nobody t blame but yuh ef yuh carry em t their *death!*" warned Deacon Smith.

"How come yuh don shut yo old big mouth n let the Reveren talk?" asked the fat woman.

"Sistah, Ah got as much right t speak as yuh!"

"Waal, don speak to me, yuh hear!"

"Somebody has t say something when ain *nobody* got no sense!"

"Man, don yuh tell me Ah ain got no sense!"

"Yuh sho don ack like it!"

"Ah got as much sense as yuh got!"

"How come yuh don use it?"

The fat sister slapped Deacon Smith straight across his face. Taylor ran between them and pried them apart. The crowd surged and screamed.

"Ef he touches Sistah Henry ergin Ahll kill im!"

"He ain got no bisness talkin tha way t a woman!"

Taylor dragged the fat woman toward the gate. The crowd followed, yelling. He stopped and faced them. They circled around, tightly, asking questions. May had hold of his sleeve. Jimmy came to him.

"Pa, theys comin!"

Taylor turned and walked across the yard with the crowd following. He took two planks and laid them upon the ends of two saw-horses and made a solid platform. He climbed up and stood in the quiet sunshine. He did not know exactly what it was he wanted to say, but whatever it was he would say it when they were quiet. He felt neither fear nor joy, just an humble confidence in himself, as though he were standing before his mirror in his room. Then he was conscious that they were quiet; he took one swift look over their heads, heads that stretched away to the street and beyond, a solid block of black, silent faces; then he looked down, not to the dust, but just a slight lowering of eyes, as though he were no longer looking at them, but at something within himself.

"Sistahs n Brothers, they tell me the Deacon Boards done voted me outta the church. Ef thas awright wid yuh, its awright wid me. The white folks says Ahma bad nigger n they don wanna have nothin else t do wid me. N thas awright, too. But theres one thing Ah wanna say. Ah knows how yuh feel erbout bein hongry. N how yuh feel is no different from how Ah feel. Yuh been waitin a week fer me t say whut yuh ought t do. Yuh been wondering how come Ah didnt tell yuh whut yuh oughta do. Waal. . . ."

He paused and looked over the silent crowd; then again his eyes, his gaze, went inward.

"Sistahs n Brothers, the reason Ah didnt say nothin is cause Ah didnt know *whut* t say. N the only reason Ahm speakin now is cause Ah *do* know. Ah know whut t do. . . ."

He paused again, swallowing. The same feeling which had gripped him so hard last night when he had been talking to Jimmy seized him. He opened his mouth to continue; his lips moved several times before words came; and when they did come they fell with a light and hoarse whisper.

"Sistahs n Brothers, las night the white folks took me out t the woods. They took me out cause Ah tol em yuh wuz hongry. They ast me t tell yuh not t march, n Ah tol em Ah wouldnt. Then they beat me. They tied me t a tree n beat me till Ah couldnt feel no mo. They beat me cause Ah wouldnt tell yuh not t ast fer bread. They said yuhd blieve everthing Ah said. All the time they wuz hepin me, all the time they been givin me favors, they wuz doin it sos *they* could tell *me* to tell *yuh* how t ack! Sistahs n Brothers, as Gawds mah judge, Ah thought Ah wuz doin right when Ah did that. Ah thought Ah wuz doin right when Ah told yuh t do the things they said. N cause Ah wouldnt do it this time, they tied me t a tree n beat me till mah blood run. . . ."

Mist covered his eyes. He heard the crowd murmuring; but he did not care if they were murmuring for or against him; he wanted to finish, to say what he had been trying so hard to say for many long hours.

"Sistahs n Brothers, they whipped me n made me take the name of *Gawd* in vain! They made me say mah prayers n beat me n laughed! They beat me till Ah couldnt membah nothin! All last night Ah wuz lying stretched out on the ground wid mah back burnin. . . . All this mawning before day Ah wuz limpin thu white folks streets. Sistahs n Brothers, Ah *know* now! Ah done seen the *sign!* Wes gotta git together. Ah know whut yo life is! Ah done felt it! Its *fire!* Its like the fire that burned me las night! Its sufferin! Its hell! Ah cant bear this fire erlone! Ah know now whut t do! Wes gotta git close t one ernother! Gawds done spoke! Gawds done sent His sign. Now its fer us t ack. . . ."

The crowd started yelling:

"Well go ef yuh go!"

"Wes ready!"

"The white folks says theyll meet us at the park!"

The fat black woman started singing:

So the sign of the fire by night
N the sign of the cloud by day
A-hoverin oer
Jus befo
As we journey on our way. . . .

Taylor got down. He moved with the crowd slowly toward the street. May went with him, looking, wondering, saying nothing. Jimmy was at his side. They sang as they marched. More joined along the way. When they reached the park that separated the white district from the black, the poor whites were waiting. Taylor trembled when he saw them join, swelling the mass that moved toward the town. He looked ahead and saw black and white marching; he looked behind and saw black and white marching. And still they sang:

"So the sign of the fire by night. . . ."

They turned into the street that led to town.

"N the sign of the cloud by day. . . ."

Taylor saw blue-coated policemen standing along the curb.

"A-hoverin oer. . . ."

Taylor felt himself moving between the silent lines of blue-coated white men, moving with a sea of placards and banners, moving under the sun like a pregnant cloud. He said to himself, They ain gonna bother us! They bettah *not* bother us. . . .

"Just befo. . . ."

Across a valley, in front of him, he could see the buildings of the town sprawled on a hill.

"As we journey on our way. . . ."

They were tramping on pavement now. And the blue-coated men stood still and silent. Taylor saw Deacon Smith standing on the curb, and Smith's face merged with the faces of the others, meaningless, lost. Ahead was the City Hall, white and clean in the sunshine. The autos stopped at the street corners while the crowd passed; and as they entered the downtown section people massed quietly on the sidewalks. Then the crowd began to slow, barely moving. Taylor looked ahead and wondered what was about to happen; he wondered without fear; as though whatever would or could happen could not hurt this many-limbed, many-legged, many-handed crowd that was he. He felt May clinging to his sleeve. Jimmy was peering ahead. A policeman came running up to him.

"You Taylor?"

"Yussuh," he said, quietly, his gaze straight and steady.

"The mayors down front; he wants to see you!"

"Tell im Ahm back here," said Taylor.

"But he wants to see the leader up front!"

"Tell im Ahm back here," said Taylor again.

The man hesitated, then left; they waited, quiet, still. Then the crowd parted. Taylor saw Mayor Bolton hurrying toward him, his face beet-red.

"Dan, tell your people not to make any trouble! We dont want any trouble, Dan. . . ."

"There ain gonna be no trouble, yo Honah!"

"Well, tell them they can get food if they go back home, peacefully. . . ."

"Yuh tell em, yo Honah!"

They looked at each other for a moment. Then the mayor turned and walked back. Taylor saw him mount the rear seat of an auto and lift his trembling hands high above the crowd, asking for silence, his face a pasty white.

A baptism of clean joy swept over Taylor. He kept his eyes on the sea of black and white faces. The song swelled louder and vibrated through him. This is the way! he thought. Gawd ain no lie! He ain no lie! His eyes grew wet with tears, blurring his vision: the sky trembled; the buildings wavered as if about to topple; and the earth shook. . . . He mumbled out loud, exultingly:

"Freedom belongs t the strong!"

EDMUND WILSON [1895-]

EDMUND WILSON has been for nearly four decades the most widely read American critic of literature, and one of the most influential. In his long, productive career he has spread his talent in so many directions that he defies classification and is regarded as a kind of unofficial dean of American letters. Though primarily a critic, he has also produced fiction, poetry, plays, contemporary history, social commentary, literary scholarship, and research into antiquities.

As a practicing critic his approach is generally historical with a social and political leaning. For him, literature is a record of life. He sees it in relation to civilization, past and present, yet always with a sense of the author behind the book, and of the book itself as a work of art worthy of close and independent analysis. In an early essay, "The Historical Interpretation of Literature" (1931), he traced his literary ancestry to the French critic Taine, for whom literature was the product of race, place, and the moment in time. Marxism has been a generating force in his writing, lending support for his concern with political and social influences. But he has never been doctrinaire or moralistic. He has explored the case-history method of Freudian criticism, symbolist criticism, and the genetic approach, and he has used the results of historical scholarship, psychology, sociology, and semantics to good advantage.

Born in Red Bank, New Jersey, he was educated at Princeton, where he edited the *Nassau Literary Magazine* and began long friendships with Scott Fitzgerald and the poet John Peale Bishop. He served in France during World War I, then returned to New York to become managing editor of *Vanity Fair.* From 1926 to 1931 he was book reviewer and editor of the *New Republic.* In 1944 he joined the staff of the *New Yorker,* continuing as book editor and contributor for many years. In the thirties Wilson was excited by Marxist ideology, traveled to Russia, reported his reactions in *Travels in Two Democracies* (1936), and wrote about the intellectual background of the Russian revolution in *To the Finland Station* (1940). In the 1960's he recorded his disillusion with Soviet Russia and saw the dream of world domination as merely another imperialistic power drive. Always a rebel against the power structure, he has done battle with the federal government over his income tax and with the censors over his *Memoirs of Hecate County* (1946), a work of fiction which was banned for many years because of its candid sexuality. In *The Dead Sea Scrolls* (1955) he combined skillful reporting with a gift for scholarly investigation. Wilson is a liberal and humanist of the older order. No expatriate or Anglophile or Russophile, he is not a nativist either. He claims to be in America, but not of it.

Wilson's reputation as a literary critic was established with *Axel's Castle* (1931), a study of symbolism in the work of Proust, Joyce, and other new writers of that time. Other distinguished books followed. *The Triple Thinkers* (1938) discussed Housman, Pushkin, and Flaubert, and included important essays on Marxism in literature, as well as the controversial "The Ambiguity of Henry James." *The Wound and the Bow* (1941) examined the relationship between genius and disease or trauma in the careers of Dickens, Kipling, and others. *Patriotic Gore* (1962) was Wilson's most thoroughly researched book, a scholarly yet colorful narrative of the literature and sub-literature of the American Civil War.

As a critic Wilson lacks a strong centralizing conception and organizing principle. Indeed, his special forte lies in his flexibility and his ability to stay abreast of the variety of tendencies in the modern literary scene. He has been called a Marxist, a Freudian, a free-lance journalist, and an impressionist, but in the totality of his accomplishment he probably has done more than any of his contemporaries to see literature as a part of the whole human problem and to write of its relation to the cultural and intellectual currents in the twentieth century.

Further reading: *The Triple Thinkers*, 1938. *The Wound and the Bow*, 1941. Sherman Paul, *Edmund Wilson*, 1967.

Symbolism

The historical interpretation of literature has long been the favorite province of scholars in our colleges and universities. Under the nineteenth-century influences of the method of science, the theory of evolution, and the example of German scholarship, literature was studied in the light of literary history or even for the sake of literary history. And literary history was usually conceived of as a branch of historical science, resting upon demonstrable facts. Of course there were many scholars, like Christian Gauss of Princeton, who employed the historical approach flexibly and imaginatively. To Professor Gauss, Edmund Wilson inscribed a letter, printed at the beginning of his *Axel's Castle:* "You will see how these essays have grown out of your lectures of fifteen years ago. . . . It was principally from you that I acquired then my idea of what literary criticism ought to be—a history of man's ideas and imaginings in the setting of the conditions which have shaped them. . . ."

First published as "A Preface to Modern Literature" in the *New Republic* in 1929, this historical-critical essay formed the opening chapter of *Axel's Castle: A Study in the Imaginative Literature of 1870-1930* (1931).

It is my purpose in this book to try to trace the origins of certain tendencies in contemporary literature and to show their development in the work of six contemporary writers. To persons already familiar with the field, my explanations in this first chapter will seem rudimentary; but I believe that it is still true in general, for reasons which I shall suggest, that the sources and fundamental principles of many of the books which have excited most discussion during the period since the War are singularly little understood. It is not usually recognized that writers such as W. B. Yeats, James Joyce, T. S. Eliot, Gertrude Stein, Marcel Proust and Paul Valéry represent the culmination of a self-conscious and very important literary movement; and even when we have become aware that these writers have something in common, that they belong to a common school, we are likely to be rather vague as to what its distinguishing features are.

We do, however, to-day as a rule have a pretty clear idea of the issues which were raised by the Romantic Movement of the beginning of the nineteenth century. We still debate Classicism and Romanticism, and when we attempt to deal with contemporary literary problems, we often tend to discuss them in those terms. Yet the movement of which in our own day we are witnessing the mature development is not merely a degeneration or an elaboration of Romanticism, but rather a counterpart to it, a second flood of the same tide. And even the metaphor of a tide is misleading: what we have to-day is an entirely distinct movement, which has arisen from different conditions and must be dealt with in different terms.

Romanticism, as everyone has heard, was a revolt of the individual. The "Classicism" against which it was a reaction meant, in the domain of politics and morals, a preoccupation with society as a whole; and, in art, an ideal of objectivity. In *Le Misanthrope*, in *Bérénice*, in *The Way of the World*, in *Gulliver's Travels*, the artist is out of the picture: he would consider it artistic bad taste to identify his hero with himself and to glorify himself with his hero, or to intrude between the reader and the story and give vent to his personal emotions. But in *René*, in *Rolla*, in *Childe Harold*, in *The Prelude*, the writer is either his own hero, or unmistakably identified with his hero, and the personality and emotions of the writer are presented as the principal subject of interest. Racine, Molière, Congreve and Swift ask us to be interested in what they have made; but Chateaubriand, Musset, Byron, and Wordsworth ask us to be interested in themselves. And they ask us to be interested in themselves by virtue of the intrinsic value of the individual: they vindicate the rights of the individual against the claims of society as a whole—against government, morals, conventions, academy or church. The Romantic is nearly always a rebel.

In this connection, it is illuminating to consider the explanation of the Romantic Movement given by A. N. Whitehead in his *Science and the Modern World.* The Romantic Movement, Whitehead says, was really a reaction against scientific ideas, or rather against the mechanistic ideas to which certain scientific discoveries gave rise. The seventeenth and eighteenth centuries were in Europe the great period of the development of mathematical and physical theory; and in the literature of the so-called Classical period, Descartes and Newton were influences as important as those of the classics themselves. The poets, like the astronomers and mathematicians, had come to regard the universe as a machine, obeying logical laws and susceptible of reasonable explanation: God figured merely as the clockmaker who must have existed to make the clock. People applied this conception also to society, which, from the point of view of Louis XIV and of the American Constitution alike, had the character of a planetary system or a well-regulated machine; and they examined human nature dispassionately, in the same lucid and reasonable spirit, to find the principles on which it worked. Thus the theorems of the physicist were matched by the geometrical plays of Racine and the balanced couplets of Pope.

But this conception of a fixed mechanical order came eventually to be felt as a constraint: it excluded too much of life—or rather, the description it supplied did not correspond to actual experience. The Romantics had become acutely conscious of aspects of their experience which it was impossible to analyze or explain on the theory of a world run by clock-work. The universe was not a machine, after all, but somethimg more mysterious and less rational.

> The atoms of Democritus,
> And Newton's particles of light
> Are sands upon the Red Sea shore,
> Where Israel's tents do shine so bright!

Blake had already contradicted contemptuously the physical theory of the eighteenth century. And to Wordsworth, the countryside of his boyhood meant neither agriculture nor neo-classic idylls, but a light never seen on land or sea. When the poet looked into his own soul, he beheld something which did not seem to him reducible to a set of principles of human nature such, for example, as La Rochefoucauld's *Maxims:* he saw fantasy, conflict, confusion. And he either set himself, like Wordsworth and Blake, to affirm the superior truth of this vision as compared to the mechanical universe of the physicists; or, accepting this mechanical universe, like Byron or Alfred de Vigny, as external to and indifferent to man, he pitted against it, in defiance, his own turbulent insubordinate soul.

In any case, it is always, as in Wordsworth, the individual sensibility, or, as in Byron, the individual will, with which the Romantic poet is preoccupied; and he has invented a new language for the expression of its mystery, its conflict and confusion. The arena of literature has been transferred from the universe conceived as a machine, from society conceived as an organization, to the individual soul.

What has really taken place, says Whitehead, is a philosophical revolution. The scientists of the seventeenth century who presented the universe as a mechanism had caused people to draw the conclusion that man was something apart from nature, something introduced into the universe from outside and remaining alien to all that he found. But a Romantic poet like Wordsworth has come to feel the falsity of this assumption: he has perceived that the world is an organism, that nature includes planets, mountains, vegetation and people alike, that what we are and what we see, what we hear, what we feel and what we smell, are inextricably related, that all are involved in the same great entity. Those who make fun of the Romantics are mistaken in supposing that there is no intimate connection between the landscape and the poet's emotions. There is no real dualism, says Whitehead, between external lakes and hills, on the one hand, and personal feelings, on the other: human feelings and inanimate objects are interdependent and developing together in some fashion of which our traditional notions of laws of cause and effect, of dualities of mind and matter or of body and soul, can give us no true idea. The Romantic poet, then, with his turbid or opalescent language, his sympathies and passions which cause him to seem to merge with his surroundings, is the prophet of a new insight into nature: he is describing things as they really are; and a revolution in the imagery of poetry is in reality a revolution in metaphysics.

Whitehead drops the story at this point; but he has provided the key to what follows. In the middle of the nineteenth century, science made new advances, and mechanistic ideas were brought back into fashion again. But they came this time from a different quarter—not from physics and mathematics, but from biology. It was the effect of the theory of Evolution to reduce man from the heroic stature to which the Romantics had tried to exalt him, to the semblance of a helpless animal, again very small in the universe and at the mercy of the forces about him. Humanity was the accidental product of heredity and environment, and capable of being explained in terms of these. This doctrine in literature was called Naturalism, and it was put into practice by novelists like Zola, who believed that composing a novel was like performing a laboratory experiment: you had only to supply your characters with a specific environment and heredity and then watch their automatic reactions; and by historians and critics like Taine, who asserted that virtue and vice were as much the products of automatic processes as alkalis and acids, and who attempted to account for masterpieces by studying the geographical and climatic conditions of the countries in which they had been produced.

Not, however, that the movement known as Naturalism arose directly from *The Origin of Species*. There had already set in, about the middle of the century, quite independent of the theory of Evolution, a reaction against the sentimentality and the looseness of Romanticism, and in the direction of the objectivity and the severity of Classicism again; and this reaction had already been characterized by a kind of scientific observation which closely corresponded to that of biological science. This reaction is seen most clearly in France. The Parnassian group of poets, who made their first appearance in the fifties—Gautier, Leconte de Lisle, Hérédia—seemed to have taken it for their aim merely to picture historical incidents and natural phenomena as objectively and accurately as possible in impassive perfect verse. Leconte de Lisle's elephants crossing the desert is a celebrated example: the elephants appear and disappear with a certain classical dignity and grandeur, and the poet leaves it at that.

It is less easy, in English poetry, to give clear examples of the reaction toward Naturalism: the English did not, after the Romantic Movement, take much interest in literary methods till toward the end of the nineteenth century. But the tendency toward what we call realism had set in, none the less: Browning, though he had, of course, nothing of the classical form of the Parnassians, was addicted to historical reconstruction of a kind more pedantic and less flamboyant than that of the true Romantics, and when he dealt with contemporary life, did so at least as realistically as any of the Victorian novelists—themselves going in Zola's direction without quite being aware of the fact. And we can see very plainly in Tennyson, who was much preoccupied with the doctrines of Evolution, something of the same exactitude of description combined with something of the same severity of verse—though with less hardness and more grace—that we find in the French poets.

> Nor wilt thou snare him in the white ravine,
> Nor find him dropt upon the firths of ice,
> That huddling slant in furrow-cloven fells
> To roll the torrent out of dusky doors:
> But follow; let the torrent dance thee down
> To find him in the valley; let the wild
> Lean-headed eagles yelp alone.

And it is interesting to compare Tennyson, in this connection, with Pope on the rare occasions (though not so rare as people sometimes suppose) when he is describing natural objects:

> The silver eel, in shining volumes roll'd,
> The yellow carp, in scales bedropp'd with gold.

These lines have the technical perfection and the precise observation of Tennyson, but they are heavier and more metallic. Pope is often, as a matter of fact, very close to the French Parnassians. The latter represent, in reality, a second classical-scientific movement, the counterpart to that represented by Pope.

But the highest development of Naturalism took place, not in poetry, but in prose. The plays of Ibsen and the novels of Flaubert are the masterpieces of this second period of modern classicism, as Racine and Swift are of the first. The art of Flaubert and Ibsen is again, like the art of the seventeenth-century writers, scrupulously non-personal and objective, and it insists upon precision of language and economy of form. Compare the lucidity, the logic and the limited number of characters of such a tragedy of Ibsen's as *Rosmersholm* with the rigorous conventions of Racine; or compare *Gulliver's Travels* with *Bouvard et Pécuchet* or *L'Education Sentimentale*. Yet, though the earlier works resemble the later ones in many obvious ways, they differ from them in this: where a seventeenth-century moralist like La Rochefoucauld would have sought to discover and set forth the universal principles of human behavior, a nineteenth-century writer like Ibsen or Flaubert has begun to study man in relation to his particular environment and time. The method of approach in both cases, however, may be described as "scientific," and it tends to lead us to mechanistic conclusions.

Now Flaubert and Ibsen both had been suckled on Romanticism. Flaubert had begun by writing a Romantic *Saint-Antoine* before he chastened it and cut it down to the more sober one which he published; and Ibsen had written in verse his Faustian *Brand* and *Peer Gynt* before he arrived at his realistic plays in prose. Each, beginning in Romanticism, had evolved for himself a new discipline and developed a new point of view. For *Madame Bovary* is not merely arranged and written differently from a novel by Victor Hugo: it also constitutes an objective criticism of a case of Romantic personality; and Ibsen was occupied all his life with situations produced by the conflict of the essentially Romantic conception of one's duty to one's own personality with the conception of one's duty to society.

But in the later prose plays of Ibsen, the trolls and ghosts of his early dramatic poems have begun to creep back into the bourgeois drawing-rooms: the Naturalist has been finally compelled to make cracks in his own mold. All that vaporous, confused and grandiose world of Romanticism had been resolutely ordered and compressed; but now the objective point of view of Naturalism, the machine-like technique which went with it, begin to cramp the poet's imagination, to prove inadequate to convey what he feels. The reader begins to chafe at the strain, and the artist begins to betray it. Huysmans described Leconte de Lisle as "the sonorous hardware man"; we remember Wordsworth's strictures on Pope. Literature is rebounding again from the scientific-classical pole to the poetic-romantic one. And this second reaction at the end of the century, this counterpart to the Romantic reaction of the end of the century before, was known in France as Symbolism.

Now in attempting to write literary history, one must guard against giving the impression that these movements and counter-movements necessarily follow one another in a punctual and well-generalled fashion—as if eighteenth-century reason had been cleanly put to rout by nineteenth-century Romanticism, which then proceeded to hold the field till it was laid by the heels by Naturalism, and as if Mallarmé and Rimbaud had then blown up Naturalism with bombs. What really happens, of course, is that one set of methods and ideas is not completely superseded by another; but that, on the contrary, it thrives in its teeth—so that, on the one hand, Flaubert's prose has learned to hear, see and feel with the delicate senses of Romanticism at the same time that Flaubert is disciplining and criticizing the Romantic temperament; and so that, on the other hand, certain members of a school, unaffected by new influences abroad, will continue to practise its methods and to exploit its possibilities further and further, when nearly everybody else has abandoned it.

I have here purposely been selecting writers who seemed to represent some tendency or school in its purest or most highly developed form. We must, however, now consider some Romantics who, in certain ways, carried Romanticism further than even Chateaubriand or Musset, or than Wordsworth or Byron, and who became the first precursors of Symbolism and were afterwards placed among its saints.

One of these was the French writer who called himself Gérard de Nerval. Gérard de Nerval suffered from spells of insanity; and, partly no doubt as a result of this, habitually confused his own fancies and feelings with external reality. He believed, even in his lucid periods—and no doubt Whitehead would approve his metaphysics—that the world which we see about us is involved in some more intimate fashion than is ordinarily supposed with the things that go on in our minds, that even our dreams and hallucinations are somehow bound up with reality. And in one of his sonnets he outdoes Wordsworth, with his "Presences of Nature in the sky" and his "Souls of lonely places," by imagining shuttered eyes coming to life in the very walls and "a pure spirit under the bark of stones."

But a more important prophet of Symbolism was Edgar Allan Poe. It was in general true that, by the middle of the century, the Romantic writers in the United States—Poe, Hawthorne, Melville, Whitman, and even Emerson—were, for reasons which it would be interesting to determine, developing in the direction of Symbolism; and one of the events of prime importance in the early history of the Symbolist Movement was the discovery of Poe by Baudelaire. When Baudelaire, a late Romantic, first read Poe in 1847, he "experienced a strange commotion." When he began to look up Poe's writings in the files of American magazines, he found among them stories and poems which he said that he himself had already "thought vaguely and confusedly" of writing, and his interest became a veritable passion. In 1852, Baudelaire published a volume of translations of Poe's tales; and from then on the influence of Poe played an important part in French literature. Poe's critical writings provided the first scriptures of the Symbolist Movement, for he had formulated what amounted to a new literary programme which corrected the Romantic looseness and lopped away the Romantic extravagance, at the same time that it aimed, not at Naturalistic, but at ultra-Romantic effects. There was, of course, a good deal in common between Poe's poetry and such Romantic poetry as Coleridge's *Kubla Khan*, as there was between his poems in prose and such Romantic prose as that of De Quincey. But Poe, by insisting on and specially cultivating certain aspects of Romanticism, helped to transform it into something different. "I *know*," we find Poe writing, for example, "that indefiniteness is an element of the true music [of poetry]—I mean of the true musical expression . . . a suggestive indefiniteness of vague and therefore of spiritual *effect*." And to approximate the indefiniteness of music was to become one of the principal aims of Symbolism.

This effect of indefiniteness was produced not merely by the confusion I have mentioned between the imaginary world and the real; but also by means of a further confusion between the perceptions of the different senses.

Comme de longs échos qui de loin se confondent . . .
Les parfums, les couleurs et les sons se répondent,

wrote Baudelaire. And we find Poe, in one of his poems, *hearing* the approach of the darkness, or writing such a description as the following of the sensations which follow death: "Night arrived; and with its shadows a heavy discomfort. It oppressed my limbs with the oppression of some dull weight, and was palpable. There was also a moaning sound, not unlike the distant reverberation of surf, but more continuous, which beginning with the first twilight, had grown in strength with the darkness. Suddenly lights were brought into the room . . . and issuing from the flame of each lamp, there flowed unbrokenly into my ears a strain of melodious monotone."

This notation of super-rational sensations was a novelty in the forties of the last century—as was the dream-like irrational musical poetry of *Annabel Lee* and *Ulalume;* and they helped to effect a revolution in France. For an English-speaking reader of to-day Poe's influence may be hard to understand; and even when such a reader comes to examine the productions of French Symbolism it may surprise him that they should have caused amazement. The medley of images; the deliberately mixed metaphors; the combination of passion and wit—of the grand and the prosaic manners; the bold amalgamation of material with spiritual—all these may seem to him quite proper and familiar. He has always known them in the English poetry of the sixteenth and seventeenth centuries—Shakespeare and the other Elizabethans did all these things without theorizing about them. Is this not the natural language of poetry? Is it not the norm against which, in English literature, the eighteenth century was a heresy and to which the Romantics did their best to return?

But we must remember that the development of French poetry has been quite different from that of English. Michelet says that in the sixteenth century the future of French literature had hung in the balance between Rabelais and Ronsard, and he regrets that it was Ronsard who triumphed. For Rabelais in France was a sort of equivalent to our own Elizabethans, whereas Ronsard, who represented to Michelet all that was poorest, dryest and most conventional in the French genius, was one of the fathers of that classical tradition of lucidity, sobriety and purity which culminated in Molière and Racine. In comparison with the Classicism of the French, which has dominated their whole literature since the Renaissance, the English Classicism of the eighteenth century, the age of Dr. Johnson and Pope, was a brief ineffective deviation. And from the point of view of English readers, the most daring innovations of the Romantic revolution in France, in spite of all the excitement which accompanied them, must appear of an astonishingly moderate character. But the age and the rigor of the tradition were the measure of the difficulty of breaking out of it. After all, Coleridge, Shelley, and Keats—in spite of Pope and Doctor Johnson—had only to look back to Milton and Shakespeare, whose dense forests had all along been in view beyond the formal eighteenth-century gardens. But to an eighteenth-century Frenchman like Voltaire, Shakespeare was incomprehensible; and to the Frenchman of the classical tradition of the beginning of the nineteenth century, the rhetoric of Hugo was a scandal: the French were not used to such rich colors or to so free a vocabulary; moreover, the Romantics broke metrical rules far stricter than any we have had in English. Yet Victor Hugo was still very far from the variety and freedom of Shakespeare. It is enlightening to compare Shelley's lyric which begins "O World! O Life! O Time!" with the poem of Alfred de Musset's which begins, "J'ai perdu ma force et ma vie." These two lyrics are in some ways curiously similar: each is the breath of a Romantic sigh over the passing of the pride of youth. Yet the French poet, even in his wistfulness, makes epigrammatic points: his language is always logical and precise; whereas the English poet is vague and gives us images unrelated by logic. And it will not be till the advent of the symbolists that French poetry will really become capable of the fantasy and fluidity of English.

The Symbolist Movement broke those rules of French metrics which the Romantics had left intact, and it finally succeeded in throwing overboard completely the clarity and logic of the French classical tradition, which the Romantics had still to a great extent respected. It was nourished from many alien sources—German, Flemish, modern Greek—and especially, precisely, from English. Verlaine had lived in England, and knew English well; Mallarmé was a professor of English; and Baudelaire, as I have said, had provided the movement with its first programs by translating the essays of Poe. Two of the Symbolist poets, Stuart Merrill and Francis Vielé-Griffin, were Americans who lived in Paris and wrote French; and an American, reading to-day the latter's *Chevauchée d'Yeldis,* for example, may wonder how, when Symbolism was new, such a poem could ever have been regarded as one of the movement's acknowledged masterpieces: to us, it seems merely agreeable, not in the least revolutionary or novel, but like something which might not impossibly have been written by Thomas Bailey Aldrich if he had been influenced by Browning. We are surprised to learn that Vielé-Griffin is still considered an important poet. But the point was that he had performed a feat which astonished and impressed the French and of which it is probable that no Frenchman was capable: he had succeeded in wrecking once for all the classical Alexandrine, hitherto the basis of French poetry—or rather, as an English reader at once recognizes, he had dispensed with it altogether and begun writing English metres in French. The

French called this "vers libre," but it is "free" only in the sense of being irregular, like many poems of Matthew Arnold and Browning.

What made Poe particularly acceptable to the French, however, was what had distinguished him from most of the other Romantics of the English-speaking countries; his interest in aesthetic theory. The French have always reasoned about literature far more than the English have; they always want to know what they are doing and why they are doing it: their literary criticism has acted as a constant interpreter and guide to the rest of their literature. And it was in France that Poe's literary theory, to which no one seems to have paid much attention elsewhere, was first studied and elucidated. So that, though the effects and devices of Symbolism were of a kind that was familiar in English, and though the Symbolists were sometimes indebted to English literature directly—the Symbolist Movement itself, by reason of its origin in France, had a deliberate self-conscious aesthetic which made it different from anything in English. One must go back to Coleridge to find in English a figure comparable to the Symbolist leader Stéphane Mallarmé. Paul Valéry says of Mallarmé that, as he was the greatest French poet of his time, he could also have been one of the most popular. But Mallarmé was an unpopular poet: he taught English for a living, and wrote little and published less. Yet, ridiculed and denounced by the public, who reiterated that his poetry was nonsense and yet were irritated by his seriousness and obstinacy, he exercised, from his little Paris apartment, where he held Tuesday receptions, an influence curiously far-reaching over the young writers—English and French alike—of the end of the century. There in the sitting-room which was also the dining-room on the fourth floor in the Rue de Rome, where the whistle of locomotives came in through the windows to mingle with the literary conversation, Mallarmé, with his shining pensive gaze from under his long lashes and always smoking a cigarette "to put some smoke," as he used to say, "between the world and himself," would talk about the theory of poetry in a "mild, musical and unforgettable voice." There was an atmosphere "calm and almost religious." Mallarmé had "the pride of the inner life," said one of his friends; his nature was "patient, disdainful and imperiously gentle." He always reflected before he spoke and always put what he said in the form of a question. His wife sat beside him embroidering; his daughter answered the door. Here came Huysmans, Whistler, Degas, Moréas, Laforgue, Vielé-Griffin, Paul Valéry, Henri de Régnier, Pierre Louis, Paul Claudel, Remy de Gourmont, André Gide, Oscar Wilde, Arthur Symons, George Moore and W. B. Yeats. For Mallarmé was a true saint of literature: he had proposed to himself an almost impossible object, and he pursued it without compromise or distraction. His whole life was dedicated to the effort to do something with the language of poetry which had never been done before. "Donner un sens plus pur," he had written in a sonnet on Poe, "aux mots de la tribu." He was, as Albert Thibaudet has said, engaged in "a disinterested experiment on the confines of poetry, at a limit where other lungs would find the air unbreathable."

What, then, was this purer sense which Mallarmé believed he was following Poe in wishing to give to the words of the tribe? What, precisely, was the nature of this experiment on the confines of poetry which Mallarmé found so absorbing and which so many other writers tried to repeat? What, precisely, did the Symbolists propose? I have called attention, in speaking of Poe, to the confusion between the perceptions of the different senses, and to the attempt to make the effects of poetry approximate to those of music. And I should add, in this latter connection, that the influence on Symbolist poetry of Wagner was as important as that of any poet: at the time when Romantic music had come closest to literature, literature was attracted toward music. I have also spoken, in connection with Gérard de Nerval, of the confusion between the imaginary and the real, between our sensations and fancies, on the one hand, and what we actually do and see, on the other. It was the tendency of Symbolism—that second swing of the pendulum away from a mechanistic view of nature and from a social conception of man—to make poetry even more a matter of the sensations and emotions of the individual than had been the case with Romanticism: Symbolism, indeed, sometimes had the result of making poetry so much a private concern of the poet's that it turned out to be incommunicable to the reader. The peculiar subtlety and difficulty of Symbolism is indicated by the name itself. This name has often been complained of as being inadequate for the movement to which it was given and inappropriate to certain of its aspects; and it may prove misleading to English readers. For the symbols of Symbolism have to be defined a little differently from symbols in the ordinary sense—the sense in which the Cross is the symbol of Christianity or the Stars and Stripes the symbol of the United States. This symbolism differs even from such symbolism as Dante's. For the familiar kind of symbolism is conventional and fixed; the symbolism of the *Divine Comedy* is conventional, logical and definite. But the symbols of the Symbolist school are usually chosen arbitrarily by the poet to stand for special ideas of his own—they are a sort of disguise for these ideas. "The Parnassians, for their part," wrote Mallarmé, "take the thing just as it is and put it before us—and consequently they are deficient in mystery: they deprive the mind of the delicious joy of believing that it is creating. To name an object is to do away with the three-quarters of the enjoyment of the poem which is derived from the satisfaction of guessing little by little: to suggest it, to evoke it—that is what charms the imagination."

To intimate things rather than state them plainly was thus one of the primary aims of the Symbolists. But there was more involved in their point of view than Mallarmé here explains. The assumptions which underlay Symbolism lead us to formulate some such doctrine as the following: Every feeling or sensation we have, every moment of consciousness, is different from every other; and it is, in consequence, impossible to render our sensations as we actually experience them through the conventional and universal language of ordinary literature. Each poet has his unique personality; each of his moments has its special tone, its special combination of elements. And it is the poet's task to find, to invent, the special language which will alone be capable of expressing his personality and feelings. Such a language must make use of symbols: what is so special, so fleeting and so vague cannot be conveyed by direct statement or description, but only by a succession of words, of images, which will serve to suggest it to the reader. The Symbolists themselves, full of the idea of producing with poetry effects like those of music, tended to think of these images as possessing an abstract value like musical notes and chords. But the words of our speech are not musical notation, and what the symbols of Symbolism really were, were metaphors detached from their subjects—for one cannot, beyond a certain point, in poetry, merely enjoy color and sound for their own sake: one has to guess what the images are being applied to. And Symbolism may be defined as an attempt by carefully studied means—a complicated association of ideas represented by a medley of metaphors—to communicate unique personal feelings.

The Symbolist Movement proper was first largely confined to France and principally limited to poetry of rather an esoteric kind; but it was destined, as time went on, to spread to the whole western world and its principles to be applied on a scale which the most enthusiastic of its founders could scarcely have foreseen. Remy de Gourmont, who was eventually to become the most distinguished critical champion of the movement, tells of his excitement, one afternoon in the eighties, at discovering the new poetry in a little magazine which he had picked up at a book-stall in the Odéon: "As I looked through it, I experienced the little aesthetic thrill and that exquisite impression of novelty which has so much charm for youth. I seemed to myself to have been dreaming rather than reading. The Luxembourg was pink with early April: I crossed it toward the Rue d'Assas, thinking a great deal more about the new literature which was coinciding for me that day with the renewal of the world than about the business which had brought me to that part of Paris. All that I had written up to that time inspired me with profound disgust. . . . In less than an hour my literary orientation was radically modified." And Yeats wrote in 1897: "The reaction against the rationalism of the eighteenth century has mingled with a reaction against the materialism of the nineteenth century, and the symbolical movement, which has come to perfection in Germany in Wagner, in England in the Pre-Raphaelites, and in France in Villiers de L'Isle-Adam and Mallarmé and Maeterlinck, and has stirred the imagination of Ibsen and D'Annunzio, is certainly the only movement that is saying new things."

We do not talk about Symbolism to-day in dealing with English literature; we do not even, as Yeats did at the end of the last century, think of writers whom he mentions as all belonging to a "symbolical movement"; yet the influence of Mallarmé and his fellow poets was felt widely and deeply outside of France, and it is difficult to understand certain of the things which have been happening lately in English literature without some knowledge of the Symbolist school. I believe, in fact, that if English and American criticism have sometimes shown themselves at a loss when confronted with the work of certain recent writers, it is partly because the work of these writers is the result of a literary revolution which occurred outside English literature. The case of the Romantic Movement was different: Wordsworth's prefaces were English manifestoes; Lockhart's attack on Keats and Byron's attack on Jeffrey were blows struck in an English civil war. But in spite of the Pre-Raphaelites, who were launched by an impulse somewhat similar to that of the Symbolists, and in spite of the English "aesthetics" and "decadents," who for the most part imitated the French without very much originality, the battle of Symbolism has never properly been fought out in English. So that whereas French writers like Valéry and Proust who have grown out of the Symbolist Movement are well understood and appreciated by French literary criticism, the critics of the English-speaking countries have often seemed not to know how to deal with writers such as Eliot and Joyce. Even when these writers have brought back into English qualities which are natural to it and resources which it originally possessed, these elements have returned by way of France and have taken on the complexion of the French mind—critical, philosophical, much occupied with aesthetic theory and tending always to aim self-consciously at particular effects and to study scrupulously appropriate means.

It has perhaps been peculiarly easy for certain of the leaders of contemporary English literature—that is, of the literature since the War—to profit by the example of Paris, because they have themselves not been English. Of the writers in English I shall discuss in this book, Yeats is an Irishman who turns almost as easily toward Paris as toward London; Joyce an Irishman who has done most of his work on the Continent and who has scarcely lived in England at all; and T. S. Eliot and Gertrude Stein are Americans living abroad. The work of these writers has been largely a continuance or extension of Symbolism. Yeats, the ablest of the *fin de siècle* group who tried in London to emulate the French, managed to make Symbolism flourish triumphantly by transplanting it to the more favorable soil of Ireland. T. S. Eliot in his earliest poems seems to have been as susceptible to the influence of the Symbolists as to that of the English Elizabethans. Joyce, a master of Naturalism as great as Flaubert, has at the same time succeeded in dramatizing Symbolism by making use of its methods for differentiating between his various characters and their varying states of mind. And Gertrude Stein has carried Mallarmé's principles so far in the direction of that limit where other lungs find the air unbreathable as perhaps finally to reduce them to absurdity. It is true, however, that under proper conditions, these principles remain valid; and both the strength and the weaknesses characteristic of much of the literature since the War derive naturally from the Symbolist poets and may already be studied in their work. The literary history of our time is to a great extent that of the development of Symbolism and of its fusion or conflict with Naturalism.

LIONEL TRILLING [1905-]

LIONEL TRILLING belongs to that group of contemporary liberal critics, influenced by the depression-economics of the thirties, for whom literature and politics are closely connected. But the newer liberalism of the forties, he felt, must be less dogmatic than the old and, above all, it must take fuller account of the aesthetic and emotional content of literature. A native of New York City, he has been a teacher, scholar, and critic of literature at Columbia University since 1931. His first book, *Matthew Arnold* (1939), revealed his interest in the tradition of English criticism and evidenced a somewhat tentative application of Freudian methods in biography. A study, *E. M. Forster* (1943), made a contribution to the revived interest in that English writer in America. Trilling has written short stories and one novel, *The Middle of the Journey* (1947), which is concerned with the conflict of ideas faced in the postwar years by liberals who could no longer accept the doctrinaire Marxism of the 1930's.

As a critic, he has written essays on Mark Twain, Sherwood Anderson, Henry James, the Kinsey Report, and the relation of Freudian concepts to literature, published in such influential periodicals as the *Kenyon Review* and the *Partisan Review*. The best of these were collected in 1950 under the title, *The Liberal Imagination*. The unifying theme of this volume was to recall liberalism to its proper function in literary criticism by emphasizing the emotional, subconscious, and imaginative areas of experience as a corrective to the tendency among social critics to reduce everything to the level of abstract ideas. *The Opposing Self* (1955) is another collection of essays giving further evidence of Trilling's use of the methods of historical and aesthetic criticism without going to the extremes of either technique. Instead, he subordinates them to devote himself to literature as an expression of man's moral life. He has been called both "divided" in his position as critic (by one reviewer) and one of the "best critical intelligences in America" (by another).

His interest in the effect of psychology upon literature has led him to write on Freud and upon such modern theories as the origin of all art in disease and neurosis. Although he has accepted some of the perceptions which Freudian criticism affords, he has likewise pointed out its deficiencies, especially its exaggeration of the element of neurosis in art and its undisguised contempt for the literary mind. Literature must be measured by literary standards, he feels, and not by an elaborate analysis of the neurotic symptoms of the writer.

Further reading: *The Liberal Imagination*, 1950. *The Opposing Self*, 1955.

Reality in America

First published in the present form in *The Liberal Imagination* (1950), this essay was based on two earlier articles in the *Partisan Review*, VII (January-February 1940) and the *Nation*, CLXII (April 1946).

I

It is possible to say of V. L. Parrington that with his *Main Currents in American Thought* he has had an influence on our conception of American culture which is not equaled by that of any other writer of the last two decades. His ideas are now the accepted ones wherever the college course in American literature is given by a teacher who conceives himself to be opposed to the genteel and the academic and in alliance with the vigorous and the actual. And whenever the liberal historian of America finds occasion to take account of the national literature, as nowadays he feels it proper to do, it is Parrington who is his standard and guide. Parrington's ideas are the more firmly established because they do not have to be imposed—the teacher or the critic who presents them is likely to find that his task is merely to make articulate for his audience what it has always believed, for Parrington formulated in a classic way the suppositions about our culture which are held by the American middle class so far as that class is at all liberal in its social thought and so far as it begins to understand that literature has anything to do with society.

Parrington was not a great mind; he was not a precise thinker or, except when measured by the low eminences that were about him, an impressive one. Separate Parrington from his informing idea of the economic and social determination of thought and what is left is a simple intelligence, notable for its generosity and enthusiasm but certainly not for its accuracy or originality. Take him even with his idea and he is, once its direction is established, rather too predictable to be continuously interesting; and, indeed, what we dignify with the name of economic and social determinism amounts in his use of it to not much more than the demonstration that most writers incline to stick to their own social class. But his best virtue was real and important—he had what we like to think of as the saving salt of the American mind, the lively sense of the practical, workaday world, of the welter of ordinary undistinguished things and people, of the tangible, quirky, unrefined elements of life. He knew what so many literary historians do not know, that emotions and ideas are the sparks that fly when the mind meets difficulties.

Yet he had after all but a limited sense of what constitutes a difficulty. Whenever he was confronted with a work of art that was complex, personal and not literal, that was not, as it were, a public document, Parrington was at a loss. Difficulties that were complicated by personality or that were expressed in the language of successful art did not seem quite real to him and he was inclined to treat them as aberrations, which is one way of saying what everybody admits, that the weakest part of Parrington's talent was his aesthetic judgment. His admirers and disciples like to imply that his errors of aesthetic judgment are merely lapses of taste, but this is not so. Despite such mistakes as his notorious praise of Cabell, to whom in a remarkable passage he compares Melville, Parrington's taste was by no means bad. His errors are the errors of understanding which arise from his assumptions about the nature of reality.

Parrington does not often deal with abstract philosophical ideas, but whenever he approaches a work of art we are made aware of the metaphysics on which his aesthetics is based. There exists, he believes, a thing called *reality;* it is one and immutable, it is wholly external, it is irreducible. Men's minds may waver, but reality is always reliable, always the same, always easily to be known. And the artist's relation to reality he conceives as a simple one. Reality being fixed and given, the artist has but to let it pass through him, he is the lens in the first diagram of an elementary book on optics: Fig. 1, Reality; Fig. 2, Artist; Fig. 1′, Work of Art. Figs. 1 and 1′ are normally in virtual correspondence with each other. Sometimes the artist spoils this ideal relation by "turning away from" reality. This results in certain fantastic works, unreal and ultimately useless. It does not occur to Parrington that there is any other relation possible between the artist and reality than this passage of reality through the transparent artist; he meets evidence of imagination and creativeness with a settled hostility, the expression of which suggests that he regards them as the natural enemies of democracy.

In this view of things, reality, although it is always reliable, is always rather sober-sided, even grim. Parrington, a genial and enthusiastic man, can understand how the generosity of man's hopes and desires may leap beyond reality; he admires will in the degree that he suspects mind. To an excess of desire and energy which blinds a man to the limitations of reality he can indeed be very tender. This is one of the many meanings he gives to *romance* or *romanticism,* and in spite of himself it appeals to something in his own nature. The praise of Cabell is Parrington's response not only to Cabell's elegance—for Parrington loved elegance—but also to Cabell's insistence on the part which a beneficent self-deception may and even should play in the disappointing fact-bound life of man, particularly in the private and erotic part of his life.[1]

The second volume of *Main Currents* is called *The Romantic Revolution in America* and it is natural to expect that the word romantic should appear in it frequently. So it does, more frequently than one can count, and seldom with the same meaning, seldom with the sense that the word, although scandalously vague as it has been used by the literary historians, is still full of complicated but not wholly pointless ideas, that it involves many contrary but definable things; all too often Parrington uses the word romantic with the word romance close at hand, meaning *a* romance, in the sense that *Graustark* or *Treasure Island* is a romance, as though it signified chiefly a gay disregard of the limitations of everyday fact. Romance is refusing to heed the counsels of experience (p. iii); it is ebullience (p. iv); it is utopianism (p. iv); it is individualism (p. vi); it is self-deception (p. 59)—"romantic faith . . . in the beneficent processes of trade and industry" (as held, we inevitably ask, by the romantic Adam Smith?); it is the love of the picturesque (p. 49); it is the dislike of innovation (p. 50) but also the love of change (p. iv); it is the sentimental (p. 192); it is patriotism, and then it is cheap (p. 235). It may be used to denote what is not classical, but chiefly it means that which ignores reality (pp. ix, 136, 143, 147, and *passim);* it is not critical (pp. 225, 235), although in speaking of Cooper and Melville, Parrington admits that criticism can sometimes spring from romanticism.

Whenever a man with whose ideas he disagrees wins from Parrington a reluctant measure of respect, the word romantic is likely to appear. He does not admire Henry Clay, yet something in Clay is not to be despised—his romanticism, although Clay's romanticism is made equivalent with his inability to "come to grips with reality." Romanticism is thus, in most of its significations, the venial sin of *Main Currents;* like carnal passion in the *Inferno,* it evokes not blame but tender sorrow. But it can also be the great and saving virtue which Parrington recognizes. It is ascribed to the transcendental reformers he so much admires; it is said to mark two of his most cherished heroes, Jefferson and Emerson: "they were both romantics and their idealism was only a different expression of a common spirit." Parrington held, we may say, at least two different views of romanticism which suggest two different views of reality. Sometimes he speaks of reality in an honorific way, meaning the substantial stuff of life, the ineluctable facts with which the mind must cope, but sometimes he speaks of it pejoratively and means the world of established social forms; and he speaks of realism in two ways: sometimes as the power of dealing intelligently with fact, sometimes as a cold and conservative resistance to idealism.

Just as for Parrington there is a saving grace and a venial sin, there is also a deadly sin, and this is turning away from reality, not in the excess of generous feeling, but in what he believes to be a deficiency of feeling, as with Hawthorne, or out of what amounts to sinful pride, as with Henry James. He tells us that there was too much realism in Hawthorne to allow him to give his faith to the transcendental reformers: "he was too much of a realist to change fashions in creeds"; "he remained cold to the revolutionary criticism that was eager to pull down the old temples to make room for nobler." It is this cold realism, keeping Hawthorne apart from his enthusiastic contemporaries, that alienates Parrington's sympathy—"Eager souls, mystics and revolutionaries, may propose to refashion the world in accordance with their dreams; but evil remains, and so long as it lurks in the secret places of the heart, utopia is only the shadow of a dream. And so while the Concord thinkers were proclaiming man to be the indubitable child of God, Hawthorne was critically examining the question of evil as it appeared in the light of his own experience. It was the central fascinating problem of his intellectual life, and in

[1] See, for example, how Parrington accounts for the "idealizing mind"—Melville's—by the discrepancy between "a wife in her morning kimono" and "the Helen of his dreams." Vol. II, p. 259. [Trilling's note.]

pursuit of a solution he probed curiously into the hidden, furtive recesses of the soul." Parrington's disapproval of the enterprise is unmistakable.

Now we might wonder whether Hawthorne's questioning of the naïve and often eccentric faiths of the transcendental reformers was not, on the face of it, a public service. But Parrington implies that it contributes nothing to democracy, and even that it stands in the way of the realization of democracy. If democracy depends wholly on a fighting faith, I suppose he is right. Yet society is after all something that exists at the moment as well as in the future, and if one man wants to probe curiously into the hidden furtive recesses of the contemporary soul, a broad democracy and especially one devoted to reality should allow him to do so without despising him. If what Hawthorne did was certainly nothing to build a party on, we ought perhaps to forgive him when we remember that he was only one man and that the future of mankind did not depend upon him alone. But this very fact serves only to irritate Parrington; he is put out by Hawthorne's loneliness and believes that part of Hawthorne's insufficiency as a writer comes from his failure to get around and meet people. Hawthorne could not, he tells us, establish contact with the "Yankee reality," and was scarcely aware of the "substantial world of Puritan reality that Samuel Sewall knew."

To turn from reality might mean to turn to romance, but Parrington tells us that Hawthorne was romantic "only in a narrow and very special sense." He was not interested in the world of, as it were, practical romance, in the Salem of the clipper ships; from this he turned away to create "a romance of ethics." This is not an illuminating phrase but it is a catching one, and it might be taken to mean that Hawthorne was in the tradition of, say, Shakespeare; but we quickly learn that, no, Hawthorne had entered a barren field, for although he himself lived in the present and had all the future to mold, he preferred to find many of his subjects in the past. We learn too that his romance of ethics is not admirable because it requires the hard, fine pressing of ideas, and we are told that "a romantic uninterested in adventure and afraid of sex is likely to become somewhat graveled for matter." In short, Hawthorne's mind was a thin one, and Parrington puts in evidence his use of allegory and symbol and the very severity and precision of his art to prove that he suffered from a sadly limited intellect, for so much fancy and so much art could scarcely be needed unless the writer were trying to exploit to the utmost the few poor ideas that he had.

Hawthorne, then, was "forever dealing with shadows, and he knew that he was dealing with shadows." Perhaps so, but shadows are also part of reality and one would not want a world without shadows, it would not even be a "real" world. But we must get beyond Parrington's metaphor. The fact is that Hawthorne was dealing beautifully with realities, with substantial things. The man who could raise those brilliant and serious doubts about the nature and possibility of moral perfection, the man who could keep himself aloof from the "Yankee reality" and who could dissent from the orthodoxies of dissent and tell us so much about the nature of moral zeal, is of course dealing exactly with reality.

Parrington's characteristic weakness as a historian is suggested by his title, for the culture of a nation is not truly figured in the image of the current. A culture is not a flow, nor even a confluence; the form of its existence is struggle, or at least debate—it is nothing if not a dialectic. And in any culture there are likely to be certain artists who contain a large part of the dialectic within themselves, their meaning and power lying in their contradictions; they contain within themselves, it may be said, the very essence of the culture, and the sign of this is that they do not submit to serve the ends of any one ideological group or tendency. It is a significant circumstance of American culture, and one which is susceptible of explanation, that an unusually large proportion of its notable writers of the nineteenth century were such repositories of the dialectic of their times—they contained both the yes and the no of their culture, and by that token they were prophetic of the future. Parrington said that he had not set up shop as a literary critic; but if a literary critic is simply a reader who has the ability to understand literature and to convey to others what he understands, it is not exactly a matter of free choice whether or not a cultural historian shall be a literary critic, nor is it open to him to let his virtuous political and social opinions do duty for percipience. To throw out Poe because he cannot be conveniently fitted into a theory of American culture, to speak of him as a biological sport and as a mind apart from the main current, to find his gloom to be merely personal and eccentric, "only the atrabilious wretchedness of a dipsomaniac," as Hawthorne's was "no more than the skeptical questioning of life by a nature that knew no fierce storms," to judge Melville's response to American life to be less noble than that of Bryant or of Greeley, to speak of Henry James as an escapist, as an artist similar to Whistler, a man characteristically afraid of stress—this is not merely to be mistaken in aesthetic judgment; rather it is to examine without attention and from the point of view of a limited and essentially arrogant conception of reality the documents which are in some respects the most suggestive testimony to what America was and is, and of course to get no answer from them.

Parrington lies twenty years behind us, and in the intervening time there has developed a body of opinion which is aware of his inadequacies and of the inadequacies of his coadjutors and disciples, who make up what might be called the literary academicism of liberalism. Yet Parrington still stands at the center of American thought about American culture because, as I say, he expresses the chronic American belief that there exists an opposition between reality and mind and that one must enlist oneself in the party of reality.

II

This belief in the incompatibility of mind and reality is exemplified by the doctrinaire indulgence which liberal intellectuals have always displayed toward Theodore Dreiser, an indulgence which becomes the worthier of remark when it is contrasted with the liberal severity toward Henry James. Dreiser and James: with that juxtaposition we are immediately at the dark and bloody crossroads where literature and politics meet. One does not go there gladly, but nowadays it is not exactly a matter of free choice whether one does or does not go. As for the particular juxtaposition itself, it is inevitable and it has at the present moment far more significance than the juxtaposition which once used to be made between James and Whitman. It is not hard to contrive factitious oppositions between James and Whitman, but the real difference between them is the difference between the moral mind, with its awareness of tragedy, irony, and multitudinous distinctions, and the transcendental mind, with its passionate sense of the oneness of multiplicity. James and Whitman are unlike not in quality but in kind, and in their very opposition they serve to complement each other. But the difference between James and Dreiser is not of kind, for both men addressed themselves to virtually the same social and moral fact. The difference here is one of quality, and perhaps nothing is more typical of American liberalism than the way it has responded to the respective qualities of the two men.

Few critics, I suppose, no matter what their political disposition, have ever been wholly blind to James's great gifts, or even to the grandiose moral intention of these gifts. And few critics have ever been wholly blind to Dreiser's great faults. But by liberal critics James is traditionally put to the ultimate question: of what use, of what actual political use, are his gifts and their intention? Granted that James was devoted to an extraordinary moral perceptiveness, granted too that moral perceptiveness has something to do with politics and the social life, of what possible practical value in our world of impending disaster can James's work be? And James's style, his characters, his subjects, and even his own social origin and the manner of his personal life are adduced to show that his work cannot endure the question. To James no quarter is given by American criticism in its political and liberal aspect. But in the same degree that liberal criticism is moved by political considerations to treat James with severity, it treats Dreiser with the most sympathetic indulgence. Dreiser's literary faults, it gives us to understand, are essentially social and political virtues. It was Parrington who established the formula for the liberal criticism of Dreiser by calling him a "peasant": when Dreiser thinks stupidly, it is because he has the slow stubbornness of a peasant; when he writes badly, it is because he is impatient of the sterile literary gentility of the bourgeoisie. It is as if wit, and flexibility of mind, and perception, and knowledge were to be equated with aristocracy and political reaction, while dullness and stupidity must naturally suggest a virtuous democracy, as in the old plays.

The liberal judgment of Dreiser and James goes back of politics, goes back to the cultural assumptions that make politics. We are still haunted by a kind of political fear of the intellect which Tocqueville observed in us more than a century ago. American intellectuals, when they are being consciously American or political, are remarkably quick to suggest that an art which is marked by perception and knowledge, although all very well in its way, can never get us through gross dangers and difficulties. And their misgivings become the more intense when intellect works in art as it ideally should, when its processes are vivacious and interesting and brilliant. It is then that we like to confront it with the gross dangers and difficulties and to challenge it to save us at once from disaster. When intellect in art is awkward or dull we do not put it to the test of ultimate or immediate practicality. No liberal critic asks the question of Dreiser whether *his* moral preoccupations are going to be useful in confronting the disasters that threaten us. And it is a judgment on the proper nature of mind, rather than any actual political meaning that might be drawn from the works of the two men, which accounts for the unequal justice they have received from the progressive critics. If it could be conclusively demonstrated—by, say, documents in James's handwriting—that James explicitly intended his books to be understood as pleas for co-operatives, labor unions, better housing, and more equitable taxation, the American critic in his liberal and progressive character would still be worried by James because his work shows so many of the electric qualities of mind. And if something like the opposite were proved of Dreiser, it would be brushed aside—as his doctrinaire anti-Semitism has in fact been brushed aside—because his books have the awkwardness, the chaos, the heaviness which we associate with "reality." In the American metaphysic, reality is always material reality, hard, resistant, unformed, impenetrable, and unpleasant. And that mind is alone felt to be trustworthy which most resembles this reality by most nearly reproducing the sensations it affords.

In *The Rise of American Civilization*, Professor Beard uses a significant phrase when, in the course of an ironic account of James's career, he implies that we have the clue to the irrelevance of that career when we know that James was "a whole generation removed from the odors of the shop." Of a piece with this, and in itself even more significant, is the comment which Granville Hicks makes in *The Great Tradition* when he deals with James's stories about artists and remarks that such artists as James portrays, so concerned for their art and their integrity in art, do not really exist: "After all, who has ever known such artists? Where are the Hugh Vereker, the Mark Ambients, the Neil Paradays, the Overts, Limberts, Dencombes, Delavoys?" This question, as Mr. Hicks admits, had occurred to James himself, but what answer had James given to it? "If the life about us for the last thirty years refused warrant for these examples," he said in the preface to volume XII of the New York Edition, "then so much the worse for that life. . . . There are decencies that in the name of the general self-respect we must take for granted, there's a rudimentary intellectual honor to which we must, in the interest of civilization, at least pretend." And to this Mr. Hicks, shocked beyond argument, makes this reply, which would be astonishing had we not heard it before: "But this is the purest romanticism, this writing about what ought to be rather than what is!"

The "odors of the shop" are real, and to those who breathe them they guarantee a sense of vitality from which James is debarred. The idea of intellectual honor is not real, and to that chimera James was devoted. He betrayed the reality of what is in the interests of what ought to be. Dare we trust him? The question, we remember, is asked by men who themselves have elaborate transactions with what ought to be. Professor Beard spoke in the name of a growing, developing, and improving America. Mr. Hicks, when he wrote *The Great Tradition*, was in general sympathy with a nominally radical movement. But James's own transaction with what ought to be is suspect because it is carried on through what I have called the electrical qualities of mind, through a complex and rapid imagination and with a kind of authoritative immediacy. Mr. Hicks knows that Dreiser is "clumsy" and "stupid" and "bewildered" and "crude in his statement of materialistic monism"; he knows that Dreiser in his personal life—which is in point because James's personal life is always supposed to be so much in point—was not quite emancipated from "his boyhood longing for crass material success," showing "again and again a desire for the ostentatious luxury of the successful business man." But Dreiser is to be accepted and forgiven because his faults are the sad, lovable, honorable faults of reality itself, or of America itself—huge, inchoate, struggling toward expression, caught between the dream of raw power and the dream of morality.

"The liability in what Santayana called the genteel tradition was due to its being the product of mind apart from experience. Dreiser gave us the stuff of our common experience, not as it was hoped to be by any idealizing theorist, but as it actually was in its crudity." The author of this statement certainly cannot be accused of any lack of feeling for mind as Henry James represents it; nor can Mr. Matthiessen be thought of as a follower of Parrington—indeed, in the preface to *American Renaissance* he has framed one of the sharpest and most cogent criticisms of Parrington's method. Yet Mr. Matthiessen, writing in the *New York Times Book Review* about Dreiser's posthumous novel, *The Bulwark*, accepts the liberal cliché which opposes crude experience to mind and establishes Dreiser's value by implying that the mind which Dreiser's crude experience is presumed to confront and refute is the mind of gentility.

This implied amalgamation of mind with gentility is the rationale of the long indulgence of Dreiser, which is extended even to the style of his prose. Everyone is aware that Dreiser's prose style is full of roughness and ungainliness, and the critics who admire Dreiser tell us it does not matter. Of course it does not matter. No reader with a right sense of style would suppose that it does matter, and he might even find it a virtue. But it has been taken for granted that the ungainliness of Dreiser's style is the only possible objection to be made to it, and that whoever finds in it any fault at all wants a prettified genteel style (and is objecting to the ungainliness of reality itself). For instance, Edwin Berry Burgum, in a leaflet on Dreiser put out by the Book Find Club, tells us that Dreiser was one of those who used—or, as Mr. Burgum says, utilized—"the diction of the Middle West, pretty much as it was spoken, rich in colloquialism and frank in the simplicity and directness of the pioneer tradition," and that this diction took the place of "the literary English, formal and bookish, of New England provincialism that was closer to the aristocratic spirit of the mother country than to the tang of everyday life in the new West." This is mere fantasy. Hawthorne, Thoreau, and Emerson were for the most part remarkably colloquial—they wrote, that is, much as they spoke; their prose was specifically American in quality, and, except for occasional lapses, quite direct and simple. It is Dreiser who lacks the sense of colloquial diction—that of the Middle West or any other. If we are to talk of bookishness, it is Dreiser who is bookish; he is precisely literary in the bad sense; he is full of flowers of rhetoric and shines with paste gems; at hundreds of points his diction is not only genteel but fancy. It is he who speaks of "a scene more distingué than this," or of a woman "artistic in form and feature," or of a man who, although "strong, reserved, aggressive, with an air of wealth and experience, was *soi-disant* and not particularly eager to stay at home." Colloquialism held no real charm for him and his natural tendency is always toward the "fine."

> ... Moralists come and go; religionists fulminate and declare the pronouncements of God as to this; but Aphrodite still reigns. Embowered in the festal depths of the spring, set above her altars of porphyry, chalcedony, ivory and gold, see her smile the smile that is at once the texture and essence of delight, the glory and despair of the world! Dream on, oh Buddha, asleep on your lotus leaf, of an undisturbed Nirvana! Sweat, oh Jesus, your last agonizing drops over an unregenerate world! In the forests of Pan still ring the cries of the worshippers of Aphrodite! From her altars the incense of adoration ever rises! And see, the new red grapes dripping where votive hands new-press them!

Charles Jackson, the novelist, telling us in the same leaflet that Dreiser's style does not matter, remarks on how much still comes to us when we have lost by translation the stylistic brilliance of Thomas Mann or the Russians or Balzac. He is in part right. And he is right too when he says that a certain kind of conscious, supervised artistry is not appropriate to the novel of large dimensions. Yet the fact is that the great novelists have usually written very good prose, and what comes through even a bad translation is exactly the power of mind that made the well-hung sentence of the original text. In literature style is so little the mere clothing of thought—need it be insisted on at this late date?—that we may say that from the earth of the novelist's prose spring his characters, his ideas, and even his story itself.[2]

To the extent that Dreiser's style is defensible, his thought is also defensible. That is, when he thinks like a novelist, he is worth following—when by means of his rough and ungainly but no doubt cumulatively effective style he creates rough, ungainly, but effective characters and events. But when he thinks like, as we say, a philosopher, he is likely to be not only foolish but vulgar. He thinks as the modern crowd thinks when it decides to think: religion and morality are nonsense, "religionists" and moralists are fakes, tradition is a fraud, what is man but matter and impulses, mysterious "chemisms," what value has life anyway? "What, cooking, eating, coition, job holding, growing, aging, losing, winning, in so changeful and passing a scene as this, important? Bunk! It is some form of titillating illusion with about as much import to the superior forces that bring it all about as the functions and gyrations of a fly. No more. And maybe less." Thus Dreiser at sixty. And yet there is for him always the vulgarly saving suspicion that maybe, when all is said and done, there is Something Behind It All. It is much to the point of his intellectual vulgarity that Dreiser's anti-Semitism was not merely a social prejudice but an idea, a way of dealing with difficulties.

No one, I suppose, has ever represented Dreiser as a masterly intellect. It is even commonplace to say that his ideas are inconsistent or inadequate. But once that admission has been made, his ideas are hustled out of sight while his "reality" and great brooding pity are spoken of. (His pity is to be questioned: pity is to be judged by kind, not amount, and Dreiser's pity—*Jennie Gerhardt* provides the

[2] The latest defense of Dreiser's style, that in the chapter on Dreiser in the *Literary History of the United States*, is worth noting: "Forgetful of the integrity and power of Dreiser's whole work, many critics have been distracted into a condemnation of his style. He was, like Twain and Whitman, an organic artist; he wrote what he knew—what he was. His many colloquialisms were part of the coinage of his time, and his sentimental and romantic passages were written in the language of the educational system and the popular literature of his formative years. In his style, as in his material, he was a child of his time, of his class. Self-educated, a type of model of the artist of plebeian origin in America, his language, like his subject matter, is not marked by internal inconsistencies." No doubt Dreiser was an organic artist in the sense that he wrote what he knew and what he was, but so, I suppose, is every artist; the question for criticism comes down to *what* he knew and *what* he was. That he was a child of his time and class is also true, but this can be said of everyone without exception; the question for criticism is how he transcended the imposed limitations of his time and class. As for the defense made on the ground of his particular class, it can only be said that liberal thought has come to a strange pass when it assumes that a plebeian origin is accountable for a writer's faults through all his intellectual life. [Trilling's note.]

only exception—is either destructive of its object or it is self-pity.) Why has no liberal critic ever brought Dreiser's ideas to the bar of political practicality, asking what use is to be made of Dreiser's dim, awkward speculation, of his self-justification, of his lust for "beauty" and "sex" and "living" and "life itself," and of the showy nihilism which always seems to him so grand a gesture in the direction of profundity? We live, understandably enough, with the sense of urgency; our clock, like Baudelaire's, has had the hands removed and bears the legend, "It is later than you think." But with us it is always a little too late for mind, yet never too late for honest stupidity; always a little too late for understanding, never too late for righteous, bewildered wrath; always too late for thought, never too late for naïve moralizing. We seem to like to condemn our finest but not our worst qualities by pitting them against the exigency of time.

But sometimes time is not quite so exigent as to justify all our own exigency, and in the case of Dreiser time has allowed his deficiencies to reach their logical, and fatal, conclusion. In *The Bulwark* Dreiser's characteristic ideas come full circle, and the simple, didactic life history of Solon Barnes, a Quaker business man, affirms a simple Christian faith, and a kind of practical mysticism, and the virtues of self-abnegation and self-restraint, and the belief in and submission to the hidden purposes of higher powers, those "superior forces that bring it all about"—once, in Dreiser's opinion, so brutally indifferent, now somehow benign. This is not the first occasion on which Dreiser has shown a tenderness toward religion and a responsiveness to mysticism. *Jennie Gerhardt* and the figure of the Reverend Duncan McMillan in *An American Tragedy* are forecasts of the avowals of *The Bulwark*, and Dreiser's lively interest in power of any sort led him to take account of the power implicit in the cruder forms of mystical performance. Yet these rifts in his nearly monolithic materialism cannot quite prepare us for the blank pietism of *The Bulwark*, not after we have remembered how salient in Dreiser's work has been the long surly rage against the "religionists" and the "moralists," the men who have presumed to believe that life can be given any law at all and who have dared to suppose that will or mind or faith can shape the savage and beautiful entity that Dreiser liked to call "life itself." Now for Dreiser the law may indeed be given, and it is wholly simple—the safe conduct of the personal life requires only that we follow the Inner Light according to the regimen of the Society of Friends, or according to some other godly rule. And now the smiling Aphrodite set above her altars of porphyry, chalcedony, ivory, and gold is quite forgotten, and we are told that the sad joy of cosmic acceptance goes hand in hand with sexual abstinence.

Dreiser's mood of "acceptance" in the last years of his life is not, as a personal experience, to be submitted to the tests of intellectual validity. It consists of a sensation of cosmic understanding, of an overarching sense of unity with the world in its apparent evil as well as in its obvious good. It is no more to be quarreled with, or reasoned with, than love itself—indeed, it is a kind of love, not so much of the world as of oneself in the world. Perhaps it is either the cessation of desire or the perfect balance of desires. It is what used often to be meant by "peace," and up through the nineteenth century a good many people understood its meaning. If it was Dreiser's own emotion at the end of his life, who would not be happy that he had achieved it? I am not even sure that our civilization would not be the better for more of us knowing and desiring this emotion of grave felicity. Yet granting the personal validity of the emotion, Dreiser's exposition of it fails, and is, moreover, offensive. Mr. Matthiessen has warned us of the attack that will be made on the doctrine of *The Bulwark* by "those who believe that any renewal of Christianity marks a new 'failure of nerve.' " But Dreiser's religious avowal is not a failure of nerve—it is a failure of mind and heart. We have only to set his book beside any work in which mind and heart are made to serve religion to know this at once. Ivan Karamazov's giving back his ticket of admission to the "harmony" of the universe suggests that *The Bulwark* is not morally adequate, for we dare not, as its hero does, blandly "accept" the suffering of others; and the Book of Job tells us that it does not include enough in its exploration of the problem of evil, and is not stern enough. I have said that Dreiser's religious affirmation was offensive; the offense lies in the vulgar ease of its formulation, as well as in the comfortable untroubled way in which Dreiser moved from nihilism to pietism.[3]

The Bulwark is the fruit of Dreiser's old age, but if we speak of it as a failure of thought and feeling, we cannot suppose that with age Dreiser weakened in mind and heart. The weakness was always there. And in a sense it is not Dreiser who failed but a whole way of dealing with ideas, a way in which we have all been in some degree involved. Our liberal,

[3] This ease and comfortableness seem to mark contemporary religious conversions. Religion nowadays has the appearance of what the ideal modern house has been called, "a machine for living," and seemingly one makes up one's mind to acquire and use it not with spiritual struggle but only with a growing sense of its practicability and convenience. Compare *The Seven Storey Mountain*, which Monsignor Sheen calls "a twentieth-century form of the *Confessions* of St. Augustine," with the old, the as it were original, *Confessions* of St. Augustine. [Trilling's note.]

progressive culture tolerated Dreiser's vulgar materialism with its huge negation, its simple cry of "Bunk!," feeling that perhaps it was not quite intellectually adequate but certainly very *strong*, certainly very *real*. And now, almost as a natural consequence, it has been given, and is not unwilling to take, Dreiser's pietistic religion in all its inadequacy.

Dreiser, of course, was firmer than the intellectual culture that accepted him. He *meant* his ideas, at least so far as a man can mean ideas who is incapable of following them to their consequences. But we, when it came to his ideas, talked about his great brooding pity and shrugged the ideas off. We are still doing it. Robert Elias, the biographer of Dreiser, tells us that "it is part of the logic of [Dreiser's] life that he should have completed *The Bulwark* at the same time that he joined the Communists." Just what kind of logic this is we learn from Mr. Elias's further statement. "When he supported left-wing movements and finally, last year, joined the Communist Party, he did so not because he had examined the details of the party line and found them satisfactory, but because he agreed with a general program that represented a means for establishing his cherished goal of greater equality among men." Whether or not Dreiser was following the logic of his own life, he was certainly following the logic of the liberal criticism that accepted him so undiscriminatingly as one of the great, significant expressions of its spirit. This is the liberal criticism, in the direct line of Parrington, which establishes the social responsibility of the writer and then goes on to say that, apart from his duty of resembling reality as much as possible, he is not really responsible for anything, not even for his ideas. The scope of reality being what it is, ideas are held to be mere "details," and, what is more, to be details which, if attended to, have the effect of diminishing reality. But ideals are different from ideas; in the liberal criticism which descends from Parrington ideals consort happily with reality and they urge us to deal impatiently with ideas—a "cherished goal" forbids that we stop to consider how we reach it, or if we may not destroy it in trying to reach it the wrong way.

CLEANTH BROOKS [1906-]

Among contemporary critics, Cleanth Brooks has been the most consistent follower of the principles of T. S. Eliot in his rejection of "biographical irrelevancies," "historical explanation," and "sociological theory" as approaches to literary criticism. As such, he has become one of the central figures in the vigorous debate over the values of the so-called New Criticism. For him the text is everything. The critic's function is to inspect it closely for subtle felicities of irony, "wit," paradox, ambiguity, and the clash of metaphors. In an early essay, "The Language of Paradox," he described poetry as "words perpetually juxtaposed in new and sudden combination," and stated that the task and challenge of the poet is to gain precision and new meaning from the paradoxical nature of language. By close textual scrutiny of a complex poem, the critic may discover levels of meaning beneath the conscious surface-intention of the poet. Like Eliot, he has traced the line of descent in modern poetry to the school of Donne and the Metaphysicals of the seventeenth century, preferring their intellectual conceits and their sense of irony to the rhythmic affirmations of romantic verse. Brooks's influence has been especially marked upon the methods of teaching literature at advanced levels. His texts, *Understanding Poetry* (1938) and *Understanding Fiction* (1943), co-edited with Robert Penn Warren, supplied a vocabulary and a technique which have had a widespread effect on the classroom analysis of difficult verse and prose. In 1947 he collaborated with Robert Heilman on a third textbook, *Understanding Drama*.

Brooks's career has been wholly within the academic world. He graduated from Vanderbilt University in 1928, went to Oxford as a Rhodes Scholar, and took his B. Litt.

degree there in 1932. While teaching literature at Louisiana State University in the 1930's he began publishing in the *Southern Review*, of which he was an editor. Since 1947 he has been a Professor of English at Yale University.

His essays published in the thirties and forties in *Poetry*, the *Kenyon Review*, the *New Republic*, the *American Scholar*, and other periodicals, have been collected in two volumes, *Modern Poetry and the Tradition* (1939) and *The Well-Wrought Urn* (1947). In *The Hidden God* (1963) Brooks analyzed the work of Hemingway, Faulkner, Yeats, Eliot, and Warren in the context of the Christian tradition.

Further reading: *Modern Poetry and the Tradition*, 1939. "The New Criticism: A Brief for the Defense," *American Scholar* (Summer 1944).

The Waste Land: An Analysis

First printed in *Modern Poetry and the Tradition* (1939), this essay has been frequently anthologized. It is still the most complete discussion of Eliot's difficult poem, which has been called the most influential poem of the twentieth century, and it serves as an excellent example of the close, analytical reading of poetry characteristic of the New Criticism. The text given here, slightly revised from the original form, is as it appeared in *T. S. Eliot, A Study of His Writing by Several Hands*, edited by B. Rajan (London, 1947).

To venture to write anything further on *The Waste Land*, particularly after the work of F. R. Leavis and F. O. Matthiessen, may call for some explanation and even apology. I am obviously indebted to both critics. The justification for such a commentary as this must be made primarily in terms of a difference of intention. Leavis is interested predominantly in Eliot's method of organization. One or two passages in the poem are treated in detail and are highly valuable for a knowledge of the "meaning" of the poem, but the bulk of the poem does not receive this kind of examination. Moreover, I believe, Leavis makes some positive errors. Matthiessen examines more of the poem in detail, and, as far as it goes, his account is excellent. But the plan of his *Achievement of T. S. Eliot* does not allow for a consecutive examination either. He puts his finger on the basic theme, death-in-life, but I do not think that he has given it all the salience which it deserves.

I prefer not to raise here the question of how important it is for the reader of the poem to have an explicit intellectual account of the various symbols, and a logical account of their relationships. It may well be that such rationalization is no more than a scaffolding to be got out of the way before we contemplate the poem itself as a poem. But many readers (including myself) find the erection of such a scaffolding valuable—if not absolutely necessary—and if some readers will be tempted to lay more stress on the scaffolding than they properly should, there are perhaps still more readers who will be prevented from getting at the poem at all without the help of such a scaffolding. Furthermore, an interest attaches to Mr. Eliot's own mental processes, and whereas Mr. Matthiessen has quite properly warned us that Eliot's poetry cannot be read as autobiography, many of the symbols and ideas which occur in *The Waste Land* are ideas which are definitely central to Eliot's general intellectual position.

The basic symbol used, that of the waste land, is taken, of course, from Miss Jessie Weston's *From Ritual to Romance*. In the legends which she treats there, the land has been blighted by a curse. The crops do not grow, and the animals cannot reproduce. The plight of the land is summed up by, and connected with, the plight of the lord of the land, the Fisher King, who has been rendered impotent by maiming or sickness. The curse can only be removed by the appearance of a knight who will ask the meanings of the various symbols which are displayed to him in the castle. The shift in meaning from physical to spiritual sterility is easily made, and was, as a matter of fact, made in certain of the legends. A knowledge of this symbolism is, as Eliot has already pointed out, essential for an understanding of the poem.

Of hardly less importance to the reader, however, is a knowledge of Eliot's basic method. *The Waste Land* is built on a major contrast—a device which is a favourite of Eliot's and to be found in many of his poems, particularly his later poems. The contrast is between two kinds of life and two kinds of death. Life devoid of meaning is death; sacrifice, even the sacrificial death, may be life-giving, an awakening to life. The poem occupies itself to a great extent with this paradox, and with a number of variations on it.

Eliot has stated the matter quite explicitly himself in one of his essays. In his "Baudelaire" he says:

> One aphorism which has been especially noticed is the following: *la volupté unique et suprême de l'amour gît dans la certitude de faire le mal.* This means, I think, that Baudelaire has perceived that what distinguishes the relations of man and woman from the copulation of beasts is the knowledge of

> Good and Evil (of *moral* Good and Evil which are not natural Good and Bad or puritan Right and Wrong). Having an imperfect, vague romantic conception of Good, he was at least able to understand that the sexual act as evil is more dignified, less boring than as the natural, 'life-giving,' cheery automatism of the modern world. . . . So far as we are human, what we do must be either evil or good; so far as we do evil or good, we are human; and it is better, in a paradoxical way, to do evil than to do nothing: at least, *we exist* [italics mine].

The last statement is highly important for an understanding of *The Waste Land.* The fact that men have lost the knowledge of good and evil keeps them from being alive, and is the justification for viewing the modern waste land as a realm in which people do not even exist.

This theme is stated in the quotation which prefaces the poem. The Sybil says: "I wish to die." Her statement has several possible interpretations. For one thing, she is saying what the people who inhabit the waste land are saying. But she also may be saying what the speaker says in *The Journey of the Magi*, . . . "this Birth was/Hard and bitter agony for us, like Death, our death/. . . . I should be glad of another death."

I

The first section of "The Burial of the Dead" develops the theme of the attractiveness of death, or of the difficulty in rousing oneself from the death-in-life in which the people of the waste land live. Men are afraid to live in reality. April, the month of rebirth, is not the most joyful season but the cruellest. Winter at least kept us warm in forgetful snow. The idea is one which Eliot has stressed elsewhere. Earlier in *Gerontion* he had written

> In the juvescence of the year
> Came Christ the tiger
> . . . .
> The tiger springs in the new year. Us he devours.

More lately, in *Murder in the Cathedral*, he has the chorus say

> We do not wish anything to happen.
> Seven years we have lived quietly,
> Succeeded in avoiding notice,
> Living and partly living.

And in another passage: "Now I fear disturbance of the quiet seasons." Men dislike to be aroused from their death-in-life.

The first part of "The Burial of the Dead" introduces this theme through a sort of reverie on the part of the protagonist—a reverie in which speculation on life glides off into memory of an actual conversation in the Hofgarten and back into speculation again. The function of the conversation is to establish to some extent the class and character of the protagonist. The reverie is resumed with line 19.

> What are the roots that clutch, what branches grow
> Out of this stony rubbish?

The protagonist answers for himself:

> Son of man,
> You cannot say, or guess, for you know only
> A heap of broken images, where the sun beats,
> And the dead tree gives no shelter, the cricket no relief,
> And the dry stone no sound of water.

In this passage there are references to Ezekiel and to Ecclesiastes, and these references indicate what it is that men no longer know: the passage referred to in Ezekiel ii pictures a world thoroughly secularized:

> 1. And he said unto me, Son of man, stand upon thy feet, and I will speak unto thee. 2. And the spirit entered into me when he spake unto me, and set me upon my feet, that I heard him that spake unto me. 3. And he said unto me, Son of man, I send thee to the children of Israel, to a rebellious nation that hath rebelled against me: they and their fathers have transgressed against me, even unto this very day.

The following passage, from Ecclesiastes xii, is not only referred to in this passage; a reference to it also is evidently made in the nightmare vision of Section V of the poem:

> 1. Remember now thy Creator in the days of thy youth, while the evil days come not, nor the years draw nigh, when thou shalt say, I have no pleasure in them; 2. While the sun, or the light, or the moon, or the stars, be not darkened, nor the clouds return after the rain: 3. In the day when the keepers of the house shall tremble, and the strong men shall bow themselves, and the grinders cease because they are few, and those that look out of the windows be darkened, 4. And the doors shall be shut in the streets, when the sound of the grinding is low, and he shall rise up at the voice of the bird, and all the daughters of musick shall be brought low; 5. Also when they shall be afraid of that which is high, and fears shall be in the way, and the almond tree shall flourish, and the grasshopper shall be a burden, *and desire shall fail* [italics mine]: because man goeth to his long home, and the mourners go about the streets: 6. Or ever the silver cord be loosed, or the golden bowl be broken, or the pitcher be broken at the fountain, or the wheel broken at the cistern. 7. Then shall the dust return to the earth as it was: and the spirit shall return unto God who gave it. 8. Vanity of vanities, saith the preacher; all is vanity.

The next section which begins with the scrap of

song quoted from Wagner (perhaps another item in the reverie of the protagonist), states the opposite half of the paradox which underlies the poem: namely, that life at its highest moments of meaning and intensity resembles death. The song from Act I of Wagner's *Tristan and Isolde,* "Frisch weht der Wind," is sung in the opera by a young sailor aboard the ship which is bringing Isolde to Cornwall. The *"Irisch Kind"* of the song does not properly apply to Isolde at all. The song is merely one of happy and naïve love. It brings to the mind of the protagonist an experience of love—the vision of the hyacinth girl as she came back from the hyacinth garden. The poet says

> . . . my eyes failed, I was neither
> Living nor dead, and I knew nothing,
> Looking into the heart of light, the silence.

The line which immediately follows this passage, "Oed' und leer das Meer," seems at first to be simply an extension of the last figure: that is, "Empty and wide the sea (of silence)." The line, however, as a matter of fact, makes an ironic contrast; for the line as it occurs in Act III of the opera, is the reply of the watcher who reports to the wounded Tristan that Isolde's ship is nowhere in sight; the sea is empty. And, though the *"Irisch Kind"* of the first quotation is not Isolde, the reader familiar with the opera will apply it to Isolde when he comes to the line "Oed' und leer das Meer." For the question in the song is in essence Tristan's question in Act III: My Irish child, where dwellest thou? The two quotations from the opera which frame the ecstasy-of-love passage thus take on a new meaning in the altered context. In the first, love is happy: the boat rushes on with a fair wind behind it. In the second, love is absent; the sea is wide and empty. And the last quotation reminds us that even love cannot exist in the waste land.

The next passage, that in which Madame Sosostris figures, calls for further reference to Miss Weston's book. As Miss Weston has shown, the Tarot cards were originally used to determine the event of the highest importance to the people, the rising of the waters. Madame Sosostris has fallen a long way from the high function of her predecessors. She is engaged merely in vulgar fortune-telling—is merely one item in a generally vulgar civilization. But the symbols of the Tarot pack are still unchanged. The various characters are still inscribed on the cards, and she is reading in reality, though she does not know it, the fortune of the protagonist. She finds that his card is that of the drowned Phoenician Sailor, and so she warns him against death by water, not realizing any more than do the other inhabitants of the modern waste land that the way into life may be by death itself. The drowned Phoenician Sailor is a type of the fertility god whose image was thrown into the sea annually as a symbol of the death of summer. As for the other figures in the pack: Belladonna, the Lady of the Rocks, is woman in the waste land. The man with three staves Eliot says he associates rather arbitrarily with the Fisher King. The term "arbitrarily" indicates that we are not to attempt to find a logical connection here.

The Hanged Man, who represents the hanged god of Frazer (including the Christ), Eliot states in a note, is associated with the hooded figure who appears in "What the Thunder Said." That he is hooded accounts for Madame Sosostris' inability to see him; or rather, here again the palaver of the modern fortune-teller is turned to new and important accounts by the poet's shifting the matter into a new and serious context. The Wheel and the one-eyed merchant will be discussed later.

After the Madame Sosostris passage, Eliot proceeds to complicate his symbols for the sterility and unreality of the modern waste land by associating it with Baudelaire's *fourmillante cité* and with Dante's Limbo. The passages already quoted from Eliot's essay on Baudelaire will indicate one of the reasons why Baudelaire's lines are evoked here. In Baudelaire's city, dream and reality seem to mix, and it is interesting that Eliot in *The Hollow Men* refers to this same realm of death-in-life as "death's dream kingdom" in contradistinction to "death's other kingdom."

The references to Dante are most important. The line, "I had not thought death had undone so many," is taken from the Third Canto of the *Inferno;* the line, "Sighs, short and infrequent, were exhaled," from the Fourth Canto. Mr. Matthiessen has already pointed out that the Third Canto deals with Dante's Limbo which is occupied by those who on earth had "lived without praise or blame." They share this abode with the angels, "Who were not rebels, nor were faithful to God, but were for themselves." They exemplify almost perfectly the secular attitude which dominates the modern world. Their grief, according to Dante, arises from the fact that they "have no hope of death; and their blind life is so debased, that they are envious of every other lot." But though they may not hope for death, Dante calls them "these wretches who never were alive." The people who are treated in the Fourth Canto are those who lived virtuously but who died before the proclamation of the Gospel—they are the unbaptized. This completes the categories of people who inhabit the modern waste land: those who are secularized and those who have no knowledge of the faith. Without a faith their life is in reality a death. To repeat the sentence from Eliot previously quoted: "So far as we do evil or good, we are human; and it is better, in a paradoxical way, to do evil than to do nothing: at least, we exist."

The Dante and Baudelaire references, then, come to the same thing as the allusion to the waste land of the medieval legends; and these various allusions drawn from widely differing sources enrich the comment on the modern city so that it becomes "unreal" on a number of levels: as seen through "the brown fog of a winter dawn"; as the medieval waste land and Dante's Limbo and Baudelaire's Paris are unreal.

The reference to Stetson stresses again the connection between the modern London of the poem and Dante's hell. After the statement, "I could never have believed death had undone so many," follow the words "After I had distinguished some among them, I saw and knew the shade of him who made, through cowardice, the great refusal." The protagonist, like Dante, sees among the inhabitants of the contemporary waste land one whom he recognizes. (The name "Stetson" I take to have no ulterior significance. It is merely an ordinary name such as might be borne by the friend one might see in a crowd in a great city.) Mylae, as Mr. Matthiessen has pointed out to us, is the name of a battle between the Romans and the Carthaginians in the Punic War. The Punic War was a trade war—might be considered a rather close parallel to the war of 1914-18. At any rate, it is plain that Eliot in having the protagonist address the friend in a London street as one who was with him in the Punic War rather than as one who was with him in the World War is making the point that all the wars are one war; all experience, one experience. As Eliot put the idea in *Murder in the Cathedral:*

> We do not know very much of the future
> Except that from generation to generation
> The same things happen again and again.

I am not sure that Leavis and Matthiessen are correct in inferring that the line, "That corpse you planted last year in your garden," refers to the attempt to bury a memory. But whether or not this is true, the line certainly refers also to the buried god of the old fertility rites. It also is to be linked with the earlier passage—"What are the roots that clutch, what branches grow," etc. This allusion to the buried god will account for the ironical, almost taunting tone of the passage. The burial of the dead is now a sterile planting—without hope. But the advice to "keep the Dog far hence," in spite of the tone, is, I believe, well taken and serious. The passage in Webster goes as follows:

> O keep the wolf far hence, that's foe to men,
> Or with his nails he'll dig it up again.

Why does Eliot turn the wolf into a dog? And why does he reverse the point of importance from the animal's normal hostility to men to its friendliness? If, as some critics have suggested, he is merely interested in making a reference to Webster's darkest play, why alter the line? I am inclined to take the Dog (the capital letter is Eliot's) as Humanitarianism and the related philosophies which in their concern for man extirpate the supernatural—dig up the corpse of the buried god and thus prevent the rebirth of life. For the general idea, see Eliot's essay, "The Humanism of Irving Babbitt."

The last line of "The Burial of the Dead"—"You! hypocrite lecteur!—mon semblable,—mon frère!"—the quotation from Baudelaire, completes the universalization of Stetson begun by the reference to Mylae. Stetson is every man, including the reader and Mr. Eliot himself.

II

If "The Burial of the Dead" gives the general abstract statement on the situation, the second part of *The Waste Land,* "A Game of Chess," gives a more concrete illustration. The easiest contrast in this section—and one which may easily blind the casual reader to a continued emphasis on the contrast between the two kinds of life, or the two kinds of death, already commented on—is the contrast between life in a rich and magnificent setting, and life in the low and vulgar setting of a London pub. But both scenes, however antithetical they may appear superficially, are scenes taken from the contemporary waste land. In both of them life has lost its meaning.

I am particularly indebted to Mr. Allen Tate's brilliant comment on the first part of this section. To quote from him, "the woman . . . is, I believe, the symbol of man at the present time. He is surrounded by the grandeurs of the past, but he does not participate in them; they don't sustain him." And to quote from another section of his commentary: "The rich experience of the great tradition depicted in the room receives a violent shock in contrast with a game that symbolizes the inhuman abstraction of the modern mind." Life has no meaning; history has no meaning; there is no answer to the question: "What shall we ever do?" The only thing that has meaning is the abstract game which they are to play, a game in which the meaning is assigned and arbitrary, meaning by convention only—in short, a game of chess.

This interpretation will account in part for the pointed reference to Cleopatra in the first lines of the section. But there is, I believe, a further reason for the poet's having compared the lady to Cleopatra. The queen in Shakespeare's drama—"Age cannot wither her, nor custom stale/Her infinite variety"—is perhaps the extreme exponent of love for love's sake—the feminine member of the pair of lovers who threw away an empire for love. But the infinite variety of the life of the woman in "A Game of Chess" *has* been staled. There is indeed no variety at all, and love simply does not exist. The function of the sudden change in the description of the carvings and paintings in the room from the heroic and magnificent to the characterization of the rest of them as "other withered stumps of time" is obvious. But the reference to Philomela is particularly important, for Philomela, it seems to me, is one of the major symbols of the poem.

Miss Weston points out that a section of one of the Grail manuscripts, which is apparently intended as a gloss of the Grail story, tells how the court of the rich Fisher King was withdrawn from the knowledge of men when certain of the maidens who frequented the shrine were raped and had their golden cups taken from them. The curse on the land follows from this act. Miss Weston conjectures that this may be a statement, in the form of parable, of the violation of the older mysteries which were probably once celebrated openly, but were later forced underground into secrecy. Whether or not Mr. Eliot intends a reference to this passage, the violation of a woman makes a very good symbol of the process of secularization. John Crowe Ransom makes the point very neatly for us in his *God Without Thunder.* Love is the aesthetic of sex; lust is the science. Love implies a deferring of the satisfaction of the desire; it implies even a certain asceticism and a ritual. Lust drives forward urgently and scientifically to the immediate extirpation of the desire. Our contemporary waste land is in a large part the result of our scientific attitude—of our complete secularization. Needless to say, lust defeats its own ends. The portrayal of "The change of Philomel, by the barbarous kind" is a fitting commentary on the scene which it ornaments. The waste land of the legend came in this way—the modern waste land has come in this way.

That this view is not mere fine-spun ingenuity is borne out somewhat by the change of tense which Eliot employs here and which Mr. Edmund Wilson has commented upon: "And still she cried, and still the world pursues." Apparently the "world" partakes in the barbarous king's action, and still partakes in that action.

To "dirty ears" the nightingale's song is not that which filled all the desert with inviolable voice—it is "jug, jug." Edmund Wilson has pointed out that the rendition of the bird's song here represents not merely the Elizabethan neutral notation of the bird's song, but carries associations of the ugly and coarse. The passage is therefore one of many instances of Eliot's device of using something which in one context is innocent but in another context becomes loaded with a special meaning.

The Philomela passage has another importance, however. If it is a commentary on how the waste land became waste, it also repeats the theme of the death which is the door to life—the theme of the dying god. The raped woman becomes transformed through suffering into the nightingale; through the violation comes the "inviolable voice." The thesis that suffering is action, and that out of suffering comes poetry is a favourite one of Eliot's. For example, "Shakespeare, too, was occupied with the struggle—which alone constitutes life for a poet—to transmute his personal and private agonies into something rich and strange, something universal and impersonal." Consider also his statement with reference to Baudelaire: "Indeed, in his way of suffering is already a kind of presence of the supernatural and of the superhuman. He rejects always the purely natural and the purely human; in other words, he is neither 'naturalist' nor 'humanist.'" The theme of the life which is death is stated specifically in the conversation between the man and the woman. She asks the question "Are you alive, or not?" and this time we are sufficiently prepared by the Dante references in "The Burial of the Dead" for the statement here to bear a special meaning. (She also asks "Is there nothing in your head?" He is one of the Hollow Men—"headpiece stuffed with straw.") These people, as people in the waste land, know nothing, see nothing, do not even live.

But the protagonist, after this reflection that in the waste land of modern life even death is sterile—"I think we are in rats' alley/Where the dead men lost their bones"—remembers a death which was not sterile, remembers a death that was transformed into something rich and strange, the death described in the song from *The Tempest*—"Those are pearls that were his eyes."

The reference to this section of *The Tempest* is, like the Philomela reference, one of Eliot's major symbols. We are to meet it twice more, in later sections of the poem. Some more general comment on it is therefore appropriate here. The song, one remembers, was sung by Ariel in luring Ferdinand, Prince of Naples, on to meet Miranda, and thus to find love, and through this love, to effect the regeneration and deliverance of all the people on the island. Ferdinand says of the song:

> The ditty doth remember my drowned father
> This is no mortal business, nor no sound
> That the earth owes. . . .

The allusion is an extremely interesting example of

the device of Eliot's already commented upon, that of taking an item from one context and shifting it into another in which it assumes a new and powerful meaning. This description of a death which is a portal into a realm of the rich and strange—a death which becomes a sort of birth—assumes in the mind of the protagonist an association with that of the drowned god whose effigy was thrown into the water as a symbol of the death of the fruitful powers of nature but which was taken out of the water as a symbol of the revivified god. (See *From Ritual to Romance.*) The passage therefore represents the perfect antithesis to the passage in "The Burial of the Dead": "That corpse you planted last year in your garden," etc. It also, as we have already pointed out, finds its antithesis in the sterile and unfruitful death "in rats' alley" just commented upon. (We shall find that this contrast between the death in rats' alley and the death in *The Tempest* is made again in "The Fire Sermon.")

We have yet to treat the relation of the title of the section, "A Game of Chess," to Middleton's play, *Women beware Women,* from which the game of chess is taken. In the play, the game is used as a device to keep the widow occupied while her daughter-in-law is being seduced. The seduction amounts almost to a rape, and in a *double entendre* the rape is actually described in terms of the game. We have one more connection with the Philomela symbol therefore. The abstract game is being used in the contemporary waste land, as in the play, to cover up a rape and is a description of the rape itself.

In the second part of "A Game of Chess" we are given a picture of spiritual emptiness, but this time, at the other end of the social scale, as reflected in the talk between two cockney women in a London pub. The account here is straightforward enough and the only matter which calls for comment is the line spoken by Ophelia in *Hamlet* which ends the passage. Ophelia, too, was very much concerned about love, the theme of conversation of the two ladies. As a matter of fact, she was in very much the same position as that of the woman who has been the topic of conversation between the two good ladies we have just heard. She had remarked too once that

> Young men will do't, if they come to't!
> By cock, they are to blame.

And her poetry (including the line quoted from her here), like Philomela's had come out of suffering. I think that we are probably to look for the relevance of the allusion to her in some such matter as this rather than in an easy satiric contrast between Elizabethan glories and modern sordidness. After all (in spite of the Marxists) Eliot's objection to the present world is not merely the sentimental one that this happens to be the twentieth century after Christ and not the seventeenth.

III

"The Fire Sermon" makes much use of several of the symbols already developed. The fire is the sterile burning of lust, and the section is a sermon, although a sermon by example only. This section of the poem also contains some of the most easily apprehended uses of literary allusion. The poem opens on a vision of the modern river. In Spenser's *Prothalamion* the scene described is also a river scene at London, and it is dominated by nymphs and their paramours, and the nymphs are preparing for a bridal. The contrast between Spenser's scene and its twentieth-century equivalent is jarring. The paramours are now "the loitering heirs of city directors," and, as for the bridals of Spenser's Elizabethan maidens, in the stanzas which follow we learn a great deal about those. At the end of the section the speech of the third of the Thames-nymphs summarizes the whole matter for us.

The waters of the Thames are also associated with those of Leman—the poet in the contemporary waste land is in a sort of Babylonian Captivity.

The castle of the Fisher King was always located on the banks of a river or on the sea shore. The title "Fisher King," Miss Weston shows, originates from the use of the fish as a fertility or life symbol. This meaning, however, was often forgotten, and so the title in many of the later Grail romances is accounted for by describing the king as fishing. Eliot uses the reference to fishing for reverse effect. The reference to fishing is part of the realistic detail of the scene—"While I was fishing in the dull canal." But to the reader who knows the Weston references, the reference is to that of the Fisher King of the Grail legends. The protagonist is the maimed and impotent King of the legends.

Eliot proceeds now to tie the waste-land symbol to that of *The Tempest,* by quoting one of the lines spoken by Ferdinand, Prince of Naples, which occurs just before Ariel's song, "Full Fathom Five," is heard. But he alters the passage from *The Tempest* somewhat, writing not, "Weeping again the king my father's wreck," but

> Musing upon the king my brother's wreck
> And on the king my father's death before him.

It is possible that the alteration has been made to bring the account taken from *The Tempest* into accord with the situation in the Percival stories. In

Wolfram von Eschenbach's *Parzival*, for instance, Trevrezent, the hermit, is the brother of the Fisher King, Anfortas. He tells Parzival, "His name all men know as Anfortas, and I weep for him evermore." Their father, Frimutel, is of course, dead.

The protagonist in the poem, then, imagines himself not only in the situation of Ferdinand in *The Tempest* but also in that of one of the characters in the Grail legend; and the wreck, to be applied literally in the first instance, applies metaphorically in the second.

After the lines from *The Tempest*, appears again the image of a sterile death from which no life comes, the bones, "rattled by the rat's foot only, year to year." (The collocation of this figure with the vision of the death by water in Ariel's song has already been commented on. The lines quoted from *The Tempest* come just before the song.)

The allusion to Marvell's *To His Coy Mistress* is of course one of the easiest allusions in the poem. Instead of "Time's winged chariot" the poet hears "the sound of horns and motors" of contemporary London. But the passage has been further complicated. The reference has been combined with an allusion to Day's *Parliament of Bees*. "Time's winged chariot" of Marvell has not only been changed to the modern automobile; Day's "sound of horns and hunting" has changed to the horns of the motors. And Actaeon will not be brought face to face with Diana, goddess of chastity; Sweeney, type of the vulgar bourgeois, is to be brought to Mrs. Porter, hardly a type of chastity. The reference in the ballad to the feet "washed in soda water" reminds the poet ironically of another sort of foot-washing, the sound of the children singing in the dome heard at the ceremony of the foot-washing which precedes the restoration of the wounded Anfortas (the Fisher King) by Parzival and the taking away of the curse from the waste land. The quotation thus completes the allusion to the Fisher King commenced in line 189—"While I was fishing in the dull canal."

The pure song of the children also reminds the poet of the song of the nightingale which we have heard in "The Game of Chess." The recapitulation of symbols is continued with a repetition of "Unreal city" and with the reference to the one-eyed merchant.

Mr. Eugenides, the Smyrna merchant, is the one-eyed merchant mentioned by Madame Sosostris. The fact that the merchant is one-eyed apparently means in Madame Sosostris' speech no more than that the merchant's face on the card is shown in profile. But Eliot applies the term to Mr. Eugenides for a totally different effect. The defect corresponds somewhat to Madame Sosostris' bad cold. The Syrian merchants, we learn from Miss Weston's book, were, with slaves and soldiers, the principal carriers of the mysteries which lie at the core of the Grail legends. But in the modern world we find both the representatives of the Tarot divining and the mystery cults in decay. What he carries on his back and what the fortune-teller was forbidden to see is evidently the knowledge of the mysteries (although Mr. Eugenides himself is hardly likely to be more aware of it than Madame Sosostris is aware of the importance of her function). Mr. Eugenides, in terms of his former function, ought to be inviting the protagonist to an initiation into the esoteric cult which holds the secret of life, but on the realistic surface of the poem, in his invitation to "a weekend at the Metropole" he is really inviting him to a homosexual debauch. The homosexuality is "secret" and now a "cult," but a very different cult from that which Mr. Eugenides ought to represent. The end of the new cult is not life, but ironically, sterility.

In the modern waste land, however, even the relation between man and woman is also sterile. The incident between the typist and the carbuncular young man is a picture of "love" so exclusively and practically pursued that it is not love at all. The scene, as Allen Tate puts it, is one of our most terrible insights into Western civilization. The tragic chorus to the scene is Tiresias, into whom perhaps Mr. Eugenides may be said to modulate, Tiresias, the historical "expert" on the relation between the sexes.

The allusions to Sappho's lines and to Goldsmith's made in this passage need little comment. The hour of evening, which in Sappho's poem brings rest to all and brings the sailor home, brings the typist to her travesty of home—"On the divan . . . at night her bed"—and brings the carbuncular young man, the meeting with whom ends not in peace but in sterile burning.

The reminiscence of the lines from Goldsmith's song in the description of the young woman's actions after the departure of her lover gives concretely and ironically the utter breakdown of traditional standards.

It is the music of her gramophone which the protagonist hears "creep by" him "upon the waters." Far from the music which Ferdinand heard bringing him to Miranda and love, it is, one is tempted to think, the music of "O O O O that Shakespeherian Rag" of "A Game of Chess."

But the protagonist says that he *sometimes* hears "The pleasant whining of a mandoline." Significantly enough, it is the music of the fishmen (the fish again as a life symbol) and it comes from beside a church (though—if this is not to rely too much on Eliot's note—the church has been marked for destruction). Life on Lower Thames Street, if not on the Strand, still has meaning as it cannot have meaning for either the typist or the rich woman of "A Game of Chess."

The song of the Thames-daughters brings us back to the opening section of "The Fire Sermon" again, and once more we have to do with the river and the river-nymphs. Indeed, the typist incident is framed by the two river-nymph scenes.

The connection of the river-nymphs with the Rhine-daughters of Wagner's *Götterdämmerung* is easily made. In the passage in Wagner's opera to which Eliot refers in his note, the opening of Act III, the Rhine-daughters bewail the loss of the beauty of the Rhine occasioned by the theft of the gold, and then beg Siegfried to give them back the Ring made from this gold, finally threatening him with death if he does not give it up. Like the Thames-daughters they too have been violated; and like the maidens mentioned in the Grail legend, the violation has brought a curse on gods and men. The first of the songs depicts the modern river, soiled with oil and tar. (Compare also with the description of the river in the first part of "The Fire Sermon.") The second song depicts the Elizabethan river, also evoked in the first part of "The Fire Sermon." (Leicester and Elizabeth ride upon it in a barge of state. Incidentally, Spenser's *Prothalamion,* from which quotation is made in the first part of "The Fire Sermon," mentions Leicester as having formerly lived in the house which forms the setting of that poem.)

In this second song there is also a definite allusion to the passage in *Antony and Cleopatra* already referred to in the opening line of "A Game of Chess."

> Beating oars
> The stern was formed
> A gilded shell.

And if we still have any doubt of the allusion, Eliot's note on the passage with its reference to the "barge" and "poop" should settle the matter. We have already commented on the earlier allusion to Cleopatra as the prime example of love for love's sake. The symbol bears something of the same meaning here, and the note which Eliot supplies does something to reinforce the "Cleopatra" aspect of Elizabeth. Elizabeth in the presence of the Spaniard De Quadra, though negotiations were going on for a Spanish marriage, "went so far that Lord Robert at last said, as I [De Quadra was a bishop] was on the spot there was no reason why they should not be married if the queen pleased." The passage has a sort of double function. It reinforces the general contrast between Elizabethan magnificence and modern sordidness: in the Elizabethan age love for love's sake had some meaning and therefore some magnificence. But the passage gives something of an opposed effect too: the same sterile love, emptiness of love, obtained in this period too: Elizabeth and the Typist are alike as well as different.

The third Thames-daughter's song depicts another sordid "love" affair, and unites the themes of the first two songs. It begins "Trams and *dusty* trees." With it we are definitely in the waste land again. Pia, whose words she echoes in saying "Highbury bore me. Richmond and Kew/Undid me" was in Purgatory and had hope. The woman speaking here has no hope—she too is in the Inferno: "I can connect/Nothing with nothing." She has just completed, floating down the river in the canoe, what Eliot has described in *Murder in the Cathedral* as

> . . . the effortless journey, to the empty land . . .
> Where the soul is no longer deceived, for there are
> no objects, no tones,
> Where those who were men can no longer turn the
> mind
> To distraction, delusion, escape into dream,
> pretence,
> No colours, no forms to distract, to divert the soul
> From seeing itself, foully united forever, nothing
> with nothing,
> Nor what we call death, but what beyond death is
> not death . . .

Now, "on Margate sands," like the Hollow Men, she stands "on this beach of the tumid river."

The songs of the three Thames-daughters, as a matter of fact, epitomize this whole section of the poem. With reference to the quotations from St. Augustine and Buddha at the end of "The Fire Sermon" Eliot states that "The collocation of these two representatives of eastern and western asceticism, as the culmination of this part of the poem, is not an accident."

It is certainly not an accident. The moral of all the incidents which we have been witnessing is that there must be an asceticism—something to check the drive of desire. The wisdom of the East and the West comes to the same thing on this point. Moreover, the image which both St. Augustine and Buddha use for lust is fire. What we have witnessed in the various scenes of "The Fire Sermon" is the sterile burning of lust. Modern man, freed from all restraints, in his cultivation of experience for experience's sake burns, but not with a "hard and gemlike flame." One ought not to pound the point home in this fashion, but to see that the imagery of this section of the poem furnishes illustrations leading up to "The Fire Sermon" is the necessary requirement for feeling the force of the brief allusions here at the end to Buddha and St. Augustine.

IV

Whatever the specific meaning of the symbols, the general function of the section, "Death by Water," is readily apparent. The section forms a contrast with "The Fire Sermon" which precedes it—a contrast between the symbolism of fire and that of water. Also readily apparent is its force as a symbol of surrender and relief through surrender.

Some specific connections can be made, however. The drowned Phoenician Sailor recalls the drowned god of the fertility cults. Miss Weston tells that each year at Alexandria an effigy of the head of the god was thrown into the water as a symbol of the death of the powers of nature, and that this head was carried by the current to Byblos where it was taken out of the water and exhibited as a symbol of the reborn god.

Moreover, the Phoenician Sailor is a merchant—"Forgot . . . the profit and loss." The vision of the drowned sailor gives a statement of the message which the Syrian merchants originally brought to Britain and which the Smyrna merchant, unconsciously and by ironical negatives, has brought. One of Eliot's notes states that the "merchant . . . melts into the Phoenician Sailor, and the latter is not wholly distinct from Ferdinand Prince of Naples." The death by water would seem to be equated with the death described in Ariel's song in *The Tempest.* There is a definite difference in the tone of the description of this death—"A current under sea/-Picked his bones in whispers," as compared with the "other" death—"bones cast in a little low dry garret,/Rattled by the rat's foot only, year to year."

Farther than this it would not be safe to go, but one may point out that whirling (the whirlpool here, the Wheel of Madame Sosostris' palaver) is one of Eliot's symbols frequently used in other poems *(Ash Wednesday, Gerontion, Murder in the Cathedral,* and *Burnt Norton)* to denote the temporal world. And one may point out the following passage from *Ash Wednesday:*

> Although I do not hope to turn again
> . . . .
> Wavering between the profit and the loss
> In this brief transit where the dreams cross
> The dreamcrossed twilight between birth and
> dying.

At least, with a kind of hindsight, one may suggest that Section IV gives an instance of the conquest of death and time—the "perpetual recurrence of determined seasons," the "world of spring and autumn, birth and dying"—through death itself.

V

The reference to the "torchlight red on sweaty faces" and to the "frosty silence in the gardens" obviously associates, as we have already pointed out, Christ in Gethsemane with the other hanged gods. The god has now died, and in referring to this, the basic theme finds another strong restatement:

> He who was living is now dead
> We who were living are now dying
> With a little patience

The poet does not say "We who *are* living." It is "We who *were* living." It is the death-in-life of Dante's Limbo. Life in the full sense had been lost.

The passage on the sterility of the waste land and the lack of water which follows, provides for the introduction later of two highly important passages:

> There is not even silence in the mountains
> But dry sterile thunder without rain

—lines which look forward to the introduction later of "what the thunder said" when the thunder, no longer sterile but bringing rain, speaks.

The second of these passages is, "There is not even solitude in the mountains," which looks forward to the reference to the Journey to Emmaus theme a few lines later: "Who is the third who walks always beside you?" The god has returned, has risen, but the travellers cannot tell whether it is really he, or mere illusion induced by their delirium.

The parallelism between the "hooded" figure who walks "always . . . beside you" and the "hooded hordes" is another instance of the sort of parallelism that is really a contrast, one of the type of which Eliot is fond. In the first case, the figure is indistinct because spiritual; in the second, the hooded hordes are indistinct because completely *unspiritual*—they are the people of the waste land—

> Shape without form, shade without colour,
> Paralysed force, gesture without motion

—to take two lines from "The Hollow Men," where the people of the waste land once more appear. Or to take another line from the same poem, perhaps their hoods are the "deliberate disguises" which the Hollow Men, the people of the waste land, wear.

Eliot, as his notes tell us, has particularly connected the description here with the "decay of eastern Europe." The hordes represent then the general waste land of the modern world with a special application to the break-up of Eastern Europe, the region with which the fertility cults were especially connected and in which to-day the traditional values are thoroughly discredited. The cities, Jerusalem, Athens, Alexandria, Vienna, like the London of the first section of the poem are "unreal," and for the same reason.

The passage which immediately follows develops the unreality into nightmare, but it is a nightmare vision which is not only an extension of the passage beginning, "What is the city over the mountains"—in it appear other figures from earlier in the poem: the lady of "A Game of Chess" who, surrounded by the glory of history and art, sees no meaning in either and threatens to rush out into the street "With my hair down, so," has here let down her hair and fiddles "whisper music on those strings." One remembers in "A Game of Chess" that it was the woman's hair that spoke:

> . . . her hair
> Spread out in fiery points
> Glowed into words, then would be savagely still.

The hair has been immemorially a symbol of fertility, and Miss Weston and Frazer mention sacrifices of hair in order to aid the fertility god.

As we have pointed out earlier in dealing with "The Burial of the Dead," this whole passage is to be connected with the twelfth chapter of Ecclesiastes. The doors "of mudcracked houses," and the cisterns in this passage are to be found in Ecclesiastes, and the woman fiddling music from her hair is one of "the daughters of music" brought low. The towers and bells from the Elizabeth and Leicester passage of "The Fire Sermon" also appear here, but the towers are upside down, and the bells, far from pealing for an actual occasion or ringing the hours, are "reminiscent." The civilization is breaking up.

The "violet light" also deserves comment. In "The Fire Sermon" it is twice mentioned as the "violet hour," and there it has little more than a physical meaning. It is a description of the hour of twilight. Here it indicates the twilight of the civilization, but it is perhaps something more. Violet is one of the liturgical colours of the Church. It symbolizes repentance and it is the colour of baptism. The visit to the Perilous Chapel, according to Miss Weston, was an initiation—that is, a baptism. In the nightmare vision, the bats wear baby faces.

The horror built up in this passage is a proper preparation for the passage on the Perilous Chapel which follows it. The journey has not been merely an agonized walk in the desert, though it is that, or merely the journey after the god has died and hope has been lost; it is also the journey to the Perilous Chapel of the Grail story. In Miss Weston's account, the Chapel was part of the ritual, and was filled with horrors to test the candidate's courage. In some stories the perilous cemetery is also mentioned. Eliot has used both: "Over the tumbled graves, about the chapel." In many of the Grail stories the Chapel was haunted by demons.

The cock in the folk-lore of many peoples is regarded as the bird whose voice chases away the powers of evil. It is significant that it is after his crow that the flash of lightning comes and the "damp gust/Bringing rain." It is just possible that the cock has a connection also with *The Tempest* symbols. The first song which Ariel sings to Ferdinand as he sits "Weeping again the king my father's wreck" ends

> The strain of strutting chanticleer,
> Cry, cock-a-doodle-doo.

The next stanza is the "Full Fathom Five" song which Eliot has used as a vision of life gained through death. If this relation holds, here we have an extreme instance of an allusion, in itself innocent, forced into serious meaning through transference to a new context.

As Miss Weston has shown, the fertility cults go back to a very early period and are recorded in Sanskrit legends. Eliot has been continually in the poem linking up the Christian doctrine with the beliefs of as many peoples as he can. Here he goes back to the very beginnings of Aryan culture, and tells the rest of the story of the rain's coming, not in terms of the setting already developed but in its earliest form. The passage is thus a perfect parallel in method to the passage in "The Burial of the Dead."

> You who were with me in the ships at Mylae!
> That corpse you planted last year in your
> garden. . . .

The use of Sanskrit in what the thunder says is thus accounted for. In addition, there is of course a more obvious reason for casting what the thunder said into Sanskrit here: onomatopoeia.

The comments on the three statements of the thunder imply an acceptance of them. The protagonist answers the first question, "What have we given?" with the statement:

> The awful daring of a moment's surrender
> Which an age of prudence can never retract
> By this, and this only, we have existed.

Here the larger meaning is stated in terms which imply the sexual meaning. Man cannot be absolutely self-regarding. Even the propagation of the race—even mere "existence"—calls for such a surrender. Living calls for—see the passage already quoted from Eliot's essay on Baudelaire—belief in something more than "life."

The comment on *dayadhvam* (sympathize) is obviously connected with the foregoing passage. The surrender to something outside the self is an attempt (whether on the sexual level or some other) to transcend one's essential isolation. The passage gathers up the symbols previously developed in the poem just as the foregoing passage reflects, though with a different implication, the numerous references to sex made earlier in the poem. For example, the woman in the first part of "A Game of Chess" has also heard the key turn in the door, and confirms her prison by thinking of the key:

> Speak to me. Why do you never speak. Speak.
> What are you thinking of? What thinking? What?
> I never know what you are thinking. Think.

The third statement made by the thunder, *damyata* (control) follows the logical condition for control, sympathy. The figure of the boat catches up the figure of control already given in "Death by Water"—"O you who turn the wheel and look to windward"—and from "The Burial of the Dead" the figure of happy love in which the ship rushes on with a fair wind behind it: *Frisch weht der Wind....*

I cannot accept Mr. Leavis's interpretation of the passage, "I sat upon the shore/Fishing, with the arid plain behind me," as meaning that the poem "exhibits no progression." The comment upon what the thunder says would indicate, if other passages did not, that the poem does not "end where it began." It is true that the protagonist does not witness a revival of the waste land; but there are two important relationships involved in his case; a personal one as well as a general one. If secularization has destroyed, or is likely to destroy, modern civilization, the protagonist still has a private obligation to fulfill. Even if the civilization is breaking up—"London Bridge is falling down falling down falling down"—there remains the personal obligation: "Shall I at least set my lands in order?" Consider in this connection the last sentences of Eliot's "Thoughts After Lambeth": "The World is trying the experiment of attempting to form a civilized but non-Christian mentality. The experiment will fail; but we must be very patient in awaiting its collapse; meanwhile redeeming the time: so that the Faith may be preserved alive through the dark ages before us; to renew and rebuild civilization, and save the World from suicide."

The bundle of quotations with which the poem ends has a very definite relation to the general theme of the poem and to several of the major symbols used in the poem. Before Arnaut leaps back into the refining fire of Purgatory with joy he says: "I am Arnaut who weep and go singing; contrite I see my past folly, and joyful I see before me the day I hope for. Now I pray you by that virtue which guides you to the summit of the stair, at times be mindful of my pain." This note is carried forward by the quotation from *Pervigilium Veneris:* "When shall I be like the swallow?" The allusion also connects with the Philomela symbol. (Eliot's note on the passage indicates this clearly.) The sister of Philomela was changed into a swallow as Philomela was changed into a nightingale. The protagonist is asking therefore when shall the spring, the time of love return, but also when will he be reborn out of his sufferings, and—with the special meaning which the symbol takes on from the preceding Dante quotation and from the earlier contexts already discussed—he is asking what is asked at the end of one of the minor poems: "When will Time flow away?"

The quotation from "El Desdichado," as Edmund Wilson has pointed out, indicates that the protagonist of the poem has been disinherited, robbed of his tradition. The ruined tower is perhaps also the Perilous Chapel, "only the wind's home," and it is also the whole tradition in decay. The protagonist resolves to claim his tradition and rehabilitate it.

The quotation from *The Spanish Tragedy*—"When then Ile fit you. Hieronymo's mad againe"—is perhaps the most puzzling of all these quotations. It means, I believe, this: the protagonist's acceptance of what is in reality the deepest truth will seem to the present world mere madness. ("And still she cried, and still the world pursues,/'Jug Jug' to dirty ears.") Hieronymo in the play, like Hamlet, was "mad" for a purpose. The protagonist is conscious of the interpretation which will be placed on the words which follow—words which will seem to many apparently meaningless babble, but which contain the oldest and most permanent truth of the race:

> Datta. Dayadhvam. Damyata.

After this statement comes the benediction:

> Shantih Shantih Shantih

The foregoing account of *The Waste Land* is, of course, not to be substituted for the poem itself. Moreover, it certainly is not to be considered as representing *the method by which the poem was composed.* Much which the prose expositor must represent as though it had been consciously contrived, obviously was arrived at unconsciously and concretely.

The account given above is a statement merely of the "prose meaning," and bears the same relation to the poem as does the "prose meaning" of any other poem. But one need not perhaps apologize for setting forth such a statement explicitly, for *The Waste Land* has been almost consistently misinterpreted since its first publication. Even a critic so acute as Edmund Wilson has seen the poem as essentially a statement of despair and disillusionment, and this account sums up the stock interpretation of the poem. Indeed, the phrase, "the poetry of drouth," has become a cliché of left-wing criticism. It is such a misrepresentation of *The Waste Land* as this which allows Eda Lou Walton to entitle an essay on contemporary poetry, "Death in the Desert"; or which causes Waldo Frank to misconceive of Eliot's whole position and personality. But more than the meaning of one poem is at stake. If *The Waste Land* is not a world-weary cry of despair or a sighing after the vanished glories of the past, then not only the popular interpretation of the poem will have to be altered but also the general interpretations of post-war poetry which begin with such a misinterpretation as a premise.

Such misinterpretations involve also misconceptions of Eliot's technique. Eliot's basic method may be said to have passed relatively unnoticed. The popular view of the method used in *The Waste Land* may be described as follows: Eliot makes use of ironic contrasts between the glorious past and the sordid present—the crashing irony of

> But at my back from time to time I hear
> The sound of horns and motors, which shall bring
> Sweeney to Mrs. Porter in the spring.

But this is to take the irony of the poem at the most superficial level, and to neglect the other dimensions in which it operates. And it is to neglect what are essentially more important aspects of his method. Moreover, it is to overemphasize the difference between the method employed by Eliot in his poem and that employed by him in later poems.

The basic method used in *The Waste Land* may be described as the application of the principle of complexity. The poet works in terms of surface parallelisms which in reality make ironical contrasts, and in terms of surface contrasts which in reality constitute parallelisms. (The second group sets up effects which may be described as the obverse of irony.) The two aspects taken together give the effect of chaotic experience ordered into a new whole though the realistic surface of experience is faithfully retained. The complexity of the experience is not violated by the apparent forcing upon it of a predetermined scheme.

The fortune-telling of "The Burial of the Dead" will illustrate the general method very satisfactorily. On the surface of the poem the poet reproduces the patter of the charlatan, Madame Sosostris, and there is the surface irony: the contrast between the original use of the Tarot cards and the use made here. But each of the details (justified realistically in the palaver of the fortune-teller) assumes a new meaning in the general context of the poem. There is then in addition to the surface irony something of a Sophoclean irony too, and the "fortune-telling" which is taken ironically by a twentieth-century audience becomes true as the poem develops—true in a sense in which Madame Sosostris herself does not think it true. The surface irony is thus reversed and becomes an irony on a deeper level. The items of her speech have only one reference in terms of the context of her speech: the "man with three staves," and "one-eyed merchant," and "crowds of people, walking round in a ring," etc. But transferred to other contexts they become loaded with special meanings. To sum up, all the central symbols of the poem head up here, but here, in the only section in which they are explicitly bound together, the binding is slight and accidental. The deeper lines of association only emerge in terms of the total context as the poem develops—and this is, of course, exactly the effect which the poet intends.

This transference of items from an "innocent" context into a context in which they become charged and transformed in meaning will account for many of the literary allusions in the poem. For example, the "change of Philomel" is merely one of the items in the decorative detail in the room in the opening of "A Game of Chess." But the violent change of tense—"And still she cried, and still the world pursues"—makes it a comment upon, and a symbol of, the modern world. And further allusions to it through the course of the poem gradually equate it with the general theme of the poem. The allusions to *The Tempest* display the same method. The parallelism between Dante's Hell and the waste land of the Grail legends is fairly close; even the equation of Baudelaire's Paris to the waste land is fairly obvious. But the parallelism between the death by drowning in *The Tempest* and the death of the fertility god is, on the surface, merely accidental, and the first allusion to Ariel's song is merely an irrelevant and random association of the stream-of-consciousness:

> Is your card, the drowned Phoenician Sailor,
> (Those are pearls that were his eyes. Look!)

And on its second appearance in "A Game of Chess" it is still only an item in the protagonist's abstracted reverie. Even the association of *The Tempest* symbol with the Grail legends in the lines

While I was fishing in the dull canal
. . . .
Musing upon the king my brother's wreck.

and in the passage which follows, is ironical merely. But the associations have been established, even though they may seem to be made in ironic mockery, and when we come to the passage "Death by Water," with its change of tone, they assert themselves positively. We have a sense of revelation out of material apparently accidentally thrown together. I have called the effect the obverse of irony, for the method like that of irony, is indirect, though the effect is positive rather than negative.

The "melting" of the characters into each other is, of course, an aspect of this general process. Elizabeth and the girl born at Highbury both ride on the Thames, one in the barge of state, the other supine in a narrow canoe, and they are both Thames-nymphs, who are violated and thus are like the Rhine-nymphs who have also been violated, etc. With the characters as with the other symbols, the surface relationships may be accidental and apparently trivial and they may be made either ironically or through random association or in hallucination, but in the total context of the poem the deeper relationships are revealed. The effect is a sense of the oneness of experience, and of the unity of all periods, and with this, a sense that the general theme of the poem is true. But the theme has not been imposed—it has been revealed.

This complication of parallelisms and contrasts makes, of course, for ambiguity, but the ambiguity, in part, resides in the poet's fidelity to the complexity of experience. The symbols resist complete equation with a simple meaning. To take an example, "rock" throughout the poem seems to be one of the "desert" symbols. For example, the "dry stone" gives "no sound of water"; woman in the waste land is "the Lady of the Rocks," and most pointed of all, there is the long delirium passage in "What the Thunder Said": "Here is no water but only rock," etc. So much for its general meaning, but in "The Burial of the Dead" occur the lines

Only
There is shadow under this red rock,
(Come in under the shadow of this red rock).

Rock here is a place of refuge. (Moreover, there may also be a reference to the Grail symbolism. In *Parzival*, the Grail is a stone: "And this stone all men call the grail. . . . As children the Grail doth call them, 'neath its shadow they wax and grow.") The paradox, life through death, penetrates the symbol itself.

To take an even clearer case of this paradoxical use of symbols, consider the lines which occur in the hyacinth-girl passage. The vision gives obviously a sense of the richness and beauty of life. It is a moment of ecstasy (the basic imagery is obviously sexual); but the moment in its intensity is like death. The protagonist looks in that moment into the "heart of light, the silence," and so looks into—not richness—but blankness: he is neither "living nor dead." The symbol of life stands also for a kind of death. This duality of function may, of course, extend to a whole passage. For example, consider:

Where fishmen lounge at noon: where the walls
Of Magnus Martyr hold
Inexplicable splendour of Ionian white and gold.

The function of the passage is to indicate the poverty into which religion has fallen: the splendid church now surrounded by the poorer districts. But the passage has an opposed effect also: the fishmen in the "public bar in Lower Thames Street" next to the church have a meaningful life which has been largely lost to the secularized upper and middle classes.

The poem would undoubtedly be "clearer" if every symbol had one, unequivocal, meaning; but the poem would be thinner, and less honest. For the poet has not been content to develop a didactic allegory in which the symbols are two-dimensional items adding up directly to the sum of the general scheme. They represent dramatized instances of the theme, embodying in their own nature the fundamental paradox of the theme.

We shall better understand why the form of the poem is right and inevitable if we compare Eliot's theme to Dante's and to Spenser's. Eliot's theme is not the statement of a faith held and agreed upon (Dante's *Divine Comedy*) nor is it the projection of a "new" system of beliefs (Spenser's *Faerie Queene*). Eliot's theme is the rehabilitation of a system of beliefs, known but now discredited. Dante did not have to "prove" his statement; he could assume it and move within it about a poet's business. Eliot does not care, like Spenser, to force the didacticism. He prefers to stick to the poet's business. But, unlike Dante, he cannot assume acceptance of the statement. A direct approach is calculated to elicit powerful "stock responses" which will prevent the poem's being *read* at all. Consequently, the only method is to work by indirection. The "Christian" material is at the centre, but the poet never deals with it directly. The theme of resurrection is made on the surface in terms of the fertility rites; the words which the thunder speaks are Sanskrit words.

We have been speaking as if the poet were a strategist trying to win acceptance from a hostile audience. But of course this is true only in a sense. The poet himself is audience as well as speaker; we state the problem more exactly if we state it in terms of the poet's integrity rather than in terms of his strategy. He is so much a man of his own age that he can indicate his attitude toward the Christian tradition without falsity only in terms of the difficulties of a rehabilitation; and he is so much a poet and so little a propagandist that he can be sincere only as he presents his theme concretely and dramatically.

To put the matter in still other terms: the Christian terminology is for the poet here a mass of *clichés*. However "true" he may feel the terms to be, he is still sensitive to the fact that they operate superficially as *clichés*, and his method of necessity must be a process of bringing them to life again. The method adopted in *The Waste Land* is thus violent and radical, but thoroughly necessary. For the renewing and vitalizing of symbols which have been crusted over with a distorting familiarity demands the type of organization which we have already commented on in discussing particular passages, the statement of surface similarities which are ironically revealed to be dissimilarities, and the association of apparently obvious dissimilarities which culminates in a later realization that the dissimilarities are only superficial—that the chains of likeness are in reality fundamental. In this way the statement of beliefs emerges *through* confusion and cynicism—not in spite of them.

RALPH (WALDO) ELLISON [1914–]

In an essay "Hidden Name and Complex Fate," Ralph Ellison, whose father named him after the American poet-philosopher, tells how he was teased as a child by neighbors calling him Ralph Waldo *Emerson.* Later, when he had chosen to become a writer, he became aware of the suggestive power of naming and felt an obligation to achieve "some of the things" his eminent namesake had achieved. His decision to write was made with great deliberation and pursued with seriousness and conscious devotion to his art and to the tradition he admired in the American authors of fiction who had preceded him, especially Mark Twain, Henry James, Hemingway, and Faulkner. Ellison has combined the writing of fiction with a career as lecturer, teacher, essayist, and critic. He has been an effective voice in the cause of Negro rights; but when he was charged by Irving Howe with not being sufficiently militant, he replied by affirming the primacy of the artist's freedom to be an artist and to be his own kind of artist, not simply a black protest-novelist following in the footsteps of Richard Wright. "The problem of becoming an artist," he wrote after the publication of his significant novel, *Invisible Man,* "is related to that of becoming a man, of becoming visible. You need a discipline far more demanding than loyalty to your racial group."

Ellison was born in Oklahoma City, the son of a construction worker who had high hopes for his second-born. Brought up in a city in the Southwest, he remained somewhat apart from the center of black activism in Harlem, nor was he subjected to the degree of racism which prevailed in the deep South. He attended public schools and went on to study music at Tuskegee Institute. Ambitious to become a composer of symphonies, he was gradually brought under the spell of literature through his reading in the library at Tuskegee. In grade school he had learned about the Negro literary movement of the twenties, reading Langston Hughes, Countee Cullen, and other poets, and becoming excited by the "glamour" of Harlem as it emerged from their poems. Later he discovered such moderns as T. S. Eliot, Ezra Pound, Sherwood Anderson, Hemingway, and Gertrude

Stein. In New York, where he had gone to pursue his musical career, he met Richard Wright, who encouraged him to publish his first book review and short story, and guided him in the study of fictional techniques through the stories of Conrad, the Prefaces of Henry James, and the letters of Dostoevsky. Ellison was also influenced at this time by the novels and theories of art of André Malraux. During the late 1930's, with the economic depression still on and the Spanish Civil War in progress, Ellison became interested in politics, especially as they concerned the Negro and civil rights. His main energies, however, were always kept for learning and practicing the art of fiction.

His career as a writer began in 1939 while he was working for the Federal Writers' Project in New York. During the 1940's he edited the *Negro Quarterly* and wrote essays and short stories on the themes of music and the race problem. In 1952 came his highly regarded novel, *Invisible Man,* a partly autobiographical narrative on the search for identity of a serious, ambitious young man who moves from his mid-South college to New York, where he experiences the difficulties of finding work in an atmosphere of race prejudice, labor strife, depression, and big-city loneliness. The narrator loses his job in a paint factory, is "discovered" by a secret Brotherhood dedicated to reforming the world's injustice, becomes disillusioned by the secrecy and invisibility of working for the Organization, and finally comes to value his own freedom and the need to "run the risk of his own humanity" in the struggle to make himself "visible." For a first novel, it showed a mature grasp of the techniques of realism as well as of methods beyond realism. Criticized for wavering between naturalism and surrealism, he said, "I didn't select the surrealism, the intensity, as an experimental technique but because reality is surreal."

Ellison's second important work is *Shadow and Act* (1964), a collection of essays, also rooted in his own life and experience. Written for such periodicals as the *New Republic,* the *New Leader, Commonweal,* the *Saturday Review,* and the *Reporter,* they cover a range of subjects, including Negro music and folklore, the relation of Negro culture to American literature, and studies in American fiction from Melville to Fitzgerald. The autobiographical essays say more about being a Negro in America, and say it better, than many of the diatribes of more militant writers, because Ellison has always sought human values behind the categories, the jargon, and the rhetoric of the cause. He tells it with conviction as it happened to him, humanized by his own background and experience.

Ralph Ellison has become eminently "visible" as a distinguished writer and critic. In 1954 he toured Germany as a lecturer. He has taught Russian and American literature at Bard College (1958-61), has been a visiting professor at Chicago and Rutgers, a Yale Fellow in American Studies, and a lecturer at the Library of Congress and elsewhere. *Invisible Man* won three national book awards and high critical acclaim. He has been working on a second novel. A black novelist, proud of his race, he has gone well beyond that label alone, perhaps because the name his father gave him implanted in his mind, long before he became aware of it, a sense of continuity between his own life and that of the great writers of the American tradition.

Further reading: *Invisible Man,* 1952. *Shadow and Act,* 1964. Harvey Breit, *The Writer Observed,* 1956.

Twentieth-Century Fiction and the Black Mask of Humanity

Written in 1946, this essay first appeared in *Confluence* (December 1953). It was prefaced by the following note, from Ellison's communication to the editors of that periodical: "When I started rewriting this essay it occurred to me that its value might be somewhat increased if it remained very much as I wrote it during 1946. For in that form it is what a young member of a minority felt about much of our writing. Thus I've left in much of the bias and short-sightedness, for it says perhaps as much about me as a member of a minority as it does about literature. I hope you still find the essay useful, and I'd like to see an editorial note stating that this is an unpublished piece written not long after the Second World War." The text used here is from *Shadow and Act* (1964).

Perhaps the most insidious and least understood form of segregation is that of the word. And by this I mean the word in all its complex formulations, from the proverb to the novel and stage play, the word with all its subtle power to suggest and foreshadow overt action while magically disguising the moral consequences of that action and providing it with symbolic and psychological justification. For if the word has the potency to revive and make us free, it has also the power to blind, imprison and destroy.

The essence of the word is its ambivalence, and in fiction it is never so effective and revealing as when both potentials are operating simultaneously, as when it mirrors both good and bad, as when it blows both hot and cold in the same breath. Thus it is unfortunate for the Negro that the most powerful formulations of modern American fictional words have been so slanted against him that when he approaches for a glimpse of himself he discovers an image drained of humanity.

Obviously the experiences of Negroes—slavery, the grueling and continuing fight for full citizenship since Emancipation, the stigma of color, the enforced alienation which constantly knifes into our natural identification with our country—have not been that of white Americans. And though as passionate believers in democracy Negroes identify themselves with the broader American ideals, their sense of reality springs, in part, from an American experience which most white men not only have not had, but one with which they are reluctant to identify themselves even when presented in forms of the imagination. Thus when the white American, holding up most twentieth-century fiction, says, "This is American reality," the Negro tends to answer (not at all concerned that Americans tend generally to fight against any but the most flattering imaginative depictions of their lives), "Perhaps, but you've left out this, and this, and this. And most of all, what you'd have the world accept as *me* isn't even human."

Nor does he refer only to second-rate works but to those of our most representative authors. Either like Hemingway and Steinbeck (in whose joint works I recall not more than five American Negroes) they tend to ignore them, or like the early Faulkner, who distorted Negro humanity to fit his personal versions of Southern myth, they seldom conceive Negro characters possessing the full, complex ambiguity of the human. Too often what is presented as the American Negro (a most complex example of Western man) emerges an oversimplified clown, a beast or an angel. Seldom is he drawn as that sensitively focused process of opposites, of good and evil, of instinct and intellect, of passion and spirituality, which great literary art has projected as the image of man. Naturally, the attitude of Negroes toward this writing is one of great reservation. Which, indeed, bears out Richard Wright's remark that there is in progress between black and white Americans a struggle over the nature of reality.

Historically this is but a part of that larger conflict between older, dominant groups of white Americans, especially the Anglo-Saxons, on the one hand, and the newer white and non-white groups on the other, over the major group's attempt to impose its ideals upon the rest, insisting that its exclusive image be accepted as *the* image of the American. This conflict should not, however, be misunderstood. For despite the impact of the American idea upon the world, the "American" himself has not (fortunately for the United States, its minorities, and perhaps for the world) been finally defined. So that far from being socially undesirable this struggle between Americans as to what the American is to be is part of that democratic process through which the nation works to achieve itself. Out of this conflict the ideal American character—a type truly great enough to possess the greatness of the land, a delicately poised unity of divergencies—is slowly being born.

But we are concerned here with fiction, not history. How is it then that our naturalistic prose—one of the most vital bodies of twentieth-century fiction, perhaps the brightest instrument for recording sociological fact, physical action, the nuance of speech, yet achieved—becomes suddenly dull when confronting the Negro?

Obviously there is more in this than the mere verbal counterpart of lynching or segregation. Indeed, it represents a projection of processes lying at the very root of American culture and certainly at the central core of its twentieth-century literary forms, a matter having less to do with the mere "reflection" of white racial theories than with processes molding the attitudes, the habits of mind, the cultural atmosphere and the artistic and intellectual traditions that condition men dedicated to democracy to practice, accept and, most crucial of all, often blind themselves to the essentially undemocratic treatment of their fellow citizens.

It should be noted here that the moment criticism approaches Negro-white relationships it is plunged into problems of psychology and symbolic ritual. Psychology, because the distance between Americans, Negroes and whites, is not so much spatial as psychological; while they might dress and often look alike, seldom on deeper levels do they think alike. Ritual, because the Negroes of fiction are so consistently false to human life that we must question just what they truly represent, both in the literary work and in the inner world of the white American.[1]

Despite their billings as images of reality, these Negroes of fiction are counterfeits. They are projected aspects of an internal symbolic process through which, like a primitive tribesman dancing himself into the group frenzy necessary for battle, the white American prepares himself emotionally to perform a social role. These fictive Negroes are not, as sometimes interpreted, simple racial cliches introduced into society by a ruling class to control political and economic realities. For although they are manipulated to that end, such an externally one-sided interpretation relieves the individual of personal responsibility for the health of democracy. Not only does it forget that a democracy is a collectivity of *individuals*, but it never suspects that the tenacity of the stereotype springs exactly from the fact that its function is no less personal than political. Color prejudice springs not from the stereotype alone, but from an internal psychological state; not from misinformation alone, but from an inner need to believe. It thrives not only on the obscene witch-doctoring of men like Jimmy Byrnes and Malan, but upon an inner craving for symbolic magic. The prejudiced individual creates his own stereotypes, very often unconsciously, by reading into situations involving Negroes those stock meanings which justify his emotional and economic needs.

Hence whatever else the Negro stereotype might be as a social instrumentality, it is also a key figure in a magic rite by which the white American seeks to resolve the dilemma arising between his democratic beliefs and certain antidemocratic practices, between his acceptance of the sacred democratic belief that all men are created equal and his treatment of every tenth man as though he were not.

Thus on the moral level I propose that we view the whole of American life as a drama acted out upon the body of a Negro giant, who, lying trussed up like Gulliver, forms the stage and the scene upon which and within which the action unfolds. If we examine the beginning of the Colonies, the application of this view is not, in its economic connotations at least, too far-fetched or too difficult to see. For then the Negro's body was exploited as amorally as the soil and climate. It was later, when white men drew up a plan for a democratic way of life, that the Negro began slowly to exert an influence upon America's moral consciousness. Gradually he was recognized as the human factor placed outside the democratic master plan, a human "natural" resource who, so that white men could become more human, was elected to undergo a process of institutionalized dehumanization.

Until the Korean War this moral role had become obscured within the staggering growth of contemporary science and industry, but during the nineteenth century it flared nakedly in the American consciousness, only to be repressed after the Reconstruction. During periods of national crises, when the United States rounds a sudden curve on the pitch-black road of history, this moral awareness surges in the white American's conscience like a raging river revealed at his feet by a lightning flash. Only then is the veil of anti-Negro myths, symbols, stereotypes and taboos drawn somewhat aside. And when we look closely at our literature it is to be seen operating even when the Negro seems most patently the little man who isn't there.

I see no value either in presenting a catalogue of Negro characters appearing in twentieth-century fiction or in charting the racial attitudes of white writers. We are interested not in quantities but in qualities. And since it is impossible here to discuss the entire body of this writing, the next best thing is to select a framework in which the relationships with which we are concerned may be clearly seen. For brevity let us take three representative writers: Mark Twain, Hemingway and Faulkner. Twain for historical perspective and as an example of how a great nineteenth-century writer handled the Negro; Hemingway as the prime example of the artist who ignored the dramatic and symbolic possibilities presented by this theme; and Faulkner as an example of a writer who has confronted Negroes with such mixed motives that he has presented them in terms of both the "good nigger" and the "bad nigger" stereotypes, and who yet has explored perhaps more successfully than anyone else, either white or black, certain forms of Negro humanity.

For perspective let us begin with Mark Twain's great classic, *Huckleberry Finn.* Recall that Huckleberry has run away from his father, Miss Watson and the Widow Douglas (indeed the whole commu-

[1] Perhaps the ideal approach to the work of literature would be one allowing for insight into the deepest psychological motives of the writer at the same time that it examined all external sociological factors operating within a given milieu. For while objectively a social reality, the work of art is, in its genesis, a projection of a deeply personal process, and any approach that ignores the personal at the expense of the social is necessarily incomplete. Thus when we approach contemporary writing from the perspective of segregation, as is commonly done by sociology-minded thinkers, we automatically limit ourselves to one external aspect of a complex whole, which leaves us little to say concerning its personal, internal elements. On the other hand, American writing has been one of the most important twentieth-century literatures, and though negative as a social force it is technically brilliant and emotionally powerful. Hence were we to examine it for its embodiment of these positive values, there would be other more admiring things to be said. [Ellison's note.]

nity, in relation to which he is a young outcast) and has with him as companion on the raft upon which they are sailing down the Mississippi the Widow Watson's runaway Negro slave, Jim. Recall, too, that Jim, during the critical moment of the novel, is stolen by two scoundrels and sold to another master, presenting Huck with the problem of freeing Jim once more. Two ways are open, he can rely upon his own ingenuity and "steal" Jim into freedom or he might write the Widow Watson and request reward money to have Jim returned to her. But there is a danger in this course, remember, since the angry widow might sell the slave down the river into a harsher slavery. It is this course which Huck starts to take, but as he composes the letter he wavers.

> "It was a close place." [he tells us] "I took it [the letter] up, and held it in my hand. I was trembling, because I'd got to decide, forever, 'twixt two things, and I knowed it. I studied a minute, sort of holding my breath, and then says to myself:
>
> "'Alright, then, I'll *go* to hell'—and tore it up, . . . It was awful thoughts and awful words, but they was said . . . And I let them stay said, and never thought no more about reforming. I shoved the whole thing out of my head and said I would take up wickedness again, which was in my line, being brung up to it, and the other warn't. And for a starter I would . . . steal Jim out of slavery again. . . ."

And a little later, in defending his decision to Tom Sawyer, Huck comments, "I know you'll say it's dirty, low-down business but *I'm* low-down. And I'm going to steal him . . ."

We have arrived at a key point of the novel and by an ironic reversal, of American fiction, a pivotal moment announcing a change of direction in the plot, a reversal as well as a recognition scene (like that in which Oedipus discovers his true identity) wherein a new definition of necessity is being formulated. Huck Finn has struggled with the problem poised by the clash between property rights and human rights, between what the community considered to be the proper attitude toward an escaped slave and his knowledge of Jim's humanity, gained through their adventures as fugitives together. He has made his decision on the side of humanity. In this passage Twain has stated the basic moral issue centering around Negroes and the white American's democratic ethics. It dramatizes as well the highest point of tension generated by the clash between the direct, human relationships of the frontier and the abstract, inhuman, market-dominated relationships fostered by the rising middle class—which in Twain's day was already compromising dangerously with the most inhuman aspects of the defeated slave system. And just as politically these forces reached their sharpest tension in the outbreak of the Civil War, in *Huckleberry Finn* (both the boy and the novel) their human implications come to sharpest focus around the figure of the Negro.

Huckleberry Finn knew, as did Mark Twain, that Jim was not only a slave but a human being, a man who in some ways was to be envied, and who expressed his essential humanity in his desire for freedom, his will to possess his own labor, in his loyalty and capacity for friendship and in his love for his wife and child. Yet Twain, though guilty of the sentimentality common to humorists, does not idealize the slave. Jim is drawn in all his ignorance and superstition, with his good traits and his bad. He, like all men, is ambiguous, limited in circumstance but not in possibility. And it will be noted that when Huck makes his decision he identifies himself with Jim and accepts the judgment of his superego—that internalized representative of the community—that his action is evil. Like Prometheus, who for mankind stole fire from the gods, he embraces the evil implicit in his act in order to affirm his belief in humanity. Jim, therefore, is not simply a slave, he is a symbol of humanity, and in freeing Jim, Huck makes a bid to free himself of the conventionalized evil taken for civilization by the town.

This conception of the Negro as a symbol of Man—the reversal of what he represents in most contemporary thought—was organic to nineteenth-century literature. It occurs not only in Twain but in Emerson, Thoreau, Whitman and Melville (whose symbol of evil, incidentally, was white), all of whom were men publicly involved in various forms of deeply personal rebellion. And while the Negro and the color black were associated with the concept of evil and ugliness far back in the Christian era, the Negro's emergence as a symbol of value came, I believe, with Rationalism and the rise of the romantic individual of the eighteenth century. This, perhaps, because the romantic was in revolt against the old moral authority, and if he suffered a sense of guilt, his passion for personal freedom was such that he was willing to accept evil (a tragic attitude) even to identifying himself with the "noble slave"—who symbolized the darker, unknown potential side of his personality, that underground side, turgid with possibility, which might, if given a chance, toss a fistful of mud into the sky and create a "shining star."

Even that prototype of the bourgeois, Robinson Crusoe, stopped to speculate as to his slave's humanity. And the rising American industrialists of the late nineteenth century were to rediscover what their European counterparts had learned a century before: that the good man Friday was as sound an investment for Crusoe morally as he was economically, for not only did Friday allow Crusoe to achieve himself by working for him, but by functioning as a living scapegoat to contain Crusoe's guilt over breaking with the institutions and authority of the past, he made it possible to exploit even his guilt economically. The man was one of the first missionaries.

Mark Twain was alive to this irony and refused such an easy (and dangerous) way out. Huck Finn's acceptance of the evil implicit in his "emancipation" of Jim represents Twain's acceptance of his personal responsibility in the condition of society. This was the tragic face behind his comic mask.

But by the twentieth century this attitude of tragic responsibility had disappeared from our literature along with that broad conception of democracy which vitalized the work of our greatest writers. After Twain's compelling image of black and white fraternity the Negro generally disappears from fiction as a rounded human being. And if already in Twain's time a novel which was optimistic concerning a democracy which would include all men could not escape being banned from public libraries, by our day his great drama of interracial fraternity had become, for most Americans at least, an amusing boy's story and nothing more. But, while a boy, Huck Finn has become by the somersault motion of what William Empson terms "pastoral," an embodiment of the heroic, and an exponent of humanism. Indeed, the historical and artistic justification for his adolescence lies in the fact that Twain was depicting a transitional period of American life; its artistic justification is that adolescence is the time of the "great confusion" during which both individuals and nations flounder between accepting and rejecting the responsibilities of adulthood. Accordingly, Huck's relationship to Jim, the river, and all they symbolize, is that of a humanist; in his relation to the community he is an individualist. He embodies the two major conflicting drives operating in nineteenth-century America. And if humanism is man's basic attitude toward a social order which he accepts, and individualism his basic attitude toward one he rejects, one might say that Twain, by allowing these two attitudes to argue dialectically in his work of art, was as highly moral an artist as he was a believer in democracy, and vice versa.

History, however, was to bring an ironic reversal to the direction which Huckleberry Finn chose, and by our day the divided ethic of the community had won out. In contrast with Twain's humanism, individualism was thought to be the only tenable attitude for the artist.

Thus we come to Ernest Hemingway, one of the two writers whose art is based most solidly upon Mark Twain's language, and one who perhaps has done most to extend Twain's technical influence upon our fiction. It was Hemingway who pointed out that all modern American writing springs from *Huckleberry Finn.* (One might add here that equally as much of it derives from Hemingway himself.) But by the twenties the element of rejection implicit in Twain had become so dominant an attitude of the American writer that Hemingway goes on to warn us to "stop where the Nigger Jim is stolen from the boys. That is the real end. The rest is just cheating."

So thoroughly had the Negro, both as man and as a symbol of man, been pushed into the underground of the American conscience that Hemingway missed completely the structural, symbolic and moral necessity for that part of the plot in which the boys rescue Jim. Yet it is precisely this part which gives the novel its significance. Without it, except as a boy's tale, the novel is meaningless. Yet Hemingway, a great artist in his own right, speaks as a victim of that culture of which he is himself so critical, for by his time that growing rift in the ethical fabric pointed out by Twain had become completely sundered—snagged upon the irrepressible moral reality of the Negro. Instead of the single democratic ethic for every man, there now existed two: one, the idealized ethic of the Constitution and the Declaration of Independence, reserved for white men; and the other, the pragmatic ethic designed for Negroes and other minorities, which took the form of discrimination. Twain had dramatized the conflict leading to this division in its earlier historical form, but what was new here was that such a moral division, always a threat to the sensitive man, was ignored by the artist in the most general terms, as when Hemingway rails against the rhetoric of the First World War.

Hemingway's blindness to the moral values of *Huckleberry Finn* despite his sensitivity to its technical aspects duplicated the one-sided vision of the twenties. Where Twain, seeking for what Melville called "the common continent of man," drew upon the rich folklore of the frontier (not omitting the Negro's) in order to "Americanize" his idiom, thus broadening his stylistic appeal, Hemingway was alert only to Twain's technical discoveries—the flexible colloquial language, the sharp naturalism, the thematic potentialities of adolescence. Thus what for Twain was a means to a moral end became for Hemingway an end in itself. And just as the trends toward technique for the sake of technique and production for the sake of the market lead to the neglect of the human need out of which they spring, so do they lead in literature to a marvelous technical virtuosity won at the expense of a gross insensitivity to fraternal values.

It is not accidental that the disappearance of the human Negro from our fiction coincides with the disappearance of deep-probing doubt and a sense of evil. Not that doubt in some form was not always present, as the works of the lost generation, the muckrakers and the proletarian writers make very clear. But it is a shallow doubt, which seldom turns inward upon the writer's own values; almost always it focuses outward, upon some scapegoat with which he is seldom able to identify himself as Huck Finn identified himself with the scoundrels who stole Jim and with Jim himself. This particular naturalism explored everything except the nature of man.

And when the artist would no longer conjure with the major moral problem in American life, he was defeated as a manipulator of profound social passions. In the United States, as in Europe, the triumph of industrialism had repelled the artist with the blatant hypocrisy between its ideals and its acts. But while in Europe the writer became the most profound critic of these matters, in our country he either turned away or was at best half-hearted in his opposition—perhaps because any profound probing of human values, both within himself and within society, would have brought him face to face with the rigidly tabooed subject of the Negro. And now the tradition of avoiding the moral struggle had led not only to the artistic segregation of the Negro but to the segregation of real fraternal, i.e., democratic, values.

The hard-boiled school represented by Hemingway, for instance, is usually spoken of as a product of World War I disillusionment, yet it was as much the product of a tradition which arose even before the Civil War—that tradition of intellectual evasion for which Thoreau criticized Emerson in regard to the Fugitive Slave Law, and which had been growing swiftly since the failure of the ideals in whose name the Civil War was fought. The failure to resolve the problem symbolized by the Negro has contributed indirectly to the dispossession of the artist in several ways. By excluding our largest minority from the democratic process, the United States weakened all national symbols and rendered sweeping public rituals which would dramatize the American dream impossible; it robbed the artist of a body of unassailable public beliefs upon which he could base his art; it deprived him of a personal faith in the ideals upon which society supposedly rested; and it provided him with no tragic mood indigenous to his society upon which he could erect a tragic art. The result was that he responded with an attitude of rejection, which he expressed as artistic individualism. But too often his rejection and individualism were narrow; seldom was he able to transcend the limitations of pragmatic reality, and the quality of moral imagination—the fountainhead of great art—was atrophied within him.

Malraux has observed that contemporary American writing is the only important literature not created by intellectuals, and that the creators possess "neither the relative historical culture, nor the love of ideas (a prerogative of professors in the United States)" of comparable Europeans. And is there not a connection between the non-intellectual aspects of this writing (though many of the writers are far more intellectual than they admit or than Malraux would suspect) and its creators' rejection of broad social responsibility, between its non-concern with ideas and its failure to project characters who grasp the broad sweep of American life, or who even attempt to state its fundamental problems? And has not this affected the types of heroes of this fiction, is it not a partial explanation of why it has created no characters possessing broad insight into their situations or the emotional, psychological and intellectual complexity which would allow them to possess and articulate a truly democratic world view?

It is instructive that Hemingway, born into a civilization characterized by violence, should seize upon the ritualized violence of the culturally distant Spanish bullfight as a laboratory for developing his style. For it was, for Americans, an amoral violence (though not for the Spaniards) which he was seeking. Otherwise he might have studied that ritual of violence closer to home, that ritual in which the sacrifice is that of a human scapegoat, the lynching bee. Certainly this rite is not confined to the rope as agency, nor to the South as scene, nor even to the Negro as victim.

But let us not confuse the conscious goals of twentieth-century fiction with those of the nineteenth century, let us take it on its own terms. Artists such as Hemingway were seeking a technical perfection rather than moral insight. (Or should we say that theirs was a morality of technique?) They desired a style stripped of unessentials, one that would appeal without resorting to what was considered worn-out rhetoric, or best of all without any rhetoric whatsoever. It was felt that through the default of the powers that ruled society the artist had as his major task the "pictorial presentation of the evolution of a personal problem." Instead of recreating and extending the national myth as he did this, the writer now restricted himself to elaborating his personal myth. And although naturalist in his general style, he was not interested, like Balzac, in depicting a society, or even, like Mark Twain, in portraying the moral situation of a nation. Rather he was engaged in working out a personal problem through the evocative, emotion-charged images and ritual-therapy available through the manipulation of art forms. And while art was still an instrument of freedom, it was now mainly the instrument of a questionable personal freedom for the artist, which too often served to enforce the "unfreedom" of the reader.

This because it is not within the province of the artist to determine whether his work is social or not. Art by its nature *is* social. And while the artist can determine within a certain narrow scope the type of social effect he wishes his art to create, here his will is definitely limited. Once introduced into society, the work of art begins to pulsate with those meanings, emotions, ideas brought to it by its audience and over which the artist has but limited control. The irony of the "lost generation" writers is that while disavowing a social role it was the fate of their works to perform a social function which re-enforced those very social values which they most violently opposed. How could this be? Because in its genesis the work of art, like the stereotype, is personal; psychologically it represents the socialization of some profoundly personal problem involving guilt (often symbolic murder—parricide, fratricide—incest, homosexuality, all problems at the base of personality) from which by expressing them along with other elements (images, memories, emotions, ideas) he seeks transcendence. To be effective as personal fulfillment, if it is to be more than dream, the work of art must simultaneously evoke images of reality and give them formal organization. And it must, since the individual's emotions are formed in society, shape them into socially meaningful patterns (even Surrealism and Dadaism depended upon their initiates). Nor, as we can see by comparing literature with reportage, is this all. The work of literature differs basically from reportage not merely in its presentation of a pattern of events, nor in its concern with emotion (for a report might well be an account of highly emotional events), but in the deep personal necessity which cries full-throated in the work of art and which seeks transcendence in the form of ritual.

Malcolm Cowley, on the basis of the rites which he believes to be the secret dynamic of Hemingway's work, has identified him with Poe, Hawthorne and Melville, "the haunted and nocturnal writers," he calls them, "the men who dealt with images that were symbols of an inner world." In Hemingway's work, he writes, "we can recognize rites of animal sacrifice . . . of sexual union . . . of conversion . . . and of symbolic death and rebirth. I do not believe, however, that the presence of these rites in writers like Hemingway is as important as the fact that here, beneath the dead-pan prose, the cadences of understatement, the anti-intellectualism, the concern with every "fundamental" of man except that which distinguishes him from the animal—that here is the twentieth-century form of that magical rite which during periods of great art has been to a large extent public and explicit. Here is the literary form by which the personal guilt of the pulverized individual of our rugged era is expatiated: not through his identification with the guilty acts of an Oedipus, a Macbeth or a Medea, by suffering their agony and loading his sins upon their "strong and passionate shoulders," but by being gored with a bull, hooked with a fish, impaled with a grasshopper on a fishhook; not by identifying himself with human heroes, but with those who are indeed defeated.

On the social level this writing performs a function similar to that of the stereotype: it conditions the reader to accept the less worthy values of society, and it serves to justify and absolve our sins of social irresponsibility. With unconscious irony it advises stoic acceptance of those conditions of life which it so accurately describes and which it pretends to reject. And when I read the early Hemingway I seem to be in the presence of Huckleberry Finn who, instead of identifying himself with humanity and attempting to steal Jim free, chose to write the letter which sent him back into slavery. So that now he is a Huck full of regret and nostalgia, suffering a sense of guilt that fills even his noondays with nightmares, and against which, like a terrified child avoiding the cracks in the sidewalk, he seeks protection through the compulsive minor rituals of his prose.

The major difference between nineteenth- and twentieth-century writers is not in the latter's lack of personal rituals—a property of all fiction worthy of being termed literature—but in the social effect aroused within their respective readers. Melville's ritual (and his rhetoric) was based upon materials that were more easily available, say, than Hemingway's. They represented a blending of his personal myth with universal myths as traditional as any used by Shakespeare or the Bible, while until *For Whom the Bell Tolls* Hemingway's was weighted on the personal side. The difference in terms of perspective of belief is that Melville's belief could still find a public object. Whatever else his works were "about" they also managed to be about democracy. But by our day the democratic dream had become too shaky a structure to support the furious pressures of the artist's doubt. And as always when the belief which nurtures a great social myth declines, large sections of society become prey to superstition. For man without myth is Othello with Desdemona gone: chaos descends, faith vanishes and superstitions prowl in the mind.

Hard-boiled writing is said to appeal through its presentation of sheer fact, rather than through rhetoric. The writer puts nothing down but what he pragmatically "knows." But actually one "fact" itself—which in literature must be presented simultaneously as image and as event—became a rhetorical unit. And the symbolic ritual which has set off the "fact"—that is, the fact unorganized by vital social myths (which might incorporate the findings of science and still contain elements of mystery)—is the rite of superstition. The superstitious individual responds to the capricious event, the fact that seems to explode in his face through blind fatality. For it is the creative function of myth to protect the individual from the irrational, and since it is here in the realm of the irrational that, impervious to science, the stereotype grows, we see that the Negro stereotype is really an image of the unorganized, irrational forces of American life, forces through which, by projecting them in forms of images of an easily dominated minority, the white individual seeks to be at home in the vast unknown world of America. Perhaps the object of the stereotype is not so much to crush the Negro as to console the white man.

Certainly there is justification for this view when we consider the work of William Faulkner. In Faulkner most of the relationships which we have pointed out between the Negro and contemporary writing come to focus: the social and the personal, the moral and the technical, the nineteenth-century emphasis upon morality and the modern accent upon the personal myth. And on the strictly literary level he is prolific and complex enough to speak for those Southern writers who are aggressively anti-Negro and for those younger writers who appear most sincerely interested in depicting the Negro as a rounded human being. What is more, he is the greatest artist the South has produced. While too complex to be given more than a glance in these notes, even a glance is more revealing of what lies back of the distortion of the Negro in modern writing than any attempt at a group survey might be.

Faulkner's attitude is mixed. Taking his cue from the Southern mentality in which the Negro is often dissociated into a malignant stereotype (the bad nigger) on the one hand and a benign stereotype (the good nigger) on the other, most often Faulkner presents characters embodying both. The dual function of this dissociation seems to be that of avoiding moral pain and thus to justify the South's racial code. But since such a social order harms whites no less than blacks, the sensitive Southerner, the artist, is apt to feel its effects acutely—and within the deepest levels of his personality. For not only is the social division forced upon the Negro by the ritualized ethic of discrimination, but upon the white man by the strictly enforced set of anti-Negro taboos. The conflict is always with him. Indeed, so rigidly has the recognition of Negro humanity been tabooed that the white Southerner is apt to associate any form of personal rebellion with the Negro. So that for the Southern artist the Negro becomes a symbol of his personal rebellion, his guilt and his repression of it. The Negro is thus a compelling object of fascination, and this we see very clearly in Faulkner.

Sometimes in Faulkner the Negro is simply a villain, but by an unconsciously ironic transvaluation his villainy consists, as with Loosh in *The Unvanquished*, of desiring his freedom. Or again the Negro appears benign, as with Ringo, of the same novel, who uses his talent not to seek personal freedom but to remain the loyal and resourceful retainer. Not that I criticize loyalty in itself, but that loyalty given where one's humanity is unrecognized seems a bit obscene. And yet in Faulkner's story, "The Bear," he brings us as close to the moral implication of the Negro as Twain or Melville. In the famous "difficult" fourth section, which Malcolm Cowley advises us to skip very much as Hemingway would have us skip the end of *Huckleberry Finn*, we find an argument in progress in which one voice (that of a Southern abolitionist) seeks to define Negro humanity against the other's enumeration of those stereotypes which many Southerners believe to be the Negro's basic traits. Significantly the mentor of the young hero of this story, a man of great moral stature, is socially a Negro.

Indeed, through his many novels and short stories, Faulkner fights out the moral problem which was repressed after the nineteenth century, and it was shocking for some to discover that for all his concern with the South, Faulkner was actually seeking out the nature of man. Thus we must turn to him for that continuity of moral purpose which made for the greatness of our classics. As for the Negro minority, he has been more willing perhaps than any other artist to start with the stereotype, accept it as true, and then seek out the human truth which it hides. Perhaps his is the example for our writers to follow, for in his work technique has been put once more to the task of creating value.

Which leaves these final things to be said. First, that this is meant as no plea for white writers to define Negro humanity, but to recognize the broader aspects of their own. Secondly, Negro writers and those of the other minorities have their own task of contributing to the total image of the American by depicting the experience of their own groups. Certainly theirs is the task of defining Negro humanity, as this can no more be accomplished by others than freedom, which must be won again and again each day, can be conferred upon another. A people must define itself, and minorities have the responsibility of having their ideals and images recognized as part of the composite image which is that of the still forming American people.

The other thing to be said is that while it is unlikely that American writing will ever retrace the way to the nineteenth century, it might be worth while to point out that for all its technical experimentation it is nevertheless an ethical instrument, and as such it might well exercise some choice in the kind of ethic it prefers to support. The artist is no freer than the society in which he lives, and in the United States the writers who stereotype or ignore the Negro and other minorities in the final analysis stereotype and distort their own humanity. Mark Twain knew that in *his* America humanity masked its face with blackness.

Poets at Mid-Century

ROBERT LOWELL [1917-]

ROBERT LOWELL is the outstanding poet of our time. In charting his career, we trace the movement of twentieth-century poetry through the two major rebellions which have sustained it. In the first, poets rejected romanticism and defended themselves against the apparent threats of scientific thought; in the second, they discovered that a new romantic expressiveness, immediacy, and sometimes even transcendent vision were for them the primary poetic qualities.

In Lowell's earlier work, such as *Lord Weary's Castle,* the influences of the first rebellion are clear. Whatever is personal and private in those poems is transmuted into the impersonal; the ideal of the artist's special awareness is approached through a density of allusion and through the poet's own occasional obsession with sin, evil, and redemption. The self who speaks in the earlier poems is a self projected totally into the poem, but one cut off from the poet's own interior life. In Lowell's later work, however, he speaks with a confessional directness as tortured neurotic, husband and lover, family historian, and political human being. When he is occasionally less successful in this mode, the finely wrought quality of all his apparently guileless outpourings becomes only more evident. The true extent of the sea-change appears.

Randall Jarrell has suggested that the typical thematic movement in these early poems is from a sense of necessity and entrapment to an awareness of freedom, possibility, and salvation. A mood of stagnation is transformed into awe and vitality. Often the movement is reversed, however; and sometimes there is no dialectical movement at all, but just a steady descent, by image and metaphor, to the core of hell.

In the later poems, if there is less exaltation, there is a greater consciousness of renewal. But the distinction between the earlier and the present Lowell ought not to be overemphasized. The later poems, stripped of the overlay of religious imagery and symbolistic armor, give us a vision of a private hell: the poet bearing his burden of sexual guilt, the poet as alcoholic, and the poet confined in a mental ward. All these explicit themes are generally elaborated in the first person and apparently direct the reader to the poet himself. Yet Lowell's possibly less spectacular artistic techniques here still reveal far more about the potential of existence than even their directness first indicates. One need only examine the shifts in tone and imagery to experience the power and honesty of these poems.

Robert Lowell is the great-grandnephew of James Russell Lowell, and a distant cousin of Amy Lowell, the cigar-smoking poetess best remembered for a handful of poems written for the Imagist revolution she briefly led with Ezra Pound. Born in Boston in 1917, Lowell spent most of his earlier years there, except for brief intervals when his father's naval career took the family to Washington and Philadelphia. He attended preparatory school at St. Mark's, where he was a student of the poet Richard Eberhart. He then studied at Harvard for two years, but his interest in poetry, stimulated under Eberhart, took him to Kenyon College. He worked there with John Crowe Ransom and Randall Jarrell, then graduated in 1940. Lowell at this time became a Roman Catholic, and the religious beliefs he rather briefly held exerted a pervasive thematic influence on his earlier poems.

During the Second World War, he twice attempted unsuccessfully to enlist. When he was finally drafted in 1943, his refusal to serve the country he believed to be no longer in danger earned him five months in the state penitentiary. He continued writing, however, and for his achievement in *Lord Weary's Castle,* he was awarded a Pulitzer Prize in 1947. He was appointed Consultant in Poetry at the Library of Congress the same year and held a Guggenheim Fellowship as well. He has received numerous other prizes and honors and has taught at a number of colleges and universities, including the State University of Iowa, Boston University, and Harvard. His first book of poems, *Land of Unlikeness,* appeared in 1944. *The Mills of the Kavanaughs* was published in 1951, *Life Studies* in 1959, and *For the Union Dead* in 1964.

Further reading: Jerome Mazzaro, *The Poetic Themes of Robert Lowell,* 1965. H. B. Staples, *Robert Lowell: The First Twenty Years,* 1962. Randall Jarrell, *Poetry and the Age,* 1953, pp.188-99.

The Exile's Return

The poem ends with a suggestion of release, or regeneration. What kinds of values do you think the poet is trying to evoke in the pattern of seasonal imagery which informs the poem? This and the three following poems are from *Lord Weary's Castle* (1946).

There mounts in squalls a sort of rusty mire,
Not ice, not snow, to leaguer the Hôtel
De Ville, where braced pig-iron dragons grip
The blizzard to their rigor mortis. A bell
Grumbles when the reverberations strip
The thatching from its spire,
The search-guns click and spit and split up timber
And nick the slate roofs on the Holstenwall
Where torn-up tilestones crown the victor. Fall
And winter, spring and summer, guns unlimber
And lumber down the narrow gabled street
Past your gray, sorry and ancestral house
Where the dynamited walnut tree
Shadows a squat, old, wind-torn gate and cows
The Yankee commandant. You will not see
Strutting children or meet
The peg-leg and reproachful chancellor
With a forget-me-not in his button-hole
When the unseasoned liberators roll
Into the Market Square, ground arms before
The Rathaus; but already lily-stands
Burgeon the risen Rhineland, and a rough
Cathedral lifts its eye. Pleasant enough,
Voi ch'entrate, and your life is in your hands.

New Year's Day

Again and then again . . . the year is born
To ice and death, and it will never do
To skulk behind storm-windows by the stove
To hear the postgirl sounding her French horn

When the thin tidal ice is wearing through.
Here is the understanding not to love
Our neighbor, or tomorrow that will sieve
Our resolutions. While we live, we live

To snuff the smoke of victims. In the snow
The kitten heaved its hindlegs, as if fouled,
And died. We bent it in a Christmas box
And scattered blazing weeds to scare the crow
Until the snake-tailed sea-winds coughed and
howled
For alms outside the church whose double locks
Wait for St. Peter, the distorted key.
Under St. Peter's bell the parish sea

Swells with its smelt into the burlap shack
Where Joseph plucks his hand-lines like a harp,
And hears the fearful *Puer natus est*
Of Circumcision, and relives the wrack
And howls of Jesus whom he holds. How sharp
The burden of the Law before the beast:
Time and the grindstone and the knife of God.
The Child is born in blood, O child of blood.

The Drunken Fisherman

Wallowing in this bloody sty,
I cast for fish that pleased my eye
(Truly Jehovah's bow suspends
No pots of gold to weight its ends);
Only the blood-mouthed rainbow trout
Rose to my bait. They flopped about
My canvas creel until the moth
Corrupted its unstable cloth.

A calendar to tell the day;
A handkerchief to wave away
The gnats; a couch unstuffed with storm
Pouching a bottle in one arm;
A whiskey bottle full of worms;
And bedroom slacks: are these fit terms
To mete the worm whose molten rage
Boils in the belly of old age?

Once fishing was a rabbit's foot—
O wind blow cold, O wind blow hot,
Let suns stay in or suns step out:
Life danced a jig on the sperm-whale's spout—
The fisher's fluent and obscene
Catches kept his conscience clean.
Children, the raging memory drools
Over the glory of past pools.

Now the hot river, ebbing, hauls
Its bloody waters into holes;
A grain of sand inside my shoe
Mimics the moon that might undo
Man and Creation too; remorse,
Stinking, has puddled up its source;
Here tantrums thrash to a whale's rage.
This is the pot-hole of old age.

Is there no way to cast my hook
Out of this dynamited brook?
The Fisher's sons must cast about
When shallow waters peter out.
I will catch Christ with a greased worm,
And when the Prince of Darkness stalks
My bloodstream to its Stygian term . . .
On water the Man-Fisher walks.

After the Surprising Conversions

For this poem, Lowell drew the idea and much of the substance from a letter written by Jonathan Edwards to Benjamin Coleman, May 30, 1735, describing the progress and effects of the religious revival of 1734–35 which Edwards' own powerful preaching had set in motion in the Connecticut Valley. A hurried postscript, dated four days later, told of "a thing of a very awful nature" that had just occurred: "my uncle Hawley, the last sabbath morning, laid violent hands on himself and put an end to his life, by cutting his own throat. He had been for a considerable time greatly concerned about the condition of his soul; till, by the ordering of a sovereign Providence he was suffered to fall into a deep melancholy, a distemper that the family are very prone to; he was much overpowered by it; the devil took the advantage and drove him into despairing thoughts; he was kept very much awake a nights, so that he had but very little sleep for two months, till he seemed not to have his faculties in his own power. . . . The coroner's inquest judged him delirious. . . ."

September twenty-second, Sir: today
I answer. In the latter part of May,
Hard on our Lord's Ascension, it began
To be more sensible. A gentleman
Of more than common understanding, strict
In morals, pious in behavior, kicked
Against our goad. A man of some renown,
An useful, honored person in the town,
He came of melancholy parents; prone
To secret spells, for years they kept alone—
His uncle, I believe, was killed of it:
Good people, but of too much or little wit.
I preached one Sabbath on a text from Kings;
He showed concernment for his soul. Some things
In his experience were hopeful. He
Would sit and watch the wind knocking a tree
And praise this countryside our Lord has made.
Once when a poor man's heifer died, he laid
A shilling on the doorsill; though a thirst

For loving shook him like a snake, he durst
Not entertain much hope of his estate
In heaven. Once we saw him sitting late
Behind his attic window by a light
That guttered on his Bible; through that night
He meditated terror, and he seemed
Beyond advice or reason, for he dreamed
That he was called to trumpet Judgment Day
To Concord. In the latter part of May
He cut his throat. And though the coroner
Judged him delirious, soon a noisome stir
Palsied our village. At Jehovah's nod
Satan seemed more let loose amongst us: God
Abandoned us to Satan, and he pressed
Us hard, until we thought we could not rest
Till we had done with life. Content was gone.
All the good work was quashed. We were undone.
The breath of God had carried out a planned
And sensible withdrawal from this land;
The multitude, once unconcerned with doubt,
Once neither callous, curious nor devout,
Jumped at broad noon, as though some peddler groaned
At it in its familiar twang: "My friend,
Cut your own throat. Cut your own throat. Now! Now!"
September twenty-second, Sir, the bough
Cracks with the unpicked apples, and at dawn
The small-mouth bass breaks water, gorged with spawn.

Memories of West Street and Lepke

This and the next two poems are from *Life Studies* (1959).

Only teaching on Tuesdays, book-worming
in pajamas fresh from the washer each morning,
I hog a whole house on Boston's
"hardly passionate Marlborough Street."
where even the man
scavenging filth in the back alley trash cans,
has two children, a beach wagon, a helpmate,
and is a "young Republican."
I have a nine months' daughter,
young enough to be my granddaughter.
Like the sun she rises in her flame-flamingo infants' wear.

These are the tranquillized *Fifties*,
and I am forty. Ought I to regret my seedtime?
I was a fire-breathing Catholic C. O.,
and made my manic statement,
telling off the state and president, and then
sat waiting sentence in the bull pen
beside a Negro boy with curlicues
of marijuana in his hair.

Given a year,
I walked on the roof of the West Street Jail, a short
enclosure like my school soccer court,
and saw the Hudson River once a day
through sooty clothesline entanglements
and bleaching khaki tenements.
Strolling, I yammered metaphysics with Abramowitz,
a jaundice-yellow ("it's really tan")
and fly-weight pacifist,
so vegetarian,
he wore rope shoes and preferred fallen fruit.
He tried to convert Bioff and Brown,
the Hollywood pimps, to his diet.
Hairy, muscular, suburban,
wearing chocolate double-breasted suits,
they blew their tops and beat him black and blue.

I was so out of things, I'd never heard
of the Jehovah's Witnesses.
"Are you a C. O.?" I asked a fellow jailbird.
"No," he answered, "I'm a J. W."
He taught me the "hospital tuck,"
and pointed out the T shirted back
of *Murder Incorporated's* Czar Lepke,
there piling towels on a rack,
or dawdling off to his little segregated cell full
of things forbidden the common man:
a portable radio, a dresser, two toy American
flags tied together with a ribbon of Easter palm.
Flabby, bald, lobotomized,
he drifted in a sheepish calm,
where no agonizing reappraisal
jarred his concentration on the electric chair—
hanging like an oasis in his air
of lost connections. . . .

Man and Wife

Consider the effect created by the color imagery in the opening lines: does it help to delineate the speaker's "mad" perspective? Does his wife's "scorching invective" serve any therapeutic purpose at the end of the poem as it becomes analogized to the Atlantic Ocean?

Tamed by *Miltown*, we lie on Mother's bed;
the rising sun in war paint dyes us red;
in broad daylight her gilded bed-posts shine,
abandoned, almost Dionysian.
At last the trees are green on Marlborough Street,
blossoms on our magnolia ignite
the morning with their murderous five days' white.
All night I've held your hand,

as if you had
a fourth time faced the kingdom of the mad—
its hackneyed speech, its homicidal eye—
and dragged me home alive. . . . Oh my *Petite*,
clearest of all God's creatures, still all air and nerve:
you were in your twenties, and I,
once hand on glass
and heart in mouth,
outdrank the Rahvs in the heat
of Greenwich Village, fainting at your feet—
too boiled and shy
and poker-faced to make a pass,
while the shrill verve
of your invective scorched the traditional South.

Now twelve years later, you turn your back.
Sleepless, you hold
your pillow to your hollows like a child;
your old fashioned tirade—
loving, rapid, merciless—
breaks like the Atlantic Ocean on my head.

Skunk Hour

(For Elizabeth Bishop)

Nautilus Island's hermit
heiress still lives through winter in her Spartan cottage;
her sheep still graze above the sea.
Her son's a bishop. Her farmer
is first selectman in our village;
she's in her dotage.

Thirsting for
the hierarchic privacy
of Queen Victoria's century,
she buys up all
the eyesores facing her shore,
and lets them fall.

The season's ill—
we've lost our summer millionaire,
who seemed to leap from an L. L. Bean
catalogue. His nine-knot yawl
was auctioned off to lobstermen.
A red fox stain covers Blue Hill.

And now our fairy
decorator brightens his shop for fall;
his fishnet's filled with orange cork,
orange, his cobbler's bench and awl;
there is no money in his work,
he'd rather marry.

One dark night
my Tudor Ford climbed the hill's skull;
I watched for love-cars. Lights turned down,
they lay together, hull to hull,
where the graveyard shelves on the town. . . .
My mind's not right.

A car radio bleats,
"Love, O careless Love. . . ." I hear
my ill-spirit sob in each blood cell,
as if my hand were at its throat. . . .
I myself am hell;
nobody's here—

only skunks, that search
in the moonlight for a bite to eat.
They march on their soles up Main Street:
white stripes, moonstruck eyes' red fire
under the chalk-dry and spar spire
of the Trinitarian Church.

I stand on top
of our back steps and breathe the rich air—
a mother skunk with her column of kittens swills the garbage pail.
She jabs her wedge-head in a cup
of sour cream, drops her ostrich tail,
and will not scare.

For the Union Dead

From *For the Union Dead* (1964).

"Relinquunt Omnia Servare Rem Publicam."

The old South Boston Aquarium stands
in a Sahara of snow now. Its broken windows are boarded.
The bronze weathervane cod has lost half its scales.
The airy tanks are dry.

Once my nose crawled like a snail on the glass;
my hand tingled
to burst the bubbles
drifting from the noses of the cowed, compliant fish.

My hand draws back. I often sigh still
for the dark downward and vegetating kingdom
of the fish and reptile. One morning last March,
I pressed against the new barbed and galvanized

fence on the Boston Common. Behind their cage,
yellow dinosaur steamshovels were grunting
as they cropped up tons of mush and grass
to gouge their underworld garage.

Parking spaces luxuriate like civic
sandpiles in the heart of Boston.
A girdle of orange, Puritan-pumpkin colored girders
braces the tingling Statehouse,

shaking over the excavations, as it faces Colonel
Shaw
and his bell-cheeked Negro infantry
on St. Gaudens' shaking Civil War relief,
propped by a plank splint against the garage's
earthquake.

Two months after marching through Boston,
half the regiment was dead;
at the dedication,
William James could almost hear the bronze
Negroes breathe.

Their monument sticks like a fishbone
in the city's throat.
Its Colonel is as lean
as a compass-needle.

He has an angry wrenlike vigilance,
a greyhound's gentle tautness;
he seems to wince at pleasure,
and suffocate for privacy.

He is out of bounds now. He rejoices in man's
lovely,
peculiar power to choose life and die—
when he leads his black soldiers to death,
he cannot bend his back.

On a thousand small town New England greens,
the old white churches hold their air
of sparse, sincere rebellion; frayed flags
quilt the graveyards of the Grand Army of the
Republic.

The stone statues of the abstract Union Soldier
grow slimmer and younger each year—
wasp-waisted, they doze over muskets
and muse through their sideburns . . .

Shaw's father wanted no monument
except the ditch,
where his son's body was thrown
and lost with his "niggers."

The ditch is nearer.
There are no statues for the last war here;
on Boylston Street, a commercial photograph
shows Hiroshima boiling

over a Mosler Safe, the "Rock of Ages"
that survived the blast. Space is nearer.
When I crouch to my television set,
the drained faces of Negro school-children rise like
balloons.

Colonel Shaw
is riding on his bubble,
he waits
for the blessèd break.

The Aquarium is gone. Everywhere,
giant finned cars nose forward like fish;
a savage servility
slides by on grease.

THEODORE ROETHKE [1908–1963]

INTERPRETATIVE analysis of Roethke's poetry may prove to be a far more difficult task than recent criticism would lead us to expect. The biographical evidence (his early and continuing love for Emerson and Thoreau) and the obsessive images in the poems (trees, plants, rocks, animals, a man, Eternity) point in the same direction, and Roethke's explicators have wasted little time debating among themselves over the theoretical and historical basis of the poems. Hence a number of studies begin and end with certain assumptions: (1) that there is an Emersonian base for Roethke's work; (2) that the Emerson who is important is the Emerson of "Nature," "The Poet," and "The Over-Soul," not the Emerson of "Illusions" and "Experience"; (3) that Roethke, therefore, is a visionary who believes in the power of poetic imagination to transcend the finite universe by penetrating to a spiritual reality within and behind the material world. Concomitant with this idealistic rooting of Roethke is a tendency to read the presiding tone and attitude of the poems as one of celebration and exaltation in the discovery of the god within and without. Given the whole movement of recent poetry and literary theory toward a recovery of our romantic nineteenth-century heritage, of what some have dared to call the Emersonian center of our literature, the claiming for Roethke of romantic définition should come as no particular shock.

There are, however, grounds for entertaining a dissenting view. On evidence external to the poems—namely, the history of ideas since about 1859—one would be warranted in concluding that if Roethke were indeed an Emersonian visionary, he was so at the expense of ignoring or disavowing the deeply anti-Emersonian shifts in philosophic and aesthetic perspective that characterize the modernist tradition. The more compelling, internal evidence, the poems themselves, suggests that Roethke neither ignored his modernist context nor disavowed it. He is a nature poet, to be sure, but the character of his sensibility will not allow an unqualified Emersonian reading of the poems. There is no community of selves in Roethke, no possibility of transcendence for the separate, isolated man. As he put it, "To try to become like God / Is far from becoming God." And, of the possibility of the natural world being a spiritual efflux from an Infinite Absolute,

> In a world always late afternoon,
> In the circular smells of a slow wind,
> I listen to the weeds' vesperal whine,
> Longing for absolutes that never come.
> And shapes make me afraid:
> The dance of natural objects in the mind,
> The immediate sheen, the reality of straw,
> The shadows crawling down a sunny wall.

Here, surely, is no sense of the continuity of self and nature, but the very opposite: a feeling of dread in the confrontation with a hostile "other" that ought to recall Camus, not Emerson.

If the otherness of nature brings terrors, it supplies comforts as well. Immersion in natural things will not provide a metaphysical consolation, but the psychological values remain, as the self, in turning *to* nature, turns *from* a miserable human context. It may, then, be the very inhumanness of nature that constitutes its prime value for the poet; that, at least, would seem to be the major implication of "Dolor." Ultimately, though, it is not nature but Roethke's view of nature that shapes and informs his metaphor. Under no illusions that nature is anything but a dead and alien realm, the poet re-creates his experience of nature by imaginatively separating it from all other experience and submitting the natural moment to the transforming effects of his craft.

Roethke was born in Saginaw, Michigan. He grew up there close to the family greenhouse that was to become a recurring symbol in his poetry. As a child, he hated school but read everything he could get his hands on. While still in grade school, he bought his own editions of Emerson and Thoreau and a subscription to the *Dial* as well. Roethke took two degrees from the University of Michigan, B.A. in 1929 and M.A. in 1936. In 1930–31 he spent a few crucial months at Harvard; there he chanced to meet Robert Hillyer, who encouraged him to submit his poems to the *New Republic* and *Commonweal.* They were promptly accepted.

As poetry was his art, teaching was his career. Beginning in 1931, he taught successively at Lafayette, Pennsylvania State (doubling as varsity tennis coach), Bennington, and the University of Washington, where he was a Professor of English from 1947 until his death. According to Arnold Stein, a colleague at Washington, Roethke was a passionate and dedicated teacher who seemed to need the classroom almost as much as he needed his art. Among his literary friends and acquaintances were W. H. Auden, William Carlos Williams, and I. A. Richards. Roethke once said that he owed more to these people as people than as thinkers, writers, or intellectual influences, and his poetry seems to validate this remark. He was honored frequently with awards, among them a Bollingen Prize and two Pulitzer Prizes. His first book of poems, *Open House and Other Poems* (1941) was followed by several others later included in *The Waking: Poems 1933–1953. The Far Field,* his last volume, was published after his death.

Further reading: R. J. Mills, *Theodore Roethke,* 1963. Karl Malkoff, *Theodore Roethke: An Introduction to the Poetry,* 1966. Arnold Stein, ed., *Theodore Roethke: Essays on the Poetry,* 1965.

Root Cellar

The poet writes, "Nothing would give up life." What has he done to make the reader understand that everything *has* life?

This and the following three poems are from *The Lost Son and Other Poems* (1948). All the Roethke poems given below are reprinted from the *Collected Poems* (1965).

Nothing would sleep in that cellar, dank as a ditch,
Bulbs broke out of boxes hunting for chinks in the
    dark,
Shoots dangled and drooped,
Lolling obscenely from mildewed crates,
Hung down long yellow evil necks, like tropical
    snakes.
And what a congress of stinks!—
Roots ripe as old bait,
Pulpy stems, rank, silo-rich,
Leaf-mold, manure, lime, piled against slippery
    planks.
Nothing would give up life:
Even the dirt kept breathing a small breath.

Weed Puller

Under the concrete benches,
Hacking at black hairy roots,—
Those lewd monkey-tails hanging from drainholes,—
Digging into the soft rubble underneath,
Webs and weeds,
Grubs and snails and sharp sticks,
Or yanking tough fern-shapes,
Coiled green and thick, like dripping smilax,
Tugging all day at perverse life:
The indignity of it!—
With everything blooming above me,
Lilies, pale-pink cyclamen, roses,
Whole fields lovely and inviolate,—
Me down in that fetor of weeds,
Crawling on all fours,
Alive, in a slippery grave.

Big Wind

What is the central, unifying metaphor of the poem? Is it an appropriate one?

Where were the greenhouses going,
Lunging into the lashing
Wind driving water
So far down the river
All the faucets stopped?—
So we drained the manure-machine
For the steam plant,
Pumping the stale mixture
Into the rusty boilers,
Watching the pressure gauge
Waver over to red,
As the seams hissed
And the live steam
Drove to the far
End of the rose-house,
Where the worst wind was,
Creaking the cypress window-frames,
Cracking so much thin glass
We stayed all night,
Stuffing the holes with burlap;
But she rode it out,
That old rose-house,
She hove into the teeth of it,
The core and pith of that ugly storm,
Ploughing with her stiff prow,
Bucking into the wind-waves
That broke over the whole of her,
Flailing her sides with spray,
Flinging long strings of wet across the roof-top,
Finally veering, wearing themselves out, merely
Whistling thinly under the wind-vents;
She sailed until the calm morning,
Carrying her full cargo of roses.

Dolor

There is an implied antithesis in this poem. What, given the context of the other Roethke poems here, might be the remedy for "dolor," or pain?

I have known the inexorable sadness of pencils,
Neat in their boxes, dolor of pad and paper-weight,
All the misery of manilla folders and mucilage,
Desolation in immaculate public places,
Lonely reception room, lavatory, switchboard,
The unalterable pathos of basin and pitcher,
Ritual of multigraph, paper-clip, comma,
Endless duplication of lives and objects.
And I have seen dust from the walls of institutions,
Finer than flour, alive, more dangerous than silica,
Sift, almost invisible, through long afternoons of tedium,
Dropping a fine film on nails and delicate eyebrows,
Glazing the pale hair, the duplicate gray standard faces.

Elegy for Jane

My Student, Thrown by a Horse

This and the following poem are from *The Waking* (1953).

I remember the neckcurls, limp and damp as tendrils;
And her quick look, a sidelong pickerel smile;
And how, once startled into talk, the light syllables leaped for her,
And she balanced in the delight of her thought,
A wren, happy, tail into the wind,
Her song trembling the twigs and small branches.
The shade sang with her;
The leaves, their whispers turned to kissing;
And the mold sang in the bleached valleys under the rose.

Oh, when she was sad, she cast herself down into such a pure depth,
Even a father could not find her:
Scraping her cheek against straw;
Stirring the clearest water.

My sparrow, you are not here,
Waiting like a fern, making a spiny shadow.
The sides of wet stones cannot console me,
Nor the moss, wound with the last light.

If only I could nudge you from this sleep,
My maimed darling, my skittery pigeon.
Over this damp grave I speak the words of my love:
I, with no rights in this matter,
Neither father nor lover.

The Waking

I wake to sleep, and take my waking slow.
I feel my fate in what I cannot fear.
I learn by going where I have to go.

We think by feeling. What is there to know?
I hear my being dance from ear to ear.
I wake to sleep, and take my waking slow.

Of those so close beside me, which are you?
God bless the Ground! I shall walk softly there,
And learn by going where I have to go.

Light takes the Tree; but who can tell us how?
The lowly worm climbs up a winding stair;
I wake to sleep, and take my waking slow.

Great Nature has another thing to do
To you and me; so take the lively air,
And, lovely, learn by going where to go.

This shaking keeps me steady. I should know.
What falls away is always. And is near.
I wake to sleep, and take my waking slow.
I learn by going where I have to go.

I Knew a Woman

This and the following poem are from *Words for the Wind* (1958).

I knew a woman, lovely in her bones,
When small birds sighed, she would sigh back at
 them;
Ah, when she moved, she moved more ways than
 one:
The shapes a bright container can contain!
Of her choice virtues only gods should speak,
Or English poets who grew up on Greek
(I'd have them sing in chorus, cheek to cheek).

How well her wishes went! She stroked my chin,
She taught me Turn, and Counter-turn, and Stand;
She taught me Touch, that undulant white skin;
I nibbled meekly from her proffered hand;
She was the sickle; I, poor I, the rake,
Coming behind her for her pretty sake
(But what prodigious mowing we did make).

Love likes a gander, and adores a goose:
Her full lips pursed, the errant note to seize;
She played it quick, she played it light and loose;
My eyes, they dazzled at her flowing knees;
Her several parts could keep a pure repose,
Or one hip quiver with a mobile nose
(She moved in circles, and those circles moved).

Let seed be grass, and grass turn into hay:
I'm martyr to a motion not my own;
What's freedom for? To know eternity.
I swear she cast a shadow white as stone.
But who would count eternity in days?
These old bones live to learn her wanton ways:
(I measure time by how a body sways).

What Can I Tell My Bones?

The poet writes, in the third section, "I'm released from the dreary dance of opposites." "Opposites" generally create tension in the person who is aware of them. One may trace through the poem the tension generated by the speaker's simultaneous commitment to his physical self and the natural world and his fear of decay and death that seems articulated to him by nature.

1

Beginner,
Perpetual beginner,
The soul knows not what to believe,
In its small folds, stirring sluggishly,
In the least place of its life,
A pulse beyond nothingness,
A fearful ignorance.

 Before the moon draws back,
 Dare I blaze like a tree?

In a world always late afternoon,
In the circular smells of a slow wind,
I listen to the weeds' vesperal whine,
Longing for absolutes that never come.
And shapes make me afraid:
The dance of natural objects in the mind,
The immediate sheen, the reality of straw,
The shadows crawling down a sunny wall.

 A bird sings out in solitariness
 A thin harsh song. The day dies in a child.
 How close we are to the sad animals!
 I need a pool; I need a puddle's calm.

O my bones,
Beware those perpetual beginnings,
Thinning the soul's substance;
The swan's dread of the darkening shore,
Or these insects pulsing near my skin,
The songs from a spiral tree.

 Fury of wind, and no apparent wind,
 A gust blowing the leaves suddenly upward,
 A vine lashing in dry fury,
 A man chasing a cat,
 With a broken umbrella,
 Crying softly.

2

It is difficult to say all things are well,
When the worst is about to arrive;
It is fatal to woo yourself,
However graceful the posture.

Loved heart, what can I say?
When I was a lark, I sang;
When I was a worm, I devoured.

The self says, I am;
The heart says, I am less;
The spirit says, you are nothing.

Mist alters the rocks. What can I tell my bones?
My desire's a wind trapped in a cave.
The spirit declares itself to these rocks.
I'm a small stone, loose in the shale.
Love is my wound.

The wide streams go their way,
The pond lapses back into a glassy silence.
The cause of God in me—has it gone?
Do these bones live? Can I live with these bones?
Mother, mother of us all, tell me where I am!
O to be delivered from the rational into the realm
of pure song,
My face on fire, close to the points of a star,
A learned nimble girl,
Not drearily bewitched,
But sweetly daft.

To try to become like God
Is far from becoming God.
O, but I seek and care!

I rock in my own dark,
Thinking, God has need of me.
The dead love the unborn.

3

Weeds turn toward the wind weed-skeletons.
How slowly all things alter.
Existence dares perpetuate a soul,
A wedge of heaven's light, autumnal song.
I hear a beat of birds, the plangent wings
That disappear into a waning moon;
The barest speech of light among the stones.

To what more vast permission have I come?
When I walk past a vat, water joggles.
I no longer cry for green in the midst of
cinders,
Or dream of the dead, and their holes.
Mercy has many arms.

Instead of a devil with horns, I prefer a serpent with
scales;
In temptation, I rarely seek counsel;
A prisoner of smells, I would rather eat than pray.
I'm released from the dreary dance of opposites.
The wind rocks with my wish; the rain shields me;
I live in light's extreme; I stretch in all directions;
Sometimes I think I'm several.

The sun! The sun! And all we can become!
And the time ripe for running to the moon!
In the long fields, I leave my father's eye;
And shake the secrets from my deepest bones;
My spirit rises with the rising wind;
I'm thick with leaves and tender as a dove,
I take the liberties a short life permits—
I seek my own meekness;
I recover my tenderness by long looking.
By midnight I love everything alive.
Who took the darkness from the air?
I'm wet with another life.
Yea, I have gone and stayed.

What came to me vaguely is now clear,
As if released by a spirit,
Or agency outside me.
Unprayed-for,
And final.

RICHARD WILBUR [1921-]

"THE FACT is that we are not always divided in spirit and that we sometimes yield utterly to a feeling or idea." In this way Richard Wilbur has suggested two apparently contradictory qualities that distinguish his poetry. Though he is an admirer of T. S. Eliot and is deeply indebted to the symbolist ideals of aesthetic autonomy, organic integrity and self-sufficiency, Wilbur has yet managed to retain his independence from the older modernists and remain open to the values of those who reject both Eliot and symbolism. Of the ironic meditative poem, the chief mode of the school of Eliot, Wilbur has said that its virtue is "that the poet speaks out of his whole nature, acknowledging the contradictions which inhere in life. The limitation of such a poem is that the atmosphere of contradiction can stifle passion and conduce to a bland evasiveness." The virtue of the dramatic poem, on the other hand, is that "it can give free expression to some one compelling mood or attitude."

Wilbur's poems are marked by the concentration of metaphor and the concern with the nature of knowledge and being that are associated with the work of Wallace Stevens, though the mixture of irony with force of "feeling or idea" represents Wilbur's own accomplishment. In "Love Calls Us to the Things of This World," the theme is broadly the one which received its classic formulation in Stevens' "Sunday Morning." In "Advice to a Prophet"—in many ways Wilbur's most significant poem, and an example of what he calls the "dramatic poem," a "free expression" of a "compelling mood or attitude"—the theme is as urgently contemporary as any of Ginsberg's, but the treatment is again reminiscent of Stevens, as the problem of the relationship between metaphor and reality is worried over. Perhaps Wilbur's outstanding quality as demonstrated in these and other poems, is his ability to retain his creative originality without severing himself utterly from tradition.

Wilbur was born in New York City, but spent his childhood in a pocket of country in northern New Jersey where his parents had leased a pre-Revolutionary stone house. His father was an artist, but Wilbur planned to follow in the footsteps of his maternal grandfather and great-grandfather by pursuing a career in journalism. At Amherst, where he took his A.B. in 1942, he was editor of the college paper. During World War II he served overseas for two years with the 36th Infantry, and it was the experience of these years, he has said, that somehow drew him away from journalism and into the writing of poetry.

After the war he did graduate work at Harvard, receiving an M.A. in English literature in 1947. In that same year he published his first book, *The Beautiful Changes and Other Poems.* Later came *Ceremony and Other Poems* (1950); *Things of This World* (1956); *Advice to a Prophet* (1961); and *The Poems of Richard Wilbur* (1963). He has taught at Harvard and Wellesley, and is now a Professor of English at Wesleyan University in Connecticut. Among the many honors he has received are the Prix de Rome and a Pulitzer Prize. In 1961 he took an extended trip to the Soviet Union as a cultural representative for the U. S. State Department, under the cultural exchange program.

As a poet who is also a university professor, Wilbur has resolved for himself the alleged conflict between the traditionalist and experimentalist views of the poet's role. He is at one with, say, Allen Ginsberg insofar as both see it as the poet's responsibility to creatively criticize the values of society; but whereas Ginsberg as alienated artist chooses to drop out in order to minimize the society's pressures (real and imagined), Wilbur as poet-citizen chooses to perform from within, deliberately taking the "risk of corruption."

Further reading: Donald Hill, *Richard Wilbur,* 1968.

Still, Citizen Sparrow

From *Ceremony and Other Poems* (1950). The poem may be said to have two parts—stanzas 1-3 and stanzas 4-6. How are they related?

Still, citizen sparrow, this vulture which you call
Unnatural, let him but lumber again to air
Over the rotten office, let him bear
The carrion ballast up, and at the tall

Tip of the sky lie cruising. Then you'll see
That no more beautiful bird is in heaven's height,
No wider more placid wings, no watchfuller flight;
He shoulders nature there, the frightfully free,

The naked-headed one. Pardon him, you
Who dart in the orchard aisles, for it is he
Devours death, mocks mutability,
Has heart to make an end, keeps nature new.

Thinking of Noah, childheart, try to forget
How for so many bedlam hours his saw
Soured the song of birds with its wheezy gnaw,
And the slam of his hammer all the day beset

The people's ears. Forget that he could bear
To see the towns like coral under the keel,
And the fields so dismal deep. Try rather to feel
How high and weary it was, on the waters where

He rocked his only world, and everyone's.
Forgive the hero, you who would have died
Gladly with all you knew; he rode that tide
To Ararat; all men are Noah's sons.

Love Calls Us to the Things of This World

What is it, exactly, that rapes "every blessed day"? What is so valuable about "laundry"?

This and the three following poems are from *Things of This World* (1956).

The eyes open to a cry of pulleys,
And spirited from sleep, the astounded soul
Hangs for a moment bodiless and simple
As false dawn.
Outside the open window
The morning air is all awash with angels.

Some are in bed-sheets, some are in blouses,
Some are in smocks: but truly there they are.
Now they are rising together in calm swells
Of halcyon feeling, filling whatever they wear
With the deep joy of their impersonal breathing;

Now they are flying in place, conveying
The terrible speed of their omnipresence, moving
And staying like white water; and now of a sudden
They swoon down into so rapt a quiet
That nobody seems to be there.
The soul shrinks

From all that it is about to remember,
From the punctual rape of every blessèd day,
And cries,
"Oh, let there be nothing on earth but laundry,
Nothing but rosy hands in the rising steam
And clear dances done in the sight of heaven."

Yet, as the sun acknowledges
With a warm look the world's hunks and colors,
The soul descends once more in bitter love
To accept the waking body, saying now
In a changed voice as the man yawns and rises,

"Bring them down from their ruddy gallows;
Let there be clean linen for the backs of thieves;
Let lovers go fresh and sweet to be undone,
And the heaviest nuns walk in a pure floating
Of dark habits,
keeping their difficult balance."

A Voice from under the Table

To Robert and Jane Brooks

How shall the wine be drunk, or the woman known?
I take this world for better or for worse,
But seeing rose carafes conceive the sun
My thirst conceives a fierier universe:
And then I toast the birds in the burning trees
That chant their holy lucid drunkenness;
I swallowed all the phosphorus of the seas
Before I fell into this low distress.

You upright people all remember how
Love drove you first to the woods, and there you
heard

The loose-mouthed wind complaining *Thou* and
Thou;
My gawky limbs were shuddered by the word.
Most of it since was nothing but charades
To spell that hankering out and make an end,
But the softest hands against my shoulder-blades
Only increased the crying of the wind.

For this the goddess rose from the midland sea
And stood above the famous wine-dark wave,
To ease our drouth with clearer mystery
And be a South to all our flights of love.
And down by the selfsame water I have seen
A blazing girl with skin like polished stone
Splashing until a far-out breast of green
Arose and with a rose contagion shone.

"A myrtle-shoot in hand, she danced; her hair
Cast on her back and shoulders a moving shade."
Was it some hovering light that showed her fair?
Was it of chafing dark that light was made?
Perhaps it was Archilochus' fantasy,
Or that his saying sublimed the thing he said.
All true enough; and true as well that she
Was beautiful, and danced, and is now dead.

Helen was no such high discarnate thought
As men in dry symposia pursue,
But was as bitterly fugitive, not to be caught
By what men's arms in love or fight could do.
Groan in your cell; rape Troy with sword and flame;
The end of thirst exceeds experience.
A devil told me it was all the same
Whether to fail by spirit or by sense.

God keep me a damned fool, nor charitably
Receive me into his shapely resignations.
I am a sort of martyr, as you see,
A horizontal monument to patience.
The calves of waitresses parade about
My helpless head upon this sodden floor.
Well, I am down again, but not yet out.
O sweet frustrations, I shall be back for more.

Beasts

In this poem the human world is seen through the lens of the animal world. Who are the true "beasts" (in the pejorative sense of the word) and why? How is one supposed to feel about the "ripped mouse"?

Beasts in their major freedom
Slumber in peace tonight. The gull on his ledge
Dreams in the guts of himself the moon-plucked
waves below,
And the sunfish leans on a stone, slept
By the lyric water,

In which the spotless feet
Of deer make dulcet splashes, and to which
The ripped mouse, safe in the owl's talon, cries
Concordance. Here there is no such harm
And no such darkness

As the selfsame moon observes
Where, warped in window-glass, it sponsors now
The werewolf's painful change. Turning his head
away
On the sweaty bolster, he tries to remember
The mood of manhood,

But lies at last, as always,
Letting it happen, the fierce fur soft to his face,
Hearing with sharper ears the wind's exciting
minors,
The leaves' panic, and the degradation
Of the heavy streams.

Meantime, at high windows
Far from thicket and pad-fall, suitors of
excellence
Sigh and turn from their work to construe again the
painful
Beauty of heaven, the lucid moon
And the risen hunter,

Making such dreams for men
As told will break their hearts as always, bringing
Monsters into the city, crows on the public statues,
Navies fed to the fish in the dark
Unbridled waters.

A Baroque Wall-Fountain in the Villa Sciarra

For Dore and Adja

Under the bronze crown
Too big for the head of the stone cherub whose feet
A serpent has begun to eat,
Sweet water brims a cockle and braids down

Past spattered mosses, breaks
On the tipped edge of a second shell, and fills
The massive third below. It spills
In threads then from the scalloped rim, and makes

A scrim or summery tent
For a faun-ménage and their familiar goose.

Happy in all that ragged, loose
Collapse of water, its effortless descent

And flatteries of spray,
The stocky god upholds the shell with ease,
Watching, about his shaggy knees,
The goatish innocence of his babes at play;

His fauness all the while
Leans forward, slightly, into a clambering mesh
Of water-lights, her sparkling flesh
In a saecular ecstasy, her blinded smile

Bent on the sand floor
Of the trefoil pool, where ripple-shadows come
And go in swift reticulum,
More addling to the eye than wine, and more

Interminable to thought
Than pleasure's calculus. Yet since this all
Is pleasure, flash, and waterfall,
Must it not be too simple? Are we not

More intricately expressed
In the plain fountains that Maderna set
Before St. Peter's—the main jet
Struggling aloft until it seems at rest

In the act of rising, until
The very wish of water is reversed,
That heaviness borne up to burst
In a clear, high, cavorting head, to fill

With blaze, and then in gauze
Delays, in a gnatlike shimmering, in a fine
Illumined version of itself, decline,
And patter on the stones its own applause?

If that is what men are
Or should be, if those water-saints display
The pattern of our areté,[1]
What of these showered fauns in their bizarre,

Spangled, and plunging house?
They are at rest in fulness of desire
For what is given, they do not tire
Of the smart of the sun, the pleasant water-douse

And riddled pool below,
Reproving our disgust and our ennui
With humble insatiety.
Francis, perhaps, who lay in sister snow

A Baroque Wall-Fountain. [1]*Areté*, a Greek word meaning roughly "virtue." [Wilbur's note.]

Before the wealthy gate
Freezing and praising, might have seen in this
No trifle, but a shade of bliss—
That land of tolerable flowers, that state

As near and far as grass
Where eyes become the sunlight, and the hand
Is worthy of water: the dreamt land
Toward which all hungers leap, all pleasures pass.

Advice to a Prophet

Author's note: "Hephaestus, invoked by Achilles, scalded the river Xanthus (Scamander) in *Iliad* xxi." This poem and the next are from *Advice to a Prophet* (1961).

When you come, as you soon must, to the streets of our city,
Mad-eyed from stating the obvious,
Not proclaiming our fall but begging us
In God's name to have self-pity,

Spare us all word of the weapons, their force and range,
The long numbers that rocket the mind;
Our slow, unreckoning hearts will be left behind,
Unable to fear what is too strange.

Nor shall you scare us with talk of the death of the race.
How should we dream of this place without us?—
The sun mere fire, the leaves untroubled about us,
A stone look on the stone's face?

Speak of the world's own change. Though we cannot conceive
Of an undreamt thing, we know to our cost
How the dreamt cloud crumbles, the vines are blackened by frost,
How the view alters. We could believe,

If you told us so, that the white-tailed deer will slip
Into perfect shade, grown perfectly shy,
The lark avoid the reaches of our eye,
The jack-pine lose its knuckled grip

On the cold ledge, and every torrent burn
As Xanthus once, its gliding trout
Stunned in a twinkling. What should we be without
The dolphin's arc, the doves return,

These things in which we have seen ourselves and spoken?
Ask us, prophet, how we shall call
Our natures forth when that live tongue is all
Dispelled, that glass obscured or broken

In which we have said the rose of our love and the
clean
Horse of our courage, in which beheld
The singing locust of the soul unshelled,
And all we mean or wish to mean.

Ask us, ask us whether with the worldless rose
Our hearts shall fail us; come demanding
Whether there shall be lofty or long standing
When the bronze annals of the oak-tree close.

She

What was her beauty in our first estate
When Adam's will was whole, and the least thing
Appeared the gift and creature of his king,
How should we guess? Resemblance had to wait

For separation, and in such a place
She so partook of water, light, and trees
As not to look like any one of these.
He woke and gazed into her naked face.

But then she changed, and coming down amid
The flocks of Abel and the fields of Cain,
Clothed in their wish, her Eden graces hid,
A shape of plenty with a mop of grain,

She broke upon the world, in time took on
The look of every labor and its fruits.
Columnar in a robe of pleated lawn
She cupped her patient hand for attributes,

Was radiant captive of the farthest tower
And shed her honor on the fields of war,
Walked in her garden at the evening hour,
Her shadow like a dark ogival door,

Breasted the seas for all the westward ships
And, come to virgin country, changed again—
A moonlike being truest in eclipse,
And subject goddess of the dreams of men.

Tree, temple, valley, prow, gazelle, machine,
More named and nameless than the morning star,
Lovely in every shape, in all unseen,
We dare not wish to find you as you are,

Whose apparition, biding time until
Desire decay and bring the latter age,
Shall flourish in the ruins of our will
And deck the broken stones like saxifrage.

ALLEN GINSBERG [1926-]

Ginsberg's commitment to his vision and art is passionate and unqualified, but his poems are filled with pain, filth, and degradation which seek from each reader a compassion directed not so much toward Ginsberg as toward the humanity, terrible though it may sometimes be, that each man must himself share.

The best-known and most talented of the "Beat" poets, Ginsberg was born in Newark, New Jersey, the son of a schoolteacher and lyric poet. He grew up in Paterson, went to high school there, and then to Columbia, graduating in 1948. Another and older Paterson poet, William Carlos Williams, remembered Ginsberg as a boy: "He was physically slight of build and mentally much disturbed by the life he encountered about him during those years after the First World War as it was exhibited to him in and about New York City. He was always on the point of 'going away'—where, it didn't seem to matter; he disturbed me, I never thought he'd live to grow up and write a book of poems. His ability to survive, travel, and go on writing astonished me." When Ginsberg did grow up, he began to lead a sometimes sensational public life as a world traveler, an experimenter with hallucinogens and narcotics, and an unabashed homosexual. He also worked at a number of weirdly assorted jobs: dishwasher, seaman in the merchant marine, spotwelder in the Brooklyn Navy Yard, night porter in a Denver department store, book reviewer for

Newsweek, and actor in films. He published *Howl and Other Poems* in 1956, *Empty Mirror* and *Kaddish and Other Poems* in 1960, *Reality Sandwiches* in 1963, and *Jukebox All'idrogeno* in 1965.

The facts of his biography and his unconventional life-style have unfortunately tended to obscure the poems, or at least to make readers more conscious of reading Allen Ginsberg than of reading poetry. Yet Ginsberg is generally a serious poet, sometimes a brilliant poet, working out of a venerable philosophical and aesthetic tradition. He is in a sense a visionary poet in the tradition of Blake, Emerson, and Whitman. As a visionary, however, Ginsberg is unable to celebrate and bless. The tension of his poetry is the tension generated when the seer confronts the world that cannot validate his visions, but befouls them. And in his frustration, that seer in turn befouls the world he sees. The poet is a "madman bum and angel beat in Time," Ginsberg writes in "Howl," and the pun implicit in "beat" suggests the paradox of his being. A visionary can glimpse what is beatific, what creates delight in existence, but a visionary can also be oppressed by a sense of the disorder and decay inherent in time. Ginsberg discovers the "archangel of soul" by making "incarnate gaps in Time and Space through/images juxtaposed," but the perception and expression of the horrible is barely relieved. The expression is created partly through the use of language which is as coarse as both some aspects of human experience and some human views of experience.

It is not possible to defend Ginsberg's every use of language, but it is important to consider the possibility of some aesthetic justification. Of course he frequently uses words simply to shock (therapeutically, he would say) or to avoid the trouble of searching out more precise terms; and when he does so, their impact is weakened. A word to which custom has assigned shock-value, if used indiscriminately and often as verb, noun, adjective, adverb, and expletive, soon loses its affectiveness in any context. Yet this language may also be Ginsberg's way of making his poetic vision "happen" in a poem. In the literature formed by the romantic tradition, images of sexual intercourse abound as metaphors for the idealistic theory that, at the deepest levels, self and nature are "married," that dualistic views are myopic, that real Being lies in undifferentiated unity. From this perspective, many of the notorious passages in Ginsberg—like the less explicit, less grossly stated images of romanticism—may be seen as renditions of the success, or failure, of poetic vision.

Howl

For Carl Solomon

All the poems reprinted here are from *Howl and Other Poems* (1956).

I

I saw the best minds of my generation destroyed by madness, starving hysterical naked,
dragging themselves through the negro streets at dawn looking for an angry fix,
angelheaded hipsters burning for the ancient heavenly connection to the starry dynamo in the machinery of night,
who poverty and tatters and hollow-eyed and high sat up smoking in the supernatural darkness of cold-water flats floating across the tops of cities contemplating jazz,
who bared their brains to Heaven under the El and saw Mohammedan angels staggering on tenement roofs illuminated,
who passed through universities with radiant cool eyes hallucinating Arkansas and Blake-light tragedy among the scholars of war,

who were expelled from the academies for crazy & publishing obscene odes on the windows of the skull,
who cowered in unshaven rooms in underwear, burning their money in wastebaskets and listening to the Terror through the wall,
who got busted in their pubic beards returning through Laredo with a belt of marijuana for New York,
who ate fire in paint hotels or drank turpentine in Paradise Alley, death, or purgatoried their torsos night after night
with dreams, with drugs, with waking nightmares, alcohol and cock and endless balls,
incomparable blind streets of shuddering cloud and lightning in the mind leaping toward poles of Canada & Paterson, illuminating all the motionless world of Time between,
Peyote solidities of halls, backyard green tree cemetery dawns, wine drunkenness over the rooftops, storefront boroughs of teahead joyride neon blinking traffic light, sun and moon and tree vibrations in the roaring winter dusks of Brooklyn, ashcan rantings and kind king light of mind,
who chained themselves to subways for the endless ride from Battery to holy Bronx on benzedrine until the noise of wheels and children brought them down shuddering mouth-wracked and battered bleak of brain all drained of brilliance in the drear light of Zoo,
who sank all night in submarine light of Bickford's floated out and sat through the stale beer afternoon in desolate Fugazzi's, listening to the crack of doom on the hydrogen jukebox,
who talked continuously seventy hours from park to pad to bar to Bellevue to museum to the Brooklyn Bridge,
a lost battalion of platonic conversationalists jumping down the stoops off fire escapes off windowsills off Empire State out of the moon,
yacketayakking screaming vomiting whispering facts and memories and anecdotes and eyeball kicks and shocks of hospitals and jails and wars,
whole intellects disgorged in total recall for seven days and nights with brilliant eyes, meat for the Synagogue cast on the pavement,
who vanished into nowhere Zen New Jersey leaving a trail of ambiguous picture postcards of Atlantic City Hall,
suffering Eastern sweats and Tangerian bone-grindings and migraines of China under junk-withdrawal in Newark's bleak furnished room,
who wandered around and around at midnight in the railroad yard wondering where to go, and went, leaving no broken hearts,
who lit cigarettes in boxcars boxcars boxcars racketing through snow toward lonesome farms in grandfather night,
who studied Plotinus Poe St. John of the Cross telepathy and bop kaballa because the cosmos instinctively vibrated at their feet in Kansas,
who loned it through the streets of Idaho seeking visionary indian angels who were visionary indian angels,
who thought they were only mad when Baltimore gleamed in supernatural ecstasy,
who jumped in limousines with the Chinaman of Oklahoma on the impulse of winter midnight streetlight smalltown rain,
who lounged hungry and lonesome through Houston seeking jazz or sex or soup, and followed the brilliant Spaniard to converse about America and Eternity, a hopeless task, and so took ship to Africa,
who disappeared into the volcanoes of Mexico leaving behind nothing but the shadow of dungarees and the lava and ash of poetry scattered in fireplace Chicago,
who reappeared on the West Coast investigating the F.B.I. in beards and shorts with big pacifist eyes sexy in their dark skin passing out incomprehensible leaflets,
who burned cigarette holes in their arms protesting the narcotic tobacco haze of Capitalism,
who distributed Supercommunist pamphlets in Union Square weeping and undressing while the sirens of Los Alamos wailed them down, and wailed down Wall, and the Staten Island ferry also wailed,
who broke down crying in white gymnasiums naked and trembling before the machinery of other skeletons,

who bit detectives in the neck and shrieked with delight in policecars for committing no crime but their own wild cooking pederasty and intoxication,
who howled on their knees in the subway and were dragged off the roof waving genitals and manuscripts,
who let themselves be fucked in the ass by saintly motorcyclists, and screamed with joy,
who blew and were blown by those human seraphim, the sailors, caresses of Atlantic and Caribbean love,
who balled in the morning in the evenings in rosegardens and the grass of public parks and cemeteries scattering their semen freely to whomever come who may,
who hiccupped endlessly trying to giggle but wound up with a sob behind a partition in a Turkish Bath when the blonde & naked angel came to pierce them with a sword,
who lost their loveboys to the three old shrews of fate the one eyed shrew of the heterosexual dollar the one eyed shrew that winks out of the womb and the one eyed shrew that does nothing but sit on her ass and snip the intellectual golden threads of the craftsman's loom,
who copulated ecstatic and insatiate with a bottle of beer a sweetheart a package of cigarettes a candle and fell off the bed, and continued along the floor and down the hall and ended fainting on the wall with a vision of ultimate cunt and come eluding the last gyzym of consciousness,
who sweetened the snatches of a million girls trembling in the sunset, and were red eyed in the morning but prepared to sweeten the snatch of the sunrise, flashing buttocks under barns and naked in the lake,
who went out whoring through Colorado in myriad stolen night-cars, N.C., secret hero of these poems, cocksman and Adonis of Denver—joy to the memory of his innumerable lays of girls in empty lots & diner backyards, moviehouses' rickety rows, on mountaintops in caves or with gaunt waitresses in familiar roadside lonely petticoat upliftings & especially secret gas-station solipsisms of johns, & hometown alleys too,
who faded out in vast sordid movies, were shifted in dreams, woke on a sudden Manhattan, and picked themselves up out of basements hungover with heartless Tokay and horrors of Third Avenue iron dreams & stumbled to unemployment offices,
who walked all night with their shoes full of blood on the snowbank docks waiting for a door in the East River to open to a room full of steamheat and opium,
who created great suicidal dramas on the apartment cliff-banks of the Hudson under the wartime blue floodlight of the moon & their heads shall be crowned with laurel in oblivion,
who ate the lamb stew of the imagination or digested the crab at the muddy bottom of the rivers of Bowery,
who wept at the romance of the streets with their pushcarts full of onions and bad music,
who sat in boxes breathing in the darkness under the bridge, and rose up to build harpsichords in their lofts,
who coughed on the sixth floor of Harlem crowned with flame under the tubercular sky surrounded by orange crates of theology,
who scribbled all night rocking and rolling over lofty incantations which in the yellow morning were stanzas of gibberish,
who cooked rotten animals lung heart feet tail borsht & tortillas dreaming of the pure vegetable kingdom,
who plunged themselves under meat trucks looking for an egg,
who threw their watches off the roof to cast their ballot for Eternity outside of Time, & alarm clocks fell on their heads every day for the next decade,
who cut their wrists three times successively unsuccessfully, gave up and were forced to open antique stores where they thought they were growing old and cried,
who were burned alive in their innocent flannel suits on Madison Avenue amid blasts of leaden verse & the tanked-up clatter of the iron regiments of fashion & the nitroglycerine shrieks of the fairies of advertising & the mustard gas of sinister intelligent editors, or were run down by the drunken taxicabs of Absolute Reality,
who jumped off the Brooklyn Bridge this actually happened and walked away unknown and forgotten into the ghostly daze of Chinatown soup alleyways & firetrucks, not even one free beer,

who sang out of their windows in despair, fell out of the subway window, jumped in the filthy Passaic, leaped on negroes, cried all over the street, danced on broken wineglasses barefoot smashed phonograph records of nostalgic European 1930's German jazz finished the whiskey and threw up groaning into the bloody toilet, moans in their ears and the blast of colossal steamwhistles,
who barreled down the highways of the past journeying to each other's hotrod-Golgotha jail-solitude watch or Birmingham jazz incarnation,
who drove crosscountry seventytwo hours to find out if I had a vision or you had a vision or he had a vision to find out Eternity,
who journeyed to Denver, who died in Denver, who came back to Denver & waited in vain, who watched over Denver & brooded & loned in Denver and finally went away to find out the Time, & now Denver is lonesome for her heroes,
who fell on their knees in hopeless cathedrals praying for each other's salvation and light and breasts, until the soul illuminated its hair for a second,
who crashed through their minds in jail waiting for impossible criminals with golden heads and the charm of reality in their hearts who sang sweet blues to Alcatraz,
who retired to Mexico to cultivate a habit, or Rocky Mount to tender Buddha or Tangiers to boys or Southern Pacific to the black locomotive or Harvard to Narcissus to Woodlawn to the daisychain or grave,
who demanded sanity trials accusing the radio of hypnotism & were left with their insanity & their hands & a hung jury,
who threw potato salad at CCNY lecturers on Dadaism and subsequently presented themselves on the granite steps of the madhouse with shaven heads and harlequin speech of suicide, demanding instantaneous lobotomy,
and who were given instead the concrete void of insulin metrasol electricity hydrotherapy psychotherapy occupational therapy pingpong & amnesia,
who in humorless protest overturned only one symbolic pingpong table, resting briefly in catatonia,
returning years later truly bald except for a wig of blood, and tears and fingers, to the visible madman doom of the wards of the madtowns of the East,
Pilgrim State's Rockland's and Greystone's foetid halls, bickering with the echoes of the soul, rocking and rolling in the midnight solitude-bench dolmen-realms of love, dream of life a nightmare, bodies turned to stone as heavy as the moon,
with mother finally °°°°°°, and the last fantastic book flung out of the tenement window, and the last door closed at 4 AM and the last telephone slammed at the wall in reply and the last furnished room emptied down to the last piece of mental furniture, a yellow paper rose twisted on a wire hanger in the closet, and even that imaginary, nothing but a hopeful little bit of hallucination—
ah, Carl, while you are not safe I am not safe, and now you're really in the total animal soup of time—
and who therefore ran through the icy streets obsessed with a sudden flash of the alchemy of the use of the ellipse the catalog the meter & the vibrating plane,
who dreamt and made incarnate gaps in Time & Space through images juxtaposed, and trapped the archangel of the soul between 2 visual images and joined the elemental verbs and set the noun and dash of consciousness together jumping with sensation of Pater Omnipotens Aeterna Deus
to recreate the syntax and measure of poor human prose and stand before you speechless and intelligent and shaking with shame, rejected yet confessing out the soul to conform to the rhythm of thought in his naked and endless head,
the madman bum and angel beat in Time, unknown, yet putting down here what might be left to say in time come after death,
and rose reincarnate in the ghostly clothes of jazz in the goldhorn shadow of the band and blew the suffering of America's naked mind for love into an eli eli lamma lamma sabacthani saxophone cry that shivered the cities down to the last radio
with the absolute heart of the poem of life butchered out of their own bodies good to eat a thousand years.

II

What sphinx of cement and aluminum bashed open their skulls and ate up their brains and imagination?
Moloch! Solitude! Filth! Ugliness! Ashcans and unobtainable dollars! Children screaming under the stairways! Boys sobbing in armies! Old men weeping in the parks!
Moloch! Moloch! Nightmare of Moloch! Moloch the loveless! Mental Moloch! Moloch the heavy judger of men!
Moloch the incomprehensible prison! Moloch the crossbone soulless jailhouse and Congress of sorrows! Moloch whose buildings are judgement! Moloch the vast stone of war! Moloch the stunned governments!
Moloch whose mind is pure machinery! Moloch whose blood is running money! Moloch whose fingers are ten armies! Moloch whose breast is a cannibal dynamo! Moloch whose ear is a smoking tomb!
Moloch whose eyes are a thousand blind windows! Moloch whose skyscrapers stand in the long streets like endless Jehovahs! Moloch whose factories dream and croak in the fog! Moloch whose smokestacks and antennae crown the cities!
Moloch whose love is endless oil and stone! Moloch whose soul is electricity and banks! Moloch whose poverty is the specter of genius! Moloch whose fate is a cloud of sexless hydrogen! Moloch whose name is the Mind!
Moloch in whom I sit lonely! Moloch in whom I dream Angels! Crazy in Moloch! Cocksucker in Moloch! Lacklove and manless in Moloch!
Moloch who entered my soul early! Moloch in whom I am a consciousness without a body! Moloch who frightened me out of my natural ecstasy! Moloch whom I abandon! Wake up in Moloch! Light streaming out of the sky!
Moloch! Moloch! Robot apartments! invisible suburbs! skeleton treasuries! blind capitals! demonic industries! spectral nations! invincible madhouses! granite cocks! monstrous bombs!
They broke their backs lifting Moloch to Heaven! Pavements, trees, radios, tons! lifting the city to Heaven which exists and is everywhere about us!
Visions! omens! hallucinations! miracles! ecstasies! gone down the American river!
Dreams! adorations! illuminations! religions! the whole boatload of sensitive bullshit!
Breakthroughs! over the river! flips and crucifixions! gone down the flood! Highs! Epiphanies! Despairs! Ten years' animal screams and suicides! Minds! New loves! Mad generation! down on the rocks of Time!
Real holy laughter in the river! They saw it all! the wild eyes! the holy yells! They bade farewell! They jumped off the roof! to solitude! waving! carrying flowers! Down to the river! into the street!

III

Carl Solomon! I'm with you in Rockland
    where you're madder than I am
I'm with you in Rockland
    where you must feel very strange
I'm with you in Rockland
    where you imitate the shade of my mother
I'm with you in Rockland
    where you've murdered your twelve secretaries
I'm with you in Rockland
    where you laugh at this invisible humor
I'm with you in Rockland
    where we are great writers on the same dreadful typewriter
I'm with you in Rockland
    where your condition has become serious and is reported on the radio
I'm with you in Rockland
    where the faculties of the skull no longer admit the worms of the senses
I'm with you in Rockland

where you drink the tea of the breasts of the spinsters of Utica
I'm with you in Rockland
where you pun on the bodies of your nurses the harpies of the Bronx
I'm with you in Rockland
where you scream in a straightjacket that you're losing the game of the actual pingpong of the abyss
I'm with you in Rockland
where you bang on the catatonic piano the soul is innocent and immortal it should never die ungodly in an armed madhouse
I'm with you in Rockland
where fifty more shocks will never return your soul to its body again from its pilgrimage to a cross in the void
I'm with you in Rockland
where you accuse your doctors of insanity and plot the Hebrew socialist revolution against the fascist national Golgotha
I'm with you in Rockland
where you will split the heavens of Long Island and resurrect your living human Jesus from the superhuman tomb
I'm with you in Rockland
where there are twentyfive-thousand mad comrades all together singing the final stanzas of the Internationale
I'm with you in Rockland
where we hug and kiss the United States under our bedsheets the United States that coughs all night and won't let us sleep
I'm with you in Rockland
where we wake up electrified out of the coma by our own souls' airplanes roaring over the roof they've come to drop angelic bombs the hospital illuminates itself imaginary walls collapse O skinny legions run outside O starry-spangled shock of mercy the eternal war is here O victory forget your underwear we're free
I'm with you in Rockland
in my dreams you walk dripping from a sea-journey on the highway across America in tears to the door of my cottage in the Western night

San Francisco 1955-56

Footnote to Howl

Holy! Holy! Holy! Holy! Holy! Holy! Holy! Holy! Holy! Holy! Holy! Holy! Holy! Holy! Holy!
The world is holy! The soul is holy! The skin is holy! The nose is holy! The tongue and cock and hand and asshole holy!
Everything is holy! everybody's holy! everywhere is holy! everyday is in eternity! Everyman's an angel!
The bum's as holy as the seraphim! the madman is holy as you my soul are holy!
The typewriter is holy the poem is holy the voice is holy the hearers are holy the ecstasy is holy!
Holy Peter holy Allen holy Solomon holy Lucien holy Kerouac holy Huncke holy Burroughs holy Cassady holy the unknown buggered and suffering beggars holy the hideous human angels!
Holy my mother in the insane asylum! Holy the cocks of the grandfathers of Kansas!
Holy the groaning saxophone! Holy the bop apocalypse! Holy the jazzbands marijuana hipsters peace & junk & drums!
Holy the solitudes of skyscrapers and pavements! Holy the cafeterias filled with the millions! Holy the mysterious rivers of tears under the streets!
Holy the lone juggernaut! Holy the vast lamb of the middle-class! Holy the crazy shepherds of rebellion! Who digs Los Angeles IS Los Angeles!
Holy New York Holy San Francisco Holy Peoria & Seattle Holy Paris Holy Tangiers Holy Moscow Holy Istanbul!
Holy time in eternity holy eternity in time holy the clocks in space holy the fourth dimension holy the fifth International holy the Angel in Moloch!

Holy the sea holy the desert holy the railroad holy the locomotive holy the visions holy the hallucinations holy the miracles holy the eyeball holy the abyss!
Holy forgiveness! mercy! charity! faith! Holy! Ours! bodies! suffering! magnanimity!
Holy the supernatural extra brilliant intelligent kindness of the soul!

A Supermarket in California

On a number of occasions Ginsberg has paid homage to Whitman. What in Whitman—formal as well as thematic—might appeal to Ginsberg? What does Ginsberg mean by Whitman's "enumerations"?

What thoughts I have of you tonight, Walt Whitman, for I walked down the sidestreets under the trees with a headache self-conscious looking at the full moon.

In my hungry fatigue, and shopping for images, I went into the neon fruit supermarket, dreaming of your enumerations!

What peaches and what penumbras! Whole families shopping at night! Aisles full of husbands! Wives in the avocados, babies in the tomatoes!—and you, Garcia Lorca, what were you doing down by the watermelons?

I saw you, Walt Whitman, childless, lonely old grubber, poking among the meats in the refrigerator and eyeing the grocery boys.

I heard you asking questions of each: Who killed the pork chops? What price bananas? Are you my Angel?

I wandered in and out of the brilliant stacks of cans following you, and followed in my imagination by the store detective.

We strode down the open corridors together in our solitary fancy tasting artichokes, possessing every frozen delicacy, and never passing the cashier.

Where are we going, Walt Whitman? The doors close in an hour. Which way does your beard point tonight?

(I touch your book and dream of our odyssey in the supermarket and feel absurd.)

Will we walk all night through solitary streets? The trees add shade to shade, lights out in the houses, we'll both be lonely.

Will we stroll dreaming of the lost America of love past blue automobiles in driveways, home to our silent cottage?

Ah, dear father, graybeard, lonely old courage-teacher, what America did you have when Charon quit poling his ferry and you got out on a smoking bank and stood watching the boat disappear on the black waters of Lethe?

Berkeley 1955

Sunflower Sutra

I walked on the banks of the tincan banana dock and sat down under the huge shade of a Southern Pacific locomotive to look at the sunset over the box house hills and cry.
Jack Kerouac sat beside me on a busted rusty iron pole, companion, we thought the same thoughts of the soul, bleak and blue and sad-eyed, surrounded by the gnarled steel roots of trees of machinery.
The oily water on the river mirrored the red sky, sun sank on top of final Frisco peaks, no fish in that stream, no hermit in those mounts, just ourselves rheumy-eyed and hungover like old bums on the riverbank, tired and wily.
Look at the Sunflower, he said, there was a dead gray shadow against the sky, big as a man, sitting dry on top of a pile of ancient sawdust—
—I rushed up enchanted—it was my first sunflower, memories of Blake—my visions—Harlem
and Hells of the Eastern rivers, bridges clanking Joes Greasy Sandwiches, dead baby carriages,

black treadless tires forgotten and unretreaded, the poem of the riverbank, condoms & pots, steel knives, nothing stainless, only the dank muck and the razor sharp artifacts passing into the past—
and the gray Sunflower poised against the sunset, crackly bleak and dusty with the smut and smog and smoke of olden locomotives in its eye—
corolla of bleary spikes pushed down and broken like a battered crown, seeds fallen out of its face, soon-to-be-toothless mouth of sunny air, sunrays obliterated on its hairy head like a dried wire spiderweb,
leaves stuck out like arms out of the stem, gestures from the sawdust root, broke pieces of plaster fallen out of the black twigs, a dead fly in its ear,
Unholy battered old thing you were, my sunflower O my soul, I loved you then!
The grime was no man's grime but death and human locomotives,
all that dress of dust, that veil of darkened railroad skin, that smog of cheek, that eyelid of black mis'ry, that sooty hand or phallus or protuberance of artificial worse-than-dirt—industrial—modern—all that civilization spotting your crazy golden crown—
and those blear thoughts of death and dusty loveless eyes and ends and withered roots below, in the home-pile of sand and sawdust, rubber dollar bills, skin of machinery, the guts and innards of the weeping coughing car, the empty lonely tincans with their rusty tongues alack, what more could I name, the smoked ashes of some cock cigar, the cunts of wheelbarrows and the milky breasts of cars, wornout asses out of chairs & sphincters of dynamos—all these
entangled in your mummied roots—and you there standing before me in the sunset, all your glory in your form!
A perfect beauty of a sunflower! a perfect excellent lovely sunflower existence! a sweet natural eye to the new hip moon, woke up alive and excited grasping in the sunset shadow sunrise golden monthly breeze!
How many flies buzzed round you innocent of your grime, while you cursed the heavens of the railroad and your flower soul?
Poor dead flower? when did you forget you were a flower? when did you look at your skin and decide you were an impotent dirty old locomotive? the ghost of a locomotive? the specter and shade of a once powerful mad American locomotive?
You were never no locomotive, Sunflower, you were a sunflower!
And you Locomotive, you are a locomotive, forget me not!
So I grabbed up the skeleton thick sunflower and stuck it at my side like a scepter,
and deliver my sermon to my soul, and Jack's soul too, and anyone who'll listen,
—We're not our skin of grime, we're not our dread bleak dusty imageless locomotive, we're all beautiful golden sunflowers inside, we're blessed by our own seed & golden hairy naked accomplishment-bodies growing into mad black formal sunflowers in the sunset, spied on by our eyes under the shadow of the mad locomotive riverbank sunset Frisco hilly tincan evening sitdown vision.

Berkeley 1955

In back of the real

This relatively simple lyric may be studied profitably as characteristic of most of Ginsberg's poems. Here, as in "Sunflower Sutra" and in "Howl," we find the poet meditating upon the homely particular, intent (as usual) in seeing even in the common things of life a more than common, sometimes even a spiritual loveliness at the core of things. Sometimes the poet can see through the filth, to the hidden beauty, sometimes he cannot: this is the central problem in Ginsberg.

railroad yard in San Jose
I wandered desolate
in front of a tank factory

and sat on a bench
near the switchman's shack.

A flower lay on the hay on
the asphalt highway
—the dread hay flower
I thought—It had a
brittle black stem and
corolla of yellowish dirty
spikes like Jesus' inchlong
crown, and a soiled
dry center cotton tuft
like a used shaving brush
that's been lying under
the garage for a year.

Yellow, yellow flower, and
flower of industry,
tough spikey ugly flower,
flower nonetheless,
with the form of the great yellow
Rose in your brain!
This is the flower of the World.

DENISE LEVERTOV [1923-]

DENISE LEVERTOV was born in London of Welsh and Russian-Jewish parents. Her mother was descended from Angel Jones of Mold, a mystic, mentioned in the poem "Illustrious Ancestors." Her father, Paul Philip Levertoff, was descended from the noted Hasid, Schneour Zalman, who figures in "Illustrious Ancestors" as "the Rav of Northern White Russia." While preparing in Königsberg for the rabbinate, Levertoff became a Christian and devoted his life thereafter toward the unification of Judaism and Christianity, writing numerous books in Hebrew, Russian, German, and English. The atmosphere of the household was liberal, intellectual, and artistic. Except for four years' study of ballet, Denise never had any formal schooling; she and her sister were educated, in the main, at home. Denise listened to the British Broadcasting Company's daily school programs, received private instruction in French, art, and music, read history on her own, and frequented the Victoria and Albert Museum and the National Gallery. The family enjoyed reading aloud, the parents to their daughters from the great masters of fiction, and the girls to each other from such English poets as Wordsworth, Keats, Tennyson, and Auden. Denise was seventeen when her first poem was published in *Poetry Quarterly* in 1940; her first book of poems, *The Double Image*, appeared in 1946.

During World War II she worked as a civilian nurse in London. After the war, in 1946-47, she was, variously, tutor, nursemaid, and bookstore employee in France, England, Holland, and Switzerland. In December 1947 she married Mitchell Goodman, a Harvard student. The Goodmans now make their home in New York.

She had her first American publication in 1948 in Kenneth Rexroth's anthology of young British poets. Her first volume of poems to be published in the United States—her second book—was *Here and Now* (1957), and it has been followed by four more: *Overland to the Islands; With Eyes at the Back of Our Heads; The Jacob's Ladder;* and *O Taste and See.* She has been poetry editor of the *Nation,* has taught at Drew, C.C.N.Y., and Vassar, and has received a number of awards, including a Guggenheim Fellowship and a citation and grant from the National Institute of Arts and Letters.

Most critics agree that Denise Levertov is a genuinely American poet, writing in the American idiom and in the Emerson-Whitman tradition of American poetry. How is it that this British-born poet of Russian and Welsh heritage can so easily merge into the Whitman stream? One may speculate that a part of the answer lies, ironically, in her Russian origins, particularly in her father's Hasidism, which Martin Buber (seeing the parallel with his own "I-Thou" concept) has described as belief in the "joy in the world as it is, in life as it is, in every hour of life in this world, as that hour is." Levertov herself has said that "Hasidism has given me since childhood a sense of marvels, of wonder. . . . The Hasidim were a little bit like the Franciscans . . . there was a recognition and joy in the physical world. And a sense of wonder at creation, and I think I've always felt something like that. . . . I think that's what poems are all about." It is not a long step from here to Whitman's joy in the actualities of life, to his sense that within and behind his experience lay a deeper mode of being.

Along with such philosophical considerations go other more purely aesthetic ones. When Levertov says that poems ought to exhibit "inner harmony," she is speaking of the poet as maker, not as seer. Indeed, the distinction between *maker* and *seer* is one of her central concerns: "I believe poets are instruments on which the power of poetry plays. But they are also *makers,* craftsmen. It is given to the seer to see, but it is then his responsibility to communicate what he sees, that they who cannot see may see. . . . I believe every space and comma is a living part of the poem and has its function." A comparison of these remarks with those of Emerson in "The Poet" and of T. S. Eliot in "Tradition and the Individual Talent" is instructive.

Most typically, as in part five of "Six Variations," Denise Levertov attempts in her poetry to communicate her sense of the immediacy of finite experience, while at the same time suggesting that "joy in the physical world" is not a mere function of seeing, but of seeing in a particular way: disorder and defilement are not denied but are transformed into harmony by the poet's vision.

Further reading: Linda Wagner, *Denise Levertov,* 1967.

Merritt Parkway

The modern "parkway" or "freeway" is an ambivalent symbol. In one sense it suggests the linkage of people ordinarily separated by great distances. Here, however, it is a figure for isolation—people caught in endless, private motion. This poem and the next are from *Overland to the Islands* (1958).

As if it were
forever that they move, that we
keep moving—

Under a wan sky where
as the lights went on a star
pierced the haze & now
follows steadily
a constant
above our six lanes
the dreamlike continuum . . .

And the people—ourselves!
the humans from inside the
cars, apparent
only at gasoline stops
unsure,
eyeing each other

drink coffee hastily at the
slot machines & hurry
back to the cars
vanish

into them forever, to
keep moving—

Houses now & then beyond the
sealed road, the trees / trees, bushes
passing by, passing
the cars that
keep moving ahead of
us, past us, pressing behind us
and
over left, those that come
toward us shining too brightly
moving relentlessly

in six lanes, gliding
north & south, speeding with
a slurred sound—

Illustrious Ancestors

The Rav
of Northern White Russia declined,
in his youth, to learn the
language of birds, because
the extraneous did not interest him; nevertheless
when he grew old it was found
he understood them anyway, having
listened well, and as it is said, "prayed
with the bench and the floor." He used
what was at hand—as did
Angel Jones of Mold, whose meditations
were sewn into coats and britches.
Well, I would like to make,
thinking some line still taut between me and them,
poems direct as what the birds said,
hard as a floor, sound as a bench,
mysterious as the silence when the tailor
would pause with his needle in the air.

With Eyes at the Back of Our Heads

This and the following poem are from *With Eyes at the Back of Our Heads* (1959).

With eyes at the back of our heads
we see a mountain
not obstructed with woods but laced
here and there with feathery groves.

The doors before us in a facade
that perhaps has no house in back of it
are too narrow, and one is set high
with no doorsill. The architect sees
the imperfect proposition and
turns eagerly to the knitter.
Set it to rights!
The knitter begins to knit.

For we want
to enter the house, if there is a house,
to pass through the doors at least
into whatever lies beyond them,

we want to enter the arms
of the knitted garment. As one
is re-formed, so the other,
in proportion.

When the doors widen
when the sleeves admit us
the way to the mountain will clear,
the mountain we see with
eyes at the back of our heads, mountain
green, mountain
cut of limestone, echoing
with hidden rivers, mountain
of short grass and subtle shadows.

To the Snake

Green Snake, when I hung you round my neck
and stroked your cold, pulsing throat
as you hissed to me, glinting
arrowy gold scales, and I felt
the weight of you on my shoulders,
and the whispering silver of your dryness
sounded close at my ears—

Green Snake—I swore to my companions that
certainly
you were harmless! But truly
I had no certainty, and no hope, only desiring
to hold you, for that joy,
which left
a long wake of pleasure, as the leaves moved
and you faded into the pattern
of grass and shadows, and I returned
smiling and haunted, to a dark morning.

The Jacob's Ladder

The ladder is a metaphor for the poem itself, its nature and value. Why the insistence that the ladder "is of stone," not "a radiant evanescence"? This and the three poems that follow are from *The Jacob's Ladder* (1961).

The stairway is not
a thing of gleaming strands

a radiant evanescence
for angels' feet that only glance in their tread, and
need not
touch the stone.

It is of stone.
A rosy stone that takes
a glowing tone of softness
only because behind it the sky is a doubtful, a
doubting
night gray.

A stairway of sharp
angles, solidly built.
One sees that the angels must spring
down from one step to the next, giving a little
lift of the wings:

and a man climbing
must scrape his knees, and bring
the grip of his hands into play. The cut stone
consoles his groping feet. Wings brush past him.
The poem ascends.

Matins

I

The authentic! Shadows of it
sweep past in dreams, one could say imprecisely,
evoking the almost-silent
ripping apart of giant
sheets of cellophane. No.
It thrusts up close. Exactly in dreams
it has you off-guard, you
recognize it before you have time.
For a second before waking
the alarm bell is a red conical hat, it
takes form.

II

The authentic! I said
rising from the toilet seat.
The radiator in rhythmic knockings
spoke of the rising steam.
The authentic, I said
breaking the handle of my hairbrush as I
brushed my hair in
rhythmic strokes: That's it,
that's joy, it's always
a recognition, the known
appearing fully itself, and
more itself than one knew.

III

The new day rises
as heat rises,
knocking in the pipes
with rhythms it seizes for its own
to speak of its invention—
the real, the new-laid
egg whose speckled shell
the poet fondles and must break
if he will be nourished.

IV

A shadow painted where
yes, a shadow must fall.
The cow's breath
not forgotten in the mist, in the
words. Yes,
verisimilitude draws up
heat in us, zest
to follow through,
follow through,
follow
transformations of day
in its turning, in its becoming.

V

Stir the holy grains, set
the bowls on the table and
call the child to eat.

While we eat we think,
as we think an undercurrent
of dream runs through us
faster than thought
towards recognition.

Call the child to eat,
send him off, his mouth
tasting of toothpaste, to go down
into the ground, into a roaring train
and to school.

His cheeks are pink
his black eyes hold his dreams, he has left
forgetting his glasses.

Follow down the stairs at a clatter
to give them to him and save
his clear sight.

Cold air
comes in at the street door.

VI

The authentic! It rolls
just out of reach, beyond
running feet and
stretching fingers, down
the green slope and into
the black waves of the sea.
Speak to me, little horse, beloved,
tell me
how to follow the iron ball,
how to follow through to the country
beneath the waves
to the place where I must kill you and you step out
of your bones and flystrewn meat
tall, smiling, renewed,
formed in your own likeness.

VII

Marvelous Truth, confront us
at every turn,
in every guise, iron ball,
egg, dark horse, shadow,
cloud
of breath on the air,

dwell
in our crowded hearts
our steaming bathrooms, kitchens full of
things to be done, the
ordinary streets.

Thrust close your smile
that we know you, terrible joy.

To the Reader

As you read, a white bear leisurely
pees, dyeing the snow
saffron,

and as you read, many gods
lie among lianas: eyes of obsidian
are watching the generations of leaves,

and as you read
the sea is turning its dark pages,
turning
its dark pages.

Six Variations

I

We have been shown
how Basket drank—
and old man Volpe the cobbler
made up what words he didn't know
so that his own son, even
laughed at him: but with respect.

II

two flutes! How close
to each other they move
in mazing figures,
never touching, never
breaking the measure,
as gnats dance in
summer haze all afternoon, over
shallow water sprinkled
with mottled blades of willow—
two flutes!

III

Shlup, shlup, the dog
as it laps up
water
makes intelligent
music, resting
now and then to
take breath in irregular
measure.

IV

When I can't
strike one spark from you,
when you don't
look me in the eye,
when your answers
come
slowly, dragging
their feet, and furrows
change your face,
when the sky is a cellar
with dirty windows,
when furniture
obstructs the body, and bodies
are heavy furniture coated
with dust-time
for a lagging leaden pace,

a short sullen line,
measure
of heavy heart and
cold eye.

V

The quick of the sun that gilds
broken pebbles in sidewalk cement
and the iridescent
spit, that defiles and adorns!
Gold light in blind love does not distinguish
one surface from another, the savor
is the same to its tongue, the fluted
cylinder of a new ashcan a dazzling silver,
the smooth flesh of screaming children a quietness,
it is all
a jubilance, the light catches up
the disordered street in its apron,
broken fruitrinds shine in the gutter.

VI

Lap up the vowels
of sorrow,
transparent, cold
water-darkness welling
up from the white sand.
Hone the blade
of a scythe to cut swathes
of light sound in the mind.
Through the hollow globe, a ring
of frayed rusty scrapiron,
is it the sea that shines?
Is it a road at the world's edge?

LEROI JONES [1934-]

LeRoi Jones was born to parents who lived comfortably in the middle of a society he later rejected because it deprived him of much more than it gave. As a result of his experience, he is determined that as many people as possible avoid a similar deprivation of the values that make life cohere and enable a man to form a sense of himself. "I mean you know how difficult and how hard it was for us," he says bluntly. "I want to make it so difficult for my son to be mediocre. Just impossible. I mean just by the example—and by that, all of our sons. Just to make it impossible for them to be without knowledge. So that a dude walking into your house will just by the very fact of it have been taught something." Jones has moved beyond his early "Beat" poetry and literature of protest; he has become involved in "cultural nationalism," a militant movement which re-creates values and life-styles in order to enhance the sense of purpose and self-esteem among America's black community.

Jones's father was a postal supervisor and his mother a social worker. He grew up in Newark, New Jersey. From high school he entered Rutgers University on a science scholarship, but, feeling like an outsider, left after a year. He transferred to Howard University, graduated in 1954 at nineteen, and entered the Air Force as an enlisted man. It was while in the service that he decided to become a writer. He had been stationed much of the time in Puerto Rico, and his experiences there and elsewhere awakened him to a sense of urgency about his future and to an awareness of the discrepancy between his potential and his accomplishment. When he was discharged from the Air Force in 1957, he returned to school, took advanced courses at Columbia and the New School for Social Research, and earned a master's degree in German literature.

For a while he lectured at Columbia, edited publications in Greenwich Village, and wrote newspaper and magazine articles on jazz. At the same time, he was developing his own idiom and technique in poetry, drama, and prose fiction. In 1961 his collection of poems called *Preface to a Twenty Volume Suicide Note* was published, and the impact of his personality and writings began to be more widely felt. He continued to support himself by teaching, and later moved from Columbia to the New School, where he taught creative writing. With the off-Broadway production of his plays *Dutchman* and *The Slave* in 1964, and the appearance in that same year of his second book of poems, *The Dead Lecturer,* he was fully launched on his controversial and productive career as poet, playwright, novelist, short-story writer, polemicist, and activist. His militant involvement in social and political affairs in Newark, where he now lives, has brought him at least as much notoriety as his poems and plays, and the results have been in some ways as creatively successful.

His work can sometimes shock, particularly when he touches on truths previously unrecognized, or experiences largely unknown, in the brutal "language of confrontation." In his poetry he is often simply obscure, yet obscure in such a way that a single phrase or image can suddenly invest an entire poem with beauty and meaning. The difficulty with Jones's poems may be partly due to the way they so characteristically grow by a process of association rather than by logic or sequence. His work can appear savage in the extreme, yet it is the savagery of an artist who can also say, "The things that I really like to do, you know, are very quiet." This apparent contradiction may create a tension that releases the creative process in him, and it may also suggest to the reader some useful insights for approaching his work.

An Agony. As Now.

This and the following poem are reprinted from *The Dead Lecturer* (1964).

I am inside someone
who hates me. I look
out from his eyes. Smell
what fouled tunes come in
to his breath. Love his
wretched women.

Slits in the metal, for sun. Where
my eyes sit turning, at the cool air
the glance of light, or hard flesh
rubbed against me, a woman, a man,
without shadow, or voice, or meaning.

This is the enclosure (flesh,
where innocence is a weapon. An
abstraction. Touch. (Not mine.
Or yours, if you are the soul I had
and abandoned when I was blind and had
my enemies carry me as a dead man
(if he is beautiful, or pitied.

It can be pain. (As now, as all his
flesh hurts me.) It can be that. Or
pain. As when she ran from me into
that forest.
Or pain, the mind
silver spiraled whirled against the
sun, higher than even old men thought
God would be. Or pain. And the other. The
yes. (Inside his books, his fingers. They
are withered yellow flowers and were never
beautiful.) The yes. You will, lost soul, say
'beauty.' Beauty, practiced, as the tree. The
slow river. A white sun in its wet sentences.
Or, the cold men in their gale. Ecstasy. Flesh
or soul. The yes. (Their robes blown. Their bowls
empty. They chant at my heels, not at yours.) Flesh
or soul, as corrupt. Where the answer moves too
quickly.
Where the God is a self, after all.)

Cold air blown through narrow blind eyes. Flesh,
white hot metal. Glows as the day with its sun.
It is a human love, I live inside. A bony skeleton
you recognize as words or simple feeling.

But it has no feeling. As the metal, is hot, it is not,
given to love.

It burns the thing
inside it. And that thing
screams.

The Liar

What I thought was love
in me, I find a thousand instances
as fear. (Of the tree's shadow

winding around the chair, a distant music
of frozen birds rattling
in the cold.
Where ever I go to claim
my flesh, there are entrances
of spirit. And even its comforts
are hideous uses I strain
to understand.
Though I am a man
who is loud
on the birth
of his ways. Publicly redefining
each change in my soul, as if I had predicted
them,
and profited, biblically, even tho
their chanting weight,
erased familiarity
from my face.
A question I think,
an answer; whatever sits
counting the minutes
till you die.

When they say, "It is Roi
who is dead?" I wonder
who will they mean?

Fiction of the Fifties and Sixties

BERNARD MALAMUD [1914-]

In one of Malamud's novels a character says of another: "He suffered, he endured, but with hope." This theme of human suffering, endurance, and aspiration is central to the fiction of a writer who has said that he refuses to accept the "colossally deceitful devaluation of man in this day," man as "fragmented, abbreviated, other-directed and organizational."

Born in Brooklyn in 1914, of Russian-Jewish immigrant stock, and growing up during the depression, Malamud was aware not only of the sufferings of his people but of what it is to be poverty-stricken in a city slum. Although his hard-working father provided him with what he has called a normal American childhood, he knew his neighborhood well, and his compassion for the poor, the bereft, the rootless, and the outcast suffuses all his work. He attended Erasmus High School in Brooklyn, received his A.B. from the College of the City of New York in 1936, and an M.A. in English literature from Columbia. Teaching has been his way of life: in the New York City night schools (1940-49), at the Oregon State University (1949-61), and since 1961 at Bennington College in Vermont, with one year as a visiting lecturer at Harvard. During these years of strenuous teaching, he as strenuously wrote short stories and novels that earned him critical acclaim, best-seller listing, and several awards including a Pulitzer Prize.

Malamud is a writer of great integrity. He says that writing must be "true," and he deplores contemporary fiction which is preoccupied with the bizarre, the psychotic, and the soul-sick because he believes that it does not give an honest picture of life. He believes that fiction should be concerned with love and beauty and hope, because these do exist even among the meanest and most insignificant of mankind. Fiction, he says, must "enflame, destroy, change the reader"; it must have emotional depth. He reaches this depth through depiction, in most of his work, of Jewish character and Jewish ways of thinking and living, much in the same way that Faulkner uses the South as symbolic of something larger than itself. The suffering and oppression of the Jewish people, their resiliency, their pride, their strong fraternal and familial bonds, their inconsistencies, absurdities, failures—all this, in Malamud's work, comes to stand for common humanity.

The Malamud "hero" is a loser. Decent, caring, well-intentioned, inept, blundering, unlucky, he moves from failure to failure, yet often manages to achieve a kind of nobility, even an occasional triumph, though it may be nothing more spectacular than facing up to a fact or a responsibility. This character, the loser, appears in Malamud's first novel, a baseball story, *The Natural* (1952), as a naive boy from the West who strikes out the big name in the game and then is himself struck out. In *The Assistant* (1957) the loser is two distinct characters, a drifter of Italian immigrant extraction and a poor Jewish grocer, whose lives as victim and victimizer, oppressor and oppressed, become intertwined until finally the assistant becomes the grocer, the Italian becomes a Jew: suffering, being common to all men, makes all men indistinguishable. In *A New Life* (1961) the loser is a Jewish professor from the East in a Western state university; tender-hearted, inept, an erstwhile drunkard, he decides to reform his department and redeem himself, but ends with no money, no job, no prospects, another man's children, and a sickly, inconstant woman whom he no longer really wants. Trapped in a "windowless prison" that is "really himself, flawed edifice of failures, each one locking up tight the one before," he submits and shoulders his burden. In *The Fixer* (1966) once again there is a loser, but this time he is loser-turned-saint, and the setting is not contemporary America but Czarist Russia. Using an actual court case, in Kiev in 1913, of a man falsely accused of ritual child-murder, Malamud transforms the central character into a symbol of the living spirit which enables men to transcend both their humanity and their inhumanity.

A humanist, Malamud has said: "If you don't respect man, you cannot respect my work. I'm in defense of the human." In this defense, he has a formidable arsenal: his control of the language and a gift for dialogue that enables him to register unerringly both Yiddish and Gentile speech-rhythms; his ability to pinpoint the essence of a character, whether forlorn ghetto shopkeeper or fatuous college professor; his versatility of range, from low comedy to satire to lyricism. Both as a student of history and as a participant in the present, he combines a profound Jewish melancholy with the conviction that "life is holy." One of his characters, the grocer in *The Assistant*, perhaps speaks for the author when he says, "Life is hard enough. Why should we hurt somebody else? For everybody should be the best, not only for you or me. We ain't animals." Since much contemporary fiction assures us that man is only an animal, Malamud's vision of man as more than that may justify the view of those who would term him a modern classicist.

Further reading: *The Magic Barrel.* Sidney Richman, *Bernard Malamud,* 1966. Harry T. Moore, ed., *Contemporary American Novelists,* 1964.

The Magic Barrel

First published in *Partisan Review* (November 1954); reprinted here from *The Magic Barrel* (1958).

Not long ago there lived in uptown New York, in a small, almost meager room, though crowded with books, Leo Finkle, a rabbinical student in the Yeshivah University. Finkle, after six years of study, was to be ordained in June and had been advised by an acquaintance that he might find it easier to win himself a congregation if he were married. Since he had no present prospects of marriage, after two tormented days of turning it over in his mind, he called in Pinye Salzman, a marriage broker whose two-line advertisement he had read in the *Forward.*

The matchmaker appeared one night out of the dark fourth-floor hallway of the graystone rooming house where Finkle lived, grasping a black, strapped portfolio that had been worn thin with use. Salzman, who had been long in the business, was of slight but dignified build, wearing an old hat, and an overcoat too short and tight for him. He smelled frankly of fish, which he loved to eat, and although he was missing a few teeth, his presence was not displeasing, because of an amiable manner curiously contrasted with mournful eyes. His voice, his lips, his wisp of beard, his bony fingers were animated, but give him a moment of repose and his mild blue eyes revealed a depth of sadness, a characteristic that put Leo a little at ease although the situation, for him, was inherently tense.

He at once informed Salzman why he had asked him to come, explaining that his home was in Cleveland, and that but for his parents, who had married comparatively late in life, he was alone in the world. He had for six years devoted himself almost entirely to his studies, as a result of which, understandably, he had found himself without time for a social life and the company of young women. Therefore he thought it the better part of trial and error—of embarrassing fumbling—to call in an experienced person to advise him on these matters. He remarked in passing that the function of the marriage broker was ancient and honorable, highly approved in the Jewish community, because it made practical the necessary without hindering joy. Moreover, his own parents had been brought together by a matchmaker. They had made, if not a financially profitable marriage—since neither had possessed any worldly goods to speak of—at least a successful one in the sense of their everlasting devotion to each other. Salzman listened in embarrassed surprise, sensing a sort of apology. Later, however, he experienced a glow of pride in his work, an emotion that had left him years ago, and he heartily approved of Finkle.

The two went to their business. Leo had led Salzman to the only clear place in the room, a table near a window that overlooked the lamp-lit city. He seated himself at the matchmaker's side but facing him, attempting by an act of will to suppress the unpleasant tickle in his throat. Salzman eagerly unstrapped his portfolio and removed a loose rubber band from a thin packet of much-handled cards. As he flipped through them, a gesture and sound that physically hurt Leo, the student pretended not to see and gazed steadfastly out the window. Although it was still February, winter was on its last legs, signs of which he had for the first time in years begun to notice. He now observed the round white moon, moving high in the sky through a cloud menagerie, and watched with half-open mouth as it penetrated a huge hen, and dropped out of her like an egg laying itself. Salzman, though pretending through eyeglasses he had just slipped on, to be engaged in scanning the writing on the cards, stole occasional glances at the young man's distinguished face, noting with pleasure the long, severe scholar's nose, brown eyes heavy with learning, sensitive yet ascetic lips, and a certain, almost hollow quality of the dark cheeks. He gazed around at shelves upon shelves of books and let out a soft, contented sigh.

When Leo's eyes fell upon the cards, he counted six spread out in Salzman's hand.

"So few?" he asked in disappointment.

"You wouldn't believe me how much cards I got in my office," Salzman replied. "The drawers are already filled to the top, so I keep them now in a barrel, but is every girl good for a new rabbi?"

Leo blushed at this, regretting all he had revealed of himself in a curriculum vitae he had sent to Salzman. He had thought it best to acquaint him with his strict standards and specifications, but in having done so, felt he had told the marriage broker more than was absolutely necessary.

He hesitantly inquired, "Do you keep photographs of your clients on file?"

"First comes family, amount of dowry, also what kind promises," Salzman replied, unbuttoning his tight coat and settling himself in the chair. "After comes pictures, rabbi."

"Call me Mr. Finkle. I'm not yet a rabbi."

Salzman said he would, but instead called him doctor, which he changed to rabbi when Leo was not listening too attentively.

Salzman adjusted his horn-rimmed spectacles, gently cleared his throat and read in an eager voice the contents of the top card:

"Sophie P. Twenty four year. Widow one year. No children. Educated high school and two years college. Father promises eight thousand dollars. Has wonderful wholesale business. Also real estate. On the mother's side comes teachers, also one actor. Well known on Second Avenue."

Leo gazed up in surprise. "Did you say a widow?"

"A widow don't mean spoiled, rabbi. She lived with her husband maybe four months. He was a sick boy she made a mistake to marry him."

"Marrying a widow has never entered my mind."

"This is because you have no experience. A widow, especially if she is young and healthy like this girl, is a wonderful person to marry. She will be thankful to you the rest of her life. Believe me, if I was looking now for a bride, I would marry a widow."

Leo reflected, then shook his head.

Salzman hunched his shoulders in an almost imperceptible gesture of disappointment. He placed the card down on the wooden table and began to read another:

"Lily H. High school teacher. Regular. Not a substitute. Has savings and new Dodge car. Lived in Paris one year. Father is successful dentist thirty-five years. Interested in professional man. Well Americanized family. Wonderful opportunity.

"I knew her personally," said Salzman. "I wish you could see this girl. She is a doll. Also very intelligent. All day you could talk to her about books and theyater and what not. She also knows current events."

"I don't believe you mentioned her age?"

"Her age?" Salzman said, raising his brows. "Her age is thirty-two years."

Leo said after a while, "I'm afraid that seems a little too old."

Salzman let out a laugh. "So how old are you, rabbi?"

"Twenty-seven."

"So what is the difference, tell me, between twenty-seven and thirty-two? My own wife is seven years older than me. So what did I suffer?—Nothing. If Rothschild's a daughter wants to marry you, would you say on account her age, no?"

"Yes," Leo said dryly.

Salzman shook off the no in the yes. "Five years don't mean a thing. I give you my word that when you will live with her for one week you will forget her age. What does it mean five years—that she lived more and knows more than somebody who is younger? On this girl, God bless her, years are not wasted. Each one that it comes makes better the bargain."

"What subject does she teach in high school?"

"Languages. If you heard the way she speaks French, you will think it is music. I am in the business twenty-five years, and I recommend her with my whole heart. Believe me, I know what I'm talking, rabbi."

"What's on the next card?" Leo said abruptly.

Salzman reluctantly turned up the third card:

"Ruth K. Nineteen years. Honor student. Father offers thirteen thousand cash to the right bridegroom. He is a medical doctor. Stomach specialist with marvelous practice. Brother in law owns own garment business. Particular people."

Salzman looked as if he had read his trump card.

"Did you say nineteen?" Leo asked with interest.

"On the dot."

"Is she attractive?" He blushed. "Pretty?"

Salzman kissed his finger tips. "A little doll. On this I give you my word. Let me call the father tonight and you will see what means pretty."

But Leo was troubled. "You're sure she's that young?"

"This I am positive. The father will show you the birth certificate."

"Are you positive there isn't something wrong with her?" Leo insisted.

"Who says there is wrong?"

"I don't understand why an American girl her age should go to a marriage broker."

A smile spread over Salzman's face.

"So for the same reason you went, she comes."

Leo flushed. "I am pressed for time."

Salzman, realizing he had been tactless, quickly explained. "The father came, not her. He wants she should have the best, so he looks around himself. When we will locate the right boy he will introduce him and encourage. This makes a better marriage than if a young girl without experience takes for herself. I don't have to tell you this."

"But don't you think this young girl believes in love?" Leo spoke uneasily.

Salzman was about to guffaw but caught himself and said soberly, "Love comes with the right person, not before."

Leo parted dry lips but did not speak. Noticing that Salzman had snatched a glance at the next card, he cleverly asked, "How is her health?"

"Perfect," Salzman said, breathing with difficulty. "Of course, she is a little lame on her right foot from an auto accident that it happened to her when she was twelve years, but nobody notices on account she is so brilliant and also beautiful."

Leo got up heavily and went to the window. He felt curiously bitter and upbraided himself for having called in the marriage broker. Finally, he shook his head.

"Why not?" Salzman persisted, the pitch of his voice rising.

"Because I detest stomach specialists."

"So what do you care what is his business? After you marry her do you need him? Who says he must come every Friday night in your house?"

Ashamed of the way the talk was going, Leo dismissed Salzman, who went home with heavy, melancholy eyes.

Though he had felt only relief at the marriage broker's departure, Leo was in low spirits the next day. He explained it as arising from Salzman's failure to produce a suitable bride for him. He did not care for his type of clientele. But when Leo found himself hesitating whether to seek out another matchmaker, one more polished than Pinye, he wondered if it could be—his protestations to the contrary, and although he honored his father and mother—that he did not, in essence, care for the matchmaking institution? This thought he quickly put out of mind yet found himself still upset. All day he ran around in the woods—missed an important appointment, forgot to give out his laundry, walked out of a Broadway cafeteria without paying and had to run back with the ticket in his hand; had even not recognized his landlady in the street when she passed with a friend and courteously called out, "A good evening to you, Doctor Finkle." By nightfall, however, he had regained sufficient calm to sink his nose into a book and there found peace from his thoughts.

Almost at once there came a knock on the door.

Before Leo could say enter, Salzman, commercial cupid, was standing in the room. His face was gray and meager, his expression hungry, and he looked as if he would expire on his feet. Yet the marriage broker managed, by some trick of the muscles, to display a broad smile.

"So good evening. I am invited?"

Leo nodded, disturbed to see him again, yet unwilling to ask the man to leave.

Beaming still, Salzman laid his portfolio on the table. "Rabbi, I got for you tonight good news."

"I've asked you not to call me rabbi. I'm still a student."

"Your worries are finished. I have for you a first-class bride."

"Leave me in peace concerning this subject." Leo pretended lack of interest.

"The world will dance at your wedding."

"Please, Mr. Salzman, no more."

"But first must come back my strength," Salzman said weakly. He fumbled with the portfolio straps and took out of the leather case an oily paper bag, from which he extracted a hard, seeded roll and a small, smoked white fish. With a quick motion of his hand he stripped the fish out of its skin and began ravenously to chew. "All day in a rush," he muttered.

Leo watched him eat.

"A sliced tomato you have maybe?" Salzman hesitantly inquired.

"No."

The marriage broker shut his eyes and ate. When he had finished he carefully cleaned up the crumbs and rolled up the remains of the fish, in the paper bag. His spectacled eyes roamed the room until he discovered, amid some piles of books, a one-burner gas stove. Lifting his hat he humbly asked, "A glass tea you got, rabbi?"

Conscience-stricken, Leo rose and brewed the tea. He served it with a chunk of lemon and two cubes of lump sugar, delighting Salzman.

After he had drunk his tea, Salzman's strength and good spirits were restored.

"So tell me, rabbi," he said amiably, "you considered some more the three clients I mentioned yesterday?"

"There was no need to consider."

"Why not?"

"None of them suits me."

"What then suits you?"

Leo let it pass because he could give only a confused answer.

Without waiting for a reply, Salzman asked, "You remember this girl I talked to you—the high school teacher?"

"Age thirty-two?"

But, surprisingly, Salzman's face lit in a smile. "Age twenty-nine."

Leo shot him a look. "Reduced from thirty-two?"

"A mistake," Salzman avowed. "I talked today with the dentist. He took me to his safety deposit box and showed me the birth certificate. She was twenty-nine years last August. They made her a party in the mountains where she went for her vacation. When her father spoke to me the first time I forgot to write the age and I told you thirty-two, but now I remember this was a different client, a widow."

"The same one you told me about? I thought she was twenty-four?"

"A different. Am I responsible that the world is filled with widows?"

"No, but I'm not interested in them, nor for that matter, in school teachers."

Salzman pulled his clasped hands to his breast. Looking at the ceiling he devoutly exclaimed, "Yiddishe kinder, what can I say to somebody that he is not interested in high school teachers? So what then you are interested?"

Leo flushed but controlled himself.

"In what else will you be interested," Salzman went on, "if you not interested in this fine girl that she speaks four languages and has personally in the bank ten thousand dollars? Also her father guarantees further twelve thousand. Also she has a new car, wonderful clothes, talks on all subjects, and she will give you a first-class home and children. How near do we come in our life to paradise?"

"If she's so wonderful, why wasn't she married ten years ago?"

"Why?" said Salzman with a heavy laugh. "—Why? Because she is *partikiler*. This is why. She wants the *best*."

Leo was silent, amused at how he had entangled himself. But Salzman had aroused his interest in Lily H., and he began seriously to consider calling on her. When the marriage broker observed how intently Leo's mind was at work on the facts he had supplied, he felt certain they would soon come to an agreement.

Late Saturday afternoon, conscious of Salzman, Leo Finkle walked with Lily Hirschorn along Riverside Drive. He walked briskly and erectly, wearing with distinction the black fedora he had that morning taken with trepidation out of the dusty hat box on his closet shelf, and the heavy black Saturday coat he had thoroughly whisked clean. Leo also owned a walking stick, a present from a distant relative, but quickly put temptation aside and did not use it. Lily, petite and not unpretty, had on something signifying the approach of spring. She was au courant, animatedly, with all sorts of subjects, and he weighed her words and found her surprisingly sound—score another for Salzman, whom he uneasily sensed to be somewhere around, hiding perhaps high in a tree along the street, flashing the lady signals with a pocket mirror; or perhaps a cloven-hoofed Pan, piping nuptial ditties as he danced his invisible way before them, strewing wild buds on the walk and purple grapes in their path, symbolizing fruit of a union, though there was of course still none.

Lily startled Leo by remarking, "I was thinking of Mr. Salzman, a curious figure, wouldn't you say?"

Not certain what to answer, he nodded.

She bravely went on, blushing, "I for one am grateful for his introducing us. Aren't you?"

He courteously replied, "I am."

"I mean," she said with a little laugh—and it was all in good taste, or at least gave the effect of being not in bad—"do you mind that we came together so?"

He was not displeased with her honesty, recognizing that she meant to set the relationship aright, and understanding that it took a certain amount of experience in life, and courage, to want to do it quite that way. One had to have some sort of past to make that kind of beginning.

He said that he did not mind. Salzman's function was traditional and honorable—valuable for what it might achieve, which, he pointed out, was frequently nothing.

Lily agreed with a sigh. They walked on for a while and she said after a long silence, again with a nervous laugh, "Would you mind if I asked you something a little bit personal? Frankly, I find the subject fascinating." Although Leo shrugged, she went on half embarrassedly, "How was it that you came to your calling? I mean was it a sudden passionate inspiration?"

Leo, after a time, slowly replied, "I was always interested in the Law."

"You saw revealed in it the presence of the Highest?"

He nodded and changed the subject. "I understand that you spent a little time in Paris, Miss Hirschorn?"

"Oh, did Mr. Salzman tell you, Rabbi Finkle?" Leo winced but she went on, "It was ages ago and almost forgotten. I remember I had to return for my sister's wedding."

And Lily would not be put off. "When," she asked in a trembly voice, "did you become enamored of God?"

He stared at her. Then it came to him that she was talking not about Leo Finkle, but of a total stranger, some mystical figure, perhaps even passionate prophet that Salzman had dreamed up for her—no relation to the living or dead. Leo trembled with rage and weakness. The trickster had obviously sold her a bill of goods, just as he had him, who'd expected to become acquainted with a young lady of twenty-nine, only to behold, the moment he laid eyes upon her strained and anxious face, a woman past thirty-five and aging rapidly. Only his self control had kept him this long in her presence.

"I am not," he said gravely, "a talented religious person," and in seeking words to go on, found himself possessed by shame and fear. "I think," he said in a strained manner, "that I came to God not because I loved Him, but because I did not."

This confession he spoke harshly because its unexpectedness shook him.

Lily wilted. Leo saw a profusion of loaves of bread go flying like ducks high over his head, not unlike the winged loaves by which he had counted himself to sleep last night. Mercifully, then, it snowed, which he would not put past Salzman's machinations.

He was infuriated with the marriage broker and swore he would throw him out of the room the minute he reappeared. But Salzman did not come that night, and when Leo's anger had subsided, an unaccountable despair grew in its place. At first he thought this was caused by his disappointment in Lily, but before long it became evident that he had involved himself with Salzman without a true knowledge of his own intent. He gradually realized—with an emptiness that seized him with six hands—that he had called in the broker to find him a bride because he was incapable of doing it himself. This terrifying insight he had derived as a result of his meeting and conversation with Lily Hirschorn. Her probing questions had somehow irritated him into revealing—to himself more than her—the true nature of his relationship to God, and from that it had come upon him, with shocking force, that apart from his parents, he had never loved anyone. Or perhaps it went the other way, that he did not love God so well as he might, because he had not loved man. It seemed to Leo that his whole life stood starkly revealed and he saw himself for the first time as he truly was—unloved and loveless. This bitter but somehow not fully unexpected revelation brought him to a point of panic, controlled only by extraordinary effort. He covered his face with his hands and cried.

The week that followed was the worst of his life. He did not eat and lost weight. His beard darkened and grew ragged. He stopped attending seminars and almost never opened a book. He seriously considered leaving the Yeshivah, although he was deeply troubled at the thought of the loss of all his years of study—saw them like pages torn from a book, strewn over the city—and at the devastating effect of this decision upon his parents. But he had lived without knowledge of himself, and never in the Five Books and all the Commentaries—mea culpa—had the truth been revealed to him. He did not know where to turn, and in all this desolating loneliness there was no *to whom,* although he often thought of Lily but not once could bring himself to go downstairs and make the call. He became touchy and irritable, especially with his landlady, who asked him all manner of personal questions; on the other hand, sensing his own disagreeableness, he waylaid her on the stairs and apologized abjectly, until mortified, she ran from him. Out of this, however, he drew the consolation that he was a Jew and that a Jew suffered. But gradually, as the long and terrible week drew to a close, he regained his composure and some idea of purpose in life: to go on as planned. Although he was imperfect, the ideal was not. As for his quest of a bride, the thought of continuing afflicted him with anxiety and heartburn, yet perhaps with this new knowledge of himself he would be more successful than in the past. Perhaps love would now come to him and a bride to that love. And for this sanctified seeking who needed a Salzman?

The marriage broker, a skeleton with haunted eyes, returned that very night. He looked, withal, the picture of frustrated expectancy—as if he had steadfastly waited the week at Miss Lily Hirschorn's side for a telephone call that never came.

Casually coughing, Salzman came immediately to the point: "So how did you like her?"

Leo's anger rose and he could not refrain from chiding the matchmaker: "Why did you lie to me, Salzman?"

Salzman's pale face went dead white, the world had snowed on him.

"Did you not state that she was twenty-nine?" Leo insisted.

"I give you my word—"

"She was thirty-five, if a day. *At least* thirty-five."

"Of this don't be too sure. Her father told me—"

"Never mind. The worst of it was that you lied to her."

"How did I lie to her, tell me?"

"You told her things about me that weren't true. You made me out to be more, consequently less than I am. She had in mind a totally different person, a sort of semi-mystical Wonder Rabbi."

"All I said, you was a religious man."

"I can imagine."

Salzman sighed. "This is my weakness that I have," he confessed. "My wife says to me I shouldn't be a salesman, but when I have two fine people that they would be wonderful to be married, I am so happy that I talk too much." He smiled wanly. "This is why Salzman is a poor man."

Leo's anger left him. "Well, Salzman, I'm afraid that's all."

The marriage broker fastened hungry eyes on him.

"You don't want any more a bride?"

"I do," said Leo, "but I have decided to seek her in a different way. I am no longer interested in an arranged marriage. To be frank, I now admit the necessity of premarital love. That is, I want to be in love with the one I marry."

"Love?" said Salzman, astounded. After a moment he remarked, "For us, our love is our life, not for the ladies. In the ghetto they—"

"I know, I know," said Leo. "I've thought of it often. Love, I have said to myself, should be a by-product of living and worship rather than its own end. Yet for myself I find it necessary to establish the level of my need and fulfill it."

Salzman shrugged but answered, "Listen, rabbi, if you want love, this I can find for you also. I have such beautiful clients that you will love them the minute your eyes will see them."

Leo smiled unhappily. "I'm afraid you don't understand."

But Salzman hastily unstrapped his portfolio and withdrew a manila packet from it.

"Pictures," he said, quickly laying the envelope on the table.

Leo called after him to take the pictures away, but as if on the wings of the wind, Salzman had disappeared.

March came. Leo had returned to his regular routine. Although he felt not quite himself yet—lacked energy—he was making plans for a more active social life. Of course it would cost something, but he was an expert in cutting corners; and when there were no corners left he would make circles rounder. All the while Salzman's pictures had lain on the table, gathering dust. Occasionally as Leo sat studying, or enjoying a cup of tea, his eyes fell on the manila envelope, but he never opened it.

The days went by and no social life to speak of developed with a member of the opposite sex—it was difficult, given the circumstances of his situation. One morning Leo toiled up the stairs to his room and stared out the window at the city. Although the day was bright his view of it was dark. For some time he watched the people in the street below hurrying along and then turned with a heavy heart to his little room. On the table was the packet. With a sudden relentless gesture he tore it open. For a half-hour he stood by the table in a state of excitement, examining the photographs of the ladies Salzman had included. Finally, with a deep sigh he put them down. There were six, of varying degrees of attractiveness, but look at them long enough and they all became Lily Hirschorn: all past their prime, all starved behind bright smiles, not a true personality in the lot. Life, despite their frantic yoohooings, had passed them by; they were pictures in a brief case that stank of fish. After a while, however, as Leo attempted to return the photographs into the envelope, he found in it another, a snapshot of the type taken by a machine for a quarter. He gazed at it a moment and let out a cry.

Her face deeply moved him. Why, he could at first not say. It gave him the impression of youth—spring flowers, yet age—a sense of having been used to the bone, wasted; this came from the eyes, which were hauntingly familiar, yet absolutely strange. He had a vivid impression that he had met her before, but try as he might he could not place her although he could almost recall her name, as if he had read it in her own handwriting. No, this couldn't be; he would have remembered her. It was not, he affirmed, that she had an extraordinary beauty—no, though her face was attractive enough; it was that *something* about her moved him. Feature for feature, even some of the ladies of the photographs could do better; but she leaped forth to his heart—had *lived*, or wanted to—more than just wanted, perhaps regretted how she had lived—had somehow deeply suffered: it could be seen in the depths of those reluctant eyes, and from the way the light enclosed and shone from her, and within her, opening realms of possibility: this was her own. Her he desired. His head ached and eyes narrowed with the intensity of his gazing, then as if an obscure fog had blown up in the mind, he experienced fear of her and was aware that he had received an impression, somehow, of evil. He shuddered, saying softly, it is thus with us all. Leo brewed some tea in a small pot and sat sipping it without sugar, to calm himself. But before he had finished drinking, again with excitement he examined the face and found it good: good for Leo Finkle. Only such a one could understand him and help him seek whatever he was seeking. She might, perhaps, love him. How she had happened to be among the discards in Salzman's barrel he could never guess, but he knew he must urgently go find her.

Leo rushed downstairs, grabbed up the Bronx telephone book, and searched for Salzman's home address. He was not listed, nor was his office. Neither was he in the Manhattan book. But Leo remembered having written down the address on a slip of paper after he had read Salzman's advertisement in the "personals" column of the *Forward*. He ran up to his room and tore through his papers, without luck. It was exasperating. Just when he needed the matchmaker he was nowhere to be found. Fortunately Leo remembered to look in his wallet. There on a card he found his name written and a Bronx address. No phone number was listed, the reason—Leo now recalled—he had originally communicated with Salzman by letter. He got on his coat, put a hat on over his skull cap and hurried to the subway station. All the way to the far end of the Bronx he sat on the edge of his seat. He was more than once tempted to take out the picture and see if the girl's face was as he remembered it, but he refrained, allowing the snapshot to remain in his inside coat pocket, content to have her so close. When the train pulled into the station he was waiting at the door and bolted out. He quickly located the street Salzman had advertised.

The building he sought was less than a block from the subway, but it was not an office building, nor even a loft, nor a store in which one could rent office space. It was a very old tenement house. Leo found Salzman's name in pencil on a soiled tag under the bell and climbed three dark flights to his apartment. When he knocked, the door was opened by a thin, asthmatic, gray-haired woman, in felt slippers.

"Yes?" she said, expecting nothing. She listened without listening. He could have sworn he had seen her, too, before but knew it was an illusion.

"Salzman—does he live here? Pinye Salzman," he said, "the matchmaker?"

She stared at him a long minute. "Of course."

He felt embarrassed. "Is he in?"

"No." Her mouth, though left open, offered nothing more.

"The matter is urgent. Can you tell me where his office is?"

"In the air." She pointed upward.

"You mean he has no office?" Leo asked.

"In his socks."

He peered into the apartment. It was sunless and dingy, one large room divided by a half-open curtain, beyond which he could see a sagging metal bed. The near side of the room was crowded with rickety chairs, old bureaus, a three-legged table, racks of cooking utensils, and all the apparatus of a kitchen. But there was no sign of Salzman or his magic barrel, probably also a figment of the imagination. An odor of frying fish made Leo weak to the knees.

"Where is he?" he insisted. "I've got to see your husband."

At length she answered, "So who knows where he is? Every time he thinks a new thought he runs to a different place. Go home, he will find you."

"Tell him Leo Finkle."

She gave no sign she had heard.

He walked downstairs, depressed.

But Salzman, breathless, stood waiting at his door.

Leo was astounded and overjoyed. "How did you get here before me?"

"I rushed."

"Come inside."

They entered. Leo fixed tea, and a sardine sandwich for Salzman. As they were drinking he reached behind him for the packet of pictures and handed them to the marriage broker.

Salzman put down his glass and said expectantly, "You found somebody you like?"

"Not among these."

The marriage broker turned away.

"Here is the one I want." Leo held forth the snapshot.

Salzman slipped on his glasses and took the picture into his trembling hand. He turned ghastly and let out a groan.

"What's the matter?" cried Leo.

"Excuse me. Was an accident this picture. She isn't for you."

Salzman frantically shoved the manila packet into his portfolio. He thrust the snapshot into his pocket and fled down the stairs.

Leo, after momentary paralysis, gave chase and cornered the marriage broker in the vestibule. The landlady made hysterical outcries but neither of them listened.

"Give me back the picture, Salzman."

"No." The pain in his eyes was terrible.

"Tell me who she is then."

"This I can't tell you. Excuse me."

He made to depart, but Leo, forgetting himself, seized the matchmaker by his tight coat and shook him frenziedly.

"Please," sighed Salzman. "*Please.*"

Leo ashamedly let him go. "Tell me who she is," he begged. "It's very important for me to know."

"She is not for you. She is a wild one—wild, without shame. This is not a bride for a rabbi."

"What do you mean wild?"

"Like an animal. Like a dog. For her to be poor was a sin. This is why to me she is dead now."

"In God's name, what do you mean?"

"Her I can't introduce to you," Salzman cried.

"Why are you so excited?"

"Why, he asks," Salzman said, bursting into tears. "This is my baby, my Stella, she should burn in hell."

Leo hurried up to bed and hid under the covers. Under the covers he thought his life through. Although he soon fell asleep he could not sleep her out of his mind. He woke, beating his breast. Though he prayed to be rid of her, his prayers went unanswered. Through days of torment he endlessly struggled not to love her; fearing success, he escaped it. He then concluded to convert her to goodness, himself to God. The idea alternately nauseated and exalted him.

He perhaps did not know that he had come to a final decision until he encountered Salzman in a Broadway cafeteria. He was sitting alone at a rear table, sucking the bony remains of a fish. The marriage broker appeared haggard, and transparent to the point of vanishing.

Salzman looked up at first without recognizing him. Leo had grown a pointed beard and his eyes were weighted with wisdom.

"Salzman," he said, "love has at last come to my heart."

"Who can love from a picture?" mocked the marriage broker.

"It is not impossible."

"If you can love her, then you can love anybody. Let me show you some new clients that they just sent me their photographs. One is a little doll."

"Just her I want," Leo murmured.

"Don't be a fool, doctor. Don't bother with her."

"Put me in touch with her, Salzman," Leo said humbly. "Perhaps I can be of service."

Salzman had stopped eating and Leo understood with emotion that it was now arranged.

Leaving the cafeteria, he was, however, afflicted by a tormenting suspicion that Salzman had planned it all to happen this way.

Leo was informed by letter that she would meet him on a certain corner, and she was there one spring night, waiting under a street lamp. He appeared, carrying a small bouquet of violets and rosebuds. Stella stood by the lamp post, smoking. She wore white with red shoes, which fitted his expectations, although in a troubled moment he had imagined the dress red, and only the shoes white. She waited uneasily and shyly. From afar he saw that her eyes—clearly her father's—were filled with desperate innocence. He pictured, in her, his own redemption. Violins and lit candles revolved in the sky. Leo ran forward with flowers outthrust.

Around the corner, Salzman, leaning against a wall, chanted prayers for the dead.

JAMES BALDWIN [1924–]

James Baldwin has become one of the most articulate and powerful literary spokesmen for the cause of Negro rights in America. He has polemicized with missionary fervor in a variety of forms, mainly prose essays, his central thesis that complete integration of the Negro into American life is inextricably bound up with realization of the democratic principles on which the nation was founded. Until this has been accomplished, he believes, American professions of liberty and equality cannot be made viable for either white or black. "I do not see how one can escape the conclusion," he wrote in 1961, "that the Negro's status in this country is not only a cruel injustice, but a grave liability." In his fiction and his two plays, as well as in his essays, Baldwin has skillfully and effectively rung the infinite changes on this prevailing idea—that the victims of segregation are as much the white race as the Negroes because the myth of white supremacy prevents them from facing their own weaknesses and hypocrisies. The thrust of his writing derives in part from his interpretation of the civil rights issue in terms of his own heroic struggle for self-identity from a poverty-stricken childhood in Harlem to his present role as an internationally known author and messiah of his people.

He was the oldest of nine children in a family which lived during the 1930's on the bare margin of subsistence and which had as its head a stepfather, a proud, bitter, even paranoid man whose harshness could not be forgiven by his children even after his death. The boy attended public schools in New York, graduating from De Witt Clinton High School where he excelled in English and was editor of the literary magazine. A homely boy with large eyes and a frail physique, he was made to feel an outcast by his more extroverted classmates, but was encouraged in his literary efforts by his teachers. At fourteen he became a Holy Roller, preaching "the Word" in competition with his clergyman stepfather. During World War II, he worked in defense plants in New Jersey, where he first experienced Jim Crow racism. In his early twenties, determined to become a writer, he moved to Greenwich Village, earning money at the usual hard jobs available to blacks, and writing nights. With essays on the Negro and book reviews, he achieved publication in *Commentary,* the *Nation,* and the *New Leader.* He was also working on a novel. In 1945, with the assistance of Richard Wright, Baldwin obtained a Saxton Trust Award, the first of many grants and fellowships in his career.

A Rosenwald Fellowship in 1948 enabled him to go to Europe, where for nine years he lived an expatriate life, in Paris and Switzerland, with occasional business trips back to his homeland. This was his real apprenticeship as a writer, a time of hard work, loneliness, and self-discovery. Mirrored in his own destiny he saw the "complex fate" of Henry James as an American writer in Europe, a fate yet further compounded for a black American. In Paris he met Camus and Norman Mailer, and came to know the work of André Gide. Often near starvation in his self-imposed exile, he completed three books: *Go Tell It on the Mountain* (1953), an autobiographical account of his boyhood and religious conversion; *Notes of a Native Son* (1955), essays on the Negro's situation and on his own life in Harlem and Europe; and *Giovanni's Room* (1956), a novel of homosexuality.

After his return to America in 1957 ("I decided to return here because I was afraid to") his reputation grew rapidly, and he began to take part in the expanding struggle over civil rights. *Nobody Knows My Name: More Notes of a Native Son* (1961) describes some of these experiences. With *The Fire Next Time* (1963) he carried on his crusade in more essays, including a discussion of the Black Muslim movement. Two plays, *Amen Corner* and *Blues for Mister Charlie,* were more propagandistic than dramatic; the latter, played on Broadway in 1964, was based on an episode of race-murder and handled racial discrimination as a disease of white society. As a lecturer to sympathetic audiences he has been profoundly influential, and his occasional appearances on radio and television programs have demonstrated his ability to hold listeners spellbound with his mellow, cultivated voice. He has been for some years a member of the national advisory board of CORE.

In Baldwin's fiction, Negro rights and homosexuality are pervasive themes. His second novel, *Another Country* (1962), is a story of sexual deviation and miscegenation. His first collection of short stories, *Going to Meet the Man* (1965), showed his ability to transmute his own experience and to write natural dialogue, though it also revealed his lack of a sure sense of form. Both his novels and his short fictions follow a fairly straightforward, documentary method drawn from the slice-of-life naturalism of the thirties.

Baldwin's strength as a writer lies in the sincerity and urgency of his convictions, in his gift for self-revelation, and in the narrative drive which has a certain mesmeric fascination, like listening to a skillful story-telling preacher. In all his writings on his reiterated subject of race relations, he has not so much offered solutions as stated movingly and dramatically, in terms of his own search for identity, how it feels to be black in America.

Further reading: *Going to Meet the Man. Notes of a Native Son.* Fern Marja Eckman, *The Furious Passage of James Baldwin,* 1966.

This Morning, This Evening, So Soon

First published in the *Atlantic Monthly* (September 1960); reprinted here from *Going to Meet the Man* (1965).

"You are full of nightmares," Harriet tells me. She is in her dressing gown and has cream all over her face. She and my older sister, Louisa, are going out to be girls together. I suppose they have many things to talk about—they have *me* to talk about, certainly—and they do not want my presence. I have been given a bachelor's evening. The director of the film which has brought us such incredible and troubling riches will be along later to take me out to dinner.

I watch her face. I know that it is quite impossible for her to be as untroubled as she seems. Her self-control is mainly for my benefit—my benefit, and Paul's. Harriet comes from orderly and progressive Sweden and has reacted against all the advanced doctrines to which she has been exposed by becoming steadily and beautifully old-fashioned. We never fought in front of Paul, not even when he was a baby. Harriet does not so much believe in protecting children as she does in helping them to build a foundation on which they can build and build again, each time life's high-flying steel ball knocks down everything they have built.

Whenever I become upset, Harriet becomes very cheerful and composed. I think she began to learn how to do this over eight years ago, when I returned from my only visit to America. Now, perhaps, it has become something she could not control if she wished to. This morning, at breakfast, when I yelled at Paul, she averted Paul's tears and my own guilt by looking up and saying, "My God, your father is cranky this morning, isn't he?"

Paul's attention was immediately distracted from his wounds, and the unjust inflicter of those wounds, to his mother's laughter. He watched her.

"It is because he is afraid they will not like his songs in New York. Your father is an *artiste, mon chou,* and they are very mysterious people, *les artistes.* Millions of people are waiting for him in New York, they are begging him to come, and they will give him a *lot* of money, but he is afraid they will not like him. Tell him he is wrong."

She succeeded in rekindling Paul's excitement about places he has never seen. I was also, at once, reinvested with all my glamour. I think it is sometimes extremely difficult for Paul to realize that the face he sees on record sleeves and in the newspapers and on the screen is nothing more or less than the face of his father—who sometimes yells at him. Of course, since he is only seven—going on eight, he will be eight years old this winter—he cannot know that I am baffled, too.

"Of course, you are wrong, you are silly," he said with passion—and caused me to smile. His English is strongly accented and is not, in fact, as good as his

French, for he speaks French all day at school. French is really his first language, the first he ever heard. "You are the greatest singer in France"—sounding exactly as he must sound when he makes this pronouncement to his schoolmates—"the greatest *American* singer"—this concession was so gracefully made that it was not a concession at all, it added inches to my stature, America being only a glamorous word for Paul. It is the place from which his father came, and to which he now is going, a place which very few people have ever seen. But his aunt is one of them and he looked over at her. "Mme. Dumont says so, and she says he is a *great actor, too.*" Louisa nodded, smiling. "And she has seen *Les Fauves Nous Attendent*—five times!" This clinched it, of course. Mme. Dumont is our concierge and she has known Paul all his life. I suppose he will not begin to doubt anything she says until he begins to doubt everything.

He looked over at me again. "So you are wrong to be afraid."

"I was wrong to yell at you, too. I won't yell at you any more today."

"All right." He was very grave.

Louisa poured more coffee. "He's going to knock them dead in New York. You'll see."

"*Mais bien sûr,*" said Paul, doubtfully. He does not quite know what "knock them dead" means, though he was sure, from her tone, that she must have been agreeing with him. He does not quite understand this aunt, whom he met for the first time two months ago, when she arrived to spend the summer with us. Her accent is entirely different from anything he has ever heard. He does not really understand why, since she is my sister and his aunt, she should be unable to speak French.

Harriet, Louisa, and I looked at each other and smiled. "Knock them dead," said Harriet, "means *d'avoir un succès fou.* But you will soon pick up all the American expressions." She looked at me and laughed. "So will I."

"That's what he's afraid of." Louisa grinned. "We have *got* some expressions, believe me. Don't let anybody ever tell you America hasn't got a culture. Our culture is as thick as clabber milk."

"Ah," Harriet answered, "I know. I know."

"I'm going to be practicing later," I told Paul.

His face lit up. "*Bon.*" This meant that, later, he would come into my study and lie on the floor with his papers and crayons while I worked out with the piano and the tape recorder. He knew that I was offering this as an olive branch. All things considered, we get on pretty well, my son and I.

He looked over at Louisa again. She held a coffee cup in one hand and a cigarette in the other; and something about her baffled him. It was early, so she had not yet put on her face. Her short, thick, graying hair was rougher than usual, almost as rough as my own—later, she would be going to the hairdresser's; she is fairer than I, and better-looking; Louisa, in fact, caught all the looks in the family. Paul knows that she is my older sister, and that she helped to raise me, though he does not, of course, know what this means. He knows that she is a schoolteacher in the *American* South, which is not, for some reason, the same place as South America. I could see him trying to fit all these exotic details together into a pattern which would explain her strangeness—strangeness of accent, strangeness of manner. In comparison with the people he has always known, Louisa must seem, for all her generosity and laughter and affection, peculiarly uncertain of herself, peculiarly hostile and embattled.

I wondered what he would think of his Uncle Norman, older and much blacker than I, who lives near the Alabama town in which we were born. Norman will meet us at the boat.

Now Harriet repeats, "Nightmares, nightmares. Nothing ever turns out as badly as you think it will—in fact," she adds laughing, "I am happy to say that that would scarcely be possible."

Her eyes seek mine in the mirror—dark blue eyes, pale skin, black hair. I had always thought of Sweden as being populated entirely by blondes, and I thought that Harriet was abnormally dark for a Swedish girl. But when we visited Sweden, I found out differently. "It is all a great racial salad, Europe, that is why I am sure that I will never understand your country," Harriet said. That was in the days when we never imagined that we would be going to it.

I wonder what she is really thinking. Still, she is right, in two days we will be on a boat, and there is simply no point in carrying around my load of apprehension. I sit down on the bed, watching her fix her face. I realize that I am going to miss this old-fashioned bedroom. For years, we've talked about throwing out the old junk which came with the apartment and replacing it with less massive, modern furniture. But we never have.

"Oh, everything will probably work out," I say. "I've been in a bad mood all day long. I just can't sing any more." We both laugh. She reaches for a wad of tissues and begins wiping off the cream. "I wonder how Paul will like it, if he'll make friends—that's all."

"Paul will like any place where you are, where we are. Don't worry about Paul."

Paul has never been called any names, so far. Only, once he asked us what the word *métis* meant and Harriet explained to him that it meant mixed blood, adding that the blood of just about everybody in the world was mixed by now. Mme. Dumont contributed bawdy and detailed corroboration from her own family tree, the roots of which were somewhere in Corsica; the moral of the story, as she told it, was that women were weak, men incorrigible, and *le bon Dieu* appallingly clever. Mme. Dumont's version is the version I prefer, but it may not be, for Paul, the most utilitarian.

Harriet rises from the dressing table and comes over to sit in my lap. I fall back with her on the bed, and she smiles down into my face.

"Now, don't worry," she tells me, "please try not to worry. Whatever is coming, we will manage it all very well, you will see. We have each other and we have our son and we know what we want. So, we are luckier than most people."

I kiss her on the chin. "I'm luckier than most men."

"I'm a very lucky woman, too."

And for a moment we are silent, alone in our room, which we have shared so long. The slight rise and fall of Harriet's breathing creates an intermittent pressure against my chest, and I think how, if I had never left America, I would never have met her and would never have established a life of my own, would never have entered my own life. For everyone's life begins on a level where races, armies, and churches stop. And yet everyone's life is always shaped by races, churches, and armies; races, churches, armies menace, and have taken, many lives. If Harriet had been born in America, it would have taken her a long time, perhaps forever, to look on me as a man like other men; if I had met her in America, I would never have been able to look on her as a woman like all other women. The habits of public rage and power would also have been our private compulsions, and would have blinded our eyes. We would never have been able to love each other. And Paul would never have been born.

Perhaps, if I had stayed in America, I would have found another woman and had another son. But that other woman, that other son are in the limbo of vanished possibilities. I might also have become something else, instead of an actor-singer, perhaps a lawyer, like my brother, or a teacher, like my sister. But no, I am what I have become and this woman beside me is my wife, and I love her. All the sons I might have had mean nothing, since I *have* a son, I named him, Paul, for my father, and I love him.

I think of all the things I have seen destroyed in America, all the things that I have lost there, all the threats it holds for me and mine.

I grin up at Harriet. "Do you love me?"

"Of course not. I simply have been madly plotting to get to America all these years."

"What a patient wench you are."

"The Swedes are very patient."

She kisses me again and stands up. Louisa comes in, also in a dressing gown.

"I hope you two aren't sitting in here yakking about the *subject*." She looks at me. "My, you are the sorriest-looking celebrity I've ever seen. I've always wondered why people like you hired press agents. Now I know." She goes to Harriet's dressing table. "Honey, do you mind if I borrow some of that *mad* nail polish?"

Harriet goes over to the dressing table. "I'm not sure I know *which* mad nail polish you mean."

Harriet and Louisa, somewhat to my surprise, get on very well. Each seems to find the other full of the weirdest and most delightful surprises. Harriet has been teaching Louisa French and Swedish expressions, and Louisa has been teaching Harriet some of the saltier expressions of the black South. Whenever one of them is not playing straight man to the other's accent, they become involved in long speculations as to how a language reveals the history and the attitudes of a people. They discovered that all the European languages contain a phrase equivalent to "to work like a nigger." ("Of course," says Louisa, "they've had black men working for them for a long time.") "Language is experience and language is power," says Louisa, after regretting that she does not know any of the African dialects. "That's what I keep trying to tell those dicty bastards down South. They get their own experience into the language, we'll have a great language. But, no, they all want to talk like white folks." Then she leans forward, grasping Harriet by the knee. "I tell them, honey, white folks ain't saying *nothing*. Not a thing are they saying—and *some* of them know it, they *need* what you got, the whole world needs it." Then she leans back, in disgust. "You think they listen to me? Indeed they do not. They just go right on, trying to talk like white folks." She leans forward again, in tremendous indignation. "You know some of them folks are *ashamed* of Mahalia Jackson? *Ashamed* of her, one of the greatest singers alive! They think she's common." Then she looks about the room as though she held a bottle in her hand and were looking for a skull to crack.

I think it is because Louisa has never been able to talk like this to any white person before. All the white people she has ever met needed, in one way or another, to be reassured, consoled, to have their consciences pricked but not blasted; could not, could not afford to hear a truth which would shatter, irrevocably, their image of themselves. It is astonishing the lengths to which a person, or a people, will go in order to avoid a truthful mirror. But Harriet's necessity is precisely the opposite: it is of the utmost importance that she learn everything that Louisa can tell her, and then learn more, much more. Harriet is really trying to learn from Louisa how best to protect her husband and her son. This is why they are going out alone tonight. They will have, tonight, as it were, a final council of war. I may be moody, but they, thank God, are practical.

Now Louisa turns to me while Harriet rummages about on the dressing table. "What time is Vidal coming for you?"

"Oh, around seven-thirty, eight o'clock. He says he's reserved tables for us in some very chic place, but he won't say where." Louisa wriggles her shoulders, raises her eyebrows, and does a tiny bump and grind. I laugh. "That's right. And then I guess we'll go out and get drunk."

"I hope to God you do. You've been about as cheerful as a cemetery these last few days. And, that way, your hangover will keep you from bugging us tomorrow."

"What about *your* hangovers? I know the way you girls drink."

"Well, we'll be paying for our own drinks," says Harriet, "so I don't think we'll have that problem. But *you're* going to be feted, like an international movie star."

"You sure you don't want to change your mind and come out with Vidal and me?"

"We're sure," Louisa says. She looks down at me and gives a small, amused grunt. "An international movie star. And I used to change your diapers. I'll be damned." She is grave for a moment. "Mama'd be proud of you, you know that?" We look at each other and the air between us is charged with secrets which not even Harriet will ever know. "Now, get the hell out of here, so we can get dressed."

"I'll take Paul on down to Mme. Dumont's."

Paul is to have supper with her children and spend the night there.

"For the last time," says Mme. Dumont and she rubs her hand over Paul's violently curly black hair. *"Tu vas nous manquer, tu sais?"* Then she looks up at me and laughs. "He doesn't care. He is only interested in seeing the big ship and all the wonders of New York. Children are never sad to make journeys."

"I would be very sad to go," says Paul, politely, "but my father must go to New York to work and he wants me to come with him."

Over his head, Mme. Dumont and I smile at each other. *"Il est malin, ton gosse!"* She looks down at him again. "And do you think, my little diplomat, that you will like New York?"

"We aren't only going to New York," Paul answers, "we are going to California, too."

"Well, do you think you will like California?"

Paul looks at me. "I don't know. If we don't like it, we'll come back."

"So simple. Just like that," says Mme. Dumont. She looks at me. "It is the best way to look at life. Do come back. You know, we feel that you belong to us, too, here in France."

"I hope you do," I say. "I hope you do. I have always felt—always felt at home here." I bend down and Paul and I kiss each other on the cheek. We have always done so—but will we be able to do so in America? American fathers never kiss American sons. I straighten, my hand on Paul's shoulder. "You be good. I'll pick you up for breakfast, or, if you get up first you come and pick me up and we can hang out together tomorrow, while your *maman* and your Aunt Louisa finish packing. They won't want two men hanging around the house."

"D'accord. Where shall we hang out?" On the last two words he stumbles a little and imitates me.

"Maybe we can go to the zoo, I don't know. And I'll take you to lunch at the Eiffel Tower, would you like that?"

"Oh, yes," he says, "I'd love that." When he is pleased, he seems to glow. All the energy of his small, tough, concentrated being charges an unseen battery and adds an incredible luster to his eyes, which are large and dark brown—like mine—and to his skin, which always reminds me of the colors of honey and the fires of the sun.

"Okay, then." I shake hands with Mme. Dumont. *"Bonsoir, madame."* I ring for the elevator, staring at Paul. *"Ciao, Pauli."*

"Bonsoir, Papa."

And Mme. Dumont takes him inside.

Upstairs, Harriet and Louisa are finally powdered, perfumed, and jeweled, and ready to go: dry martinis at the Ritz, supper, "in some *very* expensive little place," says Harriet, and perhaps the Folies Bergère afterwards. "A real cornball, tourist evening," says Louisa. "I'm working on the theory that if I can get Harriet to act like an American now, she won't have so much trouble later."

"I very much doubt," Harriet says, "that I will be able to endure the Folies Bergère for three solid hours."

"Oh, then we'll duck across town to Harry's New York bar and drink mint juleps," says Louisa.

I realize that, quite apart from everything else, Louisa is having as much fun as she has ever had in her life before. Perhaps she, too, will be sad to leave Paris, even though she has only known it for such a short time.

"Do people drink those in New York?" Harriet asks. I think she is making a list of the things people do or do not do in New York.

"*Some* people do." Louisa winks at me. "Do you

realize that this Swedish chick's picked up an Alabama drawl?"

We laugh together. The elevator chugs to a landing.

"We'll stop and say good night to Paul," Harriet says. She kisses me. "Give our best to Vidal."

"Right. Have a good time. Don't let any Frenchmen run off with Louisa."

"I did not come to Paris to be protected, and if I had, this wild chick *you* married couldn't do it. I just *might* upset everybody and come home with a French count." She presses the elevator button and the cage goes down.

I walk back into our dismantled apartment. It stinks of departure. There are bags and crates in the hall, which will be taken away tomorrow, there are no books in the bookcases, the kitchen looks as though we never cooked a meal there, never dawdled there, in the early morning or late at night, over coffee. Presently, I must shower and shave but now I pour myself a drink and light a cigarette and step out on our balcony. It is dusk, the brilliant light of Paris is beginning to fade, and the green of the trees is darkening.

I have lived in this city for twelve years. This apartment is on the top floor of a corner building. We look out over the trees and the roof tops to the Champ de Mars, where the Eiffel Tower stands. Beyond this field is the river, which I have crossed so often, in so many states of mind. I have crossed every bridge in Paris, I have walked along every *quai*. I know the river as one finally knows a friend, know it when it is black, guarding all the lights of Paris in its depths, and seeming, in its vast silence, to be communing with the dead who lie beneath it; when it is yellow, evil, and roaring, giving a rough time to tugboats and barges, and causing people to remember that is has been known to rise, it has been known to kill; when it is peaceful, a slick, dark, dirty green, playing host to rowboats and *les bateaux mouches* and throwing up from time to time an extremely unhealthy fish. The men who stand along the *quais* all summer with their fishing lines gratefully accept the slimy object and throw it in a rusty can. I have always wondered who eats those fish.

And I walk up and down, up and down, glad to be alone.

It is August, the month when all Parisians desert Paris and one has to walk miles to find a barbershop or a laundry open in some tree-shadowed, silent side street. There is a single person on the avenue, a paratrooper walking toward École Militaire. He is also walking, almost certainly, and rather sooner than later, toward Algeria. I have a friend, a good-natured boy who was always hanging around the clubs in which I worked in the old days, who has just returned from Algeria, with a recurring, debilitating fever, and minus one eye. The government has set his pension at the sum, arbitrary if not occult, of fifty-three thousand francs every three months. Of course, it is quite impossible to live on this amount of money without working—but who will hire a half-blind invalid? This boy has been spoiled forever, long before his thirtieth birthday, and there are thousands like him all over France.

And there are fewer Algerians to be found on the streets of Paris now. The rug sellers, the peanut venders, the postcard peddlers and money-changers have vanished. The boys I used to know during my first years in Paris are scattered—or corralled—the Lord knows where.

Most of them had no money. They lived three and four together in rooms with a single skylight, a single hard cot, or in buildings that seemed abandoned, with cardboard in the windows, with erratic plumbing in a wet, cobblestoned yard, in dark, dead-end alleys, or on the outer, chilling heights of Paris.

The Arab cafés are closed—those dark, acrid cafés in which I used to meet with them to drink tea, to get high on hashish, to listen to the obsessive, stringed music which has no relation to any beat, any time, that I have ever known. I once thought of the North Africans as my brothers and that is why I went to their cafés. They were very friendly to me, perhaps one or two of them remained really fond of me even after I could no longer afford to smoke Lucky Strikes and after my collection of American sport shirts had vanished—mostly into their wardrobes. They seemed to feel that they had every right to them, since I could only have wrested these things from the world by cunning—it meant nothing to say that I had had no choice in the matter; perhaps I had wrested these things from the world by treason, by refusing to be identified with the misery of my people. Perhaps, indeed, I identified myself with those who were responsible for this misery.

And this was true. Their rage, the only note in all their music which I could not fail to recognize, to which I responded, yet had the effect of setting us more than ever at a division. They were perfectly prepared to drive all Frenchmen into the sea, and to level the city of Paris. But I could not hate the French, because they left me alone. And I love Paris, I will always love it, it is the city which saved my life. It saved my life by allowing me to find out who I am.

It was on a bridge, one tremendous April morning, that I knew I had fallen in love. Harriet and I were walking hand in hand. The bridge was the Pont Royal, just before us was the great *horloge,* high and lifted up, saying ten to ten; beyond this, the golden statue of Joan of Arc, with her sword uplifted. Harriet and I were silent, for we had been quarreling about something. Now, when I look back, I think we had reached that state when an affair must either end or become something more than an affair.

I looked sideways at Harriet's face, which was still. Her dark blue eyes were narrowed against the sun, and her full, pink lips were still slightly sulky, like a child's. In those days, she hardly ever wore make-up. I was in my shirt sleeves. Her face made me want to laugh and run my hand over her short dark hair. I wanted to pull her to me and say, *Baby, don't be mad at me,* and at that moment something tugged at my heart and made me catch my breath. There were millions of people all around us, but I was alone with Harriet. She was alone with me. Never, in all my life, until that moment, had I been alone with anyone. The world had always been with us, between us, defeating the quarrel we could not achieve, and making love impossible. During all the years of my life, until that moment, I had carried the menacing, the hostile, killing world with me everywhere. No matter what I was doing or saying or feeling, one eye had always been on the world—that world which I had learned to distrust almost as soon as I learned my name, that world on which I knew one could never turn one's back, the white man's world. And for the first time in my life I was free of it; it had not existed for me; I had been quarreling with my girl. It was our quarrel, it was entirely between us, it had nothing to do with anyone else in the world. For the first time in my life I had not been afraid of the patriotism of the mindless, in uniform or out, who would beat me up and treat the woman who was with me as though she were the lowest of untouchables. For the first time in my life I felt that no force jeopardized my right, my power, to possess and to protect a woman; for the first time, the first time, felt that the woman was not, in her own eyes or in the eyes of the world, degraded by my presence.

The sun fell over everything, like a blessing, people were moving all about us, I will never forget the feeling of Harriet's small hand in mine, dry and trusting, and I turned to her, slowing our pace. She looked up at me with her enormous blue eyes, and she seemed to wait. I said, "*Harriet. Harriet. Tu sais, il y a quelque chose de très grave qui m'est arrivé. Je t'aime. Je t'aime. Tu me comprends,* or shall I say it in English?"

This was eight years ago, shortly before my first and only visit home.

That was when my mother died. I stayed in America for three months. When I came back, Harriet thought that the change in me was due to my grief—I was very silent, very thin. But it had not been my mother's death which accounted for the change. I had known that my mother was going to die. I had not known what America would be like for me after nearly four years away.

I remember standing at the rail and watching the distance between myself and Le Havre increase. Hands fell, ceasing to wave, handkerchiefs ceased to flutter, people turned away, they mounted their bicycles or got into their cars and rode off. Soon, Le Havre was nothing but a blur. I thought of Harriet, already miles from me in Paris, and I pressed my lips tightly together in order not to cry.

Then, as Europe dropped below the water, as the days passed and passed, as we left behind us the skies of Europe and the eyes of everyone on the ship began, so to speak, to refocus, waiting for the first glimpse of America, my apprehension began to give way to a secret joy, a checked anticipation. I thought of such details as showers, which are rare in Paris, and I thought of such things as rich, cold, American milk and heavy, chocolate cake. I wondered about my friends, wondered if I had any left, and wondered if they would be glad to see me.

The Americans on the boat did not seem to be so bad, but I was fascinated, after such a long absence from it, by the nature of their friendliness. It was a friendliness which did not suggest, and was not intended to suggest, any possibility of friendship. Unlike Europeans, they dropped titles and used first names almost at once, leaving themselves, unlike the Europeans, with nowhere thereafter to go. Once one had become "Pete" or "Jane" or "Bill" all that could decently be known was known and any suggestion that there might be further depths, a person, so to speak, behind the name, was taken as a violation of that privacy which did not, paradoxically, since they trusted it so little, seem to exist among Americans. They apparently equated privacy with the unspeakable things they did in the bathroom or the bedroom, which they related only to the analyst, and then read about in the pages of best sellers. There was an eerie and unnerving irreality about everything they said and did, as though they were all members of the same team and were acting on orders from some invincibly cheerful and tirelessly inventive coach. I was fascinated by it. I found it oddly moving, but I cannot say that I was displeased. It had not occurred to me before that Americans, who had never treated me with any respect, had no respect for each other.

On the last night but one, there was a gala in the big ballroom and I sang. It had been a long time since I had sung before so many Americans. My audience had mainly been penniless French students, in the weird Left Bank bistros I worked in those days. Still, I was a great hit with them and by this time I had become enough of a drawing card, in the Latin Quarter and in St.-Germain-des-Prés, to have attracted a couple of critics, to have had my picture in *France-soir,* and to have acquired a legal work permit which allowed me to make a little more money. Just the same, no matter how industrious and brilliant some of the musicians had been, or how devoted my audience, they did not know, they could not know, what my songs came out of. They did not know what was funny about it. It was impossible to translate: It damn well better be funny, or Laughing to keep from crying, or What did *I* do to be so black and blue?

The moment I stepped out on the floor, they began to smile, something opened in them, they were ready to be pleased. I found in their faces, as they watched me, smiling, waiting, an artless relief, a profound reassurance. Nothing was more familiar to them than the sight of a dark boy, singing, and there were few things on earth more necessary. It was under cover of darkness, my own darkness, that I could sing for them of the joys, passions, and terrors they smuggled about with them like steadily depreciating contraband. Under cover of the midnight fiction that I was unlike them because I was black, they could stealthily gaze at those treasures which they had been mysteriously forbidden to possess and were never permitted to declare.

I sang *"I'm Coming, Virginia,"* and *"Take This Hammer,"* and *"Precious Lord."* They wouldn't let me go and I came back and sang a couple of the oldest blues I knew. Then someone asked me to sing *"Swanee River,"* and I did, astonished that I could, astonished that this song, which I had put down long ago, should have the power to move me. Then, if only, perhaps, to make the record complete, I wanted to sing *"Strange Fruit,"* but, on this number, no one can surpass the great, tormented Billie Holiday. So I finished with *"Great Getting-Up Morning"* and I guess I can say that if I didn't stop the show I certainly ended it. I got a big hand and I drank at a few tables and I danced with a few girls.

After one more day and one more night, the boat landed in New York. I woke up, I was bright awake at once, and I thought, *We're here.* I turned on all the lights in my small cabin and I stared into the mirror as though I were committing my face to memory. I took a shower and I took a long time shaving and I dressed myself very carefully. I walked the long ship corridors to the dining room, looking at the luggage piled high before the elevators and beside the steps. The dining room was nearly half empty and full of a quick and joyous excitement which depressed me even more. People ate quickly, chattering to each other, anxious to get upstairs and go on deck. Was it my imagination or was it true that they seemed to avoid my eyes? A few people waved and smiled, but let me pass; perhaps it would have made them uncomfortable, this morning, to try to share their excitement with me; perhaps they did not want to know whether or not it was possible for me to share it. I walked to my table and sat down. I munched toast as dry as paper and drank a pot of coffee. Then I tipped my waiter, who bowed and smiled and called me "sir" and said that he hoped to see me on the boat again. "I hope so, too," I said.

And was it true, or was it my imagination, that a flash of wondering comprehension, a flicker of wry sympathy, then appeared in the waiter's eyes? I walked upstairs to the deck.

There was a breeze from the water but the sun was hot and made me remember how ugly New York summers could be. All of the deck chairs had been taken away and people milled about in the space where the deck chairs had been, moved from one side of the ship to the other, clambered up and down the steps, crowded the rails, and they were busy taking photographs—of the harbor, of each other, of the sea, of the gulls. I walked slowly along the deck, and an impulse stronger than myself drove me to the rail. There it was, the great, unfinished city, with all its towers blazing in the sun. It came toward us slowly and patiently, like some enormous, cunning, and murderous beast, ready to devour, impossible to escape. I watched it come closer and I listened to the people around me, to their excitement and their pleasure. There was no doubt that it was real. I watched their shining faces and wondered if I were mad. For a moment I longed, with all my heart, to be able to feel whatever they were feeling, if only to know what such a feeling was like. As the boat moved slowly into the harbor, they were being moved into safety. It was only I who was being floated into danger. I turned my head, looking for Europe, but all that stretched behind me was the sky, thick with gulls. I moved away from the rail. A big, sandy-haired man held his daughter on his shoulders, showing her the Statue of Liberty. I would never know what this statue meant to others, she had always been an ugly joke for me. And the American flag was flying from the top of the ship, above my head. I had seen the French flag drive the French into the most unspeakable frenzies, I had seen the flag which was nominally mine used to dignify the vilest purposes: now I would never, as long as I lived, know what others saw when they saw a flag. "There's no place like home," said a voice close by, and I thought, *There damn sure isn't.* I decided to go back to my cabin and have a drink.

There was a cablegram from Harriet in my cabin. It said: Be good. Be quick. I'm waiting. I folded it carefully and put it in my breast pocket. Then I wondered if I would ever get back to her. How long would it take me to earn the money to get out of this land? Sweat broke out on my forehead and I poured myself some whisky from my nearly empty bottle. I paced the tiny cabin. It was silent. There was no one down in the cabins now.

I was not sober when I faced the uniforms in the first-class lounge. There were two of them; they were not unfriendly. They looked at my passport, they looked at me. "You've been away a long time," said one of them.

"Yes," I said, "it's been a while."

"What did you do over there all that time?"—with a grin meant to hide more than it revealed, which hideously revealed more than it could hide.

I said, "I'm a singer," and the room seemed to rock around me. I held on to what I hoped was a calm, open smile. I had not had to deal with these faces in so long that I had forgotten how to do it. I had once known how to pitch my voice precisely between curtness and servility, and known what razor's edge of a pickaninny's smile would turn away wrath. But I had forgotten all the tricks on which my life had once depended. Once I had been an expert at baffling these people, at setting their teeth on edge, and dancing just outside the trap laid for me. But I was not an expert now. These faces were no longer merely the faces of two white men, who were my enemies. They were the faces of two white people whom I did not understand, and I could no longer plan my moves in accordance with what I knew of their cowardice and their needs and their strategy. That moment on the bridge had undone me forever.

"That's right," said one of them, "that's what it says, right here on the passport. Never heard of you, though." They looked up at me. "Did you do a lot of singing over there?"

"Some."

"What kind—concerts?"

"No." I wondered what I looked like, sounded like. I could tell nothing from their eyes. "I worked a few night clubs."

"Night clubs, eh? I guess they liked you over there."

"Yes," I said, "they seemed to like me all right."

"Well"—and my passport was stamped and handed back to me—"let's hope they like you over here."

"Thanks." They laughed—was it at me, or was it my imagination?—and I picked up the one bag I was carrying and threw my trench coat over one shoulder and walked out of the first-class lounge. I stood in the slow-moving, murmuring line which led to the gangplank. I looked straight ahead and watched heads, smiling faces, step up to the shadow of the gangplank awning and then swiftly descend out of sight. I put my passport back in my breast pocket—*Be quick. I'm waiting*—and I held my landing card in my hand. Then, suddenly, there I was, standing on the edge of the boat, staring down the long ramp to the ground. At the end of the plank, on the ground, stood a heavy man in a uniform. His cap was pushed back from his gray hair and his face was red and wet. He looked up at me. This was the face I remembered, the face of my nightmares; perhaps hatred had caused me to know this face better than I would ever know the face of any lover. "Come on, boy," he cried, "come on, come on!"

And I almost smiled. I was home. I touched my breast pocket. I thought of a song I sometimes sang, "When will I ever get to be a man?" I came down the gangplank, stumbling a little, and gave the man my landing card.

Much later in the day, a customs inspector checked my baggage and waved me away. I picked up my bags and started walking down the long stretch which led to the gate, to the city.

And I heard someone call my name.

I looked up and saw Louisa running toward me. I dropped my bags and grabbed her in my arms and tears came to my eyes and rolled down my face. I did not know whether the tears were for joy at seeing her, or from rage, or both.

"How are you? How are you? You look wonderful, but, oh, haven't you lost weight? It's wonderful to see you again."

I wiped my eyes. "It's wonderful to see you, too, I bet you thought I was never coming back."

Louisa laughed. "I wouldn't have blamed you if you hadn't. These people are just as corny as ever, I swear I don't believe there's any hope for them. How's your French? Lord, when I think that it was I who studied French and now I can't speak a word. And you never went near it and you probably speak it like a native."

I grinned. *"Pas mal. Je me défends pas mal."* We started down the wide steps into the street. "My God," I said. "New York." I was not aware of its towers now. We were in the shadow of the elevated highway but the thing which most struck me was neither light nor shade, but noise. It came from a million things at once, from trucks and tires and clutches and brakes and doors; from machines shuttling and stamping and rolling and cutting and pressing; from the building of tunnels, the checking of gas mains, the laying of wires, the digging of foundations; from the chattering of rivets, the scream of the pile driver, the clanging of great shovels; from the battering down and the raising up of walls; from millions of radios and television sets and jukeboxes. The human voices distinguished themselves from the roar only by their note of strain and hostility. Another fleshy man, uniformed and red-faced, hailed a cab for us and touched his cap politely but could only manage a peremptory growl: "Right this way, miss. Step up, sir." He slammed the cab door behind us. Louisa directed the driver to the New Yorker Hotel.

"Do they take us there?"

She looked at me. "They got laws in New York, honey, it'd be the easiest thing in the world to spend all your time in court. But over at the New Yorker, I believe they've already got the message." She took my arm. "You see? In spite of all this chopping and booming, this place hasn't really changed very much. You still can't hear yourself talk."

And I thought to myself, Maybe that's the point.

Early the next morning we checked out of the hotel and took the plane for Alabama.

I am just stepping out of the shower when I hear the bell ring. I dry myself hurriedly and put on a bathrobe. It is Vidal, of course, and very elegant he is, too, with his bushy gray hair quite lustrous, his swarthy, cynical, gypsylike face shaved and lotioned. Usually he looks just any old way. But tonight his brief bulk is contained in a dark blue suit and he has an ironical pearl stickpin in his blue tie.

"Come in, make yourself a drink. I'll be with you in a second."

"I am, *hélas!* on time. I trust you will forgive me for my thoughtlessness."

But I am already back in the bathroom. Vidal puts on a record: Mahalia Jackson, singing "I'm Going to Live the Life I Sing About in My Song."

When I am dressed, I find him sitting in a chair before the open window. The daylight is gone, but it is not exactly dark. The trees are black now against the darkening sky. The lights in windows and the lights of motorcars are yellow and ringed. The street lights have not yet been turned on. It is as though, out of deference to the departed day, Paris waited a decent interval before assigning her role to a more theatrical but inferior performer.

Vidal is drinking a whisky and soda. I pour myself a drink. He watches me.

"Well. How are you, my friend? You are nearly gone. Are you happy to be leaving us?"

"No." I say this with more force than I had intended. Vidal raises his eyebrows, looking amused and distant. "I never really intended to go back there. I certainly never intended to raise my kid there—"

"Mais, mon cher," Vidal says, calmly, "you are an intelligent man, you must have known that you would probably be returning one day." He pauses. "And, as for Pauli—did it never occur to you that he might wish one day to see the country in which his father and his father's fathers were born?"

"To do that, really, he'd have to go to Africa."

"America will always mean more to him than Africa, you know that."

"I don't know." I throw my drink down and pour myself another. "Why should he want to cross all that water just to be called a nigger? America never gave him anything."

"It gave him his father."

I look at him. "You mean, his father escaped."

Vidal throws back his head and laughs. If Vidal likes you, he is certain to laugh at you and his laughter can be very unnerving. But the look, the silence which follow this laughter can be very unnerving, too. And, now, in the silence, he asks me, "Do you really think that you have escaped anything? Come. I know you for a better man than that." He walks to the table which holds the liquor. "In that movie of ours which has made you so famous, and, as I now see, so troubled, what are you playing, after all? What is the tragedy of this half-breed troubadour if not, precisely, that he has taken all the possible roads to escape and that all these roads have failed him?" He pauses, with the bottle in one hand, and looks at me. "Do you remember the trouble I had to get a performance out of you? How you hated me, you sometimes looked as though you wanted to shoot me! And do you remember when the role of Chico began to come alive?" He pours his drink. "Think back, remember. I am a very great director, *mais pardon!* I could not have got such a performance out of anyone but you. And what were you thinking of, what was in your mind, what nightmare were you living with when you began, at last, to play the role—truthfully?" He walks back to his seat.

Chico, in the film, is the son of a Martinique woman and a French *colon* who hates both his mother and his father. He flees from the island to the capital, carrying his hatred with him. This hatred has now grown, naturally, to include all dark women and all white men, in a word, everyone. He descends into the underworld of Paris, where he dies. *Les fauves*—the wild beasts—refers to the life he has fled and to the life which engulfs him. When I agreed to do the role, I felt that I could probably achieve it by bearing in mind the North Africans I had watched in Paris for so long. But this did not please Vidal. The blowup came while we were rehearsing a fairly simple, straightforward scene. Chico goes into a sleazy Pigalle dance hall to beg the French owner for a particularly humiliating job. And this Frenchman reminds him of his father.

"You are playing this boy as though you thought of him as the noble savage," Vidal said, icily. "*Ça vient d'où*—all these ghastly mannerisms you are using all the time?"

Everyone fell silent, for Vidal rarely spoke this way. This silence told me that everyone, the actor with whom I was playing the scene and all the people in the "dance hall," shared Vidal's opinion of my performance and was relieved that he was going to do something about it. I was humiliated and too angry to speak; but perhaps I also felt, at the very bottom of my heart, a certain relief, an unwilling respect.

"You are doing it all wrong," he said, more gently. Then, "Come, let us have a drink together."

We walked into his office. He took a bottle and two glasses out of his desk. "Forgive me, but you put me in mind of some of those English *lady* actresses who love to play *putain* as long as it is always absolutely clear to the audience that they are really ladies. So perhaps they read a book, not usually, *hélas! Fanny Hill,* and they have their chauffeurs drive them through Soho once or twice—and they come to the stage with a performance so absolutely loaded with detail, every bit of it meaningless, that there can be no doubt that they are acting. It is what the British call a triumph." He poured two cognacs. "That is what you are doing. Why? Who do you think this boy is, what do you think he is feeling, when he asks for this job?" He watched me carefully and I bitterly resented his look. "You come from America. The situation is not so pretty there for boys like you. I know you may not have been as poor as—as some—but is it really impossible for you to understand what a boy like Chico feels? Have you never, yourself, been in a similar position?"

I hated him for asking the question because I knew he knew the answer to it. "I would have had to be a very lucky black man not to have been in such a position."

"You would have had to be a very lucky *man.*"

"Oh, God," I said, "please don't give me any of this equality-in-anguish business."

"It is perfectly possible," he said, sharply, "that there is not another kind."

Then he was silent. He sat down behind his desk. He cut a cigar and lit it, puffing up clouds of smoke, as though to prevent us from seeing each other too clearly. "Consider this," he said. "I am a French director who has never seen your country. I have never done you any harm, except, perhaps, historically—I mean, because I am white—but I cannot be blamed for that—"

"But *I* can be," I said, "and I am! I've never understood why, if *I* have to pay for the history written in the color of my skin, *you* should get off scot-free!" But I was surprised at my vehemence, I had not known I was going to say these things, and by the fact that I was trembling and from the way he looked at me I knew that, from a professional point of view anyway, I was playing into his hands.

"What makes you think I *do?*" His face looked weary and stern. "I am a Frenchman. Look at France. You think that I—we—are not paying for our history?" He walked to the window, staring out at the rather grim little town in which the studio was located. "If it is revenge that you want, well, then, let me tell you, you will have it. You will probably have it, whether you want it or not, our stupidity will make it inevitable." He turned back into the room. "But I beg you not to confuse me with the happy people of your country, who scarcely know that there is such a thing as history and so, naturally, imagine that they can escape, as you put it, scot-free. That is what you are doing, that is what I was about to say. I was about to say that I am a French director and I have never been in your country and I have never done you any harm—but you are not talking to that man, in this room, now. You are not talking to Jean Luc Vidal, but to some other white man, whom you remember, who has nothing do to with me." He paused and went back to his desk. "Oh, most of the time you are not like this, I know. But it is there all the time, it must be, because when you are upset, this is what comes out. So you are not playing Chico truthfully, you are lying about him, and I will not let you do it. When you go back, now, and play this scene again, I want you to remember what has just happened in this room. You brought your past into this room. That is what Chico does when he walks into the dance hall. The Frenchman whom he begs for a job is not merely a Frenchman—he is the father who disowned and betrayed him and all the Frenchmen whom he hates." He smiled and poured me another cognac. "Ah! If it were not for *my* history, I would not have so much trouble to get the truth out of you." He looked into my face, half smiling. "And you, you are angry—are you not?—that I *ask* you for the truth. You think I have no right to ask." Then he said something which he knew would enrage me. "Who are you then, and what good has it done you to come to France, and how will you raise your son? Will you teach him never to tell the truth to anyone?" And he moved behind his desk and looked at me, as though from behind a barricade.

"You have no right to talk to me this way."

"Oh, yes, I do," he said. "I have a film to make and a reputation to maintain and I am going to get a performance out of you." He looked at his watch. "Let us go back to work."

I watch him now, sitting quietly in my living room, tough, cynical, crafty old Frenchman, and I wonder if he knows that the nightmare at the bottom of my mind, as I played the role of Chico, was all the possible fates of Paul. This is but another way of saying that I relived the disasters which had nearly undone me; but, because I was thinking of Paul, I discovered that I did not want my son ever to feel toward me as I had felt toward my own father. He had died when I was eleven, but I had watched the humiliations he had to bear, and I had pitied him. But was there not, in that pity, however painfully and unwillingly, also some contempt? For how could I *know* what he had borne? I knew only that I was his son. However he had loved me, whatever he had borne, I, his son, was despised. Even had he lived, he could have done nothing to prevent it, nothing to protect me. The best that he could hope to do was to prepare me for it; and even at that he had failed. How can one be prepared for the spittle in the face, all the tireless ingenuity which goes into the spite and fear of small, unutterably miserable people whose greatest terror is the singular identity, whose joy, whose safety, is entirely dependent on the humiliation and anguish of others?

But for Paul, I swore it, such a day would never come. I would throw my life and my work between Paul and the nightmare of the world. I would make it impossible for the world to treat Paul as it had treated my father and me.

Mahalia's record ends. Vidal rises to turn it over. "Well?" He looks at me very affectionately. "Your nightmares, please!"

"Oh, I was thinking of that summer I spent in Alabama, when my mother died." I stop. "You know, but when we finally filmed that bar scene, I was thinking of New York. I was scared in Alabama, but I almost went crazy in New York. I was sure I'd never make it back here—back here to Harriet. And I knew if I didn't, it was going to be the end of me." Now Mahalia is singing "When the Saints Go Marching In." "I got a job in the town as an elevator boy, in the town's big department store. It was a special favor, one of my father's white friends got it for me. For a long time, in the South, we all—depended—on the—*kindness*—of white friends." I take out a handkerchief and wipe my face. "But this man didn't like me. I guess I didn't seem grateful enough, wasn't enough like my father, what he thought my father was. And I couldn't get used to the town again, I'd been away too long, I hated it. It's a terrible town, anyway, the whole thing looks as though it's been built around a jailhouse. There's a room in the courthouse, a room where they beat you up. Maybe you're walking along the street one night, it's usually at night, but it happens in the daytime, too. And the police car comes up behind you and the cop says, Hey, boy. Come on over here. So you go on over. He says, Boy, I believe you drunk. And, you see, if you say, No, no sir, he'll beat you because you're calling him a liar. And if you say anything else, unless it's something to make him laugh, he'll take you in and beat you, just for fun. The trick is to think of some way for them to have their fun without beating you up."

The street lights of Paris click on and turn all the green leaves silver. "Or to go along with the ways *they* dream up. And they'll do anything, anything at all, to prove that you're no better than a dog and to make you feel like one. And they hated me because I'd been North and I'd been to Europe. People kept saying, I hope you didn't bring no foreign notions back here with you, boy. And I'd say, No sir, or No ma'am, but I never said it right. And there was a time, all of them remembered it, when I *had* said it right. But now they could tell that I despised them—I guess, no matter what, I wanted them to know that I despised them. But I didn't despise them any more than everyone else did, only the others never let it show. They knew how to keep the white folks happy, and it was easy—you just had to keep them feeling like they were God's favor to the universe. They'd walk around with great big foolish grins on their faces and the colored folks loved to see this, because they hated them so much. "Just look at So-and-So," somebody'd say. "His white is *on* him today." And when we didn't hate them, we pitied them. In America, that's usually what it means to have a white friend. You pity the poor bastard because he was born believing the world's a great place to be, and you know it's not, and you can see that he's going to have a terrible time getting used to this idea, if he *ever* gets used to it."

Then I think of Paul again, those eyes which still imagine that I can do anything, that skin, the color of honey and fire, his jet-black, curly hair. I look out at Paris again, and I listen to Mahalia. "Maybe it's better to have the terrible times first. I don't know. Maybe, then, you can have, *if* you live, a better life, a real life, because you had to fight so hard to get it away—you know?—from the mad dog who held it in his teeth. But then your life has all those tooth marks, too, all those tatters, and all that blood." I walk to the bottle and raise it. "One for the road?"

"Thank you," says Vidal.

I pour us a drink, and he watches me. I have never talked so much before, not about those things anyway. I know that Vidal has nightmares, because he knows so much about them, but he has never told me what his are. I think that he probably does not talk about his nightmares any more. I know that the war cost him his wife and his son, and that he was in prison in Germany. He very rarely refers to it. He has a married daughter who lives in England, and he rarely speaks of her. He is like a man who has learned to live on what is left of an enormous fortune.

We are silent for a moment.

"Please go on," he says, with a smile. "I am curious about the reality behind the reality of your performance."

"My sister, Louisa, never married," I say, abruptly, "because, once, years ago, she and the boy she was going with and two friends of theirs were out driving in a car and the police stopped them. The girl who was with them was very fair and the police pretended not to believe her when she said she was colored. They made her get out and stand in front of the headlights of the car and pull down her pants and raise her dress—they said that was the only way they could be sure. And you can imagine what they said, and what they did—and they were lucky, at that, that it didn't go any further. But none of the men could do anything about it. Louisa couldn't face that boy again, and I guess he couldn't face her." Now it is really growing dark in the room and I cross to the light switch. "You know, I know what that boy felt, I've felt it. They want you to feel that you're not a man, maybe that's the only way they can feel like men, I don't know. I walked around New York with Harriet's cablegram in my pocket as though it were some atomic secret, in *code,* and they'd kill me if they ever found out what it meant. You know, there's something wrong with people like that. And thank God Harriet was here, she *proved* that the world was bigger than the world they wanted me to live in, I *had* to get back here, get to a place where people were too busy with their own lives, *their private lives,* to make fantasies about mine, to set up walls around mine." I look at him. The light in the room has made the night outside blue-black and golden and the great searchlight of the Eiffel Tower is turning in the sky. "That's what it's like in America, for me, anyway. I always feel that I don't exist there, except in someone else's—usually dirty—mind. I don't know if you know what that means, but I do, and I don't want to put Harriet through that and I don't want to raise Paul there."

"Well," he says at last, "you are not required to remain in America forever, are you? You will sing in that elegant club which apparently feels that it cannot, much longer, so much as open its doors without you, and you will probably accept the movie offer, you would be very foolish not to. You will make a lot of money. Then, one day, you will remember that airlines and steamship companies are still in business and that France still exists. *That* will certainly be cause for astonishment."

Vidal was a Gaullist before De Gaulle came to power. But he regrets the manner of De Gaulle's rise and he is worried about De Gaulle's regime. "It is not the fault of *mon général,*" he sometimes says, sadly. "Perhaps it is history's fault. I *suppose* it must be history which always arranges to bill a civilization at the very instant it is least prepared to pay."

Now he rises and walks out on the balcony, as though to reassure himself of the reality of Paris. Mahalia is singing "Didn't It Rain?" I walk out and stand beside him.

"You are a good boy—Chico," he says. I laugh. "You believe in love. You do not know all the things love cannot do, but"—he smiles—"love will teach you that."

We go, after dinner, to a Left Bank *discothèque* which can charge outrageous prices because Marlon Brando wandered in there one night. By accident, according to Vidal. "Do you know how many people in Paris are becoming rich—to say nothing of those, *hélas!* who are going broke—on the off chance that Marlon Brando will lose his way again?"

He has not, presumably, lost his way tonight, but the *discothèque* is crowded with those strangely faceless people who are part of the night life of all great cities, and who always arrive, moments, hours, or decades late, on the spot made notorious by an event or a movement or a handful of personalities. So here are American boys, anything but beardless, scratching around for Hemingway; American girls titillating themselves with Frenchmen and existentialism while waiting for the American boys to shave off their beards; French painters busily pursuing the revolution which ended thirty years ago; and the young, bored, perverted American *arrivistes* who are buying their way into the art world via flattery and liquor, and the production of canvases as arid as their greedy little faces. Here are boys, of all nations, one step above the pimp, who are occasionally walked across a stage or trotted before a camera. And the girls, their enemies, whose faces are sometimes seen in ads, one of whom will surely have a tantrum before the evening is out.

In a corner, as usual, surrounded, as usual, by smiling young men, sits the drunken blond woman who was once the mistress of a famous, dead painter. She is a figure of some importance in the art world, and so rarely has to pay for either her drinks or her lovers. An older Frenchman, who was once a famous director, is playing *quatre cent vingt-et-un* with the woman behind the cash register. He nods pleasantly to Vidal and me as we enter, but makes no move to join us, and I respect him for this. Vidal and I are obviously cast tonight in the role vacated by Brando: our entrance justifies the prices and sends a kind of shiver through the room. It is marvelous to watch the face of the waiter as he approaches, all smiles and deference and grace, not so much honored by our presence as achieving his reality from it; excellence, he seems to be saying, gravitates naturally toward excellence. We order two whisky and sodas. I know why Vidal sometimes comes here. He is lonely. I do not think that he expects ever to love one woman again, and so he distracts himself with many.

Since this is a *discothèque,* jazz is blaring from the walls and record sleeves are scattered about with a devastating carelessness. Two of them are mine and no doubt, presently, someone will play the recording of the songs I sang in the film.

"I thought," says Vidal, with a malicious little smile, "that your farewell to Paris would not be complete without a brief exposure to the perils of fame. Perhaps it will help prepare you for America, where, I am told, the populace is yet more carnivorous than it is here."

I can see that one of the vacant models is preparing herself to come to our table and ask for an autograph, hoping, since she is pretty—she has, that is, the usual female equipment, dramatized in the usual, modern way—to be invited for a drink. Should the maneuver succeed, one of her boy friends or girl friends will contrive to come by the table, asking for a light or a pencil or a lipstick, and it will be extremely difficult not to invite this person to join us, too. Before the evening ends, we will be surrounded. I don't, now, know what I expected of fame, but I suppose it never occurred to me that the light could be just as dangerous, just as killing, as the dark.

"Well, let's make it brief," I tell him. "Sometimes I wish that you weren't quite so fond of me."

He laughs. "There are some very interesting people here tonight. Look."

Across the room from us, and now staring at our table, are a group of American Negro students, who are probably visiting Paris for the first time. There are four of them, two boys and two girls, and I suppose that they must be in their late teens or early twenties. One of the boys, a gleaming, curly-haired, golden-brown type—the color of his mother's fried chicken—is carrying a guitar. When they realize we have noticed them, they smile and wave—wave as though I were one of their possessions, as, indeed, I am. Golden-brown is a mime. He raises his guitar, drops his shoulders, and his face falls into the lugubrious lines of Chico's face as he approaches death. He strums a little of the film's theme music, and I laugh and the table laughs. It is as though we were all back home and had met for a moment, on a Sunday morning, say, before a church or a poolroom or a barbershop.

And they have created a sensation in the *discothèque,* naturally, having managed, with no effort whatever, to outwit all the gleaming boys and girls. Their table, which had been of no interest only a moment before, has now become the focus of a rather pathetic attention; their smiles have made it possible for the others to smile, and to nod in our direction.

"Oh," says Vidal, "he does that far better than you ever did, perhaps I will make him a star."

"Feel free, *m'sieu, le bon Dieu,* I got mine." But I can see that his attention has really been caught by one of the girls, slim, tense, and dark, who seems, though it is hard to know how one senses such things, to be treated by the others with a special respect. And, in fact, the table now seems to be having a council of war, to be demanding her opinion or her cooperation. She listens, frowning, laughing; the quality, the force of her intelligence causes her face to keep changing all the time, as though a light played on it. And, presently, with a gesture she might once have used to scatter feed to chickens, she scoops up from the floor one of those dangling ragbags women love to carry. She holds it loosely by the drawstrings, so that it is banging somewhere around her ankle, and walks over to our table. She has an honest, forthright walk, entirely unlike the calculated, pelvic workout by means of which most women get about. She is small, but sturdily, economically, put together.

As she reaches our table, Vidal and I rise, and this throws her for a second. (It has been a long time since I have seen such an attractive girl.)

Also, everyone, of course, is watching us. It is really a quite curious moment. They have put on the record of Chico singing a sad, angry Martinique ballad; my own voice is coming at us from the walls as the girl looks from Vidal to me, and smiles.

"I guess you know," she says, "we weren't *about* to let you get out of here without bugging you just a little bit. We've only been in Paris just a couple of days and we thought for sure that we wouldn't have a chance of running into you anywhere, because it's in all the papers that you're coming home."

"Yes," I say, "yes. I'm leaving the day after tomorrow."

"Oh!" She grins. "Then we really *are* lucky." I find that I have almost forgotten the urchinlike grin of a colored girl. "I guess, before I keep babbling on, I'd better introduce myself. My name is Ada Holmes."

We shake hands. "This is Monsieur Vidal, the director of the film."

"I'm very honored to meet you, sir."

"Will you join us for a moment? Won't you sit down?" And Vidal pulls a chair out for her.

But she frowns contritely. "I really ought to get back to my friends." She looks at me. "I really just came over to say, for myself and all the kids, that we've got your records and we've seen your movie, and it means so much to us"—and she laughs, breathlessly, nervously, it is somehow more moving than tears—"more than I can say. Much more. And we wanted to know if you and your friend"—she looks at Vidal—"your *director,* Monsieur Vidal, would allow us to buy you a drink? We'd be very honored if you would."

"It is we who are honored," says Vidal, promptly, "*and* grateful. We were getting terribly bored with one another, thank God you came along."

The three of us laugh, and we cross the room.

The three at the table rise, and Ada makes the introductions. The other girl, taller and paler than Ada, is named Ruth. One of the boys is named Talley—"short for Talliafero"—and Golden-brown's name is Pete. "Man," he tells me, "I dig you the most. You tore me up, baby, tore me *up.*"

"You tore up a lot of people," Talley says cryptically, and he and Ruth laugh. Vidal does not know, but I do, that Talley is probably referring to white people.

They are from New Orleans and Tallahassee and North Carolina; are college students, and met on the boat. They have been in Europe all summer, in Italy and Spain, but are only just getting to Paris.

"We meant to come sooner," says Ada, "but we could never make up our minds to leave a place. I thought we'd never pry Ruth loose from Venice."

"I resigned myself," says Pete, "and just sat in the Piazza San Marco, drinking gin fizz and being photographed with the pigeons, while Ruth had herself driven *all* up and down the Grand Canal." He looks at Ruth. "Finally, thank heaven, it rained."

"She was working off her hostilities," says Ada, with a grin. "We thought we might as well let her do it in Venice, the opportunities in North Carolina are really terribly limited."

"There are some very upset people walking around down there," Ruth says, "and a couple of tours around the Grand Canal might do them a world of good."

Pete laughs. "Can't you just see Ruth escorting them to the edge of the water?"

"I haven't lifted my hand in anger yet," Ruth says, "but, oh, Lord," and she laughs, clenching and unclenching her fists.

"You haven't been back for a long time, have you?" Talley asks me.

"Eight years. I haven't really lived there for twelve years."

Pete whistles. "I fear you are in for some surprises, my friend. There have been some changes made." Then, "Are you afraid?"

"A little."

"We all are," says Ada, "that's why I was so glad to get away for a little while."

"Then you haven't been back since Black Monday," Talley says. He laughs. "That's how it's gone down in Confederate history." He turns to Vidal. "What do people think about it here?"

Vidal smiles, delighted. "It seems extraordinarily infantile behavior, even for Americans, from whom, I must say, I have never expected very much in the way of maturity." Everyone at the table laughs. Vidal goes on. "But I cannot really talk about it, I do not understand it. I have never really understood Americans; I am an old man now, and I suppose I never will. There is something very nice about them, something very winning, but they seem so ignorant—so ignorant of life. Perhaps it is strange, but the only people from your country with whom I have ever made contact are black people—like my good friend, my discovery, here," and he slaps me on the shoulder. "Perhaps it is because we, in Europe, whatever else we do not know, or have forgotten, know about suffering. We have suffered here. You have suffered, too. But most Americans do not yet know what anguish is. It is too bad, because the life of the West is in their hands." He turns to Ada. "I cannot help saying that I think it is a scandal—and we may all pay very dearly for it—that a civilized nation should elect to represent it a man who is so simple that he thinks the world is simple." And silence falls at the table and the four young faces stare at him.

"Well," says Pete, at last, turning to me, "you won't be bored, man, when you get back there."

"It's much too nice a night," I say, "to stay cooped up in this place, where all I can hear is my own records." We laugh. "Why don't we get out of here and find a sidewalk café?" I tap Pete's guitar. "Maybe we can find out if you've got any talent."

"Oh, talent I've got," says Pete, "but character, man, I'm lacking."

So, after some confusion about the bill, for which Vidal has already made himself responsible, we walk out into the Paris night. It is very strange to feel that, very soon now, these boulevards will not exist for me. People will be walking up and down, as they are tonight, and lovers will be murmuring in the black shadows of the plane trees, and there will be these same still figures on the benches or in the parks—but they will not exist for me, I will not be here. For a long while Paris will no longer exist for me, except in my mind; and only in the minds of some people will I exist any longer for Paris. After departure, only invisible things are left, perhaps the life of the world is held together by invisible chains of memory and loss and love. So many things, so many people, depart! and we can only repossess them in our minds. Perhaps this is what the old folks meant, what my mother and my father meant, when they counseled us to keep the faith.

We have taken a table at the Deux Magots and Pete strums on his guitar and begins to play this song:

Preach the word, preach the word, preach the word!
If I never, never see you any more.
Preach the word, preach the word,
And I'll meet you on Canaan's shore.

He has a strong, clear, boyish voice, like a young preacher's, and he is smiling as he sings his song. Ada and I look at each other and grin, and Vidal is smiling. The waiter looks a little worried, for we are already beginning to attract a crowd, but it is a summer night, the gendarmes on the corner do not seem to mind, and there will be time, anyway, to stop us.

Pete was not there, none of us were, the first time this song was needed; and no one now alive can imagine what that time was like. But the song has come down the bloodstained ages. I suppose this to mean that the song is still needed, still has its work to do.

The others are all, visibly, very proud of Pete; and we all join him, and people stop to listen:

Testify! Testify!
If I never, never see you any more!
Testify! Testify!
I'll meet you on Canaan's shore!

In the crowd that has gathered to listen to us, I see a face I know, the face of a North African prizefighter, who is no longer in the ring. I used to know him well in the old days, but have not seen him for a long time. He looks quite well, his face is shining, he is quite decently dressed. And something about the way he holds himself, not quite looking at our table, tells me that he has seen me, but does not want to risk a rebuff. So I call him. "Boona!"

And he turns, smiling, and comes loping over to our table, his hands in his pockets. Pete is still singing and Ada and Vidal have taken off on a conversation of their own. Ruth and Talley look curiously, expectantly, at Boona. Now that I have called him over, I feel somewhat uneasy. I realize that I do not know what he is doing now, or how he will get along with any of these people, and I can see in his eyes that he is delighted to be in the presence of two young girls. There are virtually no North African women in Paris, and not even the dirty, rat-faced girls who live, apparently, in cafés are willing to go with an Arab. So Boona is always looking for a girl, and because he is so deprived and because he is not Western, his techniques can be very unsettling. I know he is relieved that the girls are not French and not white. He looks briefly at Vidal and Ada. Vidal, also, though for different reasons, is always looking for a girl.

But Boona has always been very nice to me. Perhaps I am sorry that I called him over, but I did not want to snub him.

He claps one hand to the side of my head, as is his habit. "*Comment vas-tu, mon frère?* I have not see you, oh, for long time." And he asks me, as in the old days, "You all right? Nobody bother you?" And he laughs. "Ah! *Tu as fait le chemin, toi!* Now you are *vedette*, big star—wonderful!" He looks around the table, made a little uncomfortable by the silence that has fallen, now that Pete has stopped singing. "I have seen you in the movies—you know?—and I tell everybody, I know. *him!*" He points to me, and laughs, and Ruth and Talley laugh with him. "That's right, man, you make me real proud, you make me cry!"

"Boona, I want you to meet some friends of mine." And I go round the table: "Ruth, Talley, Ada, Pete"—and he bows and shakes hands, his dark eyes gleaming with pleasure—"*et Monsieur Vidal, le metteur en scène du film qui t'a arraché des larmes.*"

"*Enchanté.*" But his attitude toward Vidal is colder, more distrustful. "Of course I have heard of Monsieur Vidal. He is the director of many films, many of them made me cry." This last statement is utterly, even insolently, insincere.

But Vidal, I think, is relieved that I will now be forced to speak to Boona and will leave him alone with Ada.

"Sit down," I say, "have a drink with us, let me have your news. What's been happening with you, what are you doing with yourself these days?"

"Ah," he sits down, "nothing very brilliant, my brother." He looks at me quickly, with a little smile. "You know, we have been having hard times here."

"Where are you from?" Ada asks him.

His brilliant eyes take her in entirely, but she does not flinch. "I am from Tunis." He says it proudly, with a little smile.

"From Tunis. I have never been to Africa, I would love to go one day."

He laughs. "Africa is a big place. Very big. There

are many countries in Africa, many"—he looks briefly at Vidal—"different kinds of people, many colonies."

"But Tunis," she continues, in her innocence, "is free? Freedom is happening all over Africa. That's why I would like to go there."

"I have not been back for a long time," says Boona, "but all the news I get from Tunis, from my people, is not good."

"Wouldn't you like to go back?" Ruth asks.

Again he looks at Vidal. "That is not so easy."

Vidal smiles. "You know what I would like to do? There's a wonderful Spanish place not far from here, where we can listen to live music and dance a little." He turns to Ada. "Would you like that?"

He is leaving it up to me to get rid of Boona, and it is, of course, precisely for this reason that I cannot do it. Besides, it is no longer so simple.

"Oh, I'd love that," says Ada, and she turns to Boona. "Won't you come, too?"

"Thank you, mam'selle," he says, softly, and his tongue flicks briefly over his lower lip, and he smiles. He is very moved, people are not often nice to him.

In the Spanish place there are indeed a couple of Spanish guitars, drums, castanets, and a piano, but the uses to which these are being put carry one back, as Pete puts it, to the levee. "These are the wailingest Spanish cats I ever heard," says Ruth. "They didn't learn how to do this in Spain, no, they didn't, they been rambling. You ever hear anything like this going on in Spain?" Talley takes her out on the dance floor, which is already crowded. A very handsome Frenchwoman is dancing with an enormous, handsome black man, who seems to be her lover, who seems to have taught her how to dance. Apparently, they are known to the musicians, who egg them on with small cries of *"Olé!"* It is a very good-natured crowd, mostly foreigners, Spaniards, Swedes, Greeks. Boona takes Ada out on the dance floor while Vidal is answering some questions put to him by Pete on the entertainment situation in France. Vidal looks a little put out, and I am amused.

We are there for perhaps an hour, dancing, talking, and I am, at last, a little drunk. In spite of Boona, who is a very good and tireless dancer, Vidal continues his pursuit of Ada, and I begin to wonder if he will make it and I begin to wonder if I want him to.

I am still puzzling out my reaction when Pete, who has disappeared, comes in through the front door, catches my eye, and signals to me. I leave the table and follow him into the streets.

He looks very upset. "I don't want to bug you, man," he says, "but I fear your boy has goofed."

I know he is not joking. I think he is probably angry at Vidal because of Ada, and I wonder what I can do about it and why he should be telling me.

I stare at him, gravely, and he says, "It looks like he stole some money."

"Stole *money*? Who, Vidal?"

And then, of course, I get it, in the split second before he says, impatiently, "No, are you kidding? Your friend, the Tunisian."

I do not know what to say or what to do, and so I temporize with questions. All the time I am wondering if this can be true and what I can do about it if it is. The trouble is, I know that Boona steals, he would probably not be alive if he didn't, but I cannot say so to these children, who probably still imagine that everyone who steals is a thief. But he has never, to my knowledge, stolen from a friend. It seems unlike him. I have always thought of him as being better than that, and smarter than that. And so I cannot believe it, but neither can I doubt it. I do not know anything about Boona's life, these days. This causes me to realize that I do not really know much about Boona.

"Who did he steal it from?"

"From Ada. Out of her bag."

"How much?"

"Ten dollars. It's not an awful lot of money, but"—he grimaces—"none of us *have* an awful lot of money."

"I know." The dark side street on which we stand is nearly empty. The only sound on the street is the muffled music of the Spanish club. "How do you know it was Boona?"

He anticipates my own unspoken rejoinder. "Who else could it be? Besides—somebody *saw* him do it."

"Somebody saw him?"

"Yes."

I do not ask him who this person is, for fear that he will say it is Vidal.

"Well," I say, "I'll try to get it back." I think that I will take Boona aside and then replace the money myself. "Was it in dollars or in francs?"

"In francs."

I have no dollars and this makes it easier. I do not know how I can possibly face Boona and accuse him of stealing money from my friends. I would rather give him the benefit of even the faintest doubt. But, "Who saw him?" I ask.

"Talley. But we didn't want to make a thing about it—"

"Does Ada know it's gone?"

"Yes." He looks at me helplessly. "I know this makes you feel pretty bad, but we thought we'd better tell you, rather than"—lamely—"anybody else."

Now, Ada comes out of the club, carrying her ridiculous handbag, and with her face all knotted and sad. "Oh," she says, "I hate to cause all this trouble, it's not worth it, not for ten lousy dollars." I am astonished to see that she has been weeping, and tears come to her eyes now.

I put my arm around her shoulder. "Come on, now. You're not causing anybody any trouble and, anyway, it's nothing to cry about."

"It isn't your fault, Ada," Pete says, miserably.

"Oh, I ought to get a sensible handbag," she says, "like you're always telling me to do," and she laughs a little, then looks at me. "Please don't try to do anything about it. Let's just forget it."

"What's happening inside?" I ask her.

"Nothing. They're just talking. I think Mr. Vidal is dancing with Ruth. He's a great dancer, that little Frenchman."

"He's a great talker, too," Pete says.

"Oh, he doesn't mean anything," says Ada, "he's just having fun. He probably doesn't get a chance to talk to many American girls."

"He certainly made up for lost time tonight."

"Look," I say, "if Talley and Boona are alone, maybe you better go back in. We'll be in in a minute. Let's try to keep this as quiet as we can."

"Yeah," he says, "okay. We're going soon anyway, okay?"

"Yes," she tells him, "right away."

But as he turns away, Boona and Talley step out into the street, and it is clear that Talley feels that he has Boona under arrest. I almost laugh, the whole thing is beginning to resemble one of those mad French farces with people flying in and out of doors; but Boona comes straight to me.

"They say I stole money, my friend. You know me, you are the only one here who knows me, you know I would not do such a thing."

I look at him and I do not know what to say. Ada looks at him with her eyes full of tears and looks away. I take Boona's arm.

"We'll be back in a minute," I say. We walk a few paces up the dark, silent street.

"She say I take her money," he says. He, too, looks as though he is about to weep—but I do not know for which reason. "You know me, you know me almost twelve years, you think I do such a thing?"

Talley saw you, I want to say, but I cannot say it. Perhaps Talley only thought he saw him. Perhaps it is easy to see a boy who looks like Boona with his hand in an American girl's purse.

"If you not believe me," he says, "search me. Search me!" And he opens his arms wide, theatrically, and now there are tears standing in his eyes.

I do not know what his tears mean, but I certainly cannot search him. I want to say, I know you steal, I know you have to steal. Perhaps you took the money out of this girl's purse in order to eat tomorrow, in order not to be thrown into the streets tonight, in order to stay out of jail. This girl means nothing to you, after all, she is only an American, an American like me. Perhaps, I suddenly think, no girl means anything to you, or ever will again, they have beaten you too hard and kept you in the gutter too long. And I also think, If you would steal from her, then of course you would lie to me, neither of us means anything to you; perhaps, in your eyes, we are simply luckier gangsters in a world which is run by gangsters. But I cannot say any of these things to Boona. I cannot say, Tell me the truth, nobody cares about the money any more.

So I say, "Of course I will not search you." And I realize that he knew that I would not.

"I think it is that Frenchman who say I am a thief. They think we all are thieves." His eyes are bright and bitter. He looks over my shoulder. "They have all come out of the club now."

I look around and they are all there, in a little dark knot on the sidewalk.

"Don't worry," I say. "It doesn't matter."

"You believe me? My brother?" And his eyes look into mine with a terrible intensity.

"Yes," I force myself to say, "yes, of course, I believe you. Someone made a mistake, that's all."

"You know, the way American girls run around, they have their sack open all the time, she could lose the money anywhere. Why she blame me? Because I come from Africa?" Tears are glittering on his face. "Here she come now."

And Ada comes up the street with her straight, determined walk. She walks straight to Boona and takes his hand. "I am sorry," she says, "for everything that happened. Please believe me. It isn't worth all this fuss. I'm sure you're a very nice person, and"—she falters—"I must have lost the money, I'm sure I lost it." She looks at him. "It isn't worth hurting your feelings, and I'm terribly sorry about it."

"I no take your money," he says. "Really, truly, I no take it. Ask him"—pointing to me, grabbing me by the arm, shaking me—"he know me for years, he will tell you that I never, never steal!"

"I'm sure," she says. "I'm sure."

I take Boona by the arm again. "Let's forget it. Let's forget it all. We're all going home now, and one of these days we'll have a drink again and we'll forget all about it, all right?"

"Yes," says Ada, "let us forget it." And she holds out her hand.

Boona takes it, wonderingly. His eyes take her in again. "You are a very nice girl. Really. A very nice girl."

"I'm sure you're a nice person, too." She pauses. "Good night."

"Good night," he says, after a long silence.

Then he kisses me on both cheeks. *"Au revoir, mon frère."*

"Au revoir, Boona."

After a moment we turn and walk away, leaving him standing there.

"Did he take it?" asks Vidal.

"I tell you, I *saw* him," says Talley.

"Well," I say, "it doesn't matter now." I look back and see Boona's stocky figure disappearing down the street.

"No," says Ada, "it doesn't matter." She looks up. "It's almost morning."

"I would gladly," says Vidal, stammering, "gladly—"

But she is herself again. "I wouldn't think of it. We had a wonderful time tonight, a wonderful time, and I wouldn't think of it." She turns to me with that urchinlike grin. "It was wonderful meeting you. I hope you won't have too much trouble getting used to the States again."

"Oh, I don't think I will," I say. And then, "I hope you won't."

"No," she says, "I don't think anything they can do will surprise me any more."

"Which way are we all going?" asks Vidal. "I hope someone will share my taxi with me."

But he lives in the sixteenth arrondissement, which is not in anyone's direction. We walk him to the line of cabs standing under the clock at Odéon.

And we look each other in the face, in the growing morning light. His face looks weary and lined and lonely. He puts both hands on my shoulders and then puts one hand on the nape of my neck. "Do not forget me, Chico," he says. "You must come back and see us, one of these days. Many of us depend on you for many things."

"I'll be back," I say. "I'll never forget you."

He raises his eyebrows and smiles. *"Alors, adieu."*

"Adieu, Vidal."

"I was happy to meet all of you," he says. He looks at Ada. "Perhaps we will meet again before you leave."

"Perhaps," she says. "Good-by, Monsieur Vidal."

"Good-by."

Vidal's cab drives away. "I also leave you now," I say. "I must go home and wake up my son and prepare for our journey."

I leave them standing on the corner, under the clock, which points to six. They look very strange and lost and determined, the four of them. Just before my cab turns off the boulevard, I wave to them and they wave back.

Mme. Dumont is in the hall, mopping the floor.

"Did all my family get home?" I ask. I feel very cheerful, I do not know why.

"Yes," she says, "they are all here. Paul is still sleeping."

"May I go in and get him?"

She looks at me in surprise. "Of course."

So I walk into her apartment and walk into the room where Paul lies sleeping. I stand over his bed for a long time.

Perhaps my thoughts travel—travel through to him. He opens his eyes and smiles up at me. He puts a fist to his eyes and raises his arms. *"Bonjour, Papa."*

I lift him up. "*Bonjour.* How do you feel today?"

"Oh, I don't know yet," he says.

I laugh. I put him on my shoulder and walk out into the hall. Mme. Dumont looks up at him with her radiant, aging face.

"Ah," she says, "you are going on a journey! How does it feel?"

"He doesn't know yet," I tell her. I walk to the elevator door and open it, dropping Paul down to the crook of my arm.

She laughs. "He will know later. What a journey! *Jusqu' au nouveau monde!"*

I open the cage and we step inside. "Yes," I say, "all the way to the new world." I press the button and the cage, holding my son and me, goes up.

FLANNERY O'CONNOR [1925-1964]

DURING HER thirty-nine years, a life cut short by serious illness, Flannery O'Connor achieved a reputation as one of the most original and complex of the younger school of fiction writers. The puzzling and fascinating character of her art—was she essentially a satirist of degeneration in modern society, a Southern regionalist with a Faulknerian strain of violence and morbidity, a macabre humorist, a Christian allegorist?—derives in large measure from the contradictions and paradoxes of her birthright and formative years. Asked about the influences on her work, she replied, "Probably being a Catholic, and a Southerner, and a writer."

Miss O'Connor was born in Savannah, Georgia, the only child of Roman Catholic parents. She was educated at Milledgeville, where her parents lived on a dairy farm. She attended Georgia State College for Women, was art editor of the newspaper, and literary editor of the quarterly magazine, to which she contributed fiction and cartoons. Some of her stories attracted the attention of a teacher who submitted them to the Writers' Workshop of the University of Iowa, where she won a fellowship and earned an M.F.A. degree in 1947. From this point she became a dedicated writer. Her first story appeared in *Accent* in 1946; her first novel, *Wise Blood*, was published in 1952. At this period her health began to fail; but despite the crippling blood disease which confined her to the Milledgeville farm for most of her remaining years, she continued to write, carried on a correspondence with young writers, and even lectured and read her stories to university audiences in the South. Throughout these years a succession of fellowships, grants, prizes, and honorary degrees marked the ever-increasing recognition of her talent.

In an essay "The Fiction Writer and His Country" (1957) Flannery O'Connor defined the role of the Christian writer in modern life as one of finding "distortions which are repugnant to him" and making these distortions apparent to audiences used to seeing them as natural. Her method of revelation is through shock and caricature. *Wise Blood*, for instance, portrays with Kafka-esque brutality and violent exaggeration a young anti-religious army-returnee who devotes his life to evangelizing "the Church without Christ." Her second novel, *The Violent Bear It Away* (1960), is another oblique allegory of religious deviation, this time among a godless set of anti-Christian evangelists who engage in shocking perversions of the faith and mawkish parodies of the Church. In her two novels Miss O'Connor sought to depict the meaninglessness of contemporary life and the degenerate quality of contemporary belief by keeping "the sharpest eyes for the grotesque, for the perverse and the unacceptable."

Her real forte, however, is the short story, narrated in swift, bold, unsparing terms, centering on one or two characters from Southern farm or city life (Atlanta was her Babylon), and usually directed toward some ironic or violent climax. Two volumes, *A Good Man Is Hard to Find* (1955) and *Everything That Rises Must Converge* (1965), contain the best of her short fiction. Her epiphanies are often cruel and negative ones, exposing the hypocrisy and self-centeredness of otherwise well-meaning people like the embittered Mrs. May in "Greenleaf," impaled on the horns of a bull, or the genteel grandmother of "A Good Man Is Hard to Find," coldly shot down by a gangster. Harsh and unrelenting, though surfaced with comic touches and satire, many of the stories involve people who are warped and bitter toward their fellow men: "stories about original sin," she called them. Such tales as "A Circle in the Fire," "Parker's Back," "The Enduring Chill," and "Greenleaf"—all among her best—imply a major theme looming behind the grim situation: the modern world has been twisted out of shape by perversions of Christian belief and by reliance on the human ego rather than on the saving force of Christ's redemptive act. Both her corrupt and her well-disposed characters seem ripe for some apocalyptic judgment, some Christ-avenging punishment on mankind for its substitution of rationalism, humanitarianism, or selfish complacency for the pentecostal mysteries. As a writer, however, she never allowed her stories to become doctrinaire allegories of the Christian vision, but remained true to the color and reality of her Southern region and its people.

Further reading: *Three By Flannery O'Connor* (includes *Wise Blood; A Good Man Is Hard to Find; The Violent Bear It Away*). *Everything That Rises Must Converge*, with an introduction by Robert Fitzgerald, 1967. M. J. Friedman and L. A. Lawson, eds., *The Added Dimension: The Art and Mind of Flannery O'Connor*, 1966.

Greenleaf

First published in the *Kenyon Review* (Summer 1956); reprinted here from *Everything That Rises Must Converge* (1965).

Mrs. May's bedroom window was low and faced on the east and the bull, silvered in the moonlight, stood under it, his head raised as if he listened—like some patient god come down to woo her—for a stir inside the room. The window was dark and the sound of her breathing too light to be carried outside. Clouds crossing the moon blackened him and in the dark he began to tear at the hedge. Presently they passed and he appeared again in the same spot, chewing steadily, with a hedge-wreath that he had ripped loose for himself caught in the tips of his horns. When the moon drifted into retirement again, there was nothing to mark his place but the sound of steady chewing. Then abruptly a pink glow filled the window. Bars of light slid across him as the venetian blind was slit. He took a step backward and lowered his head as if to show the wreath across his horns.

For almost a minute there was no sound from inside, then as he raised his crowned head again, a woman's voice, guttural as if addressed to a dog, said, "Get away from here, Sir!" and in a second muttered, "Some nigger's scrub bull."

The animal pawed the ground and Mrs. May, standing bent forward behind the blind, closed it quickly lest the light make him charge into the shrubbery. For a second she waited, still bent forward, her nightgown hanging loosely from her narrow shoulders. Green rubber curlers sprouted neatly over her forehead and her face beneath them was smooth as concrete with an egg-white paste that drew the wrinkles out while she slept.

She had been conscious in her sleep of a steady rhythmic chewing as if something were eating one wall of the house. She had been aware that whatever it was had been eating as long as she had had the place and had eaten everything from the beginning of her fence line up to the house and now was eating the house and calmly with the same steady rhythm would continue through the house, eating her and the boys, and then on, eating everything but the Greenleafs, on and on, eating everything until nothing was left but the Greenleafs on a little island all their own in the middle of what had been her place. When the munching reached her elbow, she jumped up and found herself, fully awake, standing in the middle of her room. She identified the sound at once: a cow was tearing at the shrubbery under her window. Mr. Greenleaf had left the lane gate open and she didn't doubt that the entire herd was on her lawn. She turned on the dim pink table lamp and then went to the window and slit the blind. The bull, gaunt and long-legged, was standing about four feet from her, chewing calmly like an uncouth country suitor.

For fifteen years, she thought as she squinted at him fiercely, she had been having shiftless people's hogs root up her oats, their mules wallow on her lawn, their scrub bulls breed her cows. If this one was not put up now, he would be over the fence, ruining her herd before morning—and Mr. Greenleaf was soundly sleeping a half mile down the road in the tenant house. There was no way to get him unless she dressed and got in her car and rode down there and woke him up. He would come but his expression, his whole figure, his every pause, would say: "Hit looks to me like one or both of them boys would not make their maw ride out in the middle of the night thisaway. If hit was my boys, they would have got thet bull up theirself."

The bull lowered his head and shook it and the wreath slipped down to the base of his horns where it looked like a menacing prickly crown. She had closed the blind then; in a few seconds she heard him move off heavily.

Mr. Greenleaf would say, "If hit was my boys

they would never have allowed their maw to go after hired help in the middle of the night. They would have did it theirself."

Weighing it, she decided not to bother Mr. Greenleaf. She returned to bed thinking that if the Greenleaf boys had risen in the world it was because she had given their father employment when no one else would have him. She had had Mr. Greenleaf fifteen years but no one else would have had him five minutes. Just the way he approached an object was enough to tell anybody with eyes what kind of a worker he was. He walked with a high-shouldered creep and he never appeared to come directly forward. He walked on the perimeter of some invisible circle and if you wanted to look him in the face, you had to move and get in front of him. She had not fired him because she had always doubted she could do better. He was too shiftless to go out and look for another job; he didn't have the initiative to steal, and after she had told him three or four times to do a thing, he did it; but he never told her about a sick cow until it was too late to call the veterinarian and if her barn had caught on fire, he would have called his wife to see the flames before he began to put them out. And of the wife, she didn't even like to think. Beside the wife, Mr. Greenleaf was an aristocrat.

"If it had been my boys," he would have said, "they would have cut off their right arm before they would have allowed their maw to . . ."

"If your boys had any pride, Mr. Greenleaf," she would like to say to him some day, "there are many things that they would not *allow* their mother to do."

The next morning as soon as Mr. Greenleaf came to the back door, she told him there was a stray bull on the place and that she wanted him penned up at once.

"Done already been here three days," he said, addressing his right foot which he held forward, turned slightly as if he were trying to look at the sole. He was standing at the bottom of the three back steps while she leaned out the kitchen door, a small woman with pale near-sighted eyes and grey hair that rose on top like the crest of some disturbed bird.

"Three days!" she said in the restrained screech that had become habitual with her.

Mr. Greenleaf, looking into the distance over the near pasture, removed a package of cigarets from his shirt pocket and let one fall into his hand. He put the package back and stood for a while looking at the cigaret. "I put him in the bull pen but he torn out of there," he said presently. "I didn't see him none after that." He bent over the cigaret and lit it and then turned his head briefly in her direction. The upper part of his face sloped gradually into the lower which was long and narrow, shaped like a rough chalice. He had deep-set fox-colored eyes shadowed under a grey felt hat that he wore slanted forward following the line of his nose. His build was insignificant.

"Mr. Greenleaf," she said, "get that bull up this morning before you do anything else. You know he'll ruin the breeding schedule. Get him up and keep him up and the next time there's a stray bull on this place, tell me at once. Do you understand?"

"Where you want him put at?" Mr. Greenleaf asked.

"I don't care where you put him," she said. "You are supposed to have some sense. Put him where he can't get out. Whose bull is he?"

For a moment Mr. Greenleaf seemed to hesitate between silence and speech. He studied the air to the left of him. "He must be somebody's bull," he said after a while.

"Yes, he must!" she said and shut the door with a precise little slam.

She went into the dining room where the two boys were eating breakfast and sat down on the edge of her chair at the head of the table. She never ate breakfast but she sat with them to see that they had what they wanted. "Honestly!" she said, and began to tell about the bull, aping Mr. Greenleaf saying, "It must be *somebody's* bull."

Wesley continued to read the newspaper folded beside his plate but Scofield interrupted his eating from time to time to look at her and laugh. The two boys never had the same reaction to anything. They were as different, she said, as night and day. The only thing they did have in common was that neither of them cared what happened on the place. Scofield was a business type and Wesley was an intellectual.

Wesley, the younger child, had had rheumatic fever when he was seven and Mrs. May thought that this was what had caused him to be an intellectual. Scofield, who had never had a day's sickness in his life, was an insurance salesman. She would not have minded his selling insurance if he had sold a nicer kind but he sold the kind that only Negroes buy. He was what Negroes call a "policy man." He said there was more money in nigger-insurance than any other kind, and before company, he was very loud about it. He would shout, "Mamma don't like to hear me say it but I'm the best nigger-insurance salesman in this county!"

Scofield was thirty-six and he had a broad pleasant smiling face but he was not married. "Yes," Mrs. May would say, "and if you sold decent insurance, some *nice* girl would be willing to marry you.

What nice girl wants to marry a nigger-insurance man? You'll wake up some day and it'll be too late."

And at this Scofield would yodel and say, "Why Mamma, I'm not going to marry until you're dead and gone and then I'm going to marry me some nice fat farm girl that can take over this place!" And once he had added, "—some nice lady like Mrs. Greenleaf." When he had said this, Mrs. May had risen from her chair, her back stiff as a rake handle, and had gone to her room. There she had sat down on the edge of her bed for some time with her small face drawn. Finally she had whispered, "I work and slave, I struggle and sweat to keep this place for them and soon as I'm dead, they'll marry trash and bring it in here and ruin everything. They'll marry trash and ruin everything I've done," and she had made up her mind at that moment to change her will. The next day she had gone to her lawyer and had had the property entailed so that if they married, they could not leave it to their wives.

The idea that one of them might marry a woman even remotely like Mrs. Greenleaf was enough to make her ill. She had put up with Mr. Greenleaf for fifteen years, but the only way she had endured his wife had been by keeping entirely out of her sight. Mrs. Greenleaf was large and loose. The yard around her house looked like a dump and her five girls were always filthy; even the youngest one dipped snuff. Instead of making a garden or washing their clothes, her preoccupation was what she called "prayer healing."

Every day she cut all the morbid stories out of the newspaper—the accounts of women who had been raped and criminals who had escaped and children who had been burned and of train wrecks and plane crashes and the divorces of movie stars. She took these to the woods and dug a hole and buried them and then she fell on the ground over them and mumbled and groaned for an hour or so, moving her huge arms back and forth under her and out again and finally just lying down flat and, Mrs. May suspected, going to sleep in the dirt.

She had not found out about this until the Greenleafs had been with her a few months. One morning she had been out to inspect a field that she had wanted planted in rye but that had come up in clover because Mr. Greenleaf had used the wrong seeds in the grain drill. She was returning through a wooded path that separated two pastures, muttering to herself and hitting the ground methodically with a long stick she carried in case she saw a snake. "Mr. Greenleaf," she was saying in a low voice, "I cannot afford to pay for your mistakes. I am a poor woman and this place is all I have. I have two boys to educate. I cannot . . . ."

Out of nowhere a guttural agonized voice groaned, "Jesus! Jesus!" In a second it came again with a terrible urgency. "Jesus! Jesus!"

Mrs. May stopped still, one hand lifted to her throat. The sound was so piercing that she felt as if some violent unleashed force had broken out of the ground and was charging toward her. Her second thought was more reasonable: somebody had been hurt on the place and would sue her for everything she had. She had no insurance. She rushed forward and turning a bend in the path, she saw Mrs. Greenleaf sprawled on her hands and knees off the side of the road, her head down.

"Mrs. Greenleaf!" she shrilled, "what's happened?"

Mrs. Greenleaf raised her head. Her face was a patchwork of dirt and tears and her small eyes, the color of two field peas, were red-rimmed and swollen, but her expression was as composed as a bulldog's. She swayed back and forth on her hands and knees and groaned, "Jesus, Jesus."

Mrs. May winced. She thought the word, Jesus, should be kept inside the church building like other words inside the bedroom. She was a good Christian woman with a large respect for religion, though she did not, of course, believe any of it was true. "What is the matter with you?" she asked sharply.

"You broken my healing," Mrs. Greenleaf said, waving her aside. "I can't talk to you until I finish."

Mrs. May stood, bent forward, her mouth open and her stick raised off the ground as if she were not sure what she wanted to strike with it.

"Oh Jesus, stab me in the heart!" Mrs. Greenleaf shrieked. "Jesus, stab me in the heart!" and she fell back flat in the dirt, a huge human mound, her legs and arms spread out as if she were trying to wrap them around the earth.

Mrs. May felt as furious and helpless as if she had been insulted by a child. "Jesus," she said, drawing herself back, "would be *ashamed* of you. He would tell you to get up from there this instant and go wash your children's clothes!" and she had turned and walked off as fast as she could.

Whenever she thought of how the Greenleaf boys had advanced in the world, she had only to think of Mrs. Greenleaf sprawled obscenely on the ground, and say to herself, "Well, no matter how far they *go*, they *came* from that."

She would like to have been able to put in her will that when she died, Wesley and Scofield were not to continue to employ Mr. Greenleaf. She was capable of handling Mr. Greenleaf; they were not. Mr. Greenleaf had pointed out to her once that her boys didn't know hay from silage. She had pointed out to him that they had other talents, that Scofield was a successful business man and Wesley a successful intellectual. Mr. Greenleaf did not comment, but he never lost an opportunity of letting her see, by his expression or some simple gesture, that he held the two of them in infinite contempt. As scrub-human as the Greenleafs were, he never hesitated to let her know that in any like circumstance in which his own boys might have been involved, they—O. T. and E. T. Greenleaf—would have acted to better advantage.

The Greenleaf boys were two or three years younger than the May boys. They were twins and you never knew when you spoke to one of them whether you were speaking to O. T. or E. T., and they never had the politeness to enlighten you. They were long-legged and raw-boned and red-skinned, with bright grasping fox-colored eyes like their father's. Mr. Greenleaf's pride in them began with the fact that they were twins. He acted, Mrs. May said, as if this were something smart they had thought of themselves. They were energetic and hard working and she would admit to anyone that they had come a long way—and that the Second World War was reponsible for it.

They had both joined the service and, disguised in their uniforms, they could not be told from other people's children. You could tell, of course, when they opened their mouths but they did that seldom. The smartest thing they had done was to get sent overseas and there to marry French wives. They hadn't married French trash either. They had married nice girls who naturally couldn't tell that they murdered the king's English or that the Greenleafs were who they were.

Wesley's heart condition had not permitted him to serve his country but Scofield had been in the army for two years. He had not cared for it and at the end of his military service, he was only a Private First Class. The Greenleaf boys were both some kind of sergeants, and Mr. Greenleaf, in those days, had never lost an opportunity of referring to them by their rank. They had both managed to get wounded and now they both had pensions. Further, as soon as they were released from the army, they took advantage of all the benefits and went to the school of agriculture at the university—the taxpayers meanwhile supporting their French wives. The two of them were living now about two miles down the highway on a piece of land that the government had helped them to buy and in a brick duplex bungalow that the government had helped to build and pay for. If the war had made anyone, Mrs. May said, it had made the Greenleaf boys. They each had three little children apiece, who spoke Greenleaf English and French, and who, on account of their mothers' background, would be sent to the convent school and brought up with manners. "And in twenty years," Mrs. May asked Scofield and Wesley, "do you know what those people will be?

"*Society,*" she said blackly.

She had spent fifteen years coping with Mr. Greenleaf and, by now, handling him had become second nature with her. His disposition on any particular day was as much a factor in what she could and couldn't do as the weather was, and she had learned to read his face the way real country people read the sunrise and sunset.

She was a country woman only by persuasion. The late Mr. May, a business man, had bought the place when land was down, and when he died it was all he had to leave her. The boys had not been happy to move to the country to a broken-down farm, but there was nothing else for her to do. She had the timber on the place cut and with the proceeds had set herself up in the dairy business after Mr. Greenleaf had answered her ad. "i seen yor add and i will come have 2 boys," was all his letter said, but he arrived the next day in a pieced-together truck, his wife and five daughters sitting on the floor in back, himself and the two boys in the cab.

Over the years they had been on her place, Mr. and Mrs. Greenleaf had aged hardly at all. They had no worries, no responsibilities. They lived like the lilies of the field, off the fat that she struggled to put into the land. When she was dead and gone from overwork and worry, the Greenleafs, healthy and thriving, would be just ready to begin draining Scofield and Wesley.

Wesley said the reason Mrs. Greenleaf had not aged was because she released all her emotions in prayer healing. "You ought to start praying, Sweetheart," he had said in the voice that, poor boy, he could not help making deliberately nasty.

Scofield only exasperated her beyond endurance but Wesley caused her real anxiety. He was thin and nervous and bald and being an intellectual was a terrible strain on his disposition. She doubted if he would marry until she died but she was certain that then the wrong woman would get him. Nice girls didn't like Scofield but Wesley didn't like nice girls. He didn't like anything. He drove twenty miles every day to the university where he taught and twenty miles back every night, but he said he hated the twenty-mile drive and he hated the second-rate university and he hated the morons who attended it. He hated the country and he hated the life he lived; he hated living with his mother and his idiot brother and he hated hearing about the damn dairy and the damn help and the damn broken machinery. But in spite of all he said, he never made any move to leave. He talked about Paris and Rome but he never went even to Atlanta.

"You'd go to those places and you'd get sick," Mrs. May would say. "Who in Paris is going to see that you get a salt-free diet? And do you think if you married one of those odd numbers you take out that *she* would cook a salt-free diet for you? No, indeed, she would not!" When she took this line, Wesley would turn himself roughly around in his chair and ignore her. Once when she had kept it up too long, he had snarled, "Well, why don't you do something practical, Woman? Why don't you pray for me like Mrs. Greenleaf would?"

"I don't like to hear you boys make jokes about religion," she had said. "If you would go to church, you would meet some nice girls."

But it was impossible to tell them anything. When she looked at the two of them now, sitting on either side of the table, neither one caring the least if a stray bull ruined her herd—which was their herd, their future—when she looked at the two of them, one hunched over a paper and the other teetering back in his chair, grinning at her like an idiot, she wanted to jump up and beat her fist on the table and shout, "You'll find out one of these days, you'll find out what *Reality* is when it's too late!"

"Mamma," Scofield said, "don't you get excited now but I'll tell you whose bull that is." He was looking at her wickedly. He let his chair drop forward and he got up. Then with his shoulders bent and his hands held up to cover his head, he tiptoed to the door. He backed into the hall and pulled the door almost to so that it hid all of him but his face. "You want to know, Sugarpie?" he asked.

Mrs. May sat looking at him coldly.

"That's O. T. and E. T.'s bull," he said. "I collected from their nigger yesterday and he told me they were missing it," and he showed her an exaggerated expanse of teeth and disappeared silently.

Wesley looked up and laughed.

Mrs. May turned her head forward again, her expression unaltered. "I am the only *adult* on this place," she said. She leaned across the table and pulled the paper from the side of his plate. "Do you see how it's going to be when I die and you boys have to handle him?" she began. "Do you see why he didn't know whose bull that was? Because it was theirs. Do you see what I have to put up with? Do you see that if I hadn't kept my foot on his neck all these years, you boys might be milking cows every morning at four o'clock?"

Wesley pulled the paper back toward his plate and staring at her full in the face, he murmured, "I wouldn't milk a cow to save your soul from hell."

"I know you wouldn't," she said in a brittle voice. She sat back and began rapidly turning her knife over at the side of her plate. "O. T. and E. T. are fine boys," she said. "They ought to have been my sons." The thought of this was so horrible that her vision of Wesley was blurred at once by a wall of tears. All she saw was his dark shape, rising quickly from the table. "And you two," she cried, "you two should have belonged to that woman!"

He was heading for the door.

"When I die," she said in a thin voice, "I don't know what's going to become of you."

"You're always yapping about when-you-die," he growled as he rushed out, "but you look pretty healthy to me."

For some time she sat where she was, looking straight ahead through the window across the room into a scene of indistinct greys and greens. She stretched her face and her neck muscles and drew in a long breath but the scene in front of her flowed together anyway into a watery grey mass. "They needn't think I'm going to die any time soon," she muttered, and some more defiant voice in her added: I'll die when I get good and ready.

She wiped her eyes with the table napkin and got up and went to the window and gazed at the scene in front of her. The cows were grazing on two pale green pastures across the road and behind them, fencing them in, was a black wall of trees with a sharp sawtooth edge that held off the indifferent sky. The pastures were enough to calm her. When she looked out any window in her house, she saw the reflection of her own character. Her city friends said she was the most remarkable woman they knew, to go, practically penniless and with no experience, out to a rundown farm and make a success of it. "Everything is against you," she would say, "the weather is against you and the dirt is against you and the help is against you. They're all in league against you. There's nothing for it but an iron hand!"

"Look at Mamma's iron hand!" Scofield would yell and grab her arm and hold it up so that her delicate blue-veined little hand would dangle from her wrist like the head of a broken lily. The company always laughed.

The sun, moving over the black and white grazing cows, was just a little brighter than the rest of the sky. Looking down, she saw a darker shape that might have been its shadow cast at an angle, moving among them. She uttered a sharp cry and turned and marched out of the house.

Mr. Greenleaf was in the trench silo, filling a wheelbarrow. She stood on the edge and looked down at him. "I told you to get up that bull. Now he's in with the milk herd."

"You can't do two thangs at oncet," Mr. Greenleaf remarked.

"I told you to do that first."

He wheeled the barrow out of the open end of the trench toward the barn and she followed close behind him. "And you needn't think, Mr. Greenleaf," she said, "that I don't know exactly whose bull that is or why you haven't been in any hurry to notify me he was here. I might as well feed O. T. and E. T.'s bull as long as I'm going to have him here ruining my herd."

Mr. Greenleaf paused with the wheelbarrow and looked behind him. "Is that them boys' bull?" he asked in an incredulous tone.

She did not say a word. She merely looked away with her mouth taut.

"They told me their bull was out but I never known that was him," he said.

"I want that bull put up now," she said, "and I'm going to drive over to O. T. and E. T.'s and tell them they'll have to come get him today. I ought to charge for the time he's been here—then it wouldn't happen again."

"They didn't pay but seventy-five dollars for him," Mr. Greenleaf offered.

"I wouldn't have had him as a gift," she said.

"They was just going to beef him," Mr. Greenleaf went on, "but he got loose and run his head into their pickup truck. He don't like cars and trucks. They had a time getting his horn out the fender and when they finally got him loose, he took off and they was too tired to run after him—but I never known that was him there."

"It wouldn't have paid you to know, Mr. Greenleaf," she said. "But you know now. Get a horse and get him."

In a half hour, from her front window she saw the bull, squirrel-colored, with jutting hips and long light horns, ambling down the dirt road that ran in front of the house. Mr. Greenleaf was behind him on the horse. "That's a Greenleaf bull if I ever saw one," she muttered. She went out on the porch and called, "Put him where he can't get out."

"He likes to bust loose," Mr. Greenleaf said, looking with approval at the bull's rump. "This gentleman is a sport."

"If those boys don't come for him, he's going to be a dead sport," she said. "I'm just warning you."

He heard her but he didn't answer.

"That's the awfullest looking bull I ever saw," she called but he was too far down the road to hear.

It was mid-morning when she turned into O. T. and E. T.'s driveway. The house, a new red-brick, low-to-the-ground building that looked like a warehouse with windows, was on top of a treeless hill. The sun was beating down directly on the white roof of it. It was the kind of house that everybody built now and nothing marked it as belonging to Greenleafs except three dogs, part hound and part spitz, that rushed out from behind it as soon as she stopped her car. She reminded herself that you could always tell the class of people by the class of dog, and honked her horn. While she sat waiting for someone to come, she continued to study the house. All the windows were down and she wondered if the government could have air-conditioned the thing. No one came and she honked again. Presently a door opened and several children appeared in it and stood looking at her, making no move to come forward. She recognized this as a true Greenleaf trait—they would hang in a door, looking at you for hours.

"Can't one of you children come here?" she called.

After a minute they all began to move forward, slowly. They had on overalls and were barefooted but they were not as dirty as she might have expected. There were two or three that looked distinctly like Greenleafs; the others not so much so. The smallest child was a girl with untidy black hair. They stopped about six feet from the automobile and stood looking at her.

"You're mighty pretty," Mrs. May said, addressing herself to the smallest girl.

There was no answer. They appeared to share one dispassionate expression between them.

"Where's your Mamma?" she asked.

There was no answer to this for some time. Then one of them said something in French. Mrs. May did not speak French.

"Where's your daddy?" she asked.

After a while, one of the boys said, "He ain't hyar neither."

"Ahhhh," Mrs. May said as if something had been proven. "Where's the colored man?"

She waited and decided no one was going to answer. "The cat has six little tongues," she said. "How would you like to come home with me and let me teach you how to talk?" She laughed and her laugh died on the silent air. She felt as if she were on trial for her life, facing a jury of Greenleafs. "I'll go down and see if I can find the colored man," she said.

"You can go if you want to," one of the boys said.

"Well, thank you," she murmured and drove off.

The barn was down the lane from the house. She had not seen it before but Mr. Greenleaf had described it in detail for it had been built according to the latest specifications. It was a milking parlor arrangement where the cows are milked from below. The milk ran in pipes from the machines to the milk house and was never carried in no bucket, Mr. Greenleaf said, by no human hand. "When you gonter get you one?" he had asked.

"Mr. Greenleaf," she had said, "I have to do for myself. I am not assisted hand and foot by the government. It would cost me $20,000 to install a milking parlor. I barely make ends meet as it is."

"My boys done it," Mr. Greenleaf had murmured, and then—"but all boys ain't alike."

"No indeed!" she had said. "I thank God for that!"

"I thank Gawd for ever-thang," Mr. Greenleaf had drawled.

You might as well, she had thought in the fierce silence that followed; you've never done anything for yourself.

She stopped by the side of the barn and honked but no one appeared. For several minutes she sat in the car, observing the various machines parked around, wondering how many of them were paid for. They had a forage harvester and a rotary hay baler. She had those too. She decided that since no one was here, she would get out and have a look at the milking parlor and see if they kept it clean.

She opened the milking room door and stuck her head in and for the first second she felt as if she were going to lose her breath. The spotless white concrete room was filled with sunlight that came from a row of windows head-high along both walls. The metal stanchions gleamed ferociously and she had to squint to be able to look at all. She drew her head out the room quickly and closed the door and leaned against it, frowning. The light outside was not so bright but she was conscious that the sun was directly on top of her head, like a silver bullet ready to drop into her brain.

A Negro carrying a yellow calf-feed bucket appeared from around the corner of the machine shed and came toward her. He was a light yellow boy dressed in the cast-off army clothes of the Greenleaf twins. He stopped at a respectable distance and set the bucket on the ground.

"Where's Mr. O. T. and Mr. E. T.?" she asked.

"Mist O. T. he in town, Mist E. T. he off yonder in the field," the Negro said, pointing first to the left and then to the right as if he were naming the position of two planets.

"Can you remember a message?" she asked, looking as if she thought this doubtful.

"I'll remember it if I don't forget it," he said with a touch of sullenness.

"Well, I'll write it down then," she said. She got in her car and took a stub of pencil from her pocketbook and began to write on the back of an empty envelope. The Negro came and stood at the window. "I'm Mrs. May," she said as she wrote. "Their bull is on my place and I want him off *today*. You can tell them I'm furious about it."

"That bull lef here Sareday," the Negro said, "and none of us ain't seen him since. We ain't knowed where he was."

"Well, you know now," she said, "and you can tell Mr. O. T. and Mr. E. T. that if they don't come get him today, I'm going to have their daddy shoot him the first thing in the morning. I can't have that bull ruining my herd." She handed him the note.

"If I knows Mist O. T. and Mist E. T.," he said, taking it, "they goin to say you go ahead on and shoot him. He done busted up one of our trucks already and we be glad to see the last of him."

She pulled her head back and gave him a look from slightly bleared eyes. "Do they expect me to take my time and my worker to shoot their bull?" she asked. "They don't want him so they just let him loose and expect somebody else to kill him? He's eating my oats and ruining my herd and I'm expected to shoot him too?"

"I speck you is," he said softly. "He done busted up . . ."

She gave him a very sharp look and said, "Well, I'm not surprised. That's just the way some people are," and after a second she asked, "Which is boss, Mr. O. T. or Mr. E. T.?" She had always suspected that they fought between themselves secretly.

"They never quarls," the boy said. "They like one man in two skins."

"Hmp. I expect you just never heard them quarrel."

"Nor nobody else heard them neither," he said, looking away as if this insolence were addressed to some one else.

"Well," she said, "I haven't put up with their father for fifteen years not to know a few things about Greenleafs."

The Negro looked at her suddenly with a gleam of recognition. "Is you my policy man's mother?" he asked.

"I don't know who your policy man is," she said sharply. "You give them that note and tell them if they don't come for that bull today, they'll be making their father shoot it tomorrow," and she drove off.

She stayed at home all afternoon waiting for the Greenleaf twins to come for the bull. They did not come. I might as well be working for them, she thought furiously. They are simply going to use me to the limit. At the supper table, she went over it again for the boys' benefit because she wanted them to see exactly what O. T. and E. T. would do. "They don't want that bull," she said, "—pass the butter—so they simply turn him loose and let somebody else worry about getting rid of him for them. How do you like that? I'm the victim. I've always been the victim."

"Pass the butter to the victim," Wesley said. He

was in a worse humor than usual because he had had a flat tire on the way home from the university.

Scofield handed her the butter and said, "Why Mamma, ain't you ashamed to shoot an old bull that ain't done nothing but give you a little scrub strain in your herd? I declare," he said, "with the Mamma I got it's a wonder I turned out to be such a nice boy!"

"You ain't her boy, Son," Wesley said.

She eased back in her chair, her fingertips on the edge of the table.

"All I know is," Scofield said, "I done mighty well to be as nice as I am seeing what I come from."

When they teased her they spoke Greenleaf English but Wesley made his own particular tone come through it like a knife edge. "Well lemme tell you one thang, Brother," he said, leaning over the table, "that if you had half a mind you would already know."

"What's that, Brother?" Scofield asked, his broad face grinning into the thin constricted one across from him.

"That is," Wesley said, "that neither you nor me is her boy . . . ," but he stopped abruptly as she gave a kind of hoarse wheeze like an old horse lashed unexpectedly. She reared up and ran from the room.

"Oh, for God's sake," Wesley growled, "what did you start her off for?"

"I never started her off," Scofield said. "You started her off."

"Hah."

"She's not as young as she used to be and she can't take it."

"She can only give it out," Wesley said. "I'm the one that takes it."

His brother's pleasant face had changed so that an ugly family resemblance showed between them. "Nobody feels sorry for a lousy bastard like you," he said and grabbed across the table for the other's shirtfront.

From her room she heard a crash of dishes and she rushed back through the kitchen into the dining room. The hall door was open and Scofield was going out of it. Wesley was lying like a large bug on his back with the edge of the over-turned table cutting him across the middle and broken dishes scattered on top of him. She pulled the table off him and caught his arm to help him rise but he scrambled up and pushed her off with a furious charge of energy and flung himself out of the door after his brother.

She would have collapsed but a knock on the back door stiffened her and she swung around. Across the kitchen and back porch, she could see Mr. Greenleaf peering eagerly through the screenwire. All her resources returned in full strength as if she had only needed to be challenged by the devil himself to regain them. "I heard a thump," he called, "and I thought the plastering might have fell on you."

If he had been wanted someone would have had to go on a horse to find him. She crossed the kitchen and the porch and stood inside the screen and said, "No, nothing happened but the table turned over. One of the legs was weak," and without pausing, "the boys didn't come for the bull so tomorrow you'll have to shoot him."

The sky was crossed with thin red and purple bars and behind them the sun was moving down slowly as if it were descending a ladder. Mr. Greenleaf squatted down on the step, his back to her, the top of his hat on a level with her feet. "Tomorrow I'll drive him home for you," he said.

"Oh no, Mr. Greenleaf," she said in a mocking voice, "you drive him home tomorrow and next week he'll be back here. I know better than that." Then in a mournful tone, she said, "I'm surprised at O. T. and E. T. to treat me this way. I thought they'd have more gratitude. Those boys spent some mighty happy days on this place, didn't they, Mr. Greenleaf?"

Mr. Greenleaf didn't say anything.

"I think they did," she said. "I think they did. But they've forgotten all the nice little things I did for them now. If I recall, they wore my boys' old clothes and played with my boys' old toys and hunted with my boys' old guns. They swam in my pond and shot my birds and fished in my stream and I never forgot their birthday and Christmas seemed to roll around very often if I remember it right. And do they think of any of those things now?" she asked. "NOOOOO," she said.

For a few seconds she looked at the disappearing sun and Mr. Greenleaf examined the palms of his hands. Presently as if it had just occurred to her, she asked, "Do you know the real reason they didn't come for that bull?"

"Naw I don't," Mr. Greenleaf said in a surly voice.

"They didn't come because I'm a woman," she said. "You can get away with anything when you're dealing with a woman. If there were a man running this place . . ."

Quick as a snake striking Mr. Greenleaf said, "You got two boys. They know you got two men on the place."

The sun had disappeared behind the tree line. She looked down at the dark crafty face, upturned now, and at the wary eyes, bright under the shadow of the hatbrim. She waited long enough for him to see that she was hurt and then she said, "Some people learn gratitude too late, Mr. Greenleaf, and some never learn it at all," and she turned and left him sitting on the steps.

Half the night in her sleep she heard a sound as if some large stone were grinding a hole on the outside wall of her brain. She was walking on the inside, over a succession of beautiful rolling hills, planting her stick in front of each step. She became aware after a time that the noise was the sun trying to burn through the tree line and she stopped to watch, safe in the knowledge that it couldn't, that it had to sink the way it always did outside of her property. When she first stopped it was a swollen red ball, but as she stood watching it began to narrow and pale until it looked like a bullet. Then suddenly it burst through the tree line and raced down the hill toward her. She woke up with her hand over her mouth and the same noise, diminished but distinct, in her ear. It was the bull munching under her window. Mr. Greenleaf had let him out.

She got up and made her way to the window in the dark and looked out through the slit blind, but the bull had moved away from the hedge and at first she didn't see him. Then she saw a heavy form some distance away, paused as if observing her. This is the last night I am going to put up with this, she said, and watched until the iron shadow moved away in the darkness.

The next morning she waited until exactly eleven o'clock. Then she got in her car and drove to the barn. Mr. Greenleaf was cleaning milk cans. He had seven of them standing up outside the milk room to get the sun. She had been telling him to do this for two weeks. "All right, Mr. Greenleaf," she said, "go get your gun. We're going to shoot that bull."

"I thought you wanted theseyer cans . . ."

"Go get your gun, Mr. Greenleaf," she said. Her voice and face were expressionless.

"That gentleman torn out of there last night," he murmured in a tone of regret and bent again to the can he had his arm in.

"Go get your gun, Mr. Greenleaf," she said in the same triumphant toneless voice. "The bull is in the pasture with the dry cows. I saw him from my upstairs window. I'm going to drive you up to the field and you can run him into the empty pasture and shoot him there."

He detached himself from the can slowly. "Ain't nobody ever ast me to shoot my boys' own bull!" he said in a high rasping voice. He removed a rag from his back pocket and began to wipe his hands violently, then his nose.

She turned as if she had not heard this and said, "I'll wait for you in the car. Go get your gun."

She sat in the car and watched him stalk off toward the harness room where he kept a gun. After he had entered the room, there was a crash as if he had kicked something out of his way. Presently he emerged again with the gun, circled behind the car, opened the door violently and threw himself onto the seat beside her. He held the gun between his knees and looked straight ahead. He'd like to shoot me instead of the bull, she thought, and turned her face away so that he could not see her smile.

The morning was dry and clear. She drove through the woods for a quarter of a mile and then out into the open where there were fields on either side of the narrow road. The exhilaration of carrying her point had sharpened her senses. Birds were screaming everywhere, the grass was almost too bright to look at, the sky was an even piercing blue. "Spring is here!" she said gaily. Mr. Greenleaf lifted one muscle somewhere near his mouth as if he found this the most asinine remark ever made. When she stopped at the second pasture gate, he flung himself out of the car door and slammed it behind him. Then he opened the gate and she drove through. He closed it and flung himself back in, silently, and she drove around the rim of the pasture until she spotted the bull, almost in the center of it, grazing peacefully among the cows.

"The gentleman is waiting on you," she said and gave Mr. Greenleaf's furious profile a sly look. "Run him into that next pasture and when you get him in, I'll drive in behind you and shut the gate myself."

He flung himself out again, this time deliberately leaving the car door open so that she had to lean across the seat and close it. She sat smiling as she watched him make his way across the pasture toward the opposite gate. He seemed to throw himself forward at each step and then pull back as if he were calling on some power to witness that he was being forced. "Well," she said aloud as if he were still in the car, "it's your own boys who are making you do this, Mr. Greenleaf." O. T. and E. T. were probably splitting their sides laughing at him now. She could hear their identical nasal voices saying, "Made Daddy shoot our bull for us. Daddy don't know no better than to think that's a fine bull he's shooting. Gonna kill Daddy to shoot that bull!"

"If those boys cared a thing about you, Mr. Greenleaf," she said, "they would have come for that bull. I'm surprised at them."

He was circling around to open the gate first. The bull, dark among the spotted cows, had not moved. He kept his head down, eating constantly. Mr. Greenleaf opened the gate and then began circling back to approach him from the rear. When he was about ten feet behind him, he flapped his arms at his sides. The bull lifted his head indolently and then lowered it again and continued to eat. Mr.

Greenleaf stooped again and picked up something and threw it at him with a vicious swing. She decided it was a sharp rock for the bull leapt and then began to gallop until he disappeared over the rim of the hill. Mr. Greenleaf followed at his leisure.

"You needn't think you're going to lose him!" she cried and started the car straight across the pasture. She had to drive slowly over the terraces and when she reached the gate, Mr. Greenleaf and the bull were nowhere in sight. This pasture was smaller than the last, a green arena, encircled almost entirely by woods. She got out and closed the gate and stood looking for some sign of Mr. Greenleaf but he had disappeared completely. She knew at once that his plan was to lose the bull in the woods. Eventually, she would see him emerge somewhere from the circle of trees and come limping toward her and when he finally reached her, he would say, "If you can find that gentleman in them woods, you're better than me."

She was going to say, "Mr. Greenleaf, if I have to walk into those woods with you and stay all afternoon, we are going to find that bull and shoot him. You are going to shoot him if I have to pull the trigger for you." When he saw she meant business he would return and shoot the bull quickly himself.

She got back into the car and drove to the center of the pasture where he would not have so far to walk to reach her when he came out of the woods. At this moment she could picture him sitting on a stump, marking lines in the ground with a stick. She decided she would wait exactly ten minutes by her watch. Then she would begin to honk. She got out of the car and walked around a little and then sat down on the front bumper to wait and rest. She was very tired and she lay her head back against the hood and closed her eyes. She did not understand why she should be so tired when it was only midmorning. Through her closed eyes, she could feel the sun, red-hot overhead. She opened her eyes slightly but the white light forced her to close them again.

For some time she lay back against the hood, wondering drowsily why she was so tired. With her eyes closed, she didn't think of time as divided into days and nights but into past and future. She decided she was tired because she had been working continuously for fifteen years. She decided she had every right to be tired, and to rest for a few minutes before she began working again. Before any kind of judgement seat, she would be able to say: I've worked, I have not wallowed. At this very instant while she was recalling a lifetime of work, Mr. Greenleaf was loitering in the woods and Mrs. Greenleaf was probably flat on the ground, asleep over her holeful of clippings. The woman had got worse over the years and Mrs. May believed that now she was actually demented. "I'm afraid your wife has let religion warp her," she said once tactfully to Mr. Greenleaf. "Everything in moderation, you know."

"She cured a man oncet that half his gut was eat out with worms," Mr. Greenleaf said, and she had turned away, half-sickened. Poor souls, she thought now, so simple. For a few seconds she dozed.

When she sat up and looked at her watch, more than ten minutes had passed. She had not heard any shot. A new thought occurred to her: suppose Mr. Greenleaf had aroused the bull chunking stones at him and the animal had turned on him and run him up against a tree and gored him? The irony of it deepened: O. T. and E. T. would then get a shyster lawyer and sue her. It would be the fitting end to her fifteen years with the Greenleafs. She thought of it almost with pleasure as if she had hit on the perfect ending for a story she was telling her friends. Then she dropped it, for Mr. Greenleaf had a gun with him and she had insurance.

She decided to honk. She got up and reached inside the car window and gave three sustained honks and two or three shorter ones to let him know she was getting impatient. Then she went back and sat down on the bumper again.

In a few minutes something emerged from the tree line, a black heavy shadow that tossed its head several times and then bounded forward. After a second she saw it was the bull. He was crossing the pasture toward her at a slow gallop, a gay almost rocking gait as if he were overjoyed to find her again. She looked beyond him to see if Mr. Greenleaf was coming out of the woods too but he was not. "Here he is, Mr. Greenleaf!" she called and looked on the other side of the pasture to see if he could be coming out there but he was not in sight. She looked back and saw that the bull, his head lowered, was racing toward her. She remained perfectly still, not in fright, but in a freezing unbelief. She stared at the violent black streak bounding toward her as if she had no sense of distance, as if she could not decide at once what his intention was, and the bull had buried his head in her lap, like a wild tormented lover, before her expression changed. One of his horns sank until it pierced her heart and the other curved around her side and held her in an unbreakable grip. She continued to stare straight ahead but the entire scene in front of her had changed—the tree line was a dark wound in a world that was nothing but sky—and she had the look of a person whose sight has been suddenly restored but who finds the light unbearable.

Mr. Greenleaf was running toward her from the side with his gun raised and she saw him coming though she was not looking in his direction. She saw him approaching on the outside of some invisible circle, the tree line gaping behind him and nothing under his feet. He shot the bull four times through the eye. She did not hear the shots but she felt the quake in the huge body as it sank, pulling her forward on its head, so that she seemed, when Mr. Greenleaf reached her, to be bent over whispering some last discovery into the animal's ear.

JOHN UPDIKE [1932-]

UPDIKE IS a controversial figure. Some critics group him with the existentialists and the "alienated"; others consider him a literary conservative, a moralist, a mourner for the old Judean-Christian verities; still others dismiss him as merely clever, slick, and superficial.

He was born in Reading, Pennsylvania, in 1932. During the depression the family moved to the farm of his maternal grandparents near Shillington, Pennsylvania, a small mill and agricultural community. This boyhood environment has provided material for most of his work, and his fictional town of Olinger is the actual town of Shillington, recalled with nostalgic fidelity. As Updike puts it, "My shadow has always remained in one place."

On a scholarship at Harvard he majored in English, graduated *summa cum laude* in 1954, and spent the following year at Oxford on a Knox Fellowship at the Ruskin School of Drawing and Fine Arts. His interest in art is apparent in the pictorial quality of his prose style: he has been described as "a literary Andrew Wyeth." Upon his return to America in 1955 Updike joined the staff of the *New Yorker* as a reporter for "The Talk of the Town" column and as a writer of parodies, humorous essays, and light verse. Many of these *New Yorker* poems have been collected in *The Carpentered Hen and Other Tame Creatures* (1958) and *Telephone Poles and Other Poems* (1963). His poetry is topical, satirical, playful, with a wit and humor often missing from his prose. In 1957 he resigned from the *New Yorker* in order to devote himself to serious writing.

Critics agree that Updike's talent is immense, his skill with language unique. However, his canvas—depicting the daily lives of middle-class people in small towns and suburbia—is by some considered too narrow for his abilities, and there is disagreement about the moral and religious values of his work. Updike himself has acknowledged that, at least for a period in his life, he was sustained by the stern doctrines of the Swiss theologian Karl Barth. Unlike many of his contemporaries, Updike does not consider human life ultimately absurd, even though his characters are often contemptible and their lives insignificant. Nor does he regard faith as a myth, and mystery as mere chaos. He has the Calvinist's preoccupation with evil, and, somewhat like Hawthorne, writes of the "dark necessity" that confuses man's existence. Fumblingly, his people search for some kind of salvation or meaning. Sometimes they seek meaning through sexuality, which Updike uses metaphorically. Sometimes they seek salvation through endurance; through orderliness and integrity in a small job well done; through pity, which is "not a helpless outcry but a powerful tide that could purge the dust and rubble from every corner of the world." Updike, however, offers no explanations in philosophic terms; novelist, not preacher or teacher, he has been quoted as saying, "I don't want my fiction to be any clearer than life."

His first novel, *The Poorhouse Fair* (1959), the story of one day in a home for the aged, poses the conflict between the young administrator's efforts to create a neat, scientifically structured community, and the elderly inmates' insistence on their human individualities. *Rabbit Run* (1960) explores the theme of entrapment and again of the assertion of individuality. Its protagonist, once a high school basketball hero, scampers like a bewildered animal in the cage of his lusts, his mistaken marriage, and his dim-witted dreams of easy freedom. In *The Centaur* (1963) the Greek myth of Chiron and his son Prometheus is used to illuminate the story of a fifteen-year-old boy and his father, a small-town science teacher. Here, plainly, is autobiography in large measure, and the story, covering three crucial days in the lives of father and son, is concerned with their intelligence, awareness, isolation, and vulnerability. In *Couples* (1968) Updike moves his locale from rural Pennsylvania to a Boston suburb, and the middle-class characters are more affluent, more sophisticated than his previous ones. A minute exploration of a sexual game of chess played by ten couples of varying backgrounds, this novel, like its predecessors, is haunted by nostalgia for the past, by a sense of guilt and loss, and by the dim realization that there must be in life something better. Ironically, the serious intent of this novel—to mirror the mores of American suburbia—may have been buried beneath its popular appeal: it was an instant best-seller, and Hollywood reputedly paid half a million dollars for the film rights.

In spite of the controversy, fame, and fortune which Updike has reaped with his novels, many discerning readers contend that his genuine artistic achievement is in the short story, where in the brief moment he deals vividly and probingly with some aspect of what he terms "the little losses of life." He has been compared to Chekhov in his understated dexterity, to Henry James in his subtle searchings of complex human relationships. In his novels he has been charged with prolixity and over-writing. When his style is disciplined by the strictures of the short-story form, its virtues are best revealed: the polished sentences, the apt phrases, the fresh and imaginative imagery.

Further reading: *Pigeon Feathers and Other Stories.* N. Galakian and C. Simmons, eds., *The Creative Present,* 1963. David Galloway, *The Absurd Hero in American Fiction,* 1966.

Pigeon Feathers

First published in the *New Yorker* (August 19, 1961); reprinted here from *Pigeon Feathers and Other Stories* (1962).

When they moved to Firetown, things were upset, displaced, rearranged. A red cane-back sofa that had been the chief piece in the living room at Olinger was here banished, too big for the narrow country parlor, to the barn, and shrouded under a tarpaulin. Never again would David lie on its length all afternoon eating raisins and reading mystery novels and science fiction and P. G. Wodehouse. The blue wing chair that had stood for years in the ghostly, immaculate guest bedroom, gazing through the windows curtained with dotted swiss toward the telephone wires and horse-chestnut trees and opposite houses, was here established importantly in front of the smutty little fireplace that supplied, in those first cold April days, their only heat. As a child, David had been afraid of the guest bedroom—it was there that he, lying sick with the measles, had seen a black rod the size of a yardstick jog along at a slight slant beside the edge of the bed and vanish when he screamed—and it was disquieting to have one of the elements of its haunted atmosphere basking by the fire, in the center of the family, growing sooty with use. The books that at home had gathered dust in the case beside the piano were here hastily stacked, all out of order, in the shelves that the carpenters had built along one wall below the deep-silled windows. David, at fourteen, had been more moved than a mover; like the furniture, he had to find a new place, and on the Saturday of the second week he tried to work off some of his disorientation by arranging the books.

It was a collection obscurely depressing to him, mostly books his mother had acquired when she was young: college anthologies of Greek plays and Romantic poetry, Will Durant's *Story of Philosophy,* a soft-leather set of Shakespeare with string bookmarks sewed to the bindings, *Green Mansions* boxed and illustrated with woodcuts, *I, the Tiger,* by Manuel Komroff, novels by names like Galsworthy and Ellen Glasgow and Irvin S. Cobb and Sinclair Lewis and "Elizabeth." The odor of faded taste made him feel the ominous gap between himself and his parents, the insulting gulf of time that existed before he was born. Suddenly he was tempted to dip into this time. From the heaps of books piled around him on the worn old floorboards, he picked up Volume II of a four-volume set of *The Outline of History*, by H. G. Wells. Once David had read *The Time Machine* in an anthology; this gave him a small grip on the author. The book's red binding had faded to orange-pink on the spine. When he lifted the cover, there was a sweetish, attic-like smell, and his mother's maiden name written in unfamiliar handwriting on the flyleaf—an upright, bold, yet careful signature, bearing a faint relation to the quick scrunched blackslant that flowed with marvellous consistency across her shopping lists and budget accounts and Christmas cards to college friends from this same, vaguely menacing long ago.

He leafed through, pausing at drawings, done in an old-fashioned stippled style, of bas-reliefs, masks, Romans without pupils in their eyes, articles of ancient costume, fragments of pottery found in unearthed homes. He knew it would be interesting in a magazine, sandwiched between ads and jokes, but in this undiluted form history was somehow sour. The print was determinedly legible, and smug, like a lesson book. As he bent over the pages, yellow at the edges, they seemed rectangles of dusty glass through which he looked down into unreal and irrelevant worlds. He could see things sluggishly move, and an unpleasant fullness came into his throat. His mother and grandmother fussed in the kitchen; the puppy, which they had just acquired for "protection in the country," was cowering, with a sporadic panicked scrabble of claws, under the dining table that in their old home had been reserved for special days but that here was used for every meal.

Then, before he could halt his eyes, David slipped into Wells's account of Jesus. He had been an obscure political agitator, a kind of hobo, in a minor colony of the Roman Empire. By an accident impossible to reconstruct, he (the small *h* horrified David) survived his own crucifixion and presumably died a few weeks later. A religion was founded on the freakish incident. The credulous imagination of the times retrospectively assigned miracles and supernatural pretensions to Jesus; a myth grew, and then a church, whose theology at most points was in direct contradiction of the simple, rather communistic teachings of the Galilean.

It was as if a stone that for weeks and even years had been gathering weight in the web of David's nerves snapped them and plunged through the page and a hundred layers of paper underneath. These fantastic falsehoods—plainly untrue; churches stood everywhere, the entire nation was founded "under God"—did not at first frighten him; it was the fact that they had been permitted to exist in an actual human brain. This was the initial impact—that at a definite spot in time and space a brain black with the denial of Christ's divinity had been suffered to exist; that the universe had not spit out this ball of tar but allowed it to continue in its blasphemy, to grow old, win honors, wear a hat, write books that, if true, collapsed everything into a jumble of horror. The world outside the deep-silled windows—a rutted lawn, a whitewashed barn, a walnut tree frothy with fresh green—seemed a haven from which he was forever sealed off. Hot washrags seemed pressed against his cheeks.

He read the account again. He tried to supply out of his ignorance objections that would defeat the complacent march of these black words, and found none. Survivals and misunderstandings more farfetched were reported daily in the papers. But none of them caused churches to be built in every town. He tried to work backwards through the churches, from their brave high fronts through their shabby, ill-attended interiors back into the events at Jerusalem, and felt himself surrounded by shifting gray shadows, centuries of history, where he knew nothing. The thread dissolved in his hands. Had Christ ever come to him, David Kern, and said, "Here. Feel the wound in My side?" No; but prayers had been answered. What prayers? He had prayed that Rudy Mohn, whom he had purposely tripped so he cracked his head on their radiator, not die, and he had not died. But for all the blood, it was just a cut; Rudy came back the same day, wearing a bandage and repeating the same teasing words. He could never have died. Again, David had prayed for two separate war-effort posters he had sent away for to arrive tomorrow, and though they did not, they did arrive, some days later, together, popping through the clacking letter slot like a rebuke from God's mouth: *I answer your prayers in My way, in My time.* After that, he had made his prayers less definite, less susceptible of being twisted into a scolding. But what a tiny, ridiculous coincidence this was, after all, to throw into battle against H. G. Wells's engines of knowledge! Indeed, it proved the enemy's point: Hope bases vast premises on foolish accidents, and reads a word where in fact only a scribble exists.

His father came home. Though Saturday was a free day for him, he had been working. He taught school in Olinger and spent all his days performing, with a curious air of panic, needless errands. Also, a city boy by birth, he was frightened of the farm and seized any excuse to get away. The farm had been David's mother's birthplace; it had been her idea to buy it back. With an ingenuity and persistence unparalleled in her life, she had gained that end, and moved them all here—her son, her husband, her mother. Granmom, in her prime, had worked these fields alongside her husband, but now she dabbled around the kitchen futilely, her hands waggling with Parkinson's disease. She was always in the way. Strange, out in the country, amid eighty acres, they were crowded together. His father expressed his feelings of discomfort by conducting with Mother an endless argument about organic farming. All through dusk, all through supper, it rattled on.

"Elsie, I *know*, I know from my education, the earth is nothing but chemicals. It's the only damn thing I got out of four years of college, so don't tell me it's not true."

"George, if you'd just walk out on the farm you'd know it's not true. The land has a *soul*."

"Soil, has, no, soul," he said, enunciating stiffly, as if to a very stupid class. To David he said, "You can't argue with a femme. Your mother's a real femme. That's why I married her, and now I'm suffering for it."

"*This* soil has no soul," she said, "because it's been killed with superphosphate. It's been burned bare by Boyer's tenant farmers." Boyer was the rich man they had bought the farm from. "It used to have a soul, didn't it, Mother? When you and Pop farmed it?"

"Ach, yes; I guess." Granmom was trying to bring a forkful of food to her mouth with her less severely afflicted hand. In her anxiety she brought the other hand up from her lap. The crippled fingers, dull red in the orange light of the kerosene lamp in the center of the table, were welded by paralysis into one knobbed hook.

"Only human indi-vidu-als have souls," his father went on, in the same mincing, lifeless voice. "Because the Bible tells us so." Done eating, he crossed his legs and dug into his ear with a match miserably; to get at the thing inside his head he tucked in his chin, and his voice came out low-pitched at David. "When God made your mother, He made a real femme."

"George, don't you read the papers? Don't you know that between the chemical fertilizers and the bug sprays we'll all be dead in ten years? Heart attacks are killing every man in the country over forty-five."

He sighed wearily; the yellow skin of his eyelids wrinkled as he hurt himself with the match. "There's no connection," he stated, spacing his words with pained patience, "between the heart - and chemical fertilizers. It's alcohol that's doing it. Alcohol and milk. There is too much - cholesterol - in the tissues of the American heart. Don't tell me about chemistry, Elsie; I majored in the damn stuff for four years."

"Yes and I majored in Greek and I'm not a penny wiser. Mother, put your waggler a*way!*" The old woman started, and the food dropped from her fork. For some reason, the sight of her bad hand at the table cruelly irritated her daughter. Granmom's eyes, worn bits of crazed crystal embedded in watery milk, widened behind her cockeyed spectacles. Circles of silver as fine as thread, they clung to the red notches they had carved over the years into her little white beak. In the orange flicker of the kerosene lamp her dazed misery seemed infernal. David's mother began, without noise, to cry. His father did not seem to have eyes at all; just jaundiced sockets of wrinkled skin. The steam of food clouded the scene. It was horrible but the horror was particular and familiar, and distracted David from the formless dread that worked, sticky and sore, within him, like a too large wound trying to heal.

He had to go to the bathroom, and took a flashlight down through the wet grass to the outhouse. For once, his fear of spiders there felt trivial. He set the flashlight, burning, beside him, and an insect alighted on its lens, a tiny insect, a mosquito or flea, made so fine that the weak light projected its X-ray onto the wall boards; the faint rim of its wings, the blurred strokes, magnified, of its long hinged legs, the dark cone at the heart of its anatomy. The tremor must be its heart beating. Without warning, David was visited by an exact vision of death; a long hole in the ground, no wider than your body, down which you are drawn while the white faces above recede. You try to reach them but your arms are pinned. Shovels pour dirt into your face. There you will be forever, in an upright position, blind and silent, and in time no one will remember you, and you will never be called. As strata of rock shift, your fingers elongate, and your teeth are distended sideways in a great underground grimace indistinguishable from a strip of chalk. And the earth tumbles on, and the sun expires, and unaltering darkness reigns where once there were stars.

Sweat broke out on his back. His mind seemed to rebound off a solidness. Such extinction was not another threat, a graver sort of danger, a kind of pain; it was qualitatively different. It was not even a conception that could be voluntarily pictured; it entered him from outside. His protesting nerves swarmed on its surface like lichen on a meteor. The skin of his chest was soaked with the effort of rejection. At the same time that the fear was dense and internal, it was dense and all around him; a tide of clay had swept up to the stars; space was crushed into a mass. When he stood up, automatically hunching his shoulders to keep his head away from the spider webs, it was with a numb sense of being cramped between two huge volumes of rigidity. That he had even this small freedom to move surprised him. In the narrow shelter of that rank shack, adjusting his pants, he felt—his first spark of comfort—too small to be crushed.

But in the open, as the beam of the flashlight skidded with frightened quickness across the remote surfaces of the barn and the grape arbor and the giant pine that stood by the path to the woods, the terror descended. He raced up through the clinging grass pursued, not by one of the wild animals the woods might hold, or one of the goblins his superstitious grandmother had communicated to his childhood, but by spectres out of science fiction, where gigantic cinder moons fill half the turquoise sky. As David ran, a gray planet rolled inches behind his neck. If he looked back, he would be buried. And in the momentum of his terror, hideous possibilities—the dilation of the sun, the triumph of the insects, the crabs on the shore in *The Time Machine*—wheeled out of the vacuum of make-believe and added their weight to his impending oblivion.

He wrenched the door open; the lamps within the house flared. The wicks burning here and there seemed to mirror one another. His mother was washing the dishes in a little pan of heated pump-water; Granmom fluttered near her elbow apprehensive. In the living room—the downstairs of the little square house was two long rooms—his father sat in front of the black fireplace restlessly folding and unfolding a newspaper as he sustained his half of the argument. "Nitrogen, phosphorus, potash: these are the three replaceable constituents of the soil. One crop of corn carries away hundreds of pounds of"—he dropped the paper into his lap and ticked them off on three fingers—"nitrogen, phosphorus, potash."

"Boyer didn't grow corn."

"*Any* crop, Elsie. The human animal—"

"You're killing the *earth*worms, George!"

"The human animal, after thousands and *thousands* of years, learned methods whereby the chemical balance of the soil may be maintained. Don't carry me back to the Dark Ages."

"When we moved to Olinger the ground in the garden was like slate. Just one summer of my cousin's chicken dung and the earthworms came back."

"I'm sure the Dark Ages were a fine place to the poor devils born in them, but I don't want to go there. They give me the creeps." Daddy stared into the cold pit of the fireplace and clung to the rolled newspaper in his lap as if it alone were keeping him from slipping backwards and down, down.

Mother came into the doorway brandishing a fistful of wet forks. "And thanks to your DDT there soon won't be a bee left in the country. When I was a girl here you could eat a peach without washing it."

"It's primitive, Elsie. It's Dark Age stuff."

"Oh what do *you* know about the Dark Ages?"

"I know I don't want to go back to them."

David took from the shelf, where he had placed it this afternoon, the great unabridged Webster's Dictionary that his grandfather had owned. He turned the big thin pages, floppy as cloth, to the entry he wanted, and read

> soul . . . I. An entity conceived as the essence, substance, animating principle, or actuating cause of life, or of the individual life, esp. of life manifested in psychical activities; the vehicle of individual existence, separate in nature from the body and usually held to be separable in existence.

The definition went on, into Greek and Egyptian conceptions, but David stopped short on the treacherous edge of antiquity. He needed to read no further. The careful overlapping words shingled a temporary shelter for him. "Usually held to be separable in existence"—what could be fairer, more judicious, surer?

His father was saying, "The modern farmer can't go around sweeping up after his cows. The poor devil has thousands and *thous*ands of acres on his hands. Your modern farmer uses a scientifically-arrived-at mixture, like five-ten-five, or six-twelve-six, or *three*-twelve-six, and spreads it on with this wonderful modern machinery which of course we can't afford. Your modern farmer can't *afford* medieval methods."

Mother was quiet in the kitchen; her silence radiated waves of anger.

"No now Elsie; don't play the femme with me. Let's discuss this calmly like two rational twentieth-century people. Your organic farming nuts aren't attacking five-ten-five; they're attacking the chemical fertilizer crooks. The monster firms."

A cup clinked in the kitchen. Mother's anger touched David's face; his cheeks burned guiltily. Just by being in the living room he was associated with his father. She appeared in the doorway with red hands and tears in her eyes, and said to the two of them, "I knew you didn't want to come here but I didn't know you'd torment me like this. You talked Pop into his grave and now you'll kill me. Go ahead, George, more power to you; at least I'll be buried in good ground." She tried to turn and met an obstacle and screamed, "Mother, stop hanging on my *back!* Why don't you go to *bed?*"

"Let's all go to bed," David's father said, rising from the blue wing chair and slapping his thigh with a newspaper. "This reminds me of death." It was a phrase of his that David had heard so often he never considered its sense.

Upstairs, he seemed to be lifted above his fears. The sheets on his bed were clean. Granmom had ironed them with a pair of flatirons saved from the Olinger attic; she plucked them hot off the stove alternately, with a wooden handle called a goose. It was a wonder, to see how she managed. In the next room, his parents grunted peaceably; they seemed to take their quarrels less seriously than he did. They made comfortable scratching noises as they carried a little lamp back and forth. Their door was open a crack, so he saw the light shift and swing. Surely there would be, in the last five minutes, in the last second, a crack of light, showing the door from the dark room to another, full of light. Thinking of it this vividly frightened him. His own dying, in a specific bed in a specific room, specific walls mottled with wallpaper, the dry whistle of his breathing, the murmuring doctors, the nervous relatives going in and out, but for him no way out but down into the funnel. *Never touch a doorknob again.* A whisper, and his parents' light was blown out. David prayed to be reassured. Though the experiment frightened him, he lifted his hands high into the darkness above his face and begged Christ to touch them. Not hard or long: the faintest, quickest grip would be final for a lifetime. His hands waited in the air, itself a substance, which seemed to move through his fingers; or was it the pressure of his pulse? He returned his hands to beneath the covers uncertain if they had been touched or not. For would not Christ's touch *be* infinitely gentle?

Through all the eddies of its aftermath, David clung to this thought about his revelation of extinction: that there, in the outhouse, he had struck a solidness qualitatively different, a rock of horror firm enough to support any height of construction. All he needed was a little help; a word, a gesture, a nod of certainty, and he would be sealed in, safe. The assurance from the dictionary had melted in the night. Today was Sunday, a hot fair day. Across a mile of clear air the church bells called, *Celebrate, celebrate.* Only Daddy went. He put on a coat over his rolled-up shirtsleeves and got into the little old black Plymouth parked by the barn and went off, with the same pained hurried grimness of all his actions. His churning wheels, as he shifted too hastily into second, raised plumes of red dust on the dirt road. Mother walked to the far field, to see what bushes needed cutting. David, though he usually preferred to stay in the house, went with her. The puppy followed at a distance, whining as it picked its way through the stubble but floundering off timidly if one of them went back to pick it up and carry it. When they reached the crest of the far field, his mother asked, "David, what's troubling you?"

"Nothing. Why?"

She looked at him sharply. The greening woods cross-hatched the space beyond her half-gray hair. Then she showed him her profile, and gestured toward the house, which they had left a half-mile behind them. "See how it sits in the land? They don't know how to build with the land any more. Pop always said the foundations were set with the compass. We must try to get a compass and see. It's supposed to face due south; but south feels a little more *that* way to me." From the side, as she said these things, she seemed handsome and young. The smooth sweep of her hair over her ear seemed white with a purity and calm that made her feel foreign to him. He had never regarded his parents as consolers of his troubles; from the beginning they had seemed to have more troubles than he. Their confusion had flattered him into an illusion of strength; so now on this high clear ridge he jealously guarded the menace all around them, blowing like a breeze on his fingertips, the possibility of all this wide scenery sinking into darkness. The strange fact that though she came to look at the brush she carried no clippers, for she had a fixed prejudice against working on Sundays, was the only consolation he allowed her to offer.

As they walked back, the puppy whimpering after them, the rising dust behind a distant line of trees announced that Daddy was speeding home from church. When they reached the house he was there. He had brought back the Sunday paper and the vehement remark, "Dobson's too intelligent for these farmers. They just sit there with their mouths open and don't hear a thing the poor devil's saying."

"What makes you think farmers are unintelligent? This country was made by farmers. George Washington was a farmer."

"They are, Elsie. They are unintelligent. George Washington's dead. In this day and age only the misfits stay on the farm. The lame, the halt, the blind. The morons with one arm. Human garbage. They remind me of death, sitting there with their mouths open."

"My *father* was a farmer."

"He was a frustrated man, Elsie. He never knew what hit him. The poor devil meant so well, and he never knew which end was up. Your mother'll bear me out. Isn't that right, Mom? Pop never knew what hit him?"

"Ach, I guess not," the old woman quavered, and the ambiguity for the moment silenced both sides.

David hid in the funny papers and sports section until one-thirty. At two, the catechetical class met at the Firetown church. He had transferred from the catechetical class of the Lutheran church in Olinger, a humiliating comedown. In Olinger they met on Wednesday nights, spiffy and spruce, in the atmosphere of a dance. Afterwards, blessed by the brick-faced minister from whose lips the word "Christ" fell like a burning stone, the more daring of them went with their Bibles to a luncheonette and smoked. Here in Firetown, the girls were dull white cows and the boys narrow-faced brown goats in old men's suits, herded on Sunday afternoons into a threadbare church basement that smelled of stale hay. Because his father had taken the car on one of his endless errands to Olinger, David walked, grateful for the open air and the silence. The catechetical class embarrassed him, but today he placed hope in it, as the source of the nod, the gesture, that was all he needed.

Reverend Dobson was a delicate young man with great dark eyes and small white shapely hands that flickered like protesting doves when he preached; he seemed a bit misplaced in the Lutheran ministry. This was his first call. It was a split parish; he served another rural church twelve miles away. His iridescent green Ford, new six months ago, was spattered to the windows with red mud and rattled from bouncing on the rude back roads, where he frequently got lost, to the malicious satisfaction of many. But David's mother liked him, and, more pertinent to his success, the Haiers, the sleek family of feed merchants and innkeepers and tractor salesmen who dominated the Firetown church, liked him. David liked him, and felt liked in turn; sometimes in class, after some special stupidity, Dobson directed toward him out of those wide black eyes a mild look of disbelief, a look that, though flattering, was also delicately disquieting.

Catechetical instruction consisted of reading aloud from a work booklet answers to problems prepared during the week, problems like, "I am the ———, the ———, and the ———, saith the Lord." Then there was a question period in which no one ever asked any questions. Today's theme was the last third of the Apostles' Creed. When the time came for questions, David blushed and asked, "About the Resurrection of the Body—are we conscious between the time when we die and the Day of Judgment?"

Dobson blinked, and his fine little mouth pursed, suggesting that David was making difficult things more difficult. The faces of the other students went blank, as if an indiscretion had been committed.

"No, I suppose not," Reverend Dobson said.

"Well, where is our soul, then, in this gap?"

The sense grew, in the class, of a naughtiness occurring. Dobson's shy eyes watered, as if he were straining to keep up the formality of attention, and one of the girls, the fattest, simpered toward her twin, who was a little less fat. Their chairs were arranged in a rough circle. The current running around the circle panicked David. Did everybody know something he didn't know?

"I suppose you could say our souls are asleep," Dobson said.

"And then they wake up, and there is the earth like it always is, and all the people who have ever lived? Where will Heaven be?"

Anita Haier giggled. Dobson gazed at David intently, but with an awkward, puzzled flicker of forgiveness, as if there existed a secret between them that David was violating. But David knew of no secret. All he wanted was to hear Dobson repeat the words he said every Sunday morning. This he would not do. As if these words were unworthy of the conversational voice.

"David, you might think of Heaven this way: as the way the goodness Abraham Lincoln did lives after him."

"But is Lincoln conscious of it living on?" He blushed no longer with embarrassment but in anger; he had walked here in good faith and was being made a fool.

"Is he conscious now? I would have to say no; but I don't think it matters." His voice had a coward's firmness; he was hostile now.

"You don't."

"Not in the eyes of God, no." The unction, the stunning impudence, of this reply sprang tears of outrage in David's eyes. He bowed them to his book, where short words like Duty, Love, Obey, Honor, were stacked in the form of a cross.

"Were there any other questions, David?" Dobson asked with renewed gentleness. The others were rustling, collecting their books.

"No." He made his voice firm, though he could not bring up his eyes.

"Did I answer your question fully enough?"

"Yes."

In the minister's silence the shame that should have been his crept over David: the burden and fever of being a fraud were placed upon *him*, who was innocent, and it seemed, he knew, a confession of this guilt that on the way out he was unable to face Dobson's stirred gaze, though he felt it probing the side of his head.

Anita Haier's father gave him a ride down the highway as far as the dirt road. David said he wanted to walk the rest, and figured that his offer was accepted because Mr. Haier did not want to dirty his bright blue Buick with dust. This was all right; everything was all right, as long as it was clear. His indignation at being betrayed, at seeing Christianity betrayed, had hardened him. The straight dirt road reflected his hardness. Pink stones thrust up through its packed surface. The April sun beat down from the center of the afternoon half of the sky; already it had some of summer's heat. Already the fringes of weeds at the edges of the road were bedraggled with dust. From the reviving grass and scuff of the fields he walked between, insects were sending up a monotonous, automatic chant. In the distance a tiny figure in his father's coat was walking along the edge of the woods. His mother. He wondered what joy she found in such walks; to him the brown stretches of slowly rising and falling land expressed only a huge exhaustion.

Flushed with fresh air and happiness, she returned from her walk earlier than he had expected, and surprised him at his grandfather's Bible. It was a stumpy black book, the boards worn thin where the old man's fingers had held them; the spine hung by one weak hinge of fabric. David had been looking for the passage where Jesus says to the one thief on the cross, "Today shalt thou be with me in paradise." He had never tried reading the Bible for himself before. What was so embarrassing about being caught at it, was that he detested the apparatus of piety. Fusty churches, creaking hymns, ugly Sunday-school teachers and their stupid leaflets—he hated everything about them but the promise they held out, a promise that in the most perverse way, as if the homeliest crone in the kingdom were given the Prince's hand, made every good and real thing, ball games and jokes and pertbreasted girls, possible. He couldn't explain this to his mother. There was no time. Her solicitude was upon him.

"David, what are you doing?"

"Nothing."

"What are you doing at Grandpop's Bible?"

"Trying to read it. This is supposed to be a Christian country, isn't it?"

She sat down on the green sofa, which used to be in the sun parlor at Olinger, under the fancy mirror. A little smile still lingered on her face from the walk. "David, I wish you'd talk to me."

"What about?"

"About whatever it is that's troubling you. Your father and I have both noticed it."

"I asked Reverend Dobson about Heaven and he said it was like Abraham Lincoln's goodness living after him."

He waited for the shock to strike her. "Yes?" she said, expecting more.

"That's all."

"And why didn't you like it?"

"Well; don't you see? It amounts to saying there isn't any Heaven at all."

"I don't see that it amounts to that. What do you want Heaven to be?"

"Well, I don't know. I want it to be *some*thing. I thought he'd tell me what it was. I thought that was his job." He was becoming angry, sensing her surprise at him. She had assumed that Heaven had faded from his head years ago. She had imagined that he had already entered, in the secrecy of silence, the conspiracy that he now knew to be all around him.

"David," she asked gently, "don't you ever want to rest?"

"No. Not forever."

"David, you're so young. When you get older, you'll feel differently."

"Grandpa didn't. Look how tattered this book is."

"I never understood your grandfather."

"Well I don't understand ministers who say it's like Lincoln's goodness going on and on. Suppose you're not Lincoln?"

"I think Reverend Dobson made a mistake. You must try to forgive him."

"It's not a *question* of his making a mistake! It's a question of dying and never moving or seeing or hearing anything ever again."

"But"—in exasperation—"darling, it's so *greedy* of you to want more. When God has given us this wonderful April day, and given us this farm, and you have your whole life ahead of you—"

"You think, then, that there is God?"

"Of course I do"—with deep relief, that smoothed her features into a reposeful oval. He had risen and was standing too near her for his comfort. He was afraid she would reach out and touch him.

"He made everything? You feel that?"

"Yes."

"Then who made Him?"

"Why, Man. Man." The happiness of this answer lit up her face radiantly, until she saw his gesture of disgust. She was so simple, so illogical; such a femme.

"Well that amounts to saying there is none."

Her hand reached for his wrist but he backed away. "David, it's a mystery. A miracle. It's a miracle more beautiful than any Reverend Dobson could have told you about. You don't say houses don't exist because Man made them."

"No. God has to be different."

"But, David, you have the *evidence*. Look out the window at the sun; at the fields."

"Mother, good grief. Don't you see"—he rasped away the roughness in his throat—"if when we die there's nothing, all your sun and fields and what not are all, ah, *horror*? It's just an ocean of horror."

"But David, it's not. It's so clearly not that." And she made an urgent opening gesture with her hands that expressed, with its suggestion of a willingness to receive his helplessness, all her grace, her gentleness, her love of beauty, gathered into a passive intensity that made him intensely hate her. He would not be wooed away from the truth. *I am the Way, the Truth . . .*

"No," he told her. "Just let me alone."

He found his tennis ball behind the piano and went outside to throw it against the side of the house. There was a patch high up where the brown stucco that had been laid over the sandstone masonry was crumbling away; he kept trying with the tennis ball to chip more pieces off. Superimposed upon his deep ache was a smaller but more immediate worry; that he had hurt his mother. He heard his father's car rattling on the straightaway, and went into the house, to make peace before he arrived. To his relief, she was not giving off the stifling damp heat of her anger, but instead was cool, decisive, maternal. She handed him an old green book, her college text of Plato.

"I want you to read the Parable of the Cave," she said.

"All right," he said, though he knew it would do no good. Some story by a dead Greek just vague enough to please her. "Don't worry about it, Mother."

"I *am* worried. Honestly, David, I'm sure there will be something for us. As you get older, these things seem to matter a great deal less."

"That may be. It's a dismal thought, though."

His father bumped at the door. The locks and jambs stuck here. But before Granmom could totter to the latch and let him in, he had knocked it open. He had been in Olinger dithering with track meet tickets. Although Mother usually kept her talks with David a confidence, a treasure between them, she called instantly, "George, David is worried about death!"

He came to the doorway of the living room, his shirt pocket bristling with pencils, holding in one hand a pint box of melting ice cream and in the other the knife with which he was about to divide it into four sections, their Sunday treat. "Is the kid worried about death? Don't give it a thought, David. I'll be lucky if I live till tomorrow, and I'm not worried. If they'd taken a buckshot gun and shot me in the cradle I'd be better off. The *world*'d be better off. Hell, I think death is a wonderful thing. I look forward to it. Get the garbage out of the way. If I had the man here who invented death, I'd pin a medal on him."

"Hush, George. You'll frighten the child worse than he is."

This was not true; he never frightened David. There was no harm in his father, no harm at all. Indeed, in the man's steep self-disgust the boy felt a kind of ally. A distant ally. He saw his position with a certain strategic coldness. Nowhere in the world of other people would he find the hint, the nod, he needed to begin to build his fortress against death. They none of them believed. He was alone. In that deep hole.

In the months that followed, his position changed little. School was some comfort. All those sexy, perfumed people, wisecracking, chewing gum, all of them doomed to die, and none of them noticing. In their company David felt that they would carry him along into the bright, cheap paradise reserved for them. In any crowd, the fear ebbed a little; he had reasoned that somewhere in the world there must exist a few people who believed what was necessary, and the larger the crowd, the greater the chance that he was near such a soul, within calling distance, if only he was not too ignorant, too ill-equipped, to spot him. The sight of clergymen cheered him; whatever they themselves thought, their collars were still a sign that somewhere, at sometime, someone had recognized that we cannot, *cannot*, submit to death. The sermon topics posted outside churches, the flip, hurried pieties of disc jockeys, the cartoons in magazines showing angels or devils—on such scraps he kept alive the possibility of hope.

For the rest, he tried to drown his hopelessness in clatter and jostle. The pinball machine at the luncheonette was a merciful distraction; as he bent over its buzzing, flashing board of flippers and cushions, the weight and constriction in his chest lightened and loosened. He was grateful for all the time his father wasted in Olinger. Every delay postponed the moment when they must ride together down the dirt road into the heart of the dark farmland, where the only light was the kerosene lamp waiting on the dining-room table, a light that drowned their food in shadow and made it sinister.

He lost his appetite for reading. He was afraid of being ambushed again. In mystery novels people died like dolls being discarded; in science fiction enormities of space and time conspired to crush the humans; and even in P. G. Wodehouse he felt a hollowness, a turning away from reality that was implicitly bitter, and became explicit in the comic figures of futile clergymen. All gaiety seemed minced out on the skin of a void. All quiet hours seemed invitations to dread.

Even on weekends, he and his father contrived to escape the farm; and when, some Saturdays, they did stay home, it was to do something destructive—

tear down an old henhouse or set huge brush fires that threatened, while Mother shouted and flapped her arms, to spread to the woods. Whenever his father worked, it was with rapt violence; when he chopped kindling, fragments of the old henhouse boards flew like shrapnel and the ax-head was always within a quarter of an inch of flying off the handle. He was exhilarating to watch, sweating and swearing and sucking bits of saliva back into his lips.

School stopped. His father took the car in the opposite direction, to a highway construction job where he had been hired for the summer as a timekeeper, and David was stranded in the middle of acres of heat and greenery and blowing pollen and the strange, mechanical humming that lay invisibly in the weeds and alfalfa and dry orchard grass.

For his fifteenth birthday his parents gave him, with jokes about him being a hillbilly now, a Remington .22. It was somewhat like a pinball machine to take it out to the old kiln in the woods where they dumped their trash, and set up tin cans on the kiln's sandstone shoulder and shoot them off one by one. He'd take the puppy, who had grown long legs and a rich coat of reddish fur—he was part chow. Copper hated the gun but loved the boy enough to accompany him. When the flat acrid crack rang out, he would race in terrified circles that would tighten and tighten until they brought him, shivering, against David's legs. Depending upon his mood, David would shoot again or drop to his knees and comfort the dog. Giving this comfort to a degree returned comfort to him. The dog's ears, laid flat against his skull in fear, were folded so intricately, so—he groped for the concept—*surely*. Where the dull-studded collar made the fur stand up, each hair showed a root of soft white under the length, black-tipped, of the metal-color that had lent the dog its name. In his agitation Copper panted through nostrils that were elegant slits, like two healed cuts, or like the keyholes of a dainty lock of black, grained wood. His whole whorling, knotted, jointed body was a wealth of such embellishments. And in the smell of the dog's hair David seemed to descend through many finely differentiated layers of earth: mulch, soil, sand, clay, and the glittering mineral base.

But when he returned to the house, and saw the books arranged on the low shelves, fear returned. The four adamant volumes of Wells like four thin bricks, the green Plato that had puzzled him with its queer softness and tangled purity, the dead Galsworthy and "Elizabeth," Grandpa's mammoth dictionary, Grandpa's Bible, the Bible that he himself had received on becoming a member of the Firetown Lutheran Church—at the sight of these, the memory of his fear reawakened and came around him. He had grown stiff and stupid in its embrace. His parents tried to think of ways to entertain him.

"David, I have a job for you to do," his mother said one evening at the table.

"What?"

"If you're going to take that tone perhaps we'd better not talk."

"What tone? I didn't take any tone."

"Your grandmother thinks there are too many pigeons in the barn."

"Why?" David turned to look at his grandmother, but she sat there staring at the burning lamp with her usual expression of bewilderment.

Mother shouted, "Mom, he wants to know why!"

Granmom made a jerky, irritable motion with her bad hand, as if generating the force for utterance, and said, "They foul the furniture."

"That's right," Mother said. "She's afraid for that old Olinger furniture that we'll never use. David, she's been after me for a month about those poor pigeons. She wants you to shoot them."

"I don't want to kill anything especially," David said.

Daddy said, "The kid's like you are, Elsie. He's too good for this world. Kill or be killed, that's my motto."

His mother said loudly, "Mother, he doesn't want to do it."

"Not?" The old lady's eyes distended as if in horror, and her claw descended slowly to her lap.

"Oh, I'll do it, I'll do it tomorrow," David snapped, and a pleasant crisp taste entered his mouth with the decision.

"And I had thought, when Boyer's men made the hay, it would be better if the barn doesn't look like a rookery," his mother added needlessly.

A barn, in day, is a small night. The splinters of light between the dry shingles pierce the high roof like stars, and the rafters and crossbeams and built-in ladders seem, until your eyes adjust, as mysterious as the branches of a haunted forest. David entered silently, the gun in one hand. Copper whined desperately at the door, too frightened to come in with the gun yet unwilling to leave the boy. David stealthily turned, said "Go away," shut the door on the dog, and slipped the bolt across. It was a door within a door; the double door for wagons and tractors was as high and wide as the face of a house.

The smell of old straw scratched his sinuses. The red sofa, half-hidden under its white-splotched tarpaulin, seemed assimilated into this smell, sunk in it, buried. The mouths of empty bins gaped like caves. Rusty oddments of farming—coils of baling wire, some spare tines for a harrow, a handleless shovel—hung on nails driven here and there in the thick wood. He stood stock-still a minute; it took a while to separate the cooing of the pigeons from the rustling in his ears. When he had focused on the cooing, it flooded the vast interior with its throaty, bubbling outpour: there seemed no other sound. They were up behind the beams. What light there was leaked through the shingles and the dirty glass windows at the far end and the small round holes, about as big as basketballs, high on the opposite stone side walls, under the ridge of the roof.

A pigeon appeared in one of these holes, on the side toward the house. It flew in, with a battering of wings, from the outside, and waited there, silhouetted against its pinched bit of sky, preening and cooing in a throbbing, thrilled, tentative way. David tiptoed four steps to the side, rested his gun against the lowest rung of a ladder pegged between two upright beams, and lowered the gunsight into the bird's tiny, jauntily cocked head. The slap of the report seemed to come off the stone wall behind him, and the pigeon did not fall. Neither did it fly. Instead it stuck in the round hole, pirouetting rapidly and nodding its head as if in frantic agreement. David shot the bolt back and forth and had aimed again before the spent cartridge had stopped jingling on the boards by his feet. He eased the tip of the sight a little lower, into the bird's breast, and took care to squeeze the trigger with perfect evenness. The slow contraction of his hand abruptly sprang the bullet; for a half-second there was doubt, and then the pigeon fell like a handful of rags, skimming down the barn wall into the layer of straw that coated the floor of the mow on this side.

Now others shook loose from the rafters, and whirled in the dim air with a great blurred hurtle of feathers and noise. They would go for the hole; he fixed his sight on the little moon of blue, and when a pigeon came to it, shot him as he was walking the ten inches of stone that would have carried him into the open air. This pigeon lay down in that tunnel of stone, unable to fall either one way or the other, although he was alive enough to lift one wing and cloud the light. It would sink back, and he would suddenly lift it again, the feathers flaring. His body blocked that exit. David raced to the other side of the barn's main aisle, where a similar ladder was symmetrically placed, and rested his gun on the same rung. Three birds came together to this hole; he got one, and two got through. The rest resettled in the rafters.

There was a shallow triangular space behind the cross beams supporting the roof. It was here they roosted and hid. But either the space was too small, or they were curious, for now that his eyes were at home in the dusty gloom David could see little dabs of gray popping in and out. The cooing was shriller now; its apprehensive tremolo made the whole volume of air seem liquid. He noticed one little smudge of a head that was especially persistent in peeking out; he marked the place, and fixed his gun on it, and when the head appeared again, had his finger tightened in advance on the trigger. A parcel of fluff slipped off the beam and fell the barn's height onto a canvas covering some Olinger furniture, and where its head had peeked out there was a fresh prick of light in the shingles.

Standing in the center of the floor, fully master now, disdaining to steady the barrel with anything but his arm, he killed two more that way. He felt like a beautiful avenger. Out of the shadowy ragged infinity of the vast barn roof these impudent things dared to thrust their heads, presumed to dirty its starred silence with their filthy timorous life, and he cut them off, tucked them back neatly into the silence. He had the sensation of a creator; these little smudges and flickers that he was clever to see and even cleverer to hit in the dim recesses of the rafters—out of each of them he was making a full bird. A tiny peek, probe, dab of life, when he hit it, blossomed into a dead enemy, falling with good, final weight.

The imperfection of the second pigeon he had shot, who was still lifting his wing now and then up in the round hole, nagged him. He put a new clip into the stock. Hugging the gun against his body, he climbed the ladder. The barrel sight scratched his ear; he had a sharp, garish vision, like a color slide, of shooting himself and being found tumbled on the barn floor among his prey. He locked his arm around the top rung—a fragile, gnawed rod braced between uprights—and shot into the bird's body from a flat angle. The wing folded, but the impact did not, as he had hoped, push the bird out of the hole. He fired again, and again, and still the little body, lighter than air when alive, was too heavy to budge from its high grave. From up here he could see green trees and a brown corner of the house through the hole. Clammy with the cobwebs that gathered between the rungs, he pumped a full clip of eight bullets into the stubborn shadow, with no success. He climbed down, and was struck by the silence in the barn. The remaining pigeons must have escaped out the other hole. That was all right; he was tired of it.

He stepped with his rifle into the light. His mother was coming to meet him, and it tickled him to see her shy away from the carelessly held gun. "You took a chip out of the house," she said. "What were those last shots about?"

"One of them died up in that little round hole and I was trying to shoot it down."

"Copper's hiding behind the piano and won't come out. I had to leave him."

"Well don't blame me. *I* didn't want to shoot the poor devils."

"Don't smirk. You look like your father. How many did you get?"

"Six."

She went into the barn and he followed. She listened to the silence. Her hair was scraggly, perhaps from tussling with the dog. "I don't suppose the others will be back," she said wearily. "Indeed, I don't know why I let Mother talk me into it. Their cooing was such a comforting noise." She began to gather up the dead pigeons. Though he didn't want to touch them, David went into the mow and picked up by its tepid, horny, coral-colored feet the first bird he had killed. Its wings unfolded disconcertingly, as if the creature had been held together by threads that now were slit. It did not weigh much. He retrieved the one on the other side of the barn; his mother got the three in the middle and led the way across the road to the little southern slope of land that went down toward the foundations of the vanished tobacco shed. The ground was too steep to plant and mow; wild strawberries grew in the tangled grass. She put her burden down and said, "We'll have to bury them. The dog will go wild."

He put his two down on her three; the slick feathers let the bodies slide liquidly on one another. He asked, "Shall I get you the shovel?"

"Get it for yourself; *you* bury them. They're your kill. And be sure to make the hole deep enough so he won't dig them up." While he went to the tool shed for the shovel, she went into the house. Unlike her, she did not look up, either at the orchard to the right of her or at the meadow on her left, but instead held her head rigidly, tilted a little, as if listening to the ground.

He dug the hole, in a spot where there were no strawberry plants, before he studied the pigeons. He had never seen a bird this close before. The feathers were more wonderful than dog's hair, for each filament was shaped within the shape of the feather, and the feathers in turn were trimmed to fit a pattern that flowed without error across the bird's body. He lost himself in the geometrical tides as the feathers now broadened and stiffened to make an edge for flight, now softened and constricted to cup warmth around the mute flesh. And across the surface of the infinitely adjusted yet somehow effortless mechanics of the feathers played idle designs of color, no two alike, designs executed, it seemed, in a controlled rapture, with a joy that hung level in the air above and behind him. Yet these birds bred in the millions and were exterminated as pests. Into the fragrant open earth he dropped one broadly banded in slate shades of blue, and on top of it another, mottled all over in rhythms of lilac and gray. The next was almost wholly white, but for a salmon glaze at its throat. As he fitted the last two, still pliant, on the top, and stood up, crusty coverings were lifted from him, and with a feminine, slipping sensation along his nerves that seemed to give the air hands, he was robed in this certainty: that the God who had lavished such craft upon these worthless birds would not destroy His whole Creation by refusing to let David live forever.

SAUL BELLOW [1915-   ]

Saul Bellow was born in Lachine, Quebec, an industrial suburb of Montreal, of Russian-Jewish parents. His father, an unsuccessful small businessman, moved the family to Chicago when Bellow was nine years old, and there he grew up. Graduating in the depression year of 1937 from Northwestern University, with honors in anthropology and sociology, he worked for a while with the Federal Writers' Project, taught a little, served in the Merchant Marine during World War II, and did editorial work for the *Encyclopaedia Britannica* while establishing himself as a creative writer. Since 1946 he has combined the careers of novelist and university professor, alternating Guggenheim and Ford Foundation grants with the teaching of writing and literature at the University of Minnesota, Princeton, Bard College, and the University of Chicago, where he has been since 1963 a Professor of English and a member of the Committee on Social Thought. He has published six full-length novels, a novella (*Seize the Day,* 1956), and numerous short stories; his farce, *The Last Analysis,* had a brief run on Broadway in 1964; and he has twice received the National Book Award.

His first two novels, *Dangling Man* (1944) and *The Victim* (1947), attracted little notice, although a few critics such as Edmund Wilson discerned in them a fresh and promising talent. It was with *The Adventures of Augie March* (1953) that Bellow erupted into the front rank of the postwar generation of fiction writers. Employing the picaresque tradition that was attracting so many contemporary novelists, Bellow convoyed his ingenuous Jewish protagonist through the Chicago of his own youth on an ebullient search for racial identity and a meaningful life.

Where *Augie March* is a loose, episodic, open-ended narrative, Bellow's subsequent novels exhibit more concern with structure and more movement toward a resolution of the thematic questions they raise. *Henderson the Rain King* (1959) is the serio-comic portrait of another seeker—a man of great bulk, great wealth, and great ambition, whose soul-sickness takes him, fantastically, to Africa to become a rainmaker for a savage tribe, where amid the roaring of lions he achieves a sufficient self-understanding to return to his own world and make his individual adjustment to it. *Herzog* (1964), Bellow's biggest and most successful novel, is a confessional work, a modern *Bildungsroman* narrated in flashbacks, about a middle-aged intellectual whose separation from his first wife and his children has triggered the decline from which he seeks recovery through analyzing his false illusions and pretensions. His inquiring mind carries him to the edge of neurosis if not beyond, and his efforts to regain his mental balance and come to terms with himself are only partly successful; but in the end he finds a measure of self-acceptance without self-justification, and is able, like Henderson, to come home to the possibility of a new accommodation to life. *Mr. Sammler's Planet* (1970), another novel of ideas, with its seventy-year-old hero as a sane reference point, is a searching critique of unbridled individualism in a youth-dominated society of "desire, unlimited . . . impossible demands upon complex reality, unlimited."

Unlike many contemporary writers, Saul Bellow has never given up on the possibilities of human reason in a world gone crazily askew. Critics have tended to see in his novels, from *Augie March* to *Sammler,* an increasing progression toward the view that man, even if he cannot shape his own destiny, at least retains the ability to control the manner in which he confronts it, and thereby to challenge absurdity and chaos with a personal affirmation.

Further reading: *Herzog*. Earl Rovit, *Saul Bellow*, 1967. Irving Malin, ed., *Saul Bellow and the Critics*, 1967.

Leaving the Yellow House

First published in *Esquire* magazine (January 1958), this story is reprinted here from *Mosby's Memoirs and Other Stories* (1968).

The neighbors—there were in all six white people who lived at Sego Desert Lake—told one another that old Hattie could no longer make it alone. The desert life, even with a forced-air furnace in the house and butane gas brought from town in a truck, was still too difficult for her. There were women even older than Hattie in the county. Twenty miles away was Amy Walters, the gold miner's widow. But she was a hardier old girl. Every day of the year she took a bath in the icy lake. And Amy was crazy about money and knew how to manage it, as Hattie did not. Hattie was not exactly a drunkard, but she hit the bottle pretty hard, and now she was in trouble and there was a limit to the help she could expect from even the best of neighbors.

They were fond of her, though. You couldn't help being fond of Hattie. She was big and cheerful, puffy, comic, boastful, with a big round back and stiff, rather long legs. Before the century began, she had graduated from finishing school and studied the organ in Paris. But now she didn't know a note from a skillet. She had tantrums when she played canasta. And all that remained of her fine fair hair was frizzled along her forehead in small gray curls. Her forehead was not much wrinkled, but the skin was bluish, the color of skim milk. She walked with long strides in spite of the heaviness of her hips, pushing on, round-backed, with her shoulders and showing the flat rubber bottoms of her shoes.

Once a week, in the same cheerful, plugging but absent way, she took off her short skirt and the dirty aviator's jacket with the wool collar and put on a girdle, a dress, and high-heeled shoes. When she stood on these heels, her fat old body trembled. She wore a big brown Rembrandt-like tam with a ten-cent-store brooch, eyelike, carefully centered. She drew a straight line with lipstick on her mouth, leaving part of the upper lip pale. At the wheel of her old turret-shaped car, she drove, seemingly methodical but speeding dangerously, across forty miles of mountainous desert to buy frozen meat pies and whisky. She went to the Laundromat and the hairdresser, and then had lunch with two martinis at the Arlington. Afterward she would often visit Marian Nabot's Silvermine Hotel at Miller Street near skid row and pass the rest of the day gossiping and drinking with her cronies, old divorcees like herself who had settled in the West. Hattie never gambled anymore and she didn't care for the movies. And at five o'clock she drove back at the same speed, calmly, partly blinded by the smoke of her cigarette. The fixed cigarette gave her a watering eye.

The Rolfes and the Paces were her only white neighbors at Sego Desert Lake. There was Sam Jervis too, but he was only an old gandy-walker who did odd jobs in her garden, and she did not count him. Nor did she count among her neighbors Darly, the dudes' cowboy who worked for the Paces, nor Swede, the telegrapher. Pace had a guest ranch, and Rolfe and his wife were rich and had retired. Thus there were three good houses at the lake, Hattie's yellow house, Pace's and the Rolfes'. All the rest of the population—Sam, Swede, Watchtah the section foreman, and the Mexicans and Indians and Negroes—lived in shacks and boxcars. There were very few trees, cottonwoods and box elders. Everything else, down to the shores, was sagebrush and juniper. The lake was what remained of an old sea that had covered the volcanic mountains. To the north there were some tungsten mines; to the south, fifteen miles, was an Indian village—shacks built of plywood or railroad ties.

In this barren place Hattie had lived for more than twenty years. Her first summer was spent, not in a house, but in an Indian wickiup on the shore. She used to say that she had watched the stars from this almost roofless shelter. After her divorce she took up with a cowboy named Wicks. Neither of them had any money—it was the Depression—and they had lived on the range, trapping coyotes for a living. Once a month they would come into town and rent a room and go on a bender. Hattie told this sadly but also gloatingly, and with many trimmings. A thing no sooner happened to her than it was transformed into something else. "We were caught in a storm," she said, "and we rode hard, down to the lake, and knocked on the door of the yellow house"—now her house. "Alice Parmenter took us in and let us sleep on the floor." What had actually happened was that the wind was blowing—there had been no storm—and they were not far from the house anyway; and Alice Parmenter, who knew that Hattie and Wicks were not married, offered them separate beds; but Hattie, swaggering, had said in a loud voice, "Why get two sets of sheets dirty?" And her and her cowboy had slept in Alice's bed while Alice had taken the sofa.

Then Wicks went away. There was never anybody like him in the sack; he was brought up in a whorehouse and the girls had taught him everything, said Hattie. She didn't really understand what she was saying but believed that she was being Western. More than anything else she wanted to be thought of as a rough, experienced woman of the West. Still, she was a lady, too. She had good silver and good china and engraved stationery, but she kept canned beans and A-1 sauce and tuna fish and bottles of catsup and fruit salad on the library shelves of her living room. On her night table was the Bible her pious brother Angus—the other brother was a hell-er—had given her; but behind the little door of the commode was a bottle of bourbon. When she awoke in the night, she tippled herself back to sleep. In the glove compartment of her old car she kept little sample bottles for emergencies on the road. Old Darly found them after her accident.

The accident did not happen far out in the desert as she had always feared, but very near home. She had had a few martinis with the Rolfes one evening, and as she was driving home over the railroad crossing she lost control of the car and veered off the crossing onto the tracks. The explanation she gave was that she had sneezed, and the sneeze had blinded her and made her twist the wheel. The motor was killed and all four wheels of the car sat smack on the rails. Hattie crept down from the door, high off the roadbed. A great fear took hold of her—for the car, for the future, and not only for the future but spreading back into the past—and she began to hurry on stiff legs through the sagebrush to Pace's ranch.

Now, the Paces were away on a hunting trip and had left Darly in charge; he was tending bar in the old cabin that went back to the days of the pony express, when Hattie burst in. There were two customers, a tungsten miner and his girl.

"Darly, I'm in trouble. Help me. I've had an accident," said Hattie.

How the face of a man will alter when a woman has bad news to tell him! It happened now to lean old Darly; his eyes went flat and looked unwilling, his jaw moved in and out, his wrinkled cheeks began to flush, and he said, "What's the matter—what's happened to you now?"

"I'm stuck on the tracks. I sneezed. I lost control of the car. Tow me off, Darly. With the pickup. Before the train comes."

Darly threw down his towel and stamped his high-heeled boots. "Now what have you gone and done?" he said. "I told you to stay home after dark."

"Where's Pace? Ring the fire bell and fetch Pace."

"There's nobody on the property except me," said the lean old man. "And I'm not supposed to close the bar and you know it as well as I do."

"Please, Darly. I can't leave my car on the tracks."

"Too bad!" he said. Nevertheless he moved from behind the bar. "How did you say it happened?"

"I told you, I sneezed," said Hattie.

Everyone, as she later told it, was as drunk as sixteen thousand dollars: Darly, the miner, and the miner's girl.

Darly was limping as he locked the door of the bar. A year before, a kick from one of Pace's mares had broken his ribs as he was loading her into the trailer, and he hadn't recovered from it. He was too old. But he dissembled the pain. The high-heeled narrow boots helped, and his painful bending looked like the ordinary stooping posture of a cowboy. However, Darly was not a genuine cowboy like Pace, who had grown up in the saddle. He was a latecomer from the East and until the age of forty had never been on horseback. In this respect he and Hattie were alike. They were not genuine Westerners.

Hattie hurried after him through the ranch yard.

"Damn you!" he said to her. "I got thirty bucks out of that sucker and I would have skinned him out of his whole paycheck if you minded your business. Pace is going to be sore as hell."

"You've got to help me. We're neighbors," said Hattie.

"You're not fit to be living out here. You can't do it anymore. Besides, you're swacked all the time."

Hattie couldn't afford to talk back. The thought of her car on the tracks made her frantic. If a freight came now and smashed it, her life at Sego Desert Lake would be finished. And where would she go then? She was not fit to live in this place. She had never made the grade at all, only seemed to have made it. And Darly—why did he say such hurtful things to her? Because he himself was sixty-eight years old, and he had no other place to go either; he took bad treatment from Pace besides. Darly stayed because his only alternative was to go to the soldiers' home. Moreover, the dude women would still crawl into his sack. They wanted a cowboy and they thought he was one. Why, he couldn't even raise himself out of his bunk in the morning. And where else would he get women! "After the dude season," she wanted to say to him, "you always have to go to the Veterans' Hospital to get fixed up again." But she didn't dare offend him now.

The moon was due to rise. It appeared as they drove over the ungraded dirt road toward the crossing where Hattie's turret-shaped car was sitting on the rails. Driving very fast, Darly wheeled the pickup around, spraying dirt on the miner and his girl, who had followed in their car.

"You get behind the wheel and steer," Darly told Hattie.

She climbed into the seat. Waiting at the wheel, she lifted her face and said, "Please, God, I didn't bend the axle or crack the oil pan."

When Darly crawled under the bumper of Hattie's car, the pain in his ribs suddenly cut off his breath, so instead of doubling the tow chain he fastened it at full length. He rose and trotted back to the truck on the tight boots. Motion seemed the only remedy for the pain; not even booze did the trick anymore. He put the pickup into towing gear and began to pull. One side of Hattie's car dropped into the roadbed with a heave of springs. She sat with a stormy, frightened, conscience-stricken face, racing the motor until she flooded it.

The tungsten miner yelled, "Your chain's too long."

Hattie was raised high in the air by the pitch of the wheels. She had to roll down the window to let herself out because the door handle had been jammed from inside for years. Hattie struggled out on the uplifted side crying, "I better call the Swede. I better have him signal. There's a train due."

"Go on, then," said Darly. "You're no good here."

"Darly, be careful with my car. Be careful."

The ancient sea bed at this place was flat and low, and the lights of her car and of the truck and of the tungsten miner's Chevrolet were bright and big at twenty miles. Hattie was too frightened to think of this. All she could think was that she was a procrastinating old woman, she had lived by delays; she had meant to stop drinking, she had put off the time, and now she had smashed her car—a terrible end, a terrible judgment on her. She got to the ground and, drawing up her skirt, she started to get over the tow chain. To prove that the chain didn't have to be shortened, and to get the whole thing over with, Darly threw the pickup forward again. The chain jerked up and struck Hattie in the knee and she fell forward and broke her arm.

She cried, "Darly, Darly, I'm hurt. I fell."

"The old lady tripped on the chain," said the miner. "Back up here and I'll double it for you. You're getting nowheres."

Drunkenly the miner lay down on his back in the dark, soft red cinders of the roadbed. Darly had backed up to slacken the chain.

Darly hurt the miner, too. He tore some skin from his fingers by racing ahead before the chain was secure. Without complaining, the miner wrapped his hand in his shirttail saying, "She'll do it now." The old car came down from the tracks and stood on the shoulder of the road.

"There's your goddamn car," said Darly to Hattie.

"Is it all right?" she said. Her left side was covered with dirt, but she managed to pick herself up and stand, round-backed and heavy, on her stiff legs. "I'm hurt, Darly." She tried to convince him of it.

"Hell if you are," he said. He believed she was putting on an act to escape blame. The pain in his ribs made him especially impatient with her. "Christ, if you can't look after yourself anymore, you've got no business out here."

"You're old yourself," she said. "Look what you did to me. You can't hold your liquor."

This offended him greatly. He said, "I'll take you to the Rolfes. They let you booze it up in the first place, so let them worry about you. I'm tired of your bunk, Hattie."

He raced uphill. Chains, spade, and crowbar clashed on the sides of the pickup. She was frightened and held her arm and cried. Rolfe's dogs jumped at her to lick her when she went through the gate. She shrank from them crying, "Down, down."

"Darly," she cried in the darkness, "take care of my car. Don't leave it standing there on the road. Darly, take care of it, please."

But Darly in his ten-gallon hat, his chin-bent face wrinkled, small and angry, a furious pain in his ribs, tore away at high speed.

"Oh, God, what will I do," she said.

The Rolfes were having a last drink before dinner, sitting at their fire of pitchy railroad ties, when Hattie opened the door. Her knee was bleeding, her eyes were tiny with shock, her face gray with dust.

"I'm hurt," she said desperately. "I had an accident. I sneezed and lost control of the wheel. Jerry, look after the car. It's on the road."

They bandaged her knee and took her home and put her to bed. Helen Rolfe wrapped a heating pad around her arm.

"I can't have the pad," Hattie complained. "The switch goes on and off, and every time it does, it starts my generator and uses up the gas."

"Ah, now, Hattie," Rolfe said, "this is not the time to be stingy. We'll take you to town in the morning and have you looked over. Helen will phone Dr. Stroud."

Hattie wanted to say, "Stingy! Why you're the stingy ones. I just haven't got anything. You and Helen are ready to hit each other over two bits in canasta." But the Rolfes were good to her; they were her only real friends here. Darly would have let her lie in the yard all night, and Pace would have sold her to the bone man. He'd give her to the knacker for a buck.

So she didn't talk back to the Rolfes, but as soon as they left the yellow house and walked through the superclear moonlight under the great skirt of box-elder shadows to their new station wagon, Hattie turned off the switch, and the heavy swirling and battering of the generator stopped. Presently she became aware of real pain, deeper pain, in her arm, and she sat rigid, warming the injured place with her hand. It seemed to her that she could feel the bone sticking out. Before leaving, Helen Rolfe had thrown over her a comforter that had belonged to Hattie's dead friend India, from whom she had inherited the small house and everything in it. Had the comforter lain on India's bed the night she died? Hattie tried to remember, but her thoughts were mixed up. She was fairly sure the deathbed pillow was in the loft, and she believed she had put the death bedding in a trunk. Then, how had this comforter got out? She couldn't do anything about it now but draw it away from contact with her skin. It kept her legs warm. This she accepted, but she didn't want it any nearer.

More and more Hattie saw her own life as though, from birth to the present, every moment had been filmed. Her fancy was that when she died, she would see the film shown. Then she would know how she had appeared from the back, watering the plants, in the bathroom, asleep, playing the organ, embracing—everything, even tonight, in pain, almost the last pain, perhaps, for she couldn't take much more. How many twists and angles had life to show her yet? There couldn't be much film left. To lie awake and think such thoughts was the worst thing in the world. Better death than insomnia. Hattie not only loved sleep, she believed in it.

The first attempt to set the bone was not successful. "Look what they've done to me," said Hattie and showed visitors the discolored breast. After the second operation her mind wandered. The sides of her bed had to be raised, for in her delirium she roamed the wards. She cursed at the nurses when they shut her in. "You can't make people prisoners in a democracy without a trial, you bitches." She had learned from Wicks how to swear. "*He* was profane," she used to say. "I picked it up unconsciously."

For several weeks her mind was not clear. Asleep, her face was lifeless; her cheeks were puffed out and her mouth, no longer wide and grinning, was drawn round and small. Helen sighed when she saw her.

"Shall we get in touch with her family?" Helen asked the doctor. His skin was white and thick. He had chestnut hair, abundant but very dry. He sometimes explained to his patients, "I had a tropical disease during the war."

He asked, "Is there a family?"

"Old brothers. Cousins' children," said Helen. She tried to think who would be called to her own bedside (she was old enough for that). Rolfe would see that she was cared for. He would hire private nurses. Hattie could not afford that. She had already gone beyond her means. A trust company in Philadelphia paid her eighty dollars a month. She had a small savings account.

"I suppose it'll be up to us to get her out of hock," said Rolfe. "Unless the brother down in Mexico comes across. We may have to phone one of those old guys."

In the end, no relations had to be called. Hattie began to recover. At last she could recognize visitors, though her mind was still in disorder. Much that had happened she couldn't recall.

"How many quarts of blood did they have to give me?" she kept asking. "I seem to remember five, six, eight different transfusions. Daylight, electric light . . ." She tried to smile, but she couldn't make a pleasant face as yet. "How am I going to pay?" she said. "At twenty-five bucks a quart. My little bit of money is just about wiped out."

Blood became her constant topic, her preoccupation. She told everyone who came to see her, "—have to replace all that blood. They poured gallons into me. Gallons. I hope it was all good." And, though very weak, she began to grin and laugh again. There was more hissing in her laughter than formerly; the illness had affected her chest.

"No cigarettes, no booze," the doctor told Helen.

"Doctor," Helen asked him, "do you expect her to change?"

"All the same, I am obliged to say it."

"Life sober may not be much of a temptation to her," said Helen.

Her husband laughed. When Rolfe's laughter was intense, it blinded one of his eyes. His short Irish face turned red; on the bridge of his small, sharp nose the skin whitened. "Hattie's like me," he said. "She'll be in business till she's cleaned out. And if Sego Lake turned to whisky, she'd use her last strength to knock her old yellow house down to build a raft of it. She'd float away on whisky. So why talk temperance?"

Hattie recognized the similarity between them. When he came to see her, she said, "Jerry, you're the only one I can really talk to about my troubles. What am I going to do for money? I have Hotchkiss Insurance. I paid eight dollars a month."

"That won't do you much good, Hat. No Blue Cross?"

"I let it drop ten years ago. Maybe I could sell some of my valuables."

"What valuables have you got?" he said. His eye began to droop with laughter.

"Why," she said defiantly, "there's plenty. First there's the beautiful, precious Persian rug that India left me."

"Coals from the fireplace have been burning it for years, Hat!"

"The rug is in *perfect* condition," she said with an angry sway of her shoulders. "A beautiful object like that never loses its value. And the oak table from the Spanish monastery is three hundred years old."

"With luck you could get twenty bucks for it. It would cost fifty to haul it out of here. It's the house you ought to sell."

"The house?" she said. Yes, that had been in her mind. "I'd have to get twenty thousand for it."

"Eight is a fair price."

"Fifteen. . . ." She was offended, and her voice recovered its strength. "India put eight into it in two years. And don't forget that Sego Lake is one of the most beautiful places in the world."

"But where is it? Five hundred and some miles to San Francisco and two hundred to Salt Lake City. Who wants to live way out here but a few eccentrics like you and India? And me?"

"There are things you can't put a price tag on. Beautiful things."

"Oh, bull, Hattie! You don't know squat about beautiful things. Any more than I do. I live here because it figures for me, and you because India left you the house. And just in the nick of time, too. Without it you wouldn't have had a pot of your own."

His words offended Hattie; more than that, they frightened her. She was silent and then grew thoughtful, for she was fond of Jerry Rolfe and he of her. He had good sense and, moreover, he only expressed her own thoughts. He spoke no more than the truth about India's death and the house. But she told herself, He doesn't know everything. You'd have to pay a San Francisco architect ten thousand just to *think* of such a house. Before he drew a line.

"Jerry," the old woman said, "what am I going to do about replacing the blood in the blood bank?"

"Do you want a quart from me, Hat?" His eye began to fall shut.

"You won't do. You had that tumor, two years ago. I think Darly ought to give some."

"The old man?" Rolfe laughed at her. "You want to kill him?"

"Why!" said Hattie with anger, lifting up her massive face. Fever and perspiration had frayed the fringe of curls; at the back of the head her hair had knotted and matted so that it had to be shaved. "Darly almost killed me. It's his fault that I'm in this condition. He must have *some* blood in him. He runs after all the chicks—all of them—young and old."

"Come, you were drunk, too," said Rolfe.

"I've driven drunk for forty years. It was the sneeze. Oh, Jerry, I feel wrung out," said Hattie, haggard, sitting forward in bed. But her face was cleft by her nonsensically happy grin. She was not one to be miserable for long; she had the expression of a perennial survivor.

Every other day she went to the therapist. The young woman worked her arm for her; it was a pleasure and a comfort to Hattie, who would have been glad to leave the whole cure to her. However, she was given other exercises to do, and these were not so easy. They rigged a pulley for her and Hattie had to hold both ends of a rope and saw it back and forth through the scraping little wheel. She bent heavily from the hips and coughed over her cigarette. But the most important exercise of all she shirked. This required her to put the flat of her hand to the wall at the level of her hips and, by working her finger tips slowly, to make the hand ascend to the height of her shoulder. That was painful; she often forgot to do it, although the doctor warned her, "Hattie, you don't want adhesions, do you?"

A light of despair crossed Hattie's eyes. Then she said, "Oh, Dr. Stroud, buy my house from me."

"I'm a bachelor. What would I do with a house?"

"I know just the girl for you—my cousin's daughter. Perfectly charming and very brainy. Just about got her Ph.D."

"You must get quite a few proposals yourself," said the doctor.

"From crazy desert rats. They chase me. But," she said, "after I pay my bills, I'll be in pretty punk shape. If at least I could replace that blood in the blood bank, I'd feel easier."

"If you don't do as the therapist tells you, Hattie, you'll need another operation. Do you know what adhesions are?"

She knew. But Hattie thought, *How long must I go on taking care of myself?* It made her angry to hear him speak of another operation. She had a moment of panic, but she covered it up. With him, this young man whose skin was already as thick as buttermilk and whose chestnut hair was as dry as death, she always assumed the part of a child. In a small voice she said, "Yes, Doctor." But her heart was in a fury.

Night and day, however, she repeated, "I was in the Valley of the Shadow. But I'm alive." She was weak, she was old, she couldn't follow a train of thought very easily, she felt faint in the head. But she was still here; here was her body, it filled space, a great body. And though she had worries and perplexities, and once in a while her arm felt as though it was about to give her the last stab of all; and though her hair was scrappy and old, like onion roots, and scattered like nothing under the comb, yet she sat and amused herself with visitors; her great grin split her face; her heart warmed with every kind word.

And she thought, People will help me out. It never did me any good to worry. At the last minute something turned up, when I wasn't looking for it. Marian loves me. Helen and Jerry love me. Half Pint loves me. They would never let me go to the ground. And I love them. If it were the other way around, I'd never let them go down.

Above the horizon, in a baggy vastness which Hattie by herself occasionally visited, the features of India, her *shade*, sometimes rose. India was indignant and scolding. Not mean. Not really mean. Few people had ever been really mean to Hattie. But India was annoyed with her. "The garden is going to hell, Hattie," she said. "Those lilac bushes are all shriveled."

"But what can I do? The hose is rotten. It broke. It won't reach."

"Then dig a trench," said the phantom of India. "Have old Sam dig a trench. But save the bushes."

Am I thy servant still? said Hattie to herself. *No,* she thought, *let the dead bury their dead.*

But she didn't defy India now any more than she had done when they lived together. Hattie was supposed to keep India off the bottle, but often both of them began to get drunk after breakfast. They forgot to dress, and in their slips the two of them wandered drunkenly around the house and blundered into each other, and they were in despair at having been so weak. Late in the afternoon they would be sitting in the living room, waiting for the sun to set. It shrank, burning itself out on the crumbling edges of the mountains. When the sun passed, the fury of the daylight ended and the mountain surfaces were more blue, broken, like cliffs of coal. They no longer suggested faces. The east began to look simple, and the lake less inhuman and haughty. At last India would say, "Hattie—it's time for the lights." And Hattie would pull the switch chains of the lamps, several of them, to give the generator a good shove. She would turn on some of the wobbling eighteenth-century-style lamps whose shades stood out from their slender bodies like dragonflies' wings. The little engine in the shed would shuffle, then spit, then charge and bang, and the first weak light would rise unevenly in the bulbs.

"Hettie!" cried India. After she drank, she was penitent, but her penitence too was a hardship to Hattie, and the worse her temper, the more British her accent became. *"Where the hell ah you Hettie!"* After India's death Hattie found some poems she had written in which she, Hattie, was affectionately and even touchingly mentioned. That was a good thing—Literature. Education. Breeding. But Hattie's interest in ideas was very small, whereas India had been all over the world. India was used to brilliant society. India wanted her to discuss Eastern religion, Bergson, and Proust, and Hattie had no head for this, and so India blamed her drinking on Hattie. "I can't talk to you," she would say. "You don't understand religion or culture. And I'm here because I'm not fit to be anywhere else. I can't live in New York anymore. It's too dangerous for a woman my age to be drunk in the street at night."

And Hattie, talking to her Western friends about India, would say "She is a lady" (implying that they made a pair). "She is a creative person" (this was why they found each other so congenial). "But helpless? Completely. Why she can't even get her own girdle on."

"Hettie! Come here. Het-tie! Do you know what sloth is?"

Undressed, India sat on her bed and with the cigarette in her drunken, wrinkled, ringed hand she burned holes in the blankets. On Hattie's pride she left many small scars, too. She treated her like a servant.

Weeping, India begged her afterward to forgive her. *"Hattie, please don't condemn me in your heart. Forgive me, dear, I know I am bad. But I hurt myself more in my evil than I hurt you."*

Hattie would keep a stiff bearing. She would lift up her face with its incurved nose and puffy eyes and say, "I am a Christian person. I never bear a grudge." And by repeating this she actually brought herself to forgive India.

But of course Hattie had no husband, no child, no skill, no savings. And what she would have done if India had not died and left her the yellow house nobody knows.

Jerry Rolfe said privately to Marian, "Hattie can't do anything for herself. If I hadn't been around during the forty-four blizzard, she and India both would have starved. She's always been careless and lazy and now she can't even chase a cow out of the yard. She's too feeble. The thing for her to do is go East to her damn brother. Hattie would have ended at the poor farm if it hadn't been for India. But besides the damn house India should have left her some dough. She didn't use her goddamn head."

When Hattie returned to the lake, she stayed with

the Rolfes. "Well, old shellback," said Jerry, "there's a little more life in you now."

Indeed, with joyous eyes, the cigarette in her mouth, and her hair newly frizzed and overhanging her forehead, she seemed to have triumphed again. She was pale, but she grinned, she chuckled, and she held a bourbon old-fashioned with a cherry and a slice of orange in it. She was on rations; the Rolfes allowed her two a day. Her back, Helen noticed, was more bent than before. Her knees went outward a little weakly; her feet, however, came close together at the ankles.

"Oh, Helen dear and Jerry dear, I am so thankful, so glad to be back at the lake. I can look after my place again, and I'm here to see the spring. It's more gorgeous than ever."

Heavy rains had fallen while Hattie was away. The sego lilies, which bloomed only after a wet winter, came up from the loose dust, especially around the marl pit; but even on the burnt granite they seemed to grow. Desert peach was beginning to appear, and in Hattie's yard the rosebushes were filling out. The roses were yellow and abundant, and the odor they gave off was like that of damp tea leaves.

"Before it gets hot enough for the rattlesnakes," said Hattie to Helen, "we ought to drive up to Marky's ranch and gather watercress."

Hattie was going to attend to lots of things, but the heat came early that year and, as there was no television to keep her awake, she slept most of the day. She was now able to dress herself, though there was little more that she could do. Sam Jervis rigged the pulley for her on the porch and she remembered once in a while to use it. Mornings when she had her strength, she rambled over to her own house, examining things, being important and giving orders to Sam Jervis and Wanda Gingham. At ninety, Wanda, a Shoshone, was still an excellent seamstress and housecleaner.

Hattie looked over the car, which was parked under a cottonwood tree. She tested the engine. Yes, the old pot would still go. Proudly, happily, she listened to the noise of tappets; the dry old pipe shook as the smoke went out at the rear. She tried to work the shift, turn the wheel. That, as yet, she couldn't do. But it would come soon, she was confident.

At the back of the house the soil had caved in a little over the cesspool and a few of the old railroad ties over the top had rotted. Otherwise things were in good shape. Sam had looked after the garden. He had fixed a new catch for the gate after Pace's horses—maybe because he could never afford to keep them in hay—had broken in and Sam found them grazing and drove them out. Luckily, they hadn't damaged many of her plants. Hattie felt a moment of wild rage against Pace. He had brought the horses into her garden for a free feed, she was sure. But her anger didn't last long. It was reabsorbed into the feeling of golden pleasure that enveloped her. She had little strength, but all that she had was a pleasure to her. So she forgave even Pace, who would have liked to do her out of the house, who had always used her, embarrassed her, cheated her at cards, swindled her. All that he did he did for the sake of his quarter horses. He was a fool about horses. They were ruining him. Racing horses was a millionaire's amusement.

She saw his animals in the distance, feeding. Unsaddled, the mares appeared undressed; they reminded her of naked women walking with their glossy flanks in the sego lilies which curled on the ground. The flowers were yellowish, like winter wool, but fragrant; the mares, naked and gentle, walked through them. Their strolling, their perfect beauty, the sound of their hoofs on stone touched a deep place in Hattie's nature. Her love for horses, birds, and dogs was well known. Dogs led the list. And now a piece cut from a green blanket reminded Hattie of her dog Richie. The blanket was one he had torn, and she had cut it into strips and placed them under the doors to keep out the drafts. In the house she found more traces of him: hair he had shed on the furniture. Hattie was going to borrow Helen's vacuum cleaner, but there wasn't really enough current to make it pull as it should. On the doorknob of India's room hung the dog collar.

Hattie had decided that she would have herself moved into India's bed when it was time to die. Why should there be two deathbeds? A perilous look came into her eyes, her lips were pressed together forbiddingly. *I follow*, she said, speaking to India with an inner voice, *so never mind.* Presently—before long—she would have to leave the yellow house in her turn. And as she went into the parlor, thinking of the will, she sighed. Pretty soon she would have to attend to it. India's lawyer, Claiborne, helped her with such things. She had phoned him in town, while she was staying with Marian, and talked matters over with him. He had promised to try to sell the house for her. Fifteen thousand was her bottom price, she said. If he couldn't find a buyer, perhaps he could find a tenant. Two hundred dollars a month was the rental she set. Rolfe laughed. Hattie turned toward him one of those proud, dulled looks she always took on when he angered her. Haughtily she said, "For summer on Sego Lake? That's reasonable."

"You're competing with Pace's ranch."

"Why, the food is stinking down there. And he cheats the dudes," said Hattie. "He really cheats them at cards. You'll never catch me playing blackjack with him again."

And what would she do, thought Hattie, if Claiborne could neither rent nor sell the house? This question she shook off as regularly as it returned. *I don't have to be a burden on anybody,* thought Hattie. *It's looked bad many a time before, but when push came to shove, I made it. Somehow I got by.* But she argued with herself: *How many times? How long, O God—an old thing, feeble, no use to anyone?* Who said she had any right to own property?

She was sitting on her sofa, which was very old—India's sofa—eight feet long, kidney-shaped, puffy, and bald. An underlying pink shone through the green; the upholstered tufts were like the pads of dogs' paws; between them rose bunches of hair. Here Hattie slouched, resting, with knees wide apart and a cigarette in her mouth, eyes half-shut but farseeing. The mountains seemed, not fifteen miles, but fifteen hundred feet away, the lake a blue band; the tealike odor of the roses, though they were still unopened, was already in the air, for Sam was watering them in the heat. Gratefully Hattie yelled, "Sam!"

Sam was very old, and all shanks. His feet looked big. His old railroad jacket was made tight across the back by his stoop. A crooked finger with its great broad nail over the mouth of the hose made the water spray and sparkle. Happy to see Hattie, he turned his long jaw, empty of teeth, and his long blue eyes, which seemed to bend back to penetrate into his temples (it was his face that turned, not his body), and he said, "Oh, there, Hattie. You've made it home today? Welcome, Hattie."

"Have a beer, Sam. Come around the kitchen door and I'll give you a beer."

She never had Sam in the house, owing to his skin disease. There were raw patches on his chin and behind his ears. Hattie feared infection from his touch, having decided that he had impetigo. She gave him the beer can, never a glass, and she put on gloves before she used the garden tools. Since he would take no money from her—Wanda Gingham charged a dollar a day—she got Marian to find old clothes for him in town and she left food for him at the door of the damp-wood-smelling boxcar where he lived.

"How's the old wing, Hat?" he said.

"It's coming. I'll be driving the car again before you know it," she told him. "By the first of May I'll be driving again." Every week she moved the date forward. "By Decoration Day I expect to be on my own again," she said.

In mid-June, however, she was still unable to drive. Helen Rolfe said to her, "Hattie, Jerry and I are due in Seattle the first week of July."

"Why, you never told me that," said Hattie.

"You don't mean to tell me this is the first you heard of it," said Helen. "You've known about it from the first—since Christmas."

It wasn't easy for Hattie to meet her eyes. She presently put her head down. Her face became very dry, especially the lips. "Well, don't you worry about me. I'll be all right here," she said.

"Who's going to look after you?" said Jerry. He evaded nothing himself and tolerated no evasion in others. Except that, as Hattie knew, he made every possible allowance for her. But who would help her? She couldn't count on her friend Half Pint, she couldn't really count on Marian either. She had had only the Rolfes to turn to. Helen, trying to be steady, gazed at her and made sad, involuntary movements with her head, sometimes nodding, sometimes seeming as if she disagreed. Hattie, with her inner voice, swore at her: *Bitch-eyes. I can't make it the way she does because I'm old. Is that fair?* And yet she admired Helen's eyes. Even the skin about them, slightly wrinkled, heavy underneath, was touching, beautiful. There was a heaviness in her bust that went, as if by attachment, with the heaviness of her eyes. Her head, her hands and feet should have taken a more slender body. Helen, said Hattie, was the nearest thing she had on earth to a sister. But there was no reason to go to Seattle—no genuine business. Why the hell Seattle? It was only idleness, only a holiday. The only reason was Hattie herself; this was their way of telling her that there was a limit to what she could expect them to do for her. Helen's nervous head wavered, but her thoughts were steady. She knew what was passing through Hattie's mind. Like Hattie, she was an idle woman. Why was her right to idleness better?

Because of money? thought Hattie. Because of age? Because she has a husband? Because she had a daughter in Swarthmore College? But an interesting thing occurred to her. Helen disliked being idle, whereas Hattie herself had never made any bones about it: an idle life was all she was good for. But for her it had been uphill all the way, because when Waggoner divorced her, she didn't have a cent. She even had to support Wicks for seven or eight years. Except with horses, Wicks had no sense. And then she had had to take tons of dirt from India. *I am the one,* Hattie asserted to herself. *I would know what to do with Helen's advantages. She only suffers from them. And if she wants to stop being an idle woman, why can't she start with me, her neighbor?* Hattie's skin, for all its puffiness, burned with anger. She said to Rolfe and Helen, "Don't worry. I'll make out. But if I have to leave the lake, you'll be ten times more lonely than before. Now I'm going back to my house."

She lifted up her broad old face, and her lips were childlike with suffering. She would never take back what she had said.

But the trouble was no ordinary trouble. Hattie was herself aware that she rambled, forgot names, and answered when no one spoke.

"We can't just take charge of her," Rolfe said. "What's more, she ought to be near a doctor. She keeps her shotgun loaded so she can fire it if anything happens to her in the house. But who knows what she'll shoot? I don't believe it was Jacamares who killed that Doberman of hers."

Rolfe drove into the yard the day after she moved back to the yellow house and said, "I'm going into town. I can bring you some chow if you like."

She couldn't afford to refuse his offer, angry though she was, and she said, "Yes, bring me some stuff from the Mountain Street Market. Charge it." She had only some frozen shrimp and a few cans of beer in the icebox. When Rolfe had gone, she put out the package of shrimp to thaw.

People really used to stick by one another in the West. Hattie now saw herself as one of the pioneers. The modern breed had come later. After all, she had lived on the range like an old-timer. Wicks had had to shoot their Christmas dinner and she had cooked it—venison. He killed it on the reservation, and if the Indians had caught them, there would have been hell to pay.

The weather was hot, the clouds were heavy and calm in a large sky. The horizon was so huge that in it the lake must have seemed like a saucer of milk. *Some milk!* Hattie thought. Two thousand feet down in the middle, so deep no corpse could ever be recovered. A body, they said, went around with the currents. And there were rocks like eyeteeth, and hot springs, and colorless fish at the bottom which were never caught. Now that the white pelicans were nesting, they patrolled the rocks for snakes and other egg thieves. They were so big and flew so slow you might imagine they were angels. Hattie no longer visited the lake shore; the walk exhausted her. She saved her strength to go to Pace's bar in the afternoon.

She took off her shoes and stockings and walked on bare feet from one end of the house to the other. On the land side she saw Wanda Gingham sitting near the tracks while her great-grandson played in the soft red gravel. Wanda wore a large purple shawl and her black head was bare. All about her was—was nothing, Hattie thought; for she had taken a drink, breaking her rule. Nothing but mountains, thrust out like men's bodies; the sagebrush was the hair on their chests.

The warm wind blew dust from the marl pit. This white powder made her sky less blue. On the water side were the pelicans, pure as spirits, slow as angels, blessing the air as they flew with great wings.

Should she or should she not have Sam do something about the vine on the chimney? Sparrows nested in it, and she was glad of that. But all summer long the king snakes were after them and she was afraid to walk in the garden. When the sparrows scratched the ground for seed, they took a funny bound; they held their legs stiff and flung back the dust with both feet. Hattie sat down at her old Spanish monastery table, watching them in the cloudy warmth of the day, clasping her hands, chuckling and sad. The bushes were crowded with yellow roses, half of them now rotted. The lizards scrambled from shadow to shadow. The water was smooth as air, gaudy as silk. The mountains succumbed, falling asleep in the heat. Drowsy, Hattie lay down on her sofa. Its pads were like dogs' paws. She gave in to sleep and when she woke, it was midnight; she did not want to alarm the Rolfes by putting on her lights so took advantage of the moon to eat a few thawed shrimps and go to the bathroom. She undressed and lifted herself into bed and lay there feeling her sore arm. Now she knew how much she missed her dog. The whole matter of the dog weighed heavily on her soul. She came close to tears, thinking about him, and she went to sleep oppressed by her secret.

I suppose I had better try to pull myself together a little, thought Hattie in the morning. *I can't just sleep my way through.* She knew what her difficulty was. Before any serious question her mind gave way. It scattered or diffused. She said to herself, *I can see bright, but I feel dim. I guess I'm not so lively anymore. Maybe I'm becoming a little touched in the head, as Mother was.* But she was not so old as her mother was when she did those strange things. At eighty-five, her mother had to be kept from going naked in the street. *I'm not as bad as that yet. Thank God! Yes, I walked into the men's wards, but that was when I had a fever, and my nightie was on.*

She drank a cup of Nescafé and it strengthened her determination to do something for herself. In all the world she had only her brother Angus to go to. Her brother Will had led a rough life; he was an old heller, and now he drove everyone away. He was too crabby, thought Hattie. Besides he was angry because she had lived so long with Wicks. Angus would forgive her. But then he and his wife were not her kind. With them she couldn't drink, she couldn't smoke, she had to make herself small-mouthed, and she would have to wait while they read a chapter of the Bible before breakfast. Hattie could not bear to sit at table waiting for meals. Besides, she had a house of her own at last. Why should she have to leave it? She had never owned a thing before. And now she was not allowed to enjoy her yellow house. *But I'll keep it,* she said to herself rebelliously. *I swear to God I'll keep it. Why, I barely just got it. I haven't had time.* And she went out on the porch to work the pulley and do something about the adhesions in her arm. She was sure now that they were there. *And what will I do?* She cried to herself. *What will I do? Why did I ever go to Rolfe's that night—and why did I lose control on the crossing?* She couldn't say, now, "I sneezed." She couldn't even remember what had happened, except that she saw the boulders and the twisting blue rails and Darly. It was Darly's fault. He was sick and old himself. *He* couldn't make it. He envied her the house, and her woman's peaceful life. Since she returned from the hospital he hadn't even come to visit her. He only said, "Hell, I'm sorry for her, but it was her fault." What hurt him most was that she had said he couldn't hold his liquor.

Fierceness, swearing to God did no good. She was still the same procrastinating old woman. She had a letter to answer from Hotchkiss Insurance and it drifted out of sight. She was going to phone Claiborne the lawyer, but it slipped her mind. One morning she announced to Helen that she believed she would apply to an institution in Los Angeles that took over the property of old people and managed it for them. They gave you an apartment right on the ocean, and your meals and medical care. You had to sign over half of your estate. "It's fair enough," said Hattie. "They take a gamble. I may live to be a hundred."

"I wouldn't be surprised," said Helen.

However, Hattie never got around to sending to Los Angeles for the brochure. But Jerry Rolfe took it on himself to write a letter to her brother Angus about her condition. And he drove over also to have a talk with Amy Walters, the gold miner's widow at Fort Walters—as the ancient woman called it. The Fort was an old tar-paper building over the mine. The shaft made a cesspool unnecessary. Since the death of her second husband no one had dug for gold. On a heap of stones near the road a crimson sign FORT WALTERS was placed. Behind it was a flagpole. The American flag was raised every day.

Amy was working in the garden in one of dead Bill's shirts. Bill had brought water down from the mountains for her in a homemade aqueduct so she could raise her own peaches and vegetables.

"Amy," Rolfe said, "Hattie's back from the hospital and living all alone. You have no folks and neither has she. Not to beat around the bush about it, why don't you live together?"

Amy's face had great delicacy. Her winter baths in the lake, her vegetable soups, the waltzes she played for herself alone on the grand piano that stood beside her wood stove, the murder stories she read till darkness obliged her to close the book—this life of hers had made her remote. She looked delicate, yet there was no way to affect her composure, she couldn't be touched. It was very strange.

"Hattie and me have different habits, Jerry," said Amy. "And Hattie wouldn't like my company. I can't drink with her. I'm a teetotaller."

"That's true," said Rolfe, recalling that Hattie referred to Amy as if she were a ghost. He couldn't speak to Amy of the solitary death in store for her. There was not a cloud in the arid sky today, and there was no shadow of death on Amy. She was tranquil, she seemed to be supplied with a sort of pure fluid that would feed her life slowly for years to come.

He said, "All kinds of things could happen to a woman like Hattie in that yellow house, and nobody would know."

"That's a fact. She doesn't know how to take care of herself."

"She can't. Her arm hasn't healed."

Amy didn't say that she was sorry to hear it. In the place of those words came a silence which might have meant that. Then she said, "I might go over there a few hours a day, but she would have to pay me."

"Now, Amy, you must know as well as I do that Hattie has no money—not much more than her pension. Just the house."

At once Amy said, no pause coming between his words and hers, "I would take care of her if she'd agree to leave the house to me."

"Leave it in your hands, you mean?" said Rolfe. "To manage?"

"In her will. To belong to me."

"Why, Amy, what would you do with Hattie's house?" he said.

"It would be my property, that's all. I'd have it."

"Maybe you would leave Fort Walters to her in your will," he said.

"Oh, no," she said. "Why should I? I'm not asking Hattie for her help. I don't need it. Hattie is a city woman."

Rolfe could not carry this proposal back to Hattie. He was too wise ever to mention her will to her.

But Pace was not so careful of her feelings. By mid-June Hattie had begun to visit his bar regularly. She had so many things to think about she couldn't stay at home. When Pace came in from the yard one day—he had been packing the wheels of his horse-trailer and was wiping grease from his fingers—he said with his usual bluntness, "How would you like it if I paid you fifty bucks a month for the rest of your life, Hat?"

Hattie was holding her second old-fashioned of

the day. At the bar she made it appear that she observed the limit; but she had started drinking at home. One before lunch, one during, one after lunch. She began to grin, expecting Pace to make one of his jokes. But he was wearing his scoop-shaped Western hat as level as a Quaker, and he had drawn down his chin, a sign that he was not fooling. She said, "That would be nice, but what's the catch?"

"No catch," he said. "This is what we'd do. I'd give you five hundred dollars cash, and fifty bucks a month for life, and you let me sleep some dudes in the yellow house, and you'd leave the house to me in your will."

"What kind of a deal is that?" said Hattie, her look changing. "I thought we were friends."

"It's the best deal you'll ever get," he said.

The weather was sultry, but Hattie till now had thought that it was nice. She had been dreamy but comfortable, about to begin to enjoy the cool of the day; but now she felt that such cruelty and injustice had been waiting to attack her, that it would have been better to die in the hospital than be so disillusioned.

She cried, "Everybody wants to push me out. You're a cheater, Pace. God! I know you. Pick on somebody else. Why do you have to pick on me? Just because I happen to be around?"

"Why, no, Hattie," he said, trying now to be careful. "It was just a business offer."

"Why don't you give me some blood for the bank if you're such a friend of mine?"

"Well, Hattie, you drink too much and you oughtn't to have been driving anyway."

"I sneezed, and you know it. The whole thing happened because I sneezed. Everybody knows that. I wouldn't sell you my house. I'd give it away to the lepers first. You'd let me go away and never send me a cent. You never pay anybody. You can't even buy wholesale in town anymore because nobody trusts you. I'm stuck, that's all, just stuck. I keep on saying that this is my only home in all the world, this is where my friends are, and the weather is always perfect and the lake is beautiful. But I wish the whole damn empty old place were in Hell. It's not human and neither are you. But I'll be here the day the sheriff takes away your horses—you never mind! I'll be clapping and applauding!"

He told her then that she was drunk again, and so she was, but she was more than that, and though her head was spinning, she decided to go back to the house at once and take care of some things she had been putting off. This very day she was going to write to the lawyer, Claiborne, and make sure that Pace never got her property. She wouldn't put it past him to swear in court that India had promised him the yellow house.

She sat at the table with pen and paper, trying to think how to put it.

"I want this on record," she wrote. "I could kick myself in the head when I think of how he's led me on. I have been his patsy ten thousand times. As when that drunk crashed his Cub plane on the lakeshore. At the coroner's jury he let me take the whole blame. He said he had instructed me when I was working for him never to take in any drunks. And this flier was drunk. He had nothing on but a T shirt and Bermuda shorts and he was flying from Sacramento to Salt Lake City. At the inquest Pace said I had disobeyed his instructions. The same was true when the cook went haywire. She was a tramp. He never hires decent help. He cheated her on the bar bill and blamed me and she went after me with a meat cleaver. She disliked me because I criticized her for drinking at the bar in her one-piece white bathing suit with the dude guests. But he turned her loose on me. He hints that he did certain services for India. She would never have let him touch one single finger. He was too common for her. It can never be said about India that she was not a lady in every way. He thinks he is the greatest sack-artist in the world. He only loves horses, as a fact. He has no claims at all, oral or written, on this yellow house. I want you to have this over my signature. He was cruel to Pickle-Tits who was his first wife, and he's no better to the charming woman who is his present one. I don't know why she takes it. It must be despair." Hattie said to herself, *I don't suppose I'd better send that.*

She was still angry. Her heart was knocking within; the deep pulses, as after a hot bath, beat at the back of her thighs. The air outside was dotted with transparent particles. The mountains were as red as furnace clinkers. The iris leaves were fan sticks—they stuck out like Jiggs's hair.

She always ended by looking out of the window at the desert and lake. *They drew you from yourself. But after they had drawn you, what did they do with you? It was too late to find out. I'll never know. I wasn't meant to. I'm not the type,* Hattie reflected. *Maybe something too cruel for women, young or old.*

So she stood up and, rising, she had the sensation that she had gradually become a container for herself. You get old, your heart, your liver, your lungs seem to expand in size, and the walls of the body give way outward, swelling, she thought, and you take the shape of an old jug, wider and wider toward the top. You swell up with tears and fat. She no longer even smelled to herself like a woman. Her face with its much-slept-upon skin was only faintly like her own—like a cloud that has changed. It was a face. It became a ball of yarn. It had drifted open. It had scattered.

I was never one single thing anyway, she thought. *Never my own. I was only loaned to myself.*

But the thing wasn't over yet. And in fact she didn't know for certain that it was ever going to be over. You only had other people's word for it that death was such-and-such. How do I know? she asked herself challengingly. Her anger had sobered her for a little while. Now she was again drunk. . . . *It was strange. It is strange. It may continue being strange.* She further thought, *I used to wish for death more than I do now. Because I didn't have anything at all. I changed when I got a roof of my own over me. And now? Do I have to go? I thought Marian loved me, but she already has a sister. And I thought Helen and Jerry would never desert me, but they've beat it. And now Pace has insulted me. They think I'm not going to make it.*

She went to the cupboard—she kept the bourbon bottle there; she drank less if each time she had to rise and open the cupboard door. And, as if she were being watched, she poured a drink and swallowed it.

The notion that in this emptiness someone saw her was connected with the other notion that she was being filmed from birth to death. That this was done for everyone. And afterward you could view your life. A hereafter movie.

Hattie wanted to see some of it now, and she sat down on the dogs'-paw cushions of her sofa and, with her knees far apart and a smile of yearning and of fright, she bent her round back, burned a cigarette at the corner of her mouth and saw—the Church of Saint Sulpice in Paris where her organ teacher used to bring her. It looked like country walls of stone, but rising high and leaning outward were towers. She was very young. She knew music. How she could ever have been so clever was beyond her. But she did know it. She could read all those notes. The sky was gray. After this she saw some entertaining things she liked to tell people about. She was a young wife. She was in Aix-les-Bains with her mother-in-law, and they played bridge in a mud bath with a British general and his aide. There were artificial waves in the swimming pool. She lost her bathing suit because it was a size too big. How did she get out? Ah, you got out of everything.

She saw her husband, James John Waggoner IV. They were snowbound together in New Hampshire. "Jimmy, Jimmy, how can you fling a wife away?" she asked him. "Have you forgotten love? Did I drink too much—did I bore you?" He had married again and had two children. He had gotten tired of her. And though he was a vain man with nothing to be vain about—no looks, not too much intelligence, nothing but an old Philadelphia family—she had loved him. She too had been a snob about her Philadelphia connections. Give up the name of Waggoner? How could she? For this reason she had never married Wicks. "How dare you," she had said to Wicks, "come without a shave in a dirty shirt and muck on you, come and ask me to marry! If you want to propose, go and clean up first." But his dirt was only a pretext.

Trade Waggoner for Wicks? she asked herself again with a swing of her shoulders. She wouldn't think of it. Wicks was an excellent man. But he was a cowboy. Socially nothing. He couldn't even read. But she saw this on her film. They were in Athens Canyon, in a cratelike house, and she was reading aloud to him from *The Count of Monte Cristo.* He wouldn't let her stop. While walking to stretch her legs, she read, and he followed her about to catch each word. After all, he was very dear to her. Such a man! Now she saw him jump from his horse. They were living on the range, trapping coyotes. It was just the second gray of evening, cloudy, moments after the sun had gone down. There was an animal in the trap, and he went toward it to kill it. He wouldn't waste a bullet on the creatures but killed them with a kick, with his boot. And then Hattie saw that this coyote was all white—snarling teeth, white scruff. "Wicks, he's white! White as a polar bear. You're not going to kill him, are you?" The animal flattened to the ground. He snarled and cried. He couldn't pull away because of the heavy trap. And Wicks killed him. What else could he have done? The white beast lay dead. The dust of Wicks's boots hardly showed on its head and jaws. Blood ran from the muzzle.

And now came something on Hattie's film she tried to shun. It was she herself who had killed her dog, Richie. Just as Rolfe and Pace had warned her, he was vicious, his brain was turned. She, because she was on the side of all dumb creatures, defended him when he bit the trashy woman Jacamares was living with. Perhaps if she had had Richie from a puppy he wouldn't have turned on her. When she got him, he was already a year and a half old and she couldn't break him of his habits. But she thought that only she understood him. And Rolfe had warned her, "You'll be sued, do you know that? The dog will take out after somebody smarter than that Jacamares's woman, and you'll be in for it."

Hattie saw herself as she swayed her shoulders and said, "Nonsense."

But what fear she had felt when the dog went for her on the porch. Suddenly she could see, by his skull, by his eyes that he was evil. She screamed at him, "Richie!" And what had she done to him? He had lain under the gas range all day growling and wouldn't come out. She tried to urge him out with the broom, and he snatched it in his teeth. She pulled him out, and he left the stick and tore at her. Now, as the spectator of this, her eyes opened, beyond the pregnant curtain and the airwave of marl dust, summer's snow drifting over the water. "Oh, my God! Richie!" Her thigh was snatched by his jaws. His teeth went through her skirt. She felt she would fall. Would she go down? Then the dog would rush at her throat—then black night, bad-odored mouth, the blood pouring from her neck, from torn veins. Her heart shriveled as the teeth went into her thigh, and she couldn't delay another second but took her kindling hatchet from the nail, strengthened her grip on the smooth wood, and hit the dog. She saw the blow. She saw him die at once. And then in fear and shame she hid the body. And at night she buried him in the yard. Next day she accused Jacamares. On him she laid the blame for the disappearance of her dog.

She stood up; she spoke to herself in silence, as was her habit. *God, what shall I do? I have taken life. I have lied. I have borne false witness. I have stalled. And now what shall I do? Nobody will help me.*

And suddenly she made up her mind that she should go and do what she had been putting off for weeks, namely, test herself with the car, and she slipped on her shoes and went outside. Lizards ran before her in the thirsty dust. She opened the hot, broad door of the car. She lifted her lame hand onto the wheel. Her right hand she reached far to the left and turned the wheel with all her might. Then she started the motor and tried to drive out of the yard. But she could not release the emergency brake with its rasplike rod. She reached with her good hand, the right, under the steering wheel and pressed her bosom on it and strained. No, she could not shift the gears and steer. She couldn't even reach down to the hand brake. The sweat broke out on her skin. Her efforts were too much. She was deeply wounded by the pain in her arm. The door of the car fell open again and she turned from the wheel and with her stiff legs hanging from the door she wept. What could she do now? And when she had wept over the ruin of her life, she got out of the old car and went back to the house. She took the bourbon from the cupboard and picked up the ink bottle and a pad of paper and sat down to write her will.

"My Will," she wrote, and sobbed to herself.

Since the death of India she had numberless times asked the question, To Whom? Who will get this when I die? She had unconsciously put people to the test to find out whether they were worthy. It made her more severe than before.

Now she wrote, "I Harriet Simmons Waggoner, being of sound mind and not knowing what may be in store for me at the age of seventy-two (born 1885) living alone at Sego Desert Lake, instruct my lawyer, Harold Claiborne, Paiute County Court Building, to draw my last will and testament upon the following terms."

She sat perfectly still now to hear from within who would be the lucky one, who would inherit the yellow house. For which she had waited. Yes, waited for India's death, choking on her bread because she was a rich woman's servant and whipping girl. But who had done for her, Hattie, what she had done for India? And who, apart from India, had ever held out a hand to her? Kindness, yes. Here and there people had been kind. But the word in her head was not kindness, it was succor. And who had given her that? *Succor?* Only India. If at least, next best after succor, someone had given her a shake and said, "Stop stalling. Don't be such a slow, old, procrastinating sit-stiller." Again, it was only India who had done her good. She had offered her succor. "Het-tie!" said that drunken mask. "Do you know what sloth is? Demn you! poky old demned thing!"

But I was waiting, Hattie realized. *I was waiting, thinking, "Youth is terrible, frightening. I will wait it out. And men? Men are cruel and strong. They want things I haven't got to give." There were no kids in me,* thought Hattie. *Not that I wouldn't have loved them, but such my nature was. And who can blame me for having it? My nature?*

She drank from an old-fashioned glass. There was no orange in it, no ice, no bitters or sugar, only the stinging clear bourbon.

So then, she continued, looking at the dry sun-stamped dust and the last freckled flowers of red wild peach, *to live with Angus and his wife? And to have to hear a chapter from the Bible before breakfast? Once more in the house—not of a stranger, perhaps, but not far from it either?* In other houses, in someone else's house, to wait for mealtimes was her lifelong punishment. She always felt it in the throat and stomach. And so she would again, and to the very end. However, she must think of someone to leave the house to.

And first of all she wanted to do right by her family. None of them had ever dreamed that she, Hattie, would ever have something to bequeath. Until a few years ago it had certainly looked as if she would die a pauper. So now she could keep her head up with the proudest of them. And, as this occurred to her, she actually lifted up her face with its broad nose and victorious eyes; if her hair had become shabby as onion roots, if, at the back, her head was round and bald as a newel post, what did that matter? Her heart experienced a childish glory, not yet tired of it after seventy-two years. She, too, had amounted to something. *I'll do some good by* going, she thought. *Now I believe I should leave it to, to . . .* She returned to the old point of struggle. She had decided many times and many times changed her mind. She tried to think, *Who would get the most out of this yellow house?* It was a tearing thing to go through. If it had not been the house but, instead, some brittle thing she could hold in her hand, then her last action would be to throw and smash it, and so the thing and she herself would be demolished together. But it was vain to think such thoughts. To whom should she leave it? Her brothers? Not they. Nephews? One was a submarine commander. The other was a bachelor in the State Department. Then began the roll call of cousins. Merton? He owned an estate in Connecticut. Anna? She had a face like a hot-water-bottle. That left Joyce, the orphaned daughter of her cousin Wilfred. Joyce was the most likely heiress. Hattie had already written to her and had her out to the lake at Thanksgiving, two years ago. But this Joyce was another odd one; over thirty, good, yes, but placid, running to fat, a scholar—ten years in Eugene, Oregon, working for her degree. In Hattie's opinion this was only another form of sloth. Nevertheless, Joyce yet hoped to marry. Whom? Not Dr. Stroud. He wouldn't. And still Joyce had vague hope. Hattie knew how that could be. At least have a man she could argue with.

She was now more drunk than at any time since her accident. Again she filled her glass. *Have ye eyes and see not? Sleepers awake!*

Knees wide apart, she sat in the twilight, thinking. Marian? Marian didn't need another house. Half Pint? She wouldn't know what to do with it. Brother Louis came up for consideration next. He was an old actor who had a church for the Indians at Athens Canyon. Hollywood stars of the silent days sent him their negligees; he altered them and wore them in the pulpit. The Indians loved his show. But when Billy Shawah blew his brains out after his two-week bender, they still tore his shack down and turned the boards inside out to get rid of his ghost. They had their old religion. No, not Brother Louis. He'd show movies in the yellow house to the tribe or make a nursery out of it for the Indian brats.

And now she began to consider Wicks. When last heard from, he was south of Bishop, California, a handy-man in a saloon off toward Death Valley. It wasn't she who heard from him but Pace. Herself, she hadn't actually seen Wicks since—how low she had sunk then!—she had kept the hamburger stand on Route 158. The little lunchroom had supported them both. Wicks hung around on the end stool, rolling cigarettes (she saw it on the film). Then there was a quarrel. Things had been going from bad to worse. He'd begun to grouse now about this and now about that. He beefed about the food, at last. She saw and heard him. "Hat," he said, "I'm good and tired of hamburger." "Well, what do you think I eat?" she said with that round, defiant movement of her shoulders which she herself recognized as characteristic (*me all over,* she thought). But he opened the cash register and took out thirty cents and crossed the street to the butcher's and brought back a steak. He threw it on the griddle. "Fry it," he said. She did, and watched him eat.

And when he was through, she could bear her rage no longer. "Now," she said, "you've had your meat. Get out. Never come back." She kept a pistol under the counter. She picked it up, cocked it, pointed it at his heart. "If you ever come in that door again, I'll kill you," she said.

She saw it all. *I couldn't bear to fall so low,* she thought, *to be slave to a shiftless cowboy.*

Wicks said, "Don't do that, Hat. Guess I went too far. You're right."

"You'll never have a chance to make it up," she cried. "Get out!"

On that cry he disappeared, and since then she had never seen him.

"Wicks, dear," she said. "Please! I'm sorry. Don't condemn me in your heart. Forgive me. I hurt myself in my evil. I always had a thick idiot head. I was born with a thick head."

Again she wept, for Wicks. She was too proud. A snob. Now they might have lived together in this house, old friends, simple and plain.

She thought, *He really was my good friend.*

But what would Wicks do with a house like this, alone, if he was alive and survived her? He was too wiry for soft beds or easy chairs.

And she was the one who had said stiffly to India, "I'm a Christian person. I do not bear a grudge."

Ah, yes, she said to herself. *I have caught myself out too often. How long can this go on?* And she began to think, or try to think, of Joyce, her cousin's daughter. Joyce was like herself, a woman alone, getting on in years, clumsy. Probably never been laid. Too bad. She would have given much, now, to succor Joyce.

But it seemed to her now that that too, the succor, had been a story. First you heard the pure story. Then you heard the impure story. Both stories. She had paid out years, now to one shadow, now to another shadow.

Joyce would come here to the house. She had a little income and could manage. She would live as Hattie had lived, alone. Here she would rot, start to drink, maybe, and day after day read, day after day sleep. See how beautiful it was here? It burned you out. How empty! It turned you into ash.

How can I doom a younger person to the same life? asked Hattie. It's for somebody like me. When

I was younger, it wasn't right. But now it is, exactly. Only I fit in here. It was made for my old age, to spend my last years peacefully. If I hadn't let Jerry make me drunk that night—if I hadn't sneezed! Because of this arm, I'll have to live with Angus. My heart will break there away from my only home.

She was now very drunk, and she said to herself, *Take what God brings. He gives no gifts unmixed. He makes loans.*

She resumed her letter of instructions to lawyer Claiborne: "Upon the following terms," she wrote a second time. "Because I have suffered much. Because I only lately received what I have to give away, I can't bear it." The drunken blood was soaring to her head. But her hand was clear enough. She wrote, "It is too soon! Too soon! Because I do not find it in my heart to care for anyone as I would wish. Being cast off and lonely, and doing no harm where I am. Why should it be? This breaks my heart. In addition to everything else, why must I worry about this, which I must leave? I am tormented out of my mind. Even though by my own fault I have put myself into this position. And I am not ready to give up on this. No, not yet. And so I'll tell you what, I leave this property, land, house, garden, and water rights, to Hattie Simmons Waggoner. Me! I realize this is bad and wrong. Not possible. Yet it is the only thing I really wish to do, so may God have mercy on my soul."

How could that happen? She studied what she had written and finally she acknowledged that she was drunk. "I'm drunk," she said, "and don't know what I'm doing. I'll die, and end. Like India. Dead as that lilac bush."

Then she thought that there was a beginning, and a middle. She shrank from the last term. She began once more—a beginning. After that, there was the early middle, then middle middle, late middle middle, quite late middle. In fact the middle is all I know. The rest is just a rumor.

Only tonight I can't give the house away. I'm drunk and so I need it. And tomorrow, she promised herself, I'll think again. I'll work it out, for sure.

JOHN BARTH [1930–]

THE PYROTECHNICS and conscious experimentation of his fiction are not reflected in the academically conventional life of John Barth. He was born in Cambridge, Maryland; was educated at Johns Hopkins University (A.B. 1951, M.A. 1952); was a member of the faculty of Pennsylvania State University from 1953 to 1965, duly rising in rank from instructor to associate professor; and in 1965 became a Professor of English at the State University of New York, Buffalo. By arrangement with the university he carries a light academic load that allows him to devote much of his time to his writing, to his wife and three children—and to an occasional session with a neighborhood jazz combo (he briefly studied orchestration at the Juilliard School of Music).

As a writer, however, this "rebel along traditional lines," as he describes himself, is one of the most ebullient and energetic of contemporary experimentalists. For the artist "to be technically out of date," he feels, "is likely to be a genuine defect: Beethoven's Sixth Symphony or the Chartres Cathedral if executed today would be merely embarrassing." He criticizes the many novelists who still imitate Tolstoy or Flaubert, when they should be studying not even Joyce and Kafka, but his own contemporary idols, Samuel Beckett and Jorge Luis Borges.

And yet the earlier of Barth's five books start not far to the left of center. His first two novels are moderately conventional variants on the theme of infidelity, yet each bears a burden of shock and reveals a penchant for the grotesque which he later exhibits in abundance. Thus in *The End of the Road* (1958) the wife of a scoutmaster, pregnant by an English teacher, chokes to death on the table of an abortionist when under anesthetic she regurgitates a recent meal of sauerkraut and frankfurters. His third novel, *The Sot-*

Weed Factor (1960), is a lusty but perhaps over-long burlesque of the picaresque novel and a brilliant exercise in imitation of the eighteenth-century style. The book shows him an extraordinary virtuoso in the handling of the English sentence, running trills, rills, and variants of every imaginable kind, always with impeccable control.

There is even more of this syntactic and stylistic virtuosity in his fourth and biggest novel, *Giles Goat-Boy* (1966). An original and important work in the tradition of the absurd, it creates a world of its own, impudently comic and outrageously askew. It is a world of two campuses (cultures), East and West, each run by a nearly deified computer—both in a perpetual state of frenzied threat which never quite breaks into conflict—in which misrule and disorder grow semester by semester, ending in a vision of ceaseless and unimaginable disintegration yet to come. The central figure—Oedipus, Christ, hero, villain, scapegoat, saint—starts life believing he is a goat, battles his way into the university (West Campus) through a series of ordeals and hairbreadth adventures, ultimately wins the archetypal female, discovers the blinding mystery of his own origin—that he was sired by a computer—and ends as the sacrificial figure vainly trying to atone for the idiocies of the administration, the venality of students and faculty, the inefficiencies of the boiler room—the cacophony of a riotous society rocking steadily to ruin down the dim corridors of crazy time.

The sketch reprinted here is the first in Barth's fifth book, *Lost in the Funhouse* (1968), a volume of stories and mixed media experiments, some of which are meant to be read aloud or heard in the author's own voice as recorded on magnetic tape. "Night-Sea Journey" is also a beautiful and tender expression of one of the great preoccupations of our day: an existence freed from degrading material concerns and able to concentrate on essentials. If it is a *tour de force*, it gains much from the gradual revelation of the speaker and his situation, and originally expresses one of the ultimate verities. It is also a fit ending for this book.

Further reading: *Giles Goat-Boy*. John Barth, "The Literature of Exhaustion," *Atlantic*, August 1967.

Night-Sea Journey

First published in *Esquire* magazine (June 1966); reprinted here from *Lost in the Funhouse: Fiction for Print, Tape, Live Voice* (1968).

"One way or another, no matter which theory of our journey is correct, it's myself I address; to whom I rehearse as to a stranger our history and condition, and will disclose my secret hope though I sink for it.

"Is the journey my invention? Do the night, the sea, exist at all, I ask myself, apart from my experience of them? Do I myself exist, or is this a dream? Sometimes I wonder. And if I am, who am I? The Heritage I supposedly transport? But how can I be both vessel and contents? Such are the questions that beset my intervals of rest.

"My trouble is, I lack conviction. Many accounts of our situation seem plausible to me—where and what we are, why we swim and whither. But implausible ones as well, perhaps especially those, I must admit as possibly correct. Even likely. If at times, in certain humors—stroking in unison, say, with my neighbors and chanting with them 'Onward! Upward!'—I have supposed that we have after all a common Maker, Whose nature and motives we may not know, but Who engendered us in some mysterious wise and launched us forth toward some end known but to Him—if (for a moodslength only) I have been able to entertain such notions, very popular in certain quarters, it is because our night-sea journey partakes of their absurdity. One might even say: I can believe them *because* they are absurd.

"Has that been said before?

"Another paradox: it appears to be these recesses from swimming that sustain me in the swim. Two measures onward and upward, flailing with the rest, then I float exhausted and dispirited, brood upon the night, the sea, the journey, while the flood bears me a measure back and down: slow progress, but I live, I live, and make my way, aye, past many a drownèd comrade in the end, stronger, worthier than I, victims of their unremitting *joie de nager.* I have seen the best swimmers of my generation go under. Numberless the number of the dead! Thousands drown as I think this thought, millions as I rest before returning to the swim. And scores, hundreds of millions have expired since we surged forth, brave in our innocence, upon our dreadful way. 'Love! Love!' we sang then, a quarter-billion strong, and churned the warm sea white with joy of swimming! Now all are gone down—the buoyant, the sodden, leaders and followers, all gone under, while wretched I swim on. Yet these same reflective intervals that keep me afloat have led me into wonder, doubt, despair—strange emotions for a swimmer!—have led me, even, to suspect . . . that our night-sea journey is without meaning.

"Indeed, if I have yet to join the hosts of the suicides, it is because (fatigue apart) I find it no meaningfuller to drown myself than to go on swimming.

"I know that there are those who seem actually to enjoy the night-sea; who claim to love swimming for its own sake, or sincerely believe that 'reaching the Shore,' 'transmitting the Heritage' (*Whose* Heritage, I'd like to know? And to whom?) is worth the staggering cost. I do not. Swimming itself I find at best not actively unpleasant, more often tiresome, not infrequently a torment. Arguments from function and design don't impress me: granted that we can and do swim, that in a manner of speaking our long tails and streamlined heads are 'meant for' swimming; it by no means follows—for me, at least—that we *should* swim, or otherwise endeavor to 'fulfill our destiny.' Which is to say, Someone Else's destiny, since ours, so far as I can see, is merely to perish, one way or another, soon or late. The heartless zeal of our (departed) leaders, like the blind ambition and good cheer of my own youth, appalls me now; for the death of my comrades I am inconsolable. If the night-sea journey has justification, it is not for us swimmers ever to discover it.

"Oh, to be sure, 'Love!' one heard on every side: 'Love it is that drives and sustains us!' I translate: we don't know *what* drives and sustains us, only that we are most miserably driven and, imperfectly, sustained. *Love* is how we call our ignorance of what whips us. 'To reach the Shore,' then: but what if the Shore exists in the fancies of us swimmers merely, who dream it to account for the dreadful fact that we swim, have always and only swum, and continue swimming without respite (myself excepted) until we die? Supposing even that there *were* a Shore—that, as a cynical companion of mine once imagined, we rise from the drowned to discover all those vulgar superstitions and exalted metaphors to be literal truth: the giant Maker of us all, the Shores of Light beyond our night-sea journey!—whatever would a swimmer do there? The fact is, when we imagine the Shore, what comes to mind is just the opposite of our condition: no more night, no more sea, no more journeying. In short, the blissful estate of the drowned.

"'Ours not to stop and think; ours but to swim and sink. . . .' Because a moment's thought reveals the pointlessness of swimming. 'No matter,' I've heard some say, even as they gulped their last: 'The night-sea journey may be absurd, but here we swim, will-we nill-we, against the flood, onward and upward, toward a Shore that may not exist and couldn't be reached if it did.' The thoughtful swimmer's choices, then, they say, are two: give over thrashing and go under for good, or embrace the absurdity; affirm in and for itself the night-sea journey; swim on with neither motive nor destination, for the sake of swimming, and compassionate moreover with your fellow swimmer, we being all at sea and equally in the dark. I find neither course acceptable. If not even the hypothetical Shore can justify a sea-full of drownèd comrades, to speak of the swim-in-itself as somehow doing so strikes me as obscene. I continue to swim—but only because blind habit, blind instinct, blind fear of drowning are still more strong than the horror of our journey. And if on occasion I have assisted a fellow-thrasher, joined in the cheers and songs, even passed along to others strokes of genius from the drownèd great, it's that I shrink by temperament from making myself conspicuous. To paddle off in one's own direction, assert one's independent right-of-way, overrun one's fellows without compunction, or dedicate oneself entirely to pleasures and diversions without regard for conscience—I can't finally condemn those who journey in this wise; in half my moods I envy them and despise the weak vitality that keeps me from following their example. But in reasonabler moments I remind myself that it's their very freedom and self-responsibility I reject, as more dramatically absurd, in our senseless circumstances, than tailing along in conventional fashion. Suicides, rebels, affirmers of the paradox—nay-sayers and yea-sayers alike to our fatal journey—I finally shake my head at them. And splash sighing past their corpses, one by one, as past a hundred sorts of others: friends, enemies, brothers; fools, sages, brutes—and nobodies, million upon million. I envy them all.

"A poor irony: that I, who find abhorrent and tautological the doctrine of survival of the fittest (*fitness* meaning, in my experience, nothing more than survival-ability, a talent whose only demonstration is the fact of survival, but whose chief ingredients seem to be strength, guile, callousness), may be the sole remaining swimmer! But the doctrine is false as well as repellent: Chance drowns the worthy with the unworthy, bears up the unfit with the fit by whatever definition, and makes the night-sea

journey essentially *haphazard* as well as murderous and unjustified.

"'You only swim once.' Why bother, then?

"'Except ye drown, ye shall not reach the Shore of Life.' Poppycock.

"One of my late companions—that same cynic with the curious fancy, among the first to drown—entertained us with odd conjectures while we waited to begin our journey. A favorite theory of his was that the Father does exist, and did indeed make us and the sea we swim—but not a-purpose or even consciously; He made us, as it were, despite Himself, as we make waves with every tail-thrash, and may be unaware of our existence. Another was that He knows we're here but doesn't care what happens to us, inasmuch as He creates (voluntarily or not) other seas and swimmers at more or less regular intervals. In bitterer moments, such as just before he drowned, my friend even supposed that our Maker wished us unmade; there was indeed a Shore, he'd argue, which could save at least some of us from drowning and toward which it was our function to struggle—but for reasons unknowable to us He wanted desperately to prevent our reaching that happy place and fulfilling our destiny. Our 'Father,' in short, was our adversary and would-be killer! No less outrageous, and offensive to traditional opinion, were the fellow's speculations on the nature of our Maker: that He might well be no swimmer Himself at all, but some sort of monstrosity, perhaps even tailless; that He might be stupid, malicious, insensible, perverse, or asleep and dreaming; that the end for which He created and launched us forth, and which we flagellate ourselves to fathom, was perhaps immoral, even obscene. Et cetera, et cetera: there was no end to the chap's conjectures, or the impoliteness of his fancy; I have reason to suspect that his early demise, whether planned by 'our Maker' or not, was expedited by certain fellow-swimmers indignant at his blasphemies.

"In other moods, however (he was as given to moods as I), his theorizing would become half-serious, so it seemed to me, especially upon the subjects of Fate and Immortality, to which our youthful conversations often turned. Then his harangues, if no less fantastical, grew solemn and obscure, and if he was still baiting us, his passion undid the joke. His objection to popular opinions of the hereafter, he would declare, was their claim to general validity. Why need believers hold that *all* the drownèd rise to be judged at journey's end, and non-believers that drowning is final without exception? In *his* opinion (so he'd vow at least), nearly everyone's fate was permanent death; indeed he took a sour pleasure in supposing that every 'Maker' made thousands of separate seas in His creative lifetime each populated like ours with millions of swimmers, and that in almost every instance both sea and swimmers were utterly annihilated, whether accidentally or by malevolent design. (Nothing if not pluralistical, he imagined there might be millions and billions of 'Fathers,' perhaps in some 'night-sea' of their own!) However—and here he turned infidels against him with the faithful—he professed to believe that in possibly a single night-sea per thousand, say, one of its quarter-billion swimmers (that is, one swimmer in two hundred fifty billions) achieved a qualified immortality. In some cases the rate might be slightly higher; in others it was vastly lower, for just as there are swimmers of every degree of proficiency, including some who drown before the journey starts, unable to swim at all, and others created drowned, as it were, so he imagined what can only be termed impotent Creators, Makers unable to Make, as well as uncommonly fertile ones and all grades between. And it pleased him to deny any necessary relation between a Maker's productivity and His other virtues—including, even, the quality of His creatures.

"I could go on (*he* surely did) with his elaboration of these mad notions—such as that swimmers in other night-seas needn't be of our kind; that Makers themselves might belong to different *species*, so to speak; that our particular Maker mightn't Himself be immortal, or that we might be not only His emissaries but His 'immortality,' continuing His life and our own, transmogrified, beyond our individual deaths. Even this modified immortality (meaningless to me) he conceived as relative and contingent, subject to accidental or deliberate termination: his pet hypothesis was that Makers and swimmers *each generate the other*—against all odds, their number being so great—and that any given 'immortality-chain' could terminate after any number of cycles, so that what was 'immortal' (still speaking relatively) was only the cyclic process of incarnation, which itself might have a beginning and an end. Alternatively he liked to imagine cycles within cycles, either finite or infinite: for example, the 'night-sea,' as it were, in which Makers 'swam' and created night-seas and swimmers like ourselves, might be the creation of a larger Maker, Himself one of many, Who in turn et cetera. Time itself he regarded as relative to our experience, like magnitude: who knew but what, with each thrash of our tails, minuscule seas and swimmers, whole eternities, came to pass—as ours, perhaps, and our Maker's Maker's, was elapsing between the strokes of some supertail, in a slower order of time?

"Naturally I hooted with the others at this nonsense. We were young then, and had only the dimmest notion of what lay ahead; in our ignorance we

imagined night-sea journeying to be a positively heroic enterprise. Its meaning and value we never questioned; to be sure, some must go down by the way, a pity no doubt, but to win a race requires that others lose, and like all my fellows I took for granted that I would be the winner. We milled and swarmed, impatient to be off, never mind where or why, only to try our youth against the realities of night and sea; if we indulged the skeptic at all, it was as a droll, half-contemptible mascot. When he died in the initial slaughter, no one cared.

"And even now I don't subscribe to all his views—but I no longer scoff. The horror of our history has purged me of opinions, as of vanity, confidence, spirit, charity, hope, vitality, everything—except dull dread and a kind of melancholy, stunned persistence. What leads me to recall his fancies is my growing suspicion that I, of all swimmers, may be the sole survivor of this fell journey, tale-bearer of a generation. This suspicion, together with the recent sea-change, suggests to me now that nothing is impossible, not even my late companion's wildest visions, and brings me to a certain desperate resolve, the point of my chronicling.

"Very likely I have lost my senses. The carnage at our setting out; our decimation by whirlpool, poisoned cataract, sea-convulsion; the panic stampedes, mutinies, slaughters, mass suicides; the mounting evidence that none will survive the journey—add to these anguish and fatigue; it were a miracle if sanity stayed afloat. Thus I admit, with the other possibilities, that the present sweetening and calming of the sea, and what seems to be a kind of vasty presence, song, or summons from the near upstream, may be hallucinations of disordered sensibility. . . .

"Perhaps, even, I am drowned already. Surely I was never meant for the rough-and-tumble of the swim; not impossibly I perished at the outset and have only imaged the night-sea journey from some final deep. In any case, I'm no longer young, and it is we spent old swimmers, disabused of every illusion, who are most vulnerable to dreams.

"Sometimes I think I am my drownèd friend.

"Out with it: I've begun to believe, not only that *She* exists, but that She lies not far ahead, and stills the sea, and draws me Herward! Aghast, I recollect his maddest notion: that our destination (which existed, mind, in but one night-sea out of hundreds and thousands) was no Shore, as commonly conceived, but a mysterious being, indescribable except by paradox and vaguest figure: wholly different from us swimmers, yet our complement; the death of us, yet our salvation and resurrection; simultaneously our journey's end, mid-point, and commencement; not membered and thrashing like us, but a motionless or hugely gliding sphere of unimaginable dimension; self-contained, yet dependent absolutely, in some wise, upon the chance (always monstrously improbable) that one of us will survive the night-sea journey and reach . . . Her! *Her*, he called it, or *She*, which is to say, Other-than-a-he. I shake my head; the thing is too preposterous; it is myself I talk to, to keep my reason in this awful darkness. There is no She! There is no You! I rave to myself; it's Death alone that hears and summons. To the drowned, all seas are calm. . . .

"Listen: my friend maintained that in every order of creation there are two sorts of creators, contrary yet complementary, one of which gives rise to seas and swimmers, the other to the Night-which-contains-the-sea and to What-waits-at-the-journey's-end: the former, in short, to destiny, the latter to destination (and both profligately, involuntarily, perhaps indifferently or unwittingly). The 'purpose' of the night-sea journey—but not necessarily of the journeyer or of either Maker!—my friend could describe only in abstractions: *consummation, transfiguration, union of contraries, transcension of categories.* When we laughed, he would shrug and admit that he understood the business no better than we, and thought it ridiculous, dreary, possibly obscene. 'But one of you,' he'd add with his wry smile, 'may be the Hero destined to complete the night-sea journey and be one with Her. Chances are, of course, you won't make it.' He himself, he declared, was not even going to try; the whole idea repelled him; if we chose to dismiss it as an ugly fiction, so much the better for us; thrash, splash, and be merry, we were soon enough drowned. But there it was, he could not say how he knew or why he bothered to tell us, any more than he could say what would happen after She and Hero, Shore and Swimmer, 'merged identities' to become something both and neither. He quite agreed with me that if the issue of that magical union had no memory of the night-sea journey, for example, it enjoyed a poor sort of immortality; even poorer if, as he rather imagined, a swimmer-hero plus a She equaled or became merely another Maker of future night-seas and the rest, at such incredible expense of life. This being the case—he was persuaded it was—the merciful thing to do was refuse to participate; the genuine heroes, in his opinion, were the suicides, and the hero of heroes would be the swimmer who, in the very presence of the Other, refused Her proffered 'immortality' and thus put an end to at least one cycle of catastrophes.

"How we mocked him! Our moment came, we hurtled forth, pretending to glory in the adventure, thrashing, singing, cursing, strangling, rationalizing, rescuing, killing, inventing rules and stories and relationships, giving up, struggling on, but dying all, and

still in darkness, until only a battered remnant was left to croak 'Onward, upward,' like a bitter echo. Then they too fell silent—victims, I can only presume, of the last frightful wave—and the moment came when I also, utterly desolate and spent, thrashed my last and gave myself over to the current, to sink or float as might be, but swim no more. Whereupon, marvelous to tell, in an instant the sea grew still! Then warmly, gently, the great tide turned, began to bear me, as it does now, onward and upward will-I nill-I, like a flood of joy—and I recalled with dismay my dead friend's teaching.

"I am not deceived. This new emotion is Her doing; the desire that possesses me is Her bewitchment. Lucidity passes from me; in a moment I'll cry 'Love!' bury myself in Her side, and be 'transfigured.' Which is to say, I die already; this fellow transported by passion is not I; *I am he who abjures and rejects the night-sea journey!* I. . . .

"I am all love. 'Come!' She whispers, and I have no will.

"You who I may be about to become, whatever You are: with the last twitch of my real self I beg You to listen. It is *not* love that sustains me! No; though Her magic makes me burn to sing the contrary, and though I drown even now for the blasphemy, I will say truth. What has fetched me across this dreadful sea is a single hope, gift of my poor dead comrade: that You may be stronger-willed than I, and that by sheer force of concentration I may transmit to You, along with Your official Heritage, a private legacy of awful recollection and negative resolve. Mad as it may be, my dream is that some unimaginable embodiment of myself (or myself plus Her if that's how it must be) will come to find itself expressing, in however garbled or radical a translation, some reflection of these reflections. If against all odds this comes to pass, may You to whom, through whom I speak, do what I cannot: terminate this aimless, brutal business! Stop Your hearing against Her song! Hate love!

"Still alive, afloat, afire. Farewell then my penultimate hope: that one may be sunk for direst blasphemy on the very shore of the Shore. Can it be (my old friend would smile) that only utterest naysayers survive the night? But even that were Sense, and there is no sense, only senseless love, senseless death. Whoever echoes these reflections: be more courageous than their author! An end to night-sea journeys! Make no more! And forswear me when I shall forswear myself, deny myself, plunge into Her who summons, singing . . .

"'Love! Love! Love!'"

Index of Authors and Titles